Mapping Upper Canada 1780–1867

An Annotated Bibliography of Manuscript and Printed Maps

The early face of what is now Ontario was documented by explorers, military men, administrators, and surveyors in an extraordinary number of maps. Thousands of those maps have survived to the present – maps of the area as a whole, its regions, and its cities and towns. In this bibliography Joan Winearls offers a guide to the manuscript and printed maps of Upper Canada and Canada West from the beginning of British settlement to Confederation.

The maps depict the growing knowledge of specific areas and their components, the shape and nature of settlement patterns, the activities of the civil administration and the military, and the railway and land promotions put forward by private individuals.

Each entry includes a physical description of the map, giving information about its contents, associated documents, other editions or related maps, and the location of the map. For historians, geographers, genealogists, surveyors, archaeologists, and local history buffs this book is a unique resource.

Appendices group more than two thousand township surveys; close to three thousand plans of urban subdivisions, describing much of the evolution of towns; nautical charts of the Great Lakes; and boundary surveys. Name, subject, and title indexes are included.

JOAN WINEARLS is Map Librarian at the University of Toronto. She has published numerous articles on maps and carto-bibliography and contributed the essay on sources for *Ontario's History in Maps* by C. Grant Head and R. Louis Gentilcore.

MAPPING UPPER CANADA 1780–1867

An annotated bibliography of manuscript and printed maps

JOAN WINEARLS

UNIVERSITY OF TORONTO PRESS
Toronto Buffalo London

Toronto Buffalo London
Printed in Canada

ISBN 0-8020-2794-6

Printed on acid-free paper

Canadian Cataloguing in Publication Data

Winearls, Joan, 1937–
Mapping Upper Canada, 1780–1867

Includes bibliographical references and index.
ISBN 0-8020-2794-6

1. Ontario – Maps – Bibliography. 2. Ontario – Maps, Manuscript – Bibliography. I. Title.

Z6027.C2205 1991 016.912713 C91-093961-6

This book has been published with the help of a grant from the Social Science Federation of Canada, using funds provided by the Social Sciences and Humanities Research Council of Canada.

To

E.B., H.A., and B.K.

for their unfailing support

Contents

Preface

The history of the early mapping of Ontario has always interested me. But, when I began this project in the early 1970s, almost no bibliographical aids were available and, like another researcher before me, Marilyn Olsen, I realized that it was impossible to work on early maps with no knowledge of how extensive the original materials were. What I first envisaged as a 'quick' checklist turned into a major task and I was soon captured by the endlessly fascinating work of the bibliographer – discovering, describing, and decoding the maps. As I progressed I was sustained by a growing conviction that maps had been overlooked everywhere – dumped in corners of repositories, left uncatalogued and in poor condition, and, worst of all, neglected as historical documents. Sometimes they were overlooked because of their physical inaccessibility, but often the reason was simple ignorance of their value. Further, it became clear that even those institutions which had catalogued their holdings had not always done so with the rigour they applied to textual documents. Manuscript and printed maps were often not distinguished. Facsimiles or later transcripts were treated as if they were originals. Later 'variant states' of printed maps were treated as copies. Printed maps with significant contemporary manuscript additions had been catalogued as if the addenda were not there or as if the dates of the original map and the additional data were interchangeable. The provenance of maps had often not been recorded, and in consequence the full identification and the relationship of similar maps in different institutions had not been and possibly could never be determined.

When I began, my guess was that there would be about 3000 maps extant from the pre-1900 period. In the subsequent decade, the time span of my study shrank to the pre-1867 years as the number of maps for that period alone exploded to some 7000.

The initial steps in compiling this bibliography included writing local public libraries, university libraries, archives, historical societies, and museums in Ontario and beyond to see if these institutions had any maps. The response to these letters led to trips to Great Britain and to Washington, Chicago, and other centres in the northeastern United States. I visited Montreal and passed many weeks at the National Archives in Ottawa. As well, I visited collections in fifty-three towns in Ontario. The local visits were particularly rewarding, not only in yielding a number of interesting maps, but also in providing an unrivalled opportunity to compare the many regional and town maps with the areas themselves.

Physical examination of all actual maps was of course essential, leading me to spend many hours in such unconventional repositories as garages and attics, as well as basements and cramped offices. But the maps were always worth the trip, whether it was the opportunity to spend time looking at the attractive military maps with their delicate water-colours and artistic shaded relief or pondering changes made to states of engraved maps showing the tremendous precision of the medium, or in considering the changes in decorative designs of lithographed maps with their flowery borders and views or the excitement experienced in finding yet another printed map. Even the more everyday maps by land surveyors were rewarding because of the great care taken in their drafting and the sense they give of a well-organized routine.

In the course of my visits to over 100 repositories and the long gestation period of the work, I had an opportunity to meet and talk with many archivists, librarians, and researchers, to gain considerably from their expertise, and to be helped at every point. I wish now to thank these people.

I was indebted from the beginning to R. Louis Gentilcore and C. Grant Head, with whom I was associated in the preparation of *Ontario's History in Maps*. Their support and encouragement was vital in the early stages of my project, and they taught me many of the finer points about the historical value of early maps.

I began my research at the Archives of Ontario

and returned to it for lengthy periods over the years. I am indebted to Ian Wilson and earlier archivists for their great support. Allan MacDonald, Art Murdoch, John Mezaks, and Eugene Martel met my special requirements for access several times, and John Fortier put up with me in his area for long periods of time. Other archivists and the staff of the reading room under Leon Warmski patiently answered my queries on innumerable occasions. Dennis Jeanes and his staff and earlier Eric Carroll of the Survey Records section in the Ministry of Natural Resources gave me considerable help over many years and always managed to find me a comfortable place to work.

At the Metropolitan Toronto Library my work was greatly assisted by the resident experts, including Edith Firth, David Kotin, Christine Mosser, Sandra Alston, John Crosthwait, Bill Parker, and Nancy Biehl. Closer to home, Richard Landon, Kathryn Martyn, and all the staff of the Fisher Rare Book Library were gracious responding to innumerable requests. At the City of Toronto Archives, Victor Russell and before him Scott James, as well as Karen Teeple, Patrick Cummings, and others, helped me with my special requests on early Toronto maps and information.

Ron Logan and earlier directors of the Real Property Registration Branch, Ministry of Consumer and Commercial Relations, helped arrange for me to visit the fifty-five registry offices of southern Ontario without charge. I am also most indebted to the registrars and their assistants at all these offices who assisted me so cheerfully.

Ottawa was another major centre for my research, and over the years almost every staff member in the Cartographic Archives and Architectural Drawings Division of the National Archives assisted me in some way. My work was particularly facilitated by Betty Kidd, Gilles Langelier, and Louis Cardinal in making all sorts of special arrangements; by Tom Nagy, Robert Grandmaître, and Patrick McIntrye in the reading room; and by Brian Hallett and his staff in government records. Elsewhere in the National Archives I was assisted many times by Pat Kennedy of the Manuscript section, Tim Dube on military records, and many other staff members in government records and the reading rooms.

I wish also to acknowledge the help I received from the staff of all the public libraries, local archives, museums, and historical societies that I visited around the province. In Guelph I was particularly assisted by Elizabeth Bloomfield and Jane Turner of the Guelph Regional History project, Nancy Sadek at the University Archives, the staff of the Civic Museum, and Linda Kearns at the public library, as well as Bonnie Callen at the Wellington County Archives. In Hamilton I have to thank Carl Spadoni of Special Collections, Kate Donkin, former map librarian, McMaster University, and Margaret Houghton of the Hamilton Public Library. In Kingston William Morley and Shirley Harmer at Queen's University and in London Ed Phelps and his staff at the Regional History collection of the University of Western Ontario Library, as well as Serge Sauer of the map library, all gave me a great deal of assistance. Peter Moran of the Simcoe County Archives helped me at the very beginning and recently answered a final request. He and many others must be relieved to see the bibliography finally published. John Burtniak in St Catharines went out of his way to respond to worrying last-minute problems, as did Susan Hoffman at Kitchener Public Library. John Good of Parks Canada facilitated access to Trent Canal materials in Peterborough. In Stratford James Anderson and Lutzen Riedstra of the Stratford-Perth Archives helped on several occasions and Mark Walsh of the Windsor Public Library came through at the end with important information.

I am also indebted to the chief librarians of several public libraries for their letters of support during my early attempts to find publishing grants for the book. Grover C. Burgis, Brampton Public Library, R.C. Howell, Brockville Public Library, Norman C. McLeod, Guelph Public LIbrary, Judith McAnanama, Hamilton Public Library, Arnold Maizen, Kingston Public Library, Reed Osborne, London Public Library, Jean Orpwood, North York Public Library, Anne C. Smith, Peterborough Public Library, and Brian R. Ingram, Sault Ste Marie Public Library. David Kotin, Head, Canadian History Department, Metropolitan Toronto Reference Library, and Penny McKee, President, Ontario Library Association were equally supportive.

Elsewhere in Canada, I was greatly assisted at

different times by Claude Boudreau and Jean-Marc Garant of the Archives nationales de Québec, Carole Marley and Nellie Reiss of McGill University, and Conrad Graham of the McCord Museum, who astounded me with his rich collections of maps of Ontario. Frances Woodward and Ann Yandle of Special Collections at the University of British Columbia were most helpful in supplying me with photocopies of a mysterious atlas at the last minute, and Walter Morrison went himself to Acadia University Library and made a photograph of an important map of Toronto for me.

Abroad my work at the British Library Map Section was greatly facilitated by Helen Wallis and more latterly Tony Campbell; Yolande Hodson, John Huddy, and Sara Tyacke gave freely of their time and expertise. Peter Barber and his predecessor Hugh Cobbe responded willingly to my constant requests for information on manuscript maps. At the Public Records Office I was assisted by Peter Penfold, and more latterly Geraldine Beech, and various staff at the National Maritime Museum responded to my requests over the years. David Mann assisted me at the Admiralty Hydrographic Archives and I benefited considerably from Andrew David's extensive knowledge of early nautical charts when he did a vital piece of research there for Appendix C. Francis Herbert of the Royal Geographical Society helped at several different times.

In Washington my work at the Library of Congress was aided by Walter Ristow, Dick Stephenson, Minnie Modelski, and Gary Fitzpatrick. More recently Patrick Dempsey has responded graciously to my frantic final requests. John Wolter shared his research on nautical charts of the Great Lakes with me and I hope my work is useful to him. Ralph Ehrenberg (now at the Library of Congress) and his staff of the U.S. National Archives gave great assistance on their War of 1812 and boundary maps. Many others in the United States helped me over the years including Georgia Barnhill of the American Antiquarian Society, Susan Danforth of the John Carter Brown Library, Douglas Marshall of the William L. Clements Library, and Le Roy Barnett of the Michican State Archives. Alice Hudson and Julie Zelman of the New York Public Library went out of their way to check maps in books for me at the last minute.

Colleagues, other researchers, and friends have also come to my aid over the years. Steve Otto had the knack of finding new and important maps or information about maps all through the project. Pat Fleming's work has served as a model, and she has also been of tremendous support in many other ways. Mary Allodi shared many important parts of her research on early printing with me, found one crucial map, and was always ready to discuss our mutual areas of research. Wendy Cameron shared information on various historical projects with me, including her files on the Trent Canal, while Mary Williamson and Susan Houston often shared information from their various areas of expertise. Elizabeth Hulse has over the years made available much of her research on early printers and publishers. Friends also assisted me in many ways. In particular, Marion Magee helped me with the introduction at an early crucial grant application phase. Hugh Anson-Cartwright has helped at several points and made an important suggestion about organization early on. Finally, Ed Dahl at the National Archives of Canada has literally given me hundreds of hours of his time and has never ceased to astound me with the depth of his knowledge of cartography. Without his help I would never have been able to unlock the secrets of many of the national collections. Right to the end he was helping me to find not just new states of maps but new maps themselves.

This project has had financial support from a number of bodies: Canadian Studies Research Tools programme of the Social Science and Humanities Research Council, Ontario Heritage Foundation, McLean Foundation, and the Ontario Historical Studies Series. Publishing grants were provided by SSHRCC and the Social Sciences Federation of Canada. The University of Toronto Library has granted me several research leaves over the years and helped in many other ways. Without the support of these bodies at several points this book could never have been published.

During the latter phases of the project the grants helped me to hire a consulting editor, technical manager, and research assistants, without whom it simply would not have been finished. Richard Simpson, Anne Dondertman, Judy Donnelly, and Christy Bacque did noble work as research assistants on various aspects of the final phases including editing, finalization of appendices A and B, and the preparation of the indexes; they were ably assisted at times by Jennifer Donnelly. Elizabeth Driver did a magnificent and creative final edit and helped with that old bugbear – consistency.

I would like to thank the staff of the University of Toronto Press for the assistance given me and particularly Antje Lingner who contributed greatly to the book with the clarity of her design. Geoffrey Matthews and Jane Daire have done their usual superb job with the reference map.

I am particularly indebted to two people without whom this book might not have seen the light of day. One is my extraordinary technical manager, Gwen Peroni, who did a superhuman job, in record time, often under pressure and without complaint, and the other is my consulting editor, Mary McDougall Maude, who skilfully guided the manuscript through the many stages of the editorial process and who has been instrumental in giving the bibliography its final lucid shape.

Introduction

We all live with maps, whether they are the mental sketches that direct us about our homes, our offices, and our towns, or the more complex and concrete documents that guide us on holiday trips or in our understanding of public affairs. From the earliest days of what is now Ontario, maps were one important means by which explorers, the military, the civil administrators, surveyors, and eventually individual settlers set down new information or pursued their business. Over time, however, these maps came increasingly to be overlooked as sources of information about our past. They were difficult to store, they became separated from their accompanying texts, or if physically collected they were uncatalogued and thus inaccessible. Researchers ceased to seek out maps, and the unique information they provide remained unused. It was with the aim of making these important historical resources once more accessible to researchers that I began work on this bibliography.

Because it is a representation of an area drawn to a particular scale at a specific moment in time, a map (or series of maps) can be a crucial document for the history of that area. A map may be the only surviving record of a region for a period or the document that explains written materials. It may enable conflicting information from other sources to be reassessed or provide an interesting comparison of what was planned and what actually developed in an area. Certain kinds of maps such as hydrographic or geological charts display complex data which could be described in words only with difficulty. Some kinds of information, such as relationships of distance or size among features, are best absorbed visually.

Although the information on any map is always selective – and early maps may reflect inaccurate methods of surveying of the period, as well as the tendency to incorporate hearsay information – these early maps may nevertheless be the best source for the identification of features as named and known – of linear features such as rivers, shorelines, boundaries, and travel routes, of areal features such as forests, cleared land, urban areas and marshes, and of points such as forts or settlements or buildings.

Maps are practical documents prepared for specific purposes. Many of the first were detailed topographic surveys done by the nineteenth-century military engineers, who were working in the context of contemporary defence requirements. The needs of the civil administration were more varied, and the maps they required often reflected the narrower concerns of an individual department. At the executive level, legislative acts or a governor's decision might require a map showing the location of a boundary with another colony or country or the plans proposed for the development of a new area of the province. At the administrative level, early surveys might include only the outline of the township grid with a few bearings and physical features. As settlement progressed, the maps would be used to record land grants and sales, and thus become working office documents. The maps of public works or railway officials, for instance, would show only those features of importance to the planning and progress of such public works and railways.

The original purpose for which a map was made does of course affect its potential usefulness for historical research today. Some are far-reaching in their import, others of limited value. Together, however, the maps listed in this bibliography document the changes in Upper Canada's growth in the eighty-seven years before Confederation.

Map Collections

The maps included are held in over 150 collections, many of which are characterized by an emphasis on a special group of materials. The most important collections are discussed here. The Cartographic Archives and Architectural Drawings Division in the National Archives in

Ottawa has a substantial number of maps relating to Ontario in the pre-Confederation period. It has long held the majority of the original British military maps from the C series, the Board of Ordnance series, and the Royal Engineers Office. It has inherited many maps from various federal government departments and from the government of the Province of Canada (1841–67) pertaining to such province-wide matters as Indian lands, railways, canals and navigation, and public works. In addition the National Archives of Canada has the best overall selection of printed maps and editions of general maps for the province. Some impressive acquisitions in recent decades and a concerted effort to expand its collection make it an increasingly rich source of materials. It proved to have a number of maps that had been referred to elsewhere but never found before. For example, several of Henry Bayfield's manuscript charts of Lake Superior (see Appendix C), long known as maps 'missing' from Britain's Hydrographic Archives, made a sudden and dramatic appearance in a routine transfer of material from the Canadian Hydrographic Service to the National Archives.

The Archives of Ontario includes early and recent transfers of Department of Crown Lands maps and maps from important private collections such as the Simcoe, Talbot, and Canada Company materials. Looking at John Graves Simcoe's map collection proved an invaluable way to trace the opening up of the province and provided an interesting glimpse of the attitudes and predelictions of a British colonial administrator of the time. The Archives of Ontario's collection of printed maps, while smaller than that of the National Archives of Canada, has some unique copies including recent important transfers from the Survey Records Office of the Ministry of Natural Resources of Ontario. And it was also in this collection that a recent transfer from the Survey Records Office proved to be the original map of the early settlements on the St Lawrence done by Patrick McNiff in 1786 (**418**) – a map frequently referred to but hitherto known by most researchers only in a transcript.

The Survey Records Office still retains the main group of crown lands maps and therefore holds the largest number of maps relating to Ontario in the period. These documents, many of which are still in frequent use by officials and surveyors, include original township surveys, town plans, road and exploration surveys, compilations of surveys, maps of Indian lands, and re-surveys of disputed boundaries. This is the single most important source for early maps of the province and the one least known to researchers. Small transfers from this collection to the Archives of Ontario are made frequently (a recent transfer included most of the printed county maps), and researchers should be aware that maps showing the location OTNR assigned in the bibliography may subsequently have been moved.

The province's land registry offices (under the jurisdiction of the Ministry of Consumer and Commercial Relations) hold over 2900 subdivision plans for towns in Ontario before 1867. From 1849 on, the law required plans pertaining to land subdivision and resubdivision for the purposes of sale to be deposited with the other instruments in the local registry office. Subdivision involved dividing original farm lots to create a new town or to add land to an established town or further dividing of existing town lots or park lots into smaller parcels. The latter occurred most frequently in the larger cities. In consequence the plans in these offices, when taken together, document the thrust of urban development during the boom period of the 1850s and 1860s in a variety of interesting ways. Because of the constant use to which these registered plans were and are subject, many of them were copied by hand when the condition of the original began to deteriorate. Certified correct for legal purposes (that is, for the accurate depiction of lot dimensions and other such details), many of these copies had come to be regarded as 'originals.' Tracking down the true original sometimes proved difficult, but the reward for the researcher lies in seeing the original map and sometimes finding additional information that had been incorrectly transcribed or not transcribed at all on the copy.

The Metropolitan Toronto Library holds a small but significant group of manuscript and printed maps. The maps in the D.W. Smith Papers include a recent acquisition of an important administrative map of 1798 (**27(3)**), and the collection also has some important Canada Company maps, as well as the maps found in the library's rich book collection of Canadiana.

The local maps in the Regional History Collection of the University of Western Ontario and smaller collections such as the Waterloo Historical Society turned up some surprising and unique items. Other small but important collections in the province include those of the Simcoe County Archives, the Hiram Walker Historical Museum in Windsor, the Lennox and Addington Historical Society in Napanee, and McMaster University Rare Books Library.

Of foreign map collections, the largest and most important for pre-Confederation Ontario is that of the Public Record Office in Great Britain. This group of some 500 maps were included in despatches sent to the Colonial Office, the War Office, and the Admiralty; most come from the well-known CO 42 series of the Colonial Office. This collection is particularly important for the study of early Ontario because the maps can be related to associated documentation and thus to the policies of military and civilian officials. The Manuscript Division of the British Library (formerly part of the British Museum) has a small number of important maps, particularly those in the Haldimand and Royal United Services Institute collection. The British Library Map Room holds George III's collection of maps, the King's Topographical Collection, which includes manuscript copies of maps of features such as forts and rivers from the 1800s and Mrs Simcoe's birchbark map of Upper Canada (**18(3)**). While the United States National Archives holds very few maps of pre-Confederation Ontario, their collection is rich in boundary maps and maps relating to the War of 1812, including two incorrect plans of Kingston in 1813 (**1507**) which appear to have been drafted under the pressure of war. The U.S. Library of Congress on the other hand had several unique printed maps and an extensive collection of atlases. Other small foreign collections yielded important additional maps, such as those of the Rideau Canal in the Dalhousie collection of the Scottish Record Office (**501**).

Scope of the Bibliography

This bibliography endeavours to provide a complete list of all significant and autonomous maps (both manuscript and printed) of Upper Canada in the years between 1780 and 1867, from the beginning of effective British occupation until Confederation. The province, during this period known successively as Upper Quebec, Upper Canada, and Canada West, included all of present-day southern Ontario and parts of northern Ontario within the Great Lakes watershed, that is south of a line which extended just north of the shorelines of Lake Huron and Lake Superior (see reference map). The territory north of this was part of the Hudson's Bay Company domain and was only mapped sporadically before 1867 and specific maps for this area are not included. The latter belong more properly with a bibliography of Hudson's Bay Company mapping. The bibliography also includes the area from Lake Superior to Lake of the Woods important in boundary negotiations.

The maps cover the whole area of Upper Canada as well as its parts: regions, rivers, lakes, districts and counties, cities and towns. While maps of major parts of cities have been included, plans for individual features (buildings, cemeteries, and maps of very small parts of cities) generally have not.

Because of the vast number of military maps of towns, only those that show a good part of the town are included in the bibliography. Minor maps of parts of reserves or minor military land claims in towns have been omitted. A great many of the military maps are in the National Archives in Ottawa and can be found in the 440 classification in the *Catalogue of the National Map Collection*. Users are also referred to the 450 class in the same catalogue for maps of individual forts and other military buildings. Similar, mainly military maps are still found with despatches in the Public Record Office holdings (mainly in CO and WO series). Some of these are now being removed and filed with the maps, and a microfilm of the Public Record Office card file with map filing numbers is held in the National Archives.

Minor maps of parts of townships have also been excluded (see notes on Appendix A), as have individual maps of Indian reserves, timber leases, mining leases, and detailed engineering plans of railway lines. In many cases this last group of categories involve maps for which the bulk of material will be found after Confederation. There are also a few cases in which large groups of manuscript subdivision plans of towns have been found in libraries and archives. Generally these materials have been listed in a group together, although a few important items and all printed items are listed separately. Copies of subdivision plans from these collections as found in Appendix B have been excluded.

Of the maps which have survived in archives and libraries, about two-thirds are manuscript maps and one-third printed. Most of the manuscript maps are found separately filed in institutions, and even those related to textual material can be used as independent documents. Although certain important archival groups have been examined for maps, maps in other private and official papers have generally been excluded. Maps left in papers often serve only to illustrate the accompanying text (for example, a minor land claim) and cannot be understood separately from the text.

Printed maps from books and atlases have been included in the bibliography. The maps originally from atlases have primarily been identified from Phillips and Le Gear's *List of Geographical Atlases in the Library of Congress* (Washington 1906–) and the British Museum's *Catalogue of Printed Maps, Charts, and Plans* (15 vols, London 1967; supplement, London 1978). The maps from books and pamphlets have been identified mainly through Staton and Tremaine's *Bibliography of Canadiana* and *Supplements*. (Maps printed in periodicals and newspapers have generally been excluded.)

Books have turned out to be a very important source for printed maps of early Ontario. Unfortunately many maps were removed from books and, although some have been incorporated into map collections, others have not been found. In addition, many important maps are associated with books although it may never be clear whether they were ever bound in and actually sold with the book. The D.W. Smith map of 1800 (**30**) and William Chewett's map of 1813 (**43**) were both produced to accompany books but are generally not found bound into copies. In other cases maps were promised with books but either not published at all or only published later; the map to accompany J.C. Morgan's book of 1824, for example, was not published until 1827 (**75**). In other cases it has been difficult to date a map because, although it appears the map was intended to accompany a book, copies of likely books have been searched in vain for a copy with the map, for example, the map of the route to Red River (**884(14)**) and some maps of the Niagara Falls region (**741, 754**). There are undoubtedly maps from books that I have missed, and I would be grateful to have them brought to my attention for a supplement.

Treatment of Manuscript Maps

Although each manuscript map is a unique item and can be handled individually, it seemed more useful to link similar versions of a map together as 'related maps' and to put large groups back into the 'sets' they probably originated in. Thus different maps relating to the survey and construction of various roads are listed together (**628**), as are different versions of a manuscript map, such as 'Plan of the Organized Part of the Province ... 1797–8' (**27**). The various groups of maps showing the progress of the building of various locks along the Rideau Canal by year and month (**511**), have also been put back into the groups in which they were originally created. Manuscript transcripts are not recorded save for instances in which an original map, whose former existence can be firmly established, has disappeared. (There are some examples of such transcripts in the holdings of the land registry offices.) The decision to omit references to transcripts rests on the fact that there are a great many in existence and that these handmade copies do not reproduce the original with the exactness of camera reproduction; information can be omitted and mistranscribed. And of course a transcript lacks the style and handwriting of the original draftsman.

Treatment of Printed Maps

The printed general maps are probably the single most interesting group for bibliographers and collectors. Maps that went through many 'editions' are listed together under the first issue. Bibliographical methodology for maps is in its infancy and it is difficult to apply hard and fast terminology to the definition of an 'edition' (a conscious intent to revise and reissue) and a 'state' (a more casual and minor change). However, for practical reasons, I have listed later editions and states together somewhat following

Ralph Hyde's style as outlined in *Printed Maps of Victorian London*. Maps with changes to the title, imprint, or date, or with extensive changes to the information on the map itself, have been arranged by date as subentries (numbered (2), (3) etc) of the first listing for the map. Maps with minor changes, for example, of a few place names, have sometimes only been discussed with the last state they revise. Maps for which the date has been removed in later states and which have major changes are set out in separate subentries (see **30(12)** and **(13)** and **138(3a)** to **(9)**). Only about one-third of the printed maps in the bibliography were issued in later editions or states, and in most cases these are the major general maps issued by British, American, and sometimes Canadian commercial publishers. The cost of revising maps was so high that, although there are five states of the Tackabury map (**281**), almost all changes were made to the insets and views around the map and the map itself remained unchanged.

Some of the later British and American maps show evidence of the use of lithographic transfer. For only a few have I mentioned in notes that they may be lithographic transfers; further research needs to be done on exact printing procedures for these maps. The lithographic transfer process can be defined as the transferral of a copy of an engraved or lithographed map to a new lithographic printing surface to create a new 'plate.' Changes can then continue to be made to both the old and new plates to produce versions of the map that may be at quite different stages of revision. This results in many variant states, some of which look closer to earlier editions despite a much later date. Some evidence of the use of this process is found with James Wyld maps (**138**), W. & A.K. Johnston maps (**120**), and in the maps by Ensign & Thayer (**161, 168**). In some cases the lithographic transfer process has also been used to produce a special thematic map from a general map. The W.H. Smith Map of Canada West (**185**) is a good example – not only did it go through various revisions but railways were added to a reduced version to produce the 'Railway Map of Canada West,' which itself went through several revisions. Later on, the original plate and the 'railway plate' were used interchangeably to produce different maps, such as the geological map of Canada West (**297**).

Organization of the Bibliography

The maps, once selected, have been arranged in three main groups: Part I, general maps of the whole province; Part II, maps of regions (physical features and counties and districts); Part III, cities and towns.

Part I, about 20 per cent of the total listed, comprises maps of Upper Canada alone, maps of Upper and Lower Canada together, a few important maps of eastern Canada, usually at scales larger than 1 inch to 30 miles, and maps of large parts of Upper Canada that cover more than one region. These maps are arranged chronologically, with later editions listed under the entry for the first map. As a group, these maps – 80 per cent of which are printed – are critical for an understanding of the development of the province as a whole.

Part II, approximately 35 per cent of the total, is devoted to maps of parts of the province including administrative units and physical features, road surveys, and canals. The maps are first grouped into seven regional areas (Central, East, Huron-Ottawa, Niagara, North, South, and West) as shown on the reference map. Within each region the maps are filed chronologically. Specific names of administrative units, rivers, or roads are cross-indexed in the subject index.

Not surprisingly, the maps in Part II did not all fall neatly into the seven regions. Maps that would have covered two or more sections have been included in Part I. Generally, maps are found in the part with which they best fit, and researchers must be careful to double-check the subject index to find all pertinent maps for an area. However, the boundaries of the regions correlate closely with the growth of settlement. For instance, South is effectively the western area of the province settled before about 1826 and West covers the Huron Tract settlements and those to the north. The Huron-Ottawa area includes most of the unsettled northern areas of the districts and counties along the north shore of Lake Ontario.

The regions are generally divided along modern county lines, but many of those bisect earlier districts or counties as boundaries of districts and counties changed frequently. The reference map shows the approximate boundaries used to group regions and pre-1974 county boundaries.[1] About one-third of the maps of regions (and towns as well) are printed.

Part III, cities and towns, is by far the largest group of maps making up some 45 per cent of the total. Maps of over 700 towns are listed, filed alphabetically, and subfiled chronologically. Towns, cities, and villages are entered under the name by which they are known today, and parts of towns with community or subdivision names, whether or not they were originally separate villages, have been entered under their present designation. Cities that changed their name in 1974 are entered under the original name or names; for example, maps for Cambridge are entered separately under the three original names of Galt, Hespeler, and Preston and the modern name Cambridge is used in the index. Earlier names are indexed in the subject index. If a town for which there is a map no longer exists and the name has been removed from the gazetteer (*Gazetteer of Canada: Ontario*, 4th ed, Ottawa: Canadian Permanent Committee on Geographical Names 1988), the name is shown in parentheses (**Aboyne**). If a map shows a plan for a new town which was never established or laid out, it is entered under the name in the title with the term 'town plot' appended and the whole enclosed in parentheses (**Hardwicke town plot**).

Appendix A lists the official township plans created by surveyors under instructions from the surveyor general or Crown Lands Department and now found in the Survey Records Office and the Archives of Ontario. The plans generally consist of (1) the first or original survey, later resurveys, and some copies in the Survey Records Office; (2) office copies used to record crown patents and filed in the Patents Office (and recently transferred to the Archives of Ontario); and (3) transfers of other copies over the years from Survey Records to the Archives of Ontario. Township plans prepared by other individuals or for other purposes and any printed township plans are recorded in the appropriate regional section of the bibliography. Copies of official plans found in other places such as land registry offices, a few miscellaneous township plans from other sources in Archives of Ontario, and outline plans showing only the survey grid with no further identification or dates (as found in the National Archives) have both been omitted from the bibliography. A few maps from Indian Affairs and Survey Records at the National Archives have been listed where no other plan was found for the township. Plans for parts of townships such as the 'Partial plans' group at Survey Records Office have been omitted.

Appendix B lists the approximately 2900 registered subdivision plans for towns, or in a few cases parts of townships. The plans are arranged alphabetically and then chronologically by date of survey or, if this is unknown, by date of registration. These plans complement the listings in Part III and users should check both to find all maps of a particular town.

Appendix C lists the official nautical charts of the Great Lakes, both the manuscript surveys and the printed charts that cover Canadian waters from British and American surveys. The charts are grouped by surveys and arranged by area and chronologically. **Appendix D** lists the official maps from the international boundary surveys, according to the Treaty of Ghent (1814) and the Treaty of Washington (1842). The surveys are arranged according to the progress of the survey and grouped by British and American surveys. **Appendix E** simply lists towns by their counties (according to pre-1974 boundaries).

Emerging Themes

If the bibliography of maps is in its infancy, so too is the sophistication with which we look at and interpret maps. The maps show in graphic form how the province emerged: exploration and surveying, military and administrative concerns such as communications are some of the themes of these manuscript maps. The printed maps represent a whole new stage of development of the province and its promotion and offer an opportunity to study the transmission of information about the new province.

The mapping of towns is a fascinating subject itself with quite different imperatives, much of it related to the trends in town development in terms of areas of regional growth, the development of railways and new lines of communication, and land speculation.

Manuscript Maps

Reconnaissance and Exploration Mapping

The earliest maps are reconnaissance and exploration surveys. Since there was a need to locate the large numbers of Loyalist settlers quickly, township surveys were being laid out at the same time as shorelines and river systems were being reconnoitred. Many of the early maps range in accuracy from fast sketches to fairly precise surveys.

The first significant maps are the manuscript compilation maps made before Governor John Graves Simcoe arrived. Some, such as (**10**), were reasonably accurate and could only have been based on the smaller reconnaissance surveys such as Gother Mann's 1788 plan of Lake Huron (**7**) or the surveys of the Lake Ontario shoreline by early surveyors such as Lewis Kotte (**4, 9**).

At the same time, other maps were wildly inaccurate compilations from a variety of poorer sources such as Patrick McNiff's general plans of 1790 (**11, 12**). In the 1790s, many plans, such as the maps by Mrs Simcoe (**18, 19, 25**), were freely sketched from older maps or from descriptions by army officers. Others were painstakingly compiled by such notable surveyors as William Chewett (**16, 27, 33**) and Joseph Bouchette (**24**) into recognizable general plans of the province, plans on which officials could insert the first counties and districts with some meaning.

Some of the earliest maps found are those relating to Indian treaties. Many of these maps are sketchy. The map of ca 1799 showed areas 'conjectured to be the extent of cessions from the Indians' on the north shore of Lake Ontario (**328**). These early maps include treaty areas around Toronto, Niagara, and Penetanguishene (**313, 324, 321**) and later purchases paving the way for specific settlement projects, such as the purchase of the Huron Tract in the 1820s (**944, 946, 949, 1026**). Other plans show areas deeded to the Indians as land grants, such as the grant to the Six Nations Indians around the Grand River (**673**). There are also surveys done for the Indians themselves at St Regis and along the Grand River (**689, 448**).

Much of the reconnaissance mapping around the lower Great Lakes was concerned with defence and was done by military personnel; important surveys were made just after the War of 1812 (**464–5, 52**) but perhaps the most striking and important reconnaissance mapping was that done by military personnel in the 1840s and 1850s. The attractive maps by Colonel F.A. Mackenzie Fraser of 1840 (**123**) and Colonel John Oldfield's plans of 1843 (**136**) are the first extant plans of a series of major maps for the province which were continued in part by the general plans of the Naval and Military Commission of 1845–6 (**149**). This type of reconnaissance mapping culminated in the great Baron de Rottenburg map of about 1850 (**170**), the largest-scale map of the province produced to that date (one inch to 2 miles).

By the 1860s, possibly in anticipation of problems arising from the American Civil War, the Royal Engineers were producing the first true topographic maps for the province (**283**), and this effort continued after the Fenian raids but in the form of hasty reconnaissance surveys.

The colonial government was also interested in exploration and twice in the period mounted large expeditions to examine specific areas. The first was in the Huron-Ottawa area in the 1830s (**569–85**) to investigate the possibilities for settlement and communications (even of building a canal) in the area between Lake Huron and the Ottawa River and featured important surveys by David Thompson. These surveyors were the first to record the Muskoka Lakes and the waters between there and the Ottawa River in any detail.

Finally, Canadian interest in the acquisition of the Hudson's Bay Company territories is signalled by the important 'Map of the North West Part of Canada' by Thomas Devine in 1857 (**882**). It was followed by the maps from the several great exploring expeditions to the Red River country, those by Simon James Dawson and Henry Youle Hind (**884, 888**) and the Palliser expedition (**883**). These maps have been listed together in groups to make the sequence of the exploration clearer. The Dawson listings include both the original manuscript plans for the canoe routes from Lake Superior to Red River, the printed versions which accompany reports in both British and Canadian parliamentary sources, and the road route to be built from

Fort William to the closest river connection to the west. The emphasis in the Hind maps (**888**) on the other hand is on the geology and areas of arable land in the Rainy River area.

Township Surveys

There is an enormous amount of information in the bibliography on surveying for settlement, including information on the different forms of township surveys, problems arising from survey, survey techniques, and the impact of surveys on issues such as land tenure, road building, and boundaries. The size of townships and lots, their arrangement, and procedures for surveying were laid down in instructions issued by the governor general, Lord Haldimand, in 1783 (Gentilcore and Donkin, 3). According to them, the basic township was to be six miles square and 25 lots wide, each lot to be 120 acres. However, the size and shape of the townships began to change almost immediately, and several different survey systems were employed in southern Ontario in the period covered by the bibliography (**3**). The earliest township surveys along the St Lawrence River and the north shore of Lake Ontario (clearly evident on the general maps in the Central and East regions) were laid out in the single-front system with long narrow lots of 200 acres each, each lot only 19 chains wide. This was succeeded after the War of 1812 by the double-front system with lots of a more convenient 30 chains in width, often granted in 100-acre units so that settlers faced each other across road allowances. This system was used in the back townships north of Lake Ontario and in much of the central and southern areas. To save on costs of surveying after 1829, a different configuration was used, with lots grouped into sections surrounded by road allowances, in what are known as sectional survey systems; with the lots varying in size. These systems were used in the Huron Tract and parts of the West, in the Huron-Ottawa region, and, after 1859, in the North. The township surveys in Appendix A naturally fall into one or another of these groupings but are not specifically identified as such. The actual process of surveying depended on the dated instructions to individual surveyors for road, river, general, or town surveys, which are listed in the main sections of the bibliography, and those for township surveys, which are found in Appendix A. The references to surveyors' field notebooks are also listed with each survey and in many cases these help to date the maps.

Many of the earliest surveys show the surveying of essential baselines such as Augustus Jones' 1791 survey from the Trent River to Toronto (**316**), which determined the later orientation of all townships advancing north onto the Shield, as well as the orientation of Queen Street and thus Toronto. The fragmentary nature of these surveys is shown in the few extant surveys along the St Lawrence and Bay of Quinte (**410, 413–17**). Evidence of the piecemeal nature of early surveys is found in Patrick McNiff's important map of 1786 of 'the new settlements' (**418**), showing how few survey lines were actually run (often only the front lines of the first concessions) and suggesting how tenuous the settlers' legal rights to their land might have been until further surveying occurred. Later compilations show how the various township or road surveys tied together, such as the important plan for part of York County in about 1798 showing the road lots and the practical orientation of parts of townships to rivers and others to Yonge Street (**327**), or the printed county map of the Niagara and Gore districts of 1845 (**799**) showing the complicated fit of the irregular surveys along the Grand River and the townships of the German settlement with the more regularly surveyed townships to the east.

Land companies, such as the Canada Company, employed local surveyors to do the work. Their work in the mapping and laying out of the Huron Tract demonstrates careful planning and orderly survey, beginning with the boundaries of the tract and plans for roads (**1028, 1030**).

New survey methods were developed in the course of the intensive surveying in the Huron-Ottawa area in the 1850s, and a better plan for the recording of data in field notebooks (see **636**). In 1857 a series of maps for the area south of Lake Nipissing shows the first attempt in Ontario to use the range and township survey system, which later became the Dominion Land Survey system (**627**). Since these townships were not on the same orientation as the townships progressing northwards from Lake Ontario, the survey was later cancelled. The general progress of township surveys in the Huron-Ottawa area was closely related to the plans for colonization roads, and the sequence of surveys is clearly documented on the annual editions of the map of the Huron and Ottawa territory (**643**). The maps of the north shores south of Lakes Huron and Superior (**885–6**) show the new townships being laid out in the north from 1858 on.

Military Maps

The first group of military maps per se are those for the War of 1812, and maps pertaining to the war are arranged by year and month so that its progress can be seen. Battle plans and maps showing the movement of troops accompanied reports to headquarters. These maps are from both British and American sources, which provide different points of view, and there are interesting sequences for the battle at Lundy's Lane (or Bridgewater) (**699–702**), for the seige of Fort Erie (**703–11**), and for the Battle of the Thames or Moraviantown (**935–9**). Maps were often later made of battles to accompany memoirs. There are examples of American reconnaissance maps that are extremely inaccurate such as the two sketches marked 'incorrect' for Kingston (**1507**). There are also examples of maps that were probably captured during the war, for instance Joseph Bouchette's important map of Lake Ontario made in ca 1799 and now found in the U.S. National Archives (**28**).

There are also a few interesting maps of the Rebellion of 1837–8, including several printed plans of Navy Island produced after William Lyon Mackenzie had fled there (**769, 777**). The maps relating to the Fenian raids in 1866 are also printed, and most are from published accounts of the battles (**832–4, 837**).

Road Maps

Much of the most important mapping in the bibliography relates to the building of roads. One of the earliest maps to show a survey for a road is the 1790 plan by Jesse Pennoyer for the road from Cornwall to Kingston along the St Lawrence River (**424**); unfortunately it is partly missing. There are also early maps for Yonge Street (**327**) as planned by Governor Simcoe to open connections from York to his defensive post at Penetanguishene, and plans for Dundas Street from the Thames to the Trent River (**913, 326, 329**). Road building was interrupted by the War of 1812, but after the war maps show roads to the new military settlements around the Rideau River (**475**), and several plans signed by Thomas Talbot himself show the building of the Talbot Road from the Long Point area to the Detroit River (**925, 929–30**).

In the later period there are two main road-building initiatives. The first was toll roads built by the Board of Works in the 1840s. Its surveys include maps for roads in most of the settled parts of the province, and a few compilations show the general progress (**133, 144**). In this decade by far the largest number of roads were built in the southwest and there are maps for parts of the Brantford and London road (**969**), the London and Port Stanley Road (**963**), and the roads from London to Port Sarnia, Chatham, and Amherstburg (**966, 967–8**). Further north the Garafraxa or Owen Sound road was laid out beginning in 1837 (**1040**) and was followed by the Toronto-Sydenham (**1046, 1065**) and Durham roads. In the Huron-Ottawa region, colonization roads and township surveys accompanied the move onto the Shield. Maps of most of the major roads, such as the Opeongo Road (**603**), the Bobcaygeon Road (**623**), and the Hastings Road (**596**), are all found here. Throughout the province the series of postal maps from 1832 to 1847 (**87**) are important not just for post offices and postal routes but also as indicators of roads in use.

Canals and Navigation

Plans for canals are numerous and the nineteenth-century enthusiasm for this form of transport is reflected in the large number of maps for canals that were never built (**396, 497, 960**). Almost immediately after the War of 1812 the first plans were produced for improving navigation along the Grand River (**726**) and for building a canal around Niagara Falls (**717**). James Grant Chewett published an important map of the Welland Canal in 1823, showing the route for the canal as it was first proposed in 1818 (**730**). The extensive mapping for the Rideau Canal under the direction of Colonel John By includes the several large sets of surveys between 1827 and 1831 (**492–519**) which show the changing plans for the route and for locks and dams at various points. In the 1830s there are some interesting printed plans documenting the need for improvement of navigation in the Kawartha Lakes area (**352, 355**), and a few maps show the early detailed plans by N.H. Baird for the building of the Trent Canal (**358, 366**). General plans for improving navigation throughout the province accompanied Lieutenant-Colonel George Phillpotts' report of 1840 (**124**), and problems of navigation and harbours are dealt with in the maps of the Naval and Military Commission of 1845–6 (**149**) and in the many individual harbour plans from surveys by the Board of Works that are found in Part III.

Printed Maps

General Maps

Based on the earlier reconnaissance surveys, the first major printed map of the province, produced by D.W. Smith, the first surveyor general of Upper Canada in 1800 (**30**), gave a reasonable shape to the emerging province. It was published by William Faden, but was soon taken over by James Wyld, the elder, and went through thirteen editions or states before Confederation. This was soon followed by William Chewett's larger-scale map published by Faden in 1813 (**43**). It too was eventually taken over by James Wyld and went through six editions, many of them found in only one extant copy, but it appears to have ceased publication in the late 1830s. During the War of 1812 and later, several small maps of the province began to appear based on one or other of these early maps.

Commercial map makers relied on a variety of sources to produce new maps and, unless an author of a map did original surveys or compilations from original source materials, many maps were based on earlier printed maps of the area. In addition, the author often had nothing to do with later editions, and the publisher had to find source material for revisions. D.W. Smith, for instance, appears not to have had anything to do with the revisions of his map, and many of the later editions and states were poorly revised or not updated at all. William Chewett, on the other hand, probably contributed revision material for his own map as new information appeared regularly.

Undoubtedly one of the most important maps to be published in the first half of the century – because of its accuracy and for its impact on other map makers – was the Canada Company map of 1825–6 (**69**). The first state of 1825 was unfinished, probably because the company was delayed in receiving its charter, and the 1826 state, the finished map, adds information from the hydrographic charting of the Lake Huron coast by Henry Bayfield to produce the most accurate map of the province until the late 1850s (Olsen, p 214). The plan went through several revisions to about 1835, with the full detail of the Huron Tract added in the fifth state. Many less important map publishers copied from these major maps (particularly to produce maps for books), sometimes from out-of-date editions.

In the 1840s British publishers, such as Edinburgh publisher W. & A.K. Johnston, and James Wyld, the younger, of London, continued to produce major maps. U.S. publishers Henry Tanner, Samuel A. Mitchell, and J.H. Colton produced atlases that included maps of Upper Canada, and in Canada local engineers, surveyors, and publishers were beginning to prepare more maps for publication. Many of the local maps were still being printed in Britain, or as in Bouchette's map of 1846 (**152**), in the United States; more modest maps, such as the maps for W.H. Smith's *Canadian Gazetteer* of 1846 (**156**), were printed locally by Scobie and Balfour and others. By the 1850s growing numbers of local maps, particularly county maps and town plans, were being produced and printed by Scobie, his successor Thomas Maclear, and John Ellis in Toronto and others in Hamilton, London, and Montreal.

Finally, in the 1850s several important maps were produced by government officials or local publishers and printers. In 1857 a leading civil engineer, Thomas Keefer, prepared a fairly large map of the province for the *Canadian Directory* (**235**). In the next year Barr & Corss in conjunction with the postmaster general brought out a map showing post offices and mail routes (**245**) which was revised and reissued by Maclear in 1860. The first official map produced by the Crown Lands Department was that compiled by Thomas Devine in 1859 (**253**), which covered the area from Red River to the Gulf of St Lawrence. It showed railways, roads, and colonization roads and included various tables. Many copies were hand coloured to emphasize free grant townships and colonization roads. The map went through four other states before Confederation, two of which were reduced versions produced as lithographic transfers of the main map. The map was the first to improve on the Canada Company map (Olsen, p 214).

Two commercial publishers (the Tremaines and Tackabury) produced maps for Upper Canada at a much larger scale than the Devine map in 1862 (**280, 282**). Both were similar, and the maps are of great importance for their detail and currency.

Printed Topical Maps

Printed maps showing specific subjects first began to appear in the 1830s and 1840s. Maps were produced as early as 1836 for railways (**107, 110**), and the first railway prospectus maps appear to have been issued about 1845 (**143, 146**). However, the main period for the publication of railway maps occurred in the 1850s and 1860s. Plans were included in books giving advice to emigrants particularly during the 1830s. These include an interesting map printed by Samuel Tazewell in 1833 of the Simcoe County area with notes on costs of transportation and routes to the area (**353**). A map of missions produced by the Society for the Propagation of the Gospel in Foreign Parts in 1821 (**60**) was probably the first map to show the development of churches in Upper Canada. Others were published in books (**119, 127**), and an important map of the Presbyterian congregations was published in 1846 (**151**).

The Geological Survey of Canada was established in 1845 and it produced much of the geological mapping. Its work began in topographic mapping of the lakes and rivers in the Huron-Ottawa region (**622**) and along the north shore of Lake Huron (**881**) in an effort to produce accurate base maps for its geological surveys. The first geological maps were produced in these areas as sheets to accompany reports of progress. It is also interesting to note how quickly the Geological Survey staff were able to produce general geological compilations of all of Canada – at first a small one for the Universal Exhibition of 1855 (**204**), then a larger coloured lithograph map of 1865 (**296**), and finally the magnificent map of eastern Canada (1" to 25 miles) in 8 sections completed in 1866 but not printed until 1869. In the 1860s oil was discovered in Lambton County and approximately fifteen commercially published maps of the 'oil regions in Canada West' have been found (**999–1016**).

A school wall map of Canada appeared in 1855 (**211**), produced first by W. & A.K. Johnston in Edinburgh but later taken over by W.C. Chewett and issued in a thoroughly revised edition in 1862. Others noted as commissioned by the Education Department (see **211(2)**) may not have been produced as no copies have been found. In addition there is a map showing a proposal for setting up meteorological stations in schools (**212**).

County and District Maps

Undoubtedly the most important printed maps found in the regional section are the printed county or district maps which made their first appearance in the 1830s. The maps show each area at a particular time and document the state of township surveys, roads, railways, towns, and specific types of buildings as indicators of business and cultural development.

The first real surge in publication of district maps came in the 1840s. These were usually prepared by local surveyors and at first were printed in the United States (**371**). However beginning in 1846 Scobie and Balfour of Toronto printed and published several plans in conjunction with local surveyors. In the 1850s the maps of counties added railways and sometimes views and insets of towns. In the late 1850s and early 1860s the county landownership maps were published of the eastern areas by H.F. Walling and of the central and western counties by the Tremaines. These maps record the names of landowners for the various lots and provide detailed cultural information.

The many other types of printed maps include a significant number of tourist maps produced for Niagara Falls mainly from the 1830s on.

Mapping of Towns

The earliest town plan listed is that for Kingston in 1784 (**1498**). It shows a small town being laid out near the ruins of Fort Frontenac. Later plans in the 1780s show some attempt to lay out towns in a formal grid of lots with symmetrically placed reserves for the crown, for courthouses, jails, church, school, and markets. Soon the more formal planning concepts gave way to the reality of the wilderness, and most of these places adopted a modest rectangle of streets often devoid of any public reserves.

Most of the early towns were laid out by the government, but a few were developed privately. Brockville was developed about 1811 by William Buell around an off-centre courthouse square (**1202**) and Williamstown is shown in 1813 as earlier laid out by Sir John Johnson (**2175**). Extant maps show the gradual development of some of the early towns. Amherstburg, Kingston, Toronto, and Hamilton all have a reasonable number of plans from their first few decades.

A few important towns, such as Hamilton, Belleville, and Perth, were laid out immediately after the War of 1812. Others were probably being established in a small way at that time, but a townsite may not have been surveyed at this date. The second spurt of town building began in the mid-1820s and the 1830s to accompany the growth in population. Bytown, London, Peterborough, Guelph, and Goderich were all laid out in the 1820s while Barrie, Brantford, and Cobourg were developing in the 1830s. A model town plan was developed by government and first used for Adelaide in 1833. It was later used for Corunna, Errol, and Lindsay. The plan provided for a simple grid of streets around a central square, and the Corunna plan shows a failed attempt to introduce a more interesting diagonal pattern into the plan.

In the first decades of Upper Canada, towns emerged along the shorelines of Lakes Ontario and Erie and major river systems such as the Thames River. But by the 1820s, paralleling the opening of new townships, the thrust of town development began to move west and northwest of Toronto, and only very slowly north of the Lake Ontario shoreline and the St Lawrence River in the east.

This westward movement of town building is particularly noticeable during the boom of the 1850s. Landowners and speculators were developing new towns, subdividing lots in older towns, and often adding on town lots to increase the size of a town. The maps that resulted are called subdivision plans, and they generally show only part of a town. Most of these subdivision plans are in Appendix B, although all printed plans are also listed in the cities and towns section. Railway towns, such as Collingwood and Strathroy, and all the towns in Bruce County were laid out in this period, while places such as Owen Sound, Windsor, and Sarnia and many of the smaller villages only really developed in this decade. Of course, not all of the new subdivisions or new towns 'took' and not all of them survived, and there are often resubdivisions listed in Appendix B. Economic depression in 1857 ended much of this land speculation and there are fewer subdivision plans after that date.

The patterns of information shown for towns depend on who was making the maps. The first layout and survey by land surveyors under instructions from the Crown Lands Department shows the street and lot pattern and any reserved blocks for court-house, market, school, and mill reserves. Later plans by these civilian authorities showed changes in these patterns and often included names of patentees or notes on the status of lots granted; physical features like rivers, marshy lands, and cliffs were also noted but few buildings are shown. General plans of towns prepared by military personnel are often more detailed, showing relief, physical features, streets that have been opened, and all buildings in existence, but not lot lines. Thus manuscript landmark maps show Toronto in 1818, London in 1839, Ottawa in 1826–7, Niagara in 1817 and 1845, and Hamilton in 1842. Later, engineers and commercial publishers took over the function of the preparation of topographical plans for towns and in the 1850s there are important maps for several towns showing every building and sometimes vegation and relief. Maps that show all buildings in the town have been indexed under the heading 'towns: built-up area.'

Harbour development plans of the 1840s are documented in plans for most of the ports along Lakes Erie and Ontario. In the same way plans show canal building in some towns, such as the Welland Canal in St Catharines and Port Colborne, the construction of the Rideau Canal in Ottawa, the St Lawrence canals in Cardinal, Morrisburg, and Iroquois.

In the 1850s and 1860s the mapping of towns is dominated by subdivision plans for parts of towns and for cities such as Toronto and to a lesser extent London and Hamilton. The printed plans show the part of the town which is being subdivided and advertised for sale; some of these include cultural details such as prominent buildings, notes on the advantages of the location, views, or small location maps.

The mapping of the major cities has been described in some detail in *Ontario's History in Maps;* however, there are other useful aspects of the maps of these cities to note. Not surprisingly, there are enormous numbers of military plans for Kingston, and some of the early general plans are crucial for demonstrating the development of the town. However, in the later period there are many fewer subdivision plans for Kingston than for other cities. Ottawa grew up as a construction camp for the building of the Rideau Canal, and maps show the Lower and Upper Towns and the canal developing together, while later plans show land for the parliament buildings and a residence for the governor general.

Toronto has by far the largest number of plans. The early ones include the phase of the large formal town grid, followed by the planting of a tiny town without any reserves and the growth of this town westward along the shore. Like other towns there are few subdivision plans before 1850. The enormous number of subdivision plans in the 1850s (over 230), many of which are printed and listed in Part III, document the development of the city north along Yonge Street and to the east, as do the major general maps of 1842 (**2077**), 1851 (**2090**), and the great Boulton 'atlas' of 1858 (**2133**). The latter shows that extensive areas of the city in the northwest were laid out but not occupied at that time. Maps of Toronto also include early plans for the university, plans for the esplanade, the beginnings of railways along the waterfront, and the nucleus of park lands.

Fewer plans exist for London and Hamilton than for Ottawa and Kingston, although there are many more subdivision plans for the former two. The early plans of London are interesting because of the uncertainty displayed by officials beginning in the 1790s about where to place the actual site; finally in 1826 the decision was made to site the town east of the forks of the Thames River. Hamilton was laid out privately by George Hamilton, and several early plans recently found show the first streets and squares of the town developing from a site at the foot of the mountain (**1419, 1422**). Besides large numbers of later subdivision plans there is an interesting relief map of the city, showing proposals for water supply in 1856, which emphasizes the dominance of the Niagara escarpment (**1439**).

Maps of smaller towns show a wide variety of themes. The plans for Brantford, laid out after the Indian surrender of land in 1830, show the impediment to town development caused by irregular tracts running across the survey grid. The plans for Barrie show the development of the town in several separate areas over time, beginning with the government plot of Kempenfeldt surveyed in 1812, a second town site on another government plot at the foot of the Penetanguishene Road, and the gradual joining up of these two areas. In the same way, the maps for Windsor show the original reserve and survey for the town of Sandwich, laid out in 1797, and the development of the town of Windsor proper from the long narrow farm lots further up-river over three decades later. The two parts of the town did not join up until well after Confederation.

It is not possible here to discuss all the themes found on the maps nor to do justice to the work of early map-makers who have left this wealth of information to us. However, these brief comments may serve to guide users to maps that will meet their particular needs.

Description of the Record

Each numbered entry gives in sequence: the date of the plan; the bibliographical statement giving details of title, authorship, publishing; physical description; additional information; and present location (as the samples below indicate).

Sample 1 (manuscript map)

1→ **170** *[1850]* ←2

3→ Map of the Principal Communications in Canada West Compiled from the most authentick sources, actual Surveys, District maps, etc. etc. by Major Baron de Rottenburg Asst. Quarter Mr. Genl.

4→ Col ms in 12 sheets 372 x 588 cm 1" to 2 miles Watermark: 'JAMES WHATMAN TURKEY MILL KENT 1831'

5→ Endorsements (on title sheet): 'Quartermaster General 2932 Dec 30 1868'; stamp on sheet 12 'Dept of Militia and Defence Survey Division'

6→ The most detailed topographic map of the province to date; macadamized, planked, common co, and principal travelled roads all distinguished; distances and notes on condition of roads given; relief and swampy land are shown; cleared land is shown in London Twp, in part of the Niagara Peninsula, and in the eastern part of the province; gives numbers of men and horses that can be billetted in each place; the list of 'authorities consulted' includes printed and ms maps from 1836 to about 1848; the map is dated 1850 from a note that a road was opened in the summer of 1849 and the fact that Rottenburg was promoted to Lt Col in Nov 1850; however, much of the area may have been surveyed by 1848 as a letter of 8 Apr 1862 to REO Kingston refers to a 'Military Sketch of part of the Districts of Gore and Niagara by Major de Rottenburg AQMG 12th May 1848' (not found) that may be a sketch for it (OOA RG 8 I/1566 p 120); the map is not up to date for twps and roads are poorly shown in areas for which source maps and reports not listed; (Holmden 3826; *OHIM* 6.4; Olsen 106 and pp 166–75).

7→ OOAMA (NMC 12437)

Sample 2 (printed map)

1→ **235** *[1857]* ←2

3→ MAP / OF THE / PROVINCE OF CANADA / FROM / Lake Superior to the Gulf of St. Lawrence / CORRECTED FROM INFORMATION OBTAINED BY THE / GEOLOGICAL SURVEY UNDER THE DIRECTION OF / SIR W.E. LOGAN / AND / PREPARED FOR THE CANADA DIRECTORY / Thos. C. Keefer C.E. MONTREAL / ROBERT BARLOW / Draughtsman. / Geo. Matthews Litho. Montreal.

4→ Print (lith) sometimes hand col 57 x 86 cm 1" to 25 miles

6→ Issued separately and in *The Canada Directory for 1857–58* (Montreal: John Lovell 1857), at end of vol 2 (OOA), and in F.X. Garneau, *History of Canada* 2nd ed rev (Montreal: Printed and published by John Lovell 1862), 1:frontis (*Bib Can* 2459, Dionne 994); shows railways completed, in progress, and projected; twps north to line Draper, Macaulay, Bexley to Anstruther, Wollastonnorth to Airy, Murchison, Bangor to Brudenell, Algona to Rolph; colonization roads; a printed flyer entitled 'References to Map' found at beginning of vol I of *The Canada Directory* lists sources: Bayfield's charts, surveys of rivers in the Huron-Ottawa area by Sir W.E. Logan (1857) (**622**), and 'the remainder from Bouchette [see **152**] & other authorities'; also noted: 'The MAP ... may be had ... at ... Publisher Price 75c. mounted $1.50'; described as 'An entirely new map of Upper and Lower Canada ...' in a prospectus for *The Canada Directory for 1857–58* issued in Feb 1857 (*Bib Can* 8542); (Olsen 115).

7→ GBL (70615 (22)) OLU OMSA OOA OOAMA (NMC 24953) OTAR OTMCL OTUTF USDLC

---

1 *Entry Number*
The consecutive number assigned to each map in the bibliography.

2 *Date*
The date is the date of production or of publication of the map. If a manuscript map is known to be a later copy, the original date is followed by the date of copying in parentheses, 1820 (1842). If a map was made over a period of time, the beginning and ending date are given separated by a dash, 1820–3. Dates known from another source but not on the map are given in square brackets, [1820]; if the date is still uncertain a question mark is added, [1820?].

3 *Bibliographical Statement*
For all maps the title, statement of authorship, and publishing or preparation information is transcribed for each item exactly as found on the map in terms of linear order and punctuation. For manuscript maps with many author signatures, the signatures and statements associated with them are transcribed in order of date where present. For printed maps, upper and lower case letters and line endings are indicated but not lettering style. A double slash precedes parts of the author or imprint statements found in areas of the map other than the title block or cartouche, such as below the lower margin. A printed map with significant manuscript additions is entered with a shortened title if an unannotated version of the printed map is also listed. Endorsed titles for manuscript maps are given in supplied quotation marks.

4 *Physical Description*
The physical description includes format and technique, size, scale, watermark, and endorsements.
Format and technique Maps are indicated as Ms (manuscript) or Print (printed) followed by the printing technique used: Print (lith). In a few cases where the printing method cannot be determined, the term 'Print' alone is used. Colour, if present, is indicated in the following ways: 'Col lith,' a map printed in colours; 'Col ms,' a manuscript map in colour; 'Print (lith), hand col,' a printed map coloured by hand. If the map is produced on a substance other than paper (e.g., linen), has parts missing, or is printed but with manuscript additions (ms adds) these facts are cited.
Size The map is measured in centimetres to the nearest whole centimetre (oriented as it is read) from top to bottom and then from side to side. Manuscript maps are measured to the edge of written information. (If the mapped information is distributed very unevenly over the map the measurement is made to the edge of the paper.) On printed maps the measurement is made to the outer edge of printing.
Scale The scale is stated as given on the map in statement form or as measured from a bar scale in the units indicated: statute miles, chains, or feet. If it is not shown on the map, the term 'scale not given' is used, save in the case of a few general maps where it has been computed from latitude or by comparison with another map. Square brackets indicate the use of such computations.
Watermark Watermarks that are names and dates are transcribed from the map as found and shown between quotation marks. Most watermarks have been verified in the Gravell and Miller catalogues and Churchill (see references), and inferred letters and names are shown in brackets. Watermarks have been found on many early printed maps and manuscript maps from all periods but unfortunately many are obscured by map-backing materials and are not fully legible.

5 *Endorsements*
All relevant endorsements, numbers, or stamps on the map are transcribed and appear in supplied quotation marks after the term 'Endorsements'; manuscript marks are cited first and set off from the following stamps by a semicolon. Abbreviations used with endorsements are keyed in the abbreviations list.

6 *Annotation*
Elements in the annotation include, in order: statement of provenance in the few cases where it is known and not clear from the location and other references; a list of insets, or views, or additional data such as lists, tables, charts; for printed maps found in books or atlases, a reference to the work(s), and for manuscript maps removed from an archival record group, a reference to the original location where known; for manuscript maps the date and description of

survey instructions (SI) and field notebook (FN) references and dates are given at the beginning of notes. A brief description of the content of the map, extent of area if necessary, and annotations on the map is followed by bibliographical comments on similar maps, variations in title, dating problems, historical context and sources of further information, and in parentheses at the end of notes, reference numbers for the map in other bibliographies and catalogues.

7 *Location*

The last item in the entry gives the present location of a manuscript map or the locations of a printed map. Official location symbols as established by the National Library are used and keyed on page xxxi. Unique call numbers are given for manuscript maps and for printed maps where known. For maps in the National Archives of Canada and Ontario Ministry of Natural Resources, numbers assigned in microfilming are used rather than call numbers (NMC 16431; SR 4562). All locations in the major repositories are given for printed maps, but only the location of the item seen is given for maps in books and atlases.

Appendices and Indexes

Appendix A Township Plans

	Date of Instructions	Date of Map	Surveyor and Signature	Endorsements and Notes	Location
	CAYUGA				
A389	15.11.1830	6.1.1831	Lewis Burwell	'Q51' '1112'; pt; Indian surrender, marshes, mill seat, Delaware Council House and mission school, a few names; FN 107	OTNR (SR 748)

The plans are organized alphabetically by name of township, chronologically within that grouping, and numbered (**A1**). The information for each map includes township name, date of original survey instructions where known, date of plan (dates in square brackets are inferred), names of surveyors and any other authorizing signatures, notes, and location. The form of notes is as follows: endorsements, original township number or range of numbers, part of townships shown (N pt or concession no), other features included (settlements, roads, marshes), scale if other than 40 chains to 1 inch, the field notebook number, for example, 'FN107' or 'FN6–127' for material in 'Written volumes' (for further information on the field notebooks see Gentilcore and Donkin especially p 25–7) (the location OTAR is shown for field notebooks transferred from OTNR and now in OTAR RG 1 CB-1); present location and Survey Records (SR) micro numbers, if present.

The names of surveyors are as taken from the map and, in a few cases, special notes on their function are given in notes. The name of the actual or probable surveyor is on the first line; names on the next lines are those of officials authorizing or copying the plan and this function is indicated by 'Copy' or 'dr' or the abbreviation of their position 'AC/CL' (assistant commissioner, Crown Lands). Although many township plans are undated, particularly the office or working copies, every attempt has been made to determine the original survey and the copies relating to it and to place them in the correct date sequence. It should be noted, however, that since many plans were working copies for offical purposes they had later additions made through the years (as shown in the notes). Precise dating is therefore virtually impossible in many cases.

Cross references for names of all townships and combined surveys of several townships can be traced through the Subject Index.

Appendix B Registered Subdivision Plans

	Date of survey	Date of regist.	Surveyor	Owner	Description and notes	Location
	BURLINGTON					
B380	17.6.54	21.7.54	Henry Winter	D. Torrance	'Wellington Square'; L Ontario north to Caroline St, Brant St to Martha St, schedule of owners; part of plan missing; 2ch	Halton 20 R.P.12

The registered subdivision plans of towns in Appendix B are arranged alphabetically by town name and then chronologically for each town. The entry consists of name of town, an item number prefixed by B, date of survey, date of registration, name of surveyor, name of owner of the land being subdivided, description of the exact location of the survey by lot and concession or extent of streets, other cultural detail shown, scale, name of registry office, and plan number.

Abbreviations such as 'E Hurontario St' are standard survey references to the survey fabric for different groups of lots and concessions in townships that would otherwise have the same numbers and are as found on official surveys today. Printed plans are listed in brief in this appendix and are fully described in Part III, Towns; the reference number indicates where they will be found. Railway and street names are as taken from the actual plan and have not been verified elsewhere. Some plans were never registered and were not given a registered plan number. These are designated (no R.P. #). The date of survey is as found in the title or in a certification statement by the surveyor and/or the owner of the property being subdivided. The date of registration is as taken from a certified statement signed by the registrar. In some cases these dates are not on the map but found on a list of plans in the registry office and are then placed in square brackets. Every effort was made to find the original plan but if only transcripts seem to have survived these are noted. When the term 'now known as' occurs concerning a street name, the information was taken from the plan itself.

Appendix C Nautical Charts

This appendix includes entries for the official nautical charting of the Great Lakes by both the British government and the U.S. government. Both manuscript and printed charts are included. The charts are organized in sets and within each set by region or date or chart number. The sets are as follows:

Great Britain

(1) Manuscript maps from the Report on the Surveys and Lakes of Canada (Report 82 from Owen to Croker), 1815 – arranged by region and original map number
(2) Manuscript maps from the Survey of the Great Lakes under Capt. W.F.W. Owen and Lt Henry Bayfield, 1816–25 – arranged by region and dates of survey
(3) Printed charts from the Survey of the Great Lakes 1828 – arranged by chart number and date of later states

United States

(1) Printed charts from the U.S. Survey of the Northern and Northwestern Lakes 1852 – arranged by date of publication

Further notes on the charts, related textual matter and dating problems are found with each set as appropriate.

Appendix D International Boundary Surveys

The appendix covers the official international boundary mapping for Upper Canada under the 6th and 7th articles of the Treaty of Ghent (1814) and the later Treaty of Washington (1842). The maps are arranged in groups according to the progress of the surveys and beginning with preliminary surveys in the south subarranged by date. These are followed by the official boundary maps for the south or atlases as found in the Public Record Office, Great Britain, and the U.S. National Archives, Washington. Similar groups then follow for the north. These sections are followed by a section listing copies of boundary maps and later maps, a few of which are printed. Again this latter group is arranged chronologically.

Appendix E Towns of Upper Canada Arranged by County

This appendix groups towns in the bibliography from Part III and Appendix B by county names according to pre-1974 boundaries. Since so many plans for towns were found, this appendix should facilitate the work of the researcher who is interested in seeing what towns in a particular county were mapped in the period.

Indexes

Three indexes are included.

The Name Index includes the names of all the people involved in the making of the map, namely, surveyors, draughtsmen, engravers, authors, publishers, printers, and authorizing such as military or civilian administrators. The reference given is by citation number rather than page.

The Subject Index covers general themes specifically indicated in the titles of maps, such as railways and individual railways, roads and names of specific roads, harbours, Indian lands and treaties. Names of places indexed include those no longer used and other names used at the time the map was made. To facilitate access, names of all towns are indexed to bring together for users both the maps of towns in the text and those from Appendix B. However, no attempt has been made to index all the data on the maps, a well-nigh impossible task. For example, names of people for whom land was subdivided have not been included.

The Title Index includes a short title of all printed maps and all atlases and books and printed reports that contain maps.

Location Symbols

France

FPA	Service historique de l'Armée, Paris–Vincennes
FPBN	Bibliothèque nationale, Département des cartes et plans

Great Britain

GBC	University Library, Cambridge
GBE	National Library of Scotland, Edinburgh
GBEr	Scottish Record Office, Edinburgh
GBEXr	Devon County Record Office, Exeter
GBL	British Library, London
GBLmm	National Maritime Museum, London
GBLpro	Public Record Office, London
GBLrg	Royal Geographic Society, London
GBO	Oxford University, Bodleian Library, Oxford
GBTAUh	Hydrographic Archives, Taunton

Canada

British Columbia

BVAU	University of British Columbia Library

Manitoba

MWHBC	Hudson's Bay Company Archives, Winnipeg
MWPA	Provincial Archives of Manitoba, Winnipeg

Nova Scotia

NSHP	Nova Scotia Public Archives, Halifax
NSWA	Acadia University, Wolfville

Ontario

OBBM	Brant County Historical Museum, Brantford
OBEH	Hastings County Historical Society, Belleville
OCHAK	Chatham-Kent Museum, Chatham
OFEC	Wellington County Museum, Fergus
OFF	Fenelon Falls Public Library, Fenelon Falls
OG	Guelph Public Library, Guelph
OGAL	Cambridge Public Library, Cambridge
OGM	Guelph Civic Museum, Guelph
OGOHC	Huron County Pioneer Museum, Goderich
OGU	University of Guelph, Guelph
OH	Hamilton Public Library, Hamilton
OHAN	Hanover Public Library, Hanover
OHMA	Archives and Special Collections Division, McMaster University, Hamilton, Ontario
OK	Kingston Public Library, Kingston
OKIT	Kitchener Public Library, Kitchener
OKITD	Doon Pioneer Village, Kitchener
OKQ	Queen's University, Kingston
OKQAR	Archives, Queen's University, Kingston
OL	London Public Library, London
OLI	Lindsay Public Library, Lindsay
OLU	University of Western Ontario, London
OMSA	Simcoe County Archives, Minesing
ONF	Niagara Falls Public Library, Niagara Falls
ONHI	Niagara Historical Society, Niagara-on-the-Lake
ONLAH	Lennox and Addington Historical Society, Napanee
ONLAM	Lennox & Addington Museum, Napanee
OOA	National Archives, Ottawa
OOAK	Oakville Public Library, Oakville
OOAKM	Oakville Museum, Oakville
OOAMA	Cartographic Archives and Architectural Drawings Division, National Archives, Ottawa
OORA	Orangeville Public Library, Orangeville
OORI	Orillia Public Library, Orillia
OOWM	County of Grey - Owen Sound Museum, Owen Sound
OPETC	Trent Canal Office, Peterborough
OPETCM	Peterborough Centennial Museum and Archives, Peterborough
OPETHS	Peterborough Historical Society, Peterborough
OPM	Perth Museum, Perth
OSINH	Norfolk Historical Society, Simcoe
OSTCB	Brock University, St Catharines
OSTPA	Stratford-Perth Archives Board, Stratford
OTAR	Archives of Ontario, Toronto
OTAR(P)	Archives of Ontario, Land Patents, Toronto
OTC	University of Toronto, Faculty of Education, Toronto
OTCR	Ontario, Ministry of Culture and Recreation, Toronto
OTCTAR	City of Toronto, Division of Records and Archives, Toronto

OTHB	Toronto Historical Board, Toronto
OTL	Legislative Library of Ontario, Toronto
OTMCL	Metropolitan Toronto Reference Library, Toronto
OTNR	Ontario Ministry of Natural Resources, Survey Records Branch, Toronto
OTRMC	Royal Ontario Museum, Canadiana Department, Toronto
OTUAR	University of Toronto Archives
OTUMA	University of Toronto, Map Library, Toronto
OTUTF	University of Toronto, Thomas Fisher Rare Book Library, Toronto
OWHM	Hiram Walker Historical Museum, Windsor

Quebec

QMBN	Bibliothèque nationale de Québec, Montréal
QMM(L)	McGill University, McLennan Library, Lande Collection, Montreal
QMMRB	McGill University, Department of Rare Books and Special Collections, Montreal
QMMMCM	McCord Museum, McGill University, Montreal, Quebec
QQA	Archives nationales du Québec, Québec
QQERT	Ministère de l'énergie et des ressources du Québec, Terres et forêts, Québec
QQS	Séminaire de Québec, Québec

United States of America

USCSmH	Henry E. Huntington Library, San Marino, California
USDLC	Library of Congress, Washington, District of Columbia
USDNA	National Archives, National Archives and Records Service, Washington, District of Columbia
USICHi	Chicago Historical Society, Chicago, Illinois
USKyLoF	Filson Club, Louisville, Kentucky
USMA	Amherst College, Amherst, Massachusetts
USMH	Harvard University, Cambridge, Massachusetts
USMiD	Detroit Public Library, Detroit, Michigan
USMiMtpT	Central Michigan University, Mount Pleasant, Michigan
USMiU	University of Michigan Library, Ann Arbor, Michigan
USMiU-C	University of Michigan, William L. Clements Library, Ann Arbor, Michigan
USMWA	American Antiquarian Society, Worcester, Massachusetts
USN	New York State Library, Albany, New York
USNB	Buffalo and Erie Historical Society, Buffalo, New York
USNBuHi	Buffalo and Erie County Historical Society, Buffalo, New York
USNIC	Cornell University, Ithaca, New York
USNN	New York Public Library, New York, New York
USPBMW	Moravian College, Bethlehem, Pennsylvania
USPP	Free Library of Philadelphia, Philadelphia, Pennsylvania

Ontario, Ministry of Consumer and Commercial Relations, Registry Offices

Registry Office	*Location*
Brant 2	Brantford
Bruce 3	Walkerton
Dufferin 7	Orangeville
Dundas 8	Morrisburg
Durham 40	Oshawa
Elgin 11	St Thomas
Essex 12	Windsor
Frontenac 13	Kingston
Glengarry 14	Alexandria
Grenville 15	Prescott
Grey 16	Owen Sound
Grey 17	Durham
Haldimand 18	Cayuga
Halton 20	Milton
Hastings 21	Belleville
Huron 22	Goderich
Kent 24	Chatham
Lambton 25	Sarnia

Registry Office	*Branch*
Lanark 26	Almonte
Lanark 27	Perth
Leeds 28	Brockville
Lennox 29	Napanee
Middlesex 33	London
Middlesex 34	Glencoe
Newcastle 10	Bowmanville
Niagara 30	St Catharines
Niagara 59	Welland
Norfolk 37	Simcoe
Northumberland 38	Colborne
Northumberland 39	Cobourg
Ottawa-Carleton 5	Ottawa
Oxford 41	Woodstock
Peel 43	Brampton
Perth 44	Stratford
Peterborough 45	Peterborough
Port Hope 9	Port Hope

Registry Office	*Branch*
Prescott 46	L'Orignal
Prince Edward 47	Picton
Renfrew 49	Pembroke
Russell 50	Russell
Simcoe 51	Barrie
Stormont 52	Cornwall
Toronto 63	Toronto
Toronto 64	Toronto
Toronto 66	Toronto
Victoria 57	Lindsay
Waterloo 58	Kitchener
Waterloo 67	Cambridge
Wellington 60	Arthur
Wellington 61	Guelph
Wentworth 62	Hamilton
York Region 65	Newmarket

Abbreviations

AC	assistant commissioner
AC/CL	assistant commissioner of crown lands
adds	additions
App	appendix
approx	approximately
appt	appointed
ASG	acting surveyor general
b.	born
B	brigadier
BF	broken front
bldgs	buildings
B↑O	Board of Ordnance
btwn	between
BW	Board of Works
c	copyright
ca	circa
c & c	crown and clergy
Capt	captain
C/CL	commissioner of crown lands
Cdr	commander
CE	civil engineer
C.E.	Canada East
cert	certified
CLD	Crown Land(s) Department
CLO	Crown Lands Office
Co.	company
co(s)	county(ies)
Col	colonel
col ms	coloured manuscript
con(s)	concession(s)
CREO(C)	Commanding Royal Engineers' Office (Canada)
C.W.	Canada West
d.	died
DPS	deputy provincial surveyor
dr	drawn
DS	deputy surveyor
E	east
ea	each
ed(s)	edition(s), editor(s)
engrav	engraving, engraved, engraver
et al.	and others
etc	etcetera
exam	examined
f	folio
ff	following
fig(s)	figure(s)
FN	field notebook
frontis	frontispiece
Gen	general
geog	geographical
Gov	governor
govt	government
GSC	Geological Survey of Canada
GTR	Grand Trunk Railroad
GWR	Great Western Railroad
HMSPO	Her Majesty's State Paper Office
IASR	Indian Affairs Survey Records
IGF	inspector general of fortifications
Is	island
L	lake
L.C.	Lower Canada
lith	lithograph, lithographed, lithographer
LS	land surveyor
Lt	lieutenant
Lt Col	lieutenant colonel
Lt Gov	lieutenant governor
Maj	major
ms/mss	manuscript/manuscripts
ms adds	manuscript additions
N	north
n.g.	not given
no(s)	number(s)
oblit	obliterated
O.C.	order in council
opp	opposite
orig	original
p/pp	page/pages
PAC	Public Archives of Canada
PLS(s)	provincial land surveyor(s)
pt	part, partial
QMG(O)	Quarter Master General('s Office)
R	river
rd(s)	road(s)
rec'd	received
Regt(s)	regiment(s)
REO	Royal Engineers' Office
Rev	reverend
R.P.	registered plan
R.R.	railroad
ry(s)	railway(s)
S	south
S & D	surveyor & draughtsman
SG	surveyor general
sgd	signed
SGO	Surveyor General's Office
SI	survey instructions
SR	Survey Records
SS	senior surveyor
SS&D	senior surveyor & draughtsman
st(s)	street(s)
surv	surveyed
TE	topographical engineer
twp(s)	township(s)
U.C.	Upper Canada
vol(s)	volume(s)
W	west
WD	Western District

Bibliography

ARCHIVAL SOURCES

Canada

Acadia University, Wolfville, N.S. (NSWA)
William Inglis Morse Collection of the 8th Earl of Dalhousie Papers

Archives of Ontario, Toronto (OTAR)
MS 178 Municipal Records, Town of Niagara
MS 385 Toronto City Council Papers
MU 275 Blanchard, Harry D., Collection
MU 1052 Sir Sandford Fleming Collection
MU 1805–949 Mackenzie-Lindsay Papers
 A 9 Maps
MU 1532–7 Jarvis-Powell Papers
MU 2782–808 Simcoe, John Graves, Papers
 MS 83 Letterbook, 1792–3
 MS 517 Canadian Letterbooks
MU 2968–82 Thompson, David, Journals
MU 3279 Selkirk, Thomas Douglas, Earl of, Papers
MU 3514 Andrew Merrilees Collection
MU 5810 (MS 393) Baird, N.H., Papers
 A-6 Trent Canal
Canada Company Records
 B 2 Surveys and field notes
 TRHT Topographical Register of the Huron Tract
Horwood Collection
RG1 Records of the Ministry of Natural Resources
 A Offices of Surveyor General and Commissioner of Crown Lands
 I-1 Letters Received by the Surveyor-General, 1766–1913 (MS30, 626)
  Vol 1, pp 151–7, 'List of Maps Delivered to His Excellency Lieut Governor Simcoe from the Survr Genls Office Quebec ... 22 June 1793'
 I-6 Letters Received, Surveyor General and Commissioner, 1786–1905
 I-7 Subject Files, 1790–1890
 II Reports and Statements
  1: Vol 2, pp 942-87, D.W. Smith, 'Report upon Glebes & Commons ... 13th Jany 1802'
 B Financial Services Branch
 IV Survey Accounts
 C Lands Branch
 I-2 Orders-in-Council, 1793–1864
 III-1 Notices of Sales of Crown Lands
 CB Surveys Branch
  1 Survey diaries and field notes, originals and copies
  Instructions to Lands Surveyors (MS 31)
RG2 Dept. of Education Records
 C6C Chief Superintendent Incoming Correspondence
Map Section
 Canada Company Atlas
 Canada Company Maps
 Simcoe Map Collection
 Talbot Map Collection
 T.W. Nash, Plans of Kingston

City of Toronto Archives (OTCTAR)
John George Howard Collection
Department of Public Works Records

Hiram Walker Historical Museum (OWHM)
Hands Papers
Wilkinson Collection

McMaster University, Dept of Rare Books and Special Collections, Hamilton (OHMA)
Wentworth County Court House Map Collection

Metropolitan Toronto Library, Toronto (OTMCL)
William Allan Papers
E.W. Banting Map Collection
Denison Papers
John George Howard Papers
David William Smith Papers

National Archives of Canada, Ottawa (OOA, OOAMA)
MG 23 HII 6 Berczy Papers, German Company
MG 24 D2 Martin Peter Hayes Papers
MG 23 HI 1 McDonald-Stone Family Papers
MG 24 D 39 James McLaren Company Papers
MG 19 F1 Claus Family Papers
MG 21 B1-232 Haldimand Papers (transcripts)
MG 24 B1 Sandford Fleming Papers
MG 24 B31 Henry Chapman Collection
MG 24 I9 Hamnet Pinhey Hill Collection
MG 26 A Sir John Alexander Macdonald Papers
MG 29 C101 A.P. Sherwood Papers
MG 30 D 49 Joseph Burr Tyrrell Papers
RG 1 Executive Council: Quebec, Lower Canada, Upper Canada, Canada, 1764–1867
 E1 Minute-books (state matters)
 E3 Upper Canada: submissions to the Executive Council, state matters
 E15 Audit records
 L3 Land Petitions, Upper Canada and Canada, 1791–1867
 L4 Land Board Records, Upper Canada, 1764–1804
RG 5 Civil and provincial secretaries' offices: Upper Canada and Canada West
 A1 Upper Canada sundries

C1 Provincial secretary's numbered correspondence files
RG 7 Governor General's Office
G 12 Letter books of despatches to the Colonial Office
RG 8 British military and naval records
I C series (British military records)
II Ordnance Records
RG 11 Department of Public Works
A Board of Works records
1 Correspondence in subject files
2 Registers and indexes
3 Minutes, letter-books, and reports
vol 135 Surveyors instructions
4 Records of individual committees, commissions, and projects, 1827-60
B Department of Public Works, 1821–1967
1 Registry Records, 1826–1880
Registered Correspondence
Unnumbered Correspondence and Documents

Cartographic Archives and Architectural Drawings Division (OOAMA)
RG 8M British military and naval records: Maps
RG 10M Department of Indian Affairs: Maps
RG 11M Department of Public Works: Maps
RG 45M Geological Survey of Canada: Maps
85601/26 Collection of the 9th Earl of Dalhousie
A.E. MacDonald Collection
Kingston Planning Board Map Collection

Niagara Historical Society, Niagara-on-the-Lake (ONHI)
George Ball Papers

Ontario, Ministry of Natural Resources, Survey Records Branch, Toronto (OTNR)
Field Notebooks, originals and photocopies
Field Notes 'Written Books,' originals
Instructions to Land Surveyors, originals (mfm at OTAR MS 31)

Queen's University Archives, Kingston (OKQAR)
Cartwright Papers

Simcoe County Archives, Minesing (OMSA)
Clarke Papers

Trent Canal Office, Peterborough (OPETC)
Trent Canal Atlas and map collection

Great Britain

Admiralty, Hydrographic Archives, Taunton (GBTAUh)
Catalogues, accessions registers

British Library, London (GBL)
Add Mss 21661-892 Official correspondence and papers of Sir Frederick Haldimand, 1758-85
Add Ms 23618 Lt Col C. Hamilton Smith Collection
Add Ms 57707 Royal United Services Institution Collection

Devon County Record Office, Exeter (GBEXr)
John Graves Simcoe Collection

National Library of Scotland, Edinburgh (GBE)
46.10.2 Sir George Murray Papers

National Maritime Museum, Greenwich (GBLmm)
Grenville Map Collection

Public Record Office, London (GBLpro)
Admiralty
Adm 7 Accounting Department registers, returns, and certificates: Miscellanea, 1563–1871
Colonial Office
CO 5 America: Original Correspondence
CO 6 America, British North: Original Correspondence, 1816–68
CO 42 Canada: Original Correspondence, 1700–1922
CO 384 Emigration: Original Correspondence, 1817–96
CO 700 Maps and Plans: Maps, 17th to 19th century
Foreign Office
FO 5 General Correspondence (before 1906): America, United States of, Series II, 1793–1905
FO 925 Maps and Plans
Public Record Office, Private Papers
PRO 30/35 Carmichael Smyth Papers, 1805–37, 1860
Treasury
T 62 Miscellanea: Maps and Plans, Series I
War Office
WO 1 Correspondence: In-letters, 1732–1868
WO 44 Ordnance Office: In-letters, 1682–1873
WO 55 Ordnance Office: Miscellanea, 1568–1923
WO 78 Miscellanea: Maps and Plans, 1627–1946

Scottish Record Office, Edinburgh (GBEr)
GD45 Dalhousie muniments

United States

Filson Club, Louisville, Ky (USKyLoF)
Journal of Capt Robert B. McAfee

Michigan, University of, William L. Clements Library, Ann Arbor (USMiU-C)
John Graves Simcoe Papers
Clinton Papers

National Archives, Washington, D.C. (USDNA)
Cartographic Branch
R76 Records relating to International Boundaries
RG 77 Department of Defense, Department of the Army, Records of the Office of the Chief of Engineers
Civil Works Map File
Fortifications Map File

PRINTED SOURCES

Note: Abbreviations for frequently cited printed sources are included in this list and cross-referenced to the full entry.

Allodi, Mary. *Printmaking in Canada: The Earliest Views and Portraits/Les Débuts de l'estampe imprimée au Canada: vues et portraits*. Toronto: Royal Ontario Museum 1980

Allodi, Mary, and Rosemarie Tovell. *An Engraver's Pilgrimage*. Toronto: Royal Ontario Museum 1989

The American War of Independence, 1775–83: A Commemorative Exhibition Organized by the Map Library and the Department of Manuscripts of the British Library. London: The British Library 1975

Armstrong, Frederick Henry, ed. *Handbook of Upper Canadian Chronology and Territorial Legislation*. Rev. ed. Toronto: Dundurn Press 1985

Arthur, Eric. *Toronto, No Mean City*. 3rd ed, revised by Stephen A. Otto. Toronto: University of Toronto Press 1986

Association of Canadian Map Libraries. *Facsimile* [series]. No. 1– . Ottawa 1976–

Association of Ontario Land Surveyors. *Manual Relating to Surveys and Surveyors*. Willowdale, Ont. 1973

– *Report* [and] *Proceedings*. Vol 1– . 1885– . Various issues contain biographies of provincial land surveyors.

Bald, W. Clever, ed. *Patrick McNiff's Plan of the Settlements at Detroit, 1796*. Ann Arbor, Mich.: University of Michigan Press 1946

Belden, H., & Co. *Illustrated Atlas of the County of Bruce*. Toronto: H. Belden & Co. 1880; Port Elgin, Ont.: Ross Cumming 1970

– *Illustrated Historical Atlas of the Counties of Essex and Kent*. Toronto: H. Belden & Co. 1880–1; Port Elgin, Ont.: Ross Cumming 1973

– *Illustrated Atlas of the County of Simcoe*. Toronto: H. Belden & Co. 1881; Port Elgin, Ont.: Ross Cumming 1970

– *Illustrated Historical Atlas of the County of Huron, Ont*. Toronto: H. Belden & Co. 1879; Owen Sound, Ont.: Richardson, Bond & Wright 1972

Bib Can see *A Bibliography of Canadiana*

A Bibliography of Canadiana, Being Items in the Public Library of Toronto, Canada, Relating to the Early History and Development of Canada. Edited by Frances M. Staton and Marie Tremaine. Toronto: Toronto Public Library 1934. Two supplements. 1: Edited by Gertrude M. Boyle, assisted by Marjorie Colbeck. Toronto Public Library 1959; 2: Edited by Sandra Alston, assisted by Karen Evans. Vol 1, beginnings to 1800; vol 2, 1801–49; vol 3, 1850–67. Toronto: Metropolitan Toronto Library Board 1985–9 (Cited as *Bib Can*)

Bigger, Charles Albert. 'Catalogue of Maps and Plans of Date Prior to 1867 in Possession of Ontario Government at Toronto, ca. 1890.' 3 vols. Typescript. Copy at OTNR

Bishop, Olga. *Publications of the Government of the Province of Canada, 1841–1867*. Ottawa: National Library of Canada 1963

– *Publications of the Province of Upper Canada and of Great Britain Relating to Upper Canada, 1791–1840*. Toronto: Ontario Ministry of Citizenship and Culture 1984

Bladen, M.L. 'Construction of Railways in Canada to the Year 1885.' In *Contributions to Canadian Economics* V (1932):43–55

Bloomfield, Elizabeth, et al., comps. *Inventory of Primary and Archival Sources: Guelph and Wellington County to 1940*. Guelph: Guelph Regional Project, University of Guelph 1989

British Museum. *Catalogue of Printed Maps, Charts and Plans*. 15 vols. London 1967. Ten-year supplement, 1965–74. London 1978

– *Catalogue of the Manuscript Maps, Charts and Plans and of the Topographical Drawings in the British Museum*. 3 vols. London 1844–61

Brown, Ron. *Ghost Towns of Ontario*. Vol I. Langley, B.C.: Stagecoach Publishing Co. 1978. Vol 2: *Northern Ontario and Cottage Country*. Toronto: Cannonbooks 1983

Brun, Christian, comp. *Guide to the Manuscript Maps in the William L. Clements Library*. Ann Arbor, Mich.: University of Michigan Press 1959

Buisseret, David, ed. *From Sea Charts to Satellite Images: Interpreting North American History through Maps*. Chicago: University of Chicago Press 1990

Cameron, Wendy, and Mary McDougall Maude. 'Essays and Research Papers on the History of the Trent-Severn Waterway.' 2 vols. Research study prepared for Parks Canada, 1987–8

Campbell, Marjorie Freeman. *A Mountain and a City: The Story of Hamilton*. Toronto: McClelland and Stewart 1966

Canada Book Auctions. [Catalogue]: auction sale 135, November 18, 1981. Toronto: Canada Book Auctions 1981

Canada, Public Archives. *Annual Reports*. Ottawa 1872–

Canada (Province), Department of Crown Lands. *Report*. Ottawa 1857–67

– Legislative Assembly. *Appendix to the ... Journals of the Legislative Assembly of the Province of Canada, 1841–59* (Cited as JLA)

– Legislative Council. *Journals [and Appendix] of the Legislative Council of the Province of Canada, 1841–67*. (cited as JLC)

– Parliament. *Sessional Papers*. 1860–1866 (Cited as SP)

Canadian Institute for Historical Microreproductions. *Canada, the Printed Record: A Bibliographic Register with Indexes to the Microfiche Series*. [Ottawa 1981–8] (Microfiches are cited as CIHM.)

Carter, Floreen. *Place Names of Ontario*. 2 vols. London: Phelps Publishing 1985

Casey, Magdalen, comp. *Catalogue of Pamphlets in the*

Public Archives of Canada, with Index. I:1493–1877.
Catalogue of the National Map Collection, Public Archives of Canada, Ottawa, Ontario. 16 vols. Boston: G.K. Hall 1976 (Cited as *NMC Cat*)
Catalogue of the Public Archives Library. 10: *Chronological List of Pamphlets, 1493–1876.* Boston: G.K. Hall 1979
The Celebrated Collection of Americana, Formed by the Late Thomas Winthrop Streeter, Morristown, New Jersey. 8 vols. New York: Parke Bernet Galleries 1966–70 (Cited as *Streeter*)
Churchill, W.A. *Watermarks in Paper.* Amsterdam: Menno Hertzberger & Co. 1935
CIHM *see* Canadian Institute for Historical Microreproductions
Classen, H. George. *Thrust and Counterthrust: The Genesis of the Canada-United States Boundary.* Toronto: Longmans 1965
Côté, Joseph Olivier, and N.O. Côté. *Political Appointments and Elections in the Province of Canada from 1841 to 1865 ... Appendix from 1st Jan 1866 to 30th June 1867.* 2nd ed enlarged. Ottawa 1918
Cruikshank, Ernest A. *The Settlement of the United Empire Loyalists on the Upper St Lawrence and Bay of Quinte in 1784.* Toronto: Ontario Historical Society 1934
Currier & Ives: A Catalogue Raisonné ... 1834–1907. Introduction by Bernard F. Reilly, Jr. Detroit: Gale Research Co. 1983
David, Andrew, and Tony Campbell. 'Bibliographical Notes on Nineteenth-Century British Admiralty Charts.' In *The Map Collector* 26 (1984):9–14
Dawson, Irene. 'The Dawson Route, 1857–1883: A Selected Bibliography with Annotations.' *Ontario History* LIX (1967):47–55
DCB see *Dictionary of Canadian Biography*
Dean, W.G., ed. *Economic Atlas of Ontario.* Toronto: University of Toronto Press 1969
Denison, Jean. *Main Street: A Pictorial History of Erin Village.* Cheltenham, Ont.: Boston Mills Press 1980
Dictionary of Canadian Biography. 12 vols to date. Toronto: University of Toronto Press 1966– (Cited as *DCB*)
Dionne, Narcisse-Eutrope, comp. *Inventaire chronologique.* 5 parts. Quebec: Royal Society of Canada 1905–12. Part 4: *Inventaire chronologique des cartes, plans, atlas relatifs à la Nouvelle-France et à la province de Québec, 1508–1908.*
Doughty, Arthur G., and McArthur, Duncan A., eds. *Documents Relating to the Constitutional History of Canada, 1791–1818.* Ottawa: Public Archives of Canada 1914
Dow, Charles Mason, comp. *Anthology and Bibliography of Niagara Falls.* 2 vols. Albany: State of New York 1921
Evans, Lois C. *Hamilton: The Story of a City.* Toronto: Ryerson Press 1970
Ferrier, W.F. *Annotated Catalogue of and Guide to the Publications of the Geological Survey of Canada, 1845–1917.* Ottawa: Geological Survey of Canada 1920
Firth, Edith G., ed. *The Town of York, 1793–1815: A Collection of Documents of Early Toronto.* Toronto: Champlain Society and University of Toronto Press 1962
– *The Town of York, 1815–1834: A Further Collection of Documents of Early Toronto.* Toronto: Champlain Society and University of Toronto Press 1966
Fleming, Patricia Lockhart. *Upper Canadian Imprints 1801–1841: A Bibliography.* Toronto: University of Toronto Press in co-operation with the National Library of Canada 1988
Gagnon, Philéas, comp. *Essai de bibliographie canadiennne; inventaire d'une bibliothèque comprenant imprimés, manuscrits, estampes, etc., relatif à l'histoire du Canada et des pays adjacents.* 2 vols. Quebec 1895–1913
Ganton, Isobel K. 'The Development of the Military Reserve, Toronto, 1792–1862.' 1975. Unpublished
– and Joan Winearls. *Mapping Toronto's First Century, 1787–1884: Exhibit Texts.* Toronto: Prepared by the Royal Ontario Museum and the University of Toronto Library 1984
Gazetteer of Canada: Ontario/Répertoire géographique du Canada: Ontario. 4th ed. Ottawa: Geographical Services Division, Canada Centre for Mapping for the Canadian Permanent Committee on Geographical Names 1988
Gentilcore, R. Louis, and Kate Donkin. *Land Surveys of Southern Ontario: An Introduction and Index to the Field Notebooks of the Ontario Land Surveyors, 1784-1859.* Toronto: University of Toronto Press 1973
– and C. Grant Head, comps. *Ontario's History in Maps.*Toronto: University of Toronto Press 1984 (Cited as *OHIM*)
Gilroy, Marion, comp. *Catalogue of Maps, Plans and Charts in the Public Archives of Nova Scotia.* Halifax 1938
Goggin, Daniel T. *Preliminary Inventory of the Records Relating to International Boundaries (Record Group 76).* Washington: National Archives 1968
Gravell, Thomas L., and George Miller. *A Catalogue of American Watermarks, 1690–1835.* New York: Garland 1979
– *A Catalogue of Foreign Watermarks Found on Paper Used in America, 1700–1835.* New York: Garland 1983
Great Britain, Admiralty, Hydrographic Department. *Catalogue of Charts, Plans and Views, Published by Orders of the Lords Commissioners of the Admiralty ... with the Prices ...* London 1839–80
– Parliament. *House of Commons, Parliamentary Papers, 1801–1900.* [Microfiche]. Cambridge: Chadwyck-Healey 1980–2
Green, Ernest. 'Township No 2 – Mount Dorchester – Stamford.' In Ontario Historical Society, *Papers & Records* XV (1929):248–338
'The Grenville Collection of Maps.' In W.H. Robinson *Catalogue (no 70).* London 1940, 185–8
Gundy, H. Pearson. 'Samuel Oliver Tazewell, First Lithographer of Upper Canada.' In *Humanities Association Review* 27, 4 (fall 1976):466–83

Guillet, Edwin Clarence, ed. *The Valley of the Trent*. Toronto: Champlain Society 1957

Hahn, Josephine. *Home of My Youth: Hanover*. [Hanover: The Author 1947?]

Haig, Robert. *Ottawa: City of the Big Ears*. [Ottawa: Haig and Haig Publications 1970]

Hamil, Fred Coyne. *The Valley of the Lower Thames, 1640–1850*. Toronto: University of Toronto Press 1951

Harper, J. Russell. *Early Painters and Engravers in Canada*. Toronto: University of Toronto Press 1970

Harris, R. Cole, ed., and Geoffrey G. Matthews, cartographer. *Historical Atlas of Canada*. I: *From the Beginning to 1800*. Toronto: University of Toronto Press 1987

Harris, Robin. 'The Beginning of the Hydrographic Survey of the Great Lakes and the St. Lawrence River.' In *Historic Kingston: Transactions of the Kingston Historical Society for 1965* (1966), 24–39

Herbert, Francis. '*The London Atlas of Universal Geography* from John Arrowsmith to Edward Stanford ...' *Imago Mundi* 41 (1989):98–123

High Ridge Books. *Catalogue 15: Rare and Unusual Maps from the 18th and 19th Centuries*. Rye, NY: High Ridge Books 1987?

Historical Atlas of the County of Wellington, Ontario. Toronto 1906; Belleville, Ont.: Mika 1972

History of Elderslie Township. Chesley, Ont.: Elderslie Historical Society 1977

A History of Harriston: A Commemorative Book for the Harriston Centennial. Mildmay, Ont.: Town Crier 1978

Holmden, H.R., comp. *Catalogue of Maps, Plans and Charts in the Map Room of the Dominion Archives*. Publications of the Canadian Archives, no 8. Ottawa 1912

Hulse, Elizabeth. *A Dictionary of Toronto Printers, Publishers, Booksellers and the Allied Trades, 1798–1900*. Toronto: Anson-Cartwright Editions 1982

Hunter, Andrew F. *A History of Simcoe County*. 2 vols. Barrie, Ont.: County Council 1909; repr. in 1 vol, Barrie: Historical Committee 1948

Indian Treaties and Surrenders from 1680 to 1890. 2 vols. Ottawa: Department of Indian Affairs 1891

Jackson, John N. *St. Catharines, Ontario: Its Early Years*. Belleville, Ont.: Mika 1976

– and John Burtniak. *Railways in the Niagara Peninsula*. Belleville, Ont.: Mika 1978

Jackson, Peter, ed. *John Tallis's London Street Views, 1838–40*. London: Natali & Maurice in association with the London Topographical Society 1969

JHA see Upper Canada, House of Assembly, *Appendix to the Journal* ... and *Journal*

JLA see Canada (Province), Legislative Assembly, *Appendix to the ... Journals*

JLC see Canada (Province), Legislative Council, *Journals [and Appendix]* ...

Johnson, Leo A. *The History of Guelph, 1827–1927*. Guelph: Guelph Historical Society 1977

Johnston, Charles Murray, ed. *The Valley of the Six Nations: A Collection of Documents on the Indian Lands of the Grand River*. Toronto: Champlain Society and University of Toronto Press 1964

Jones, Gwen. *Black Gold Built Bothwell*. Bothwell: Bothwell Times 1967

Karpinski, Louis C. *Bibliography of the Printed Maps of Michigan, 1804–80*. Lansing, Mich.: Michigan Historical Commission 1931

Karrow, Robert W., ed. *Checklist of Printed Maps of the Middle West to 1900*. 14 vols in 12. Boston: G.K. Hall 1981–3

Koerner, Alberta G. Auringer, comp. *Detroit and Vicinity before 1900: An Annotated List of Maps*. Washington: Library of Congress 1968

Lajeunesse, Ernest J., ed. *The Windsor Border Region, Canada's Southernmost Frontier: A Collection of Documents*. Toronto: Champlain Society and University of Toronto Press 1960

Lande, Lawrence, comp. *Lawrence Lande Collection of Canadiana in the Redpath Library of McGill University*. Montreal: Lawrence Lande Foundation for Canadian Historical Research 1965. Supplement: *Rare and Unusual Canadiana: Supplement to the Lande Bibliography*. Montreal: McGill University 1971

LC Atlases see *List of Geographical Atlases*

List of Geographical Atlases in the Library of Congress, with Bibliographic Notes. 8 vols. Washington: Government Printing Office 1909–74 (Cited as *LC Atlases*)

Looking Back: The Story of Fergus through the Years. [Fergus, Ont. ca 1983]

Loyalist Settlements, 1783–1789, The Land: Maps and Sketches 1783–1800. Toronto: Ministry of Citizenship and Culture 1985

Lysons, Sir Daniel. *Early Reminiscences*. London: John Murray 1896

MacPherson, Ian. *Matters of Loyalty: The Buells of Brockville, 1830–1850*. Belleville, Ont.: Mika 1981

Maddick, Heather, comp. *County Maps: Land Ownership Maps of Canada in the 19th Century/Cartes de comtés: cartes foncières du Canada au XIXe siècle*. Introduction by Joan Winearls. Ottawa: National Map Collection 1976

Malinski, Richard. 'The Importance of the "Map of Cabotia" in the Early Nineteenth Century Mapping Sequence of Eastern Canada.' Unpublished M.A. thesis, University of Alberta, Edmonton 1973

Maps and Plans in the Public Record Office. 2: *America and West Indies*. Edited by P.A. Penfold. London: HMSO 1974 (Cited as *PRO Cat*)

Mathews, Hazel Chisholm. *Mark of Honour*. Toronto: University of Toronto Press [1965]

– *Oakville and the Sixteen: The History of an Ontario Port*. Toronto: University of Toronto Press 1953

May, Betty, comp. *County Atlases of Canada: A Descriptive Catalogue*. Ottawa: National Map Collection 1970

McGechaen, Alexander, and Coolie Verner. *Maps in the Parliamentary Papers by the Arrowsmiths: A Finding List*. London: Map Collectors Circle 1973– . no 88, 89

McKenzie, Ruth, ed. *The St Lawrence Survey Journals of Captain Henry Wolsey Bayfield, 1829–1853*. Vol I. Toronto: Champlain Society 1984
Michigan, University of, William L. Clements Library. *Research Catalog of Maps of America to 1860 in the William L. Clements Library*. 4 vols. Boston 1972
Miller, Warren C. *Vignettes of Early St. Thomas: An Anthology of the Life and Times of its First Century*. St Thomas, Ont.: Sutherland Press 1967
Morris, James Lewis. *Indians of Ontario*. Toronto: Department of Lands and Forests 1943
Morris, John A. *Prescott, 1810–1967*. Prescott: *Prescott Journal* [1969]
Morrison, Walter K. 'Manuscript Maps from the Earl of Dalhousie's Library Located at Dalhousie and Acadia Universities, in the Nova Scotia Museum and in the National Archives of Canada.' In *Association of Canadian Map Libraries Bulletin* 63 (June 1987):1–11
Murray, Florence B., ed. *Muskoka and Haliburton, 1615–1875: A Collection of Documents*. Toronto: Champlain Society and University of Toronto Press 1963
Nagy, Thomas L. *Ottawa in Maps: A Brief Cartographical History of Ottawa*. Ottawa: National Map Collection 1974
National Union Catalog Pre-1956 Imprints [and Supplement]. 754 vols. London and Chicago: Mansell and American Library Association 1968–81 (Cited as *NUC*)
New York Public Library. *Dictionary Catalog of the Map Division*. 10 vols. Boston 1971
Niagara Falls, Canada: A History of the City and the World Famous Beauty Spot. Niagara Falls Ont.: Kiwanis Club, 1967
Nicholson, N.L., and L.M. Sebert *The Maps of Canada: A Guide to Official Canadian Maps, Charts, Atlases and Gazetteers*. Folkestone, Kent: Wm. Dawson & Sons 1981
Nicholson, Norman. *The Boundaries of Canada, Its Provinces and Territories*. Ottawa: Queen's Printer 1954
NMC Cat see *Catalogue of the National Map Collection*
North America at the Time of the Revolution: A Collection of Eighteenth Century Maps. Introductory notes by Louis de Vorsey, Jr. Part II. Lympne Castle, Kent: Harry Margary 1974
Norwood Then & Now. Norwood, Ont. [1978?]
NUC see *National Union Catalog*
OHIM *see* Gentilcore, Louis R., and C. Grant Head, comps
O'Leary, P.M. 'Inventaire des cartes, plans ... conservées au département des terres de la province de Québec, Québec 30 mai 1909.' Unpublished. Copy in OOAMA
Olsen, Marilyn Beatty Mackenzie. 'Aspects of the Mapping of Southern Ontario, 1783–1867.' Unpublished M.Phil. thesis, University of London 1968
Ontario, Department of Public Records and Archives. *Report, 1905–33*. Toronto 1906–34 (Cited as Ontario Archives, *Report*)
Ontario, Ministry of Consumer and Commercial Relations. *The Ontario Conveyancer's Directory, Land Registry and Sheriff's Offices, Arranged Alphabetically According to Territorial Divisions*. Toronto 1975
Ontario Historic Sites, Museums, Galleries and Plaques. Toronto: Heritage Conservation Division, Ministry of Culture and Recreation 1978
Otto, Stephen A. *Maitland: 'A Very Neat Village Indeed.'* Erin, Ont.: Boston Mills Press 1985
Page & Smith. *Illustrated Historical Atlas of the County of Wentworth, Ont*. Toronto 1875; Dundas, Ont. 1971
Page, H.R., & Co. *Illustrated Historical Atlas of the County of Middlesex*. Toronto 1878; Sarnia, Ont.: E. Phelps 1972
Parker, B.A. 'The Niagara Harbour and Dock Company.' In *Ontario History* XXXII, 2 (1980):93–100
Parsell, H., & Co. *Illustrated Atlas of the County of Waterloo*. Toronto: H. Parsell & Co. 1881; Owen Sound, Ont.: Richardson, Bond & Wright 1972
Passfield, Robert. *Engineering the Defence of the Canadas: Lt Col John By and the Rideau Canal*. Parks Canada Manuscript Report 425. Ottawa: Parks Canada 1980
– 'A Wilderness Survey: Laying Out the Rideau Canal, 1826–1832.' In *Journal of the History of Canadian Science, Technology and Medicine* 24 (1983):80–97
Peters, Harry T. *America on Stone*. New York: Doubleday, Doran & Co. 1931
Phillips, P. Lee, comp. *List of Maps of America in the Library of Congress Preceded by a List of Work Relating to Cartography*. Washington: Government Printing Office 1901
Places in Ontario: Their Name Origins and History. 3 vols. Belleville, Ont.: Mika 1977–83
Pope, J.H. *Illustrated Historical Atlas of the County of Halton Ont*. Toronto: Walker & Miles 1877
Preston, Richard Arthur, ed. *Kingston before the War of 1812: A Collection of Documents*. Toronto: Champlain Society and University of Toronto Press 1959
PRO Cat see *Maps and Places in the Public Records Office*
Radford, P.J., & Co. *Americana Catalogue* 27 (Nov. 1980). London: P.J. Radford & Co. 1980
Reps, John. *Views and Viewmakers of Urban America: Lithographs of Towns and Cities in the United States and Canada*. Columbia, Mo: University of Missouri Press 1984
Reville, F. Douglas. *History of the County of Brant*. Brantford, Ont.: Brant Historical Society and Hurley Printing Co. 1920
Ristow, Walter William. *American Maps and Mapmakers: Commercial Cartography in the Nineteenth Century*. Detroit: Wayne State University Press 1985
Robertson, John Ross. *The History of Freemasonry in Canada*. 2 vols. Toronto: Morang 1900

– *Robertson Collection: Catalogue of the Maps and Plans of the Town of York, Upper Canada, 1788–1834, and of York after Being Incorporated as the City of Toronto, from 1834–1908*. Toronto 1908
Robinson, Percy James. *Toronto during the French Régime: A History of the Toronto Region from Brûlé to Simcoe 1615–1793*. Toronto: Ryerson Press 1933
Ross, A.H.D. *Ottawa Past and Present*. Toronto: Musson [1927]
Russell, Peter. *The Correspondence of the Honourable Peter Russell with Allied Documents* ... Edited by E.A. Cruikshank and A.F. Hunter. 3 vols. Toronto: Ontario Historical Society 1932–6
Sebert, L.M. 'The Lost Townships of Duncan Sinclair and Hugh Savigny.' In *Ontario Land Surveyor*, fall 1983, 4–5
Simcoe, Elizabeth Posthuma. *Mrs. Simcoe's Diary, with Illustrations from the Original Manuscript*. Edited by Mary Quayle Innis. Toronto: Macmillan 1965
Simcoe, John Graves. *Correspondence, with Allied Documents Relating to his Administration of the Government of Upper Canada*. Edited by E.A. Cruikshank for the Ontario Historical Society. 5 vols. Toronto 1923–31.
Smith, David William. *A Short Topographical Description of His Majesty's Province of Upper Canada, in North America, to Which is Annexed a Provincial Gazetteer*. London: W. Faden 1799; repr. Wakefield, Eng.: S.R. Publishers 1969
Smith, W. Randy. *The Early Development of Three Upper Canadian Towns: Barrie, Holland Landing and Newmarket*. Toronto: York University, Department of Geography 1977
Smith, William Henry. *Smith's Canadian Gazetteer; Comprising Statistical and General Information Respecting All Parts of the Upper Province, or Canada West*. Toronto: H. & W. Rowsell 1846; repr. Toronto: Coles Canadiana Collection 1970
Source List of Manuscripts Relating to the U.S.A. and Canada in Private Archives Preserved in the Scottish Record Office. London: Swift (P&D) Ltd. 1970
SP see Canada (Province), Parliament, *Sessional Papers*
Statutory History of the Steam and Electric Railways of Canada, 1836–1937. Ottawa: J.O. Patenaude 1938
Stelter, Gilbert A. 'Charles Prior's Report of the Founding of Guelph.' In *Historic Guelph, the Royal City* 21 (1981–82):38–62
– 'Combining Town and Country Planning in Upper Canada: William Gilkison and the Founding of Elora.' In *The Country Town in Rural Ontario's Past, Proceedings of the 6th Annual Agricultural History of Ontario Seminar 1981*. [Guelph, Ont.]: University School of Part-time Studies and Continuing Education, University of Guelph 1982
– 'John Galt as Town Booster and Builder.' In *John Galt, Reappraisals*. Edited by Elizabeth Waterston. Guelph: University of Guelph 1975
Stevens, Henry, and R. Tree. 'Comparative Cartography.' In R.V. Tooley, *The Mapping of America*. London: Holland Press 1980
Stewart, J. Douglas, and Ian E. Wilson. *Heritage Kingston*. Kingston: Queen's University 1973
Stone, Patricia. 'The Publishing History of W.H. Smith's *Canada: Past, Present and Future*, a Preliminary Investigation.' In *Papers of the Bibliographical Society of Canada* XIX (1980):38–68
Story, Norah. *The Oxford Companion to Canadian History and Literature*. Toronto: Oxford University Press 1967
Streeter see The Celebrated Collection of Americana ...
Taylor, John H. *Ottawa: An Illustrated History*. Toronto: James Lorimer and the Canadian Museum of Civilization 1986
Ten Cate, Adrian. *Brockville: A Pictorial History*. Kingston: Hanson & Edgar ca 1972
Toronto Public Library. *Map Collection of the Public Reference Library of the City of Toronto, Canada*. Toronto 1923
Trout, John M., and E. Trout. *The Railways of Canada for 1870–1*. Toronto: Monetary Times 1871
Twyman, Michael. 'A Directory of London Lithographic Printers, 1800–1850.' In *Journal of the Printing Historical Society* 10 (1974–5):1–57
Upper Canada, House of Assembly. *Appendix to the Journal*. 1835–39/40 (Cited as JHA)
– *Journal [and appendix]*. 1825–34 (Cited as JHA)
Wadsworth, Unwin & Brown. *Illustrated Historical Atlas of the County of Oxford, Ontario*. Toronto: Walker & Miles 1876; Owen Sound, Ont.: Richardson, Bond & Wright 1972
Walker & Miles. *Illustrated Atlas of the County of Wellington* ... Toronto: Walker & Miles 1877; Owen Sound, Ont.: Richardson, Bond & Wright 1972
Walling, Henry Francis. *Tackabury's Atlas of the Dominion of Canada*. Montreal: G.N. Tackabury 1875
Warkentin, John, and Richard I. Ruggles, eds. *Manitoba Historical Atlas: A Selection of Facsimile Maps, Plans and Sketches from 1612 to 1969*. Winnipeg: Historical and Scientific Society of Manitoba 1970
Weaver, John C. *Hamilton: An Illustrated History*. Toronto: J. Lorimer 1982
Whebell, C.F.J. 'Printed Maps of Upper Canada, 1800–1864: A Select Bibliography.' In *Ontario History* XLIX (1957):139–44
– 'Two Polygonal Settlement Schemes from Upper Canada.' In *Ontario Geographer* 12 (1978):85–92
Wolter, John. 'Official Charting of the Great Lakes 1815–1970.' 1980. Unpublished
Zaslow, Morris. *Reading the Rocks: The Story of the Geological Survey of Canada, 1842–1972*. Toronto and Ottawa: Macmillan and Department of Energy, Mines and Resources and Information Canada 1975

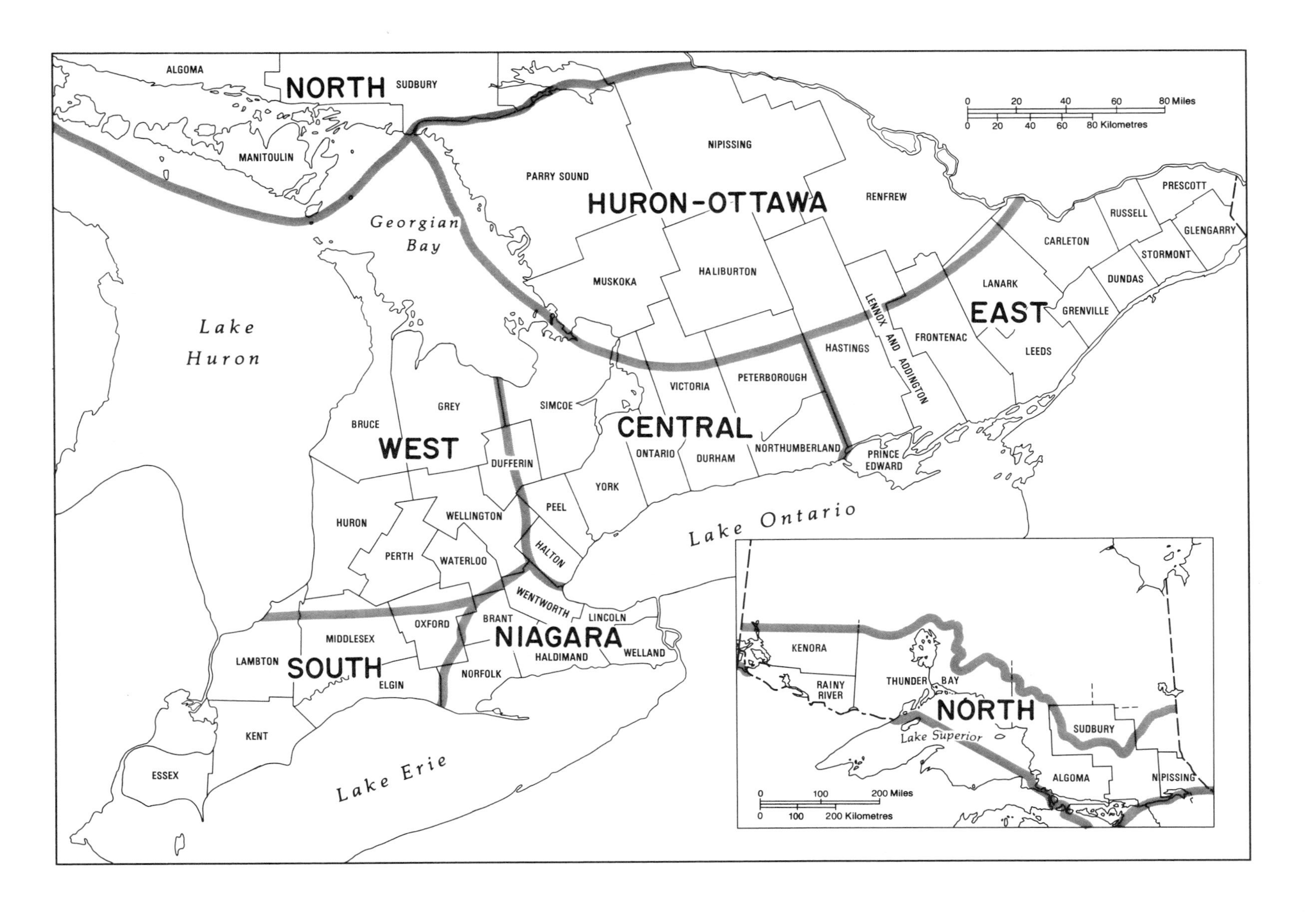

Approximate boundaries for regions in Part II
and pre-1974 county and district boundaries for Ontario

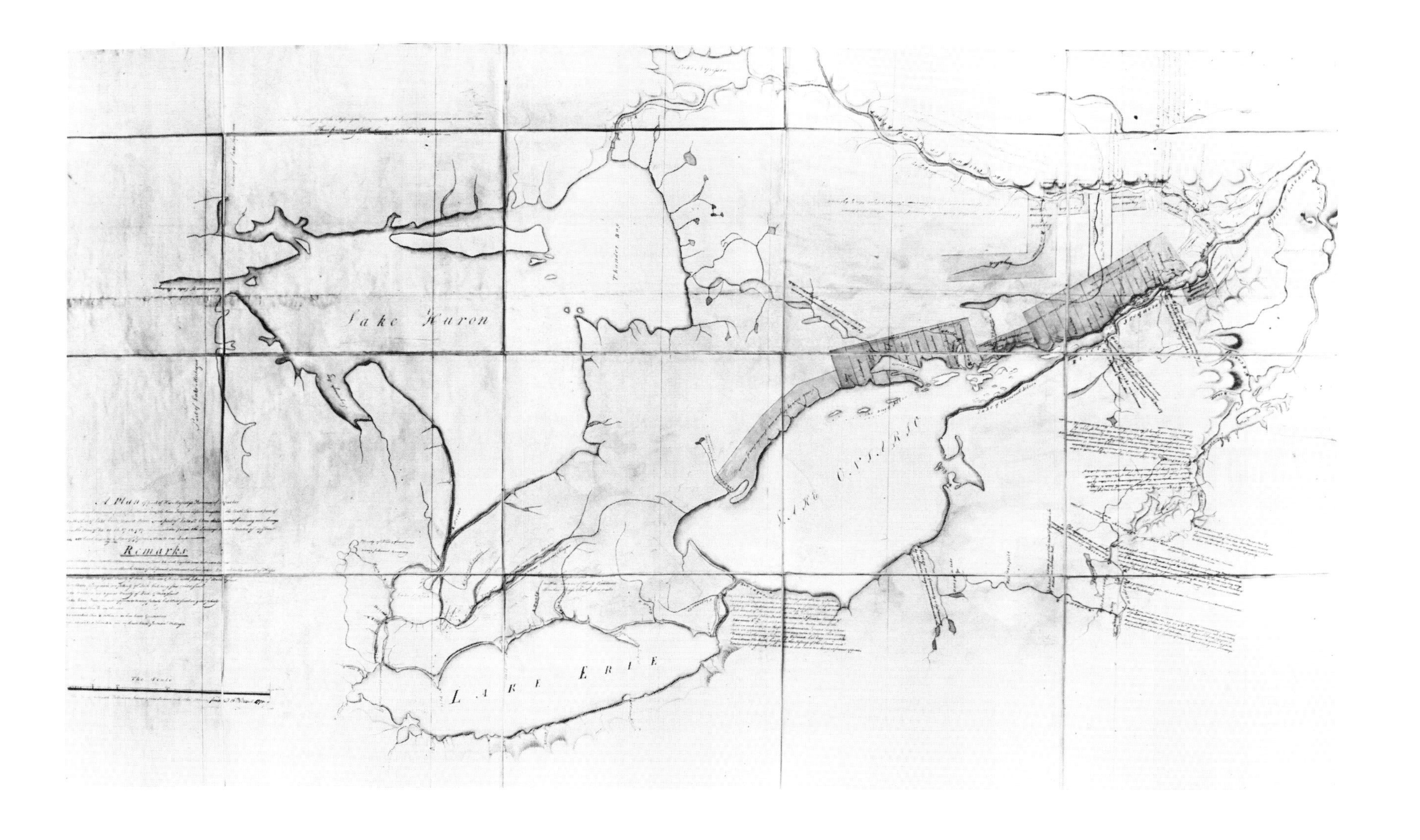

11(3) 'A Plan of Part of His Majesty's Province of Quebec.' Probably made by Patrick McNiff in 1790, this inaccurate rendering of the province was obviously not based on the available reconnaissance maps.
National Maritime Museum, Greenwich, Grenville Collection

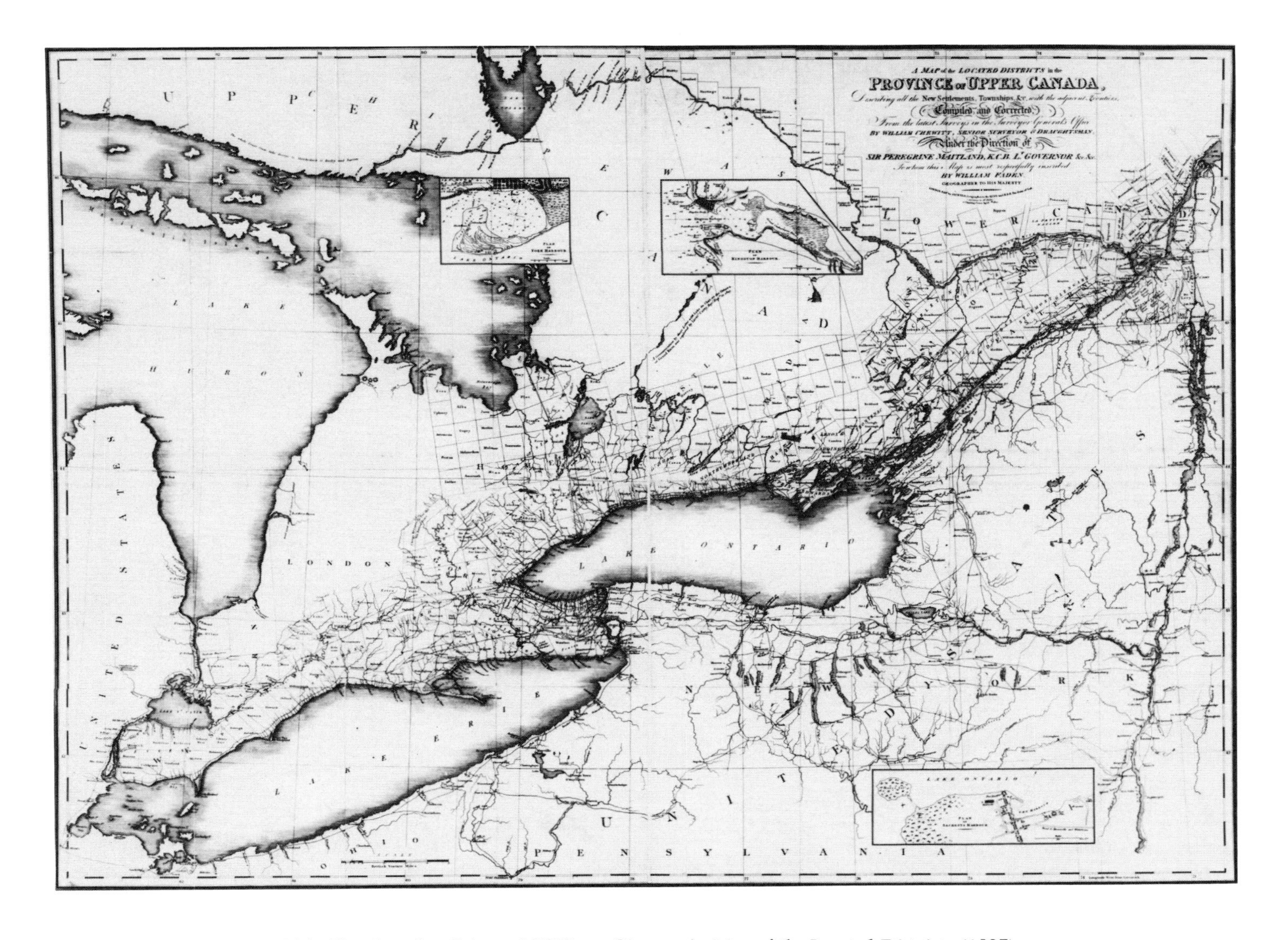

43(4) The fourth edition of William Chewett's *Map of the Located Districts* (1825) is similar in content to the Canada Company maps of 1825–6 (69) but the Lake Huron coast in later editions was never corrected. *National Archives of Canada (NMC 11234)*

185(2b) The second state of W.H. Smith's *Map of Canada West* (1856) shows the advance of settlements and the first surge of railway building. *National Archives of Canada (NMC 11256)*

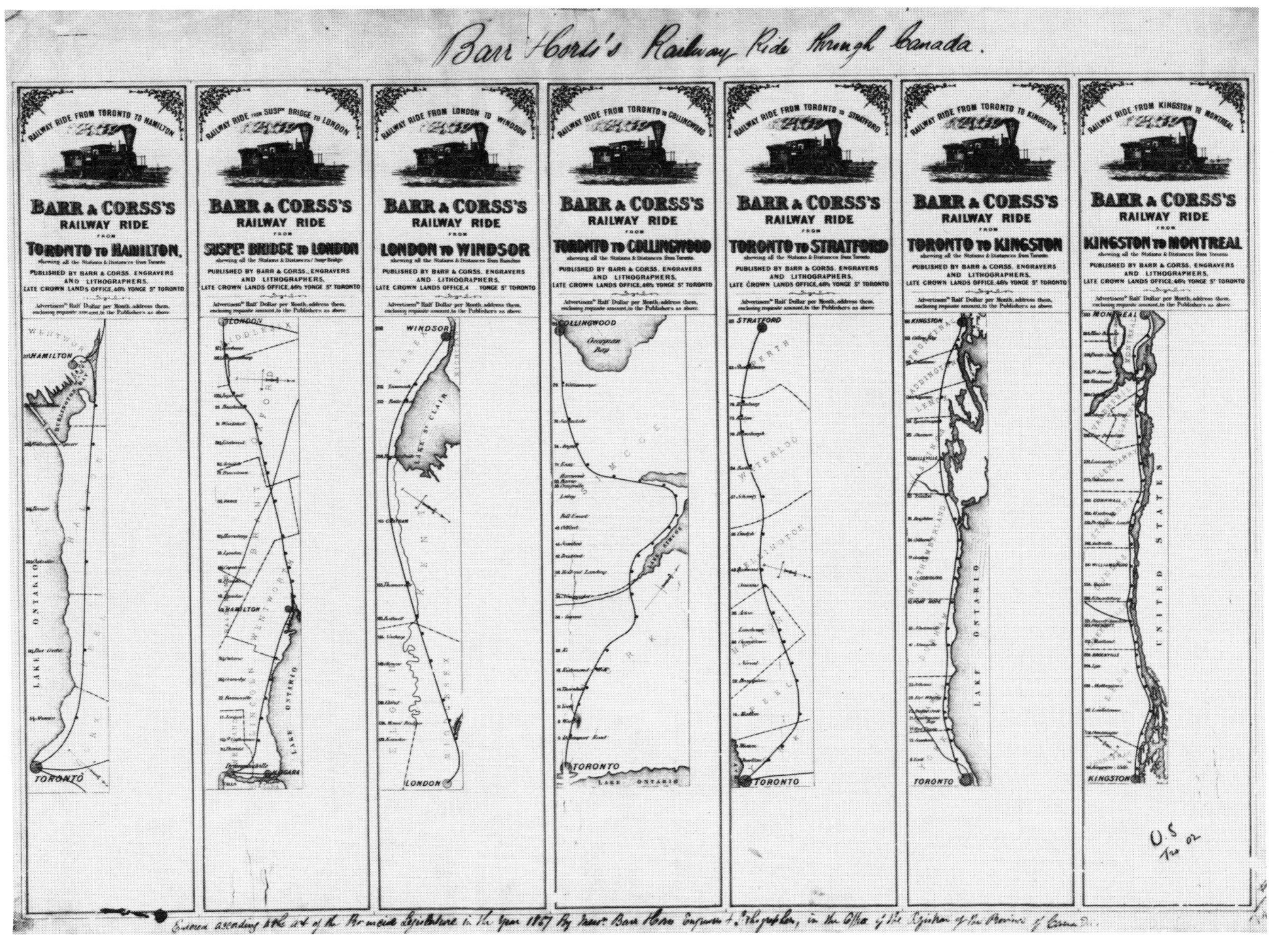

239 This copyright registration copy made in 1857 of *Barr & Corss's Railway Ride* is the only one known and the map may not have been published.
National Archives of Canada (NMC 24952)

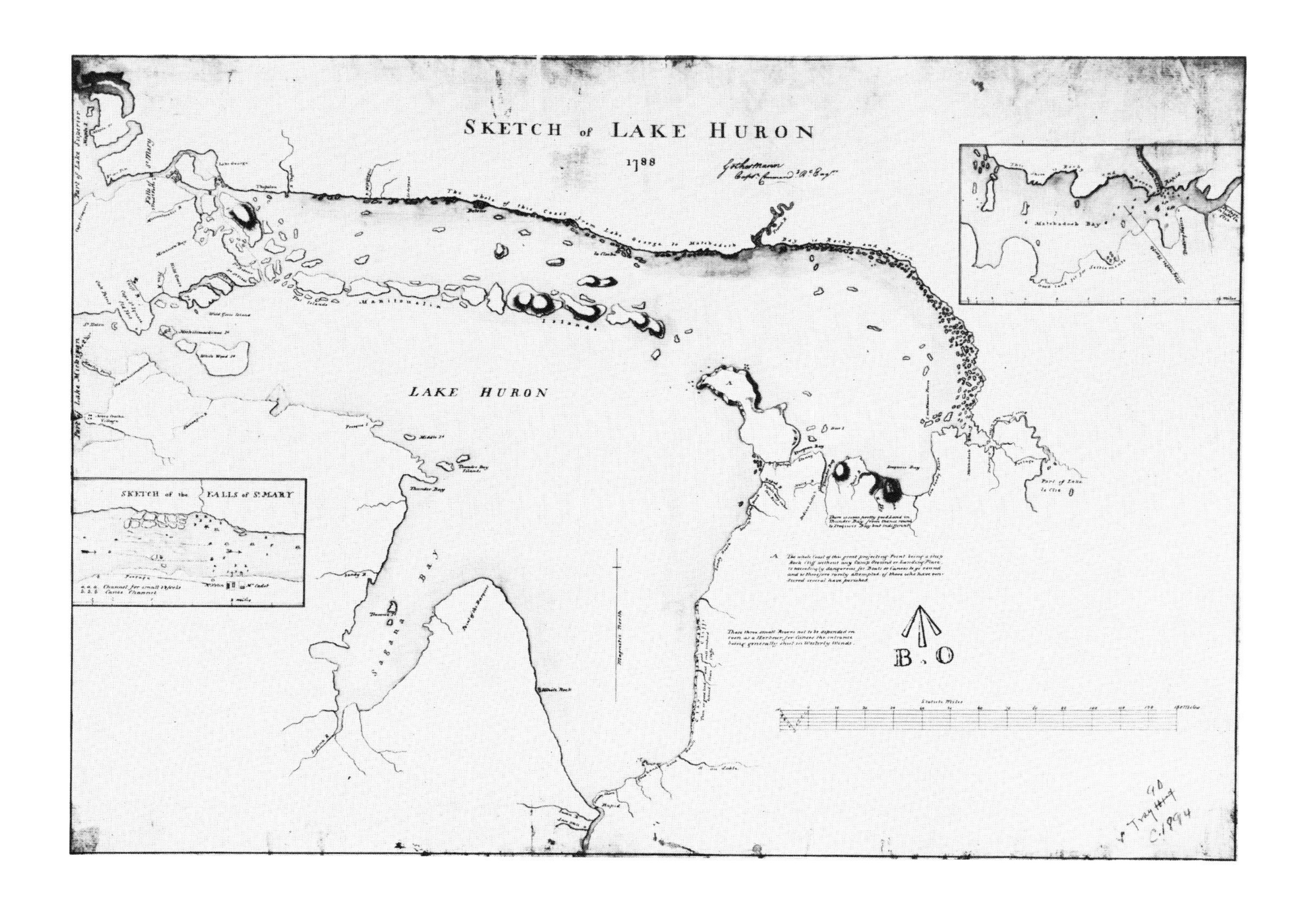

7(4) This 'Sketch of Lake Huron' from Gother Mann's survey of 1788 was used for years as a source for general maps, particularly for delineating Manitoulin Island and the north shore.
National Archives of Canada (NMC 18558)

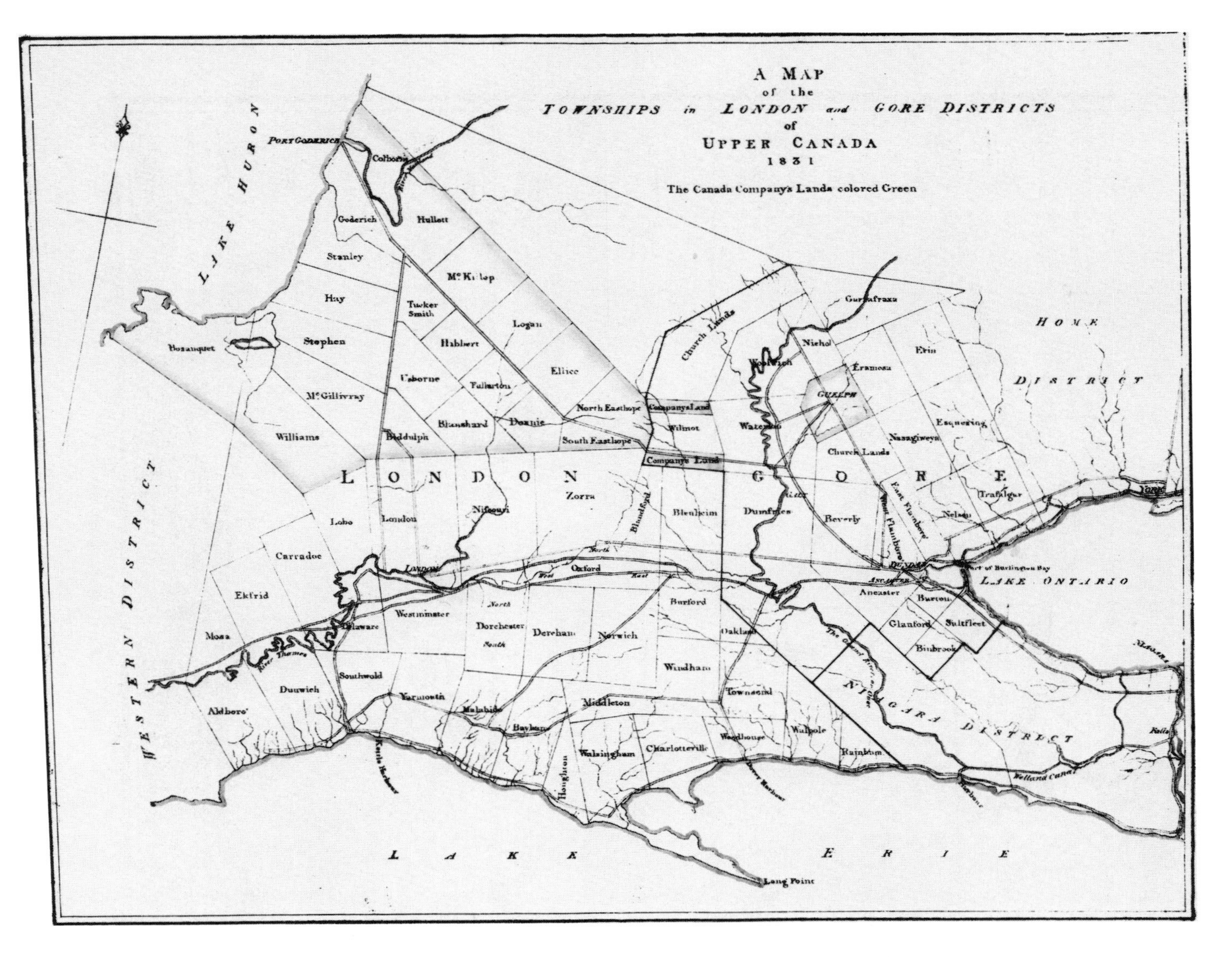

81 A printed map of 1831, probably prepared in England, showing the Canada Company's land and the Huron Tract. The map shows the orientation of the townships based on the tract boundaries and gives a good idea of roads before the great road-building decade of the 1840s.
Metropolitan Toronto Reference Library (Baldwin Room, Bain Collection, BR JB fo 912.713 S52)

A CHART, shewing the Interior Navigation of the DISTRICT of Newcastle, Upper Canada, and the proposed improvements on the Otanabee River &c.
Drawn by F.P. Rubidge, and engraved by T. Evans, for the Cobourg Star.

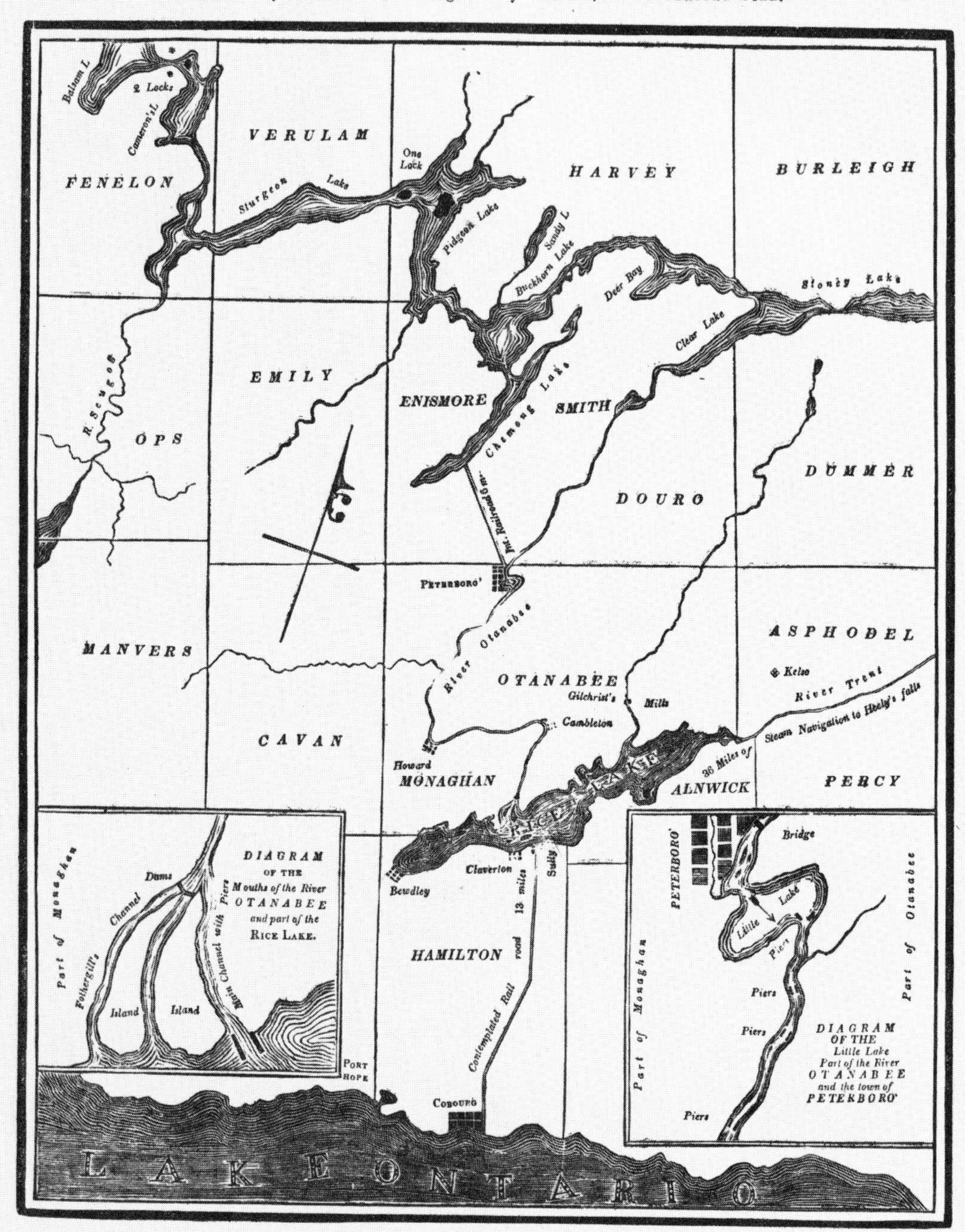

TABLE of DISTANCES.

COBOURG to RICE LAKE - - - - 18 Miles, Land carriage.	CHEMONG thro' SMITH, ENNISMORE, HARVEY, VERULAM, OPS,
RICE LAKE to PETERBORO' - - - 25 By Steam-boat.	CARTWRIGHT and FENELON, 81 Miles by Steam boat.
PETERBORO' to CHEMONG LAKE - - 7 Miles Land carriage.	RICE LAKE to Heeley's falls in Seymour, 35 Miles, by Steam-boat,

352(2) One of the few wood-engraved maps prepared in the period, this map of part of the Newcastle district (ca. 1833) highlights proposed road and water communications in the Trent river system.
National Archives of Canada (NMC 3052)

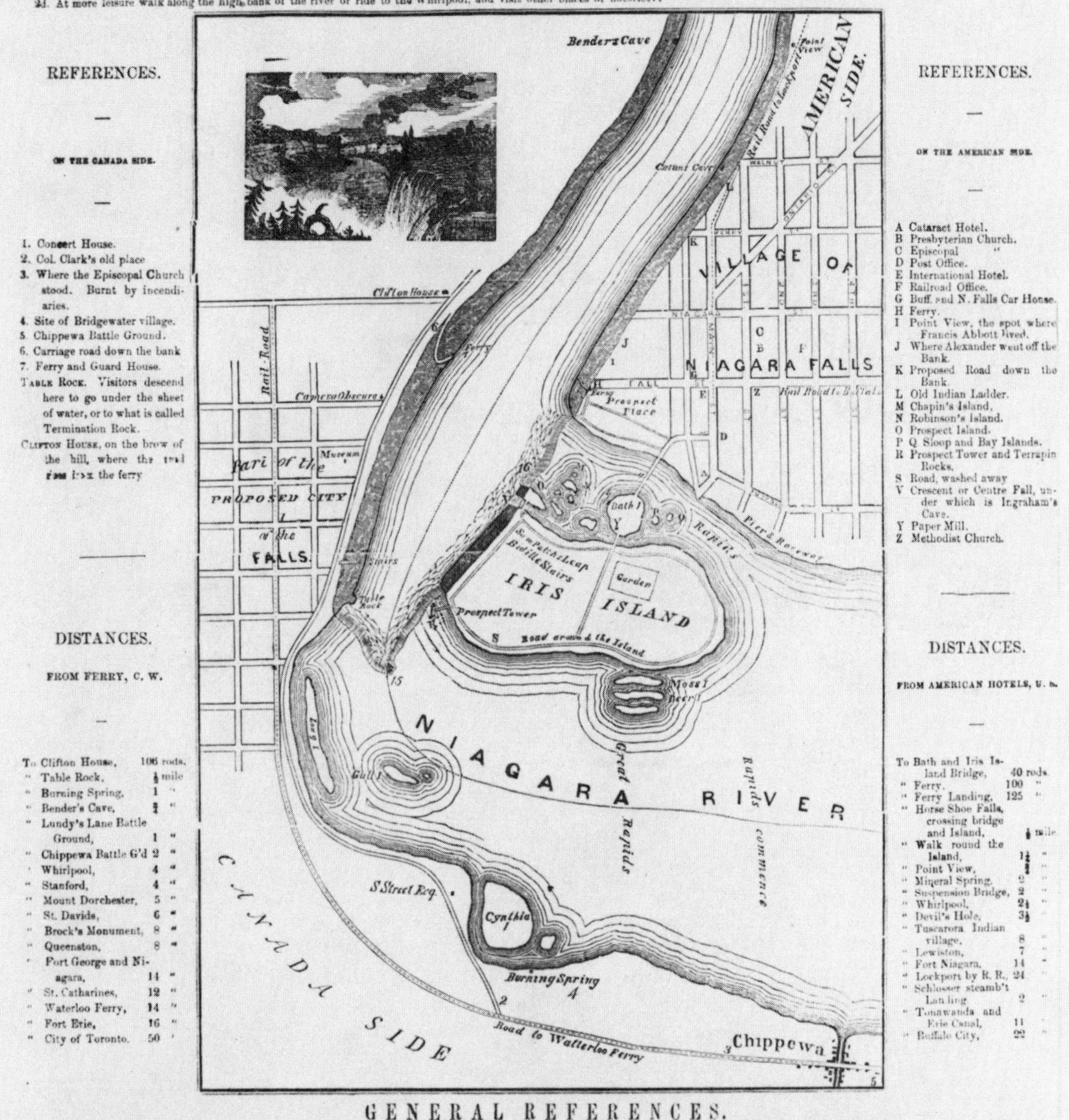

803(2) This map of Niagara Falls from Andrew Burke's *Descriptive Guide ... to Niagara Falls* (1854) was one of the many maps prepared for books on Niagara Falls.
As often was the case, it was redrawn from an earlier map and revised from an earlier plate.
Thomas Fisher Rare Book Library, University of Toronto Library

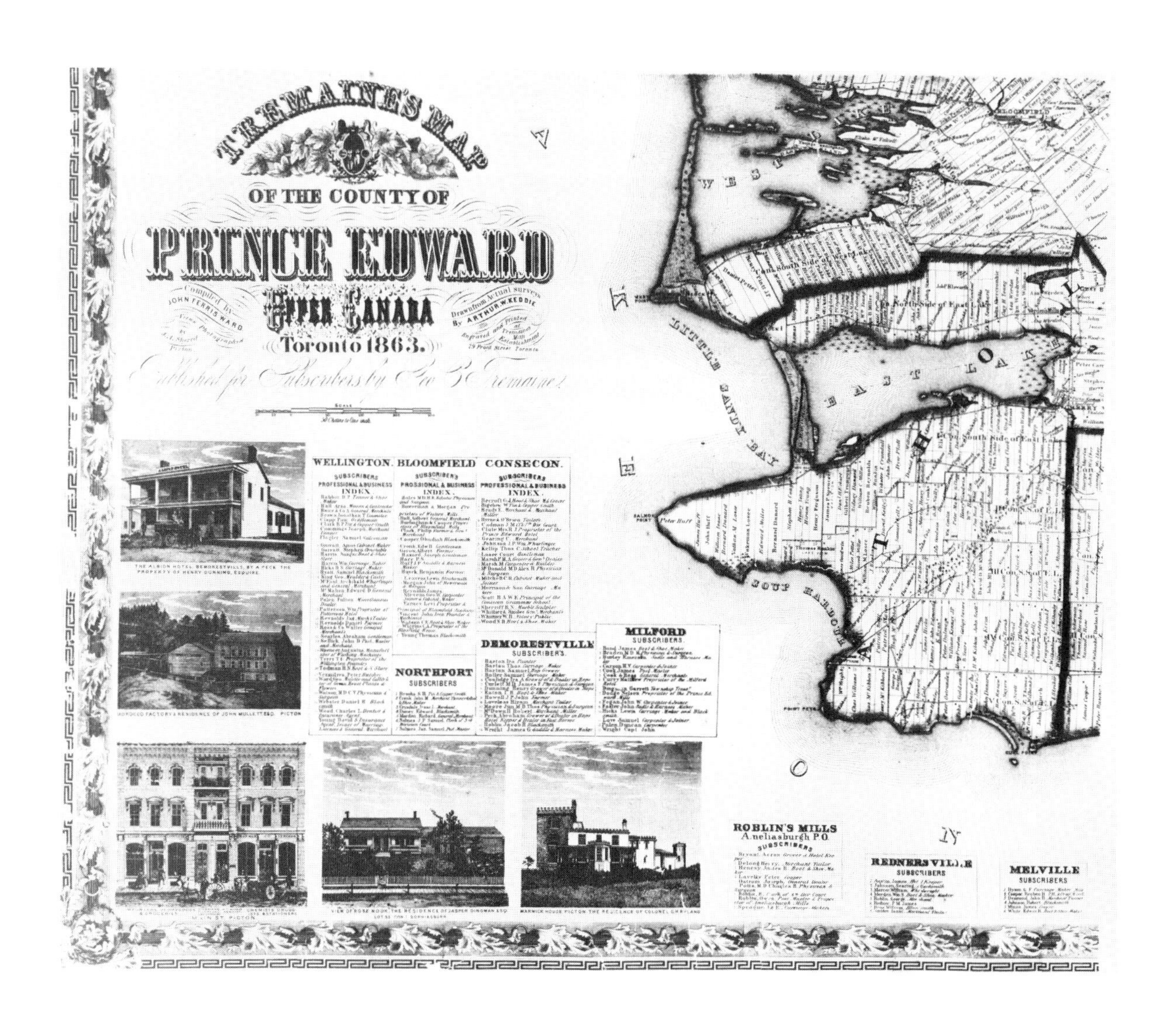

564 This part of one of the county landownership maps by the Tremaines shows the typical features of their style – the farm lots with names of owners or tenants, the views of buildings in towns and the subscribers' directories, and the decorative title block and border.
National Archives of Canada (NMC 19020(3))

1005(2) One of a series of printed maps showing the 'oil lands' in Lambton, Kent, and Middlesex counties in the 1860s. New towns such as Oil Springs, Petrolia, and Bothwell developed because of the discovery of oil, and new roads and railway lines were built to these points. One version of this map was printed on linen.
Thomas Fisher Rare Book Library, University of Toronto Library

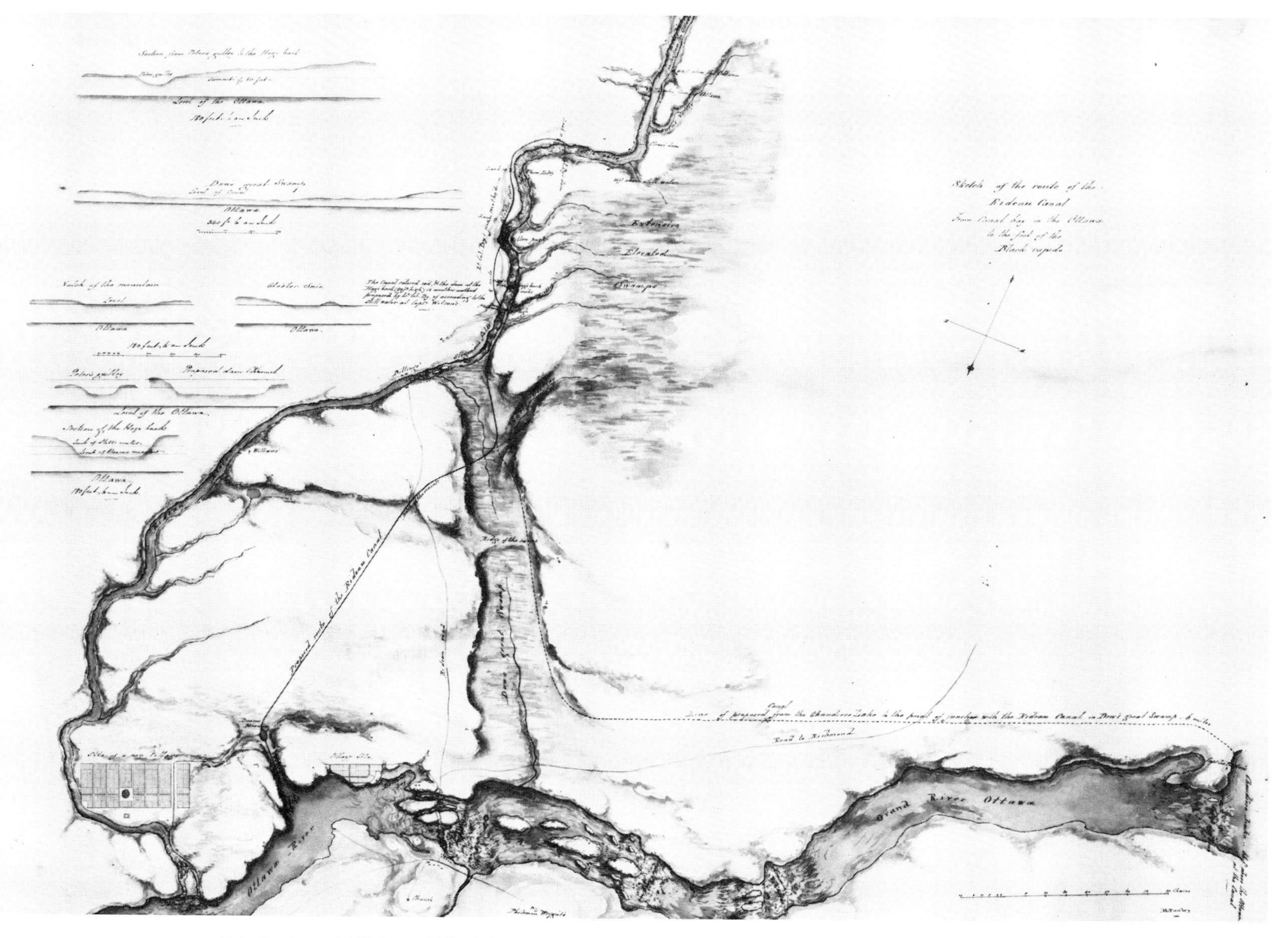

488 A plan of 1826 or 1827 of Ottawa showing early proposals for the Rideau Canal route and the sites and extent of development of both Lower Town and Upper Town.
National Archives of Canada (NMC 97797)

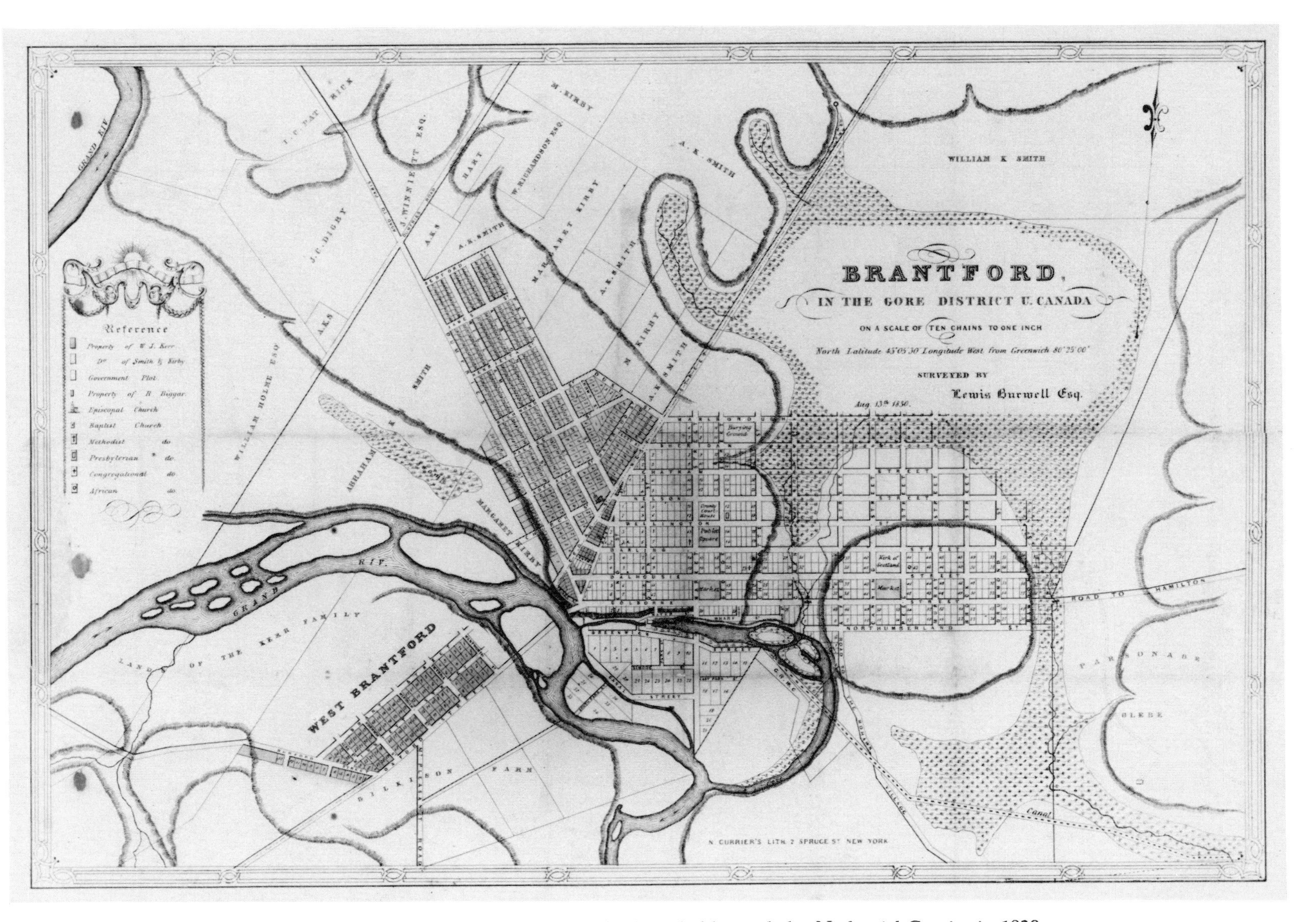

1193 An attractive printed plan of Brantford, probably made by Nathaniel Currier in 1839, showing the central part laid out by government and the subdivision surveys around the perimeters.
Archives of Ontario (AO 228)

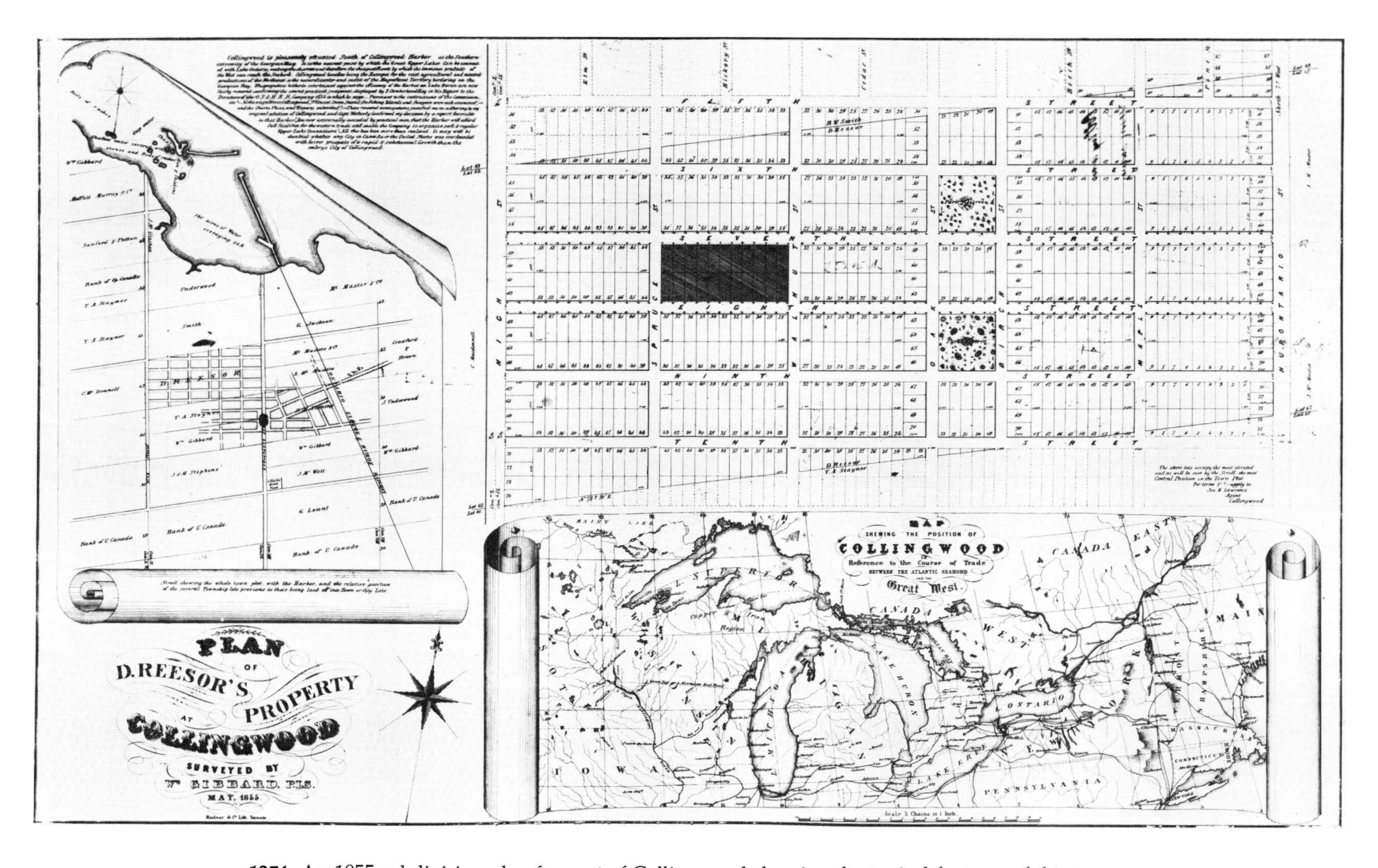

1274 An 1855 subdivision plan for part of Collingwood showing the typical features of this type: the lot plan for the subdivision with reserves for parks, the inset map locating the property, the general plan showing rail and water connections for trade, and the notes on the advantages of the property.
National Archives of Canada (NMC 23888)

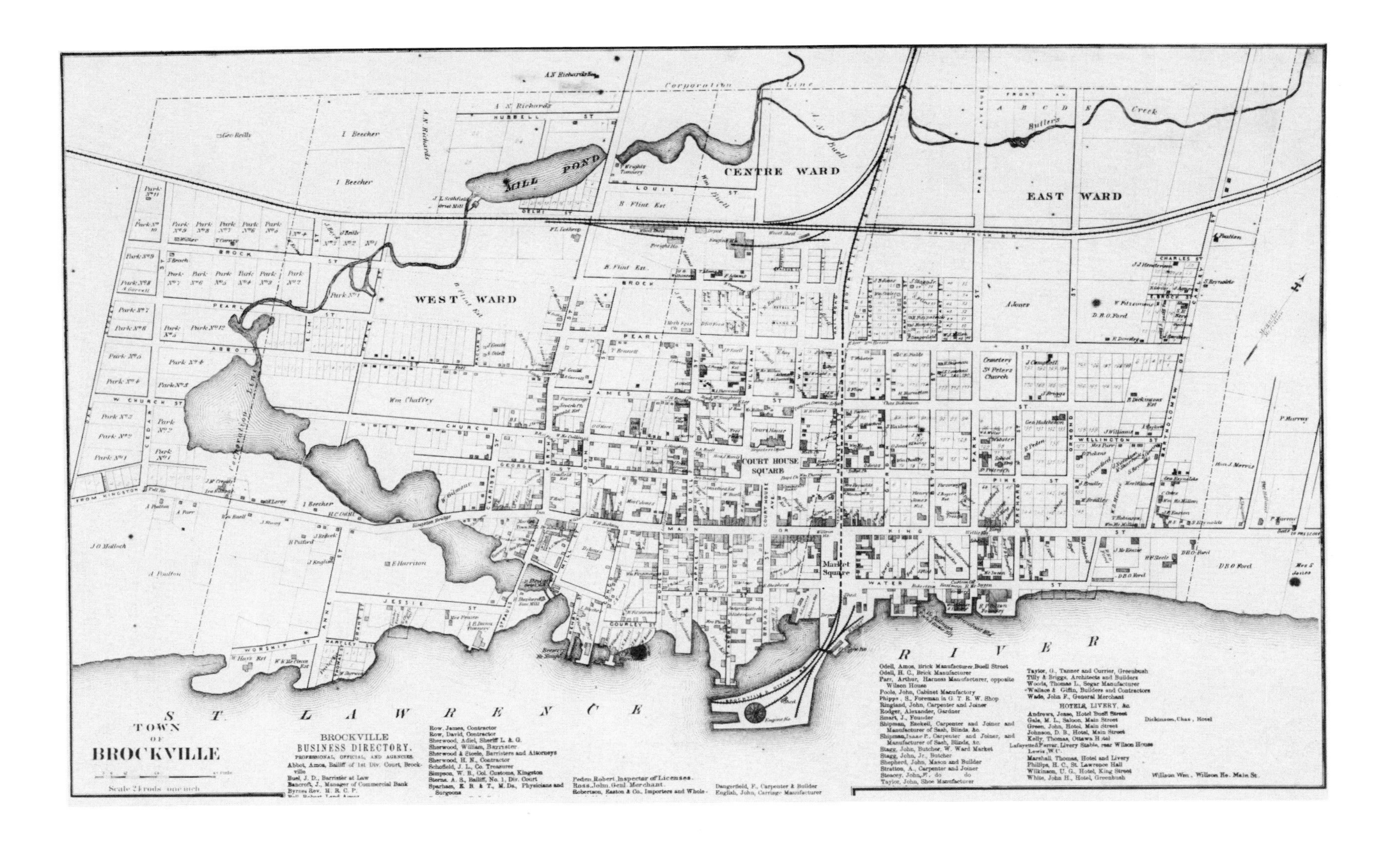

557(2) This plan of Brockville in 1861 from the Walling map of Leeds and Grenville emphasizes the urban core and the developed area of the town since all the buildings are shown and names of occupants or types of businesses are marked.
National Archives of Canada (NMC 17007(4))

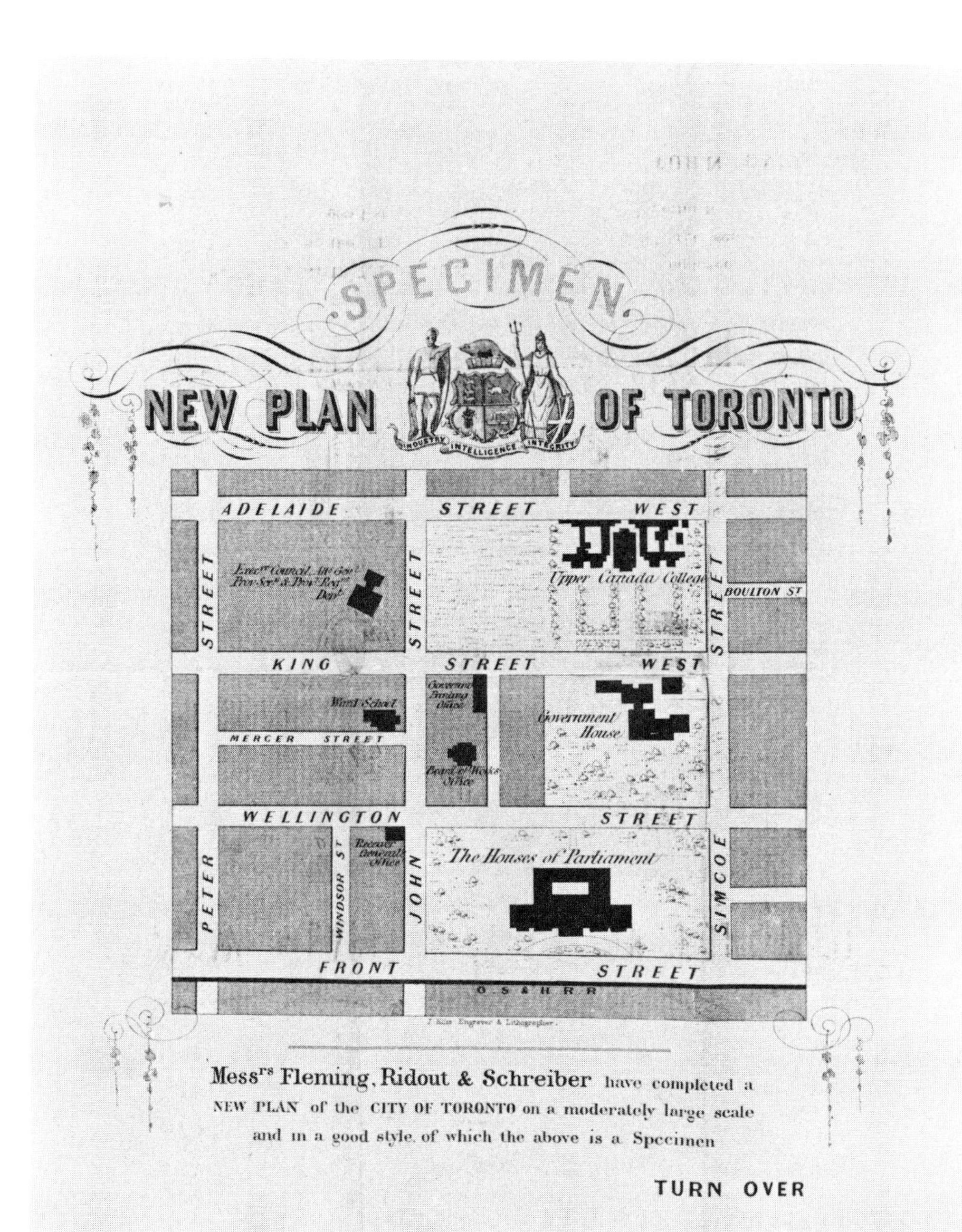

2131 One of the few samples of prospectuses for maps surviving from the period. It advertises an important map of Toronto of 1857 which showed major buildings in detail and built-up areas in a grey pattern. It also included information on a fire-alarm system and zones for cab tariffs.
Archives of Ontario (MU 1052 Env 70)

2215 This plan of York Township in 1851 by J.O. Browne shows the extent of the urban growth, the roads leading into Toronto, the development of small villages and the large amount of land in the farm lots still under forest cover.
Metropolitan Toronto Reference Library (Map Room, 912.71354 B68)

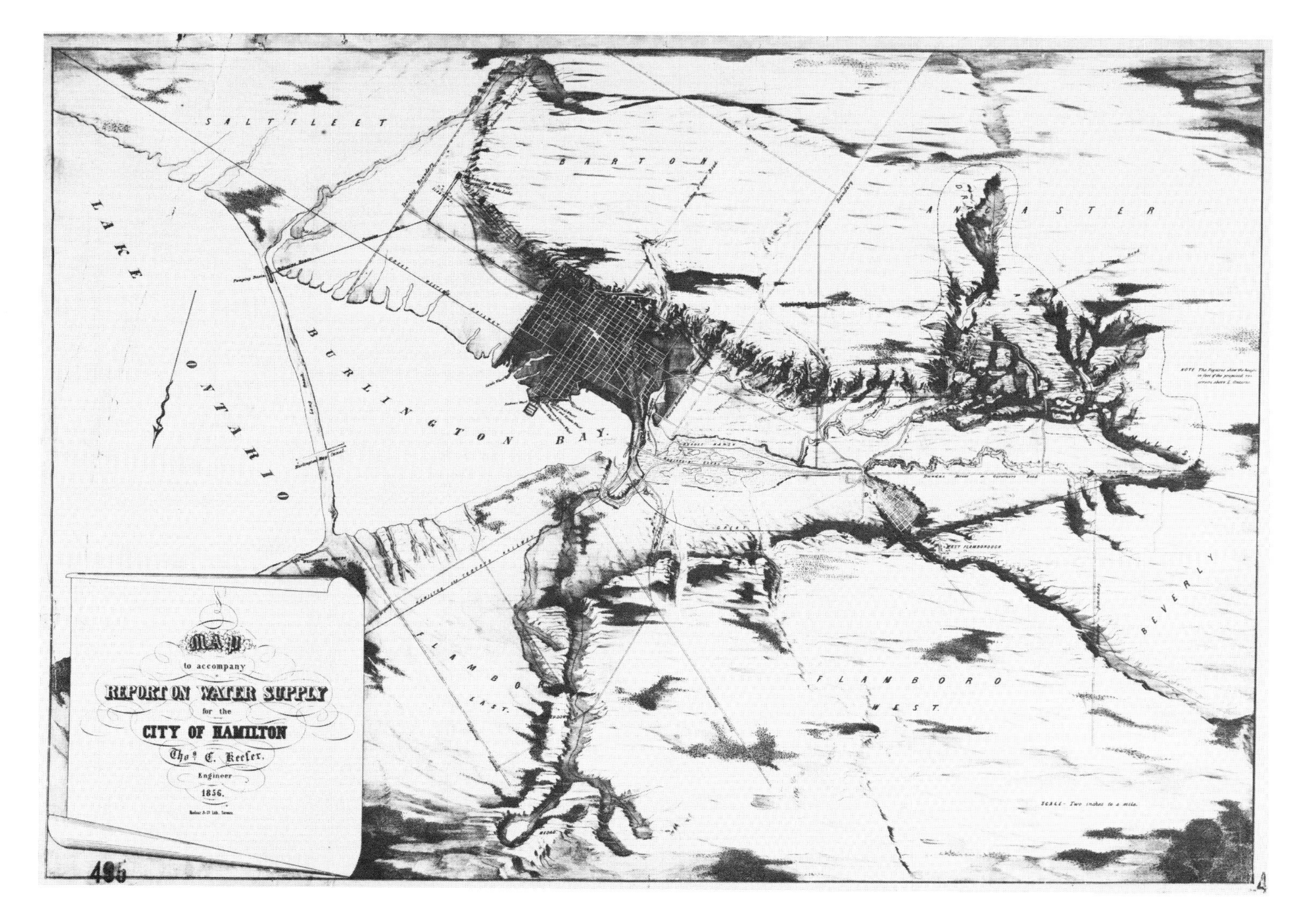

1439 An unusual bird's-eye view showing relief in the Hamilton area, made by Thomas Keefer in 1856 to accompany his report on water supply. Oriented to the south, the map emphasizes the escarpment below which Hamilton and other towns developed.
National Archives of Canada (NMC 21999)

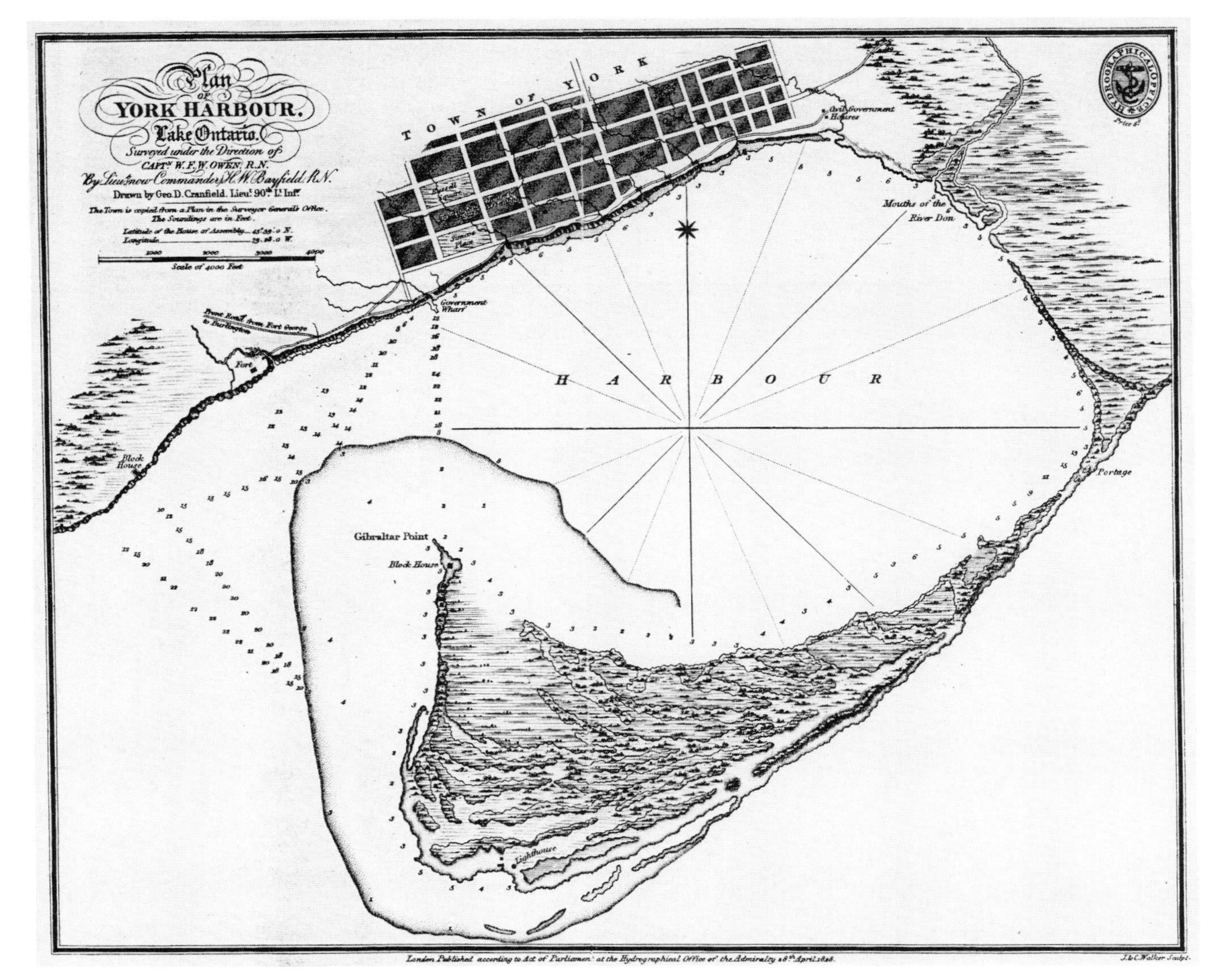

C118 *Plan of York Harbour*. The first state of the British Admiralty chart 337, published in 1828, showing the town and harbour as it existed at the time of the survey in 1817.
Hydrographic Archives, Ministry of Defence (Navy), Taunton, England

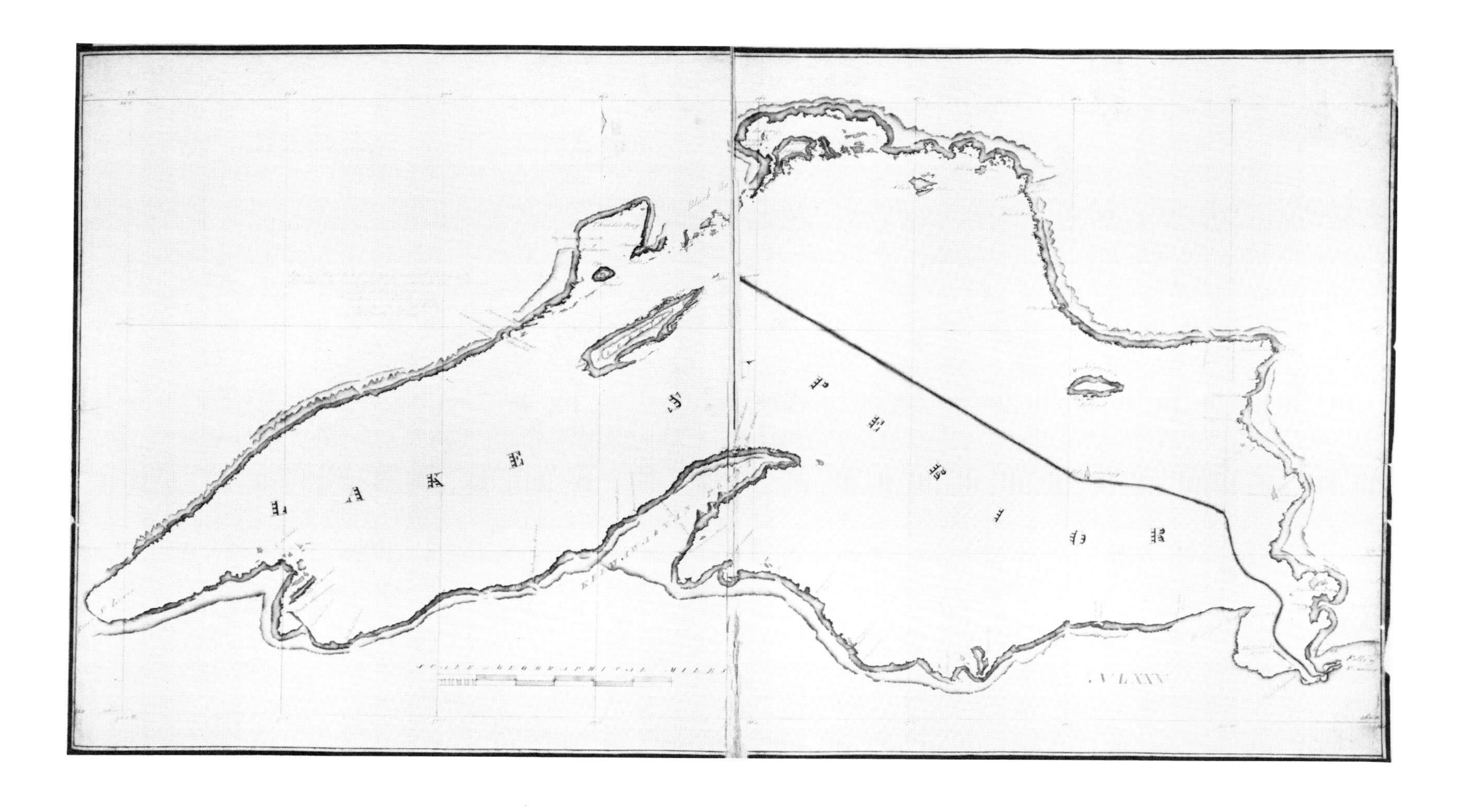

D17, Plate LXXV Lake Superior from David Thompson's copy of the official boundary surveys of 1826. Only part of the boundary line is shown since the Pigeon River was not accepted as the line of demarcation to the west until 1842.
Archives of Ontario (AO 226)

Part I

General

1 *[1782]*
A MAP of the / BRITISH COLONIES in / North America / WITH THE / Roads, Distances, Limits and Extent of the / SETTLEMENTS, / Humbly Inscribed to the Right Honourable / the Earl of Halifax, / And ... / The Lords Commissioners for Trade & Plantations, / By ... / Jno. Mitchell. // Printed for Jefferys and Faden ... at the corner of St. Martin's Lane, Charing Cross, LONDON. Thos. Kitchen Sculp. Published by the Author, Feb 13th 1755 ... / [5th ed 1775, with ms additions to 1782]
Print (engrav) with ms adds 197 x 140 cm 1" to 30 miles
The printed map is the 1775 ed of Mitchell's map with the addition of boundary lines by Richard Oswald in 1782; the red line and other annotations show the British interpretation of the boundaries as concluded in the Preliminary Articles of Peace, 1782, which ended the American War of Independence; in the Upper Canada area the red line shows the international boundary through the Great Lakes and west of L Superior via a 'Long Lake' and a river system south of 'Caministiquia or Trois Rivieres' to Lake of the Woods; other lines shown are conflicting interpretations of the boundary of the Hudson's Bay Co. territories, French and English interpretations of the boundaries by the Treaty of Utrecht, the boundary of the Province of Quebec by the Quebec Act of 1774, and Indian lands as of 1763; the map played an important role in later international and inter-provincial boundary demarcations; photoreproduction in OOAMA (NMC 10098); (*The American War of Independence ... a Commemorative Exhibition* (1975), 96, 154; *North America at the Time of the Revolution*, Part II; *OHIM* 2.13; Stevens and Tree, 87).
GBL (K.118.d.26 (K.Top CXVIII 49.b))

---

2 *1782*
A New & / Accurate MAP of the / PROVINCE / of / CANADA, / in / NORTH AMERICA; / from the latest and best Authorities. // Political Mag. July 1782. // London Published as the Act directs, 31st July 1782, by J. Bew, Pater Noster Row.
Print (engrav) 26 x 34 cm Scale not given
In *The Political Magazine* (1 July 1782), 441; a roughly drawn map of the rivers and lakes from L Superior to beyond Quebec; a combination of French, Indian, and English place-names; Indian tribes.
OOAMA (NMC 113491) OTAR OTMCL

---

3 *[1783–99]*
[Proposed plans for township layout in Upper Canada]
Col mss Sizes vary Scales vary
The plans are based on different sizes of twp with different lot sizes and numbers of cons and lots; road allowances are also shown; the earlier elaborate plans for reserves were only implemented in one or two cases, whereas the later chequered plan became the basis for the crown and clergy reserve system in Upper Canada; the plans are as follows:

(1) *[1783]*
[A proposed plan for a township and town layout]
Col ms 53 x 76 cm 1" to 2000 yds
In Sir Guy Carleton to Gov Parr of New York 30 Oct 1783 (GBLpro CO 5/3 pp 282–3); shows a layout for a town fronting on the water surrounded by 'King's Common' park lots and reserves and twp or farm lots; 'References In each Square of half a mile there are 8 lots of 20 Acres. Each lot is 220 yards in Front and 440 in depth.'
GBLpro (CO 5/3 pp 282–3)

(2) *1789*
Plan of a Town and Township of Nine Miles front by Twelve Miles in depth proposed to be situated on a River or Lake Agreeable to the Tenth Article of the Rules and Regulations for the Conduct of the Land Office Department of 17th February 1789 By order of His Excellency The Right Honourable Lord Dorchester.
1" to 80 chains
Originally accompanied Dorchester's no 25 to Grenville of 27 May 1790 (GBLpro CO 42/67 f 427); shows a town on one side surrounded by common, park lots with reserve for glebe to north, and reserves in the corners; a similar plan on a larger scale of 1" to 40 chains further sgd 'Quebec 3d March 1790 John Collins D.S.G.' is in GBLpro (CO 700 Canada 47 (1)); there is also a copy in OOAMA (NMC 272) endorsed 'B↑O,' 'Z28/65,' and '(278)' (*OHIM* 4.10) and another copy in OOAMA (NMC 273) with the same endorsements as NMC 272 but sgd 'Ts Chamberlaine Nov 28th' [in pencil]: '1789' (*PRO Cat* 1686, 1689).
GBLpro (CO 700 Canada 47 (1); MPG 45)
OOAMA (NMC 272–3)

(3) *1789*
Plan of a Town and Township of Ten Miles Square proposed for an Inland Situation agreeable to the Tenth Article of the Rules and Regulations for the Conduct of the Land Office Department of the 17th Feby 1789 By Order of His Excellency Lord Dorchester.
1" to 80 chains
Originally accompanied Dorchester's no 25 to Grenville of 27 May 1790 (GBLpro CO 42/67 f 433); shows the town in the centre surrounded by common, park lots; and with glebe reserves beyond and other reserves at the corners; also a similar plan at 1" to 40 chains further sgd 'Quebec 3d March 1790 John Collins D S G' (GBLpro CO 700 Canada 47 (2)); and a copy in OOAMA (NMC 275) endorsed 'B↑O' 'Z28/65' and '278' and a copy (NMC 276) with the same endorsements further sgd 'Ts Chamberlaine'; (*OHIM* 4.11; *PRO Cat* 1688–9).
GLBpro (CO 700 Canada 47 (2); MPG 46)
OOAMA (NMC 275–6)

(4) *1789*
Plan of Nine Townships Agreeable to the Tenth Article of the Rules and Regulations for the Conduct of the Land Office Department of Feby 1789 showing the Reservations for the Crown 'A' By Order of His Excellency The Right Honorable Guy Lord Dorchester.
1" to 3 miles
Originally accompanied Dorchester's note 25 to Grenville of 27 May 1790 (GBLpro CO 42/67 f 435; shows the combination of plans for twps on a river and those inland; also a plan at 1" to 1 mile further sgd 'Quebec May 24th 1790 John Collins Esq.' (GBLpro CO 700 Canada 47 (3) and photoreproduction in OOAMA (NMC 29336)); there are also two copies in OOAMA (NMC 278–9) endorsed 'B↑O,' 'Z28/65,' and '(278),' with one further sgd 'Thos Chamberlaine Decr 15th' (*PRO Cat* 1687, 1689).
GBLpro (CO 700 Canada 47 (3); MPG 47)
OOAMA (NMC 278–9)

(5) *1791*
Plan of Two Townships of Ten Miles Square; on each side of the Main Branch of the River Rideau beginning at the Forks. By Order of the Board Williamsburg 28th March 1791 (Signed) W Chewit D.P. Surveyor. True Copy by [Sgd] Jn Fdk Holland
1" to 1 mile
Originally enclosed in a minute of the Land Committee 5 Aug 1791 (GBLpro CO 42/85 p 337) and also a copy in Clark to Dundas no 6, 1 Nov 1791 (GBLpro CO 42/8 f 669); shows a town plot, common, and glebe reserves at one side of the junction of two twps; further reserves at the corners; schoolmaster's reserve; the plans are early proposals for Marlborough and Oxford twps; (*PRO Cat* 1559).
GBLpro (CO 42/85 p 337; MPG 432)

(6) *1792*
Plan of Four Inland Townships exhibiting the Reserves proposed to be Located for the Church and for the future disposition of the Crown: Intended as an Explanation of the Report of the Surveyor Genl & Deputy Surveyr Genl of the 24th September 1792
Shows four twps each with 10 cons and 28 lots and with groups of reserves for the crown and clergy at the intersection of the four twps and further reserves in the corners.
OOAMA (NMC 18260)

(7) *1792*
Plan of a River Township Exhibiting the Reserves proposed to be located for the Church & for the future disposition of the Crown intended as an explanation of the Report of the Surveyor Genl & Dy Surveyor General of the 24th Sept. 1792
1" to 40 chains
Shows a proposal for three areas of crown and clergy reserves at the rear of a twp of 12 cons and 28 lots.
OOAMA (NMC 18261)

(8) *1792*
Sketch of a Township of nine miles in front by twelve miles in depth, supposed to be situated on a River or Lake, laid out into Farm Lots of about 200 Acres each, agreeable to the 10th Article of the Rules & Regulations for the Conduct of the Land Office Department of 17 February 1789, so far as it relates to farm lots; Shewing in what manner two sevenths of the Lands may be reserved for the Clergy & for Government. [Sgd] D.W. Smith Actg Surveyor General Upper Canada 1792. [Endorsed title]: 'The Original Cheqd Plan appd by the Council in 1792' 'No 1'
Shows the alternating plan for crown and clergy reserves adopted for use in Upper Canada (*OHIM* 4.12) (OTMCL D.W. Smith Papers B-5 p 131); also a copy called 'The Chequered Plan for a Township of nine miles ...,' undated but originally included in Simcoe's no 17 of 16 Sept 1793 (GBLpro CO 42/317 p 17) (*PRO Cat* 1382), photoreproduction in OOAMA (NMC 7430).
GBLpro (MPG 93) OTMCL (D.W. Smith Papers B-5 p 131)

(9) *1793*
Plan No 4 The Lots coloured red are reserves for the Crown those coloured black reserves for the Church. N.B. The above Diagram is considered to be conformable to that described in the Extract from the Secretary of State's letter dated 2d October 1793
Shows reserves in blocks in alternate rows with a note indicating that this method only produced 84 and not 96 reserves [as in Diagrams 1–3, which are lacking] and others had to be added.
OOAMA (NMC 281)

(10) *[1793]*
Upper Canada The Township of Darlington. A chequered Plan, Designed to Accommodate Eleven Townships on the North Shore of Lake Ontario, whose base lines were run in 1791; Each 9 miles in front by 12 miles in depth ... shewing in what manner two Sevenths of the Lands may be reserved for the Government & Clergy [Sgd] D W Smith Actg Surveyor General.
1" to 1 mile Endorsements: 'No 2'
Originally enclosed in Simcoe's no 17 of 16 Sept 1793 (GBLpro CO 42/317 p 17); an alternating plan for reserves; (*PRO Cat* 1450).
GBLpro (MPG 94)

(11) *1794*
Plan D ... Plan E the lots coloured red are proposed reserves for the Crown ... I certify that this Diagram was approved of by the Governor and Council ... this tenth day of October 1794. [Sgd] Williams C Ex. C
2 col mss 1" to 1 mile
Originally enclosed with committee reports of 10 and 30 Oct 1794 (GBLpro CO 42/100); both show plans for alternating reserves for twps of 12 cons and 28 lots, but Plan E is a very complicated system and was never used; photoreproductions in OOAMA (NMC 7431–2); (*PRO Cat* 1696).
GBLpro (MPG 467–8)

(**12**) *1795*
The Chequered Plan Diagram A ... The Chequered Plan Discriminating the Reserves of the Crown from those of the Clergy ... Diagram B on the Principle of the Chequered Plan ... Diagram B on the principle of the Chequered Plan and discriminating the Reserves of the Crown from those of the Clergy
4 col mss Sizes vary Scales vary
In 'Report on the Reserved Lands of Upper Canada [Sgd] D W Smith Actg Sur General Upper Canada Surveyor General's Office Upper Canada 9th November 1795' in Simcoe's no 5 to Portland, 22 Dec 1795 (GBLpro CO 42/320 pp 69–72); copies of the 2nd and 4th plans were also included in Hunter's no 11 of 25 July 1800 (GBLpro CO 42/325 pp 159, 161); shows various systems for reserves for twps of 14 cons and 24 lots or for 10 cons and 35 lots; tables for each system.
GBLpro (CO 42/320 pp 69–72; CO 42/325 pp 159–61)

(**13**) *1799*
Project for a Township to be laid off in blocks Containing 1400 Acres, of which 1000 Acres may be granted – Copy W.C. [Sgd] D.W. Smith Actg Sur General. 23d March 1799 Approved in Council & order to be Carried into Execution [Sgd] Peter Russell
Shows a simple chequered plan in a twp of 12 cons and 28 lots with road allowances between each con and after every 5th lot.
OTMCL (D.W. Smith Papers B-9 p 233)

---

4 *[1784–5]*
Plan of the North Side of Lake Ontario from Cataraque to Niagara as surveyed by order of His Excellency General Haldimand Governor and Commander in Chief in and over the Province of Quebec &c&c&c by Mrss Kotte and Peachey Deputy Surveyors under the Direction of Samuel Holland Esqr Surveyor General with Niagara River surveyed by Lieut Tinling 29th Regt Acting Engr.
Col ms 122 x 285 cm 1" to 11/4 miles
Shows the north shore of the lake from about Niagara Falls east to Carleton Is in the St Lawrence R; shows mouths of rivers along shore, the Bay of Quinte, and place-names many of which are in French; shows the twps in the Bay of Quinte and Kingston area; 'General Return of the People's Names Referring to the Anexed [*sic*] Plan' lists settlers by lot and con no for 'Seigneurie no 1 – no 4' [Kingston, Ernestown, Fredericksburgh, Adolphustown]; No 1 twp [Niagara] is also laid out; line of Indian land purchased from the Indians parallel to the Niagara R is marked 'Johnson 9th May 1781'; although the 1789 plan (**9**) indicates that the north shore survey was done in 1783, it appears from the list on **10** and (**2**) below that the north shore was not completed until 1784 and the Niagara R was surveyed in 1785; a letter from Samuel Holland to Lt Gov Hope of 28 Dec 1785 indicates the above surveys have been done (Ontario Archives, *Report 1905*, 399–400); (*OHIM* 3.1).
OTAR

Related maps

(**2**) *[1784–5]*
The North Side of Lake Ontario From Cataraque to Niagara Surveyed by Order of His Excellency General Haldimand under the direction of Samuel Holland Esqr Surveyor General in the Year 1784 – Copied from an Original by Lieutt Augustine Prevost R.F. [Sgd] Samuel Holland Survr Genl.
Col ms 143 x 293 cm 1" to 11/4 miles
Endorsements: 'No 23'
'N.B. The River Niagara surveyed by Lt. Tinling the other parts by Messrs Kotte and Peachey'; similar to the plan above except the map extends south to about Fort Erie and the Indian purchase line is marked 'Tract purchased for the Crown by Coll Johnson 9th May 1781'; the plan is L-shaped and does not include the area where the list of names is given on the other plan.
OTAR

---

5 *1785*
[Map of Upper Canada showing communication from Lake Ontario to Lake Huron by Lake LaClie]
Col ms 26 x 33 cm 1" to 50 miles Watermark: '... TAYLOR'
Enclosed with Benjamin Frobisher's letter to Henry Hamilton 2 May 1785 and further enclosed in Lt Gov Hamilton's letter no 3, 6 June 1785 (GBLpro CO 42/47 p 655); the map shows the whole province and Cataraqui, Niagara, and Detroit forts and Toronto are marked; the carrying place from Toronto to L LaClie [L Simcoe] and from there to L Huron are marked as straight lines; Rice L is named; Trent R and a few other rivers shown with several rivers flowing into the Ottawa R; notes on distances and navigability of L Simcoe and rivers from there to L Huron; Frobisher indicates in his letter that until a survey is done from the Bay of Quinte to L Simcoe, not enough is known of the possibilities of the Trent R route in comparison to the Toronto portage (Guillet, 132–6); (*OHIM* 6.13; *PRO Cat* 1380).
GBLpro (MPG 426)

---

6 *1785*
Plan of part of a projected communication from Cataraquoui to Lake Huron Quebec April 7th 1785 [Sgd] John Collins, D. Surveyor Genl 1785
Col ms 19 x 46 cm 1" to 4 miles
In Lt Gov Hamilton's of 7 Apr 1785 to Sydney (GBLpro CO 42/47 pp 397–9); shows the L Ontario shore from Carleton Is to Presqu'ile; part of Collins's survey of 1785 to L Huron (in the letter the final plan is promised later); shows various English place-names along the shore and houses around Cataraqui, along the mainland by the Bay

of Quinte, and at the east end of Prince Edward Is; Mohawk settlement; (*PRO Cat* 1467).
GBLpro (CO 42/47 p 397)

Related maps

(**2**) *1792*
[Map of north shore of Lake Ontario, the Trent River, and Rice Lake] [Sgd] John Collins D S G Quebec 5th May 1792
Col ms 18 x 26 cm Scale not given Watermark: 'J WHATMAN'
Enclosed in Lt Gov Simcoe's no 8 of 26 May 1792 to Dundas (GBLpro CO 42/316 p 117); the sketch accompanied '1785, Proceedings on my route from Kingston to Lake Huron [Sgd] John Collins Esq. Quebec 5th May 1792' and is an extract from his survey of July 1785, in this case showing a salt spring on the Trent R that Simcoe was interested in exploiting; Collins was instructed to make the survey to L Huron on 22 May 1785 by Henry Hamilton, the instructions probably arising from Frobisher's map (**5**) and report of 2 May (Ontario Archives, *Report 1905*, 371); the plan shows carrying places, falls, rapids, portages; notes on the route, nature of the land and trees, and suitability of terrain for roads; also a copy of this map and report in OTMCL (D.W. Smith Papers B-9 p 39); no map of the full route from the 1785 survey has been found although the results of the survey are shown on the District of Nassau plans, 1790 (**315**); (*PRO Cat* 1381).
GBLpro (MPG 91) OTMCL (D.W. Smith Papers B-9 p 39)

---

7 *1788*
Sketch of Lake Huron [Sgd] Quebec 6th Decr 1788. Gother Mann Captn Commandg Rl Engrs Plan E
Col ms 52 x 75 cm 1" to 14 miles Endorsements: 'Case 40 No 29'; stamp 'HMSPO'
Insets: 'Falls of St Mary' 1" to 1/2 miles, 'Matchadosh Bay' 1" to 11/4 miles; since this plan is marked 'Plan E,' it may be the original accompanying Gother Mann's report of 6 Dec 1788 enclosed in Dorchester's no 58 of 24 Oct 1790 (GBLpro CO 42/70 pp 41ff); Mann received instructions to make the journey and survey of the defences of the lakes from Lord Dorchester on 29 May 1788 (a copy of the report is in the District of Nassau Papers (OTAR RG 1 A-VII vol 29), cited incorrectly as John Collins's report in Ontario Archives, *Report 1905*, 347–63); shows rivers, islands, portages; notes on shorelines and navigability problems; place-names, relief, Indian settlement; Michilimackinac, soundings, settlement, small vessels' channel, and canoe channel at St Marys R on insets; for Mann's other plans, see **669**, **905**, **1111**, **1499**, **2011**; photoreproduction in OOAMA (NMC 21704); (*PRO Cat* 1468).
GBLpro (CO 700 Canada 38E)

Related maps

(**2**) *1788*
Sketch of Lake Huron 1788 [Sgd] Gother Mann Captn & Commandg Rl Engrs
Col ms 52 x 71 cm 1" to 14 miles Watermark: '... LONIAL' Endorsements: '399'; stamp 'HMSPO'
Enclosed with Lord Dorchester's no 58 of 24 Oct 1790 (GBLpro CO 42/12 f 805); differs only slightly from above map; one inset has a different title: 'Sketch of the Falls of St Mary' 1" to 1/2 mile; [Matchedash Bay] with different scale: 1" to 21/2 miles; photoreproduction in OOAMA (NMC 21703); (*PRO Cat* 1469).
GBLpro (MPG 272)

(**3**) *1788*
Sketch of Lake Huron. 1788 [Sgd] Circumnavigated by Gother Mann Captn Commandg Rl Engrs in Canada
Col ms 52 x 74 cm 1" to 14 miles Endorsements: stamps 'IGF' 'B↑O'
Insets: 'Sketch of the Falls of St Mary' 2" to 1 mile; 'Sketch of Matchadosh Bay' 1" to 21/2 miles; similar to copies above; (Holmden 1894; *OHIM* 6.17).
OOAMA (NMC 18557)

(**4**) *1788*
Sketch of Lake Huron 1788 [Sgd] Gother Mann Captn Commandg Rl Engrs
Col ms 52 x 74 cm 1" to 14 miles Endorsements: 'B↑O'
Very similar to third map above but lacking an indication of relief near Matchedash Bay; (Holmden 1894).
OOAMA (NMC 18558)

(**5**) *1788*
Sketch of Lake Huron taken in 1788
Col ms (pt missing) 52 x 76 cm 1" to 14 miles Endorsements: '813' '8'
Insets: 'Sketch of the Falls of S. Mary,' 1" to 1 mile, 'Matchadash Bay'; similar to above surveys, less finished and with minor variations; probably the plan listed in 'State of the Surveyor General's Office York ... 7th January 1807, Appendix A' as 'Plan of Lake Huron ... supposed to be from Col. Manns R. Engrs' (Ontario Archives, *Report 1905*, 511).
OTAR (SR 5925)

---

8 *1789*
Plan of the New Settlements from Point à Bodet to Niagara, comprehending the Carrying Places, the Rivers and Lakes to Lake Huron [Sgd] W Chewett D.P.S. and Draughtsman
Col ms 51 x 119 cm 1" to 6 miles Endorsements: 'New Settlements above Montreal Walsingham 1789' [with book-plate], 'Ext. of Mr James Greys letter ... 10 Sep/89 No 13'
Shows a better outline for the Bay of Quinte than 1784–5 plan and shows area from L Huron at Penetanguishene to Lancaster Twp, south to

Niagara; Toronto and carrying place, and portage marked; shows the Trent R system and portages to 'L LaClie' [Simcoe]; Indian and English place-names; the following twps named and/or numbered: Lancaster to Elizabethtown, Kingston Twp; Adolphustown, Fredericksburgh, Ernestown, and one unnamed twp north of the latter; notes in another hand about names of various military personnel with land grants and notes on distances from Montreal; photo-reproduction in OOAMA (NMC 117659).
GBL (Add Mss 31,866.1 (289b))

Related maps

(2) *[1789]*
Plan of the New Settlements from Point a Bodet to Niagara comprehending ... Huron W Chewett DPS and Draughtsman
Col ms 46 x 122 cm 1" to 6 miles
Very similar to plan above without the endorsements and notes.
GBLmm (Grenville Map no 64 case 75A)

---

9 *1789*
A Survey of Lake Ontario done by H. Laforce of the Naval Department & Lewis Kotté Assistant Engineer The North Shore in 1783 and the East and South Shores in 1789 by Order of His Excellency The Rt. Honble Lord Dorchester Governor and Commander in Chief Etc. etc. Copied from the Original Survey in the Drawing Room of the Engineers Department at Quebec by Wm Hall Draughtsman [Sgd] Examined Gother Mann Captn Commandg Rl Engrs
Col ms 123 x 288 cm 1" to 1 1/2 miles
Endorsements: stamp 'HMSPO'
Insets: 'Toronto Bay' 1" to 2000 ft, 'Kingston Harbour' 1" to 13 chains, 'Plan of the Entrance of the Harbour of Oswego' 1" to 200 ft; shows the shoreline with rivers, marshes, cliffs, sand-bars; Indian and English place-names; bldgs at Toronto shown at site of French fort; a translation of Laforce's journal is in Dorchester's no 58 of 24 Oct 1790 (GBLpro CO 42/70 pp 75ff); shows a better shoreline for the Bay of Quinté than 1784–5 map **(4)** but Toronto harbour is the same; photorepro-duction in OOAMA (NMC 26918); (*PRO Cat* 1514).
GBLpro (CO 700 Canada 40)

---

10 *1790*
A Map of Part of Canada for the use of His Majesty's Secretary of State Compiled in the Surveyor General's Office Pursuant to an Order in Council of the 22nd day of February 1790 Quebec this 1st day of October 1790 [Sgd] Samuel Holland Surveyor General, John Collins D.S.G.
Col ms 130 x 341 cm 1" to 6 miles Endorsements: stamp 'HMSPO'
Notes: 'Remarks This Map being a compilation from separate Surveys they are mentioned here by Command, for a test of its authenticity and in justice to the Acting Surveyor who shall be found to have merit by the accuracy of their work' (includes a complete list of twp and regional surveys to date with names of surveyors and dates), 'The District of Hesse laid down from Sketches no Surveys having been as yet reported to the Surveyor General's Office,' and 'The Niagara River from the Falls to Fort Erie, Lakes Erie and St. Clair and part of Lake Huron, are taken from sketches only'; the map shows the area from about Quebec west to include Upper Canada; depicts 37 twps in Upper Canada, named but some not yet surveyed; besides the twps shown on **11**, twps are now shown on the north shore of Niagara Peninsula; the Trent R system is shown to L LaClie, a few settlements are shown; 'The South side of Lake Ontario from Niagara to Carleton Island is only Sketched'; this or (3) below is probably the map referred to as having been sent to England in the minutes of the Land Committee of 4 Jan 1791 (Ontario Archives, *Report 1905*, 432); the accuracy is discussed in Olsen, 69–81, map 2; (*PRO Cat* 1690).
GBLpro (CO 700 Canada 44)

Related maps

(2) *1790*
A Map of Part of Canada ... 1st day of October 1790.
Col ms 126 x 348 cm 1" to 6 miles Endorsements: stamp 'B↑O'
Similar to map above but lacks Holland's and Collins's signatures; notes and lists of surveyors and surveys are the same; (Holmden 287).
OOAMA (NMC 35540)

(3) *1790*
Map of Part of Canada from Bay De La Val and Island of Barnaby in the River St. Lawrence to the Lakes Huron and Erie
Col ms 61 x 119 cm 1" to 18 miles Endorsements on back: 'Canada Case 37 no 48'; stamp 'HMSPO'
A note indicates 'This Map is a reduction from the Map of Six British Statute Miles to an Inch compiled in the Surveyor General's Office pursuant to an Order in Council of the 2nd Febry 1790 for the use of His Majesty's Secretary of State dated at Quebec 1st Octr 1790. Signed Samuel Holland Surveyor, John Collins D.S.G.'; shows the same information and notes as first map above; (*PRO Cat* 1691).
GBLpro (CO 700 Canada 45)

(4) *1791*
[A Map of the Province of Quebec, comprehending the Districts of Gaspé, Quebec, Three Rivers, Montreal, Luneburgh, Mecklenburgh and Nassau, the Provinces of Nova Scotia and New Brunswick ... in which are laid down the several Seigniories to facilitate a division of the country, for the purpose of an equal representation of the people in a House of Assembly. Compiled & drawn by command of

His Excellency, by Saml Holland, Surveyor-General Quebec, August 1791.] Compiled & drawn by Jn. Fredk. Holland 1791.
Col ms in 10 sheets Ea 126 x 92 cm 1" to 6 miles
Provenance: Nine sheets received from the Library of Parliament in 1967, the tenth sheet was already in OOAMA (Canada, *Archives Report* (1969), 57); the title is taken from the original slip-case now lost; the map is similar to (1) above but only shows Upper Canada to west end of L Ontario; twps are named and shown along the St Lawrence and Bay of Quinte, and from Niagara west along the south shore of L Ontario; the Trent R connection to L Simcoe is shown and the portage to Rice L and the Toronto portage.
OOAMA (NMC 11736)

---

11 *1790*
Plan of Part of His Majesty's Province of Quebec, from Montreal Westward; Part of the Ottawa River, the River Iroquois, as far as Kingston, the South Shore and Part of the North Shore of Lake Erie, Detroit River and part of Lake St Clair, delineated from my own Surveys, made in the Years, 1784, 1785, 1786, 1787, 1788, 1789. The remainder from the Surveys and Sketches of different persons. ... Finished 16th March 1790
Col ms 75 x 113 cm 1" to 15 miles Endorsements: stamp 'HMSPO'
A very inaccurate plan particularly for the western peninsula; the east and north coasts of L Huron, the south shore of L Ontario, and some of L Nipissing marked in yellow as 'inserted from Indian and other sketches'; the red lines 'shew extent of the present Settlements at and near Detroit in the District of Hesse'; shows churches, garrisons, and Indian villages; twps surveyed are shown in very inaccurate locations from Lancaster to Elizabethtown, Sidney to Kingston, and certain areas between are marked as areas settled by the Loyalists but twps not named; settlements of Loyalists on the Rideau R and Ottawa R shown but twps not named; the map is in a more formal hand than maps below but all were probably drawn by Patrick McNiff; photoreproduction in OOAMA (NMC 117660); the accuracy is discussed in Olsen, 58–69, map 1; (*PRO Cat* 85).
GBLpro (CO 700 Can 48)

Related maps

(**2**) *[1790]*
[Sketch of the eastern part of Upper Canada]
Col ms 75 x 93 cm Scale not given Watermark: 'I TAYLOR'
This is an untitled draft for the eastern part of the above map and shows the area from about Long Point east; remarks and legend not included; otherwise, shows the same twp notes and names as plan above.
OTAR (Simcoe Map 446981)

(**3**) *1790*
A Plan of Part of His Majesty's province of Quebec ... Iriquois ... from my own surveys made in the years 1784, 1785, 1786, 1787, 1788 and 1790, the remainder from the surveys and sketches of different persons ... finished 16th March 1790 [Sgd illegible]
Col ms 76 x 127 cm 1" to 15 miles
Very similar to first map except with an additional note that parts marked in red [including the twp areas along the Rideau, Thames, and Detroit rivers] 'Shew the Settlements made since June 84 with Loyalists and disbanded Troops'; more notes and detail in L Champlain area than on plans above; 'McNiffe' is either signed or endorsed across top part of map.
GBLmm (Grenville Map no 66 case 75B)

---

12 *[1790]*
Sketch of Lake Erie, Detroit River, Lake St. Clair & Part of Lakes Huron & Ontario intended to shew the Extravagant Claims to Lands in the District of Hesse By Patrick McNiff D.P.S. Copied from an Original, by Lieut John Fredk Holland Ry R N.Yk [Sgd] Samuel Holland Surveyor Genl
Col ms 49 x 67 cm Approx 1" to 15 miles
Endorsements: '937' '7' 'Sketch shewing extravagant claims of sundry persons in the vicinity of Detroit'
Shows the area from Niagara to Detroit in a considerably distorted shape; shows R La Tranche [Thames R], Grand, and Chippewa rivers and several others; shows Fort Erie, Detroit, Toronto, Point Pelee, Long Point, and 'Point au Pin' (noted as good harbour); shows tracts claimed by Mr Caldwell, A. Grant, and Schieffelin, and 'different persons' in the western end of the province and along major rivers; several names shown on the Detroit side, rivers shown along the south shore of L Erie; 'Loyalists' noted along the south shore [Essex Co area]; notes on the land; shows some similarity in outline to 1790 plan (**11**) but fewer rivers shown; probably the map Henry Motz instructed the Land Board of Hesse to make 19 Jan 1790 (Ontario Archives, *Report 1905*, 35); (*OHIM* 4.9).
OTAR

Related maps

(**2**) *[179?]*
[Untitled] James Bramall Toosey copied this not from an actual survey
Col ms 66 x 75 cm 1" to 15 miles Endorsements on back: 'Hesse Indian Claims J.G.S. ...'
The map is copied from McNiff's plan above but with the addition of notes on terrain and land for settlement from McNiff's later survey of 1791 (**910**).
OTAR (Simcoe Map 446701)

---

13 *[ca 1790]*
[Sketch of the Great Lakes area]
Col ms 22 x 37 cm Approx 1" to 55 miles
Watermark: 'CURTEIS & SONS'
A distorted version of Upper Canada similar to

McNiff's maps of 1790 (**11, 12**); identifies Cataraqui, Toronto, Niagara Falls, Fort Erie, Grand R, R La Tranche [Thames R], and Detroit; Hesse and Nassau [districts] shown north of L Huron; faint pencil notes about navigability of R La Tranche; on back notes on bearings for vessels in Great Lakes, Detroit, Mackinac, and Taquina Bay with distances initialled 'A R'; a fragment (probably the upper right corner) of a larger map since there is a margin on the top and right side.
OTAR (Simcoe Map 451191)

Related maps

(**2**) *[ca 1790]*
[Sketch map of the Great Lakes area west to the Mississippi River]
Col ms 46 x 46 cm Approx 1" to 53 miles
Two-thirds of this map (the northeastern portion) is very similar to (**1**), suggesting that plan above may originally have existed in this complete version; there is also a similar untitled plan in GBLpro, 24 x 36 cm, endorsed 'Case 44 no 7' and marking Hesse and Nassau in the area north of L Huron (*PRO Cat* 159).
GBLmm (Grenville Map no 68 case 75B) GBLpro (CO 700 Canada 62)

---

14 *1791*
Sketch / of the / WESTERN COUNTRIES / of / CANADA / 1791.
Print (engrav) 21 x 30 cm 1" to 90 geog miles
In John Long, *Voyages and Travels of an Indian Interpreter and Trader* (London: Printed for the author 1791), opp [1] (*Bib Can* 597; OONL (CIHM 36367)); shows the area from the Mississippi to the Saguenay R and from L Erie to James Bay; lakes north of L Superior 'according to the reports of the Indian Traders'; 'New Settlements' noted along R Cataraqui [St Lawrence R]; Ft Michilimackinac, Ft Detroit, and Ft Frontenac or Cataraqui shown; Indian tribes; NMC 6966 is a photoreproduction of a redrawn version of the map, original not located.
OOAMA (NMC 16098) OONL OTMCL

Later editions and states

(**2**) *1791*
SKETCH / of the / WESTERN COUNTRIES / of / CANADA / 1791. / WESTLICHES / CANADA // C. Reichard del et Sculps:. Brauns.
Print (engrav) 29 x 29 cm 1" to 90 geog miles
In John Long, *See und Land-Reisen* (Hamburg: B. Gottlob Hoffmann 1791); place-names are in English.
USDLC

(**3**) *1791 [1794]*
CARTE / des Pays situes à l'Ouest du / CANADA / 1791 // Gravé par P.F. Tardieu
Print (engrav) 21 x 30 cm 1" to 90 geog miles
In John Long, *Voyages chez differentes nations sauvages de l'Amerique Septentrionale* (Paris: Chez Prault [1794]), opp 17 (*Bib Can* 4759); the map has been reengraved with all place-names translated into French; otherwise, shows the same information as the English ed above.
OTMCL

---

15 *[1792]*
[Sketch map of Upper Canada and lands to west and south]
Col ms 21 x 25 cm 1" to 55 miles Watermark: 'J WHATMAN'
In Lt Gov Simcoe's no 5 of 10 March 1792, no 1, to Dundas about Indian lands recommended to be purchased (GBLpro CO 42/316 p 64); at same scale but different coast profile and rivers to the fragment in the Simcoe Map Collection (**13**) and containing later information; shows the settlements proposed on L Huron: one at Matchedash Bay and one at the base of the Bruce Peninsula; 'Brants Grant,' 'Huron Reserve of Detroit'; shows forts and Navy Hall at Niagara; shows areas south of the Thames, Trent, and Rideau rivers purchased from the Indians; shows the area from the Falls of St Mary east; (*OHIM* 4.1; *PRO Cat* 87).
GBLpro (MPG 90)

---

16 *[1792–3] (1795)*
Plan of the Province of Upper Canada, divided into Counties; by Order of His Excellency John Graves Simcoe Esqre, Lt Governor and Commander in Chief of the same, &c. &c. &c. Drawn by His Excellencys most Obedient and most Humble Servant. [Sgd] W. Chewett D.P. Surveyor Wm Chewett D.P. Surveyor
Col ms 68 x 128 cm Approx 1" to 13.3 miles
Endorsements: stamp 'HMSPO'
Originally enclosed in Simcoe's no 24 to Portland of 29 July 1795 (GBLpro CO 42/319 p 281); shows the 19 counties and ridings as proclaimed on 16 July 1792 including Essex, Kent, Suffolk, Norfolk, Lincoln in four ridings, York in east and west ridings, Durham, Northumberland, Hastings, Lennox, Addington, Prince Edward, Frontenac, Leeds, Grenville, Dundas, Stormont, Glengarry; [Ontario Co] covering the islands in the St Lawrence is not named; boundaries in the west extend north to the Thames R, and east of the Trent R they extend north to the Ottawa R; rivers and L LaClie partly drawn; Trent R system and L Huron shore after plan of 1788 (**7**) are shown; the map is considerably more accurate in outline than earlier efforts (Olsen, 82–93, map 6); a close copy in GBLpro (CO 700 Canada '59 dup') shows minor variations and lacks Chewett's signature; since it does not show York (named provincial capital in Aug 1793) or the survey of Long Point by Chewett in the summer of 1793, probably drawn in late 1792 or early 1793; reference to considerable work in drafting general maps is recorded in Chewett's journal and a plan was delivered to the Lt Gov's office on 2 Nov 1792 (OTAR RG 1 CB-1 vol 42); the original map was probably copied about July 1795

for dispatch to Portland (OTAR RG 1 A-I-1 vol 51 p 987); a printed facsimile of the transcript by Brigly of 'No 59 Dup' is found in Doughty and McArthur (at end); (*PRO Cat* 1383); there is also a copy in GBTAUh (C122 Aa2) with identical title and endorsed 'Copied 12 Jan [missing] ... for Secretary [missing].'
GBLpro (CO 700 Canada 59) GBTAUh (C122 Aa2)

Related maps

(2) *[1792–3?]*
A Map of the Province of Upper Canada.
Col ms 43 x 79 cm 1" to 20 miles
A reduced version and less finished than the plan above; shows the same counties, rivers, coastline configuration, and place-names; part of Michigan peninsula cut off on the left; photoreproduction in OOAMA (NMC 117662).
GBLmm (Grenville Map no 70 case 75B)

---

17 *[1793?]*
[Sketch map of Upper Canada and surrounding area]
Col ms 24 x 37 cm 1" to 50 miles
Shows a sketch of the province with various places including Toronto, Niagara, Kingston, Iroquois Bay, Sturgeon Bay, Thunder Bay, and Bay of Quinte; later adds in a different ink include completion of shape of L Simcoe, Toronto's name corrected to York, Penetanguishene Rd and military site, and corrections to shapes of islands in L Huron (north shore); L Huron is from plan of 1788 (**7**); a note indicating that one river runs underground and communicates with the La Tranche [Thames] R is initialled 'H'(?); (Brun, no 11, p 3).
USMiU-C (Simcoe Papers)

---

18 *[1793]*
[Sketch of Upper Canada showing proposed towns and military roads]
Col ms 20 x 30 cm 1" to 50 miles
Enclosed with Lt Gov Simcoe's letter of 19 Oct 1793 in his report no 19 of 27 Jan 1794; (GBLpro CO 42/318 p 6); a duplicate was enclosed with copy of report dated 23 Feb 1794 (GBLpro CO 42/318 p 54); shows the towns of York, Oxford, London, Chatham, [Charlotteville], and settlement at Penetanguishene Bay as proposed by Simcoe; also shows military roads planned or under construction including [Yonge St] from York to L Simcoe, [Dundas St] from York to London, and a road from London to Long Point; counties named; probably drawn by Mrs Simcoe; photoreproduction in OOAMA (NMC 49482); (*PRO Cat* 1385).
GBLpro (CO 42/318 p 54; MPG 95)

Related maps

(2) *[1793?]*
[Sketch map of the Great Lakes and eastern United States]
Col ms 58 x 63 cm 1" to 40 miles
Note: 'Proposed towns are coloured Red'; shows some similarity in shape for Upper Canada and the same information about planned towns and roads except road from London to Long Point not shown; (*OHIM* 3.8).
OTAR (Simcoe Map 446292)

(3) *[1794]*
Sketch of Upper Canada
Col ms on birchbark 19 x 29 cm Scale not given
Sent to England as a presentation copy for the Prince Regent probably in 1794; shows the planned towns and names of counties established in 1792; routes from York to Burlington Bay and to Oxford, York to Kingston, part of [Yonge St], a route from Chatham to Pointe aux Pins; route from Kempenfelt Bay to Penetanguishene; drawn by Mrs Simcoe and reproduced in *Mrs Simcoe's Diary* (1965), between 92–3; photoreproduction in OTAR; (*The American War of Independence ... a Commemorative Exhibition* (1975), no 199).
GBL (Map K.Top CXIX.15)

(4) *[1793?]*
[Sketch of Upper Canada]
Col ms 20 x 29 cm 1" to 50 miles
Endorsed: 'one of the earliest maps'; keys 'Proposed Towns ... Red' and 'Proposed Military Roads dotted in yellow' (colours appear faded or not shown but Dundas St to Oxford, and Yonge St shown); shows Chatham, London, Oxford, York, Queenston, Kingston, and Navy Hall; 'Pennandatashene Bay'; the plan appears to date from 1793 and may be by Mrs Simcoe.
Private Collection

---

19 *1794*
Chart of part of Upper and Lower Canada June 1794
Col ms in 2 sheets Approx 56 x 109 cm Approx 1" to 35 miles
Shows the area from Quebec to the Mississippi R and L Superior; 'Proposed towns by Col Simcoe coloured Blue' include as listed Chatham, London, Oxford, York, Burlington Bay, Long Point, 'Pennatikansheen Bay'; 'Proposed Military Roads coloured Yellow' include Burlington Bay to London, London to Long Point, and Yonge St; L LaClie [Simcoe] and Long Point have very inaccurate shapes although drawn after Simcoe's Oct 1793 trip to Penetanguishene and the survey of Long Point in the summer of 1793; 'Posts on the American side of the Treaty line' are listed; two other routes shown from Chatham to L Erie.
GBLmm (Grenville Map 65 case 75B)

---

20 *1794*
A NEW MAP / OF / UPPER & LOWER / CANADA / 1794. // Published October 10, 1794, by J. Stockdale Piccadilly. Geor: Allen sculpt
Print (engrav) 18 x 23 cm Scale not given
In Jedidiah Morse, *The American Geography*, new ed (London: John Stockdale 1794), opp iii (*Bib Can* 4786, *LC Atlases* 1361); depicts a poor shape for

Upper Canada and the only river shown is 'New River' [Thames R]; few place-names; from Anticosti to L Winnipeg, and L Erie to James Bay; (OOAMA MacDonald Collection 512 (NMC 93316)).
OOAMA (NMC 93316) OMSA OTMCL USDLC

Later editions and states

(2) *1798*
A NEW MAP / OF / UPPER & LOWER / CANADA / 1798. // Published Novr 10th 1798 by J. Stockdale Piccadilly.
Print (engrav) 17 x 23 cm Scale not given
In Isaac Weld, *Travels through the States of North America* (London: John Stockdale 1799), I: opp 175 (*Bib Can* 4789), and in the 2nd ed (London 1799) (GBL 10408.ee.9), and in the 3rd ed (London: John Stockdale 1800) (*Bib Can* 709), and in the 4th ed (London 1801) (Lande 891), and the 4th ed (London 1807), I: opp 305 (OOA); from the same plate as above map but with a few changes; 'New River now R Thames,' 'Jonstown,' Kingston, York, Falls of Niagara, and 'Clie Lake' [Simcoe] all named; (OOAMA MacDonald Collection 513 (NMC 93317)); the map does not appear in the French ed of Weld but a smaller version entitled 'NOUVELLE CARTE / DU CANADA / SUPÉRIEUR ET INFÉRIEUR.' appears as an inset on the larger folding map in *Voyage au Canada* (Paris [1800]), at end (*Bib Can* 710).
GBL OOA OOAMA (NMC 93317) OTAR OTMCL QMM(L) QMMMCM USDLC

(3) *1800*
A NEW MAP / OF / UPPER & LOWER / CANADA // nach dem Englischen original gestochen von C. Jattnig
Print (engrav) Approx 17 x 22 cm Scale not given
In Isaac Weld, *Reisen durch die Staaten von Nordamerika* (Berlin 1800), at end (OONL; CIHM 41987); redrawn from the English ed with names generally in English.
OONL

(4) *1801*
NEUE KARTE / von Ober und Unter / CANADA // Joh. Stenger sc.
Print (engrav) 17 x 22 cm Scale not given
In Isaac Weld, *Reisen durch die Staaten von Nordamerika* (Berlin und Hamburg 1801), after 475 (Lande S2305); the map has been reengraved from the 1798 ed with major place-names translated into German.
QMM(L)

(5) *1802*
Nieuwe Kaart / van / OPPER en NEDER / CANADA / 1798.
Print (engrav) Approx 17 x 22 cm Scale not given
In Isaac Weld, *Reizen door de Staaten van Nord-Amerika* (Den Haage 1802), II: opp 25 (OONL; CIHM 42004); redrawn from the English ed with Dutch place-names.
OONL

(6) *1819*
Carta del / CANADA' / Superiore ed inferiore / nel Viaggio di Weld. // A. Stucchi dis. ed inc.
Print (engrav) 16 x 19 cm Scale not given
In Isaac Weld, *Viaggio nel Canada* (Milano: Tipografia di Giambattista Sonzogno 1819), I: opp 272 (Lande 892; III: frontis, OTUTF); reengraved from 1798 ed with major place-names translated into Italian; the Lande copy lacks engraver's statement.
OTUTF QMM(L)

---

21 *1794*
[Plan of Upper Canada showing Simcoe's journeys and other surveys] Surveyor Genls Office Newark 23rd Octr 1794 [Sgd] W Chewett
Col ms 75 x 153 cm 1" to 4 miles Watermark: 'J WHATMAN'
Originally enclosed in Lt Gov Simcoe's no 2 of 23 Oct 1794 to the Duke of Portland in which he summarizes his plans for the defence and settlement of Upper Canada (GBLpro CO 42/318 pp 343ff); shows the communications and journeys between York and L Simcoe, and York, Thames R, and L St Clair made in 1792–4; Yonge St, 'Continuation of Dundas St' shown from York to Oxford and London; the Six Nations Indian lands shown along the Grand R; Chewett's survey of Long Point in the summer of 1793 is shown; sites of Chatham, London, Dorchester, and Oxford shown, and site of proposed block to be purchased north of London; note in pencil: 'I was forced to detain the man until I could finish the Plan W Chewett'; (*PRO Cat* 1384).
GBLpro (MPG 98)

---

22 *[1794?]*
Plan of Ye North Shore of Lake Ontario from York to Oswegatchie [Sgd] A: Aitkin D. Syr.
Col ms 53 x 296 cm 1" to 2 miles Watermark: 'J WHATMAN'
Note on back: 'North Shore of Lake Ontario ... U Canada unfinished'; all of the twps are named and located from York to Elizabethtown but boundaries are not shown; many rivers shown and named; Scarborough bluffs; 'Portage to Rice Lake' is shown between Hope and Hamilton twps; the plan is unfinished but was probably prepared before the survey of Presqu'ile by Aitken in Sept 1795 and after the town of York was laid out in the summer of 1793.
OTAR (Simcoe Map 446487)

---

23 *1795*
Map of the Country Westward of Lake Ontario to the River Mississippi and Southward to the 37° of North Latd intended more immediately to shew the Frontier Boundary between the United States and the Indian Tribes; as expressed in their Treaty of the 3d August 1795: with the particular Grants or Concessions in favor of the United States as therein described. [Sgd] Quebec 25th Octbr 1795 Gother Mann Lt Coll Commandg Royal Engineers.

Col ms 132 x 181 cm 1" to 14 miles Endorsements: stamp 'HMSPO'
Originally accompanied Dorchester's no 71 of 26 Oct 1795 to Portland (GBLpro CO 42/104 p 429); note: 'This Map is compiled partly from Hutchin's Map of the Western parts of Virginia, Pennsylvania and partly from authorities in the Engineer's Drawing Room at Quebec'; shows most of Upper Canada from the St Lawrence R and west to the Mississippi R and south to Virginia; most detail is shown for the American regions; the shape of Upper Canada is very similar to the [1795] map (**24**) except that Manitoulin is shown as a series of islands similar to earlier maps; portages and routes to L Simcoe shown from Simcoe's trip; a few routes or boundaries are shown around the Thames R; York, Kingston, Navy Hall, and an 'old Indian village' at Rondeau marked; (*PRO Cat* 2053).
GBLpro (CO 700 No Am Col Gen 25)

Related maps

(**2**) *1800*
Map of the Country Westward of Lake Ontario to the Rr Mississippi ... By Lt Wm Hall Royal Arty and J.B. Duberger 1800. [Sgd] Gother Mann Col. Commandg Rl Engrs Quebec 3 Novr 1800.
Col ms 127 x 174 cm 1" to 14 miles
Similar to the map above and containing the same note on sources; additions for Upper Canada include Fort George, a portage from L Ontario to Rice L, and more routes shown around the Thames R.
GBL (Maps 23.b.2)

---

24 *[1795?]*
Plan of Upper Canada Compiled from the Latest Surveys & best Observations
Col ms 55 x 85 cm Approx 1" to 30 miles(?) Watermark: 'J WHATMAN' Endorsements: 'N 12' '965'
The outline appears to be based on the 1792–3 Chewett map (**16**) but with corrections to shape of L Simcoe from the surveys there in late 1793 (although the orientation is wrong); Manitoulin Is has been revised and more islands are shown in L Erie; routes are shown from York to L Simcoe, Burlington Bay to the Thames R; red lines are shown from Kingston along the north shore of L Ontario and along Niagara R and the north shore of L Erie to Long Point, and from Point Pelee around the shore to the Windsor area, possibly showing coast surveys; only a few rivers are shown and almost no place-names, suggesting plan is unfinished; observations of latitude and longitude are given for Kingston by Kotte, for Niagara by Ellicot, and for Detroit from earlier sources; the shape of L Ontario and the style is very similar to **28** and **443**, and the map may be by Lt Joseph Bouchette who was noted as making a map of Upper Canada during the winter of 1794–5 (*DCB* VII:95).
OTAR (SR 5980)

---

25 *[1795]*
[Sketch map of Upper Canada showing the routes Lt Gov Simcoe took on journeys between March 1793 and September 1795]
Col ms 48 x 80 cm 'about 20 mile to an Inch'; Watermark: 'J WHATMAN'
Shows the routes that are listed on the map; 'on foot from Niagara to Detroit and returned ... March 8, 1792' [i.e., 1793] (cf. Simcoe, *Correspondence*, 1:288–93); 'on foot & canoe York-Gloucester Bay & L Huron & back by Oct 1793'; 'York to the Thames R & to Detroit & to the Miamis & returned May 5th 1794'; 'York to Kingston by open boat arrived Dec 5 1794'; 'Niagara to Long Pt on foot & in boats & returned Sept 1795'; lists of distances and further notes given; a section of the map along L Ontario has been cut out and replaced; established and proposed towns shown; Dundas St, Yonge St; a few county and riding names, and a rough grid of twps shown at the eastern end of the province; several different inks have been used, which may indicate the plan was compiled over some time, and erasures of information are apparent in some parts; the shape of the province has been improved over 1793 maps (**18**); probably by Mrs Simcoe since the notes are of a personal nature, e.g., 'This country was with hazard & difficulty explored by Lt G Simcoe'; (*OHIM* 3.10).
OTAR (Simcoe Map 445090)

Related maps

(**2**) *[1795?]*
[Sketch map of Upper Canada] [Endorsed title]: 'Chart of N. America designed under the Orders of my Lieut Genl Simcoe and sent to me while he was Governor there'
Col ms 31 x 44 cm Scale not given
Provenance: gift of David McCord to QMMMCM; the outline and place information are very similar to those on Mrs Simcoe's map above; the routes of journeys are shown and listed, the proposed towns marked in red, and the same notes indicate York and Chatham are begun, Dundas St laid out from Oxford to the Bay of Quinte and nearly finished from Oxford to Burlington Bay; however, on this map Dundas St is shown considerably inland from York and extending to the border with Lower Canada; this map also has many more notes on water and land routes to Penetanguishene and along the St Clair and Ottawa rs, on harbours, and on the Indians; the official referred to is possibly the Duke of Portland, secretary of state for the Home Department from 1794 to 1801, Lord Grenville or Lord Dorchester to all of whom Simcoe sent dispatches during 1794–6 (cf. Simcoe, *Correspondence*); the main part of the map was probably drawn by Mrs Simcoe but the additional notes may be by Lt Gov Simcoe or someone else.
QMMMCM

---

26 *1796*
Map of the Provinces of Upper and Lower Canada, comprehending also the Provinces of New Brunswick, Nova Scotia; the islands of Cape Breton, and St. John: with part of New England and extending westward to the River Mississippi Compiled & Drawn at Quebec 1796 by Lt. W. Hall R. Arty under the direction of Lt. Col. Mann Royal Engineers
Col ms 93 x 238 cm 1" to 20 miles Endorsements: 'B↑O' 'IGF'
A detailed compiled map for eastern Canada; sources for the various parts of Upper Canada cited including 'Plan of Part of the Province of U.C. by McNiff' (see **11**) for the north shore of L Erie and L St Clair area, the communication to Matchedash from a sketch by Pilkington (see **317**), the part north of L Superior from A. Arrowsmith, L Huron from Gother Mann (see **7**); the districts and co lines according to 1791 Act 'are laid down on this map from a Plan of the organized part of Upper Canada (see Q 11)' (probably a copy of **16**); shows proposed canals between the Thames and the Grand R and between the Grand and the Chippewa; notes on lake navigation and inland routes and portages; photoreproduction in OOAMA (NMC 29041); (*PRO Cat* 156).
GBLpro (CO 700 Canada 60A)

Related maps

(**2**) *1798*
Map of the Provinces of Upper and Lower Canada ... Compiled & Drawn at Quebec 1798 by Lt. W. Hall Rl Arty & J.B. Duberger Draftsman, under the direction of Colonel Mann Rl Engrs
Col ms 96 x 244 cm 1" to 20 miles Endorsements: stamps 'B↑O' 'IGF'
Shows the same information and same shape for Upper Canada but lacks comments on sources; (*PRO Cat* 157).
GBLpro (CO 700 Canada 60B)

---

27 *[1797?]*
[Endorsed title]: 'Upper Canada the first & second organization of the Province'
Col ms 52 x 74 cm Approx 1" to 20 miles
Watermark: 'J WHATMAN' Endorsements: '964'
Shows the new districts created in 1798: Western, London, Niagara, Home, Midland, Johnstown, and Eastern (proclaimed in 1800, Armstrong, 160), and the 'present' limits between these districts and between the counties created in 1792; since county and district lines were projected to the northern part of the province, there is considerable clashing between lines; twps are shown and numbered but no key given; Ontario Co, covering the islands in eastern Ontario, is named; the map shows the major towns established or (proposed), including Sandwich, Amherstburg, (Colchester), Chatham, (London), Middleton, (Dorchester), (Oxford), Charlotteville, Queenstown, Newark, York, Markham, Gwillimbury, (Gloucester), Newcastle, Adolphustown, (Vesey), Kingston, Augusta, Johnston, and Cornwall; blocks of crown and clergy reserves, Indian land; Dundas St from Oxford to the boundary with Lower Canada, Yonge St; since the twps are shown in similar fashion to (2) but the map does not show the new counties, it is possibly an earlier draft per correspondence of 25 Apr 1797 (OTAR RG 1 A-I-1 Bk 15 pp 43–4 (MS 30 reel 3)); a transcript was printed in Ontario Archives, *Report 1905*, cxvi; a rough drawing and L Simcoe and other shorelines very inaccurately shown; (Olsen 14).
OTAR

Related maps

(**2**) *1798*
A Plan of the Organized Part of the Province of Upper Canada, according to a Bill which has passed the two Houses, and reserved for the Signification of the Royal Pleasure – [Sgd] D W Smith, Chief Surveyor of Lands Actg as Surveyor General Upper Canada
Col ms Approx 55 x 84 cm 1" to 20 miles
In President Russell's no 40 of 11 Aug 1798 to the Duke of Portland (GBLpro CO 42/323 p 5); the report includes 'Reference From the Numbers on the Plans for the Names of the Townships &c.' on pp 6–9; the outline of the province is the same as on plan above; shows the new districts as listed above and the same twps with the same nos; shows the new counties of Oxford, Middlesex, Haldimand, Prescott, Russell, Carleton, and Simcoe; the boundaries of the former counties have been readjusted to the new ones and aligned with the twp boundaries; projected District of Newcastle; the new district boundaries are also shown as they have been realigned to the orientation of the twp surveys and to the new counties; Suffolk and Ontario cos deleted; a few places, reserves, and Yonge St and Dundas St shown; a transcript of this map was 'Lithographed to Accompany the Report on Canadian Archives for 1891, ... (Canada, Public Archives, *Annual Report ... 1891* (Ottawa 1892)); (Olsen 15?).
GBLpro (CO 42/323 p 5)

(**3**) *[1798]*
Plan of the Organized part of the Province of Upper Canada as divided into Districts Counties Ridings and Townships according to a Bill passed the two houses and which has received the Royal Approbation.
Col ms 42 x 135 cm 1" to 10 miles Endorsements: '180'; printed paste-on: '180. Original Map of Upper Canada, divided into districts, prepared for the Surveyor-General about 1798'
Provenance: owned by James Bain, D.C.L., Toronto, and given to OTMCL in 1980; folded into binding with D.W. Smith book-plate, on spine: 'Upper Canada Settlements'; the map is in William Chewett's hand; shows the same districts, counties, and twps as (**2**) but shows only the more

southerly, settled part of the province; the map is at a larger scale and shorelines are more carefully and accurately drawn than the other plans; the twps are named on the map; early settlements and (town plots) shown as follows: Sandwich, Amherstburg, Chatham, (London), (Oxford), (Dorchester), Ft Welland, Ft Erie, Queenstown, Newark, York, (Gwillimbury), (Newcastle), Kingston, Johnston, Cornwall; projected district of Newcastle shown; (not in Olsen).
OTMCL (D.W. Smith Papers)

(**4**) *1799 (1800)*
A Plan of the organised Part of the Province of Upper Canada, according to a Bill which has passed the ~~two~~ [*sic*] Upper Houses, and reserved for the Signification of the Royal Pleasure. Surveyor General's Office, Upper Canada 28th August 1799. For the Acting Surveyor General (Signed) Chewett & Ridout. Copied in the Engineer's Drawing Room Quebec by Lieut Wm Hall Rl Arty [Sgd] Gother Mann Coll Commandg Rl Engrs Quebec 3d Novr 1800.
Col ms 56 x 78 cm 1" to 20 miles Watermark: 'J WHATMAN 1791' Endorsements: '43.10.9.55'
The word 'Upper' has been added and 'two' crossed out in the title; shows the districts, counties, and ridings as in (2) above; 152 twps shown, most named in a table; 'The names of the townships are taken from a plan in the Engineers Drawing Room, Quebec'; the 'projected District of Newcastle' is shown (created from the eastern part of the Home District in 1802); photoreproduction in OOAMA (NMC 21351); (Olsen 16).
GBL (Maps 23.b.3 (no 18))

---

28 *[1799?]*
A Plan of Lake Ontario Compiled by [Sgd] Jos Bouchette Lieut 1st Battn Rl [VR?]to His Excellency Peter Hunter Esqr Lieutenant General of His Majesty's Forces Lieut Governor and Commander in Chief of the Province of Upper Canada &c&c&c
Col ms 69 x 115 cm 1" to 8 miles
Insets: 'Plan of the Different Channels Leading from Kingston into Lake Ontario Surveyed and sounded by [Sgd] Jos. Bouchette' 1" to 40 chains, 'A Plan of York Hr Sounded by [Sgd] J Bouchette' 1" to 20 chains, 'Plan of Nicholas and Egg Id Surveyed and bounded by [Sgd] Jos. Bouchette' 1" to 20 chains; eight watercolour views are arranged around the dedication including 'Navy Bay,' 'Navy [Hall],' '[Ft] Levy,' 'Niagara [Ft],' '[K]ingston,' 'York,' [Ft York], and 'Sodus [Bay]'; remarks on currents, nautical hazards, etc, at Oswego, sailing directions for Niagara and York harbours; a few other points; place-names are different from other maps; probably prepared after Bouchette became a lieutenant in the Royal Canadian Volunteer Regiment in 1797 and presented to Lt Gov Hunter early in his governorship (*DCB* VII:95).
USDNA (RG 77 dr 113 sheet 1)

---

29 *[1800]*
CHARTE / der neuen Niederlassungen / in / OBER CANADA / nach der Smythschen Charte / reducirt / von / I.C.M.R. ... / 1800.
Print (engrav) 19 x 31 cm Scale not given
In *Allgemeine geographische Ephemeriden* (Weimar: Verlag des Industrie-Comptoirs 1800), 6:334; a redrawing reduced in scale of Smith's 1800 map (**30**); some names in German.
USDLC

Later editions and states

(**2**) *[1800?]*
CHARTE / Der neuen Niederlassungen / in / OBER CANADA / nach der Smythschen Charte / reducirt / von / I.C.M.R.
Print (engrav) Approx 19 x 31 cm Scale not given
Redrawn with different letter styles in title and on map; a spelling error 'West District' on map above has been corrected; photoreproduction in OOAMA (NMC 119059; MacDonald Collection 513A). Original not located

---

30 *1800*
A MAP / of the Province of / UPPER CANADA, / describing / ALL THE NEW SETTLEMENTS, TOWNSHIPS, ETC. / WITH THE COUNTRIES ADJACENT, FROM / Quebec to Lake Huron. / Compiled at the Request of / HIS EXCELLENCY MAJOR GENERAL JOHN G. SIMCOE, / FIRST LIEUTENANT GOVERNOR, By David William Smyth Esqr. / Surveyor General. / LONDON, Published by W. FADEN, Geographer to HIS MAJESTY and to H.R.H. the PRINCE OF WALES. / Charing Cross, April 12th 1800. / Accompanied with a topographical Description / price 10s. & 6d.
Print (engrav), sometimes hand col Ea 57 x 87 cm [Approx 1" to 23 miles]
The first printed map of Upper Canada; to accompany Smith's *A Short Topographical Description of His Majesty's Province of Upper Canada* (London 1799) (*Bib Can* 734); shows twps, towns, settlements, forts, Dundas St, Yonge St, and two proposed canals to unite the Thames and Grand rivers and at Presqu'ile; the counties and districts are those of Simcoe's in 1792 and the map was probably first prepared during his term and before 1796 (cf. Whebell, *Printed maps* ...), but has some later additions; shows Dundas St from London to Kingston; the overall shape is similar to **24** except Long Point oriented more correctly and there are changes to position of certain features (Bruce Peninsula shown 1° further east); most towns or proposed towns as in plan **27** except Markham, Gloucester, Vesey deleted and shows approx the same number of twps; OOAMA MacDonald Collection 444 (NMC 98186) folding into cover with title in ms 'Upper Canada'; (Dionne 775; Holmden 2765; *OHIM* 3.14); a comparison of this map and **16** is found in Olsen, 93–112, map 17).
GBL (70640(2)) OOAMA (NMC 15289; 15290; 98186) OTAR OTMCL USDLC

Later editions and states

(**2**) *1813*
— Accompanied with a topographical Description. / Second Edition / 1813.
Counties revised to those of 1798; districts now shown: Eastern, Johnstown, Midland, Newcastle, Home, Niagara, London, and Western; a few twps have been added; some county names misspelled, e.g., 'Lenox and Haddington'; the shoreline has been enhanced by addition of linework; (Holmden 2768; Olsen map 20).
GBL (70640(20)) OOAMA (NMC 15292–3)

(**3**) *1818*
— / Second Edition / 1818.
The west coast of the Michigan peninsula has been drawn in; Gore District has been added as well as twps on the north shore of the Ottawa R in Lower Canada; (Holmden 2771; Olsen map 21; OOAMA MacDonald Collection 450 (NMC 119062)).
OOAMA (NMC 15295; 119062) OTAR OTMCL USDLC

(**4**) *1831*
— By David William Smyth / Esqr Surveyor General. / LONDON, Published by JAS WYLD Geographer to His MAJESTY. / Charing Cross April 12. / 1831. Watermark (GBL and USDLC): 'RUSE & TURNERS 1828'
Change to imprint only; GBL copy has '45' and OOAMA '49' stamped on back at upper corner; (Olsen map 22; OOAMA MacDonald Collection 454 (NMC 119045), 455 (NMC 119065)).
GBL (70640(68)) OOAK OOAMA (NMC 119045; 119065) USDLC

(**5**) *1835*
— COMPILED FROM THE ORIGINAL DOCUMENTS / in the / SURVEYOR GENERAL'S OFFICE. / LODON, [*sic*] / Published by JAS. WYLD, Geographer to HIS MAJESTY. / CHARING CROSS EAST. / 1835.
OOAMA (NMC 15296, 95872) folding into sleeve with cover-title: 'JAS. WYLD & SON (Successors to MR. FADEN.) Geographer to His Majesty ... CHARING CROSS (EAST) nearly opposite Northumberland House ...'; scale bar added; shows a major improvement in the shape of L Huron and the Bruce Peninsula; additions of twps in the Huron and Simcoe districts and north of L Ontario; addition of Bathurst District; OTUTF copy with cover-title 'JAMES WYLD (Successor to MR. FADEN ...' and in ms 'E.B.B. Upper Canada ...'; (Olsen map 23; OOAMA MacDonald Collection 462, 463).
GBL (70640(64)) OKQ OOAMA (NMC 15296; 94069; 95872) OTUTF

(**6**) *1838*
— Geographer to HER MAJESTY. / CHARING CROSS EAST. / 1838.
Two states:
(6a) Shows a few new place-names and roads; OOAMA (NMC 15297) copy has '49' stamped on back; OTUTF, OTMCL, and OOAMA copies (OOAMA MacDonald Collection 471 (NMC 119068) and NMC 15298) fold into sleeve with same cover-title as 1835 above except 'Geographer to HER Majesty ... 4 Doors from Trafalgar Square.'
OOAMA (NMC 15297–8; 119068) OTAR OTMCL OTUTF QMM (L)
(**6b**) Additional rivers and lakes are shown in the Huron-Ottawa territory, a proposed railway is shown from Hamilton to London, and 'Indian Territory' is indicated in the area north of 'Lands Belonging to the Crown' and the Huron Tract; (OOAMA MacDonald Collection 472 (NMC 119044), 470 (NMC 119067)); the map also appeared in Wyld's *A New General Atlas of Modern Geography* (London [1840]) (*LC Atlases* 6091; GBL (maps 35.f.4, plate 49)); (Olsen (maps 24 and 25) describes two maps for 1838 at slightly different scales; Gagnon, I:4959).
GBL (70640(6), (65)) OOAMA (NMC 119044; 119067) OTAR USDLC

(**7**) *1841*
— 1841.
The same as (6b); (Olsen map 26).
OOAMA (NMC 15299) USDLC

(**8**) *1842*
— 1842.
Also appeared in Wyld's *A New General Atlas of Modern Geography* (London [1842]), plate '59' (*LC Atlases* 6096); cos added: Halton, Huron, Lanark; districts added: Brock, Talbot, Colborne, Dalhousie, Victoria; one OOAMA copy folding into cover with same imprint as (6a); (not in Olsen).
OOAMA (NMC 15300; 8923) OTMCL USDLC

(**9**) *1843*
— 1843.
The shape of L Nipissing has been changed and names added along the French R; 'Darley' and Somerville twps added; (not in Olsen).
OOAMA (NMC 15301) OTMCL

(**10**) *[ca 1845]*
— (date removed from title).
Same as 1843 map; also appeared in Wyld's *A New General Atlas of Modern Geography* (London [1852]), plate '59' (*LC Atlases* 808).
OOAMA (NMC 15302) USDLC

(**11**) *1846*
— 1846.
The same as 1843 map; (Olsen map 27).
GBL (70640(1)) OOAMA (NMC 21377) OTAR

(**12**) *[1854]*
— (date removed from title).
Also in Wyld's *A New General Atlas of Modern Geography* (London [1854]), plate '59' (GBLrg); a legend for railways and canals has been added; twps have been added to the base of the Bruce Peninsula and in a line from Harvey to Palmerston twps in the Newcastle and Midland districts; railway shown as built from Niagara Falls to St

Catharines and proposed from there to Windsor; possibly proposed railway lines from Toronto to Hamilton, Toronto to Montreal, and Guelph to Stratford also shown; (Dionne 956; Olsen map 28?; OOAMA MacDonald Collection 480 (with '59' on back) (NMC 119047) and 481 (NMC 119046)).
GBLrg OOAMA (NMC 119046–7) OTUTF

(13) *[ca 1862]*
— LONDON, Published by JAS. WYLD, Geographer to HER MAJESTY. / CHARING CROSS EAST.
Twps have been added in the Bruce Peninsula and drawn in with some named north to Macaulay, Airy, Murchison, and Chewett to Papineau in the Huron-Ottawa area, east of L Nipissing, and east of Sault Ste Marie; Muskoka and Opeongo rds and a road on the north shore of L Huron are shown; railways now shown as built; county names are all shown but district names not deleted; probably revised from printed plans of 1860 (**886**) and 1861 (**643**); OOAMA (NMC 15304) folding into cover with imprint 'JAMES WYLD Geographer to HER Majesty 457 Strand ...' and inscribed 'Comdr. J.F. Rushton ...'; (Olsen map 29?).
OOAMA (NMC 15304; 51376)

---

31 *[1800?]*
A MAP / of the Province of / UPPER CANADA, / describing ... By David William Smyth ... / LONDON ... W. FADEN ... April 12th 1800 [with ms adds of routes]
Print (engrav) with ms adds Approx 57 x 87 cm [Approx 1" to 23 miles]
Ms adds to a copy of **30(1)**; the routes are those of Simcoe's journeys to the Thames R and north to Matchedash Bay; ms adds possibly added much later.
OTAR (Simcoe Map 446764)

---

32 *[1800?]*
A MAP / of the Province of / UPPER CANADA, / describing ... By David William Smyth ... LONDON ... W. FADEN ... 1800 [with ms adds]
Print (engrav) with ms adds 57 x 87 cm 1" to 23 miles
Ms adds to a copy of **30(1)**; sgd on the back: 'John Duncan Campbell'; on the front a point is marked in the area between Black and Talbot rivers east of L Simcoe with note: 'I visited this place in the year 1800.'
OTAR

---

33 *[1801–2?]*
By Order of His Excellency Peter Hunter Esquire, Lieutenant General Commanding His Majesty's Forces in Upper and Lower Canada; & Lieutenant Governor of His Majesty's Province of Upper Canada. This Map of the organized part of the Province of Upper Canada, is Compiled and Corrected from Surveys in the Surveyor Generals Office, By His Excellencys Authority; Agreeably to the Latest division of the Province. [Sgd] David William Smith Surveyor Generale Wm Chewett Senr Surr & Draftsn
Col ms 117 x 165 cm 1" to 9.5 miles
Inset: 'Plan of the Town of York being the Seat of Government of Upper Canada.'; shows the districts and counties as of 1798; shows the same no of twps as on the 1797–8 maps (**27**) but more are now named; similar in outline to the 1800 map (**30(1)**) except the L Huron shoreline has been revised; the inset shows the extension of the town of York laid out west to Peter St in 1798; shows blockhouse, government bldgs, Russell Square and Simcoe Place; probably made before the 'projected Newcastle Dist' shown on map was created in 1802; Dundas St shown from York to Bay of Quinte and west from Burlington; Yonge St; (*OHIM* 3.13; Olsen, 119, map 7, links this map to Chewett's map of 1813 and dates it 1805).
OTAR (Canada Co. Maps no 189 shelf 5)

---

34 *1805*
A Map / of the PROVINCE OF / UPPER CANADA. // Published May 20th 1805.
Print (engrav) hand col 22 x 19 cm Scale not given
In D'Arcy Boulton, *Sketch of His Majesty's Province of Upper Canada* (London: Printed by C. Rickaby 1805), opp [viii] (*Bib Can* 781).
OOA OTMCL USNN

---

35 *1807*
A / NEW MAP / OF / UPPER & LOWER / CANADA, FROM THE LATEST AUTHORITIES. / BY JOHN CARY, Engraver. / 1807. // LONDON: Published by J. Cary Engraver & Map-seller No 181 Strand Decr 1st 1807.
Print (engrav) 46 x 52 cm 1" to 37 miles
Issued in J. Cary, *New Universal Atlas* (London: Printed for J. Cary 1808), [plate] no 53 (GBL; *LC Atlases* 714; Phillips, 194); some copies have plate no pasted on; probably also issued separately; includes northern parts to James Bay; shows districts, cos, major places, and some roads such as Dundas St; based on **30(1)**; (Dionne 790).
GBL GBLpro OKQ OOAMA (NMC 8512–5; 113507) OTAR (SR 81248) USDLC

Later editions and states

(2) *1811*
— 1811. // London: Published by J. Cary ... April 28, 1811.
Also issued in J. Cary, *New Universal Atlas* (London 1811), [plate] no 53 (*LC Atlases* 6031, GBL (Maps 40.f.11); same as 1807 ed but GBL map has no plate no; there is also a copy with ms adds showing boundary line re Treaty of 1783 and boundaries of the Indian territory (GBLpro FO 925/1407).
GBL (70615(17)) GBLpro (FO 925/1407) OMSA OOAMA (NMC 8516) OTMCL USDLC

(3) *1819*
— 1819. // London: Published by J. Cary ... Jany 1st 1819.

Also issued in J. Cary, *New Universal Atlas* (London: Printed for J. Cary 1819), [plate] no 54 (GBL; *LC Atlases* 736); same as 1807; (OOAMA MacDonald Collection 516 (NMC 6979)).
GBL OOAMA (NMC 6979) USDLC

(4) *1821*
— 1821. // London: Published by J. Cary ... Jany 1st 1821.
Pasted on back: '54'; same as 1807 ed; (OOAMA MacDonald Collection 517 (NMC 113506)).
OOAMA (NMC 113506, 24687)

(5) *1824*
— 1824. // London, Published by J. Cary Engraver & Map-Seller No 86 St James Str April 1st 1824.
In J. Cary, *New Universal Atlas* (London: 1824–[5]), [plate] no 54 (*LC Atlases* 745); plate no pasted on back of sheet; same as 1807 ed.
USDLC

(6) *1825*
— 1825. // London: Published by J. Cary Engraver & Map-seller No 86 St James Str.
The map is the same as the 1807 ed.
OOAMA (NMC 116818)

---

36 *1808*
CANADA. / BY JOHN CARY. // London: Published by J. Cary Engraver & Map-Seller No 181 Strand Octr 1st 1808 / 60.
Print (engrav) hand col 23 x 29 cm 1" to 130 miles
A reduction of Cary's 1807 map (**35(1)**) with the same information; (OOAMA MacDonald Collection 515).
OOAMA (NMC 122065)

---

37 *[ca 1810]*
A MAP / of the Province of / UPPER CANADA, / ... By David William Smyth ... LONDON ... W. FADEN ... April 12th 1800 [with ms adds showing proposed settlements and roads]
Print (engrav) with ms adds 57 x 87 cm [Approx 1" to 23 miles]
Shows 'Proposed new road from York to Amherstburgh' [Talbot Rd in part] with note that from Aldborough Twp west it may take one of two possible routes, 'Proposed new tract of road from R Trent to Kingston,' the area for a proposed settlement of 'Highlanders' north and west of Toronto and L Simcoe, revisions to L Huron shoreline, Mohawk lands; settlements of Loyalists and Americans shown by differently coloured dots (difficult to distinguish); SI for the Talbot Rd were first issued in 1809; photoreproduction in OOAMA (NMC 15291); base from printed map (see **30(1)**); (*PRO Cat* 158).
GBLpro (CO 700 Canada 61)

---

38 *1812*
TO THE OFFICERS OF THE ARMY AND THE CITIZENS OF THE UNITED STATES / This / Map / OF / UPPER AND LOWER CANADA. / and United States contigious / Contracted from the Manuscript surveys of P.F. / Tardieu / Is respectfully Inscribed by the publick's / most Obedient Servant / Thomas Kensett // Copy right secured and entered according to Act of Congress November 4th 1812 / Engraved by A. Doolittle New-Haven / and T. Kensett Sculp Cheshire Connect
Print (engrav) 35 x 46 cm Scale not given
A rough map showing the area from Quebec to L Superior and south to the Ohio R; twps are numbered and indexed in a table 'Reference to the Townships in Canada'; counties and districts shown; the map is in several states and appears to have been partially or completely re-engraved each time as the line patterns in the lakes vary on all states seen and there are many other variations; the final order of the states has not been fully determined but the possible sequence is shown below; the variations that show the differences for each state are described in each entry; this state (OOAMA (NMC 6977)) has wavy lines along the shores of the lakes and the boundary is only partly drawn through the lakes; 'unsurveyed land' is noted in the Huron-Bruce co area; (Karpinski 13)
(1b) The OTUTF copy appears to be a 2nd state of this plate; the wavy lines in the lakes have been erased and replaced with straight lines.
OOAMA (NMC 6977) OTUTF USDLC USMWA

Other editions and states

(2) *1812*
... Contracted from the manuscript survey of P.F. / Tardieu / ... Inscribed by the public's / ... // Copy-right secured and entered according to Act of Congress November 4th 1812 / Engraved by T. Kensett Cheshire / & A. Doolittle New-Haven.
The imprint has changed, the words 'survey,' 'publick's,' and 'copy-right' have been corrected or changed in title and imprint; a different wavy line pattern is shown throughout the lakes and the boundary is drawn more fully; the New Hampshire boundary line has been added and 'unsurveyed forests' not 'land' shown in the Huron-Bruce area.
USMH USMWA Private Collection

(3) *1812*
... Contracted from the Manuscript surveys of P.F. / Tardieu / ... // Coppy right secured and entered according to Act of Congress November 4th 1812 / Kensett Sculp. Cheshire / Connt
A heavy pattern of straight lines is shown well into the centre of the lakes with a ghost print visible; the imprint has changed; the words 'surveys,' 'public's,' and 'coppy right' are used in the title and imprint; 'Watenan Village' in Indiana and 'Canadian Honse' near L Abitibi incorrectly spelled.
GBE USMH

(4) *1812*
... This / Map / O[space]F / ... Manuscript surveys ... / most Obedient Servant / THOMAS KENSETT

// Coppy-right secured and entered according to Act of Congress November 4th 1812 / Kensett Sculp. Cheshire Connt.

A wavy line pattern is shown filling in the lakes but no boundary is shown through the lakes; Parts of the title and 'Coppy-right' in the imprint changed; 'Watenau Village' and 'Canadian House' now shown correctly.
OTAR USMiMtpT USMWA

(**5**) *1815*
To the Officers of the Army and Citizens of the United States This Map of Uppeer [*sic*] and Lower Canada and United States Contigious contracted from the Manuscript Survey of P.F. Tardieu is respectfully Inscribed by the publics most Obedient Servant Daniel Lee 1815.
Ms 37 x 49 cm Scale not given
Shows the same information as and possibly traced from a state of the Kensett map above.
USMA

---

39 *[1812–14]*
A / CORRECT MAP / of the / SEAT OF WAR, / Published by / JOHN CONRAD // Philadelphia Published as the Act directs by John Conrad and Fielding Lucas Baltimore
Print (engrav) 41 x 58 cm Approx 1" to 40 miles
Shows the area from Upper Canada to Lower Canada and south to Washington; twps named; the Moravian village on the R Thames or La Tranche is marked; a few roads; shows a very poor shape for Upper Canada.
USICHi

---

40 *1813*
CANADA // Published Jany 1st 1813 by S. & G. Neele, Strand / Neele sculp / XL.
Print (engrav) 22 x 29 cm Approx 1" to 130 miles
In *Neele's General Atlas ... Engraved by Samuel & George Neele* (London: Published by the engravers 1813), plate XL (OOAMA); a few place-names, rivers, lakes.
OOAMA

Later editions and states

(**2**) *1819*
— // Published Jany 1st 1819, by Pinnock & Maunder Strand / Neele sculp / XL.
Possibly from G. Pawley, *General Atlas* (London: S. & G. Neele 1819), and possibly also in the 1822 ed (Tooley, 492); the same as the 1813 ed.
OOAMA (NMC 7105)

---

41 *1813*
A MAP / EXHIBITING THE FRONTIERS / of / CANADA / and the / UNITED STATES; / intended to Illustrate / The Operations of the British & American Armies. / LONDON: Printed for C. SMITH, Mapseller & Publisher, 172, Strand. / Octr 1st 1813.
Print (engrav) sometimes hand col 51 x 76 cm 1" to 25.3 miles
Inset: 'A Sketch of the Coast of North America from the River St Lawrence to Chesapeake Bay.' approx 1" to 75 miles; forts, main towns, rivers, and many roads shown; (Holmden 292; Karpinski 20; Olsen map 9; *PRO Cat* 163).
GBLpro OOAMA (NMC 48908) OTMCL USDLC

---

42 *1813*
A MAP / of the / AMERICAN LAKES / and / ADJOINING COUNTRY, / the present SEAT OF WAR between / Great Britain & the United States. / Done in part, from a Sketch of the late / Major General Sr Isaac Brock. / LONDON: / Published Jany 21. 1813, by Luffman, 377, Strand.
Print (engrav) 20 x 41 cm 1" to 50 miles
Watermark: 'EDMEADS & PINE ... 1798'
OOAMA copy: 'Price 1s.6d the sheet 2s. in a case'; shows Upper Canada and part of Lower Canada and area south to Albany and Portland; only a few places shown in Upper Canada including Johnstown, Ft Frederick, Ft George, Queenston, Ft Erie, York, [Oxford], London, and Amherstburg; issued separately and also bound with other maps in [*Cities, Harbours, Forts, etc, by John Luffman 1801–16*] (OTMCL); (Holmden 1697 1/2; Karpinski 23).
OOAMA (NMC 6756–7) OTMCL

---

43 *1813*
A MAP of the LOCATED DISTRICTS in the / PROVINCE OF UPPER CANADA, / Describing all the New Settlements, Townships, &c. with the adjacent Frontiers; / Compiled and Corrected, / From the latest Surveys in the Surveyor General's Office / BY WILLIAM CHEWITT SENIOR SURVEYOR & DRAUGHTSMAN; / Under the Direction of Francis Gore Esqr Lieutenant Governor &c. &c. / To whom this Map is most respectfully inscribed / BY WILLIAM FADEN, / Geographer to His Majesty & to His Royal Highness the Prince Regent. / Charing Cross, January 1st 1813. // Published Jany 1, 1813, by W. Faden, Charing Cross. / Cooper sculp.
Print (engrav) hand col 83 x 116 cm 1" to 12.5 miles
D.W. Smith's *A Short Topographical Description of His Majesty's Province of Upper Canada* was revised by Francis Gore and published by W. Faden, London, in 1813 to accompany this new map (see *Bib Can* 736); the twps, cos, and districts are the same as those on the 2nd ed of Smith's map (**30(2)**) and the map is similar in shape although the L Ontario shoreline has been corrected and a few lakes to the north have been revised; (Holmden 2767; *OHIM* 2.18; Olsen, 113–28, map 8; OOAMA MacDonald Collection 444, 446).
OKQ OOAMA (NMC 48603–5) OTAR OTMCL OTUTF QMM(L) USDLC

Later editions and states

(**2**) *1819*
— Charing Cross, October 1st 1819. / Second Edition. // Published Octr 1, 1819 by W. Faden, Charing Cross. / Cooper sculp.

Insets added: 'PLAN / OF / YORK HARBOUR' approx 1" to 3/4 mile, 'PLAN / OF / KINGSTON HARBOUR' 1" to 3/4 mile, 'PLAN / OF / SACKETTS HARBOUR' 1" to 550 yds; a few twps in the Grand R tract are named and a few places added; Wentworth Co, Gore and Niagara districts added; Lord Selkirk's purchase at the mouth of the Grand R shown; (Olsen map 11).
GBLrg

(3) *1821*
— BY WILLIAM FADEN, / GEOGRAPHER TO HIS MAJESTY. / Charing Cross, August 3rd 1821. / Third Edition.
Imprint below border trimmed or deleted; the inset of York Harbour has been moved to the right; 'Note the Townships bounded by a Red line were laid out during the Government of the late Duke of Richmond'; several twps added north of the Thames; all twps shown in York and Simcoe cos west to line Luther to Zero; twps north of L Ontario added to line Mariposa to Emily, Marmora to Oso, Dalhousie to March; shorelines have been revised in the St Clair R, Georgian Bay, and Penetanguishene areas, and north of Balsam L from Lt Catty's exploration in 1819; the insets of York and Kingston show more roads; (not in Olsen).
GBC

(4) *1825*
— Under the Direction of / SIR PEREGRINE MAITLAND, K.C.B. Lt. GOVERNOR &c. &c. / To whom this Map is most respectfully inscribed BY WILLIAM FADEN, / GEOGRAPHER TO HIS MAJESTY. / LONDON, Pub'd by JAs. WYLD, Geographer to the KING and H.R.H. The Duke of York. / (successor to Mr. Faden) / 5 Charing Cross, April 5th 1825. // Cooper sculp.
The Bruce Peninsula, L Huron shoreline, and a few other rivers and lakes have been revised; twps added to line from Eldon to Palmerston north of L Ontario; Ottawa District and Halton Co added; (Holmden 2107; Olsen map 12; OOAMA MacDonald Collection 451 (NMC 119063, 452 (NMC 119064)).
OOAMA (NMC 11234; 119063–4) OTMCL USDLC

(5) *1836*
— Compiled and Corrected, / From the latest Surveys in the Surveyor General's Office. / LONDON, / PUBLISHED BY JAMES WYLD, GEOGRAPHER TO THE KING. / Charing Cross East. / 1836. // Cooper sculp.
Twps have been added in the Huron tract to line from Colborne to North Easthope twps and in the east to line from Lavant to Torbolton and McNab to Horton twps; Welland and Rideau canals and a few new places shown; York has been changed to Toronto on the map and in the title of the inset; (Gagnon I-4460; Olsen map 13; OOAMA MacDonald Collection 464 (NMC 119066).
GBLrg OOAMA (NMC 119066) OTAR OTMCL

(6) *1838*
--- PUBLISHED BY JAMES WYLD, GEOGRAPHER TO THE QUEEN / Charing Cross East. / 1838
Part of imprint and date has changed, otherwise the same as (5) with minor additions and changes; photoreproduction in OOAMA.
GBLpro (FO 925/1916)

---

44 *1813*
A MAP OF / Upper and Lower CANADA / WITH PART OF THE / United States Adjoining. / Comprising the present seat of War / Taken from the best authorities by / J.G. Hales Geogrphr. Ec. of Portsmouth N.H. / 1813 / Wightman Sc. Boston.
Print (engrav) Approx 53 x 81 cm Approx 1" to 28 miles
Described from photoreproduction copy; shows twps in Canada and roads, connecting points, and routes from United States; (Nova Scotia, Public Archives, *Catalogue*, 22).
NSHP USMH

---

45 *1813*
[Map of Upper and part of Lower Canada and the adjoining United States] [Sgd] [Cha?] Taylor fecit 1813
Col ms 43 x 67 cm Scale not given
Shows places and rivers in Upper Canada and places, rivers, and roads in the United States; a few notes on good harbours and landing places; place-names in the north in French; the outline is very similar to Smith's plan of 1800 (see **30(1)**).
USCSmH

---

46 *1813*
Map of / UPPER CANADA, / describing / ALL THE NEW SETTLEMENTS, TOWNSHIPS &c. / WITH THE COUNTRIES ADJACENT, FROM / Quebec to Lake Huron. / Compiled at the Request of / HIS EXCELLENCY MAJOR GENERAL JOHN G. SIMCOE, / FIRST LIEUTENANT GOVERNOR, / By David William Smyth Esqr. / Surveyor General. / With additions and corrections from Hollands three sheet Map. / NEW YORK Published by PRIOR & DUNNING / 1813. / Engraved by Jas. D. Stout.
Print (engrav) sometimes hand col 55 x 85 cm [1" to 22.9 miles]
To accompany *A Gazetteer of the Province of Upper Canada* (New York: Prior and Dunning 1813) (*Bib Can* 735, Dionne 802, Lande 2209); a close copy of the Smith 1813 edition (**30(2)**) with adds in the United States and Lower Canada; Lande copy folded in covers with title: 'MAP OF CANADA PUBLISHED by PRIOR & DUNNING 111 Water Street, New York, 1813'; (Holmden 2769; Olsen map 19).
GBL OOA OOAMA (NMC 15294) OTAR OTMCL QMM(L) USDLC

---

47 *[ca 1813]*
[Map of Upper Canada showing districts, counties, and townships]
Col ms 59 x 145 cm Scale not given Endorsements: 'No 99'; stamp 'CREOC'
Shows Upper Canada south of the Bruce Peninsula and the north end of L Simcoe; main places, roads, some twps and districts shown; an unfinished map but very similar to W. Chewett's map of [1801–2?] (**33**) and showing the same twps but with a few later adds from the War of 1812 such as Prescott and [Willow Creek depot] north of Kempenfelt Bay.
OOAMA (NMC 11235)

---

48 *1814*
A MAP OF / CABOTIA: / Comprehending / THE PROVINCES OF / UPPER AND LOWER CANADA, NEW-BRUNSWICK, AND / NOVA-SCOTIA, WITH BRETON ISLAND, NEWFOUNDLAND, &c. / And Including also, / THE ADJACENT PARTS OF THE UNITED STATES. / Compiled from a great Variety of Original Documents. / BY JOHN PURDY. / PUBLISHED 12TH. OCTOBER, 1814, BY JAS. WHITTLE AND RICHD. HOLMES LAURIE, No 53, FLEET STREET, LONDON. // Engraved by THOMSON & HALL, 14 Bury Str. Bloomsby
Print (engrav) on 4 sheets Ea 60 x 78 cm 1" to 23 miles
Insets: 'General Sketch of / the GRAND LAKES &c.' 1" to 130 miles, 'ENVIRONS / of / QUEBEC' approx 7/8" to 1/2 mile, 'THE BANKS of the RIVER ST LAWRENCE, from THE ISLE OF ORLEANS to LAKE ST FRANCIS, On an Enlarged Scale' 1" to 10 miles, 'FRONTIER of NIAGARA &c.' 1" to 2 miles, 'Continuation of / HUDSON'S RIVER / to New-York.' 1" to approx 13 miles, [Is of Newfoundland], 'ENVIRONS of ST JOHN'S / NEWFOUNDLAND.' 1" to 1/2 mile, 'THE / PROVINCE / of / NOVA-SCOTIA, / With Part of / NEW-BRUNSWICK, &c. / On an Enlarged Scale. / PRINCIPALLY from SURVEYS / Made by / HIS MAJESTY'S OFFICERS / and / SURVEYORS.' 1" to 15 miles, 'HARBOUR / of / HALIFAX' 3/4" to 2 miles, 'HARBOUR OF ST JOHN, / NEW BRUNSWICK.' 1" to 2 miles; additional imprints found along edges of the northeast, southeast, and southwest sheets; shows districts, cos, twps, and places for Upper Canada principally derived from the Smith map of 1813 (see **30(2)**); a cartobibliographical analysis of the map is found in Malinski, *The Importance of the 'Map of Cabotia'*; (Olsen map 30; OOAMA MacDonald Collection 393).
GBL (70615 (18)) GBLrg OOAMA (NMC 18323, 23569) USDLC USMiU-C

Later editions and states

(2) *1821*
— BY JOHN PURDY. / LONDON: PUBLISHED, 1st SEPTR 1821, BY RICHARD H. LAURIE, No 53, FLEET STREET. // Improved Edition with Additions.
Print (engrav) 123 x 159 cm
From the same plate and showing mainly the same information for Upper Canada as on the 1814 map; a few name changes including L 'Temiscaming'; a few names corrected and adds to inset of the 'Grand Lakes'; (not in Olsen).
OOAMA (NMC 109843) USDLC

(3) *1825*
— / LONDON: PUBLISHED, 1st Sept. 1821, BY RICHARD H. LAURIE, No 53, FLEET STREET. // Improved Edition, with Additions, 1825. [Paste-on addition to OTMCL copy]: 'Sold by JAMES WYLD, (Successor to Mr FADEN). / GEOGRAPHER. / To HIS MAJESTY & to His Royal Highness the DUKE of YORK. / 5 Charing Cross, Opposite Northumberland House.'
The shape of Pelee Is has been changed and some notes added; (Olsen map 31).
OTMCL USDLC

(4) *1828*
— LONDON: PUBLISHED 15th May 1828, BY RICHARD H. LAURIE, No 53, FLEET STREET. // Improved Edition, with Additions.
LC has the two east sheets only and lacks most of coverage for Upper Canada; (Malinski, Section III, State 4).
USDLC

(5) *1828*
— / LONDON: PUBLISHED, June 4th 1828, BY RICHARD H. LAURIE, No 53, FLEET STREET. // Improved Edition, with Additions.
Twps shown north to Eldon to Clarendon and from Luther to Zero; L Erie and L Huron shorelines have been redrawn; Welland and Rideau Canals and roads added; note added about the Canada Co. lands and Huron Tract; adds and changes have been made to Niagara inset and to 'Grand Lakes' inset; most of the changes to the map appear to be derived from the Canada Co. map (**69(2)**); (Olsen map 32?; *PRO Cat* 170).
GBLpro (CO 700 Canada 83) OOAMA (NMC 17298) USDLC USICN

(6) *1838*
MAP OF THE / VICE-ROYALTY OF CANADA; / Comprehending / THE PROVINCES OF / UPPER AND LOWER CANADA, ... / BY JOHN PURDY. / LONDON: PUBLISHED, August 4th 1838, BY RICHARD H. LAURIE, No 53, FLEET STREET. // Improved Edition with Additions
The shoreline of upper L Huron and Manitoulin Is has been revised; relief and more rivers shown in the Huron-Ottawa region; the twps have been added in the Huron Tract to line Colborne-N Easthope; places added; (Olsen map 33; *PRO Cat* 182).
GBL (70615 (19)) GBLpro (CO 700 Canada 92)

(7) *1850*
MAP OF THE / VICE-ROYALTY OF CANADA: ... / LONDON: PUBLISHED, AUGUST 4TH 1850, BY

RICHARD H. LAURIE, No 53, FLEET STREET. // Improved Edition with Additions.
(Olsen map 34); map not seen.
GBLrg

49 *[1814?]*
A NEW IMPROVED / MAP / of the / SEAT OF WAR // D. Haines fc.
Print (engrav) 35 x 45 cm 1" to 45 miles
In *History of the American War of 1812*, 3rd ed (Philadelphia: M'Carty & Davis 1817), frontis (USDLC, USNN); possibly also issued separately; inset: [L Superior, L Michigan, L Huron] 1" to 120 'American Miles'; shows the southern part of Upper Canada and the U.S. south to Washington; depicts a very inaccurate shoreline; places include towns and twp names; (Karpinski 35 lists map as 1815; Phillips, 877, suggests some states of map have an imprint of 1814).
OTMCL USDLC USNN

50 *1815*
MAP / of the Provinces of / UPPER & LOWER / CANADA / with the adjacent Parts of the / UNITED STATES OF AMERICA &c. / Compiled from the latest Surveys and Adjusted from the most recent and / Approved Astronomical Observations by / Joseph Bouchette. // Published as the Act directs, Augst 12th 1815, by W. Faden, Geographer to HIS MAJESTY & to HIS ROYAL HIGHNESS the PRINCE REGENT, Charing Cross, London. / Engraved by J. Walker.
Print (engrav) 76 x 123 cm Scale not given
Published to accompany Bouchette's *Topographical Description of the Province of Lower Canada* (London: W. Faden 1815) (*Bib Can* 1031) and in the French ed (*Bib Can* 1030) but not found in these works; includes four views, two in Upper Canada: 'View on Lake Ontario' and 'VIEW of the GRAND PORTAGE on LAKE SUPERIOR'; dedication statement to the Prince Regent at lower left; map covers area from the Mississippi R to Nova Scotia and from Washington to James Bay; twps and shape similar to the Smith map (1813) (**30(2)**); roads, cos, districts, and relief shown; (Dionne 814; Gagnon, I:4411–12; Holmden 2934; Lande 1589; Nova Scotia, Public Archives, *Catalogue*, 22; Olsen map 35; OOAMA MacDonald Collection 449).
NSHP OOAMA (NMC 18392) OTAR OTMCL QMM(L) USDLC

51 *[1815?]*
Sketch, shewing the North & South Land, and Water communication from Fort Erie to Niagara to York, to Penetanguishene & by Cabots Head to Fort Gratiot & Pt Edward – Copy from Capt Owen's R.N.
Col ms 57 x 63 cm Scale not given Endorsements: 'Y36' '794'
Probably copied from map 29a, 29d, (**C34, C37**) and others in Owen's survey of 1815; shows the connections from Ft Erie west through L Erie and L Huron to the Penetanguishene area, road from York to Holland R, and the Penetanguishene Rd; relief.
OTAR (SR 7118)

52 *1815*
[Endorsed title]: 'Townships on the North Coast of Lake Erie from the Surveyor Generals Office York U. Canada' G.B. 18 Septr 1815
Col ms 63 x 131 cm 1" to 4 miles
Shows all the twps of the London and Western districts from the Grand R west to the Detroit R and north to Chatham, London, Oxford, and Burford twps, all roads and houses of settlers along rivers and roads, marshes, names of places and some settlers; a star symbol may indicate places to bivouac troops and horses; this map is one of a series of important military reconnaissance maps, others described below; the Talbot Rd is shown from Woodhouse to Dunwich Twp and from there a trail is shown along L Erie shore to Sandwich; probably by G. Brock as in (2) below.
GBTAUh (B796 Aa2)

Related maps

(2) *1815*
The London & Western Districts of Upper Canada. 1815. G. Brock A.Q.M.G.
Col ms 79 x 117 cm 1" to 4 miles Watermark: 'C WILMOTT 1814'
Inset: 'Post at Drummond's Island' approx 1" to 500 yds; shows same area and is very similar to the plan above but in a more finished style and with the following changes: Shawanese, Blandford, and Blenheim twps have been added, road locations seem to have been drawn more carefully and are in slightly different positions; more place-names and names of settlers are shown along rivers and roads and particularly along the Grand R; the boundary of the London and Western District is shown between Aldborough and Orford twps, the 'Long Woods' Rd and 'Governors Road' are named.
QMMRB (Hardinge Papers)

(3) *[1815?]*
[Endorsed title]: 'Map of Grand River &c. Map of River Niagara &c. &c.'
Ms in 2 sheets 33 x 80 cm and 40 x 80 cm [1" to 4 miles] Watermark: 'J BATES 1812'
Generally fits to east of above map; shows the area of the Niagara Peninsula and west to the Grand R, roads and distances, names of some landowners, houses, rivers, ferries, fords.
QMMRB (Hardinge Papers)

53 *[1816?]*
CANADA &c. / S. Lewis del. H.S. Tanner fc.
Print (engrav) hand col 21 x 27 cm Scale not given
In F. Lucas, *A New and Elegant General Atlas* (Baltimore: F. Lucas, Jr [1816?]), plate no 32 (*LC Atlases*

3542), and in [1817] ed (USDLC); only a few rivers and major places shown from Sault Ste Marie to New Brunswick; (OOAMA MacDonald Collection 399 (NMC 119056)).
OOAMA (NMC 119056) USDLC USNN

---

54 *[1817?]*
A Map of the Eastern part of the Province of Upper Canada; A Map of the Western part of the Province of Upper Canada.
2 col mss 44 x 90 cm and 50 x 66 cm 1" to 10 miles
Watermark: 'J WHATMAN 1816' Endorsements: 'Left by Col Pilkington on his going to Gibraltar in 1818'; stamp 'B↑O'
Dated from watermark and endorsement; shows twps, districts, roads and other routes; west sheet from Whitby Twp to Detroit, east sheet from Burlington Bay to eastern boundary; (Holmden 2772, 2773; Olsen map 44).
OOAMA (NMC 21359; 20917)

---

55 *1817*
PLAN / of the PRINCIPAL SETTLEMENTS of / UPPER CANADA / 1817.
Print (engrav) sometimes hand col 19 x 70 cm [1" to 23 miles] Endorsements: 'With Col Pilkington's Compl. to Col Rowley 22 May 1817'; stamp 'B↑O'
Shows Upper Canada south of north end of L Simcoe, main roads, twps, places; there is a copy in GBLpro (*PRO Cat* 1391) sgd in ms 'Robt Pilkington Woolwich' and endorsed '4G' with twps from Goulburn west to Bathurst and the settlement on the Rideau at Richmond added in ms; the map was probably drawn by Pilkington but bears some similarity to the Smith 1800 map (**30(2)**); (Olsen map 41?).
GBLpro (CO 700 Canada 77) OOAMA (NMC 21352)

Later editions and states

(**2**) *1817*
— [No change in title]
Endorsements: stamp 'B↑O'
Scale bar, eight twps north of L Ontario and Newcastle and Niagara districts added; Rice L redrawn.
OOAMA (NMC 21356)

(**3**) *[ca 1820?]*
— [No change in title]
20 x 70 cm
Information has been drawn in to the north extending beyond border; L Huron corrected; all twps shown in York-Simcoe cos (Home District); twps in the east and the river communication explored by Lt Catty in 1819 added; GBLpro copy has further ms adds of towns and forts; (*PRO Cat* 1392).
GBLpro (MPG 490) OTAR

(**4**) *1820*
PLAN / of the PRINCIPAL SETTLEMENTS of / UPPER CANADA. / 1820. // G.E. Madeley del. / C. Ingrey Lithog. 310 Strand.
Print (lith) 22 x 65 cm 1" to 23 miles
In *Summary of Information Relative to the Canadian Company. 1824.* (London: Printed by A. & R. Spottiswoode [1824]), opp 1st p (*Bib Can* 1337); also found in John Galt's report of 27 Apr 1824 about 'Canadian Land Co' (GBLpro CO 42/396 p 55); the map is very similar to the [ca 1820?] ed but it is a redrawn lithographed version; imprint trimmed off on OOAMA copy; twps added Eldon to Palmerston and north to McNab; (Olsen map 42).
OOAMA (NMC 14069) OTMCL

(**5**) *1830*
PLAN / of the PRINCIPAL SETTLEMENTS of / UPPER CANADA / 1830.
Print (engrav) 19 x 70 cm 1" to 23 miles
Twps added in the Huron tract north to Colborne to North Easthope twps and in the east from Mara to Burleigh, Douro to Belmont, Fitzroy and Torbolton twps; some rivers added and redrawn; the area of the map has been reduced to the original border in (2) above; (Olsen map 43).
OTMCL USDLC

---

56 *1819*
Plan of the central part of the Province of Upper Canada Shewing the seat of War in the Years 1812, 1813, & 1814. York 1st May 1819. [Sgd] J.G. Chewett D.S.
Col ms 63 x 97 cm 1" to 5 miles
A detailed map showing the area from Hamilton Twp on north shore of L Ontario to Southwold Twp, London District; most detail is shown for the York Co area and the Niagara Peninsula; 'Remarks' keys 'Actions, Roads, Causeways and Bridges, Bye Roads and Paths, Mills'; shows the Niagara escarpment and Oak Ridges moraine, all the numbered creeks on the north and south shores of L Ontario, twps, cos, names of some settlers along roads; (Holmden 2774).
OOAMA (NMC 18556)

---

57 *[1820?]*
CANADA // Drawn & engraved by J.H. Franks, Liverpool // Engraved for D. Blowe's View of America
Print (engrav) 20 x 24 cm 1" to 40 miles
In Daniel Blowe, *A Geographical, Commercial, and Agricultural View of the United States of America* (Liverpool: Henry Fisher [1820?]), opp 715 (*Bib Can* 7042); major places, rivers, and lakes.
OTMCL

---

58 *1820*
MAP / of / UPPER CANADA / Engraved for Statistical Account. // Published by Longman & Co. Paternoster Row, Dec. 1, 1820. / Neele & Son fc. 352 Strand.
Print (engrav) 36 x 49 cm [Approx 1" to 20 miles]
Insets: 'PLAN / OF / KINGSTON HARBOUR' approx 1" to 11/4 miles, 'PLAN / OF / YORK HARBOUR, etc' approx 1" to 11/4 miles, 'Sketch of

the Practicable courses of the / GRAND COMMERCIAL CANAL OF ST LAWRENCE, / with its Junctions' 1" to 81/2 miles; diagram: 'Mode of laying out Land in Canada'; probably a proof state since Gourlay describes having an ed of the map 'thrown off in November 1820' and sent to Upper Canada for adds and corrections (*Statistical Account of Upper Canada* (1822), I:[i]); shows twps and districts, plans for laying out new lands with towns at regular intervals; various plans for canals in eastern Upper Canada.
Private Collection

Later editions and states

(2) *1821*
— // Published by Longman & Co. Paternoster Row, Dec. 1, 1821. / Neele & Son fc. 352 Strand.
Print (engrav) 36 x 49 cm [Approx 1" to 20 miles]
Watermark (OTMCL copy): 'SMITH 1818'
In Robert Gourlay, *Statistical Account of Upper Canada* (London: Simpkin and Marshall 1 Jan 1822), I: frontis (*Bib Can* 1254); new twps 'laid out under the Duke of Richmond,' added in a different lettering style; these new twps are the same as those in the Chewett 1821 ed (**43(3)**) as are revisions to shoreline and rivers; 'Little York' has been added and the 'Natural & proper & politic boundary' with the United States is labelled in New York State; (*OHIM* 2.20, 7.2; Olsen map 45).
OOA OTMCL USDLC

---

59 *[1820]*
Plan / of the / PRINCIPAL SETTLEMENTS / of UPPER CANADA // Published January 1, 1821, by Baldwin, Cradock & Joy, London. / J.C. Russell sculpsit, Sydenham
Print (engrav) 12 x 40 cm 1" to 40 miles
In *A Few Plain Directions for Persons intending to Proceed as Settlers to ... Upper Canada ... with a Map* (London: Baldwin, Cradock and Joy 1820), frontis (*Bib Can* 4859; Casey I–1084); similar to and a reduced version of 1817 plan of same title (**55(2)**).
OOA OTMCL

---

60 *[1821]*
THE PROVINCE OF / UPPER CANADA.
Print (engrav) 20 x 32 cm 1" to 35 miles Watermark (USDLC copy): 'J WHATMAN TURKEY MILL 1821'
In *A Sermon Preached before the Incorporated Society for the Propagation of the Gospel in Foreign Parts* (London: Printed by S. Brooke 1821), frontis (Casey I–1108); shows towns and villages having churches, those without churches, and churches where there are no towns; twps and main roads indicated; the outline is based on Smith's 1818 ed (**30(3)**) but a few twps and revisions have been added; there is a separate copy in GBC (Maps C.6b3.81.3) with ms adds showing missions operated by Society for the Propagation of Christian Knowledge and Society for the Propagation of the Gospel.
GBC OOA USDLC

Later editions and states

(2) *[1838]*
THE PROVINCE OF / UPPER CANADA. //
Engraved by W. Collard.
In Wm Waddilove, *The Stewart Missions* (London: J. Hatchard & Son 1838), frontis (*Bib Can* 2235; Casey I–1684); the map is from the same plate as that above.
OOA OTMCL

---

61 *1822*
[The north shore of Lake Erie, the Niagara River, Lake St Clair and area] Deputy Quarter Master Generals Office Quebec 29th March 1822 [Sgd] [illegible] W.R.D.
Col ms Approx 60 x 140 cm
Shows soundings along shores, named twps, roads and trails, marshy lands, notes, including some on navigation.
GBEr (GD 45/3/545/65)

---

62 *[1823]*
PART [*sic*] / OF PART OF THE / PROVINCE / of / UPPER CANADA / Organized, / TAKEN FROM THE MOST RECENT COMPILATIONS &c. / PUBLISHED & / ENGRAVED BY / David Smillie & Son, / QUEBEC.
Print (engrav) 79 x 137 cm 1" to 10 miles
Shows the more southern part of the province north to the Bruce Peninsula; shows most of the same twps as found on the 1825 state of the Canada Co. map (see **69(1)**) and the shoreline, rivers and lakes, relief features, and roads are also very similar to that map; names of districts and cos; the map was engraved by Smillie in 1823 from a copy of an official plan that hung in the House of Assembly, made by David William Smith, a law student; correspondence in newspapers indicated that this was an unauthorized publication and only one copy has been found; the title was probably meant to be 'Plan of part ...' (Allodi and Tovell, 35–6).
QQS

---

63 *[1823]*
Plan / of the / PRINCIPAL SETTLEMENTS / IN / UPPER CANADA, / According to the latest Surveys / to 1823. / DRAWN BY CLAUDIUS SHAW, / Deputy Provincial Surveyor. // C. Hullmandel Lithography.
Print (lith) 25 x 67 cm 1" to 20 miles
Twps shown north to line Sombra and St Clair, and from Ekfrid to Zorra, Zero to Luther, and east to Orillia; also east of L Simcoe north to line from Harvey to Palmerston and Torbolton to Lavant; districts; similar to and possibly copied from **55 (4)**.
QMMRB

64 *1823–4 (1826)*
(Copy) Skelton Map shewing the situation of all the forts or Military Positions and the Ordnance Depots in the two Canadas with their Names and Distances from each other and from Montreal or Quebec dated June 9th 1824 [Sgd] E.W. Durnford Colonel Commg Rl Engrs Canada [Commanding Royal Engineer's Office, June 22nd 1826, Quebec.]
Col ms 74 x 125 cm 1" to 24 miles Endorsements: stamp 'B↑O'
Last part of signature statement now obliterated and supplied from Holmden; this may be a later copy of a general plan originally accompanying 'Report on the Present State of the New and Old Works of Fortifications and Buildings ... throughout the Canadas by E.W. Durnford Lt Col Commg Rl Engrs Canada 24 Sept 1823' (OOA RG 8 II vols 80–2); the map lists various military fortified areas and includes a list of bldgs at each place; (Holmden 296; Olsen map 58); the detailed plans accompanying the report are mainly of bldgs and not listed here; all plans are in OOAMA and most are listed in Holmden; general maps with endorsements, and Holmden and/or *NMC Catalogue* references are as follows:
'No 20' 'U.' Prescott ... (Signed) D Bolton Lieut Royl Engrs ...; (Holmden 2382, 2383). (NMC 4336)
'No 22' and 'No 23'; Kingston; (Holmden 1798).
'No 24' 'Y' ... York ...; (Holmden 2684, 2680–3). (NMC 4444)
'No 25' 'Z' 'No 26' 'AA'; Niagara, Fort George, and Fort Mississauga; (Holmden 2019; *NMC Catalogue* 7: 575–8, 581–2). (NMC 15014)
'No 27' 'BB' ... Fort Erie ...; (Holmden 1653, 1654). (NMC 3806)
'No 30' 'EE' ... Burlington Heights ...; (Holmden 1540, 1541). (NMC 3739)
'No 28' 'CC' ... Chippawa Creek ...; (Holmden 1568, 1569). (NMC 3768)
'No 29' 'DD'; Queenston; (*NMC Catalogue* 7:648).
'No 32' 'GG' Amherstburgh; (Holmden 1481–3).
'No 34' I; St Joseph; (*NMC Catalogue* 7:651).
OOAMA (NMC 3739, 3768, 3806, 4336, 4444, 11739, 15014)

---

65 *[1824]*
CANADA. // Published by A. Finley Philada. / Young & Delleker Sc. / 5.
Print (engrav) hand col 22 x 29 cm 1" to 38 miles
In Anthony Finley, *A New General Atlas* (Philadelphia: A. Finley 1824), plate 5 (*LC Atlases* 4314); the same map also appeared in later eds of the atlas: (1825) (GBL (Maps 39.d.13, plate 5)), (1829) (*LC Atlases* 752), (1830) (*LC Atlases* 755), (1831) (*LC Atlases* 760), (1833) (*LC Atlases* 3551); a few rivers, places, and districts shown.
GBL USDLC

---

66 *[1824]*
PLAN OF A TOWNSHIP, TEN MILES SQUARE.
Print (typeset) 18 x 19 cm Scale not given
In Edward Talbot, *Five Years Residence in the Canadas* (London: Longman, Hurst, Rees, Orme, Brown and Green 1824), 2:208–9 (*Bib Can* 1299); 'this plan exhibits the division of a Township into Concessions and Lots, each Lot containing 200 Acres'; shows 'public roads' and crown and clergy reserves.
OTMCL

Related maps

(2) *[1825]*
CATARACTES DE NIAGARA. [and] DETAIL / DES CHUTES [and] KINGSTON [and] YORK. // Canada Pl. 2 // Gravé par Ambroise Tardieu.
Print (engrav) 15 x 24 cm Scale not given
In Edward A. Talbot, *Cinq années de séjour au Canada* (Paris: Boulland et Compagnie 1825), 3: at end (*Bib Can* 7137) (OOA), and in his *Voyage au Canada ... ornée de cartes gravées par Ambrose Tardieu* (Paris: 1833), 2: at end (*Bib Can* 1300); the imprint may have been trimmed off in the 1833 ed seen; the Niagara maps are on a plate with maps of York and Kingston; this map does not appear to have accompanied the English ed (1824).
OOA OTMCL

(3) *1833*
Plan de la Division d'un District de Dix Milles Concessions et en Lots
Print 18 x 19 cm Scale not given
In Edward Talbot, *Voyage au Canada* (Paris: A la Librairie centrale 1833), 2: at end (*Bib Can* 1300); shows the same information as (1) above.
OTMCL

---

67 *[1824]*
Sketch of the manner in which a Township is laid out in Upper Canada. // G.E. Madeley del. // C. Ingrey Lithog 310 Strand
Print (lith) 35 x 25 cm Scale not given
In *Summary of Information Relative to the Canadian Company. 1824.* (London: A. & R. Spottiswoode [1824]), opp 1st p (*Bib Can* 1337), and enclosed with John Galt's report of 27 Apr 1824 about the 'Canadian Land Co.' (GBLpro CO 42/396 p 55); shows the same twp plan as that on the Canada Co. map, with 15 cons and 26 lots, crown and clergy reserves, and road allowances.
GBLpro (CO 42/396 p 55) OTMCL

---

68 *1825*
Amer. Sep. HAUT CANADA ET MICHIGAN No 42 // Dressée et Dessinée par Ph Vandermaelen / Desée sur pierre et Lithé par H. Ode et Ph Lippens Avril 1825.
Print (lith) 46 x 51 cm Scale not given
In Philippe Vandermaelen, *Atlas universel de geographie ... Lithographié par H. Ode. Bruxelles, 1827. Quatrieme partie – Amer. Sept.* (*LC Atlases* 749); (OOAMA); shows out-of-date information for the province; probably copied from the Smith 1800 map (see **30(1)**); population and also area figures for the province given; this sheet covers most of Upper Canada; (Olsen map 46).

Other sheets are as follows:
(2) Amer. Sept. PARTIE DES ETATS-UNIS. No 43 ... Mars, 1825. [southeastern part]
(3) AMÉR. SEP. PARTIE DE LA NOUVELLE BRETAGNE. No 33. [Lake of the Woods area]
(4) AMÉR. SEP. PARTIE DE LA NOUVELLE BRETAGNE. No 34. [north of L Superior]
(5) AMÉR. SEP. PARTIE DE LA NOUVELLE BRETAGNE. No 35. [south of James Bay]
OOAMA USDLC

---

69 *[1825]*
A Map / OF THE / PROVINCE / of / UPPER CANADA / and the Adjacent Territories in / North America / COMPILED BY JAMES G. CHEWETT, / Assistant Draftsman under the direction of / Thomas Ridout Esqr Surveyor General / OF THE PROVINCE / Shewing the Districts, Counties and Townships / in which are situated the Lands purchased from the / CROWN / BY THE / CANADA COMPANY. / Incorporated 1825. // Engraved by I.S. Cox, for the Canada Company.
Print (engrav) in 3 sheets hand col 98 x 176 cm 1" to 8.2 miles
List of board members: Chairman: Charles Bosanquet, Deputy Chairman: William Williams, Directors: Robert Biddulph, Richard Blanshard, Robert Downie, John Easthope, Edward Ellice, John Fullarton, Chas David Gordon, William Hibbert Jun., John Hodgson, John Hullett, Hart Logan, Simon McGillivray, James Mackillop, John Masterman, Martin Tucker Smith, Henry Usborne, Auditors: Thos Starling Benson, Thos Poynder, Thos Wilson, John Woolley, Secretary: John Galt; 'List of Commissioners appointed by the King to ascertain the value of the Crown & Clergy Reserves'; diagram: 'Sketch of the manner in which a Township is laid out in Upper Canada'; dedication statement to George IV; three tables of distance; coat of arms unfinished; northern line of twps: St Clair, Sombra to Zone, Mosa to Zorra, Wilmot, Woolwich, Luther to Zero, Matchadash to Thorah, Eldon to Palmerston, Lavant, Darling, McNab; also copy in OOAMA (MacDonald Collection 453, NMC 113165); (Olsen map 48).
OOAMA (NMC 11232; 113165) OTMCL

Later editions and states

(2) *[1826]*
— Incorporated 1826. // Engraved by I.S. Cox for the Canada Company. // LONDON: Published for the CANADA COMPANY by C. SMITH & SON, 172 Strand.
Watermark (USDLC copy): 'J WHATMAN 1826'
Board members as in 1825 ed; added information: coat of arms completed, symbols added in twps in which the Canada Co. has lots or blocks of land, note added in the Huron area: 'The Company's Territory to be selected in these districts ...'; twp sketch moved to lower left corner; L Huron shoreline corrected from surveys of Lt Bayfield; Horton Twp added; relief shown by hachures; 'list of Commissioners ...' deleted; Welland Canal added; OOAMA (NMC 11231) originally sectioned to fold in case with imprint: 'SOLD BY C. SMITH, MAPSELLER 172 STRAND, LONDON.' and endorsed 'P. Maitland'; copy in private collection folding into cover with title: 'PLAN / OF / UPPER / CANADA 1827'; advertised as 'New map of Upper Canada by Chewitt just published and for sale by H.H. Cunningham no 28 St Paul St' in *Canadian Courant* (Montreal) 8 Apr 1826; (*OHIM* 2.19; Olsen map 50).
OGU OKQ OOAMA (NMC 18562, 11231) OTAR OTMCL OTUTF USDLC Private Collection

(3) *[1827?]*
— [Title, etc, unchanged]
Provenance: formerly OTMCL Banting Collection; line of 'proposed Rideau Canal' and 'Grenville Canal' added; ms adds on OOAMA copy in John MacDonald's hand shows Huron Tract, proposed roads, and Guelph Twp.
OOAMA (NMC 23129) USDLC

(4) *[1827–9?]*
— [Title, etc, unchanged]
Changes: the boundary of the Huron Tract is drawn in with statement 'THE HURON TRACT GRANTED BY THE CROWN TO THE CANADA COMPANY,' 'Land belonging to the Crown' indicated below and above it, Goderich Twp is located, and drainage in the area including the Maitland R and R aux Sables is shown.
OTMCL (West sheet only)

(5) *[1830]*
— [Title, etc, unchanged]
Watermark (OTAR copy): 'J WHATMAN 1829'
Board members changed: Deputy Gov: E. Ellice, Directors dropped: R. Blanshard, E. Ellice, C.D. Gordon, J. Hodgson, S. McGillivray, J. Masterman, Director added: C. Franks, Secretary: N.S. Price; twps in the Huron Tract filled in to line Colborne-North Easthope; OTAR copy has 'Guelph twp' in ms; more roads added in western portion; (Lande S1451).
OTAR QMM (L)

(6) *[1831–2]*
— [Title, etc, unchanged]
Board members changed: Deputy Gov Charles Franks, Director dropped: C. Franks, Auditors: James Gooden added and Benson and Wilson dropped; Guelph Twp added; OOAMA copy has many ms adds and changes with twps shown north to Saugeen to Sydenham, places and roads added, Rideau Canal corrected.
OOAMA (NMC 23130)

(7) *[1835]*
— [Title, etc, unchanged]
Watermark (OTAR copy): 'J WHATMAN 1834'
Board members changed: Directors dropped: J. Fullarton, H. Usborne, Directors added: Thos Stokes, F.H. Mitchell, Auditor added: J. Woolley, Secretary changed: John Perry; twps added:

Plympton, Warwick, Enniskillen, Brooke, Moore, and Sarnia; 'Toronto' replaces York; Bytown has been added; Guelph Twp and town of Guelph added with road from Burlington and the final route of the Rideau Canal indicated; OOAMA (NMC 119072) is copy of west sheet only; (Canada Book Auctions 18 Nov 1981, [Catalogue], Item 119 now in OTCR).
OOAMA (NMC 119072) OTAR OTCR

Copies with ms adds:

(**8**) *[1825–ca 1836]*
— [Printed map is 1825 edition]
Ms adds: pasted-on add shows twps in the Huron Tract to line Colborne-Ellice; other ms adds show 'proposed canal from Thames to Point au Pins,' 'Toronto late York,' Welland and Rideau canals, road from Cobourg to Rice L, 'Wilberforce to be inserted,' five new twps in Renfrew, 'the places where the Navigation of the River St Lawrence is interrupted'; photoreproducton in OOAMA (NMC 26916); (*PRO Cat* 1395).
GBLpro (CO 700 Canada 81)

(**9**) *[1826–ca 1838]*
— [Printed map is 1826 edition]
Ms adds: twps added in [Lambton Co] and in the Huron Tract to line Colborne-North Easthope; Brock and Talbot districts; twp names changed: Zero to St Vincent, Java and Merlin to Nottawasaga, Alta to Collingwood; twps added: Bexley, Somerville, Ross-Pembroke; Ottawa R and Rideau Canal line revised; another copy in GBL has only minor adds (GBL Maps 32.d.7); photoreproduction in OTUM.
GBL (Maps 32.d.6–7)

(**10**) *[1826–4?]*
— [Printed map is 1826 edition]
Ms adds: twps: Ashfield, Wawanosh, Derby to Minto, Maryborough, and Mornington; Wellington, Huron, and Dalhousie districts added; shoreline corrected near Owen Sound; copy endorsed on back: 'Honble D. Daly'; (Lande S1450).
QMM(L)

---

70 *[ca 1825]*
MAP OF THE / PROVINCE / OF / UPPER CANADA / Shewing the organized part thereof and the adjacent Country / Compiled by James G. Chewett / Assistant Draughtsman / under the direction of THOMAS RIDOUT Surveyor General / Dedicated by permission to His Excellency / Sir Peregrine Maitland K.C.B. &c. &c. &c. / LIEUTENANT GOVERNOR / During whose administration / a very large proportion of the Territory has been Organized / By His obliged and most obedient / Humble Servant / Thos Ridout Survr. Genl. // New York, Printed by S. Maverick 73 Liberty St. // Engraved by D.W. Wilson N. York
Print (engrav) 61 x 92 cm 1" to 16 miles
The map is similar to the Canada Co. [1825] map (**69(1)**) in terms of shape and general information, and is possibly the map advertised as in preparation in *Upper Canada Gazette* 23 June 1823 to Nov 1824; table of distances from York added in ms; OTAR copy has ms adds of new twps, cos, and districts to about 1838, and is inscribed 'Surveyor Genl Office'; proposed [Welland] Canal shown in early position (see **730**); OTAR (SR 81257) has ms adds showing Indian land surrenders and a transcript of this map 'Office Copy map shewing position of Indian surrenders according to accompanying Schedule' endorsed '733' is in OOAMA (NMC 15966); (Olsen map 53?).
OTAR OTAR (SR 81257)

Later editions and states
(**2**) *[1828?]*
— By ... / Thos Ridout / Survr. Genl. With the latest Surveys and additions / in the Surveyor Generals Department // New York, Printed by S. Maverick, 73 Liberty St. / Engraved by D.W. Wilson N. York.
Twps added in the Huron Tract to line Colborne to North Easthope with note 'Canada Company' and in the east from Madawaska to Pembroke; the Ottawa R has been drawn in further north and the Trent R system has been revised; the Rideau and Welland canals are both shown, but Bytown not named; first part of imprint trimmed off on OTUTF copy; probably issued before Ridout died early in 1829.
OTMCL OTUTF

---

71 *1825*
UPPER AND LOWER / CANADA. // London: Published by C. SMITH, 172 Strand January 1825. / Pickett sculpt / 49.
Print (engrav) hand col 27 x 37 cm 1" to 78 miles
Watermark: 'T EDMONDS WYCOMBE'
Based on Smith 1800 map no (**30(1)**) in shape; shows Dundas St, districts, cos, and places.
OOAMA (NMC 9835)

Later editions and states

(**2**) *[1826]*
— [The date has been removed]
Watermark (OOAMA copy): 'T EDMONDS WYCOMBE'
In Charles Smith, *New General Atlas* (London: Printed for C. Smith 1826), plate 49 (*LC Atlases* 6056) and also in the 1830 ed (*LC Atlases* 6067); the map is the same as the 1825 ed.
OOAMA (NMC 23299) USDLC

---

72 *1826*
Outline Map to Illustrate a Report to His Grace The Duke of Wellington, relative to His Majesty's North American Provinces, by a Commission of which Major General Sir J. Carmichael Smyth was President Lieutenant General Sir George Hoste Captain Harris Members 1825 Compiled by S.B.

Howlett Inspector General's Office Feb. 24th 1826.
Col ms 55 x 166 cm 1" to 23 miles Endorsements: 'For Report see Reports / 107'; stamps 'IGF' 'B↑O'
Inset: 'Map of Kingston & Vicinity' 1" to 5 miles, also an inset of Halifax; shows the area from Sault Ste Marie to Nova Scotia; a note indicates that some later adds were made to the map; shows boundaries as claimed by the British and the Americans in the northeast (Maine-New Brunswick, Lower Canada); shows the Rideau and Welland canals and other water communications; shows roads and proposed new roads with reference to pp 102 and 128 of the report of 1825, which is found in OOA RG 8 II vol 6; (Holmden 297).
OOAMA (NMC 17063)

---

73 *1826–7*
[Canada Company diagrams of the districts of Upper Canada, certified correct by Thos Smith in 1826 and 1827]
8 vols of col ms maps Ea 68 x 85 cm Ea 1" to 40 chains

Contents:

(1) Canada Company Diagrams of the Eastern and Ottawa Districts [Certified correct and sgd] 'Tho Smith London 30th September 1826'; 21 leaves of individual twp maps; map of the districts listed in the index is missing; maps show twp survey grid and Canada Co. lands in green; notes on some maps: 'reduced and printed' and on others 'not to be copied'; maps interleaved with sheets to list 'purchasers' (very few names).

(2) ... Johnston District. [Certified correct and sgd] 'Tho Smith Accountant London 30th September 1826'; 19 leaves of twp maps; map of the districts (part of general map of 1826, **69(2)**); same information as volume above.

(3) ... Gore & Niagara Districts [Certified correct and sgd] 'London 20th March 1827 Tho Smith'; 17 leaves of twp maps; map of the districts (part of **69(2)**); on index page: 'John Thomson Fecit.'

(4) ... Bathurst District [Certified correct and sgd] 'London 14 June 1827 ... Tho Smith'; 20 leaves of twp maps; map of the district (part of **69(2)**); on index page: 'John Thomson Fecit.'

(5) ... Midland District [Certified correct and sgd] 'London 14th June 1827 Tho Smith'; 26 leaves of twp maps; map of the districts (part of **69(2)**); on index page: 'John Thomson Fecit'; notes on a few maps about size of lots.

(6) ... Home District [Certified correct and sgd] 'London 27 July 1827 ... Tho Smith'; 40 leaves of twp maps; map of the districts (part of **69(2)**); on index page: 'John Thomson Fecit.'

(7) ... Newcastle District [Certified correct and sgd] 'London 27 July 1827 ... Tho Smith'; 28 leaves of twp maps; map of the districts (part of **69(2)**); on index page: 'John Thomson Fecit.'

(8) ... Western District [Certified correct and sgd] 'London 27 July 1827 ... Tho Smith'; 20 leaves of twp maps; map of the districts (part of **69(2)**); on index page: 'John Thomson Fecit.'
OTMCL (Canada Co. Papers)

---

74 *1827*
Map / of the / BRITISH POSSESSIONS / in / NORTH AMERICA, / Compiled from Documents in the / COLONIAL DEPARTMENT, / To accompany the report of the / EMIGRATION COMMITTEE. // THIRD REPORT ON EMIGRATION. 6 // 550 / Ordered by the House of Commons to be Printed, 29th June 1827. / A. Arrowsmith sculpt / Luke Hansard & Sons, Printer
Print (engrav) 41 x 66 cm Approx 1" to 38 miles
Inset: 'THE ISLAND OF / NEWFOUNDLAND / Divided into / Three Districts'; prepared to accompany *Third Report from the Select Committee on Emigration from the United Kingdom: 1827 ... Ordered ... to be Printed 29 June 1827. 550.* (*Bib Can* 7169 (map missing); HCPP V (1826–7), after 890, in OTU (mfe)); shows twps as on the Canada Co. map of 1826 (see **69(2)**) with a key to numbered twps in the Niagara District; shows twps where 2024 Irish emigrants were settled by Peter Robinson [Peterborough area] in 1825 and twps in the Bathurst District where 568 Irish were settled by Robinson in 1823; reference keys canals executed or projected, towns with Protestant and Roman Catholic churches and those without, etc; table on population and trade; OOAMA (NMC 44367) is a facsimile copy by the Irish Academic Press.
Original not located

Later editions and states

(2) *1828*
— THIRD REPORT ON EMIGRATION . 6 // Ordered to be Printed, 19th Feby 1828. / A. Arrowsmith, Sculpt.
Print (lith) hand col 40 x 66 cm Approx 1" to 38 miles
Shows the same information as map above and from the same plate; not found with British Parliamentary Papers (McGechaen, 10).
GBLrg OTMCL

(3) *1834*
BRITISH POSSESSIONS / IN / NORTH AMERICA. / from the Report / OF THE / EMIGRATION COMMITTEE / of / 1827. / CORRECTED TO 1834 // London Published by Longman & Co Paternoster Row, April 1834 / Engraved by S. Hall 13 Bury Strt Bloomsby
Print (engrav) 36 x 65 cm 1" to 48 miles
Reengraved from the 1827 map without the emigration data or the key to churches and canals; twps added north to Colborne-Ellice, Luther-Zero, and Eldon-Palmerston.
OOAMA (NMC 19846) USDLC

(4) *[183?]*
BRITISH POSSESSIONS / IN / NORTH AMERICA, / WITH PART OF THE UNITED STATES, / COMPILED FROM / OFFICIAL SOURCES. // London, Published by Longman & Co Paternoster Row. / Engraved by S. Hall Bury Strt. Bloomsby
Print (engrav) 37 x 64 cm 1" to 48 miles
Insets: 'PLAN / of the / CITY AND HARBOUR / of / MONTREAL' and 'PLAN / of the / CITY AND HARBOUR / of / QUEBEC'; reengraved from (3) with the addition of insets and the title moved to the lower right; otherwise, information the same.
OOAMA (NMC 6992)

---

75 *1827*
A Map OF / The New Settlements / and Townships in / UPPER & LOWER CANADA, / COMPILED BY LIEUT J.C. MORGAN late 2nd BATN R.M. / Dedicated by permission to / Vice Admiral Sir Geo. Cockburn G.C.B. &c&c. / Published and Sold for the Author as an accompaniment to / THE EMIGRANTS GUIDE. / Jany 1827. / BY C. Smith & Son, Mapsellers No 172 Strand // James & Josiah Neele sculp 352 Strand.
Print (engrav) hand col 55 x 74 cm Scale not given
The map was meant to accompany Morgan's *The Emigrant's Note Book and Guide* (London: Longman, Hurst, Rees, Orme and Brown 1824) as mentioned in the preface, but was apparently not issued with the book (*Bib Can* 1326); based on the Smith 1818 ed (**30(3)**) with the addition of Bathurst District (shown as a co) and twps north to Lavant to Fitzroy.
USDLC

---

76 *[1827]*
MAP of the TOWNSHIPS in the PROVINCE OF UPPER CANADA. // Ingrey & Madeley, Lithog. 310 Strand.
Print (lith) 25 x 42 cm Approx 1" to 32 miles
Pasted in front of some copies of *Diagrams of the Townships in Upper Canada* I (**77**); inset: 'Sketch of the manner in which a Township is laid out in Upper Canada'; also in *Lands in Upper Canada to be Disposed of by the Canada Company* (York: Geo. Gurnett 1830), frontis (*Bib Can* 7231); based on the Canada Co. [1825] map (**69(1)**); three tables of distance, coat of arms; across Huron Tract: 'The Company is to have 1 million acres selected in these Districts'; (Olsen 56?).
OOAMA (NMC 48369) OTMCL OTUTF

Later editions and states

(2) *[1828]*
— [Same title, etc]
26 x 41 cm
Redrawn to appear in *Lands in Upper Canada to be Disposed of by the Canada Company ... 1st Feb 1828* (London: Marchant, Printer, Ingram-Court), 4 pp, map at end (*Bib Can* 7185); boundary of the Huron Tract 'granted by Government to the Canada Company'; crown lands shown north and south of this.
OTMCL

(3) *[1830]*
MAP OF THE TOWNSHIPS IN THE PROVINCE OF UPPER CANADA // C. Ingrey Lithog. 310 Strand.
Print (lith) 22 x 38 cm 1" to 36 miles Watermark: 'J WHATMAN 1830'
Redrawn to appear on broadside: *Lands in Upper Canada to be Disposed of by the Canada Company* (London: Marchant, Printer, Ingram-Court); also with a letter from Price to Hay 19 Feb 1830 enclosing a 'New Prospectus' (GBLpro CO 42/410 p 48); three tables of distance; boundary of Huron Tract marked and crown land; inset deleted: 'Sketch of the manner in which a township is laid out'; (Holmden 2761).
GBLpro (CO 42/410 p 48) OLU OOAMA (NMC 5117) USDLC

(4) *[1831]*
MAP OF THE TOWNSHIPS IN THE PROVINCE OF UPPER CANADA.
Print (lith) 24 x 39 cm 1" to 50 miles
Redrawn to appear on broadside: *Lands in Upper Canada to be Disposed of by the Canada Company* (London: Marchant, Printer, Ingram-Court 1831) (*Bib Can* 1630); inset: 'HURON TRACT / BELONGING TO THE / CANADA COMPANY / On a larger Scale than the above.' approx 1" to 12.5 miles; two tables of distance; 'Reference to the townships in the Niagara District'; twps in the Huron Tract shown north to Colborne to North Easthope; shows a corrected L Huron shoreline after the map of 1826 (see **69(2)**); also found bound in front of OKQ copy of *Diagrams of the Townships in Upper Canada* I (**77**), and in William Hickey, *Hints on Emigration to Upper Canada* (Dublin: William Curry, Jr 1831) (*Bib Can* 1583, Casey I–1326), and in William Cattermole, *Emigration* (London: Simpkin and Marshall [1831?]) (*Bib Can* 1632).
OKQ OOA OTMCL

(5) *1832–42*
The same map as (4); appeared in *Emigration; Letters from Sussex Emigrants* (Petworth and London: John Phillips, and Longman & Co. 1833) (OONL, CIHM 35220); it also appeared in the broadside: *Lands in Upper Canada* (1832) (OTMCL, OOAMA (NMC 5119), USDLC), and in an ed (1833) (OGU), and (1835) (GBC and OLU copies with adds of names of Moore, Enniskillen, Sarnia, and Plympton twps and a few other places; OTMCL copy of 1835 ed without adds), and (1837) (USDLC, OLU), and (1839) (GBL, QMM(L), OTMCL); it probably appeared in an 1841 ed of the broadside printed by Marchant, Singer & Smith as listed in Alfred van Peteghem Encan-Auction [Catalogue] 18 Nov 1987 (original not located); the map also appeared in R.M. Martin, *History of the British Colonies* (London: Cochrane

and McCrone 1834–5), III: opp 540 (*Bib Can* 5033); and in Canada Co., *A Statement of the Satisfactory Results which have Attended Emigration to Upper Canada* (London: Smith, Elder & Co 1841), frontis (*Bib Can* 2445), and in the 3rd ed (1842) (Casey I–1860), and the 4th ed (1842) (*Bib Can* 5226); also in John Strachan, *Journal of the Visitation of the Diocese of Toronto* (London: Richard Clay 1841), frontis (*Bib Can* 7649).
GBC GBL OGU OLU OOA OOAMA (NMC 5119) OONL OTMCL QMM(L) USDLC

---

77 *[1827–8?]*
DIAGRAMS / OF THE / Townships / IN / UPPER CANADA, / SHEWING THE LOTS PURCHASED FROM / HIS MAJESTY'S GOVERNMENT, / BY THE / Canada Company. / VOL. I .... VOL. II
2 vols prints (liths) some hand col 199 maps ea approx 40 x 23 cm Scales not given Watermarks: mostly 'RUSE & TURNERS' with dates 1823–26

Vol I:

[Frontis]: MAP of the TOWNSHIPS in the PROVINCE of UPPER CANADA. // Ingrey & Madeley, Lithog. 310 Strand
26 x 43 cm 1" to 30 miles ([1827], see **76**(1)).

[Following frontis]: vol I / INDEX / OF THE TOWNSHIPS IN THIS VOLUME [3–p alphabetical list of twps]

[Following index of twps]: PLAN / of the Townships in the / EASTERN, Ottawa, JOHNSTOWN, / Bathurst Midland / and NEWCASTLE DISTRICT // Ingrey & Madeley Lithog 310 Strand
23 x 39 cm

[Following map]: INDEX / TO THE / Plan of the Townships / IN THE / EASTERN ... NEWCASTLE DISTRICTS. vol I [lists twps numbered 1–97]

The plans are on leaves numbered in ms; most have as titles printed twp names although a few twp names are in ms and some have the name of the district added in ms or in print; on map 1 in ms: 'The lots to be purchased by the Company are colored Green'; the maps are generally as follows (titles as transcribed from maps): 1, Lochiel; 2, Lancaster; 3, Roxborough; 4, Finch; 5, Winchester; 6, Mountain; 7, Williamsburgh; 8, Hawkesbury; 9, Caledonia; 10, Plantagenet (front); 11, Plantagenet (rear); 12, Alfred; 13, Cambridge; 14, Russell; 15, Cumberland; 16, Gloucester; 17, Clarence; 18, Osgoode; 19, Edwardsburgh; 20, S Gower; 21, N Gower; 22, Oxford; 23, Marlborough; 24, Wolford; 25, Montague; 26, Elizabeth town; 27, Yonge; 28, Lansdown; 29, Leeds; 30, Kitley; 31, Bastard; 32, N Crosby; 33, S Crosby; 34, Burgess; 35, Elmsley; 36, Nepean; 37, Goulburn; 38, March; 39, Huntley; 40, Torbolton; 41, Fitz-roy; 42, Pakenham; 43, Beckwith; 44, Drummond; 45, Bathurst; 46, N Sherbrooke; 47, S Sherbrooke; 48, Ramsay; 49, Lanark; 50, Dalhousie; 51, Darling; 52, Lavant; 53, Pittsburgh; 54, Loughborough; 55, Portland; 56, Palmerston; 57, Camden (east); 58, Richmond; 59, Sheffield; 60, Kaladar; 61, Tyendinaga; 62, Thurlow; 63, Sidney; 64, Hungerford; 65, Huntingdon; 66, Rawdon; 67, Marmora; 68, Madoc; 69, Elzevir; 70, Lake; 71, Halowell [*sic*]; 72, Murray; 73, Cramahe; 74, Haldimand; 75, Hamilton; 76, Seymour; 77, Percy; 78, Alnwick; 79, Otanabee; 80, Monaghan; 81, Asphodel; 82, Belmont; 83, Dummer; 84, Douro; 85, Smith; 86, Emily Gore; 87, Methuen; 88, Burleigh; 89, Harvey; 90, Hope; 91, Cavan; 92, Clarke; 93, Manvers; 94, Emily; 95, Mariposa; 96, Cartwright; 97, Darlington.

Vol II:

[Title-page]: DIAGRAMS ... Canada Company. / VOL. II

[Frontis]: MAP of the TOWNSHIPS ... Ingrey & Madeley, Lithog. 310 Strand [1827]

[Following frontis]: VOL. II / INDEX / of the Townships in this volume. [3–p alphabetical list of twps]

[Following index of twps]: PLAN / of the Townships in the / HOME, Niagara, GORE, / London & Western / DISTRICTS.
23 x 39 cm

[Following map]: INDEX / TO THE / Plan of the Townships / IN THE / HOME ... WESTERN DISTRICTS / vol II [lists twps in which the company has land, numbered 1–102]

The plans are as described above and numbered as follows: 1, Whitby; 2, Reach; 3, Brock; 4, Georgina; 5, Scott; 6, Uxbridge; 7, Whitchurch; 8, Pickering; 9, Scarborough; 10, Markham; 11, E Gwillimbury; 12, N Gwillimbury; 13, King; 14, Vaughan; 15, York; 16, Toronto; 17, Gore of Toronto; 18, Etobicoke; 19, Chinguacousy; 20, Caledon; 21, Albion; 22, Thorah; 23, Mara; 24, Orillia; 25, Tay; 26, Medonte; 27, Oro; 28, Tiny; 29, Flos; 30, Vespra; 31, Mulmur; 32, Tosorontio; 33, Essa; 34, Innisfil; 35, W Gwillimbury; 36, Tecumseth; 37, Adjala; 38, Mono; 39, Amaranth; 40, Trafalgar; 41, Esquesing; 42, Erin; 43, Garrafraxa; 44, Eramosa; 45, Nasagiweya [*sic*]; 46, Nelson; 47, Flamborough E and W; 48, Beverly; 49, Glanford; 50, Binbrook; 51, Crown Reserve for the Co of Lincoln, now called Wilmot; 52, Crown Reserve for the Six Nations land; 53, Caistor; 54, Windham; 55, Rainham; 56, Walpole; 57, Woodhouse; 58, Townsend; 59, Charlotteville; 60, Walsingham; 61, Middleton; 62, Houghton; 63, Nissouri; 64, Zorra; 65, Blenheim; 66, Oxford; 67, Burford; 68, Dereham; 69, Norwich; 70, Bayham; 71, Malahide; 72, Yarmouth; 73, Southwold; 74, Dunwich; 75, Aldborough; 76, Delaware; 77, Westminster; 78, Dorchester; 79, London; 80, Lobo; 81, Carradoc; 82, Ekfrid; 83, Mosa; 84, Orford; 85, Howard; 86, Harwich; 87, Chatham; 88, Raleigh; 89, Tilbury E; 90, Tilbury W; 91, Romney; 92, Dover; 93, Camden; 94, Zone; 95, Dawn; 96, Sombra; 97, Mersea; 98, Gosfield; 99, Colchester; 100, Malden; 101, Sandwich; 102, Maidstone and Rochester; most sets are bound in two vols with

title: 'DIAGRAMS / OF / UPPER CANADA' and Canada Co. coat of arms on the cover.
GBL OOAMA OTAR (Canada Co. Papers A-4-3 vols 6–11) OTMCL (Canada Co. Papers L 31)

Other states

(2) *[1827?]*
Some sets of diagrams appear to be slightly earlier than the sets described above; OTUTF copy lacks the two maps 'Plan of the Townships in the Eastern...' and 'Plan of the Townships in the Home ... Districts' and the indexes that accompany them, but includes 'Vol I / LIST OF THE DISTRICTS / In this Volume, with the Townships in which the Company have Lands. / EASTERN DISTRICT ... OTTAWA ... JOHNSTOWN ... BATHURST ... MIDLAND ... NEWCASTLE.' and 'VOL. II. / List of the Districts in this Volume, with the Townships in which the / Company have Lands. / HOME DISTRICT ... GORE ... NIAGARA ... LONDON ... WESTERN DISTRICT.'; it also lacks a copy of the general map in vol II; the set has the book-plate of 'Thomas Poynder,' company auditor from 1825 to 1835 or later; the OTCR copy lacks title-pages in both vols; it also lacks the printed index of the twps and the maps; a ms list of twps (3 pp) is included as well as a ms 'List of the Districts with the Townships in which the Company have lands Eastern ... Western District' (6 pp); the leaves of maps are numbered consecutively 1–199 and the two vols are bound in one; there are also sets in four or five vols grouped by titles on binding: 'Diagrams of the Eastern, Ottawa, Johnston & Bathurst districts,' '... Midland & Newcastle,' '... London & Western,' '... Home District & Gore,' '... Home, Gore & Niagara Districts' (OTAR, OTMCL); these lack printed title-pages and the printed preliminary general maps and indexes, but have ms lists of twps and many ms adds; these may be working copies since the OTMCL copy of the Eastern ... Bathurst districts vol is endorsed 'Superintendents Copy for 1827–1828' and there are ms adds and interleaved sheets with notes on sales.
OTAR (Canada Co. Papers A-4-3 vols 1–3, 5) OTCR OTMCL OTUTF

(3) *[1830–1?]*
Copies with adds to the basic vols:
vol I of OKQ copy has 'MAP OF THE TOWNSHIPS IN THE PROVINCE OF UPPER CANADA' from broadside *Lands in Upper Canada* (1831) (see **76**(4)) added in front; vol II of OKQ copy and 'Home District & Gore' vol of a set in OTAR similar to four- to five-vol set in (2) above have the add of 'TOWNSHIP OF GUELPH Gore District C. Ingrey' (see **1034**), 'TOWN OF GUELPH Gore District C. Ingrey' (see **1394**), 'TOWNSHIP OF GODERICH. / Huron Tract // C. Ingrey' ... (see **1033**), 'HURON TRACT. / Town of Goderich. / C. Ingrey' (see **1373**); probably dated [1830?] at the earliest since Ingrey appears to work alone from that time (Twyman, 36); map 52 in the contents is now named Goderich but the Township of Guelph map appears with that number and 52A is the Town of Guelph map.
OKQ OTAR (Canada Co. Papers A-4-3 vol 4)

---

78 *[1828]*
Map / of part of the Province of / UPPER CANADA / Shewing the Territory situate in the London / and Western Districts lately purchased by / Government from the Indians and the Block / or Tract of 1,100,000 Acres part thereof selected by / THE CANADA COMPANY / in lieu of the / Clergy Reserves. // Ingrey & Madeley, Lithog. 310 Strand.
Print (lith) 30 x 47 cm 1" to 8 miles Watermark: (USDLC copy) '1825'; (OOA copy) '1828'
Possibly issued separately (GBLpro, USDLC), but also in *Lands in Upper Canada to be Disposed of by the Canada Company ... 1st Feb 1828* (London: Marchant, Printer, Ingram-Court), 4 pp, map at end (*Bib Can* 7185); and in *Letters from Settlers in Upper Canada* (London: Marchant, Printer, Ingram-Court 1833), frontis (Casey I–1407); one GBLpro copy is with memorandum in McGillivray to James Stephen of 1 Apr 1828 that directs the Surveyor General to lay out the boundary of the tract per agreement with company 28 March 1828 (GBLpro CO 42/409 p 114), and another copy was removed from GBLpro CO 384/20 f 134); shows the area from York to Sombra twps and from Long Point to the Huron Tract; the latter is designated 'The Huron Tract granted by the Crown to the Canada Company'; also shows twps, districts, Niagara escarpment, clergy reserve for the Six Nations Indians, main roads; location of Goderich; (*PRO Cat* 1404).
GBLpro (CO 42/409 p 114; MPG 990) OGL OOA OTMCL USDLC

---

79 *1829*
The Within Diagrams represent the principle upon which Townships have been surveyed in Upper Canada and the allotment of two sevenths reserved for the Crown and Clergy together with the allowance for roads
4 col ms Ea 25 x 18 cm Scale not given
In Peter Robinson's 1157 to Hay of 31 March 1829 (GBLpro CO 42/390 pp 297–301); the plans are for different twp survey systems and are as follows:

'No 1 Diagram of a Township 9 by 12 miles containing 2/7 allotted for Crown and Clergy 18,500 ... Roads 1392'

'No 2 Diagram of a Township ... Roads 2444'

'No 3 Diagram of a Township ... Clergy – 19,600 ... Roads 1392'

'No 4 Diagram of a Township ... Clergy 19,800 ... Roads 1556'

Diagrams 1 and 2 are for 10-con twps with lots 20 chains by 100 chains containing 200 acres; Diagram 3 is for a twp of 14 cons and 200-acre lots each 29 chains by 69 chains, 40 links; Diagram 4 is

for 11-con twps and 200-acre lots each 30 chains by 66 chains, 67 links.
GBLpro (CO 42/390 pp 297–301)

---

80 *[183?]*
Upper Canada / F.C. Sibbald.
Ms 61 x 48 cm Scale not given Endorsements: 'Map of Upper Canada copied by Frank Mr. Sibbald'
An unfinished map showing a combination of early 19th-century names for cos and districts, also locating twps laid out in the 1830s.
OTAR (Simcoe Map 445335)

---

81 *1831*
A MAP / of the / TOWNSHIPS in LONDON AND GORE DISTRICTS / of / UPPER CANADA / 1831
Print (lith) 29 x 37 cm Scale not given Watermark: 'KILLEEN 1823'
Note below title: 'The Canada Company's Lands Colored Green'; shows area from York to the Huron Tract; the twps are shown in the London and Gore districts and Huron Tract only; shows major roads, twps north to Colborne on the west and Garafraxa, and clergy reserve lands; a rough litho; see also **99** for a later version of this map.
OTMCL (James Bain Collection)

Related maps

(2) *1833*
A Map of the Townships in the London and Gore Districts of Upper Canada 1833 [Sgd] Robt Jno Pilkington Sep. 3 1833
Col ms 30 x 36 cm Scale not given
Very similar to plan above with the Canada Co. land in green, main roads, and twps; appears to be a ms copy of the printed map.
GBL (Add Mss 31357.H)

---

82 *1831*
Map of / UPPER AND LOWER CANADA / WITH THE / Adjacent States. // London, Published by Josh. Cross 18 Holborn (opposite Furnivals Inn) June 1st 1831.
Print (engrav) hand col 39 x 65 cm Scale not given
In John W. Bannister, *On Emigration to Upper Canada*, new ed (London: Published by Joseph Cross 1831), frontis (Casey I–1323; *Bib Can* 7247); shows area east to Nova Scotia; Huron Tract named but twps not laid out; twps as in the Canada Co. map of [1826] (**69(2)**); 'Reference for the Names of the Townships in Niagara Distrt.'
OOA OTMCL

Later editions and states

(2)
Map of / UPPER AND LOWER CANADA / WITH THE / Adjacent States. / 1832.
The date has been changed and added to the title, and the imprint deleted.
GBL (70615(75))

(3) *1832*
Map of / BRITISH NORTH AMERICA / WITH THE / Adjacent States. / 1832.
1" to 50 miles
The title has been changed; more lakes and rivers are shown in the Huron-Ottawa area and a line of hills is shown by hachures south of L Nipissing.
OOAMA (NMC 10125)

(4) *1835*
A Map of / UPPER and LOWER / CANADA, / OR / BRITISH NORTH AMERICA / WITH THE / Adjacent States. // London, Published by Josh. Cross 18 Holborn (opposite Furnivals Inn) 1835.
Part of cover pasted on back with list: 'Travelling maps published by James Wyld and Son...'; same as (3) for Upper Canada area.
GBL (Maps C.7.b.48) OOAMA (NMC 14697)

(5) *1838*
— 1838 / London, Published by Josh. Cross 18 Holborn (opposite Furnivals Inn) 1838.
Toronto named.
USCSmH

(6) *1839*
— 1839 / London, Published by Josh. Cross – 1839.
The same as 1838.
OOAMA

(7) *1842*
— [Date deleted] / London, published by Josh. Cross – 1842.
The same as 1838.
GBL (70615(20)) USDLC

(8) *1848*
— London, Published by J. Cross & Son, 18 Holborn (opposite Furnival's Inn) 1848
'Railroads completed and those in progress' have been added; GBL accession stamp '31 Jy 54.'
GBL (70615(4))

---

83 *[1831]*
Projected Plan of Four Townships / FOR / EMIGRANT SETTLEMENTS / in the British Colonies of North America
Print (engrav) 28 x 21 cm 1" to 4 miles
Inset: 'Project of Settlement' 1" to 1 mile; in Joseph Bouchette, *British Dominions in North America* (London: Henry Colburn and Richard Bentley 1831), 2: opp 222 (OOA), and in the later ed (London: Longman, etc 1832) (*Bib Can* 1627, 4968); shows crown and clergy reserves together in blocks at the outside corners of the twps; main village reserve in the centre where twps meet, with area for expansion and surrounded by common; plan for interconnecting clearings of settlers and placement of log huts.
OOA OTMCL

---

84 *1831*
Rough Diagram of the Province of Upper Canada shewing the vacant Lands by J.G. Chewett ... S.G. Office 2nd September 1831.
Col ms Approx 43 x 94 cm Scale not given

In Colborne to Viscount Goderich 5 Sept 1831, no 36, Miscellaneous 2712 (GBLpro CO 42/394 p 81); based on the Canada Co. map (**69(5)**); 'List of Lands surveyed shewing the number of acres in each Township exclusive of forfeited lands'; 'Statement of Lands to be surveyed if found necessary'; also shows 'unextinguished Indian rights,' twps to be surveyed the following winter, areas being surveyed and those where agents are locating settlers, routes to three areas; (Olsen map 55).
GBLpro (CO 42/394 p 81)

---

85 *1831*
To / His Most Excellent Majesty / King William IVth / This Map of the Provinces of / LOWER & UPPER CANADA, / Nova Scotia, New Brunswick, Newfoundland & Prince Edwards Island. / WITH A LARGE SECTION OF THE UNITED STATES, / Compiled from the latest & most approved Astronomical Observations, Authorities & recent Surveys, / IS WITH HIS MAJESTY'S MOST GRACIOUS & SPECIAL PERMISSION / Most humbly & gratefully dedicated by / His Majesty's most devoted & Loyal Subject / Joseph Bouchette Junr / Deputy Surveyor General, of the Province of Lower Canada. / ENGRAVED BY J. & C. WALKER, BERNARD STREET, RUSSEL SQUARE. // Published as the Act directs by James Wyld, Geographer to the King Charing Cross London May 2nd 1831.
Print (engrav) 96 x 188 cm 1" to 14 miles
Insets: 'The / GULF OF ST LAWRENCE, / shewing / the Geographical position / of the / PRINCIPAL HEADLANDS, / laid down from the most / recent Astronomical Observations' and 'The / BRITISH DOMINIONS / in / NORTH AMERICA.'; noted as produced to accompany Joseph Bouchette's *British Dominions in North America* (London: 1831) on p xiii of preface (CIHM 42807), but not found with the text vols; shows twps north to Colborne to Ellice, Luther to Zero, Matchadash to Rama, Eldon to Palmerston, Lavant to Horton; Welland and Rideau canals and roads shown with some named; 'Reference' keys twps in which the Canada Co. have lots and blocks, post towns, villages, canals, and boundaries; the list of authorities includes surveys of S. Holland, Capt Owen and Capt Bayfield, Lt Col Bouchette, and surveyors on the Boundary Commission for the Treaty of Ghent; similar to and based on the Canada Co. map for Upper Canada (see **69(5)**); OOAMA (NMC 48942) folding into cover marked 'Bouchette's Canada'; OOAMA also has a copy originally owned by Lord Durham (NMC 113504); (Olsen map 36).
GBL (70615 (2)) OOAMA (NMC 48942, 113504) OTMCL USDLC

---

86 *[1832]*
MAP / OF / UPPER AND LOWER / CANADA. / J. Netherclift Lithog: // London, Published by Effingham Wilson, Royal Exchange.
Print (lith) 32 x 54 cm Approx 1" to 35 miles
In Andrew Picken, *The Canadas as They at Present Commend Themselves ... With a Map* (London: Effingham Wilson 1832), at end (*Bib Can* 1731 lacks map, OOA) and in Joseph Pickering, *Inquiries of an Emigrant*, 4th ed (London: Effingham Wilson 1832), frontis (OKQ, CIHM 47244); shows twps laid out in Huron Tract, main roads, districts; similar in outline to Cross's map of 1831 (**82(1)**); Dionne 865; photoreproduction in OOAMA (NMC 6987).
OKQ OOA

---

87 *1832*
Map of Upper and Lower Canada including New Brunswick, part of Nova Scotia etc. Exhibiting the Post Towns and Mail Routes the latter being distinguished agreeably to the Reference below so as to indicate the frequency of the mails passage Octr 1832 / A true copy [Sgd] T A Stayner D P M Gl Govt Post Office Quebec.
Col ms 70 x 195 cm 1" to 14 miles
Shows post routes, post towns with names, frequency of mail service along routes; refers to tables of routes A and B, and Table C listing offices with distance from Quebec and postage rates, all of which are lacking; see also later maps below; (not in Olsen; Dionne 863).
OOAMA (NMC 11933)

Related maps

(2) *1839*
Map of Upper and Lower Canada, including New Brunswick, part of Nova Scotia etc. Exhibiting the Post Towns & Mail Routes; the latter being distinguished agreeably to the Reference below, so as to indicate the frequency of the mail's passage. Compiled under the direction of T.A. Stayner Esqr D.P.M.G. by J. Adams 1832, corrected to the 1st January 1839.
Col ms 75 x 193 cm 1" to 14 miles
The map has the same notes, information on post routes and frequency as map above; tables A, B, and C are again lacking; routes have been extended into the Huron District, further north of L Ontario, and increased between Kingston and Ottawa; (Olsen map 59).
OOAMA (NMC 40462)

(3) *1839*
[Same title and signatures]
A nearly identical copy with added notes on duties and the potential of trade with the American West via canals; photoreproduction in OOAMA (NMC 11740); (*PRO Cat* 176).
GBLpro (CO 700 Canada 96)

(4) *[1847]*
Map of Upper and Lower Canada including New Brunswick, part of Nova Scotia &c. Exhibiting the Post Towns & Mail Routes General Post Office Quebec T.A. Stayner D.P.M.Gl Jan [uary 1847].

Col ms, pt of lower half missing 74 x 209 cm 1" to 14 miles

Date supplied from earlier records at OOAMA; similar to earlier maps above but explanation is lacking; shows post offices and names, routes; routes increased in area northwest of Toronto to Owen Sound with a water route shown to Manitoulin Is and St Joseph Is, and more routes north of L Ontario; (Olsen map 60).

OOAMA (NMC 11742)

---

88 *[1832]*

MAP / of / UPPER CANADA / Exhibiting the / Districts & Counties / FOR / McGREGOR'S / BRITISH AMERICA // W.H. Lizars Sculpt.

Print (engrav) 12 x 20 cm Scale not given

In John McGregor, *British America* (Edinburgh: William Blackwood; London: T. Cadell 1832), 2: opp 521 (*Bib Can* 1721); shows districts, main roads, notes on forests, location of Canada Co. lands.

OOAMA (NMC 16088) OTMCL

---

89 *1832*

NORTH AMERICA / Sheet III / UPPER CANADA / With Parts of / NEW YORK, PENNSYLVANIA AND MICHIGAN. / Published by the Society for the Diffusion of Useful Knowledge. // Published September 1st 1832 by Baldwin & Cradock 47 Paternoster Row London // J. & C. Walker Sc.

Print (engrav) hand col 32 x 44 cm 1" to 28 miles

This is Pt XXVI of XXVIII original paper parts each with own cover and title, the last published Oct 1832 (GBL Maps 177.j.1); also in Society for the Diffusion of Useful Knowledge, [*A Series of Maps Modern and Ancient* (London: Baldwin & Cradock 1829–37)], plate [120] (*LC Atlases* 6062); –, *A Series of Maps* ... (London: Published by the Society Dec 1840) (OTAR (Simcoe Map 446275a)); –, *Maps of the Society for the Diffusion of Useful Knowledge* (London: Chapman & Hall 1844), 2: plate [132] or [129] (*LC Atlases* 794 and 6100, OTUTF, GBL, OOAMA); –, *Maps of the Society* ... (London: C. Knight 1849), 2: plate [132] (*LC Atlases* 6109); shows Western, London, Gore, Niagara, Home, Newcastle, Midland, Bathurst, Johnston, Ottawa, Eastern districts, cos, main roads (some named), rivers, places; (OOAMA MacDonald Collection 457–60).

GBL OKQ OMSA OOAMA (NMC 2858) OTAR OTUTF USDLC

Later editions and states

(2) *1832*

— // Published September 1st 1832 by Chapman and Hall, 186, Strand, London. // J. & C. Walker Sc.

The same as plan above; (Karpinski 114).

USDLC USMiU

(3) *[1844]*

— // London, Charles Knight & Co. 22, Ludgate Street // 132 // J. & C. Walker Sc.

In an untitled atlas of maps that includes an 'Index to the Principal Places in the World with Reference to the Maps of the Society for the Diffusion of Useful Knowledge,' (London: Charles Knight and Co. 1844) (OTMCL); and in *Maps of the Society* ... (London: Charles Knight and Co. 1844), 2: plate 132 (OOAMA), and in a new ed (London: C. Knight 1846–51), 2: plate 132 (*LC Atlases* 4326), and (London: 1846) (GBL Maps 38.e.9); shows same information as the first 1832 issue above.

GBL OOAMA OTMCL USDLC

(4) *1852*

— // London Charles Knight Jany 1st 1852 // 132 // J. & C. Walker Sc.

In Society for Diffusion of Useful Knowledge, *General Atlas* (London: G. Cox [1853]), 2: plate 132 (*LC Atlases* 811); same information as 1832 map.

USDLC

(5) *1853*

— // London, George Cox, Jany 1st 1853 // 132

In Society for the Diffusion of Useful Knowledge, *General Atlas* (London: George Cox [1854]), 2: plate 132 (OOAMA); map same as 1832 but legend added for railways and those projected, roads, and canals; no railways shown.

OOAMA

(6) *1857*

— // London, Edward Stanford, 6 Charing Cross. // 132 // J. & C. Walker Sc.

In *The Cyclopaedian or Atlas of General Maps Published under the Superintendance of the Society for the Diffusion of Useful Knowledge* (London: Edward Stanford 1857), plate 33 (GBL Maps 40.d.36); in *Portfolio Atlas* [cover-title] (GBL Maps 41.d.16); and in *The Family Atlas ... by SDUK* (London: Edward Stanford 1857), plate 55 (GBL Maps 40.e.20).

GBL OOAMA USDLC

(7) *1860*

... Sheet III / WEST CANADA ...

In *The Cyclopaedian Atlas of General Maps ... SDUK* (London: Stanford 1860), plate 33 (GBL Maps 40.d.37); *The Family Atlas* (London: Stanford 1860), plate 62 (GBL Maps 40.e.21); *The Complete Atlas ... SDUK* (London: Stanford 1860), plate 132 (GBL Maps 38.e.13); *Atlas of North and Central America, Selected from the Maps Designed by the Society for the Diffusion of Useful Knowledge* (London: Edward Stanford 1861), [No 5] (GBL Maps S102 (5)); *Atlas of Modern Geography* (London: Stanford 1861), plate 114 (GBL Maps 41.e.6); *The Cyclopaedian or Atlas of General Maps* (London: Stanford 1862), plate 33, with '33' in upper right and '132' deleted from bottom margin (GBL Maps 41.d.1); and in SDUK, *The Family Atlas* (London: E. Stanford 1863), plate 62 (printed on map) (*LC Atlases* 3559); map shows addition of main railways, projected north shore railway from Ottawa R to north shore of L Huron, Ottawa and Opeongo Rd and other colonization roads.

GBL USDLC

(8) *[1865]*
— // London, Edward Stanford 6, Charing Cross. // J. & C. Walker Sc. // 33
In SDUK, *The Cyclopaedian or Atlas of General Maps* (London: Edward Stanford 1865), plate 33 (GBL Maps 41.d.2); SDUK, *The Family Atlas* (London: Edward Stanford 1865), plate 62 (OOAMA, GBL Maps 41.e.1); Ottawa and Opeongo Rd shown extended to French R; plate no changed to 62 in *The Family Atlas*.
GBL OKQ OOAMA

---

90 *1832*
NORTH AMERICA / Sheet IV LAKE SUPERIOR / Reduced from the Admiralty Survey // Published under the Superintendance of the Society for the / Diffusion of Useful Knowledge. // Published Novr 1st 1832 by Baldwin & Cradock 47 Paternoster Row London. // J. & C. Walker Sculpt
Print (engrav) hand col 32 x 40 cm 1" to 28 miles
In Society for the Diffusion of Useful Knowledge, [*A Series of Maps Modern and Ancient* (London: Baldwin & Cradock 1829–37)], plate [121] (*LC Atlases* 6062); also in *Maps of the Society for the Diffusion of Useful Knowledge* (London: Chapman & Hall 1844), 2: plate [130] or [133] (*LC Atlases* 794 and 6100, GBL, OOAMA), and in atlas of same title (London: C. Knight 1849), 2: plate [133] (*LC Atlases* 6109, OOAMA MacDonald Collection 456 (NMC 119060)); shows international boundary and lakes and rivers emptying into L Superior.
GBL OOAMA (NMC 119060) USDLC

Later editions and states

(2) *1832*
— // Published Novr 1st 1832 by Chapman and Hall, 186, Strand, London. // J. & C. Walker Sculpt.
The same as map above.
OKQ

(3) *[1844]*
— // London, Charles Knight & Co 22, Ludgate Street // 133 // J. & C. Walker Sculpt
In *Maps of the Society* ... (London: Charles Knight and Co. 1844), 2: plate 133 (OOAMA), in a new ed (London: C. Knight 1846–51), 2: plate 133 (*LC Atlases* 4326), and in (London 1846) (GBL Maps 38.e.9); shows the same information as first map above.
GBL OOAMA USDLC

(4) *1853*
— // London: George Cox, Jany 1st 1853. // 133 // J. & C. Walker Sculpt.
In SDUK, *General Atlas* (London: G. Cox [1853]), 2: plate 133 (*LC Atlases* 811), and (London: George Cox [1854]), 2: plate 133 (OOAMA); same as (1).
OOAMA USDLC

(5) *[1861]*
— // London, Edward Stanford, 6 Charing Cross. // 133 // J. & C. Walker Sculpt.
Found separately with copyright stamp '5 No 6.1.'
GBL (Maps 33.d.5)

---

91 *1832*
UPPER CANADA &C. / BY J. ARROWSMITH // London, Pubd 15 Feby 1832, by J. Arrowsmith, 33 East St. Red Lion Square. / 41.
Print (engrav) 61 x 49 cm 1" to 34 miles
Shows roads, districts, cos, twps to line Colborne to North Easthope, Zero to Luther, and Eldon to Palmerston; from Philadelphia to James Bay and from west end L Superior to Montreal; 1 in '41' in ms, possibly changed from 40.
OOAMA (NMC 21362)

Later editions and states

(2) *1834*
— // London, Pubd 15 Feby 1834, by J. Arrowsmith, 33 East St. Red Lion Square. / 41.
In J. Arrowsmith, *The London Atlas* (1842), plate 41 (GBL Maps 43.f.23); also map of the same date with address changed to '35 Essex Street Strand' in J. Arrowsmith, *The London Atlas* ([London: J. Arrowsmith 1832–46]), 4: plate 41 (*LC Atlases* 764, OTAR); same as 1832 map; *The London Atlas* was first issued in 1834 and (2) was probably the earliest state included in it (Herbert, 99ff).
GBL OOAMA (NMC 21364) USDLC

(3) *1837*
— // London, Pub'd 15 Feby 1837, by J. Arrowsmith, 35 Essex Street, Strand. / 41.
Issued separately mounted with map entitled: 'LOWER CANADA, NEW BRUNSWICK, NOVA SCOTIA ... BY J. ARROWSMITH. / 42'; also in *The London Atlas* (London: Arrowsmith 1835–[7?]), plate 41 (GBL Maps 41.f.7); the same as 1832; GBLpro copy has ms adds showing post office, postal routes and frequency of service (*PRO Cat* 181).
GBL GBLpro (CO 700 Canada 90)

(4) *1838*
— // London, Pubd 15 Feby. 1838, by J. Arrowsmith, 10 Soho Square. / 41.
In J. Arrowsmith, *The London Atlas* (London: J. Arrowsmith 1840), plate 41 (*LC Atlases* 4322); also some separately issued copies with same date and earlier address '35 Essex Street Strand' (OOAMA (NMC 88456), OTAR, GBL, USDLC); also a separately issued map with 'Sold by G. Cruchley MapSeller & Publisher, 81 Fleet St. ... from 38 Ludgate St. London' pasted over imprint and mounted with map entitled 'LOWER CANADA ... 42' (OTAR); OOAMA (NMC 25232 and 88456) mounted with 'LOWER CANADA ... 42'; the twps of Darley and Somerville have been added; (OOAMA MacDonald Collection 469).
GBL OMSA OOAMA (NMC 25232, 88456–7) OTAR USDLC

(5) *1842*
— // London, Pub'd 15 Feby 1842 by J. Arrowsmith, 10 Soho Square. / 41.

In J. Arrowsmith, *The London Atlas* (London: J. Arrowsmith 1842 [i.e., 1844], plate 41 (OOAMA); same as 1838.
OTAR OOAMA (NMC 48757) USDLC

(6) *1846*
— // London, Pubd 15 Feby 1846, by J. Arrowsmith, 10 Soho Square. / 41.
Published separately and also mounted with Lower Canada map and folding into cover entitled: 'CANADA, &c. / John Arrowsmith ...' (OOAMA MacDonald Collection 409); also in J. Arrowsmith, *The London Atlas* (London: J. Arrowsmith 1842–[50]), plate 41 (*LC Atlases* 789); same as 1838.
OKQ OOAMA (NMC 21381) OTAR OTMCL

(7) *1853*
— // London, Pubd 15 Feby. 1853, by J. Arrowsmith, 10 Soho Square./ 41.
In J. Arrowsmith, *The London Atlas* (London: J. Arrowsmith 1842–[53]), plate 41 (*LC Atlases* 790); same as 1838; also in *The London Atlas* (1858) (*LC Atlases* 4339); twps have been added to the base of the Bruce Peninsula; GBLpro copy has later ms adds showing railways completed and in progress (*PRO Cat* 209).
GBLpro (CO 700 Canada no 105) USDLC

---

92 *1833*
MAP / OF THE / BRITISH NORTH AMERICAN / PROVINCES / and / ADJOINING STATES/ 1833 // Published as the Act directs by W. Blackwood Edinburgh, 1833 // Engd by J. Moffat
Print (engrav) hand col 40 x 67 cm 1" to 50 miles
In Adam Fergusson, *Practical Notes Made during a Tour in Canada*, 2nd ed (Edinburgh: Blackwood; London: T. Cadell 1834) (*Bib Can* 1641; Dionne 874); shows Upper and Lower Canada and area east to Nova Scotia; similar to the Cross map of 1831 (**82(1)**); there is also a copy in OFF that has been annotated: 'John Langton is in Fenelon and Verulam Township of Newcastle Dist 44.3 Lat 78.3 Long.'; reproduced in W.A. Langton, *Early Days in Upper Canada* (Toronto: 1926), on endpapers.
OFF (Langton Papers) OTMCL

---

93 *[1833]*
Map of / UPPER & LOWER CANADA, / with the DISTRICTS & TOWNSHIPS / into which the Provinces are divided.
Print (lith) 34 x 52 cm Scale not given
In [Francis Fairplay], *The Canadas as They Now Are ... With a Map showing the Position of Each Township, a Point of the Utmost Consequence to the Settler* (London: James Duncan 1833), frontis (*Bib Can* 1638, Casey I–1398); inset: 'Diagram of a Township shewing the Crown and Clergy Reserves'; notes about the map in the text; twps numbered, indexed, and described in Pt 2 of text; a very rough sketch; also found in Fairplay's *A Map of the Canadas* (London: Printed for the Author 1834), at end (QQS, CIHM 49950); the index to the numbered twps forms most of the text.
OOA OTAR OTMCL QQS

---

94 *1833*
SKETCH / of Part of / UPPER AND LOWER CANADA / with reference to the / PROPOSED MILITARY DISTRICTS // Drawn for the United Service Journal by L.J. Hebert and Printed by B. King No 11 Charlotte Street Rathbone Place // London Published for Henry Colburn by R. Bentley 1833.
Print (lith) 26 x 38 cm 1" to 58 miles
Insets: Fig 1 [southwest part of Upper Canada with routes] 1" to 23 miles, Fig 2 [Niagara Peninsula with index to locations] 1" to 20 miles, Fig 3 [Montreal region] 1" to 8 miles; in *United Service Journal* 1833; three districts outlined in Upper Canada; Fig 1 shows routes to a centre midway between L Erie, L Huron, and Detroit R.
USDLC

---

95 *1833*
UPPER CANADA. // Entered according to Act of Congress, in the year 1833, by Illman & Pilbrow, in the Clerk's Office of the District Court for the Southern District of New York. / 47.
Print (engrav) hand col 28 x 31 cm 1" to 36.5 miles
In David Burr, *A New Universal Atlas* (New York: D.S. Stone [1835?]), 'plate 31' (in ms) (*LC Atlases* 771, 1379a); shows districts and some cos, places, main roads; (OOAMA MacDonald Collection 461 (NMC 119054)).
OKQ OOAMA (NMC 119054) USDLC

Later editions and states

(2) *[1840]*
— [Copyright statement deleted] / 47.
In Jeremiah Greenleaf, *Universal Atlas* (Brattleboro, Vt.: 1840); OOAMA copy MacDonald Collection 474 (NMC 119051) has '31' in upper left margin; identical to 1833 map.
OOAMA (NMC 119051) USDLC

(3) *[1842]*
WEST PART / OF CANADA. // 31.
In J. Greenleaf, *A New Universal Atlas*, new ed rev (Brattleboro, Vt.: G.R. French 1842), plate 31 (*LC Atlases* 784); L Nipissing enlarged; many new twp and town names in the Huron District, Simcoe Co, and north of L Ontario; more rivers and lakes shown in Huron-Ottawa area.
USDLC

(4) *[1848]*
— [Title the same]
In J. Greenleaf, *A New Universal Atlas*, new ed ([Brattleboro, Vt., and Boston]: 1848), plate 31 (USNN); revisions to boundary lines of districts and cos; several district and co names added.
USNN

---

96 *[1833–4]*
UPPER / CANADA. // Published by H.S. Tanner, Philadelphia. // TANNER'S UNIVERSAL ATLAS // 3 1/2
Print (engrav) hand col 30 x 38 cm Approx 1" to 32 miles
In H.S. Tanner, [*A New Universal Atlas* (Philadelphia: Published by the author 1833–4)], plate 3 1/2 (*LC Atlases* 4320); and in 1836 (GBL Maps 40.d.8) and 1839 eds of the same atlas (*LC Atlases* 774, 6086); inset: [L Superior] 1/2" to 30 miles; districts: Western, London, Gore, Niagara, Home, Newcastle, Midland, Johnstown, Bathurst, Ottawa, Eastern; shows cos, main roads (some named), Rideau and Welland canals; since 'Toronto' is named, the map may have been made in 1834; (OOAMA MacDonald Collection 465 (NMC 119052)).
GBL OOAMA (NMC 119052) USDLC

Later editions and states

(2) *[1842]*
— // Published by H.S. Tanner, Philadelphia. Tanner & Disturnell, 124 Broadway, New York.
In H.S. Tanner, *A New Universal Atlas* (Philadelphia: Carey & Hart 1842–[3]), plate 3 1/2 (*LC Atlases* 788), and in another ed (1843) (*LC Atlases* 6099); a few place-names and a legend for railways and canals added; shows 'Wilberforce Tract' just northwest of London; (OOAMA MacDonald Collection 473 (NMC 119053)).
OOAMA (NMC 119053) USDLC

(3) *[1844]*
CANADA WEST / FORMERLY / UPPER / CANADA. // Published by Carey & Hart, Philadelphia. // TANNER'S UNIVERSAL ATLAS. // 4.
In H.S. Tanner, *A New Universal Atlas* (Philadelphia: Carey & Hart 1844), plate 4 (*LC Atlases* 4324); same as [1842] ed.
USDLC

(4a) *1844*
— CANADA WEST / FORMERLY / UPPER CANADA // Entered according to Act of Congress, in the Year 1844, by Carey & Hart in the Clerks Office of the Eastern District of Pennsylvania. // 4.
Issued separately and in H.S. Tanner, *A New Universal Atlas* (Philadelphia: Carey & Hart 1845), plate 4 (OOAMA); capitals, important towns, common towns added to legend.
OKQ OOAMA

(4b) *1844 [1846?]*
— [Title etc the same]
In H.S. Tanner, *A New Universal Atlas* (Philadelphia: S.A. Mitchell 1846), plate 4 (*LC Atlases* 3553); districts added: Huron, Brock, Talbot, Wellington, Simcoe, Colborne, Victoria, Dalhousie.
OKQ OOAMA USDLC

(5) *1846*
— / PUBLISHED BY S. AUGUSTUS MITCHELL, / N.E. Corner of Market & 7th Streets, 1846. // Entered according to Act of Congress, in the Year 1846, by H.N. Burroughs in the Clerks Office of the Eastern District of Pennsylvania. // 4.
Print (lith) 31 x 39 cm Approx 1" to 32 miles
Issued separately folding with cover-title: 'West Canada' (OTAR), and in S.A. Mitchell, *A New Universal Atlas* (Philadelphia: S.A. Mitchell 1846), plate 4 (*LC Atlases* 6103); map same as (4b) above but border is different; (Olsen map 81?; OOAMA MacDonald Collection 475 (NMC 119057); 476 (NMC 119058)).
GBL OKQ OOAMA (NMC 119057–8) OTAR USDLC

(6) *1847*
— [Date in the title changed to 1847]
In Mitchell's *A New Universal Atlas* (Philadelphia: S.A. Mitchell 1847), plate 4 (*LC Atlases* 6104); map same as (4b) above.
USDLC

(7) *1848*
— [Date in title changed to 1848]
In Mitchell's *A New Universal Atlas* (Philadelphia: S.A. Mitchell 1848), plate 4 (*LC Atlases* 6106); map same as (4b) above.
USDLC

(8) *[1849]*
— / PUBLISHED BY S. AUGUSTUS MITCHELL, N.E. corner of Market & 7th Streets. // 4.
In S.A. Mitchell, *A New Universal Atlas* (Philadelphia: S.A. Mitchell 1849), plate 4 (*LC Atlases* 797, OOAMA); also in *A New Universal Atlas* (Philadelphia: Thomas, Cowperthwait & Co. 1850) (*LC Atlases* 800), and in the 1851 ed published by Thomas Cowperthwait (*LC Atlases* 805); map same as (4b) above; (OOAMA MacDonald Collection 477).
OKQ OOAMA OTMCL USDLC

(9a) *1850*
— / PUBLISHED BY THOMAS, COWPERTHWAIT & CO. /No 253 Market Street Philadelphia. // Entered according to Act of Congress in the year 1850, by Thomas, Cowperthwait & Co. in the Clerk's Office of the District court of the Eastern District of Pennsylvania. // 4.
L Superior inset deleted and two new insets added: 'THE CITY OF / TORONTO / AND ITS ENVIRONS' approx 1" to 3 miles, 'VICINITY / OF / THE FALLS / OF / NIAGARA' approx 1" to 9 miles; district names dropped; cos added: Bruce, Lambton, Huron, Perth, Waterloo, Halton, Wentworth, Peterborough, Renfrew; railways and proposed railways in Niagara inset.
OKQ

(9b) *[1851]*
— [Same title and imprint as above]
In *Mitchell's New Atlas of North and South America* (Philadelphia: Thomas, Cowperthwait & Co. 1851), plate 4 (*LC Atlases* 1179), and in S.A. Mitchell, *A New Universal Atlas* (Philadelphia: Thomas, Cowperthwait & Co. 1852) (*LC Atlases* 807, OOAMA), and the 1853 ed (*LC Atlases* 809); adds: cos of Grey, Wellington, Victoria, Ontario,

and Peel and a railway from Niagara Falls to Windsor; (OOAMA MacDonald Collection 478 (NMC 119071)).
OOAMA (NMC 13215; 119071) OTAR OTMCL USDLC

(9c) *[1854]*
— [Same title and imprint as above]
In S.A. Mitchell, *A New Universal Atlas* (Philadelphia: Cowperthwait, Desilver & Butler 1854) (*LC Atlases* 813, OOAMA), and the ed of 1855 (Philadelphia: Cowperthwait Desilver & Butler 1855) (*LC Atlases* 6118), and the 1856 ed (Philadelphia: C. Desilver 1856) (*LC Atlases* 4336); several more railway routes added; (OOAMA Macdonald Collection 479 (NMC 119061)).
OOAMA (NMC 119061) USDLC

(10) *1856*
— / PUBLISHED BY CHARLES DESILVER / No 251 Market Street Philadelphia. // Entered according to Act of Congress in the year 1856 by Charles Desilver in the Clerks Office of the District Court of the Eastern District of Pennsylvania. // 4.
In S.A. Mitchell, *A New Universal Atlas* (Philadelphia: C. Desilver 1857) (*LC Atlases* 823), and in the 1858 ed (*LC Atlases* 4340), and the 1859 ed (Philadelphia: C. Desilver 1859) (OOAMA); same as (9c) above; (OOAMA MacDonald Collection 488).
OOAMA USDLC

(11) *1856 [1859]*
— [Address in title changed to: 'No 714 Chestnut Street Philadelphia.']
In S.A. Mitchell, *A New Universal Atlas* (Baltimore: Cushing & Bailey 1859) (*LC Atlases* 6135); a railway has been added from London to Saugeen; 1859 was the last ed of the *New Universal Atlas* (Ristow, 313).
USDLC

---

97 *1834*
CANADA. // Hewett, sculp // 30.
Print (engrav) 18 x 24 cm Scale not given
In *Counsel for Emigrants* (Aberdeen: John Mathison 1834), frontis (*Bib Can* 5023); shows area from L Superior to New Brunswick, L Erie to James Bay; a few place-names.
OTMCL

---

98 *[1834]*
CANADA / AND / PART OF / THE / UNITED STATES // J. HALL, Lithog. Edinr. // Published by JOHN MATHISON, Broad Street Aberdeen.
Print (lith) 26 x 41 cm Approx 1" to 50 miles
In *Sequel to the Counsel for Emigrants* (Aberdeen: John Mathison 1834), frontis (Casey I-1460), and in *Counsel for Emigrants* (Aberdeen: John Mathison 1834), frontis (*Bib Can* 5023, map missing); and in 2nd ed (Aberdeen: John Mathison 1835) (CIHM 18819, Dionne 882); table of distances from Toronto to Montreal; cos, places, Canada Co. lands.
OOA

---

99 *1834*
A MAP / OF THE / TOWNSHIPS IN THE LONDON AND GORE DISTRICTS / OF / UPPER CANADA. / Shewing Mr Brydone's route in 1834, by a dotted line / marked by the side of the Road on which he travelled. // Straker Litho: George Yd Lombard St London
Print (lith) 29 x 36 cm 1" to 17 miles
In James M. Brydone, *Narrative of a Voyage with a Party sent out from Sussex in 1834 by the Petworth Emigration Committee* (Petworth and London: John Phillips and Effingham Wilson 1834), frontis (*Bib Can* 7342); redrawn from the map of 1831 (see **81**) with the addition of more information on roads; shows the areas from the Niagara Peninsula and York to approximately Chatham; twps named, a few names of settlers, and twps 'where Sussex emigrants are settled' are marked.
OTMCL

---

100 *[1834]*
MAP OF THE TOWNSHIPS IN THE PROVINCE OF UPPER CANADA [With ms adds showing areas where Sussex emigrants are settled]
Print (lith) with ms adds 24 x 38 cm 1" to 50 miles
In *The Emigrant's Informant or a Guide to Upper Canada* (London: G. Cowie and Co. 1834), frontis (*Bib Can* 1767); the Petworth emigration scheme; the printed map is the same as the 1831 ed of **(76(4))**.
OTMCL

---

101 *[1834]*
MAP OF THE TOWNSHIPS IN THE PROVINCE OF UPPER CANADA. [With ms adds showing 'The schemes of the proposed land Companies for purchasing lands in Upper Canada...']
Print (lith) with ms adds 24 x 38 cm 1" to 50 miles
In Colborne's no 72 Miscellaneous of 2 Dec 1834 (GBLpro CO 42/423 p 227); the desired lands are in the Indian territory north of the Huron Tract and along the Ottawa R and west to Georgian Bay; the ms adds are overlaid on the printed map **(76(4))**.
GBLpro (CO 42/423 p 227)

---

102 *1834*
MAP OF / UPPER CANADA // For Montgomery Martin's History of the British Colonies Vol iii – Possessions in N. America // Published by J. Cochrane & Co. 11 Waterloo Place Pall Mall Novr 1834. // Drawn & Engraved by J. & C. Walker.
Print (engrav) hand col 12 x 18 cm 1" to 78 miles
In Martin, *History of the British Colonies* (London: Cochrane and McCrone 1834–5), III: opp 187 (*Bib Can* 5033).
OTMCL

Later editions and states

(2) *1836*
— // For Montgomery Martin's History of the British Colonies Vol i – Possessions in N. America

// Published by John Mortimer, 2 Wigmore Street, Cavendish Square, 1836 // Drawn & Engraved by J. & C. Walker.
In Martin, *History of Upper and Lower Canada* (London: John Mortimer 1836), between 262 and 263 (*Bib Can* 1794); map is the same as 1834.
OTMCL

(3) *1836*
— [Vol no deleted] // Published by G.B. Whitaker & Co. Ave Maria Lane London 1836. // Drawn & Engraved by J. & C. Walker.
In Martin, *History of Upper and Lower Canada* (*Bib Can* 1795), and in the same author's *History, Statistics and Geography of Upper and Lower Canada*, 2nd ed (London: Whitaker & Co. 1838), after 264 (*Bib Can* 1796); same as 1834 ed.
OTMCL

---

103 *1834*
NEW TRAVELLING / and Commercial Map of the / CANADAS, / From the Sault of St. Marie to the River Saguenay, AND A LARGE SECTION OF THE UNITED STATES OF AMERICA; / Compiled from the latest Surveys & most approved Authorities. Dedicated by permission to Commodore Robert Barrie, C.B. &c. &c. &c. / By his Obliged Obedient Humble Servant / DAVID TAYLOR, R.N. / March 1834. / ENGRAVED BY S. STILES & CO. NEW YORK.
Print (engrav) hand col 79 x 120 cm Approx 1" to 23 miles
Some copies fold into cover with title: 'Travelling Map of the Canadas'; twps, cos, districts, and roads named; tables of distances; a letter from Taylor to Joseph Bouchette in Sept 1833 asks permission to add his name to the list of sources, and states that he served under Barrie as a master from 1827 to 1831 (QMMRB); High Ridge Books, Catalogue 15, item 45, cites Streeter 3848 copy with advertising slip for J.H. Colton at 4 Spruce St, New York; (Dionne 877; OOAMA MacDonald Collection 519; Olsen map 62).
GBL (Maps 12.b.52) OOAMA (NMC 11700; 16874) OTAR OTMCL OTUTF USDLC USNN

---

104 *[1835]*
UPPER & LOWER / CANADA. // 61.
Print (engrav) hand col 19 x 25 cm Scale not given
Insets: 'CITY OF / MONTREAL' and 'CITY / OF / QUEBEC.'; in T.G. Bradford, *A Comprehensive Atlas* (Boston: W.D. Ticknor; New York: Wiley & Long c1835) (*LC Atlases* 770), and in an 1836 ed, plate [61] (USDLC); shows area from London to New Brunswick; districts, cos, canals; (OOAMA MacDonald Collection 520 (NMC 119055)).
OOAMA (NMC 119055) USDLC

---

105 *1836*
CHART / OF / LAKE ONTARIO. / From Actual Survey / BY / AUGUSTUS FORD U.S.N. / Entered according to Act of Congress in the Year 1836 by Augustus Ford in the Clerks Office of the District Court of the Northern District of New York. / N. Curriers Lith 148 Nassau St. N.Y.
Print (lith) 62 x 140 cm Approx 1 1/2" to 5 [nautical miles?]
Shows the nature of the shoreline and bottom, soundings, lighthouses, shoals, 'salmon fishery,' settlements, Indian villages, roads, and twps; the orientation of Toronto harbour is wrong and the shape of the lake is somewhat inaccurate, particularly at the western end.
OOAMA (NMC 11314) USDLC

---

106 *1836*
Chart / OF / LAKE ONTARIO / From Actual Survey by / AUGUSTUS FORD U.S.N. / Lith. of Sarony & Major 117 Fulton St. N. York, / on Stone by G. Haring. // Published by Henry Adriance, Oswego. // Entered according to Act of Congress in the year 1836 by Augustus Ford, in the Clerk's Office of the District Court of the Northern District of New York.
Print (lith) 42 x 94 cm Scale not given
Shows similar information to map above and possibly reduced from it.
GBL (70540(2)) USDLC

---

107 *1836*
MAP / OF THE / GREAT LAKES. / York [1]St Oct 1836. H.J. Castle Lith Toronto.
Print (lith) 32 x 50 cm Approx 1" to 30 miles
A crudely drawn map extending from Sault Ste Marie to Kingston; twps, districts, several roads; proposed railway routes and distances shown with notes on routes; probably the map described as showing 'the most favourable points of termination for the Railroad' [City of Toronto and L Huron Railroad] and advertised by Castle in the *Patriot* 11 Oct 1836 (Fleming, 307; Holmden 1696, 1697).
OOAMA (NMC 9833)

---

108 *1836*
Map OF UPPER CANADA G.W. Boynton Sc. // Entered according to Act of Provincial Legislature in the year 1836 by Walton & Gaylord in the Clerk's Office of the Court of King's Bench for the District of St. Francis // Z. Thompson Del.
Print (engrav) hand col 14 x 26 cm Approx 1" to 47 miles
Issued attached to cover with 'Map / OF / LOWER CANADA. // Z. Thompson Del. / Bourne Sc. / Entered ... 1835 by Walton & Gaylord ...'; shows twps in the Huron Tract, districts, some cos, canals.
OTAR QMMMCM

---

109 *[1836]*
UPPER & LOWER / CANADA. // London, C. SMITH & SON 172 Strand. // 49.
Print (engrav) hand col 37 x 57 cm 1" to 42 miles
In Charles Smith, *Smith's New General Atlas* (London: C. Smith & Son 1836), plate 49 (*LC*

Atlases 6078); shows districts, cos, twps in the Huron Tract and to a line Zero to Luther and Eldon to Darling.
OMSA OOAMA (NMC 6996) USDLC

Later editions and states

(2) *1839*
— // London, C. SMITH & SON 172 Strand. / 1839. // 49.
In Smith's *New General Atlas* (London: Charles Smith & Son 1839), plate 49 (OTMCL); map is the same as the [1836] ed.
OTMCL

(3) *[1842?]*
— // London, C. SMITH & SON 172 Strand. // 51 / 52.
Watermarks: '1840' 'WHATMAN 1844' (atlas); 'J WHATMAN 1846' (MacDonald Collection 518, NMC 105517)
Also in Smith's *New General Atlas* (London: Charles Smith 1852), plate 51–2 (OOAMA); the Lower Canada-Maine boundary line (1842) has been added in print; hand-colouring for the boundary has also been added on the later issues with 1844 and 1846 watermarks.
OOAMA OOAMA (NMC 6930; 105517)

---

110 *1837*
A / MAP / AND / PROFILE / of the / N. & DETROIT RIVER'S / RAILROAD
Print (engrav) 23 x 79 cm 1" to 8 miles, [Profile]: 1" to 200 ft vertical
In *Report of the Engineer upon the Preliminary Surveys for the Niagara & Detroit Rivers Railroad* (May 1837), frontis (OOA); shows the 'Eastern Tangent' from Ft Erie to Simcoe and St Thomas, and 'Western Tangent' from St Thomas to Chatham, Ft Malden, and Sandwich; 'Explanation of Map' printed on pasted slip on title-page keys 105 twps shown; the Talbot Rd shown from Grand R to Sandwich; the company was incorporated with a charter of 20 Apr 1836 but the line was not built (Trout and Trout, 55); (Fleming 1109).
OOA (Pamph 1837 (21))

---

111 *[1837]*
Map of / BRITISH NORTH AMERICA, / With the Adjacent States. / FOR / DUNCUMB'S EMIGRANT'S ADVOCATE.
Print 32 x 51 cm Scale not given
In John Duncumb, *The British Emigrant's Advocate* (London: Simpkin & Marshall 1837), opp ii (*Bib Can* 2056); a map drawn freehand showing considerable distortion in shapes; extends from L Superior to Quebec City and Boston; shows twps, roads, proposed railway.
OTMCL

---

112 *1837*
MAP / OF / UPPER CANADA. / Shewing the Proposed Routes of Rail Roads, / for the purpose of extending the Trade of the Province. / DEDICATED, / TO HIS EXCELLENCY, SIR FRANCIS BOND HEAD, K.G.H. & G. AND PRUSSIAN M.O.M. / Lieut. Governor of U.C. / By his Humble devoted Servant, / JOHN SMYTH, / CITY OF TORONTO. / 1837. / N. Currier's Lith N.Y. / James Hamilton D.R.G. Delineant // N. Currier's & son [illegible] Nassau Cor. of Spruce St. N.Y.
Print (lith) 66 x 97 cm 1" to 23.5 miles
Several proposed railways shown: part of route from Boston to Mississippi R, Toronto to London indicated as 'Proposed Railroad Smiths Railroad,' Toronto to Saugeen shown via 'Smyths route'; twps numbered and indexed; drawing of a train; the plan for publication of the map was announced by John Smyth in *The Patriot* 22 Aug 1836; (*OHIM* 6.32; Olsen map 64).
GBL (70640(5)) OTMCL

---

113 *1837*
A / NEW & CORRECT MAP / UPPER-CANADA / Compiled from the latest information / PUBLISHED BY T. & M. BUTLER / No 159 Main Street Buffalo. // 1837.
Print (engrav) 41 x 51 cm Scale not given
Shows cos, 'townships wherein the Canada Co have lands for sale,' post towns and villages, canals, roads; 'Table of distances by water'; in the Huron-Ottawa area: 'This part is imperfectly known except to the Traders'; (not in Olsen).
OTUTF USNN

---

114 *1837–40*
Roads along the Frontiers [Sgd] P.J. Bainbrigge Royal Engineers Chatham U.C. 1838
Ms sketchbook 19 x 12 cm Scales vary or not drawn to scale
Sketch maps of various road connections in Upper and Lower Canada interleaved with notes on distances and routes; maps are dated from 1837 to 1840; 18 maps show routes for Upper Canada including those between most major centres west of Toronto to the Detroit and St Clair rivers and as far north as Goderich, the Niagara Peninsula, and Yonge St to Penetanguishene; (*OHIM* 6.2); a plan of the western part of the province by P.J. Bainbrigge was enclosed with a letter of 24 Dec 1840 (GBLpro WO 44/37 f 30) and a plan of the Niagara District of 30 Sept 1841 was enclosed in GBLpro (WO 46/37 f 119).
GBLpro (MPH 902(3) Pt 1; MR 1929 (1)) OOAMA

---

115 *[1838]*
MAP / Shewing the most / direct Commercial Route, / FROM THE / ATLANTIC via L ONTARIO, / to the Province of / UPPER CANADA, / the North Western States & Territories / and to the MISSISSIPPI / T. & C. Woods Lith: 18 Wall St. J. Price Script. 83 Columbia St. N.Y.
Print (lith) 30 x 58 cm Scale not given
In James Buchanan, *A Letter to the Right Honorable the Earl of Durham* (1838), frontis (*Bib Can* 2130);

shows area from Cape Cod to the Mississippi and from Ohio R to L Nipissing; Great Western Railroad and Toronto & Huron Railroad shown with ship connection Oswego to Hamilton to connect the route; distance and time chart from New York.
OOAMA (NMC 6779) OTMCL

---

116 *1838*
UPPER CANADA // Engraved by G.W. Boynton // Entered according to Act of Congress, in the year 1838, by T.G. Bradford in the Clerk's Office of the District Court of Massachusetts. // III.
Print (engrav) hand col 29 x 36 cm Approx 1" to 32 miles
In Thomas Bradford, *An Illustrated Atlas, Geographical Statistical, and Historical of the United States* (Boston: Weeks, Jordan and Co. [1838]), plate 3 (*LC Atlases* 11028), and another ed (Philadelphia: E.S. Grant & Co. [c1838]), plate 3 (*LC Atlases* 1381); also in Samuel Goodrich, *A General Atlas of the World* (Boston: C.D. Strong 1841), plate [5] (*LC Atlases* 6092), and in Bradford and Goodrich, *A Universal Illustrated Atlas* (Boston: C.D. Strong 1842), plate 4 (*LC Atlases* 783); some maps have '5' in margin; shows districts (Western, London, Gore, Niagara, Home, Newcastle, Midland, Johnstown, Eastern, Ottawa, Bathurst), cos, a few places; (Olsen map 65; OOAMA MacDonald Collection 466–8).
OKQ OMSA OOAMA (NMC 2865–6) OTAR USDLC

---

117 *1838–9*
UPPER CANADA / WEST PART / Compiled & Drawn in Transfer Lithography by L.J. Hebert and Printed / at the Lithographic Establishment Quarter Master Generals Office / Horse Guards Feby. 1838. [and] UPPER CANADA / CENTRAL PART. / Drawn in Transfer Lithography by L.J. Hebert / Printed at the Lithographic Establishment / Quarter Master General's Office Horse Guards. [and] UPPER CANADA / EAST PART / Compiled and Drawn in Transfer Lithography by L.J. Hebert and / Printed at the Lithographic Establishment Quarter Master Generals / Office, Horse Guards; January 1839.
3 prints (liths) Ea approx 36 x 44 cm or 53 x 61 cm 1" to 8 miles
'West Part' shows Western District and west part of London District; 'Central Part' includes Niagara, Gore, part London, south part of Home and Newcastle districts; 'East Part' includes part of Newcastle and Midland, Dalhousie, Johnstown, Ottawa, and Eastern districts; twps named but boundaries not shown; roads, canals, mills; GBTAUh holds the west part only; (Dionne 893; Olsen map 67).
GBTAUh (L1211 Aa1) OOAMA (NMC 14021–2, 21365) USDLC

---

118 *[1839]*
EASTERN DISTRICTS // Vol I p. 291 ... CENTRAL DISTRICTS // Vol I p. 301 ... WESTERN DISTRICTS // Vol I p. 312 ... // S. Hall // PUBLISHED BY OLIVER & BOYD, EDINBURGH // A. Wright.
3 prints (wood engrav) Ea 16 x 9 cm Scale not given
In Hugh Murray, *An Historical and Descriptive Account of British America ... Six Maps by Wright* (Edinburgh: Oliver & Boyd 1839) (*Bib Can* 2295), and in the 2nd ed (1839) (*Bib Can* 2296); shows twps and main roads.
OTMCL

---

119 *[1839]*
MAP / OF / UPPER CANADA: / specifying the various Stations occupied by MISSIONARIES of the CHURCH of ENGLAND. // Lithographed For the Upper Canada Clergy Society, by J. Netherclift, 23 King Wm. St. West Strand.
Print (lith) 29 x 41 cm 1" to 32 miles
Inset: 'PLAN of the GRAND RIVER TRACK: / with the Stations occupied by the Rev. B.C. Mill (see adjoining Page of the Report)' 1" to 7.5 miles; in *Second Report of the Upper Canada Clergy Society* (London: G. Norman 1839) (Casey I–1738), and in the *Third Report* (London: G. Norman 1840) (OTMCL); 'Reference – Eight sources whence the missionaries are sent out' specifying the societies or government that support them; 'churches built but not provided with Clergymen'; (Olsen map 66).
OOA OTMCL

---

120 *[ca 1840]*
CANADA // Edinburgh, W. & A.K. Johnston; Glasgow, Robert Weir; Lumsden & Son. // Engraved by W. & A.K. Johnston.
Print (engrav) hand col 50 x 61 cm 1" to 40 miles
Shows districts of Home, Gore, London, Niagara, Western, Newcastle, Midland, Bathurst, Johnston, Ottawa, and Eastern; shows roads including the Goderich Rd, canals, block belonging to the Canada Co; (OOAMA MacDonald Collection 521 (NMC 119048)).
OOAMA (NMC 119048)

Later editions and states

(2) *[1843?]*
CANADA / BY A.K. JOHNSTON F.R.G.S. // John Johnstone and W. & A.K. Johnston Edinburgh. Robert Weir and James Lumsden & Son Glasgow. // Engraved by W. & A.K. Johnston // NATIONAL ATLAS 38.
In A.K. Johnston, *The National Atlas* (Edinburgh: J. Johnstone and W. & A.K. Johnston 1843), plate 38 (GBL Maps 41.f.10); twps are now named but without boundaries and are shown north to Colborne to Easthope and from Harvey to Palmerston.
GBL

(3) *[1844]*
[Same title as above]
In A.K. Johnston, *The National Atlas* (Edinburgh: J. Johnstone and W. & A.K. Johnston 1844), plate 38 (*LC Atlases* 4323; OOAMA), and in an 1846 ed of the atlas (OOAMA, *LC Atlases* 4325), an 1845 ed (GBL Maps 45.e.13), and an 1850 ed (Edinburgh and London: W. Blackwood & Son 1850) (*LC Atlases* 799); twps are shown north to Ashfield, Mornington, and Maryborough and from Minto to Derby, Bexley, and Somerville; a line of hills added in the north and some relief by hachures; references to some twps by no; stipple pattern added in water bodies.
GBL USDLC OOAMA OMSA

(4) *[1845–9?]*
[Changes as noted below]
Print (lith) 51 x 62 cm
(4a) A lithographic transfer but with imprint removed below the margin (OOAMA (NMC 24938)); (4b) a lithographic transfer with 'LITHOGRAPHED EDITION' added above the title but retains the imprint below margin; in *The National Atlas Lithographic Edition* (Edinburgh: W. & A.K. Johnston; New York: G.P. Putnam [1849]); (*LC Atlases* 6108, OOAMA *Atlas* and NMC 24940); both show the same information as (3).
OOAMA (NMC 24938, 24940) USDLC

(5) *[1849?]*
[Above title printed in red] 'LITHOGRAPHED EDITION' [and in red below margin] 'EDINBURGH: JOHN JOHNSTONE W. & A.K. JOHNSTON AND COWAN & CO. GLASGOW LUMSDEN & SON
Print (lith)
In *The National Atlas* (Edinburgh: W. & A.K. Johnston and Cowan & Co.; Glasgow: James Lumsden & Son [c1849–54] (OOAMA) (GBL Maps 41.f.12); shows the same information as (3) but cos and shoreline are shown in red.
GBL OOAMA

(6) *[1854]*
CANADA / BY A.K. JOHNSTON F.R.G.S. // Engraved by W. & A.K. Johnston // NATIONAL ATLAS / 38.
Print (steel engrav)
In A.K. Johnston, *The National Atlas* (Edinburgh: Cowan & Co. [1854] (*LC Atlases* 4335), and later eds of the same atlas: (Edinburgh: W. & A.K. Johnston 1855) (*LC Atlases* 6117) and (Edinburgh: W. & A.K. Johnston 1857) (OTMCL); shows the same information as (3).
OTMCL USDLC

(7) *[1855?]*
CANADA / BY A.K. JOHNSTON // Engraved by W. & A.K. Johnston // NATIONAL ATLAS 38.
Print (steel engrav?)
Similar to (6) but with railways added to about 1855.
OOAMA (NMC 51363)

---

121 *[1840]*
CANADA. / divided into / COUNTIES AND RIDINGS, / as per / UNION BILL. // John Arrowsmith.
Print (lith) hand col 32 x 72 cm 1" to 40 miles
In Great Britain, Colonial Office, *Copies or Extracts of Correspondence relative to the Reunion of the Provinces of Upper and Lower Canada ... Ordered to be Printed 23d March 1840* ([London 1840]) (*Bib Can* 2365); some copies found separately and some lack Arrowsmith's name; shows Upper and Lower Canada; districts and cos named; ridings shown with hand-coloured boundaries per Union Act (Great Britain, 3 and 4 Vict, cap 35 (1840)); (Dionne 900).
OOAMA (NMC 26165) OTAR OTMCL

Related maps

(2) *[1840]*
UPPER CANADA, in Counties and Ridings, as at Present Divided.
Print (lith) hand col 31 x 41 cm Approx 1" to 41 miles
From the same source as map above (*Bib Can* 2365); districts and cos named; ridings shown with hand-coloured boundaries; shows ridings per Act of 1833 (3 Wm IV, cap 16) (Armstrong, *Handbook*, 150; Holmden 2783).
OOAMA (NMC 26167) OTAR OTMCL

---

122 *[ca 1840]*
[Map of part of Upper Canada by Anne Langton]
Col ms 33 x 46 cm 1" to 14 miles
Shows the area from Waterloo Twp to the St Lawrence R and north from Georgian Bay to the Ottawa R; most twps named and boundaries shown; relief shown including the Oak Ridges moraine and Niagara escarpment; notes on water communication north of twps from Eldon to Palmerston; several twps shown with asterisks (denoting land held by Canada Co.); similar to and possibly copied from the Canada Co. map **(69(2))**; probably made soon after Anne Langton arrived in Canada in 1837.
OFF (Langton Papers)

---

123 1840
Parts of the Brock Western, London, Gore, Niagara, & Home Districts, with the Huron Tract Upper Canada Copied from the original compilation by Colonel Mackenzie Fraser, Asst Qr Mr Genl Upper Canada by C.J. Colville Lt 85th Lt Infy Certified a true Copy [Sgd] F.A. Mackenzie Fraser Colonel Asst. Q M. Genl Upper Canada Toronto 2 April 1840
Col ms 76 x 167 cm Approx 1" to 3 miles
Watermark: 'J WHATMAN ... 1837[?]'
This and the maps below appear to be part of an overall military survey of the province carried out ca 1840; the legend keys 'Roads which tho' often far from good may be considered as militarily passable at all seasons,' 'Roads generally but not

at all seasons passable by guns,' and 'Bad roads and bridle-paths'; roads are named; tolls, inns, mills, rivers, schools, and post offices shown; relief by shading; names of a few landowners; view of a sailboat near a shore sgd 'A.C.S. 1840'; the map covers the area from Toronto west to L Huron but terminates south of London; the part to the south appears to be missing.
OOAMA (NMC 15179)

Related maps

(2) *1840*
Parts of the Home & Newcastle Districts Upper Canada Copied from the original compilation by Colonel Mackenzie Fraser, Asst Qr Mr Genrl Upper Canada By C.J. Colville Lt 85th Lt Infy Certified a true copy [Sgd] F.A. Mackenzie Fraser Colonel Asst Q. M. Genl. Upper Canada
Col ms 76 x 191 cm Approx 1" to 3 miles
Watermark: 'J WHATMAN ... 1838'
View: 'Toronto U.C. C.J. Colville 1840. C.I.C. 1840.'; includes the same legend as map above, and the same information and relief are shown; the map fits with (1) but the part to the east appears to be missing; possibly the map referred to as received on 8 Apr 1862 by the REO Kingston to assist with the 1862 surveys (OOA RG 8/1566 p 120).
OOAMA (NMC 16911)

---

124 *1840*
[Plans to accompany Lt Colonel Phillpotts' Report on the Inland Navigation of the Canadas. with letter to the Inspector General dated 12th Feby 1840]
10 col mss Sizes vary Scales vary
Title from statement on Pls 1–3 below; originally bound together with title '22 Plans Received with Lt. Col. Phillpotts's letters of 12th Feby 1840 and 5th May 1841, relative to his first and second Reports on the Inland Navigation of the Canadas. Book 33' (Holmden 3819); Phillpotts's first report of 21 Dec 1839 and second report of 3 Aug 1840 are in GBLpro (CO 42/498); all maps have 'B↑O' stamp; the maps relating to Upper Canada are as follows:

Pl 1 Map of Lower and Upper Canada Together with the Northern part of the United States of America Shewing the different Routes between the Vast Tract of Country bordering upon the Upper Lakes and the Atlantic Ocean To accompany ...
135 x 76 cm 1" to 32 miles
Keys canals, roads, proposed canal and railways and macadamized roads for Canada and the U.S.; (Olsen map 69).
OOAMA (NMC 34153)

Pl 2 Plan of a part of The River St Lawrence Shewing all the Canals required between Kingston and Montreal as well as the position of the Ottawa and Rideau Canals. to accompany ...
76 x 174 cm 11/2" to 1 mile Endorsements: stamp 'IGF'
Shows the St Lawrence Canal from Long Sault to past Cornwall and the Rideau Canal; canals required opp Ogden's Is, at Iles Galoppes and Farrens Pt.
OOAMA (NMC 15610)

Pl 3 Plan of the Niagara Frontier Shewing the General Line of the Welland Canal To accompany ...
76 x 111 cm 1" to 1 mile Endorsements: stamp 'IGF'
Shows present canal line, line proposed for sloops, and one for steamboats between Thorold and St Catharines; proposed connections of feeder line to Grand R and Fork Creek Harbour.
OOAMA (NMC 29139)

Pl 4 Plan of a part of the line of the Welland Canal Shewing the intended deviation Between St Catharines and Thorold
57 x 158 cm 1" to 4 chains
Notes: 'deviation proposed by Messrs Baird and Killaly for Schooner navigation' and 'deviation proposed by Lt Colonel Phillpotts if the Canal be enlarged for the Navigation of Steam Boats'; 22 locks proposed; names of owners affected; (*OHIM* 6.28).
OOAMA (NMC 34150)

Pl 5 Plan of the River St Lawrence between Prescott and Cornwall – shewing in yellow the parts of the River which require to be improved
44 x 228 cm 13/4" to 1 mile
Areas to be improved include Farrens Pt, Le Rapid Plat, Les Galoppes, and Pt Cardinal.
OOAMA (NMC 15427)

Pl 6 Plan of the Proposed Improvements at Les Galoppes and Point Cardinal Suggested by Mr Mills
51 x 80 cm Scale not given
[Two profiles]: 1" to 400 ft horizontal and 1" to 20 ft vertical for proposed canals at these points.
OOAMA (NMC 15423)

Pl 7 (Copy) Plan of the Proposed Improvement at the Rapide Plat Suggested by Mr Mills
56 x 131 cm 1" to 400 ft
[Profile]: 1" to 20 ft vertical; three possible routes shown and profile covers routes 2 and 3; route 1 proposed by Mr Clowes and Mr Barrett.
OOAMA (NMC 15425)

Pl 8 Plan of the Proposed Improvement at Farren's Point Suggested by Mr Mills
44 x 56 cm 1" to 400 ft
[Profile]: 1" to 20 ft vertical.
OOAMA (NMC 3795)

Pl 9 PLAN / of the / ST LAWRENCE CANAL / Passing the LONG SAUT / By order of the / BOARD OF COMMISSIONERS / Appointed under the Act Chap. XVIII ... By J.B. Mills Civil Engineer / Stodart & Currier's Lithy. New-York. / S. Keefer 1835
Print (lith) with ms adds 68 x 130 cm Scale not given

Ms notes on the state of the building of various locks as of 1839 including parts completed, parts to be excavated; (see **524**).
OOAMA (NMC 29141)

Pl 10 (Copy) 5 Cross Sections of that part of the Saint Lawrence Canal which has been made along the Rapids of the Long Saut, shewing the Geological formation of the Banks ... Drawn under the direction of Lieut. Col. Phillpotts, R.E. By Samuel Keefer Assistant Engineer St. L. Canal. June 1839.
Col ms in 2 pts, pt 2 missing 51 x 77 cm 1" to 15 ft
Shows station nos 24 and 54.
OOAMA (NMC 15424)

Pl 21 (Copy) Sketch of Presqu'ile Bay shewing the Canal Proposed to open a communication for large Steamers between it and the Bay of Quinte – To accompany ...
51 x 75 cm 1" to 40 chains
Shows the proposed Murray Canal; two possible positions shown with estimates for each; town of Newcastle.
OOAMA (NMC 29143)

Related maps

(2) *1842*
Sketch / OF THE LINE OF / WATER COMMUNICATION, / FROM THE FORT OF / LAKE ERIE TO MONTREAL; / To accompany Coll Phillpotts Report on the / CANAL NAVIGATION OF THE / CANADAS. / 1842. // John Weale, 59, High Holborn, London, 1842 // J.R. Jobbins, lith. 3, Warwick Ct Holborn // J.R. Jobbins del.
Print (lith) 64 x 80 cm Approx 1" to 12 miles
In Phillpotts's 'Report on the Canal Navigation of the Canadas,' *Gt. Brit. Corps of Royal Engineers. Professional Papers Quarto Series* (1842), 5:140–93 (OOA); shows the Rideau, Welland, and St Lawrence canals, rivers, lakes, and a few place-names; OTAR copy has ms changes to the title in which 'Canal' is changed to 'Inland' and '1842' changed to '1840.'
OOA OTAR

---

125 *1840*
SKETCH of the CANADAS / shewing the relative Positions of the / several / Military Posts. // Lithd. at the Rl Engr Press. / [in ms?] Montreal. 26th Novr 1840.
Print (lith) with ms adds 35 x 85 cm Approx 1" to 27 miles Endorsements: 'To accompany Report by Lt Coll Oldfield K.H. Comg Rl Engr in the Canadas, dated 14th Nov 1840' 'In 209 24 Decr' '40 Lower Canada'
Originally filed with report in GBLpro (CO 42/312 pp 527–8); tables of numbers of men per the four districts: Western, Niagara, Montreal, Quebec; military posts on the Rideau Canal; in ms: 'proposed posts are tinted green existing red'; 'the Temporary Posts are not included'; (*OHIM* 2.11; Olsen map 70; *PRO Cat* 1408).
GBLpro (MPG 99)

---

126 *[1842]*
CANADA // London Published for the Proprietors by Geo. Virtue, 26 Ivy Lane // W. Hughes.
Print 20 x 24 cm Approx 1" to 70 miles
Inset: 'PART OF NEW BRUNSWICK and NOVA SCOTIA on the same scale'; in N.P. Willis, *Canadian Scenery Illustrated* (London: George Virtue 1842), pt 6: opp 77 (*Bib Can* 7673); shows area from Hamilton east only; railways; some places illustrated by views are underlined in the text; also published with imprint '... // JAMES S. VIRTUE LONDON // ...' in the American ed (New York: Virtue and Yorston [1842?]) 1: opp 1 (*Bib Can* 5251).
OOAMA OTMCL

---

127 *1842*
DIOCESE OF / TORONTO // LONDON, PRINTED FOR THE SOCIETY FOR THE PROPAGATION OF THE GOSPEL, NOV 1842. // Drawn & Engraved by J. Archer // III.
Print (engrav) hand col 22 x 28 cm 1" to 45 miles
In *Colonial Church Atlas* (London: Printed for the Society for the Propagation of the Gospel in Foreign Parts 1842), plate III (*LC Atlases* 4159, OTMCL); legend keys churches located, table of areas with population and number of clergy; approx 59 churches shown; imprint trimmed off on OTMCL copy.
OTMCL USDLC

Later editions and states

(2) *1843*
— LONDON, PRINTED FOR THE SOCIETY FOR THE PROPAGATION OF THE GOSPEL, FEB. 1843. // ...
In John Strachan, *A Journal of Visitation to the Western Portion of his Diocese* (London: Sold by Rivingtons, Hatchard and Burns 1844), frontis (OONL, CIHM 47609); the same as 1842.
OONL

(3) *[1845]*
— [Date removed in imprint]
In *Colonial Church Atlas* (London: Printed for the Society for Promoting Christian Knowledge 1845), plate III (OOAMA), and in John Strachan, *A Journal of Visitation to the Western Portion of his Diocese* 3rd ed (London: Printed for the Society for the Propagation of the Gospel 1846), frontis (*Bib Can* 2550); the same as 1842; the imprint has been trimmed off the map in the Strachan book.
OOAMA OTMCL

(4) *[1848]*
— // LONDON PUBLISHED BY THE SOCIETY FOR PROMOTING CHRISTIAN KNOWLEDGE // Drawn & Engraved by J. Archer.
In Ernest Hawkins, *Annals of the Diocese of Toronto* (London: Printed for the Society for Promoting Christian Knowledge 1848), frontis (*Bib Can* 2909); the same as 1842.
OTMCL

(5) *[1853]*
— / / LONDON PUBLISHED BY THE SOCIETY FOR PROMOTING CHRISTIAN KNOWLEDGE ...
Archer / VII
In *Colonial Church Atlas* (London: Printed for the Society for Promoting Christian Knowledge 1853), plate VII (OOAMA); most of legend except for churches deleted; over 60 churches are marked; base map same as (1).
OOAMA

---

128 *1842*
Map of part of the Niagara, Gore, London and Talbot Districts Showing the Townships, principal roads, Towns, Villages and streams of Water ... outlined from Materials furnished by Colonel G. A. Wetherall C.B.K.H. by Sir J.E. Alexander K.I. S 14 Regt London, Canada West, 1842
Ms 42 x 55 cm Approx 1" to 4 miles
Shows twps, roads, towns, inns, sawmills; mileages shown on some roads; the map is similar to and roughly adjoins (2) below.
GBLrg

Related maps

(2) *[1842?]*
Map of the Western District [Sgd?] Alexander
Ms 45 x 55 cm [Approx 1" to 4 miles]
Shows twps north to Sarnia to Warwick in the Western district.
GBLrg

---

129 *[1842?]*
[Map of Upper and Lower Canada]
Print (wood engrav) 10 x 18 cm Scale not given
In *Emigration to Canada ... Chambers Information for the People No. 17* (Edinburgh: W. & R. Chambers [1842?]), on 258 (*Bib Can* 7661); shows cos, major roads and places.
OTMCL

---

130 *1842*
New Map of the United Province of Canada With The New Municipal Districts Divisions from the Lake Superior to the Gulf of St Lawrence and a large Section of the United-States by N. Bazire 1842.
Col ms 81 x 110 cm 1" to 27 miles
Provenance: USDLC, received from U.S. Coast and Geodetic Survey Library in 1914; references: districts, cos, twps, large towns, fortifications, canals, railways, roads.
USDLC

---

131 *1842*
Sketch to accompany Coll Oldfield's Memoranda of the 14th of Decr 1842 as called for by His Excellency the Commander of the Forces for the Occupation of the existing Works of Defence in Canada [Sgd] J. Oldfield Colonel Staff Commandg Royl Engineer in Canada 14 December 1842 / [in print] Lithographed at the Royal [Engrs] Press / Montreal [26th Novr] 1840 / [in ms] [Sgd] R I Pilkington Draftsman.
Print (lith) with col ms adds 37 x 86 cm Approx 1" to 28 miles Endorsements: 'Canada Military Posts and Barrack Accommodation Col Oldfield 14 Dec. 1842.' 'B 155'; stamps 'B↑O' 'IGF'
Title mainly in ms; the printed base is the same as **125** except imprint has been moved to lower right, a printed table of permanent barracks accommodation has been added, and other tables deleted; works of defence, permanent barracks, and hired barracks all shown in ms; (Holmden 3941).
OOAMA (NMC 24936)

---

132 *[1842]*
Upper Canada West Part ... Central Part ... East Part Drawn by Lt. Lysons D.A. Q.M.G. [Sgd] Charles Gore D.Q.M.G.
3 col mss Ea 36 x 44 or 52 x 61 cm Approx 1" to 8 miles Endorsements: '43' '44' '45'
Withdrawn from GBLpro T.62/8; infantry, cavalry, volunteers, and artillery stations located; names of regiments, roads, and notes on conditions; sheets appear to be traced from the printed maps of 1838–9 (**117**); Sir Daniel Lysons described his surveying work in the Niagara region in 1841 in *Early Reminiscences* (1896), 119; tables of barrack accommodation 'as of Returns 1st Jany 1842'; (Olsen map 68; *PRO Cat* 1411).
GBLpro (MPD 11)

---

133 *[ca 1842–3]*
Map of the London Brock Talbot and Part of the Huron Districts
Col ms in 3 sections 98 x 168 cm [1" to 2 miles]
Endorsements: stamps 'BW' '505'
Shows the twps and survey grid for Middlesex, Oxford, and Norfolk cos with the various roads being built by the Board of Works; one of first of several compiled reference maps of the western part of the province prepared by the Board of Works; possibly by Peter Carroll as noted in map below.
OOAMA (NMC 21613)

Related maps

(2) *1842*
Map of the County of Oxford District of Brock. Copied from Mr Peter Carroll's Map. 1842
Col ms 61 x 75 cm 1" to 2 miles Endorsements: stamps 'BW ...' '509'
(SI (BW) no 43, 12 Feb 1842); probably a copy of part of above map; shows similar information to (1) with more emphasis on stage road to Brantford through Woodstock with connections via Sodom to Ingersoll.
OOAMA (NMC 21927)

(3) *[1842?]*
Map of the London and Western Districts In The Province of Canada, as subdivided into Lots

according to the original Surveys, and shewing the several roads made or Improved by the Provincial Board of Works. Compiled by F.P. Rubidge, Draftsman.
Col ms 96 x 172 cm [1" to 2 miles] Endorsements: stamps 'BW ...' '518'

Shows all the area from Middlesex Co and the southern part of the Huron District west and southwest, roughly where (1) ends, as instructed to be made on 12 Feb 1842 (as above); shows survey grid including twps in the Huron Tract only, partly surveyed roads, clergy reserves, and Canada Co. lands.
OOAMA (NMC 16910)

(4) *1843*
Map No 3 To accompany Report on macadamized District Roads in Canada West, dated St Catharines 22d April 1843 and Signed David Thorburn, Francis Hall. [ms adds on]: Map of the Home & Simcoe Districts ... 1841
Print (lith) with ms adds 100 x 70 cm [1" to 200 chains] Endorsements: stamp [BW] '433'

The printed base map is **371**; ms adds although not keyed probably show open roads (some named) and ms figures the number of people in each twp (Holmden 2152).
OOAMA (NMC 21375)

---

134 *1843*
CHART / of / LAKE ERIE / DRAWN BY / ROBT HUGUNIN. / 1843. // Lith. of Hall & Mooney, Buffalo. // Entered according to Act of Congress, in the year 1843 by Robert Hugunin in the Clerk's Office of the District Court of the United States for the Northn Dist. of N. York.
Print (lith) 49 x 85 cm 1" to 7 miles

Note: 'N.B. the line of the Northern Coast was taken from an English Survey ordered by the Board of Admiralty' (probably the published chart of 1828 (**C114**); shows relief along shoreline, soundings, boundaries; (Karpinski, 730).
USDLC

---

135 *1843*
Map / OF / CANADA / SHEWING GENERALLY / THE SEVERAL PUBLIC WORKS COMPLETED OR NOW IN PROGRESS; / As embraced & authorized by IIIrd & IVth Victoriae Cap: 28; / Also / EXHIBITING THE DIFFERENT LINES OF ROADS UNDERTAKEN BY THE RESPECTIVE DISTRICTS. // J. Arrowsmith lith. // 595 Ordered by the House of Commons to be Printed 21 August 1843. // James & Luke J. Hansard Printers. // PAPERS RELATING TO PUBLIC WORKS. (CANADA)
Print (lith) 67 x 104 cm Scale not given

From Great Britain, Colonial Office, *Public Works (Canada) Return to an Address ... for Copy of the Act of the Parliament of Canada in 1841 appropriating of Colonial Monies for the ... Public Works* (London 1843), at back (*Bib Can* 7689); shows roads and canals in progress by the government; various districts; schedule of the estimates and costs of the works with indication of work done or expected completion date, sgd in facsimile 'Hamilton H. Killaly President Board of Works'; OOAMA copy in 2 sheets, lacking all the imprint (possibly trimmed), but with addition of '37' and '38' on east and west sheets, respectively; photo-reproduction of GBLpro map in OOAMA (NMC 24939); (Olsen map 71; *PRO Cat* 187).
GBLpro (CO 700 Canada 101) OOAMA (NMC 24937) OTMCL

---

136 *1843*
Map of the Province of Canada Compiled from the Reconnoitring Plans of the Several districts made as directed by Paragraph 7 of the Standing Orders issued by Col. Oldfield K.H. Commanding Royl Engineer For the guidance of the Royal Engr Department in Canada in June 1839. Compiled & Drawn by R.I. Pilkington Draftsman [Sgd on each sheet] J. Oldfield Colonel Staff Comg Royal Engineer in Canada 1 May 1843.
Col ms in 3 sheets 103 x 372 cm 1" to 6 miles
Endorsements: stamps 'B↑O' 'IGF'

On west sheet: 'Compiled and Drawn by Fredrc Torrens Captn 23rd Fusiliers Assistant Rl Engr'; on central sheet: (L Scugog to province boundary) 'R.I. Pilkington Draftsman'; inset: 'Sketch shewing the proposed Water Communication between the Ottawa River and Lake Huron' approx 1" to 27 miles; shows military posts, settlements, roads with comments on surface, rivers, relief; three tables of distances; on inset two different routes are shown: the Ottawa R, L Nipissing, and the French R route and a more southerly route between the Madawaska R and Balsam L; east sheet shows Lower Canada; (Holmden 3942).
OOAMA (NMC 11741)

Related maps

(2) *[1843]*
Map of the Province of Canada Compiled from the Reconnoitring Plans of the Several Districts made as directed by Par 7 of the Standing Orders issued by Colonel Oldfield KH Commanding Royal Engineer for the guidance of the Royal Engineer Department in Canada in June 1839
Col ms in 2 sheets Ea 102 x 122 cm 1" to 6 miles

Provenance (OTMCL): ownership label with coat of arms and name 'Col. Oldfield K.H. Colonel, R.E.'; the central sheet for the east half of Upper Canada is missing; west sheet shows the same information as (1) above except the drafting statement and Oldfield's signature lacking and table has been placed in the centre.
OTMCL

(3) *1843*
Map of the Province of Canada ... [as in first map above] [Sgd] J. Oldfield ... 1 Jany 1843
Col ms in 2 sheets Ea 103 x 125 cm 1" to 6 miles
Endorsements: 'No 417-1' '417-3'; stamp 'CREOC'

The central sheet is again missing; the west sheet

has later ms adds showing railway lines including the Northern Ry from Toronto to Collingwood; otherwise, the map is the same as maps above and was possibly the original from which (1) was copied.
OOAMA (NMC 18309)

---

137 *1843*
MAP OF THE TOWNSHIPS IN THE PROVINCE OF UPPER CANADA [with ms adds showing the 'Great Northern & Great Western Railways & Plank Roads 1843']
Print (lith) with ms adds 24 x 39 cm 1" to 50 miles
The printed base (**76(5)**) is from an ed of broadside: *Lands in Upper Canada* [text and imprint trimmed off]; ms adds: three proposed railways and four plank roads; the railway from Toronto to Saugeen noted as 'to be pushed for by Toronto'; the Great Western Ry shown going through Hamilton to the west and northeast is noted as 'to be pushed for by Hamilton'; (*OHIM* 6.33).
OOAMA (NMC 2872)

---

138 *1843*
THE / PROVINCE / OF / CANADA / BY / JAMES WYLD / GEOGRAPHER TO THE QUEEN / and / H.R.H. PRINCE ALBERT / CHARING CROSS EAST LONDON / 1843. // Published by JAS. WYLD, Charing Cross East, London, March 3rd 1843.
Print (engrav) 61 x 94 cm [1" to 26.3 miles]
Shows Upper and Lower Canada with twps in Upper Canada shown north to line Colborne to North Easthope, Luther to St Vincent, Matchedash to Rama, Darley to Somerville, Emily to Palmerston, Lavant to Kenmore; districts, cos, roads, relief; OOAMA MacDonald Collection 523 (NMC 88405) folding into case with title: 'MAP / OF / THE PROVINCE / OF / CANADA, / AND PART OF THE / UNITED STATES; / WITH THE / RAILWAYS, / ROADS AND CANALS. / BY / JAMES WYLD, / GEOGRAPHER TO THE QUEEN / AND H.R.H. PRINCE ALBERT, / CHARING CROSS, EAST, LONDON, / Four Doors from Trafalgar Square'; (Olsen 123).
GLBpro GBLrg OOAMA (NMC 88082, 88405) OTMCL

Later editions and states

(**2**) *1845*
— [Date in title and imprint changed to 1845]
OOAMA MacDonald Collection 524 (NMC 88083) folding into cover with same title as above; the map is the same as 1843.
OOAMA (NMC 88083)

(**3a**) *[1848]*
— [Dates removed from title and imprint]
Print (lith)
In James Wyld, *An Emigrant's Atlas* (London: J. Wyld [1848]) (*LC Atlases* 3304); a lithographic transfer from the same map as 1843.
USDLC

(**3b**) *[1849]*
— [Title as in (3a)]
Print (lith)
In *A Popular Atlas of the World* (London: J. Wyld 1849) (GBL Maps 45.f.8); a lithographic transfer; twps have been added north to Lavant to Westmeath.
GBL

(**4**) *[ca 1850]*
— [Title as in (3a)]
Print (lith) Endorsements: stamp in upper left corner '38'
A lithographic transfer; lakes and rivers added in Huron-Ottawa territory; twps added to line Madawaska to Bromley, Ashfield, and Wawanosh; lakes and rivers added north and east of L Nipissing and in Lower Canada; Newcastle District named and moved to proper place; Wellington and Huron districts and Waterloo Co added.
OOAMA (NMC 97957)

(**5**) *[ca 1851]*
— [Title as in (3a)]
Print (engrav)
Twps have been added to the base of the Bruce Peninsula; the name Bruce has been added but in letter style for a district; OOAMA copy folding into slip-case with the same title as (1) and (2); the addition of twps and the list of maps advertised on the back suggest this map may have been updated to about 1851.
OOAMA (NMC 94067)

(**6**) *[1851?]*
— CHARING CROSS EAST, AND / MODEL OF THE EARTH, LEICESTER SQUARE. / LONDON. // Published by JAS WYLD, Charing Cross East, London.
Print (engrav)
Pasted on the back: '65'; probably published soon after the 'Model of the Earth' was completed in May 1851 (Hyde, 3); the map is the same as (5).
OOAMA (NMC 8925)

(**7**) *[1854?]*
— [Title as in (6)]
Print (engrav)
OOAMA MacDonald Collection 528a (NMC 88084) folded into slip-case with title: 'MAP / OF / THE PROVINCE / OF / CANADA, / ...' as in (1) and (2); railways shown as built or planned: Toronto-Hamilton-Windsor, Niagara Falls-Hamilton and Toronto-Montreal, Buffalo-Brantford-Guelph, Toronto-Guelph, Toronto-Barrie-Collingwood, Woodstock-Port Dover, London-Port Stanley, Port Hope-Lindsay, Brockville-Smith Falls-Perth, Ottawa-Prescott, Ottawa-Renfrew; twps added north to Wilberforce to Brougham; Grey, Perth, Lambton, Elgin, and Renfrew cos added; Port Franks has been moved to proper location; USDLC copy endorsed 'G.A. Moncrieff S.I.G.R. 18/12/61'; QMMMCM copy does not include Ottawa-Renfrew railway.
OOAMA (NMC 88084) OTMCL QMMMCM USDLC

(8) *[1858?]*
— [Title as in (6)]
Print (engrav)
OOAMA copy folding into slip-case with the same title as (7); railways added: Brantford to Goderich, Guelph-Stratford-Sarnia, London-Sarnia; New Brunswick-Lower Canada boundaries are marked in hand-colouring [1851, demarcated 1853–5] (Nicholson, 60, 95).
OOAMA (NMC 24357)

(9) *[ca 1860]*
— CHARING CROSS EAST / LONDON // LONDON, PUBLISHED BY JAMES WYLD, GEOGRAPHER TO THE QUEEN, CHARING CROSS EAST, 457 STRAND & 2 ROYAL EXCHANGE.
Print (lith)
Additions: inset: [New Brunswick, Nova Scotia, Newfoundland] approx 1" to 72 miles, the border has been broken at the bottom to include New York and Long Is; Ottawa named; New Brunswick–Lower Canada boundary printed on; OOAMA MacDonald Collection 522 (NMC 88085) folding into cover with title as in (7); OOAMA (NMC 22443) has ms adds of railways to about 1869.
GBL OKQ OOAMA (NMC 88085; 22443)

---

139 *[1844]*
CANADA. // Drawn & Engraved by J. Gellatly, Edinr // Published by Armour & Ramsay, Montreal.
Print (lith) hand col 22 x 28 cm 1" to 80 miles
In *Armour & Ramsay's Canadian School Atlas*, [2nd ed] (Montreal: Armour & Ramsay 1844), map 10 (*Bib Can* 7718), and in *The Canadian School Atlas, intended as an Accompaniment to Gouinlock's Geography* (Toronto: Hugh Scobie 1846) (*Bib Can* 5317); shows districts, some cos, a few place-names.
OTMCL

---

140 *1844*
A MAP / OF / CANADA / COMPILED FROM THE LATEST AUTHORITIES / BY / EDWARD STAVELEY, CIV. ENGR / 1844. / Engd by W. & A.K. Johnston, Geographers & Engravers to the Queen, Edinr.
Print (engrav) hand col 48 x 94 cm Approx 1" to 28 miles
Insets: 'ISLAND / OF / MONTREAL' 1" to 4 miles, 'QUEBEC / AND ITS ENVIRONS' and 'VICINITY / of the / FALLS / of / NIAGARA' and 'KINGSTON / and its / ENVIRONS' 1" to 6 miles, 'TORONTO / and its ENVIRONS' 1" to 3.2 miles; a folding copy at OKQ has pasted on to cover: 'Map of Canada, DRAWN AND ENGRAVED FOR ARMOUR & RAMSAY, PUBLISHERS, MONTREAL. 1844.'; railways, canals, cos, districts, twps shown north to line Ashfield, Wawanosh, Mornington, Maryborough, Minto to Derby, Bexley to Somerville, Harvey to Palmerston, Lavant to 'Pemberton'; (Lande 2224; Olsen map 72).
OKQ OOAMA (NMC 22581–3; 48943) QMM(L) USDLC USNN

Later editions and states

(2) *1845*
— STAVELEY, CIV. ENGR / MONTREAL, / 1845. // Engd by W. & A.K. Johnston, Geographers & Engravers to the Queen, Edinr / for ARMOUR and RAMSAY, Montreal.
Cover-title on two folding copies: 'Armour & Ramsay's Map of Canada 1845'; map is the same as 1844; (Dionne 1845; Olsen map 73).
OOAMA (NMC 24941) OTAR USDLC

(3) *1846*
— [Date changed in title to 1846]
Cover-title on OOAMA copy: 'ARMOUR & RAMSAY'S / MAP OF CANADA / 1847'; map is the same as 1844; (Olsen map 74; OOAMA MacDonald Collection 526 (NMC 119070)).
OOAMA (NMC 17941; 119070) OTMCL USDLC USNN

(4) *1848*
— [Date changed in title to 1848]
Issued separately and in *The Canadian Guide Book with a Map of the Province* (Montreal: Armour & Ramsay 1849), at end (*Bib Can* 2975; Lande 1637); same as 1844; USDLC copy has ms adds showing railways in operation, under construction, and proposed in 1855; photoreproduction in OOAMA (NMC 24943); (Dionne 926; Olsen map 75).
OTMCL QMM(L) USDLC

(5) *1851*
— [Date changed in title to 1851]
Issued separately and in *The Canadian Guide Book with a Map of the Province* (Montreal: Armour & Ramsay 1849) (Casey I–2131); twps added to the base of the Bruce Peninsula; two railways shown: Niagara Falls-Windsor and London-Sarnia; part of OOAMA (NMC 17165) copy is missing; OOAMA (NMC 48940) has ms adds of railways proposed, under construction, or in operation in 1855; (Olsen map 77).
OOA OOAMA (NMC 48940; 17165) OTAR OTMCL USDLC

(6) *[1856]*
— [Date deleted]
Issued separately and in *The Canadian Tourist Accompanied by a Map of the British American Provinces* (Montreal: Hew Ramsay [1856]) (Casey I – 2585); legend removed; Georgian Bay, French R, L Nipissing, and Manitoulin Is drawn in; route of proposed [Georgian Bay] Ship Canal; two colonization roads; railways shown, railways under construction: Woodstock and Pt Dover, London-Pt Stanley, Toronto-Stratford, Pt Hope to Ops Twp; Brockville to Ottawa R; (Olsen map 78?).
GBL (70615 (24)) OOA OOAMA (NMC 24954)

141 *[1845]*
[Canada] / Pubd. by R.W.S. McKay.
Print 11 x 75 cm Scale not given
In Robert Mackay, *The Traveller's Guide to the River St. Lawrence and Lake Ontario* (Montreal: Published by Robert W.S. Mackay, Lovell and Gibson Printers 1845), frontis (*Bib Can* 5300, OOA); shows shoreline from L Erie to Quebec with twps and a few places named; imprint trimmed off on OTMCL copy.
OOA OTMCL

---

142 *1845*
CANADA / WEST // Entered according to Act of Congress in the year 1845 by Sidney E. Morse and Samuel Breese in the Clerks Office of the Southern District of New York.
Print (col wax engrav) 31 x 40 cm 1" to 30 miles
Inset: [L Superior] 1" to 70 miles; in *Morse's North American Atlas* (New York: Harper & Brothers 1842–[5]), plate 3 (*LC Atlases* 1228, OOAMA); shows canals, railways, districts, twps north to Ashfield, Wawanosh, Mornington, Maryborough, Minto to Derby, Matchedash, Bexley, Somerville, Harvey to Palmerston, Lavant to Pembroke; Huron-Ottawa area reported as hardwood and fertile land.
OOAMA (NMC 116811) USDLC

Later editions and states

(2) *[1856]*
CANADA WEST.
In Charles W. Morse, *Morse's General Atlas* (New York: D. Appleton & Co. 1856), plate [8]; changes: inset removed, twps added to the base of the Bruce Peninsula, district names removed, co names inserted; a few railways shown; title moved and reengraved and registration statement deleted.
USDLC

---

143 *[1845]*
CITY OF TORONTO / AND / LAKE HURON / RAILWAY. // Madeley lith. 3 Wellington St. Strand. // [On back]: CITY OF TORONTO AND LAKE / HURON RAILWAY. // Prospectus. // T.C. Savill, Printer 4, Chandos Street, Covent Garden.
Print (lith) 22 x 36 cm on sheet 38 x 48 cm Scale not given
Broadside (3pp) with cover-title: 'City of Toronto and Lake Huron Railway ... August 6th 1845'; on back of OOAMA copy in ms: 'Issued by / Alex G. Gilkison / 27 Gordon St. / Glasgow'; ms note on OTMCL copy: 'Recd 9th Sepr 1845 corrected to 9th July 1846'; shows the area of the Great Lakes and northeastern U.S.; the route is shown from Toronto to Goderich via Guelph and Stratford with railway connections to Niagara R, Boston, and Montreal, and Portland Ry; the railway was incorporated in 1836 but not built, revived in 1845 and reincorporated in 1849 as the Toronto Simcoe and Lake Huron Union Railroad (Trout and Trout, 54).
OTMCL (William Allan Papers box 7/S123)
OOAMA (NMC 120182)

---

144 *[ca 1845]*
Map of a portion of the Province of Upper Canada Shewing the Improved Roads
Col ms 125 x 402 cm Approx 1" to 200 chains
Endorsements: stamp [BW] '423'
Shows the area from Kingston west, but twps and information only shown along shore between Kingston and York and not all twps shown in Western District; the legend keys plank, stone, graded, and common roads; roads are named and toll-gates shown; includes general plan of toll-house and gate; shows the following roads built by the Board of Works: Kingston and Napanee, Port Hope to Rice L, East York and West York, Yonge St, Port Dover and Hamilton, Hamilton and Brantford, Woodstock and London, Bradford and Barrie, Barrie and Penetanguishene, Coldwater, L Scugog, London and Pt Stanley, London and Sarnia, London and Chatham, Rondeau, Maidstone Cross, Sandwich, and Amherstburgh; later than 1843 map (**133(4)**) since more roads shown as completed.
OOAMA (NMC 23281)

---

145 *1845*
[Map of Canada showing improvements in navigation] Office of the Board of Works. 1845 F.P. Rubidge Draftd.
Col ms 72 x 106 cm 1" to 25 miles Endorsements: '467' 'In 583 Canada military'
Withdrawn from GBLpro WO 1/555 pp 467–8; shows Welland and Rideau canals, canals on the St Lawrence, projected communication on the Trent system, tables of statistics on canals and locks; (*PRO Cat* 195).
GBLpro (MPHH 671 (3))

---

146 *1845*
MAP / OF / PART OF CANADA, / SHOWING / THE LINE OF THE PROPOSED / RAILROAD / FROM TORONTO TO PORT SARNIA, / WITH / BRANCHES / TO / HAMILTON & GODERICH. // Lowe Sc. Toronto // British Canadian, Extra, Toronto, Thursday August 7, 1845.
Print (wood engrav) 25 x 36 cm Scale not given
Shows twps, plank or macadamized roads and main roads; proposed railway line.
OTMCL (William Allan Papers box 7 S123)

---

147 *1845*
OBER- (UPPER-) / CANADA / 1845. // MEYER'S – HANDATLAS // Aus der Geographischen Graviranstalt des Bibliographischen Instituts zu Hildburghausen Amsterdam Paris u. Philadelphia. // No 55
Print (lith) hand col 31 x 37 cm 1" to 32 miles
Inset: [Lake Superior] 1/2" to 30 miles; in Carl

Joseph Meyer, *Meyer's Handatlas* [Hildburghausen Bibliographisches Institut 1848?], II: no 55 (USMiU-C); the map is based on the Tanner-Mitchell map (**96(2)**); in English.
OOAMA (NMC 51854) USMiU-C

Later editions and states

(2) *1849*
— 1849. // MEYER'S - AUSWANDERUNGS - ATLAS v. N.A. // Aus der Geographischen ... // No 16.
In Meyer's *Auswanderings – Atlas ... der Westlichen Hemisphaere* (Hildburghausen [1858]) (USNN); the same as 1845.
OMSA USNN

(3) *1850*
— 1850. // MEYER'S - GROSSER ZEITUNGS - ATLAS // Aus der Geographischen ... // No 50.
The same as 1845.
OKQ

---

148 *[ca 1845]*
[Sketch map of parts of Home, Gore, Simcoe districts]
Ms 109 x 175 cm Scale not given
An unfinished sketch map showing the twp survey grid and roads; some towns shown but few place-names; some roads are named in the Waterloo area; the Sunnidale Rd and Hurontario St from Barrie to Nottawasaga as found on a map of 1845 (**383**) is shown but not named.
OTAR (SR 8190)

---

149 *1845–6*
[Maps drawn to accompany the reports of the Naval and Military Commission dated 1845–6 by 'W.C.E. Holloway Colonel Com. R. Engr & Edward Boxer Captain R.N.']
23 col mss Sizes vary Scales vary
Most maps are dated 29 Jan 1846 and accompany 4th report; the maps are listed individually in *PRO Cat* and catalogue nos given below; the maps are all sgd by Holloway and Boxer as in the title above; OOAMA has photoreproductions of all plans, which are cited below as NMC; all original plans are found in GBLpro (WO 1); note at beginning of maps in 1846 report: 'Canada 1846 Military vol. 3 maps to accompany Reports of Coll Holloway and Captn Boxer 1845 and 1846 Commander in Chief Maps enclosed in letters 25 Augt 1845 and 11 April 1846' (GBLpro WO 1/556 9–32, 223–46 and WO 55/880 f 322ff).

Plans from the 1845 reports relating to Upper Canada are as follows:

32 Canada No I General Plan Shewing the Land and Water communications between Kingston and Rivière du Loup as well as the Communications between the boundary line of the United States and the River St Lawrence compiled from various sources Drawn to accompany the joint Report of Colonel Holloway C.B. Comg Royal Engineer in Canada & Captain Boxer C.B. Royal Navy Addressed to His Excellency the Commander of the Forces under date 17th Feby 1845. [Sgd] W.C.E. Holloway Colonel Comg Rl Engrs Edward Boxer Captain R.N. Drawn by J. Woods Lieut 81st Regt Asst Royl Engr.
106 x 237 cm 1" to 6 miles
Shows the area from Kingston east to Rivière du Loup; with the same information as 31 below except twp boundaries and names have been added; accompanied the 2nd report in letter of 25 Aug 1845 (GBLpro WO 1/553 pp 241–64); NMC 7003; there are also plans of Kingston and St Mary's R, etc, with Holloway's report of 12 June 1845 in GBLpro (WO 55/879 f 189 and WO 880 f 52); (*PRO Cat* 1760).
GBLpro (WO 1/553 (32))

Plans from the 1846 reports relating to Upper Canada are as follows:

9 Plan of the River St. Lawrence between Prescott and Cornwall. Drawn to accompany ... (Copy) John Desborough Lieut Rl Artillery Assistant Royal Engineers
54 x 123 cm 1" to 1000 yds Watermark: 'H B 1840' Endorsements: '12' '2' '15' 'No 2'
Shows canals, locks, proposed canals, settlements and bldgs, soundings; NMC 3268; (*OHIM* 6.22; *PRO Cat* 1577); there is also a plan of 1846 showing this area in Nov 1838 with position of British ships, originally accompanying letter of 13 Feb 1846 (GBLpro PRO 30/9/16/13 f 28)
GBLpro (MPI 479)

10 Reconnaissance of the Roads from Gannanoqui on the St. Lawrence to the Rideau Canal and from Collins Bay to the Rideau Canal on the Westward. Drawn to accompany ... (Signed) E.Y.W. Henderson Lt Royal Engineers R.W. Piper Lt 46th Regt A.R.E.
89 x 96 cm 1" to 1 mile Endorsements: 'No 3' '13' '16'
Shows roads, dams, mills and areas of cleared land; NMC 2878; (*PRO Cat* 1412).

11 Reconnoitring Sketch shewing the Communications from the St. Lawrence Frontier between Gananoque and Jones or Tonnewanta Creek. Drawn to accompany ... Copy F. King Lt Royal Engineers.
57 x 68 cm 1" to 1 mile Endorsements: '17' '14' 'No 4'
Shows roads, mills, settlements, cleared land; NMC 2877; (*PRO Cat* 1460).

12 Military Reconnaissance of the Frontier Between Point Iroquois and Jones Creek on the St Lawrence and Beckett's landing and the 1st rapids on the Rideau Canal. Drawn to accompany ... (Signed) E.Y.W. Henderson Lieut Royal Engineers (Copy) R.W. Piper Lt 46th Regiment A.R.E.
88 x 109 cm 1" to 1 mile Endorsements: '18' 'No 5' '15'
Shows roads with comments on condition, proposed road from Prescott to Kemptville

'surveyed but not opened,' Prescott and Brockville with some bldgs in red [brick or stone?]; islands and shorelines noted as 'not correct as the Plan was merely formed to accompy a Reconnoitring Report upon the Roads'; NMC 2876; (*PRO Cat* 1413).

13 Sketch of Collin's Bay Drawn to accompany ... [Sgd] Hampdon Moody Lt R.E. 25/25/46.
57 x 43 cm Approx 1" to 600 yds Endorsements: '19' 'No 6' '16'
Shows soundings; relief along shoreline; NMC 3781; (*PRO Cat* 1448).

14 Chart of Tonnewanta or Jones Creek shewing its capabilities as a Gunboat Harbour. Drawn to accompany .... Copy John Desborough Lieut R Artillery Assistant Rl Engineers
53 x 83 cm 6" to 1 mile Endorsements: '22' '18' 'No 1' 'DR/592'
Note: 'Soundings in red taken under direction of Captn Boxer R.N. 4th Septr 1844'; shows mouth of creek near Brockville, mills, international boundary; NMC 3267; (*PRO Cat* 1598).

15 Chart of part of the River St Lawrence Shewing the relative position of Sheriffs Point proposed Gun boat Harbour at Gananoqui and the American inlet French Creek Drawn to Accompany ...
83 x 56 cm 6" to 1 mile Endorsements: '22' 'No 2' 'DR/591'
'Soundings were taken ... 3d Sept. 1844'; relief by shading; boundary; NMC 3269; (*PRO Cat* 1461).

16 Plan showing the position of Hare Island and its capabilities for affording shelter for Gun Boats. Drawn to accompany ... Copy John Desborough Lieut Rl Artillery Assistant R Engineers
44 x 53 cm 6" to 1 mile Endorsements: '20' '24' 'No 3 copied' 'DR/593'
'Soundings were taken ... 2nd Septr 1844'; also shows Gage Is; NMC 4166; (*PRO Cat* 1459).

17 Chart of the Bay of Quinté and of the South shore of Prince Edwards County Lake Ontario. surveyed by the Hydrographic Department under the direction of Captain William FitzWilliam Owen Royal Navy in the years 1815 and 1816. Drawn to accompany ... (Copy) R.W. Piper Lt 46th Regt A.R.E.
77 x 165 cm 1 1/2" to 2000 yds Endorsements: '22' 'No 4' 'DR/594'
Insets: 'McDonalds Cove or Grog Harbour' and 'Plan of Presque'Isle Harbour' (1 1/2" to 1/4 mile) sgd 'Edward Boxer Captain R.N.'; both insets initialled 'R.W.P. Lt 46th Regt A.R.E.'; a note indicates that soundings were taken on 17 Sept 1845 under the direction of Boxer; NMC 2874; (*PRO Cat* 1521).

18 Plan of Cobourg Harbour with soundings copied from a Plan at the Board of Works Drawn to accompany ... (Copy) R.W.P. Lt 46th Reg. A.R.E.
48 x 45 cm 1" to 100 ft Endorsements: '26' 'No 5' 'DR/612'
Shows some soundings taken by Boxer on 15 Sept 1845; piers and recent improvements; probably copied from plan of 1835–41 (**1259**); NMC 3779; (*PRO Cat* 1447).

19 Plan of Port Hope Drawn to accompany ... (Copy) R.W. Piper Lt 46th Regt A.R.E.
57 x 45 cm 1" to 160 ft Endorsements: '27' '24' 'No 6' 'D.R./595'
Shows soundings by Boxer 15 Sept 1845, harbour, piers, relief; also a copy of the same title: '(Copy) R.G. Pilkington Draftsman 21st Apl 1846. [Sgd] W.C.E. Holloway Colonel Com: R Engrs' originally filed with GBLpro WO 1/544 f 223; NMC 14026; (*PRO Cat* 1549, 1550).

20 Chart of the Harbour of Windsor Copied from a plan at the Board of Works. Drawn to accompany ... (Copy) R.W.P. Lt 46th Reg. A.R.E.
90 x 54 cm 1" to 3 chains Endorsements: '28' '25' 'No 7' 'D.R./613'
Shows soundings 15 Sept 1845; probably copied from plan of 1843 (**2164**) [Whitby]; NMC 5003; (*PRO Cat* 1618).

21 Sketch of Toronto shewing the Harbor & the relative positions of the present & proposed Defences Drawn to accompany ...
138 x 160 cm 1" to 900 ft Endorsements: 'No 8' '29' '26'
Shows soundings by Boxer on 12 Sept 1845, most of the city north to about [Eglinton Ave], shaded relief, ravine systems, roads, turnpikes, block-houses, and other bldgs; bldgs in red [brick or stone?]; harbour and island shown in detail; notes on vegetation and cleared land; NMC 4401; (*PRO Cat* 1611).

22 Port Credit Copied from a plan at the Board of Works. Drawn to accompany ... (Copy) R.W.P. Lt 46th Regt A.R.E.
45 x 28 cm 1" to 4 chains Endorsements: '30' '27' 'No 9' 'D.R./610'
A note states that Port Credit and Oakville both have the capabilities of a harbour for gunboats but a plan of Oakville could not be found, and entrances to both harbours require dredging and widening; military reserve shown on east bank; bldgs and streets; NMC 4319; (*PRO Cat* 1542).

23 Sketch of Burlington Bay, Hamilton and its vicinity. Drawn to accompany ... R.W. Piper Lt 46th Regt A.R.E.
45 x 84 cm 3/4" to 1/4 mile Endorsements: '28' '31' 'No 10' 'D.R/347'
Shows soundings taken by Boxer, Desjardins Canal, a cut in Burlington Beach being made, a few streets and bldgs and names of owners on outskirts of Hamilton, relief by shading; NMC 3740; (*PRO Cat* 1442).

24 Sketch of 20 Mile Creek Drawn to accompany ... R.W. Piper Lt 46th Regt A.R.E.
38 x 24 cm 3" to 1 mile Endorsements: '32' '29' 'No 11' 'DR/600'
Shows piers at entrance of creek noted as in ruins, relief, roads; NMC 4143; (*PRO Cat* 1613).

25 Port Dover Copied from a plan at the Board of Works. Drawn to accompany ... R.W. Piper Lt 46th Regt A.R.E.
28 x 45 cm 1" to 125 ft Endorsements: '33' 'No 16' 'DR/611'
Shows soundings taken by Boxer 9 Sept 1845; note that piers being extended by the Board of Works; NMC 4323; (*PRO Cat* 1545).

26 Plan Showing the Condition of the Harbor of Port Dalhousie In 1845 and the Proposed Improvements. A. Jukes Delt. Drawn to accompany ... [Sgd] C.E.
56 x 67 cm 1" to 200 ft Endorsements: '34' '12' 'D.R/597' 'rel Ellis/446'
Shows soundings taken by Boxer 8 Sept 1845; shows the same information as the Board of Works plan of 1845 (**1848**); NMC 4320; (*PRO Cat* 1544).

27 Plan Showing the Condition of the Chippewa Cut Before and After the Late Improvements [Sgd] W.C.E. Holloway Colonel Comg Rl Engrs.
44 x 53 cm Scale not given Endorsements: '35' '32' 'No 13' 'D.R./500' 'rel. Mil/446'
Shows the condition of the harbour in 1844, improvements made in 1845, the proposed new improvements; soundings taken by Boxer 7 Sept 1845; NMC 3771; (*PRO Cat* 1446).

28 Plan Shewing the Condition of the Harbour of Port Colborne in October 1845. Drawn to accompany ... [Sgd] [illegible] Lewis Leslie Del.
68 x 44 cm 1" to 200 ft Endorsements: 'No 14' '36' '33' 'D.R./599' 'Re Misc/446'
Shows soundings by Boxer on 5 Sept 1845; probably copied from the same source as 1845 plan (**1842**); NMC 4317; (*PRO Cat* 1541).

29 Plan Shewing the Condition of the Harbour of Port Maitland in October 1845. Drawn to accompany ... A. Jukes Delt.
68 x 47 cm 1" to 200 ft Endorsements: '37' 'No 15'
Shows soundings, piers, lighthouse, breakwater, some bldgs; probably copied from the same source as 1845 plan (**1865**); NMC 6179; (*PRO Cat* 1547).

31 [39?]
Part of Canada West Shewing the communications both by land and water through-out the Western Province, also the relative positions of the several posts &c referred to in the 4th Report of the Naval & Military Commission Dated 29th Jany 1846 [Sgd] Edward Boxer Captain R.N. W.C.E. Holloway Colonel Comg Rl Engrs. J.E. Alexander Knt Capt. 14th Regt & Assist. Engr 27/3/46.
170 x 85 cm 1" to 6 miles Endorsements: 'Enclosure in Lord Fitzroy Somerset Letter 11 June 1846 Canada Military 35A DR 417'
A slightly later general plan summarizing the survey; shows the area from Gananoque to the Detroit R and north to Owen Sound; some relief by shading covering the south part of Niagara escarpment; notes on the terrain, swamps; shows all roads and some trails, towns and settlements including Indian villages; NMC 2879; (*PRO Cat* 1414).
GBLpro (WO 1/556 9–29, 39)

---

150 *1846*
A MAP OF CANADA ... BY EDWARD STAVELEY, ... 1845 ... [with ms adds]: denoting the line of Canals for facilitating Commerce and conveyance of Government supplies' [Sgd] W.C.E. Holloway Colonel Com R. Engrs.
Print (engrav) with ms adds 48 x 94 cm 1" to 28 miles
With attached letter entitled 'D.R./676 List of Canals in the Province of Canada ... To accompany the Commg Royl Engrs letter to the Inspector General of Fortifications dated 12th September 1846 No. 651 and with reference to the Commg Royl Engrs former letter Dated 25th March 1846 No 538'; on folding cover: 'I.G.F.'s Office'; OOAMA (MacDonald Collection 525); a similar map illustrating Col Holloway's report on canal navigation in the Canadas of 25 March 1846 is in GBLpro WO 55/880 f 400 (GBLpro MR1000 (39)).
GBLpro (MR1000 (39)) OOAMA (NMC 119069)

---

151 *[1846]*
Map of CANADA West / EXHIBITING THE STATIONS OCCUPIED BY / The Presbyterian Church / Presented To The Colonial Committee of the Free Church of Scotland / THROUGH THE REVD JAMES BEGG / BY / their humble Servant / Thomas Alexander of Cobourg.
Print (col lith) 52 x 76 cm Scale not given
A table 'Presbyterian Church of Canada in 1846' lists stations and names of ministers and congregations without ministers; twps coloured green show area covered by a minister, twps coloured brown where 'ministers or missionaries are required.'
OTAR

---

152 *1846*
MAP OF / THE PROVINCES OF / CANADA, / NEW BRUNSWICK, NOVA SCOTIA, / Newfoundland and Prince Edward Island. / WITH / A LARGE SECTION / OF THE UNITED STATES AND EXHIBITING THE / BOUNDARY / OF THE / British Dominions in North America. / ACCORDING TO THE TREATY OF 1842. / Compiled from the latest and most approved Astronomical observations Authorities and recent Surveys. / by Joseph Bouchette Depy Survr Genl L.C. / 1846.
Print (engrav) 120 x 220 cm 1" to approx 14 miles
Unfinished proof state; lacking most place-names in Upper Canada, titles for insets, hatching and stipple along shores, table, imprint, and registration statements; border unfinished; OOAMA copy has ms adds showing some roads including Owen Sound Rd, Penetanguishene Rd,

and locks along the Trent R; presumably prepared before the Oregon boundary treaty of 15 June 1846, which is marked on the 'British Dominions' inset on (2); a prospectus for the map sgd Robert W.S. Mackay was first published in the *Globe* (Toronto) 3 Oct 1845; (Olsen map 38?).
OOAMA (NMC 17400)

Later editions and states

(**2**) *1846*
— ACCORDING TO THE TREATIES OF 1842 & 6. / by Joseph Bouchette ... 1846. // Entered according to Act of Congress in the Year 1846 by Joseph Bouchette in the Clerk's Office of the District Court of the Southern District of New York
Print (engrav) in 6 sheets Ea 60 x 74 cm Watermark on accompanying sheet: 'AFONWEN 1843'
With copyright registration sheet appended in ms: 'Bouchette's Map of Canada &c. The enclosed Engraved Map has been deposited in this Office by Joseph Bouchette, Esqr of Montreal, the Author, for the purpose of securing the Copyright thereof, ... Montreal 29th July 1846 [Sgd] R.D. Tucker Registrar'; the map has now been finished except that the symbols in the explanation are not shown, the title on the L Superior inset is not finished (see (3) for titles of insets), and the imprint and actual Canadian registration statement not shown.
OOAMA (NMC 119073)

(**3**) *1846*
— 1846. // Engraved by / SHERMAN & SMITH / New York. // Entered according to Act of the Provincial Legislature in the Year 1846 by Joseph Bouchette in the Office of the Registrar of the Province of Canada. Entered according to Act of Congress ... New York.
Print (engrav) some hand col 120 x 220 cm 1" to approx 14 miles
Originally printed in six sheets with registration statements found on the edges of each sheet; insets: 'THE / BRITISH DOMINIONS / IN / NORTH AMERICA.,' 'MAP OF THE / NIAGARA DISTRICT / by Joseph Bouchette D.S.G.' 1" to 6 miles, 'MAP OF / LAKE SUPERIOR / Reduced from the Hydrographical Surveys of / Capt. Bayfield R.N. / by Joseph Bouchette D.S.G.' 1" to 28 miles, 'MAP OF / NEWFOUNDLAND / by Joseph Bouchette D.S.G.,' 'ENVIRONS / OF / MONTREAL / by Joseph Bouchette D.S.G.' 1" to 6.5 miles; the map is a revised and redrawn version of the 1831 map (see **85**) but extending further east to include all of Nova Scotia and with many revisions and additions; Manitoulin Is, parts of the L Huron shore, and L Nipissing have been revised; more lakes and rivers are shown in the L Timiskaming area and in the Huron-Ottawa territory; twps are shown to Ashfield-Wawanosh, Minto-Derby, Matchedash-Rama, and Eldon to Palmerston; 'explanation' keys macadamized and post roads, canals, railways, common roads, post towns and villages; authorities consulted are as in the 1831 map; table of population of cos 1836–44, cities for 1844, and province for 1846; (Olsen map 37; OOAMA MacDonald Collection 408).
GBL (69917 (19)) OOAMA (NMC 22610, 48910) OTAR OTMCL USDLC

(**4**) *1852*
— [Date in title changed to 1852]
'Proposed railroad' has been added to legend but no changes to railways on west part of map; GBLpro copy has ms adds showing changes to co and district names, new twps added in the Bruce area, and railways and proposed railways to 1865; (Olsen map 39; *PRO Cat* 208).
GBLpro (CO 700 Canada 104) OTAR

(**5**) *1853*
— [Date in title changed to 1853]
Shows the same information as 1852 map; (Olsen map 40).
OTAR

---

153 *[1846?]*
MAP OF THE TOWNSHIPS IN CANADA WEST. // J. Arrowsmith.
Print (engrav) 24 x 38 cm 1" to 43 miles Watermark (OOA, OTAR loose copy): 'RUSE & TURNER 1845'
Issued in Canada Co., *A Statement of the Satisfactory Results which have attended Emigration to Upper Canada*, 5th ed (London: Smith, Elder and Co. 1846), frontis (*Bib Can* 2762, Casey I–2053); inset: Huron Tract belonging to the Canada Company, 1" to 28 miles; note on map: 'The small map which the Canada Company have hitherto been accustomed to publish with their yearly prospectus and of which upwards of 93,000 impressions have at different times been circulated, having in some degree become obsolete in consequence of the rapid extension of improvement, the formation of new roads and the multiplication of townships during the last few years in Canada West, the Company have thought it right on the present occasion to substitute the above sketch, reduced from a travelling map of the province on an enlarged scale which has been corrected from recent surveys made under the direction of the Company's officers in Canada and which the Company have now in course of publication by Mr. John Arrowsmith of Soho Square.'; a revision of **76(5)** with more rivers in the Huron-Ottawa area, a better shape for the province, the addition of Ashfield, Arthur, and Wawanosh twps and Wellington, Colborne, Victoria, Talbot, and Brock districts, and the retention of the two distance tables and the inset; the map 'in course of publication ...' may possibly be **155**.
OOA OTMCL

Later editions and states

(**2**) *1849*
— [Title, etc, unchanged]
On broadside: *Lands in Canada West, to be disposed of by the Canada Company* (London: Marchant Singer & Co., Printers, Ingram-Court 1849); twps

added: Maryborough, Wellesley, Peel, Mornington, and Minto to Derby.
OLU OTAR

154 *1846*
SMITH'S / Commercial and Travelling / MAP / OF / CANADA WEST, / Compiled expressly for / SMITH'S / CANADIAN GAZETTEER / 1846.
Print (lith) 38 x 53 cm 1" to 23 miles
Prepared to accompany W.H. Smith, *Smith's Canadian Gazetteer ... With a Map of the Upper Province Compiled Expressly for the Work, in which are Laid Down All the Towns and Principal Villages* (Toronto: Published for the author by H. & W. Rowsell 1846), frontis with pp [i]–x 'References to the Map' (OTUTF); twps and places are numbered and indexed in book; twps shown north to line Ashfield, Wawanosh, Derby to Minto, Bexley, Somerville, Harvey to Palmerston, Pembroke to Lavant; (Olsen map 82).
OKQ OOAMA (NMC 21379) OTAR OTUTF

Later editions and states

(2) *1847*
SMITH'S / Commercial AND Travelling / MAP OF / CANADA WEST, / COMPILED EXPRESSLY FOR / SMITH'S / CANADIAN GAZETTEER / 1847. / Published by H. Rowsell, Toronto.
Print (engrav) 38 x 52 cm Approx 1" to 23.5 miles
Issued separately with cover-title: 'Smith's Travelling Map of Canada West with Table of distances' (OOAMA); also in *Smith's Canadian Gazetteer* 'First edition, third issue' (Toronto: Published for the author by H. & W. Rowsell 1846), frontis (*Bib Can* 2805), and in another 1846 ed of the book (OOA), and in another ed (Toronto: Published for the author by Henry Rowsell 1849), after title-page (*Bib Can* 2806); the map has been redrawn in a finer style to show the same twps as the 1846 map above, which are now all named; district towns, other towns and villages and roads are shown; (Olsen map 83).
OOA OOAMA (NMC 9849) OTMCL

155 *184[6–9?]*
[CANADA] London, Pubd. [blank]th. May 184[blank], by J. Arrowsmith 10 Soho Square.
Print (engrav) in 2 sheets 134 x 206 cm 1" to 15.5 miles
GBLpro copy has label on back: 'UPR CANADA JOHN ARROWSMITH'; a map of the eastern part of Canada at a larger scale than Arrowsmith's earlier map (see **91**); the shape of coastlines, lakes, and rivers, as well as twps in Upper Canada, are very similar to Bouchette's map of 1846 (see **152**); more twps are shown than on Arrowsmith's smaller map, 1846 ed (**91(6)**); Ashfield and Wawanosh twps west to Minto to Derby added; and more lakes and rivers shown in the Huron-Ottawa country; imprints are found on the west sheets only (OOAMA and GBLpro); a proof state since date is incomplete; possibly the map described as 'in course of publication' by Arrowsmith on **153**; (*PRO Cat* 184; Olsen 105).
GBLpro (CO 700 Canada 97) OOAMA (NMC 116794)

Later editions and states

(2) *1854*
— London, Pubd. 3rd Jany 1854, by J. Arrowsmith 10 Soho Square.
Print (engrav) in 3 sheets 134 x 206 cm 1" to 15.5 miles
Sectioned and folding into cover with title: 'CANADA &c. / JOHN ARROWSMITH, / 10 SOHO SQUARE, LONDON'; shows the same information and from the same plates as (1) except that the New Brunswick/Canada boundary has been changed [per act of 1851]; (OOAMA MacDonald Collection 412).
OOAMA (NMC 105116)

(3) [1858–60?]
— London, Pubd. [blank] May 18 [blank] by J. Arrowsmith 10 Soho Square
2 imprints on west sheets; twps in Bruce Co area added to base of peninsula; railways added throughout Canada West to ca 1860; the twps north of L Ontario and rivers and lakes in the Huron- Ottawa area are the same as on the 1854 edition; many twps added north of Ottawa R; somewhat unevenly revised and probably about 1858–60 since twps not shown in Bruce peninsula or in Huron- Ottawa area; the map was later taken over by Edward Stanford and reissued in 1880; see OOAMA (NMC 105112); photoreproduction in OOAMA (NMC 119074).
QQA

156 *[1847]*
Copy. / Plan. / Shewing the different SURRENDERS made by the INDIANS in UPPER CANADA to the CROWN // MATTHEWS LITH
Print (lith) 30 x 35 cm Scale not given
In 'Report on the Affairs of the Indians in Canada' in *JLA* (1847), App T opp 57 (OTUTF); shows all the major surrenders in Upper Canada with names of tribes, dates, and sums of money expended; also shows current Indian reserves.
OOAMA (NMC 10823) OTUTF

157 *1847*
MAP AND PROFILE / of the / GREAT WESTERN RAILWAY / CANADA WEST / 1847 / C.B. Stuart: Engineer of Location. // C.L. Beard, delt. // Lith. of P.S. Duval
Print (lith) hand col 30 x 46 cm 1" to 14 miles horizontal; 1" to 1000 ft vertical
In Charles B. Stuart, *Report on the Great Western Railway, Canada West* ([n.p.]: 1 Sept 1847), frontis (*Bib Can* 2850; Casey I–2085); shows the rail line from Niagara Falls to Windsor with a branch to Port Sarnia; names of twps and major roads; profile shows the route from Niagara Falls

to Windsor; there is also a general plan in the same work entitled 'MAP / of the Route of the / GREAT WESTERN RAILWAY / SHEWING ITS CONNECTION WITH OTHER PUBLIC WORKS / Projected and Completed // [C.]L. Beard del Lith of P.S. Duval'; shows area from Mississippi R to Atlantic coast with connecting railways.
OOA OTMCL

Related maps

(2) *[1851]*
MAP AND PROFILE / OF THE / GREAT WESTERN RAILWAY / CANADA WEST / C.R. Stuart Engineer of Location // Martin & Hood lith [?] Gt Newport St. / No I
Print (lith) Size not known 1" to 14 miles
[Profile]: 1000 ft to 1" vertical;In *The Great Western Railway Canada Prospectus May 1851* (London: Printed by T. Breitell) (OOA, CIHM 63691), and in a prospectus issued in June 1851 (OOA, CIHM 63692); redrawn from map above; shows main line Hamilton to Windsor, western branch to Sarnia, eastern branch to Niagara Falls, and connections to Toronto, etc, and U.S.; also includes general maps: 'SKETCH shewing the Connections of / THE GREAT WESTERN RAILWAY OF CANADA / With the System of Main Trunk lines of Railway / PROJECTED THROUGH CANADA, NEW BRUNSWICK AND NOVA SCOTIA / also THE CONNECTION ... UNITED STATES OF AMERICA / NO II' and 'SKETCH / Shewing the Connection / of the Eastern & Western Termini of / THE GREAT WESTERN RAILWAY OF CANADA. / with Railways in the United States, already in highly remunerative operation. / No III.'
OOA

---

158 *1847*
[Map in] TORONTO AND GODERICH / RAILWAY. / Prospectus / Brown's Printing Establishment, Yonge Street, Toronto. //
[Text sgd] ... H.J. Boulton Chairman January 23rd, 1847
Print (wood engr) 16 x 27 cm Scale not given
On p [3] (*Bib Can* 2877); shows the area from Toronto to Port Sarnia and Goderich and from London to about Proton Twp; proposed railway shown as a straight line between Toronto and Goderich; names of twps, main roads.
OOAMA (NMC 122066) OTMCL

---

159 *[1847]*
MAP OF THE TOWNSHIPS IN CANADA WEST [with ms adds showing railway lines]
Print with ms adds 24 x 28 cm 1" to 43 miles
In City of Toronto and Lake Huron Railroad Co., *General Statement ... and Remarks upon the Railroad Interests of Western Canada* ([Toronto 1847]), attached to p 4 (*Bib Can* 5341); the base map is the same as **153**; ms adds show proposed original Toronto line, Toronto line in union with the Great Western line; United line and other railway connections with the United States; line of trade from Atlantic to upper Great Lakes region.
OTMCL

---

160 *1847*
MAP OF UPPER CANADA / Copied by permission from the Canada Company's Map engraved by Arrowsmith / Lithographed & Published by / SCOBIE & BALFOUR, / Toronto 1847.
Print (lith) 24 x 38 cm 1" to 43 miles
In *Scobie & Balfour's Canadian Almanac ... for the Year 1848* (Toronto: Printed and published by Scobie & Balfour 1847), opp 3 (*Bib Can* 2871); inset: 'HURON TRACT / belonging to the CANADA COMPANY' 1" to 27 miles; twps to line Ashfield, Wawanosh, Derby to Minto, Bexley, Somerville, Harvey to Palmerston; twps north to Colborne-North Easthope; a lithographic transfer of a revised state of **153** with a new title and the same as the 1849 ed except the note has been deleted; a copy with ms adds was originally filed in GBLpro (WO 55/1618).
GBLpro (MPHH 697 (15) pt1) OTAR OTMCL

Later editions and states

(2) *[1849]*
— CANADA, / With the latest additions, arranged and corrected for / SCOBIE & BALFOUR'S CANADIAN ALMANAC, / 1850. // Scobie & Balfour Lithog. Toronto.
In *Scobie & Balfour's Canadian Almanac ... for the Year 1850* (Toronto [1849]), frontis (*Bib Can* 2871); twps added to the base of the Bruce Peninsula; all cos named; the almanac was advertised in the Toronto *Globe* as published on 29 Oct 1849.
OLU OTAR OTMCL

(3) *1850*
— arranged and corrected for the / MUNICIPAL MANUAL FOR UPPER CANADA. / 1850 // Scobie & Balfour Lithog Toronto.
In *Scobie & Balfour's Municipal Manual for Upper Canada for 1850* (Toronto: Scobie & Balfour 1850), frontis (*Bib Can* 3106), and in the 2nd ed (Toronto: Hugh Scobie 1851), frontis (*Bib Can* 3207); the same as [1849] above.
OTMCL

(4) *1852*
— arranged and corrected for / HUGH SCOBIE, / TORONTO 1852. // Hugh Scobie Lithog. Toronto.
'Railroads in progress' are shown.
OOAMA (NMC 2898)

---

161 *1848*
Map of / CANADA / EAST AND WEST. / NEW YORK, / Published by / ENSIGNS & THAYER, / 36 Ann Street. / D. Needham, Buffalo, N.Y. 1848. / No 12 Exchange St. / Drawn & Engraved by / J.M. Atwood N. York. // Entered according to Act of Congress in the year 1848 by Ensign's & Thayer in the Clerk's office of the District Court of the United States for the Southern District of New York.
Print (lith) hand col 72 x 103 cm 1" to 18 miles

Inset: 'MAP OF / NOVA SCOTIA / AND / NEW BRUNSWICK. / Showing the Route of Steamers from / HALIFAX TO BOSTON'; portraits of Queen Victoria and Prince Albert with a coat of arms and motto; 'Explanations' [legend]: districts, cos, capitals of districts, railways, canals; shows some roads but no railways; twps north to the base of the Bruce Peninsula and in the east north to Bexley, Somerville, Harvey to Palmerston, and Lavant to Pembroke; decorative scroll-work border; (Dionne 925).
OLU OTMCL USDLC

Later editions and states

(2) *1849*
— / 50 Ann Street. / D. Needham, Buffalo, N.Y. 1849. / No. 12 Exchange St. / Drawn & Engraved by / J.M. Atwood, N. York. // Entered ... 1848 by Ensign's & Thayer ...
Same as 1848.
OTAR

(3) *1850*
— ENSIGN & THAYER, / 50 Ann Street. / & 12 Exchange St. Buffalo, N.Y. 1850. // [as above]
Same as 1848.
OTAR

(4) *1852*
— NEW YORK, / Published by / HORACE THAYER & CO. / 50 Ann Street / & 127 Main St. Buffalo N.Y. 1852. / Drawn ... [as above]
Same as 1848.
OTAR

(5) *1853*
— [Date in title changed to 1853] Drawn ... // Printed by D. McLellan, 26 Spruce St. N.Y.
Changes: a table 'Population of Counties' added; more place-names; railways shown: Toronto-Montreal, Toronto-Hamilton, Niagara Falls-Hamilton-London-Windsor, Toronto-Guelph-Goderich, Toronto-Barrie-Penetanguishene, Prescott-Ottawa; proposed railways: London-Sarnia, London-Stratford, Buffalo and Lake Huron, Toronto-Peterborough-Hawkesbury.
OTMCL

(6) *1853*
— HORACE THAYER & CO. / Corrected to March 1853, / for the Supplement to / THE CANADA DIRECTORY. / Drawn & Engraved by J.M. Atwood, N. York. // Entered ... 1848 by Ensign's & Thayer ...
66 x 97 cm
The table 'Census of 1852 by Counties' replaces the earlier table; probably issued with *A Supplement to the Canada Directory ... Accompanied by a Map of Canada* (Montreal: Robert W. Stuart Mackay 1853) (*Bib Can* 3150 lacking map); notes in the directory give the price of the map and book and the map alone; a note on p 6 indicates 'the map was more costly than expected' and gives new prices including cost of map coloured; the map is the 'only one yet published which gives the present Geographical divisions of the Province in counties, townships and railways already chartered or for which charters applied.'; shows railways built or being built; railways proposed: London-Pt Stanley, Marmora-Belleville.
OOAMA (NMC 11744)

(7) *1853*
— NEW YORK / Published by / THAYER, BRIDGMAN & FANNING, / 156, WILLIAM STREET. / Corrected to 1853 for / MACKAY'S CANADA DIRECTORY. / Drawn ... [as above]
The same as (6) above.
OOAMA (NMC 21069)

(8) *1853*
— 156 WILLIAM STREET, / & 8 Exchange St., Buffalo New York 1853. / Drawn & Engraved by / J.M. Atwood New York / Entered ... 1848 by Ensign's & Thayer ... // Printed by D. McLellan 26 Spruce St. N.Y. // Entered ... 1853 by Thayer, Bridgman & Fanning in the Clerk's office of the District Court of the United States for the Southern District of New York.
70 x 102 cm
Changes: Toronto-Guelph-Goderich railway deleted, as is the proposed Marmora-Belleville line; Toronto-Stratford-Sarnia line and line to Collingwood shown as completed; the decorative border design changed, enlarging print area.
OOAMA (NMC 22313)

(9) *1854*
— NEW YORK, / Published by / ENSIGN, BRIDGMAN & FANNING. / 156 WILLIAM STREET, / 1854. Drawn ... [as above]
Changes: the coat of arms and motto have been changed; proposed railways: Stratford to Saugine [*sic*]; proposed Hawkesbury-Kingston railway deleted; railways built: Woodstock-Pt Dover, London-Pt Stanley, Brockville-Pembroke.
OLU OOAMA (NMC 11745)

(10) *1855*
— [Date changed to 1855] ... D. McLellan, Print 26 Spruce St. N.Y.
A few place-names and roads added.
OKQ OOAMA (NMC 13207)

(11) *1855*
— 1855. / D. & J. McLellan Lith 26 Spruce St. N.Y. // Entered ... 1848 by Ensign's & Thayer ...
Scale bar added to inset: 1" to 33 miles; more place-names in Bruce and Grey cos; proposed railway Peterborough to Kingston dropped.
OOAMA (NMC 13208) OTAR OTMCL

(12) *1856*
— [Date changed to 1856]
The same as (11).
OOAMA (NMC 7039)

(13) *1857*
— [Date changed to 1857 and printing statement dropped]
The same as (11).
OTAR

(14) *1860*
— 1860. / Entered according to Act of Congress in the year 1853 by Thayer, Bridgman & Fanning in the Clerk's Office of the District Court of the United States for the Southern District of New York.
Changes: new twps added in the Bruce Peninsula east of L Nipissing and in the Huron-Ottawa area north to Macaulay, Bexley to Anstruther, north to Airy-Murchison, and in a line north to Rolph.
OOAMA (NMC 11747)

(15) *1861*
— [Date changed to 1861 in title] / Entered according to Act of Congress in the year [obliterated] by Ensigns & Thayer ... [as found on (11)]
Positions of some railways corrected; twps shown in line Stephenson to Richards and north to Clara; numbered twps south of L Nipissing shown; decorative border changed.
OOAMA (NMC 7050)

(16) *1864*
— [Date changed to 1864 in title]
Map is the same as the 1861 state.
GBL (70615 (28))

---

162 *1848*
A NAUTICAL / CHART / of the North Shore of / LAKE ERIE, / FROM POINT ABINO UP TO PT PELEE ISLANDS / By Capt Alexr McNeilledgel / of / PORT DOVER C.W. / June 1848. Accompanied with Sailing Directions / Copy-Right secured. / Lith. of Hall & Mooney, Buffalo N.Y.
Print (lith) hand col 27 x 124 cm 1" to 41/2 miles
Provenance: OSINH map presented by author to Customs Dept, Port Dover, 24 Apr 1854; soundings, details of shoreline, relief; ms adds of drawings of ships made by the author; probably prepared to accompany but not found in his *Sailing Directions and Remarks Accompanied with a Nautical Chart of the North Shore of Lake Erie* (Buffalo: Jewett, Thomas & Co. 1848) (OOA); (CIHM 46276).
OSINH

---

163 *[ca 1848]*
Plan of the Province of Upper Canada [showing administrative and electoral divisions]
Col ms 98 x 161 cm [1" to 8 miles]
An unfinished map showing cos, districts, and electoral divisions, the latter possibly as being planned for revision in 1849; notes on some twps indicating they are in one co for municipal, and in another for electoral purposes; twps shown north to Ashfield, Wawanosh, Derby to Minto, Bexley to Somerville, Harvey to Palmerston, Blithfield to Pembroke; base map is a tracing of the Canada Co. map of [1825] **(69)** with symbols indicating the twps in which the company has land.
OTAR

---

164 *1849*
CANADA
Print (wax engr) 12 x 21 cm 1" to 80 miles
In Sidney E. Morse, *A System of Geography for the Use of Schools* (New York: Harper & Bros 1849), 14 (OOAMA), and in *Morse's School Geography* (New York: Harper & Bros 1854), 14 (OOAMA), and in the 1863 ed of the latter (OOAMA); shows Upper Canada east to Quebec; districts and places shown on 1849 ed; co names have replaced districts in the 1854 ed; the 1863 ed is the same as 1854.
OOAMA

---

165 *1849*
SKETCH MAP / of / CANADA WEST. // J.E.A. delt // London, Henry Colburn 1849 // S. Hall sculpt. // To face Chap. 1, Vol 1.
Print (lith) 10 x 16 cm Scale not given
In James E. Alexander, *L'Acadie* (London: Henry Colburn 1849), 1: opp 131 (*Bib Can* 2950); shows major places and rivers.
OTMCL

Later editions and states

(2) *1852*
SKETCH MAP / of / CANADA WEST. // J.E.A. delt London, Colburn & Co 1852. S. Hall sculp. // To Face Chap 1. Vol 2.
Print (lith) 10 x 16 cm Scale not given
In Richard Bonnycastle, *Canada as It Was, Is and May Be* (London: 1852), 2: frontis (*Bib Can* 2825); from the same plate as map above.
OTMCL

---

166 *[ca 1849]*
WEST / CANADA // The illustrations by H. Warren, & Engraved by Robt Wallis. // J. & F. TALLIS, LONDON, EDINBURGH & DUBLIN. // The Map, Drawn & Engraved by J. Rapkin.
Print (steel engrav) hand col 26 x 33 cm 1" to 42 miles
Views: Indian hunting buffalo, two beaver, an otter, Indians encamped, 'FALLS OF NIAGARA'; twps shown in the Huron District north to Ashfield and Wawanosh and in the east to a line from Harvey to Palmerston; cos and districts shown; OOAMA copy has 'Indian Territory' named in Huron area; designated 'first state first issue' in P.J. Radford, *Americana Catalogue*, no 27 (Nov 1980); Tallis's maps were being produced from about 1847 on and J. & F. Tallis were in business together until Dec 1849 (P. Jackson, 18, 21).
GBL (70640(42)) OKQ OOAMA (NMC 27543) QMMMCM

Related maps and later editions and states

(2) *[1853?]*
— [Same title and imprint]
In R.M. Martin, *The British Colonies* (London and New York: The London Printing and Publishing Co. [and] J. & F. Tallis [1853?]), I: between 28 and 29 (OTUTF); dedication in vol II is dated Apr 1853;

views of Indian hunting and two beaver replaced with 'KINGSTON' and seal of the province of Canada; 'Crown lands' and 'Indian Territory' now noted in the Huron District.
OTUTF

(**3**) *[1851–4?]*
— / JOHN TALLIS & COMPANY, LONDON & NEW YORK. // ...
In R.M. Martin, *Tallis's Illustrated Atlas, and Modern History of the World* (London and New York: Tallis & Co. 1851), plate [67] (*LC Atlases* 804), and in Martin's *The Illustrated Atlas and Modern History of the World* (London and New York: J. & F. Tallis [1857]), plate [45] (*LC Atlases* 822), and in Martin's *The British Colonies* (London and New York: The London Printing & Publishing Co. [1851–7?]), I: between 28 and 29 (*Bib Can* 3009) or opp 105 (OOA); the map is the same as (2); John Tallis & Co. was a business name used from 1851 to 1854 (Brown, 196); (OOAMA MacDonald Collection 483).
OKIT OKQ OLU OOA OOAMA (NMC 2888, 10671, 105076) OTAR OTMCL USDLC

(**4**) *[1853–6?]*
— // THE LONDON PRINTING AND PUBLISHING COMPANY // ...
Maps with this imprint are found in copies of Martin's *The British Colonies* ([1853?]), his *The Illustrated Atlas* ([London: J. & F. Tallis 1853]), plate 66 (OOAMA), his *British Possessions in North America* (London: London Printing and Publishing Co. [1850?]), [plate] '66' (*Bib Can* 5451), and his *Tallis Illustrated Atlas* (1851) (USDLC); some maps (except that in *Bib Can* 5451) show twps filled in to the base of the Bruce Peninsula; a few railways have been added; the London Printing and Publishing Co. was formed 15 Dec 1853 (P. Jackson, 22).
OKQ OOA OOAMA OTMCL USDLC

---

167 *1850*
CHART OF LAKE HURON, / REDUCED FROM SURVEYS BY / Captain Bayfield R.N. / WITH ADDITIONS BY / LIEUT. F. HERBERT R.N. / PUBLISHED BY PERMISSION / OF THE / Lords Commissioners of the Admiralty. / By HUGH SCOBIE, / TORONTO, 1850. / Hugh Scobie, Lith.
Print (lith) 94 x 89 cm Approx 1" to 6.66 miles
Soundings, place-names, navigation aids; nature of shoreline; rivers; a few mills, portages, Indian villages and missions, and mines shown along coast; list of distances and bearings; this or a later issue was advertised by Scobie in *British Colonist* (Toronto) 21 May 1851 as dated 1851 and just published and for sale.
GBTAUh (L7635 1d) OTAR OTMCL

---

168 *1850*
Map / of / CANADA / EAST AND WEST. / NEW YORK, / Published by / ENSIGN & THAYER, / 50 Ann Street. / & 12 Exchange St. Buffalo, N.Y. 1850. // Entered according to Act of Congress in the year 1848 by Ensign's & Thayer in the Clerk's Office of the District Court of the United States for the Southern District of New York.
Print (lith) hand col 57 x 71 cm 1" to 18 miles
This is a smaller folding ed with cover and on thinner paper of **161(3)**; Lower Canada has been inset at the same scale in the lower right corner and the inset of Nova Scotia, etc, deleted; the portraits and coat of arms have also been deleted; table: 'Population ... Canada West in 1848'; distances and notes on the province affixed to the cover; (OOAMA MacDonald Collection 527 (NMC 119049)).
OOAMA (NMC 22086, 119049)

Later editions and states

(**2**) *1853*
— NEW YORK, / Published by / HORACE THAYER & CO. / 50 Ann Street, / & 127 Main St. Buffalo, N.Y. 1853. // Entered ... 1848 by Ensign's & Thayer ...
Same as 1850; title and information are similar to **161(4)**; (OOAMA MacDonald Collection 528 (NMC 119050)).
OOAMA (NMC 119050) OTAR USDLC

(**3**) *1853*
— / Published by / THAYER, BRIDGMAN, & FANNING / 156 WILLIAM STREET. / Corrected to 1853, for / MACKAY'S CANADA DIRECTORY. / Printed by D. McLellan 26 Spruce St. N.Y. // Entered ... 1848 by Ensign's & Thayer ... / Entered ... 1853 by Thayer, Bridgman & Fanning ...
The 'Census of 1852 by Counties' has been added; cover-title: 'Map of Canada East & West with travelling chart'; OTMCL copy includes a sheet listing railway fares, Crown Lands agents, co registrars, canals, with imprint 'Compiled and Published by Robert W.S. Mackay Montreal.'; the railways are the same as the large map ed (**161**(6) and (7)).
OKQ OTMCL USDLC

(**4**) *1853*
— / 156 William Street. / NEW YORK, / 1853. Printed by D. McLellan ... [as above]
Content similar to **161**(6) and to (3) above.
OTAR

(**5**) *1854*
— / NEW YORK, / Published by / ENSIGN, BRIDGMAN & FANNING. / 156 WILLIAM STREET, / 1854. // Printed by D. McLellan ... [as above]
Similar to no **161**(9).
OOAMA (NMC 21957)

(**6**) *1854*
— / & 8 Exchange St., Buffalo, N.Y. / [added before date]
Same as (5).
OOAMA (NMC 21956)

(7) *1855*
— [as (5) above with date changed to 1855]
OOAMA copy has cover-title: 'Map of Canada East & West' with list of maps for sale by 'Ensign Bridgman & Fanning 156 William St. corner of Ann, New York'; same as (5) above but also similar to **161**(10); (OOAMA MacDonald Collection 529).
OOAMA (NMC 21860)

(8) *1862*
— / NEW YORK, / Published by / ENSIGN, BRIDGMAN & FANNING. / 156 William Street, / 1862. // Entered ... in the year 1857 by Ensign Bridgman & Fanning in the Clerk's Office of the District Court ... Southern District of New York.
Print (lith) 84 x 63 cm 1" to 20 miles
The map has been enlarged to incorporate some features of the larger version: the coat of arms and the portraits of Queen Victoria and Prince Albert; new insets: [L Superior] 1" to 76 miles, [L Ontario] 1" to 36 miles, [L Huron] 1" to 35 miles, [L Erie] 1" to 48 miles, [L Michigan] 1" to 62 miles; view: 'VIEW OF NIAGARA FALLS'; four tables show the population of Canada West and East in 1861 and railways in both parts of the province; 'Historical Sketch of Canada'; twps are shown in the Bruce Peninsula and north to a line Stephenson to Richards and McKay to Clara and south of L Nipissing.
OTAR

(9) *1865*
— [Date changed in title to 1865]
The same information, insets, and features as (8).
GBL (70615 (30)).

---

169 *[1850]*
A / MAP OF THE LAKES AND RIVERS / ILLUSTRATED ON / BURR'S SEVEN MILE MIRROR.
Print (wood engrav with typeset names) 18 x 9 cm Scale not given
In William Burr, *Descriptive and Historical View of Burr's Moving Mirror of the Lakes* (Boston: Dutton & Wentworth, Printers 1850), opp frontis (*Bib Can* 5427); a rough sketch of the Great Lakes and St Lawrence R as far as the Saguenay R; major towns located.
OTMCL

Later editions and states

(2) *[1854]*
— ILLUSTRATED ON THE SEVEN MILE MIRROR.
In J. Perham, *Descriptive and Historical View of the Seven Mile Mirror of the Lakes* (New York: Baker, Godwin & Co. 1854), after title-p (*Bib Can* 5645); the same base map as the 1850 ed but no place-names are shown.
OTMCL

---

170 *[1850]*
Map of the Principal Communications in Canada West Compiled from the most authentick sources, actual Surveys, District maps, etc. etc. by Major Baron de Rottenburg Asst. Quarter Mr. Genl.
Col ms in 12 sheets 372 x 588 cm 1" to 2 miles
Watermark: 'JAMES WHATMAN TURKEY MILL KENT 1831' Endorsements (on title sheet): 'Quartermaster General 2932 Dec 30 1868'; stamp on sheet 12 'Dept of Militia and Defence Survey Division'
The most detailed topographic map of the province to date; macadamized, planked, common co, and principal travelled roads all distinguished; distances and notes on condition of roads given; relief and swampy land are shown; cleared land is shown in London Twp, in part of the Niagara Peninsula, and in the eastern part of the province; gives numbers of men and horses that can be billetted in each place; the list of 'authorities consulted' includes printed and ms maps from 1836 to about 1848; the map is dated 1850 from a note that a road was opened in the summer of 1849 and the fact that Rottenburg was promoted to Lt Col in Nov 1850; however, much of the area may have been surveyed by 1848 as a letter of 8 Apr 1862 to REO Kingston refers to a 'Military Sketch of part of the Districts of Gore and Niagara by Major de Rottenburg AQMG 12th May 1848' (not found) that may be a sketch for it (OOA RG 8 I/1566 p 120); the map is not up to date for twps and roads are poorly shown in areas for which source maps and reports not listed; (Holmden 3826; *OHIM* 6.4; Olsen 106 and pp 166–75).
OOAMA (NMC 12437)

---

171 *[1850?]*
MAP OF / THE PROVINCES OF / CANADA ... by Joseph Bouchette ... 1846 [with ms adds on railways and canals]
Print (engrav) with ms adds 120 x 220 cm Approx 1" to 14 miles
Proposed railways and canals added to the map in ms; includes two sheets of notes and tracings made from the map to show railways in the Ottawa and Montreal areas; notes entitled 'Statement of Railways in Canada completed or in progress to accompany the Commg Rl Engrs letter no 176 ... [Sgd] Henry Vavasour Col Comg Rl Engineers Canada Montreal 8th August / 50' and 'List of Canals in the Province of Canada ... To accompany the Comg Rl Engineer's letter to the Inspector General of Fortifications dated 21st May 1847 No. 835 (Signed) R.I. Pilkington Draftsman'; (*PRO Cat* 200).
GBLpro (CO 700 Canada 101B)

---

172 1850
MAP OF THE RAILWAYS TO BE CONSTRUCTED TO ESTABLISH THE ABLE-BODIED POOR IN CANADA.

Print (lith) 18 x 38 cm Approx 1" to 120 miles
In *A Plan for the Systematic Colonization of Canada ... by an Officer of Rank* (London: Hatchard & Son 1850), after 56 (Casey I–2190); shows a large area of land in the north accessed by proposed railways with note 'millions of acres of the finest land for the Irish'; a railway is planned to run from L Simcoe and Cobourg across Canada East to L St John.
OOA

---

173 *[ca 1850?]*
PRINCIPAL CITIES & PORTS IN CANADA / KINGSTON / TORONTO / MONTREAL / QUEBEC // Drawn & Engraved by / G.H. Swanston Edinr. // A. Fullarton & Co London & Edinburgh
4 maps on 1 sheet (lith) 24 x 14 cm Scales not given
In *Gazetteer of the World or Dictionary of Geographical Knowledge* (London [1850]–6), 2:232 (USDLC, USNN); the maps are redrawn from insets on the Staveley maps (see **140**).
OOAMA (NMC 48747) USNN USDLC

---

174 *[1850]*
WESTERN & CENTRAL PARTS / OF THE / VALLEY / OF THE / ST LAWRENCE. / To Illustrate the Excursions. // Day & Son, Lithrs to the Queen
Print (lith) 28 x 48 cm Scale not given
In John J. Bigsby, *The Shoe and Canoe* (London: Chapman and Hall 1850), 1: opp 352 (*Bib Can* 1426); main rivers, lakes, roads, and places named.
OTMCL

---

175 *1850–1*
SKELETON MAP / Shewing in Vermillion the relative positions of the Ordce Properties and / Military Reserves in Canada West, exclusive of those along the Rideau / Canal, and more fully detailed on the accompanying Plans, enumerated below, viz – ... [Sgd in facsimile] Henry Vavasour Col Comg R1 Engineers Canada 26 October 1850 R I Pilkington Draftsman. / Drawn in Transfer Lithogy by J.G. Kelly and Printed at the Lithographic Establishment, / Quarr Mastr Genls Department, Horse Guards, January 1851.
Print (lith) hand col 40 x 53 cm Scale not given
A ms list in alphabetical order accompanies the general map; withdrawn from GBLpro WO 78/1047; a ms note on the map reads: '13,2, and 6 given over to Supt for Enrolled Pens'; (Olsen 107; *PRO Cat* 1415).
GLBpro (MPH 126 (1))
The individual lithographed maps 2–30 are listed in the title and are described separately below; 15, 22, and 27 are on same sheet as 5; most have the same imprint and signatures as shown above with a few variations as noted; only the first also indicates 'Transfer Lithogy'; notes on dates of purchase or patent; all GBLpro copies are filed in MPH 126 (2–30); (Holmden 2786 a–cc).

No 2 / PENETANGUSHENE / Plan of the Naval and Military Reserves / Drawn in Transfer Lithogy ... January 1851.
39 x 30 cm 1" to 1900 ft (Holmden 2330).
GBLpro OOAMA (NMC 4299)

No 3 / SIMCOE DISTRICT / Sketch shewing the relative position of the Military Reserve, Lot 27, Con 9, Township of Flos, ... Shewing / also the Naval and Military Reserves at Penetangushene ... January 1851
30 x 39 cm 1" to 260 chains reserve according to 'Patent dated 6th Sepr 1848'; (Holmden 2331).
GBLpro

No 4 / POINT EDWARD / Plan of the Military Reserve, Content called 641 Acres. / ... January 1851
39 x 31 cm 1" to 780 ft (Holmden 2532).
GBLpro

No 4 [2nd] / AMHERSTBURG / Plan shewing the arrangement for the Settlement of the Pensioners // Henry Vavasour / Col Comg Rl Engineers / Canada / R.I. Pilkington / Draftsman / 3rd June 1851
43 x 55 cm 1" to 200 yds Various notes and ms adds; (Holmden 1492).
OOAMA (NMC 3698)

No 5 / WINDSOR. / Plan of the Government Property.
15 x 19 cm 1" to 350 ft [Printed on sheet with]:

No 15 / LYONS CREEK. / Plan shewing Military Reserve
15 x 19 cm 1" to 335 ft

No 22 / SNAKE ISLAND. / Plan of Military Reserve
15 x 19 cm 1" to 118 ft

No 27 / BROCKVILLE, / GRANTS ISLAND / Plan of Military Reserve / ... Copy / [Sgd in facsimile] W F Lambert / Lieut Rl Engrs / ... Drawn in Lithogy ... March, 1851.
15 x 19 cm 1" to 68 ft
GBLpro OOAMA (NMC 4996)

No 6 / AMHERSTBURG / Plan of the Military Reserve ... / Bois Blanc Island / Drawn in Lithogy ... January 1851.
30 x 38 cm 1" to 300 ft (Holmden 1491).
GBLpro OOAMA (NMC 3697)

No 7 POINT PELEE / Sketch of the Military Reserve / ... January 1851.
30 x 39 cm 1" to 7000 ft (Holmden 2354).
GBLpro OOAMA (NMC 4312)

No 8 / RONDEAU / Plan of Military Reserve. / ... Copy / [Sgd in facsimile] W.F. Lambert / Lieut Rl Engrs / August 2nd / 1850. ... January 1851.
30 x 38 cm 1" to 5500 ft (Holmden 2587).
GBLpro OOAMA (NMC 4372)

No 9 / CHATHAM / Plan of the Military Reserves / ... January 1851.

30 x 39 cm 1" to 500 ft (Holmden 1555).
GBLpro OOAMA (NMC 3760)

No 10 / LONDON. C.W. / Plan of the Military Reserve / ... Lambert ... 4th July 1850. / Drawn in Lithogy ... February 1851.
30 x 39 cm 1" to 320 ft (Holmden 1948).
GBLpro OOAMA (NMC 4066)

No 11 / TURKEY POINT / Plan Shewing the proposed boundary to the Military Reserve. / ... Drawn in Lithogy ... Feby 1851.
30 x 38 cm 1" to 4000 ft (Holmden 2753).
GBLpro OOAMA (NMC 4497)

No 12 / PORT MAITLAND. / Plan of the Naval and Military Reserves. / ... Drawn in Lithogy ... February 1851.
30 x 39 cm 1" to 2000 ft
GBLpro

No 13 / FORT ERIE. / Plan of the Military Reserve. / ... Drawn in Lithogy ... February 1851.
30 x 39 cm 1" to 3400 ft (Holmden 1657).
GBLpro OOAMA (NMC 3811)

No 14 / CHIPPAWA. / Plan of the Military Reserve ... Feby 1851.
30 x 39 cm 1" to 260 ft (Holmden 1574).
GBLpro OOAMA (NMC 3372)

No 16 / QUEENSTON. / Plan of the Military Reserve, total content called 175 Acres. / ... Feby 1851.
30 x 38 cm 1" to 750 ft Shows bldgs; railway; ruins; proposed grant for Queenston Suspension Bridge Co.; (Holmden 2398).
GBLpro OOAMA (NMC 4351)

No 17 / NIAGARA. / Plan of the Military Reserve / ... February 1851.
26 x 53 cm 1" to 485 ft (Holmden 2035).
GBLpro OOAMA (NMC 4212)

No 18 / SHORT HILLS. / Plan of the Ordnance Property / ... Copy W.F. Lambert ... July 17th 1850. / Drawn in Litho by T.K. King ... February 1851.
30 x 39 cm 1" to 450 ft (Holmden 2036).
GBLpro OOAMA (NMC 3584)

No 19 / BURLINGTON HEIGHTS, C.W. / Plan shewing the Military Reserve. / ... Lambert ... July 6th 1850. / Drawn in Lithogy ... Feby 1851.
38 x 30 cm 1" to 900 ft
GBLpro

No 20 / TORONTO. C.W. / Plan shewing the Military Reserves / containing about 182 Acres. / exclusive of the portion leased to the Corporation. / ... Copy W.F. Lambert ... August 29th 1850 – / Drawn in Lithogy ... March 1851.
30 x 39 cm 1" to 300 yds There is also a similar but ms 'Plan of the Military Reserves ... [Sgd] R.I. Pilkington Draftsman Oct 1850.'; (Holmden 2723) .
GBLpro OOAMA (NMC 4471)

No 21 / CAPE VESEY. MARYSBURG. C.W. / Plan of Military Reserve / Copied from Hd Qr Plan by John Desborough Lieut Rl Artillery Asst Rl Engr Feby 7th 1845 [Sgd in facsimile] John Y. Moggridge Lieut Rl Engineers 30th July 1850. / ... C.O. Streatfield Lt Col ... 1st August 1850.
30 x 39 cm 1" to 150 chains
GBLpro

No 23 / KINGSTON. / Horseshoe Island. / Plan of Military Reserve. Copied from Lieut. Sedley's Plan, dated 28th Novr 1849. [Sgd in facsimile] George F. Dawson Lieut R.E. 29th July 1850. / ... C.O. Streatfield Lt. Col. ... 1st August 1850. / Drawn by T.K. King in Litho. ... February 1851.
31 x 39 cm 1" to 390 yds (Holmden 1865).
GBLpro OOAMA (NMC 3940)

No 24 / KINGSTON. / Plan of the Ordnance Property / South half of Lot No 16 [Sgd in facsimile] George F Dawson Lieut. R.E. 27 July 1850. C.O. Streatfield Lt Col. ... 27 July 1850. ... February 1851.
39 x 30 cm 1" to 500 ft (Holmden 1865).
GBLpro OOAMA (NMC 3936–7; 3947–9)

No 25 / KINGSTON C.W. / Plan of Ordnance Property on western side / of / Harbour. [Sgd in facsimile] Charles Sedley Lieut R.E. ... C.O. Streatfield Lt Col ... 1st August 1850 ... February 1851.
30 x 38 cm 1" to 650 ft (Holmden 1865).
GBLpro OOAMA (NMC 3943)

No 26 / KINGSTON, C.W. / Plan of Ordnance Property / Eastern side of Harbour [Sgd in facsimile] John Y. Moggridge ... 26th July 1850. ... C.O. Streatfield ... 27 July 1850. ... February 1851.
30 x 39 cm 1" to 700 ft (Holmden 1865).
GBLpro OOAMA (NMC 3945–6)

No 28 / PRESCOTT, C.W. / Plan of Military Reserve / [Sgd in facsimile] George F. Dawson Lieut R.E. 30th July 1850; C.O. Streatfield Lt Col ... 1st August 1850; ... Feby 1851
38 x 30 cm 1" to 300 ft (Holmden 2385).
GBLpro OOAMA (NMC 4339)

No 29 / CORNWALL, C.W. / Plan shewing the Military Reserve. / [Sgd in facsimile] Copy W.F. Lambert ... July 24th 1850 ... 1851.
30 x 38 cm 1" to 730 ft
GBLpro

No 30 / FIGHTING ISLAND. / Plan shewing Military Reserve. / ... Copy / W Lambert Lieut Rl Engrs. / ... Feb 1851
30 x 39 cm 1" to 2550 ft (Holmden 1629).
GBLpro OOAMA (NMC 3797)

---

176 *[1850–2]*
[Maps from W.H. Smith, *Canada Past Present and Future ... Containing Ten County Maps, and One General Map of the Province, Compiled Expressly for the Work* (Toronto: Thomas Maclear [1850–2]), 2 vols]
11 prints (lith) Sizes vary Scales vary

Vol I:

(1) Counties of / ESSEX, KENT / AND LAMBTON.
27 x 21 cm 1" to 9 miles Opp [1].
OOAMA (NMC 2896) OTAR OTMCL OWHM

(2) Counties of / MIDDLESEX, / OXFORD, / AND NORFOLK, / Toronto, Thomas Maclear.
21 x 27 cm 1" to 8.5 miles Opp 85.
OOAMA (NMC 2892) OTMCL

(3) Counties of / LINCOLN, HALDIMAND, WELLAND, / WENTWORTH AND HALTON. / Toronto, Thomas Maclear.
28 x 22 cm 1" to 7.5 miles Opp 153.
OTMCL

Vol II:

(4) Counties of / YORK AND SIMCOE. / Toronto, Thomas Maclear.
21 x 28 cm 1" to 12 miles Opp [1] or in I: opp 270; (OOAMA MacDonald Collection 499).
OOAMA (NMC 2890) OTMCL

(5) Counties of / WATERLOO, / HURON, PERTH, / AND / BRUCE. Toronto. Thomas Maclear.
22 x 22 cm 1" to 10 miles Opp 90.
OOAMA (NMC 2891) OTMCL

(6) Counties of / PETERBOROUGH, / DURHAM, / AND / NORTHUMBERLAND.
21 x 27 cm 1" to 8 miles Opp 199.
OOAMA (NMC 2295) OTMCL

(7) Counties of / HASTINGS, FRONTENAC, / LENNOX AND ADDINGTON.
21 x 27 cm 1" to 11.5 miles Opp 241.
OOAMA (NMC 2899) OTMCL

(8) County of / PRINCE EDWARD. / Toronto. Thomas Maclear.
21 x 27 cm 1" to 5.5 miles Opp 256.
OOAMA (NMC 2897) OTMCL

(9) Counties of / LANARK AND RENFREW, / CARLETON AND LEEDS, / AND GRENVILLE. / Toronto, Thomas Maclear.
27 x 21 cm 1" to 11.5 miles Opp 316.
OTMCL

(10) Counties of / PRESCOTT AND RUSSELL, / AND STORMONT, DUNDAS, / AND / GLENGARRY. / Toronto. Thomas Maclear.
21 x 27 cm 1" to 8 miles Opp 375.
OTMCL

(11) MAP OF / CANADA WEST OR UPPER CANADA, / COMPILED FROM / Government Plans, Original Documents, and Personal Observation. / BY / William H. Smith, / Author of the Canadian Gazetteer for Canada / PAST, PRESENT, AND FUTURE. / TORONTO. / Published by Thomas Maclear, / 1852.
44 x 58 cm Approx 1" to 23 miles
Sometimes found in I: between viii and [ix] or in II: opp title-p (OTMCL); see also **185** for later eds and other issues of this map; at least some of the maps were issued with parts of the work beginning in Nov 1850 and later published in two vols in 1851 and 1852 (*Bib Can* 3310, 3311); for a full bibliographical analysis and list of many locations see Patricia Stone, 'The Publishing History of W.H. Smith's *Canada: Past, Present and Future*'; the co maps show plank and gravelled roads; twps, towns, and miscellaneous cultural detail; locations other than OTMCL are for loose sheets; the co maps were probably produced by 1851 since the cos of Elgin and Grey (established 1851) are not shown.
OOAMA (NMC 105075) OTAR OTMCL OWHM

---

177 *[1850–3]*
Map of Part of / CANADA WEST, / COMPILED FROM THE MOST RECENT AUTHORITIES AND SURVEYS, / for Scobie's Canadian Almanac for 1851, / Being the commencement of a complete Map of the entire Province the continuous portions of which will be published in successive Almanacs for future years. / / H. Scobie, Lith. Toronto
Print (lith) 39 x 47 cm 1" to 8.5 miles
Central and northwest sheet; found separately or in *Scobie's Canadian Almanac ... for ... 1851* (Toronto: Hugh Scobie [1850], frontis (*Bib Can* 2871); imprint lacking on some copies; shows area from York Co west and north of Hamilton; shows twps, travelled roads, post offices, relief; twps to the base of the Bruce Peninsula; more rivers shown in south; (OOAMA MacDonald Collection 482).
OOAMA (NMC 2887) OTAR OTMCL

The three other sheets in the set are as follows:

(2) *[1851]*
— / For Scobie's Canadian Almanac for 1852. / Being the Continuation of a Complete map of the Entire Province / the remaining portions of which will be published in / successive Almanacs for future years.
48 x 35 cm
Southwest sheet; in *Scobie's Canadian Almanac ... for ... 1852* (Toronto: Hugh Scobie [1851]) (OTUTF); depicts area from Niagara to Windsor; shows same information as in the first sheet, and railways in progress.
OLU OTAR

(3) *[1852]*
— / for Scobie's Canadian Almanack for 1853.
31 x 49 cm
Central sheet; in *Scobie's Canadian Almanac ... for ... 1853* (Toronto: Hugh Scobie [1852]) (OTUTF); OTMCL copy bound in the almanac for 1852; depicts area from Toronto to Kingston and north to line Harvey-Palmerston twps; shows same information as the first sheet, including railways proposed.
OLU OTAR OTMCL OTUTF

(4) *[1853]*
— / for Scobie's Canadian Almanack for 1854.
33 x 44 cm
Eastern sheet; in *Scobie's Canadian Almanac ... for 1854* (Toronto: Hugh Scobie [1853]), frontis (*Bib Can* 2871); shows area from Kingston east, twps

north to line to Palmerston, Brougham to Wilberforce; railways; (OOAMA MacDonald Collection 485).
OOAMA (NMC 2902) OTAR OTMCL

178 *[1851]*
Map of Part of / CANADA WEST, / COMPILED FROM THE MOST RECENT AUTHORITIES AND SURVEYS, / Shewing the line of the Ontario Simcoe and Huron Union Railroad as / approved by authority from Toronto to Barrie. // H.Scobie, Lith. Toronto.
Print (lith) 40 x 47 cm 1" to 8.5 miles
The title and line for the railway (Toronto-Nottawasaga Bay) have been overprinted on the central and northwestern sheet of Scobie's four-part map [1850–3] (**177(1)**); the map was advertised as published 19 Sept 1851 (*British Colonist*).
OTAR

Related maps and later editions and states

(**2**) *[1852]*
MAP / showing the Routes between / BOSTON, NEW-YORK / AND THE / NORTH WEST / VIA / TORONTO / and the / GEORGIAN BAY. / DRAWN BY D. VAUGHAN. // Lith of Rich[d] H. Pease.
Print (lith) 44 x 73 cm Approx 1" to 62.5 miles
In *Report by the Chief Engineer ... Ontario Simcoe and Huron Railroad Union Company* (Toronto: Hugh Scobie 1852), frontis (*Bib Can* 3300); shows area from Nova Scotia to Mississippi R; few place-names shown in Upper Canada but Hythe is marked as connecting port for a railway; 'Proposed Grand Trunk Rail Road' shown from Halifax to Toronto; route of the railway Toronto to Collingwood, various other connecting lines shown in U.S., and GWR from Niagara to Detroit.
OTMCL

(**3**) *[1853]*
Map of Part of / CANADA WEST, / Shewing the / Ontario Simcoe & Huron Union Rail-Road. / As constructed to Barrie and the Routes examined / thence to the waters of Lake Huron &c. // H. Scobie Lith. Toronto.
Print (lith) 40 x 47 cm 1" to 8.5 miles
Issued with *Report by the Chief Engineer ... of the Ontario Simcoe & Huron Railroad Union Company, February 1853* (Toronto: Hugh Scobie 1853) (OTAR); from the same plate as first map above but with changes to the title; the railway line shows part constructed and routes proposed for northern section to Penetanguishene, Nottawasaga R, Sydenham, etc; the population and assessed value of land for twps in Bruce, Grey, York, Simcoe, Halton, and Peel are given; ms adds on OOAMA copy show proposed routes of other railways.
OOAMA (NMC 15677) OTAR (Pamphlets 1853 box 1)

(**4**) *1853*
MAP / Showing the Routes between / New York Boston Washington / AND THE / NORTHWESTERN STATES AND MINERAL REGIONS / VIA / TORONTO / THE / ONTARIO SIMCOE & HURON RAILROAD / and the / GEORGIAN BAY / 1853. / Hugh Scobie, Lith. // Toronto Jan. 1853
Print (lith) 43 x 65 cm 1" to 60 miles
A redrawing of (2) above and in the same report as (3); shows same area as (2); shows connecting routes in the U.S. and proposed O.S. & H. Railroad with connections from Collingwood and Saugeen; shows GTR and GWR.
OTAR

179 *[ca 1851]*
[Map of townships in Home, Simcoe, and Wellington districts showing proposed county boundaries and proposed roads]
Col ms with pt printed 99 x 149 cm 1" to 200 chains
Part of map formed from 1841 printed map of Home and Simcoe districts (**371**), and the area from there to L Huron in ms with twps laid out north to Ashfield to Arran and Wellesley to Sydenham; proposed roads shown including Wawanosh Rd and 'projected line of road from the district of Gore to the mouth of the Saugeen R, Saugeen Rd'; boundaries of York, Simcoe, and Ontario cos added in ms (14 and 15 Vict, cap 5 (1851)); road lots along Toronto-Sydenham Rd also shown.
OTAR (SR 8913)

180 *1851*
MAP / shewing the Line / of / THE MONTREAL, OTTAWA, AND KINGSTON TRUNK LINE / RAILWAY COMPANY. / and through BYTOWN, GEORGIAN BAY, GODERICH AND WINDSOR. / By / P. Fleming Civil Engineer / APRIL 1851 // T. IRELAND LITHY. MONTREAL.
Print (lith) 36 x 52 cm Scale not given
A rough sketch showing the route proposed and connections to the U.S. and eastern seaboard; (Dionne 940).
OOAMA USMH

181 *1851*
Map / SHOWING THE LINE OF THE / CANADA GRAND TRUNK / RAILWAY / FROM QUEBEC TO WINDSOR / 1851 / G. Matthews' Lith. Montreal
Print (lith) 32 x 57 cm Scale not given
In *Report of the Committee on the Montreal and Kingston Section of the Grand Trunk Railway ... 4th March 1851*, at back (OOA Pamph 1851(39)); shows area from Nova Scotia to Michigan and the northeastern U.S.; shows the line of the GTR from Montreal to Toronto, Hamilton, London, and Windsor with branch to Sarnia; other lines shown to Bytown and Georgian Bay and connecting lines to the U.S.; table of distances; (Dionne 940).
OOA

182 *1852*
[Plans of all ordnance, barrack, naval and other government buildings called for by Inspector Gen of Fortifications, Circular 421, 12 Apr 1851]
18 col mss Sizes vary 1" to 50 ft to 1" to 100 yds
Most plans are sgd by M.C. Dixon, Col Commanding Royal Engineers, Canada, as well as others; most plans have 'B↑O' stamp; described in Holmden 4102 as '30 Plans of Government Buildings Circular 421.' The plans for Canada West are as follows: [13] Kingston C.W. [East side] ... H.M. Dockyard ... 25th Sept 1852 (NMC 22437); Kingston Plan of the Eastern Side of the Harbour ... 15th June 1852 (NMC 17526); [14] Kingston, Plan of the Western Side of the Harbour ... 15th June 1852 (NMC 17525); [15] Kingston ... Royal Artillery & Tete de Pont Barracks ... 15th June 1852 (NMC 17527); [16] Prescott ... 15th June 1852 [inset]: '... Grants Island' (NMC 17528); [17] Toronto C.W. [old fort] ... 15th June 1852 (NMC 17529); [18] Toronto C.W. [old fort and new barracks] ... 15th June 1852 (NMC 17530); [19] Niagara C.W. ... 15th June 1852 (NMC 17531); [20] Niagara C.W. ... 15th June 1852 (NMC 17532); [21] London C.W. ... 15th June 1852 (NMC 17533); [22] Amherstburgh C.W. ... 15th June 1852 [inset: ... Bois Blanc Is] (NMC 17534); [23] Chatham C.W. ... 15th June 1852 (NMC 17535); [24] Windsor Canada West ... 15th June 1852 (NMC 17536); [25] Penetanguishene ... 15th June 1852 (two copies: NMC 17537, 4301); [27–8] Bytown C.W. Guardroom and Hospital [and] Barracks; [29–30] Rideau Canal Plans Elevations and Sections of the Blockhouses and Defensible Guardhouses on the Line (NMC 17541–2).
OOAMA (NMC 4301; 17525–37; 17541–2; 22437)

---

183 *1852*
Index Map to the Territorial Divisions Act of Upper Canada Compiled and drawn in the Surveyors Branch West of the Crown Land Department [Sgd] By Thomas Devine Surveyor & Draftsman Crown L. Department Quebec April 1852
Col ms 104 x 145 cm 1" to 8 miles
Shows the cos and twps established by Territorial Divisions Act (14 and 15 Vict, cap 5 (1851)); 'O.C. 31 January 1853'; later adds to 1856 show islands surrendered in the St Lawrence R, L Ontario, L Erie, Georgian Bay, L Simcoe, and adjoining inland lakes; later adds show lands surrendered by the Indians to July 1856.
OTAR

---

184 *[1852]*
LAKE ONTARIO, / Reduced From the Surveys of Capt. Owen R.N. & A. Ford U.S.A. / With additions by / LIEUT. FREDK HERBERT R.N. / Published by / Hugh Scobie, Lith. / TORONTO.
Print (lith) 50 x 69 cm Approx 1" to 7.6 miles
Variation of compass in 1850; soundings, navigation aids; nature of shoreline; plank or macadamized roads along shore and north from various places along shore; advertised as just published in *British Colonist* 30 March 1852.
GBTAUh (L8696, 49b) OTAR

---

185 *1852*
MAP OF / CANADA WEST OR UPPER CANADA, / COMPILED FROM / Government Plans, Original Documents, and Personal Observation. / BY / William H. Smith, / Author of the Canadian Gazetteer for Canada / PAST, PRESENT, AND FUTURE. / TORONTO. / Published by Thomas Maclear, / 1852.
Print (lith) 44 x 58 cm Approx 1" to 23 miles
Issued in Smith's *Canada Past, Present, and Future* (*Bib Can* 3310, 3311, see **176**) and separately issued folded with cover-title: 'CANADA WEST' (OTMCL); the map covers the area from the end of Drummond Is east to Montreal and from L Nipissing to the south shore of L Erie; twps are shown to the base of the Bruce Peninsula and north to line from Harvey to Palmerston and Blithfield to Pembroke; railways shown including Niagara Falls to Windsor, Toronto to Barrie, Prescott-Bytown; legend keys railways, plank and gravelled roads, canals; boundaries of cos also shown; a coat of arms is at upper centre; title at centre right; (Olsen map 84; OOAMA MacDonald Collection 484).
OOAMA (NMC 105075) OTMCL

Later editions and states

(2a) *1852*
— [Title, etc, unchanged]
Railways added: Toronto-Guelph-Stratford with extension to London and Sarnia; and Buffalo, Brantford and L Huron railway; found in some copies of W.H. Smith, *Canada Past, Present, and Future* (*Bib Can* 3310, 3311).
OTMCL

(2b) *1852*
— [Title, etc, unchanged]
Hand col 67 x 88 cm
A border surrounding the map has been pasted on in parts to include views and statistics: 'VIEW OF KINGSTON C.W.,' 'VIEW OF COBOURG, C.W. F.C. Lowe Sculp,' 'VIEW OF LONDON, C.W. F.C.L.,' 'PORT HOPE,' 'QUEENSTON SUSPENSION BRIDGE F.C.L.,' 'BROCKVILLE, C.W.'; tables on the statistics of Canada from the census of 1852, including population by origin and religion, lists of educational establishments, distances, canals, average produce per acre, etc; the map is the same size and has same information as (2a) above.
OOAMA (NMC 11256)

(3) *1855*
— / BY / William H. Smith. / Author of Canada / PAST PRESENT AND FUTURE / WITH / ALTERATIONS and ADDITIONS / to the present time for the / CANADIAN ALMANAC / 1855. / Maclear & Co. Toronto.
34 x 49 cm

Found separately and in *Maclear & Co's (late Scobie's) Canadian Almanac ... for ... 1855* (Toronto: Maclear & Co. [1854]), after 2 (*Bib Can* 2871); this is the first of the smaller versions of the map: the map area has been reduced on all sides, the coat of arms deleted, the title has been dropped to the lower right, and scale and legend moved to left of title; this size was used for later eds in the *Canadian Almanac* and for the railway map; adds of railways: Barrie-Collingwood, Belleville-Peterborough, Peterborough-Cobourg, Port Hope-Lindsay and line to Beaverton, Grand Trunk RR Hamilton to Montreal; (Holmden 2795; Olsen map 85 or 86).
OOAMA (NMC 2907) OTAR OTMCL

(**4**) *1855*
— Personal Observation. / TORONTO / Published by / Maclear & Co. / 1855.
The map is as (1) above in layout and has the same information as (3); (Olsen map 85 or 86).
GBL OTMCL OTUMA

(**5**) *1856*
— [The same title as (1) with imprint]: TORONTO. / Published by Maclear & Co. / 1856.
The map is the same as (4); (Olsen map 87).
GBL (70640(11)) OKQ USDLC

(**6**) *1857*
THE / RAILWAY MAP / OF / CANADA WEST, / Including the latest surveys / FOR THE / CANADIAN ALMANAC / Published by Maclear & Co / TORONTO, / 1857. [Small edition]
Found separately and in *The Canadian Almanac ... for ... 1857* (Toronto: Maclear and Co. [1856]), after 194 (*Bib Can* 2871); similar to (3) but the coat of arms has been redrawn and placed in the upper centre, drawing of a train added bottom centre, legend moved to right, and 'proposed railrods' [*sic*] added; railways enhanced to be more legible, twps named in the Bruce Peninsula; a version of this map without title and train also appeared in Catherine Traill, *The Canadian Settler's Guide*, 7th ed (Toronto 1857), opp app, entitled 'From Maclear's Canadian Almanac Our Railway Policy Its Influence and Prospects' and with note: 'Compare this map with its predecessor issued in 1852 ... and it will be seen that our railways then embraced those only ... in process of Construction or projected.' (*Bib Can* 3489); London-St Thomas and Brockville-Perth rys; distances by water shown; (*OHIM* 6.35; Olsen map 88 or 89).
OKQ OOAMA (NMC 2910; 2908) OTAR OTMCL

(**7**) *1857*
— surveys / Published by Maclear & Co. TORONTO / 1857. [Small edition]
Changes: coat of arms not shown; otherwise, the same as (6); (Olsen map 88 or 89).
OTAR

(**8**) *1857*
— surveys / Published by Maclear & Co. / TORONTO / FOR ALEXANDER INGLIS / 28 Quay / ABERDEEN / 1857 // Maclear & Co, Publishers of several Statistical & Topographical Works on Canada, Booksellers, 16 King Street East, Toronto. [Small edition]
Twps added in the Huron-Ottawa area to line Airy, Murchison to Brudenell, Macaulay, Galway to Anstruther, and east of L Nipissing; Ottawa-Opeongo Rd route shown from Renfrew to Georgian Bay; coat of arms deleted; otherwise, similar to (6).
OOAMA (NMC 2909)

(**9**) *1857*
— [Title the same as (1) and (2) with change in imprint]: TORONTO. / Published by Maclear & Co. / 1857.
The map is in the style of (1); a few rivers added south of L Nipissing and L Opeongo redrawn; (Olsen map 88 or 89).
OTMCL

(**10**) *1858*
MAP OF / CANADA WEST. / CORRECTED FOR THE / CANADIAN ALMANAC / 1858. Published by Maclear & Co / TORONTO. [Small edition]
Found separately and in *The Canadian Almanac ... for ... 1858* (Toronto: Maclear & Co. [1857]) (*Bib Can* 2871); the train has been removed and a decorative border added; otherwise, similar to (8); legend has been shifted to left again; (Olsen map 90).
OOAMA (NMC 2912) OTAR OTMCL

(**11**) *1864*
EMIGRATION / MAP OF / CANADA / WESTERN SECTION / 1864.
In [A.C. Buchanan], *Canada. For the Information of Intending Emigrants* (Quebec: Printed by J. Blackburn 1864), at back (*Bib Can* 4294; CIHM 23114); the larger version with the coat of arms at the top; title, legend, and scale at lower right; twps extended north to line Stephenson to Richards, Mowat to Blair and on the north shore of L Huron to Gladstone and Bright; 'List of Various Railway Stations Western Section of the Province and their Respective Distances' (stations listed by railway line) at lower right; Belleville-Peterborough railway deleted; Smiths Falls to Renfrew railway added; townships added north of Ottawa R to Merritt; colonization rds shown.
OTMCL

(**12**) *1865*
EMIGRATION / MAP OF / CANADA / WESTERN SECTION / 1865. / W.C. CHEWETT & CO. Lith TORONTO. C.W.
Similar to (11) with the addition of a few more twps north of the Ottawa R; change to shape of Montreal and island, additions of names of some colonization rds; proposed railway extension Lindsay to Beaverton; (Olsen map 92).
OTAR

(**13**) *[1865]*
POCKET MAP / of / UPPER CANADA, / Corrected to the latest Surveys. / Lithographed,

Printed & Published / by / W.C. CHEWETT & Co. / TORONTO.

Cover-title: 'CHEWETT'S Map of UPPER CANADA Corrected to the latest Surveys. 1865 TORONTO. W.C. CHEWETT & CO.'; the same as (12) except 'List of Railways' deleted; (Olsen map 93).
OTMCL

(14) *1865*
MAP OF CANADA WEST, Engraved & Published in the Canadian Almanack for 1865 by W.C. CHEWETT & Co TORONTO. [Small edition]

Found separately and in *The Canadian Almanac ... for ... 1865* (Toronto: W.C. Chewett & Co. [1864]) (*Bib Can* 2871); title across top, list of railways; shows the same information for smaller area as (12); (OOAMA MacDonald Collection 494).
OKQ OOAMA (NMC 105071) OTAR OTMCL

---

186 *1852*
MAP OF THE / BASIN OF THE ST. LAWRENCE / SHOWING ALSO THE NATURAL AND ARTIFICIAL / Routes between the Atlantic Ocean / AND THE / INTERIOR OF NORTH AMERICA / BY / THOMAS C. KEEFER / for I.D. Andrews Report to Hon. Thomas Corwin, / SECRETARY OF THE TREASURY, / 1852. LITHOGRAPHED AND PRINTED BY D. MCLELLAN, / 26 Spruce St. New York.
Print (lith) 88 x 190 cm Scale not given

Shows two projected routes for railways from the Atlantic to the Mississippi R going through Montreal, Peterborough, and Sarnia; names of cos and major towns marked with population figures.
OTAR

---

187 *[1852]*
MAP / OF THE / TORONTO AND GUELPH / RAILWAY / SHEWING THE TOWNSHIPS IN CONNECTION WITH IT / and the / PROPOSED WESTERN EXTENSION / OF THE SAME / Walter Shanly Engineer in Chief / Hugh Scobie Lith. Toronto. // drawn by J.O.Browne
Print (lith) 47 x 77 cm 1" to 4 miles

In Walter Shanly, *Report on the Preliminary Surveys of the Toronto & Guelph Railway* (Toronto: Brewer M'Phail & Co. 1852), frontis (Casey I–2345); shows the area from Toronto to Goderich and south to Elgin Co; extension of railway from Guelph to Stratford, London, and Goderich; table of distances; GWR line Niagara-Hamilton-London; (Holmden 2864).
OOA OOAMA

---

188 *1852–3*
MAP / of the Western Division of / UPPER CANADA / Compiled from the most recent authorities & surveys / Lithographed and Published / By / HUGH SCOBIE, / TORONTO / 1852. / Copyright Secured / Entered According to law in the office of the Registrar of the Province of Canada, / 1852.
Print (lith) hand col 93 x 69 cm Approx 1" to 8.5 miles

The west sheet of a revised and redrawn ed of Scobie's four-part map issued from 1850 to 1853 (**177**); 'Explanation' keys travelled roads and plank, gravel, and macadamized roads (some named); railways completed and in progress, post offices, co towns, villages, boundaries of cos and twps; also shows relief, marshy lands; margin on right deleted to allow mounting with east sheet; advertised as just published 8 Apr 1852 (*British Colonist*); Buffalo-Brantford, Niagara Falls-Hamilton-Windsor, Toronto-Barrie railways; (Holmden 2792, 2793; Olsen map 94).
OOAMA (NMC 19516; 24342) OTAR OTMCL

The eastern sheet is as follows:

(2) MAP / of the / Eastern Division / OF / UPPER CANADA, / Compiled from the most recent authorities and surveys / Lithographed and Published / By / HUGH SCOBIE / TORONTO, / 1853. / Copyright Secured / Entered According to Law in the Office of the Registrar of / the Province of Canada / 1853.
93 x 69 cm

Margin on left deleted to allow mounting with west sheet; information shown as on west sheet; also shows Prescott-Ottawa railway line, proposed Toronto-Kingston line, and proposed Peterborough-Kingston line with branch to Belleville; advertised as published on 26 Aug 1853 in the *British Colonist* (Toronto); (Olsen map 94).
OOAMA (NMC 21383) OTAR OTMCL

Later editions and states

(3) *1854*
MAP / of Canada West or / UPPER CANADA / Compiled from the most recent authorities & surveys / by Donald McDonald / Lithographed and Published / BY MACLEAR & Co. / LATE / HUGH SCOBIE, / TORONTO / 1854. // COPYRIGHT SECURED / Entered According to Law, in the Office of the Registrar of the Province of Canada, 1852.
91 x 137 cm 1" to 8.5 miles

The map has been produced from the same plates as the west and east sheets above but the title has been deleted on east sheet and rivers and lakes added; a few railways and roads added; 'Proposed Central Trunk Ry line' and 'Surveyed line of Proposed Toronto and Kingston Railway' on east part do not continue across to west half; railways added: Brockville-Perth-Carleton Place, Barrie-Collingwood, Brantford-Goderich, Stratford-Sarnia, Woodstock-Pt Dover, Toronto-Guelph-Stratford; (Holmden 2794; Olsen map 95).
OOAMA (NMC 48606)

---

189 *1852–9*
[Verification plans for military or ordnance reserves] Canada ... Plan shewing the Boundaries as marked on the ground, of the Military Reserve

belonging to the Ordnance at ... [Most sgd] Surveyed by F.F. Passmore ... [verified by] Berdoe A. Wilkinson Lt R.E. ... Alexr Gordon Lt Col Dist Commg Royal Engineer Canada West ... M.C. Dixon Col Comg Royal Engineers Canada
23 col mss Sizes vary Approx 1" to 2–5 chains
Endorsements: stamp 'B↑O' (on most maps)
Most plans were surveyed from 1851 on and survey date and final date are given below; plans show boundaries of reserve, ordnance and other bldgs of stone, brick, or wood, and often parts of adjoining towns; each plan has a text with description and contents of the survey; names of surveyors and endorsement stamps are given below if they vary from above.

The plans are as follows:

(1) Chippawa ... Surveyed ... 1851 ... 12th Sept. 1853 (Holmden 1576).
OOAMA (NMC 19786)

(2) Chippawa ... Surveyed ... 1851 ... A.R. Vyvian Crease, Lt R.E. 29 Oct 1851
OOAMA (NMC 3773)

(3) Fort Erie ... Surveyed ... 1852 ... 3rd October 1853
OOAMA (NMC 11363)

(4) Fort Erie ... Surveyed ... 1852 ... 15th April 1854 Endorsed: 'CREOC' 'No 124'
OOAMA (NMC 16784)

(5) Fort Erie... Surveyed ... 1852 ... 12 April 1855 (Holmden 1659).
OOAMA (NMC 16795)

(6) Kingston ... Lots 23, 24 Con 1 Twp of Kingston ... Verified ... Lt. Farrell ... 1853 ... 1st Novr 1853 Endorsed: 'CREOC' 'No 153' '276–21'
OOAMA (NMC 11385)

(7) Kingston Fort Henry ... Lt Farrell 1853–4 ... 9th Novr 1854 Endorsed: 'REO' 'No 127'
OOAMA (NMC 11386)

(8) Kingston City of Kingston ... Surveyed by Mr Thomas Fraser Gibbs, ... 1859 ... 31st July 1860 Endorsed: 'CREOC' 'No 275' '255–22'
OOAMA (NMC 2403)

(9) Kingston No 1 Canada Cataraqui Reserve [lot 16, con 1, twp of Kingston]. ... Charles Walkem ... 1859 ... 7th Feb 1859 Endorsed: '276–48'
OOAMA

(10) Kingston Mills ... Surveyed Mr T.F. Gibbs ... 1853 ... 18th January 1854 Endorsed: 'CREOC' 'No 155'
OOAMA

(11) London ... Surveyed ... 1853 ... 2d October 1854 Endorsed: 'CREOC' 'No 123' (Holmden 1939).
OOAMA (NMC 11854)

(12) London ... Surveyed ... 1853 ... 12 April 1855
OOAMA (NMC 11855)

(13) Niagara ... Surveyed ... 1852 ... 11 March 1853 Endorsed: 'CREOC' 'No 146'
OOAMA (NMC 11403)

(14) Owen Sound ... Surveyed by Mr Charles Rankin ... 1854 ... 12 April 1855 Endorsed: 'CREOC' 'No 119'
OOAMA (NMC 11423)

(15) Penetanguishene ... [twps of Tay and Tiny] ... Surveyed by Mr John Emerson ... 1852 ... 12th Sept 1853
Copy at OTNR (SR 81009).
OOAMA (NMC 11426)

(16) Point Pelee ... Surveyed by Mr John A. Wilkinson ... 1851 ... 17th Feby 1853 Endorsed: 'CREOC' 'No 35'

(17) Prescott ... Surveyed by Mr T.F. Gibbs ... 1854 ... 26th August 1854
OOAMA (NMC 19777)

(18) Queenston ... Surveyed by Mr William Hawkins ... 1854 ... 31 July 1854 Endorsed: 'CREOC; 'No 129'
OOAMA (NMC 11434)

(19) St Josephs Island of Biquabigong ... Surveyed by Mr. T.N. Molesworth ... 1853 ... 12th April 1855 Endorsed: 'B↑O' 'Plan No 2' [and copy] 'CREOC' 'No 118'
(Holmden 1737).
OOAMA (NMC 11440–1)

(20) St Josephs [Island] Surveyed by Mr T.N. Molesworth ... 1854 ... 12 April 1855 Endorsed: 'B↑O' 'Plan No 1' [and copy] 'CREOC' 'No 117'
OOAMA (NMC 11438–9)

(21) Toronto ... Surveyed by Mr Sandford Fleming ... 1852 ... 4th June 1853 Endorsed: 'CREOC' 'No 38'
OOAMA (NMC 11448)

(22) Toronto ... Surveyed by Mr Sandford Fleming ... 1852 ... 12 Sept 1853 Endorsed: 'B↑O' 'Toronto F 51'
OOAMA (NMC 11449)

---

190 *[1853]*
Endorsed title: 'Atlas containing maps of the Counties of Upper and Lower Canada laid before the Legislature of the Province of Canada in the year 1853 by the Crown Lands Department' [On most maps]: By Thomas Devine Surveyor & Draftsman, C.L.D. Montreal Matthews Lith
1 vol of 85 lith maps 44 x 29 cm Most maps 1" to 8 miles
Title as endorsed in ms on copies 2 and 3 (OOAMA); on maps 61, 83: 'Thos Devine, Surveyor & Draftsman, C.L.D.'; on maps 65, 69: 'Matthews Lith' or 'G. Matthews' Lith' or 'Matthews Lith Montreal'; no scale given on most maps, a few at 1" to 6 miles or 1" to 14 miles; copy 2 (OOAMA) has 3 pp in ms at front entitled 'Index of Counties Upper & Lower Canada 1853'; map nos sometimes added in ms; 42 maps from no 44 to 85 are for individual cos of Canada West; each map is entitled with name of co except 65, 'Northerly part of the County of Simcoe'; the cos are arranged geographically from east to west; maps show roads or routes that may be for postal delivery; ms note on OTAR copy of map of Ontario Co indicates Georgina 'In Cy of York by

16 Vict c 96 1853'; BVAU has a copy endorsed 'A. Todd Esq with Mr Rolph's respects' with a ms list of cos and ms adds of names of M.P.s from 1857 to 1867; (Dionne IV:942 gives date [1852]).
BVAU OOAMA OTAR OTMCL OTUMA QMBN USDLC

---

191 *[1853]*
MAP OF THE / GREAT WESTERN RAILWAY OF CANADA, / WITH THE / PROPOSED BRANCH TO PORT SARNIA – / THE HAMILTON & TORONTO RAILWAY, / AND / THE CONNECTING LINES EAST & WEST / THROUGH THE UNITED STATES / AND CANADA. // MARTIN & HOOD, LITH. 8, GT NEWPORT ST. LONDON
Print (lith) hand col 38 x 73 cm Scale not given
Shows the GWR, the proposed Hamilton and Toronto Railway and proposed Port Sarnia Branch and connecting lines; shows area from Kingston to Michigan and south to Cleveland; OOAMA copy has many other railways added in ms; (Olsen 109).
OOAMA

---

192 *1853*
Map / OF THE / St. Lawrence & Ottawa Grand Junction Railway, / WITH ITS PROPOSED / EXTENSION TO LAKES SIMCOE & HURON / forming the Line of a / CANADA CENTRAL RAILWAY / SHEWING ALSO THE / Connection between Canadian & American Railways, / AND THEIR / RESPECTIVE GAUGES. / 1853.
Print (lith) 40 x 54 cm Approx 1" to 28 miles
In *Reports of the Directors and Chief Engineer of the St. Lawrence and Ottawa Grand Junction Railway Company* (Montreal: Printed by John Lovell 1853), frontis (*Bib Can* 3389), and in French ed (*Bib Can* 3388); shows area from Penetanguishene to Pennsylvania, New York and Boston; gauges of various railways, population of cos; proposed railway runs from the Ottawa R to Kemptville, Peterborough, and Goderich; connecting railways.
OTMCL

---

193 *1853*
Montreal Herald / RAILWAY MAP OF CANADA. / 1853. / G. Matthews' Lithography.
Print (lith) 27 x 73 cm Approx 1" to 28 miles
Shows lines built, those proposed, and connections with the United States; list of railways with miles completed, under construction, and chartered; (Olsen 108).
OOAMA (NMC 51811) OTAR

Later editions and states

(2)
RAILWAY MAP OF CANADA. / 1853.
Adds of co boundaries and a railway line running west from Port Huron, Michigan; (Holmden 3823).
OOAMA (NMC 51812) OTAR OTMCL USMH

---

194 *1853*
ROUTES FROM ALBANY / TO / NIAGARA FALLS, BUFFALO / AND / MONTREAL. // NORTHERN ROUTE. / U.S. MAIL LINE / AND / AMERICAN EXPRESS LINE // ONTARIO & ST LAWRENCE STEAM-BOAT COMPANY'S / STEAMERS / BAY STATE, ONTARIO, NORTHERNER, CATARACT, NIAGARA, LADY OF THE LAKE, / NEW YORK / AND / ROCHESTER
Print (lith) 19 x 27 cm Scale not given
In *The Ontario and St. Lawrence Steamboat Company's Hand-Book for Travelers to Niagara Falls* (Buffalo: Jewett, Thomas & Co. 1853), tipped in at front (*Bib Can* 3299); view of the Niagara Falls; steamer route shown from Prescott via Kingston, Toronto to Lewiston; shows the southern part of Canada West and New York State and Montreal, with railway and canal connections.
OTMCL

---

195 *1854*
Canada Sketch map Shewing the positions of the Military & Naval Reserves agreeably to the request of His Excellency the Lieut. General Commanding dated 12th October 1854 – To accompany the Commanding Royal Engineer's Letter in reply thereto dated Montreal 31st Octr 1854. [Sgd] W.R. Ord Comg R1 Engrs Coll on Staff Montreal 31 Octr 1854. Charles Walkem Surveyor & draftsman 29th Octr 18[54].
Col ms 55 x 128 cm Approx 1" to 18 miles
Endorsements: 'F15'; stamp 'IGF'
Accompanied a letter from W.R. Ord about the ordnance lands that should be retained and those that can be surrendered (OOA RG 8 I/468 p 271); ordnance and naval posts numbered and key is found with letter; shows location of pensioners, railways completed, under construction, or proposed; (Holmden 3794; Olsen 110).
OOAMA (NMC 11746)

---

196 *1854*
CANADA WEST / OR / UPPER CANADA / PUBLISHED BY J.H. COLTON. No 86 CEDAR ST. NEW YORK. / 1854. // Entered according to Act of Congress, in the Year 1853, by J.H. Colton, in the Clerks Office of the District Court of the United States for the Southern District of New York.
Print (lith) hand col 31 x 40 cm 1" to 32 miles
Insets: 'WOLF ISLAND / AT THE COMMENCEMENT OF THE / RIVER ST LAWRENCE.' 1" to 8 miles, 'VICINITY OF THE / WELLAND CANAL / & NIAGARA FALLS:'; shows twps to the base of the Bruce Peninsula and north to a line Bexley, Somerville, Harvey to Palmerston, Brougham to Wilberforce; also shows cos, common roads, canals, villages, co towns; railways shown as completed: Niagara Falls-Windsor, Buffalo-Paris, London-Pt Stanley, Toronto-Guelph-Paris, Toronto-Barrie, Port Hope-Peterborough, Cobourg-Peterborough, Prescott-

Bytown; proposed railways: Barrie-Collingwood, Guelph-Stratford-Sarnia, Paris-Goderich, Stratford-London, London-Sarnia, Kingston-Peterborough-Lindsay-Penetanguishene, Peterborough-Belleville, Hamilton-Toronto-Montreal; decorative scroll-work border; the eds below are grouped first by date and after 1855 by publisher.
USDLC

Later editions and states

(2) *[1854]*
— / PUBLISHED BY J.H. COLTON & Co. No. 172 WILLIAM ST. NEW YORK // Entered ... 1853 by J.H. Colton ...
In *Colton's Atlas of the World* (New York: J.H. Colton and Co. ... Pt 2, entered ... 1854 by J.H. Colton); changes: railways shown completed: Hamilton-Montreal, Beaverton-Lindsay-Peterborough-Belleville, Brockville-Ottawa R, Woodstock-Pt Dover, Niagara Falls-Dunnville-Simcoe; railways proposed: Simcoe-St Thomas-Amherstburg, Stratford-Saugeen; Peterborough-Kingston deleted.
USDLC

(3) *1855*
— NEW YORK. / 1855 // Entered ... 1853 by J.H. Colton.
The map is the same as (2).
OOAMA (NMC 2906)

(4a) *1855*
— [Date removed from title] // Entered according to Act of Congress in the Year 1855 by J.H. Colton in the Clerks Office of the District Court of the United States for the Southern District of New York.
In George W. Colton, *Colton's Atlas of the World* (New York: J.H. Colton and Co.; London: Trübner and Co. 1855), 1: plate [6] (*LC Atlases* 6116); the same as (3).
USDLC

(4b) Copy with the add of 'No. 6' at bottom right, Barrie-Collingwood railway shown completed, railway line from Pt Huron west, and sometimes with 'Clks' instead of 'Clerks' in registration statement; also in *Colton's Atlas of the World* (New York: 1856) (*LC Atlases* 816, OOAMA).
OOAMA USDLC

(4c) In *Colton's Atlas of America* (New York: 1856) (*LC Atlases* 10269); railway line from Pt Huron relocated north to go to La Peer and proposed railway Guelph to Saugeen and Guelph-Sydenham; (OOAMA MacDonald Collection 486).
OOAMA (NMC 105277) USDLC

(4d) Also in G.W. Colton, *Colton's General Atlas* (New York: J.H. Colton & Co.; London: Trübner 1857 and 1858) (*LC Atlases* 6129, 827), and in 1859 ed (OTMCL) with [plate] 'No. 9' added bottom right, road Hamilton-Pt Dover, decorative border replaced by plain border.
OOAMA (NMC 105277) OTMCL USDLC

Maps produced with Johnson imprints after 1855:

(5a) *1855 [1859]*
CANADA WEST / OR / UPPER CANADA / PUBLISHED BY JOHNSON & BROWNING, 172 WILLIAM ST. NEW YORK. // Entered ... 1855 by J.H. Colton ... / No 6.
In *Colton's General Atlas* (New York: J.H. Colton & Co.; Johnson & Browning 1859); railways shown as completed: London-Sarnia, Paris-Goderich; new railways shown in Michigan; proposed railway Collingwood to Sydenham; decorative border.
USDLC

(5b) *1855 [1859?]*
Colton's / CANADA WEST / OR / UPPER CANADA / PUBLISHED BY JOHNSON & BROWNING, ... Entered ... 1855 by J.H. Colton ... No 6
Shows the same information as (5a).
OKQ OOAMA (NMC 16402)

(5c) *[1860]*
JOHNSON'S / UPPER CANADA / BY / JOHNSON & BROWNING.
In A.J. Johnson, *Johnson's New Illustrated ... Family Atlas* (Richmond, Va.: Johnson and Browning, formerly (successors to J.H. Colton and Company) 1860), plate [11a] (*LC Atlases* 6140); the decorative border has been changed and registration statement deleted; information the same as (5a); (OOAMA MacDonald Collection 417, NMC 105725).
OOAMA (NMC 105725) USDLC

(5d) *[1862]*
[Same title as (5c)] // 18.
In *Johnson's ... Family Atlas* (New York: Johnson & Browning 1862), plate 18 (*LC Atlases* 4343, OOAMA); plate no added at lower right and Stratford-Sarnia railway shown as completed; twps added north to Stephenson-McClintock and Richards to Rolph and in the Bruce Peninsula.
OOAMA USDLC

(5e) *[1862]*
— / BY / JOHNSON AND WARD. // 18.
In A.J. Johnson, *Johnson's New Illustrated ... Family Atlas* (New York: Johnson & Ward 1862) (*LC Atlases* 837), and in eds for 1863, 1864, and 1865 (*LC Atlases* 840, 843, and 4345); shows the same information as (5d) except that both of the 1862 eds lack the railway line to La Peer in Michigan shown on earlier and later eds; OOAMA (NMC 16413) has a different border.
OOAMA (NMC 16413, 22591) USDLC

(5f) *[1866]*
— / BY / A.J. JOHNSON, NEW YORK. // 18.
In A.J. Johnson, *Johnson's New Illustrated Family Atlas* (New York: A.J. Johnson 1866) (*LC Atlases* 4346) shows the same information as (5e).

Maps produced with Colton imprints after 1855:

(6a) *[1860]*
Colton's / CANADA WEST / OR / UPPER CANADA / PUBLISHED BY J.H. COLTON / NO. 172 WILLIAM ST, NEW YORK // Entered ... 1855 by J.H. Colton ... // No 6
In J.H. Colton, *Colton's General Atlas* (New York: J.H. Colton 1860) (*LC Atlases* 4342); information the same as (5a) with the add of the Stratford-Sarnia railway shown as completed.
OTAR USDLC

(6b) *1862*
CANADA WEST / OR / UPPER CANADA / PUBLISHED BY J.H. COLTON, ... No. 6
In *Colton's General Atlas* (New York: J.H. Colton 1862); (GBL Maps 40.e.16); twps have been added north to line Stephenson to McClintock and Richards to Rolph and are shown in the Bruce Peninsula; similar to (5d).
GBL

(6c) *[1863]*
— / BY J.H. COLTON – No. 172 WILLIAM ST. NEW YORK // No. 18.
In G.W. Colton, *Colton's General Atlas* (New York: J.H. Colton 1863) (USDLC), and in another ed (New York: J.H. Colton; London: Bacon & Co. 1864) (*LC Atlases* 6148); shows the same information as (6b).
USDLC

(6d) *[1864]*
Colton's / CANADA WEST / OR / UPPER CANADA / PUBLISHED BY J.H. COLTON &c – No 172 WILLIAM ST. NEW YORK // No. 5
In G.W. Colton, *Colton's Atlas of America* (New York: J.W. Colton 1864) (*LC Atlases* 1182, 1386); shows information the same as (6b).
USDLC

---

197 *[1854]*
COLLINS' / Railway & Emigrants Map / OF / CANADA / AND / LOWER PROVINCES OF / BRITISH NORTH AMERICA. // London: H.G. Collins, 22 Paternoster Row.
Print (lith) hand col 38 x 59 cm 1" to 40 miles
Accompanied by 4-p pamphlet, *Emigration to the British North American Colonies Official Parliamentary Papers. (Presented to Both Houses of Parliament by Command of Her Majesty, 1854)* (USDLC); shows twps as of the 1830s north to Colborne-Ellice, Zero-Luther, Eldon-Palmerston; several railways also shown.
OOAMA (NMC 7047) USDLC

---

198 *[1854]*
DISTANCE MAP / of / UPPER CANADA / Compiled from the latest authorities / by Robert W. Stewart McKay. // J. Walker s.
Print (engrav) 14 x 21 cm Scale not given
In Robert Mackay, *The Stranger's Guide to the Cities and Principal Towns of Canada* (Montreal 1854), opp 81 (*Bib Can* 3453); distances are reckoned from Montreal, Kingston, and Toronto proceeding west; shows railways, cos, major towns.
OTMCL

---

199 *[1854]*
[Geological map of part of Canada West and Michigan] Engraved for the Canadian Journal by John Ellis Toronto
Print (lith) with ms adds 33 x 46 cm Approx 1" to 30 miles
Accompanies W.E. Logan, 'On the Physical Structure of the Western District of Upper Canada,' *The Canadian Journal* III, no 1 (Aug 1854): 1–2 (OTUTF); shows twp boundaries, rivers, and a few places; 14 geological groups are shown by the add of ms colouring.
OTUTF

---

200 *1854*
Mail Route Paris to Wilmot thro Canning Richmond Drumbo Washington & Chesterfield for 1 Nov 1854– [and title on back]: No 3 Skeleton Map shewing Mail Routes and Post Offices in Western Division
Col ms 51 x 39 cm Scale not given Watermark: 'MONIERS 1850'
Shows the area from Niagara north to Toronto and Penetanguishene and west to Owen Sound; a part further west of this appears to be missing; shows many more routes than mentioned in the first title; routes are classified in three colours but no key is given; map appears to show main routes, and possibly new routes or extensions of old routes; main centres shown by size; possibly originally part of a set but no other sheets found.
OOAMA (NMC 2901)

---

201 *[1854?]*
MAP / OF THE / GREAT WESTERN RAILWAY / OF / CANADA. / SURVEYED BY MR. JOHNSON. // S. Rutter Lith. Adams Ct. Old Broad St. London.
Print (lith) hand col 35 x 45 cm Scale not given
Shows connections created by the Great Western Ry, which opened for traffic during 1853 and 1854, west to St Louis and east to New York and Boston.
OOAMA (NMC 15678–9)

---

202 *[1854]*
MAP / Shewing the route of the Proposed / SOUTH WESTERN RAILWAY / AND THE RAILWAY SYSTEM / of / SOUTHERN AND WESTERN CANADA. // Lithog'd at the Spectator Office Hamilton
Print (lith) 31 x 92 cm Scale not given
In H.B. Willson, *The Proposed Hamilton and South-Western Railway* (Hamilton: Printed at the Spectator Office 1854) (Casey I–2467); the proposed Hamilton and South Western Ry route goes from Hamilton to Simcoe, Pt Stanley, and Amherstburgh; legend keys other railways in

operation, in course of construction, and proposed.
OOA

---

203 *[1855]*
CARTE / DU / CANADA / G. Matthew's Litho. Montreal // Carte pour servir à l'Intelligence du Canada par J.C. Taché.
Print (lith) 14 x 47 cm Approx 1" to 10 lieues de France
In *Canada at the Universal Exhibition of 1855. Printed by Order of the Legislative Assembly* (Toronto: Printed by John Lovell 1856), after 407 (*Bib Can* 3512), and in *Le Canada et l'Exposition universelle de 1855* (Toronto 1856), after 408 (*Bib Can* 5702), and in J.C. Taché, *Esquisse sur le Canada considéré sous le point de vue economiste* (Paris: Hector Bossange 1855) (*Bib Can* 3613); cos are numbered and are indexed on p [67] of the latter essay, which is also found in the general vols above.
OTMCL

---

204 [1855]
Carte Géologique du CANADA par W.E. Logan // Gravée chez Erhard Schieble, R. Bonaparte 42/ Chromolith Lemercier Paris - Plantrou Lith.
Print (col lith) 13 x 29 cm 1" to 150 miles
In Wm E. Logan, *Esquisse géologique du Canada pour servir a l'intelligence de la carte géologique* (Paris: Hector Bossange 1855) (*Bib Can* 8428); the map (published only in French) and the book (appeared in French and English eds) were prepared for the Universal Exhibition, Paris, 1855; *Bib Can* and other bibliographies report map missing in the octavo version of this work in French and English eds but map did not accompany those eds (see Ferrier, 202; *Bib Can* 3512); shows geological formations in detail from L Superior to Nova Scotia, list of sources; later assigned GSC no 396; (Zaslow, 58–9).
OTMCL

---

205 *[1855]*
A MAP / OF / CANADA ... BY EDWARD STAVELEY ... 1851 ... [with ms adds showing railways]
Print (engrav) with ms adds 49 x 92 cm 1" to 28 miles
Shows railways 'in operation or will be this year (1855)'; proposed lines: Belleville-Peterborough-Penetanguishene, Woodstock-Pt Dover, London-Pt Stanley; printed base map is the same as (**140(5)**).
OOAMA

---

206 *[1855]*
MAP / OF / CANADA / G Matthew's Litho Montreal // Map for the Assistance of the reader of the Essay on Canada by J.C. Taché Esqr.
Print (lith) 14 x 47 cm 1" to 10 French leagues
In *Canada at the Universal Exhibition of 1855* (Toronto: John Lovell 1856), after 407 (OTUTF); also in *Sketch of Canada: Its Industrial Condition and Resources* (Paris: Hector Bossange 1855), [67], with index to cos as in **203** above.
OTUTF

---

207 *1855*
Map / OF CANADA WEST OR / UPPER CANADA / COMPILED FROM THE MOST RECENT AUTHORITIES & SURVEYS. / Showing RAILWAYS completed and in progress to this date. / Canada Company's Office / Toronto 1st July, 1855. // DAY & SON, LITHRS TO THE QUEEN, LONDON.
Print (lith) 43 x 66 cm 1" to 17 miles
List of railways with mileages completed, under construction, and chartered; shows plank and gravel roads, post offices, twps to the base of the Bruce Peninsula and north to line Bexley, Somerville, Harvey to Palmerston, Brougham to Wilberforce, cos; OTAR also has three copies in Canada Co. Map Collection with ms adds showing nos of acres of available lands in various twps; (Olsen 111).
GBLrg OTAR (Canada Co Maps pkg 18 no 206)

---

208 *[1855?]*
MAP / OF THE / BUFFALO, BRANTFORD & GODERICH RAILWAY, / WEST CANADA; / WITH ITS CONNECTIONS. // Royston & Brown 40 Old Broad Street, London.
Print (lith) 23 x 54 cm Scale not given
Inset: 'MAP / OF / LAKES HURON, SUPERIOR / & MICHIGAN, / on a smaller scale'; also shows the Great Western Ry line and connections in New York and Pennsylvania; the name was changed to Buffalo and Lake Huron Railway in 1856 (*Statutory History ... Railways* (1938)).
OTAR

---

209 *1855*
MAP / OF THE / PROVINCE OF CANADA, / AND THE / LOWER COLONIES, / SHEWING THE CONNECTION BY STEAM NAVIGATION WITH / New York, Pennsylvania, Ohio, Indiana, Illinois, Michigan, Wisconsin & Minnesota, / AND WITH EUROPE BY THE ROUTE / OF THE / RIVER ST LAWRENCE AND THE GREAT LAKES, / SHEWING ALSO THE / CONNECTION BY RAILWAYS & CANALS WITH / NEW ENGLAND, MISSISSIPPI & MISSOURI RIVERS, IOWA & NEBRASKA. / Prepared For the / Canadian Commissioners of the Paris Exhibition / BY / Thos C. Keefer, C.E. / Montreal, 1855. / Matthews' Lith Montreal
Print (lith) 63 x 97 cm Scale not given
Inset: 'PROFILE OF ST LAWRENCE RIVER & LAKE NAVIGATION FROM ANTICOSTI TO FOND-DU-LAC, LAC SUPERIOR ...' 1" to 50 miles, 1" to 100 ft vertical; in J.S. Hogan, *Canada: An Essay* (Montreal: B. Dawson; London: Sampson, Low 1855), frontis (OTUTF); also with A. Morris, *Canada and Her Resources* (Montreal:

John Lovell 1855), frontis (OTUTF); shows railways in operation, in progress, and those proposed; canals; major place-names; L Superior to Newfoundland; railway connections in the United States.
OTUTF

---

210 *1855*
New Chart / OF LAKES / MICHIGAN, HURON / and / ST CLAIR, / Compiled from the latest & most reliable Surveys / by / CAPT M. CALDWELL, BUFFALO / 1855.
Print (lith) 51 x 67 cm 1" to 15 miles
Shows area from Detroit R to Sault Ste Marie; courses and direction indicated across lakes.
USDLC

---

211 *1855*
New Map of / BRITISH NORTH AMERICA, / Comprising / UPPER AND LOWER CANADA, / NOVA SCOTIA, NEW BRUNSWICK, / Prince Edward's Island and Cape Breton. // EDINBURGH. / W. & A.K. Johnston, Engravers & Geographers to the Queen. / 1855.
Print (lith) 105 x 126 cm 1" to 14 miles
Sectioned and folding into cover with title: 'JOHNSTONS' / EMIGRATION / MAP / OF / CANADA'; inset: 'NOVA SCOTIA, / NEW BRUNSWICK, / North East part of Canada, / Prince Edwards Island & Cape Breton.' 1" to 25 miles; 'Table of Explanation' keys districts, cos, twps, co towns, towns and villages, railways; a large print wall map; shows twps north to Matchedash, Rama, Carden, Bexley, Somerville, Harvey to Lake, Wicklow to Brudenell, and Fraser to Rolph; twps east of L Nipissing are shown; relief; (Olsen 113?).
OOAMA (NMC 51930) OTUTF

Later editions and states

(2) *1855*
BRITISH NORTH AMERICA, / COMPRISING / UPPER AND LOWER CANADA, / NOVA SCOTIA, NEW BRUNSWICK, / Prince Edward's Island and Cape Breton, / FOR THE USE OF PUBLIC SCHOOLS IN UPPER CANADA. / EDINBURGH, / W. & A.K. Johnston, Engravers & Geographers to the Queen. / 1855 / Public Schools Depository for Upper Canada Educational Department, Toronto.
Print (lith) hand col 104 x 122 cm 1" to 14 miles
One of the three maps referred to in *Journal of Education, Upper Canada* IX, no 3 (1856): 42–3, as commissioned by the Educational Department for use in schools; the map is identical to one above but title has been changed and 'Public Schools Depository ...' statement has been added with coat of arms.
OTAR

(3) *[ca 1862]*
MAP OF / BRITISH NORTH AMERICA, / Comprising / UPPER AND LOWER CANADA, / Nova Scotia, New Brunswick, / British Columbia, / AND THE ISLANDS OF / PRINCE EDWARD, NEWFOUNDLAND / AND / VANCOUVER. / Prepared under the Supervision of the Educational Department / FOR THE USE OF THE / PUBLIC SCHOOLS OF UPPER CANADA. / W.C. CHEWETT & CO. LITH. TORONTO.
Print (lith) 107 x 229 cm Approx 1" to 14 miles
Insets: 'Map of the Southern Part / OF / BRITISH NORTH AMERICA / FROM / Lake Superior to the Pacific Ocean,' [Map of North America and connections with Europe], Island of Newfoundland; the map has been extended to the east; twps have been added north to line from Stephenson to Richards, Wallbridge to Balaklava and Robinson, along the Magnetawan R, and along the north shore of L Huron; colonization roads; railways added: Hamilton-Toronto, London-Sarnia; Toronto-Peterborough-Belleville-Kingston Ry deleted; shows Biddulph and McGillivray twps as part of Middlesex Co (1862); (Olsen 114).
OOAMA (NMC 21864)

---

212 *[1855]*
OUTLINE MAP OF / UPPER CANADA / Showing the proposed / METEOROLOGICAL STATIONS / in connexion with the / GRAMMAR SCHOOLS / To illustrate Mr Hodgins' paper, read 26th January 1856. [i.e., 1855] / before the Canadian Institute. // Maclear & Co Lith. Toronto.
Print (lith) 41 x 54 cm Scale not given
Accompanies J.G. Hodgins, 'Memorandum on the Steps which have been Taken by the Educational Department to Establish a System of Meteorological Observation throughout Upper Canada,' *Canadian Journal* III, no 17 (Dec 1855): opp 407 (OTUTF); 'Read before the Canadian Institute, January 1855'; shows proposed chief stations in senior grammar schools and others in junior grammar schools; proposed grammar schools also shown.
OTMCL OTUTF

---

213 *1855*
Skeleton Map / SHEWING THE POSITION OF / THE GREAT SOUTH WESTERN / RAILWAY OF CANADA, / AND ITS CONNECTION / WITH OTHER LINES.
Print (lith) 28 x 74 cm Scale not given
In *Great Southwestern Railway of Canada Extract from a Report Made in 1855. W. Wallace C.E.*, at back (OOA Pamph 1855(42)); shows the proposed railway from Niagara Falls and Ft Erie to Dunnville, Simcoe, St Thomas, Amherstburg and Windsor; GTR, GWR, Buffalo and L Huron Railway and other connecting lines shown from L Michigan to Boston.
OOA

---

214 *[ca 1855]*
[Sketch map of Upper Canada showing ports and water routes from the Great Lakes to the Atlantic]
Col ms 44 x 56 cm Scale not given Watermark: 'J WHATMAN ... 1852'
Notes indicate distance and desirability of various routes; route from Upper Lakes via a canal from Georgian Bay to the Ottawa R 'is 540 miles and is the communication wanted.'
OOAMA (NMC 2886)

---

215 *[1856?]*
CANADA / MAP of / BROCKVILLE & OTTAWA RAILWAY // Baily Bros Royal Exchange E.C.
Print (lith) 31 x 38 cm Approx 1" to 23 miles
Shows area from Toronto to Montreal and north to Pembroke; proposed extension of Ottawa and Brockville Ry to Georgian Bay shown probably as part of proposal for line from L Huron to Quebec (1856) (*Statutory History ... Railways* (1938)); Prescott and Ottawa Ry shown and other connecting lines; OTMCL copy lacks imprint.
OTAR OTMCL

---

216 *[1856]*
CANADA. / WEST SHEET. // Printed in Colours by Schenck & Macfarlane, Edinburgh. // Published by A. & C. Black, Edinburgh. // Drawn & Engraved by J. Bartholomew, Edinburgh. // 3.
Print (col lith) 56 x 42 cm 1" to 38 miles
Inset: 'ENVIRONS OF / MONTREAL' 1" to 15 miles; found separately and in *Black's Atlas of North America* (Edinburgh: Adam and Charles Black 1856), plate 3 (*LC Atlases* 1385; OOAMA); also in Black's *General Atlas of the World*, new ed (Edinburgh 1859), plate XLVI (GBL Maps 53.f.12); twps shown to the base of the Bruce Peninsula and north to a line from Harvey to Palmerston; railways shown: Toronto-Guelph, Toronto-Barrie, Niagara Falls-Windsor, London-Pt Stanley, Woodstock-Pt Dover and connection to Niagara Falls, Brockville-Ottawa R, Prescott-Ottawa, Belleville-Peterborough-Beaverton; Buffalo-Paris.
GBL OOAMA (NMC 7040) USDLC

Later editions and states

(2) *[1856?]*
— [Mounted with] CANADA, / NEW BRUNSWICK, NOVA SCOTIA &c. / EAST SHEET. / ... // [pasted on sheet in place of publishing statement] BY G. CRUCHLEY, MAP SELLER & PUBLISHER, 81 FLEET STREET from 38 LUDGATE STT. LONDON ...
56 x 83 cm
The same as [1856].
OOAMA (NMC 48945)

(3) *[1860]*
— / [Below bottom margin at left]: // Drawn & Engraved by [at right]: J. Bartholomew, Edinburgh. / [at centre]: Published by A. & C. Black, Edinburgh. Printed in Colours by Fr. Schenck Edinburgh. // WEST SHEET. 42.
In J. Bartholomew, *Black's General Atlas of the World* (Edinburgh: A. & C. Black 1860), plate 42 (*LC Atlases* 829); adds of railways: Paris-Goderich, London-Sarnia, Stratford-Sarnia, Barrie-Collingwood; L Nipissing has been redrawn and lakes and rivers added in the area.
USDLC

(4a) *[ca 1860?]*
CANADA, / NEW BRUNSWICK, NOVA SCOTIA &c. / B. DAWSON & SON, MONTREAL. // Printed by W.S. McFarlane, Lithogr Edinburgh // Drawn & Engraved by J. Bartholomew, Edinburgh
Print (lith) hand col 54 x 80 cm 1" to 40 miles
Combines east and west sheet of earlier map; inset added: 'NEWFOUNDLAND'; shows the same information and possibly a lithographic transfer of (3); (Olsen 118).
OOAMA (NMC 44426)

(4b) *[186?]*
— B. DAWSON & SON, MONTREAL. // Drawn & Engraved by // J. Bartholomew, Edinburgh.
Inset added: 'UNITED STATES / & CANADA.'; otherwise, shows same information as (4a).
OOAMA (NMC 8926)

(5a) *[1865]*
CANADA / AND NORTHERN / UNITED STATES / BY J. BARTHOLOMEW F.R.G.S. / [below bottom margin at left]: // Engraved & Printed in Colours by [at right]: J. Bartholomew Edinburgh. [at centre]: Published by A. & C. Black, Edinburgh // WEST SHEET. 42.
In *Black's General Atlas of the World*, new ed (Edinburgh: Adam and Charles Black 1865) (GBL (Maps 39.e.22); OOAMA); proposed railways added to legend; twps extended into the Bruce Peninsula and north to line Stephenson-Fraser and east of L Nipissing.
GBL OOAMA

(5b) *1867*
NEW MAP / OF / CANADA, / NEW BRUNSWICK, NOVA SCOTIA / DAWSON BROTHERS, MONTREAL. / 1867 // Engraved & Printed by // J. Bartholomew, Edinburgh.
Inset for U.S. and Canada deleted; shows the same new twps as [1865] map and possibly a lithographic transfer.
OOAMA (NMC 24961)

---

217 *[1856?]*
MAP / OF / BUFFALO & LAKE HURON / RAILWAY / AND CONNECTIONS. / MACLURE & MACDONALD, LITHRS. 20 ST VINCENT PLACE, GLASGOW.
Print (lith) 27 x 45 cm Approx 1" to 73 miles
Shows the location of the railway and the main connections in Upper Canada and northern United States; GWR, GTR, and connection to Detroit shown; the railway changed its name to this form in 1856 and was fully opened in 1858.
OTAR

---

218 *1856*
MAP OF / CANADA / SHEWING THE / Railway's / COMPLETED IN PROGRESS AND PROJECTED / to Accompany the / CANADA / RAILWAY AND STEAM-BOAT / GUIDE. / TORONTO / Published for the Proprietor / BY / MACLEAR & CO. / 1856 // Maclear & Co. Liths Toronto C.W.
Print (lith) 45 x 67 cm Scale not given
Found separately and in *The Canada (Monthly) General Railway and Steam Navigation Guide ... No 2, 1st July 1856* (Toronto: Maclear & Co. 1856), frontis (*Bib Can* 3648); covers the area east to Quebec and connections with the United States; shows towns, villages, and railways projected: Galt to Saugeen, London-Sarnia, Port Dover-St Thomas-Amherstburg, Lake Huron, Pembroke, and Quebec Junction railway.
OOAMA (NMC 21384) OTMCL

---

219 *1856*
MAP / of part of / CANADA WEST / SHEWING THE LINES OF RAILWAY IN CONNECTIONS WITH THE / UNITED STATES / 1856. Drawn by Charles L. Beard. H.Gregory Lith. Hamilton
Print (col lith) 46 x 67 cm 1" to 14 miles
Shows railways completed and in progress in the southwestern part of the province; one OOAMA copy (NMC 21385) has ms adds showing the proposed line of the Great South Western Ry [incorporated 1858?] from Niagara Falls to Windsor with four alternate lines for parts including No 1 under the 'old charter,' and also a 'loop line,' 'projected in the Great Western Railway Office which scheme was taken home by Mr Brydges on his late visit to England'; it also has the printed add of the Lake Erie, Wabash, and St Louis Ry; north arrow moved to left, legend moved to upper right, and coat of arms added above; OOAMA (NMC 109693) shows add of London and St Mary's ry to Southampton.
OOAMA OOAMA (NMC 21385, 109693)

Later editions and states

(2) *1856*
Map / of the railway system of part of / CANADA WEST / SHEWING THE EASTERN AND WESTERN CONNECTIONS WITH THE / UNITED STATES / prepared for the / HAMILTON & PORT DOVER RAILWAY COMPANY / 1856. / H. Gregory Lith, Hamilton C.W. // Drawn by Charles L. Beard
Print (col lith) 28 x 66 cm 1" to 14 miles
In Hamilton and Port Dover Railway, *Report* (Hamilton: 1856), at back (OOA Pamph 1856(1)); derived from the bottom part of same plate as map above; adds of some railways and changes to shoreline; OOA copy shows Great Southwestern Ry in ms.
OOA OOAMA

---

220 *1856*
Map of the / GREAT WESTERN RAILWAY OF CANADA, / AND ITS CONNECTION WITH / RAILWAYS IN CANADA & THE UNITED STATES OF AMERICA. / 1856. // Martin & Hood lith. 8 Gt. Newport St. London
Print (lith) 45 x 76 cm Approx 1" to 17 miles
Shows the GWR and the Sarnia branch, railways completed and in course of construction; a few place-names; shows part of the United States south and west.
OTAR

---

221 *[1856]*
SKELETON MAP / SHEWING THE POSITION OF THE PROPOSED / TORONTO AND GEORGIAN BAY CANAL / WITH REFERENCE TO THE TRADE OF THE GREAT WEST / WITH THE ATLANTIC PORTS, MONTREAL / QUEBEC, BOSTON, NEW YORK PORTLAND / &c. &c. / Prepared by M.P. Hayes for the Committee.
Print (lith) 17 x 50 cm Scale not given
In *Report of the Toronto Board of Trade ... and Report on the Toronto & Georgian Bay Canal* (Toronto: Thompson & Co. Printers 1856), frontis (*Bib Can* 3614); depicts area from St Paul to Boston; shows statistics on trade at Chicago, distances between points, canal proposed between Georgian Bay and L Simcoe and between L Simcoe and the Humber R mouth, new canal at Sault Ste Marie; see **396**.
OTMCL

---

222 *[1856]*
[Sketch of the St Lawrence River and eastern Great Lakes showing canals, railways, population of cities, and location of building yards] [Sgd] [J?] Taylor Master R.N.
Col ms 72 x 107 cm Approx 1" to 20 miles
Shows Welland, Rideau, and Cornwall canals; 'finished railroads useful for transferring stores': Hamilton-Sandwich, Toronto-Collingwood; Toronto-Kingston-Brockville railways shown as unfinished; note that 'population of Toronto at least 20,000 less than 60,000 shown, S.E.H.'; dated from listing in GBTAUh catalogue.
GBTAUh (D2212 Aa3)

---

223 *[1856?]*
SKETCH / Shewing the position of / THE HAMILTON & TORONTO RAILWAY / IN THE GRAND TRUNK LINE OF CANADA / And its connection with other Lines / IN THE UNITED STATES. // Martin & Hood, lith. 8, Gt Newport St London
Print (lith) 34 x 38 cm Scale not given
Shows northeastern North America with the GTR and GWR lines and connections to the east, west, and south; branch to Port Sarnia shown; the Hamilton and Toronto Railway Co. was incorporated in 1852 and opened in 1856 (Trout and Trout, 97).
OOAMA OTAR

---

224 *1857*
Canada and Adjacent Provinces Shewing the Central Position of the City of Ottawa Compiled for the City Council by W.A. Austin P.L.S. & C.E.
Col ms 64 x 127 cm 1" to 47 miles Endorsements: '454' '323' '5646–1857 (from the Mayor of Ottawa)' 'Duplicate'
Originally accompanied a memorial from the City of Ottawa to the Queen requesting that Ottawa be made the capital (GBLpro CO 42/611 f 328); shows eastern Canada and part of New England with present and proposed railway connections to Ottawa, 'Proposed Huron and Ottawa Canal,' table of distances; shows natural resources, particularly timber and copper mining to the north and west and 'Interior Fertile Tract of 41/2 millions of Acres'; (*PRO Cat* 218); there is also another map accompanying a memorandum of 18 May 1857 about the selection of Ottawa as capital in (GBLpro CO 880/1 f 317 (*PRO Cat* 219).
GBLpro (MR 404 (3); MPGG 71 (2))

Related maps

(2) *1857*
MAP / Shewing the extent of the Connections Formed by the / RAILWAY / UNITING / LAKES ERIE AND ONTARIO. / Maclear & Co. Liths. Toronto C.W.
Print (lith) Size not known Scale not known
Inset: 'Map / SHOWING WELLAND RAILWAY / with adjoining Country and local connections'; accompanied a memorandum by Sir F.B. Head on the reasons why Toronto should be selected as capital 18 Oct 1857 (GBLpro CO 42/612/398); map shows area from St Paul to Minnesota and Philadelphia north; the inset is trimmed and only a small part of the Welland railway at the north end is shown.
GBLpro (CO 42/612 p 398)

---

225 *[1857]*
CANADA / AND / LOWER PROVINCES OF BRITISH AMERICA // LITHD ADAMS & GEE / MIDDLE STREET WEST SMITHFIELD
Print (lith) Size not known Scale not given
In *Report of Mr Charles Hutton Gregory C.E. ... upon the Works of the Grand Trunk Railway Company of Canada* (London: Waterlow and Sons 1857), at end (QMBN, CIHM 45460); shows area from L Superior to Halifax and various railway connections in Canada West including 'Montreal & Toronto' and 'Toronto & Sarnia.'
QMBN

---

226 *1857*
CANADA, / NOVA SCOTIA & NEW BRUNSWICK &c. // Charles Magnus / IMPORTER AND PUBLISHER / AMERICAN & EUROPEAN / PRINTING ESTABLISHMENT. / No 12 Frankfort Str. NEW YORK.
Print (lith) 66 x 75 cm 1" to 50 miles
Inset: 'NEW MAP / OF / UPPER CANADA / 1857 Engraved by Chas. Nolte' 1" to 23 miles; nine pictorial views including 'VIEW FROM BELOW TABLE ROCK' and 'NIAGARA FALLS UNITED STATES & CANADA' and four views of cities: Toronto, Hamilton, Montreal, Quebec; inset map is based on Maclear map **185(6)**, but includes a railway from Fort Erie to Simcoe-St Thomas and proposed from there to Amherstburg, and there are changes in the legend; twps to base of Bruce Peninsula and from Harvey to Palmerston.
OOAMA (NMC 44427) USNIC

---

227 *[1857]*
CANADA / WEST
Print (wax engrav) 13 x 16 cm Approx 1" to 70 miles
In C.G. Colby, *The Diamond Atlas ... The Western Hemisphere* (New York: S.N. Gaston 1857), after 44 (*LC Atlases* 1180), and in another ed (New York: Morse & Gaston 1857) (*LC Atlases* 4338), and in C.G. Colby, *The World in Miniature ... The Western Hemisphere* (New Orleans: A.B. Griswold 1857), after 44 (*LC Atlases* 820), and in a later ed (New Orleans: Bloomfield & Steel 1861) (*LC Atlases* 1181); cos and twps are indexed on the page opp the map; shows railways, proposed railways, canals.
USDLC

---

228 *[1857]*
DIAGRAM / SHEWING THE PROPOSED ROUTE / OF THE / TORONTO & OWEN SOUND / Central Railway. // LITHOGRAPHED BY J. ELLIS 8 KING ST TORONTO. C.W.
Print (lith) 61 x 47 cm Approx 1" to 8.5 miles
In Kivas Tully, *Engineer's Report in Reply to the Communication from the Mayor of Owen Sound ... on the Proposed Toronto and Owen Sound Central Railway Route* (Toronto: Thompson & Co. 1857) (*Bib Can* 5778; Casey I–2650); shows the area approx from Toronto to L Huron and Owen Sound; shows twps, places, the proposed Northwest Railway from Hamilton to Southampton, also branch lines from the Toronto and Owen Sound Ry to Southampton and Penetangore [Kincardine].
OOA OTMCL

---

229 *1857*
THE GRAND TRUNK RAILWAY OF CANADA. / 1857. // Litho. Waterlow & Sons, London.
Print (lith) 37 x 61 cm Scale not given
Printed on back of broadside: *Grand Trunk Railway of Canada ... Tariff of Passenger Rates ... Free Grants of Land ... Fully Described in the Canadian News Published in London of Feb 4th 1857 and Their Site is Marked on the Map of the Railways of Canada Issued as a Supplement to that Publication*; shows Grand Trunk in Canada East and West and connections with the United States; list of 'Principal Stations on Grand Trunk line'; also a copy 'In Mr Kernaghan's July 7/59 6322/59' (GBLpro CO 42/611 f 163); (Olsen map 80?; *PRO Cat* 222).
GBLpro (MR 404(1)) OTMCL

Later editions and states

(2) *1857*
— [Title same]
The same map without text on back in *Letter of a Canadian Merchant on the Prospects of British Shipping in Connection with the Grand Trunk Railway of Canada* (London 1858), frontis (Casey I-2716).
OOA

(3) *1857*
— [Added above top margin]: // ISSUED AS A SUPPLEMENT TO THE CANADIAN NEWS ... // Published at No. 11 Clements Lane Lombard Street, London, ...
Print (col lith) 40 x 62 cm
Without text on back; a note on the 'site of the Canadian Government free grants of land' is printed in red across the top of the sheet; information same as on (1) and (2).
OTAR

---

230 *[1857]*
THE / HARBOURS AND PORTS / OF / LAKE ONTARIO, / IN A SERIES OF CHARTS / ACCOMPANIED BY A DESCRIPTION OF EACH ... / BY EDWARD M. HODDER M.D. / COMMODORE OF THE ROYAL CANADIAN YACHT CLUB / TORONTO: / MACLEAR & CO., 16 KING STREET EAST / 1857.
20 maps on 16 prints (liths) in 30 p book Sizes vary Scales not given
Title from title-p of book (*Bib Can* 3737); maps for Ontario are as follows: 'TORONTO HARBOUR,' 'LIVERPOOL / or PICKERING HARBOUR [and] PORT OF OSHAWA,' 'WHITBY HARBOUR,' 'Port Darlington,' 'PORT HOPE [and] COBOURG HARBOUR,' 'PRESQUE'ISLE / HARBOUR,' 'KINGSTON HARBOUR,' 'MOUTH / of / Niagara River,' 'PORT DALHOUSIE,' 'BURLINGTON CANAL [and] PORT of OAKVILLE,' 'Plan / of intended / Harbour of Refuge / and Docks at / Port Britain / Township of Hope Canada West 1857'; each plan shows soundings, wharves, piers, lighthouses; note indicates plans are compiled from 'The charts of Capt Owen and Lieut Herbert' as well as personal observations.
OTMCL

---

231 *1857*
LAKE ONTARIO, / AND THE / Surrounding Country, Showing all the great / ROUTES OF TRAVEL &c. New York Published by J. Disturnell MDCCCLVII // J DISTURNELL, Publisher and Dealer in MAPS, GUIDE BOOKS etc.
Print (lith) 9 x 15 cm Scale not given
In *The Picturesque Tourist* (New York: J. Disturnell 1858), opp 126 (*Bib Can* 5821); view: 'NIAGARA From below TABLE ROCK'; shows road and railway routes around L Ontario, in the Niagara Peninsula, and north to L Simcoe.
OTMCL

---

232 *1857*
MAP AND PROFILE / OF THE VALLEY OF THE ST LAWRENCE RIVER & LAKE COUNTRY EXTENDING FROM LAKE SUPERIOR TO THE GULF OF ST LAWRENCE. // NEW YORK, / Published by / J. DISTURNELL, / 1857.
Print (lith) 48 x 76 cm Approx 1" to 65 miles
In *A Trip through the Lakes of North America* (New York: J. Disturnell 1857) (*Bib Can* 3720; Dionne 977); inset: 'PROFILE OF St LAWRENCE RIVER & LAKE NAVIGATION FROM QUEBEC TO FOND DU LAC, LAKE SUPERIOR 1650 miles' 1" to 60 miles, 1" to 200 ft vertical; shows canals, railways, telegraph lines, steamboat lines, stage routes.
OTMCL USMiU

---

233 *[1857?]*
A MAP / OF / CANADA / COMPILED FROM THE LATEST AUTHORITIES / FOR / THE GRAND TRUNK RAILWAY / OF / CANADA.
Print (lith) hand col 49 x 92 cm 1" to 28 miles
Shows the GTR line and connecting lines built and in course of construction; the map is from the same plate as **140(6)** with the following changes in railways: Pt Hope-Lindsay, Cobourg-Peterborough, Buffalo-Goderich are shown as completed; Stratford-London, Woodstock-Pt Dover, and Brockville-Smith Falls, under construction; (Olsen map 76?).
OTAR

---

234 *1857*
MAP / OF THE / GRAND TRUNK RAILWAY / OF / CANADA, / Showing its Connections with / RAILWAYS / IN THE UNITED STATES. // ENGRAVED BY J.W. ORR N.Y.
Print (wood engrav) 16 x 30 cm 1" to 150 miles
On broadside: *Tariff of Passenger Rates via the Grand Trunk Railway of Canada ... January 1857. Clapp Matthews & Co's Steam Printing House Buffalo.* (OOA Pamph 1857 (2)); shows Canada and the northeastern U.S. with railways in operation and in progress.
OOA (Pamph 1857 (2))

---

235 *[1857]*
MAP / OF THE / PROVINCE OF CANADA / FROM / Lake Superior to the Gulf of St. Lawrence / CORRECTED FROM INFORMATION OBTAINED BY THE / GEOLOGICAL SURVEY UNDER THE DIRECTION OF / SIR W.E. LOGAN / AND / PREPARED FOR THE CANADA DIRECTORY / Thos. C. Keefer C.E. MONTREAL / ROBERT BARLOW / Draughtsman. / Geo. Matthews Litho. Montreal.
Print (lith) sometimes hand col 57 x 86 cm 1" to 25 miles
Issued separately and in *The Canada Directory for 1857–58* (Montreal: John Lovell 1857), at end of vol 2 (OOA), and in F.X. Garneau, *History of Canada* 2nd ed rev (Montreal: Printed and published by John Lovell 1862), 1: frontis (*Bib Can* 2459; Dionne

994); shows railways completed, in progress, and projected; twps north to line Draper, Macaulay, Bexley to Anstruther, Wollaston north to Airy, Murchison, Bangor to Brudenell, Algona to Rolph; colonization roads; a printed flyer entitled 'References to Map' found at beginning of vol I of *The Canada Directory* lists sources: Bayfield's charts, surveys of rivers in the Huron-Ottawa area by Sir W.E. Logan (1857) (**622**), and 'the remainder from Bouchette [see **152**] & other authorities'; also noted: 'The MAP ... may be had ... at ... Publisher Price 75c. mounted $1.50'; described as 'An entirely new map of Upper and Lower Canada ...' in a prospectus for *The Canada Directory for 1857–58* issued in Feb 1857 (*Bib Can* 8542); (Olsen 115).
GBL (70615 (22)) OLU OMSA OOA OOAMA (NMC 24953) OTAR OTMCL OTUTF USDLC

---

236 *1857*
MAP OF UPPER CANADA / Shewing the Proposed / LAND AGENCY DIVISIONS. / G. Matthews Lith. Montreal. // Crown Lands Office Toronto 30th March 1857. / [Sgd in print] Joseph Cauchon Commissioner of Crown Lands
Print (lith) 79 x 98 cm 1" to 14 miles
In *Appendix to Report of the Commissioner of Crown Lands, 1856*, Part II *Maps of Canada* (Toronto: Printed by Stewart Derbishire & George DesBarats 1857) (OOAMA, OTAR); four divisions proposed; co boundaries and twps also shown; 'Note. This Map which is designed chiefly to shew the Agency Divisions is not a recent compilation; details will be more accurately shown in the map mentioned in the accompanying Report which is being prepared from the latest surveys–'; refers to **253**; (Holmden 2787, 2788; Olsen 119; OOAMA MacDonald Collection 490).
OOAMA (NMC 48922) OTAR OTMCL USDLC

---

237 *[1857]*
[Panoramic view from Niagara Falls to Quebec] DRAWN BY ALFRED R. WARD / BOSTON, U.S. // ENGD. BY JOHN ANDREW. / BOSTON U.S.
Print (lith) 300 x 18 cm Scale not given
In Wm Hunter, *Hunter's Panoramic Guide from Niagara Falls to Quebec* (Boston: J.P. Jewett & Co. 1857), frontis (*Bib Can* 3664); includes bird's-eye views of towns, scenery, falls, roads; railways shown; connecting routes to other places noted; pictures of people, ships, etc; the preface is dated 'Stanstead, C.E. Oct 25, 1856'; also in *Hunter's Panoramic Guide from Niagara Falls to Quebec* (Montreal: Hunter & Pickup, John Lovell 1860), frontis (*Bib Can* 3665, part of map missing); also in Hunter and Pickup's *Panoramic Guide from Niagara Falls to Québec* (Montreal 1866), at end (Casey I–3387).
OOA OTMCL

---

238 *[1857?]*
Plan shewing the Naval Reserves
Col ms 61 x 93 cm Scale not given Endorsements: 'Recd 13 May 1857'; stamp 'Hydrographic Office'
Reserves and acreages are given for Kingston, Penetanguishene, Grand R, Isle aux Noix, and Montreal.
GBTAUh (D2596 Aa3)

---

239 *[1857]*
RAILWAY RIDE FROM ... BARR & CORSS'S / RAILWAY RIDE / FROM / ... shewing all the Stations & Distances from ... / PUBLISHED BY BARR & CORSS, ENGRAVERS / AND LITHOGRAPHERS, / LATE CROWN LANDS OFFICE, 46 1/2 YONGE ST. TORONTO.
Print (lith) 59 x 85 cm Scale not given
Endorsements: in ms 'Barr & Corss's Railway Ride through Canada. Entered according to the act of the Provincial Legislature in the year 1857 by Messrs Barr & Corss Engravers & Lithographers in the Office of the Registrar of the Province of Canada'
Seven route maps on panels ea 58 x 11 cm, with the same title and imprint except for the different route names, and each repeated twice on the panels as follows: '... TORONTO TO HAMILTON,' '... SUSPEN. BRIDGE TO LONDON,' '... LONDON TO WINDSOR,' '... TORONTO TO COLLINGWOOD,' '... TORONTO TO STRATFORD,' '... TORONTO TO KINGSTON,' and '... KINGSTON TO MONTREAL'; the distances are shown on each panel from Toronto, Suspension Bridge, or Hamilton; each route map has a view of a train and a note: 'Advertisements Half Dollar Per month...'; distances between stations along line shown; the map was advertised for sale 'may be had separate ... or the whole in one sheet' in the *Daily Colonist* (Toronto) 22 Sept 1857.
OOAMA (NMC 24952)

---

240 *[1857]*
Sketch of part of Canada West to Accompany Preliminary Report / on the projected Northwest or Saugeen Railway. / by Sandford Fleming Engineer. / Maclear & Co Lith. Toronto.
Print (col lith) 33 x 18 cm Scale not given
In S. Fleming, *Preliminary Report on the Projected Northwest Railway of Canada* (Toronto: Blackburn's City Steam Press 1857), frontis (*Bib Can* 3722, Casey I–2628); shows the area from Toronto and Hamilton to the Bruce Peninsula; 'The coloured portion shows the extent of Country whose trade may be considered tributary to the North-West Railway ...'; proposed route is not shown but coloured area extends from Guelph to Huron Twp and Owen Sound.
OOA OTMCL

---

241 *1857*
UPPER OR WESTERN / AND / LOWER OR EASTERN / CANADA. / BY PROF. H.D. ROGERS & A. KEITH JOHNSTON F.R.S.E. // Entered in Sta. Hall London & according to act of Congress in the Year 1857 by H.D. Rogers in the Clerk's Office of the

District Court of Massachusetts. // London, John Murray, Albemarle Street, Edinburgh W. & A.K. Johnston. // Engraved by W. & A.K. Johnston, Edinburgh. // ATLAS OF UNITED STATES &c. // 4.
Print (lith) hand col 34 x 43 cm 1" to 54.5 miles
In H.D. Rogers and A.K. Johnston, *Atlas of the United States of North America, Canada, New Brunswick* (London: Edward Stanford [1857]) (*LC Atlases* 3670; OOAMA); co boundaries, railways, places; (Dionne 976).
OOAMA USDLC

---

242 *1858*
CHART OF / LAKE SUPERIOR / COMPILED FROM THE / United States & English Government Surys / BY / Parkinson & Smith Civil Engineers / BUFFALO. / 1858. / Lith. by H. Gerlach, 204 Washington St. Buffalo N.Y. Printed at Sage & Sons Lith. Establishment, Buffalo N.Y. Entered according to Act of Congress A.D. 1858 by Parkinson & Smith in the Clerks Office of the Northern District of New York
Print (lith) 69 x 126 cm 1" to 8 miles
Note certifying the plan as correct and sgd by ships' captains experienced in navigating L Superior 'Cleveland March 24, 1858'; shows soundings along shore, nature of shoreline, shoals, lighthouses, comments on land; (Karpinski 830).
USDLC

---

243 *1858*
CITY OF / HAMILTON, C.W. / ITS POSITION AND CONNECTIONS / BY RAIL AND WATER / 1858 / MATTHEWS LITH MONTREAL
Print (lith) 22 x 34 cm Scale not given
Pasted on back of broadside: *Hamilton, Canada West, January, 1859 An Association for Scientific and Literary Purposes Has Recently Been Formed in This City ... Thos. C. Keefer, Corresponding Secretary.* (OOAMA, USDLC); shows the area from the Great Lakes to New Brunswick and south to Washington; railways and major places.
OOAMA USDLC

---

244 *1858*
GRAND TRUNK RAILWAY OF CANADA WITH ITS BRANCHES & CONNECTIONS; [and] CENTRAL POSITION OF TORONTO IN CANADA // Barr & Corss Litho. Toronto
2 prints (liths) Ea 11 x 17 cm Scale not given
In Toronto City Council, *Toronto: The Grounds upon Which Are Based Her Claims to Be the Seat of Government of Canada* (Toronto: Thompson & Co. printers 1858), opp 21 and 27, respectively (*Bib Can* 3861); the maps are almost identical except that the first one includes a railway line up the Ottawa R, the Grand Trunk route is shown with a heavier line, and the provinces are named Upper and Lower Canada rather than 'Province of Canada' as on the second map.
OTMCL

---

245 *1858*
MAP / OF / CANADA WEST, / SHEWING THE / POST OFFICES & MAIL ROUTES. / Prepared by Order of the Post Master General. / 1858. / LITHOGRAPHED BY BARR & CORSS. / TORONTO. // H.F. Hayward, Del.
Print (col lith) 112 x 172 cm 1" to 6.6 miles
Names of twps printed in red; shows towns and postal routes between post offices, but no legend; (Holmden 2789; Olsen 120).
OOAMA (NMC 48612) OTMCL USDLC

Later editions and states

(2) *1860*
— Prepared by Order of the Post Master General. / BY / JOHN DEWE, / Post Office Inspector. / 1860. // Printed by Maclear & Co. Toronto.
The following has been added and keyed in a legend: co towns, money order offices, telegraph stations, railway stations; postal routes have been revised and extended; (Holmden 2790; Olsen 121).
GBL (70642(10)) OOAMA (NMC 21065) USDLC

(3) *[1858?]*
MAP / OF / CANADA WEST, / SHEWING THE / POST OFFICES ... 1858 ... [with ms adds showing the electoral divisions]
Print (lith) with ms adds 111 x 168 cm 1" to 6.6 miles
The printed map is the same as **245(1)** with the addition of electoral divisions and possibly proposed new divisions.
OTAR

---

246 *1858*
KARTE / von / CANADA / mit besonderer Rücksicht auf / die angesiedelten und der Ansiedelung erschlossenen Theile / nach dem neusten Material. / Berlin, Verlag der Nicolaischen Buchhandlung, / 1858. // Lith. Anst.v. Leopold Kraatz in Berlin.
Print (lith) 32 x 51 cm ca 1" to 60 miles
In *Canada, Eine Darstellung ... Nebst einer Karte von Canada* (Berlin: Verlag der Nicolaischen Buchhandlung, 1858) frontis). (*Bib Can* 8643); a roughly drawn map of the area from L Superior to New Brunswick; shows major places in English with many misspelled or inaccurate; railways shown fairly accurately but including a projected railway from Ottawa to Sault Ste Marie parallel to the Opeongo Rd and projected to Vancouver; 'Eisen Wke' marked near Hastings.
OTMCL

---

247 *1858*
[Map of the Great Western Railway from Toronto and Niagara Falls to Windsor]
Print (lith) in 3 sheets 16 x 61 cm, 23 x 63 cm, and 16 x 63 cm Scale not given
In Great Western Railway, *Rules and Regulations* (Hamilton: John Harris 1858), frontis (*Bib Can* 3817); sheet 1: 'TORONTO BRANCH' and 'MAIN

'MAIN LINE' [from Desjardins Junction to Longwood]; sheet 3: 'MAIN LINE' [from Glencoe to Windsor]; each sheet includes two profiles for part of line, with mileages.
OTMCL

248 *[1858]*
MAP OF UPPER CANADA / Shewing the Proposed / LAND AGENCY DIVISION [with ms adds showing administrative boundary changes]
Print (lith) with ms adds 74 x 98 cm 1" to 14 miles
Boundary of temporary judicial districts of Nipissing and Algoma shown (20 Vict, cap 60, 1857 [1858]); several twps are shown as attached to the north parts of Victoria, Peterborough, and Hastings cos by 22 Vict cap 14 [1858]; the printed base is the same as **236**.
OOAMA (NMC 14099)

249 *1858*
MAP / showing the / NIAGARA & DETROIT RIVERS RAILWAY / AND ITS CONNECTION WITH THE / RAILWAYS OF CANADA / and the / UNITED STATES OF AMERICA. / JAMES C. STREET, CHIEF ENGINEER. / 1858 / Drawn by Charles L. Beard H. Gregory Lith: Hamilton, C.W.
Print (lith) 88 x 205 cm 1" to 25 miles
Shows area from Nova Scotia to the Great Lakes and south to Washington; note refers to the line of railway as 'projected but not built'; also shows GTR, GWR, Buffalo & Lake Huron, Ontario Simcoe & Huron Railroad, Ottawa and Prescott, Brockville and Ottawa, Port Hope-Lindsay, and Cobourg-Peterborough lines; figures of estimated population per co as of 1857 given.
OOAMA

250 *1858*
Upper Canada County Map. [Sgd] T. Devine Crown Land Department Toronto January 1858 [blank space] Commissioner Crown Lands / T. Devine C.L.O.
Col ms 113 x 128 cm 1" to 8 miles
Shows cos, land agency divisions as proposed in 1857 (**236**); railways, twps north to line of Macaulay, Draper to Brudenell, Algona to Rolph, numbered twps south of the Mattawa R.
OTAR

251 *[ca 1859]*
CANADA EAST & WEST. // Published by Charles Magnus & Co. / STATIONERS & PUBLISHERS NEW YORK PRINTING ESTABLISHMENT. / Office No 12 Frankfort St.
Print (lith) hand col 56 x 75 cm Approx 1" to 24 miles
Insets: 'GREAT WESTERN RAILWAY OF CANADA.' and 'GRAND TRUNK RAILWAY OF CANADA.'; [Canada East and West and the eastern United States also with inset]: 'NEW BRUNSWICK / and / NOVA SCOTIA'; view: 'ROYAL MAIL MONTREAL & QUEBEC to LIVERPOOL'; shows railways completed and in progress, proposed Niagara Falls-St Thomas rail line; shows similar information to that of 1857 map (**226**) except twps now shown in the Bruce Peninsula and east of L Nipissing.
OOAMA (NMC 24955)

252 *[1859]*
CANADA WEST, / AND PART OF / CANADA EAST. // Drawn by J.W. Lowry F.R.G.S. // BLACKIE & SON, GLASGOW, EDINBURGH & LONDON. // Engraved by J.W. Lowry London. // No. LXIX.
Print (lith) 34 x 50 cm 1" to 33 miles
Inset: 'Environs of Montreal'; found separately as a folding map bound with Lower Canada map and with cover-title: 'ROUTE MAP / OF / CANADA, NOVA SCOTIA, / AND NEW BRUNSWICK / from Blackie and Son's Imperial Atlas' (GBL Maps 28.bb.48); note on GBL copy: 'Rec'd 13 Jy 59'; also in W.G. Blackie, *The Imperial Atlas of Modern Geography* (London 1860), plate LXIX (GBL Maps 41.d.14; *LC Atlases* 3556); twps to the base of the Bruce Peninsula but unnamed, roads, railways.
GBL (Maps 28.bb.48) USDLC

253 *1859*
GOVERNMENT MAP OF / CANADA, / from Red River to the Gulf of St. Lawrence / Compiled by Thomas Devine P.L.S. / Head of Surveys / Upper Canada Branch / CROWN LANDS DEPARTMENT. / NOVEMBER 1859. // THOMPSON & CO. PRINTERS & PUBLISHERS, QUEBEC & TORONTO // Rae Smith Engraver & Printer 71 Nassau Str. New York U.S.A.
Print (lith) sometimes hand col 74 x 166 cm 1" to 29.4 miles
Inset: [Polar projection of the Northern Hemisphere]; twps are numbered and keyed in 'Tabular List of the Counties in Upper Canada with the Townships composing the same alphabetically arranged'; 'Tabular List of the Counties in Lower Canada with the Parishes therein ... Surveyors Branch Quebec 26th October 1859'; 'List of the various Railway Stations ... and distances'; notes on timber types and locations, and minerals; a list of sources includes nine maps and groups of maps or surveys consulted; shows cos, twps in the Bruce Peninsula but not named, twps north to line Stephenson to Robinson, numbered twps east and south of L Nipissing, railways, common roads, colonization roads, canals; many copies hand-coloured to show free-grant twps and colonization roads; the map was announced as ready in Dec 1859 in Canada (Province), Dept of Crown Lands, *Report ... 1859* (Quebec: Thompson 1860), 10; (Dionne 985; *OHIM* 2.22; Olsen 122).
GBL (70615(25)) OOAMA (NMC 17078) OTAR OTUTF QMM(L) USDLC

Later editions and states

(1b) *1861*
Reduced Copy of the / GOVERNMENT MAP OF / CANADA / Compiled by Thomas Devine P.L.S. / Head of Surveys U.C. / Department of Crown Lands 1861 // Rae Smith Engraver & Printer 71 Nassau Str. New-York U.S.A.
43 x 66 cm
The map area has been reduced to Sault Ste Marie on the west, to 48° on the north, 70° on the east, and on all sides by removing all the tables; the Gaspé area has been inset; possibly a lithographic transfer from map above; shows the same information as the 1859 map except the Parry Sound Rd has been added; also issued in [William Hutton], *Canada: A Brief Outline of Her Geographical Position*, 3rd ed (Quebec: Printed by John Lovell 1861), after title-p (*Bib Can* 3743, Casey I–2921); (*PRO Cat* 1423).
GBLpro OOA OOAMA (NMC 26649–50) OTAR OTMCL OTUTF

(2a) *1862*
GOVERNMENT MAP OF / CANADA, / FROM LAKE SUPERIOR TO THE GULF OF ST LAWRENCE / WITH THE OUTLINES OF / NEW BRUNSWICK, NOVA SCOTIA, PRINCE EDWARD ISLD. &c. &c. / BY / THOMAS DEVINE F.R.G.S. &c. / HEAD OF SURVEYS / UPPER CANADA BRANCH / DEPARTMENT OF CROWN LANDS / 1862 // Rae Smith Engraver & Printer 71 Nassau Str. New York U.S.A.
75 x 126 cm
Inset: [Eastern Canada and Newfoundland] replaces inset on 1859 ed; the map is from the same plate as 1859 ed but has been reduced on the west to show only half of L Superior; the list of Upper Canada cos, notes on minerals and sources, and the legend have been dropped; twps now named throughout and added in the Bruce Peninsula; numbered twps south of L Nipissing have been deleted; detail added for northern New Brunswick; this is probably the map referred to as 'the Official Map' on title-p of *Letters from Canada*, 10th ed (Quebec 1862), and on title-p of a later ed (London 1863) (*Bib Can* 4156, 4157).
OOAMA (NMC 48746)

(2b) *1862–3*
REDUCED COPY / of the / GOVERNMENT MAP OF / CANADA / Compiled by Thomas Devine, F.R.G.S. &c. / Head of Surveys / UPPER CANADA BRANCH / D.C.L. / 1862.63 / [at head of title]: Department of Crown Lands, / The Honorable William McDougall, / Commissioner &c. // Rae Smith Engraver ...
44 x 66 cm
The map, which is similar to (1b), contains the same information and is probably a lithographic transfer from (2a); it has been extended to 49° north in the east to include the Chicoutimi area, and the Gaspé inset has been made smaller; printer statement moved and lacking on some copies; also issued in *Canada. Information for Immigrants ... With Map Shewing the Newly Surveyed Townships, Colonization Roads, Etc. of Canada ... Commissioners of Crown Lands* (Quebec: Printed by Hunter, Rose & Lemieux 1862), at end (*Bib Can* 8987), and in 1863 ed (OOA Pamph 1863 (11)); copies in books do not include Rae Smith imprint.
OOA OOAMA (NMC 8523) OTAR OTMCL

(3) *1867*
[Title as in (2a)] DEVINE F.R.G.S. etc. / SURVEYOR – IN – CHIEF / FOR UPPER CANADA / DEPARTMENT OF CROWN LANDS / 1867 // Department of Crown Lands, / Honorable Alex Campbell Commissioner // Rae Smith Engraver ...
75 x 126 cm
The map has the same layout and information as (2a) with adds: the complete twp grid is shown for the Huron-Ottawa territory and a few more twps named; numbered twps east of L Nipissing deleted; OOAMA copy has ms adds showing later electoral divisions.
OOAMA (NMC 11752) OTAR

---

254 *[1859]*
MAP OF / CANADA WEST / exhibiting all the / POST OFFICES. / Compiled & Engraved expressly for the / CANADIAN ALMANAC / FOR / 1860 / BY / MACLEAR & CO. / TORONTO.
Print (lith) 32 x 47 cm Scale not given
Found separately and in *The Canadian Almanac ... for ... 1860* (Toronto: Maclear & Co. [1859]), after 2 (*Bib Can* 2871); shows railways, cos, twp boundaries, and named post offices or towns with post offices.
OKQ OTMCL

Later editions and states

(2) *1863*
— / POST OFFICES. / COUNTIES, TOWNSHIPS, RAILROADS, / AND / Free Grant Roads, / Republished by Authority / 1863 // W.C. Chewett & Co. Lith. Toronto, C.W.
38 x 53 cm 1" to 22.2 miles
A redrawn and larger scale version of map above with the addition of many post offices and twps in the Huron-Ottawa area; 'List of the Counties in Upper Canada, with the townships comprising the same, alphabetically arranged'; (Olsen map 91).
OTMCL

---

255 *1859*
Part of South Shore of Lake Huron Surveyed and drawn under the direction of Capt. Geo. G. Meade T.E. By H.C. Penny H. Gillman F.M. Speed and G.E. Swinscoe 1859.
Col ms 75 x 125 cm 1:16,000 Endorsements: 'L Huron Map no 40 Sable R to C. Ipperwash L Huron s shore Enc to H.'; stamp 'Hydrog Dept Admir. Original Document 29 May 1902'
Possibly a ms draft or a copy of one for the U.S.

printed chart of 1861 (see C136); shows soundings and isolines for 6, 12, and 18 ft of water; nature of the shoreline and bottom.
GBTAUh (B8309.16n)

256 *[1859]*
PROVINCE OF CANADA / (Western Sheet) / BY KEITH JOHNSTON, F.R.S.E. // Engraved & Printed // by W. & A.K. Johnston. / KEITH JOHNSTON'S GENERAL ATLAS.
Print (col lith) hand col 44 x 57 cm 1" to 32.5 miles
OTAR and GBL copies issued folded and mounted with plate 43 (Eastern Sheet), with cover-title: 'Canada from Keith Johnston's Royal Atlas' (OTAR, GBL (Maps 4.aa.24)); GBL copy endorsed 'Rec'd 15 Au 59'; OTAR inside cover quotes from reviews, one published in 1860; shows co boundaries, canals, relief, railways: Toronto-Stratford-Sarnia, Toronto-Montreal, Toronto-Collingwood, Niagara Falls-Hamilton-Windsor with extensions to Toronto and Sarnia, London-Pt Stanley, Buffalo-Goderich, and smaller connections between Pt Hope-Lindsay and Peterborough, Cobourg-Peterborough, Brockville-Arnprior, Prescott-Ottawa.
GBL (Maps 4.aa.24) OTAR

Later editions and states

(2) *[1861]*
— [Added imprint and number] // William Blackwood & Sons Edinburgh & London // 42
In A.K. Johnston, *The Royal Atlas of Modern Geography* (Edinburgh and London: W. Blackwood & Sons 1861), plate 42 (*LC Atlases* 835; OOAMA); the first ed of this atlas (Tooley, 341); the same as map above; also in a later ed of the atlas (Edinburgh and London: W. Blackwood & Sons 1865 [i.e., 1864]) (OOAMA (NMC 10504); OTUTF; USDLC), with the add of a few place-names; and in another ed (Edinburgh and London: W. Blackwood & Sons 1867) (OOAMA, OTMCL, USDLC), with the add of more place-names, extension of co boundaries into the Huron-Ottawa area, and a colonization road; (OOAMA MacDonald Collection 416).
OOAMA OOAMA (NMC 10504; 105726)
OTMCL OTUTF USDLC

257 *[1860?]*
BRITISH NORTH AMERICA / SHEET II WEST / CANADA / WITH PART OF / UNITED STATES. / COMPILED BY J. HUGH JOHNSON F.R.G.S. // A. FULLARTON & CO. EDINBURGH, LONDON & DUBLIN // Engraved at Stanford's Geographical Establishment 6 Charing Cross, London.
Print (col lith) 41 x 52 cm Approx 1" to 38 miles
In G.H. Swanston, *The Companion Atlas to the Gazetteer of the World* (Edinburgh: A. Fullarton & Co. [1852–60]), no 19 (*LC Atlases* 832, GBL (Maps 42.f.7)), and in *The Royal Illustrated Atlas of Modern Geography* (London and Edinburgh: A. Fullarton & Co. [1854–62]), pt 18 (*LC Atlases* 838, GBL (Maps 42.f.5)); 17 railways are keyed and named in the railway list, which varies between the two atlases; shows cos, places, relief; OOAMA (NMC 16361) has '32' pasted in upper left and right corners; a note in the Swanston atlas indicates binding was completed 1 Nov 1860 but the sheet may have been printed earlier.
GBL OOAMA (NMC 7049; 16361)
USDLC

258 *1860*
Canada Sketch Map shewing the extent of the Canada Engineer Command and the Railroad Steamboat and Telegraphic Communications between the several Stations. To accompany C.R.E.'s letter to I.G.F. dated 26th January 1860. No 49 [Sgd] A. Storer Lieut R.E. 25th January 1860 H. Servante Coll R.E. Canada.
Col ms 72 x 150 cm Approx 1" to 18 miles
Endorsements: 'See Montreal 6/191 S.B.H. 28/4/60' 'F105'; stamp 'B↑O'
Shows table of distances, military posts under the War Dept and those under the provincial government, locations of pensioners; (Holmden 3827; Olsen 127).
OOAMA (NMC 11748)

259 *[1860]*
THE DISPATCH ATLAS / UPPER CANADA // Weekly Dispatch Atlas 139, Fleet Street. // Drawn & Engraved by T. Ettling, 3 Red Lion Square, Holborn. // E. Weller Lithogr
Print (lith) 31 x 44 cm 1" to 32 miles
In *Cassell's General Atlas* (London: Cassell, Petter and Galpin [1860]), plate [48] (OOAMA), and in *The Dispatch Atlas* (London: 'Weekly Dispatch' Office 1863), plate [201] (*LC Atlases* 839, GBL (Maps 45.e.10)); stamped on the plate in the latter: 'Weekly Dispatch Sunday Augt 12th 1860'; shows cos, railways finished and unfinished, roads including some colonization roads and relief, railways in progress: Belleville-Peterborough-Penetanguishene, Arnprior-Pembroke, part of Hamilton-Pt Dover, Niagara Falls-Simcoe-St Thomas-Amherstburg, Lindsay-Beaverton.
GBL OLU OOAMA USDLC

Later editions and states

(2) *1865–[6]*
UPPER CANADA // LONDON PUBLISHED BY CASSELL, PETTER & GALPIN, LA BELLE SAUVAGE YARD, LUDGATE HILL E.C. // 42.
Print (lith) 31 x 44 cm 1" to 32 miles
In *Cassell's General Atlas* (London: Cassell Sept 1865–[6]) (GBL (Maps 43.f.8)); note on paper cover indicates it is to be completed in 10 monthly parts; the same as map above.
GBL

260 *[1860]*
Hamilton as it should be. / [and] Hamilton as Messrs Brydges & Baker want to have it

Col ms 32 x 39 cm Scale not given
Provenance: OOA Buchanan Papers; a rough sketch showing Hamilton as the railway centre for southwestern Ontario with the GWR, the Buffalo & L Huron Ry, Hamilton & Saugeen Ry, and Great Southwestern all starting from it or connecting through it; other railways shown with branch lines to Hamilton; the second title refers to inset showing main focal point as Toronto; (*OHIM* 6.34).
OOAMA (NMC 2915)

---

261 *1860*
MAP OF / CANADA WEST / IN / COUNTIES. // Entered according to Act of Congress in the year 1860 by S. Augustus Mitchell Jr. in the Clerk's Office of the District Court of the U.S. for the Eastern District of Penna. // 8.
Print (lith) hand col 27 x 34 cm 1" to 40 miles
In: (1) S.A. Mitchell, *Mitchell's New General Atlas* (Philadelphia: S.A. Mitchell, Jr 1860), plate [6] (OKQ (loose sheet), USDLC); shows co boundaries, railways, and proposed railways: London-Sarnia, Toronto-Peterborough-Kingston, Pt Hope-Lindsay-Penetanguishene; Brockville-Pembroke;

(2) another issue of the 1860 ed of the atlas (*LC Atlases* 831); the number '8.' has been moved from margin to near the title and the registration statement has been redrawn with 'U.S.' deleted and 'Pennsylvania' written in full; a railway has been added from St Mary's to Pt Stanley; loose sheet also in OOAMA (NMC 2914);

(3) in the 1861 ed of the atlas (OOAMA); the map is as in (1);

(4) in the 1862 ed of the atlas (*LC Atlases* 3558); 'U.S.' added to registration statement; as (2) but the following railways are shown as completed: London-Sarnia, Pt Hope-Beaverton, Brockville-Ottawa R;

(5) in the 1863 ed of the atlas (*LC Atlases* 6145); the map is the same as (4);

(6) in the 1864 ed of the atlas (*LC Atlases* 6150); the registration statement has been redrawn and more place-names added; (OOAMA MacDonald Collection 493 (NMC 105072));

(7) in the 1865 ed of the atlas (*LC Atlases* 846, OKQ (loose sheet)); many place-names have been added in the Bruce-Grey area and north of L Ontario;

(8) in the 1866 ed of the atlas (*LC Atlases* 848); the proposed Toronto-Peterborough-Kingston railway has been deleted.
OKQ OOAMA (NMC 2914; 105072) USDLC

Later editions and states

(9) *1867*
— // Entered according to Act of Congress in the year 1867 by S. Augustus Mitchell Jr. in the Clerks Office of the District Court of the U.S. for the Eastern District of Pennsylvania. // 9.
In S.A. Mitchell, *Mitchell's New General Atlas* (Philadelphia: S.A. Mitchell, Jr 1867) (*LC Atlases* 850); the same information as (8) above but the decorative margin and registration statement have been changed.
OTMCL USDLC

---

262 *1860*
MAP OF CANADA WEST SHEWING THE POST OFFICES ... 1860 ... [with ms adds showing Indian surrenders and reserves]
Print (lith) with col ms adds 110 x 172 cm 1" to 6.6 miles Endorsements: 'Enclosure no 3 in 11035 /60' 'With Resp. Rec. 26/11/1860'
In R.J. Pennefather's report of 1 Nov 1860 to the Duke of Newcastle (GBLpro CO 42/624 p 311); reserves shown in Tuscarora, Tyendinaga, Delaware, Anderdon, Sarnia twps, and in Hastings Co, Christian Is, Cape Croker, and three other locations in the Bruce Peninsula; boundaries of ceded lands shown sometimes with dates of cession; the printed base map is **245(2)**; (*PRO Cat* 1421).
GBLpro (MR 635)

Related maps

(2) *1860*
[Title the same with ms adds showing Indian surrenders and reserves] [Endorsed]: 'True Copy of Original attached to the Report by R.J. Pennefather Superintendent of Indian Affairs Addressed to the Duke of Newcastle and dated India Dept Quebec Nov 1st 1860 (Colonial Office Mark '11035 Canada recd. 26th Nov. 1860') Stanford's Geogl Estabt'
An official copy of the plan above, presumably to be kept in Canada.
OTAR

---

263 *[1860]*
MAP OF / CANADA. / WITH PART OF NEW BRUNSWICK & NOVA SCOTIA. / Shewing the Line of / GRAND TRUNK RAILWAY / AND ITS CONNECTIONS. / BY KEITH JOHNSTON F.R.S.E. // Engraved & Printed // W. & A.K. Johnston, Edinburgh.
Print (col lith) 45 x 114 cm 1" to 32.5 miles
Issued separately with cover-title: 'BRITISH PROVINCES OF NORTH AMERICA. 1860.' (OTMCL, USDLC); inset: 'GENERAL VIEW OF THE NORTH ATLANTIC WITH PART OF THE COASTS OF EUROPE & NORTH AMERICA. (From Photograph of Terrestrial Globe)'; a smaller version of map without the inset is in Grand Trunk Ry of Canada, *Report for 1859* (London: Waterlow 1860), frontis (46 x 84 cm) (*Bib Can* 3906); the Grand Trunk Ry has been overprinted in red with mileages along the line from Detroit to Richmond, Quebec, and with branches to Trois Rivières, Rivière du Loup, and Portland, Maine; otherwise, the map is the same as **256(2)**.
OTMCL USDLC

264 *1860*
[Map of the valley of the Ottawa] compiled by A.J. Russell Agent in charge of the Upper Ottawa Territory, Ottawa 1st Sept 1860.
Col ms 101 x 166 cm 1" to 12 miles Watermark on text: '1859'
Accompanies 'Map of the Valley of the Ottawa Distinguishing the Occupied Parts of it from the Uninhabited and the Surveyed from the Unsurveyed and Comparatively Unknown ...' and 32-p 'memorandum descriptive of the Ottawa Country'; the map covering Canada West and part of Canada East appears to be unfinished and shows rivers, lakes, co boundaries, railways, and drainage basins; settled localities in the Ottawa valley only are shaded a darker brown than unsettled areas; twps shown to line Airy-Fraser to McKay, Petawawa, and Buchanan; colonization roads; Russell's theory was that the Ottawa country should be reserved for timber exploitation and settlement should go further west; (Monk Bretton Books [Toronto], *Catalogue* 2 [1975]).
OOAMA (NMC 25630)

---

265 *1860*
MAP / OF / UPPER & LOWER / CANADA, / COMPILED FROM THE / MOST RECENT AUTHORITIES, / SHOWING THE BLOCKS OF LAND FOR SALE. / & THE FREE GRANT ROADS / ON EITHER SIDE OF WHICH ARE / GOVERNMENT LANDS / TO BE DISPOSED OF IN / 100 & 200 ACRE LOTS. // London, Edward Stanford, 6, Charing Cross.
Print (lith) hand col 55 x 86 cm 1" to 30 miles
In *The Canadian Settlers' Guide*, 10th ed (London: Edward Stanford 1860) (*Bib Can* 3891); roads named in ms and railways enhanced in ms; shows cos, places, notes on the location and cost of 'The Government Lands.'
OTMCL

---

266 *1860*
MAP / OF / Upper Canada / OR / CANADA WEST / Compiled from the most recent authorities & surveys. / TORONTO, / 1860. / Engraved & Published by Maclear & Company.
Print (col lith) with hand col 94 x 141 cm 1" to 8 miles
Inset: 'THE NORTH SHORE / OF / LAKE HURON' 1" to 12 miles; OOAMA copy folding with cover-title: 'MAP OF UPPER CANADA. Price, $4.'; twps are shown in the Bruce Peninsula and north to line Stephenson-Richards, McKay-Clara; shows roads, railways; tables: 'Electoral Divisions, Canada West. Con. Stats Canada Cap 2. Secs 8 and 9' and 'Distances by Railway.'; redrawn from the 1854 map (see **188(2)**); (Olsen map 96; OOAMA MacDonald Collection 491).
OOAMA (NMC 105115) OTAR

Later editions and states

The main part of the map was reissued in four parts without revisions for successive issues of the *Canadian Almanac* as follows:

(2) *[1860]*
MAP / OF PART OF / CANADA WEST / Engraved Expressly for the / CANADIAN ALMANAC / 1861.
39 x 44 cm
In *The Canadian Almanac ... for ... 1861* (Toronto: Maclear & Co. [1860]), opp 3 (*Bib Can* 2871); covers the northwestern area between Toronto and L Huron and north to the top of the Bruce Peninsula; 'the complete map of Canada West, on this scale may be had at the Publishers, King Street, Toronto.'
OOAMA (NMC 2919) OTMCL

(3) *[1861]*
[Date in title changed to 1862] / Published by W.C. Chewett & Co / TORONTO // 6.
49 x 33 cm
In *The Canadian Almanac ... for ... 1862* (Toronto: W.C. Chewett & Co. [1861]) (*Bib Can* 2871); covers area from Durham Co east to Frontenac Co and north to part of Renfrew.
OTAR OTMCL

(4) *[1862]*
[Date in title changed to 1863, '6' deleted]
32 x 65 cm
In *The Canadian Almanac ... for ... 1863* (Toronto: W.C. Chewett & Co. [1862]), opp 3 (*Bib Can* 2871); covers area from Stratford south to L Erie west of the Niagara R; (Holmden 2137, 2791).
OOAMA (NMC 2921) OTMCL

(5) *[1863]*
[Date in title changed to 1864]
38 x 37 cm
In *The Canadian Almanac ... for ... 1864* (Toronto: W.C. Chewett & Co. [1863]), opp title-p (*Bib Can* 2871); covers area from Kingston east.
OTMCL

---

267 *1860*
[Plan of Grand Trunk Railway station grounds]
6 prints (liths) Ea 45 x 70 cm or smaller Scales vary
In *Report of Mr. Thomas E. Blackwell ... of the Grand Trunk Railway of Canada. For the year 1859* (London: Waterlow & Sons 1860) (*Bib Can* 3906); includes 'MAP OF / CANADA ...' as described above (see **263**).
The following station plans relate to Ontario:
(8) 'GRAND TRUNK RAILWAY / PRESCOTT JUNCTION STATION / Waterlow & Sons Lith. London' 1" to 200 ft
(9) 'G.T.R. / BROCKVILLE STATION / Waterlow & Sons. Lith. London' 1" to 100 ft
(10) 'G.T.R. / Plan / OF / KINGSTON STATION. / Waterlow & Sons Lith. London' 1" to 100 ft
(11) 'COBOURG STATION. / TOWNSHIP OF HAMILTON. / Waterlow & Sons Lith. London' 1" to 100 ft

(12) 'TORONTO. / CANADA WEST. / Waterlow & Sons Lith. London' 1" to 12 chains

(13) 'PLAN / OF / SARNIA AND PORT HURON. / Waterlow & Sons Lith. London' 1" to 800 ft

Except for the Toronto map, the plans show only a small area around the stations, with all bldgs identified and other railway lines; Toronto is described more fully under (**2137**).
OTMCL

---

268 *[1860?]*
STANFORD'S / MAP OF / CANADA / NEW BRUNSWICK, NOVA SCOTIA / PRINCE EDWARD & BRETON ISLANDS / extending from the / GULF OF ST LAWRENCE TO LAKE SUPERIOR / and including the adjacent parts of the / UNITED STATES / FROM NEW YORK TO CHICAGO / with the / RAILWAYS, ROADS & CANALS. / LONDON, EDWARD STANFORD 6 CHARING CROSS.
Print (lith) 80 x 146 cm 1" to 28.5 miles
Shows cos but not twps; colonizaton roads including Ottawa and Opeongo Rd, Peterson Rd, Sault Ste Marie Rd, Muskoka Rd, Bobcaygeon Rd, Pembroke and Mattawan Rd; free-grant lands in blocks as shown on 1859 map (see **253**); shows the north-south oriented twp survey south of L Nipissing (1857), which is also shown as free-grant land; (Olsen 34).
GBL (70615 (29)) OOAMA (NMC 24904)

---

269 *[1860–1]*
MAP / OF / Upper Canada / OR / CANADA WEST / Compiled from the most recent authorities & surveys // Published by / GEO. R. & G.M. TREMAINE / Engravers, Lithographers, / MAP PUBLISHERS &c. &c. / 288 King Street, East, / TORONTO.
Print (lith) Approx 83 x 130 cm Scale not given
Insets: 'THE NORTH SHORE / OF / LAKE HURON.' 1" to 12 miles, [North Monaghan and Otonabee twps with names of owners]; view: 'Residence of MARK DURNHAM [*sic*] / Ashburnham'; the main map is similar to the Holden map (see **277**) but shows more places and not as many roads; shows railways, twps north to Stephenson to Richards and Balaklava and twps south of L Nipissing; the twp inset map also shows schools, mills, churches, bldgs; list of subscribers; probably published in 1860 or 1861 when the Tremaines were listed at that address (Hulse, 265); described from photoreproduction in OOAMA (NMC 21475).
Private Collection

---

270 *1861*
CHART OF THE LIGHTS / on the / LAKE COAST OF THE UNITED STATES / Published by the order and under the direction / of the / U.S. LIGHT HOUSE BOARD / Prepared at the Office of the Survey of the Northern and Northwestern Lakes / under the supervision of / CAPT. GEO. G. MEADE, TOP'L ENG'RS. / 1861.
Print (lith) hand col 68 x 114 cm 1" to 9.5 miles
Covers Lakes St Clair, Erie, Ontario, and the Upper St Lawrence R; a legend keys 12 classes of lights including English lights and discontinued lights; for United States various types of light including coloured, flashing, and those of different sizes; (*PRO Cat* 2105).
GBLpro (FO 925/1661/3)

Later editions and states

(**2**) *[1861?]*
[Chart of the lights on the lake coast of the United States ... Lake Huron] Lith. of J. Bien 180 Broadway N.Y.
Print (lith) hand col 92 x 56 cm 1" to 9 miles
Shows the same classes of light including English lights for L Huron; (*PRO Cat* 1473).
GBLpro (FO 925/1661/4)

---

271 *1861*
CONLIN, BONNEY & CO.'S / NEW MAP OF UPPER CANADA / OR / CANADA WEST / Compiled from the latest County Maps / AND OTHER LOCAL AND OFFICIAL SURVEYS / BY THE PUBLISHERS John S. Conlin, Samuel B. Bonney, James E. Hynes. / Toronto. / 1861.
Print (lith) hand col 110 x 168 cm Approx 1" to 6.8 miles
Insets: 'TOWN OF / COBOURG' 1" to 20 chains, 'PLAN OF THE / TOWNSHIP OF HAMILTON / County of Northumberland' 1" to 50 chains, 'THE NORTH SHORE OF LAKE HURON with part of the OTTAWA & HURON TERRITORY.' 1" to 30 miles; view: 'NEW PARLIAMENT BUILDINGS OTTAWA, C.W.'; table: 'Population of Cities, Towns, Villages, Counties and Townships in Canada West from the Census Returns of 1861.'; shows twps north to line Stephenson-Richards, cos, co towns, villages, post offices, telegraph stations, money order offices, railways, roads; the inset map of Hamilton Twp shows names of landowners or tenants, and houses, churches, schools, mills, etc; advertisements for businesses in Hamilton Twp are also included; (Olsen 126).
OOAMA (NMC 11255) OTAR

---

272 *1861*
THE GRAND TRUNK RAILWAY OF CANADA. / 1857. / [With ms adds]: 'Railways amended to 1861 (Private) Lord Clarence Paget with Mr Wm Kernaghan's Compts Log of "Dean Richmond" on Lakes Canals & St Lawrence.
Print (col lith) with ms adds 37 x 61 cm Scale not given Endorsements: 'D5587 Shelf' 'Nad. for Mr. Kernaghan ... in Jany 62' 'Jany 4 1861.'; stamp 'Hydrographic Office'
The log and another note on iron shipments of L Superior are from newspapers; note on the advantages of railways to Collingwood and

Goderich to control trade as the St Clair R is 'frozen until 10 March or 1 Apl'; printed base map is the same as **229**; (*PRO Cat* 223).
GBLpro (MR 1823(5))

273 *1861*
Map of the / GREAT WESTERN RAILWAY OF CANADA, / WITH THE VARIOUS LINES OF RAILROAD / IN CONNECTION WITH IT. // Martin & Hood lith, 8 Gt Newport St London
Print (lith) 23 x 35 cm Scale not given
In Great Western Ry of Canada, *Reply of the President and Directors to the Report of the Committee of Investigation* (London 1861) (OOA Pamph 1861 (46)); shows the GWR from Niagara to Windsor and Sarnia and the Hamilton and Toronto branch; other railways connecting with the northeastern U.S. and Lower Canada shown.
OOA

274 *1861*
Map of / THE LAURENTIAN LAKES, / to illustrate "Raspberry Moon", / by / John Hoskyns Abrahall, M.A. // E. WELLER, LITH RED LION SQUARE, LONDON // December, 1861.
Print (lith) hand col 25 x 30 cm Approx 1" to 70 miles
In Abrahall's *Western Woods and Waters* (London: Longman, Green 1864), after 406 (*Bib Can* 6083); covers area from the Great Lakes to Kingston; shows route of tour, boundary of Laurentian watershed, place-names.
OTMCL

275 *1862*
CANADA / CANALS & LAKES // Drawn by E.J. Powell Hydrographic Office, February 1862. // Malby & Sons Lith.
Print (lith) hand col 32 x 65 cm 1" to 35 miles
GBLpro copy originally from Adm 7/624; shows railways (some named), canals and locks; some forts; (*PRO Cat* 236).
GBLpro (MR 1823(6))

276 *1862*
Map / ILLUSTRATING THE / COURSE AND COMPARATIVE MAGNITUDE / OF THE PRINCIPAL CHANNELS OF THE / GRAIN TRADE OF THE LAKE REGIONS / 1862. by [Sgd in facsimile] Arthur Harvey F.S.S. Statistical Clerk Finance Dept Quebec // Duncan & Co. Lith Montreal
Print (col lith) 36 x 46 cm Scale '200,000,000 bus. [bushels] to 1 Inch'
In Harvey's 'The Grain Trade – Extract from a Paper on "The Graphical Delineation of Statistical Facts" ... Read before the Society 21st January 1863' (OOA), offprint from 'The Grain Trade of the Lake Regions,' *Transactions of the Literary and Historical Society of Quebec 1863*, new series, [2]:71–4 (OTMCL); extends from L Michigan to Quebec and Boston; shows the movement of grain by a line proportional in width to the amount moving between points; rail movements also shown; import figures given for certain ports in Canada West; also in *Reports on the Ottawa and French River Navigation Projects* (Montreal: John Lovell 1863), at end (Casey I–3067).
OOA OTMCL

277 *1862*
NEW MAP OF / UPPER CANADA / OR / CANADA WEST / Compiled from the latest County Maps / AND OTHER LOCAL AND OFFICIAL SURVEYS / BY THE PUBLISHERS / JOHN H. HOLDEN, / TORONTO. / 1862 ... // Geo R. & G.M. Tremaine Lith, St Lawrence Buildings / Toronto.
Print (lith) hand col 111 x 172 cm 1" to 7 miles
Insets: 'THE / North Shore of Lake Huron / with part of the / OTTAWA & HURON TERRITORY.' 1" to 30 miles, 'Plan / of the City of / KINGSTON' 1" to 18 chains, 'Plan / of the Township of / CRAMAHE C.W. / BY / J.H. Holden / TORONTO. / ...'; views: 'NEW PARLIAMENT BUILDINGS, OTTAWA C.W.' and 10 views of commercial bldgs and residences in Colborne; on the main map a legend keys cos, twps, cities, important towns and co towns, villages, post offices, railways, canals, roads, telegraph stations, and money order offices; table of railway stations in Canada West showing distances; population of towns, cos, and twps from 'Census Returns of 1861'; in Cramahe inset map the names of owners or tenants are shown in lots; business directory for Colborne; the printing statement is found with the twp inset map; part missing in lower left and right on OTAR copy; photoreproduction in OOAMA (NMC 20480).
OTAR

278 *1862*
[Plans to accompany 'Report of the Commissioners ... the Defences of Canada']
7 col mss, 2 prints (liths) with ms adds Sizes vary Scales vary
(OOAMA RG 8M 82303/23 items 1, 2, 4–10); a printed version of the report (marked '0185 Printed at the War Office' [ca Sept 1862]) is located in OOA (RG 8 II vol 18), and the report is also in GBLpro (WO 33/11); the report was also published commercially and dated 1 Sept 1862 in *Report of the Commissioners Appointed to Consider the Defences of Canada, 1862* (London: Eyre & Spottiswoode 1862) (*Bib Can* 4108; OOA 1862(33)); no maps are included in the printed version although all the maps are described; (Holmden 3998).

The plans relating to Ontario are as follows (all col mss unless otherwise noted):

'Plan no 1' MAP OF / CANADA. / ... Shewing the Line of / GRAND TRUNK RAILWAY [with ms adds showing military districts]

Print (col lith) 45 x 114 cm 1" to 32.5 miles
In ms shows four districts, proposed sites for permanent and temporary works, defensive positions, naval establishments; printed map is from same plate as **263** except inset and area east of 63° deleted and overprint of railway in red not shown.
OOAMA (NMC 26831)

Plan No 2 TACKABURYS' MAP / OF / CANADA WEST / ... 1862 ... [with ms adds showing defensive works and transportation]
Print (lith) 187 x 160 cm 1" to 6 miles
Endorsements: stamp 'IGF'
A ms legend keys proposed permanent works, temporary works, and entrenched positions, naval establishments, canals, railways, and gravelled roads; the permanent military reserves include Guelph, the naval establishments include Belleville; entrenched positions are proposed around London, west of Chatham, west of Paris, Queenston, St Catharines, Hamilton, St Marys, and Kingston Mills; shows the Bradford and Georgian Bay Ship Canal route (Burr route); (see **280(1)**).
OOA OOAMA (NMC 26833)

Plan No 4 Plan of the Harbour of Goderich on Lake Huron Surveyed and drawn by F.A.Wise, July, 1861.
59 x 94 cm 1:2,400 or 1" to 200 ft
'Sites of Proposed Temporary Works' are shown; shows harbour with soundings, two piers, proposed extensions, and dredging, relief, bldgs along shore; very similar to other copies of plans by Wise except more bldgs are named (see **1388**).
OOAMA (NMC 26834)

Plan No 5 [Sarnia and Port Huron]
69 x 50 cm 1" to 800 ft
Shows site of proposed permanent work at Point Edward; also shows GWR and depot in Sarnia, and GTR and depot in Point Edward, with railway bldgs; the map has been copied from a printed map; see **1948**.
OOAMA (NMC 13012)

Plan No 6 A survey of the River Detroit by Capt W.F.W. Owen and Assistants 1815.
27 x 28 cm 1" to 1 nautical mile
Shows proposed permanent works at Fort Malden and on Bois Blanc and temporary works also on Bois Blanc; the map is copied from printed nautical chart 331 (see **C113 (2)**).
OOAMA (NMC 26835)

Plan No 7 Plan of Guelph & Neighborhood Sketched by J H Satterthwaite Lieut R.E. 3/9/62
35 x 40 cm 4" to 1 mile
'Site of proposed fortified place of arms' on hill north of town; 'site of proposed outwork' on hill south of town; shows main streets and bldgs, relief by contours, wooded areas, roads, and railways.
OOAMA (NMC 26836)

Plan No 8 The Niagara Frontier and Welland Canal From Sketches by Captn Stotherd & Lieutt Price Rl Engineers
84 x 67 cm 1" to 1 mile
Shows sites of 'Place of Arms Short Hills,' proposed works at Fort Erie, Chippewa, and opp Black Rock, Port Dalhousie, and Port Colborne; sites of entrenched camps and batteries at Queenstown, Fort Mississauga, and position at Thorold; relief, wooded areas, towns, roads, railways.
OOAMA (NMC 26837)

Plan No 9 Plan of Hamilton: C.W. and surrounding Country. Compiled and Surveyed by J. Heriot Maitland. Captn Rl Engineers. 27th October 1862.
67 x 68 cm 2" to 1 mile
Shows area from Wellington Square [Burlington] and Waterdown east to Stoney Creek; site of proposed tower at entrance to Burlington Bay and site of proposed defensive position east of Hamilton; relief, wooded areas, railways, roads, towns; a few major bldgs.
OOAMA (NMC 26838)

Plan No 10 Reconnaissance of the Environs of Kingston. Canada West Surveyed by Lieut. Storer R.E. for the Defence Commission of 1862
112 x 101 cm 4" to 1 mile
Shows the various towers and fortifications including Cedar Is, Fort Henry, Fort Frederick, shoal tower, market battery, Murney tower, military hospital, Tête de Pont barracks, Artillery Park; relief, wooded areas, major bldgs, streets, railways, macadamized roads, roads unfit for traffic.
OOAMA (NMC 26839)

---

279 *[1862?]*
[Sketch of the River St Lawrence, Lakes Ontario and Erie showing canals]
Col ms 44 x 143 cm Scale not given
Originally from GBLpro Adm 7/624 and from the same source as **275**; shows the Desjardins, Welland, Rideau, St Lawrence, and Ottawa canals with size of locks for each; (*PRO Cat* 236).
GBLpro (MR 1823(1))

---

280 *1862*
TACKABURY'S MAP / OF / CANADA WEST / Drawn from Government and Special Local Surveys by / H.F. WALLING / PUBLISHED BY / R.M. & G.N. TACKABURY / LONDON, CANADA WEST. / 1862. / ENGRAVED ON COPPER PLATES / BY D. GRIFFING JOHNSON.
Print (lith) hand col Approx 155 x 191 cm 1" to 6 miles
Insets (city maps all at 1" to 1650 ft): 'HAMILTON Drawn from actual survey by W. Haskins, City Engineer,' 'KINGSTON,' 'LONDON Reduced from Plan of Actual Survey made by S. Peters

P.L.S.,' 'OTTAWA,' 'TORONTO,' 'MAP OF THE BRITISH POSSESSIONS IN NORTH AMERICA Taken by permission from the Map of J.H. COLTON 1862,' 'CLIMATOLOGICAL MAP OF CANADA WEST ... by LORIN BLODGETT' 1" to 38 miles, 'GEOLOGICAL MAP OF CANADA WEST, Compiled from the Surveys of SIR WM. E. LOGAN ... 1862'; views: 'AMERICAN FALL, NIAGARA,' 'HAMILTON, C.W.,' 'THE HORSE SHOE FALL NIAGARA,' 'KINGSTON, C.W.,' 'LONDON C.W.,' 'MONTREAL, C.E.,' 'NIAGARA FALLS, CANADA SIDE,' 'OTTAWA, C.W.,' 'SUSPENSION BRIDGE, NIAGARA RIVER,' 'TORONTO,' 'UNIVERSITY OF TORONTO'; tables: 'Population of the Cities and Counties of Canada West, Census of 1861,' 'Time-table' (times in various world cities compared to Ottawa), table of distances; shows railways and those proposed, canals, road allowances, opened roads, schools, churches, post offices, co seats, telegraph stations, money order offices, swamps, colonization roads; twps are shown north to a line Stephenson to Richards and a block southeast of L Nipissing, but not all are subdivided; in an advertisement dated 30 Oct 1862 and entitled 'The Rival maps.' in *Canadian Almanac for 1863*, [293] (*Bib Can* 1871), the Tremaines stated that the Tackabury map was corrected from their own (see **289**); (*OHIM* 2.24; Olsen map 129 and p 188–99).
OOAMA (NMC 16697, 23449) OTAR OTMCL OTNR

Later editions and states

(**2**) *1863*
— [Date in title changed to 1863]
154 x 191 cm
Inset map added centre left: 'NORTH WEST PART / OF / CANADA WEST.' 1" to 12 miles; dates in the other inset maps changed to 1863 and scale added to 'BRITISH POSSESSIONS ...' 1" to 275 miles; a few more twps shown as subdivided in Huron-Ottawa area; view of 'LONDON C.W.' replaces that of Montreal; view in top centre moved and 'NIAGARA FALLS CANADA SIDE' placed lower; coat of arms moved to left of title; proposed railways deleted from legend and gravel roads added.
Private Collection

(**3**) *1864*
— [Date changed in title to 1864]
The date 1864 replaces 1862 in the insets of the climatological map, the geological map, and the map of British possessions; a few views have been moved; more of Manitoulin Is is shown; border has been changed; (Olsen map 130).
GBL (70640(8)) OSINH USDLC

(**4**) *1865*
— [Date changed in title to 1865]
Inset maps now dated 1865.
OTUTF

(**5**) *1866*
— [Date changed in title to 1866 and 'ENGRAVED ... JOHNSON' statement deleted] [Embossed on map]: 'G.W. & G.B. COLTON & CO. / PUBLISHERS OF / MAPS / ATLASES etc / 173 WILLIAM ST. N.Y.'
Endorsements: (USDLC) 'Furnished from the Engineer Bureau War Department June 25th 1866'
Dates changed to 1866 in the inset maps; photoreproduction in OTUM.
USDLC

---

281 *1862*
Track Chart of Lake Huron. [Sgd] Wm Gibbard P.L.S. May 1862.
Col ms on linen 94 x 97 cm 1" to 8 miles
Endorsements: 'Forwarded to Adml Washington by Capn [Blythsea?] Decr 2nd 1862' 'Decr 2 1862'; stamp 'Hydrographic Office'
Shows islands, lighthouses, 'Free port line' around Manitoulin Is, steamboat tracks along shore, ports at which 'Kaloolah & Valley City' called in 1862.
GBTAUh (D6172.Aa3)

Related maps

(**2**) *1862*
Track Chart of Lake Superior. [Sgd] Wm Gibbard P.L.S. May 1862
Col ms 72 x 135 cm 1" t 8 miles Endorsements: 'Decr 2 1862'; stamp 'Hydrographic Office'
Shows islands, points, harbours, lighthouses, steamboat tracks.
GBTAUh (D6171.Aa3)

---

282 *1862*
TREMAINE'S MAP / OF / UPPER CANADA / COMPILED & DRAWN BY GEO. R. TREMAINE / Assisted by A. Jones, Esq., / From Original Surveys & Government Plans. / ENGRAVED, PRINTED & PUBLISHED / BY / GEO. C. GEO. R. & G.M. TREMAINE, / No. 79, FRONT STREET, / TORONTO / 1862.
Print (lith) hand col Approx 166 x 229 cm 1" to 5 miles
Insets: 'HAMILTON' 1" to 23 chains, 'KINGSTON' 1" to 25 chains, 'LONDON' 1" to 35 chains, 'TORONTO' 1" to 23 chains, 'OTTAWA' 1" to 25 chains, 'GEOLOGICAL MAP / OF / UPPER CANADA, / Compiled from information furnished the / PUBLISHERS / by SIR W. LOGAN, Director of the / GEOLOGICAL SURVEY OF CANADA,' 'Plan / OF THE / ALGOMA DISTRICT, / BEING PART OF THE / NORTH SHORE OF LAKE HURON / Showing the new Townships divided into / FARM LOTS' 1" to 12 miles; views (in Toronto): 'NORMAL SCHOOL,' 'OSGOODE HALL,' 'PROVINCIAL LUNATIC ASYLUM,' 'UNIVERSITY OF TORONTO,' 'PROVINCIAL EXHIBITION BUILDING'; 'TABLE OF / Railway & Telegraph Stations in Upper Canada' (with distances); 'Population of Upper Canada CENSUS ... OF 1861'

(including 'London from Special Census Mar. 1862'); 'METEOROLOGICAL TABLE'; 'TIME TABLE'; some copies have 'Names of Subscribers for the City of Toronto & County of York' (GBL, OTMCL, USDLC); shows roads, road allowances, principal travelled roads, railways, canals, post offices, villages without post offices, list of free-grant roads; twps are shown north to line Stephenson to Richards, McKay to Maria and ranges south and east of L Nipissing, but not all are subdivided; co boundaries; the map as described here was advertised in a *Prospectus of a Large and Elaborate Map of Canada West (Messrs Geo R. & G.M. Tremaine, of Toronto: December 21st, 1860,* 3 pp (OTAR); (Olsen 128 and pp 188–99).
GBL (70640 (40)) OOAMA (NMC 11259) OTMCL USDLC

Later editions and states

(2) *1862*
— GEO. R. TREMAINE / from Original Surveys & Government Plans. / Published by GEO. C. TREMAINE, / TORONTO / 1862
156 x 219 cm
The map has been reduced in size, particularly on the bottom edge and left side where the decorative border has been relocated around it; the insets of towns and the geological map have been deleted to be replaced by views; new views: 'CITY OF HAMILTON,' 'CITY OF KINGSTON,' 'CITY OF LONDON,' 'CITY OF OTTAWA,' 'CITY OF TORONTO,' 'NIAGARA FALLS,' 'PARLIAMENT BUILDINGS OTTAWA,' or 'CAPITAL AT OTTAWA' (OTNR copy), 'PASSENGER SUSPENSION BRIDGE QUEENSTON & BROCKS MONUMENT,' 'SUSPENSION BRIDGE AT CLIFTON,' 'TRINITY COLLEGE, TORONTO'; the tables have been deleted and replaced with: 'LIST OF MONEY ORDER OFFICES' and 'POPULATION of the Cities, Towns, Townships & Villages of CANADA' (table includes more towns including Yorkville and some figures different from above map); Guilford Twp now subdivided; otherwise, map is the same as state above; the map took a prize at the Provincial Exhibition of 1862 (see *Journal of the Board of Arts & Manufactures for U.C.* (1862), 364); OOAMA (NMC 85088) has views in different positions and view of Provincial Exhibition bldg has been deleted; alphabetical list of telegraph stations added; (*OHIM* 2.23 and 4.32).
OLU OOAMA (NMC 85088) OTAR OTNR USDLC

---

283 *1862–7*
[Topographic maps of parts of Canada West]
Ms and printed Sizes vary 1" to 1 mile
Topographic mapping or military sketch mapping done during the American Civil War of areas near the boundary that could be invaded (Nicholson and Sebert, 15); see the two maps of 1866, which show location of surveys (**300, 304**); some of the maps were printed and these are listed with the ms maps from which they were copied; a few maps are at scales larger than 1" to 1 mile; the maps relating to Canada West are listed by date and region below:

(**1a**) *1862*
Plan of Hamilton C.W. and surrounding country Compiled and surveyed by J. Heriot Maitland Capt. Royal Enginrs 27th October 1862
Col ms 67 x 69 cm 1" to 800 yds Endorsements: 'Mar 81 312'; stamp 'Intelligence Branch Militia Dept. Canada'
Shows the area from Stoney Creek to Ancaster and Waterdown; relief by shading; roads and toll points; cleared and wooded land; spot heights; major bldgs or landmarks located and named; town layouts shown; railways; there is a copy with the same title accompanying **278** (Plan 9) with added defence information; (Holmden 1708).
OOAMA (NMC 21074)

(**1b**) *1862*
Hamilton Compiled and Surveyed by J. Heriot Maitland, Captn Rl Engineers 27th October 1862. Copied from a Drawing lent by the War Office Jany 15th 1864
Col ms on tracing paper 52 x 72 cm 1" to 800 yds Endorsements: 'Jany 7 1865'; stamp 'Hydrographic Office'
Shows the same information and possibly copied from plan above, also water pipelines, filtering basin, Desjardins Canal.
GBTAUh (D7895,Tm)

(**1c**) *1865*
PLAN / OF / HAMILTON, C.W. / AND / SURROUNDING COUNTRY / Compiled and Surveyed by / J. Heriot Maitland. Capt Royal Engineers / 27th October 1862. // Zincographed at the Topographical Department of the War Office Southampton / Colonel Sir Henry James R.E. F.R.S. &c. Director. / 1865
Print (zincograph) hand col 67 x 69 cm 1" to 800 yds Endorsements: stamp (GBO copy) 'Topographical Department War Office Oct 26 1866'
Based on plans above but the contours have been added and printed in brown; rock drawing and hachures also added.
GBO

(**2a**) *1862*
The Niagara Frontier and Welland Canal From Sketches by Captn Stotherd & Lieutt Price Rl Engineers
Col ms 84 x 67 cm 1" to 1 mile
'Plan no 8' accompanying the 'Report of the Commissioners ... the Defences of Canada'; shows the same topographical information as Hamilton plans (1a–1c) above; the proposed defence sites marked; also listed with 1862 report (**278** (Plan 8)).
OOAMA (NMC 26837)

(**2b**) *1865*
NIAGARA FRONTIER. From Sketches by Capt. Stotherd & Lieut Price Rl Engineers & Capt. & Lieut. Colonel Henry Malet 1st Battn Grenr Guards in 1862–3. PLAN 2 // Zincographed at the Topographical Department of the War Office Southampton / Colonel Sir Henry James R.E. F.R.S. & Director. / 1865.
Print (zincograph) hand col 94 x 66 cm 1" to 1 mile Endorsements: stamps (GBO copy): 'Topographical Department War Office Sep 7 1865' (OOAMA copy): 'QuarterM. G. Horse Guards Mar 18 1869' 'Dept Militia & Defence Mar 4 1910'
Shows the same topographical information as plan (2a) above as well as the proposed defensive sites; includes part of Malet's survey west of Jordan (3a); OOAMA (NMC 45968) copy has later ms notes dated 1867 on the number of men and horses that can be accommodated at various places; (Holmden 2038).
GBO OOAMA (NMC 54254–5, 45968)

(**3a**) *1863*
Military Sketch of part of the Shore of Lake Ontario between Hamilton and Port Dalhousie [Sgd] Henry Malet Captain & Lt. Colonel 1st Batta Gren'r Guards. 1863
Col ms 50 x 96 cm 1" to 1 mile Endorsements: stamps 'Quartermaster General May 19, 1865' 'Dept of Militia & Defence Survey Division 1903 5 177'
Note: 'The Country East of 20 mile Creek is from a Sketch by Captain Stotherd R.E. made in 1862' (see (2a)); legend keys roads, cleared land and woods, marshes, churches and meeting houses, stone or brick houses and wooden houses, forges, GWR and Hamilton & Port Dover Ry (unfinished); relief is shown by shading and rock drawing; all bldgs appear to be shown; (Holmden 2115).
OOAMA (NMC 21066)

(**3b**) *1865*
HAMILTON. From a Sketch by Captain & Lt Colonel Henry Malet 1st Battn Grenr Guards, 1863. PLAN 1 // Zincographed at the Topographical Department of the War Office Southampton / Colonel Sir Henry James R.E. F.R.S. & Director, / 1865
Print (zincograph) hand col 93 x 66 cm 1" to 1 mile Endorsements: stamp (GBO copy) 'Topographical Department War Office Sep 7 1865'
Shows most of the same area as the ms map (3a) above; relief by hachures, field outlines.
GBO

(**3c**) *1865*
NIAGARA FRONTIER. From a Sketch ... 1865
The same as (3b) except for change in title.
OOAMA (NMC 54252–3)

(**3d**) *1865*
NIAGARA FRONTIER. From Sketches by Capt. Stotherd & Lieut Price Rl Engineers 1862. PLAN 3. // Zincographed at the Topographical Department of the War Office Southampton / Colonel Sir Henry James R.E. F.R.S. &c. Director / 1865.
Print (zincograph) hand col 88 x 65 cm 1" to 1 mile Endorsements: stamp (GBO and OOAMA copies) 'Topographical Department War Office Sep 7 1865'
Shows the area around Fort Erie only; shows the same topographical information as all plans above; (Holmden 2037).
GBO OOAMA (NMC 54256–7)

(**4**) *1863*
Plan of the Environs of Kingston Canada. Embracing a Circuit of about five miles round Fort Frederick From a Reconnaissance by Lieut Storer R.E. in 1862 and other Sources [Sgd] A. Storer Lieut R.E. 11th September 1863
Col ms 114 x 118 cm 4" to 1 mile Endorsements: stamps 'REO Kingston' 'No 861' '1263' '277–3' '1425'
Shows area from Ferris Pt to Gates Is and north to Kingston Mills; relief; roads, railways, main bldgs; similar to plan **278** (Plan 10).
OOAMA (NMC 11387)

(**5a**) *1864*
MAP / of the / TOWNSHIP / OF / YORK / ... 185 [blank] [with ms adds sgd] M.H. Synge Lt Col. R.E. Oct 64 Drawn by Lt. Turner R.E.
Print (engrav) with col ms adds 66 x 64 cm 1" to 40 chains
Ms adds to printed map (**2214(4)**); showing routes followed by Col Jervois in 1864, batteries located, relief added, breach forming Toronto island has been added; (Holmden 2726); there is also a map of Toronto showing existing defences and lithographed at the Topographical Depot of the War Office, 1864 to accompany report of Col Jervois of Jan 1865 originally in GBLpro (WO55) 2281 (not seen).
GBLpro (MPH 1111(1)) OOAMA (NMC 26683)

(**5b**) *1865*
Rapid Reconnaissance Sketch by Lt. H.F. Turner Royl Engrs to accompany Report called for by D.C.R.E. ... April 1865 Sigd M.H. Synge Lt. Col. D.C.R.E. Toronto 20th Oct 65
Print (engrav) with col ms adds 66 x 63 cm 1" to 40 chains
Similar ms adds to the same printed map as that in (5a) with addition of further drawing of terrain on east and west edges; proposed sites for works tinted yellow; notes about island, soundings, bridges.
QMMMCM (5593)

(**6a**) *1865*
[Topographical survey of the roads between Kingston and Peterborough] Zincographed at the Topographical Department of the War Office Southampton. / Colonel Sir Henry James R.E. F.R.S. &c. Director. / 1865
3 prints (zincographs) Ea 98 x 64 cm or 69 x 101 cm or smaller 1" to 1 mile Ea sheet endorsed: 'Canada/Ontario Dist 27 sheet 1 .. 2 .. 3' and 'Sheet 1 ... Sheet 2 ... Sheet 3 Kingston to Peterborough'; stamp (GBO copy) 'Topographical Department War Office Oct 16 1865'

A road reconnaissance with relief by contours, woods, farm fields, bldgs, mileages along route; sheet 1 shows area from Kingston to Gull L (Sheffield Twp), sheet 2 shows the area from Bridgewater to Flinton north of Bay of Quinte, and sheet 3 shows area from Trenton and Belleville to Peterborough; in OOAMA (NMC 4012) there is what is possibly a ms copy of the Kingston portion of this map (noted as made in 1864) sgd 'Copied C. Walkem S & draftsman Montreal Octr 1865.'
GBO

(6b) *1865*
[Reconnaissance of the road from Perth to Ottawa] Zincographed at the Topographical Department of the War Office Southampton, / Colonel Sir Henry James R.E. F.R.S. &c. Director, / 1865
Print (zincograph) 97 x 64 cm 1" to 1 mile Endorsements: stamp (GBO copy) 'Map Room Intelligence Branch War Office Ontario Dist 27a'
A survey of the route Perth-Franktown-Richmond-Ottawa; relief by contours, woods, fields, and bldgs shown.
GBO

(7) *1867*
[Topographic surveys made after the Fenian raids]
11 Col mss Sizes vary 1" to 1 mile or larger
The surveys cover part of the eastern area of the province including Kingston and part of Haldimand and Welland cos, the Niagara Peninsula, the area around London, and the Toronto region; these surveys were all made in 1867 but the work continued after 1867 when other areas, such as the rest of the Toronto region, were done; the plans show relief by shading, cleared and wooded areas, roads with comments on condition, many bldgs with indication of those in stone, brick, or wood, and many named; all plans are in OOAMA and are as follows:

(7a)
Part of the Counties of Glengarry and Prescott Surveyed by E. Stanley Creek Lt 23rd Roy Welsh Fusiliers 26th 1867
Col ms 78 x 54 cm Endorsements: '2158'; stamps 'Quartermaster General Montreal Sep 27 1867' 'Dept of Militia & Defence S.D. Ottawa Nov 8 1910'
Shows Lochiel, Hawkesbury, and Lancaster twps.
OOAMA (NMC 43068)

(7b)
Survey of part of Glengarry Ontario taken with Prismatic Compass [Sgd] A.J. Shuttleworth Lieut R.E. 1867
Col ms 78 x 54 cm Endorsements: '2156'; stamps 'Quartermaster General Horse Guards Mar 18 1869' 'Dept. of Militia & Defence S.D. Ottawa Nov 8, 1910'
Shows Kenyon and Charlottenburgh twps.
OOAMA (NMC 43069)

(7c)
Part of a Survey of Upper Canada during the Summer of 1867 by A.J. Shuttleworth Lieut. Royl Art.
Col ms 53 x 55 cm Endorsements: '2150'; stamps 'Quartermaster General Horse Guards Mar 18, 1869' 'Militia & Defense Ottawa Survey Div. Nov 8, 1910'
Shows Alfred, Longueuil, and Caledonia twps.
OOAMA (NMC 43081)

(7d)
Sketch by Hatton Turner, R.B. In the Summer of 1867. Printing by J. Brophy. Sapper. R.E.
Col ms 95 x 65 cm Endorsements: '2162' 'x/1007'; stamps 'Quartermaster General Montreal Recd Jan 3 1868' 'Dept of Militia & Defence Ottawa Survey Division 1910'
Shows Cambridge, Plantagenet S, Finch, Roxborough, and Cornwall twps; also gives statistics for each twp on the number of people and animals, and number of acres cleared and uncleared; shows 'The Connaught Settlement' and 'English Ridge.'
OOAMA (NMC 19021)

(7e)
Sketch of a portion of the Country near Kingston [Sgd] T Glancy Lieut R.E. 12th April 1867
Col ms 72 x 118 cm 4" to 1 mile Endorsements: '277–11' 'a/374'
Relief by grey wash; treed areas; roads, houses, Kingston to Kingston Mills and Grass Creek; GTR (pencil notes indicate first and second positions); similar to (4).
OOAMA (NMC 20026)

(7f)
Part of the Counties of Haldimand and Welland Surveyed between 4th June and 29th August 1867 by Captain H.M. Moorsom Rifle Brigade
Col ms on tracing paper 37 x 61 cm Endorsements: stamps 'Quarter Master General Montreal' 'Quarter Master General Horse Guards recd Mar 18 1869' 'Dept Militia and Defence Ottawa 1910'
Page nos given to description of roads in report (not found); (Holmden 1702).
OOAMA (NMC 3287)

(7g)
London C.W. Sketch of Country. Sketched by R. Armstrong Lieut R.E. 8.7.67
Col ms 57 x 45 cm 6" to 1 mile Endorsements: 'London C.W. 4 Reconnaissance Plans Lt Armstrong R.E.'
Shows the area west of the Thames R and the city in 1st and 2nd cons of London Twp; topographic detail including table of number of acres under various crops; bldgs classed according to space available for billetting men and horses.
OOAMA (NMC 24190)

(7h)
London Canada Sketch made Rapidly on Horseback to accompany Descriptive Report
Col ms (bottom half missing) 28 x 53 cm [6" to 1 mile] Endorsements: '352–1' 'J 2/123'
Shows the area to the north of (7g) in approx con 5, London Twp.
OOAMA (NMC 4063)

(7i)
[Topographical map of the northeast part of the Niagara Peninsula] [Sgd] W.L. Geddes Captn 53 Regiment 1867
Col ms 43 x 43 cm 1" to 1 mile Endorsements: stamps 'Quarter Master General Horse Guards Mar 18 1869' 'Dept. of Militia & Defense Ottawa Survey Division 1910'
Shows area from Stamford Twp and Niagara Falls to Port Dalhousie; relief by shading; cleared and wooded land; roads, railways, 19 bridges located and described; houses, mills; towns and bldgs listed with indication of the number of men and horses that can be billeted; descriptions of roads and creeks.
OOAMA (NMC 3560)

(7j)
Toronto District Sketch Sheets of a Reconnaissance of the Country between the rivers Humber and Etobicoke from the shore of Lake Ontario to Dundas Street on the North. [Sgd] H.J.W. Gehle Lt R.E. 16/7/67
Col ms 79 x 96 cm 6" to 1 mile Endorsements: '3' 'J2/71'
Shows relief by shading, wooded land, roads, railways, major buildings.
OOAMA (NMC 26685)

(7k)
(Copy) Sketch of a Reconnaissance in the County of York, Township Etobicoke, between the Humber & Etobicoke River, N. of Dundas Street [Sgd] H.J.W. Gehle Lt R.E. 16/10/67
Col ms 66 x 99 cm 6" to 1 mile
Also another copy further signed 'F.C. Hassard Col R.E. 21/10/67' (NMC 26682)
OOAMA (NMC 26681-2)

---

284 *1863*
CANALS OF CANADA
Print (wood engrav) 10 x 17 cm Scale not given
In *Eighty Years' Progress of British North America* (Toronto: L. Stebbins 1863), 170 (*Bib Can* 4237); includes Canada West and east to Montreal; canals named and keyed.
OTMCL

---

285 *1863*
Chart / OF / LAKE ONTARIO / Compiled from Surveys made by / CAPT OWEN & LIEUT. HERBERT, R.N. / AND / CAPT A. FORD, U.S.N. / with the / HARBOURS AND PORTS OF THE LAKE / Surveyed by / EDWARD M. HODDER, ESQRE M.D. / Commodore of the Royal Canadian Yacht Club. / Lithographed, Printed & Published by W.C. CHEWETT & CO. TORONTO, 1863. // Entered according to Act of the Provincial Legislature in the Year of our Lord One thousand eight hundred and sixty-three by W.C. Chewett & Co. in the Office of the Registry of the Province of Canada.
Print (col lith) 60 x 86 cm 11.25" to 1° latitude
Endorsements: (GBTAUh D6493Aa.3 copy) 'Presented to the Hydrographic Office by the Surveyor See his letter dated 20 July 63 to Secy'; stamp (OOAMA copy) 'IGF'
Insets of harbours include the following for Ontario: 'WHITBY HARBOUR,' 'PRESQUE'ISLE HARBOUR,' 'PORT OF OAKVILLE,' 'PORT DALHOUSIE,' 'PORT DARLINGTON,' 'MOUTH OF NIAGARA RIVER,' 'TORONTO HARBOUR,' 'KINGSTON HARBOUR,' 'BURLINGTON BAY CANAL,' 'PORT OF OSHAWA,' 'PORT HOPE,' 'COBOURG,' 'PICKERING OR LIVERPOOL'; also seven insets of harbours in the United States; shows lighthouses, soundings, nature of shoreline.
GBTAUh (D6493Aa.3 and D8823.Tf) OOAMA (NMC 18910)

Later editions and states

(2) *1866*
[Date changed in title to 1866 and placed on line below]
A few changes have been made: Outer Drake and Inner Drake Is renamed False Duck and Timber Is, respectively, the Presqu'ile light is shown in a different position on the main map, and a darker blue is used to enhance shoreline; (Holmden 1911).
OOAMA (NMC 18909)

---

286 *[1863]*
MAP / OF / CANADA / AND BORDERING TERRITORIES / SHOWING PROPOSED SHIP NAVIGATION / FROM LAKE HURON TO MONTREAL BY THE / FRENCH RIVER AND OTTAWA / AS COMPARED WITH THAT / BY THE / GREAT LAKES / ACCOMPANYING REPORT OF WALTER SHANLY C E / FRENCH RIVER AND OTTAWA NAVIGATION. // G. Matthews Litho Montreal
Print (lith) 31 x 51 cm Scale not given
In *Reports on the Ottawa and French River Navigation Projects* (Montreal: John Lovell 1863), at end (*Bib Can* 4260; Casey I-3067); shows the area from L Superior to Nova Scotia and south to New York; the route is highlighted in ms: French R, Ottawa, Montreal, L Champlain to Albany and New York; shows railways and a few places.
OOA OTMCL

---

287 *1863*
Map of Canada West Shewing the Number of Volunteer Corps in each Military District / Militia Department Quebec Feby 1863 [Sgd] J.S. Macdonald Minister of Militia. Examined &c. [Sgd] Thos. Devine Head of Surveys U.C.
Col ms in 2 sections 90 x 205 cm 1" to 6 miles
Rifle, infantry, cavalry, and artillery corps located; shows field batteries, military districts, cos, railways; (Olsen 131).
OOAMA (NMC 11253)

---

288 *1863*
MAP OF THE / LAKE REGION & / ST. LAWRENCE VALLEY // Lith by HATCH & CO 29 William St. N.Y. // No. 2
Print (lith) 29 x 47 cm 1" to 65 miles
In *The Niagara Ship Canal* (New York: 1863) (*Bib Can* 9128); shows the Erie Canal and connection to proposed U.S. canal around Niagara R, and in Canada 'Proposed Line of the Ottaway Slack Water Navigation'; Welland Canal shown but no other place-names or features for Canada West.
OTMCL

289 *1863*
MAP OF THE / LAKE REGION, ST LAWRENCE VALLEY / AND / SURROUNDING COUNTRY. / NEW YORK; / Published by J. Disturnell. // PRINTED BY LANG & COOPER, 117 FULTON ST N.Y.
Print (lith) 35 x 65 cm Scale 1" to 65 miles
In J. Disturnell, *The Great Lakes or Inland Seas of America* (New York: 1863), at back (QQS; CIHM 44380), and in the 1865 ed of the same book (Karpinski 255); shows the area from the Saguenay to beyond L Superior and south to Washington; concentric circles show distances from Mackinac Is; railways; major places.
QQS

290 *[1864]*
CANADA. / (WEST SHEET.) / BY J. BARTHOLOMEW, / F.R.G.S. // GEORGE PHILIP & SON LONDON & LIVERPOOL // 41.
Print (col lith) 62 x 53 cm 1" to 30 miles
In J. Bartholomew and W. Hughes, *Philips' Imperial Library Atlas* (London: George Philip & Son 1864) (GBL (Maps 46.f.1)); shows Canada West and part of Canada East, railways, cos, place-names; a prospectus dated Feb 1862 is inserted in front of GBL atlas.
GBL OOAMA

291 *1864*
CHART / OF / LAKE HURON, / with enlarged Plans of the principal HARBORS AND PORTS ON THE LAKE, / compiled from Surveys made by / CAPTN W.H. BAYFIELD, R.N. / AND / CAPTN G.G. MEADE, U.S. TOPL ENGS / revised and the most recent information added under the direction / of the / CROWN LANDS DEPARTMENT OF CANADA. / 1864. / Lithographed Printed & Published by W.C. / CHEWETT & CO. TORONTO.
Print (col lith) 75 x 92 cm 8" to 1° latitude
Insets: 'HARBOR OF OWEN SOUND,' 'MOUTH OF THE RIVER SEVERN,' 'PRESQU'ILE, Harbor of Refuge,' 'FALSE PRESQU'ILE Harbor of Refuge,' 'HEAD OF ST CLAIR RIVER / COLLINGWOOD HARBOR,' 'GODERICH HARBOR,' 'CHANTRY ISLAND AND ENTRANCE TO RIVER SAUGEEN'; list of Canadian lighthouses; soundings; navigational hazards, bearings, table of distances for small boats and steamboats; insets show piers, lighthouses, hazards, type of bottom and shore, layout of towns, soundings.
OLU

292 *1864*
[Map series for eastern Canada and northeastern United States produced by the Ordnance Survey]
Constructed and Engraved at the ORDNANCE SURVEY OFFICE Southhampton in 1864, Colonel Sir Henry James R.E. F.R.S. M.R.I.A. &c. Director
6 prints (engrav) Ea 92 x 58 cm 1" to 10 miles
Provenance: OOAMA received with transfer of Geological Survey of Canada maps; the six sheets covering Canada West are entitled as follows (each with same imprint as above): 'DETROIT,' 'TORONTO,' 'KINGSTON,' 'ST. MARY,' 'NIPISSING,' 'OTTAWA'; shows area from L Superior east to Quebec and south to Boston; the maps show detailed cultural information including rivers and lakes, places, post offices, railways, cos; a bordering sheet, 'SUPERIOR,' is also indicated but has not been found; the series appears to be comprised of at least 14 sheets of which eight are in OOAMA.
OOAMA (NMC 51486–93)

293 *1864*
SKETCH – MAP OF THE GEOLOGICAL FORMATIONS OF WESTERN CANADA.
Print (wood engrav) 9 x 16 cm Scale not given
In E.J. Chapman, *A Popular and Practical Exposition of the Minerals and Geology of Canada* (Toronto: W.C. Chewett and Co. 1864), 202, fig 249 (*Bib Can* 4304); the key to the geological formations is found on p 203.
OTMCL

294 *[1864]*
UPPER CANADA. // Printed in Colours by W.H. McFarlane Edinr.
Print (lith) hand col 10 x 15 cm 1" to 80 miles
In *British North America* (London: Religious Tract Society [1864]), opp 58 (*Bib Can* 9165); places, cos, railways.
OTMCL

295 *[1865]*
Colton's / CANADA WEST / OR / UPPER CANADA / PUBLISHED BY J.H. COLTON – No 172 WILLIAM ST. NEW YORK. // No 19 // No 20.
Print (lith) hand col 44 x 67 cm 1" to 23 miles
Stamped on the map: 'PUBLISHED 1865' (USDLC); in G.W. Colton, *Colton's General Atlas* (New York: J.H. Colton 1865) (OOAMA), and in the 1866 ed (*LC Atlases* 6155); text on verso; twps are shown north to line Stephenson to Richards, with blocks south of L Nipissing and north of L Huron; roads shown and some named; railways including proposed lines: Stratford-Saugeen, Simcoe-St Thomas-Windsor, Lindsay-

Penetanguishene; proposed [canal?] route shown Toronto-L Simcoe-Nottawasaga Bay.
OOAMA USDLC

296 *1865*
GEOLOGICAL MAP OF CANADA / and the adjacent regions including parts of other / BRITISH PROVINCES and of the UNITED STATES / the Geology of Canada being derived from the results of / THE CANADIAN GEOLOGICAL SURVEY / that of the other British Provinces from the labors of / Dr J.W. Dawson Prof James Robb. J.B. Jukes and others / while that of the United States is compiled under the authority of / Prof. James Hall / From various sources mentioned in the accompanying text. / BY / SIR W.E. LOGAN F.R.S. / Director of the Geological Survey of Canada. / 1864. // Drawn by R. Barlow Montreal. / Engraved by A.W. Graham. Montreal / Printed in Colors at Stanford's Geographical Establishment, London, 1865.
Print (col lith) 22 x 49 cm 1" to 125 miles
In Geological Survey of Canada, *Report of Progress from its Commencement to 1863. Atlas of Maps and Sections* (Montreal: Dawson Brothers 1865), [Map I] (*Bib Can* 4217; OOAMA), and also in Commission Géologique du Canada, *Rapport de progrès* ... (Montréal: Dawson Frères 1865), [Map I] (*Bib Can* 4218; OOAMA); 30 classes of geology shown; the text includes extensive notes about the maps and their production and includes a list of source maps and surveys and notes on the geology; a note accompanying vol I of the *Report of Progress* indicates that, though planned for 1863, the publication would be delayed; later assigned GSC publication no 53 (Ferrier, 13).
OOAMA OTMCL

Related maps

(2) *[1865]*
GEOLOGICAL SURVEY OF CANADA / Sir W.E. Logan F.R.S. Director / MAP / Showing the distribution of various / SUPERFICIAL DEPOSITS / BETWEEN / LAKE SUPERIOR AND GASPE // Stanford's Geographical Establishment London
Print (col lith) 13 x 22 cm 1" to 125 miles
[Map VI] in the same sources as above; seven classes of sand and gravel; later assigned GSC publication no 58 (Ferrier, 13).
OOAMA OTMCL

297 *[1865]*
GEOLOGICAL MAP / OF / CANADA WEST, / giving / THE FORMATIVE STRUCTURE OF THE PROVINCE, / with / Townships, Counties, Lakes, Rivers, Cities, / Towns, Roads, Railroads &c. / by / / HENRY WHITE, P.L.S. / Lithographed & Published by W.C. Chewett & Co. / TORONTO.
Print (col lith) 44 x 57 cm 1" to 22 miles
In Henry White, *Geology, Oil Fields and Minerals of Canada West* (Toronto: W.C. Chewett & Co. 1865), at back (OTUTF); the geological information and title is overprinted on **185(14)**, original title deleted); a red line is used to show boundaries of geological formations across the province.
OTUTF

298 *1865*
TREMAINE'S / MAP OF THE / BRITISH PROVINCES, / CANADA, NEW BRUNSWICK, AND NOVA SCOTIA / Prince Edward Island, / WITH THE ADJACENT BORDER STATES. / Compiled and drawn from the latest and best authorities by G.W. and G.B. Colton / PUBLISHED FOR SUBSCRIBERS BY / GEORGE C. TREMAINE, TORONTO. / 1865
Print (lith) hand col 86 x 176 cm 1" to 25 miles
Insets: 'NEWFOUNDLAND' 1" to 50 miles, 'BRITISH NORTH AMERICA' 1" to 300 miles, 'MAP OF THE GREAT NORTHWEST' 1" to 50 miles; tables: 'POPULATION OF CANADA, 1861' (by co); twps shown north to Stephenson to Richardson and block south of L Nipissing; railways, co boundaries; shows area west to include L Superior.
OTMCL

299 *1865*
WALKER'S MAP / OF / UPPER CANADA / COMPILED BY THOS. WALKER C.E. / BEAMSVILLE, C.W. / 1865.
Print (lith) hand col 81 x 99 cm 1" to 14 miles
Tables: 'Money order offices,' 'County Population' (1861), 'Population of Cities and Towns' (1861), 'List of Telegraph Stations,' 'List of Division Courts and Court Clerks,' 'Ports of Entry,' 'County Grammar Schools,' lists of railways and branches for the following: Great Western, Grand Trunk, Buffalo & Lake Huron, Northern, Welland, London & Pt Stanley, Port Hope, Lindsay & Beaverton, Cobourg & Peterboro, Prescott & Ottawa, Brockville & Ottawa; shows twps north to line Stephenson to Burns and Fraser to Rolph, and some shown on the north shore of L Huron; also Land Agency divisions and some colonization roads; (Olsen 133).
GBL (70640 (9))

300 *1866*
Canada Sketch Map – Showing the Existing Surveys (prepared with reference to papers 38115/30) see my minute of 17/8/65 [Sgd W.F.D.?] Jervois [initialled] H.T. 7/8/66 G.J. 25/7/66 W.F.D.J. 17/8/66.
Col ms 54 x 86 cm 1" to 19 miles Endorsements: stamp 'Canada No 4088'
Shows area covered by 'existing maps ... most of which are published,' 'Fortification Surveys now in progress under dir. Col Jervois,' and areas to be surveyed in future; coverage of co maps by Tremaines and Walling shown and notes on availability of other published maps for districts and towns; (*PRO Cat* 1425).
GBLpro (WO 78/4652)

301 *[1866]*
FREE / PUBLIC SCHOOL / LIBRARY MAP / OF UPPER CANADA / Shewing the Municipalities and School Sections in which Libraries have been / supplied by the U.C. Educational Depository. // Lithographed by / W.C. CHEWETT & CO. / TORONTO.
Print (lith) hand col 22 x 56 cm Scale not given
In *Annual Report of the Normal, Model, Grammar and Common Schools in Upper Canada ... 1866 ... by the Chief Superintendant of Education* (Ottawa: Hunter Rose 1867), after 16 (*Bib Can* 2759); colour added by hand to show individual libraries in twps and whole twps covered.
OTMCL

---

302 *1866 (1869)*
GEOLOGICAL MAP OF CANADA / AND THE ADJACENT REGIONS, INCLUDING PARTS OF OTHER / British Provinces and of the United States. / THE / GEOLOGY OF CANADA / BEING DERIVED FROM THE RESULTS OF / THE CANADIAN GEOLOGICAL SURVEY / ... BY / SIR W.E. LOGAN, F.R.S. &c. / Director of the Geological Survey of Canada. / 1866 // Compiled and Drawn by / ROBERT BARLOW, SURVEYOR & DRAUGHTSMAN, / Montreal. // Engraved on Steel / by JACOBS and RAMBOZ, / Paris. / GUSTAVE BOSSANGE, / Paris Agent.
Print (steel engrav) hand col in 8 sections 144 x 238 cm 1" to 25 miles Endorsements on OOAMA (NMC 104195): '(Canada) 65' 'No 197' 'Recd Feb 10 1870'; stamp 'Quartermaster General Montreal'
Shows the area from L Winnipeg to Newfoundland and south to New York; geology hand-coloured over printed key and extends just north of L Superior and throughout Upper Canada; 33 classes of geology in seven main and four subclasses; the base information of rivers, lakes, and twps summarizes the work of the Geological Survey in topographic surveying in the province before Confederation; map not printed until 1869 and later assigned GSC publication no 65 (Ferrier, 197); (Olsen 136; Zaslow, 89).
OOAMA (NMC 104195, 48946–7) OTAR OTMCL

---

303 *1866*
MAP / OF A PART OF / CANADA WEST, / SHEWING THE ROUTE FOR THE PROPOSED / TORONTO AND OWEN SOUND / CENTRAL RAILWAY, / And its Connections / by / J.W. TATE, C.E. / W.C. CHEWETT & CO. LITH. TORONTO.
Print (lith) Size not known Scale not given
In *Report on the Proposed Route of the Toronto & Owen Sound Central Railway 1866* (Peterborough: Robert Romaine [1866]), at back (Casey I–3362); shows area from Toronto and Hamilton to L Huron and north; the proposed railway is shown from Toronto to Orangeville with a line to Owen Sound and another to Malta in Bruce Twp; other railways and connections; photoreproduction in pamphlet, original not seen.
OOA

---

304 *[1866]*
[Map of Canada West and part of Canada East showing progress of topographic mapping]
Col ms on linen 55 x 90 cm Approx 1" to 17 miles
Enclosed with dispatch of 11 June 1866 by Lt Gen J. Michael about progress of Survey of Canada (GBLpro CO 42/661 p 304); similar to **300** but less detailed; shows areas in which some mapping is in progress: Niagara Peninsula, area east of Ottawa-Prescott, track from Perth to Ottawa and from Kingston to Peterborough; notes on scales and state of publication; (Olsen map 138; *PRO Cat* 1424).
GBLpro (MPG 263)

---

305 *1866*
[Map of the southwestern part of Canada West]
D.W. Greany Capt & A.D.C.
Col ms 38 x 55 cm 1" to 9 miles Endorsements: 'I hereby certify that this is one of many plans or charts found with and captured from the Fenians at Fort Erie year 1866 [E.J. Brule] S.D.F.O.'
A sketch map showing rivers, roads, and railways.
OOAMA (NMC 2924)

---

306 *1866*
MAP / Shewing the Lines and Stations / IN / BRITISH NORTH AMERICA AND THE UNITED STATES / OF THE / Montreal Telegraph Company / 1866. / Hugh Allan, President. / PREPARED BY PLUNKETT AND BRADY, ENGINEERS / MONTREAL. // DRAWN BY / Jno. Johnston // ROBERTS & REINHOLD CHROMO-LITH. PLACE D'ARMES, MONTREAL C.E. // Entered according to Act of the Provincial Legislature in the year 1866 by Plunkett & Brady in the Office of the Registrar of the Province of Canada.
Print (col lith) 58 x 188 cm 1" to 20 miles
Shows the area from L Michigan to Nova Scotia and south to Boston; Montreal Telegraph Co. lines shown with connecting lines; distances marked along lines; railways and major colonization roads marked in the Huron-Ottawa area.
OTAR

---

307 *1866*
SCHONBERG'S / MAP OF / CANADA WEST. // Entered according to Act of Congress in the year 1866 by Schonberg & Co. in the Clerk's Office of the District Court of the United States, for the Southern District of New York.
Print (lith) hand col 28 x 37 cm 1" to 30 miles, '1:1,900,800 of Nature'
In Schonberg & Co., *Standard Atlas of the World* (New York 1867) (USNN); co boundaries shown, place-names, railways, and relief.
USDLC USNN

---

308 *1867*
GEOLOGICAL MAP / OF THE / GOLD REGIONS / OF / CANADA WEST / BY / HENRY WHITE P.L.S. / Author of the Geology Oil-fields and Minerals of / CANADA WEST / Maclear & Co. Publishers 17 King St West / TORONTO
Print (lith) hand col 28 x 37 cm Scale not given
In Henry White, *Gold Regions of Canada* (Toronto: Maclear & Co. 1867), opp 7 (*Bib Can* 4642); shows the area from Toronto east and north to Georgian Bay and the Ottawa R; shows twps, railways, colonization roads; shows major geological boundaries; some mines named.
OTMCL

---

309 *1867*
GRAND TRUNK RAILWAY. / AND ITS CONNECTIONS. / J. Walker Sc.
Print (lith) 10 x 18 cm Scale not given
In *The International Railway Guide ... 1867 October* (Montreal: Montreal Printing & Publishing Co. [1867]), 17 (*Bib Can* 4596); shows routes, stations, and connecting railway routes for eastern Canada and northeast U.S.; the other maps relating to Upper Canada in the guide are listed below.
OTMCL

Related maps

(**2**) *1867*
MONTREAL / AND / TORONTO. / INTERNATIONAL R.W. GUIDE.
Print (lith) 10 x 18 cm Scale not given
On p 21 of the guide.
OTMCL

(**3**)
TORONTO, BUFFALO AND DETROIT. / INTERNATIONAL RAILWAY GUIDE.
Print (lith) 10 x 18 cm Scale not given
On p 27 of the guide.
OTMCL

---

310 *1867*
JOHNSON'S / CANADA WEST / PUBLISHED BY / A.J. JOHNSON, NEW YORK. // Entered according to Act of Congress in the Year 1867, by A.J. Johnson, in the Clerks Office of the District Court of the United States for the Southern District of New York. // 17. // 18.
Print (lith) hand col 43 x 61 cm 1" to 20 miles
Endorsements (USDLC copy): 'Copyright Library Dec 23 1867'; deposit stamp and 'June 14 1867' '526'
Inset: 'NIAGARA RIVER / AND VICINITY' 1" to 10 miles; similar to Colton's map **295** but smaller and includes less area north of L Huron; 'geographical index' on verso; OOAMA copy has '18' and '19' in upper margin; shows cos, twps north to line Stephenson to Richards, with a block south of L Nipissing and on the north shore of L Huron; some railways shown and named, roads shown, and colonization roads named.
OOAMA (NMC 2928) OTAR USDLC

---

311 *[1867]*
Map / SHEWING PROPOSED ROUTES / of the / TORONTO, GREY & BRUCE, / AND / TORONTO & NIPISSING / RAILWAYS. / Being part of / CHEWETT & CO'S. MAP / OF / ONTARIO. / W.C. CHEWETT & CO. LITH. TORONTO
Print (lith) 41 x 49 cm Scale not given
In G. Laidlaw, compiler, *Reports & Letters on Light Narrow Gauge Railways ... with Remarks on the Advantages to be Derived by the Counties of Bruce, Grey, Victoria, Ontario ... from Direct Railway Communication with Toronto* (Toronto: Globe Printing 1867), frontis (Casey I–3466; *Bib Can* 9609); shows area from L Erie and Niagara Peninsula to the French R; and from L Scugog to L Huron; Toronto Grey & Bruce Ry shown to Mount Forest and then to Owen Sound with possible branch lines to Kincardine and Southampton; the Toronto and Nipissing is shown to Coboconk and to Franklin Twp; the report recommends light gauges for these routes.
OOA OTMCL

---

312 *1867*
SKETCH / OF / part of CANADA shewing / projected / "Grey and Simcoe" / and / "Toronto, Grey & Bruce" Railways. / Being Copy of Map published with / FLEMING'S REPORT on North Western Railway
Print (lith) 32 x 18 cm Scale not given
In F.W. Cumberland, *Railways to Grey* (Toronto: Globe Printing Co. 1867), frontis (*Bib Can* 4566); from the same plate as Fleming's 1857 map, (**228**); the two proposed railway routes from Angus to Walkerton and Toronto to Durham and Walkerton added.
OTMCL

Part II

Regions

Central

313 *[1788?]*
[Endorsed title]: 'Toronto Purchase in 1787.'
Col ms 50 x 33 cm [Approx 1" to 2 miles]
Endorsements: 'Q 43' '1092'
Shows the 28 by 14 mile block purchased from the Indians in 1787 and reconfirmed in 1805, from the Don R to the Etobicoke R, and the Toronto portage along the Humber R north to the Holland R; A. Aitken did the original surveying for the purchase boundaries in 1788 (*Indian Treaties*, Treaty No 13, I:32ff; Robinson, 247–54).
OTNR (SR 2485)

Related maps

(2) *[ca 1790]*
[Endorsed title]: 'Plan of the purchase made from the Indians at Toronto in the year 1787' Copied from an Original by Lieut Augustine Prevost R.F. [Sgd] Samuel Holland.
Col ms 127 x 44 cm 1" to 2 miles Endorsements: '1048'
Includes the Toronto purchase as shown on the above map but also the area from the Holland R to Matchedash Bay and purchases from the Indians in the L Huron area.
OTNR (SR 5913)

(3) *1795*
Plan of the Purchase made from the Indians at Toronto on Lake Ontario in the District of Nassau in the year 1787. Quebec 15th Jany 1795. We hereby certify that this plan is truly copied from the original [Sgd] Gother Mann, Lt Col Command Rl Engrs, John Collins, D.S.G., Wm. Hall Draughtsman.
Col ms 112 x 47 cm 1" to 2 miles Endorsements: 'LVIII Entd' 'H.H. M.[iles]'
Shows the same area and information as (2); modern place-names added later.
QMMMCM (4816)

---

314 *[179?]*
Sketch of the Tongue of Land (Coloured Green) in the Forks of Holland River [and] Survey of Holland River from the Landing at Pine Fort to the entrance of Lake Simcoe – Copy W.C.
2 col ms maps on 1 sheet 74 x 35 cm 1" to 10 miles and 1" to 40 chains Endorsements: 'Q 26' '1058'
The first map shows lands at the forks and to east of river 'claimed under the Cessions in 1784, 1787 & 1788' and Yonge St and Gwillimbury town plot; the second map shows the river in detail and 'Pine Tree Landing' at the 'Forks'; since Yonge St and Gwillimbury are not shown on the second map, it may have been drawn earlier.
OTNR (SR 2481)

---

315 *1790*
A Plan of the District of Nassau in the Province of Quebec For the [use] of His Majesty's Governor and Council Compiled in the Surveyor General's Office Pursuant to an Order in Council of the 22nd day of February 1790 [Sgd] Samuel Holland Surr Genl John Collins D. [S.]
Col ms 165 x 134 cm 1" to 2 miles
Shows the district from the Niagara Peninsula to L Simcoe and east to the Trent R and Bay of Quinte; lists surveys from which the map was compiled: Kotte, Peachey (1784), Tinling and Collins (1785); shows plan for twp at Toronto with 42 lots in 7 cons and town plot with reserves; detail on water communications from L Ontario via Toronto and the Trent R system to L Simcoe; notes on portages and nature of land; fronts of eight twps shown from Hamilton to Niagara Falls; Sidney and Thurlow twps shown; the twp layout at Toronto differs from **2010** and the position for the town is closer to Aitken's on **2012**.
OTAR

Related maps

(2) *[1790?]*
District of Nassau Copied from an original in the Engineers Drawing Room [Sgd] Samuel Holland Surveyr Genl.
Col ms 144 x 148 cm 1" to 2 miles Watermark: 'J WHATMAN' Endorsements: 'PH 256' '1075'
Inset: [Niagara R]; similar to the above map except omits most of Niagara Peninsula, and a small part on the east, but includes the connections to L Huron via Matchedash Bay; the detailed notes on the Trent system are those from Collins's trip to L Huron of 1785, and some are the same as notes on above plan; inset shows Indian purchase along the Niagara R and a twp planned below Navy Hall; (Robinson, 230, and Guillet, 139–41, list three copies of this map but the third one is the general map of 1790 (**10**).
OTAR (SR 17515)

---

316 *[1791]*
An accurate Plan of a Survey [words missing] of the River Trent (Head) [words missing – North shore?] of Lake Ontario to Toronto [words missing].
Col ms in 2 parts 39 x 112 cm and 37 x 107 cm 1" to 80 chains Endorsements: '1019'
Later note: 'This appears to be DPS Augustus Jones' original Plan ... 18th October 1856 [Sgd] Andrew Russell S.S. & D.'; a note indicates that part of Darlington, all of Clarke and Hope, and part of title are wanting; (SI 22 Feb 1791 to A. Jones to survey the front lines of a row of twps from boundary of land purchased from the

Indians at the R Trent to Toronto; OTNR FN 835 13 Sept 1791); shows the front line and broken front and sometimes several cons of the following twps: 'Dublin' [York], 'Glasgow' [Scarborough], 'Edinburgh' [Pickering], 'Norwich' [Whitby], 'Bristol' [Darlington], Hamilton, Haldimand, Cramahe, Murray; also shows 'carrying place' at Bay of Quinte and front line of Sidney Twp; note on lot sizes.
OTNR (SR 5803)

Related maps

(2) *[1791?]*
Plan of Eleven townships fronting on Lake Ontario beginning at the River Trent and extending westerly to Toronto as laid out and surveyed by Augustus Jones Dy PL Survr / A true copy by Jn Fk Holland [Sgd] Samuel Holland Surveyr Genl.
10 col mss size varies 1" to 80 chains
The individual maps were meant to be fitted together as co and twp names often cross several maps. The maps were endorsed and sgd by A. Russell, probably in 1856. They are as follows:

[1] [Endorsed title]: 'York Home Dist' 'Township of Dublin' 'Y 30' '847' OTNR (SR 2391)

[2] [Endorsed title]: 'Scarborough Home Distt Partial – Copy of Jones Plan ... [Sgd] A. Russell S.S. & D.' 'Y28' OTNR (SR 2051)

[3] [Endorsed title]: 'Pickering Home Distt Partial – Copy of Jones Plan ... [Sgd] A. Russell S.S. & D.' 'Y 29' '762' OTAR

[4] [Plan with title as above shows Whitby and Darlington] 'Z 19' '849' OTNR (SR 2320)

[5] [Endorsed title]: 'Clarke Distt of Newcastle (Partial)' 'Z 14' OTNR (SR 9369)

[6] [Endorsed title]: 'Hope District of Newcastle (Partial) Copy of Jones Plan ... [Sgd] A. Russell S.S. & D.' 'Z 15' '918' OTNR (SR 1328)

[7] [Endorsed title]: 'Hamilton Distt of Newcastle (Partial) Copy of Jones Plan ... [Sgd] A. Russell S.S. & D.' 'Z 16' '950' OTNR (SR 1249)

[8] [Endorsed title]: 'Haldimand Distt of Newcastle (Partial) Copy of Jones Plan ...' 'Z 17' OTNR (SR 1234)

[9] [Endorsed title]: 'Cramahe Distt of Newcastle ...' 'Z 18' '716' OTAR (SR 825)

[10] [Endorsed title]: 'Murray Distt of Newcastle (Partial) Copy of Jones Plan ...' 'Z no 13' '834' OTNR (SR 1728)

The plans are basically the same as OTNR (SR 5803) but on 3, 4, and 6–10 notes indicate the twps have been granted to various individuals by Orders in Council from 6 Oct 1792 to 22 June 1793.
OTAR OTNR (SR 825; 1234; 1249; 1328; 1728; 2051; 2320; 2391; 9369)

---

317 *1793*
Sketch of the Communication from York on Lake Ontario to Glouscester or Matchidash Bay Lake Huron taken by Lt Pilkington of the Royl Engineers and Alexr Aitken Dpy Surveyor in Octr 1793 [Sgd] Alex Aitkin D Syr York Oct 1793.
Col ms 120 x 59 cm 1" to 2 miles
Shows Lt Gov Simcoe's journey in that year from York to Penetanguishene, his route north via the Humber and Holland rivers to L Simcoe and the Severn R, and back along a more easterly route; encampment points and dates; shows proposed route for Yonge St and three trails from L Simcoe to Penetanguishene; fine pencil grid for tracing; (*OHIM* 3.9).
OTAR (Simcoe Map 446288)

Related maps

(2) *[1793?]*
[Title is the same as above map but signature is lacking]
Col ms 117 x 56 cm 1" to 2 miles
Shows the same information as above map.
GBLmm (Grenville Map no 71 case 75B)

(3) *[1793?]*
Sketch of a Route from York Town on Lake Ontario to Penetangasheen on Lake Huron – Upper Canada. by Lt Pilkington in the Year 1793.
Ms 137 x 60 cm [1" to 2 miles] Endorsements: stamps 'B↑O' 'IGF'
Similar to (1) except only some encampment points and dates are marked and notes on navigation vary slightly; there is also a copy sgd 'Copied by [Sgd] Thos H. Blakiston Lieut– Royl Engrs 15th Decr 1817' and endorsed 'B↑O' and 'IGF' (OOAMA (NMC 16827)); (Holmden 2134).
OOAMA (NMC 11273; 16827)

(4) *1793 (1800)*
A Sketch taken on a Journey with His Excellency Colonel Simcoe in 1793. Done by Mr Aitkin, Upper Canada. – [Sgd] Gother Mann Coll Commandg Rl Engrs Quebec 1800.
Col ms 126 x 50 cm 1" to 2 miles
Similar to (1) but does not show encampments; part of the area on the east is cut off and proposed Yonge St not shown; a few additions.
GBL (Maps 23b3)

(5) *[1793]*
[Two sketch maps showing area between York and Matchedash Bay]
2 col mss 31 x 13 cm and 31 x 17 cm 1" to 8 miles
Probably by Mrs Simcoe (cf. her diary 25 Oct 1793 in which she describes such a map: 'I send a map to elucidate the Governor's journey ... the western side of the Lake is drawn from Mr. Pilkington's sketches, the eastern from former accounts'); both show routes and one indicates the route and campsites of Lt Gov Simcoe in 1793 (*Mrs Simcoe's Diary* (1965), 108).
OTAR (Simcoe Papers Letterbook 36)

318 *[1794?]*
Road & Communication from York to Nottawasaga Bay. Copy W.C.
Col ms 134 x 53 cm 1" to 2 miles Endorsements: 'Y 35' '974'
(SI to A. Jones 12 Apr 1794 and A. Aitken 25 Apr 1794, 15 Aug 1794 to survey Yonge St and lay out road lots); shows Yonge St laid out to Gwillimbury with one-mile posts marked and road lots; comments on the state of the road; shows trails from L Simcoe to Penetanguishene, portage routes and area purchased from the Indians by John Collins.
OTAR

Related maps

(**2**) *1794*
[Endorsed title]: 'Road & Communication from York to Matchadash or Gloucester Bay' Copied from a Plan of Scale four Miles to One Inch Surveyor Genls Office Newark 22nd August 1794 [Sgd] W Chewett.
Col ms 72 x 47 cm [1" to 4 miles] Endorsements: 'Y 11' '783'
A smaller-scale map than that above with little information; shows Yonge St as a line angling southeast to York harbour, town of York and huts of Queen's Rangers, portages, and water communication from L Simcoe to Matchedash Bay; there is also a fragment of a map in OTAR(P) (C 44) showing trail between L Simcoe and Matchedash Bay with the same notes as (1).
OTAR (SR 7225) OTAR(P)

(**3**) *[1796?]*
A Survey of Yonge Street from York Harbour to Holland River the communication into Lake Simcoe, opened fit for a Sleighing Road being 33 Miles and 53 Chains Copy W.C.
Col ms 64 x 53 cm 1" to 40 chains Endorsements: 'Y 17' '816'
A more detailed survey than (1) with slightly different locations of lakes and rivers crossing Yonge St; shows relief, marshes, mileages along line to Pine Tree at Holland R, and the road as opened by the Queen's Rangers in 1796 (cf Firth, I:27).
OTAR (SR 349)

---

319 *1794*
Sketch of the Harbour of Prisque Isle. in the County of Northumberland Upper Canada [Sgd] A. Aitken June 1794
Col ms 48 x 60 cm 1" to 400 yards
A rough sketch showing soundings at the mouth and routes into the harbour, relief of shoreline, and sand-bars.
OTAR (Simcoe Map 445086)

Related maps

(**2**) *1795*
Plan of the Harbour of the Prisque Isle de Quinté Surveyed by Order of His Excellency Lieutenant Governor Simcoe in September 1795 with the Soundings laid down in feet by [Sgd] A. Aitken Depy Syr Midland District.
Col ms 38 x 57 cm 1" to 1/2 mile Endorsements: 'No 8' '897' 'Newcastle Harbour'
(SI 26 Sept 1795 to survey and reserve a town plot in vicinity of Presqu'ile); a rough plan showing a different configuration of shoreline from above map; note 'Prisque Isle Reserved for a town' [proposed town of Newcastle]; shows soundings at entrance and nature of shoreline.
OTNR (SR 1919)

(**3**) *1795*
Plan of the Harbour of Presque Isle de Quinté ... By A. Aitken Depy Syr Middland District – Copied from the Original by Mr Wm Chewitt. Surveyr Genls Office Newark 21st Octr 1795 [Sgd] D W Smith Actg Sur Genl.
Col ms 57 x 74 cm 1" to 1/2 mile
This is a more finished copy of (2) showing the same information but including more of the coast of Prince Edward Co.
OTAR (Simcoe Map 445789)

---

320 *1795*
Plan of Dundas Street, on the North Side of Lake Ontario, from Burlington Bay, to the River Trent – Surveyor Genls Office Newark 18th November 1795 [Sgd] D W Smith Actg Surveyor General
Col ms in 6 sheets 84 x 373 cm 1" to 1 mile
(SI 18 July 1795 to A. Jones to continue Dundas St from York to Bay of Quinte); shows the line for the road with type of terrain, road ends at Burlington with footpath connection to Coote's Paradise and then starts again west of there.
OTAR (Simcoe Map 445091)

---

321 *1795*
Sketch of the Indian Purchase at Penetangushene (Sigd) A. Aitkin Dy Survr. A true Copy from the Original – Niagara 26th May 1795 W. Johnson Chew for Keepr I.D.
Col ms 53 x 38 cm Scale not given
Originally enclosed with letter from Joseph Chew of 9 Oct 1797 to Capt James Green that included a requisition for stores to pay the Chippewas for the recent purchase of Penetanguishene and two plans (OOA RG 8 I/250 pp 208–17); shows the Penetang peninsula and Nottawasaga Bay with purchase line drawn across base; note indicates 'sold for £100 Quebec currency in goods 19th May 1795'; map is signed by four Indian chiefs and witnessed by 'J. Givens Lt.,' 'George Cown,' 'Alex Aitken Dy Survr,' and 'Wm. Johnson Chew Store Keepr I.D.' (Holmden 2309; *Indian Treaties*, Treaty No 5 (1795, confirmed 1798), I:15ff).
OOAMA (NMC 4276)

Related maps

(**2**) *1797*
Sketch of the Indian Purchase at Penetangushene, (coloured with Lake) (Signed) A. Aitken Dy Survr Copy D.W. Smith Actg Sur Genl 21 September 1797

Peter Russell President &c &c &c Montreal 2d Octr 1797 Exd Joseph Chew S.I. A True Copy W. Claus Supt I.D.
Col ms 66 x 42 cm Scale not given Endorsements: 'B 974'
A copy of the above map with the same notes and copies of signatures and from the same original source; (Holmden 2310).
OOAMA (NMC 4295)

---

322 *1796*
Letter B [Markham township] Newark 3th [*sic*] Nov 1796 [Sgd] William Berczy
Col ms 40 x 58 cm Scale not given
Originally from Berczy Papers, German Co. (OOA MG 23 H116); shows the king's reserves and occupied lots in cons I–V and boundary of the 64,000 acres given to the German Co.; notes indicate lines run by Iredell and clearing of part of the R Nen [Rouge R] for navigation in June 1795; Berczy notes on map that he hopes to make the river navigable further upstream; (Holmden 2542).
OOAMA (NMC 3510)

---

323 *1796*
Plan of Six hundred Acres of Land appropriated under an Order of Council for Richd Barnes Tickell Esqr – Surveyr Genls Office Upper Canada 16th June 1796 – W.C. [Sgd] D W Smith Actg Sur General
Col ms 31 x 16 cm Scale not given
Shows Nen R [Rouge R] with marsh at the mouth, and land in lots 34 and 35, con I, Pickering Twp and lot 1 in Scarborough Twp.
OTAR (Simcoe Map 445088)

---

324 *1797*
[Endorsed title]: 'Jones Lines from the River Etobicoke (Partial) meant to enclose the Toronto Purchase' [Sgd] York 20th June 1797 A. Jones D.P.S.
Col ms 81 x 48 cm 1" to 80 chains Endorsements: 'Q 33' '1070'
(SI 27 Nov 1795); the boundary of the Toronto purchase runs from the mouth of the Etobicoke R north 28 miles, east 14 miles then south to Yonge St; shows points where Humber R and footpath intersect boundary; shows Yonge St and grid of survey lines parallel to Yonge St in pencil north of mile 14.
OTNR (SR 987)

Related maps

(2) *[1805?]*
Plan of the Purchase about York from the Etobicoke. Copy W.C.
Ms 81 x 54 cm 1" to 80 chains Endorsements: 'Q 36' '1069'
Later endorsed title: 'Toronto Purchase (Home Distt) in 1817' and note 'Copy of Jones plan'; a more finished copy of the above map; shows town line of Whitchurch/Markham twps but lacks survey grid; this and plan below possibly made in 1805 when Indian treaty reconfirmed (*Indian Treaties*, Treaty No 13, I:34–5; see also **313**).
OTNR (SR 2480)

(3) *[1805?]*
[Endorsed title]: 'Toronto Purchase Eastern Boundary Line.'
Col ms 75 x 51 cm Scale not given Endorsements: 'Q 37' '1068'
Shows the eastern boundary starting just east of the Don R, north 28 miles across Yonge St then west and south; a lake is shown in a different position from (2).
OTNR (SR 2478)

---

325 *[1797]*
Plan of the Block of Land between Burlington Bay and Tobicoak. Copy W.C. [Endorsed title]: 'Mississaga Tract.'
Ms 70 x 53 cm 1" to 2 miles Endorsements: 'Q 8' '1060'
Shows a rectangular block along the lake from Etobicoke R, crossing the Credit R and Sixteen Mile and Twelve Mile creeks to Burlington Bay, that was to be purchased from the Indians; indicates surveyed road line for Dundas St; survey lines blocked in for two cons; shows Capt Brant's land north of Burlington; this plan appears to be included on a list of plans delivered to the Surveyor General 5 June 1797 (OTAR RG 1 A-I-1 vol 15 no 54); (*Indian Treaties*, Treaty No 14 (1806), I:37ff).
OTNR (SR 5929)

Related maps

(2) *[1806?]*
Sketch of the Tract purchased from the Mississague Indians [Sgd] C.B. Wyatt Surv. Genl.
Col ms 24 x 46 cm 1" to 2 miles Endorsements: 'S 394' 'G 468'
Similar to (1).
OOAMA (NMC 3296)

(3) *1806*
Plan of the Tract of Land to be purchased from the Missisague Indians [Endorsed title]: 'Purchase from the Missassagas in 1806. Reduced Plans – Drawn by T. Ridout.'
Col ms 40 x 64 cm 1" to 160 chains
(SI 31 Jan 1805 to S. Wilmot; OTAR FN 777 28 June 1806); shows the south part of the area from Nelson to Toronto twps, 'old road to York,' and Dundas St marked as a straight line; shows Indian reserves along the Credit R, Twelve Mile and Sixteen Mile creeks.
OTNR (SR 5743)

(4) *1806*
Purchase from the Mississague Indians in the year 1806.
Col ms 31 x 46 cm Scale not given Endorsements: 'Q 17' '1093'
The same as (3) except 'old' road not marked.
OTAR (SR 354)

(5) *[1806?]*
[Endorsed title]: 'Mississaga Tract.'
Col ms 75 x 51 cm Scale not given Endorsements: 'Q 18' '1061'
South part similar to (1) and (2) but also shows a large triangular tract to the north named 'Mississague Tract'; (*Indian Treaties*, Treaty No 13a (1805, 1806), I:35ff, 47ff, and No 19 (1818)).
OTAR (SR 2477)

---

326 *[1798?]*
Plan of the Upper Road from the Kings Mill on the River Humber, to the Landing at Mordens head of Cootes Paradise laid out by Mr [Jones?] Copied W.C.
Col ms 36 x 189 cm 1" to 40 chains Endorsements: '791'
(SI 11 July 1798 to A. Jones); shows Dundas St, relief, and intersections with rivers; below 'mountain' two routes angle south to Burlington Bay; shoreline and survey grid added in pencil.
OTAR (SR 81026)

---

327 *[1798?]*
[Endorsed title]: 'Yonge Street L Ontario shewing the communication from York to Lake Simcoe with a project for settling the French Royalists' [Sgd] D W Smith Actg Sur Genl Approved [Sgd] Peter Russell. Copy W.C.
Col ms 73 x 63 cm 1" to 2 miles Endorsements: 'Y 3' '767'
Twps named north to King, Whitchurch, and Gwillimbury and east to Uxbridge, Pickering, and Whitby; notes on the state of surveys; lots surveyed in west part of Whitchurch with indication of those settled; some road lots on Yonge St; Gwillimbury town plot located and note about finding a spot for town plot of 'Windham' on Cook's Bay; this appears to be a plan for allotting the twps of Uxbridge, Gwillimbury, and part of Whitchurch, and land north of Whitby for the Count de Puisaye's settlement and was probably made about Dec 1798 (Russell, *Correspondence* 2:321); (*OHIM* 4.14).
OTAR (SR 5512)

---

328 *[ca 1799]*
Sketch coloured Lake conjectured to be the Extent of the Cessions from the Indians to the Crown on the North side of Lake Ontario, not including Matchadash. The two small spots coloured Green are those which the President wishes should be purchased. [Endorsed title]: 'Cessions from the Indians on the North shore of Lake Ontario 1784, 1787 & 1788.' Copy W.C.
Col ms 38 x 53 cm 1" to 10 miles Endorsements: 'Q 38' '1059'
Shows the area from L Simcoe to the Bay of Quinte, and the Toronto Purchase '1787'; the two areas to be purchased are that in the forks of the Holland R and a small area west of the mouth of Etobicoke R; twps named north to King, Whitchurch, and Gwillimbury; note about twps on north shore of L Ontario: 'the front line of these eleven townships were surveyed in 1791 and are now located'; probably from the end of President Russell's tenure; (*OHIM* 4.3).
OTAR

---

329 *[1799–1800]*
[Map showing the survey for Dundas St from York to the River Trent by John Stegmann]
Col mss in 7 sheets ea 51 x 209 cm or smaller 1" to 20 chains
(SI 29 Apr 1799, 14 June 1799, 29 June 1799; OTAR FN 173 16 Dec 1800); detailed survey showing route, survey grid, relief, swamps, and sometimes older road line and alternate routes; the sheets are as follows:

(1) [York-Scarborough twps] [Sgd] John Stegmann Dy Surveyor. Endorsements: 'No 10' '830' OTAR (SR 81034)

(2) Plan of the New Road through the Township of Scarborough Corrected agreeable to an Seconde Survey August the 2nd 1800 [Sgd] John Stegmann Dy Surveyor. Endorsements: '874' Road follows a more northerly route than on (1). OTAR (SR 81025)

(3) [Pickering] 'I am positive that the Road passing through this Town is true by the Concessions [Sgd] John Stegmann Dy Surveyor.' Endorsements: 'Y 6' '765' OTAR (SR 81030)

(4) [Whitby-Darlington ... Sgd] John Stegmann Dy Surveyor. Endorsements: '876' OTAR (SR 81035)

(5) [Clarke-Hope ... Sgd] John Stegmann Dy Surveyor. Endorsements: 'Z 3' '883' OTAR (SR 81029)

(6) [Hamilton-Haldimand] Endorsements: '884' OTAR (SR 5560)

(7) [Cramahe-Murray] Endorsements: 'Z 20' Shows 'new road to foot of rapids or place for the Bridge' at the Trent R. OTAR (SR 81028)

OTAR (SR 5560; 81025; 81028–30; 81034–5)

---

330 *[ca 1800]*
[Sketch of the front of Murray and Cramahe townships and the town plot for Newcastle]
Ms 29 x 38 cm Scale not given Watermark: 'GOLDING & SNELGROVE 1799'
A rough sketch showing a few bldgs, mills with names at 'Oconsacon,' the outlet to L Ontario, and house of A. Willens; Murray Twp named but not subdivided.
OOAMA (NMC 3308)

---

331 *[1802]*
Plan of 7800 Acres of Land in the Township of Pickering in Upper Canada of which 6600 Acres ... are the property of the Honble D.W. Smith Esqr Surveyr Genl including 4800 acres ... granted to his Father the late Lieut Colo Smith 5th Regmt and 1200

Acres ... the property of his Daughter Miss Anne Smith [Sgd] W Chewitt Senr Surveyr & Dftsman
Col ms 41 x 30 cm 1" to 1 mile
Land is in cons 1–6; also shows Dundas St and names of other owners; part of a series of maps of D.W. Smith's land prepared by W. Chewett in 1802; there is also an earlier plan 'Projection of 4800 Acres of Land Submitted for Major Genl Smith in Township No 9 ... 21 June 1793' in OOAMA (NMC 3585) (Holmden 2654).
OOAMA (NMC 3585) OTMCL (D.W. Smith Papers B-15 p 44a)

---

332 *1808*
[Sketch map showing a road route from Kempenfelt Bay to Penetanguishene and other communications in the area] [Sgd] Chewet & Ridout A.S.G. 12th Feby 1808
Ms 67 x 50 cm Scale not given Watermark: 'J WHATMAN'
This is probably the diagram (or copy) for the survey of the Penetanguishene Rd which was issued with the instructions of 12 Feb 1808 to Saml Wilmot; shows road line from mid-point along the shore of Kempenfelt Bay in a straight line to Penetanguishene Bay; shows the bearing for the road and an estimate of work: 'say about 31 1/2 mile to be blazed'; notes on the land at both ends of the road line; shows portages, mill sites, and boundaries of Indian purchase; notes on the navigability of rivers.
OMSA (Clarke Papers A2 (974–96))

Related maps

(2) *1808*
A Plan Representing Lake Simcoe and the River Matchadash Communication to Gloucester Bay on Lake Huron not by actual Survey. – Shewing a line Surveyed for a Road between Kempenfelt Bay on Lake Simcoe and Penetangushene Harbour on Lake Huron by order of His Excellency Lieutenant Governor Gore Esquire &c&c&c. bearing date the 12th Feby 1808 [Sgd] Saml S. Wilmot Dy Surveyor March 23d 1808.
Col ms 96 x 76 cm 1" to 160 chains
(OTNR FN vol 5 pp 181–3 27 June 1808); shows a road line running north from a point just east of the west end of Kempenfelt Bay; shows mileage points, swamps, relief, and diversions along line; notes on navigability of rivers flowing into L Simcoe; one other road line shown in south part, and area further west noted as potential for road line; twps shown south of L Simcoe to King to Uxbridge.
OTAR (SR 7128)

(3) *[1808?]*
[Endorsed title]: 'Communication betwn Kempenfelt Bay & Penetangushene shewing Nottawa[sa]ga Bay & River.'
Col ms 65 x 75 cm Scale not given Endorsements: '778'
An unfinished sketch showing road roughed in from Kempenfelt Bay to Penetanguishene diverging around two lakes; relief.
OTAR (SR 7213)

(4) *[1808] (1815)*
[Sketch map of the area from York to Penetanguishene showing the line for a road from Kempenfelt Bay to Penetanguishene] Copied by [Sgd] [illegible] Saunderson D.S. Q.M. Genl Q Mr Genls Office March 13th 1815.
Ms 115 x 52 cm Scale not given
North half of map shows road location in a straight line as '28 miles' and other notes as on (1); the south half shows Yonge St with survey data along line and named twps on either side.
GBE (Sir George Murray Papers 46.10.2/105)

---

333 *1811*
Sketch from Cook's Bay, on Lake Simcoe, to Penetangushene, on Lake Huron, shewing the Tract proposed to be purchased (shaded black) with the contents thereof, upon medium calculation. [Sgd] Surveyor Genl Office York, Upper Canada 5 June 1811 Thos Ridout Surveyr Genl
Col ms 36 x 39 cm 1" to 4 miles Watermark: 'CHILTON MILLS 1805' Endorsements: 'Enclosure Mark C/ in Dispatch No 2'
Shows the tract from Kempenfelt Bay to Penetanguishene Bay that was purchased in 1815, the Penetanguishene Purchase of 28,800 acres (1795), and an area from L Couchiching to Matchedash Bay 'Purchase by the Depy Surveyr Genl of the late Province of Quebec 150,720 Acres' (1785); relief, swamps.
OOAMA (NMC 3323)

Related maps

(2) *1811*
Endorsed title]: 'C. Plan of a Tract of Land intended to be purchased from the Chippawa Indians in Upper Canada Containing about 250,000 acres for 400 Halx Currency' [Sgd] Surveyor Genl Office York U.C. 5 June 1811 Thos Ridout Surveyr Genl
Col ms 43 x 55 cm 1" to 4 miles
Enclosed in letter from Brock to Liverpool dated 23 Nov 1811 (GBLpro CO 42/351 p 127) with memorial from the Northwest Co. of 5 Nov 1810 requesting the land purchase to open a route from L Simcoe to Georgian Bay with town plots at either end; similar to plan above; shows earlier purchases and agreements; describes other documents relating to this purchase and indicates boundary; shows a survey line for a road and Indian path from Narrows to Matchedash Bay.
GBLpro (CO 42/351 p 127)

(3) *[1811?]*
Sketch from Holland River on Lake Simcoe, to Penetangushene on Lake Huron, shewing the Tract proposed to be Purchased coloured Yellow with the contents thereof upon a medium calculation being

250,000 Acres [Endorsed title]: 'The Penetangushene Purchase & proposed Purchase'
Col ms 67 x 42 cm 1" to 4 miles Endorsements: '1064' 'Q27'

Similar to plans above but includes area south to King to Uxbridge twps; shows earlier purchases, area west of Holland R and line of proposed purchase as containing 207,715 acres, Indian path to L Huron; correction made to shoreline of Kempenfelt Bay; later note on variation of compass at end of Kempenfelt Bay by Birdsall.
OTAR

(4) *1815*
Plan of the intended Purchase situated between Kempenfelt Bay on Lake Simcoe, and the Penetangushene Purchase on Lake Huron (coloured Yellow) containing upon a medium calculation 250,000 Acres [Sgd] Surveyor General's office York, Upper Canada 13th November 1815. Thos Ridout Surveyor General.
Col ms 57 x 49 cm 1" to 4 miles Endorsements: 'Memo for file 21543 & 2423 Ont. Jany 1956' 'F 4128'; stamp 'IASR'

Similar to (3) above; also shows relief, swamps, falls on the Matchadash R [Severn], route from L Simcoe to Matchedash Bay, Indian path and carrying place; the official plan for the purchase; (*Indian Treaties*, Treaty No 16 (1815), I:42ff).
OOAMA (NMC 4817)

---

334 *1811*
A Sketch of two Villages to be Surveyed one on the North Shore of Kempenfeldt Bay on Lake Simcoe and the other on the East Shore of Pennetangushene Harbour on Lake Huron. Yonge Street 23d Octr 1811 [Sgd] Saml S. Wilmot Dy Surveyor.
Ms on 2 sheets 109 x 48 cm 1" to 40 chains

A diagram for survey probably issued with instructions (SI 29 Aug 1811, 25 Oct 1811, 28 Oct 1811 to Saml Wilmot); shows a line opened for a 'road of Communication [Penetanguishene Rd] between Kempenfeldt Bay on L Simcoe and Pennetangushene Harbour on L Huron N 30° W 34 3/4 miles'; road appears to be opened for 10 miles north of bay; shows other lines opened in winter and June 1808; shows a boundary line for unnamed village [Kempenfeldt].
OMSA (Clarke Papers A-2 (975–74))

Related maps

(2) *1812*
A Plan Shewing the Survey of a Road of Communication, and one Concession on each side thereof, and the situation of a Village on each end of the Street shewing the Waters of Lake Simcoe and Huron [sketched?] Surveyed by order of His Excellency Fracis [*sic*] Gore Esquire Lieutenant Governor &c &c &c dated the 29th August 1811 [Sgd] Jany 1812 Saml S. Wilmot Dy Surveyor.
Col ms 67 x 190 cm 1" to 40 chains Endorsements: 'No 20'

(OTNR FN 578 31 Dec 1811); shows road with road lots and village plots at each end, and boundary of land purchased from the Indians; notes on terrain, vegetation, and surveys; names added later in road lots; there is also a copy in OTAR (SR 8544) with a slight variation in the title but without the addition of names and endorsed '1032.'
OTAR (SR 8544; 86753)

(3) *1815*
Plan By actual Survey of the Street of Communication between Kempenfelt Bay on Lake Simcoe, and Penetangushine Harbour on Lake Huron and one Concession on each side therof made out by the particular request of Angus Shaw Esquire, Agent to the North West Company. Copied by [illegible] Saunderson D.S. Q M Genel Q Mr Generals Office March 15th 1815.
Ms 72 x 95 cm 1" to 80 chains

Shows road with survey data along it and boundary of concession on either side but no lots; village plots; see also **C41** for a copy of this plan that shows road with lots and two village plots.
GBE (Sir George Murray Papers 46.10.2/106)

---

335 *[1817]*
[Endorsed title]: 'Land between Kempenfeldt Bay and Notawasaga Creek 1833'
Col ms 27 x 21 cm Scale not given

Originally accompanied a letter from Claus to Lt Col Addison of 30 Mar 1817 about the proposed purchase of land from the Indians (OOA RG 8 I/261 p 129); the date in the endorsed title is incorrect; shows boundaries of purchases from the Indians with dates, including block purchased in 1785, and purchase line to the west in 1815; land east of the Nottawasaga R is labelled 'No 1' and to the west on a line from the Holland R to Collingwood is 'No 2'; proposed road from Kempenfelt Bay to Penetanguishene is shown; (Holmden 1746); there is also a map for this area and approximate date showing Indian purchases in OOA (MG19 (F1) vol II p 33).
OOAMA (NMC 72396)

---

336 *[1818]*
Plan of the Route Between Robinson's, foot of the long rapids River Trent, and the head of that River, or mouth of the Rice Lake. Surveyed in May 1817, by Lieut Smith 70th Infy
Col ms 90 x 73 cm 3" to 1 mile Watermark: 'JAMES WHATMAN TURKEY MILL KENT 1818'

Provenance: OOAMA 85601/31 Collection of the 9th Earl of Dalhousie; a survey of the route and parallel to Percy Reach, and Mill Creek between the Trent R and Rice L; shows bldgs and names of settlers, types of trees; relief by colour wash; see also **C70–1**.
OOAMA

---

337 *1819*
Copy of a Survey taken by Captain Owen Royal Navy of Nottawasage Bay – Penetanguishene Harbour &c. in Lake Huron ... (Signed) W.R. Payne Capt Royl Engineers W.R.P. Commanding Royal Engineers Office Quebec June 26 1819
Col ms 52 x 68 cm 'Supposed Scale Two Miles to one Inch' Endorsements: 'I 19'; stamps 'B↑0' 'IGF'
Shows areas to be reserved for defences and a mill site in Penetanguishene and Nottawasaga Bay, Penetanguishene Rd to L Simcoe and connections from Kempenfelt Bay to Nottawasaga Bay, and at Kempenfelt Bay area to be reserved for a mill and other purposes; there is another copy at OOAMA (NMC 22697) further sgd 'Commanding Royal Engineers Office Quebec June 10, 1828' and endorsed: 'No 269' and stamp 'REO'; the base map is a copy of map of 1815 (**C37**); (Holmden 2094).
OOAMA (NMC 17910; 22697)

---

338 *[182?]*
[Map of townships of Darlington, Clarke and Hope] [Sgd] Saml S. Wilmot Surveyor.
Ms 30 x 40 cm 1" to 4 miles Watermark: 'I ANNANDALE 1819'
Shows roads including two running north to Cavan Twp, survey grid, and 'Darlington Mills.'
OTAR

---

339 *1820*
Sketch shewing the situation of the Gore of Toronto
Col ms 30 x 46 cm 1" to 5 miles
Sketch 'C' to accompany a report on 'Lands Proposed to be Sold to defray the annual charge of Presents to the Indians in payment for the Tracts purchased of them ...' in Maitland to Bathurst, 8 March 1820 (GBLpro CO 42/365 p 86); shows the area proposed to be laid out for settlement between Chinguacousy and Toronto twps, and Vaughan and York twps – '2000 acres.'
GBLpro (CO 42/365 p 86)

---

340 *[1821]*
[Endorsed titles]: 'No 1 Wilmots Sketch, of the interior Communication from Lake Simcoe to Sturgeon Lake.' [and] 'No 2 Wilmots Sketch of the interior Communication from Sturgeon Lake to Clear Lake &c. Copy from Mr Wilmot's Sketch.'
2 mss ea 32 x 83 cm 1" to 80 chains Endorsements: 'No 9 Z' '818' [and] 'Z 31' '819'
Maps fit together to form one; shows outlines of twps, lakes, rivers, exploration lines, and comments on bad and good land for settlement; prepared to accompany Wilmot's diary and field notes about an exploration for a road from L Simcoe (OTAR RG 1 CB1 FN 743, 744 28 July 1821).
OTAR (SR 7162; 5826)

---

341 *[1821]*
Sketch of the Water Communication between Crow Lake and Deer Bay. Copy from Captain McAulay's Sketch by J.G.C.
Ms approx 54 x 100 cm 1" to 1 mile Watermark: 'WHATMAN 1818'
Accompanies 'Copy of Report of Capt Macaulay R.E. on Part of the Water Communication between the Bay of Quinty and Lake Simcoe with Sketch of Survey 29 October 1821' in Maitland's No 57 of 19 March 1822 (GBLpro CO 42/368 p 73); shows the area from Crow L in Marmora Twp to Deer Bay and the south part of Lower Buckhorn L; iron ore noted on edge of Crow L; points shown on map keyed in report; portages; outlines of three twps shown in south part.
GBLpro (CO 42/368 p 73)

Related maps

(2) *[1821]*
Sketch of the Water Communication between Crow Lake and Deer Bay.
Col ms 68 x 99 cm 1" to 1 mile Watermark: 'J WHATMAN 1811'
Shows the same information as plan above; (Holmden 1591).
OOAMA (NMC 21711)

---

342 *1825*
Plan of Roads, Paths, Churches, Meetinghouses, Saw & Grist Mills Drawn in Consequence of a Circular from the Survr Genl Office 6th December 1824 Signed 17 March 1825 ... John Goessmann Dy Surveyor.
Ms 55 x 63 cm 1" to 2 miles Endorsements: 'Y 26' '799'
There is no key to information but roads, mills, and churches can be distinguished; gives data for York, Markham, Vaughan, and Albion twps, but other twps in York Co left blank; possibly unfinished.
OTNR (SR 2387)

---

343 *1825*
A Sketch accompanying a letter reporting the situation of the South River & the probable impracticality of uniting it with Lake Simcoe by a Canal Signed J. Walpole Lt Royal Engrs Fort George 22 Octr 1825 Commanding Royal Engineers Office Quebec 18th Novr 1825 [Sgd] E.W. Durnford Colonel Comg Royal Engrs
Col ms Approx 40 x 50 cm 1" to 4 miles
With his letter to Capt Melhuish of 22 Oct 1825 (GBLpro WO 55/863 pp 277–9); shows the southern Matchedash R and North and South rivers flowing into Matchedash Bay.
GBLpro (WO 55/863 p 277)

Related maps

(2) *1826*
Sketch showing the description of ground between Lake Simcoe & the South River to accompany a

Letter dated at York 25 Sept 1826 in which a Route by the North River is reported to be only of consideration. York U.C. 25th Sept. 1826 (Signed) J. Walpole Lt R. Engrs Copied [Sgd] Will R. Eaton.
Col ms 40 x 49 cm 1" to 4 miles
Originally accompanied Walpole's report to Lt Col R. Wright Commg Royal Engrs, 25 Sept 1826, on his survey to select a route for a canal between L Simcoe and Georgian Bay in the Matchedash Bay, Gloucester Pool area (PAC RG 8 I vol 428 pp 52–63); there is a copy of the map and report in GBLpro (WO 55/863 p 368); the map is further sgd '9th Novemr 1826 E.W. Durnford Col Comg Rl Engrs'; shows two proposed routes, one from L Simcoe and one from L Couchiching to South R [Matchedash]; shows good line for road to North R, and suggests latter as a better route for canal; notes on navigability, falls, portages.
GBLpro (WO 55/863 p 368) OOAMA (NMC 3324)

---

344 *1826*
Sketch showing the situation of the Townships of Merlin and Java, – containing about 60,000 Acres exclusive of Reserves for Crown & Clergy J.G.C. [Sgd] Surveyr Genl Office York 8 March 1826 Thos Ridout S.G.
Col ms 20 x 15 cm Scale not given
Originally enclosed with land petition from the Board for the General Superintendant of Education to reserve some new twps for school revenue (OOAMA RG 1 L3 E 14 no 50 (1826)); shows the location of the proposed twps of Merlin and Java later laid out as Nottawasaga Twp (SI 9 Aug 1832 and 23 March 1833); also shows Hurontario Rd, portage from Kempenfelt Bay to Nottawasaga R and the twps of Sunnidale, Mulmur, Osprey and 'Alta' [Collingwood].
OOAMA (NMC 53762)

---

345 *1827*
Plan of the Survey of a Route for a Road between Guelph and York passing through Streetsville on the River Credit and representing three different Routes proceeding from thence (Streetsville) to Dundas Road ... And also representing the Route surveyed for the Hon. L. Comp. also the Route proposed by Mr John Scarlett & James McNab together with a Representation on enlarged Scales 1 of the Village of Streetsville 2 of a Section of rough ground in the Route leading through Streetsville representing a deviating Route 3 of the village of McNab on the Credit. Executed f. T. St[evenson?] A.D. 1827
Ms (top edge missing) 36 x 96 cm 1" to 120 chains
Three insets: 'Representation of ... the village contemplated ... by James McNab' [Norval] 1" to 40 chains, 'Representation ... of a section of the Route being impractible ...' 1" to 40 chains 'Representation of the situation of Streetsville on the Credit in respect to the proposed route ...' 1" to 4 chains; shows routes including route presumably proposed by the Canada Co. through Eramosa, Nassagaweya, Esquesing, Toronto, Etobicoke, and York twps; tables of distance by each route; details on terrain and cleared land; attributed to Thomas Stevenson (see Firth, ... 1815–34 2:302).
OTMCL (E.W. Banting Collection)

Related maps

(2) *1827*
Sketch of the late exploring of a Route from Guelph to York with additional exploration for the use of Mr John Scarlet of the Township of York. Executed by [Sgd] John Goessman D.S. York A.D. 1827.
Col ms 26 x 101 cm 1" to 120 chains Endorsements: 'Y 21' '861'
Shows the same area as above map and the three road lines with the adopted line in the middle described as 'Road between York & Guelph as at present practicable for Waggon'; some information on the land.
OTAR (SR 5813)

(3) *[1828?]*
Map shewing the lines explored to ascertain the most eligible route for a Road from Guelph to York. John Thomason Fecit.
Col ms 28 x 99 cm 1" to 120 chains Endorsements: 'Y 38' '862'
Shows the various routes with proposed amendments, the middle line is as shown on (2) but with further amendments proposed; this is later than (2).
OTAR (SR 5814)

---

346 *[1828]*
Plan shewing the relative situation of the Town of Newcastle, and the Peninsula in Concesn C joining to the main Land on Lot No 35 in the B Concessn of Murray, laying opposite to Lots No 33 & 34, being the situation to which the Petitioners, pray to have the Town of Newcastle removed – W.C.
Col ms 26 x 41 cm 1" to 40 chains
Originally accompanied one of several land petitions, that of James Lyons in 1825 asking that the area revert to farm lots as it has not been settled (OOA RG 1 L3 L 14/111), or that of E. Buller in 1828 asking for a town site in compensation for other land (OOA RG 1 L3 B 15/106); also shows canal reserve in Murray and another reserve in Cramahe; (Holmden 1986, 1993).
OOAMA (NMC 3309)

---

347 *[1829]*
Route from Younge St. to Penetanguishene from Phelps Inn to Eaton's[?].
Ms 32 x 20 cm Scale not given
Originally accompanied Capt Phillpotts's letter of 18 May 1829 in which he reports that the road is in very bad shape and 'should be cleared for waggons immediately' (OOA RG I E3 vol 435 p 179); distances given along route; shows bridges, a

few mills with names of owners, route to Barrie town site; (Holmden 2313).
OOAMA (NMC 3325)

---

348 *1830*
Plan of Part of the County of Simcoe Shewing the Townships adjacent to the Penetangushine Road. Surveyor Genls Office York Feby 28th 1830 [Sgd] W Chewett Actg Surveyr Genl / J.G.C.
Col ms 94 x 62 cm 1" to 2 miles
The 'Explanation' keys lots patented, lots located before 8 May 1829, lots located by Peter Robinson since then, lots on which settlement duty performed, lots reserved for Indians and other purposes, and lots with mill seats; shows twps of Tecumseth, Essa, Vespra to Tiny and Tay, Orillia to Mara, Innisfil, and W Gwillimbury, town plots of Barrie and Penetanguishene, a few roads; (Holmden 2326).
OOAMA (NMC 21993)

---

349 *[ca 1830]*
[Plan of the south parts of the townships of Vespra, Oro, and Orillia]
Col ms 36 x 130 cm Scale not given Watermark: 'WHATMAN ... 182[3 or 5]'
Shows the survey grid and the line of a road along the shore of L Simcoe but angling north between cons XII and XIII in Oro and then east into Orillia; probably an earlier location of the [Ridge] road than **354** [ca 1833] (see Hunter, I:93); possibly a fragment of a larger map.
OTAR (SR 5314)

---

350 *1832*
Plan of Presque Isle Point in Newcastle District [Sgd] C. Rankin D.S. July 31st 1832.
Ms 66 x 58 cm 1" to 20 chains Endorsements: 'No 34' '981'
(SI 21 Dec 1831); shows the 'town plot of Newcastle' with burying ground and hospital square on the periphery, relief and marshy areas, and boat harbour by island; soundings off the point have been added later by J.G.C.; table of contents of types of land; the town plot, which is in outline only, was first proposed in 1795 but never occupied (see **346**, **1650**).
OTAR

Related maps

(2) *[1832]*
Plan of Presque Isle Bay, Newcastle Dist. [Sgd] C. Rankin D.S.
Ms 55 x 59 cm 1" to 20 chains Endorsements: 'No 14' '760' 'Newcastle No 14 received from the Crown Land Office 25th June 1844 A.R.' 'Vide Report C.L.O. 6th Jany 1840 No 292'
(OTNR FN 385, 809 1 Aug 1832); the plan is similar to (1) but shows a slightly larger area including front cons of Cramahe and Murray twps.
OTNR (SR 222)

(3) *1848*
Plan of Presque Isle Point. Crown Land Department Surveyors Office West Montreal April 1848. [Sgd] Andrew Russell S & D.
Col ms 79 x 65 cm 1" to 20 chains
This is the same as (2) with a few pencilled notes on land and municipal boundaries added later.
OTNR (SR 5535)

---

351 *1832*
[Plan of Smith and Harvey townships showing New Line of Road and the place for a bridge across the Otonabee River] Planned and Surveyed By [Sgd] J. Huston Depty Prov. Surr Novembr 1832.
Col ms (part missing) 39 x 46 cm 1" to 40 chains
Endorsements: '917'
Shows line for a road through cons XV to XVIII in Smith Twp to cross Otonabee R above Buckhorn L and then turning west through cons VIII to XI of Harvey Twp to Sandy L, and then heading north; part missing at top left; Capt Hicks's house on shore of Sandy L is shown.
OTNR (SR 6042)

---

352 *[1832?]*
Steam Navigation in the Interior of the Newcastle District. F.P. Rubidge Cobourg Nov 20.
Col ms 70 x 53 cm Scale not given
Insets: [1] 'Diagram representing The Mouths of the River Otanabee.' and [2] 'Diagram Shewing The Little Lake, part of the River Otanabee, and the Town of Peterboro.'; shows the area from Fenelon east to Burleigh Twp and south to L Ontario; twps, settlements, mills, and navigability of most rivers indicated; many pencilled comments on the land and the settlement taking place: 'much absentee land,' 'Catholic Irish – industrious and doing well'; shows roads and proposed railroads from Cobourg to Rice L and from Peterborough to Mud L; Cobourg and Peterborough shown; probably made in 1832 since (2) and (3) below appear to be based on it; (Holmden 1988).
OOAMA (NMC 21617)

Related maps

(2) *[1833?]*
A CHART, Shewing the Interior Navigation of the DISTRICT / of Newcastle, Upper Canada, and the proposed improvements on the Otanabee River &c. / Drawn by F.P. RUBIDGE, and engraved by T. EVANS, for the COBOURG STAR.
Print (wood engrav with typeset title) 33 x 23 cm Scale not given
Insets: [1] 'DIAGRAM / OF THE / Mouths of the River / OTANABEE / and part of the / RICE LAKE.' and [2] 'DIAGRAM / OF THE / Little Lake / Part of the River / OTANABEE and the town of / PETERBORO'; based on the ms map above but provides much less detail; shows the contemplated railway from Cobourg to Rice L; table of distances by land and river (steamboat); (Holmden 1992).
OOAMA (NMC 3052)

(**3**) *[1833]*
A CHART, / SHEWING THE / INTERNAL NAVIGATION / OF THE / DISTRICT OF NEWCASTLE, / And the proposed improvements on the / OTONABIE RIVER. / Drawn by F.P. Rubidge, ... Engraved by T. Evans.
Print (wood engrav with typeset title) 27 x 22 cm [Approx 1" to 6 miles]
In James G. Bethune, *A Schedule of Real Estate in the Newcastle District* (Cobourg: Printed by R.D. Chatterton 1833), frontis (*Bib Can* 1761; Fleming 691); the insets are the same as on (2); this map is from the same block as (2) except the title has been changed and the table of distances has been relocated; the real estate was to be offered at auction 1 Aug 1833 (changed to 29 Aug).
OTMCL

(**4**) *[1836]*
Chart shewing the Interior Navigation of the Districts of Newcastle / and Upper Canada.
Print (wood engrav) 12 x 17 cm Scale not given
In C.P. Traill, *The Backwoods of Canada* (London: Charles Knight 1836), opp 164 (*Bib Can* 1922, 1923, 7436), and in the following other eds: (1840), opp 146 (*Bib Can* 1924), (London: M.A. Nattali 1846) (*Bib Can* 1925), and 3rd and 4th eds, (London: Charles Knight 1838 and 1839) (*Bib Can* 7509, 7551); the map is based on (2) but has numbered locations for the information keyed at the bottom.
OTMCL

---

353 *1833*
[Map of part of Simcoe County showing roads and projected roads] Survr General's / Office York U.C. / 1833 / S.O. Tazewell Lithr.
Print (lith) 28 x 42 cm Scale not given
Shows the twps of Nottawasaga, Sunnidale, Flos, Vespra, Oro, Mulmur, Tosorontio, Essa, and Innisfil, towns and town reserves in Sunnidale [Rippon and Hythe], roads including new road to Sunnidale and 'proposed new road to Lake Huron'; notes at the bottom give the distances between points and costs of transportation by road and water from York; possibly related to the publication of *Information for the Use of Persons emigrating to Upper Canada* ... Surveyor Generals Office York 30th November 1832 (Toronto: R. Stanton, 1832) (*Bib Can* 1755; Fleming 676) which was supposed to include a plan but this is lacking in all copies seen; one copy accompanied a letter of Wm R. Hopkins, 8 Feb 1834, about a land dispute (GBLpro CO 42/418 p 214); map described in the *Patriot* 28 June 1833; (Holmden 1634).
GBLpro (CO 42/418 p 214) OOAMA (NMC 3327)

---

354 *[ca 1833]*
[Endorsed title]: 'Plan of Oro Surrounding tps. on Lake Simcoe U.C.'
Col ms 27 x 38 cm Approx 1" to 2 miles
Shows parts of Flos, Medonte, Vespra, Oro, Orillia, Mara, Essa, and Innisfil twps, the line of road from Barrie to Nottawasaga Bridge, Penetanguishene and Coldwater rds, the villages of Barrie, Kempenfeldt, and Shanty Bay, the names of settlers along the shore in Oro and the 'new line of road' [Ridge Rd]; Oro is noted as 'thickly settled'; plan probably dates from 1833 or a little earlier, before the Sunnidale Rd was extended beyond Nottawasaga Bridge but after the settlement of half-pay officers along the shore in 1831 (Hunter, 2:137–42); (Holmden 2161).
OOAMA (NMC 3326)

---

355 *1833*
PLAN / OF / THE COURSE OF / THE / RIVER TRENT. / Shewing the IMPROVEMENTS Proposed. / BY ORDER OF / HIS EXCELLENCY / Sir John Colborne K.C.B. / &c. &c. &c. / 1833. Drawn by D.J. Estry & J. Overend S.O. Tazewell Lithr / Survr Genls Dept York U.C.
Print (lith) hand col 57 x 44 cm 1" to 120 chains
Shows Asphodel, Percy, Seymour, and Murray twps and Trent R system with numbered points for proposed cuts or locks; 'Abstract Estimate 61 Miles & 365 Ft Lockage'; heights of lifts given; OOAMA copy has a ms endorsement: 'F.P. Rubidge del. N.H. Bairds Civil Engineer U.S. C.E. L.'; (Holmden 2583).
OFF OOAMA (NMC 4117)

---

356 *1833*
Plan shewing the Portage Road and Indian Reserve with the Improvements thereon from Lake Simcoe to Coldwater a distance of 14 miles. By William Hawkins, Deputy Surveyor. [Sgd] William Hawkins Deputy Surveyor York March 20th 1833.
Col ms 82 x 65 cm 1" to 40 chains Endorsements: 'Q 52' '1123'
Inset: 'The Narrows' 8" to 1 mile; (OTNR FN 771 27 March 1833); shows the reserve and road in parts of Orillia, Oro, and Medonte twps, bldgs and clearings with names of settlers, 'The Coldwater Establishment,' and licences of occupation.
OTNR (SR 6795)

Related maps

(**2**) *1833 (1842)*
Plan shewing the Indian Reserve from Lake Simcoe to Coldwater Taken from the Plan of William Hawkins Deputy Surveyor Dated York March 20th 1833. Drawn by A. Larue Land Surveyor D'ftsman Kingston 25 June 1842.
Col ms 82 x 52 cm 1" to 40 chains
An outline copy from the earlier plan of the survey grid and Indian reserve boundary; shows clergy reserves and notes on sales of sections of the

Indian reserve; another copy at OTMCL is the same except it lacks the notes.
OTMCL

---

357 *1833*
Plan shewing the route of a road from Kempenfeldt Bay thro' the Townships of Vespra & Essa to Sunnidale 10 mls & 73chs. Vespra 16th April 1833 [Sgd] C. Rankin.
Col ms 32 x 154 cm 1" to 20 chains Endorsements: '773'
Route for the Sunnidale Rd is shown from the bay to the Nottawasaga R at the south boundary of Sunnidale; note by Rankin that only a small part is cleared; shows terrain, vegetation, marshes, gullies, and streams requiring bridges (Hunter, I:92–3).
OTNR (SR 5326)

Related maps

(2) *[1834]*
Plan of a Road through the township of Sunnidale shewing the different pieces of causey etc. [Sgd] C. Rankin.
Col ms 91 x 60 cm 1" to 40 chains Endorsements: 'Y 14' '890'
(SI 30 May 1833 to survey road line from town plot at boundary of Essa and Sunnidale twps [Rippon] to a favourable point on L Huron for a town); shows the road along boundary between Essa and Sunnidale and then north through Sunnidale to 'Village plot just laid out by C.R.' at mouth of Nottawasaga R [Hythe]; notes on causeways required and work allotment for contractors.
OTAR (SR 7224)

---

358 *1833–5*
[Plans from the survey for improvements to navigation from the Trent River to Lake Simcoe by N.H. Baird]
11 col mss sizes vary scales vary
Baird surveyed the lower part of the system from the mouth of the Trent R to Rice L in 1833 and from Rice L to L Simcoe with a detour down the Scugog R in 1835; Baird's SI and correspondence for the survey, from June 1835 to March 1836, are found in OOA RG 1 E15 B vol 87; the plans are bound into an atlas with later plans of surveys and improvements to parts of the system (OPETC); Baird's report to Colborne of 28 Nov 1833 is in *JHA* (1833–4), App, and his fuller report of Dec 1835 is in *JHA* (1836), App 12.

The plans from 1833 are as follows:

[1] Plan of the Rapids on the River Trent From its Mouth to the First Navigable Water. Shewing the Improvements proposed. By Order of His Excellency Sir John Colborne, K.C.B. 1833. F.P. Rubidge Delt. N.H. Baird Civil Engineer [Sgd] N.H. Baird Civil Engineer
Col ms 70 x 210 cm 1" to 10 chains Endorsements: stamp 'BW'
Inset: 'Section of the River Trent' [Drawings of Dams I–VIII] 1" to 70 ft; the main map shows the location of nine dams and locks up to Frankford; relief, marshes, treed areas, names of mills, and some landowners; section indicates the level of the Bay of Quinte dated 'October 1833'; piers of bridge shown at mouth of R Trent.
OPETC ('Atlas' plate 2)

[2] [Longitudinal profile from Percy Lake to Crow Bay and Sections] duplicate 5 Oct 1833 [Sgd] N.H. Baird 1833
Col ms 70 x 360 cm 1" to 10 chains Endorsements: stamp 'BW'
Shows 'Section 2d across the Portage at Chisholm's Rapids, Section 3rd from Percy Landing to Crow Bay, Section 4th from Crow Bay to the summit of Healey Falls, Section 6th Crooks Mills'; level of Rice L above the Bay of Quinte.
OPETC ('Atlas' plate 3)

The plans from 1835 are as follows:

'No 1' Plan of Part of Otonabee River from Rice Lake Upwards shewing the Improvements proposed to render the same available for the purposes of Navigation By Order of His Excellency Sir John Colborne K.C.B. Lieutenant Governor 1835. N.H. Baird Civil Engineer 1835. F.P.R. Surveyed August 3 F.P. Rubidge 1835 [Sgd] N.H. Baird Civil Engineer M.I.C.E.L. 1835
Col ms in 2 parts 65 x 425 cm 1" to 4 chains Endorsements: stamp 'BW'
Inset: 'mouth of the River Otonabee' at Rice L; covers the area from Station 202 east, i.e., from Rice L to Monaghan Twp and Robinsons Is; shows relief, marshes, rapids, names of settlers along shore, mills, and mill dams, walls in place, proposed locks and dams and proposed canal route through Peterborough; joins with 'No 2.'
OPETC ('Atlas' plate 10)

'No 2' Plan of the several portions of the River Otonabee from Clear Lake to Rice Lake requiring Improvement on the Projected Route for a Water Communication from the Bay of Quinte to Lake Simcoe, shewing the operations required to render the same Navigable. By order of His Excellency Sir John Colborne, K.C.B. N.H. Baird Civil Engineer 1835. F.P. Rubidge D.P.S. Fecit. [Sgd] N H Baird Civil Engineer M.I.C.E.L. 1835
Col ms 33 x 480 cm 1" to 4 chains Endorsements: stamp 'BW'
Shows Young's Mill and Rapids, Douro and Smith Shallows, Kitchiwannoe L, Herriots Mill down to Rapids and Station 203; an attractive drawing of the river showing rapids, relief, and proposed dams and locks; joins with 'No 1.'
OPETC ('Atlas' plate 9)

'No 3' Buckhorn Rapids Hall's Mill shewing the operations proposed to overcome the Obstructions at this place By Order of His Excellency Sir John Colborne K.C.B. Lieutenant Governor &c &c &c 1835 N.H. Baird Civil Engineer. F.P. Rubidge D.P.S. fecit [Sgd] N.H. Baird Civil Engineer M.I.C.E.L. 1835

Col ms 66 x 81 cm 1" to 11/2 chains Endorsements: stamp 'BW'

Shows rapids, proposed dams and locks.

OPETC ('Atlas' plate [1b?], linen transcript plate 11)

'No 4' Bobcaygeon Rapids shewing the alterations required to render the Navigation available on the contemplated scale of Improvement by Order of His Excellency Sir John Colborne K.C.B. Lieutenant Governor &c&c&c 1835. N.H. Baird Civil Engineer M.I.C.E.L. 1835

Col ms 64 x 165 cm 1" to 11/2 chains

Endorsements: stamp 'BW'

Shows lock, canal, and dam from Lock Is to Dam Is.

OPETC ('Atlas' plate 14)

'No 5?' Plan of part of Scugog River at Purdy's Mill Shewing the effect the removal of the Dam would have upon the Navigation by order of His Excellency Sir John Colborne K.C.B. Lieutenant Governor 1835.

Col ms 64 x 146 cm 1" to 1 chain Endorsements: '387'

This plan is a transcript copy; 'Longitudinal Section from the Level of Sturgeon Lake to the Summit Level of Scugog Lake taken in November 1835' 1" to 15 chains; 'Transverse Section of the Scugog River Showing the Extent of Dam required of the lower extremity of Mr. Purdy's property' [Lindsay] 1" to 10 chains; shows proposed lock and waste weir at west end and bldgs and mills at east end.

OPETC ('Atlas' plate 19)

'No 6' Balsam Rapids. shewing the Works required to overcome the same, and to connect Cameron and Balsam Lakes, by order of His Excellency Sir John Colborne, K.C.B. Lieutenant Governor &c&c&c 1835. N.H. Baird Civil Engineer. F.P. Rubidge D.P.S. [Sgd] N.H. Baird Civil Engineer M.I.C.E.L. 1835

Col ms 41 x 126 cm 1" to 1.5 chains

Shows proposed canal, lock, and three sites on which dam may be placed.

OPETC ('Atlas' plate 15)

'No 7' The Proposed Line of Communication between Balsam Lake and Lake Simcoe By Order of His Excellency Sir John Colborne K.C.B. &c&c&c N.H. Baird Civil Engineer 1835. F.P. Rubidge D.P.S. Scripsit [Sgd] N.H. Baird Civil Engineer M.I.C.E.L. 1835 [another title] Diagram of the Country between Balsam Lake and Lake Simcoe taken from J.S. Smith's plan of Survey in 1834.

Col ms 66 x 96 cm 1" to 40 chains Endorsements: stamp 'BW'

Shows proposed route of canal overland for 16 miles from Balsam L to the lower Talbot R, Balsam L Rd in Thorah Twp, and area surveyed east of there by J. Smith (see **580**).

OPETC ('Atlas' plate 16)

'No 8' A Plan made from actual survey of the Talbot River from its confluence with Lake Simcoe. shewing the Improvements proposed to render the same available for the intended communication from the Bay of Quinte By Order of His Excellency Sir John Colborne K.C.B. &c&c&c N.H. Baird Civil Engineer 1835. F.P. Rubidge D.P.S. 1835 [Sgd] N.H. Baird Civil Engineer M.I.C.E.L. 1835

Col ms 49 x 351 cm 1" to 2 chains Endorsements: stamp 'BW'

Shows proposed canal, lock, and two piers at the river's mouth; rapids, depths.

OPETC ('Atlas' plate 17)

'No 9?' Longitudinal Section of the Line of the Proposed Water Communication from Rice Lake to Lake Simcoe, In Continuation of the Trent Navigation From the Bay of Quinte. shewing the Improvements required 'to connect those Lakes.' By Order of His Excellency Sir John Colborne K.C.B. Lieutenant Governor. 1835. N.H. Baird Civil Engineer M.I.C.E.L. [Sgd] N.H. Baird Civil Engineer M.I.C.E.L. 1835

Col ms 30 x 1000 cm Approx 1" to 40 ft

Endorsements: stamp 'BW'

Shows 110 miles of profile to L Simcoe with gaps in some sections; relief, trees, proposed locks and dams; see also the general plans of [1836] (**366**).

OPETC ('Atlas' plate 4)

---

359 *1834*

A MAP OF THE DISTRICT OF NEWCASTLE: / UPPER CANADA. / 1834. // Designed by G. Smart Esqr. // Engraved by Rd Barrett Port Hope.

Print (lith) 35 x 47 cm 1" to 6 miles

Inset: 'PLAN of the proposed CANAL / from / RICE LAKE to LAKE ONTARIO'; shows area from Eldon to Burleigh and Methuen twps, with roads and settlements; 'A Statistical Table of the District of Newcastle Upper Canada' lists towns and twps with number of churches and post offices, population figures for 1817 and 1833, table of distances; a proposed canal enters L Ontario at Port Hope; (Holmden 1994).

OOAMA (NMC 4799)

---

360 *1834*

ORILLIA / Home District / H. Bonnycastle del / S.O. Tazewell lithr / City of Toronto. U.C. 1834.

Print (lith) 37 x 24 cm Scale not given

Shows survey grid, rivers, north and south divisions of twp, bordering twps; (not in Holmden, but Holmden 1633 describes map of Flos Twp that has not been found although apparently printed; see Tazewell's report of 11 Feb 1834 (OTAR RG 1 A-I-7 box 9)).

OOAMA (NMC 4101)

---

361 *[ca 1834]*

[Sketch of the Simcoe County area]

Col ms 24 x 31 cm Scale not given Watermark: 'S EVANS & CO 1831'

Shows twps from St Vincent to Artemisia, Melancthon to East Gwillimbury and north to Matchedash; also shows the Penetanguishene Rd, Sunnidale Rd, Coldwater Portage, 'Portage' from

Barrie into Vespra to Nottawasaga R, Barrie, Penetanguishene, Village [Orillia], and the town plot of Hythe; possibly made about 1834 when Hythe laid out.
OTAR

---

362 *1835*
Plan of the Country between Lake Ontario and Rice Lake shewing the most eligible Route for a Rail Road from Cobourg to the Waters of the Newcastle District By Order of the Board of Directors N.H. Baird C.E. M.I.I.C.E. 1835 F.P. Rubidge D.P.S. [Sgd] N.H. Baird M.I.C.E.L. Cobourg 10 Octr 1835
Col ms 165 x 64 cm 1" to 20 chains Endorsements: stamp 'BW'
Shows the proposed route of the Cobourg Railroad (incorporated 1834; see Trout and Trout, 54) to 'Cochrane's,' then east and west proposed routes, then a west route to Claverton and an east route to 'Steam Boat Landing'; table of distances via the different routes; relief, spot heights, names of a few mills, travelled roads; the plan for the Cobourg railway as surveyed by Baird in 1835; some of his reports, etc, for the survey are found in OTAR (MS 393 C-1).
OPETC ('Atlas' plate 8)

---

363 *1835*
Plan Shewing the Reserve on the Portage Road from the Narrows to Coldwater belonging to the Indians coloured Red, also the Blocks No 1, 2 & 3, coloured Brown, proposed to be added thereto by Mr Anderson S.I.A. in his letter to Colonel Givens C.S.I.A. dated 13th February 1835 J.G.C. 1st May 1835 S.G.O. [Sgd] S.P. Hurd S.G.
Col ms 60 x 98 cm 1" to 40 chains Endorsements: 'YQ 35' '801'
Shows the Indian reserve lying on either side of the 'Portage Rd' in part of Medonte, Orillia, and Oro twps; three blocks are proposed to be added: two adjacent to the reserve and one south of the reserve; also shows a proposed road running north from Oro to Coldwater but west of the Indian reserve; there are also two untitled plans in OOAMA showing part of Medonte, Oro, and Orillia twps, the Coldwater Rd, lots and some houses: 'IASR F4154' [183?] (NMC 3518) and 'IASR F4162 [Sgd] R.B. Sullivan Survr Genl ... 25th April 1839' (NMC 22124).
OOAMA (NMC 3518; 22124) OTAR (SR 6746)

---

364 *[ca 1835]*
Townships in the Newcastle District open for Settlement [Sgd] J.G. Chewett.
Col ms 51 x 55 cm Scale not given Endorsements: '804'
Shows the area from L Ontario north to the twps from Georgina and Thorah east to Methuen; shows the villages of Lindsay, Fenelon Falls, Rokeby [Bobcaygeon], Bridgenorth, Peterborough, Keene, Cobourg, Port Hope, and a few others unnamed; a few roads are shown; a rough, possibly unfinished plan.
OTAR (SR 5564)

---

365 *1835 [1836?]*
Rough Sketch of part of Nottawasaga made by order of His Excellency Sir John Colborne in the summer of 1835 by [Sgd] R.H. Bonnycastle Capt. Roy Eng Western Di[st] 11th Feby 18[36?]
Col ms 75 x 130 cm 1" to 1/2 mile Endorsements: stamp 'B↑O'
Shows the mouth of the Nottawasaga R with a proposed line for a canal south through [Jacks] lake to meet the river again; shows the nature of the coastline, 'Penetanguishene Portage,' and the location of Bonnycastle's camps with dates; part of the title is missing and some information has been erased and replaced at a later date; an early plan for a canal in conjunction with the City of Toronto and Lake Huron Railroad in 1836 (Hunter, I:160); (Holmden 2095).
OOAMA (NMC 16912)

---

366 *[1836]–66*
Diagram of the Water Communication through the Home and Newcastle Districts From Lake Huron to the Bay of Quinte. With the Cobourg Rail Road connecting Rice Lake with Lake Ontario Compiled by F.P. Rubidge Land Surveyor Cobourg [Sgd] N.H. Baird Civil Engineer [oblit]
Col ms 71 x 131 cm Scale not given
Shows the area from Nottawasaga Bay east to Tyendinaga Twp on the Bay of Quinte, and the railway route from Cobourg to Rice L; later additions in red by G.F. Baillairgé (see (2) below) show the sections for the canal on the Trent system; routes, rise, and cost estimates; Sections I–V to Rice L has 37 locks; shows Sections I–V from Rice L to L Simcoe with 12 locks; other later notes show the Port Hope & Lindsay Ry; note by the Severn R 'not surveyed or estimated for by Mr Baird'; Baird and Rubidge drew this large map ca 1836 to show plans for the Trent navigation as well as for the Cobourg railway, and other data was added in 1866 (see plans of 1833–5, **358**) (Cameron and Maude).
OPETC ('Atlas' plate 1)

Related maps

(2) *1836–66*
Diagram of the Inland Water Communication From Lake Huron to the Bay of Quinte. With the Cobourg Railroad connecting Rice Lake with Lake Ontario. Compiled by F.P. Rubidge, Land Surveyor, Cobourg for N.H. Baird C.E. in 1836. Notes in red respecting works, constructed up to 7 Feb 1866, added by G.F. Baillairgé.
Col ms 84 x 132 cm 1" to 3 miles Endorsements: '156'; stamp 'BW'
The map is similar to the one above and the later additions are the same; note: 'For further information concerning the Works marked on this

Diagram See the Tabular Statement shewing the Nature of the Works and of the Water Communication on the River Trent and its Tributaries dated and signed by me on 6th February 1866 and transmitted to Secretary of Public Works with my report of 28th Feb 1866. Ottawa 28th Feb 1866 G.F. Baillairgé' (OOA RG 11 B1 (a) vol 191 subject 14); the map has some further later additions not on plan above.
OOAMA (NMC 16777)

367 *1836*
Plan of the Proposed Railway between The City of Toronto and Lake Simcoe to accompany a second report made Feby 12th 1836 by Thos Roy.
Col ms (upper corner missing) 387 x 99 cm 1" to 1200 ft
Letters and accounts for the survey by Thomas Roy are in the Allan Papers; shows a detailed route for the Toronto and Lake Huron Railroad (incorporated Apr 1836; see Trout and Trout, 54) from York to Holland R with notes on mileages, terrain, names of landowners and rivers; there are also detailed plans of the route of the railway from Toronto to Tecumseth Twp and Nottawasaga R (1" to 6 chains); 'Profile' and plans 'Site for a Village in the Township of Etobicoke' and 'Tecumseth Village' both showing proposed depots for the railway are filed with other engineering plans in portfolio 'Original plans and drawings Toronto and Lake Huron R.R. 1838.'
OTMCL (William Allan Papers)

368 *[1838]*
PLAN / of the / REVD F. OSLER'S / LOCATION / at / TECUMSETH / & / WEST GUILLEMBURY. // Lithographed by Jas Wyld, Charing Cross East, London.
Print (lith) 18 x 21 cm [Approx 1" to 3.5 miles]
In *The First Report of the Upper Canada Clergy Society* (London: Printed by G. Norman 1838), opp 24 (*Bib Can* 2234); shows churches, schools, residences, and open roads; the legend indicates the frequency of services and sunday schools at various churches and schools.
OTMCL

369 *[1838]*
SKETCH OF THE COUNTRY ROUND TORONTO
Print (wood engrav) 12 x 10 cm Scale not given
In *An Impartial and Authentic Account of the Civil War in the Canadas* (London: J. Saunders, Jr, Stevens and Pardon, Printers [1838]), Pt II:126 (*Bib Can* 5124; Casey I–1666); a location map showing twps, roads, and relief; 'Montgomerie's' is roughly located.
OOA OTMCL

370 *[184?]*
[Road from Cooksville south to Lake road] [and] Sections of Road from Dundas Street to Port Credit called Cooksville and Lake Shore Road
2 mss ea 104 x 35 cm or smaller 1" to 6 chains and 1" to 300 ft, 1" to 100 ft vertical Endorsements: stamp [BW] '414' (on sections)
The map shows Indian line and Indian reserve, wooded areas and clearings, and several bldgs in Cooksville; the sections show culverts and small creeks; possibly connected with work on the West York Rd completed by 1847 ('Report ... Public Works ... 1847' in *JLA* (1848), App N).
OOAMA (NMC 8844; 70938)

371 *1841*
MAP / of the / HOME & SIMCOE DISTRICTS / CANADA. / Compiled from the Township Maps in the Surveyor General's Office by / C. RANKIN ESQ. / of the Surveyor General's Department / Toronto 1st March 1841 Miller's Lith.
Print (lith) 101 x 119 cm 1" to 200 chains
Shows the area west to Owen Sound and twps St Vincent, Euphrasia, Collingwood, Luther, and Amaranth; shows twps with survey grid, roads (some named), towns, and post offices; 'On this Map each Township is by itself perfect, shewing all the Concessions, Lots &c. In regard to the meeting of the Corners or Concession lines of adjoining Townships, it may be (from irregularity of different Surveys etc) that in some instances on the ground, they will differ a little from the appearance here – in like Manner the Roads (represented by the dotted lines) may occasionally vary a little as to their manner of crossing lots. Besides these Roads there are many others in the older settled townships as – Whitby, Markham, Vaughan, Toronto, etc. opened on the Government Allowances between Concessions & Lots, as indicated by the heavy lines and new Roads are constantly being opened in most of the Townships ...'; shows the line of road from Oakville to Owen Sound with notes on terrain [Garafraxa Rd]; advertised for sale in the *Toronto Patriot* from 29 Oct 1841 until March 1842; OOAMA (NMC 11272) has ms adds showing 'the road from Toronto to Saugine Surveyed for the Board of Works. 1842. W.H.' (Holmden 1713); OTAR and OLU copies have later ms adds showing railways; OMSA copy has ms adds of 'Sheriffs sale of Land for Taxes'; (Holmden 1713, 1715; *OHIM* 4.21).
OLU OMSA OOAMA (NMC 11272; 17638)
OTAR OTMCL

372 *1841*
Sketch of the Outlets of Black's & Annis's Creeks in the Township of Whitby. Shewing the Proposed Sites for Harbours. Surveyed by George Saunders D.P.S. 1841 N.H. Baird Civil Engineer
Col ms 48 x 64 cm 1" to 10 chains Endorsements: 'Sketch referred to in my Report 11th [illegible] [Sgd] N.H. Baird Civil Engineer Cobourg 13th September 184[1?]'; stamps 'BW' '631'
Shows two piers and further proposed pier and bridge, 'New road from 'Skue's Corners'

[Oshawa], 'Road from Farwell's Corner,' shoreline, sand-bars, and soundings; Baird's report on his survey for the Board of Works is found in OTAR (MS 393 E-6).
OOAMA (NMC 4962)

---

373 *[1841]*
[Sketch of the region from Toronto to the River Trent] N.H. B[aird].
Ms 39 x 48 cm Scale not given
With report 'River Trent and Inland Waters of the District of Newcastle' in Sir George Arthur's report on the economy of the province, 2 March 1841 (GBLpro CO 42/476 p 104); shows locks built, proposed, or being built on the Trent R system; also shows intended harbours in Clarke and Darlington twps; list of distances; the report discusses the communication routes by land and canals between Penetanguishene and Kingston, and gives a description of works to improve navigation on lakes and rivers.
GBLpro (CO 42/476 p 104)

---

374 *1842*
Map of the Country between Rice Lake and Lake Ontario shewing the Line of Proposed Plank Road. From Actual Survey By N.H. Baird C.E. April 1842 Drawn by J. Lyons. Plan referred to in Report of this date [Sgd] N.H. Baird Civil Engineer. Eng. Office Cobourg 26 [?] 1842
Col ms 98 x 61 cm 1" to 40 chains Endorsements: stamps 'BW' '442'
(BW SI 8 Feb 1842 to survey for best line for road from Rice L to L Ontario and later extension to Peterborough); shows Port Hope, Cobourg, road to Peterborough from Port Hope with branch to Rice L at Bewdley, and 'Bosket route' further to the east from Kingston Rd to the New Landing; a possible road line is also shown from Cobourg with a few deviations around 'Prospect Hill' in Hamilton Twp; the first and second reports (8 Oct 1842) of the Select Committee on the road are in *JLA* (1842), App 10; (Holmden 2154);.
OOAMA (NMC 22082)

Related maps

(2) *1842*
[Proposed road lines between Rice Lake and Lake Ontario] Mapped and Surveyed By [Sgd] John Huston Depty Prov. Surveyor September 1842.
Col ms 92 x 53 cm 1" to 30 chains Endorsements: stamps 'BW' '443'
Shows Hope and Hamilton twps and generally includes less detail than plan above; shows the same road route as on (1) to Rice L at Black's Landing; also shows road line to the east with notes indicating swampy parts; (Holmden 2155).
OOAMA (NMC 22083)

(3) *[1852?]*
[Road lines and proposed road lines between Rice Lake and Lake Ontario]
Col ms 83 x 57 cm [1" to 40 chains]
In 'A Series of Diagrams ... Illustrative of the Various Local Improvements ... Completed by the Board of Works ... Samuel Keefer 1844,' plate 60 (OOAMA RG 11M 85603/40); covers the same area as plans above but with later information; shows Port Hope and Cobourg with boundaries as of Incorporation Act [1850]; shows western 'line of road improved and graveled by the Board of Works' (completed 1846, OOA RG 11 A3 vol 137 no 77), 'Bosket line for Road' and a deviation west of it 'Newton line of Road' 'Line surveyed by N.H. Baird' (along Hamilton/Hope boundary), proposed branch road to Cobourg, 'Toronto & Kingston Mail Road,' 'Road formerly known as Dundas St,' 'Common travelled Rd to Rice Lake' (from Cobourg), and 'Proposed Railroad Route' from Cobourg to halfway along Rice L [Cobourg & Peterborough Railway Co. incorporated 1852]; 'Gulls Island Light House,' steamboat landing shown at Bewdley.
OOAMA (NMC 16962)

---

375 *[1842]*
Plan and Section of Two Routes for Secton B of the Rouge Hill McAdamized Road [and endorsed title]: 'Plan and Section of Rouge Hill R.A. Maingy No 309'
Col ms 51 x 70 cm 1" to 2 chains Endorsements: stamps 'BW' '367'
Two sections: 1" to 40 ft; shows two possible routes around the hill, points to be bridged, with notes on advantages of one route sgd 'Robt A. Maingy'; Maingy wrote letters to the Board of Works on the matter in early 1842 (OOA RG 11 A2 vol 93); (Holmden 1339).
OOAMA (NMC 22767)

Related maps

(2) *1843*
Plan and Section of the Kingston Road from the Rouge Hill to the Eastern Boundary of the Township of Whitby [Sgd] St Catharines 22d April 1843 David Thorburn, Francis Hall [and title] No 1 Plan of Section of unfinished Part of Toronto East Road from Rouge Hill to the District Boundary [Sgd] Francis Hall
Col ms 25 x 378 cm 1" to 10 chains, 1" to 50 ft vertical Endorsements: stamp [BW] '432'
Shows the line of road with all bldgs marked including inns, churches, etc; section shows 'grades proposed to be adopted in the General Estimate F.H.'; line around Rouge Hill not shown.
OOAMA (NMC 78509)

(3) *1845*
Plan of the Rouge-Hill with the several lines of Road. Office of the Board of Works. 1845 [and] Section of Mr Keefer's Line
Col ms 57 x 83 cm 1" to 100 ft
In Samuel Keefer, 'A Series of Diagrams ... 1844' (OOAMA RG 11M 85603/40); (BW SI to J. Lyons 19 Apr 1845 refers to Keefer's line and plan for long bridge and further surveying of parts of line);

shows three different lines for the Rouge Hill including Maingy's line to the north with two bridges, 'present travelled road' to the east with one bridge, and Keefer's line to the south with plan for elevated bridge and side cutting on hill.
OOAMA (NMC 16964)

---

376 *1843*
Plan of the Proposed Road from Bradford To Barrie Surveyed pursuant to Instructions from The Honorable H.H. Killaly Presdt. Board of Works. [Sgd] William Hawkins Kingston Feb. 1843.
Col ms 169 x 111 cm 3" to 1 mile, 1" to 200 ft vertical Endorsements: stamps 'BW' '392'
Addressed to 'The Honorable Hamilton H. Killaly President Board of Works &c &c &c Kingston'; indicates mileages along road, relief, and marshes; profile of section between Bondhead and Barrie and Bondhead and Holland R.
OOAMA (NMC 22609)

---

377 *1843*
Road from the Narrows to Coldwater Surveyed under the Authority of the Honble The Board of Works May 1843. [Sgd] William Hawkins [Belleville?] July 1843.
Col ms 33 x 197 cm 4" to 1 mile Endorsements: stamps 'BW' '421'
Shows the present travelled road from the Narrows between L Simcoe and L Couchiching to Coldwater [Coldwater Rd]; places noted where it could be altered to shorten it and costs listed; distances for each section; bridges, relief, houses.
OOAMA (NMC 21994)

---

378 *[1844?]*
Survey of the Sixteen – Mile – Creek Copy Office of the Board of Works
Col ms 60 x 85 cm 1" to 2 chains Watermark: 'J WHATMAN TURKEY MILL 1844' Endorsements: stamps 'BW' '408'
Shows old road and new proposed line with lengths; new bridges are shown further downstream; connecting routes to Toronto, Dundas St, Hamilton, and Oakville.
OOAMA (NMC 21804)

Related maps

(2) *[1844?]*
Survey of the 16 Mile Creek
Col ms 89 x 143 cm 1" to 2 chains Endorsements: stamp '408'
This plan covers a larger area and shows a few more bldgs along the road; shows bearings of survey line for new route and deviation line west of river.
OOAMA (NMC 17968)

---

379 *[1845]*
[Chart of shoreline from Nottawasaga Bay to Rennies Bay] [Sgd] J. Harper
Ms 38 x 26 cm 1" to 2 miles
Originally with James Harper's letter of 15 Nov 1845 to Capt Boxer (GBLpro Adm 7/626); soundings, points, and bays named; nature of shoreline, relief, portages and roads across Penetang peninsula shown; (*PRO Cat* 1462).
GBLpro (MPII 6(1))

---

380 *1845*
[Plan of the Road through Reach, Brock, and Thorah townships] [Sgd] James Lyons, Sept [illegible 1]845.
Col ms 162 x 50 cm 2" to 1 mile Endorsements: stamps 'BW' '441'
Shows the road going north through middle of twps to mile 31 with a branch road to Scugog, present travelled road, proposed route following con lines, sections presently planked, other roads through Beaverton; the Windsor and Scugog Rd was finished in 1846 (OOA RG 11 A3 vol 137 no 160 27 Feb 1847).
OOAMA (NMC 21924)

Related maps

(2) *1846*
Map, shewing the continuation of the Windsor-Harbour and Lake Scugog Road to the Narrows of Lake Simcoe. Surveyed by James Lyons. C.E. Septr 1845. Office of the Board of Works. 1846.
Col ms 52 x 131 cm 1" to 80 chains Endorsements: BW '527'
Includes the information on map above but also shows the road terminating at Atherley in Mara Twp, and is at a smaller scale; also a copy at OOAMA with the same title but no signature or date, stamped BW '401' (NMC 22118); (Holmden 2899).
OOAMA (NMC 16830; 22118)

---

381 *1846*
Plan of the Country between Presqu'Isle Harbour and the Bay of Quinte shewing the proposed Cut for a Canal. March 1846. (Signed) James Lyons.
Col ms 70 x 133 cm [8" to 1 mile]
Profile: 1" to 10 chains, 1" to 20 ft vertical; accompanied report by Samuel Keefer, E.B.W., 8 Apr 1846 (OOA RG 11 A1 11/68–11); shows the location for the [Murray] canal, marshy areas, and an alternative exit to Twelve O'Clock Point on the Quinte side; (Holmden 2389).
OOAMA (NMC 11316)

---

382 *1846*
Plan of the River Trent between Widow Harrisn [*sic*] and the Bay of Quinte Shewing the Proposed Improvement. March 1846 'Signed' James Lyons. Board of Works 1846. Copy. [and] Section ... [Sgd] James Lyons March 1846
2 col mss 89 x 49 cm and 21 x 168 cm 1" to 20 chains, 1" to 20 ft vertical
(BW SI 7 Oct 1845 to survey the Trent Canal and estimate routes and need for locks); shows the

route of canal from Bay of Quinte to above Frankford with rough positions of proposed locks; relief.
OPETC ('Atlas' pp 21, 22)

Related maps

(**2**) *1846*
Plan of the River Trent between Crow Bay and Percy Landing Shewing the Proposed Improvements March 1846 [Sgd] James Lyons [and] Section ... [Sgd] James Lyons March 1846
2 col mss ea 71 x 50 cm 1" to 20 chains and 1" to 10 chains, 1" to 20 ft vertical
Shows canal route with locks from Percy Landing to Myers Mills and from there past Ranney Falls to Crowe Bay; proposed slides at Crowe Bay.
OPETC ('Atlas' pp 25, 26)

(**3**) *1846*
Plan of the River Trent between Heeley's Falls and Crow Bay Shewing the Proposed Improvement March 1846 [Sgd] James Lyons
Col ms 49 x 75 cm 1" to 10 chains
'Section': 1" to 5 chains, 1" to 20 ft vertical; shows proposed slide and canal and four dams.
OPETC ('Atlas' p 31)

---

383 *1846*
Sketch of part of the Simcoe District Shewing the Road from Barrie to Nottawasagua. Office of the Board of Works, 1846.
Col ms 35 x 50 cm 1" to 200 chains Endorsements: [BW] '437'
Shows the Sunnidale Rd in Vespra and Sunnidale twps and its junction with Hurontario St in Nottawasaga Twp.
OOAMA (NMC 3328)

---

384 *1847*
MAP AND PROFILE / of RAILWAY from PETERBOROUGH to PORT HOPE / Scobie & Balfour, Lith. Toronto.
Print (lith) 37 x 34 cm 1" to 6 miles
In *Engineer's Report and Statistical Information, Relative to the Proposed Railway from Port Hope to Peterboro* (Port Hope: Printed by William Furby 1847), after title-p (*Bib Can* 2864; Casey I-2088); includes a profile; shows area from Darlington to Murray and from Eldon to Methuen twps, the proposed Peterboro' and Port Hope Railway (incorporated 1846; see Trout and Trout, 55) and branch to Millbrook with major roads, towns, and heights in area, 'practicable line of railway to Lakes Simcoe and Huron' and 'Proposed course for railway from Toronto to Kingston.'
OOA OTMCL

---

385 *1848*
MAP OF THE / NEWCASTLE & COLBORNE / DISTRICTS. / Compiled from / Maps of the original Surveys and the best Authorities / by Sandford A. Fleming, Surveyor. / Published by Scobie & Balfour, Lith.. Toronto 1848.
Print (lith) 88 x 81 cm 1" to 2 miles
'Explanations': road allowances, post offices, mills, schools, principal travelled roads, plank and gravelled roads, proposed railways; twp and district boundaries; shows the proposed railway Toronto-Kingston (ending at Port Hope), and the proposed Peterboro' and Port Hope Railway with branch to Millbrook; also 'contemplated line of railway from Peterboro to Lake Huron'; includes statistical table of the districts, table of population of towns and villages, table of distances between towns by various routes; OTAR copy has later ms adds showing co boundaries and Brighton twp as of 1851; advertised as published in *British Colonist* (Toronto) 16 Feb 1848.
GBL (70645(80)) OOAMA (NMC 11263)
OPETCM OTAR OTUTF

---

386 *1849*
Map of the damaged lands ... Newcastle District ... Surveyed & Drawn by James Lyons C.E. & D.S. July 1849
6 col mss sizes vary 1" to 5 chains
(SI 18 Oct 1848 to survey certain lands purchased by the Dept of Public Works and drowned as a result of dam construction); the maps show the extent of flooding from the Trent Canal with lot and con nos and names of landowners affected; the maps are as follows:
No I twp of Seymour (cons II and III, lots 20–6)
No II twp of Murray (cons IX and X, lots 1–5)
No III gore of Seymour (lots 10–15)
No IV twp of Seymour (con I, lot 6; con XIII, lot 14)
No V twp of Murray (cons VIII–IX, lots 22–7)
No VI twp of Seymour (con I, lot 22)
OPETC ('Atlas' pp 27, 23, 28, 29, unpaged, 30)

Related maps

(**2**) *1849 (1864)*
[Maps of damaged lands in the townships of Seymour and Murray, Newcastle District caused by the construction of Public Works. Surveyed and Drawn by J. Lyons C.E. & D.S. July 1849]
Department of Crown Lands Quebec 26th Novr 1864 [Sgd] Andrew Russell Assist. Commissioner.
6 col mss on linen sizes vary 1" to 5 chains
Copies of maps made in 1849 as follows:
No I '16092/64' (SR 78271); No 2 (dated 31 July 1865) '16093/65' (SR 78266); No III '16092/65' (SR 78268); No IV '10150' and '16093/65' (SR 78270); No V (SR 78267); No VI (SR 78269).
OTNR (SR 78266–71)

---

387 *[185?]*
[Sketch of the township of Orillia and surrounding area showing the Coldwater Road and the Matchedash Road] [Sgd] J. Ardagh M.L. Orillia
Ms 35 x 25 cm Scale not given
Shows Matchedash, Tay, Medonte, Oro, and Orillia twps; Coldwater Rd runs from Orillia to

Coldwater and Sturgeon Bay; a note indicates that the Municipality of Orillia includes the twp of Matchedash and the north and south division of Orillia; possibly drawn after 1850 when the twps were united for municipal purposes (Hunter, I:265).
OTAR

---

388 *[1850?]*
[Plan of Part of the Penetanguishene Road in the townships of Tiny and Tay] [Sgd] John Ryan Engineer
Col ms 33 x 102 cm 1" to 20 chains Endorsements: stamps 'BW' '438'
Shows the area from the Penetanguishene town plot south to road lot 83; note indicates 'ends contemplated improvements begins improvements done under late Contract'; shows proposed deviations from road line and part labelled 'Mr Gzowski's last selected line' and 'portion left unfinished by contractor'; some lot owners named; Ryan is reported working on the finishing of this road during 1850 ('Report ... Public Works 1850' in *JLA* (1851), App T).
OOAMA (NMC 2202)

---

389 *1851*
Plan of the County of Ontario Drawn by William Powson of Manchester Township of Reach Draughtsman 30th August 1851.
Col ms 93 x 59 cm 1 1/4" to 3 miles
Endorsed in same hand: 'Map or Plan referred to in the Petition praying that the Village of Brooklin be named as the Site for the County Town of Ontario'; shows the county from Whitby to Rama, Pickering to Georgina twps, and Scugog Twp; population and assessed value given for each twp; roads; shows proposed line of railway running east-west just south of Brooklin.
OOAMA (NMC 21925)

---

390 *[1853?]*
MAP / OF THE COUNTY, AND RIDINGS, / of / YORK / CANADA WEST, / By Act of Parliament, 12° Victoriae Cap. 78, 1849. / Drawn & Engraved from Official Surveys by John Ellis & Co. / 8 King Street, Toronto. / Including the Two New Counties, ONTARIO & PEEL / Divided & Set off 15° Vicae Cap 5, 1851.
Print (engrav) 79 x 68 cm 1" to 200 chains
Insets: 'CITY AND PORT OF TORONTO' and 'HARBOUR OF PORT CREDIT. Scale 10 chs.'; shows the survey grid, roads with some named, places, railways, and stations (Grand Trunk, Hamilton & Toronto Railway, Ontario Simcoe & Huron Railway [also named the Northern]); insets show names of streets and lots; Toronto map bounded by Carleton Ave on the north, by River St on the east, and Niagara St on the west; shows churches, a few schools and markets, Northern Railway depot, line of Esplanade and proposed infill (1853); shows Georgina Twp as part of York Co (16 Vic 96 1853).
OOAMA (NMC 48662) OTAR (SR 2392)

---

391 *1853*
MAP / of the / COUNTY OF SIMCOE / revised and improved / By / W. GIBBARD P.L.S. / 1853. // Hugh Scobie Lith.
Print (lith) 83 x 55 cm 1" to 200 chains
Shows towns and villages, post offices, railways, travelled roads, survey grid; shows six types of mill (saw, steam saw, grist, steam grist, grist and saw, carding and fulling mills) with names of mill owners; distance table; 'Abstract from Census Rolls of Co. of Simcoe for Jany 1852 prepared by John Alexander Esq. Census Commr'; 'Boundaries & Streams Copied from large Maps in Registrars office were not laid down from Actual Survey'; population table for towns.
OTAR

Later editions and states

(2) *1853*
[Title as above but added within bottom right-hand margin]: Wm. Gibbard C.E. & P.L.S. / Collingwood Harbour / Sept. 1853.
Note about boundaries and streams changed: 'Where the boundaries and streams have not been laid down from actual Survey they have been copied from the large Government map in the Registrars Office.'
GBL (70684(2)) OKQ OOAMA (NMC 3329) OTAR (SR 2640) OTMCL

---

392 *1854*
MAP OF THE / TOWNSHIP OF MARKHAM / IN THE / County of York / ACCORDING TO A RE-SURVEY MADE UNDER INSTRUCTIONS FROM THE MUNICIPALITY BY GEORGE McPHILLIPS, P.L.S. IN 1853–54 / LITHOGRAPHED BY J. ELLIS, TORONTO.
Print (lith) 65 x 76 cm 1" to 40 chains
The 'Reference' keys six denominations of churches, saw and grist mills; shows survey grid and subdivision boundaries, cleared land, and all bldgs including barns; names of owners.
OTMCL

---

393 *1855*
Map of the Port Hope, Lindsay and Beaverton Railway [Sgd] Roswell G. Benedict Chief Engineer May 1855
Col ms 146 x 93 cm 1" to 1 mile
Shows the area from Hope Twp to Darlington and north to Thorah to Verulam twps; shows mileages for the railway from Port Hope to Beaverton and stations; also shows GTR.
OOAMA (NMC 17849)

---

394 *[1856?]*
MAP / of the County of / PEEL, / CANADA WEST / COMPILED BY / CHAS UNWIN & A.B. SCOTT / P.L. SURVEYORS, PROVINCIAL CHAMBERS. / TORONTO. / LITHOGAPHED [*sic*] BY J. ELLIS 8 KING ST. TORONTO. C.W.
Print (lith) 95 x 65 cm 1" to 1 mile
Legend shows four types of mill, travelled roads, post offices, grammar schools, boundaries of school sections, ward boundaries; distance tables; survey grid; railways; GTR and Toronto & Hamilton Railway; the map was advertised as soon ready for publication in the *British Colonist* (Toronto) 12 Aug 1856; (Holmden 2305).
OOAMA (NMC 19789) OTAR (SR 2645; 86905)

---

395 *1856*
MAP / OF THE TOWNSHIP OF / ESQUESING / County of Halton / PROVINCE OF CANADA, / COMPILED FROM VARIOUS SURVEYS / BY / Charles McCarthy / 1856. // [missing] Maclear & Co. Toronto C.W.
Print (lith) Approx 100 x 68 cm 1" to 2500 ft
Shows survey grid, lot sizes, and names of owners, wards, school sections 1–16, towns, and railways with names; photoreproduction in OTAR.
Private Collection

---

396 *[1856–7?]*
MAP / Shewing the Several Proposed Routes / OF THE / HURON AND ONTARIO / SHIP CANAL / Between the / CITY OF TORONTO & LAKE HURON. / KIVAS TULLY C.E. Toronto / Chief Engineer / R.B. MASON C.E. CHICAGO / Consulting Engineer. // LITHOGRAPHED BY J. ELLIS, TORONTO.
Print (lith) hand col 102 x 70 cm 1" to 21/2 miles
Legend keys lines of watershed, railways in operation, railways projected; shows four projected routes or partial routes for the canal: route 1 via the Humber R, Holland R to Kempenfelt Bay then to the Nottawasaga R to Georgian Bay; route 2 takes the northern part via L Couchiching and the Severn R; route 3 runs from the Humber R through Kleinberg and Bolton to the Nottawasaga R to Georgian Bay; route 4 proposes a connection from the Holland R directly to the Nottawasaga R; mileages of proposed routes shown and water supply required; proposed Toronto & Owen Sound Central Railway shown (incorporated 1857), and the proposed extension of the Ontario Simcoe & Huron Railroad to Beaverton; the Toronto and Georgian Bay Canal Company was incorporated on 1 July 1856 (19–20 Vict Cap 118); it is possible that this was an early state of the map with an earlier name for the canal as there is a circular letter explaining advantages of and requesting subscriptions towards the survey of the proposed Ontario & Huron Ship Canal by M.P. Hayes in 19 Sept 1855 (OTAR MSS (Misc) 1855 no 4).
OTAR OTMCL

Later editions and states

(2) *[1858?]*
MAP / Shewing the Several Proposed Routes / OF THE / TORONTO & GEORGIAN BAY / SHIP CANAL / ... Toronto ... J. ELLIS, TORONTO
The name of the canal in the title has been changed; found separately and in R. Mason, *The Georgian Bay Canal. Reports of Col. R.B. Mason ... and Kivas Tully* (Chicago: 1858), frontis (*Bib Can* 8673; Casey I–2715); accompanied by profile: 'TORONTO / AND / GEORGIAN BAY / Ship Canal / PROFILES. / KIVAS TULLY ... R.B. MASON ... / DRAWN BY FRED W. BARBER. / LITHOGRAPHED BY J. ELLIS, TORONTO. 1" – 5000 ft, vertical scale 1" – 200 ft'; profile lacking in copies of reports seen; except for change in title the map is the same as above; (Holmden 2810).
OOA OOAMA (NMC 43038; 21701) OTAR OTMCL

Related maps

(3) *[1858?]*
PROSPECTUS MAP / Shewing the position of the Proposed / TORONTO & GEORGIAN BAY / SHIP CANAL, / AS THE SHORTEST ROUTE BETWEEN / THE / NORTHWESTERN PORTION OF THE UNITED STATES, / and the / Atlantic Ocean. / KIVAS TULLY, TORONTO / Chief Engineer. COL. R.B. MASON, CHICAGO / Consulting Engineer. / LITHOGRAPHED BY J. ELLIS TORONTO.
49 x 85 cm Scale not given
Shows Great Lakes and United States northeast canal route and railways; (Holmden 2809).
OOAMA (NMC 21700)

(4) *1858*
Toronto and Georgian Bay Canal Detailed Plan Shewing cut from John Jacks Lake to the Nottawasaga River [Sgd] Kivas Tully Civil Engineer Toronto Jany 15th 1858.
Col ms on linen 37 x 130 cm 1" to 500 ft
Shows the proposed cut from lake to river and from there to the mouth of the river at Nottawasaga Bay; Boys' Mill; relief.
OTMCL

(5) *[1858]*
[Map of Nottawasaga River from the village of Hythe to the Bay showing a proposed cut through to Jacks Lake]
Col ms on linen 37 x 132 cm 1" to 500 ft
Shows a slightly different area from (4); shows soundings in the river, piers at Nottawasaga Bay, 'Boys' S.S. Mill,' and street plan of Hythe.
OTMCL

---

397 *[1858]*
[Map accompanying petition of the Cobourg & Peterborough Railroad Company]
Print (lith) hand col 76 x 46 cm Scale not given
In 'Return to an Address ... Petition ... by the Cobourg and Peterborough Railroad Company Praying for the Disallowance of a Certain By-law

of the Municipality of the Town of Peterborough ... 11th June 1858' (*JLA* (1858), App 53) (OTL, OTUTF); shows area from Ops to Douro and south to Clarke to Haldimand twps, Cobourg & Peterborough Railway line, and Port Hope, Lindsay & Beaverton Railway line; petition was to fight the proposal of the latter to build a branch from Millbrook to Peterborough, which they contended would be intolerable competition.
OOAMA OTL OTUTF

---

398 *[1858?]*
PLAN OF THE / COUNTY OF VICTORIA / CANADA WEST, / AND OF THE TOWN PLOT OF / FENELON FALLS. / W. Francis Lithographer Engraver & Printer / 12 Grays Inn Lane, Holborn, London W.C.
Print (lith) 53 x 70 cm Scale not given
Insets: [Location map including Upper Canada and New York State], 'TOWN PLOT OF FENELON FALLS'; four views: 'Cameron's Lake from the Church Hill,' 'The Falls from the Bend. Steamer Ogemah at Wharf,' 'Sturgeon Lake from the Church Hill,' 'Bridge and [Niagara] Falls from Clifton House'; twps north to Eldon, Bexley, and Somerville laid out and other twps are named north to Macaulay and Muskoka Rd line; from Macaulay, Draper to Stanhope twps in the north to Mariposa to Smith twps in the south; inset of Fenelon Falls shows names of streets; notes on the advantages of locating in Fenelon Falls, advantages for tourists and settlement generally in the county; distances; probably made about 1858 when the northern twps were added to Victoria Co but before the survey of Macaulay and Draper in that year.
OOAMA (NMC 43084)

---

399 *1858*
TREMAINE'S MAP / OF THE / COUNTY OF HALTON / CANADA WEST. / COMPILED & DRAWN BY GEO. R. TREMAINE FROM ACTUAL SURVEY / OAKVILLE PUBLISHED BY GEO C. TREMAINE 1858. / LITHOGRAPHED BY J. ELLIS, TORONTO.
Print (lith) 147 x 116 cm 1" to 40 chains
Includes 21 views of public and commercial bldgs and residences; subscribers directories; shows survey grid and subdivision boundaries, names of owners and/or tenants, roads, railways, schools, churches, and mills; two drawings of trains on railway lines; OTAR copy inscribed 'from J.F. Ward, Napanee, Ontario.'
OLU OOAMA (NMC 14503) OTAR USDLC

---

400 *1859*
TREMAINE'S MAP / OF THE / COUNTY OF PEEL. / Canada West. / COMPILED & DRAWN BY GEO. R. TREMAINE FROM ACTUAL SURVEY. / TORONTO, Published by G.R. & G.M. TREMAINE, 1859. / LITHOGRAPHED BY J. ELLIS, 8 KING ST. / Toronto C.W.
Print (lith) hand col 165 x 126 cm 1" to 50 chains
Insets (all at 1" to 10 chains unless otherwise noted): Alton, Bolton 1" to 8 chains, Brampton, Cheltenham, Cooksville, Mono Mills, Springfield 1" to 8 chains, Streetsville; 20 views of commercial and residential bldgs; 'Explanations': railways, plank and gravel roads, common roads, schools, tin shops, churches, water, saw, steam and grist, and woollen mills, cabinet and shoe shops; survey grid and subdivision boundaries; names of owners and/or tenants; insets show streets, lot nos, and many bldgs, some with names; subscribers directories.
OOAMA (NMC 13820) OTAR (SR 2637; 14105)

---

401 *[1860?]*
PLAN / OF THE SOUTH QUARTER OF LOT 11 / IN THE 2nd CONCESSION OF / HOPE / Maclear & Co Lith Toronto.
Print (lith) 62 x 89 cm 1" to 1 chain
Plan is based on **B1048** but is endorsed 'In Chancery Fraser v. Hastings Exhibited in Settling advertisements of Sale this 21st Dec 1860'; shows lots on York Rd, Hastings and Thomas sts; several bldgs marked with names; this plan was registered 15 Jan 1861.
Port Hope 9 (R.P. Hope 9)

---

402 *1860*
RETURN. – INDIAN DEPARTMENT, CANADA // [Land purchased from the Indians in Simcoe County] No. 595. Ordered by the House of Commons, to be printed, 25 Aug. 1860. / Henry Hansard Printer
Print (lith) hand col 30 x 37 cm Scale not given
In Canada, Indian Dept, *Return ... for Copies or Extracts of Correspondence ... respecting Alterations in the Organization of the Indian Department in Canada ... 25 August 1860*, opp 31 (OOA Pamph 1860 (41)); shows the 'Penetanguishene Purchase, 1798' and a block between L Couchiching and Matchedash Bay purchased in 1785; also shows block from L Simcoe to Penetanguishene purchased 18 Nov 1815.
OOA

---

403 *1860*
TREMAINE'S MAP / OF THE / COUNTY OF ONTARIO, / UPPER CANADA. / Drawn by John Shier Esq. P.L.S. & County Engineer. / PUBLISHED BY GEO. C. TREMAINE. TORONTO, 1860.
Print (lith) hand col 168 x 116 cm 1" to 50 chains
Inset: [twps of Thorah, Mara, and Rama at a smaller scale]; 13 views of public and commercial bldgs; 'Explanations' keys railways, gravel roads, common roads and road allowances not open, post towns, and 15 types of bldgs; survey grid and subdivision boundaries; shows names of owners

and/or tenants and bldgs of subscribers; a few mills and names of estates; lists of co officers; subscribers directories.
OOAMA (NMC 14104; 43076) OTAR USDLC

404 *1860*
Tremaine's Map / OF THE County OF YORK CANADA WEST, / COMPILED AND DRAWN BY / GEO. R. TREMAINE / FROM ACTUAL SURVEYS / TORONTO / PUBLISHED BY GEO. C. TREMAINE / 1860.
Print (lith) hand col 170 x 136 cm 1" to 60 chains
Inset: 'PLAN / OF the City OF / TORONTO.'; 10 views of public and commercial bldgs; 'Explanations': common roads, macadamized and plank roads, road allowances not open, railways, places with and without post offices, churches, schools, graveyards, steam saw, water saw, grist, and woollen mills, tin shops, cabinet and shoe shops; shows survey grid and boundaries of subdivisions; names of owners and/or tenants, houses of subscribers and names of estates; subscribers directories; inset shows Toronto south of Bloor St, major streets, major bldgs located and keyed; fire alarm information; parks, cemeteries; advertisement on map for 'Tremaine's Map Establishment 164 King St. East 2nd and 3rd flats.'
GBL (70691(4)) OOAMA (NMC 13819) OTAR (SR 86911)

Later editions and states

(2) *[1860?]*
[Title, etc, the same]
Two variant states have been identified; one lacks the inset for Toronto and some of the subscribers directory in the upper centre and right corner (OOAMA (NMC 22104)); a facsimile in OOAMA (NMC 15361) lacks all the subscribers directory in upper centre and right corner; original of facsimile not located.
OOAMA (NMC 22104)

405 *1861*
MAP / OF THE COUNTIES OF / NORTHUMBERLAND DURHAM, / PETERBOROUGH & VICTORIA. / COMPILED FROM / Actual Surveys and re-Surveys, / By E.C. Caddy, P.L. Surveyor & C.E. / COBOURG, 1861. / LITHOGRAPHED BY J. ELLIS, TORONTO, C.W.
Print (col lith) 198 x 134 cm 1" to 100 chains
View: 'Victoria Hall, Cobourg'; survey grid and places; 'Explanations' pasted on to sheet: railways, travelled roads, post offices, steam saw, saw, steam grist, and grist mills; railway distance table within cos; remarks on surveys in some twps; red printing is for railway lines, possibly postal routes and riding boundaries; 'N.B. Where the Paper has stretched in the Blue or Red Ink the Black dots indicate the true course'; OOAMA copy has ms adds showing the Burleigh Rd.
OOAMA (NMC 18018) OTAR OTMCL

406 *1861*
TREMAINE'S MAP / of the / COUNTY OF DURHAM / UPPER CANADA. / DRAWN BY JOHN SHIER Esq. P.L.S. C.E. / ASSISTED BY Mr JOHN F. WARD. / Published by / GEO. C. TREMAINE, / TORONTO / 1861
Print (lith) hand col 132 x 150 cm 1" to 50 chains
Twenty-five views of public and commercial bldgs and residences; views of towns; 'Explanations': railways, gravel roads, common roads, road allowances not opened, post towns and villages, churches, schools, grist, saw, steam saw mills, tanneries, carriage shops, oat mills, blacksmith shops, copper shops, stores, private residences; shows survey grid and boundaries of subdivisions; names of owners and/or tenants; subscribers' houses shown; names of estates; subscribers directories; OTAR (SR 2651) is a copy of the north half of map only; (*OHIM* 4.48).
GBL (70654(1)) OOAMA (NMC 11474) OTAR OTAR (SR 2651)

Later editions and states

(2) *1861*
[Title is the same] Engraved Printed Colored and Mounted by / Geo. R. & G.M. TREMAINE / Map Publishers &c. / 288 King St. E. Toronto C.W.
The map is the same as that above but an imprint has been added within bottom inner margin at left.
GBLrg

407 *1863*
PLAN OF SURVEY / FOR / GEORGIAN BAY CANAL / THROUGH THE / DIVIDING RIDGES / OF THE / COUNTY OF ONTARIO / TO ACCOMPANY REPORT OF SEPTEMBER 3rd 1863. / [Sgd in facsimile] Thos C. Keefer. / W.C. Chewett & Co. Lith. Toronto C.W.
Print (col lith) 72 x 100 cm 1" to 5 miles
Inset: 'HEAD WATERS / ADJOINING THE / SOURCES OF GULL RIVER.'; Profile: 'COMPARISON OF THE SUMMIT CUTTINGS IN THE HUMBER AND SCUGOG ROUTES.' 1" to 1600 ft, 1" to 120 ft vertical; accompanies *Report of Thomas C. Keefer esq. C.E. of Survey of Georgian Bay Canal Route to Lake Ontario by Way of Lake Scugog ... Ordered by the Council of Ontario, June Session 1863.* (Whitby: W.H. Higgins 1863) (*Bib Can* 4248); shows the area from Halton Co to Georgian Bay and Sydney to Airy twps; shows the route for the canal from L Simcoe to L Scugog and then partly by river connections to east Whitby Twp to lake and feeder from Balsam L; shows earlier proposed routes via the Humber R (see **396**); notes volume of water from feeder; correction note that Port Whitby inadvertently omitted; there is also a ms copy of the map without the printing statement in OOAMA (NMC 59332).
OTMCL

408 *[1865]*
MAP / OF THE / COBOURG & PETERBOROUGH / AND / Marmora Railways, / CANADA WEST. / W.C. CHEWETT & CO. LITH. TORONTO.
Print (col lith) 44 x 39 cm Scale not given
Issued with *Prospectus. Cobourg & Peterborough and Marmora Railways* (Cobourg: Printed at the 'World' Office 1865), folded at back (*Bib Can* 6144); shows area from Hamilton to Sidney north to Douro to Lake twps; shows the line with branch to Millbrook and 'proposed branch' from Trent R to Marmora L; GTR also shown.
OTMCL

East

409 *[1783]*
The Mohawks from Lachine have pitched upon this Tract of Land and Wish Government to give them a grant for it in lieu of their lands in the Mohawk Country usurped by the Rebels
Ms Approx 22 x 26 cm Scale not given
Endorsements: 'A Design or Description of the Lands the Mohawks of Lachine pitched upon in Lake Ontario delivered in Decemr. 1783'
A rough sketch of L Ontario oriented to the south with the Bay of Quinte area disproportionately enlarged; the large block of land is on the mainland, north of the Quinte peninsula; Fort Frontenac, Toronto, Niagara, and American places named; a possible mill site on a river is noted; the Mohawks were granted a smaller part of this area in 1793 (*Indian Treaties*, Treaty No 3 1/2 (1793), I:7ff).
GBL (Add Mss 21829/30)

---

410 *[1783]*
[Sketch from Kingston to the Bay of Quinte with the plan for the first three townships]
Col ms Approx 40 x 90 cm 1" to 1 mile
Endorsements: 'Plan which was received with Capt. Sherwood's Journal'
Shows the outline and front two cons of 'First Township' [Kingston], the outline and front con of 'Second Township' [Ernestown], and the front con and outline of 'No 3' [Fredericksburgh]; outlines of shore and north of the Quinte peninsula shown, blocks and nos for twps roughly marked based on frontages of 12–15 miles; note: 'Supposing 2370 acres of land to a Township the Bay of Quinty will admit of settling 3415 Familys at 120 acres each, on the North Side, the tongue on the South Side suppose it to make six townships ... will admit of the settling of 1857 families the Isle Tonte ... will make two Townships and settle at least 250 familys ...'; Kingston and Ernestown were first surveyed in 1783, Fredericksburgh in 1784 (see list on 1790 plan, **10**); this was Sherwood's plan for survey which accompanied his '...Journal from Montreal to Lake Ontario,' 19 Sept–23 Oct 1783 (GBL Haldimand Papers; OOA transcript B169 pp 15–23, 29–30); (Preston, xv, 39; Cruikshank, 25–9).
GBL (Add Mss 21829/74–5)

Related maps

(2) *[1784?]*
[Endorsed title]: 'Plan of the Settlement at the Bay of Quinte' [Sgd?] Henry Holland
Col ms 68 x 102 cm Scale not given Watermark: 'J WHATMAN' Endorsements: 'Presented to the United Services Museum by Lt. Humphrey 88th Regt' '41, Draw 28 Sec 2, No 355'
A more finished version of plan above; shows area from Grand Is to the Sandbanks on the west side of the Quinte peninsula, [Kingston] twp, [Ernestown, Fredericksburgh, and Adolphustown] twps, with glebes in the centre of each; a few notes in a different hand and corrections to the shape of Ducks Is and False Ducks Is; soundings along North Channel and into Mohawk Bay; Henry Holland, Kotte, Peachey, and Tuffie surveyed Fredericksburgh and Adolphustown in 1784 (1790 plan, **10**).
GBL (Add Mss 57710.3)

---

411 *[1783]*
Sketch from Montreal to Lake Ontario
2 ms maps on 1 sheet 49 x 72 cm 1" to 10 miles and [approx 1" to 23 miles] Endorsements: '1199'
The first plan shows a detailed sketch of the Rideau, Ganonoque, and Petite Nation rivers with carrying places, falls, and notes: 'The Rivers du Rideau & Ganannoncoui will be Navigable for Batteaux in time of High Water at all Places Except the Falls & Carrying Places Marked'; the second map is a general map of the area between the Ottawa and St Lawrence rivers with various place-names along rivers; probably the original by Lt Gershom French who surveyed the area in 1783 and whose journal (29 Sept 1783 to 29 Oct 1783) was enclosed in a letter from Haldimand to Lord North 6 Nov 1783 (GBLpro CO 42/46 pp 7ff).
OTAR (SR 7115)

Related maps

(2) *1783 (1794)*
Sketch from Montreal to Lake Ontario – Copy from Lieut G. French, Surveyor Genls Office Newark 26th August 1794 [Sgd] W Chewett [and] [Map of the Rideau & Petite Nation Rivers] Copy from Lieut G. French's Sketch [Sgd] W Chewett
2 col mss on 1 sheet 40 x 61 cm 1" to 10 miles and [approx 1" to 23 miles] Endorsements: 'No 2' '780' 'Communicaton with the St Lawrence & Ottawa Rivers, by the Rivers Petite Nation & Rideau'
The same base information as above with the addition (on the detailed plan) of Lt French's places of encampment and 'excursions'; comments on the nature of the land for settlement, and portages to the St Lawrence R; the general plan includes notes on the land along the Rideau and Ottawa rivers.
OTAR (SR 7085)

---

412 *1783*
Surveyed by Order of His Excellency General Haldimand Governor and Commander in Chief of the Province of Quebec &ca &ca &ca. A Township or Tract of Land of Six Miles square lying and being in the Province aforesaid, Situate on the North side of Lake Ontario near the Ancient Fort Frontenac ... Surveyed the 27th day of October 1783 (Signed) John Collins D.S.G1
Col ms 77 x 88 cm 1" to 1/4 mile Watermark: 'W WILMOTT'
Originally enclosed in Gov Haldimand's no 25 of 18 Nov 1783 (no 1) to Lord North (GBLpro CO 42/46 p 25); (SI 11 Sept 1783 from Haldimand to John Collins to survey various twps including [Kingston] and reserve town plot); shows the twp of Kingston laid out in seven cons and 25 lots of 120 acres each from the Cataraqui R west across the Little Cataraqui R to Bay Tonegeyon; the survey is described with notes on the quality of land, road allowances along every con and after every eighth lot, Ft Frontenac, Major Ross's house, and hospital; (*OHIM* 4.8; *PRO Cat* 1476).
GBLpro (MPG 424)

---

413 *[1784?]*
Plan of the Townships No 1 and 2 above Cataraqui
Col ms 60 x 113 cm 1" to 40 chains Endorsements: 'B 48' 'Quebec Plan'
Shows Kingston and Ernestown twps with seven cons in each and a glebe in the centre; shows the increase in the size of lots in Kingston to 200 acres each, the addition of the glebe, and the renumbering of cons and lots (see the original plan for Kingston, **412**); includes list 'General Return of the Peoples Names Refering to the Anexed Plan.'
OTAR (SR 5976)

Related maps

(2) *[1784?]*
Plan of the Townships or Seigniory's of No 3 and No 4 Situated on the Bay of Quinty. The Front Line of No 3 was Surveyed by John Collins Deputy Surveyor General, Hay Bay and the Appanee River by Mr Louis Kotte Deputy Provincial Surveyor and No 4 by Mr James Peachey Lieut Heny Holland and Lieut Saml Tuffie Deputy Surveyors. Sam Tuffie
Col ms 59 x 93 cm 1" to 40 chains Endorsements: 'N 34' 'Quebec Plan B 44' 'Tuffies Plan' '1784'
This plan appears to be in the same hand as the one above and has the same layout including 'General Return of the People's Names Refering to the Annexed Plan'; shows Fredericksburgh and Adolphustown twps, both surveyed in 1784 by Kotte, Peachey, Holland, and Tuffie (see 1790 plan, **10**); surveys include glebes, two town plots, shoreline in detail, marshes; notes on size of lots.
OTNR (SR 5557)

---

414 *[1784?]*
[Plan of Towns]hips or Seigniory's from Point Bodette on Lake St Francis to above Oswagatchey including Point Moullee Township with No 1, 2, 3, 4, 5, 6 7 and 8. [Sgd] Samuel Holland.
Col ms 46 x 168 cm 1" to 11/4 miles Watermark: 'J WHATMAN' Endorsements: '2' 'Handed to me by Mr C. Walkem 6/11 [18]71 H.H. Miles'
Note: 'The Front of the Several Townships layed out, by Mr Louis Kotte, Deupt Provl Surveyor, and the River au Rasine with the Lots there on, and the concessions line by Mr Patk McNiff Deupt Surveyor, agreeable to the Order of His Excelly General Haldimand to Samuel Holland, Surveyor General.'; shows the twps from Lancaster to Elizabethtown, each laid out in seven cons with glebes in the centre; Indian lands shown between twps 1 and 2 and in part of twp 6; names of grantees (officers) inserted in about a quarter of the lots; 'N.B. The lots in front Occupied by Major Gray and Lieut I.F. Holland were ceded by the Indians after the Township was surveyed' [southeast part of twp 2]; New Oswegatchy is shown in twp 7 and New Johnstown in twp 2 [Cornwall].
OTNR (SR 7064)

Related maps

(2) *[1784?]*
Plan of the Townships or Seigniory's from Point Bodette on Lake St Francis to above Oswagatchey including Point Mouille Township with No 1, 2, 3, 4, 5, 6, 7 and 8.
Col ms 50 x 390 cm 1" to 11/4 miles Endorsements: 'No 49' '1017'
In the same hand and shows the same information as above map but with more notes and 'General Return of the People's Names Refering to the Anexed Plan'; this list gives names for grantees in about the first three cons; notes on bearings for the twps; a later note sgd by Thomas Devine calls this an 'important Upper Canada Plan & Schedule'; these two plans are probably later than **415**.
OTAR (SR 8906)

---

415 *[1784?]*
[Endorsed title]: 'River St Lawrence from Point à Bodet to the Long Sault'
Col ms 46 x 165 cm [1" to 40 chains]
From Point à Bodet to twp 8 past Point au Baril; shows Lake [Lancaster] Twp and twps 1 and 2 [Charlottenburgh and Cornwall] in outline only; shows sight lines at the east end, relief along the shoreline, Johnstown town plot.
OTAR (SR 7056)

Related maps

(2) *[1784?]*
[Plan of the St Lawrence River from Isle au Long Sault to Point au Baril] Copied from a Plan of Mr Lewis Kotte D.P.S. [Sgd] W.C.
Col ms 44 x 273 cm 1" to 40 chains Endorsements: '1086'

This plan fits with the one above and shows the outlines only of twps 3 to 8 [Osnabruck to Elizabethtown]; relief along shoreline; many place-names in French; Isle du Fort Levy; Lewis Kotte and Patrick McNiff surveyed the fronts of twps from Charlottenburgh to Matilda in 1784 (see 1790 plan, **10**) and these plans probably date from early parts of these surveys.
OTAR (SR 6003)

---

416 *[1784–5?]*
[Endorsed titles]: 'Survey from Pt Frederic to the 8th Township by Cotté' [and] 'River St Lawrence North shore from Elizabethtown to Pt Frederick' [Sgd] L. Kotté
2 ms maps 34 x 40 cm and 49 x 106 cm 2" to 1 mile Watermark on 2nd map: 'J WHATMAN' Endorsements: 'No 19' '759'
An unfinished plan of the shoreline with no place-names; the two maps fit together to cover the area as described in titles; first plan is further endorsed 'By Kotté'; in a letter to Hope on 28 Dec 1785 Samuel Holland states that Kotte has surveyed all the front lines of the twps from Pointe Beaudette to the Bay of Quinte (Ontario Archives, *Report 1905*, 399); this or (2) is probably the same as 'Plan of Part of the River St Lawrence from Oswegatchie to Cataraqui surveyed by Lewis Kotté' in 'List of Maps ... 1793' (OTAR RG 1 A-I-1/1, 151–7).
OTAR (SR 1887; 5998)

Related maps

(**2**) *[1785?]*
Survey from Oswegatchie to Cataraqui. Copied from an Original, by Lieut Augustine Prevost R.F. [Sgd] Samuel Holland Surveyr Genl
Col ms 35 x 149 cm 2" to 1 mile Endorsements: 'No 13' '872'
Similar to Kotte outline in above map but nine lines of boundaries of twps to be surveyed are dotted in; nature of land noted; shows the area from Toniata R at the west boundary of twp 8 to Cataraqui.
OTAR (SR 6821)

(**3**) *[1785?]*
Plan of the Communication from Township No 8 to Cataraqui as Surveyed by Mr Louis Kott Dept Provl Survr. Sam'l Tuffie.
Col ms 46 x 68 cm 1" to 1 1/3 miles Watermark: 'J WHATMAN' Endorsements: 'Presented to the United Services Museum by Lieut. Humphrey 88th Regt.' 'A 28/13 34 Draw 28 Sect 2'
Shows the shoreline and islands; relief shows the west boundary of twp 8 to Cataraqui; a more finished plan than those above; Samuel Tuffie surveyed the east side of the Cataraqui R in 1785 with W. Chewett and may have prepared this presentation copy after this and Kotte's surveys (see surveys listed on **10**).
GBL (Add Mss 57707/8)

---

417 *[1785?]*
[Plan of the townships from Kingston to the Bay of Quinte]
Col ms 54 x 120 cm Scale not given Endorsements: '1020'
A fragment possibly of a larger plan extending further east, west, and south; two different inks and handwritings; shows outlines of twp 1 [Kingston] west to twps 5 [Marysburgh] and 6 [Sophiasburgh]; twps 7 [Ameliasburgh] and 8 [Camden] shown north of 2 and 3; each twp shows a glebe in the centre; comments on the terrain; note: 'Carrying Place from the Head of the Bay of Quinty to Lake Ontario' is the same as on Collins's survey of 1785 (**6**); Sophiasburgh and Marysburgh were both surveyed partially in 1784 and 1785 but twp 8 [Camden] was not surveyed until 1787; also shows shoreline to east and twp 8 on the St Lawrence; the lack of detail on the plan suggests this is from the earlier date; probably related to SI Oct 1785 to L. Kotte for surveying of several groups of cons on the Quinte peninsula; Kotte surveyed Ameliasburgh in 1785 (see list on **10**).
OTAR

---

418 *1786*
A Plan [of part of the] New Settlements on the North bank of the South-west branch [of the St] Laurence River commencing near Point au Bodett on La[ke St Fra]ncis and extending westerly along the said North bank to the west boundary of [twp] 5. Laid down from the Latest Surveys & observations By [Sgd] Patrick McNiff. November the 1st 1786
Col ms (pts missing) 71 x 326 cm 1" to 40 chains
Shows the twps from Lancaster to the west boundary of Matilda; dotted lines mark where con lines have been run with road line along the shoreline (SI for road 18 June 1785); the main outline is in black with later additions including title in brown; names of grantees are shown in most lots in two inks and handwriting styles – the main group of names is in black with new names inserted in brown, possibly in McNiff's hand; a few names are crossed out; 'Remarks' includes notes on the type of land in each twp; double lines indicate road allowances at twp boundaries and halfway across running north-south; shows the town plot of 'Johnstown' [Cornwall] and Indian land between twps 1 and 2; the plan was used in a court case and is endorsed 'G Filed 30th Oct 1854 ... Exhibit No 2 Charlottenburgh vs. [?]McDonald Filed in Court this 14 May 1884'; many transcripts of this plan exist and a letter on file with those in OOAMA indicates that the plan was finally returned to the Ontario Dept of Lands and Forests in 1933 or 1934 (letter from C.H. Fullerton, surveyor general of Ontario, 24 March 1941); (*OHIM* 3.2).
OTAR (SR 11081)

---

419 *[1787?]*
[Plan of Part of 2nd, 3rd, 10th (Richmond) & 11th (Camden) townships [Sgd] L. Kotté D.P.S.
Col ms 53 x 24 cm 2" to 1 mile Endorsements: '1201' 'B52'
Shows the upper part of 2nd twp [Ernestown], 3rd to 7th cons, 3rd twp [Fredericksburgh], and 1st to 4th cons in (11th) twp [Camden], and the lower part of the 10th twp [Richmond]; the twp numbering has changed from the plan of [1785?] (**417**); names are shown in the front cons of both Camden and Richmond twps but the latter shows no other cons; Richmond and Camden were first laid out in 1787, Camden by Kotte and Richmond by John Collins (see list on **10**), and this plan probably dates from these surveys.
OTAR

---

420 *1787*
Remarks on River Gananoque 23rd April 1787 [Sgd] Patrick McNiff Surveyor. [Endorsed title]: 'Sketch of the River Gananoque left by Mr. Ogden 28 Dec. 1787.'
Col ms 44 x 31 cm 1" to 10 chains
Shows rapids, falls, remarks on portages, fields, treed areas; names of two landowners near St Lawrence R; (Holmden 2530).
OOAMA

---

421 *1788*
[Map of the proposed division line for Upper and Lower Canada]
Ms 38 x 46 cm 1" to 6 miles Watermark: 'I TAYLOR' Endorsements: 'D'
Originally with Lord Dorchester's nos 94 and 95 of 8 Nov 1788 to Lord Sydney showing the proposed boundary between Upper and Lower Canada (GBLpro CO 42/62 f 153); shows the seigneuries of Vaudreuil, 'New Longeuil,' and Soulanges in Lower Canada and twps from Lancaster to Matilda on the St Lawrence and eight unnamed twps plotted along both shores of the Ottawa R; (*PRO Cat* 1685).
GBLpro (MPG 428)

---

422 *1788*
Plan of Part of the Grand (or Ottawa) River fronting the Townships of Chatham, Hawkesbury, Grenville & Carrmarthen Surveyed in 1788 by Patk McNiff
Col ms in 4 sheets 320 x 42 cm 1" to 20 chains Watermark: 'J WHATMAN'
Shows lots fronting on the river and names of grantees in Hawkesbury and Longueuil twps; shows both sides of the river.
OOAMA (NMC 25377)

---

423 *[1789?]*
Plan of the River Rideau in the District of Luneburg together with a line from thence Southeast to the River St Lawrence surveyed in [blank space] by James Rankin
Col ms Approx 35 x 65 cm 1" to 40 chains
Endorsements: 'A7' '112' 'Projection from Township on the River Rideau No 1'
(SI 4 June 1789 to survey the south side of the Ottawa R to the mouth of the Rideau R and then 40 miles southeast and from there to run traverse line to the St Lawrence); shows the Rideau R with lots along the east side and the mouth at the Grand R (Ottawa); possibly cut off at the south end; similar to no 11 in 'List of Maps ... 1793' (OTAR RG 1 A-I-1/1, 151–7).
OTAR (SR 1104)

Related maps

(2) *[1789?]*
[Endorsed title]: 'Communication Edwardsburg, Line from the St Lawrence to the Rideau (by Rankin) – Partial'
Col ms 32 x 65 cm Scale not given Watermark: 'J WHATMAN' Endorsements: 'No 12' '788'
Shows the traverse line near Indian land and part of Edwardsburgh Twp to the south branch of Rideau R; 'Rr La Vielle Gallelle' shown near the St Lawrence; the two maps seem to fit together although they are not in the same hand.
OTAR (SR 5810)

---

424 *1790*
Plan of a Road leading from Cornwall to Kingston Laid out by order of His Excellency The Right Honorable Guy Lord Dorchester Governor General &c &c &c. Surveyed in the Year 1790. by [Sgd] Jesse Pennoyer D.P. Surveyor
Col ms 50 x 105 cm 1" to 80 chains Endorsements: 'R 45'
(SI issued to W. Chewett 4 June 1789 to survey for the road line; similar instructions reissued to Pennoyer on 20 June 1790; OTAR FN 336 [1790]; FN 337 1 July–7 Dec 1789 for the Osnabruck to Coteau du Lac section is in OTAR (RG 1 CB-1 box 36)); only part from Pittsburg to Yonge Twp, the west half of this survey, has survived and map is cut off part way through the name Luneburg; the road line is shown from mile 106 at Toniata Creek to mile 150 at Kingston; shows survey grid for twps, relief, and marshes along the line.
OTAR (SR 81038)

Related maps

(2) *[1790?]*
Plan of a Road Surveyed by Jesse Pennoyer in 1790 Copied from an Original by Lieut John Fredk Holland Ry Rt NYk [Sgd] Samuel Holland Surveyr Genl
Col ms 42 x 246 cm 1" to 1 mile Endorsements: '972'
This copy of Pennoyer's original shows most of the road but the part from Osnabruck Twp to Cornwall Twp is still missing; the fronts of twps from Pittsburgh to Osnabruck are named except for twps 10 and 9 between Lansdown and Eliza

bethtown [Escott and Yonge]; survey grid not shown; mileages are noted along the line from 47 on the east to 146 at Cataraqui Bay.
OTAR (SR 81036)

---

425 *[1790?]*
A Plan of the District of Luneburg in the Province of Quebec for the Use of His Majesty's Governor and Council Compiled in the Surveyor General's office Pursuant to an Order in Council of the 22nd day of February 1790.
Col ms Size not known 1" to 2 miles
The original plan has not been found; however, a transcript entitled 'Reduced Copy of A Plan of the District of Luneburg, ... 1790 G.B. Kirkpatrick delt.' made probably in the latter part of the nineteenth century is in OTAR; shows twps from Lancaster to Leeds and projected twps: Cumberland, York, Plantagenet, Alfred, Gloucester, and Clarence on or near the Ottawa or Rideau rivers; some of the twps include reserves for towns in centre or along river as in 1789 maps (see **3, 423**); probably another copy of no 1 in 'List of Maps ... 1793' (OTAR RG 1 A-I-1/1, 151–7) that includes notes on errors in the location of the Ottawa R twps and distances between points; remarks include dates of survey and surveyors from 1784 to 1789; shows Johnstown (surveyed by W. Chewett in 1789) and 'New Oswegatchie' but not Cornwall; (*OHIM* 7.1).
OTAR (transcript)

Related maps

(**2**) *[1792?]*
A Plan of the District of Luneburg. [Sgd] Copied from an Original in the Engineers Drawing Room Samuel Holland Survyr Genl
Col ms 125 x 143 cm 1" to 2 miles
Similar to plan above; shows the whole extent of Luneburg including the twps laid out south and north of the Ottawa R; shows the twps of Alfred, Plantagenet, Cumberland, York, and, below the last two, Gloucester and Clarence as they were either partly surveyed or planned for completion in 1789 (see (1) above); Hawkesbury is also shown but clashing with [Lochiel] in the rear of Lancaster Twp; the northern twps portray early plans for a twp with a town plot surrounded by park lots, common, and crown and clergy reserves; the twps along the Ottawa R and Gloucester Twp on the Rideau R include the town plots fronting on the river, whereas the other two include the town plots in the centre (*OHIM* 4.11); shows the surveyed twps along the St Lawrence from Lancaster to Elizabethtown, a gap (not on the 1790 plan above), then Lansdowne and Leeds; Charlottenburgh and Cornwall are shown extended into what became Kenyon and Roxborough (as shown on 1790 plan above); co lines for Leeds, Grenville, Dundas, Stormont, and Glengarry have been added as of the Proclamation of July 1792; 'New Oswegatchy' is shown in Augusta Twp, a blank town plot [Johnstown] in Edwardsburgh and 'New Johnstown' [Cornwall]; boundary line with Lower Canada named; the plan may date from several periods but probably not later than 1792 as the Ottawa R twps were surveyed in their final positions from about 1792 on and new twps were being laid out between the St Lawrence and Ottawa rivers from 1791 (see App A); transcript of this plan reproduced in Ontario Archives, *Report (1905)*, cii.
OTAR

---

426 *1790*
A Plan of the District of Mecklenburg in the Province of Quebec for the use of His Majesty's Governor and Council. Compiled in the Surveyor General's Office. Pursuant to an Order in Council of the 22nd day of February 1790 [Sgd] Samuel Holland Survr Genl [Sgd] John Collins D.S.G.
Col ms 103 x 99 cm 1" to 2 miles
Shows the area from Lansdowne Twp and the boundary of Mecklenburg in Leeds Twp to the west boundary of Sidney Twp and the Trent R; shows twps or partial twps laid out as follows: Leeds, Pittsburgh, Kingston, Ernestown, Fredericksburgh, Adolphustown, Richmond, Camden, Thurlow, Sidney, and parts of Marysburgh, Sophiasburgh, Ameliasburgh, and unnamed cons laid out on the south coast of the Quinte peninsula; a list of surveys, surveyors, and dates is the same as on the 1790 general plan **10**; shows the Mohawk Settlement beside Richmond, a few mills; glebes shown in all twps; town plots shown in Fredericksburgh and Adolphustown; Cataraqui [Kingston town plot]; 'the carrying place from the Head of the Bay of Quinte to Lake Ontario'; the 'hill commanding a harbour which is protected from the wind' marked in legend appears not to be shown; Richmond Twp is not in its final form; probably similar to no 2 in 'List of Maps ... 1793' (OTAR RG 1 A-I-1/1, 151–7) that notes errors in plotting of Richmond Twp.
OTAR

Related maps

(**2**) *[1792?]*
Plan of the District of Mecklenburg. Drawn in the Engineers Office & finished in the Surveyor Generals Office from an Original by Lieut. John Fredk Holland Ry R N Yk [Sgd] Samuel Holland Surveyr Genl
Col ms 98 x 92 cm 1" to 2 miles Endorsements: '932'
This plan shows the same base information as the other but adds the names of counties by Proclamation of 16 July 1792: Leeds, 'Frontignac,' Addington, Lennox, Hastings, Prince Edward, and the short-lived Ontario Co consisting of Amherst Is and Wolfe Is (Armstrong, *Handbook*, 152); Rawdon and Huntingdon twps are shown north of Sidney and Thurlow, probably as proposed since they were not surveyed until 1797 (see App A);

Richmond is not laid out and is squeezed between the Mohawk land and Camden Twp; more place-names are shown than on the earlier plan.
OTAR

427 *1790*
[Sketch of the township of Charlottenburgh showing the manner in which lots have been laid out]
Ms 10 x 13 cm Scale not given
With copy of Report of the Land Committee Quebec, 19 Feb 1790, further enclosed in Dorchester's no 33 to Grenville, 7 June 1790 (GBLpro CO 42/68 f 182); the sketch shows that some blocks of lots front on the R au Raisin and some on the St Lawrence, a method described in the report as unsuitable for laying out the twp since some would receive less than 200 acres because of the river and would need to be compensated elsewhere; the twp was later resurveyed so that all cons fronted on the St Lawrence.
GBLpro (CO 42/68 f 182)

428 *1791*
Plan de la Riviere Rideau depuis la jonction des deux Branches aux environs d'onze milles et de la Devanture de la Seigneurie de Marlborough. Arpentés dans l'Année 1791. par ordre de Son Excellence le Tres Honorable Guy Lord Dorchester Capitaine Général et Gouverneur en Cheff &c &c by Theod De Pencier. par [Sgd] Theodor de Pencier Deputé Arpenteur Provincial
Col ms 37 x 137 cm 1" to 20 chains Endorsements: 'N 16' '986'
(SI 14 Feb 1791 Theodore Depencier to survey Marlborough Twp); shows the traverse of the Rideau R in front of Oxford and Marlborough twps and 1st con of Marlborough.
OTAR (SR 7059)

Related maps

(2) *1791*
Plan of two Townships of ten miles square, on each side of the main branch of the River Rideau, beginning at the Forks – By order of the Board, – Williamsburg 28th March 1791 [Sgd] W. Chewett D.P. Surveyor
Col ms 59 x 50 cm 1" to 1 mile
Shows two unnamed twps [Marlborough and Oxford] on both sides of river; lots are numbered along the river; glebe, schoolhouse, and reserve A are shown fronting on the river in each twp; this plan is clearly related to Depencier's survey, and is either a projection or later copy; (Holmden 2552).
OOAMA (NMC 3511)

429 *1791*
Plan of part of the Division Line between the Districts of Luneburg and Mecklenburg. Osnabruck 23rd December 1791 [Sgd] W. Chewett D.P. Surveyor Luneburg
Ms 19 x 98 cm 1" to 20 chains Endorsements: '952'
The line is shown for only seven miles, first crossing the Thames [Gananoque] R, then running north; note that work stopped at a lake seven miles from Thames R as Aitken was unwell, 'we were forced to postpone the business untill his recovery or some future period'; relief and mileage points marked along line; plan described in 'List of Maps ... 1793' (OTAR RG 1 A-I-1/1, 151–7).
OTAR (SR 5817)

Related maps

(2) *1791*
Plan of part of the Division Line between the Districts of Luneburg and Mecklenburg, by William Chewitt and Alexander Aitkin, Deputy Provincial Surveyors. Surveyed in the Year 1791. Copied from an Original by Lieut John Fredk Holland Ry Rt N Yk [Sgd] Samuel Holland Surveyr Genl
Col ms 29 x 96 cm 1" to 20 chains Endorsements: 'No 24' '953'
Note: 'Meridian otherwise the division Line between Luneburgh & Mecklenburgh at the mouth of the Thames, formerly the River Gannanoqui'; a copy of above plan without the notes.
OTAR (SR 8609)

430 *1791*
The Property of Sir John Johnson Bart Surveyed in the Months of August, September and October 1791 by [Sgd] J Pennoyer D.P.S.
Col ms, pt missing 49 x 106 cm 1" to 10 chains
(OTNR FN 501 1791); shows property on the east and west sides of the Thames [Gananoque] R; notes indicate that 1000 acres were laid out in 1789 and 2300 acres in the rear were laid out by order 4 Oct 1791; notes and part of map depicting area west of the river are missing; there is a copy of part on east side of river by W. Chewett endorsed '775' and 'No 1' (OTAR).
OTAR (SR 5973) OTAR

431 *[1791?]*
[Endorsed title]: 'River Petite Nation Partial'
Col ms 58 x 46 cm Scale not given Watermark: 'J WHATMAN' Endorsements: 'No 21' '774'
(SI 22 Feb 1791 to James Rankin to proceed to the Petite Nation R and mark out a twp [Cambridge] 10 miles square); shows the river with rapids at the junction with the Grand [Ottawa] R; shows a survey line from the south to the Ottawa R; the configuration of this line and the river are the same as on Rankin's plan of Cambridge Twp (**A325–7**); a later note indicates 'This River falls in the Township of Plantagenet.'
OTAR

432 *1791 (1795)*
700 Acres of Lands, the Property of Joel Stone Esqr. surveyed in the month of October 1791 by (Signed) J. Pennoyer D.P.S. A true Copy Johnstown, 4 July

1795 – (Signed) Lewis Grant, D. Survr Eastn Distr A Copy [Sgd] D.W. Smith Actg Sur Genl
Col ms 61 x 41 cm 1" to 10 chains Watermark: 'C PATCH 1794'
Shows property on the west side of the 'Gannonoque River'; the lot boundaries are described; a further note indicates the potential of the river mouth for a harbour; rapids are shown; (Holmden 2581); there is a copy of the plan by Lewis Grant endorsed 'No 22' and '777' in OTAR (SR 7060).
OOAMA (NMC 3101) OTAR (SR 7060)

---

433 *1792*
General Plan of the District of Luneburg Compiled from the Several Plans in my possession, on which are laid down the names of the Officers who have drawn Land in this District, formerly belonging to the Corps serving in the Province of Quebec. To His Excellency Governor Simcoe, This Plan is most humbly presented. By ... [Sgd] W Chewett Surveyor for the District of Luneburg Osnabruck 7th February 1792.
Col ms 83 x 239 cm 3/4" to 1 mile Endorsements: 'District of Lunebourg & 3 maps Gananoqoi Iles au Baril & Bay of Quinté & Presq'isle'
Twps named except for nos 9 and 10 [Yonge and Escott]; shows the southern part of the district from Leeds Twp and Co to Lancaster Twp and Glengarry Co; shows mills 'where built and building' and names of owners; notes on parts of twps not laid out; surveyed lines shown with data on relief and terrain; shows town plots for Johnstown and Cornwall but a note indicates the latter is not laid out; (*OHIM* 3.3).
OTAR (Simcoe Map 446889)

---

434 *[1792]*
Sketch of the River St Lawrence, from the Cedres, to Lake Ontario
Col ms 31 x 227 cm 1" to 2 miles Watermark: 'J WHATMAN'
Originally enclosed in Simcoe to Dundas 4 Nov 1792 (GBLpro CO 42/317) in which he comments, 'I beg to send a Map of the River St. Lawrence that in case of a Treaty being entered into with the States, it may plainly appear of what consequence it is to render it effectual & permanent that the British Boundary should enclose the Islands of the St Lawrence'; shows the river, islands, route for ships, twp and co names and boundaries; French and English names for large islands; a note indicates that the plan is probably fairly accurate in Glengarry and Grenville but from there to Kingston is about 'eight miles too great in distance'; Cornwall, Johnstown, and Kingston shown; a reproduction of the plan with letter is in Simcoe, *Correspondence* I:246–9; photoreproduction in OOAMA (NMC 21842); (*PRO Cat* 1568).
GBLpro (MPG 92)

Related maps

(2) *[ca 1792]*
[Endorsed title]: 'Sketch of the river St Laurence from the Cascades to Oswegathy with plans of Lake Champlain ... 13' 'Part of the St. Lawrence'
Col ms 37 x 137 cm Approx 1" to 2 miles Watermark: 'J WHATMAN'
An unfinished plan showing the boundaries of twps 1 to 9 and Lancaster along the St Lawrence; islands in front are named; comments on land and timber for masts; notes on some of the twps indicate the number of families that can be or are being settled there, e.g., twp 9, 500 families; names have been pencilled in including Johnstown and Cornwall; rapids in river; base information is similar to above map which may have been compiled from this one.
OTAR (Simcoe Map 446219)

---

435 *[1793]*
[Plan of the boundaries of townships from north of Matilda to Cornwall]
Col ms 74 x 101 cm 1" to 120 chains Endorsements: 'No. 5' '776'
Possibly part of survey by Hugh McDonell (SI 1 Sept 1793) of boundary lines for twps west, north, and east to the Ottawa R; (OTNR FN 252 [1793]); shows boundaries of Mountain, Winchester, and Finch twps and the continuation of line on the east side of St Regis Indian land to the Ottawa R, crossing the Petite Nation R; shows survey data along lines and crown and clergy reserves.
OTNR (SR 5522)

---

436 *[ca 1793–5]*
[Endorsed title]: 'Midland District'
Col ms 46 x 127 cm Scale not given Watermark: 'J WHATMAN' Endorsements: '6'
An unfinished plan showing the north shore of L Ontario from Presqu'ile to about Yonge Twp; the twps of Kingston, Portland, Loughborough, and Pittsburgh are named; other twps are pencilled in west of these in orientations that were not used; only three place-names are given on the east side of Bay of Quinte; possibly a plan for survey since Loughborough was partly laid out in 1792 or 1793 (SI 16 Oct 1792); the outline for Presqu'ile is better than on the Mecklenburg map of [1792?] (**426(2)**) although the rest of the shoreline is similar to latter.
OTAR (SR 5981)

---

437 *1794*
By order of the Honl David William Smith Esqr Actg Surr General in the Province of Upper Canada, The above Six Townships on River Radeau [*sic*] and Part of the Waters of River Thames, was Surveyed in the Year of our Lord, one Thousand Seven Hundred and Ninety Four, By Wm Fortune D.P.S.
Col ms 99 x 68 cm 1" to 80 chains Endorsements: 'No 4' '878'

(SI 1 Sept 1793; OTNR FN 311 12 Aug 1794); in the title, Thames is crossed out and 'now Gananoqui' inserted; shows the surveyed outlines of the twps of Bastard, Kitley, Wolford, Burgess, Elmsley and Montague; distances noted along lines.
OTNR (SR 5493)

---

438 *1794*
[Map showing part of Marysburgh township] A. Aitken D Sr 1794
Ms 54 x 76 cm 1" to 220 yds
Shows the north part with high land, bluffs, and 'Pt Pleasant' marked; soundings off shore and 'road from Lake Ontario to the Bay of Quinté' shown.
OTAR (Simcoe Map 445790)

---

439 *1794*
Sketch of les Isles au Barrel ... A. Aitken, July 1794
Ms 60 x 48 cm 1" to 400 ft
A sketch of part of the Brock Group of islands opp Elizabethtown Twp in the St Lawrence considered by Simcoe to be important points for defence (along with Ft Levy) as noted in a letter 5 Sept 1794 to Lord Dorchester (Simcoe, *Correspondence* III:42); soundings shown around the islands; one island is noted as 'supposed to command the passage of the River.'
OTAR (Simcoe Map 445336)

Related maps

(2) *1794*
Sketch of the Ruins of Fort Levy with the Soundings taken in fathoms. A.A. 1794
Ms 59 x 47 cm 1" to 400 ft
By A. Aitken; shows Ft Levy on Chimney Is below [Prescott]; also shows Garden Is, relief, and soundings.
OTAR (Simcoe Map 446223)

(3) *[1794]*
Sketch of les Isles au Barrill. [Endorsed titles]: 'Isles du Baril Partial' [and] 'Isle du Fort Levy (Partial)'
2 col mss on 1 sheet 111 x 37 cm 1" to 400 ft
Endorsements: 'No 27' '871'
These sketches are unfinished but appear to be by Aitken; very similar to (1) and (2) above; only outlines are shown but soundings are the same.
OTAR (SR 5811)

(4) *[179?]*
Sketch of Les Isles au Barri D.F.
Col ms 34 x 28 cm 1" to 400 ft
Rough outlines of the islands, soundings, and part of the mainland; note indicates 'islands are about 130 yards in length and from 80 to 90 in breadth, composed almost entirely of Granite rock and about 15 feet high in the middle'; similar to (1) above and possibly a contemporary copy.
QMMMCM (3530)

---

440 *1795*
Plan of the Tongue of Land laying between a part of Ottawa River and part of the river Saint Lawrence including the Seigniories New Longueil, of Rigaud, Vaudreuil and Soulange. Quebec 4th August 1795. Surveyor General's Office [Sgd] Samuel Holland Survr General. Wm VondenVelden.
Col ms 49 x 71 cm 1" to 2 miles Endorsements: 'Fr. Lord Dorchesters dated 10th Septr 1795 to Lieut Govr Simcoe'
Shows the four seigneuries and boundaries with the twps of Hawkesbury and Lancaster; bearings; a descriptive text on the boundary between Upper and Lower Canada and the history of the land granting and survey is given; there is also a copy with the same title and date but further sgd 'Copy Wm Hall Lt R Arty' enclosed in Lord Dorchester's no 63 of 19 Sept 1795 (GBLpro CO 42/104 p 297) (*PRO Cat* 1955; GBLpro (MPG 433)).
OTAR (Simcoe Map 446491) GBLpro (MPG 433)

Related maps

(2) *1795*
Plan of part of the Land laying between a part of the Ottawa River, and part of the River St Lawrence, including the Seigniories of Rigaud, New Longueuil, and the Township of Newton. Surveyor General's Office Upper Canada 7th October 1795. [Sgd] D W Smith Actg Sur Genl
Col ms 43 x 66 cm 1" to 2 miles
Similar to plan above except more bearings given and Newton Twp shown; extensive notes on original intention of location of boundary re Order in Council August 1791, sgd 'With a Report from the Surveyor Generals Office, Upper Canada 7th October 1795 [Sgd] D W Smith'; a copy of the report was sent from Simcoe to Dorchester on 25 Oct 1795 with a copy of this sketch (Simcoe, *Correspondence* IV:112) (*OHIM* 2.12); the 1791 act relating to the boundary was incorrect, which led to later problems (Nicholson, 22).
OTAR (Simcoe Map 446291)

(3) *[180?]*
Copy of part of a Plan of the Province from which it is supposed the boundary between the Provinces of Lower and Upper Canada was founded.
Col ms 31 x 45 cm Scale not given Watermark 'T STAINS 1800'
Shows the boundary between the Seigneury of Vaudreuil and the Seigneury of 'Villchauve and Longuille' and Upper Canada; (Holmden 3881).
OOAMA (NMC 7372)

---

441 *[ca 1795]*
[Plan of townships on the Ottawa River showing conflicting survey lines]
Col ms 85 x 194 cm [1" to 40 chains]
Endorsements: '496'
Shows the area from line run from 'Mons. de Lotbegniere and Rigaud's seigneuries' to [Plantagenet Twp]; shows the front two cons for Hawkesbury and Plantagenet, and cons 3 to 4 for Alfred; conflicting lines shown around Longueuil; various other lines run; estimates of area; probably

done between the survey of Alfred and Plantagenet by James Rankin in 1789 (see list on 1790 plan, **10**) and survey of Alfred, Plantagenet, and Hawkesbury by W. Fortune in 1797 (see App A); this plan is probably by W. Chewett.
OTAR (SR 6778)

---

442 *1795*
Sketch of the Gananoque Johnstown 17th June 1795 [Sgd] Lewis Grant D Surveyor Eastern District
Col ms 68 x 47 cm 1" to 2 miles Endorsements: 'No 23' '776'
Probably surveyed by Grant under instructions of 15 Sept 1794 to survey J. Sherwood's land at the mouth of the Gananoque; shows part sketched from a canoe and that taken from an Indian plan of the river; notes on making carrying places 2 to 6 and 8 navigable and the need for locks at carrying places 1, 7, and 9.
OTAR (SR 2405)

---

443 *[1796?]*
Plan of the Different Channels leading from Kingston to Lake Ontario. With the Rocks, Shoals, & Soundings &c&c Surveyed & Drawing [*sic*] by [Sgd] Jos. Bouchette 2nd Lieut Rl N.
Col ms 63 x 97 cm 1" to 20 chains Endorsements: '915'
Shows area from Isle Tonty and Forest Is south of Little Cataraqui to Kingston; shorelines with nature of bottom, soundings, sailing routes; views: sketch of a ship following a route, sailors taking soundings; shows streets in town of Kingston and bldgs on Point Frederick; similar to inset map on **28**; after 1794 when Bouchette was made a 2nd lieutenant and probably 1796 as per his dating of the printed plan (4) and his date on (2).
OTAR (SR 5965)

Related maps

(2) *1796*
Plan of Nicholas & Egg Ids on Lake Ontario with the Rocks, Shoals & Soundings &c. Surveyed by [Jos Bouchette] 1796
Ms 33 x 42 cm 1" to 15 chains
Part of title and scale missing; soundings, anchorages.
GBTAUh (205 Aa2)

(3) *[1796]*
Plan of the Different Channels leading from the Lake into Kingston Harbour with the Rocks Shoals & Soundings thereof Surveyed & drawn by Joseph Bouchette.
Col ms 45 x 52 cm 1" to 40 chains
Similar to (1) above but at a smaller scale; shows the nature of the shoreline, soundings; navigational courses; 'Tonegeyon Bay' and 'Little Cataraqui' marked, also many islands and place-names.
OTAR (Simcoe Map 445785)

(4) *1796 (1815)*
PLAN / of / The Different Channels, / Leading from / KINGSTON to LAKE ONTARIO; / Surveyed by / Josh Bouchette. / 1796. // Published by W. Faden Charing Cross 12th Augst 1815. J. Walker Sculp.
Print (engrav) 22 x 26 cm 1" to 60 chains
In Joseph Bouchette, *A Topographical Description of the Province of Lower Canada* (London: W. Faden 1815), opp 603 (*Bib Can* 1031), and in the French ed (Londres: W. Faden 1815), opp 625 (*Bib Can* 1030); a reduced and simplified version of (1) and (3) above.
OTMCL

---

444 *[1798?]*
[Endorsed title]: 'Projected by Alexr Aitken Deputy Surveyor of Midland District [Sgd] J.G. Chewett'
Col ms (bottom right missing) 64 x 121 cm Scale not given Endorsements: '840'
This appears to be a compilation made by Aitken (who died in 1799 (*DCB* IV:12–13)) of surveys to date in the district; shows the survey grid for Leeds, Pittsburgh, Kingston, Loughborough, Portland, Ernestown, Fredericksburgh, Camden, Richmond, Marysburgh, Sophiasburgh, Hallowell, Ameliasburgh, Thurlow, Sydney, Murray, Hungerford, Huntingdon, Rawdon, Cramahe, and Percy, all at least partly surveyed before 1797; also the surveyed town site for Newcastle at Presqu'ile (SI 14 Sept 1797 to A. Aitken); various military reserves and posts; several boundary lines (not keyed); title is as supplied by Chewett some years later.
OTAR (SR 5984)

---

445 *[1802]*
Plan of 600 Acres in the Township of Ameliasburgh, in Upper Canada – The Property of Mrs Anne Smith, Widow of the late Lieut. Colonel Smith, 5th Regmt [Sgd] W Chewett Senr Surveyor & Dftmn
Col ms 41 x 31 cm Scale not given
The property is part of lots 111–14, 2nd con; shows portage to Bay of Quinte, barrier beach, and proposed canal; a copy of the description of the property by A. Aitken, 1799, accompanies plan.
OTMCL (D.W. Smith Papers B15 f 11)

---

446 *[1805]*
[Plan of boundary line between Upper and Lower Canada] [Sgd] Joseph Bouchette Dy S. Genl
Col ms 48 x 63 cm 1" to 2 miles Watermark: 'BUDGEN 1800'
Notes by Bouchette about the original boundary delineation as of 1791, an explanation of how the error crept in and the true intent of the original proclamation; shows the original boundary line and corrected line, original idea of shore of Ottawa R and boundaries of seigneuries of Rigaud, New Longueuil, Vaudreuil, Soulange and twp of Newton; a transcript was reproduced to accompany Doughty and McArthur, 56; there is

also a small plan of part of Lancaster as surveyed by Joseph Fortune in 1806 showing probable boundary as requested by Rev. Alexr McDonell (OOAMA (NMC 7373)) and a 'Plan of the Seigniories of Rigaud and New Longueuil ... 1806 ... true copy 29th Dec 1819' (OOAMA (NMC 11837)) with details from the Lower Canada side, and there is a later 'Plan of the Seigniories of New Longeuil and Rigaud ... 10th April 1810 [Sgd] Jos Bouchette S. Genl' marking the boundary in detail OOAMA (NMC 17839); (Holmden 3882).
OOAMA (NMC 14702; 7373; 17839; 11837)

---

447 *1807*
Plan by R Sherwood Esq of a water communication from the waters of the Gananoque to South Lake as he came himself in Sept 1807 in Birch Canoe
Ms 32 x 20 cm Scale not given Watermark: 'E MORGAN TROY'
Provenance: OOA H.S. MacDonald Papers; shows the route north and then west to South L; 'Furnace Road'; portages.
OOAMA (NMC 59326)

---

448 *1809*
Plan and Survey of the Indian Reservation Land commonly called Nutfield, the property of the St. Regis Indians, situated and lying in the County of Glengarry in the Eastern District Province of Upper Canada bounded in front or southerly by the St Lawrence, northerly by the Township of Plantagenet, easterly by the Townships of Charlottenburg and Kenyon and westerly by the Townships of Cornwall and Roxburg ... Surveyed at the Request of the Indian Chiefs of St Regis by me [Sgd] Jeremiah McCarthy Senr Dy Surveyr for the Provinces of Lower & Upper Canada Indian Land County of Glengarry 31st September 1809
Col ms 58 x 225 cm 1" to 25 chains
Detailed plan showing swamps, roads, houses, description of survey; list of tenants on lots and yearly rent; notes on survey discrepancies and land claims of Indians; accompanied by J. McCarthy's 1809 survey notes and two reports by Thos. Ridout 4 Sept 1811 and 30 Jan 1817, rejecting Indian land claims; map was certified by 10 Indian chiefs 29 June 1811.
OTAR

Related maps

(2) *1821*
Map of the Indian Reservation in the County of Glengary, Eastern District and Province of Upper Canada by McDonald & Browne to The Honorable William McGillevray. 1821.
Col ms 75 x 63 cm 1" to 1/2 mile Endorsements: '1113' 'Q 30'
(SI 5 Dec 1821 to resurvey land in the St Regis Reserve); shows trees, rocks, marsh, mills, roads, cleared areas; table of notes on each con and lot; encroachments on lots noted.
OTNR (SR 2644)

(3) *1848*
Map of the Indian Reservation County of Glengarry Eastern District Province of Canada [Sgd] John S. Bruce D.P.S. 1848.
Col ms 73 x 58 cm 1" to 40 chains Endorsements: 'Q 82'
Similar to 1821 map except names of owners added; list of owners of some lots; burial ground; (OTNR FN 833, 834 14 June 1848); also a plan marked 'Copy T. Devine C.L.D.' 28 Feb 1849, endorsed 'C57' at OTAR(P); the reservation was surrendered to the Crown in 1847 (*Indian Treaties*, Treaty No 57 (1847), I:136ff).
OTNR (SR 2472)

---

449 *[181?]*
Chart of the Bay of Quinte and part of Lake Ontario
Ms (part missing) 48 x 67 cm 1" to 13/4 miles
Endorsements: 'Copy of Harbor plan made by an officer of the Royal Navy'
An unfinished plan of the area between Kingston and Adolphustown; concentric circles show distances from Kingston; nature of the shoreline; shows Bath, Napanee R, and Knapps Pt on Wolfe Is and Simcoe Is; possibly drawn after the War of 1812.
OOAMA (NMC 4806)

---

450 *[181?]*
No 1 [Map of the St. Lawrence River from Collins Bay to Grenadier Is]
Col ms 40 x 57 cm 1" to 2 miles Watermark: 'STACE(?) CO' Endorsements: '849'; stamp 'R.E.O. Kingston'
A fragment of what was probably a whole survey of the river, the rest of which has not been found; shows area from Kingston to about Mallorytown; the shape of the islands differs from the Duberger plan of 1813 (**457**) but the names are in English; shows the following islands: Wolfe or Long, Howe, Gage, Garden, and Carlton; 'Old Ship Channel'; roads.
OOAMA (NMC 4135)

---

451 *[181?]*
[Sketch of townships from Edwardsburgh to Leeds showing towns, roads, and mills] [Endorsed title]: 'Augusta'
Ms 42 x 139 cm Scale not given Endorsements: '771'
A rough sketch; shows Brockville, Prescott, and Johnstown; several mills including W. LaRu's mill pond, Tricky's mill, Charles Jones's mill pond, Jones's mill, Daniel Jones's back mill pond, and Buell's mill; mill ponds exaggerated in size; road to Kitley and Bastard; bridges; probably made after 1810 when Prescott was established (Morris, 16).
OTAR (SR 5497)

452 *[1813]*
EAST END of LAKE ONTARIO. // H.S. Tanner fc.
Print (engrav) 17 x 11 cm 1" to 10 miles
In John Melish, *A Military and Topographical Atlas of the United States* (Philadelphia: Printed by G. Palmer Nov 1813), opp 18 (*Bib Can* 6922; *LC Atlases* 1346), and in the 1815 ed (Philadelphia: G. Palmer 1815), opp 18 (*Bib Can* 6980); map shows the area from Oswego on the American coast to Kingston; twps, cos, roads, settlements, islands.
OTMCL USDLC

---

453 *[1813?]*
The River St. Lawrence from Point Massena to Point L'Ivrogne by Joseph Bouchette Survr General L. Canada
Col ms 35 x 75 cm 1" to approx 4/5 mile
Watermark: 'J WHATMAN 1811' Endorsements: '1813'
Shows the lower part of the river from just west of Cornwall to part of Lower Canada; names of rivers, places, mills, twps, islands; a road shown along shore has names of some settlers marked along it; (*PRO Cat* 1569).
GBLpro (CO 700 Canada 73)

---

454 *1813 Feb*
General Survey of the River St Lawrence &c from Quebec to Montreal – From Original British Documents, left unfinished by the late Genl Montresor Engineer General – Furnished to the Am. government by Mr Tatham Feb 3rd 1813 – (Copy from T. Stephenson's J.G.T. [Endorsed title]: 'West sheet River St Lawrence Tatham'
Ms 39 x 137 cm (west sheet) 1" to 1 league
Notes: 'Central Washington July 25 1813. This Part from Montreal to Lake Ontario was added from an original in Genl Montresor's public collection by order of the Hon. J. Armstrong Secy at War by (Signed) Wm Tatham'; this is the west sheet of a three-sheet set and is an early, fairly rough survey with place-names in French; possibly done by Lt Carleton in 1768 who is described as surveying 'The St Lawrence Islands from the Cedars to Lake Ontario' (see list on 1790 plan, **10**); the information is clearly fairly old but a few corrections may have been made; copy attributed to Joseph Gilbert Totton (USDNA).
USDNA (RG 77 Dr 113-81/2)

---

455 *1813 Oct*
Sketch of the Entrance into Lake Ontario Upper Canada Octr 15 1813
Col ms 37 x 46 cm 1 1/4" to 2 miles Watermark: '... BATH 180[?]'
Shows the American side in more detail than the Canadian side; from Sacketts Harbour to Watertown and Brownsville with roads; shows Kingston, fort at Point Henry, and bldgs at Point Frederick; ship channels; the town plan of Kingston is inaccurate and the plan was obviously not made from a reconnaissance survey (see also Kingston, **1507**).
USDLC

---

456 *1813 [Nov?]*
The East End of Lake Ontario with the River of St Lawrence to Salmon Creek. Drawn on a Scale of Eleven twentieths of an Inch to a Mile 1813.
Ms 48 x 200 cm 1" to 1 mile Endorsements: 'Received from Com. Chauncey'; stamp 'Engr Dept. U.States Topl Bureau'
Shows the area from Kingston to Cornwall with soundings, ship channels, and boundary south of river; sketch of Kingston, Brockville, and other towns; shows the position of British and American troops at Crysler's Farm and Gen Wilkinson's troops at the Salmon R south of St Regis Is.
USDNA (RG 77 AMA 30)

---

457 *1813 Nov*
[Map of the St Lawrence River between Pointe au Baudet and Kingston] J.B. Duberger Novr 1813
2 col mss ea 30 x 93 cm 1" to 4 miles
Endorsements: stamp 'R E Office Quebec No 600'
Two close copies showing twp boundaries, settlements, bldgs, names of islands; both plans show Gananoque R, the blockhouse, and falls but only second plan identifies them; second plan also shows 'Crystler's Farm' [*sic*]; the names of islands in front of Kingston are in French suggesting earlier sources; ship channels shown.
OOAMA (NMC 21837–8)

---

458 *1813 Nov*
Sketch of the Action at Williamsburg, Upper Canada between A Detachment of the Centre Division of the British Army under the Command of Lieut Coll Morrison 89 Regiment and A Division of the American Army under Brigr Genl Boyd on the 11th November 1813. M.C.
Ms 24 x 35 cm 1" to 1/4 mile
Shows the position of various regiments at the Battle of Crysler's Farm: the Royal Artillery under Capt Jackson, the 49th and 89th regiments, the Canadian Voltigeurs under Maj Heriot, and the American infantry, cavalry, and gunboats, and the British gunboats; the positions of the Canadian Voltigeurs and the Indian warriors are shown at the beginning and end of battle; photoreproduction at OOAMA.
Original not located

---

459 *1814*
EAST END / of / LAKE ONTARIO / and / RIVER ST LAURENCE / From / KINGSTON TO FRENCH MILLS / Reduced from an Original Drawing / in the / NAVAL DEPARTMENT / By John Melish. H.S. Tanner Sc. // PHILADELPHIA, Published by JOHN MELISH 1st October 1814.
Print (engrav) sometimes hand col 47 x 57 cm 1" to 5 1/2 miles
In John Melish, *A Military and Topographical Atlas*

of the United States (Philadelphia: Published by John Melish 1815), at end (*Bib Can* 6980; *LC Atlases* 1347), and in *A General Collection of Maps* (Philadelphia 1824), No [24] (*LC Atlases* 6053); shows the river from Kingston to Cornwall with twps named on both sides, routes in the river, soundings, and towns; disposition of British and American troops at Crysler's Farm; (*PRO Cat* 1516).
GBLpro OKQAR OTMCL USDLC

Related maps

(2) *1814*
MAP / of the / RIVER ST LAWRENCE / AND ADJACENT COUNTRY / From Williamsburg to Montreal / FROM AN ORIGINAL DRAWING / in the / War Department. / J. Melish del. H.S. Tanner sc. // PHILADELPHIA, Published by JOHN MELISH, 1st October 1814.
Print (engrav) 43 x 62 cm 1" to 43/4 miles
At end of the Melish 1815 atlas cited above and no [25] in the 1824 publication; shows only a small part of Upper Canada; road along shore; 'Sir John Johnson's Mills' at 'R. Raisin'; notes and legend refer to U.S. and Lower Canada; (*PRO Cat* 1386).
GBLpro OTMCL USDLC

---

460 *[1815]*
[Sketch of communications along the St Lawrence River from Kingston to Montreal] Tracing from a Survey by the Surveyor General
Ms in 5 sheets 78 x 324 cm Scale not given
A military reconnaissance sketch showing all settlements, roads, and ship channels on both sides of the river; block houses, forts, major mills, houses; distance tables are given for 20 places along the river; a note indicates that since the plan is mainly to show water communication, the con roads are not laid down; note: 'French Mills on Salmon River where General Wilkinson and the remainder of his Army retreated with precipitation from the British side on the 12th November 1813'; a note in OOAMA indicates this plan may be by R. Sherwood from report of 25 Jan 1815 (see also **C45**).
GBE (Sir George Murray Papers 46.10.2 (101, 102))

---

461 *1815*
A SKETCH of the BATTLE / at / CHRISTLERS FARM / WILLIAMSBURG / UPPER CANADA / 11th Novr 1813. // Published by W. Faden Charing Cross Augst 12th 1815. // J. Walker Sculpt.
Print (engrav) 11 x 19 cm 2" to 3/4 mile
In Joseph Bouchette, *Topographical Description of the Province of Lower Canada* (London: W. Faden 1815), opp 638 (*Bib Can* 1031), and in the French ed, *Description topographique de la province du Bas Canada* (Londres: W. Faden 1815), opp 661 (*Bib Can* 1030); shows the positions of the troops on both sides, fields, houses, relief, road.
OTMCL

---

462 *[1816]*
PART / of the / RIVER ST LAWRENCE // H.S. Tanner // vol III Page 187 // No 7
Print (engrav) 11 x 19 cm 1" to 1 mile
In James Wilkinson, *Diagrams and Plans Illustrative of the Principal Battles ... in Memoirs of My Own Times* (Philadelphia: Abraham Small 1816), Map 7 (*LC Atlases* 1344); shows Matilda Twp during part of the War of 1812 with British battery and point east of that proposed by Gen Armstrong for a post to command river; 'See his letter Aug 8th 1813 ...'; point on U.S. side west of Hamilton where cavalry crossed 8 Oct 1813.
OTMCL USDLC

---

463 *1816*
Part of the River St Lawrence from East Bay to the lower point of Isle de Rapid plat by actual Survey 1816 [Sgd] J. Anderson, I. Roberdeau U.S. T. Engineers. Roberdeau del.
Ms 60 x 90 cm 31/2" to 1 mile Endorsements: stamp 'Engr Dept U States Topl Bureau'
Note: 'apparently prepared with a view to fortifying Point Iroquois (on the American side opposite Point au Pins) & west of Hamilton village'; inset of Point Iroquois and section; a British battery is noted as destroyed by Gen Wilkinson in 1813.
USDNA (RG 77 AMA31)

Related maps

(2) *[1816]*
Sketch of the River St Lawrence from East Bay Creek downards by [Sgd] J. Anderson, I. Roberdeau U.S. T. Engineers
Ms 37 x 56 cm Approx 1" to 48 chains
Endorsements: 'D 36'
Shows the same area as above plan with a section across Point Iroquois; notes indicate that the latter is higher than Pointe aux Pins upon which the British were to erect a battery; the British battery is actually shown to the east; the shoreline differs from above map but was probably prepared at the same time.
USDNA (RG 77)

---

464 *1816*
Plan of the Rideau River from its mouth to the Head of Long Island (Sigd) J. Jebb Lt Royl Engrs June 20th 1815 [6?] True Copy, J.B. Duberger Junr 28th June 1815 [6?]
Col ms 42 x 206 cm 6" to 1 mile Watermark: 'J WHATMAN 1815'
Originally accompanied J. Jebb's letter and report to Lt Col Nicoll 8 June 1816 and further enclosed in Lt Gen Wilson's letter 2 July 1816 (GBLpro CO 42/166 p 331); shows 12 points along river for locks and a 'dam Head for retaining the water' on west side Long Is; rapids, falls, heights of water; dimensions of dams and locks; two roads shown, one noted as 'cut in the Winter of 1815'; photoreproduction in OOAMA (NMC 4988); (*PRO Cat* 1560).
GLBpro (MPG 457(2))

Related maps

(2) *1816*
Plan of the Mouth of the River Rideau and Project for improving the Communication (Signed) J. Jebb Lt Royl Engr 8th June 1816
Col ms 50 x 74 cm 1" to 100 ft
'Section' 1" to 50 ft, 1" to 10 ft vertical; shows basin on the Rideau for securing boats and stores; proposed wharf for boats, landing places on the Ottawa R, and communications between the two rivers; relief; filed with correspondence as cited in (1); photoreproduction in OOAMA (NMC 3270).
GBLpro (MPG 457(3))

(3) *1816*
(Copy) No 2 Plan of the Rideau River from its mouth to the Head of Long Island. (Signed) J. Jebb Lt Rl Engineers June 20th 1816. With a letter to Lt. Col. Durnford dated Kingston 22 June 1816.
Col ms on tracing paper 41 x 198 cm 6" to 1 mile
Watermark: 'JOHN HAYES 1814' Endorsements: '60' 'F 49' 'Ordnance Admiralty & Railway Lands Canada Record 689'; stamps 'B↑O' 'IGF'
OOAMA map originally accompanied Jebb's letter and report of the same date (OOA RG8 IB vol 1915); a copy of first map above with additional notes on soundings and the rate of current sgd by J. Jebb; note: 'See Lt Colonel Durnford's letter to Lt General Mann dated 7th May 1817'; also an undated copy in OTNR (SR 2679); 'Copy Sketch of the Rideau ...' endorsed '790'; the originals by J. Jebb do not seem to have survived.
OOAMA (NMC 21791) OTNR (SR 2679)

---

465 *1816*
Plan of the Water communication from Kingston to the Grand River (Signed) J. Jebb Lt Royal Engineers July 8th 1816 (Copy) No 1
Col ms in 2 sheets 78 x 234 cm 1" to 1 mile
Watermark: '1814' Endorsements: 'F49'; stamps 'IGF' 'B↑O'
Originally accompanied Jebb's letter and report of 14 July 1816 to Lt Col Durnford (OOA RG 8 IB vol 1915); later note: 'See Lt. Colonel Durnford's letter to Lt. General Mann dated 7th May 1817'; shows the Irish Creek route for a canal on the Rideau; shows twps, settlements, roads, rivers, rapids, swamps, etc; 'Direction of new road from Brockville to Perth (via Koyle's)' and 'road cut in winter of 1815' along the Rideau R from Montague Twp to Nepean Twp; 'Direction of the new road from Perth Settlement to Kingston'; notes in pencil showing lock bldgs at Black Rapids were probably added in 1828; (Holmden 2410).
OOAMA (NMC 16814)

Related maps

(2) *1816 (1826)*
Plan of the Water Communication from Kingston to the Grand River By J. Jebb Lieut R.Engineers, July 8th 1816. Copied by A. Gibbs Decembr 1826.
Col ms in 2 sheets 67 x 238 cm 1" to 1 mile
Endorsements: stamps 'R.E. Office No 5'
Shows the same information as above map.
OOAMA (NMC 21941)

(3) *[1816]*
Sketch of the Water Communication from Kingston to the Grand River Signed J. Jebb Lt Royl Engrs [endorsed title]: 'No 3 Copy General Sketch of the Water Communication from Kingston to the Ottawa or Grand River (Sigd) J. Jebb Lt Royl Engineers'
Col ms 79 x 236 cm 1" to 1 mile Watermark: 'J WHATMAN TURKEY MILL' Endorsements: '979'
Shows the same information as (1) above.
OTAR (SR 7131)

(4) *[1816?]*
[Endorsed title]: 'No 7 Communication between Kingston and the mouth of the River Rideau by Jebb'
Col ms 82 x 231 cm 1" to 1 mile Watermark: 'J WHATMAN' Endorsements: '975'
Shows the same information as (1) above; possibly done a little later as note has been changed to 'Line of Road laid out from Perth to Kingston' and the road is shown to Perth, not just to the Narrows; original sgd by Jebb does not seem to have survived.
OTAR (SR 7119)

---

466 *1816*
Plan shewing the Intended Purchase in rear of the Settlement in the District of Johnstown [and endorsed title]: 'D Sketch of projected purchase from the Indians of a Tract of Land West of the River Rideau'
Col ms 20 x 26 cm 1" to 10 miles
In a letter from Col Claus, deputy superintendent Indian Affairs, to Capt Ferguson, resident agent, 22 Feb 1816 enclosed in Gore to Drummond 23 Feb 1816 about the purchase (GBLpro CO 42/357 p 45); related to the purchase of 1819 (*Indian Treaties*, Treaty No 27 (1819), I:62ff); shows area from the St Lawrence R to the Ottawa R, and from Kingston to Edwardsburgh Twp; the area to be purchased covers the twps of Bathurst, Drummond, Beckwith, and two unnamed twps to the east and west; there is also a copy with the same title but without the endorsement in OOAMA (NMC 13505); (Holmden 1741).
GBLpro (CO 42/357 p 45) OOAMA (NMC 13505)

---

467 *[1816?]*
[Sketch of Cornwall Island, St Regis Island, Hog Island, and mainland shores of the St Lawrence River]
2 mss Ea 35 x 26 cm Scale not given Watermark of (1): 'S.C. 1805'
Provenance: part of a collection of maps of Maj D.B. Douglass; two similar untitled and unfinished maps of the same area; the first black and white plan shows 'Amer Commandr Camp,' 'British Commandr Camp,' and 'Observatory' on St Regis Is; a survey line is shown running north-

south through islands and another along mainland at St Regis; church and house drawn in at St Regis; a title oval is blank; the second plan is a more finished version of the first and shows the bldgs and camp in colour, vegetation, but no names; probably related to the boundary surveys beginning in 1816 since Douglass was an astronomical surveyor for the U.S. Party (see App D).
USDLC

Related maps

(**2**) *[181?]*
Sketch of the St. Lawrence River from Lake Ontario to Grenadier Island below the Thousand Islands; continuation thence down to St. Regis. D.D.
2 mss 28 x 126 cm and 23 x 118 cm 2" to 3 geog miles
Although attributed in pencil note to J.B. Duberger with possible date between 1788 and 1798, D.D. may refer to D.B. Douglass (see plan above); shows Kingston, Point Henry, and Johnstown, most other place-names in French; ship channel, batteau channel shown.
QMMMCM (5589, 5589.1)

---

468 *1818*
PART / of / LAKE ONTARIO / and of the / RIVER ST LAWRENCE / from an actual Survey / by / Captn W.F.W. Owen R.N. / 1816 // Published as the Act directs 11th May 1818, by Willm James // J. Walker Sculpt // To face p 131 vol 1st // Plate II
Print (engrav) 24 x 59 cm 1" to 3 miles
Insets: 'PLAN / of / KINGSTON HARBOUR / Plate IV' 1 1/4" to 1 mile, '[Sackets Harbour] Plate III' 1" to 575 yds; in William James, *A Full and Correct Account of the Military Occurrences of the Late War* (London: Printed for the author 1818), opp 131 (*Bib Can* 1058); based on the ms survey (**C58**); soundings; a few roads, relief, marshes.
OTMCL

---

469 *[1818]*
Sketch of the Rideau Settlement with the New Townships and others in its vicinity. Copied W.R.D.
Col ms on tracing paper 44 x 56 cm Scale not given
Originally with 'Report on the Military Settlement in the Neighbourhood of the Rideau Pointing Out the Communication Which May Be Established in That Direction between Lachine and Kingston by Lt Col Francis Cockburn 26 Nov 1818' (GBLpro CO 42/182/21); shows twps from Sherbrooke Twp to Gloucester Twp and Kingston to Edwardsburg; Perth, Richmond, and other places marked; some names of settlers, bldgs, etc; shows roads connecting with Kingston, Gananoque, Brockville, Ft Wellington, and 'New Johnstown' [Johnstown]; proposed road to Perth from Kingston; photoreproduction in OOAMA (NMC 1553); (*PRO Cat* 2839).
GBLpro (MPG 484)

---

470 *1819*
[Map of Glengarry County showing names of lot owners] 1819
Ms 141 x 107 cm Scale not given
Note: 'Supposing the County of Glengarry to contain 18 concessions and each concession 83 lots of 200 acres the number of lots would be 1494'; shows names (some with 'N.D.' beside them) in about 85 per cent of lots; St Regis Indian Reservation shown on the west side; boundary with Lower Canada; (Bigger, I:63).
OTAR

---

471 *1819*
[Endorsed title]: 'Map of the River St Lawrence from Kingston to Point au Pin, 70 Miles downwards including the Thousand Islands ... The survey was made in 1819 – the pencilled line running among the Islands & along the River marked the Boundary between the States & U. Canada'
Col ms 53 x 200 cm 1" to 2025 yds Endorsements: stamps 'Topographical Department War Office Oct 23 1887 81/2' 'Canada Ontario Dist 2' 'Canada District 42'
Originally from GBLpro WO 78/1051; notes: 'these Islands and the Shores of the River ... are very accurately laid down on this map, as may be ascertained by reference to the maps of Commodore Owen and of the Boundary line Commission maps, in possession of Government, but not on the same Scale'; the map was probably drafted in 1819; includes notes on types of settlements along river, e.g., 'many dutch families hereabout'; geological notes; navigational note with references to the War of 1812; old forts and Ft Wellington shown; the pencilled boundary line has been enhanced in red with date '20/3/69' and the title was probably added at the same time; (*PRO Cat* 1575); (see also **D1(2–4)** and **D2**).
GBLpro (MR 296(2))

---

472 *1819*
Mohawk Tract, S.G.O. 28 Dec 1819 [Sgd] T. Ridout S.G.
Ms on tracing paper 42 x 27 cm 1" to 2 miles
Endorsements: 'Q2' '1091'
Shows the tract between Richmond and Thurlow twps; 'Angousola Rr now the Shannon'; 'Mohawk Settlement' shown by shore; 'present road travelled' on shore and a proposed road; a similar map, lacking only the roads and endorsed 'Q7' and '1094,' is entitled 'Mohawk Tract (Sketch) Bay of Quinté. Copy W.C. now Tyendinaga' (42 x 36 cm); SI for Tyendinaga Twp were issued in Feb 1820.
OTNR (SR 2429; 2436)

Related maps

(**2**) *[1820]*
Sketch showing the situation of the Mohawk Tract Plan A
Col ms approx 30 x 44 cm 1" to 5 miles

Accompanies a memorandum on 'Lands proposed to be sold to defray the annual charge of Presents to the Indians for the Tracts purchased of them ...' in Maitland to Bathurst 8 May 1820 (GBLpro CO 42/365 p 84); shows the same tract of land as in above map; the tract was purchased from the Indians in 1820 and was laid out as Tyendinaga Twp.
GBLpro (CO 42/365 p 84)

(**3**) *1820*
[Endorsed title]: 'Plan shewing the land on the Mohawk Tract (Bay of Quinté) purchased from the Indians' [Sgd] Surveyor Generals office York U.C. 12 July 1820 Thos Ridout Surveyr Genl
Col ms 41 x 53 cm 1" to 80 chains
Shows the tract '33,280 acres,' location of Mohawks, and line of road; (Holmden 1511; *Indian Treaties*, Treaty No 24 (1820), I:54ff).
OOAMA (NMC 3650)

---

473 *[182?]*
Military Settlements / OF / Upper Canada / Bourne Sc.
Print (engrav) 19 x 11 cm Scale not given
Shows the area from the St Lawrence R to Lavant and Fitzroy twps at the Ottawa R and from March Twp west to Dalhousie Twp; Bathurst and Johnstown districts, and Carleton and Leeds cos shown; locates Perth, Lanark, Richmond, and the Rideau and Mississippi rivers and lakes.
OOAMA (NMC 15712)

---

474 *[182?]*
Plan of the Division of the two Districts, viz. Midland & Newcastle Districts, to form one in the centre of the two viz. The District of Maitland ...
Ms 39 x 51 cm Scale not given Watermark: 'FELLOWS 1819'
Note describes proposed boundary 'commencing ... on the Eastern Boundary lines of the Townships of Tydendenaga and Hungerford, thence northerly running on the lines between Murray and Cramahe, Seymour & Percy and so on as far northerly as necessary'; further note: 'Division line of the Intended District Should it be requested by petition'; the proposed boundary would have taken in two more western twps (Murray and Seymour) than that of the eventual District of Victoria established in 1837; shows twps as far north as Marmora and Madoc surveyed in 1819 and 1820; (Holmden 2766).
OOAMA (NMC 3080)

---

475 *[182?]*
Sketch of the Water Communication from Kingston to the Grand River
Col ms 41 x 50 cm 1" to 4 miles
Shows twps, settlements, roads from Kingston to Edwardsburgh, north to Bytown, west to 'Twp no 1' and North Crosby Twp; shows some of the same information as on 1816 maps above (**465**) including 'road cut in the summer of 1816' (from Kitley Twp (Koyles) to Perth) and 'road cut in the winter of 1814' [i.e., 1815] (along Rideau R); the twps of the military settlement around Perth are shown as 'No 1–4'; 'Bytown' is marked; probably dates from the early 1820s; (Holmden 1757).
OOAMA (NMC 3198)

---

476 *1821*
[Plan of Hungerford, Sheffield, Hinchinbrooke, and Bedford townships] Surveyor Generals Office York 24 May 1821 [Sgd] Thos Ridout Surveyr General
Col ms 67 x 161 cm Scale not given
(SI to Samuel Benson 18 June 1821 to survey these twps); a projected plan of survey to accompany instructions; note: 'This plan to be returned to the Surveyor Genls Office'; notes on lines and bearings to be surveyed.
OTAR

---

477 *1821*
[Plan of the Military Settlement north of the Rideau River] A Q Master Generals Office, Quebec 16th February 1821 (Copied) W.R. Dickson D.A.Q.M.G.
Col ms 77 x 130 cm 1" to 120 chains Watermark: 'J WHATMAN TURKEY MILL KENT 1818'
Shows 12 twps north of the Rideau R; N Sherbrooke to March Twp and S Sherbrooke to Nepean Twp; Richmond 'village commenced Spring 1818,' Perth 'village commenced [Aug?] 1816,' and Lanark 'commenced Autumn 1820'; shows road from Richmond Landing (Ottawa) to Richmond, Franktown, Perth, and Lanark and two connecting roads south to Kingston and Brockville; names of settlers along roads; (Holmden 2419).
OOAMA (NMC 11274)

Related maps

(**2**) *1821*
[Plan of the Military Settlement north of the Rideau River] [Sgd] Dy Qr Mr General's Office Quebec 28th May 1821 W.R. Dickson D A Q M Genl
Col ms 69 x 120 cm 1" to 120 chains Watermark: 'J GREEN ... 1815'
Originally enclosed with Dalhousie's no 46 to Bathurst 14 June 1821 (GBLpro CO 42/187); very similar to above map but more names of settlers shown along roads; routes between Richmond, Franktown, Perth, and road to Brockville from Franktown are different and a road from Perth to Brockville has been added; photoreproduction in OOAMA (NMC 15539); (*PRO Cat* 1495).
GBLpro (MR 137)

---

478 *[1821]*
Sketch / Map of the Townships, / Upper Canada / From Montreal on the St Laurence / to Lake Ontario. / and to Mansfield on the Ottawa. J.H. Glasgow Litho: Props.
Print (lith) 76 x 23 cm Approx 1" to 24 miles
In Robert Lamond, *A Narrative of the Rise and Progress of Emigration ... to the New Settlements in Upper Canada ... With a Map of the Townships*

(Glasgow: Printed by James Hedderwick 1821), frontis (Casey I-1093); from Montreal west to Sidney and Rawdon twps; twps on the north bounded by Rawdon to Bedford, and Dalhousie to Almonte [Ramsay]; names of districts, roads.
OOA OTAR

---

479 *1822*
[Map of the townships of Lancaster, Lochiel, and Hawkesbury, part of Kenyon and Charlottenburgh] By Angus Cattenoch Deputy Surveyor Nov 29th 1822
Col ms 173 x 112 cm 1" to 40 chains Endorsements: 'No 5 B' '684'
(SI 20 Sept 1822 to resurvey west boundary of Lancaster and Lochiel twps and other lines between there and the Ottawa R; OTNR FN 489 9 Oct 1822); shows the conflicting lines from earlier surveys; roads, a few bldgs and owners, swampy areas.
OTNR (SR 11097)

---

480 *1822*
Plan showing the relative situation of the Town of Lancaster, Lochiel and Hawkesbury, with the Seigy of New Longueuil, the Townp of Newton the Seigy of Rigaud according to the Lines of separation carried into operation by Joseph Bouchette Esqr Surveyr Genl of Lower Canada, between the Provinces of Lower and Upper Canada – where the said Lines would have been fixed according to the Proclamation of the 18th November 1791 and where the said Lines should have been fixed according to the French Grants A & B also the tract of Land which will be cut off from the Province of Upper Canada provided the said Lines carried into operation by Mr Bouchette from the Cove West of the Pointe au Baudet, on Lake St Francis to Point Fortune, on the Ottawa or Grande River should be found correct and established and the tract that will be cut off from the Province of Lower Canada, provided the Western Limits of the Seigneuries of New Longueuil and Rigaud are deemed to be the Lines of separation between the said provinces, according to the true intent and meaning of the said French Grants A & B. York S.G. Office 21st October 1822 [Sgd] W Chewett Senior Surveyr & Draftsman
Col ms 83 x 94 cm 1" to 80 chains Endorsements: 'No 3' 'No 21'
Names of owners along boundary in Lancaster; 'Fair plan'; there is also a plan 'Seigneuries of Messrs De Lotbinière & De Longueuil, showing the same' demonstrating the conflicting boundary lines and with extensive notes sgd '21st October 1822 W. Chewett' in OTAR (SR 2064); a brief discussion of the boundary problem in 1822 and 1823 is found in OTAR RG 1 C-I-2 in a letter of 21 Oct 1822 from W. Chewett to Council where he indicates he is sending a report, three plans, and respective papers on the boundary between Upper Canada and Lower Canada (OOA RG 1 E1 Land Bk L pp 289–343).
OTAR (SR 5489)

Related maps

(**2**) *[1822]*
[Plan showing the relative situation ... correct and established]
Col ms 86 x 99 cm 1" to 80 chains Watermark: 'J WHATMAN 1818' Endorsements: '1029'
A draft for the more finished plan above, with scale not marked and not sgd and dated; in addition to the shorter title, plan lacks some of the detail of above map.
OTAR (SR 5496)

(**3**) *[1822?]*
[Endorsed title]: 'Projection Lancaster Lochiel & Hawkesbury [illegible] Line run by Joseph Bouchette Surveyor General of Lower Canada
Col ms 178 x 98 cm Scale not given Endorsements: 'No 2c'
Shows various lines according to Joseph Fortune's survey for 18th con, Lancaster and Hawkesbury, Caledonia, seigneury of Pointe à l'Original and 'Mr. Bouchette's boundary' between Rigaud and Newton; several cons and lot lines are shown in three or four different locations; some names of owners; note 'See Fair plan & report' refers to first map above.
OTAR (SR 8919)

(**4**) *[1822?]*
[Sketch showing conflicting boundary lines] Upper & Lower Canada
Col ms 81 x 62 cm [Approx 1" to 1 mile]
Shows names of owners of lots in Lancaster Twp and conflicting boundary lines crossing their property; crown and clergy reserves and a few improvements noted; unfinished but probably dates from the period of the above surveys; there is also a plan (OOAMA (NMC 25345)) prepared from Bouchette's survey by David Thompson and William Macdonald to accompany a petition regarding encroachment of Lower Canada on Upper Canada (OOA RG 1 L3 D13 no 41 1822).
OOAMA (NMC 25345) OTAR (SR 5494)

---

481 *[1823?]*
'PART OF THE RIVER ST. LAWRENCE'
Print (engrav) 8 x 18 cm Scale not given
Title from phrase on map; enclosed in a letter from Planta to Horton of 26 Jan 1824 about problem of British access to navigation channels after boundary changes and further enclosed in Barclay to Canning 24 Feb 1824 (GBLpro CO 42/201 p 44); the points marked on the map are keyed in the letter; islands named; oriented to the south; (Holmden 2557, 2560) (see also **D18**).
OOAMA

---

482 *[1823]*
A Sketch showing the Connection between the Head Waters of the Mississippi flowing into the Ottawa and those of the Moira & Salmon Rivers emptying into the Bay of Quinte ascertained by John Smith Junr on an exploratory survey undertaken by

directions of Charles Hayes Esqre [and endorsed title]: 'Communication from the Marmora Iron Works on the Rr Trent, to Lanark, on the Rr Mississippy'
Ms 50 x 74 cm 1" to 4 miles Endorsements: 'Z10' '967'
A letter from John Smith to Charles Hayes of 8 July 1823 encloses a detailed report of his journey from Marmora to Lanark and return (OTAR RG 1 A-6 vol 7); shows rapids, falls, and notes along the north and south branches of the Mississippi R, the Salmon R, and east and west branches of the Moira R; shows proposed line of road going into Marmora Iron Works from Trent R, possibly added later.
OTAR (SR 7074)

---

483 *[1824]*
Map of the proposed Canal for uniting Lake Ontario with the River Ottawa by way of the Rivers Cataracquay, Gananoque and Rideau surveyed in the years 1823 and 1824 by Mr Samuel Clowes Civil Engineer, and compiled from the minutes of actual survey by Mr Reuben Sherwood Land Surveyor under the direction of the Commissioners of Internal Navigation
Col ms 63 x 140 cm 1" to 2 miles
[Profile] 1" to 8 miles; probably accompanied Clowes report of 1825 in OOA RG 5 A1 vol 70 D37269–37326; the proposed entrance into the Ottawa R is below Rideau Falls and the route above Chaffey's Mills goes by Indian and Loon lakes; 45 points for works are marked along the route; swampy areas are shown; the report was also printed in *Third General Report ... Commissioners of Internal Navigation 5 Feb 1825* (*Bib Can* 1380); (Holmden 2421).
OOAMA (NMC 11962)

---

484 *[1824]*
THE / Perth, Lanark & Richmond / SETTLEMENTS / - DISTRICT OF BATHURST UPPER CANADA: / with part of / THE ADJACENT COUNTRY./ / A. Bell delint / / Engd by C. Thomson Edinr
Print (engrav) 20 x 22 cm 1" to 8 miles
In William Bell, *Hints to Emigrants* (Edinburgh: Printed for Waugh and Innes 1824), frontis (*Bib Can* 1274); shows the area from Kingston to Matilda twps and from Lavant to Torbolton twps; the towns of Perth, Lanark, and Richmond are shown with roads connecting them to each other, to villages to the south, and to the Ottawa R; (*OHIM* 4.16); also another map in the same work opp p 73: 'Township of DRUMMOND Ten miles square, / / A. Bell Delint / / C. Thomson Sc. Edinr' (15 x 16 cm), 'This sketch shows how a township is divided into Concessions & lots.'
OTMCL

---

485 *1825*
A MAP / OF PART OF THE / PROVINCE / OF / UPPER CANADA / Shewing the proposed route for a Canal / to unite the waters of Lake Ontario / WITH THE OTTAWA RIVER / from actual survey / by order of the Commissioners of Internal Navigation / appointed by / His Excellency Sir Peregrine Maitland K.C.B. LIEUTENANT GOVERNOR &c. &c. &c. / Under authority of an act of the Provincial Parliament / COMPILED BY / James Grant Chewett / Draftsman. / 1825 / Engraved and Printed by Saml. Maverick N. York.
Print (engrav) 83 x 119 cm 1" to 4.25 miles
Inset: [profile of route from L Ontario to the Ottawa R]; this may be a proof state as it lacks any names along the Rideau Canal route, names in other areas, and the fine line work along the shoreline; shows roads, proposed roads, and other canals along the St Lawrence R; only the west part of this version seems to have survived.
OOAMA (NMC 36608)

Other editions and states

(2) *1828*
[Title statement the same]
Additions: inset: 'PLAN of BY-TOWN / and of the / OUTLET OF THE RIDEAU CANAL / Now in Progress under the Direction / OF THE ROYAL ENGINEERS / 1828'; [profile of St Lawrence R from Johnstown to Cornwall with note]: 'Scale of Elevation & Distance [1" to 5 miles], the same with the above Section taken from Mr. Clowes Report. York Augt 12th 1828. J.G.C.'; the inset shows the canal entering the Ottawa R above Rideau Falls in Canal Bay with note: 'now constructing by the Royal Engineers'; the route of the whole canal is the same as that on Clowes's map but 52 points are marked for works instead of 45; a note indicates that information north of Frontenac Co is from J. Smith's survey [1823] (**482**); (Holmden 2776).
OOAMA (NMC 38518) OTAR OTUTF

(3) *[1828?]*
[Title statement the same]
Additions: Col By's and Lt Pooley's houses have been added to the inset, a road is shown west of the bridge at the canal, and a few place-names have been added to the main map; land was surveyed for Pooley in March 1828 (see **1730**).
OOAMA (NMC 11233) OTMCL

---

486 *1825 (1827)*
Sketch of the Water Communication between Kingston and the Ottawa River Canada Referred to in Sir J.C. Smyth's Report dated 1825. Copied by S.B. Howlett Inspector General's Office 21st May 1827
Col ms approx 39 x 52 cm Scale not given
With the 'Report of the Joint Committee Appointed to Confer upon the Improvement of

the Internal Navigation April 6th 1825' (GBLpro CO 42/375 p 218); a small location sketch showing the Rideau R and connecting lakes that became part of the canal route; covers the area from Kingston to Cornwall and north to the Ottawa R; Smyth made two reports to the Master General and Board of Ordnance on 9 Sept 1825 (GBLpro WO 55/1551) and on 14 March 1826 (GBLpro WO 44/18) on estimates of the cost of the canal and accepting Samuel Clowes's route (Passfield, *Engineering the Defence of the Canadas*).
GBLpro (CO 42/375 p 218)

---

487 *1826*
Plan of the Proposed Canal from Kingston on Lake Ontario to the Ottawa River By order of the Commissioners appointed by His Excellency Sir Peregrine Maitland K.C.B. Lieut. Governor &c. &c. under Authority of an Act of the Provincial Parliament. Copy by (Signed) James G. Chewett. York Nov 4th 1826. Copy P. Durnford 2[?] March 1827 [Sgd] E.W. Durnford Col. Comg Rl Engr Canada 17 Augt 1827
Col ms 72 x 129 cm 1" to 2 miles Endorsements: 'AA1'; stamps 'IGF' 'B↑O'
[Profile]: 1" to 8 miles; note: 'This Plan shows the line of Canal as proposed by Mr Clowes'; 52 points for works are marked; the plan has less detail than the printed plan (**485(2)**) and the profile is at a smaller scale; locates route and lock nos; mills, falls, rapids; (Holmden 2422).
OOAMA (NMC 11306)

Related maps

(**2**) *1826 (1827)*
Plan of the Proposed Canal ... Copy by (Signed) James G. Chewit York Novr 4th 1826. Copy P. Durnford 18th Mar. 1827
Col ms 77 x 131 cm 1" to 2 miles Watermark: 'JAMES WHATMAN TURKEY MILL KENT 1823' Endorsements: 'Rideau Canal by Clowes Report'
Provenance: OOAMA Collection of the 9th Earl of Dalhousie; the same as plan above.
OOAMA (NMC 103921)

---

488 *[1826–7]*
Sketch of the Route of the Rideau Canal from grand entrance Bay to the foot of the Black Rapids
Col ms 66 x 100 cm 1" to 22 chains Endorsements: 'No. 3'; stamp 'REO'
Seven sections 1" to 180 ft or 1" to 340 ft; possibly by John McTaggart as it shows his survey completed in Dec 1826 for the straight route of the canal from the first eight locks to the 'Notch of the Mountain' (Passfield, 'Wilderness Survey'); layout for upper and lower Bytown shown; relief; two proposed dams; also shows 'line of proposed Canal from the Chaudiere Lake to the point of Junction with the Rideau Canal in Dows Great Swamp'; proposed bridges across the Chaudière Falls.
OOAMA (NMC 21762)

Related maps

(**2**) *[1826–7]*
Sketch of the route of the Rideau Canal From Canal bay in the Ottawa to the foot of the Black rapids H. Pooley
Col ms 54 x 105 cm 1" to 22 chains Watermark: 'J WHATMAN TURKEY MILL 1823'
Provenance: OOAMA Collection of the 9th Earl of Dalhousie (85601/26); similar to plan above and including seven sections; shows 'Lt Col By's first method' [for the Rideau Canal] and shows more detail and possibly later plans for canal with locks around Hogs Bank and from 'Gloster Shore' to 'Col By's dam'; locks and dams; shows the same plan for Lower Town labelling it 'Site of a new Village' and Upper Town marked as 'Village Site' as in plan above; shows proposed bridges; 'line of proposed canal from the Chaudiere Lake'; the map probably dates from late 1826 or early 1827 (Taylor, 14; Haig, 59–74).
OOAMA (NMC 97797)

---

489 *[ca 1827]*
[Endorsed titles]: 'Bathurst Johnstown & Midland Distt' [and] 'Eastern District Chewett'
2 col mss 91 x 63 cm and 65 x 97 cm 1" to 4 miles and approx 1" to 1.5 miles
Two unfinished compilation plans possibly drafted by James Chewett when preparing his printed plan of 1825–8 (**485**); the first map is at the same scale as the printed plan and twps are shown to area north of Palmerston to Huntley, but not named; mills are located in several twps; roads are shown in the south part; Rideau Canal is marked in the south only; the map extends from Bay of Quinte to the Rideau R and Prescott and matches the edge of information on the second plan, but latter is at a larger scale; the eastern plan shows the area east of the Rideau R and Bytown, and from Matilda Twp to the east; all twp grids shown and named; since the Ottawa District (1816) is not named and the Rideau Canal is not shown, part of this plan may be earlier.
OTAR

---

490 *[1827?]*
[Plan of Cataraqui Creek] Copy from the Diagram received from York John Burrows Overseer of Works
Col ms 28 x 58 cm 1" to 40 chains Endorsements: '330'
Shows section 23 of the canal; names of owners; (Holmden 1759).
OOAMA (NMC 11895)

---

491 *[1827 Aug?]*
Plan of the Cataraqui Creek from Brewers Lower Mill to Kingston Mills. Scaled and Laid down by Order and under the Command of Lt Coln By Commanding Royal Engineer Rideau Canal. [Sgd] John Burrows O Works & Kings Surveyor

Col ms in 4 sections 70 x 460 cm 1" to 200 ft
Endorsements: 'K13' '168'; stamps 'REO'
Shows the proposed dam at Kingston Mills, points where excavation is to be commenced and where 'Mr. Clows has commenced excavation' and where marshy areas will be flooded; shows the preliminary survey of the river completed by Aug 1827.
OOAMA (NMC 13203)

---

492 *[1827 Oct]*
[Plans accompanying reports of 25 Oct 1827, all sgd 'John By Lt Colonel Royl Engrs Comg Rideau Canal July 8th 1827' and 'E.W. Durnford Col Commg Rl Engineers Canada 17 Augt 1827' or '25th October 1827']
21 col mss Sizes and scales vary Endorsements: stamps 'IGF' 'B↑O'
Varying dates from above are noted in listing below.

(**1**) [General] General Plan of the Rideau Canal from Kingston Bay to the Ottawa.
74 x 234 cm [1" to 1 mile] Endorsements: 'AA 18'
Forty-seven dams, locks, or works marked; proposed cut between Mud L and Rideau L shown; three stations for sappers shown.
OOAMA (NMC 16826)

(**2**) [Section 1] Sketch shewing the proposed line of the Rideau Canal from the River Ottawa to the Head of Long Island with the position of various works required to complete the navigation for 44 miles carrying the level of the Canal 144 feet above the level of the Ottawa [Sgd] Wm. Smith Lt Royal Artillery Asst Engineer ... John By ... 7th July 1827, E.W. Durnford Comg Rl Engrs Canada 17th Aug. 1827.
127 x 71 cm 1" to .375 miles Endorsements: 'AA17'
'Section showing the natural state of the ground between the Beaver Meadow and the Notch of the Mountain' 1" to 100 ft; old and 'new town partly built'; shows 'proposed line of Canal to connect Lake Chat with the Rideau,' the revised route of canal following the natural gully, and the notch in the mountain by Dow's Swamp.
OOAMA (NMC 16813)

(**3**) [Section 1] Plan Elevation and Sections of the Works in Canal Valley and Entrance Bay Ottawa River as proposed by Lt Coln By Commanding Royal Engineer A No 1 ... [Sgd as in AA17]
64 x 181 cm 1" to 35 ft Endorsements: 'AA12'
Consists of: 'Ground Plan of the Locks in Canal Valley,' 'Longitudinal Section of the first 8 Locks in Canal Valley with the elevation of the East side of the Valley and Bay,' 'Longitudinal Section of Canal Valley,' Section of Basin.'
OOAMA (NMC 17261)

The other 18 plans are briefly listed as follows: [Section 1]: 'Sections ... Entrance Bay ... Hogsback ... AA16' (NMC 21885); '... Mound ... Dow's Great Swamp ... AA15' (NMC 21884); 'Hogs Back ... AA14' (NMC 21883); '... Long Island ... Black Rapids ... AA13' (NMC 21882); [Section 2]: 'Oxford Snie ... Hurds Shallows ... 25th October 1827 ... AA19' (NMC 21875); [Sections 3, 4]: 'Nicholson's ... Clow's Quarry ... AA30' (NMC 21890); [Section 5]: 'Merricks Mills ... AA29' (NMC 21889); [Section 6]: 'Maitland's Rapids ... AA22' (NMC 21878); [Sections 7, 8, 9]: 'Old Slys ... Phillip's Bay ... Edmond's ... AA24' (NMC 21880); [Section 10]: 'Smith's Falls ... AA27' (NMC 21887); [Section 11]: 'First Rapids ... AA26' (NMC 21886); [Section 13]: 'Narrows ... AA28' (NMC 21888); [Section 15]: 'Chaffee's Mills ... AA23' (NMC 21879); [Section 16]: 'Davis's Mills ... AA31' (NMC 21891); [Section 17]: 'Jones's Falls ... AA32' (NMC 21892); [Section 18]: 'Round Tail ... AA 25' (NMC 21881); [Sections 20–2]: 'Jack's Rifts ... Bellidors Rifts ... Brewer's Lower Mills ... AA 20' (NMC 21876); [Section 23]: 'Kingston Mills ... AA 21' (NMC 21877); (Holmden 2435–53).
OOAMA (NMC 16813; 16826; 17261; 21875–92)

---

493 *1827 Nov 20*
Plan and Section of the First Eight Locks of the Rideau Canal Canal Bay and Valley Ottawa River Lt Coln J. By Commanding Royal Engineers [Sgd] John By Lt Colonel Royl Engrs Comg Rideau Canal Upper Canada 20th November 1827
Col ms 242 x 69 cm Scale not given
Similar to map of 7 July (AA12) (**492(3)**) except this extends north to Ottawa R and beyond road that crosses canal, Col By's house and one other drawn more prominently, barracks bldg west of canal entrance, and a slightly different configuration around some locks and stone-filled areas; there is also a series of 'Plans and Sections the Large Lock ... [Sgd] John By ... 1st December 1827' in OOAMA (NMC 14701, 21871–4).
OOAMA (NMC 14701; 21871–4) OTRMC

---

494 *[1827–8]*
[Plan of the route of the Rideau Canal from Bytown to Hogsback]
Col ms 66 x 167 cm 1" to 600 ft
Attributed to Thomas Burrowes and the first accurate map of the route of the canal through Natural Gully and the planned route through Dow's Great Swamp from a survey in the winter of 1827–8 (Passfield, 'Wilderness Survey,' 84); bldgs and streets shown in Bytown.
OOAMA (NMC 17005)

---

495 *1827[30?]*
Outline Map showing the Water-Communications between Kingston & Montreal 1827. Compiled from various documents and corrected to this date. [Sgd] Saml. B. Howlett Chief Draftsman.
Col ms 75 x 145 cm 1" to 4 miles Endorsements: 'Lt Pooley from the Rideau Canal examined this map in 1828 and considered it correct. The memorandum were added in March 1830.'; stamps 'IGF' 'B↑O'
A note on the building of the Lachine Canal is sgd

'McTaggart 1829'; memoranda relating to the water communication between Montreal and Kingston include details on locks and dams on the Ottawa R, Lachine Canal, and Rideau Canal; Rideau Canal route is shown with dams and lock sites marked; (Holmden 1808).
OOAMA (NMC 11229)

---

496 *[1828?]*
The Ottawa River between the Long Sault and the Chaudiere Lake [Sgd] E Frome Lieut R. Engrs
Col ms 60 x 98 cm 1" to 2 miles Watermark: 'J WHATMAN TURKEY MILL KENT'
Endorsements: 'AA42'; stamps 'B↑O' 'IGF'
Shows the twps of Hawkesbury to Goulburne [*sic*], Chaudière L and twps on the Lower Canada side; details of shore, islands, bldgs, roads; shows Upper and Lower Bytown, road to Richmond and road up the Rideau R; upper part of Rideau Canal shown; later note 'about 1828'; (Holmden 2460).
OOAMA (NMC 23673)

---

497 *[1828]*
[Plan of part of the Rideau Canal from Cataraqui Bridge to Brewers Lower Mills]
Col ms in 3 sections 78 x 448 cm 1" to 330 ft
Relief, wooded, and swampy areas; triangulation lines along route of canal; possibly drawn by Thomas Burrowes; proposed second lock at Kingston Mills was planned in 1828 and shows lands to be flooded by proposed dam; (Passfield, 'Wilderness Survey' 91, 97).
OOAMA (NMC 17112)

---

498 *[1828]*
[Plan of part of the Rideau Canal from Round Tail to Bellidors Rifts]
Col ms in 2 sections 54 x 223 cm 1" to 330 ft
Endorsements: '182'; stamp 'REO'
An unfinished partial plan, possibly by Thomas Burrowes; relief, wooded areas; shows excavation underway in 1828 and a lock at Brewers Upper Mills proposed that year (Passfield, 'Wilderness Survey' 91, 97).
OOAMA (NMC 13201)

---

499 *1828 Jan 28*
Plan of the Cataraqui Creek from Brewers Lower Mill to Kingston Mill Scaled and Surveyed by Order of Lt Coln By Commanding Royal Engineers Rideau Canal Janry 28 1828 John Burrows A.O.W.
Col ms 64 x 97 cm 1" to 800 ft Endorsements: stamps 'IGF' 'B↑O
Relief, wooded, and swampy areas; (Holmden 2434).
OOAMA (NMC 21894)

---

500 *1828 Feb*
Map of a proposed new Road to lead from Prescott to the Rideau River, by John Booth Depy Prov Surveyr. Prescott 5 Feby 1828
Ms 62 x 49 cm 1" to 1 mile
Shows route through Augusta and Oxford twps to connect with the Rideau R; relief, swamps, survey grid.
OTMCL (E.W. Banting Collection)

---

501 *1828 May 5*
[Plans and estimates for the Rideau Canal each sgd] John By Lt Colonel Royl Engrs Comg Rideau Canal 5th May 1828
36 col ms and 2 accompanying sheets Most at 1" to 200 ft
Remarks and estimates noted on each plan; availability of limestone and sand; some plans signed 'H.I. Savage Capt. R.E.,' others unsigned; maps show proposed locks, dams, and land and rapids to be flooded; frequent references are made to Mr Clowes's more costly proposals to cut and excavate; six plans cover section 1 and there is one plan each for sections 2–23; general and special plans are as follows:

(1) 'Sketch of the Line of the Rideau Canal from By Town to Kingston. 3 sheets No 1 ... No 2 ... No 3 ...' 1" to 9 miles; with 'Section thro the Line of the Canal from Ottawa River to Ontario Lake' and 'Plan & Elevation of the Line of Bridges erected at the fall's over the Chaudiere Ottawa River [Sgd] H.I. Savage Capt R.E.' 1" to 200 ft; Estimate.

(2) 'Plan & Elevation of the line of Bridge's erected at the falls over the Chaudière Ottawa River [Sgd] H.I. Savage Capt R.E.' (1" to 300 ft) and estimate sgd 'John By ... 5th May 1828'; similar to other plans of the bridges (see also Ottawa **1725**).
GBEr (GD 45)

---

502 *1828 June 26*
Plan and Section by actual Survey of the Rideau River and part of the Ottawa River from Kettle Island to the Black Rapids Showing the Line of the Rideau Canal from Entrance Bay to the Black Rapids Lt Col By Commanding Royal Engineer [Sgd] John By Lt Colonel Royl Engrs Comg Rideau Canal 26th June 1828
Col ms 126 x 314 cm 1" to 400 ft Endorsements: 'AA2'; stamp 'B↑O'
Shows all the bldgs along Rideau St in Lower Bytown and Wellington St in Upper Bytown; bridges, roads, and bldgs at Chaudière Falls; route through Natural Gully and mound in 'Dows Great Swamp'; bldgs and names of occupants along route; shows the same route for canal as **494** but at a larger scale; reproduced in *Ottawa in Maps*, 3; there is also a 'Plan of the approved Locks ... 8th July 1828' 'AA9' in OOAMA (NMC 21893) (Holmden 2433); there are also three plans for dam and locks at Black Rapids 'AA5,' Long Is 'AA3,' and Old Sly's Rapids 'AA4,' all probably from 1828, in OOAMA (NMC 14272, 21895, 21870) (Holmden 2427–9).
OOAMA (NMC 14272; 17345; 21870; 21893; 21895)

---

503 *1828 June 28*
Map of the St. Lawrence between Kingston and Lake St Peter Shewing the back water communication proposed on the Rideau & Ottawa Rivers also the Frontier towards Lake Champlain on each side of the Richilieu to explain the Report of the committee appointed to assemble in Canada & formed according to the 12 Article of Instructions dated 27th March 1828 ... 23rd July 1828 [Sgd] Edwd G W. Fanshawe Lt Colonel Rl Engineers G.G.Lewis Lt Colonel Royal Engineers
Col ms and pt printed 92 x 212 cm 1" to 2 2/3 miles Endorsements: 'A11'; stamps 'IGF 'B↑O'

Notes on map: 'Compiled from Bouchettes Map of Lower Canada, the Canada Company Map of Upper Canada and filled in from Sketches and information by the Officers & Engineers employed in Canada. The St Lawrence from Lake Ontario to Lake St Francis is reduced from the Survey of the Commissioners to settle the boundary line,' 'This Map is not submitted as an Accurate Survey but as a Compilation from the best Sources ... and Information which the Committees could procure in the Country, to accompany their Report to the Master General of the Ordnance dated Quebec 23rd July 1828'; the printed part is from Bouchette's *Topographical Map of the Province of Lower Canada* (1815); the Upper Canada part is ms and shows area west to Kingston; main roads, places, inns, cleared land, locks on the Rideau Canal as built to date, table of distances; the committee was set up to verify By's estimates and approve the changes he recommended while also conducting a reconnaissance survey of the whole area (Passfield, *Engineering the Defence of the Canadas*); the main report by Sir James Kempt and Lt Cols Fanshawe and Lewis was submitted 28 June 1828 and is in GBLpro WO 44/19 p 361; (Holmden 2458).
OOAMA (NMC 17079)

Related maps

(**2**) *1828*
Outline of the Country from Kingston to Olivers ferry along the route of the Rideau Canal, and from Kingston to Brockville, with the roads leading upon the Canal from the St. Lawrence; Accompanying a report of a reconnaissance made in pursuance of the orders of the Commissioners of whom Lt Genl Sir James Kempt K.C.B. &c &c &c is President [Sgd] J.Walpole Lt Royal Engineers 22 June 1828
Col ms 114 x 94 cm 1" to 1/2 mile Endorsements: 'AA33'; stamps 'IGF' 'B↑O'

Roads are classed to distinguish those leading to canal communication and good roads; notes on the terrain and extent of settlement; route of canal; table of distances; (Holmden 1755).
OOAMA (NMC 11230)

(**3**) *[1828]*
Sketch of the country between the Rivers Petite Nation and Rideau. to his Excellency Lt Genl Sir James Kempt KCB &c &c &c [Sgd] W Denison Lt Rl Engrs [Endorsed date]: 'About June 1828'
Col ms 65 x 98 cm 3/8" to 1 mile Watermark: 'J WHATMAN TURKEY MILLS 1825' Endorsements: 'AA35'; stamps 'IGF 'B↑O'

Shows roads including those traversed by surveyor; similar to but showing area just east of first map above; rivers with rapids and falls, depths of streams, some settlements named including 'Dutch settlement' and 'McDonald's settlement,' mills, taverns; (Holmden 2423).
OOAMA (NMC 21360)

(**4**) *[1828?]*
Sketch of the South Nation River
Col ms 82 x 33 cm 1" to 2 miles and 4" to 1 mile Watermark: 'SMITH & ALL [NUTT] 1818' Endorsements: 'AA45'; stamps 'IGF' 'B↑O'

Oriented to the south; shows the river from its mouth at the Ottawa and inland a few miles; later pencil notes sgd 'S.B.H[owlett]' correct the scale and indicate that the first scale must be for the length of the river and the second for the breadth; mills and names of some settlers noted; Holmden assigns the plan to 'about 1828'; this river is included on (2) above; (Holmden 2463).
OOAMA (NMC 21805)

(**5**) *[1828]*
Sketch of the road between Cornwall and Hawkesbury Lt Coll Fanshawe Rl Engrs [Sgd] W Denison [Endorsed date]: 'About June 1828'
Col ms 47 x 50 cm 3/8" to 1 mile Endorsements: 'AA34'; stamps 'IGF' 'B↑O'

Shows road connections from Cornwall to Hawkesbury with various side roads, and roads along the St Lawrence including 'Dundas St.' fairly far inland, towns, mills, swampy land, names of some settlers; (Holmden 1587).
OOAMA (NMC 2848)

---

504 *1829 Feb 5*
Plan of the Line of the Rideau Canal Lt. Coln. By Commanding Royal Engineers John Burrows Overseer of Works. [Sgd] John By Lt Colonel Royl Engineers Comg Rideau Canal 5th February 1829
Col ms 61 x 95 cm 1" to 4 miles Endorsements: '19 L'

Originally accompanied Sir James Kempt's letter of 1 Apr 1829 (GBLpro CO 42/223); [section between L Ontario and Ottawa R] 1" to 8 miles horizontal, 1" to 60 ft vertical; points for works marked; roads, settlements, mills; table showing dimensions of locks and dams, estimates of costs, size of excavations; 'Contingencies and Difference of Estimate caused by Enlarging the Locks'; civil and military establishments; photoreproduction in OOAMA (NMC 51959); (*PRO Cat* 1554).
GBLpro (MPG 51)

---

505 *1829 March 7*
Maps No 1 to No 4. Shewing the Lands adjacent to the route of the Rideau Canal By W Chewett York January 29th 1829 [Ea sheet sgd] Surveyor Generals Office York 7th March 1829 W Chewett Actg Surveyr Genl

4 col ms Ea 74 x 130 cm or smaller 1" to 40 chains
Endorsements: '835' '838' '843' '845'

Portions taken for canal, clergy and crown land reserved for canal, lands purchased or settled for by arbitration, parts taken by Col By for canal or military; location of Ordnance boundary stones; later additions include references from later plan sgd 'D Bolton ... 29th Augt 1842'; there is also a transcript in OOAMA (NMC 16824) of plan 4 from a set dated 19 Aug 1828, 11 Aug 1829 and originally sgd by John By 28 Jan 1830, but no other parts or originals have been found.
OTNR (SR 2680–2; 86887)

---

506 *1829 May*
[Pittsburg township] Rough Copy from the Office Plan. Surveyor General's Office (Signed) W. Chewett Actg Surveyor Genl dated Surveyor Generals Office 30th May 1829
Ms 41 x 27 cm 1" to 40 chains

Originally from GBLpro WO 44/29 pp 682–3; shows Ft Henry and names of owners in lots of the third con next to the military reserve; 'N.B. The shore of the military reserve ... must be scaled and the number of Acres reported therein'; there is also a copy further sgd 'Royal Engineers Office Kingston U. Canada 30th Novr 1829 R.H. Bonnycastle Capt R1 Engrs' (39 x 25 cm); (*PRO Cat* 1443–4).
GBLpro (MPHH 47 (13–14))

---

507 *1829 June 18*
[Plans and sections showing the construction and reconstruction at Hogsback between Oct 1826 and 18 June 1829] [Each sgd] John By Lt Colonel Royl Engrs Comg Rideau Canal 18th June 1829
11 col mss Ea 1" to 50 ft

The nine maps show the original site, the dam as first built, as partly destroyed three times by flooding, and as rebuilt each time; reproduced in *OHIM* 6.24; there is also a partial set of these maps in OOAMA (NMC 12892 (18–26)) all sgd 'John By Lieut Colonel Royl Engrs Comg Rideau Canal 18 March 1830' with variations in nos 4, 5, 8, and lacking 6 and 9; there also appear to be copies of these originally filed with abstracts of expenditure to 1831 in GBLpro WO44/26 ff 253–62.
GBLpro (MPH 1083 (5–16)) OOAMA (NMC 12892 (18–26); 26715–23)

---

508 *1829 June 24*
Diagram of parts of the Townships of Nepean & Gloucester showing the Rideau Canal from the Ottawa to the Hogs Back Lt Col By Comg R1 Engrs [Sgd] John By Lt Colonel Royl Engrs Comg Rideau Canal 24th June 1829
Col ms 54 x 43 cm Scale not given

Provenance: Board of Ordnance; shows streets, lots and owners, marshy areas, leases, timber channels, and the canal from first eight locks to Section 1; (Holmden 2216, 2517).
OOAMA (NMC 3203)

---

509 *1829 Aug 11*
Works at Long Island Part of 1st Section Lt Coln By Comg R1 Engineer Rideau Canal. Certified that the portions of Land described on this Plan are requisite for the service of the Rideau Canal. [Sgd] E.W. Durnford Colonel Commandg R1 Engineer Canada 11th Augt 1829. No 5
Col ms 54 x 67 cm Scale not given Endorsements: 'No 109'; stamps 'REO'

Shows two areas of land required and names of owners.
OOAMA (NMC 21896)

---

510 *1829 Sept 9 (1830)*
Plan of the Line of the Rideau Canal Lt Coll By Commanding Royal Engineers. Copied 3 [Apr?] 1830 [Sgd] John By Lt Col R.E.Comg Rideau Canal 9 Septr 1829
Col ms 41 x 82 cm 1" to 4 miles

Section numbers for canal shown, roads, section from Kingston to Bytown; 'Table of Computed distances on the line of the Rideau Canal'.
GBLrg

---

511 *1830 March 18*
[Plans and estimates on the state of the works on the Rideau Canal] [Sgd] John By Lt Colonel Royl Engrs Comg Rideau Canal March 18th 1830 [or] Jan 11th 1830
51 col mss Sizes vary Ea at 1" to 330 ft [exceptions noted]

Plans show relief, works completed and proposed, boundaries of land required for canal purposes, and notes on some sheets; the plans for the Black Rapids part of Section 1 to Section 11 are sgd by By 'Jan 11th 1830'; some plans also sgd with 1829 dates and some are unsigned and undated; each plan accompanied by 'Report on the State of works; ... showing the probable sums and time required ... as also the reasons for Excess of Estimate'; the plans are as follows: [Section 1]: 'First Eight Locks ...' and 'Sections No 9 ... 24 Oct 1829 ...' 4 sheets (NMC 12892/8–11); '... proposed excavations for a curve ... No 11' (NMC 12892/12); 'Sections ... First Eight Locks to the Hogs Back ...' 'No 13' 'No 14' 2 sheets (NMC 21974, NMC 12892/14, 15); '... Hartwells ... No 15' (NMC 12892/16); '... Hogs Back ... [and sections]' 'No 27' 'No 28' 2 sheets (NMC 12892/27, 28); '... Hogs Back ...' 'No 3' 'No 4' 'No 29' 2 sheets (NMC 12892/29); ... 'Black Rapids ... Decr. 20th 1829 ... No 31' (NMC 12892/31); '... Long Island ... 10 Dec. 1829 ... No 33' (NMC 12892/33); [Section 2]: 'Burrits Rapids Novr 7th 1829 ... No 35' (NMC 12892/35); [Sections 3, 4]: 'Clows quarry and Nicholson's Rapids ... Octr. 22 1829 ... No 37' (NMC 12892/37); [Section 5]: 'Merricks Mills ... 17 Oct. 1829 ... No 40' (NMC 12892/40); [Section 6]: 'Maitlands Rapids ... Oct. 18 1829 ... No 42' (NMC 12892/42); [Section 7]: 'Edmonds Rapids ... No 44' (NMC 12892/44); [Section 9]: 'Old Slys Rapids ... No 46' (NMC 12892/46); [Section 10]: 'Smiths Falls

... No 48' (NMC 12892/48); [Section 11]: 'First Rapids ... No 50' (NMC 12892/50); [Section 13]: 'Upper Narrows ... No 52' (NMC 12892/52); [Section 14] 'Isthmus ...' 'No 54' and 'Sections ...' 'No 59' 2 sheets (NMC 12892/54–5); [Section 15]: 'Chaffey's Mills ... No 57' (NMC 12892/57); '... Chaffey's Mills ... No 58' (NMC 12892/58); [Section 16]: 'Davis' Mills ... No 60' (NMC 12892/60); [Section 17]: 'Jones Falls [Sgd] John Burrows ...' 'Nos 62–66' 6 sheets (NMC 12892/62–7); [Sections 19–23]: 'Brewers Upper Mill ... Round Tail To Kingston Mills Cataraqui Creek [nos 1–10]' 'Nos 68–70, 73–74' (NMC 12892/68–73, 75–6, 78–9).
OOAMA (NMC 12892/8–12, 14–16, 27–29, 31, 33, 35, 37, 40, 42, 44, 46, 48, 50, 52, 54–5, 57–8, 60, 62–7, 68–73, 75–6, 78–9; 21974).

---

512 *1830 June 12*
Section of the Rideau Canal Shewing the Estimated expence of the whole work, the am't Expended to the 1st of June 1830. The Lands Purchased, the Crown & Clergy Reserves Required &c. Lt Coln By Comg Rl Engineer [Sgd] John By Lt Colonel Royl Engrs Comg Rideau Canal 12th June 1830.
Col ms 69 x 129 cm Not to scale Endorsements: stamps 'IGF' 'B↑O'
Vertical scale of section 1" to 100 ft; section shows heights and steps required; also plans with same title except date 1 July 1830 and sgd 8 July 1830, stamp 'B↑O' (Holmden 2468–9) in OOAMA (NMC 16816); and plan 1 July 1830 but sgd 12 July 1830, stamp 'J27' in OTNR (SR 2684); also a copy in OOAMA (NMC 11305) sgd 'Surveyor General's office, Montreal 23 July 1844 ... Thomas Parke Surveyr Genl'; (Holmden 2493).
OOAMA (NMC 11305; 16815–6) OTNR (SR 2684))

---

513 *1830 July 8*
Plan of the Line of the Rideau Canal shewing the Situation of the Fall Lt. Col. B[y] Commg Royal Engineers [Sgd] John By Lt. Colonel Royl Engrs Comg Rideau Canal 8th July 1830
Ms 43 x 53 cm 1" to 5.3 miles [Endorsed title]: 'Plan & Sections Rideau Canal'
Note on map: 'Canada – Ordered by the House of Commons to be Printed February 1831' (see (2) below and removed from GBLpro PRO 30/35 p 13); line of canal heights; sections numbered; relief, roads, settlements; photoreproduction in OOAMA (NMC 3205); (*PRO Cat* 1555).
GBLpro (MPI 157)

Related maps

(2) *1831*
PLAN / OF THE / LINE OF THE RIDEAU CANAL / Shewing / THE SECTION OF EACH WORK. / Lt Coln By Comg Royal Engineers. // John Burrows / Overseer of Works / [Sgd in facsimile] John By / Lt Colonel Royl Engrs / Comg Rideau Canal / 8th July 1830. // Ordered by the House of Commons to be Printed, February 1831. / James and Luke G. Hansard & Sons, Printers. / A. Arrowsmith lithog // WATER COMMUNICATION IN CANADA. 5
Print (lith) 32 x 68 cm Approx 1" to 5 1/2 miles
In *Canada Canal Communication. Return to an Address ... for Copies of the Correspondence between the Treasury, the Secretary of State for the Colonies and the Ordnance of the Canal Communication in Canada ... Ordered ... to Be Printed, 10 February 1831* ([London 1831]), Plan 5 (*Bib Can* 1646); probably prepared from the ms map above; sections in the same work: '4. Hog's Back LONGITUDINAL SECTION ... TRANSVERSE SECTION Shewing the Dam after it had given – way. ... J. Basire lith.' and '6. SECTION OF THE LINE OF THE RIDEAU CANAL. ...' 1" to 160 ft vertical; OOAMA copy has imprint partly trimmed; (Holmden 3992, 2480; *OHIM* 6.25).
GBLpro OOAMA (NMC 3204; 3213; 109434) OTMCL USDLC

---

514 *[1831]*
Rough Sketch of the Rideau Canal from the Ottawa River to Lake Ontario by Captain J.E. Alexander H.R. late 16t.h M.R.G.S. M.R.A.S.re
Col ms 63 x 81 cm Scale not given Endorsements: 'For the Royal Geographical Society' 'A278'
Shows the extent of the canal, locks, roads, and towns; in his book *Transatlantic Sketches* (London: R. Bentley 1833) (*Bib Can* 1623) the author describes his trip from Kingston to Bytown in 1831.
GBLrg (S/S75)

---

515 *1831*
To / His most Excellent Majesty, / KING WILLIAM IV, / this / Topographical Map / of the / DISTRICT OF MONTREAL, / Lower Canada, / Exhibiting THE New Civil Division / of the District into Counties pursuant to a recent Act of the Provincial Legislature: also a large section of Upper Canada / Traversed by THE Rideau Canal, / IS / WITH HIS MAJESTY'S / Gracious and Special Permission / most humbly & gratefully dedicated by / His Majesty's most devoted & Loyal Canadian Subject, / Joseph Bouchette, / His Majesty's Surveyor General of the Province and Lieutt Colonel C.M. / ENGRAVED BY J & C. WALKER 47 BERNARD STREET RUSSEL SQUARE / Published by James Wyld, Geographer to the King, Charing Cross, London, May 2nd 1831.
Print (engrav) 96 x 226 cm Approx 1" to 2.66 miles
Inset: 'CONTINUATION / of the / RIDEAU CANAL / from / Rideau Lake at / A to KINGSTON.' [and sections] 'Scale of Elevation & Distance, the same with the above Section taken from Mr Clowes Report York Augt 14th 1828. J.G.C.' 1" to 2 miles vertical; shows Upper Canada as far west as Carleton and Lanark cos; roads, relief, cleared areas indicated by field pattern; mills, churches, and schools located; asterisks indicate twps in which the Canada Co. has land; the elevation inset at a reduced scale and most of

the rest of west part of map are from Chewett's map of 1825 (1828 state) (**485(2)**) except that the final route of the Rideau Canal with locks and dams has been added; (*PRO Cat* 1728); there is also a copy of the map in GBLpro (*PRO Cat* 1719) that could be a proof copy since the relief is lacking, the inset is unfinished, and the title is lacking.
GBLpro (CO 700 Canada 87; FO 925/1244)
OOAMA (NMC 16835) OTAR OTMCL

---

516 *1831 Jan 8*
Plan of the Line of the Rideau Canal Lt. Col. By Comg Rl Engineers [and] Section of the Line of the Rideau Canal [Sgd] John By Lt Colonel Royl Engrs Commg Rideau Canal 8th January 1831 John Burrows Fecit
Col ms 64 x 98 cm Scale not given Endorsements: 'No 14 This belongs to the Military Secretary's Office [Sgd] J Glegg'
Shows the route of the canal with sections numbered; section shows heights and levels; roads, settlements; table on amount spent and estimated for completion and abstract of the estimate and further notes about estimates sgd by By; also a close copy in OTAR.
OOAMA (NMC 23351) OTAR

---

517 *1831 Jan 22*
Plan Shewing the Waters through which the Route of the Rideau Canal are to pass. Lt. Coln By Comg Rl Engineer [Sgd] John By Lt Col Royl Engrs Comg Rideau Canal 22nd January 1831; Section of the Rideau Canal Lt Col By Comg Rl Engineer [Sgd] John By Lt Col. Royl Engrs Comg Rideau Canal
3 col mss Ea 53 x 72 cm or smaller 1" to 1 mile Endorsements: stamp on section 'B↑O'
Two sheets from Bytown to First Rapids, Section 11, are in OOAMA; a sheet covering Kingston to Section 18 is in OKQ; a middle sheet is missing; each sheet has title and note 'The Waters (Generally) are Copied from the Surveyor Generals Plan and may be considered correct only where intersected by concession lines'; shows sections numbered, lands required for the canal, relief, canal works; parts that may include 'B↑O' stamp cut out of two of the sheets.
OKQ OOAMA (NMC 21980; 21982)

---

518 *1831 Jan 22*
[Plans of the state of the works on the Rideau Canal] [Sgd] John By Lt Coll Rl Engrs Commg Rideau Canal 22nd January 1831
Col mss Size varies Most at 1" to 330 ft [exceptions noted] Endorsements: stamps on some sheets 'B↑O'
Provenance: some sheets at OOAMA have a paste-on over a small square hole marked 'Certified genuine original map of the Rideau Canal'; OOAMA sheets at some point bound into an atlas entitled 'John By. Report on the State of Work on the Rideau Canal 1831'; other sheets at OTAR and OKQ also with small hole where B↑O stamp may have been; plans show locks, dams, etc, completed and proposed, lands required for the canal; all plans are sgd by By on 22 Jan 1831 and most plans are also sgd 'John Burrows O.W.'; Section 5 appears to be missing; the general plan is as follows: [General] 'A Map of Upper Canada Shewing the Route of the Rideau Canal Lt Coln John By Commanding Rl Engineer Rideau Canal. Drawn by John Burrows O.W.,' 2 sheets, scale not given; the general plan covers central and eastern parts of province and is based on the Canada Co. map (**69(2)**); it shows roads, twps, districts, cos; also a 'Section ... sheet signed by John By' but undated in OOAMA (NMC 21981).
OOAMA (NMC 26663, 26714, 21981)

Other plans are as follows: [Section 1]: 'First 8 Locks ...' (NMC 21976); '... Sections ... [and] Plan West side of the First Eight Locks ... 11 Nov. 1831' 'BB12' 'No 66' 'B↑O' (Holmden 2476, 2479) (NMC 11304, 17423); '... Sappers Bridge ...' 'B↑O' 'No 6' (NMC 21978); '... Natural Gulley ... No 14' '(2)' (NMC 21977); '... Dows Swamp ... (3)' (NMC 21986); '... Sections ... first eight Locks [to] the Hogs Back ...' '4' '(9)' (NMC 21974); '... Hogs Back ...' 'No 4' '(4)' 'B↑O' (NMC 21975); '... Black Rapids ... No 15' (NMC 21985); '... Long Island ... No 11' (NMC 21983); [Section 2]: 'Burrits Rapids ... No 9' (NMC 21951); [Sections 3, 4]: 'Nicholson's Rapids & Clows Quarry ... No 23' (NMC 19503); [Section 6]: 'Maitlands Rapids ... No 15' (NMC 19502); [Section 7]: 'Edmonds Rapids ... Map 2' (NMC Atlas (NMC 26664)); [Section 9]: 'Old Slys Rapids ... Map 3' (NMC Atlas (NMC 26665)); [Section 10]: 'Smiths Falls ...' (NMC 21979); [Section 11]: 'First Rapids ... Map 4' (NMC Atlas (NMC 19333)); [Section 13]: 'Narrows ...' (OTAR); [Section 14]: 'Isthmus ... Map 5' (NMC Atlas (NMC 26668)); [Section 15]: 'Chaffey's Mills ...' (NMC 21984); [Section 16]: 'Davis' Mills ...' (NMC Atlas (NMC 26667)); [Section 17] 'Jones' Falls ... Map 7' (NMC Atlas (NMC 26666), OTAR); [Sections 19–23]: 'No 1 Brewers Upper Mill and Round Tail' accompanied by 'Report ...' 1 sheet (OKQ); '... Brewers Upper to Brewers Lower Mills ... No 2 ... Map 8' (NMC Atlas (NMC 26669)); '... Brewers Lower Mill and the Cataraqui Creek ... No 3 ... Map 9' (NMC Atlas (NMC 21950)); '... Cataraqui Creek ... No 4–9 ... Map 10–Map 15' 6 sheets (NMC Atlas (NMC 26670–5)); [Sections 21, 22]: 'Kingston Mills ... No 4 ... Accompanied by Report ...' (OKQ).
OKQ OOAMA (NMC 11304; 17423; 19333; 19502–3; 21950–1; 21974–9; 21983–6; 26663–75; 26714) OTAR

---

519 *1831 March*
[Plans of the Rideau River and Lake, etc, surveyed in Feb 1830 and 1831 all sgd] J L Victor Captn R.E. 1831
Col mss Sizes vary 4" to 1 mile
The plans show the rivers and lakes on the Rideau Canal route with dams and locks where built; only the following plans have been found:

No 2 Plan of part of the Rideau Lake and River from Olivers Ferry to the first Rapids and of the River Tay from Perth ... 'REO No 17' OOAMA (NMC 21969)

No 5–6 Plan of the Rideau River from Olmsteads to ... Long Island OOAMA (NMC 21967–8)

[No 7?] [Plan of the Rideau River] from the head of Long Island to the Black Rapids and of the River Jacques from Richmond OOAMA (NMC 21970)

OOAMA (NMC 21970; 21967–8)

---

520 *1832*

Appendix No 11 OUTLINE MAP / shewing the / WATER COMMUNICATIONS / between / KINGSTON AND MONTREAL / 1832. / Compiled by Saml B. Howlett, Chief Draftsman,/ Inspector General's Office. // REPORT FROM COMMITTEE RESPECTING THE RIDEAU CANAL. // 570. Ordered by the House of Commons to be Printed, 29th June 1832. / James and Luke G. Hansard & Sons, Printers. S. Arrowsmith, lithog.

Print (lith) 29 x 58 cm Approx 1" to 7 3/4 miles

In *Report from the Select Committee ... Canal Communications in Canada. 1832* ... 570 ... 29th June 1832 (*HCPP* V 1831–2, 71) (OTU(mfe)); shows the line of the canal, rivers, lakes, and towns; sections numbered and named; also shows Ottawa R navigation works including Grenville and Lachine canals; facsimile in OOAMA (NMC 14592).

Original not seen

---

521 *1832*

Plan Exhibiting the Relative Situation of Towns Roads & Waters in the Bathurst and Johnstown Districts. York May 3rd 1832 [Sgd] J.W. McNaughton Dy Surveyor

Col ms 70 x 50 cm 1" to 5 miles Endorsements: '704'

Shows all the twps laid out, settlements, post offices, roads in Leeds, Grenville, Carleton, and Lanark cos, and twps numbered I, II, and III north of McNab and Horton along the Ottawa R in what is now Renfrew Co.

OTAR (SR 3488)

---

522 *1833*

A Map / OF THE / Townships / IN THE / DISTRICT OF BATHURST / IN THE / PROVINCE of UPPER CANADA / compiled from actual surveys and a personal knowledge of localities, and dedicated / with permission to / His Excellency Sir John Colborne K.C.B. / LIEUTENANT GOVERNOR / &c &c &c / BY / Francis Henry Cumming / late 104th Regt /1833

Print (lith) hand col 156 x 109 cm 1" to 1 1/2 miles

Inset: 'A PLAN of the TOWN of PERTH'; the map, lithographed by Samuel O. Tazewell, appears to be the largest one he printed; 'Reference' keys co boundary, road allowances, and con lines, 'cross roads authorized by the Court of General Quarter Sessions'; the latitude of Rideau R, Franktown, and Perth shown; various types of mill indicated; surveyed twps shown north to McNab but Horton, Ross, Westmeath, and Pembroke named but not laid out; the inset shows streets named and market square; a later notice of sale of map at £1 each is found in the *Bathurst Courier* 10 July 1835; (Holmden 1507).

OOAMA (NMC 16828)

---

523 *1835*

MAP / of the / DISTRICT OF PRINCE EDWARD, / Exhibiting an outline of the manner / in which it was originally laid out / into Townships, Concessions and lots, / BY / PUBLIUS V. ELMORE. / 1835. / Engraved by S. Stiles & Co. N. York.

Print (engrav) 62 x 79 cm 1" to 90 chains

'Reference' keys boundary lines of twps, con lines showing road allowances, allowances for roads between lots, public highways and mail roads, towns and villages; a note refers to a clash between first con of Sophiasburg and gore of Ameliasburgh; also shows relief, mills with names of owners, churches with denomination; (Holmden 2390).

OOAMA (NMC 21628) OTAR (SR 86915) OTMCL

Related maps

(2) *1850*

[Date in title changed to 1850 and 'N.York' deleted]

The same as 1835.

OTAR

(3) *1859*

MAP / of the / COUNTY OF PRINCE EDWARD ... ELMORE. / 1859. Printed by J. Ellis Toronto.

Print (lith) 62 x 80 cm Approx 1" to 90 chains

The map, though slightly larger, is a lithographic transfer from the original plate with changes in title and imprint but otherwise the same as 1850.

OTAR

---

524 *1835*

PLAN / of the / ST LAWRENCE CANAL / Passing the LONG SAUT / By Order of the / BOARD OF COMMISSIONERS / Appointed under the Act Chap. XVIII 3rd Year William IV for / The Improvement of the Navigation of the River Saint Lawrence / By J.B. Mills / Civil Engineer / Stodart & Currier's Lithy New-York // S. Keefer 1835.

Print (lith) 73 x 130 cm Scale not given

Mill's report on the proposed route is in 'Report of the Commissioners Appointed to Superintend the Improvement of the Navigation of the River St Lawrence 14 Jan 1835' (*JHA* (1835) App 7); inset: 'Cross-Section' 1" to 40 ft vertical, approx 1" to 1 mile; 'View of Mr Harvey's works on Section No 1 Long Saut Wm Roebuck del. Stoddard & Currier's Lith.'; shows the area of Long Sault, Sheeks,

Barnhart's, and Cornwall islands, the canal and roads; some names of owners on the Canadian side; locks numbered.
GBL OOAMA (NMC 15619; 29141)

525 *1836*
MAP / of the / MIDLAND & PRINCE EDWARD / DISTRICTS, / Exhibiting the manner in which they have been subdivided / into Counties, Townships, Concessions and Lots, / Compiled principally from actual Surveys, / BY PUBLIUS V. ELMORE. / Printed & Published at Hallowell, U.C. / 1836. / Engraved by S. Stiles & Co. N.Y.
Print (engrav) 78 x 103 cm 1" to 160 chains or 2 miles
The legend is the same as that for the Prince Edward District map of 1835 (**523**); the map shows mills with names of owners, churches with denominations, courthouses, steamboat landings; some of the churches and other cultural details on the earlier map have been left off and others added; the bridge to Big Is, which was not on the 1835 map, is shown; OTAR has two copies, one with ms adds showing the counties as of 1838 or later since Peterborough is included.
OOAMA (NMC 21614) OTAR OTAR (SR 81255) OTMCL

526 *[184?]*
[Sketch map of part of Augusta and Edwardsburgh townships showing roads, mills, and names of landowners]
Col ms 37 x 56 cm Scale not given
An untitled fragment possibly lacking a western part; shows Prescott, road from Johnstown to Spencer Mills, and the boundary of Johnstown District; names of owners are shown by their houses; many roads are shown.
OTAR

527 *[184?]*
[Townships in the Bathurst District]
Col ms 122 x 75 cm Scale not given
Shows twps from Burgess to Montague north to 'Pimbroke' [*sic*]; all twps named and laid out; some roads shown; possibly a compilation drawn after J. Richey's survey of the five twps of Bagot, Blithfield, Admaston, Bromley, and Stafford as per SI 24 Dec 1838.
OTAR (SR 5969)

Related maps

(2) *1842*
Plan of part of the Bathurst District shewing the Townships 1,2,3,4 and 5 which have been recently surveyed and reported to this Office. Copied from Mr Bouchette's By [Sgd] A LaRue Land Survr & Drftsn. Surveyor Generals Office Kingston 20th August 1842 [Sgd] Thomas Parke Survr Genl
Col ms 53 x 48 cm Scale not given Endorsements: '966'
Twps 1–5 (Bagot, Blithfield, Admaston, Bromley, and Stafford) are shown west of line McNab to Pembroke; lakes, rivers, and places are marked; shows a smaller area than plan above.
OTAR (SR 7544)

528 *1841–2*
Plan of the Country between the Rivers St Lawrence & Ottawa and the Rideau Canal Reconnoitred by Order of His Excellency the Commander of the Forces & under the direction of Coll Oldfield. K.H. Commd Royl Engr in Canada. 1841. [Sgd] by Hampdon C.B. Moody Lieutt Roy. Engineers
Col ms in 8 sheets 189 x 291 cm 1" to 1 mile
Endorsements: 'Received with the Commg Royal Engineers' letter No 41 dated 24th May 1842.'; stamp 'B↑O'
Inset: 'Index Map' [for the eight sheets]; covers the area from the junction of the Ottawa and St Lawrence rivers west to a semicircle connecting Kingston and Bytown; a major military reconnaissance map and the most detailed for the area to date. 'References' keys summer roads, winter roads, footpaths, locks of stone and wood, tunnels, stone and wooden bridges, churches, villages, blockhouses, windmills, water mills, rapids, proposed posts (temporary and permanent); note: 'The settlements were not sketched in the Field but from Recollection & are intended only to give a general idea of the settlement of the country'; cleared areas are shown by a yellow and forests by a blue-green tint; one of the source maps used for Oldfield's general map of 1843 (**136**); (*OHIM* 6.3; Holmden 2490).
OOAMA (NMC 17853)

529 *[1842]*
Plan of the Military and Post Road between the River St. Lawrence and the Ottawa To accompany Report [Sgd] James Cull. [Endorsed title]: 'Culls Map of Lancaster Road'
Col ms 58 x 39 cm Scale not given
Provenance: OOAMA RG 11M 81203/5 item 1; removed from OOA RG 11 vol 51; (SI (BW) 21 Oct 1841 for the completion of the road from L'Orignal to the St Lawrence); shows the route from Lancaster to Alexandria, Vankleeks Hill, Hawkesbury, L'Orignal, and Caledonia Springs; distances are shown via various routes; also shows Dundas St, connections to Greenfield and the Cornwall to Lancaster road; notes about the work done (first 11 miles).
OOAMA (NMC 18054)

Related maps

(2) *1842*
Map of the St. Lawrence and Ottawa Military Road, completed under the direction of the Board of Works of the Province of Canada: This Map Constructed from Actual Survey; By the Superintendant [Sgd] Jas West Deputy Surveyor and District Surveyor Eastern District, Cornwall 8th December 1842.

Col ms 131 x 66 cm 1" to 80 chains Endorsements: stamps 'BW' '410'
Shows the route and other roads, also villages, mills, post offices, and some bldgs; table of distances; (Holmden 2151).
OOAMA (NMC 11226)

---

530 *1843*
MAP / of / DALHOUSIE DISTRICT / Compiled from the most accurate Surveys / BY / Donald Kennedy, / District Surveyor. / BYTOWN, Febr. 3rd 1843. Willis & Probst, Lith. 2 Wall St N. York
Print (lith) hand col 85 x 59 cm 1" to 11/2 miles
Shows the area from Marlborough Twp east to Osgoode and Gloucester twps and northwest to Fitzroy Twp; survey grid; road allowances and roads; 'Statistical Table of the District' with figures by twp for 1842 and blank spaces for 1843–52; the towns have been added in ms.
OOAMA (NMC 18893)

Related maps

(2) *[184?]*
[Endorsed title]: 'Carleton County'
Col ms 61 x 92 cm [1" to 1.5 miles] Endorsements: stamps 'BW' '507'
An unfinished map that is very similar to the above; the same roads and some of the same physical features are shown; this may be the ms from which the printed map was made or it may be traced from the printed map; (Holmden 1593).
OOAMA (NMC 29471)

---

531 *1844*
Canada Outline Map Shewing the Water Communications between Kingston & Montreal ... With reference to Report to His Excellency the Commander of the Forces, from the Commanding Royal Engineer, & Captain Boxer C.B. Royal Navy dated 9th October 1844. [Sgd] W.C.E. Holloway Colonel Comg Rl Engrs, J.E. Alexander Captn 14th Regt & Assist Rl Engrs Copied by L.J. Hebert Quarter Master Generals Office Horse Guards Decr 1844
Col ms 37 x 57 cm 1" to 7.5 miles Endorsements: 'A'
Accompanies Sir A. Jackson's letter to Lord Fitzroy Somerset 28 Oct 1844 (GBLpro WO 1/541 p 112); shows the Rideau and St Lawrence canals with numbers keyed in the accompanying memorial of 23 Sept 1844 from merchants trading on the line of the Ottawa and Rideau rivers and canals about improvements to hazards, dredging, and locks that they desire; there is also a copy of a similar map originally enclosed in Holloway & Boxer's report to IGF of 9 Oct 1844 (GBLpro WO44/49 f 7); photoreproduction in OOAMA (NMC 5040).
GBLpro (WO 1/541 p 112; MPH 701(1))

---

532 *[1845?]*
[Map of part of the counties of Hastings, Lennox and Addington, Frontenac, Leeds and Lanark]
Col ms 84 x 69 cm Scale not given Endorsements: stamp [BW] '510'
Part of a map that probably extended further east; possibly related to Richard Birdsall's SI of 30 June 1845 to explore for a road line from the Kingston area to Allumettes on the Ottawa R or to James Lyons's SI of 11 Oct 1847 to decide on the routes recommended by Birdsall starting in Ernestown Twp; lakes and rivers are shown and twps named and sometimes laid out; shows the Rideau Canal; there is a dotted line for a road from McNab Twp to Allumettes; possibly a plan for the Bytown and Pembroke Rd; Tudor to Clarendon twps not laid out.
OOAMA (NMC 21902)

---

533 *1845*
[Map of the Mouth of the Gananoque River] Copy. Office of the Board of Works 1845
Col ms 47 x 68 cm 1" to 880 ft Endorsements: (stamps) 'BW' '551'
Shows area from Howe Is to Corn Is in the St Lawrence R and 'steamboat track (Cn McIntyre)' and soundings, shoals, and nature of shoreline.
OOAMA (NMC 4813)

---

534 *[1845?]*
A Map of the Proposed Route for a Plank Road [from Prescott to Kemptville and Milo Barton's]
Col ms 58 x 46 cm Approx 1" to 2 miles
Shows little information except 'present condition of road established'; old road, twp outlines, rivers, and towns shown.
OOAMA (NMC 2830)

Related maps

(2) *1846*
A Map of the Line for a plank road between Prescott and M. Barton's Surveyed by order of the Board of Works [Sgd] Francis Jones D.P.S. 14th March 1846
Col ms 89 x 58 cm Scale not given
Shows the route from Prescott through Oxford (on the Rideau) Twp, S Gower, and to lot 5, con V, in Osgoode at Milo Barton's where it joins a north road and a road that goes southeast.
OTAR

---

535 *1845*
A Map of the St Lawrence and Bytown Road Surveyed by order of the Board of Works. Septr 1845 Signed John S. Bruce D.P.S.
Col ms 40 x 122 cm 1" to 80 chains Endorsements: stamp [BW] '446'
Shows the whole road as it was surveyed via Osgoode and Winchester twps to intersect road to Prescott from Milo Barton's; (BW SI 31 July 1845); in addition there are two larger-scale plans covering the area of Carleton and Dundas cos with

the same titles and BW stamps (ea 127 x 51 cm or smaller, 1" to 40 chains); (Holmden 2157–9).
OOAMA (NMC 11222–4)

---

536 *[1845]*
[Map of the St Lawrence River from Johnstown to Cornwall showing the Canals]
Col ms 50 x 210 cm Approx 1" to 2.3 miles
Endorsements: 'No 10'
Originally enclosed with Report of Capt. Frederick Warden R.N. of 27 Jan 1846 (GBLpro Adm 7/625); shows Les Galopes, Point Iroquois, Rapide Plat, and Farren's Point canals and Cornwall Canal with six locks; rapids located; travelled road and places marked along shore; (*PRO Cat* 1576).
GBLpro (MR 1052(7))

---

537 *1846*
Bytown and Pembroke Road Sketch shewing proposed routes [and] ... Copy Board of Works 1846
2 col mss 34 x 77 cm or smaller Scale not given
Endorsements: stamps [BW] '444' and '97'
(BW SI 3 July 1846 to Thomas Keefer to survey and report on road from Bytown to Pembroke); shows the established road to Lake des Chats and several different routes proposed for area from there to Pembroke, in Lanark Co and north to the Bonnechere R; the two maps are the same; (Holmden 2141–2).
OOAMA (NMC 21378)

---

538 *[1846]*
Map of Bytown & L'Orignal Road by James West D.P.S. Original Map [Sgd] Thomas C. Keefer Engr Ott. Works
Col ms 45 x 222 cm Scale not given Endorsements: 'Appendix LL Thurs 8 July 1847'; stamp [BW] '447'
(BW SI 7 June 1845 to James West to survey regarding the improvement of road from L'Orignal to Bytown); this or plan below probably prepared to accompany (but not printed with) a report by Keefer on the road dated 8 July 1847 in *JLA* (1847) App LL; shows the present road with mileages and some bldgs and proposed new route; unfinished; (Holmden 2114).
OOAMA (NMC 14287)

Related maps

(2) *[1846?]*
Copy of Mr West's sketch of the Line of Road established by him between Bytown and L'Orignal
Col ms 38 x 215 cm Scale not given
Provenance: OOAMA RG 11M 81203/5 item 2; shows the road from Bytown, Gloucester Springs, and the Nation R to Hattville; mileages, names of settlers.
OOAMA (NMC 18056)

---

539 *[1846]*
[Map of road from Rigaud to Vankleeks Hill and Caledonia Springs with branches to L'Orignal and Hawkesbury]
Col ms 26 x 58 cm Scale not given Endorsements: stamps 'BW' '418'
Mills, burying ground, and a few names of owners; another copy of the map is in OOA RG 5 C1 no 1707 1846.
OOAMA (NMC 3317)

---

540 *1846*
Sketch of the Proposed Line of Road from the Rideau to the Boncher shewing the old Road and the alterations made by Malcolm McPherson D.P.S. April 1846.
Col ms 49 x 118 cm Scale not given Endorsements: stamps 'BW' '445'
(BW SI 23 June 1845); shows the route from Smiths Falls to Elmsley, Drummond, Lanark, Ramsay, Darling, Pakenham, and Bagot and McNab twps; survey grid, swampy areas; notes on alternative routes and costs, i.e., to cross new bridge on the Madawaska in McNab; (Holmden 2156).
OOAMA (NMC 14281)

---

541 *[185?]*
[Endorsed]: 'Unfinished Reconnoitring Map Capt. Freeth R.E.'
Col ms 142 x 370 cm Scale not given
Shows the communications and settlements between the Ottawa and St Lawrence rivers and from the boundary west to Kingston; mills; travelled roads; a major reconnaissance survey not listed as a source on the Rottenburg map but probably prepared soon after; Freeth became a captain on 29 Dec 1849; (Holmden 2424).
OOAMA (NMC 120812)

---

542 *1850*
Sketch of part of Canada / showing the Rail Roads, / Completed & Projected. / Published for the MONTREAL HERALD, May 1850.
Print (lith) 17 x 25 cm Scale not given
Shows area from Brockville east to include the Eastern twps.
QMMRB

---

543 *1851 (1861)*
Canada Rideau Canal Index Plan Shewing the Whole of the Ordnance Lands on the line of the Rideau Navigation between Bytown and Kingston Mills. Compiled from Various Departmental Records & Surveys of Lock Stations made in 1847, 1848.8.9 & 50 Drawn and Compiled under the directions of The Commg Royal Engineer in Canada (signed) by Nelson Walker Surveyor & Draftsman Rl Engr Dept 16th Septr 1851 from a tracing by (Sig) Hy Adams Ottawa 29th Novr 1861 T Bruce Draftn
Col ms on linen 43 x 120 cm 1" to 2 miles
Provenance: OOAMA received from McGill University Archives 26 Nov 1914; keys 21 plans of parts of the canal; shows drowned lands, lands left dry, ordnance property surveyed and not surveyed; table of lands and waters acquired by the Ordnance; there is also a similar but undated map

entitled 'Rideau Canal, Canada, index plan' (QMMMCM (3594)); an untitled undated plan in OOAMA approx 1" to 132 ft, endorsed 'BW 449' (Holmden 2407) showing the whole extent of the canal lands and marking drowned lands, may also date from 1847–50 surveys described above.
OOAMA (NMC 14339) QMMMCM (3594)

---

544 *1851*
MAP / SHEWING THE CONNECTION OF THE OTTAWA COUNTRY, WITH / the Seaports of the / NEW England States & New York / BY MEANS OF THE / BYTOWN & PRESCOTT RAILWAY. / Walter Shanly Engineer / 1851. Matthews' Lith. Montreal.
Print (lith) 47 x 64 cm Scale not given
In Walter Shanley, *Reports on the Preliminary and Locating Surveys of the Bytown and Prescott Railway* (Toronto 1853), frontis (*Bib Can* 3390) (Casey I–2401); shows the area from Belleville east to part of Canada East, Boston and Albany, New York; railway connections with Ogdensburgh Railroad and others to Boston.
OOA OTMCL

---

545 *[1852]*
Geological Map of a Part of CANADA, / To Illustrate Mr W.E. Logan's Paper / on the Foot-tracks in the Potsdam Sandstone // Quart. Journ. Geol. Soc. Vol. VIII. Pl. VI.
Print (lith) hand col 19 x 29 cm 1" to 13.7 miles
In W.E. Logan, 'On the Footprints Occurring in the Potsdam Sandstone of Canada,' *Quarterly Journal of the Geological Society of London* VIII (August 1852), bound at end (*Bib Can* 3278); shows the area from the Madawaska R to Brockville and Bytown to Montreal; formations classified and localities with trackmarks shown.
OTMCL

---

546 *[1852]*
MAP / of the / UNITED COUNTIES / of / LEEDS AND GRENVILLE / Compiled by / Wm Sherwood. // Hugh Scobie, Lith Toronto
Print (lith) 56 x 81 cm 1" to 150 chains
Shows twps, towns, rivers, lakes, etc; 'References' keys twp boundaries, macadamized and plank roads with names, other roads, line of railway, and the Rideau Canal; table gives 'Population of the United Counties of Leeds and Grenville in 1852' by twps and towns; the line of the St Lawrence and Lake Huron Railway is shown.
OOAMA (NMC 78546) OTAR

Later states and editions:

(2) *1852*
MAP / of the / UNITED COUNTIES / of / LEEDS AND GRENVILLE / Compiled by / Wm Sherwood. / 1852. // Hugh Scobie Lith. Toronto.
Print (lith) 56 x 81 cm 1" to 150 chains
The date has been added to the title; map is the same as above.
GBL OTAR

---

547 *1853–4 (1856)*
SURVEYS OF THE PRINCIPAL RAPIDS / OF THE / RIVER ST LAWRENCE / BETWEEN PRESCOTT AND LAKE ST LOUIS. / made under the Instructions of the Commissioners of Public Works. / by Messrs Maillefort and Raasloff. / SUBMARINE ENGRS IN 1854. / Office of Public Works, Toronto 1856 / G. Matthews Litho Montreal.
Prints (liths), 5 maps on 4 sheets Ea 1" to 9 chains
The sheets are as follows:

(1) DIVISION. / MAP-No 1. / GALOPS-RAPID. [and] DIVISION. / MAP-No 2. / SURVEY OF A PORTION / NORTH CHANNEL. / OF THE / LONG SAULT RAPIDS. 45 x 57 cm

(2) SURVEY OF THE RAPIDS / OF THE / RIVER ST LAWRENCE / BETWEEN PRESCOTT AND LAKE ST LOUIS / made under the Instructions of the Commissioners of Public Works / by Messrs Maillefort and Raasloff / SUBMARINE ENGRS IN 1854. DIVISION 3. / from Lake St Francis to Pointe au Diable comprising the Coteau Rapids. / G. Matthews Litho. Montreal 33 x 97 cm

(3) ... DIVISION 4. / from Pointe au Diable to Pointe au Moulin / comprising the Cedar Rapids. / G. Matthews Litho. Montreal 33 x 84 cm

(4) SURVEY ... IN 1853. DIVISION 5. / from Pointe au Moulin to Lake St. Louis comprising the Split Rock & Cascades Rapids. / G. Matthews Litho: Montreal. 32 x 126 cm
All are in *Maps, Reports, Estimates, etc, Relative to Improvements of the Navigation of the River St Lawrence ... Laid before the Legislative Assembly...* (Toronto: Printed by John Lovell 1856) (*Bib Can* 3635, OOAMA) and show soundings, steamboat channels, canals with locks, dams, obstructions to be removed; other notes on survey.
OOAMA OTAR OTMCL OTUTF

Related maps

(2) *[1854]*
Map No 1 Survey of a portion of the Galoppe Rapids River St Lawrence [and] Map No 2 Survey of a portion of the North Channel of the Long Sault Rapids River St Lawrence
2 col mss 63 x 95 cm and 62 x 173 cm 1" to 3 chains
Endorsements: stamps 'BW' '625..654'
The maps show information similar to that on (1) and (2) above; Map No 1 has a pencilled title and also date and names of surveyors as in (1) above, suggesting that these were the ms maps from which the final maps were reduced for publication.
OOAMA (NMC 21840; 22911)

---

548 *[1856]*
MAP / OF THE / COUNTY OF HASTINGS / AND / ADJOINING TOWNSHIPS. / Compiled from Actual Surveys & / THE LATEST AUTHORITIES / BY / W.R. ELMORE, C.E. / Snyder, Black & Sturn 92 William St. N.Y.
Print (lith) 126 x 113 cm 1" to 100 chains
Inset: 'P.V. Elmore's Road Line towards Ottawa River ('Hastings Free Grant Road')'; views: 'COURT HOUSE & JAIL, BELLEVILLE,' 'EPISCOPAL METHODIST SEMINARY / BELLEVILLE ERECTED 1855'; a very detailed map; advertised for sale in the *Napanee Standard* Oct 1856; shows the co as far north as Belmont to Kaladar and Lake twps; legend keys plank and gravel roads, road allowances, located railway lines, railways built; churches, post offices, schools, mills; names of owners; tables of population and distance, electoral divisions; list of bldgs in Belleville; 'Grand Junction Georgian Railway'; proposed tram road to Marmora from Belleville.
OOAMA (NMC 13206) OTAR (SR 86902; 92317)

549 *1856*
MAP / OF THE / UNITED COUNTIES / OF / LANARK & RENFREW / COMPILED FROM MAPS & DOCUMENTS IN THE OFFICE OF / THE COUNTY CLERK / AT PERTH C.W. / BY GEORGE ELLIS G.I.C.E. LONDON / Civil Engineer and Surveyor / 1856. / G. Matthew's Litho: Montreal.
Print (lith) Approx 118 x 60 cm 1" to 2 miles
Top part of OTAR copy is damaged and part missing; shows twps from Burgess to Montague, north to Pembroke, west to Sherbrooke, and Brougham to Alice; boundaries, railways, roads; survey grid, villages, town plots, some mills; some roads named; shows the Brockville & Ottawa Railway to Castleford with a branch to Perth.
OOAMA (NMC 19016) OTAR

550 *1856*
PLAN OF / RIVER ST LAWRENCE / BETWEEN PRESCOTT AND MONTREAL. / SHEWING THE RAPIDS, AND PROVINCIAL CANALS, / TO IMPROVE THE NAVIGATION. / Drafted by H.H. Killaly, Junr Office of Public Works Toronto, 1856. / George Matthews Lith. Montreal.
Print (lith) 51 x 521 cm 1" to 1/2 mile
Found with report cited in **547** but not listed in contents; shows relief by hachures along shoreline; canals, locks numbered, rapids, towns; (Holmden 2572).
GBTAUh (D8108 37f) OTAR OTMCL OTUTF

551 *[1857]*
Map of the Counties of / CARLETON AND RUSSELL / WITH A CORRECT MAP OF / THE / CITY OF OTTAWA. / COMPILED FROM THE MOST / ACCURATE SURVEYS BY W.A. AUSTIN P.L.S. C.E. // LITHOGRAPHED BY J. ELLIS, TORONTO. // 'W.A. AUSTIN & Co. / Land Agents Provincial Land Surveyors / Civil Engineers etc. OTTAWA C.W.'
Print (lith), 2 maps on 1 sheet Ea 57 x 78 cm 1" to 2 miles and 1" to 8 chains
Map sometimes found in two sheets with very large margin at bottom or top and sometimes found folding in two parts into cover suggesting that co map and city map were also issued separately; shows survey grid for twps, some relief; sources listed include: 'Crown Lands Dept., Mr Wells map now constructing, Ordnance Dept., Plans of the Corporation, Surveys of J.D. Slater, J.A. Snow and Donald Kenedy [*sic*]'; also shows Rideau Canal and Ottawa & Prescott Railway; city map shows streets with names, falls, and relief by hachures; Rideau Canal and view of Rideau Falls and city boundary; presumably made before Alphonso Wells died on 31 Oct 1857 and before ms copy made from Ottawa part in Apr 1858 (**1762**); OOAMA (NMC 29051) is north sheet for co only; (Holmden 1558, 1559, and 2165 (for Ottawa section only)).
OKQ OOAMA (NMC 11475; 19361; 29051) OTAR

552 *[1858]*
MAP / of the County of / HASTINGS / AND ADJOINING TOWNSHIPS / SHEWING THE ROUTE OF THE PROPOSED / MARMORA AND BELLEVILLE / RAILWAY. / Engraved by Maclear & Co. Toronto.
Print (lith) 84 x 62 cm 1" to 2 miles
In Marmora and Belleville Railway Company, *Marmora Railroad: Chairman's remarks and Engineers Report* (Belleville 1858), at front (*Bib Can* 5808); a detailed map showing macadamized roads with names, churches, schools, mills, iron ore and lithographic stone locations, railways; shows subdivided twps north to Methuen to Tudor and outlines of Wollaston, Limerick and Grimsthorpe.
OTAR OTMCL

553 *1859*
Plan of Cape Vesey Ordnance Reserve in the Township of Marysburgh Surveyed by J.J. Haslett Provl Land Surveyor A.D. 1859. Examined and compared with field book Nov. 4th 1859. J.W.B.
3 col mss on 1 sheet 50 x 77 cm 1" to 20 chains
Endorsements: 'No 9' '15566 /59'
(OTNR FN 1017 30 Aug 1859); the first map shows land parcels, cleared and wooded land, and former boundaries of various squatters; the second map shows 'Diagram of Chain Lines'; the third map has been pasted on later and is partly illegible but it seems to show names of owners or leasees keyed to a list with the contents of the lot.
OTNR (SR 5912)

554 *1859*
Plan of the Boundary Line between Upper and Lower Canada ... No 1 St Lawrence Section ... No 2 Ottawa Section ... No 3 ... Newton Section [All sgd]

Toronto 15th August 1859 (Signed) E.T. Fletcher P.L.S. True Copy Crown Lands Office Quebec 22nd October 1859 [Sgd] P W Vankoughnet Commissioner
3 col mss Ea 101 x 67 cm or smaller 1" to 20 chains
Endorsements: '1533 of 59'
Detailed surveys of the line with bearings, measurements, etc; title of first sheet varies: 'Plans of a Reconnaissance of the boundary line ...' (OOAMA (NMC 44609–11)); also a set sgd 'Department of Crown Lands Surveying Branch East Quebec 14th Feby 1862 Andrew Russell Assist Commr' with slightly different lines (OOAMA (NMC 44106–7, 27570)) (Holmden 3927–9); also a set 'Performed in pursuance of Instructions from the Department of Crown Lands dated Quebec 15 July 1862 (Sigd E.T. Fletcher S.S.D.C.L. [Sgd] 4th March 1863 Andrew Russell Asst Commissioner' (OOAMA (NMC 44108, 44612–13)); there is also a set of plans dated 1859–61 by Fletcher as listed in P.M. O'Leary's 'Inventaire des cartes, plans ... conservées au Département des terres de la province de Québec, Québec 30 mai 1909' (Maps B1a, b, d–h, B2, B2b); OTNR has transcripts of some of the Quebec plans (SR 3235, 3239, 4158, 5183).
OOAMA (NMC 44106–8; 44609–13; 27570) QQERT

---

555 *1860*
Map of / THE UNITED COUNTIES OF / FRONTENAC / LENNOX AND ADDINGTON / Canada West / From actual Surveys under the Direction of / H.F. WALLING / PUTNAM & WALLING, PUBLISHERS / KINGSTON, C.W. / 1860 / Entered according to Act of the Provincial Legislature in the Year of our Lord 1860 by the Proprietors, H.F. Walling & D.P. Putnam of Kingston, in the Western District, in the Office of the Registrar of the Province of Canada.
Print (lith) hand col 150 x 151 cm 1" to 400 rods
Thirty insets of towns at 1" to 100 rods or larger: Barriefield (60 rods), Bath (40 rods), Battersea (60 rods), Centreville (50 rods), Clark's Mills (50 rods), Colebrooke (40 rods), Croydon (80 rods), Elginburg (80 rods), Enterprise (80 rods), Garden Is (40 rods), Harrowsmith (40 rods), Inverary (80 rods), Kingston (35 rods), Kingston Station (50 rods), Lower Landing, Amherst Is (80 rods), Marysville (60 rods), Mill Haven (80 rods), Morven (100 rods), Napanee (30 rods), Newburgh (40 rods), Odessa (40 rods), Portsmouth (60 rods), Roblin (80 rods), Selby (80 rods), Sydenham (60 rods), Tamworth (30 rods), Violet (100 rods), Waterloo (60 rods), Wilton (80 rods), Yarker (50 rods); eight views of public and commercial bldgs and residences; table of distances within cos, business directory; Clarendon and Anglesea Twp not laid out; in rural areas bldgs are shown with names of occupants; in the northern twps only names of owners given; insets of towns show bldgs with type of business and/or name of occupant; a prospectus advertised 'For Sale at $5.00 Proposed Map of Frontenac, Lennox & Addington. Subscribers Wanted... Henry F. Walling no. 90 Fulton St. New York' in *Napanee Standard* 18 March 1858.
OOAMA (NMC 11476; 49420) OTAR (SR 92343)

---

556 *1860*
PLAN / of the County of / HASTINGS / BY / R.L. INNES, ESQR C.E. / Published by M. Bowell. / For the / Hastings Directory. / 1860–61. / W.A. Little, Lith. Montreal
Print (lith) 72 x 47 cm 1" to 2 miles
Prepared for *Directory of the County of Hastings ... 1860–61* (Belleville: Mackenzie Bowell 1860) (*Bib Can* 3976); shows the twps with survey grid north to Lake and Tudor; roads and railways named; towns, schools, mills, factories; shows the location of iron ore and iron works near Marmora and lithographic stone; table of distances.
ONLAH OTMCL

Related maps

(2) *1865*
PLAN / of the County of / HASTINGS / BY / H.A.F. MACLEOD, ESQ C.E. & P.L.S. / for the Hastings Directory. / 1864–65. // W.A. LITTLE LITH MONTREAL
Print (lith) 77 x 58 cm 1" to 3 miles
Inset: 'PLAN OF THE / VILLAGE OF MARMORA / THE PROPERTY OF THE / MARMORA IRON WORKS.' 1" to 10 chains; in *Directory of the County of Hastings ... 1864–65* (Belleville: Mackenzie Bowell 1865), frontis (*Bib Can* 3976), redrawn at a smaller scale but with similar information to plan above.
OOAMA (NMC 22286) OTAR OTMCL

---

557 *1861*
Map of / THE UNITED COUNTIES OF / LEEDS AND GRENVILLE / Canada West / From actual Surveys under the Direction of / H.F. WALLING / PUTNAM & WALLING PUBLISHERS / KINGSTON, C.W. / 1861. Surveys by / O.W. GRAY, Topl Engr / Albert Davis S.S. Southworth Geo. B. Sanford / Assistants
Print (lith) hand col 152 x 158 cm 1" to 1 mile
Thirty-one insets of towns (all at 1" to 40 rods unless otherwise noted): Adams, Addison, Bishop's Mills, Brockville (1" to 24 rods), Burritts Rapids, Charleston, Delta, Easton's Corner, Edwardsburgh, Elgin, Escott, Farmersville, Frankville, Gananoque, Greenbush, Harlem, Kemptville, Lyn, Lyndhurst or Furnace Falls, Maitland, Mallorytown (1" to 80 rods), Merrickville (1" to 30 rods), Morton, Newboro, North Augusta, Oxford Mills, Portland, Prescott (1" to 32 rods), Spencerville, Toledo, Westport; six views of public and commercial bldgs and residences; 'Explanations' keys side lot lines, con lines; open roads, twp lines, railways, tenant houses, schools, blacksmith shops; business directories; table of distances, 'Statistics Population 1861'; in rural areas bldgs

are shown with name of occupant; insets of towns show bldgs with type of business and/or name of occupant.
OOAMA (NMC 17007) OTAR USDLC

Later editions and states

(2) *1861–2*
[The title, etc, is the same but the date has been changed to '1861–2']
The map is the same as the 1861 map.
OLU OOAMA (NMC 11856; 17384)

---

558 *[1861?]*
PLAN / of the United Counties of / PRESCOTT AND RUSSELL. / Compiled by order of the County Council. / Saml T. Abbott Evans Provl Land Surveyor &c. &c. / L'ORIGNAL C.W. // MACL[EAR & CO. LITH. ?]
Print (col lith) 87 x 136 cm 1" to 1 mile
Lower right corner missing from OTAR copy; 'Reference' keys town or twp halls, post offices, churches with denomination, schools, chief travelled roads, inns with names of proprietors, government road allowances, side lines, unoccupied lots; notes on conflicting surveys of some twp boundaries with lines as surveyed in 1856–7 and 1858; the map was probably being prepared while Evans was articling with Robert Hamilton in L'Orignal in 1859–60, but may not have been published before he became a provincial land surveyor on 14 Jan 1861.
OTAR (SR 86913)

---

559 *1862*
MAP OF THE COUNTIES OF / STORMONT, DUNDAS, / GLENGARRY, PRESCOTT / & RUSSELL / CANADA WEST. / From Actual Surveys under the direction of / H.F. WALLING / PUBLISHED BY D.P. PUTNAM / PRESCOTT C.W. / 1862 / Surveyed & drafted by / O.W. GRAY, / ASSISTED BY / ALBERT DAVIS, S.S. SOUTHWORTH
Print (lith) hand col 151 x 156 cm 1" to 1 mile
Twenty-one insets of towns (all at 1" to 40 rods unless otherwise noted): Alexandria, Aultsville, Cornwall, Cumberland (1" to 80 rods), Dalhousie, Dickinson's Landing (1" to 60 rods), Dixon's Corners, Hawkesbury (1" to 60 rods), Inkerman, Iroquois, Lancaster, Lancaster Station (1" to 20 rods), L'Orignal, Martintown, Milleroches, Morrisburgh, Moulinette, North Plantagenet, North Williamsburgh, Vankleek Hill, Williamstown, four views of businesses; public bldgs and residences; business directories; table of distances; statistics tables for each co (by twp); bldgs with names of occupants; insets of towns show bldgs; type of business and/or occupant. OC copy has an additional inset of the town of Chesterville.
GBL (70685(1)) OC OOAMA (NMC 21998; 53146) OTAR USDLC

---

560 *1862*
Sketch Showing Proposed new road near the Village of Lancaster; North Shore of Lake St Francis Surveyed by Order of the Dept of Public Works. Lachine Canal Office Montreal, Septr 1862. Suptg Engr
Col ms on linen 63 x 155 cm 1" to 400 ft
Endorsements: '96' 'Contract No 2559' 'in No 60920'; stamp [BW] '403'
'Profile of New Road' 1" to 10 ft vertical; shows the drowned land affecting the old road near the shore; 'proposed new road' is further inland and follows a con line.
OOAMA (NMC 21476)

---

561 *1863*
MAP / OF THE COUNTIES OF / LANARK AND RENFREW / CANADA WEST. / From actual surveys under the direction of / H.F. WALLING. / PUBLISHED BY D.P. PUTNAM; / PRESCOTT; C.W. / 1863 / Surveyed and Drawn by / O.W. GRAY; Civil Engineer. / ASSISTED BY: ALBERT DAVIS; S.S. SOUTHWORTH.
Print (lith) hand col 104 x 141 cm 1" to 1 1/2 miles
Insets: Northern part of Renfrew County 1" to 3 miles, [Raglan and Radcliffe twps] 1" to 5 miles; 36 insets of towns (most at 1" to 60 rods unless otherwise noted): Adamsville, Almonte (40 rods), Appleton, Arnprior (40 rods), Ashton, Beachburgh, Burnstown, Calderson [Balderson], Campbelltown (30 rods), Carleton Place (40 rods), Clayton (40 rods), Cobden, Douglas, Egansville, Ferguson's Falls, Franktown (40 rods), Harper's Corners, Hopetown, Innisville, Lanark (40 rods), McDonald's Corners, Middleville, Osceola, Pakenham (30 rods), Pembroke (55 rods), Perth (30 rods), Playfair's Mills, Port Elmsley, Prospect, Renfrew (40 rods), Sand Point, Smiths Falls (40 rods), Watson's Corners, Westmeath, White Lake, and Chapeau, Quebec; six views of public and commercial bldgs and residences; 'Explanations' keys roads; side and con lines; tenant houses; schools; houses; churches; business directories; population statistics for 1861; in rural areas bldgs shown with name of occupant; insets of towns show bldgs, type of business and/or occupant; (Holmden 1932).
OOAMA (NMC 21920) OTAR (SR 92345; 88277; 88386) USDLC

---

562 *1863*
MAP / of the County of / CARLETON / CANADA WEST / from Surveys under the Direction of H.F. WALLING. / Published by D.P. PUTNAM; / PRESCOTT; C.W. / 1863. / Surveyed and Drawn by / O.W. GRAY; Civil Engineer. / ASSISTED BY ALBERT DAVIS S.S. SOUTHWORTH
Print (lith) hand col 134 x 131 cm 1" to 1 mile
Thirteen insets of towns (all at 1" to 40 rods unless otherwise noted): Antrim, Ashton, Bell's Corners, Burritts Rapids, Carp, Fitzroy Harbor (30 rods), Kenmore, Lewisville (30 rods), Metcalf, North

Gower, Ottawa (50 rods), Richmond, Wellington; nine views of public and commercial bldgs and residences; 'Explanation' keys roads; side and con lines; tenant houses; schools; churches; population statistics for Ottawa and Carleton cos; table of distances; business directories; in rural areas bldgs shown with name of occupant; insets of towns show bldgs, type of business and/or occupant; also a copy at OTAR (SR 92344) in which outer lines of the border are lacking; (Holmden 1557; *OHIM* 4.29).
OOAMA (NMC 14834; 20794) OTAR (SR 86912; 92344) USDLC

---

563 *[1863]*
MAP / SHEWING THE POSITION OF THE / CANADA LEAD MINES / LANSDOWNE; C.W. // W.A. Little; Lith.
Print (lith) 12 x 18 cm Scale not given
In *Reports on the Property of the Canada Lead Mining Company ... Lansdowne* (24 Oct 1863), at end (OOA Pamph 1863(32)); shows the area from Kingston to Lansdowne; shows 'Canada Lead Mines' and direction of formation south to Rossie Lead Mines in upper New York State.
OOA

Related maps

(**2**) *[1863]*
PROPERTY OF THE / CANADA LEAD MINING COMPANY // W.A. Little Lith C. Robb M.E.
Print (lith) 20 x 10 cm 1" to 15 Chains
From the same source as (1) above; shows site on the Gananoque R in con VIII, lots 3 and 4, Lansdowne Twp; lead veins and mine shafts.
OOA

---

564 *1863*
TREMAINE'S MAP / OF THE COUNTY OF / PRINCE EDWARD / UPPER CANADA / Toronto 1863. / Compiled by JOHN FERRIS WARD. / Views Photographed / by / J.A. Sherrif / Picton. / Drawn from Actual Surveys / By ARTHUR W. KEDDIE / Engraved and Printed / at / Tremaine's / Map / Establishment / 79 Front Street. Toronto. / Published for Subscribers by Geo. C. Tremaine
Print (lith) hand col 126 x 156 cm 1" to 50 chains
Inset: Picton 1" to 10 chains; 13 views of public and commercial bldgs and residences; 'Explanations' keys roads; road allowances not opened; twp boundaries; post offices; churches; Friends meeting houses; schools; water; steam saw, and grist mills; tanneries; blacksmith shops; private residences; lighthouses; names of owners and/or occupants of lots; most bldgs shown in rural areas; names of estates; subscribers directories; 'Population from the Census of 1861'; co officers; inset shows bldgs, type of business and/or occupant.
OOAMA (NMC 19020) OTAR (SR 92639; 92341) USDLC

---

565 *1866*
A / GEOLOGICAL MAP / OF THE / MADOC / GOLD REGIONS / BY / HENRY WHITE P.L.S. // G.B. Ware Lithogrs 16 Toronto St Toronto // Toronto Dec 24 1866
Print (col lith) and hand col 44 x 37 cm Scale not given
On cover: 'Toronto: G. Mercer Adam, Publisher'; shows the area from Rawdon to Hungerford twps north to Lake to Tudor twps; survey grid; names of mines and locations of minerals; the map is coloured for the main geological formations; roads; notes on geology.
OTAR

---

566 *1867*
GEOLOGICAL MAP / OF THE / GOLD REGIONS / OF / MADOC / BY / HENRY WHITE P.L.S.: / Author of the Geology; Oil fields and Minerals of Canada West / Maclear and Co Publishers 17 King St West / TORONTO
Print (lith) hand col 40 x 53 cm Scale not given
In Henry White, *Gold Regions of Canada* (Toronto: Maclear & Co. 1867), frontis (*Bib Can* 4642); covers a larger area than the 1866 map above (**565**); shows Asphodel to Burleigh twps and Hungerford to Tudor twps; and mines and the locations of gold and other minerals; general geological formations shown; compared with the 1866 map, there are fewer notes on mineral locations in the Madoc and Marmora areas and some mines have been deleted.
OTMCL

Huron-Ottawa

567 *[ca 1790]*
Plan of the Ottawa or Grand River. Copied from an original by Lieut John Fredk Holland Ry Rt NYk [Sgd] Samuel Holland Surveyr Genl.
Col ms 81 x 184 cm 1" to 6 miles
Note: 'N.B. Not from Actual Survey'; shows the area from Montreal and the St Lawrence R to L Nipissing, the French R, and L Huron; many parts inaccurate in position and shape; shows portages; possibly similar to No. 25 in 'List of Maps ... 1793' (OTAR RG 1 A-I-1/1, 151–7).
OTAR (SR 6677)

---

568 *[1826] (1828)*
Sketch of the Ottawa River from the mouth of the Bonchere to the Pond deux Joachims a distance of one hundred miles by order of His Excellency Sir Peregrine Maitland K.C.B. Lieutenant Governor.
Col ms 73 x 128 cm 1" to 2 miles
Note: 'This Plan to be returned to [Sgd] J.G. Chewett 19th Augt 1828'; a more finished plan than (2) and includes more comments and observations and some incorrect place-names; note: 'At the Upper End of Lake du Chat ends the Surveyed land on the Ottawa River. The distances on this Sketch are measured by the run of the Canoes with a common Watch in the months of May and June 1826 by J.G. Chewett'.
OTAR (SR 5891)

Related maps

(**2**) *1826 (1828?)*
Sketch of the Ottawa River from the mouth of the Bonnechere to the Pond deux Joachims distance one hundred miles / By order of His Excellency Sir Peregrine Maitland K.C.B. Lieutenant Governor &c&c&c by [Sgd] J.G. Chewett June 1826 [Sgd] Copy by J.G. Chewett December 1828.
Col ms 73 x 128 cm 1" to 2 miles Endorsements: 'S 32'
Shows rapids, falls, nature of the riverbank, comments on timber and lumbering, longitude and latitude observations, the boundary between the Bathurst and Midland districts, a few survey lines.
OTAR (SR 11067)

---

569 *1826*
[Endorsed title]: 'Sketch shewing modes of communication between Lake Simcoe and the Ottawas Report of Henry Briscoe Lt R.E.' Commanding Royal Engineers Office Quebec 28th Octr 1826
Col ms 54 x 43 cm 1" to 8 miles
The map originally accompanied 'Report of a Survey ... to Examine the Water Communication between Lake Simcoe and the River Ottawa [by] Henry Briscoe 16th Oct 1826' (OOA RG 8 I/428 pp 81–5); shows Briscoe's and Ensign Durnford's route from the Severn R through Sault du Sauvage, L Baptiste, and unnamed rivers and lakes to Rapides des Allumettes on the Ottawa R; the route explored by Capt Catty from the Talbot to the Madawaska R and to the Ottawa is also shown; Briscoe probably explored the Muskoka lake and river system to Opeongo L and the Petawawa R (cf. Murray, xlvii); (Holmden 2109); also an untitled copy further sgd '9th Novr 1826 E.W. Durnford Col Comg Royl Engrs Canada' accompanying copy of his report in GBLpro WO 55/863 p 377.
GBLpro (WO 55/863 p 377) OOAMA (NMC 2845)

---

570 *1826*
Sketch shewing the situation of the Black River and the communication from its source to the Talbot (Signed) W B Marlow Lieut Royal Engineers Septr 22d 1826 W M Smith Lieutt Royal Artillery Copied [Sgd] M.O.R. Wilson.
Col ms 43 x 51 cm 1" to 8 miles
Originally accompanied Lts Marlow and Smith's report of 22 Sept 1826 to Col J.R. Wright on the survey of the Black R (OOA RG 8 I/428 pp 64–76); shows the Black R entering the Severn R north of L [Couchiching] and connections eastward to a junction with the Talbot R, Balsam L, and further connections to the Madawaska R; the Talbot route is named 'Captain Catty's Former Route to the Ottawa'; falls, rapids, and portages shown but no other place-names given; (Holmden 1516); there is also a copy of the plan further sgd 'Commanding Royal Engineers Office Quebec 9 Novr 1826 E.W. Durnford Col Comg Rl Engrs Canada' accompanying a copy of Marlow's report (GBLpro WO 55/863 p 359).
GBLpro (WO 55/863 p 359) OOAMA (NMC 2844)

---

571 *1827*
Route explored by Lieuts Briscoe R.E. & Greenwood R.A. 1 Octr 1827 (signed) H. Briscoe Lieut Royal Engineers [Sgd] E.W. Durnford Col Comg Rl Engineers Canada ... 20th Novr 1827
Col ms Size unknown 1" to 10 miles
With Briscoe's report 13 Oct 1827 (GBLpro WO 55/864 p 377); shows his route by the Madawaska R, earlier routes, and those of others.
GBLpro (WO 55/864 p 377)

---

572 *1827*
Sketch of the Waters between Lake Simcoe & the Ottawa River taken between the 19th August and the 6th of October, accompanied by Lt Walpole, Royal Engineers. [Sgd] J.G. Chewett York 19th October 1827
Col ms 76 x 340 cm Approx 1" to 11/4 miles
Inset: 'Sketch shewing the Route, by Lt Catty in the year 1818 by Lt Briscoe in the Year 1826 and 1827, and by Lt Walpole in the Year 1827 by J.G. Chewett'; shows the route taken from Talbot R through Balsam L and Gull L through [Kashagawigamog, Head, Drag, and Miskwabi lakes] to the York R branch of the Madawaska R and to the Ottawa R; rapids, falls, portages shown; numbers marked along the route are probably observation points.
OTAR (SR 7584)

Related maps

(2) *1827*
Sketch A sketch of the waters on the route passed thro' in 1819 by Captn Catty and in 1827 by Lt J. Walpole Royal Engrs York 12th Nov 1827 (Sigd) J Walpole Lieut Royal Engrs ... 27th Novr 1827 [Sgd] E.W. Durnford Col Comg Rl Engineers Canada
Col ms Size unknown 1" to 2000 yds
With Walpole's report 12 Nov 1827 (GBLpro WO 55/864 p 374); also Sketch B sgd J. Walpole, 1" to 8 miles (GBLpro WO 55/864 p 378); shows connections south to Kingston.
GBLpro (WO 55/864 pp 374, 378)

---

573 *1829*
[Map showing the proposed line of a canal between Lake Huron and the Ottawa River] (Signd) John By Lt Colonel Royl Engrs Commandg Rideau Canal 16th March 1829. Commanding Royal Engineers Office Quebec 2nd April 1829. Copy.
Col ms 37 x 47 cm 1" to 15 miles
Originally accompanied 'Observations on the Advantages of a Canal from the Ottawa to Lake Huron with Information Collected respecting Its Practibility by Charles Shirreff January 1829' enclosed in a letter by Lt Col By and further enclosed in Durnford to R.E. Office Quebec (OOAMA RG 8 I/48 p 18); shows a route by the Petawawa R, Trout L, and connecting rivers to L La Vieille, then by the Moose R to L Huron (cf. Murray, xlix); (Holmden 2110).
OOAMA (NMC 2852)

Related maps

(2) *1831*
MAP / of the Territory between the / OTTAWAS RIVER & LAKE HURON / Illustrative of the Paper on / the Topography of that Country / BY ALEX R SHIRREFF ESQ. / Compiled for the 2nd Vol. Transactions of / the Literary & Historical Society of Quebec. / May 1831. – by William Henderson.
Print (lith) 21 x 26 cm 1" to 25 miles
In A. Shirreff, 'Topographical Notices of the Country Lying between the Mouth of the Rideau and Penetanguishene on Lake Huron' in *Transactions of the Literary and Historical Society of Quebec* ser 1, 2 (1831), 243–309 (OOA); 'Note. The Ottawa Rr and the Lakes and rivers between Ottawa and Gloucester Bay are delineated from Mr Shirreffs Map of his exploring survey laid down by that Gentleman from his sketches taken on the spot. Lake Nipissing and the extensive Country between that Lake and the Rivers Severn and Madawaska are also inserted from information of various kinds obtained by Mr. Shirreff in 1829. W.H.'; Shirreff explored the route shown on his father's map above but judged the L Nipissing route to be best for a canal (cf.Murray, xlix); photoreproduction in OOAMA (NMC 2856).
OOA

(3) *1834*
Sketch of the Routes between Bytown & Penetanguishene by the Ottawa, Nesswabic & Muskoka rivers [Sgd?] Maria Knowles July 2nd 1834.
Col ms 41 x 76 cm 1" to 10 miles Endorsements: '2927 Canada'
Originally accompanying a letter sgd by Lord FitzWilliam and others addressed to Thomas Spring-Rice 24 June 1834 (GBLpro CO42/254); shows a more northerly area than the 1831 map but includes the same note; 'Waters marked in colours have been traversed and sketched. The rest is laid down from Indian charts and other information'; shows in pink the area north of Muskoka L, Opeongo L, and the Petawawa R that Lord FitzWilliam and others requested for colonization and to establish trading links between the Ottawa R and L Huron; (*PRO Cat* 1406).
GBLpro (MPG 506)

---

574 *[183?]*
[Endorsed title]: 'Lake Huron and Routes to it from L.C.'
Ms on tracing paper 57 x 44 cm 1" to 10 miles
Shows the area from the Ottawa R to L Huron and routes from the Mississippi R to Nesswabic R, and Muskoka R to L Huron; the twps of Pakenham, Horton, and MacNab are named; latitude lines pencilled in; dotted lines show connections in the area of the north branch of Muskoka R, Roulet L to L Nipissing by the South R, and 'Amable du Fongs [*sic*] Creek,' 'Abeonga Lakes,' 'Pittowois' [Petawawa] R; notes indicate good hardwood; similar to **573(3)** and in a different hand from **576**.
OOAMA (RG 16M 77803/32 no 1)

---

575 *[183?]*
[Plan of the Ottawa River from Grand Calumet to Deep River]
Col ms 65 x 183 cm Scale not given

A rough tracing of an earlier map, possibly unfinished and with some later information; shows the mouths of the Indian and Muskrat rivers opp Rapides des Allumettes, 'River Pittowoise' [Petawawa], Chalk R, and Sturgeon L; Ft William and Ft Coulonge located on the Lower Canada side; note: 'the distances from one place to another as usually reckoned commencing at the foot of Calumet Island and running upward are as under stated ...'; 'Adams Mill' is located on Grand Allumette Is and 'John Egan & Co.' noted in the area.
OTAR (SR 5483)

---

576 *[183?]*
[Sketch of Muskoka River and part of Lake Huron]
Ms on tracing paper 42 x 52 cm 1 1/4" to 1 minute of latitude Watermark: 'J WHATMAN TURKEY MILL 1817'
An early sketch of the 'Muskoko R' up to the 12th fall; each fall described and height given, e.g.: 'The 1st Fall the descent is 15 ft. about 3 miles from Lake Huron; Vessels can come to it'; a note by the mouth of the Muskoka R indicates it is 'a short 100 Miles from Toronto of which 48 miles by Land and 40 Miles by Lakes Simcoe and Huron'; possibly related to David Thompson's plan (see **582(2)**) or to the exploration surveys in the area in the 1830s.
OOAMA (RG 16M 77803/32 no 3)

---

577 *1831*
Sketch of the 100,000 acre tract in the Newcastle District lately ordered to be Surveyed, shewing the route taken in exploring, the different points of observation from tops of highest bushes etc etc York Jany 6th 1831 [Sgd] C. Rankin D.S.
Col ms 47 x 61 cm 1" to 80 chains Endorsements: 'C 1' '753'
(SI 22 Nov 1830 to survey and lay out tract on the same principle used for L Huron area; OTAR FN 57 Jan 1831); shows the area north of Eldon and Fenelon twps with survey grid and observation points along main exploration line; note: 'Extensive uncultivable plains limestone near the surface and small growth of poplar, cedar and pine bushes no timber for building or fencing etc.'
OTAR (SR 591)

---

578 *[1832]*
Sketch of Ottawa River from Rideau Falls up to River Mississippi, Lac Des Chats [Endorsed on back]: 'Ottawa River from Lacs Chats to Rideau Falls N.H. Baird 1832'
Col ms 65 x 52 cm Scale not given Watermark: '... 1827' Endorsements: 'A 45'; stamps 'B↑O' 'IGF'
Shows Fitzroy, Torbolton, Huntley, March, Nepean, and Gloucester twps; rivers, relief along shoreline; a few mills located on rivers near Les Chats Rapids; (Holmden 2261).
OOAMA (NMC 29472)

Related maps

(2) *1832*
Plan of proposed improvements for the passage of timber at the Chaudiere 1832 [Sgd] N H Baird Civil Engineer M.I.C.E.L. 1832
Col ms 49 x 123 cm 1" to 60 ft Endorsements: 'A 45'; stamp 'B↑O'
Shows the old timber slide and the proposed new slide and regulating weir, dam, and timber channel on the south side of the river; (Holmden 2168).
OOAMA

---

579 *1835 (1836)*
Plan of an Exploration made Easterly of Lake Huron under the Command of Lieut Carthew R.N. by William Hawkins D.P.S. Pursuant to Instructions from the Surveyor General Dated at Toronto 18th June & 15 July 1835 [Sgd] William Hawkins Dpy Surveyor Toronto February 1836.
Col ms 97 x 65 cm 1" to 3 miles Endorsements: '921'
(OTAR FN 458–9 1835–6); shows the survey of the exploration line that was the continuation of the boundary line between the Home and Newcastle districts run 78 miles north from the east side of Rama Twp; five lateral excursions at various mileages shown; the reports of Lt Carthew and Wm Hawkins were printed in *JHA* (1836–7) App 37, pp 1–8 and 43ff (cf. Murray, 1).
OTAR (SR 5554)

---

580 *1835*
Plan shewing the line of Road marked out & established between Lake Simcoe & Balsam Lake: A line of Level run between the South Branch of the Talbot River & Balsam Lake, also the Indian Reservation on Balsam Lake, by Command of His Excellency Sir John Colborne K.C.B. Lieutt Governor. 24 May 1835 [Sgd] Jn Smith Junr Deputy Surveyor.
Ms 68 x 115 cm Scale not given Endorsements: 'Y 13'
Inset: 'Section of the Ground between the South Branch of the Talbot and Balsam Lake' 1" to 300 ft, 1" to 20 ft vertical; (SI 24 Sept 1834; OTNR FN 248 1834–5); shows the Portage Rd line, mill site, and summer portage from Balsam L to Talbot R.
OTNR (SR 6561)

---

581 *1835 (1836)*
Sketch of Courses to accompany Captn Baddeley's Report upon a portion of the Lake Huron Territory traversed by him while attached to an Exploring Party acting under the Orders of His Excellency Major Genl Sir John Colborne K.C.B. 1835 No 1.
Col ms 123 x 76 cm 1" to 1 mile Endorsements: '926'
Shows the route followed from L Couchiching east and north along the Black R to Muskoka R to point reached after 1 Sept (Muskoka L and Falls); shows

course of Carthew and Hawkins; notes on routes; Baddeley's 'Exploring Report' dated 8 March 1836 (OTAR RG 1 CB-1 box 25); (cf. Murray, 1 and 74).
OTAR (SR 7070)

---

582 *[1837]*
[Canoe route from Lake Huron to the Ottawa River] no. 1 [Lake Huron to Muskoka River to 79° 20′ W Sgd] David Thompson // no. 2 [Forked Lake to Galeary Lake to 78° 20′ W Sgd] David Thompson // no. 3 [Galeary Lake to Madawaska River 77° 20′ W Sgd] David Thompson // no. 4 [Madawaska River to Ottawa River to 76° 20′ W Sgd] David Thompson.
4 col mss No 1: 95 x 127 cm, nos 2–4: ea 75 x 129 cm 1" to 1 mile
Falls, rapids, portages, and longitude/latitude lines shown; falls are numbered from L Huron, and points where readings were taken are noted; the route is marked through lakes and rivers and described in detail in Murray, lii; Thompson's 'Report on the Survey of the Rivers, Lakes ... etc, from Lake Huron to the Ottawa R ... Aug 1837' and 'Astronomical Observations' are in OTAR David Thompson Papers; the latter report and 'Report on the Examination of the Ottawa River, the Muskrat Lake and River, etc ...' were printed in the 'Report of the Commissioners ...' (see **583(3)**).
OTAR OTAR (SR 7921 (Map no 1))

Related maps

(2) *[1837] (1842)*
[Map of the Muskoka River from Lake Huron to Cross Lake by David Thompson]
Col ms 104 x 160 cm Scale not given
Accompanied by a letter from David Thompson 10 March 1842 to the Governor General endorsed 'Country between Lake Huron & the Ottawa River - reports result of his observations when surveying line for a canal in 1837' originally filed in OOA RG11 A1 vol 79 file 10; the map is similar to and covers area of sheets 1 and part of 2 above; falls with heights and rapids numbered from L Huron for 110 miles; route through lakes; the letter urged the importance of building a canal to route commerce from L Huron to Montreal and opening the land for agricultural settlement.
OOAMA (NMC 119075)

(3) *1844*
To His Excellency the Right Honorable Lord Metcalfe etc. etc. a Chart of the lower part of the Muskoko River, from actual survey by [Sgd] David Thompson
Ms 49 x 49 cm Scale not given
Enclosed in Thompson's memorial to Metcalfe asking that a survey be made of the east side of L Huron as he is confident of future settlement there (OOA RG 1 L3 T3 no 23 1844); similar to pt of sheet 1 in (1) and west pt of (2); includes a table of heights of various falls; (Holmden 1975).
OOAMA (NMC 8907)

---

583 *1837 (1838)*
Exploration of the Rivers Maganetawang and Pittoiwais: Taken pursuant to Instructions from the Honble John Macauley Survr Genrl Captn Baddely R. Engrs & John S. Cartwright Esqr By William Hawkins Dy Surveyor. 1837. [Sgd] William Hawkins Dy Surveyor Toronto 8th Feb 1838 No 1 [and] [Ottawa River from Isle aux Allumettes to Lake Nipissing] Exploration taken pursuant to Instructions ... [Sgd] William Hawkins Dy Surveyor Toronto Feby 183[8] No 2. [and] [Lake Nipissing to Lake Huron via the French River] Exploration Pursuant to Instructions ... Sgd William Hawkins Dy Surveyor Toronto Feb 1838 No 3
3 col mss Ea 341 x 74 cm or smaller 1" to 1 mile
One of the three surveys made under authority of 'An Act to Provide for a Survey of the Ottawa River...together with the Country and Waters Lying between that River and Lake Huron' (7 William IV c 57 4 March 1837); the maps show falls, rapids, portages, relief, comments on land and timber, and points from which geological specimens were taken.
OTAR (SR 5982, 6719, 7084)

Related maps

(2) *1837*
Profiles Exhibiting the Comparative difference of two routes from Lake Huron to the Ottawa River both terminating at the northerly end of the Allumette Island; viz. by the French River Lake Nipissing; and by the River Maganetawang thence entering the source of the Pettawais River. Explored in the Summer of 1837 By William Hawkins Dy Sur.
Col ms 51 x 73 cm 1" to 5 miles, 1" to 200 ft vertical Endorsements: '944'
Shows the Magnetawan route at 340 ft above L Huron compared with 75 ft for the L Nipissing route.
OTAR

(3) *1837 [1838?]*
Sketch of part of the Ottawa River Illustrative of a Report thereon from an examination in Septr 1837 by William Hawkins Dy Survr.
Col ms 73 x 53 cm 1" to 4 miles Endorsements: '815'
Shows the area from Bytown to the mouth of the Petawawa R; this smaller-scale version or a similar map may have accompanied Hawkins's report of 2 Feb 1838; the report (but not the map) was printed in 'Report of the Commissioners on the Survey of the Ottawa River, etc,' *JHA* (1839) App, vol 2, pt 1 87–117.
OTAR (SR 7080)

---

584 *[1837(1838?)]*
Map Shewing the Country and Waters, North and East of Lake Huron, Commencing at French River, By Order of the Commissioners Appointed under the Authority of an Act 'to provide for a Survey of the Ottawa River and the Country bordering on it,

together with the Country and Waters lying between that River and Lake Huron' By their Obt Sert [Sgd] David Taylor.
Col ms 73 x 100 cm 1" to 4.75 miles Endorsements: '931'
Inset: [profile of route between L Huron and the Ottawa R via Turtle L]; shows the survey via L Nipissing, Turtle L, and the Mattawa R to the Ottawa R; falls, rapids, portages; Taylor's ms report is found in OTAR RG 1 CB-1 box 29; the 'Diary of Mr. Taylor July 12th 1837 – Oct. 7, 1837' was printed with the 'Report of the Commissioners on the Survey of the Ottawa River' (see **583(3)**).
OTAR (SR 7113)

---

585 *[1841]*
[Endorsed title]: 'Map drawn by Indians on birch-bark and attached to a tree to show their route to others following them, found by Capt. Bainbrigge Rl Engineers at the 'ridge' between the Ottawa and Lake Huron. May 1841.'
Ms on birchbark mounted on paper 10 x 38 cm Not drawn to scale
Also a tracing on paper by Bainbrigge; shows a river, lake, encampment, and route followed; area not identified; 'Forwarded to the United Service Institution in the hope that it may show young officers how small an effort is needed to acquire that most useful art, Military Sketching since even Savages can make an intelligble [*sic*] plan.'
GBL (RUSI(Misc))

---

586 *1845 (1846)*
[Map of the Mattawa River] 'Copy' of Survey by W.E. Logan, Provincial Geologist 1845. Board of Works, 1846.
Col ms in 2 pieces 48 x 227 cm 1" to 1 mile
Traverse lines shown; portages, rapids, differences in water levels; types of rock, settlements.
OOAMA (NMC 14270)

Related maps

(2) *[1845]*
[Map of the Mattawa River endorsed]: 'Sir W.E. Logan 1845?'
Col ms 47 x 225 cm 1" to 1 mile Endorsements: '0961'
Shows the river with locations of camps from 16 Sept to 9 Oct [1845]; notes on geology along the river; twp names have been pencilled in including: Head, Maria, Clara, Cameron, Papineau, Calvin, Bonfield, and Ferris; traverse lines are marked along the river; longitude and latitude lines and compass variations are marked; (Zaslow, 44).
OOAMA (RG 45M 83403/21 D-V-2032)

---

587 *1845*
Plan of the Petewawis River Surveyed pursuant to Instructions bearing date at the Crown Timber Office Bytown 22nd Jany 1845 [Sgd] John Robertson Depy Provl Surveyor.
Col ms 127 x 51 cm 1" to 40 chains
Shows the area from Boyd Twp to Fitzgerald and White twps; river surveyed in three sections with observation points marked; rapids, trails.
OTAR (SR 6026)

---

588 *1845*
Diagram of a Section of the Petawawe River, Scaled in June 1845 By J.J. Roney P.L.S.
Col ms 47 x 73 cm 1" to 40 chains
Shows the area south of Cedar L to Peter's L and L Dawson, and to Little Nipissing L south of area shown on Robertson's survey (**587**).
OTAR (SR 7275)

---

589 *1845*
Diagram of Surveys Performed on the Ottawa, between the months of Jany & April 1845. In accordance with Instructions from Crown Timber Office, Bytown. J.J. Roney D.P.S.
Col ms 65 x 79 cm 1" to 80 chains
Shows surveys along Bissett Creek, Grant Creek, and Bennett's Creek in and near Maria Twp; names of timber licensees, tree types, relief.
OTAR (SR 7068B)

---

590 *1845*
General Plan of the vicinity of the Chats' Rapids, Ottawa River. From a survey by [Sgd] Thomas Keefer C.E. Office of the Board of Works, 1845.
Col ms 136 x 117 cm 1" to 20 chains Endorsements: stamps 'BW' '478'
Inset: 'Enlarged Plan of the Mississippi Snye with the Bar at the entrance of the River Mississippi' 1" to 275 ft; shows Fitzroy Twp, Chats L and Chaudière L on the Ottawa R; shows steamboat route and ferry connection and proposed roads to landings; proposed dam and timber slides shown on the Mississippi Snye; also another similar map with same title but showing only the lower half (endorsed stamp: '488')(NMC 19514); (Holmden 2289).
OOAMA (NMC 11839, 19514)

Related maps

(2) *1845*
Plan of the Mississippi Snye, And the Portages and Ferry connecting the Navigation From Lake Chaudiere to the Chats' Lake. Compiled from the Original and Partial Surveys. Office of the Board of Works 1845.
Col ms 76 x 110 cm 1" to 12 chains Endorsements: stamps 'BW' '538'
'Profile from the Mouth of the Snye to the Site of the Dam.' 1" to 10 ft vertical; shows high and low water levels 1845, Fitzroy Harbour with bldgs, roads, relief; notes on obstructions and surveys by Walton and Nagle; (Holmden 2283).
OOAMA (NMC 14278)

(3) *1845*
Mississippi Chenail [and] Profile of the Mississippi Snye 1845.

Col mss, 2 sheets and profile 30 x 102 cm, 37 x 93 cm, 23 x 75 cm 1" to 275 ft and 1" to 20 chains, 1" to 12 ft vertical Endorsements: '521'
From Chaudière L to L des Chats on the Ottawa R; shows dams, rapids, falls; side cuttings and excavations to create channel near the rapids; water level as of 'Oct 45.'
OOAMA (NMC 21720–1)

---

591 *[1847]*
Map of Bissetts Creek. Surveyed under instructions from the Crown Land Deptt by Hugh Falls D.P.S.
Col ms 60 x 43 cm 1" to 40 chains Endorsements: '47'
(SI 23 Feb 1847 to H. Falls to survey Bissett and Bennett's creeks [Maria Twp]; OTAR FN 49 Sept 1847).
OTAR (SR 6021)

Related maps

(2) *[1847]*
Plan of Bennetts Creek Surveyed by Hugh Falls P.L.S.
Col ms 45 x 44 cm 1" to 40 chains Endorsements: '48'
(OTAR FN 49 Sept 1847); shows 13 miles of creek beginning at its mouth at the Ottawa R.
OTAR (SR 7138)

---

592 *1847*
Plan and Survey of the River Madawaska a tributary of the Ottawa beyond the Surveyed Lands commencing at the Southwesterly boundary of the Township of Blithfield under Instructions bearing date 19th January 1847 [Sgd] Duncan McDonell, Greenfield Dy Provl Surveyor.
Col ms 74 x 437 cm [2" to 1 mile]
(OTAR FN 511 29 Nov 1847); shows the area from Blithfield Twp to Bark L and Opeongo L; stations for observations marked, bearings, falls, rapids, and other rivers noted; names of squatters.
OTAR (SR 11070)

---

593 *1847*
Plan of Part of the Mattawan and Amable du Fonts Rivers Surveyed under instructions from the Crown Land Department by Duncan Sinclair DPS [Sgd] July 16th 1847 Duncan Sinclair Provl Survr.
Col ms 165 x 65 cm 1" to 40 chains Endorsements: 'No 43' '3094/47'
(SI 30 Jan 1847; OTAR FN 1992 14 July 1847); shows L Manitou and the Amable du Fond R to its junction with the Mattawa R; falls, mileages along river, mill sites, shanties, tree types; part of the survey of the Mattawa and its tributaries.
OTAR (SR 7062)

Related maps

(2) *1848*
Plan of the River Mattawan and its Tributaries Surveyed under Instructions from the Crown Land Department. By Duncan Sinclair P.L.S. [Sgd] Duncan Sinclair Provincial Land Surveyor Carillon June 21st 1848.
Col ms 200 x 193 cm 1" to 40 chains
(OTAR FN 1991 24 June 1848); the finished plan of the whole survey; shows the survey of the Mattawa R from Trout L to the Ottawa R and tributaries Amable du Fond R, Potois Creek, Kaibushokang R, and Maskinonge R; relief, mileages, traverse lines along rivers.
OTAR (SR 92315)

---

594 *1847*
Sketch of Part of Ottawa & Pettewauwe Rivers. Pettewauwe River February 27th 1847.
Col ms 54 x 42 cm 1" to 40 chains Endorsements: '1019/47'
(SI 19 Jan 1847 to J.R. McDonell to survey the Petawawa R may relate to this plan); shows the area at the junction of the Petawawa and Ottawa rivers; shows some bldgs and cleared land.
OTAR (SR 3185)

---

595 *1847*
York River Surveyed and drawn by [Sgd] Thomas Devine P.S. Montreal 5th June 18[47].
Col ms 78 x 133 cm 1" to 40 chains Endorsements: '42'
(SI 19 Jan 1847; OTAR FN 1994 27 Apr 1847); shows area from its mouth at the Madawaska R to mile 40 and also part of Little Mississippi R and Egan's R; rapids; mill sites; clearings.
OTAR (SR 7090)

---

596 *1848*
Plan of a Survey of Exploration & Road extending Northwesterly from the Settlement in the rear of the Township of Madoc in the Victoria District to a distance of eighty miles towards the Ottawa River by P.V. Elmore, P.L.S. Belleville July 1848.
Col ms 76 x 410 cm 1" to 40 chains Endorsements: 'Z37'
(SI 8 July 1847; OTNR FN 862 10 Aug 1848); the original exploratory survey for the Hastings Rd; road line is shown with deviations from Madoc to [Airy and Murchison twps] passing Bell's and Haslett's exploring lines; notes on construction needed.
OTAR (SR 7819)

Related maps

(2) *1852*
Plan of a Tier of Lots laid out from the Rear Boundary of the Township of Madoc towards the Ottawa River by P.V. Elmore P.L.S. 1851 and 1852.
Col ms, pt missing 45 x 377 cm Scale not given Endorsements: 'B40'
(SI 22 Jan 1851; OTNR FN 2214 30 Dec 1854); lots laid out from Wollaston and Limerick to Airy and Murchison twps; part to south missing.
OTNR (SR 1298)

(3) *1862*
Plan of the new line for the Hastings Road in Tudor C.W. [Sgd] John A. Snow Provl Land Surveyor Hull December 23rd 1862.
Col ms 83 x 258 cm 1" to 10 chains
From Millbridge to con XIX in Tudor; swamps, clearings; shows new line to replace old line on the west side of twp.
OTAR (SR 8474)

(4) *1863*
Plan of the Hastings Road extending from the southern boundary of Tudor to the northern boundary of Monteagle By [Sgd] J.J. Haslett P.L.S. April 20th 1863.
Col ms 47 x 270 cm 1" to 40 chains Endorsements: 'R58a'
The south part of the road with lot nos is shown; mill and village site on the York R in Faraday Twp; date on map is in pencil.
OTNR (SR 6572)

(5) *1864*
Plan of Lots on Elmore's Road Line Department of Crown Lands Quebec May 1864 [Sgd] Andrew Russell Asst Commissioner. Belleville Augst 5 1864 [Sgd] Henry A.F. MacLeod Provl Land Surveyor.
Col ms 44 x 380 cm 1" to 40 chains
(OTNR FN 2225 5 Aug 1864); from Tudor and Lake twps to Airy and Murchison twps; replanted posts marked; note about error on original survey.
OTNR (SR 4744)

---

597 *1848*
A Plan of the River Mississippi and its branches from the Township of Palmerston to their respective sources Surveyed by John S. Harper P.L.S. 1848 Examined A.R. [Sgd] J.S. Harper P.L.S.
Col ms 100 x 132 cm 1" to 40 chains
(SI 19 Jan 1847); a south fork is shown from Palmerston Twp by Cross L to Clarendon L, and two northerly forks are shown ending in Mazinaw L; traverse lines and stations marked; mileages; mill sites; a few comments on rocks and trees.
OTAR (SR 10901)

---

598 *1848*
Plan of the survey of the westerly part of an Exploring Line Extending from the Bathurst to the Home District with the Survey of the Road and Township Divisions Executed in connection therewith. [Sgd] Bytown 6th September 1848 Robert Bell Provl L Surveyor.
Col ms 440 x 73 cm 1" to 40 chains Endorsements: 'Bell's Road line'
(SI 9 July 1847 to survey and lay off double cons fronting on line; OTAR FN 1895 6 Sept 1848); line is shown following best ground, and twps I–VII north and south of line are marked [from Sabine and McClure to Macaulay and Draper twps] from Bark L west to Home District boundary; 'town site' [Muskoka Falls] shown at Great Falls.
OTAR (SR 7525)

Related maps

(2) *1848*
Plan of the Eastern part of a line of road and exploration extending from the Bathurst District to the Home District Surveyed by John J. Haslett P.Ld. Surveyor 1848.
Col ms 83 x 295 cm 1" to 40 chains
(SI 9 July 1847; OTAR FN 928 May 1848); shows survey line from west boundary of Bromley Twp through twp V to twp I north and south of the road line [Wilberforce and Grattan to Lyell and Wicklow twps]; line deviates around obstructions to mile 219; notes on land, trees, mill and village sites, relief, swamps, squatters; straight exploring line also shown; the Bell/Haslett line was not developed as a road.
OTAR (SR 7104)

---

599 *1848*
Sketch D shewing the projected townships adjacent to the Midland & Bathurst Districts. Crown Land Department Surveyor's Office West Montreal May 1848.
Col ms 40 x 38 cm Scale not given
Originally accompanied a memo from J.H. Price, commissioner of crown lands, to the Governor General 17 June 1848 requesting permission to open the 'wastelands' for settlement in twps and road lots (OOA RG 1 L3 C4 no 251 (1848)); shows two north-south tiers of twps to be developed west of Admaston and Bromley twps; Bell's line and Elmore's exploring lines shown; (Holmden 1971).
OOAMA (NMC 3045)

---

600 *1848*
Survey of the Bonnechere River Montreal 22nd July 1848 By [Sgd] J McNaughton Provl Surveyor.
Col ms 98 x 324 cm 1" to 40 chains
(SI 29 Jan 1847; OTAR FN 797 24 July 1848); shows area from Bromley Twp to Golden L, Round L to beyond Opeongo L and to J.J. Roney's surveyed line; traverse lines and mileage points; relief, swamps, settlers, trails marked; Hudson's Bay Co. post on Golden L.
OTAR (SR 7931)

---

601 *1850*
Sketch B [showing projected means of communication between the Ottawa River and Lake Huron] Crown Lands Department Toronto 6th Decr 1850 [Sgd] J.H. Price Comr of Crown Lands.
Col ms 45 x 56 cm Scale not given
Originally accompanied a memo to the Governor General requesting permission to develop a road from the Ottawa R to Opeongo L to open up the area for lumbering and settlement (OOA RG 1 L3 S6 no 19 (1850)); shows road line with a branch to Bell's line; also shows a tract at rear of Palmerston and Clarendon twps to be detached from the Midland District and attached to the Bathurst District;

Elmore's line is shown opening communication from the old settlements; free-grant road lots are mentioned in the memo; (Holmden 2518).
OOAMA (NMC 2884)

---

602 *1852*
Plan of the Southern Limit of the Tract annexed to the United Counties of Lanark and Renfrew C.W. by 12 Vic. Cap 94 Montreal 31st March 1852 [Sgd] A. Wells Provl Survr Examined [Sgd] A Russell.
Col ms 33 x 101 cm 1" to 40 chains Endorsements: 'B35'
(SI 29 March 1851; OTAR FN 1924 31 March 1852); shows boundary between Miller, Clarendon, S Canonto, and Palmerston twps.
OTAR (SR 5805)

Related maps

(**2**) *1853*
Plan of the Western Limit of the Tract Annexed to the United Counties of Lanark and Renfrew (southern section) by 12 Vic. Cap. 49 Montreal 31st March 1852 [Sgd] A. Wells Provl Survr Examined [Sgd] A Russell.
Col ms 32 x 192 cm 1" to 40 chains Endorsements: 'B36'
(OTAR FN 1924 31 March 1924); from the north end of Clarendon and Barrie twps to Brudenell and Sebastopol twps and Bell's line; relief, swamps, other exploratory survey lines.
OTAR (SR 5801)

(**3**) *1853*
Plan of part of the outlines of the Counties of Lanark & Renfrew Surveyed under instructions from the Comr of Crown Lands dated 15th October 1852, Point Fortune July 25th 1853 [Sgd] Duncan Sinclair Provl Land Surveyor Examined A.R.
Col ms 294 x 127 cm 1" to 40 chains Endorsements: 'B 44'
(SI 15 Oct 1852 to Sinclair to complete Wells's survey of tract, prolong boundary to the Ottawa R, and survey south bank; OTAR FN 1682 28 July 1853); shows the area from the northern part of the western boundary of S and N Algona twps to the Ottawa R; notes on land and timber; relief.
OTAR (SR 37756)

(**4**) *1853*
Part of the Ottawa River from the Joachim down. Surveyed April 1853 by [Sgd] Duncan Sinclair P.L.S. Point Fortune Augst 7th 1853. A true copy [Sgd] Duncan Sinclair P.L.S.
Col ms 101 x 37 cm 1" to 40 chains Endorsements: '4956/53'
Mileage markers start at mile IV at the Joachim and go south to mile XXII; some bldgs and names of settlers.
OTAR

---

603 *1852*
Plan of the Survey of the Ottawa & Opeongo Road Bytown 16th August 1852 [Sgd] Robert Bell P.L. Surveyor. Section No. 1 [Opeongo Lake east to mile 26] ... Section No. 2 [Mile 27 to mile 50] ... Section no. 3 [Mile 57 to mile 99 at Ottawa River]
3 col mss 66 x approx 300 cm 1" to 40 chains Endorsements: 'B38' 'B39' 'B40'
(SI 23 Dec 1850; OTNR FN 2203 16 Aug 1852); exploring line with mileages, relief, swamps, type of trees; lots laid out along road, lot sizes shown.
OTNR (SR 7159; 7180)

Related maps

(**2**) *1854*
Plan of the Survey of the Ottawa & Opeongo Road, (From Lake Opeongo to the 27th mile of the Survey of 1851 & 2) and Shewing the Proposed Village Site at Lake Opeongo. [Sgd] Bytown 10th May 1854 – A.H. Sims [and] Part of the Ottawa & Opeongo Road. From the 27th Mile to the 57th Mile. Ottawa & Huron Roads Bytown 10th June 1854. [Sgd] A.H. Sims Supt.
2 col mss 67 x 149 cm and 66 x 159 cm 1" to 40 chains Endorsements: 'Z 46' 'Z 48'
(OTNR FN 2230 10 May 1834); shows relief, vegetation, lots, exploring line and distances; profile of the Madawaska R; note indicates change in road route to a crossing at the narrows instead of at the south end of Opeongo L.
OTAR OTNR (SR 6419)

(**3**) *1864*
A part of the Townships of Sherwood Radcliffe Hagarty & Brudenell Shewing the lots fronting on the Ottawa and Opeongo Road. [Sgd] Pembroke February 2nd 1864 William Bell Provl Land Surveyor.
Col ms 56 x 88 cm 1" to 20 chains Endorsements: 'R34'
(OTNR FN 2205 31 Dec 1863, FN 2208 4 Feb 1864); shows deviation of 'present road' from original line; shows lot numbers, dimensions, and sizes; cleared lands, swamps, beaver meadows.
OTNR (SR 6553)

---

604 *1853*
Map of exploration of French River and Lake Nipissing Shewing Indian Reserves Nos: IX, X and XIII under the treaty of Septbr 9th A.D. 1850. [Sgd] J. Stoughton Dennis P.L.S. Weston 14th May 1853.
Col ms 57 x 84 cm 1" to 3 miles Endorsements: 'L.H. No 27'
Shows reserves with names of bands, villages, cornfields, rapids, falls, types of tree, and relief; survey notes.
OTNR (SR 2413)

---

605 *1853*
Mattawan & Nipissing Road Surveyed under instructions dated Crown Lands Office 16th Septbr 1853. Point Fortune December 17th 1853 [Sgd] Duncan Sinclair Provl Land Surveyor. Examined A.R.
Col ms 72 x 250 cm 1" to 40 chains Endorsements: 'Z 39' 'CLO 7708/53'

(OTAR FN 2234 17 Dec 1853); shows road line from the Ottawa R south of the Mattawa R to L Nipissing; relief, swamps; another proposed road line is shown further south.
OTAR (SR 8208)

Related maps

(2) *1855*
Plan of the Mattawan-Nipissing Road with the Subdivision of Lots thereon. Surveyed under Instructions from the Crown Land Department dated 3rd July 1854 by [Sgd] Duncan Sinclair Provl Land Surv Point Fortune July 31st 1855.
Col ms 71 x 216 cm 1" to 40 chains Endorsements: 'Z 53'
Shows lines run and those still to be run; road lots laid out and numbered from Papineau Twp to L Nipissing; also shows three proposed twps: Collins (including a town plot), Chewett, and Nipissing; mill sites and three branch road lines running west from Collins Twp also shown.
OTAR (SR 7307)

(3) *1856*
Mattawan Nipissing Roads and Farm Lots Surveyed in 1855 & 6 under instructions dated 3rd July 1854 by D. Sinclair [Sgd] Ottawa Augt 5th 1856 Duncan Sinclair Provl Land Surveyor.
Col ms 87 x 251 cm 1" to 40 chains Endorsements: '361'
(OTAR FN 2235 5 Aug 1856); shows the three-prong road system continuing to L Nipissing but no road lots laid out at that end; exploring line from Opeongo L shown and a survey line to the south parallel to road line; the survey grid for the three roads was later rescinded.
OTAR (SR 8535)

---

606 *[1853]*
Plan shewing the Survey of a line for Road from the Township of Hinchinbrooke to the River Madawaska. Examined [Sgd] A.R.
Col ms 128 x 74 cm 1" to 2 miles Endorsements: 'Z38'
Probably by Thomas Gibbs; (SI 11 Oct 1852; OTNR FN 2239 1853); shows the area from Kingston to the Madawaska R with road connections in the south; lots laid out along surveyed road line [Frontenac Rd] from Hinchinbrooke to Miller and Matawatchan twps; comments on land and trees.
OTAR (SR 7071)

Related maps

(2) *1859*
Survey of parts of the townships of Hinchinbrooke, Olden and Clarendon, on the Frontenac Road C.W. Part I ... Survey of the South Westerly Parts of the Township of Miller and Matawatchan, on the line For Road leading from the County of Frontenac, to the Madawaska River, C.W. Part II [both Sgd] Thomas Fraser Gibbs Provl Surveyor Kingston 11th June 1859.
2 col mss 202 x 65 cm and 64 x 238 cm 1" to 40 chains Endorsements: 'No 10' '1215/60' 'No 11'
(SI 19 Apr 1858 to lay out free-grant lots on road in Clarendon, Miller, and Matawatchan, and to survey side roads from Olden to Madawaska R; OTNR FN 1306, FN 1479 1859); shows free-grant lots, all twps laid out, relief, vegetation along survey lines; 'newly opened road from Mississippi' in Miller Twp.
OTNR (SR 6551; 6577)

(3) *1865*
Plan shewing part of Frontenac Road Line. June 26th 1865 [Sgd] Thos Byrne P.L. Surveyor.
Col ms 40 x 76 cm 1" to 40 chains Endorsements: '9579/65'
Shows the road from Brule L to Madawaska R in Miller and Matawatchan twps.
OTNR (SR 6574)

---

607 *1853*
Topographical View of the Country lying Southward of Muskako River. [Sgd] James W. Bridgland P.L. Surveyor Toronto January 31st 1853. Examined A.R.
Col ms 85 x 105 cm 1" to 100 chains Endorsements: 'B56'
(SI 2 Jan 1852 to explore for a road line north to Muskoka R); shows exploring lines from the Talbot R to Muskoka R and a line south of Muskoka R running west to Georgian Bay; swamps, tree types, comments on land; shows L Couchiching, Severn R, Orillia, and Indian village.
OTAR (SR 11085)

Related maps

(2) *1853*
View of the Harbour at the Mouth of Muskako River [Sgd] James W. Bridgland P.L. Surveyor Toronto Feb 4th 1853.
Col ms 54 x 75 cm 1" to 5 chains Endorsements: 'B57'
Relief, traverse lines, channel to Severn R.
OTAR (SR 5775)

---

608 *1854*
Part of the Ottawa and Huron Tract, Shewing the Projected Roads from the Ottawa [Sgd] Bytown 1st June 1854 A.H. Sims.
Col ms 83 x 160 cm 1" to 4 miles Endorsements: 'Z52'
Inset: 'Huron & Ottawa Tract' [southwest part] 1" to 14 miles; shows Bell's Rd line, Elmore's Rd line [Hastings Rd], Ottawa and Opeongo, Pembroke and Mattawan, and Nipissing and Mattawan road lines; proposed line from the latter to the mouth of the French R, exploring line from Opeongo L to L Nipissing, and proposed line from Opeongo L to the mouth of the Magnetawan R.
OTAR (SR 6056)

---

609 *1854*
Plan of part of York River, commencing at the Floodwood Jam. [Sgd] John A. Snow Provl Land Surveyor Hull July 14th 1854.
Col ms 67 x 180 cm 1" to 40 chains Endorsements: 'No 58' '4927/55'
Shows the area on the river from east of Elmore's Rd line to Bell's line; traverse lines, mileage points, trails, notes on land and timber; portage route to Otonabee R system.
OTAR (SR 7082)

Related maps

(2) *1854*
Plan of part of the Madawaska River [Sgd] John A. Snow Provl Land Surveyor Hull July 14th 1854.
Col ms 67 x 202 cm 1" to 40 chains Endorsements: 'No 56'
(OTNR FN 1987 8 Aug 1854); shows area from Elmore's Rd line [Hastings Rd] west to Lake of Two Rivers, Cache L, and L Caroline; shows connections south via Otter Creek to the York R; traverse lines.
OTAR (SR 7078)

---

610 *1854*
Plan of the River Petawawa, From its mouth to a mile above the 3rd Chute. With the position of Town Plot, Mill Sites etc. Surveyed under Instructions from the Commissioner of Crown Lands, Dated Quebec 18th Feby 1854. L'Orignal 18th Sept 1854 [Sgd] Robert Hamilton Prov. Land Surveyor. Exd A.R.
Col ms 69 x 88 cm 1" to 8 chains Endorsements: 'B45'
Inset: 'Profile of the River Petawawa From its mouth to a mile above the 3rd Chute' 1" to 8 chains, 1" to 20 ft vertical; (OTNR FN 1643 18 Feb 1854); four mill sites, town plot [Petawawa] at mouth of river, with a few clearings and bldgs; dams, booms; also a copy at OTAR (SR 7088) endorsed 'Copy ... Millsites etc [Sgd] Andrew Russell Assistant Commissioner Department of Crown Lands Quebec 15th April 1861'; similar to the earlier plan but lacks profile and some notes.
OTAR (SR 7088) OTNR (SR 7305)

---

611 *1854*
Plan of the Survey of the Pembroke & Matawan Road (from the River Matawan to Deux Joachim) [Sgd] John A. Snow Provl Land Surveyor Hull February 4th 1854. Examined A.R. [and] Plan of the Survey of the Pembroke & Mattawan Road (from near Pembroke to Deux Joachim.) Ottawa & Huron Roads Bytown 1st June 1854 [Sgd] A.H. Sims Survr.
2 col mss 68 x 286 cm and 56 x 224 cm 1" to 40 chains Endorsements: 'Z41' 'C.L.D. 1082/54'
(SI 16 Sept 1853; OTNR FN 2231 16 March 1854); titles of maps are typeset and printed; shows routes considered, relief, comments on trees and land; lots are shown on the north part; the south part was surveyed partly by R. Hamilton and partly by A.H. Sims; sources for the outlines of rivers are noted.
OTNR (SR 6368; 8219)

Related maps

(2) *1863*
Plan of Lots on Part of the Mattawan and Pembroke Road City of Ottawa February 1863 [Sgd] Duncan Sinclair Provl Land Surveyor.
Col ms 37 x 111 cm 1" to 40 chains Endorsements: 'R29'
(SI 28 July 1862 to retrace road line between Maria Twp and mouth of the Mattawa R; OTNR FN 2237 17 Feb 1863); road lots and road shown from Papineau Twp to Clara Twp; contents of lots.
OTNR (SR 1595)

---

612 *1855*
[Lake Nipissing and connecting rivers] Copied from Mr. Logan's Map Scale 1 mile to one Inch Crown Land Department Quebec 23d July 1855 T.D. [Sgd] Joseph Cauchon Commr Crown Land
Col ms 81 x 117 cm 1" to 1 mile
Falls and rapids marked; longitude and latitude lines drawn in; some notes on rock types; copied from the surveys of Logan and Murray between 1845 and 1854 (Zaslow, 44, 50–3).
OTAR (SR 5999)

Related maps

(2) *[1855?]*
[Muskoka River] Drawn by [Sgd] T.Devine C.L.O.
Col ms 92 x 124 cm [Approx 1" to 1' latitude]
Endorsements: 'No 45'
Shows similar information to that above with notes on timber and some relief; shows the area from Lake of Bays west to L Muskoka and L Huron; note about the position of Capt Bayfield's lines of longitude 'which we have the authority of Capt. Bayfield to state are 4' too far west.'; possibly related to ms plans for **622(2)** surveyed 1853.
OTAR (SR 7897)

---

613 *[1855?]*
[Map of the French River between Lake Huron and Lake Nipissing]
Col ms 27 x 99 cm Scale not given
Dated from note: 'Copied for Crown Timber Office January 23rd 1856'; shows falls and rapids, which are numbered; currents, heights of falls.
OTAR

---

614 *1855*
Plan of Islands in the River Otanabee and its lakes Surveyed by John J. Haslett Provincial Ld Surveyor A.D. 1855 Part I ... [Part II].
2 col mss 132 x 91 cm and 122 x 135 cm 1" to 40 chains Endorsements: 'No 61' 'No 62'
(SI 6 Nov 1854 to survey islands in Trent R, and Otonabee R and lakes system, and estimate value; OTNR FN 2170 10 Dec 1855); Part I locates islands

in Somerville, Fenelon, and Verulam twps, and Part II, in Douro, Smith, Ennismore, Dummer, Burleigh, and Harvey twps; islands numbered and sometimes named; settlements.
OTNR (SR 8034; 16087)

Related maps

(2) *1863*
Copy of part of Haslett's Plan of Islands in the River Otanabee and its lakes. Depart. of Crown Lands Quebec April 21st 1863 [Sgd] Andrew Russell Assist. Commr.
Col ms 70 x 118 cm 1" to 40 chains
A copy of Part II; also a copy at OOAMA (NMC 3160) probably made in the 1860s, endorsed 'Copy of part of P.L.S. John Haslett's Plan of Islands in the Otanabee'and showing Iron's Is, Fox Is, and others in the west end of Buckhorn L.
OOAMA (NMC 3160) OTNR (SR 7202)

---

615 *1855*
Plan of part of York River and its Southern Tributaries, Egan's River, Hudson's Creek & Allen's Creek together with the Head Waters of the E. & W. Branches of Crow River & Buckhorn Branch of Ottanabe River, Tributaries to the St. Lawrence [Sgd] John A. Snow Provl Land Surveyor Hull May 1st 1855.
Col ms 67 x 195 cm 1" to 40 chains Endorsements: 'No 59'
Title is typeset and printed; includes a greater area on the east and the south than the 1854 survey; traverse lines, notes on land, trees, relief; some settlers named.
OTAR (SR 7091)

Related maps

(2) *1855*
Plan of the Head Waters of the Madawaska River, and the Head Waters of the Muskoka River, A Tributary to Georgian Bay. [Sgd] John A. Snow Provl Land Surveyor Hull May 1st 1855.
Col ms 66 x 149 cm 1" to 40 chains Endorsements: 'No 57'
(OTNR FN 1986 44:120); shows the area from Galeary L west to South R, L Louisa, north branch Muskoka R to Lake of Two Rivers, and the middle and south branches of the Muskoka R ending in L Travers [Smoke L]; printed title.
OTAR (SR 6043)

(3) *1855*
Plan of Papineau Creek, A Tributary to the York River. [Sgd] John A. Snow Provl Land Surveyor Hull May 1st 1855.
Col ms 68 x 100 cm 1" to 40 chains Endorsements: 'No 60'
Shows the area from the York R to L St Peter near Bell's line.
OTAR (SR 7081)

---

616 *1856*
Map of Line Run Northerly from Burleigh Rapids in the County of Peterborough Shewing the Country explored. February 9th 1856 [Sgd] John Reid Provl Land Surveyor. Examined 31 March 1856 [Sgd] Thos Devine.
Col ms 151 x 56 cm 1" to 40 chains Endorsements: 'Z 55' '1998/56'
(SI 23 Nov 1854 to M. Deane (later J. Reid) to survey an exploring line from Burleigh Rapids to Elmore's line; OTAR FN 1915 15 Feb 1856); shows the line run north from Burleigh Rapids for 55 miles.
OTAR (SR 7820)

Related maps

(2) *1861*
Burleigh Road [Sgd] James W. Fitzgerald Prov. Land Surveyor Peterboro Sept 12th 1861.
Col ms 265 x 106 cm 1" to 40 chains Endorsements: 'PH 257' 'B 13'
(SI 9 Aug 1860 and 24 Dec 1860 to survey road from Burleigh Rapids to Peterson Rd line; OTNR FN 2215 9 Sept 1851); shows road line running through Burleigh, Anstruther, Chandos, Monmouth, Cardiff, and Dudley twps; comments on land, swamps, relief.
OTNR (SR 17507)

---

617 *1856*
Map of the North Shore Georgian Bay shewing the position of the various islands examined for the Indian Department 1856. [Sgd] Toronto Decr 1st 1856 Napier & Herrick P.L.S.
Col ms 74 x 68 cm Scale not given
Provenance: OOAMA RG 10M 76703/9 no 128; shows the area around Parry Is and harbour; relief; clearings, rivers; main islands named; there is also a map in OTAR that is possibly a copy made in 1876 and annotated 'tracing compared 29/3/76 P.B.S.'
OOAMA (NMC 12974) OTAR

---

618 *1856*
Map of the outlines of the Townships of Abinger Effingham Denbigh and Ashby. Ernesttown April 22nd 1856 [Sgd] A.B. Perry P.L.S. Wm. R. Rombough P.L.S.
Col ms 125 x 71 cm 1" to 80 chains Endorsements: 'Z59'
(SI 24 Oct 1854 to Perry, 22 July 1855 to Wm Rombough; OTNR FN 902 22 Apr 1856, FN 2227 22 Apr 1856); also shows Anglesea subdivided and Barrie not subdivided; road lots along Addington Rd; notes on tree types and land capability; notes on earlier surveys.
OTNR (SR 6726)

---

619 *1856 (1864)*
Ottawa and Georgian Bay Railway Exploration. Note The above Exploration was made by the undersigned in the year 1856 at the Instance of Walter Shanly Esquire the object being as set forth

in his letter of Instructions dated 27th September 1856 'rather for the purpose of ascertaining the Nature of the Country as respects its adaptability to settlement than with any view to establishing facts bearing on the feasibility of Railway Construction' and this plan is hereby certified to be an accurate copy of the original supplied to Mr Shanly. Toronto, December 12th 1864 [Sgd] B.W. Gossage P.L. Surveyor
Col ms 61 x 591 cm 1" to 1/2 mile
Shows the main survey line beginning at Georgian Bay and intersecting with the Magnetawan R at several points then touching Opeongo L and east from there to the Ottawa R; shows mileages, types of land and vegetation with comments; also shows north-south sidelines explored.
OTAR (SR 11064)

---

620 *1856*
Plan Camden & Madawaska Road Lots. Ernesttown April 22nd 1856 [Sgd] A.B. Perry Provincial Land Surveyor. Examined [Sgd] A. Russell
Col ms part missing 218 x 67 cm 1" to 40 chains
Endorsements: 'Z 58'
Inset: 'Plan of Part of Addington Road'; (SI 16 Sept 1853 to examine road line traced by Birdsall, and return on Gibb Frontenac Rd line, consider if both roads should be used; 24 Oct 1854 to lay out lots on road line and outlines of twps; OTNR FN 2227 19 Aug 1856); shows Addington Rd line with lots from north boundary of Kaladar Twp to Ashby, Denbigh, and Lyndoch twps; comments on land and trees.
OTNR (SR 8220)

Related maps

(2) *[1856]*
The Addington Road. [Endorsed title]: 'Lots on the Addington Road A.B. Perry.'
Col ms 46 x 188 cm 1" to 40 chains Endorsements: 'Z 56'
Similar to other map but not in the same hand; notes about locations and copying to 15 May 1856; refers to above plan as the original.
OTNR (SR 4582)

---

621 *1856*
Plan of an Exploration Line on South side of the French River between Lakes Nipissing and Huron Surveyed under instructions from the Crown Lands Department dated 23rd Jany 1856. By [Sgd] Duncan Sinclair P.L.S. Toronto May 19th 1856.
Col ms 68 x 356 cm 1" to 40 chains Endorsements: 'Z 60'
(OTAR FN 1909 30 May 1856); shows swamps, relief, portages, notes on Indian reserves.
OTAR (SR 7182)

Related maps

(2) *1857*
Copy of Sinclair's Plan of an Exploration Line on South Side of the French River between Lakes Nipissing and Huron Crown Lands Department Toronto 31st July 1857 Certified a true copy Assist Commissr of Crown Lands.
Col ms 68 x 337 cm 1" to 40 chains
Shows the line with mileage points but lacks notes and survey data.
OTAR (SR 7207)

---

622 *1857*
GEOLOGICAL SURVEY OF CANADA. / Sir Wm E. Logan F.R.S. Director. / INDEX OF THE PLANS, / SHOWING THE EXPLORATIONS / between the / EAST SHORE OF LAKE HURON / and the / OTTAWA. / G. Matthew's Litho. Montreal
Print (lith) 29 x 51 cm 1" to 10 miles
In Geological Survey of Canada, *Report of Progress for the Years 1853–54–55–56* (Toronto: John Lovell 1857), opp 86; later assigned GSC publication no 15 (Ferrier, 9); shows the sheet layout for the surveys of the Magnetawan, Muskoka, and Petawawa rivers, and the Bonnechere R to Gull L system; (Holmden 2799); the individual plans were issued in *Plans of Various Lakes and Rivers between Lake Huron and the River Ottawa, to Accompany the Geological Reports for 1853–54–55–56*. (Toronto: John Lovell 1857) (see **881** for French R, L Nipissing, Mattawa R, and part of Ottawa R).

The plans are as follows:

(1) GEOLOGICAL SURVEY OF CANADA / Sir Wm E. Logan F.R.S. Director // TOPOGRAPHICAL PLAN / OF THE / RIVER BONNECHERE & S.W. BRANCH OF THE MADAWASKA / WITH / A SKETCH OF THE / HEADWATERS OF THE OTTONABEE / by A. Murray Esq. / Asst Provl Geologist / 1853 / G. Matthews' Lith. Montreal. / Sheet 1 ... Sheet 2 ... Sheet 3 ... Sheet 4
4 prints (liths) Ea 56 x 86 cm 1" to 80 chains
Shows the Bonnechere R from Chats L on the Ottawa R to Clear L and Golden L; shows also the Madawaska R, Shawashkong R [York R] to Papineau L and southwest to Drag L, and Gull L and R system to Balsam L; comments on geology, land, timber, and soils; these plans were later assigned GSC publication nos 35–8 (Ferrier, 10); (*OHIM* 5.3). OOAMA (NMC 21453–6)

(2) GEOLOGICAL SURVEY OF CANADA / Sir Wm E Logan F.R.S. Director // TOPOGRAPHICAL PLAN / OF THE / RIVERS MUSKOKA & PETEWAHWEH / by A. Murray Esqr. / Asst Provl. Geologist. / 1853. / G. Matthews Lith. Montreal. / Sheet 1 ... Sheet 2 ... Sheet 3 ... Sheet 4 ... Sheet 5
5 prints (liths) Ea 56 x 86 cm 1" to 80 chains
Shows L Huron to L Muskoka and Muskoka R, Marys L to Oxtongue L, Canoe L to Petawawa R at Cedar L and down the river to Upper Allumette on the Ottawa R; falls, rapids, types of rock, bearings, dates of encampments; GSC publication nos 30–4 (Ferrier, 10); (Holmden 2537–41).
OOAMA (NMC 21448–52)

(3) GEOLOGICAL SURVEY OF CANADA / Sir WM E. Logan F.R.S. Director // TOPOGRAPHICAL PLAN / OF THE / RIVER MEGANATAWAN / by A. Murray Esq. / Asst Provl Geologist. / 1854 / G. Matthews Lith. Montreal / Sheet 1 ... Sheet 2
Prints (liths), 3 maps on 2 sheets Ea 56 x 86 cm 1" to 80 chains
Shows the Magnetawan R from its mouth at L Huron to [Sand L]; shows the same information as the other plans; GSC publication nos 28–9 (Ferrier, 10); (Holmden 2535–6). OOAMA (NMC 21446–7) OOAMA (NMC 21446–56) OTAR USDLC

Related maps

(2) *[1853–7]*
[Topographical maps of the Muskoka, Petawawa and Bonnechere Rivers A. Murray]
12 ms Ea approx 65 x 90 cm 1" to 80 chains
These are final drawings for the printed plans nos (1) and (2) above (GSC publication nos 30–8) but in 12 sheets.
OOAMA (RG 45M 83403/21 B 30–8)

---

623 *1857*
Map of Exploration in the rear of the County of Victoria Part I [Sgd] M. Deane P.L.S. Lindsay 21st April 1857 Examined 26 Feby 1856 [i.e., 1858] T. Devine ... Part II [Sgd] M. Deane P.L.S. Lindsay 25th April 1857. Examined May 30th 1857 J.W.B.
2 col mss 190 x 55 cm and 55 x 150 cm 1" to 40 chains Endorsements: 'Z 54' 'Z 62'
(SI 23 Oct 1854 to J. Reid (transferred to Dean 15 Nov 1854) to run line from Somerville to Bell's line; OTNR FN 1926); Pt I [Bobcaygeon Rd] shows road line and lots through Lutterworth and Snowdon twps to Hindon and Stanhope twps and Bell's line with survey data and deviations; Pt II shows an exploring line [Bell's line?] running west on a bearing of N 72 W to the Muskoka R and traverses run north and south of this; survey data on main line.
OTAR (SR 7083; 7112)

Related maps

(2) *1858*
Plan of lots on the Bobcaygeon Road from Somerville to Bell's Line. Lindsay 7th Sept 1858 [Sgd] M. Deane P.L.S. Examined Oct 5th 1858 J.W.B.
Col ms 34 x 153 cm 1" to 40 chains Endorsements: 'No 51' '10157/58'
(SI 22 March 1858; OTNR FN 2210 7 Sept 1858); shows numbered lots and some alternate road routes.
OTNR (SR 5829)

(3) *1862*
Re-Survey Free Grants Bobcaygeon Road [and] Free Grants, Bobcaygeon Road Surveyed under instruction dated the 31st July 1861 [Both sgd] J. Stoughton Dennis P.L.S. Toronto 15th July 1862. Examined 11th October 1862.
2 col mss 55 x 99 and 53 x 102 cm 1" to 20 chains Endorsements: 'R 24' 'R 25' '14345, 11166 & 10352/62'
(OTNR FN 2212 15 July 1862); a further survey to lay out lots along the road line, the first map showing the part from Lutterworth and Snowdon twps to Hindon and Stanhope, and the second part the area north of Bell's line for two twps; there is a copy in OTAR of the northern part '[Sgd] Depart. of Crown Lands Quebec Oct 27th 1862 Wm McDougall Commr' endorsed 'PH 257' that, in addition, shows line located by Mr Brady in Ridout and Sherborne twps; (*OHIM* 4.26).
OTAR OTNR (SR 6828; 6606)

---

624 *1857*
Map of the Chats Islands Ottawa River Sd [Sgd] Thos. E. Norman C.E. Nov 15th 1857.
Col ms on linen 63 x 92 cm 1" to 400 ft
(BW SI 14 Aug 1857 to survey the Ottawa from Lac des Chats down, re leasing of various mill sites); indicates the height above water in Big Bay for various points on land and islands; Egan and Co. sawmill, various dams, chutes, slides, and falls shown; some owners named; detailed maps of Chats Is and L by Norman for 1857–9 are found in OOAMA (see *NMC Cat* II:404–9); there is also an untitled map of the Ottawa R from Chats L to Bytown at 1" to 8 chains in OOAMA, which originally accompanied OOA RG 5 I no 195918 of 25 Aug 1854.
OOAMA OTAR

Related maps

(2) *1858*
Plan of the River Madawaska From Arnprior to Lot No 3 on the 11th Concession Township of MacNab [Sgd] Thos. E. Norman C.E. March 2nd 1858.
Col ms 61 x 106 cm 1" to 400 ft Endorsements: stamp [BW] '1024'
Sawmill, bridge, landing chute, lot nos, relief along shore; a ms copy on linen is nearly identical.
OOAMA (NMC 20014; 20015)

---

625 *1857*
Map of the OTTAWA AND HURON TERRITORY. Crown Lands Office Toronto March 17th 1857. [Sgd in facsimile] Joseph Cauchon Commissioner.
Print (lith) 87 x 135 cm 1" to 4 miles
Issued with *Appendix to Report of Commissioner of Crown Lands, 1856*, Part II *Maps of Canada* (Toronto 1857), Map 6 (OOAMA); the first general map of this newly developing area to be published by government; shows area from Severn R and Talbot R east to Anstruther and Brougham twps, north to the Ottawa R and L Nipissing; shows roads and exploring lines as follows: Bobcaygeon, Hastings, Addington, Frontenac, Opeongo, Mattawa and Nipissing, Pembroke and Mattawan road lines, and Unwin's exploring lines from the Severn R to the Muskoka Rd line and R; other exploring lines; (Holmden 1724, 1725).
OLU OOAMA (NMC 11257) OTAR USDLC

626 *1857*
A Map of the Survey of the North Westerly Outlines of the Townships of Galway, Cavendish & Anstruther [Sgd] M. Deane P.L.S. Lindsay 11th May 1857. Examined and compared with field notes June 1st 1857 J.W.B.
Col ms 147 x 55 cm 1" to 40 chains Endorsements: 'B43'
(SI 24 Oct 1856; OTAR FN 890 11 May 1857); shows north boundary of the twps with traverse lines running north and south across them; relief, drainage, comments on land and trees.
OTAR (SR 6767)

Related maps

(2) *1857*
Map of exploration in the Township of Galway, Part I [Sgd] Lindsay 11th May 1857 M. Deane P.L. Surveyor.
Col ms 30 x 46 cm 1" to 40 chains Endorsements: 'B44'
Shows layout of lots in con A, Galway, and lots on the east side of Somerville Twp as described in SI 24 Oct 1856; Part II is missing.
OTAR (SR 4102)

---

627 *1857*
Outlines of Townships Nos 1 & 2 South of Lake Nipissing U.C. Surveyed by H.P. Savigny P.L.S. Octr 1857 [Sgd] Hugh P. Savigny P.L. Surveyor No 5.
Col ms 80 x 57 cm 1" to 40 chains
(SI 17 Aug 1857 and 25 Aug 1857 to H. Savigny and D. Sinclair to lay out a range of twps south of L Nipissing along a due north principal meridian line); shows the principal meridian line for the survey south to South R, and twps 1 and 2 laid out west of this; this appears to be the first attempt to employ what later became the Dominion Land Survey system in southern Ontario (see Sebert, 'The Lost Townships ...').
OTAR (SR 5920)

Related maps

(2) *1858*
Rough Plan of the Nipissing and Mattawan Base Line East of Principal Meridian With Explorations [Sgd] March 1858 Duncan Sinclair Provl Land Survr.
Ms 35 x 212 cm 1" to 40 chains
Shows the east-west baseline for the range of twps; twps 1–6 are shown north of baseline; other survey lines shown; comments on land.
OTAR (SR 5802)

(3) *1858*
Exploration Survey of Territory South of Lake Nipissing U.C. Surveyed by H.P. Savigny P.L.S. May 1858 [Sgd] Hugh P. Savigny P.L. Surveyor.
4 col mss Ea 120 x 60 cm or smaller 1" to 40 chains
Contents: 'Sheet no 1 and 2 Embracing Southern Extension of Principal Meridian and part of Western Exploration Line. Examined Aug 23, 24 1858 J.W.B.' and 'Sheet No 3 and 4 Embracing Western Meridian Line and part of Western Exploration Line. Examined Aug 23, 24 1858 J.W.B.'; (OTAR FN 1917 17 July 1858); shows relief, trees, bearings, and mileage points along survey line.
OTAR (SR 5916–19)

(4) *1858*
Plan of a Range of townships south of Nipissing & Mattawa Surveyed under instructions from the Commissioner of Crown Lands dated 25th August 1857. [Sgd] Ottawa June 1858 Duncan Sinclair Provl Land Surveyor.
Col ms 74 x 223 cm 1" to 40 chains Endorsements: 'No 52'
(OTAR FN 1921 22 June 1858); the finished plan of survey of the six twps north of the east-west baseline, south of Nipissing Twp to Papineau Twp; detailed classing of forest land; burnt land, portage roads, rocky land; shows lines run and those projected; the twps are numbered in 36 blocks from southeast corner.
OTAR (SR 7033)

(5) *1859*
Plan of Township Outlines South of Lake Nipissing U.C. Surveyed by H.P. Savigny P.L.S. March 1859. [Sgd] Hugh P. Savigny Provl Land Surveyor.
Col ms 66 x 92 cm 1" to 40 chains Endorsements: '7142/59'
(SI 27 Oct 1858; OTAR FN 1920 19 July 1859); shows twp 1 east and west of Principal Meridian in Ranges 2 and 3 south of east-west baseline; survey data along lines; these north-south oriented twps were later annulled and new twps laid out beginning in 1874 (AOLS *Manual* 4.1).
OTAR (SR 5921)

---

628 *1857*
Plan of Preliminary Survey for a Road from Lake Simcoe to the Great Falls of Muskoka River [Sgd] Toronto February 20th 1857 Chas Unwin P.L. Surveyor. Crown Lands Department Toronto Examined Oct 28th 1857 J.W. Bridgland.
Col ms 67 x 205 cm 1" to 40 chains Endorsements: 'Y50'
(SI 11 Oct 1856; OTAR FN 1989 26 Feb 1857 and 7 Sept 1857); shows line from the Narrows and east side of L Couchiching through Mara and Rama twps to Severn R to Great Falls, Muskoka R, and Bell's line; station nos, survey data; exploration line for Muskoka Rd.
OTAR (SR 6555)

Related maps

(2) *1857*
Plan of Exploration from Orillia to the Great Falls of Muskoka River [Sgd] Chas Unwin Provincial Land Surveyor Toronto September 7th 1857
C.L. Dept. Toronto Examined Oct 28th 1857
J. Bridgland. J.R. Jack del.
Col ms 72 x 213 cm 1" to 40 chains Endorsements: 'Y 51' '7123/57'

(OTAR FN 1989 7 Sept 1857); road line now placed on west side of L Couchiching, then north past Sparrow L to most southerly part of L Muskoka and to the Great Falls; other exploring lines and town plot at Great Falls shown, shape of some lakes corrected.
OTAR (SR 8154)

(3) *1859*
Plan Shewing Lots as Laid out on the Severn and Muskoka Road. [Sgd] C. Rankin Owen Sound 23rd May 1859.
Col ms 96 x 68 cm 1" to 40 chains Endorsements: 'No 2'
(SI 18 Nov 1858); shows road lots laid out in Morrison Twp with names of a few owners, and road line in Muskoka Twp; table of contents of lots; also a copy in (OTAR(P)) sgd 'Department of Crown Lands Quebec 29th Dec 1860 Andrew Russell Assistant Commissioner' showing names in the two twps; also a plan showing the survey for the road in Muskoka and Morrison twps by C. Rankin 4 Aug 1859 'No 2' in OTAR (SR 2071).
OTAR(P) OTAR (SR 2071) OTNR (SR 6564)

(4) *1860*
Tracing shewing Survey of Muskoka Road through Draper & Macaulay [Sgd] J. Stoughton Dennis P.L.S. 1st Sep 1860.
Col ms 63 x 36 cm 1" to 40 chains
Shows the continuation of the road north to mile 12; mileages, relief, swamps, notes.
OTAR (SR 11110)

(5) *1861*
Plan of Muskoka Road Line North of Grand Falls [Sgd] To The Honble P.M. Vankoughnet Commr Crown Lands Quebec J. Stoughton Dennis P.L.S. Toronto 19th Apl 1861. Examined July 18th 1861.
Col ms 75 x 179 cm 1" to 40 chains Endorsements: '60'
(SI 26 June 1860 and 6 Aug 1860; OTAR FN 2211 19 Apr 1861); shows road line from Macaulay Twp past Marys L between Vernon L and Fairy L then east to Bobcaygeon Rd; shows relief, rapids, notes on land and timber; also shows exploration line from Parry Sound to Bobcaygeon Rd.
OTAR (SR 6634)

---

629 *[ca 1857]*
[Sketch map showing the Opeongo Road and the supposed height of land]
Col ms 32 x 25 cm Scale not given
Shows twps north to Airy-Murchison and Fraser, Sabine, Lyell, and N Algona, McClure east to Ross; supposed height of land shown as line from Olden Twp to Faraday Twp; a rough line of road, which may be the Mississippi Rd surveyed in 1858, is shown from Canonto to Monteagle and Herschel twps; the Opeongo Rd is shown east of Airy Twp.
OOAMA (NMC 2885)

---

630 *1858*
Plan of the Mississippi Road Line, Hull 31st May 1858 [Sgd] John A. Snow Provl Land Surveyor Examined July 1st 1858 James W. Bridgland.
Col ms 69 x 274 cm 1" to 40 chains Endorsements: 'No 50'
(SI 21 Aug 1857; OTNR FN 2236 31 May 1858); shows route of the road from the Hastings Rd in Dungannon Twp to Palmerston Twp; shows relief, swamps, types of tree, mill sites, portages, other roads, and a few names of settlers.
OTNR (SR 6571)

---

631 *1858*
Plan of the Third Chute River Bonnechere situated on Lot No IV, Con VIII, Township of Bromley Surveyed by [Sgd] William Wagner Civil Engr Ottawa 16th March 1858.
Col ms 60 x 76 cm 1" to 1 chain
Includes two profiles and shows relief, mills, booms, slides, dam, and bridge.
OTAR

---

632 *1858*
Plan of Township boundaries north of the counties of Victoria and Peterborough [Sgd] John Lindsay P.L.S. Toronto February 8th 1858.
Col ms 102 x 195 cm 1" to 40 chains Endorsements: 'E 58' '1125/58'
(SI 18 Aug 1857; OTNR FN 1912); shows the outline of eight twps in two tiers from Snowdon and Minden east to Cardiff and Harcourt; survey data along lines.
OTNR (SR 8818)

Related maps

(2) *1858*
Plan of Boundary Lines of Townships North of the Counties of Peterboro and Victoria [Sgd] Jas. W. Fitzgerald Provincial Surveyor St Mary's June 1st 1858.
Col ms 116 x 198 cm 1" to 40 chains Endorsements: 'E 57' '11/568'
(SI 28 Sept 1857; OTNR FN 2236 31 May 1858); shows eight twps in two tiers north of above map, from Minden and Stanhope east to Harcourt and Bruton; comments on land, trees, swamps, relief; the line between these twps became the Peterson Rd; six of these twps were later sold to the Canadian Land and Emigration Co. for settlement.
OTNR (SR 16904)

---

633 *1858*
[Plans of the Ottawa and French River Survey] [All sgd] Ottawa Survey Engineers' Office Pembroke 27th February 1858 Certified [Sgd] James Stewart Resident Engineer W. Shanly Chief Engineer.
6 col mss Ea 171 x 209 cm or smaller 1" to 400 ft Endorsements: '5784/15'
Shanly was instructed on 22 July 1856 to survey the Ottawa R as a major route for commerce; his

'Report on Ottawa and French River Navigation ... 22 March 1858' is in OOA RG 11 A4 vol 145; shows surveys of the lower Mattawa R, and Amable du Fond R, R des Vases, and Trout L; shows water levels at various dates, and observation points marked from 1 to 695 on traverse lines; the R des Vases – Trout L sheet is stamped [BW] '361'; note: 'compiled from ordinary compass traverses and is not so reliable ... levels are accurate'; detailed maps by Shanly, Clarke, and Stewart from this survey for parts of the Ottawa R are found in OOAMA (see *NMC Cat* II:404–9).
OOAMA (NMC 59334; 59343–7)

Related maps

(2) *[1858]*
Map of the Province of Canada shewing the proposed Ship Navigation from Lake Huron to Montreal by French River and Ottawa as compared with that by the Great Lakes.
Ms on linen Approx 75 x 10 cm 1" to 16 miles
[Profile] 1" to 200 ft vertical; shows cos, railways, and canals; profile shows area of difficult navigation between L Nipissing and the Ottawa R.
OOA (RG 11 A4 vol 145)

(3) *1858*
[Triangulation survey of the Mattawa River] [Sgd] Ottawa Survey Engineer's Office. Pembroke 27th February 1858. James Stewart, Resident Engineer W. Shanly, Ch. Engineer.
5 mss Ea 85 x 135 cm 1" to 400 ft
Shows the survey with tables of data at various points.
OOAMA (NMC 59343–7)

(4) *1860*
The Mouths of French River on Lake Huron. Enlarged Copy of Bayfield's Survey of 1822: [Sgd] Thos. C. Clarke Engineer Ottawa Survey Jan 2d 1860.
Col ms 28 x 48 cm 1" to 1 mile
Provenance: OOA J.B. Tyrrell Papers; shows main channel with a proposed lock at Petite Dallas; old trading post at the Key; further instructions to the engineers on the Ottawa survey were issued 13 and 16 Nov 1858 to assess the amount of canalizing required and the practicability of raising L Nipissing to summit level as proposed by Shanly; maps (3), (4), and (5) were prepared to accompany 'Report Ottawa and French River Navigation Thos C. Clarke, Engineer ... Jan 2, 1860' (in OOA RG 11 A4 vol 145).
OOAMA (NMC 3120)

(5) *1860*
Summit between Nipissingue and Trout Lakes. [Sgd] Thos. C. Clarke Engineer Ottawa Survey Jan 2d 1860 [and] E.R. Blackwell Engineer Nipissingue Division Ottawa Survey. W.H.C.
Col ms 46 x 74 cm 1" to 1/4 mile Endorsements: stamp [BW] '321'
[Profiles]: 'Ojibwaysippi route 4.19 miles' and 'Des Vases route 6.69 miles' both 1" to 30 ft vertical; both routes are shown in detail with lakes and widths of rivers; relief; also a copy further endorsed '(Copy) Office of Public Works Quebec June 1862 E.[T]' (NMC 20277); (Holmden 2090).
OOAMA (NMC 20276–7)

(6) *1860*
Western Outlets of French River [Sgd] E.R. Blackwell Engineer Nipissingue Division Ottawa Survey; Thos. C. Clarke Engineer Ottawa Survey Jan 2d 1860.
Col ms 104 x 109 cm 1" to 100 ft
Four dams located with sections.
OOAMA (NMC 11324)

(7) *1860*
Ottawa Canal Survey / GENERAL MAP AND PROFILE / of the Proposed Line of Navigation for Connecting / THE RIVER ST LAWRENCE WITH THE GEORGIAN BAY, LAKE HURON. / by the Valleys of / THE OTTAWA, THE MATTAWAN, LAKE NIPISSINGUE, AND THE FRENCH RIVER. / from Actual Survey. / Office of Public Works Quebec January 22nd 1860.
Print (lith) 71 x 89 cm 1" to 12 miles
[Profile] 1" to 200 ft vertical; from *Return to an Address ... of the Recent Survey and Report of the Engineers on the Ottawa Ship Canal. Quebec 19th March 1860* (Quebec: Printed by order of the Legislative Assembly 1860), at back (Casey I–284); shows the route of the canal from the French R through L Nipissing, Mattawa R, and Ottawa R to Montreal; height of land shown; profile shows distances and route in detail; four sources listed for the map including Thomas Clarke's surveys.
OOA OOAMA (NMC 21683)

---

634 *[1858?]*
Sketch of part of the county of Victoria with the proposed Route for a Colonial Road [Sgd] John K. Roche Provincial Land Surveyor.
Col ms 110 x 44 cm 1" to 120 chains Watermark: 'J WHATMAN ... 1857.'
Shows the proposed road from Lindsay crossing the Portage Rd in Eldon Twp and going straight north to Draper Twp; this was later developed as the Victoria Rd; the map was probably made in early 1858 as Roche surveyed Draper Twp in 1857 and Laxton Twp (not subdivided on this map) after receiving survey instructions 24 Aug 1858; Roche died in 1859; twps and settlements shown.
OOAMA (NMC 11352)

---

635 *1859*
Map of the Lavant and Darling Road Line [Sgd] John A. Snow Provl Land Surveyor Hull February 3rd 1859. Examined Feby 18th 1859 J.W.B.
Col ms 48 x 119 cm 1" to 40 chains
(SI 12 Nov 1858 to begin survey at mile 10 on Mississippi Rd and run road line from Palmerston to Lavant; OTNR FN 2233 12 Feb 1859); shows the road line through Palmerston, Lavant, and Darling

twps; clearings, swamps, relief, notes on land, and names of settlers.
OTNR (SR 6826)

636 *1859*
MINDEN [Twp with sample of page from field notebook endorsed]: 'The above form of Field Book is respectfully submitted for the approval of the Hon. P.M. Vankoughnet, Commissioner of Crown Lands, by Thomas Devine, Senior Surveyor &c. Upper Canada Surveyors Branch. Approved 2nd April 1859. P.M. Vankoughnet, Commissioner.'
Print (lith), map and diagram on 1 sheet 17 x 36 cm Scale not given
In *The Canadian Settlers' Guide*, 10th ed (London 1860), opp 196 (*Bib Can* 3891); shows Minden as a sample twp survey with survey grid, rivers, relief, swamps, tree types, etc; the survey was split into left and right parts and distance nos along line refer to the text, which describes the area shown; the sample field note style was known as the 'split-line method' and first recorded in OTNR SI 2 Apr 1859 (see 'Devine, Thomas,' in *DCB* XI: 256–7); this map was also printed with text in *Daily Leader* (Toronto) 16 Apr 1860.
OTMCL

637 *[186?]*
[Plan of the eastern part of the Huron-Ottawa territory and adjacent areas to the southeast]
Col ms 132 x 118 cm Scale not given
Unfinished; shows three exploring lines: Bell's line, Hastings Rd line, and the Addington Rd line; shows twps surveyed in the southern part and twps outlined and named from Lake to Palmerston, north to Airy and Murchison to Wilberforce.
OTAR

638 *[186?]*
[Sketch of the Mattawa River and part of the Ottawa River]
Ms on linen 29 x 48 cm 1" to 4 miles
Shows Whitefish Bay with Hudson's Bay Co. post opp it; beginning of Canoe R-Lost L-Pelican L connection; portages, chute.
OOAMA

639 *[186?]*
[Sketch of the Petawawa River, and lakes and rivers between there and the Madawaska River]
Col ms on tracing paper 41 x 65 cm 1" to 2 miles
Shows relief, portages, rapids, falls, names of lakes and rivers, a timber road, some depots, and the line of a route south and west of the Petawawa R.
OOAMA (NMC 3162)

640 *1860*
Plan of Bobcaygeon and Nipissing Exploring and Road Line From Bell's Line to Lake Nipissing [Sgd] Crosbie Brady P.L. Surveyor Lindsay 1st September 1860.
Col ms 431 x 78 cm 1" to 40 chains Endorsements: 'R 56'
(SI 19 May 1859 to J.K. Roche transferred to Brady); shows the exploring line crossing Lake of Bays, Muskoka R, Oxtongue L, and Magnetawan R to L Nipissing; shows Sinclair's baseline south of L Nipissing; twps I and II north and I to III south of line; swamps, relief, comments on land.
OTAR (SR 5210)

641 *1860*
Plan of Part of the River Severn as surveyed under instructions from the Crown Land Department Dated 25th November 1859. [Sgd] John Lindsay Provl Land Surveyor February 14th 1860
2 col mss Ea 87 x 115 cm 1" to 20 chains
Endorsements: 'S No 13' 'S No 14'
(SI 25 Nov 1859 to survey from mouth of Severn R to southwest angle of Morrison Twp; OTAR FN 1985 4 Apr 1860); Section I shows Matchedash Bay, Gloucester Pool, Six Mile L, and mouth and part of Severn R; Section II shows area along river through Matchedash Twp to survey point 186 and 'Mr. Browne's line'; traverse lines, mileages, bearings, notes on trees, shoreline, mills, etc.
OTAR (SR 7912; 7930)

Related maps

(2) *1860*
Plan of part of [the] River Severn [Sgd] John Lindsay Provl Land Surveyor 1860.
Col ms 45 x 49 cm 1" to 1 mile Endorsements: 'S15'
Possibly a reduction of or working sketch for the larger map; shows the same area and information with survey points 1–33 marked along Severn R.
OTAR (SR 7087)

642 *[1860?]*
Plan of the County of Victoria with the proposed system of roads.
Col ms 57 x 51 cm Scale not given
Shows the area from Mariposa Twp to Emily Twp north to Carden, Laxton, and Somerville twps; shows proposed [Victoria] road north from Lindsay to Eldon and Carden twps along two alternate routes; shows the 'Bowerman line' [Cameron Rd] on the east side of Balsam L; also shows railway to Lindsay and an east-west road through Fenelon Falls; work began on the Victoria and Cameron rds in 1861 (Murray, 189).
OOAMA (NMC 4820)

643 *1861*
GOVERNMENT MAP / of part of the / HURON AND OTTAWA TERRITORY / UPPER CANADA / Compiled under the direction of / Thomas Devine F.R.G.S. etc. / Head of Surveyors Branch / U.C. / 1861 // Rae Smith Engraver & Printer 71 Nassau St. N.Y. // [in part of map area]: DEPARTMENT OF CROWN LANDS / Quebec April 1861 / P.M. Vankoughnet / Commissioner.

Col print (lith), some hand col 52 x 84 cm 1:316,800 [1" to 5 miles]
Shows the area from L Simcoe to Parry Sound on the west and from Thorah Twp east to Palmerston Twp and north to Rolph Twp on the Ottawa R; shows all twps as surveyed or outlined and named to date; shows all colonization roads: Bobcaygeon, [Burleigh], Hastings, Addington, Frontenac, Mississippi, [Victoria], Muskoka, Peterson, Opeongo, Parry Sound, Pembroke and Mattawan, and Bell's exploration line; details of terrain along survey lines; oriented slightly to northwest; one OTAR copy (SR 7644) has later ms adds of possible timber licences and drainage areas; endorsed on back of OTAR copy (SR 1359): 'S.G.O. Quebec, 21st June 1861.'
OTAR (SR 1359; 7644) OTUTF

Later editions and states

(2) *1861*
[Same title but 'DEPARTMENT OF CROWN LANDS ... Commissioner' deleted]
The Departmental imprint in map area has been replaced by outline of L Muskoka, L Joseph, L Rosseau, and adjacent drainage system; also issued with *Remarks on Upper Canada Surveys* (Quebec 1862) (*Bib Can* 4113); (Holmden 2796; *OHIM* 4.25).
GBL (70664(3)) OOAMA (NMC 21474) OTAR OTMCL

(3) *1862–3*
[Date in title changed to 1862–63; added at head of title]: 'Department of Crown Lands, / Honorable Wm. McDougall / Commissioner.'
Issued with *Report of the Commissioner of Crown Lands of Canada for the Year 1862* (Quebec 1863) (*Bib Can* 6043) and *Remarks on Upper Canada Surveys* (Quebec 1863) (*Bib Can* 4214); the following twps are now shown as subdivided: Clarendon, Matawatchan, Chandos, Cavendish, part of Monmouth and Cardiff, Monteagle, Harcourt, Dudley, Dysart, Longford, McLean to Sherborne, Brunel, and Sherwood; (Holmden 1726).
OOAMA (NMC 21487) OTAR OTMCL OTUTF

(4) *1863–4*
[Date in title changed to 1863–4]
Changes: a legend has been added showing symbol for colonization roads; the Parry Sound Rd line has been relocated south to L Rosseau; twps subdivided: Limerick, Monmouth, Cardiff are shown completed, and part of Guilford, Harburn, Bruton, Havelock, Eyre, Clyde, Jones, and Monck; road lots are shown in the north part of Lyell between Opeongo Rd and Hastings Rd; (Holmden 1727).
OOAMA (NMC 21478)

(5) *1866*
... / Thomas Devine F.R.G.S. &c. Surveyor in Chief / U.C. 1866 // ... Department of Crown Lands / Honorable Alex. Campbell Commissioner.
Print (lith) 77 x 87 cm
Map issued separately and with Canada, Dept of Crown Lands, *Remarks on Upper Canada Surveys* (Ottawa: Hunter, Rose & Co. 1867), at end (*Bib Can* 9544); extensive changes: the bottom part of the map is from the same plate as 1863–4 but the map area has been extended north to French R, L Nipissing, and the Mattawa R; the title has been moved to the upper right; twps have been added for Simcoe Co and survey grids shown for Watt, Cardwell, Humphry and McDougall twps; road lots on the Parry Sound Rd are shown in Franklin, Herschel, Wollaston, Dungannon, Carlow, Raglan, and part of Wylie twps; in the north the road line and lots are laid out to L Nipissing; [Rosseau Rd] called 'Campbell Road'; parts of twps and the road line are shown along the Ottawa R; Mattawan Twp and the three road lines with lots on the Mattawan and Nipissing Rd are also shown.
OOAMA (NMC 16698)

---

644 *1861*
Map Shewing details of Exploration of Townships owned by the Canada Land & Emigration Co. in Canada [Sgd] B.W. Gossage P.L.S.
Col ms on tracing paper Approx 90 x 75 cm 1" to 1 mile
With 'Report on Preliminary Examination of Canadian Land & Emigration Cos Townships Canada 1861 [Sgd] B.W. Gossage ... 31st December 1861' (OTAR RG 1 CB-1 box 14 (FN 810)); shows the 10 twps with comments on the land, soil, trees along survey lines.
OTAR (RG 1 CB-1 box 14)

---

645 *1861*
Plan of Exploration Line from Parry Sound to Bobcaygeon Road [Sgd] To the Honble P.M. Vankoughnet Commr of Crown Lands Quebec J. Stoughton Dennis P.L.S. Toronto 19th Apl 1861. Examined July 18th 1861.
Col ms 75 x 269 cm 1" to 40 chains Endorsements: '59'
(Possibly SI 6 Aug 1860); shows line run to mile 49 from Parry Sound to Bobcaygeon Rd; lateral traverse lines shown; swamps, relief, comments on land and timber; an early plan for a more northerly route for the Parry Sound Rd; see also **647**.
OTAR (SR 7157)

---

646 *1862*
MAP / OF THE COUNTY OF / RENFREW / COMPILED FROM / AUTHENTIC MAPS AND DOCUMENTS / BY ANDREW BELL / Civil Eng: & Surveyor / Douglas, Sept 1862 // W.C. CHEWETT & CO LITH. TORONTO.
Print (lith) 58 x 49 cm 1" to 4 miles
Legend: travelled roads, railway, proposed railways; shows mills, post offices, proposed railway from McNab Twp to Pembroke, table of distances; 'Populations marked on the map are

taken from the last Census – the value is taken from the revised assessment roll of 1861.'
OOAMA (NMC 22310)

---

647 *1862*
Plan of the Parry Sound and District Line Exploration Surveys under instructions from the Department of Crown Lands dated 31st July 1861 [Sgd] J. Stoughton Dennis P.L.S. Toronto 15th July 1862. O. Jones.
Col ms 87 x 153 cm 1" to 40 chains Endorsements: '10352/62'
(OTAR FN 1902 15 July 1862); map in two parts: one part shows where road will meet Muskoka Rd line, other part shows exploration line from L Rosseau to Parry Sound; other exploration and lateral surveys shown with data along survey lines.
OTAR (SR 7798)

Related maps

(**2**) *1862*
Plan Shewing Exploring Lines between Lake Rosseau and Muskoka Road Line Under Instructions from the Dept of Crown Lands. Dated 31st July 1861. [Sgd] J. Stoughton Dennis P.L.S. Toronto July 15th 1862.
Col ms 88 x 113 cm 1" to 40 chains Endorsements: 'No 68' '10352/62'
(OTAR FN 1902 15 July 1862); shows exploration lines and alternative lines for the Parry Sound Rd east of L Rosseau and to point where it would join Muskoka Rd line (SI 31 July 1861); Dennis located this part of road (his other surveys were for exploration only) (cf. Murray, 198).
OTAR (SR 8075)

(**3**) *1863*
Plan of the Parry Sound Road Line [Sgd] James A. Gibson P.L.S. Parry Sound May 1863.
Col ms 69 x 198 cm 1" to 40 chains
(SI 18 Dec 1862 (cf. Murray, 198)); shows road line in detail deviating around obstructions; Dennis's exploring lines shown; pencil adds show lots and projections for twp surveys.
OTAR (SR 8224)

(**4**) *1866*
Plan of Parry Sound Road as posted for farm lots Surveyed by [Sgd] J.L.P. O'Hanly P.L. Surveyor Ottawa 10th August 1866. Examd 19th Octr 1866.
Col ms 64 x 131 cm 1" to 40 chains Endorsements: '11293/66' 'R 38'
(SI 7 Sept 1865; OTNR FN 2226 10 Aug 1866); shows lots from Watt Twp to [McDougall] Twp; shows poor, rocky, fair, and average land; notes on progress of building of road.
OTNR (SR 6578)

(**5**) *1867*
Parry Sound Road Department of Crown Lands Ottawa 11th Feby 1867 [Sgd] A Russell Assistant Commissioner.
Col ms 41 x 150 cm 1" to 40 chains
Shows road with lots from north boundary of Watt Twp to McDougall Twp and Parry Sound; crosses S. James's exploring line.
OTAR

---

648 *1862*
Outlines of Townships Hagarty, Richards, Burns & Sherwood
Col ms 99 x 92 cm 1" to 40 chains
Probably drawn by Robert Hamilton who received the instructions to survey these outlines (SI 30 Apr 1860) and who submitted field notes (OTNR FN 1263 1 Nov 1862); shows relief, swamps, nos, and some road allowances.
OTNR (SR 8686)

---

649 *1863*
Map exhibiting all the Recent 'Colonization Roads' in Canada West [Sgd] Department of Crown Lands Quebec 31 Dec 1863 Andrew Russell Assistant Commissioner
Col ms 102 x 95 cm Scale not given
All roads named and located; projected extensions shown including Lavant and Darling rds, Mississippi Rd (extending west to L Simcoe), Renfrew and Addington Rd (connecting to Opeongo Rd), Elezevir and Kaladar Rd (connecting to Addington Rd), and Campbell line from Parry Sound Rd to L Nipissing; Cameron Rd; Burleigh Rd; connecting roads and railways to southern part of province shown.
OOAMA (NMC 11254)

---

650 *1863*
Plan of the Production of the Victoria Road Through the Townships of Lonford [*sic*] & to the Peterson Road in the Township of Oakley [Sgd] Peter S. Gibson Prov. Land Surveyor Willowdale 18 Jany 1863.
Col ms 64 x 44 cm 1" to 40 chains
Shows the road line for the northern part from Digby to Oakley twps to meet Peterson Rd line; table of distances, notes on land and tree types.
OTNR (SR 6370)

---

651 *1863*
Trace Shewing proposed road line connecting Opeongo & Hastings Roads [Sgd] A.G. Forrest P.L.S. October 10th 1863
Col ms on linen 26 x 87 cm 1" to 40 chains
(SI 29 Sept 1862); shows road with road lots in Lyell and Jones twps at the north end of Bark L, and from lot 123 on the Opeongo Rd to lot 58 on the Hastings Rd; relief, swamps, etc.
OTAR

---

652 *[1863–4?]*
GOVERNMENT MAP of part of the HURON and OTTAWA TERRITORY ... 1863–4 [with ms additions giving comments on the nature of the land]
Print (lith) with ms adds 53 x 83 cm 1:316,800 [1" to 5 miles]

Detailed comments written in each surveyed twp indicating amount and location of good land and soil for agricultural settlement or timber exploitation; probably compiled by Thomas Devine from surveyors' field notes and other sources (cf. *DCB* XI:256); there is also an unfinished map in OTAR (99 x 190 cm, 1" to 80 chains) that is possibly a working draft for this map and shows twps in the north end of Victoria and south part of [Haliburton] cos with comments written in for some twps on the nature of the land for settlement and timber possibilities; (*OHIM* 5.4).
OTAR OTAR (SR 7168)

Related maps

(2) *[1863–4?]*
GOVERNMENT MAP of part of the HURON and OTTAWA TERRITORY ... 1863–4 [overprinted with 3 classes of land capability]
Col print (lith)
The colour is used to indicate areas of the three classes as indicated in legend: [1] 'Rough Rocky land, Timber principally Hemlock and Scrubby Pine,' [2] 'Fair Land, Sandy Soil, Mixed Timber, but generally Pine in Townships East of Hastings Road,' [3] 'Good Land, Hardwood Timber generally'; shows data for surveyed twps from approximately north of line from Mara Twp to S Canonto Twp, to south of line from Stephenson Twp to Fraser Twp; the map is described in *Report of the Commissioner of Crown Lands, Canada, for 1863* (Quebec 1864); (*OHIM* 5.5).
OOAMA (NMC 21477) OTMCL

---

653 *[1863–4?]*
PLAN OF / DUDLEY / in the / COUNTY OF PETERBOROUGH / CANADA WEST. / THE PROPERTY OF THE / CANADIAN LAND & EMIGRATION COMPANY (Limited) / OF LONDON, – ENGLAND. // W.C. Chewett & Co Lith. Toronto.
Print (lith) 71 x 50 cm 1" to 40 chains
'Note. Applications for Purchase of Lots to be addressed to Frederic T. Roche Agent for the Company 148 Duke Street, Toronto, Canada West.'; one of the 10 twps in the Haliburton area purchased by the Canadian Land and Emigration Co. (incorporated 1861) from the government; the twps were surveyed by B.W. Gossage for the company in 1862 and 1863; the twp plans were published to encourage land sales, probably in 1863–4, but some may have been reissued later; each plan was a copy of the ms twp plan (see App A) and all are at the same scale as (1); each shows the survey grid, lot sizes, contents of lots with an indication of relief, swampy areas, and sometimes roads; this plan also shows 'Burleigh road line'; the eight plans with Roche listed as agent at 148 Duke St were probably issued first as Roche was at a different address in *Mitchell's Toronto Directory for 1864–5* and Chas J. Blomfield is listed at the Toronto address below in *Mitchell's General Directory for ... Toronto* (1866); many OOAMA copies are from the Mossom Boyd Collection and have ms adds about lumbering; other OOAMA copies are found in RG 45M 83403/21 E series; (see also Murray, lxxvi ff).
OOAMA (NMC 22043) OTMCL

The other twp plans are as follows:

(2) PLAN / OF / DYSART, / COUNTY OF PETERBOROUGH, / CANADA WEST. / THE PROPERTY OF THE / CANADIAN LAND & EMIGRATION COMPANY Limited / OF LONDON-ENGLAND. // W.C. CHEWETT & Co. LITH. TORONTO.
Print (lith) 67 x 50 cm
'Applications ... Roche ... 148 Duke Street ...' (OTMCL copy); OOAMA copy has following statement pasted over the Roche information: 'applications for Lots to be made to CHAs J. BLOMFIELD, Secretary to the Company. / TORONTO BANK BUILDINGS, TORONTO.'; (*OHIM* 4.27).
OOAMA (NMC 22045) OTMCL

(3) PLAN / OF / EYRE, / COUNTY OF PETERBOROUGH / CANADA WEST. / THE PROPERTY OF THE / CANADIAN LAND & EMIGRATION COMPANY Limited / OF LONDON – ENGLAND. // W.C. CHEWETT & CO. LITH: TORONTO.
Print (lith) 75 x 52 cm
'Applications ... Roche ... 148 Duke Street ...'
OTMCL

(4) PLAN / OF / GUILFORD / COUNTY OF PETERBOROUGH / CANADA WEST / THE PROPERTY OF THE / CANADIAN LAND & EMIGRATION COMPANY (Limited) / OF LONDON, – ENGLAND. // W.C. CHEWETT & Co. LITH. TORONTO
Print (lith) 68 x 52 cm
'Applications ... Roche ... 148 Duke Street ...' (OTMCL copy); imprint trimmed off OOAMA copy; OOAMA copy has later agent's statement pasted over the Roche information: 'Applications ... to CHAs J. BLOMFIELD Secretary to the Company, / TORONTO BANK BUILDINGS, TORONTO.'
OOAMA (NMC 22081) OTMCL

(5) PLAN / OF / HARBURN, / COUNTY OF PETERBOROUGH / CANADA WEST. / THE PROPERTY OF THE / CANADIAN LAND & EMIGRATION COMPANY (Limited) / OF LONDON, ENGLAND. // W.C. CHEWETT & Co LITH. TORONTO.
Print (lith) 70 x 50 cm
'Applications ... Roche ... 148 Street ...' (OTMCL copy); OOAMA copy has Roche's name crossed out and 'Chas Jas. Blomfield Manager or Alexr Niven' added in ms [ca 1868].
OOAMA (NMC 22084–5) OTMCL

(6a) Plan of the Township / OF / HARCOURT / IN / THE County OF / PETERBOROUGH / (CANADA WEST.) / The Property of the / CANADIAN LAND & EMIGRATION COMPANY (Limited) OF LONDON, - ENGLAND.
Print (lith) 64 X 49 cm
'Applications ... to Roche ... 148 Duke Street ...'
OTMCL

(6b) [1865–6?]
PLAN / OF / HARCOURT, / COUNTY OF PETERBOROUGH, / CANADA WEST. / THE PROPERTY OF THE / CANADIAN LAND & EMIGRATION COMPANY, Limited, / OF LONDON - ENGLAND. / W.C. CHEWETT & CO. LITH. TORONTO
Print (lith) 66 x 52 cm
'Applications for lots to be made to CHAs J. BLOMFIELD Secretary to the Company, / TORONTO BANK BUILDINGS, TORONTO or to CHAs R. STEWART Resident Agent of the / Company at HALIBURTON'; a redrawing of the map showing mostly the same information but lacking names of some of the lakes.
OOAMA (NMC 22087)

(7) PLAN / OF / HAVELOCK, / COUNTY OF PETERBOROUGH, / CANADA WEST. / THE PROPERTY OF THE / CANADIAN LAND & EMIGRATION COMPANY Limited / OF LONDON, - ENGLAND. // W.C. CHEWETT & Co LITH. TORONTO.
Print (lith) 70 x 52 cm
'Applications ... Roche ... 148 Duke Street ...' (OTMCL, OOAMA (NMC 22091)); OOAMA (NMC 22092) has paste-on addition [1867 or 8?]: 'Applications ... to CHAs J. BLOMFIELD Manager of the Company Peterborough.'
OOAMA (NMC 22091–2) OTMCL

(8) Plan of the Township / OF / LONGFORD / IN / THE County OF / VICTORIA / (CANADA WEST). / The Property of the CANADIAN LAND & EMIGRATION COMPANY (Limited) OF LONDON, - ENGLAND.
Print (lith) 62 x 50 cm
'Applications ... Roche ... 148 Duke Street ...'
OOAMA (NMC 22109) OTMCL

(9) PLAN / OF / BRUTON, / IN THE / COUNTY OF PETERBOROUGH, / CANADA WEST. / THE PROPERTY OF THE / CANADIAN LAND & EMIGRATION COMPANY (Limited) / OF LONDON - ENGLAND.
Print (lith) 63 x 50 cm Trimmed at bottom margin
'Applications for Purchase of Lots to be addressed to Frederic T. Roche, Agent for the Company Corner of Wellington and John Stts TORONTO Canada West'; issued in 1864 or 1865 when Roche was at this address.
OOAMA (NMC 22025)

(10) PLAN / OF / CLYDE, / IN THE / COUNTY OF PETERBOROUGH, / CANADA WEST. / THE PROPERTY OF THE / CANADIAN LAND & EMIGRATION COMPANY (Limited) / OF LONDON - ENGLAND.
Print (lith) 72 x 50 cm Trimmed at bottom margin
'Applications ... to Frederic T. Roche, / Agent for the Company Corner of Wellington and John Stts TORONTO Canada West.'
OOAMA (NMC 4826; 22025; 22043; 22045; 22081; 22084–5; 22087; 22091–2; 22109) OTMCL

---

654 *1864*
Plan of Proposed Road [Cameron Rd] Line from Laxton to Head of Gull Lake [Sgd] Crosbie Brady County Surveyor Lindsay June 22nd 1864.
Col ms 40 x 65 cm 1" to 40 chains
Shows the extension north from Laxton Twp to Lutterworth Twp along Gull R and L.
OTAR

---

655 *1865*
No 1 Plan of Survey Line No 1 from Township of Stephenson to the Georgian Bay ... No 2 Plan of Survey Line No II from Lake Joseph to the Magnetawan River ... No 3 Plan of part of the Magnetawan River [All sgd] under instructions from the Department of Crown Lands dated 23rd February 1864. Silas James P.L.S. Newton Brook Jan 27th 1865
3 col mss 40 x 184 cm and 263 x 38 cm and 61 x 535 cm 1" to 40 chains (Nos 1 and 2) 1" to 10 chains (No 3) Endorsements: '1578/65'
(SI 23 Feb 1864 to survey baselines for twp and traverse Magnetawan R; OTAR FN 2384 24 Jan 1865); maps 1 and 2 were baselines for future twp development along the south line of Cardwell, Humphrey, and Conger twps and running north between Conger and Humphrey for about six twps; map 3 follows the river east from Byng Inlet to survey line II; relief, swamps, comments on timber and land.
OTAR (SR 7106; 6599; 11071)

---

656 *[ca 1865]*
Parry Sound Region Projected Sketch [ms additions to part of] GOVERNMENT MAP of part of the HURON and OTTAWA TERRITORY ... 1862–3.
Col print with ms adds 49 x 29 cm 1:316,800 [1" to 5 miles]
Shows a proposal for laying out six new twps that were surveyed from 1866 on: Cardwell, Humphry, Conger, Monteith, Christie, and Foley.
OTAR

---

657 *1865*
Plan of part of the County of Renfrew, Showing the proposed Site for a Branch Road leading from Springtown on the Madawaska to the Opeongo Road Being the 2nd Section of the projected Madawaska Road. Surveyed and Examined under Instructions from the Crown Lands Department, dated Quebec, June 20th, 1864. Pembroke March 1st 1865 [Sgd] S.T. Abbott Evans Provl Land Surveyor.
Col ms 68 x 102 cm 1" to 40 chains
(SI 20 June 1864 to examine road from Springtown

to intersection of Frontenac Rd with Madawaska R with view to a road between Brougham and Matawatchan); shows the twps of Bagot, Admaston, Brougham, and Grattan and the existing line of road and recommended directions; notes on obstructions and lengths; cleared land; some names of settlers.
OTAR (SR 6559)

---

658 *1865*
Plan of Survey of Lakes Rosseau and Nipissing Road Line. Section from Lake Rosseau to the XV Mile Post ... Section from XV Mile Post to River Magnetewan. [Both sgd] J. Stoughton Dennis P.L.S. Toronto Nov 30th 1865.
2 col mss 127 x 375 cm and 119 x 274 cm 1" to 10 chains
(SI 14 Oct 1864 for [the Rosseau Rd]); shows the road line from L Rosseau and the Parry Sound Rd line, crossing the Parry Sound and Bobcaygeon exploration line, and Ottawa and Georgian Bay Railway exploration line to mile 33 at Magnetawan R; relief, swamps, notes on trees and land.
OTAR (SR 16901; 16099)

Related maps

(2) *[1866?]*
Projected Plan Lots on the Road Line between Lakes Rosseau and Nipissing.
Col ms on linen 86 x 315 cm 1" to 40 chains
Shows 218 numbered lots along the route; shows Savigny's exploration lines south of L Nipissing; probably the projection for the survey below.
OTAR (SR 7603)

(3) *1867*
Plan of Lots on Rosseau and Nipissing Road [Sgd] James W. Fitzgerald Provl Land Surveyor Peterborough June 1867.
Col ms 325 x 47 cm 1" to 40 chains Endorsements: 'B 42'
(SI 20 Aug 1866); shows road lots 1–218 from Humphry and Cardwell twps to L Nipissing; relief, swamps.
OTNR (SR 8874)

---

659 *1865*
[Sketch of part of Rama and Mara townships showing proposed lines for the Monck Road] Copy [Sgd] John A. Snow Provl L. Surveyor. [illegible] 15th July 1865.
Col ms on linen 65 x 65 cm Scale not given Endorsements: '10402/65'
Provenance: OTAR Colonization Road Papers; shows three proposed routes for the western end of the Monck Rd in Rama and Mara twps, including 'Mr. Gibson's line'; shows the Beaverton Rd and the travelled road along shore of L Couchiching; swampy areas; names of some landowners.
OTAR

---

660 *[ca 1866]*
Peterborough [in pencil]: A MacDonald P.L.Surveyor
Col ms on linen 137 x 94 cm 1" to 100 chains
Shows the area bounded on the south by Ennismore and Harvey twps to Methuen Twp and on the north by Stanhope Twp to Bruton Twp; shows Bobcaygeon, Burleigh, Peterson, and Monck rds.
OOAMA

---

661 *1866–7*
Plan of the River Ottawa from ... Reduced from the maps of the Ottawa Ship Canal Survey deposited in the Department of Public Works also from other documents in the Dep't of Crown Lands Exhibiting the line of boundary between Upper and Lower Canada in reference to the islands in the said river. The Said line of Boundary being the Red Line referred to in the approved Report of Council dated 21st July 1866. Department of Crown Lands Ottawa [Sgd] A. Campbell Commiss'r ... Joseph Bouchette Dy Surv Genl June 24 ... June 29, 1867
5 col mss on linen Sizes vary 1" to 40 chains
The five sections cover the river from Point Fortune to the Mattawan R and the Head of L Temiscamingue; a memo sgd by Joseph Bouchette 29 June 1867 lists acts pertaining to the boundary and principles involved in assigning islands to Upper Canada or Lower Canada; a further note indicates that the Ottawa R boundary plans were sgd and approved by A. Campbell and one set sent to Upper Canada Branch and the other to the Lower Canada branch; there is a set listed as in Quebec in O'Leary, 'Inventaire' (B3c, B8(1–4), B8a, B9, B9a).
OTAR OTNR (SR 3237; 7710; 8764; 8799; 8816)
QQERT

---

662 *1867*
Plan of Mill Site on Magnetawan River. [Sgd] Fitzgerald & Bolger Provl Land Surveyors Peterboro June 11th 1867.
Col ms 39 x 42 cm 1" to 10 chains Endorsements: '8860/67'
Shows a mill site opp the Indian reserve at the mouth of the river near Byng Inlet; relief of shoreline, meadow, notes about site selected by Messrs Dodge.
OTNR (SR 2703)

---

663 *1867*
Plan shewing a location for milling purposes situated on Byng Inlet – Georgian Bay accompanying the application of Eli C. Clark [Sgd] V.B. Wadsworth Prov. L. Surveyor – Toronto July 2nd 1867.
Col ms 58 x 76 cm 1" to 3 chains Endorsements: '34a' '11053/67'
Inset: 'Diagram shewing the connection of the survey with the westerly boundary of the Indian reserve' 1" to 40 chains; shows a mill site west of the Indian reserve; relief, survey lines, bearings.
OTNR (SR 2700)

Niagara

664 *[178?]*
Plan of a Survey from Fort Niagara to the Landing Place above the Falls; shewing the exact Distance between both Places as also the different Turnings & Windings of the River & Road. (Signed) Wm Hill. Copied from an Original by Lieut Augustine Prevost R.F. [Sgd] Samuel Holland Surveyr Genl
Col ms 51 x 92 cm 2" to 1 mile Endorsements: 'Y No 8'
Shows both sides of the river with Fort Niagara on the American side; notes about the siege of the fort in 1759; shows sites for landing, portages, mills, roads along the shore, relief; the original map by Wm Hill and endorsed 'C30' and '1006' is also in OTAR (SR 215) and may date from the 1770s.
OTAR (SR 215, 7900)

---

665 *1781 [178?]*
Sketch of a Tract of Land purchased of the Missasagas for His Majesty by Col. Guy Johnson at Niagara 9th May 1781. Copied from an original by Lieut Augustine Prevost R.F. [Sgd] Samuel Holland Survr Generl.
Col ms 40 x 28 cm 1" to 4 miles Watermark: T BUDGEN Endorsements: 'Q 19' '1096'
Boundary line of tract is shown running parallel to the river about 15 to 20 miles west; few places noted except 'Little Niagara' on American side at the falls, and Fort Erie; (*OHIM* 4.2); *Indian Treaties*, Treaty No 381 (1781), III.
OTAR

---

666 *[1783]*
The River line from Niagara falls to the four mile pond on the West side of Lake Enterio [*sic*] with its courses & windings. [Endorsed title]: 'New Settlement Niagara.'
Col ms 32 x 104 cm Scale not given
Originally accompanied a letter from Lt Col Butler to Haldimand of 21 March 1783 (GBL Add Mss 21765 f 326); shows four cons laid out fronting on Niagara R south to Mountain line and west to Four Mile Creek; names are inserted in the front row and a few behind and to the south; the town is partly laid out with two rows of lots behind 'Rangers Barrick' and Navy Hall, and names are inserted in most lots; no reserve is shown; the plan is by Allan Macdonell and he filed his account for surveying the area on 24 Apr 1783 (cited in Mathews, *Mark of Honour*, 88, 189).
GBL (Add Mss 21829 f 71–2)

---

667 *[1783?]*
[Sketch of the area west of the Niagara River showing the Grand River and the Delaware villages]
Col ms 18 x 24 cm Scale not given
Shows Niagara with 'Rangers' bldgs, Fort Erie, Chippawa Creek, and boundary of 'Late Purchase from the Mississaugas' (1781); at west end of L Ontario 'Naghiadiron'; probably dates from the same period as (**666**) above.
GBL (Add Mss 21829 f 73)

---

668 *[1787?]*
[Niagara Township]
Col ms 45 x 38 cm Scale not given Endorsements: 'Plan B' [and] 'B' 'Plan taken From Old Quebec Plan used in Shubal Welton Trial' 'With W 25 State Papers Shubel Welton Papers About 1784 or earlier'
Originally with OOA RG 1 E 1 vol 49 pp 33–62 and Series E3 vol 91–4 case W 25 pp 65–205; shows the twp as surveyed by Philip Frey in 1787; land reserved by Crown extends across north part on L Ontario shore; Frey enclosed twp plan and report in letter of 18 Sept 1787 to John Collins (Ontario Archives, *Report 1905*, 308); shows many name changes and names differ from (2) below; (Holmden 2005; *OHIM* 4.7).
OOAMA (NMC 3556)

Related maps

(**2**) *[1787?]*
[Niagara Township]
Col ms 49 x 38 cm Scale not given Endorsements: 'A' 'Plan taken from the old Quebec Plan used in the Shubel Welton trial ... circa 1784'
From same source as in (1) above; twp with names; Rangers' Barracks; names of landowners including Lt Pilkington, John Secord, Col Butler, Jacob Servos, Philip Frey; Navy Hall; some names shown on reserve; some names crossed out and later adds; indications of 'certificate' issued and disputed lots; (Holmden 2004?).
OOAMA (NMC 3555)

---

669 *1788*
Plan of the River from Niagara to Fort Schlosser [Sgd] Quebec 6th Decr 1788 Gother Mann Captn & Commandg Rl Engr.
Col ms 28 x 93 cm 1" to 1/2 mile Endorsements: stamps 'HMSPO' 'Case 42 No 50'
Removed from a copy of Mann's report enclosed with Dorchester's no 58 of 24 Oct 1790 (GBLpro

CO 42/70 p 41ff); shows Navy Hall opp Fort Niagara and a road on the east side of river south to Fort Schlosser; two points marked near 'landing place' on east side but not explained; relief by shading; 'Niagara Falls 150 feet high'; (*PRO Cat* 1502); also a plan of the same title marked 'Plan C' with slight variations from above (GBLpro (CO 700 Canada 38C 'dup')); photoreproductions in OOAMA (NMC 26922–3).
GBLpro (CO 700 Canada 38C; 38C 'dup')

Related maps

(**2**) *1788*
[Same title as above]
32 x 97 cm Endorsements (on back): 'No 6' 'Z 28/70'; stamp 'B↑O'
Similar to plan above except Navy Hall is not shown, other roads are shown near Fort Schlosser, and the line of escarpment is shown across the peninsula; 'Falls' marked; (Holmden 2057).
OOAMA (NMC 26862)

---

670 *1788*
Plan of the Townships laid out in the Settlement of Niagara since the 11th June 1787. P.R. Frey Surveyed in 1788 by F.R. Frey.
Col ms 47 x 123 cm 1" to 80 chains Endorsements: '989' 'N 31'
Shows part or all of twps nos 1–8 [Niagara, Grantham, Leath, Clinton, Grimsby, Saltfleet, Barton, Stamford] laid out from Niagara R to west end of L Ontario and south to Chippawa R; shows Four, Eight, Twelve, Twenty, and Forty Mile creeks, and mills near the first three; shows 'Lenox Town' [Niagara], Garrison Line, and glebes in twps nos 1–3; considerable topographical detail is shown for Barton (twp 8); relief by shading and hachures; there is also a 'Copy [Sgd] Jos. Bouchette [illegible] Survr General' endorsed '994' at OTAR (SR 7137) that shows the same information; the latter presumably made after 1804 when Bouchette became Surveyor General.
OTAR (SR 5911; 7137)

---

671 *[1788?]*
Township No 2
Col ms 46 x 42 cm Scale not given Endorsements: 'Niagara Chain Reserve Papers 1791 or earlier'
Shows the lots in the twp and names added in all lots; marshes; number of acres indicated in some lots; later adds of names or word 'dispute' in some lots; Stamford Twp was surveyed in late 1787 and early 1788 by Philip Frey and Augustus Jones (Ontario Archives, *Report 1905*, 308, 344); since names have been added in lots, this plan might have been made later in 1791 by Augustus Jones (Green, 265–6; (Holmden 2011).
OOAMA (NMC 3624)

---

672 *[1789?]*
[Bertie Township] [Endorsed title]: 'Survey of Quaker Township as made by Mr. Chapman 1789'
Col ms 29 x 37 cm Endorsements: 'Niagara Chain Reserve Papers 1789' 'Fort Erie Township'
Shows the outline of Bertie Twp and Fort Erie; note indicates the northern part of the twp 'is so very wet that it will Scarce ever be fit for cultivation'; Bertie was first surveyed in 1788 by Augustus Jones (Ontario Archives, *Report 1905*, 346); (Holmden 2006).
OOAMA (NMC 3381)

---

673 *[1791]*
[Endorsed titles]: 'The Six Nation Indian Lands Southeasterly part Gr. River Niagara District' [and] 'The Six Nations Lands, Northerly part, Grand River – Distt of Gore.'
2 col mss 138 x 35 cm and 73 x 95 cm 1" to 1 mile Endorsements: 'Q 23' [and] 'Q 24' '1040'
Unfinished plans probably from surveys by Augustus Jones; the southern plan shows the boundary line of Indian reserves and bearings, Indian villages, and the names of a few settlers; the northern plan shows the area from Deer Creek to four falls north of the forks on the Grand R and the east, west, and northern boundary lines of the tract; the grant to the Six Nations was made in 1784 and 1793 (*Indian Treaties*, Treaty No 106 (1784) and No 4 (1793), I:9ff and 251ff).
OTAR (SR 6947; 81039)

Related maps

(**2**) *[1791?]*
Plan of a Tract of Land situate in the District of Nassau reserved for the Mohawk Indians and others agreeable to an Order of the Governor in Council of the 4th January 1791 – Taken from Mr. Jones Plan of the settled part of that District.
Col ms 49 x 126 cm 1" to 80 chains Endorsements: '1069'
(OTNR FN 835 1791); shows the area south of the Mohawk village to L Erie; shows much of the same information as on the southern plan above but includes a few places not shown and more footpaths (to Long Point, to L Ontario, and to the R 'Trench' [Thames]); lacks some notes found on plan above.
OTAR (SR 5776)

---

674 *[1793]*
[Endorsed titles]: 'Nth Shore L[ake Erie] from Ft Erie [to] Gd River Har[bour]' [and] 'Long Pt Bay with Soundings (Sketched)'
2 col mss 36 x 117 cm and 61 x 90 cm Scales not given Watermark on 2nd: 'J WHATMAN'
Endorsements: '837' [and] '946' 'No 13'
(SI 9 June 1793 to W. Chewett to survey from Fort Erie to mouth of Grand R and to look for suitable site for town and fortifications on point opp Presqu'ile); the plans match along the shore and both are in Wm Chewett's hand; shows the nature of the shoreline, soundings, and marshy areas; names of squatters; Chewett surveyed along shore 3 June–3 Aug 1793 and on 18 Sept he delivered a

sketch from Fort Erie to Long Point (possibly (1), (3), or (4)) to Aitken (W. Chewett diary 1792–5 OTAR RG 1 CB-1 box 42).
OTAR (SR 8632; 8895)

Related maps

(2a) *[1793?]*
Plan of a Sketch of the Grand River and Bay with the Soundings
Col ms 54 x 125 cm 1" to 10 chains Endorsements: 'No 15'
Unfinished and part of title in pencil; this is probably the original survey made by Chewett to go with (1) above, and shows soundings and shoreline; however, added information shows two naval reserves east of river, one with a note dated Oct 1820; grid lines for tracing and note 'Copy this (Sketch) made for the Board of Ordinance 25th April 1835. H.L.'; see (2b) below.
OTAR (SR 7076)

(2b) *1835*
Sketch of the mouth of the Grand River with Soundings on Lake Erie. Surveyor General's Office, Toronto U.C. 25th April 1835. Copy Henry Lizars [Sgd] S.P. Hurd S.G. (Certified a True Copy) P.J. Bainbrigge Lt Royl Engrs 25th July 1836.
Col ms 57 x 100 cm 1" to 40 chains [i.e., approx 1" to 10 chains] Endorsements: stamps 'B↑O' 'IGF'
Endorsed 'mouth of Grand River Capt. Bonnycastle 26 June 1837 E20'; a copy of (2a) except lacks notes around naval reserves; (Holmden 1690).
OOAMA (NMC 21688)

(3) *1793*
Plan of a Sketch from Fort Erie along the North Shore of Lake Erie round Long Point to where it joins the main Land with the Soundings [Sgd] Niagara 28th August 1793 W. Chewett.
Col ms 85 x 213 cm 1" to 1 mile Endorsements: stamp 'HMSPO'
Inset: 'Plan of a Sketch of the Grand River and Bay with the Soundings' 1" to 10 chains; originally endorsed in Simcoe's no 18 of 20 Sept 1793 (GBLpro CO 42/317 pp 283ff); a more finished copy of the original survey (see (1) and (2a) above) with the addition of notes along the shore; Patterson's, Nanticoak, Sangass, and Stoney creeks all noted as good harbours for batteaux; no comments on Grand R as potential for harbour on inset; this inset shows the survey before the addition of later notes as in (2a) above; (*PRO Cat* 1452).
GBLpro (CO 700 Canada 57)

(4) *[1793]*
[Plan of the L Erie shoreline from Fort Erie to Long Point]
Col ms 27 x 78 cm 1" to 4 miles Watermark: 'R WILLIAMS ...'
A smaller version of the main survey (1) above.
OTAR (Simcoe Map 446695)

---

675 *[1793?]*
[Sketch Map of the Niagara Peninsula, Lower Grand River and part of the River Thames]
Col ms 32 x 44 cm Scale not given Watermark: '[J WHAT]MAN'
A sketch, possibly drawn by Mrs Simcoe after Lt Gov Simcoe's return from his trip from Niagara to Detroit (cf. *Mrs. Simcoe's Diary* (1965), 88, 10 March 1793; shows rivers, present road from Thames to L Ontario, and a proposed road north of this [Dundas St]; 'Sleigh road from the Indian village' on the Grand to Burlington Bay; boundaries of Indian lands and Indian villages.
OTAR (Simcoe Map 445786)

---

676 *[1793–5?]*
[Sketch of the south shore of Lake Ontario from Niagara River to Forty Mile Creek]
Ms 17 x 13 cm Scale not given
A small sketch oriented to the west; all rivers shown but not named; fort at Niagara, Navy Hall and four other bldgs shown; possibly by Mrs Simcoe.
GBEXr (Simcoe Collection 1038M F1/III)

---

677 *[1795?]*
[Endorsed on back]: 'County of Lincoln'
Col ms 104 x 148 cm Scale not given
Shows and names all the twps from Barton to Newark [Niagara], Gainsborough to Stamford, and Crowland and Humberstone to Willoughby and Bertie, but survey grid not shown; indicates rivers, swamps, and the Niagara escarpment; shows a few trails, bldgs and names, and east boundary of the Six Nations Indian land; many of the twps were instructed to be laid out in 1791 and others in 1795.
OTAR (Simcoe Map 446887)

---

678 *[1795?]*
The front of Two Townships at Long Point [and] The front of three Townships on the North Shore of Lake Erie [Sgd on both maps] D W Smith Actg Sur Genl.
2 col mss in 5 numbered sheets partly joined 34 x 99 cm [and] 37 x 154 cm 1" to 1/2 mile
Shows the front three cons of five twps [Walsingham, Charlotteville, Woodhouse, Walpole, Rainham]; terrain and marshes noted and a town plot proposed at Turkey Point [Charlotteville]; bearing on west sheet 'by Mr. Hambly's instrument' and on east sheet 'by Mr. Hambly's ... [and] Mr. Aitken's instrument' (SI 15 July 1795 to A. Aitken to lay out a row of twps from Long Point to boundary of Indian lands at Grand R and to mark a town plot); Hambly was later instructed to complete the survey of three twps on 30 Nov 1795, but he may have assisted Aitken earlier when these plans were probably made; the maps are in two different hands.
OTAR (Simcoe Map 446497 a–b)

679 *1795*
[Sketch of Turkey Point] Done in the Surveyor General's Office Upper Canada 12th October 1795 [Sgd] D.W. Smith Actg Sur General J.G.S.
Ms 40 x 36 cm 1" to 1 mile
In Lt Gov Simcoe's 29 to Portland (GBLpro CO 42/319 p 330) with a note indicating that this is the site he has fixed on for a town at Long Point and for position of blockhouse and pier for protection of shipping; shows blockhouse and wharf and place 'where ships or wharfs may be constructed,' as well as town site [Charlotteville].
GBLpro (MPG 1173)

---

680 *1796*
Sketch of the Communications between Lake Ontario & Lake Erie
Col ms 32 x 107 cm 1" to 1 mile Endorsements: '29L' 'D'
Originally in Lord Dorchester's no 87 of 16 Apr 1796 to the Duke of Portland about matters of defence (GBLpro CO 42/105 p 154); 'References' shows blockhouses, guardhouses, storehouses, wharves, etc, built for troops at Fort Erie, at mouth of Chippawa R and at Queenston in 1791, and those ordered to be built at Niagara in 1796; former landing place at Queenston shown; (*PRO Cat* 1504); also a close copy of this map in GBLpro (MPG 39) endorsed 'D' from the same source (*PRO Cat* 1505).
GBLpro (MPG 36; 39)

---

681 *1798*
AN EYE SKETCH / of the / FALLS OF NIAGARA // London Published by J. Stockdale Piccadilly 16th Novr 1798. Neele sculpt.
Print (engrav) 16 x 22 cm 1 1/2" to 2 furlongs
Inset: [location map of Niagara Peninsula and Upper New York State]; in Isaac Weld, *Travels through the States of North America* (London: Printed for John Stockdale 1799), opp 308 (*Bib Can* 4789); the map shows both falls in detail, the American named 'Fort Schlosser Fall'; Table Rock, Indian ladder and Simcoe's ladder on west side and road from L Ontario to L Erie with Wilson's tavern located.
OTMCL

Later editions and states

(2) *1798*
[Same title] // I. Weld Delt. ...
In Isaac Weld, *Travels ...*, 2nd ed (London: Printed for John Stockdale 1799), II, and in the 3rd ed (London: Printed for John Stockdale 1800), II: opp 118 (*Bib Can* 709), and in the 4th ed (London: J. Stockdale 1800), 378 (USDLC), and in the 4th ed (1807), II: opp 118 (OHM, CIHM 49846).
OHM OTMCL

(3) *1802*
SCHETS / Van de / WATERVALLEN / van / NIAGARA
Print (engrav) 17 x 22 cm Approx 1 1/2" to 2 stadion
In Isaac Weld, *Reizen door de staaten van Noord-Amerika* (Den Haage 1802), III: opp 343 (*Bib Can* 711) or II: opp 348 (OONL, CIHM 42004); redrawn from the English ed.
OONL OTMCL

---

682 *[1799]*
[Map of the Niagara Falls area] [Sgd] John Stegmann Dy Surveyor.
Col ms 128 x 149 cm 1" to 3 chains Endorsements: '1187'
(SI 13 Nov 1798 to survey from Table Rock to Chippawa R along the shore of the Niagara R noting the boundary of the military reserve north of the Chippawa R and the position of the high road); shows both falls and relief in detail; survey lines and points including north boundary of Mr Swayze's licence of occupation; shows roads, several houses, improved land, Burches's and Canby's mills, Wilson's, Stegmann's, and Fairbank's houses, and boundary of military land.
OTAR

Related maps

(2) *1797 [i.e., 1799] (1836)*
Plan of the Reserve from the Chippewa to Table Rock Surveyed by John Stegman Deputy Surveyor 1797 [i.e., 1799] (Copy) J.G. Chewett Surveyor General Office 17th May 1836.
Col ms 65 x 160 cm 1" to 3 chains Endorsements: stamps 'B↑O' 'IGF'
This appears to be a copy of only part of the information on the original map since a later note indicates that data in red on the original (1) was added from it in 1892; (Holmden 2061).
OOAMA (NMC 22196)

---

683 *1801*
Long & Turkey Points as taken from an Eye Sketch with the actual Soundings & Bearings in Septr 1801 ... Capt Cowan
Ms 22 x 36 cm Scale not given
A rough, inaccurate sketch showing incorrect orientations for some of the features.
OTAR (MU 1537 maps)

---

684 *[1801]*
PLAN / de la CATARACTE de NIAGARA / et de l'Isthme qui separe les lacs / Erie et Ontario. // Gravé par P.F. Tardieu, Place de l'Estrapade No. 18 / Ecrit par Giraldon. // Pl. VI. Tom. II. Pag 131.
Print (engrav) 21 x 44 cm 1" to 3 miles
In M.G.S. de Crèvecoeur, *Voyage dans la haute Pensylvanie* (Paris: Maradon 1801), 2: opp 131 (*Bib Can* 6801); shows places including 'Newark,' 'Queenstown,' Fort Chippeway, and Fort Erie, roads, relief, settlements.
OTMCL

---

685 *[1802]*
Plan of 206 Acres in the Township of Newark otherwise called Niagara including 4 Acres in the

Town of Niagara in Upper Canada. The property of the Honble D.W. Smith Esqre Surveyr Genl [Sgd] W Chewett Senr Surveyr & Dftsman.
Col ms 41 x 29 cm Scale not given
Shows Smith's lots as well as the boundary of the military reserve in Niagara, Fort George, and Navy Hall; creeks are named and roads shown in the twp.
OTMCL (D.W. Smith Papers B-15 p 37)

686 *[1803]*
Local de Niagara. [and] Coupe de la Chute prise sur le milieu de la Rivière // Pl. III, en regard à la page 112.
2 prints (engrav) 6 x 36 cm and 9 x 36 cm 1" to 1200 toises
In C.F. Volney, *Tableau du climat et du sol des Etats-Unis d'Amérique* (Paris: Courcier 1803), 1: opp 112 (*Bib Can* 723); shows a few places and roads; the Niagara R is called 'Fleuve St Laurent' and Queenston is 'Kouinston.'
OOA OTMCL

Related maps

(2) *1804*
The Falls of Niagara with the adjacent Country. // London Published April 1st 1804 by J. Johnson St Pauls Church Yard // J. Bye Sculpsit // Fig 2 [and] Section of the Fall in the middle of the River. // Fig 1 // [At top right] Pl III to face p 99.
2 prints (engrav) 6 x 35 cm and 9 x 35 cm 1" to 1200 toises and 1" to 100 ft
In C.F. Volney, *View of the Climate and Soil of the United States of America* (London: Printed for J. Johnson 1804), opp 99 (*Bib Can* 724); reengraved from the French ed with English place-names; names corrected to Niagara R and Queenston, and 'Mrs Simcoe's ladder' is shown; (Phillips, 546).
OOA OTMCL

687 *[1803]*
Plan and Discription [*sic*] of a Stripe [*sic*] of Land above the Falls of Niagara, surveyed by Geo: Lowe Overseer of Works
Col ms 33 x 37 cm 1" to 4 chains
Originally with Capt Nicholl's report of 17 June 1803 concerning Isaac Swayze's petition to build a mill (OOA RG 8 I/383 p 58); a survey of the parcel with dimensions; (Holmden 2015).
OOAMA (NMC 3176)

688 *[1807]*
[Endorsed title]: 'Bridgewater Mills 1807'
Ms 26 x 42 cm Scale not given
Originally with 'Land Papers, Privy Council Office' (OOA RG 1) but exact location not found; shows the area near the Fort Erie reserve and the Niagara R; new and old ferry route from Black Rock on United States side; (Holmden 1530).
OOAMA (NMC 3177)

Related maps

(2) *1807*
[Endorsed titles]: 'A Plan of Survey from Chippawa to Bridgewater Mills 1807' [and] 'Bridgewater Mills 1807 A'
Ms 33 x 84 cm Scale not given
Probably from the same source as above; a rough plan with bearings and a few bldgs marked; (Holmden 1564).
OOAMA (NMC 21727)

(3) *[1807?]*
Plan Shewing the Mill Scite, prayed for by Benjamin Hardison, James Macklem and John Fanning [Sgd] W Chewett Senr Surveyr & Drftsmn
Col ms 33 x 85 cm 1" to 3 chains
Probably from the same source as above; shows Chippewa Creek with military reserve and several bldgs; locates Bridgewater Mills, mill race, 'McGill and Canby's Upper Boundary,' and three other mill sites; note in river 'course of rafts'; (Holmden 1575).
OOAMA (NMC 21726)

689 *1807*
A Survey of the Grand River, from the North West line, to the Forks about twenty Miles, the course taken on the River when froosen [*sic*] and and [*sic*] Containing as the lines are laid down, about 125.486 acres of Land, ... [Sgd] by A. Jones D.P.S. Surveyed in February 1807 –
Ms 38 x 55 cm 1" to 1 mile
Originally filed with a lease dated 4 June 1801 from Joseph Brant and the Six Nations Indians to Charles Anderson for 450 acres of land for 999 years (OOA RG 10/106 p 378); the plan shows the area from the northwest purchase line (west from Burlington Bay) at the Upper Falls up the river to the Forks; notes on rivers, relief, and vegetation.
OOAMA (NMC 3109)

690 *1810*
No IV Upper Canada, Plan of Niagara River by A. Gray Asst Qr Mr Genl Quebec 22d Decr 1810.
Col ms in 2 sheets 62 x 164 cm 1" to 1 mile
Watermark: 'J WHATMAN 1801'
Endorsed 'This Plan is from a Survey by Lieut. Gray, assisted by some local Surveys obtained on the Spot. [Sgd] Q.M. Genls Office Quebec 1st June 1811. James Kempt Q.M. Genl N. America'; a topographical map for a few miles east and west of the river; shows vegetation, relief, clearings, roads, and towns; bldgs are shown in towns and along roads; shows proposed road from Fort Erie to Niagara, portages at Chippawa R and Queenston.
OOAMA (NMC 21728)

691 *1812*
A map of the Country contiguous to the Niagara River (Copied from a map in the possession of Major Genl Lewis 1812

Ms 81 x 53 cm 1" to 1 mile Endorsements: stamp 'Engr Dept U. States Topl Bureau D 29'
Shows the locations of American camps at the beginning of War of 1812 including Gen Van Rensselaer's near Lewiston, Gen Smyth's north of Buffalo, and Col Winder's camp; notes on Grand Is claimed by both sides and Navy Is inhabited by British subjects; roads and towns shown on both sides of river.
USDNA (RG 77 AMA 24)

---

692 *1812*
VIEW of the COUNTRY / round the / FALLS OF NIAGARA // Drawn by J. Melish // J. Vallance F.S.A. Sculpt.
Print (engrav) 17 x 10 cm Approx 1" to 5 1/3 miles
This small map showing the Niagara R with settlements and roads first appeared in Melish's *Travels through the United States of America* (Philadelphia: Printed for the author ... T. & G. Palmer 1812), II: opp 318 (*Bib Can* 878); it also appeared in later eds of this work, (Philadelphia: G. Palmer 1815) and (Philadelphia, London: George Cowie; Dublin: John Cumming 1 May 1818), II: after 488 (*Bib Can* 879) (Melish/Vallance imprint has been deleted); in Melish's *A Military and Topographical Atlas of the United States* ([Philadelphia: Printed by G. Palmer Nov 1813?]), opp 11 (*Bib Can* 6922, *LC Atlases* 1346), and in another ed (Philadelphia: John Melish, G. Palmer printer 1815), opp 11 (*Bib Can* 6980, *LC Atlases* 1347); in Melish's *Description of the British Possessions in North America* ([Philadelphia: T. & G. Palmer 1813?]), opp 21 (*Bib Can* 953); and in Melish's *Geographical Description of the United States*, new ed (Philadelphia 1822), 188 (GBL).
GBL OTMCL USDLC

---

693 *1813*
MAP / of the / STRAIGHTS OF NIAGARA / from Lake Erie to Lake Ontario. / 1813. / Published by Prior & Dunning N. York, / Drawn by I.H. Eddy N. York / Robbinstone & Son. Sc.
Print (engrav) 38 x 18 cm 1" to 2 miles
Inset: 'Vertical Section of the great slope which occasions the Falls' 1" to 1 mile, 1" to 450 ft vertical; in *Gazetteer of the Province of Upper Canada* (New York: Prior & Dunning 1813), opp entry for Niagara (*Bib Can* 735, map missing; OTUTF); shows the river with forts, towns, roads, and Indian villages on either side; some houses and names of settlers; the map was copied in several later works; see plan below and (**718**).
GBLpro (CO 700 Canada 71) OTUTF

Later editions and states

(**2**) *[1816]*
[same title but date and imprint statements deleted] // No 15
In James Wilkinson, *Diagrams and Plans Illustrative of the Principal Battles ... in Memoirs of My Own Times* (Philadelphia: Abraham Small 1816), map 15 (*LC Atlases* 1344); the map is from the same plate as the 1813 ed but with the addition of some roads, battle sites in the War of 1812, and the positions of camps and troops at various times; a key to sites in the war has been added at right.
OTMCL USDLC

---

694 *[1813]*
Plan of the English Fort George. [Endorsed on back]: Major Vanderventer Plan of the British Fort George.
Ms 43 x 27 cm Scale not given
Accompanied by a two-page description '(Signed) C. Van De Venter'; shows the blockhouse, magazine, officers' quarters, guardhouse, etc, relief of the area, and a wharf; the text describes the fort and the best ways to attack it.
USDNA (RG 77 dr 113 sh 51/2)

---

695 *[1813]*
[Sketch of Burlington Heights]
Ms 39 x 33 cm 1" to 10 chains
With letter from Lt Col R.H. Bruyeres to Sir George Prevost of 4 Sept 1813 indicating the barracks to be built there before the rainy season (OOA RG 8 I/387 p 106); the proposed barracks are shown at the north and south ends of the sand spit; the commissariat stores, magazine, and house also shown; (*OHIM* 2.7).
OOA (RG 8 I/387 p 106)

---

696 *[1814 July 5]*
[Endorsed title]: 'Battle of Chippewa Engineer of Genl Brown the position of the two Armies at certain periods during the action'
Ms 45 x 69 cm [Approx 1" to 1/8 mile]
A rough pencil sketch with notes on the positions of commanders and their troops at various points during the engagement, including B Gen Scott, B Gen Ripley, Maj Gen Porter, and Capt Towson's Artillery; shows British and American Indian allies and American encampment after the battle.
USDNA (RG 77b map file dr 154 sh 42–24)

---

697 *[1814 July 12]*
Plan of Niagara Frontier
Col ms 52 x 65 cm 1" to 1 1/2 miles
In Sir George Prevost no 170 to Earl of Bathurst 12 July 1814 recording the loss of Fort Erie and defeat at Chippawa (GBLpro CO 42/157 p 24); insets: 'Fort Erie' 1" to 300 ft, 'Chippawa' 1" to 450 ft; the general map shows road connections on both sides of the river, bldgs, and forts; the insets show all the military bldgs, fortifications, and size of barracks; photoreproduction in OOAMA (NMC 3170).
GBLpro (MPG 456 (1))

---

698 *1814 July 21*
Plan of Niagara Frontier. Engineers Office – Montreal Copied by George Williams R.M.S.D. 21st July 1814

Col ms 67 x 196 cm 1" to 1/2 mile Watermark: 'J WHATMAN 1811' Endorsements: 'no 93' 'P 3 D. 20 P No 543 D U'; stamp 'CREOC'
Oriented to the west; shows the river, escarpment, forts, roads on both banks, Col Murray's landing north of Queenston and Maj Gen Ryall's [Riall] landing at Black Rock and north of Queenston.
OOAMA (NMC 18466)

---

699 *[1814 July 25]*
[Endorsed title]: 'Action at Lundy's Lane'
Ms 68 x 48 cm [Approx 1" to 200 ft]
Relief by hachures and shading; notes on positions of troops at different points during the battle; shows Genls Scott and Brown's positions, the British Artillery in position, and Col Morrison of the British 89th Regt retreating after the third attack.
USDNA (RG 77 dr 154 sh 42–27)

---

700 *[1814 July 25]*
[Endorsed title]: 'Lundy's Lane [illegible] the relative situation of the two Armies at the time the order was given by Major Genl Brown to Col. James Miller to attack and carry the British Battery on the height.'
Col ms 62 x 39 cm [Approx 1" to 700 ft]
A smaller-scale plan than the above showing various positions of British troops and positions of Gen Scott, Gen Ripley, Col Jessup, and Col Nicholas, and other American troops; relief by shading.
USDNA (RG 77 dr 154 sh 42–27B)

---

701 *1814 July 25*
Plan of part of the Niagara Frontier shewing the Communications from thence to the 15 mile Creek July 1814 H Q Montreal [Sgd] Ph. Hughes Lt Col. Comg Rl Engr.
Col ms 54 x 72 cm Scale not given
Inset: 'Sketch of the action fought on the night of 25th July 1814 near the Falls of Niagara between a British force under Lieut. Genl Drummond and an American force under Major Genl Brown by G.A. Eliott D.A.Q.M.Gl' 6" to 1 mile; shows the area from Fifteen Mile Creek to Chippewa Creek at the Niagara R; shows escarpment, wooded and cleared areas, roads, some houses and names of settlers; inset shows the Battle of Lundy's Lane with position of troops at different times and notes.
OOAMA (NMC 21586)

Related maps

(**2**) *[1814 August 16]*
Plan of part of the Niagara Frontier
Ms 53 x 73 cm 1" to 1 mile Endorsements: 'No 3'; stamps 'B↑O' 'IGF'
Inset: 'Sketch of an Action fought on the night of the 25th July 1814 near the Falls of Niagara between a British Force under Lieutt General Drummond and an American Force under Majr General Brown by G.A. Eliott Dy A Q Gl' 6" to 1 mile; originally accompanied Lt Col Hughes's letter to Lt Gen Mann dated 16 Aug 1814 in GBLpro WO 55/860 pp 105–6; similar to above plan but some wooded areas drawn in more detail and in a more finished manner; the inset shows the same positions; (Holmden 2066).
OOAMA (NMC 18559)

---

702 *[1814 July–Aug]*
Sketch of an action fought on the Night of the Twenty-fifth of July 1814, near the Falls of Niagara between a British Force under Lieut Genl Drummond and an American Force under Major Genl Brown.
Col ms 32 x 41 cm Scale not given
Originally in Prevost's no 183, 5 Aug 1814, to Earl Bathurst enclosing Lt Gen Gordon Drummond's report of the engagement (GBLpro CO 42/157 pp 116–18); shows the locations of each regiment of both sides and Indians in their 1st and 2nd positions at Lundy's Lane; relief shown by hachures and shading; the positions are slightly different from those shown on (**701**) (*OHIM* 2.8).
GBLpro (MPG 456 (2))

---

703 *[1814 July–Aug]*
[Endorsed title]: 'Strait of Niagara from Fort Erie to Chippewa'
Ms 81 x 66 cm 1" to 700 yds
Inset: [The River Niagara by Fort Erie with various distances between points and batteries]; shows the position of two batteries near Black Rock commanded by Lt Col Towson and Capt Archer, the position of the Battle of Chippawa on 5 July 1814 and other military positions and activities in July and Aug including the positions of British Maj Gen Riall and B Gen Scott; shows forested land, shore road, and houses.
USDNA (RG 77 dr 142 sh 2)

---

704 *1814 Aug*
Plan of the Country round Fort Erie Shewing the Entrenchments &c thrown up by the Enemy in August 1814 Position the 8th Augt 1814 – Phh Hughes Lt Col Comg Rl Engr. J.B. Duberger Junr Augt 27th 1814.
Ms 37 x 53 cm 1 ft to 1 mile Endorsements: 'B 132'; stamps 'B↑O' 'IGF'
Originally accompanied a letter to Lt Gen Mann dated Montreal 7 Oct 1814 in GBLpro WO 55/860 p 106; 'References': 'Entrenchments thrown up by Enemy around Fort, Abbatis by Enemy and British, Batteries,' position of part of British Army, enemy's schooners; relief, forested areas; (Holmden 1645).
OOAMA (NMC 3803)

---

705 *1814 [Aug–Sept]*
Chart Illustrative of the Siege & Defence of Fort Erie. Campaign of 1814. [Sgd] D.B. Douglass U.S. Engineers.

Col ms 60 x 186 cm 3" to 200 yds Endorsements: 'N.Y. Topl Plan to Illustrate the Siege of Fort Erie 1814 Capt Douglass D32'; stamp 'Engr Dept U States Topl Bureau'

Includes key to various locations, bastions built by the enemy before the surrender of 3 July and during the siege; shows the positions of American troops after the siege and bastions erected by them; also shows batteries and blockhouses constructed by Lt Gen Drummond during the unsuccessful British siege of 16 Aug to 17 Sept 1814; relief by shading, vegetation, roads in the area.
USDNA (RG 77 dr 154 sh 43–13)

Related maps

(2) *[1816]*
SIEGE & DEFENCE OF FORT ERIE / Drawn by D.B. Douglass U.S. Engineer. Engraved by J. Vallance.
Print (engrav) 21 x 39 cm 1" to 175 yds

In John Lewis Thomson, *Historical Sketches of the Late War between the United States and Great Britain*, 2nd ed (Philadelphia: Thomas DeSilver and others 1816), opp [303] (*Bib Can* 1078); shows the siege and defence of Aug 1814 and the position of British troops to the north; actions are keyed in a note under the map; based on map above.
OTMCL USDLC

---

706 *1814 Aug–Sept (1815)*
Plan of the Attack made upon Fort Erie (Upper Canada) by the Right Division of the British Army, under the Command of Lt Genl Drummond in August and Septr 1814 [Sgd] George Philpotts Lieut Royl Engineers, Capt Romilly Comg Rl Engineers Niagara Frontier. G. Nicolls Lt Col. Cg Rl Engineers in Canada Quebec 27th July 1815.
Ms (upper right corner missing) 87 x 56 cm 1" to 150 yds Endorsements: stamps 'B↑O' 'IGF'

Shows the area of the British camp, entrenchments, and the fort; roads, cleared and forested areas; batteries shown with distances; (Holmden 1883).
OOAMA (NMC 22340)

---

707 *1814 Aug–Sept (1815)*
Plan of the Operations of the British Army, in front of Fort Erie, in the Months of August & Septembr 1814 under the Command of Lieutenant General Sir Gordon Drummond, Knight Commander of the Bath &c. &c. Copied from the Original of Lieut [W.A.] Nesfield by Geo. D. Cranfield D.A.Q.M. Genl. Kingston. Upper Canada. 3d May 1815.
Col ms 59 x 50 cm 1" to 200 yds

'Reference': shows Fort Erie as it was when taken by the Americans, additional works raised by the American Army, Major Buck's Rd, roads cut by the British Army; also shows entrenchments, fortifications and batteries and picquets on either side of the river; position of troops.
OOAMA (NMC 22341)

---

708 *1814 Aug–Sept*
[Sketch showing the situation of Fort Erie and position of forces for the attack by the British] [Sgd] J.B. Glegg Major & Asst Adjt Genl 1814.
Ms 61 x 49 cm 1" to 200 yds

Shows the area from Snake Hill past Fort Erie and British lines to headquarters of Lt Gen Drummond further down the Niagara R; Indian camp, camp and artillery park, picquets, trails, fortifications by the British; shows the same layout for entrenchments and possibly a field sketch for plan above; may be in the same hand but lacks the details around the fort itself.
OOAMA (NMC 4857)

---

709 *1814 Sept 6*
[Endorsed title]: 'Map of Fort Erie Canada made by the Brother of Gen. Zebulon Montgomery Pike who was killed there' [and] '[Engagement?] ft by the British ... Septr 6th 1814.'
Col ms 32 x 39 cm Scale not given

A rough sketch of the fort with its artillery and other defences with the position of American troops and a note on the attack by the British on 14 Aug 1814.
USICHi

---

710 *[1814 Oct 4]*
[Map of area between Fort Erie and Fort George on the Niagara River] A.W. R.E.
Ms 31 x 47 cm 1" to 2 1/3 miles

Originally with Lt Gen Sir G. Prevost no 197 of 4 Oct 1814 to Earl Bathurst about deployment of troops along the river (GBLpro CO 42/157 p 241); shows locations of regiments along the river and headquarters of various commanders; roads and names of some settlers; (*PRO Cat* 1507).
GBLpro (MPG 456)

---

711 *[1814 Nov]*
[Endorsed title]: 'Fort Erie as left by the Enemy.' [Sgd] Sam Romilly Lieut Rl Engineers.
Ms 20 x 32 cm Scale not given

Enclosed in Romilly's letter to Lt Gen Drummond dated Chippawa 10 Nov 1814 (OOA RG 8 I/686 p 143) in which he describes the conditions of the fortifications after the battle; shows the state of fortifications, lines destroyed and those left intact; relief, forested areas, roads; (Holmden 1646).
OOAMA (NMC 70956)

---

712 *1815 (1818)*
Grand River Entrance by Messrs Harris & Vidal Marine Surveyg Department under Capt W.F.W. Owen R.N. November 1815 Lake Erie Royl Engineer's Drawing Room Quebec 24th June 1816 J.B. Duberger R.My.S.D. [Sgd] Quebec 24th June 1818 G Nicholls Lt Coll R1 Engineers
Ms 42 x 53 cm Approx 1" to 80 yds Endorsements: stamps 'B↑O' 'IGF'

The plan is based on the Owen 1815 survey but this map is at a larger scale (see **C21–2**); shows the

entrance with the sandbanks in detail, the nature of the shore, and soundings; 'The New Naval Settlement' is shown on the east bank; (Holmden 1679).
OOAMA (NMC 3110)

713 *[1815]*
Map of the Niagara District in Upper Canada, by Lieutenant W.A. Nesfield, drawn partly from Survey, & from documents obtained from the Qr Mr Genls Department.
Col ms 56 x 82 cm Approx 1" to 3 miles
Enclosed with Owen's report to Croker no 82 (CO 42/172 p 15); oriented to the south; an important general map of the Niagara Peninsula and area west to Long Point as it was just after the War of 1812; shows the Niagara escarpment, swamps, roads, villages, forts, and battle sites; 'Reference': shows main roads, logged roads and Bye roads, mills; some houses and names of settlers shown; (*PRO Cat* 1390); photoreproduction in OOAMA (NMC 21587; *OHIM* 6.1); also listed in **C19**.
GBLpro (MPG 62)

714 *[1816]*
Battle of / BRIDGEWATER / View 1st // vol. I // No 12; ... / View 2nd // vol. I // No 13; ... / View 3rd // vol. I // No 14; ... / View 4th // vol. I No a 14.
4 prints (engrav) Ea 18 x 18 cm 1" to 200 yds
In James Wilkinson, *Diagrams and Plans Illustrative of the Principal Battles ... in Memoirs of My Own Times* (Philadelphia: Abraham Small 1816), maps 12–14a (*LC Atlases* 1344); shows the action at Lundy's Lane of 25 July 1814; shows three different positions of troops and movements later that night; roads, bldgs, relief.
OTMCL USDLC

715 *[1816]*
[Endorsed]: 'Country between Lakes Erie & Ontario from the Falls of Niagara' 'America Fort. Part of Upper Canada.'
Col ms 36 x 69 cm Scale not given Watermark: 'S & C 1805' Endorsements: stamp 'Engr Dept U. States Topl Bureau I. 25'
A reconnaissance map showing the area from the Niagara R to Grand R, Mohawk village, and 'Fairchilds Creek'; note by the Grand R: 'N.B. The English have selected this River as being the most convenient for wintering their vessels and are now (1816) erecting locks, arsenals etc.'; shows rivers, marshes, roads with distances between settlements or settlers; several houses shown with names of settlers.
USDNA (RG 77 AMA 5)

716 *[1816?]*
Inner and Outer Bay's of Long Point Surveyed by order of the Admiralty in 1816.
Ms 33 x 52 cm 1" to 11/2 miles Endorsements: stamps 'BW' '553'
The map is related to the Admiralty survey of 1816 (see **C76**) and the printed chart (see **C116**); shows soundings, type of shoreline and bottom, Long Point and mainland from Walsingham to Walpole twps; town plot of Charlotteville and Fort Norfolk and other points marked along shore; a pencil grid indicates it has been used for copying; (Holmden 1954).
OOAMA (NMC 3124)

717 *1818*
An Accurate Plan of the Level of the Land between Chippawa and the Twelve Mile Creek taken on the 28th September 1818 by George Keefer and Wm Hamilton Merritt Esquires with the assistance of Capt Decew Mr Hale Davis Cook and a number of the Inhabitants the results of which has shown us that it is practicable to unite the two Waters by means of a Canal at a Moderate expense being about 2 miles Distant and having 17 feet fall and only about 30 feet deep. [Sgd Wm Hamilton Merritt] [pt missing]
Ms 27 x 140 cm Scale not given
Shows part of Twelve Mile Creek near Capt Decew's and profile from there to Mr Cowan's house at Chippawa; figures from estimates on back (part missing); later note on back calls this 'Tracing of the First Survey of the Old Welland Canal.'
OOAMA (NMC 103849)

718 *1818*
MAP / OF THE / STRAITS OF / NIAGARA / From Lake Erie / to Lake Ontario // Published as the Act directs, by William James, May 11th 1818. // H. Mutlow Sculp. // Plate I // to face title of Vol. I.
Print (engrav) 40 x 18 cm 1" to 2 miles
Inset: 'Vertical Section of the great slope which occasions the Falls' 1" to 1 mile, 1" to 450 ft vertical; in William James, *A Full and Correct Account of the Military Occurrences of the Late War* (London: Printed for the author 1818), frontis (*Bib Can* 1058); the map is reengraved from Wilkinson's map (**693(2)**), but the title has been moved to the lower left, section placed in upper right, and two roads going west have been added near Chippawa; some of Wilkinson's letter references have been deleted and some moved slightly; in the introduction, James states that he is indebted to Wilkinson for this plate as well as three others; James's imprint statement is lacking on all but USDLC copy.
OOA OTMCL OTUTF USDLC

719 *1818*
THE / NIAGARA / FRONTIER. // London, Published by Longman, Hurst, Rees, Orme & Brown, Paternoster Row, May 20th 1818. Engraved by Sidy Hall, 14 Bury Stt Bloomsby.
Print (engrav) 20 x 25 cm Approx 1" to 12 miles
In Francis Hall, *Travels in Canada and the United*

States, in 1816 and 1817 (London 1818), frontis (*Bib Can* 1096); a small but detailed map of the Niagara Peninsula; shows roads cleared and forested areas, Indian settlements, some bldgs and relief.
OTMCL

---

720 *1818*
A plan, of part of the Grand River on which Messrs Nelleses, Youngses, and Huff's Lands are Situate. 3rd April 1818 by Samuel Ryckman Depty P. Surveyor.
Col ms 42 x 32 cm 1" to 80 chains
Enclosed with a petition for a crown patent for land purchased by Nelles and others from Capt Brant along the Grand R in 1788 (OOA RG 8 I/262 p 64); shows boundaries of the lands in question and that of Indian land on the southern part of the Grand R; (Holmden 1684).
OOAMA (NMC 3112)

---

721 *1818*
[Sketch of Fort Erie] Royal Engineers' Drawing Room Quebec 31st January 1818 [Sgd] A. Walpole Lt R Engr E.W. Durnford Lt Col. Commg Rl Eng
Col ms 45 x 32 cm 1" to 400 ft
Accompanied a letter from Lt Col Durnford about the need for a government wharf (OOA RG 8 I/402 p 39); shows fort and other fortifications, relief, road, a few houses; some numbered points, mostly houses, not keyed; also shows positions of both sides during action in 1814; (Holmden 1649).
OOAMA (NMC 3804)

---

722 *[1819?]*
Plan shewing the Lands granted to the Six Nation Indians situated on each side of the Grand River or Ouse commencing on Lake Erie Containing about 674,910 Acres W.C.
Col ms 76 x 45 cm 1" to 4 miles Endorsements: 'Q 41' '1053'
Shows the area from L Erie to beyond Nichol Twp; shows the boundaries of the Grand R Indian land and Blocks 1–4 noted now as Dumfries, Waterloo, Woolwich, and Nichol twps, respectively, originally sold to various individuals in 1798; also shows Block A or No 5, and B or No 6 near L Erie; shows bearings of the boundaries and the road to the Thames; 'To be kept to copy from W.C.'; probably made early in the 1800s but including later information about twp surveys to 1819.
OTAR (SR 6962)

Related maps

(2) *1821*
[Same title as above] [Sgd] Surveyr Genl Office York 2nd Febry 1821 Thos Ridout Surveyr General.
Ms 61 x 44 cm 1" to 4 miles
Enclosed in Lt Gov Sir Peregrine Maitland's Dispatch No 16 of 22 Feb 1821 to Earl Bathurst with copies of many early documents on Indian lands (GBLpro CO 42/366 p 62); there is also a copy at OOAMA (NMC 3114) from OOA RG 8 I/263 p 68a with documents reviewing Indian complaints that certain of their lands were being illegally alienated; the map is a copy of the other plan with the addition of names of twps on the east from Beverly to Nelson and Binbrook to Saltfleet, and Blenheim on the west and the crown and clergy reserves on the east, north and west for the county of Lincoln, and the Six Nations Lands; (Holmden 1688).
GBLpro (MPG 1174) OOAMA (NMC 3114)

(3) *1836*
[Same title as (1)] Copy J.G.C.
Ms 67 x 51 cm 1" to 4 miles
With a report by Sir Francis Bond Head and the Executive Council of 18 Aug 1836 on Nelson Cozen's claim to land in the area (GBLpro CO 42/492 p 215); a sketchy copy of (2) with a copy of the extract of the description of land (Block 4) as deeded 7 Dec 1792; twps of Guelph and Puslinch are now shown in part of the crown and clergy reserve lands; some of the early names of the settlers on the Grand R have been left off; (*OHIM* 4.5).
GBLpro (CO 42/432 p 215)

---

723 *[1819]*
THE / STRAITS OF NIAGARA. / ENGRAVED for DARBY'S TOUR. / W. Hooker Sc.
Print (engrav) 17 x 38 cm 1" to 2 miles
Inset: 'VERTICAL SECTION of the GREAT SLOPE which occations [*sic*] the FALLS.'; in William Darby, *A Tour from the City of New-York to Detroit* (New York: Kirk & Mercein and others 1819), opp 155 (*Bib Can* 1136); the map is reengraved from the Prior and Dunning map of 1813 (**693**) with the addition of a few battle sites.
OOAMA OTMCL

---

724 *[1820]*
Map / OF PART OF / NIAGARA RIVER // D.W. Wilson Sc. Albany
Print (engrav) 29 x 11 cm Approx 1" to 20 miles
In Elkanah Watson, *History of the Rise, Progress ... of the Western Canals in the State of New York* (Albany: D. Steele 1820); shows area from Ft Erie to Grand Is, road on Canadian side, and canal surveyed in 1816 along U.S. side of Niagara R.
USNN

---

725 *[ca 1820]*
[Map of the area between the Thames River, Dumfries Mills, and part of the Credit River] Drawn by Absalom Shade of Dumfries; from the information of Travellers who have explored this part of the Province.
Col ms 53 x 45 cm 1" to 5 miles
Shows height of lands, rivers, falls, marshes, notes on areas of good land, the outlines of Dumfries (surveyed in 1817), Waterloo and Woolwich twps; certain tracts of land not identified; possibly made about 1820 when the Dumfries Mills in [Galt] were built (cf. Parsell, ... *Waterloo*, 8); (Holmden 1694).
OOAMA (NMC 3113)

---

726 *1820*
Plan 1. Mouth of the Grand River. (Signed) J.E. Portlock Lieut Royal Engineers. Commanding Royal Engineers Office. Quebec March 1, 1820 [Sgd] J. Jebb [Lt Royal Engineers] [and] (Copy) Sections to accompany Plan 1 (Signed) ... 1820 J. Jebb.
Col ms in 3 pieces 53 x 79 cm 1" to 176 yds
Watermark: 'J GREEN 1815.'
[Section]: 1" to 264 ft, 1" to 20 ft vertical; with Portlock's remarks to accompany the three plans about the possibility of a canal to connect Lakes Ontario and Erie (OOA RG 8 I/39 p 81ff); Plan 1 shows the desirability of improving the harbour at the mouth of the river; relief, vegetation, bldgs shown on the east bank, roads; (Holmden 1685, 2550).
OOAMA (NMC 21686–7)

The other plans are as follows:

(**2**) Lower Rapids of the Grand or Ouse River Plan 2 (Signed) J.E. Portlock Lieut Royal Engineers. Commanding Royal Engineers Office Quebec March 9, 1820 [Sgd] J. Jebb (Copy)
Col ms 66 x 271 cm Approx 1" to 176 yds
Watermark: 'J GREEN 1815.'
(OOA RG 8 I/39 p 104; vol 403 pp 135–40); shows relief, trees, houses, roads and line for sections; the sections are apparently missing; (Holmden 1686).
OOAMA (NMC 14267)

(**3**) Sections to accompany Plan 3 J.E. Portlock Royal Engineer. Commanding Royal Engineers Office Quebec Feb 22d 1820 [Sgd] J. Jebb (Copy)
Col ms 69 x 224 cm 1" to 528 ft, 1" to 20 ft vertical (OOA RG 8 I/39 p 104); sections are between Chippawa Creek and L Ontario crossing Beaver, Taylor, Twenty Mile, and Forty Mile creeks; Portlock commented that there might not be enough water for a canal and suggested that a road from the Grand to Forty Mile Creek might also be suitable; the map is lacking and appears not to have accompanied the original report; (Holmden 1567 describes sections only).
OOAMA (NMC 21685)

---

727 *[1821]*
GROUND SKETCH / OF / NIAGARA FALLS, / the / RAPIDS, AND VICINITY. / by / R.G. / for statistical account of U. Canada. // Neele & Son fc. 352 Strand.
Print (engrav) 19 x 11 cm Scale not given
In Robert Gourlay, *Statistical Account of Upper Canada* (London: Simpkin & Marshall 1 Jan 1822), I: opp 66 (*Bib Can* 1254); shows relief, cleared and forested areas, roads and battle sites in War of 1812.
OTMCL

---

728 *[1821]*
Sketch / of / Practicable Water Communications / between / LAKES ERIE AND ONTARIO, / by R.G. / for Statistical Account of Upper Canada. / Neele & Son Sculp. 352 Strand.
Print (engrav) 19 x 22 cm Approx 1" to 7.4 miles
Inset: 'Section / of the / GRAND NIAGARA CANAL, / between / Chippawa Creek and Queenston.'; in Robert Gourlay, *General Introduction to Statistical Account of Upper Canada* (London: Simpkin & Marshall 1822), frontis (*Bib Can* 1253); shows 'Government Canal Course' (for the Welland Canal from Twenty Mile Creek through Clinton, Gainsborough, and Wainfleet twps to L Erie) and Gourlay's proposals for 'Practicable Navigation Cut' between Forty Mile Creek and Grand R and another between Twenty Mile Creek and Grand R; also shows 'Grand Niagara Canal' (from Queenston to the Chippawa R and from the latter to L Erie in Wainfleet Twp); several other practicable canal routes also shown including two in Thorold Twp; shows relief, falls, mills, twps; Gourlay notes in 'Explanation of the Map' that it was engraved in Oct 1820 but that other data added later suggesting existence of an earlier state (see no **58**); there is also a ms tracing of this map in USDLC (Peter Force Map Collection no 723).
OTMCL

---

729 *1822*
[Endorsed title]: 'Roads in Barton, Glanford, Ancaster &c &c &c' [Sgd] Saml Ryckman Depty Surveyor 16th March 1822.
Col ms 58 x 63 cm [1" to 1 mile?] Endorsements: 'Y9' '782'
Shows the area from the Mohawk village on the Grand R to Burlington Bay with the twps; [Hamilton] and [Ancaster] villages shown; many roads and saw and grist mills shown.
OTNR (SR 6377)

---

730 *[1823]*
MAP / of the / PROPOSED CANAL / through the DISTRICT of NIAGARA and GORE / to form a junction of Lakes / ERIE AND ONTARIO / by the GRAND RIVER / Compiled from Actual Survey / BY ORDER OF THE / COMMISSIONERS / of / INTERNAL NAVIGATION / BY / James G. Chewett // Maverick, sculp.
Print (engrav) 56 x 77 cm 1" to 2 miles Watermark: 'J WHATMAN 1794'
In Upper Canada, Commissioners of Internal Navigation, *First Report* [York: Printed by order of the House of Assembly 1823], frontis (*Bib Can* 1303; Fleming 209); shows the early proposal of 1818 (Jackson, *St. Catharines*, 177–8) for the canal to follow route from the Grand R in Canborough Twp through Caistor, Gainsborough, and Clinton twps crossing Twenty Mile Creek and then west below the escarpment to exit at Burlington Bay; this route is also described in the *First Report* above; a profile of the route at 1" to 4 miles and 1" to 250 ft vertical is also included; a feeder is shown from further up the Grand R to enter the canal near Oswego Creek; shows locations of proposed locks, relief, marshes, all roads, and settlements; a separate loose copy in OTMCL has later ms adds

showing a proposed alternate route 'Welland Canal cut,' which was the actual route used; (Holmden 2044; *OHIM* 6.26).
OOAMA (NMC 19506) OTAR OTMCL OTUTF

---

731 *1824*
THE / STRAITS of NIAGARA / From a Map by Mr Darby. // London, Published by Baldwin, Cradock & Joy, Paternoster Row, June 1824. Engraved by Sidy Hall, Bury Strt Bloomsby // Page 406.
Print (engrav) 17 x 36 cm 1" to 2 miles
Inset: 'VERTICAL SECTION of the GREAT SLOPE which occasions the FALLS.' approx 1" to 1 mile, 1" to 450 ft vertical; in [William Blane], *An Excursion through the United States and Canada* (London: Printed for Baldwin, Cradock and Joy 1824), opp 406 (*Bib Can* 1276), and in his *Travels through the United States and Canada* (London: Baldwin & Co. 1828), opp 404 (USDLC); a reengraved copy of the Darby map of 1819 (**723**).
OTMCL USDLC

---

732 *[1825]*
A Plan of the Erie and Ontario Junction or Welland Canal. / For the purpose of uniting the great Lakes of Canada by a Navigable Communication around the Falls of Niagara, with a map of the adjacent territory. Compiled From actual Survey by / order of the President and Directors of the Welland Canal Company, by George Keefer, Jun. – Redrawn and engraved for the New-York Albion.
Print (wood engrav with typeset title) 15 x 26 cm Scale not given
In *Colonial Advocate* 15 Dec 1825; OTAR copy includes text 'An interesting Extract from the report of the select Committee of the House of Assembly of Upper Canada on the Welland Canal company's affairs'; shows the main proposed route via Twelve Mile Creek to the Chippawa R with a route to the Chippawa from the Grand R a few miles above its mouth (Route No 1); shows feeders nos 1 and 2 around the Grand, 'Route 2' connecting to L Erie in Wainfleet Twp, and 'Route No 3' proposing a connection from the Grand to Oswego Creek; also shows the proposed line to the town of Niagara, distances, names of twps and settlements.
OTAR (MU 1805–1949 A-9 box 118)

Later editions and states

(**2**) *[1826?]*
A PLAN of the Erie and Ontario Junction or Welland Canal, for the purpose of uniting the great Lakes in / Canada by a navigable communication round the Falls of Niagara, with a map of the adjacent territory. Compiled / from actual survey by Mr. George Keefer, Junior.
16 x 26 cm
On half of a circular from Colonial Advocate Office, dated York [in ms] 'Feby 23rd,' 182'6,' to 'Mr Jonah Brown' [asking for payment of half a year's subscription]; the map is from the same block as plan above but the title has been reset; (*OHIM* 6.27).
OOAMA (NMC 3005)

---

733 *[1826]*
MAP of the DISTRICT of NIAGARA in UPPER CANADA / Shewing the Course and a Section of the / WELLAND CANAL / Compiled from Actual Survey by order of the Directors. // Jardine & Co Lithogr. 1 Birchin Lane.
Print (lith) 29 x 31 cm Approx 1" to 5 miles
In *The Report of the President and Directors of the Welland Canal Company* (York, U.C.: Robert Stanton 1826), frontis (*Bib Can* 1418); shows the route of the canal and forks from L Ontario to the Chippawa or Welland R and west to the Grand R; relief, names of twps, major rds; the 'Survey of Lands appropriated to the Use of the Welland Canal Company' [ca 1826–34] comprising 84 plans and descriptions of parcels is found in the Welland Canal Papers from the St Lawrence Seaway Authority on microfilm at OTAR (MS 191).
OTMCL

---

734 *[1826]*
Part of the Township of Trafalgar Copied by J.G. Chewett [Sgd] Surveyr Genl Office York 30 Decr 1826 Thos Ridout Survr Genl
Col ms 23 x 14 cm 1" to 40 chains
Shows Indian reserve and lands to be sold along Twelve Mile Creek; (Holmden 2742).
OOAMA (NMC 53779)

---

735 *[1827]*
[Niagara Falls] and [Niagara River and vicinity]
2 prints (engrav) 9 x 9 cm and 9 x 7 cm Scale not given
In John de Ros, *Personal Narrative of Travels in the United States and Canada in 1826* (London: William Harrison Ainsworth 1827), opp 167 and 176 (*Bib Can* 7164); also in the 2nd ed (1827) (*Bib Can* 1392), and in the 3rd ed (1827), opp 140 and 154 (*Bib Can* 1393); small maps with a few points, roads, etc, marked.
OTMCL

---

736 1827
No 8 Sketch of the Isthmus or Belt of Niagara Shewing the situation of the New Fortress [Sgd] R.H. Bonnycastle Capt R.E. Rl Engrs Office Quebec 20th Novr 1827 [Sgd] E.W. Durnford Col. Comg Rl Engineers Canada.
Col ms 53 x 74 cm 1" to 2 miles Watermark: 'J WHATMAN TURKEY MILL 1825' Endorsements: 'BB 53'; stamps 'B↑O' 'IGF'
Shows the site for a new military establishment near 'Short Hills' on top of the escarpment in Pelham Twp; also shows the Welland Canal, roads, and twps; (Holmden 2080 h8).
OOAMA (NMC 21588)

Related maps

(2) *1827*
No 2 Plan of that part of the Short Hills in the District of Niagara called the Mountain shewing those Lots or grants of land in the 5th, 6th & 7th concessions of the Township of Pelham ... which are near the Site of the New Fortress as proposed in the Report of M. General Sir James Carmichael-Smyth. [Sgd] R H Bonnycastle Captn Royal Engineers Rl Engineers Office Quebec 20th Novr 1827 E.W. Durnford Col Comg Rl Engineers Canada
Col ms 55 x 67 cm 1" to 440 ft Endorsements: 'BB47'; stamps 'IGF' 'B↑O'
Shows the plan for two star-shaped forts; relief by hachures; farms, fields, and lot lines with names of owners; (Holmden 2080B); there is a plan in OOAMA (NMC 22143) 'No 1 Sketch of that part of the Short Hills ... on which it is proposed to construct the New Fortress ... 20th Novr 1827' endorsed 'BB46,' 'IGF,' and 'B↑O' that is similar to above without lots (Holmden 2080); also a plan in OOAMA (NMC 22146) showing cleared and forested land in the area with notes on soil.
OOAMA (NMC 22143–4; 22146)

(3) *1827*
No 3 Plan of Comparison of that part of the Short Hills ... on which it is proposed to erect a Fortress [Sgd] R.H. Bonnycastle ... E.W. Durnford ... 20th Novr 1827
Col ms 53 x 68 cm 1" to 220 ft Endorsements: 'BB48'; stamps 'IGF' 'B↑O'
Shows the proposed site for the forts in detail; relief by hachures and contour lines; (Holmden 2080C).
OOAMA (NMC 22145)

---

737 *1827*
A Survey of the ground with the differences of level to the extent of 1000 yards around a site on the eastern bank of the River Ouse distant 18 miles from its mouth proposed to be occupied by a large sized Redoubt for the protection of a Naval Depot. [Sgd] J. Walpole Lieut. R. Engineers 21 August 1827 Upper Canada. [Sgd] Rl Engineers Office Quebec 20th Novr 1827 E.W. Durnford Col Comg Rl Engineers Canada.
Col ms 77 x 102 cm 1" to 200 ft Watermark: 'JAMES WHATMAN TURKEY MILL KENT 1820' Endorsements: 'Pl. 1 BB 54'; stamps 'B↑O' 'IGF'
On the Grand R; redoubt is sketched in proposed position, relief is shown by spot heights suggesting contour lines; marshy ground; (Holmden 1687A).
OOAMA (NMC 11321)

---

738 *[1828]*
MAP of the NIAGARA PENINSULA / Shewing the Course and a Profile of the / WELLAND CANAL. / Connecting Lakes Erie and Ontario by / SHIP NAVIGATION. // George Keefer Jnr. 5th Jan: 1828 / A. Doolittle Sc.
Print (engrav) 22 x 37 cm Scale not given
[Profile] 1" to 4 miles; in Wm Merritt, *Account of the Welland Canal* ([N.p. 1828]), frontis (*OOA Pamph* 1828 (9)); offprint from *American Journal of Science* XIV (1828), 159–68; shows line of canal from Port Dalhousie to Welland/Chippawa R and connecting to the Grand R north of mouth; shows names of twps and a few roads in the peninsula; reproduced in Jackson, *St. Catharines*, 361.
OOA

---

739 *[1828]*
Map of the Survey of Sundry Lots on Burlington Beach in the District of Gore, by Order of The Honorbl Thomas Ridout Surveyor General of the Province of Upper Canada; dated 15th December A.D. 1827. Surveyed and Executed by [Sgd] John Goessman Dy Survyr. [also entitled] Plan of Port Huskisson.
Col ms 66 x 129 cm 1" to 2 chains Endorsements: 'No 56'
(SI 15 Dec 1827 to survey several lots on Burlington Beach and to lay out roads, lots, and reserves on each side of the canal as projected; OTNR FN 328 21 Jan 1828); shows cut through beach for canal; 'Explanations' keys various bldgs including houses, barns, warehouses, etc, Canada Co. land, road.
OTNR (SR 29)

---

740 *1828*
Plan of the Grand River / & Location of 6 Nations of Indians, / as found settled, by the Revd Rt Lugger, / February 20th 1828. // Lake, Token-house Yard.
Print (lith) 22 x 34 cm 1" to 2 miles
In *Report by a Committee of the Corporation, Commonly Called the New England Company, of Their Proceedings for the Civilization and Conversion of Indians* (London: J.R. Lake printer 1829), opp 44 (*Bib Can* 1540); shows various Indian and white settlements with names of people and tribes; schools built and proposed roads; shows Grand R from its mouth to 'Davies Hamlet' [about Brantford]; the map was drawn by the Rev Lugger; a copy was enclosed in Gibson to Hay 18 Nov 1829 (GBLpro CO 42/227 f 278); (*OHIM* 4.6; *PRO Cat* 1465).
GBLpro (CO 42/227 f 278) OTMCL

---

741 *[1829?]*
MAP / of a part of the / NIAGARA RIVER / and Plan of the Proposed / HARBOUR AT BLACK ROCK // W.A. Bird del. // Balch, Rawdon & Co. fc.
Print (engrav) 18 x 31 cm 1" to 2000 ft
Originally enclosed with a memo of 11 May 1829 from Gen P. Porter to Sir John Colborne requesting that stone be taken from the Canadian side to build a mole at Black Rock (OOA RG 1 E3 vol 63 pp 44–9); on United States side shows Upper Village of Black Rock and Lower Village; a pier is

shown from Squaw Is south to Bird Is and canal from Buffalo Creek; Towson's Battery and Fort Erie shown on Canadian side; also a ms copy of the plan at OOAMA (NMC 3173) with the addition of a new ferry to Canadian side and a bridge over the canal and old ferry shown; (Holmden 2029).
OOAMA (NMC 3173; 59331)

---

742 *1829*
Plan of the Cut at Mouth of River Welland By Geo. Keefer Jnr Asst Engineer. St. Catharines 4th March 1829.
Col ms 30 x 30 cm 1" to 4 chains Watermark: 'G WILMOT[T?] 1827'
'Cross Section of Canal' 1" to 20 ft; shows two lines for the cut near the Niagara R; military ground and fort shown beyond lines; 'old Drawbridge'; there is also an undated plan of the same title showing how the cut on the east side encroaches on the military reserve (QMMMCM).
OOAMA (NMC 5236) QMMMCM

---

743 *[183?]*
Plan of the Skinner, Ellsworth & Forsyth Tracts at Niagara Falls
Col ms 35 x 42 cm 1" to 10 chains
Shows lot nos and some pencilled notes about the tracts; a few bldgs are shown including 'Museum' and 'Pavilion' and 'Tower' on Goat Is; shows parts of lots 143–6, 159, 160, 173–5 in Stamford Twp.
OTMCL

---

744 *1830*
Garrison Line run by Order of Major Campbell 29th Regt 11th June 1787 by P.R. Frey [Sgd] Surveyr Genls Office York 12th April 1830 W Chewett Actg Surveyr Genl.
Ms 12 x 24 cm Scale not given
With Colborne's report to Murray no 23 Miscellaneous of 16 Apr 1830 (GBLpro CO 42/391 p 159) about the leasing of military lands not required for military purposes; shows the area from Niagara R west to about Four Mile Creek and from the mouth south to Navy Hall and the boundary line of the military reserve; the Garrison line is shown on Frey's plan of 1788 (see **670**) but no original of this plan has been found.
GBLpro (CO 42/391 p 159)

---

745 *1830*
MAP of the DISTRICT of NIAGARA in UPPER CANADA / shewing the Course and a Section of the / WELLAND CANAL / Compiled from Actual Survey by order of the Directors // Published by J. Millar 23 St. James's Street 1830.
Print (lith) hand col 29 x 31 cm Approx 1" to 5 miles
[Section] 1" to 5 miles, 1" to 250 ft vertical; in Ogden Creighton, *General View of the Welland Canal* (London: Printed for J. Miller 1830) (*Bib Can* 1574); shows the revised route of the canal with additional canal built around the Welland R; the map is redrawn from that of 1826 (**733**) with deletion of former canal connection and lock at Misener's Mill; Gravelly Bay now marked.
OOA OTMCL

---

746 *[ca 1830]*
[Plan of part of the Niagara Peninsula showing the Welland Canal]
Col ms 92 x 68 cm Scale not given Watermark: 'JAMES WHATMAN TURKEY MILL ... 1827'
An unfinished plan showing twps, survey grid, settlements, roads, forts, some mills, and the Welland Canal; the canal is shown from Port Dalhousie to the link with the Chippawa R and the feeder to the Grand R is shown; two possible routes for the extension of the canal to the south are marked – one to exit at Gravelly Bay and one to exit further west in 'Graniells Bay'; the more easterly exit was chosen and the extension was opened in 1833.
OTMCL

---

747 *[1831]*
Description of Harbour at mouth of Grand River or Port Maitland – Lake Erie.
Col ms 33 x 25 cm Scale not given
With a petition from the Welland Canal Co. dated Dec 1831 for a Crown grant of the water lots within the harbour the company is building near the naval reserve (OOA RG 1 L3 W17 no 22 1831); shows naval depot and reservation and the harbour with a survey description; the petition for one lot was denied because of the proximity to the naval reserve; (Holmden 1693).
OOAMA (NMC 3116)

---

748 *1831*
NIAGARA RIVER (from Lake Erie to Lake Ontario, 36 miles.) / ... by Geo. Catlin / in 1827.
Print (lith) 28 x 22 cm Scale not given
Probably from George Catlin *Views of Niagara* ([Baltimore]: 1831) (USMiU-C, USNN); shows places, roads on either side of the river; 'ancient shore of Lake Ontario,' and of Niagara R; oriented to the south; inset shows area covered on map below.
OOAMA (NMC 120091)

Related maps

(2) *1831*
Catlin's Survey & model of NIAGARA in the year 1827. // G.J. Poore & Co lithogr L'pool. / J. Gow, Script.
Print (lith) 30 x 22 cm Scale not given
Inset: 'Horizontal Section and Elevation of the Model, with Geological Features.'; a high level view of a model of the falls area from the same source as above; shows the two falls with notes on heights and depths; bldgs named; roads; 'alluvial

bank or terrace ...'; distances across river shown; Catlin's painting of the model is reproduced in Buisseret, on cover and at 284.
OOAMA (NMC 120090)

---

749 *1831*
Plan of part of the Lands of the Six Nations Indians as surveyed by order of their Superintendant John Brant Esqr dated at the Mohawk Village the 20th day of April 1831. by [Sgd] Lewis Burwell Dy Surveyor Brantford 31st October 1831.
Col ms 65 x 98 cm 1" to 40 chains Endorsements: '1082' 'B12'
(OTNR FN 69, 31 Oct 1831); shows the area northwest and west of Brantford to Dumfries, Burford, and Blenheim twps; roads, survey grid, clearings, marshes, some names of owners.
OTNR (SR 6961)

---

750 *[1831]*
Sketch of / NIAGARA RIVER / between / Queenston & Chippewa // Engraved by J & C Walker.
Print (engrav) 20 x 23 cm 1" to 1 mile
Inset: 'VERTICAL SECTION' 1" to 475 ft vertical; in Joseph Bouchette, *The British Dominions in North America* (London: Henry Colburn and Richard Bentley 1831), I: opp 140 (OOA), and in the later ed (London: Longman, Rees, Orme, Brown, Green, and Longman 1832) (*Bib Can* 1627, 4968); relief by hachures, rapids, roads, some bldgs identified.
OOA OTMCL

---

751 *[1832?]*
No 1 Rough Sketch of the Welland Canal from The Welland River to Lake Ontario [and] No 2 ... from The Welland River to Lake Erie [both sgd] by Capt. J.E. Alexander H.R. late 16th L M.R.G.S. M.R.A.S.Ve.
2 col ms Ea 64 x 82 cm 2" to 1 mile
Shows the canal with locks, bridges, and names of owners along route; relief, marshy areas; includes cross-section; probably drawn after Alexander's first trip to North America in 1831 and just after he transferred to the 42 Highland Regiment in 1832.
GBLrg

---

752 *1833 (1846)*
Long Point Inner and Outer Bay Soundings taken in 1833. Copy from Harriss.
Col ms 55 x 71 cm Approx 3/4" to 1000 yds
Endorsements: 'No 2'
'Enclosure to the Report of Capt Frederick Warden R.N. of 27 Jan 1846' (GBLpro Adm 7/625); John Harris surveyed the Long Point area in mid-1815 (Harris, 33) (see **C94**) but retired from the Hydrographic service soon after; therefore, the plan appears to originate from the earlier date with additions in 1833; shows lighthouse on the end of the point that fell down by erosion of sand; line of coast in 1790; ruins of old blockhouse at Turkey Point; a proposed lighthouse shown; soundings, marshy areas, trees, settlements along shore; (*PRO Cat* 1497).
GBLpro (MR 1052(10))

---

753 *[1833]*
[The Niagara Peninsula showing the Welland Canal] D.[J.] Estry Del. Tazewell lith. Survr Genls Dept York U.C.
Print (lith) 44 x 57 cm Scale not given
'Profile of the Canal according to the present Levels'; shows the canal through to Port Colborne with the feeder to Dunnville; table of distances via canal and feeder; a proposed cut and new shorter feeder are shown closer to mouth of Grand R; the northern and southern route of a proposed side cut to the town of Niagara are shown; the escarpment is shown by hachures; Tazewell listed 200 copies on hand as of 21 Mar 1834 (OTAR RG 1 A-1-7 box 9).
OTMCL

---

754 *[1834?]*
Map / OF / NIAGARA FALLS / AND / VICINITY.
Print (engrav) 23 x 30 cm 1" to 1/3 mile Watermark: 'WHATMAN ... 1830'
Inscribed 'Wm Cromwell Goat Island Niagara Falls [illegible] 15th 1834'; shows the falls, Goat Is, and the river upstream; streets and canal shown in Niagara Falls, New York, and 16 bldgs indexed; distances between various points; a few bldgs on Canadian side identified.
OTUTF

---

755 *1834*
[Part of Twenty Mile Pond and outlet to Lake Ontario] [Sgd] Geo. Rykert D.P.S. St Catharines 24th July 1834.
Col ms 63 x 83 cm 1" to 5 chains Endorsements: 'No 1' '858'
Shows outlet and bridge and sand beaches.
OTAR (SR 7214)

---

756 *1834 (1835)*
Plan of Burlington Heights Surveyed by Lewis Burwell D.P.S. in 1834. Surveyor Generals Office, Toronto, U.C. 12th May 1835 Copy – Henry Lizars
Col ms 62 x 46 cm 1" to 10 chains Endorsements: 'J 8' '943'
Endorsed 'See Descriptions Nos L.O. 156 and 166'; endorsement refers to Licences of Occupation to John Simpson of 12 Apr 1834 (L.O. 156) and to Allan Napier McNab 8 Nov 1834 (L.O. 166); shows relief, roads to Dundas St and to Toronto; batteries; Desjardins Canal.
OTAR (SR 81002)

Related maps

(2) *1834 (1836)*
Plan of Burlington Heights ... Surveyor General's Office Toronto U.C. 23rd April 1835. Copy Henry

Lizars [Sgd] S.P. Hurd S.G. (Certified as a true copy) [Sgd] P J Bainbrigge Lt. R.E. 4th Augt 1836.
Col ms 60 x 48 cm 1" to 10 chains Endorsements: 'Burlington Heights Capt Bonnycastle 20 June 1837'; stamp 'B↑O'
Shows the same information as above with the addition of copies of the text of the two licences of occupation; (Holmden 1544); also a copy: 'Plan of Burlington Heights ... Surveyor General's Office 23rd April 1835. Certified a true copy [Sgd] P.J. Bainbrigge, Lt. R.E. 14th August, 1836' endorsed 'REO,' '38,' and 'Can V 20' (QMMMCM (3628)); and a copy: 'Copy No 2 Plan of Burlington Heights ... 1834 Copy J.G.C. Surveyor Generals Office Toronto 19th January 1837 [Sgd] J W Macaulay Survr Genl endorsed 'A.R.,'; 'REO,' and '88' (QMMMCM (3629)); also a plan marked 'Copy No 3' with the same title stamped '254' and 'A.S.' (QMMMCM (3653)).
OOAMA (NMC 3849) QMMMCM (3628–9; 3653)

---

757 *1834*
Sketch shewing the Reserve at Burlington Heights. Surveyor General's Office, 12th Dec'r 1834 Signed J.G. Chewitt. Copied from the sketch sent with Col. Rowan's letter dated 16th Dec. 1834. Royal Engineers Office, Toronto 19th Decr 1834 [Sgd] R.H. Bonnycastle Capt. W.D.
Col ms 33 x 21 cm 1" to 40 chains Endorsements: '30 6 Reserve Hamilton' 'A.W.'; stamp 'REO'
Shows parts of Barton, Ancaster, Flamborough East and West twps, military reserve, Desjardins Canal, and licence of occupation to A. McNab.
QMMMCM (3626)

---

758 *[1835?]*
[Map of Niagara Falls and Niagara River showing Goat Island and Porter's Bridge]
Col ms 26 x 30 cm Scale not given
Provenance: USDLC attributed to Major D.B. Douglass, ca 1835; the plan was acquired with his collection of maps in 1836.
USDLC

---

759 *1835*
Map / OF / NIAGARA FALLS / AND VICINITY / BY H.A. PARSONS / Published by O.G. STEELE, Buffalo. // Copy Right Secured [and] Map / OF / NIAGARA RIVER / AND PARTS ADJACENT. / BY H.A. PARSONS. / Published by O.G. STEELE, Buffalo. // Engraved by J.G. Darby, Buffalo, N.Y.
2 prints on 1 sheet (engrav) 30 x 18 cm and 30 x 19 cm on sheet 30 x 38 cm Scale not given
Inset: 'SECTION of the SLOPE which occasions the FALLS' 1" to approx 2 miles, 1/2" to 350 ft vertical; in Horatio Parsons, *A Guide to Travellers Visiting the Falls of Niagara*, 2nd ed (Buffalo: Oliver G. Steele 1835), frontis (*Bib Can* 1909, CIHM 42509); shows the area of the falls with streets and some houses on the United States side and some bldgs and lot lines on the Canadian side; the map of river shows roads, battle sites, relief; 'Proposed City of the Falls'.
OSTCB OTMCL

Later editions and states

(2) *[1836]*
[Same titles, imprints, etc]
In Horatio Parsons, *The Book of Niagara Falls ... Accompanied by Maps*, 3rd ed (Buffalo: Oliver G. Steele 1836), frontis (*Bib Can* 7431, QMBN, CIHM 40062); also in the 5th ed revised and enlarged (Buffalo: Steele & Peck 1838) (OKQ, CIHM 49434); from the same plate as the 1835 ed.
OKQ OTMCL QMBN

(3) *[1855–6]*
[Same title] Published Expressly for BURKE'S Descriptive Guide / 1855 // Copy Right Secured. [and] Map / OF / NIAGARA RIVER ... PARSONS / 1855 // Engraved by J.G. Darby, Buffalo, N.Y.
2 prints on 1 sheet (lith) Ea 31 x 18 cm
In *Burke's Descriptive Guide or the Visitors Companion to Niagara Falls* (Buffalo: Andrew Burke 1855) (OSTCB, CIHM 18269), and in a later ed with cover-title 'Burke's Illustrated Guide to Niagara Falls for 1856 ... Enlarged Edition' ([New York 1856]), between 6 and 7 (OTAR, USDLC, CIHM 22587); the map is a lithographic transfer from the same plate as the 1835 map and slightly larger; the Steele imprint has been deleted and the date on the later map; some bldgs deleted and other bldgs and canal on American side added; references to the location of four bldgs added; the Niagara R map is the same; the same map may also have appeared in the 1857 ed of *Burke's Descriptive Guide* (*NUC pre-1956 imprints* 85:367).
OSTCB OTAR USDLC

---

760 *[1835]*
Map / of / NIAGARA FALLS / AND / Vicinity // T. Physick lithr Manchester.
Print (lith) 30 x 17 cm Scale not given
In W. Fleming, *Four Days at the Falls of Niagara* ([Manchester]: Gillet printer [1835?]), frontis (*Bib Can* 1886); the book is a journal for part of June and July 1835 and possibly published later; the map is similar to and possibly reengraved from Parsons (**759(1)**); however, town plot on United States side and survey grid on Canadian side not shown; Termination Rock is located and Terrapin Bridge named; cliffs in relief, tourist sights.
OTMCL

Later editions and states

(2) *1840*
[Title is the same]
Print (lith) 30 x 17 cm
In W. Fleming, *Four Days at Niagara Falls in North America* (Manchester: Printed by Love & Barton 1840) (Casey I–1764); the same as the earlier ed.
OOA

---

761 *1835*
Plan of part of the Grand River shewing the Indian Lands apportioned to the G.R.N. Co at each Lock and Dam, denoted by a red margin. Surveyed by order from the Surveyor General's Office bearing date at Toronto the 16th day of February 1835. by [Sgd] Peter Carroll D.P. Surveyor Oxford 26th March 1835.
Col ms 56 x 114 cm 1" to 20 chains Endorsements: 'Q 40' '1078'
(OTNR FN 424 13 Apr 1835); shows the area from the Port Dover Rd crossing south to the Talbot Rd crossing, and Seneca and Oneida twps; shows towing path along east shore, bldgs with names of owners, mills, stores, etc; Indian Council House; two proposed routes to Port Dover west of river; a later note initialled 'J.W.M.' indicates a disagreement between the Grand River Navigation Co. and the surveyor about the south boundary of Cayuga Twp (15 June 1836).
OTNR (SR 7061)

---

762 *1835*
Plan of the Military Reserve at Burlington [Sgd] H.O. Crawley Lieut. R. Engineers 11th March, 1835
Col ms 42 x 26 cm 1" to 10 chains Endorsements: stamps 'REO' '770 I'
Shows the bldgs and boundary of the reserve on the spit between Coote's Paradise and Burlington Bay; relief, forested areas, roads; licence of occupation to A. McNab.
QMMMCM (3620)

---

763 *1835*
Plan of the Mount Pleasant Tract in the Township of Brantford Surveyed by [Sgd] Lewis Burwell Dy Surveyor Brantford 23rd Octr 1835
Col ms 36 x 55 cm 1" to 20 chains Endorsements: 'I 21'
Shows lot nos, dimensions, and sizes for the part of Brant Twp south of Brantford; some owners named.
OOAMA (NMC 3389)

Related maps

(**2**) *1838*
Plan of the Mount Pleasant and Phelps Tracts. As surveyed and reported upon in 1835. Including Lot No Five in the Second Range East which was Surveyed in 1837. Brantford 22d August 1838 [Sgd] Lewis Burwell Dy Surveyor.
Col ms 36 x 55 cm 1" to 20 chains
Shows names of occupants or owners; note that lots in the second and third ranges were settled and improved by squatters; notes about encroachments on lots owned by Kerr.
OOAMA (NMC 3392)

---

764 *1836*
[Map of the Niagara River area]
Print (lith) 39 x 18 cm 1" to 2 miles
In Solomon van Rensselaer, *A Narrative of the Affair of Queenstown: in the War of 1812* (New York: Leavitt, Lord & Co., etc 1836), frontis (*Bib Can* 929); 'References' includes the locations of Gen van Rensselaer's camps, various batteries, routes and crossing place on 12 Oct 1812.
OTMCL

---

765 *[1837]*
Plan and Section of a Ship Canal from Lake Erie to the Niagara River at the Village of Waterloo, by Tho. Roy Civil Engineer.
Col ms 67 x 99 cm 1" to 400 ft, section: 1" to 48 ft vertical Watermark: 'J WHATMAN 1833'
Endorsements: 'Proposed Canal at Entrance of Niagara Capt Bonnycastle 28 June 1837 F 20'; stamps 'B↑O' 'IGF'
The canal with locks is shown close to the shore between Fort Erie and the village of Waterloo on Niagara R; shows terrain, soundings, nature of river bottom, rapids, wharves, Fort Erie military reserve boundary, and previous location for canal further north; (Holmden 2053).
OOAMA (NMC 21731)

Related maps

(**2**) *[1837?]*
Plan of a Canal between Fort Erie and Waterloo by Thos Roy.
Col ms 67 x 99 cm 1" to 400 ft Watermark: 'J WHATMAN 1832'
'Section of the line of Canal as originally laid out' 1" to 24 ft vertical; this is similar to the other plan except the section is in more detail including bottom sediments, floodgates, etc, and the lock at Waterloo has a different shape; whereas other parts of the map are unfinished, the town plot of Fort Erie has been added; (Holmden 1642).
OOAMA (NMC 21732)

---

766 *1837*
Plan of a Ship Canal from the Niagara River to the Welland Canal. Made to accompany a Report by [Sgd] Thos Roy. Jany 6th 1837.
Col ms 77 x 134 cm 1" to 2400 ft Endorsements: stamp 'B↑O'
'Section of the line of Canal' 1" to 1200 ft, 1" to 200 ft vertical; shows a proposed line for a canal from the town of Niagara to intersect the Welland Canal at Thorold; (Holmden 2054); Roy's report of the same date is found in OTAR (MS 393 A-4-b).
OOAMA (NMC 11293)

---

767 *1837*
Plan of the Present Route of the Welland Canal. From Lake Ontario, to Lake Erie. (From actual Survey.) Shewing the works in their present situations, with the Deviatios [*sic*] proposed thereon. By order of the Board of Directors. 1837. Surveyed by F.P. Rubidge D.P.S. under the direction of N.H. Baird H.H. Killaly Civil Engineers.
Col ms 74 x 305 cm 1" to 16 chains Endorsements: stamp [BW] '693'

'Note The deviations and Improvements proposed are delineated by the red tinting [Sgd] N.H. Baird Hamilton H. Killaly'; shows the 18 locks and proposed deviations to the present route; all engineering works shown; some of Baird's reports for this survey are found in OTAR (MS 393 A-4-a); the published report by Baird and H.H. Killaly, *Report on the Present State and Proposed Deviations and Improvements of the Welland Canal* (1838), is found in OTMCL (*Bib Can* 5112).
OTAR

Related maps

(2) *[1837]*
Welland Canal from actual Survey, Section First Comprising from Lake Ontario, to the Village of Thorold, ... Welland Canal Section Second from Thorold to the Aqueduct ... Welland Canal Section Third from below the Aqueduct to its Conflux with Lake Erie &c By Order of the Board of Directors. Surveyed by F.P. Rubidge D.P.S. under the direction of N.H. Baird H.H. Killaly Civil Engineers.
Col ms 129 x 124 cm 1" to 4 chains
A separate title and author statement is found for each of the sections; 'Note The proposed Improvements and Deviations are delineated on the Plans by the red tinting, subject to local modifications [Sgd] N.H. Baird Hamilton H. Killaly.'; these are the more detailed plans from which the above reduced plan was prepared; all locks, dams, weirs, etc, are shown in detail; relief, length of locks, and heights; notes on locks 'in repair,' proposed deviations, excavation, building of piers and locks, etc.
OOAMA (NMC 11848)

---

768 *1837*
[Endorsed]: 'The Welland Canal Capt. Bonnycastle 28th June 1837.'
Col ms (pt missing) 50 x 61 cm Scale not given
Watermark: 'S. & A. BUTLER, U.S.' Endorsements: 'F 19'; stamps 'IGF' 'B↑O'
'[Section] of the Canal according to the present levels. 1" to 2 miles'; endorsed 'Private Plan. To be returned.'; shows the completed canal with proposed cut at end of feeder to Port Maitland and a northern and southern proposed route to the town of Niagara; shows the escarpment, twps named, and settlements; 'Table of distances' along canal and feeder; (Holmden 2886).
OOAMA (NMC 21589)

---

769 *1838*
ACKERMANN'S / Authentic Plan / of / NAVY ISLAND, the village of CHIPPEWA, / AND THE / Niagara River, / with the Principal Objects of Interest / in the Vicinity of the / SEAT OF WAR / IN / UPPER CANADA. / From Actual Survey. / 1838. // G.T. delt. // LONDON, PUBLISHED 6TH FEBY 1838, BY R. ACKERMANN, AT HIS ECLIPSE SPORTING GALLERY, 191 REGENT ST.
Print (engrav) hand col 32 x 19 cm
Shows the location of the steamboat 'Caroline' burnt 29 Dec 1837 opp Fort Schlosser; 'Brocks Monument' and a few other bldgs located; hand-coloured key to British possessions and United States; (Holmden 1571); also a map 'MAP / of / NAVY ISLAND. U.C. ... at which Place / the / Steamboat Caroline / was Burnt by the Royalists ... N. Currier's ... N.Y.' reproduced in *Currier & Ives*, 436; original not located.
OOAMA (NMC 59330)

---

770 *[1838]*
[Map of Niagara Falls and vicinity]
Print (lith) 14 x 20 cm Scale not given
In Guillaume Blouet, *Chutes du Niagara. Niagara Falls* (Paris: Delpech, 1838), on title-p (*Bib Can* 2043); place-names in French; oriented to the west; more detail is shown for the United States side; relief, tourist attractions.
OTMCL

---

771 *1838*
MAP / OF THE / RIVER NIAGARA / AND VICINITY, / By / D. Jay Browne. / T. Moore's Lithography, / Boston. / 1838. // Surveyed & drawn under the direction of the East Boston Timber Co.
Print (lith) 35 x 30 cm 1" to 21/2 miles
Shows twps, towns, railways including line from Chippawa to Queenston and 'Niagara & Detroit Railroad,' canals including Welland Canal and feeders; railways and survey grid on U.S. side.
USNN

---

772 *1838*
[Map of the Road from Queenston to Sixteen Mile Creek] [Sgd] Francis Hall Civil Engineer 23d Feby 1838.
Col ms 55 x 700 cm Approx 1" to 40 ft
Endorsements: stamp 'BW'
Part of the Queenston and Grimsby Rd; shows road as planned and actual route via St Davids and St Catharines; distances, shows bldgs with names of owners, relief, trees, bridges, culverts.
OOAMA

---

773 *[1838]*
[The Niagara River and vicinity]
Print (wood engrav) 13 x 9 cm Scale not given
In *An Impartial and Authentic Account of the Civil War in the Canadas* (London: J. Saunders [1838]), 172 (*Bib Can* 5124, Casey I–1666); shows places along the Niagara River including Navy Is.
OOA OTMCL

---

774 *1838*
Plan of Navy Island [Sgd] H.O. Crawley Lieut Rl Engineers Chippewa 19 Jany 1838.
Ms 23 x 38 cm 1" to 400 yds Endorsements: 'Navy Island Case N.1 No 7' 'No 411'; stamps 'REO'
Shows the island four days after W.L. Mackenzie vacated after the Rebellion of 1837; relief, trees, bldgs; 'Rebel Hospital' shown on Grand Is and batteries located on Canadian side opp Navy Is.
OOAMA (NMC 4202)

Related maps

(2) *[1838]*
Sketch of Navy Island.
Endorsements: 'No 116'; stamp 'REO'
The same as above with a few more notes: distance measurements from shore, currents in river, and point on island where 'schooner may come within 10 ft of this shore'; also an untitled undated plan from the Wm. Gourley Papers OOA (MG 24 G20 p 4840–1).
OOAMA (NMC 4203; 8764)

775 *1838*
[Rough sketch of the roads from Cayuga to Chippewa] (Signed) R.J. Barou Major Royal Engineers Evan's Tavern 13 Miles from Port Dover 7th Nov 1838. (A True Copy) F.A. Mackenzie Fraser Colonel Asst Q.M. Genl.
Ms 32 x 40 cm Scale not given
To accompany F.A. Mackenzie Fraser's report on roads in the vicinity 13 Nov 1838 (OOA RG 8 I/277 p 68); includes notes on the lengths of various roads, those passable in winter and in summer, the lake road in winter and various problems with it; (Holmden 2781).
OOAMA (NMC 3007)

776 *1838*
Sketch of Ryerse's Creek 25th November 1838 [Sgd] C. Mackenzie Capt Rl Engrs.
Ms 18 x 23 cm Scale not given
Map is filed with the 2nd report from Capt Mackenzie to Col Halkett about the defence of the port at 'Ryerse's Creek' (OOA RG 8 I/446 p 101); shows relief, bridge, various bldgs at mouth, and 'sketch of proposed basin'; routes to Simcoe and Port Rowan.
OOA (RG 8 I/446 p 101)

777 *1838*
SKETCH / of the / NIAGARA RIVER / LONDON / Published by Jas Wyld, Geographer to the Queen Charing Cross East. / 1838 // [in decorative script] J W
Print (engrav) 29 x 18 cm 1" to 2.5 miles
Shows the whole river with places and main roads on both sides; 'Navy Island McKenzie's Camp'; battle sites of the War of 1812.
GBL (74190(8)) OOA (Pamph 1838 (67))

778 *[1839]*
MAP OF / NIAGARA FALLS, / and / ADJOINING SHORES. / Lith. of Hall & Mooney, Buffalo. // MAP OF NIAGARA FALLS. / AND GUIDE TABLE. / Being a complete Directory and Guide to the Falls and vicinity, for remark on the spot or for reference at home.
Print (lith) 39 x 30 cm Scale not given
Insets: 'A Bird's eye View of Niagara Strait' and 'THE WHIRLPOOL.'; in Samuel de Veaux, *The Falls of Niagara* (Buffalo: William B. Hayden 1839), frontis (*Bib Can* 2257) (see also **779** below), and in *Legend of the Whirlpool* (Buffalo: Press of Thomas & Co. 1840) (Casey I–1763); key to many bldgs located on the American and Canadian sides; distances from the ferry, Upper Canada, and from American hotels; 'Directions to Hasty Travellers'; shows the village of Niagara Falls and 'part of the proposed city of the Falls'; relief.
OOA OTMCL

Later editions and states

(2) *1841*
MAP OF / NIAGARA FALLS, / AND / ADJOINING SHORES / BUFFALO / Faxon & Read. / 1841. // MAP OF NIAGARA FALLS, / AND GUIDE TABLE ...
Print (lith) Size not known Scale not given
Inset: 'THE WHIRLPOOL'; in de Veaux's *The Travellers Own Book to Saratoga Springs, Niagara Falls and Canada* (Buffalo: Faxon & Read 1841) (QML, CIHM 58908) and possibly in editions for 1842, 1843, 1844, 1845, and 1846 and in the 1847 edition (USNN); from the same plate as map above with the same tables around the side and similar information on the map; the bird's-eye view has been deleted, the title has been redrawn and moved, and the secondary title reset.
QML USNN

779 *1839*
MAP / OF / NIAGARA RIVER, / &C.
Print (woodcut) Approx 16 x 10 cm Scale not given
In Samuel de Veaux, *The Falls of Niagara* (Buffalo: William B. Hayden 1839), frontis (Casey I–1746; CIHM 35067; OTUTF); a roughly executed woodcut with major places, roads, and railways marked on both sides of the river; a few names added from typeset; this is a different map from that found in the OTMCL copy of the book (see **778**).
OOA OTUTF

780 *1839*
Plan of that portion of the Indian lands on the Grand River situate between the mouth of Fairchilds Creek and the Township of Cayuga, shewing the different parcels which have been granted to claimants under 999 year leases and other conveyances from the Six Nations Indians. Also the parcels granted to the Grand River Navigation Company – School Lots &c &c &c. Brantford 5th February 1839 [Sgd] Lewis Burwell Dy Surveyor.
Col ms 63 x 127 cm 1" to 40 chains Endorsements: '1080'
Shows the Indian lands south of Brantford; shows the Grand River Navigation Co. parcels from survey by Peter Carroll in 1835 (see **761**) totalling 160,000 acres; boundaries of other parcels with numbers; shows town plot of Cayuga, Onondaga Mission School and Council House, Tuscarora Mission Lot, church parsonage lot, and other

Indian settlements and trails; note indicates that lots laid out on road leading from Grand R to Hamilton not as yet surrendered to Crown.
OTNR (SR 5884)

781 *[1839]*
VIEW of the COUNTRY / round the / FALLS of NIAGARA // J. Vallance Sculpt
Print (engrav) 8 x 11 cm Scale not given
'Section of Country between Lakes Erie and Ontario'; in *The North American Tourist* (New York: A.T. Goodrich [1839]), opp 118 (*Bib Can* 7547); shows battle sites, roads, places; the map is a redrawn and smaller version of the one first published by Melish in 1812 (**692**).
OTMCL

782 *1840*
Military Reserve, Burlington Heights, surveyed by Vincent Biscoe, Capt. Royal Engineers, December 21st 1840
Col ms 42 x 27 cm 8" to 1 mile Endorsements: 'Office Copy' 'No 95' 'A.Y.'
Shows the remains of blockhouse, a few other bldgs and the ordnance boundary; relief by hachures; roads to Dundas and Wellington Square; Sir Allan McNab's land.
QMMMCM (3627)

783 *[1840]*
NIAGARA RIVER / and / PARTS ADJACENT. [and] NIAGARA FALLS / and / VICINITY. / Lith of Hall & Mooney, Buffalo
2 prints on 1 sheet (lith) 14 x approx 18 cm Scales not given
In *Steele's Book of Niagara Falls*, 8th ed (Buffalo: Oliver G. Steele 1840), frontis (QMBN, CIHM 42250), and possibly also in the 9th ed (1846) and in the 10th ed (1847) (USPP); the preface indicates that the book is a revision of H.A. Parson's work first published in 1835 (see **759**) with new maps specially prepared; the first map shows places, twps, and roads; the falls map shows Clifton, Drummondville, proposed City of the Falls, Village of Niagara Falls, and bldgs.
QMBN USPP

784 *1840*
No 42 Sketch of the Niagara District by Capt Stehelin R.E. March 1840.
Col ms 59 x 76 cm 1" to 1 mile Watermark: 'J WHATMAN TURKEY MILL 1830' Endorsements: 'P No 560 V 93' 'No 95' stamps 'CREO'
A general reconnaissance sketch of the area from the Welland Canal to the Niagara R; relief, cleared and wooded areas; locks on the canal; roads including some comments on their state; shows hotels, taverns, mills, names of some settlers, and houses.
OOAMA (NMC 21590)

785 *1840*
Sketch of the Principal Roads in the Niagara District shewing in yellow the Site of the "Proposed Fortress" Signed P.J. Bainbrigge Lt Roy Engineers dated Septr 16, 1840 [Sgd] Hampden C B Moody Lt Royl Engrs Novr 20th 1840
Col ms Size not known Scale not given
Endorsements: 'No 1 Received with the Comg Rl Engrs letter (no 199) to the Inspector General of Fortifications ... 20th Novr 1840'
With letter in GBLpro WO 44/36 p 214; shows twps, main roads with distances marked; villages shown with nos of houses; Welland Canal; relief; proposed fortress at Short Hills.
GBLpro (WO 44/36 p 214)

Related maps

(2) *1841*
Sketch of the Principal Roads in the Niagara District Shewing in Yellow the site of the Proposed Towers [Sgd] Lt Pilkington Draftsman. J. Oldfield Lt Colonel Commanding Rl Engineers in Canada 30th September 1841
Col ms Size not known 1" to 1 mile Endorsements: 'to accompany estimate dated 4th Oct 1841' 'recd with letter No 155 of 4th Octr 1841'; stamp 'B↑O'
Shows several towers for defence instead of the fortress; the other information on the plan is the same as plan above.
GBLpro (WO 44/37 p 119)

786 *[1841?]*
Map of the Brantford and Hamilton Road
Col ms 66 x 125 cm 1" to 40 chains Endorsements: stamp [BW] '393'
'Sections of the Plank Road' and 'Sections of the McAdamized Road' both at 1" to 25 chains, 1" to 100 ft vertical; shows road line in detail with relief, marshes, other roads crossing; total length of plank road 10 miles, 32 chains; established by act in 1837, the main part of the road was built in the late 1830s and early 1840s but repairs were not completed until 1846 (Bishop, *Publications ... Upper Canada*, 222–3; OOA RG 11 A3 vol 137 no 77 1 Dec 1846).
OOAMA (NMC 11241)

787 *1841*
Sketch of Burlington Bay and its vicinity shewing in yellow the proposed Cantonment [Sgd] J Oldfield Lt Colonel Commanding Royal Engineers in Canada 19 Sept 1841
Col ms Approx 1" to 1/2 mile Endorsements: stamp 'B↑O'
Accompanies estimate for a defensible cantonment in Burlington Heights with ordnance and commissariat depots for the Queenston District with no 155 of 4 Oct 1841 (GBLpro WO 44/37 p 133); shows the layout for Hamilton, and area north and south of Burlington Bay; roads, places, canal, relief.
GBLpro (WO 44/37 p 133)

788 *1842*
MAP OF / NIAGARA STRAIT / AND / PARTS ADJACENT. / 1842 // COPYRIGHT SECURED // Carson Albany [and] CHART / OF THE / FALLS. / 1842 // COPYRIGHT SECURED // Carson Albany.
2 prints (liths) 12 x 7 cm and 11 x 7 cm Scale not given
In *Pictorial Guide to the Falls of Niagara* (Buffalo: Press of Salisbury and Clapp 1842), [14] (*Bib Can* 5244); settlements, roads, a few names of owners, 'Proposed City of the Falls'; chart shows tourist attractions near the falls.
OTMCL

Later editions and states

(2) *1844*
MAP OF / NIAGARA STRAIT / AND / PARTS ADJACENT. / 1844.
Print (lith) 13 x 8 cm Scale not given
In O.L. Holley, editor, *The Picturesque Tourist* (New York: J. Disturnell 1844), between 176 and 177 (*Bib Can* 7745; PACL); also in J. Disturnell, *Western Traveller* (New York: Disturnell 1844), between 56 and 57 (*Bib Can* 7734), and in *Peck's Tourist Companion* (Buffalo: William B. & Charles E. Peck 1845), between 16 and 17 (Bib Can 7805; OTUTF), with added imprint 'COPYRIGHT SECURED, Engraved for Peck's Tourists Companion, Carson Albany'; all three books also include 'CHART OF / NIAGARA FALLS, / THE / SHORES & / ISLANDS. / 1844 /'; this last map with same title but lacking date also appeared in Hulett, *Every Stranger His Own Guide to Niagara Falls* (Buffalo 1844), frontis (*Bib Can* 7747) with another map 'NIAGARA FALLS / and / VICINITY // Lith of Hall & Mooney, Buffalo' (print (lith), 13 x 8 cm, scale not given); the maps show relief along river and the Niagara Escarpment; main places, a few roads.
OOA OTMCL OTUTF

---

789 *1842*
[Plan of the townships of Gainsborough, Clinton No 5, Caistor, Grimsby No 6, Saltfleet No 7] Surveyor Generals Office Kingston 23rd June 1842 [Sgd] Thomas Parke Survr Genl.
Col ms 55 x 76 cm Scale not given
Shows the survey grid and conflicting survey lines; notes indicate the lines surveyed by Hambly in 1794, the 1st con of Grimsby and Saltfleet surveyed on 10 Oct 1808 by A. Jones, and the line surveyed by Jones in 1796.
OTAR

---

790 *1843*
Burlington Beach Surveyor General's Office Kingston 27th June 1843 [Sgd] Andrew Russell S & D.
Col ms 35 x 56 cm 1" to 40 chains Endorsements: 'No 100'
Shows 'Port Huskisson,' the Desjardins Canal, and the road; Wellington Square [later Burlington] located on the north shore; shows the spit of land between Cootes Paradise and Burlington Bay.
OTAR (P)

---

791 *[1843]*
Plan of part of the Dover Road shewing the proposed position of the toll gates between Hamilton and Caledonia [Sgd] W. Shaw.
Col ms 26 x 122 cm Scale not given Endorsements: stamps 'BW' '400'
Shows the main route and some variant routes and three toll gates proposed; relief; houses and inns along road; areas macadamized and planked; probably about 1843 as SI 25 Jan 1843 issued to W. Walker to lay out lots along road and town plot at the Grand R with W. Shaw mentioned as engineer of road; the road was built between 1842 and 1845 (*JLA* (1846) App N); OOAMA also has three plans for the mountain section of the road: 'Plan of the Mountain Section of the Hamilton and Port Dover Plank Road.' endorsed 'BW' and '399' with profile 1" to 20 ft vertical; 'Plan & Profile of the Mountain Section Hamilton & Dover Road through the Property of R. Hamilton Esqre [Sgd] W Shaw W.D.H.' endorsed 'BW' and '399'; and 'Plan of proposed route for descending the mountain Hamilton & Dover Road [Sgd] Hamilton 14th April 1845 W Shaw.' endorsed 'BW' and '399' with profile 1" to 50 ft vertical; also another copy with same title as last cited but with signature 'Wm Bu[tler] Hamilton.'
OOAMA (NMC 11227)

---

792 *[1843?]*
[Sketch of the Niagara Peninsula]
Ms 21 x 25 cm Scale not given
An inaccurate sketch of the area between the Six Nations Indian lands and the Niagara R; shows the Welland Canal to L Erie, the 'South Talbot Road' ending at Short Hills, and the Hamilton and Port Dover Rd, all too far east; the town of Niagara is incorrectly located part way down the Niagara R; possibly dates from 1843 when the Hamilton and Port Dover Rd was being built, but pre-1844 when Caledonia was laid out; (Holmden 1674).
OOAMA

---

793 *1843*
Sketch shewing the Indian lands on the Grand River originally granted to the Six Nations and the several surrenders of the same by them made to the Crown. Surveyor General's Office Kingston 16 February 1843 [Sgd] Thomas Parke Survr Genl.
Col ms 69 x 54 cm 1" to 4 miles
Shows the original grant of 14 Jan 1793 and the surrenders: 15 Jan 1798 and 5 Feb 1798 of the northern Blocks 1–4 and the Blocks 5 or A and 6 or B near the mouth of the Grand R east side, 19 Nov 1809 of [Sherbrooke Twp] to William Dickson, 19 Apr 1830 of site of Brantford, 19 Apr 1831 of the

north part of Cayuga, 8 Feb 1834 of the residue of Cayuga, Dunn, and pt of Moulton and Canborough twps, and 18 Jan 1841 of the residue of all lands along the Grand R (see *Indian Treaties* I, II); the twps are named; also a copy at OTAR(P) with the same title (endorsed: '174' 'Q 71') and later notes about patents.
OTAR(P) OTAR (SR 5979)

---

794 *1844*
Map of an Experimental Survey for a Branch from the Welland Canal to the Town of Niagara Oct 1844 [Sgd] S.P.[Power?] Jas D. Sla[ter] Ass.
Col ms (pt missing) 67 x 116 cm 1" to 20 chains
Endorsements: 'No 20'; stamps 'BW' '75'
Insets: [2 profiles] 1" to 2 chains, 1" to 20 ft vertical; with note 'profile of red line marked A from that of the Blue line marked B will not differ much'; 'Proposed plan of Lock'; 'Section of Canal'; shows two proposed routes A and B, B follows Swamp Rd; Mr Shanly's route is also pencilled in to join canal at locks 12 and 13; B line includes proposed locks and culverts; table of estimated costs.
OTAR

---

795 *1844*
[A plan of the front concessions of the townships along the Niagara River] E.Y.W.H.[enderson] Lieutenant Royal Engineers November 16th 1844.
Col ms 41 x 155 cm 1" to 45 chains Watermark: 'J WHATMAN TURKEY MILL 1840' Endorsements: 'No 380' 'Case K no 10'; stamp 'REO'
Shows the section of the bank that is military reserve; towns, forts, roads, treed areas.
OOAMA (NMC 21851)

Related maps

(2) *1850*
Niagara Sketch of the Military Reserves extending from Chippewa to the debouché of the Niagara River into Lake Ontario, distinguishing in yellow such part of 'the one chain' in width on top of the bank, as may be surrendered to the Provincial Government; the remainder tinted red being actually required for purposes of defence. As called for by the Military Secretary's letter, dated 16th May 1850. [Sgd] R.I. Pilkington Draftsman Hd Qr Royl Engr Office. 21st May 1850. [Sgd] Henry Vavasour Col. Comg Rl Engineers Canada 21 May 1850.
Col ms 29 x 44 cm 1" to 96 chains Endorsements: 'No 12' 'E 1739' '12'; stamp 'CREOC'
The boundary is shown as it affects the town of Niagara, Niagara and Stamford twps, and the two proposed suspension bridges to the United States side; also a copy at OOAMA (NMC 3009) on tracing paper with same title but signatures as follows: '(sigd) R.I. Pilkington Draftsman. 21st May 1850. John Moggridge Lieut Rl Engineers 21st June 1850.' (endorsed 'REO' 'No 394.')
OOAMA (NMC 3010; 3004)

(3) *1852*
Sketch of part of the Niagara River shewing the portion of Ordnance Chain Reserve, colored red applied for by the St Catherines, Thorold & suspension Bridge Road Company. 27/9/52. [Sgd] W. [T.?] Renwick Captain R.E. 4 Novr 1852.
Col ms on tracing paper 45 x 56 cm 1" to 4000 ft
Watermark: 'J GREEN & Sons 1848' Endorsements: 'To accompany my report of 6th Novr 1852. [Sgd] Alexr Gordon Lt Colonel Royal Engineers.' 'No. 11' 'R 6667' 'rel. CW/122'; stamp 'CREOC'
Shows area along bank from Niagara Falls to Niagara Suspension Bridge at Queenston applied for by the company; heights of cliffs on both sides of river given; roads and distances.
OOAMA (NMC 3154)

---

796 *1844*
Welland Canal. Plan of the Harbour at Chippewa Shewing its Condition in May 1844 The improvements executed during that season and those which will hereafter be required to render the harbour safe and easy of access. [Sgd] S. Power Engr W.C. December 24th 1844.
Col ms 45 x 57 cm 1" to 100 ft Endorsements: stamps 'BW' '589'
Detailed notes sgd by Power on the engineering work to correct the crooked and too narrow channel and estimate of cost; shows work executed in 1844 (excavation and fill on Hog Is) and future work required; (Holmden 1573).
OOAMA (NMC 3770)

---

797 *[1845]*
BIRDS-EYE VIEW OF THE FALLS OF NIAGARA & ADJACENT COUNTRY, COLOURED GEOLOGICALLY. / London, John Murray, Albemarle Street 1845. // Day & Haghe lithrs to the Queen. // pl. 1 [and] MAP OF THE / NIAGARA DISTRICT // Pl. III.
2 prints (liths) hand col 16 x 30 cm and 17 x 9 cm
Not to scale and scale not given
In Sir Charles Lyell, *Travels in North America* (London: John Murray 1845), I: frontis and opp 30 (*Bib Can* 2538), and in the 2nd ed (London 1855), I: frontis and II: opp 30 (*Bib Can* 8430); and in his *Travels in North America in the Years 1841–2* (New York: Wiley and Putnam 1845), I: frontis and opp 24 (*Bib Can* 2539); the bird's-eye view shows the geological layers and the map shows six geological formations and section on both sides of the Niagara R.
OTMCL

---

798 *1845 (1846)*
The Desjardins Canal Showing the Proposed enlargement Nov. 1845. Board of Works 1846 (copy) R Pilkington Draftsman [Sgd] W.C.E. Holloway Colonel Comg R E
Col ms Size not known Scale not known
Enclosed with the 'Commg Rl Engrs letter to the IGF' 20 July 1846, no 616 (GBLpro WO 44/45 p 40).
GBLpro (WO 44/45 p 40)

---

799 *1845*
MAP / of the / NIAGARA, GORE, AND WELLINGTON DISTRICTS, / (including also the Southern Front of the HOME DISTRICT,) / CANADA. / Compiled from the Township Plans in the Surveyor Genl's Office, / by C. RANKIN, D.S. / Toronto, 18th June 1845. / Lith. of Hall & Mooney.
Print (lith) 81 x 106 cm 1" to 200 chains
The map is bounded on the west, north, and east by the twps of Walpole, Tuscarora, Brantford, Dumfries, Waterloo, Wilmot, Wellesley, Peel, Garafraxa, Caledon, King, and Whitby; detailed survey grid for all twps with lot nos; villages, towns, and roads; 'NOTE' describes Welland Canal, some roads in Niagara District, villages not shown, and notes on survey in Brantford area; description of electoral districts; there is also a copy in OOAMA (NMC 11225) with ms adds showing the Niagara Escarpment and types of rock.
OOAMA (NMC 11225) OTAR (SR 81258) USDLC

---

800 *[1846]*
Map of the Welland Canal Shewing Its position with regard to the Niagara Frontier and the Adjoining Townships [Sgd] S Power
Col ms Size not known Scale not given
In Capt Warden's letter of 16 Feb 1846 (GBLpro Adm 7/626 p 132); shows the canal, feeders, locks, proposed canal to town of Niagara, roads, distances; notes on lake harbours.
GBLpro (Adm 7/626 p 132)

---

801 *1847*
Map shewing Old and New Roads at Jordan. [Sgd] Samuel Keefer Engr in C. 28th June 1847
Col ms 60 x 75 cm 1" to 4 chains
'No 18 Profile of Old Road' and 'Profile of New Road' both at 1" to 30 ft vertical; originally with 'No 2838 Report of S. Keefer Queenston Grimsby Road' (OOA RG 11 vol 10, docket 2838); shows old road passing through Jordan and crossing Twenty Mile Creek; new road diverts to the west along the escarpment and crosses Twenty Mile Creek south of town; several bldgs shown and identified including tannery and store; relief.
OOAMA (RG 11M 82303/38)

---

802 *[1847]*
NIAGARA RIVER / and / PARTS ADJACENT. // E. Wild, Sc.
Print (engrav) 9 x 16 cm Scale not given
In William Barham, *Descriptions of Niagara* (Gravesend: Published by the compiler [1847]), opp 173 (*Bib Can* 2822); shows twps, relief, roads, and places.
OTMCL

---

803 *[1849]*
MAP OF / NIAGARA FALLS / AND / ADJOINING SHORES. / Being a complete Directory and Guide to / the Falls and vicinity, for remark on the / spot, or for Reference at Home. // MAP OF NIAGARA FALLS / AND / GUIDE TABLE.
Print (lith) 33 x 25 cm Scale not given
In *The Niagara Falls Guide* (Buffalo: A. Burke 1849) (USDLC, CIHM 50142), copyright note J. Faxon, 1848, and also in another ed (Buffalo: J. Faxon, 1850), frontis (*Bib Can* 8083); the map is redrawn from that in de Veaux (1841) (**778(2)**) but shows essentially the same information except inset not included; key to references on map; distance tables; 'Directions to Hasty Travellers.'
OTMCL USDLC

Later editions and states

(2) *[1852]*
MAP OF / NIAGARA FALLS, / AND / ADJOINING SHORES. // MAP OF NIAGARA FALLS / AND / GUIDE TABLE. / BEING A COMPLETE GUIDE TO THE FALLS AND VICINITY, FOR REMARK ON THE SPOT, OR FOR REFERENCE, AT HOME.
Print (lith) 33 x 25 cm Scale not given
In *Burke's Descriptive Guide ... to Niagara Falls* (Buffalo: Andrew Burke 1852), frontis (*Bib Can* 8180), and probably also in the 1853 ed (*NUC Pre-1956 Imprints* 85:367); map is from the same plate as above but titles have been redone; includes the same references as those above.
OTMCL

(3) *[1854]*
[First title deleted] MAP OF NIAGARA FALLS, / ... FOR REFERENCE AT HOME.
Print (lith) 32 x 24 cm Scale not given
In *Burke's Descriptive Guide ... to Niagara Falls* (Buffalo: Andrew Burke 1854), opp preface (OTUTF); the first title has been replaced with a view of the falls but the map is from the same plate as maps above.
OTUTF

---

804 *[1849?]*
[A map of the District of Niagara showing water communications and roads]
Print (lith) with ms adds 45 x 55 cm Scale not given
With petitions from Duncan McFarland M.P.P. 21/23 Feb 1849 asking for a change in location of the district town (OOA RG 5 C1/250 no 440 1849); 'Explanations' keys a long list of road and water routes; twps, places, roads, and Welland Canal shown; 'Proposed military road from Hamilton to Port Robinson ... to Fort Erie'; ms adds show boundaries of the cos of Lincoln and Welland; circle shown around [Welland] presumably as central location for district town.
OOAMA (NMC 3008)

---

805 *1850*
MAP OF / NIAGARA FALLS / AND / VICINITY. / Engraved expressly for 'Burke's Descriptive Guide' / by Hall & Co. Buffalo // Press of Jewett, Thomas & Co. Buffalo

Print (lith) Size not known Scale not given
In *Burke's Descriptive Guide ... to Niagara Falls* (Buffalo: Andrew Burke 1850) (USDLC, CIHM 29866); similar to Burke's map (**803(1)**) in terms of information; a few bldgs keyed.
USDLC

---

806 *1850*
Map of the Otterville and Port Dover Road 1850. Richard Burrowes Del.
Col ms 61 x approx 245 cm 1" to 20 chains
Shows the road from Norwich Twp in Oxford Co via Delhi and Simcoe to Port Dover on L Erie; relief, trees, marshes, villages marked along route.
Norfolk 37 (no R.P. number)

---

807 *[1850]*
[Niagara Falls] // Day & Son, lithrs to the Queen
Print (lith) 11 x 16 cm Scale not given
In John Bigsby, *The Shoe and Canoe or Pictures of Travel in the Canadas* (London: Chapman and Hall 1850), 2: opp 325 (*Bib Can* 1426); shows the location of particular falls and geological formations: 'American Fall,' 'Ribbon Fall,' 'Table Rock,' and 'alluvial terrace'; treed areas, international boundary.
OTMCL

---

808 *[1852]*
F.H. JOHNSON'S / NEW MAP / of / NIAGARA FALLS and RIVER, / showing all the / PROMINENT POINTS ADJACENT. / Niagara Falls, N.Y.
Print (lith) 23 x 29 cm Scale not given
In F.H. Johnson, *A Guide for Every Visitor to Niagara Falls* (Rochester: D.M. Dewey [1852]), frontis (OONL, CIHM 37216) (map missing in *Bib Can* 8212); shows Drummondville and Clifton House; key to bldgs; the same map appeared in Johnson's *Every Man His Own Guide at Niagara Falls* (Rochester: D.M. Dewey [1853?]), frontis (*Bib Can* 8073; Casey I–2957; OONL; CIHM 22357) with the addition of the Erie and Ontario Railroad and a view of the falls.
OOA OONL OTMCL

---

809 *[1853]*
Burlington Heights Plan shewing tinted yellow, the portion of land containing about 10 acres, applied for by the Hamilton & Toronto Railway Co 4 August 1853. A, the site the Company desires to occupy temporarily, for the purpose of excavating Ballast and material for forming an embankment across the Desjardins Canal ... To accompany the Commanding Royal Engineers letter to the Inspector General of Fortifications dated 3 Novr 1853 No. 205 [Sgd] R.I. Pilkington Draftsman
Col ms on tracing paper 44 x 55 cm 1" to 400 ft
Watermark: 'J WHATMAN 1851' Endorsements: 'No 1' 'rel 8/2002'; stamp 'REO'
Shows the boundary of ordnance land, old Desjardins Canal, and 'new cut for canal'; five cross-sections showing levels of railway line; shows the 30 acres occupied by the GWR and Desjardins Canal; there is also an unfinished, unsigned copy of this map at OOAMA (NMC 3742) endorsed 'CREOC' and 'No 45/1 No 1.'
OOAMA (NMC 3741–2)

---

810 *1853*
HACKSTAFF'S / NEW MAP / of / NIAGARA FALLS AND RIVER / Published by / W.E. TUNIS & Co.
Print (lith) 17 x approx 25 cm Scale not given
In *Hackstaff's New Guide Book of Niagara Falls; Illustrated with a New Map* (Niagara Falls: W.E. Tunis & Co. 1853), frontis (OLU, CIHM 50020); shows the area of the falls with an index to bldgs on the U.S. side; a few bldgs and railways shown on the Canadian side; similar to F.H. Johnson's map of 1852 (see **808**).
OLU

---

811 *1853*
MAP OF / THE VICINITY OF / NIAGARA FALLS / FROM ACTUAL SURVEYS BY SAMUEL GEIL AUTHOR OF MAPS OF / NIAGARA, ORLEANS AND CAYUGA COUNTIES, N.Y. &c. / Published by S. GEIL & I.L. DELP, No 15, Minor St Philada // Entered According to Act of Congress in the year 1853 by Samuel Geil in the Clerk's Office of the District Court of the Eastern District of Pennsylvania.
Print (lith) 60 x 76 cm Scale not given
Shows the area from Queenston/Lewiston south to Grand Is and west to Thorold and Port Robinson and twps of Stamford, Willoughby and Crowland; shows names of occupants and houses on Canadian side and in Niagara Co and Grand Is, New York; roads, railways, some major bldgs located in towns; 13 views of the falls, the river, and prominent bldgs.
USDLC

---

812 *[1854]*
CARTE / des / CHUTES du NIAGARA // Lith. Gendre aux Bercles à Neuchatel // Pl. 1
Print (lith) 1" to 100 metres
In E. Desor, *Les cascades du Niagara et leur marche retrograde* (Neuchatel: Henri Wolfrath 1854), opp 12 (Casey I–2435); shows 'Chute Canadienne' and American Falls and bldgs on the shore; also includes a profile of the Niagara R.
OOA

---

813 *1854*
Plan of Long Point in Lake Erie C.W. Surveyed under instructions from the Honourable the Commissioner of Crown Lands dated February 28 1853 and January 19th 1854; By Provincial Land Surveyor James Black. Examined T.D. 3rd Sept. 55.
Col ms 34 x 126 cm 1" to 40 chains Endorsements: 'B 76'
Shows bearings of survey lines, marsh, and trees;

lot nos and sizes; shoreline in twp of Walsingham and on Long Point has reserve two chains wide for fishing stations.
OTNR (SR 5303)

---

814 *1855*
MAP / OF THE / COUNTY / OF / HALDIMAND. / Drawn and Compiled from the Government Maps with latest surveys, / BY / WILLIAM OWEN. / CALEDONIA, C.W. / 1855. / MOONEY & BUELL LITH. BUFFALO.
Print (lith) 85 x 127 cm Scale not given
Insets: 'Plan of the Town of Cayuga,' 'Plan of the Town of Dunville' [*sic*], 'Plan of the Town of Caledonia'; four views of bldgs; shows the survey grid in detail with lot nos, acreage, and notes; roads are named; railways; towns; a few names of owners; insets show streets with names and subdivisions; OOAMA copy is damaged and lacks insets.
OOAMA (NMC 16780) OTAR

---

815 *[1855]*
PLAN OF OPERATIONS ALONG THE NIAGARA FRONTIER. [and] DIAGRAM OF THE BATTLE OF QUEENSTON
2 prints (wood engrav) Ea 20 x 12 cm Scale not given
In G. Auchinleck, *A History of the War* (Toronto: Maclear & Co. 1855), pp 97–8 (*Bib Can* 8397); references to battle sites of War of 1812 along river and to points in Queenston.
OTMCL

---

816 *[1855]*
TUNIS' / NEW MAP / of / NIAGARA FALLS and RIVER, / showing all the / PROMINENT POINTS ADJACENT. / Niagara Falls N.Y.
Print (lith) 23 x 29 cm Scale not given
View of the falls; in *Tunis's Topographical and Pictorial Guide to Niagara* (Niagara Falls: W.E. Tunis 1855), opp frontis (*Bib Can* 5692; OLU; CIHM 63228; USNN), and in the 1856 ed (OONL; CIHM 62052; USNN) with many changes and additions; shows the falls, river, islands, points on the Canadian side, and Niagara Falls, New York; the map is redrawn from the F.H. Johnson map (**808**).
OLU OONL OTMCL USNN

---

817 *1856*
MAP / OF THE / COUNTY OF NORFOLK / CANADA WEST / Published by GEORGE C. TREMAINE, / KINGSTON, C.W. / 1856. / The Map Engraved by / D. & J. McLELLAN, NEW YORK CITY / from Drawings by / WALSH & MERCER, P.L.SRS SIMCOE. /The Views Engraved from / Ambrotypes taken by / GEORGE R. TREMAINE.
Print (lith) hand col 146 x 140 cm 1" to 60 chains
Shows survey grid, names of owners and/or tenants; 27 views of residences, commercial and public bldgs; 'explanations' keys railways, roads in the survey and roads not in survey, plank and gravel roads, grist mills, steam sawmills, water sawmills, tanneries, woollen factories, breweries, distilleries, foundries, 'The Celebrated Lyndoch Mineral Springs,' and post offices; subscribers directory; the first co map published by the Tremaines; a variant copy with four views in different positions and an additional subscribers directory is in OOAMA (NMC 21963); (Holmden 2040).
OOAMA (NMC 15345; 21963) OSINH OTAR

Related maps

(2) *1857*
[Same title but date changed to 1857]
131 x 136 cm
The map is the same but only 20 of the views have been included and two small miscellaneous subscribers directories added; the border has been changed to reduce the size of the printed area.
OLU

---

818 *[1856–8?]*
Map of the Counties of / WENTWORTH / part of / BRANT, / and / LINCOLN, / HALDIMAND, / WELLAND / Drawn & Engraved by ELLIS & Co. / 8 King Street / TORONTO.
Print (engrav) 42 x 73 cm Scale not given
Shows the survey grid, canals, roads and road allowances, and railways: the Buffalo to Brantford (1856), Chippawa to Niagara (1854), GWR to Niagara Falls and to Hamilton and west; suspension bridges at Queenston and at Niagara Falls shown; probably prepared after 1856 and before 1859 when Welland Railway was completed and while Ellis was at address listed (Bladen, 44; Hulse, 93).
OTAR OTUTF

Related maps

(2) *[1859–66?]*
[Same title but address of printer changed]: '11 King Street.'
The railway from Fort Erie to Niagara, the Welland Railway (1859), Merrittsville, and Clifton have been added; railway lines have been enhanced and stations added; since Ridgway is now marked, the map may date from the Fenian raids (1866); Ellis is listed at this address from 1859 on (Hulse, 93).
OOAMA (NMC 21585)

---

819 *1858*
CHART / OF / Niagara River / SHOWING CROSSINGS / FOR THE PROPOSED / INTERNATIONAL BRIDGE / FROM ACTUAL SURVEY / BY / W.S. SMITH, CIVIL ENGINEER. Published by J. SAGE & SONS, Buffalo. // Entered according to Act of Congress A.D. 1858 by J. Sage & Sons in the Clerks Office of the North'n Dist. Court of New York.
Print (lith) 48 x 84 cm Scale not given

Inset: 'PROFILES OF CROSSINGS' 1" to 100 ft, 1" to 60 ft vertical; shows nine proposed locations for bridges, mostly around Fort Erie; rock and gravel bottom areas of river shown, currents.
GBL (69930(5))

820 *1858*
COPY / OF PART OF P.L.S. KIRKPATRICK'S PLAN / OF / GRIMSBY / (Marked 'B8') / Crown Lands Department / Toronto 23th [*sic*] July 1858. / Certified a true copy. / [Sgd in facsimile] Andrew Russell / Assist Commissioner. Maclear & Co. Lith. Toronto.
Print (lith) 34 x 57 cm 1" to 40 chains
Shows conflicting survey lines in cons VII, VIII, and IX, and gore between cons VII and VIII; locations of Hambly's, McDonnel's, and Rykert's lines; a copy of **A835** dated 29 May 1841; OOAMA copy lacks imprint.
OOAMA (NMC 3622) OTAR

821 *[1858?]*
MAP / OF / NIAGARA RIVER / at the City of Buffalo / Shewing proposed Bridge Crossings & Ship Canal // Maclear & Co. Liths Toronto C.W.
Print (lith) 30 x 46 cm Scale not given
Shows two sites for a bridge, one north of Fort Erie and one at Fort Erie crossing to United States; shows Black Rock Harbour, Erie Canal, Buffalo & L Huron R.R.; shows a 'Ship Canal proposed as compensation for the destruction of River Navigation' from west of Fort Erie to Niagara R opp Squaw Is.
OOAMA (NMC 3171)

822 *[ca 1858]*
Map of the Counties of Haldimand & Welland
Col ms 55 x 76 cm Scale not given Watermark: '... [WHATMAN] ... KENT 1835' Endorsements: stamps 'BW' '541'
Possibly an unfinished plan of the area with roads and proposed railways marked; the Hamilton-Port Dover Rd is shown to the north boundary of Walpole Twp and dotted in from there north; two proposed railway lines shown from Fort Erie to the Grand R in North Cayuga Twp; Welland Canal railway line (1857) shown and GWR from the Niagara R to Hamilton and Toronto; the Buffalo & L Huron Railway is shown from Fort Erie to Brantford (Trout and Trout, 35–6).
OOAMA (NMC 21910)

823 *[1858]*
NIAGARA RIVER, / FROM / LAKE ERIE TO LAKE ONTARIO
Print (wood engrav) 12 x 8 cm Scale not given
Inset: 'NIAGARA FALLS / AND VICINITY'; in *The Falls of Niagara* (London, etc: T. Nelson & Sons 1858), frontis, and in the 1860 ed (*Bib Can* 8657, 8810); sketch maps showing roads, railways, suspension bridge.
OTMCL

824 *1858*
TREMAINE'S / MAP OF THE / COUNTY OF BRANT / CANADA WEST / Compiled and Drawn by GEO. R. TREMAINE from the Surveys of / LEWIS BURWELL Esq. P.L.S. / BRANTFORD / Published by / GEO. C. TREMAINE / 1858. / Engraved and Printed by D & J. McLellan, 26 Spruce Street, New York.
Print (lith) 130 x 166 cm 1" to 40 chains
Thirty-one views of public and commercial bldgs and residences; subscribers directory and list of co officers; 'Explanations' includes railways, plank and gravel roads, common roads, water, steam, grist mills, school houses; survey grid; names of owners and/or tenants.
OOAMA (NMC 27315; 19019)

Related maps

(2) *1859*
[Same title but the date has been changed to 1859]
The map is the same as the 1858 ed but the captions have been changed on four views and there are several changes in the subscribers directory.
GBL (70650 (1)) OOAMA (NMC 27314) OTAR (SR 2638)

825 *1859*
MAP / OF THE / COUNTY OF WENTWORTH / Canada West. / COMPILED FROM AUTHENTIC SURVEYS, / BY / ROBERT SURTEES CIVIL ENGINEER / and Published by / HARDY GREGORY LITHOGRAPHER & ENGRAVER / HAMILTON / 1859. // Entered in the Office of the Registrar of the Province of Canada, in the year 1859 by HARDY GREGORY according to Act of the Provincial Legislature.
Print (lith) 102 x 156 cm 1" to 50 chains
Thirty views of businesses and residences; 'Reference' includes twp boundaries, ward divisions, macadamized plank roads and original con roads, post offices, residences, schools, churches, four types of mill, foundries, survey grid, railways; shows names of owners in lots; table of areas of original lots by twp; photoreproduction in OOAMA (NMC 3340).
OH OTAR (SR 2653)

826 *1860*
Plan of Ordnance Property Burlington Heights in the City of Hamilton As surveyed under Instructions from the Commissioner of Crown Lands Dated 20th November 1859 [Sgd] Toronto 20th Feb 1860 J Stoughton Dennis P.L.S.
Col ms 48 x 109 cm 1" to 5 chains Endorsements: '3547/60'
(SI 20 Nov 1859); relief shown and treed areas; Cootes Paradise; GWR and Hamilton & Toronto Ry; cemetery; nursery; Sir A. McNab's land.
OTNR (SR 5741)

Related maps

(**2**) *1861*
Plan of Ordnance Property Burlington Heights Department of Crown Lands Quebec January 1861 [Sgd] Andrew Russell Assistant Commissioner.
Col ms 56 x 98 cm 1" to 3 chains
Shows the boundary of the property with GWR and Hamilton & Toronto Ry, cemeteries, lots, a few names.
OTAR(P)

---

827 *1860*
Plan of Ordnance Property known as the Short Hills Farm Being Lots 5 and 6 in the 6 Concession of Pelham County of Welland C.W. [Sgd] J. Stoughton Dennis P.L.S. Toronto 2d March 1860. Examined and Compared with Duplicate J.W.B.
Col ms 94 x 64 cm 1" to 200 links Endorsements: '3547/60'
(SI 20 Nov 1859); shows boundary of property and cleared and wooded land in the area; some bldgs and names of owners; the survey accounts for this and plan above (**826**) are found in OTAR RG 1 B-IV box 10 nos 20 and 24.
OTNR (SR 6797)

---

828 *1862*
Toronto District Canada West Sketch Showing the position of a 3 Gun Battery erected December 1861 to defend the entrance to Burlington Bay near Hamilton. [Sgd] H.F. Turner Lt R.E. del. 25/10/62 S.D. Robertson [illegible] D.C. R Eng 29.10.62. J.P. Maquay Cap R.E. D.C.R.E. 26.3.66.
Col ms on tracing paper 44 x 55 cm Approx 1" to 575 yds
Battery is located just north of the canal; two lighthouses shown; roads.
OOAMA (NMC 3743)

---

829 *1862*
TREMAINES' MAP / OF THE COUNTIES OF / LINCOLN AND WELLAND / CANADA WEST, / Compiled and Drawn from Actual Surveys / by the Publishers / GEO. R. & G.M. TREMAINE / St. Lawrence Buildings / TORONTO / 1862
Print (lith) hand col 125 x 179 cm 1" to 50 chains
Twenty-six views of public and commercial bldgs and residences; subscribers directories; explanations: railways, travelled roads, common roads, post offices, schools, churches, four types of mill, battlegrounds; survey grid, names of owners and/or tenants; 'Lincoln & Welland' hand-stamped on some copies; OTAR copy has 28 views and only 'Welland' stamped on map.
OOAMA (NMC 19014) OSTCB OTAR

Related maps

(**2**) *1862*
[Same title]
There are now 33 views shown and a scale bar has been added; several subscribers directories have been moved; the Sumner view has been removed.
OTAR (SR 92319)

---

830 *1863*
MAP / OF THE COUNTY OF / HALDIMAND / CANADA WEST / Compiled & drawn by the Publisher / W Jones / Toronto, / 1863. / Engraved & Printed at Tremaine's Map Establishment No 79 Front Street, Toronto.
Print (lith) hand col 111 x 166 cm 1" to 50 chains
Inset: 'MAP OF / CANADA WEST or UPPER CANADA, / TO ACCOMPANY / THE Map OF THE County / 1" to 12 miles'; 22 views of public and commercial bldgs and residences; 'Explanation': railways, boundary of wards; subscribers directory and table of census data; names of owners; a few schools and churches shown; the inset is from (**185(10)**); photoreproductions in OTAR and OOAMA.
GBL (70661(1))

---

831 *1865*
SKETCH MAP / SHEWING THE PROPOSED / INTERNATIONAL BRIDGE / AND ITS / UNION RAILWAY EXTENSION. / 1865. // Maclure Macdonald & MacGregor Lithrs London
Print (col lith) 39 x 50 cm Scale not given
Mainly shows the Buffalo side with streets, railway depots and the proposed union depot and International Bridge Railway line; shows street grid for Fort Erie, bridge, connections to Erie and Niagara Ry, and GWR, GTR and Buffalo Brantford & Goderich Ry; ferry.
OOAMA (RG 19M 82303/24 item 1)

---

832 *[1866]*
[In ms] 'Denison's map of the position at Limeridge' // J. Ellis, Lith King St East Toronto.
Print (lith) with ms adds 21 x 26 cm 1" to 250 yds
In G. Denison, *The Fenian Raid on Fort Erie* (Toronto: Rollo & Adam 1866), at back (*Bib Can* 6209); shows the road to Fort Erie and Garrison Rd; various positions of troops.
OTMCL

---

833 *1866*
MAP / Illustrating / the / FENIAN RAID, / JUNE, 2nd 1866. / Published by W.C. CHEWETT & Co. / TORONTO // W.C. Chewett & Co. Lith. Toronto.
Print (lith) 27 x 19 cm Scale not given
In *The Fenian Raid at Fort Erie, June the First and Second, 1866* (Toronto: W.C. Chewett & Co. 1866), frontis (*Bib Can* 4497); shows various locations of Fenian camps and Col Peacocke's camps; landing place of Fenians and 'point where they fled'; notes on movements; shows twps east from Wainfleet to Louth; railways and canals, roads.
OTMCL

Related maps

(**2**) *1866*
Enlarged Plan of / GROUND at LIMERIDGE, / shewing the position of the / COMBATANTS, / and of those who fell in the SKIRMISH / June 2nd 1866 / Engraved expressly to Accompany / THE FENIAN RAID, / from Actual Survey of the Ground by / a Staff Officer. / W.C. Chewett & Co Lith. Toronto.
Print (lith) 31 x 36 cm 1" to 220 yds
In same source as above; shows Ridge Rd, Garrison Rd, various positions of remains of battle, names of farm owners; positions occupied along Ridge Rd numbered and described in the account.
OTMCL

---

834 *1866*
MAP / OF THE / FIELD OF COMBAT, / AT / LIMESTONE RIDGE, / PUBLISHED IN THE NARRATIVE OF / ALEXANDER SOMERVILLE, / AT / HAMILTON, CANADA WEST.
Print (lith) 40 x 25 cm 1" to 825 ft
In Alex Somerville, *Narrative of the Fenian Invasion of Canada* (Hamilton: Published for the author by Joseph Lyght 1866), frontis (*Bib Can* 4538, Casey I-3395); shows area from 'Ridgeway Station' to Stephensville Rd west of Fort Erie; various positions marked, houses, woods.
OOA OTMCL

---

835 *[1866]*
[Map of the Niagara Peninsula]
Print (wood engrav) 15 x 28 cm Scale not given
In *Canada Gazette* ([Ottawa]) Saturday 23 June 1866, 2146 (*Bib Can* 4478, OTUTF); locates Fenian camp north of Fort Erie and places mentioned in the accompanying account ('New Germany,' 'Ridgway'); railways, main roads, Welland Canal.
OTMCL OTUTF

---

836 *1866*
Peninsula of Niagara. E.H. Fletcher December 8 1866.
Col ms 32 x 43 cm Scale not given
A general location map of the Niagara area extending west to Charlotteville and North Dumfries twps; places, railways, twps; (Holmden 2039).
OOAMA (NMC 3011)

---

837 *1866*
[Plan of the Battle of Ridgeway]
Print (lith) 19 x 21 cm 1" to 250 yds
In George Denison, *History of the Fenian Raid on Fort Erie* (Toronto: Rollo & Adam; Buffalo: Breed, Butler & Co. 1866) (*Bib Can* 4490); shows disposition of troops of various regiments including the Trinity College Co. and Fenians east and west of Ridge Rd between Garrison Rd and road to Fort Erie.
OTMCL

---

838 *1866*
THAT PART OF CANADA NOW / invaded by / FENIANS. / W.C. Chewett & Co / TORONTO. / June 2nd 1866.
Print (lith) 23 x 18 cm Scale not given
Includes the Niagara Peninsula and the area from Hamilton to Toronto; twp names, railways, canals; note at Fort Erie 'Fenian position,' places, roads.
OTMCL

---

839 *[1867]*
GRAND RIVER NAVIGATION
Print (wood engrav) 18 x 32 cm 1" to 5 miles
In *Report on Grand River Navigation by the Board of Trade of Brantford* (Brantford: 1867), frontis (*Bib Can* 6246); shows the river from Paris to L Erie, with navigational works numbered; twps named.
OTMCL

---

840 *[1867]*
[Map of the Fenian movements near Fort Erie]
Harrison & Sons Lith
Print (lith) Size not known Scale not given
In *Correspondence Respecting the Recent Fenian Aggression upon Canada, Presented to Both Houses of Parliament ... February 1867* (London: Printed by Harrison and Sons 1867), opp 16 (*HCPP* (1867) XLVIII 561 (OTU (mfe)); accompanied J.S. Dennis's report of 4 June 1866 about the defeat of the Fenians at Ridgeway; shows area from Niagara R to Welland Canal and from L Erie to Chippawa; shows points referred to in dispatch including location of Ridgeway, Fenian camp, roads, and railways.
Original not located

North

841 *[1788?]*
[Sketch of Manitoulin Island, the North Channel, and St Marys River]
Col ms 37 x 50 cm Scale not given Endorsements: '1008'
Possibly a fragment of a larger map extending further east; similar to the general plan of L Huron made in 1788 (**7**); shows a rough shape for Manitoulin Is, a few place-names on other islands; 'Falls of St. Mary,' 'I. St. Joseph'; 'Old Michilimaquinacabre Croche Village' shown south of the straits of Mackinac.
OTAR

---

842 *[1788?]*
Sketch of the Falls or Rapids at St. Mary's [and Matchedash Bay]
Ms 40 x 31 cm Scale not given Watermark: 'C TAYLOR ...' Endorsements: 'Z 47/9'; stamp 'B↑O'
Inset: [Matchedash Bay] 1" to 21/2 miles; the map is a copy of the insets on (**7**); the main map shows the houses of Nolin and Cadot on the United States side; (Holmden 2609).
OOAMA (NMC 3246)

---

843 *1794*
A Sketch of the North Shore of Lake Superior collected from the Journal of a Coasting Survey and remarks made by Lieut. Bennett of the 8th Regiment. [Sgd] P. McNiff Detroit Octobr 1794
Col ms 53 x 109 cm 1" to 8 miles Endorsements: 'No 16'
Shows the route of the survey with bearings and distances; many place-names in French; shows relief and comments on the nature of the shoreline; shows the area from the Falls of St Mary to 'Grand Portage'; 'Copper Mines' are shown on shore south of Montreal R with a note indicating work to extract metal had stopped; accompanied a letter to D.W. Smith dated 19 Oct 1794 in which McNiff says he is sending this sketch and one of St Marys River to help Smith in his efforts to publish a map of Upper Canada.
OTAR

---

844 *[1794?]*
Sketch of the River St Mary's from the Detour, or its junction with Lake Huron to the Falls of St. Mary's and thence to the Entrance of Lake Superior. Copy W.C.
Col ms 95 x 76 cm 1" to 2 miles Watermark: '... WHATMAN ...' Endorsements: '948' 'No 9 Communication St. Mary's River from the Detour on Lake Huron to entrance of Lake Superior (Sketch)'
Shows Muddy L, L George, Falls of St Mary, 'Pt aux Pins or Fort Gloster,' L Superior; boat channel to falls and channel leading to French R, Matchedash, etc; relief and nature of shoreline; bearings of main channel; notes including references to Indians travelling from Michilimackinac to the falls in one day and about the south side of the falls, 'flat bottomed vessels twenty or thirty Tons are frequently taken up, and down'; possibly related to 1794 survey for L Superior and copy of plan sent to Smith (see **843**).
OTAR (SR 6443)

---

845 *1796*
Plan of part of the Strait, and the Fall of St. Maries situated between Lake Superior, and Lake Huron. Surveyed by Order of the North West Company in the Summer 1796, by Theodore Depincier under the inspection of Lieut Brice of the Royal Engineers. Copy W.C.
Col ms 43 x 82 cm 1" to 500 ft Endorsements: 'No 19' '814'
Shows the north and south side of the strait with various islands, channels, triangulation lines, and traverse lines along the shore; roads and bldgs shown on both sides; 'Remarks – the perpendicular Ht of the Fall ... is 15 feet 10 inches The length of the Road made on the carrying place ... half a mile ... The length with the proposed addition for the conveniency of Carts for loading of Boats ... 3/4 miles.'
OTAR (SR 7132)

Related maps

(2) *1797 (1852)*
Plan of the Falls of St Mary between Lake Huron & Lake Superior Surveyed by Order of the Northwest Company by Theodore de Pincier 1797. Copy – [Sgd] R.I. Pilkington Draftsman 26 August 1852
Col ms 52 x 69 cm 1" to 160 yds Watermark: 'I.H. SAUNDERS & Co. 1846' Endorsements: 'No 3'; stamp 'CREOC'
Similar to the above plan with statement on height of falls 'Signed A. Brice'; shorelines are the same; a few twps added on north shore; roads and bldgs as on plan above; 'Lot no 2 house and Lot claimed by Mr Cotte'; 'drag road for canoes'; (*OHIM* 6.18).
OOAMA (NMC 21799)

---

846 *[1796]*
Sketch of the Streights of St Mary between Lake Huron & Lake Superior with part of the Coast of Lake Huron and Michilimacinac
Col ms 56 x 62 cm 1" to approx 11/4 leagues or approx 33/4 miles

Inset: 'Sketch of the Falls of St Mary' 1" to 1/2 mile; endorsed on back: 'In Lord Dorchester's no 87 to the Duke of Portland' of 16 Apr 1796 accompanying a letter about trading with the Indians (GBLpro CO 42/105 p 154); shows the fort at Michilimackinac and 'old fort' on the mainland opp; two trading houses and portage at St Marys, several ship and canoe channels; the inset is the same as the inset on **7**; photoreproduction in OOAMA (NMC 21798); (*PRO Cat* 1583).
GBLpro (MPG 34)

Related maps

(**2**) *[1796]*
Upper Canada 33L. Sketch of the Streights of St Mary between Lake Huron & Lake Superior with part of the Coast of Lake Huron & Michilimacinack
Col ms 56 x 63 cm 1" to 11/4 leagues
Endorsements: 'D'
Endorsed on back: 'In Lord Dorchesters No 87 to the Duke of Portland' (see reference above); this plan is similar to above except the inset is not included and the 'old fort' not located; photoreproduction in OOAMA (NMC 21797); (*PRO Cat* 1583).
GBLpro (MPG 40)

---

847 *[1796–8?]*
Scetch of the Straits of St Mary between Lake Huron & Lake Superior by A. Bryce Lieut Rl Engrs July 1798
Col ms 61 x 69 cm 1" to 21/4 miles Endorsements: stamps 'Canada Ontario Dist 1, 81/1'
'Topographical Department War Office Oct 23 1887'
Note about nature of survey and bearings: 'This Sketch is laid down from bearings ... Surveyed' [as in title of (2)], '(Signed) Alexr Bryce Lieut Rl Engrs'; shows place-names, canoe tracks, and ship channels; withdrawn from GBLpro WO 78/1051; photoreproduction in OOAMA (NMC 21349); although dated 1798, the information is the same as on the 1796 plan described below except bldgs are shown at the Falls of St Marys; (*PRO Cat* 1584).
GBLpro (MR 196(1))

Related maps

(**2**) *1796 (1816)*
Sketch of the Straits of St Mary between Lake Huron and Lake Superior laid down from bearings of the Principal Points, and computed distances; excepting a few places which have been more particularly surveyed. July 1796 (Signed) Alexr Bryce Lieutt Corps Royal Engineers. Rl Engineers Drawing Room Quebec 5th May 1815 [Sgd] G. Nicolls Lt Coln Rl Engineers. Engineers Office Quebec 1815. [Sgd] G. Nicolls Lt. Coln Cg Rl Engineers. Quebec 24th June 1816
Col ms 46 x 72 cm 1" to 21/4 miles Watermark: 'J WHATMAN 1807' Endorsements: 'No 2' 'G272'; stamps 'B↑O' 'IGF'
Shows the same information as map above with the addition of Fort St Joseph on St Joseph Is 'destroyed by the Americans in 1813 G.N.' and an extract from a letter of Capt Payne 24 Feb 1816 indicating that 'there is a good channel on the east side of Drummond Is called False Detour'; (Holmden 2604).
OOAMA (NMC 8906)

---

848 *1797*
Map Shewing part of North America Comprehended between 46° & 54° of North Latitude & between 83° to 103° of West Longitude Containing Lake Superior the Communication & Chain of Lakes from the Grand Portage to Lake Winnipeg ... Taken from Astronomical Obervations by Mr Thompson Surveyor &c to the Said Company & Adjusted and Copied by Jos. Bouchette in the Year 1797
Ms 51 x 98 cm Scale not given
'Company' refers to the North West Co. and its posts are shown; relief by grey wash; canoe routes.
GBTAUh (186 Aa3)

---

849 *1797*
Sketch of the Military Post on the Island of St. Joseph in Lake Huron shewing the proposed arrangement for Buildings to be erected thereon. 24th of August, 1797
Col ms 27 x 40 cm 1" to 1000 ft Endorsements: 'LXI Entd'
The map is sgd on the verso 'W.E. Glegg Royl Engrs' who may have been the owner; the proposed bldgs are shown and keyed; there is also a map (QMMMCM 3605) entitled 'Plan of the Post on the Island of St. Joseph in Lake Huron, 1799 No 3' (col ms, 48 x 29 cm, 1" to approx 133 ft) that shows the proposed bldgs, present bldgs, and 'Section through the Face of a Bastion ...' 1" to 8 ft; this plan may, however, have been made much later.
QMMMCM (7688, 3605)

Related maps

(**2**) *1800*
Plan of the Post on the Island of St. Joseph in Lake Huron Copied in the Engineer's Drawing Room Quebec by J.B. Duberger in 1800. [Sgd] Gother Mann Coll Commandg Rl Engrs.
Col ms 59 x 90 cm 1" to 200 ft Watermark: 'J WHATMAN 1794' Endorsements: '43.10.9.52'
Insets: [plan of the fort] 1" to 50 ft; 'Section through the Platform' 1" to 8 ft; 'Section through the Picketing' 1" to 4 ft, 1" to 15 ft vertical; similar to the maps above but a more finished plan and including two more sections and more details on temporary bldgs to be removed; shows blockhouse, bakehouse and kitchen, guardhouse, platform for guns; other bldgs and roads.
GBL (Maps 23.b.3 (15))

---

850 *1798 ([1825?])*
[Map of route from Lake Superior to the Lake of the Woods] Sketched from my Survey in 1798. [Sgd] David Thompson

Ms 84 x 106 cm Scale not given
Provenance: OOAMA Tiarks Papers Map 15 and a note on a separate piece of paper indicates that map belongs to Dr Tiarks and not to the Foreign Office; shows the route via the Grand Portage and Pigeon R via Dog L; the St Louis R connection to the Mississippi R and north through Vermilion L and R to Rainy L also shown; a note indicates that the only communication known prior to 1783 was this route, which is described as a 'commercial communication'; David Thompson's notes for the 1798 survey are in OTAR (MU 2968–82), but this map was probably drafted later; there is also a photoreproduction in OOAMA (NMC 6061) of a ms map entitled 'Approximate Map of the Old and New route from Lake Superior to the Lake of the Woods. by D. Thompson Astronr' that shows the old or southern route via the Grand Portage and Pigeon R and the new route from Fort William via Dog R and L, Sturgeon L, 'Lake of the Thousand Isles,' L LaCroix to Rainy R and L, and Lake of the Woods, and gives lengths of portages and notes on rock types; the source of the photoreproduction has not been identified; the map may date from the 1825 boundary survey.
OOAMA (NMC 11695)

---

851 *1802*
Lake Superior copied from a Plan in possession of S. McTavish, Esq. Surveyed by Mr. Thompson, Astronomer & Surveyor employed by the N.W. Company, 1802.
Ms in 2 sheets 49 x 123 cm Scale not given
Endorsements: 'C.S.' 'W 16/11/71 H.H.M.'
An outline plan with a few major points marked; shows Fort Charlotte south of Thunder Bay and Kaministiquia R; note in pencil, 'The projection of this plan very ill drawn'; David Thompson conducted surveys in the area in 1798 and his field notes are in OTAR (MU 2968–82).
QMMMCM (4834)

---

852 *1802*
Sketch of the Entrance of the River Kamanistiqua Lat: 48d..21' North. Lon: 89d..20' West [and] Sketch of Thunder Bay and the adjacent Coast of Lake Superior [Sgd] July 23rd 1802 R.H. Bruyeres Captn Royl Engrs
Col ms 37 x 21 cm Scale not given
Originally with Bruyeres's report to Lt Gen Hunter of 10 Sept 1802 on the trading establishment at Kaministiquia R (and St Marys) (OOA RG 8 I/382 p 220); the larger-scale plan shows the old French fort and establishment and house and areas cleared by New Co. and fort and houses and area cleared by the North West Co.; the smaller-scale map has a few places marked; (Holmden 2531).
OOAMA (NMC 3137)

---

853 *1802*
Sketch of the North Shore contiguous to the Falls of St Mary shewing the Improvements made by the North West Company. 8th July 1802 [Sgd] R.H. Bruyeres Captn Royl Engrs.
Col ms 23 x 38 cm 1" to 500 ft
Originally with Bruyeres's report to Lt Gen Hunter 10 Sept 1802 on the trading establishment founded at Falls of St Mary (OOA RG 8 I/382 p 219); shows the portage road and road for dragging canoes, two canals, and lock; various bldgs keyed including house and lot claimed by Mr Cotté; (Holmden 2608).
OOAMA (NMC 3248)

Related maps

(2) *[1803]*
Sketch of the North Shore at St. Mary's
Col ms 26 x 41 cm 1" to 250 ft
With a letter of 29 Dec 1803 from F. Richardson to Maj Green about land the North West Co. wished to occupy at St Mary's R (OOA RG 8 I/363 p 37); similar to plan above but shows smaller area around falls and indicates the road marked out by Lt Brice and road marked by 'F.R & Co. and their Assoc.'; also shows grounds requested by F.R & Co. and certain houses now being built; old 'NWC canal'; upper landing.
OOAMA

---

854 *1816*
Plan of the Indian Territories Comprehended between the 46th and 53rd Degrees of North Latitude and the 90th and 101st Degrees of West Longitude from Greenwich By [Sgd] Jos. Bouchette Survr Genl
Col ms 158 x 74 cm Approx 1" to 10 miles
Originally enclosed in Bouchette's report of 7 Dec 1816 re concerns about the forthcoming boundary survey (GBLpro CO 6/1/379); shows the area from L Superior west to parts of Manitoba and North Dakota; shows the water route from Fort William via Dog L and also via Knife L, Crooked L, Cross L to Rainy R and L; (*PRO Cat* 100).
GLBpro (MR 108)

---

855 *1818*
[Sketch of area from L Superior to L Winnipeg and York Factory] True Copy Wm Sax D.P. Surveyor April 1818
Col ms 35 x 23 cm 1" to 70 miles Endorsements: 'No 2'
Originally in GBLpro CO 42/181 f 318; shows the height of land between L Superior and Lake of the Woods and between L Winnipeg and Hudson Bay; rivers and lakes named; (*PRO Cat* 593).
GBLpro (MPG 43)

---

856 *1818*
A Sketch of the passage from Drummonds Island in Lake Huron to the Falls of St Mary & to Lake Superior taken by Maj General Macomb in 1818

Col ms 53 x 42 cm 1" to 2 miles Endorsements: stamp 'Engr Dept U. States Topl Bureau'
Includes two profile views of the shoreline; shows 'Fort St. Joseph destroyed during the late war' and the British post on Drummond's Is; rough indication of terrain; notes about commanding point on the west shore.
USNA (RG 77 0–10)

---

857 *1826*
[Endorsed title]: 'Outline of Portlock Harbour Lake Huron' [and] 'Portlock Harbour, Lake Huron Lieut. Portlock 25th February 1826'
Ms 60 x 52 cm Scale not given Watermark: '... BASTED MILL 1813' Endorsements: 'A 29'; stamps 'B↑O' 'IGF'
Accompanied by A.W. Robe's letter of 25 Feb 1826 to Lt Col Ellicombe, R.E., stating that Lt Portlock is the author of this map and of (2) below; an unfinished copy with pencil grid lines and pin pricks for copying; shows St Joseph Channel and present-day Coatsworth, Dawson, and Portlock islands; Portlock Harbour, which was opp the north end of Dawson Is, is not named on the map but is shown on the hydrographic chart of 1848 (**C105(2)**); (Holmden 2369).
OOMA (NMC 22742)

Related maps

(**2**) *[1826]*
Portlock Harbour on the North Shore of Lake Huron
Col ms 119 x 93 cm 1" to 300 ft Endorsements: stamp 'B↑O'
This is a more finished map with relief shown by colour wash; Portlock Harbour is not located on map and name Portlock added in pencil; (Holmden 2368).
OOAMA (NMC 17873)

---

858 *[1827]*
[River communication between La Cloche and Temiscamingue District posts by John McBean, Chief Factor, Huron District]
Ms 33 x 22 cm Approx 1" to 7.5 miles
Shows rivers and lakes between L Huron and the height-of-land, Wanapitei L and the Spanish R; McBean was centred at La Cloche.
MWHBC (D5/22 f 257)

---

859 *1837*
Part of the Island of St. Joseph. Copy [Sgd] J.G. Chewett S.G. Office 22nd July 1837
Col ms 28 x 57 cm 1" to 40 chains
Originally with a land petition (OOA RG 1 L1 R8 no 32 1837); shows the south part of the island with lot nos and sizes and a few names of owners; (Holmden 1735).
OOAMA (NMC 4379)

---

860 *1845*
Lake Huron Enlarged from Captn Bayfield's Chart & other Plans. By P.L. Morin, P.L. Surveyor, and Draughtsman. 1845
Col ms 141 x 288 cm Scale not given
Inset: [map of the Falls of St Mary, Village of St Mary, Canada, and Fort Brady, U.S.]; shows longitude and latitude and grid lines for copying; shows area from Penetanguishene and the Bruce Peninsula to Sault Ste Marie; Indian reserves shown and numbered; mining locations; timber location with comments on trees.
OTAR (SR 16092)

---

861 *1847*
GEOLOGICAL MAP / of the / LAKE SUPERIOR LAND DISTRICT / in the / State of Michigan. Prepared PURSUANT TO AN Act of Congress APPROVED / MARCH 1st 1847 ENTITLED "AN Act to ESTABLISH A NEW Land District / AND TO PROVIDE FOR THE SALE OF MINERAL LANDS IN THE / STATE OF Michigan" / BY / J.W. FOSTER & J.D. WHITNEY U.S. GEOLOGISTS / J. Ackerman Lithr 379 Broadway N.Y.
Print (lith) hand col 65 x 96 cm 1" to 11 miles
Hand-coloured to show geological formations; the geology of the north shore is laid down from the author's observations as well as those of Logan, Bayfield, and Mather; also shows the location of copper, iron, silver, and marble mines with those abandoned noted; shows the coast area in Canada on either side of Sault Ste Marie.
USDLC

---

862 *1847*
[Portion of Lake Huron showing La Cloche Island] [Sgd] T. Bouthillier Crown Land Department, Montreal 28 October 1847
Col ms 51 x 41 cm Approx 1" to 2.5 miles
Watermark: 'J. WHATMAN TURKEY MILL 1846'
A. Vidal surveyed the front of Hudson's Bay Co. land at LaCloche on 25 June 1847 (see **864** below).
MWHBC (D 5/20 f 414)

---

863 *1847*
Sketch of St Mary's Island and of the adjoining portion of The River, north of the Sault St Mary, on which is shown the Line of the Proposed Canal. Hamilton H. Killaly C.E. A.M. 1846. Department of Public Works, April 1847. G.F. Baillairgé Drafd
Col ms 52 x 70 cm 1" to 5 chains
'Longitudinal Section in the Line of the Proposed Canal' 1" to 10 ft vertical; from a report by H.H. Killaly on improving the communication between Lakes Superior and Huron by means of a canal of 30 March 1847 (OOA RG 5 Cl/200 1846–7 file 16,554); (SI (BW) to Killaly 19 Sept 1846 to ascertain possibility of ship canal at St Mary's); shows the first and second locks and proposed entrances at each end of canal; 12 points are numbered but not keyed on map or in report; soundings; Hudson's Bay Co. post.
OOAMA (NMC 19628)

Related maps

(2) *[1847?]*
Plan of position of proposed canal. Sault Ste Marie
Col ms 129 x 260 cm 1" to 2 chains Endorsements: 'Q8'
Shows canal reserve on St Mary's Is and two cross-sections; Hudson's Bay Co. post with bldgs and portage road; a later note attributes the plan to 'Rubidge.'
OOAMA

(3) *1852*
Location of the proposed canal at Sault Ste Marie. Surveyed August 1852 Samuel Keefer Chf. Engr. P.W. Tom Stafford Rubidge Asst. Engr. F.P. Rubidge Drft.
Col ms 129 x 250 cm 1" to 2 chains
Prepared to accompany Keefer's reports on the Sault Ste Marie Canal of 19 Aug and 24 Nov 1852; shows the proposed canal on St Mary's Is; rapids; also shows Hudson's Bay Co. post and bldgs and portage route around the town.
OOAMA

(4) *[1852]*
Survey and Sketch of the Bar in Lake George (with soundings taken by Tom S. Rubidge) [Sgd] Samuel Keefer C.E. P.W.
Col ms 53 x 65 cm 1" to 400 ft Endorsements: 'Enlarged Portion with Soundings'; stamp [BW] '539'
'See A.B. General Chart F.P.R'
OOAMA (NMC 21699)

---

864 *1848*
Map of the Hudson's Bay Company's Tracts at the Mississaga and La Cloche Rivers. Lake Huron. Surveyed and Drawn by Alexander Vidal P.LS. 1848. 'Original plan' [Sgd] [illegible]
2 ms maps on 1 sheet 57 x 43 cm 1" to 40 chains Endorsements: 'No 11' '1140/49'
(A. Vidal's survey of Hudson's Bay Co. land at LaCloche on 25 June 1847 is mentioned in SI to A. McDonald 13 Oct 1854; OTNR FN 369 16 March 1849); shows triangulation lines and observation points around shore; Hudson's Bay Co. bldgs.
OTNR (SR 7125)

---

865 *1848*
[Map to accompany Quebec and Lake Superior Mining Association Report 1847–8] G. & W. ENDICOTT'S LITH. 59 BEEKMAN ST. N.Y.
Print (lith) 35 x 23 cm Approx 1 1/4" to 1 mile
In Quebec and Lake Superior Mining Association, *Report 1847–8*, at back (*Bib Can* 2866); shows the north point of St Joseph Is and Desbarats, Hincks, Keating, and Cuthbertson twps; shows Bruce Mines, Portlock Harbour, and St Joseph North Channel; notes on rock types and probable locations of veins of ore.
OTMCL

---

866 *[1849]*
PLAN / of part of / The Bruce Mines. / Shewing the Mineral Veins. / Surveyed by W.E. Logan, Esqr F.G.S. / Drawn by James Cane, C.E. / MATTHEWS' LITH.
Print (lith) 40 x 51 cm 1" to 2 chains
In Geological Survey of Canada, *Report on the North Shore of Lake Huron* (Montreal: Printed by Lovell & Gibson 1849), frontis (*Bib Can* 2964, OOA); shows direction of lodes, location and depths of shafts, bldgs and roads, pier to offshore island, and wharves.
OOA OOAMA (NMC 3731) OTMCL

Related maps

(2) *[1849]*
A Plan of the / whole of the Location of the / BRUCE MINES / the Property of the / MONTREAL MINING COMPY / Containing 6400 Acres. // G. MATTHEWS' LITH
Print (lith) 52 x 29 cm 1" to 40 chains
In same source as above; mining lease boundary shown from Ottertail L to Thessalon R; types of rock, lodes, shafts with names shown by the shore.
OOA OOAMA (NMC 3732) OTMCL

---

867 *[1849]*
Sketch map Shewing the position of the Bruce and Mica Bay Copper Mines, near the Sault St. Mary [by Major Sir James Alexander].
Col ms 30 x 22 cm 1" to 13.5 miles
Withdrawn from Lt Gen William Rowan's dispatch of 24 Nov 1849 about sending troops to guard miners against violence from Indians (GBLpro WO 1/vol 561 f 43); rivers, a few places, and mines shown; (*PRO Cat* 1582).
GBLpro (MPHH 672(1))

---

868 *[185?]*
[Endorsed title]: 'Copy of Bayfield's Lake Superior M P No 4'
Col ms 84 x 177 cm Scale not given
The shore area is coloured for about four geological formations but no key is given; possibly a draft used in making the printed map of 1858 (**885**), although the scale of this one is larger.
OTAR (SR 6426)

---

869 *1850*
LAKE / OF THE / WOODS. / Reduced from a Map made from actual survey by / David Thompson. Astr to the Boundary Commission. // Day & Son, lithrs to the Queen.
Print (lith) 23 x 22 cm 1" to 8 geog miles
In J.J. Bigsby, *The Shoe and Canoe* (London: Chapman and Hall 1850), 2: opp 294 (*Bib Can* 1426); shows place-names, the international boundary line by the Treaty of Ghent, and portages.
OTMCL

---

870 *[1850]*
[Map of the north shore of Lake Huron showing geology attributed to A. Murray]
Col ms on 3 sheets 120 x 98 cm Approx 1" to 1 mile
Shows the whole extent of the north shore from L George east to the Bruce Peninsula and Nottawasaga Bay; geology formations shown by colours but there is no key; notes on rock types; longitude and latitude lines shown; some topography is shown uncertainly with lines of rivers dotted in; probably prepared after 1849 when Murray completed a survey of the coast of L Huron (Zaslow, 52).
OOAMA (RG 45M 83403/21/D-V-1470)

---

871 *1850*
Plan of the Spanish River. Crown Land Department Montreal 16 October 1850 [Sgd] Jean Langere[t]?
Ms, part missing 61 x 105 cm 1" to approx 2.6 miles
Shows rapids, portages, falls, currents, Hudson's Bay Co. posts and Indian villages.
OTAR (SR 7093)

---

872 *1850*
Systems of Dykes. // OUTLINES OF LAKE SUPERIOR // A. Sonrel on stone // Tappan & Bradford's Lithy
Print (lith) 12 x 17 cm Scale not given
In Louis Agassiz, *Lake Superior* (Boston: Gould, Kendall, and Lincoln 1850), opp 428 (*Bib Can* 3044); six dyke systems located and most are on the north shore; glacial scratches and direction indicated.
OTMCL

---

873 *1852*
Rough Sketch of the Island of St. Joseph Lake Huron and Vicinity shewing in red proposed Military Reservations [Sgd] W.T. Renwick Capt R.E. 30/9/52. To accompany my Report of 6 Octr 1852. [Sgd] Alexr Gordon Lt Colonel Royal Engineers
Col ms 55 x 44 cm 1" to 2000 yds Endorsements: 'rel C.W./129' 'No 10/1'; stamp 'CREOC'
Shows four proposed military reserves around the island including the old garrison ground at the south end; relief and rough contours given; shows ship channel and United States Ship Channel, and Canada-United States boundary; proposed reserves 'with reference to C.R.E. letter to I.G.F. dated 11th Novr 1852 No 66.'
OOAMA (NMC 4381)

Related maps

(2) *1852*
Rough Sketch of the old Garrison Ground at The Island of St. Joseph's [Sgd] W.T. Renwick Capt R.E. 1 Oct 1852 – To accompany my Report of 6 Octr 1852 [Sgd] Alexr Gordon Lt. Colonel Royal Engineers
Col ms 44 x 27 cm 1" to 400 yds Endorsements: 'Rel. C.W. 129' 'No 2' 'No 10/2'; stamp 'CREOC'
Shows site of fortifications at the south end of the island, line of old clearance 1827, old military reserve and proposed boundary; boundary with United States.
OOAMA (NMC 4380)

---

874 *1853*
Lake Superior, / BY / LIEUT HENRY WR. BAYFIELD / Assisted by / Mr. Philip Ed Collins Mid. / between the Years 1823 & 1825 / Crown Lands Department. / Quebec 12th March 1853. / Certified a true Copy / John Rolph, / Commissioner / of / Crown Lands. // Matthews Lith
Print (lith) hand col 53 x 99 cm Scale not given
Originally accompanied 'Report of the Special Committee on the Magdalen Islands, and the Western Part of This Province above Lake Huron' (*JLA* (1852–3), App 222); shows the lake with numbered mining reserves on north shore around Fort William, Nipigon Bay, Michipicoten Is and nearby shore, and Mamainse; 'The Mining Locations are edged yellow and numbered to correspond with the Tabular Return in Appendix U to Journals of Legislative Assembly for 1851.'
OOAMA (NMC 26756)

Related maps

(2) *1853*
Sketch of Lake Superior, shewing the / supposed Northern and Western Limits / of this Province in that direction. / G. Matthews' Lith. // Crown Lands Department / Quebec, 12th March 1853. / Certified a true Copy. / T.D. [Sgd in facsimile] John Rolph / Commissioner of Crown Lands.
Print (lith) hand col 35 x 51 cm Scale not given
From the same source as map above; the boundary line between Canada and the United States is shown in L Superior and along the Pigeon R; the supposed height of land and boundary of the province is shown to the north; Dog R and Whitefish R located.
OOAMA (NMC 4283)

---

875 *1855*
MAP / OF THE / ST MARY'S RIVER / FROM LAKE SUPERIOR TO LAKE HURON / Compiled from the U.S. Government Surveys / (from the Records of the U.S. Land Office) / BY LIEUT A.L MAGILTON U.S.A. / 1855. // ENGRAVED & PRINTED BY J.H. COLTON & Co. 172 WILLIAM ST N.Y. / FOR SAMUEL WHITNEY OF SAULT DE ST MARIE.
Print (lith) 47 x 64 cm Approx 1" to 2 3/4 miles
Cover-title on OTMCL copy: 'Map of the St. Mary's River S Whitney.'; on the Canadian side shows Hudson's Bay Co. post at Sault Ste Marie and Indian village at Little L George; 'old Fort St. Joseph'; international boundary; shows more information on the American side including towns, rivers, survey grid; (Karpinski 804).
OOAMA (NMC 43049) OTMCL

876 *[1855]*
Plan of Exploration of the North Shore of Lake Huron By Albert Pellew Salter P.L.S.
Col ms 135 x 665 cm 1" to 1 mile Endorsements: '240' 'Exploration North of Lake Huron A.P. Salter 1855'
(OTNR FN 1916 4 Feb 1856); an unfinished and unsigned plan showing the results of some of Salter's exploratory surveys in July to Nov 1855; shows the area from L Nipissing and the French R west to Sault Ste Marie; shows several exploration lines, Indian reserves, and mining locations; camps located; relief, villages, falls and rapids; indication of vegetation and land types.
OTAR (SR 16909)

---

877 *1855–6*
[Plans of Hudson's Bay Company property, north shore of Lake Superior and Lake Huron]
7 col mss on 6 sheets Various sizes 1" to 40 chains
(SI to A. McDonald 13 Oct 1854 to survey Hudson's Bay Co. property and lay out some tracts on north shores of L Huron and L Superior; for Fort William and St Marys R see **1349** and **1954**.

The plans are as follows:

(**1**) A Sketch showing the relative positions of Gull River and the Hon. Hudson's Bay Company's Post on Lake Neepigon [Sgd] Alexander McDonald Land Surveyor Neepigon 10 January 1855 [on sheet with]: Map Shewing the coast about the Hon. Hudson's Bay Coy's Post on Lake Neepigon [Sgd] Alexander McDonald Land Surveyor Neepigon 10 January 1855
Ea 22 x 25 cm
Both are rough sketches with place-names.
OTNR (SR 1358)

(**2**) Map of the Hudson's Bay Company's Property at Pic. Surveyed and drawn by Alex. McDonald. 1855. Montreal 9 Mar 1856 [Sgd] Alexander MacDonald Provincial Land Surveyor. Examined [Sgd] A.Russell
69 x 50 cm Endorsements: 'LS. No 40'
Shows boundary of property with bearings, triangulation lines along shores; relief.
OTNR (SR 7105)

(**3**) Map of the Hudson's Bay Company's Property at Michipicoton Surveyed and Drawn by Alex. McDonald 1855. Montreal 9 May 1856 [Sgd] Alexander MacDonald Provincial Land Surveyor Examined [Sgd] A. Russell
68 x 50 cm Endorsements: 'LS. No 41'
Boundary of Hudson's Bay Co. property at mouth of river; boundary of another surveyed tract shown; traverse lines along river.
OTNR (SR 7121)

(**4**) Map of the Hudson's Bay Company's property at Angenwang Surveyed and Drawn by Alex. McDonald 1855. Montreal 9 May 1856 [Sgd] Alexander MacDonald Provincial Land Surveyor Examined [Sgd] A.Russell
68 x 51 cm Endorsements: 'LS. No 42' '8288/556'
Shows the bearings and boundary of Hudson's Bay Co. property at mouth of the Angewang R [Agawa R].
OTNR (SR 7120)

(**5**) Map of the Hudson's Bay Company's property at Mississauga Surveyed and Drawn by Alex. McDonald 1856. Montreal 9 May 1856 [Sgd] Alexander MacDonald Provincial Land Surveyor. Examined [Sgd] A. Russell
50 x 68 cm Endorsements: 'LH. No 29'
Shows the property at the mouth of the Mississagi R at L Huron and area between Baie de Calumet and Fox Is; Indian reserve.
OTNR (SR 7123)

(**6**) Map of the Hudson's Bay Company's property at La Cloche Surveyed and Drawn by Alex. McDonald 1856. Montreal 9 May 1856 [Sgd] Alexander MacDonald Provincial Land Surveyor. Examined [Sgd] A Russell
68 x 51 cm Endorsements: 'LH. No 30'
Bearings and boundary of property, relief; 'See P.L.S. Vidal's plan of survey of the shore L.H. No 11' (1848) (**864**).
OTNR (SR 7109)

---

878 *1856*
MAP OF / ST. JOSEPH ISLAND / LAKE HURON / DRAWN & LITH. By T. Devine C.L.O. / Crown Lands Department / Toronto Augt 1856 / A.R
Print (lith) 48 x 51 cm 1" to 1 mile
Inset: [location map] 1" to approx 3.6 miles; based on the twp survey by T.N. Molesworth of Feb 1856 (**A1709**); copies are found with land petitions in OOA RG 1 L3 R8 no 32 1857 and I no 9, no 10; shows the survey grid; OTUTF copy has ms adds about clearing and request for lots, and note: 'The Sale will take place at the Crown Lands Office, on Monday the Fifteenth September, next' [1856]; (Holmden 1738).
OKIT OOAMA (NMC 22773) OTUTF

---

879 *[ca 1856]*
[Map of the north shore of Lake Huron between Thessalon and Whitefish Falls]
Col ms 79 x 263 cm 1" to 90 chains
An unfinished plan showing boundaries of Indian reserves, falls, rapids, heights of land; note indicates lines 'according to P.S. Dennis's' survey per SI 19 Aug 1851; 'Saw mill now being erected by M. Sabroit'; a note refers to MacDonald's plan of 1856 (**877(5)**, **(6)**).
OTAR (SR 5989)

---

880 *1856*
REDUCTION OF PLAN OF EXPLORATION OF THE NORTH SHORE OF LAKE HURON BY / ALBERT PELLEW SALTER P.L.S. / Thos Devine S & D / G. Matthews Litho. Montreal // Crown Land Department / TORONTO 15th APRIL 1856. / [Sgd in facsimile] Joseph Cauchon / Commissioner of Crown lands

Print (lith) 53 x 101 cm 1" to 6 miles
In *Report Made to the Crown Lands Department by Albert Pellew Salter Esq. P.L.S. upon the Country Bordering upon the North Shore of Lake Huron* (Toronto: John Lovell 1856), frontis (OTUTF); shows the area from L Nipissing to Sault Ste Marie; shows the same information as the large ms plan (**876**) except lines of survey, mineral locations, and Indian reserve boundaries not distinguished; dotted lines show boundaries of differing land types; (Holmden 1900).
OOAMA (NMC 19788) OTUTF

Later editions and states

(**2**) *1857*
No 7 / REDUCTION OF MR SALTER'S PLAN of Exploration OF THE NORTH SHORE OF LAKE HURON / By T. Devine C.L.O. / Maclear & Co. Lith. Toronto // Crown Lands Department / A.R Toronto Feby 1857 [Sgd in facsimile] Joseph Cauchon / Commissioner of Crown Lands
Print (lith) 45 x 130 cm 1" to 6 miles
In *Appendix to Report of the Commissioner of Crown Lands 1856, Part II, Maps of Canada* (Toronto: Printed by Stewart Derbishire & George DesBarats 1857) (OOAMA); and in French ed of 1857 (OOAMA); the map has been extended at the west end to show part of the L Superior shore; from the same plate as the 1856 map above with a different title and the following changes: mineral locations are now designated, some Indian reserves added, and numbers given; shows exploration line from Sturgeon R west to mile XXX at Spanish R and many more rivers and lakes added; (Holmden 1901).
OOAMA (NMC 11320) OTMCL

---

881 *1857*
GEOLOGICAL SURVEY OF CANADA / Sir Wm Logan F.R.S. Director / INDEX TO THE PLANS / SHOWING THE EXPLORATIONS / On the NORTH SHORE OF LAKE HURON. / AND THENCE EASTWARD / to the OTTAWA. Geo. Matthews, Lithographer Montreal.
Print (lith) 19 x 48 cm 1" to 10 miles
In Geological Survey of Canada, *Report of Progress for the Years 1853–54–55–56* (Toronto: John Lovell 1857), opp 166 (*Bib Can* 2568); an index map for sheets 1–11 of survey from Spanish R to Mattawa R and Ottawa R; index map later assigned GSC publication no 14 (Ferrier, 9); the plans themselves are found in Geological Survey of Canada, *Plans of Various Lakes and Rivers between Lake Huron and the River Ottawa to Accompany the Geological Reports for 1853–54–55–56* (Toronto: John Lovell 1857) (*Bib Can* 2568); the plans are each approx 55 x 85 cm and all at 1" to 80 chains; each plan has at head of title: 'GEOLOGICAL SURVEY OF CANADA / Sir Wm E. Logan F.R.S. Director'; the plans show the rivers and lakes, rapids, falls; the plans were later assigned GSC publication nos 17–27 (Ferrier, 9–10); the plans are as follows:

(**1**) TOPOGRAPHICAL PLAN / OF THE / SPANISH RIVER / by A. Murray Esqr / Asst Provl Geologist / 1848 / G. Matthews Lith. Montreal / Sheet 1
(Holmden 2630). OOAMA (NMC 21435)

(**2**) GEOLOGICAL SURVEY OF CANADA / Sir Wm. E. Logan F.R.S. / TOPOGRAPHICAL PLAN / OF PART OF THE / SPANISH AND WHITE FISH RIVERS / by A. Murray Esqr / Asst Provl Geologist / 1848–56 / G. Matthews Lith. Montreal / Sheet 2
(Holmden 2631). OOAMA (NMC 21436)

(**3**) TOPOGRAPHICAL PLAN / OF THE MOUTH OF THE / WHITE FISH RIVER / by A. Murray Esqr / Asst Provl Geologist / 1856, 7 / G. Matthews Lith. Montreal / Sheet 3
(Holmden 2892). OOAMA (NMC 21437)

(**4**) TOPOGRAPHICAL PLAN / OF PART OF / WAHNAPITAE RIVER / AND OF / WAHNAPITAEPING AND ADJOINING LAKES: / by A. Murray Esqr / Asst Provl Geologist / 1856. / G. Matthews Lith. Montreal / Sheet 4
(Holmden 2875). OOAMA (NMC 21438)

(**5**) TOPOGRAPHICAL PLAN / OF PART OF THE / WAHNAPITAE RIVER &c. by A. Murray Esqr / Asst Provl Geologist / 1855–6 / G. Matthews Lith. Montreal / Sheet 5
(Holmden 2876). OOAMA (NMC 21439)

(**6**) TOPOGRAPHICAL PLAN / OF PART OF THE / FRENCH AND WAHNAPITAE RIVERS / by A. Murray Esqr / Asst Provl Geologist. / 1847, 1855–56–57 / G. Matthews Lith. Montreal / Sheet 6
(Holmden 2877). OOAMA (NMC 21440)

(**7**) TOPOGRAPHICAL PLAN / OF PART OF THE / STURGEON RIVER / by A. Murray Esqr / Asst Provl Geologist / 1856. / G. Matthews Lith. Montreal / Sheet 7
(Holmden 2638). OOAMA (NMC 21441)

(**8**) TOPOGRAPHICAL PLAN / OF PART OF / LAKE NIPISSING AND STURGEON RIVER / by A. Murray Esqr / Asst Provl Geologist / 1854–55–56 / G. Matthews Lith. Montreal / Sheet 8
(Holmden 1905). OOAMA (NMC 21442)

(**9**) TOPOGRAPHICAL PLAN / OF PART OF THE / FRENCH RIVER. / by A. Murray Esqr / Asst Provl Geologist / 1854–55–56 / and / 1847. / G. Matthews Lith Montreal / Sheet 9
(Holmden 1669). OOAMA (NMC 21443)

(**10**) TOPOGRAPHICAL PLAN / OF PART OF / RIVER MATTAWA, / by Sir W.E. Logan F.R.S. &c. / Provl Geologist / 1845. / AND PART OF / LAKE NIPISSING: / by A. Murray Esqr / Asst Provl Geologist / 1854 / G. Matthews Lith. Montreal / Sheet 10
(Holmden 2533). OOAMA (NMC 21444)

(**11**) TOPOGRAPHICAL PLAN / OF THE / RIVERS OTTAWA AND MATTAWA / by Sir W.E. Logan F.R.S. &c. / Provl Geologist / 1854 / G. Matthews Lith. Montreal / Sheet 11
(Holmden 2534). OOAMA (NMC 21445)
OOAMA (NMC 21435–45) OTAR OTMCL USDLC

Related maps

(2) *[1856]*
[Topographical plan of part of Lake Nipissing and Sturgeon River by A. Murray]
Col ms 94 x 123 cm 1" to 80 chains Endorsements: 'Surveys between River Ottawa, & Lake Huron by A. Murray, Lake Nipissing' 'Plan 1812'
A ms draft to the same scale for printed sheets 5, 8, 9, 10 (see above); shows L Nipissing, Mammanitigong R and branches, and Sturgeon R with Restoule L pencilled in; geological notes similar to those on the printed plan; revisions have been made to shoreline and these are as on printed plan; (Zaslow, 69).
OOAMA (RG 45M 83403/21 B-24-1)

---

882 *1857*
Map / OF THE NORTH WEST PART / OF / CANADA / INDIAN TERRITORIES & HUDSON'S BAY / Compiled & Drawn by Thos Devine Provincial Land Surveyor & Draftsman / by Order of the / HONE JOSEPH CAUCHON, / Commissioner of Crown Lands / Crown Lands Department / TORONTO MARCH, / 1857. / Maclear & Co Lith Toronto.
Print (lith) 158 x 141 cm 1" to 40 miles
Found separately and in *Appendix to Report of the Commissioner of Crown Lands 1856, Part II Maps of Canada* (Toronto: Derbishire and Desbarats 1857) (OOAMA OTMCL OTUTF); an important map for northwestern Ontario, although it covers the whole of western Canada and the Arctic; shows exploring lines, railways, and major roads for area from Toronto to the north and west; geological notes; mineral locations; notes on land particularly with reference to agriculture, e.g., 'grain producing district' noted in the bend of Lake Sal [Seul] and 'large quantities of rich land' noted near Rainy L and Lake of the Woods; shows conflicting boundaries of Upper Canada and Hudson's Bay territory as of Treaty of Utrecht, British claims, etc; lines of winter temperatures equal to those of Kingston shown; sources; (see 'Devine, Thomas,' in *DCB* XI:256–7; Warkentin and Ruggles, 154–5).
OOAMA OTMCL OTUTF

Related maps

(2) *1857*
... / Published by / S. DERBISHIRE & G. DESBARATS / Printer to the Queen's Most Excellent Majesty.
Print (lith) hand col
With the addition of Derbishire imprint and a legend and hand colouring for geological formations including copper-bearing rocks, Silurian, Crystalline, and Devonian formations for Ontario portion.
GBL (Maps 23.d.8) OOAMA (NMC 19515) OTMCL OTUTF USDLC

(3) *1857*
MAP / of the / North West Part of / CANADA, / HUDSON'S BAY & INDIAN TERRITORIES / Drawn by Thos Devine, / by Order of / The Honble Joseph Cauchon / Commr. of Crown Lands. / Toronto / March 1857. // SELECT COMMITTEE ON THE HUDSON'S BAY COMPANY // John Arrowsmith Litho. / Nos 224 & 260 (Sess. 2) / Ordered by the House of Commons to be Printed 31st July & 11th August, 1857. / Henry Hansard, Printer
Print (col lith) 48 x 65 cm 1" to 133 miles
A reduced version of the large map showing the same information and the coloured geological formations; accompanies Great Britain House of Commons *Report from the Select Committee on the Hudson's Bay Company ... 1857* (*HCPP* 1857 (II) XV, 572–6 (OTU mfe)); Holmden 3769.
OOAMA (NMC 7041

---

883 *[1857]*
[Maps and plans from Capt John Palliser's report of 1857]
4 col mss Size varies Scales vary
Originally with report from Capt Palliser, no 6157, 14 July 1858, in GBLpro CO 6/29 f 93ff; the maps relating to Ontario are as follows:
(a) [Endorsed title]: 'Sketch map White Fish River on the Kaministaquoia R. Ft. William. Lower 17 Miles. [Sgd] John Palliser Esq. June 1857'
35 x 55 cm 1" to 1/2 mile
Shows camps, nature of terrain, probable route back on the 16th [June].
(b) [Endorsed title]: 'Map and Section Shewing the structure of the Kakabeka Falls. River Kaministiquoia. J.H. 1857.'
16 x 23 cm Scale not given
(c) [Endorsed title]: 'Sketch Map on the Lakes on the Sturgeon Rivers, Upper Sturgeon Lake – H.B.Cos. Territories [Sgd] John Palliser Esq. June 1857. Lower 10 miles.'
55 x 37 cm Scale not given
Routes, camps, notes on terrain and trees.
(d) [Sketch map and section of Rainy Lake to Lake Superior route] J.H. 1857
16 x 23 cm Scale not given
Geological notes including strikes, rock types, and glacial markings; both (a) and (d) are probably by James Hector, the geologist with the expedition whose first general report on the geology of the country dated Dec 1857 was included with Palliser's above (*DCB* XI:661ff); (*PRO Cat* 1418).
GBLpro (MPG 395 (1, 4, 12, 14))

Related maps

(2) *[1857–8]*
Part of route of the exploring expedition under command of Captain Palliser ... 1857 and 1858] Thomas Blakiston Lieut Rl Artillery. Copied by E. Oulet October 1858
3 col mss Sizes vary Scales not given
Marked as received 'E 5th/10/58'; the maps

relating to Ontario are as follows and show lakes, rivers, portages, routes, etc:
(a)'Sheet 1' [Lake Superior to Rainy R]
(b)'Sheet 2' [Fort Frances to Winnipeg R]
(c)'Sheet 3 Map and Section Shewing the structure of the Kakabeka Falls River Kaministiquoia'
Sheets (a) and (c) are similar to sheets (1b) and (1d) above.
GBLrg (Canada S/S40)

(3) *1859*
Sketch / of the Lower portion of / WHITE FISH RIVER / by / John Palliser, Esqr / 1857. // John Arrowsmith, Litho. 1859.
Print (lith) 30 x 18 cm 1" to 1 mile
This and the other plans described in this entry accompanied *Exploration – British North America; Papers relating to the Exploration by Captain Palliser ... Presented ... by Command of Her Majesty June 1859* (London: Eyre and Spottiswoode 1859) (*Bib Can* 3928); this plan shows the river entering the Kaministiquia R at 48° 21'N and 89° 47'W; camps of 13–15 June [1857] located; notes on tree types; rapids, falls; a note indicates that map not made from exact measurements vis-à-vis distances; the other plans include an untitled plan of Sturgeon L, 'John Arrowsmith Litho. 1859,' showing camp of 28 June [1857] and two routes through the lake, two untitled plans numbered 'Sh1' and 'Sh2' showing route from L Superior to Winnipeg R with geological cross-sections, and 'Map and Section / showing the Structure of the / KAKABEKA FALLS. / River Kaministoquoia [Sgd in facsimile] J. Hector 1858 John Arrowsmith. Litho. 1859'; the plans are the printed versions of (1) above; the first and second maps are also found in GBLpro FO 925/1951 (1,2) (*PRO Cat* 1617, 1593).
GBLpro (FO 925/1951(1, 2)) OTMCL

---

884 *1857 Dec*
Plan of the Canoe Route from Fort William Lake Superior to Fort Garry Red River [Sgd] W.H.E. Napier Fort Garry Red River Decb. 10th 1857
Col ms on linen 43 x 1354 cm 1" to 1 mile
Endorsements: '354/58'
(SI to S.J. Dawson 18 July 1857 to make an exploratory survey from L Superior to Red River); the largest scale ms plan that shows the route followed on the 1857 survey; shows route from Fort William via the Kaministiquia R, Great Dog L and Dog R, Savanne R system, Lac des Milles Lacs, Sturgeon L and R, Pine L, Namakan L to Rainy L, Rainy R, Lake of the Woods, Rat Portage, Winnipeg R to L Winnipeg and Red R to Fort Garry; gives bearings and shows Hudson's Bay Co. posts and forts; other ms plans from the 1857 survey are listed below.
OTAR (SR 6041)

Related maps

(2) *1857 Dec*
Section of Canoe Route between Fort William and Red River as surveyed in August 1857 [Sgd] W.H.E. Napier Red River Settlement Decr 10th 1857
Col ms 65 x 879 cm 1" to 2 miles, 1" to 100 ft vertical Endorsements: '4849/58'
Section of the route as described above; portages and rapids shown; there is also a copy of this plan at OTAR, col ms on linen, with the same title '(Sgd) W.H.E. Napier.'
OTAR (SR 5452) OTNR

(3) *1857 Dec*
Map of the Winter Route by the North from Fort Frances to the Rat Portage shewing also the Usual Canoe-Route by Rainy River and the Lake of the Woods [Sgd] W.H.E. Napier Red River Settlement Decr 10th 1857.
Col ms 63 x 82 cm 1" to 4 miles
Shows the canoe route by Rainy R, Lake of the Woods, and Rat Portage into Winnipeg R called 'Usual Canoe Route' and with note 'this is undoubtedly the best route to be pursued in going to Red River [Sgd] Geo Gladman'; shows international boundary line, route explored by Napier through Rainy L and a more northerly route from Rainy L through to Rat Portage via L Agachewana, Lac de l'Eau Clair into the northeast corner of Lake of the Woods and Lac des Poissons Blancs; 'The survey of this portion of the Country was made by Mr Napier alone – and in my opinion, should be inserted in any map which it would be thought proper to publish. Geo Gladman.'; also shows northwest corner of Lake of the Woods and road line under exploration to Red River.
OTAR (SR 6000)

(4) *1857 Dec*
Plan shewing Canoe Route between the Lake of the Woods and Fort Garry by the Winnipeg River also the Direct Line under Exploration between Fort Garry and the N W Corner of the Lake of the Woods [Sgd] W.H.E. Napier Red River Settlement Decr 10th 1857
Col ms 75 x 108 cm 1" to 4 miles
Similar to (3) above except shows the whole area west to Fort Garry; shows 'Usual Canoe Route,' direct road line under exploration, and the more northerly canoe route described above.
OTAR (SR 6002)

(5) *1857 Dec*
Plan Shewing the Proposed Route from Lake Superior to Red River Settlement S.J. Dawson Red River December 1857
Col ms 78 x 158 cm 1" to 8 miles Endorsements: 'No 58 of 288'
A reduction of (1) above with the route proposed in 1857 consisting of the road from Fort William to L Shebandowan and river route via Dog L, Savanne R, Lac des Milles Lacs to Rainy L, Rainy R and Lake of the Woods; the more northerly connection at Lake of the Woods is not shown; supposed direction of discharge of Lac des Milles Lacs shown; mining locations have been added later;

shows more southerly river system to the west by Arrow L and connections to L Nipigon; also a copy at GBL entitled 'Proposed Route from Lake Superior to Red River Settlement (signed) S.J. Dawson Red River December 1857,' col ms on tracing paper at the same scale with the same information.
GBL (Map 70200 (6)) OTAR (SR 5957)

(6) *1858 May*
Plan / SHEWING THE PROPOSED ROUTE FROM / LAKE SUPERIOR TO RED RIVER / SETTLEMENT / COMPILED FROM MESSRS DAWSON & NAPIERS MAPS. / T. Devine Surveyor Branch West / Crown Lands Department / Toronto 29th May 1858. / Andrew Russell Assistant Commissioner. / Maclear & Co. Liths. Toronto.
Print (lith) 86 x 148 cm 1" to 8 miles
Insets: 'PROFILE OF CANOE ROUTE / AS HANDED IN BY PROFESSOR HIND' 1" to 10 miles, 1" to 600 ft vertical, 'PLAN / OF THE COUNTRY BETWEEN / RED RIVER SETTLE-MENT / AND THE / LAKE OF THE WOODS / (Signed) S.J. DAWSON ...' 1" to 8 miles; in *Report on the Exploration of the Country between Lake Superior and the Red River Settlement* (Toronto: John Lovell 1858) (*Bib Can* 3791, map missing; OTUTF) and in the French ed (1858); shows the northern canoe route from Fort William via Kaministiquia R, Dog L, Savanna R, Lac des Milles Lacs, Rainy L, and Rainy R to Lake of the Woods and from there straight to Fort Garry; part of the river route north of Rainy R to Lake of the Woods shown and indicated as 'This route explored by Mr Napier' (see (3)); essentially the same and at the same scale as (5) showing the results of the 1857 survey, with the addition of Hind's profile the same as that on (**888(2)**); the first printed plan showing results of the survey.
OLU OTAR OTMCL OTUTF USDLC

(7) *1858 May (1859)*
PLAN / Shewing the Proposed Route from / LAKE SUPERIOR / to / RED RIVER SETTLEMENT / Compiled from the / Maps of Messrs Dawson and Napier / T. Devine, Surveyor Branch West, / Crown Lands Department / Toronto, 23rd May 1858. / [Sgd in facsimile] Andrew Russell Assistant Commissioner. / [J. Arrowsmith Lith]
Print (lith) hand col, trimmed below border 38 x 63 cm Scale not given
Insets: 'Plan / of the Country between / RED RIVER SETTLEMENT / and the / LAKE OF THE WOODS / (Signed) / S.J. Dawson' 1" to 18 miles, 'Profile of Canoe Route as handed in by Professor Hind'; in Great Britain, Colonial Office, *Papers Relative to the Exploration of the Country ... June 1859* (London: Eyre and Spottiswoode 1859), in *HCPP* 1859 (II), XXII:after 643 (OTU (mfe); *Bib Can* 3908); the route is enhanced in red; the map is a reduced version of plan (6); also enclosed in GBLpro FO 925/1855; (*PRO Cat* 1419).
GBLpro (FO 925/1855) OOAMA (NMC 6074) OTMCL

(8) *[1858?] Dec*
Plan of part of the region explored and surveyed by S.J. Dawson and his party
Col ms on linen 74 x 149 cm Approx 1" to 4 miles
Shows the area from Thunder Bay to Fort Frances and the southern and northern canoe route systems; shows road lines including 'Russell's line' from Kaministiquia R to Green Flint L and from the river to Dog L; also shows the 'located line of road' to Dog L and two exploratory lines east and north of this; probably shows the results of survey in 1858 as L.A. Russell's work is mentioned in the 1859 report by Dawson (see (12) and (13)) and the road route was located in 1858; other plans that appear to date from the 1858 surveys are listed below.
OTAR (SR 8073)

(9) *[1858?]*
[Map of Muskaig Lake and River, Dog River, Savanne River and portage]
Ms 98 x 66 cm Approx 1" to 1 mile Endorsements: '526'; stamp 'BW'
Possibly plan referred to by J.F. Gaudet in letter of 23 Dec 1858 in which he gives a description of this portage and one described in (4); the letter is reproduced in Dawson, *Report on the Exploration* (1859), 31 (see (12) and (13)).
OOAMA

(10) *[1858?]*
[Map of LaSeine River, Eagle's Nest Lake and Kamanatikojiwan Lake]
Ms 98 x 66 cm 1" to 500 ft Endorsements: '525'; stamp 'BW'
Portages, rapids in area east of Rainy L; probably from the same source as (9).
OOAMA

(11) *[1858?]*
[Map of Dog River and Dog Lake]
Ms 98 x 67 cm Scale not given Watermark: 'J WHATMAN TURKEY MILL 1856' Endorsements: stamps '524' 'BW'
Shows the various survey lines for the road from Fort William including 'Dog Portage,' 'Pointe des Meurons Line,' 'L.A. Russell's Line,' 'Current River Line,' and 'Savanne Line' cutting across Dog R; Dawson notes that Gaudet made a survey of the Dog R and L in 1858 (Dawson, *Report* (1859), 39) (see (12) and (13)); a dam has been pencilled in at an outlet of Dog L but was not built until 1867.
OOAMA

(12) *[1859]*
PLAN / SHEWING THE REGION EXPLORED / BY / S.J. DAWSON AND HIS PARTY / between / FORT WILLIAM, LAKE SUPERIOR / AND THE / GREAT SASKATCHEWAN RIVER, / From 1st of August 1857, to 1st November 1858. / Lithographed by J. Ellis, Toronto
Print (lith) 112 x 202 cm 1" to 10 miles

In S.J. Dawson, *Report on the Exploration of the Country between Lake Superior and Red River*, 2nd ed (Toronto: John Lovell 1859) (*Bib Can* 3885); also issued in *JLA* (1859), App 36, and in *Rapport sur l'exploration de la contrée située entre le lac Superieur et la colonie de la rivière Rouge* (Toronto: John Lovell 1859) (OOAMA); shows the rivers and lakes and the northern canoe route, with the alternate north route above Rainy R as surveyed by Napier, and the southern canoe route via the Grand Portage and Pigeon R, Arrow L with an alternate north route via Sturgeon L and R; shows the straight exploring line to Fort Garry 'as drawn in February 1858'; the first edition of the 1859 report was apparently issued without maps (I. Dawson, 48).
OOAMA (NMC 11867) OTAR OTMCL USDLC

(**13**) *[1859]*
PROFILE OF ROUTE BY THE GRAND PORTAGE AND PIGEON RIVER FROM LAKE SUPERIOR TO RAINY LAKE. / [Sgd in facsimile] S.J. Dawson / C.E. in charge Red River Expedition / [and] PROFILE OF ROUTE BETWEEN LAKE SUPERIOR AND RAINY LAKE BY THE KAMINISTIQUIA AND RIVER LA SEINE. [Sgd in facsimile] S.J. Dawson. / [as above] // LITHOGRAPHED BY J. ELLIS, TORONTO.
Print (lith) hand col 61 x 166 cm 1" to 4 miles, 1" to 200 ft vertical
Profiles of the two routes as described in (12) and found in the same report.
OOAMA (NMC 24368) USDLC

(**14**) *[1863?]*
PLAN OF PART / OF THE / RED RIVER ROUTE, / SURVEYED AND EXPLORED / BY / S.J. DAWSON AND PARTY IN 1858. / W.C. Chewett & Co. Lith. Toronto.
Print (col lith) 70 x 145 cm 1" to 4 miles
Possibly related to Sandford Fleming, *Memorial of the people of Red River* (Quebec: Hunter, Rose and Co. 1863) (OTUTF); the report describes a scheme for a road based on Dawson's 1857–8 survey; map shows northern and southern canoe routes with middle connections from Lac La Croix to Lac des Milles Lacs; rapids, falls, portages; located route of road; other exploratory lines; W.C. Chewett and Co. was in business from 1861 to 1869 (Hulse, 56).
OTAR OTMCL

---

885 *1858*
CROWN LAND SURVEY / OF / CANADA / The Honble P.M. Vankoughnet Commissioner. / PLAN OF THE NORTH SHORE OF LAKE SUPERIOR / Compiled from Bayfields Chart. ... / Engraved by Maclear & Co. Toronto. // Exd / T. Devine / S. Surveyor / Crown Lands Department / Toronto 15th April 1858 / [Sgd in facsimile] P.M. Vankoughnet Commissioner of Crown Lands
Print (lith) 67 x 97 cm 1" to 6 miles
The map covers the area from Pigeon R to below Mica Bay; shows shoreline in detail with soundings around islands; rivers and lakes near the shore; international boundary line is shown and Isle Royale; mining lease tracts shown; OTAR copy (SR 6451) has ms adds showing bearings along shoreline and map has been extended by ms adds of adjoining areas to increase size to 84 x 117 cm.
OTAR OTAR (SR 6451)

Later editions and states

(**2**) *1860*
CROWN LAND SURVEY ... Maclear & Co. Toronto. / Crown Lands Department / Quebec 15th April 1860. / [Sgd in facsimile] P. M. Vankoughnet / Commissioner of Crown Lands. / Exd / T. Devine / Head of Surveys / U.C.
Print (lith) 67 x 98 cm 1" to 6 miles
The map is from the same plate with considerable additions in the Thunder Bay area including the addition of Fort William and Paipoonge Twp with survey grid; exploring lines and rivers shown to Dog L; 'Mr. Dawsons Road to Dog Lake' is added; OTMCL copy has ms adds showing Indian reserves, mining locations, blocks owned by the Hudson's Bay Co., and locations liable to forfeiture and described for patents; OTNR copy has similar col ms adds and in ms 'Department of Crown Lands Quebec Septr 12th 1863 Commissioner.'
OTAR (SR 5924) OTMCL

(**3**) *1863*
DEPARTMENT OF CROWN LANDS. / The Honorable Wm McDougall Commissioner / PLAN OF THE NORTH SHORE OF / LAKE SUPERIOR / 1863. / W.C. Chewett & Co. Lith. Toronto. // H.F. Hayward Draftsman. // Department of Crown Lands / Quebec January 1863 / [Sgd in facsimile] Wm McDougall / Commissioner. / Examined / [Sgd in facsimile] T. Devine / Head of Surveys / U.C.
Print (col lith) 66 x 79 cm 1" to 9 miles
The map has been redrawn and reduced in scale and extends from Pigeon R further south to just east of Sault Ste Marie; shows the surveying line inland from the shore from St Marys R to the Dawson Rd; mileages noted for each section; shows twps around Sault Ste Marie north to Kars and Fenwick and east to Chesley, part of L Nipigon, sidelines from main exploring line back from shore; Neebing Twp and Fort William town plot; (Holmden 1926; *OHIM* 5.1).
OOAMA (NMC 16776) OTAR OTMCL

(**4**) *1866*
DEPARTMENT OF CROWN LANDS, / The Honorable Alex. Campbell Commissioner / PLAN OF THE NORTH SHORE OF / LAKE SUPERIOR / 1866. W.C. Chewett & Co. Lith. Toronto. / H.F. Hayward Draftsman. // Department of Crown

Lands, Ottawa 1st January 1866 [Sgd in facsimile] Alex Campbell Commissioner. / Examined [Sgd in facsimile] T. Devine Surveyor in Chief U.C.
Print (col lith) 64 x 78 cm 1" to 9 miles
Twp surveys extended north to Mamainse to Palmer and Herrick to Archibald twps; added legend for mining locations and Indian reserves both colour-printed on map.
OOAMA (NMC 21809) OTMCL

---

886 *1858*
CROWN LAND SURVEY / OF / CANADA / The Honorable L.V. Sicotte Commissioner / TOPOGRAPHICAL PLAN / OF THE NORTH SHORE OF / LAKE HURON / Shewing P.L.S. Albert P. Salter's recent Survey. / Engraved by Maclear & Co. Toronto. // Compiled & drawn by Thomas Devine / Surveyor and Draftsman, Surveyor's Branch West. / Joseph Bouchette. Deputy Surveyor General. / Crown Lands Department / Toronto 15th April 1858. / L.V. Sicotte / Commissioner of Crown Lands.
Print (lith) 58 x 131 cm 1" to 6 miles
Shows the area from L Nipissing west to Batchawana Bay, L Superior; shows twps surveyed to date, the Nipissing and Mattawan colonization rd; the survey of St Joseph Is and two twps surveyed north of St Marys R; shows the survey line from Sturgeon R west to Batchawana Bay and exploring sidelines with comments on the land, timber, and rock types; some mineral locations; relief, soundings along shore; list of 'authorities' gives survey sources used in the compilation of the map; title is at bottom right; (Holmden 1902).
OOAMA (NMC 16722) OTAR (SR 6450, 81225)

Later editions and states

(2) *1860*
CROWN LAND SURVEY / OF / CANADA / The Honble P.M. Vankoughnet Commissioner. / TOPOGRAPHICAL PLAN / OF THE NORTH SHORE OF / LAKE HURON / ... Devine / Head of Surveys / Upper Canada. / Crown Lands Department / Quebec 15th April 1860. / P.M. Vankoughnet / Commissioner of Crown Lands
Print (lith) 57 x 128 cm 1" to 6 miles
The same plate as plan above with changes; more twps are shown surveyed from St Marys north to Kars, Fenwick, and east to MacDonald; seven twps are shown along the north shore; Great Northern Rd line shown from Goulais Bay east to Spanish R with proposed extension to Nipissing Twp; OTMCL copy has ms adds showing Indian reserves, mining locations, blocks belonging to Hudson's Bay Co., locations liable to forfeiture and locations described for patents.
GBL (70120(4)) OOAMA (NMC 11319) OTAR (SR 81224) OTMCL

(3) *1862*
PART OF THE / NORTH SHORE / OF / LAKE HURON / SHEWING THE NEW TOWNSHIPS SUBDIVIDED / INTO / FARM LOTS. / Engraved by W.C. Chewett & Co. Toronto C.W. // Compiled & drawn under the / direction of Thomas Devine / Head of Surveys U.C. / Department of Crown Lands / Quebec, January 1862.
Print (col lith) 48 x 77 cm 1" to 6 miles
The map is from the same plate but has been reduced in size on the east by including the area from Collins Inlet west only and on the south by deleting the part south of Manitoulin Is; the title has been redrawn and moved to the upper left centre of plan; the names of twps on the north shore have been added; appeared separately and in *Remarks on Upper Canada Surveys* (Quebec: Hunter, Rose & Lemieux 1862) (OOA Pamph 1862(12))
OOA OOAMA (NMC 27230) OTAR

(4) *1863*
Department of Crown Lands. / The Honble Wm McDougall, Commissioner. / PLAN OF PART OF / THE NORTH SHORE OF / LAKE HURON / shewing the / SUBDIVISION OF THE NEW TOWNSHIPS, / W.C. Chewett & Co. Lith Toronto / Department of Crown Lands / Quebec, January 1863. [Sgd in facsimile] Wm McDougall / Commissioner, / Examined / T. Devine, / Head of Surveys / U.C.
Print (col lith) 46 x 78 cm 1" to 6 miles
From the same plate as (3) but the title has been redrawn, more survey data has been added for Manitoulin Is, and includes comments on the land, Indian clearings, and proposed roads; road is proposed through the Garden R area east and north of St Marys R; found separately and in *Report of the Commissioner of Crown Lands of Canada, for the Year 1862* (Quebec: Hunter Rose & Co. 1863) (*Bib Can* 6043); one OTAR copy has ms adds of rivers, twps, mills, and post offices in the Spanish R area; (Holmden 1903).
OOAMA (NMC 21601) OTAR

(5) *1866*
CROWN LAND SURVEY / OF / CANADA / The Honble Alex Campbell Commissioner. / TOPOGRAPHICAL PLAN / OF THE NORTH SHORE OF / LAKE HURON / Shewing recent Surveys. / [Sgd in facsimile] Department of Crown Lands, / Ottawa, 1st January, 1866. / Alex. Campbell Commissioner. / Examined / T. Devine / Surveyor in Chief / U.C.
Print (col lith) 59 x 129 cm 1" to 6 miles
From the same plate as (2) with the title at the lower left; more twps have been added to area around Batchawana Bay and twps are shown five deep along north shore; Great Northern Rd connects to road to Parry Sound and extension proposed east to L Nipissing; several more twps shown south of L Nipissing and the six north-south-oriented twps removed (see **627**); several twps laid out on Manitoulin Is; mining locations and Indian reserves are shown in colour; OTAR copy has ms adds of islands in pencil and comments.
OOAMA (NMC 16723) OTAR (SR 4608) OTMCL

---

887 *[1858]*
GEOLOGICAL SURVEY OF CANADA. / Sir W.E. Logan F.R.S. Director. / PLAN / SHOWING THE DISTRIBUTION OF THE / HURONIAN LIMESTONE / BETWEEN / ROOT RIVER AND BRUCE MINES / G. Matthew's Lith Montreal
Print (lith) 13 x 30 cm 1" to 5 miles
Issued with Geological Survey of Canada, *Report of Progress for the Year 1857* (Toronto: John Lovell 1858), opp 26 (*Bib Can* 2568); shows the area from Thessalon R to beyond Sault Ste Marie; notes on the various locations of limestone; later assigned GSC publication no 42 (Ferrier, 11).
OOAMA OTMCL

Related maps

(2) *[1847–58]*
[Manuscript drafts for the printed map 'Plan showing the distribution of the Huronian Rocks']
5 black-and-white or col mss Sizes vary Most at approx 1" to 1 mile
The plans are as follows:
An untitled outline draft of the printed map area to L George only, endorsed '0 137–(13)' and with some geological notes and boundaries in place; 'Geological Plan of a portion of the Huronian formation in the country surrounding Echo Lake North Shore of Lake Huron by Alexr. Murray Esqre Assist Provl Geologist' [and section], endorsed '0813' and with nine classes of geology shown; 'Plan showing the Distribution of the Huronian Rocks between Rivers St. Mary and Missisague' 1" to 3 miles, endorsed '0813'; a final draft to scale for the printed map showing geology, etc, title, and scale in pencil; [map and two sections across Campement d'Ours Is] endorsed '013,' sections at 6" to 1 mile; with seven classes of geology shown and notes on sections; and [geological plan of area from Pt Thessalon to the mining claims] endorsed '0813' and showing geological formations.
OOAMA (RG 45M B 48 1-5)

---

888 *1858*
Map No 1 To Accompany a Report on a Topographical and Geological Exploration of the Canoe Route between Fort William and Lake Superior and Fort Garry and Red River and also of the Valley of Red River north of the 49th Parallel [Sgd] Henry Youle Hind February 6th 1858
Col ms on linen 93 x 875 cm 1" to 2 miles
Endorsements: 'No(274) of 1858 PSO'
A copy of the report is found in OOA RG 5 C1 vol 932; shows the results of Hind's work as member of the 1857 Canadian Exploring Expedition; sections: (Ontario) 'No 1 Great Dog Portage' and 12 others of areas around Red R; shows heights of land, rapids, falls, rivers and lakes, and rock samples; the northwest point of Lake of the Woods is shown in a different location than on the other plans of 1857; shows the canoe route by the Kaministiquia R, Great Dog L, and Lac des Milles Lacs with many notes on the terrain, portages, etc; also shows the southern route via Pigeon R; the line from the Kaministiquia R to Arrow L is noted as 'route examined by Henry Gladman 1857/8 and found to be good Geo. Gladman'; there is also a 'Profile of Kaministiquia Route' and 'Profile of Pigeon River Route' in Hind's *Narrative of the Canadian Red River Exploring Expedition of 1857* (London: Longman, Green 1860), II: opp 267 (*Bib Can* 3820).
OTAR (SR 7961) OTMCL

Related maps

(2) *1858*
Map No 2 Geological Sketch of the Canoe Route from Fort William – Lake Superior to Fort Garry – Red River and the Valley of the Red River. [Sgd] Henry Youle Hind February 6th 1858
Col ms on linen 76 x 175 cm 1" to 10 miles
Endorsements: 'PSO No 274'
'Profile of Canoe Route' 1" to 600 ft vertical; shows several classes of geology as well as structural features along the northern canoe route; probable height of land; 'Conventional line' shown north-south through Pickerel L.
OTAR (SR 7959)

(3) *1858*
Map No 3 Shewing the areas of arable land on the canoe route from Fort William-Lake Superior to Fort Garry-Red River and the Valley of the Red River [Sgd] Henry Youle Hind February 6th 1858 No 274 of 158 P.S.O.
Col ms 55 x 170 cm 1" to 10 miles
Shows arable land with tree types or prairie between Rainy L and Lake of the Woods and at Red R; height of land; similar notes by Gladman as on (1) above.
OTAR (SR 6001)

(4) *[1858?]*
MAP / TO ACCOMPANY / REPORT / on the / Canadian Red River Exploring Expedition. / by [Sgd in ms]: 'H.Y. Hind' / Maclear & Co Liths Toronto.
Print (lith) with ms adds 41 x 80 cm 1" to 16 miles
Provenance: OOAMA, received from J.J. Murphy Estate 1 Sept 1936; 'PROFILE OF CANOE ROUTE / Maclear & Co Liths Toronto' 1" to 10 miles, 1" to 600 ft vertical; the printed base appears to be unfinished and was possibly prepared to accompany Hind, *Report on a Topographical and Geological Exploration of the Canoe Route between Fort William ... and Fort Garry* (Toronto: Derbishere and DesBarats 1858) or *Reports of Progress ... Assiniboine and Saskatchewan Exploring Expedition* (Toronto: John Lovell 1859), but was not included with those reports; ms notes in black on routes and forts possibly by Hind; later notes in red discuss preferable routes including Dog L route with the steamer recommended by Dawson and the Arrow L route recommended by Hector and Palliser and Hind; 'Fort William Route' [Dog L route]

'abandoned in 1861 for want of a steamer'; later notes about routes of Canadian troops in 1870–1.
OOAMA (NMC 113510)

(5) *1858*
No 1 Map of the Pigeon River Route between Lake Superior & Rainy Lake. According to the Survey under the 6th and 7th Articles of the Treaty of Ghent. To Accompany Report No 2 [Sgd] James A. Dickinson June 5th 1858 Henry Youle Hind
Col ms in 2 sheets 37 x 200 cm Scale not given
A detailed plan of the southern canoe route along or near the international boundary; rapids, falls, portages, and camps marked; possibly map described as accompanying but not printed in H.Y. Hind's *Reports of Progress ... Assiniboine and Saskatchewan Exploring Expedition* (Toronto: John Lovell 1859).
OOAMA (NMC 21073)

(6) *1860*
Assiniboine & Saskatchewan Exploring Expedition. // Map of the Boundary Line between / BRITISH AMERICA & THE UNITED STATES, / showing the Proposed Route from / Fort William to Arrow Lake, thence to Rainy Lake. / via / The Old North West Company's Route / (For details see Chapter XXI) // J. Arrowsmith, Litho. 1860.
Print (lith) hand col 31 x 80 cm 1" to 6.3 miles
In Henry Hind, *British North America; Reports of Progress ... Assiniboine and Saskatchewan Exploring Expedition Presented to Both Houses of Parliament ... August 1860.808* (London: Eyre & Spottiswoode 1860), at back (*Bib Can* 3913) and in *HCPP* 1860, XLIV:729 (OTU (mfe)); shows the rapids, falls, portages on the southern river system as in plan above; relief by hachures; 'Proposed Cart Road to Arrow Lake' from area north of Fort William; the map is also found in GBLpro CO 6/32; (*PRO Cat* 1422).
GBLpro (MPG 267) OTMCL

---

889 *1859*
GEOLOGICAL SURVEY OF CANADA. / Sir W.E. Logan F.R.S. Director. / PLAN SHOWING THE DISTRIBUTION OF THE / HURONIAN ROCKS / BETWEEN / RIVERS ST MARY AND MISSISAGUE
Print (lith) 38 x 59 cm 1" to 3 miles
Issued with Geological Survey of Canada, *Report of Progress for the Year 1858* (Montreal: John Lovell 1859), opp 104; has key to 10 classes of rock types along the north shore; shows copper veins, mining locations, twps, and exploration lines; later assigned GSC publication no 48 (Ferrier, 12).
OOAMA (NMC 81529)

---

890 *1859*
Plan of Exterior Lines of Townships North of Base Line on the North Shore of Lake Huron. [Sgd] Arthur Jones Prov. Land Surveyor Mattawa May 30th 1859. Examined 4th July 1859 J.W.B.
Col ms 73 x 129 cm 1" to 40 chains Endorsements: 'No 8' '7656/59'
(OTNR FN 1911 27 May 1859); shows Deroche to Hodgins twps and Jarvis to Anderson twps north of the L George area; part of Indian reserve, sugar bush, and Garden R area; Indian guide's track from L Huron.
OTNR (SR 5928)

---

891 *1859*
TOWNSHIP No 2 NORTH RANGE 25 WEST / AWE'RES. / Crown Lands Department / Surveyors Branch West. / Toronto 1st June 1859. / [Sgd in facsimile] P M Vankoughnet / Commissioner. / Exd / T. Devine L. Surveyor. // Maclear & Co. Liths Toronto
Print (lith) 48 x 40 cm 1" to 40 chains
(SI to A.P. Salter and J. Johnson of 12 May 1858 to survey the twps No 1 N and S and No 2, range 25, and twps 1 N and S, range 26); shows the survey grid, Indian reserve, several lakes and the Root R.
OOAMA (NMC 14087) OTUTF

Related maps

(2) *1859*
TOWNSHIPS No 1 NORTH AND SOUTH RANGE 25 WEST / TARENTORUS // Crown Lands Department / Surveyors Branch West / Toronto, 1st June 1859. / [Sgd in facsimile] P M Vankoughnet / Commissioner. / Exd / T. Devine / L. Surveyor
Print (lith), pt trimmed 50 x 38 cm 1" to 40 chains
Imprint may have been trimmed off; shows the survey grid, the Sault Ste Marie park lots survey, McKay's road, wooded areas, burnt land, mineral location.
OOAMA (NMC 14087) OTUTF

(3) *1859*
TOWNSHIPS Nos 1 NORTH AND SOUTH RANGE XXVI WEST. // Crown Lands Department / Surveyor's Branch West. / Toronto, 1st June 1859 / [Sgd in facsimile] P M Vankoughnet / Commissioner / Exd / T. Devine. / L Surveyor. // Maclear & Co. Liths Toronto C.W.
Print (lith) 47 x 36 cm 1" to 40 chains
Shows the survey grid, wooded areas, and types of tree, sugar camps, burnt land, village of Ste Marie and Hudson's Bay Co. post.
OTUTF

---

892 *1860*
Plan of Great Northern Road between Goulais and Mississaga Rivers with branches to Sault Ste Marie District of Algoma Surveyed by A.P. Salter P.L.S. Assisted by James Johnston P.L.S. 1859 [Sgd] Chatham February 9th 1860 Albert Pellew Salter Provl Surveyor Examined Mar 29th 1860 J.W.B.
Col ms 125 x 317 cm 1" to 40 chains
(SI were issued to Salter on 31 May 1859 and 13 July 1859 to survey the road from Sault Ste Marie to Goulais Bay and along north shore of L Huron, and on 12 Aug 1861 to survey from Bruce Mines to

outlet of Ottertail L; OTAR FN 748 10 Feb 1860); shows the road route east to mileage 69 at Mississagi R; comments on land along the line; Indian reserves, mining licences; Bruce Mines and Wellington Mines shown; two branches shown to Sault Ste Marie.
OTAR (SR 37759)

Related maps

(2) *1860*
Plan of Great Northern Road between Mississaga River and Range line No 6 West District of Algoma Surveyed by A.P. Salter P.L.S. Assisted by James Johnston P.L.S. 1859 Chatham February 9, 1860 [Sgd] Albert Pellew Salter Provin Surveyor. Examined March 29th 1860 J.W.B.
Col ms 127 x 353 cm 2" to 1 mile
Shows the route east from Missassague R to Spanish R, mileages, types of tree, and notes on terrain.
OTNR (SR 37730)

(3) *1863*
Plan of part of the Great Northern Road between Goulais and Thessalon Rivers and branches to Goulais Bay St Mary and Bruce Mines. January 22nd 1863 [Sgd] Albert Pellew Salter Superintendent of Colo: Roads Algoma District
Col ms 87 x 249 cm 1" to 40 chains
Shows the western part of the road on the north shore of L Huron as built to date; 'Explanation' keys finished road, road chopped out, road ditched, bridges, culverts; list of distances.
OTNR (SR 8584)

---

893 *1861*
Plan of Exploration of Goulais River [Sgd] Josph Wm Burke PLS March 1861
Ms 68 x 247 cm 1" to 40 chains Endorsements: 'G 10'
(SI 23 June 1860 to make an angular survey of the Goulais R from twp 3, N range 26 W, to its source and connect with Salter's exploration line; OTNR FN 1899 8 Feb 1861); shows 112-mile traverse along the river to present-day Goulais L; trail to Mississaga Crossing.
OTAR (SR 7055)

---

894 *[1861]*
[Plan of the north shore of Lake Huron from Garden River to east of La Cloche]
2 col mss 58 x 127 cm and 65 x 128 cm 1" to 2 miles
The two untitled and unsigned maps join to make a plan of the whole shore; the western plan shows Thompson Twp (laid out in 1861) and Lefroy, Rose, and Patton twps located but not laid out (all surveyed in 1861); shows mining leases and names of companies; the eastern map shows Salter, Esten, and Spragge twps all surveyed in 1861; both maps are in the same hand.
OTAR (SR 6421) OTNR (SR 6448)

---

895 *[1864?]*
TOPOGRAPHICAL PLAN / OF THE NORTH SHORE OF / LAKE HURON ... 15th April 1860 [with ms adds showing 'Projected Exploration Line for Road']
Print (lith) with ms adds 57 x 128 cm 1" to 6 miles
Ms adds show road projected from Gibsons Mill at Parry Sound to Spanish R to join the 'Great Northern Road'; printed base map is (**886(2)**).
OTAR (SR 6738)

Related maps

(2) *1865*
Plan of Exploration-Line between Spanish River and Parry-Sound [Sgd] James W. Fitzgerald Provl Land Surveyor Sept. 1865
Col ms 138 x 728 cm 1" to 40 chains Endorsements: 'R 35'
(SI to survey line from Parry Sound to complete line of Great Northern Road at Spanish R); comments on timber, type of land, rocks, and relief along survey line; shows mining lands, Indian reserve, mills, villages; 'projected line to connect village of Killarney with great northern road.'
OTAR (SR 37758)

---

896 *1865*
GEOLOGICAL SURVEY OF CANADA / Sir W.E. Logan F.R.S. Director / MAP / Showing the distribution of the / HURONIAN ROCKS / BETWEEN / RIVERS BATCHEHWAHNUNG and MISSISSAGUI // Compiled & Drawn by R Barlow. Montreal Engraved by A.W. Graham // Printed in Colors at Stanford's Geographical Establishment, London 1865
Print (col lith) 21 x 29 cm 1" to 8 miles
Issued with Geological Survey of Canada, *Report of Progress from Its Commencement to 1863; Atlas of Maps and Sections* (Montreal: Dawson Brothers 1865), [Map III] (*Bib Can* 4217), and in the French ed (*Bib Can* 4218); shows 13 classes of geological formations for part of Manitoulin Is, the north shore, and part of the hinterland; survey grid; later assigned GSC publication no 55 (Ferrier, 13).
OOAMA OTMCL

Related maps

(2) *1863*
[Map of area from Little Lake George to north of Batchawana Bay with geological notes, attributed to A. Murray, 1863]
Ms 1" to 1 mile Endorsements: '0220–(30)'
Shows twps of Tarentorus, Korah, Pennefather, Dennis, Fenwick, Kars, and Tilley and traverse lines along the Goulais R; notes on geology, types of rock, and boundaries of geological formations; one of the source sketches for the printed plan above.
OOAMA (RG 45M 83403/21/D-V-4016)

---

897 *1865*
Map of the Outlines of the Townships of Tilley, Archibald, Tupper and Havilland, together with the subdivisions of Tilley and part of Havilland Algoma District C.W. Surveyed in accordance with Instructions issued by the Crown Land Department dated Quebec Oct 28th 1864. Dec. 5th 1864. April 25th 1865. Mount Forest, Upper Canada September 1865 [Sgd] Hugh Wilson P.L.S.
Col ms 100 x 66 cm 1" to 40 chains Endorsements: 'No 8'
(OTNR FN 1821 Sept 1865); shows lot sizes and contents of a group of twps being laid out around Batchawana Bay; rivers, lakes, and notes on terrain; 'Begley's Copper Location' shown in Tilley.
OTNR (SR 5568)

---

898 *[1865]*
MAP / Showing the Water Communications / and Comparative Distances / From LAKE SUPERIOR to the / IRON MARKETS. / OAKLEY & TOMPSON LITH. 46 WATER ST. BOSTON.
Print (lith) 35 x 43 cm Scale not given
In *Peter Bell Iron Company, Lake Superior* (Boston: 1865), frontis (*Bib Can* 9374); shows the location of mining area east of L Superior and Michipicoton Bay and connections to Marquette and to southwestern Canada West.
OTMCL

---

899 *[1865]*
PLAN / OF LAKE / HURON / Showing the principal Steamboat / ROUTES
Print (lith) 43 x 27 cm Approx 1" to 28 miles
Inset: 'PLAN / OF THE INDIAN RESERVE / on the Island / OF / GREAT MANITOULIN / Showing the Oil Wells Thereon' 1" to 6 miles; in *Great Manitoulin Oil Company, Prospectus* (Montreal: J. Starke & Co. 1865), frontis (*Bib Can* 9341); main map shows location of island, shipping routes, and railway connections in the southwestern part of province; the inset shows the oil region at eastern end of island.
OTMCL

---

900 *1865*
Plan showing the mouths of the Rivers Montreal and Metabetchuan, and also points A and B the latter established by P.L.S. Duncan Sinclair, and the former by the Undersigned, in accordance with instructions from A.J.Russell Esq. Crown Timber Agent, Ottawa to Mr Sinclair dated March 11th 1865. [Sgd] Pembroke Apl 17th 1865 Joseph White P.L.S.
Col ms 42 x 52 cm 1" to 10 chains
Shows the Montreal R flowing into L Timiskaming.
OTAR (SR 7597)

Related maps

(2) *1867*
Additional No 1 Plan of the River Montreal Surveyed & Explored under instructions from The Commissioner of Crown Lands Dated Ottawa 20th September 1866 [Sgd] A.G. Forrest Provl Land Surveyor Ottawa 18th November 1867
Col ms 100 x 102 cm 1" to 40 chains Endorsements: 'R 43'
(SI 18 Sept 1866 to explore each side of river for 3 miles; OTNR FN 1990 18 Nov 1867); the survey covered the area up river from Sinclair and White's survey of the mouth; shows L Timiskaming to the south and latitude 47.56N marked; comments on timber, soil, relief, etc, along survey lines.
OTNR (SR 16903)

---

901 *[1866?]*
[Map of Manitoulin Island]
Ms 143 x 225 cm Scale not given Endorsements: '1865–66'
Provenance: OOAMA Bell Collection; shows the twps of Billings, Howland, Assiginack, Bidwell, Tekhumah, and Sheguiandah as all or partly laid out; portages; notes on Indian villages; clearings; probably drawn in 1866 as it shows the same twp grid as in (**886(5)**) with the addition of Tekhumah surveyed in 1866; Robert Bell's 'Report on the Geology of Grand Manitoulin ...' is in Geological Survey of Canada, *Report of Progress from 1863 to 1866* (Ottawa: 1867).
OOAMA (NMC 17347)

---

902 *1866*
[Map of the northern part of Canada West]
Department of Crown Lands Ottawa 1866. Assistant Commissioner.
Col ms on linen 28 x 39 cm Scale not given
The projected plan for an exploration line from Montreal R and L Superior; the line is routed due east from Michipicoten Bay; shows the area from L Nipissing to L Superior and to L Temiscaming; the Great Northern Road from Sault Ste Marie is shown running north and west.
OTAR

Related maps

(2) *1867*
Plan of the Montreal River and Lake Superior Exploratory Line Done under Instructions from the Hon. the Commissioner of Crown Lands Dated at Ottawa 11th Septr 1866 [Sgd] Duncan Sinclair Provl Land Surveyor Ottawa June 24th 1867
Col ms 137 x 321 cm 1" to 1 mile Endorsements: 'M 29a'
(SI 18 Sept 1866 to survey east part of the exploration line; OTNR FN 1922 24 June 1867); shows the general survey of the line along the east shore of L Superior from approx 85°W to Montreal and Matawatchan rivers; relief, notes along survey lines; mining locations.
OTAR (SR 37733)

(**3**) *1867*
Plan of the Western End of Exploratory Line from Michipicoten Bay on Lake Superior east towards the Montreal River As Surveyed by A.P. Salter and R. Gilmour P.L. Surveyors A.D. 1867. [Sgd] Robert Gilmour P.L.S. Albert Pellew Salter P.L.S. Chatham July 3rd 1867
Col ms 126 x 381 cm 1" to 40 chains Endorsements: 'M 85a'
Inset: 'Sketch, shewing Mr Salter's explorations from Lake Huron northerly to Exploration Line in Lat. 47.56N' 1" to 3 miles; (SI 31 Sept 1866 to survey the western part of the line from Michipicoten to Montreal R; OTAR FN 1923 4 July 1867); shows the survey line to mile 84; relief by hachures; notes on terrain, soil, trees; Salter's north line is shown from the mouth of the Mississaga R.
OTAR (SR 37757)

903 *[1866?]*
Map Received from P.L.S. Herrick shewing Exploration line of Road from Manitowaning to Michael's Bay Manitoulin Island
Col ms on tracing paper 81 x 93 cm Scale not given Endorsements: '1528'; stamp 'IASR'
Shows two alternate routes for road, surveyed twps, comments on the soil, timber, etc; the proposed road is shown on the 1866 north shore plan (**886(5)**) and Assiginack and Tekhumah twps, which were surveyed in 1864 and 1866, respectively, are both shown.
OOAMA (NMC 22506)

---

904 *1867*
Plan showing the six miles of the Red River Road made in 1867. [Sgd] John A. Snow Provl Land Surveyor. Overseer of Works Hull 20th Nov. 1867.
Col ms 59 x 173 cm 1" to 40 chains Endorsements: '12982/67'
Shows the road from Red R depot further north along shore from Fort William to meet the exploring line from the mission on the Kaministiquia R at mile 9; two other exploratory lines shown and 'Transportation Co' portage route to Dog L; notes along the survey lines on timber, terrain, distances, etc.
OTAR (SR 6673)

South

905 *1788*
Plan of the Entrance of the River from Lake Erie to Detroit [Sgd] Quebec 6th Decr 1788 Gother Mann Captn Commandg Rl Engrs
Col ms 93 x 55 cm 1" to 600 yds Watermark: 'J WHATMAN' Endorsements: stamp 'HMSPO'
Originally accompanied Mann's report on defences and enclosed in Dorchester's no 58 to Grenville of 24 Oct 1790 (GBLpro CO 42/70 pp 41ff) (*PRO Cat* 2535); shows the area from L Erie to Turkey Is; wooded areas, marshy areas, soundings, and nature of shoreline and river bottom shown; shows Ft Malden with public works, naval yard around it, and 'ground reserved for the Crown'; below and set back from shore 'Proposed town' [Amherstburg] with square grid and reserves shown; Isle de Pierre and Isle au Bois Blanc reserved for crown, fortifications shown on the latter; 'A' point on shore opp Bois Blanc is noted as the best situation for a post in Mann's report (Ontario Archives, *Report 1905*, 358); (Koerner 17).
GBLpro (CO 700 Canada no 38D)

Related maps

(**2**) *[1788]*
[Title the same]
Col ms 93 x 53 cm 1" to 600 yds Watermark: 'J WHATMAN' Endorsements: stamp 'B↑O'
Shows the same area as above but omits the fort and plan for town and area reserved for crown; (Holmden 1601, 1480).
OOAMA (NMC 20791)

---

906 *[179?]*
Actual Survey of the Narrows betwixt the Lake Erie and Sinclair [Endorsed]: 'Two Plans of Detroit by P. McNiff.'
Col mss on 2 sheets 53 x 146 cm and 53 x 75 cm 1" to 600 yds
A very finished plan unlike McNiff's other work; shows swamps, soundings, lots, and bldgs on both sides of the river; the place-names are in French with notes in English; includes 'Schedule of Lots ...' listing the names of the French settlers on both sides of the river; 'Huron village and fields' and 'Ottawa Burying Place' shown; although in English, it is very similar to Collot's map of 1796 (below) and both may be based on the same sources including an earlier map by Chaussegros de Léry for lots and names of settlers (discussed below); the shape of the fort shown at Detroit predates Fort Lernoult (built in 1778); however, south part of this map may also be based on Mann's plans of 1788 (**905**) as it shows point 'A' for a post and the same shapes of islands in the river including a small island not on the Collot map; there is also a note: 'The Gentleman who marked the Soundings of the River on this map says he has reason to believe there is good depth of water through this Channel west of Grosse Isle and also in that marked C near the lower end of Grosse Isle', (however, point 'C' is not marked); the plan was probably prepared by McNiff between 1790 and 1792, but the information predates his plan of Amherstburg of 1792 (see **1112**); (*OHIM* 3.7).
OTAR (Simcoe Map 446700A and B)

Related maps

(**2**) *1796 [i.e., 1798?]*
Plan Topographique du Détroit Et des eaux qui forment la jonction du Lac Erie avec le Lac Saint-Clair. Dressée pour l'intelligence des Voyages du Gal Collot dans Cette partie du Continent en 1796
Col ms 193 x 145 cm 3" to 1 mile or 7" to 2000 toises
Endorsements: stamp 'Ministere de la Guerre Depôt de la Guerre, Archives'
An attractive plan showing relief, wooded areas, cleared and settled areas on both shores of the river, and soundings; views: 'Vue de la Ville et Fort du Detroit' and 'Vue du Fort Erie'; includes 'Liste des Lots de Terre situés sur la Rive E. de la Rivière [opp Detroit], 'Liste des Lots situes de ce côte de la Rivière' [at Detroit], and 'liste des Lots situés sur la rive Sud de la Rivière' opp Turkey Is [lists of settlers]; place-names are all in French; the lists are very similar to those on above map with the same number of lots and identical names; Lajeunnesse infers that this map is copied from the Chaussegros de Léry survey of ca 1754 with the addition of later information (Lajeunesse, lvii; *Historical Atlas of Canada* I: plate 41), but the exact source map has not been identified; the maps are also attributed to Philip Joseph L'Etombe, French consul general at Philadelphia; new fort commenced by the English opp Bois Blanc [Ft Malden] noted; dated 1798 in Koerner 20 and Bald, [1]; there is also another plan of the same title in Archives du Dépôt des Cartes et Plans de la Marine (FPBN Pf no 61/3g), but it lacks the bottom part from part of Grosse Isle south and there are no views; (Holmden 1603); photographs of both maps and a possible unidentified source map are in OOAMA (NMC 3096; 3097; 116581).
FPBN (Pf no 61/3g) (FPA 7B61)

---

907 *1790*
Plan of Part of the East Shore of Lake Erie in the District of Hesse from Point Pele to Detroit River

with the names of the Proprietors inserted in the Lots including likewise a Tract of Land, reserved for the Huron Indians Surveyed in 1790 by Patk McNiff
Col ms 73 x 151 cm 1" to 40 chains Endorsements: '990' '1325'

Shows the area from Point Pelee to Turkey Is in the Detroit R; shows the boundaries of the Huron Tract as surveyed 14 Aug 1790, Indian cornfields at 'R Cannards'; an old entrenchment and proposed fort opp Bois Blanc Is; names of owners in lots to the south with a note indicating large marsh surveyed for Wm and James Caldwell in July 1789; shows the fronts of the two connected twps on L Erie [Colchester and Gosfield] as surveyed by Thomas Smith in 1787 and the 12 extra lots surveyed by McNiff by 10 Sept 1790 (Ontario Archives, *Report 1905*, 73); village plot in Colchester; names of settlers shown in all lots were possibly added up to Apr 1791; similar to **908**.
OTAR (SR 6558)

---

908 *1791 Jan*
A plan of part of the District of Hesse commencing near Point Pelê in the North Shore of Lake Erie and extending from thence along the waters edge to the Entrance of River la Tranche on the East shore of Lake St Clair & from the entrance of the said River up to the 2d Fork of the same delineated from actual survey made in the years of 1789 & 1790 by Patrick McNiff Dty Surveyor January 1791
Col ms in 5 sheets 22 x 104 cm, 66 x 37 cm, 115 x 37 cm, 29 x 61 cm, 108 x 37 cm Scale not given

A rough survey in sheets that fit together at irregular angles; comments on land and nature of shoreline; Sheet 1 endorsed 'Detroit shore No 1'; Sheet 2 endorsed 'Bois Blanc' with note on the boundary of Indian lands 'marked on the 13th and 14th Augt 1790 [Sgd] Patrick McNiff Dy Surveyor'; shows the Huron cornfields at R Canards and proposed fort opp Bois Blanc Is; a few tracts surveyed with names of settlers; Sheet 3 shows area from Fighting Is to Peach Is and R, endorsed 'L Erie and the La Tranche'; shows several survey lines and houses along the shore; there is a small gap (possibly destroyed) between Sheets 3 and 4, and a note is partly missing; comments on the French and Indian settlements up the R Ruscom; shows area from R au Puce to beyond Point au Roche; Sheet 5 endorsed: 'River la Tra[nche from] its mouth to the [second Fork] J.G.S.'; shows Indian burying places and settlements, battle sites, trails; houses shown along river, village site marked at junction with McGregor Creek [Chatham]; this plan (or a copy) is described as delivered to the Land Board of Hesse on 25 Jan 1791 (Ontario Archives, *Report 1905*, 97).
OTAR (Simcoe Maps 446892–5)

Related maps

(**2**) *[1791]*
A Plan of part of the District of Hesse in two Separate parts commencing near Point Pele on the North shore of Lake Erie and Extending from thence along the Waters Edge to the Entrance of River La Tranche on the East Shore of Lake St Clair and from the Entrance of the Said River up to the Second Fork of the same. Delineated from actual Surveys made in the Years 1789 and 1790 By Patrick McNiff Depy Surveyor. Copied from an Original in the Engineers Office [Sgd] Samuel Holland Surveyr Genl
Col ms in 7 sheets Size varies 1" to 40 chains

A copy of a more finished plan but showing most of the same information as the above with the addition of names in lots; possibly the plan delivered to the Land Board of Hesse 19 Mar 1791 (Ontario Archives, *Report 1905*, 105); the sheets were once joined together but later separated and are as follows:

[No 1] 'Gosfield East (Partial)' Copied from an Original in the Engineers Office [Sgd] Samuel Holland Surveyr Genl.
Endorsements: 'X 8' '893'
Shows Point Pelee and the 12 lots surveyed by McNiff to add to the lots 1–97 in the two connected twps.
OTAR (SR 1122)

'No 2 Colchester and Gosfield'
Endorsements: 'X9' '957'
Shows 97 lots with names and notes dated 'Spring 90'
OTAR (SR 796)

'No 3 Huron Reserve and Malden (Partial)'
Endorsements: 'X10' 'Q68' '1055'
Notes on surveys in 1788 and 1790; shows names of owners south of Huron Reserve; Huron cornfields; proposed fort opp Bois Blanc Is.
OTAR

'No 4 Sandwich from Fighting Island to Detroit'
Endorsements: 'Q 12' '1066'
This part has the title for whole map as cited above; shows 'houses and farms under Improvements'; 'From A to B is a space settled sometime hence by Canadians under Indian grants ... there are scarcely any of them but what exceed the limits specified in their Deeds'; shows Indian huts and parts inserted from sketches marked in yellow; names in all lots.
OTAR (SR 2025)

'No 5 St Clair Lake from Bloody Bridge to River aux Puces (Partial)'
Endorsements: 'No 11' '901'
Shows Hog Is, Peach Is, and Grand Marsh.
OTAR (SR 910)

'No 6 St Clair Lake from Belle River, to River La Tranche (Partial)'
Endorsements: 'X11' '856' 'D'
Note about site of battle between the 'Chippewas and Senekees.'
OTNR (SR 2492)

'No 7 River Thames (Partial)'
Endorsements: 'X4' '936'
Shows the area up to the town site for [Chatham]:

'this is the most convenient Situation for a village'; some names of owners.
OTAR (SR 7092) OTAR OTNR

---

909 *1791 Apr (1793)*
Plan of River La Tranche from its Entrance up to the end of the first Township unto entrance of the Branch whereon Clark's Mills are Built from Actual Surveys made in April 1791 [Sgd] Patrick McNiff Depy Surveyor Western District Detroit 5th Decemr 1793
Ms 38 x 92 cm 1" to 40 chains
Shows lots along the river only, with names of occupiers of land and improved land; houses; notes on areas claimed by various people; lots on the river numbered to 24 just before Clark's Mill; a note indicates that this is the 'original' of the 1791 survey and since there are fewer names than on the 1793 survey below (**912**), it would seem to date from 1791.
OTNR (SR 91245)

---

910 *1791 May*
A Plan of Lake Erie Detroit River part of Lake St Clair and River La Tranche from Actual Surveys made in the Years 1789, 1790 & 1791, That part of Lake St Clair and all River St Clair Coloured Yellow is copied from Capt Henry Ford's Coasting Survey; The Inland parts Coloured Yellow are Inserted from Indian and other Sketches; The uncoloured part from Long Point to Fort Erie Copied from old French Surveys By [Sgd] Patrick McNiff Asst Engineer Detroit, May 1791.
Col ms 76 x 154 cm 1" to 4 statute miles
Shows all of L Erie and the first part of the Thames R; a somewhat distorted map, particularly the shapes for Long Point and the lake, also with an incorrect orientation of the Six Nations tract along the Grand R; some relief, with notes on both sides of the lake about terrain, trees, etc; notes below the title signed by McNiff describe islands in the Detroit R and comment on potential for settlement; shows windmills along the Detroit R and proposed settlements along the Detroit and the Thames rivers; proposed towns [Amherstburg, Chatham] shown; (*OHIM* 3.6).
OTAR (Simcoe Map 446890)

---

911 *[1791] Dec*
[Part of the River Thames from Lake St Clair to the Second Fork]
Col ms 38 x 131 cm 1" to 40 chains Watermark: 'EDMEADS & PINE' Endorsements: 'Course of River La Tranche Ex. 11 Feb 1792. Transmitted by Lt Governor Simcoe 16 March 1792'
Originally with Simcoe to Dundas 7 Dec 1791 (GBLpro CO 42/316): 'I am happy to have found in the Surveyor's office an actual Survey of the River La Tranche ... I have but little doubt but that its communication with the Ontario & Erie will be found to be very practicable'; similar to the Thames parts of plans made in 1791 including note about site for [Chatham] (see **908**); shows 'Indian burial place,' abandoned Indian village, trails along the river; houses shown on both sides; types of tree; mill seats noted on South branch; 'the huts on the Banks of the River marked Red are small Settlements without authority many abandoned'; (*PRO Cat* 1956); map and text reproduced in Simcoe, *Correspondence* I:90–1).
GBLpro (MPG 89)

Related maps

(2) *[1791]*
[Part of the River Thames from Lake St Clair to the Second Fork]
Col ms 38 x 115 cm [1" to 40 chains]
Similar to plan above and to **908** with the same notes, types of tree, and houses.
GBLMM (Grenville Map no 63 Case 75A)

---

912 *1793*
Survey of the River Thames formerly River La Tranch from its Entrance or confluence with Lake St Clair to the upper Delawar Village: from the entrance to the 12th Lot of the 3rd Township was Surveyed Two Years hence from the 12th Lot of the 3d Township to the upper village surveyed in April and May 1793 By [Sgd] Patrick McNiff Detroit 25th June [1793]
Col ms 320 x 45 cm 1" to 40 chains Endorsements: 'X2' '1185'
(SI 12 Nov 1792 to P. McNiff and A. Jones to survey the river and town plot at the forks, and to look for a connection with the Grand R); McNiff surveyed the western part to this point; shows the river from L St Clair to about [Delaware] Twp; shows relief, fields, types of tree, marshes, Indian villages, cornfields, trails; shows town site [Chatham] with a mill, Moravian village with road to latter, and road to Kettle Creek; twp names have been pencilled in along the Thames: Dover/Raleigh, Chatham/Harwich, and Camden/Howard; shows the front lots 1 to 24 along the river only for these twps; more names are shown in lots than on **909**.
OTNR (SR 7089)

---

913 *1793*
[Sur]vey of the Road from Burlington Bay to the River Ouse; opened by the Queen's Rangers; in September & October 1793. Copied from an original by Mr Augustus Jones, D.P.Survr Surveyor Generals Office; Province of Upper Canada, 15th day of December, 1793, [Sgd] D W Smith Acting Surveyor General
Col ms 27 x 261 cm Scale not given
An attractive sketch showing the road route to the Grand R, relief, and notes on the land through which the road passed; boundary of Six Nations Indian lands; two reserves; mileages noted; SI 19 Dec 1792 were issued to A. Jones to explore for a route from Thames R to Burlington Bay.
OTAR (Simcoe Map 445998)

Related maps

(**2**) *[1793]*
[Dundas Street from Burlington to the River Ouse] Copy W.C.
Col ms 51 x 131 cm 1" to 20 chains Endorsements: '977'
A more detailed plan than (3) showing the road below the mountain in Flamboro E Twp to the landing at Mordens at the head of Burlington Bay as well as four strip maps showing details of the route to the Grand R; bridging points, boundary of Indian lands; a later note indicates that the plan is compiled from A. Jones's and L. Grant's survey of the road from Burlington to the Thames (SI 17 March 1793); Grant's field notes dated 22 Apr to 24 June 1793 are in OTNR (FN 174); Jones's field notes are in OTNR (FN 298 1793 and FN 340 26 Apr 1793) and OTAR (FN 393 Feb 1793).
OTAR (SR 81027)

(**3**) *[1793]*
[Map of the River Thames from Lake St Clair to Oxford, and the road from Oxford to Burlington Bay]
Col ms in 4 sheets 54 x 442 cm, 105 x 150 cm, 38 x 152 cm, 38 x 54 cm 1" to 40 chains Watermark: 'BUDGEN' Endorsements: 'Canada Case 37 No 51'; stamp 'HMSPO'
Originally enclosed in Simcoe's no 18 to Dundas of 20 Sept 1793 (GBLpro CO 42/317 p 283) (Simcoe, *Correspondence* II:56); an important detailed map of the river and road connection; shows Simcoe's route to Detroit from Niagara Feb 1793; a note on the road 'as marked and about to be opened' indicates the map dates from the fall of 1793 or before (see (1) above); notes on land, Indian settlements, Indian purchases, and boundaries; shows Moravian settlement, site of 'New London,' and site of 'Oxford'; photoreproduction in OOAMA (NMC 14905); (*OHIM* 7.23; *PRO Cat* 1597).
GBLpro (CO 700 Canada 58)

(**4**) *[1793?]*
[Plan of Dundas Street from Burlington Bay to the River Thames] Copied W.C.
Col ms 44 x 177 cm 1" to 1 mile
Probably from Jones's and Grant's survey (SI 19 March 1793) for a road line and to lay out a twp south of the road; shows road from Burlington Bay to Indian line at the Grand R with lots laid out; shows road line continuing to the Thames beyond Indian lands with road lots; outlines of a twp [Burford] just west of the Grand R; other twps pencilled in along road line probably at a later date; note: 'A copy of this Plan was sent to the Council Office on the 19th Augt 1800 ... W.C.'
OTAR (SR 81031)

(**5**) *[1793?]*
River Thames
Col ms 31 x 112 cm Scale not given Endorsements: '881'
A fragment showing area from below Lower Forks to Middle and Upper Forks; a pencilled note attributes the plan to 'A Jones 1793'; possibly from his surveys in Jan and Feb 1793 (FN 389); shows strip along river and site for London with high land noted; road is partly shown between 'Oxford' and London.
OTAR (SR 5807)

(**6**) *[1793?]*
[Plan of Dundas Street from Burlington Bay to 'Oxford']
Ms in 2 sheets 46 x 302 cm Scale not given
Possibly an incomplete map that may have extended to cover the Thames R; the road from Burlington is shown with mileage markers; relief and trails shown including route Simcoe took from Niagara to Detroit in Feb 1793; a few twp names pencilled in on both sides of road; a town and twp reserve shown at 'Oxford.'
GBLMM (Grenville Map no 69 case 75B)

---

914 *[1794]*
Plan shewing the communication between Lake Ontario and Lake St Clair by way of the River Thames Copy W.C.
Col ms 48 x 118 cm 1" to 4 miles Endorsements: 'X4' '873'
Shows details and a better configuration for Long Point after survey in 1793; shows continuation of Dundas St from Burlington to the Upper Forks and 'Oxford.'
OTAR (SR 11141)

Related maps

(**2**) *1794*
[Communication between Long Point and the Thames River] Surveyor Genls Office Newark 10th Sepr 1794 [Sgd] W Chewett
Col ms 54 x 119 cm 1" to 4 miles Endorsements: 'L. Erie by Chewitt'
The road, river, and shoreline for Long Point are identical to plan above with additions; shows planned road from London to Turkey Point, boundary between Home and Western districts; boundary of proposed purchase from the Indians at London; river systems in the Grand R area shown in detail; Chatham and Moravian village, town sites at 'Oxford,' London, Dorchester, and roads to various points; twps named; shows the same information for this area as the larger plan of 23 Oct 1794 (see **21**) except the latter does not show the road to Turkey Point.
OTAR (Simcoe Map 446704)

---

915 *[1795?]*
Part of the River Thames [Sgd] D W Smith Act Sur General
Col ms 38 x 54 cm 1" to 40 chains
Shows a small area of the Thames R from the twp of Delaware to Allan's mill west of London town site; note: 'The Lots 2 and 4 with their broken fronts washed Pink are those petitioned for by Mr Allan' (the lots are marked 'R'); there was a

controversy over Ebenezer Allan's land claims and the issue was settled 4 Oct 1795 (Simcoe, *Correspondence* II:99); other landowners shown in area; roads to Kettle Creek, path from Mohawk village, and 'Delawares' marked.
OTAR (Simcoe Map 446904)

---

916 *1795*
Plan of the River Thames from the Upper Forks to its entrance into Lake St Clair. Copied from the original Surveys of Messrs Jones and McNiff Surveyor Genls Office Newark 7th Novr 1795 [Sgd] D W Smith Actg Sur. General Wm Chewett, Senr Surveyr U.C.
Col ms 72 x 306 cm 1" to 1 mile Endorsements: 'River Thames & four plans of Chatham' [later drawing on back with date]: 'August 2d 96'

A detailed, attractive map of the river from L St Clair to the site for 'Oxford'; twps are marked; comments on the land, marshes, relief; shows Indian villages including Moravian village, Chatham showing bldgs, various roads; sites for London, Dorchester, and 'Oxford'; 'Allan's Mill'; shows a different proposed orientation for Dorchester and a larger Chatham and London than on the [1794] map (**914(2)**); shows proposed continuation of Dundas St from Oxford to London; tables of distances; (*OHIM* 3.11).
OTAR (Simcoe Map 446698)

Related maps

(**2**) *[1795?]*
Survey of the River La Tranche or Thames from its entrance or confluence with Lake St Clair to the Upper Forks: delineated by a Scale of Forty Gunters Chains to one Inch collected from plans by Mr. McNiff and Mr. Jones [Sgd] D.W. Smith Actg Surveyor General Upper Canada
Col mss in 3 sheets Size varies 1" to 40 chains

The first sheet (SR 7920) extends from the mouth of the Thames to Orford Twp and has the title of the whole map; shows the proposed site for Chatham with potential mill site, etc; notes on land capability for wheat and corn; oak, ash, maple, and black walnut tree types located; 'Point Chenal Ecarté'; note: 'The Space between the Yellow Lines on each side of the River represents a Sketch of all the woodland anywise convenient to the River near which the Plain ends on the south side'; the other maps show the area from Orford Twp to beyond Delaware village (SR 16902) and from west of proposed 'New London' to past proposed site for Dorchester (SR 7684); the latter includes a 'Table shewing the Distances from the Delaware Village on the River Thames to the Proposed Site of "Oxford" ... Collected from Mr. Jones Report'; shows Gov Simcoe's route to Detroit in February 1793; various trails; later notes added showing where Tecumseh was killed in War of 1812; the part from 'Dorchester' to 'Oxford' appears not to have survived.
OTAR (SR 7684; 7920; 16902)

(**3**) *[1795?]*
Survey of the River La Tranche or Thames ... D.W. Smith Actg Surveyor Genl Upper Canada. (Copy) Engrs Drawg Room Quebec
Col ms in 5 sheets 68 x 451 cm 1" to 40 chains
Watermark: 'J WHATMAN 1794' Endorsements: 'No 1065'; stamp 'CREOC'

A copy of (2) above with the same notes; a part on the west end is missing, including the area from Chatham to the mouth of the river; (*OHIM* 7.28 (part)).
OOAMA (NMC 21347)

(**4**) *[1795?]*
Plan of the River Thames Copied by A. Aitken D.P. Syr
4 col mss 71 x 460 cm 1" to 40 chains

Shows a similar configuration of the river with proposed towns, routes, and notes as in (3) above; more relief shown along riverbanks; includes the area from the mouth of the Thames to the forks where the site for Dorchester was located, but Dorchester is not labelled; a street grid for New London has been added between the oxbow and the forks.
GBLMM (Grenville Map no 63A case 75A)

---

917 *1795*
A Sketch of Part of the Western District for Mr Iredell Sur Gen Office Newark 2 Aug 95 D W Smith Asst. Surv Genl
Col ms 53 x 75 cm Approx 1" to 6 miles
Endorsements: '900'

Probably related to SI of 2 Aug 1795 to Iredell in which he is sent 14 plans of twps and areas in the Western District, as well as instructions to survey Chatham; shows Indian villages, old and new footpaths from Chatham town site to Point aux Pins and to the west; shows boundary of purchase line of land from the Moravian Indians on the Thames R due west to the mouth of the St Clair R; shows twps from Detroit R to Camden and Howard twps including Malden Twp 'granted to the Indian officers and others.'
OTAR (SR 5871)

---

918 *[1795]*
A Sketch of the River Thames, from the Delaware Village to the Upper Forks. Surveyor Generals Office Upper Canada 22d March 1793 D.W. Smith Act Surveyor General. A True Copy of the Original in my Possession Exd [Sgd] Joseph Chew S.I.A. [Sgd] A. McKee D.S.G.I.A.
Col ms 45 x 37 cm 1" to 4 miles

Originally with letter from Joseph Chew to Thomas Coffin of 26 Nov 1795 enclosing plans of intended purchases from the Indians (OOA RG 8 I/248 p 391); shows the boundary of the area to be purchased and a copy of a treaty agreement signed 29 Sept 1795 by P. Selby A.S.I.A., T. McKee Lt 60th Regt, Charles Reaume Interpreter, and six Indian chiefs; the purchase area eventually became Treaty No 6 with the Chippewas (7 Sept 1796)

(*Indian Treaties*, I:17ff); shows also a proposed twp at the Forks, 12 miles square; proposed road to London from Oxford town site to the east; various Indian villages and trails; (Holmden 2578).
OOAMA (NMC 4113)

Related maps

(**2**) *1795*
We the Chiefs of the Chippawa Nation do hereby agree with Alexander McKee Esquire Deputy Superintendant General and Deputy Inspector General of Indian Affairs ... that for the Consideration of Eight Hundred pounds Quebec Currency Value in Indian Goods, we will execute a regular Deed for the Conveyance of the Lands hereon marked Red to His said Majesty being Twelve Miles Square and adjoining the uppermost line at Channail Ecarte ... This agreement signed by us on the bank of the River Thames formerly known by the name of the River La Tranche this Twenty ninth day of September 1795. [Sgd by six Chippewa chiefs] In the presence of us P. Selby A.S.I.A. T. McKee Lt. 60th Regt Charles Reaume, Interpreter. A true Copy of the Original in my possession [Sgd] A McKee D.S.G.I.A.
Col ms 37 x 67 cm 1" to 10 miles
With the same letter as above map; shows a small block north of Chenal Ecarte and along the St Clair R that eventually became Treaty No 7 of 7 Sept 1796 (*Indian Treaties*, I:19ff); also shows the large purchase of much of the southwestern part of the province south of the Thames R of 19 May 1790, Treaty No 2 (*Indian Treaties*, I:1) and a small tract on the Detroit R marked 'Cession 7 June 1784 Ind. Officers Land'; the Huron reserve is shown to the north and the 'Huron Church' reserve further up; a block on L Erie is marked 'Lately called the two connected Townships'; (Holmden 1721; *OHIM* 4.4).
OOAMA

---

919 *[1795]*
Two Sevenths of certain old Townships in the Western District set apart for the Crown & the Clergy as specified on this Plan.
Col ms 27 x 44 cm 1" to 10 miles
In D.W. Smith to Simcoe, 'Report on the Reserved Lands Upper Canada,' 9 Nov 1795 (OTAR Simcoe Papers, env 44 p 18, MS 517 reel 8), and copy enclosed in Simcoe's no 34 to Portland of 22 Dec 1795 (GBLpro CO 42/320 p 75); 'The Tracts colored with Indian Ink are reserved for the Clergy and those with Lake for the Crown'; shows the proposal for two interior blocks of reserves in the twps of Malden, Colchester, Gosfield, Mersea, Sandwich, Raleigh, Harwich, Howard, Orford, Dover, Chatham, and Camden; these twps were laid out before the chequerboard plan came into use.
GBLpro (CO 42/320, p 75) OTAR (Simcoe Papers MS 517 reel 8)

---

920 *1796*
The above is a Plan of a Tract of Land called the Huron Reserve, situate on the River Detroit, Western District and Province of Upper Canada, Containing Twenty-three thousand six hundred and forty acres; – [Sgd] A. Iredell Depy Surveyor W. District. Detroit Feby 20th 1796.
Col ms 55 x 42 cm 1" to 40 chains Endorsements: 'Q3' '1057'
The Indian reserve that later became Anderdon Twp; notes on the nature of the land and types of tree; Huron village; names of some settlers.
OTNR (SR 2425)

---

921 *1797*
The above is a plan of a Meridian Line, in the Township of Malden, Situate on Lots No 7 & 8 (the property of Captain Cowan) about half a mile from the Bank of the River Detroit; – [Sgd] A. Iredell D.S. W.D. September 20th 1797
Ms in 2 sheets 53 x 73 cm and 68 x 59 cm 1" to 1 chain Endorsements: 'No 23' '928'
Notes on the timber of the monuments and the marking of such by the burying of halfpennies and a lead plate marked 'I G Simcoe Lieut Govr U.C. ...'
OTNR (SR 7420)

---

922 *1800*
A Map of Sandwich with the position and situation of the Lands of William Park and Meldrum and Park; together with Notes and references Inscribed for William Park Esq. 30th Dec 1800
Col ms 34 x 48 cm 1" to 40 chains
Shows the area from lot 1 to lot 77 on the Detroit R with names, town of Sandwich, lot A and lots 1 to 56 in 2nd con; extensive notes on early French settlement sgd 'T. Smith' and notes on conflicting survey lines; (Holmden 2612).
OOAMA (NMC 3600)

---

923 *1803*
Plan de la Riviere du Detroit qui Separe le Lac Ste Claire d'avec le Lac Erié Reduit et dessiné par Georges de Bois St Lyr anc. offr français 1803
Col ms 26 x 49 cm 1" to approx 1 lieue commune
Watermark: 'BUDGEN'
Inset: 'Plan Particular and detaillé du Fort du Detroit' 1" to 17.5 toises; relief, vegetation, French place-names; shows 'Habitations' on the Canadian side between 'Ruisseau de la vielle Reine' and 'Riviere aux Dindes'; 'Village de Hurons,' 'Village des Outaouis'; similar to a much earlier plan by J.N. Bellin in *Le petit atlas maritime* (1764), I: no 12, except that the details of the bldgs of the town in the inset are different, more are keyed, and the Jardin du Roi is shown in greater detail; attributed by USICHi to Gen George Collot who lived near the Bois St Lyr in France.
USICHi

---

924 *[1803?]*
Plan of the River Thames from the Moravian Grant to Lot No 5, commonly called, the Reserve near Chatham Copy W.C.
Col ms 44 x 85 cm 1" to 40 chains Endorsements: 'A4'
Shows lots 6 to 24, Chatham, and 1 to 18, Camden, fronting on the river and extending back several cons; crown and clergy reserves are in four blocks north of river; 'Note the unlocated part of Chatham, Reserved for the Earl of Selkirk' [1803]; (Story, 755).
OTAR(P)

---

925 *1804*
Sketch of the proposed Road through the District of London supposed to be about Ninety Miles [Sgd] Thomas Talbot [etc] Commissioners
Ms Size not known Scale not given Endorsements: 'A'
With documents of 14 and 19 Sept 1804 related to proposed road (OOA RG 1 E3 vol 87); shows twps from Townsend, Aldborough, and north to the Thames R; [Talbot] road is proposed starting at the Grand R and gradually approaching the L Erie shore in Yarmouth Twp; rivers shown and notes on nature of land.
OOA (RG1 E3 vol 87)

---

926 *1809*
The Mouths of River St Clair with the Islands and Channels ascertaining the main navigable waters which divide that part of His Majesty's Dominions from the United States. [Sgd] Thos Smith, Upper Canada Decr 1809
Col ms 54 x 75 cm Approx 1" to 1 mile
Endorsements: 'No 4' '803'
Inset: [Baldoon Settlement] 1" to 20 chains; shows boundary of tract purchased from the Chippewas in 1790 including 'Shawanese twp'; swampy, wooded areas and details on shoreline; names of a few settlers; statistics on marshy and dry parts of islands; soundings; navigable waterways; inset includes an 'Extract of Patent no. 1 to the Earl of Selkirk' with survey description, and shows mansion, calf pasture, sheep-folds, brickyard, wooded areas, area divided up into fields and numbered, Chippewa settlement, and paths.
OTAR

---

927 *1810*
No. VII Upper Canada. Plan of Detroit River by A. Gray Asst Qr Mr Genl Quebec 7th Decr 1810 / [Endorsed title]: 'This Plan is from a Survey by Lieut. Gray, aided by Some local Surveys obtained in Upper Canada [Sgd] James Kempt Q M. Genl N. America, Q M. Genls Office, Quebec 1st June 1811.'
Col ms in 2 sheets 75 x 197 cm 1" to 600 yds
Watermark: 'JAMES WHATMAN. TURKEY MILL KENT 180[?]'
Provenance: OOAMA Plimsoll Edwards Estate; an attractive plan of the river and adjacent land; shows vegetation, marshy areas, soundings, forts, dockyards, roads, cleared land, bldgs; shows layout of Amherstburg, Sandwich, and Detroit; 'Ottawa Burying Ground.'
OOAMA (NMC 20970)

---

928 *[1810]*
[Plan of the area from Aldborough Twp to Oxford Twp, south of the Thames River]
Ms 37 x 47 cm Scale not given Watermark: 'JOHN HALL 1808'
From memorial of S.Z. Watson of 19 Apr 1810 petitioning to obtain land for prospective immigrants from Lower Canada (OOA RG 1 L3 W9 no 67 (1810)); shows Southwold Twp, which Watson wanted, as well as new tract 'from 15 to 18 miles in width' between Yarmouth and Houghton [Malahide and Bayham twps]; [Talbot Rd] leading from Port Talbot to the Grand R shown; (Holmden 1882).
OOAMA (NMC 4111)

---

929 *[ca 1810]*
[Sketch of area from Long Point to Orford Twp showing a road]
Col ms in 2 sheets 18 x 228 cm [Approx 1" to 1.25 miles]
A fragment with part trimmed; shows pt of the [Talbot] road with mileage points 1 to 85 marked and the following twps named: Walsingham, Houghton, Yarmouth, Southwold, Dunwich, Aldborough, Orford; probably made before Malahide and Bayham twps were surveyed in 1811.
OOAMA (NMC 14277)

---

930 *[1810–15]*
The Road opened from Nanticoak Creek Westward fifty two and an half miles – [Sgd] Thomas Talbot Commissr for Roads in the District of London
Col ms 19 x 132 cm Scale not given Watermark: '1801' Endorsements: 'J8' '870'
Shows part of the [Talbot Rd] running from [Walpole Twp] west to Kettle Creek and [Yarmouth Twp]; swamps and rivers crossed; parts of the road were surveyed by M. Burwell in 1809–10 and this part is shown on maps of 1815 (see **52**); the west part shown here extends beyond Kettle Creek on 1810 map above (**929**).
OTAR (SR 81037)

---

931 *[1812?]*
Plan of the American Forts and Possessions in the Environs of the Head of Lake Erie. Jno Le Breton Lieut Royl Nfd Reg't.
Col ms 59 x 73 cm 1" to 3.3 miles Watermark: '1811'
Provenance: OOAMA Plimsoll Edwards Estate; shows Fts Seneca and Stevenson and old fort on the Miami R on the U.S. side; shows wooded areas, swamps, cleared land, houses, and roads on both sides of the river.
OOAMA (NMC 21693)

---

932 *[1812?]*
River Detroit
Col ms 66 x 49 cm 1" to 1 mile Watermark: 'J WHATMAN' Endorsements: 'No 18' '935'
Shows settlements and forts on the British and American sides, and pencil addition of American redoubt and fortified camp north of Sandwich; landing place of Americans opp Hogs Is 5 July 1812; note: 'Detroit Surrd 16th Aug 1812'; British camp shown north of R aux Canards; note: 'Intended communication between Detroit, Point au Playe and the Islands explored by Army Surveyr cutting off the Peninsula'; possibly an American military map.
OTAR

---

933 *[1812]*
[Sketch of the Detroit River showing engagements in 1812] [Endorsed on back]: 'Sketch of Detroit &c.'
Col ms 46 x 36 cm Scale not given Watermark: 'G R WARD 1808' Endorsements: 'Enclosed in John Hale's letter to Lord William Amherst Quebec 12 Sept 1812'
Shows place where the Indians were supposed to land, where they did land and take up positions, and where Tecumseh defeated the enemy (Battle of Brownstown, 5 Aug 1812); other troop locations shown including Capt Muir's position; notes on distances on the map and probability that it was not done to scale; (Brun 732).
USMiU-C

---

934 *[1812?]*
[Sketches of the delta of the St Clair River and the Detroit River showing roads and settlements]
2 col ms on 1 sheet 62 x 38 cm 1" to 2 miles Endorsements: '902'
Two unfinished sketches showing towns, forts, relief, and roads on both sides of the rivers; the Detroit R map shows similar information to **932**.
OTAR (SR 4745)

---

935 *[1813]*
Harrisons Victory. A Plan of the Order of Battle, in Action fought on the Banks of the Thames in Upper Canada, on the [blank space] between the Americans commanded by Genl Harrison & the British Comd by Genl Proctor – In Which The British were completely Defeated. Sketched from the Report of General Harrison of the 9 Oct. as published in the Gazette of the 27th by [Sgd] Edw Roche
Col ms 21 x 22 cm Scale not given Watermark: 'J & C Co.'
Battle of the Thames or Moraviantown 5 Oct 1813; shows positions of British regiments, Indians, and American troops (Trotter's Brigade, Johnston's Mounted Cavalry, and others); relief, swamps.
USIChi

---

936 *1813*
MAP / OF / Detroit River / and / ADJACENT COUNTRY, / From an Original Drawing, / by a British Engineer. / H.S. Tanner Sc. / / Entered as the Act Directs / / PHILADELPHIA: Published by John Melish, Chestnut Street, 26 August 1813.
Print (engrav) 59 x 45 cm 1" to 1 mile
In John Melish, *A Military and Topographical Atlas of the United States* (Philadelphia: Printed by G. Palmer 1813), part 2, opp 18 (*Bib Can* 6922), and in the ed of 1815 (Philadelphia: Published by John Melish, G. Palmer, printer 1815) (*Bib Can* 6980; *LC Atlases* 1347), and in *A General Collection of Maps* (Philadelphia, 1824), Map [7] (*LC Atlases* 6053) (imprint trimmed off); shows the area from the entrance at L St Clair to L Erie; relief by hachures; towns, settlements, roads, forts, batteries; point where the British army landed south of Detroit 16 Aug 1812.
OTMCL USDLC

---

937 *[1813]*
A Representation of the Genl. Action by Col. Johnson's Regt and Governor Shelbys' Troops on the River Thames under Genl Harrison October 5th 1813 ...
Ms 27 x 20 cm Scale not given
In 'Journal of Capt Robert B. McAfee 19 May 1813–May 1814' (USKyLoF); shows the Thames R from Arnold's Mill to Moraviantown; shows battleground, location of the British regiments, Indians, and various U.S. regiments; a note indicates the battleground is enlarged in proportion to rest of map to show it in detail; (*OHIM* 2.9).
USKyLoF

---

938 *1814*
No 1 Part of the River Thames Upper Canada. [Sgd] Gust Williams 9 Augt 1814
Col ms 33 x 98 cm Scale not given Endorsements: stamps 'IGF' 'B↑O'
Originally 'accompanying Lt. Col. Hughes letter to Lt. General Mann dated 16th August 1814' (in GBLpro WO 55/860 pp 104–5); inset: [map of southwestern part of province showing location of River Thames]; shows route that Americans followed to Moraviantown in Oct 1813, position of British troops, and note that Tecumseh was killed by the enemy; relief, notes on trees; inset shows twps, roads; (Holmden 2580).
OOAMA (NMC 21814)

---

939 *[1814]*
[Sketch of Longwood near Delaware showing the action in which Captain Baden of the 89th Regt and his men were surrounded and shot down on 4 March 1814]
Col ms 30 x 20 cm 1" to 30 yds
Accompanied a letter from John LeBreton to Capt Foster, military secretary, of 8 March 1814 with details on the retreat (OOA RG 8 I/682 p 232).
OOAMA (NMC 68557)

---

940 *1815*
A Topographic Chart of the mouth of Detroit River With the Islands and Adjacent Country Surveyed Desig[ned] and Executed [in] March 1815 By [Edward] W Miller 3rd Lieutenant. 2nd Regt U.S. Riflemen in p[ursua]nce of an order from [Major] William Henry Puthoff [2nd] Regt U.S. Rifle[men]
Ms 108 x 66 cm [Approx 1" to 1/4 mile] Endorsements: stamp 'Engr Dept U. States Topl Bureau'
Shows relief, swamps, notes on riverbank areas; spot heights; forts, batteries, roads, settlements, treed areas; notes on whether armed troops, horses, and artillery can pass; encampments of Indians; sand-bars, navigational hazards in river; some information may come from earlier sources.
USDNA (RG 77:03)

---

941 *1816*
Map of Detroit River
Col ms 29 x 21 cm 1" to 2 miles Endorsements: '262' 'K26'
Originally from (GBLpro FO 5/115 p 262); note: 'Inclosure (No 5) in Mr. Bagot's despatch (No 46) Decr 3 1816'; an outline sketch showing Sandwich, Amherstburg, Ft Malden, boundary with U.S., and towns on U.S. side; (*PRO Cat* 2538).
GBLpro (MPK 26)

---

942 *1817*
The Entrance of Detroit River from Lake Erie Arranged from a Survey made by Order of Major Puthoff, late of the Rifle Corps for Major General Macomb West Point July 1817 [Sgd] T Roberdeau U.S. T. Engineers
Col ms 41 x 62 cm 2" to 1 mile
Shows the area from Brownstown to end of Turkey or Fighting Is; shows location of American and British troops at the Battle of Brownstown 5 Aug 1812; more detail on American side including 'Great Military Road'; Canadian side shows Ft Malden, [Amherstburg], and town and two French villages with roads, and notes on thickness of forest re troop movement.
USMiD

---

943 *[1819]*
ENVIRONS of / DETROIT / Engraved for / DARBY'S TOUR. // W. Hooker Sc.
Print (engrav) 28 x 16 cm Scale not given
In William Darby, *A Tour from the City of New-York to Detroit* (New York: Kirk and Mercein and others 1819), opp 185 (*Bib Can* 1136); shows area from Sandusky Bay to L Huron and from west of Detroit R to Point Pelee; names of twps, etc, but more detail in U.S.
OTMCL

---

944 *[1819]*
[Endorsed title]: 'Tract of Land on North Side of River Thames Taken from "Proposals for Survey No 61 – 1819"'
Ms 24 x 21 cm Scale not given
Probably from OOA RG 1 L3 or L5 but exact location not found; shows two tracts north of the Thames R west of London containing '937 & 1/2 sq miles proposed for survey by advertisement of 30th June 1819'; 'Mr Arthur's track' also indicated from Baldoon to London; (Holmden 2582).
OOAMA (NMC 4109)

Related maps

(2) *[1820?]*
[Map of the area between the Thames River and Ausable [La Sable] River showing town plots, townships, and reserves]
Col ms 26 x 41 cm Scale not given
Probably from OOA RG 1 L3 or L5 but exact location not found; shows area from Rochester Twp to the Ausable R, east to clergy reserve north of Blandford and Blenheim twps, south to Norwich Twp; shows blocks to be surveyed as in 1819 plan above; shows two large blocks west and north of the others, '712,000 acres' and '2,391,000 acres,' and six small blocks in red, which may be proposed Indian reserves; L St Clair called 'Lake Simcoe'; the southern part of this area was purchased from the Indians in 1819 (see **947**); (Holmden 2577).
OOAMA (NMC 4108)

---

945 *1820*
Map of the Road through the Long Woods from Delaware to the Moravian Grant and of the River Thames from the S.W. Angle of London to the Oil Spring, near the Boundary between the London and Western Districts ... Also the Tract between the Road and the River with a part of Township C N.W. of the Road, and a part of Township A on the Thames. By Order from the Surveyor Generals Office bearing date the 19th day of January 1820. [Sgd] Dy Surveyors Office Port Talbot 16th June 1820 M. Burwell Dy Surveyor
Col ms 58 x 188 cm 1" to 40 chains Endorsements: 'No 20'
(OTNR FN 98, 191–3 1820); shows survey grid with crown and clergy reserves, mill seats, swamps, contents of lots, and a few names of settlers.
OTNR (SR 86975)

---

946 *[1820]*
Sketch submitted by Crawley the Lieut [illegible] in July 1819. [With] Additions at this time.
Ms 32 x 39 cm Scale not given
Accompanies 'Lands Proposed to be Sold to Defray the Annual Charges of Presents to the Indians ... in Conformity to Your Lordships Despatch No. 39 of 30th May 1819' in Maitland to Earl Bathurst 8 March 1820 (GBLpro CO 42/365 p 85); shows area from Dereham Twp to L St Clair and the block of land along the Longwoods Rd north of the Thames above Delaware Twp to

Howard Twp; shows 65 lots south of the Longwoods Rd that would bring in £370; other notes about the road location and Indian reserves.
GBLpro (CO 42/365 p 85)

---

947 *1821*
[Map showing boundary of Indian purchase north of the Thames] Surveyor Generals Office York, Upper Canada 24 July 1821. [Sgd] Thos Ridout Surveyr General. Office Copy.
Col ms 33 x 42 cm 1" to 4 miles Endorsements: 'Q48' '1095'
Shows the boundary of Treaty No 21 with the Chippewas of 9 March 1819; shows small blocks reserved for Indians in Carradoc and [Zone] twps, and north of Sombra Twp; (*Indian Treaties*, I:49ff).
OTNR (SR 2502)

---

948 *1824*
Map of a Road, and Lots adjoining through the Reserves of London and Westminster, near the forks of the Thames: by Order from the Surveyor General's Office, bearing date at York, the 26th day of January 1824. Dy Surveyors Office Port Talbot 31st Decemr 1824 [Sgd] M. Burwell Dy Surveyor
Col ms 43 x 33 cm 1" to 40 chains Endorsements: 'No 22'
(SI 26 Jan 1824); shows the south part of London Twp and the north part of Westminster Twp; 100-acre lots shown on road from lot 31, 1st con, Westminster Twp, to Thames R, and along road allowance between lots 16 and 17 to front of 3rd con, London Twp; shows crown and clergy reserves, names in road lots, Wortley Rd.
OTAR(P)

---

949 *1826*
Map Shewing the boundaries of the Reserves made by the Chippewa Indians, in the tract of Land lately purchased from them by Government in the London and Western Districts. – By Order from the Surveyor General's Office, bearing date at York, the 31st day of July 1826 – by [Sgd] M. Burwell Dy Surveyor Deputy Surveyor's Office, Port Talbot, 30th December 1826
Col ms, pt missing 64 x 151 cm 1" to 80 chains Endorsements: '1186'
(OTNR FN 124 30 Dec 1826); shows the area near the L Huron shore from Ausable R south to St Clair R; major survey outlines connecting with Lobo and London twps, and four reserves shown along shore; indication of settlement without authority along the St Clair R; the area was purchased from the Indians in 1825 (*Indian Treaties*, Treaty No 27 1/2, I:65).
OTNR (SR 5740)

---

950 *1828*
Map of the foot of Lake Huron and part of the River St Clair By Order from the Surveyor General's Office bearing date at York the 31st day of July 1826. Deputy Surveyor's Office Port Talbot 17th May 1828 [Sgd] M. Burwell Dy Surveyor
Col ms 104 x 74 cm 1" to 40 chains Endorsements: 'Q 60' '1087'
Shows lots fronting on St Clair R and lakeshore; notes on locations where houses erected, clearings, Chippewa Indian reserves, swamps; proposed twp boundaries; note that numbers correspond with statistical table E and names of occupants found in FN 776 (OTAR RG 1 CB1 box (6)).
OTAR (SR 6435)

---

951 *[ca 1830]*
[Map of part of the London District showing roads and townships]
Ms 48 x 40 cm Scale not given Watermark: 'G WILMOT[T?] 1828'
Shows the outlines of the twps of Burford, Oakland, and those in Norfolk Co; location of various villages and roads including 'present road to Grand River at Brantford' (from Simcoe); new road to be examined between 'Middleton St' along the south boundary of Windham Twp, and east of Simcoe; (Holmden 1681).
OOAMA (NMC 3307)

---

952 *1830*
Point Edward Surveyed by Order from the Surveyor Generals Office bearing date at York the 13th day of April 1829. [Sgd] Roswell Mount Dy Surveyor Dr Surveyors Office Carradoc 30th January 1830
Col ms 81 x 57 cm 1" to 8 chains Endorsements: '852'
Profiles: 'Three Profiles of Levels taken upon Point Edward' 1" to 8 ft; surveyed by Mount while surveying Moore and Sarnia twps; shows swamps, clearings, heights; Ft Gratiot and two lighthouses shown on U.S. side.
OTNR (SR 2042)

Related maps

(2) *1836*
[Title as above] (Copy) J.G. Chewett Surveyor Generals Office Toronto 27th April 1836 (Signed) J. Radenhurst. T.G.W. Eaststaff Draughn.
Endorsed 'Plan No 5 To accompany the Report of the Commanding Royal Engineers to His Excellency the Lieut Governor of Upper Canada on the subject of the Military Reserves dated 18th July 1836 [Sgd] G Nicolls Colonel Comg Rl Enginrs Canada' (from GBLpro CO 42/431); the same as original above; (*PRO Cat* 1539).
GBLpro (MPG 762(5))

---

953 *[1831?]*
[Plan of townships and roads in the Western and London districts]
Col ms 46 x 53 cm Scale not given Endorsements: '803'
Twps are shown north to Plympton, Warwick, Adelaide, Lobo, and London; only part of the survey grid is shown for Plympton to Adelaide

twps, which were laid out between 1829 and 1833; shows Commissioners Rd, Longwoods Rd, Talbot Rd N, Talbot Rd E (east of Dunwich Twp); extension of Commissioners Rd west of Woodhull's Bridge; in Lobo Twp 'Road to the new Survey' goes west to Warwick Twp; other roads not named; reserves.
OTAR (SR 81040)

---

954 *1832*
TOWNSHIP OF MOORE / Surveyor Generals Office / 22nd October 1832 // Tazewell Print [part illegible]
Print (lith) 23 x 23 cm 1" to 120 chains
Shows the survey grid, 'Cn' [crown] and 'Cy' [clergy] reserves marked; 'Double Front' [survey system] shown in one area; Indian reserve; print very light and/or faded; (Holmden 1972).
OOAMA (NMC 3530)

Related maps

(2) *1832*
TOWNSHIP of Moore / Drawn & Lithographd From Canadian Stone by S.O. Tazewell / Surveyor General's Office York / Octr 25th 1832
Print (lith) 26 x 24 cm Scale not given
Redrawn from the earlier map with scale slightly larger than (1), a north arrow has been added, the 't' of 'Double Front' has been cut off, and printing is darker; (Holmden 1973).
OOAMA (NMC 3529)

---

955 *[1833]*
ENNISKILLEN / Home District [*sic*] / Tazewell del & lith Toronto
Print (lith) 25 x 22 cm 1" to 120 chains
Shows the survey grid, rivers, etc; map oriented to north but 'East' is incorrectly located above top and bottom boundaries; the twp was in the Western District, not the Home District; the original twp survey plan for Enniskillen is dated 8 Jan 1833 (see **A653**).
OOAMA (NMC 53740)

---

956 *[1833]*
Township of Moore Surveyor General's Office York U.C. [Initialled] S.P.H.
Col ms 51 x 28 cm 1" to 100 chains
Originally with correspondence from S.P. Hurd about a useful style of plan and the value of producing lithographed copies (OOA RG 1 E3 vol 44 p 132); shows twp outline with cons and lots numbered in the margin but no reserves shown; blank table below map for notes on each con and lot about soil and timber, water communication, and mill sites; 'General Remarks' regarding limestone, clay, minerals, etc; an attempt to develop a style of plan for recording data for office records.
OOAMA (NMC 3531)

---

957 *1834*
For the Steamboat, Menesetunk Chart of the navigation between Lake Erie and the Port of Goderich. Canada Company's Office. City of Toronto, 16th June 1834 Henry Lizars
Col ms on linen in 2 sheets 193 x 66 cm 1" to 2 miles Endorsements: stamp [BW] '537'
'Accompanied by a Letter of this date'
Shows the shore area from Point Pelee to Goderich; soundings, channels; notes on nature of the shore, shoals, rivers; the upper map sheet is offset to the west; probably a later copy of the original, which has not been found; (Holmden 2113).
OOAMA (NMC 18003)

---

958 *1834*
Plan of Road connecting the Long-Woods' Road with the Village of Colborne in the Chippewa Indians' Reservation, Township of Carradoc (Signed) Henry James Castle, D.P.S. Surveyor General's Office, Toronto, 19th Sepr 1834. – Copy, – Henry Lizars. [Sgd] S.P. Hurd S.G.
Col ms 55 x 74 cm Scale not given Endorsements: 'No 10'
(OTNR FN 99 4 Oct 1833); shows road allowance and part blazed; shows block of land surrendered by the Chippewas 5 Feb 1834; lots open for land sales; Chippewa clearing; town plot of Colborne.
OTNR (SR 6524)

---

959 *1834*
[Sketch of Lands near Port Sarnia]
Ms 23 x 39 cm Scale not given
Accompanying a letter by R.V. Vidal to the Earl of Limerick 30 Oct 1834 about a matter of land being sold under current price (GBLpro CO 42/424 p 516); shows the area north of Port Sarnia with survey grid, marsh, some names of owners.
GBLpro (CO 42/424 p 516)

---

960 *1835*
Longitudinal Section of the Proposed Route of Canal from the Grand River to the River Thames Surveyed by R.A. Maingy Mining and Civil Engineer 1835 [Sgd] Robt A. Maingy Mining & Civil Engineer
Ms Size not known Scale not given
Section divided into 11 parts; shows only approximate route; names of owners whose land crossed; crosses Horner Creek, Mud Creek, and ends at junction of Cedar Creek with Thames R beyond road to Woodstock; the map of this proposed canal route has not been found; Maingy's *Report on the Practicability of Connecting the Grand River with the River Thames by Means of a Canal* was published in Brantford in 1835 (*Bib Can* 5059; Fleming 842), but does not contain maps; photoreproduction in OTAR.
Private Collection

961 *[184?]*
A Rough Outline of Parts of the Western District
Col ms 54 x 75 cm 1" to 3 miles Watermark: '... EDMONDS 1837'
Shows area west of Zone/Orford twps to Sombra Twp and south; roads shown and named including Talbot Rd, Centre Rd, road from Sandwich to Chatham and from Amherstburg east, Communication Rd from Chatham to Rondeau; Baldoon.
OTMCL (E.W. Banting Collection)

---

962 *[184?]*
Section of the river Thames at Delaware
Ms 25 x 41 cm 1" to 80 ft, 1" to 10 ft vertical
Endorsements: 'In No 113 C.S. Gzowski Sec of River Thames at Delaware'
Shows plan for bridging the river at Delaware; depths of water, notes on highest and lowest watermarks; probably related to the building of the London and Chatham Rd begun in 1842 and mostly finished by 1846 (OOA RG 11 A3 vol 137 no 77, 1 Dec 1846).
OOAMA

---

963 *1840*
Map of the London and Port Stanley Plank Road 1840
Col ms 51 x 78 cm 1" to 1 mile Endorsements: stamp [BW] '389'
The road follows the westerly route shown on (2).
OOAMA (NMC 21368)

Related maps

(2) *[1842?]*
Survey of a Road from London to St. Thomas
Col ms 48 x 134 cm 1" to 40 chains Endorsements: stamp [BW] '388'
Several possible routes are shown including 'present travelled road,' 'line first surveyed,' 'proposed union of North Road with town line'; shows lines that have been explored; proposed bridges and other lines; 'line selected by the Hon. H.H. Killaly'; shows routes through to Port Stanley; possibly connected with (BW) SI 24 Jan 1842 to James Cull about Killaly's preferred routes; there is also a plan (OOAMA (NMC 3662)) entitled 'Road from Five Stakes to St Thomas' (1" to 20 chains and BW '435') showing the town of St Thomas, Kettle Creek, the Talbot Rd, and a new route for part of the London-Port Stanley Rd.
OOAMA (NMC 3662; 11228)

(3) *[1848?]*
Map of the Port Stanley Road
Col ms 59 x 256 cm 1" to 20 chains Endorsements: stamp '420'
Date '1848' given in pencil; appears to show an alternate route near Port Stanley; the London and Port Stanley Rd was completed in 1844 and this map may show later road changes (OOA RG 11 A3 vol 136 no 277).
OOAMA (NMC 11258)

---

964 *[ca 1840]*
[Plan of Essex County]
Col ms 61 x 73 cm 1" to 11/2 miles Watermark: 'J WHATMAN TURKEY MILL 1826' Endorsements: '1030'
An unfinished plan showing the survey grid for Essex Co and crown and clergy reserves; shows the subdivision of the Huron Reserve (1835) and Anderdon Twp (1836); only a few place-names; Talbot Rd and Malden Rd.
OTAR (SR 86908)

---

965 *1840*
Plan of the Rondeau to accompany a Report upon the practicability of constructing a Canal from thence to the River Thames made by Command of His Excellency the Lieutenant Governor [Sgd] Thos Roy C. Eng. Toronto Novr 12th 1840
Col ms 55 x 71 cm 1" to 2400 ft Endorsements: stamps 'BW' '609'
A rough sketch showing the proposed line of canal from mouth of Indian Creek to the northwest; feeder canal; Antrim in Howard Twp marked with note that the mouth of the creek would form a good small harbour; Communication Rd and Talbot St dotted in; (Holmden 2586).
OOAMA (NMC 22090)

Related maps

(2) *1840 [1846?]*
Plan of the Rondeau Harbour. (Signed) Thomas Roy C.E. Toronto Novr 12th 1840. Copy.
Col ms 55 x 71 cm 1" to 2400 ft
Accompanied Capt Warden's report of 27 Jan 1846 (GBLpro Adm 7/625); shows the marsh, 'prairies,' government reserve at Pointe aux Pins, road to harbour, soundings, Canada Co. land; proposed line of canal; (*PRO Cat* 1562).
GBLpro (MR 1052(6))

---

966 *1840*
Plan shewing the most eligible route for a road from the town of London to Port Saraia [*sic*] for the information of His Excellency the Lieutenant Governor Sir George Arthur K.G.H. &c &c &c. Surveyed per order of the Surveyor General The Honorable R.B. Sullivan By (Signed) John McDonald Dy P. Surveyor (signed) James Cull Civil Engineers Toronto 23rd June 1840 copy [Sgd] J.G. Chewett Surveyor Genls Office Toronto Septem 1840 [Sgd] [K] Cameron S.G.
Col ms 50 x 115 cm 1" to 11/2 miles Endorsements: stamp [BW] '387'
(SI 8 Nov 1839 to John McDonald to do an exploratory survey, and 15 Jan 1840 to R. Maingy and J. McDonald to survey the road line; shows most eligible route for a road and deviations from it as 'presently travelled'; (Holmden 2146).
OOAMA (NMC 14292)

Related maps

(2) *[1842]*
A Map of the different lines of Road between London & Port Sarnia
Col ms 28 x 53 cm 1" to 3 miles Endorsements: stamp [BW] '387'
Shows the old road from London following the Egremont Rd line and the 'new road laid out by Mr Cull' (showing a slightly different route in Warwick and Plympton twps); 'direct road well settled from Port Sarnia to Carradoc'; construction on the road began in late 1841 and this map may relate to further Board of Works SI to Walter Lawson of 11 March 1842 to survey route from London to Warwick; (Holmden 2145).
OOAMA (NMC 2827)

(3) *[1843–4?]*
Map of the Line of Road from London to Port Sarnia
Col ms 47 x 131 cm 1" to 11/2 miles Endorsements: stamp [BW] '387'
The London and Port Sarnia Rd was begun in 1841 and completed in 1844 (OOA RG 11 A3 vol 136 no 277); (Holmden 2147).
OOAMA (NMC 11242)

---

967 *[1840]*
Roy's Map of proposed road from Amherstburgh to Sandwich and Sandwich to Chatham
Col ms, pt missing 67 x 98 cm Scale not given Endorsements: stamp [BW] '522'
(SI 29 July 1840 to Thomas Roy to survey a road line from Amherstburg to Sandwich to Chatham; shows the road line in detail with mileages; road follows old Sandwich St, then through the middle of Maidstone, Rochester, Tilbury E and W, and Raleigh twps, then along town line to Chatham; other roads that are partially, fully, or recommended to be open; rivers, swamps.
OOAMA (NMC 21366)

Related maps

(2) *[ca 1845?]*
Map of the Line of road from Chatham to Sandwich and from Maidstone Cross to Amherstburgh
Col ms 55 x 156 mm 1" to 1 mile
The Chatham to Sandwich Rd begun in 1842 was noted, as finished in 1847 ('Report ... Public Works ... 1847,' *JLA* (1848), App N).
OOAMA (NMC 21342)

(3) *[ca 1845?]*
Map of the Line of Road from Chatham to Sandwich Maidstone Cross and Amherstburg
Col ms 57 x 204 cm 1" to 60 chains Watermark: 'J WHATMAN ... 1839'
This is similar to (2) above but looks unfinished and neither the marsh nor rivers are coloured in; mileage points.
OOAMA

---

968 *[1842?]*
Plan of the London and Chatham Road
Col ms 65 x 163 cm 1" to 40 chains Endorsements: stamp [BW] '391'
(SI (BW) 11 March 1842 to Mr Billyard to make a survey of the road with sections); shows the line of road in detail including proposed road and old roads; deviations for hills; costs for each section for grubbing, clearing, grading, excavation, bridging, and culverts.
OOAMA (NMC 78511)

Related maps

(2) *[1842?]*
Sections of the Part of London and Chatham Road Through the towns of Mosa and Part of Ekfrid
Col ms 48 x 149 cm 1" to 400 ft, 1" to 20 ft vertical Endorsements: stamp [BW] '474'
Shows the area from mile 24 to mile 36 only, with areas to be excavated and filled to help level the road.
OOAMA (NMC 21922)

---

969 *1842*
Plan shewing the Proposed Routes of the Brantford and London Plank Road W.D.H. April 1842 [Sgd] W.M. Shaw
Col ms 45 x 95 cm 1" to 60 chains Endorsements: stamp [BW] '390'
(SI 28 Jan 1842 to examine country for line of road between Brantford and London); shows the survey for the eastern part through Brantford, Burford, and East Oxford twps; shows other roads and names of some owners; there is also a copy with the same title but no signatures, the same BW number, and more colouring (Holmden 2150; NMC 21371); (Holmden 2148, 2150).
OOAMA (NMC 21370–1)

Related maps

(2) *1842*
Plan Showing the Proposed Routes for the Woodstock and London Plank Road [Sgd] W.M. Shaw [in pencil]: 1842
Col ms 50 x 93 cm Scale not given Endorsements: stamp [BW] '406'
Shows the western part of the road partly following the stage road and partly on a new route; Governors Rd, relief, and swamps shown.
OOAMA (NMC 21373)

(3) *[1845?]*
Map of the London and Brantford Plank Road
Col ms 54 x 94 cm 1" to 11/2 miles Endorsements: stamp [BW] '390'
'Sections of the line of the road from London to Woodstock' 1" to 200 ft, 1" to 20 ft vertical; 'Sections of the line of road from Woodstock to Brantford'; shows the road as completed with planked and macadamized parts; relief by hachures, swamps; the road follows the river closely from Woodstock to London; (Holmden 2149).
OOAMA (NMC 21372)

(**4**) *[1845?]*
Plan shewing the line of Plank Road between London and Woodstock. T.S. Gore C.E. delr.
Col ms 66 x 112 cm 1" to 55 chains Endorsements: stamp [BW] '406'
Shows the western part of road with the planked part indicated; relief shown by formlines; the London and Brantford Plank Rd was completed in 1846 (OOA RG 11 A3 vol 137 no 77 1.12.1846).
OOAMA (NMC 14132)

---

970 *1843*
SKETCH / of Part of the / WESTERN and LONDON DISTRICTS / CANADA WEST. // Lithogd at the Press of H. Scobie, Toronto.
Print (lith) 17 x 20 cm 1" to 14 miles
On broadside: *The Canada Company Having Had Numerous Inquiries ... upon the Western District ... Canada Company's Office, Frederick Street, Toronto, 5th June, 1843* (*Bib Can* 2571); possibly the earliest map printed by Scobie since his lithographic press was first advertised in Oct 1843 (*Canadian Mercantile Almanack for 1844* (OTUTF)); shows twps in which the Canada Co. had blocks for sale; total number of acres for sale per twp; roads.
OTMCL

---

971 *[1843–4?]*
Map of the Chatham and Rond-Eau Road also Rond-Eau Harbour
Col ms 54 x 75 cm 1" to 80 chains Endorsements: stamp [BW] '606'
Inset: 'Town Plot' [Shrewsbury] 1" to 20 chains; (SI BW 26 Jan 1843 to Mr Billyard to survey for a road route from Chatham to Rondeau); shows the road south from Chatham along the Raleigh/Harwich twp line, then cutting diagonally southeast through Harwich to the east end of Rondeau; Talbot St and other roads shown; clergy reserve and Canada Co. block shown; swampy land shown in front of the town plot; shows the 1843 plan for Shrewsbury (see **1966**); the road was not finished until 1847 (OOA RG 11 A3 vol 137 no 574 27.3.1848).
OOAMA (NMC 22089)

---

972 *[1844?]*
Diagram of the Townships in the Vicinity of London. shewing the several Roads diverging therefrom: as constructed or improved by the Board of Works. F.P. Rubidge Draftd
Col ms 63 x 57 cm 1" to 2 miles Endorsements: stamp [BW] '63'
Inset: 'Plan of Port Stanley Harbour with part of the Town Plot.' 1" to 5 chains; in 'A Series of Diagrams ... Samuel Keefer Engr 1844' (OOAMA RG 11M/58603/40/no 63); shows the twps from Ekfrid to London, Dunwich to Malahide, and north to N Dorchester; shows survey grid, swamps, etc; London and Port Sarnia Rd; London, Brantford, and Woodstock Rd; London, Chatham, and Sandwich Rd; line of road (by BW) London to Port Stanley, south to Five Stakes; other roads and many villages located; inset shows new piers, town from river west to George and William sts, and east to Main and Bridge sts; bldgs shown, some named.
OOAMA (NMC 16965)

---

973 *1844*
Plan of the Entrance to the Rondeau Harbour as taken immediately after the Storm of the 18th Oct 1844 ... [Sgd] C.S. Gzowski Engineer
Col ms 38 x 67 cm 1" to 4 chains Endorsements: stamp [BW] '610'
Shows the works proposed to be erected at the entrance with list of timber requirements and estimate of cost.
OOAMA (NMC 4371)

---

974 *[1845]*
[Sketch map of Isle au Bois Blanc showing relative heights by contour lines and the location of Fort and Town of Amherstburg] [F.F.W.30/8/45]
Col ms 42 x 78 cm 1" to 100 yds Watermark: 'J WHATMAN TURKEY MILLS 1840' Endorsements: '218'; stamp 'REO'
Signature and date on map are no longer legible (supplied by OOAMA) who attribute maps to Francis Wyatt Overseer of Works; shows contours on the island with one-foot intervals counted from high points of land; three blockhouses.
OOAMA (NMC 22222)

---

975 *[1846]*
MAP / OF THE / TALBOT, BROCK, / AND / LONDON DISTRICTS, / CANADA. / Compiled from the Township Maps in the Surveyor General's Office, / by / CHARLES RANKIN ESQR. / Published by Henry Rowsell, / TORONTO. / Scobie & Balfour, Toronto Lith:
Print (lith) 73 x 114 cm 1" to 200 chains
Explanations: travelled roads, plank roads, survey grid, road allowances, villages, a few mills; roads named and connecting roads to Hamilton shown; rivers shown only across survey lines; note indicates William Twp is owned by the Canada Co. and is attached to London District; Normandale and Port Rowan incorrectly located; advertised as just published in *British Colonist* 13 Oct 1846.
GBL (70645(79)) OLU OOAMA (NMC 14274) OTAR

---

976 *1846*
Map of the / TALBOT DISTRICT / from / Actual Surveys / by / THOMAS W WALSH / Deputy Provincial Surveyor / Simcoe / 1846. / Scobie & Balfour Lith. / Toronto. // J. Hauer, Lith.
Print (lith) 54 x 89 cm 1" to 120 chains
[Legend] indicates main roads, roads opened and travelled, post offices, saw and grist mills; shows

the complete survey grid, names of roads, twps, settlements; 'Table of distances from Simcoe'; noted as published as of 11 Nov 1846 in *British Colonist* (Toronto).
GBL (70645(78)) OKQMA OOAMA (NMC 21646) OTAR

---

977 *1847*
MAP / of the / WESTERN DISTRICT / CANADA. / Compiled from the Township Maps in the Surveyor Generals Office by / CHARLES RANKIN ESQ. / 1847. / Scobie & Balfour, Lith: Toronto
Print (lith) 87 x 77 cm 1" to 200 chains
Shows the twps, survey grid, roads named, and proposed roads; rivers, marshes, 'prairies,' mills, salt springs, oil springs, town plots, post offices; extensive note in upper left about the size of lots in Sandwich Twp and in Gosfield and Colchester twps, and problems with lot boundaries; also lists islands belonging to the U.S. and British; note about various windmills in the old French settlements in Malden, Sandwich, and Dover; battleground, Indian reserves; advertised by Charles Rankin as 'about to be published on the 20th January 1847' (*British Colonist* 4 Jan 1847); (Holmden 2785).
OOAMA (NMC 11326) OTAR OTMCL

Later editions and states

(2) *1847*
[Title, etc, the same] // J Hauer
Print (lith) 87 x 76 cm 1" to 200 chains
The margin has been placed closer to the map to reduce the size, and the marsh symbol has been changed.
OW

---

978 *1847*
MAP / of the / WESTERN DISTRICT / IN THE / PROVINCE OF CANADA, / with part of the adjoining / STATE OF MICHIGAN / By / WILLIAM BILLYARD AND RICHARD PARR / Civil Engineers. / Scobie & Balfour, Lith: Toronto. / Entered according to ACT of the PROVINCIAL LEGISLATURE / in the Year of Our Lord One Thousand Eight Hundred and Forty Seven / by the Proprietors WILLIAM BILLYARD and RICHARD PARR / of Chatham in the Western District, in the Office of the Registrar of the PROVINCE OF CANADA. // J. Hauer Lith
Print (lith) hand col 169 x 126 cm 1" to 120 chains
'Explanation': boundaries of Essex and Kent cos (the latter including present-day Lambton), roads made by BW, 'Bye Roads' laid out by orders of Quarter Sessions and District Council, grist, saw, and windmills, post offices, lighthouses; also shows survey grid, names of main roads, street grid of major towns, marshy areas; three distance tables by various routes; the map is on a larger scale than that by Rankin (**977**), shows more roads, and includes Bosanquet Twp; advertised as lithographed by Scobie and Balfour and published by Billyard and Parr on 16 Jan 1847 in *British Colonist* (Toronto) (*Bib Can* 5383); one copy in OLU has ms adds with some lots coloured.
OLU OOAMA (NMC 59348) OTAR (SR 92318)

---

979 *1848*
Plan of roads in Sarnia [Sgd] Philo D Salter P.L.S. Sept 30th 1848
Col ms 49 x 70 cm Scale not given Watermark: 'J WHATMAN TURKEY MILL 1846'
Shows the area between Perch R and Call drain in Sarnia Twp; bearings of two roads shown; twp drains and bridges noted.
OWHM

---

980 *1848 (1853)*
Sketch of St Claire Rr near Sarnia. Signed – J.E. Alexander Knt. A.D. 10/8/48. Copy [Sgd] R.I. Pilkington Draftsman 5 Sept. 1853
Col ms 28 x 44 cm [Approx 1" to 250 yds]
Watermark: 'J WHATMAN 1851' Endorsements: 'No 23/3'; stamp 'CREOC'
Shows the rough location of Sarnia and Fort Gratiot with proposed tower and batteries at several points; proposed canal on American side.
OOAMA (NMC 3242)

---

981 *1850*
Sketch of part of the London township. [Sgd] Nath. Steevens Lt XX Regt 1850.
Col ms 68 x 65 cm 2" to 1 mile Endorsements: '92'
A very attractive and detailed military map; 'Reference': 'roads practicable for troops and guns at all seasons, those generally so, and bridle roads and footpaths,' bridges, frame, log, stone, and brick bldgs; mills, barns, farm boundaries, houses with names of some owners; some major bldgs keyed; relief by colour wash, cleared land, tree types; areas with 'stumps' noted in London; (*OHIM* 7.31).
OLU

---

982 *1852*
MAP / OF THE / COUNTY OF OXFORD, / Drawn By / T.S. SHENSTON, / Census Commissioner, / From Rough Drafts Furnished / BY THE ENUMERATORS. / 1852. / Lith. of Hall & Mooney, Buffalo.
Print (lith) 52 x 55 cm 1" to 130 chains
Found separately and in Shenston's *The Oxford Gazetteer ... to which is Added a Map of the County, Compiled Expressly for the Work* (Hamilton, C.W. 1852), at back (*Bib Can* 3308, 8245); 'Explanations'; saw, steam saw, and grist mills, plank or gravel roads, railway, survey grid, a few names of residences, post offices, churches; one copy in OOAMA has ms adds proposing changes to the electoral divisions.
OOAMA (NMC 19836–7) OTMCL OTUTF

---

983 *1854*
Map and Profile / OF A / PROPOSED LINE OF RAILWAY / FROM / PORT DOVER TO ST THOMAS. / R.G. BENEDICT C.E. / 1854. // Lith. of Snyder, Black & Sturn 37 Fulton St. N.Y.
Print (lith) in 2 sheets Ea 23 x 69 cm [Approx 1" to 2 miles]
Shows line and profile from Port Dover to St Thomas as it crosses twp boundaries, creeks, etc; towns and villages shown.
OOAMA

---

984 *1855*
MAP / of the County of / MIDDLESEX. / Compiled from the Township Maps / BY SL PETERS, P.L.S. AND C.E. / 1854–5. / Charles Grebner Lith. Buffalo.
Print (lith) hand col 74 x 109 cm 1" to 100 chains
'Explanation': co roads, railways in operation and in course of construction, projected railways, villages, toll-gates, taverns, churches, GWR, and stations; also shows survey grid.
OLU OTAR OTMCL

---

985 *[1855]*
PLAN / OF THE / ELGIN SETTLEMENT / IN THE / TOWNSHIP OF RALEIGH / COUNTY OF KENT / CANADA WEST / Maclear & Co. Lith. Toronto
Print (lith) 85 x 57 cm Scale not given
Found with *Sixth Annual Report of the Directors of the Elgin Association ... 5th Day of September 1855* (Toronto: Printed at the Globe Book and Job Office 1855) (OTLUC); shows settlement from Thompson St to Granville St on either side of Centre Rd; main bldgs keyed and located including Rev W. King's house, and mission church and school; houses are shown and keyed and only some lots are built upon; notes about the founding of the settlement in 1850.
OLU OTLUC

---

986 *1857*
TREMAINE'S / MAP OF / OXFORD COUNTY / CANADA WEST. / Published by GEO. C. TREMAINE, KINGSTON / 1857. / Engr. by Ch. Nolte. / DRAWN BY W.G. WONHAM, P.L.S. & CO. ENGINEER. / Engraved by D & J. McLellan, New York City. / Views Ambrotyped by Geo. R. Tremaine.
Print (lith) hand col 147 x 175 cm 1" to 60 chains
Insets (scale noted where given): Beachville 1" to 10 chains, Burgessville, Drumbo, Embro 1" to 10 chains, town of Ingersoll 1" to 20 chains, Innerkip 1" to 10 chains, Mount Elgin, Norwichville 1" to 10 chains, Otterville 1" to 10 chains, Plattsville 1" to 10 chains, Princeton 1" to 10 chains, Springford, Thamesford 1" to 10 chains, Tillsonburgh 1" to 10 chains, Washington, town of Woodstock 1" to 20 chains; 34 views of commercial, residential, and public bldgs; legend keys four types of mill, plank and gravel roads, railways, and post offices; names of owners and/or tenants shown in lots; subscribers directory; list of co officers and clerks of the division courts; 'Engr. by Ch. Nolte' refers to the title and not to the map.
GBLrg OLU OOAMA (NMC 19486) OTAR (SR 2652)

---

987 *[1858]*
MAP OF THE / COUNTY OF ESSEX / Compiled and Engraved / expressly for the / CANADIAN ALMANAC / 1859 / MACLEAR & CO. PUBLISHERS / 17 & 19 King St. East / TORONTO.
Print (lith) 36 x 48 cm Scale not given
In *The Canadian Almanac ... for the Year 1859* (Toronto: Maclear and Co. [1858]) (OTUTF); shows the survey grid, roads (some named), some mills, GWR and 'Proposed Southern Railway.'
OTAR OTUTF

---

988 *1858*
Plan No 1 to accompany Report on Pier in Pigeon Bay [Sgd] William Scott C.E. 11 March 1858 Traced from Billiards [*sic*] & Parrs Map of the Western District
Col ms on tracing paper 42 x 62 cm 1" to 11/2 miles
Endorsements: stamp [BW] '584'
Shows the proposed Pier A between Leamington and Sturgeon Creek; Point Pelee Light also shown and [boat] 'Launching Ways'; map traced from **978**.
OOAMA

---

989 *[1858]*
MAP / OF PART OF / CANADA WEST, / [Printed and pasted on]: SHEWING THE / NIAGARA & DETROIT RIVERS RAILWAY
Print (lith) with ms adds 36 x 66 cm 1" to 8 miles
The new title covers the original printed title: 'Shewing the Woodstock and Lake Erie Road to Port Dover and Dunnville'; the railway line is shown in ms beginning at Niagara Falls and Fort Erie and ending at Windsor and Amherstburg; the map shows the area south of Goderich to Toronto and is derived from the southern part of the 1852 map (see **188**) with some changes; legend at left shows travelled roads, plank or macadamized roads, railways in progress, population of twps, and assessed value for twps in Oxford, Norfold, and Haldimand cos; a railway line is added in print from Woodstock to Port Dover and Dunnville; the title may have been changed when the railways were amalgamated under this name in 1858 (*Statutory History*, 413).
OOAMA (NMC 2917)

---

990 *[1858]*
PLAN / OF PART OF THE TOWNSHIPS OF / ORFORD & ZONE. / IN THE COUNTY OF KENT, / Shewing the Lands lately surrendered to the Crown by the / DELAWARE INDIANS. / Maclear & Co. Lith. Toronto C.W.
Print (lith) Approx 76 x 58 cm 1" to 30 chains

'These Lands will be offered for Sale by Public Auction at the City of London C.W. on Wednesday the 15th September 1858 ...'; shows a small part of Zone Twp from north of the Thames R to the Longwoods Rd, and the north part of Orford Twp; shows Indian reserve in Orford with the Indian village, church, burying ground, and 'Tecumseth house'; lot nos, swampy land.
OTAR OTUTF

---

991 *1859*
Plan of Clergy lot letter C Southwold, Showing the position of the quantity of Land now claimed by each Squatter Provincial Land Surveyor's Office St Thomas C.W. [Sgd] 2nd November 1859 Daniel Hanvey Provl Land Surveyor
Ms 145 x 45 cm 1" to 2 chains Endorsements: 'No 27' '2359/60' '1687/61'
Note: 'This is the proper and correct Plan to be deposited in the Office of the Honble Commissioners of Crown Lands ...'; names of squatters and acreage held.
OTNR (SR 7799)

---

992 *1860*
PLAN / OF THE / ELGIN SETTLEMENT / IN THE / TOWNSHIP OF RALEIGH, / COUNTY OF KENT, / CANADA WEST.
Print (lith) 25 x 20 cm Scale not given
On broadside: *Fugitive Slaves in Canada. Elgin Settlement ... Wm King Robt Burns ... July 1860* (OOA Pamph 1860 (64)); shows cons 8–14, lots 6–12 of Raleigh Twp with lots of 50 acres each; houses shown on most lots, other bldgs keyed including Rev Wm King's house, mission church, school, Buxton P.O., mills, etc; main settlement at King St and Centre Rd; notes.
OOA (Pamph 1860 (64))

---

993 *1861*
Plan of the Two Creeks on Lake Erie. Surveyed and drawn by F.A. Wise. Sept 1861
Col ms 95 x 62 cm 1" to 500 ft Endorsements: stamp [BW] '310'
In Romney Twp south of Talbot Rd; shows the creeks, nature of the beach and shorelines, soundings in L Erie; trees, swampy areas; 'Moses Warner House.'
OOAMA (NMC 26679)

Related maps

(2) *1861*
[Same title] Surveyed in Sept 1861 by F.A. Wise [Sgd] John Page Chf Engr P. Works
Col ms 60 x 54 cm 1" to 400 ft Endorsements: stamp [BW] '519'
The plan shows the same information as above map; (Holmden 1890).
OTAR

---

994 *1861*
Plan Shewing the State of the Entrance into Rondeau Harbour Surveyed and drawn by Fred. A. Wise August 1861.
Col ms 59 x 84 cm 1" to 400 ft Endorsements: 'W Gibbard 1861'; stamp 'Hydrographic Office Decr 2 1862'
Shows sand shoal, pier, and soundings; there is also a very similar plan in OOAMA (RG 11M 86703/16 no 269) (Holmden 2592).
GBTAUh (D 6174.Aa3) OOAMA (NMC 96442)

---

995 *1862*
Plan of Point Pelee shewing the Reservations Required for Timber Preservation Light-house Keepers' Residence & containing 516 acres [Sgd] A.B. Perry P.L.S. Violet C.W. April 24th 1862.
Col ms 83 x 53 cm 1" to 20 chains Endorsements: 'In No 58430'
Light-keepers' houses, Indian graves, claims of occupants; descriptions of trees; bearings; also a photoreproduction in OOAMA (NMC 4313) of a plan on linen with same title but dated 24 Apr 1862 and endorsed '12224/66.'
OOAMA (NMC 4313) OTNR (SR 1912)

---

996 *1862*
PLAN / OF THE / MAPLE GROVE ESTATE / IN THE TOWNSHIP OF / DELAWARE / THE PROPERTY OF / DEAN TIFFANY ESQR. / Canada West / 1862 // The Property of Dean Tiffany Esqr, / ... March 8th 1862 / B. Springer P.L.S. / ... Surveyed and Drawn by / S. Peters / P.L.S. / LONDON. / Octr 1862. // Lith, by Phillips & Evans, London C.W.
Print (lith) 47 x 57 cm 1" to 5 chains
Notes on the size of the estate and bldgs as advertised for sale, about 270 acres '... Total value $41,000'; shows the house, orchard, garden, cattle sheds, sawmills, dwellings, deer park, sugar bush; note by S. Peters: 'I have frequently visited the Maple Grove Estate ... and have no hesitation in pronouncing it one of the best farms I have seen in Western Canada'; the property was on the Thames R near Delaware village; no registered plan was found; an interesting plan showing the layout of a farm estate in the 1860s.
OLU

---

997 *1862*
TREMAINES / MAP / OF THE / COUNTY OF MIDDLESEX / CANADA WEST. / COMPILED & DRAWN FROM ACTUAL SURVEYS / BY THE PUBLISHERS / Geo. R. & G.M. Tremaine. / 1862 / St Lawrence Buildings. / TORONTO C.W.
Print (lith) 131 x 187 cm 1" to 60 chains
Inset: 'Improved / COPPER PLATE / MAP OF / CANADA WEST / to / Accompany / TREMAINES' MAP / OF THE / County of Middlesex' approx 1" to 23 miles; the inset is derived from an edition of Maclear's map of Canada West (see **185(10)**); insets of towns:

'APPIN,' 'CARLISLE,' 'DELAWARE,' 'GLENCOE,' [Komoka], 'LONDON,' [Melbourne], 'NAIRN,' 'NAPIER,' 'NEWBURY,' 'STRATHROY,' 'WARDSVILLE'; 26 views of residences, public and commercial bldgs; explanation keys railways, gravel and common roads, post offices, school houses, churches, sawmills, steam sawmills, grist mills, and woollen mills; subscribers directories; names of owners and/or tenants; Mount Brydges spelled incorrectly on directory in copies held by OOAMA, OL, and OLU.
OL OLU OOAMA (NMC 19018) OTAR

---

998 *1863*
MAP / OF THE / TOWNSHIP OF LONDON, / Canada West. / CORRECTED FROM ACTUAL SURVEY, LITHOGRAPHED & PUBLISHED / By / SAML PETERS, P.L.S. & C.E. / 1863.
Print (lith) hand col 74 x 56 cm 1" to 50 chains
'Explanations' keys railways, gravel roads, bldgs, churches, school houses, school sections; names of landowners; many mills, churches, and other bldgs identified; wards; nos of school sections added in ms.
OLU

---

999 *1863*
Sketch shewing the position of the flowing wells at Enniskillen by Sandford Fleming Esqr Feby 29th 1863
Ms 18 x 22 cm Scale not given Watermark: 'JOYNSON'
Shows names of wells, test wells, wells first discovered, gum beds, boundary of oil area; Oil Springs village; (*OHIM* 5.10).
OTMCL

Related maps

(2) *[1863]*
Sketch shewing the position of the flowing Wells at Enniskillen. // W.C. Chewett & Co. Lith. Toronto
Print 18 x 22 cm 1" to 30 chains
In Sandford Fleming 'Notes on the Present Condition of the Oil Wells at Enniskillen,' *Canadian Journal* new series XLV (May 1863): 246–9 (OTMCL); based on ms plan above.
OTMCL

1000 *1864*
Plan of the Pointe aux Pins at the Rond'Eau Surveyed by Provincial Land Surveyor Henry Lawe under instructions from the Commissioner of Crown Lands, dated June the 27th 1864. [Sgd] Henry Lawe P.L.S. Dunnville Sepr 8th 1864
Col ms 52 x 37 xm 1" to 40 chains Endorsements: 'No 15'
(SI 17 June 1864 to subdivide land south of 'Rond'eau' into farm lots; OTNR FN 1693 6 Sept 1864); a detailed plan of the shoreline and marsh, with bearings and lots; 'Lac à la Pointe aux Pins.'
OTAR (SR 1983)

Related maps

(2) *[1864?]*
Plan of the Pointe aux Pins Township of Harwich Lake Erie Canada West H. Lawe [In pencil]: 'Henry Lawe PLS Dunnville Sept 8 1864'
Col ms 38 x 39 cm 1" to 40 chains
This may be an unfinished plan or a sketch for survey as the shoreline has a very rough shape and no survey grid is shown on the mainland; relief, swamp, and trees shown.
OTAR (SR 1984)

1001 *1864*
TREMAINE'S MAP / OF THE COUNTY OF / ELGIN / CANADA WEST, / Compiled and Drawn by / GEORGE R. TREMAINE. / PUBLISHED FOR THE SUBSCRIBERS ONLY / ST. THOMAS. / 1864. / Engraved and Printed at Tremaine's Map Establishment No 79 Front St. Toronto.
Print (lith) hand col 89 x 198 cm 1" to 60 chains
Endorsements: GBL accession stamp on GBL copy '20 Jy64'
Inset: 'MAP OF / UPPER CANADA. / to accompany / THE MAP OF THE COUNTY.'; insets of towns: 'AIREY or NEW GLASGOW,' 'AYLMER,' 'FINGAL,' 'IONA,' 'PORT BURWELL,' 'PORT STANLEY,' 'ST THOMAS,' 'SPARTA,' 'UNION,' 'VIENNA,' 'WALLACETOWN'; five views of public and commercial bldgs and residences; subscribers directory; names of owners and/or tenants; the inset map is from the same plate as the Maclear map (see **185(10)**; photoreproduction in OOAMA (NMC 15349).
GBL OTAR

1002 *[1864–5?]*
PLAN / OF THE / COUNTY OF LAMBTON, C.W. / Shewing the Principal / OIL SPRINGS. [imprint cut off?]
Print (lith) 64 x 62 cm Scale not given
Shows the survey grid, plank and other roads, railways, post offices, and oil wells (named); OMTCL copy has ms adds outlining several lots with notations about sales; the plan is at a larger scale than the Ellis maps (**1005**) and is not from the same plate; imprint deleted on OTMCL copy; since the map does not show the plank road from Sarnia to Oil Springs, the GWR through Bothwell, or the branch line to Oil Springs (authorized in 1863 and built 1866), it was probably made between 1864 and 1865; this may be 'Ellis' Pocket Map of the County of Lambton, the Principal Oil Bearing Districts' advertised in J.D. Edgar, *Manual for Oil Men* (Toronto: Rollo and Adam 1866).
OTMCL

1003 *[1865]*
GEOLOGICAL MAP / of / THE OIL REGIONS / IN / CANADA WEST, / by / HENRY WHITE, P.L.S. / Lithographed and Published by W.C. Chewett & Co / TORONTO.

Col print (lith) 58 x 55 cm 1" to 5 miles
Profile: 'Longitudinal sketch exhibiting at one view the various Geological Formations comprising the under strata of Canada West ...' In Henry White, *Geology, Oil Fields and Minerals of Canada West* (Toronto: W.C. Chewett and Co. 1865), at back; shows the area from Hay and Usborne twps south to St Thomas and west; geological formations; 'Anticlinals,' 'Synclinals,' 'Hamilton formation,' 'Corniferous formation,' 'Portage and Chemung formation'; survey grid, roads, and railways.
OTUTF

1004 *[1865]*
MAP / OF THE CANADA OIL DISTRICTS. / ENGRAVED FOR THIS WORK.
Print (wood engrav) 15 x 9 cm Scale not given
In [J.F. Tyrrell], *The Oil Districts of Canada* (New York 1865), frontis (*Bib Can* 6190); shows Lambton Co and part of Kent Co from Chatham to Orford; roads, schools, post offices.
OTMCL

1005 *1865*
MAP / OF THE / CANADA / OIL LANDS / Compiled from reliable sources / AND ENGRAVED BY JOHN ELLIS JR / TORONTO, / 1865. // Lithographed and Published by Jno Ellis, King Street, Toronto.
Print (lith) hand col 87 x 70 cm 1" to 200 chains
Inset: 'DIAGRAM / OF THE / HAMILTON AND HELDERBERG / Formations / COMPILED FROM THE / GEOLOGICAL REPORTS OF SIR W.E. LOGAN' approx 1" to 22 miles; 'Explanations' at upper left: twp boundaries, plank roads, travelled roads, railways, schools, churches, post offices, town halls, stations; notes: 'Oil Region of Canada its Geological Features, Deduced from Sir W.E. Logan's Reports'; shows Lambton, Kent, part of Middlesex, and Elgin cos.
OTMCL

Later editions and states

(2) *1865*
[Same title and imprint]
Cover title (OTUTF): 'OIL LANDS / OF / CANADA'; cover-title (OTAR): 'CANADA OIL LANDS'; inset added: 'ENLARGED / PLAN OF / BOTHWELL' 1" to 50 chains; 'Explanations' has been moved to upper right; OTAR copy printed on linen; (Gagnon, I:4445).
OTAR OTUTF

(3) *1866*
[Date in title changed to 1866]
Print (lith) on linen, hand col 86 x 71 cm
From the same plate but title and note moved and imprint reengraved leaving a gap between 'Ellis,' and 'King Street'; inset of [Enniskillen Twp] showing oil wells added; 'Diagram of Hamilton ...' has been redrawn; decorative border and legend removed; street layout of Bothwell added to inset; the rest of London Twp has been added on the right and London redrawn in more detail; this or one of the earlier editions is probably the map advertised as 'Ellis Complete Map of the Canada Oil Lands' in J.D. Edgar, *Manual for Oil Men* (1866); (*Bib Can* 6213).
OTUTF

1006 *1865*
MAP / OF THE / OIL REGIONS, / IN THE VICINITY OF / BOTHWELL, / C.W. / December, 1865. / / UNWIN & DYAS, P.L. SURVEYORS, BOTHWELL. // W.C. CHEWETT & CO. LITH. TORONTO. // McMILLAN'S MAP
Print (lith) 30 x 52 cm 1" to 60 chains
'Price 50 cents'; view of oil well; shows the area from Thamesville to Wardsville on either side of the Thames R; names of owners of lots; wells.
OLU

Related maps

(2) *1866*
MAP / OF THE / OIL REGIONS, / IN THE VICINITY OF / BOTHWELL, / C.W. / MAY, 1866. // Murdock Hanning Peterson & Brodie Civil Engineers & P.L. Surveyors, Oak Street Bothwell C.W. // W.C. Chewett & Co. Lith. TORONTO // McMILLAN'S NEW MAP FOR MAY, 1866
Print (lith) 43 x 69 cm 1" to 50 chains
Similar to 1865 map but not from the same plate; shows a larger area to the south including parts of Orford, Zone, Aldborough, Euphemia, and Mosa twps; includes a different drawing of oil rig and station; more names of owners are shown and the Indian reserve is subdivided; more wells are shown; OOAMA copy endorsed 'Map To the Editor of the Telegraph, Montreal C.W.'
OOAMA (NMC 21479)

1007 *1865*
Map of the / Petroleum District / OF CANADA WEST. / Compiled by John Kennedy C.E. / 1865. / Montreal, C.E.
Print (lith) 58 x 43 cm 1" to 1 1/2 miles
Shows Plympton Twp to Dawn, Zone, Orford, and Aldborough Twp, and Mosa to Warwick Twp; survey grid, roads, and railways; some lots are hand-coloured.
QMMMCM

1008 *[1865?]*
OIL REGIONS IN CANADA WEST. Compiled by J.P. Donnelly. // Schönberg Co, New York.
Print (lith) hand col 57 x 62 cm 1" to 1 1/2 miles
Shows Lambton Co and Zone Twp with Bothwell Station; survey grid, many towns and villages; roads, oil wells; notes on location of oil on the surface and presence of 'gumbeds'; shows proposed and surveyed branch line of the Great Western (Canada) railway to Oil Springs (built in 1866); plank road from Oil Springs to Port Sarnia.
OOAMA (NMC 24030) OTAR

1009 *1865*
PLAN / OF PROPERTY BELONGING TO THE / BOTHWELL / LAND & PETROLEUM CO. (LIMITED) / Shewing Portions for Sale by Auction / ON THE 23RD NOVEMBER 1865. // Surveyed by Provl Land Surveyors Albert Pellew Salter. Peters & Niven and Unwin & Dyas // Lith. Spectator Office, Hamilton. J.D. Evans P.L.S. DELT.
Print (lith) 51 x 69 cm 1" to 10 chains
Shows subdivision of part of lots 10–21 south of Longwoods Rd, and lots 1–17 north of Longwoods Rd, Zone Twp; shows Bothwell from GWR to Walnut St, and Catharine St to Peter St; names of landowners, oil wells.
OTAR

1010 *[ca 1865]*
PLAN / OF THE / ELGIN SETTLEMENT / IN THE / TOWNSHIP OF RALEIGH / COUNTY OF KENT / CANADA WEST / Forster and Co. Lith: Dublin
Print (lith) with ms adds 83 x 55 cm Scale not given
References to public bldgs; names given in lots in ms with sums of money still owing and some noted as paid; 'Settlement ... containing about 200 families ... about 1000 Souls'; probably earlier than plan below.
OOAMA (NMC 26689)

Later editions and states

(2) *[1866?]*
PLAN / OF THE / ELGIN SETTLEMENT / IN THE / TOWNSHIP OF RALEIGH, / COUNTY OF KENT, / CANADA WEST. // J.S. WILSON LITHR 28 ANN ST BIRMN
Print (lith) 71 x 47 cm Scale not given
In A.M. Harris, *A Sketch of the Buxton Mission and Elgin Settlement, Raleigh, Canada West* (Birmingham: J.S. Wilson [1866?]), at back (*Bib Can* 9455; Casey I–3368); note: 'The Elgin Association was incorporated by Act of Parliament 10th August 1850 for the Social and Moral Improvement of the Colored Population of Canada'; shows Rev King's house, church, post office, school, store, mills, shops, etc; shows farm lots of 50 acres each with houses; drawings of houses on lots, treed areas; con roads are named; 'Settlement ... containing about 250 families embracing about 1200 Souls'; shows village of [Buxton]; dates in text indicate plan is probably 1866.
OOA OTAR OTMCL

1011 *1865–6*
ELLIS' NEW MAP / OF THE CANADA OIL LANDS / Pocket Edition / 1865 // J. ELLIS LITHR. TORONTO.
Print (lith) 60 x 43 cm 1" to 200 chains
Cover-title: '[Title as on map ...] 1866. Lithographed by J. Ellis, Toronto.'; [on back of cover]: 'MAP OF THE / CANADA OIL LANDS / DRAWN & COMPILED BY / John Ellis Jr. / Toronto.'; from the same plate as the 1865 and 1866 maps (**1005**) but covers only Lambton Co and the north part of Kent Co; survey grid, railways named; many oil wells at Bothwell, Oil Springs, and Petrolia, schools, churches, roads named; OTAR copy endorsed 'J.C. Tarbutt' inside cover; (*OHIM* 5.11).
OTAR OTUTF

1012 *1866*
DYAS & BAIKIE'S / MAP OF THE / OIL REGION / IN THE VICINITY OF / TILSONBURG / C.W. / WITH A SKETCH SHOWING THE TILSONBURG ANTICLINAL. / UNWIN, DYAS, FORNERI & BAIKIE, / Provincial Land Surveyors, / Tilsonburg, C.W. / (Office over Post Office.) // March, 29th, 1866. // W.C. CHEWETT & CO. LITH. TORONTO
Print (lith) 53 x 85 cm Scale not given
Inset: 'SKETCH / of part of / CANADA WEST, / showing the position / of the / OIL DISTRICT OF TILSONBURG, / AND THE / TILSONBURG ANTICLINAL' 1" to 60 chains; shows twps of Dereham, S Norwich, Bayham, Middleton and the north part of Walsingham; rivers with relief along shores; roads; several wells marked around Tillsonburg; inset shows geological formations; 'Offices at Bothwell, Toronto, Delaware & Glencoe.'
OLU

1013 *[1866?]*
ELLIS' NEW MAP OF / ENNISKILLEN.
Print (lith) 38 x 25 cm 1" to 100 chains
From the same plate as the inset on **1005(2)** with the addition of more of Dawn Twp and a scale bar; survey grid, oil wells, a few names of companies such as 'Crescent Petroleum Association'; bldgs identified in Petrolia and Oil Springs; this is probably the map of Enniskillen advertised in J.D. Edgar, *Manual for Oil Men* (Toronto 1866).
OTUTF

1014 *[1866]*
MAP OF THE / CANADA OIL LANDS, / DRAWN & COMPILED BY / John Ellis Jr / Toronto.
Print (lith) 28 x 44 cm Scale not given
Inset: 'Map of the / TOWNSHIP OF LONDON.'; in J.D. Edgar, *Manual for Oil Men ... (With a New and Correct Map of the Oil Districts, by J. Ellis, Junr.* (Toronto: Rollo and Adam 1866), frontis (*Bib Can* 6213); from the same plate as **1005(2)** but only shows the area from Sarnia to Wardsville on the Thames R, and south to Dresden.
OTMCL

1015 *[1866]*
PLAN / OF PART OF THE / BENNETT FARM, / being Lot 24, Con. XV, / TOWNSHIP OF ORFORD, / KENT. / Unwin & Dyas, P.L. SURVEYORS, / BOTHWELL, C.W. // W.C. CHEWETT & CO. LITH. TORONTO.
Print (lith) 39 x 44 cm 1" to 3 chains

A subdivision plan certified 8 Jan 1866, registered 22 Feb 1866; shows lot nos, dimensions and sizes, relief, and 'Lester Well Tanks.'
Kent 24 (R.P. 169)

1016 *[1866]*
PLAN / OF THE SWALWELL FARM / being Lot No 17, River Range, / TOWNSHIP OF ZONE, / KENT. / Unwin & Dyas, / P.L. Surveyors &c. / BOTHWELL, C.W. // W.C. CHEWETT & CO. LITH. TORONTO
Print (lith) 52 x 59 cm 1" to 4 chains
Inset: 'SKETCH / Shewing the Position / OF THE / SWALWELL FARM.'; a subdivision plan certified 20 Nov 1866 and registered 24 Nov 1866; shows property of Messrs Williams, Wells, and Conro, G. Pope, and Adrian Oil Co.; relief, oil wells identified; inset shows other wells in surrounding areas.
Kent 24 (R.P. 161)

West

1017 *[1795]*
Plan for setting apart one Seventh of Land for the Crown equal to one Seventh set apart for the Protestant Clergy, of Eighteen Townships in the County of Lincoln, containing about 71,680 Acres.
Col ms Approx 27 x 44 cm 1" to 10 miles
In 'Report on the Reserved Lands Upper Canada,' 17, enclosed in D.W. Smith to Lt Gov Simcoe 9 Nov 1795 (OTAR Simcoe Papers env 44 ms 517 reel 8); shows the crown block laid out north of Blandford and Blenheim twps and the clergy block laid out north of Beverly and Flamborough twps; shows the area south to the town of 'Oxford' and Dundas St; the area was set aside as compensation for lack of reserves in the co of Lincoln; a copy of the map was enclosed in Lt Gov Simcoe's no 34 to the Duke of Portland 22 Dec 1795 (GBLpro CO 42/320 p 74); (*OHIM* 413).
GBLpro (CO 42/320 p 74) OTAR (Simcoe Papers MS 517 reel 8)

Related maps

(2) *[1795]*
Plan for setting apart one Seventh of Land, for the Protestant Clergy of 18 Townships in the County of Lincoln, containing about 71,680 acres.
Col ms Approx 44 x 27 cm 1" to 5 miles
Appeared as p 16 of the 'Report on the Reserved Lands...' cited above and a copy was also included in Simcoe's no 34 to Portland as cited above; shows clergy reserve at a larger scale than above and is divided into parts, each named for a twp in Lincoln Co; number of acres indicated.
GBLpro (CO 42/320 p 74) OTAR (Simcoe Papers)

1018 *[ca 1810]*
A Map of the Townships of Waterloo and Wolwich [*sic*] U.C.
Ms Size not known Scale not given
Shows lots in the north part of Waterloo Twp numbered 1–284 and those in Woolwich Twp numbered 1–130; names shown in all lots; the area that became Waterloo Twp was conveyed to the German Co. in 1805 and most of 'Woolwich' was conveyed to them in 1807 (Johnston, lx–lxi); photoreproduction in OTAR.
Private Collection

1019 *1819*
(Copy) Plan of Part of the River aux Sables (Signed) H.H. Willson Lieut. Royal Engrs 25th Sepr 1819 Commanding Royal Engineers Office – Quebec Nov. 11 1819.
Col ms 51 x 79 cm 1" to 2000 ft Watermark: 'JOHN HAYES 1814'
Lt Willson's report of 27 Sept 1819 is found in OOA RG 8 1B/1916; shows the river at its mouth at the lower end of L Huron and a short way upstream with soundings and wooded areas along shore; (Holmden 1137).
OOAMA (NMC 21793)

1020 *[1820]*
[Sketch showing the crown reserves for the Six Nations Indians and for the County of Lincoln]
Ms 30 x 45 cm Scale not given
Sketch 'D' accompanying 'Memorandum-Lands Proposed to be Sold to Defray the Annual Charge of Presents to the Indians ... Re Despatch No. 39 of 26th May 1819' in Lt Gov Maitland to Earl Bathurst 8 March 1820 (GBLpro CO 42/365 p 87); shows the two blocks of land proposed for sale in the District of Gore, which later became Guelph and Wilmot twps; also shows Waterloo, Woolwich, and Nichol twps, and the clergy reserves for the Six Nations Indians for Lincoln Co.
GBLpro (CO 42/365 p 87)

1021 *[1820?]*
[Township of Waterloo]
Col ms 58 x 69 cm 1" to 60 chains
Shows Bechtel's, Biehn's, and Beasley's tracts, names of owners, roads.
OKITD

1022 *[1824]*
Map to accompany Dr BIGSBY'S PAPER ON the Geography and Geology of LAKE HURON. // J.J. Bigsby del. // B.R. Baker Lithog. // C. Hullmandel's Lithography. // Transactions of the Geological Society 2d Series Vol I Pl XXXI.
Print (lith) 39 x 44 cm Scale not given Watermark (OTMCL copy): 'FELLOWS & SONS 1821'
In John Bigsby, *Notes on the Geography and Geology of Lake Huron* (London: Printed by Richard Taylor 1824), at end (*Bib Can* 1275); an outline map of L Huron with names of islands; a note on p 177 of the text indicates the source: 'The accompanying map is a reduced copy with additons of one four times this size compiled by David Thompson Esq. British Astronomer under the 6th and 7th articles of the Treaty of Ghent from surveys made by himself and by Captain Owen R.N. from a map of the lake by Mr. Smith late Surveyor General of Canada.'
GBLrgs OTMCL

1023 *1826*
Sketch shewing a situation in the London District in the rear of Zorra containing about 49,786 Acres, exclusive of Reserves for Crown & Clergy J.G.C. [Sgd] Surveyor Genls Office York 8 March 1826 Thos Ridout S.G.
Col ms 15 x 12 cm Scale not given
Originally accompanied land petition from the Board for the General Superintendent of Education to reserve some new twps for school revenue (OOA RG 1 L3 E14 no 50 1826) and shows an area proposed for survey.
OOAMA

1024 *[ca 1827]*
[Plan of the mouth and part of the Maitland River]
Col ms in 3 pieces 53 x 59 cm Scale not given
An untitled survey showing the islands, low land, and a sand-bar near the mouth of the river; possibly done by or at the time of Mahlon Burwell's survey in 1827.
OTMCL (E.W. Banting Collection)

1025 *1827*
[Endorsed title]: Road from Beverly to Guelph: Copied from Mr M. Burwell's Plan of Survey. Guelph 17th Sepr 1827 W.C. 6th Octr 1827.
Ms 70 x 37 cm 1" to 40 chains Endorsements: '784'
(SI 10 July 1827 to survey road from E and W Flamborough twps to strike road line of the Canada Co.); shows the exploration line for a road from rear of E and W Flamborough twps and Beverly Twp north to the south boundary of Guelph Twp; notes on land and relief; shows Aboukir Rd.
OTAR (SR 5815)

Related maps

(2) *1828*
Plan of the line of Road through the Southern Block of Clergy Reserves in the District of Gore Surveyed in April 1828 by [Sgd] David Gibson Dpy Surveyor.
Col ms 59 x 32 cm 1" to 40 chains Endorsements: '786' 'Y23'
(SI to David Gibson to continue where Burwell left off; OTNR FN 592); shows the same area as Burwell's map but the actual road line has been surveyed and is shown deviating around swamps and obstructions.
OTAR (SR 5827)

(3) *1828*
Plan of the Line of Road through the Southern Block of Clergy Reserves in the District of Gore copy from the Plan of Survey made in April 1828 by David Gibson Depy Surveyor W Chewett 1828 Surveyr Genl Office York 18 May 1828 [Sgd] Thos Ridout S Genl.
Col ms 60 x 33 cm 1" to 40 chains Endorsements: 'Y27' '761'
A projected plan for a further survey of the same road to lay out lots along the road and lines to be run east and west of it; 'Plan to be returned ... [Sgd] T. Ridout.'
OTAR (SR 1929)

1026 *1827*
The Tract purchased by [Government from] the Chippewa Indians in the London & Western Districts in the year 1825 in which the Canada Co[mpany's purchase of] the 1000000 of acres is bordered with red. [Sgd] John McDonald Dy Surveyor Guelph 15th December 1827.
Col ms, pt missing 63 x 105 cm 1" to 4 miles
Endorsements: '1162'
Shows the results of the 1827 survey; shows the area from Toronto Twp west to L Huron with the boundaries of the purchase, twps laid out including Guelph Twp, and the outlines of twps west of this to Wilmot, Woolwich, and Nichol; McDonald's route for the York Rd and three proposed routes for road from Guelph to L Huron; routes of earlier exploration under Wm Dunlop; 'Proof Line,' 'Purchase Line,' and Bridle Rd as surveyed by Burwell and McDonald in 1827; the first of several general maps of the Huron Tract by John McDonald, this one a draft before his road survey of 1828; also a plan in OTAR (Canada Co. Paper Minutes of the Court of Directors 17 Dec 1827) showing the boundaries of the Huron Tract and other lands south and north purchased from the Indians with accompanying descriptions.
OTAR (SR 6959)

1027 *1828*
Map of the T[own]ship of Guelph [Sgd] [J W] McDonald [missing] Surveyor Guelph [missing] 1828.
Col ms, pt missing 97 x 98 cm 1" to 20 chains
Endorsements: 'Exhibit F ... 21 May 1853'; stamp [Canada Co. Coat of Arms] 'No 3'
Notes indicate that survey was commenced by George Tiffany and finished by McDonald 'according to a Diagram which was furnished me' and that a number of lots in Division D and G were to be altered on ground: 'See the former map of 1827' and 'J.W.D. Contents – 42338 acres'; shows roads from Waterloo to Eramosa, roads to York and Woolwich; town plot of Guelph shows Woolwich, Quebec, McDonell, Market, and Waterloo sts with park lots on west; also a rough tracing of this map in OTAR (Canada Co. Maps pkg 5 no 61) entitled 'Map Guelph Township J.C.W. Daly 1831' with watermark '1827' and names of owners in most lots; the 1827 map has not been found.
OTAR OTAR (Canada Co Maps Pkg 5 no 61)

Related maps

(2) *[1828?]*
Map of the Township of Guelph as altered to the different divisions at the request of Mr Thomas [Lount?]
Col ms 84 x 98 cm 1" to 20 chains Watermark: '1820'

Shows names of owners, road from Waterloo, and road to Eramosa; Woolwich, Quebec, McDonell, Market and Waterloo sts are shown in the town but the rest is blank and possibly unfinished; in John McDonald's hand and similar to map above.
OTMCL (E.W. Banting Collection)

1028 *1828 Jan–May*
Map of the Tract of Land purchased by Government from the Chippewa Indians in the year 1825 in the London and Western Districts: Upon which is [kno]wn from actual Survey, the Northern Boundary of the Purchase, the shore of Lake Huron a line for a road [from] Guelph towards Burlington Bay, and the rivers, brooks, rills and swamps as found on an exploring expedition for the Canada Company. By Orders from the Surveyor Generals Office, bearing date at York, the 6th July, the 10th July, and the 31st August 1827. To which is added with great submission, a line, in the neighbourhood of which it is believed a Canal may be made to connect the waters of Lake Huron, with those of Lake Ontario. by [Sgd] M. Burwell Dy Surveyor York 7th January 1828.
Col ms 65 x 100 cm 1" to 4 miles Endorsements: '1164'
(OTNR FN 776 17 May 1828); shows the tract from the north boundary of Sombra Twp, east to Guelph and north; also includes Guelph block east to L Ontario and south to Grand R; shows line for a road from Guelph to L Huron, various proof lines with notes and a proposed canal route from Menestunk R through Guelph to L Ontario; other maps from M. Burwell's part of the 1827 survey are listed below.
OTAR (SR 6943)

Related maps

(**2**) *1828*
[Endorsed title]: 'Road in Southern Block Clergy Reserve marked clergy for Lincoln County' Deputy Surveyor's Office Port Talbot 17th May 1828. [Sgd] M Burwell Dy Surveyor.
Col ms 66 x 85 cm 1" to 40 chains Endorsements: 'No I.' '1166'
(OTNR FN 588); shows the twps north of Guelph to Garafraxa and the survey of a line for [Aboukir] road; other road lines, purchase line; there is also a similar map sgd by T. Ridout of 10 May 1828 endorsed 'Y-27' in OTAR (SR 1929).
OTAR (SR 5991; 1929)

(**3**) *1828*
Map Parts of the Purchase Line, Proof Line, Shore of the Lake and River Menestunk. Deputy Surveyor's Office, Port Talbot, 17th May 1828 [Sgd] M Burwell Dy Surveyor.
Col ms 56 x 86 cm 1" to 40 chains Endorsements: 'No III' '1169'
Shows the proof line from the rear of Wilmot Twp to L Huron and the purchase line to the north with mileages; notes on the proper location of the latter; traverses along shore of L Huron and mill seat noted; the proof line was noted as the one 'to correspond with the Provisional Agreement of 26th April 1825.'
OTNR (SR 2423)

(**4**) *1828*
[Traverse of part of the shore of Lake Huron] Deputy Surveyors Office, Port Talbot 17th May 1828 [Sgd] M. Burwell Dy Surveyor.
Col ms 55 x 85 cm 1" to 40 chains Endorsements: 'No IV' '1171'
Shows the shore from Ausable R to station 39 at Goderich.
OTAR (SR 7116b)

(**5**) *1828*
Proof Line as Surveyed for the Canada-Company in 1827. Deputy Surveyor's Office, Port Talbot 17th May 1828. [Sgd] M Burwell Dy Surveyor.
Col ms 57 x 86 cm 1" to 40 chains Endorsements: 'No V' '1170'
(OTNR FN 744 20 March 1828); shows only the surveyed line with indication of swamps and terrain, 'Chippewa Indian deer fence.'
OTAR (SR 5894)

1029 *[1828] [Sept?]*
A Map of the River, Aux Sables in the London & Western Districts, Granted to the Canada Company, Surveyed by order of John Galt Esqr [Sgd] Samuel Smith Dy Surveyor.
Col ms 129 x 73 cm Scale not given Endorsements: OTMCL: 'In Chancery Brewster v. The Canada Company Exhibit No 5 ... 21 July 1853.'
Shows the area from Lobo Twp to the mouth of the river in L Huron; lines run by Rosewell Mount, Mahlon Burwell, and Asa Townshend with mileages; mill sites, marshes, Indian paths, and settlements; the FN books for Smith's survey of the river are dated 29 July 1828 and 21 Sept 1828 (OTAR Canada Co. Records ms 564).
OTMCL (E.W. Banting Collection)

1030 *1828 Dec*
Draft of the Huron Tract belonging to the Canada Company shewing the Communication Road from Guelph to Goderich Harbour opened through the Tract by the Company in the summer of 1828 and proposed by Mr Galt as the Base of two Tier of Townships [Sgd] John McDonald Dy Surveyor Guelph 10th December 1828.
Col ms 41 x 64 cm 1" to 4 miles Watermark: '1820'
Shows the area from Guelph to L Huron and the survey of the southern route for a road as shown on McDonald's 1827 map (**1026**) with some changes in Waterloo and Wilmot; 'tavern places marked at the request of Mr Galt'; twps in the tract are outlined and named after Canada Co. directors, e.g., Horton Twp (later Colborne); note about amount of land in Wilmot Twp sgd 'JGC 20th Dec 1828'; the Canada Co. coat of arms has been stamped above the title; (Holmden 1723).
OOAMA (NMC 3301)

Related maps

(2) *1828 Dec*
[Same title as (1)] (Signed) John McDonald Dy Surveyor Guelph 10th December 1828 Copy [Sgd] J G Chewett 20th Decr 1828.
Col ms 44 x 63 cm 1" to 4 miles Endorsements: '1167'
A copy of and very similar to (1) with the addition of 'taverns to be' marked along the road.
OTAR (SR 6580)

1031 *1829*
Draft of the Huron Tract belonging to the Canada Company Showing The Communication Road from Goderich by Wilmot with the Tier of Lots on each side thereof And the Line of Road communicating therefrom to the Talbot Settlement, together with a tier of Lots in like manner on each side and a proposed arrangement of the Townships by which almost all abut on these two Roads. Copy for the Surveyor General's Office per order of the C C Commissioners by [Sgd] John McDonald Dy Surveyor Canada Company's Office York 16th December 1829.
Ms 44 x 50 cm 1" to 4 miles
(SI 29 Dec 1828 to lay out lots along road from Wilmot to Goderich; OTNR FN 762 9 March 1829); the twps are named but not as yet laid out; Indian reserves; shows the road lots along road to Goderich and along road to 'town' [London] from east end of Goderich Twp; tavern places marked; Horton now named Colborne Twp; (*OHIM* 4.19).
OTAR (SR 4750)

1032 *1829–31*
Draft Shewing the Townships based on the Huron Road and also The Range of Lots laid out on both sides thereof from the Township of Wilmot to the Township of Goderich agreeable to the Order of John Galt Esquire Superintendant for the Canada Company under instructions from The Honble Thomas Ridout Sury General by John McDonald Dept. Surveyor Guelph 28th February 1829. Additional Survey IInd & IIIrd Concessions Northerly & Southerly of the above Road between the above Townships of Wilmot & Goderich Executed in the Summer of 1830 per order of the Canada Company Commissioners by John McDonald Dy Surveyor. Surveyor Generals Office York 12th February 1831 [Sgd] John McDonald Dy Surveyor.
Col ms 61 x 240 cm 1" to 40 chains Endorsements: 'No 20' '1138'
(OTNR FN 762–3 12 Feb 1831); shows survey data along road, part presently opened, and notes on the intention to keep deviations to a minimum; taverns, mills, mill sites, connecting roads; shows proposed town plots along road, which were never laid out: 'Friern Barnett,' 'Appin,' 'Howich,' 'Alipore,' 'Balangeigh,' and 'Ross'; sold lands indicated.
OTNR (SR 6576)

Related maps

(2) *1830–1*
Road Line from the Township of London to the Township of Goderich with the Tier of Lots laid out per fronts on both sides. [Sgd] John McDonald Dy Surveyor Canada Company's Office York 2nd March 1830 Additional Survey IInd & IIIrd Concessions Easterly & Westerly of the above Road Line between the above Townships of London & Goderich Executed in the Summer of 1830 per order of The Canada Company Commissioners by John McDonald Dy Surveyor. Surveyor Generals Office York 12th Feby 1831 [Sgd] John McDonald Dy Surveyor.
Col ms 40 x 190 cm 1" to 40 chains Endorsements: 'No 20' '1136' 'For the Surveyor Generals Office by order of the Commissioners'
(OTNR FN 756 10 Sept 1830); shows the 'London Road' line from the twp of London going north between McGillivray and Biddulph twps to Goderich Twp; survey posts, bearings.
OTNR (SR 6614)

(3) *[1831?]*
[Plan of the Huron Tract showing the two communication roads]
Ms 103 x 54 cm Scale not given
An untitled fragment in John McDonald's hand showing lot nos, rivers, etc.
OTMCL (E.W. Banting Collection)

1033 *[ca 1830?]*
TOWNSHIP OF GODERICH. / Huron Tract. // C. Ingrey, lithog. 310, Strand.
Print (lith) 28 x 17 cm Scale not given
Found in one OTAR copy of *Diagrams of the Townships in Upper Canada* (see **77(3)**); shows survey grid and reserve for town; contents of lots listed with ms note indicating plan is from Gibson's survey of 1828–9 'vide Report of David Gibson 1829.'
OTAR (Canada Co. Records A-4-3 vol 3)

1034 *[ca 1830?]*
TOWNSHIP of GUELPH. / Gore District. // C. Ingrey, Lithog. 310, Strand.
Print (lith) 41 x 29 cm Scale not given
Shows the survey grid, the town as laid out west of river, and town reserve; rivers; main roads; found in one OTAR copy of *Diagrams of the Townships in Upper Canada* (see **77(3)**); also a copy in OTAR with imprint trimmed and ms adds: 'Contents 42,338 acres of which there remains for sale 30th January 1832 17,000 acres' sgd 'J W McDonald'; sold(?) lots indicated by shading.
OTAR (Canada Co. Records A-4-3 vol 4)

1035 *1832*
Huron Tract / belonging to the / CANADA COMPANY // Printed for the use of Emigrants // Tazewell lith. Kingston U.C. 1832.
Print (lith) hand col 21 x 27 cm 1" to 12.5 miles

Shows the twps, road connections, Goderich, and swampy lands in the northern parts of Logan and Ellice twps; crown land and Indian territory are shown to the north; (Holmden 1720).
OOAMA (NMC 2860)

1036 *1834*
Plan of the Survey of the Northern Boundary of the Canada Company's Huron Tract in the London District. Taken pursuant to Instructions from the Surveyor General's office bearing date at Toronto 12th Aug. 1834 [Sgd] Rich Birdsall D Surveyr [Sgd] William Hawkins D Surveyor [Sgd] Samuel P Hurd Esqr Surveyor General.
Col ms 73 x 129 cm 1" to 100 chains Endorsements: 'No I' '1133'
(OTNR FN 766 25 Nov 1834); shows the 'Huron Road' to Goderich and the 'Proof Line' (the northern boundary of twps from Colborne to North Easthope); a recommended location for a town plot north of Goderich is shown in [Ashfield] Twp.
OTAR (SR 5867)

Related maps

(2) *[1834]*
Plan of the Survey of the Northern Boundary of the Canada Company's Huron Tract in the London District Shewing also the Unsurveyed Lands North of it, together with a proposed Road through the same, and a new method of laying out Townships thereon [Sgd] Richd Birdsall DyS. William Hawkins D.S.
Col ms 76 x 132 cm 1" to 100 chains Endorsements: 'No 2' '1135'
(OTAR FN 765, 767 26 Nov 1834); this is similar to above map except it shows more area to the north, with a proposed road from the corner of Woolwich and Wilmot twps to L Huron at the point recommended for a town plot north of Goderich [Port Albert]; land to the north of the line is shown with another twp and a further boundary line; 'Proposed Method of Laying out Townships' [the 1000-acre sectional system] (see Weaver, 16) is shown north and south of new proposed road.
OTAR (SR 5881)

1037 *1834*
Sketch of the Fishing islands above the Saugink River called the [blank] Islands about ninty mills [*sic*] north of Goderich. [Sgd] David Smith 5th Feby 1834.
Ms 38 x 31 cm 1" to 2 miles
The islands are numbered; 'Brocks camp' and 'Chife Point' are shown on shore.
OTAR

1038 *1834*
[Sketch of the northern boundary of the Canada Co.'s Huron Tract, and land to the north] Survey Generals Office Toronto 29th Novr 1834 [Sgd] J.G. Chewett S.P. Hurd S.G.
Ms 52 x 30 cm 1" to 8 miles
Enclosed in a letter from R. Birdsall and W. Hawkins to S.P. Hurd 21 Nov 1834 and further enclosed with Colborne's no 72, 2 Dec 1834 (GBLpro CO 42/423 p 228); shows the block north of the boundary as 3,418,579 acres 'subject to the Clergy Seventh'; shows surrendered and unsurrendered Indian lands and twps from Luther to Zero [St Vincent].
GBLpro (CO 42/423 p 228)

1039 *[1836?]*
Map of the Huron Tract. Drawn by D. McDonald.
Col ms 72 x 128 cm Scale not given Endorsements: stamps 'BW' '520'
Shows twps laid out as follows: Bosanquet, Williams, Stanley, Tuckersmith, Goderich, Colborne, Easthope, South Easthope, and Guelph; lots shown along Huron Rd, London Rd, and Lake Rd; shows the towns of Guelph, Stratford, Goderich, and Bayfield; other twps not laid out or part laid out along road lines; probably made after the survey of most of the twps in 1835 and before Biddulph was surveyed in March 1836.
OOAMA (NMC 11243)

1040 *1837*
Plan of a Line for Road from Owen Sound to Garafraxa and propsd thence to Oakville [Sgd] C. Rankin D.S. Toronto 13th Novb 1837.
Ms 132 x 74 cm 1" to 2 miles Endorsements: '831'
(SI 28 Apr 1837 to explore line for a road from Oakville to Owen Sound to run west of Luther and Artemisia twps; OTNR FN 754 [1837] RG 1 CB-1 box 29); shows the whole route (61 miles) from Garafraxa to Owen Sound and a proposed line for continuation to Oakville; relief, comments on the land, swamps; surveyed and unsurveyed twps shown; the first general plan for the Garafraxa or Owen Sound Rd.
OTAR (SR 6557)

Related maps

(2) *[1837]*
Plan of the Road from Owen's Sound to Garafraxa [Sgd] C. Rankin D.S.
3 ms maps Ea 74 x 53 cm 1" to 20 chains
Endorsements: [1] 'Y42a' '820'; [2] 'Y42b' '821'; [3] 'Y42c' '823'
Shows the road line in detail from Owen Sound to 53-mile point; relief, comments on land, mill sites.
OTAR (SR 7219; 7220; 7221)

(3) *1840*
Diagram for Survey at Owen's Sound on the line of Road from Garrafraxa Surveyor General's Office Toronto 8th July 1840 [Sgd] J.G. Chewett R.B. Sullivan Surv Genl.
Col ms, pt missing 60 x 51 cm 1" to 50 chains
(SI 6 July 1840 J. McDonald to lay out lots on road line); the projection for the survey showing the north end with town reserve and several cons laid

out on both sides of road in [Derby] and [Sullivan] twps.
OTAR

(4) *1841*
Sketch showing the position nearly of the Line of Road from the Township of Garrafraxa to Owen's Sound and the manner in which the lots are laid out on both sides thereof Kingston 28th October 1841 [Sgd] John McDonald Dy Surveyor.
Col ms 96 x 53 cm 1" to 2 miles Endorsements: 'Y40' '1860'
Also shows good mill and village sites, reserves, etc; also a copy with the same title and note 'Copied by [Sgd] Andrew Russell Surveyor General's Office Kingston 17th November 1841 A true copy [Sgd] Thomas Parke Survr Genl' 42 x 87 cm (SR 6653).
OTAR (SR 6653; 7212)

(5) *1842*
Plan of the Owens Sound Road and Tier of Lots on both sides thereof from the Township of Sydenham to the Township of Arthur [Sgd] John McDonald Dy P. Surveyor Goderich 21st June 1842.
Col ms 220 x 37 cm 1" to 40 chains Endorsements: 'No 44' 'Office Copy'
(OTNR FN 755); a more detailed plan of the road and road lots; swamps, good mill and village sites; names of patentees; also a similar map in OTNR (SR 6565), but without names and a few different notes, with same title but dated '2nd July 1842' (188 x 40 cm, endorsed '683').
OTAR(P) OTNR (SR 6565)

(6) *[1842?]*
Diagram shewing the Continuation of the Road to Owens Sound
Col ms 77 x 54 cm 1" to 40 chains
A fragment of a road survey through a twp showing road lots 1–107; location not identified.
OTAR (SR 6616)

(7) *1846*
Diagram of the proposed Road from Garrafraxa to Owen Sound [Sgd] J.G. Chewitt S.G. Office July 8 1846.
Col ms, top pt missing
A fragment showing Garafraxa Twp and part of another twp, possibly meant to show the continuation of the road south through Garafraxa Twp.
OTAR

(8) *[ca 1846?]*
Sketch of the Road from Dundas to Owen's Sound. 107 1/2 miles. Copied from Plan in the Surr General's Office.
Col ms 119 x 73 cm 1" to 200 chains Watermark: 'J WHATMAN TURKEY MILL ... 1843'
Endorsements: stamp '440'
Shows sections of road open and travelled, sections in poor condition (Arthur Twp), and those expensive to build (north of Arthur); 'Dundas to Arthur opened and travelled'; area south of Owen Sound opened by Telfer; shows other lines of roads and connecting roads; Hawkins line of road from Saugeen to Toronto.
OOAMA (NMC 16831)

1041 *1837*
Plan shewing the Lands purchased by Government from the Indians to be laid out into Townships [Sgd] J.G. Chewett S.G. Office 13th June 1837.
Ms 94 x 65 cm Scale not given Endorsements: '770'
Shows the area from Waterloo Twp to the Bruce Peninsula and from Luther to St Vincent Twp; shows the original orientation proposed for Ashfield and a new proposal as surveyed; line between old and new purchase from the Indians and Indian reserve in the peninsula; notes about survey of Ashfield sgd and approved by J.W. Macaulay and F.B.H. 14 June 1837; new twps numbered 1–22; the land acquired from the Indians in Treaty No 45 1/2 (9 Aug 1836) (see *Indian Treaties*, I:113).
OTAR (SR 5978)

Related maps

(2) *1843*
(Copy) Plan shewing ... 1837 Surveyor General's Office Kingston 14th July 1843 [Sgd] Thomas Parke Survr Genl.
Col ms 79 x 41 cm Scale not given
Reduced from map above but shows only the Indian purchase line, boundary of the reserve, and Ashfield and Wawanosh twps; originally accompanied letter from T. Parke of Executive Council respecting Indian petition for a more southerly location for the reserve boundary line (OOA RG 1 L3 W2 no 29 1843); (Holmden 1722).
OOAMA (NMC 18902)

1042 *1837*
Sketch of the Proposed District of Wellington 1837
Ms Approx 20 x 10 cm Scale not given
With a petition against the proposed creation of the district and enclosed with a dispatch from F.B. Head of 26 May 1837 (GBLpro CO 42/438 p 149); shows proposed district from Wilmot and Waterloo twps to Proton and Melancthon twps.
GBLpro (CO 42/438 p 149)

1043 *1839*
[Map of roads and those proposed between Goderich and Ashfield townships] [Sgd] William Hawkins Dist Agent Goderich 10 Jany 1839 [To] The Commissioners of the Canada Company &c &c Toronto.
Col ms 40 x 32 cm 1" to 1 mile Watermark: 'W WARREN 1838'
Hawkins's plan and report were enclosed in the Surveyor Gen's report to the Lt Gov of 29 Apr 1840 (OOA RG 1 E3 vol 3 pp 190ff 'E3/3'); shows two proposed routes from Goderich north to Ashfield; three other roads proposed to be opened in Ashfield; town plot [Port Albert] and inn

shown at Nine Mile R; notes on the distances of the two routes and parts opened.
OOAMA (NMC 3302)

1044 *[ca 1839]*
MAP OF THE TOWNSHIP / OF / GODERICH, / HURON TRACT. // C. Ingrey lithog. 131, Fleet St London.
Print (lith) 42 x 29 cm 1" to 1 mile
One of five lithographed maps of twps in the Huron Tract showing the survey grid, main roads, towns, notes on mill sites, and road communications; the maps appear to have been prepared to advertise land for sale and were probably made soon after the last surveys of the twps (1838); Ingrey was at this address in 1838–9 (Twyman, 36).
OTAR (Canada Co Records TRHT 238, 238A)

The other maps are as follows:

(2) MAP OF THE TOWNSHIP / OF / HULLETT, / HURON TRACT. // C. Ingrey lithog, 131, Fleet St London
39 x 30 cm
OTAR (Canada Co Records TRHT 241)

(3) MAP OF THE TOWNSHIP / OF / NORTH AND SOUTH EASTHOPE. / HURON TRACT // C. Ingrey, lithog, 131, Fleet St. London
38 x 37 cm
Shows Stratford, Huron Rd, road to Oxford, Long Point Iron Works, and Port Burwell.
OTAR (Canada Co Records TRHT 244)

(4) MAP OF THE TOWNSHIP / OF / TUCKERSMITH / HURON TRACT //
Lithographed by C. Ingrey 131 Fleet Street London
38 x 30 cm
Shows grist and sawmills on Silver Creek and road to them.
OTAR (Canada Co Records TRHT 242)

(5) MAP of the TOWNSHIP / OF / WILLIAMS / HURON TRACT // Lithographed by C. Ingrey 131 Fleet Street London
30 x 46 cm
OTAR (Canada Co Records TRHT 254)

(6) There are also 14 ms twp maps in TRHT, undated but at the same scale and showing the same information as the printed maps; these are as follows: Colborne (240), Stanley, McKillop, and Logan (all unnumbered), Ellice (243), Downie (246), Hibbert (247), Usborne (248), Bosanquet (249), Biddulph (250), McGillivray (251), Hay (252), Stephen (253), West Williams (255).
OTAR (Canada Co Records TRHT 240, 243, 246–52, 255)

1045 *1839*
SKETCH / of / THE GHEGHETS ISLANDS. / NORTH OF THE SAWGINE RIVER.
Print (lith) 40 x 61 cm Scale not given
In *Report of the Huron Fishing Company 1839* (London: Printed by Smith and Ebbs [1839]), at end, enclosed with letter 9 March 1842 from Morgan Hamilton to T.W. Murdoch, Esq., about good harbours in the area (GBLpro CO 42/493 p 208); 'Notes of Gheghet's Islands Lake Huron November 6, 1838 John Macdonald D.P.S.,' on pp 14–15 of report; shows the company's boundary, shoals, hauling grounds, wooded areas; description of terrain on mainland.
GBLpro (CO 42/493 p 208)

1046 *1842*
Map of the Proposed Road from Toronto to Saugine, Lake Huron. Surveyed Pursuant to Instructions from the Honorable the President of The Board of Works. &c &c &c [Sgd] William Hawkins, Surveyor. [Toronto July 184(2?)]
Col ms 66 x 97 cm 1" to 5 miles Endorsements: stamp [BW] '371'
Place and date supplied from Holmden; (SI (BW) 17 Oct 1841 from Killaly to Wm Hawkins refers to Hawkins's report on the Saugeen Rd); shows a proposed route from the Holland R through W Gwillimbury, Tecumseth, Adjala, Tosorontio, Mulmur to the northeast corner of Melancthon twps and west to the mouth of the Saugeen R; road is shown in sections from 1 to 10 with mileages; other proposed roads shown including [Sunnidale]-Owen Sound, road from Goderich to cross Saugeen Rd, and road from Sydenham [Owen Sound] to Saugeen; line of railway surveys in 1836 near the Sunnidale Rd shown; 'Mem. The Townships are laid down from Rankins map ... that part of line in the unsurveyed Land is Laid down to a scale of 6 mi p. Inch: there is some discrepancy in the two parts – discovered too late for correction W.H.'; (Holmden 2144).
OOAMA (NMC 21369)

Related maps

(2) *1842*
MAP / of the / HOME & SIMCOE DISTRICTS / ... 1841 ... [with ms adds] 'The Red-line Shows the Road from Toronto to Saugine – Surveyed for the Board of Works – 1842. W.H.'
Print (lith) with ms adds 100 x 118 cm 1" to 200 chains
Shows approximately the same route as map above but with more detail in the southeastern part; the route is shown up Yonge St to Bondhead and Barrie and west through Essa to Melancthon, then crossing Beaver R to southwest corner of Euphrasia and in a direct line to Saugeen; ms notes on the land in unsurveyed parts; the first part of the route was not implemented and eventually the Toronto-Sydenham Rd was laid out from Mono to the Garafraxa Rd; (Holmden 1713).
OOAMA (NMC)

(3) *1843*
Copy of part of Mr Hawkin's Plan of a line for a Road from Toronto to Saugeen. Surveyor General's Office Kingston 14th July 1843 [Sgd] Thomas Parke Survr Genl

Col ms 42 x 53 cm Scale not given
Originally with letter from T. Parke to the Executive Council in response to Order in Council 5 July 1843 respecting the boundary line of the Saugeen Indian reserve (OOA RG 1 L3 W2 no 29 1843); shows Hawkins's line for a road to Toronto and proposed road to Owen Sound (from Saugeen to Sullivan Twp); proposed south boundary of reserve in line due west from Owen Sound as desired by government, in line from Owen Sound to Saugeen as desired by Indians, and as line was finally agreed upon; (Holmden 2128).
OOAMA (NMC 3273)

(4) *1843*
Sketch of the Retrace of a part of Mr Hawkins 'Line for a Road to connect Toronto with the mouth of the River Saugeen Toronto Octr 20th 1843 [Sgd] J.S. Dennis D.S.
Col ms 46 x 75 cm 1" to 1 mile Endorsements: 'Y 47' '782'
The line is drawn from point intersecting Owen Sound Rd to L Huron with mileages marked from Saugeen Twp to Sullivan Twp where it intersects Owen Sound Rd.
OTNR (SR 6609)

(5) *1850*
South-Half of the Saugeen Road 22768 acres. Surveyed in the year 1850 [Sgd] Allan Park Brough P.L.S.
Col ms 31 x 175 cm 1" to 30 chains Endorsements: 'B 54' '751/51'
(SI 20 May 1850 to survey road lots on road from Maryborough to Brant Twp); road angles through twps of Minto and Carrick to the southwest boundary of Brant Twp; shows lots laid out and survey information; vegetation and terrain; references to field notes and other plans; this road is named the 'Elora Road' on the 1855 map (see **1078**).
OTNR (SR 5328)

1047 *1842 (1845)*
A Plan and Profile of the Road Recently Surveyed through the Wellington District from Puslinch in the District of Gore to the Village of Arthur. Surveyed by Order of the Wellington District Council. By Robert W. Kerr District Surveyor August 1842. (Copy) Office of the Board of Works – 1845.
Col ms 71 x 268 cm 1" to 20 chains Endorsements: stamps 'BW' '404'
[Profile] 1" to 250 ft vertical; shows the exploration line and the road as surveyed from Aboukir Rd in Puslinch Twp and Guelph, through the twps of Guelph, Nichol, and [Peel Twp] to Arthur; vegetation, relief, etc, shown; Scotch Block Rd and Woolwich and Nichol Rd and other roads shown.
OOAMA (NMC 78510)

1048 *1842*
A Plan of the proposed Road through the Township of Garrafraxa. Surveyed by order of the Wellington District Council. by Robert W. Kerr. District Surveyor – September 1842.
Col ms 44 x 118 cm 1" to 40 chains
Shows proposed road between Amaranth and Nichol twps along side road 5/6; a new line for road between Guelph and Fergus.
OTAR

1049 *1842*
Sketch A exhibiting a proposed line of road between the Wellington District and the mouth of the River Saugin with a projected division of the land adjacent in townships. Surveyor General's Office Kingston 30th April 1842 [Sgd] Thomas Parke Survr Genl
Col ms 67 x 103 cm 1" to 4 miles Endorsements: '844'
Shows a proposed road from Woolwich Twp north between Wellesley/Peel and Maryborough/Mornington twps and angling north and west to Saugeen harbour; also shows the Owen Sound Rd with twps named on either side and south connection to Oakville and joining with Aboukir Rd to Guelph; in the northern area Ashfield, Wawanosh, Arthur, Luther, St Vincent, Euphrasia, and Collingwood twps are laid out; 'proposed road Owen Sound to Saugeen' pencilled in; notes on shoreline; shows Huron Rd and London Rd; only part of the route shown was used for the Saugeen Rd; Mornington, Maryborough, Wellesley, and Peel twps designated in crown reserve land.
OTAR (SR 5964)

1050 *1842*
Sketch B exhibiting a projected subdivision of the tract of Clergy Reservations for the Six Nations Indians' lands and Huron tract. Surveyor General's Office, Kingston 30th April 1842.
Col ms 85 x 58 cm 1" to 1 mile Endorsements: '768'
Shows the first proposed subdivision for the twps of Maryborough, Peel, Mornington, and Wellesley; proposed line of road from Woolwich Twp to the mouth of the Saugeen R with 50-acre lots on each side and proposed line of road from Owen Sound Rd to Fergus with 50-acre lots; plans listed below varied according to the position of their boundaries within the tract.
OTAR

Related maps

(2) *1843*
Plan of the outboundaries of the Clergy Reservation for the Six Nations Indians Lands and the Huron Tract. Brantford 11th February 1843. Surveyed by William Walker Deputy P. Surveyor.
Col ms 76 x 54 cm 1" to 80 chains Endorsements: 'B20' '346'

(SI 13 Oct 1842 to survey four twps out of the tract and trace NW boundary line of tract); shows the boundary with a note indicating west line is too far west; swamps and vegetation along boundary lines noted; roads and two 'coloured settlements' noted.
OTAR (SR 5935)

(3) *1843*
Diagram of a projected survey of a township on the south-easterly part of the Clergy Reservation for the Six Nations Indians' Lands of Huron Block. Surveyor Generals' Office Kingston 7th March 1843 [Sgd] Thomas Parke Survr Genl.
Col ms 52 x 41 cm 1" to 80 chains
Shows a projected subdivision for Wellesley Twp.
OTAR

(4) *1843*
Diagram of a projected survey & subdivision of the Clergy Reservations for the Six Nations Indians Lands & Huron Tract. Moved in Council 31st March 1843 [Initialled] E.T. C.E.C.
Col ms 99 x 65 cm Approx 1" to 80 chains
The final plan for the subdivision of the four twps; Wellesley and Peel ordered to be laid out immediately.
OTNR (SR 2503)

1051 *1842*
This Plan is intended to represent a Road, laid out in the month of October in the year of our Lord one thousand eight hundred & forty two Leading from the Village of Waterloo, (in the township of Waterloo) to the Village of Arthur, in the Township of Arthur, Surveyed by [Sgd] Joel Good, Surveyor of Highways.
Col ms 42 x 287 cm 1" to 20 chains
Shows line of proposed road from Jacob Snider's Mill in Waterloo north through Woolwich Twp and crown and clergy land to Arthur; survey grid, mills, other roads, relief.
OTAR

1052 *1843*
Plan Shewing the Unsurveyed Crown Lands South of Owens Sound Compiled principally for the purpose of laying down a proposed line of Road between Ashfield and the Saugine Road. [Sgd] William Hawkins Agt Huron District Kingston March 1843. [Sgd] The Honorable Robert B. Sullivan etc. etc. Kingston.
Col ms 68 x 88 cm 1" to 4 miles Endorsements: stamps 'BW' '439'
Shows the area from Goderich to Toronto and north to the base of the Bruce Peninsula; shows surveyed twps, the Garafraxa or Owen Sound Rd, and the Huron Rd; shows a plan for the several tiers of twps near L Huron parallel to the lake, with a road from Ashfield to Saugeen between the first and second tier of twps; also a first proposal for the [Toronto-Sydenham Rd] running directly from [Southampton] to the southeast corner of Osprey Twp; shows three proposed town plots of which only Southampton was laid out; (Holmden 2153).
OOAMA (NMC 21374)

1053 *[1844]*
SKETCH / OF THE / HURON DISTRICT, / IN WHICH THE CANADA COMPANY HAVE ABOUT / 1,000,000 Acres of Land. / AND OF SOME OF THE / ADJACENT TOWNSHIPS, / SHOWING THE ROADS THERETO, / DISTANCES, AND POST OFFICES. // RICHARDSON, BUFFALO.
Print (wood engrav and typeset) 15 x 19 cm 1" to 14 miles
On leaflet, *Lands in Canada West, (Late Upper Canada.) ... Canada Company's Offices Frederick-Street, Toronto and Goderich, 21st May 1844. Printed at the Patriot Office, Toronto* (OOA Pamph 1844(6)); shows twps in the Huron Tract and east to Hamilton and south to L Erie; explanations key; boundary of company lands; grist and sawmills, leading roads, and taverns on route from Hamilton to Goderich.
OOA (Pamph 1844(6))

Later editions and states

(2) *1847*
[Title as above]
On leaflet, *Lands in Canada West, (Late Upper Canada.) ... Canada Company's Office, Frederick-Street, Toronto, January 21, 1847. Printed at the Toronto Patriot Office.* The map is the same as 1844 above.
USDLC

(3) *1852*
SKETCH / OF THE / CANADA COMPANY'S / HURON SETTLEMENT, / CONTAINING ABOUT / 1,000,000 ACRES OF LAND, / AND OF SOME OF THE ADJACENT TOWNSHIPS, / Showing the Roads thereto, Distances & Post Offices. // RICHARDSON, BUFFALO.
Print 15 x 19 cm 1" to 14 miles
On leaflet, *Lands in Canada West ... Canada Company's Office ... Toronto and Goderich 30th April 1852. H. Rowsell Printer King Street Toronto* (OOA Pamph 1852(30)); the title has been changed but the map is the same as that of 1844; there is also a reference to a plan of the Huron settlement on leaflet, *Lands in Canada West ... [London] Marchant, Singer & Co. 1852* (leaflet advertised in Canada Book Auctions, *Auction Sales [Catalogue] No. 135 Nov. 1981*, item 115), but the leaflet has not been located.
OOA (Pamph 1852(30))

1054 *1845*
PLAN / OF THE / TOWNSHIP OF NICHOL. / Canada West. // Alexr Dingwall Fordyce Jr delt 1845 // F. Schenck Lith. & Print. Edinr
Print (lith) 46 x 64 cm 1" to 1/2 mile

Insets: 'PLAN / of the Village of / FERGUS. / 1845' 1" to 5 chains, 'PLAN / of the Village of ELORA. / 1845' 1" to 5 chains, 'SKETCH / shewing the situation / of the Township of / NICHOL'; views: 'FERGUS, from Belleside, Mr Ferrier's W.H.T. 1845' and 'Village of ELORA, with Falls of the Grand River W.H.T. 1845'; main map shows survey grid, cleared land, names of owners, roads, houses, and description of twp for prospective settlers; insets show village streets, bldgs, and names of owners.
OFEC OKIT

Related maps

(2) *1845 (1852)*
[Same title]
Print (lith) with ms adds 46 x 64 cm 1" to 1/2 mile
Possibly an earlier state as initials and dates on views are lacking; OTAR (SR 1764) also includes ms adds about boundary of Elora as in 'Territorial Divisions Bill' [1851]; ms note referring to 'plan of Village as lithographed by Scobie' (see also **1307** (Elora)), and boundary marked in letter to Hon F. Hincks, 'Position believed to be actually staked out for Village and Park lots Village of Elora,' 'boundary described March 1852.'
OTAR (SR 1764)

1055 *[ca 1845]*
Proposed County of Waterloo [and] Part of the Road surveyed by order of the Wellington District Council running thro' the Townshp. of Peel [and] Part of the Road surveyed by the Wellington District Council (and adhered to by Government) running thro' the unsettled parts of the Township of Nichol.
3 col mss on 1 sheet 47 x 38 cm (Scale for second map only) 1" to 40 chains Watermark: 'J.G. REE ... & SON 1835'
The first map shows the Waterloo Co including rows of twps on both sides of Owen Sound Rd to Owen Sound, and shows the road surveyed in the twp of Peel to Arthur; the other maps show the details of the road survey; although Waterloo Co was created in 1838, the northern twps were only added to the co in 1845.
OTAR

1056 *1846*
MAP OF THE / HURON DISTRICT / and of the Townships of / BOSANQUET IN THE WESTERN AND WILLIAMS IN THE LONDON DISTRICTS / Compiled From the Maps of the original Surveyors / by Donald McDonald Esqr. / Toronto / 1846. / Published by / Scobie & Balfour Lith: / Toronto. // I. Hauer L.
Print (lith) 85 x 87 cm 1" to 160 chains
In upper right corner: notes on who surveyed twps and 'Explanations': cons, lots, road allowances, roads opened by Canada Co., boundaries of twps, grist and sawmills, merchant shops, churches, and schools contributed towards by Canada Co., inns; statistics on population, cultivated lands, and schools; shows twps north to line from Colborne to N Easthope and Ashfield and Wawanosh; the map was advertised for sale in *British Colonist* (Toronto), 4 Jan 1847.
OTAR

Later editions and states

(2) *1846*
MAP / OF THE / HURON DISTRICT / and of the Townships of / Bosanquet in the Western and Williams in the London Districts. / Compiled / from the Maps of the original Surveyors / by Donald McDonald, Esqr. / Toronto / 1846. / Published by / Scobie & Balfour, Lith: / Toronto. // I. Hauer Lith.
The title has been reengraved with different ornamental lettering and a table of distances added to the left of the title; OTAR also has a copy cut into sections and pasted in a book with ms adds of twps west to Sarnia and Moore, and notes on locations of roads, inns, etc, dated 1850 and 1851.
OOAMA (NMC 21611; 48644; 47601) OTAR OTMCL USDLC

(3) *[1855?]*
[Title as in (2) above]
A printed paste-on in one sheet has been added showing the twps of Morris, Gray, Elma, Turnberry, Howick, and Wallace, covering the notes and explanations in the northeast corner; OTAR copy has the above with the addition of Mornington Twp; OTAR also has a separate printed sheet of the latter twp with top and right margin only; the latest twp to be surveyed was Wallace in 1855.
OLU OTAR

(4) *[1856]*
MAP / OF PART OF THE / COUNTY OF HURON / Published BY MACLEAR & Co. / Toronto.
Print (lith) 44 x 49 cm Scale not given
The same as OTAR copies in (3) above with the change in title and with the addition of the name 'Rr Maitland'; the map is noted as being reissued by Maclear with addition of twps as listed in (3) (including Mornington) in *British Colonist* (Toronto), 18 Apr 1856.
OTAR (SR 86907)

1057 *1846*
[Plans of mill-sites on the Owen Sound Road all sgd] C. Rankin D.S.
7 col mss on 4 sheets Sizes vary 1" to 5 chains Watermark on sheet 4: '... WHATMAN ... 1844'
(SI 4 Aug 1845 to survey mill sites on the road from Arthur to Owen Sound); the maps are as follows:

[1] No 1 Plan of Crown Lots Nos 25 and 26 in the 1st Concessions of Glenelg and Bentinck the former on the East and latter west of Garafraxa Road, shewing the position of the mill Ground etc.

[Sgd] C. Rankin D.S. 20th Feby, 1846 [and] 'No 2' Plan of Crown Reserve in the townshps of Arthur, Egremont and Normanby shewing the traverse of the river therethro' and its capacity as a mill site ... 23d Feby 1846 [Endorsements]: 'B21' '549'
OTNR (SR 2708)

[2] No 3 Plan of Crown Lots Nos 18 & 19 in the 1st Concessions of Holland & Sullivan shewing so much of the traverse of the river as includes the most favourable Site for a Mill 26 Feby 1846 [and] No 4 Plan of Crown Lots Nos 6 & pt of 5 in the 1st Concessions of Glenelg & Bentinck shewing the Supposed Mill Site on a small scale 26th February 1846 [Endorsements]: 'B 22' '504'
OTNR (SR 1830)

[3] No 5 Plan of Crown lots Nos 16 1st Concessions of Glenelg & Bentinck Shewing the traverse of the North branch of the Saugin thro' those lots ... Feby 26th 1846 [and] No 6 Plan of Crown lots Nos 26 1st Concessions of Egremont and Normanby shewing the traverse of the Creek – a branch of the Saugin. No mill site ... Feby 26th 1846. [Endorsements]: 'B23' '502'
OTNR (SR 2710)

[4] No 7 Plan of Crown Reserve Nth 1/2 of 28 & S1/2 29 on both sides of Garafraxa Road Township of Arthur shewing the traverse of the four mile Creek etc No Good Mill Site ... 26th Feby 1846 [Endorsements]: 'B24' '503'
OTNR (SR 2709)

1058 *1847*
Plan of the Indian Line or Division line between the Indian & Crown Lands. Toronto 8th Jany 1847 [Sgd] C. Rankin. Examined A.R.
Col ms 57 x 150 cm 1" to 40 chains Endorsements: 'Q80' '1077' 'F 4171'; stamp 'IASR'
(OTNR FN 617 18 Jan 1847); shows the area from Sydenham [Owen Sound] west to the Saugeen R at L Huron; notes on the survey line; note about a possible town reserve at the mouth of the Saugeen: 'it seems to possess no particular advantages without a harbour'; Indian village, cornfields, and trails; shows the more southerly boundary line favoured by the Indians; OTNR SR 5933 has the same title but is dated '9th Jany 1847.'
OOAMA (NMC 21382) OTNR (SR 5933)

1059 *1847*
Plan / OF THE TOWNSHIPS & BLOCK OF LAND / Intended to Constitute the / NEW DISTRICT OF PEEL. / Attached to Petition from the Inhabitants / of the Townships of North & South Easthope &c. / Huron District, June 1847. / MATTHEWS' LITH. / Drawn by J.G. Kirk D.P.S. / Stratford / Huron District. J.J.E.L.
Print (lith) 31 x 18 cm Scale not given
On broadside: *Division of the Huron District, C.W. Statement of Facts* (1847), leaf 2 (*Bib Can* 2842); the twps to be included are as follows: Blanshard, Hibbert, Fullerton, Downie, Gore of Downie, Logan, Ellice, N and S Easthope; block of government lands northwest of Mornington, Maryborough, and Wellesley; also shows the road leading from Stratford to Hamilton; most of the area later became Perth Co.
OTMCL

1060 *1847*
Sketch of Boat Cove or Little Harbor on the East Coast of Lake Huron, Surveyed by Alexander Vidal P.L.S. 1847
Col ms 45 x 58 cm 1" to 5 chains
Inset: 'Sketch of part of the East Coast of L Huron. By Alexander Vidal, P.L.S. October 1847.' 1" to 2 miles; (SI 11 May 1847 to examine harbour near Cape Hurd); shows relief, soundings, nature of bottom, marshy areas of present-day Johnston Harbour.
OTAR (SR 7130)

1061 *1847*
Sketch of the River Saugin for about 5 miles up from its mouth from actual Survey by [Sgd] C. Rankin D.S. Toronto 9th Jany 1847
Col ms 64 x 99 cm 1" to 10 chains Endorsements: 'Q81' '1076'
Shows Indian village, cornfields, and sawmill; Indian path to Owen Sound, relief.
OTAR (SR 7010)

1062 *1847*
Survey from Wawanosh to Mornington by [Sgd] A. Wilkinson Pro: Land Surveyor Sandwich 21st October 1847.
Col ms 55 x 197 cm 1" to 40 chains Endorsements: 'B28'
(SI 8 May 1847 to A. Wilkinson to survey con of double lots on line from Mornington to Wawanosh and along shore of L Huron; OTNR FN 2238 1847); shows survey, road line, and also a trial line of proposed railway from Turnberry and Morris twps to Wallace and Elma twps.
OTNR (SR 6550)

Related maps

(2) *[1847] (1848)*
Part of the North Shore of Lake Huron Crown Lands Department Montreal Jany 1848.
Col ms 52 x 200 cm 1" to 40 chains Endorsements: 'C 47' 'X4-33' 'P8-14'
(SI 8 May 1847); shows the shore survey in Huron, Kincardine, Bruce, and Saugeen twps; relief; this map is probably a later copy of the survey.
OTAR

(3) *1847*
Survey on the shore of Lake Huron by [Sgd] A. Wilkinson Pro: Land Surveyor Sandwich 21st October 1847.
Col ms 55 x 210 cm 1" to 40 chains Endorsements: 'B30'
(SI 21 Sept 1847 to lay off lots along shore to extent of two twps; OTNR FN 1623 22 Nov 1847); shows

Con A and about three other cons inland for the same areas as (2); relief.
OTNR (SR 6663)

1063 *1848*
[Map of the Wellington and part of the Huron and Simcoe districts] Crown Lands Department Surveyor's Office West Montreal April 1848 [Sgd] T Devine S.D. [Initialled] A.R.
Col ms 80 x 102 cm 1" to 200 chains
A compiled plan showing the state of various twp surveys and road development; shows the Brant Rd [Durham Rd] as projected and the line for the Toronto and Sydenham Rd; also shows Saugeen Rd and Hurontario St; notes about surveys and roads to 1851.
OTAR (SR 5970)

1064 *1848*
Plan of the East Part of the Durham Road Surveyed 1848 by David Gibson Prov: Surveyor Examined A.R.
Col ms 57 x 186 cm 1" to 40 chains
(SI 25 June 1848 to survey east part of road line from Nottawasaga to mouth of Penetangore R; OTNR FN 745 June 1849); shows the surveyed road line from the east end to the town of Durham; survey grid, abandoned plank road.
OTNR (SR 6552)

Related maps

(2) *1849*
[Plan of western part of Durham Road] [Sgd] Allan Park Brough P.L.S. 1849
Col ms 53 x 75 cm Scale not given Endorsements: 'B36' 'No 3' '1292/50'
(SI 23 June 1848 to survey west part of road line from rear of 3rd con in Bentinck Twp to Kincardine Twp; OTNR FN 746 11 June 1850); shows distances along road line and a town reserve in Brant Twp.
OTNR (SR 6825)

(3) *[185?]*
[Plans showing the Durham and other roads in Greenock and Kincardine twps]
2 col mss 46 x 187 cm and 46 x 151 cm 6" to 1 mile
Endorsements: 'B32' 'B33'
Relief, swamps, tree types.
OTNR (SR 6602; 6579)

1065 *1848*
Sketch C. shewing the projected Road from Toronto to Lake Huron. Crown Land Department Surveyors Office West Montreal 4 May 1848 [Initialled] A.R.
Col ms 42 x 52 cm Scale not given
Originally with proposals for surveys sgd 'J.H. Price 17 June 1848' (OOA RG 1 L3 C4 no 251 1848); shows 'proposed road' [Toronto and Sydenham Rd] running diagonally from Melancthon Twp to Holland Twp; also a projected road [Durham Rd] from Nottawasaga and Osprey Twp to Greenock and Kincardine twps; also shows Wawanosh Rd, Saugeen Rd, Owen Sound Rd, Hurontario St, and Albion Rd; districts named; (Holmden 2126).
OOAMA (NMC 2882)

Related maps

(2) *1850*
Plan of the Toronto and Sydenham Road [Sgd] C. Rankin P.L.S. Toronto 30th January 1850
Col ms 272 x 75 cm 1" to 4 chains Endorsements: 'B 51'
(OTNR FN 760–1 30 June 1850); shows road in the area from Melancthon Twp to Sydenham Twp where it meets Garafraxa Rd; relief, vegetation, swampy areas along survey lines; lot nos; rivers.
OTNR (SR 6556)

1066 *1848*
[Township of Nichol] [Sgd] Mary Grant ... Nov 11 1848
Col ms Size not known Scale not given
Shows names of owners, cleared land, and a description of the twp in a letter on the back; shows Elora and Fergus; reproduced in Stelter, 'Combining Town and Country Planning,' 21.
OFEC

1067 *1850*
Plan shewing the unsurveyed Portions of Osprey, Artemesia, & Glenelg and suggesting their division on the same plans as the adjoining townships of Nottawasaga Collingwood etc. March 6th 1850 [Sgd] C. Rankin.
Col ms 42 x 47 cm Scale not given
Shows the area from Nottawasaga west to Garafraxa Rd and north to Sydenham and St Vincent twps; shows proposed twp surveys and Toronto and Sydenham road lots.
OTAR

1068 *1850*
Projected Plan for the subdivisions of the townships of Kincardine Brant & Bentinck Approved by O.C. 7th May 1850 Crown Land Department Toronto May 2nd 1850 T.D. [Sgd] J.H. Price Com Crown Lands
Col ms 39 x 52 cm 1" to 200 chains
Also shows surveys along Garafraxa Rd and Durham Rd, outlines the twps of Bruce, Elderslie, and Sullivan, and shows the town plots of Penetangore [Kincardine] and Durham.
OTAR

1069 *[ca 1852]*
MAP OF THE TOWNSHIP / OF / GUELPH / D. McD. / / Lithog. H. Scobie, Toronto.
Print (lith) 30 x 36 cm 1" to 53.6 chains
Shows blocks A to E and G and the Woolwich, Eramosa and Waterloo rds; town of Guelph shown with streets, built-up area, and park lots; OOAMA copy was enclosed with a petition for the enlargement of the town of Guelph and proposed boundaries are shown with the built-up area

marked in ms (OOA RG 5 Cl no 731 1854); the plan was probably made in the early 1850s prior to the railway but after the subdivision of park lots in the north.
OLU OOAMA (NMC 3464) OTAR (SR 1156)

1070 *1852*
MAP / of the Township of / WOOLWICH / made by Joel Good / For the Municipal Council / of the Township of Woolwich / A.D. 1852 / Hugh Scobie Lithr.
Print (lith) 57 x 75 cm 1" to 40 chains
Shows the survey grid of lots, cons, and blocks, and the German Co. Tract; OOAMA copy has ms adds possibly showing roads.
OKIT OOAMA (NMC 53782)

1071 *1852*
Plan of a Strip of Land (red & yellow borders) lately surrendered by the Saugeen Indians as divided into 47 farm lots. Shewing also by the yellow line the route marked out for road through [illegible] ... Sydenham O.S. January 1852 (Signed) Charles Rankin Crown Lands Department Quebec Dec 1852 Certified a true copy [Sgd] John Rolph Commr of Crown Lands
Ms 39 x 122 cm 1" to 40 chains Endorsements: 'F4170'; stamp 'IASR'
Shows Southampton, Indian village, sketch for the layout of Arran, Sydenham; part of road 'now opened and travelled' between Southampton and Sydenham; quantities in lots; shows lots laid out along 'Indian boundary of 1846' (see **1058**).
OOAMA (NMC 3370)

1072 *[1852]*
Sketch Shewing the Durham Road West of the Garafraxa Do [and] Sketch Shewing the Owen's Sound & Toronto Roads and part of the Durham Do [Both sgd] C. Rankin.
2 col mss Ea 77 x 50 cm 1" to 200 chains
Endorsements (both maps): '1824/52'
The maps fit together with a slight overlap at Garafraxa Rd; first map shows Durham Rd to Penetangore [Kincardine] with mileages and the area from there to Owen Sound; second map shows the area from Chinguacousy to Garafraxa with the Albion Rd to Mono Mills and the Toronto and Sydenham Rd from Melancthon to Owen Sound; there is also a similar but untitled map in OTMCL of the whole area in Charles Rankin's hand, 74 x 97 cm, also showing free-grant road lots and the boundaries of twps affected by the Durham Rd.
OTAR OTMCL

1073 *1853*
ARRAN / 1853 / Crown Land Department / QUEBEC
Print (lith) 65 x 44 cm 1" to 40 chains
Shows the twp outline and survey grid; L Arran.
OTAR

1074 *1853*
Chart of the Mouth of the River Saugeen and adjacent Shore of Lake-Huron O.S. & H.R.R. Extension Survey 1853.
Col ms 71 x 101 cm 1" to 12 chains Endorsements: stamp [BW] '573'
Shows soundings and bathymetric contours in L Huron; nature of bottom; government reserve of 600 acres shown south of village of Saugeen [Southampton]; two piers shown on Chantry Is; railway line and pier in reserve; also a plan (NMC 26680) with same title, 73 x 107 cm, endorsed '(Copy)' and [BW] '571'; (Holmden 2575).
OOAMA (NMC 26561, 26680)

Related maps

(2) *1853*
Chart of the Fishing Islands, Lake Huron. Extension Survey. Ontario, Simcoe & Huron R.R. 1853. Surveyed in June 1853 by Sandd Fleming.
Col ms on linen 75 x 111 cm 1" to 12 chains
Endorsements: stamp 'BW 533'
Shows soundings, marshy areas, and bathymetric contours; (Holmden 1630).
OOAMA (NMC 16789)

(3) *1853*
Chart of the Fishing Islands, Lake Huron Extension Survey Ontario Simcoe & Huron Railroad 1853
Col ms on linen 66 x 101 cm 1" to 12 chains
Endorsements: 'From Dept of Transport 1939' '11594/66' '38'
Possibly a copy of (2) with information on fishing added; islands named; boundaries of areas with seine and gill nets; reefs, sand-bars.
OOAMA

1075 *1854*
Map of a part of the river Maitland where the road allowance between the Canada Company's Land and the Crown Lands Cross it, showing proposed deviation of road and site for bridge [Sgd] Wm Perceval County Surveyors Office Goderich March 22nd/ 54
Col ms 49 x 74 cm 1" to 2 chains Endorsements: '2412/54'
Covers the area of Wawanosh, Colborne, and Hullett twps and includes a profile of the site.
OOAMA

1076 *1855*
Board of Public Works Survey of the mouth of Saugeen River. January 24th 1855 (Signed) A.G. Robinson C. Engineer
Col ms on linen 61 x 148 cm 1" to 400 ft
Endorsements: '572'
Inset: 'Levels of Bank on south side of River chaining same as in Traverse'; shows soundings in river and offshore; various survey lines from Chantry Is to village of Southampton west shore; pier.
OOAMA (NMC 11297)

1077 *1855*
MAP / OF THE / COUNTIES / OF / GREY AND BRUCE / CANADA / by C. RANKIN D.S. / January 1855. / Maclear & Co Lith. Toronto.
Print (lith) 67 x 95 cm 1" to 200 chains
Inset: 'THE / INDIAN PENINSULA / from / Capt. Bayfield's chart' approx 1" to 8 miles; shows the survey grid of twps to the base of the Bruce Peninsula; roads with names, including projected roads; village plots and those proposed; Indian villages and reserves; OOAMA has copyright deposit copy with (in ms): 'Entered according to Act of the Provincial Legislature in the year of one thousand, eight hundred and fifty-five, by C. Rankin in the Office of the Registrar of the Province of Canada.'; (Holmden 1698; *OHIM* 4.21).
OOAMA (NMC 21850) OTAR

Later editions and states

(2) *1855*
[Title is the same]
Note: *'Copyright secured'* and a memorandum have been added below title; the memorandum comments on the size of lots in some twps, and describes the boundary line between cos and the twp demarcation along the Toronto and Sydenham Rd.
OTAR OTMCL OTUTF

(3) *[1856]*
[Title is the same]
68 x 99 cm
Inset: 'THE / INDIAN PENINSULA / as divided / INTO TOWNSHIPS.'; the main map now shows Amabel and Keppel twps subdivided (as surveyed in 1856) and the inset shows the boundaries of twps and the town plots of Hardwicke, Adair, Oliphant, and Wiarton.
GBL (70660(1)) OOAMA (NMC 48655) OTAR (SR 2636, 2643)

1078 *1855*
MAP / of the County of / WELLINGTON / Province of Canada West. / Compiled from Various Surveys by / E.H. KERTLAND Esq. Civil Engineer & P.L.S. / 1855 / Engraved by Maclear & Co. Lith. Toronto
Print (lith) hand col 95 x 96 cm Approx 1" to 1 1/4 miles
Shows survey grid, gravel roads (some named), other roads, towns, town plots, division court boundaries, taverns, railways; one OTAR copy has later ms adds showing Toronto, Grey and Bruce Railroad telegraph lines; OOAMA (NMC 48666) folded and in cover, with title: 'KERTLAND'S / MAP / OF THE COUNTY OF / WELLINGTON'; the map was described as nearly ready for publication in *British Colonist* 26 Oct 1855.
GBL (70689(2)) OOAMA (NMC 19781; 48666) OTAR (SR 2639) OTMCL

1079 *1855*
PLAN OF TOWN LOTS / in / NORTH EASTHOPE / near / SHAKSPERE [*sic*] / Lot 26 Concession 1st North Easthope / Maclear & Co. Lith Toronto // John Tully / Architect & P.L.S. / Toronto July 1st 1855.
Print (lith) 26 x 83 cm 1" to 2 chains
Notes on sizes of lots.
Perth 44 (RP 279)

1080 *1855*
PLAN / SHEWING / SUBDIVISION OF LOTS 3, 4 AND 5 IN / Division C. / TOWNSHIP OF GUELPH / SURVEYED FOR / JAMES WEBSTER ESQRE / BY / M.C. Schofield P.L.S. / May 1855. / Maclear & Co. Lith Toronto.
Print (lith) on linen 43 x 61 cm 1" to 4 chains
The name of owner has been added in ms and original name cut out; shows subdivision into five 10-acre lots between Guelph/Puslinch town line and York Rd and bounded to the south by the Eramosa R; certified by registrar 25 Nov 1865 and attached to a deed; notes on relief and vegetation.
OGM OGU

1081 *1856*
MAP OF SURVEY IN THE TOWNSHIP OF GUELPH. / FOR WILLIAM ALEXANDER Esq. / Messrs. Schofield & Hobson P.L.Ss. Berlin, C.W. / 1856 // Maclear & Co Lith.
Print (lith) 53 x 68 cm 1" to 2 chains
Shows a subdivision along Silver Creek Rd, Alexander St, and Paisley Block Rd by the GTR; residences of Wm Alexander and Thomas Sandilands shown with landscaping.
OGM

1082 *1856*
Map of the / SAUGEEN INDIAN PENINSULA / SHEWING THE TOWNSHIPS OF / ALBEMARLE, KEPPEL, / & AMABEL. / County of Bruce. / Province of Canada. // Published under Authority of the Indian Department of Canada / by DENNIS & BOULTON, / Surveyors & Land-Agents, TORONTO. / SAGE & SONS LITH. BUFFALO, N.Y.
Print (lith) 80 x 61 cm [1" to 1 mile]
Note: 'The undersigned offer their services as Agents to parties desiring to invest in the Indian Reserve Lands ... DENNIS & BOULTON. / Toronto, July 31st, 1856.'; further notes on sales of lands at public auction on 2 Sept and on terms and conditions of settlement; shows survey grid, Indian reserves, town plots of Oliphant, Adair, and Wiarton, roads, vegetation, trails; site of 'Indian Council of 1855.'
OOAMA (NMC 21388) OTUTF

Later editions and states

(2) *[1856?]*
[Title, etc, the same]

Scale bar and statement added to the centre bottom of the map.
OTNR (SR 5533)

1083 *1856*
Map of the / SAUGEEN INDIAN PENINSULA / shewing the Townships of / EASTNOR, LINDSAY, / & / ST. EDMUND. / County of Bruce Province of Canada. / Surveyed & Published under Authority of the Indian Department of Canada by Dennis & Boulton, Surveyors & Land / Agents, TORONTO. / SAGE & SONS LITH. BUFFALO, N.Y.
Print (lith) 63 x 92 cm 1" to 1 mile
Inset: 'Map showing the / General Position of the Peninsula'; note: 'The undersigned offer their services ... [sgd as in **1082** above] July 31st, 1856' but includes a longer explanation; shows survey grid, swampy and treed areas, town plots of Bury [Tobermory], Hardwicke, etc, roads; 'These valuable Wild Lands will be sold at public auction from time to time ... There will be no settlement conditions'; latter statement crossed out in ms on OTMCL, OOAMA, and OTAR copies; (Holmden 2621).
GBL (70645(81)) OLU OOAMA (NMC 21867) OTAR (SR 2049) OTMCL

Later editions and states

(**2**) *[1856?]*
[Title, etc, the same]
The sentence 'There will be no settlement conditions' has been removed.
OTAR OTUTF

(**3**) *[1856?]*
Map of the Saugeen Indian Peninsula shewing the Townships of Eastnor, Lindsay, Albemarle, Keppel & Amabel St. Edmund. Surveyed & Published under Authority of the Indian Department of Canada by Dennis & Boulton Surveyors & Land Agents Toronto.
Ms 93 x 169 cm Endorsements: stamp [BW] '502'
A ms copy of the two printed maps (**1082(1), 1083(1)**) on one sheet with copies of notes; the sentence 'There will be no settlement conditions' is not present.
OOAMA (NMC 21389)

1084 *1856*
[Map of the Saugeen or Bruce Peninsula showing Indian reserves] (Enclosed in Lord Elgin's Despatch No 66 – 18th Decr 1854, to Secretary of State) / (To face page 14) // PAPER – INDIAN DEPARTMENT (CANADA) // J Arrowsmith, Litho // No 247 Ordered by the House of Commons, to be Printed 2 June 1856. / Henry Hansard, Printer
Print (lith) 32 x 20 cm Scale not given
In Great Britain, Colonial Office, *Indian Department (Canada). Return to an Address ... Dated 28 April 1856 ... Respecting Alterations in the Organization of the Indian Department* ([London 1856]) (*Bib Can* 3660); shows Indian lands surrendered in 1851 and later, reserves, and villages; the Bruce Peninsula was surrendered by Treaty No 72 (30 Oct 1854) (*Indian Treaties*, I:195ff).
OTMCL

1085 *1856*
Plan shewing the mouth of the River Au Sable and adjoining coast. [Sgd] Ridout & Schreiber Engineers Nov. 1856
Col ms 72 x 122 cm 1" to 200 ft Endorsements: stamps [BW] '561' '22'
Shows soundings, nature of shoreline, borings made at mouth of the [Sauble] R and in channel, piers drawn in pencil; Indian reserve on north shore.
OOAMA (NMC 16775)

1086 *1857*
MAP / OF THE / COUNTY OF BRUCE / SHEWING THE / LATELY SURVEYED TOWNSHIPS / IN THE / Saugeen Indian Peninsula / CANADA WEST. / Lithographed and Published by H. Gregory, Hamilton C.W. 1857. // Entered according to Act of the Provincial Legislature in the year of our Lord 1857 / by Hardy Gregory in the Office of the Registrar of the Province of Canada
Print (lith) 50 x 83 cm 1" to 3 miles
Coat of arms above title; survey grid for all twps except [Sarawak]; Indian reserves and villages; town plots, those proposed, some named; major roads, some named; shows Owen Sound and twps to the south; shows Keppel Twp as part of Bruce Co; (Holmden 1533; *OHIM* 4.23).
OOAMA (NMC 21869)

1087 *1857*
PLAN / OF / PARK LOTS, FARM LOTS / AND / MILL SITES, / BEING SUBDIVISIONS OF LOTS 4 AND 5 IN THE 3RD CONCESSION OF / PILKINGTON. / THE PROPERTY OF / THE REVD ARTHUR PALMER / Maclear & Co. Lith. / TORONTO / Edwin H. Kertland C.E. & P.L.S. Elora 25th August 1857
Print (lith) with ms adds 59 x 84 cm 1" to 3 chains
Mill property; first certified 20 Dec 1860.
Wellington 61 (RP 140)

1088 *[1857]*
PLAN OF / PARK LOTS / laid out on Lot No 5 in the seventh Concession, Division C, / IN THE TOWNSHIP OF GUELPH. / FOR MR J.T. LESLIE BY FRANCIS KERR P.L.S. // LITHO. BY J. ELLIS, TORONTO
Print (lith) 58 x 82 cm 1" to 2 chains
Based on Wellington S 61 (RP 48) of Jan 1857; oriented to northeast; lots along Speed R and west of Eramosa Rd; a few bldgs.
OTAR

1089 *1857*
PLAN OF / THE TOWNSHIPS OF / AMABEL, KEPPEL, ALBEMARLE / & / SARAWAK. / INDIAN DEPARTMENT / Toronto August 1857. / Examined July 1857/ T. Devine / C.L.O. // Maclear & Co Lith. Toronto
Print (lith) hand col 89 x 62 cm 1" to 1 mile
'Note The Lots Colored are already sold' (only a small part); Indian reserves, and reserves for fishing stations; town plots of Adair, Oliphant, Wiarton, and Brooke.
OLU

1090 *[1857]*
[Sketch of the area from Toronto to the Bruce Peninsula showing the County of Bruce]
Col ms on linen 35 x 20 cm Scale not given
Originally accompanied a petition of 11 Apr 1857 giving reasons for the selection of Southampton as County Town as the most central town in the county (OOA RG 5 C 1/508 'No 621 of 1857'); shows twps, towns, roads.
OOAMA

Related maps

(2) *[1858]*
Map of the present settled part of the County of Bruce [Sgd] Latham B Hamlin C.E. P.L. Surveyor
Ms 48 x 64 cm 1" to 3 miles
Originally accompanied a petition of 14 Sept 1858 requesting that Paisley be selected as County Town (OOA RG 5 C 1/583 'No 1852 of 1858'); shows twps, towns, and town plots for S Bruce; 'east and west line dividing the county into two equal parts' bisects the lower half of the co south of Kincardine.
OOAMA (NMC 3274)

(3) *[1858]*
Map of the County of Bruce Section A
Col ms 47 x 59 cm Scale not given
Originally accompanied a petition of 29 Sept 1858 recommending Inverhuron as the County Town because of its harbour and its central position (OOA RG 5 C1/584 'No 1907 of 1858'); shows the population north and south of a line running between Bruce and Kincardine twps and through Greenock Twp to the Durham Rd.
OOAMA (NMC 3275)

1091 *1858*
Map / of the / TOWNSHIP OF GUELPH / IN THE / County of Wellington, / COMPILED AND PUBLISHED / BY / HOBSON AND CHADWICK / Provincial Land Surveyors Guelph. / 1858. / Maclear & Co. Liths Toronto // Fred J. Chadwick del.
Col print (lith) 83 x 116 cm 1" to 20 chains
Shows the survey grid, roads, school sections, schools, names of lot owners, and a few bldgs; lot nos and railways shown in red; streets and wards shown in town of Guelph.
OGM OG OTAR

1092 *[186?]*
Plan of the County of Waterloo
Col ms on linen 43 x 47 cm 1" to 150 chains
Shows the North Riding (Wellesley, Woolwich, and part of Waterloo Twp including Berlin), South Riding (Wilmot, Dumfries, and part of Waterloo Twp); main roads and other roads; railways including GTR and GWR; the North and South ridings went into effect for the 5th Parliament in 1854 (Coté, 93), but this plan probably dates from the 1860s.
OOAMA (NMC 3334)

1093 *1861*
MAP / of the County of / WELLINGTON, / Canada West. / Published by Guy Leslie, / and / Charles J. Wheelock P.L.S. / ORANGEVILLE / 1861. / LITH. by W.C. CHEWETT & CO. / TORONTO.
Print (lith) hand col 160 x 160 cm 1" to 60 chains
Insets (plans of towns): 'ABOYNE,' 'ELORA,' 'FERGUS,' 'GUELPH,' 'KINNETTLES,' 'ORANGEVILLE,' 'SALEM'; 10 views of public and commercial bldgs and residences; shows the survey grid, roads and road allowances, mills, schools, churches, and names of owners or occupants; insets show streets with some bldgs named; list of subscribers for twps, towns, and those outside the county.
OGM OKIT OOAMA (NMC 13205) OTAR USDLC OTUTF

1094 *1861*
TREMAINE'S MAP / OF THE / COUNTY OF WATERLOO / Canada West. / Compiled & Drawn from Actual & Original Surveys by the Publishers / GEO. R. & G.M. TREMAINE / TORONTO, 1861. / ENGRAVED, PRINTED COLORED & MOUNTED / By the Publishers / At their Map Establishment 288 King St. East / TORONTO.
Print (lith) 133 x 145 cm 1" to 50 chains
Insets (plans of towns): 'AYR,' 'BADEN,' 'BERLIN,' 'BRIDGEPORT,' 'CONESTOGO,' 'DOON,' 'GALT,' 'HAMBURG,' 'HAWKSVILLE,' 'PRESTON,' 'WATERLOO,' 'WELLESLEY'; 34 views of public and commercial bldgs and residences; explanations: railways, travelled common roads and road allowances not opened; tract names and boundaries, churches, school houses, grist, saw, and steam sawmills, blacksmiths' shops, names of post offices, towns and villages without post offices; shows names of landowners or tenants and no of acres; subscribers lists; OKIT and OOAMA copies have a different caption on a view of some commercial bldgs in Galt.
GBL (70687(1)) OKIT OOAMA (NMC 11350–1) OTAR (SR 2641)

Other editions and states

(2) *[1860?]*
[Partial map without title, endorsed on back]: 'Township of Waterloo' [Sgd] O.J. Klotz
Print (lith) 56 x 67 cm 1" to 50 chains
This appears to be a proof copy without insets and views of Waterloo Twp part of the map possibly sent to Otto Klotz, Senior, for corrections; there are a few different printed names in lots, and acreages are not printed though some have been added in ink; Bloomingdale village is not shown.
OKIT

1095 *1862*
Map of Part of the Townships of Bosanquet Stephen and McGillivray Surveyed under instructions from the Canada Company Mitchell March 27th 1862 [Sgd] Wm Rath P.L. Surveyor
Col ms 69 x 102 cm 1" to 40 chains
Shows lots around L Burwell and L Smith, travelled roads, marshes; later notes and certifications about surveys of 1865, 1872; also a copy of the map with the same notes.
OTAR (Canada Co. Maps pkg 2 no 163, 167)

1096 *1862*
NEW MAP / OF THE / COUNTY OF / HURON / CANADA WEST. / COMPILED AND DRAWN FROM ORIGINAL PLANS AND / ACTUAL SURVEY / BY / R.W. HERMON, P.L.S. / Published by R.W. Hermon, R. Martin and L. Bolton, 1862. / MAYNE P.O. T'P. WALLACE. / LITH: BY W.C. CHEWETT & CO. / TORONTO. C.W.
Print (lith) 161 x 133 cm 1" to 80 chains
Insets of towns (all at 1" to 12 chains except where noted): 'AILSA CRAIG,' 'ALBERT' 1" to 8 chains, 'BAYFIELD' 1" to 8 chains, 'BLUEVALE,' 'CLINTON,' 'EGMONDVILLE,' 'EXETER,' 'GODERICH,' 'HARPURHEY,' 'HOWICK (LEECHVILLE),' 'LUCAN (MARYSTOWN),' 'LUCKNOW,' 'WINGHAM' 1" to 16 chains, 'WROXETER'; 13 views of public and commercial bldgs; legend keys railways, gravel and common roads; churches with denomination, four types of mill, schools with nos, post offices, and names of landowners shown; insets show streets with major bldgs, some named, and wards in larger towns; subscribers directory, lists of county and other officials, distance table, census returns for 1861.
OOAMA (NMC 17425; 16433) OTAR (SR 92342)

1097 *1863*
SUTHERLAND'S MAP / OF THE / COUNTY OF PERTH / DRAWN FROM / Original Surveys / BY JAMES S. KENNEFICK C.E. 1863. // Lithographed by BRETT & Co. 83 Nassau St. N.Y.
Print (lith) 49 x 61 cm 1" to 160 chains
Shows the survey grid, railways named; list of post offices; towns shown prominently, many with earlier names.
OOAMA OTAR OTMCL

1098 *1864*
Plan of the Fisher's Mill Property Being composed of Parts of Lots Nos 11, 12 & 13 of Richard Beasley's Lower Block Township of Waterloo ... By James Pollock, P.L.S. Galt 10th March 1864
Col ms 63 x 79 cm 1" to 2 chains
'Compiled partly from Descriptions and partly from actual survey for and at the instance of William Cooke, Esquire.'; shows various bldgs, mills, roads, mill pond, and vegetation.
OGUA

1099 *1867*
Plan of part of Artemisia. showing roads established by by-law of Township Council. Drawn by Provl Surveyr Wm Spry. I hereby certify this to be a true plan ... of the Roads numbered I, II III, IV & V ... for the Municipality of the Township of Artemisia ... [Sgd] Wm Spry C E & Provl Surveyor Owen Sound May 30. 1867
Col ms 95 x 62 cm 1" to 10 chains
Includes the area of cons IX to XIV and lots 21 to 28; shows and describes roads; town of Eugenia with streets named, names of some landowners, and five mill reserves.
OTNR (SR 6075)

Part III

Towns and Cities

(ABBOTSFORD town plot)

1100 *1854*
Plan of Survey of Part of Abbotsford Laid out into Acre Lots, the Property of Lockhart Duff. [Sgd] Thos Allen Blyth P.L.S. Hamilton June 1854.
Col ms 54 x 49 cm 1" to 2 chains
Provenance: Wentworth Co Court House maps no 62 dr 2; a plan for subdivision on part of lot 57, con I, Ancaster Twp, south of plank road; lots laid out along George and Lockhart sts; the subdivision is shown on the Wentworth Co map of 1859 (**825**) but is not shown on the co atlas (Page & Smith, ... *Wentworth* (1875)).
OHMA (map 7628)

(ABOYNE)

1101 *1855*
PLAN / of the Village of / ABOYNE / IN THE TOWNSHIP / OF / NICHOL WELLINGTON COUNTY / Surveyed for Messrs Allan & Geddes. / Edwin Henry Kertland / CIVIL ENGINEER AND P.L. SURVEYOR / Elora, 17th August 1855. / Maclear & Co. Lith. Toronto.
Print (col lith) 90 x 66 cm 1" to 2 chains
Shows the area from Gilkison St to beyond Union St, and from Bartlett St to the Grand R and Union St; shows town and park lots with sizes and lot nos; part of lots 21 and 22, con XIII, Nichol Twp; town disappeared in late 19th century; (Brown, *Ghost Towns* I:74); (see also **B2**).
OFEC OTAR Wellington 61 (R.P. 88)

(ADAIR town plot)

1102 *1856*
Plan of the Town Plot of Adair on Hope Bay in the Township of Albemarle [Sgd] Toronto 1st March 1856 J. Stoughton Dennis P.L.S.
Col ms 107 x 107 cm 1" to 4 chains
Provenance: OOAMA RG 10M 76703/9 no 183; shows the plan for the town on the west side of Hope Bay in cons VIII, IX, and X; shows town lots with a centre square and radial streets from Bay St to Home St and from Grafton St to Cliff St; park lots beyond; relief by hachures; a later note indicated 'Plan cancelled see File 11,577' with notes about land sales in 1889.
OOAMA (NMC 13011)

ADELAIDE

1103 *1833*
Village Plot of Adelaide. Surveyed by order from the Surveyor General's Office bearing date at York the 2nd day of February 1833. By [Sgd] Peter Carroll Dy Surveyor. Oxford 20th March 1833. To Samuel P. Hurd Esquire Surveyor General &c &c &c York.
Col ms 47 x 61 cm 1" to 3 chains Watermark: 'J WHATMAN 1830' Endorsements: 'A 4'
(SI 2 Feb 1833 to survey and layout town plot; OTNR FN 2 20 March 1833); shows a town plot of four streets north of Dundas St and five cross streets, with a square laid out on part of lot 11, con II, north of Egremont Rd, Adelaide Twp; note: 'N.B. The land south of the Main Road belongs to T. Radcliff Esq. J.W.M.'; the street names have been added later; Henry St to Joseph St, and Egremont St to Prince's St; a few bldgs shown at south end of town; also an undated plan in OTAR: 'Village Plot of Adelaide Surveyed by Peter Carroll Deputy Surveyor. One tier of lots South of the Road Surveyed for T. Radcliff Esquire.' showing the same layout and a few bldgs, and a copy (OTAR(P)): 'Village – plot of Adelaide (Signed] Peter Carrall [*sic*] Surveyor General's Office Toronto 24th Octr 1834 Copy [Sgd] Henry Lizars.' endorsed 'No 4' and showing the same layout with streets named and names of patentees.
OTAR OTAR(P) OTAR (SR 4642)

Related maps

(2) *1837*
Adelaide. Copy J.G. Chewitt S G Office 14th June 1837. Surveyor General's Office Toronto 19th June 1837 [Sgd] J W Macaulay Surv Genl.
Col ms 50 x 34 cm 1" to 3 chains
(SI 22 Apr 1845 to J. O'Mara to lay off a range of lots on the south side of St George's Square); shows the new lots per SI; later notes to 1849 describe areas to be reserved for churches; note 29 July 1844 about changes to square.
OTAR

ADOLPHUSTOWN

1104 *1799*
Plan & Survey of the Village of Adolphus Town formerly called Hollandville laid out into Acre Lots in June 1799 Signed Alexr Aitken Dpy Surveyor Midland District Copy W.C. S.G.O. 13th Augt 1799 & Report.
Col ms 53 x 75 cm 1" to 4 chains Endorsements: '1190' 'A 1'
Shows the original survey for the town on lots 22–26, con I, Adolphustown Twp; shows six east-west streets and eight north-south streets; shows extent of 'Old Survey'; one lot on each side of Front St, houses and barns keyed to owners names, and irregular fence lines; relief, swampy areas, land being improved; travelled roads.
OTAR (P)

Related maps

(2) *[1799?]*
Adolphustown.
Ms 44 x 75 cm 1" to 4 chains Endorsements: 'A 2' '1191'

Similar to (1) but more of a sketch and lacks reference, although some names are shown; possibly the original or another copy by Aitken; there is also a plan showing reserves in D.W. Smith's 'Report upon Glebes & Commons ... 1802.'
OTAR (P)

1105 *1825*
Adolphustown December 15th 1825 [Sgd] P V Elmore Depy Surveyor.
Col ms 50 x 75 cm 1" to 4 chains Endorsements: 'No 1'
(SI 9 June 1825 to resurvey town plot); shows the town plot with names in all lots, roads, bridges, and more houses than on the earlier plans; note referring to boundary of John Spencer's land has almost faded; names, etc, added to approx 1836; orchards.
OTNR (SR 10)

1106 *[ca 1850]*
Village of Adolphustown
Ms 39 x 73 cm 1" to 4 chains Watermark: '1848'
Shows the original streets and lots and the conflicting claims of several lot owners along the main road and eastern part; original lot, street, and fence lines; possibly accompanied a land petition but original source not found; (Holmden 1460).
OOAMA (NMC 3668)

1107 *1856*
Adolphustown J.W.B. Crown Lands Office, Toronto 9th July 1856 [Sgd] E.P. Taché Acting for Commissr of Crown Lands
Col ms 61 x 82 cm 1" to 4 chains
Shows the town plot in ranges A–E and 30 lots; swamp along shore; no street names given; initials in lots: 'W.C.,' 'B.S.,' and 'Rev. J.D.'
OTAR

ALMONTE

1108 *1839*
Map of Ramseyville Surveyed by H. Falls June 1839
Col ms 56 x 43 cm 1" to 2 chains Watermark: 'J WHATMAN TURKEY MILL 1837.' Endorsements: 'Almonte formerly Ramsayville, Original Plan when laid out in building lots by H. Falls Jr. P.L.S. 1839. Signed by Daniel Shipman Proprietor of the Lands. Presented by John Menzies Registrar.'
Shows the first survey of the town on the southwest side of the Mississippi R from Perth St to Union St, and from the river to Country St; some street names appear to have been changed later; table of bearings; a few owners; (Holmden 2401).
OOAMA (NMC 3670)

ALTON

1109 *1857*
PLAN / of the Village of / ALTON / situated in Lots 22 and 23 in 3rd and 4th Concessions West of / Hurontario Street / IN THE / TOWNSHIP OF CALEDON. / Charles J. Wheelock P.L.S. & C.E. / Orangeville / November 1857. / Maclear & Co. Liths Toronto.
Print (lith) hand col 93 x 66 cm 1" to 2 chains
Inset: 'SKETCH OF PART / OF THE / COUNTY OF PEEL / Shewing the position of / ALTON'; 'Longitudinal Section shewing the available Fall of Water at each Privilege shown on place'; shows the town from Thomas to John St, and Chisholm to Edmond and King sts; proprietors' names; block and lot nos added in red; many bldgs shown, most identified; treed areas; (see also **B36**).
Peel 43 (R.P. CAL-5)

ALVINSTON

1110 *1853*
Projected Plan of Town Plot of Alveston in Brooke to accompany instructions. Crown Lands Department, Quebec 11 May 1853 Certified a true copy [Sgd] John Rolph Comr of Crown Lands [Initialled] T.D.
Col ms 34 x 24 cm Scale not given
Pt of lots 20–22, cons V and VI, Brooke Twp; probably accompanied SI 11 May 1853 to S. Smith to outline and subdivide half of the town plot; shows Bear Creek and boundary only of town plot, including two lots already sold.
OTAR

Related maps

(2) *1855*
Map of Alveston in the Township of Brooke as Surveyed by Saml Smith P.L.S. By Order of the Commissioner of Crown Lands Bearing Date Quebec May 12th 1854 August 28th 1855. [Sgd] Samuel Smith P.L. Surveyor Alveston August 28th 1855.
Col ms 129 x 88 cm 1" to 4 chains Endorsements: 'A 198'
(OTNR FN 881 29 Dec 1855); certified correct by surveyor 'May 12th A.D. 1854'; shows the town as projected, laid out from Franklin St to Wellington St and Durham St to Albert St; town lots in the southwest, park lots mainly in north and east; 'reference': 'timbered swails [*sic*],' willow marshes, reserves, relief, mills and mill dam.
OTNR (SR 8781)

(3) *1856*
Alveston Crown Lands Office Toronto March 1856 J.W.B. Commissioner of Crown Lands.
Col ms 124 x 76 cm 1" to 4 chains Endorsements: 'Office Copy' 'No 118'

Shows the same layout and general information as (2) but without the relief.
OTAR (P)

AMHERSTBURG

1111 *1788*
Plan D Plan shewing the Situations proposed for a Town and Naval Yard opposite the Isle aux Bois Blanc near the entrance of the Narrows leading from Lake Erie to Detroit, with the works necessary for the protection of the same, and to command the Navigable Channel. [Sgd] Quebec 6th Decr 1788 Gother Mann Captn Commandg Rl Engrs
Col ms 89 x 50 cm 1" to 600 yds Endorsements: 'B T Map 42/50'; stamp 'HMSPO'
Accompanied Gother Mann's report of 6 Dec 1788; possibly removed from copy of report with Dorchester's no 58 of 24 Oct 1790 (GBLpro CO 42/70 pp 41ff); shows Bois Blanc Is, Grosse Isle (part), and shore opp; fort and naval yard reservations located on mainland; shows a layout for the town and twp with town lots, common, park lots, farm lots, and reserves, similar to 1788 plan for Toronto (**2011**); fortifications on Bois Blanc Is; there is a similar plan, but showing more of the river, from the same report (see **905**); (*PRO Cat* 2535).
GBLpro (CO 700 Canada 38D (2))

Related maps

(**2**) *[1788]*
Plan shewing the Town and Township, proposed opposite the Isle au Bois Blanc, near the entrance of the Narrows from Lake Erie, to Detroit, with the reservations for the Crown (coloured Yellow) for Works, Naval-yards &ca. [and] Plan showing the situations proposed for a Town and Naval Yard opposite of Isle aux Bois Blanc near the entrance of the Narrows leading from Lake Erie to Detroit with the works necessary for the protection of the same and to command the Navigable Channel
Col ms 83 x 124 cm 1" to 600 yds Watermark: 'J WHATMAN' Endorsements 'C 49' 'Proposed Township opposite Isle au Bois Blanc ... with the Reservation of the Crown in 1787 [illegible] by H. Got[her Mann] ...'; stamps 'B↑O' 'IGF'
Shows a larger area than the above map including more to the south and east, and the far shore of Detroit R; 'Sketch of Intended Fort & Reserve'; shows town as in above plan with note: 'N.B. The town & township is here laid out half a mile too much to the northward. The Town ought to lay between the points a.a [i.e., further south]'; the twp is shown as extending from R aux Canards on north to same distance beyond fort to the south; soundings, comment on shoreline and bottom of river; (Holmden 1465).
OOAMA (NMC 16823)

1112 *1792*
Plan shewing the Town and Fort Proposed to be made opposite the Isle au Bois Blanc near the Entrance of Detroit River and Soundings as found in May 1790 [Sgd] Patrick McNiff Asst Engineer Detroit April 1792
Col ms 77 x 55 cm 1" to 600 yds
Shows area from entrance to river to end of Grosse Isle; soundings; the town plot is shown further to the south than the 1788 plan (**1111**) but with the same layout of town lots and a twp boundary beyond an area reserved for crown; the fort and fortifications are shown in a more finished state to the north of town including 'old Breast work and ditch'; Indian reserve; relief.
OTAR (Simcoe Map 446982)

1113 *1796*
Plan of Ground at mouth of Detroit River. (Amherstburg) Capt Wm Mayne 8th Sept 1796
Col ms 30 x 47 cm 1" to 4 chains Watermark: 'J WHATMAN'
In Capt Mayne's letter to Capt Green, military secretary, of 8 Sept 1796 (OOA RG 8 I vol 382 p 46); shows a plan for a town of 326 lots proposed by Col Caldwell on his own land in lot 3, Malden Twp; proposed canal across the front near the Detroit R; reserve for public square; notes in letter indicate lots could sell well to British persons wanting to leave Detroit and also that lots for merchants were needed along the water; this proposed location and plan for the town was never used (Lajeunesse, cxxvi); (Holmden 1605).
OOAMA (NMC 3678)

1114 *1796*
1796 Plan of part of the Entrance of the Streights from Lake Erie leading to Detroit; shewing the Situations for Buildings ordered to be erected.
Col ms 55 x 61 cm 1" to 200 yds Endorsements: 'D'
Enclosed in Lord Dorchester's no 87 to the Duke of Portland 16 Apr 1796 (GBLpro CO 42/105 f 167); shows the fort and outer fortifications and military bldgs keyed; situations for batteries noted on Bois Blanc Is; soundings; 'Supposed South boundary of Indian Lands' and 'Proposed Boundary of Land to be reserved for Government extending across Indian land and Capt. Bird and Capt. Caldwell's land'; soundings; 'Scite for Naval yard'; there is also a transcript of a similar plan sgd 'Quebec 25th Jany 1796 Gother Mann Lt Col. Commnandg Rl Engr' in OTMCL but original has not been identified; (*PRO Cat* 1437).
GBLpro (MPG 35)

Related maps

(**2**) *[1796]*
[Plan of the Fort and reserved lands at mouth of the Detroit River]
Col ms 54 x 64 cm 1" to 200 yds Watermark: 'J WHATMAN 1794' Endorsements: stamps 'B↑O' 'IGF'

This plan shows most of the same information as plan above except that Indian boundary marked as 'South boundary ...'; (Holmden 1464).
OOAMA (NMC 22220)

1115 *1797*
Plan shewing the Site of the Military Post of Amherstburg, and the Land reserved for Government, by Colonel Mann, as it falls on the Huron Reserve, and the Lots in the Township of Malden. July 24th 1797 Sign'd A. Iredell D.S. W.D. Copy W.C.
Ms 32 x 42 cm 1" to 200 yds Endorsements: '806' 'No 17'
Shows lots in the twp 'No 1 reserved by the Patentees of said Township,' and No 2 and No 3 claimed by Capt Bird and Capt Caldwell, respectively; shows dimensions of blocks, a few bldgs; a pier on lot 2 and an old retrenchment and present military entrenchment in lots 2 and 3; there is also a similar plan with the same title and scale and further sgd 'C.B. Wyatt Surv Genl.' in OOAMA (NMC 3679) (Holmden 1467), and a copy with same title enclosed in Mr President Grant's no 18 of 8 Apr 1806 (GBLpro CO 42/341 p 66) further sgd 'True copy [Sgd] C.B. Wyatt Surv Genl April 9th 1806' .
GBLpro (CO 42/341 p 66) OOAMA (NMC 3679) OTNR (SR 8111)

1116 *1797–9*
Sketch of the Post at Amherstburg By Lt Cooper Rl Engrs 1797 Also the Works of Defence Ordered to be constructed in 1799 [Sgd] Gother Mann Coll Commandg Rl Engrs
Col ms 64 x 97 cm 1" to 200 ft Watermark: 'J WHATMAN 1794' Endorsements: stamps 'B↑O' 'IGF'
Shows the first layout for the town within the south boundary of the military reserve and beyond the naval yard; shows about 27 lots, three or four streets, and a few bldgs; shows the fort to the north with blockhouse, storehouse for Indian Dept, and magazine; soldiers' huts; Indian boundary and 'Vestige of an Indian entrenchment'; probably shows the town as it looked in 1797 and early 1798 (Lajeunesse, cxxvi); (Holmden 1471).
OOAMA (NMC 14963)

Related maps

(2) *1800*
Sketch of the Post at Amherstburg Upper Canada with a Plan & Sections of the Works of Defence. Engineers Drawing Room Quebec. Copied by Lt Wm Hall Rl Arty & J.B. Duberger in 1800. [Sgd] Gother Mann Coll Commandg Rl Engrs
Col ms 61 x 140 cm 1" to 200 ft Watermark: 'J WHATMAN 1794'
Insets: 'Section through the Picketing forming the Curtains' 1" to 4 ft, 1" to 12 ft vertical, 'Section through ye Batteries of the Fort' 1" to 8 ft, 1" to 16 ft vertical; an attractive presentation copy showing the same information as (1) with the addition of the sections; the magazine is shown in a different position in fort; relief by shading; photoreproduction in OOAMA (NMC 15360).
GBL (Maps 23.b.3 (19))

1117 *1799*
Sketch of the Military Post at Amherstburg shewing the Situation of the Public Buildings and of the New Town. [Sgd] Wm Backwell Lt R. Engineer's June 1799.
Col ms 32 x 40 cm 1" to 80 yds Watermark: 'COLES 1795' Endorsements: 'First Set' '... New Town, With a reference to the Names of the Holders of Lots'
This map and (2) below were enclosed in Capt McLean's letter of 26 June 1799 (OOA RG 1 E3 vol 1 p 3); shows the town plot with lots as expanded to three streets north-south and two streets east-west; key to a few bldgs in town and various civilian and military bldgs outside of town; (Holmden 1468).
OOAMA (NMC 3682)

Related maps

(2) *[1799]*
[Amherstburg] Reference to the Holders of Lots
Col ms 32 x 40 cm 1" to 90 ft Watermark: 'COLES 1795'
Shows the town with First, Second, and Third sts named, all the lots, and names of owners in each lot; lots are numbered 1–27 or more on both sides of streets; blockhouse, burying ground; a few lots reserved; a few bldgs; the plan is redrawn and the reference to names, etc, given in Lajeunesse, cxxviii and 226; (Holmden 1469).
OOAMA (NMC 3681)

(3) *[1800]*
[Amherstburg] Reference to the Holders of Lots
Ms 30 x 40 cm 1" to 90 ft
Enclosed with Capt Maclean's letter to Maj Green, military secretary, of 5 June 1800 showing lots for building on military reserve per Gen Prescott, 1800 (OOA RG 8 I vol 272 p 29); the map is essentially the same as (2) above but a few names have been added in blank lots; (Holmden 1472).
OOAMA (NMC 3683)

1118 *1804*
Sketch of the Military Post of Amherstburg Shewing the Situation of the Rope Ground applied for by Messrs Mills and Gilkison 1804
Col ms 31 x 49 cm 1" to 75 yds Watermark: 'PORTAL & BRIDGES 1794'
Accompanies the memorial of Mills and Gilkison of 17 Apr 1804 to Lt Gov Hunter enclosed in Lt Col Vincent's letter of 1 Sept 1804 (OOA RG 8 I vol 254 p 230); shows two positions for rope walk around fort and town; fort and town with references to 29 military bldgs; town extends back to 7th range, and plan shows many houses and

bldgs including those built and partly built; relief by shading; (Holmden 1473).
OOAMA (NMC 3684)

1119 *1808*
[Amherstburg showing Capt Bird's improvements]
Col ms 26 x 44 cm Scale not given
In the memorial of Elizabeth Bird, widow of the late Lt Col Bird, of 5 Feb 1808 claiming compensation for his improvements (GLBpro CO 42/348 p 221); shows Fort Malden, Amherstburg, and various military and civilian bldgs including Capt Bird's houses.
GBLpro (CO 42/348 p 221)

1120 *1819*
Plan of the Town Plot of Amherstburg [Sgd] H.H. Willson Lieutt Royl Engrs 17th Augst 1819
Col ms 51 x 40 cm 1" to 200 ft Watermark: 'JOHN HAYES 1814'
Originally with a later petition about a water lot (OOA RG 1 L3 A 7 no 14 1853); shows the street and lot outline of the town only; six north-south cross streets are now shown; lanes are dotted in; military reserve shown to the north; (Holmden 1476).
OOAMA (NMC 3688)

Related maps

(2) *1819*
Plan Shewing the present extent of the Military Reserve at Amherstburg, the Town Plot, and the part of the Mily Reserve, as originally laid out, granted to Willm Caldwell. [Sgd] H.H.Willson Lieutt Royl Engrs 17th Augst 1819
Col ms on tracing paper 40 x 48 cm 1" to 200 yds Watermark: 'JOHN HAYES 1814'
With the same source as above; shows original boundary line of military reserve and town plot outline within it; boundary of Huron reserve; part of military reserve granted to W. Caldwell (south of town); also shows David Cowan's and Caldwell's lands east of reserve; (Holmden 1477).
OOAMA (NMC 3687)

(3) *1820*
Reference to the Old Numbers in Amherstburg as Reported by the Commissioners. This Reference to accompany the Plan of Amherstburg transmitted to the Surveyor General's office by T.S. ... T. Smith D.S. 5th Dec 1820.
Col ms 39 x 27 cm Scale not given Watermark: 'FELLOWS 1812'
On back: 'Topographical Index to the Old Numbers in the Town of Amherstburg W.D.'; accompanied the same source as (1) above; note: 'The old numbers as reported by the Commissioners are marked by a circle'; shows old and new lot nos for town from Dalhousie St east to George St and from Richmond St to Simcoe St; church; Berczy Macon & Co.; the plan mentioned is probably **1121** (1) or (2) below; (Holmden 1478).
OOAMA (NMC 3689)

1121 *[1820]*
The Town of Amherstburg Western District Surveyed by order dated 29th May 1820 Thos Smith Dep. Sur.
Col ms pt missing 54 x 120 cm [1" to 100 ft]
Endorsements: 'A 3'
(OTNR FN 19 29 May–July 1820); shows the town from Dalhousie (formerly Maitland) St to Wolfe St and from Richmond St to Simcoe St; shows English graveyard and church, and Roman Catholic church; wharves; old and new lot nos shown; 'The Figures in Red Ink are agreeable to the Original plan ... [and] agreeable to the original location tickets York 9th Nov [1820?] [Sgd] J. B. Askin'; names are shown in lots to about King St; extensive notes about names and descriptions of some lots; photoreproduction in OTAR(P).
OTNR (SR 97961)

Related maps

(2) *[1820?]*
Office Plan of the Town of Amherstburg Western District Surveyed by order dated 29th May 1820 Copy from Mr Thos Smith's Plan
Col ms 57 x 105 cm 1" to 100 ft Endorsements: 'No 2'
Shows the same information as plan above including note by Askin, but names now shown in all lots with many changes; includes the same note of 9 Nov 1820; there is also a plan 'Amherstburgh. Copy J.G. Chewett' showing an outline of town plot only in OTNR (SR 6682).
OTAR(P) OTNR (SR 6682)

(3) *1836*
Amherstburgh. Surveyor General's office, Toronto, 11th August, 1836. Copy Henry Lizars [Sgd] J Radenhurst. Office Copy C.C.L.O. Toronto 13th Augt 1836.
Col ms 75 x 95 cm Scale not given
Shows the same layout as (1) above with note by Askin; adds include reserves for Roman Catholic church and notes about sale of lots east of Seymour and King sts.
OTAR

1122 *[1822]*
Amherstburgh [Sgd] Henry Briscoe Royl Engineers
Col ms 26 x 18 cm 1" to 300 ft
Enclosed in a memorial from Wm Stanton, deputy assistant commissioner gen, to Lt Gov Maitland 18 Sept 1822 (OOA RG 8 I/274 p 58); shows military reserve and boundary between Huron reserve and twp of Malden; notes on conditions of bldgs; (Holmden 1479).
OOAMA (NMC 3690)

1123 *[ca 1825?]*
[Part of Amherstburg]
Ms 61 x 38 cm Scale not given Watermark: 'KILN 1821'
Shows the town extending to Sections I–VIII with only Maitland [Dalhousie] St and Bathurst St

named; shows Episcopal church and open ground for burying ground; tanyard by river.
OTMCL (E.W. Banting Collection)

1124 *1827*
Sketch of the position of Amherstburgh Fort in Upper Canada [Sgd] R.H. Bonnycastle Capt Royal Engineers. J.R. Wright Lt Col. Rl Engineers. Rl Engineers Office Quebec 20th Novr 1827 E.W. Durnford Col. Comg Rl Engineer Canada.
Col ms 67 x 96 cm Approx 1" to 165 yds
Endorsements: 'BB 65'; stamps 'B↑O' 'IGF'
'Sections' 1" to 20 ft vertical; shows 'scite of old Fort' and 'present ruinous work as altered by the Americans'; shows 'Town of Malden' and a few houses and fortifications on Bois Blanc Is; relief; a note indicates sketch of ground from papers at REO, Quebec; (Holmden 1486).
OOAMA (NMC 22221)

Related maps

(2) *1827*
Sketch of the Position of Amherstburgh shewing the projected defences, 1827.
Col ms 54 x80 cm 1" to 150 yds
Shows the same information as plan above and includes same notes.
QMMMCM (3592)

1125 *1828*
Plan shewing the Military Reserve, in the North West corner of the Townp of Malden; and in the Western part of the Cession from the Indians in 1800 adjoining thereto – Office copy, 28th Octr 1828 [Sgd] W. Chewet S Sy D
Col ms 47 x 49 cm 1" to 200 yds Endorsements: '808' 'No 10'
Shows relative location of town and military reserve; shows later adds for park lots in northeast corner beyond reserve to Jan 1849; note indicates a copy was made for 'Ordinance 16th April 1835 H.L.' and there is a copy of this date '[Sgd] TGW Eaststaff' and further endorsed 'B↑O' and 'Capt Bonnycastle 28 June 1837 B 136' in OOAMA (NMC 3508) (Holmden 1488).
OOAMA (NMC 3508) OTNR (SR 81013)

1126 *[ca 1830]*
The Town of Amherstburgh
Ms Size unknown Scale not given
Shows the town with streets laid out to Section 11 and streets named east to King St; names shown in most lots to King St; shows military ground and line of the reserve on the southeast according to military plan; also shows a line further west that was supposed to be boundary between reserve and Mr Cowan's land; photoreproduction at OOAMA (NMC 8730).
Private Collection

1127 *1835*
Sketch of part of the Military Reserve at Amherstburg Upper Canada showing the mode in which it is proposed to let the Ordnance premises now occupied by the Establishment there, agreeably to the Honble Boards' Orders of 8th May 1835 Royal Engineers Office Toronto U.C. 16th Octr 1835 (Signed) R.H.B. Capn R.E. Westn Distt U.C. (Signed) Guss Nicolls Colonel Commandg Royal Engineer, Canada Quebec 14th December 1835. ... T.G.W. Eaststaff Draugn
Col ms 57 x 44 cm 1" to 200 ft [i.e., 300 ft]
To accompany the report of the Commanding Royal Engineer to the Lt Gov on the subject of the military reserves, 18 July 1836, no 4 (GBLpro CO 42/431); shows 'present' Fort Malden, old fort, and ruins; hospital, school, stores, commandant's house, and lots to be let around bldgs along the river; (*PRO Cat* 1438).
GBLpro (MPG 762(4))

1128 *1838*
Sketch of the Island of Bois Blanc shewing the position of the Block House ordered to be erected by the Comg Royal Engineer's letter dated 15th November 1838. [Sgd] Vincent Biscoe Capt Royl Engrs December 6th 1838. R.J. Barou Major R Engrs Commg W.D. 17/12/38
Col ms 28 x 45 cm 1" to 170 yds
Enclosed in Col Halkett's letter 18 Dec 1838 to Col Rowan, military secretary, asking approval to erect blockhouses (OOA RG 8 I vol 446 p 136); shows the streets of the town, fort, roads along shore, and major bldgs; notes on the blockhouses and state of repair; three blockhouses located on island; (Holmden 1733).
OOAMA (NMC 3692)

1129 *[1838]*
Town of Amherstburg [Sgd] Vincent Biscoe Captn R.E.
Ms 50 x 39 cm 1" to 200 ft Endorsements: '195' '53' '92'; stamp 'REO'
Shows the town east to Wolfe St; English graveyard and two Roman Catholic graveyards shown (including one across Kempt St); names of owners; probably made at the same time as plan above (**1128**).
OOAMA (NMC 3677)

1130 *1840*
Plan shewing the Position of Fort Amherstburg on the Military Reserve, The Blockhouses on the Island of Bois Blanc and the Town of Amherstburg. Copy [Sgd] Hampdon C G Moody Lieut Roy Engineers Decr 1840
Col ms 37 x 42 cm 1" to 200 yds Endorsements: 'No 2'; stamp 'B↑O'
Shows the town with street outline extending east to about South Victoria St; three blockhouses shown on Bois Blanc Is in slightly different

positions from those on 1838 map (**1128**); lighthouse, fort.
OOAMA (NMC 3693)

1131 *1847*
Plan of the Rear Parts of Lots 1 and 2 in the Front Concession of Anderdon Western District subdivided into Park Lots [Sgd] Albert Pellew Salter D.P.S. Sandwich February 22nd 1847 Examined A.R.
Ms 44 x 45 cm 1" to 4 chains Endorsements: 'A 162'
(SI 29 Jan 1847); shows park lots east and north of town; lot nos and sizes; there is a copy in OTAR(P) without Salter's name but sgd 'Crown Lands Department Surveyors Branch West Montreal Jany 1848. True Copy.' and endorsed 'No 76' and '128' and with addition of names.
OTAR(P) OTNR (SR 6047)

1132 *1851*
Amherstburg, C.W. Plan shewing the arrangement for the settlement of the Pensioners. Copied from plan (sig'd) R. Pilkington Draftsman, John Y. Moggridge, Lieut R. Engineers, 6 June 1851
Col ms 40 x 55 cm 1" to 200 yds
Shows the town, fort, military reserve, and Bois Blanc Is; shows area to be laid out for pensioners beyond reserve and fort to east; leased areas and areas to be leased in future; areas reserved and leased on island; list of leases the same as printed plan (**175(No 4)**).
QMMMCM (7705)

Related maps

(**2**) *1852*
Amherstburg. Canada West Cottage Lots of Enrolled Pensioners on Military Reserve. The Survey of Reserve taken by Lieut De Moleyns R. Engineers and copied November 1852 by [illegible initials] Moore. Captain & Staff Officer Toronto Canada West
Col ms 49 x 65 cm 1" to 200 yds Endorsements: '9366/58' 'No 20'
Similar to (1) except shows location of cottages on lots, and cottages built; proposed lots for school and various officers' and sergeants' quarters shown; trees planted; two drawings: 'front elevation of Pensioners Cottage' and 'Ground Floor Plan.'
OTAR

(**3**) *1858*
Plan of Cottage Lots of Enrolled Pensioners on the Military Reserve Town of Amherstburg. Surveyed by John A. Wilkinson Provincial Land Surveyor under instructions from the Honorable the Commissioner of Crown Lands dated 7th September 1858. Sandwich 12th October 1858 [Sgd] John A. Wilkinson P.L.S.
Col ms 52 x 62 cm 1" to 4 chains Endorsements:'A No 4'
(OTNR FN 884 25 Oct 1858); shows the block of cottage lots around Fort, Alma, St Arnaud, and William sts; names of owners shown in lots.
OTNR (SR 81007)

1133 *[1859?]*
Plan Shewing the Locality of the Reserve in Malden lately occupied as a Lunatic Asylum
Col ms 60 x 70 cm Approx 1" to 4 chains
Shows the military reserve with parts sold or leased and names, and part reserved for pensioners; part proposed to be purchased for asylum at old fort; area from Richmond St north to William St; (Holmden 1487).
OOAMA (NMC 22218)

Related maps

(**2**) *1860*
Map of Lunatic Asylum Reserve Park and Lots at the Town of Amherstburg C.W. Surveyed by Samuel Brodie P.L.S. 1860.
Col ms 58 x 94 cm 1" to 2 chains Endorsements: '0 100'
Similar to (1) above but lots also laid out east of Sandwich St and south of Park St; a 'Copy' at OTNR (SR 6860) is dated 18 Jan 1860 and sgd 'Andrew Russell Assistant Commissioner Exd T.D.'
OTNR (SR 6856, 6860)

1134 *1863*
Plan of Subdivision of part of the Ordnance Reserve Amherstburgh. Surveyed by order of the Honorable The Commissioner of Crown Lands. Amherstburgh Septr 22 1863 [Sgd] O. Bartley P.L.S.
Ms 10 x 22 cm 1" to 4 chains Endorsements: '12705/63' '0 101'
Shows the area west of Dalhousie St and north of Richmond St; lot nos and sizes; two bldgs.
OTNR (SR 81004)

(AMSTERDAM)

1135 *1837*
Survey of a Village Plot Bordering on the West Branch of the Holland River on the rear or westerly part of Lots no 19 & 20 in the 2nd Concession (Old Survey) of the Township of West Gwillimbury signed George Lount Dy Surveyor 16th Jany 1837 Surveyor General's Office Toronto 31st January 1837 [Sgd] J W Macaulay Surv Genl.
Col ms 34 x 49 cm 1" to 2 chains
(SI 23 Dec 1836 to lay off the town plot of Amsterdam on lot 19, con II, on both sides of the Holland R); shows 12 lots on both sides of river with bridge causeway; lot nos; notes on sales; the 'Old Survey' is now part of King Twp; also a copy entitled 'Amsterdam Surveyed by George Lount D.P.S.' and endorsed 'No 3' with the addition of trails and names of patentees (OTAR(P)).
OTAR OTAR(P)

1136 *1854*
Town Plot of Amsterdam County of York. Bradford February 1854 [Sgd] John Ryan C.E. P.L.S. Exd A.R.
Col ms 55 x 76 cm 1" to 4 chains Watermark: 'J WHATMAN ... 1854' Endorsements: 'A 189' '2010/54'
(OTNR FN 883 8 March 1854); the town plot has been considerably expanded since the 1837 survey; shows Utrecht St to Erasmus St, Rubens St west to river, and Hague St to both sides of Rotterdam St; railway; park lots of five acres and town lots along railway; margin of swamp and dry land; outline of old town plot; a few bldgs identified; a town plot (Mannheim) is also shown laid out to the north; also a copy in OTAR(P): 'Town plot of Amsterdam Office Plan Crown Lands Department Quebec 1st April 1854 Certified a true copy T.D. [Sgd] A.N. Morin Commissioner Crown Lands.' endorsed 'No 102' with the addition of names of patentees.
OTAR(P) OTNR (SR 7012)

1137 *1866*
Town Plot of Amsterdam. Department of Crown Lands Ottawa, August 31st 1866 [Sgd] A. Russell Assistant Commissioner.
Col ms 51 x 72 cm 1" to 40 chains Endorsements: '14551/66'
Shows the same layout as 1854 with the addition of bridges, a few bldgs, and the 'Plank Road to Holland Landing'; the town did not develop, reverting to farm lots, and in 1869 was patented to a lumbering company (Hunter, 2:14).
OTNR (SR 7014)

ANGUS

1138 *1857*
PLAN / of the Town of / ANGUS / THE PROPERTY OF / W. PROUDFOOT AND J.T. BUSH / COMPOSED OF LOTS 30 & 31 / [Third] Concession [of] Essa / AND PART OF LOTS 30 & [31] in the 4TH. / W.E. Yarnold P.L.S. February 16th 1857. Maclear & Co. Liths Toronto C.W.
Print (lith) hand col 68 x 95 cm 1" to 3 chains
Inset: 'PART OF THE COUNTY OF SIMCOE.' [showing the location of Angus]; views: sawmill, engine house, grist mill; store at Angus 'the property of Jonas T. Bush'; 'tavern at Angus erected by Mr Harper'; shows the area between the Nottawasaga and Pine rs; Curtis property including mill; from Centre St to the south marked in green; streets named, lot nos and sizes, railway; names added in ms.
OMSA

(ANNAN)

1139 *[1856]*
PLAN / OF THE TOWN / OF / ANNAN / SITUATED ON PART OF LOTS Nos XI & XII in the XI / CONCESSION WESTERN DIVISION TOWNSHIP OF ASHFIELD / AND PART OF LOT XXIX, LAKE RANGE CONCESSION / IN THE AFORESAID TOWNSHIP & COUNTY / Herbert Dixon Esqre Proprietor. // Molesworth & Weatherald P.L. Surveyors Saml Peters Lith. London C.W.
Print (lith) hand col 54 x 70 cm 1" to 3 chains
Weatherald and John sts to Thomas and Herbert sts; lots for sale mainly along Dundas and John sts: 'will be sold by Auction at one o'clock P.M. on Thurs. 16th Octr 1856'; the plan was registered 18 Oct 1856; the village was shown in the co atlas (Belden, ... *Huron* (1879)); see also **B49**.
Huron 22 (R.P. 5 Ashfield)

(ANTRIM)

1140 *1834*
A Map of Antrim Surveyed for Robt Wm & James Ruddle By Samuel Smith P.D.S. 1834.
Col ms 48 x 68 cm 1" to 2 chains Endorsements: 'A 115' '599'
A village laid out at the mouth of Big Creek in Howard Twp; on west Lake St to Patrick St, William St to Anthony St; on east Erie St to St Andrew St, Colborne St to Robert St; intended harbour, market-place, school ground, church, public ground, reserved lots, relief; the village functioned as a port according to *Smith's Canadian Gazetteer* (1846); a note about the potential for a harbour appears on map of 1840 (**965**).
OTNR (SR 6071)

1141 *1867*
Plan of Broken Lots Nos 94, 95 & 96 and the Village of Antrim South of Talbot Street Township of Howard Kent The Property of The Revd Mr Massingberd [Sgd] Sherman Malcolm P.L. Surveyor 'Rond Eau' May 1867.
Col ms 68 x 102 cm 1" to 5 chains Watermark: 'J WHATMAN 1864' Endorsements: 'Exhibit 33 S.C.O. Kent Court Brown vs. Cull ... 9.4.45'
Shows the same streets as map above with church lot and public ground; names of landowners of large lots, including Massingberd; not shown in co atlas (Belden, ... *Kent* (1881)).
OLU

ARTHUR

1142 *1842*
Plan of the Reserve in the southern extremity of the Township of Arthur as laid out into Town and Park Lots [Sgd] John McDonald Dy P. Surveyor Goderich 21st April 1842.
Col ms 63 x 75 cm 1" to 5 chains
(OTNR FN 27 22 July 1842); shows the triangular town bounded by Catharine, Wells, and Eliza sts;

town lots are in the area bounded by Frederick, Catharine, and Eliza sts and park lots beyond; recommended reserve for market and burial ground; contents and lot dimensions; mill pond and dam, some bldgs; also a copy entitled 'Arthur with the Park Lots. by John McDonald D.P.S. 1842 Office Copy Surveyor General's Office Kingston a true copy.' and endorsed 'C 11' with the additions of names of patentees (OTAR(P)), and a copy entitled 'Town of Arthur. Crown Lands' Department Montreal 24th June 1846 A.R.' with the addition of burial ground and mill reserve (OTAR).
OTAR OTAR(P) OTNR (SR 6497)

1143 *1855*
PLAN OF PART / OF THE TOWN OF / ARTHUR / Surveyed for Andr Mitchell Esqr / May 1855. / Maclear & Co. Lith. Toronto.
Print (lith), pt missing at bottom Approx 51 x 43 cm 1" to 4 chains
Shows the area between Catharine, Frederick, and Eliza sts; lots to be sold are shaded; bldgs shown, some identified; mill dam and mills; note about sale 1 June 1855 with part missing.
OKIT

1144 *[1857]*
Plan of Lots / IN THE / VILLAGE OF ARTHUR / THE PROPERTY OF ANDREW MITCHELL ESQRE / [Sgd in facsimile] W & A Boultbee / P.L. Surveyors / Arthur. / LITHOGRAPHED BY J. ELLIS 8 KING ST. TORONTO, C.W.
Print (lith) with ms adds 56 x 70 cm 1" to 2 chains
Shows subdivision between Frances, John, and Catherine sts around mill pond; also shows the rest of the town to Frederick and Eliza sts; some bldgs shown mainly along George St; a slip attached to map reads: 'Sale of lots ... will take place on the ground, on the 15th September next,'; the same as **B66** which is probably a transcript of this map.
OTAR

ATHERLEY

1145 *[ca 1843]*
Plan of the Town of / ATHERLEY. J. Ellis fc. Toronto.
Print (engrav) 23 x 27 cm 1" to 5 chains
Fitzroy Place to Marlborough St, Paget St north to Winchester St; Mountjoy and Market squares; 'The Property of Ogden Creighton Esq. Toronto'; 'Lots £7–10 each'; 'Front Lots £10 each'; ms adds indicate lots sold on condition of building; the map was possibly prepared and printed about 1843 when Creighton apparently laid out the town (*Smith's Canadian Gazetteer* (1846), 7).
OTAR

AVENING

1146 *[186?]*
PLAN OF THE VILLAGE OF / AVENING / LAID OUT ON LOT No V THIRD CON. OF / THE TOWNSHIP OF NOTTAWASAGA / The Property of W.H. Thornbury Esqre.
Print (lith) 42 x 50 cm 1" to 2 chains
Stayner St west to mill pond, Robertson St north to William, John, and Simcoe sts; lot nos and sizes, grist and sawmills; Thornbury built his mill in 1860 and the property was probably laid out then or soon after (Hunter, 2:247–8); the village is not shown on the general maps of 1862 (**280**, **282**).
OMSA

AYTON

1147 *1855*
Projected Plan of the Town Plot of Ayton in the Township of Normanby T Devine Astd by P.L.S. Gibson. Crown Lands Department Quebec 5th April 1855 Certified a true Copy [Sgd] Joseph Cauchon Comm. Crown Lands.
Col ms 44 x 33 cm 1" to 30 chains
(SI 5 Apr 55 to Q. Johnstone to subdivide town reserve of Ayton into town and park lots, and mill site); shows a mill site and streets in lots 14, 15, 16, con IX, Normanby Twp; George to Victoria St and Helena to Caroline St; town and park lots; proposed road.
OTAR

Related maps

(**2**) *1855*
Plan of Ayton. Comprising Lots numbers fourteen fifteen and sixteen in the ninth and tenth concessions of the Township of Normanby in the county of Grey Surveyed under instructions from the Honourable the Commissioner of Crown Lands, dated April the 5th 1855. Quintin Johnstone Provincial Land Surveyor. Examined T. Devine C.L.O.
Col ms 76 x 62 cm 1" to 4 chains Endorsements: 'A 197' '6140/55'
(OTNR FN 909 13 July 1855); laid out as described in (1) but mill site not marked; table of lot sizes sgd 'A. Russell'; also a copy in OTAR(P) 'Ayton Crown Lands Office Toronto 16th April 1856 [Sgd] Joseph Cauchon Commisr of Crown Lands.' with the addition of names.
OTAR(P) OTNR (SR 6072)

BADEN

1148 *1856*
Plan [of the] Village [of] Baden in [the] Township [of] Wilmot County of W[ater]loo, C.W. as sur[veyed for] Jacob B[ec]k Esq. 1[856?] Drawn by J.

Hobson, Provincial Land Surveyor Berlin, C.W. April A.D. 1856.
Col ms, pt missing 53 x 88 cm 1" to 2 chains
Shows the town from Snyders Rd to William St and from Brewery St to Queen St; GTR and station; mill and mill pond; some bldgs; related to R.P. 627 (**B86**); photoreproduction in OTAR.
Private Collection

(BALAKLAVA)

1149 *[1860]*
PLAN / OF / BALAKLAVA / COMPRISING LOTS No 30 & 31 CONCESSIONS C & D / OF THE / TOWNSHIP OF CARRICK / Surveyed for John Shennan / BY / E.H. KERTLAND C.E. & P.L.S. // Maclear & Co Lith. Toronto
Print (lith) 71 x 92 cm 1" to 2 chains
Shows the town laid out from Lucan to Peter sts and Taylor to Butchard sts; park lots on either side of town lots; grist mill reserve; a few bldgs including church and cemetery; R.P. was certified by owner 8 March 1860; still shown in the co atlas (Belden, ... *Bruce* (1880)) but had disappeared from maps by the end of the century; see also **B87**.
OOAMA (NMC 21080) Bruce no 3 (R.P. 29)

(BALLINARD town plot)

1150 *1856*
MAP OF PARK LOTS / LAID OUT IN / BALLINARD / IN THE / TOWNSHIP OF GUELPH / AND / County of Wellington, / FOR / JOHN C. CHADWICK Esq. / Henry Strange P.L.S. // Maclear & Co Liths. Toronto
Print (lith) 55 x 80 cm 1" to 2 chains
Shows lots on either side of Ballinard Ave between Chadwick Rd and the Galt & Guelph Railway and Waterloo Rd, about one mile from Guelph; shows residence and bldgs of Chadwick and his woodland; note indicates sale to take place in 1856 with day and month left blank; related to R.P. 47 (**B909**) of 11 Oct 1856; village is not shown on the co map of 1861 (**1093**).
OGM OGU

BARRIE

1151 *1811*
A Sketch of the outlines of a Village on the North Shore of Kempenfelt Bay on Lake Simcoe; Surveyed and laid down by order of the Surveyor Generals Office bearing date the 29th Augst 1811 [Sgd] Saml S. Wilmot Dy Surveyor J.G.C. To be returned ... [Sgd] T. Ridout S.G. 28 Jany 1812.
Col ms 47 x 66 cm 1" to 4 chains Endorsements: 'No 26' '1200'
(SI 25 Oct 1811 to choose site for town, one mile by 1/2 mile on north side of Kempenfelt Bay at end of Penetanguishene Rd, and to survey outlines); the outline is shown and was probably completed by Wilmot in 1811; the streets are shown and named as in (2) below but were possibly added later; the first site for part of what became Barrie on either side of the Penetanguishene Rd, lot 22, 6th con, twp of Vespra and southeast corner of Oro.
OTNR (SR 1399)

Related maps

(**2**) *1812*
Project for a Village on Kempenfeldt Bay [Sgd] Surr Genl Office York U.C. 28 Jany 1812. [Sgd] Thomas Ridout Sur Genl.
Col ms 49 x 67 cm 1" to 4 chains Endorsements: 'A 38' '1338'
The plan for the town shows Front, 2nd to 5th, and Rear sts running east-west, and seven unnamed cross streets; bearing of purchase line and Penetanguishene Rd shown; relief; the projection may have accompanied the survey instructions; lots shown with dimensions.
OTAR(P) OTNR (SR 1399)

(**3**) *1812*
Plan of a Village on Kempenfelt Bay on Lake Simcoe 1st July 1812 [Sgd] Sam S. Wilmot Dy Surveyor.
Col ms 47 x 66 cm 1" to 4 chains Endorsements: 'No 24'
(SI 20 Jan 1812 to survey town plot; OTNR FN 478 4 July 1812); the original survey for the town of 'Kempenfeldt'; shows the same streets as on the projection but these have been named O'Brien to Hewson St, Davis to Steel St; relief; the street names appear to have been added later.
OTAR(P)

(**4**) *1837*
Kempenfeldt. Copy [Sgd] J.G. Chewett S.G. Office 6th June 1837. [Sgd] Surveyor General's Office Toronto 12th June 1837 J W Macaulay Surv Genl.
Col ms 43 x 67 cm 1" to 4 chains
Shows the same streets and names as in (3) but also many later additions of names of owners, many of whom own large blocks of land.
OTAR

1152 *1833*
Plan of the Town of Barrie In the Township of Vespra and County Simcoe and in the West half of Lot 24 – 4th Concession of Vespra by Wm Hawkins D.S. [Sgd] William Hawkins Depy Surveyor Surveyor General's Office York 15th May [1833].
Col ms, pt missing 59 x 82 cm 1" to 11/2 chains
Endorsements: 'No 8' '618'
(SI 6 Apr 1833 to lay out town lots on same principle as Adelaide (see **1103**); OTNR FN 40 23 May 1833); the first survey for Barrie proper on the government reserve two miles to the west of 'Kempenfeldt'; shows an irregularly shaped town bounded by Dunlop St at the water to Macdonell St at the north, and from Bayfield St east to Poynts and Sampson sts; shows a main square bisecting

Mulcaster and Collier sts; treed areas and meadow, cleared land; bldgs identified, including 'small log houses built for the accommodation of Emigrants'; fenced areas, lime-kilns, drains, 'Edgar's wharf'; notes on lot sizes and houses.
OTNR (SR 19)

Related maps

(2) *1833*
PLAN of the TOWN of BARRIE / Home District / U.C. / Tazewell del. & lithr York. U.C. From Candn. Stone 1833.
Print (lith) 20 x 24 cm Scale not given
A reduced plan based on the original survey; shows the same layout of streets as on (1) above, lots numbered; square is now labelled 'Market Place'; (Holmden 1499).
OOAMA (NMC 3704)

(3) *1837*
Barrie. Copy J G Chewitt Surveyor General's Office Toronto 31st May 1837 [Sgd] J W Macaulay Surv Genl.
Col ms 50 x 64 cm 1" to 1 1/2 chains
Shows the same streets as in (1) but Bayfield St is called Bedford St; names have been added in lots and water lots; reserves added with dates of Orders-in-Council: gaol and court-house (1844), burial ground (1838), two glebe lots (1836), Wesleyan Methodist Society (1837), reserve for school and several others undesignated; also an undated plan in OTAR(P): 'Town of Barrie Copy J.G.C.' endorsed 'No 21' and similar to (3) except town is shown extending further east as far as Berczy St and later notes added; also a copy in OOAMA (NMC 22227): 'Town of Barrie. Copy Geo. Shaw. [Sgd] Thomas Parke Survr Genl Surveyor Genrals Office Kingston 20th April 1842.' 1" to 2 1/4 chains, similar to (3).
OOAMA (NMC 22227) OTAR OTAR(P)

1153 *1842*
Diagram of the Lots A, B and C in the Township of Vespra. Surveyor General's Office Kingston 25th July 1842. [Sgd] Thomas Parke Surr Genl.
Col ms on tracing paper 50 x 82 cm Scale not given Endorsements: '615'
A rough survey of the area east of Barrie providing the first extension of the town; notes on land and terrain, bearings along shore, Indian landing; 'Course of Mr Bettridges Road,' 'one large lot separates it from Barrie' '25 acres adjoining Barrie in 1/4 acre lots the property of Charles Berczey.'
OTNR (SR 22)

Related maps

(2) *[1842]*
Diagram of the Extension of the Town of Barrie into Town & Park Lots.
Col ms 47 x 68 cm 1" to 4 chains Endorsements: '617'
A projected plan for the layout of the extension with notes on lot sizes and street widths; streets roughly marked but not named; shows connection with Surrey and Water sts.
OTNR (SR 20)

(3) *1842*
Survey and Extension of the town of Barrie on Lots A B C in the County of Simcoe November 1842 [Sgd] Saml Richardson D.P.S.
Col ms 40 x 58 cm 1" to 4 chains Endorsements: 'A 132' '614'
(OTNR FN 226 4 Jan 1843); the actual survey for the extension as per SI 25 July 1842; shows the streets from Duckworth east to Puget St, and from Kempenfeldt St to Napier St; Nelson Square, St Vincent Square, Duckworth Place, and Codrington Place shown; town lots and part lots shown; also a copy in OTAR(P): 'Extension of the Town of Barrie by Samuel Richardson D.P.S. 1842 Office Copy Surveyor Generals Office Kingston January 1843 A true copy [Sgd] Andrew Russell S & D.' endorsed 'No 20' with the addition of names of patentees; and a copy in OTAR: 'Addition to the Town of Barrie. Surveyor General's Office Kingston 16th October 1843 [Sgd] Thomas Parke Survr Genl.' with later additions regarding the reserves for grammar school (1844), Presbyterian church (1844), and Agricultural Society (1845).
OTAR OTAR(P) OTNR (SR 21)

1154 *1847*
Plan of proposed Road from the Main Street, Barrie, thro' the Government Lands to the S.E. Corner of Lot No 4 in the 1st Concession West of Penetanguishene Road.
Col ms 32 x 70 cm Scale not given Watermark: 'T EDMONDS 1842' Endorsements: '1394/47'
Originally with OOA RG 1 L3 B4 no 78 1847; shows a proposal for the extension of Market St from gaol and court-house, to cut across Duckworth St at Napier St and run diagonally north to intersect with the Penetanguishene Rd; the western diagonal was built but not the eastern; (Holmden 1501).
OOAMA (NMC 3705)

1155 *1848*
Plan of the Town Plot of Barrie and adjacent Crown Lands (within the red border) shewing a propos'd plan of division of those Crown lands into Park lots Toronto 8th Jany 1848 ... [Sgd] C. Rankin D.S.
Col ms 76 x 109 cm 1" to 4 chains Endorsements: 'A 165'
(SI 18 Oct 1847 for a reconnaissance survey of crown land reserved for park lots); shows the original town, the extension to the east, and part of 'Kempenfeldt'; the park lots are planned to the north of the extension and of Kempenfeldt, and also a few to the west of this; notes about roads.
OTAR

Related maps

(2) *1848*
Plan of Park Lots (within the red borders) on the

westerly part of lot No 1 and on lots Nos 2&3 in the 1st concession and on the N.E. 1/4 of No 23 – 4th Concession of Vespra. Toronto April 1848 [Sgd] C. Rankin D.S. Examined A.R.
Col ms 85 x 132 cm 1" to 4 chains Endorsements: 'A 166'
(SI 16 Feb 1848 to subdivide into park lots; OTNR FN 38 19 Apr 1848); shows the park lots surveyed as proposed; proposed road from Napier St at Duckworth jogging up to Steel St at Puget St, in a different proposal than that on 1847 plan (**1154**); Penetanguishene Rd connection to the west shown; names of some landowners; swampy lands; also an undated copy (OTAR(P)): 'Park lots in the Township of Vespra Copy T. Devine C.L.D.' endorsed 'No 20' and '1203' and with the addition of names in the lots; and a later plan (OOAMA (NMC 11362)): 'Park Lots within the red border as laid off on the westerly part of lot No 1 and on lots Nos 2 & 3 in the 1st Concession of Vespra. [Sgd] T. Devine S & D Crown Lands Department Quebec 9th Decr 1853. Commr of Crown Lands.' originally with a land petition (OOA RG 1 L3 H7 no 37 1854); and a copy of part of (2) in OOAMA showing the park lots north of extension and Kempenfeldt; (Holmden 2873).
OOAMA (NMC 11362) OTAR(P) OTNR (SR 7722)

1156 *1853*
PLAN / of the / BARRIE STATION / Laid out / by / ROBERT ROSS P.L.S. / for the Proprietor / JACOB JACOBS / 1853. / H. Scobie Lith. Toronto.
Print (lith) 40 x 63 cm 1" to 4 chains
A subdivision plan for the west part of Allandale west of the station from Baldwin to Alfred St and from Adelaide St north to the town line; related to R.P. 30 (**B102**), which shows only the east part.
OMSA

1157 *1854*
PLAN / OF / BUILDING LOTS / IN THE TOWN OF / BARRIE / THE PROPERTY OF / James Patton / laid out by / WILLIAM GIBBARD / January 1854 / Scobie's Lith. Toronto. / Wm Gibbard C.E. & P.L.S.
Print (lith) 64 x 81 cm 1" to 5 chains
Shows a subdivision from Bayfield to Berczy St north of James and Worsley sts to above Wellington St; the rest of the town is shown from Cook St west to Frances St, Bradford Rd, and Rose St; major bldgs named; names of owners of large properties; relief, railways, wharves; notes on the advantages of the town; related to part of R.P. 31 (**B104**); OTAR also has a partial copy of the central area of the map with ms adds showing sale of lots, new bldgs, and names of owners.
OMSA OTAR

1158 *1855*
PLAN / OF TOWN LOTS LAID OUT / AT THE / BARRIE RAILWAY STATION / TO BE SOLD BY PUBLIC AUCTION / JANUARY 31st 1855 / AT THE TOWN OF / BARRIE. / Survey made by Robert Ross P.L.S. // Maclear & Co. Lith. Toronto.
Print (lith) 44 x 55 cm Scale not given
Shows a subdivision north of the station running from the bay west to Thompson St, south of Ross St; lot nos and those to be sold indicated, time and place of sale noted; possibly related to R.P. 25 (**B103**).
OMSA

BAYFIELD

1159 *[183?]*
Map of Bayfield
Ms on tracing paper 22 x 20 cm Scale not given
Watermark: 'GEORGEM ... CORO ...'
Shows an early plan for the town to the south of the Bayfield R with Market Square in the centre and streets radiating out from it; one major radial to southwest ends in a square, but this radial does not show on later plans; lots are laid out and numbered along Main St and square, and to the north and east along river; lots are not laid out in south and southwest section and some lots on west are not numbered; Old Goderich Rd and New Goderich Rd shown crossing river at two bridges; mills along river; a few other bldgs; park lots shown in row along the south end; the town plot was apparently laid out when de Tuyll bought the land in 1832 (*DCB* VIII:900).
OOAMA

1160 *1840*
PLAN / of the / TOWN and ESTATE of BAYFIELD / in the / Townships of Goderich and Stanley / in the / County of Huron in the London District / Province of Upper Canada / the property of the / Baron de Tuyll / Containing together about / 4000 ACRES / By J. McDonald Dy Provincial Surveyor / Goderich 1st October 1840. / Surveyed by D. Smith Huron County Surveyor
Print (lith) 68 x 51 cm 1" to 10 chains
Shows the same layout of town lots as in (**1159**), also shows de Tuyll's land in part of the twps laid out into park lots and small farm lots; relief, mills; some bldgs and occupied lots shown in town; there is also a ms copy with the same title, etc, sgd 'A true Copy A. Wilkinson P.L.S.' in OTAR Wilkinson Papers (M292) with all lots numbered.
OTAR (Canada Co. Papers TRHT 234)

1161 *1856*
PLAN OF LOTS ADJOINING THE TOWN OF BAYFIELD / AND SITUATED ON THE WESTERLY PORTION OF LOT No 4 IN THE BAYFIELD CONCESSION / TOWNSHIP OF GODERICH. / THE PROPERTY OF JOSHUA CALLOWAY ESQUIRE / Molesworth & Weatherald C.E. & P.L.S. / Maclear & Co Toronto, C.W.

Print (lith) 55 x 75 cm 1" to 4 chains
'Note The property will be offered for Sale by Auction on the Ground on [in ms] "Friday 29th August 1856" ...'; shows a subdivision north of the Bayfield R at mill pond and old bridge, and west of road to Goderich; shows part of original town to south, new road to Goderich, bridge; related to R.P. 541 (**B125**), registered 13 May 1857.
OTAR

1162 *[1856]*
Plan / of / TEN VALUABLE BUILDING LOTS / FRONTING ON / MAIN STREET AND MARKET SQUARE / AND / situated in the very centre of the / RAPIDLY INCREASING / TOWN OF BAYFIELD / Enlarged Plan / OF / PROPERTY TO BE SOLD / Surveyed by / Molesworth and Weatherald C.E. / Provincial Land Surveyors. // Maclear & Co. Liths Toronto
Print (lith) 54 x 76 cm 1" to 20 ft
Inset: 'PLAN / OF / PART OF THE TOWN OF / BAYFIELD / SHOWING POSITION OF PROPERTY / TO BE SOLD.' 1" to 10 chains; the lots are on Main St at Market Square; plan was certified as surveyed by 22 Sept 1856; (see also **B123**).
Huron 22 (R.P. 145)

1163 *1856*
Plan / OF THE / TOWN OF BAYFIELD / IN THE / Township of Stanley and County of Huron / THE PROPERTY OF / the Hon Malcolm Cameron. / Drawn by T.N. Molesworth, C.E. and P.L.S. / 28th January 1856.
Print (col lith), pt trimmed 84 x 59 cm 1" to 4 chains
Shows the town fully laid out in town lots within the block from Cameron St north to Bayfield Terrace and from Huron Terrace east to Sarnia St; the southwest radial has disappeared; all lots are numbered; lots have also been added north of Bayfield Terrace; roads to London and Port Sarnia marked; (*OHIM* 7.5).
OTNR (SR 16)

1164 *[1856]*
PLAN OF THE TOWN OF BAYFIELD / SHEWING THE POSITION OF 56 VALUABLE TOWN LOTS / THE PROPERTY OF MESSRS STARK & HAMILTON. // Surveyed by Molesworth and Weatherall [*sic*] / Civil Engineers and P.L.Ss / Maclear & Co. Lith Toronto
Print (lith) 77 x 55 cm 1" to 4 chains
The plan was registered on 17 Dec 1856; lots on Hamilton and Stark sts at the south end of town; shows the streets in the rest of the town also; (see also **B124**).
Huron 22 (R.P. 146)

1165 *1857*
Plan of the Harbour of Bayfield, in the County of Huron. November 1857. ... [Sgd] John Denison P.L.Surveyor & Civil Engr Bayfield, 25th November 1857.
Col ms on tracing paper 54 x 80 cm 1" to 132 ft
Endorsements: stamp [BW] 'No 309'
Inset: 'Section at mouth of River' 1" to 66 ft, 1" to 40 ft vertical; shows the river to mill dam, harbour with piers, proposed dredging and retaining wall, high water line, roads, lighthouse; there is also a 'Plan of the Bayfield Harbour. June A.D. 1858' 1" to 66 ft, showing 'designed harbour road' and area designed for dock and lumber yards in OOAMA (NMC 22230).
OOAMA (NMC 22229–30)

1166 *[1858]*
Plan of part of the Town of Bayfield surveyed by T.N. Molesworth Provincial Land Surveyor.
Ms 36 x 49 cm 1" to 2 chains Endorsements: 'in N. 38971 of 1858 C. of P.W.'
Originally with a letter from John Denison of 14 June 1858 about a site for a lighthouse (OOA RG 11 A 1 a vol 33 no 38971 1858); shows town from Bayfield Terrace to the river; shows proposed lines for co road up the bluff and harbour road below bluff.
OOAMA (NMC 3707)

BEAVERTON

1167 *[1853]*
BEAVERTON. / A / PLAN OF MILL-SITE & LOTS IN THE VILLAGE OF BEAVERTON, / Being part of Lot 15 and Broken Lot 16 in the 6th Concession of the Township of THORAH, / LAKE SIMCOE, / AS LAID OUT BY F.F. PASSMORE, Esq. P.L.S. // Lithographed by J. Ellis, Toronto.
Print (lith with typeset title) 53 x 78 cm 1" to 2 chains
'This Mill Site ... is valuable from its proximity to the Lake ... A Public Sale will be held at the Auction Rooms of Wakefield & Coate, Toronto. EDWARD SHORTISS. Toronto 1st October, 1853.'; shows lots on Main St to lake, south of Beaver R; bldgs shown east of lake in established part of town; proposed wharf, stone dam, and mill.
OTUTF

BELLEVILLE

1168 *1811*
Plan of a Tract of Land (coloured yellow) purchased from the Mississaga Indians and known by Lots Number Four in the 1st and 2nd Concessions of the Township of Thurlow in the Midland District. Province of Upper Canada. – containing 428 acres. Surveyor Genl Office York U.C. 6 Septr 1811. [Sgd] Thos Ridout Surveyr Genl
Col ms Approx 26 x 41 cm 1" to 20 chains
With agreement sgd by James Givens, agent, and chiefs in Isaac Brock's no 2 to Lord Liverpool 23 Nov 1811 (GBLpro CO 42/351 p 135); a note

indicates that the land on both sides of the Moira R near its mouth was needed for mill sites for a populous neighbourhood; shows a narrow strip of land and names of landowners surrounding it.
GBLpro (CO 42/351, 135)

Related maps

(2) *1816*
Plan shewing the relative situation of the Indian Burying Ground, in the Township of Thurlow [with later title] Belleville & Park Lots in Thurlow projection for the Survey. Surveyor Generals Office York U.C. 5 August 1816 [Sgd] Thos Ridout Surveyr Genl.
Col ms, possibly pt missing 33 x 41 cm 1" to 20 chains
Shows the long narrow strip from the bay and east of the lower Moira 'reserved for the Indian Burying Ground'; original adjacent lot owners; a later addition shows town plot of Belleville, glebe, clergy reserve, and other park lots laid out across the whole area; the Indians surrendered some 428 acres in the area to the crown on 5 Aug 1816 and *Indian Treaties*, Treaty No 17, 1:45 includes a copy of this map.
OTNR (SR 3566)

(3) *[1816?]]*
Plan shewing the relative situation of the Indian Burying Ground in the Township of Thurlow
Col ms 22 x 42 cm 1" to 20 chains Endorsements: 'Q 50' '1090'
This map is similar to the one above and was probably made at the same time; however the burying ground is not specifically located.
OTNR (SR 2412)

1169 *[1812]*
Project for laying out a Town on Lot No 4 in front of the Township of Thurlow.
Col ms 33 x 80 cm 1" to 4 chains Endorsements: 'A 119' '605'
Shows the proposed layout for town east of the river; notes on size of lots and streets; 'Singleton River now the Moira'; old baseline; Mayer's Mills and McNabb's Mills shown.
OTNR (SR 17)

Related maps

(2) *1812*
Sketch of a plot for a Town to be laid out on Lot No 4 in the front of the Township of Thurlow S.G.O. 5 June 1812 Copy [Sgd] T. Ridout S.G.
Ms 33 x 79 cm 1" to 4 chains
The same as (1) above without the note about the old baseline; the carrying out of the survey may have been delayed because of the War of 1812 (see plan below).
OTAR

1170 *1816*
A Plan of the Town Plot on the Mississauga Reservation at the River Moira First Concession of the Township of Thurlow [Sgd] River Moira April 24th 1816 Saml S. Wilmot Dy Surveyor.
Col ms 66 x 178 cm 1" to 2 chains Endorsements: 'A 5' '604'
(SI 3 March 1816 to survey and lay out village and to note existing bldgs); shows the town laid out east of river from the bay and Wharf St north to Mill St between Front and Rear St; relief, roads, three bridges; 45 bldgs indexed including residences, stores, breweries, mills, etc; lot nos; also a later plan in OTAR(P): 'Copy. Plan of the Town Plot at the River Moira on Lot No 4 in the 1st Concession & Broken Front of the Township of Thurlow Surveyed by Mr Saml S. Wilmot Dy Surveyor 24th April 1816 Surveyor Genls Office York 12th July 1816 [Sgd] Thos Ridout Surveyr Genl.' with the addition of names of patentees.
OTAR(P) OTNR (SR 7730)

1171 *1817*
[Plan of the mouth of the Moira River] Clarke 8th July 1817 [Sgd] Saml S. Wilmot Dy Surveyor
Col ms 1" to 4 chains Endorsements: 'Q21'
Shows part of lots 3 and 4, Thurlow Twp, various survey lines, dams, mills, bldgs, bridge, the Mississauga Reservation; improved land and fence lines.
OTNR (SR 5491)

1172 *1817*
Plan shewing the Survey of lot No 4 in the 2nd Concession of the Township of Thurlow laid into five acre Park Lots [Sgd] Decr 31st 1817 Sam'l S. Wilmot Dy Surveyor
Col ms 78 x 29 cm 1" to 4 chains Endorsements: 'No 49'
Shows park lots on either side of Park St between the 2nd and 3rd cons; names; note re Order in Council 28 Aug 1818; later notes about vacant land given to S. Wilmot [1818?] and lots returned to commissioner of crown lands in 1842; photoreproduction in OTAR(P).
OTNR (SR 2412)

1173 *[1845]*
Plan / OF / THE TOWN OF / BELLEVILLE / COUNTY OF HASTINGS, / AND /DISTRICT OF / VICTORIA / BY / John J. Haslett, D.P. Survr / J. Ellis & Co. fc. 8 King St. Toronto.
Print (engrav) 97 x 72 cm 1" to 3 chains
Shows the town from Dundas and Bridge sts west of river to Ann St and north to Front, Park and Mill sts; all bldgs shown, some named; names of owners, large estates, and landscaping shown around houses; OOAMA has a transcript of a sale advertisement from a newspaper dated Belleville, 25 Oct 1845, but source for this not found; exhibited at the Toronto Society of Arts, 2nd Exhibition 1848 (see *Catalogue* (OTUTF)).
OTNR (SR 7729)

1174 *1860*
PLAN / OF THE / TOWN OF BELLEVILLE, / BY / R.L. INNES, ESQR. C.E., / PUBLISHED BY / M. BOWELL / FOR THE / HASTINGS DIRECTORY. / 1860–61. // W.A. Little Lith Montreal.
Print (lith) 39 x 35 cm 1" to 10 chains
In *Directory of the County of Hastings ... 1860–61* (Belleville 1860), after 104 (*Bib Can* 3976); shows the town east and west of the river, streets named, schools, lot nos; various churches, major bldgs shown; 'Flint's Steam S Mills'; 'Bogarts Steam S Mills'; proposed Marmora railway; oriented to west; (*Bib Can* 3976).
OTAR

Related maps

(**2**) *1864*
PLAN / OF THE / TOWN OF BELLEVILLE / PUBLISHED FOR THE / HASTINGS DIRECTORY / BY R.L. INNES, C.E. / 1864 65. // W.A. LITTLE, LITH. MONTREAL.
Print (lith) 35 x 36 cm 1" to 10 chains
In *Directory of the County of Hastings ... 1864–65* (Belleville 1865), opp 68 (*Bib Can* 3976); a redrawn plan but very similar to (1) above; this map is oriented to the north and the title has been relocated to the bottom; a table of distances from Belleville to 25 places and a description of the North and South Ridings of Hastings have been added; the town is shown bounded by Thurlow/Sidney town line on the west, the Episcopal Methodist College on the north, and the GTR station grounds and Victoria St on the east.
OOAMA (NMC 3710)

1175 *1861*
Plan of Part of the Town of Belleville Shewing a portion of the Gore Lots in said Town By [Sgd] John Emerson P.L. Surveyor Belleville Sept 1861.
Col ms 182 x 33 cm 1" to 1 chain Endorsements: '12937/61' 'B 5' '11854/61'
Shows lots off Church St from Wharf St to Mill St along the Moira R; conflicting survey lines; grammar school and hospital are shown; contents of lots; also a reduced plan in OTAR(P) of the same title but sgd 'Department of Crown Lands Quebec Nov 11th 1861 [Sgd] Andrew Russell Assist Commissioner.' 1" to 4 chains.
OTAR(P) OTAR (SR 5832)

BELMORE

1176 *[1856?]*
BELMORE IN THE TOWNSHIP OF TURNBERRY AND COUNTY OF HURON. / Maclear & Co. Lith Toronto. / Surveyed by – / T.N. Molesworth C.E. / Provincial Land Surveyor.
Print (col lith) 66 x 89 cm 1" to 2 chains
Shows the town at the junction of Turnberry, Howick, Culross, and Carrick twps; William St to Howick St, John St to Culross St; 'Victoria Square' public reserve, and reserve for tannery and mill; 'Saw and Grist-Mill are now in course of erection by the proprietor [Francis W. Irwin] within a short distance of the Townplot'; probably laid out ca 1856 when the post office was opened with Irwin as first postmaster (Carter, I:90).
OTNR (SR 23)

(BENDERVILLE town plot)

1177 *1856*
PLAN OF TOWN LOTS / Adjacent to the / VILLAGE of ARTHUR, / COUNTY OF WELLINGTON / The Property of / G.H. BENDER, ESQR / W. Boultbee P.L.S. // Lith: Spectator Office, Hamilton C.W. [Sgd in ms] Wm Boultbee P.L. Surveyor Hamilton Augst 15th 1856.
Print (lith) 62 x 85 cm 1" to 2 chains
A subdivision plan for a town on part of lots 3 and 4, con II, twp of Luther, east of Arthur; shows the streets from King St to Hastings St, and Cedar St to Nelson St and market square and foundry reserve; the site is shown on the 1861 co map (**1093**) and on the co atlas (Walker and Miles, ... *Wellington* (1877)).
Wellington 60 (no R.P. number)

BETHANY

1178 *1867*
Plan of Village Lots Laid Out on Lot No 23 in the 8th Concession of the Township of Manvers Surveyed for Christopher Fell By M. Deane P.L.S. [Sgd] Lindsay 11th Decr 1867 M. Deane P.L.S.
Col ms 34 x 41 cm 1" to 2 chains
Provenance: received from Municipal Village Hall, Bethany; this would appear to be the same as R.P. Manvers 6 (**B234**).
OTAR

BLYTH

1179 *[1855]*
PLAN OF THE TOWN OF BLYTH / SITUATED ON LOT 42 1st CONCESSION OF THE TOWNSHIP OF WAWANOSH AND THE SOUTH HALF OF LOT 1 IN THE 9th CONCESSION / OF THE TOWNSHIP OF MORRIS IN THE COUNTY OF HURON CANADA / Surveyed by / William Percival C.E. / Provincial Land Surveyor. / Maclear & Co Lith. Toronto. // [Certification statement] William Percival / Provincial Surveyor / Goderich, Dec. 7, 1855.
Print (lith) 58 x 84 cm 1" to 4 chains
Inset: [Location map of Huron Co]; certified as copy of a plan registered 29 Dec 1855 (**B253**); shows town laid out on both sides of river, Queen

St, Wilson St south to Mill St, road line between cons 1 and 2, Wawanosh, west to Wellington St; (Holmden 1518).
OOAMA (NMC 22238)

BOBCAYGEON

1180 *1833 (1860?)*
Town Plot of Verulam. Mapped and Survey'd in October 1833 By J. Huston Depty Prov Survr. Copy Office of Public Works. Quebec, July 20th 1860.
Col ms on linen 46 x 61 cm 1" to 3 chains
Endorsements: 'No 48240'; stamp 'Dept. of Public Works Canada 157'
Shows first part of town as laid out for Thomas Need on the south side of the river on lot 15, con X, on part of Bobcaygeon Is; the town is shown in seven ranges east-west and 16 lots north-south; 'Reference': intended site for sawmill, the lock, line of canal, mill reserve, falls of Bobcaygeon, McConnell's Inn; the original plan of 1833 appears not to have survived; however, there are six undated plans of this same area regarding a later land dispute in OTAR (Thomas Need Papers); (Holmden 2872).
OOAMA (NMC 3716)

1181 *1837*
Map of a Town Plot in the X Concession and XVI Lot of Verulam By [Sgd] John Reid Dy Surveyor October 2nd 1837. Named Rokeby by His Excellency Sir Francis B. Head Bt 14th November 1837.
Col ms 38 x 65 cm 1" to 3 chains Endorsements: 'A 111' '690'
(SI 30 Aug 1837 to lay out town plot on lot 16, con X, corresponding to plan of lot 15 by Geo. Boulton; OTNR FN 604 2 Oct 1837); shows government town plot on the north side of the river from East St to West St with Bond and Francis sts running east-west between Kent to Head sts; streets line up with those on south side, which is named 'Rokeby as surveyed by Huston D.P.S.'; canal shown but no locks; bridge on Joseph St; also a copy in OTAR(P): 'Rokeby. Office Copy [Sgd] J.G. Chewett S.G. Office 17 Nov 1837.'; the OTAR(P) plan also shows streets south of river with note that the land is private property, Queen St is shown to the north with some lots above it, and the plan is marked as cancelled.
OTAR(P) OTNR (SR 289)

1182 *1859*
Plan of the town plot of Rokeby, Lot 16, Con X, Verulam. [Sgd] William Drennan P.L. Surveyor Peterborough March 4th 1859.
Col ms 46 x 55 cm 1" to 4 chains Endorsements: 'No 52'
(SI 2 Dec 1858 to subdivide into town and park lots lot 16, con 10, Verulam; OTNR FN 388 1859); a resurvey of north part of town; shows the town north of river from West St to East St and to North St, but some streets in a different configuration; streets east of John (Joseph, Bobcaygeon, Helen, and Ann) are angled to the northeast or northwest; South St south of river is shown; canal and lock, bridges, slide wharf, a few bldgs; also a copy in OOAMA (NMC 4851): 'Rokeby in the Township of Verulam. Crown Land Department Toronto 31st March 1859 [Sgd] Andrew Russell Assistant Commissioner.' with a few names added; and in OTAR(P) a 'Copy of plan of the Town Plot of Rokeby "now village of Bobcaygeon" Crown Lands Department Quebec 2nd December 1859 [Sgd] Andrew Russell Assistant Commissioner.' with all names of patentees added; also a copy at OTNR (SR 291) sgd 'Departmt of Crown Lands Quebec Nov 29th 1860 Asst Commissioner.'
OOAMA (NMC 4851) OTAR(P) OTNR (SR 290–1)

1183 *[186?]*
Map Bobcaygeon
Ms on linen 55 x 65 cm Scale not given
Provenance: Mossom Boyd Collection; a sketch showing the town on the south side of the river from Portland east to Need St, and from Boyd St south to beyond John St; names of some owners, squatters, some houses and bldg material; reserve for burial ground; mills, mill reserve; shows the same canal, bridges, dam, lock, and road across river as on 1859 plan (**1182**).
OOAMA (NMC 70939)

BOLTON

1184 *[1856?]*
MAP / OF / NUNNVILLE / ADJOINING / BOLTON. / BEING THE EAST HALF OF THE LOT No VII CON VII OF / ALBION, / In the / COUNTY OF PEEL. / Surveyed and draughted by / T.C. Prosser, P.L.S. Collingwood. / Maclear & Co. Lith Toronto.
Print (lith) 66 x 51 cm 1" to 2 chains
A subdivision east of Bolton on the Humber R; cleared areas; a few bldgs shown; names of owners; plan was registered 22 Aug 1856 (see also **B260**).
Peel 43 (R.P. ALB–4)

BOTHWELL

1185 *1866*
PLAN / OF THE / TOWN OF BOTHWELL, / TOWNSHIP OF ZONE, / COUNTY OF KENT, / CANADA WEST. / COMPILED FROM ACTUAL SURVEY & ORIGINAL PLANS / BY / UNWIN, DYAS & FORNERI, P.L. SURVEYORS. / JUNE 1866. // Published by / UNWIN, DYAS & FORNERI / AND / RICHD. McMILLAN, / BOTHWELL, C.W.

Print (lith) Size not known 1" to 5 chains
Inset: 'PETER / STREET / CONTINUED / Scale, 8 Chains to an Inch.'; shows the town from the GWR grounds and George St northwest to Beech St, Jane to Catharine St and south to Peter St; reproduced in Jones, *Black Gold Built Bothwell*, chap 2.
Original not located.

BRADFORD

1186 *1853*
Extension Bradford Town Plot County of Simcoe Bradford September 1853 [Sgd] John Ryan C.E. P.L.S. Exd [Initialled] A.R.
Col ms 59 x 61 cm 1" to 4 chains Endorsements: 'A 190'
Shows the extension from Holland St to Holland R and the town plots of Amsterdam and Manheim across the river; lots, margin of swamp, dimensions, acreages, railway; also shows many bldgs, wharf, mill, tavern, and Canada Co. land in Amsterdam; also a copy in OTAR(P): 'Office Copy Extension of Bradford Town Plot County of Simcoe Crown Lands Department Quebec April 1854 [Sgd] A.N. Morin Commr Crown Lands.' endorsed 'No 99' and showing lots between Bridge St and Tecumseth St and the Bradford Flax Co. land.
OTAR(P) OTNR (SR 42)

1187 *1857*
PLAN / OF / THE TOWN OF / BRADFORD / SHEWING PRESENT SUBDIVISIONS / Compiled by / JOHN RYAN C.E. / P.L.S. / Yonge St. January 1857. / Maclear & Co. Lith Toronto.
Print (lith) 92 x 135 cm 1" to 5 chains
A compiled plan of the town; from Canton St to Victoria St, and Toronto St east to Station St, and on the west Victoria Terrace to Holland St at Alma and Albert sts; to the east is the Ontario Simcoe and Huron Railroad and depot and the 'Government town plot' with lots along Bridge and Tecumseth sts to river; Amsterdam and Manheim shown across the river; churches, schools, mills; related to R.P. 122 A (**B284**).
OTAR(P)

BRAMPTON

1188 *[1850?]*
Brampton
Col ms 46 x 60 cm 1" to 250 ft
Shows lots and streets laid out mainly from east of Hurontario St to Scott St, from south of Queen St north to Ellen St and west to George St; related to and probably made at the same time as the compiled plan R.P. BR-2 (July 1850) (**B290**); (Holmden 1519).
OOAMA (NMC 22247)

1189 *[1855]*
PLAN / OF / BUILDING AND VILLA LOTS / IN THE TOWN / OF BRAMPTON / Being / The Property of Samuel Patterson Esq. / Chas Unwin P.L.S. / Maclear & Co. Lith. Toronto.
Print (lith) 72 x 50 cm 1" to 2 chains
A subdivision in the northwest sector of town from Main St or Centre Rd to Scotch St, and Irish St to English St; some bldgs shown with landscaping; 'Sale to take place on the premises on Tuesday Novr 13th.' [1855]; see also **B297**.
Peel 43 (R.P. BR-9)

BRANTFORD

1190 *1830*
Plan of the Indian Surrender and Village Plot of Brantford as surveyed by order of His Excellency the Lieut Governour and under the Superintendence of John Brant Esqr Superintendent of the Six Nations of Indians Brantford 15th June 1830 by [Sgd] Lewis Burwell Dy Surveyor Exd S.G.O. 24th Decemb 1830 – Copied [Sgd] W Chewett A S Genl
Col ms 37 x 49 cm 1" to 10 chains Watermark: 'J WHATMAN TURKEY MILLS 1828' Endorsements: 'Q 49' 'H32'
Shows the unnamed streets of the village per map of 1830 below (**1191**); shows Indian lands, and large lots outside the village owned by John and Jacob Brant, Wm K. Smith, and J. Wood; 'Mohawk Parsonage Glebe'; an earlier plan by Lewis Burwell of 22 Oct 1829 is cited in Reville, 85, but has not been located.
OTNR (SR 33)

1191 *1830*
Plan of the Village of Brantford. Surveyed by Order of His Excellency the Lieutenant Governour and under the superintendance of John Brant Esquire Superintendant of the Six Nations of Indians, during the months of March, April, May and June 1830. by [Sgd] Lewis Burwell Dy Surveyor, Brantford June 15th 1830.
Col ms 69 x 158 cm 1" to 2 chains Endorsements: 'No 7'
(OTNR FN 68 June 1830); shows the town laid out from river north to Nelson St and south of river to Canal St, and from Rawdon St west to West St [Cedar St]; shows bridge, mills, reserve on river, mill sites; squares reserved for market, public square, court-house, Kirk of Scotland, Church of England; names of owners added, some at a later date.
OTNR (SR 32)

Related maps

(2) *[183?]*
Plan of the Town of Brantford. Copy Thos Allen Blyth D.P.S.
Col ms 76 x 132 cm 1" to 2 chains Watermark:

'JAMES WHATMAN TURKEY MILL KENT [182?]9' Endorsements: 'F 4175'; stamp 'IASR'
Shows the same layout for town and the river as in (1); names of owners given and vacant lots noted; canal, sawmill, grist mill, reserves; certain blocks east of Clarence St and between Dalhousie and Wellington sts numbered 1–9; probably made after 1836 when Blyth became a P.L.S.
OOAMA (NMC 11361)

1192 *1834*
Map of Brantford in the District of Gore by [Sgd] Lewis Burwell Dy Surveyor April 1834
Col ms 89 x 175 cm 1" to 2 chains Endorsements: '969'
The village plot has now been extended north to Marlborough St and east of Rawdon to Aylmer and Maitland sts; shows the village south to river; a few bldgs identified.
OTNR (SR 8759)

Related maps

(**2**) *1846*
Brantford. Reduced Copy by [Sgd] J.G. Chewett S.G. Office 28th June 1837 Surveyor Generals Office Toronto 29th June 1837 J.W. Macaulay Surv Genl
Col ms 75 x 134 cm 4/5 inch to 2 chains
Provenance: OOAMA RG 10M 76703/9 no 265); shows the town as extended in 1834 with the addition of lots laid out in square, reserved for Church of England; canal; also copy of 31 Jan 1846, reduced, 1" to 4 chains, 'IASR 1690' (OOAMA (NMC 22248)); and a copy dated 24 Feb 1848 (OOAMA (RG 10M 76703/9 no 262, NMC 13069); and a later copy, 'Brantford. Department of Crown Lands Quebec March 18th 1863. Compd E.T. [Sgd] Andrew Russell Assist. Commissioner' endorsed 'IASR' and 'F 4188' (OOAMA (NMC 22250)).
OOAMA (NMC 13069; 13131; 22248; 22250)

(**3**) *1849*
Brantford Copy T.Devine Crown Land Department Surveyors Office Toronto 19th December 1849 [Sgd] J.H.Price Commissioner of Crown Lands
Col ms 53 x 86 cm 1" to 4 chains Endorsements: 'No 79'
Shows the same layout as (1) above; the Wilkes tract is shown running diagonally across the town.
OTAR(P)

1193 *[1839?]*
BRANTFORD / IN THE GORE DISTRICT U. CANADA / SURVEYED BY / Lewis Burwell Esq. / Aug. 13th 1830. / / N. CURRIER'S LITH. 2 SPRUCE St NEW YORK
Print (lith) hand col 38 x 56 cm 1" to 10 chains
OTAR copy inscribed on cover 'Presented by James Wilkes Esq. to David Thorburn Commissioner Six Nations Indian Lands 10th June 1846' (provenance: OTAR Wilkes Papers); shows the 1834 survey of the town with the addition of subdivisions by W.J. Kerr south of the Grand R from Oxford to Brant St, and Burford to Wentworth St; by R. Biggar between West and Cedar sts to river; by Smith and Kerby northwest of Cedar St to Bedford St, and from Dumfries to Duke St; these subdivisions are shown on the twp plan dated 1839 (see **A254**) and the date in the title was perhaps meant to be 1839; Currier was at Spruce St from 1838 but made few maps after 1840 (Ristow, 296); 'Reference' keys the various properties, the 'Government Plot,' and the Episcopal, Baptist, Methodist, Presbyterian, Congregational, and African churches; roads named; marshy lands.
OBBM OTAR OTMCL

1194 *1840*
Extract from the Plan of the Town of Brantford showing in a red dotted margin the twenty acres of ground leased by the Indians to Marshall Lewis, and sold by him to Nathan Gage, lying south of the old travelled Road, now Colborne Street and fronting the Grand River. – Also two other parcels of uplands, and also within red dotted margins, conveyed by Asahe Hulbert to the said Nathan Gage ... Brantford 6th October 1840 [Sgd] Lewis Burwell Dy Surveyor
Col ms on tracing paper 53 x 41 cm 1" to 2 chains
From petition (OOA RG 1 L3 G22 no 73 1840); also shows lands Gage acquired from Jedediah Jackson; the Lewis land is between mill cove and river, and crosses the canal; the land from Hulbert is the Wilkes tract; notes sgd by N. Gage about certain lots; (Holmden 1522).
OOAMA (NMC 3722)

Related maps

(**2**) *1848*
Plan of part of the Town of Brantford, shewing within this Red margin, a parcel of 47 1/2 acres of Land claimed by Nathan Gage Esqr a Lease from certain Chiefs (John Hill and others) of the Five Nations Indians to John A. Wilkes Esqr. Brantford 28th July 1848. [Sgd] Lewis Burwell Dy Surveyor
Col ms 119 x 18 cm 1" to 2 chains Endorsements: 'No 1516'; stamp 'IASR'
Endorsed 'With my Report on Nathan Gage Esqr. claim 22d Feby 1849 [Sgd] D. Thorburn I. Commr'; map shows the diagonal parcel originally leased to John Wilkes, from Darling St to beyond Marlborough St; additional notes on claims by Mr Gage for parts of church lands; also a plan from the same source (NMC 22288): 'Part of the Town of Brantford showing the lots granted to Nathan Gage.' endorsed 'IASR' and 'F 4138' and showing area south of Dalhousie St to canal, Canal St and Wilkes tract from Colborne St north, notes and descriptions of Gage's claims, 'old fording place,' and 'original road before the building of the bridge.'
OOAMA (NMC 3723; 22288)

1195 *1847*
Plan of the Town of Brantford, in the District of Gore. Shewing the completion of the Survey. by [Sgd] William Walker Dy P. Surveyor. Brantford 11th Feby 1847
Col ms 66 x 98 cm Scale not given
Shows the extension of the government survey north six streets to Alice St; park lots laid out; town lots shown west of Clarence to Queen St; the Wilkes tract is shown running diagonally north-east from Darling St; shows area between canal and river; public cemetery; also a copy dated 24 Feb 1848 (OOAMA RG 10M 76703/9 no 262; NMC 13069); and a copy of (1): 'Plan of the Town of Brantford ... Brantford 23d May 1849. Copied by William Walker D.P.S. David Thorburn' 1" to 4 chains, endorsed 'IASR' and 'No 1691' and with the additions of notes about status of lots and a few names (OOAMA (NMC 22249)).
OOAMA (NMC 22249; 31069) OTNR (SR 34)

Related maps

(2) *1852*
Copy of part of D.P.S. Wm Walker's Plan of Brantford Office copy Crown Lands Department Quebec Dec 1852 T.D. [Sgd] Andrew Russell S & D
Col ms 58 x 79 cm 1" to 4 chains Endorsements: 'No 82'
Shows the northern part of town from Chatham St to Alice St with town lots and park lots as in (1); shows Wilkes tract; names added in many lots.
OTAR(P)

1196 *1852*
MAP / of the Town of / BRANTFORD / COUNTY OF BRANT / Canada West / drawn from New Surveys by / MARCUS SMITH. / 1852 / Based on the Original Survey of the Town by / Lewis Burwell Esqr / Published by C.L. HELLIWELL, Hamilton. // ENGRAVED AND PRINTED AT / FERD. MAYER'S LITHOGRAPHY / No 93 William St N.Y.
Print (lith) hand col 81 x 108 cm 1" to 5 chains
Inset: 'PORTION OF THE TOWN ENLARGED.'; views: 'JOHN KERBY [residence],' 'PUBLIC SCHOOL,' and 'TOWN HALL'; shows the town south of Alice St and east of Bedford St, west of Maitland St and south of river to Burford and Walnut sts; shows all bldgs with major ones named; relief, canal, Grand River Navigation Co. land; names of owners of large lots and names of subdivision surveys; inset shows area north to Dalhousie St only.
OBBM OOAMA (NMC 11355)

1197 *[1856]*
PLAN / of / BUSH HILL & OAKLEY PARK / The Property of / GEO. S. WILKES ESQ. / L. Mooney Lith. Buffalo
Print (lith) 65 x 54 cm Scale not given
In ms: 'Copy Registered March 13 1856' and 'This Property is composed of Lots Numbers 26,27,28,29 and 30, in the Third concession of the Township of Brantford. Surveyed for the Proprietor by O. Robinson'; shows area east of Buffalo, Brantford and Goderich Ry and gravel road to Paris, on both sides of Elm and Cypress sts and along Crescent St; names of owners; probably related to R.P. 31 (**B320**).
Private Collection

1198 *1857*
MAP OF / EAGLE PLACE / SOUTH BRANTFORD / BEING PART OF LOT NO. 2 / EAGLE'S NEST / Township of Brantford / F.T. WILKES ESQ. PROPRIETORS. / T. Cheesman C.E. & P.L.S. // Maclear & Co. Lith. Toronto / 1857
Print (lith) 54 x 67 cm 1" to 3 chains
Ms note indicates plan is substitute for that made by O. Robinson (R.P. 36 of 16 Aug 1854); area bounded by river, canal, lots on Eagle Ave and Row to Brighton Row and Mohawk Rd; centre of town shown north of canal; a few bldgs; see also **B316, B324**.
Brant 2 (R.P. 35(2))

1199 *1857*
VALUABLE / PROPERTY FOR SALE, / IN THE FLOURISHING / TOWN OF BRANTFORD, C.W. // FOUR ACRES OF LAND / In the Town of Brantford, adjoining the ERIE & LAKE HURON RAILWAY DEPOT, / on the West Side of Sydenham Street, and has been divided into Lots (as here given), upon which Property are three houses, ... For particulars, &c apply to Mr. J.R. MOUNTJOY, Toronto. Toronto, 12th May, 1857. // BLACKBURN'S CITY STEAM PRESS, 63 YONGE STREET, TORONTO
Print (typeset) 52 x 35 cm 1" to 1 chain
Shows area from railway to Hughsons Alley and Usher St and Sydenham St to St John St; added in ms are the number of feet on each lot; sgd 'Brantford June 24th 1857 O. Robinson P.L.Surveyor.'; this plan forms part of a set of mainly ms maps from 1847–81 of the Brant co area, many sgd by O. Robinson (OOAMA acc no 85602/596).
OOAMA (NMC 88460)

BRIGHTON

1200 *1848*
Plan of the Reserve for a town plot on Freeman's Point in the township of Murray. Surveyed by J.K. Roche Provincial Land Surveyor. 1st August 1848.
Ms 71 x 51 cm 1" to 4 chains Watermark: 'JAMES WHATMAN TURKEY MILLS 1845'
Probably the projected plan for the survey to accompany the second instructions (see (2)) as the streets have been pencilled in but not named; some bldgs shown; road to Freeman's Point, road from Presqu'ile to Carrying Place; relief, swampy areas, sawmill, other roads; the first plan for Gosport, now part of Brighton.
OTNR (SR 99)

Related maps

(2) *1848*
Plan of the Town Plot of Gosport Township of Murray. [Sgd] John K. Roche Provincial Land Surveyor 3 October 1848.
Col ms 96 x 65 cm 1" to 2 chains Endorsements: 'A 168'
(SI 12 July 1848 and 22 Aug 1848 to survey and subdivide into bldg lots the town plot at Freeman's Point; OTNR FN 289 7 Oct 1848); shows the survey of the town from Bay to Queen St, and Blake to Lambton St; includes road to Presqu'ile, and mill pond and mills; swampy areas; some bldgs identified; also a later copy in OTAR(P): 'Plan of Brighton formerly Gosport Crown Land Department Surveyors Office West Montreal March 1854 [Sgd] Andrew Russell S & D.' endorsed 'No 77' and with the addition of some names of patentees, 'Brighton' in the title added later.
OTAR(P) OTNR (SR 115)

(BRISTOL)

1201 *[1836?]*
Copy of a Plan of part of the Town of Bristol Laid out by Robert Ross Dy Surveyor w/in Part of Lot 24 in the 6th Con. Vespra.
Ms 33 x 41 cm Scale not given
Shows a plan for a subdivision west of Barrie bounded by Colborne, Queen, and Princess sts; various reserves for market block, etc; the subdivision apparently was not implemented (Hunter, 1:48) and there is no registered plan; town lots in Bristol were being advertised for sale in the *Patriot* (Toronto) in October 1836.
OMSA

BROCKVILLE

1202 *1811*
Plan of the Village of Elizabethtown the Property of William Buell Esq. into Town Lots of which the following have been disposed of prior to the delineation of this Plan and were made with the [consent?] of the Purchasers ... Elizabethtown, 12th September 1811 [Sgd] Jeremiah McCarthy [and] Plan and Survey of Williamstown in the Township of Elizabethtown Founded by William Buell Esquire Proprietor of the said Town Plot.
Col ms Size unknown 1" to 100 ft Endorsements: 'F 57'
'This Plan traced from a photograph of the original in the possession of J.D. Buell Esqr ... Decr 21st 1881 ... Willis Chipman O.L.S.'; shows the nucleus of the town laid out on both sides of the King's Highway and between the properties of Daniel Jones on the west and Charles Jones on the east; a street leads north to Court House Square and a grid of three north-south streets and about five east-west streets is shown south of the King's Highway; about 20 blocks of land, some with houses, are shown and keyed with names of owners; orchards; reproduced in MacPherson, 14.
Original not located.

1203 *1816*
Plan of the Village of Brockville being part of the property of William Buell Esq. situated in front of a part of his Lands and laid out in lots according to this plan into Town lots of which the following have been disposed of prior to the delineation of this plan and marked with the initials of the Purchasers Names ... Taken from Actual Survey [Sgd] Andrew N. Buell. Brockville September 25th 1816.
Col ms Size unknown 1/2" to 100 ft
Streets named: Court Ave, Broad St, St Andrew St, Commonwealth St, Return St; shows fewer streets laid out south of King's Highway but a complete grid of streets is now shown north of highway; major property owners keyed as well as major bldgs, orchards, and houses; a photoreproduction is in OOAMA (NMC 70948), and in Ten Cate, 31.
Original not located

1204 *1827*
Plan of the Island referred to in Mr. Flint's Petition, and the adjacent part of Brockville. [Endorsed title:] 'Enclosed in Petition for License of Occupation 1827.'
Col ms 36 x 39 cm 1" to 200 ft
Detached from land petition of Billa Flint of 20 Mar 1827 requesting island opp town (OOA RG 1 L3 vol 556 no 16); shows the area from Court House Square to the shore between St George's St [Broad St] and Notre Dame St; Flint's property, with wharves shown at foot of St Andrew's St and a proposed wharf shown on [Refugee] island opp; bldgs and inns; (Holmden 1531).
OOAMA (NMC 3728)

1205 *1833 (1850)*
Brockville Copied from John Booth's plan of 1833 Crown Land Department Toronto 10th September 18[50] T.D.
Col ms 66 x 84 cm 1" to 200 ft Endorsements: 'No 20'
Shows the outline of the town and streets from the water to two streets north of Church St and from Perth to Ford St; shows the court-house, churches, market, mill pond, burying ground; irregular lots on some streets; later changes; the 1833 original plan has not been found.
OTAR(P)

1206 *1853*
MAP / OF / BROCKVILLE / Canada West / 1853. / Published by WALL & FORREST New York.
Print (lith) hand col 75 x 117 cm 1" to approx 275 ft or 16 rods
Inset: 'Messrs Coleman & Cos / TANNERY, &c. /

Situated in the Village of LYN near BROCKVILLE' 1" to 24 rods; 10 views of residences and businesses 'from Daguerre by Spencer'; 'list of subscribers'; shows the town from west boundary beyond Perth St to Plank Road and from the water north to beyond GTR and Hubbles mill pond; all bldgs shown and major ones named; names of owners of large properties; mills, mill ponds, treed areas.
OTNR (SR 50)

1207 *1854*
Map of part of Brockville Canada West Showing the River Frontage 1854.
Col ms on linen 70 x 91 cm 1" to 200 ft
Endorsements: 'No 22'
Shows the town from the water to Court House Square; a few bldgs shown; a few later notes.
OTAR(P)

1208 *1860*
Map of the Property of James L Schofield Esqr near the Town of Brockville. Surveyed in Septr 1860 By Samuel Hazlewood.
Col ms 64 x 91 cm 1" to 100 ft
Shows a subdivision west of Perth St, and from GTR to Frederick St with lots from Havelock to Frederick St and a few south of Hubbell St; some names of owners; mill pond and mills; line of high water traced 'from a map by H. Lillie P.L.S.'; detailed plan of estate with bldgs and landscaping.
OTAR

BRONTE

1209 *[1833]*
Plan of town plot on 12 Mile Creek 4th Concsn Trafalgar. Surveyed by William Hawkins D.P.S. Bronté (Indian Lands).
Col ms 55 x 80 cm 1" to 4 chains Endorsements: 'No 5'
(OTNR FN 690 3 Apr 1834); shows the town from Lake and Ontario St north to Chalmers St, East St to beyond Mississauga St on other side of river; lots intended for farm and park lots; areas cleared by D. Donovan and Mrs Belyea; depths in creek and lake; some bldgs shown possibly added later, and later additions of names; endorsed '1834' and 'original'; some town lots were advertised for sale on 21 Apr 1836 (OTAR RG 1 C-III-1 vol 2); also a copy in OTAR(P): 'Bronte Office Copy [Sgd] J.G. Chewett.' endorsed 'No 58' and with added notes about Bronte Harbour Co. lands of 1842, 1843, and 1848.
OTAR(P) OTNR (SR 26)

Related maps

(2) *1834*
Bronte 12 Mile Creek Town Plot Surveyor Generals Office copy from Mr Hawkins plan [Sgd] 28th July 1834 J.G.C.
Col ms 56 x 68 cm 1" to 4 chains
Provenance: OOAMA RG 10M 76703/9 no 272; shows the same layout of streets and lots with some names and many later additions; there is also a copy sgd '25 Apr 1839 R.B. Sullivan Survr Genl' showing names of patentees at the time in OOAMA (RG 10M 76703/9 no 279, NMC 13134).
OOAMA (NMC 13115; 13134)

1210 *1848*
Copy of P.L.S. J.S. Dennis's Plan of Bronte. Crown Land Department Surveyors Office West Montreal November 1848 True Copy. A.R. [Sgd] T. Bouthillier.
Col ms 59 x 70 cm 1" to 4 chains Endorsements: '1983'; stamp 'IASR'
Certified as an exact copy of plan of survey and inspection made under instructions of March 1848, '(Signed) Jno Stoughton Dennis P.S. Toronto Aug 10th 1848'; shows town plot and streets as originally surveyed; low land, marsh, lot sizes; Bronte Harbour Co. lands; many later additions of notes.
OOAMA (NMC 22255)

1211 *1864*
Plan of Survey made to determine the Easterly Boundary of the Town of Bronte in the 4th Con. of the Township of Trafalgar Pursuant to Instructions dated 4th of April 1864 from Andrew Russell Esqre Asst Comr C. Lands by W. Hawkins P.L.S. [Sgd] William Hawkins P.L.S. Toronto 30 June 1864.
Col ms 125 x 74 cm 1" to 4 chains Endorsements: '18301/64' 'B 15'
(SI refers to an earlier survey by Winter; OTNR FN 76 1864); line cuts across East St; treed areas.
OTNR (SR 7695)

BURLINGTON

1212 *1856*
PLAN / of / BUILDING AND PARK LOTS / IN THE / VILLAGE OF BURLINGTON / adjoining the WELLINGTON SQUARE STATION of the / HAMILTON AND TORONTO RAILWAY / 1856 / H. Gregory Lith. Hamilton. [and] [WELLINGTON SQUARE]
2 prints (lith) on 1 sheet 94 x 63 cm 1" to 200 ft
Shows the village to be established north of Wellington Square on the railway; railway to beyond Burlington St, Brant St east to Nelson St; station; a few bldgs on estates; printed slip pasted on: 'This Property will be sold by Auction [in ms]: "On Wednesday 20th July 1856 on the ground" Best & Green Auctioneers, Hamilton'; the other map shows Wellington Square from the lake north to Caroline St, and Locust St east to Martha St; all bldgs shown including A.M. Chisholm's house; no registered plan and subdivision not shown on plan below (**1213**) or in co atlas (Pope, ... *Halton* (1877)).
OTAR

1213 *1858*
MAP / of the / BRANT BLOCK, / IN THE / Township of Nelson Co Halton, / By / WINTER & ABREY. / Provincial Land Surveyors. / Maclear & Co. Lith: Toronto.
Print (lith) hand col 81 x 60 cm 1" to 12 chains
Inset: 'Nelson Representing the location of the Brant Block, by Winters & Abrey P.L. Surveyors, Milton Feby 11th 1858 [on a location map of Nelson and Brant Block in central south Canada West]'; inset: 'PLAN / OF / WELLINGTON SQUARE, / ENLARGED. 1" to 2 chains'; the main map shows the blocks and nos in the Brant Block and the names of owners including 'Heirs of late Wm Sinclair' and 'Heirs of the late Kerr'; the Hamilton and Toronto railway is shown with the Wellington Square station; the inset shows the town from Water St to Caroline St, and Martha St to Brant St; lot nos and sizes.
OTAR

1214 *1864*
[Map of ...] WELLINGTON SQUARE / TOWNSHIP OF NELSON / [COUNTY – OF] – HALTON // Drawn By G. Brockitt Abrey P.L.S. Milton June 20 1864.
Print (lith), pt missing 61 x 94 cm Approx 1" to 2 chains
A compiled plan of the town with all the subdivisions shown; surveys of A. Bates, W. Bates, and Torrance; first part of title missing on R.P. copy; see also **B381**.
Halton 20 (R.P. 39)

CALEDONIA

1215 *[1844] March?*
Diagram Showing the proposed Reservation for the Town of Caledonia.
Col ms 54 x 75 cm 1" to 4 chains Endorsements: '1669'; stamp 'IASR'
Shows the proposed boundary of the town with bldgs and boundaries of land already occupied by various individuals around the intersection of the Brantford to Dunnville Rd and the Hamilton and Port Dover Rd; also shows the village of Seneca at the east end, north of river; towing path; this is probably R. Wells's original plan; also a copy of the same title sgd 'Surveyor Generals Office Kingston, 20th March 1844. A true copy of R. Wells Plan in the office of the Chief Superintendent of Indian Affairs [Sgd] Thomas Parke Survr Genl.' and endorsed '1114' (OTNR (SR 43)).
OOAMA (NMC 22262) OTNR (SR 43)

1216 *1844 October*
A Plan of the Village of Caledonia surveyed by order of Thomas Parke Esqre, Surveyor General etc. West Flamboro October 15th 1844 [Sgd] James Kirkpatrick D.P. Surveyor.
Col ms 65 x 87 cm 1" to 4 chains Endorsements: 'Q 69' '1115'
(SI 12 Apr 1844 and 5 Aug 1844 to survey and subdivide lands on or near plank rd and those in rear into park lots; OTNR FN 800 18 Oct 1844); shows the town laid out from Moray St to Orkney St and Kincardine St to Ross St north of river, and Forfar to Linlithgow and Haddington and Berwick to Bute St south of river; five squares laid out; marshy areas; some bldgs shown; Grand River Navigation Co. land shown on north and south bank at west side of town; town and park lots with nos and sizes; also a copy: 'Caledonia. By James Kirkpatrick D.P.S. 1844. Surveyor General's Office Montreal 5th March 1845 A true copy [Sgd] Thomas Parke Survr Genl.' endorsed 'IASR' and 'F 4176' with the addition of some notes on sales and some names of owners (OOAMA (NMC 22263)); (*OHIM* 7.7).
OOAMA (NMC 22263) OTNR (SR 44)

Related maps

(2) *1845*
Town Plot of Caledonia Exhibiting the boundaries of the different claimants [Sgd] James Kirkpatrick P.D. Surveyor July 1845
Col ms 64 x 95 cm 1" to 4 chains
Provenance: OOAMA (RG 10M 76703/9 no 263); shows the same layout of streets and lots with boundaries of large lots and names of owners; Grand River Navigation Co. land.
OOAMA (NCM 13070)

CANFIELD

1217 *1855*
Plan of the Town Azoff in the Township of North Cayuga County of Haldimand By [Sgd] Edmd DeCew P.L. Surveyor Cayuga 14th August 1855 [Sgd] David Thorburn Special Commissioner Examined T.D. C.L.O. Sept 1855.
Col ms 43 x 59 cm 1" to 2 chains Endorsements: 'Q 88'
Streets laid out above Talbot St to Retallack St and from Emma to Raglan St east of corner of 1st con north and south lot X; burying ground, school lot; Buffalo, Brantford & Goderich Railroad cuts diagonally through plot; also a copy with same title, and statement: 'Deposited by David Thorburn ...' (R.P. 5937); also a copy of the same date, etc, in OOAMA (RG 10M 76703/9 no 257, NMC 13081).
Haldimand 18 (R.P. 5937) OOAMA (NMC 13081) OTNR (SR 6491)

(CAPE RICH)

1218 *1856*
CAPE RICH / THE PROPERTY OF D. McLAREN, TOWNSHIP OF ST. VINCENT, COUNTY OF

GREY. / SURVEYED by Wm GIBBARD, AUGUST 1856. / Maclear & Co Lith Toronto C.W. / Wm GIBBARD P.L.S. / AUGUST 1856.
Print (lith) 83 x 55 cm 1" to 2.5 chains
Inset: 'SCROLL / SHEWING THE POSITION OF CAPE RICH / IN REFERENCE TO THE STEAMBOAT COMMUNICATION / BETWEEN COLLINGWOOD AND OTHER PLACES TO THE WEST.'; shows the town with streets and lots as laid out; steamer wharf; soundings; post office closed in 1920 and name deleted 1945 (Carter, I:192).
Grey 16 (no R.P. number)

CARDINAL

1219 *[1848?]*
Map / of the TOWN of / ELGIN / JOHNSTOWN DISTRICT / CANADA WEST. / Surveyed by James West, / Provl Land Surveyor, Civil Engr &c / District Surveyor Eastn District. / Matthews' Lith.
Print (lith) 85 x 53 cm 1" to 80 ft
Shows the town laid out from Lewis St east to Jessup St along the St Lawrence; houses shown along Dundas St; some bldgs identified; canal and lock around Galops Rapids; 'reservation for mill purposes'; note: 'The Terminus of the Boston and Ogdensburgh Rail Road is Only about 7 miles distant. The whole of this property with the Water Power ... is for sale ... Apply to James Jessup, Brockville, Canada West.'; R.P. Cardinal 7 (**B417**) was registered 18 Oct 1848 and appears to be a transcript of this map; OOAMA copy has ms adds of names of owners in all lots; (Holmden 1622).
OOAMA (NMC 23892) OTNR (SR 92)

1220 *[1857]*
Map of the Town of Elgin Johnstown District Canada West. Surveyed by James West, Provl Land Surveyor ... Remark This Copy shows the Mill Race as laid out on the 14th May 1857 on the North Side of the Left Lock. [Sgd] G.F. Baillairgé.
Ms on linen 91 x 53 cm 1" to 80 ft Endorsements: stamps 'BW' '593'
A close copy of the printed map (**1219**) with dimensions of proposed mill race, proposed mill, and mill site shown.
OOAMA (NMC 23891)

CATARAQUI

1221 *1852*
Sketch of the part of the Village of Waterloo situated on the front of Lot No 16 3rd Concession Township of Kingston delineating The situation and dimensions of the two Tracts of Land ... between the front of the Lot and the Road to Purday's Mills; – The one Edward Cooks and the other David Purdy; but principally designed to Exhibit the part of Cook's Tract ... [Sgd] William H. Kilborn Provincial L. Surveyor Kingston 24th September 1852.
Ms 50 x 39 cm 1" to 2 chains
Provenance: OOAMA Kingston Planning Board map no 8; shows village, lots, and owners along 3rd Concession Rd, road to Dundas Mills, Loughborough and Portland Rd; description and contents of two tracts.
OOAMA (NMC 4515)

CAYUGA

1222 *1833*
Rough Plan of the Town of Cayuga situate on the Grand River on Talbot Road South in the County of Haldimand in the District of Niagara, Surveyed by order of the Surveyor General by [Sgd] Lewis Burwell Dy Surveyor Cayuga Grand River 5th June 1833
Col ms 51 x 79 cm 1" to 4 chains Endorsements: 'F 4131'; stamp 'IASR'
(SI 23 March 1833 to survey town plot on Grand R in Cayuga Twp on principle of Brantford); shows a town plot from Winniett St on the east side to beyond Delaware St on the west, and from Chippawa to Norton St on the east and from Talbot Rd north on the west; town lots on the east and park lots on the west; some unnamed streets and park lots shown at outer edges; shows church and burying ground, marshy areas, cornfields, drowned land, co court reserves; notes; also an untitled and unfinished plan endorsed 'A 14' and '629' and showing similar streets to above but unnamed, and marshy areas (OTNR (SR 46)).
OOAMA (NMC 22269) OTNR (SR 46)

1223 *1834*
Town Plot of Cayuga Surveyed by Order of S.P. Hurd Esquire Surveyor General dated York 23d Apl 1833. by [Sgd] Lewis Burwell Dy Surveyor. Brantford 4th March 1834.
Col ms 71 x 95 cm 1" to 4 chains Endorsements: 'No 10' '619'
(OTNR FN 105 4 Apr 1834); shows more named streets than the 1833 map, from Winniett St west to Dixon St across river, from Clench St to Philip St on west, and Indian St to Joseph St on east; co court-house, market, school lot, common; public and church burying grounds; proposed bridge at King St; also a copy: 'Town of Cayuga situate on the Grand River on Talbot Road south County of Haldimand District of Niagara Surveyed by Lewis Burwell Dy Surveyor Cayuga, Grand River 5th [June] 1833 Copy JGC.' endorsed 'No 15' and showing same layout as 1834 plan above with later additions of names in lots on east side of river and reserves for Municipal Corporation (OTAR(P)); and a copy in OOAMA (NMC 22279): 'Cayuga by Lewis Burwell D.P.S. 1833 Surveyor General's Office, Montreal 8th Novr 1844, A true

copy [Sgd] Thomas Parke Survr Genl.' endorsed 'IASR' (stamp) and 'F 4126' with the additions of names and notes on lots.
OOAMA (NMC 22279) OTAR(P) OTNR (SR 6807)

1224 *1842*
Plan of that part of the town of Cayuga lying upon the west side of the Grand River in the County of Haldimand [Sgd] E & J De Cew P.L. Surveyors Cayuga 11th August 1842.
Col ms 68 x 62 cm 1" to 4 chains Endorsements: '1526'; stamp 'IASR'
Shows a different layout for the town west of the river; the River Rd has been extended diagonally from near the river to cross the Talbot Rd west of Delaware St; streets and some lots oriented to River Rd but unnamed; notes across much of new layout: 'not subdivided.'
OOAMA (NMC 22280)

1225 *1843*
Plan of the Village of Cayuga on the Grand River in the Niagara District Canada. December 4th 1843 to Saml P. Jarvis Esqre Chief – Superintendent of Indian Affairs by [Sgd] Robert Wells.
Col ms 63 x 92 cm 1" to 4 chains Endorsements: '1675'; stamp 'IASR'
A very detailed map showing the town plot layout as in earlier plans with reserves for school, market, churches, etc, as well as later irregular development; east of Winniett St irregular lots cut across town grid; from Chippawa St to Soho St 'proposed subdivision'; names of owners and indication of areas cleared, bldgs; table of total area cleared by squatters, by government, and in town plot; bridge, relief, Indian cornfields; town on west side is shown as in 1834 plan (**1223**) with a few lots and roads cutting across.
OOAMA (NMC 22281)

1226 *1851 June*
Map of that part of the Town of Cayuga in the County of Haldimand lying upon The East Side of the Grand River by Edmund DeCew P.L.S. Cayuga June 3rd 1851.
Col ms 66 x 58 cm 1" to 4 chains Endorsements: '1676'; stamp 'IASR'
Shows the town from Latham St to Joseph St and from river east to Monture St; the court-house is not shown and Ottawa St is shown as extending through the court-house grounds.
OOAMA (NMC 22283)

1227 *1851 October*
Plan of that part of the Town of Cayuga lying upon the east side of the Grand River in the County of Haldimand by [Sgd] Edmd DeCew P.L.S. Cayuga 21st October 1851.
Col ms 64 x 67 cm 1" to 4 chains
(OTNR FN 331 15 Nov 1851); similar to above plan (**1226**) but shows court-house and grounds, markets, town hall, school lot, grammar school, burying ground, churches; several reserve blocks; also a copy: 'Plan ... 1851. Indian Office Cayuga 21st Octr 1851 [Sgd] David Thorburn Special Commissioner.' endorsed 'IASR' (stamp) and '1685' (OOAMA (NMC 22282)); and a copy: 'Cayuga Copy of DeCew's Plan East side of Grand River Office Copy Crown Lands Department Quebec 31st January 1853 [Sgd] Andrew Russell for the Commissioner of Crown Lands.' endorsed 'No 83' but not showing court-house, although names of patentees added (OTAR(P)).
OOAMA (NMC 22282) OTAR(P) OTNR (SR 91259)

1228 *1856*
Plan of water lots in the Town of Cayuga by [Sgd] Edmd DeCew P.L.S. David Thorburn I. Comr. Cayuga 11th Septr 1856. A Survey under instructions from the Indian Department [Sgd] A Russell.
Col ms 56 x 46 cm 1" to 2 chains Endorsements: 'A 216'
Water lots shown along Ouse St from Norton St to Tuscarora St on east side of river; lot nos and dimensions, notes; there are two copies in OOAMA (NMC 3745, 3746) both entitled 'Plan of water lots in the Town of Cayuga. Cayuga 11th September 1856 [Sgd] Edmd De Cew P.L.S. David Thorburn S. Comr.'; NMC 3745 is endorsed 'IASR' and 'F 4180'; NMC 3746 is endorsed '1686' and has notes on sales of water lots to 1863.
OOAMA (NMC 3745–6) OTNR (SR 45)

1229 *1867*
Plan of that part of the Town of Cayuga lying west of the Grand River according to the Plan and Field notes of Lewis Burwell P.L.S. dated A.D. 1833 Surveyed by Edmund DeCew Provincial Land Surveyor. Cayuga 25th March 1867. Drawn by John DeCew Cayuga.
Col ms 63 x 45 cm 1" to 4 chains Endorsements: [IASR] '1687'
Shows the west part of town from Dixon St to river and Clench to Philip St; 'Note 25 March 1867 ... Mr Burwell PLS did not post off any Streets west of Delaware Street –with no traces of survey except outside limits of the plot –'; shows east part of town to Seneca St.
OOAMA (NMC 4853)

CHARLESTON

1230 *1835*
Map of the Town of Charleston Situate on lots no 21 & 22 in the 9th Conn of Yonge formerly Escott as Surveyed by John Booth Dep Pl Surveyor in July 1835.
Ms 32 x 19 cm 1" to 140 ft
Shows the town from Bay St to St Andrew St, and Hill St to William St; lot nos and sizes; some

names on lots; related to Leeds 28 (R.P. 103) except streets and lots extend further east and west in the latter.
OTAR (MU 275)

(CHARLOTTEVILLE)

1231 *[1793?]*
Charlotteville
Col ms 42 x 33 cm 1" to 20 chains Endorsements: 'A 13' '627'
(SI 9 June 1793 to W. Chewitt to find suitable site for fortification and town on point opp Presqu'ile [Long Point]); shows town plot and proposed streets as in [1798] plan below (**1232**); shows the area from Charlotteville to Turkey Point; land including 'Mabee's old house is to be reserved for Lt. Governors future disposal'; improved land by Mabee, fields, and 'valuable fishery occupied by squatters'; a later addition and note shows the 'Normandale and Fredericksburgh Plank Road.'
OTNR (SR 58)

1232 *[1798]*
Submitted for the Commencement of the Town of Charlotteville. D.W. Smith A.S.G. Copy W.C. Approved Peter Russell.
Col ms 52 x 36 cm 1" to 4 chains Endorsements: 'A 12' '621'
(SI 6 Feb 1798 and 15 Sept 1798 to T. Welch to ascertain and sketch suitable site for town on ground immediately above point on hill above Mabee's house and commence survey of town); two survey points and baseline noted as 'Mr Aitken's'; streets laid out from Court St east to Grave St, and shoreline north to Back St; reserves in centre for church, pound, market, school, schoolmaster, parson, and at boundary of town for gaol, court-house, and burying ground; Mabee's old house; relief; also a copy in OTNR (SR 57): 'Plan for the commencement of the town of Charlotteville [Sgd] D W Smith A.S.G.' endorsed 'No 16' and with the addition of later notes, names, and dates of patentees, and note on a grant to Mr Brock in 1812 and lots returned for sale 13 Jan 1853; there is also a plan showing reserves for glebe and commons in D.W. Smith's 'Report upon Glebes & Commons ... 1802.'
OTAR (RG 1 A-II-1 vol 2 pp 942–87) OTNR (SR 56–7)

1233 *1815*
Town of Charlotteville [Sgd] Surveyor General's Office York 29 July 1815. Thos Ridout Survr Genl.
Col ms 63 x 49 cm 1" to 4 chains Endorsements: 'A 11' '628'
Shows the same layout of the town as the 1798 plan (**1232**) but a few names have been added on shore lots and lots on river are not shown; a later note by J.W. Macaulay, 7 Sept 1837.
OTNR (SR 59)

1234 *1853*
Plan of Lot No 14 in Concession A, Charlotteville, as laid out into a town-plot, park-lots and glebe. Park-lots & Glebe Surveyed & Town Plot Re-surveyed by James Black P.L.S. June 1853. Examined [Initialled] A.R.
Col ms 82 x 40 cm 1" to 4 chains Endorsements: 'A 185'
(SI 29 Jan 1853 to subdivide block of land in rear of town plot into 5-acre park lots); shows park lots in ranges A and B north of Back St, and above Normandale and Fredericksburg Rd north of glebe; streets and lots shown in town plot; also a copy in OTAR(P) with the same title, 'Plan ... glebe. Crown Lands Department Quebec Dec 1853 [Sgd] A.N. Morin Commissioner of Crown Lands,' endorsed 'No 97'; although resurveyed at this late date, Charlotteville was described as a ruin in 1823 having been abandoned after the War of 1812 (Brown, I:84); not shown on co map of 1856 (**817**).
OTNR (SR 55)

CHATHAM

1235 *1794*
A Survey of Part of the River Thames, called Chatham Upper Canada 1794.
Col ms on 2 sheets Ea 38 x 54 cm 1" to 150 ft
Inset: [three sections across river] 1" to 15 ft; this sketch is mentioned in Simcoe's letter of 13 Oct 1794 to Lt Adye about the building of a blockhouse (Simcoe, *Correspondence*, III:127); shows the site of town, the point designated for military reserve, and sections for area where blockhouse to be built; relief.
OTAR (Simcoe Map 446696–7)

1236 *1795*
The above is a plan of the Town of Chatham, situate on a fork, of the River Thames, in the Western District and Province of Upper Canada; [Sgd] Abraham Iredell Depy Surveyor Western District Detroit Novr 1st 1795
Col ms 48 x 37 cm Scale not given Endorsements: 'A 9' '634'
(SI 2 Aug 1795 to find point where four twps intersect, lay out row of lots near military grounds, and subdivide into town plot); shows the town as laid out into 114 lots with military ground, church and gaol reserve; lots are one acre in size; further notes given on measurements in the survey; 'Clark's House & Mill'; there is also a later copy of this plan entitled '[Chatham] Detroit 1st Nov 95 (Signed) A. Iredell,' probably copied by Charles Rankin (OTMCL (E.W. Banting Collection)).
OTMCL (E.W. Banting Collection) OTNR (SR 49)

Related maps

(2) *1795*
Plan of the Town of Chatham. Situate on a fork of the River Thames in the Western District and

Province of Upper Canada ... Copied from an Original, by Mr Abram Iredell, Depy Surveyr., Western District dated Detroit Novr 1st 1795. Surveyr Genls Office Newark 24th Novemr 1795 W.C. [Sgd] D W Smith Actg Sur General.
Col ms 42 x 55 cm 1" to 10 chains
Shows the same information as (1); there is also a plan showing reserves for Chatham in D.W. Smith's 'Report upon Glebes & Commons ... 13th Jany 1802'; (*OHIM* 3.12).
OTAR (Simcoe Map 446287) OTAR (RG 1 A-II-1 vol 2 pp 942–87)

1237 *1821*
Plan of the Town of Chatham. Copy W.C. [Sgd] Survey Genl Office York 6 Septr 1821 T. Ridout Surveyr Genl
Col ms 37 x 43 cm Scale not given Endorsements: 'A 6' '630'
Shows the survey by Iredell in 1795 but with the addition of notes by Ridout in connection with resurvey of 1823; lots marked D are granted; notes on sizes of lot; 'church and burial ground at north end of river lots'; only a few streets named; the town was to be resurveyed as it had not been settled after the 1795 survey and survey markers had disappeared (Hamil, 139).
OTNR (SR 48)

1238 *[1822?]*
Town of Chatham A Sketch shewing the principle upon which the Town of Chatham is to be commenced (The Lots are to contain one acre each. The two situats [*sic*] marked S will afford Sites for Public Squares whenever the Town is enlarged. J.H. [and endorsed title:] 'Plan of the Town of Chatham W.D. U.C. 1822'
Ms 26 x 36 cm 1" to 10 chains
Provenance: OWHM Hands Papers; shows the 114 lots laid out south of river by Iredell, with military reserve; McGregors Mills; notes on back about deeds of land; initials in title may refer to James Hands and probably map described in Hamil, 14.
OWHM (M64))

1239 *1823*
Plan of the Town of Chatham. Surveyed by Order from the Surveyor General's Office, bearing date of 8th day of October 1821. York 23rd March 1823. [Sgd] M Burwell Dy Surveyor
Col ms 59 x 66 cm 1" to 5 chains Endorsements: 'No 11'
The resurvey of the town but essentially only of the original part laid out by Iredell; shows 114 lots from the river south to Wellington St; many later additions regarding lots deeded and names added; plan also shows later surveys and changes as follows: lots returned by Peter Robinson, 4 Apr 1829, lots returned 10 Sept 1832, park lots laid out by A. McIntosh, 22 Feb 1838, survey by Wilkinson, 23 Aug 1843; many names added later.
OTNR (SR 53)

1240 *[1833–4?]*
Plan of the Town / of / Chatham / Copy from Mr Burwells plan of Survey // Lithographed for Peter Robinson Esqr [illegible] Surveyor Genl Office / [Sgd in facsimile: H.W.L. or S.O.T.?]
Print (lith) 17 x 24 cm 1/2" to 5 chains
Originally from OOA RG 1 L3 B 5 119 1849; note: 'The Lots marked thus S were returned to the Honble Peter Robinson CC 4 April 1829'; note probably refers to lots to be put on sale in the town as advertised in May 1833 by Peter Robinson, commissioner of crown lands (Hamil, 211); the 'S' is shown in lots later subdivided by McIntosh in 1834; shows the layout of the Burwell survey with military reserve; the map was enclosed with petitions in a land dispute that involved the original purchase of lots in 1834 based on this map; the initials are unclear and refer either to Henry W.(?) Lizars or Samuel O. Tazewell; (Holmden 1551).
OOAMA (NMC 3755, 3756)

1241 *1834*
Plan of the Town of Chatham [Sgd] A.J. McIntosh P.D. Surveyor Chatham 4th Sept 1834
Ms 34 x 49 cm 1" to 5 chains Endorsements: 'A 8' '663'
(SI 19 June 1834 to divide and mark off water lots in front of lots 94, 97, 98, 101, 102); shows area at west end, west of military reserve; subdivision of lots listed.
OTNR (SR 50)

Related maps

(2) *1834*
Plan of the Town of Chatham. Copy – Henry Lizars. Surveyor General's Office, Toronto, 22nd Sepr 1834.
Col ms 58 x 74 cm 1" to 5 chains Endorsements: 'A 7' '636'
Shows the subdivision of lots as in plan above but more of the town is shown with streets named; reserves for churches; a few owners.
OTNR (SR 47)

1242 *1835*
Plan shewing the Military Reserve adjoining the Town of Chatham, on the River Thames (signed) 'J.G.C. 16th April 1835' Surveyor General's Office, Toronto U.C. 12th May 1835, Copy – Henry Lizars
Col ms 48 x 32 cm 1" to 44 yds Endorsements: '885' 'No 11'
Shows the military reserve as west of William St and between Gaol and Colborne St; boundary, dimensions, bearings; 'Copy ... made for the Board of Ordnance 16th April 1835 H.L.'
OTNR (SR 81012)

Related maps

(2) *1835 (1837?)*
Plan shewing the Military Reserve adjoining the Town of Chatham, on the River Thames. J.G.C. 16th April 1835 (signed) S.P. Hurd S.G. (Certified as a

true Copy T.G.W. Eaststaff Draugn
Col ms 46 x 32 cm 1" to 44 yds Endorsements: 'Chatham – Military Reserve Capt Bonnycastle 18 June 1837 B 136'; stamps 'B↑O' 'IGF'
The same as the plan above; (Holmden 1552).
OOAMA (NMC 3758)

1243 *1836 (1838)*
Sketch shewing the situation of the Barracks proposed to be built on the Military Reserve at Chatham U.C. Copied 1st June 1836 Richard Birley Tempy Clk R.E. Dt Toronto U.C. (Signed) Vincent Biscoe Captain R. Engineers May 26th – 1838.
Ms on tracing paper 27 x 39 cm 1" to 330 ft
Shows positions for soldiers' and officers' barracks, stores, hospital, guardroom, cookhouse, palisades; proposed bridge at Gaol St; shows area from Wellington St to Water St, and Princess St to beyond forks; (Holmden 1553).
OOAMA (NMC 3757)

1244 *[1838]*
Plan Shewing the Park Lots Surveyed adjoining the Town of Chatham By Alex John McIntosh P.L. Surveyor
Ms 40 x 52 cm 1" to 5 chains Endorsements: 'A 124' '631"
(SI 9 June 1837 to survey two ranges of park lots in town reserve south of Wellington St); shows the park lots laid out, and large blocks between them and the town owned by two religious denominations; this is the survey dated 22 Feb 1838 on 1823 plan (**1239**).
OTNR (SR 51)

1245 *1840*
Plan of Part of the Town of Chatham in the Western District as surveyed and laid off by [Sgd] John A. Wilkinson D.P.S. Sandwich 20th June 1840.
Col ms 41 x 51 cm 1" to 5 chains Endorsements: 'A 122' '632'
(SI 23 March 1840 to lay out town lots in blocks remaining in town reserve in Raleigh and Harwich twps); shows the extension of the town lots south to Park St from Wellington St; park lots further south; original town not shown; some later notes about lots.
OTNR (SR 52)

1246 *1841*
Town of Chatham. March 17th 1841. Copy A. Wilkinson
Ms 33 x 41 cm 1" to 1 mile [i.e., 10 chains]
Originally from OOA RG 1 L3 B5 no 119 1849; shows the original town with the 1840 extension and park lots; also shows a few lots laid out from Wellington St west to line between Raleigh and Harwich twps; from the same petition as map of [1833–4?] (see **1240**); (Holmden 1554).
OOAMA (NMC 3759)

1247 *1845*
Plan of Lot No 1 in the 2nd Con. Harwich Subdivided into Park Lots each containing 10a.1r.9p. [Sgd] Albert Pellew Salter D.P. Surveyor Sandwich Septr 22nd 1845.
Col ms 37 x 49 cm 1" to 4 chains Endorsements: 'A 141' '647'
Shows 20 park lots south of Park Ave and east of line between Harwich and Raleigh twps; also a copy in OTAR: 'Park Lots adjoining the Town of Chatham Crown Lands' Department Montreal 28th February 1846. A.R.' with notes on sales and mounted with a more general map without title that shows the whole town and later notes about 1862; and a copy in OTAR(P): 'Park Lots in Harwich adjoining the Town of Chatham. Office Copy Crown Lands Department Montreal December 1846 True Copy [Sgd] Andrew Russell S & D.' endorsed 'No 98' and with the addition of names.
OTAR OTAR(P) OTNR (SR 128)

1248 *[1854]*
PLAN OF THE TOWN / OF / CHATHAM NORTH / Showing the subdivision of part of Lot No 24 Dover East & Part of No 2 Chatham known as the "TAYLOR FARM." // Surveyed by R. Parr P.L.S. & Salter & Jones P.L.S. Lith by Compton, Gibson & Co. Buffalo
Print (lith) 63 x 100 cm 1" to 2 chains
Shows area between Thames R and Forest St, and Robert and Victoria sts; streets to the west and south shown; major bldgs including Royal Exchange, barracks, registry office, gaol, court-house; marked lots 'will be sold at Public Auction on the ground on Tuesday 10th October [1854] next'; related to R.P. 8 and 11 (**B451, B455**); R.P. 4 (Kent 24) (**B454**)is a transcript of printed plan.
Original not located

1249 *[1856]*
PLAN / OF THE / COMMON SCHOOL LAND / IN THE / TOWN OF CHATHAM, / as subdivided into / BUILDING LOTS, / by A.P. SALTER & CO. P.L.S. // J.G. SHERRIFF, Draughtsman
Print (lith), trimmed 49 x 69 cm 1" to 1 chain
Shows a subdivision for Wellington St to town line between Harwich, Raleigh, and Park sts; common school and playground; Catholic Church and 'Seceders Church'; the same as R.P. 14 surveyed 25 Nov 1856 (**B458**).
Kent 24 (R.P. 14(2))

1250 *1860*
Plan / OF THE / TOWN OF CHATHAM / COMPILED FROM ACTUAL SURVEY / BY / Salter and Johnston P.L.S. and C.E. / A.D. 1860. / Engraved by Fuller & Bencke, Victoria Hall. Toronto. // Fuller & Bencke, Lith: Vict: Hall, Toronto, C.W.
Print (lith) 110 x 78 cm 1" to 6 chains

Four views of streets, river, and a bldg; shows the town from Sandys St east to McGregor St and from Mercer St north to Forest St; major bldgs are keyed and indexed, all bldgs shown, many identified; large estates shown with landscaping; photoreproduction in OTAR.
OTMCL

(CHEVIOT)

1251 *1856*
PLAN / OF / MOSCOW / SITUATED ON LOTS NUMBERS 18, 19 AND 20, / in the Fourteenth Concession of Culross / IN THE COUNTY OF / BRUCE / Surveyed 1856. / by / George McPhillips P.L.S. // Maclear & Co Lith. Toronto.
Print (col lith) 96 x 66 cm 1" to 2 chains
Inset: [location map of western part of province]; shows the town from Queen St north to Park St, and Main St to Peter St; town lots in centre, park lots to north; saw and grist mill; town was shown in the co atlas (Belden, ... *Bruce* (1880)) but seems to have died out in the early part of the 20th century (Carter, I:226).
OTAR

CHIPPAWA

1252 *[1796?]*
Plan shewing the Ground proposed to be reserved for Government, and situation for the Barracks and Stores at the entrance of the Chippewa Creek. Signed Gother Mann Capt Commandg Rl Enginrs.
Col ms 64 x 41 cm 1" to 100 ft Endorsements: 'No 18' '961'
Shows boundary, King's storehouse and wharf, fort, and a few other bldgs; fenced areas, Indian burial places, 'proposed situation for the Merchants Storehouse and wharf,' proposed road and bridge across river; fence lines; probably made in 1796 as were similar plans for Niagara and Amherstburg; also a copy in OTNR (SR 7223) with same title sgd 'Copied by Wm Chewett.' and with watermark 'J WHATMAN' and endorsed 'No 14' and '962'; this copy was made in the 1790s and bears a note indicating that a copy of it was 'made for Board of Ordnance 11th April 1835 H.L.'; and a copy of this latter plan in OOAMA (NMC 3767) further sgd '(Copy) J.G.C. – 16th April 1835 (signed S.P. Hurd S.G.) Certified as a true Copy T.G.W. Eaststaff Draugn.'; it has watermark '1834,' is endorsed 'B↑O' and 'IGF,' and has notes on a licence of occupation of part of the military reserve, 14 Apr 1819; (Holmden 1570).
OOAMA (NMC 3767) OTAR (SR 7223; 81010)

1253 *1798*
Descriptions of some lots proposed to be laid out at Fort Chippawa for the convenience of Trade Province of Upper Canada, Township of Stamford and Home District Fort George 1798 [Sgd] Robt Pilkington Capt Lieut Royal Engrs.
Col ms 38 x 54 cm Approx 1" to 1 1/2 chains
Endorsements: 'LX Entd'
Shows the military reserve on both banks of the Chippawa R at its mouth; bldgs; a few names in lots.
QMMMCM (3612)

Related maps

(2) *1798*
Plan shewing the situation, and dimensions approved for bldg lots, for merchants and Traders, on the King's reserved Land at Fort Chippewa in Upper Canada. 1798. W. Hall Lt Rl Ary [Sgd] Gother Mann Coll Commandg Rl Engrs.
Col ms 33 x 48 cm 1" to 1 chain, 60 links
Boundary of reserve, blockhouse, several other bldgs, bridge; lots 1 to 4 for merchants; 'Robt Hamilton & Co.' on lot 1.
GBL (Maps 23.b.3(8))

(3) *1798*
Plan showing the situation & dimensions proposed for Building lots for Merchants & Traders in the Kings reserved land at Fort Chippawa in Upper Canada (Signed) Gother Mann Coln Commandg Rl Engrs Quebec 30 June 1798 Approved (signed) Robt Prescott.
Col ms 39 x 50 cm 1" to 160 chains Watermark: 'C WILMOTT 1797'
From Col McDonell's letter, 10 Aug 1798, granting permission to Thomas Clark to occupy a lot at Chippawa (OOA RG 8 I vol 272 p 13); shows the same information as (2) but Thomas Clark's name added to lot 2, and Thomas Dickson's to lot 3; (Holmden 1637).
OOAMA (NMC 6187)

1254 *1799 (1824)*
[Part of the Niagara River at the River Welland or Chippawa] Copy from a Plan of Survey by John Stegmann Deputy Surveyor. J.G.C. Surveyor Genl Office York 14th February 1824 [Sgd] Thos Ridout Sur Genl.
Col ms 46 x approx 200 cm 1" to 3 chains
Enclosed in Lt Gov Sir P. Maitland's dispatch no 148 of 26 July 1824 about claim of Mr Robert Randal to a piece of land on the Niagara R granted to the Honourable Thomas Clark (GBLpro CO 42/373 p 28); shows the site with five lots for merchants shown and described, a few bldgs, roads, mills; the survey was probably the one made by Stegmann under SI 13 Nov 1798 (see **682**).
GBLpro (CO 42/373 p 28)

1255 *[1841]*
Trace of Chippewa Harbour
Ms 37 x 36 cm 1" to 100 ft Endorsements: '1841 H.H. Killaly'
Originally from OOA RG 8 I but exact location not found; shows Chippewa Cut by 'Old Fort' on Hog Is; built up ground formed by materials excavated from cut; (Holmden 1572).
OOAMA (NMC 3769)

1256 *1861*
Military Reserve. Lyons' Creek (included within the pink margin) Township of Willoughby County of Welland U.C. (Sgd) F.F. Passmore Provl Land Surveyor Toronto Sept 24th 1861
Col ms 44 x 64 cm 1" to 2 chains Endorsements: '16870/61'
Shows sites of old fort, battery, bridge; boundary of reserve at junction of Lyons Creek and Chippawa Creek; distances between various points; present steam sawmill outside boundary, and other bldgs shown.
OTNR (SR 5742)

CLIFFORD

1257 *[1857?]*
PLAN / OF / THE VILLAGE OF / MINTO / COMPRISING LOTS 59 & 60 IN CONCESSIONS C & D OF / THE TOWNSHIP OF MINTO / Surveyed for Chas. Allan & Jas. Geddes / BY E.H. KERTLAND / Maclear & Co. Lith. Toronto
Print (col lith) 89 x 63 cm 1" to 3 chains
Registered 26 Jan 1857; shows the subdivision from Main St to James St, and Brown St to Howick St; lot nos and sizes; road connections to Hamilton and Southampton and the Elora and Saugeen Rd are shown; 'village of Minto' also shown on the south side of the Red R; see also **B477**.
OFEC Wellington 60 (R.P. 78)

COBOURG

1258 *183[5?]*
Diagram of the Clergy Reserve No XV in the Broken Front Concession B Township of Hamilton District of Newcastle. [Sgd] F.P. Rubidge Deputy Provincial Surveyor Cobourg 183[5?]
Col ms, pt missing 65 x 42 cm 1" to 2 chains Endorsements: 'No 4' '757'
Diagram for the survey showing boundary and position of some lots, names of some owners, bldgs; the area is between Division and Darcy sts.
OTNR (SR 1247)

Related maps

(**2**) *[1835]*
The Clergy Reserve Lot no 15 in the Broken Concession B in the Township of Hamilton N.D. F.P. Rubidge.
Col ms, pt missing 65 x 42 cm 1" to 2 chains Endorsements: 'No 14'
(OTNR FN 354 26 Oct 1835); shows the subdivision of area between East St and beyond Church St south of Dundas [King] St; clergy reserve lands; names in lots; table of lots belonging to church and to G.M. Boswell; note that copy made for 'Comr Crown Lands' 3 Aug 1836; also a copy with same title, with note on lots for the church and Mr Boswell 'Signed F.P. Rubidge D.P.S. vide O.C. 3rd July 1834,' and endorsed '(956)' and 'Commr Crown Lands Office Plan 3rd Aug 1836.' (OTAR(P)); and copy in OTNR (SR 67) sgd 'Surveyor General Office Montreal 10th October 1842 A true copy.' and endorsed 'A 136' and '624.'
OTAR(P) OTNR (SR 66–7)

1259 *1835–41*
Plan of Cobourg Harbor with Proposed Improvements 1835 [Sgd] Francis Hall Civil Engineer Cobourgh 11th May 1835 [Sgd] Samuel Keefer C.E. Board of Works Kingston 19th July 1841.
Col ms 51 x 48 cm 1" to 100 ft Endorsements: 'No 1' '82'; stamps 'BW' '655'
Shows harbour with proposed changes to shape and orientation of a few bldgs shown on shore; two piers and additional pier proposed; Keefer's additions include a new part to map, soundings taken 17 July 1841, and notes about existing and proposed works; a second copy on linen is the same except it lacks Hall's signature.
OOAMA (NMC 3778; 11899)

1260 *1842*
Plan of Cobourg Harbour with Soundings by N.H. Baird C.E. – May 1842. Surveyed and Drawn by J. Lyons, under the direction of N.H. Baird C.E. [missing] [Sgd] N.H. Baird Civil Enginr.
Col ms 75 x 75 cm 1" to 3 chains Endorsements: '82'; stamps 'BW' '656'
[Four sections], each 1" to 66 ft, 1" to 20 ft vertical; shows the piers in the two outer positions as on earlier plan; soundings taken between 30 May and 4 June 1842; high water line in 1836 and 'present' one, filled areas; proposed developments shown; town is shown on east and west.
OOAMA (NMC 22312)

1261 *[1847]*
PLAN of the TOWN / OF / COBOURG / By Order of the Board of Police. / From actual Survey, Registered Deeds, and / the most Correct, information. / by / SANDFORD A. FLEMING, C.E. / Scobie & Balfour, Lith: Toronto. // J. Hauer Lith:
Print (lith) 104 x 80 cm 1" to 5 chains
Provenance: OOAMA copy from OOA MG45; shows the town from the lake north to White St, and Burnham St east to Darcy St; lot nos, block nos, and main bldgs shown including churches, schools, industrial structures, mills, mill sites; 'only the best Buildings are laid down'; proposed

streets, table of distances, names of some owners; 'Historical Description of Cobourg'; population revised from Incorporation Act 1846; 'Plank and gravel roads are now being constructed through the Town to be extended to Rice Lake, Port Hope and Grafton.'; advertised for sale in the *Cobourg Star* 17 Nov 1847.
OOAMA (NMC 11366)

1262 *[1856]*
PLAN / of the / COBOURG STATION / Grand Trunk Railway / OF / CANADA / Dennis & Boulton / Surveyors. / Maclear & Co. Liths Toronto. C.W.
Print (lith) 50 x 70 cm 1" to 2 chains
Related to R.P. 9 of 26 Nov 1856 (**B507**); shows the area from Station to Campbell St, and Division St to east of Cobourg & Peterborough Railway; lots, station bldgs; attached to map is printed notice: 'This Valuable Property will be sold by auction on the ground on Wednesday November 16, [1856] Maclear, Thomas & Co. Printers 16 King Street East, Toronto.'
OTUTF

1263 *1857*
PLAN OF THE / BUCK & McKAY / PROPERTIES, IN THE TOWN OF / COBOURG. / 1857 / LITHOGRAPHED BY J. ELLIS 8 KING ST TORONTO. C.W.
Print (lith) 76 x 52 cm 1" to 50 ft
Seminary St to GTR depot; Cobourg & Peterborough Railway to George St; note that Victoria Square in the centre of subdivision to be used as a park by surrounding inhabitants; see also **B506**.
Northumberland 39 (R.P. Cobourg 10)

1264 *1858*
PLAN / of the Town of / COBOURG, / WITH ITS LIMITS. / HANNAFORD & LLOYD C.E. COBOURG, 1858. / LITHOGRAPHED BY J. ELLIS, TORONTO.
Print (col lith) 132 x 103 cm 1" to 4 chains
Shows the town now extended east to Cottesmore St, west to West St, and north to White St; all bldgs shown with major bldgs named; names of owners of large lots; advertised as a new map planned by John H. Lloyd in the *Cobourg Star* 20 Jan 1858 and on 28 Apr 1858 noted as lithographed but town crest to be corrected.
OOAMA (NMC 23964) OTAR OTMCL

(COLBORNE) (Middlesex Co)

1265 *1830*
Map of Colborne Being a plot of ground surveyed and laid out into lots for the permanent settlement and civilisation of the Chippewa and Munsee Indians; on the River Thames in the Township of Carradoc. Under the direction of Joseph B. Clench, Esq. Superintendent &c. &c. &c. Dy Surveyor's Office Carradoc 11th July 1830 by [Sgd] Roswell Mount Dy Surveyor.
Col ms 62 x 81 cm 1" to 10 chains Endorsements: 'Q 39' '1120'
Ranges 1–3 and part of range 4, Carradoc Twp north of Thames R; shows a layout for town plot with streets named including 'Union Square'; sites for houses shown at front of lots on flats by the river; shows 'Munsee village' with wigwams, names of some Indians, burial grounds, and cornfields nearby; only 'Munseytown' is mentioned in *Smith's Canadian Gazetteer* (1846); street grid still shown on the co atlas (Page, ... *Middlesex* (1878)) but not named.
OTNR (SR 717)

COLBORNE (Northumberland Co)

1266 *1862*
Plan of the Village of Colborne Township of Cramahe Canada West Surveyed September 1862 ... as incorporated by Bylaw of the County Council of the United Counties of Northumberland and Durham, No 117 dated 11th December 1858. Colborne 15th January 1863 J.H. Reid P.L. Surveyor.
Col ms 67 x 101 cm 1" to 4 chains Endorsements: 'No 23' '1011/63'
(SI for municipal survey 14 May 1862); shows the area from the GTR station north to Park St, and between road allowances for lots 26/27 and 32/33; streets named, some bldgs shown and named, some names of owners; mills; related to R.P. 17 (**B520**).
OTNR (SR 6810)

COLCHESTER

1267 *[1839]*
Plan of Octagonal Village of 32 Houses, – with School-house in the centre. [Sgd] R.A. Lachlan Late Major 17th Artillery & Sheriff W.D.
Col ms 39 x 28 cm 1" to 4 chains
A proposal for the layout of the town plot of Colchester originally enclosed in Robert Lachlan's letter to Sir George Arthur 28 Sept 1839 (OOA RG 5 A1 vol 230 pp 126102); an ideal plan for a town showing lots and houses for 32 different trades or craftsmen 'to restrain idle speculation'; lots radiate out from a central square where the schoolhouse is situated; 'the front of each side of the octagon measures 110 yards, which, divided into four bldg lots, gives a front of 27 1/2 yards to each lot; – and each cottage or house is supposed to be situated 1 chain or 22 yards retired from, and in the centre of the front of each lot ... The component parts of the population desirable are specified on each lot'; shows roads and a method for extension of the plan; the plan was never adopted; (*OHIM* 7.4; Whebell 'Two Polygonal Settlement Schemes ...').
OOAMA (NMC 3667)

1268 *[1841]*
Plan of the Town-Plot in Colchester as surveyed and laid out by [Sgd] John A. Wilkinson Depy Provl Surveyor.
Ms 107 x 34 cm 1" to 4 chains Endorsements: 'A 161'
(SI 7 Nov 1839 and 16 Aug 1841 to lay out town and park lots; OTNR FN 131 21 Oct 1841); shows a grid layout of streets from L Erie to [Ogden St] and [Dunn to Daly sts]; streets not named; church, graveyard, bldgs; road to St Thomas and Amherstburg cuts across town grid; height of bank at L Erie; irregular fence lines shown north of town plot.
OTNR (SR 6841)

Related maps

(2) *[1841?]*
Town and Park Lots in Colchester, Copy [Sgd] J.G. Chewett.
Col ms 66 x 34 cm 1" to 4 chains Endorsements: 'No 61'
Inset: 'Park Lots Reduced Copy' shows the same layout as (1) above but streets now named, park lots shown on inset, and names added on most lots; notes on plan suggest date of original survey above was 27 Dec 1841.
OTAR(P)

1269 *[1843]*
Colchester
Col ms 74 x 26 cm 1" to 4 chains
Inset: [glebe and park lots] 1" to 12 chains; accompanied a petition of the minister and members of the Church of England at Colchester about land for a church (OOA RG 1 L3 C 3 no 2 1843); shows the town as it was laid out from Dunn to Daly St, and Ogden St to L Erie.
OOAMA (NMC 4856)

COLLINGWOOD

1270 *1853*
Chart of Collingwood Harbor Lake Huron. To Accompany Report [Sgd] Fred. W. Cumberland Chief Engineer Toronto. February 1853.
Col ms 63 x 95 cm 1" to 10 chains Endorsements: stamps [BW] '659' 'Survey made in October and November 1852'
Shows the harbour and site for the northern terminus of the railway; depths shown by contours; breakwater, pier, navigation lights; Hurontario Mills on east side, road to Boy's steam mill; printed reports by the Chief Engineer of the railway were issued for 1852 and 1853 (*Bib Can* 3300) but they do not contain maps; (Holmden 1584).
OOAMA (NMC 23887)

1271 *1853*
PLAN / of / TOWN LOTS AT COLLINGWOOD / AT THE / TERMINUS OF THE NORTHERN RAILROAD / TOWNSHIP OF NOTTAWASAGA COUNTY OF SIMCOE / THE PROPERTY OF JOHN S. WALLACE ESQ. / 1853 // Hugh Scobie, lith.
Print (lith) 49 x 66 cm 1" to 10 chains
Shows lots and streets laid out from road to harbour to Toronto St, and Victoria St to Wellington St; 'will be sold by Public Auction on Saturday the 11th of June 1853, by Messrs Wakefield and Coate ... King Street, Toronto'; wharves, breakwater, eastern harbour entrance; railway terminus to the southeast; based on R.P. 39 (see **B525**).
OTUTF

1272 *1854*
PLAN / OF THE PROPERTY OF / MESSRS McMASTER, PATERSON, HAMILTON, & ROBINSON. / AT / COLLINGWOOD / LAKE HURON / THE NORTHERN TERMINUS, OF THE ONTARIO SIMCOE & HURON RAILROAD / SURVEYED 1854 BY / William Gibbard. // Wm Gibbard P.L.S. / October 1854 // Miller's Lith. cor. Trinity Pl. & Thames St. New York.
Print (lith) 67 x 100 cm 1" to 200 ft
Inset: 'PLAN / OF / COLLINGWOOD HARBOUR / AND ADJACENT COUNTRY / Shewing the advantageous position / OF MESSRS McMASTER, PATERSON, HAMILTON / AND ROBINSON'S / LOTS. 1" to 20 chains'; 'VIEW OF COLLINGWOOD HARBOUR J. Bornet del.'; 'Cross Section on Minnesota Street from the Lake'; 'Cross Section on Palmerston Street from the Lake'; shows the area from the water south to St Clair St, and from Pine St east to Parker St at the harbour; bldgs shown on sold portions are identified; Ontario Simcoe and Huron Railroad terminal; shows plans for Napoleon Crescent, Alma Circus, and Turkish Crescent, which were later changed; reserve for market block generally below high water mark; related to R.P. 55 (**B533**); oriented to the south.
OTAR OTNR (SR 7028)

1273 *1855*
O.S. & H.R.R. Plan of Collingwood Harbour in the Township of Nottawasaga.
Col ms on linen 17 x 48 cm 1" to 20 chains
Endorsements: '5683/55'
Originally accompanied a petition for water frontage from con VII, lot 43, to con X, lot 48 (OOA RG 1 L3 08 no 4 1855); shows cons and lots fronting on harbour, piers, and breakwater.
OOAMA (NMC 3780)

1274 *1855*
PLAN / OF / D. REESOR'S PROPERTY / AT / COLLINGWOOD / SURVEYED BY / Wm. GIBBARD, P.L.S. / MAY, 1855. / Maclear & Co Lith. Toronto.

Print (lith) 58 x 96 cm 1" to 3 chains
Insets: 'Scroll showing the whole town plot, with the Harbour, and the relative positon / of the several Township lots previous to their being laid off into Town or City Lots' and 'MAP / SHEWING THE POSITION OF / COLLINGWOOD / IN / Reference to the Course of Trade / BETWEEN THE ATLANTIC SEABOARD / AND THE / Great West.'; shows lots laid out from Hurontario St west to High St, and from Fifth St to 10th St; two squares reserved for parks; town inset shows railway and major landholders in area but no other streets; OOAMA copy has ms adds to inset of more streets south of Reesor property; notes on advantages of Collingwood harbour; related to R.P. 45 (**B531**).
OOAMA (NMC 23888) OTAR

1275 *1855*
PLAN / OF THE / PROPERTY OF C. JACKSON ESQ. / M.P.P. / AT / COLLINGWOOD / SURVEYED BY / Wm GIBBARD P.L.S. / August 1855.
Print (lith), trimmed at margin 63 x 82 cm 1" to 3 chains
Inset: 'PLAN / OF / COLLINGWOOD / Shewing the Surveys already made / and / THE EXTENT OF HARBOUR WORKS COMPLETED / up to Augt 1855. / also / THE ADVANTAGEOUS POSITION / OF / MR JACKSON'S PROPERTY'; includes sections on Hurontario St and east side of Minnesota St with average rises; shows area from Hume St to beyond Francis St, east of Hurontario St; reserves around railway terminus; 'Market Block'; inset shows owners of various blocks of land in town and other streets laid out; piers, breakwaters; related to R.P. 39 (**B526**); imprint possibly trimmed off.
OMSA

1276 *[1856]*
PLAN / OF / 55 Valuable Building Lots / IN THE TOWN OF / COLLINGWOOD, / Being part of Lot 40, in the South half of the Tenth Concession of the Township of Nottawasaga. MACDONALD & CO., / Auctioneers. // Blackburn's City Steam Press, 63 Yonge Street, Toronto.
Print (typeset) 51 x 70 cm 1" to approx 27 ft
Shows the area from Douglas St south to Tecumseth St, and from Ann St to Nile St; 'Messrs MacDonald having received instructions from Mr. Blackburn and Mr. I. Faulkner ... the Proprietors will offer for sale 55 Building Lots ... at their Auction Rooms, 61 Yonge Street, Toronto on Saturday 10th of May [1856]'; notes on the advantages of the site; related to R.P. 51 (**B530**).
OMSA

1277 *1856*
PLAN OF TOWN LOTS / IN / COLLINGWOOD / AS LAID OUT ON LOT No 45. 10 CON. NOTTAWASAGA / Surveyed for / JAMES PATTON Esq. & S.M. SANFORD, Esq. / by Henry Creswick P.L.S. / JUNE 1856. // Maclear & Co Lith Toronto, C.W.
Print (col lith) 68 x 96 cm 1" to 6 chains
Insets: 'MAP of the COUNTIES of SIMCOE and GREY / Shewing part of the line of the Ontario Simcoe & Huron R.R. / and the / POSITION OF COLLINGWOOD' and 'MAP SHEWING POSITION OF COLLINGWOOD / in the / direct line of travel from the Seaboard to the / WESTERN STATES and LAKE SUPERIOR COUNTRY.'; 'Sale by Wakefield, Coate & Co., at their Toronto Auction Mart, on Friday, August 1, 1856,'; shows streets and bldgs in town and new subdivision; 'section of levels taken from High Water on Main Street'; harbour area and breakwaters; distances from Toronto to Collingwood on railway; notes on the advantages of the town: 'The Growth of all Towns in Canada (unless turned aside by some natural obstruction) is in a westerly direction.'
OMSA

1278 *1858*
Chart / OF / COLLINGWOOD / HARBOR, / AND ITS CONNECTIONS. / BY / WILLIAM GIBBARD, / C.E. & P.L.S. / Collingwood April 1858 // LITHOGRAPHED BY J. ELLIS, TORONTO.
Print (lith) 69 x 90 cm 1" to 10 chains
Inset: 'SCROLL SHEWING THE POSITION OF COLLINGWOOD IN CONNECTION WITH TORONTO AND THE GREAT WEST'; shows soundings, two wharves, breakwaters, lighthouses, nature of bottom near shore, sailing directions for harbour; shows streets and major bldgs identified near shore; inset shows most of the Great Lakes with distance table, routes, sailing directions.
GBTAUh (D6170 Aa3) OOAMA (NMC 24034) OTAR

1279 *1867*
Collingwood Harbour Sketch shewing relative positions of proposed batteries near the Railway Depot & on Fisherman's Point. [Sgd] H.J.W. Gehle Lt R.E. 18/5/67 F.C. Hassard Lt. Col. D.C.R.E.
Col ms on linen 69 x 71 cm 1" to 6 chains
Endorsements: 'On A/371'
Shows west and east batteries and soundings, channels, piers, shoals, and shore roads.
OOAMA (NMC 22318)

CONESTOGO

1280 *1856*
MAP OF PART / of the Village of / CONESTOGO / IN THE / TOWNSHIP OF WOOLWICH, COUNTY OF WATERLOO, C.W. / AS SURVEYED FOR / GEORGE DAVIDSON Esqr / BY / Schofield & Hobson P.L.SS. / Berlin C.W. / 1856. / Maclear & Co. Liths Toronto.

Print (lith) hand col 52 x 67 cm 1" to 2 chains
Shows streets, houses, mill pond, mills, mill races, Lutheran church ground, cabinet factory, a few names of owners; no registered plan has been found.
OKIT

CONSECON

1281 *1853 (1866)*
Plan of Consecon Village. Copy from plan of John J. Haslett's prepared A.D. 1853 Correct copy [Sgd] Robert L Innes March 17th 1866.
Col ms on linen 78 x 93 cm 1" to 2 chains
Shows lots on both sides of Consecon Creek on Main, Mill, Albert, Division sts, and Queen to Store St; some bldgs named; mills, dams, churches, some names of owners, and notes on land sold and held; related to R.P. Consecon 1 (**B541**) but the latter shows a smaller area.
OTAR

COOKS MILLS

1282 *1848*
[Endorsed title]: Plan of Village Lots at Cooks Mills on Lot No 11 4th Conn Crowland Aug 25 1848 [Sgd] James West [?]
Col ms 52 x 41 cm Scale not given Watermark: 'WEBSTER 1833'
Shows lots along Main Rd; names of patentees, notes on deeds 1836–50; notes on survey.
OTAR(P)

COPETOWN

1283 *[1856?]*
PLAN OF THE / Village of COPETOWN / As laid out by Saml C. Ridley Esqr / T.A. Blyth P.L.S. // Lith: Spectator Office, Hamilton C.W.
Print (col lith) 68 x 49 cm 1" to 100 ft
'COPETOWN' has been pasted over another name, which cannot be identified; Copetown was shown on the county map of 1859 (**825**); shows the town from Prince St to GWR; various bldgs identified, Elliott's mill pond; probably published in 1856 as plan was certified correct by owner 4 Oct 1856; see also **B548**.
Wentworth 62 (R.P. 342)

CORNWALL

1284 *1792 Jan*
Plan of part of the Town of Cornwall, formerly called New Johnstown, as laid out and located by Mr Louis Kotte Surveyor, sent from Mr Patrick McNiff Surveyor at Detroit by order of Council of the 12th April 1790, and received by the Board for the Land Office Department the latter end of the Summer 1791, with which he did not send the State of the Locations he made, nor his own Remarks thereon, enlarged from a Scale of 10 Chains to one Inch to that of three to two Inches, to insert the Original Proprietors Names, in order that the Board for the Land Office Department, May proceed to a full Investigation of the same ... Osnabruck 15th January 1792. [Sgd] W Chewett D.P. Surveyor Luneburg Examined with the original 17th August 1792 [Sgd] W Chewett [Sgd] Williamsburg 28th April 1795 W Chewett Senior Surveyr Eastern District.
Col ms 51 x 135 cm 2" to 3 chains Endorsements: 'No 1' 'A 16' 'It must be supposed from Mr McNiffs not having sent any Record, remark or Explanation relative to the part of the Town Located, since Mr Kotte made his Locations, that he never kept any, although it was Customary at the time he was Surveyor of the District, to give Tickets of Location.'
This appears to be an enlarged copy of the resurvey by P. McNiff in 1790 with the addition of later signatures and notes; 'The red lines shew the new survey under the Authority of Lord Dorchester and His Excellency Lieutenant Governor Simcoe, – The black lines shew the Old Survey under the Authority of His Excellency Lieut Governor Haldimand and are lots of 2/5ths of an acre, located to sundry persons who are entered on this plan by Sir John Johnston and Major Holland and are the only original nominees in the whole of this Town plot – The numbers in red Ink are made to correspond with the acre Lots on Plan No 2'; shows the original survey with the smaller town lots around the perimeters of squares and the centres left empty, and the double set of diagonal streets in the east and west sides of town; the main lots are lettered, streets not named; red lines show the new survey of 6-acre blocks subdivided into six lots each; this or the plan below may be no 13 in 'List of Maps ... 1793' (OTAR (RG 1 A-I-1 vol 1 p 151–7).
OTNR (SR 7031)

Related maps

(2) *1792*
Plan of part of Town of Cornwall ... Tickets of Location. Osnabruck 5th January 1792. Copied from an Original by Lieut Augustine Prevost R.F. [Sgd] Samuel Holland Survy Genl (Signed) William Chewett D.P. Sr Luneburg.
Col ms 68 x 140 cm 2" to 3 chains Endorsements: 'A 15' '637'
An enlarged contemporary copy of McNiff's resurvey with the names in black pertaining to the old survey and without the later note and signatures of the above.
OTNR (SR 7026)

1285 *1792 Feb 7*
Plan for the better regulating and laying out the Town of Cornwall, formerly called New Johnstown, in the District of Luneburg, shewing the project on which it was [first settled] and that approved by the Board for the Land Office Department in the Year 1790, making it nearly correspond with the Plan Ordered by His Excellency Guy Lord Dorchester in Councill the 17th February 1789, in consequence of which, an Investigati[on] was ordered but which was never carried into execution, the Board having business of more importance under their consideration. To ... Lieut Governor Simcoe This Plan is most humbly presented by [Sgd] W Chewett Surveyor, Osnabruck 7th Feby 1792, District of Luneburg.
Col ms 102 x 98 cm 1" to 3 chains
Note: 'it will be perceived by this plan that every one of the proprietors have more than they were originally entitled to, either by monopoly or by enclosure and none of them have Certificates of Location or Deeds and people are enclosing and improving without authority'; shows the original small town lots, fenced areas, houses, and names of occupants; also shows how the actual settlement conflicts with the original reserves, diagonal streets, etc; note that schoolhouse and parsonage now on reserve for public square must be removed to their proper situation; original reserves for market, court-house, workhouse, church, etc, shown; (*OHIM* 3.5).
OTAR (Simcoe Map 446888)

Related maps

(2) *1792 Feb 17*
[Plan for the better] regulating and laying out the Town [of Cornw]all formerly called New Johnstown; in the district of Luneburg making it nearly Correspond with the Plan approved by His Lordship in Council the 17th Feby 1789. Agreeable to an order of Council of the 19th April 1790 [Sgd] W Chewett Surveyor for the District of Luneburg Osnabruck 17th Feb 1792. Examined [Sgd] W Chewett Actg Survey Genl for the Province of Upper Canada Osnabruck, 18th Augt 1792 – Williamsburg 28th April 1795 [Sgd] W Chewett Senior Surveyr Eastern District. [Later title added]: Plan of the Town of Cornwall laid out by an order of the Board of Investigation dated Stormont 24th April 1795, and finished agreeable to the approved Plan the 15th August 1795. Williamsburg 29th August 1795 [Sgd] W Chewett Senior Surveyor Eastern District.
Col ms 72 x 95 cm 1" to 3 chains Endorsements: 'No 17' 'A 1'
Shows the new survey into larger town lots, six to a square, from Water St to 9th St and Marlborough St to Cumberland St; reserves, bldgs, and old fences still shown: 'Notice has been given to the Inhabitants of this Town to lay all their fences in a proper line agreeably to the present boundaries and to throw down all the old Buildings that are in or interfere with the Streets'; some names of patentees added later but a later note refers to Patent Plan 'Office Plan no 12' (**1286(2)**).
OTNR (SR 79)

(3) *1795*
Plan for the better regulating and laying out the Town of Cornwall, formerly called New Johnstown in the District of Luneburg shewing the project on which it was first settled and that at present approved by the Board making it [n]early correspond with the Plan approved by His Lordship in Council the 17th February 1789. [Later title added]: Plan of the Town of Cornwall laid out by an Order of the Board of Investigation dated Stormont the 2nd April 1795 and finished agreeable to the Approved Plan the 15th August 1795 – ... Williamsburg 29th August 1795 [Sgd] W. Chewett Senior Surveyr Eastern District.
Col ms 122 x 80 cm 1" to 3 chains Endorsements: 'A 17' 'No 2' '621'
Similar to (1), lacking some signatures and dates but having original diagonal streets drawn in and bearing note about encroachment; there is also a plan showing reserves for Cornwall in D.W. Smith's 'Report upon Glebes & Commons ... 13th Jany 1802.'
OTAR (RG 1 A-II-1 vol 2 pp 942–87) OTNR (SR 7021)

1286 *1832*
Town of Cornwall in the County of Stormont [Sgd] Surveyr Genls Office York 16th January 1832 W. Chewet Actg Surveyr Genl.
Col ms 82 x 59 cm 1" to 4 chains Endorsements: '2637/62'
Shows the original streets and reserves for church, parsonage, school, court-house, workhouse, hospital, market-place, and public squares; names of owners have been added on most lots in the centre and south of town.
OTNR (SR 7023)

Related maps

(2) *[1832?]*
Town of Cornwall Office Plan Copy from Wm Chewett's Survey by J.G.C.
Col ms 76 x 65 cm 1" to 4 chains Endorsements: 'No 12'
Similar to plan above but with the addition of note from the earlier plans about the need to move the school and parsonage from the public square; names of patentees have been added with notes dated 1819, 1839, and 1842; only the church reserve still exists in present-day Cornwall.
OTAR(P)

(3) *1837*
Cornwall Copy [Sgd] J.G. Chewett S.G. Office 19th June 1837 [Sgd] Surveyor Generals' Office Toronto 19th June 1837 J W Macaulay Surv Genl.
Col ms 74 x 56 cm 1" to 4 chains
A copy of the 1832 plan with indications of lots

patented, leased, and notes about some sold; notes about waterfront leases; position of Cornwall Canal added later.
OTAR

CORUNNA

1287 *1836*
Diagram for a Town Plot on the River St Clair Township of Moore. [Sgd] Surv Generals Office Toronto 20 July 1836 J Radenhurst
Ms 28 x 42 cm Scale not given
Lot 8, con 11, Moore Twp; shows a plan with two diagonal streets crossing in a central square and some lots laid out to front on the radial streets in the central portion of the town; 'N.B. Should the Diagonal Roads not be approved of I see no better way than to continue upon the principle of the 1st 2nd and 3 Ranges J.G.C.'; the sketch probably originally accompanied SI 20 Aug 1836 (see (2) below); earlier SI to P. Carroll of 26 Apr 1835 to lay out town appear not to have been carried out.
OTAR

Related maps

(2) *1836 (1837)*
Plan of the Town of Corunna in the Township of Moore in the Western District Surveyed and laid out by John A. Wilkinson Deputy Provincial Surveyor Sandwich 1st Novr 1836. W.R. Wood. delin. Sandwich W.D. 1837.
Col ms 53 x 41 cm 1" to 4 chains Endorsements: '622' 'A 110'
(SI 20 Aug 1836 to J. Wilkinson to lay out the town on lots 59–62 fronting the St Clair R; OTNR FN 138 10 Nov 1837); the town is shown as on the plan above with lots numbered and dimensions given; street names pencilled in later; 'N.B. This Plan has been disapproved by His Excellency the Lieutenant Governor and orders sent to Mr. Wilkinson to amend it 20th May 1837 J.W.M.'; (*OHIM* 7.6).
OTNR (SR 62)

1288 *1837*
Corunna as Surveyed by me the 20th June 1837 [Sgd] John A. Wilkinson Deputy Surveyor
Col ms 45 x 40 cm 1" to 4 chains Watermark: 'JAMES WHATMAN TURKEY MILLS KENT 1833'
(OTNR FN 139 20 June 1837); shows the resurvey for the town in a regular grid and without diagonal streets as noted on (2) above; Beresford St east to Colborne St, Cameron St north to Beckwith St; shows St George's Square in the centre, and reserves for market-place on the shore and towards the rear of the plot; also a copy in OTAR(P): 'Corunna Copy enlarged [Sgd] J.G. Chewett S.G. Office 3rd July 1837 Office Copy.' 1" to 3 chains, endorsed 'No 59a' and with names of patentees added and notes about sale of some land to Major Bowen; and a copy in OTAR: 'Corunna Copy [Sgd] J.G. Chewett S.G. Office 12th July 1837. [Sgd] Surveyor General's Office Toronto 15th July 1837 J W Macaulay Surv Genl' 1" to 3 chains, with notes on sales of front and other lots.
OTAR OTAR(P) (OTNR (SR 64))

1289 *1854*
Projected plan for the subdivision of the residue of the Town Plot of Corunna C L D 21st June 1854 (signed) A.N. Morin
Col ms 56 x 38 cm Scale not given Endorsements: 'B'
Shows a plan for the survey of the area from Colborne St east to Queen St, and Cameron St to Beckwith St; probably accompanied SI (see (2) below).
OTAR

Related maps

(2) *1854*
Plan of the residue of the Town Plot of Corunna Surveyed by P.D. Salter P.L.S. October 1854. Examined A.R.
Col ms 47 x 67 cm 1" to 4 chains Endorsements: 'A 192'
(SI of 22 June 1854 to P.D. Salter to subdivide residue into acre lots and trace rear lines of subdivision; OTNR FN 1070 28 Nov 1854); shows the layout of area as in plan above except block south of Hill St is blank; a few names added in pencil; table of cultivated and uncultivated acres; 'Returned [for] sale 20th November 1854'; also a copy: 'Part of Corunna Crown Lands Department Quebec 30th December 1854 [Sgd] Andrew Russell for the Commr Crown Lands.' endorsed 'No 105' and with names added to all lots (OTAR(P)).
OTAR(P) OTNR (SR 63)

CRAIGHURST

1290 *[1859?]*
PARK & TOWN LOTS, / LAID OUT ON / LOT FORTY-ONE, FIRST CONCESSION OF THE TOWNSHIP OF / MEDONTE, / FOR THE / HON. JAS. PATTON & HEWITT BERNARD, ESQ., / By Henry Creswicke, P.L.S.
Ms (with typeset title) 63 x 45 cm 1" to 2 chains Watermark: 'J WHATMAN TURKEY MILLS 1854'
Endorsements: '1002' 'App. 2446 Patton & Bernard'
Shows streets and lots laid out from Penetanguishene Rd to Third St, and lots also on both sides of Centre St; various bldgs named at corner of the Penetanguishene Rd and town line; related to R.P. 91 of 1859 (**B554**).
OTAR

CRANBROOK

1291 *1856*
Plan of the Town of Cranbrook laid out on lots 11, 12, 13, 14, 15 in the XIth Conn Township of Grey County of Huron C.W. [Sgd] Wm Rath Provl

Surveyor Dated Mitchell 5th October 1856. Examined J.W.B.
Col ms 57 x 77 cm 1" to 4 chains Endorsements: 'A 212'
(SI 31 May 1856 and 2 July 1856 to lay out into town and park lots and mill site; OTNR FN 1077 15 Oct 1856); shows town laid out between South and North sts, and from 15/16 sideroad to West St; park lots on the east and north; mill reserve; quarry sites, stores, post office, school, and a few cleared areas with bldgs; SR 86567 is a close copy; also a copy: 'Cranbrook In the Township of Grey J.W.B. Crown Lands Office Toronto 16th Jan. 1857 [Sgd] Joseph Cauchon Commissioner of Crown Lands' endorsed 'No 123' and with the addition of names of patentees (OTAR(P)).
OTAR(P) OTNR (SR 75; 86567)

CREEMORE

1292 *1853*
CREEMORE / THE / PROPERTY OF / EDWARD WEBSTER / LAID OUT FOR THE PROPRIETOR / into quarter & half acre Lots / BY / WILLIAM GIBBARD / Dec. 1853. // Wm. Gibbard C.E. & P.L.S.
Print (lith) 56 x 77 cm 1" to 5 chains
Shows the town from Napier St to Louisa St, and John St to William St; key to 18 bldgs including mills, stores, etc; notes on the advantages of the town site.
OTAR

DORCHESTER

1293 *[186?]*
Plan of Dorchester water power by Wm McClary P.L.S. and C.E.
Col ms 38 x 102 cm 1" to 5 chains
Shows GWR station and railway line near Thames R; streets named; possibly made after 1861 when the post office was named Dorchester (Carter, I:353); part north of river named Frampton and part to south named Edwardsburg and Dorchester Station P.O. on co map of 1862 (**997**).
OLU

DOUGLAS

1294 *1859*
Plan of the Town of Douglas, The Property of John G. Malloch Esq., On Lots 3, 4 and 5 in the 8th Con. of the Township of Bromley. Drawn by Andrew Bell C.E.
Ms 77 x 54 cm 1" to 3 chains
Inset: 'Map of the County of Renfrew' 1" to 8.5 miles; the ms plan from which the printed plan below was prepared; shows the town from High St to Robertson St, and Queen St to Edward St; mills, dam, slide, proposed bridge; other bldgs shown and named; description of the town, its industries, and advantages dated '... Douglas March 18th, 1859'; note beside inset: 'Make the town of Douglas rather larger & more conspicuous'; based on R.P. 1 (**B597**).
OOAMA (NMC 18058)

Related maps

(2) *1859*
PLAN OF THE / TOWN OF DOUGLAS / THE PROPERTY OF JOHN G. MALLOCH ESQ. / ON LOTS 3, 4 AND 5 IN THE 8th CON: OF THE TOWNSHIP OF / BROMLEY. / DRAWN BY ANDREW BELL C.E. // Fuller & Bencke, Liths Victoria Hall, Toronto.
Print (lith) 83 x 54 cm 1" to 3 chains
Inset: 'MAP / OF THE COUNTY OF / RENFREW.' 1" to 8.5 miles; shows the same information as the ms plan, and the map, inset, and location of items such as the note dated 'Douglas March 18th 1859' are almost exactly the same; an added note makes the case for choosing Douglas as the co town because it is the most central; the letters of the title are much larger and more ornamental in style than on the ms map and a coat of arms has been added.
OOAMA (NMC 21083) OTAR

DRUMBO

1295 *1857*
PLAN / of Maitland Fisher's Survey of part of the Village of / Drumbo in the Township of Blenheim in the County / of Oxford Being the North East quarter of Lot No 13 / in the 6th Concession of the Said Township // Thos Allchin, P.L. Surveyor & C.E. / Canning, C.W. [Sgd in ms] 'Canning Augt 17th 1857 Thos Allchin P.L.S.'
Print (lith) with ms adds 74 x 61 cm (trimmed to margin) 1" to 2 chains
Shows the town from Oxford St to South St, and Wilmot St to Henry St; some bldgs named including 'Sadlery Shop,' store, and Baptist church lot; see also **B614**.
Oxford 41 (R.P. 104)

DUNDAS

1296 *1800*
No 1 Project for the Subdivision of the Village of Coots Paradise, into 40 lots for store houses; under the idea, that the Creek runs nearly Strait, [Sgd] D W Smith Actg Sur Genl Approved in Council Nov 11th 1800 [Sgd] J Elmsley
Col ms 32 x 19 cm Scale not given
Shows the town laid out on both sides of the river with Dundas St shown by the shore on both sides; two squares shown opp each other in the centre 'for the general purposes of lading and unlading';

the town is sited between East and West Lane with four lots on either side of squares and 12 lots north of Flamborough St and south of Ancaster St; (*OHIM* 7.24).
OTMCL (D.W. Smith Papers B-9 p 363)

Related maps

(2) *1800–1*
No 2 Project for the Subdivision of the Village of Coots Paradise into lots for store houses, under the probability that the creek winds in its course [Sgd] D W Smith A S G1 Approved in Council Novr 11th 1800 [Sgd] J Elmsley Addenda 28 April 1801 by his Honor the Chief Justice in Council D W S.
Col ms 32 x 20 cm Scale not given
Follows the same plan as the other but the river, streets, and lots form a V-shape towards the south; the addenda indicate the sites for the church, gaol, court-house, and parsonage; (*OHIM* 7.25).
OTMCL (D.W. Smith Papers B-9 p 361)

1297 *1801*
Plan of the Village near Coots Paradise. This Survey made per order of the Surveyor Generals office bearing Date May the first and performed by John Stegmann D.P. Surveyor 1801
Col ms 53 x 37 cm 1" to 2 chains Endorsements: 'No 13'
(SI 19 May 1800 to survey village at east end of Dundas St at marsh); shows the actual survey for the river, which flowed diagonally; South St to North St, East St to West St; the reserves are in a position somewhat similar to **1296(2)** above; relief; North and South quays shown; the actual location of the river created a need to angle Meadow Lane, Pound Lane, and Mill Lane on the south side, and resulted in an extra tier of lots near the river; names of patentees added in all lots, eradicating some reserves; photoreproduction in OTAR(P); there is also a plan showing reserves for Cootes Paradise in D.W. Smith, 'Report upon Glebes & Commons ... 13th Jany 1802.'
OTAR (RG 1 A-II-1 vol 2 pp 942–87) OTNR (SR 97960)

Related maps

(2) *1801 (1844)*
Coote's Paradise by [Sgd] John Stegmann 1801 Surveyor General's Office Montreal 8th October 1844. A true copy.
Col ms 53 x 37 cm 1" to 2 chains Endorsements: '69' '623'
Shows the street outline and lot nos as in (1) above; relief south of river.
OTNR (SR 72)

1298 *1827*
Map of the Town of Dundas including Coots Paradise. Copy from Mr Valentine Gill's Plan of Survey by J.G. Chewett 1827
Col ms 44 x 63 cm Scale not given Watermark: 'J WHATMAN TURKEY MILL 1825' Endorsements: 'G 13' '710' 'PF 74'
Shows the two villages as they developed side by side – the earlier town plot of Cootes Paradise as it was laid out in 1801 with the addition of bldgs and the village of Dundas developing around the mills to the west and at the junction of Bridge and York sts; shows lots laid out along [King] St, the Desjardins Canal and Basin, and connecting roads on all sides; bldgs identified by function or owner; North St, St Georges St, and Dundas St connect Cootes Paradise with Dundas; (*OHIM* 7.26).
OTNR (SR 85)

1299 *1851*
MAP / of the TOWN of / DUNDAS / in the Counties of / WENTWORTH AND HALTON / Canada West. / Surveyed & Drawn by Marcus Smith / 1851. /PUBLISHED BY THE AUTHOR.
Print (lith) hand col 70 x 106 cm 1" to 250 ft
Views: 'Town-Hall' and 'Merchants Exchange Hotel'; [portrait] 'James Coleman Esqr Mayor of Dundas'; a very detailed map showing the town from the GWR to South St, and from Head St to East St; all bldgs are shown, most named; names of owners; cleared land and treed areas distinguished; escarpment.
OHMA

1300 *[1855]*
PLAN / OF / PART OF THE TOWN / OF / DUNDAS / IN THE / TOWNSHIP OF WEST FLAMBORO / Surveyed for Messrs Allan & Mathieson. / BY J. MACKINTOSH P.L.S. / H. Gregory Eng. & Lith. Dundas.
Print (lith) 83 x 60 cm 1" to 2 chains
Shows lots from Park St to GWR, and from Sydenham St west to beyond Princess St; bldgs, churches, and a few businesses shown; free-stone quarry north of railway; a flyer about the auction has been pasted on below title: '... for Sale by Public Auction on Friday, the 28th September 1855 about 250 town and park lots ... [and] Lime and free stone quarries ... Dundas 5th September 1855.'; notes on value of property and terms of sale; related to R.P. 1446 of 1855 (**B625**).
OOAMA (NMC 22327)

DURHAM

1301 *1849*
Plan of the town plot of Durham Wellington District Canada West. Surveyed in 1849 by [Sgd] David Gibson Prov: Land Surveyor. Examined A.R.
Col ms 56 x 79 cm 1" to 4 chains Endorsements: 'A 170'
(SI 9 Oct 1848 and 21 Dec 1848 to survey and subdivide into town and park lots the town plot at the intersection of Owen Sound and Durham rds; OTNR FN 181 4 Sept 1849); shows the town laid out from Durham Rd to South St, and Rock St to

West St; laid out partly from school lands; mills, stores, and a few other bldgs; reserve for Presbyterian church; shows a road diversion around Saugeen Hill; also a copy: 'Plan of Durham Garafraxa Road Crown Land Department Toronto 5th January 1850 T.D. [Sgd] J.H. Price Commissioner of Crown Land.' endorsed 'No 78' and with the addition of names of patentees (OTAR(P)).
OTAR(P) OTNR (SR 84)

1302 *1855*
Durham [Sgd] W [Winkler?] August 4th 1855
Col ms 90 x 65 cm 1" to 5 chains Watermark: 'J WHATMAN TURKEY MILL 1855'
Shows the development of the town north of Durham Rd to John and Jackson sts, and from Elizabeth St to James St, and south of South St to road line between lots 27 and 28 east and west of Garafraxa Rd; two reserves are shown south of Presbyterian church lands, some town lots are marked as sold.
OOOAMA (NMC 26619)

ELDORADO

1303 *[1867]*
Plan and Section / OF PART OF THE SOUTH HALF OF / LOT NO 18 CONCESSION V / TOWNSHIP of MADOC / COUNTY OF HASTINGS / C.W. / SURVEYED & DRAWN BY MURDOCH REID & UNWIN P.L. SURVEYORS, / FOR / HUGH R. FLETCHER & T.D. LEDYARD // LITHOGRAPHED BY J. ELLIS 8 KING ST TORONTO C.W.
Print (lith) Size unknown 1" to 2 chains
Inset: 'MADOC and adjoining TOWNSHIPS.'; [profile] 1" to 20 ft vertical; relief; names of mines; 'line of levels' shown in profile; plan was certified by owners Nov 1867; R.P. 121 is a reduced photoreproduction and original not located; see also **B664**.
Hastings 21 (R.P. 121)

ELORA

1304 *1832*
Plan of the Village of Elora Situated at the Falls of the Grand River in the Townships of Nichol and Woolwich in the District of Gore Surveyed for William Gilkison Esqr and James Crooks Esquire by [Sgd] Lewis Burwell Dy Surveyor. Brantford 10 November 1832 Copied from the Original
Col ms 67 x 49 cm 1" to 2 chains
'Profile of the Ground to be excavated for the Mill Privileges at the Falls of the Grand River' 1" to 1 chain; shows the town from Nichol St to Carleton Place by the Grand R and from Waterloo St to Guelph Rd; names on lots and some initialled by Gilkison family members; reserve by the river; notes on the situation of the village and the lots; key to points at the falls; bldgs shown; lots laid out west of Guelph Rd for James Crooks; a portrait of Burwell has been pasted onto the map; for further details on the first survey of Elora see Stelter, 'Combining Town and Country Planning ...' (1981).
OFEC

1305 *[1850–1?]*
PLAN / OF THE VILLAGE OF / ELORA / COMPRISING / Lots Nos 1, 2 and 3 Broken front on the North side of the Grand River / AND LOTS NOS. 1,2 AND 3 BROKEN FRONT ON THE SOUTH SIDE OF THE GRAND RIVER / in the Township of / NICHOL. / Hugh Scobie Lith. // Surveyed by Edwin H. Kertland Civil Engineer & P.L.S. Elora
Print (lith) 78 x 49 cm 1" to 4 chains Endorsements (OTNR copy): 'A 175'
OTNR copy has ms adds: 'Description of this Plan' and 'Description of so much of this Plan as is bounded by Purple line in accompanying Plan of Township [Sgd] Edwin Henry Kertland ...' (see **1054(2)**); shows the town from Colborne St to South Queen St, and Kertland St to Queen Rd; park lots also to the south; mills, church square, market square; list of bldgs and occupations of inhabitants; 'In 1850 the population of Elora is 400.'; R.P. 56 of 12 July 1851 is a transcript (**B670**).
OTNR (SR 91)

1306 *1851*
Plan of the village ground of Elora in Nichol as divided into village and Park Lots – Proposed to be annexed to the Pilkington Tract, Woolwich, according to application made to Parliament in the Session of 1850; Containing 9761/2 Acres Including Water [Sgd] Edwin Henry Kertland C.E. & P.L.S. Elora 5th April 1851.
Col ms 52 x 32 cm Scale not given Endorsements: 'A 176'
Shows the town with town lots on both sides of the Grand R with park lots beyond; streets not named; a note states 'See correct plan A 177,' which is a plan of part of the area originally in Portfolio E' OTNR (SR 9691).
OTNR (SR 90, SR 9691)

1307 *1853*
PLAN / of a part of the / TOWN OF ELORA, / Hugh Scobie Lith. Toronto. / J. Macintosh P.L.S. / Elora July 12th 1853.
Print (lith) 59 x 47 cm 1" to 4 chains
Shows the area from Cameron St to Colborne St, and Water St east to Cecilia and Kertland sts; the subdivision shows lots north of George St, town lots on part of market-place, and lots between Waterloo and Arthur sts; a note indicates the survey of north side of river was taken from Kertland's survey (see plan **1305** above) and south (west of Arthur St) from Percival's survey (no

registered plan); note indicates sale by auction 29 July and 9 Sept 1853; later ms notes about sales.
OOAMA (NMC 21085) OTAR

1308 *[1855]*
TOWN / OF / ELORA / Compiled from the / SURVEYS OF BURWELL / Kertland, Percival and Macintosh P.L.Ss / BY / W.S. GILKISON C.E. / Maclear & Co. Lith. Toronto C.W.
Print (lith) hand col or col printed 96 x 63 cm Scale not given
Ms adds on OTAR copy: 'lots col'd Red will be offered for Sale this day 4th Octr 1855,' indicating a few lots south and west of river and around Kertland St; map shows the area from Guelph Rd east to beyond Kertland St, and from road allowance in front of 1 con north to beyond Mathieson St; many bldgs identified; drawings of trees; decorative title block; one OFEC copy is colour-printed.
OFEC OKIT OOAMA (NMC 21072) OTAR

1309 *1856*
[Elora] // Edwin H. Kertland C.E. & P.L.S. / [missing] 1856. // Maclear & Co. Lith. Toronto
Print (lith), top half missing Approx 50 x 45 cm 1" to 3 chains
Shows part of Elora from Guelph Rd east to Waterloo St, and beyond Queen St to Fergus Rd and further north; Victoria Circus and various other crescents shown in plan; a few bldgs; title missing on R.P. 111 copy (see **B672**).
Wellington 61 (R.P. 111)

EMBRO

1310 *[185?]*
PLAN of NORTH EMBRO, / BEING COMPOSED of part of lot 13, in the 5th CONCESSION,/ Township of Zorra, Co of Oxford. SUBDIVIDED INTO PARK & BUILDING LOTS / By W. McMillan P.L.S. / For the Proprietors Messrs Colin Munroe, Levi Fowler & Jas Ferguson. // Spectator Office Hamilton, C.W.
Print (lith) 53 x 92 cm 1" to 2 chains
Shows the area from the mill pond to Wallace and Monroe Sts, and from road allowance between 4/5 cons east to Waverly St and 5/6 con road allowance; relief, lot nos and sizes; certified by owners and surveyor but not dated; see also **B682**.
Oxford 41 (R.P. 131)

1311 *[1856]*
PLAN OF / NORTH EMBRO. / Being composed of part of Lots Nos 13 & 14. / IN THE FIFTH CONCESSION / Township of Zorra / COUNTY of OXFORD. / Subdivided into Park and Building Lots, / By LEATHER and ROBINSON. / for the Proprietors, / MESSRS J. FERGUSON C. MUNROE & L. FOWLER. // [Lith ... Spectator] Office, Hamilton C.W.
Print (lith), pt missing at edge, with ms adds 58 x 66 cm 1" to 3 chains
Shows subdivision from Scott St to North St, and on both sides of Waverly St to con lines 4/5 and 5/6; mill pond, mill; certified by surveyor and owner 20 Nov 1856; ms note about size of certain lots 14 May 1861; see also **B681**.
Oxford 41 (R.P. 81)

ERIN

1312 *1852*
Plan of the Village of Erin, Being composed of a part of the Easterly halves of Lots Nos 13, 14 and 15 in the 9th Concession, also a part of the Westerly halves of Lots nos 14 and 15 in the 10th Concession of the Township of Erin in the County of Wellington and in the Province of Canada West. ... This Plan was made on the 13th day of November 1852 by C. Kennedy L.S. Esquesing
Print (lith) Size not known 1" to 1 chain
'This Village took its commencement several years since. Surveying done at sundry times in small portions by Chas Kennedy Licensed Surveyor.'; the town is shown from Hill St to Church St, laid out on both sides of Main St to William and John sts, and to mill ponds and river; mills, town hall, three bridges; Wellington 61 (R.P. 61) is a transcript of this map; reproduced in Jean Denison, *Main Street ... Erin Village* (1980), 5; see also **B704**.
Original not located

ERINDALE

1313 *1847*
Plan and Section of the River Credit at the Village of Springfield Dundas Street Toronto 28 April 1847
Col ms 48 x 74 cm 1" to 200 ft Endorsements: stamp [BW] '535'
'Cross Section' 1" to 50 ft, 1" to 10 ft vertical; [profile] 1" to 200 ft, 1" to 20 ft vertical; relief by hachures; shows a route to be bridged along Dundas St with houses on either side; heights given along profile; road to Streetsville shown.
OOAMA (NMC 22803)

ERROL

1314 *1835*
Errol Plan of the Town Plot in Plympton in the Western District. Surveyed by Order from the Surveyor General's Office bearing date Toronto 21st April 1835. Oxford 8th July 1835 By [Sgd] Peter Carroll D.P. Surveyor. To Samuel P. Hurd Esquire Surveyor General &c&c&c Toronto.
Col ms 64 x 80 cm 1" to 2 chains Watermark: 'JAMES WHATMAN TURKEY MILLS 1827'
Endorsements: 'A 18' '642'

(SI 26 Apr 1835 to lay out lots 14–17, Plympton Twp on L Huron, based on the plan for Adelaide; OTNR FN 205 15 July 1835); the triangular town is bounded by L Huron and Colborne, Egremont, and Maitland sts; Kings Square is in the middle with reserves for church and court-house; the four or five streets each way are at angles to the triangular boundary; similar to Adelaide (see **1103**); some town lots were advertised for sale on 7 Apr 1836 (OTAR RG 1 C-III-1 vol 2); also a copy at OTAR(P): 'Town of Erroll Western District Copy J.G. Chewett S.G.O. Office' endorsed 'No 8' and with a few names of patentees added; this copy has later notes dated 1840, 1855, and relief; and a copy in OTAR: 'Erroll [Sgd] Copy J.G. Chewett S.G. Office 12th June 1837 [Sgd] Surveyor General's Office Toronto 12th June 1837 J W Macaulay Surv Genl.' with a few more names added.
OTAR OTAR(P) OTNR (SR 89)

1315 *1855*
Map of Errol in the Township of Plympton County of Lambton Canada West Surveyed in August 1855 under Instructions from the Honble the Commissr of Crown Lands By P.S. Donnelly P.L.S. Examined with the diary A.R. Examined March 1856 T.D.
Col ms 66 x 54 cm 1" to 4 chains Watermark: 'JAMES WHATMAN 1855' Endorsements: 'A 203'
(SI 22 June 1855 to verify Carroll's town plot survey and subdivide into park lots south of Egremont Rd; OTNR FN 1159 16 Oct 1855); shows the original town plot and streets, with park lots laid out on both sides of the street running south of Egremont Rd; also a copy: 'Errol Crown Lands Office Toronto April 4th 1856 [Sgd] Joseph Cauchon Commissr of Crown Lands J.W.B.' endorsed 'No 108' and with the addition of names (OTAR(P)).
OTAR(P) OTNR (SR 88)

ETOBICOKE TWP

1316 *1796*
Reservn attached to the Sawmill on the Humber 7 July 1796 Surveyed by Augustus Jones W.C.
Col ms Approx 25 x 33 cm 1" to 2 chains Endorsements: 'No 21' '891'
Shows Humber R with rapids, mill pond, road, proposed bridge, sawmills; S. Fisher property; reserve for king's mill; relief; inset appended showing location of property and with further notes by T. Ridout, 25 July 1811; there is also a 1799 survey of the land attached to the king's sawmill on the Humber in OOA (RG 1 E3 vol 34 pt 2, 98).
OTNR (SR 994)

1317 *1834*
Plan of the King's Mill-Reserve situate in the Township of Etobicoke and Home District by William Hawkins D.P.S. [Sgd] William Hawkins D.P.S. Toronto 19th Aug 1834
Col ms (pt missing) 60 x 81 cm 1" to 10 chains Watermark: 'WHATMAN ... 1832' Endorsements: 'B73' '712'
(OTNR FN 245); shows clearings with bldgs including mill; lot sizes, roads; meadows and marshes; some names of owners.
OTNR (SR 991)

Related maps

(2) *[1834?]*
[Endorsed title]: 'King's Mill Reserve'
Col ms 41 x 69 cm 1" to 10 chains Endorsements: 'No 9'
Shows a smaller area than (1); lots 1–9, ranges I–V; shows Fisher's property and various kinds of mills; clearings; and bldgs shown; later notes and names of owners; title missing.
OTAR (SR 988)

1318 *1838*
Reserve at the mouth of the Humber, in Etobicoke, Divided into about five-acre Lots [Sgd] H.J. Castle D.P.S. Toronto 19th January 1838
Col ms 40 x 60 cm 3/8" to 1 chain
(SI 3 Jan 1838); shows subdivision west of bridge at mouth of river; relief; sandbanks; wooded land; there is also another plan of the reserve dated 12 May 1840 in (OOA RG 1 L3 E22 no 19 (1840)).
OTNR (SR 997)

1319 *1847*
Proposed / VILLAGE / of / ST ANDREWS / on Lot 33 Con's A & B / Etobicoke / Dennis / D.S. / May 1847
Print (lith) Approx 30 x 40 cm 1" to 2 chains
Shows lots laid out along the Albion Rd and con line between A and B; several bldgs shown, many across boundary lines; Donaldson's Shop, Conal's Inn, and Coulter's Shop and Inn shown; several ms adds including names of owners; based on R.P. 6 (**B715**); photoreproduction in OTAR.
Private Collection

1320 *1856*
MAP / OF THE TOWNSHIP / OF / ETOBICOKE, / IN THE COUNTY OF / YORK, / COMPILED BY CHARLES UNWIN PROVINCIAL LAND SURVEYOR, / PROVINCIAL CHAMBERS, / TORONTO. / 1856. / LITHOGRAPHED BY J. ELLIS TORONTO, C.W.
Print (col lith) 71 x 45 cm 1" to 40 chains
Shows the detailed survey grid for the twp with lot nos, names of landowners, roads, railways, town, and mills; outline of surveys, and names and nos of cons printed in red; also hand-colouring to distinguish areas; the map was advertised for sale in the *British Colonist* (Toronto) 11 Apr 1856.
OTMCL OTNR (SR 986)

1321 *1856*
PLAN / OF THE TOWN OF / MIMICO / IN THE TOWNSHIP OF ETOBICOKE / & ADJOINING THE RAILWAY STATION. / Within 8 Minutes Ride of Toronto. / [Sgd in facsimile] J.O. Browne / Civil Engineer P.L.S. / Toronto Jany 14th, 1856 / LITHO J. ELLIS TORONTO
Print (lith) 93 x 68 cm 1" to 4 chains
Shows lots laid out on both sides of Toronto & Hamilton Railway from the lake and Lakeshore Rd to Sydenham St, and west to Windsor St and con line; larger villa lots shown east of 'Mimocoke Creek.'
OTAR

1322 *[1857]*
PLAN OF PART / OF THE / VILLAGE OF LAMBTON / IN THE / COUNTY OF YORK // DENNIS BOULTON & Co / D.P. SURVEYOR'S. / LITHOGRAPHED BY J. ELLIS TORONTO
Print (lith) 47 x 68 cm 1" to 4 chains
Shows lots along Frederick, William, John, Dundas, and Lambton sts west of the Humber R to road allowance between cons A and B; related to R.P. 234 of 1857 (**B724**).
OTMCL

EUGENIA

1323 *1856*
Plan of Eugenia in the Township of Artemesia and County of Grey Surveyed in 1856. [Sgd] George McPhillips P.L.S. Examined Oct 24th 1856 J.W.B.
Col ms 112 x 82 cm 1" to 4 chains Endorsements: 'A 213' '9907/56'
(SI 23 May 1856 to subdivide town plot reserve into town and park lots and mill sites; OTNR FN 1163 21 Oct 1856); town laid out from South St to North St, and from East St to West St; relief in detail including comments on 'perpendicular rock'; five mill reserves shown and four other reserves; park lots at south and north ends of town; falls and rapids shown; also a copy in OTNR (SR 7013): 'Eugenia. J.W.B. Crown Lands Office Toronto 21st Jan 1857 [Sgd] Joseph Cauchon Commissioner of Crown Lands.' with watermark: 'J WHATMAN TURKEY MILLS 1856'; this copy is an outline plan with names of streets and lot nos only; and a copy in OTAR(P): 'Eugenia in the township of Artemisia. J.W.B. Crown Lands Office Toronto Jan. 26th 1857 [Sgd] Joseph Cauchon Commissioner of Crown Lands' endorsed 'No 125' and with the addition of names.
OTAR(P) OTNR (SR 7013; 7016)

FENELON FALLS

1324 *1854*
PLAN OF THE / TOWN PLOT / of / FENELON FALLS / Township of Fenelon / COUNTY OF / VICTORIA / (LATE) / COLBORNE DISTRICT. / 1854. James Wallis / MERINO PETERBORO C.W. / Proprietor // Edwd C. Caddy P.L.S. // Lithographed by J. Ellis, Toronto.
Print (lith) 53 x 74 cm 1" to 4 chains
View of town sgd 'J Gillespie'; shows Cameron L with river, mills, mill race and dam, bridge; town laid out from Francis St to Princes St and beyond, and from Clifton St west to line between lots 24 and 25; some bldgs including Marysboro Lodge shown; notes on distances and transportation links from other places and advantages of town; the same as R.P. 19P (**B735**).
OTNR (NMC 22330)

1325 *[186?]*
A Plan of the Town Plot of Fenelon Falls M Deane P.L.S.
Col ms 72 x 62 cm 1" to 4 chains
Shows the original town as laid out east of the Fenelon R in 1854; shows more streets south of Clifton St to Elgin St and a few park lots; west of river shows Elliott St to West St, and South St to King St; shows bridge, grist and sawmills, falls, relief, market square, parsonage; a few names of owners; probably before 1867 as some development west of river already shown on the 1861 co map (see **405**).
OTAR

FERGUS

1326 *[1847]*
PLAN OF THE TOWN OF FERGUS CANADA WEST / as laid out for Sale By M.C. SCHOFIELD Deputy Provincial Surveyor. Fr. Schenk, Lith. Edinburgh. / Axr D.F. Junr Delt.
Print (lith) 66 x47 cm 1" to 300 ft
Inset: 'Part / of / CANADA-WEST / (shewing the situation of / FERGUS.)'; six views of churches, manses, town from the east and south; shows the town laid out from Hill St south to Wellington St, and from Breadalbane St to Gowrie St; shows churches, glebes, mills, park lots; a description of the advantages of the town refers to 1847 as 'this year'; nature of the riverbank; the town was laid out in 1833 by Adam Ferguson and James Webster (*Smith's Canadian Gazetteer* (1846), 58).
OTNR (SR 102)

1327 *[1847]*
PLAN / of the / VILLAGE OF FERGUS / TOWNSHIP OF NICHOL / WELLINGTON DISTRICT / Canada West. / Scobie & Balfour, Lith / Toronto.
Print (lith) 59 x 39 cm Scale not given
Some lots west of Tower St by the river now shown as reserved; OOAMA copy has ms note about the right of proprietors to open new streets dated 'Fergus 15 Septr 1847.'; probably also made from Schofield's survey as it shows much of the

same detail and the same streets as plan above (**1326**).
OOAMA (NMC 3796)

1328 *1853*
Plan / OF PART / OF THE TOWN OF / FERGUS / 1853. / W. Armstrong / Hugh Scobie Lith Toronto
Print (lith) 74 x 56 cm 1" to 200 ft
Inset: 'Part / of / CANADA WEST (shewing the situation of FERGUS.)'; note: 'Valuable Property To be sold by Auction on 6th July ... Lots marked X already sold Population of village over 500.'; shows the east end of town from Tower St to beyond Herrick St, and from Hill St to Wellington St; some bldgs including churches; inset shows railway connections from Toronto to Barrie, Owen Sound, and Saugeen, Toronto to Sarnia, and Guelph to Owen Sound; OOAMA copy has ms notes and colouring of some lots in south part: 'shaded lots for Sale by Geo. D. Ferguson without Building Obligations'; possibly related to R.P. 77 (see **B740**).
OFEC OOAMA (NMC 22334; 26373) OTNR (SR 101)

1329 *[1853]*
PLAN OF PART / OF / FERGUS // Hugh Scobie Lith. Toronto
Print (lith) 75 x 55 cm 1" to 200 ft
The plan is from the same plate as **1328** with some later changes; new town lots have been added north of Hill St, and area east of Cameron St further subdivided; inset has been replaced with park lots and marked 'A.D. Ferrier's Survey'; OOAMA also has copy without name of Ferrier survey and with ms adds between river and Patrick St, including bldgs, names, and possibly a line for a railway (NMC 22332).
OFEC OOAMA (NMC 22331–2) OTAR

1330 *[1854]*
MAP / of part of the Town of / Fergus / Surveyed by W.H.Barker, C.E. // Lithog'd. at the Spectator Office Hamilton.
Print (lith) 70 x 53 cm Scale not given
Shows a subdivision east of the town from Herrick St to Barker St and Lamond St, and from Hill St south to Union St; shows mill property and Glenlivet Distillery; notice pasted on bottom: 'sale of lands by Public Auction on Thursday the 12th of October next' dates map as 1854; proposed bridge shown at Tom St and bridge at Gartshore St.
OFEC OOAMA (NMC 22333)

1331 *[1856?]*
PLAN / OF PART OF / FERGUS / CANADA WEST / FRANCIS KERR C.E. & P.L.S. / Guelph./ Maclear & Co. Liths. Toronto C.W. // Drawn by Alexander W. Simpson P.L.S. &c.
Print (lith) 56 x 83 cm 1" to 200 ft Endorsements: 'Novr 1856'
Shows the same subdivisions as **1330** but extends further west to Gowrie St to show Adam Fergusson's and A.D. Ferrier's houses, and shows area from about St George St south; shows more bldgs than other plan, including Mr Cadenhead's and J. Lamond Smith's houses; shows bridges at Tom St and Gartshore St; 'Note the Lots coloured Green shows the property of Mr Gartshore'; copy produced in *Looking Back* is endorsed 'Novr 1856'; Simpson became a provincial land surveyor in Apr 1856.
OFEC OTAR

1332 *1856*
Plan of Part / OF THE VILLAGE OF / FERGUS / AND / SOUTH KINNETTLES / SURVEYED FOR THE HONBLE / ADAM FERGUSSON, GEO. D. FERGUSSON / AND / JOHN WATT Esqrs / BY / Messrs Schofield & Hobson, P.L.S. / 1856 // Maclear & Co. Lithrs Toronto
Print (lith) 55 x 80 cm 1" to 4 chains
Shows the area from Queen St and the Grand R to beyond Elora St and between Tower and Black sts; some names of owners; St Andrew's Church; related to R.P. 77 (**B740**).
OFEC

FITZROY HARBOUR

1333 *1840*
Fitzroy Harbour A Copy of John Robertson D.P. Surveyor 1840
Col ms 44 x 53 cm 1" to 6 chains Endorsements: 'With the Chas & Robt Shirriff Papers 1841'
Possibly from OOA RG 1 L3 but exact location not found; shows the town between the Carp R and the harbour, clay ridge, various mills, and mill pond; 'small canal for deals,' timber slide; streets unnamed, bldgs shown along canal or by the river or harbour.
OOAMA (NMC 3799)

1334 *1840*
Plan of the Town Lots of Abercrombie as laid out at Fitzroy Harb. 1840
Ms 34 x 40 cm Scale not given
A sketch shows the town from Victoria St to Ottawa R and from Wellington Rd to Mississippi Snye; drawings of three churches; market squares; relief; prices in some lots; steamboat landing; dam.
OTAR (MU 5810)

FLORENCE

1335 *[ca 1856?]*
PLAN OF THE TOWN OF FLORENCE IN THE TOWNSHIPS OF EUPHEMIA, ZONE, AND GORE OF CAMDEN. // Surveyed by A.P. Salter P.L.S. / Maclear & Co Lith Toronto
Print (lith) 68 x 79 cm 1" to 2 chains

Shows the area from Fansher St to Victoria and Mary sts, and Alfred St to Sydenham R; shaded lots indicated as sold; all bldgs shown and indicated by business or name of owner; Kirbey & Knapps Saw Mill; distances marked to GWR and GTR stations; possibly laid out in 1856 or later when post office name changed to Florence (Carter, 2:1259).
OTAR

FORDWICH

1336 *1856*
A Plan of the Town Plot of Fordwich In the Township of Howick Surveyed in Accordance with an order in Council dated the 30 April 1856 Laid out in Town and Park Lots according to instructions from the Crown Lands Department Dated 31st May 1856 Francis Jones Provincial Land Surveyor
Ms 97 x 64 cm 1" to 4 chains Endorsements: 'A 206'
A pencil drawing of the town showing streets from West St to East St, and North St to South St; size of lots marked; 'Mark the limits of the Mill site on this plan. A.R.'; probably the plan for survey accompanying the first set of instructions (see (2)).
OTNR (SR 6381)

Related maps

(2) *1856*
Plan of Fordwich (Township of Howick) Surveyed agreeably to instructions from the Crown Land Department dated 21st July 1856. [Sgd] Francis Jones Provincial Land Surveyor Examined 7th Oct. 1856 T.D.
Col ms 80 x 64 cm 1" to 4 chains Endorsements: 'A 211' '9029/56'
(SI 31 May 1856 and 21 July 1856; OTNR FN 1192 24 Sept 1856); shows the same street outline as above with more detail added; town lots between Helena and Victoria sts, park lots beyond; most of area around Maitland R reserved for mill site; a few names of owners; also a copy: 'Fordwich in the Township of Howick Crown Lands Office Toronto 10th Jan 1857 [Sgd] Joseph Cauchon Commissioner of Crown Lands. J.W.B.' endorsed 'No 121' and with the addition of names of patentees (OTAR(P)).
OTAR(P) OTNR (SR 103)

(FORESTVILLE town plot)

1337 *1848*
Plan of the Village of Forestville laid out for Enoch Pixley on a part of Lot Number 1 in the 3rd Concession of North Dorchester in the fall of 1848 by [Sgd] Wm McClary P.L. Surveyor
Col ms 43 x 63 cm 1" to 1 chain Watermark: '... J WHATMAN ... 1847'
A plan for a town that was never put into effect and for which no registered plan exists; there are two similar copies of this map in OLU, and the second one has '1849' in place of '1848' in title.
OLU

FORT ERIE

1338 *1798*
Plan shewing the Situation & Dimensions proposed for building Lots for Merchants & Traders on the King's reserved Land at Fort Erie in the Province of Upper Canada. (Signed) Gother Mann Col: Commg Rl Engrs Quebec 30th June 1798. Approved (Signed) Robt Prescott. By Order of the Commander in Chief (Signed) James Green My Secy
Col ms 43 x 52 cm 1" to 1 1/2 chains
In Col McDonell's letter of 20 Aug 1798 regarding permission to Thomas Clark to occupy a lot (OOA RG 8 I/272 p 8); shows 12 lots for merchants along shore south of Fort Erie; shows bldgs in the fort and a few others; names of some occupants of the lots; there is also an untitled, undated plan in OOAMA (NMC 5258) endorsed 'G M No 41' and showing the same lots and old fort by the water and with a plan and sections for the new fort similar to those on 1803 plan (see **1339**); (Holmden 1641, 1643).
OOAMA (NMC 3800; 5258)

1339 *1803*
Plan of the Situation of Fort Erie with the New Works & Buildings proposed Vide Reports of this Date. Submitted by [Sgd] Gother Mann Coll Commandg Rl Engr Quebec 1st Aug 1803
Col ms 52 x 39 cm 1" to 100 ft Watermark: 'WHATMAN 1801'
Inset: 'Section of proposed Works' 1" to 10 ft; in Gother Mann's letter of 1 Aug 1803 enclosed in Lt Gen Hunter's no 42 of 17 Aug 1803 to Lord Hobart (GBLpro CO 42/333 p 122); shows the old fort in ruins and proposed new fort and fortifications, barracks, guardhouse, and officers' quarters; king's store and merchant's store shown; relief by colour wash; there is also a contemporary copy in OOAMA with the same title and with watermark 'WILLIAMS 1801.'
GBLpro (MPG 1171) OOAMA (NMC 3801)

1340 *1814*
[Endorsed title]: Fort Erie as left by the Enemy. [Sgd] Sam Romilly Capt Rl Engineers
Ms 20 x 32 cm Scale not given
Enclosed in Romilly's letter to Lt Gen Drummond of 10 Nov 1814 describing the fort (OOA RG 8 I/686 p 143); shows the state of fortifications, lines destroyed and those left after the Americans retired from Fort Erie on 5 Nov 1814; (Holmden 1646).
OOAMA (NMC 3804)

1341 *1818*
[Sketch of Fort Erie showing the British siege of Fort Erie in 1814] Royal Engineers' Drawing Room Quebec 31st January 1818 A. Walpole Lt. R. Engr E.W. Durnford Lt Col. Commg Rl Eng Copy
Col ms 45 x 32 cm 1" to 400 ft
Enclosed in Durnford's letter of 31 Jan 1818 to Lt Col Addison about rebuilding of wharves (OOA RG 8/402 p 39); shows the fort and various batteries and fortifications in the area and bldgs on the shore road; (Holmden 1649).
OOAMA (NMC 3804)

1342 *1819*
The Military Reserve at Fort Erie. Niagara April 19th 1819 [Sgd] A. Walpole Lt R.E. Henry Vavasour Capn Comg Royl Engineers N.D.
Col ms 52 x 80 cm 1" to 400 ft
Enclosed in Durnford to Major Bowles of 4 May 1819 about encroachments on the reserve and a key to these (OOA RG 8 I/405 pp 63–7); shows the fort, the old American lines, and the boundary of the reserve; relief, vegetation; various lots and bldgs are shown encroaching on the reserve; (Holmden 1652).
OOAMA (NMC 22342)

Related maps

(2) *1819*
Plan of the encroachments on the Military Reserve at Fort Erie, Niagara April 19th 1819 [Sgd] A Walpole Lt RE, Henry Vavasour Capt Comg Royl Engineers N.D.
Col ms on tracing paper 51 x 41 cm 1" to 40 ft
Watermark: 'JOHN HAYES 1814'
Originally in the same source as above; diagrams of individual lots with names of occupants; bldgs keyed in grey and pink; (Holmden 1650).
OOAMA (NMC 3805)

1343 *1852*
Fort Erie Bertie Plan of Military Reserve. Land applied for by the Brantford & Buffalo Railroad Company ... Line of Proposed railroad marked in Yellow across the Reserve. Copied by A.R. Vyvian Crease Lt R.E. 10/1/52. W. Renwick Capt R.E. 7.2.52
Col ms on tracing paper 90 x 56 cm 1" to 6 chains Endorsements: 'To accompany Captain Renwicks Report dated 7th February 1852' '342'; stamp 'REO'
Two proposed lines for railway shown, the second 'as per plan recd in R.E.O Toronto 27/2/52 from the Company'; also shows proposed ship canal, ruins of fort, planned railway depot, mill site; town development shown north of ordnance boundary on Niagara R; there are also two plans showing the military reserve per order 19 Nov 1850, one in QMMMCM (3632), and one in OOAMA (NMC 22343) further dated 18 Nov 1851.
OOAMA (NMC 11343; 22343–4) QMMMCM (3632)

1344 *1853*
[Plan of Fort Erie showing military reserve and the line of the Brantford and Buffalo Railroad] [Sgd] William Wallace Engineer. Forwarded with my report of 1st February 1853. [Sgd] Alexr Gordon Lt Col: Royal Engineers.
Col ms 36 x 57 cm 1" to 12 chains Endorsements: 'No 16'; stamp 'CREOC'
Shows part of the town, a few bldgs by the river, railway terminal, ferry wharf.
OOAMA (NMC 3812)

1345 *1855*
PLAN / OF / BUILDING LOTS / in the / TOWN OF / FORT ERIE / CANADA / Opposite to the City of Buffalo and at the Terminus of the / BUFFALO, BRANTFORD AND GODERICH RAILWAY / The property of Alexander Douglas Esq. / 1855. / H. Churchill, Surveyor Fort Erie & 328 Main Street Buffalo / Compton Buffalo
Print (lith) 60 x 71 cm Scale not given
Shows a subdivision from the terminus of the railway and Niagara St to North St and Garrison Rd to Bertie St; relief; bldgs shown along the water and Queen St as owned by William Wallace; mill race and mill, engine house; a few notes in lots; related to R.P. 504 (**B766**).
OTAR

1346 *1858*
Military Reserve Fort Erie Shewing the Location of the Enrolled Pensioners 1858. [Sgd] F.F. Passmore Provincial Land Surveyor Toronto October 14th 1858. This Plan amended by adding Lot letter 'D' Lake Shore range from survey performed under Instructions dated the 26th of November 1858. [Sgd] F.F. Passmore Provincial Land Surveyor Toronto, Decr 16th 1858.
Col ms 62 x 85 cm 1" to 5 chains Endorsements: 'F No 12'
Shows the pensioners' lots numbered at the north end of the reserve and east of the railway, with names; railway and spur to Niagara R marked 'Proposed dock and railway'; ruins of fort, shoreline, and perimeter roads shown.
OTNR (SR 5888)

1347 *1861*
Plan of the Subdivision of the Military Reserve Fort Erie Township of Bertie County of Welland 1861 [Sgd] F.F. Passmore Provl Land Surveyor Toronto Septr 7th 1861
Col ms 62 x 95 cm 1" to 5 chains Endorsements: 'E No 67' '14335/61' '16869/61'
Shows the subdivision from the river to Helena St and Garrison Rd; dimensions and sizes of lots shown, some irregularly shaped; names of owners and some bldgs shown; relief, ruins of fort; Buffalo Brantford and Lake Huron Railroad shown; also a copy: 'Plan of the Subdivision of the Military Reserve Fort Erie Department of Crown Lands

Quebec Jany 1862 [Sgd] Andrew Russell Asst Commissioner' endorsed 'F 11a' (OTAR(P)).
OTAR(P) OTNR (SR 5887)

FORT WILLIAM

1348 *[1816]*
[Plan of lots around Fort William on the Kaministiquia River] [on back: plan of the fort and buildings]
2 mss on 1 sheet 22 x 37 cm 1" to 20 chains Scale not given Watermark: 'J WHATMAN 1812'
Shows the river, fort, and lots under cultivation; burying ground; notes on the height of land and location of Northwest Co. land and XY Co. land; plan of fort and bldgs is in pencil on the back; the plans are attributed to Lord Selkirk and probably drawn in 1816 when he was at Fort William (*DCB* V:267); a note on the plan is dated '1815'; photoreproductions in OOAMA (NMC 3815, 3816).
OTAR (MU 3279)

1349 *1855*
Map of the Hudson's Bay Company's Property at Fort William. Surveyed and Drawn by Alex. McDonald, 1855. Montreal 9 May 1856 [Sgd] Alexander MacDonald Provincial Land Surveyor. Examined A. Russell
Col ms 68 x 55 cm 1" to 40 chains Endorsements: 'L.S. No 39'
(SI 13 Oct 1854 to A. MacDonald to survey Hudson's Bay Co. property at various places); shows the Hudson's Bay Co. post with bldgs and the Roman Catholic mission; McKay's Mountain shown with relief in colour wash; bearings of boundary of land.
OTNR (SR 7126)

1350 *[1857?]*
Plan of Fort William Reserve. Chief Peau de Chat First Lake Superior Reserve. [Sgd] James W. Bridgland P.L.S. Examined A.R.
Col ms 54 x 79 cm 1" to 40 chains Endorsements: 'L.S.P. No 34'
In addition to the reserve, the plan shows Fort William and the Roman Catholic mission in detail with houses and wigwams; vegetation, terrain indicated along survey lines and shore; McKay's Mountain shown in relief by hachures and wash; 'alluvial islands claimed by the H.B. Co.'
OTNR (SR 2438)

Related maps

(2) *1857*
Fort William Reserve Chief Peau de Chat. Crown Lands Department Toronto 18th July 1857 Commissionr of Crown Lands.
Col ms on linen 64 x 73 cm Scale not given Endorsements: '590'
Similar to plan above except the Hudson's Bay Co. post and Roman Catholic mission not shown in detail, and lacks the notes.
OOAMA (NMC 22347)

1351 *1860*
Townplot of Fort William L. Superior [Sgd] [illegible and endorsed later]: T.W. Herrick 1860
Col ms, pt missing 64 x 76 cm 1" to 4 chains Endorsements: 'F No 13'
(SI 6 June 1859 and 10 June 1859 to T. Herrick to subdivide tract on Kaministiquia R into town and farm lots; OTNR FN 1572 23 July 1860); shows the town laid out between Hector and Edward sts, and Chief and Rebecca sts; park lots above Rebecca St behind Roman Catholic mission on other side of river; bldgs; relief; possibly dated 10 July 1860 in missing part (Bigger, 1:59); also a copy: 'Town Plot Fort William L. Superior Department of Crown Lands Quebec January 31st 1861 [Sgd] Andrew Russell Assistant Commissioner.' with the addition of names of patentees (OTAR(P)).
OTAR(P) OTNR (SR 94)

FRANKTOWN

1352 *1819*
A Plan of the Village of Franktown District of Bathurst Surveyed Sept. 1819 Josias Richey Dy Surv
Col ms 26 x 36 cm 1" to 10 chains Endorsements: 'No 20'
Part of con III, lot 11, Beckwith Twp; blocks numbered, a few streets named; later additions and names to ca 1826.
OTNR (SR 98)

GALT

1353 *1852*
Plan of the Mackenzie Block adjoining the Incorporated Village of Galt Canada West Surveyed & [dr]a[wn] By James Black P.L.S. 1852.
Col ms 58 x 53 cm Scale not given
Shows a subdivision from Union St to John St and from Elgin St to Chalmers St west of Crown St; names of owners; related to R.P. 443 (**B786**).
OTMCL

1354 *1853*
PLAN / OF VILLAGE LOTS / IN THE VILLAGE / OF / Galt / WATERLOO COUNTY / Lithographed by J. Ellis, Toronto. // ... J. MACKENZIE, Proprietor / JAMES BLACK, Provincial Land Surveyor / November 2nd, 1853.
Print (lith) 43 x 70 cm 1" to 1 chain
Shows a subdivision from Bruce St to road between 10th and 11th cons and from Chestnut St to Cameron St; lot nos and sizes; names of owners added in ms; related to R.P. 441 (**B787**).
OTAR

1355 *1856*
PLAN / OF / BUILDING LOTS / IN THE / Town of Galt, / WATERLOO COUNTY. / 1856. / ... [Sgd in facsimile] J Mackenzie Proprietor / James Pollock P.L.S. Galt 27th May 1856. // Lith. Spectator Office, Hamilton, C.W.
Print (lith) 43 x 67 cm 1" to 1 chain
Subdivision of area from Pollock Ave to Pine St and McNaughton Ave and from Fiddes Ave and Spruce St east; names of owners added in ms; lot sizes; related to R.P. 442 (**B792**).
OTAR

1356 *1856*
PLAN OF THAT PART / OF THE / ESTATE OF THE LATE HON. ROBERT DIXON / situate in the Town of Galt / CANADA. / [Sgd in facsimile] Jas Webster & Co Proprietors / M.C. Schofield & Hobson P.L. Surveyors &c. / Dennis & Boulton Agents Toronto May 1856 // LITHOGRAPHED BY J. ELLIS. TORONTO.
Print (lith) hand col 79 x 65 cm 1" to 2 chains
Shows the area from the Grand R to macadamized road north of Portland St, and from Samuelston St to GWR; notice of sale of lots with terms on 17 June [1856] and also the sale of the Galt Mills; many bldgs shown in the developed part of town; related to R.P. 447 (**B788**).
OKIT OKITD

1357 *1867*
Map / OF THE / TOWN OF GALT / COUNTY OF WATERLOO, / COMPILED FOR THE CORPORATION / BY / JAMES POLLOCK, / Provincial Land Surveyor / 1867. / W.C. CHEWETT & CO. LITH. TORONTO
Print (lith) 148 x 121 cm 1" to 2.5 chains
A very detailed map of the town showing all streets and all bldgs, many identified; wooded areas, roads, railways; names of owners of large holdings, layout of estates and landscaping shown; wards; cemeteries; shows the area on both sides of the Grand R from South St to beyond Samuelston St and from Sprague and Osborne sts to Macadamized road.
OCL OKITD OTAR

GANANOQUE

1358 *1794*
Plan and Section of the Ganonnoque [Sgd] Alex. Aitken D. Syr Kingston Augt 4th 1794.
Col ms 93 x 60 cm 1" to 300 ft Endorsements: '3 maps Gananoqui, iles du Baril, Bay of Quinte.'
Shows the mouth of the Gananoque R with soundings also given; relief; saw and grist mill located upstream.
OTAR (Simcoe Map 445791)

1359 *1815*
Sketch of the Garrison of Gananoque and Parts adjacent July 14th 1815. [Endorsed]: 'No 12 Sketch and Description of Buildings in Charge of the Barrack Departm at Gananoque'
Ms 35 x 47 cm Scale not given Watermark: 'J RUMP 1813 ...'
Originally enclosed in letter of Deputy Barrack Master Gen to Major Foster, military secretary, 7 Aug 1815, on the state of barracks in Canada (OOA RG 8 I/555 p 68); identifies 26 bldgs and parts of fortifications; falls, bridge, slide for timber, roads; (Holmden 1670).
OOAMA (NMC 3825)

1360 *[1818]*
Plan of the property of Sir Johnson [*sic*] Bart
Ms Size unknown 1" to 160 ft
Enclosed in letter of Sir John Johnson to Lt Col Addison, military secretary, 21 March 1818; shows the village of Gananoque laid out in a grid of three streets each way east of river; town lots at the front, park lots to the rear; 12 military bldgs and others are keyed; proposed canal on the Gananoque R, mill house, blockhouse, etc; streets not named; OOAMA copy is photoreproduction and original is with letter in OOA RG 8 I, but location not found.
OOAMA (NMC 3826)

1361 *[ca 1850?]*
A Plan of the Town of Gananoque in the Township of Leeds and District of Johnston [Sgd] William H. Deane Prov Land Surveyor
Col ms 65 x 119 cm 1" to 3 chains Watermark: 'J WHATMAN TURKEY MILL 1847' Endorsements: stamps 'BW' '500'
Shows the town laid out from South St to North St and from the river east to William and East sts; west of river from St Lawrence to King, Main, Market, and Tanner sts and unnamed streets; all bldgs shown, many identified; some names of owners and landscaping of estates shown; proposed canal.
OOAMA (NMC 15193)

1362 *1858*
Supplementary Plan of part of the town of Gananoque The Property of W.S. Macdonald Esquire. 1858. Gananoque 15 November 1858. [Sgd] W.H. Deane Prov. Land Surveyor
Col ms on linen 66 x 90 cm 1" to 1 1/2 chains
Note on this plan indicates that it shows subdivisions as shown on R.P. 105 (**B795**), described as blocks J, C, N, M, and O (6 June 1853) with certain changes in other lots and streets; the plan also shows the subdivision of the mill reserve as shown on the earlier plan; related to R.P. 111 of 15 Nov 1858, which also has the same note (**B797**); shows area from the river west to Maple St and on the east lots along Stone and Mill sts north to Brock St; various businesses identified including machine shop, nail works, etc.
OTNR (SR 86558)

GARDEN RIVER

1363 *1866*
Plan of Shingcuicouse at Garden River C.W. [Sgd] Wilson & McGee Provincial Land Surveyors Mount Forest C.W. December 1866.
Col ms 64 x 98 cm 1" to 4 chains Endorsements: 'S 37'
(SI 20 Aug 1866 to lay out and subdivide the town plot of Shingcuicouse; OTNR FN 1741 26 Dec 1866); shows the town at the junction of the 'River St Mary' and Little L George with lot sizes and streets, swampy and wooded areas, relief; 'Sault & Bruce Road'; houses, other bldgs, cemetery, and wharves; also a copy sgd '19th June 1867 A. Russell Assistant Commissioner' in OOAMA (RG 10M 76703/9 no 173).
OOAMA (NMC 13058) OTNR (SR 302)

GEORGETOWN

1364 *1854*
PLAN / OF / GEORGETOWN / IN / ESQUESING / COUNTY OF HALTON / Chisholm Miller P.L.S. / Georgetown Jan. 1854 / Maclear & Co Lith. Toronto. (Late Hugh Scobie)
Print (lith) 67 x 88 cm 1" to 3 chains
Shows the town with streets named, major bldgs identified; mill pond, various mills, factories; GTR and station; names of landowners of large estates; (see also **B803**).
Halton 29 (no R.P. number)

GLEN ALLAN

1365 *[1854 or 5?]*
PLAN / OF / ALLANSVILLE / COMPRISING LOTS 5 & 6 IN THE 2nd & 3th [*sic*] CONCESSIONS / OF THE TOWNSHIP OF / PEEL / Surveyed for G. Allan / by / E.H. KERTLAND / Maclear & Co. Lith. Toronto
Print (col lith) 48 x 56 cm 1" to 2 chains
Shows the area from Wellesley St to the 'Canistoga R' and Church St to Ghent St; shows lot nos and sizes, some bldgs identified; possibly the first subdivision for the town and laid out before **1366** in 1854 or 5; no registered plan.
OKIT

1366 *1855*
PLAN / OF A PORTION OF / ALLANSVILLE, / LAID OUT FOR / MR David Ghent / by Edwin Henry Kertland, C.E. & P.L.S. / Elora 19th Novr 1855. / Lith. Spectator Office, Hamilton C.W.
Print (lith) 43 x 56 cm 1" to 1 chain
Shows streets and subdivision between 'Canistoga R' and Main St, and east to beyond Mary St; lots shaded are offered for sale; this plan was never registered; (see also **B812**).
Wellington 60 (R.P. 62)

1367 *[1857]*
PLAN / OF / GLEN ALLAN / formerly Allansville, / COUNTY / OF / WELLINGTON / [Sgd in facsimile] Edwin Henry Kertland C.E. & P.L.S. Elora / LITHOGRAPHED BY J. ELLIS TORONTO.
Print (lith) 84 x 64 cm 1" to 3 chains
Certified by the owner 22 Jan 1857; includes two views of parts of the town; shows the area from Maryborough St to George St, and Wellesley and Peel sts to Ghent St; relief by hachures; many bldgs shown south of Main St including sawmill, grist mill, tannery; lot nos and sizes; see also **B813**.
Wellington 60 (R.P. 60)

GLEN MILLER

1368 *1854*
PLAN / OF THE VILLAGE OF / ST ALBANS / on LOT LETTER – A / SECOND CONCESSION OF SIDNEY / in the / COUNTY OF HASTINGS / the property of / D.M. GILKISON ESQ. / Maclear & Co. Lith / J.S. Peterson P.L.S. Sept. 1854
Print (lith) 51 x 80 cm 1" to 2 chains
Provenance: OOAMA copy from Gilkison Papers in OOA; shows the lots and streets laid out from Colborne to George's St, and Peterson to Downing St; a few mills along the Trent R; (see also **B818–9**).
Hastings 21 (R.P. 111; 111A) OOAMA (NMC 22768)

GLEN ROSS

1369 *[1859?]*
GLEN ROSS / SITUATED ON LOTS 8, 9 & 10, / IN THE / 8th & 9th CONCESSION / OF THE TOWNSHIP OF / SIDNEY. / Maclear & Co. Lith. Toronto.
Print (lith) 94 x 119 cm 1" to 2 chains
Streets laid out from Bay to Church St, and Green to Way St, lots numbered; shows land owned by Stevenson and Way at the north end, and by Ross, Stuart, and Cumming by the canal and Trent R; mill sites, saw, grist, carding, and fulling mills; dam and timber slide; a few other bldgs shown; 'Mt Murney' shown by hachures; related to R.P. 94 of July 1859 (**B820**).
OTNR (SR 86559)

GODERICH

1370 *1827*
Plan of the Harbour at the mouth of the River Menesetunk on Lake Huron as Surveyed for the Canada Company by [Sgd] M. Burwell Dy Surveyor. Deputy Surveyor's Office, Port Talbot 28th December 1827
Col ms 81 x 62 cm 1" to 4 chains Endorsements: '1165'

Shows relief, soundings, boat channel; description of trees and marshy areas at the mouth of the river; shows the site for Goderich before survey.
OTAR (SR 7063)

1371 *1827–8*
Plan of Goderich Harbour copied from a Plan by M. Burwell Esquire Dy Surveyor [Sgd] John McDonald Dy Surveyor Guelph 18th December 1827.
Col ms 63 x 56 cm 1" to 4 chains
The map of the river and harbour is similar to 1827 plan above (**1370**), but part of the town plot by the river is shown including crescent and diagonal streets; the plan possibly dates from 1828 as Samuel Smith mentions on 15 July 1828 that the town plot had been drawn for Charles Prior (OTAR MU 2839 box 3 FN and diary of survey 1828).
OTMCL (E.W. Banting Collection)

1372 *1829*
Plan of the Town of Goderich Laid out on the principle of a Proforma Plan made under the direction of John Galt Esquire late Superintendant of the Affairs of the Canada Company by John McDonald Dy. Surveyor York August 1829
Col ms 66 x 82 cm 1" to 4 chains
Shows the first part of the town laid out around Market Place from [Britannia St] north; the eight streets radiating from Market Place are named North, Northeast, East St, etc; Lighthouse St also named; east-west streets are all numbered; lots numbered; company's bldg and reserves shown; 'York 30th October 1829 There is an increase in the No. [of lots] from its being considered proper to halve the Reserves around the Market Place for the purpose of opening them for sale.'; a pencilled layout between bluff and river has note: 'to be laid out as thought most advisable hereafter.'
OTAR (Canada Co. Maps pkg 4 no 110)

1373 *[1830?]*
HURON TRACT. / Town of Goderich // C. Ingrey, Lithog. 310. Strand
Print (lith) 20 x 20 cm Scale not given
Shows the streets with the radials from the central square named; shows the town as in the survey of 1829 (see **1372**); OTAR copy has ms notes: 'Reserve for Goderich Town ... 1458 Acres per David Gibson's Survey 1828/9'; also a ms list of the number of acres in various parts of town; oriented to the east.
OTAR (Canada Co. Papers A-4-3 vol 3)

1374 *1831*
PLAN / of the Town of / GODERICH / UPPER CANADA / Founded by the Canada Company / 1829. / Lat. 43° 46m. N Long. 81° 53m. W // Reduced by F. Cattlin. // Engraved by J. & C. Walker.
Print (engrav) 19 x 20 cm 1" to 16 chains
In Joseph Bouchette, *British Dominions in North America* (London: Henry Colburn & Richard Bentley 1831), 1: opp 117 (OOA), and in a later ed (London: Longman, Rees, Orme, Brown, Green & Longman 1832) (*Bib Can* 1627, 4968); the plan is a reduction and more generalized version of McDonald's plan above (**1372**), without lots; same streets are named, relief shown along river; (*OHIM* 7.16).
OOA OTMCL OTRMC

1375 *[ca 1840]*
Map of the Town and Harbour of Goderich
Col ms 65 x 85 cm 1" to 4 chains
Shows the original town with streets still numbered; streets now laid out down ravine to harbour; pier and piling in harbour; jail, court-house, general burying ground, Presbyterian church, Methodist chapel, church and ground on bluff by crescent; shows some lots by roman numerals and coloured green; list of purchasers of lots 1–328; the plan appears to predate Kirk's plan of 1844 (**1379**).
OTAR (Canada Co. Maps pkg 4 no 24)

1376 *1841*
Sketch of the Survey of the Proposed mill race and the livel [*sic*] in the Town and township of Goderich Designed by John Longworth Esqr and Executed by David Smith county Surveyor 4th May 1841
Col ms 53 x 113 cm 1" to 4 chains
Shows streets and bldgs along shore, bridges and channels of rivers; points along mill race numbered, distances and heights given.
OTMCL (E.W. Banting Collection)

1377 *[1842?]*
[Goderich]
Ms 47 x 71 cm Scale not given
Note: 'Received 18 Feby 1843 with letter of 21 Jany'; shows streets of original town plot pencilled in; shows lots designed to be laid out along the flats below top of bank; islands and pilings in harbour.
OTAR (Canada Co. Papers TRHT 225)

1378 *[ca 1843]*
[Plan of Goderich harbour and Maitland River]
Ms 1" to 4 chains Endorsements: stamps 'BW' '596'
Reference keys two Martello towers, five gun batteries, and brewhouse; 'The above batteries purposed to be erected by Colonel Love for the defence of the Harbour and Town'; two piers and piling in river shown; a few depths; plan done before breastwork built, as shown on 1844 map (**1379**); 'Canada Companys Flagstaff.'
OOAMA (NMC 22366)

1379 *1844*
Map of the Town and Harbour of Goderich J.G. Kirk D.P.S. 1844
Col ms 61 x 87 cm 1" to 4 chains
Shows the town as originally laid out but streets all named; Brittania St to Gloucester Terrace, L

Huron east to Maitland Rd; relief, bridges, two piers, and breastwork along river; market-place, Canada Co. office; lot nos in roman and arabic; related to R.P. 1 of Sept 1844 (**B823**).
OTAR (Canada Co. Atlas)

Related maps

(2) *[1856?]*
Plan of the Town of Goderich Certified Correct [Sgd] T.N. Molesworth Provincial [Land Surveyor] 1st April [1856]
Col ms 70 x 115 cm 1" to 4 chains
The plan is similar to Kirk's plan above and was certified by registrar as the map filed Sept 1856 (R.P. 457) (**B830**) but as not agreeing with map previously filed by Mr Jones, commissioner (see (3) below); plan differs in small details but does not show later information such as railways; no breakwater shown.
OTAR (Canada Co. Maps pkg 4 no 114)

(3) *1858*
Map of the Town and Harbour of Goderich Certified a correct copy of the Map of Goderich placed in the Registrar's Office ... by T.M. Jones Esq. [Sgd] Molesworth & Weatherald C.E.'s Provincial Land Surveyors 16th January 1858.
Col ms 62 x 90 cm 1" to 4 chains
Similar to Kirk's plan (1) above and probably a later copy of the plan mentioned in (2) above as 'previously filed by Mr. Jones'; shows breastwork across island in river.
OTAR (Canada Co. Maps pkg 4 no 139)

1380 *[185?]*
Plan of the Town of Goderich
Col ms 74 x 98 cm 1" to 5 chains
Shows a similar layout and information to the 1844 plan; Canada Co. lots are marked in red; two piers and breakwater shown.
OTAR (Canada Co. Maps pkg 4 no 60)

1381 *1852*
Plan of the Town of Goderich shewing its extended boundary – as prayed for in the memorial – and also the extended boundaries of the Several Wards – the whole according to the accompanying descriptions. Drawn by (Signed) T. Nepean Molesworth C.E. & P.L. Surveyor Signed W.A. Lewis Mayor Crown Lands Department Quebec 26th May 1852 Certified a true Copy T.D. [Sgd] John Rolph Commissioner of Crown Lands
Col ms 44 x 68 cm 1" to 10 chains
From petition for extension of boundary (OOA RG 5 no 54 1852); desired boundary runs from L Huron south to town to lot 107, Maitland con, and lots 2 and 3, Maitland con; north of this are 'ten acre accommodation lots'; petition is also to extend boundaries of four wards.
OOAMA (NMC 3836)

1382 *1853*
Plan of part of the Town of Goderich As Surveyed June 1853 by [Sgd] Wm Perceval C.E. P.L.S.
Ms on tracing paper 33 x 49 cm 1" to 4 chains
Shows the area from the Canada Co. office and streets to the harbour; contents of lots.
OTAR (Canada Co. Maps pkg 4 no 161)

1383 *1853*
PLAN / of the / TOWN AND HARBOUR / OF / GODERICH ... Showing the Lots offered for disposal by / The Canada Company, / on the 14th October, 1853. // NARINE & Co LITH. 7 BROAD ST N.Y.
Print (lith) 42 x 55 cm 1" to 10 chains
Shows town with new lots laid out south to Thomas St, from Elizabeth St to Eldon St, and Huron Rd to Maitland Rd, and Walnut St to Maple St; four wards shown; town boundary is as petitioned for in 1852; 'Notice This sketch plan ... merely made to afford intending purchasers a general view of the locality of the Lots ... Toronto 7 September 1853'; OTAR copy (54) shows the railway line in ms; OTAR copy (205) shows lots to be offered in Oct and remaining undisposed lots in ms; south extension cut out of (54) copy; OTAR copy (57) shows lots still owned by Canada Co. in 1919.
OOAMA OTAR (Canada Co. Maps pkg 4 nos 54, 57, 59, 205)

1384 *1856*
Plan / OF TWELVE VALUABLE BUILDING LOTS / IN ELGIN and VICTORIA STREETS, / Fronting on all the Leading Roads; / and very near the centre of the / TOWN OF GODERICH / THE PROPERTY OF IRA LEWIS ESQUIRE, / To be Leased by Auction or Otherwise ... Projd and Drawn by / T.N. Molesworth / Civil Engineer and P.L. Surveyor / January 1856 / Maclear & Co. Lith Toronto
Print (lith) 58 x 89 cm 1" to 20 ft
Inset: 'PLAN / OF / PART OF THE TOWN OF / GODERICH / SHEWING POSITION OF PROPERTY / TO BE LEASED.'; a resubdivision of lots between Elgin, Picton, and Victoria sts; see also **B829**.
Huron 22 (R.P. Goderich 6)

1385 *1857*
PLAN OF THE TOWN OF GODERICH / Showing the position of 60 Valuable Town Lots / THE PROPERTY OF MESSRS R. & T. MACINDOE ROBERTSON. / Molesworth & Weatherald / C.E.S. & P.L. Surveyors Goderich May 1st 1857
Print (col lith) 57 x 92 cm 1" to 4 chains
Inset: 'ENLARGED PLAN / OF / MESSRS ROBERTSON'S / PROPERTY TO BE SOLD. / 1" to 66 ft' ; shows a subdivision from Brittania Rd to Oxford St, and from Regent St to Toronto St; see also **B831**.
Huron 22 (R.P. Goderich 458)

1386 *1859*
Plan of Goderich Harbour and part of the River Maitland with certain Lands and premises sold by the Canada Company to the Buffalo and Lake Huron Railway Co. Drawn under the direction of J. Macdonald Esqre by T.N. Molesworth PLS & CE Copied by Wm Armstrong CE Toronto (Signed) Fred Widder Commissioner Toronto 3rd June 1859 (Signed) R.S. Carter Director & Gen. Manager B & L. H Ry Co. 3rd June 1859
Col ms 75 x 112 cm 1" to 4 chains
Shows the shore and streets nearby; parcels in green presumably those to be sold; number of acres and dimensions; certified as copy of registered plan R.P. 462 (**B834**).
OTAR (Canada Co. Maps pkg 4 No 147)

1387 *[1859?]*
Plan of the / TOWN AND HARBOUR / OF / Goderich. // Waterlow & Sons Lith. London
Print (col lith) 38 x 48 cm 1" to 10 chains
There is also a copy at OTAR (Canada Co. Maps pkg 4 no 217) with ms adds '(Signed) T. Weatherald C.E. & P.L.S. Oct 22d 1861' and with the addition of north pier, breakwater in river, elevator, and costs of construction; shows the town from Brittania Rd to river and lake with the line of the Buffalo & Lake Huron Railway and passenger station; lots belonging to Canada Co.; Platts Mills and Goderich Mills named; probably related to and made after plan above.
OTAR (Canada Co. Maps pkg 4 nos 222, 222A)

1388 *1861*
Plan of the Harbour of Goderich on Lake Huron Surveyed and drawn by F.A. Wise
Col ms 61 x 94 cm 1" to 200 ft
'The Soundings were taken in the beginning of the month of July 1861'; relief by grey wash; vegetation; mills, various bldgs by river, piers, cribwork, ice-breaker; similar to map with 1862 report (see **278** (Plan No 4)) except more soundings and fewer bldgs are shown; also a copy in GBTAUh (D6188 Aa3) with the same title dated 'July 1861' and endorsed 'Recd H.O. Dec 1862' and including a view: 'Sketch of the Harbour of Goderich from a Point below the English Church [Sgd] F.A. Wise.'
GBTAUh (D6188 Aa3) OOAMA (NMC 58329)

1389 *1863*
Plan of Glebe Lot Situate on Falls Reserve on the Maitland River Township of Goderich
Col ms on vellum 35 x 43 cm 1" to 5 chains
Shows a reserve of 100 ft along river near Huron Rd; map is on the back of a deed conveying parcel to the Church Society of the Diocese of Huron dated 3 June 1863.
OTAR (Canada Co. Maps pkg 4 no 55)

GORRIE

1390 *1856*
MAP / OF THE VILLAGE OF / HOWICK / LAID OUT ON LOTS 5 & 6 IN THE 8th CONCESSION OF THE / TOWNSHIP OF HOWICK / COUNTY OF HURON / FOR THE PROPRIETORS / EDWD LEECH & BROTHERS & GEORGE & ROBERT GREER / BY / Wm Rath Provincial Land Surveyor ... [Sgd and certified in facsimile by surveyor] 15th May 1856
Print (col lith) 94 x 62 cm 1" to 2 chains
Inset: [location map]; 'Profile of Victoria Street' 1" to 2 chains, 1" to 48 ft vertical; shows William St to James St, Alma St to Nelson St; lot nos and sizes; mill pond, dam, and mills on Maitland R; table of areas of properties; notes on roads, mill sites, etc; certified by owners in ms; see also **B843**.
Huron 22 (R.P. Howick 2)

GOULAIS BAY

1391 *[1860]*
Plan of the Town of Aupaquash being Section 27 in Townp No 3 North, Range 26 west [Sgd] Josph Wm Burke P.L.S.
Col ms 59 x 87 cm 1" to 4 chains Endorsements: 'A 13' '15763/60'
(SI 3 May 1860 to subdivide town plot at Goulais Bay into town and park lots); the town plot was laid out east of the present-day town but west of the Goulais R; a note on plan indicates the subdivision was cancelled in 1907; shows the town from William St east to Patrick St, and Maud St north to Victoria St; town lots on the west, park lots on the east; swampy land, burnt land; lot nos; also a copy: 'Plan of Town Plot of Apaquosh. Department of Crown Lands Quebec July 1861 [Sgd] Andrew Russell Ass. Commissioner.' endorsed 'IASR' and 'No 649' (OOAMA (NMC 22223)); and a copy: 'Aupaquash. Department of Crown Lands Quebec Augt 9th 1864 [Sgd] Andrew Russell Assist Commissioner' (OTAR (SR 11)); and a copy: 'Town Plot of Apaquosh Department of Crown Lands Ottawa April 30th 1866 [Sgd] Andrew Russell' (OTAR(P)).
OOAMA (NMC 22223) OTAR(P) OTNR (SR 11; 6503)

GOWANSTOWN

1392 *1856*
MAP / OF PART / OF / COWANSTOWN / COMPRISING LOTS No 1 & 2 IN THE 9th CONCN OF THE TOWNSHIP OF WALLACE & PART OF LOT No 1 IN THE 9th CONCN OF MARYBOROUGH / Surveyed for / Charles Cowen Esqre & the Revd G. Moore. // By Edwin Henry Kertland C.E. & P.L.S. Elora 21 November 1856. / Maclear & Co. Liths Toronto C.W.

Print (col lith) 104 x 91 cm 1" to 2 chains
With typeset printed advertisement of lots for sale pasted on map; shows the area from Nelson St to Bishop St and Front St to beyond Centre St; some bldgs identified along Front St; includes decorative feature of large red star above title; post office established as Gowanstown in 1863 (Carter, I:468).
OFEC

GUELPH

1393 *[1828–9]*
Plan of Guelph
Col ms 67 x 69 cm 1" to 4 chains Endorsements: 'No 8 Guelph v. Can Company ... referred to in depositions of Fredk Madden 23d April 1853'
The plan appears to be in John McDonald's hand and was probably copied from George Tiffany's plan in 1828; shows town lots 1–about 975 and Waterloo, Market, McDonell, Quebec, and Woolwich sts; other streets shown but not named; includes 'List of persons who have taken up Town Lots in Guelph' (names for lots 1–220); an overlay sgd 'April 8th 1829 By J. McNaughton' changes the plan for the focal point, reduces open space, and places boundary around the priory land (see Stelter, 'John Galt,' 31, 38–9); a further overlay sgd 'Canada Company Offices York 6th Decr 1833' shows a few more lots along the river, some renumbered; Clarence Place deleted, amount of land for Catholic church square reduced, and more lots laid out.
OTMCL (E.W. Banting Collection)

1394 *[1830?]*
TOWN OF GUELPH, / Gore District. // C. Ingrey, lithog. 310 Strand.
Print (lith) 20 x 20 cm Scale not given
Shows streets, lots, and squares with a few streets named near focal point; market ground and market house, St Patrick's and two other churches shown; two bridges shown; 'Office,' [priory bldg], and site of 'Maple' [tree]; the plan is essentially the same as the original 1828–9 plan without the 1829 revision (see **1393**); probably printed in 1830 or slightly later when Ingrey was in business alone.
OTAR (Canada Co. Papers A-4-3 vol 4 p 53a)

1395 *1831*
PLAN / of the Town of / GUELF / UPPER CANADA / Founded by the Canada Company / 1827. // Reduced by F. Cattlin. // Engraved by J. & C. Walker
Print (engrav) 19 x 20 cm 1" to 16 chains
In Joseph Bouchette, *British Dominions in North America* (London: Henry Colburn & Richard Bentley 1831), I: opp 118 (OOA), and in a later ed (London: Longman, Rees, Orme, Brown, Green & Longman 1832) (*Bib Can* 1627, 4968); appears to be a reduced and simplified version of the Ingrey plan above (**1394**); shows market ground and bldg, St Patrick Square, 'general burying ground,' three churches; Clarence Place; Woolwich and Waterloo sts; Tiffany's plan of May 1827 appears not to have survived, but Bouchette's plan is referred to as an accurate version of it (Stelter, 'Charles Prior's Report,' 41, 48); (*OHIM* 7.17).
OOA OTMCL OTRMC

1396 *[ca 1833]*
Plan of the Town of Guelph [and endorsement]: 'No 12 Guelph vs The Can Company The Exhibit marked No 12 referred to in depositions of Donald McDonald 23d April 1853 A J'
Col ms 65 x 89 cm Scale not given
Note: 'Mem. 1st May 1830 No of first new lots to be 1058'; shows the streets as amended in 1829, town lots in the west and north removed and replaced with 99 park lots; from Wellington St to London Rd, and Edinburgh St to Speed R; Nelson Crescent added but western square and circle deleted; three churches shown including St Patrick's and St Andrew's, schoolhouse, grist mill, sawmill, three bridges; a red line surrounds block between Woolwich, Windham, and Quebec sts; shows extra lots by the river per 1833 additions (on **1393**); a pencilled addition extends Suffolk St west and town lots laid out (a subdivision of Sept 1853 (see **1401**); the basic plan appears to date from the early 1830s with various later additions.
OTAR (Canada Co. Maps pkg 5 no 141)

1397 *[1843–6?]*
Plan of / PARK LOTS / FOR SALE NEAR THE TOWN OF / GUELPH / Lithog. H. Scobie, Toronto
Print (lith) 28 x 24 cm 1" to 8 chains Watermark: 'J MORBEY & Co 1842'
Shows lots on the north side of the Speed R east of Eramosa Rd; gaol and court-house shown on Woolwich St; some names of owners given; this appears to be an early plan by Scobie possibly prepared soon after he advertised his lithographic press in 1843 (see **970**); the subdivision differs from proposal on 1847 plan (**1399**) and the lines of park lots differ from those on the township plan of ca 1852 (**1069**).
OKIT

1398 *1847*
Plan of the Town of Guelph According to the Surveys thereof under the directions of the Canada Company. Toronto 27th March 1847 [Sgd] J. McDonald Dy P Surveyor
Col ms on tracing paper 67 x 64 cm Scale not given
Endorsements: 'No 26'
Shows the town as originally surveyed with 1058 town lots between Fleet St and Yorkshire Rd and 99 park lots to boundaries of town; only a few streets named between Woolwich and Waterloo sts; shows churches including St Andrew's, St Patrick's, and St George's, grist and sawmills, school-house, market house, burying ground, mill

reserve, tannery ground; three bridges; the printed plan below (**1399**) was probably based on this map, although more information is shown on the latter.
OTNR (SR 117)

1399 *1847*
PLAN OF THE TOWN / OF / GUELPH / By Donald McDonald / October 1847. // Scobie & Balfour, Lith. Toronto
Print (lith) 34 x 44 cm 1" to 8 chains
Shows the original town with 1058 town lots and 99 park lots, streets named, major bldgs shown including Scotch church, English church, Roman Catholic church and lot, schoolhouse and lot, burying ground, market-place, priory, grist-mill land, a few other churches, court-house and gaol; 'town pumps'; table showing the number of types of bldgs and occupations in Guelph in 1843, 1846, and 1847; a subdivision east of the river from Eramosa Rd to Budd St and north to Metcalfe St is noted as owned by John McDonald, and plan is 'principally proforma and ... may ... undergo some alterations ...'; this subdivision did not develop, although the southeastern part retained the same street layout; the plan was advertised as just published in the *British Colonist* (Toronto) 18 Jan 1848; (*OHIM* 7.18).
OG OGM OGU OTAR

1400 *[1853?]*
PLAN OF TOWN LOTS. / Guelph / as Staked out by F. Kerr, Provl. Land Survr / Lithographed by J. Ellis, Toronto
Print (lith) 45 x 41 cm 1" to 3 chains
Provenance: OOA Sir John A. MacDonald Papers; from Toronto & Guelph Grand Trunk Railway Depot at Waterloo St to Huskisson and Crawford sts and proposed Queen St and York Rd; 'application to be made to Jas Webster Esqre, Guelph ...'; similar to R.P. 113 of 3 July 1856 (**B876**) (reproduced in Johnson) except the orientation of Huskisson and Crawford sts is different and the layout of lots and streets around Bridge and Neeve sts differs; some of these lots were probably those owned by MacDonald and advertised for sale in Nov 1855 (Johnson, 158–9, 182–3).
OOAMA (NMC 3843)

1401 *1853*
PLAN / Shewing the Subdivision of Park Lots / 4, 5, 11, 12, 13, 26, 27, 28, 29, 36, 37, 48 & 49. / IN THE / TOWN OF GUELPH / FRANCIS KERR P.L.S. / Guelph Sept 1853. // Hugh Scobie Lith. Toronto
Print (lith) 44 x 54 cm 1" to 2 chains
Shows a subdivision from Gladwin St to Suffolk St W, and from Edinburgh Rd to Yorkshire Rd; OKIT copy has ms adds showing 'The intended Galt & Guelph Railway Station' between Raglan and Sultan Sts; 'Sale at 2 p.m. 28 Sept at Guelph'; related to R.P. 29 of 1855 (**B875**).
OKIT

1402 *1854*
PLAN OF LOTS / IN THE / TOWN OF GUELPH, / FOR SALE BY G.S. TIFFANY, ESQ. // Printed at The Advertiser Office, Guelph
Print (typeset) 24 x 39 cm 1" to 2 chains
The plan was certified by Francis Kerr, surveyor, 16 Dec 1854; shows a subdivision from Clarence to Kerr St, and Woolwich St to the Speed R; 'Sale of these valuable lots by Auction ... on Saturday 21st October 1854'; R.P. 18 (Wellington 61) (**B857**) is a transcript.
Original not located

1403 *[1854?]*
PLAN OF THE ESTATE / OF / MR. ROBERT THOMPSON / ADJOINING THE TOWN OF GUELPH, / IN THE COUNTY OF WELLINGTON
Print (typeset) 43 x 27 cm 1" to 2 chains
Shows a subdivision from Speed R southeast to Charles St, and from Mary St to the Guelph to Dundas Rd; 'Race to Gow's Tannery'; 'Victoria Place Reserve'; the subdivision is shown on the 1855 map (**1405**) and the lots are described as laid out and sold in July 1854 (Johnson, 181); related to R.P. 37 (**B878**).
OTAR

1404 *1855*
MAP / OF / PART OF BROKEN FRONT LOT NO. 5 DIVISION F, / IN THE TOWN OF GUELPH, / AS LAID OUT FOR JOHN THORP, ESQUIRE: / BY / M.C. SCHOFIELD, P.L.S. / 1855
Print (lith) 47 x 67 cm 1" to 50 ft
Lots on both sides of Brockville St between York St and Eramosa R; (see also **B871**).
Wellington 61 (R.P. 24)

1405 *1855*
MAP / OF THE TOWN OF / GUELPH, / FROM RECENT SURVEYS AND ORIGINAL MAPS. / PUBLISHED BY J. SMITH, GUELPH. / Drawn by Fred: J. Chadwick, May 1855. Lithographed by John Ellis, Toronto.
Print (lith) 76 x 103 cm 1" to 6 chains
Shows the town as it had developed from Victoria Rd southwest to Silver Creek Rd, and from Forest St west to beyond Speedvale Ave; major bldgs named; GTR bisects the main square of town; Galt and Guelph Railway shown terminating at station west of Edinburgh St; OOAMA copy has ms adds showing a proposal for three wards to accompany petition of 20 Nov 1855 (OOA RG 5 C1 no 1457 1855), plan endorsed 'A Plan of Guelph showing the proposed division into Wards and population of each Jno Smith'; this petition was withdrawn and a new petition for four wards submitted on 27 Dec 1855 (OOA RG 5 C1 no 1617).
OOAMA (NMC 26374)

Later editions and states

(**2**) *[1856]*
[Same title and date]

Print (col lith) 76 x 103 cm 1" to 6 chains
A coloured overprint in brown has been added showing the four wards of Dec 1855 (see (1) above), streets, and town boundary; (*OHIM* 7.19).
OTAR OTMCL

1406 *1855*
Map / SHEWING THE POSITION / OF LOTS LAID OUT IN THE TOWN OF GUELPH / FOR / GEORGE J. GRANGE AND ADAM J. FERGUSSON ESQUIRES / By / M.C. SCHOFIELD, P.L.S. / 1855. Maclear & Co. Lith. Toronto C.W.
Print (lith) 52 x 82 cm 1" to 200 ft
Inset: [plan of Guelph showing the location of the lots]; shows lots from Edinburgh St to Alma St south of Paisley Rd as laid out by Grange around the Galt & Guelph Railway station and GTR station, and lots east of Edinburgh St laid out by Fergusson; the lots were advertised for sale 6 Jan 1855 in the *Guelph Advertiser TriWeekly* (Johnson, 182); related to R.P. 27, 28 (**B870, B873**); there is a ms note on OTNR copy about owners' right to open streets; R.P. 28 is reproduced in Johnson, 184.
OGM OTAR OTNR (SR 118)

1407 *1855*
PLAN / OF / BUILDING LOTS / Laid out in the / TOWN OF GUELPH / For JOHN MITCHELL Esq. / Fras. Kerr P.L.S. / Maclear & Co. Lith. Toronto. / Fras. Kerr P.L.S. Guelph July 1855.
Print (lith) 46 x 63 cm 1" to 2 chains
Shows lots from Perth to King sts and from Eramosa Rd to past Spring St north of the Speed R; shows other streets south of the river to Woolwich St; a few bldgs shown and identified; a notice about sale of lots in 1855 has day and month left blank; the same as R.P. 40 (**B885**).
OGM

1408 *1855*
PLAN OF LOTS / IN / THE TOWN OF GUELPH, / SHOWING THE VICINITY OF BOTH / RAILWAY STATIONS, / AND THE PRINCIPAL ROADS TO THEM. / Surveyed for Mr. BUCKLAND by HENRY STRANGE, Esq. P.L.S. / 1855. // PRINTED AT THE "ADVERTISER" OFFICE, GUELPH
Print (typeset) 87 x 60 cm 1" to 3 chains
Shows lots laid out on Bodiam, Sussex, Buckland, Heathfield, and Elliott sts north of London Rd and 'Road newly made leading to Paisley Block and West End'; also shows area to Paisley St, the Galt and Guelph Ry Station, and GTR Station; related to R.P. 30 (**B860**).
OGU

1409 *1855*
TYRCATHLEN / the Property of the / REVD ARTHUR PALMER / in the / TOWN of GUELPH / Laid out into Building Lots / BY / WM. HASKINS P.L.S. / September 1855
Print (col lith) 64 x 88 cm 1" to 66 ft
Lots along Queen, Palmer, and Arthur sts west of Grange St and north of the Speed R; proposed bridge at Grange St; court-house shown on Woolwich St; related to R.P. 32 (**B869**); reproduced in Johnson, 115.
OGM

1410 *[1856]*
Map of / FREDERICK GEORGE'S SURVEY OF LOTS / AND / HYDRAULIC PRIVILEGES / FOR THE TOWN OF / GUELPH. / COUNTY OF WELLINGTON. // SCHOFIELD & HOBSON P.L.S.'s // Maclear & Co. Liths Toronto.
Print (lith) 60 x 93 cm 1" to 1 chain
'Sale of this valuable property ... will take place on the ground on the [in ms]: 15th day of May 1856'; shows mill pond on the Speed R and lots on either side from Cardigan St to Perth St and Eramosa Rd to Wood St; drawings of mills; shows dams, hydraulic canal, bridges; identification of bldgs and residence of F. George; some names of owners.
OGU

1411 *[1856]*
PLAN OF LOTS / IN THE FOURTH [in ms]: 'Third' RANGE, DIVISION A, / IN THE TOWN OF GUELPH, / BELONGING TO W.D.P. JARVIS, ESQ. AND MR. ROBERT SCOTT, / SURVEYED BY W. HASKINS, PROVINCIAL SURVEYOR, &C. // PRINTED AT THE "ADVERTISER" OFFICE, GUELPH
Print (typeset) 55 x 42 cm 1" to 1 chain
Shows lots along Augusta St, Emilia St, and unnamed street to 'Woolwich Rd'; related to R.P. 36 of 8 Sept 1856 (**B879**).
OTAR (MU 1532–7)

1412 *1856*
Plan of Subdivision of Lots Nos 63 & 64 in the Town of Guelph Canada West. 1856 Alexr. W. Simpson P.L.S. Del.
Col ms 57 x 59 cm 1" to 80 ft
Shows lots along Woolwich and River sts; bldgs in area shown including gaol, court-house, and registry office.
OGM

Related maps

(2) *1856*
PLAN / OF SUBDIVISION OF / LOTS Nos 63 and 64 / IN THE / TOWN OF GUELPH / Canada West. / 1856. / F. KERR P.L.S. / Maclear & Co Liths Toronto C.W. // Drawn by Alexander W. Simpson P.L.S. &c.
Print (lith) 62 x 68 cm 1" to 80 ft
Based on ms plan above but with some additions; GTR line and station added; town hall; 'New Stone Block' of bldgs marked along McDonell and Windham sts; major commercial and public bldgs identified.
OGM

1413 *1860*
PLAN / Of Lots Laid Out for / G.M. STEWART, ESQ. / In the Town of Guelph. / 1860. // Guelph, 15th October, 1860. FRED J. CHADWICK, P.L.S.
Print (typeset) 50 x 68 cm 1" to 1 chain
'These splendid Villa Sites will be offered for sale ... 1st of November, 1860'; shows the area from King St to beyond Delhi St and from Eramosa Rd west to Spring St; related to R.P. 133 (**B895**).
OGL

1414 *1862*
MAP / of the / TOWN OF GUELPH / IN THE / COUNTY OF WELLINGTON / CANADA WEST / Compiled From Recent Surveys and Original Plans / BY / THOMAS W. COOPER C.E. & P.L.S. / W.C. CHEWETT & CO. LITH. TORONTO. / 1862.
Print (lith) 138 x 130 cm 1" to 4 chains
Inset: [central area from Woolwich to Norfolk to McDonell sts]; six views of town, public bldgs including town hall and residences; shows the town from York Rd to north limit and from the southwest to the southeast boundary; all lots shown; all bldgs shown and major ones named; railways; some names of owners; all bldgs identified in inset.
OGM

(GWILLIMBURY town plot)

1415 *[1800]*
Project for the Town Plot of Gwillimbury laid out into Acre lots of 2 chains front by 5 chains in depth [Sgd] D.W. Smith Actg Surv General.
Col ms 53 x 76 cm 1" to 10 chains Endorsements: 'A 22' '646'
The projected plan for the town probably prepared after Stegmann's twp survey reserving town plot in 1800; shows the town to be laid out on lots 110–115 with five streets east of and parallel to Yonge St and four to five cross streets; reserves for court-house, church, market, school, poor-house, and other reserves for officials, gardens, the public, burying ground, and hospital; notes on navigability of the river and location of the swamp; the laying out of the town is referred to in OOA (RG 1 E3 vol 58 p 64 (1800)); there is also a plan showing reserves for Gwillimbury in D.W. Smith's 'Report upon Glebes & Commons ... 13th Jany 1802.'
OTAR (RG 1 A-II-1 vol 2 pp 942–87) OTNR (SR 112)

Related maps

(**2**) *[180?]*
Project for the Town Plot of Gwillimbury, laid out into Acre Lots of 2 chains front, by 5 chains in depth. ... Copy W.C.
Col ms 53 x 76 cm 1" to 10 chains Watermark: 'WHATMAN' Endorsements: 'A 21' '645'
Shows the same plan for the town but later notes added about lines to be surveyed, bearings, the further survey of the river and area between it and the town; the later notes were probably related to Wilmot's survey of 1811 (see **1416**).
OTNR (SR 111)

1416 *1811*
A Plan of the Vilage [*sic*] of Gwillimbury Surveyed by order of His Excellency Francis Gore Esqre Lieutenant Governor &c. &c. &c. April 9th 1811 [Sgd] Saml S. Wilmot Dy Surveyor.
Col ms 60 x 162 cm 1" to 4 chains Endorsements: 'No 21'
(SI 30 Jan 1811 to survey the village of Gwillimbury commencing at the limit between lots 110 and 111); shows the town laid out partly according to the projection but shifted one range east because of the marshy land near the river and extended two lots further north; lots laid out west of Yonge St to compensate for this (W.R. Smith, 25); East St and Pond St to marsh and river and Hospital St to several unnamed streets; shows a similar layout for reserves for court-house and clerk, church and parson, market and pound, and school and schoolmaster; farm lot reserves; many later notes about patents including a note indicating that the most southerly part of the town plot was taken over by Holland Landing to the south; also a later copy:'Gwillimbury Part East & West [Sgd] Copy J.G. Chewitt S.G. Office 17th June 1837 [Sgd] Surveyor General's Office Toronto 19th June 1837 J W Macaulay Surv Genl' (OTAR).
OTAR OTNR (SR 137)

1417 *1847*
Town Plot as Resurveyed of Gwillimbury, Holland River. [Sgd] to Thos Baines Esquire Crown Lands Agt Toronto – Weston July 27th 1847 J. Stoughton Dennis D.S.
Col ms 39 x 59 cm 1" to 4 chains
Only the streets from Yonge to Ramsay, and Church to School St are shown in this resurvey; three streets to the east and two west of Yonge have been deleted; school, market, and church blocks are still shown; a few houses and names of owners shown; block by the river owned by the 'N.W. Compy'; notes on survey; Gwillimbury was never really settled (W.R. Smith, 24ff) and it was shown only as crown land on the co map of 1860 (see **404**).
OTAR

HALIBURTON

1418 *[1864?]*
TOWN PLOT / OF / HALIBURTON, / IN THE / TOWNSHIP OF DYSART / CANADA WEST / THE PROPERTY OF THE CANADIAN LAND & EMIGRATION COMPANY (Limited) / OF LONDON, – ENGLAND. // W.C. CHEWETT & CO. LITH. TORONTO.

Print (lith) 84 x 53 cm 1" to 4 chains
Shows the town plot with lot nos and streets, mill reserve, and 'clearing' on the edge of Head L; OTNR copy has printed paste-on: 'Applications for lots to be made to CHAS J. BLOMFIELD Secretary to the Company, TORONTO. BANK BUILDINGS, TORONTO – or to CHAS R. STEWART Resident Agent of the Company at HALIBURTON.'; this copy also has a ms note indicating 'The Sawmill and forge have been at work for some months. A building for a store and trading House has also been erected and is in operation but Mr Stewart has not yet notified me on what lot – [Sgd] Chas. Jas. Blomfield Sec. Toronto May 6/65'; plan probably published in 1864 after survey in 1862 or 1863 (Murray, cx, 279–80, 377–8).
OTAR OTMCL OTNR (SR 86576) OTUTF

HAMILTON

1419 *[1816–?]*
Town of Hamilton District of Gore
Ms 40 x 32 cm Scale not given Watermark: 'BEVAN 1814'
A rough sketch showing the first survey for Hamilton; shows 12 blocks of 80 lots laid out between unnamed streets [King St to Peel St and James St to Mary St]; two reserves marked in centre; shows road to Bellevue, George Hamilton's house; shows land belonging to Rich Springer, Jno Springer, N. Hughson, 'Ferguson,' 'Kirkendall,' and R. Beasley, and 'Lowrie farm' and McAfee's Inn; Hamilton bought the land in 1815, probably laid the town out soon after, and it became district town in 1816 (Weaver, 16–17; Campbell, 51–3); the north part between King and Main may have been laid out first, the southern part appearing a year or so later (Evans, 80); (*OHIM* 7.33).
OTMCL

1420 *1829*
Plan of Hamilton. Hamilton July 23d 1829 [Sgd] Lewis Burwell Dy Surveyor
Col ms 48 x 34 cm 1" to 2 chains
Shows the town plot as originally laid out and extended to one more street and lots at both the north and south ends; streets unnamed; shows new court-house [being built] and market square (added by George Hamilton in 1828–9) (Weaver, 16); a later note on [church] reserve indicates it was regranted to George Hamilton by Order in Council 23 Sept 1831.
OTMCL

1421 *1830*
Hamilton Burford February 12th 1830 [Sgd] Lewis Burwell Depty Surveyor
Col ms 66 x 98 cm 1" to 2 chains
Provenance: OHMA Wentworth Co Court House Maps no 118 dr 5; shows the town and property of George Hamilton with Robert Land property on lot 12 and James Crook property shown to the west; shows King, Main, Bond, Charles, James sts.
OHMA (Maps 7677/8)

1422 *1830–67*
[Maps of Hamilton and Wentworth co from the Wentworth County Court House collection]
40 col mss and five prints (liths) Sizes vary Scales vary
The 40 pre-1867 plans (only part of the set) appear to be mainly unregistered subdivision-type plans, possibly originating in the Wentworth Co Registry Office and acquired by McMaster University in the 1970s; the set includes an important general plan of 1830 (see **1421**), a general plan of 1833 related to **1423**, and five printed plans listed separately (see nos **1437**, **1441–2**, **1446–7**).
OHMA

1423 *1833*
Hamilton [Sgd] James Kirkpatrick Deputy Surveyor May 20th 1833.
Col ms 66 x 47 cm 1" to 2 chains
Shows the town as in the 1829 map (**1420**) with the addition of three new streets and lots to the south; town is bounded by Jarvis, George, Mountain, Robert, and Hannah sts; court-house, church, and market shown; areas of lots given; a similar plan with names of owners and showing built-on lots is in OHMA (Map 7453).
OTMCL

1424 *1834*
Plan shewing the relative situation of the Wharfs and Store Houses of Mr. Hughston and Mr Gunn in the Town of Hamilton on Burlington Bay in the District of Gore [Sgd] Lewis Burwell Dy Surveyor. Hamilton 1st December 1834.
Col ms 78 x 65 cm 1" to 1 chain Endorsements: 'No 22' '648'
Shows the area from John St west to McNab St on the bay; relief and swampy areas shown.
OTNR (SR 124)

1425 *1836*
A PLAN OF / the town of / HAMILTON / UPPER CANADA / Reduced & Compiled / from / VARIOUS SURVEYS / in 1836 by Alexr McKenzie. / Surveyor. // [part missing] Lithog. New York
Print (lith) 73 x 58 cm 1" to 6 chains
Shows the area from Queen St to Wellington St, and from Burlington Bay and Bay St to Mountain Rd and con 4, Barton; shows the town boundaries, streets, and subdivided areas with key to owners subdividing; blocks not subdivided shown with names of owners; transcript copy in OH.
Original not located

1426 *1837*
PLAN / of the / TOWN OF HAMILTON, / CANADA WEST, / Reduced and Compiled from /

VARIOUS SURVEYS, / in 1837 by / JOSHUA LIND / Surveyor / Lith: of Hall & Mooney Buffalo N.Y.
Print (lith) Approx 81 x 40 cm 1" to 6 chains
Shows the town laid out from the mountain to the bay and Queen St east to boundary at road allowance lots 12/13 Barton Twp; streets named; lot nos; market places; a few blocks of land with names of owners; wharves; key to 7 churches and 4 public bldgs; shows the same subdivisions as **1425**; photoreproduction in OH.
Original not located

1427 *1841*
Sketch of the Survey of part of lot no. 15 in the 3d Concessn of the Township of Barton being a part of the Town of Hamilton in the Gore Dist [Sgd] T Allen Blyth D P Surveyor Oct 1 1841
Ms 40 x 32 cm 1" to 2 chains
Shows two lots west of James St and south of Hunter St; notes on the back indicate part or all 'for H. Archd Kerr.'
OTAR

1428 *1842*
Plan of the Town of Hamilton District of Gore Canada 1842. E.T.H.A. 2042
Col ms 49 x 70 cm 6" to 1 mile
An attractive military-style map showing the town and environs in 1842; shows area from the bay to beyond the mountain, and area from Land's wharf to canal to Dundas, and High Road to London and Brantford; relief by shading; all rivers, roads, cleared land; all bldgs shown with indication if brick or frame; names of major landowners; shows 'Corktown' southeast of King and John sts; wharves, names of some industries; 'Dundurn'; although considerable subdivision and extension of town limits had occurred, the area developed is mainly between Park and Mary sts, and Peel and Henry sts; (*OHIM* 7.41).
OH

1429 *1845*
Sketch of the Surveys of Lots Nos 13, 14 and 15 in the Broken Front on Burlington Bay in the Township of 'Barton' and 'Town of Hamilton' [Sgd] Thos Allen Blyth D.P.S. Hamilton June 9th 1845
Col ms 58 x 50 cm 1" to 4 chains Endorsements: 'G.D. No 35'
Shows the area between the eastern boundary and McNab and Bay sts; various wharves shown with names of owners; water lots with owners' names include two being applied for; names of owners of large lots to the south include Ferguson, Hughson, McNab, etc.
OTNR (SR 27)

1430 *1846*
Map of the Bay and Harbour in front of The City of Hamilton in the Gore District Shewing the Public Thoroughfare and the Water Lots adjoining the same, Also the front part of the City as far up as King Street and likewise including Burlington Heights Surveyed by order from the Honble Comr of Crown Lands dated Montreal. Hamilton 30th June 1846. [Sgd] Peter Carroll P.L. Surveyor
Ms 114 x 152 cm 1" to 4 chains Endorsements: 'A 156' '1035' 'PH 251'
(SI 27 Feb 1846 to survey all provincial harbours with regard to development of a system of laying out water lots); shows the harbour and surrounding area from King St north and from road allowance, lots 12/13, to Cootes Paradise and around to north shore; Desjardins Canal and proposed new line of canal through the Heights; relief in detail by hachures, nature of shoreline, water lots; a few major bldgs shown; also a copy: 'Plan of the Bay and Harbour ... Burlington Heights Surveyed by Peter Carroll D.P.S. 1846 J Cane Dtsn Crown Land Department Montreal Septr 1846' endorsed 'No 20' and with later changes and additions made to harbour area (OTAR(P)).
OTAR(P) OTNR (SR 16088)

1431 *1846*
Plan of the Survey of part of the Town of 'Hamilton' fronting on Burlington Bay [Sgd] Thos Allen Blyth D.P.S. Hamilton Feby 1846
Col ms 53 x 69 cm 1" to 4 chains
Shows area from Mary and Simcoe sts to the water; wharves, names of owners, and a water lot applied for by Calvin Cook & Co[?] at the top of Burlington St.
OTNR (SR 6739)

1432 *1847*
Map shewing the surveys made for the Location of the Great Western Railway through Hamilton City, Burlington Bay & Heights. 1847. C.B. Stuart, Engineer of Location. C.L. Beard Del.
Col ms 70 x 125 cm 1" to 500 ft
The line is shown crossing bay on the east, then along Burlington Heights, and over the road to Dundas; Desjardins Canal and Dundas Marsh and Creek shown; relief by colour wash; streets named; wharves.
OTNR (SR 5426)

1433 *1847*
PLAN / OF SURVEY OF LOTS IN THE / CITY OF HAMILTON / C.W. / THE PROPERTY OF / H.B. WILLSON ESQ. / 1847. / Scobie & Balfour Lithographers Toronto [Sgd in facsimile] Thos Allen Blyth P.L.S. Hamilton Oct 27th 1847
Print (lith) 55 x 86 cm 1" to 100 ft
Shows the area from Peel St to Willson St, and Wellington St east to Emerald St; related to R.P. 223 of which there are two versions, one being a transcript of this printed plan (**B931**).
OH

1434 *1850–1*
MAP / of the City of / HAMILTON / in the County of Wentworth / Canada West / Surveyed and drawn by / MARCUS SMITH. / 1850–1 // Mayer & Korft's Lith. 93 William St. N.Y. // Entered according to Act of the Provincial Legislature in the year 1851 / by Marcus Smith in the office of the Registrar of the Province of Canada
Print (lith) 112 x 105 cm 1" to 400 ft
Inset: 'CENTRAL PORTION OF CITY ENLARGED.' approx 1" to 200 ft; views: 'Dundurn / The Residence of Sir A.N. MACNAB,' 'COURT HOUSE,' 'CHRIST CHURCH / (Episcopal) Revd J.G. GEDDES – Pastor'; shows the town from the front of con 4, Barton, and from line between lots 20 and 21 to line between lots 10 and 11; relief, wooded areas, landscaping of estates, names of subdivision surveys to date, cemeteries; all bldgs shown, many identified; names of owners of large lots; inset shows area from Tyburn St to Gore St, and from Bay St to Mary St, with owners or businesses identified for all bldgs.
OOAMA (NMC 11371)

Later editions and states

(2) *1851*
MAP / of the City of / HAMILTON / ... MARCUS SMITH. / 1850–1 / Published by the Author. / SECOND EDITION. // ENGRAVED AND PRINTED AT / FERD. MAYER'S LITHOGRAPHY / No 93 William St. N.Y. // Entered ... Province of Canada.
Print (lith) 106 x 99 cm 1" to 400 ft
From the same plate as the 1st ed above; shows the same information, inset, and views but the border has been changed.
OTAR

1435 *1851*
A Plan of Lot No 16 in the 1st or broken front Concession of the Township of Barton in the City of Hamilton By Robert W. Kerr D.P.S. 1851
Col ms, pt missing 64 x 94 cm 1" to 100 ft
Shows lots from Queen St to Bay St and from Concession St to the bay; relief, swamps; shows land deeded to GWR; part of George S. Tiffany's survey as shown on map of 1850–1 (**1434**).
OTNR (SR 6392)

1436 *1852*
Plan of Lot No 17 broken front on Burlington Bay and part of Lot No 17 in the 3rd Conn of the Township of Barton now in the City of Hamilton taken from a plan made by Thos A. Blyth D.P.S. purporting to be a true copy of a survey made by Hugh Black D.P.S. in September 12th 1833 to which is added the red lines exhibiting the proposed site of the Great Western Rail Road By [Sgd] Robert W. Kerr D.P. Surveyor ... Copied Hamilton March 26th 1852 [Sgd] Robt W. Kerr D.P.S.
Col ms 62 x 58 cm 1" to 2 chains Endorsements: 'A 191'
Shows the route of the railway along the shore and across the water; 'part of route would go across Ferrie's property who is claiming the water lots affected.'
OTNR (SR 125)

1437 *1854*
PLAN / OF LOTS, IN THE / CITY OF HAMILTON / The Property of / V.H. TISDALE, ESQ. / Surveyed by T.A. Blyth P.L.S. / Maclear & Co. Lith. Toronto / 1854
Print (col lith) 82 x 56 cm 1" to 50 ft
Provenance: OHMA Wentworth Co Court House Maps no 1 dr 1; from Emerald St to Steven St, and Wilson St to King St; house of 'R.R. Smiley Esqr.'; 'This Property will be sold by Auction ... 25th day of September inst ...'; probably a printed version of R.P. 125 (**B959**).
OHMA (Maps 7683, 7688)

1438 *[1855?]*
PLAN OF VILLA AND PARK LOTS / MOUNTAIN CRESCENT, / HAMILTON. The Property of Wm Leggo Esqr AS LAID OUT BY ARMSTRONG C.E. TORONTO. / From Surveys by T.A. Blyth D.P.S. / J. Ellis Lith: Toronto.
Print (lith) 51 x 84 cm 1" to 4 chains
Shows lots laid out from 5th Con Rd to Strongman Rd and the mountain, and from James St to road allowance between lots 10 and 11; some names of owners, some houses shown; relates to R.P. 29 of 1855 (**B940**; see also **B968**).
Wentworth 62 (R.P. 124)

1439 *1856*
MAP / to accompany / REPORT ON WATER SUPPLY / for the / CITY OF HAMILTON / Thos C. Keefer / Engineer, / 1856. / Maclear & Co. Lith. Toronto.
Print (lith) 66 x 93 cm 2" to 1 mile Endorsements (on OOAMA copy): stamp [BW] '495'
An attractive relief drawing simulating a bird's-eye view of the area from Saltfleet Twp west to Ancaster Twp and north to Waterdown; shows pumping basin, main distribution reservoir south of 'Slabtown,' pipelines, proposed reservoir locations in Ancaster Twp, railways, roads, streets; prepared to accompany Keefer's *Report on the Supply of Water to the City of Hamilton* (Montreal: John Lovell 1856) (*Bib Can* 3668; CIHM 15393), but not found with these copies of report.
OOAMA (NMC 21999) OTAR OTMCL

1440 *[1856?]*
MAP / to accompany / REPORT ON WATER SUPPLY ... HAMILTON [with ms adds showing geology]
Print (lith) with ms adds 66 x 93 cm 2" to 1 mile Endorsements: 'Sir W.E. Logan Geological Survey of Canada'
The ms adds show the survey grid in red, geological boundaries, and rock types; shows

'everinal,' chert, bitumen, dolomite, drift, and 'supposed outcrop'; locates Webster's Falls, Spencer's Falls, and West Flamborough village.
OOAMA (NMC 22380)

1441 *1856*
[Part of the Beasley Farm in the City of Hamilton] as laid out into Lots for / THE HON. M. CAMERON / BY THOS. A BLYTH P.L.S. GEO. B. SPENCER AGENT. / H. Gregory Lith, Hamilton
Print (lith), pt missing 86? x 63 cm 11/4" to 100 ft
Provenance: OHMA Wentworth Co Court House Maps no 12, 265 book 2; an inset shows the location of the property but some of title is missing; shows area from Paradise Rd on the west limit of town to meadow land, and from King St to 5th St; 'This Extensive Sale will take place on the Ground on Wednesday 1st October 1856 ... Best & Green Auctioneers'; the printed version of R.P. 34 of 1 Oct 1856 (**B977**).
OHMA (Map 7694)

1442 *1856*
PLAN / OF BUILDING LOTS in the / CITY OF HAMILTON / advertised / TO BE SOLD BY PUBLIC AUCTION, / on the ground on Monday 23, June 1856 at noon / by the Proprietor / J. Richard Thomson Esquire / Thos. A. Blyth P.L.S. / Hamilton. / H. Gregory Lith. Hamilton J.T. NOTTLE, AGENT.
Print (lith) 54 x 47 cm 1" to 100 ft
Provenance: OHMA Wentworth Co Court House Maps no 10 book 1; from Wellington St to Emerald St, and from Duke St to Main St.
OHMA (Map 7454)

1443 *1856*
PLAN OF VILLA & PARK LOTS / OF ABOUT 2 ACRES EACH / MOUNTAIN CRESCENT / HAMILTON / THE PROPERTY OF E.M. HARRIS & W.H. PARK ESQR / H. Gregory Lith. Hamilton. / Thos A. Blyth P.L.S. / Hamilton May 2, 1856.
Print (col lith) 71 x 51 cm 1" to 3 chains
View: 'Residence on Lot No 4'; shows a subdivision from Mountain Drive to North Lane, and from Wellington St to road allowance between lots X and XI; shows a crescent, treed areas; a few bldgs with names of owners; related to R.P. 231 (**B976**); a plan at OHMA (Map 7676) shows the south half of this survey and was probably an early draft for R.P. 231.
OOAMA (NMC 22381)

1444 *1857*
PLAN / OF PROPERTY BELONGING TO / MESSRS HOLDEN & PAPPS / IN THE CITY OF / HAMILTON / W. BOULTBEE / P.L. SURVEYOR &c. / HAMILTON C.W. 30th APRIL 1857.
Print (lith), pt missing 57 x 82 cm? 1" to 20 ft
Inset: 'PLAN / OF PART OF THE CITY OF / HAMILTON / SHEWING PROPERTY BELONGING TO MESSRS HOLDEN & PAPPS' 1" to 100 ft; shows lots on both sides of Grove St east of Liberty St, and along Aurora St south of Mills St to Jane St; imprint probably trimmed off; see also **B980**.
Wentworth 62 (R.P. 120)

1445 *1858*
MAP / of the City of / HAMILTON, / Canada West / Published by Wm A. Shepard. / FOR THE HAMILTON DIRECTORY. / 1858. / H. Gregory Lith Hamilton
Print (lith) 33 x 38 cm Scale not given
In *City of Hamilton Directory 1858* (Hamilton: Printed at the Christian Advocate printing house 1858), frontis (*Bib Can* 3799); shows the city from Wentworth St west to Cootes Paradise, and from Markland St to the bay; major bldgs named including churches, schools, banks, hotels, and businesses; wharves named.
OTMCL

1446 *[1858?]*
Plan / of Survey of Lots in / the CITY of / HAMILTON, / and adjacent thereto. / The Property of / [Thomas] STINSON, ESQ.R / T.A. Blyth, P.L.S. / / [Lith.?] Spectator [Office, Hamilton?]
Print (lith), pt missing 83 x 52 cm 1" to 70 ft
Provenance: OHMA Wentworth Co Court House Maps no 18 dr 6; shows lots in two areas, from King St to Willson St, and Wentworth St to beyond Steven St, and from Ida St to Main St, and Burris St to Burlington St; 'Market House Site'; related to R.P. 43 and 225 of 1858 (**B983–4**).
OHMA (Map 7640)

1447 *[ca 1860]*
PLAN / OF LOTS / THE PROPERTY OF / Hutchinson Clark / and / Burton & Sadler. / ON / Victoria Avenue / And Opposite / The Foundry of / McQuesten & Co / Lith. Spectator Office, Hamilton C.W.
Print (lith) 77 x 57 cm 1" to 50 ft
Provenance: OHMA Wentworth Co Court House Maps no 8 dr 4; shows a subdivision from GWR to George St, and from Victoria Ave to Balaclava St; not shown as subdivided on the co map of 1859 (see **825**).
OHMA (Map 7639)

1448 *1862*
Toronto District Canada West Sketch of Hamilton shewing the Positions of Buildings hired by the War Department for the Accommodation of Troops [Sgd] I.D. Robertson Lt R Engrs 5/8/62 [Sgd] J. Heriot Maitland Capt R Engrs 14-7-62
Col ms 44 x 55 cm 1" to 100 yds
Shows area from Margaret and Locke sts, east to John and Cannon sts, south to Duke St; shows Artillery Park barracks with bldgs including officers' quarters, other barracks, MacNab St barracks, school, hospital.
OOAMA (NMC 3855)

1449 *1865*
MAP / OF THE CITY OF / HAMILTON, / REGISTRY OFFICE WENTWORTH / 1865. // L. Ennecker Lith Hamilton C.W.
Print (lith) 78 x 97 cm Scale not given
Shows the city from Wentworth St west to Paradise Rd and from Markland St to the bay; indexes 49 subdivision surveys of sections of the city to date with names of subdividers; 'The Numbers in Survey's XIX, XXIV, and XXVI are taken from McKenzie's Map' (see **1425**) of 1836; photoreproduction in OOAMA.
USDLC

HANOVER

1450 *1856*
PLAN / OF / ADAMSTOWN / the Property of / H.P. ADAMS & JOHN HAHN Esqrs / To be Sold by Auction at Hunter's Tavern / Durham on 2d day of April 1856 / Maclear & Co Lith. Toronto
Print (lith) 1" to 2 chains
Shows the town laid out on either side of the Durham Rd and south to William St, and west of the Bentinck and Brant Rd to Church St; mills shown to north on the Saugeen R; reproduced in Hahn, 15.
OHAN

(HARDWICKE town plot)

1451 *1857*
Plan of the Town Plot of Hardwicke on Stokes Bay in the Township of Eastnor [Sgd] J. Stoughton Dennis P.L.S. Toronto Jany 1 1857
Col ms 121 x 96 cm 1" to 4 chains Endorsements: '1523'; stamp 'IASR'
Shows a town laid out in 462 lots from Colbourne Rd to the water, and Barsham St north to Burgoyne St; south of the present site of the town of Stokes Bay; still shown as a town plot on co atlas (Belden, ... *Bruce* (1880)).
OOAMA (NMC 11373)

HARRISBURG

1452 *1856*
Map of the Village / OF / HARRISBURG / Late / FAIRCHILDS CREEK STATION / County of Brant, C.W. / Surveyed & Laid out for the Proprietors / MESSRS J & D.M. OSBORNE OF HAMILTON, / by James Pollock P.L.S. / Galt 2nd June 1856 / LITH. SPECTATOR OFFICE, HAMILTON, C.W.
Print (lith) hand col 62 x 80 cm 1" to 2 chains
Shows the area from Spence St north to con 2, and from gore of Beverly west to Gilbert St; this plan is related to Brant 2 (R.P. 63, 65 (1st), and 71 (**B1026, B1028–9**)) but shows more streets laid out; tinted lots are those on R.P. 65 and 71; certified by owners in ms as amended on this plan and with name change from Dumfries, 10 July 1856; some bldgs shown.
Brant 2 (R.P. 65 (2nd))

HARRISTON

1453 *[1859?]*
HARRISTON / Comprising Lots 85, 86 & 87 / CONCESSIONS C & D / TOWNSHIP OF MINTO. / Maclear & Co. Lith Toronto. // Surveyed by E.H. Kertland / C.E. & P.L.S.
Print (lith) 88 x 65 cm 1" to 2 chains
Shows the area from Pellissier St to William St and George St to Margaret St; sites for tannery, brewery, chair factory, distillery, town hall, and court-house; sawmill property, fairground, mill race, cemetery, a few bldgs, and bridge shown; although the first lots may have been laid out in 1855–6 (*History of Harriston*), this plan may have been made about 1859 as OTAR copy endorsed 'Elora 1st Novr 1859' and piece of paper attached has postmark 'Elora Sp 17 1859 CW'; town shown on the co map of 1861 with seven bldgs (see **1093**); (see also **B1030**).
OTAR Wellington N 60 (R.P. 26)

(HARTFIELD)

1454 *1856*
MAP / OF / HARTFIELD VILLAGE / IN THE TOWNSHIP OF GUELPH, COUNTY OF WELLINGTON / THE PROPERTY OF / MR. THOS. CARD / AS DIVIDED INTO BUILDING AND PARK LOTS / by HENRY STRANGE ESQR P.L.S. / AUGUST 1856. / Maclear & Co Lith. Toronto C.W.
Print (lith) 56 x 70 cm 1" to 2 chains
A typeset notice about sale on 11 Sept 1856 has been pasted on; shows village laid out at the intersection of the Woolwich Rd and the Owen Sound Rd with town and park lots on Union, Hartwell, and Card sts; 'Hartwell House residence of Mr Card' is shown; related to R.P. 49 (**B1032**); the village was still shown as part of lots 18–21, Section D, in *Historical Atlas of the County of Wellington* (1906).
OGL

HASTINGS

1455 *1839*
Plan of the Survey of the East half of Lot No 4 in the 7th Con and broken Lot No. 4 in the 8th Conn Asphodel [Sgd] Richd Birdsall D Surveyor 3 Oct 1839
Ms Approx 38 x 48 cm Scale not given
Shows the town of Hastings (Crooks Rapids) on the Trent R with three east-west and two north-

south streets; new bridge, sawmill, and roads in the area; there are photoreproductions of the map in OTAR and OOAMA (NMC 3371).
Private Collection

1456 *1861*
PLAN of the VILLAGE / OF / HASTINGS. / IN THE COUNTY OF / NORTHUMBERLAND & PETERBORO: / Embracing part of (Lot 14 in the 4th and 13 & 14 in the 1st Concessions of PERCY and) Lots 4 in the 7th, & 8th, Cons, Asphodel. / the Property of HENRY FOULDS. Also part of / Lot, No. 5 in the 8th Con. of Asphodel, the Property of / TIMOTHY COUGHLAND / November, 1861. / Tremaine's Lith. Toronto C.W.
Print (lith), pt missing Approx 58 x 61 cm 1" to 5 chains
Shows the town from the Trent R north to Division St, and from William St to Nelson St; bridge, mills, and other bldgs all identified; certified as surveyed by Thomas J. Dennehy, provincial land surveyor, Oct 1864 and partly related to R.P. 13 (**B1037**; see also **B1038**).
Northumberland 38 (R.P. 33)

(HASTINGS town plot)

1457 *[ca 1856–8?]*
PLAN of Lots in the / VILLAGE OF HASTINGS / being part of Lots 15 & 16 in the Township / of Luther County of Wellington / THE PROPERTY OF / G. H. BENDER ESQRE / [Signed in facsimile] Wm Boultbee P.L.S. / Hamilton C.W. / H. Gregory Lith. Hamilton C.W.
Print (lith) 63 x 95 cm 1" to approx 42 ft
Inset: 'MAP / of part of Canada / Shewing the position of / The Village of / HASTINGS'; shows a town plot with streets from Arthur St to Main St (Luther/Proton town line) and from Wellington St east to Buchanan St; foundry and steam mill reserves; probably made after 1855 when Boultbee became a provincial land surveyor and after 1856 when H. Gregory was established in Hamilton (Hulse unpub); not shown on co map of 1861 (see **1093**) or co atlas (Walker and Miles, ... *Wellington* (1881)); see also **B1035**.
Wellington 60 (no R.P. number)

HAWKESBURY

1458 *[1832]*
Copy Plan and Survey of the Hawkesbury Mills and the property adjoining belonging to George Hamilton Esqr Shewing parts of Lots No 6, 7, 8, 9, 10, 11 & 12 in the broken front of 1st Concession of the Western Division of the Township of Hawkesbury and the Islands laying in front of the same ... (Signed) Duncan McDonell Dy Surveyor
Col ms on linen 111 x 46 cm 1" to 4 chains
Boundaries of various properties including those of George Hamilton and Thomas Mears; bldgs and lots with names of owners; mill site and pond, dock; notes and reference to McDonell's report 14 Jan 1832; a later copy, original not found.
OTNR (SR 5186)

1459 *1852*
Plan of the Shore of the Ottawa River and adjacent Islands, lying in front of Lots No 8, 9, 10, 11 & 12 in the 1st Concession of the Township of West Hawkesbury U.C. [Sgd] Robert Hamilton P.L.S. 16th Augt 1852
Col ms 33 x 42 cm 1" to 8 chains Watermark: 'E.A. GORDON 1852'
A sketch of the site of the village of Hawkesbury at the intersection of several roads from L'Orignal, Vankleek Hill, and Point Fortune leading to the mills and islands.
OOAMA (NMC 4167)

HAWKESTONE

1460 *1859*
PLAN / of the Village of / HAWKSTONE / IN THE / TOWNSHIP OF ORO / and lands adjacent belonging to the / HONBLE JAMES PATTON. / Surveyed by H. Creswicke P.L.S. / 1859. / Maclear & Co. Lith. Toronto
Print (lith) hand col 53 x 77 cm 1" to 20 chains
Insets: 'PLAN OF / HAWKSTONE.' and 'MAP / of the / COUNTY / OF / SIMCOE.'; the main map shows parts of cons X–XIV, lots 20–26, on Carthew Bay with lots and names of owners including many owned by Patton and Capt Charles Bell; the inset shows the town from Mill to Lally St and from Main to Robinson St with grist and sawmills; notes on the advantages of Hawkestone lots already sold and businesses in place; OTAR copy has ms adds showing lots sold, some further bldgs located, and notes on the site.
OMSA OTAR

HAWKESVILLE

1461 *1856*
PLAN / OF PART OF / HAWKSVILLE / TOWNSHIP OF WELLESLEY / County of Waterloo. / Surveyed for Gabriel Hawk Esqr / John Grant / P.L. Surveyor / July 1856. / Maclear & Co. Lith. Toronto C.W.
Print (lith) 67 x 48 cm 1" to 2 chains
Shows the area from Woolwich and Huron Rd east to Hamilton St and Peel St south to road allowance between cons 11 and 12; notice of sale at auction 2 Oct 1856 by W.P. Newman and Co. Agents; terms of sale; (see also **B1043**).
Waterloo 58 (R.P. 626A)

HESPELER

1462 *1858 Jan*
Diagram showing limits of the proposed Village of New Hope in the Township and County of Waterloo C.W. 1858. Schofield & Hobson P.L. Surveyors &c. Berlin C.W. 26th Jan 1858
Col ms 47 x 60 cm 1" to 10 chains
Both this and the related plan below were originally filed with a petition for incorporation as a village by C. Nahrgang, James Jackson, and Jacob Hespeler of 28 Jan 1858 (OOA RG 5 Cl/543 no 331 1858); shows Queen, Adam, and Cooper sts, Puslinch Rd, and Woolwich and Guelph Rd; J. Hespeler's mill pond, survey grid, boundary; no town lots or bldgs shown.
OOAMA (NMC 4859)

Related maps

(2) *1858 July*
Copy of Diagram Showing limits of the proposed Village of Hespeler in the Township and County of Waterloo C.W. 1858. Crown Lands Office Toronto July 1858 [Sgd] Andrew Russell Asst Commissioner
Col ms on linen 39 x 63 cm 1" to 10 chains
Shows the same information as the other plan, with boundary marked more clearly; notes that the name is being changed to Hespeler as indicated in a later document filed with the above petition; the petition for incorporation was approved 12 July 1858.
OOAMA (NMC 4170)

(HIAWATHA town plot)

1463 *[1819]*
Town Plot of Otanabee
Ms 20 x 25 cm Scale not given Endorsements: 'contt 1720 acres' 'Petition from Mr. Anderson to be confirmed in title to land wh. he now occupies'
Originally with petition from Anderson (OOA RG 1 L3 A 12 no 90 1819–20); shows area bounded on west by Otonabee R, 'Mr Anderson's improvements' on the east shore, and the boundaries of the town plot to east and north of this; the town plot was marked on the early twp maps (see **1494–5**) and was sometimes referred to as 'Indian Village'; OOAMA (NMC 3575) is another untitled sketch of the village from the same source; (Holmden 2547).
OOAMA (NMC 3574–5)

1464 *1820*
A True Plan of Capt Andersons Land in the Town Reservation in the Township of Otonibee with a Sketch how I should recommend a Town to be laid in the said Reservation by [Sgd] Richd Birdsall Dy Surveyor Rice Lake June 9th 1820
Col ms 41 x 27 cm 1" to 6.5 chains Endorsements: 'C7' 'PE66'
Shows a plan for a town west of Capt Anderson's of six streets each way with market square in the centre and reserves for church, court-house, and jail at the north end; 'Town reservation 1620 Acres.'
OTNR (SR 10743)

1465 *[1828?]*
A Plan of Part of the Town Plot reserved in the Township of Otonibee
Col ms 60 x 82 cm 1" to 4 chains Endorsements: 'No 36'
Shows the final form of the town plot of 10 east-west streets and six north-south streets, and lots; town is shown east of the Otonabee R and Capt Anderson's land, and the back street is 65 chains east of the river; '1 1/2 chains to be reserved from the Lake for Road'; later additions in pencil are nearly illegible.
OTNR (SR 86586)

Related maps

(2) *1828*
PLAN / of Town Reservation in the township of / Otonibee containing 1,120 acres which is now granted / for the use of the Rice Lake Indians under the / Superintendance of the Revd Richd Scott. / ... Surveyed by Richd Birdsall. Depy Surveyor. July 1828.
Print (lith) 17 x 24 cm 1" to 50 chains
In Corporation for the Promoting and Propagating the Gospel of Jesus Christ in New England, *Report* (London: J.R. Lake printer 1829), opp 44 (*Bib Can* 1540); a reduced version of the ms survey above, with the same information.
OTMCL

1466 *1840*
Sketch of a Survey made for the Rice Lake Indians of Broken Lots no. 3, 4 and 5 in the 10th Concession of Otonabee, Newcastle District. Sepr. 1840 [Sgd] Thomas I Dennehy D.P.S.
Ms 13 x 15 cm Scale not given
A small map showing the Indian village plot, number of acres in lots, and Smith's house; this location is slightly further east than earlier town plot.
OTMCL

1467 *1855*
The Village of Indiana Rice Lake [and] Rough Sketch of part of Lots Nos 3 & 4 in the 10th Con. of the Township of Otonabee At the Indian Village Rice Lake – by order of the Chief Paudash by [Sgd] Thomas J. Dennehy P.L. Surveyor Sep. 13th 1855.
Ms 42 x 33 cm 1" to 2 chains Endorsements: '494'; stamp 'IASR'
Shows a railway bisecting a town of about five streets, two of which are named (Queen St and Albert St); lot nos and sizes, names of owners; road on the left described as 'travelled Road from

Hiawatha to Peterborough'; 'Railroad Reserve for Depot' shown at bottom of plan; this village site is not shown on co map of 1861 (see **405**); original 'Indian reserve & village' shown to west.
OOAMA (NMC 4364)

HILTON BEACH

1468 *1855*
Projected Plan of the Town Plot of Hilton. [Sgd] Crown Lands Department Quebec 11th June 1855 Joseph Cauchon Commr Crown Lands. [Sgd] T. Devine
Col ms 46 x 38 cm 1" to 10 chains
Shows the plan for the town including named streets, wharf, and reserve.
OTAR

Related maps

(2) *1855*
Plan of the Town of Hilton in St Joseph Island Lake Huron. Surveyed by T.N. Molesworth Provincial Land Surveyor. Examined November 1855 T.D.
Col ms 64 x 88 cm 1" to 4 chains Endorsements: 'A 109'
(SI 11 June 1855 to subdivide town into bldg and park lots; OTNR FN 1299 25 Oct 1855); shows the town laid out as planned from Cedar and First sts to Tenth St, and West St to East St; lot nos, wharf, reserve, some bldgs, and cleared land shown; relief; also a copy: 'Hilton J.W.B. Crown Lands Office Toronto Oct 8th 1856 [Sgd] Joseph Cauchon Commissioner of Crown Lands.' endorsed 'No 119' and with addition of names of patentees (OTAR(P)); and a copy: 'St. Joseph J.W.B. Crown Lands Office Toronto 31st Jan. 1857 [Sgd] Joseph Cauchon Commissioner of Crown Lands.' endorsed 'No 124' (OTAR(P)); the latter is similar to others except some street names have been changed and park lots are shown around town.
OTAR(P) OTNR (SR 1316)

(HYTHE town plot)

1469 *1834 Sept*
Plan of the Town of Hythe near the Mouth of the Nottawasaga River Sunnidale Home Dist. Sept 1834 C.R. D.S.
Ms 53 x 74 cm 1" to 3 chains Endorsements: 'No 32'
(SI 30 May 1833 to C. Rankin to survey road from town plot in Essa/Sunnidale to a favourable point on L Huron for a town; OTNR FN 473 8 Oct 1834); the survey of lots 3 and 4, cons XV and XVI, Sunnidale, at the mouth of the Nottawasaga R; shows the town laid out between John and Helen sts, and Joseph St to Wellington and Ann sts; shows sites for a market, a public bldg, and bridge; a few names of patentees have been added; later note indicates that the town plot was abandoned and sold in 1904 except three patented lots; notes on relief, soils, nature of land, depths in river.
OTAR(P)

Related maps

(2) *1834 Oct*
Pla[n] of the Tow[n Plot of Hythe] near the Entrance o[f the] Nottawasaga Rivr Sunnidale, Home Distt (signed) C.R. D.P.S. Surveyor General's Office, Toronto, 8th Octr 1834, Copy – Henry Lizars.
Col ms, pt of title missing 54 x 69 cm Scale not given Endorsements: 'A 43' '650'
Similar to earlier plan with a few differences: shows the proposed streets, lot nos, 'proposed road to Collingwood and St Vincent'; Indian graves, road to Barrie; Water and Portage sts are the only streets named; shows the reserves for market, public bldg, and site for bridge; also two copies similar to (1): 'Hythe Copy [Sgd] J.G. Chewett S.G. Office 20th June 1837 [Sgd] Surveyor General's Office Toronto 23rd June 1837 J W Macaulay Survr Genl' (OTAR) and 'Hythe by C. Rankin D.P.S. 1834 Surveyor General's Office Montreal 16th October 1844. A true copy.' endorsed 'A 137' and '649' and with the road to Barrie marked (OTAR (SR 134)).
OTAR OTNR (SR 134–5)

(Indian village, Credit River)

1470 *[1821]*
Plan Shewing the intended Indian Village at the Credit Surveyed by J.G. Chewett
Col ms 32 x 52 cm 1" to 3 chains Endorsements: 'Q 44' '1116'
(OTNR FN 672 13 Oct 1821); laid out on lots 6, 7, 8, range III, Mill Block, Credit Indian Reserve, Toronto Twp; shows one main street roughly parallel to Dundas St, and four cross streets; block of lots in two tiers laid out on bluff on west side of river, with church and school lot; Indian place of worship; 'Capt. Johns'; roads to Dundas St, York, and the Head of the Lake shown; the Mississaugas were moved to the Grand R in 1847 and the village fell into disuse; Chewett sent the plan and field notes in a letter to Thomas Ridout 13 Oct 1821 (OTAR RG 1 A-I-1 vol 44 book 40 p 217).
OTAR (SR 76)

Related maps

(2) *1847*
Sketch of the Mill Block River Credit Canada, To T.G. Anderson Esquire Sup. Indian Affairs Toronto [Sgd] Jno Stoughton Dennis D.S. September 1847
Col ms 52 x 73 cm 1" to 6 chains
Provenance: OOAMA RG 10M 76703/9 no 283; shows the Indian village with unnamed streets and reserves between the Middle Rd and the Credit R; Mill Block boundary; Indian mill, dam;

shows the reserves for market and public bldg and site for bridge.
OOAMA (NMC 13096)

(INDIANA)

1471 *1843*
Sketch of the Lots adjoining the Village of Indiana, in Township Number Two, Shewing the different Improvements thereon. Shewing the proposed Reservation as marked within the dotted line. June 1843
Col ms 50 x 37 cm 1" to 10 chains Endorsements: '1682'; stamp 'IASR'
Shows the proposed Indian reservation, which includes the town site of Indiana; names of claimants of many irregularly shaped lots; areas claimed cut across survey grid; Grand River Navigation Co.'s land on both sides of river and canal shown; front of lots 8–11, River Range, Seneca Twp.
OOAMA (NMC 4176)

1472 *1844 Apr*
Sketch of the Town Plot at Indiana. Surveyor General's Office Kingston 16th April 1844 [Sgd] Thomas Parke Survr Genl
Col ms 70 x 49 cm 1" to 4 chains Endorsements: 'Q 74' '1109'
Shows canal, Grand River Navigation Co.'s land, and boundary of Indiana between two large lots along the river; towing path.
OTAR (SR 141)

1473 *1844 Oct*
A Plan of the Village of Indiana surveyed by order of Thomas Parke Esquire Surveyor General. West Flamboro October 15th 1844 [Sgd] James Kirkpatrick D.P. Surveyor
Col ms 61 x 62 cm 1" to 4 chains Endorsements: 'Q 73' '1110'
(SI 5 Aug 1844 to subdivide into town and park lots; OTNR FN 800 18 Oct 1844); town is laid out on both sides of Grand River Navigation Co.'s land on the east from Brant to Jones and Johnson sts, to Albert St and square, and on the west to Winniett and York sts; canal, sawmill, grist mill, towing path; also a copy of the plan at OTNR (SR 140) '(Signed) James Kirkpatrick D.P. Surveyor' and endorsed '1111'; and a copy at OTAR(P): 'Indiana Surveyed by James Kirkpatrick D.P.S. 1844 Surveyor Generals' Office Montreal 11th Novr 1844 A true copy [Sgd] Andrew Russell S & D. / Office Copy.' endorsed 'No 96' and with names of patentees shown in all lots.
OTAR(P) OTNR (SR 139)

1474 *1845*
Town Plot of Indiana Exhibiting the boundaries of the different claimants [Sgd] James Kirkpatrick P.D. Surveyor July 1845
Col ms 54 x 67 cm 1" to 4 chains Endorsements: '1681'; stamp 'IASR'
Names and boundaries of claimants' lands are shown irregularly across the street layout on east and west; canal, sawmill, grist mill, deeded land; there is also a copy in OOAMA (RG 10M 76703/9 no 373, NMC 13348).
OOAMA (NMC 22391; 13348)

INGERSOLL

1475 *1848*
Plan of a part of Lot number 19 in the Broken front of West Oxford laid out into Village Lots for Daniel Carroll Esqr as an addition to the Village of Ingersoll. January 1848. [Sgd] Wm McClary P.L. Surveyor
Ms 52 x 74 cm 1" to 2 chains Watermark: 'J WHATMAN TURKEY MILL 1847'
From the Thames R to Commissioners Rd, and from Carroll St to McCarthy St; mill pond and race, grist mill, and fulling mill; similar to R.P. 13 (**B1073**).
OLU

1476 *1855*
Sketch of part of the Village of Ingersoll by W.G. Wonham P.L.S. 1855
Col ms 27 x 39 cm 1" to 132 ft
Originally accompanied a petition (OOA RG 1 L3 and L 8 no 1 1855); shows the depot lands of the GWR and part of river required to be leased by them west of bridge at Thames St; shows lots along Victoria St; (Holmden 1732).
OOAMA (NMC 4177)

1477 *1856*
MAP / OF / INGERSOLL / Canada West, / by / W.G. WONHAM P.L.S. / 1856. / LITH. BY J. SAGE & SONS BUFFALO
Print (lith) 89 x 118 cm 1" to 4 chains
Endorsements (OTAR copy): 'Index to Plans' 'No 26'
Shows the town extending from Holcraft Rd to 4th con line N Oxford; and from Harris and Pemberton sts to Ingersoll St; all bldgs shown, some identified; names of some owners beside houses or properties including W.G. Wonham's house; OTAR copy has ms adds showing three wards.
OTAR (SR 92347)

INVERHURON

1478 *1853*
Plan of that part of Bruce proposed to be appropriated for a village site. [Sgd] Chisholm Miller P.L.S. Norval Esquesing Janry 17th /53
Ms 59 x 47 cm 1" to 10 chains Endorsements: 'B 61'
Shows the site and the boundary of the town plot

for Inverhuron, lots 1–10, Lakeshore Range, and lots A, B, C, cons I and II, Bruce Twp, on the 'Little Sable R'; shows the nature of the shoreline and soundings offshore, marshy areas, hardwood trees; some areas cleared, bldgs shown; 'stations' on shore possibly for surveying or fishing; surveyed by Miller during his survey of Bruce Twp (SI 16 July 1852).
OTNR (SR 138)

1479 *1855*
Plan of the Town Plot of Inverhuron Surveyed by C. Miller P.L.S. Norval April 13th 1855 [Sgd] Chisholm Miller P.L.S.
Col ms 62 x 110 cm 1" to 5 chains Endorsements: 'A 195'
(SI 20 Oct 1854 to subdivide town plot and set up mill sites according to D. Gibson's report; OTNR FN 1339 12 Apr 1855); shows town laid out from Douglas St to McNabb St, and William and Russell sts to Albert St; park lots east of Albert St; shows three mill sites, cleared and fenced areas with names of occupants, marshy areas across streets, meadows, and proposed reserves; relief.
OTNR (SR 6472)

Related maps

(2) *1855*
Inverhuron T. Devine Crown Lands Department Quebec 8th June 1855 [Sgd] Joseph Cauchon Commissioner Crown Lands.
Col ms 62 x 100 cm 1" to 5 chains Endorsements: 'No 20'
Shows the same layout as above plan with the addition of names of patentees; an advertisement dated 25 June 1857 says that certain lots will be offered for sale on 29 June by the Crown Lands Dept; a note indicates that much of the town north of Caley St was later cancelled and became Inverhuron Provincial Park.
OTAR(P)

INVERMAY

1480 *1856*
PLAN / OF THE TOWN PLOT OF / INVERMAY / TOWNSHIP OF ARRAN / COUNTY OF BRUCE. / Maclear & Co. Lith. Toronto. January 1856.
Print (lith) 56 x 89 cm 1" to 3 chains
Inset: [location map showing Bruce and Grey cos]; shows the streets and lots laid out, and a few bldgs; saw and grist mill location on the Ausable R; see also **B1123**.
Bruce 3 (R.P. 15) OLU

(INVERNESS town plot)

1481 *[185?]*
Plan of the Village of Inverness being the subdivision of Lot No 1 First Concession Flamboro East as laid out for A. Chisholm Esq. by [Sgd] Thos. A. Blyth P.L.S.
Col ms 60 x 70 cm 1" to 1/2 chain
Provenance: OHMA Wentworth Co Court House no 56 dr 6; subdivision for a town that did not go into effect; shows streets from Argyle St to Ontario St, and Flamboro St to Hamilton St and Nelson Gravel Rd; shows the GWR, wooded areas, and some bldgs; there are pencil notes for some changes in the title including the addition of 'County of Wentworth' and a note '300 copies,' which suggests the plan was about to be printed; probably prepared after 1855 when the GWR was built, but the town is not shown on the co map of 1859 (see **825**).
OHMA

JOHNSTOWN

1482 *1790*
Plan of the New Town ordered to be laid out on the Land lately purchased from the Indians, situated in the Township of Edwardsburg, in the District of Luneburg, called Johnstown [Sgd] W. Chewett D.P. Surveyr for the District of Luneburg 18th March 1790
Col ms 64 x 79 cm 1" to 200 ft Watermark: 'J WHATMAN' Endorsements: '1001'
Shows the southern part of the town with town lots of one acre as laid out in the fall of 1789; Ernest St east to Sophia St, and from Water or 1st St to 6th St; reserves for church, hospital, market-places, public squares, and fortifications just east of river; relief, marshy land, bridge across river; names of patentees in two bottom blocks; 'The streets in bistre only want about three days work to be finished but a sudden fall of snow on the 3rd November 1789 prevented any further prosecution of the business.'; 'Upon the nearest calculation the remaining part of the Town and Town Parks will require one hundred and forty-four Days Work to compleat the whole.'
OTNR (SR 142)

Related maps

(2) *1790*
Plan of the Town Plot of New Johnstown and a lot of one Thousand Acres for Messrs Lorrimier ... Agreeable to the order of Council the 25th Augt 1790. Quebec 27th Augt 1790 (Sign'd) John Collins D.S.G.
Ms 48 x 40 cm Scale not given
With documents regarding Lorimier's claim before the Executive Council (OOA RG 1 L1 Land Book B pp 16–17); shows the outline of the town plot, the reservation for defence, boundary of land purchased from the Indians, town parks, and boundary of Lorimier's land; transcript in NMC (NMC 3784); (Holmden 1995).
OOA (RG 1 L1 Land Bk B pp 16–17)

1483 *1791*
Plan of the Town of Johnstown in the Township of Edwardsburg with the Town Parks laid out to the end thereof in the Year 1790. Cornwall 9th April 1791 [Sgd] W. Chewitt D.P.S. [part illegible or missing]
Col ms 81 x 101 cm 1" to 400 ft Watermark: 'J WHATMAN' Endorsements: '991'
The survey has been finished with 6th to 11th sts laid out; the key to locations for reserves specifies them in more detail than the earlier plan; church, parsonage, school, gaol, and court-house; workhouse, hospitals, markets, public squares, crown reserves, and town parks reserved for schoolmaster and minister; meeting-house, saw and grist mill shown; shows the diagonal lot on the west belonging to Messrs Lorrimier, and the west boundary of land purchased from the Indians; town lots are four to a block; the park lots are north and partly to the east of the town plot; relief, marshy land, nature of shoreline; also a copy with same title further sgd 'Copied from an Original by Lieut John Fredk Holland Ry Rt N Yk [Sgd] Samuel Holland Surveyr Genl.' and endorsed 'A 23' and '1208' (OTNR (SR 144)).
OTNR (SR 144; 6468)

Related maps

(2) *1792*
Plan of the Town of Johnstown situated in the Township of Edwardsburg in the District of Luneburg, with the Town Parks laid out to the end thereof in the year 1790. To His Excellency Governor Simcoe This Plan is most humbly presented By His Excellency's most obedient and most humble servant [Sgd] W Chewett Surveyor District of Luneburg Osnabruck 7th Feby 1792.
Col ms 81 x 120 cm 1" to 400 ft
Similar to (1) above but includes a pencilled list of names of patentees for the front lots; possibly the plan in 'List of maps ... 1793' no 14 (OTAR RG 1 A-I-1/1, 151–7).
OTAR (Simcoe Map 445788)

1484 *1795*
Plan of Johnstown with the Town Parks that were laid out in the year 1790, for making Entries, and Erasures, by order of the Land Board for the District of Luneburg. [Sgd] Cornwall 13th December 1790 W Chewett. D.P. Surveyor for the District of Luneburg; [Sgd] Examined W Chewett Acting Surveyor for the Province of Canada Osnabruck 18th [?] 1792; [Sgd] Williamsburg 28th April 1795, 29th August 1795 W Chewett Senior Surveyor Eastern District
Col ms 98 x 170 cm 1" to 200 ft Endorsements: 'A 24'
The map shows the streets and reserves as in plan of 1791 (**1483**) but several houses and bldgs now shown including the 'Gaol & Courthouse' on the waterfront in the centre of the town; names are shown in the front four blocks and in the park lots; many later additions and changes to names made up to 1821 at least; land in front of the town and on both sides is crown reserve; also a copy in OTAR(P): 'Johnstown with the Town Parks adjoining.' endorsed 'No 23' and 'Office Plan'; similar to the plan first described but the only bldgs shown are the gaol, court-house, saw and grist mill and there are later notes and names of patentees added up to the 1850s; there is also a plan showing reserves for Johnstown in D.W. Smith's 'Report upon Glebes & Commons ... 13th Jany 1802.'
OTAR OTAR(P) OTAR (RG 1 A-II-1 vol 2 pp 942–87)

1485 *1849 Feb*
Map of the Crown Lands in rear of Johnstown as divided into Park Lots. Surveyed under instructions from the Crown Lands Department, dated 21st July 1848 by [Sgd] Jas West Provl Land Surveyor, Johnstown, Feby 1849. Examined [Initialled] A.R.
Col ms 68 x 48 cm 1" to 10 chains Endorsements: 'B 19'
(SI 9 Jan 1847 to subdivide certain reserved lands adjacent to the town; OTNR FN 476 March 1849); shows the area north of the town of lots 29–31 with names of owners, small lots laid out on range southwest and southeast of Kemptville Rd, and 30 park lots laid out northeast of town directly above original park lots; names of landowners of large lots; roads, treed areas, and marshy land; also a copy: 'Park Lots. Crown Lands. [Johnstown] Johnstown District. Crown Land Department Montreal May 1849 True Copy. T.D.' but does not show vegetation or names of owners in new lots (OTNR (SR 143)); and a copy: 'Johnstown Park Lots Crown Lands Department Toronto March 1850 Office Copy T.D. [Sgd] Andrew Russell S & D' endorsed 'No 81' and with names of patentees shown in all lots (OTAR(P)).
OTAR(P) OTNR (SR 143; 145)

KARS

1486 *1857*
Plan of Kars Survey June 1857
Ms on linen 60 x 35 cm 1" to 100 ft
Shows the town on the east end of lot 23, con 1, N Gower; streets are shown from Rideau R and Wellington St to Ann St, and Rideau St to unnamed street beyond Nelson St; mill and wharf; related to R.P. 7 (**B1134**).
OOAMA (NMC 70945)

(KATESVILLE)

1487 *1856*
PLAN / of the Village of / KATESVILLE, / IN THE TOWNSHIP OF METCALF, IN THE / COUNTY OF MIDDLESEX. / THE PROPERTY OF ALEXR CAMPBELL ESQRE / 1856. / Surveyed by Walsh &

Mercer P.L. Surveyors Simcoe. // Lithographed by J. Ellis Toronto.
Print (lith) Approx 89 x 62 cm 1" to 11/2 chains
Shows the town as laid out from Caradoc St to Metcalfe St and Sydenham R and Maitland St to Sandwich St on lot 17, con II, Metcalfe; town was listed in *Smith's Canadian Gazetteer* (1846) and is shown on the co map of 1862 (**997**) but not in the co atlas (Page, ... *Middlesex* (1878)); this plan was later cancelled; R.P. 116 is a photoreproduction, original not seen.
Middlesex 34 (R.P. 116, photoreproduction)

KEMPTVILLE

1488 *1855*
MAP OF PART OF / NORTH KEMPTVILLE, / Laid down by actual Survey by / FRANCIS JONES, P.L.S. Sept. 22nd. 1855. // KEMPTVILLE PRINTING OFFICE.
Print (typeset) 42 x 57 cm 1" to 110 ft
Includes a drawing of a train, steamboats, and bldgs to show 'Business part of Kemptville'; shows streets from Gower St to Concession Rd; King St to south branch of Rideau R; names of owners of large properties outside the town; R.P. 6 has the ms add of Alma St as extension of Victoria St; see also **B1150**.
Grenville 15 (R.P. 5, 6)

1489 *1862*
Plan of the Village of Kemptville Shewing the position of the lots and parcels of land in the Municipality. Surveyed Compiled and examined by [Sgd] John Burchill Pro. Land Surveyor. Mirickville 31st March 1862
Col ms 65 x 55 cm 1" to 4 chains Endorsements: 'K No 24' '5130/62' '6223/62' 'Municipal Survey No. 158'
(SI 10 Oct 1861); shows the whole town bounded on the north and south by the Queen's Highway, on the east by the Ottawa & Prescott Railway, and on the west by Alfred St; mill pond; proposed market square and fairground; burial ground; bridges; there is also a copy of the plan in Grenville 16 filed as R.P. Kemptville 11; notes on locations of survey monuments.
Grenville 16 (R.P. Kemptville 11) OTNR (SR 5880)

Related maps

(**2**) *1862*
Plan of the Village of Kemptville Shewing the position of the lots and parcels of land in the Municipality. Surveyed, compiled and examined by John Burchill Pro: Land Surveyor Merrickville 31st March 1862
Ms 113 x 97 cm 1" to 2 chains
Shows an enlargement of plan above and the same layout with the addition of some names of owners; notes on the town, including information on the subdivision surveys, size of lots, and lots left unsold sgd by John Burchill.
OOAMA (NMC 80789)

KESWICK

1490 *1824*
Plan of the town of Keswick near Roaches Point on Lake Simcoe in North Gwillimbury Surveyed between the 8th June and the 16th July 1824 by [Sgd] James G. Chewett D.P.S.
Col ms 60 x 81 cm 1" to 21/2 chains Endorsements: 'No 25'
(SI 3 June 1824 to survey town plot in rear of Roaches Point in parts of lots 21 and 22); shows the layout of the town from Mossington to Raines St and Roaches Point to Kennedy St; orchard, garden, marshy land, names of settlers; later changes and additions to names; also a later copy: 'Keswick. in North Gwillimbury. Copy [Sgd] J.G. Chewett S.G. Office 1st June 1837 [Sgd] J.W. Macaulay Surv. Genl' endorsed 'A 113' and '1337' and with addition of a few names, bldgs, and note about a clearing of swamp (OTNR (SR 151)).
OTAR(P) OTNR (SR 151)

1491 *1859*
Plan shewing that portion of Lot No 22 in the rear of the Townplot of Keswick. in the 2nd Con. of the Township of North Gwillimbury in the county of York. [Sgd] John Lindsay P.L.S. Toronto June 6th 1859 Examd June 1859 [Initialled] J.W.B.
Col ms 34 x 73 cm 1" to 8 chains Endorsements: 'No 7'
(SI 20 May 1859 to define boundary of town plot); shows the boundary of the town and a portion of land to the rear.
OTNR (SR 149)

1492 *1861*
Copy of part of the Town Plot of Keswick, Crown Land Department Quebec Sept. 23d 1861.
Col ms on linen 31 x 92 cm 1" to 21/2 chains
Shows part of town from Roaches Point to Kennedy St and from Raines to Chewett St; lot nos.
OTNR (SR 150)

KINCARDINE

1493 *[1850]*
Plan of the town of Penetangor on Lake Huron [Sgd] A.P. Brough D.P.S. Examined [Initialled] A.R.
Col ms 73 x 104 cm 1" to 4 chains Endorsements: 'A 171' 'In 1292/50'
(SI 15 June 1849 to subdivide plot into bldg and park lots and to lay out mill sites; OTNR FN 746 11 June 1850); shows the town laid out from Huron Terrace and Goderich St to Huron Rd, and

from Bruce Ave to Durham St; lot nos, relief, four reserves for mills, burial ground; the name Penetangor in the title has been crossed out and Kincardine written in, when name changed on 1 Jan 1858; also a copy: 'Penetangore Crown Land Department Quebec 10 December 1851 [Sgd] John Rolph Commissioner of Crown Lands' endorsed 'No 107' and showing market squares (OTAR(P)); and a copy: 'Copy of Penetangore Crown Land Department Quebec February 1852 Certified a true copy [Sgd] T. Devine S & D [Sgd] John Rolph Commissioner of Crown Lands' endorsed 'No 84' and with names of owners added throughout (OTAR(P)); there are also two untitled plans in OTAR showing the Penetangore R and town lots, one with Durham Rd survey by 'Mr Brough' and the other endorsed 'A.B.' and '1977.'
OTAR OTAR(P) OTNR (SR 170)

1494 *[ca 1855?]*
Survey of the Coast at Penetangore Township of Kincardine
Col ms on linen 71 x 66 cm Scale not given
Endorsements: stamps 'Public Works' '648'
The town and river are shown back to Victoria St and from Albert to Durham St; soundings and line of levels along river; part of piers built; two alternative plans for completing piers are shown; predates plan below since no piers have been built and mouth of river is shown as in 1850 plan.
OOAMA (NMC 43127)

1495 *1857*
Map / OF THE TOWN OF / PENETANGORE / Canada West / by / SIMPSON & HAMLIN / LAND SURVEYORS & CIVIL ENGINEERS / H. Gregory, Lith. Hamilton C.W. / 1857
Print (lith) 98 x 93 cm 1" to 5 chains;
Insets: 'PLAN / OF THE PROPOSED HARBOUR / at / PENETANGORE' 1" to 3 chains, 'MAP / of the / COUNTY OF BRUCE' 1" to 40 chains; shows the same streets as in 1850 map (**1493**); area to the north named 'Williamsburgh' and 'Mount Forrest'; bldgs shown, some named; various mills, distillery, tannery, steam chair factory, 'Durham Market'; relief along river and lakeshore; plan for harbour shows two inner basins created within river loop by dredging; north and south pier shown as built with a cut to the river; OOAMA copy accompanied a petition (OOA RG 5 C1 no 1957 of 1858).
OOAMA (NMC 17874)

KING CITY

1496 *[1854]*
Plan / OF THE / VILLAGE OF KING / ONE OF THE PRINCIPAL STATIONS / OF THE / Northern Railway / SITUATE ON LOTS / 3, 4 AND 5 IN THE THIRD CONCESSION / OF THE FLOURISHING / TOWNSHIP OF KING / M[aclear? & Co Lith Tor]onto (La[te Hugh Scobie)]
Print (lith) 45 x 82 cm 1" to 2 chains
Ms adds: 'Tuesday 4th day of July [1854] Sale on the ground at 11 o'clock A.M.'; probably the printed version of R.P. 109 (**B1162**); the latter was prepared by J. Stoughton Dennis and registered 30 Jan 1855; shows the town laid out from road allowance between cons 3 and 4, west to Ontario Simcoe and Huron Railway line, and from line between lots 2 and 3 to road allowance between lots 5 and 6; passenger and freight stations shown; streets and lot nos.
OTAR

KINGSTON

1497 *[1783]*
[Endorsed]: 'Plan des environs de Catarakui, recu du Major Ross le 12 Sepr.' Drawn by J.F. Holland
Col ms 60 x 79 cm 1" to 200 ft
Shows a survey of Point Frederick and Point Henry; relief, wooded and marshy areas, soundings, no place-names; probably sent with Major Ross's letter of 3 Sept 1783 to Haldimand; (Preston, xliii, 34); photoreproduction in OOAMA (NMC 3875).
GBL (Add Mss 21829 f 12–13)

Related maps

(**2**) *[1783]*
Point Frederick and Point Henry] [Sgd] W. Tinling Assistant Engineer
Col ms Approx 46 x 50 cm 1" to 400 ft
A similar survey of the points but without soundings; shows the heights of land on Point Henry with two points marked (A and B); the plan appears to be the main one referred to in Ross's letter to Haldimand of 3 Sept 1783 in which he points out that Point Frederick would not be a good site for a town because it is commanded by Point Henry; he recommends a fort at A on Point Henry with a town below and a naval establishment at B on east side of Point Frederick (Preston, 34); photoreproduction in OOAMA (NMC 3876).
GBL (Add Mss 21829 f 77)

1498 *1784*
Plan of old Fort Frontenac and Town Plot of Kingston. Quebec 15th Octr 1784 (Sign'd) Fredk Haldimand. Surveyed by Jn Fdk Holland. Copied from an Original by Lieut John Fredk Holland Ry Rr N. Yk [Sgd] Samuel Holland Surveyr Genl
Col ms 90 x 101 cm 1" to 1 chain Endorsements: 'No 22'
Insets: [elevations of officers' and soldiers' barracks being built] 1" to 20 ft; 'Reference' keys the bldgs in the French fort including barracks, 'King's Houses,' hospital, storehouses, inhabitants' houses, and [Col] 'Bradstreet's Works' [not shown]; shows part of the first layout of the town,

three streets by one street, and blocks of 12 lots between; 'Note the first Town Lots and Streets are to be laid down as expressed upon the Plan ... each lot being 66 x 132. The remaining Ground to be laid out in the same manner according as the Shape of the Ground will admit of and be drawn for together'; the town was probably laid out in 1783 as Haldimand's instructions for the 'Survey of the Neck intended for the Town Plot' were issued to Collins 11 Sept 1783 (Cruikshank, *Settlement*, 8–9) and Major Ross sent a plan of the state of the works at Cataraqui on 3 Nov 1783 (OOA Haldimand Papers B-126 f 69); however, the title naming it Kingston may not have been added until after 1788 when town was so named (*Heritage Kingston*, 39); probably no 18 in 'List of maps ... 1793' (OTAR RG 1 A-I-1/1, 151–7); (*OHIM* 2.2); OOAMA has a transcript copy initialled 'G.F.W.' and lacking some information.
OTAR

Related maps

(2) *[1784?]*
Plan of Old Fort Fron[tenac] and Town Plot of Ki[ngston] Surveyed by John F. Holland Quebec 15 Oct 1784. Copied from an Original by John Fredk. Holland Ry Rr N. York (Sd) Samuel Holland Deputy Surveyor General
Col ms 24 x 31 cm '1/3 true size'
A reduced version of (1) above but shows the same information; the 'K' marking Bradstreet's works is now marked at the end of ruins of the French fort; this plan appears to have been drawn later than plan above and may be a later copy of 1784 original; (not in surveys list); (*OHIM* 7.34).
OTAR

1499 *1788*
Sketch of Kingston Harbour, with the Neck reserved for a Town Lot with its Common. [Sgd] Quebec 6th Decr 1788 Gother Mann Captn Commandg Rl Engrs Plan A
Col ms 50 x 33 cm 1" to 1000 ft Watermark: 'J WHATMAN'
Originally with Mann's report on defences of 6 Dec 1788 (GBLpro CO 42/12 f 807); shows Point Montreal [Frederick], Point Henry, a town plot above Point Frederick, and town commons to the north; The west side of the harbour is shown with Fort Frontenac but no town lots shown; the town plot is probably the one proposed by Holland in his letter of 23 July 1783 (Preston, 26–7); batteries; point C marked as high point for fortifications on Point Henry; photoreproduction in OOAMA (NMC 3878); (*PRO Cat* 1479).
GLBpro (MPG 273)

Related maps

(2) *1788*
Sketch of Kingston Harbour with the Neck reserved for a Town Lot with its Common. Quebec 6th Decr 1788 [Sgd] Gother Mann Captn Command. Rl Engr
Col ms 54 x 34 cm 1" to 1000 ft Endorsements: stamps 'B↑O' 'Z 28/70' 'No 5 Sketch of Kingston Harbour'
Shows the same information as (1) above; (Holmden 1767).
OOAMA (NMC 3879)

(3) *1788 (1790)*
Sketch of Kingston Harbour The Ground reserved for the purposes of Government: for Public Works, Buildings, Naval Yard etc. is colour'd yellow. [Sgd] Quebec 6th Decr 1788 Gother Mann Captn and Commandg. Rl. Engr
Col ms 40 x 30 cm 1" to 13 chains Endorsements: stamp 'HMSPO'
Originally filed with 'Lord Dorchesters letter no 58 of 24th Oct 1790' (GBL pro CO 42/70 41ff); another version of (1) and (2), at a slightly larger scale; shows the same points as other plans except commons not marked ; soundings; shows a different configuration of coastline and islands; photoreproduction in OOAMA (NMC 3877); (*PRO Cat* 1480).
GBLpro (CO 700 Canada 38A)

1500 *1789*
[Sketch for the survey at Point Frederick]
Col ms 21 x 34 cm Scale not given
With 'Instructions proposed for the Surveyor at Kingston ... The Extent of the Survey to be agreeable to the Annexed Sketch ... [Sgd] Gother Mann Captn Commandg Rl Eng Quebec 19th Octr 1789. Approved and the Surveyor General to give the proper orders for carrying it into Execution Quebec 19th October 1789 [Sgd] Dorchester'; two pages of documents and a sketch of Point Frederick and Point Henry; 'N.B. The Coloured part of this Sketch, shows the ground to be surveyed by Mr Aitken'; ground for bldg lots shown above Point Frederick; also a copy in OOAMA (Kingston Planning Board maps 12, NMC 3881).
OOAMA (NMC 3881; 7084)

Related maps

(2) *[1789?]*
[Endorsed title]: 'The Harbours of Point Frederick and Henry (partial)'
Ms 48 x 97 cm Scale not given Endorsements: 'No 10' '934'
An unfinished plan showing coastlines; two blocks drawn in on Point Frederick, one representing the naval yard; possibly a draft for the survey described as 'Plan of the Points Henry & Frederick with the Coves Haldimand and Hamilton ... Surveyed in 1789 by Alex Aitken,' no 17 in 'List of maps ... 1793' (OTAR RG 1 A-I-1/1, 151–7).
OTAR (SR 7919)

(3) *[1794?] 1815*
Plan of Points Frederick and Henry, showing the Coves Haldimand & Hamilton on the East side of

the Harbour of Kingston. Copied from an original plan of Mr. James Toosey (Signed) Samuel Holland Surveyor General Surveyor General's Office York 10 Augst 1815 Signed Thos Ridout Surveyor Genl Copy / Drawing Room Kingston 8th September 1815 [Sgd] George Williams R.M.S.D.
Col ms 73 x 95 cm 1" to 200 ft Endorsements: 'No 140 277–6'; stamp 'REO'
Note: 'No 1 Copied from one in the possession of His Excellency Sir Frederick Robinson ... G.W.'; possibly from an original by A. Aitken who made a survey of Point Frederick as noted in his diary 13 Feb 1794 (OTAR RG 1-CB-1 box 43); shows Point Frederick with dockyard, old wharf, provision stores, area reserved for battery, type of soil; Point Henry noted as 'Reserve for the Crown'; the outline and a boundary of naval yard are similar to plan (2) above and probably copied from a similar but finished original.
OOAMA (NMC 22422)

1501 *[ca 1789–ca 1885]*
[Maps from the Kingston Planning Board Collection]
95 mss Sizes vary Scales vary
The collection includes some general plans but most are plans of small areas in the town or subdivision plans; many of the plans are undated; plans of the whole town, or significant plans of large sections have been listed separately; OOAMA has a list of the collection arranged by the numbers found on the maps (1–97).
OOAMA

1502 *[179?]*
Town of Kingston. [Sgd] Alexr Aitken D.P. Syr
Col ms 76 x 53 cm 1" to 200 ft Endorsements: 'A 34'
Shows the 262 lots of the first survey of the town and lots to 306 east of Barrack St; shows the area from Front to Rear St, from West St to two streets east of Cross St, and to north garrison and church reserves; Government House, lots reserved for Indian store, schoolhouse and lots for schoolmaster, areas reserved for public bldgs, quarry, Fort Frontenac; many later additions to the plan to 1834 including water lots and 'Johnsonville.'
OTNR (SR 165)

Related maps

(**2**) *[179?]*
Part of Kingston
Col ms 51 x 74 cm Scale not given Endorsements: 'A 35' '658'
Shows the streets only (unnamed) of the original town and lots 263–90 above Brewery St; list of owners keyed to most lot nos on the plan; front lots A–F along shore shown with lot A reserved for A. Aitken; possibly prepared by Aitken (d 1799) and probably from the same period as plan above; there is also a plan showing reserves for Kingston in D.W. Smith's 'Report upon Glebes & Commons ... 13th Jany 1802.'
(OTAR RG 1 a-II-1 vol 2 pp 942–87) OTNR (SR 164)

1503 *[1790]*
Plan shewing the Ground opposite the Town of Kingston to be reserved for the Crown: on which no settlement is to be made, Buildings erected; or Timber cut but by the authority, and for the Purposes of Government.
Col ms 32 x 38 cm 1" to 40 chains Watermark: 'J CRIPPS'
Originally with report of the Land Committee of 21 May 1790 about the reserve for naval purposes, but based on Mann (**1499**) (GBLpro CO 42/69 pp 338 ff); the areas immediately around Point Frederick and Point Henry are to be reserved for 'Public works, Buildings, and Naval yard,' etc; parts further away are to be reserved for 'Firewood, Timber, and Garden-Ground'; lots laid out above reserve; saw and grist mill located up river; photoreproduction in OOAMA (NMC 4862); (*PRO Cat* 1477).
GBLpro (MPG 430(2))

Related maps

(**2**) *[1790]*
No 2 [Point Frederick and Point Henry]
Col ms 31 x 38 cm Scale not given Endorsements: '22' '23'
A larger scale plan of the areas immediately around the points; shows dockyard on east side of Point Frederick, with tip reserved for a battery; a town plot is shown further up peninsula; old wharf, soil good for cultivation, marshy ground; stores and bldgs; land held by A. Aitken and Mr Cartwright to the north; from the same report as (1) above with statement that plan shows current situation of May 1790 and may conflict with reservation for naval purposes; photoreproduction in OOAMA (NMC 4862).
GBLpro (MPG 430(1))

(**3**) *1790*
No 3 [Same title as (1)]
Col ms 33 x 42 cm 1" to 40 chains Watermark: 'I TAYLOR'
Endorsed: 'In the observations of the Comg Engineer of the 6th March 90 respg Point Frederick near Kingston'; from Land Board Mecklenburg District Minutes and Records (OOA RG 1 L4 vol 7); shows the same information as (1) above with the addition of name Archibald McDonell written on a lot to the east.
OOAMA (NMC 3883)

(**4**) *1790*
No 2 Plan of Point Frederick &c. A.A. D.P.S.
Col ms 32 x 37 cm 1" to 10 chains Endorsements: 'In the Report of the Land Office Board for Mecklenburg of 8th Feby 90'
From the same source as (3); shows the same

information as (2); there is also a copy marked 'No 2 [without title] A.A. D.P.S.' at OKQ (Cartwright Papers box I folder 7) showing the same information; (Preston, 155–6 and 158–9).
OKQ OOAMA (NMC 3886)

1504 *1807*
Plan of the late Survey of the Town of Kingston Being the part Colored yellow. December 26th 1807 [Sgd] Saml S. Wilmot Dy Surveyor
Col ms 35 x 63 cm 1" to 2 chains Endorsements: 'A 29' '652'
Shows the area from Garrison Garden and Barrack St to William St; only Rear St named to northwest; lots 290–342 laid out to north, and names inserted, e.g., 'Sir John Johnson no 1.'
OTNR (SR 157)

Related maps

(2) *1808*
A Plan of a Part of the Town of Kingston surveyed by order of His Excellency Francis Gore Esquire Lieutenant Governor &c &c &c [Sgd] January 7th 1808 Saml S Wilmot Dy Surveyor.
Col ms 65 x 62 cm 1" to 2 chains Endorsements: 'A 28' '656'
Insets: [two plans of bearings of survey lines], each 1" to 1 chain; shows the area northwest of the garrison ground for six streets; only Grave St named; 'Sir John Johnson no. 1 property'; burying ground; various garden plots; some points not keyed; related to plan above, and both appear to be resurveys.
OTNR (SR 159)

1505 *[ca 1809?]*
[Part of the Town of Kingston]
Col ms 72 x 140 cm Approx 1" to 80 ft
Endorsements: '750'
Shows much of the town from about Water St to Rear St and West St to North St; reserve for market-place and church; names of owners and lot nos; many later notes from about 1807 to 1822.
OTNR (SR 6501)

1506 *1810*
Plan of the Town of Kingston shewing the Military Reservations. [Sgd] Chewett & Ridout Actg Surveyor Genl York 5th Octr 1810
Col ms 77 x 62 cm 1" to 200 ft
Shows the streets laid out from Shore St to Rear St and to 'hospital reservation' and 'garrison garden,' and from West St to beyond Bay St; Fort Frontenac and bldgs identified; gaol, court-house, church and yard, market-place, public school, and schoolmaster's lots all marked; unlocated land behind plot 'only fit for a quarry'; names of owners and houses shown; note: 'Additional Reference with the names of the Proprietors inserted on the Plan to make it answer as a Copy of the two Plans delivered to His Excy Lieut Govr Gore on the 22nd October 1815'; this note refers to plan of 1815 (see **1510**); additional information is for two areas along shore 'Resd for Fortification 21st Octr 1815'; there is also a later copy of part of this plan made in 1857 in OOAMA (NMC 3888), which originally accompanied a land petition (OOA RG 1 L3 R8 no 27 1857).
OTNR (SR 6487)

1507 *[1813?]*
Plan of Kingston in U. Canada. a loose sketch from hearsay. [and endorsed]: 'Incorrect 1st Sketch'
Ms 52 x 41 cm Approx 1" to 1/2 mile
An incorrectly oriented sketch of town drawn by the Americans during the war; shows streets, Navy Point, relief, and wooded areas; references key pickets, batteries, types of land, places 'where troops are paraded in case of alarm'; 'Route by which to avoid pickets' and 'a good landing area'; photoreproduction in OOAMA (NMC 15702).
USDNA (RG 77 dr 154 42-16A)

Related maps

(2) *[1813?]*
[Endorsed title]: 'Plan of Kingston in Upper Canada. Incorrect 2nd Plan'
Col ms 56 x 42 cm Scale not given Watermark: 'J WHATMAN 1808'
A larger-scale sketch of town, Point Frederick, and Point Henry but still wrong in orientation; key to military sites with number of guns and men; relief and vegetation shown but note that cleared land, fences, and distances not designated; photoreproduction in OOAMA (NMC 15700); there is also a rough sketch of the fortifications at Kingston: 'Kingston garrison in July 1711 effective men ...' (USDNA RG 107B-118(7); photoreproduction in OOAMA (NMC 120575).
USDNA (RG 77b dr 154 42-16; RG 107B-118(7))

1508 *1814*
Plan of Kingston and its vicinity [Sgd] J.B. Duberger Junr [Jany? 8th? 1814]
Col ms 61 x 142 cm 1" to 1/4 mile Endorsements: stamps 'B↑O' 'IGF'
Originally accompanying Lt Col Hughes's letter to Lt Gen Mann dated 16 Aug 1814 (GBLpro WO 55/860 pp 104–5); shows the area from Collins Bay east to Cedar Is near Point Henry; roads, bldgs, relief by grey wash, wooded areas; marshy land; fortifications noted as 6250 feet long on the west side; blockhouses nos 1–5 and burying ground outside the defences; date illegible on map and supplied from Holmden; (Holmden 1770).
OOAMA (NMC 11377)

Related maps

(2) *[1814]*
Plan of Kingston and its Vicinity [Sgd] J Kilborn
Col ms 63 x 139 cm 1" to 1/4 mile Endorsements: 'No 3 277–5' 'No 2'; stamp 'REO'
Similar to other plan and showing the same information; burying ground is marked as 'New';

also a plan in GBTAUh (187 Aa2) of the same title and scale but undated and with note: 'Distance round the line of Defence is [6250] feet.'
GBTAUh (187 Aa2) OOAMA (NMC 11376)

(3) *[1814?]*
[Plan of Kingston and vicinity]
Col ms 28 x 37 cm 1" to 1/2 mile
An untitled, unsigned sketch that appears to be a reduction of the plans above; shows same area and information with note that line of defence is '2083 yrd 1 foot.'
GBE (Sir George Murray Papers 46.10.2 no 104)

1509 *1814*
Plan of Kingston Surveyor Generals office York Upper Canada 12th March 1814 (Signed) Thos Ridout Surveyor Genl Copy W.C. (Copy) J. Kilborn
Col ms 48 x 89 cm 1" to 200 ft Endorsements: 'A 37' '659'
Shows town south of Rear St and from West St to one street beyond Bay St; lots have been added to 336 north of Rear St; 'Reference' keys Government House, Indian store, schoolhouse and lot, lots reserved for various purposes, and 'since granted as per schedule'; areas reserved for public bldgs and quarry; area proposed for hospital; houses shown; later additions regarding water lots; there is also a copy in OOAMA (NMC 3889) dated 3 March 1857, which originally accompanied a land petition (OOA RG 1 L3 R8 no 27 1857).
OTAR(P)

1510 *1815*
Plan of the Town of Kingston shewing the Military reservations also the unlocated land being principally only fit for a Quarry [Sgd] W. Chewett S S & D. Surveyor General's Office York Upper Canada October 21st 1815 [Sgd] Thos Ridout Surveyr Genl
Col ms 92 x 69 cm 1" to 200 ft
With a memorial against the transfer of the government seat from York to Kingston because of the cost of establishing government officials and the lack of free land, enclosed in Gore to Earl Bathurst 31 Oct 1815 (GBLpro CO 42/356 p 153); shows the town laid out in lots and streets as in 1814 plan above; Fort Frontenac and bldgs, hospital reservation, Garrison Garden, church, market-place reserve, gaol, school; shows all bldgs and names of owners in lots including water lots; (*OHIM* 7.35).
GBLpro (CO 42/356 p 153)

Related maps

(2) *1815*
Plan of the Town of Kingston shewing its environs three miles on the East and West sides thereof and six Miles to the Northward of said Town ... [Sgd] W. Chewett S.S.D. Surveyor Generals Office York Upper Canada October 21st 1815 [Sgd] Thos Ridout Surveyr Genl
Col ms 46 x 63 cm 1" to 1/2 mile
From the same source as above and showing that all the lots in the twp of Kingston have been located and the small area reserved for the town; 'Note This Plan is Copied from that of the Surveyor of the Midland District the late Alexr Aitken [possibly no **1502 (1)** or similar] but it is apprehended that the Northern boundary of the Military Reserve will fall on or near to the dotted line as it appears by the Plan delivered by the late Surveyor Genl of the Province of Quebec in the Year 1792 to Lieut Governor Simcoe' possibly **426 (2)**); shows the military reserve and the unlocated part of town; Gore agreed that the plans showed little available land and York remained the capital at this time (*Heritage Kingston*, 52–3).
GBLpro (CO 42/356 p 154)

1511 *1817*
A Plan Rough of a part of the Town and Township of Kingston Novr 5th 1817 [Sgd] Saml S Wilmot Dy Surveyor
Ms 85 x 124 cm 1" to 2 chains Endorsements: '687'
(SI 8 Aug 1817 to lay out twelve lots in Kingston of 1 to 5 acres each; OTNR FN 367 31 Dec 1827); lots shown on both sides of Grave St; names of some landowners nearby; notes about problems with older survey lines.
OTNR (SR 6483)

Related maps

(2) *1817*
Plan shewing the late Survey in the Town of Kingston Decr 31st 1817 [Sgd] Saml S. Wilmot Dy Surveyor
Col ms 61 x 36 cm 1" to 2 chains Endorsements: 'A 32' '651'
Shows a smaller area than plan above of area around Store St where West and North sts meet; Sir John Johnson's land shown.
OTNR (SR 156)

(3) *1818*
Rough Plan shewing the late Survey in the Town of Kingston. March 24th 1818 [Sgd] S.S. Wilmot Dy Surveyor
Col ms in 2 sheets 65 x 81 cm 1" to 2 chains
Endorsements: 'A 31' '653' '654'
Area from below Montreal St to West and North sts; shows glebe, graveyard straddling North St; Sir John Johnson's and Mrs Anne Earle's land; Artillery Park; several bldgs; the two plans were intended to form one map; and an undated copy: 'Kingston partial' endorsed 'A 33' and '660' and with the addition of names of owners (OTNR (SR 160)).
OTNR (SR 158; 160; 167)

1512 *1817–20*
A Plan of Kingston. Surveyed and Drawn by Lieut: Smith 70th Infy Surveyed in 1817. Drawn in 1820.
Col ms 56 x 91 cm 1" to 440 ft Endorsements: '3L' 'Lt. Colonel Cockburns Dy Qm General'

An attractive map of the town and Forts Frederick, Henry, and Mississauga; shows naval establishment, hospital, dockyards, artillery yard, Murney's Battery; all bldgs, town streets, and roads in the area are shown; relief by shading; (*PRO Cat* 1483).
GBLpro (CO 700 Canada no 78)

1513 *[ca 1818]*
Kingston
Col ms 66 x 56 cm 1" to 3 chains Endorsements: 'No 27'
Shows the town bounded by North and West sts; streets shown in the west, north to Rear St, and filled in northeast of Rear and Garden sts; Garrison Garden; garrison bldgs; shows market square 'per O.C. 28 Aug 1818'; many later additions; some illegible early notes.
OTAR(P)

1514 *1824*
Plan of Kingston Upper Canada shewing the site proposed for constructing a bridge between that place and Fort Henry. [Sgd] Rl Engrs Office Quebec 8th May 1824 E.W. Durnford Lt Col. Commg Rl Engrs Canada
Col ms 52 x 81 cm 1" to 400 ft Endorsements: stamps 'B↑O' 'IGF'
Shows the town and all its bldgs, Forts Frederick and Henry; all military bldgs identified, army distinguished from naval bldgs; endorsed 'With Lt Col Durnford's letter to Lt Genl Mann dated 17th May 1824' (in GBLpro WO 55/861 p 214); relief by shading; proposed bridge shown to Point Frederick; a few later pencilled notes; (Holmden 1799).
OOAMA (NMC 16105)

1515 *[1827]*
No 8 Sketch of Points Henry & Frederick shewing the situations on which it might be advisable to construct additional Towers
Col ms 66 x 100 cm 1" to 300 ft Watermark: 'J WHATMAN TURKEY MILL ... 1825'
Endorsements: 'AA61'; stamps 'B↑O' 'IGF'
Shows the 'present' military and naval bldgs and four proposed towers; Barriefield; relief by hachures and grey wash; dated 1827 by Holmden; (Holmden 1807h).
OOAMA (NMC 22425)

1516 *[1827?]*
Plan of the Ground around No 5 Block House shewing the Outline of a Proposed Work with a Casemated keep for 200 men as recommended by the Engineer Commissioners
Col ms 113 x 85 cm 1" to 100 ft Endorsements: 'AA62'; stamps 'B↑O' 'IGF'
Shows the area from Brewery St to West St; Artillery Park; shows plan for enlarged blockhouse at Cross and Bay sts and north of town; bldgs and owners shown; area 'deemed advisable to be purchased by the government'; proposed work shown; 'old French village'; relief by wash; Holmden dates map 1827; (Holmden 1811).
OOAMA (NMC 11379)

Related maps

(2) *1831*
Plan of the Ground round No 5 Blockhouse shewing the lots belonging to the Estate of the late Magdalen Ferguson which have been claimed and recommended to be conditionally granted to Mr Wm Kerr and Mrs Elizabeth Farley. [Sgd] Rl Engineer Office Kingston 22nd Novr 1831 J.R. Wright Lt Col. Comg Rl Engineer Upper Canada. H.O. Crawley Lieut Rl Engineers Novr 22nd 1831.
Col ms 111 x 77 cm 1" to 100 ft
Originally with (GBLpro WO 44/21 f 59); shows the same area and shows the extent of town lots, bldgs, and grounds that 'it might be advisable for government to purchase'; Presbyterian, Catholic, and Episcopalian burying grounds lie partly within clergy reserve near blockhouse; shows a different configuration for the blockhouse than on above map; photoreproduction in OOAMA (NMC 22429); (*PRO Cat* 1485).
GBLpro (MR 502(4))

1517 *1828–9*
A Survey of the Ground to the extent of 4000 yards in the Vicinity of the Dock-Yard at Kingston Upper Canada as ordered in the summer of 1828 by the Committee of which His Excellency Lieut General, Sir James Kempt, G.C.B. &c &c &c was President. (Signed) J.R. Wright Lieut Col. Royal Engineers (Signed) J. Walpole Lieut Royal Engineers Royal Engineers Office – Kingston Novr 7 – 1828. Commanding Royal Engineers' Office Quebec Septr 1829 [Sgd] E.W. Durnford Col Commandg Rl Engrs [Canada?]
Col ms 106 x 144 cm 1" to 400 ft Endorsements: stamps 'B↑O' 'IGF'
A detailed, attractive plan showing the town and forts; relief by hachures and grey wash; wooded and marshy areas, roads; all bldgs shown in town and in forts; a note indicates plan is duplicate of 16 Feb 1829; a later addition is noted: 'The Contour lines shown in pencil copied from Col. Oldfield's Plan dated 26 June 1841 (D3) J N 17 Feby 1843'; (Holmden 1822).
OOAMA (NMC 11380)

1518 *1829*
Map of the Northern & Eastern Boundary of the Military Reserve Adjoining Fort Henry Township of Pittsburgh, U.C. Surveyed by Order of His Excellency Sir John Colborne K.C.B. by J.S. McDonald D.P.S. Under the inspection of Captn Bonnycastle R.E. MDCCCXXIX. Drawn by J.S. McDonald D.P.S. 1829 [Sgd] John S. McDonald Dy Pl Syr. Examined and Certified [Sgd]

R.H. Bonnycastle Captain Royal Engineers 18 Oct 1829
Col ms 67 x 100 cm [1" to 100 yds] Endorsements: '863'
Shows conflicts along the survey lines with notes; land occupied by Col Lightfoot; village of Barriefield and Fort Henry shown; shows the erroneous boundary marked by Chewett in 1821; there are two copies of the plan originally filed with GBLpro WO 44/29 f 685 and 684 and marked 'Copy Rl Engr Office Kingston U.C. 18th Novr 1829' and '(Copy) Royal Engineer Office Kingston U. Canada [Sgd] R.H. Bonnycastle Captain Royl Engrs'; (*PRO Cat* 1537).
GBLpro MPHH 47 (15–16) OTNR (SR 5906)

1519 *1829*
Plan showing in yellow the Works proposed for the defence of Kingston Upper Canada. Drawn to illustrate the Committee's Report dated 84 Pall Mall, 24th Octr 1829. Drawn by S.B. Howlett 24th October 1829. Copied by J. Nightingale 19th Novr 1829
Col ms in 2 sheets 55 x 153 cm 1" to 130 yds
Endorsements: 'No 1' 'A42'; stamps 'B↑O' 'IGF'
Several towers, redoubts with fortifications at Murney's Point, and new plans for Fort Henry are proposed; shows whole town and major military and other bldgs in Kingston and the forts; later notes added to 1846 including note that ordnance property is shown from Lt Col Ward's plan dated 26 Jan 1842 (see **1531**); relief by hachures and grey wash; there are two other plans with similar titles and a few different notes in OOAMA (NMC 22427, 3907); NMC 3907 is a rough sketch; (Holmden 1823–4, 1843).
OOAMA (NMC 3907; 11381; 22427)

1520 *1829*
Survey of Kingston U Canada & its Dependencies with a projected Work submitted for consideration of General Mann in connection with Colonel Durnford's Report dated 4 Sepr 1829 instead of that already recommended for Point Henry including a Tower & Battery at that immediate point; and the Sites for advanced Towers as Numbered 1,2,3,4,& 5 together with the situation of the Pentagonal Tower already approved to be erected on the Kingston side of the Harbour &c whether this new work is or is not approved Commanding Royal Engineers Office - Quebec 4 Sepr 1829 [Sgd] E.W. Durnford Col. Comg Rl Engrs Canada
Col ms 53 x 120 cm 1" to 400 ft Endorsements: 'A 47'; stamps 'B↑O' 'IGF'
Sections; shows the area of the military establishment in town and the two forts with sight lines; spot heights; proposed bridge to Point Frederick; the letter from Durnford to Ellicombe of 4 Sept 1829 is in GBLpro WO 55/866 pp 302–14.
OOAMA (NMC 22426)

1521 *[183?]*
[Kingston showing area from Montreal Rd to School St]
Col ms 60 x 75 cm Scale not given
Shows most of the town with streets named; lot nos to 262; military redoubts shown with firing ranges; names of owners of large lots to the north including Ferguson land conveyed to late Charles Stuart and property of Wm Kerr and Mrs Farley.
OTNR (SR 11541)

1522 *[183?]*
[Kingston showing names of lot owners]
Col ms 70 x 143 cm Scale not given Endorsements: 'No 211' '688'
Shows the town and all the streets, but no bldgs; names of owners in lots; also shows Commanding Officers' Quarters; burying ground; market-place, church; jail and court-house plot shown as subdivided.
OTAR (SR 6499)

1523 *[1832]*
Town / of / KINGSTON. // Burrows Survr del. / Tazewell, Lithr
Print (lith) hand col 58 x 48 cm 1" to 4 1/2 chains
A rough lithograph, the first map printed by Tazewell and the first map lithographed in Upper Canada; shows the town laid out between West St and North St; streets named, lot nos shown; major bldgs named, list of hotels; drawings of the *John By* and one other ship in the harbour; the plan was being made during the latter part of 1831 since the *Kingston Chronicle* of 5 Nov 1831 notes it would be ready in the ensuing week but publication was not announced until 14 Jan 1832; reproduced in *Heritage Kingston*, 170; (Gundy, 468–9).
OTAR

1524 *1835*
Plan No 1 Fort Henry Kingston, Upper Canada to accompany Colonel Nicoll's letter to the Inspector General of Fortifications No 42 dated 18th August 1835. T.G.W. Eaststaff Draugn [Sgd] Gusts Nicolls Colonel Comg Rl Engineers Canada Rl Engineers Office Quebec 18th August 1835
Col ms 65 x 93 cm 1" to 200 ft Endorsements: stamp 'B↑O'
Originally accompanied letter 18 Aug 1835 in GBLpro WO 55/872 pp 173–191; relief by shading and spot heights; soundings; shows Fort Henry and Fort Frederick with the commissariat establishment, dockyard, and other military bldgs; (Holmden 1837).
OOAMA (NMC 22430)

1525 *1838*
Sketch Showing the proposed site of the Ordnance Establishment at Kingston 30 March 1838.
Col ms 26 x 41 cm Scale not given
Enclosed in Maj Bonnycastle's letter to Col Rowan, military secretary, 11 June 1839 (OOA RG 8 I/448

p 177); shows the present ordnance establishment near Fort Henry on Navy Bay and the proposed site near Cataraqui Bridge on Point Frederick behind dockyard; bldgs noted in grey (stone) and pink (brick); (Holmden 1840).
OOAMA (NMC 3917)

1526 *[184?]*
[Endorsed title]: 'Part of Kingston City'
Ms 20 x 32 cm Scale not given Watermark: '...1842'
Shows the area from North Bagot St to Division St and Main and Picard sts to Colbourne St; names in some lots.
OTAR

1527 *[184?]*
Plan of a Tract of Land Belonging to the Honble Joh[n Mac]aulay As Surveyed by (Signed) George Bruce D.P.S. Kingston October 1841 [certified a correct copy] [Sgd] William Kilborn D.P.S. Kingston 29th December 1841
Ms 43 x 55 cm 1" to 1 chain
Shows lots from Union St to Stuart St, and Barrie St to Arch St; later notes about sales with names, 1843–7; has same title and similar to OOAMA copy (Kingston Planning Board Map no 94, NMC 3923).
OOAMA (NMC 3923) OTAR (T.W. Nash Collection)

1528 *1840*
Plan of the southerly part of the town of Kingston shewing the projected extension of the Streets adjoining Park Lots no 1 and 2 across those lots and Lot no 25 in conformity with the adjoining part of the Town and also with the Streets already laid out and designed to be laid out on Lot No 24 1st Concession township of Kingston, together with the laying into town lots the land between said backs. By the Order and Direction of the Court of Common Council of the Town of Kingston. Kingston 14th October 1840. (Signed) William H. Kilborn Depy P. Surveyor copied by [A. Larue?] Junr Surveyor and Drftsmn
Col ms 61 x 84 cm 1" to 2 chains Endorsements: '655'
Shows the area between Queen St and Grave St, and continuation of Barrie St to George Okill Stuart's lot; shows seminary, kirk, and various houses.
OTNR (SR 161)

1529 *1841*
Plan shewing the Contours of the Ground within the Military Radius around Proposed Redoubts No 3,4 & 5 Kingston required by the Insp Genls letter of 22d Feby 1841 No 1779. Royl Engrs Office Kingston 16th June (Signed) G. Whitmore Capt. Royl Engrs. [Sgd] J. Oldfield Lt Colonel Comg Royal Engineers in Canada 16 June 1841
Col ms 107 x 122 cm 1" to 50 yds Endorsements: 'D3'; stamps 'B↑O' 'IGF'
'To accompany Lt Coll Oldfields letter no. 100 26th June 1841'; original proposed positions and present proposal for positions; part lot 23 near clergy reserve and Herchmer's farm; also a reduced copy at OOAMA (NMC 3932) sgd 'J N 17 Feby 1845' 1" to 400 ft (Holmden 1852), which shows unnamed streets at west and north end of town; (Holmden 1846).
OOAMA (NMC 11382)

1530 *1841*
Sketch of Proposed Improvements for Kingston now the Capital of Canada Submitted to the consideration of all Her Majesty's Subjects by their Humble Servt [Sgd] Robt F. Gourlay Kingston Sepr 8 1841.
Col ms 66 x 53 cm Scale not given
Note: 'This Copy respectfully presented to the Merchants of Quebec November 22 1841 – by R.F.G.'; a rough sketch showing a proposal for two major approach roads ending at a square for government bldgs behind a 'Campus' reserve at Brock St between Montreal 'Avenue' and Clergy and Barrie sts; Montreal St is marked as 'North Approach'; a few major bldgs shown; newspaper clippings appended testifying to Gourlay's merits and one of 16 Aug 1841 written by Gourlay explaining the scheme (*Heritage Kingston*, 130–1); (Holmden 1847; *OHIM* 7.44).
OOAMA (NMC 22432)

1531 *1842*
No 1 Plan shewing the different Lots contained within a radius of 609 yds in front & 300 yds in rear of Proposed Defenses at Kingston together with such buildings as have been erected since 1842. [Sgd] B. Wilkinson Capt Royal Engineers 16th November 1842 To Accompany Colonel Oldfield's letter No 127 dated Novr 26th 1842 referring to paragraphs 1 to 4. [Sgd] J. Oldfield Colonel Staff Commg Royal Engineers in Canada 29 November 1842. (Copy) R.I. Pilkington Draftsman
Col ms 84 x 65 cm 1" to 100 yds Endorsements: '43 E 89' 'F 5' '1191'; stamps 'B↑O' 'IGF'
The north and west part of town from L Ontario to road to Toronto, and Brewery St to Cataraqui R; shows all bldgs within range, and stone, brick, and wooden bldgs, and those erected since 2 Nov 1840; notes on land leases; redoubts nos 3, 4, and 5; (Holmden 1851a–c); other plans related to this survey include: 'No 2 Sketch shewing the Lots in the Village of Barriefield ... [Sgd] B Wilkinson Capt Royal Engineers 16th November 1842.' (OOAMA (NMC 17439)), 'No 3 Kingston Plan shewing the extent of Ground to be purchased in and around the Town ...' (OOAMA (NMC 17438)), 'No 4 Village of Barriefield Kingston. Plan shewing the extent of ground to be purchased ...' (OOAMA (NMC 3929)).
OOAMA (NMC 3929; 17437–9)

1532 *1842*
Part of the Harbour of Kingston. Shewing the position of the Shoals adjacent to the town. &c Copy. Office-Board of Works. Surveyed by F.P. Rubidge 1842. Drafted by A.K.
Col ms 73 x 121 cm 1" to 2 chains Watermark: 'JAMES WHATMAN TURKEY MILL KENT [1839?]' Endorsements: stamps 'BW' '563'
Shows soundings and bathymetric tints, bridge to Point Frederick, naval dockyard, ship channel, wharves, and names of owners; (Holmden 1753).
OOAMA (NMC 16821)

Related maps

(2) *1847*
Plan of part of the City of Kingston shewing the position of the Shoal in the Harbour, between Johnson and Union Streets extended, with accurate soundings. [Sgd] Thomas Fraser Gibbs Deputy Prov. Surveyor Kingston 13th February 1847. [Sgd] J Mann Lieut Royl Engr 12th March 1847
Col ms 75 x 53 cm 1" to 2 chains Endorsements: 'No 77 277–12'; stamp 'REO'
Shows area from waterfront and Union St to Clarence St with wharves and names of owners; patents; soundings and table of stations; also a copy at OOAMA sgd 'R.I. Pilkington Draftsman 31st May 1847' and with the line of the original shore added, enclosed with land petition (OOA RG 1 L3 K4 no 67 1847); (Holmden 1854).
OOAMA (NMC 21434; 22436)

1533 *[1843]*
A DIAGRAM, / Exhibiting the true Boundaries and Lines of Survey of Lots Nos 23, 24 and 25, in the 1st Concession of the Township of Kingston / in Contradistinction to the Erroneous and Defective ones. / / Peabody Sc.
Print (wood engrav) 24 x 19 cm Scale not given
In George Stuart, *Mentoriana* (Kingston: Printed at the Herald Office 1843), frontis (*Bib Can* 2618); shows 10 different boundary lines around the lots from various 'correct' and 'erroneous' surveys from 1783 on; property owned by Grass and Herchmer also shown; Stuart's book was about 'establishing the true boundaries and lines of survey on a permanent basis and thereby securing the rights of land in the original patents to the Loyalists and their Heirs.'
OTMCL

1534 *1843*
Kingston. Plan of all the Government Land on the Eastern Side of Kingston Harbour Canada Showing the proposed Site of the Several Works which were designed by the Committee of 1829 for the occupation of the position upon this Side of the Harbour. ... Prepared in obedience to the Inspector General of Fortifications Letter of the 3rd March 1843 [Sgd] E Y H Henderson Lieut Royl Engrs July 31st 1843 Wilkinson Capt District Royal Engineer 31st July 1843 [Sgd] W.C.E. Holloway Colonel Comg R Engrs
Col ms 170 x 171 cm 1" to 150 ft Endorsements: stamps 'B↑O' 'IGF'
'To accompany Col. Holloway's Letter No 77 of 8th August 1843'; a detailed, contoured plan of Point Frederick and Point Henry; contours except where wooded; quarries; notes on original shapes for redoubts and final form; new position for tower on Cedar Is.
OOAMA (NMC 27592)

Related maps

(2) *1845*
Reduced from contoured Plan of Point Henry (FF 10) for the purpose of putting the Contours upon the general Plan of Kingston (A 43) J.N. 31st Decr 1845
Col ms 65 x 69 cm Scale not given
A rough sketch reduced from (1) above; irregular contour interval; there is also a plan in OOAMA 'Tracing from Record contoured Plan ...' showing site proposed for tower on Cedar Is in 1843 and position as built in 1850; (Holmden 1853).
OOAMA (NMC 22435)

1535 *1845*
Plan of the Boundary Line between the Town and Township of Kingston showing the subdivisions of the parts adjoining the eastern portion of the same: as the whole was retraced and surveyed by the undersigned Surveyor – September 1845. (Signed) A. Wells D.P.S. By L.P. Morin Draughtsman C.L.O.
Col ms 59 x 157 cm 1" to 2 chains
Inset of lot 24 showing original boundary line, 1" to 4 chains; shows the boundary running through lot 25 west of Union and Johnson sts; also a copy of plan at OKQ inscribed 'September 1844 [i.e., 1845?]' and 'Crown Lands Department Toronto Oct 28th 1858 [Sgd] Andrew Russell Assistant Commissioner' and which was later used in a court case (1879); original lots 24 and 25, twp from Montreal Rd to Division St and Barrie St, and from L Ontario to north boundary; conflicting lines 'Picardville'; also a copy with same title and dated 'Sept. 1846 [Sgd] A. Wells D.P.S.' showing the same information (OTNR (SR 1422)).
OKQ OTNR (SR 1422; 5958)

1536 *1845*
Plan of the Front of the North Easterly part of the Town of Kingston extending from Barrack Street to the Northern Limit of the Town and Exhibiting a Water lot embracing the whole of said front, Laid down from actual Survey. Kingston Aug 31st 1845 [Sgd] William H. Kilborn Depy P. Surveyor [Sgd] R.H. Bonnycastle Lt. Col. R.E. B Wilkinson Capt R.E. 31st May 1845
Col ms 53 x 77 cm 1" to 2 chains Endorsements: 'M 44 and No 39' '933' 'rel CW/315'

Shows the town with streets and various government lots, bldgs, barracks, bridge, wharves, etc; also a copy in OOAMA (NMC 16609) endorsed 'Kingston' and 'No 75 276–.'
OOAMA (NMC 16609) OTNR (SR 163)

1537 *1849*
Kingston Plan shewing the portions of Ordnance Property tinted green exchanged for Water Lot J tinted yellow by Deeds dated 11th May 1848. Agreeably to the Boards Order dated 24th December 1846 M/1532. To accompany the C.R.E. Letter to the I.G.F. dated 31st March 1849 No 1265 [Sgd] W.C.E. Holloway Colonel Comg Rl Engrs R.I. Pilkington Draftsman
Col ms 41 x 56 cm 1" to 3 chains Endorsements: 'DR/884' '179'; stamps 'IGF' 'B↑O'
Shows the area of town to Bagot St on west and William St on south; military bldgs identified and indexed; ordnance, government, and private property; water lots and piers; (Holmden 1859).
OOAMA (NMC 3938)

1538 *[185?]*
Portsmouth Harbour and Property Adjacent.
Col ms on linen 52 x 54 cm 1" to 2 chains
Endorsements: stamp [BW] '791'
Shows pier and wharves with names of occupants; town hall, stores, bakeries, hotels, marine railway, tannery, brewery, penitentiary property; soundings.
OOAMA

1539 *1850*
PLAN / OF THE / City and Liberties / OF / KINGSTON / Delineating severally the Wards and Lots, with the Streets, Wharves / and Principal Buildings / Compiled by Thomas Fraser Gibbs, Provincial L. Surveyor. / 1850. / Hugh Scobie Lith. Toronto.
Print (lith) 93 x 63 cm 1" to 6 chains
View: 'FRONT ELEVATION OF THE CITY HALL'; shows streets named, the westerly boundary of the city proper [Gordon St] and the northerly boundary; beyond are the western and northern liberties; all bldgs are shown and major ones named; most of the settlement is still within Barrie and North sts but pockets of subdivision have occurred beyond; names of owners of large lots; parks, cemeteries; reproduced in *Heritage Kingston*, 196; OOAMA copy has ms adds showing military land; (*PRO Cat* 1491).
GBLpro (CO 700 Can 103(1)) OOAMA (NMC 21043) OTAR OTNR (SR 6493)

1540 *1850*
Survey of Kingston C.W. Embracing a circle of about two miles round the Tete du Pont Barracks and shewing the Contours Soundings and Ships Course on entering the Harbour. Surveyed by Lieuts Morrison and Moggridge Royal Engineers Drawn by [Sgd] John Y. Moggridge Lieut Rl Engineers 25th June 1850. [Sgd] C.O. Streatfield Lt Colonel Royal Engineers 25th June 1850 Henry Vavasour Col Comg Ryl Engineers Canada 5 August [1850]
Col ms 107 x 183 cm 1" to 400 ft Endorsements: stamp 'B↑O'
Accompanied by '[List of] Armament of Works, Accommodation for Troops, Magazines, Blockhouses, Towers ... [Sgd] John Y. Moggridge Lieut Rl Engineers ... 5 August 1850'; a large and attractive plan; shows relief by shading, wooded areas, roads, spot heights, and soundings; all bldgs shown in town and bldgs and forts classed by bldg material; notes about redoubts and towers per proposal of 1829 and new line of defence per 'Col. Holloway's letter to the I.G.F. dated 12th June 1845 No 357'; (Holmden 1864); also a plan of similar title and same dates, endorsed 'REO' and 'Kingston No 757 277–8' (OOAMA (NMC 14268)); and a copy: '(True Copy) A.R. Clarke Lt Rl Eng March 1853' endorsed 'No 15 277–8' and 'CREOC' (NMC 26089).
OOAMA (NMC 3944; 14268; 14273; 26089)

1541 *1852*
PLAN / DESIGNED TO SHEW THE MANNER IN WHICH THE FRONT OF THE / WEST HALF OF LOT NUMBER XVIII IN THE 1st CONCESSION OF / KINGSTON / the Property of Francis Manning Hill, Esquire / IS LAID OUT INTO BUILDING LOTS, IN EXTENSION / of the / VILLAGE OF PORTSMOUTH, / ADJOINING THE CITY OF KINGSTON / Hugh Scobie Lith. Toronto. / Thomas Fraser Gibbs Prov. L. Surveyor Kingston 17th November 1852
Print (lith) 42 x 30 cm 1" to 3 chains
Shows the area from Front St to 'Aberchallader' and west of King St to 'Woodstone,' the property of Jas Hopkirk, Esq.; lot nos and sizes; names of owners; (see also **B1185**).
Frontenac 13 (no R.P. number)

1542 *1854*
PLAN / DESIGNED TO SHEW THE SOUTH EAST PART OF LOT NO XXII, IN THE FIRST CONCESSION OF / KINGSTON / SITUATED BETWEEN UNION STREET AND THE CONTINUATION OF KING STREET / With the manner in which it is laid out into Building Lots, being the Property of / ARCHIBALD JOHN MACDONNELL ESQRE // Lith by Bien & Sterner 90 Fulton St. N.Y. // Thomas Fraser Gibbs, Prov. L. Surveyor / Kingston 9th March 1854
Print (lith) 52 x 41 cm 1" to 4 chains
Lots on Collingwood and Nelson sts; houses, names of owners; related to R.P. B4 (**B1189**).
ONLAH

1543 *1854*
PLAN / OF PART OF / KINGSTON / DESIGNED TO SHEW THE LOTS LAID OUT ON JOHNSON, CENTRE, PARK AND OTHER STREETS / THE PROPERTY OF A.J. MACDONNELL, ESQ. / 1854.

Print (lith) 58 x 41 cm 1" to 4 chains
Shows the area from Union St to Princess St and Nelson/Collingwood sts west to Regent St; bldgs shown at Princess and Victoria sts; some lots added in ms with ms title: 'Plan showing the situation of the Range of Lots laid out on Collingwood, Nelson, Princess, Johnson and Union Streets Kingston the property of Archibald John MacDonnell [Sgd] Thomas Fraser Gibbs Provl Land Surveyor Kingston 15th May 1854'; based on R.P. A2 (**B1190**); also a copy at OOAMA (Kingston Planning Board Map no 31, NMC 3955) with the ms adds and title partly trimmed.
OOAMA (NMC 3955) OTAR

1544 *1854*
PLAN / SHEWING THE SITUATION OF THE RANGE OF LOTS LAID OUT ON / COLLINGWOOD, NELSON, PRINCESS, JOHNSON AND UNION STREETS. / KINGSTON / the property of / THE HON. JOHN A. MACDONALD & DAVID SHAW ESQ. / [Sgd in facsimile] Thomas Fraser Gibbs Prov. L. Surveyor Kingston 15th May 1854
Print (lith) 57 x 42 cm 1" to 4 chains
Names of owners, bldgs shown in the area; related to R.P. A2 (**B1190**).
ONLAH

1545 *[1856?]*
Canada Naval Reserves – Kingston Harbour [Sgd] [J?] Taylor Master R.N.
Col ms 44 x 75 cm Scale not given Endorsements: stamp 'HO 30 Jul 56'
Shows Point Frederick with bldgs erected in naval grounds and dockyard, and 'spaces & slips once in existence'; Fort Henry, military and ordnance lands shown.
GBTAUh (D2213 Aa3)

1546 *[1856?]*
PLAN / OF THE PROPERTY OF / JAMES HOPKIRK ESQ. / AT / KINGSTON. / Thomas Fraser Gibb / P.L.S. / Kingston. Maclear & Co Lith. Toronto
Print (lith) 61 x 42 cm 1" to 3 chains
Shows the area from Front St to Aberchallader St and from MacDonald St west; names of owners; houses shown; also shows 'Rockwood ... now purchased by Government for a Lunatic Asylum' (1856) (*Heritage Kingston*, 153); shows Dr Sampson's property below Front St with note that government may purchase it for a reformatory for juvenile delinquents; see also **B1197**.
Frontenac 13 (R.P. 47)

1547 *1857*
Kingston and its vicinity Ontario 1857
Col ms on linen 85 x 90 cm Approx 5.3" to 1 mile
Shows the streets and major bldgs and the boundaries of the ordnance reserves; GTR; four points north and east of Fort Henry marked but not keyed; photoreproduction in OOAMA (NMC 15005); (*PRO Cat* 1492).
GBLpro (CO 700 Canada 103(2))

1548 *1859*
Hand Trace shewing Her Majesty's Dockyard; Fort Henry and Fort Frederick, at Kingston, Upper Canada. [Sgd] C.F. Skyring Lt. Col. R.E. [illegible] 6th May 1859.
Col ms 54 x 80 cm 1" to 400 ft Endorsements: stamps 'HO' 'May 30 1859'
Shows the boundaries of ordnance and naval lands, and bldgs including those in the town; relief; note: 'Some additions have been made to this tracing from a plan lent by the War Office, which plan appears to be a copy of the Original from which this was traced at Kingston [Sgd] E.J. Powell June 1st 1859.'
GBTAUh (D4676 Ael)

Related maps

(**2**) *[1859]*
Kingston C.W. Plan of the Naval property, shewing the existing Buildings, Wharfs, etc. etc.
Col ms 58 x 105 cm Scale not given Endorsements: stamps 'HO' 'May 30 1859'
Inset: 'Part of the Township of Pittsburgh 1" to 20 chains'; index to 36 bldgs in naval reserve at Fort Frederick; attributed in GBTAUh catalogue to 'Lieut. Col. Skyring 1859.'
GBTAUh (D4675 Ael)

1549 *1865*
MAP / OF THE CITY OF / KINGSTON / COUNTY OF FRONTENAC / CANADA WEST. / BY JOHN C. INNES / CITY ENGINEER / 1865. / SNYDER, BLACK & STURN, 92 WILLIAM ST., NEW-YORK./ Published and sold by John Creighton, City Book Store.
Print (lith) 99 x 138 cm 1" to 4 chains
Views: 'COURT HOUSE,' 'CITY HALL,' 'CUSTOM HOUSE,' 'POST OFFICE,' 'CITY BOOK STORE,' 'CRIMINAL LUNATIC ASYLUM,' and [view of the waterfront]; 'Reference' keys ward divisions, sewers constructed, hydrants, gas lamps, and spot heights above L Ontario; streets named; all bldgs shown and major bldgs identified; ordnance lands, wharves, railways; names of estates and some lot owners; 'Land purchased by the City for the purpose of erecting a City Jail and House of Refuge' north of Pine and Division sts; OOAMA (NMC 17877) has ms adds to 1881 re railways.
OKIT OKQ OOAMA (NMC 17877; 21076)

(KINNETTLES)

1550 *1855*
MAP / OF PART OF THE / VILLAGE of KINNETTLES / TOWNSHIP OF NICHOL / County of Wellington / Surveyed for Alexander

Harvey Esq. / M.C. SCHOFIELD P.L.S. / 1855. / Maclear & Co. Lith. Toronto.
Print (lith) 53 x 73 cm 1" to 2 chains
Related to R.P. 57 (**B1211**); shows the village laid out from Grand R to Elora and Fergus sts and from Pellissier St to Sebastian St; mill race and pond, water lots; the village still appears on the co atlas (Walker & Miles, ... *Wellington* (1877)) but disappeared at the end of the 19th century (Carter, I:619).
OOAMA (NMC 22465)

KIRKFIELD

1551 *1865*
Plan of the Village of Kirkfield. [Certified as correct and sgd] Geo. Gibson P.L.S. Woodville April 20th 1865. [Certified correct by owners and sgd] Jacob Belfry, Alexander Munro, John McKenzie Woodville April 10th 1865
Ms 48 x 63 cm 1" to 2 chains
Part of lots 41–44 con N and S of Portage Rd in Eldon Twp; shows Nelson St and Portage Rd and lots laid out along King and Water sts; all bldgs shown including sawmill; no registered plan similar to this found.
OTAR

KITCHENER

1552 *1853*
PLAN / OF / LOTS FOR SALE / IN THE / TOWN OF BERLIN / H. Scobie Lith Toronto W. Armstrong / 1853
Print (lith) 55 x 77 cm 1" to 264 ft
Views: 'BERLIN FROM THE SOUTH / LOWE' and 'COURT HOUSE BERLIN'; shows the area laid out and bounded by King, Styx, Wellington, Lancaster, and Queen sts; shows a few bldgs including town hall, court-house, and residences of A.C. Weber and Henry Eby; GTR and station; see also 1853–4 plan below (**1553**).
OKIT OTUTF

1553 *1853–4*
Map / of part of the / TOWN / OF / BERLIN, / CAPITAL OF THE COUNTY OF WATERLOO C.W. / Surveyed for / GEORGE JOHN GRANGE, ESQ. / BY / M.C. SCHOFIELD, P.L.S. / 1853–54 / Lith of Compton & Gibson 161 Main St Buffalo
Print (lith) 62 x 80 cm 1" to 8 chains
Four views of co court-house, King St, Waterloo and mill, and Bridgeport and mill, each sgd 'W.H.E.N. Del.'; the same as on **1554**; lots are shown from Gaukel to Napier sts south of King St, and north of King St from Railway and Ahrens sts to Shanly and Palmers sts; a notice indicates that the sale will take place on [added in ms]: 'Tuesday the 31st day of October 1854'; major bldgs identified in centre and large properties, nurseries, mills shown; related to Waterloo N 58 (R.P. 374–7) of 10 Oct 1854; this map includes the subdivision shown on the 1853 plan but extends the lots beyond King and north of Wellington sts and more streets and bldgs are shown south of Queen St; reproduced as ACML Facsimile no 91 (1982).
OOAMA (NMC 19554)

1554 *1855*
MAP / OF THE / TOWN / OF / BERLIN, / CAPITAL OF THE COUNTY OF WATERLOO C.W. / DRAWN / FROM ACTUAL SURVEY AND ORIGINAL MAPS / BY / M.C. SCHOFIELD, P.L.S. / 1855 / Lith of Compton Main St Buffalo.
Print (lith) 60 x 80 cm 1" to 8 chains
Four views of parts of town each sgd 'W.H.E.N. Del.' and the same as those on **1553** above; a compilation plan of whole town from Cameron to Shanley sts and from Strange to Lancaster sts; GTR and station and some other bldgs identified, some names of owners.
OKIT

1555 *1855*
MAP / of the Village / OF / BERLIN / Previous / to its being incorporated / 1855 / Lith by Compton 209 Main St. Buffalo
Print (lith) 55 x 65 cm 1" to 4 chains
Shows the central part of town from Water St to Cameron St and Church St to Pine St; churches, hotels, court-house, jail, and other bldgs identified; many names of owners; Berlin was incorporated 1 Jan 1854; the information possibly dates from 1853 since the subdivision around the GTR is not shown.
OKITD

1556 *1855*
PLAN OF PART OF THE / TOWN LOTS IN BERLIN, / FOR SALE / ON THURSDAY, THE 30TH AUGUST, 1855 / BY F.E. MARCON, ESQ.
Print (lith) 42 x 53 cm 1" to 25 ft
Lots on Weber, Victoria, and Water sts; the same information as R.P. 389 and filed with it (see **B1219**).
Waterloo N 58 (R.P. 389 [2])

1557 *1856*
PLAN OF LOTS / Drawn / from M.C. Schofields Map of the / TOWN OF BERLIN / 1856 / Alexander W. Simpson C.I. and P.L.S. over Best & Green's / HAMILTON. / Maclear & Co Lith. Toronto
Print (lith) with ms adds 68 x 96 cm 1" to 2 chains
'The Lots coloured red, will be sold by Auction by Best & Green on the property'; the lots are between Victoria and Shanly and Adam sts and from Upper King St to St Leger St; the subdivision amends R.P. 374–7 of 1853–4 (**B1213**) by creating more lots around the station and deleting a few on Shanly St to allow for a new street; related to R.P. 378 (1859) (**B1229**); about one-quarter of original lots on 1853–4 plan to be sold.
OOAMA (NMC 43129)

1558 *1856*
PLAN / OF THE / VILLAGE OF BRIDGEPORT / IN THE / TOWNSHIP & COUNTY / OF / WATERLOO, C.W. / AS SURVEYED FOR / MESSRS SHOEMAKER, TAGGE, EBY, DEVITT & FERRIER / BY / Schofield & Hobson P.L.S. / BERLIN, C.W. / 1856
Print (lith) 55 x 77 cm Scale not given
Imprint may have been trimmed off; shows the layout of the village including all bldgs; many businesses identified and names of landowners; several mills, ponds, and races shown; related to R.P. 577 (**B1220**); the village of Bridgeport was listed in *Smith's Canadian Gazetteer* (1846) and was annexed by Kitchener in 1973 (Carter, 2:1063).
OKIT

LANARK

1559 *1824*
Village of Lanark Lanark Military Settlement 29th March 1824 [Sgd] W. Marshall S & D
Ms 34 x 53 cm 1" to 2.5 chains Endorsements: 'No 31'
Shows the town site of 40 town lots on the Clyde R from Argyle to Cannings sts and from Hillier to Owen sts; reserved lot; names of settlers.
OTAR(P)

Related maps

(2) *1824*
Plan of the Village of Lanark with the Park Lots Adjoining Lanark 29th March 1824 [Sgd] W. Marshall S & D
Ms 33 x 53 cm 1" to 10 chains Endorsements: 'No 28'
Shows the town site with 40 lots and a central reserve surrounded by 32 park lots to the north and larger lots east and south of town; names and notes.
OTAR(P)

1560 *1834*
Plan of the Village of Lanark with the Park Lots adjoining (signed) W. Marshall. Surveyor General's Office, Toronto. 2nd Octr 1834, Copy – Henry Lizars.
Col ms 58 x 76 cm 1" to 5 chains Endorsements: 'A 40' '662'
The same layout as in the 1824 survey above (**1559** (2)) but shows only street outline with names and mill; also a copy: 'Lanark. with the Park Lots. Copy of a Plan signed Wm Marshall P.L.S. Surveyor General's Office Montreal 8th January 1845 [Sgd] Thomas Parke Survr Genl' (OTAR); and a copy (OTNR (SR 181)): 'Plan of the Village of Lanark with the Park Lots adjoining [Initialled] J.W.B. Crown Lands Office Toronto 15th June 1856 [Sgd] Joseph Cauchon Commissr of Crown Lands' endorsed 'A 207.'
OTAR OTNR (SR 180–1)

LINDSAY

1561 *1833 (1837)*
[Lindsay] Mapped and Surveyed by [Sgd] J. Huston Depty Prov. Survr. July 1833 [and later title] Town Plot [of] Lindsay in Ops so called by Order of His Excellency Sir Francis Bond Head vide Letter from Government House dated 22nd September 1837 [Initialled] J.W.M.
Col ms 49 x 70 cm 1" to 3 chains Endorsements: 'No 35'
(SI 23 May 1833 to survey and lay out town on lots 20 and 21, con 5; OTNR FN 263 July 1833); shows the layout of streets with Queen's Square in the centre; streets were named in 1837 and town extends from Prince St to Sussex St and Durham St to Francis St; many later notes and additions of names; includes note that northern boundary of town does not agree with J.K. Roche's survey (1846); also another copy: 'Ops now Lindsay [Sgd] Copy J.G. Chewett [Sgd] Surveyor General's Office Toronto 31st May 1837 J W Macaulay Surv Genl' with the addition of lots granted for churches, burying ground, and reserves in 1844, 1846, etc, and with a few names added (OTAR); and a copy: 'Lindsay by J. Huston D.P.S. 1833. Surveyor General's Office Montreal 17th October 1844. A true copy.' endorsed 'A 138' and '1318' and showing only streets (OTNR (SR 175)); also a later copy of this survey in OTNR (SR 174): 'Lindsay [Initialled] J.W.B. Crown Lands Office Toronto 14th June 1856 [Sgd] Joseph Cauchon Commissr for Crown Lands' endorsed 'A 208' and with lot nos also given.
OTAR OTNR (SR 174–6).

1562 *1846*
Plan of the Town Plot of Lindsay and the Park Lots adjacent. 1846 [Sgd] John K. Roche Provincial Land Surveyor 6 July 1846. Examined [Initialled] A.R.
Col ms, pt missing 58 x 87 cm 1" to 3 chains Endorsements: 'A 148' '2989/46'
(SI 12 May 1846 to survey park lots and boundary lines of town and park lots; OTNR FN 307 8 July 1846); shows park lots west of town from Albert St to Alfred St; shows part of town cleared and that still forest; bldgs shown around centre; Queen's Square subdivided; streets named; mill, locks; also a copy (OTNR (SR 173)): 'Town Plot of Lindsay and the Park Lots adjacent. J. Cane Dts. Crown Land Department Montreal August 1846.' endorsed 'A 163' and '663' with lot lines erased from Queen's Square, and showing two travelled roads, mill bridge, and locks; and a copy (OTNR (SR 179)): 'Town Plot of Lindsay and the Adjacent Park Lots. Crown Land Department Montreal August 1846 [Sgd] Andrew Russell S & D' endorsed 'No 93' and with the addition of names in park lots.
OTNR (SR 173; 177; 179)

Related maps

(2) *1848*
Plan of the Park Lots of Lindsay. Crown Lands Department Surveyors Office West. Montreal November 1848. True Copy.
Col ms 60 x 52 cm 1" to 40 chains
Shows the park lots only with areas cleared and names of owners; also a plan of the same title sgd 'Montreal 29th Nov 1848 J M Price Commissioner of Crown Lands' in OTNR (SR 6046).
OTNR (SR 178; 6046)

1563 *1854*
Plan of the Subdivision of Lots Nos 20 & 21 in the 6th Concession of Ops forming part of the town of Lindsay. [Certified by surveyor and sgd] John K. Roche Provincial Land Surveyor Port Hope 6 March 1854.
Col ms 45 x 74 cm 1" to 4 chains
Similar to R.P. 15P (**B1278**) in showing a subdivision from Lindsay to Verulam sts and from Melbourne St to above Queen St, but with added information indicating a grist and sawmill, bldgs on Kent St, and the route surveyed for the St Lawrence and Lake Huron Railroad; railway depot on R.P. not shown on this map.
OLI

1564 *1860*
PLAN / OF THE / TOWN OF LINDSAY / COUNTY OF VICTORIA / CANADA WEST. 1860. M. Deane P.L. Surveyor. Maclear & Co. Lith. Toronto.
Print (lith) 103 x 76 cm 1" to 5 chains
Views: 'Residence of J. Knowlson Esq.' and 'Keenan's Buildings, Kent Street'; shows the extent of the town as it had expanded to east, south, and north from Wellington St to beyond George St, and Angeline St east to Verulam St; all bldgs shown and these are mainly confined to the centre and river areas; some development along King and Queen sts east of river; Queen's Square is now Market Square; town hall and 'Lockup' also shown; Port Hope, Lindsay and Beaverton Railway property and lines; names of many owners.
OOAMA (NMC 43133) OTAR Victoria 57 (R.P. 10)

LITTLE CURRENT

1565 *1866*
Plan of Town Plot of Shaftesbury in the Township of Howland Manitoulin Island [Sgd] David C. O'Keeffe Provincial Land Surveyor Hamilton August 1866
Col ms 62 x 96 cm 1" to 4 chains Endorsements: 'S 34'
(SI 28 Aug 1865 to subdivide town plot; OTNR FN 1723 Sept 1866); shows the town laid out from Cockburn St to Water St and Hayward St to Russell St; marshy areas; cleared areas; a few bldgs and names of owners; later additions; also a copy: 'Town Plot of Shaftesbury Manitoulin Island Department of Crown Lands Ottawa 1867 Assistant Commissioner H. Lawe' (OTAR(P)); and a copy sgd '5th Feby 1867 A Russell Asst Commissioner' and with names of owners and later additions in OOAMA RG 10M 76703/9 no 213 (NMC 13052).
OOAMA (NMC 13052) OTAR(P) OTNR (SR 292)

LIVERPOOL

1566 *1853*
PLAN / of / BUILDING LOTS IN THE TOWN OF / LIVERPOOL / [Township of ?] PICKERING / 1853. F.F. Passmore D.P.S. Lithogd by Hugh Scobie.
Print (lith), pt missing 84 x 54 cm 1" to 4 chains
Shows the town from Stafford St to Grafton St, and Bath St to Hope St; Pickering harbour and wharf; coat of arms of Liverpool; notes on the advantages of town indicate that survey for GTR has been made; see also **B1297**.
Durham 40 (R.P. H-50057)

LOCKERBY

1567 *[1857?]*
PLAN / OF THE / TOWN OF LOCKERBY / IN THE / TOWNSHIP OF ELDERSLIE / in the / County of Bruce / GEO. JARDINE AND CO. PROPRIETORS. / Surveyed by Gilmour and Lynch Provincial Land Surveyors. / And Agents. // Maclear & Co Lith. Toronto. C.W.
Print (col lith) 90 x 61 cm 1" to 3 chains
Endorsements: 'In 10454'
Inset: 'Sketch / Shewing part of / COUNTY OF BRUCE.'; shows the layout of the town from Alexander St to the Queen's Rd, and from Bomarsund St east to beyond mill and John St; three mill reserves, grist and sawmill, mill race; lot nos and bldgs shown; inset map shows position of town on Elora Rd; a ms note about lot subdivision is sgd 'Francis H. Lynch P.L.S.'; possibly laid out in 1857 when the post office was established (*History of Elderslie Township*, 46, 64); Gilmour and Lynch advertised their partnership from 13 June 1856 to about March 1858 in the *Daily Colonist* (Toronto).
OTNR (SR 6045)

LONDON

1568 *[1793]*
Birds eye view of the Site of the Forks with a project for a town
Ms 10 x 15 cm Scale not given
Shows Simcoe's proposed site for London selected

in March 1793 west of the forks and south of the Thames R in the area first reserved for the town; the sketch shows a plan for long rows of bldgs without cross streets; bldgs are keyed as follows: 'Mrs Simcoe's intended villa,' square for Governor's house and intended bldgs, principal streets and rows of houses, public terraces, meadows, gardens; road from Niagara, bridge and road to Detroit; (*OHIM* 7.29).
OTAR (Simcoe Papers env 17 [1793])

1569 *[1793]*
The Site of London. Compiled field Notes of Mr. A. Jones by Lewis Grant D.P.S. Copy. [Initialled] W.C.
Col ms 37 x 53 cm 1" to 20 chains Watermark: 'J WHATMAN' Endorsements: 'X 6' '892'
A site plan showing the island formed by the ox-bow in the river: 'the greatest body of water runs through the new formed passage at the neck of the Island which seems formerly to have been a peninsula'; relief, old Indian cornfields, plains, notes on the depth and width of river, etc; mill seat located on northwest branch; possibly done under SI to Jones of 12 Nov 1792 or to Jones and Grant of 19 March 1793 regarding surveys of the Thames R; there are also two plans showing the proposed reserves for village, common, and glebe in D.W. Smith, 'Report upon Glebes & Commons ... 13th Jany 1802.'
OTAR (RG 1 A-II-1 vol 2 pp 942–87d) OTNR (SR 189)

1570 *1816*
London [showing site] Submitted for Glebe & Commons [and] Site for the City Copy [Sgd] T Ridout S Genl Surv Genls Office 2d March 1816
Ms 26 x 19 cm 1" to 80 chains
Accompanied a report on petitions for land with note that proposed site interferes with patented lots in broken front lots 25–33, Westminster Twp (OOA RG 1 L3 W 11 no 21 1817); a sketch showing the site for the city as a square centred on the forks and bisecting the ox-bow in the river; the reserve for glebe and commons blocks are in the area east of the site between the forks; (Holmden 1944; *OHIM* 7.30).
OOAMA (NMC 15582)

1571 *1826*
Town Plot in the Township of London, in the London District. Surveyed by Order from the Surveyor General's Office bearing date at York, the 22nd day of March 1826. by [Sgd] M. Burwell Dy Surveyor. Dy Surveyor's Office Port Talbot 29th June 1826.
Col ms 75 x 64 cm 1" to 3 chains Endorsements: 'A 41' '665'
(SI 22 March 1826 to survey and lay out lots in town plot of 1/2 acre each; OTNR FN 406 May 1826); shows the first survey for the town as laid out east of the forks, on a different site from 1816 (**1570**); the town extended from Thames St east to Clarence St and from South St to North St; relief, marshy areas, ox-bow, and open meadows shown; some lot nos given; streets not named; also an undated copy in OTAR(P): 'Town of London Copy from Mr. Burwell's Plan of Survey by J.G.C.' endorsed 'No 29' and with the later addition of Wellington St on the east and Furnival Terrace on the south and many other later additions including names, bldgs, and mill reserve (1833).
OTAR(P) OTNR (SR 188)

Related maps

(2) *1826*
Town Plott, in the Township of London in the London District. Copied from M. Burwell's Plan of Survey dated th June 1826. W.C. [Sgd] Thos Ridout Surveyr Genl Surveyor Generals Office York 12th October 1826
Col ms 76 x 66 cm 1" to 3 chains
Shows the same layout as above but street names pencilled in and shows names of people located by Thomas Talbot with dates in the 1830s and early 1840s.
OTAR (Talbot Maps bk D/15)

1572 *[ca 1830]*
Plan of Laying out the ground of Publick Square London
Ms 53 x 32 cm [1" to 24 ft]
Shows the plan for the square between King, Ridout, Dundas, and Thames sts; court-house, jail and jail yard, Mechanics' Institute; yard and seminary are shown surrounded by gardens and paths.
OLU

1573 *[1833]*
Plan of a Piece of Ground including and to accompany a Mill Site on the south side of the town of London in the London District, containing 28 acres. [Sgd] C. Rankin D.S.
Col ms 66 x 62 cm 1" to 2 chains Watermark: 'J WHATMAN, TURKEY MILLS ...' Endorsements: 'A 39' '664'
(SI 24 Nov 1832 to survey mill sites in London; OTNR FN 283 28 Jan 1833); shows the area from York St south to Grey St and from Richmond St to Thames St; all of the area along river is reserved for mill site; a natural canal used as mill race, site for mill house and bridge, and streams shown.
OTNR (SR 187)

1574 *[1836]*
Town of London
Col ms 58 x 58 cm 1" to 10 chains Endorsements: 'No 30' 'Peter Carroll'
(OTNR FN 504 18 March 1836); this may be Carroll's original plan for the 'new survey' of London in 1835–6; it shows the extension of the town particularly to the north to Huron St, to the east to Adelaide St, and two streets south to Trafalgar St; also shows the park lots on the west

side of the river to Wharncliffe Highway, churches, burial ground, and 'Smithfield,' as well as other later additions, names, notes, etc; a notice of sale for the 'Town and Park Lots lately surveyed' was issued on 21 Apr 1836 (OTAR RG 1 C-III-1 vol 2).
OTNR (SR 86581)

Related maps

(2) *1836 (1837)*
London. (Enlarged) [Sgd] J.G. Chewett S.G. Office May 30th 1837
Col ms 119 x 66 cm 1" to 5 chains Endorsements: 'A 116'
Shows the enlargement of the town from Peter Carroll's 'New Survey' of 1835–6; later additions to 1842 show school reserves (1836, 1842) and infantry and artillery barracks (reserve) (1839); also shows Blackfriar's Bridge and Westminster Bridge, mill pond, and other reserves; a few names; also a copy dated 14 and 19 June 1837 '[Sgd] J W Macaulay Survr Genl' of which the top part is missing (SR 190).
OTAR(P) OTNR (SR 190)

1575 *1839*
Sketch of the Position of London. U.C. Novr 1839. [Sgd] by Wm Eyre Majr 73d Regt.
Col ms Size not known 6" to 1 mile
View: 'Sketch of the Court House'; relief by grey wash; indications of wooded areas; shows town from Waterloo and Wellington sts to the river; all bldgs are marked and military bldgs, churches, and court-house keyed; bridges; roads on outskirts shown.
OLU

1576 *[1840?]*
London & Park Lots
Col ms 130 x 78 cm 1" to 5 chains Endorsements: 'A 107'
Inset: 'Park Lots adjoining the Town of London' 1" to 10 chains; the main map shows the area from Trafalgar St to Huron St and from the river to Adelaide St; reserves are shown and names have been added in the centre and north; the inset shows park lots west of Wharncliffe, north and south of Oxford St, and on both sides of Frances St with names added.
OTAR(P)

Related maps

(2) *1840*
Park Lots adjoining the Town of London Copy [Sgd] W. Hawkins S.G.O. 11 May 1840 [and] [Plan of London]
2 col mss mounted on 1 sheet 95 x 112 cm 1" to 10 chains Endorsements: '685'
The first plan shows the park lots as in plan above; the second plan shows London from Grey St north to Huron St, and from the river to Adelaide St; school reserves, market square, Episcopal church and land; reserved area between Mark Lane and Waterloo St 'under the Superintendance of Col Talbot' [later the military reserve]; only a few names in lots.
OTAR(P)

(3) *1844*
London Park Lots. Surveyor General's Office Kingston 8th January 1844 a true copy [Sgd] Thomas Parke Survr Genl
Col ms 53 x 58 cm 1" to 10 chains
Shows the park lots west of the river as well as lots east of the river to Talbot St, lot nos and sizes, notes on sales.
OTAR

1577 *[ca 1840]*
[London with the park lots]
Col ms 76 x 58 cm Scale not given
Shows the same street layout as the 1836 plan including the park lots west of the river; a detailed plan with many notes; shows military square and market square marked out by Sir George Arthur and 'New London Bridge' (1840); notes about squares for Agricultural Society and school reserve; 'streets opened and travelled upon constantly'; churches named, inns and taverns; notes about squatters on lots in 1837; other bldgs; (Bremner, 24).
OTAR

Related maps

(2) *[184?]*
Map of the Town of London
Col ms 76 x 51 cm Scale not given
This map is similar to map above but lacks the park lots and details of the 'old survey,' and incorporates some later additions to 1849; shows school reserves, Smithfield, burying ground, and agricultural reserves; other squares and reserves subdivided; shows London and Port Stanley Rd, London and Brantford Plank Rd, and Sarnia Rd; new bridge now called Wellington St Bridge.
OTAR

1578 *1840–1*
London Canada West Drawn by Wm. Robinson 1840 + 1841
Col ms 49 x 60 cm 1" to 13 chains
An attractive detailed plan showing the town from the river to Huron St and east to Adelaide St; reserves, glebe for St Paul's Church; park lots and roads shown south and west of the river; names of owners of large lots; military reserve and bldgs, school reserve; Smithfield; Episcopal church; improved land on the fringe is shown; lots are tinted various colours but no key given.
OLU

1579 *[1844?]*
Plan of the Town of London
Col ms 82 x 63 cm 1" to 10 chains Watermark: 'J WHATMAN TURKEY MILL 182[7?]'
Endorsements: stamps 'BW' '496'
Shows streets and lots including park lots west of the river; agricultural reserve and reserves for market and schools shown; Smithfield; Arthur St is pencilled in and glebe lot is shown subdivided; New London Bridge is pencilled in and the jail block is shown as subdivided (1844) (see **B1306**).
OOAMA

1580 *1846*
Plan of part of the Town of London in the London District Shewing the reservation for a millsite in front of lots no. 25 and 26 on York Bathurst & Horton Streets. Surveyed by ord[er of] the Hon. The Comr of Crown Lands dated Montreal 31st January 1846. By [Sgd] Peter Carroll P.L. Surveyor. Examined [Initialled] A.R.
Col ms 86 x 60 cm 1" to 2 chains Endorsements: 'A 149'
(OTNR FN 507 4 July 1846); shows the area from Simcoe St to King St and Thames St to Ridout St, Balkwill's mill site, and several other bldgs.
OTNR (SR 186)

1581 *1846*
PLAN / OF THE TOWN OF / LONDON / CW / Published by Thos Craig, London, / 1846. / Scobie & Balfour Toronto Lith
Print (lith) on tissue paper 58 x 40 cm 1" to 1/4 mile
Shows the streets with names, the river, and a few major bldgs.
OOA (MG 29 B1 vol 45 f 312)

1582 *1848*
Plan of Town Lots Laid out upon Glebe Lot Number 13 in Concession C in the Township of London for the Church Wardens of Saint Pauls Church as an addition to the Town of London June 1848 by [Sgd] Wm McClary P.L. Surveyor
Col ms 63 x 100 cm 1" to 2 chains
Shows the area from Adelaide St to Colborne St, and East Dundas St to Trafalgar St; a subdivision for which a registered plan has not been found; note about earlier surveys by Peter Carroll and certain adjustments to survey; boundary of land leased to Harper.
OLU

1583 *[1850–2]*
PLAN / of the town of / LONDON. / C.W. / Published by ROBERT REID, Bookseller / Dundas Street, London. // John P. Hall Lith. Buffalo
Print (lith) 112 x 62 cm 1" to 5 chains
Shows the town north and east of the river to Regent St and Adelaide St; major bldgs shown and named; large estates indicated with bldgs and landscaping; 'Jail Reserve Sold in small lots in 1846'; military reserve shown with bldgs; Court House Square shown with court-house, Mechanics' Institute, and grammar school; GWR line and depot; Hall is listed in business from 1850–2 (Peters, 203) and Reid was listed as a bookseller in London in 1850 (*The Canada Directory* (Montreal: John Lovell, 1851)); (Holmden 1937).
OOAMA (NMC 14275)

1584 *1853*
Plan / OF BUILDING LOTS / The Property of / COLONEL ASKIN / ON THE NORTH SIDE OF / OXFORD STREET / in the Town of / LONDON C.W. / Survey'd by / Messrs Leather & Robinson / August. 1853. / Hugh Scobie Lith Toronto.
Print (lith) 56 x 39 cm 1" to 2 chains
Shows the area from Oxford St to St James St, and from the river to the Port Sarnia Rd; inn, mills, and travelled way along river; relief; related to R.P. 65W (**B1340**).
OLU

1585 *1853*
Plan / of part of Lot No 6 East of the Wharncliff Highway, / in the Township of Westminster, / laid out as an addition to the Town of London, by Saml Peters, P.L. Surveyor./ For the Proprietors H.C.R. Becher, G. Macbeth, L. Ridout & J.G. Horne Esqrs / 1853. / Hugh Scobie, Lith.
Print (lith) 39 x 44 cm 1" to 2 chains
Shows the area from the river to Wharncliffe Rd with lots along Stanley, Becher, and Macbeth sts; relief, Westminster Bridge, and 'Proposed Suspension Bridge' shown; 'Auction on 1st July 1853 on the Ground'; related to R.P. 26 (**B1331**).
OTUTF

1586 *1853*
Plan of part of the Town of London shewing actual Quantity of Land taken from Glebe Lot No [1]3 Concession C by Mr Carroll's Survey of 1835–6. [Sgd] Saml Peters P.L. Surveyor London C.W. Jany 31st 1853
Col ms 72 x 51 cm 1" to 4 chains
Shows the area taken from the glebe along Colborne St between Trafalgar and Simcoe sts; also shows the area north to Dundas St, and from Wellington to Adelaide sts, and GWR; (Holmden 1949).
OOAMA (NMC 4866)

1587 *1854*
PLAN OF LANDS / Situated on Maitland Street, from Dundas to North and Duke Streets, in the Town of London. / THE PROPERTY OF L. LAWRASON, ESQ.,/ As Surveyed into Building Lots, by Messrs. LEATHER & ROBINSON; to be sold at the 'City Auction Mart' on MONDAY, 19th JUNE 1854, at Twelve O'clock, by EDWARD EMERY, Auctioneer. // Talbot & Siddons, printers, London.
Print (typeset) 30 x 36 cm 1" to approx 110 ft
Endorsed 'No 27 Lawrasons Survey City'; shows

lots for sale and also 'Lauriston,' the residence of L. Lawrason, Esq., and Lauriston Cottage, residence of W.L. Lawrason; also three sketches of other bldgs; related to R.P. 66E (**B1357**).
OLU

1588 *1854*
Plan / of part of Lot No. 7 / East of the Wortley Road / in the Township of / WESTMINSTER. / known as the Carfrae Farm / laid out into Building Lots / by Messrs Leather & Robinson / for / Thomas Craig Esqre / 1854 / SAML PETERS LITH.
Print (lith) 39 x 48 cm 1" to 2 chains Endorsements: 'No 26'
Shows the area from Bruce St to beyond the Thames R; names of landowners given and lot sizes, various bldgs; 'Sketch of Victoria Bridge as Contracted for and to be erected on or before 15th Septr 1854'; 'For Sale by Auction on Wednesday 10th May 1854 at Emery's Auction Mart Dundas Street'; possibly superseded by R.P. 92 1855 (**B1379**), which shows a later subdivision of the same lot for W. Winslow.
OL

1589 *1854*
Plan of Property in and near the / Town of London / as laid out in Building Lots by Saml Peters P.L.S. / for the Proprietors Messrs W & D. Glass. / 1854
Print (lith), trimmed along bottom 39 x approx 48 cm 1" to 2 chains
Shows the area from Dundas St to Simcoe St, and James St to sideline between lots 10 and 11; notes indicate that property beyond belongs to St Paul's Church and 'Front Lots recently sold at £5 per foot'; partly related to R.P. 23 (**B1330**).
OLU

1590 *1855*
MAP / OF THE / CITY / OF / LONDON / CANADA WEST. / Surveyed and Drawn by S. Peters, P.L.S. & C.E. / 1855 // PRINTED IN COLOR BY MOONEY & BUELL / BUFFALO.
Print (col lith) 141 x 94 cm 1" to 4 chains
View: 'COVENT GARDEN MARKET. / BUILT A.D. 1853–4 S. PETERS, Architect.'; a detailed plan of the city showing the area from Huron St to Hamilton Row and Trafalgar St, and from Adelaide St west to Wharncliffe Highway; all bldgs shown and many identified; names and estates of large landowners; many businesses identified; ward nos; photoreproduction in OOAMA (NMC 15046).
OLU

1591 *1855*
Plan of [the] SOUTH PART OF / LOT No 12 CONN. C / ADJOINING THE CORPORATION OF THE / CITY OF LONDON / as laid out into Building Lots by / Saml Peters and Chas L. Davies P.L.Ss / London July 1855. / S. PETERS LITH.
Print (lith) 47 x 38 cm 1" to 150 ft Endorsements: 'B 4'
Shows a subdivision from Hamilton Rd to Nightingale Ave, and from Adelaide St east to Marmora St; related to R.P. 110 (**B1390**).
OLU

1592 *1856*
MAP / OF THE CITY OF / LONDON / SURVEYED AND DRAWN / BY / SAML PETERS, P.L.S. / Published by / GEO. RAILTON / FOR THE LONDON DIRECTORY / 1856. // [Sgd in facsimile] Samuel Peters Lith / London C.W. March 1856
Print (lith) 38 x 27 cm 1" to 16 chains
Originally issued with *Railton's Directory for the City of London C.W. ... Also a Map of the City. 1856. 1857.* (London: Printed by Hunter & Culbert 1856), frontis (OTAR; *Bib Can* 3684, map missing); shows the city from Trafalgar to Huron sts and from the river east to Adelaide St; 39 major public bldgs and businesses keyed and located; seven wards shown; GWR, GTR, and Port Stanley Railway; government reserve, [military reserve], and 'Lake Horn' shown; (*OHIM* 7.38).
OLU OTAR

1593 *1856*
Ordnance Ground – London, C.W. William R. Best City Engineer London C.W. December 1856.
Col ms 101 x 67 cm 1" to 2 chains
Shows the ordnance land between Dundas and Piccadilly sts, and between Mark Lane and Waterloo St; shows hospital, officers' quarters, commissariat, drill ground, Roman Catholic church, English church, and grammar school ground; (Holmden 1941).
OOAMA (NMC 24501)

Related maps

(2) *1856*
Ordnance Ground in London C.W. William R. Best City Engineer London C.W. Decr 26th 1856
Col ms 94 x 61 cm 1" to 2 chains
Similar to map above except that a gore of land north of Bond St and between Mark Lane and Church St now indicated as 'land proposed to be purchased by the City for School purposes and drill ground proposed to be purchased by the City for a park'; (Holmden 1940).
OOAMA (NMC 24500)

1594 *1856*
PLAN / OF PART OF THE / Estate / OF / COLONEL ASKIN / Situated in the Township of Westminster / Close adjoining / TO THE / CITY OF LONDON / CANADA WEST / Shewing the Subdivisions into Building Lots / As Surveyed by / MESSRS LEATHER & ROBINSON / 1856. // Cloak, Practical Lithographer, Dundas St London, C.W.
Print (lith) 68 x 103 cm Scale not given
Shows the area from Westminster Bridge to Bruce St and from the city east of the Thames R to the

London and Port Stanley Rd; shows lot nos, large estates with names of owners, several bldgs; a few ms adds indicate lots sold and a school on lot 59, Section F.
OLU

1595 *1856*
PLAN / OF PROPERTY IN THE CITY OF / LONDON / PROPOSED TO BE SOLD BY / Dr. J.W. Kermott / 1856./ S. Peters P.L.S. & Lith.
Print (lith) 43 x 36 cm 1" to 40 ft Endorsements: 'No 16'
Shows the area southeast of St James and Maitland sts; lot nos and dimensions.
OLU

1596 *1856*
PLAN OF PROPERTY / IN THE CITY OF LONDON, / To be Sold by Auction, by Mr. G. Emery, on Thursday, June 5, 1856, / Under Order of the Court of Chancery for Upper Canada. / / Blackburn's City Steam Press, 63 Yonge Street, Toronto. / / In Chancery Re Healey
Print (typeset) 26 x 38 cm Approx 1" to 21 ft Endorsements: 'No 11'
The property is shown at York and Clarence sts.
OLU

1597 *1857*
Plans showing those Lots in the Township of London County of Middlesex which have been subdivided into Building and Park Lots, also the Name and Survey of each Proprietor with an accompanying reference to each Map containing the Number, Frontage, Depth and Acreage of each Lot or Subdivision. Compiled from Original Maps by W. Pigott Civil Engineer & Land Surveyor In Accordance with a resolution passed by the Municipal Council of the Township Feb: 1857
Col ms atlas of 19 maps and text on [64 pp] Ea page approx 66 x 48 cm 1" to 4 chains [exceptions noted]
Provenance: Middlesex 33 Registry Office; the atlas includes 'Plan of the Township of London 1857, W. Pigott Civil Engineer & L. Surveyor London C.W. March 1857.' (ms on linen, 98 x 70 cm, 1" to 40 chains); the atlas provides a detailed survey of subdivision in the twp but outside the city boundary, and includes survey grid, railways, roads, and names of owners; 18 of the 19 plans are arranged to cover various cons and lots in the twp and alternate with text that includes statistics on lot sizes and other details.
OLU

1598 *1859*
Map of the City Mills Homstead London C.W. 1859 Sam Peters P.L.S. London C.W.
Col ms on linen 48 x 45 cm 1" to 2 chains Endorsements: 'A 1'
Shows the area from Thames R and Queen St/Ridout St east, and from Grey St to Horton St; bldgs on mill reserve shown and original course of river; gives names of original owners of various blocks: J.K. Labatt, Wm Balkwill, R. Carfrae, T. Craig, S.H. Graydon.
OLU

1599 *1862*
Rough Sketch of Ground in vicinity of London C.W. [Sgd] H. Tovey Lieut R.E. del 11/12/62 E.W. Hewitt Capt R.E. 11/12/62
Col ms 97 x 96 cm 4" to 1 mile
Shows inhabited parts of city and main streets; gravel and con roads; cleared and forested land; relief by hachures and form lines, spot heights; 'sites which command London, therefore necessary to occupy'; there is also another map (NMC 17876) with the same title but no signatures and endorsed 'London Canada West Reconnaissance Map 1864 D 10 B↑O'; it shows the same information and is more finished than the other plan (Holmden 1938).
OOAMA (NMC 17875–6)

1600 *1863*
PLAN / OF THE / CITY OF LONDON / Shewing all the Public Buildings &c &c Published with / S.W. MURPHY's / Directory of London / FOR / 1863–4.
Print (lith) 57 x 38 cm Scale not given
Probably issued with S.W. Murphy, *City of London Directory for 1863–4 together with a Plan of the City* (London: C.W.T. Evans Printer 1863) (OLU, map missing); shows the town from the Thames R north to Huron St and from the river east to Adelaide St; major bldgs shown and identified; shows a few streets west of river from Blackfriar's St to Oxford St.
OLU

1601 *1864*
Plan of N.W. quarter of Lot No 11 and part of the N. half of Lot No. 12 in the First Concession of the Township of London as Surveyed by Samuel Peters P.L.S. for W. Carling Esqre & the Hon. J. Carling Novr 1864. Saml Peters P.L. Surveyor 14th Decr 1864.
Col ms 64 x 51 cm 1" to 3 chains Endorsements: 'B 1'
Provenance: Murphy & Moore Architects; shows the area east of Adelaide St and south of Oxford St; various lots are shown and names of owners given including property belonging to Noble English below Gt Market St.
OLU

1602 *1865*
London. C.W. drawn by [Sgd] H F Turner Lt R.E. [Sgd] Wm Emory Cap R.E. 14/12/65 DCRE
Col ms on tracing paper 19 x 32 cm 6" to 1 mile
Endorsements: 'Rel 1/950' '127/503' '48' '10'
Shows the town with streets named from area north of GWR to Piccadilly and east of river to

beyond Wellington St; military bldgs identified and also Royal Exchange, 'Tower of London,' prison, Crystal Palace Barracks.
OLU

1603 *1867*
London Canada P.O. Site Plan of Barracks [Sgd] F.C. Hassard Lt Colonel R Engrs Toronto 13 Decr 1867. Plan of London Copied. Position of Barracks corrected with reference by R.M. Armstrong Lt R.E. 23.10.67
Col ms on linen 67 x 46 cm 1" to 270 ft
Endorsements: '348–43'
Shows the area from Thames R to Waterloo St and from the GWR at York St to Mill St and Pall Mall; military and private bldgs of brick and wood shown; piped water supply, wells, drains, cess-pools, fire tanks, etc; index to all bldgs and functions; also shows 'portions of military reserve of which occupation is resumed.'
OOAMA (NMC 22473)

LURGAN

1604 *1855*
Plan of the Town of Alma in the Township of Huron County of Bruce Surveyed in 1855 by E.R. Jones P.S. Examined Nov 1855 T. Devine
Col ms 55 x 67 cm 1" to 4 chains
(SI 2 May 1855 to subdivide town plot of Alma into mill site and town lots; OTNR FN 880 16 Oct 1855); shows the town lots 18–22, Lake Range, twp of Huron, as laid out from Arthur to Lake sts and from North to St Arnaud sts; lot nos and sizes; Pine R and mill reserve shown with relief; also a copy: 'Alma Crown Lands Department Toronto 17th January 1856 [Sgd] Joseph Cauchon' endorsed 'No 109' and with names of patentees added and some later changes (OTAR(P)).
OTAR(P) OTNR (SR 6498)

1605 *1867*
Plan shewing improvements on Lots 18, 19, 20, 21 & 22, Lake Range, Tp. of Huron Previous to the Survey of the Village of Alma. Correct from Survey [Sgd] Latham B. Hamlin P.L.S. etc. Surveyed November 1867 J. Ross Jack Del.
Col ms 53 x 46 cm 1" to 4 chains
Cleared land and 'improvements' shown around the Pine R with some names of claimants of lots or parts of lots.
OTNR (SR 14)

(LURGAN town plot)

1606 *[1855?]*
VILLAGE OF LURGAN IN THE COUNTY OF BRUCE / CANADA WEST / FORMING PART OF LOTS 6,7 & 8 IN THE CONCESSION A OR LAKE RANGE OF THE TOWNSHIP OF HURON AND BEING THE PROPERTY OF / HENRY C. GAMBLE ESQR. / Molesworth & Weatherald C.E.'s / Provincial Land Surveyors. // Maclear & Co. Lith. Toronto
Print (col lith) 58 x 96 cm 1" to 4 chains
Inset: 'SKETCH / of part of the Counties of Bruce and Huron Shewing the position of / LURGAN.'; this town plot was laid out privately and considerably further south (shown at Point Clark on the inset) of Alma, which later changed its name to Lurgan; shows streets from Ontario St north to Huron St and from Park St to Lake and Mill sts; park lots located beyond; market reserve, mill reserve with location of mills, hotels; proposed harbour with projected breakwater; soundings; there is no registered plan and the town plot did not develop; probably made in 1855 or earlier as Alma is not shown on inset map.
OTAR

LYNDHURST

1607 *[186?]*
Map of Lyndhurst
Col ms on linen 66 x 76 cm Scale not given
Shows the area from mill reserve to Water St, and lower mill pond to Ford St and beyond, bridge to Lansdowne Station; carding mill, English church property, other churches, cemeteries, residence and grist and sawmill of 'John Roddick Dep. Reeve'; note about a natural ravine falling towards Mill L.
OOAMA

MADOC

1608 *1858*
Plan of the northern part of the village of Hastings laid out on the West half of lot No 2 and a part of the west half of No. 1 in the 6th Con. of the Township of Madoc County of Hastings Belonging to the Estate of the late Colin Russel Esq. Surveyed by Samuel M. Benson P.L. Surveyor December 1858. [J?]B.B.
Col ms 78 x 56 cm 1" to 2 chains
Shows the town from Front or Division St to north of Nelson and Park sts; Metcalfe St east to Wellington St; Presbyterian church, Wesleyan Methodist church, and Catholic church shown as well as town hall and mill site; 'Old Mill dam' and house and barn of Jos. Bateman also shown; related to R.P. 105 of 1864 (**B1460**), which may have confirmed this earlier survey.
OTAR

Related maps

(**2**) *1858*
Plan of the / NORTHERN PART OF THE VILLAGE OF / HASTINGS / THE PROPERTY OF THE ESTATE OF THE LATE COLIN RUSSEL, ESQR OF

MONTREAL. / LAID OUT IN THE WEST HALF OF LOT NO 2 AND A PART OF WEST HALF OF / NO. 1 IN THE 6TH CONCESSION OF THE TOWNSHIP OF MADOC. / Surveyed for MRS SARAH RUSSEL / OF MONTREAL. BY SAMUEL M. BENSON / P.L. SURVEYOR OF BELLEVILLE C.W. / December 1858. / W. Little Lith Montreal.
Print (lith) 61 x 52 cm 1" to 2 chains
Based on the ms plan above and shows the same information except that the 'Old Mill dam' and the Bateman house and barn have not been included.
OTAR

MAITLAND

1609 *[1862?]*
Plan of the village of Maitland
Ms 25 x 18 cm Scale not given
Shows the town laid out on lot 30, con I, twp of Augusta, from Mill St to Main St and St Lawrence R, and on both sides of Richmond St; names of owners or occupants in lots; plan accompanied deeds and legal documents dated 1862.
OTAR (RG 1 C-IV Augusta p 333)

(MALTA)

1610 *[1856]*
MALTA, TOWNSHIP AND COUNTY OF BRUCE. // Lith. & printed in Colors by Maclear & Co. Toronto C.W. [Sgd in ms] Dennis & Boulton Surveyors
Col print (lith) 61 x 91 cm 1" to 3 chains
Inset: 'SKETCH / Shewing the Situation of / MALTA AND ITS HARBOUR / As enlarged from original Plan of Bruce in the / possession of the Crown Land Department.' 1" to 20 chains; based on R.P. 1 of 1 Jan 1856 (**B1466**); shows town plot from Cayley to MacGregor St, and Lakeshore Rd to Franklin and Front sts, on lots 34–9, Front Range, twp of Bruce; a few mills, post office; wharf; notes on advantages of site for a harbour and route connections; although shown in co atlas (Belden, ... *Bruce* (1880)), a note indicates that the town, which adjoined Port Bruce, was abandoned after a major fire some years earlier.
OTMCL

MALTON

1611 *[1855]*
PLAN / OF THE / VILLAGE OF MALTON / IN THE / COUNTY OF PEEL / CANADA / Maclear & Co. Lith. Toronto. Dennis and Boulton Surveyors & Agents
Print (lith) 87 x 62 cm 1" to 1 1/2 chains
Shows the town laid out from Holderness St to Beverley St and from Cattrick St to plank road leading to L Huron; the GTR station grounds and land go diagonally through the town; a few streets are parallel to the line; some smaller streets run perpendicularly to it; lot nos; similar to R.P. Tor 4 of 5 Oct 1855 (**B1467**); a few bldgs are shown and identified at Brayshaw's Corners at the east end of town; notes on the advantages of the town; (Holmden 1961).
OOAMA (NMC 43140)

Later editions and states

(2) *[1856–7?]*
MALTON / Maclear & Co Lith Toronto
Print (col lith) 75 x 61 cm [1" to 100 ft]
Shows the same layout of streets, GTR line and grounds, and bldgs at Brayshaw's Corners as on map above; small drawings locate Church of England, Methodist church, and Baptist church; some lots marked in colour possibly still for sale; reserves for Mechanics' Institute, grammar school, and market block now marked in former town lots; station bldgs now shown.
OTAR (MU 3514/1)

MANOTICK

1612 *1863*
Copy Plan [No 18] of that part of the Village of Manotick Laid out by Richard Tighe the elder, John Tighe and Richard Tighe the younger Situated on the west bank of the Rideau River opposite Long Island on Lot number 2 in the Broken Front or Concession A of the Township of North Gower in the County of Carleton. ... Surveyed and drawn by Joseph M.D. Cromwell Provincial Land Surveyor January 1863
Col ms 61 x 94 cm 1" to 66 ft
Shows the town from Rideau R and Elizabeth St to Anne St, and Catherine St to Tighe St; a few names of owners; a copy of R.P. 18 (**B1476**) but possibly copied later than 1863.
OOAMA (NMC 26170)

MAPLE

1613 *1853*
PLAN / OF / RUPERT TOWN, / ADJOINING / THE / RICHMOND HILL / STATION / OF THE / ONTARIO, SIMCOE / AND / HURON RAILROAD / [Sgd in facsimile] J.O. Browne P.L.S. / Toronto Aug. 18th 1853 / Compton & Co. Buffalo
Print (lith) 88 x 60 cm 1" to approx 39 links
Shows the layout of a village on part of lot 21 of con 3 of Vaughan Twp on both sides of the railway; see also **B1477**.
Toronto 64 (R.P. 72)

1614 *[1853]*
Plan of the New Village of Maple. at the Richmond Hill Station of the O.S. and H.U. Railroad Township of Vaughan. Hugh Scobie Lith

Print (lith) 34 x 51 cm 1" to 200 ft
Shows lots along Richmond St east and west of the railway station; this plan was registered 17 Sept 1853 and shows the same information as R.P. 79 of 2 Oct 1853 (**B1479**); title and information from R.P. 73 which is a transcript (see **B1478**).
Original not located

MARKDALE

1615 *1866*
A diagram of the Mill Reserve as Surveyed in the Original Survey. Durham June 11th 1866
Col ms on linen 80 x 44 cm 1" to 4 chains
Inset: 'Diagram shewing the Plot of hilly land proposed to be purchased by D. McDonald of Priceville being that part edged Red containing 11 – acres.'; shows the Saugeen R with saw and grist mill, and streets from Mill St to Terry St; lots 54 and 1–5 also shown with names of owners.
OOAMA (NMC 43141)

MARMORA

1616 *1826–8*
Plan of the Marmora Iron Works in Upper Canada late the property of Chas Hayes Esqre 1826
Col ms 45 x 40 cm 1" to 2 chains
Inset: 'Plan and Elevation of the New Bridge constructed over the Crow River at the Marmora Iron Works Upper Canada 1828' 1" to 32 ft; shows all the bldgs associated with the ironworks and these are numbered but no key is given.
OTAR

MEAFORD

1617 *[1845]*
Plan for the survey of the Town Plot (of Meaford) at the mouth of the Big Head River in the Township of St Vincent
Col ms 34 x 55 cm Scale not given
The projection for the survey showing streets and lots; pinpricks for tracing; probably issued with SI 26 Apr 1845 described below; shows streets from Miller to Parker St and from Huron to Pearson St.
OTAR

Related maps

(2) *1845*
Plan of the Town Plot of Meaford. Surveyed by William Gibbard D.P.S. 1845. [Sgd] Wm Gibbard D.P.S. Septr 3rd 1845
Col ms 50 x 75 cm 1" to 4 chains Endorsements: 'A 139'
(SI 26 May 1845 to survey town plot at the mouth of Big Head R and establish north and south boundaries; OTNR FN 524 24 March 1846); shows the village laid out from Miller to Parker sts, and from Pearson to Huron sts; lot nos and sizes, bearings, and relief shown; shows Winthuysen Square, three reserves at mouth of river, and some water lots; later note about Rankin's southern boundary of the town plot per his report 9 Sept 1846; the south boundary cuts across part of Miller and Boucher sts; no bridges are shown; also a copy: 'Meaford Surveyed by William Gibbard P.L.S. 3rd September 1845 Crown Lands Department Montreal October 1845 [Sgd] Andrew Russell S & D' endorsed 'No 95' and with the additions of names and other later changes (OTAR(P)); and a copy: 'Meaford. Surveyed by Wm Gibbard P.L.S. 1845. Crown Lands Department Montreal 18th March 1846. A true copy [Initialled] A.R.' with a few later notes and names to 1851, but no bridges shown (OTAR); there is an advertisement for a government sale of some town lots in Meaford on 25 March 1847 (OTAR RG 1 C-III-1 vols 1–5).
OTAR OTAR(P) OTNR (SR 198)

1618 *[1856]*
Plan of part of the Town of Meaford shewing the Government Reserve. The above plan was made by P.L.S. Donovan under my directions and I find it to be accurate and to agree with my original Notes [Sgd] Wm Gibbard P.L.S.
Col ms 41 x 32 cm 1" to 4 chains
Originally with a land petition about the building of a public wharf (OOA RG 1 L3 S8 no 25 1856); shows the town south of the river and three streets only to the north; the government reserve extends along the shore of the bay and along part of the river; proposed wharf, a few bldgs and names; (Holmden 1964).
OOAMA (NMC 4085)

1619 *1859*
Plan of Town Plot of Meaford. [Sgd] Thomas Donovan Civil Engineer Provincial Surveyor. Meaford St. Vincent. February 26th 1859. [Examined] T. Devine
Col ms, pts missing 99 x 66 cm Approx 1" to 2 chains
Shows the town from the bay to Boucher St on the south and to Miller St on the west; similar to [1856] plan above (**1618**); shows several mills, bldgs, bridges, reserved areas, flooded land, and land belonging to J.T. Purdy; proposed harbour and pier are shown as well as water lot; there is also an undated, unsigned plan in OTAR endorsed 'Meaford Town' and showing high and low ground, two bridges, and location of 'Big Head's grave.'
OTAR OTNR (SR 6020)

1620 *1864*
PLAN / OF / TOWN LOTS ADJOINING / MEAFORD, / BEING THE SUBDIVISION OF LOT XV CON IV / TOWNSHIP OF / ST. VINCENT. / The Property of Cyrus R. Sing Esqr 1864 / / Thos

Donovan Civil Engineer / and Provincial Surveyor / Meaford Jany 15th 1864 // LITHOGRAPHED BY J ELLIS TORONTO
Print (lith) 100 x 60 cm Scale not given
Inset: 'SCROLL / Shewing part of the Township / OF / ST VINCENT.'; shows all of the town as originally laid out including Winthuysen Square; the subdivision lies east of St Vincent St and from Boucher St to Kildare St; all bldgs shown and many identified with names of owners; mill pond and mills; Indian camp; drawings of some bldgs and ships in the harbour; related to R.P. 77 (**B1500**); notes on the advantages of the town and terms of sale of lots.
OOAMA (NMC 43142) OTAR

MERRITTON

1621 *1855*
MAP / OF / WELLAND CITY / THE PROPERTY OF THE / WELLAND CANAL LOAN COMPANY. / 1855. / Lithographed by J.Ellis, Toronto.
Print (lith) 70 x 98 cm Scale not given
Inset: 'MAP OF THE NIAGARA DISTRICT'; also found with OOA RG 5 C1 no 1056 1856; shows the area from Grantham/Thorold twp line and Hamilton St north to Cherry St, and road allowance cons 8/9 and Division St east to Ann and Pine sts; the GWR depot and a few bldgs shown; reserve for church; the inset shows railways including proposed Southern Canada Railroad, locks 11–21 on the Welland Canal, twps, and mills; remarks on the advantages of the town for industry, shipping, etc; OOAMA (NMC 22875) endorsed 'Hon. Wm. H. Merritt' on back and with ms adds on the sale of land and water-power 20 May 1855 and notes added to 'Remarks' on the possibility of a new branch of the GWR being built from there north.
OOAMA (NMC 22875; 52345)

MILLBANK

1622 *1857*
MAP / of the Village of / MILLBANK, / TOWNSHIP OF / MORNINGTON, / COUNTY OF PERTH. / SURVEYD FOR THE PROPRIETORS MESSRS RUTHERFORD & SMITH. / 1857. / LITHOGRAPHED BY J. ELLIS, TORONTO
Print (lith) 59 x 84 cm 1" to 2 chains
Shows the village laid out from Wellington St to King St, and Stratford St to Mornington St; shows Smith's Creek and various mill ponds and mills including a proposed steam grist and sawmill; lot nos and a few other bldgs shown; (see also **B1516**).
OOAMA (NMC 43147) Perth 44 (R.P. 260)

(MILLEROCHES)

1623 *1830*
Sketch of the Rapids and part of the Village of Milleroches in the Eastern District and Township of Cornwall. By William Browne. D Survr 1830
Col ms 32 x 53 cm 1" to 30 yards
Originally accompanied a land petition (OOA RG 1 L3 R 16 no 58 1831); shows the rapids and island with a planned new road on the island; the settlement is shown on the mainland with various bldgs identified: grist mill, fulling mill, carding machine, store; horse-way for towing boats, dam; the area was flooded for the St Lawrence Seaway in the late 1950s; (Holmden 2097).
OOAMA (NMC 4186)

MINDEN

1624 *1860*
Plan of Town Plot Being Composed of Lot III Concession A Minden R.T. Burns P.L. Surveyor. 1860. Town Plot of Brunswick [in pencil]: 'Minden' Certified Correct [Sgd] Robert T. Burns Provincial Land Surveyor.
Col ms 52 x 80 cm 1" to 2 chains Endorsements: 'B No 2'
(SI 19 Oct 1860 to establish remaining boundary of town plot in Minden Twp and subdivide into lots; OTNR FN 983 30 Jan 1861); shows the village laid out from Bobcaygeon Rd to Queen's Line with lots on both sides of Newcastle and Prince sts; relief, wooded areas, cleared land, and a few bldgs by the Gull R and bridge; also a copy: 'Minden Haliburton County Copies from P.L.S. R.T. Burns' Plan. Department of Crown Lands Quebec Mar 9th 1864 [Sgd] Andrew Russell Asst Commissioner' endorsed 'M 22A' and with some names of owners added (OTAR(P)); and a copy: 'Agents Copy of Town Plot of Minden. Department of Crown Lands Quebec March 1864 [Sgd] Andrew Russell Assist Commissioner. Comp'd E.T.' with lot nos and streets only.
OTAR(P) OTNR (SR 107; 7032)

MITCHELL

1625 *1842*
Lots surveyed in the Town Plot of Mitchell June 18th 1842.
Col ms on tracing paper 42 x 38 cm 1" to 4 chains
Shows the town with three streets south of Huron Rd and five cross streets (unnamed); shows two large lots on both sides of Huron Rd at Thames R reserved for mills; planned mill race is surveyed north of town; a few lots along Huron Rd coloured green; map '230A' is a copy.
OTAR (Canada Co. Papers TRHT 230 and 230A)

1626 *[1843–4?]*
Plan / der Stadt / MITCHELL / in / Logan Township / Huron District / Canada West / Nord America
Print (lith) 25 x 42 cm Scale not given
Endorsements: 'No 2'
Shows the town as laid out above (**1625**) with lots numbered 1–142 but streets not named; a few bldgs along Huron Rd; survey posts and route of mill race shown; notes in German about the route from New York to Mitchell and to Goderich and Stratford.
OTAR (Canada Co. Papers TRHT 229)

1627 *1845*
Map of the Town of Mitchell Surveyed November 1845 by J.G. Kirk D.P. Survy
Col ms 80 x 60 cm 1" to 4 chains
Shows the extension of the survey of the town subdividing lots 14–17, con 2, twp of Logan, and lots 24–27, con 2, twp of Fullarton, with town lots added north of the Huron Rd and park lots added to the north and south; streets are laid out from Napier to Wellington, and Mitchell Rd to the 2nd con line, Logan; shows the mill pond and new mill dam and a few other bldgs; there is also a copy with the same title in OTAR (Canada Co. Maps pkg 6 no 142); also a similar map with the same title, on tissue paper, endorsed 'Recd with le[tter?] 13 Decr 1845 No 6' in OTAR (Canada Co. Papers TRHT no 226), which shows town lots numbered 1–499 and park lots numbered 1–41.
OTAR (Canada Co. Papers Atlas, TRHT 226, Maps pkg 6 no 142)

1628 *1853*
PLAN OF MITCHELL // Toronto, September 7, 1853. Lithographed by J. Ellis, 8 King St
Print (lith) 38 x 28 cm Scale not given
'"NOTICE" / This Sketch-Plan of the Village of Mitchell is merely made to afford intending purchasers a General View / of the locality of the Lots offered for disposal. It in no manner pretends to any precision; nor will the Canada Company consider themselves bound in any way by this Plan'; shows layout and lots as on the 1845 plan (**1627**).
OPM OTAR (Canada Co. Papers TRHT no 228)

1629 *1859*
Map of the Town of Mitchell Stratford October 1858 [Sgd] Joseph Kirk Prov. Land Surveyor Canada Companys Office Toronto Feby 16 1859 [Sgd] Fred Widder Commissioner
Col ms 95 x 64 cm 1" to 4 chains
Certified by registrar as copy of plan R.P. 339 (**B1552**); shows the same layout as on the 1845 plan with the addition of the Buffalo & Lake Huron Railroad line as of 2 May 1859.
OTAR (Canada Co. Maps pkg 6 no 143A)

1630 *1862*
Map of an extension of the Village of Mitchell Subdividing Lots 23, 28 and 29 in the 1st Concession of the Township of Fullarton into Park Lots Dated Mitchell 5th June 1862 [Sgd] Wm Rath P.L. Surveyor Canada Company's Office Toronto Octr 9 1862 [Sgd] J B Robinson Commissioner
Col ms 66 x 98 cm 1" to 4 chains
Certified by registrar as a copy of R.P. 341 (**B1554**); shows the town layout and the new park lots at the southeast and west of town numbered 53–93.
OTAR (Canada Co. Maps pkg 6 no 140)

MORAVIANTOWN

1631 *1793*
Grundriss von Fairfield in Ober Canada [and] Fairfield in Ober Canada August 1793
2 mss Size not known Scale not given
Shows the original village of Fairfield established by the Moravian missionaries in 1792 on the north side of the Thames R (pt lots 3–4, con VII, Zone Twp); both maps show two sets of lots separated by a width of ground and houses with names of settlers or functions; the second map also shows relief and marshy land, road to Detroit, and notes in German; described from photoreproductions in OOAMA (NMC 2138; 2139).
USPBMW

1632 *1814 (1830)*
Action fought in front of Moravian Town 1814
Col ms 19 x 29 cm Scale not given
Provenance: GBL Collection of Lt Col C. Hamilton Smith; endorsed on original cover: 'Lt-Col C.H. Smith 22nd July 1830.' and '(British under Maj. Gen Proctor; 41st Reg. a few Newfoundland Fencibles and Artillery 550. Indians under Tecumseh 1100. 1650. American under General Harrison about 5000 best troops.)'; shows British and American troop positions at the Battle of the Thames, Oct 1813; relief, forested and cleared land; road from Detroit to Burlington; shows the town with houses; probably drawn from memory in 1830.
GBL (Add Mss 23,618 f 50)

1633 *1814*
A Plan of Moravian Town on the River Thames in Upper Canada inhabited by Hostile Indians of the Delaware tribe containing Sixty or Seventy Houses – which we burnt
Ms 27 x 20 cm Scale not given
In 'Journal of Capt Robert B. McAfee, 19 May 1813–21 May 1814'; shows the main street of the village with lots, houses, and a few fields; church, gardens, cornfields, and pastures identified; shows the cabin in which McAfee lodged 5–7 Oct 1813 before the village was burnt; after the war the village was rebuilt on the south shore of the Thames and named New Fairfield (*Ontario Historic Sites* (1978)); (*OHIM* 2.10).
USKyLoF

MORRISBURG

1634 *[ca 1840]*
[Morrisburg]
2 mss 53 x 38 cm and 73 x 57 cm Scales not given
Provenance: OTAR received from St Lawrence Development Commission; the first plan shows Union, Lock, Church, Maple, and Ellen sts north and south of the Queen's Highway; names in most lots; lots 1–37 north of Queen's Highway also shown; the second plan shows most of the same area but at a larger scale and with lot nos and dimensions; since the Rapide Plat Canal (built 1844) is not shown, these plans probably were made in the late 1830s or early 1840s.
OTAR

MOUNT FOREST

1635 *1853*
Plan Exhibiting a proposed subdivision of the Town Plot of Mount Forest in the Townships of Arthur Egremont & Normanby Francis Kerr P.L.S. Guelph August 1853
Col ms 57 x 84 cm 1" to 5 chains
(SI 24 June 1853 to survey outlines and project subdivision into town lots, mill site, park lots, etc); shows the river, town boundary and other surveyed lines, and layout for streets; two positions given for the Garafraxa Rd, one from Rankin's plan and one from McDonald's plan (**1040**); two bldgs and a spring are shown.
OTAR

Related maps

(2) *1853*
Plan of the Town Plot of Mount Forest. Francis Kerr P.L.S. Guelph November 1853. Examined 6th March 1854 [Initialled] T.D.
Col ms 68 x 101 cm 1" to 4 chains Endorsements: 'A 186'
(SI 6 Sept 1853 to complete survey and lay out square, markets, school, churches, etc; OTNR FN 288 2 Dec 1853); shows the village from Sligo Rd to McDonald St beyond the Saugeen R, and from Cork and Perth sts to London Rd; shows market square, mill lots, lot nos and sizes, a few areas cleared with names of settlers and a few bldgs; public cemetery; also a copy: 'Mount Forest Office Copy Crown Lands Department Quebec 25 March 1854 [Sgd] A.N. Morin Commr Crown Lands' endorsed 'No 94' and with the addition of names of patentees (OTAR(P)).
OTAR(P) OTNR (SR 204)

1636 *1855*
PLAN / of a Portion of / MOUNT FOREST / In The / Township of Arthur // The Property of Messrs Allan & Geddes Elora. // Surveyed by / E.H. Kertland Civil Engineer & P.L.S. / 1st DECEMBER, 1855.
Print (lith) 58 x 98 cm 1" to 2 chains
Shows a subdivision on the south edge of the town from Bentley St to Wellington St; shows mill pond, Maitland R [Saugeen R], sawmill, flouring mill, mill race and dam, chair factory, cloth-factory site, and distillery site; a ms note: 'Property of Allan McAllan Esqr Toronto ... 24th February 1857' refers to a change in ownership when the plan was filed in the registry office; see also **B1600**.
Wellington 60 (R.P. 16(1))

MUSKOKA FALLS

1637 *1864*
Plan of Muskokaville Township of Draper 1864. Lindsay 2nd May 1864 [Sgd] W.H. Deane Prov. Land Surveyor.
Col ms 55 x 84 cm 1" to 4 chains Endorsements: 'No 24'
(SI 13 July 1863 and 20 Aug 1863 to subdivide town plot into town and park lots; OTNR FN 1520 2 May 1864); shows the town from Joseph St to George St and from First St to Twelfth St; relief is shown in detail including Upper Falls, Middle Falls, and Grand Falls; bridge along Muskoka Rd; cleared areas, marshy land; post office, churches, tavern, graveyards, town hall and market sites; the town plot site had been reserved in 1847–8 by Bell while surveying a line from the Bathurst District (see **598** and Murray, 147).
OTNR (SR 199)

NAPANEE

1638 *1834*
Diagram of a town plot in the East Half of Lot Number XX In the Seventh Concession of Fredericksburg, in the Midland District. Surveyed September 1834. F.P. Rubidge Cobourg
Ms 64 x 89 cm 1" to 2 chains Endorsements: 'A 20' '625'
Inset: [town plot at a larger scale]; 'This Plot is named Clarkville by order of His Excellency Sir Francis B. Head 12th June 1837 [Initialled] J.W.M.'; (SI 1 July 1834 to lay out the town; OTNR FN 309 8 Oct 1834); shows the layout of this village south of the Napanee R and east of the town of Napanee, roads, houses, and a few names of owners; shows area from Front St to Rear St, and Main St to West St; the inset shows the street names and lot nos and the nature of the land.
OTNR (SR 54)

Related maps

(2) *1844*
Office Copy. Clarkville with the Park Lots by F.P. Rubidge Surveyor General's Office Montreal 5th October 1844 A true copy
Ms 69 x 33 cm 1" to 2 chains Endorsements: 'No 68'

Inset: [park lots on part of lots 20 and 21] 1" to 10 chains; shows the same layout as above; inset shows park lots south of Rear St and bisected by the road to Kingston; also a copy in OTAR: '[Clarkville ca 1850]' 1" to 10 chains, mounted on board with **1640** of ca 1855; and another copy in OTAR: 'Clairville. Crown Land Office Toronto 24th April 1856 [Sgd] Joseph Cauchon Commissr of Crown Lands [Initialled] J.W.B.' 1" to 2 chains, with inset: [location map] 1" to 10 chains; this OTAR copy also shows roads in the area, bldgs in Napanee proper, and mills, dams, and bridges on the Napanee R; and another copy in OTAR: 'Clarkville. Crown Lands Office Toronto 10th July 1856 [Sgd] E.P. Taché Acting for Commisr of Crown Lands. [Initialled] J.W.B.' 1" to 10 chains, showing only part of area from lot 19 to 22.
OTAR OTAR(P)

1639 *1854*
PLAN / OF THE VILLAGE OF / UPPER NAPANEE. Drawn by G.S. Clapp P.L.S. / June 1854 / LITHOGRAPHED BY J. ELLIS KING ST / TORONTO.
Print (lith), pt trimmed Approx 31 x 39 cm 1" to 2 chains
Shows the area west of the original town of Napanee, from the river north to Dundas St and from Hessford St to Union St; this plan was not registered.
Lennox 29 (R.P. 29)

1640 *[ca 1855]*
Plan of the Village of Clarksville
Col ms 46 x 28 cm 1" to 3 chains
Shows a subdivision on the west half of lot 20, con 7 of Fredericksburg Twp as laid out for John Clark by John Ryder and related to R.P. 12 registered in 1850 (**B1605**); the streets are not named; since it also shows the east boundary of the incorporated village of Napanee (1855), the plan was probably made in 1855 or later; mounted on board with **1638(2)** above; (*Places in Ontario* III:14).
OTAR

1641 *[1859?]*
Cartwrightville
Col ms 69 x 42 cm 1" to 3 chains
Shows a subdivision laid out along Camden Rd at the east end of Napanee and north of river, with town lots between Front and Church sts and park lots beyond; there is no registered plan for Cartwrightville but it is shown on R.P. 82, which was prepared for R.J. Cartwright (**B1606**); not shown on the co map of 1860 (**555**); a few names of owners.
OTAR

1642 *1859*
PLAN / OF / NAPANEE / COMPILED BY / A.B. Perry P.L. Surveyor / 1859. / Lith. Spectator Office Hamilton C.W.
Print (lith) 68 x 103 cm 1" to 3 chains
Views: [railway bridge over river], 'Corner Dundas & Centre Streets,' and 'Napanee Mills'; shows the town from Napanee R to Graham St and from Hessford St in Upper Napanee east to include Cartwrightville east of GTR line and depot; shows various bldgs along river including mills, factories, churches, market, school lot, etc; probably based on compiled plan R.P. 82 (**B1606**); there is also a ms copy of this plan in OOAMA (NMC 11396) without the views and printing statement, endorsed 'Dept. of Public Works Canada' and '176 – D2'; (Holmden 1977).
ONLAH

1643 *1864*
Sketch showing with a Red Colour Lots situate in the Town of Napanee belonging to the estate of the late Wm Aitken Esqre M.D. 1864
Col ms 38 x 56 cm Scale not given
Shows the area from Robert St to Centre St, and Water St to Bridge St; note: 'To be sold at auction on Monday Septr 5th 1864'; notes about the sales of various lots from 1864–8; Campbell House is shown and there are notes about the building of other houses in the vicinity.
ONLAH

1644 *1867*
Part of Clarkville ... Violet Jany 1867 [Sgd] A.B. Perry P.L. Surveyor
Col ms 50 x 26 cm 1" to 1 chain
Shows the dwelling and other bldgs of the late Daniel Roblin on lots 80, 81, 84–5 north of the road to Kingston on the west half of lot 20, con 7, Fredericksburg Twp.
OTAR

NELSON

1645 *1855*
PLAN / Of that part of / HANNAHSVILLE, / in the Township of Nelson, / laid out into lots / By / J.D. PRINGLE, ESQ'R. / Thos Allen Blyth, Esq. P.L.S. / Hamilton Febry. 26th 1855. // Lith. Spectator Office, Hamilton
Print (lith) 40 x 54 cm 1" to 50 ft
Shows lots on Dundas and James sts east of plank rd; various bldgs shown and identified including stores, blacksmith shop, school, post office, tavern, town hall, houses, barns, and 'Mr Hopkins family vault'; see also **B1614**.
Halton 20 (R.P. 48)

(NEW ABERDEEN)

1646 *1856*
MAP / of the Village of / NEW ABERDEEN / AND PART OF TOWNSHIP LOTS 10, 11, 12 AND 13 OF / BEIHN'S TRACT / IN THE / TOWNSHIP

AND COUNTY OF WATERLOO C.W. / AS LAID OUT FOR THE PROPRIETOR / George Davidson Esq. / BY / SCHOFIELD & HOBSON P.L.SS / Berlin June 1856. / Maclear & Co. Lith. Toronto.
Print (lith) hand col 72 x 85 cm 1" to 3 chains
Shows a town plot west of Strasburg, with named streets, lot nos, some bldgs including flour and sawmills, and two mill ponds; a few names of owners; shown on the co map (**1094**) and the co atlas (Parsell, ... *Waterloo* (1881)); (see also **B1616**).
OKIT Waterloo N 58 (R.P. 640)

NEWBURGH

1647 *1835*
A Plan of the Village of Newburgh On Lot No 16 First Con. of Camden Surveyed by [Sgd] Wm J. Fairfield Dpty Surveyor Aprl 1835
Col ms 52 x 39 cm Approx 1" to approx 2 chains
Originally accompanied a land petition about a land dispute in the village (OOA RG 1 L3 G18 no 188 1835); shows a mill yard, saw and grist mills on the Napanee R; names of owners; (Holmden 1984).
OOAMA (NMC 4206)

NEWBURY

1648 *1855*
Plan of part of the village of Newbury at the Wardsville Station of the Gt W. Railway being Lot No 16 in the 2nd Conn of the Township of Mosa The Property of the Canada Company Novr 1855 [Sgd] Saml Peters P.L.S. London C.W. Novr 10th 1855
Col ms 74 x 55 cm 1" to 3 chains
Shows five north-south and five east-west unnamed streets east of Omara to Durham sts; the GWR bisects the southern part and town lots are shown here and on the west.
OTAR (Canada Co. Maps pkg 14 no 174)

NEWCASTLE

1649 *[1857–8]*
PLAN / OF THE TOWN OF / NEWCASTLE, / IN THE TOWNSHIP OF CLARKE. / THE PROPERTY OF THE HON. GEO. S. BOULTON. / Compiled from the Plans of the late John Huston Dept. Surveyor by J.K. Roche P.L. Surveyor / BARR & CORSS, ENGRAVERS & LITHOGRAPHERS 46 1/2 YONGE STREET, TORONTO.
Print (lith) 48 x 147 cm 1" to 3 chains
Shows the whole town from L Ontario to Monro St, and between Mill Pond and North St and Arthur St on the east; shows reserve for courthouse, lot nos and a few names of owners; the plan was made during the period 1857–8 when Barr and Corss were in partnership (Hulse, 15).
OTUTF

(NEWCASTLE town plot)

1650 *1797*
Projection for the Town of Newcastle in Acre Lots S.G.O. 13th Septemr 1797 [Sgd] D W Smith A.S.G. [Sgd] Approved Peter Russell [Endorsed title]: His Honor the President Plan of Newcastle approved 13 Septr 1797
Col ms 27 x 37 cm Scale not given
Shows the plan for a town on the north side of the Presqu'ile Peninsula in three long rows with reserves at various points; from the harbour and Water St to 2nd, 3rd, and Glebe sts and from Grave St east to West Passage, East Passage, and the street at east end; reserves for church, prison, school, market, hospital, parson, glebe, burying ground, and common; A. Aitken had been instructed to choose and reserve the site in SI of 26 Sept 1795.
OTMCL (D.W. Smith Papers B-9 p 202)

Related maps

(2) *1797*
Plan of Newcastle in the Home District Surveyed in November 1797 by Alexr Aitken Dpy Syr
Ms 53 x 75 cm 1" to 4 chains Endorsements: 'No 33'
(SI 14 Sept 1797 to survey the town using Water St as a base with the front of the town occupying about 3/4 mile); the town was substantially as shown in the projection; the reserves are shown between lots throughout the rectangular town; further reserves for government are shown on the main peninsula and a reserve for a quay to the west; three lighthouses were added to the map later; and a copy: 'Plan of Newcastle In the Home District, each Lot one Square acre. Surveyed in November 1797 by Alexr Aitken Depy Surv. Copy W.C.' endorsed 'A 45' and '667' and lacking the later additions (OTNR (SR 220)).
OTNR (SR 220–1)

(3) *[183?]*
Town of Newcastle
Ms 45 x 68 cm Scale not given Watermark: '... WHATMAN ...' Endorsements: 'A 47' '666'
Shows an enlarged plan for the town but with the same layout and reserves; a few names added in lots, one dated 1832; possibly a copy made for or by C. Rankin when surveying Presqu'ile in 1832 (SI 29 Dec 1831); the town was never settled (see **350**) and was no longer shown on the 1848 district map (see **346**, **385**) and later maps.
OTNR (SR 219)

NEW HAMBURG

1651 *1854*
PLAN / of the Village of / HAMBURGH / TOWNSHIP OF WILMOT / AND / COUNTY OF WATERLOO, C.W. / as surveyed for / Geo. Davidson Esqr / BY / M.C. Schofield, P.L.S. /

Maclear & Co. Lith. / Toronto. / 1854
Print (lith) 53 x 67 cm 1" to 4 chains
Shows the village from Bleams Rd to James St, and Nith R to Victoria St; all bldgs shown (most are along Peel and Wilmot sts) and many are identified; index to businesses and public bldgs on various lots; drawing of a church; GTR and station; lot nos; related to R.P. 532A (**B1638**); photoreproduction in OKIT.
Private Collection

1652 *1856*
PLAN / of Building Lots in the / TOWN OF HAMBURG / County of Waterloo / The Property of D.G. MACDONALD, ESQR / Surveyed by / BRISTOW & FITZGERALD / Provincial Land Surveyors &c. / Brampton September 15th 1856. // Maclear & Co Lith Toronto C.W.
Print (col lith) 74 x 96 cm 1" to 60 ft
Inset: 'SKETCH / OF THE / TOWN OF HAMBURG / Shewing the Position of the Property / D.G. MACDONALD ESQR'; shows the area from Elizabeth St to Bleams Rd, and Nith R to Main St; some bldgs shown; inset shows all streets and bldgs in town; see also **B1639**.
Waterloo N 58 (R.P. 532B)

NEWMARKET

1653 *1853*
PLAN / OF / W.A. CLARK'S PROPERTY / IN THE TOWN OF / NEW MARKET / LAID OUT FOR THE PROPRIETOR / into Building Lots / by / Wm Gibbard P.L.S. / October 1853. / Hugh Scobie Lith: Toronto. // Wm Gibbard P.L.S. October 1853.
Print (lith) 66 x 55 cm 1" to 300 ft
Shows the area from Huron St south to Cotters Mill Pond and from Church St to Cedar St; all bldgs are shown on streets already laid out; 'OS & H Railroad'; major bldgs identified; names of owners of large lots; related to R.P. 103 (**B1646**).
OTUTF

1654 *[ca 1855]*
Town of Newmarket Compiled from Plans in the Registry Office
Col ms on linen 67 x 79 cm 1" to 4 chains
Shows the town with streets and the subdivisions of Gibbard (Geo. Lount), Passmore (W.A. Clark), Dennis & Henry; the plan was probably compiled after the Dennis survey of June 1855; shows the town boundary.
OTAR

1655 *1860*
Plan of building lots in the village of Newmarket the property of the Hon' Henry J. Boulton [Sgd] Dennis & Gossage P.L. Surveyors August 1860
Col ms 38 x 74 cm 1" to 2 chains
Shows lots on part of lot 93, con I, Whitchurch Twp, on Eagle St, and Boulton St west of Main St; lots sold are indicated; Episcopal church and mill pond also shown; later note about indenture of 1 Jan 1865 between H.J. Boulton, Eliza Boulton, and John Dennis; photoreproduction in OTAR.
Private Collection

1656 *1862*
PLAN / OF THE VILLAGE OF / NEWMARKET / SHEWING PRESENT SUBDIVISIONS. / COMPILED BY / S.W. HALLEN, P.L.S. / 1862. / JOHN ELLIS, LITHOGRAPHER ETC. 8, KING ST. WEST TORONTO.
Print (lith) 72 x 98 cm 1" to 3 chains
Shows the town from Elm St north to Huron St and from Niagara St to Cedar St; Northern Railroad; shows six subdivision surveys to date; all bldgs shown and many identified; some names of owners.
OOAMA (NMC 43148) OTAR

(NEW OSWEGATCHIE)

1657 *[178?]*
Plan of the Town Plot in the 7th Township Redrawn by Dunn Grant, Town Clk
Ms 32 x 42 cm Scale not given Endorsements: 'No 133'
(OTNR FN 380 25 June 1784); note on plan indicating that it was delivered to the Surveyor General by Samuel Sherwood, M.P., on 8 July 1801; shows the town plot on lots 14, 15, and part 16 of the front of Augusta Twp with the church commons in the centre, lots 1–155 on the west, and 1–167 on the east; the town was laid out by June 1784 by Capt Justus Sherwood (FN 380 (25.6.1784)); and the field notes were also signed by Duncan Grant Town Clerk (OTAR RG1 CB-1 Box 43 FN 375); the town reserve is shown on twp plans of 1795 and later with the name New Oswegatchie; later notes added to the 1840s; the town was listed in D.W. Smith, *A Short Topographical Description of ... Upper Canada* (1799); this plan was probably made in the 1780s when Augusta was still known as the 7th twp; there is also a plan for reserves in the town plot of 'Augusta' in D.W. Smith's 'Report ... 1802' (OTAR RG1-A-II-1 vol 2, pp 942–77); (Otto, *Maitland*, 1).
OTAR (RG 1 A-II-1 vol 2, pp 942–87) OTNR (SR 6070)

Related maps

(**2**) *1804 (1843)*
Copy of the Town Plot of Augusta (Copy) Surveyor Genls Office 1st Augt 1804 for the Surveyor Genl Signed Chewett & Ridout
Col ms 43 x 54 cm Scale not given Endorsements: 'P226/43'
Originally accompanied a land petition (OOA RG 1 L3 B 3 no 113 1843); shows the same layout as (1) but later additions indicate that most of the lots belong to Judge Sherwood, the Rev Robert Blakey,

belong to Judge Sherwood, the Rev Robert Blakey, and the government; in the petition Blakey wishes to purchase all the undisposed lots; the original map of 1804 has not been found.
OOAMA (NMC 4077)

(3) *[180?]*
Town Plot of Augusta
Ms 30 x 34 cm Scale not given
Shows the streets and lots numbered 1–167 as in earlier plans; shows church commons and burying ground and the church, which was built in 1809.
OTAR

(4) *1844*
Town Plot of Augusta Surveyor General's Office Kingston March 29th 1844 Enlarged from a Plan by Dunn Grant Town Clk
Col ms 66 x 86 cm Scale not given Endorsements: 'No 67'
Shows the town plot bounded on the south by the St Lawrence R and on the north by 4th St and lots 1–167; east and west streets unnamed; much of the west part is noted as granted to Rev Robert Blakey 28 Aug 1832; church common in centre shown but not church probably because it burned in 1840 and the 'blue' church was not erected until 1845; the village was never really settled and is known today as Blue Church.
OTAR(P)

NIAGARA FALLS

1658 *1819*
Plan of the Government reservation on the Niagara River, with the Island adjacent, from the Honourable Thomas Clark's grant to the brink of the Falls ... Stamford, Niagara District 3d November 1819 [Sgd] John Burch Land Surveyor
Col ms 59 x 50 cm 1" to 2 chains Endorsements: 'No 29' '887'
Shows the site that eventually became part of Niagara Falls and land belonging to John Hardy, Samuel Street, Timothy Skinner, and Francis Ellsworth; also road from Messrs Clark and Street's mills, Portage Rd, houses and other bldgs, and lot boundaries; later notes.
OTAR (SR 81006)

1659 *1831*
Plan Shewing the Military Reserve at the Falls of Niagara Surveyed by command of His Excellency Sir John Colborne K.C.B. Lieutenant Governor &c &c &c [Sgd] J.G. Chewett Surveyor York 8th October 1831
Col ms 71 x 125 cm 1" to 5 chains Endorsements: '841'
Shows the military reserve along the bank and lots granted to Philip Bender, James Forsyth, and Francis Ellsworth; shows roads and proposed road for visiting the falls, museum, Forsyth's Inn, Ontario House, Wright's stairs at Table Rock, and ferry; description of land grants and later notes to 1852; an attractive, detailed plan; relief by shading; also a copy with the same title and further sgd '(Copy) 20th April 1836 J.G.C. Surveyor Generals Office J. Radenhurst Toronto 20th April 18[36] Certified to be a true Copy [T.G.W. Eaststaff?]'; this copy is similar to the earlier plan except Forsyth's Inn is now marked 'Pavilion'; (Holmden 2085).
OOAMA (NMC 11404) OTAR (SR 6745)

1660 *1834*
Plan of the Military Reserve at the Falls of Niagara Surveyed Septr 1834 by Messrs Burwell Keating & Hawkins. Drawn by William Hawkins D.P.S. [Sgd] William Hawkins D.P.S.
Col ms 61 x 92 cm 1" to 10 chains Endorsements: '868'
Four sections shown at vertical scales of 1" to 1 chain; relief by shading and hachures; the sections are shown to the edge of the cliff and from above to below the falls; bldgs shown at Chippewa and Niagara rds and the 'Sworn Line' or Concession Rd, along Lundy [Lane], and in lots 146, 143 [Drummondville]; Ontario House, Pavilion Hotel, assembly rooms, museum, and hydraulic works located; roads and survey grid; also a copy in OOAMA (NMC 22535) with the same title further sgd '(Copy) J.G. Chewett Surveyor Genl Office 20 April 1836 (Signed) J. Radenhurst (Certified as a true Copy) [Sgd] T.G.W. Eaststaff Draugn,' endorsed 'B↑O,' with some variations and showing less on the south end (Holmden 2084); and another copy in OOAMA (NMC 4217): 'Copy of a Copy of a plan obtained from the Crown Land Office by Rt Pilkington draftsman' endorsed 'REO'; and later copy in OTNR (SR 5586): 'Plan shewing the Military Reservation at the Falls of Niagara' endorsed '866' with a note indicating 'That part of the Reserve along the top of the bank of the Niagara River in front of Lots 145 up to 191 surrendered by the Board of Ordnance 1st October 1852.'
OOAMA (NMC 4217; 22535) OTAR (SR 5586; 6748)

1661 *1838*
MAP / OF / NIAGARA FALLS / AND VICINITY // Published by J. Sutherland, 12, Calton Street, Edinburgh.
Print (lith) 30 x 18 cm Scale not given
In *The Stranger's Guide through the United States and Canada* (Edinburgh: John Sutherland 1838) (OTLS); the map is redrawn from the Parsons/Burke map (see **759**) and shows Clifton and City of the Falls on the Upper Canada side and Village of Niagara Falls with bldgs and streets on the American side; hotels; tourist sights.
OTLS

Related maps

(2) ***1838***
MAP / of / NIAGARA RIVER / and Parts Adjacent // Published by J. Sutherland, 12 Calton Street,

Print (lith) 30 x 19 cm Scale not given
From the same source as map above; a close copy of the Parsons/Burke map (see **759**).
OTLS

1662 *1838*
Sketch of Drummondville Shewing in red the Houses etc. hired for the Accommodation of Troops. Sd W.H. Roberts Lieut R.E. Royal Engineer Office Toronto U.C. Copied Rd Birley Tem. Clk. 22nd Augt 1838 Compared and ready for Transmission 1st Sept 1838 H Ry. Copy forwarded with return dated 1 Sept. 1838
Col ms 37 x 48 cm 1" to 100 yds Watermark: 'J COLES 1836' Endorsements: 'No 428'; stamp 'REO'
Shows the village with all the houses and names of many owners; number of men and horses that can be accommodated and other notes.
OOAMA (NMC 3790)

1663 *1841*
Environs of Niagara Falls showing Crown Reserve and claim of James Windeat 1841
Ms 53 x 43 cm Scale not given
Originally with a petition for a licence of occupation (OOA RG 1 L3 W 1 no 63 1841); shows the falls and the bldgs on top of the bluff including that of James Windeat; (Holmden 2034).
OOAMA (NMC 4218)

1664 *1854*
Map / of the / VILLAGES / of / BELLEVUE, NIAGARA FALLS / AND / ELGIN / T.D. JUDAH, CIVIL ENGINEER. / 1854 / Lith. of Compton & Gibson, 161 Main St Buffalo. // Entered according to Act of Congress AD 1854 by Theodore D. Judah in the Clerks office of the District Court of the Northern Dist of New York
Print (lith) 76 x 105 cm 1" to 400 ft
'SECTION of STRATA along the NIAGARA RIVER from LAKE ONTARIO to LAKE ERIE'; 'SECTION OF FALLS ABREAST'; 'Two Views from Vista Cottage Bellevue The Property of T.D. Judah'; shows the falls and relief along shores, the city of Elgin from Welland St to Morrison St, and Stamford and Pelham sts to the river; shows City of the Falls; Zimmerman estate and Clifton House; railways, some bldgs identified.
USDLC

1665 *[1854–5?]*
Map of the / VILLAGES / of / NIAGARA FALLS, & NIAGARA CITY. / NEW YORK / THE VILLAGE OF / ELGIN, AND THE CITY OF THE FALLS / CANADA WEST. / 185 / J.H. Bufford's Lith. Boston
Print (lith) 35 x 52 cm 1" to 800 ft
The plan is very similar to the 1854 plan and possibly a reduction from it but does not show lots in Elgin or Bellevue; this appears to be a proof state as the date is uncompleted.
OOAMA (NMC 4219)

1666 *1855*
DRUMMOND HILL, / LAID OUT ON PART OF LOTS Nos. 131 & 142 IN THE TOWNSHIP OF STAMFORD, / The residence of the late Major Leonard, as an addition to the / TOWN OF DRUMMONDVILLE. / by Jas W. Fell P.L.S. for the Proprietors Sepr / 1855. [Sgd in facsimile] Chippawa Sept. 4th 1855. James W. Fell Prov. Land Surveyor
Print (lith) 55 x 74 cm 1" to 2 chains
Shows the area west of Drummondville with lot nos and sizes; in ms: 'To be sold by Auction October the 9th 1855'; shows the same layout as R.P. 2 (**B1661**) with lot no 142 corrected to 125.
Niagara S 59 (no R.P. number)

1667 *1857*
CORPORATIONS / OF / NIAGARA FALLS / AND / NIAGARA CITY, N.Y. / & CLIFTON, C.W. / From actual Surveys by FRANK FRENCH & E. C. SMITH, Civil Engineers. / Published by J.H. FRENCH, 8 S. Syracuse St. / SYRACUSE, N.Y. / 1857. // Entered according to Act of Congress in the year 1857 by J.H. French in the Clerk's Office of the District court of the Northern District of N. York. // Lith. of Friend & Aub, 332 Old No 80) Walnut St. Phila.
Print (lith) 145 x 129 cm 1" to 300 ft
On the Canadian side shows all streets, houses, and other bldgs, with lot nos, names of owners; relief by hachures, etc, wooded areas; five of the 29 views show the Canadian side; notes on the town of Clifton; shows the Zimmerman estate; part was reproduced in *Niagara Falls, a history*, 404.
GBO ONF OSTCB

NIAGARA-ON-THE-LAKE

1668 *[ca 1790?]*
Plan of Part of Lake Ontario & of the River Niagara with some Tracts laid down opposite the Fort. Surveyed [blank] by [blank]
Col ms 51 x 73 cm 1" to 20 chains Watermark: 'J WHATMAN' Endorsed: 'No 22' '1005'
A sketch map showing boundaries of Mississauga Point and Fort, ground behind Navy Hall for works of 400 square yds [site of Fort George] surrounded by a reserve of 800 yds, Rangers' barracks, and Fort Niagara; 'Division Line between the Settlements and the Land reserved for Public Bldgs' to the south of the town; about the same date as **1669** and before work commenced on Fort George in 1796.
OTAR (SR 214)

1669 *1790*
[Endorsed title]: 'Sketch of Lower Part of Niagara River 1790'
Col ms 90 x 110 cm 1" to 200 ft Watermark: 'J WHATMAN' Endorsed: stamps 'B↑O' 'IGF'
Shows Fort Niagara on the American side with bldgs and relief, Navy Hall, Rangers' barracks,

Mississauga Point with plan of fortifications, boundary of reservation, and reserve for a fort to the south [Fort George] with note 'ground within 800 yards of the Fort to be reserved for Government'; roads and several bldgs shown along shore; marsh; latitudes for Niagara and Fort Erie given with date '1790'; (Holmden 2008).
OOAMA (NMC 17879)

1670 *[1792?]*
Rough Sketch of the Town of Newark
Col ms 37 x 38 cm Scale not given Endorsements: 'A 46' 'No 4'
(SI of 14 Feb 1791 and 22 Feb 1791 to Augustus Jones to mark out the town plot of Lenox); name changed to Newark in 1792 by Lt Gov Simcoe; the plan shows 412 lots of the first survey with a list of names on the back for 37 lots; various squares of four lots each reserved; no streets are shown or named.
OTNR (SR 225)

1671 *1794*
Survey of the Town of Newark in the Township of Newark, County of Lincoln Province of Upper Canada ... The outlines of this Town, Adjoining the Reservation west of Navy Hall, made thus by directions of the Land Board on the 24th of June 1791 – a Boundary having been fixed betwixt this Town (then called Lincoln) with works reserved for Government, by the Engineer and the Deputy Surveyor ... Surveyor Genls Office Newark 5th Sepr 1794 [Sgd] W. Chewett. Examined 6 Decr 1794 D.W. Smith Actg Sur Genl
Col ms 75 x 104 cm 1" to 200 ft Endorsements: 'A 42' '898'
(OTNR FN 548 A. Iredell 4 Sept 1794?); notes indicate that this survey allows for 1/7 allotment of land for reserves east of Lt Col Butler's land, unlike the previous survey above (**1670**); shows the 412 park lots and 64 town lots; streets not named, reserves for church, parsonage, school, workhouse, market, gaol and court-house, hospitals, etc; Mississauga Point noted as reserved for works south to King St.
OTNR (SR 6478)

Related maps

(2) *[1798?]*
Town of Newark now Niagara Copy W.C.
Col ms, pt missing 75 x 104 cm 1" to 200 ft Endorsements: 'No 34' 'Plan no 86'
Shows the town laid out from Anne St to Queen St and from King St west to water; cross streets are not named; the town lots are between Queen and Front sts west of King St; shows the same layout as the other plan with the later addition of names; the town's name changed to Niagara in 1798.
OTAR(P)

(3) *[1855?]*
Town of Niagara. Copied by J. Innes
Col ms 69 x 98 cm 1" to 200 ft Watermark: 'J WHATMAN 1855'
This is a copy of the 1794 plan showing the same streets and area reserved for works by Mississauga Point; nature of shoreline, location of river flowing through town shown in detail.
OTNR (SR 6418)

1672 *1796*
1796 Plan of the Entrance of Niagara River shewing the Positions for the Buildings, to be erected on the West Shore of the River at Navy Hall, and on the high Ground behind it –
Col ms 62 x 87 cm 1" to 200 ft Endorsements: 'D'
In Lord Dorchester's no 87 to the Duke of Portland of 16 Apr 1796 (GBLpro CO 42/105 f 169); shows the plans for Fort George and proposed storehouse for commissary general, proposed ordnance store and quarters for troops, and proposed powder magazine, all ordered to be erected; also shows situations for batteries and kitchens; relief, marshy land, boundary of military reserve, and other bldgs; (*PRO Cat* 1503); copy in OOAMA (NMC 23039); also a plan in GBLpro (MPG 41) with the same title as MPG 37 above, endorsed '23L'; MPG 41 is from the same source and similar to MPG 37 except officers' kitchens also ordered to be erected and more detail shown for Niagara Fort on the other side of river; there is also a transcript of a similar plan sgd 'Quebec 25th Jany 1796 Gother Mann Lt Coll Command. Rl Engr' in OTMCL but exact original has not been identified.
GBLpro (MPG 37; 41) OTMCL

1673 *[1796?]*
Plan of the Ground on the West Side The Entrance of Niagara River Exhibiting the Reservations for Military Purposes.
Col ms 73 x 128 cm 1" to 200 ft Endorsements: 'Left by Coll. Pilkington on his going to Gibraltar 1818'; stamp 'B↑O'
Shows the boundary of the military reserve with description; [Fort George] is shown with bldgs planned or as being built in 1796; relief; further endorsement on back [partly illegible]: stamp 'IGF' and 'West side of Entrance Niagara River between lakes Erie & Ontario 1793'; the base map may have been an earlier plan with additions made to 1796 or later; dated from (2) below; (Holmden 2074).
OOAMA (NMC 11397)

Related maps

(2) *1796*
From a 'Plan of the Ground on the West Side the Entrance of the Niagara River exhibiting the Reservations for Military Purposes' by Robt Pilkington Lt Royal Engrs in Sepr 1796 No 5 [Endorsed title]: 'Military Reservn of Missassaga Point'
Col ms 44 x 52 cm 1" to 62 yds Endorsements: '888'
Shows the town near the Mississauga reserve boundary north of Fort George, and Queen,

Prideaux, and King sts; another OTAR copy (SR 81021) has the same title but is unfinished and shows only a group of houses; it is endorsed 'No 1' and '958'; another OTAR copy (SR 81020) has the same title and shows only 'His Honor [Peter Russell] the Administrator's House 750 Yards from the Block-House'; it is endorsed 'No 8' and '867.'
OTAR (SR 81018) OTNR (SR 81020–1)

1674 *1798*
Plan of the House and premises of the Honble D.W. Smith. Newark Upper Canada. December 1798 [Sgd] Robert Pilkington Capt Royal Engineers
Col ms 41 x 53 cm 1" to 30 ft
Originally with 'Proceedings of a Board of Survey ... 11 Dec 1798 ... to estimate the value of the house and premises of the Honorable DW Smith' about the possibility of purchasing the bldg and land for a school; enclosed 'In Mr Prest Russell's No 55 of 12 February 1799' (GBLpro CO 42/324 p 80); shows lots 65, 66, 103, and 104 between Johnson St and Gage St at King St; shows the stable barn, root house, pond, pump, well, and landscaping as well as the house; another plan in same source shows plan and elevation of the house.
GBLpro (MPG 1169(1–2))

1675 *1799*
Plan of Fort George Upper Canada shewing the Works of Defence ordered to be constructed in 1799.
Col ms 94 x 89 cm 1" to 200 ft Watermark: 'J WHATMAN 1794' Endorsements: 'FF7'; stamp 'IGF'
A reference keys military bldgs including blockhouse, magazine, hospital and kitchen, officers' quarters, guardhouse, storehouses, and wharf; also shows perimeter of Fort George, Navy Hall, bldgs for the Indian Dept, Fort Niagara, and reservation at Mississauga Point; relief by grey wash, roads, and other bldgs in area; (Holmden 2014); also a copy in OOAMA (NMC 16811) with the same title and date, watermark: 'J WHATMAN 1794' and endorsements: 'P 1 D20 P No 542 D C,' 'CREOC,' 'No 88.'
OOAMA (NMC 16811; 17880)

Related maps

(2) *1799*
Plan of Fort George Upper Canada shewing the Works of Defence order'd to be constructed in 1799 [Sgd] Gother Mann Coll Commandg Rl Engrs Engineers Drawg Room Quebec, Wm Hall Lt Rl Ay J.B. Duberger
Col ms 92 x 90 cm 1" to 200 ft Watermark: 'J WHATMAN 1794'
Insets: 'Section through the Picketing forming the curtains' 1" to 4 ft, 'Section through the Batteries of the Fort' 1" to 8 ft, 1" to 18 ft vertical; a more attractive presentation copy showing the same information as (1) above but with the addition of the sections; OOAMA has a photoreproduction (NMC 43149).
GBL (Maps 23.b.3(14))

1676 *[ca 1800]*
[Town plan of Niagara with names]
Col ms, pt missing 60 x 70 cm Approx 1" to 200 ft
Endorsements: 'No 20'
Shows the streets and some bldgs and names of original grantees; from Anne St to Front St but side streets not named; probably drawn by Wm Chewett; 'D.W.S.' noted beside many names; some later additions including note dated Aug 1851 regarding grants of D.W. Smith; there is also a plan showing reserves for Niagara in D.W. Smith's 'Report upon Glebes & Commons ... 13th Jany 1802' (OTAR RG 1 A-II-1 vol 2 p 942).
OTNR (SR 218)

1677 *1802*
Plan shewing the situation & dimensions proposed for Building Lots for Merchants and Traders on the King's reserved Land near Fort George in the Province of Upper Canada. Submitted by [Sgd] Gother Mann Coll Commandg Rl Engrs Quebec 10th Novr 1802
Col ms 43 x 93 cm 1" to 200 ft Watermark: 'T STA[INS] 1797'
Originally accompanied a letter from Col Mann to Lt Gen Hunter of 20 Nov 1802 (OOA RG 8 I/272 p 80); shows 18 lots for merchants on low land by the river between Navy Hall and Mississauga reserve; 'Site of Fort George,' other bldgs, and roads shown; relief by grey wash; there is also another copy in OOAMA (NMC 19553); (Holmden 2064, 2063).
OOAMA (NMC 19552–3)

1678 *1810*
No V Upper Canada Plan of Niagara by A. Gray Asst Qr Mr Genl Quebec 20th Novr 1810 This Plan is from a Trigonometrical Survey by Lieut: Gray [Sgd] Q.M. Genls Office Quebec 1st June 1811 James Kempt Q M Genl N.America
Col ms 85 x 131 cm 1" to 100 yds Watermark: 'J WHATMAN 1801'
An attractive, large-scale plan of the town of Niagara, Fort George, Fort Niagara, and the surrounding area; shows all bldgs in town and in forts, some named including churches, courthouse, prison, Indian Council House; trees are shown and relief, roads, and rivers; pin holes for tracing at corners of bldgs and along roads.
OOAMA (NMC 19551)

1679 *1816*
Plan of a Fort proposed to be erected at Mississauga Point. [Sgd] John Smyth Lieut Royl Engrs Feby 19th 1816 [Sgd] Quebec 8th April 1816 G. Nicolls Lt Col. Comg Rl Engineers in the Canada's
Col ms 79 x 118 cm 1" to 200 ft Endorsements: stamps 'IGF' 'B↑O'

'Section through ABCD' 1" to 20 ft; shows the star-shaped plan for Fort Mississauga with 14 bldgs keyed, the streets of the 'Town of Newark wantonly burned by the Americans in 1813,' Fort George as it was before the war and as altered by the Americans, the state of Fort Niagara in Feb 1815, lots for merchants as laid out in 1802, and shops and yard established during the war; (Holmden 2071).
OOAMA (NMC 17884)

Related maps

(2) *1816*
Plan of a Fort proposed to be erected at Mississaugue Pt by [Sgd] Lt Col Nicolls Cg Rl Engineers Quebec – Royl Engineers Drawg Room J.B. Duberger Junr 1816 Cadet &c &c
Col ms 75 x 114 cm 1" to 200 ft
Includes the section and the same information as the plan above except for the addition of a memorandum: 'The Site of the Fort as shown in this Plan is different from that marked on the ground in the Autumn of 1815 it having been placed further back from the Lake & the Tower brought into the center of the Flat Bastion.'
OOAMA (NMC 17882)

(3) *1816*
Plan of a Fort proposed to be erected at Mississauga Point [Sgd] Quebec 8th April 1816 G. Nicolls Lt Coln Comg Rl Engineers in Canada
Col ms 81 x 120 cm 1" to 200 ft
Originally accompanied dispatch (GBLpro CO 42/166); very similar to the plans above; 'The Soundings and Bar of Niagara are copied from a Plan surveyed & drawn by Mr Chillingworth master of H.M.S. St. Lawrence 1815'; photo-reproduction in OOAMA (NMC 15019); (*PRO Cat* 1509; *OHIM* 2.6).
GBLpro (MR 127)

1680 *1817*
Plan of Forts George, Mississaga and Niagara, the Military Reserves, and the Town of Newark. by H.H. Willsons Lieut Royl Engrs 2nd May 1817 (signed) Henry Vavasour Capn Comg Royal Engr Niagara Frontier. Royal Engineers Office Quebec Novr 19 – 1818
Col ms 83 x 107 cm 1" to 100 yds Endorsements: 'No 6'; stamps 'B↑O' 'IGF'
A detailed map showing the forts, ruins of Fort George, the American lines and other military bldgs, relief, treed areas and clearings, Indian Council House; shows all the streets and bldgs in town, various proposed fortifications for Fort Mississauga, and reserve boundaries as proposed by Col Nicolls and Col Durnford; (Holmden 2073).
OOAMA (NMC 16999)

1681 *1817*
Town of Niagara. Copy / York U.C. May 3rd 1817 Copied from a Plan in the Surveyor Genls Office Sigd Geo. Phillpotts Lt R.E.
Col ms 22 x 22 cm 1" to 800 ft
Accompanying a letter from Henry Vavasour to Lt Col E.W. Durnford of 2 June 1819 concerning the selling of lots 65, 66, and 203–4 originally owned by D.W. Smith (OOA RG 8 I/405 p 159); also shows streets, lot nos, and reserve for works at Mississauga Point; (Holmden 2020).
OOAMA (NMC 19556)

1682 *[1819]*
Fort George showing location for tan yard [Sgd] H Vavasour Captn Ryl Engineers [5th Jan 1819]
Ms 15 x 30 cm 1" to 100 yds
Enclosed in H. Vavasour to Maj Bowles of 5 Jan 1819 regarding request of Mr Grier for land to erect a tan-yard OOA RG 8 I/273 p 168); shows a rough sketch of the area, and Fort George, church, Navy Hall, roads, hills, and several possible sites for the tan-yard; (Holmden 1664).
OOAMA (NMC 70953)

1683 *1819*
The Military Reserve at Fort George. [Sgd] Niagara March 24th 1819 Arthur Walpole Lieut R Engrs Henry Vavasour Capn Comg Rl Engineers [illegible]
Col ms 41 x 87 cm 1" to 300 ft
Accompanying letters from Col Durnford and Lt Col Bruyeres about encroachments on the military reserve (OOA RG 8 I/403 p 140); shows the military establishment from Fort Mississauga to Fort George with relief, cleared areas, roads and paths, Butler's barracks, Indian Council House, inns, Navy Hall; bldgs by the shore including Engineers' establishment; shows Fort George as rebuilt and part to the south in ruins; shows encroachments near both forts; (Holmden 2076).
OOAMA (NMC 22531)

1684 *1823*
Plan of Town Lots Laid out upon the Plains between Fort George & Niagara. Which it is proposed to exchange for lands required in the vicinity of the projected fort on Mississaga Point [Sgd] Henry Vavasour Capn Royl Engineers February 1st 1823
Col ms 53 x 61 cm 1" to 200 ft Endorsements: 'No 7' '955'
Shows the town, streets, and many bldgs; shows the new streets to the northeast from Castlereagh St to Ricardo St, and King St to Lieven St, with 46 new lots; many notes on lots to be exchanged, reserved, sold, etc, and those leased from government; there is also a copy in OTNR (SR 217) initialled 'J.G.C.' and endorsed 'No 57' and '954,' which includes more notes; also an unfinished sketch copy in OTNR (SR 212) entitled 'A copy from Capt. Vavasour Royl Engineers Plan of Part of Niagara' and endorsed 'No 9' and '851,' showing only outlines of streets and relief.
OTNR (SR 216–7; 212)

1685 *1823*
[Town of Niagara] Copied from a Plan of Niagara by Claudius Shaw D.P.S. Niagara May 9th 1823
Ms 45 x 57 cm 1" to 6 chains
A rough sketch showing the town with streets, a few named, 412 lots, forts, rivers, heights of land; 'Crooks Estate'; related to and probably copied from R.P. 10 Co of the same date (**B1669**).
OTMCL

1686 *1824*
[Sketch of part of the town of Niagara] With a memorial for permission to establish a Brewery near Navy Hall 1824
Col ms 16 x 31 cm 1" to 100 yds
Accompanying a memorial from Francis Hall, John Kidd, and Dr Walter Telfer of 13 Dec 1824 to Sir P. Maitland requesting land to erect a steam mill, brewery, distillery, and other works (OOA RG 8 I/517 p 74); shows a site near Navy Hall and the wharf, also the proposed line of a canal, roads, and other bldgs in vicinity; (Holmden 2026).
OOAMA (NMC 70995)

1687 *[1829]*
Plan of part of the military reserve adjoining the Town of Niagara shewing the manner in which it has been laid out in Lots and the part desired by the Roman Catholic Congregation. G.H.
Col ms 32 x 41 cm 1" to 200 ft
Originally accompanied letter of J.R. Wright, commanding Royal engineer, of 6 Sept 1829 about the congregation's request for land (GBLpro WO 44/29 f 572); the block wanted by the Roman Catholic Church is between Davy and Wellington, Byron, and Picton sts; also shows lots exchanged by James Crooks for land near the military reserve, and two lots east of King St by the shore reserved for military; shows Fort George, Navy Hall, and trails cutting across the new town grid; (*PRO Cat* 1499).
GBLpro (MPHH 47(12))

1688 *1829*
Plan of part of the Town of Niagara shewing the Lots in the vicinity of the Market Place belonging to Government [Sgd] George Phillpotts Capt Royal Engrs R.E. Office Ft George 23rd Decr 1829
Col ms 36 x 24 cm Scale not given Watermark: 'WEATHERLEY & CO. 1820'
Accompanied a petition for lots for a market square for the town of Niagara (OOA RG 1 L3 B 2 no 92 1842); shows the area from Gage St to Prideaux St and from King St east four streets; notes about the ownership of lots 65, 66, 103, and 104 originally granted to D.W. Smith and purchased for site of government house; (Holmden 2028); also a map in OOAMA (NMC 4169): 'Sketch showing part of the Town of Niagara Copy [Initialled] J.G.C. 11th March 1839' accompanying the same petition and showing lots applied for on John St and Queen St at King St, 'granted for the market lots.'
OOAMA (NMC 4169, 19555)

1689 *1831*
Plan Shewing the Survey of the Military Reserve at Niagara. 17th Augt 1831 [Sgd] J.G. Chewett
Col ms 65 x99 cm 1" to 3 chains
Shows the town including new streets laid out around Fort George, although only in effect to Alava St, with another block added below Castlereagh St; also shows a new layout of park lots and streets oriented to the shore below Fort George; shows the bldgs in the forts and land exchanged with Crooks near Fort Mississauga; (Holmden 2081).
OOAMA (NMC 22532)

1690 *1833*
[Plan of Niagara with the military reserves] Royal Engineers Office Quebec 20th April 1833 [Sgd] Gusts Nicolls Colonel Comg Rl Engineers Canada
Col ms 43 x 79 cm Scale not given
Originally accompanied correspondence on the Niagara Dock and Harbour Co. (GBLpro WO 44/29 f 521); shows streets and bldgs near Fort George and along the shore; boundary of the military reserves, and areas released for public or private use; Niagara Dock Co. land, hospital and military bldgs shown and note 'occupied by a detachment of the 66th Regt'; photoreproduction in OOAMA (NMC 22539); (*PRO Cat* 1498).
GBLpro (MPHH 47(11))

1691 *1833*
Plan of the Town and Reserve at Niagara Surveyed 1832 By J.G. Chewett Surveyor & Draftsman Surveyor General's Office Surveyor General's Office York U.C. 31st January 1833 [Sgd] S.P. Hurd S.G.
Col ms 64 x 99 cm 1" to 4.5 chains Endorsements: '889'
Shows the whole town with streets named, military reserves and forts, proposed reserve for hospital and barracks; relief shown along shoreline; names of some owners; notes about later copying of plan.
OTNR (SR 6388)

1692 *1833*
Sketch shewing the extent of the Ground given to the Niagara Harbour & Dock Company by an Act of Parliament of Upper Canada passed 16th March 1831. [Sgd] Royal Engineers Office York U.C. 5th Oct 1833 R.H. Bonnycastle Capt Rl Engr Western District
Col ms Approx 30 x 60 cm 1" to 300 ft
In Colborne to Goderich 4 March 1833 about government land at the east end that should not be included in the act (GBLpro CO 42/414 p 124); 'Compared with that Sketch dated Comg Royl Engs Office Quebec Sept 5th 1832 I.G.H.E.' (note

refers to a sketch not found); shows the area along the shore below Front and Ricardo sts with the boundary by the act and proposed boundaries of company land; 'the red border refers to the former Sketch'; shows marshy land that the company is excavating; names of owners or lessees.
GBLpro (CO 42/414 p 124)

Related maps

(2) *[1833]*
Sketch shewing the Ground given to the Niagara Harbour & Dock Company by an Act of Parliament of Upper Canada, passed 16th March 1831
Col ms 22 x 40 cm Approx 1" to 4.5 chains
Endorsements: 'This map belongs to J.A. Clark Niagara C.W.'
Shows the same information as plan above; the plan appears to have been based partly on **1691** as a note indicates that the scales are the same.
ONHI

1693 *1835*
Sketch of the Military Reserve at Niagara Shewing the mode in which it is proposed to let the Ordnance premises now occupied by the establishment. (signed) Guss. Nicolls Colonel Commandg Royal Engineer Canada Royal Engineers Office Quebec 14th Decr 1835 T.G.W. Eaststaff Draugn
Col ms 44 x 110 cm 1" to 300 ft
Endorsed 'No 1 To accompany the Report of the Commanding Royal Engineer to His Excellency the Lieut. Governor of Upper Canada on the subject of the Military Reserves dated 18th July 1836' (GBLpro CO 42/431 p 19); shows the town and all reserves, Mississauga reserve, and J. Crook's former lots; Niagara Harbour and Dock Co. land and land granted to English and Catholic churches; shows land to be leased south of Fort George (noted as laid out by Lt Pilkington in 1796); (*PRO Cat* 1500); there is also a copy in OOAMA (NMC 14283) with the same title, showing the same information, and sgd 'R.H. Bonnycastle Capn Royal Engineer's Westn District. ... [Sgd] T.G.W. Eaststaff Draugn'; there is also a 'Plan of the military reserve and town of Niagara in 1834 sgd R.H. Bonnycastle Capt R.E. 5 Aug 1834 ... 1835' originally from GBLpro WO 44/28 f 86–7).
GBLpro (MPG 762(1) MPH 1084 (1–2)) OOAMA (NMC 14283)

1694 *1837*
Plan of a portion of the Town of Niagara Shewing the Lots adjoining Mississaugua Reserve which have been built upon, also the Lots which have been granted, but not built upon. Royal Engineer Office Toronto 11th Nov. 1837 (Sd) Geo: Stoughton Clerk of Works (Signed) F.H. Baddeley Captn Royal Engineers Western Distt. ... (Copy) Jno Sloane Clerk of Works Kingston 17th Novr 1837 [Sgd] R.H. Bonnycastle Capt & Major Comg Royl Engrs U.C. forwarded with letter of same date to Commanding Royal Engineer Canada
Col ms 45 x 58 cm Scale not given Endorsements: 'No 23 Case V' 'No 382'; stamp 'REO'
Shows the area from John St and King St to the water and the Mississauga reserve; lots are keyed: those built on, number of houses, lots enclosed but not built on, and reserves.
OOAMA (NMC 4211)

1695 *[184?]*
[Plan of the town of Niagara by Charles Hall, surveyor]
Ms, pt missing 33 x 26 cm Scale not given
Watermark: 'W TANNER 1838'
Provenance: ONHI George Ball Papers; shows the streets named and the lot nos in the town; note indicates plan is copied from an earlier plan of 1826 that has not survived; names of owners shown.
ONHI

1696 *[1840]*
Niagara: Plan of part of the Military Reserve.
Col ms 46 x 57 cm 1" to 300 ft
Endorsed on back: '1840'; shows the part of town along the river with encroachments on military lands and grants to various people; lands granted to Niagara Dock Co.; ruins of Fort George and Royal Engineers' offices and other bldgs identified.
OMMMCM (3610)

1697 *1843*
Niagara Plan of the Military Reserves bounded Green, showing the lots tinted yellow which are required by the Commissioner of Crown Lands. ... (Signed) W.C.E. Holloway Colonel Comg Rl Engrs To accompany Col. Holloway's letter no. 82 of 12th August 1843 Copy J. Nightingale 16th Septr 1843
Col ms 59 x 97 cm 1" to 300 ft
The land was required by the trustees of the Niagara District School and was at the corner of the barrack ground next to proposed cricket ground; lots wanted in exchange by the ordnance were near Fort Mississauga.
OOAMA (NMC 43151)

1698 *1845*
Plan of Niagara Shewing the boundaries of the Town according to the Act of Incorporation Passed March 29th 1845.
Col ms 72 x 126 cm 1" to 5 chains
An attractive, detailed plan showing all the streets, bldgs, and lots of the town with Fort Mississauga and the ruins of Fort George; settlement is confined to Ricardo St to dock and Dock Co.'s land and along Picton, Queen, Platoff, and Johnson sts at King St; four wards shown; Queenston Rd is shown across garrison reserve; boundaries described per act.
OTAR

1699 *1845*
Plan of the Town of Niagara Including the Survey made by Captn Vavasour R.E and that portion ... set off from the Estate of Walter H. Dickson [illegible] also that of the Niagara Harbour & Dock Company Compiled from the latest & most authentic surveys by [Sgd] David Thompson Junr 6th January 1845
Col ms Size not known 1" to 30 perches
Shows the town from Castlereagh St to Water St, and King St to Lieven St; lot nos and some street names including small lots in front of Ricardo St; irregular streets and lots are shown south of town and east of King St; photoreproduction in OTAR (MS 178 reel 17).
ONHI

1700 *[ca 1850]*
Copy of Plan of the Niagara Harbour and Dock Co. Property at Niagara [ca 1850]
Ms Size not known Scale not given
Shows area from Byron St to the river and from the Erie & Niagara Railway to beyond Nelson St; blocks, wharves, slips, lots shown below Ricardo St; possibly a transcript; photoreproduction in OTAR (MS 178 reel 17); also reproduced in Parker, 93.
ONHI

1701 *1852*
A Sketch of the Military Reserve about Navy Hall, shewing (in red margin) the land petitioned for by the Mayor and Corporation of the Town of Niagara. (Niagara. August 26. 1852) (Signed) F.F. Passmore Provincial Surveyor Toronto. copy. [Sgd] R.I. Pilkington Draftsman 25 Sepr 1852
Col ms 44 x 55 cm 1" to 4.5 chains Watermark: 'J WHATMAN 1851' Endorsements: 'No 5 R 7052 E/1748'; stamp 'CREOC'
Shows a block of land laid out into lots east of Alava St to Collingwood St, north of Byron St; shows the proposed boundary for the military reserve, Butler's barracks and other military bldgs, and names of owners in the area.
OOAMA (NMC 4216)

1702 *[1853]*
Niagara ... portion tinted red containing about 96 acres to be retained by the Ordnance, The portion edged Vermilion ... is proposed to be given up for the settlement of the Pensioners, ... The portion tinted purple may be used by the Pensioners for Pasturage only, ... [Sgd] R.I. Pilkington Draftsman ...
Col ms 44 x 56 cm 1" to 4 chains Watermark: 'J WHATMAN 1851' Endorsements: 'No 41'; stamp 'CREOC'
The title has been crossed out and a second titled added: 'Plan showing the portion edged Vermilion proposed to be given up for the settlement of the Pensioners containing about 145 acres and which is drawn from recollection, the original plan having been destroyed at the late fire [Sgd] R. I. Pilkington Draftsman 14 June 1853'; the area referred to is on the garrison reserve around Fort George; a proposed line for the Erie and Ontario Railroad across the garrison reserve is shown; the location of telegraph posts also shown.
OOAMA (NMC 4215)

1703 *1853*
Niagara Sketch shewing the relative position of Forts Mississauga & Niagara. [Sgd] Chas Walkem Surveyr & draftsman R.E. departt Montreal March 1853
Col ms 54 x 85 cm 1" to 200 ft
Shows Fort Mississauga and Ricardo and Front sts, a few bldgs along the shore; Fort Niagara shown on the United States side.
OOAMA (NMC 22533)

1704 *1853*
Plan of Part of the Government Reserve at Niagara. (Signed) F.F. Passmore Provincial Land Surveyor Toronto. March 24 1853. Copied from the original by [Sgd] R.S. Beatson Captain R.E. Quebec 12th April 1853.
Col ms 43 x 53 cm 1" to 300 ft Endorsements: 'No 32' 'rel CW/409/563' 'R 7251' 'M 280'; stamp 'CREOC'
Shows the proposed Erie & Ontario Railroad through the military reserve by Fort George and Butler's barracks; boundary of reserve.
OOAMA (NMC 4214)

1705 *1863*
Plan of that part of the Town of Niagara known as the Niagara Dock Property [Sgd] Geo. Rykert Provincial Surveyor St Catharines Decr 1863
Col ms 52 x 98 cm 1" to 100 [ft] Endorsements: '16454/65' '5531 5190/65' 'Plan A as referred to in the Report of Mr. Solc Genl Cockburn Dec. 6 1865'
Shows the area from Fort George to King St and from Byron St to the water; note indicates areas to be leased to the Dock Co., those to be exchanged by the War Dept for other land, and boundary of the Dock Co. land; all bldgs shown in the area including machine shops, the Erie and Ontario Railroad, private bldgs, hotels, names of lot owners.
OTNR (SR 6378)

NILESTOWN

1706 *1855*
[Plan of village lots situated in the village] of Nilestown being composed of part of the north half of Lot No 1 in the first Consn of the Township of Westminster 1855, Dn by W. Pigott London C.W.
Col ms 46 x 62 cm 1" to 80 ft
Shows a subdivision on both sides of Hamilton Rd west of town line between London and Dorchester with notes indicating that part is in Sage's survey and part in Burdick's survey; some bldgs shown.
OLU

NORWOOD

1707 *[184?]*
Plan of the Town Plot of Norwood in the Township of Asphodel, Colborne District. On the property of J.A. Keeler Esq.
Col ms 49 x 65 cm 1" to 4 chains
Endorsed on back: 'P.M. Grover Esq. Norwood C.W. Plan of Village Lots By Parcel Post 244'; the plan is related to R.P. Norwood 1 of 15 Feb 1853 (**B1691**) and shows the same layout of lots; probably drawn in the 1840s with later changes to 1850s as Colborne District in the title is crossed out; shows area Queen St to Wellington St, and Oak St to Belmont St; Mill, Cedar, and Queen sts are shown in original and corrected positions; names are given in some lots but in some cases these are different from the R.P.; the sawmill and grist mill are drawn in more detail than on the R.P.; carding mill, pond, and quarry are pencilled in; proposed mill race to Cedar St (not shown on R.P.) is shown; some later additions of names dated to 1859; the title used on the two later maps (see **1708**) has been pencilled in to left of title; Keeler originally laid out the town in 1833 (*Norwood Then and Now*, 5).
OTUTF

1708 *1856*
Plan of the Town of Norwood as laid out on Lots Nos 16, 17, 18, 19 & 20, in the VIIIth & IXth Concessions of Asphodel. Being the property respectively of P.M. Grover, Esquire, and Mrs. E.J. Gilchrist. Survey extended by P.V. Elmore, P.L.S. August 1856
Col ms 97 x 87 cm 1" to 4 chains
Shows the town as extended beyond the earlier plans; on the west from Oak St to Balsam St, Spring St has become Pine St and been extended, Ridge St has become Napoleon St, and Wellington St has been extended parallel to latter; lots have been added from Queen St south to Pringle St and between Wellington St and Queen St, and Belmont St has been extended; all bldgs are shown and are found mainly along Peterborough and Belmont sts; a few names are given; public square, town hall, grammar school, mills, and residence of P.M. Grover shown; plan is not registered.
OTUTF

Related maps

(**2**) *[1856?]*
PLAN / OF THE TOWN OF / NORWOOD / AS LAID OUT ON LOTS NOs 16, 17, 18, 19 & 20 / IN THE VIITH & IXTH CONCESSIONS OF / Asphodel. / Being the property respectively of / P.M. GROVER, ESQUIRE, / and / MRS. E.J. GILCHRIST. / SURVEY EXTENDED / by / P.V. Elmore, P.L.S. / AUGUST [blank]
Print (lith) 98 x 91 cm [1" to 4 chains]
The printed map is a close copy of the ms map except the date and scale statement have not been included; the title is positioned as in the ms but has slightly less decorative lettering; views: 'BALSAM FARM HOUSE. / Residence of P.M. Grover, Esq. // J. Gouinlock' and 'GRIST & FLOURING MILL / Thomas Buck, Esq. Proprietor, NORWOOD C.W.'; since the year in the date was omitted and no printer is given, this may be a proof copy and the plan may never have been published.
OTUTF

NOTTAWA

1709 *1856*
Plan / OF THE SUBDIVISION OF / LOT 37 IN THE 8 CON OF NOTTAWASAGA / ON HURONTARIO STREET, / NEAR THE TOWN OF / COLLINGWOOD. / Toronto Aug 1856. Dennis & Boulton Surveyors & Agents for the Sale. // Maclear & Co Lith. Toronto
Print (lith) hand col 47 x 66 cm 1" to 3 chains
Shows town and park lots laid out at the north end of Nottawa east of Hurontario St, including mill property on the Nottawasaga R; a pasted addition indicates that the sale will take place 'At Montgomery's Hotel, Collingwood On Tuesday 14th October 1856 ... J.H. Lawrence Auctioneers.'
OMSA

OAKVILLE

1710 *1833*
Plan of Oakville Situated on part of Lots Nos 13, 14, 15, 16 in the 3rd Concession and also part of Lots Nos 12, 13, 14, 15, 16 in the 4th Conc or Broken Front South of Dundas Street, Lake Ontario, Township of Trafalgar, County of Halton, District of Gore, Province of Upper Canada. Oakville Property of William Chisholm Esqr of Nelson. H.J. Castle fecit. Dep. Survr 20th July 1833.
Col ms 60 x 76 cm 1" to 4 chains Endorsements: ['A 106'?]
Shows the first survey for the town extending from [Brock] St to Allan St and from the harbour to [Rebecca] St on both sides of the river; the streets are laid out but few named; shows shipyard, steamboat and sloop being built, bridge, wharf, and a few other bldgs; a sawmill and grist mill are shown further up the creek; the St Catharines and Niagara Central Railway line has been added later; the lots were advertised as for sale on 24 June 1833 in the *Patriot* (Toronto); (Mathews, 37).
OTNR (SR 228)

Related maps

(**2**) *1833*
Town of / OAKVILLE / Situate on Lake Ontario 16 Mile Creek / Gore District U.C. / H.J. Castle Depty Survr // S.O. Tazewell delr & lithr York U.C. / 1833.

Print (lith) 26 x 51 cm 1" to 6 chains Endorsements (OTNR copy): '671' ['A 112'?]
A slightly simplified and smaller-scale version of the above map; the river is cut off on the north at the edge of the lots; the bldgs, wharf, and boats are as in the other plan.
OOAKM OTNR (SR 227)

1711 *1835*
Plan of Oakville Township of Trafalgar Upper Canada. 1835. Edwd B. Palmer. Oakville deled October 1835.
Col ms 35 x 55 cm 1" to 300 ft
Shows the town extending further to the north on the east side to Palmer St; two piers shown surrounding harbour; shipyard and bridge and 'Intended Dam' shown to cross the creek at Rebecca St; streets named; a few names of owners; Market Block and George's Square and a few other reserves; (Holmden 2100).
OOAMA (NMC 4226)

1712 *1837 June*
Map / of / The Town / of OAKVILLE / TOWNSHIP of TRAFALGAR / GORE DISTRICT / UPPER CANADA / 1837. // Edwd B. Palmer Draftsman &c. Oakville 2nd June 1837.
Ms (with printed title) 51 x 69 cm 1" to 4 chains
The plan was certified by Robert W. Kerr 1 Jan 1850; shows the town extended to Bond St on the west and to Shedden St on the east; relief by hachures and marshy areas shown; reserves for Scotch church, George's Square, and public cemetery; shipyard and mill dam shown in river (see also **B1696**); a plan of 1 Aug 1836 by Robert W. Kerr is described on R.P. 34 and cited by Mathews, 39, but has not been found.
Halton 20 (R.P. 1)

1713 *1837 Sept*
Map of the Property of W. Chisholm Esq. at the Mouth of the Sixteen Mile Creek Township of Trafalgar U.C. 1837. E.B. Palmer Draftsman, Oakville U.C. 20 Sept 18[37?]
Col ms Approx 44 x 29 cm Scale not given
Shows the town and streets on both sides of the river and area north of town to lots 12–17 of the third con south of Dundas St; shows the areas of the town mortgaged by Chisholm to J. Forsyth, J.H. Dunn, and others to raise money to build the dam across the creek between 1831 and 1837 (Mathews, 87ff) ; shows land on the west formerly owned by James Brock and now owned by John Terry; a photoreproduction is in OTAR.
OOAKM

1714 *1863*
PLAN OF THE / town of / OAKVILLE / IN THE COUNTY OF HALTON / Canada West. / Published by MICHAEL HUGHES, 1863. / TREMAINE'S LITH. TORONTO.
Print (lith) with hand col 86 x 92 cm 1" to 4 chains
Includes six views of town hall and market bldgs, residences, and businesses; shows the town from Front and Walker sts to beyond the Hamilton & Toronto Railway and from Second St west to beyond Brock St; major bldgs named, names of owners of large lots; lot nos, list of subscribers, wards; treed areas, Episcopal church and cemetery, Catholic and public cemetery, railway depot.
OTAR

Related maps

(2) *[1863]*
Plan of the town of Oakville in the County of Halton Canada West
Col ms on linen 90 x 99 cm Scale not given
Endorsements: stamps 'Dept of Public Works Canada 121' 'D23'
A ms copy of the printed plan lacking some bldgs and views.
OOAMA (NMC 11398)

OLIPHANT

1715 *[1856?]*
Plan of the Town Plot of Oliphant [Sgd] C. Rankin
Ms 70 x 102 cm 1" to 6 chains
Provenance: OOAMA RG 10M 76703/9 no 184; shows the town lots laid out from Mary to Merry sts and from bay to Bryant St with park lots beyond; notes on terrain, vegetation, and islands; Rankin's field notes are in OTNR (FN 1762 22 May 1856).
OOAMA (NMC 13011)

ORANGEVILLE

1716 *1856*
PLAN OF PART / OF THE PROPERTY / OF / JESSE KETCHUM JUNR ESQR / SITUATED IN THE / VILLAGE OF ORANGEVILLE / TOWNSHIP OF MONO / CANADA WEST. / APRIL 1856.
Print (lith) 57 x 81 cm 1" to 3 chains
Inset: 'A SECTION OF WESTERN CANADA EXHIBITING THE POSITION OF ORANGEVILLE WITH ITS PRINCIPAL TRIBUTARY THOROUGHFARES.'; shows a subdivision of the town from Broadway to 5th Avenue and from 6th St E to 3rd St W; trees and named bldgs are shown along Broadway, mills are shown to south in developed part of town; views: 'Proposed plan of Dwelling [obliterated] Jesse Ketchum Jrn [obliterated]' and 'Plan of Chambers'; also shows plan for a park with lake between S and N Park St and mill races along boundaries of some new lots.
OORA

ORILLIA

1717 *1840*
Town plot of Orillia. Plan of Town plot on Lots No 7 & 8 in the 5th Con. S. Orillia. Toronto Jany 1840 [Sgd] Saml Richardson D.P.S.
Col ms 44 x 65 cm 1" to 4 chains Endorsements: '669'
(SI 2 Nov 1839 to survey and lay out town fronting on the Bristol Channel; OTNR FN 271 Jan 1840); shows the town as first laid out from Bay St to West St, and Mississaga St to North St; bldgs are numbered but not keyed; lot nos; a few names have been added to lots; also a copy: 'Plan of Town plot on Lots Nos 7 and 8 in the 5th Concession of Southern Orillia. Toronto Jany 1840 signed Saml Richardson D.P.S. Copy S.G. office' endorsed 'No 2370' 'IASR' in OOAMA (NMC 3963); also a copy dated 28 Aug 1845 in OOAMA (RG 10M 76703/9 no 333, NMC 13176).
OOAMA (NMC 3963; 13176) OTNR (SR 233)

Related maps

(2) *1847*
Town Plot of Orrillia [*sic*] Crown Land Department Montreal July 1847 A true copy [Sgd] T.D. D.B. Papineau C.C.L.
Col ms 63 x 48 cm 1" to 4 chains Endorsements: 'F 4169'; stamp 'IASR'
Shows the same layout as the 1840 plan but lots renumbered, Market Square has been created, and names have been added to all lots with many later changes; and a copy: 'Orillia Office Copy Surveyor General's Department Kingston 27th October 1847 [Sgd] Andrew Russell S & D' endorsed 'No 92' and with names (OTAR(P)).
OOAMA (NMC 4874) OTAR(P)

1718 *[1852?]*
VILLAGE LOTS / IN / THE TOWN OF / INVERMARA. / the Property of / JNO. THOMSON ESQ'R. / IN THE SOUTHERN DIVISION OF THE TOWNSHIP OF / ORILLIA, / IN THE COUNTY OF / SIMCOE / / Scobie's Lithography Toronto.
Print (lith) 44 x 52 cm 1" to 4 chains
A subdivision for a town southeast of the village of Orillia at the Narrows; shows the streets from Thistle St to L Simcoe, and Fawn St to the Narrows; lots numbered; swing bridge and causeway; 'line of Grand Junction Railway as Surveyed' [incorporated 1852]; ms adds include certain marked lots near bridge and note on a wharf; there is no registered plan for Invermara; shown separately on the co atlas (Belden, ... *Simcoe* (1881)) but it eventually became part of Orillia (*Statutory History*, 220).
OOAMA (NMC 22547)

OSHAWA

1719 *[1857?]*
PLAN / OF LOTS 12, 13, & 14 IN THE 3RD CONCESSION OF / TOWNSHIP OF WHITBY. / THE PROPERTY OF / J.W. GAMBLE ESQ M.P.P. / Unwin & Jack / P.L. Surveyors and Land Agents / Provincial Chambers / Toronto. / Litho. J. Ellis Toronto.
Print (lith) with ms adds 94 x 51 cm 1" to 4 chains
Shows a subdivision plan for area; original road allowance displaced by river and new roads shown; relief by hachures along riverbank; park lots; the plan was registered on 7 Apr 1866 but was made between Oct 1856 and May 1858 when Unwin and Jack advertised their partnership (*Daily Colonist* (Toronto); see also **B1763**.
Durham 40 (R.P. H–50001)

OTTAWA

1720 *1822*
Town Plot of Sherwood. 5th July 1822 [Sgd] Levius P. Sherwood Jn LeBreton
Ms 31 x 60 cm 1" to 4 chains
Attached to a deed from John LeBreton to L.P. Sherwood in 1822 for a strip of land in the area; shows the town plot of unnamed streets laid out on the LeBreton Flats, part of broken front con, Nepean, lot 40, along shore; Sherwood advertised lots for sale in the *Perth Independant Examiner* 26 Aug 1828, calling it 'the town of Sherwood formerly Richmond Landing, west of Bytown' (Ross, 172–3); photoreproduction in OOAMA (NMC 3974).
OOA (MG 29 C101)

1721 *[1823]*
[Sketch of lots between Rideau River and Richmond Landing] G.A. Eliot Br Maj 68th Regt
Col ms 20 x 32 cm 1" to 20 chains
Accompanied Maj G.A. Eliot, 'Remarks on the Best Position for a Military Depot ... Sept 1823' (OOA RG 8 I/274 p 87); the plan shows lots claimed by Mr Henry Fraser in the area being surveyed by Eliot for a fortified village under instructions from Lord Dalhousie; (Holmden 2208).
OOAMA (NMC 79949)

Related maps

(2) *1824*
Sketch of the Government Purchase in the Township of Nepean by Major Eliot 68th Regt
Col ms 20 x 30 cm 8" to 1 mile
Accompanied Maj Eliot, 'Remarks on the Purchase at the Falls of the Rideau 1824' (OOA RG 8 I/274 p 91); shows part of lots A and B on either side of Sleigh Bay purchased for government, crown reserve near Rideau Falls, and south to lot C; Richmond Landing; (Holmden 2209).
OOAMA (NMC 3541)

1722 *[1825]*
[Sketch of the Ottawa River at Chaudière Falls showing Wrightstown and Richmond Landing]
Col ms 24 x 36 cm Scale not given Watermark: 'GREEN 1815'
With a letter from Maj G.A. Eliot to George Hillier, civil secretary, of 15 Feb 1825 about petition of Wm Morris for a mill site and dam in front of the landing (OOA RG 5 A1 vol 70); shows the LeBreton, Sherwood, and Sparks properties on the south side, the government purchase between the road and the river, and Sleigh Bay; shows bldgs on either side of river, cleared and wooded areas; road to Richmond; reproduced in Nagy, 1; (Holmden 2206).
OOAMA (NMC 3163)

1723 *[1826]*
Plan of Village near the Shier Falls in the Township of Nepean Laid out under the orders of Lt Col By
Col ms Size not known Scale not given
Shows the town laid out in the Upper Town area between the Ottawa R and [Wellington St] and from the canal west to the Chaudière Falls; dated by and reproduced in Ross, 95.
Private Collection

1724 *[1826–7?]*
Sketch of the proposed bridges and roadway across the Ottawa at the Falls of the Chaudiere and the Dams constructed for rendering the Timber Channel navigable for Rafts &c. H. Pooley R.E.
Col ms 51 x 59 cm 1" to 100 ft
Provenance: OOAMA Collection of the 9th Earl of Dalhousie 85601/29; an attractive plan of the road route with indication of bridges and dams to be built and areas of rapids and falls; relief by colour wash; similar to plans below (**1725**) but probably slightly earlier.
OOAMA

1725 *1827*
Plan and Elevation of a Bridge at the Falls of the Chaudiere erected in 1827 under the Superintendence of Lt Coll John By Commanding Royal Engineer Rideau Canal [Sgd] John By Lt Colonel Royl Engrs Comg Rideau Canal 25th October 1827
Col ms 71 x 125 cm 1" to 40 ft Endorsements: stamps 'B↑O' 'IGF'
Notes: 'This Bridge is the first land communication that has been effected between Upper and Lower Canada and will be the means of causing the trafic [*sic*] from Kingston to Montreal to pass on the north side of the river' and 'Expence of Bridges £2724'; relief by colour wash; shows the islands, falls, and channels over which the bridge passed; section shows construction method in detail; (Holmden 2466).
OOAMA (NMC 16822)

Related maps

(**2**) *[1827]*
Plan & Elevations of Bridges at the Falls of Chaudiere Erected in 1827 ... [Sgd] John Burrows Dy Provl Surveyor
Col ms 67 x 122 cm 1" to 40 ft Watermark: 'JAMES WHATMAN TURKEY MILL KENT [date illegible]'
Similar to (1) although some features including bridge route in plan are slightly different in shape and a few more details on water courses given; darker colour wash used; probably in a different hand from plan above; includes the same note about the first land communication with slightly different wording.
OOAMA (NMC 16832)

(**3**) *[1827–8?]*
A Plan and Elevation of Bridges on the Ottowa [*sic*] at the Chaudiere Falls W. Cartan Lt 79 Highrs
Col ms 39 x 61 cm 1" to 80 ft Watermark: '[WHAT]MAN TURKEY MILL KENT 1825'
Endorsements on pasted label: 'From the Library of George, 9th Earl of Dalhousie ... Wm. Inglis Morse Collection'
Inset: [elevation] shows rafting channel, East Channel, Great Kettle; shows vegetation, rock embankments, and bridges in detail.
NSWA

(**4**) *[1827–8]*
Plan of The Line of Bridges & Road over the Chaudiere Falls. Ottawa River. [Sgd] Lt Col By Commanding Rl Engineers. John Burrows Overseer of Work
Col ms 68 x 95 cm 1" to 60 ft Endorsements: '3914'
The route is closer to those on the 1827 plans but houses shown and Firth's tavern.
OOAMA (NMC 12261)

(**5**) *1828*
Plan and Elevation of a Bridge ... John Burrows Octr 10. 1828 [Sgd] John By Lt Colonel Royal Engineers Comg Rideau Canal 19th October 1828
Col ms 65 x 98 cm 1" to 60 ft Endorsements: stamps 'B↑O' 'IGF'
Similar to plans above but houses drawn on Ottawa side and route has changed again at the Ottawa end; (Holmden 2456).
OOAMA (NMC 23381)

(**6**) *1828*
Plan & Section of the Line of Bridges Over the Chaudiere Falls Lt Col By Commanding Rl Engineer [Sgd] John By Lt Colonel Royal Engineers Comg Rideau Canal 22nd November 1828 John Burrows Overseer of Works
Col ms 65 x 97 cm 1" to 60 ft
Accompanied a letter from Col By to Colborne of 25 May 1829 about construction of a timber slide (GBLpro CO 42/388 f 341–2); shows the same information as (4); (*PRO Cat* 1879–80).
GBLpro (MPGG 75)

(7) *1830*
Plan and Section of the Chaudiere Falls Ottawa River and the Line of Bridges over the Same Lt Coln By Comg Rl Engineers. John Burrows Overseer of Works [Sgd] John By Lt Colonel Royl Engrs Comg Rideau Canal 8th July 1830
Col ms 73 x 129 cm 1" to approx 60 ft
Endorsements: stamp 'B↑O'
Relief by colour wash; slides, mills, etc; section shows construction plan of bridges; Mrs Firth's tavern similar to (4) but larger area and more roads and timber slides shown; (Holmden 2467).
OOAMA (NMC 16833)

(8) *1827 (1831)*
PLAN and ELEVATION of the UNION BRIDGES – OTTAWA RIVER near the FALLS OF CHAUDIERE in 1827. // Mr Burrows Land Survr fecit. // Day & Haghe lithogrs to the King, 17, Gate St Linc. Inn Fds
Print (lith) 19 x 26 cm 1" to 200 ft
In Joseph Bouchette, *The British Dominions in North America* (London: Henry Colburn and Richard Bentley 1831), 1: opp 82 (OOA), and in the 2nd ed (London: Longman, Rees, Orme, Brown, Green & Longman 1832), 1: opp 82 (*Bib Can* 1627; 4968); oriented to the northwest; bridges are described in legend; a reduced version possibly of (4) or (7).
OTMCL OTRMC

1726 *[1827]*
Plan of Lots 39 & 40 in the Broken Front to the South of the Timber Channel at the Chaudiere Falls [Sgd] John By Lt Coll Rl Engrs Comg Rideau Canal
Col ms 61 x 46 cm 1" to 200 ft
Enclosed with a letter of 30 Jan 1827 from Col Darling to Col Durnford about a claim by Sherwood to a mill site by the lower dam (GBLpro CO 42/411 p 323); shows relief, roads, and proposed roads; legend keys land reserved for fortifications, and dams and timber channel built by order of Lord Dalhousie in 1826–7; proposed dam to divert water to ravine where mill to be built; land purchased from Sherwood to secure approaches to bridges.
GBLpro (CO 42/411 p 323)

Related maps

(2) *1828*
Plan of Lots 39 and 40 ... [Sgd] John By ... 11th August 1828
Col ms 42 x 52 cm 1" to 200 ft
Originally accompanied a land petition (OOA RG 1 L3 S no 3 (3rd series no 8) 1828); some of the land is noted as appropriated for the Rideau Canal in note sgd 'J.B.'; two sites for mills noted as sold and rented; sgd 'L.P. Sherwood August 3rd 1844'; (Holmden 2228).
OOAMA (NMC 3876)

1727 *[1827?]*
[Plan of part of Lower Bytown]
Ms 60 x 77 cm 1" to approx 1.33 chains
Watermark: 'RUSE & TURNER 1817'
Shows the area between Sussex St and King St, and St Patrick St and Rideau St, with lots and some names of owners; notes on prices and dates of deeds '1827' and '1829'; a note by Holmden in 1921 indicates he partially restored lines that were obliterated and identifies this as 'original plan for Bytown'; (Holmden 2199).
OOAMA (NMC 22552)

1728 *1827*
[Sketch of Bytown and the Chaudière Falls, Ottawa River, showing land taken and road opened by Col By for the Rideau Canal]
Ms 32 x 20 cm Approx 1" to 360 ft Watermark: '... 1827' Endorsements: '16 Nov 27 Col By to Wm Sherwood with a Sketch within'
Originally from OOA RG 1 L3 S no 1 (2nd series no 29) 1827; proposed dam and mill site, bridges, timber slide; shows land in LeBreton Flats area on south shore taken for canal; (Holmden 2212).
OOAMA (NMC 79950)

1729 *[1827–8?]*
Rough draft of the Ground between Dows Swamp on the Rideau Canal, & the Chaudiere Lake Alexr Shirriff
Col ms 23 x 37 cm Approx 1" to .7 mile
Watermark: '... 1827'
Provenance: OOA RG 1, removed from Miscellaneous Papers S series U.C.; shows lots settled; Richmond Rd; red lines mark possible proposed canal to Chaudière L; shows the town sketched near canal; mound by Dow's Swamp.
OOAMA (NMC 79951)

1730 *1828 July 2*
Diagram of a piece of land Near the entrance of the Rideau Canal. [Sgd] John Burrows Dy Provl Surveyor July 2nd 1828. His Excellency Lt General Sir James Kempt K.C.B. Lt. Colonel Fanshawe Royl Engrs & Lt Colonel Lewes Royl Engrs have ordered that no buildings should be erected on this high ground [Sgd] John By Lt Colonel Royl Engrs Comg Rideau Canal 5th July 1828.
Col ms 50 x 65 cm 1" to 85 ft Endorsements: 'Pro 15' 'No 53'
Area between Canal Valley and Sussex St; also shows 'Piece of Land Surveyed for Lt Pooley March 21st 1828 Area 8.1.11 A.R.P.'; relief, surrounding lots, and bldgs; (Holmden 2213); also a map in OTNR (SR 2685) with the same title: '(copy) [Sgd] J.G. Chewett 3rd Decr 1828' endorsed 'No 20' and '938' and showing the same information.
OOAMA (NMC 4804) OTNR (SR 2685)

1731 *1829*
Plan of the Proposed Improvements in the Timber Channel At the Chaudiere Falls by Lt Col By Commanding Royal Engineers [Sgd] John By Lt Colonel Royl Engrs Comg Rideau Canal 1st January 1829. John Burrows Overseer of Works.

Col ms 97 x 64 cm 1" to 60 ft Endorsements: stamps 'BW' '683'

Two longitudinal sections, 1" to 20 ft vertical; a plan for works in four locations along the channel on the south side of the river; shows other channels with dams and 'lost channels'; (Holmden 2197).
OOAMA (NMC 21865–6)

Related maps

(2) *1832*
Plan of the proposed improvements for the passage of timber at the Chaudiere 1832 [Sgd] N H Baird Civil Engineer 1832 M.I.C.E.L.
Col ms 50 x 124 cm 1" to 60 ft Endorsements: stamp 'B↑O'

Proposed works shown in yellow including proposed slide; Firth's Inn; roads from Richmond and Bytown.
OOAMA (NMC 16829)

1732 *1831*
[Plan of Upper and Lower Bytown] John Burrows O.W. [Sgd] John By Lt Col. Rl Engrs Comg Rideau Canal 22nd [Jan] 1831
Col ms 69 x 106 cm 1" to 350 ft

An attractive and detailed map showing all streets and houses in Lower Bytown from Sussex St to several streets beyond King St and Rideau St to Murray St, and from Wellington to Victoria sts east and west of Kent St in Upper Bytown; government property and barracks shown and Rideau Canal; some bldgs named and some names of owners of large lots; bridges over the Chaudière, timber slides, and roads shown; there was also a later copy at OOAMA made in 1858 and indicating original date of plan above as 22 Jan 1831 and sgd 'Copy (Signed) J. Nightingale Assistant Draftsman Inspector Generals Office 8th April 1858. A true copy (Signed) Saml B. Howlett Chief Draftsman War Office Whitehall Gardens 8th April 1858'; however, only later transcripts of this copy appear to have survived; there is mention of a plan of Dec 1830 showing all the bldgs in Ross (preface), but this has not been found.
OOAMA (NMC 14284)

1733 *[1831]*
Sketch of / BYTOWN / OTTAWA RIVER / Founded in 1826. // Reduced by F. Cattlin. Engraved by J. & C. Walker.
Print (engrav) 18 x 21 cm Scale not given

In Joseph Bouchette, *The British Dominions in North America* (London: Henry Colburn and Richard Bentley 1831), 1: opp 80 (OOA), and in the 2nd ed (London: Longman, Rees, Orme, Brown, Green & Longman 1832), 1: opp 80 (*Bib Can* 1627; 4968); shows the area from the Rideau R in Lower Town to the Scotch church in Upper Town on Wellington St; relief along banks; streets named; ferry to Hull.
OOA OOAMA OTMCL (NMC 15506)

1734 *1836*
Sketch of the Channel of the Ottawa River at the Chaudiere Falls shewing the Stone wall built by Coll By across the old Timber Channel and the Ravine or Gully in which Captn Le Breton states that he intended to form a mill site by excavating a Channel ... [Sgd] Rl Engineers Office Kingston 1st Feby 1836 J.R. Wright Lt Col. Comg Rl Engineers Upper Canada. (Copy) H.O. Crawley Lieut R. Engineers 1st Feby 1836
Col ms 39 x 56 cm 1" to 200 ft

Relief by colour wash, roads, falls, bridges, channels; land purchased by government from Sherwood; description of proposed mill pond by LeBreton; (Holmden 2220).
OOAMA (NMC 3980)

1735 *1838*
Plan of By Town Shewing the Proposed Fortifications Land taken from Mr Sparks Lot No C in Conn C also Crown Reserve O [Sgd] John Burrows Clerk of Works & Eng 25/8/38 [Sgd] D. Bolton Major Senior Royal Engineer Rideau & Ottawa Canal 25th Augt 1838
Col ms 63 x 107 cm 1" to 5 chains

Shows the proposed extensive fortifications west of the canal on Citadel Hill with military bldgs keyed; shows streets and bldgs in both parts of town and two possible sites for a court-house; shows names of owners of large lots including John By, LeBreton, Sherwood, and Sparks, and various purchases; (Holmden 2221; Nagy, 7; *OHIM* 7.37); there is also a later plan of 7 March 1841 showing land to be retained for military purposes originally with WO 44/49 f 575.
GBLpro (MPH 1155(1)) OOAMA (NMC 18913)

1736 *[184?]*
By-Town [and plan of part of Lower Bytown]
2 mss 48 x 42 cm and 48 x 73 cm Scales not given

Two undated maps showing parts of Lower Bytown with names of owners in lots; the first shows the area from Augusta St to Wurtemburg St, Ottawa St to Rideau St, and the second shows the area from King St to Augusta St, and Ottawa St to Rideau St, with the Wesleyan chapel and school; (Holmden 2202–3).
OOAMA (NMC 3973; 8879)

1737 *[184?]*
Plan of Lot No. 40 Concession A, Nepean, Part of Bytown.
Col ms 99 x 70 cm 1" to 125 [links]

Shows the area from Broad St to con road C, Rideau Front, and Victoria Terrace to Montreal St; names of owners in lots; canal; Board of Works site.
OOAMA (NMC 3969)

1738 *1840*
Plan of Bytown with some of the adjoining 200 acre Lots. [Sgd] Anthony Swalwell Depy Pl Surveyor Sepr 4th 1840.
Col ms 76 x 77 cm 1" to 8 chains Endorsements: stamps 'BW' '514'
Shows the area from the Rideau R to Chaudière Falls and from north of Rideau St to lot H; streets named and major bldgs identified; relief; names of some owners of larger lots; shows the main road around Barrack Hill; graveyard; oriented to the south.
OOAMA (NMC 21868)

1739 *1842*
Plan of Bytown and the adjacent lots &c. Shewing their relative situation thereto July 14th 1842. Joseph Kirk D.P.S.
Col ms 62 x 79 cm 1" to 8 chains
An attractive, detailed plan showing all streets, the survey grid, major bldgs and military bldgs; some bldgs shown in New Edinburgh; names of owners of large lots; relief; various subdivisions of land by Sparks, Col By, Besserer, and government shown; differs in subdivisions and other details from printed plan of 1842 (**1740**); (Holmden 2224).
OOAMA (NMC 23382)

1740 *1842*
PLAN / OF / BYTOWN / WITH ITS LIMITS / Shewing the exact Situation / of every / STREET & LOT / Drawn to a Scale of 6 Chains to the Inch / by / Donald Kennedy, / District Surveyor. / Dec. 4th 1842. // WILLIS & PROBTS. LITHO 2, WALL ST N. YORK
Print (lith) 61 x 85 cm 1" to 6 chains
Untitled view of the Union Suspension Bridge across the Ottawa R; [profile of the first eight locks of the Rideau Canal]; shows the town as it had developed north of road allowance between lots C and D to [Cathcart] St in Lower Bytown and east to the Rideau R, and from Kent St west to about [Broad] St in Upper Bytown; government land and land owned by N. Sparks shown in between; New Edinburgh is shown laid out between Rideau St and McKay St and for four blocks north to south; lands owned by estate of Col By shown to the south; NMC 19056 (from OOA MG 24 A66) folding into cover with ms title 'Plan of Bytown, otherwise City of Ottawa, 1842' and shows Col By's land in colour; (Holmden 2227); there are also two later ms transcripts of the map made by Joseph Aubé about 1920, both with a different view entitled 'UNION SUSPENSION BRIDGE ON THE OTTAWA RIVER AT BYTOWN Engraved for the "Ottawa Citizen. Jos. Aubé"' (OOAMA (NMC 22556–7)).
OOAMA (NMC 19056) OTNR (SR 8912)

Later editions and states

(2) *[184?]*
[Title is the same]
Area between St Andrew's St and Thos MacKay's property on the Ottawa has now been laid out in streets and lots.
OTNR (SR 232)

1741 *1842*
Plan of Part of Lower Bytown shewing the Concession line or Road between Concessions C & D Township of Nepean shaded yellow [Sgd] D Bolton Maj Royl Engr R & O Canal 1 Sept 1842 [Sgd] J. Burrows C Works 1/9/42
Col ms 57 x 91 cm 1" to 200 ft Endorsements: 'no 33'; stamp 'REO'
Inset: 'Sketch from the Surveyor Generals Plan shewing the Crown Reserve O being in two Concessions'; the road allowance cuts across lots from Rideau St to St Patrick St west of Cumberland St at an angle; shows area between Rideau Canal and river; (Holmden 2226).
OOAMA (NMC 22555)

1742 *1843*
Plan of Bytown Called for by the Boards Order dated 24th Febry 1843 0/1304 Surveyed by Lieutt White Royal Engineers. Royal Engineer Office Bytown 8th Septr 1843 [Sgd] H.A. White Lieut Rl Engineers 8th Septr 1843. [Sgd] Fras Ringler Thomson Major [illegible]
Col ms 301 x 182 cm 1" to 100 ft Endorsements: 'no 103'; stamp 'REO'
Shows all the streets, lot nos, and all bldgs; stone, wooden, and brick bldgs distinguished; canal and locks shown in detail; military bldgs identified; boundaries of ordnance and canal lands; fenced areas shown in Lower Bytown and road allowance cutting across lots; relief by hachures; no streets shown south of Rideau or south of Sparks St; also a copy (NMC 14285); (Holmden 2492; *OHIM* 7.36); there is also a 'Sketch of Bytown and of the Rideau Canal from the Hogs Back to the Ottawa River copied by R. Pilkington ...' to accompany letter of 19 March 1844 in GBLpro WO 44/45 f 479).
GBLpro (MPH 918(19) OOAMA (NMC 14285; 20054)

1743 *[1845?]*
Barrack Field [and plan of Upper Bytown] D.B.
Col ms 30 x 105 cm 1" to 200 ft
Shows Upper Bytown north of Wellington St with Scotch kirk and Methodist chapel; boundary of barrack field and Rideau Canal land shown.
OOAMA (NMC 18912)

1744 *1845*
Plan of lot C in Concessn C Township of Nepean belonging to N. Sparks Esqr. [Sgd] Anthony Swalwell Depy Provl Surveyor By Town April 22. 1845
Col ms 49 x 122 cm 1" to 2 chains Endorsements: stamps 'Received May 15 1845' '123'
Accompanied a petition by N. Sparks about his rights to this land enclosed in Lord Metcalfe's no

260 to Lord Stanley 27 Apr 1845 (GBLpro WO 1/552); shows the areas claimed by Sparks and ordnance land; shows the canal basin, locks, and some bldgs; photoreproductions in OOAMA (NMC 15342; 43158); (*PRO Cat* 1534).
GBLpro (MPHH 459)

1745 *1845*
Plan shewing the sites of the bridges of Communication across the Ottawa River, Between Hull and Bytown which were built under the direction of Col. By Surveyed and Drawn John S. McDonald. Bellows Bay Sepr 4 1845
Col ms 74 x 132 cm 1" to 80 ft Endorsements: stamps 'BW' '382'
[Section] 1" to 20 ft vertical; shows the bridges, slides, piers in detail; bldgs; OOAMA also has 'Plan of the Timber Chenail ...' of this date (NMC 22558) and a 'Plan and Profile of the New Slides ...' (NMC 23380).
OOAMA (NMC 18914)

1746 *[1845]*
Projected plan of part of Bytown 14th Nov. [1845] [Sgd] M. McDermott C.E. & Dy Sr
Col ms 41 x 62 cm 1" to 2 chains Endorsements: 'A 144' '608'
(SI 21 July 1845 to verify division lines between lots O and A in con C and D, and to survey outlines of remainder of lot O); shows a diagram for survey of area from Cathcart St to the Ottawa R and Rideau R; 'This subdivision into blocks or streets will leave the Greatest Number of houses untouched M.McD.'; later references mention (3) and (4) below; also in OTNR (SR 6376): 'Plan of Part of lot letter O in Concessions C and D of Nepean showing the chain lines improvements and subdivision into bldg lots. 14th Nov 1845 [Sgd] Mich McDermott C.E. & D.P.S.' endorsed 'A 152' and showing a street plan overlaid on the existing layout of irregular lots and lines at an angle with most houses fitting into old system.
OTNR (SR 38; 6376)

Related maps

(2) *1846*
Projected Plan for the subdivision of Lot Letter O Bytown into Building Lots. Crown Lands Department Montreal 20th January 1846 [Sgd] D.B. Papineau C C L A.R. Approved by O.C. 21st January 1846
Col ms 58 x 71 cm 1" to 2 chains Endorsements: '609'
A note refers to the actual survey done by Bell (see (4) below); shows streets from Cathcart to McKay, and Rideau Terrace to Sussex St, Metcalfe and Cathcart squares, and area set apart for a market by 'O.C. 19th March 1846'; lot nos.
OTNR (SR 41)

(3) *1846*
Plan of the Survey of the subdivision of Lot Letter O Bytown Into Building lots. by [Sgd] Robert Bell D.P. Surveyor Bytown 3rd Augt 1846. Examined A.R.
Col ms 47 x 66 cm 1" to 2 chains Endorsements: 'A 151'
(OTNR FN 86 5 Aug 1846); shows the actual survey and streets as in (3); Metcalfe and Cathcart squares are shown and a site for a market between Boteler and Bolton sts on Dalhousie St; area reserved for wharves along the Ottawa R; lot nos; there is also a copy in OOAMA (NMC 3993) endorsed 'A 150' and showing fence lines and bldgs running counter to survey, which accompanied a petition; another copy (NMC 3994) also accompanying a petition; a copy in OTAR: 'Lot Letter O Bytown 24th October 1846' with later additions; and a copy in OTAR(P) of 1847 endorsed 'No 101' and with the addition of names.
OOAMA (NMC 3993–4) OTAR OTAR(P) OTNR (SR 37)

1747 *1846*
Plan of Lot No 39 in Concession A on the Ottawa River in the township of Nepean. And projected subdivision of the lot. [Sgd] Robert Bell D.P. Surveyor Bytown 19th August 1846. Examined A.R.
Col ms 47 x 36 cm 1" to 4 chains Endorsements: 'A 153' '607'
An unfinished plan showing outline only of the area south of the Chaudière Falls and west of Broad St.
OTNR (SR 35)

Related maps

(2) *1846*
Plan of the survey of the subdivision of Lot No 39 in Con A. on the Ottawa River, township of Nepean [Sgd] Robert Bell D.P. Surveyor Bytown 16th Sept 1846. Examined A.R.
Col ms 49 x 55 cm 1" to 2 chains Endorsements: 'A 154' '611'
Shows the area from Oregon St south to beyond Ottawa St, and from Broad St west to West St; Dept of Public Works site is shown north of Oregon St; part claimed by Nicholas Sparks; later notes about patents; there is also a copy in OTNR (SR 39): 'Lot No 39 in Con A Nepean ...' dated Dec 1846 and endorsed '612'; and a copy in OTAR(P): 'Office Copy Lot No. 39 Dec. 1847' endorsed 'No 75' and '61.'
OTAR(P) OTNR (SR 39–40)

1748 *1847*
Bytown Plan from actual survey shewing the true side lines between Lots B and C in Concession C. Township of Nepean (in Red) and the manner in which Wellington and Rideau Streets are laid out. Royal Engineer Office Bytown, 19th June 1847. (Signed) Frs. Ringler Thomson Lt Coll Royal Engineers. [Sgd] N. Walker Draftsman R.E.O. 14/6/47.
Col ms 45 x 244 cm 1" to 2 chains Endorsements: 'S.P. No 22/A L.B. 64/74'

Shows bldgs abutting on Wellington and Rideau sts, and area east to Rideau R; (Holmden 2237).
OOAMA (NMC 18901)

1749 *[1847]*
[Green Island] [Sgd] Thos C Keefer D.P.S.
Col ms 28 x 45 cm 1" to 2 chains
(OTNR FN 308 3 Feb 1848); shows the island in the Rideau R between Lower Bytown and New Edinburgh; notes on the difference between high and low water and heights of the Ottawa and Rideau rivers Sept 1847; two mill lots shown on island; bridges; Rideau Falls; tables of bearings; the island was advertised for sale by government on 4 Jan 1848 (OTAR RG 1 C-III-2 vol 3); there is also a copy of Keefer's plan dated Nov 1847 with a note that island placed in charge of Dept of Public Works 21 Nov 1853 (OTNR (SR 7124)).
OTAR (SR 9848) OTNR (SR 7124)

1750 *1847*
Plan Shewing the Town Lots on the Ordnance Property on Lot B, Concession D, Township of Nepean also the present occupation of the Ground. [Sgd] Bytown 6th Feb. 1847 Michael McDermott C.E. and Provincial Land Surveyor
Col ms 44 x 109 cm 1" to 2 chains Endorsements: 'no 77' 'S.P. Bytown No 17'; stamp 'REO'
Shows the area from Rideau St to Ottawa St, King St to Rideau R; shows Anglesea Square and burial grounds for four denominations; houses shown with names of owners, shows fence lines often running counter to the lot lines; stone and wooden houses; ordnance boundary stones; (Holmden 2235).
OOAMA (NMC 18911)

1751 *1847*
Sketch shewing (Colored in Yellow) a vacant spot of ground belonging to the Ordnance at Bytown which is considered eligible for the site of a Church of England and Ireland. Royal Engineer Office Bytown, 28th July 1847 (Signed) Frs. Ringler Thomson Lt Col. Rl Engineers
Col ms 28 x 44 cm 1" to 2 chains Watermark: 'RUSE & TURNERS 1847' Endorsements: 'S.P. No. 25/A L.B. 64/101'
Shows the area between the Senior Royal Engineers' quarters east of the canal and Sussex St; other bldgs, locks, and quarry shown; (Holmden 2175).
OOAMA (NMC 3992)

1752 *1848*
Bytown Plan shewing the land belonging to the Ordnance on the Barrack Hill with the relative position of Wellington and Rideau Streets. Royal Engineer Office Bytown, 2nd June 1848 (signed) Charles E. Ford Captn Rl Engineers (Signed) F.W. King Lieut. Rl. Engineers 2nd June 1848.
2 col mss 55 x 145 cm 1" to 2 chains Endorsements: 'S.P. No 37/A ...' 'S.P. No 38/A ...'
'Sections of Barrack Hill'; shows officers' quarters, barracks, ruins, stables, and bldgs around canal, basin, and waste weir; relief by colour wash; (Holmden 2241, 2242).
OOAMA (NMC 14100)

1753 *1848*
Plan of Upper Bytown Shewing the Boundaries as marked on the ground and laid out agreeably to the M.G. and Board's order, dated the 23rd April 1845. M/1238. [Sgd] Michael McDermott C.E. and Provincial Land Surveyor Bytown 17th July 1848 Fred A. King Lieut Rl Eng. 29th July 1848 Royal Engineer Office Bytown 5 Aug 1848 Charles E. Ford Capt R. Engineers
Col ms 95 x 128 cm 1" to 2 chains Endorsements: 'S.P. No 40/A' 'Plan No 1 Part Second'
Shows the area between Wellington St and the Ottawa R and from the canal to the road to the Chaudière bridges; military bldgs identified and brick, stone, and wood bldgs distinguished; (Holmden 2243); also a copy in OTNR (SR 5892); there is also another survey of the same title but sgd 'Alfred Driscoll Provincial Surveyor 26 Septr 1850 [Sgd] Fred W. King Lieut Rl Eng 26th Septr [1850] Royal Engineer Office Bytown 28th Septr 1850 [Sgd] Charles E. Ford Capt Rl Engineers' (OOAMA (NMC 22402)).
OOAMA (NMC 17885; 22402) OTNR (SR 5892)

1754 *1848*
Plan shewing the part of Lot No 39 Broken Front Concession A on the Ottawa River claimed by Nicholas Sparks Esquire. Crown Lands Department Surveyor's Branch West Montreal. February 1848 [Sgd] John Macdonald A.R. T. Devine Drftms.
Col ms 70 x 65 cm 1" to 2 chains Watermark: 'J WHATMAN 1842' Endorsements: '610'
Shows the area from the Dept of Public Works land to beyond Ottawa St and from Broad St to West St; shows an area from Richmond St to beyond West St claimed by Sparks and part already cleared by him.
OTNR (SR 36)

1755 *[1849?]*
Plan of Bytown Called for by Seth Thomas Esq. Junior Ordce Storekeeper
Col ms 64 x 118 cm 1" to 4 chains
Shows the streets in Lower and Upper Bytown and Barrack Hill with bldgs; military bldgs identified; probably made while Thomas was in Bytown between 1846 and 1850; (Holmden 2232).
OOAMA (NMC 16790)

1756 *1851*
Chaudiere Islands Bytown as Surveyed out into Building and Hydraulic Lots under the orders of the Commissioners of Public Works by Messrs Bell and Russell Provl Land Surveyors 1851
Col ms 48 x 74 cm 1" to 1 chain Endorsements: stamp [BW] '457'

Shows the lots on Chaudière, Victoria, Albert, and Amelia islands; shows Bridge St, proposed new bridge, old bridge, and present road; Union Suspension Bridge; proposed future continuation of mill race across part of Chaudière Is; (Holmden 2172).
OOAMA (NMC 22563)

Related maps

(2) *1852*
Plan of the Chaudiere Islands Bytown Surveyed in 1851 by the Undersigned by Order of the Dept of Pubc Works Signed Robert Bell P.L. Surveyor Signed A.J. Russell Prov. Land Surveyor Signed Samuel Keefer Chf. Engr P.W. Quebec 6th May 1852
Col ms 73 x 126 cm 1" to 1 chain Endorsements: stamp 'Dept of Public Works Canada no 208'
'Section ...' 1" to 20 ft vertical; shows the same survey and names of owners in lots; proposed flumes and dams; remarks on construction problems, geology, amount of discharge at various points; also a copy on linen at OOAMA (NMC 22401): 'Copied from the Original by Chas. McCarthy Examined F.P. Rubidge A.S.P.W.'; there is also a plan at OOAMA (NMC 22564) by D. Sinclair of 9 Sept 1852, under SI of 23 Aug 1852 which shows some of the lots only on the islands; (Holmden 2247).
OOAMA (NMC 22400–1; 22564)

1757 *1851*
Rideau Canal. Plan of Lower Bytown from a Survey made by the Royal Engineer Department in August 1850 and in April 1851. [Sgd] Nelson Walker Surveyor & Dftsmn Rl. Engr Dept. 17th May 1851. [Sgd] Fred W. King Lieut R.E. 17th May 1851
Col ms 88 x 197 cm 1" to 85 ft Endorsements: 'no 61'; stamp 'CREOC'
Shows the area from George St to Bolton St, and Wurtemberg St to Sussex St; all bldgs are shown; some names of owners; later note about survey lines: 'C.R.O.'s Mem. of 5th Octr 1852 S.B. Tanell Lt. R.E. 11th Novr 1852'; also a copy at OOAMA (NMC 22403): 'Copied by H. Williams Lt Royal Engrs 31st December 1852'; (Holmden 2515).
OOAMA (NMC 21960; 22403)

1758 *[1852–4?]*
Bytown Plan shewing edged Vermilion, the land retained for Defensive purposes in the Lower Town, distinguishing Purple, the land proposed to be surrendered to the Provl Govt Light Yellow to be leased in 2 or 3 portions – Dark Yellow 14 Building Lots – Green land already disposed of. [Sgd] R.I. Pilkington Draftsman
Col ms 28 x 44 cm 1" to 4 chains Watermark: 'RUSE & TURNER 1851' Endorsements: 'no 20/1'; stamp 'CREOC'
Shows the area from Sussex St to the canal to be retained for defence, but 14 bldg lots shown and other lands to be leased; shows land around canal to be turned over to government of the province; land leased to Bytown and Prescott Ry 16 Apr 1852; Royal Engineers' quartermaster's house shown as destroyed by fire; shows the streets of the lower town.
OOAMA (NMC 4000)

1759 *[1853]*
Part of Kennedy's Plan of / BYTOWN. / Certified as Correct by Mr Bell. / MATTHEW'S LITH. // No 4
Print (lith) 52 x 74 cm Scale not given
In *Report on the Petition of W.L. Mackenzie Acting Executor to the Estate of the Late Robert Randall* (Quebec: Printed by Rollo Campbell 1853), opp 16 (*Bib Can* 3343); a rough copy of the plan of 1842 (**1740**) with blocks of land in lots 39 and 40, con A, Nepean, marked as belonging to Messrs Sherwood and LeBreton.
OTMCL

Related maps

(2) *[1853]*
Plan of Lots 40. Con I and 40 Con: A Nepean / and 39 in said Concessions in part. / Certified by Mr. Bell, Surveyor to be Correct. // No 3
Print (lith) 30 x 41 cm Scale not given
In the same source as plan above; shows the area of the lots with the Chaudière Islands, bridges, timber slides, etc; Mr Firth's tavern.
OTMCL

1760 *1853*
Sketch in explanation of A.J. Russell and H. Merrills Report of the [?]th April 1853, To The Honorable The Commissioners of Crown Lands on the necessity for certain reserves on Lot No 39 Range A. Ottawa Front Nepean Crown Timber Office Bytown 9th April 1853 (Signed) A.J. Russell
Ms 108 x 72 cm 1" to 8 chains Endorsements: stamp 'Public Works no 454'
Reserves required for slides and site of proposed canal around the Chaudière Falls; shows bridge to Hull and area east to Lower Bytown; relief; (Holmden 2192).
OOAMA (NMC 43160)

1761 *1857*
Plan / OF THE / CITY OF OTTAWA / COMPILED FROM THE BEST AUTHORITIES / ON A SCALE OF 8 CHAINS TO AN INCH / BY / WILLIAM WAGNER, / CIVIL ENGINEER & PROVINCIAL LAND SURVEYOR OTTAWA, / August. 1857. // BARR & CORSS ENGRAVERS & LITHOGRAPHERS 461/2 YONGE STREET, TORONTO.
Print (col lith) 61 x 85 cm 1" to 8 chains
'VIEW OF THE MANUFACTURING ESTABLISHMENTS AT THE CHAUDIERE FALLS / from an Ambrotype by Lockwood, Centretown / Litho Barr and Corss'; shows the streets from Broad St to the Rideau R, and two unnamed streets south of Jacob St to Ottawa R; lot

nos; relief by hachures; some bldgs named; Chaudière Falls with dams, booms, etc; city limits; similar to the Ottawa map by W.A. Austin (**551**) but shows less subdivision into lots; advertised for sale by Maclear and Barr & Corss 13 Apr 1858 in the *Daily Colonist* (Toronto).
OOAMA (NMC 43161; 47863) OTMCL OTNR (SR 8817)

1762 *1858*
Plan of the City of Ottawa shewing the position of the buildings available for legislative and departmental accommodation. Ottawa April 1858 [Sgd] W.A. Austin & Co. Engineers Architects &c&c
Col ms on linen 64 x 90 cm [1" to 8 chains]
A ms copy of the Austin printed map of Ottawa (**551**); shows seven locations of bldgs along Sussex, Wellington, and Sparks sts.
OOAMA (NMC 22568)

1763 *1859–61*
Plan of part of Lower Town Ottawa [Sgd] Toronto Oct 28th 1859 J. Stoughton Dennis P.L.S. Amended plan according to my report to the Honble the Commissioner of Crown Lands dated 8th May 1861 [Sgd] J Stoughton Dennis P.L.S. Approved [Sgd] P M Vankoughnet Commr Crown Lands Quebec 10th May 1861
Col ms in 2 parts Ea 65 x 165 cm 1" to 2 chains
Endorsements: 'A5 630 & 632'; stamp 'Admiralty & Railway Ordnance Lands Canada'
Shows the area from Rideau St to Cathcart St in Lower Town, and Sussex St to Wurtemberg St; bldgs in stone, brick, frame, poor frame, and log shown; lots sold by the ordnance indicated; Roman Catholic, Wesleyan Methodist, Presbyterian, and Episcopalian cemeteries shown; ordnance reserve; there are also copies of the western part of map of 2 Mar 1861 (OTAR(P)), 30 Sept 1861 (OTNR (SR 5793)), and 18 Feb 1862 (OTAR(P)).
OOAMA (NMC 43163–4) OTAR(P) OTNR (SR 5793)

1764 *1860*
Plan of Survey of Subdivision of the East half of Lot no 40 First Concession Township of Nepean Surveyed at the request of the Hon: Geo: Sherwood By Alfred Forrest Provincial Land Surveyor Ottawa 1860 (True Copy) signed A.H. Forrest
Print (lith) with ms adds 38 x 126 cm 1" to 2 chains
A subdivision plan showing unnamed streets and with town lots at the north end and park lots to the south; Ottawa city limits marked and road to Long Is; Sherwood's name added in ms in several lots.
OTAR

1765 *[1860]*
The Plan referred to in the Humble Petition of James Manger Holmes & others to Her Majesty the Queen. [Endorsed]: 'Nov./1861'
Col ms on linen 44 x 60 cm Scale not given
Provenance: Hill Collection; shows the land owned by Col By now belonging to Charles Willm By, land taken in 1826 for the canal from the land purchased by By; land originally taken from Nicholas Sparks but restored to him ca 1844 except part required for canal; the plan accompanied petition claiming land owned by By and not now required for canal purposes; the date is that on the copy of the judgment (OOA MG 24 I 9 6275–83).
OOAMA (NMC 4005)

1766 *1861*
PLAN / OF PART OF THE / CITY OF OTTAWA. // Park Lots / Being composed of Lot 7 in the Gore of Gloucester / to be laid out in accordance with the annexed Diagram ... Ottawa City January 1861. // Maclear & Co. Liths Toronto C.W.
Print (lith) 47 x 75 cm 1" to 8 chains
Shows the subdivision east of the Rideau R to 'Road from the Interior to the Ottawa & L'Orignal Road,' and from John St to Peter St; also shows part of Lower and Upper Bytown with 'Site for ViceRegal Residence' as originally planned just east of the canal; a few major bldgs including Parliament Bldgs; note on advantages of site indicates that area is outside of Ottawa and free from taxes, yet close to city centre; reproduced in Nagy, 21; the layout of the Parliament Bldgs added in pencil.
OOAMA (NMC 22570)

1767 *1861*
Plan of part of Upper Town Ottawa. Department of Crown Lands Quebec Septr 26th 1861. Assistant Commissioner [not sgd]
Col ms 68 x 101 cm 1" to 2 chains Watermark: '... WHATMAN 1858'
Shows the area from Wellington St to the Ottawa R and from reserve east of the Rideau Canal to beyond Water St; shows bldgs in stone, brick, and frame and boundaries of ordnance reserve.
OTNR (SR 5787)

Related maps

(2) *1861*
Plan of part of Upper Town Ottawa Department of Crown Lands Quebec February 1861. [Sgd] Andrew Russell Assistant Commissioner
Col ms 62 x 92 cm 1" to 2 chains
Shows similar information for the same area; ordnance land and bldgs on Barrack Hill marked.
OTAR(P)

1768 *1861*
Plan shewing the subdivision of the property belonging to Joseph Hinton Esqre Ottawa Signed George F. Austin Provl Land Surveyor Ottawa 17th Sept 1861 traced W.A.A. Office of W.A. Austin & Co. P.L. Surveyors C. Engineers etc. Ottawa C.W.
Col ms 65 x 90 cm 1" to 25 links

Shows lots on Bellevue Terrace at con line and Queen and Albert sts.
OOAMA (NMC 22569)

1769 *1861*
'Projected' Plan Shewing Proposed Subdivision of Ordnance Lands Ottawa [Sgd] Wm Ryan Thistle 7 September 1861. Thistle Provl Land Surveyor Ottawa
Col ms 64 x 94 cm 1" to 4 chains Endorsements: 'No 65'
Shows the plan for subdivision of the area by Dows L and Rideau Canal, con C, lot I; owners of large lots in the area named; 'Forrest & Thistle' crossed out in title.
OTNR (SR 5870)

Related maps

(2) *1861*
Plan shewing subdivision of Ordnance Lands being part of the West half of Lot 40 Con I Ottawa Front. The Easterly portion of Lots I & K Con. B. Rideau Front and part of Lot K. Con C. Rideau Front Township of Nepean As Surveyed by W. Ryan Thistle P.L.S. [Sgd] Wm Ryan Thistle Ottawa December 8/1861.
Col ms 55 x 77 cm 1" to 4 chains Endorsements: 'No 9' '16580/61'
Shows the subdivision as planned on map above; 'Examined & Copied for Ordnance & Agent Jan 16th 1862 J.W.B.'
OTNR (SR 5890)

1770 *[1863]*
[Map of the Ottawa area]
Col ms 42 x 44 cm Scale not given
Provenance: endorsed 'Map from Customs, 1863 fyle 599' [OOA RG 16]; shows the streets and lots of Ottawa, New Edinburgh, and Hull on the north side of the river; lot A in Gloucester Twp is marked in green and Point Gatineau is marked in red.
OOAMA (NMC 4233)

1771 *[1864]*
[Map of the MacKay Estate, part of the city of Ottawa, and part to be acquired for the Governor General's residence]
Print (lith) with ms adds 45 x 82 cm 1" to 8 chains
Originally enclosed in F.P. Rubidge's letter of 2 Apr 1864 to J.B. Brown, secretary Public Works (OOA RG 11 9B no 1028 vol 277 p 894); ms adds show proposed bridge, New Edinburgh and 'area which can be acquired' to the east of this, and 'proposed private station for Govr Genl'; the base is probably an early black-and-white proof for plan of the MacKay Estate (**1773(1)**) since the lettering is the same, but it has a little less detail and lacks title and views; there are also plans of 5 Apr (NMC 79961), 18 July, 27 Sept (NMC 79960), and 31 Oct (NMC 43166) from the same source showing further surveys and proposed work on the property.
OOAMA (NMC 43166–7, 79960–1)

1772 *1864*
Plan Shewing actual and proposed subdivision of portion of the 'By' Estate City of Ottawa [Sgd] Messr A.G. & A.H. Forrest Provl Land Surveyor Ottawa 23d Aug/ 64
Col ms on linen 75 x 95 cm 1" to 2 chains
Shows the area from Maria St to Biddy St, and Bank St to Concession Rd, as already laid out; the area from Biddy St to Halliford St between Esther St (continuation of Bank St) and Concession Rd proposed to be surveyed; lots being sold are marked; also second copy at OOAMA.
OOAMA (NMC 22571–2)

1773 *1864*
Topographical Map / OF THE / MACKAY ESTATE, / Shewing the divisions into / PARK, VILLA, AND VILLAGE LOTS, / and the position of the same with relation to the / CITY OF OTTAWA. / 1864 / [Sgd in facsimile] Thos C. Keefer / C.E. & P.L.S.// W.C. CHEWETT & CO LITH. TORONTO
Print (col lith) 45 x 88 cm 1" to 8 chains
Views: 'NEW EDINBURGH, FROM RAILWAY BRIDGE.' and 'MAIN FALL, RIVER RIDEAU'; an attractive chromolithograph showing the area from the Parliament Bldgs to the Mackay Estate beyond New Edinburgh; the Rideau Hall Domain is marked 'Residence of the Governor General'; shows lots, wooded areas, and roads on the estate and proposed roads; relief, streets named; major bldgs shown; (Nagy, 23–4).
OOAMA (NMC 17613) OTAR

Related maps

(2) *[1864]*
PARK AND VILLA LOTS / ON THE / MACKAY ESTATE AT OTTAWA // W.C. Chewett & Co. Lith. Toronto C.W.
Print (lith) 13 x 20 cm on sheet 37 x 22 cm Scale not given
Shows the same layout as plan above; description of advantages of the area including note that Thomas C. Keefer, C.E., laid out the roads and lots; prospective purchasers are to apply to Keefer and Robert Surtees; possibly prepared after plan above as a cheaper version to advertise lots for sale.
OOAMA (NMC 4234)

1774 *1865*
Plan of Part of Lower Town Ottawa Department of Crown Lands Ottawa 30th November 1865 [Sgd] Andrew Russell Assistt Commissr
Col ms 65 x 90 cm 1" to 2 chains
Shows the area from King St east to the Rideau R and from Rideau St north; Anglesea Square; cemeteries; a few names.
OTAR(P)

OTTERVILLE

1775 *[1857?]*
Map of Part of the Village / OF / OTTERVILLE / IN THE TOWNSHIP OF / SOUTH NORWICH / Shewing lots 8 & 9 in the 8th & 9th Concessions / the property of Gilbert Moore. / Charles L. Beard del. H. Gregory Lith. Hamilton
Print (lith) 64 x 93 cm 1" to 300 ft
Shows the area from Dover St to McQueen and Warren sts, and Carden St to the road allowance of the 9/10 con; some bldgs are shown to the south in the established part of town; shows two mills and proposed dam and mill race; Stover's sawmill and mill pond; includes a large extension of the town east of the railway, which is shown on the 1857 co map (**986**); see also **B1813**).
Oxford 41 (no R.P. number)

OWEN SOUND

1776 *1840*
Sydenham Plan of a Village Plot near the head of Owen's Sound – Lake Huron. Toronto Decb 11th 1840 C. Rankin D.S.
Col ms 58 x 86 cm 1" to 2 chains Endorsements: 'A 130' '696'
(SI 8 July 1840 to lay out lots in tract of land in vicinity of road line); shows the town plot as first laid out around a mill site on the Sydenham R and south of the bay; Murdoch St to river, and Baker St and Le Marchand Place to Campbell St; the town is mainly on the east side of the river; Indian trails and clearings, relief, marshes, a few names of squatters; also a copy: 'Sydenham by C. Rankin D.P.S. 1840. Office Copy. Surveyor General's Office Kingston 30th June 1843 A true copy [Sgd] Andrew Russell S & D.' endorsed 'No 20' and with the addition of names in the central and northern area (OTAR(P)); and a copy: 'Sydenham. Surveyed by C. Rankin, D.P.S. Office copy Surveyor General's Office Kingston 7th October 1843. A true copy [Sgd] Thomas Parke Survr Genl' with the pencilled addition of new streets at the north end and some names (OTAR).
OTAR OTAR(P) OTNR (SR 336)

1777 *1841*
Plan of Part of the Tract lately Surveyed at the head of Owen's Sound – Lake Huron. shewing particularly the traverse of the Rivers and the position of the best Mill Scites thereon. C. Rankin Toronto janry 7th 1841
Col ms 100 x 67 cm 1" to 10 chains Endorsements: '989'
Shows the boundary of the town reserve to include all of part west of Garafraxa Rd north of lot 14 in Sydenham and Derby twps, west to all of II con, Derby, and east of 12 con, Sydenham; mill sites and falls shown in Sydenham, and Pottawatomi R; relief, marshy land; streets are shown as in the 1840 plans but unnamed.
OTAR (SR 1831)

1778 *1846*
Plan of Sydenham town plot in the townships of Sydenham & Derby [Sgd] C. Rankin D.S. Toronto 1st Feby 1846
Col ms 63 x 97 cm 1" to 4 chains Endorsements: 'A 146' '698'
(SI 5 June 1845 to survey unsurveyed portion of town plot into lots); shows the extension of the town and some park lots to Garafraxa Rd and Staveley St, North St, West St, and south to Dease St; also shows Newash Indian village, mill reserves, proposed reserve for public pleasure-grounds, market, and Block B proposed for military reserve; relief and marshy areas; later notes about the boundary of the town as of 15 March 1847, and 1856; also a copy: 'Sydenham town plot Crown Lands Department Surveyors Branch West Montreal Dec 1847 A True Copy [Sgd] Andrew Russell' endorsed 'No 91' and with the addition of names and many later notes (OTAR(P)).
OTAR(P) OTNR (SR 8903)

1779 *1846*
Plan of the Town Reserve of Sydenham Toronto Feby 1st 1846 [Sgd] C. Rankin D.P.S.
Col ms 95 x 66 cm 1" to 12 chains Endorsements: 'A 147'
Shows the area of the town with the boundary encompassing con 10, Sydenham, ranges I–XI, and around Garafraxa Rd, and con 3, Derby, ranges I–III, west of river; shows the extension to the town as in the plan above (**1778**) but more park lots are shown; also shows the proposed reserve for pleasure-grounds, the proposed military reserve, mill reserve, and a reserve for lighthouse; Indian village; rocky high bluffs indicated and soundings given in the bay.
OTNR (SR 337)

Related maps

(**2**) *[1847]*
MAP / of the / TOWN RESERVE / of / SYDENHAM. / Scobie & Balfour, Lith: Toronto.
Print (lith) 86 x 62 cm 1" to 12 chains
Prepared from (1) above and incorporating most of the information except a few notes have been deleted; another copy at OTAR has ms adds of names of owners in most lots on the edge of the town; the map was advertised as just published on 25 May 1847 in the *British Colonist* (Toronto).
OTAR OTAR (SR 92647)

(**3**) *1856*
Sydenham Crown Lands Office Toronto 21st June 1856. Commissr. of Crown Lands Joseph Cauchon. Office Copy. J.W.B.
Col ms 86 x 67 cm 1" to 40 chains [i.e., 1" to 12 chains]

A copy of (1) above with the two ordnance reserves as designated in 1853 and some later additions of mill reserve.
OTAR

1780 *1849*
Part of the Town Plot of Sydenham Owen's Sound Shewing (red shaded) a tier of lots lately laid off on the East side of Marsh Street as ordered by the Crown Lands office 6th June 1849. C. Rankin D.S.
Col ms 42 x 57 cm 1" to 4 chains Endorsements: 'A 169'
Shows area from Marsh St to Water St and Peel St to Canning St east of river; houses shown and some names; notes indicate that several lots already settled by squatters; lots on Marsh St and some park lots were offered for sale on 3 July 1851 (OTAR RG 1 C-III-1 vol 5); and an undated copy: 'Part of the Town Plot of Sydenham ... Marsh St Sigd C. Rankin D.S.' (OTAR).
OTAR OTNR (SR 335)

1781 *1851*
Plan of part of the Town Reserve of Sydenham (Owen's Sound) Shewing the Military Reserve. In Reference to C.R.L.'s memorandum dated 16th November 1850. Traced from a Plan in the Crown Lands' Office. S. Freeth Capt R.E. 20th February 1851.
Col ms 49 x 61 cm 1" to 12 chains Endorsements: 'No 43/2'; stamp 'CREOC'
Shows the upper part of town from Division St to proposed military reserve in Block B north of North St and park lots beyond; also shows the Indian village of Newash, proposed public pleasure-ground, trails, marsh, etc.
OOAMA (NMC 4884)

1782 *1853*
Sydenham Owen's Sound Shewing the Military Reserve [Sgd] W.R. Renwick Captain R.E. 8 Sep 1853 Traced W.I. Fennell Lt R.E.D.
Col ms 88 x 56 cm 1" to 12 chains Endorsements: 'No 43' 'Rel. CW/ 520 & 574 ... 675 R. 7759'; stamp 'CREOC'
Sections at 1" to 100 ft vertical; shows all of the town plot with details of the two military reserves, areas cleared, etc; relief, drainage, comments on geology, depths in harbour; radius line from military reserve; sections are across harbour and along shore to show positions of bluffs; lighthouse point.
OOAMA (NMC 19839)

1783 *1854*
PLAN / OF TOWN LOTS IN / SYDENHAM / OWEN SOUND / 1854. / THE PROPERTY OF JOHN MCNAB. / Litho: J. Ellis King St Toronto / [Sgd] F.F. Passmore Provl Land Surveyor Toronto.
Print (lith) 52 x 74 cm 1" to 2 chains
A subdivision of lots 12–15, 17, 19 on Bay St east of the harbour; relief, treed areas; see also **B1814**.
OOAMA (NMC 43210) Grey 16 (R.P. 2)

1784 *1856*
Plan of Military Block B in the town plot of Sydenham as subdivided. Owen's Sound Sept 10th 1856 [Sgd] C. Rankin P.L.S.
Col ms 74 x 52 cm 1" to 4 chains Endorsements: 'No 210'
(SI 13 Jan 1852 to subdivide squatters' land left vacant by earlier survey into park and town lots, the residue of Block B; OTNR FN 299 17 Sept 1856); from Bay St to Rear St, North St north to Albert St, the subdivision of block between the two ordnance reserves in the northeast part of town; streets named and lots numbered; grammar school; also a copy: 'Military Block B. Sydenham Office Copy Crown Lands Department Toronto 22nd September 1856 [Sgd] Joseph Cauchon Comr Thomas Devine' endorsed 'No 120' (OTAR(P)).
OTAR(P) OTNR (SR 338)

1785 *[1857]*
PLAN / of the Town of / OWEN SOUND / COUNTY OF GREY / Maclear & Co Lith. Toronto. / Rankin & Spry P.L.Ss
Print (lith) 85 x 60 cm 1" to 12 chains
Shows the town including an area laid out south of 'Potawotamie R' to lot 14, Superior and Regent sts between Bay and Rear sts, and east between Adelaide and Victoria sts; shows several subdivisions west, south, and east of extended town; various reserves for grammar school, public pleasure-ground, ordnance reserve; a few small drawings of public bldgs; relief, mills; OOAMA copy has stamp: 'Dept of Public Works Canada'; the map was advertised for sale at Maclear's in the *Daily Colonist* (Toronto) 20 Oct 1857.
OOAMA (NMC 19797) OOWM OTUTF

Related maps

(2) *1858*
Plan of the Town Plot of Owen Sound County of Grey (Signed) Rankin & Spry Surveyors [Sgd] Feb. 18th 1858. Copied from actual Survey A.G. Robinson C Engr
Col ms 126 x 96 cm 1" to 8 chains Endorsements: stamps 'BW' 'No. 492'
Shows the town on the east side with streets and lots; relief, public and military reserves, grammar school lots, mills, and swampy areas; shows the Indian village of Newash; probably copied from the printed plan or a common original but lacks two of the subdivisions shown to the southeast and the north.
OOAMA (NMC 16792)

1786 *1857*
Plan of the townplot of Brooke in the township of Sarawak [Sgd] Edwin Henry Kertland C E & P.L.S. Elora 12 June 1857. Surveyed under instructions from the Indian Department [Sgd] A Russell. Examined 11 July 1857 Thos Devine

Col ms 78 x 99 cm 1" to 4 chains Endorsements: 'A 222'
(OTNR FN 227, 293 20 June 1857); shows the subdivision of part of the Indian reserve lands on the west side of the harbour; from Sound St and Raglan St west to West St, and from Ann St north to Caughnawaga St; town lots are laid out on the eastern part with park lots to the west; St George's Square, Queen's Square, and a few bldgs are shown including church and parsonage; relief; also a later copy in OTAR(P): 'Town of Brooke Surveyed by Edwin Henry Kertland P.L.S. 1857 Department of Crown Lands Quebec June 30th 1862 [Sgd] Andrew Russell Asst Commissioner.'
OTAR(P) OTNR (SR 7726)

Related maps

(2) *1857*
A 222. / PLAN / OF THE TOWN PLOT OF / BROOKE / IN THE TOWNSHIP OF / SARAWAK. / Indian Department / Toronto, August 1857. / Edwin Henry Kertland C.E. & P.L.S. / Elora 12 June 1857. // Maclear & Co. Liths Toronto. // Examined 11 July 1857. / Thos Devine. / C.L.O.
Print (lith) 74 x 98 cm 1" to 4 chains
Based on (1) above and showing the same information.
OLU

1787 *1858*
Plan shewing (within the red border) the outline of the Town of Owen Sound, as now incorporated, and the position &c of the adjacent Town Plot of Brooke (within the yellow border), proposed to be added to, or included within the corporation &c. and also shewing by the yellow dotted line the portion of the Bay or Sound desired to be included &c. Owen's Sound 12th May 1858 [Sgd] C.Rankin P.L.S.
Col ms on linen 93 x 81 cm 1" to 12 chains
Originally accompanied a petition for the enlargement of the town (OOA RG 5 C1 no 965 1858); shows streets and lots of Brooke and main streets and boundary of original Sydenham part; the harbour boundary runs from the north point of Brooke at the shore to the point beyond the military reserves.
OOAMA (NMC 11424)

1788 *1859*
Plan of Part of Owen Sound Town Plot for the purpose of shewing the bank of River in front, with the opportunity for setting a road of any particular breadth on the top of the bank. April 2d 1859 [Sgd] C. Rankin P.L.S.
Ms 46 x 99 cm 1" to 2 chains
Originally accompanied a petition for a road (OOA RG 1 L3 W9 no 11 1859); a survey along the east bank of the river past the steamboat basin; description of bldgs between proposed road and river; relief; (Holmden 2298).
OOAMA (NMC 22691)

1789 *[186?]*
Part of O Sound shewing high streets C.R.
Col ms on linen 73 x 29 cm Scale not given
Shows lot nos and streets with heights of land by contours and spot heights.
OTMCL (E.W. Banting Collection)

1790 *1865*
Plan Shewing the proposed extension of the limits of the corporation of the town of Owen Sound in the county of Grey July 12th 1865 [Sgd] C. Rankin P.L.S. Copy C.R. July 12th 65
Col ms 52 x 44 cm 1" to 25 chains
Note: 'A Copy of this presented by me – through the Mayor Mr. Stephens to the Corporation – 27th Augt 1866 C.R.'; shows an extension to include the east half of the harbour or bay; description of proposed extension; town plot of Brooke, twp of Sarawak and Indian lands marked also.
OTMCL (E.W. Banting Collection)

PAISLEY

1791 *1855*
Plan of the Proposed Sub-division of the Town Plot of Paisley in the Townships of Elderslie and Greenock in the County of Bruce. Fras Kerr P.L.S. Guelph February 1855
Col ms 41 x 71 cm 1" to 10 chains Endorsements: 'B 74'
(SI 21 Oct 1854 to make a preliminary survey of reserve); shows the town on lots 52–56, con A, Greenock, and cons A and B, lots 11–15, Elderslie, on the Saugeen Rd; streets from Canrobert to North St, and Kertch St to Baumersund St; relief, sawmill and mill race on the Mud R; Saugeen R also shown; various bldgs shown; lot nos; note refers to 'Order in Council July 1856 permitting Orchard, Rowe, Hodge and Valentine to purchase the respective portions edged yellow & green'; also a copy: 'Projected Plan of Paisley Crown Lands Department Toronto 19th July 1856 [Sgd] E.P. Tache Actg Commr C.L.' with land allotted to the four landowners as named above (OOAMA (NMC 70950)); and a copy: 'Paisley. Crown Lands Department Quebec 26th July 1856' (OTAR).
OOAMA (NMC 70950) OTAR OTNR (SR 256)

1792 *1856*
Plan of the Town-plot of Paisley in the townships of Elderslie and Greenock. Francis Kerr P.L.S. Guelph 1856. Alex W. Simpson, del.
Col ms 79 x 100 cm 1" to 4 chains Endorsements: 'A 214' '10568/56' '11497/56'
(SI 17 Sept 1855 to lay out town plot; OTNR FN 1616 22 Oct 1856); shows the town as laid out according to the 1855 plan; relief, dam, mills, and names of owners as specified on 1855 plan; 'Returned for sale 26th December 1856 A.R.'; and a copy: 'Paisley by F. Kerr 1856' with watermark: 'J WHATMAN 1855' (OTAR (SR 7720)); and a

copy: 'Paisley in the Townships of Elderslie & Greenock J.W.B. Crown Lands Office Toronto 6th Jan 1857 [Sgd] Joseph Cauchon Commissioner of Crown Lands' endorsed 'No 122' and with the addition of notes indicating area reserved for 'Crown' and 'School' (OTAR(P)).
OTAR(P) OTNR (SR 7720; 7724)

1793 *[1858]*
PLAN OF THE TOWNPLOT OF PAISLEY. / Surveyed for the Crown Lands Department by / Francis Kerr, P.L.S. Lithographed for and published / by Gilmour & Lynch, P.L. Surveyors Paisley.
Print (lith) 78 x 100 cm 1" to 4 chains
Shows the same layout of streets as on 1856 plan (**1792**), but many more bldgs shown and some identified including Valentine's Mills, Valentine's Arms, British Hotel, school, Rowe's Tavern; originally accompanied a petition of 21 Sept 1858 asking that Paisley be made the co town (OOA RG 5 C1 vol 912 letter no 1852 of 1858).
OOAMA (NMC 11425)

Later editions and states

(**2**) *[1859?]*
[Title, etc, the same]
From the same plate as above with the addition of a few more bldgs including the Caledonian Hotel and different position and shape for St Andrew's Church (erected 1859).
OOAMA (NMC 16793)

PARIS

1794 *1847*
Plan of the Town of Paris In the Townships of Dumfries, Brantford District of Gore. Thomas Allchin Deputy Provincial Surveyor drawn by F. Herbst 1847
Col ms 47 x 64 cm 1" to 4 chains Endorsements: stamp [BW] 'no 491'
Shows the town from Smith's Creek to Grand River St and Grand R, and Church St to Grand River St on the west side of the Grand R and both sides of Smith's Creek; bridges, a few major bldgs; (Holmden 2302).
OOAMA (NMC 22692)

PENETANGUISHENE

1795 *1794–5*
Sketch of the Harbour of Penetangushene taken in Octr 1794 by A. Aitken Dpy Syr [and] Sketch of the Indian Purchase at Penetangushene (Coloured with Lake) Copy W.C.
2 col mss on 1 sheet 67 x 42 cm 1" to 1/2 mile and 1" to 2 miles Endorsements: 'Q 16' '1065'
(SI 12 Sept 1794 regarding locating sites at either end of road being surveyed from Yonge St to Matchedash Bay); the larger-scale map shows the harbour and relief of shoreline; the other plan shows the block of land acquired from the Indians in 1795, various place-names, and the 'French ruins.'
OTNR (SR 2489)

Related maps

(**2**) *1794*
Sketch of the Harbour of Penetangushene with the Soundings laid down in fathoms taken by Alexr Aitken Dpy Surveyor in 1794
Ms Approx 46 x 54 cm 1" to 1/2 mile
With Lt Gov Simcoe's letter no 10 to the Duke of Portland, 10 Nov 1794, urging the establishment of a military post at the site to counteract American establishments on L Huron (GBLpro CO 42/319 p 28A); shows the same outlines as the above plan with the addition of a spot marked on the west side as 'the proper situation for a town being the highest land' and islands reserved for naval purposes.
GBLpro (MPG 1173(1))

1796 *1811–12*
A Sketch of the out lines of a Village on the East Shore of Pennetangushine Harbour on Lake Huron, surveyed, by Order of the Surveyor Generals Office, bearing date the 29th Augst 1811. [Sgd] Saml S. Wilmot Dy Surveyor
Col ms 47 x 65 cm 1" to 4 chains Endorsements: 'A 52' '676'
(SI 29 Aug 1811 and 25 and 28 Oct 1811 to designate area for a town at the end of the Penetanguishene Rd; SI 28 Jan 1812 to lay out town plot and number lots from south boundary); shows a grid of seven streets by seven streets (unnamed) laid out, and lots numbered along the front 1–23; relief, sandy beach, place where vessels may unload; this plan appears to include the 1812 survey of the town plot.
OTNR (SR 247)

1797 *1815 (1816)*
Plan of Penetanguishene Harbour and Works projected for the Defence of the intended Dock-Yard by (Signed) W.R. Payne Capt Royal Engrs Feby 1815 Royl Engrs Drawg Room true Copy [Sgd] J.B. Duberger Junr Quebec 24th June 1816 [Sgd] G Nicolls Lt Coll Rl Engineers
Col ms 69 x 65 cm 1" to 300 ft Endorsements: stamps 'BO' 'IGF'
Shows the area of harbour and port north of town site; proposed fort, blockhouses, batteries; references to present bldgs; relief, roads, etc; also in OOAMA (NMC 4888): 'Plan of the Harbour of Penétanguisheen Taken Octr 1815 by Captn W.F.W. Owen ... 24th June 1816 G. Nicolls' (Holmden 2306), a copy of **C38**.
OOAMA (NMC 4888; 17810)

1798 *[1833]*
Plan of Town Lots Laid off at Penetangushine (Home Dist) in continuation of the Scite of the Present village by C.R.
Col ms 42 x 54 cm 1" to 6 chains Endorsements: 'A 53' '675'
Inset: 'Plan shewing the relative situation of Town Lots laid out at Penetangushine (Home Dist) in continuation of the Present Village. C.R.' 1" to 20 chains; (SI 30 March 1833 to Charles Rankin to lay out the town plot nearer the establishment than present site on the request of inhabitants; OTNR FN 579 17 May 1833); the present village is shown extending to Penetanguishene Rd; the continuation is shown to the north, on the east side of the harbour; Water St and 2nd to 4th sts are named; the inset shows the new town lots and the military and naval reserves to the north; new barrack, government storehouse, and arsenal shown; 'Proposed Site of Fort' indicated on an island.
OTNR (SR 250)

1799 *1835*
Plan of Naval and Military Reserves at Penetangushine Surveyor General's Office, Toronto U.C. 8th April 1835. Projected J.G. Chewett
Col ms 64 x 48 cm 1" to 20 chains Endorsements: '959' 'Office Plan'
Two naval and military reserves are shown on west side of harbour and one on the east; shows the street layout of the old village, and extension from Water St to Poyntz St and west to West St; also a grid of lots on the west side of harbour; later addition shows proposed reserves; sawmill on creek at mouth; also copy at OOAMA (NMC 4889) with same title, sgd '18th April 1835. (Copy) – Henry Lizars (Signed) S.P. Hurd S.G. Certified as a true Copy T.G.W. Eaststaff Draugn,' endorsed 'B↑O,' and with additions of notes of 1835 about a licence of occupation, and of 20 Nov 1852 about portions of military reserves to be retained for use of ordnance (Holmden 2329); and another copy at OOAMA (NMC 4297): 'Copy No 2 Projection Plan of the Naval and Military Reserves at Penetanguishene Copy J.G.C. Surveyor General's Office Toronto 19th January 1837 [Sgd] J W Macaulay Survr Genl' endorsed 'REO' and '272.'
OOAMA (NMC 4297; 4889) OTNR (SR 248)

1800 *1837*
Penetangushine. Projected Copy [Sgd] J.G. Chewett S.G. Office 23rd June 1837. Surveyor General's Office Toronto 23rd June 1837 [Sgd] J W Macaulay Survr Genl
Col ms 44 x 63 cm 1" to 4 chains
Shows the town as laid out in 1833 from Penetanguishene Rd west to Scott St and from the water to Pointz St, and the new part east of Penetanguishene Rd from Nelson to Fox St and Simcoe to Barrack St; some names and notes in lots; also a copy with same title and date, endorsed 'No 64' and 'Office Copy' and with the addition of names and some notes (OTAR(P).
OTAR OTAR(P)

1801 *1851*
Penetanguishene Plan shewing the arrangement for the Settlement of the Pensioners ... Signed Henry Vavasour, Col Comg Rl Engrs Canada Signed Rl Pilkington Draftsman 26th June 1851
Col ms 55 x 43 cm 1" to 20 chains Watermark: 'RUSE & TURNER 1846' Endorsements: 'No 31'; stamp 'B↑O'
Parts to be laid out for pensioners; area reserved for naval purposes; roads; bldgs, some identified.
OOAMA (NMC 4300)

1802 *1851*
Plan of Mill Reserve Penetanguashene Surveyed by Hugh P. Savigny P.L.S. Barrie 2nd May 1851
Col ms 46 x 33 cm 1" to 4 chains
Originally accompanied a petition (OOA RG 1 E3 C no 6 no 70); shows the area west of Centre St extending west to con line, and the position of three mills along the river leading into the bay; (Holmden 2332).
OOAMA (NMC 4298)

1803 *1855*
Plan of the eastern part of the Town Plot of [Pe]netanguishene. Surveyed By H.P. Savigny P.L.S. 1855. [Sgd] H.P. Savigny Prov. Land [Surveyor]. Examined 24 January 1856 [initialled] T.D. Surveyor
Col ms 64 x 89 cm 1" to 4 chains
(SI 31 May 1855 to survey the residue of the town plot into town and park lots and lengthen streets east of Penetanguishene Rd as surveyed by Rankin (1833) and west of the road as surveyed by Richardson (SI 18 May 1829); OTNR FN 1640 12 Nov 1855); shows town lots laid out from Nelson St to Fox St and from Penetanguishene Rd and Simcoe St to Barrack St; park lots beyond this; shows a few bldgs; 'road travelled at present' bisects some lots; cleared areas; also a copy of same title sgd 'Crown Lands Office Toronto Feby 26th 1856 [Sgd] Joseph Cauchon Commissr of Crown Lands J.W.B.' and endorsed 'No 110' and with the addition of names (OTAR(P)).
OTAR(P) OTNR (SR 245)

1804 *1855*
Plan of the western part of the town-plot of Penetanguishene Surveyed by H.P. Savigny P.L.S. 1855.
Col ms 58 x 72 cm 1" to 4 chains Endorsements: 'A 205'
(SI 31 May 1855 as described in **1803** above; OTNR FN 1640 12 Nov 1855); shows town lots laid out from the Penetanguishene Rd west to Centre and Pointz sts with park lots to West St; also a copy with same title sgd 'Crown Lands Office Toronto Feby 25th 1856 [Sgd] Joseph Cauchon Commissioner of Crown Lands J.W.B.' and

endorsed 'No. 111' and with the addition of some names and bldgs (OTAR(P)).
OTAR(P) OTNR (SR 251)

1805 *1856*
PLAN OF TOWN LOTS / IN / PENETANGUISHENE / LAID OUT ON LOT No 115 IN THE 1st CONCESSION / OF THE / TOWNSHIP OF TAY. / the Property of / S. JEFFERY & A. DUNLOP Esqrs / Surveyed by / H.P. SAVIGNY P.L.S. 1856. / Maclear & Co. Lith. Toronto C.W.
Print (lith) 68 x 97 cm 1" to 3 chains
An untitled inset shows the location of the property in the town and bldgs with some identified; the main map shows the area east of Penetanguishene Rd, north of Edward St, and south of the continuation of Robert St; notes on the advantages of the town; drawing of the paddle-steamer *Collingwood* by C. Wood.
OMSA

1806 *1857*
Plan of Subdivision of Lot E. Town of Penetanguishene Sept 1857. [Sgd] Hugh P. Savigny P.L. Surveyor. Examined Aug. 20th 1858 J.W.B.
Ms 26 x 39 cm 1" to 4 chains Endorsements: 'A 206'
Shows the area bounded by Penetanguishene Rd, Robert St, Fox St, and Brock St.
OTNR (SR 246)

1807 *[1857?]*
PLAN / OF / TOWN LOTS / THE PROPERTY / OF / JNO. LEYS ESQRE / AT / PENETANGUISHENE // UNWIN AND JACK / P.L. Surveyors & Land Agents / Provincial Chambers / TORONTO C.W. // Maclear & Co Liths Toronto C.W.
Print (lith) 58 x 87 cm 1" to 20 chains
Insets: 'SKETCH / OF / Penetanguishene / Shewing / LOCATION OF LOTS' 1" to 2 chains, 'MAP / Shewing THE POSITION of / PENETANGUISHENE / IN / Reference to the Course of Trade / BETWEEN THE ATLANTIC SEABOARD / and the / Great West.'; shows a subdivision from Edward St to road allowance, lots 115/116, and from Dunlop St to road allowance, cons I/II, at the southeast corner of town; inset shows projected railway Whitby to Penetanguishene; Unwin and Jack's partnership was advertised from 25 Oct 1856 to about May 1858 in the *Daily Colonist* (Toronto).
OOAMA (NMC 97277)

1808 *1858*
Plan of the Reformatory Prison Farm near Penetanguishene [Sgd] John Lindsay Provl Land Surveyor Penetanguishene November 22nd 1858.
Col ms 56 x 63 cm 1" to 4 chains Endorsements: 'P No 2'
(OTNR FN 1638 18 Feb 1859); shows the farm covering the area of the naval and military reserve on the east side of the bay; shows the ordnance store, graveyard, old hospital, and barracks; the reformatory prison yard is designated to displace the officers' barracks; pensioners' lots, private bldgs, and relief and wooded land also shown.
OTNR (SR 249)

1809 *[1859] (1860)*
Copy of P.L.S. Lindsay's plan of Pensioners 3 acre lots near Penetanguishene in the township of Tay. Crown Lands Department Quebec June 1860 [Sgd] Andrew Russell Assistant Commissioner
Col ms 68 x 77 cm 1" to 4 chains Endorsements: 'No 13'
Shows the area south of the reformatory prison farm from Don St to Navy St and from harbour to the road allowance between cons I and II; lot nos and sizes and some names added; two lots reserved for Church of England; the original plan dated 18 Feb 1859 and endorsed 'PN 64' appears not to have survived (Bigger, 2:64); also a later copy: 'Copy of Pensioners 3 acre Lots Penetanguishene Surveyed 1859 by John Lindsay P.L.S. Department of Crown Lands Quebec Augt 14th 1863 [Sgd] W B McDougall Commissioner' endorsed '13' (OTAR(P)).
OTAR(P) OTNR (SR 2501)

PERTH

1810 *[1816]*
Plan of the Town of Perth on the River Tay – laid out on Lot No 2 – 1st Conn of the Township of [Drummond] in the District of Johnstown. ... [Sgd] Samuel Ridout
Ms on tissue paper, pts missing 46 x 42 cm 1" to 4 chains Watermark: 'J WHATMAN 1811' Endorsements: '673'
(OTNR FN 41 John Booth 2 Jan 1817); a note with parts missing begins: 'His Excellency Lieut Governor Gore w[ho visited] in October 1816 was pleased to signify his pleasure that Lot No 3 in the same Concession ...'; the note indicates that lot 3 was given to town and lot 4 reserved as a glebe; shows the town from the river south to Robinson St and from Wilson St east to Sherbrooke St; two reserves for public purposes; government office is located southeast of Harvey and Gore sts.
OTAR(P)

1811 *1821*
Perth. James H. Powell, Secretary, Superintendent
Ms 67 x 49 cm 1" to 200 ft Endorsements: 'No 37'
Endorsed with partially obliterated statement about the survey '... letter of January 29th 1821 ... Feby 10th 1821'; shows an enlarged town plot from South St to North St, and Wilson St to Irwin St; town extended to east and a bit to the north and south; 'containing 400 acres lot nos 3 and 4 1st Concession Township Drummond'; names in the

lots with many later changes and one note dated 1839; photoreproduction in OTAR(P).
OTNR

Related maps

(2) *[ca 1830]*
Town Plot of Perth Surveyed by James H. Powell
Col ms 71 x 47 cm 1" to 200 ft Endorsements: 'A 155' '674'
Shows the same streets as (1) above; also shows church, court-house, and school lot near market site; probably made after 1827 as it shows church lots divided for the Catholics, Episcopalians, and Presbyterians as per SI 27 Nov 1827 to Owen Quinn; also a later copy in the 1850s: 'James H. Powell Secretary Superintendent Containing 400 acres lots No 3 & 4 1st Concession Township Drummond. Copied by J. Innes.' with watermark: 'J WHATMAN TURKEY MILL 1854' (OTNR (SR 3524)).
OTNR (SR 257; 3524)

1812 *[1822?]*
Perth 1822
Col ms 36 x 48 cm Scale not given
Shows streets, lots with nos, brick and frame houses, roads, wooded areas; some names of owners and all bldgs; three bridges; superintendent's office; landscaping of estates; Wilson St east to town line; 2nd con line beyond Foster St to Scotch line; the date 1822 on the map may be a later endorsement.
OPM

1813 *[1824]*
Perth // A. Bell Delint C.Thomson Sculpt Edinr
Print (engrav) 16 x 16 cm 1" to 15 chains
In William Bell, *Hints to Emigrants* (Edinburgh: Printed for Waugh and Innes 1824), opp 74 (*Bib Can* 1274); streets named, 10 major bldgs, and areas shown and indexed including 'rising ground reserved for govt,' 'Parade ground for the Militia,' 'the Superintendants office.'
OTMCL

1814 *1837*
Perth Copy [Sgd] J.G. Chewitt S G Office 20th June 1837. [Sgd] Surveyor General's Office Toronto 23rd June 1837 W Macauley Survr Genl
Col ms 57 x 50 cm 1" to 2.66 chains
Shows the same street layout as the 1821 plan (**1811**); notes on sales of lots; two bridges shown along Gore St.
OTAR

PETAWAWA

1815 *1854*
Plan of Town Plot mouth of River Petawawa With proposed Subdivision into Lots. Surveyed under Instructions from the Commissioner of Crown Lands Dated Quebec 18th Feby 1854 [Sgd] Robert Hamilton Prov. Land Surveyor. L'Orignal 13th Sept 1854 Copied for R. Hamilton P.S. 7 Dec 1854. Examined A.R.
Col ms 65 x 45 cm 1" to 4 chains Endorsements: 'B 46'
(SI 18 July 1854 to survey river for three miles from mouth for best location of town plot and survey outlines; OTNR FN 1643 18 Sept 1854); shows the layout of the town with streets from Allumette L to Victoria St, and East St to West St; shows lots, a mill site and public square, names of a few owners, improved land, and relief.
OTNR (SR 253)

Related maps

(2) *1857*
Plan of the Petawawa Town Plot. Surveyed under Instruction from the Commissioner of Crown Lands, Dated Toronto 21st June 1856, [Sgd] L'Orignal 30th Novr 1857. Robert Hamilton Prov. Land Surveyor.
Col ms 65 x 49 cm 1" to 4 chains
The finished survey for the town per SI 21 June 1856 with all streets named, lot nos, dimensions, and areas; bldgs and names of owners shown; the Pembroke and Mattawan Rd and A. Montgomery's property shown in detail.
OTNR (SR 252)

PETERBOROUGH

1816 *1825*
Plan of the Survey of a part of the Town Plott in the Township of Monaghan. Surveyed by Order of the Honble Thos Ridout Surveyor General by Richd Birdsall Depy Surveyor Asphodel 3rd Decr 1825
Col ms 73 x 108 cm 1" to 5 chains Endorsements: 'No 38'
(SI 18 Oct 1825 to survey the town plot in Monaghan; OTNR FN 581 10 Dec 1825); shows the area laid out in town lots from the Otonabee R to Aylmer St and from Townsend St to McDonell St, and beyond this areas laid out in park lots; part of lot 10, con 13, Monaghan; many later additions and changes particularly in the area of park lots.
OTNR (SR 238)

Related maps

(2) *1825*
Plan of the Survey of that part of the Town Plott in the Township of Monaghan as laid out in half Acre Lots. Surveyed by Order of The Hon. Thos Ridout, Surveyor Genl by Richd Birdsall Depy Surveyor. Asphodel 9th Decr 1825
Col ms 48 x 68 cm 1" to 3 chains Endorsements: 'A 49'
Shows the town proper as on map above, some bldgs shown; reserves for depot, market, burial ground, public properties; a few names of owners; and a copy in OTAR(P): 'Town of Peterborough

Copy from Mr. Birdsall's Plan of Survey. Office Plan.'
OTAR(P) OTNR (SR 242)

1817 *1833*
Diagram of the Town Reservation of Peterborough shewing the Surveyed and unsurveyed Land By [Sgd] J. Huston Depty Prov Survr Septbr 1833
Col ms 48 x 71 cm and addition 15 x 16 cm 1" to 5 chains Endorsements: 'No 39'
(SI 27 May 1833 to lay out remaining part of the reserve); the town has been extended north and west to Smith and Park sts; the unsurveyed part of reserve is shown south of Townsend St; many additions and later changes of names; two later notes indicate that block between Charlotte St and King St shown incorrectly on this plan but correctly on 1825 plan (**1816**), and two conflicting positions for Park St and Smith St have been noted (see **1819**); also a copy with the same title, sgd 'A true Copy Surveyor General's Office Kingston July 21st 1843 [Sgd] Thomas Parke Survr Genl' and with addition of mill site, reserves for school, churches, etc (OTAR).
OTAR OTNR (SR 239)

1818 *1836*
Part of Peterborough By [Sgd] John Huston Depty Surveyor 30th May 1836
Col ms 33 x 20 cm 1" to 3 chains
Originally accompanied a petition for water frontage from reserved lands to add to mill property (OOA RG 1 L3 S 20 no 110 1837); shows the southeast part of town from Charlotte St to Townsend St east of George St; (Holmden 2335).
OOAMA (NMC 70951)

1819 *1845*
Plan of Part of Peterborough shewing the True Position of Park Street. by John Reid Dy Provl Surveyor 29 Octr 1845
Col ms 82 x 29 cm 1" to 5 chains Endorsements: 'A 140'
(SI 1 Oct 1845 to verify western boundary (Park St) as surveyed by Birdsall and Huston; OTNR FN 582 29 Oct 1845); shows the correct position of Park St with jog between Sherbrooke St and Dalhousie St; shows streets, numbered lots, table of sizes for irregular lots.
OTNR (SR 240)

Related maps

(2) *1846 (1847)*
Map of Smith Street in Peterboro' by John Reid D P Surveyor January 26th 1846. Exd A.R.
Col ms 36 x 50 cm 1" to 5 chains Endorsements: 'A 145'
(SI 18 Dec 1845 to verify north boundary of town (Smith St) with regard to original survey by Wilmot of 1818); several positions are shown for Smith St; a note: 'This survey is erroneous See Mr. Reid's report of 4th May 1847'; the final later adjustment of the line is also shown; shows the whole town with table of broken lots on Smith St.
OTNR (SR 241)

1820 *[1846]*
[Map of Peterborough by Sandford Fleming]
Col ms 68 x 83 cm Scale not given
Provenance: endorsed 'Fleming Collection No 145' (OOA (MG 29)); this is an untitled, unfinished ms draft made by Fleming for the production of his printed map below; the plan shows streets in red, bldgs and other detail in black, relief by hachures, and trees drawn in detail; bridge and dam; the bldgs are exactly as shown on the printed map but none are named and no other names are shown; the shoreline is shown as corrected at Wolfe St and four small bldgs appearing at the end of Brock St are not shown on the printed plan; part of a border is drawn in faintly on one side.
OOAMA (NMC 25416)

Related maps

(2) *1846*
PLAN of the TOWN / of / Peterborough / CANADA WEST / Surveyed in the Spring of 1846 by / [Signature in facsimile] Sandford Arnot Fleming. Scobie & Balfour Lithog. Toronto on Stone by S.A. Fleming.
Print (lith) 85 x 67 cm 1" to 4 chains
View: 'View of the Courthouse'; shows the streets from the Otonabee R west to Park St, from Townsend St to Smith St (including variations in position of the latter), east of the river to Stewart St, and from Maria St north to beyond Elizabeth St; all bldgs are shown and major ones named including mills, churches, schools, wharves, etc; relief by hachures; all lots shown including irregular parcels; OOAMA copy has ms adds showing extension of town to south and east; the plan was published by Sept 1846 (OOA MG 29 vol 45 folder 312).
OOAMA (NMC 17889) OPETHS OTAR

1821 *1846*
Peterborough J.C.Dts Crown Land Department Montreal August 1846 A.R. A true copy [Sgd] D.B. Papineau C.C.L.
Col ms 53 x 81 cm 1" to 3 chains Endorsements: stamp [BW] '498'
A plan drawn by James Cane showing the town and streets from the river west to Park St including the jog in the latter, from Townsend St to Smith St; an unsurveyed portion is shown to the south.
OOAMA (NMC 22707)

1822 *[185?]*
[Map of Peterborough showing proposed extension]
Col ms, pt missing 118 x 123 cm Scale not given
Shows a proposal for the extension of the town to the north to take in some mills along the river, to the west to take in the park lots, and to the south

to the con line; the village of Ashburnham is shown east of river; two dams, the Ashburnham bridge, and bridge at locks shown; the streets in town are named and several lots in green; the proposal shows approx the same area but different boundary lines from that of 1854 below.
OTAR

Related maps

(2) *1854*
Diagram of the proposed limits of the Town of Peterboro' [Sgd] Jas Stevenson Mayor Thos White Jr Town Clerk
Col ms on linen 123 x 74 cm Scale not given
Originally accompanied a petition from the Municipal Council to extend limits to include the park lots on the south and west, a portion of the twp of Smith on the north, and 'Peterborough East' in the twp of Otonabee on the east, and to divide town into four wards (OOA RG 5 C1/421 no 1272 1854); the rough map shows proposed boundary and north, south, east, and centre wards; streets named; Cobourg & Peterboro' Railway; the petition was presented again in 1856 but the extension was not granted until the 1870s.
OOAMA (NMC 11427)

1823 *1851*
Diagram of the 12th Lot in the 12th Concession of Monaghan as laid out into Park Lots Augt 4th 1851 Copy by John Reid P.L.Surveyor
Col ms 42 x 35 cm 1" to 5.5 chains
Shows lots 1–7 and 11–21 with a few deeded; 'proposed new Gravelled Road'; related to R.P. 110 (**B1895**).
OOAMA (NMC 3525)

1824 *[1855]*
A Diagram of the south part of the Town of Peterborough and some of the Town Parks
Col ms 41 x 25 cm Scale not given
Originally accompanied a land petition from the town about boundaries of 14 May 1855 (OOA RG 1 L1 P 9 no 20 1855); shows the area south of Townsend St with note: 'land eligible for the contemplated cemetery'; also shows marshy land, areas liable to flooding south of town, and a road approved by the District Council; (Holmden 2340).
OOAMA (NMC 4305)

1825 *1855*
Improvements in the town of Peterboro' [Sgd] Geo A Stewart May 14th 1855
Col ms 53 x 70 cm 1" to 2 chains
Shows the area at the south end of town from George St to Park St and from Hospital Point to Wolfe St; shows proposals for engineering improvements to reduce marshy land and divert river into the Otonabee; proposed breastwork across river along George St.
OTNR (SR 243)

Related maps

(2) *1855*
A true copy of a plan for laying out the unsurveyed land south of the Town of Peterborough (Lately purchased by the Town Council) submitted to the Town Council of the town of Peterborough on the 14th May 1855 by Geo. A. Stewart Esq. P.L.S. Town Clerk Council Office Town of Peterborough May 16th 1855
Col ms 51 x 79 cm Scale not given
Originally accompanied petitions about the reclaiming of a swamp and about squatters (OOA RG 1 L3 P8 no 12 filed with P9 no 20 1855); shows the same information as (1) above; (Holmden 2337).
OOAMA (NMC 43195)

1826 *1857*
PLAN OF LOTS / LAID OUT ON – THE PROPERTY / KNOWN AS / CLONSILLA HILL / OWNED BY / Stafford F. Kirkpatrick Esq. / Situated on part of the South Quarter of Lot No 12 in / the Thirteenth Concession / OF THE / TOWNSHIP OF MONAGHAN / IMMEDIATELY ADJOINING / THE TOWN OF PETERBOROUGH. // LITHO. BARR & CORSS. TORONTO
Print (lith) 46 x 60 cm 1" to 2 chains
In ms on plan: 'From a Survey by John Reid Esqre P.L.S. Peterborough March 1857'; views: 'Peterborough from Mr Kirkpatricks Residence' and 'Residence of Mr. Kirkpatrick'; Peterborough 45 (R.P. 9Q (Monaghan)) (**B1892**) is a photoreproduction.
Original not located

1827 *[1859]*
[Plan of Peterborough showing ward divisions]
Col ms on linen 87 x 56 cm Scale not given
Originally with a petition about a possible extension to town limits of 14 Apr 1859 (OOA RG 5 C1 vol 914 no 699 1859); shows the town limits and park lots outside town; boundaries of south, centre, north, and east wards shown in different locations from proposal of 1854 (**1822(2)**).
OOAMA (NMC 43196)

1828 *[186?]*
Plan shewing part of The Stewart Estate Peterboro'
Ms Size not known 1" to 4 chains
Shows the area of part of lots 1, 2, 3, con 12, Douro, from Otonabee and Smith-town Rd to John St, and Brock St to Mill's Station; shows the Peterboro & Chemong Railway, a bridge on the town line road, and mill dam; Langton's mills, Boswell's mills, Glen Morrison mills, village of Blythe; many bldgs are shown and names of owners; Stewart's mill lots are shown; photoreproduction in OOAMA (NMC 4307).
Private Collection

1829 *[1866]*
MAP / OF THE / BEAVERMEAD PROPERTY / AT / PETERBOROUGH, C.W. / FORMERLY THE PROPERTY / OF THE LATE / JUDGE HALL / Comprising Lot No 28, and part of Lot No 27 in the 12th Concession, / and parts of Lots No 26, 27 & 28 in the 13th Concession, / IN THE TOWNSHIP OF / OTONABEE. / Shewing the Subdivision of said Property into Park / and Building Lots by / Clementi & Nicholl. / W.C. Chewett & Co. Lith. Toronto.
Print (lith) 52 x 76 cm Scale not given
Shows the property near the Otonabee R with relief, treed areas, house, lock, swamp, and Beaver Meadow Creek; lot nos and divisions; related to R.P. S-7a (Ashburnham (no 5 Otonabee)) (**B1906**).
OOAMA (NMC 22703) OTAR

PICTON

1830 *[1833]*
TOWN OF / PICTON / UPPER CANADA. // SURVEYED AT THE REQUEST / OF / The Revd Wm Macaulay / BY / William McDonald // H. Bonycastle [*sic*] & J. Overend del. Tazewell Lithr / Govt Lithc Press. / York U.C.
Print (lith) 46 x 70 cm 1" to 5 chains
Shows the original town as laid out south and east of the harbour; from King's St and Bridge St to Mount St, and Western St to Church St; streets named and lots numbered; relief by hachures; village of Hallowell shown across the river; some bldgs shown by the river; OTNR copy is endorsed 'A 121' and '679' and has ms adds showing various reserves for market and court-house and note about con road to south 'which ought to be thrown open'; R.P. has ms note: 'as Before 1825 – submitted until a correct plan can be furnished by a D.P.S.'; a block of streets shown to the east was never developed; probably printed by Tazewell in 1833 as 100 copies were noted in stock in Tazewell's report of 16 Feb 1834 (OTAR RG 1 A-1-7 box 9); (Holmden 2343).
OOAMA (NMC 22709) OTNR (SR 254) Prince Edward 47 (R.P. Picton 1)

1831 *[ca 1840]*
Plan of town plot as laid out on lot No. four first concession north of the carrying place in the township of Hallowell belonging to the Estate of the late Corey Spencer, by P.V. Elmore
Ms 29 x 39 cm Scale not given
Endorsed 'Matilda Spencers Map'; shows an area north and west of the harbour from Main St to Water St, and James St to the end of Centre St; block nos and lot nos; names of owners in lots; a subdivision plan but no registered plan has been found; (Holmden 1703).
OOAMA (NMC 4309)

1832 *[1841]*
Chart of Picton Bay P.V.Elmore
Col ms 32 x 44 cm 1" to 132 ft Endorsements: 'Taken from State Papers P. 4 1841'
Shows the area that was proposed to be made into a harbour for steamboats; various wharves with names of owners; (Holmden 2344).
OOAMA (NMC 4310)

1833 *1857*
Chart of Picton Harbour From the Steam Grist mill to the Bridge. Office of Public Works August 1857.
Col ms 59 x 123 cm 1" to 80 ft Endorsements: stamp [BW] '591'
Soundings in feet and inches at high water are given; many bldgs along shore are identified including customs house, McAulay's granary, wharves, etc.
OOAMA (NMC 19770)

PINE GROVE

1834 *1843*
Plan of the Village Plot of Vaughanville on Lots 9 & 10 7th Conn of Vaughan Toronto July [7th? 1843?]
Col ms 45 x 76 cm 1" to 2 chains
A subdivision on the east branch of the Humber R, west about four streets; streets unnamed; road to Yonge St; present travelled road to Kingston; shows several mills, mill race and pond, drawings of houses, taverns, churches; 'orchard reserve' lot; shown on the Rottenburg map of 1850 (see **170**) as Pine Grove Mills or Vaughan; not in *Smith's Canadian Gazetteer* (1846).
OTAR

(PLUMBPORT town plot)

1835 *1858*
Map of Plumbport Laid out on part of Lot No 33 in the 1st Concession of Edwardsburgh, the property of Capn Isaac Plumb, Surveyed in August 1858; by [Sgd] Jas West Provl Land Surveyor and C.E.
Col ms 48 x 69 cm 1" to 60 ft Watermark: 'J WHATMAN 1854'
Shows a town laid out from Mary St to 'Road to the Pine Grove and Rock of Truth' and with lots along King St or Queen's Highway just north of the St Lawrence R; drawing of windmill; Wharf St and two wharves shown; not shown on co map of 1861 (**557**).
OOAMA (NMC 15373)

POOLE

1836 *1855*
Map of the Town of Poole in the County of Perth C.W. Surveyed by Joseph Kirk Prov. Land Surveyor, November 12th 1855. Examined Nov 1855 Thos Devine

Col ms 60 x 79 cm 1" to 4 chains Endorsements: 'A 202'

(SI 8 May 1855 to subdivide town plot into mill site and town lots; OTNR FN 384 12 Nov 1855); shows streets from South St to North St beyond Smith's Creek, and Leopold St to Adelaide St; town lots from Creek St to Alfred St and park lots beyond; Black Creek and Smith's Creek are shown with springs and a mill site; relief; some areas cleared; a school and a few bldgs shown; also a copy: 'Poole [Sgd] T. Devine Crown Lands Department Toronto 13th January 1856 [Sgd] Joseph Cauchon Commr Crown Lands' with a few names of owners of large blocks added (OTNR (SR 5515)); and a later copy: 'Office Plan Town of Poole Department of Crown Lands Quebec March 1862 [Sgd] Andrew Russell Assistt Commissioner' with the addition of names (OTAR(P)).

OTAR(P) OTNR (SR 271; 5515)

PORT ALBERT

1837 *1840*

Proposed Plan for Surveying the Town Plot in Ashfield. To The Honorable The Surveyor General &c &c &c Toronto [Sgd] William Hawkins D.S. Ashfield 3 Apr 1840

Col ms 40 x 66 cm 1" to 6 chains

(SI 8 June 1840 to lay out into town and park lots the town plot of Albert; OTNR FN 32 15 Sept 1840); endorsed 'Diagram of Survey Approved in Council 21st May 1840 ... R.B. Sullivan S.G. [Sgd] J.G. Chewett ... This Plan to be returned with the Plan of Survey J.G.C.'; proposes six streets parallel to L Huron and eight cross streets for town lots on both sides of river, and two diagonal streets from river to outer edge of park lots; Market Square; mill and harbour reserves.

OTNR (SR 4)

Related maps

(2) *[1840]*

Plan of the Town of Albert in the Township of Ashfield. Copy S.G.O.

Col ms 54 x 76 cm 1" to 4 chains Endorsements: 'A 123' '603'

Differs from proposal on (1) above; shows the town as laid out from L Huron to Harrison St with only five streets parallel to lake, and from South St to North St in a more southerly position; only the south diagonal road, 'London Road,' is as planned and some reserves are in different positions; sawmill; site for grist mill; reserve for a burial place; relief; proposal for channel in harbour; also a copy: 'Plan of the Town of Albert in the Township of Ashfield Copy S.G.O' endorsed 'No 62' and with the addition of names (OTAR(P)); and a copy: 'Town Plot of Ashfield. Crown Land Department Surveyors Branch West Montreal Nov 1847 A true copy [Sgd] T. Bouthillier A.R.' (OTAR).

OTAR OTAR(P) OTNR (SR 7018)

PORT BRITAIN

1838 *[1856]*

Plan / of / Port Britain Harbour, / TOWNSHIP OF HOPE, / County of Durham, / CANADA WEST. / Blackburn Delt.

Print (lith) 17 x 28 cm 1" to 500 ft

In *Prospectus of the Port Britain Harbour Company* (Toronto: Blackburn's City Steam Press 1856), frontis (*Bib Can* 3682); shows area south of the GTR and station on lots 21 and 22 and south of Lakeshore Rd; mill, mill dam, and bldgs.

OTMCL

(PORT BRUCE)

1839 *1858*

Chart of Baie du Dard [Sgd] Alexander Sproat Provincial Land Surveyor. Southampton 25th Septr 1858

Col ms 65 x 89 cm 1" to 4 chains Endorsements: stamps 'Department of Public Works Ottawa' '534'

Shows a harbour opp con VIII or Lake Range, lots 30–40, in Bruce Twp; Main St and Wellington St identified; soundings, shoal; (Holmden 1498); although shown in Belden, ... *Bruce* (1880), a note indicates that town (which adjoined Malta) was abandoned after a major fire years before.

OOAMA

PORT BURWELL

1840 *[1840]*

Sketch of the Piers and Basin at Port Burwell Harbour Shewing part of the Village Plot. [Sgd] M Burwell Dy Surveyor

Col ms 30 x 47 cm 1" to 3 chains Watermark: 'SEVAN'S & Co, 1831'

Shows Otter Creek with old channel, canal, basin, dam, piers, and line of old shore; shows streets, rectory block, church and rectory, post office, and custom house; notes: 'Lighthouse to be completed by the Contractors on 15th July 1840' and 'harbour land to be surrendered to Crown.'

OOAMA (NMC 4316)

PORT COLBORNE

1841 *[1837–8]*

A Map of Port Colborne, the termination of the Welland Canal on Lake Erie. Copied by permission from a plan drawn by H.H. Killaly A.M. CEngr. Copied by order of [illegible]

Col ms 74 x 128 cm 1" to 45 yds Endorsements: 'No 84'

Shows the front part of the village of Port Colborne with houses, streets, relief, and 'proposed eastern pier' and 'intended enlargement of western pier'; probably from Killaly's and N.H.

Baird's survey of the Welland Canal enlargement in 1837–8 (*DCB* X:403).
OOAMA (NMC 11428)

1842 *1845*
Plan Shewing the Condition of the Harbour of Port Colborne in October 1845. and the Improvements in Progress. Lewis J. Leslie Del.
Ms 70 x 48 cm 1" to 200 ft
Originally in 'Report of Capt. Frederick Warden R.N. of 27 Jan 1846' (GBLpro Adm 7/625 (5)); shows a configuration in the harbour different from the earlier plan (**1841**); shows site of destroyed old pier, entrance to the Welland Canal, soundings, roads, bldgs; (*PRO Cat* 1540).
GBLpro (MR 1052(5))

1843 *[1862?]*
Map of part of the Village of Port Colborne
Col ms 63 x 131 cm 1" to 2 chains Endorsements: stamp 'Hydrographic Office Decr 2 1862'
Shows streets from the Buffalo and Lake Huron Railroad to L Erie; bldgs; basin, locks, and piers shown on the Welland Canal; high water mark; a note in GBTAUh indicates plan received from or made by W. Gibbard.
GBTAUh (D6175 Aa3)

PORT CREDIT

1844 *[1798]*
Survey of a piece of Ground for use of Public House at the River Credit – Containing about Six Acres and thirty three Perches. – Surveyed according as the Boundarys were marked by Capt. Claus A – Indian Affairs and the principal Chiefs of the Messissague Nation, 31st May 1798 – Signed A. Jones D.P.S. Copy W.C. [and] Credit Reserve etc. Copy W.C.
2 col mss on sheet 30 x 76 cm 1" to 4 chains [and] 1" to 10 chains Endorsements: 'Q 25' '1052'
The main map shows a few survey markers and 'proposed place to erect a bridge'; the smaller map shows lots along the shore with some names of owners.
OTNR (SR 2421)

1845 *[1835–7]*
Plan of the Survey of Port Credit. A Village Plot at the mouth of the River Credit, on the Indian Reserve laid out by order from the Surveyor General. Dated 20 June 1835. Surveyed and Executed by your Obedient Servant [Sgd] Robert Lynn D.P.Surveyor.
Col ms 48 x 64 cm 1" to 4 chains Endorsements: 'No 9'
(SI 20 June 1835 to lay out town lots); shows the area for town laid out on the west bank from Front St to Park St and from the river west to Joseph St; church and market reserves; bridge over river, government reserve, and inn shown on east side and Harbour Co. land and 'canal in progress' through a bar across mouth of river; projected park lots at north end of town with later note: 'not surveyed 11th November 1837 [Sgd] Robert Lynn'; Indian land is shown above this; survey possibly completed in 1837.
OTNR (SR 262)

Related maps

(2) *[1835–7]*
[Title and signature the same]
Col ms 50 x 63 cm 1" to 4 chains Endorsements: 'No 20'
Shows the same layout and information as (1) above; 'Note Surveyed 11 November 1837 Robert Lynn D.P.Surveyor Original Plan filed in Survey Branch April 1931'; note was probably taken from note about park lots on (1) above; also an undated copy: 'Port Credit [Sgd] Humphrey Young' endorsed 'A 118' and '68' and with the same layout (OTNR (SR 261)).
OTAR(P) OTNR (SR 261)

(3) *[1835?]*
[Title and signature the same]
Ms 47 x 63 cm 1" to 4 chains Endorsements: '4166'; stamp 'IASR'
Shows the same layout and information as (1) above; a description of the village site is added and a note indicating that the first sale of lots was held at the Court-House, Toronto, on Friday 28 Aug [1835] and including a list of owners, lot nos, and prices paid; also a later copy in OOAMA (NMC 4318): 'Port Credit Copy [Sgd] J.G. Chewitt Surveyor Genls Office Toronto 25th April 1839 [Sgd] R.B. Sullivan Sur. Genl' endorsed 'F4167' and 'IASR'; also a copy dated 28 Aug 1844 in OOAMA RG 10M 76703/9 no 284 (NMC 13094).
OOAMA (NMC 4318; 13094; 22719)

(4) *1843*
Plan of the Town Plot of Port Credit shewing the Improvements upon each Lot since the Sale in 1835 and the Names of the Occupants [Sgd] Robert Wells Toronto September 1843 Canada
Col ms Size not known 1" to 2 chains Endorsements: '1553'
Provenance: OOAMA RG 10M 76703/9 no 286; shows bldgs, names of owners; wharves, canals, piers in L Ontario; bridge; government reserve on east side; uncleared land marked.
OOAMA (NMC 13095)

1846 *1846*
Plan of the extension of the Town Plot of Port Credit, Canada. To T. Bouthillier Esq. Crown Lands Dept. Montreal [Sgd] J.S. Dennis D.S. Toronto April 14th 1846
Col ms 41 x 64 cm 1" to 4 chains Endorsements: 'Q 79'
(SI 12 March 1846 to subdivide extension of town plot into bldg lots; OTNR FN 804 30 Apr 1846); shows the extension of the town east of the river and streets from Port St north to Queen St, and Brock and Lot sts to Huron St; relief, marshy areas; formation of shingle across mouth of river,

canal, warehouses; houses and bldgs shown in original town plot; a note indicates that an area is reserved by Board of Works until completion of dam; some later changes and additions of owners' names; there is also a copy sgd 'J.S. Dennis June 10th 1846' in OOAMA (RG 10M 76703/9 no 281 (NMC 13089).
OOAMA (NMC 13089) OTNR (SR 267)

Related maps

(2) *1850*
Port Credit Crown Land Department Toronto April 1850 Office Copy [Sgd] J H Price Commissioner of Crown Lands
Col ms 46 x 63 cm 1" to 4 chains Endorsements: 'No 80'
Shows the same layout as plan above with the addition of names of owners in the eastern part; there is also a plan of 1" to 2 chains sgd 'Dennis & Boulton Surveyors Toronto 15 Apl 1856' in OOAMA (RG 10M 76703/9 no 285 with some names of owners and notes.
OOAMA (NMC 13112) OTAR(P)

PORT DALHOUSIE

1847 *1839*
Port Dalhousie Situated at the termination of the Welland Canal Lake Ontario. Surveyed under the Superintendance of Captain Mackenzie R.E. By William Hawkins Dy Survr Jany 1839 [Sgd] William Haw[kins Deputy Surveyor Toronto? ... illegible]
Col ms 64 x 99 cm 1" to 4 chains Endorsements: stamps 'REO' '240'
Shows several streets and all bldgs along the main road in 'Village of Dalhousie'; soundings, heights above lake level, relief, trees.
OOAMA (NMC 22720)

1848 *1845*
Plan showing the condition of the harbour of Port Dalhousie in 1845 and the Proposed Improvements
Ms 57 x 69 cm 1" to 200 ft Endorsements: 'No 1'
Originally in 'Report of Capt. Frederick Warden R.N. of 27 Jan. 1846' (GBLpro Adm 7/625); shows the present harbour and old canal route; outer harbour and 'proposed new harbour & canal route'; 'Abbey's ship yard'; detailed soundings; shows the same information as **149(26)**; (*PRO Cat* 1543).
GBLpro (MR 1052(8))

Related maps

(2) *[1845?]*
Plan of Port Dalhousie Showing the present Harbour & proposed improvements Lewis L. Leslie del.
Ms 53 x 79 cm 1" to 200 ft Endorsements: '36'
In 'A Series of Diagrams, Plans, Illustrative of the Various Local Public Improvements ... Completed by the Provincial Board of Works ... Samuel Keefer Engr 1844' (OOA RG 11M 85603/40 no 5); similar to (1) above; also shows present and new towing path, Collector's Office Lock No 1.
OOAMA (NMC 16937)

1849 *1858*
Plan of the Village of Dalhousie in the County of Lincoln Canada West as laid out for N. Pawling Esqr. 1858
Col ms Size not known Scale not known
Shows the town laid out from the canal mouth west to beyond Church St and from L Ontario south to Main St; pond and part of canal; lots, piers, dams and locks around canal; Nathan Pawling advertised lots for sale in his new town plot on 5 Apr 1826 (Aloian, 6); map reproduced in Aloian, 7.
Original not located

1850 *[1862]*
Plan of Port Dalhousie Harbour.
Col ms 64 x 127 cm 1" to 100 ft Endorsements: stamp 'Hydrographic Office Decr 2 1862'
Shows piers, lock 1 on the Welland canal, dam, and bldgs; soundings; other bldgs shown in village; a note in GBTAUh indicates map received from or drawn by W. Gibbard.
GBTAUh (D6173 Aa3)

PORT DOVER

1851 *1838*
Town of Port Dover 22d Novr 1838 [Sgd] Colin Mackenzie Capt R.E.
Ms 35 x 26 cm Scale not given
With 2nd report about Port Dover by Capt Mackenzie, R.E., to Col Haskett, military secretary, 24 Nov 1838 (OOA RG 8 I/446 p 96); a rough sketch of the river, swamp, etc, showing piers and a few bldgs; points for defensive works identified; (Holmden 2369).
OOAMA (NMC 4322)

1852 *[1849]*
Port Dover
Col ms 43 x 66 cm 1" to 2 chains Watermark: 'J WHATMAN TURKEY MILLS' Endorsements: stamp [BW] '566'
Shows the area from the river and Harbour St west to Clinton St, and St George St to Bridge St; shows two piers, bridge, plank road to Hamilton; proposed new basin and new line of beach as of Jan 1849 as on (2) below; land owned by Israel W. Powell, Moses C. Nickerson, and J.B. Crouse.
OOAMA (NMC 4321)

Related maps

(2) *[1849]*
Port Dover Harbour
Col ms 32 x 94 cm 1" to 60 ft Endorsements: stamp [BW] '565'

'Enlarged View' 1" to 20 ft and 'Enlarged Section' 1" to 4 ft; shows the harbour area in more detail with area proposed to be dredged for new basin; piers shown with new work; 'Line of Beach & Soundings 6th Jan 1849.'
OOAMA (NMC 22722)

PORT ELGIN

1853 *[1854]*
MAP / of / PORT ELGIN / County of Bruce / C.W.
Print (lith) 47 x 87 cm 1" to 6 chains
Shows the area from L Huron and Huron St east to Albert St, and Emma St north to River St; the numbered lots are between Mill St and Market St west of Goderich St; note: 'The Numbered Lots will be sold by Auction at Port Elgin (at Staffords Tavern) on Friday October 20th' [1854]; also shows reserves, public square, a few bldgs including Benj. Shantz Saw and Grist Mills; 'Proposed Stratford & Huron Railway'; OOAMA copy is addressed in ms on back 'to The Honble Wm Cayley Inspector General Quebec C.E. ... Quebec L.C. Mar 7 1855.'
OOAMA (NMC 22723)

1854 *1857*
MAP / OF / PORT ELGIN / IN THE / County of Bruce, / Messrs Stafford, Shantz, Hilker, Bricker & Siefert Proprietors / KERTLAND & SPROAT C.E. & P.L.S. / PORT ELGIN 2 MARCH 1857. / Maclear & Co. Lith. Toronto
Print (col lith) 79 x 119 cm 1" to 4 chains
Inset: 'MAP / SHEWING THE POSITION OF PORT ELGIN / in / Reference to the Course of Trade / BETWEEN THE ATLANTIC SEABOARD / AND THE / Great West.'; shows the town laid out covering a larger area than earlier plan (**1853**) – from Elizabeth St to Catherine St, and Kertland St to Lehnan St; a few major bldgs are named and mill pond and mills shown; route of proposed Stratford and Lake Huron Railroad; description of the advantages of the site; town lots are in the area shown on the earlier plan and park lots beyond; related to R.P. 11 (**B1982**).
OOAMA (NMC 11431)

PORT FRANKS

1855 *1851 July*
Plan of the Town Plot of Port Franks on the River Aux Sables Bosanquet Goderich 31st July 1851
Col ms on tissue paper, pts missing 50 x 73 cm 1" to 4 chains Endorsements: 'Recd 15 Dec 1851 with no 45'
Shows unnamed streets around harbour at the mouth of river with market square in the centre; some land around harbour reserved.
OTAR (Canada Co. Papers TRHT 233A)

1856 *1851 Nov*
Map of the Town of Port Franks In the Township of Bosanquet Engineers Office Goderich 18th November 1851 David [Smith] Civil [Engineer?]
Col ms, pt missing 48 x 81 cm 1" to 4 chains
Shows 10 streets east-west and eight streets north-south; blocks are numbered 1–43 and lots, 1–16, in each block; soundings, relief; shows more streets and lots than plan above (**1855**).
OTAR (Canada Co. Papers TRHT 233)

1857 *1854*
Map of the Town of Port Franks In the Township of Bosanquet Engineers Office Goderich 6th Sept 1854 [Sgd] David Smith Civil Engineer & Surveyor
Col ms 61 x 97 cm 1" to 4 chains
The plan shows a layout with lot and block nos similar to the plan above (**1856**); notes added on lots that have been sold.
OTAR (Canada Co. Maps pkg 7 no 172)

(PORT HEAD town plot)

1858 *1855*
Plan of Port Head Harbor Opposite lots 31, 32, 33, 34, 35 Lake Range Townp of Kincardine and at nearly half distance from G[oderi]ch to Southampton. [Certified correct and sgd] John Denison P.L.S. & Civil Engineer Goderich 7th December 1855
Ms 69 x 49 cm 1" to 4 chains
Shows the proposed town from Harbour St to Argyle St, and King St to Queen St and beyond; soundings in harbour, shoals, and sandbanks; probably related to R.P. 5 (**B1985**); not shown on the co map of 1857 (see **1086**) and post office closed by 1861 (Carter, 2:150).
OOAMA (NMC 22724)

PORT HOPE

1859 *1842*
Port Hope Harbour 1842 By R.W.Smart
Ms 27 x 19 cm Scale not given Endorsements: stamps 'BW' '626'
Shows two bldgs by the harbour, two piers, soundings, and channel.
OOAMA (NMC 70952)

1860 *1846*
Plan of Port Hope Harbour and the plan for a New Harbour Surveyed and Planned by Peter Fleming January 1846
Col ms 67 x 87 cm 1" to 160 ft Endorsements: stamp [BW] '627'
(SI (BW) 24 Oct 1845 to survey harbour to complete works); shows the present harbour configuration, works proposed by Fleming, and those proposed by the Board of Works; a note indicates

that Mr Keefer's plan for the inner harbour is the same as that proposed by Fleming; mills, storehouses, etc, are identified by the harbour and the location of the town is noted to the north; there is also a col ms copy at OOAMA (NMC 22725) with the same title and the addition of '(Copy) Office of the Board of Works,' 76 x 60 cm, 1" to 160 ft, stamp '628'; (*OHIM* 7.10).
OOAMA (NMC 22738; 22725)

Related maps

(2) *[1851]*
Plan / of / PORT HOPE HARBOUR / and a Plan for a New Harbour. / Surveyed and Planned by Peter Fleming / January 1846. / MATTHEWS' LITH. / (Copy) Office of the Board of Works.
Print (lith) hand col 44 x 56 cm 1" to 160 ft
The printed version of the ms map NMC 22725 above, but only of the area from the boundary of the Harbour Co.'s land to the harbour; a few details also omitted; this plan was printed to accompany Canada (Province), Department of Public Works, *Return to an Address ... Dated 12th May 1849 on the Subject of a Survey of the Harbour [Port Hope] ... the Instructions Given to Peter Fleming ... together with His Survey, Reports, Plans* in *JLA* (1851), App BB (OTUTF).
OTAR OTNR (SR 22725) OTUTF

1861 *1846*
Reconnoitring Sketch of the Ground in the neighbourhood of Port Hope shewing its capability for the Defence of the proposed Harbour. [Sgd] C.G. Gray Lt. Rl Engrs 22/5/46.
Col ms on tracing paper 52 x 81 cm 1" to 12 chains
Endorsements: 'Mil C.W./714' 'D.R./ 693'
Withdrawn from GBLpro WO 1 vol 544 f 225; shows the town west of the river and inland from the harbour, proposed harbour, Methodist chapel and Episcopal church, mill dam, relief by hachures, treed areas; (*PRO Cat* 1848).
GBLpro (MPH 53(2))

1862 *1853 [i.e., 1854]*
MAP / OF / PORT HOPE. / CANADA WEST, / Published BY / WALL & FORREST / Engineers & Surveyors / 250 Pearl Stt./ NEW YORK / 1853. / Lith. of Geo. E. Leefe 225 Fulton St N.Y.
Print (lith) hand col 105 x 74 cm 1" to 16 rods
Views: 'Town Hall,' 'Residence of H.H. Meredith Esq.,' 'Residence of Wm Sisson Esq.,' 'Residence of N. Kirchhoffer, Esq.'; shows the town from the harbour to Cumberland and Bedford sts and from Victoria St to street leading to mill of Meredith Moulson; all bldgs shown and many identified including churches with denominations, wharves, schools, stores, hotels, etc; 'proposed Grand Trunk Railroad' and 'Port Hope and Lindsay Railroad'; Wall & Forrest advertised on 22 Oct 1853 that they were making a survey but the map was not placed before the Town Council until 15 Apr 1854 (see the *Port Hope Commercial Advertiser* for these dates); 'List of subscribers.'
OOAMA (NMC 20024) OTAR

1863 *1855*
Plan of Port Hope Harbour [Sgd] Thos. C. Clarke Engineer Feby 19th 1855
Col ms 58 x 91 cm 1" to 100 ft Endorsements: stamp [BW] '629'
Shows the area from King St west to John St and from harbour north to Market Square and Augusta St; shows the old and new harbour, new channel, and marine railway no 1 and 2; index to bldgs in the port area; relief, harbour depths shown by contours; (Holmden 2366; *OHIM* 7.11).
OOAMA (NMC 19769)

1864 *1859–62*
Plan of Port Hope Harbour June 1859 [Sgd] Geo. A. Stewart C.E. & P.L.S. Port Hope C.W.
Col ms 79 x 42 cm 1" to 100 ft Endorsements: stamp 'Hydrographic Office Decr 2 1862'
Shows old harbour and new channel to Smith's Creek; new harbour dredged with depths shown; shows the position of a sand-bar in 1859 and 1862; piers, railways, projected piers, boundary of wharf area, streets shown in harbour area.
GBTAUh (D6176 Aa3)

PORT MAITLAND

1865 *1845*
Plan Shewing the Condition of the Harbour of Port Maitland in October 1845. L.I. Leslie Del.
Ms 70 x 47 cm 1" to 200 ft Endorsements: 'No 4'
Originally enclosed in report of Capt Frederick Warden, R.N., of 27 Jan 1846 (GBLpro Adm 7/625(4)); soundings; shows piers, lighthouse, and breakwater; some bldgs; probably from the same source as Holloway Boxer plan (**149(29)**); (*PRO Cat* 1546).
GBLpro (MR 1052(4))

1866 *1848*
Port Maitland Sketch of Land referred to in Mr Farrell's Letter to Hd Quarter R.O. and my Report dated June 1848 [Sgd] George C. Page Lt Col R.E.
Ms 25 x 42 cm 1" to 10 chains Watermark: 'J WHATMAN TURKEY MILL 1840' Endorsements: '259'; stamp 'REO'
A rough sketch showing the mouth of the Grand R with naval depot, lighthouse, harbour, area requested by Mr Farrell across from naval depot, a church and a few other bldgs, squatters.
OOAMA (NMC 4327)

1867 *1855*
Port Maitland. Prepared by [Sgd] Andrew Hood Provl L Surveyor Dunnville 11th Aug 1855 Indian Office Cayuga 10th Septr 1855 [Sgd] D Thorburn I. Commr

Col ms 60 x 50 cm 1" to 3 chains Endorsements: 'F4181'; stamp 'IASR'
Shows the west side of the Grand R and the Welland Canal, marshy lands, relief, bldgs and a few names of owners.
OOAMA (NMC 22740)

1868 *[1856?]*
[Endorsed title]: 'Canada Naval Reserves' ... [Sgd] [J?] Taylor, Master, R.N.
Col ms 26 x 37 cm Scale not given Endorsements: stamp 'Hydrographic Office No 30 July 1885'
A note indicates plan received in Hydrographic Office 29 July 1856; 'Port Maitland and the Grand River so far as Dunville 4 miles from the Entrance will contain room for a large fleet of light draught of water.'
GBTAUh (D2213a Aa3)

1869 *[1862?]*
Plan of the Harbour of Port Maitland
Col ms 53 x 46 cm 1" to 200 ft Endorsements: stamp 'Hydrographic Office Decr 2 1862'
Shows the Grand R and the Welland Canal with pier and soundings in the entrance, remains of naval depot bldgs on the east shore, location of naval depot for provincial steam vessels during disturbance of 1837, 1838, 1839; a note indicates that this branch of the Welland Canal is open three weeks earlier in year than Port Colborne; a note in GBTAUh catalogue indicates plan as '(tr.) [traced?] G.A. Stewart.'
GBTAUh (D6177 Aa3)

PORT PERRY

1870 *1854*
PLAN / OF THE / TOWN OF PORT PERRY / In the / Sixth Con: of Reach / COUNTY OF ONTARIO / Province of / CANADA / Maclear & Co. Lith: Toronto / (Late Hugh Scobie) // J. Stoughton Dennis / P.L. Surveyor / Jany: 1854.
Print (lith) 57 x 65 cm 1" to 3 chains
Shows the town from Water St at L Scugog to Simcoe St and from Shanly and Barclay sts to beyond Cotton St; bldgs are shown on lots that are shaded; mills; present shoreline, marshy wooded areas, and water lots shown; notes on the advantages of the town; related to R.P. H-50020 (**B2011**); advertised for sale in the *British Colonist* 14 Apr 1854.
OTMCL OTNR (SR 270)

(PORT POWELL)

1871 *1846*
PLAN / OF / PORT POWELL / 1846.
Print (lith) 54 x 77 cm Approx 1" to 135 chains
Shows a village on Sturgeon Bay on L Huron in Tay Twp near present-day Waubashene; Murray St to William St, and Ridout St to Bleecker St; ms notes indicate that lots are for sale: 'apply to John Ridout Esqr County York Register Office or to Grant Powell Esqr Civil Secty Office Toronto'; other ms notes indicate names of purchasers; shown as Tayport on the 1853 co map (see **391**) and still shown as Port Powell on the co atlas (Belden, ... *Simcoe* (1881)); however, the town did not survive (Hunter, I:48).
OMSA

Related maps

(2) *1846*
Plan of Tayport 1846 [Sgd] J G Howard Architect
Col ms 21 x 35 cm Scale not given
Shows spit of land with a pier and town laid out behind it from Murray St to Albert St and Elisabeth St to Bleecker St.
OTAR (MU 1537/1085)

PORT STANLEY

1872 *1842*
Map of the Harbour and Creek at Port Stanley in the London District Shewing the several divisions of property adjoining the same. Surveyed by order of the Honble H.H. Killaly Prest of the Board of Works. By [Sgd] Peter Carroll D.P. Surveyor West Oxford 15th Augt 1842.
Col ms 67 x 66 cm 1" to 5 chains Endorsements: stamp [BW] '637'
(SI 23 July 1842 to survey harbour at Port Stanley and boundaries of Mr Bostwick's property); shows the town from Erie to George St on the west, and Main and Bridge St to Matilda St on the east; bldgs are shown and some identified; lots shown along Kettle Creek; College Lot D with proposed site for a church; roads, relief, piers; (Holmden 2370).
OOAMA (NMC 22741)

1873 *1843*
Plan of the Town of Port Stanley [Endorsed title]: 'No ... Plan of the Town Plot and College Lot at Port Stanley 1843'
Col ms 49 x 73 cm 1" to 4 chains Endorsements: stamp [BW] '644'
Shows a layout for the town similar to the 1842 plan above (**1872**).
OOAMA (NMC 4970)

1874 *[1845]*
Plan of the Harbour and part of the Town of Port Stanley Copy from J. Coll C.E.
Col ms 47 x 70 cm 1" to 65 ft Endorsements: 'No 8'
Originally from report of Capt Frederick Warden, R.N., of 27 Jan 1846 (GBLpro Adm 7/625(2)); streets are shown on the west shore and many bldgs on the east shore; new line of pier, soundings; (*PRO Cat* 1551).
GBLpro (MR 1052(2))

1875 *1852*
Plan of Port Stanley [Sgd] W.D. Hales Jany 5th/52
Col ms 55 x 76 cm 1" to 2 chains Endorsements: stamp [BW] '629'
Shows the proposed excavation for the inner basin in the area of Water St and 'Mr. Keefer's limit'; streets and lot nos, relief, and marshy areas also shown; (Holmden 2371).
OOAMA (NMC 19764)

1876 *[1854–5?]*
Town of Port Stanley Townships of Yarmouth and Southwold
Col ms 45 x 60 cm [Approx 3" to 1 mile]
Shows the proposed route of the London and Port Stanley Railway (incorporated 1853, line completed 1856); shows streets on both sides of the creek and inland to East Main St and the village of Selborne, 'gravelled road,' relief, marshy areas, lots affected by the railway.
OLU

PORT TALBOT

1877 *1813*
Map of Colonel Talbots Farm That which is contained within the yellow margin is his cultivated land. Port Talbot 16th June 1813 [Sgd] Lewis Burwell
Col ms 43 x 56 cm 1" to 5 chains
Later note: 'This is the first Plan I ever made ... being 19 years of age Brantford 21st February 1852 [Sgd] Lewis Burwell P.L. Surveyor'; shows the fort at the mouth of the river on the east bank; roads leading to upper, back, and lakeshore settlements; shows bldgs including house, registry office, and Mahlon Burwell's house; relief; the village did not develop and is not listed in *Smith's Canadian Gazetteer* (1846); (*OHIM* 7.12).
OOAMA (NMC 4330)

PRESCOTT

1878 *1810*
Map of the Town of Prescott in the Township of Augusta District of Johnstown Upper Canada The Property of Edward Jessup Esquire. Surveyed in the Year 1810 by [Sgd] J Kilborn Dp.P. Surveyor [Sgd] H. Walker – J. Kilborn
Col ms 44 x 58 cm 1" to 2 chains
Shows the town laid out in a grid of seven streets by six streets, from Water St north to Wood St and from East St to West St; lot nos and sizes.
OTAR

1879 *1816 (1821)*
Plan of Fort Wellington and Prescott Septr 6th 1816 (Signd) J. Jebb R. Engrs Received from Lt Col. Du[rnford] 7th [May] 1817 letter to Lt Genl Mann
Col ms 47 x 56 cm 1" to 90 ft Endorsements: 'No 3' 'I 3'; stamps 'B↑O' 'IGF'
Shows the fort and 18 bldgs keyed; some bldgs shown in town; wooded areas; (Holmden 2378).
OOAMA (NMC 4343)

Related maps

(2) *1816 (1821)*
Plan of Fort Wellington and Prescott (Signed) Sept 6, 1816 J.J. R.E. [Sgd] E.W.Durnford Lt Col. Comg Rl Engrs Canada Commanding Royal Engineers Office Novr 15 1821 Quebec [and] Plan shewing the proposed Site of a new Commissariat, Wharf & Store at Fort Wellington '
Col ms 43 x 54 cm 1" to 200 ft
Accompanying the estimates of the Royal Engineers for 1822 (OOA RG 8 I/410 p 43); the base plan shows the same information as (1) above; the planned store and wharf are shown at the east end of town; also shows block of land and bldg below hospital; bldgs of town shown along highway and to present commissariat store and wharf; (Holmden 2379).
OOAMA (NMC 4342)

1880 *1816*
Sketch of Prescott and Environs (Signed) J. Jebb Lt Royl Engrs 29th Jany 1816 Royl Engr Drawg Room Quebec 28th March 1816 J.B. Duberger Junr
Ms 42 x 54 cm 1" to 200 ft
From Lt Col Nicoll's letter to Maj Foster, military secretary, of 28 March 1816 regarding the property of Mr Jessup (OOA RG 8 I/556 pp 129–30); shows most land owned by Jessup except for a few lots along the King's Highway; the town is not shown as laid out, although a few bldgs are indicated; Fort Wellington and bldgs occupied by government to the north and stockade shown to the west; wooded areas.
OOAMA (NMC 4333)

Related maps

(2) *1816*
Sketch of part of the Town of Prescott Copied from a Map in the possession of the Executors of the late Mr Jessup March 14th 1816 Signed J. Jebb Lt Royl Engrs J.B. Duberger Junr Quebec [illegible] 1816
Ms 42 x 27 cm 1" to 2 chains
From the same source as above; only the eastern part of town is shown as laid out in a grid of six streets east-west and two streets north-south; Water St to Wood St, East St and Edward St; names are shown in lots south of Henry St; the stockade occupies part of East St; a few bldgs.
OOAMA (NMC 4341)

1881 *1823*
Plan of the Government Property at Fort Wellington &c. In the Town of Prescott Upper Canada Shewing the Lots as now marked out & prepared to be disposed of (Signed) D. Bolton Lieut Royl Engineers Quebec June 20th 1823 A Copy [Sgd] E.W. Durnford Lt Col. Comg Rl Eng Quebec 20 June 1823

Ms 51 x 40 cm 1" to 200 ft
From Lt Col Durnford's letter of 19 June 1823 to Col Darling, military secretary (OOA RG 8 I/416 p 691/2); shows the town from East St to Edward St and from High St to Upper St, with a settlement to the west around Water and Centre sts; lots to be disposed of are numbered 7–12 along East St and 13–16 (park lots) north of fort and ordnance land; (Holmden 2381).
OOAMA (NMC 4335)

Related maps

(**2**) *1823 (1837)*
Survey of the Government Property at Fort Wellington in the Town of Prescott Upper Canada shewing the Lots now marked out and prepared to be disposed off. [*sic*] Copy of original Survey (signed) E.W. Durnford Col. Comg R. Eng. (Signed) D. Bolton Lieut R.E. Royal Engineer's Drawing Room July 1st 1823. Surveyor Generals Office April 1837 Copy J.G. Chewett
Ms 69 x 41 cm 1" to 200 ft Endorsements: 'No 41' '38'
Shows the same information as the map above with the addition of notes about patents and a description of the lots; there is also a plan of 24 Sept 1823 adding lots sold (see **64**); and a later plan by 'H.O. Crawley ... 13th July 1839,' 'REO 960–6' (OOAMA (NMC 4337)); and one of 15 Feb 1842 showing the same area but with the fort in more detail (OOAMA (NMC 113488)); (Holmden 2382).
OOAMA (NMC 4337; 113488) OTAR(P)

1882 *[ca 1830]*
Map of Prescott Upper Canada Drawn by James West Depy Provl Surveyor Matilda
Col ms, pt missing 46 x 67 cm [1" to 2 chains]
Endorsements: 'A 51'
Shows the same layout as the 1810 survey with streets named and lot nos and sizes; reserves for English church, Roman Catholic church, Presbyterian church, and Methodist church; a few names of owners including H. Walker and Mr Norton; West became a provincial land surveyor in 1825.
OTNR (SR 276)

1883 *1834*
Town of Prescott. Copy J.G.C. S.G.O. 10 Jany 1834
Col ms 63 x 74 cm 1" to 2 chains Endorsements: 'No 42'
Shows the town as extended west two streets to Ann St and north to James St; Court House Square; names in water lots, later additions; also a copy: 'Prescott. Crown Lands Department Montreal December 1846 True Copy' endorsed '682' and 'A163' (OTNR (SR 275)).
OTAR(P) OTNR (SR 275)

1884 *1838*
Battle of Prescott Novr 13th 1838
Ms Size not known Scale not given
From Maj Maclean's report of 14 May 1839 to Sir J. Colborne on his conduct at Prescott (OOA RG 8 I/750 p 75); shows the fortifications at Fort Wellington with boats opp fort and Ogdensburgh; positions numbered on both shores but not keyed on map; the original is in OOA (MG24 B31) and a copy in OOA RG 8; photoreproduction in OOAMA (NMC 70947).
OOA (MG24 B31; RG 8 I/750 p 75)

1885 *[1854?]*
Map of Prescott embracing the Several Additional Surveys
Col ms 64 x 97 cm Scale not given
Shows the town laid out west to Sophia St and north to Matilda St; railway line runs through Matilda St; names of streets and some notes on lots; possibly unfinished; probably a little later than **1886** as it shows more streets, but railway does not appear to be finished.
OTAR

1886 *[ca 1854]*
Map shewing the Proposed Terminus of the Bytown & Prescott Railway in connection with the Ordnance Property at Prescott signed W Shanly Chief Engineer
Col ms 44 x 81 cm 1" to 400 ft Endorsements: '14'
Includes a section at 1" to 100 ft and a view of Fort Wellington; shows the 'Located Line of Bytown and Prescott Railway' and 'proposed terminus' in the area to be filled between Edward St and land in front of the fort; shows the town plot with streets north to Wood St and west to Sophia St; Shanly was chief engineer on the railway from 1851 to 1854; there is also a plan showing the land to be leased to the Bytown & Prescott Railway sgd 'R.I. Pilkington Draftsman 12 January 1853' (OOAMA (NMC 4340)).
OOAMA (NMC 22744; 4340)

1887 *1859*
Plan of Ordnance Property in the Town of Prescott As Surveyed under instructions from the Crown Lands Department Dated 11th May 1859. [Sgd] B.W. Gossage P.L. Surveyor Toronto December 24th 1859.
Col ms 85 x 48 cm 1" to 2 chains
Shows the town from the river north to Wood St and the Powell Estate, and from Boundary St to East St; shows the fort, the Ottawa and Prescott Railway Co. with engine house, freight house; names of some owners; a copy of the plan with the same title, endorsed 'B/4416,' and originally from OOA RG 8 I, is in OOAMA (NMC 19751); OOAMA also has a copy marked '960–1.'
OOAMA (NMC 19751) OTNR (SR 5782)

1888 *[1860?]*
[Map of part of Prescott showing lots laid out]
Col ms 56 x 39 cm Scale not given
Shows the area from the river to the GTR station

ground and from West St to Ann St; lots are marked between James St and Railway Ave and from West St to St Lawrence St, and some names of owners are shown; station bldgs; similar to R.P. Prescott 7 of Oct 1860 (**B2030**), which was laid out for H.D. Jessup by James West.
OTAR

PRESTON

1889 *1851*
Plan of the Boundaries of the Intended Incorporation of the Village of Preston. Township of Waterloo By [Sgd] James Pollock Provincial Surveyor. Galt 26th June 1851
Col ms 49 x 69 cm 1" to 10 chains Endorsements: 'A 180'
Shows the village laid out between the Speed R and Grand R from William St southwest to Hamilton St; major bldgs located on either side of King St including churches, schools, post office, courthouse, mills, printing office, distillery, etc; mail route to Berlin, Goderich; 'commencement of Dundas & Waterloo turnpike'; shows Joseph and John Erb's village lots; the boundary includes an area considerably larger than the town; (*OHIM* 7.13).
OTNR (SR 277)

1890 *[1856]*
MAP / of Building Lots / VILLAGE OF PRESTON / GIRDLESTONE & MADDISON, Agents, / Hamilton. / Surveyed & laid out by James Pollock, P.L.S. // Lith. Spectator Office, Hamilton C.W.
Print (lith) hand col 56 x 69 cm 1" to 50 ft
Shows lots along Victoria Ave, Hespeler St, and Union St, and the area from the travelled road from Galt, New Hope, and Guelph west to Galt & Guelph Railway; a note pasted on indicates 'This Property will be sold by Auction on Wednesday ... 28th May 1856 ... on the ground by Best & Green.'; based on R.P. 526 of 14 Dec 1855 (**B2034**).
Waterloo 67 (R.P. 526 (2))

1891 *[1856]*
TOPOGRAPHICAL / Map OF THE Village / OF / PRESTON / IN THE COUNTY OF WATERLOO / CANADA WEST. / By N. Booth D.P.S. & C.E. / Lith of J. Knayer, Preston C.W.
Print (lith) 84 x 81 cm 1" to 4 chains
Shows the town from the Grand R to the mills on the Speed R and Joseph Erb's property and from east of the Galt & Guelph Railway to the Speed R; all bldgs shown with names of owners; town hall, cloth factory, school, churches, cemeteries, distillery, mills; the *Berlin Telegraph* 18 Jan 1856 noted that J. Knayer was in Preston printing maps and views.
OKITD OOAMA (NMC 13209)

Related maps

(2) *[1859?]*
TOPOGRAPHICAL / Map / of the Village of / PRESTON / in the County of Waterloo / CANADA / by N. BOOTH D.P.S. & C.E. / Maclear & Co Lith. Toronto
Print (lith) 74 x 80 cm (trimmed) 1" to 4 chains
The plan was certified as correct by N. Booth and James Pollock on 9 Mar 1859 but statement refers to an original survey for Jacob Hespeler in 1854; shows much of the same information as plan above and probably redrawn from it; various subdivision surveys indicated; all bldgs shown with names of owners and businesses; shows major estates, railways, relief, and treed areas; see also **B2039**.
Waterloo S 67 (R.P. 520)

1892 *[1857?]*
KLOTZ's BLOCK / IN THE / VILLAGE OF PRESTON / Laid out into Building Lots for and at the instance of / OTTO KLOTZ Esqr / By James Pollock P.L.S.
Print (lith) 57 x 42 cm 1" to 2 chains
Shows lots laid out from Laurel St to Middle St, South St to North St, and Clark St to Hespeler St; a subdivision north of original town and west of Galt & Guelph Railway and station; owners shown; based on R.P. 528 (2) of 11 July 1857 (**B2035**).
Waterloo S 67 (R.P. 528)

1893 *[1857?]*
PLAN OF VILLAGE LOTS. / RAILWAY-STATION, PRESTON. / Lith. Spectator Office, Hamilton.
Print (lith) 49 x 78 cm 1" to 2 chains Endorsements: 'E-No-10'
Shows the Galt & Guelph Railway and lots laid out on Hespeler St and Clark St, and Wellington St to Union St; 'proposed branch to Berlin' refers to the Preston and Berlin Railway incorporated in 1857 (*Statutory History*, 493); relief and a few bldgs shown; see also**B2036**.
Waterloo S 67 (R.P. 524)

1894 *1866*
Map of the Village of Preston in the County of Waterloo Canada West Otto Klotz Conveyancer delt
Col ms 87 x 81 cm 1" to 4 chains
Certified as correct and as prepared for the Municipality of Preston in accordance with the Act of Registration of Titles and sgd 'James Pollock Provl Land Surveyor Preston 28th December 1866'; streets named from Grand R to Cyrus St; Galt & Guelph Railway and lots shown; names of original subdivision surveys; names of present owners; also shows the GTR, mills, mill races and ponds; the same as registered plan of 28 Dec 1866 (**B2042**).
OKITD

PRICEVILLE

1895 *1852*
Town Plot of Grovesend. Crown Land Department, Quebec 16th July 1852 [Sgd] John Rolph Commissioner of Crown Lands
Col ms 26 x 37 cm Scale not given
Shows the boundary of the town plot in lots 1–5, con I, north and south of Durham Rd in Artemisia Twp, and lot 54, con I, north of Durham Rd in Glenelg Twp.
OTAR

1896 *1853*
Plan of Priceville by David Gibson Prov: Land Surveyor 1853. Examined A.R.
Col ms 87 x 62 cm 1" to 4 chains Endorsements: 'B 56'
(OTNR FN 300 12 March 1853); shows the town lots laid out from John St to Mill St, and Artemisia St to Glenelg St south and west of the Saugeen R; park lots are shown south of Torry St; mill reserve with location of mill, race, and dam; relief, swampy areas; also a copy: 'Priceville. Crown Lands Department Quebec 11th Decr 1854 [Sgd] A.N. Morin Commissioner of Crown Lands' endorsed 'No 104' and lacking some of the detail but with the addition of names (OTNR (SR 274)); and a copy: 'Priceville Crown Lands Office Toronto June 12th 1856 [Sgd] Joseph Cauchon Commisr of Crown Lands' endorsed 'No 117' and with the addition of names in all lots (OTAR(P)).
OTAR(P) OTNR (SR 273)

PUTNAM

1897 *1863*
Plan of the Village of Putmanville being composed of a part of Lot No IV – Concession B in the Township of North-Dorchester in the County of Middlesex. as resurveyed by Wm McClary, P.L.S. for Thos Putman, Esqre November 1863. W.B. Leather. [Certified correct] London C.W. Decr 1863 [Sgd] Wm McClary P.L.S.
Col ms 39 x 61 cm 1" to 2 chains
The town is laid out with lots along Main, Marshall, Thames, and Malahide sts; mill pond; 'Note – This Village Plot was Surveyed and laid out by Charles W. Connor, in the Year 1848 and the resurvey made by Wm McClary P.L.S. was a verification survey for the purpose of getting a Correct Plan made for registration'; the same as R.P. 192 (**B2056**).
OLU

QUEENSTON

1898 *[1793?]*
[Sketch of Queen's Town Harbour] Surveyed & Drawn by [Sgd] Joseph Bouchette
Col ms 11 x 10 cm 1" to 10 chains
Shows the harbour, Hamilton's house, King's store, Rangers' barracks, 'Ship's Course'; 'Remarks It is very requisite for vessels bound to this Port to follow the East side of this River as far as the Point A from thence, bearing directly across to the wharf will bring them safe into the Harbour. Vessels leaving the wharf will sometimes get into the whirlpool which will occasion the vessels to veer round several times'; probably drawn in late 1792 or 1793, soon after Simcoe established the Queen's Rangers there (Simcoe, *Correspondance* I:247).
OTAR (Simcoe Map 445085)

1899 *[1796?]*
Plan shewing the Ground reserved for Government at the Landing Place on the west side of the Niagara River, and the proposed situation for Wharf, Stores, etc. (Signed) Gother Mann Capt Commandg Rl Engrs
Col ms 62 x 81 cm 1" to 200 ft Endorsements: 'No 16' '864'
Shows bldgs by the river, guardhouse, proposed wharf and store, names of a few occupants, road and proposed road, and the long narrow reserve extending inland; also a similar map at OTNR (SR 81003) with the same title and endorsed 'No 24' and '960'; probably made in 1796 as were similar plans for Niagara and Amherstburg (see **1672** and **1114**).
OTNR (SR 81003; 81022)

Related maps

(2) *1835*
Military Reserve at Queens Town, Niagara. Plan Shewing the Ground reserved for Government ... Surveyor General's Office Toronto Upper Canada, 15th April 1835, Copy, – Henry Lizars S.P. Hurd Surv. Genl. T.G.W. Eaststaff Draugn
Col ms 67 x 83 cm Scale not given
Endorsed 'No 2 To Accompany the Report of the Commanding Royal Engineer to His Excellency the Lieut Governor of Upper Canada on the subject of the Military Reserves dated 18th July 1836 [Sgd] G Nicolls Colonel Comg Rl Engineers Canada' (GBLpro CO 42/431 f 21); a later copy of (1) above; photoreproduction in OOAMA (NMC 22753); (*PRO Cat* 1552); and copy with same title as (1) further sgd 'Surveyor General's Office Toronto, Upper Canada 16th April 1835. (Copy) Henry Lizars (signed) S.P. Hurd S.G. Certified as a true Copy [Sgd] T.G.W. Eaststaff Draugn' and endorsed 'B↑O' (Holmden 2082) (OOAMA (NMC 22752)).
GBLpro (MPG 762(2)) OOAMA (NMC 22752)

1900 *1798*
Plan shewing the situation & Dimensions proposed for building lots for Merchants & Traders on the King's reserved Land near the West Landing on the Niagara River in the province of Upper Canada. (Signed) Gother Mann Col Commg Rl Engrs Quebec

30th June 1798 Approved (Signed) Robt Prescott By order of the Commander in Chief (Signed) James Green Mil. Secy
Col ms 43 x 53 cm 1" to 1.4 chains
In Col McDonell's letter of 10 Aug 1798 enclosing permission for a bldg lot to Thomas Clark at Queenston (OOA RG 8 I/272 p 19); oriented to the west; shows Robert Hamilton & Co. occupying one of the lots; storehouse; 'A Range of Log Buildings' [Rangers' barracks]; also shows roads, cliff, and two small lakes to the west; (Holmden 2012); and a copy in OTAR: 'Plan shewing the situation ... Appd (Signed) Robt Prescott'; this copy lacks the final signature and was possibly made at a much later date; and a plan in GBL (Maps 23.b.3 (13)) of the same title further sgd '1798 Wm Hall Lt R. Arty [Sgd] Gother Mann Coll. Commandg Rl Engrs'; the GBL map is an attractively finished plan with the same information; photoreproduction in OOAMA (NMC 4208).
GBL (Maps 23.b.3 (13)) OOAMA (NMC 4347) OTAR

1901 *[1817?]*
A Plan of the Position of Queenston [Sgd] Jno. C. Alexander Lieut Royl Engrs Henry Vavasour Capt Comg Rl Engrs N.F.
Col ms 76 x 87 cm 1" to 500 ft Endorsements: '141' 'Queenston & Country adjacent'; stamp 'REO'
Shows streets and bldgs in town, barracks, fuel yard, 'position where Brock fell'; boundaries of fields, roads, relief by hachures and wash, treed areas, ravines, etc; dated from copy below.
OOAMA (NMC 22750)

Related maps

(2) *1817*
Plan of the Military Reserve, Queenston. (Signed) Jno. C. Alexander, Lieut. Royal Engineers, 1817. (Signed) Henry Vavasour, Capt. Comg. Rl. Engrs. Niagara Frontier. [Sgd] R.H. Bonnycastle, Capt. R.E. Western District U.C.
Col ms 45 x 78 cm 1" to 500 ft Endorsements: 'Case No. 3, No. 11'
Shows part of the area and the same information as plan above and appears to be a copy of it with the addition of later notes, the railroad, and revision of streets; 'License of Occupation to James Secord Senr March 1st 1820 by P. Maitland ... [Sgd] H.O. Crawley Lieut. R. Engineers.'
QMMMCM (1411)

1902 *1818*
[Plan of Government Wharf at Queenston] (signed) Jno. C. Alexander Lt. R.E. Signed H. Vavasour Capt Comg Royl Engr N.F. Royal Engineers Drawg Room Quebec 31st Jany 1818 [Sgd] J.B. Duberger Junr [Sgd] E.W. Durnford Col. Comg Rl Eng / Copy /
Ms 19 x 27 cm 1" to 200 ft
Enclosed with a request for use of part of the wharf by Mr Kirby in Durnford's letter to Lt Col Addison, military secretary, 31 Jan 1818 (OOA RG 8 I/273 p 107); a small sketch showing the wharf, relief, and roads in the area; (Holmden 2395).
OOAMA

1903 *1819*
Plan of the Military reserve at Queenston [Sgd] A. Walpole Lt R.E. Niagara May 6th 1819 [Sgd] Henry Vavasour Capn Ryl Engineers
Col ms 26 x 38 cm 1" to 500 ft
Accompanied a report of Lt Col Durnford of 23 Apr 1819 concerning encroachments on the military reserves (OOA RG 8 I/403 p 137); shows the long, narrow reserve along the shore and west to part of the road to St David's; shows the front street in town with a few bldgs and names of owners; relief; (Holmden 2397).
OOAMA (NMC 4349)

1904 *[1831–5?]*
A Plan of the Village of Queenston Drawn from Actual Survey Presented to the Honble John Hamilton By his very Obedient Servant [Sgd] John W. Benn C.E.
Col ms 92 x 65 cm 1" to 100 ft
Shows the town from King St to Front St, and York St to the river; shows the military reserve, wharf, king's store, barracks, school, log house and tavern, relief, bridge over gully; probably made in the early 1830s, after Hamilton became a member of the Legislative Council (1831) (*DCB* XI:378) but before the Erie and Ontario Railroad was built (1835–9) (Trout and Trout, 56).
OSTCB

1905 *1838*
Military Reserve at Queenston & in the Township of Niagara Surveyed Novr 1838. William Hawkins Dy Survr
Col ms 93 x 64 cm 1" to 4.5 chains Endorsements: 'No 35' '1194'
Shows the boundary of the reserve with several notes on bearings, deeds, names of owners, etc; bldgs shown and some named, shows cleared areas, orchard, relief, streets and several roads; also a copy: 'Military Reserve at Queenston, Township of Niagara, Surveyed, Nov. 1838 William Hawkins Dt. Survr. Copy Fras. Nisbet' (QMMMCM (1114)).
OTNR (SR 6929) QMMMCM (1114)

1906 *[184?]*
[Sketch of Queenston with lots laid out]
Col ms 65 x 102 cm 1" to 4 chains Watermark: 'JAMES WHATMAN TURKEY MILLS KENT ...'
This appears to be an unfinished plan for subdivision, the only name being 'Niagara River'; lot nos and sizes shown surrounding a large house on point overlooking river; list of all lots and acreages; instructions on how to finish the map, e.g., 'ink in pencilled lines,' 'colour roads, lots A&B pink, C blue.'
OOAMA (NMC 22749)

1907 *1840*
Queenston; To accompany the Perambulation Report, June 1840. Surveyed by W. Hawkins, 1838. (Copy) J. Collard. Niagara, 1840.
Col ms 42 x 65 cm 1" to 4.5 chains Endorsements: 'From Niagara Office No. 142'
Shows the boundaries of the reserve, streets, bldgs and some identified; roads, the Queenston-Chippawa Railroad; there is also a plan of 1844 and one of 1849 of the military reserve, both showing the encroachments of the Erie and Ontario Railroad (QMMMCM 3631 and 1113).
QMMMCM (1113; 3624; 3631)

1908 *1841*
Plan of Queenston and the Heights showing the site of the proposed work [Sgd] P.J. Bainbrigge, Lt. R.E. J. Oldfield Lt Colonel Commanding Rl Engineers in Canada 30th Sept 1841 (Copy) S. Westmacott Lt R.E. 25th Sepr 1841
Col ms 112 x 87 cm Approx 1" to 400 ft
Endorsements: stamp 'B↑O'
Accompanied estimate of cost in letter no 155 of 4 Oct 1841 (GBLpro WO 44/37 pp 166ff); 'Sections showing the proposed Tower'; shows relief along escarpment and river; contours marked on the hill; old redoubt and battery; roads, bldgs.
GBLpro (MR 1929(4, 5))

1909 *1850*
Queenston, C.W. Survey of part of the Ordnance Property occupied by the Queenston Suspension Bridge Company and required to be surrendered by the Ordnance in virtue of an Act of the Provincial Legislature. (Copy) (Signed) S. Freeth, Capn R.E. 26th Nov. 1850.
Col ms 33 x 28 cm 1" to 2 chains
Shows a small tract of land near Front St; there is also a plan of 1851 showing the line of the bridge with notes on layout (QMMMCM 3630).
QMMMCM (3618; 3630)

1910 *1859*
Plan of Part of the Ordnance Reserve Fronting on the Niagara River at Queenston Canada West [Sgd] B.W.Gossage P.L. Surveyor Toronto September 23rd 1859
Col ms 61 x 120 cm 1" to 2 chains
Inset: 'Sketch shewing Fishing Stations North of the Village of Queenston' 1" to 16 chains; shows the area by the river from wharf and steamboat landing to water lot 19; suspension bridge; some names of owners; wooded areas.
OTNR (SR 6928)

(RACEY VALE town plot)

1911 *[1866]*
PLAN / OF / RACEY VALE / BEING LOT No 16 IN THE 15th CONCESSION / TOWNSHIP OF ORFORD. / COUNTY OF KENT / SITUATED IN THE CENTRE OF THE CELEBRATED / BOTHWELL OIL REGION / THE PROPERTY OF / RACEY & BROTHER, CLINTON, C.W. / AS SURVEYED BY / A.P. SALTER, / P.L. SURVEYOR / CHATHAM, C.W. // Brown & Bautz, Hamilton
Print (lith) hand col 56 x 51 cm 1" to 4 chains
Inset: 'SKETCH / SHEWING THE POSITION / OF / RACEY VALE / IN THE / BOTHWELL OIL DISTRICT.'; the plan was certified correct by the surveyor 20 March 1866; shows the subdivision of the area into lots, relief, sketch of a refinery and well; the inset shows many wells on both sides of the Thames R; no longer shown on the co atlas (Belden, ... *Kent* (1881)); see also **B2059**.
Kent 24 (R.P. 171)

RATHO

1912 *1857*
MAP / OF / TOWN AND VILLA LOTS / AT / RATHO, / In the Township of Blandford, County of Oxford, the property of / Messrs. Peat, Elliot & Sellers. / William Smith, Provincial Land Surveyor, / WOODSTOCK. / May 2nd, 1857. / Printed at the Gazetteer Office, Woodstock.
Print (typeset) 56 x 93 cm Approx 1" to 132 ft
Shows the town laid out from Green St to Galt St, and James St to Elm St on both sides of the Buffalo, Brantford & Lake Huron Railway; a few bldgs are shown; 'This Property will be sold by Public Auction, on Tuesday May 26th ...'; description of the town and notes on the advantages of the site; OOAMA copies both have ms adds indicating prices of lots and some names of purchasers; (*OHIM* 7.14).
OOAMA (NMC 43202; 43352)

RENFREW

1913 *[1857]*
Plan of the Town of Renfrew / THE PROPERTY OF WILLIAM ROSS, Esq: / ON Lots 13 IN THE 1ST AND 2ND CON. OF THE TOWNSHIP OF HORTON. / DONALD KENNEDY PRACL. ENGR / Bytown Febr. 16th 1854. / Maclear & Co Lith. Toronto.
Print (lith) Size not known 1" to 2 chains
Two views of town with bldgs indexed, both sgd 'Eastman Ottawa'; shows the town from Bonnechere R to Bruce St, and Baldwin St east to Bourette St; lot nos and sizes; grist and sawmills, slides, flume, bridge, reserves for public square, co bldgs, 'Prescot Road'; the notes on the advantages of the town sgd 'Renfrew, June 1857' include the hope that Renfrew will become the co town when it soon separates from Lanark; the plan shows the same areas as R.P. 8 of 16 March 1854 (**B2067**) but the latter was subdivided by J.S. Harper for Frances Hincks; photoreproduction in OOAMA (NMC 4362). Original not located

RICHMOND

1914 *[1819?]*
Plan of the Village of Richmond situate in the Township of Goulburn district of Johnstown province of Upper Canada. Surveyed under Instructions of Thomas Ridout Esquire Surveyor General of said province in the year of our Lord 1818. by [Sgd] J Fortune Dy Pl Surveyor
Col ms 54 x 47 cm 1" to 4 chains Watermark: 'W Turner & Sons' Endorsements: 'A56' '689'
(SI 17 Sept 1818 to survey the town plot of Richmond; OTNR FN 277 3 Feb 1820); shows the town laid out on lot 26, con 6, Goulburn Twp, with nine streets north-south and seven streets east-west, from King St to Queen St, and Ottawa St to Perth St; some park lots numbered; area north of Ottawa St owned by George Lyon; some names of owners; surveyed from 24 Dec 1818 to 20 Jan 1819; also a photoreproduction at OOAMA (NMC 4368) of a similar map owned by Richmond Village.
OTNR (SR 288)

Related maps

(2) *[1819] (1859)*
Plan of the Village of Richmond in the Township of Goulburn Copied from J. Fortune's Plan by [Sgd] W.A. Austin P.L. Surveyor Ottawa October 21st 1859.
Col ms 85 x 90 cm 1" to 5.5 chains
Shows the town as originally laid out from King St to Queen St, and Ottawa St to Perth St; park lots as numbered by Fortune 1–37 north-south and 1–20 east-west; shows land owned by G. Lyon and other family members.
OOAMA (NMC 11435)

1915 *1825*
Town of Richmond & Park Lots in the Township of Goulburn Bathurst District A reduced copy from Mr. Fortunes Plan By J.G.C. Decemr 14th 1825.
Col ms 91 x 76 cm 1" to 4.5 chains Endorsements: 'No 43'
Shows the same layout of town lots as 1819 plan (**1914**), now surrounded by long, narrow park lots on four sides running perpendicular to town-site square; reserves for Presbyterian and Catholic churches, church ground, and government reserve; with later renumbering of park lots according to 'Original Plan sent to this office 23rd Dec 1833'; park lots are numbered 1–40 north-south and 1–20 east-west; names have been added in lots.
OTAR(P)

1916 *1837*
Richmond Copy [Sgd] J.G. Chewitt S.G. Office 21st June 1837. Surveyor General's Office Toronto 23rd June 1837 [Sgd] J W Macaulay Surv Genl
Col ms 64 x 74 cm 1" to 4 chains
Shows the town proper, the park lots to east and west, and only part of the north and south park lots; school, churches; many notes about deeding of lots to 1846.
OTAR

(RIPPON town plot)

1917 *1833*
Plan of the town of Rippon Situate in the 1st Concession of Sunnidale, Lots 22 & 23 Surveyed by William Hawkins Dpy Survr 1833. [Sgd] William Hawkins Deputy Surveyor Surveyor General's Office York U.C. August 21st 1833
Col ms 80 x 62 cm [1" to 3 chains] Endorsements: 'A 61' '691'
(SI 30 May 1833 to Wm Hawkins about a road line from bridge on the Nottawasaga to an undecided point on L Huron for a town plot; OTNR FN 603, 3 Sept 1833, and 647, 2 Dec 1833); shows town from Sunnidale Rd to Drummond St, and Maitland St, and west to Simcoe St between sideline for lots 21/22 and lots 23/24, con 1, Sunnidale; Victoria Square; although still shown as a town plot on the co atlas (Belden, ... *Simcoe* (1880)), the town was not listed in *Smith's Canadian Gazetteer* (1846) and never developed; also a copy: 'Town Plot of Rippon late, Nottawasaga being part of Lot No 23 1st Con. Sunnidale. Surveyed 1833. [Sgd] William Hawkins Toronto' endorsed 'No 45' and with some later notes about ownership (OTNR (SR 285)); and a copy with the same title, endorsed 'No 59' and with a few notes on patents (OTNR (SR 286)); and a later copy: 'Rippon late, Nottawasaga in township of Sunnidale. Copy [Sgd] J.G. Chewett S.G. Office 7th June 1837. Surveyor General's Office Toronto 12th June 1837 [Sgd] J W Macaulay Surv Genl' (OTAR).
OTAR OTNR (SR 285; 286; 287)

RIVERSDALE

1918 *1856*
PLAN OF RIVERSDALE / in the / TOWNSHIP OF GREENOCK / Surveyed for G. Cromar Esq. / BY / EDWIN HENRY KERTLAND C.E. & P.L.S. / Elora 20 January 1856. // Maclear & Co Lith. Toronto Canada West
Print (lith) hand col 46 x 80 cm 1" to 2 chains
Inset: [location map]; shows the town laid out from Teesdale St to Christopher St, and James St to Sylvan St, on part of lots 29 and 30, con 1, Greenock; the inset shows the Owen Sound Rd, the Durham Rd, and other road connections to town; see also **B2079**.
OTAR Bruce 3 (R.P. 6)

ROCKWOOD

1919 *1856*
PLAN / OF THE VILLAGE OF / ROCKWOOD / IN THE / TOWNSHIP OF ERAMOSA, / COUNTY OF WELLINGTON / ON THE / PROPERTY OF H. STRANGE. / Surveyed by H. Strange P.L.S. / October 1856. // Maclear & Co. Lith. Toronto
Print (lith) hand col 49 x 65 cm 1" to 4 chains
Shows streets and lots in three areas from Main St to Caspell St, and Frederick St to Carroll St, and Dowler St to Fall St, Rock St to Shanly/Division sts and GTR station, and Queen St to Main St, Jackson St to Gzowski St west of the station; bldgs are shown on lots coloured pink and are mainly around mills at Harris and Main sts and west along Main St; a slip pasted on indicates 'This property will be sold on the 5th December, 1856'; see also **B2082**.
OTAR Wellington 61 (R.P. 150)

ROSSEAU

1920 *1866*
Plan of the Town Plot of Helmsley in the fifth Con. of Humphry. [Sgd] William Robert Aylsworth P.L. Surveyor. Tamworth 20th Aug 1866.
Col ms 76 x 37 cm 1:3168 Endorsements: 'H 30' (SI 15 May 1866 to subdivide town plot into town lots; OTNR FN 1298 20 Aug 1866); shows the town from Water St to Confederation St, and to Lock St; relief, clearings; lot nos and sizes.
OTNR (SR 119)

ROTHSAY

1921 *1855*
MAP / OF THE VILLAGE OF / MARYBOROUGH / COMPRISING PART OF LOTS No 10 / IN 13th & 14th CONCESSION OF / MARYBOROUGH / Surveyed for Messrs Allan & Geddes / BY / EDWIN HENRY KERTLAND CIVIL ENGINEER P.L.S. / Maclear & Co.
Lith. Toronto. Elora 27th November 1855.
Print (col lith) 61 x 87 cm 1" to 2 chains
Shows the town from Nelson St to Queen St at 'Canistoga' [Conestogo] R, and King St to Paul St and beyond; park lots are shown on both ends of town; site for steam grist and sawmills, tannery site; lot nos and sizes; see also **B2089**.
Wellington 60 (R.P. 70)

ST CATHARINES

1922 *1836*
MAP / of the VILLAGE of / ST CATHARINES / Surveyed by / Robt A. Maingy Civil Engineer / 1836
Print (lith) 42 x 64 cm Scale not given
Inset: 'Elevation of the Hydraulic Ditches'; shows the town laid out from the Welland Canal north to North St, and east to beyond Geneva St; shows lots and some bldgs along canal and at junction of Ontario, St Paul's, and Yates sts; the elevation shows the levels of the various mill races; see also **B2095**.
Niagara 30 (R.P. 77 (City))

1923 *1852*
MAP / OF THE / TOWN / OF / ST CATHARINES / CANADA WEST / Surveyed drawn & published by / MARCUS SMITH. / 1852. // A. Kollner's Lithc. Establt Phila
Print (lith) hand col 67 x 126 cm 1" to 3 chains
View: 'Town Hall'; shows the town as it has been extended to the south of the Welland Canal and on the east to beyond Pace St and slightly to the north; all bldgs are shown with major ones named and some names of owners; the layout of large estates shown; shows the canal and locks in detail; includes a description of the Welland Canal and the town and its advantages for location.
OOAMA (NMC 11436, 16796) USDLC

1924 *[ca 1855]*
PLAN OF BUILDING LOTS / NEAR THE / G.W. Railway Depot / ST CATHARINES. / BEING PART OF LOTS 19 & 20. 7th CONN / GRANTHAM. / PROPERTY OF A.E. RYKERT, ESQ. // LITHOGRAPHED BY J. ELLIS, TORONTO
Print (lith) hand col 43 x 62 cm 1" to 132 ft
Shows a subdivision from George St to Union St and from con rd north to macadamized rd southwest of original town; lots coloured green are probably those for sale; the subdivision is not on the 1852 map and was probably laid out soon after the GWR station was built and the line opened from Niagara to Hamilton in Nov 1853 (Bladen, 47); see also **B2103**.
Niagara 30 (no R.P. number)

Related maps

(2) *[1857]*
PLAN OF BUILDING LOTS / AT THE / GREAT WESTERN RAILWAY, / DEPOT, / ST CATHARINES, / The Property of / J.C. RYKERT. / LITHOGRAPHED BY J. ELLIS. TORONTO.
Print (Lith) 64 x 99 cm 1" to 2 chains
From Charles St to Welland Canal and Thomas Merritt estate to GWR station; many bldgs shown on Hainer and St Paul sts; ship-yard; names of owners; certified correct by owner in Oct 1857.
Niagara 30 (R.P. 74A)

ST GEORGE

1925 *1836*
Plan of the Village of St George in the Township of Dumfries District of Gore and Province of Upper Canada Brantford 4th October 1836 [Sgd] Lewis Burwell Dy Surveyor
Col ms 66 x 54 cm 1" to 2 chains

Shows the town at the intersection of High, Beverly, Dumfries, and Brantford sts; several bldgs shown including businesses, grist mill, mill pond, residences and some names of owners.
OBBM

ST JACOBS

1926 *1857*
MAP / OF THE / VILLAGE OF ST JACOBS / TOWNSHIP OF / WOOLWICH, / COUNTY OF WATERLOO. C.W. / SURVEYED FOR / GEORGE W. EBY ESQ. / by / Schofield & Hobson P.L.S.s / 1857. / Maclear & Co. Liths Toronto.
Print (col lith) 56 x 77 cm 1" to 3 chains
Shows town from Young St to Park St, and Conestogo R to Clerkenwell St; many bldgs shown including mills, furniture factory, cloth factory, tannery, etc; reserve for a church.
OKIT

(ST JOSEPH town plot)

1927 *1854*
Sketch A Projected Plan for the subdivision of the Town Plot of St Joseph. Crown Lands Department Quebec 18th April 1854 [Sgd] A N Morin Commissioner of Crown Lands
Col ms 57 x 46 cm 1" to 10 chains
(SI to T.N. Molesworth of 18 Apr 1854 to subdivide into bldg and park lots); shows the proposal for the town on part lots 11–17, con A, and Huron and Neebish cons, St Joseph Twp; shows streets and lots, reserve for square, military reserve; note: 'Name the Streets & post the lanes on the Street but do not run the lines in the lanes; To be returned with your plan of survey.'
OTAR

Related maps

(2) *1855*
Plan of the town of St Joseph in St Joseph Island. Lake Huron. Surveyed by T.N. Molesworth, Provincial Land Surveyor. Examined Decr 1855 [Sgd] T. Devine
Col ms 77 x 92 cm 1" to 4 chains Endorsements: 'A 200'
Inset: 'Plan of Park Lots Nos XI to XX Town of St Joseph situated on Victoria Street between Inkerman Road and the front of Conn A'; (OTNR FN 1299 25 Oct 1855); shows the town laid out according to plan on (1), from Water St to Quebec St, and Walnut St to Cedar St, in town lots; park lots extend east and north to Inkerman Rd and Victoria St; relief, marshy areas; cleared land; also a copy: 'St Joseph J.W.B. Crown Lands Office Toronto 7th Feby 1857 [Sgd] Joseph Cauchon Commissioner of Crown Lands' with streets and lots only (OTNR (SR 6384)).
OTNR (SR 6384; 7685)

1928 *1866*
Plan of the subdivision in farm lots of the Town plot of St Joseph, St Joseph's Island. C.W. [Sgd] Wilson & McGee Provincial Land Surveyors. Mount Forest C.W. December 1866. Examd with field notes 15th Feby 1867.
Col ms 46 x 46 cm 1" to 40 chains Endorsements: '36'
(OTNR FN 1794 26 Dec 1866); shows the cancelling of the town plot and the reversion to farm lots of lots 11–20, con A, and part Huron and Neebish cons, twp of St Joseph; the military reserve is shown and two wharves; wooded and marshy lands; also a copy: 'Plan ... St Joseph St Josephs Island. Department of Crown Lands Ottawa, 28th May 1867. [Sgd] A. Russell Assistant Commissioner' (OTNR (SR 321)).
OTNR (SR 320–1)

ST MARYS

1929 *1858*
MAP / OF / ST MARY'S / COUNTY OF PERTH / Canada West. / Compiled from original Surveys by I.K. Clendenin P.L.S. / and other authentic sources. / BY / W.G. TOMKINS C.E. / A.D. 1858. / Maclear & Co. Liths Toronto
Print (lith) 80 x 103 cm 1" to 6 chains
View: 'TROUT CREEK VIADUCT L. & ST MARY'S R.R. / as seen from Stratford Road'; shows the town from Birtch St to Charles St, and Francis St to Victoria St and Front St; major bldgs shown and named; names of owners of large lots; railways.
OTNR (SR 7926)

1930 *1866*
Sketch of a Hasty Reconnaissance of the town of St Mary's C.W. [Sgd] R.M. Armstrong Lieut. R.E. 19.1.66
Col ms on linen 42 x 47 cm Approx 1" to 750 yds
Shows the main streets of the town, a few houses, connecting roads; GTR shown from Sarnia and London to Stratford; relief; areas marked in yellow but not keyed.
OOAMA (NMC 4382)

ST THOMAS

1931 *1821*
Map of the Town of St Thomas [Sgd] Dy Surveyor's Office Port Talbot 25th Septembr 1821 [Sgd] M. Burwell Dy Surveyor
Col ms 46 x 57 cm 1" to 2 chains
Shows streets and lots from river to road allowance beyond Church St and to old government road allowance along Kettle Creek to the north; relief; some names of owners; canal leading to grist mill; also a redrawn copy deposited 1 March 1826 '[Sgd] Copied by J.G.C.'
Elgin 11 (no R.P. number)

1932 *1830 (1860)*
[Map of part of St Thomas] by [Sgd] Roswell Mount Dy Surveyor Dated at Port Talbot 3d March 1830 ... Copied 28 March 1860
Col ms 46 x 38 cm Scale not given
'Copied from a map ... of the Property of Lucius Bigelow ... being part of Lot No 46 South of Talbot Road East'; shows properties along Kettle Creek including mill dam and old and new race; roads.
Elgin 11 (no R.P. number)

1933 *1838*
Maps and Profile of the Village of St Thomas Drawn by Danl Hanvey Dy. P. Surveyor Dy Surveyors Office St Thomas 6th March 1838
Col ms 61 x 72 cm 1" to 2 chains
Inset: 'Plan of Lots No 7 & 8 & Part of No 6 fronting on Talbot Street by Daniel Hanvey Deputy Surveyor' 1" to 32 ft; two views of houses; an attractive map showing the area from river to west and south of Queen St; several bldgs shown; bridges shown in profile; possibly the map and views described in Robertson, *History of Freemasonry in Canada* I:988.
Elgin 11 (no R.P. number)

1934 *[1854]*
Map / of part of the / TOWN / of / ST THOMAS, / THE CAPITAL OF THE COUNTY OF ELGIN C.W. / Showing the property of / MESSRS. WHITE, MITCHELL & SOUTHWICK. / Surveyed by / DANIEL HANVEY, P.L.S. // Lith. of Compton & Gibson 161 Main St Buffalo
Print (lith) 51 x 86 cm 1" to 100 ft
Shows the area west of the London & Port Stanley Railway to Hincks St, and Eliza St north to Talbot St; blocks A–W; school lot and Catholic church shown; Compton & Gibson were at this address in 1854 (Peters, 145); plan was probably certified by owners on 1 July 1854; see **B2159**.
Elgin 11 (R.P. 3)

1935 *[1855?]*
Map / OF / PART OF THE TOWN / of / ST THOMAS, / SHOWING THE PROPERTY / OF / ELTHAM PAUL, ESQ. / As surveyed by DANIEL HANVEY, P.L.S. / Compton, Gibson & Co. 209 Main St Buffalo.
Print (lith) 89 x 53 cm 1" to 100 ft Endorsements: 'No 24'
Shows the area from Southwold St at Kettle Creek to Walnut St on north, and Euclid St on east to 'Gravelled Road' on west; blocks 1–21, A–D; Kettle Creek, mill dam and pond, race to mill and from mill, flouring mill, a few bldgs with names of owners dated 1851; possibly published 1855 when Compton moved to address listed (Peters, 145).
OLU

1936 *1855*
Plan of the present and contemplated limits of the incorporated Village or Town of St Thomas, County of Elgin, C.W. by [Sgd] Daniel Hanvey Provincial Land Surveyor Provincial Land Surveyor's Office, St Thomas C.W. 15th August A.D. 1855
Col ms 89 x 62 cm 1" to 5 chains
Shows the town within cons VIII and IX, lots 1–4, Yarmouth Twp; shows the boundary but no streets of town; area to be extended is the part north and east of the east branch of Kettle Creek; London & Port Stanley Railway; price per acre of surrounding farmland.
OOAMA (NMC 43205)

1937 *1856*
PLAN / OF ADDITION TO THE TOWN OF / ST THOMAS / Being East Part of South Half / of Lot No 4 in the 9th Concession / Township of Yarmouth / Made by S. Peters P.L.S. / For the Proprietor Thomas Hodge Esqre / 1856. // [Sgd in facsimile] Saml Peters Lith. / London C.W.
Print (lith) hand col 49 x 38 cm 1" to 132 ft
Shows the area from Talbot St to Nolan St and Hodge St, and White's and Mitchell's survey east to Alma and Balaklava sts; 'To be Sold by Auction on Saturday June 7th 1856 Edward Emery Auctioneer'; no registered plan has been found.
OLU

SALEM

1938 *1856*
PLAN / OF THE / VILLAGE OF SALEM / SURVEYED AND DRAWN / FOR / MESSRS WISSLER, ERB AND KEITH. / BY EDWIN HENRY KERTLAND ESQ. C.E. & P.L.S. / Elora, 18th April, 1856 / Maclear & Co. Lith. Toronto
Print (col lith) 67 x 82 cm 1" to 2 chains
Shows the village from William and Wissler sts to Matheson St, and Victoria and Ann sts to Bridge St, on part of con 11, twp of Nichol, including lot XVII; R.P. 75 (**B2174**) is a transcript copy of this printed plan.
OOAMA (NMC 19812)

SALTFORD

1939 *1834*
Sketch of the Village of Gairbraid in the township of Colborne Huron District 30th December 1834 [Sgd] David Smith
Col ms 44 x 53 cm Scale not given
Shows the village across the Maitland R from Goderich; sts named and a few bldgs shown.
OGOHC

SANDHURST

1940 *1823*
A plan of the Village Plot of Fredericksburgh Surveyed in 1823. [Sgd] W. Conger Depy Pro. Surveyor

Col ms 70 x 53 cm 1" to 2 chains Endorsements: 'A 19' '643'
(SI 10 Jan 1823 to resurvey town plot 40 chains from the Bay of Quinte between lots 9 and 10, con I S, Fredericksburgh; OTNR FN 408 2 Apr 1825); shows the village from George St to King St, and Apsley St to Bathurst St; burying ground and church; a few houses shown with names of owners; marshy areas; road through town; table of lots; SI were issued to J. Ryder on 11 Nov 1809 to resurvey original plot laid out by Capt Sherwood but no plan has been found.
OTNR (SR 97)

Related maps

(2) *1823*
A plan of the Village Plot of Fredericksburgh. Surveyed in August and September 1823. by [Sgd] W. Conger Pro Depy Sur.
Col ms 75 x 58 cm 1" to 2 chains Endorsements: 'No 19'
Shows the same layout as plan above but with several additions; shows 18 houses, names of owners and bldgs keyed; lot nos with an indication if deeded; various irregular boundaries showing fenced areas, some with names of owners and uses, e.g., pasture; names are shown in most lots.
OTNR (SR 96)

1941 *1856*
Fredericksburgh [Sgd] T. Devine Crown Lands Department Toronto July 1856 [Sgd] Joseph Cauchon Comm. Crown Lands
Col ms 74 x 65 cm 1" to 2 chains
Shows the outline of streets and lots as on **1940** but none of the other detail or names are shown.
OTAR

SARNIA

1942 *1838*
PORT SARNIA. / H.J. Castle lithog. / 5th Feby 1838, / Toronto.
Print (lith) Approx 40 x 28 cm 1 3/4" to 3 chains
Shows the village from the water and Irongate St to Mechanic St, and on both sides of Lochiel St; lot nos; a church and a few other bldgs shown; photoreproduction in OOAMA (NMC 4383).
Original not located

1943 *[185?]*
A Chart of the River St Clair and the adjacent Country at Port Sarnia (Copy)
Col ms on linen 107 x 71 cm Scale not given
Endorsements: [BW] '531'
Shows part of Port Sarnia from lot 77 to Point Edward and lot 65; streets, churches, court-house, and burial ground.
OOAMA (NMC 43108)

1944 *1852*
Plan of the addition to the Town of Port Sarnia on the Tract ceded by the Indians September 1852. Surveyed and drawn by Alexander Vidal
Col ms 61 x 39 cm 1" to 2 chains Endorsements: 'Q 84'
Shows an extension of the town to the south with Christina and Victoria sts connecting the new part to the old; shows Front St to Brock St, Wellington and Nelson sts, lot nos, fences; several houses with names of owners including that of 'Chief J. Wawanosh'; Indian land is shown to the south; a later addition indicates the line of the 'Great Western Railway' along the shore.
OTNR (SR 258)

Related maps

(2) *[1853]*
ADDITION TO THE TOWN OF / PORT SARNIA / ON THE TRACT CEDED BY THE INDIANS / September 1852.
Print (lith) 51 x 29 cm 1" to 2 chains
A printed version of (1) above but lacking part of the area on the right and some of the detail; lot nos; shows 'D. Wawanosh's house, S. Marsden's house, and P. Salt's house'; OOAMA copy is endorsed 'IASR 4132'; OTAR(P) copy is endorsed 'No 89' and has a ms statement below title: 'Crown Lands Department Quebec Sept. 1853 A.N. Morin C.C.L. Crown Land Lithographic Press'; it also includes additional names in ms and a piece pasted on to the map to include the R St Clair.
OOAMA (NMC 22777) OTAR(P) OTNR (SR 259)

1945 *1853*
Plan of the Park Lots adjoining the Town-plot of Port Sarnia, Surveyed and drawn by Alexander Vidal, P.L.S. 1853. Original Plan [Sgd] Alexander Vidal Provl Land Surveyor. Exd A.R.
Ms 36 x 53 cm 1" to 6 chains Endorsements: 'Q 85'
The park lots are shown east of the town on both sides of Wellington east of Brock St; the Indian reserve is shown to the south; and a later copy: 'Park Lots adjoining the Town Plot of Port Sarnia J.W.B. Crown Lands Office Toronto 5th March 1857 [Sgd] Joseph Cauchon Commissioner of Crown Lands' endorsed 'No 126' (OTAR(P)).
OTAR(P) OTNR (SR 260)

1946 *[1854]*
PORT SARNIA. / Plan of a continuation of the Town. / Comprising Lots 70 & 71 Front Con. Township of Sarnia. / The Property of the Heirs of the late Henry Jones, Esqr. / AND KNOWN AS / THE MAXWELL ESTATE. / SURVEYED BY P.D. SALTER, ESQ. P.L.S. / Lithog'd at the Spectator Office Hamilton.
Print (lith) 68 x 98 cm 1" to 4 chains
Shows an extension of the town to the north beyond the London Rd with town lots from Water St to Parker St, and from Exmouth St to Maxwell

St, and R St Clair to Ham St; a few churches, jail, burial grounds; the town of Port Huron is shown across the river; notes on the advantages of the town and statement that lots to be sold by auction but date not given; R.P. Sarnia 3 is a transcript of this map and was certified by the surveyor on 8 Nov 1854 (**B2159**).
OOAMA (NMC 19039)

1947 *1855*
[Map of Sarnia showing ordnance property] [Sgd] W R Ord Col Cg Rl Eng. Montreal 31 Jan 1855.
Col ms 71 x 95 cm 1" to 4 chains Endorsements: 'Rel CW/1275' '1397'
Accompanied Col Ord's letter no 55 to the Inspector General of Fortifications dated 13 Aug 1855 (OOA RG 8 I/1407 p 351); shows the boundaries of the ordnance property at Point Edward and a proposed site for a tower; shows the railway connection to the North Michigan Railway.
OOAMA (NMC 22778)

1948 *[1859?]*
MAP OF / PORT HURON, SARNIA & GRATIOT / PORT HURON & GRATIOT, ST. CLAIR CO. MICHIGAN. / SARNIA, LAMBTON CO. CANADA WEST. / Drawn upon a Scale of 400 feet to an Inch & Published by I.D. CARLETON, Surveyor & Land Agt. / Port Huron, Mich. / Lith. by J. Sage & Sons, Buffalo N.Y.
Print (lith) 140 x 104 cm 1" to 400 ft
Shows the GTR, GWR, and two ferries between the towns; shown streets and lot lines in Sarnia; promotional notes and inset showing railway connections with the American mid-west; dated from Karpinski (*Checklist* 5:596; Karpinski 599); also a ms copy with the streets, railways, and the notes in OOAMA (NMC 21785).
USDLC USMiHi

1949 *1867*
BIRDS EYE VIEW OF THE CITY OF / PORT HURON, / & GRATIOT. / ST CLAIR CO. MICHIGAN 1867 / SARNIA & POINT EDWARDS. / LAMBTON CO. CANADA WEST // Chicago Lithographing Co. 158 & 154 Clark St. Chicago. // Drawn & Published by A Ruger Battle Creek, Mich.
Print (col lith) 50 x 72 cm Not drawn to scale
The view shows mostly the American side but streets are named in Sarnia and Point Edward, and bldgs shown; nine bldgs keyed; photoreproduction in OOAMA (NMC 4385); (Reps, *Views* no 1859).
USDLC

SAULT STE MARIE

1950 *1846*
Plan of the Town of St Mary's at the Falls of the River St Mary near Lake Superior. Surveyed and drawn by [Sgd] Alexr Vidal P.L.S. under instructions from the Crown Lands' Department, dated 3rd June 1846. Alexr Vidal del. Octr 1846. Examined A.R.
Col ms 60 x 90 cm 1" to 4 chains Endorsements: 'A 159'
Inset: [profile of portage] 1" to 5 chains, 1" to 20 ft vertical; (SI 4 Dec 1845 to survey location for a town plot and park lots and SI 3 June 1846 to subdivide the town plot; OTNR FN 616 19 Oct 1846); shows the town laid out from East St to Gore St, Bay St to Wellington St, Gore St to West St, and Portage St to Cathcart St; shows enclosures of Hudson's Bay Co. settlers, cleared land, and bldgs; island in front noted as granted to H.M. Ordnance; proposed reserves for public purposes; corrections to survey shown; also a copy at OTNR on linen without Vidal's signature (SR 3526); also a copy: 'Town of Sault Ste Marie Office Copy by Thomas Devine S & D. Crown Land Department Surveyors Branch West Montreal Dec 1847 A.R.' endorsed 'No 72' but with the addition of names in all lots (OTAR(P)).
OTAR(P) OTNR (SR 324; 3526)

Related maps

(2) *1846*
Plan of the Park Lots adjoining the Town of St Mary's surveyed and drawn by [Sgd] Alex Vidal P.L.S. under instructions from the Crown Lands Department dated 19th June 1846. Alexr Vidal del. October 1846. Examined A.R.
Col ms 60 x 87 cm 1" to 10 chains Endorsements: 'A 160'
(SI 19 June 1846 to survey park lots; OTNR FN 616 19 Oct 1846); shows a larger area than (1) above and shows the American town; shows park lots east of East St in con 1 and to the north; Hudson's Bay Co. land; custom-house reserve; Roman Catholic church lot and burying ground; cultivated land; relief, types of trees, bldgs; also a copy: 'Office Copy Park lots adjoining the Town of St Mary's Crown Lands Department Surveyors Branch West Montreal December 1847 By Thos. Devine' endorsed 'No 73' (OTAR(P)).
OTAR(P) OTNR (SR 323)

1951 *1847*
A Plan of part of the Town-Plot of St Mary's and of the adjacent Islands, shewing the lands claimed by the Hnble the Hudson's Bay Company. and its present inclosures. Surveyed and drawn by me, [Sgd] Alexander Vidal. Provl Land Surveyor June 22nd 1847.
Col ms 48 x 61 cm 1" to 4 chains
Shows the Hudson's Bay Co. claim to much of the western end of the town plot and its enclosure around its old establishment along a small river at John St; boundary of cleared lands; site of old mill, dam, mill race and flume; a later note indicates that the company was granted most of the western part of town, area to north, and islands in river on 3 July 1854.
OTNR (SR 325)

1952 *1847*
Plan of the Islands at the Falls of the River St Mary. Shewing the contemplated Mill Sites. Surveyed by [Sgd] Alexander Vidal P.L.S. June 19th 1847.
Col ms on tracing paper 49 x 65 cm 1" to 4 chains
'Section along the line on the Large Island' 1" to 10 ft vertical; (SI 11 May 1847 to survey islands at St Mary's for mill sites); eight proposed mill sites are shown on the islands; old mill site, dam, race and flume shown; Hudson's Bay Co. warehouse and wharf; portage road.
OTNR (SR 7117)

Related maps

(2) *1847*
Plan of the Mill Sites and Islands at the Falls of the River Ste Mary Surveyed and Drawn by Alexander Vidal P.L.S. June 1847.
Col ms 46 x 68 cm 1" to 4 chains Endorsements: 'A 161' 'With 1019/48'
'Profile of the ground on the line through the middle of St Mary's Island.' 1" to 10 ft vertical; boundaries of the respective mill sites shown, and boundary between canal reserve and mill sites; area reserved for canal with later note 'O.C. 24th March 1851'; reserve for ordnance on the island shows Hudson's Bay Co. post, part of town, and portage along shore; also a copy: 'Mill Sites and Islands at the Falls of the River St Mary Surveyed & drawn by A. Vidal P.L.S. Crown Lands Department Surveyors Office West Montreal April 1848 Copy – Devine' (OTAR (SR 7542)).
OTAR (SR 7542) OTNR (SR 2707)

1953 *[ca 1854]*
Townships XLVII North Ranges I East & I West / INCLUDING THE TOWN OF / SAUT DE STE MARIE / MICHIGAN / ALSO THE VILLAGE OF / SAUT DE STE MARIE / CANADA WEST / Copied from British and United States Surveys / BY LIEUT. A.L. MAGILTON U.S.A. ENGRAVED & PRINTED / BY / J.H. COLTON & CO. / 172 William St New York / FOR / SAMUEL WHITNEY. / SAUT DE STE MARIE.
Print (lith) 78 x 121 cm 1" to 1/4 mile
Includes a bird's-eye view of the American town; shows the street grid without names for the Canadian town and Episcopalian church, hotel, and windmill; shows greater area on the United States side and smaller area on the Canadian side than plan above; United States Ship Canal appears to be only roughly shown; earlier than **1955** and before U.S. canal was opened in 1855; (*OHIM*, 173).
OTAR

1954 *1855 (1856)*
Map of the Hudson's Bay Company's property at Sault de Ste Marie Surveyed and drawn by Alex. McDonald 1855. Montreal 9 May 1856 [Sgd] Alexander MacDonald Provincial Land Surveyor. Examined [Sgd] A.Russell
Col ms 50 x 68 cm 1" to 10 chains Endorsements: 'L.H. no 28'
(SI 13 Oct 1854 to survey Hudson's Bay Co. posts on L Huron and L Superior); shows the western part of town and extensive land there and to the north owned by the company; bldgs; portage road; relief, vegetation; traverse of river by the post.
OTNR (SR 7107)

1955 *1855*
PLAN OF THE TOWN / OF / SAUT DE STE MARIE / CANADA WEST / ENGRAVED & PRINTED / FOR / SAMUEL WHITNEY / SAUT DE STE MARIE / BY / J.H. COLTON & Co / NEW YORK // PLAN OF THE TOWN / OF / SAUT DE STE MARIE / MICHIGAN // Entered according to Act of Congress in the Year 1855, by J.H. Colton, in the Clerk's Office of the District Court of the United States for the Southern District of New York
Print (lith) 62 x 78 cm 1" to 10 chains
Shows the town from West St to East St, and north to Wellington and Cathcart sts; shows bldgs, which are located mainly along the shore, including the Episcopalian church; the American city shows streets, ship canal, and a few bldgs; there is also a deposit copy in USDLC that is identical but with date of registration changed in ms to 1856 and endorsed on back '501 Deposited in Clerk's Office for Dist New York Feb 18th 1856.'
OOAMA (NMC 22787; 43208) USDLC

SCARBOROUGH TWP

1956 *[1855]*
PLAN / OF LOTS FOR SALE IN / SCARBORO' VILLAGE. / BEING THE S.E. PART OF LOT 19, CONCESSION D THE PROPERTY OF MR ISAAC STONER. / J. Ellis Lith: Toronto.
Print (lith) 53 x 71 cm 1" to 100 ft
Certified by surveyor in ms, sgd 'F.F. Passmore Provl Surveyor,' and registered 3 Jan 1856; shows the area south of Nelson St and west of the Markham Plank Rd to Beachell St; GTR and station; a few names of owners; see also **B2198**.
Toronto 64 (R.P. 142)

1957 *[ca 1860]*
MAP / of the / TOWNSHIP OF SCARBORO / In the County of York and Province / of / CANADA / BY C.J. WHEELOCK C.E. / Lith. of F[uller & Bencke?]
Print (col lith) 68 x 57 cm 1" to 35 chains
Shows the complete survey grid with names of owners in the lots; boundaries of wards and school sections; schools, inns, mills, churches; blacksmith; drawings of four ships in lake; published between 1858 and 1862 when Fuller & Bencke were in partnership (Hulse, 102).
OTAR

(SEYMOUR town plot)

1958 *1835*
Town Plot in Seymour Shewing the part proposed to be Surveyed on Lot No 16 in the XI Concession (Clergy) coloured with a red margin, also No 16 in the 12 Concession and the connection with the Canada Company's Lot No 15 in the 12 Concession. Surveyor Genls Office 15 June 1835 [Sgd] J.G. Chewitt
Col ms 65 x 50 cm 1" to 6 chains Endorsements: 'A 168' '694'
Shows a town plot with streets 'to be surveyed' on the north shore of river in con XI, lots 15 and 16, for park lots and town reserve shown in lot 14, con XII; this extensive town plot appears not to have been laid out since it does not appear on later twp plans (see **A1781–4**); Healey's Falls was developed on part of the site.
OTNR (SR 312)

SHAKESPEARE

1959 *1855*
PLAN / of part of the Town of / SHAKESPEARE / IN THE / COUNTY OF PERTH / AS SURVEYED FOR JOHN GALT ESQ. / BY / C.L. Davies P.L.S. / June 1855. / Maclear & Co. Lith. Toronto
Print (lith) 48 x 65 cm 1" to 3 chains
Shows the southwest corner of the village around the station; streets named and note indicates 'The Sale will take place on the ground 11th July 1855'; Bell's Corners is shown in the northeast; the same as R.P. 334 (**B2214**).
Perth 44 (no R.P. number)

SHANNONVILLE

1960 *1839*
Plan of Shannonville Surveyed for George Auldjoc [Sgd] Saml M. Benson D.P. Surveyor. Belleville 10th Octr 1839.
Col ms 56 x 48 cm 1" to 2 chains
A note indicates the plan was 'Registered June 21st 1872'; shows the village from George St west to Colborne St, and Arthur St south to Young St, on both sides of the Salmon R; bridge at Dundas St and two inns, a mill, and a store shown.
OTAR

1961 *1843*
This is a Plan of lots laid out at Shannon Ville for the Mohawk Indians on part of Lots Nos 5 and 6 in the 1st Concession of Tyendinaga [Sgd] Saml M. Benson D.P. Surveyor Belleville June 13th 1843.
Col ms 34 x 48 cm 1" to 2 chains
Shows a further subdivision of the south side of the river from Queen St to Howard and [Brock] sts, and [King] St west to Gore St, altering part of survey on 1839 map (**1960**); seven bldgs shown.
OTAR

1962 *1846*
This is a Plan of part of the Village of Shannonville laid out on the South Easterly side of the Salmon River on part of Lots number five and Six in the first concession South of the Road in the Township of Tyendinaga. Belleville June 12th 1846 [Sgd] Saml M. Benson D.P. Surveyor
Col ms 44 x 58 cm 1" to 2 chains Endorsements: 'I 57'
Shows the area from Queen St to Brock St, and King St to Gore St, and the same lots as on the 1843 map with a few notes on sales and a few bldgs added; 'premises of George Auldjo' and 'lands leased to George Auldjo Esqr.'; 'premises of Philip Ham'; also a copy with the same title, etc, endorsed 'No 103' and with the addition of names (OTAR(P)); and a copy: 'Copy of a Plan of a Village laid out on part of Lots Nos 5 and 6 in the 1st Concession (South of the Road Tyendinaga) for the Mohawk Indians, on the East Side of the Salomon Rr. Shannonville, Surveyed in 1843 [Sgd] Saml M. Benson D.P.S. New Map dated June 12th 1846' with prices added to lots (OTAR); and a copy: 'This is a plan ... Tyendinaga Signed S.M. Benson D.P. Surveyor. Belleville June 12th 1846. Crown Lands Department Quebec 9th October 1853 Certified a true copy T.D. [Sgd] John Rolph Commissioner of Crown Lands' endorsed 'IASR 2051' and with further notes on sales (OOAMA (NMC 4400)).
OOAMA (NMC 4400) OTAR OTAR(P) OTNR (SR 340)

1963 *[ca 1850]*
[Shannonville]
Ms 20 x 33 cm Scale not given
Shows area south of the Salmon R from Queen St to Young St, and King St to Gore St, in a layout similar to the 1843 (**1961**) and 1846 (**1962**) maps; names have been added in some lots and some bldgs are shown.
OTAR

1964 *1855*
Plan of Town lots laid out on part of the North half of Lot number four in the second concession South of the Road in the Township of Tyendinaga in the county of Hastings [Sgd] Saml M. Benson P.L. Surveyor Belleville July 12th 1855. [Endorsed title]: 'Townsite of Kimmerly Tyendinaga I.R. near Shannonville'
Col ms 47 x 54 cm 1" to 2 chains Endorsements: 'No 1527'; stamp 'IASR'
Shows the village from the Salmon R south to Raglan St, and the road to Shannonville and Queen St east to Dickson St; a description is given of progress in constructing houses along Queen St, with names of owners, etc; also a later copy: 'Plan of Lots laid out on part of Lot No IV IInd Con. of Tyendinaga By S.M. Benson P.L.S. [Certified by surveyor as surveyed in 1855 and sgd] Saml M. Benson P.L. Surveyor Belleville July 23rd 1862. [Endorsed title]: Shannonville in Tyendinaga'

endorsed 'no. 1527' and 'IASR' and with names of owners added on some lots (OOAMA (NMC 7086); and a copy: 'Plan of Village Lots Surveyed by me in 1855 on a part of Lot No. 4 in the 2nd Concession South of the Road in the Township of Tyendinaga in the County of Hastings Situate about one fourth of a Mile South West of Shannonville on the South East side of the Salmon River Belleville July 23d 1862 [Sgd] Saml M. Benson' (OTAR).
OOAMA (NMC 4183; 7086) OTAR

SHEGUIANDAH

1965 *1866*
Plan of Town-Plot of Sheguiandah Manitoulin Island [Sgd] David C. O'Keeffe Provincial Land Surveyor Hamilton Augt 1866
Col ms 60 x 67 cm 1" to 4 chains Endorsements: 'S 33'
(OTNR FN 1734 24 Sept 1866); shows the town laid out from Anderson St to beyond Campbell St and Assickinac St, to Lindsay and Macaulay sts and Palmerston and McDougall sts along the shore; town lots in the centre part; Indian burying grounds and clearings.
OTNR (SR 313)

Related maps

(2) *1867*
Plan of Town Plot of Sheguiandah Manitoulin Island. Department of Crown Lands Ottawa 2nd May 1867 [Sgd] A. Russell Assistant Commissioner Henry Lawe
Col ms 61 x 68 cm 1" to 4 chains
Shows the same layout as plan above with addition of three mill sites on river, relief, treed areas, and marshy land; there is also a copy of the 1867 plan with later additions in OOAMA (RG 10M 76703/9 no 374; NMC 13349).
OTNR (SR 7469)

SHREWSBURY

1966 *1843*
Rough Plan of the Government Reservation for a Town Plot at the Intersection of the Communication Road with the Lac à la Pointe aux Pins in the Township of Harwich ... [Sgd] M. Burwell Dy Surveyor Port Talbot 24 October 1843.
Ms Size not known 1" to 6 chains
Shows a plan for a town west of marsh with 15 north-south streets and four east-west streets on both sides of Communication Road; reserves for church, gaol and court-house, and market square.
OTAR (RG1 C-1-1 vol 8)

1967 *1846*
Plan of the town of Shrewsbury Surveyed under the Authority of the Crown Land Department, as per Instructions dated 20th Feby and 12th June 1846. By [Sgd] Richr Parr Provl Land Surr Chatham C.W. Octr 22nd 1846.
Col ms 58 x 71 cm 1" to 4 chains Endorsements: 'A 167'
(SI 20 Feb 1846 and 12 June 1846 to verify outlines of town plot on the Rondeau and subdivide town plot into bldg lots; OTNR FN 629 1846); town is shown from Nelson St to Kent St and from water to Cathcart St in Harwich Twp; lots laid out mainly on both sides of Brock St; road and lots to L Erie 'recommended by Board of Works Reserved for Public purposes'; marshy area in front of town by shore shown; reserves for market, church, gaol and court-house; 'Intended Plank Road'; plan differs from proposed plan of 1843 (**1966**); some town lots were advertised in a government sale on 29 Mar 1848 (OTAR RG 1 C-III-1 vol 3); also a copy: 'Office copy Shrewsbury County of Kent Crown Land Department Surveyors Branch West Montreal Nov. 1847 True copy A.R.' endorsed 'No 74' and with the addition of names in all lots (OTAR(P)); and another copy: 'Shrewsbury. Crown Lands Department Surveyors Branch West Montreal December 1847. A.R.' (OTAR).
OTAR OTAR(P) OTNR (SR 293)

1968 *[1846?]*
Plan of the Town Plot of Shrewsbury on the Rond'eau Bay Township of Harwich in the Western District
Col ms 53 x 73 cm 1" to 4 chains Watermark: 'J WHATMAN TURKEY MILL 1845' Endorsements: stamp [BW] '501'
Shows the same layout and information as (**1967**) above with the addition of school reserve; street lines sketched in to the bay appear to show plan to reclaim marsh from Brock St east to William St and part of Kent St.
OOAMA (NMC 22796)

SIMCOE

1969 *[1840?]*
Plan of Part of the Village of Simcoe Copied from the original drawn by Lewis Burwell Esqr (the property of George Kent) [Sgd] by F.L. Walsh
Ms 27 x 68 cm 1" to 2 chains
Originally with a land petition about church lands (OOA RG 1 L3 S no 3 (2nd series) no 2 1843); shows the town from Peel St to Patterson's Creek and mill pond, and Colborne St to Norfolk St; Kent's brewery; a few names of owners.
OOAMA (NMC 4409)

Related maps

(2) *1840*
Plan shewing the relative situation of five acres of ground being the South East corner of Lot No 14 in the Gore of Woodhouse, with the Town of Simcoe known as the Clergy Block; reserved from the

Church of England. Shewing also the subdivisions of the same into Town lots for the purpose of Sale ... a True Copy [Sgd] Lewis Burwell Dy Surveyor Brantford 15th June 1840
Col ms 33 x 20 cm 1" to 1 chains Watermark: 'Newton 1838'
From the same source as above; Colborne St to Norfolk St, and Peel St to Robinson St; boundary of clergy block; (Holmden 2625).
OOAMA (NMC 4408)

1970 *[1854]*
PLAN OF THE LANDS / OF / MESSRS WILSON & WALSH / ADJOINING THE / SIMCOE, / Depot & Station Grounds of the Woodstock & / Lake Erie Railway & Harbour Company. / Laid out into Lots by / THOS W. WALSH, P.L.S. / Compton, Gibson & Co. Buffalo
Print (lith) 46 x 63 cm 1" to 21/2 chains
Shows the area from John St to Mill St, and Windham town line to mill pond; shows the lands purchased by the Railway and Harbour Co. for a depot and station; however, the railway was not built at this time; possibly published in 1854 when Compton and Gibson were in partnership (Peters, 145); see also **B2228**.
Norfolk 37 (no R.P. number)

SINGHAMPTON

1971 *1856*
Kelvin. Wm. Gibbard P.L.S. Nov 3rd 1856
Ms 23 x 34 cm Scale not given
Endorsed 'Copy of Gibbards Plan of Kelvin'; shows Clyde, Union, Bell, Yuill, and Queen sts; part of lot 9, con A, Osprey Twp; related to R.P. 261 (**B2230**).
OTMCL

1972 *1856*
PLAN OF TOWN PLOT / OF / SINGHAMPTON / ON THE MAD RIVER / AS LAID OUT ON LOT No 18 12. CON. NOTTAWASAGA 1856. / THE PROPERTY OF / CYRUS R. SING & JOSIAH R. SING / SURVEYED / by / THOMAS DONOVAN P.L.S. 1856 // Maclear & Co. Liths Toronto
Print (lith) 61 x 90 cm 1" to 2 chains
Inset: 'MAP / COUNTIES OF SIMCOE AND GREY / Shewing the Position of the Town of Singhampton / on the Mad River / Township of Nottawasaga / Thomas Donovan / Civil Engineer P.L.S. / Meaford St Vincent'; shows the village from Victoria St to Collingwood St, and Roger St to Mill St; mill pond and mill sites; description of the advantages of the town; small drawings of several bldgs including 'English Church'; similar to R.P. 92 (**B2231**; see also **B2232**).
Grey 17 (R.P. 251)

SMITHS FALLS

1973 *1833*
Map of Township Lots number one and two in the 4th Concession of the Township of Elmsley; Including a plot of the Village of Wardsville Smiths Falls Upper Canada. 27th April 1833 Surveyed and laid down [Sgd] By John Booth Depy Pl Surveyor
Col ms 72 x 54 cm 1" to 200 ft
Shows the village from canal basin to John St, and James St to Fly St, and the town line of Elmsley/Montague twps; two streets laid out south of river; two locks on Rideau Canal shown and dam and weirs; lots owned by William Simpson and Abel R. Ward shown; later note indicates that Main, Mary, By, and Centre sts closed after 1833 but before lots sold; another later note indicates that some lots west of Mill St and north of William St laid out in June 1858, sgd '12th July 1858 John Booth'; there is also a 'Plan of Smith's Falls' 1" to 330 ft accompanying letter of 7 Jan 1833 (GBLpro WO 44/15) and showing areas for proposed erection of houses.
GBLpro (MPH 1097(3)) OTAR

1974 *[ca 1835?]*
Map of the Government property at Smith's Falls
Col ms 66 x 53 cm 1" to 3 chains
Shows locks, dams, and mills, and most of street layout as in the 1833 plan (**1973**); streets shown north only to Mary St; bldgs shown by the river; roads to Merrickville, Carleton Place, Perth, Brockville; (Holmden 2414).
OOAMA (NMC 22799)

1975 *1857*
Village of Smiths Falls. C.M.C.
Col ms 61 x 66 cm Scale not given Endorsements: stamp [BW] '490'
Shows the town from Mill St to Clark St, and Shaw St to Montague St; shows names of owners in northeast part and development of town east of town line or Queen St; also a copy at OOAMA (NMC 22800) without title but endorsed 'No 190 of /57 referred to in letter from Reeve of Smith's Falls ...' and showing a proposed addition to the town east of Queen St, which was not granted (OOA RG 5 C1/500); text indicates maps made by Francis Jones, PLS.
OOAMA (NMC 22798; 22800)

SOMBRA

1976 *1854*
Village of Sombra surveyed by P.D. Salter P.L.S. 1854
Ms on linen 46 x 51 cm 1" to 2 chains
Originally accompanied a petition for a water lot (OOA RG 1 L3 F 9 no 12 1855); shows water lots on river opp Water St and near Forsyth and

George sts with names of owners; (Holmden 2626).
OOAMA (NMC 4417)

SOUTHAMPTON

1977 *1850 Oct*
Sketch of a projected subdivision of the Town plot of Saugeen Called Southampton into Building and Park Lots. Crown Lands Department Toronto 2nd October 1850
Col ms 81 x 86 cm 1" to 10 chains
Shows the plan for the town with streets and town lots shown to street 4, 0, and J from the lake; park lots to be behind these; blocks numbered; relief, river shoreline.
OTAR

1978 *1850 Dec (1851)*
Plan of Part of the Projected Town-plot of Southampton. Surveyed December 1850 By Robert F. Lynn Provl Land Surveyor and Civil Engineer. Drawn by J.M. Hearle 1851
Col ms 71 x 119 cm 1" to 4 chains Endorsements: 'A 178' 'B47'
(SI 23 Sept 1850 to subdivide town plot into bldg and park lots dependent on site for harbour; make reserves, traverse for mill sites, and find sites for bridges, commercial blocks); shows the part of the town from L Huron and Lake St with reserve, and from Wellington St north to River St; reserves for public square, court-house; park lots shown east of Grenville St; some streets do not extend east beyond small lake at Victoria St; proposed canal and harbour shown across mouth of Saugeen R; relief.
OTNR (SR 7686)

1979 *1851*
Plan of Part of the Town Plot of Southampton in the Township of Saugeen 1851.
Col ms on tracing paper 76 x 62 cm Scale not given Endorsements: 'A 183'
One of several plans from 1851 showing surveys in different parts of the town plot area; shows street and lot layout further to the east from Victoria St, and public square by the lake east to Carlisle St, and from H St [Arthur] south and east of Norfolk St; reserves shown for widow and orphan asylum, laundry yard and gardens, hospital, town hall and police station, Mechanics' Institute, market, school, seminaries and temperance hall; flats and marshy land shown and piers; a later endorsement is sgd 'Exhibit E ... R.F. Lynn 26/8/57 In Chancery Saugeen Church Society'; there is also a rough, undated map at OTAR entitled 'Part of Southampton-Saugeen' (43 x 40 cm), which may be a projection for the layout of this part of town.
OTAR OTNR (SR 6740)

Related maps

(2) *1851*
Rough Sketch of part of the Town Plot of Southampton in the Township of Saugeen. by [Sgd] Robert F. Lynn July 3rd 1851.
Col ms on tracing paper 43 x 71 cm 1" to 4 chains
Shows an extension of the town to the northeast from H St [Arthur] north to the Saugeen R and from Carlisle St east to street 21; flumes for 12 mill sites shown and projected basin and mill race; flats in river, rapids, reserve for public square.
OTNR (SR 6374)

(3) *1851*
Plan of part of the Town Plot of Southampton, in the Township of Saugeen laid out into farm lots. 1851. [Sgd] Robert F. Lynn Provincial Land Surveyor & Civil Engineer.
Col ms 70 x 54 cm 1" to 10 chains Endorsements: 'B 50'
(SI 20 June 1851 to subdivide part of town reserve into farm lots); shows the area east of street 13 and south of street H [Arthur] to the river in cons 13–15 and part of broken con 16 as laid out in farm lots, although originally reserved for town; flats, marshy areas, details on the river and nature of shoreline; 'Returned for sale 7th April 1852.'
OTNR (SR 2045)

(4) *1851*
Plan of the Town of Southampton in the Township of Saugeen. Survey'd Augst 1851 by Robert F. Lynn. Provincial Surveyor & Civil Engineer.
Col ms 150 x 228 cm 1" to 4 chains Endorsements: 'A 179'
(OTNR FN 1763–4 5 May 1852); shows the fullest extent of the town as laid out in 1851; from Peel St and Arthur St on the south to the Saugeen R, and east to street 13; shows relief, marshy areas, flats and soundings in lake and river, and 12 mill sites; 'projected canal basin & harbour'; various reserves; ruins of Indian sawmill; names of patentees have been added later.
OTNR (SR 86598)

1980 *1852–6*
Copy of Dp Sr R. Lynn's Plan of Southampton West Part Crown Lands Department Quebec 5th August 1852 [Sgd] Andrew Russell S & D
Col ms 89 x 63 cm Scale not given Endorsements: 'No 87'
One of a series of copies showing the parts of the original surveys for the town; shows the first part of the town laid out from L Huron and Front St east to Norfolk St and from Peel St to Augusta St; public square and other reserves shown; park lots are shown east of Grenville St and south of Clarendon St; basin and harbour are not shown; names have been added later.
OTAR(P)

Related maps

(**2**) *1852*
East part of Southampton Office Copy from D.S. Lynn's Plan Crown Lands Department Quebec 6th August 1852 [Sgd] Andrew Russell
Ms 65 x 98 cm 1" to 4 chains Endorsements: 'No 88'
Shows the area north of Augusta and Arthur sts to Saugeen R and mill sites, and east to Robert St; school lands, reserves, and names are added.
OTAR(P)

(**3**) *1856*
Office Copy Southampton South Part Crown Lands Office Toronto 23rd July 1856 [Sgd] Joseph Cauchon Commissr of Crown Lands
Col ms 68 x 102 cm 1" to 4 chains Endorsements: 'No 112'
Shows a similar area to (1) above from Peel St north to river, and east of L Huron to Carlisle St, but cuts off one street south of Augusta and extends one street east of Norfolk St; 'projected canal basin & harbour' includes two piers; public and school reserves.
OTAR(P)

(**4**) *1856*
Office Copy Southampton North Part Crown Lands Office Toronto 25th July 1856 [Sgd] Joseph Cauchon Commssr of Crown Lands
Col ms 69 x 99 cm 1" to 4 chains Endorsements: 'No 113'
Shows the same area as (2) above but with fewer names; one more public reserve is shown and later additions are shown southeast of Carlisle and Arthur sts.
OTAR(P)

1981 *1856*
Plan of town and park lots as laid out on the North or Indian side of the Saugeen River in continuation of the Town Plot of Southampton. [Sgd] C. Rankin P.L.S. Feby 9th 1856
Col ms 104 x 66 cm 1" to 6 chains Endorsements: 'A 215' '10119/56'
(OTNR FN 1762 22 May 1856); shows the survey of lots on the north side of the river in former Indian lands; Rankin St north to Conway St, and L Huron east to Craig St and Copway Rd; town lots in southwest and park lots east of Division St and north of Oak St; Indian village and cornfield at eastern end; relief; also a copy dated 'Septr 1856' with many later additions in OOAMA (RG 10M 76703/9 no 192, NMC 13054); also a copy: 'Southampton in the Township of Amabel J.W.B. Indian Lands Crown Lands Office Toronto March 3rd 1857 [Sgd] Joseph Cauchon Commissr of Crown Lands' endorsed 'No 127' (OTAR(P)).
OOAMA (NMC 13054) OTAR(P) OTNR (SR 7700)

1982 *1857*
Copy of Plan of Custom House and A reserves in Southampton. Crown Lands Office Toronto 20th July 1857 [Sgd] Andrew Russell Asst Commissr of Crown Lands.
Col ms 49 x 33 cm 1" to 4 chains
(SI 4 May 1857 to R. Gilmour to survey reserve A at the mouth of the Saugeen and custom-house reserve); shows part of the main developed area of the town from High St to the river and from L Huron to Huron St; all bldgs and fenced areas shown with many encroaching on streets.
OTNR (SR 317)

1983 *1857*
MAP / OF / SOUTHAMPTON / COMPILED FROM THE ORIGINAL SURVEY AND / MAPS, / BY SPROAT & HAWKINS ENGINEERS & SURVEYORS / Southampton. / JULY 30TH 1857. / LITHOGRAPHED BY J. ELLIS, TORONTO.
Print (col lith) 67 x 88 cm 1" to 8 chains
Shows the town from L Huron to Carlisle and Robert sts, and from Peel St to Saugeen R and north to Copway and Craig sts; shows town lots, reserves, and park lots; bldgs are shown and some identified; commercial bldgs are concentrated north of High St and west of Victoria St; Indian reserve and village, mills; some copies have ms adds on prices, dimensions of lots; some copies uncoloured.
OKQ OOAMA (NMC 23750) OTAR OTNR (SR 6401, 7675)

1984 *[ca 1857]*
PLAN / OF / Village and Park Lots / ADJOINING THE TOWN PLOT OF / SOUTHAMPTON / IN THE / TOWNSHIP OF SAUGEEN AND COUNTY OF BRUCE / Joseph Gilbert Esqr Proprietor. / GILMOUR AND LYNCH / P.L. Surveyors & Land Agents Southampton. / Maclear & Co Liths Toronto, C.W.
Print (col lith) 62 x 90 cm 1" to 3 chains
Inset: 'SKETCH OF PART / OF THE / TOWNSHIP OF SAUGEEN / SHEWING THE POSITION OF TOWN AND PARK LOTS / FOR SALE / The Property of J. Gilbert Esqr.' 1" to 40 chains; shows a subdivision east of Southampton and east of the Saugeen and Goderich Rd on both sides of the Saugeen and Elora Rd; Saugeen St to Gilbert St and Joseph St to Helena St; Victoria Hotel and a few bldgs shown; the inset locates the roads, Port Elgin, and Elmbank; probably later than plan above, but no registered plan has been found; Gilmour and Lynch advertised their partnership in the *Daily Colonist* (Toronto) June 1856–Feb 1858.
OTNR (SR 16015)

STONEY CREEK

1985 *1856 (1865)*
Plan of Six Park Lots Containing About 4 acres each being part of the Lake View Farm Stoney Creek The Property of Henry Sanders Esq. H. Gregory Lith Hamilton T.A. Blyth P.L.S. Hamilton May 7 1856 Copy 8th August 1865.
Print (lith) Size not known Scale not given
Shows the lots near road between lots 24 and 25 west; 'Ontario House'; 'Canada House'; names of owners; Wentworth 62 (R.P. 309 (old 42)) (**B2282**) is a ms copy; lithographed original not seen.
Original not located

STRATFORD

1986 *1834 (1839)*
Plan of the Town of Stratford on Avon in the Huron Tract Copy from John McDonald Dy P. Surveyor's Plan dated May 1834 D. McD. Canada Company's Office Toronto Decr 1839
Col ms, pt missing 81 x 64 cm 1" to 4 chains
Endorsements: 'B'
Keys the part surveyed in Ellice, N Easthope, Downie, Gore of Downie, and S Easthope twps; shows the town as first laid out with town lots from Avon St to Caledonia St, Nelson St to Birmingham St, and Brunswick St to Water St; mill pond, mill reserve, grist and sawmill shown; reserve for burying ground and church; street names appear to have been added later; also a copy with the same title, with a note indicating that street names are those selected by James C.W. Daly, and dated 25 Dec 1841 (OSA); and a copy: 'Map of the Town of Stratford' endorsed 'C' and without street names (OTAR (Canada Co. Maps pkg 8 no 4)).
OSTPA OTAR (Canada Co. Maps pkg 8 no 3, 4)

1987 *[184?]*
Sketch of part of the plan of the Town of Stratford – I hereby certify that this is a correct Sketch of the Roads as originally laid out and that the present Road through Stratford has been the travelled Road since the year 1833 to the entire exclusion of the Original Road on which the Stratford Mills are built [Sgd] [David] Smith District Surveyor H.D.
Col ms on tracing paper 46 x 62 cm Scale not given
The 'Road' referred to is Huron St, which diverged from straight line of original survey around the mill pond, dam, and mills; 'The dotted Lines Show the Road as originally Surveyed and the Colouring as in its present position [Sgd] Chas Widder'; shows the centre of Stratford; prepared between 1841 and 1829 when the Huron District was in existence.
OSTPA

1988 *[1848]*
PLAN OF THE / TOWN OF / STRATFORD / By Donald McDonald. / Scobie & Balfour Lith. Toronto.
Print (lith) 76 x 65 cm 1" to 4 chains
Shows the town from Cambria St to Britannia Rd, and St Vincent St to Niles St, as originally laid out in 1834; most bldgs shown; foundry drawn in perspective; 'Statistics of the Town of Stratford 1st May 1848' includes number of bldgs in brick, stone, frame, and log, number of people in different trades, number of stores, churches, hotels, schools, etc, population given as 627; exhibited at the Toronto Society of Arts, Second Exhibition, 1848 (exhibition catalogue in OTUTF); (Holmden 2637).
OOAMA (NMC 22805) OSTPA

1989 *1851*
Plan of Property / IN THE TOWN OF / STRATFORD / BELONGING TO / WILLIAM MACKENZIE ESQ / LITHOGRAPHED BY J. ELLIS TORONTO. // [Sgd in facsimile] F.F. Passmore / Provl Land Surveyor / Toronto / March 15/53
Print (lith) 46 x 71 cm 1" to 3 chains
Shows subdivision from Cambria to St David's sts, and Nelson St to Victoria Rd, and Guelph to Downs sts, and east of Niles St; lot nos; a few names added in ms; related to R.P. 55 (**B2290**).
OTAR

1990 *1852*
Map of the Town of Stratford on Avon Drawn by T.N. Molesworth C.E. & P.L.S. Goderich 22nd July 1852
Col ms 80 x 64 cm 1" to 4 chains
Shows the town streets, town lots and park lots, and reserves as in original survey of 1834.
OTAR (Canada Co. Atlas O.S. 17/24)

1991 *1853*
PLAN / OF / BUILDING LOTS / FOR SALE / At / STRATFORD / Hugh Scobie Lith. Toronto C.W. J.O. Browne P.L.S. Toronto September 2d 1853
Print (col lith) 36 x 50 cm Approx 1" to 3 chains
Shows a subdivision in the southeastern part of the town from Brunswick St to Guelph St, and Nelson St to Toronto and Sarnia Railway Station; see also **B2292**.
Perth 44 (no R.P. number)

1992 *[1853?]*
PLAN OF PART / of the / TOWN / of / STRATFORD / [Sgd in facsimile] Joseph Kirk Provincial Land Surveyor // Lithographed by J. Ellis. Toronto
Print (lith) 56 x 77 cm 1" to 4 chains
Shows a subdivision from Guelph St to Ontario St and from Front St to eastern boundary of town; the reserve for the GTR depot is shown between Douro and Falstaff sts and GTR line is shown; Buffalo, Brantford & Goderich Railway and depot are also shown; shows an early plan for streets around the railway station, later superseded by

the lot layout on the 1855 (**1996**) and 1856 (**1997**) plans; some street names also different; note on terms of sale indicates Messrs Arnold and Robinson are the proprietors.
OTAR (Canada Co. Maps pkg 8 no 6)

1993 *[1853]*
PLAN OF / SUBDIVISION OF PARK LOTS / in the Town of / STRATFORD / BELONGING TO WILLIAM MACKENZIE ESQ. / [Sgd in facsimile] J.O. Browne P.L.S. / Toronto // Lithographed by J. Ellis, Toronto
Print (lith) 44 x 68 cm 1" to 80 ft
Subdivision of park lots 440–442 from Caledonia Rd to Britannia Rd, and Thomas St to St George's St; lot nos; names of some owners added in ms; related to R.P. 52 of 8 Apr 1853 (see **B2291**).
OTAR

1994 *1854*
Map of Part of the Town of Stratford Comprising that portion Surveyed by the Canada Co. From the Original Maps and Surveys by [Sgd] Joseph G. Kirk P.L.S. Canada Company's Office Toronto 19th September 1854. [Sgd] Fred Widder Commissioner
Col ms 82 x 86 cm 1" to 4 chains
Shows the area from Galt St north to Princes St, and Front St west to John St, with town lots on both sides of Erie, Huron, and Ontario sts and park lots beyond; a few lots added north of Water St; certified as a copy of compilation plan filed 12 Oct 1854 as R.P. 20 (**B2293**); copy in OTAR (Canada Co. Maps pkg 8 no 5).
OTAR (Canada Co. Papers TRHT 227, pkg 8 no 5)

1995 *1855*
PLAN / of part of Park Lot No 452 / in the / TOWN OF STRATFORD / COUNTY OF PERTH, / AS / Surveyed by John DeC. O'Grady P.L.S. / Stratford August 1855.
Print (lith), trimmed to margin 46 x 60 cm 1" to 1 chain
Inset: 'Sketch of Centre / of STRATFORD / August 1855.' 1" to 800 ft; a subdivision of original park lot on the southeast part of town; shows the area from Victoria St to St David's St and Downie Rd; the inset is a sketch of the town with railways and stations, main bldgs, and names of subdivision surveys; see also **B2299**.
Perth 44 (no R.P. number)

1996 *1855*
PLAN / OF PART OF THE / TOWN / OF / STRATFORD / JOHN TULLY / ARCHITECT & P.L.S. / Maclear & Co. Lith Toronto / 1855. // [Signature in facsimile] John Tully Architect & P.L.S. Toronto, July 3rd 1855.
Print (lith) 56 x 67 cm 1" to 4 chains
Shows a subdivision on the east side of town from Ontario St to Park St and from Front St east to Main St and beyond; shows the GTR and depot and the Buffalo, Brantford & Goderich Railway; ms note: 'Sale on the ground on Tuesday July 24/55 E. Emory Auctioneer'; R.P. 47 (**B2296**) is a transcript copy of this plan; lots are shown between Shakespeare St and Guelph St; area below depot reserved for warehouses; see later changes to plan (**1997**).
OLU

1997 *1856*
PLAN / OF PART OF THE TOWN OF STRATFORD. / 1856. // LITHOGRAPHED BY J. ELLIS 8 KING ST TORONTO C.W.
Print (lith) 61 x 91 cm 1" to 4 chains
Inset: [location maps showing position of Stratford and railway lines in the province]; shows the same subdivision as the 1855 plan above (**1996**) but some lots are hachured indicating they are either for sale or have been sold at the earlier auction noted above; block nos added; lots are no longer shown between Shakespeare St and Guelph St; Buffalo, Brantford & Goderich Railway called the Buffalo & Lake Huron in the inset; lots are shown but not numbered between Brunswick St and Water St from west of Front St to Nile St.
OLU

1998 *1857*
MAP / OF THE / TOWN OF STRATFORD / CAPITAL OF THE COUNTY OF PERTH / COMPILED FROM REGISTERED PLANS AND RECENT SURVEYS / BY / Charles James C.E. / 1857. // LITH by / J. SAGE & SONS / Buffalo N.Y.
Print (lith) 84 x 111 cm 1" to 6 chains
Shows the town from Catharine St to Princes St and from Main St to beyond John St; lot nos, names of subdivision surveys, owners of large lots; GTR and Buffalo & Lake Huron rys.
OSTPA OTAR OTAR (Canada Co. Maps pkg 8 no 1)

1999 *1863*
Plan of part of the Town of Stratford C.W. being subdivision of lot B in the second concession of the Gore of Downie Stratford April 1863 ... [Sgd] Joseph G. Kirk Prov Land Survy
Col ms 55 x 41 cm 1" to 4 chains
Shows area on south end of town south of Gore St to road allowance between 2nd and 3rd cons and east of Erie Rd; shows 20 park lots, oat mill of 'Kenedy Parker & Co.,' and property of J.C.W. Daly.
OTAR (Canada Co. Maps pkg 8 no 2)

STRATHROY

2000 *1862*
Plan / of Addition to the Village of / STRATHROY, / Being part of the North West quarter of / Lot No 12 / 10th Concession, Township of / CARADOC. / 1862. / Samuel Peters, P.L.S. London. Phillips & Evans, Lith. / London C.W.
Print (lith) 54 x 39 cm 1" to 2 chains
Shows a subdivision south of GWR depot grounds

between Princess St and County Rd; ms adds on one copy indicate that lots are to be sold by A.H. Kittridge, Strathroy, and note prices of lots sold; ms adds on another copy indicate terms of payment and mark some lots as sold; similar to R.P. 177 (**B2334**).
OLU

STREETSVILLE

2001 *[1856]*
A NEW PLAN OF / STREETSVILLE / FROM ACTUAL SURVEY & CAREFUL REFERENCE TO ORIGINAL PLANS & DOCUMENTS PUBLISHED FOR SUBSCRIBERS BY [Sgd in facsimile] Bristow Fitzgerald & Spencer // LITHOGRAPHED BY J. ELLIS, TORONTO
Print (lith) 65 x 140 cm Approx 1" to 4 chains
The map was enclosed with a petition of 8 July 1856 from the residents of Streetsville for incorporation: '... map of the said Village has lately been made at the request of your Petitioners ... a lithographed plan of the village according to these dimensions is in course of preparation' (OOA RG 5 C 1 vol 483 no 1101 1856); a compilation plan of the village showing streets and lots in part of lots 1–7 in west half of con 4 west of Hurontario St, and east half of con 5 west of Hurontario St; bldgs shown with names of owners; mills, relief; the map appears to be a proof print: scale is noted in pencil, notes direct engraver to add a house and a north arrow, the name Streetsville is added after the surveyors' names, and places for views indicated.
OOAMA (NMC 11443)

Later editions and states

(2) *1856*
A NEW PLAN OF / STREETSVILLE / FROM ACTUAL SURVEY & CAREFUL REFERENCE TO ORIGINAL PLANS & DOCUMENTS PUBLISHED FOR SUBSCRIBERS BY [Sgd in facsimile] Bristow, Fitzgerald & Spencer Streetsville July 16th 1856. // LITHOGRAPHED BY J. ELLIS, TORONTO.
Print (lith) hand col 65 x 139 cm 1" to 4 chains
Views: 'VIEW AT CORNERS OF QUEEN & MAIN STREETS A. Bristow Delt.' and 'ONTARIO MILLS & PART OF WEST END OF STREETSVILLE A. Bristow Delt.'; the finished version of the map; includes views, scale, and the rest of the imprint; the plan is related to R.P. STR-4 (**B2344**).
USDLC

(SUDBURY town plot)

2002 *1854*
Town Plot of Sudbury Township of Nottawasaga [Sgd] John Ryan C.E. P.L.S. Yonge Street Holland Landing December 1854.
Col ms 76 x 55 cm 1" to 4 chains Endorsements: 'A 193'
Inset: 'Longl. Sectn Batteau Creek' 1" to 264 ft, 1" to 20 ft vertical; (SI 11 May 1853 to survey outlines and project the subdivision of half of area into mill site, town lots, and park lots); shows a town plot on lots 38, 39 of con VI on Batteau Creek; Regent St to James St, and King St to West St; reserves for church, market, hospital, mill site, burying ground; the profile of river includes mill sites 3 and 4 but a note indicates only one good mill site (No 1) 'Examined April 1855 T.D.'; overflow on mill site shown and note about adjustment to be made to lots; roads to Hurontario mills and clearing also shown; also a later copy in OTAR(P): 'Sudbury Crown Lands Department Quebec 19th April 1855 [Sgd] Joseph Cauchon Commr Crown Lands T. Devine' endorsed 'No 106' and with the addition of names of patentees; this copy has reserve for 'Presbyterian Congregation of Collingwood,' but section not included; and another later copy in OTAR(P): 'Sudbury Crown Lands Office Toronto Feby 1856 [Sgd] Joseph Cauchon Commissr of Crown Lands. J.W.B.' with the addition of some names.
OTAR(P) OTNR (SR 333)

THAMESVILLE

2003 *1856*
PLAN / OF / TECUMSEH / in the County of / Kent / 1856 / David Sherman Esqre Proprietor / John O'Mara P.L.S. / Saml Peters Lith / London C.W.
Print (lith) 79 x 54 cm 1" to 250 ft
Shows the town from Jane St to Thames R, and Priscilla St to Lamila St, market grounds south of railway, church land, and graveyard; shows position of battle of Moraviantown and Tecumseh's line of retreat from Fort Malden; description of the town and its advantages for settlement; R.P. 144 (**B2371**) is a transcript of the printed map, original not seen.
Kent 24 (R.P. 144)

THORNBURY

2004 *[1852]*
Plan of the town plot of Thornbury Township of Collingwood County of Grey [Sgd] William Gibbard Prol Land Survr Exd A.R.
Col ms 90 x 62 cm 1" to 4 chains Endorsements: 'A 184'
(SI 1 July 1851 and 20 Feb 1852 to make a preliminary survey of reserve for town plot in the twp of Collingwood; OTNR FN 660 1852); shows town on lots 32–34, con 9 and 10, from Russell St to Peal St, and Bay St to Duncan St, with town lots north of Louisa St; bearings; mill site on the Beaver R; also

a copy: 'Plan of the Town-Plot of Thornbury Crown Lands Department Quebec 2nd Dec 1853 [Sgd] A.N. Morin Commissioner of Crown Lands' endorsed 'No 86' (OTAR(P)).
OTAR(P) OTNR (SR 341)

2005 *[186?]*
Part of the Village of Thornbury. shewing proposed site of pier.
Col ms 66 x 75 cm 1" to 100 ft Endorsements: stamp [BW] '664'
Shows the Beaver R, old channel, and line of former beach; present bluff and beach position; proposed wharf; King, Huron, Elma, and Bridge sts shown; shows a different configuration for mouth of river from that of original survey.
OOAMA (NMC 19811)

THORNHILL

2006 *1859*
MAP /OF / THORNHILL / including the First Concessions of / the Townships of / MARKHAM AND VAUGHAN / IN THE / COUNTY OF YORK. // John [Rat?]cliffe / Land Surveyor / Thornhill / 1859
Print (lith) hand col, pt missing Approx 88 x 65 cm 1" to 10 chains
The town is shown on both sides of Yonge St from Elgin St to above Centre St, and Church St to west of Yonge St; bldgs shown and names of owners; mills, churches, and treed areas; lots 26–35 east and west of Yonge St; later annotation for Supreme Court of Ontario, *Watson v. Jackson*, Exhibit 22, 19 Nov 1873.
OTAR

THOROLD

2007 *[1855]*
PLAN / OF PART OF THE / VILLAGE OF THOROLD / AND PART OF THE / TOWNSHIP LOTS NUMBER 17 & 18. / Maclear & Co. Liths Toronto.
Print (col lith) 49 x 63 cm 1" to 100 ft
Certified by surveyor Geo. Z. Rykert, 10 Dec 1855; shows the village from Elgin St to Mill St, and Pine St to Sydenham St; Keefer's mill, reserve for public square; Roman Catholic church; names of owners of large lots; see also **B2383**.
Niagara S 59 (R.P. 892)

2008 *1856*
Plan of David Hoover's Lots part of Lot No 15 of the Township of Thorold, Township of Townsend County of Norfolk 29 Sept 1856
Ms 25 x 41 cm Scale not given
Note above title: 'Elizabeth Ann Hoover'; a rough plan showing Regent St to Peter St, and Wellington St to Chapel St, with names of owners in all lots; related to R.P. 893 (**B2385**).
OOAMA (NMC 4429)

(THORPVILLE town plot)

2009 *1856*
PLAN OF THE / VILLAGE OF THORPVILLE, / Composed of part of Lot 1, in the ninth Concession, / NICHOL, / And part of Lot 15, in the First Concession of / PILKINGTON, COUNTY OF WELLINGTON, C.W. / Surveyed for John Thorp, Esq., by Schofield and Hobson P.L.S. / 1856 // PRINTED AT THE "ADVERTISER" OFFICE, GUELPH
Print (lith) 50 x 72 cm 1" to 66 ft
Shows lots on both sides of the Woolwich Rd at 8/9 con rd; small drawings are included of two houses and a school; the land was advertised for sale in the *Guelph Advertiser TriWeekly* 18 June 1856; see also **B2387**.
Wellington 61 (R.P. 93)

TORONTO

2010 *1788*
Plan of the Harbour of Toronto with a proposed Town and settlement 1788
Col ms 81 x 59 cm 2" to 1 mile Endorsements: 'D'
Originally enclosed in Lord Dorchester's no 87 to the Duke of Portland, 16 Apr 1796 (GBLpro CO 42/105 f 163); has a similar layout to (**2011**) except that it shows a larger area with twp lots, and an explanation indicates that lots around common are 'town parks,' lots beyond are farm lots, laid out in 30 lots in 5 cons; lots in four corners of twp reserved for public purposes; point 'A' is location for fortifications per Capt Mann's report; peninsula shown in outline only; a later note says, 'Copied from a Plan of Mr Collins it does not agree with the survey made by L. Kotté in 1783. (plan I.24 Engrs D.R.) Kotté's Survey agrees with one taken in 1793 by J. Bouchette. Chateau.'; this note probably refers to the shore and harbour surveys by Kotte and Bouchette (see **4** and **2013**); plan for town is as in Mann's (**2011**) and not as described in Firth, ... *1793–1815*, 21; GBLpro (MPG 38) is another copy with slightly different title, '... with the Town and Settlement. 1788,' and endorsed '27L' and 'D'; it is from the same source and includes the same information and notes; photoreproduction in OOAMA (NMC 22814; 22815); (*PRO Cat* 1601).
GBLpro (MPG 33; 38)

2011 *1788*
Plan of Torento [*sic*] Harbour with the proposed Town and part of its Township [Sgd] Quebec 6th Decr 1788 Gother Mann Captn & Commandg Rl Engrs

Col ms 37 x 54 cm 2" to 1 mile Endorsements: 'Case 42 no 50'; stamp 'HMSPO'
Accompanying Mann's report on defences (no 38F) of 6 Dec 1788 and enclosed in Dorchester's no 58 of 24 Oct 1790 (GBLpro CO 42/70 pp 41ff); shows an early plan for the laying out of Toronto centred on the shore between the Humber R and the Don R, east of the 'Ruins of a trading fort'; shows a square town with town lots and reserves, surrounded by a common and six ranges of park lots; ground by the shore is reserved; shows the peninsula, the 'Road' or Toronto Portage to Lake LaClie [Simcoe]; soundings; point 'A' near trading post noted in report as best situation for fortifications; magnetic variation; photoreproduction in OOAMA (NMC 6188); there is also a copy in OOAMA (NMC 4434) with the title as in (2) but similar to this map, endorsed 'B↑O' and 'Z28/70'; (Holmden 2651; *OHIM* 7.48; *PRO Cat* 1600).
GBLpro (Co 700 Canada no 38 (B)) OOAMA (NMC 4434)

Related maps

(2) *1788*
Plan of Torento [*sic*] Harbour with the proposed town and part of the Settlement. [Sgd] Quebec 6th Decr 1788 Gother Mann Captn Commandg Rl Engrs
Col ms 34 x 51 cm 2" to 1 mile Watermark: 'J WHATMAN' Endorsements: 'Plan B'; stamp 'HMSPO'
From the same source as plan above (GBLpro CO 42/70 f 147); shows the same information as plan above with some slight changes including different positions for title, north arrow, and scale, and more detailed vegetation on island and around [Humber] R; photoreproduction in OOAMA (NMC 4433); (*PRO Cat* 1599).
GBLpro (MPG 431)

2012 *1788*
Plan of Toronto by Alexr. Aitkin 1788.
Col ms 35 x 81 cm 2" to 1 mile
Shows two outer boundaries for a town and possibly twp, somewhat further to the east than the other 1788 maps (see Firth, ... *1793–1815*, xxxii); shows the Nichingguakokonk R [Don] as navigable a short way for a boat, the 'Toronto River' [Humber], and carrying place to 'Lake LaClie'; shows the west boundary of land purchased from the Indians at Tobecoak R; 'Place fit for a fort' is shown east of old fort; Aitken was ordered to survey at Toronto by Collins on 7 July 1788 and referred to the plans in letter of 15 Sept 1788 (Robinson, 166–8, 252), and his survey is listed on the 1790 plan (**10**); Aitken was surveying for the Toronto purchase and noted that he laid out the town plot further to east than plan he received later (probably a pro forma town similar to one of the other 1788 plans above (**2010–11**)); therefore, not based on Mann as stated in Firth, ... *1793–1815*, 21; shoreline is similar to plan by LaForce and Kotte (1789) (see **9**).
OTAR (Simcoe Maps 446486)

Related maps

(2) *1788*
Plan of Toronto Surveyed by A. Aitken in 1788
Col ms 35 x 91 cm 1" to 40 chains
A slightly larger and more finished map than plan above but with essentially the same information; more details on terrain and shoreline; new site for a fort is not shown; this or plan above may be no 19 in 'List of Maps ... 1793' (OTAR RG1 A-I-1/1, 151–7).
OTAR (Simcoe Maps 445787)

2013 *1792*
Plan of Toronto Harbour With the Rocks, Shoals & Soundings Thereof Surveyed & Drawn by [Sgd] Joseph Bouchette 15th Novr 1792
Col ms 50 x 53 cm 1" to 20 chains Endorsements: 'Presented to the City by Mr Willoughby P. Cole, a descendant of Governor John Graves Simcoe of Upper Canada ... May 28th 1934'
Bouchette's first survey of the peninsula and harbour; shows the island and shoreline; ship drawn in harbour; Blacksmith's house and Toronto fort marked to the west; 'Remarks on the problem of navigation in the Harbour'; decorative wind-rose and north arrow; (Robinson, 185).
OTCTAR (520)

Related maps

(2) *[1793]*
Plan of Toronto Harbour with the Rocks, Shoals & Soundings &c. Surveyed & Drawn by [Sgd] J. Bouchette.
Col ms 35 x 44 cm 1" to 20 chains
The survey of the peninsula and shoreline is similar in outline to plan above, with the addition of four points as noted in Simcoe's letter to Clarke of 31 May 1793 (quoted in Firth, ... *1793–1815*, 3–4); shows a proposed fortification on the western tip of the peninsula, the town plot for York 3/4 mile square, smaller and further east than 1788 plans, a site for barracks just west of the town, and a place for dockyards south of the mouth of the Don R and on the neck of the peninsula; blacksmith's house and 'old Toronto Fort' marked to the west; (Holmden 2653; *OHIM* 7.49).
OOAMA (NMC 4436)

(3) *[1794 (1813?)]*
A Plan of York Harbour in Upper Canada Survey'd by [Sgd] Jos. Bouchette.
Col ms 48 x 69 cm Scale not given Watermark: 'J WHATMAN 1813'
Shows a similar survey of the peninsula and shoreline; notes on the harbour and navigation include 'Remarks during the Winters of 1793 and 1794'; references to points where the schooner 'Anandaga' [*Onondaga*] cast away and afterwards raised in the autumn of 1793 by Bouchette; town of York with boundary shown; 'Castle Francis named by Genl Simcoe'; garrison of York; a later

copy of a survey of 1794 by Bouchette but sgd by him; there is also a copy on tracing paper with the same GBTAUh no; another copy in GBTAUh (191 Aa2) cannot be located.
GBTAUh (P31 Aa1 (2 copies) and 191 Aa2)

(4) *(1815)*
PLAN / of / YORK HARBOUR / by / Josh. Bouchette. // Published by W. Faden Charing Cross August 12th 1815. // J. Walker Sculpt.
Print (engrav) 14 x 22 cm Approx 1" to 42 chains
In Joseph Bouchette, *Topographical Description of the Province of Lower Canada* (London: W. Faden 1815), opp 605 (*Bib Can* 1031), and in the French ed (Londres: W. Faden 1815), opp 627 (*Bib Can* 1030); and in his *The British Dominions in North America* (London: Henry Colburn and Richard Bentley 1831), I: opp 88 (OOA), and in another ed (London: Longman, Rees, Orme, Brown, Green & Longman 1832), I: opp 88 (*Bib Can* 1627, 4968); the outline of the shoreline and peninsula are similar to the Toronto inset on Bouchette's plan of L Ontario (see **28**); shows the location of the schooner 'Anandaga' [*Onondaga*] as raised in late 1793; the stylized block outline for the town shows development to about 1797 and the garrison blockhouse on the east side of the creek (built 1797) is shown.
OOA OOAMA (NMC 48307) OTMCL OTRMC USDLC

2014 *[1793?]*
Plan of a Town proposed for the seat of Government with its Reference
Col ms 30 x 18 cm Scale not given Endorsements: 'Home District York Partial' '16' 'W. Chewitt. Plan proposed for the seat of Government with its Reference'
Shows a formal plan for a square town with reserves marked for crown: government, upper and lower houses, barracks, public offices, church, parsonage and schoolhouse, gaol and court-house, public squares, market-places, church yards, hospitals, workhouses; similar to early plans for other towns, particularly the plan for New Johnstown; the endorsements indicate that it was prepared for York, possibly for Lord Dorchester, about 1793 but never put into effect; (Firth, ... *1793–1815*, 23; *OHIM* 7.3).
OTAR

2015 *[1793]*
Plan of York Harbour Surveyed by order of Lt Govr Simcoe [Sgd] by A. Aitken D [Syr?] 179[3]
Col ms 51 x 74 cm 1" to 20 chains Endorsements: 'B.T. Map Case 44 no. 49 Canada 60'; stamp 'HMSPO'
Originally enclosed in Simcoe's no 18 to Dundas of 20 Sept 1793 (GBLpro CO 42/317 p 283); shows the peninsula and shoreline from the Don R east with the mouths of 'many rivers and creeks'; the shoreline and island differ from Bouchette's early plans (see **2013**); the Don R shown a considerable way inland; shows the east-west survey baseline for Toronto [Queen St]; farm lots 1–41 marked off in the first con; town plot of 10 blocks shown by small creek west of the Don R; 'References' marks 'Proposed Block House to Command the entrance to Harbour' (on the peninsula), a proposed battery, proposed barracks for the Queen's Rangers, and a point from which view is taken; reserved land marked west of town.
GBLpro (CO 700 Canada no 60)

Related maps

(2) *1793*
Copy of a Plan of York Harbour with the soundings, Shoals &c. surveyed by Order of Lt Governor Simcoe by A. Aitken D. Surveyor 1793 the Soundings taken by Mr Bouchette
Col ms 32 x 68 cm 1" to 20 chains Watermark: 'W J'
Similar to (1) but a sketchier plan; keys proposed blockhouse, battery and barracks; (Brun 143).
USMiU-C (Clinton Papers map 28)

(3) *1800*
Plan of the Harbour of York. Engrs Drawing Room Quebec Wm Hall Lt Rl Arty [Sgd] Gother Mann, Coll Commandg. Rl Engrs Quebec 1800.
Col ms 48 x 68 cm 1" to 20 chains Watermark: 'J WHATMAN' Endorsements: '43.10.9.54'
Similar to (1); shows the town plot, location for barracks, mouths of creeks, and same configuration for island; photoreproduction in OOAMA (NMC 4438).
GBL (Maps 23.b.3(17))

2016 *[1793–4?]*
Plan of Castle Frank Farm
Col ms in 2 sheets 116 x 49 cm 1" to 4 chains
A rough sketch showing the area from the mouth of the Don R and the marsh north to Castle Frank at the top of the 1st con; locations for marked Castle Frank house, J. and G. Playter's houses, and Mr Scadding's [burnt down late Jan 1794]; road; Mrs Simcoe mentions going to locate place for house on 29 Oct 1793 and bldg commenced in 1794 (*Mrs. Simcoe's Diary* (1965), 110); there is also a plan at OTAR (SR 402) entitled 'Castle Frank' and endorsed 'Y 16' and '754'; it shows the north part only, but the Playter houses are not shown and Castle Frank is not named.
OTAR (Simcoe Maps 446905)

2017 *1796*
Sketch of the Ground for Public Buildings [York]
Col ms 32 x 40 cm Scale not given Endorsements: 'His Honor the Administrator 3 Octr 96 York public Buildings'
An unfinished sketch of area west of original town showing the boundaries of area reserved for public bldgs; some bldgs, a road, two bridges, and shoreline shown; further note: '3d October 1796 This Reserve for public Buildings at York ordered.'
OTMCL (D.W. Smith Papers B-9 pp 133–4)

2018 *1797*
Plan submitted by Order of His Honor The President for the enlargement of York The Blocks washed red are already surveyed the unsurveyed part is projected in acre lots with a few exceptions [Sgd] D W Smith ASG [Endorsed title]: 'His Honor the President Mr Russell, 9 June 1797 Plan of York as amended by Him'
Col ms 30 x 57 cm Scale not given
Shows the original town of 10 blocks from Ontario St with extension west to York St and north to Lot St [Queen]; shows the reserves for court-house, market, gaol, church, hospital, and school, and smaller reserves for sheriffs, clerk, gaolers, parson, doctors, and schoolmaster; street names pencilled in; includes changes to allow Market, Newgate, and Hospital sts to join new town with old; (*OHIM* 7.50).
OTMCL (D.W. Smith Papers B-9 pp 173–4)

Related maps

(**2**) *1797*
Plan for the enlargement of York as amended by Order of His Honor the President projected in Lots containing an acre more or less. [Sgd] D.W. Smith ASG 10 June 1797. In Council at York June 10th 1797 [Sgd] Peter Russell. [Endorsed title]: 'His Honor the Prest 10th June 1797 approval of the Town plot of York – addition'
Col ms 29 x 50 cm Scale not given
The final version of plan above showing through streets and open space left below market; names have been added later in lots with dates to 1798 and many initialled 'P.R.'; reserves for personnel crossed out and some names inserted; (*OHIM* 7.51).
OTMCL (D.W. Smith Papers B-9 pp 217–20)

(**3**) *[1798?]*
[Endorsed title]: 'His Honor the Presdt approval of the Town Plot of York. 2d addition' [Sgd] Approved Peter Russell Copy W.C.
Col ms 30 x 54 cm [Approx 1" to 100 yds]
Shows the second addition from York St west to Peter St and the garrison, and north to Lot St [Queen]; two large lots 'Submitted for Russell Square' and 'Submitted for Simcoe Place'; 10 acres submitted for a college in the northwest corner of the garrison reserve; names in some lots, one marked '24 July 1798'; some reserves on the front and lot reserved for burying ground below college reserve; Russell is noted as building on Simcoe Place in a letter of June 1798 (Firth, ... *1793–1815*, 225); (*OHIM* 7.52).
OTMCL (D.W. Smith Papers B-9 pp 223–4)

2019 *1798*
[Map of part of York Township showing a lot of about 183 acres on the east side of the Humber River] [Sgd] S.G.O. 31 Jany 1798 D.W. Smith A.S.G
Col ms 19 x 31 cm Scale not given Endorsements: 'Upper Canada Executive Council State Papers H 1 1798.'
Probably from OOA RG 1 E3 but exact location not found; shows lot 41, 1st con from the bay; marshy areas; a mill marked on the west bank to the north; 'Indian wedding' marked on the east bank and 'St. Johns' house marked on L Ontario [J.B. Rousseau]; (Holmden 2657).
OOAMA (NMC 47968)

2020 *1798*
Part of the Town of York Home District
Col ms 19 x 33 cm Scale not given Watermark: '... 1796'
Endorsements: 'W. Chewitt's Examination of Lot Street Dev. 98' '10'
Shows a deviation along Hospital St from Yonge St east to Caroline St to avoid marshy ground and a creek; names of adjoining lot owners.
OOAMA (NMC 47967)

2021 *1798*
A Return of the Locations in the Town of York S.G.O. 17th Nov 1798 D. Smith A.S.G. Copy W.C.
Col ms 53 x 76 cm Scale not given
Shows the town from Ontario St west to Peter St and from the waterfront to the fronts of lots north of Lot St [Queen]; lot nos and names of owners in many lots including the park lots; rivers not named; Russell Square and Simcoe Place shown.
OTNR (SR 408)

2022 *[1798?]*
York
Ms 38 x 102 cm Scale not given Endorsements: 'A67'
Shows the town from Ontario St to Peter St and from the waterfront to above Lot St [Queen]; reserves for school, hospital, gaol, church, market, and court-house are shown; shows names of owners of town lots and park lots to the north; Simcoe Place and Russell Square shown; Duchess St not shown continuing through to New St; a few water lots shown; old parliament bldgs not shown; similar to general plan of 1798 (see **2021**).
OTAR(P)

2023 *1799 (1905)*
Sketch of the Town of York made for Wm Willcocks Esq by permission of his Honor the President the 23rd July 1799 For the Acting Surveyor Genl [Sgd] Chewett & Ridout
Ms Size not known Scale not given
A general plan of the town with streets, lots, and names of owners; also shows hospital, school, church, gaol, market, and court-house; notes on the history of ownership of some park lots north of Queen St; OTMCL has a transcript made in 1905 and endorsed '20 G.T.R & C.P.R. Toronto 23 Oct 1905'; a blueprint copy is in OTAR.
Original not located

2024 *[1799]*
Yonge Street Branches. York, the Pinnacle Copy from Stegmann's S.G.O. 14th August 1779 [i.e., 1799] W.C.
Col ms 76 x 49 cm 1" to 4 chains Endorsements: 'Y 15' '817'
(SI 15 Feb 1799 to open a road upon line 23/24, con 2, Humber to Yonge St, to foot of hill at Pinnacle, to Castle Frank Creek, and around Poplar Plains); shows the Pinnacle in lot 23 owned by Peter Russell and lots 21 and 22 owned by D.W. Smith; three new roads to Yonge St shown as built or projected.
OTAR (SR 401)

Related maps

(2) *[1799?]*
Branches of the Yonge Street Communication Copy W.C.
2 col ms on 1 sheet 76 x 27 cm Endorsements: 'Y 19' '785'
The top map shows the Humber Rd to the 3rd con line west of Yonge St, lots 21, 22, 23, and Poplar Plain Hill; the bottom one shows Castle Frank Creek, land to be cleared around the Pinnacle, road to 'Poplar Plain Hill,' and two bridges.
OTAR (SR 389)

2025 *[ca 1800]*
Plan shewing the plots that are too much in depth at York [Sgd] D.W. Smith A.S.G.
Ms 19 x 50 cm Scale not given Endorsements: 'Plan of York No 4' '89'
Shows 'Part of the land surveyed by W. Chewitt for Public Purposes' on both sides of King St west of New St, and the houses of Messrs John, Berry, and Kendrick on the east side of New St where blocks of old town are too deep; 'Govt House Grounds' shown on right; (Holmden 2648).
OOAMA (NMC 4437)

2026 *[1801]*
Sketch of a part of the Town of York ... This seconde Examination done by order of the Honorable John Elmsley Esquire and performed by [blank]
Col ms 39 x 51 cm Scale not given Endorsements: 'A75' '732'
Shows the area between Lot St and Front St, and Peter St and Toronto St, and indicates lots that are cleared, those with no work done, with brush cut and burnt, etc; examination of lots probably prepared in early 1801 after the order to clear lots of 4 Sept 1800 (cited on (2)); 77 lots appear to have been cleared; method for enforcing clearing described in letter from Elmsley to Hunter of 6 March 1801 (Firth, ... *1793–1815*, 54).
OTNR (SR 407)

Related maps

(2) *1801*
Sketch of the part of the Town of York West of Toronto Street ... this survey made by order of the Surveyor General's Office bearing date April the 23rd 1801 John Stegmann
Col ms 40 x 67 cm Scale not given Endorsements: 'A 74' '740'
Shows the further progress of clearing the town lots per the order of 4 Sept 1800; 112 lots are now noted as cleared.
OTNR (SR 387)

2027 *[1802]*
Plan of Maryville, at the East end of the City of York in Upper Canada, containing about 16 1/4 Acres The property of the Honble D W Smith Esqre Surveyor General [Sgd] W Chewett Senr Surveyr & Dftsmn
Col ms 41 x 32 cm [1" to 2 chains]
In a volume of plans drawn for Smith by W. Chewett 28 Apr 1802; shows the layout of his estate between King St and road north of Duchess St east of Ontario St; roads, creeks, etc; there is also a plan in the same source of 'Maryville Lodge ...,' which shows the floor plan of the house, stables, servants' quarters, vegetable gardens, orchards.
OTMCL (D.W. Smith Papers B-15 pp 86–7)

2028 *[1802]*
Plan of 916 1/4 Acres in the Township of York in Upper Canada. The property of the Honble D.W. Smith Esqre Surveyr Genl Including Park Five, which contains about 100 Acres, & 16 Acres at the East end of the City of York, on which is the Lodge lately called Maryville [Sgd] W. Chewett Senr Surveyr & Dftsmn
Col ms 30 x 41 cm Scale not given
Shows the whole town from the garrison to Ashbridges Bay east of the Don R and north to the 3rd con from the bay; shows peninsula and marsh at mouth of Don R; major bldgs or sites marked including Government House, Simcoe Place, and Russell Square; also shows his properties in con II, and con III, lots 6, 20; copies of deeds dated 1796–9; note indicates plans prepared especially for Smith and sgd 'W Chewett Sen Surveyr & Dftsmn 28th April 1802.'
OTMCL (D.W. Smith Papers B-15 f 72)

2029 *1802*
[Reserves for the town and township of York]
Col ms Approx 34 x 40 cm Scale not given
In D.W. Smith's 'Report upon Glebes & Commons ... 13th Jany 1802' (OTAR RG 1 A-II-1 vol 2 p 987); shows the town and twp as far west as lot 18, con I, east of the military reserve and north to the 3rd con; shows three glebe reserves in con 2 and 3 and commons reserve in con 3; government park reserve shown east of town; Castle Frank.
OTAR (RG 1 A-II-1 vol 2 p 987)

2030 *[1802]*
A Sketch shewing the Land Occupied by John Small Esqre upon the Reserve, appropriated for the Govt house at York, by his Excellency Lt Govr Simcoe [Sgd] D W Smith Sur Genl

Col ms 25 x 25 cm Scale not given
Accompanies a letter from Smith to Lt Gov Hunter of 25 May 1802 explaining the origins of Small's claim (OTMCL D.W. Smith Papers B-9 p 311); shows Small's improvement on King St east of Princess and Ontario sts; the two wings of the first Government House are sketched to the southeast; reproduced in Arthur, 3rd ed (1986), 32; a copy without the signature and endorsed 'A 83' and '730' is in OTNR (SR 399); another later copy with Smith's signature and 'Copy Surveyr Gen. Office York 16 Decr 1805 [Sgd] C.B. Wyatt Surv Genl' is in OOAMA (NMC 48021); it was enclosed with Small's land petition to reclaim part of his property (OOA RG 1 L3 S8 no 60); (Holmden 2663).
OOAMA (NMC 48021) OTMCL (D.W. Smith Papers B-9 p 311) OTNR (SR 399)

2031 *1810*
The Red line shewes the situation of a Road from York to Mr Ashbridges [Sgd] Saml S. Wilmot Dy Surveyor 1810.
Col ms 37 x 123 cm 1" to 10 chains Endorsements: 'Y 18' '772'
Shows the eastern extension of King St angling north to cross the Don R at the bridge on Kingston Rd; relief.
OTAR (SR 5318)

2032 *1810*
Sketch of Lots No 15 & 16 in the Broken Front of the Township of York. Copied from John Stegmann's Plan. W.C. [and] Sketch shewing two projects for laying out the Reserve for the Government Buildings at the East end of the Town of York with the relative situation ... W.C. 7th Decr 1810.
Col ms 73 x 35 cm [Approx 1" to 9.5 chains] Endorsements: 'A 86' '741'
A small sketch showing the first proposal for laying out lots east to the Don R; notes indicate that the first project will give 62 lots and the second, 50 lots, with lots reserved for the government bldgs; the base plan was probably copied from those Stegmann did while surveying for road in 1799–1800 (see **329**); shows Scadding's land and land owned by John Small and F.G. Simcoe.
OTNR (SR 391)

2033 *1811*
A Plan Shewing the Survey of the land Reserved for Government Buildings, East end of the Town of York, Surveyed by order of His Excellency Francis Gore Esquire Lieutenant Governor &c &c &c bearing date the 18th day of Decr 1810. Feby 25 1811 [Sgd] Saml S. Wilmot Dy Surveyor
Col ms 83 x 56 cm 1" to 4 chains Endorsements: 'A 99' '743'
Shows the area east of Ontario St to bridge where King St crosses Don R and north to the 5th con; government house shown enclosed within boundary for reserve; blockhouse shown; shows the proposed 4-acre lots with figures denoting estimated yearly rent, sgd 'T Ridout S.G.'; the survey was not implemented and the land was granted to the new hospital in 1819 and laid out in 1830 (see **2059**); there is also a plan in OOAMA (NMC 4442) for part of area showing land to be attached to the legislative bldgs and sgd '24 Apl 1819 T. Ridout,' but a new site for the parliament bldgs was chosen further west.
OOAMA (NMC 4442) OTNR (SR 390)

2034 *[1811]*
Sketch of the relative situation of the Land adjoining the Town of York, in the possession of George Crookshank Esqre, under permission from His Excelly Lieut Genl Hunter Governor and Commander in Chief, of Upper Canada
Col ms 33 x 42 cm Scale not given
Accompanied a petition from Crookshank for the land of 31 Sept 1811 (OOA RG 1 L3 C no 10 no 46 1811); shows the area between Front St and Lot St west of John St; the lot in question falls within the 1000 yd range of the guns at Fort York; (Holmden 2664).
OOAMA (NMC 4439)

2035 *1813*
Sketch of the ground in advance of and including York Upper Canada by Geo: Williams R.M.S.D. Novr 1813.
Ms 28 x 97 cm Scale not given Endorsements: 'No 6'; stamps 'IGF' 'B↑O'
Accompanying Lt Col Hughes's letter to Lt Gen Mann dated 16 Aug 1814 (GBLpro WO 55/860 pp 104–5); an attractive military plan of York showing the open streets, paths, all bldgs with some identified, and indications of landscaping and cleared land; shows the remains of ship *Sir Isaac Brock* burnt in 1813 and the destruction of middle part of government bldgs in burning of York 27 Apr 1813; reproduced in Firth, ... *1793–1815*, opp lxxxi; (Holmden 2668).
OOAMA (NMC 22819)

2036 *1814 June 24*
A Plan of the Town and Harbour of York. John S. Kitson. Lieut R. Engrs 24 June 1814
Col ms 70 x 87 cm 1" to 10 chains Watermark: 'BUDGEN 1803' Endorsements: 'no 98' '544' 'U'; stamp 'CREOC'
Shows the town and harbour with all streets and bldgs; some military bldgs and sites indexed; relief.
OOAMA (NMC 22821)

2037 *1814 July 27*
Plan of the Town and Harbour of York George Williams Royl Military Surveyor &c. 27 July. 1814
Col ms 63 x 95 cm 1" to 10 chains Endorsements: 'C 57 no 7'; stamps 'IGF' 'B↑O'
Accompanying Lt Col Hughes's letter to Lt Gen

Mann dated 16 Aug 1814 (GBLpro WO 55/860 pp 104–5); shows the town and the peninsula with relief, all streets, paths, and bldgs; 'References' key 30 military bldgs; shows the rebuilding of Fort York and other blockhouses (Firth, ... *1793–1815*, xciv); similar to **2036** but a more finished map; (Holmden 2665).
OOAMA (NMC 21771)

2038 *[1815]*
Government Buildings at York. [Sgd] P. Van Cortland Depy B.M. Genl
Ms 37 x 47 cm 1" to 60 ft Watermark: 'J. RUMP 1813'
Originally enclosed in a letter from van Cortland to Maj Foster, military secretary, giving description of bldgs of 7 Aug 1815 (OOA RG 8 I/555 p 71); lists and locates the bldgs in the fort; (Holmden 2646).
OOAMA (NMC 4440)

2039 *1816*
Plan of the Harbour, Fort and Town of York, the Capital of Upper Canada March 16th 1816. [Sgd] Quebec 24th June 1816 G. Nicolls Lt. Col. Rl Engineers. Royl Engrs Drawing Room Quebec J.B. Duberger Junr
Col ms 74 x 93 cm 1" to 10 chains Endorsements: 'No 6'; stamps 'IGF' 'B↑O'
Originally enclosed with letter from Nicolls to Mann of 24 June 1816 (GBLpro WO 55/860 pp 182–7); shows the town and harbour with various points marked from the War of 1812; point of landing of Americans shown; 'The Battery O had all Guns and were made use of on the 27th April except the one at the marsh. Government bldgs and blockhouse were Burnt by the Americans as were many others'; ruins 'proposed to be destroyed' of old French fort; shows streets and bldgs; soundings; (Holmden 2670).
OOAMA (NMC 17441)

Related maps

(**2**) *1816*
Plan of the Fort at York, Upper Canada, shewing its state in March 1816. [Sgd] Royl Engineers Drawg Room, Quebec 16th Feby 1816, J.B. Duberger Junr. Quebec, 24th June 1816, G. Nicolls, Lt. Col. Rl Engineers
Col ms 34 x 38 cm 1" to 60 ft Endorsements: 'No 7'; stamps 'IGF' 'B↑O'
Shows the fort as rebuilt after the war; bldgs in and outside the fort keyed; also shows crater by the lakeshore caused by explosion of powder magazine in 1813; (Holmden 2671).
OOAMA (NMC 23139)

2040 *[1817]*
Plan of York Surveyed and Drawn by Lieut. Phillpotts Royal Engineers
Col ms on tracing paper 55 x 65 cm 6" to 1 mile Endorsements: 'I 15' 'No 6'; stamps 'IGF' 'B↑O'
Accompanying copy of letter from Lt Col Addison to Maj Henderson dated 20 June 1817 and included in Lt Col Durnford's letter to Lt Col Mann dated Quebec, 20 June 1819; a rough sketch of the town and peninsula showing relief, cleared land, and treed areas; streets and all bldgs shown in town; sight-lines from island to mainland marked in red; possibly traced from another original of 1817; (Holmden 2674).
OOAMA (NMC 17440)

Related maps

(**2**) *1818 (1823)*
Plan of York Surveyed and Drawn by Lieut. Phillpotts Royal Engineers. 24th May 1818. Commandg Royal Engrs Office Quebec Septr 24th 1823 [Sgd] George Phillpotts Lieut. Royl Engineers
Col ms 56 x 63 cm 6" to 1 mile Endorsements: 'BB 37'; stamps 'IGF' 'B↑O'
An attractive final draft of plan above and showing the same information; cleared and wooded land, streets, paths, and bldgs; bldgs in military reserve are numbered but no key given; an outline copy of this plan accompanied report of 1823 (see **64**); the plan has been copied several times and is incorrectly dated 1838 in Holmden and 1828 in other sources; transcript published in Canada, House of Commons, *Sessional Papers*, (1906), vol 7 pt III; (Holmden 2712; *OHIM* 7.53).
OOAMA (NMC 17026)

2041 *1817*
Plan of York. Surveyed in 1817 by Lieut. Smith 70th Regt. E.A. Smith pinxit.
Col ms 56 x 75 cm 8" to 1 mile
Provenance: (Morse Collection of 9th Earl of Dalhousie maps); a military reconnaissance map of the town and harbour showing mainly the area below Lot St; shows a slightly different street and ravine configuration from that of Phillpotts (**2040**) and the peninsula differs considerably; shows three wharves, officers' barracks at Gibraltar Point, some houses of residents or major bldgs marked; the court-house is shown north of Hospital St and east of Yonge St.
NSWA

2042 *1817*
Plan shewing the Reservation for the Garrison of York Coloured with Lake [Sgd] Surveyor Generals Office York U.C. 25th June 1817. Thos. Ridout Surveyr. General. Wm Chewett S.S. & D.
Col ms 30 x 65 cm 1" to 10 chains Endorsements: 'Taken from Series "S"'
(SI 25 Apr 1817; OTNR FN 679 1817); shows the boundary of the garrison reserve by Order in Council 3 June 1817 west of Peter St; shows present garrison, site of old garrison, and 'old Fort Toronto'; shows blockhouse on Lot St and property of James Brock beyond reserve; there is also a 'Sketch of the Military Reserve at York with the arcs laid down at 1000 yds ... [Sgd] J.P. Catty'

of ca 1820 (OOAMA NMC 4431) and another contemporary plan showing lots west of the military reserve (OOAMA NMC 4430); there is also 'A Rough Plan of the Survey of a part of the Garrison Reservation by Richard Birdsall. Sept 13th 1820 ...' (OTNR SR 356).
OOAMA (NMC 4430–1; 4441) OTNR (SR 356)

2043 *1818*
The Hospital Reserve in the Town of York containing Six Acres – [Sgd] Survey Genl Office York 21 Sept. 1818 Thos Ridout Survey Genl
Ms 29 x 20 cm Scale not given Endorsements: 'Taken from S.G. Correspondence 1818'
Shows the subdivision of the area between Hospital St and Newgate St west of Church St; (Holmden 2672).
OOAMA (NMC 48022)

2044 *[1818]*
Town of York W.C. [9 June 1818]
Ms 43 x 124 cm 1" to 4 chains Endorsements: 'No 53'?
Dated from 'Ontario Register of Plans' (OTNR) and probably 'No 53' in Bigger, III:33; shows the town from Ontario St to west side of the garrison reserve and from waterfront to Lot St; names of owners in all lots including park lots; note that areas east of Parliament St granted in trust to Chief Justice Robinson and others 9 June 1818; school reserve 1818; shows government bldgs; later additions to about 1827 including some of water lots and Law Society land; an office copy is also noted in Ontario Register of Plans above but has not been found.
OTAR(P)

2045 *1819*
[Part of York east of Parliament St] York 26th June 1819; [Sgd] Reuben Sherwood Depy Surveyor
Ms 40 x 61 cm 1" to 2 chains Endorsements: 'A 71' '735'
Shows lots between Parliament St and West St, Park St, and along King St, with names; relief of area east to the bridge over the Don R.
OTNR (SR 406)

2046 *1819*
[Part of York from Newgate to Richmond St and from Upper George St to Church St] Surveyor Genls Office York 1819 [Sgd] T. Ridout Survey Genl
Ms 41 x 65 cm 1" to 50 ft Endorsements: 'A 79' '737'
Shows the reserves south of Newgate St for court-house and gaol and college square and church square; names of owners in other lots; later notes to 1824.
OTNR (SR 396)

Related maps

(2) *1829*
Plan of Survey Shewing the School Reservation in the Town of York divided into Lots: Surveyed York 24th April 1829 [Sgd] J G Chewett Deputy Surveyor
Col ms 28 x 38 cm 1" to 70 ft Endorsements: 'A 84'
Shows the subdivision from Richmond St to Newgate St and from Church St to New St; March St (now Stanley) shown east-west; two schools located; names in most lots.
OTNR (SR 395)

2047 *1820*
The Eastern part of College Square or School reserve Surveyed by order of Thomas Ridout Esqr Surveyr Genl between the 28th March and 1st of April 1820 by [Sgd] Richd Birdsall Depy Surveyor York April 1st 1820
Ms 47 x 60 cm 1" to 40 ft Endorsements: 'A 80' '736'
Shows the subdivision of block between Church St and New St south of Richmond St; there is a similar map at OTNR (SR 405) with added signature 'Surveyr Generals Office York 5 April 1820 Thos Ridout Surveyr Genl' and endorsed 'A 81' and '738.'
OTAR (SR 404) OTNR (SR 405)

2048 *[1820]*
[Plan E showing 100 lots and Plan F, 28 Lots, in the town of York]
2 ms 33 x 52 cm and 46 x 60 cm Scale not given
In 'Memorandum Lands Proposed to be Sold for the Endowment of a Royal Invalid Asylum' enclosed in Maitland to Earl Bathurst of 8 Mar 1820 (GBLpro CO 42/365 pp 78–81); 'F' shows the block from Richmond St to Newgate St and from Upper George St to Church St; 'Space for Court House & Gaol' below Newgate St; 'E' shows the area from Parliament St east to Sumach St with lots on both sides of King St; names of some purchasers shown on both maps.
GBLpro

2049 *1820*
[Plan of the 'Church Reservation' and vicinity] The numbered Lots Surveyed by Order of Thos Ridout Esqr Surveyr Genl by [Sgd] Richd Birdsall Depy Surveyor York April 20th 1820
Ms 47 x 59 cm 1" to 40 ft Endorsements: 'A 82' '734'
Shows the lots east of the reserve to New St between Newgate St and King St; 'Waterloo House' shown and some names of owners.
OTNR (SR 400)

2050 *[ca 1820]*
Plan Shewing the Building & Water Lots in front of the Town of York proposed for Sale to defray the expense of Building a Quay. J.G.C.
Col ms 45 x 52 cm 1" to 1 chain Endorsements: 'A 101' '733'
Shows the area from Yonge St to Church St, and Market St to the waterfront; water lots shown with two owned by the Honourable Thomas Scott and

Wm Cooper, others for sale; former shoreline; also a tracing in OTAR marked 'A 101'; also another early 'Plan showing the Subdivision of lots number nine South of King and North of Market Streets ... J.G. Chewett 10th Septemr 1830' in OTNR (SR 388).
OTAR OTAR (SR 388; 403)

2051 *[ca 1820]*
[Sketch of part of York east of Yonge St]
Ms 41 x 52 cm Scale not given
An unfinished sketch of town with street names; new names for some streets: Duke formerly Duchess St, King formerly Duke St; church and market squares; college square and hospital reserve both shown as subdivided but 'School Reservation' remains blank.
OTAR

2052 *1821*
Diagram for the Survey of Lot No 13 with the Broken front 1st Con: Township of York. Sur General's Office 15 January 1821 [Sgd] Thos Ridout Surveyr Genl
Ms 36 x 33 cm 1" to 10 chains Endorsements: 'To be returned to this Office with the fair Plan of Survey'
(SI J. Huston 15 Jan 1821 to lay out estate of Mathias Brown into parcels of 10 acres each); in 1st con from the bay east of town; shows 14 lots; there is also another early subdivision plan in the area: 'Plan of the Survey of Lot No 12 in the 1st Conc ... 1824 by [Sgd] John Goessmann' showing a subdivision for John Beverly Robinson (OTAR).
OTAR

2053 *[ca 1825]*
[Town of York]
Col ms 48 x 112 cm Scale not given Endorsements: '746' 'A66'
An unfinished plan of the town from Parliament St to Peter St; a few bldgs have been sketched in with names in pencil; shows court-house, St James Church, district school, council chambers shown in temporary position after fire of 1824 east of Simcoe Place (Arthur, 3rd ed (1986), 30); government house, commissariat stores, fort, and military reserve; old French fort; a red boundary marks the area east of town to the Don R; relief, marshy areas.
OTNR (SR 6471)

2054 *1827*
Plan of the Town of York. Corrected. By J.G. Chewett 1827 [Sgd] Surveyor Generals Office York 7th Decemr 1827 Thos Ridout Surveyr General
Col ms 66 x 130 cm 1" to 4 chains Watermark: '... WHATMAN ... 1825' Endorsements: '129'
A large-scale plan showing streets and some major bldgs including Bank of Upper Canada, post office, various churches, school, gaol and court-house, House of Assembly and public offices, Government House and other government offices including Council; garrison reserve and bldgs; map probably has later additions since Osgoode Hall shown but not named (built 1829–30) and Upper Canada College is shown in Russell Square (built in 1830); Chewett was involved in designs for the former (*DCB* IX, 128–9); several wharves; (Holmden 2688).
OOAMA (NMC 16819)

2055 *1827*
Sketch of the Military Reserve at York shewing the position of such of the Government Buildings &c. as are situated at the dist. of several hundred yards from the Fort. R. Engrs Office York March 31. 1827 [Sgd] J. Walpole Lieut. Roy. Engrs [Sgd] George Phillpotts Capt. Commg R. Engrs. West. Dist.
Col ms 33 x 51 cm 1" to 220 yds Watermark: 'JOHN HAYES 1814' Endorsements: '17' '22 Can U'; stamp 'REO'
Bldgs numbered and keyed; shows boundaries of blocks of land on northeast corner of reserve.
OOAMA (NMC 4445)

2056 *1828*
Plan Shewing the Land purchased for Kings College in the Township of York. Reduced and Copied from plan of J.G. Chewett Deputy Surveyor June 1828 by Richd Brassington Capt
Col ms Scale not given
Shows streets of the town with names, park lots 5–15, 'College Avenue' and site for King's College north of present-day College St; names of owners adjoining including D. Boulton, W.D. Powell, and J.B. Robinson, all of whom sold the north portions of their lands for the site; rivers, 'Sandy Mill'; photoreproduction in OTUAR.
Private Collection

2057 *1830*
Garrison Ground [York] in the occupation of the Honble George Crookshank. Copy from a Plan in possession of the Honble George Crookshank by J.G. Chewett York 25: March 1830
Col ms 37 x 48 cm Scale not given Watermark: 'J BUDGEN 1823'
Accompanied a petition for a lease of the land from Crookshank because of his improvements (OOA RG 1 L3 C 16 no 5 1830); shows the area west of Peter St in the southeast corner of reserve, next to wood-yard and below property of John McDonnell; (Holmden 2691); there is also a copy at GBLpro accompanying a memorial from Crookshank to Sir George Murray of 7 Apr 1830 asking for a lease (GBLpro CO 42/392 p 140).
GBLpro (CO 42/392 p 140) OOAMA (NMC 4447)

2058 *[ca 1830]*
Plan of York & adjacencies
Ms 20 x 32 cm Scale not given Watermark: 'T EDMONDS 1829'
Dates noted on the back: '21 Novr, 31 Dec, 31 Jany,

29 July, 31 March, 30 April, 6th May'; shows the area from the waterfront to the top of the 2nd con from the bay, and from the Don R to the Humber R; names of lot owners of the park lots and in the two cons; town of York and garrison shown; 'Dundas St.' and 'Road to Yonge St.' marked towards the east; 'Road to Coopers Mills.'
OTAR

2059 *1830*
Plan shewing the Survey of part of the Park East of the Town of York into 1/2 Acre Lots by Command of His Excellency Sir John Colborne Lieutenant Governor &c &c &c By James G. Chewett Surveyor York June 21st 1830.
Col ms 56 x 66 cm [1" to 2 chains] Endorsements: 'A 72'
Shows the subdivision east of Parliament St to the Don R with lots off King St and South Park St, and south to marsh; old roads, fence lines, and bldgs conflict with new survey; brickyards, reserve for market; later additions to ca 1833.
OTNR (SR 394)

Related maps

(2) *1830*
Rough Plan Shewing the Park Lots East of the Town & the valuation thereon in Red Ink as supposed to be reasonable by Order of the Trustees by [Sgd] J.G. Chewett York 21st September 1830
Ms 61 x 69 cm Scale not given Endorsements: 'A 73'?
Shows the same layout with names added to ca 1832 in half the lots and values written in all lots.
OTAR(P)

(3) *[183?]*
[Endorsed title]: 'Toronto Park Reserve' 'Plan by J.G. Chewett'
Ms 69 x 50 cm Scale not given Endorsements: 'A 76'
Lots laid out to two streets north of North Park St; two lots designated as 'Catholic' and 'Episcopal O.C. 3rd Nov 1831'; bridge across Don R; there is also an earlier 'Plan of Lots surveyed by J.G. Chewett York October 1828' showing lots at Centre Rd and Cross St east of Parliament (OTAR).
OTAR OTAR(P)

2060 *1830*
Town of York [Sgd] Surveyor Genls Office York 14th July 1830
Ms 39 x 127 cm Scale not given
Shows the whole town from the area east of Parliament St to the garrison reserve and from Lot St to the waterfront; street names and former names; all lots shown; names of owners in larger lots; shows subdivision south of King St and east of Parliament St; water lots shown; a few bldgs or reserves for bldgs shown; Upper Canada College; blueprint transcript of plan endorsed 'SCO Toronto v. Kingston [?] This is exhibit 2 referred to in the examination of Tracy LeMay ... 16 day of Sept 1914 ... 8 in the Supreme Court of Ontario'; described from blueprint (OTMCL), original not found; also a map at OTNR (SR 6469) entitled 'Town of York' (35 x 133 cm), scale not given, endorsed 'A 69' and '749'; the OTNR map is similar but appears unfinished, lacks names in lots, and area east of Parliament St south of Palace St not laid out.
OTNR (SR 6469)

2061 *1831*
Plan of Survey of the Lands for Lease to the York Garrison in the Township of York Home District [Sgd] York 25th May 1831 J.G. Chewett Surveyor
Col ms 68 x 111 cm [1" to 4 chains] Endorsements: 'No 1' '747'
Shows streets laid out south of Lot St and west of Brock St to the garrison, and four blocks of lots laid out west of Garrison Creek; bldgs in garrison; road allowance along shore; military reserve is shown as laid out per final plan of 1837 (**2064(15)**).
OTNR (SR 6074)

2062 *1833 Jan*
Plan of York U.C. Surveyed and Drawn by Lieut Phillpotts Royl Engineers. Copy by J.G. Chewett [Sgd] S.P. Hurd S.G.
Col ms 61 x 91 cm 6" to 1 mile
Accompanied letter from Colborne to Goderich, 23 Jan 1833, about the selling of some garrison lands and bldg a new fort further west (GBLpro CO 42/414 p 87); a copy of the plan of 1818 without bldgs (see **2040(2)**), but with the addition of notes on number of acres in parts of the military reserve and distances within the reserve and to the peninsula; a few roads in west part of town shown as now opened and two names of lessees shown at east end of reserve; there is also a copy of plan at GBLpro from WO 44/29 f 487 (MPHH 47(7)), further sgd 'Copy S.B.H. Inspector General's Office 4th May 1833'; photoreproduction in OOAMA (NMC 22824); (*PRO Cat* 1606).
GBLpro (CO 42/414 p 87, MPHH 47(7))

Related maps

(2) *1833*
Sketch of the ground Plan of a projected Place d'Armes for York, Upper Canada on the Plain, between the present ruined Work and the ancient French Fort Toronto. Royal Engineers Office Western District York U.C. January 21st 1833 [Sgd] R H Bonnycastle Capt Royl Engineers Western District
Ms 43 x 53 cm 1" to 60 ft Endorsed: 'For ... Sir John Colborne...' 'B 6' 'J/24'
Enclosed in Colborne's letter as cited in (1); GBLpro also has a copy endorsed 'No 3,' and a copy endorsed 'Copy J Nightingale, Drawing Room 3d May 1833' and 'B↑O' from GBLpro WO 44/29 f 500 and 488 (MPHH 47(9) and (8)); a plan for a five-sided fort with bldgs identified;

photoreproductions in OOAMA (NMC 8858; 8859); (*PRO Cat* 1605).
GLBpro (CO 42/414 p 87; MPHH 47(8, 9))

2063 *1833 Aug*
Plan of the Position of York Upper Canada as it exists in 1833, with a project for its defence. No 1. From the original Royal Engineer Office York Upper Canada 29th August 1833 R.H. Bonnycastle Captain Royal Engineers Western District U.C. ... No 1 of 31st October
Col ms 63 x 138 cm 6" to 1 mile Watermark: 'JAMES WHATMAN TURKEY MILL KENT 18[?]'
Endorsements: stamp 'REO'
Inset: 'Sketch of the Ground Plan of a projected Place d'Armes for the position of York ... Jany 21st 1833.' 1" to 60 ft; the main map shows the town streets and major bldgs, roads, relief along shoreline and peninsula, sandbanks, treed areas and marshy lands, proposed site of new Place d'Armes, soundings in bay, proposed line of canal near Don R, two new bridges over the Don R, proposed barracks; oriented to the south; inset is similar to **2062(2)** above; many later notes and additions including soundings, 1835, and a draft for the title of the more finished map below (2); note in title suggests this is a copy of another plan, which has not survived.
OOAMA (NMC 11446)

Related maps

(2) *1833 Oct*
No 1 Plan of the Town and Harbour of York Upper Canada and also of the Military Reserve Showing the site of the new Barracks and Work around them, as proposed to be erected near the Western Battery. Royal Engineer Office York U. Canada 31st Octr 1833 – (Signed) R H Bonnycastle Captn Royl Engrs Senr Off. Western District U.C. E.J. Ford Lt Royal Engineers Decr 5th 1833. Royal Engineers Office Quebec 24th Decr 1833 Gusts Nicolls Colonel Comg R Engineer Canada
Col ms 72 x 127 cm 1" to 300 yds Watermark: 'J WHATMAN TURKEY MILL KENT 1832'
Endorsements: stamp 'B↑O'
A more finished version of plan above without the inset for the projected Place d'Armes; oriented to the south; shows the streets named and major bldgs of the town; peninsula shown with relief, marshy and sandy areas; soundings in harbour; site for proposed new fort with a different shape from that in (1) and **2062(2)** ; proposed cut in sand-bar at neck of peninsula; steamboat route; many notes on terrain and areas being opened up for settlement; there is also a copy at GBLpro from WO 44/29 f 486 (MPHH 47(6)) entitled 'Sketch of the Town and Harbour of York ... Western Battery. Copied from Plan No 1 ... 24th Decr 1833. J.N. Inspector General's Office 26th July 1834' (*PRO Cat* 1606); photoreproduction in OOAMA (NMC 22825); (Holmden 2701).
GBLpro (MPHH 47(6)) OOAMA (NMC 16818)

(3) *1833 Oct*
No 2 Plan of Comparison shewing in yellow, the site of the new Barrack and Work around it at A; the Wharf B, and Tower C, proposed for the defence of the entrance of the Harbour of York, the Capital of Upper Canada and a chief Port for commerce on the Lake Ontario to be proceeded upon, if approved, as means shall be furnished from the Sale of that part of the Military Reserve given up for the improvement of the Town. Royal Engineer Office York, Upper Canada 31st October 1833 (Signed) R.H. Bonnycastle Capn Royl Engineers Western District U.C. Royal Engineer Office 24 Decr 1833. [Sgd] Gusts Nicolls Colonel Comg Rl Engineers Canada.
Col ms 76 x 133 cm 1" to 90 yds Watermark: 'J WHATMAN TURKEY MILL KENT 1832'
Endorsements: stamp 'B↑O'
Shows the area from Simcoe St to the old French fort; streets and major bldgs named; shows soundings in harbour and notes about proposed pier; design for proposed new fort is similar to that on (2); shows 'proposed plan of the new addition to the Town of York' – a layout for the military reserve similar to but differing slightly from printed plan of Nov 1833 (see **2064(2)**); proposed church is shown in circle; (Holmden 2701); there is also a plan for the pier from GBLpro WO 44/29 f 501 (MPHH 47(10)): 'Sketch of the Garrison of York shewing the Site ... for ... the proposed Pier for the Improvement of the Harbour of York ... 15th March. 1833 [Sgd] G Nicolls' (*PRO Cat* 1604); photoreproduction in OOAMA (NMC 5435).
GBLpro (MPHH 47(10)) OOAMA (NMC 16817)

2064 *1833*
With the exception of the Lots on the Bay shore and those on Dundas or Lot Street coming under the head of Sections A and C this Plan is merely a Proposed Sketch of an intended addition to the Town of York. His Excellency not having yet decided upon the Internal Arrangement. [Sgd] H.J. Castle Dep. Surv. 26th Nov. 1833
Col ms 36 x 54 cm 1" to 400 ft Endorsements: 'A 102' '723'
The first plan of layout for the military reserve lands; shows results of a partial survey for the lots (those numbered) on the bay and Lot St (*Upper Canada Gazette* 31 Oct 1833) and a projection for the rest; proposes a circle at Bathurst and King sts with radiating lots, two crescents along boundaries; shows the two burial grounds in squares; streets from new town do not connect with established part of town; a few names of owners or lessees of adjoining lots; wharf; proposed esplanade along front; this and the following maps are discussed in Ganton (unpub).
OTNR (SR 359)

Related maps

(2) *1833*
With the exception of the Lots on the Bay shore / and those on Dundas or Lot street coming under the

head of Sections A and B [in ms: C] this PLAN is / merely a Proposed Sketch of an intended / addition to the Town of York. His Excellency / not having yet decided upon the Internal Arrangements. // H.J. CASTLE Dep. Survr. Novr. 26th 1833 // Surrr Genls Dept York. U Canada
Print (lith) 46 x 60 cm 1" to 200 ft Endorsements: stamp 'B↑O'
Probably copied by transfer lithography from a slightly different version of ms plan above; shows minor variations on lot layout; in ms on print: names of owners and prices paid for lots 'sold by public Auction on the 25th of Nov. 1833'; Adelaide St is sketched to connect with town; many ms notes about houses built or to be demolished; note: 'perhaps for Government House' in lots 9–13 by shore; probable sites for church and market; the plan was lithographed by Tazewell and described in the *Patriot* (Toronto) 26 Nov 1833; (Holmden 2700; *OHIM* 7.54).
OOAMA (NMC 5035)

(3) *1834*
Plan of ye proposed New Town of York. U.C. on ye late Military Reserve. Henry James Castle Dep. Survr 14th Jany 1834
Col ms 76 x 79 cm 1" to 200 ft
Enclosed in letter from J. Colborne to W. Hay of 16 Jan 1834 (GBLpro CO 42/418 p 87); shows a considerable change in planning; the circle has been replaced by squares for church, park, and the market on Newgate St; all streets shown continuing through from town; most lots shown as smaller; lots sold with prices and notes about possible prices of others by H.J. Castle.
GBLpro (CO 42/418 p 87)

(4) *1834*
Plan of the Proposed – New – Town in the late Military Reserve York, U.C. Henry James Castle Depy Survr York U.C. Feby 20 1834.
Col ms 59 x 91 cm 1" to 200 ft Endorsements: 'A 97' '744'
(OTNR FN 670 18 June 1834); similar to (3) except church square design changed and Niagara St slightly further west; includes same notes on lots; (*OHIM* 7.55).
OTNR (SR 393)

(5) *[1834]*
Plan of part of York U.C.
Col ms 23 x 37 cm Scale not given Endorsements: 'O.S. 13' 'Plan no 37'
Shows a proposal for the layout of Government House reserve and area to the west, with streets Picton, Pellew, and Ponsonby, and from King St to St George Terrace; square in the centre called 'the Alameida'; plan for Government House; prepared after (4) and before (6); (Holmden 2647; *OHIM* 7.56).
OOAMA (NMC 48341)

(6) *1834*
Government / Second Sale of LOTS in / the / CITY OF TORONTO / May 1834 / Commissioner of Crown Lands Office / Toronto May 5th 1834 // H.J. Castle Dy. Surveyor 5th May 1834. // H.W.J. Bonnycastle del.
Print (lith) 42 x 55 cm 1" to 300 ft
Shows several changes of lot sizes and positions of streets including deletion of curving road on east, Government House reserve enlarged, Brock St shifted eastwards, Wellington Place is shown as different shape from proposed 'Alameida' (see (5)), Niagara St is shown less curved, north-south streets named, and Market Square shifted; (Holmden 2703).
OOAMA (NMC 5038) OTMCL OTNR (SR 10044)

(7) *1834*
Plan of lands, lately surveyed adjacent to Toronto Garrison. Surveyor General's office, Toronto 17th Novr 1834, Copy – Henry Lizars.
Col ms 42 x 74 cm 1" to 4 chains Endorsements: 'No 2' 'A 90' '726'
Notes: 'This Plan was copied from the plan dated June 11th 1834 – Surveys by Messrs Chewett & Hawkins laid down upon it' and 'Block D E & Easterly Block A Surveyed by Messrs Chewett & Hawkins J.G.C. S.G. Office 19th Novr 1834' and 'Lots 19, 20 ... 24 in line of Market Street West of the Military Burial Ground together with the Block in front were surveyed by W Hawkins 3rd Dec 1834 J.G.C.'; similar to (6) except some street names added, e.g., Stewart St, and Lot St renamed Egremont St; slight reorientation of a few lots.
OTNR (SR 343)

(8) *1835*
Plan of the Military Reserve at Toronto U.C. R.E. Office Toronto 20th Feby 1835
Col ms 53 x 124 cm 1" to 300 ft Endorsements: '39'
Accompanying enclosure on lands sold from Bonnycastle to Colborne of 18 Aug 1835 (GBLpro CO 42/426 p 209); shows changes: Niagara St moved further west, church shown on west side of square, part of Brock St reduced and called Albuera St beside government reserve; shows the military reserve with proposed site of new barracks and proposed boundary south of Lot St (Egremont); proposed extension to pier.
GBLpro (CO 42/426 p 209)

(9) *1835*
Plan of Re-Survey of a part of the Military Reserve City of Toronto. [Sgd] William Hawkins Dy Surveyor Toronto June 5 1835 Copy of No 1, 2, and 3 compiled and dated the 18th Novr 1836 sent to the Royal Engineers Office Nov 1836 J.G.C.
Col ms, pt missing 55 x 77 cm 1" to 4 chains Endorsements: 'No 3' 'A 91' '72'
Shows Government House reserve further south and bisected, with east side occupied by Crookshank; proposed church at the west end of Victoria Square; lots north of King St not shown; a later note indicates that copy was compiled from this map and others to make (12).
OTNR (SR 342)

(10) *1835*
No 2, Plan of the part of the Military Reserve given up for the benefit of the Town of Toronto, Upper Canada, as laid out in 1835 – Royal Engineers Office Quebec – Sepr 22nd 1835. [Sgd] Gusts Nicolls Colonel Comg Rl Engineer Canada. T.G.W. Eaststaff Draugn
Col ms 32 x 42 cm 1" to 600 ft
Enclosed in Byham to Hay of 14 Dec 1835 (GBLpro CO 42/428 pt I); shows land sold to June 1835; proposed church in square moved to east side; photoreproduction in OOAMA (NMC 4449); (*PRO Cat* 1609).
GBLpro (MPG 658)

(11) *1836*
GOVERNMENT / Second Sale of Lots in ye / CITY of TORONTO / Commissioner of Crown Lands Office / Royal Engineer Office / Toronto 9th Novr 1834 and 25th Octr 1836 / Copy of attested Plan / by R H Bonnycastle / Captn Royl Engrs' // Henry James Castle D.P.S. Toronto June 13 1834 / H.J. Castle, del.
Print (lith) 43 x 52 cm 1" to 300 ft
Accompanies report by Bonnycastle keying lots sold in four different sales (GBLpro CO 42/431 p 319); shows the streets and lots as in plan (7), but with ms adds to 14 Nov 1836; square with church now named Victoria Square; printed plan dates from June 1834 with later ms adds; parts of title are in ms but this is difficult to distinguish on copies found; also a copy with minor ms changes to signature from GBLpro WO 44/29 f 314 (MPHH 47(2)), photoreproduction in OOAMA (NMC 4452); (*PRO Cat* 1610).
GBLpro (MPG 1224; MPHH 47(2))

(12) *1836*
Part of the City of Toronto compiled from a Plan dated York 25th May 1831 by J.G. Chewett from a Plan dated – 19th Novr 1834 & 3rd Decemr 1834 by J.G. Chewett & Wm Hawkins and also from a Plan dated in June 1835 by Wm Hawkins Surveyor Genls Office Toronto 10th Novr 1836 [Sgd] J.G. Chewett [Sgd] J. Radenhurst
Col ms 45 x 65 cm Scale not given Endorsements: 'A 89' '725'
Note indicates that Brock St has been opened; Niagara St not shown north of King St; lots shown in all blocks west to Tecumseh St; Victoria Square not named; compiled plan from **2061** and from (**1**)–(**3**) and (9).
OTNR (SR 344)

(13) *1836*
PLAN / OF / LANDS LATELY SURVEYED, / adjacent to Toronto Garrison. / (Signed) Henry James Castle / D.P.S. / Toronto 11th June 1834. / Surveyor General's Office / Toronto, 28th Feby 1835. / Copy. // Copy from a Plan marked "Attested Copy, R.H. Bonnycastle Captn Royal / Engineers, Western District, U.C. 25th Octr 1836" and "Commissioner of Crown / Lands Office, Toronto, Novr 9th 1834 & 25th Octr 1836 ... 2nd Sale 18th Novr 1834" / and "Final Approved Plan By Command ... R.H. Bonnycastle, Captn Royal / Engineers, Western District, U.C. ... R.E., Office. Toronto. 14th November 1834 / & 25th October 1836. / S.G.O. Toronto 10th Novr 1836" J. Radenhurst. / Copy by H.J. Castle. Lithog. York Street. Toronto.
Print (lith) 34 x 51 cm 1" to 300 ft Endorsements: [Sgd] 'R.H. Bonnycastle Capt Royal Engineers' (OOAMA (NMC 5036)) and 'BW' '912' (OOAMA (NMC 5037))
The reserve for Government House has been deleted and Clarence Square and some lots laid out; church is again at the west end of Victoria Square; all lots now numbered; also a copy at OOAMA (NMC 4453) endorsed 'Capt Bonnycastle 28 June 1837,' 'B↑O,' and 'E 17' and showing lots paid for by 20 May 1837; (Holmden 2704).
OOAMA (NMC 5036–7; 4453)

(14) *1836*
Government Sale of Lots in the City of Toronto Commissioner of Crown Land's Office Toronto. Novr 9th 1834 & 25th Oct 1836. Copy of Final approved Plan By Command (Signed) R.H. Bonnycastle Capt R.E. Westn District Royal Engrs Office Toronto U.C. 14th Novr 1834 & 25th Octr 1836. from attested copy Signed R.H. Bonnycastle Captn Royl Engrs West. District 25th Octr 1836. [Sgd] Gust Nicolls Colonel Comg Rl Engineers Canada Quebec 28th Novr 1836 (True Copy) P Bainbrigge Lt R.E. 28th Novr 1836. H.J. Castle del.
Col ms 37 x 56 cm 1" to 300 ft
Originally from GBLpro WO 44/29 f 332; notes on the disposition of the lots at five sales to 12 Nov 1836; shows lots sold earlier now enclosed and some also built upon; mainly a copy of (11); also a copy of the eastern part in OOAMA (NMC 48023) entitled 'Copy of Final Approved Plan by Command ... 25th Octr 1836. [Sgd] G. Nicolls ... 8 December 1836 ...' and showing lots sold at auction 12 Nov 1836; (*PRO Cat* 1610).
GBLpro (MPHH 47(4)) OOAMA (NMC 48023)

(15) *1837*
Toronto Military Reserve. Resurvey by Wm Hawkins Dy. Surveyor. By order of His Excellency Sir Francis B. Head Lieut. Governor U. Canada &c &c &c as laid out in Town Lots on the east of the Ravine. [Sgd] To the Honble John Macaulay Surveyor General &c&c&c Toronto William Hawkins Dy Surveyor Toronto 18th Feby 1837 [Certified and sgd] R.H. Bonnycastle Captn Royal Engineers Western District U.C. 21st Feby 1837
Col ms 67 x 101 cm 1" to 4 chains Endorsements: 'Approved and ordered to be the plan on which all deeds grants or locations are to be founded ... 21st Feby 1837' 'No 55'
The final official plan for the area with lots numbered, names of owners, and notes; Clarence Square and McDonnell Square named; there is also a copy at QMMMCM (5660) sgd 'T Renwick Capt R.E. 18 August 1844' and endorsed 'REO'

and '262'; also a copy originally accompanying Col Dixon's letter of 30 Oct 1852 (GBLpro WO 44/48).
GBLpro (MR 1024 (41)) OTNR (SR 348)
QMMMCM (5660)

(16) *1837*
Toronto Military Reserve as laid out by Captn Bonnycastle Royal Engineers and Resurveyed by William Hawkins Dy. Surveyor ... Feby 21st 1837. William Hawkins Dy Surveyor Toronto March 1837.
Col ms 58 x 91 cm 1" to 4 chains Endorsements: stamps 'B↑O' 'IGF'
A copy of (15) above to show streets and lot nos only; notes about grants of public squares; there is a copy of this plan at OTAR on linen and endorsed '5331/63'; (Holmden 2711; *OHIM* 7.57).
OOAMA (NMC 22826) OTAR

(17) *1837*
Plan Shewing the corrections and alterations made in a Resurvey of the Military Reserve Toronto By Order of His Excellency Sir Francis B. Head Lieut Governor U. Canada &c&c&c William Hawkins Dy. Surveyor To the Honble John Macaulay Surveyor General &c&c [Sgd] William Hawkins Dy Surveyor Toronto 9th March 1837.
Col ms 63 x 82 cm 1" to 4 chains Endorsements: 'No 2' 'A 37' '728'
Shows conflicts in surveys of H.J. Castle and W. Hawkins of June 1835; shows adjustment to part of King St, Wellington Place, and Douro St; also a copy dated 21 May 1862 at OTNR (SR 81008).
OTNR (SR 345; 81008)

(18) *[184?]*
Sketch of the late Garrison Reserve copied from the Survey of Wm Hawkins Esquire P.L.S.
Ms 43 x 56 cm Scale not given Watermark: 'J WHATMAN TURKEY MILL 1839'
Provenance: OOA Hayes Papers; includes notes on various denominations occupying squares including Society for the Propagation of the Gospel in Foreign Parts; the Fitzgibbon property is noted as 'now Hospital Block'; 'Market Square granted to the City'; 'Lot St. now Queen St.' suggests a date after 1843 (Arthur, 3rd ed (1986), 288).
OOAMA (NMC 4455)

2065 *1834*
City of Toronto by J.G. Chewett Surveyor Generals Office 24th June [1834?] [Sgd] S.P. Hurd S.G.
Col ms, pts missing 66 x 126 cm 1" to 3 1/2 chains
Shows the area from waterfront to just north of Richmond St and from Parliament St to new town beyond Peter St; hospital and school reserves, goal, court-house, and church; 'Market leases' shown; area reserved below Front St for 'Public Walk'; in west part of town sites for House of Assembly, public offices, Government House, hospital, and Upper Canada College; wards; public wharf and soundings.
OTMCL

Related maps

(2) *1834*
City of Toronto and Liberties by J.G. Chewett Surveyor Generals Office 24th June 1834 [Sgd] S.P. Hurd S.G.
Col ms, pt missing 65 x 110 cm 1" to 20 chains
Shows area from water to top of 1st con and from lot 1 west to lot 41 on the Humber R; shows similar information for centre of town as (1); on the west shows 'proposed addition to the City under Survey' (around Garrison); 'Burial Ground & Park Reserve' shown north of Lot St and east of Parliament St; King's College site marked at the top of College Avenue; some subdivisions shown north of Lot St; possibly unfinished; shows five wards: St Patrick's, St George's, St David's, St Lawrence, St Andrew's.
OTMCL

2066 *1834*
CITY of TORONTO / The Capital of Upper Canada / 1834 / Respectfully dedicated to / HIS EXCELLENCY SIR JOHN COLBORNE / K.C.B. &c.&c.&c. / by H.W.J. Bonnycastle / and Lithographed by S.O. Tazewell
Print (lith) 50 x 116 cm 1" to 7 chains
Inset: 'City and Liberties' approx 3/4" to 1 mile; oriented to the south; streets named; lots shown including subdivisions north of Lot St; shows major bldgs: Osgoode Hall, Upper Canada College, 'Parliament House,' 'Government House,' and site for new Government House; proposed esplanade; table listing places in Upper Canada and distance table from Toronto to various places by water or by land; the plan was probably based on the 1833 plan (**2063(2)**), which was drawn by Henry Bonnycastle's father; the first separately published map of the city; Tazewell was noted as in process of lithographing the map in the *Patriot* (Toronto) 11 Apr 1834.
OTRMC

2067 *1834*
[Endorsed title]: 'Toronto in 1834 This map was drawn in the year 1834, from his own measurements, by Alpheus Todd, LL.D. C.M.G. late librarian of the Parliament of Canada, then a lad of 13 years of age.' By Master Alpheus Todd, No 85 Newgate St. Toronto / Opposite the Brewery
Print (engrav?) Approx 14 x 26 cm Scale not given
Shows the area from Lot St to bay, and Peter St to Chapel and Windmill sts; over 50 bldgs shown and keyed to reference; the plan was noted as an engraving just published in the *Colonial Advocate* (Toronto) 22 May 1834; a transcript of the plan made by J. Ross Robertson is in OTMCL; a facsimile was printed by Rolph Smith & Co., Toronto, in 1884 and issued under the auspices of the Semi-Centennial Celebration Committee (OTMCL); the title is a later endorsement but the author statement may be from the original.
Original not located

2068 *1834*
The Water Lots in front of No 13 to 33 & 42 & 43 have been disposed to the extent of the Blue Shade. The Water Lots from No 13 to 33 & 42 & 43, extending beyond the blue shade, to the outer dotted line to be given to proprietors with privilege to build on Front Street Conditionally. Lots L, M, N, O, P, Q, R, S to be Sold Conditionally. J.G. Chewett S.G. Office 20 June 1834.
Col ms 29 x 49 cm Approx 1" to 4 chains
Endorsements: 'A100' '720'
Shows area from Yonge St east to Caroline St; names of owners of water lots; water areas proposed for reclamation; 'Proposed esplanade.'
OTNR (SR 351)

Related maps

(2) *1834*
Plan shewing the proposed work in front of the City of Toronto [Sgd] Surveyor Genls Office Toronto 6th Decr 1834 J.G. Chewitt
Col ms 42 x 72 cm Scale not given Endorsements: 'A 70' '727'
Shows the same area as (1) with land to be added in front of Front and Palace sts, and areas for further extension of land for building lots; water lots already granted as in (1).
OTNR (SR 357)

2069 *1835*
Plan of Building Lots situate at the East End of Toronto, Township of York. [Sgd] William Hawkins Dy Surv Toronto 11 May 1835.
Ms 44 x 55 cm 1" to 1 chain Endorsements: 'A 78' '722'
Shows the area east of Parliament St to Mill St, and between King St and Palace St; two insets show the area between Sumach, Lot, and King sts and the area south to the bay with a windmill, both at 1" to 3 chains.
OTNR (SR 347)

2070 *[1835]*
[Endorsed title]: 'Toronto by J.G. Chewett'
Col ms 74 x 130 cm 1" to 800 ft Endorsements: 'A 172'
'Section of the Channel of Toronto Harbour [and pier showing] work completed [and] proposed addition of 200 ft'; water-line noted as of 1835; shows the whole city and the Liberties attached to St George's Ward, St Andrew's Ward, St Patrick's Ward, and [added later] St John's Ward; boundaries shown east of Yonge, but wards not named; notes on the channel and piers dated 1834 and 1835; possibly unfinished but also later additions; shows several subdivisions north of Queen St and east of Yonge St and a few abutting on Queen St to the west; shows final layout of the military reserve.
OTNR (SR 362)

2071 *1836*
Plan of Building Lots in the City of Toronto the Property of the Hon: Peter McGill. Surveyed September 1836 by Robert Lynn D.P. Surr [Sgd] Robert Lynn P.L.S.
Col ms 78 x 59 cm 1" to 100 ft
Shows a subdivision from Lot St to Gerrard St and from Yonge St to Dalhousie St; drawing of McGill cottage and garden; creeks; 'The New Normal School Block,' added about 1850, deletes some of the subdivision at the north end.
OTMCL (Howard Papers 917)

2072 *1837*
[Plan of the Law Society ground and lots owned by Chief Justice Robinson] To the Honble John Macaulay Surveyor General &c &c &c [Sgd] William Hawkins Dy Surveyor Toronto 22 May 1837.
Col ms 47 x 33 cm 1" to approx 60 ft
Endorsements: 'A 103' '719'
Shows Osgoode Hall and a half-acre given to government by Robinson on east side of Osgoode St; a few streets; OTNR (SR 398) also has a copy sgd 23 May 1837; there is also a photoreproduction in OTAR of an undated ms (original not found): 'Plan of Land the Property of The Honorable John Beverley Robinson Chief Justice &c. Toronto' showing the area from Lot St to house and property north of Head St, from College Ave to Sayre St, Law Society ground and Osgoode Hall; the undated ms is later than SR 353 as lots are shown; it is related to R.P. 147 (**B2408**).
OTNR (SR 353; 398)

2073 *1837*
Toronto. [Sgd] J.G. Chewett S.G. Office 12th June 1837; Surveyor General's Office Toronto 12th June 1837 J W Macaulay Survr Genl
Col ms 38 x 132 cm 1" to 6 chains
Shows the town with streets named and lots shown; site for new gaol at Palace and Parliament sts; water lots under grant, area granted in trust for a public walk; proposed esplanade; a later addition of the 1850s shows the railway line crossing the waterfront from the northwest.
OTMCL

Related maps

(2) *1837*
Proposed Plan of Improvement in front of the City of Toronto. Toronto 14th May 1837 [Sgd] J.G. Chewett. R.H. Bonnycastle Major & Capt R. Engs Comg in U.C. 14th May 1837
Col ms 37 x 128 cm Approx 1" to 6 chains
Endorsements: 'A98'
Shows the town and waterfront south of Lot St; reference keys areas where shoreline and water lots to be extended; storehouses to be erected, water lots already granted, proposed walk and proposed baths, Ontario Terrace; note indicates 'copy of this plan sent with instructions to J.G. Howard P.L.S. March 1845.'
OTNR (SR 5323)

(3) *1839*
Proposed Plan of Improvement ... 1837 [copy with additions]
Col ms 37 x 132 cm Endorsements: 'A98'
Shows the same information as (2) with red lines added showing grant of land to Corporation per Minute in Council 17 Aug 1837; a note about the patent and descriptions is sgd 'S.G. Office 30th March 1839 J.G. Chewett'; there is also a transcript of this map at OTMCL: 'Copy of part of the Plan of improvements to be made in front of the City of Toronto showing the water lots granted to the City Corporation in terms of a Minute in Council bearing date the 17th day of August 1837 Surveyor Generals Office Toronto 30th March 1839 True Copy (Signed) J.G. Chewitt [Sgd] a true copy A.J. Brunel D.P.L. Surveyor May 29th 1860'; and a printed version at OTMCL with same title, without the Chewett and Brunel signatures, with imprint 'Rordans and Carter, Law Stationers & Lithographers Toronto.,' and further endorsed 'In Chancery Worts v. Toronto ... 30th March 1860'; the three plans show the eastern part of the waterfront and indicate lots given to city by patent of 1840.
OTAR(P) OTMCL

(4) *[1840?]*
The City of Toronto
Col ms 47 x 57 cm 1" to 6 chains
Shows the area from Bathurst St to Berkeley St with the streets south of Lot St; the same information for waterfront as on (2) except shows area 'now granted to the Corporation' (1840); also shows piece of land granted by Boulton for the St Patrick's market and details of lots around St Lawrence market.
OTCTAR (J.G. Howard Collection 85–10)

2074 *[ca 1837]*
[Toronto and vicinity showing roads]
Col ms 75 x 129 cm 1" to 24 chains Endorsements: 'Y45'
Shows the south half of York Twp north to about [Lawrence Ave]; shows all streets in the city and subdivision streets north of Queen St; shows con road allowances beyond the city and travelled roads marked in brown, many cutting across survey grid.
OTAR (SR 7728)

2075 *1838*
Sketch of the neighbourhood of Toronto shewing the position of the Block Houses. [Sgd] Royal Engineer's Office Toronto U.C. 15th Decr 1838. Rd Birley R.E. Dt delt
Ms 63 x 61 cm Scale not given
Originally accompanied a letter of 15 Dec 1838 from Maj Barou about suitable positions for blockhouses (OOA RG 8 I vol 446 p 151); a sketch showing area from Lot St north to Davenport and ravine and from Bathurst St to Don R; shows streets, some lots and houses; blockhouses 1–7 shown on Lot St and Bloor St; site of university; some names of owners; there is also an earlier plan of a proposal for blockhouses at the same points, with notes and costs, watermark: 'G MUNN 1837,' originally accompanying Maj Barou's letter of 4 Nov 1838 (OOA RG 8 I vol 446 p 71, NMC 19465); (Holmden 2713–4).
OOAMA (NMC 10022; 19465)

2076 *1840*
Plan shewing the position of the Ground belonging to King's College, also showing the site of proposed magnetic observatory at Toronto, erected since the 6th May 1839. – [Sgd] W.C. Ward Lt. Col. R. Engrs 25 Sept 1840
Col ms 40 x 26 cm 1" to 12 chains Watermark: 'J MORBEY & Co 1838' Endorsements: 'No1' '10'; stamp 'B↑O'
Shows the site west of Yonge St and north of present-day College St, and proposed 'Road to Observatory'; shows College Ave and south part of park lots 9–14; some names of owners; streets of town to south; (Holmden 2716a).
OOAMA (NMC 4456)

2077 *1842*
Topographical Plan / OF THE / CITY AND LIBERTIES / OF / TORONTO / In the Province of Canada / Surveyed Drawn & Published by / JAMES CANE, TOPHL ENGR / 1842 / Dedicated / by special permission / To His Excellency The Rt. Hon / SIR CHARLES BAGOT, G.C.B. / GOV'R GEN'L OF BRITISH N. AMERICA / by his / VERY OBEDIENT, HUMBLE & DEVOTED SERVT / James Cane
Print (engrav) 101 x 90 cm 1" to 7 chains
A view of the Toronto waterfront is shown below map; the city's coat of arms is top centre; shows the city from the former military reserve to the Don R and from the waterfront north to [Bloor St]; streets named, all bldgs shown, major bldgs in detail with ground-plans and important ones named; shows landscaping of large estates; ravines and treed areas; 'Reference' lists churches, public bldgs, and banks; 'Locality' lists prominent societies and facts about the city including population of various groups, but the numbers and locations have not been added; Cane asked for patronage from the city on 1 Aug 1842 but later withdrew his request (OTAR MS 385); the City Council discussed purchasing copies of Cane's plan in Dec (City of Toronto Council meetings, Minutes, 12 Dec 1842 (OTCTAR)).
OOAMA (NMC 16801) OTCTAR OTMCL

2078 *[ca 1845]*
MAP OF THE PROPERTY OF / THE HONBLE J.S. MACAULAY / SITUATED ON YONGE STREET. / TORONTO // Lithg by H. Scobie, Toronto
Print (lith) 25 x 20 cm [1" to 2 chains]
Shows lots laid out along Teraulay, Jeremy, Anne, and James sts surrounding Macaulay's estate west

of Yonge St; Terauley Town is shown south of Jeremy St; reproduced in Arthur, 3rd ed (1986), 89, with note that it shows Teraulay Cottage in 1845; R.P. 45 of Jan 1850 (**B2426**) shows the final lot layout for this area.
OTMCL

2079 *1846*
Chart of the North Shore of Toronto Harbour, and Plan of the Wharves and Storehouses, &c &c Surveyed by Mr John G. Howard D.P. Surveyor, Toronto 1846. [Sgd] John G. Howard Surveyor August 17th 1846.
Col ms 59 x 168 cm 1" to 5 chains Endorsements: 'A 157'
Insets: 'Queen's wharf & soundings,' 'Section of Breastwork' 1" to 8 ft, 'Section of the Bank at the end of different streets,' 'Section of the Banks of the Government Creek at the Bridge...'; shows the area from King St to the harbour and from Don R to the new garrison; 15 wharves are named and keyed; soundings along shore and wharves; OTCTAR (Map 82) lists an earlier plan by Howard of the harbour from surveys Jan to Oct 1835, but the plan appears to be lost.
OTNR (SR 410)

Related maps

(2) *1846*
Toronto Harbour [Sgd] John G. Howard D.P. Surveyor August 17th 1846
Col ms on tracing paper 45 x 160 cm 1" to 4 chains Endorsements: 'A 158'
Shows the same area with a plan for an esplanade beyond the water lots and with insets of two alternative methods of embaying along the new shoreline; shows old shoreline, wharves with names of owners, and bldgs.
OTNR (SR 6477)

2080 *1846*
Plan of Lots 39, 40 and 41 1st Con Township of York Surveyed March 1846 J.G. Howard D.P. Surveyor
Col ms 75 x 55 cm 1" to 3 chains, 75 links
Shows the area east of the Humber R; much of it owned by Howard; relief, marshy land, bearings; contents of lots; Lake Rd shown with several bldgs; also: 'Plan of Lots 39, 40 & ... Shewing the new line of Road through 40 & 41, 1847 [Sgd] John G. Howard D.P. Surveyor July 10th 1847' endorsed 'H49' and showing the new road along the Humber R and other road surveys by Dennis and Rankin (OTNR (SR 6543)); and: 'Plan of the Subdivision of Lot 39 and E. part 40 in Br'kn FR'T and 1st Con. FR'M Bay in York [Sgd] Jno. Stoughton Dennis D.S. Toronto Feby 24th 1849' endorsed 'B 45' and showing lots, good land, relief, marshy areas, and road laid out by Howard (OTNR (SR 409)); also a later copy in OTNR (SR 392) of 12 June 1851 that lacks some of the information.
OTAR (SR 6827) OTNR (SR 392; 409; 6543)

2081 *1846*
Toronto C.W. Sketch shewing the Harbour and Ordnance Property, with the Encroachments on the latter ... C.G.G. Lt R.E. 11/7/46 ... J.D. 31/7/46
Col ms 64 x 128 cm 1" to 264 yds Endorsements: 'no 287'; stamp 'REO Kingston'
Two small plans: 'Toronto C.W. Plan of the Old Fort and adjacent Buildings' 1" to 80 ft, and 'Plan of the New Barracks' 1" to 80 ft, both sgd 'C.G.G. Lt R.E. 20 & 24/7/46'; shows the area from the military reserve to Simcoe St south of Queen St and encroaching bldgs with names of owners; shows peninsula and soundings in harbour.
OOAMA (NMC 11444)

2082 *1847*
PLAN / of several / BUILDING LOTS / near YORKVILLE Yonge Street / The Property of W.B. Jarvis, Esqr / Scobie & Balfour Lithog. // [Sgd in facsimile] Kivas Tully Civil Engineer &c. / Toronto Novr 10th 1847.
Print (lith) 22 x 33 cm 1" to 132 ft
Shows a subdivision east of Yonge St with lots on both sides of Murray St north of 'Rosedale'; Jarvis's estate.
OTAR

2083 *1847*
SKETCH / of / Lots to be sold on Kingston road / BY / J.M. STRACHAN ESQ. / Toronto / April 1847. / J.S.D. / D.S.
Print (lith) 57 x 22 cm Scale not given
Shows a subdivision on the Kingston Rd and part of lot 11, con 1, twp of York; with lots on Audley, Methven, and Clifford sts; related to R.P. 'Strachan Plan' (**B2421**).
OTAR

2084 *1847–8*
Topographical Plan of the City of Toronto from actual measurement Presented to the Mayor & Corporation of the City of Toronto By [Sgd] F.W. Barron Master, Principal U.C. College ...J.G. Howard Drawing Master
Col ms 121 x 172 cm Scale not given
Note: 'Names of Boys Engaged in the Survey and Compilation of this Plan VIIth form 1847: Palmer G., Evans G.M., Barber G.A., Beaver J.F., Armour J., Hutton J., Harris C., Ryan J.; 1848: Freer C., Grier J.C., Simpson C.P., Baines E.R., Watson J.H., Eliot C.E., Tyner R.J., Clark A.M., Morris J.H., ...'; a large, unfinished plan of the city from the waterfront to [Bloor St] and from Garrison Creek to Parliament St; all streets are shown and some named; treed areas; bldgs generally shown from Queen St south and some are named; subdivisions of some lots shown; a few names of owners.
OTHB

2085 *1849*
West Part of Toronto. [Sgd] William Hawkins Dy Surveyor Toronto 20 Decr 1849.

Col ms 28 x 44 cm 1" to 9 chains Watermark: 'MORBEY & SAUNDERS 1845' Endorsements: 'T 835'

Accompanying a memorial of 29 Dec 1849 for a licence of occupation for part of the garrison lands enclosed in letter of 16 Jan 1850 to Maj Talbot (OOA RG 8 I/72 p 65); shows the area west of Brock St to end of ordnance lands; shows blocks A and B on either side of Lunatic Asylum, the areas requested; licence of occupation to James Duffy on shore at west end; site of proposed church in Victoria Square shown; (Holmden 2722).
OOAMA (NMC 4457)

2086 *[ca 1850]*
CITY OF / TORONTO / CANADA WEST.
Print (lith) on tracing paper 24 x 39 cm Scale not given

An unfinished map; streets are shown north to [Bloor St] but not all named; many major bldgs drawn in but only some identified including Lunatic Asylum (built 1846–9) (Arthur, 3rd ed (1986), 91).
USDLC

2087 *[1850]*
Plan of the Peninsula shewing the Streets and Lots Toronto [Sgd] [illegible] John G. Howard [illegible] J.G. Howard Architect & City Surveyor Toronto
Col ms 52 x 63 cm 1" to 8.8 chains Endorsements: 'See Minutes Dec 24th 1850'

Shows a proposal for laying out Toronto Is into streets and lots; many of the proposed areas were actually under water; photoreproduction in OTNR (SR 86700).
OTCTAR (Map 669)

2088 *[1850–1]*
[Plans for the improvement of Toronto Harbour by Sandford A. Fleming]
24 col mss Size varies Scale varies Endorsements: 'Sa.F' (on many plans)

Some of the ms plans for Fleming's paper (see (2)) are in OOAMA (nos 1–5, 9–10, 14–16, 18–20, 25 (NMC 4459–69; 22829–31)); plans show the changing shape of the peninsula or island by wave action through time.
OOAMA (NMC 4459–69; 22829–31)

Related maps

(2) *1853*
[Plans accompanying 'Toronto Harbour: Its Formation and Preservation' by Sandford Fleming]
Prints (liths) 14 maps on 2 sheets Size varies Scale not given

In *Canadian Journal* II (Dec 1853–4), 105–7, 226–30, figs 9–15, 16–22 (OTAR); shows formation of shoreline, harbour, and island from 1796 to 1853; the printed form of some of the maps above.
OOAMA (NMC 4472) OTAR OTUTF

2089 *1851*
Plan of the intended Site of the New University at Toronto [Sgd] J.O. Browne P.L.S. January 1851 Toronto
Col ms 70 x 124 cm 1" to 80 chains

An attractive plan showing the site for Trinity College fronting on Queen St in park lot 22; relief, marshy areas, and ravine, treed slopes, and species of tree; table of arable land, pasture, broken ground, woodland, and water.
OTMCL

2090 *1851*
TOPOGRAPHICAL PLAN / OF THE / CITY OF TORONTO, / IN THE PROVINCE OF CANADA, / From actual Survey, by J. STOUGHTON DENNIS, Provin'l Land Surveyor. / Drawn and Compiled by / SANDFORD A. FLEMING, / Provin'l Land Surveyor. / 1851. // THIS PLAN IS MOST RESPECTFULLY DEDICATED / TO THE WORSHIPFUL THE / MAYOR, ALDERMEN, AND COMMONALTY / OF THE / CITY OF TORONTO, / BY THE AUTHOR. / PUBLISHED BY HUGH SCOBIE, ADELAIDE BUILDINGS, KING STREET EAST. / TORONTO. / Engraved on Stone by Sandford A. Fleming, Land Surveyor, 67, Yonge Street.
Print (lith) 66 x 89 cm 1" to 12 chains

Inset: 'THE / HARBOUR OF TORONTO, / and / ADJOINING COAST, / Reduced from / FLEMING'S CHART. / 1851.'; views: 'BANK OF MONTREAL,' 'RICHD ST. WESLEYAN,' 'ST LAWRENCE HALL,' 'THE CITY HALL,' 'BANK OF B.N. AMERICA,' 'KNOX'S,' 'ST GEORGE'S,' 'COMMERCIAL BANK,' 'UPPER CANADA COLLEGE,' 'UNITED PRESBYTERIAN,' 'OSGOODE HALL,' 'HOLY TRINITY,' 'PROVL LUNATIC ASYLUM,' 'BANK OF UPPER CANADA,' 'ST MICHAEL'S,' 'ST ANDREW'S'; shows streets, major ones named, and all lots; ravines, treed areas; shows the area from the waterfront to Bloor St and from the Don R to [Dufferin St]; list of public bldgs and places of worship; the ms draft plan was first exhibited by J.G. Howard at the Toronto Society of Arts First Exhibition 1847; it was later taken over by J.S. Dennis and subscribers solicited by Scobie & Balfour (*British Colonist* 9 Mar 1848) and was finally finished and engraved by Sandford Fleming (OOA MG45, diary 1848–51) and published 9 Aug 1851 (*British Colonist*); the views were by Thomas Young and engraved by John Allanson (*DCB* VIII:14).
OOAMA (NMC 44116) OTAR OTMCL OTNR (SR 6486)

2091 *[1852]*
[I]ncorporated Village of Yorkville in the County of York and Province of Canada. Drawn from an actual Survey by G.P. Liddy Late of the Engineering Department of the Ordnance Survey of Great Britain and Ireland Provincial Land Surveyor, Civil Engineer etc. Geo. P. L[iddy]

Col ms 79 x 90 cm 1" to 3 chains Watermark: 'J WHATMAN ... 184[5?]'
An attractive plan of the newly incorporated village north of Bloor St and on both sides of Yonge St; wooded areas, fields, streets, lots; list of all owners keyed to map; bldgs also keyed and brickyards shown; shows an early rectangular plan on part of the Rosedale estate superseded by the 1854 subdivision (**2107**); possibly plan listed in 'Ontario Register of Plans' (OTNR) as 'A181' and '1852' and 'For Incorporation'; Yorkville was incorporated 1 Jan 1853.
OTNR (SR 7017)

2092 *1852*
PLAN / OF THE / PROPOSED RAILWAY TERMINI / IN CONNECTION / WITH THE / Harbour of the City / OF / TORONTO. // Engraved by Jno Ellis Toronto / Drawn by J.O. Browne
Print (engrav) 25 x 78 cm 1" to 500 ft
In Walter Shanly, *Report on the Preliminary Surveys of the Toronto & Guelph Railway* (Toronto 1852) (Casey I–2345); shows the plan for the route of the line into Toronto across the garrison reserve and along the waterfront; shows the area from Queen St south and east to George St; shows area to be filled and connections to new piers along waterfront; copy in OTAR has ms adds showing 'land claimed by the O.S & H.R. Co. or nearly one half the Water Lots, granted ... to the Corporation Toronto Feb 18th 1853'; an additional note marks 'land proposed to be filled by the Toronto & Guelph Railway Co.'; (Holmden 2865; *OHIM* 7.61).
OOA OTAR

2093 *[1852?]*
PLAN / of the subdivision into / Lots of a / TRACT IN THE CITY OF TORONTO / Part of the Estate / of the late ALEX. WOOD ESQ. / Situate upon Park Lots / 7 and 8 / 1st Con. from the Bay. / York. J. Stoughton Dennis P.L.S. Hugh Scobie Lith. Toronto.
Print (lith) 51 x 64 cm 1" to 60 ft
Insets: 'SKETCH / OF / LOTS AT THE / Corner of / King and Princess Strs.' and 'SKETCH / OF / Lots at the corner / of / King and Frederick / STREETS' and 'PLAN / OF WATER LOT'; the main area is a subdivision from Yonge St to Church St and from Maitland St to Wood St; the insets show further lots for sale; the water lot is between Frederick St and George St; 'To be sold at the rooms of Wakefield and Coate on the 29th of Sepr'; related to R.P. 34 of 2 Dec 1851 (**B2436**).
OTUTF

2094 *1852*
Sketch of a Design for Laying Out the North Shore of the Toronto Harbour in Pleasure Drives Walks and Shrubbery For the recreation of the Citizens. [Sgd] John G. Howard City Surveyor June 18th 1852. C.L.O. 29 Nov 1852 [Initials illegible]
Col ms 26 x 75 cm 1" to 200 ft
Accompanied documents from the City of Toronto petitioning for water lots and frontage for public park, etc (OOA RG 1 L3 T7 no 8 1852 and filed with RG 1 E5/11 1853 no 189); shows proposal for drive and parkland from York St to Bathurst St; railway shown ending at Queen's Wharf at foot of Bathurst St; Royal Engineers' office shown at foot of Peter St; (Holmden 2729; *OHIM* 7.60).
OOAMA (NMC 4974)

Related maps

(2) *1852*
Sketch of a Design ... [Sgd] John G. Howard City Surveyor July 5th 1852
Col ms 25 x 149 cm 1" to 250 ft
Shows the same layout as the earlier plan but with additions on the east end showing wharves, and a 'New line of Esplanade' in front of proposed drive and park on the west in harbour area near route of railway line; 'Old line of Esplanade' on the east is shown closer to the shore; from the same source as (1); (Holmden 2730).
OOAMA (NMC 11447)

(3) *[1851]*
Part of the City of Toronto Shewing the Proposed Public Improvement by the Harbour Commissioners
Col ms 24 x 39 cm Scale not given
With a memorial of 8 Apr 1851 from the Harbour Commissioner requesting area to be filled for quays and construction of esplanade, in the same source as (1) above; shows shoreline and area to be filled in between Bay St and Yonge St; owners of lots; warehouses and proposed line of esplanade; (Holmden 2728).
OOAMA (NMC 4473)

(4) *1853*
Copy of part of D.S. J.G. Howards Plan of the North Shore of the Toronto Harbour. Crown Land Department Quebec March 1853.
Col ms 27 x 74 cm 1" to 4 chains
From the same source as (1–3); shows the waterfront from Bathurst St to Yonge St with existing shoreline and wharves; there is also a copy of **2064(15)** with the same title and further sgd 'True Copy [Sgd] R.I. Pilkington Draftsman 8th Octr 1852. M Dixon Colonel' and a partial copy from OOA RG 1 L3 T7 no 21 1852 (Holmden 2731, 2710) (NMC 22827, 4454); both show land along shore 'Reserved for the Public as a promenade ... Ontario Terrace.'
OOAMA (NMC 4454; 4973; 22827)

2095 *1853*
GENERAL PLAN OF ARRANGEMENTS / for / RAILWAY TERMINI in the CITY OF TORONTO / WITH PROVISION FOR PUBLIC WALKS / Referred to in Letter From a member of the

Canadian Institute – see page 233. // Hugh Scobie Lith, Toronto
Print (lith) 17 x 39 cm 1" to 12 chains
'SECTION / across Proposed Terrace & General Railway Approach' 1" to 40'; in *Canadian Journal* I, no 10 (May 1853), opp 233 (OTMCL); shows the city from Queen St south following 1851 plan (see **2094(3)**); shows a plan for new wharves, winter harbour; proposed eastern and western terraces and a small park; notes about wharves intended for railways and public purposes; the design for the railway approach is similar to **2098(1)**.
OTMCL

2096 *1853*
PLAN OF / BUILDING LOTS / ON MCMAHON, / SEATON AND BEECH STREETS, / TORONTO. / FOR SALE BY AUCTION, / At the Rooms of Wakefield & Coate, King St. / on Tuesday, September 27, 1853, at 2 o'clock P.M. // Lithographed by J. Ellis 8 King St.
Print (lith) 26 x 43 cm 1" to 60 ft
Shows lot nos and sizes on the subdivision north of Queen St and east of Sherbourne St; related to R.P. 82 (**B2460**); orchard noted at Queen St.
OTUTF

2097 *1853*
PLAN OF BUILDING LOTS / ON THAT PROPERTY COMMONLY KNOWN AS MERCER'S BLOCK OF SIX ACRES / BOUNDED BY KING, PETER, WELLINGTON AND JOHN STREETS. TORONTO / Feby 12 1853. / Hugh Scobie Lith. Toronto. // John G. Howard / C.E. & D.P. Surveyor
Print (lith) 57 x 78 cm 1" to 35 ft
Shows the area from King St to Wellington St and from Peter St to John St; see also **B2445**.
Toronto 63 (R.P. 57)

2098 *1853*
Plan of Esplanade in connection with the Grand Trunk and other railways [Sgd] Submitted with the Report No 9 of the Standing Committee on Wharves & Harbours and adopted by the Common Council of the City of Toronto November 3 1853. Mayors Office Toronto. Toronto November 4 1853 T.G. Powers Mayor
Col ms on linen 42 x 151 cm 1" to 250 ft
Endorsements: 'No 6 City Front showing the different lines of the Esplanade' 'Plan of Esplanade CSG & Co's estimate of 7th Octr 1853'
Shows the waterfront from Wellington St to harbour; a note further explains that proposed line for esplanade is that on which Gzowski's tender was based; shows existing wharves only; another undated and untitled plan shows proposed new quays and design for railway quay.
OTAR (Horwood Collection 1650)

Related maps

(2) *1854 [1853?]*
Plan of the Waterfront of the City of Toronto shewing the Proposed line of esplanade in connection with the Grand Trunk and other Railway lines
Col ms Approx 58 x 170 cm 1" to 100 ft
Endorsements: 'A 187'
A copy of 'A 187' was attached to the contract of 4 Jan 1854 with Gzowski and Co., contractors; there is a transcript in OTMCL marked 'GTR & CPR Toronto Exhibit 9 ... 23rd Oct 1905 Property of Pl'FFs ... 20th Oct 1904'; shows esplanade line on east end only, merging with railway line; carriage road further out; original plan 'A187' not found.
Original not located

(3) *1853*
Copy of part of the Plan of the Waterfront of the City of Toronto shewing the proposed line of esplanade in connection with the Grand Trunk and other Railway Lines. Crown Lands Department Quebec November 1853 (Signed A.N. Morin Commissioner of Crown Lands. Certified to be a true copy [Sgd] Charles Walkem Surveyor & Draftsman R.E. Dept 14th Decr 1853.
Col ms 58 x 170 cm 1" to 100 ft Endorsements: 'No 49'; stamp 'CREOC'
Probably a copy of the original of (2) above; shows the area south of Front St from Simcoe St to Brock St; bldgs along existing waterfront; area to be reclaimed and proposed 'Carriage Road'; 'O.S. & H.R. goods stations.'
OOAMA (NMC 22832)

(4) *[1855]*
ROUGH SKETCH / OF / MR SHANLEY'S / Proposed / LINE FOR / Toronto & Guelph Rail Co. / 21 May 1852. / Maclear & Co. Lith. Toronto
Print (lith) 20 x 31 cm Scale not given
In *Report of Select Committee ... of the City of Toronto to Whom was Referred the Contract for the Esplanade and the Esplanade Bill before the Legislature* (Toronto: Maclear, Thomas & Co. 1855), frontis (*Bib Can* 3616); with seven other plans showing different locations of line including Howard's line and line of esplanade on which C.J. Gzowski & Co. tender of 7 Oct 1853 is based, and the line in course of construction or contract line; the plans show the waterfront from Bathurst St to Yonge St with the various proposed lines.
OTMCL

2099 *1853*
PLAN / OF THE / CROOKSHANK ESTATE / North of Queen Street / In the City of Toronto / Province of Canada. / Hugh Scobie Lith. Toronto. // J. Stoughton Dennis / P.L.S. / April 1853
Print (lith) 77 x 39 cm 1" to 6 chains
Shows area from Hope St to beyond Bathurst St and from Queen St to [Bloor St]; the first subdivision plan for the estate in 418 lots; 'SECTION through BATHURST STREET Shewing slope of land towards Bay'; also shows Queen's Wharf with intended docks on either side; west city market shown; 'Remarks This magnificent

property will be sold ... on Thursday the 26th of May ... Toronto April 18 1853, J.M. Strachan, W.J. Fitzgerald.'
OTAR OTMCL

Related maps

(2) *1855*
PLAN / OF THE / CROOKSHANK ESTATE / North of Queen Street / IN / The City / OF / TORONTO. / Maclear & Co. Lith. Toronto
Print (lith) hand col 90 x 55 cm 1" to 3 chains
'The Crookshank Estate Closing Sale of the Estate on Tuesday the 5th day of June 1855 ... [Sgd] James M. Strachan, W.J. Fitzgerald. Wakefield, Coate & Co. Auctioneers'; lots coloured (mostly south of College St) are indicated as sold; lots north of College St still being sold; north of Harbord St the lots have been resubdivided and area called 'Seaton Square'; an inset shows area from north city limits to Davenport Rd; (*OHIM* 7.64).
OOAMA (NMC 22837) OTMCL

(3) *[1856]*
PLAN / OF / THAT PART OF THE / CROOKSHANK ESTATE / FRONTING ON / BATHURST STREET / AND THE NORTH LIMIT OF THE / CITY OF TORONTO. // Maclear & Co Liths Toronto C.W.
Print (col lith) 73 x 60 cm [1" to 100 ft]
'This valuable Property will be sold by Public Auction ... 28th May 1856 ... Messrs Wakefield & Coate ... apply to Dennis & Boulton Church Street Toronto'; inset: 'SKETCH / SHEWING THE POSITION / OF THE / PROPERTY TO BE SOLD'; shows the first subdivision for the area north of [Bloor St] to Seaton St and from Bathurst to Hope St; Seaton Square is now shown as laid out north of Bloor rather than to the south as in (2); notes stress the advantages of the lots for 'tradesmen & mechanics' since they are outside the city limits and the taxes are lower.
OTAR (MU 3514/26)

(4) *1857*
PLAN OF THE CROOKSHANK ESTATE NORTH OF QUEEN ST / IN THE CITY OF / TORONTO. / Maclear & Co. Liths Toronto C.W. / [Sgd in facsimile] J.O. Browne / Civil Engineer P.L. Surveyor / Toronto Feby 25th 1857
Print (lith) hand col 56 x 90 cm 1" to 3 chains
Shows the further subdivision of the unsold larger lots into smaller lots; 'The Crookshank Estate The Residue ... will be offered ... at the Auction Rooms of Messrs Wakefield Coate & Co. on Saturday the 25th day of April ... the Property has recently been subdivided into smaller Lots for the convenience of Mechanics, Tradesmen and Others.'
OTUTF

(5) *1857*
PLAN OF PART OF THE CROOKSHANK ESTATE / TORONTO. / Maclear & Co. Lith. Toronto. // Dennis Boulton & Co. / Surveyors etc. / 167 King St. West Toronto.
Print (lith) 42 x 67 cm 1" to 130 ft
From north city limit [Bloor St] north to Hammond St, and between Hope St and Bathurst St; shows a further subdivision of the northern part of the estate now extending north two streets from Seaton St; lots to Seaton St appear to be sold; related to R.P. 219 of 30 July 1857 (**B2563**); 'The lots will be sold at the prices marked until the 1st October, 1857 when 10 per cent will be added.'
OOAMA (NMC 22842) OTAR OTMCL

(6) *[1864]*
[Lots for sale on the Crookshank estate] / W.C. Chewett & Co. Lith. Toronto C.W.
Print (lith) 47 x 15 cm Scale not given
In *The Mechanics & Labourers Almanack, 1864 and 'The Crookshank Estate' Advertiser* (Toronto: W.C. Chewett & Co. [1864]), after 43 (*Bib Can* 4339); shows a layout similar to (3) but the text indicates that, although all lots sold in 1857, many lots reverted to original purchaser James Strachan because of the commercial crisis in that year; lots were being offered for resale at auction on 14 May 1864.
OTMCL

2100 *1853*
PLAN / OF THE NEW VILLAGE / of / SEATON / SITUATED AT THE NORTH / CITY LIMIT / & / Near the New Parliament Buildings / CITY OF TORONTO / PROVINCE OF CANADA / 1853. // John Tully P.L.S. King St. Toronto June 27, 1853
Print (lith) 85 x 58 cm 1" to 150 ft
Shows a subdivision from Bloor St to Davenport Rd, Bathurst St to Coleman St; Seaton Square and Market Square shown; names of a few landowners; 'This Property will be sold by Auction ... on Tuesday the 9th August next'; this plan appears to have been superseded by the 1857 plan of part of the Crookshank estate (**2099(4)**).
OOAMA (NMC 22833; 43217)

2101 *[1853?]*
[Plan of Toronto]
Col ms 55 x 79 cm 1" to 12 chains Watermark: 'T H SAUNDERS & CO 1848' Endorsements: 'no 56'; stamp 'CREOC'
Shows the streets and major bldgs of town south of about Dundas St; military bldgs shown in red; shows the Lunatic Asylum and Trinity College, Ontario Simcoe and Huron Railway, and other railway lines planned; proposed infill and new docks.
OOAMA (NMC 43215)

2102 *[1853]*
PLAN / of / VILLA LOTS / Near the / RAILWAY STATION / ON THE / Trunk Line / in the Village of / WESTON / Hugh Scobie Lith. // J. Stoughton Dennis P.L.S.
Print (lith) 45 x 57 cm 1" to 4 chains
Note: 'Notice The above valuable Lots will be sold at the rooms of Messrs Wakefield and Coate on

Thursday the 8th of September ...' [1853]; shows the area near the Humber R between the GTR and St Phillip's Church; names of purchasers shown in some lots.
OTAR

2103 *1853–4*
Plan of the Viceregal Park and other grounds in the City of Toronto the Property of the Provincial Government. 1854 [Sgd] F.F. Passmore Provl. Land Surveyor October 21 1853
Col ms 130 x 75 cm 1" to 2 chains Endorsements: stamp [BW] '493'
Inset: 'Lot 22 in the 2nd Con. from the Bay'; shows College Ave from Queen St and from Yonge St, boundary of park, with relief, creek, treed areas, Magnetic Observatory and King's College; 'Report & Description' of survey gives table of areas owned by various groups including the provincial government; a pencil sketch shows an early plan for University College; there is also a 'Plan of the University Park in the City of Toronto 1854' showing existing bldgs or those under construction and others added later, in OTAR (Horwood Collection 626(2)); (Holmden 2733).
OOAMA (NMC 11452) OTAR (Horwood Collection 626(2))

Related maps

(2) *1859*
[Plan of the University Park]
Col ms 52 x 77 cm [1" to 2 chains] Endorsements: 'No 735 of 1859'
Note: 'Within the Red margin is the land leased to the Corporation of Toronto for a "Public Park" ... Lease dated January 1st 1859.' (see also R.P. D 18 (**B2602**)); shows University College, The Asylum, The Medical School, The Observatory; and a few other bldgs; relief by colour wash; treed areas; 'Site of proposed statue of her Majesty'; proposed botanic garden.
OTUAR (A65-0001-20)

(3) *[ca 1859?]*
Plan of a Portion of the University Grounds and Avenues set apart for a Public Park (Signed) John Langton, Vice Chancellor Countersigned (Signed) James H. Morris Reg.
Col ms on linen 65 x 75 cm 1" to 2 chains
Possibly a tracing from (2) without all the smaller bldgs or relief; list of contents included.
OOAMA (NMC 22836)

2104 *1854*
[Diagrams to accompany] Report on the Preservation and Improvement of Toronto Harbour, by Henry Youle Hind
3 prints (liths) Ea 47 x 75 cm or smaller Scales vary
In *Reports on the Improvement and Preservation of Toronto Harbour. Published by Authority of the Harbour Commissioners* (Toronto: Thomas Maclear & Co. 1854) (OTAR); sheet 1: 'Diagram to illustrate the First Premium Report. Maclear & Co. Lith. Toronto.' includes nos 1, 2, 4, 5, 8, 10; sheet 2: '... no 6'; sheet 3: '... No 9 Maclear & Co Lith Toronto'; the diagrams show the erosion around the Scarborough Bluffs and the build-up of sediment on the peninsula; Hind concluded that the only practicable location for a navigable canal to improve harbour was across the western part of the island.
OTAR (Pamphlet no 33)

2105 *1854*
Plan / of / PART OF THE / CITY OF TORONTO / Shewing the / TOWN LOTS ON BELLEVUE / For Sale by / THE TRUSTEES FOR / THE DENISON ESTATE / March 1854. // J. Stoughton Dennis P.L.S. // Maclear & Co. Lith Toronto
Print (lith) 55 x 48 cm 1" to 6 chains
Shows lots laid out from Queen St to Bloor St and from Major St to Lippincott St; notes on the advantages of the site indicate that lots are near the new Parliament Bldgs and Government House 'about to be erected'; shows the early plan by Cumberland and Ridout for the Parliament Bldgs never put into effect (Arthur, 3rd ed (1986), 307); related to R.P. 65 and 112 (**B2454**, **B2464**); (ACML Facsimile Map Series no 121 (1986)).
OOAMA (NMC 22835) OTMCL

2106 *1854*
Plan / of / PART OF THE / CITY OF TORONTO / Shewing the / VILLA LOTS ON COLLEGE ST: / For Sale by / THE MESS'RS: JARVIS / March 1854. // J. Stoughton Dennis / P.L.S. / Maclear & Co. Lith. Toronto
Print (lith) 55 x 48 cm 1" to 6 chains
The same base plan as above (**2105**) has been used to show Jarvis's lots for sale between Borden St and Major St; Denison estate is shown to west and south; also includes the plan for the Parliament Bldgs as on **2105**; note indicates that lots not sold privately 'will be offered at Public Auction on Thursday the 15th day of June next at Messrs Wakefield & Coates Rooms ...'; related to R.P. 87 (**B2466**).
OTAR OTUTF

2107 *1854*
PLAN / OF / ROSE-PARK / BEING A SUBDIVISION / of the / ROSEDALE ESTATE / ADJOINING THE / City of Toronto, / CANADA. / Lithographed by J. Ellis Toronto, / CANADA. [In ms certified correct by] J. Stoughton Dennis P.L.S. [and owner] G. Duggan Jr. 28th December 1854
Print (lith) 65 x 88 cm 1" to 100 ft
Inset: [Rosedale in relation to the city to the south]; shows the first curvilinear subdivision for Rosedale, and an early example of this type of urban design in Canada (Ganton and Winearls); from Yonge St east to Crescent Rd and from Park Rd to Murray St; relief along ravines; wooded areas; Rosedale Villa, Vinery, gardens; this is the original R.P. 104 (**B2429**), now in OTAR; there is a ms copy of the plan on linen with the same title and possibly sgd by Dennis in OTMCL.
OTAR OTMCL

2108 *1854*
VILLA LOTS FOR SALE / ON THE / MOSS PARK ESTATE / TORONTO / THE PROPERTY OF / G.W. ALLAN ESQ. / [Sgd in facsimile] J.O. Browne P.L.S. Toronto April 23rd 1854.
Print (lith) 85 x 43 cm 1" to 60 ft
Shows area from George St to Sherbourne St, and Wilton Crescent to Gerrard St; related to R.P. 150 (**B2512**); shows roads on Moss Park estate to the south.
OOAMA (NMC 22834) OTMCL

2109 *1855*
CITY AND BAY OF TORONTO (YORK IN 1812).
Print (wood engrav) 19 x 11 cm Scale not given
In G. Auchinleck, *A History of the War* (Toronto: Maclear & Co. 1855), 146 (*Bib Can* 8397); a note indicates that the map shows Toronto 'as it is now' but woods are shown as they were 'to mark the difficulty which attended military movements generally'; key to places, garrison, ships, and business part of York in 1812.
OTMCL

2110 *1855*
PLAN / OF / BUILDING LOTS FOR SALE / UPON THE / HOMEWOOD ESTATE / TORONTO. Maclear & Co Lith. Toronto
Print (lith) 47 x 61 cm 1" to 100 ft
'SKETCH OF PROPOSED STYLE OF BUILDING' to be built on the site and two floor plans shown; from Church St to Sherbourne St and from Bloor St to third street to the south; bldgs and names of a few owners shown north and south of Bloor; blockhouse; 'Terms ...upon application to the subscriber at his office, Ontario Hall Church Street, Toronto. J.O. Browne Civil Engineer and P.L. Surveyor Toronto, June 2nd 1855'; both OOAMA and OTMCL copies have the surveyor's signature below title in ms: 'J.O. Browne P.L.S. Toronto June 8th 1855.'
OOAMA (NMC 4891) OTAR OTMCL

2111 *1855*
PLAN / OF / LOTS AT YORKVILLE / TO BE SOLD / BY AUCTION. / AT / WAKEFIELD AND COATE'S ROOMS, / ON / Tuesday 29th May, 1855, / AT TWELVE O'CLOCK. [and] PLAN OF LOTS ON GLOUCESTER STREET / To be Sold ... May 29th, at Twelve O'Clock [and] PLAN OF BUILDING LOTS, / ON / King, Tecumseth, Adelaide and West Streets, / TO BE SOLD / BY AUCTION, / AT THE ROOMS OF / MESSRS. WAKEFIELD, COATE & Co., / IN TORONTO, ON / Tuesday, 29th May, 1855, at noon.
3 prints (typeset) on 1 sheet 46 x 58 cm Scales not given
The first plan shows lots fronting on Yonge St; the second plan shows lots on Gloucester St near Yonge St; the third plan shows 30 lots and is based on R.P. 126 (**B2498**).
OTAR

2112 *1855*
PLAN OF LOTS / on the North East corner of / KING AND BATHURST STREETS / Maclear & Co. Lith. Toronto. Sandford Fleming, Surveyor April 14th 1855.
Print (lith) 46 x 62 cm 1" to 15 ft
Certified in ms by the owners J.G. Brown, Sandford Fleming, and S.M. Jarvis on 14 Apr 1855; not registered until 1868; see also **B2487**.
Toronto 63 (R.P. D 41)

2113 *1855*
PLAN / OF PARK LOT, / No 2, / in the City / OF / TORONTO, / The Property of A.H. St. Germain, Formely [*sic*] belonging / to Captn Irvin and Mr James Francis ... Toronto, May 10th 1855.
Print (lith) 43 x 56 cm 1" to 20 ft
Shows the subdivision at the corner of Pine St and King St E with lot nos, existing bldgs, and trees; 'This very valuable property will be sold ... at the Auction Mart of Wakefield Coate & Co. on Tuesday the 15th May 1855 ...'; related to R.P. 118 (**B2490**).
OTMCL

2114 *1855*
PLAN OF THE PROPERTY OF / THE HONBLE W.H. DRAPER, / Situated on the corner of / YORK STREET, / AND / WELLINGTON STREET, / TORONTO. / Lithographed by J. Ellis / TORONTO
Print (lith) 50 x 77 cm 1" to 20 ft
Shows lots on the northwest corner of Wellington St and York St; bldgs shown with names of owners including Chewett's Bldgs; 'to be sold by Auction ... by Messrs Wakefield, Coate & Co. 20th June, 1855'; see also **B2487**.
Toronto 63 (R.P. D 37)

2115 *1855*
PLAN / OF / VILLA SITES AT "THE WILLOWS" / THE RESIDENCE OF / the HONBLE J.H. PRICE / being Lot No 1 in the 1st Concession west of Yonge Street / TOWNSHIP AND COUNTY OF YORK / TORONTO / 1855 // Maclear & Co Lith. Toronto / [Sgd in facsimile] John Tully / Architect & P.L.S. / July 11th 1855 Toronto
Print (lith) 39 x 53 cm 1" to 8 chains
Shows lots along present-day Eglinton Ave; a note indicates area as 3 1/2 miles from Toronto and 1 1/2 miles east of the Northern Railway.
OTUTF

2116 *1856*
Part of Toronto T.D. Crown Lands Department Toronto October 1856 Commissioner Crown Lands
Col ms 64 x 99 cm 1" to 4 chains
Shows the area from Queen St to Front St, and York St to Niagara Rd; location of various churches, squares, some important bldgs; wharf; possibly unfinished.
OTNR (SR 8862)

2117 *[1856]*
PLAN OF / BUILDING LOTS, / ON NORTHERN PORTION OF LOT No 3 IN THE / CITY OF TORONTO, / The Property of The Honble Christopher Widmer. / Archd M. Barr Lithog. Toronto
Print (lith) 53 x 77 cm 1" to 100 ft
From Parliament St to McMahon St, and East St to Nassau St; the plan was certified as correct in ms and sgd 'Sandford Fleming Provl Land Surveyor Toronto 5th June 1856'; see **B2526**.
Toronto 63 (R.P. 185)

2118 *1856*
Plan of Part of Lots Nos 15 and 16 in the First Concession from the Bay in the township of York & County of York, Canada West. Sold by Charles Scadding Esqr To the Corporation of the City of Toronto, 1856.... [Sgd] John Tully Architect & P.L.S. King Street east Toronto Decr 9 1856
Col ms on linen 69 x 102 cm 1" to 3.3 chains
Provenance: City of Toronto Finance Department; certified by J.B. Robinson, mayor, and H. and C. Scadding as the plan referred to on the conveyance of 30 Dec 1856; shows the area from the Don R east to Old Mill Rd north of Kingston Rd; also shows the area from Parliament St east to Winchester St/Don Mills Rd; several parcels of land shown and 'road to Scaddings Flats.'
OTCTAR

2119 *1856*
PLAN OF PROPERTY ON SIMCOE STREET / AND WELLINGTON STREET / WEST OF YORK STREET TORONTO / TO BE SOLD BY PUBLIC AUCTION AT THE ROOMS OF MESSRS WAKEFIELD & COATE ON THURSDAY 16 OCT. 1856. / at 12 o'Clock [Sgd in facsimile] Dennis & Boulton Surveyors
Print (lith) 55 x 71 cm 1" to 30 ft
Shows area from Front St to Wellington St, and Simcoe St to York St; a proposed street is shown between Wellington and Front sts and still shown as proposed on 1862 plan (see **2139**) but never built; 'Wellington Terrace' is shown and two property owners.
OOAMA (NMC 22838)

2120 *1856*
PLAN / OF / SUNNYSIDE / THE PROPERTY OF / GEO. H. CHENEY ESQ. / June 1856. / Maclear & Co. Lith. Toronto C.W.
Print (lith) 62 x 77 cm 1" to 1 chain
Shows an area north of Lakeshore Rd to the Hamilton & Toronto Railway and west of [Dufferin] St; various bldgs, gardens, paddocks, and stables shown and notes indicate further sites for bldgs, stables, etc; reservations for roads; see also **B2530**.
Toronto 63 (R.P. 175)

2121 *1856*
PLAN / OF THE / ELMSLEY VILLA ESTATE / IN THE CITY / OF / TORONTO, / The Property of A.M. Clark, Esq., / AS DIVIDED INTO LOTS FOR SALE. / J.O. Browne, / Toronto, 12th June, 1856 / Civil Engineer, P.L.S. / 1856 / BLACKBURN'S CITY STEAM PRESS, YONGE STREET, TORONTO
Print (typeset) 70 x 64 cm 1" to 45 ft
Shows Elmsley Villa and the subdivision northwest of Yonge St and College St, from Yonge St to Surrey Place and College Ave to Breadalbane St; related to R.P. 159 (**B2525**).
OTAR

2122 *[1856?]*
Plan of the Proposed Improvements on part of the Ordnance Reserve Toronto [Sgd] Dennis & Boulton Surveyors. O. Jones del.
Col ms 51 x 92 cm 1" to 3 chains Watermark: 'J WHATMAN TURKEY MILL 1854'
Shows an early subdivision plan for the ordnance reserve, i.e., the area between Niagara St and the GTR line and north to Adelaide St; the old fort was to be removed and a subdivision laid out called 'Grosvenor Railton' with various parklands, a botanical garden, and museum north of the Hamilton & Toronto Railway line; the plan predates (2) below; (*OHIM* 7.59).
OOAMA (NMC 19783)

Related maps

(2) *1856*
PLAN / OF PART OF THE / ORDNANCE RESERVE / TORONTO / Dennis Boulton & Co. Surveyors. / 1856. / Maclear & Co. Lith. Toronto.
Print (lith) 62 x 52 cm 1" to 100 ft
View: 'TRINITY COLLEGE, FRONT ELEVATION'; shows a new plan of subdivision for area west of Garrison Creek to beyond Strachan Ave and from Wellington St to Queen St; copies are found in black and white and with the view in upper centre (OTAR, OOAMA (NMC 22840–1)); OOAMA (NMC 22839) and OTUTF copies are colour-printed in green with the view in the upper left; (Holmden 2737, 2734).
OOAMA (NMC 22839–41) OTAR OTUTF

(3) *1858*
Map Shewing the Position of the Ordnance Lands in the City of Toronto. 1858. [Sgd] Toronto 15 June 1858 W.S. Boulton P.L.S.
Col ms 64 x 97 cm Scale not given
Shows the area from John St west to Strachan Ave, and Front St to Queen St; an unfinished sketch; shows streets, wharves; old and new garrisons; Lunatic Asylum pencilled in; there is also an earlier plan of 1843 showing site proposed for the Lunatic Asylum, accompanying Col Holloway's letter of 18 July 1843 (GBLpro WO 46/44 f 162).
GBLpro (MPH 1142) OTMCL

(4) *1858*
PLAN / of part of the / ORDNANCE RESERVE / TORONTO / DENNIS & GOSSAGE SURVEYRS / 1858. // LITHOGRAPHED BY J. ELLIS TORONTO

Print (col lith) 58 x 76 cm 1" to 100 ft
Views: 'Trinity College' and 'The Provincial Exhibition Building / Toronto 1858.'; shows the area from Wellington St to Queen St and from Garrison Creek to the Lunatic Asylum; the same lots as those on the 1856 map are being offered for sale together with a block of lots at King, Wellington, and Ordnance sts; 'Sale at the rooms of Wakefield Coate & Co. on Wednesday the 15th December 1858'; Ontario Simcoe & Huron Railroad cuts through the area.
OTAR OTAR (SR 86708)

(5) *1862*
Plan of the Ordnance Reserve at Toronto Canada [Sgd] J. Stoughton Dennis P.L.S. Toronto 28th Feb. 1862. Owen Jones Del / 62
Col ms 69 x 100 cm 1" to 200 ft
Shows the area from Bathurst St to west city limit at Dufferin St, and from Queen St south to waterfront; GTR, GWR, and Northern Railway lines and bldgs, Queen's Wharf, Provincial Lunatic Asylum; shows area subdivided around Strachan Ave and Exhibition Grounds and bldgs.
OTNR (SR 5904)

2123 *[1856?]*
PLAN / OF THE / RUNNYMEADE ESTATE / NEAR THE CARLTON STATION / of the / GRAND TRUNK RAILWAY / IN THE / TOWNSHIP OF YORK / Maclear & Co Lith Toronto. / Dennis & Boulton / Surveyors & Agents.
Print (col lith) 48 x 66 cm 1" to 4 chains
Shows lots laid out from Victoria St to Jane St, and Louisa St to Davenport Rd; shows bldgs at the corner of Dundas St and Victoria St; probably related to R.P. 166 of 1 Aug 1856 (**B2533**).
OTAR (MU 3514/p–25)

2124 *[1856]*
PLAN / of the Subdivision of the / DEER PARK PROPERTY, / ON / YONGE STREET, / Being part of Lot 21 in 3rd Con. from Bay, / Township of York. / Maclear & Co. Lith Toronto.
Print (lith) 51 x 61 cm 1" to 1 chain
Shows area from Yonge St west to the W.A. Baldwin property with lots along Mount, Heath, and Gordon sts; names of owners of large lots adjoining; certified in ms by surveyor Sandford Fleming and proprietor John G. Brown 16 Sept 1856; see also **B2538**.
Toronto 63 (R.P. 181)

2125 *1856*
PLAN, / Shewing the Situation of the 2 Lots, to be Sold on the 13th November, 1856. // In Chancery. / GOODWIN vs. WILLIAMS. // Blackburn's City Steam Press, 63 Yonge Street, Toronto
Print (typeset) 46 x 36 cm Approx 1" to 12 ft
Shows the two lots west of Spadina Ave and north of Queen St with a bldg adjacent, but exact area unidentified.
OTUTF

2126 *[1856?]*
PLAN / Shewing the Subdivision / OF THE PROPERTY OF / JOHN EWART ESQ / ON SPADINA AVENUE / TORONTO / Maclear & Co. Lith Toronto. [Sgd in facsimile] Dennis & Boulton Surveyors
Print (lith) 62 x 44 cm 1" to 50 ft
Shows area from North Huron St to Spadina Ave and from Heyden St to [Bloor] St; some pencilled notes including prices and name of one owner; Dennis & Boulton are listed in partnership in *Brown's Toronto General Directory* (Toronto: Maclear & Co. 1856).
OTUTF

2127 *[1857?]*
CITY / OF / TORONTO / C.W. // Lith of Chs Magnus 12 Frankfort St. N.Y.
Print (lith) 15 x 20 cm Scale not given
Below imprint to the right is printed 'Toronto ... 18 ...' and opp is a vignette of boy in sailor-dress suggesting that map was part of letterhead; date is filled in on one copy 'August 10th 1857'; major streets named; some areas hachured, probably indicating the outline of the built-up area; a few major bldgs named; old and new garrison; Northern, Hamilton and Toronto, and GTR railways shown; Magnus is described as a 'lithographer particularly of letterheads' and is only noted at this address from 1858 on (Peters, 269 and plate 95).
OTMCL Private Collection

2128 *[1857]*
PLAN OF / BUILDING LOTS / IN THE / CITY OF TORONTO / The Property of / THOMAS BRUNSKILL ESQRE / Maclear & Co. Lith. Toronto. // Fleming, Ridout & Schreiber / Engineers & Surveyors
Print (lith) 44 x 59 cm 1" to 100 ft
Shows a subdivision from Parliament St west to McMahon St and from Nassau St to East St; also lots on Gloucester and Wellesley sts; related to Toronto 63 (R.P. 198) of Apr 1857 (**B2552**).
OTUTF

2129 *1857*
PLAN / of / BUILDING LOTS ON PARLIAMENT AND WINCHESTER STREETS. / THE PROPERTY OF JOHN O'DONOGHOE ESQR / TORONTO / 1857./[Sgd in facsimile] John Tully Architect & P.L.S. King Street east Toronto September 3rd 1857.
Print (lith) 48 x 68 cm 1" to 25 ft
Shows lot sizes and dimensions; see also **B2567**.
Toronto 63 (R.P. D 62)

2130 *1857*
Plan of Building Lots / ON / YONGE STREET AT YORKVILLE, / NEAR ROSE PARK TORONTO. / THE PROPERTY OF / MESSRS J. BUGG AND R. ROBINSON. / 1857 / LITHOGRAPHED BY J. ELLIS KING ST TORONTO / [Sgd in facsimile]

John Tully / Architect & P.L.S. / King Street (east) Toronto / April 16th 1857
Print (lith) 60 x 51 cm 1" to 40 ft
Shows lots along Grimsby and Price sts east of Yonge St; names of owners of large lots adjoining; see also **B2553**.
Toronto 63 (R.P. 208)

2131 *1857*
PLAN / OF THE / CITY OF TORONTO / CANADA WEST / 1857 // PUBLISHED BY FLEMING RIDOUT & SCHREIBER / LITHOGRAPHED BY J. ELLIS 8 KING ST. TORONTO C.W.
Print (lith) 83 x 142 cm 1" to 396 ft
Shows the city from the waterfront to Bloor St and from Don R to Dufferin St; streets named and the built-up or subdivided area shown by hatched lines; a small sketch map shows three 'zones' for carts and cabs with tariff for hauling materials and people; major bldgs located and named; wharves identified; wards; table of fire-alarm system; OOAMA (NMC 11961) copy has parts missing; a prospectus issued on 17 Jan 1857 describes the plan as completed and to be published immediately for subscribers (OTAR MU 1052 env 70); (Holmden 2736).
OOAMA (NMC 11961) OTMCL

2132 *[1857?]*
SUBDIVISION / OF PART OF THE / GIVENS ESTATE / CITY OF TORONTO / UNWIN & JACK / Provincial Land Surveyors / Provincial Chambers / TORONTO. // Maclear & Co. Lith. Toronto.
Print (lith) 88 x 56 cm 1" to 150 ft
Inset: 'SKETCH SHEWING THE ADMIRABLE SITUATION OF THE PROPERTY / in the / CITY OF TORONTO' 1" to 25 chains; shows a subdivision from Dundas St to Bloor St and from Denison St east to Shaw St; inset shows streets, railways, and names of estates in the west half of the city; also shows the 'new University' and University College; plan probably made in 1857 but R.P. D 29 of May 1857 (**B2558**) only registered the lots south of Harrison St, and subdivision shown on 1858 map (**2133**) but not shown on 1862 plan (**2139**); Unwin & Jack advertised their partnership from Oct 1856 to about May 1858 in the *Daily Colonist* (Toronto).
OTAR

2133 *[1858]*
[Atlas of Toronto] [Imprint on most sheets]: Surveyed & Compiled by W.S. & H.C. Boulton Toronto. / Lithographed & Published by Jno Ellis 8, King Street.
30 or 31 prints (col liths) Ea approx 100 x 70 cm 1" to 100 ft
OTAR and OOAMA copies also include on separate sheet 'INDEX / Map of the / CITY OF TORONTO' (32 x 62 cm); covers the area from the waterfront to Bloor St and from Don R to Dufferin St; streets named and all bldgs shown; explanation keys first-class brick and stone houses, second-class brick and stone ... and brick houses covered with wood, all shown in red, three classes of frame house shown in grey; key to fire alarm by wards; location of fire hydrants; relief; sheets numbered I–XXX and sheets VIII, XVII, XVIII, XIX lack imprints; W.S. Boulton asked the City Council for patronage for the 'atlas' early in 1858 (City of Toronto Council meetings, Minutes, 22 Feb 1858 (OTCTAR)); W.S. Boulton described the work proposed and called for further information in *Daily Colonist* (Toronto) 8 March 1858; Messrs Boulton & Ellis received a diploma for the work at the Upper Canada Provincial Exhibition 1858–9 (*Transactions of the Board of Agriculture* III (1858–9): 197; (*OHIM* 7.62).
OOAMA OTAR OTMCL

2134 *[1858]*
Map of the / CITY OF TORONTO. / Canada West / LITHOGRAPHED BY J. ELLIS, TORONTO.
Print (lith) 32 x 57 cm Scale not given
In G.P. Ure, *The Hand-book of Toronto* (Toronto: Lovell and Gibson 1858), frontis (*Bib Can* 3868); shows the city from the harbour to Bloor St and from the Don R to the Lunatic Asylum; vignettes of 24 bldgs as described in preface; 'The beautiful map of the City ... has been engraved by Mr Ellis, engraver expressly for this work and it contains a feature never before displayed in any Canadian map, that of giving a microscopic representation of public bldgs upon sites which they respectively occupy. This has of course considerably increased the expense of the work but it has also enhanced its value' (p iv).
OTCTAR (518) OTMCL

2135 *[1858?]*
PLAN OF THE CITY OF TORONTO / Published by / James Bain 37 King St. East / Drawn by Chas Unwin P.L. Surveyor York Chambs. / Maclear & Co Liths Toronto.
Print (lith) 50 x 64 cm Scale not given
Some copies folding into cover with title: 'Plan of Toronto J. Bain King Street East'; shows the city from the waterfront to Bloor St and from Don R to Dufferin St; major bldgs named and indexed; built-up or subdivided area indicated by hatched lines; wards named; fire-alarm system; shows University College, and 'Site of New Jail & Industrial Farm' on Elm St (construction began in 1858 (Arthur, 3rd ed (1986), 146)); Provincial Exhibition bldgs and Lunatic Asylum; Union Railway Station; Bain was at this King St address between 1857 and 1859; (Hulse, 10).
OOAMA OTAR OTCTAR (200) OTMCL OTNR (SR 5398) OTUTF

2136 *[1859?]*
PLAN OF WATER LOTS IN THE CITY OF TORONTO. / Rordans and Carter, Law Stationers & Lithographers Toronto
Print (lith) 20 x 54 cm Scale not given
Shows area from 'The Old Fort' to the Don Station at Beachell St, and from Wellington and Palace sts to the waterfront; major bldgs named and owners of wharves and bldgs named; Ontario Simcoe & Huron Railway, GTR, GWR, Union Railway Station; part of the same base as **2135** with ward names moved.
OTMCL

2137 *[1860]*
TORONTO. / CANADA WEST. / Waterlow & Sons, Lith. London
Print (lith) 40 x 69 cm 1" to 12 chains
In *Report ... of Mr Thomas E. Blackwell ... of the Grand Trunk Railway Company of Canada for ... 1859* (London: Waterlow & Sons 1860) (*Bib Can* 3906); shows the city from the waterfront to Bloor St and from the Don R to Dufferin St; major built-up or subdivided areas shown by hatched lines; major bldgs shown and identified; Union Station and GTR line, freight depot, and lands shown; also shows Ontario Simcoe & Huron Railway and depot grounds, and Hamilton and Toronto or GWR.
OOAMA (NMC 22852) OTMCL

2138 *1862*
Plan of Rusholme The Property of G.T. Denison Esq. City of Toronto. [Sgd] Toronto May 1862 Unwin & Miles P.L. Surveyors
Col ms 66 x 41 cm 1" to 3 chains
Shows the area west of Dovercourt Rd between Bloor and Dundas sts; shows the house and grounds attached, and various other bldgs; additional subdivision shown in pencil in the south part.
OTMCL (Denison Papers)

2139 *1862*
PLAN / OF / THE CITY OF / TORONTO / showing / THE GOVERNMENT SURVEY and the / Registered SUBDIVISION into LOTS according to / Plans filed in the Office of the City Registrar / Compiled and drawn from surveys made expressly for the purpose by / H.J. BROWNE / under the direction of / J.O. BROWNE / CIVIL ENGINEER AND P.L. SURVEYOR. / 1862 // FULLER & BENCKE LITH. TORONTO. // Published by J.O. & H.J. Browne at 17 Masonic Hall Toronto. Printed by Fuller & Bencke Victoria Hall Toronto. 'Entered according to Act of the Provincial Legislature in the Year 1861 ... in the Office of the Registrar of the Province of Canada.'
Print (lith) 92 x 169 cm 1" to 330 ft
An important reference map showing the city from the waterfront to Bloor St and from the Don R to Dufferin St; 'Explanation' keys boundaries of wards, park lots, public bldgs, residences and offices, registered plan nos and lot nos; major bldgs named; relief, estates with landscaping; proposed streets; names of wharves; note sgd by registrar indicating all subdivisions copied from registered plans.
OOAMA (NMC 16921) OTAR OTMCL

2140 *1862*
Sketch of Toronto Harbour showing the Entrance Channels, soundings position of the Batteries etc. 1862. [Sgd] H.F. Turner Lt. R.E. del. 19/7/62. C.D. Robertson Lt. Col. D.C.R.E. 29.10.62 J.P. Maguay Cap. R.E. 26/6/66
Col ms 28 x 45 cm 4" to 1 mile Watermark: 'J WHATMAN 1854'
Shows the waterfront and island, lines of fire from fort and gun emplacements, new channel between island and mainland on east with note that it is continually changing, soundings, parts 'washed away in last 5 years.'
OOAMA (NMC 4477)

2141 *1864*
Plan of Lots Numbers 35, 36 & 37 First Con. Township of York. Feby 1864.
Col ms 65 x 53 cm 1" to 4 chains
Provenance: City of Toronto Parks department; shows area that later became High Park; relief by shading, ravines, Grenadiers pond; shows John Howard's land, Colborne Lodge, and farm on lot 37; lot 38 owned by John Ellis; lot 35 subdivided into large lots with notes on price per acre; names of owners and other bldgs shown including the Cheney Estate. There is also in OTCTAR a copy of a similar plan without date 'by J.G. Howard Esqr P.L. Surv' with endorsement 'This Plan belongs to John Ellis Swansea P.O.'
OTCTAR

2142 *1866*
CITY OF TORONTO / COMPILED FROM SURVEYS / made to the present date / 1866. / Lithographed, Printed & Published by W.C. Chewett & Co. 17 & 19 King St. East, Toronto.
Print (lith) 46 x 81 cm 1" to 12 chains
Shows the city from harbour to Bloor St, and between the Don R and Dufferin St; streets named and indexed; major bldgs identified; notes on numbering of houses and lots, and fire-alarm bells; wooded areas and ravines shown.
OOAMA (NMC 25145) OTMCL

2143 *1867*
Plan of Part of Toronto Shewing the Sites of the Several Barracks, Offices &c. [Sgd] F.C. Hassard Lt. Col. C Rl Eng. 1st Mil Dist. 4th Decr 1867.
Col ms 59 x 171 cm Approx 1" to 260 ft
Endorsements: '581–101' '933'
Inset: 'Plan of Crystal Palace'; shows the ordnance reserve east to Yonge St, south of Queen St; index to ordnance bldgs and construction materials;

shows drains and water-pipes in ordnance reserve area, and other major bldgs in area.
OOAMA (NMC 43219)

TRAVERSTON

2144 *1856*
MAP / OF / WAVERLEY / TOWNSHIP OF GLENELG COUNTY OF GREY / As surveyed for / MESSRS SCHOFIELD & COLLIER / by / Henry Strange P.L.S. / December 1856. / Maclear & Co. Lith Toronto.
Print (lith) 69 x 43 cm 1" to 3 chains
Shows the layout of a village on lots 9–10, con 9, Glenelg Twp; from South St to North St, and Milton St to East St; town lots are shown to south of the Rocky Saugeen R and majority are shown as sold; shows names in many lots, mills, factories, and Mr T. Collier's house.
OTAR

TRENTON

2145 *1832*
PLAN / of the / MOUTH of the TRENT / Shewing the Situation / for the / Proposed Bridge / by N.H. Baird Civil Engineer / M.I.C.E.L. 26th October 1832. // Tazewell Lith: / Canadian Stone // Survr. General's Office York.
Print (lith) 34 x 39 cm 1" to 100 ft
Shows the bridge upstream with piers and measurements, and 'breakwater (in middle) if ice should allow'; on west side of river shows old wharf, inn, ferry, Mr Robinson's store and a few other bdlgs, wharf, and pier; on east side shows wharf and pier and road to Kingston and Marmora.
OTAR

2146 *1834*
Diagram of a Town Plot, near the mouth of the River Trent called the Town of Trent port Situated on Lot No Two, in the First Concession of The Township of Murray. Surveyed May 1834 by Frederick Preston Rubidge D.P.S. F.P. Rubidge D.P.S. Cobourg 1834.
Ms 65 x 93 cm 1" to 1 1/2 chains Endorsements: 'No 48'
(SI 12 Apr 1834 to survey and lay out town plot at the mouth of the Trent R; OTNR FN 295 5 June 1834); shows the town plot laid out from Dundas St to Pinnacle St, and Front St to Rear St, fronting on the river but set back from the shore; intended road to wharves and new bridge shown; bridge has been built further downstream by old wharves and not as shown on **2145**; some bldgs and paths shown cutting across new street grid; later additions and names to the 1860s; also a copy: 'Trent. Situated on Lot No Two ... Copy J.G.C. Surveyor Genls Office 9th Augt 1834' endorsed 'A 63' and '680' and with some lots and streets pencilled in between Front St and the water (OTNR (SR 367); also a copy: 'Trent-Port. Copy [Sgd] J.G.Chewitt S.G. Office 1st June 1837. Surveyor General's Office Toronto 12th June 1837 W. Macaulay Surv Genl' with a few added notes and names and lots deeded to the Catholic Church and the Church of England (OTAR).
OTAR OTNR (SR 367–8)

2147 *1852*
Plan of the proposed incorporation of the Village of Trenton by River Trent 10 May 1852 (Signed) J.S. Peterson P.L.S. [Sgd] John Rolph Crown Land Department Quebec 20th September 1852 Certified a true Copy T.D.
Col ms 34 x 40 cm Approx 1" to 10 chains
With a petition of the inhabitants requesting incorporation of the village, which was approved 23 Sept 1852 (OOA RG 5 C1/366 no 1489 1852); shows the proposed boundary of the town and survey grid only to include all of broken front Block A in 1st con, Sidney, south half of lots 1 and 2, 1st con, Murray, on the east side of the river, and lots 1 and 2, 1st con, Murray, west side of the river; note indicates that Trentport and Annewood to be named Trenton.
OOAMA (NMC 4495)

TROWBRIDGE

2148 *1856*
Plan of the town of Toubridge Composed of lots 6 & 7, 2 & 3 Cons in the Township of Elma County of Perth [Sgd] Crown Lands Department Toronto Sepr 1856 signed Joseph Cauchon C C L Joseph Kirk Prov Land Surv
Col ms 98 x 64 cm 1" to 4 chains
'Projected plan' possibly issued with the first set of instructions 31 May 1856; shows a few streets laid out but only West St and North St named; proposed market-place; burying ground crossed out; mill pond, sawmill, and a few other bldgs; signature is in pencil.
OTAR

Related maps

(2) *1857*
Map of the Town of Toubridge in the Township of Elma. Surveyed by Joseph Kirk Prov. Land Surveyor Feby 6th 1857
Col ms 89 x 55 cm 1" to 4 chains Endorsements: 'A 213'
Inset: 'Plan shewing the quantity of land overflowed by mill dam in Lots No 8 in the 2nd Con. and Lots 15 and 16 in the 1st Con.' 1" to 6 chains; (SI 6 Sept 1856 to subdivide town and park lots and mill sites; OTNR FN 1824 6 Feb 1857); shows the actual survey of the town with streets named from South St to North St, and East St to West St; proposed market square and proposed

burial ground; shows clearings and some bldgs and mill reserve on the Maitland R; the Stratford-Saugeen Railroad line cutting diagonally through the town was added later; also a copy: 'Toubridge in the Township of Elma Copy of PLS Kirk's plan of Survey. Crown Lands Department Toronto 27th May 1857 [Sgd] E.P. Taché Commr Crown Lands' endorsed 'No 128' and with an excerpt from a newspaper appended '20th August 1857 notice that undermentioned village and park lots to be offered for sale by Auction 24th Sept next' (OTAR(P)); also a copy: 'Toubridge. Crown Lands Department Toronto 6th June 1857 [Sgd] E.P. Taché Acting Commissioner of Crown Lands' (OTNR (SR 6505)).
OTAR(P) OTNR (SR 369; 6505)

TULLAMORE

2149 *1856*
PLAN / OF BUILDING LOTS / IN THE / VILLAGE OF TULLAMORE / The Property of / I.M. CHAFEE ESQ. / Surveyed by / MESSRS. BRISTOW AND FITZGERALD PROVINCIAL LAND SURVEYORS &c. / BRAMPTON NOV 20th 1856. / Maclear & Co. Lith. Toronto.
Print (lith) 57 x 83 cm 1" to 66 ft
Shows a subdivision of part of lot 17, VIIIth con, gore of Toronto, and part of lot 17, VI con, east of Hurontario St in Chinguacousy Twp; King St and King William St shown with some bldgs and names of owners; the printed version of R.P. CH-4 (**B2643–4**).
Peel 43 (TOR G-2)

(TUSCARORA town plot)

2150 *1843*
Diagram Showing the Indian improvements on the River lots at Tuscarora June 1843
Col ms 36 x 46 cm 1" to 10 chains Endorsements: '1670'; stamp 'IASR'
Shows cleared areas with number of acres, boundaries and names of Indians on lots 48–62; proposed village reserve of 90 acres is shown across lot 49–51; road, council house, and church.
OOAMA (NMC 4513)

2151 *1844*
Sketch of the Town Plot at Tuscarora. Surveyor General's Office Kingston 17th April 1844 [Sgd] Thomas Parke Survr Genl
Col ms 37 x 55 cm 1" to 4 chains Endorsements: 'Q75' '1103'
Shows the boundary of the town plot on the Grand R with road and towing path.
OTNR (SR 372)

Related maps

(**2**) *1844*
Tuscarora Village Surveyed by [Sgd] James Kirkpatrick D.P.Surveyor West Flamboro October 15th 1844
Col ms 40 x 30 cm 1" to 4 chains Endorsements: 'Q 72' '1102'
(SI 5 Aug 1844 to subdivide Tuscarora town plot into lots and park lots; OTNR FN 800 18 Oct 1844); shows the actual survey for the village with streets laid out from William St to Edward St and from John St to David St; park lots north of Henry St, which is the through road from Brantford to Dunnville; school, church, and a few other bldgs; also a copy: 'Tuscarora. Surveyed by James Kirkpatrick D.P.S. 1844. Surveyor General's Office Montreal 9th Novr 1844. A true copy' endorsed '1100' (OTNR (SR 86707)); and another copy with the same title but dated '12th Nov. 1844 Office copy' (OTNR (SR 370)).
OTNR (SR 370–1; 86707)

2152 *1845*
Town Plot of Tuscarora Exhibiting the boundaries of the clearances of the different claimants [Sgd] James Kirkpatrick P.D. Surveyor July 1845
Col ms 47 x 34 cm 1" to 4 chains Endorsements: '1678'; stamp 'IASR'
Shows the town plot with church, school, commons, a few bldgs, and names of occupants; boundaries of six clearances shown cutting across the town.
OOAMA (NMC 4498)

(VAIL POINT town plot)

2153 *1862*
Track Survey of Government Reserves at Vail's Point in the townships of St Vincent and Sydenham County of Grey. and diagram of proposed subdivision. [Sgd] Wm Gibbard P.L.S. Colld Jany 1862.
Col ms on linen 50 x 57 cm 1" to 4 chains
A survey and projection for the town with a few streets laid out but in a different orientation to final survey (2); some lines have been corrected on this plan; triangulation lines from lots 40–1 north to the point and location of reserves; reserves for fishing stations; proposed wharf; houses and some names of owners.
OTNR (SR 86712)

Related maps

(**2**) *1862*
Vails-Point Plan of subdivision of part of lot 41. XII concession St Vincent and Lot 1 Broken Front Concession Sydenham. [Sgd] Wm Gibbard P.L.S. March & April 1862. Examined by Mr. Bridgland
Col ms 47 x 72 cm 1" to 4 chains Endorsements: 'No 1'
(SI 15 Feb 1862 to subdivide into town and park lots; OTNR FN 1842 26 Apr 1862); shows the final survey of the town from Lysons St to Water St, and between Wharf and Galt St, also Cromarta St and lots to the west along harbour; site for wharf,

reserves, and small-boat harbour shown; some soundings and bldgs shown; also a copy: 'Plan of Vail Point Department of Crown Lands Quebec March 24th 1864 [Sgd] Andrew Russell Asst Commissioner' (OTAR(P)); town plot no longer appears on the co atlas (Belden, ... *Grey* (1880)).
OTAR(P) OTNR (SR 373)

WALKERTON

2154 *[1857]*
Village Plot / OF / WALKERTON / Between Lots 25 & 32 in 1st Concession North & South of / Durham Road / BRANT / Property of J & W. Walker. / Maclear & Co. Lith Toronto. / David Gibson P.L.S.
Print (lith) 61 x 51 cm 1" to 4 chains
Shows the village laid out north and south of the Durham Rd from South St to Saugeen R, and north of river from Silver Creek and sideline to Durham Rd, and east to Robinson St; note on dimensions and sizes of lots; some bldgs including hotel, post office, and mills; related to R.P. 7 (**B2690**).
OOAMA (NMC 22869) OTAR OW

WALTERS FALLS

2155 *1857*
Plan of Town Lots adjoining the village of Walters Falls Township of Holland County of Grey John Hewlett Esq. Proprietor Surveyed by Archd McNab P.L.S. April 16th 1857 [Certified by surveyor and sgd] Archd McNab P.L.S.
Col ms 50 x 71 cm 1" to 2 chains
Shows the village laid out on part of lot 3, con 12, Holland Twp; from side-road between lots 3 and 4 north to Owen Sound St, and Head R west to James St; market square; park lot and Walter's property shown to the north.
OTNR (SR 86711)

WARWICK

2156 *1836*
Plan of the Town Plot in Warwick in the Western District. Surveyed by Order from the Surveyor General's Office bearing date Toronto 28th July 1836. By [Sgd] Peter Carroll D.P. Surveyor Oxford 14th Sept 1836. To John Radenhurst Esquire Actg Surveyor General &c &c &c Toronto.
Col ms 67 x 46 cm 1" to 4 chains Endorsements: 'A 64' '757'
(SI 28 July 1836 to survey the town plot on lot 10, 1st con, south of Egremont Rd, twp of Warwick); shows the town from William St to Egremont Rd, and Park St to Camden St; Guy Square; school reserve and church; Plank Rd to Port Sarnia; park lots on the south side; also a copy: 'Town of Warwick in the Western District. Copy J.G.C.' endorsed 'No 50' and with the addition of notes about lots and patents to 1850 (OTAR(P)); and a later copy: 'Town of Warwick in the Western District. Copied by J. Innes' with watermark: 'J WHATMAN TURKEY MILL 1855' (OTNR (SR 86706)).
OTAR(P) OTNR (SR 378, 86706)

WATERDOWN

2157 *1856*
Plan of Village Lots in Waterdown being composed of portions of Lots 5, 6, 13 & the whole of 14 lying on the north side of John Street and on the easterly side of Main Street as shown on the Plan of Waterdown by Henry Winter P.L.S. Surveyed by J Mackintosh P.L. Surveyor Oct 1856
Ms 36 x 36 cm 1" to 1 chain
Provenance: Wentworth County Court House plan 34 book 2; a subdivision plan certified by the owner Moses Kelly, 8 Dec 1860, and registered 8 Dec 1860, but not in Wentworth 62; plan referred to in title is probably R.P. 'Old 47' of 26 Aug 1854 (**B2726**).
OHMA

WATERLOO

2158 *1855*
MAP / OF THE VILLAGE OF / WATERLOO / AND PART OF THE TOWN OF BERLIN / LAID OUT FOR / JOHN HOFFMAN ESQUIRE / BY / M.C. SCHOFIELD, P.L.S. / 1855. / Maclear & Co. Lith. Toronto
Print (lith) 63 x 67 cm 1" to 4 chains
Extends south and east of Hoffman survey from Hannah St south and Waterloo St, and north of Erb St to Church and Elgin sts, Water, King, and Queen sts; all bldgs shown including J. Hoffman's residence, GTR station, mills, mill pond Waterloo Nursery; Mount Hope Cemetery; photoreproduction in OOAMA (NMC 4517) with ms adds 'Extra Notice Please Return this map to M.C.Schofield as soon as possible who is required to refer to it quite often Berlin 9th June 1864.'
OKITD

2159 *1855*
PLAN / OF / John Hoffman's Survey / OF PARTS OF LOTS NUMBERS 14 AND 15 / IN / WATERLOO C.W. / 1855.
Print (lith) Size not known 1" to 6 chains
Shows a subdivision from mill pond and Erb St to Green St, and Queen St and Mary St to Caroline and Park sts; shows cemetery, mill square, public square, a few names of owners; based on R.P. 385 (**B2729**); photoreproduction in OOAMA (NMC 4516).
Original not located

(WAUBUNO)

2160 *1855*
PLAN OF THE TOWN / OF / WAUBUNO, / SITUATE IN THE TOWNSHIP OF DORCHESTER IN THE COUNTY / OF / MIDDLESEX, / BEING COMPOSED OF LOTS 2 & 3 / IN THE 3D CONN / NORTH SIDE OF THE RIVER THAMES. / The property of / T.G. RIDOUT ESQR / Laid out by W. McCLARY ESQR P.L.S. & C.E. / 1855. // ARCHD BARR, ENGRAVER & LITHOGRAPHER, TORONTO
Print (lith) hand col 76 x 58 cm 1" to 200 ft
Printed inset pasted on bottom right corner: 'Map / SHEWING THE / TOWN OF WAUBUNO.' 1" to 200 chains; shows a town plot between the Thames R and Creek with mill site at the top; grist mill; GWR station bldgs and line; market ground; site of ancient Indian village in southeast; shown on the co map (see **997**) but no longer shown on the co atlas (Page, ... *Middlesex* (1878)); see also **B2749**.
Middlesex 33 (R.P. 128)

WEST MONKTON

2161 *1857*
PLAN OF THE TOWN PLOT / OF / WESTMONCTON / in the Township of Elma on Lot No 16 in the XVIII Con. County of Perth. / As surveyed for / E. WINSTANLEY Esq. / by KERTLAND AND GILKISON. / C.E. & P.L.S. / H. Gregory Lith. Hamilton
Print (col lith) 69 x 51 cm 1" to 2 chains
Shows the town laid out from Madison St to Queen St and from Winstanley St to Yonge St; mills and a few businesses shown; Market Square; see also **B2774**.
Perth 44 (R.P. 272)

WHITBY

2162 *1835*
Plan of / Big Bay Harbour / Surveyed by order of His Excellency / Sir John Colborne K.G.B. / Lieutenant Governor / &c. &c. &c. / Toronto 16 March 1835, / [Signature in facsimile] J.G. Chewitt / Hugh Richardson // Lithographed / for / Parliament / of U. Canada. / 1835. / Tazewell, Lithr. / Toronto.
Print (lith) 69 x 50 cm 1" to 88 yds
Shows a town plot of six streets east-west and five streets north-south and a few bldgs, marshy areas, nature of shoreline, soundings; two wharves and a long pier or breakwater shown; a railway is shown from Mr Walsh's bldg to shore across the marsh.
OTAR

2163 *1838*
Windsor Harbour. Lake Ontario. F.P. Rubidge Delt from Survey by J.J. Dennehy D.P.S. Cobourg 1837. Soundings by N.H. Baird Civil Eng. To The Commissioners for the Improvement of Windsor Harbour by [Sgd] N.H.Baird Civil Engineer M. I.C.E.L. 13th Jany 1838
Col ms 90 x 96 cm 1" to 3 chains
Various proposals are described for piers in the harbour and note about first and second estimates; the town is laid out only on the east side from Front St north to first con rd, and John St west three streets to Colborne St; some bldgs shown and owners identified; distillery, brewery, warehouses, etc; (Holmden 2896).
OOAMA (NMC 17899)

2164 *1843*
Windsor Harbour as constructed by the Board of Works in 1843. Office of the Board of Works
Col ms 81 x 58 cm 1" to 3 chains Endorsements: stamp '59'
With 'A Series of Diagrams, Plans, Elevations ... Illustrative of the Various Local Public Improvements ... Completed by the Provincial Board of Works ... Samuel Keefer Engr 1844' (OOA RG 11M 85603/40 no 26); shows the same layout for town as in 1838 map (**2163**); a causeway 'made from deposit of dredging machine' is extension of Richmond St to warehouse at end of point of land to meet eastern pier; east and west breakwaters and piers, lighthouse; (*OHIM* 7.9).
OOAMA (NMC 16959)

Related maps

(2) *1843–4*
Plan of the Town and Harbour of Windsor in the Home District Drawn By John Shier 1843 Soundings taken January 1844 By John McIntyre Supert
Col ms 76 x 60 cm 1" to 200 ft Endorsements: stamps 'BW' '618'
Shows the bldgs and streets of town close to water and around railway; shows the same layout for piers, etc, as 1843 map but a dotted line suggests inner eastern pier unfinished; notes on engineering work to be done in connection with breakwaters and piers to be built; (Holmden 2895).
OOAMA (NMC 22880)

2165 *[ca 1848]*
Town and Harbour of Windsor
Col ms 39 x 64 cm 1" to 4 chains
Endorsed on back: 'Sketch of Water Lots Windsor Harbour'; shows lots being developed by the eastern breakwater and lots requested by J. Welsh and C. Lynde; shows streets north to King St and from John St to Colborne St; roads proposed to be made by Mr Perry; a note on a later map (**2171**) indicates Lynde was refused a lot and Welsh granted small lots in 1847–8; (Holmden 2894).
OOAMA (NMC 4523)

2166 *[1849?]*
Plan of a portion of Windsor Harbour Shewing the Position of the Forwarding Establishment of James Rowe & Co.
Ms 26 x 33 cm 1" to 1 1/2 chains Endorsements: stamps 'BW' '617'
Shows water lots, warehouses, bridge to pier, and proposed slip; 'platforms built by P. Perry for piling lumber' and Perry's new warehouse built in 1849 as noted on later map below (**2171**); there is also a plan of 26 Feb 1848 showing land owned by Welsh Rowe & Watson at 'Port Whitby' in OTAR; also a 'Plan of the town and Harbour of Windsor in the Home District 1843' 1" to 200 ft, in the Baird Papers at OTAR (MS 393 B-2-b reel 6) with notes about work in progress on the harbour.
OOAMA (NMC 4521) OTAR OTAR (MS 393 B-2-b reel 6)

2167 *[ca 1853]*
'WINDSOR HARBOUR'
Print (lith) 115 x 47 cm 1" to 4 chains
Title from name on the map; shows the streets laid out from Colborne St to John St south of King St, and lots to the north along William St and Plank Rd; north of this is jail and court-house and Perry's Corners; the harbour is shown as of the 1844 construction plans but part of eastern pier not shown; probably not made before 1853 when work on the co court-house began; possibly unfinished as a proper title and imprint are lacking and few names are shown on the map; (*OHIM* 7.8).
OTAR OTUTF

2168 *1854*
PLAN / OF / TOWN AND PARK LOTS / Laid out on Lots Nos 29 and 30, in the 2nd Concession of the / TOWNSHIP OF WHITBY / OCTOBER 1854. / Maclear & Co. Lith Toronto / John Shier P.L.S. / Whitby
Print (lith) 77 x 46 cm 1" to 4 chains
Shows a subdivision in the northern area of the town from Dundas St north to road allowance between cons 2 and 3, and from D'Hillier St to Cochrane St; mill pond; see also **B2783**.
Durham 40 (R.P. H-50045)

2169 *1855*
PLAN / OF PART OF THE / TOWN OF WHITBY, / LAID OUT ON THE SOUTH EAST QUARTER, / OF LOT No 27 IN THE 1ST CONCESSION, / OF THE / TOWNSHIP OF WHITBY. [Sgd in facsimile] John Shier P.L. Surveyor Whitby May 26th 1855
Print (lith), pt trimmed Approx 53 x 25 cm 1" to 3 chains
The printed version of R.P. H-50047 (**B2860**) showing lots from King St to Third St and Brock St, Plank Rd to Centre St; 'N.B. Those lots marked X previously sold'; part of this subdivision appears to be shown on the [ca 1853] plan above (**2167**); the imprint may have been cut off; see **B2785–6**.
Durham 40 (no R.P. number)

2170 *[1856]*
PLAN / of the / WHITBY STATION / Grand Trunk Railway / OF / CANADA / Dennis & Boulton Surveyors / Maclear & Co. Lith. Toronto.
Print (lith) 57 x 78 cm 1" to 100 ft
Inset: 'Sketch shewing / the / GENERAL POSITION / of the / PROPERTY'; a subdivision plan of area from King St to Watson St, and John St to Whitby St; bldgs are shown; notice pasted on: 'This Desirable Property will be sold by auction on the ground on Monday 10th November next ...'; based on R.P. H-50036 of 10 Nov 1856 (**B2795**).
OTAR

2171 *1865*
Plan of Whitby Harbour Formerly called Windsor Harbour Quebec 23rd May 1865 G.F. Baillairgé.
Col ms 98 x 60 cm 1" to 5 chains Endorsements: stamp [BW] '633'
Shows the town from Front St to King St, and east to John and Henry sts; Richmond St is extended south as causeway and streets are laid out on the east end and on Water St along the water; various water lots and names and dates of owners given; shows inner or eastern pier built from end of causeway to east breakwater; listing with dates for work done in the harbour since the 1840s; there is also a small, untitled plan endorsed 'BW 588' showing the Rowe warehouse and water lots, probably made in the early 1860s (OOAMA (NMC 4522)).
OOAMA (NMC 43238; 4522)

WIARTON

2172 *1855*
Plan of the town Plot of Wiarton [Sgd] C Rankin 1855
Col ms 89 x 91 cm 1" to 6 chains
Provenance: OOAMA RG 10M 76703/9 no 193; shows the town laid out between line between cons XXI and XXII to line between cons XXIII and XXIV and from the bay and Lions St west to park lots beyond Dawson St; later additions of file nos in lots; relief; Rankin's field notes are in OTNR (FN 1762 22 May 1856).
OOAMA (NMC 13014)

Related maps

(2) *[185?]*
Plan of the Town Plot of [Wiarton] C.R.
Col ms 75 x 55 cm 1" to 6 chains Watermark: 'J WHATMAN'
Shows streets on south and west side of bay from Dawson to Taylor sts, and Jenny to Mary sts; lots numbered; Indian reserve.
OTMCL (E.W. Banting Collection)

WIDDER

2173 *1855*
MAP OF THE TOWN OF WIDDER, / FORMERLY PINEHILL / IN THE TOWNSHIP OF BOSANQUET. / SURVEYED BY S. PETERS P.L.S. / 1855. // Maclear & Co. Lith. Toronto
Print (lith) 71 x 57 cm 1" to 2 chains
Inset: [location map]; shows the town laid out from Blyth St to Henry St, and Bosanquet St to Whitby St; relief by hachures along shore of Ausable R; bldgs located and identified particularly along Frank St; shows blacksmith's shop, barn, shoeshop, tavern, etc; inset shows twps from L Huron to London and the GTR, GWR, and roads; related to R.P. Bosanquet 2 (**B2804**).
OOAMA (NMC 43359)

WILLIAMSFORD

2174 *1859*
Plan of the village plot of Williamsford as laid out on Lots 18 & 19, 1st Concession of Holland and Lot 19, 1st Concession of Sullivan County of Grey. February 15th 1859 Rankin & Spry P.L.S.'s
Col ms 51 x 76 cm 1" to 4 chains Endorsements: 'No 33' 'No 2'
(SI 2 Dec 1858 to C. Rankin to subdivide into town and park lots; OTNR FN 1873 21 Feb 1859); shows town laid out from South St to Orr St, and East St to West St; town lots are on both sides of Garafraxa Rd from Gordon St to Salter St; mill site and mill pond on the north branch of the Saugeen R; clearings with bldgs and names; also a copy: 'Copy of Williamsford Surveyed by Rankin & Spry P.L.Srs 1859. Department of Crown Lands Quebec Augst 7th 1863 [Sgd] Andrew Russell Asst Commissioner' endorsed 'No 34' and with names added (OTAR(P)).
OTAR(P) OTNR (SR 380)

WILLIAMSTOWN

2175 *1813*
Plan and Surv[ey] of the Village of Williamstown North and South Banks of the River aux [Raisins] Charlottenburgh County of Glengarry Eastern District being part of the [Estate of the] Honble Sir John Johnson Surveyed and allotted and laid out into Town Lots [agreeable to] the Annexd Plan Surveyed [illegible] thereof Deputy Provincial Surveyor Williamstown 20th May 1813 [Sgd] Jeremiah McCarthy
Col ms 80 x 61 cm 1" to 2 toises? Endorsements: 'No 31' 'The Fair Place of Williamstown Containing 12 Acres'
Shows William St with lots on the south side of the river, and John and Warren sts on the north side; church and Church St and other bldgs on the north and east side; shows Sir John Johnson's land, Alexander Mackenzie's land, and another estate; list of lot nos and names of lessees; photoreproduction also in OOAMA (NMC 26878).
OOAMA

2176 *1831*
A Plan of Williamstown and Domain By [Sgd] Jno McGillis Apr 1831
Col ms 129 x 73 cm 1" to 2 chains
Shows area from Church St to Bethune St, and St Mary's St to Warren St; shows the same street layout as 1813 plan (**2175**) but all bldgs shown; shows two mills and mill races, cleared and wooded land, and two fields, 'Domain of H. McGillis Esqr,' and fairground.
OOAMA (NMC 11769)

(WINDHAM town plot)

2177 *[1799]*
Plan of a Village or intended Settlement of the French Royalists, beginning at No 51 Yonge Street and extending up the same to No 63 Containing in all 84 Lots of about 50 acres each – Copy W.C.
Col ms 75 x 39 cm 1" to 20 chains Endorsements: '752' 'Windham, a Village on Yonge Street, settled by the French Royalists under Comte de Puisaye.'
(SI to A. Jones 2 Dec 1798 to survey 1000 acres for town of Windham and common around it for the Comte de Puisaye and trace line from nearest con on Yonge St to it); shows a subdivision into long lots numbered 1–40 and 1–44 on both sides of Yonge St; relief, rivers, two lakes; the plan is in two parts pasted together with the top apparently a projection for the layout and the bottom the proper survey.
OTNR (SR 383)

WINDSOR

2178 *1797*
The above is a plan of the late purchase called the Huron Reserve containing 1078 Acres purchased ... [Sgd] A. Iredell D.S. W.D. July 12th 1797
Col ms 76 x 53 cm 1" to 10 chains
From 'Report on the L[and] from the Church Rec'd from the Sur Genl Office 10th July 1799/ Surveyor Gen Reports accompanied with the Petitions' (OOA RG 1 L3 L no 4 no 65); further notes: 'remaining unpurchased 61 acres – The Town Lots containing one acre each. ... that part of the town coloured red is Mr Hands improved Lands ... Mr. Pajas improvement ... within the dotted line'; shows the triangular town of Sandwich as first laid out from Russell St to Peter St, and Detroit St to South St; marshy areas; windmill; (Holmden 1717); also a similar plan: 'Plan of the late Purchase, called the Huron Reserve Containg [*sic*] 1078 Acres. Copy W.C.' with watermark: 'J WHATMAN' and endorsed 'Q 14' and '1056' (OTNR (SR 2495)).
OOAMA (NMC 22776) OTNR (SR 2495)

2179 *[1798?]*
Project for the Subdivision of Sandwich – Copy W.C. [Sgd] Approved Peter Russell
Col ms 53 x 38 cm 1" to 10 chains Watermark: 'J WHATMAN' Endorsements: 'A 58' '693'
Shows a projection for a considerable enlargement to the original plan; extends three blocks south along the front to End St, and then to Back St, with town lots in the centre and park lots on both sides; other park lots laid out to the east and along Centre Rd; later note about a boundary problem; reserve along shore; some marked points not keyed.
OTNR (SR 298)

Related maps

(2) *1798*
Town of Sandwich The above is a plan of the Town of Sandwich the Part Lot[s] Messrs Pajas and Hands Claims and the Reserve ... [Sgd] A. Iredell D.S. W.D. Chatham August 20th 1798 Exd by Mr. Iredell Plan SGO York 9th July 1800 W.C.
Ms 54 x 43 cm 1" to 10 chains Endorsements: 'No 47'
(SI 9 March 1798 to survey addition to town plot of Sandwich and the park lots); shows the town as projected from Detroit St to End St, and back to Peter and Back sts; reserve 'as yet not purchased from the Indians'; many later names added; also a copy: 'Plan of the Town of Sandwich, the Park Lots, Messrs Pajas and Hand's claims, and the Reserve. Copy W.C.' endorsed 'A 57' and '692' and with dimensions added to park lots (OTNR (SR 299)); also a later copy of Iredell's survey: 'Town of Sandwich. Copied by J. Innes' (OTAR); there is also a plan for reserves for the town of Sandwich in D.W. Smith's 'Report upon Glebes and Commons ... 13th Jany 1802.'
OTAR OTAR(P) OTAR (RG 1 A-II-1 Vol 2 p 942–87) OTNR (SR 299)

2180 *[182?]*
Plan of the Town of Sandwich Enlarged Copy W.C.
Ms 43 x 67 cm 1" to 4 chains Endorsements: 'No 46'
Shows the town essentially as laid out in 1798 with the addition of names and later notes to the 1840s.
OTAR(P)

Related maps

(2) *1837*
Sandwich Copy [Sgd] J.G. Chewitt, Surveyor General's Office Toronto 31st May 1837 J W Macaulay Survr Genl
Col ms 41 x 65 cm 1" to 4 chains
Shows the same layout as 1798 with the addition of later notes about sales and names of owners.
OTAR

2181 *1853*
Plan of part of the Town of Windsor in the Township of Sandwich Canada West Surveyed in 1853 by P.S. Donelly P.L.S.
Col ms 65 x 55 cm 1/2" to 1 chain
A subdivision plan for Windsor proper further upriver than Sandwich; shows area from London St to river, and Ferry St to proposed River St; wharves, etc; notes indicate that this plan is taken from Donnelly's plan of the François Baby estate with list of heirs and lots apportioned (R.P. 120 (**B2818**)).
OWHM

Related maps

(2) *1853*
PLAN / of part of the / TOWN OF WINDSOR / in the / TOWNSHIP OF SANDWICH / CANADA WEST / Surveyed in 1853 by / P.S. Donelly P.L.S. // Lith by R. Bürger, Detroit
Print (lith) 60 x 46 cm 1" to 133 ft
A printed version of plan above except that wharves are not shown.
OWHM

2182 *1853*
PLAN / of part of the / TOWN OF WINDSOR / on the / RIVER DETROIT / being on / Lot No 82 according to Iredell & No. 83 according to McNiff / in the / FIRST CONCESSION TOWNSHIP OF SANDWICH / Subdivided in to Town Lots by / P.S. Donnelly P.L.S.
Print (lith) 72 x 42 cm 1" to 145 ft [i.e., 66 ft]
Inset: [map showing ferry connection from the foot of Goyeau St to Woodward Ave, Detroit] and [profile from docks to Park St]; 'Application to be made to S S Macdonell Windsor Decr 20th 1853'; subdivision is from river to Park St and on both sides of Goyeau St; ravine and outlet of 'Grand Coulee'; notes on advantages of site; based on R.P. 93 of Nov 1853 (**B2822**).
OTAR

2183 *1853*
Plan of the Indian Reserve in the Town of Sandwich as surveyed by Wm McClary P.L.S. under instructions from the Indian Department bearing date Augst 27th 1853. [Sgd] Wm McClary P.L. Surveyor. Exd A.R.
Col ms 55 x 76 cm 1" to 2 chains Endorsements: 'Q 86'
Shows the subdivision of the small reserve at the north end of Sandwich from Huron Church Line to Detroit St; names of owners, bldgs, relief; drawing of Huron church; also a copy: 'Plan of the Indian Reserve ... bearing date Augst 27th 54 [i.e., 1853?] [Sgd] Wm McClary P. Surveyor' but shows Roman Catholic chapel north of Huron Church Line (OLU); and: 'Indian Reserve Town of Sandwich Crown Lands Department Quebec 4 July 1854 [Sgd] A.N. Morin Commr Crown Lands' endorsed 'No 85' (OTAR(P)).
OTAR(P) OTNR (SR 2410) OW

2184 *1854*
PLAN / of the Front part of Lot No 84 First Concession / TOWNSHIP of SANDWICH / COUNTY OF ESSEX Forming part of the / VILLAGE OF WINDSOR SUBDIVIDED BY P.S. DONNELLY P.L.S. / Windsor 1854
Print (lith), trimmed 70 x 62 cm 1" to 176 ft
Shows lots laid out on Windsor Ave from Sandwich St to Barrack Square with park lots north of the square; the same as R.P. 94 (**B2826**).
OWHM

2185 *1855*
MAP OF / part of the / Town of Windsor / COUNTY OF ESSEX / CANADA WEST / INCORPORATED JANUARY 1ST 1854. // S.D. Elwood & Co. Stationers, Detroit / Lith of W. Felt & Co. N.Y. 1855.
Print (lith) Size not known 1" to 400 ft and 1" to 200 ft
Shows streets of part of the town from Aylmer St to beyond Goyeau St; GWR and Depot shown; birdseye view of Detroit; original not seen.
OW

2186 *1855*
PLAN / of part of / LOT No LXXIX in the 1ST CONSN / TOWNSHIP OF / SANDWICH / in the Village of Windsor / According [to a plan of] the Estate of the late Francis Baby Esqre, / drawn [by P.S. Donnelly] Esqre P.L.S. and subdivided into Buil / ding lots by [Leather &?] Robinson for the Trustees, Charles Baby / James Baby and James Dougall Esqre for Alfred Baby Esqre / Septbr 7th 1855 William Ro[binson P.L.S.?] // Lith. by R. Bürger No 91 Macom [Detroit?]
Print (lith), pt missing Approx 43 x 54 cm 1" to 48 ft
A subdivision from Windsor St to lane beyond Church St, and London St to lane beyond Park St; parts missing in title and supplied from R.P. 78 (**B2829**) of the same date, which is probably a transcript of this printed map.
OWHM

2187 *[1856?]*
MAP OF PART OF THE / TOWN / OF / WINDSOR / in the County of Essex, / CANADA / WEST. // Lithographed by J. Ellis Toronto C.W.
Print (lith) 58 x 91 cm 1" to 200 ft
Shows the subdivision of part of the Rankin farm on part of lot 86; lots along Mercer and Victoria sts and on cross street south from Sandwich to Erie sts; shows surrounding streets and railway terminal bldgs, etc; related to Essex 12 (R.P. 122) of 24 May 1856 (**B2832**); describes the subdivision and refers to the benefits of the Reciprocity Treaty [1854]; 'For terms of Sale apply to Arthur Rankin Esq.'
OWHM

2188 *1857*
MAP OF / The / Town of Windsor / COUNTY OF ESSEX / CANADA WEST. / Including all Surveys to Date; Drawn & Reduced by / CHAS. PINNEY ESQ. CIVIL ENGINEER &c. / JUNE 1857. // Maclear & Co. Lith. Toronto.
Print (col lith) and hand col 121 x 81 cm 1" to 300 ft
Shows the town from Detroit R and Sandwich St to Tecumseh Rd, and from Bruce St to Aylmer Ave; northwest and southwest limits of corporation; bldgs and railways shown along shore; some proposed streets and proposed site for a church; three wards have been added in ms in 1865 and coloured by hand (see **2190(2)**).
OTAR OTNR (SR 6678) OW

2189 *[1862?]*
PLAN / OF THE / Property of / James Dougall Esqre / FORMING PART / OF THE / TOWN OF WINDSOR / CANADA WEST / G. Matthews's Litho. Montreal
Print (lith) 59 x 92 cm 1" to 100 ft
Shows a subdivision from Detroit R to Chatham St and Ferry St to Bruce Ave; also shows the area north to Elliott St; common free school, church, custom-house, ferry, GWR station and docks also shown; this plan appears to be the same as an inset on R.P. 81 of 10 Dec 1862 (**B2838**).
OWHM

2190 *1865*
Sketch of the Town of Windsor Actual Subdivision into Wards. Windsor 28th June 1865. O. Bartley P.L.S.
Col ms on linen 44 x 41 cm 1" to 100 ft
Originally with OOA RG5 C1 no 946 1865, a petition for the revision of wards with the map here showing actual subdivision of wards and proposed new wards (see (2) below) with more equal population; the boundaries of the existing wards are as follows, from the west: Ward I ends at Pellissier Ave, Ward II ends at Aylmer Ave and north, and Ward III at town limits; the following population figures are given: 1100 for Ward I, 2544 for Ward II, 276 for Ward III; the streets and development of the town are much as in the 1857 map (**2188**).
OOAMA (NMC 4995)

Related maps

(2) *1865*
Sketch of the Town of Windsor proposed subdivision into wards. Windsor 28th June 1865. O. Bartley P.L.S.
Col ms 44 x 41 cm 1" to 1000 ft
The proposed new boundaries call for Ward I to end at Goyeau St and Ward II to end at Mercer St, giving a population of 1500 for Ward I, 1400 for Ward II, and 1000 for Ward III; number of acres are given for each ward.
OOAMA (NMC 4994)

WINGHAM

2191 *1857*
Plan of the Town of Wingham in the Township of Turnbery and County of Huron. Surveyed and Drawn by T.N. Molesworth C.E. Provincial Land Surveyor. Examined & returned January 1857.
Col ms 77 x 133 cm 1" to 4 chains Endorsements: 'A 217' '11770/56'
(SI 31 May 1856 (26 Aug 1856) to subdivide projected town plot into town and park lots and traverse river for mill site; OTNR FN 397 12 Dec 1856); shows the town laid out mainly west of the river from South St to North St, and West St to Josephine St, with park lots to the north and northwest; mill reserve along Maitland R; Eugenie and Victoria squares; reserve for burying ground and schools; also a copy: 'Wingham Turnberry as surveyed by T.N. Molesworth P.L.S.' endorsed 'No 20' (OTAR(P)).
OTAR(P) OTNR (SR 6044)

2192 *1857*
Townplot of Wingham Plan of Park Lots East of Josephine St Surveyed and Drawn by T.N. Molesworth C.E. Provincial Land Surveyor. Examined & Returned January 1857 T.D. J.W.B. 14th May 1857
Col ms 68 x 79 cm 1" to 8 chains Endorsements: 'A 218'
Shows the area from North St to South St, and Josephine St to East St east of the river; park lot nos and dimensions; clearings, marshy lands, relief; some bldgs are shown; 'Diagonal Road' angles south from John St; also a copy: 'Wingham Park Lots Turnberry [Sgd] Crown Lands Department Toronto January 1857 Commr Crown Lands.' endorsed 'No 20a' and with later note written across plan, 'This part of Turnberry is sold in farm lots.' (OTAR); and a copy: 'Park Lots in the town of Wingham J.W.B. Crown Lands Office Toronto 14th March 1857 [Sgd] Joseph Cauchon Commissioner of Crown Lands.' (OTNR (SR 374)); and a copy: 'Town Plot of Wingham Park Lots East of Josephine Street I.R.I. Crown Lands Department Toronto October 1857 [Sgd] Andrew Russell Asst Commissioner' endorsed 'A 213' (OTNR (SR 375)).
OTAR OTNR (SR 374–5; 6048)

2193 *1861*
Plan of part of Wingham Town Plot and Mill Reserve. [Sgd] Andrew Bay Provincial Land Surveyor 3d December 1861
Col ms 56 x 39 cm 1" to 4 chains Endorsements: 'W 25'
(SI 24 Oct 1861 to lay out limits of mill reserve); shows the area from Helena St east to Minnie St, and Albert St south to mill reserve.
OTNR (SR 377)

WINONA

2194 *[1854?]*
Plan / of the Village of / Ontario / Shewing the Village, & Villa Lots therein. / the property of / The Hon. John Willson / T.A. Blyth. D.P.S. / Lithog'd at the Spectator Office, Hamilton.
Print (lith) 97 x 63 cm Scale not given
Shows the village laid out from Esplanade to Railway St and GWR property, and East Ave to West Ave; shows Margaret and Sophia sts, and John St runs east-west across McLaren property shown in plan below (**2195**); probably precedes plan below.
OOAMA (NMC 22895)

2195 *1855*
Plan / OF / ONTARIO / 10 miles East of Hamilton / According to the SURVEY / made by / T.A. BLYTH, P.L.S.
Print (lith) 59 x 42 cm 1" to 4 chains
View: 'LAKE HOUSE / ONTARIO W. Boultbee Archt' 1" to 12 ft; originally from *Prospectus of a Joint Stock Company for the Purpose of Erecting a Hotel at the Village of Ontario ... 1 August 1855* (Hamilton: 'Spectator' Office 1855) (OOA Pamphlet 23 (1855)); shows the same street and lot layout as on the other plan (**2194**) but W.P. McLaren property is shown and hotel is located on the property; John St deleted; pier; related to R.P. 310 (**B2847**).
OOAMA (NMC 5060)

WINTERBOURNE

2196 *1854*
MAP / OF THE / VILLAGE OF WINTERBOURNE, / TOWNSHIP OF WOOLWICH, / County of Waterloo, / CANADA WEST, / as laid out for sale by / W.H. Lanphier Esqre / 1854 / M. Schofield / P.L.S.
Print (lith) 43 x 46 cm 1" to 3 chains
Shows the village laid out between Katharine St and the Grand R; some bldgs identified; see also **B2848**.
Waterloo N 58 (R.P. A-12)

2197 *1855*
PLAN / OF PART OF / THE VILLAGE OF / WINTERBOURNE / TOWNSHIP OF WOOLWICH / County of Waterloo / CANADA WEST. / As laid out for / SHERIFF DAVIDSON / 1855. / Maclear & Co. Lithr Toronto. // M.C. SCHOFIELD P.L.S.
Print (lith) 52 x 67 cm 1" to 2 chains
Shows lots north and part south of Castania St east of the Grand R, mills and mill ponds; drawing of grist mill and Scotch church; several other bldgs identified; see also **B2849**.
Waterloo N 58 (R.P. 598 and A-20)

2198 *1855*
PLAN / OF THE VILLAGE OF / WINTERBOURNE / IN THE / TOWNSHIP OF WOOLWICH. / Surveyed for Messrs Allan & Mathieson. // Surveyed and drawn by / J. Mackintosh P.L.S. / Winterbourne April 28th 1855. // Maclear & Co. Lith. Toronto
Print (col lith), pt trimmed 75 x 55 cm 1" to 2 chains
Shows area from Peel St to Lanphier St, and Grand R to Katharine St; mill dam, town and park lots, market-place, mill property, school site; see also **B2850**.
Waterloo N 58 (R.P. 598)

WOODSTOCK

2199 *1830*
Plan of a Town plot in the township of North Oxford London District. Oxford 20th Jany 1830 [Sgd] C. Rankin D.S.
Col ms 30 x 55 cm 1" to 4 chains Endorsements: 'A 48' '670'
(SI C. Rankin 4 Aug 1829 to survey and lay out a town at the upper forks of the Thames on lots 28, 29, and 30, North Oxford Twp; FN 561 of 16 Jan 1830); a town plot surveyed between the sideline for lots 27/28, Dundas St, and the Thames R; the streets and lots are laid out; shows relief, marshy land, trees, cleared land with names of settlers, some bldgs, and orchards; a note indicates that the town plot was cancelled and the land granted as a farm lot by fiat of 20 March 1834; the town was just west of present-day boundary of Woodstock.
OTNR (SR 236)

Related maps

(**2**) *1830*
Sketch shewing the Town Reservation at the Upper Forks of the River Thames, and the Town Plot already surveyed, accompanied by a Report; – by order from the Surveyor General's Office bearing date at York the 31st day of March 1830 – Dy Surveyor's Office Port – Talbot 30th April 1830. [Sgd] M. Burwell Dy Surveyor. To William Chewett Esquire Acting Surveyor General &c. &c. &c. York
Col ms 41 x 50 cm 1" to 40 chains
Originally from OOA RG 1 but exact location not found; shows a town grid of 10 north-south and three east-west streets, west of the forks; the area east of the forks and north and south of Dundas St in Blandford Twp is shown as reserved; squatters are noted in various areas near the river and along Dundas St; travelled roads, Hatch's mill.
OOAMA (NMC 3311)

2200 *1833*
Plan of the Town of Woodstock in the Township of Blandford London District [Sgd] C. Rankin. York 2 Jany 1833
Col ms 67 x 98 cm 1" to 3 chains Endorsements: 'No 51'
(SI to L. Burwell 2 July 1832 and 1 Dec 1832 to lay out town plot in the reserve of Blandford at the upper forks of the Thames R; OTNR FN 726 23 Aug 1833); shows the first survey for the eventual town, east of the forks on lot 2, con 5, Blandford; Dundas St north to Vincent St, and Thames R east to Riddle St; square shown at Vansittart St between Barwick, Drew, and Mary sts; Roman Catholic church land; names of owners; a later note indicates reserve between Bexley St and Givens St for church endowment (27 Nov 1834), and area north of Barwick St added later: 'This is proposed to be laid out on same plan as that now surveyed'; Capt Drew's land shown to northeast.
OTNR (SR 384)

Related maps

(**2**) *[183?]*
Town of Woodstock Copy J.G.C.
Col ms 62 x 80 cm 1" to 3 chains
Noted as copied from C. Rankin's survey of 1833 with additions in Bigger, III:47; shows the same information as the Rankin plan with the streets north of Barwick only sketched in and the same note about the endowment land for church (1834); a few names of owners.
OTAR (SR 6069)

(**3**) *1837*
Woodstock. Copy [Sgd] J.G. Chewett, Surveyor General's office Toronto 31st May 1837 [Sgd] J W Macaulay Survr Genl.
Col ms 67 x 94 cm 1" to 3 chains
Shows the area surveyed by Rankin with the area north of Barwick St indicated for the Petworth Emigrants and Capt Drew's land; Dundas St to Vincent St, and the river to Riddle St; names of some owners and notes; later notes refer to correspondence about ownership of Capt Drew's land ('Letter from S.G. 23rd Sep. 1844'); church and Presbyterian church lands; court-house square; marshy lands.
OTAR

2201 *1834*
Part of the Town Plot of Blandford by [Sgd] Peter Carroll D.P. Surveyor. Oxford 12th July 1834.
Col ms on tracing paper 46 x 78 cm 1" to 3 chains Endorsements: 'A 65' '613'
Note: 'The red margin shows the part which was surveyed for the Petworth Emigrants ... Order from the Surveyor General's Office the 19th day of June 1834.'; shows the area from Barwick St north to 1st, 2nd, and 3rd sts with eight east-west streets shown; shows the Thames R to the southwest and two streets south of Barwick; names are added to most of these lots, and houses are shown as well as two improved areas.
OTNR (SR 24)

2202 *1834 (1841)*
Town of Woodstock Shewing the fiveacre lots Surveyed in June 1834 for the Petworth Emigrants By [Sgd] Peter Carroll
Col ms 77 x 55 cm Scale not given Endorsements: 'A 65'
Dated 22 Jan 1841 in Bigger, III:47; shows the town from Dundas St north to street beyond Vincent St, and from Riddle St west to Yeo St; the area reserved for the Petworth Emigrants is shown from Barwick St to Vincent St and from Riddle St west to Winniett St; names are shown in these larger park lots north of Barwick, bldgs are shown, and notes on amount of land cleared by the owner; some names of earlier or original owners; Capt Drew's land is shown across part of western half.
OTAR(P)

2203 *1854*
Plan of Part of the Gore of Oxford formerly the Property of Colonel A.W. Light as surveyed by W.G. Wonham P.L.S. [Certified by surveyor] Sept 12 1854
Ms 61 x 89 cm Approx 1" to 2 chains
The map is probably a copy of R.P. 55 (**B2864**); park and town lots are shown south of Main St and GWR, and between Macadamized Rd on the west and line between E Oxford and the gore; shows blocks north of area from Queen St to Dundas St to Mill St, Givens and Winniett sts; photoreproduction in OTAR.
Private Collection

2204 *1855*
MAP / OF THE TOWN OF / WOODSTOCK / Canada West / from the / SURVEYS OF W.G. WONHAM P.L.S. / by / CHARLES L. BEARD. / 1855. / LITH. COMPTON 209 MAIN ST. BUFFALO N.Y. // Entered according to Act of the Provincial Legislature in the year of our Lord 1855 by Charles Lockey Beard in the office of the Registrar of the Province of Canada
Print (lith) 83 x 100 cm 1" to 5 chains
Views: 'New Jail' and 'Matsons Hotel'; shows the town from Hall St north to boundary north of Vincent St, and from Thames R east to Stafford St; major bldgs shown and identified; a note indicates that frame bldgs not shown; area northwest of Dundas and Riddle sts described as the 'Town plot,' but not built on except for public bldgs between Light and Graham sts; names of subdivision surveys shown; most bldgs are shown along Dundas St and to the south; GWR and station; names of some landowners shown; OLU copy has ms adds showing wards and 'proposed new channel for creek' from Finkle's mill pond.
OLU OOAMA (NMC 16798) OTAR

2205 *1855*
PLAN / of part of the / TOWN OF WOODSTOCK / the property of Thomas J. Cottle Esqr / W.G. Wonham P.L.S. / 1855. / Maclear & Co. Lith Toronto
Print (lith) 69 x 42 cm 1" to 3 chains
Shows the area from Dundas St north to Vincent St, and Huron St west to Riddell St; residence of Thos J. Cottle, 'Altadore,' shown in the centre bounded by Percival, York, Henry, and Wellington sts; a few bldgs shown; terms of purchase indicate that 'persons erecting a Brick House of the value of £250. may ... have the time of payment extended to fifteen years'; date of sale left blank; related to R.P. 49 (**B2865**).
OLU

2206 *1857*
MAP / OF TOWN AND PARK LOTS / ADJOINING THE TOWN OF / WOODSTOCK. / the Estate of the Late / JOSEPH CLARKE ESQ.RE / 1857 / Saml Peters Lith / London C.W.
Print (lith) hand col 78 x 53 cm 1" to 150 ft
The plan was certified by the surveyor, William Smith, and owner; lots shown north of Dundas St along Clarke St; see also **B2877**.
Oxford 41 (R.P. 174)

2207 *1857*
MAP / OF / TOWN AND PARK LOTS / AT / DOUGLASVILLE / In The Township of East Oxford, / Adjoining the Town of / WOODSTOCK, / The Property of / MESSRS. WILSON, DOUGLAS & KINTREA. / 1857. William Smith, / Provincial Land Surveyor, / WOODSTOCK, Jan. 29, 1857. / Printed by George Laycock at the Book & Job Printing Office of the / WOODSTOCK GAZETTEER. [and] MAP / OF / TOWN AND PARK LOTS / AT / DOUGLASVILLE, / IN THE TOWNSHIP OF BLANDFORD, / Adjoining the Town of / WOODSTOCK, / The Property of Messrs / WILSON, DOUGLAS & KINTREA. / 1857.
2 prints on 1 sheet (typeset) 47 x 45 cm and 90 x 14 cm on sheet 91 x 60 cm [Approx 1" to 1.3 chains]
The first map shows streets and lots from Watt St and GWR to Dundas St, and Catharine St to Frederick St, and the second plan shows lots extending along Lamport St from Dundas St to con 2, Blandford; some bldgs shown and drawing of a train and two carriages shown on GWR line; 'price £5, for 300 copies' printed below imprint on first title.
OTAR

2208 *[1857?]*
PLAN / OF PART OF THE / TOWN OF WOODSTOCK / THE PROPERTY OF / J.G. VAN SITTART ESQR / as surveyed by / W.G. WONHAM P.L.S. / H. Gregory, Lith. Hamilton C.W.
Print (lith) 56 x 37 cm 1" to 1 chain
Shows the area from Dundas St to East St, and Marlborough St east to road allowance between lots 18/19; also shows property of Rev Wm Bettridge and Henry de Blaquiere along Dundas St;

later inscription for court case 'Barnacle vs Cameron 6th July 1877'; not shown on 1855 plan above (**2204**).
OTAR

WROXETER

2209 *[1856?]*
WROXETER / Situated on Lots 26, 27, and 28, / IN CONCESSION A IN THE TOWNSHIP OF HOWICK / in the / County of Huron. / Maclear & Co Lith. Toronto.
Print (lith) 21 x 31 cm 1" to 3 chains
Inset: 'MAP / of the Counties of / HURON PERTH GREY / & BRUCE.'; also a copy originally filed with a petition about title to land of Jan 1857 (OOA RG 1 L3 P no 8 no 38 1857); shows a rectangular plan for the town from Market north to Huron St, and town line Turnberry/Howick east to Erie St; court-house and square; mill block and mills; certain lots along Centre St indicated as sold and names given; notes on advantages of the town including numbers of mechanics' dwellings and workshops being erected; inset shows position on the road from London to Southampton, other connecting roads, and the Buffalo & Lake Huron Railway to Goderich; (Holmden 2901).
OOAMA (NMC 43361)

2210 *1860*
Plan of Wroxeter in the Township of Howick County of Huron Laid out on Lots 26 and 27 Concession A (Signed) Andrew Bay Provincial Land Surveyor and Civil Engineer 17th March 1860
Col ms on tracing paper 63 x 46 cm 1" to 3 chains
Shows a layout for the town different from the plan above (**2209**); the town is laid out around the north-south Centre St but diagonals lead to the south (St Andrew's Terrace and Howick Rd) and to the north across mill pond (James Terrace and Gibson's Ave); Ontario St and Ottawa St run parallel at east and west ends of town; several bldgs named including Gibson's sawmill; mill yard; related to R.P. Wroxeter 1 (**B2886**).
OTAR

2211 *[1860]*
Wroxeter as laid out by Andr Bay Esq P.L.S. on south half Lot 26 – Lot 27 and north part of Lot 28 in Con A Township of Howick
Col ms on linen 49 x 40 cm Scale not given
Endorsements: 'Hon. Jas. Patton Plan of Wroxeter'
Shows the same layout for the town as the 1860 plan above (**2210**) but the street names have been changed; the layout and street names are the ones used and appear in the co atlas (Belden, ... *Huron* (1879)); Presbyterian church and English church burial grounds.
OTAR

WYEBRIDGE

2212 *[186?]*
Plan of Pts lots 93 and 94 Con 1 Tiny
Col ms on linen 27 x 40 cm Scale not given
Mill site and mills outlined in red with note: 'Property on which loan is asked ...'; shows Mill St and Centre St east of Penetanguishene Rd; about 15 bldgs shown including dwellings, woollen mill, storehouses, stables, etc; possibly later than R.P. 97 of 1864 (**B2888**).
OTAR

WYOMING

2213 *1862*
Plan / OF THE TOWN PLOT OF / WYOMING, / Situated on Lots 15 & 16 in the 2nd Concn of the / Township of / PLYMPTON. / The Property of / Wm Spencer Esqr. / Surveyed by W.G. Wonham P.L.S. 1862. // Phillips & Evans Lith. London C.W.
Print (lith) Approx 50 x 35 cm 1" to 5 chains
Shows a subdivision from Isabella St [in ms] to Superior St on both sides of GWR and Main St, and Toronto St to London St; related to R.P. Wyoming 2 (**B2890**); photoreproduction in OTAR.
Private Collection

YORK TWP

2214 *1850*
Plan of the Boundry [*sic*] Line between the Townships of York & Scarborough With the Adjoining Lots Surveyed for the Municipalities of York and Scarborough Under Instructions from the Commissioner of Crown Lands by D. Gibson & W. Smith Provl Surveyors 1850. [Sgd] David Gibson ... William Smith Prov. Land Surveyor
Col ms 144 x 48 cm 1" to 20 chains Endorsements: 'B 7' '3146 50'
Shows relief, creeks, treed areas, roads, and bldgs along the line; bearings.
OTNR (SR 5959)

2215 *1851*
MAP / of the / TOWNSHIP / OF / YORK / in the County of York Upper Canada, / 1851 / Compiled and Drawn by J.O. Browne FSA. Civil Engineer & D.P. Surveyor. / Toronto. / Engraved & Printed by Jno Ellis, 8, King St.
Print (engrav) 66 x 64 cm 1" to 40 chains
Shows the whole of the twp with lots and cons numbered and the streets of Toronto shown; shows cleared and forested land, roads, and all bldgs in rural areas and villages outside the city; schools, churches, mills, and estates identified; the map was first announced as in preparation and to be published by Scobie & Balfour in the *British Colonist* (Toronto) 19 June 1848 and was still being advertised by them on 4 Dec 1849.
OTMCL

Later editions and states

(**2**) *1851 [1853?]*
[Title the same]
Additions include Government House and Parliament Bldgs in the city, several new subdivisions north of Bloor St and the additions of bldgs and names of houses, e.g., Rosedale, Russell Hill, Deer Park, a few new roads.
OTLS (Riddell Collection)

(**3**) *1851 [1853?]*
[Same title]
Railway lines added including GTR and Toronto and Guelph Railway; scale bar added; the position of 'Davenport House' and 'Russell Hill' moved; a few other minor changes.
OTNR (SR 2385)

(**4**) 1851 [1853–4?]
[Same title]
GTR depot added; a few other additions and changes of bldgs and names; the number one in the date appears to have been erased; OOAMA copy has later ms adds to 1864 (see also **283(5a)**).
OOAMA (NMC 26683)

2216 *1852*
A / PLAN OF PART OF LOT No 4 / First Concession from the Bay / TOWNSHIP OF YORK / The property of the late / James Browne Esqr. / Toronto. [Sgd in facsimile] F.F. Passmore / Provincial Surveyor / Augt 22. 1852
Print (lith) 29 x 68 cm 1" to 6 chains
Shows small lots along Kingston Rd and Danforth Rd, and 10-acre lots behind these; ravines, horse paths; related to R.P. 47 (**B2442**).
OOAMA (NMC 3666) OTMCL (Howard Papers 727)

2217 *1853*
J.A. DONALDSON'S LOTS WESTON. / [Sgd in facsimile] J. Stoughton Dennis / P.L.S. / Weston Jany 4th / 1853
Print (lith) 24 x 58 cm 1" to 4 chains
Shows the area from Humber R to the road allowance between cons 3/4 and from the 5/6 side-road to 6/7 side-road; Toronto & Guelph Railway Station and line; a few names of owners; related to R.P. 50 (**B2899**).
OOAMA (NMC 4520)

2218 *1856*
BALMORAL / AT THE / Weston Station / OF THE / NORTHERN RAILWAY. / [Sgd in facsimile] Dennis & Boulton Surveyors & Agents // Lithographed by J. Ellis / Toronto. / ... WAKEFIELD, COATE & CO. / Auctioneers / or DENNIS & BOULTON, Agents, / Toronto, May 31st, 1856.
Print (lith) 52 x 77 cm 1" to 2 chains
Inset: 'Diagram showing the situation of Balmoral' 1" to 1 mile; shows lots from Fisher St to Main St and from Balmoral St to road allowance between cons 3/4; Railway Station Ground; inset shows the Ontario Simcoe & Huron Railway, plank roads, and mills on the Humber R; '... property will be sold at Public Auction ... on Friday the 13th day of June next ...'; OTAR copy has ms adds of names of some purchasers; related to R.P. 162 (**B2906**).
OOAMA (NMC 22226) OTAR

2219 *[1856]*
[Park lots for suburban gardens and villa residences, Balmoral Avenue, Weston]
Print (lith) 23 x 110 cm 1" to 3 chains
Inset: 'MAP SHEWING THE RELATIVE POSITION OF THE / BALMORAL AVENUE PROPERTY / with the Village of Weston and the Stations on the Northern & Grand Trunk Railways' 1" to 4 miles; in a prospectus of the same title sgd 'John Maulson, King Street East, Toronto, August 1, 1856,' frontis (*Bib Can* 5725); map probably printed by Maclear & Co. as cover-title and vignette are noted as 'engraved by Maclear ...'; shows subdivision at road between cons 3/4, and Weston at road between cons 4/5 and north of travelled side-road between lots 5 and 6; inset shows 'contemplated omnibus road between the two stations'; OOAMA has trimmed copy without inset (NMC 22212).
OOAMA (NMC 22212) OTMCL

2220 *[1856]*
PLAN / OF / Building Lots in the Village / OF YORK MILLS / OTHERWISE KNOWN AS HOGG'S HOLLOW. / THE PROPERTY OF / J. & W. HOGG. Dennis and Boulton Surveyors and Agents. / LITHOGRAPHED BY J. ELLIS 8 KING ST TORONTO C.W.
Print (lith) Approx 67 x 49 cm 1" to 100 ft
Shows lots along Yonge St, John St, Mill St, and side-road between lots 10 and 11; mill pond, mills, brickyards, two churches and other bldgs named; appended to it is advertisement for sale by auction on Wed 5 Nov 1856: 'Apply to J. & W. Hogg York Mills or W. Hogg & Co. 122 Yonge Street, Toronto ... Wakefield Coate & Co. Auctioneers ... Toronto 29th Oct. 1856'; related to R.P. 204 and 246 (**B2911**, **B2918**); photoreproduction in OTAR.
Private Collection

2221 *1858*
Plan of Lots 1,2,3,4 and 5 in the 2nd Concn from the Bay township of York [Sgd] William Hawkins P.L.S. Toronto 27 Septr 1858. To the Honourable The Commissioner of Crown Lands Toronto.
Col ms 65 x 96 cm 1" to 10 chains Endorsements: 'B 78' 'Municipal Survey no 91'
Shows the area west of the town line between York and Scarborough twps; relief, rivers, bldgs, names of owners; Danforth Plank Rd.
OTNR (SR 84724)

Appendix A

Township Plans

	Date of Instructions	Date of Map	Surveyor and Signature	Endorsements and Notes	Location
	ABINGER				
A1	27.6.1857	21.5.1859	A.B. Perry	'No 5'; vegetation indicated along survey lines, Abinger Rd, Snow's Mississippi Rd line, sawmill, mill site; FN 868	OTNR (SR 434)
A2		–.11.1860	Andrew Russell AC	'3'; marshes, roads, names on E and W pts, later changes	OTAR(P)
	ADELAIDE				
A3	30.5.1831	–.9.1831	Peter Carroll	'B17'; pt: cons 1–2 N and S of Caradoc to L Huron Rd; a few names	OTAR
A4		29.12.1831	Peter Carroll	'No 1'; office copy with names, c & c reserves, adds to 1851; FN 190	OTNR (SR 438)
A5		29.12.1831 4.2.1833	Peter Carroll copy J.G.C. S.P. Hurd	'C1'; c & c reserves, names in pencil	OTAR(P)
A6	29.5.1832	[1831–2]	Peter Carroll copy J.G.C.	C & c reserves, marshes; FN 4	OTAR
A7		–.7.1843	Thomas Parke	Includes Metcalfe Twp, reserves, notes; scale n.g.	OTAR
	ADJALA				
A8	4.2.1820	19.6.1820	Sam'l M. Benson	'B2' '237'; c & c reserves, marshes, trails; scale n.g.; FN 5	OTNR (SR 436)
A9		19.6.1820	S.M. B[enson]	A few names, c & c reserves, trails; scale n.g.	OTAR
A10		19.6.1820	Sam'l M. Benson	'No 1' 'office copy'; many adds to 1844	OTNR (SR 437)
A11		[182?]	Copy J.G. Chewett	'1506'; c & c reserves, marshes	OTAR
A12		–.7.1843	Thomas Parke	Survey grid, reserves; scale n.g.	OTAR
	ADMASTON				
A13	24.12.1838	–.–.1842	Josias Richey	'B26' '238'; c & c reserves, vegetation, drainage; scale n.g.; FN 6	OTNR (SR 440)
A14		[184?]	–	'No 38' 'office plan'; c & c reserves, names	OTAR(P)
A15	29.1.1847	14.3.1848	J.W. McNaughton	'B29'; lots fronting on Bonnechere R of Admaston and Bromley twps; FN 78	OTNR (SR 439)

A16		–.5.1848	Copy T.D. J.H. Price C/CL	'No 42'; lots on Bonnechere R with names	OTAR(P)
A17		–.11.1848	Copy [T.] Devine	'No 43'; lots fronting on Bonnechere R in Admaston and Bromley twps	OTAR(P)
	ADOLPHUSTOWN				
A18	1783	1784	James Peachey, Lewis Kotte, Henry Holland, Samuel Tuffie	'Twp No 4' '1012' 'No 34[?]'; glebe, town plot, names	OTAR
A19		[1784]	James Peachey, Lewis Kotte, Henry Holland, Samuel Tuffie	'No 3' 'Quebec Plan'; names, glebe, town plot	OTAR
A20		[1784]	James Peachey, Lewis Kotte, Henry Holland, Samuel Tuffie	'1013' 'No 45'; town plot, names	OTAR
A21		[179?]	W. Chewett copy Charles Chambers Samuel Holland	'No 2'; town plot, names	OTAR
A22		[179?]	–	'1510'; outlines, town plot; scale n.g.	OTAR
A23		28.6.1856	J.W.B. E.P. Taché	Outlines	OTAR
	ALBERMARLE				
A24	–	20.11.1857	C. Rankin Andrew Russell AC	'B86'; Adair town plot, some names, marshes, copy	OTAR(P)
	ALBION				
A25	15.5.1819	25.10.1819	J.G. Chewett	'B1' '231'; marshes, relief, a few names; FN 8–143	OTNR (SR 441)
A26		27.10.1819	–	'A3'; c & c reserves, names, notes 1818; scale n.g.	OTAR(P)
A27		27.10.[1819?]	–	'A2'; c & c reserves, names, notes 1818 and 1825; scale n.g.	OTAR(P)
A28		[182?]	James Chewett copy W.C.	'1519' 'A8'; c & c reserves, marshes, relief	OTAR
A29		[182?]	–	'A1' 'Office Plan'; c & c reserves, reference to new office plan 1827 (**A30**)	OTAR(P)

	Date of Instructions	Date of Map	Surveyor and Signature	Endorsements and Notes	Location
A30		11.9.1827	James Chewett copy W.C. T. Ridout	'No 3' 'Office plan'; names, many changes	OTAR(P)
	ALDBOROUGH				
A31	18.8.1797	[1797?]	[Wm Parren Lawe]	'1512'; note re size of lots and 'Gore-'; scale n.g.	OTAR
A32		[180?]	–	'No 4'; c & c reserves, names; scale n.g.	OTAR(P)
A33	4.5.1803	[17.11.1803]	Wm. Hambly	'No 2'; names, meadows, adds to 1851; FN 12	OTNR (SR 447)
A34		8.6.1811	Thos Ridout SG	Outline, marshes, note: 'no locations made under Col Talbot,' projected plan	OTAR
A35	8.6.1811	24.10.1811	Mahlon Burwell	'B1' '232'; Talbot Rd W through 'twp A'; FN 10	OTNR (SR 446)
A36		16.3.1821	[Sgd] Thomas Talbot	'A1'; c & c reserves, names on some lots, lots certified as located by Talbot	OTAR(P)
A37		[182?]	J. Chewett	'No 47' 'office copy'; marsh, rivers	OTAR (SR 445)
A38		29.5.1832	S.P. Hurd SG	Pt; outline, reserves, a few names, projection for survey; scale n.g.	OTAR
A39	23.12.1831 29.5.1832	–.4.1832 –.5.1832	Peter Carroll W.C. Chewett	'No 3'; notes on renumbering of lots, c & c reserves, names, roads, many adds; FN 8, 9, 11	OTNR (SR 442)
A40		–.7.1843	Thomas Parke SG	Survey grid, notes on survey, reserves; scale n.g.	OTAR
A41		4.9.1844	M. Burwell	'No 48'; c & c reserves, Talbot Rd, Long Wood Rd, later notes	OTAR (SR 443)
A42	22.7.1850	10.12.1850	Daniel Hanvey	'B49'; pt: cons A–VII; names, cleared land; FN 13	OTNR (SR 444)
A43		10.12.1850 18.5.1854	Daniel Hanvey CLD A.N. Morin C/CL	'No 60'; pt: outline only cons 1–7	OTAR(P)
A44		5.3.1853	CLD	Pt; reduced from Hanvey's plan **A42**, town of Wardsville; scale n.g.	OTAR
A45		5.3.1853	C/CL	Pt; Wm Parren Lawe's line reduced from Hambly's survey; scale n.g.	OTAR
A46		10.12.1850 –.1.1854	Daniel Hanvey T. Devine CLD A.N. Morin C/CL	'No 69'; pt: cons 1–7; Furnival Rd, reserves, some names	OTAR(P)

	ALFRED				
A47	4.6.1789	[1789?]	J. R[ankin?]	'A18' '8' 'Twp no 3'; pt: Ottawa R lots only; names, dates 1789 with names, school reserves, adds to 1819; scale n.g.	OTAR (SR 449)
A48		[1789?]	–	'A17' 'Twp no 3 S side Grand R'; pt: river lots only, names; scale n.g.	OTAR (SR 454)
A49		14.8.1792 28.4.1795	Wm. Chewitt Wm. Chewitt exam	'A16'; pt; names; scale n.g.	OTAR (SR 453)
A50	11.10.1796	[20.7.1797]	W. Fortune	'B2' '233'; pt: Ottawa R lots; clergy reserve, marshes; scale n.g.; FN 348	OTAR (SR 451)
A51		[1797?]	Copy W.C.	'1514'; marshes, relief, strip of vacant land	OTAR
A52	2.11.1815	–.1.1816	Jos. Fortune	'B4' '234'; pt: 2 or 3 front cons laid out in Alfred and Plantagenet; Petite Nation R, marshes; 80 ch; FN 218	OTNR (SR 448)
A53		–.–.1820	Wm. Browne	'B5'; pt; c & c reserves, burnt land, 'windfall,' trails, canal site, a few names; scale n.g.; FN 793	OTNR (SR 452)
A54		14.5.1821	Thos. Ridout SG	'17'; c & c reserves, names, later adds	OTAR (SR 450)
A55		[182?]	Jeremiah McCarthy, J. Fortune, W. Browne	Shows Alfred and Plantagenet; pts surv by each surveyor shown, duplicate plan; scale n.g.	OTNR (SR 5585)
A56		[182?]	W.C.	'16'; names, c & c reserves, later changes, notes 1840 and 1843	OTAR(P)
A57	8.2.1829	17.1.1829	Copy W.C.	'1518'; Great Swamp, rd to Chesseres Mills, burnt land	OTAR
	ALGONA, N and S				
A58	27.5.1856 22.12.1856	7.2.1857	J.L.P. O'Hanly	'B53'; S pt; roads, trails, settlement, clearings, some names, proposed rd route; FN 1807	OTNR (SR 458)
A59		22.6.1857	J.W.B. CLD P. VanKoughnet AC/CL	'No 51'; S pt; names	OTAR(P)
A60		18.7.1857	J.L.P. O'Hanly	'B55'; N pt; clearings, relief, a few names, roads, trails; FN 1592	OTNR (SR 455)
A61		25.7.1857	Andrew Russell AC	S pt; copy for agent	OTAR (SR 457)
A62		–.–.1857 10.10.1857	J.L.P. O'Hanly Andrew Russell AC/CL	'No 62' 'Copy of B55' (**A60**); N pt: on the river and lake only; names	OTAR(P)
A63		8.10.1857	Andrew Russell	'A11'; N pt; scale n.g.	OTAR

	Date of Instructions	Date of Map	Surveyor and Signature	Endorsements and Notes	Location
	ALICE				
A64	12.6.1854	-.-.1854	John Morris	'B49'; clearings, houses, travelled rds, land classed for settlement; FN 875	OTNR (SR 459)
A65		25.5.1855	T. Devine Joseph Cauchon C/CL	'No 47'; names, later changes	OTAR(P)
A66	11.8.1860	8.12.1860	H.O. Wood	'A11'; pt; roads, marsh; FN 876	OTNR (SR 460)
	ALLAN				
A67	15.8.1866	-.5.1867	Francis Bolger	'No 17'; marshes, relief, portages; FN 879	OTNR (SR 461)
	ALNWICK				
A68	-	6.9.1811	W.C. exam Thos Ridout	'A1' '9'; names; c & c reserves	OTAR (SR 467)
A69		[181?]	-	'No 1'; names, notes 1820 and 1856; scale n.g.	OTAR(P)
A70	24.-.1826	29.5.1826	Richd. Birdsall	'No 2'; c & c reserves, names, marshes, adds to 1856; FN 37	OTNR (SR 463)
A71	-	-.6.1835 8.7.1835	Fred Preston Rubidge adds Henry Lizars	'Q45' '1127'; pt: cons 1–2 intended for an Indian settlement; rd, conflicting survey lines; 10 ch; FN 322	OTNR (SR 464)
A72		-.6.1835	F.P. Rubidge copy J.G.C.	'Q46' '1122'; reduced copy of pt of cons 1–2 for Indian settlement; 20 ch	OTAR (SR 465)
A73		-.8.1843	Thomas Parke SG	Reserves, survey grid; scale n.g.	OTAR
A74		[1845]	-	'No 3' 'office copy'; c & c reserves, names, Indian lands, notes 1834–60; scale n.g.	OTAR(P)
	AMABEL				
A75	-	-.-.1856	C. Rankin	'B80'; Indian paths and reserves, town plots, mill lot, marsh, copy; FN 2983	OTNR (SR 468)
A76		-.12.1856	Joseph Cauchon C/CL	'No 71'; town plots Oliphant and Wiarton, names, mill lot on Sauble R, Indian reserves	OTAR(P)
	AMARANTH				
A77	4.2.1820	1823	Hugh Black	'B3' '230'; c & c reserves; FN 222	OTNR (SR 469)

A78		–.–.1823	Hugh Black	'No 2'; c & c reserves, marsh, names, notes 1842, 1844, and 1851	OTAR(P)
A79		[1823?]	–	'1508'; c & c reserves, marshes	OTAR
A80		–.7.1843	Thomas Parke SG	Reserves, survey grid; scale n.g.	OTAR
	AMELIASBURGH				
A81	–.10.1785	[1785]	Lewis Kotte	'1021'; pt: Bay of Quinte S shore lots in Ameliasburgh and Sophiasburgh; some names	OTAR
A82		[1785?]	–	'A2'; pt: Bay of Quinte S shore in Ameliasburgh and Sophiasburgh; all names; scale n.g.	OTAR
A83		[1785?]	Copy [sgd] Samuel Holland	'N5'; pt: names in 3 cons S of Bay of Quinte only; scale n.g.	OTAR(P)
A84		–.4.1794	A. Aitken	'C3'; pt: 'Carrying Place' lots; 20 ch	OTAR
A85		[1794?]	–	'No 45'; c & c reserves, names; scale n.g.	OTAR(P)
A86		[1794?]	[A. Aitken]	'No 44'; names, many with dates of 1796 and 1797, adds to 1846	OTNR (SR 478)
A87	4.4.1816	26.5.1816	S.S. Wilmot	'B1' '228'; pt: resurvey of pt cons 2–6; FN 16	OTNR (SR 475)
A88		30.6.1816	Samuel S. Wilmot	'B2' '227'; pt: resurvey cons 1–6; mill, marshes, roads, fences in con 1	OTNR (SR 474)
A89		30.6.1816	Sam'l S. Wilmot	'B41' '229'; pt: resurvey cons 1–6; marshes, very similar to 'B2' (**A88**)	OTNR (SR 472)
A90		31.1.1818	[S. Wilmot]	'B3'; a few names, relief, marsh; FN 321	OTNR (SR 473)
A91		[182?]	Copy W.C.	'C1'; notes on survey lines 1811, 1823, and 1835	OTAR (SR 470)
A92		[182?]	Copy W.C.	'No 1'; names, c & c reserves, notes on the road allowances 22.10.1825 W.C.; scale n.g.	OTAR(P)
A93	20.2.1839	–.–.1839	P.V. Elmore	'B38'; resurvey; 50 ch	OTNR (SR 471)
A94		–.8.1843	Thomas Parke SG	Survey grid, reserves; scale n.g.	OTAR
	AMHERST ISLAND				
A95	–	–.1.1790	Alexr Aitken Samuel Holland	'949'; outline only, no lots shown; 1/2 mile	OTNR (SR 483)
A96		–.–.1790	Alex'r Aitken copy [sgd] Samuel Holland	'No 25'; outline only, formerly 'Isle Tonté,' marsh; 1/2 mile	OTAR (SR 484)

	Date of Instructions	Date of Map	Surveyor and Signature	Endorsements and Notes	Location
	ANCASTER				
A97	23.5.1793	[1793?]	[A. Jones?]	'A1'; names, notes 1799, 1811, and 1816; scale n.g.; FN 366	OTAR(P)
A98		[1794?]	D.W. Smith	'1513' 'C1'; notes on boundaries, outlines; 80 ch	OTAR
A99		20.8.1811	Exam T. Ridout	'No 1'; names; conflicting boundary lines	OTNR (SR 95572)
A100		–.7.1843	Thomas Parke	Survey grid; scale n.g.	OTAR
	ANDERDON				
A101	27.7.1835	6.4.1836	Peter Carroll	'B7' '226'; names, mill site, stone quarry, area to be sold, notes, former Huron reserve; FN 21	OTNR (SR 480)
A102		[1836?]	P. Carroll	'No 36' 'Office Copy'; names, mill site, reserve for Indians, town of Amherstburgh, later changes	OTAR(P)
A103		14.6.1837	Copy W.C. J.W. Macaulay SG	Pt; subdivision of Huron reserve Sept 1836, names, notes on benefits from sales; scale n.g.	OTAR
	ANGELSEA				
A104	9.2.1857	12.1.1858	Thomas Fraser Gibbs	'A' 'No 3'; pt: E 11 lots on Addington Rd, marsh, contents; FN 889	OTNR (SR 485)
A105		–.6.1858	Andrew Russell AC/CL	Pt: lots on the Addington Rd only; names	OTAR(P)
A106		[1858]	[T.F. Gibbs]	Addington Rd, Skootamatta R	OTAR (SR 486)
	ANSON				
A107	6.10.1858	30.7.1859	Crosbie Brady	'No 7'; marshes, M. Deane's exploring line; FN 891	OTNR (SR 481)
A108		26.5.1860	Andrew Russell AC	A few names, exploring line, later changes	OTAR(P)
	ANSTRUTHER				
A109		7.11.[1859?]	–	'A23' 'Projected plan to accomp. Instructions'; outlines; scale n.g.	OTAR
A110	16.11.1859	7.12.1860	James W. Fitzgerald	'A12'; marshes, road; FN 892	OTNR (SR 490)
A111		23.1.1862	Andrew Russell AC/CL	Some names, many later changes	OTAR(P)

	ARRAN				
A112	8.4.1851	1.11.1851	C. Rankin	'B52'; marshes, Saugeen Rd; FN 28	OTNR (SR 499)
A113		17.1.1852	C. Rankin	'Q83'; strip in Arran and Derby surrendered by Indians and subdivided, several rd routes, Sydenham and Southampton town plots, marshes, Indian villages; FN 774	OTNR (SR 498)
A114		–.2.1854	T.D. A.N. Morin C/CL	'No 59'; names	OTAR
	ARTEMESIA				
A115		8.4.1850	C/CL	'Sketch A' 'Copy sent to Rankin with instructions'; diagram for survey showing surrounding area in Artemesia and Osprey; scale n.g.	OTAR
A116	11.5.1850	28.1.1851	C. Rankin	'B48'; marshes, relief, roads, Priceville town plot; FN 898	OTNR (SR 500)
A117		21.8.1851	T.D. J.H. Price C/CL	'No 30'; Priceville and Eugenia town plots, marshes, names	OTAR(P)
	ARTHUR				
A118		8.7.1840	R.B. Sullivan SG	'C12'; diagram for survey; 50 ch	OTNR (SR 5540)
A119	8.7.1840	18.1.1841	John McDonald	'B13'; E pt and rd survey; contents, marshes; FN 24	OTNR (SR 493)
A120		18.1.1841 [1846?]	John McDonald	'C11'; town plot, school lands, table of lots, copy	OTAR(P)
A121		–.4.1842	John McDonald	'B14'; gov't reserves for towns, marshes, rd survey, rivers dotted in; FN 27	OTNR (SR 492)
	ASHBY				
A122	27.10.1856	14.12.1857	Thomas Fraser Gibbs	'A No 2'; marshes, tree types, comments on land, falls, rapids; FN 900	OTNR (SR 502)
A123		–.4.1858	Thomas Gibbs CLO	'No 1'; pt later annulled, later changes	OTAR(P)
	ASHFIELD				
A124	10.2.1836	21.7.1836	Wm. Hawkins	'B22' '226'; pt: lots 1–33, cons 1–13, S pt Ashfield and W Wawanosh; c & c reserves; FN 29	OTNR (SR 507)
A125	26.1.1838	23.6.1838	Wm. Hawkins	'B25' '255'; c & c reserves, complete relief, marshes, reserve for town plot; FN 30	OTNR (SR 506)

	Date of Instructions	Date of Map	Surveyor and Signature	Endorsements and Notes	Location
A126		30.7.1838	Wm Hawkins copy J.G. Chewett	'No 57' 'office copy'; school lands, c & c reserves, names, town reserve, as surveyed by Hawkins in 1836 and 1838; notes 1839	OTAR(P)
A127		[1838?]	–	'1617' 'office copy'; c & c reserves, marsh	OTAR (SR 508)
A128		–.7.1843	Thomas Parke	Survey grid, c & c reserves, town of Albert; scale n.g.	OTAR
A129	8.5.1847	21.10.1847	A. Wilkinson	Pt: rear and Wawanosh; town reserve, relief, marshes; FN 1323, 2238	OTNR (SR 6569)
A130		–.11.1847	A.R. D.B. Papineau	Survey grid; rivers	OTAR
	ASPHODEL				
A131		27.4.1820	T. Ridout	'Township of Asphodel to be surveyed'; sketch for survey; scale n.g.	OTAR
A132	27.4.1820	14.7.1820	R. Birdsall	'No 3'; names, contents; FN 33	OTNR (SR 504)
A133		14.7.1820	R. Birdsall	'B2' '224'; c & c reserves, rapids, marshes	OTNR (SR 503)
A134		29.7.1820	Richard Birdsall	'B1' '223'; mill seats, c & c reserves, marshes	OTAR (SR 505)
A135		–.7.1843	Thomas Parke	Survey grid; reserves; scale n.g.	OTAR
	ASSIGINACK				
A136	13.11.1863	30.12.1864	John Grant	'No 15'; marshes, later notes; FN 899	OTNR (SR 510)
	AUGUSTA				
A137	–	15.11.1789	Ed Jessup, Jeremiah McCarthy, W. Chewett	'No 36' '1014'; surveyed in 1785 and 1787, names, office copy indicating alterations from orig survey	OTNR (SR 517)
A138		17.10.1792	W. Chewett	'No 2'; names, marshes, later notes to 1843	OTAR(P)
A139		11.12.1794	W. Chewett	'C2'; conflicting survey lines	OTNR (SR 513)
A140	–.4.1795	[1795]	John Stegmann	'B2' '222'; pt: cons 6–11; marshes, Petite Nation R; scale n.g.; FN 1–1	OTNR (SR 514)
A141		27.4.1795 29.8.1795	W. Chewett	'A1' 'New Oswegatchie town'; glebe, names, clergy reserve, notes about 6th con survey; scale n.g.	OTAR(P)
A142		[1795?]	–	'C1' '1509'; N boundary according to Fortune and Stegmann	OTAR (SR 515)

A143		[1795?]	–	'C18' '1516'; pt: cons 1–3; 2 plans: No 1 copied from plan held by Land Board with survey traces marked, No 2 resurvey; scale n.g.	OTAR (SR 516)
A144		[1795?]	–	'No 1'; glebe, New Oswegatchie town, names, notes re error in con 2, road, 2 mills; scale n.g.	OTAR(P)
A145	15.5.1809	15.6.1810	Reuben Sherwood	'B1' '221'; earlier survey lines, commons, notes on lot sizes; FN 34, 36	OTNR (SR 518)
A146		[181?]	–	'787'; roads, houses in cons 1–5, road to the Rideau, Fort Wellington; scale n.g.	OTAR (SR 519)
A147		[185?]	–	Lots 3–5, con 1 N, town of Prescott and park lots, shows area of a fire, burying ground; scale n.g.	OTAR
A148		22.6.1854	Jas West	Rd allowance btwn lots 6 and 7, con 1 and other lines, names; scale n.g.	OTAR
	AWERES				
A149	12.5.1858	21.1.1859	Albert P. Salter, Jas. Johnston	'No 6' 'A No 10'; amounts of land and water, boundary of crown/Indian lands; FN 1810	OTNR (SR 524)
A150		2.4.1859	CLD	A few names, many later changes	OTAR(P)
A151		9.9.1863	Andrew Russell AC/CL	Outline, Indian reserve	OTAR
A152		9.9.1863	Andrew Russell AC	Survey grid, Indian reserve	OTAR
	BAGOT				
A153	24.12.1838	18.4.1840	Josias Richey	'B27' '239'; marshes, c & c reserves, note re clergy reserve 13.5.1842; FN 795	OTNR (SR 529)
A154		[184?]	–	'Office Plan'; c & c reserves, names, later changes	OTAR(P)
	BANGOR				
A155	26.10.1858	1858-9	Edwin H. Kertland	'No 1'; pt: cons I–VII; Hastings and Opeongo rds; FN 920	OTNR (SR 86718)
A156		–.6.1860	Andrew Russell	Pt; free grants on Hastings and Opeongo rds, names	OTNR (SR 5531)
A157		–.7.1860	Andrew Russell AC/CL	'B3'; free grants on Hastings and Opeongo Junction Rd	OTAR
A158	19.10.1860	15.9.1861	Edwin H. Kertland	'B4' '11983/61'; pt: cons VII–XIV; Hastings Rd, clearings, marshy lands, relief; FN 919	OTNR (SR 533)
A159		–.12.1861	Andrew Russell AC/CL	'No 2' 'Office Plan'; names, many later changes	OTAR(P)

	Date of Instructions	Date of Map	Surveyor and Signature	Endorsements and Notes	Location
	BARRIE				
A160	1.10.1856	12.6.1857	A.B. Perry PLS	'B59'; Addington Rd, trails; FN 924	OTNR (SR 539)
A161		-.10.1857	Andrew Russell AC/CL	'No 62'; Addington Rd, names, later changes	OTAR(P)
	BARTON				
A162	–	[178?]	–	'No 6' 'twp no 8'; lots 1–25, cons I-VIII, names, note on existence of settlement further west but not yet surveyed; scale n.g.	OTAR(P)
A163		25.10.1791	A Jones copy JFK Holland [sgd] Sam'l Holland D.W. Smith ASG	'A7'; pt: 9 cons, and 4 cons and BF E Flamborough; names; FN 835 (pt)	OTAR (SR 543)
A164		[1791?]	–	'C2' '1504'; outline; 20 ch	OTAR (SR 542)
A165		25.1.1812	Exam T. Ridout	'No 26'; names	OTAR (SR 541)
A166		29.10.1834	Lewis Burwell	Pt: Burlington Heights and con II; parcel of 50 acres, road; 20 ch; FN 84	OTAR
	BASTARD				
A167	11.10.1796	19.10.1797	Lewis Grant	'No 4'; names, c & c reserves, marshes; FN 233	OTNR (SR 546)
A168	9.1.1812	6.1.1816	R. Sherwood	'B13' '241'; c & c reserves; FN 486	OTNR (SR 545)
A169		[1816?]	–	'No 3' 'Office Plan'; c & c reserves, names, notes 1818, 1828, and 1848	OTAR(P)
	BATHURST				
A170	24.2.1816	[1816]	William Graves	'PF1' '705'; front cons and sideline; FN 42	OTNR (SR 549)
A171		[1816]	[D. McDonnell?]	'A2' 'Township No 1 Perth Settlement'; names, c & c reserves, later notes 1816, 1817, and 1821; FN 80	OTAR(P)
A172		-.1.1817	R. Sherwood	'B1' '240'; c & c reserves, beaver meadow, marshes, relief	OTNR (SR 548)
A173		[1817?]	R. Sherwood	'Q5'; names	OTAR (SR 550)
A174		[182?]	R. Sherwood copy J.G.C.	'No 1'; c & c reserves, names, later notes 1843	OTAR(P)

A175		[182?]	Copy T.F. Gd late Gleny Regt	'1405' 'C1'; outline, c & c reserves	OTAR
A176		–.8.1843	Thomas Parke SG	Survey grid; scale n.g.	OTAR
	BAYHAM				
A177	–	–.–.1809	Mahlon Burwell	'No 3' 'Bayham Malahide and Houghton shewing the Road'; c & c reserves, names, Talbot Rd; FN 513	OTAR
A178		[1810]	[Mahlon Burwell]	'No 5'; c & c reserves, names, Talbot Rd, note 4.4.1820; scale n.g.; FN 43	OTNR (SR 559)
A179		[182?]	M. Burwell?	Names of those located by T. Talbot to 1830	OTAR (Talbot BkD/10)
A180		–.7.1843	Thomas Parke SG	Survey grid; scale n.g.	OTAR
	BECKWITH				
A181	24.2.1816	–.1.1817	R. Sherwood	'B2' '1243'; c & c reserves; marshes; 1816–17 surveys: FN 9–98 and possibly FN 41, 44, 46, 80, 238	OTNR (SR 566)
A182		–.1.1817	R. Sherwood	'A1'; c & c reserves, some names, notes 1818 and 1827	OTAR (SR 567)
A183		[1817?]	[R. Sherwood?]	E and W divisions, names indicating name of regiment or 'emigrant'; scale n.g.	OTAR(P)
A184		[182?]	R. Sherwood copy J.G.C.	'No 2' 'Office plan'; c & c reserves, names, marshes, notes 1826, 1843, and 1845	OTAR(P)
A185		–.8.1843	Thomas Parke SG	Survey grid; scale n.g.	OTAR
	BEDFORD				
A186	18.6.1821	19.7.1824	Sam'l M. Benson	'B4'; a few names, relief; FN 47	OTNR (SR 568)
A187		[1824?]	Copy W.C.	'No 3'; c & c reserves, names, notes 1824, many later changes	OTAR(P)
A188		–.8.1843	Thomas Parke SG	'B10'; survey grid, Indian lands; scale n.g.	OTAR
	BELMONT				
A189	15.11.1821	–.–.1823	Henry Ewing	'No 5'; contents, names, c & c reserves; FN 48	OTNR (SR 573)
A190		[1823?]	Copy J.G.C.	'1402'; c & c reserves, marshes	OTAR
A191		–.7.1843	Thomas Parke SG	Survey grid, reserves; scale n.g.	OTAR
A192		16.4.1851	J.S. Peterson	'B31'; pt: cons 1–5	OTNR (SR 575)

	Date of Instructions	Date of Map	Surveyor and Signature	Endorsements and Notes	Location
A193	23.5.1851	22.11.1852	John K. Roche	'B36'; resurvey, roads, various exploration lines; FN 941	OTNR (SR 572)
A194		26.–.1857	John K. Roche copy	Roads, exploration lines, irregular survey grid	OTAR (SR 574)
	BENTINCK				
A195	28.8.1845	15.12.1845	Alex Vidal	'B26'; pt: also Glenelg Twp; Owen Sound Rd, cedar swamps, open meadows; FN 323	OTNR (SR 581)
A196		5.3.1846	A.R. CLD	Pt: also Glenelg Twp; Owen Sound Rd and lots	OTAR
A197		10.8.1847	Andrew Russell S&D CLD	'No 40'; pt: cons I–III west of Garafraxa Rd; names, school lots	OTAR(P)
A198	23.6.1848	–.1.1849	Allan Park Brough	'B39'; also includes Brant Twp; relief, marshes, town plot reserve; 1/2 mile; FN 747	OTNR (SR 3565)
A199	25.6.1850	30.4.1851	John S. Dennis	'B52'; contents, marshes, meadow, relief; FN 944	OTNR (SR 582)
A200		8.7.1851	T.D. Andrew Russell for C/CL	'No 32' 'Office Plan'; roads, town plot of Durham, names	OTAR(P)
	BERTIE				
A201	–	[179?]	–	'No 1'; names, glebe, Fort Erie, ordnance reserve with revision of shoreline, later changes; scale n.g.	OTAR(P)
A202		[179?]	–	'A2' 'rec'd by D.W. Smith from Land Board'; names; scale n.g.	OTNR (SR 584)
A203		–.1.1811	Copy W.C. exam Thos Ridout	'A1'; names, crown reserve	OTNR (SR 585)
A204	21.12.1821	28.5.1828	M. Burwell	'B7'; pt; survey monuments, roads, Fort Erie, mills, Niagara R detail; FN 52	OTNR (SR 586)
	BEVERLY				
A205	16.8.1797	[179?]	[J. Stegmann?] copy W.C.	'A2' 'office copy'; names, c & c reserves	OTNR (SR 599)
A206	26.9.1836	10.12.1836	James Kirkpatrick	'G5' 'PF32'; pt: cons 8–10; clearings with names, marshes, notes on survey; FN 799	OTNR (SR 601)
A207		–.7.1843	Thomas Parke SG	Survey grid, reserves; scale n.g.	OTAR

A208	22.5.1843 –.6.1843	–.8.1843	P.V. Elmore	'No 1'; cons 6–10; resurvey, notes on surveys; 20 ch	OTNR (SR 8917)
A209		–.8.1843	P.V. Elmore copy cert J. Cauchon	'C13' '1488/59' 'No 2 plan'; cons 6–10; resurvey lines, old lines, names, occupants; 20 ch	OTAR (SR 602)
A210		–.8.1843	P.V. Elmore	Pt: gore; resurvey, notes; scale n.g.	OTNR (SR 597)
A211		–.8.1843	–	'No 2'; similar to **A208**; 20 ch	OTAR (SR 603)
A212		5.12.1843	Thos Parke SG	'C15' '1403'; pt: boundary btwn lots and gores cons 6–10; names; 20 ch	OTAR (SR 596)
A213		[1843?]	–	'No 3'; c & c reserves, names, notes 1843, 1851, and 1858; scale n.g.	OTAR(P)
A214		5.3.1853	Andrew Russell SS CLD	Conflicting survey lines, resurvey, notes on new boundaries; scale n.g.	OTNR (SR 600)
	BEXLEY				
A215	–	–.–.1835	John Huston	'B11' '244'; c & c reserves, town resurvey; 30 ch; FN 58	OTNR (SR 589)
A216		[1835?]	J. Huston	'Q4' '1125'; 'Indian lands'; 8 ch	OTNR (SR 590)
A217		–.–.1835	John Huston copy J.G. Chewett	'No 4' 'Office Copy'; notes 1829, 1838, 1851, and 1855, names, c & c reserves	OTAR(P)
	BIDDULPH				
A218	–	16.3.1836	John McDonald	'No 3' '1137'; for Canada Co.; FN 59	OTNR (SR 592)
A219		[1836?]	[J. Mcdonald?]	Contents of I–III surveys, some names; photoreproduction of original; scale n.g.	OTAR (Canada Co. Atlas)
	BIDWELL				
A220	12.11.1863	8.7.1864	Joseph Hobson	'B16'; marshes, relief; FN 946	OTNR (SR 594)
	BILLINGS				
A221	27.12.1866	30.5.1867	Francis Bolger	'B24'; relief, Indian gardens; FN 952	OTNR (SR 608)
	BINBROOK				
A222	–	25.10.1791	Augustus Jones copy Lt John Fredk Holland Samuel Holland [sgd] D.W. Smith ASG	'A6' 'Township No 11'; 1000-acre lots; names; FN 366	OTNR (SR 97933)

	Date of Instructions	Date of Map	Surveyor and Signature	Endorsements and Notes	Location
A223		25.10.1791	Augustus Jones copy Lt John F.K. Holland [sgd] Samuel Holland	'No 5'; 1000-acre lots, some subdivided from 1809, names in cons I–IV only	OTAR(P)
A224	16.10.1810	[1810]	[S. Wilmot]	'No 4'; cons 1–4, 7–10; some large blocks, names, later notes; scale n.g.; FN 62	OTAR(P)
A225		[181?]	–	Roads, mills, settlements	OTAR
A226		–.7.1843	Thomas Parke SG	Survey grid; scale n.g.	OTAR
	BLANDFORD				
A227	27.9.1823	[1824?]	[A. Millar] copy J.G.C.	'No 8'; c & c reserves, names, copy sent to Hon T. Talbot 16.5.1826, later changes; FN 324	OTAR(P)
A228		16.5.1826	Thos Ridout SG	Names; c & c reserves	OTAR (Talbot BkC/9)
A229	21.7.1832	16.1.1833 29.8.1844	Lewis Burwell copy SGO	'1404'; pt: also Oxford Twp, upper forks Thames R; govt reserves, clearings, improvement by squatters; 20 ch; FN 63	OTAR
A230		–.7.1843	Thomas Parke SG	Survey grid, reserves; scale n.g.	OTAR
A231		11.3.1844	Thomas Parke SG	'1502'; survey grid, reserves	OTAR
	BLANSHARD				
A232	–	21.1.1839	John McDonald	'24' '1143'; contents, mill sites, roads, marshes; FN 66	OTNR (SR 624)
A233		21.1.1839	John McDonald D. McDonald	Marshes, contents, roads, some names	OTAR (Canada Co. Atlas)
	BLENHEIM				
A234	15.11.1794	1.8.1795	Abraham Iredell	'No 6'; c & c reserves, names; FN 209	OTNR (SR 625)
A235	20.1.1798	[1798]	John Stegmann	'B3'; marshes, meadows, windfall, reserves; FN 1–89, 3–366	OTNR (SR 627)
A236		[182?]	Copy J.G. Chewett	'C37' '1505'; c & c reserves, names, marshes, 'Canada Co' in crown reserves	OTAR (SR 626)
A237		[182?]	Copy J.G. Chewett	Marshes, c & c reserves	OTAR
A238		–.7.1843	Thomas Parke SG	Survey grid, reserves; scale n.g.	OTAR

	BLITHFIELD				
A239	24.12.1838	[1840]	Josias [Richey]	'B28' '241'; c & c reserves, mill sites, marshes; FN 795	OTNR (SR 629)
A240		[1840?]	–	'No 39' 'Office Plan'; c & c reserves, some names, later changes	OTAR(P)
	BOSANQUET				
A241	–	4.2.1835	John McDonald	Marshes, Indian reserves and villages, contents of I and II surveys; scale n.g.	OTAR (Canada Co. Atlas 3)
A242		4.9.1835	John Mcdonald copy G. Burgess	'No 2'; for Canada Co., road, Indian reserve, marshes; FN 67	OTNR (SR 623)
A243		25.4.1861	John Macdonald copy CLD	Indian reserves, many later changes	OTAR(P)
	BRANT				
A244		–.6.1849	[A.P. Brough?] CLD	Pt: also Bentinck Twp; Durham Rd lots, town plot reserve; FN 747	OTAR
A245	20.5.1850	–.–.1850	Allan Park Brough	'B55'; contents, relief, marshes, road, town reserve; 2 in = 1 mile; FN 758	OTNR (SR 637)
A246		20.11.1851	T.D. Andrew Russell S&D CLD	'No 56'; names	OTAR(P)
A247	24.1.1857	–.3.1857	Francis Kerr	'B84' '2646/57'; pt: subdivision of reserve; also Greenock Twp; FN 325	OTNR (SR 9564)
	BRANTFORD				
A248	20.4.1831	26.1.1833	Lewis Burwell	'B11' '1130'; N pt; a few names, marshes, roads, villages; FN 69, 70	OTNR (SR 97629)
A249		[1833?]	Copy J.G.C.	'No 2' 'office plan'; N pt; names, roads, town of Brantford showing centre pt only, 6 sts N–S	OTAR(P)
A250		22.8.1838	Lewis Burwell	'Q57' '1081'; Mt Pleasant, Phelps and Douglas tracts; names, roads, villages; various scales	OTNR (SR 646)
A251		1.9.1838	Lewis Burwell	'Q56'; pt; Oneida mission, school lots, Wesleyan Methodist mission lot, names, roads; various scales	OTNR (SR 644)
A252		5.9.1838	Lewis Burwell copy Alex'r Burwell	'Q59' '1171'; names, clearings, Mohawk Church lot, roads, Grand R Navigation Co. property and canal; 20 ch	OTNR (SR 648)

	Date of Instructions	Date of Map	Surveyor and Signature	Endorsements and Notes	Location
A253		7.12.1838	Copy J.G. Chewett	'1521' 'B28'; pt: area N of Brantford; names of owners, 999-year leases	OTAR
A254		6.4.1839	Copy J.G. Chewett	'No 20' 'corrected from earlier surveys including Burwell's'; marshes, roads, some bldgs located and identified, names, town of Brantford with west extension, irregular lots	OTAR(P)
A255	–	25.10.1842	William Walker	'Q65' '1128'; Oxbow Tract, boundaries of sections, pencilled names, relief; 10 ch; FN 71	OTNR (SR 642)
A256		25.10.1842 18.11.1854	W. Walker A.N. Morin C/CL	'No 34'; Oxbow Tract; 10 ch	OTAR(P)
A257		24.3.1843	William Walker	'Q66'; alteration to Burch Tract survey, names; 20 ch; FN 568	OTNR (SR 647)
A258		–.4.1845	Lewis Burwell	Pt: lot 1, Kerr Tract; bearings, notes; scale n.g.	OTAR
A259	19.5.1845	20.12.1845	William Walker	'Q77'; names, Eagles Nest Tract, ranges S of Hamilton Rd; 20 ch; FN 73	OTNR (SR 649)
A260		29.9.1848	Lewis Burwell David Thorburn	Brant Tract, description, names, roads; 20 ch	OTNR (SR 643)
A261		–.2.1849	Copy T. Devine Andrew Russell S&D CLD	'No 39'; survey of residue of twp, N and E of Grand R, names; 20 ch	OTAR(P)
A262		7.12.1853	Lewis Burwell	Pt: lot 4 1st range S of Brantford-Hamilton Rd; Brant Tract; scale n.g.	OTAR
	BROCK				
A263	4.11.1817	22.5.1817	Sam'l S. Wilmot	'A4'; names, c & c reserves, marshes; FN 326	OTNR (SR 664)
A264		[1817?]	S. Wilmot copy W.C.	'C2' '1520'; c & c reserves, marshes	OTAR (SR 666)
A265		[182?]	S. Wilmot copy J.G.C.	'No 4' 'office plan'; names, marshes, later changes	OTAR(P)
A266	28.11.1828	27.4.1829	John Galbraith	'B4' '249'; pt: 14th con line; c & c reserves, marsh; FN 74	OTNR (SR 665)
A267		–.7.1843	[Thomas Parke] SG	Survey grid, reserves, pt missing; scale n.g.	OTAR

	BROMLEY				
A268	24.12.1838	[1841?]	[J. Richey?]	'No 36'; c & c reserves, marsh, names; FN 77	OTAR(P)
A269		–.–.1844	Josias Richey	'B24' '248'; c & c reserves, marshes; scale n.g.	OTNR (SR 670)
A270		23.8.1848	Copy T.D. J.H. Price C/CL	'B31'; lots fronting Bonnechere R, survey grid; scale n.g.	OTAR
	BROOKE				
A271	28.6.1832	20.4.1833	Samuel Smith	'B1'; c & c reserves, marshes, relief; FN 327	OTNR (SR 669)
A272		[1833?]	Copy J.G.C.	'No 1'; c & c reserves, names, later notes 1834 and 1842	OTAR(P)
A273		–.7.1843	Thomas Parke	'B32'; survey grid, reserves; scale n.g.	OTAR
	BROUGHAM				
A274	11.4.1851	–.–.1851	Wm. Campbell	'B32'; pt; clearings, marshes, roads; FN 980	OTNR (SR 652)
A275		–.1.1853	T. Devine CLD A.N. Morin C/CL	'B33' 'No 44' 'Office Copy'; pt: N and NE only laid out; 'Ottawa and Opeongo exploring line'	OTAR
A276		29.3.1853	T.D. Andrew Russell S&D CLD	'No 44' 'Office Plan'; pt: lots in NE portion only; pt Opeongo Rd with lots, trails; scale n.g.	OTAR(P)
	BROWN				
A277	24.8.1866	15.5.1867	M. Deane	'B23'; outlines, trees, marshes, burnt land, comments on land; FN 2334	OTNR (SR 5263)
	BRUCE				
A278		[1851]	–	Shoreline, survey ranges, tracing of pt of projected plan	OTAR
A279	8.4.1851	–.–.1852	A.P. Brough copy Thomas Devine	'B60' 'from A.P. Brough's field notes'; W pt; FN 224	OTNR (SR 656)
A280	16.7.1852	17.1.1853	Chisholm Miller	'B59'; E pt; marshes, beaver meadow, relief; FN 988	OTNR (SR 657)
A281		7.9.1854	David Gibson	Cons I–II and Lakeshore range; proposed subdivision for a village [Inverhuron]; 10 ch	OTAR
	BRUDENELL				
A282	12.6.1856	15.4.1857	H.O. Wood	'B56'; clearings, marshes, rd survey; FN 987	OTNR (SR 658)
A283		3.8.1858	Andrew Russell AC	'No 2' 'office copy'; names, roads	OTAR(P)

	Date of Instructions	Date of Map	Surveyor and Signature	Endorsements and Notes	Location
A284		10.9.1858	CLD	'35'; pt; shows branch rd from Madawaska R to Opeongo Rd in con IX	OTAR
A285	4.8.1862	21.12.1863	Wm. Bell	'R33'; pt: lots on Ottawa and Opeongo Rd; cleared land, marshes, roads, relief, contents; 20 ch	OTNR (SR 7174)
	BRUNEL				
A286	7.6.1861	16.6.186[2?]	J.P. Vansittart	'B9' '8721/62'; relief, marshes; FN 986	OTNR (SR 659)
	BRUTON				
A287	10.9.1862	1.5.1863	B.W. Gossage	Marshes, relief, roads; FN 989	OTNR (SR 660)
	BUCHANAN				
A288	19.6.1854	–.9.1855	James Lyons	'B52'; rd survey, burnt land, slides, several other roads, note: 'erroneous see Hamilton's plan'; FN 225 (OTAR)	OTAR (SR 673)
A289		25–6.8.1856	J.W.B. Joseph Cauchon C/CL	'B38'; Government Rd, survey grid, 2 copies	OTAR
A290	1.12.1856	30.4.1857	Robert Hamilton	'B56' 'B No 1'; Pembroke and Mattawan Rd, erroneous survey lines; FN 1001	OTAR (SR 672)
A291		6.2.1858	Andrew Russell AC	'No 61'; names, roads, many later changes	OTAR(P)
	BURFORD				
A292	–	[1792]	D.W. Smith ASG	'1500' 'C5'; twp granted to Abraham Dayton by O.C. 24.11.1792, notes, reserves; 80 ch	OTAR
A293		15.1.1795	Augustus Jones	'No 7'; c & c reserves, names, marshes; FN 298	OTAR(P)
A294	20.1.1798	[1798]	John Stegmann	'B2' '250'; c & c reserves, marsh, roads, former survey lines; FN 3–345	OTNR (SR 675)
A295		[180?]	W.C.	'1501' 'C4'; c & c reserves	OTAR
A296		[182?]	Copy J.G. Chewitt SG	Marshes, c & c reserves	OTAR
A297		–.7.1843	Thomas Parke SG	Survey grid, reserves; scale n.g.	OTAR
A298		–.10.1846	CLD	'1523' 'C43'; survey grid	OTAR
A299	–	3.6.1852	John Rolph C/CL	Resurvey, orig surv J. Stegmann 1798, road, marshes	OTAR

	BURGESS, N and S				
A300	9.1.1812	[1812]	Reuben Sherwood	'No 5'; names, notes on surveys; FN 79	OTNR (SR 680)
A301		25.8.181[?]	T. Ridout SG	'No 29' '29'; names, notes 1816 and 1843, many later changes	OTAR(P)
A302		-.8.1843	Thomas Parke SG	'B41'; N pt; survey grid, reserves; scale n.g.	OTAR
	BURLEIGH				
A303	14.2.1822	[1822]	A. Miller	'No 6'; c & c reserves, marshes; FN 1003	OTAR (SR 678)
A304		17.11.1837	Copy J.G. Chewett	'No 7' 'Office Copy'; c & c reserves, names in S half, marshes	OTAR(P)
A305		-.7.1843	Thomas Parke SG	Survey grid, reserves; scale n.g.	OTAR
A306	9.1.1864	12.10.1864	James W. Fitzgerald	'B21'; old and new surveys, rd with free grant lots, portages, marshes, relief; FN 48M	OTNR (SR 677)
A307		7.5.1866	Andrew Russell AC	Names, many later changes	OTAR(P)
	CAISTOR				
A308	26.11.1794	[1794–5]	[T. Welch?] [A. Iredell?]	'No 3'; c & c reserves, names, description of the survey and size of lots, roads; scale n.g.; FN 89, 329	OTAR(P)
A309		20.9.1811	Exam T. Ridout	'A4' '30'; names; road from Grand R	OTNR (SR 6317)
A310		[181?]	–	Pt: also Grimsby Twp; names of owners, roads; scale n.g.	OTAR
A311		-.7.1843	Thomas Parke SG	Survey grid, reserves; scale n.g.	OTAR
A312	10.8.1847	23.10.1848	Thomas Allchin	'B10'; pt: line btwn cons I and II; roads, mills, houses, marshes; 20 ch; FN 88	OTNR (SR 689)
	CALEDON				
A313	15.5.1819	25.10.1819	J.G. Chewitt	'B5' '360'; E pt; a few names, marshes, mill seat, c & c reserves; FN 8–120	OTNR (SR 694)
A314	18.6.1819	27.10.1819	S. Ryckman	'A6' 'A7' Caledon East and West, '32' '31'; names, c & c reserves, bearings; scale n.g.; FN 90	OTNR (SR 693)
A315		[1820?]	S. Ryckman J.G. Chewett copy J.G.C.	'C3'; W pt by Ryckman and E pt by Chewett; c & c reserves, marshes, pin holes for tracing	OTAR
A316		[1820?]	S. Ryckman J.G. Chewett copy J.G.C.	'No 6' 'office copy'; W pt by Ryckman, E pt by Chewett; c & c reserves, marshes	OTAR(P)

	Date of Instructions	Date of Map	Surveyor and Signature	Endorsements and Notes	Location
A317		–.7.1843	Thomas Parke SG	Survey grid, reserves; scale n.g.	OTAR
	CALEDONIA				
A318	22.3.1806	29.10.1807	Jos Fortune	'14'; c & c reserves, marshes, a few names; 60 ch; FN 91	OTNR (SR 697)
A319		7.9.1826	T. Ridout	'13' 'rec'd from Land Board'; also shows seigneury Pointe a L'Orignal; names, c & c reserves, later notes 1808 and 1809; 60 ch	OTAR(P)
A320	12.9.1828	15.12.1828	Angus Cattanach	'B7'; resurvey, marshes, road, notes on surveys	OTNR (SR 696)
A321		18.12.1828	Angus Cattanach	'B6' '363'; pt; resurvey, former surveys, road; scale n.g.	OTNR (SR 695)
A322	3.10.1829	1828–9	Angus Cattanach	'B8' '361'; notes on earlier surveys, marshes; FN 92, 93	OTAR (SR 698)
A323		[183?]	Copy J.G. Chewett	Survey details for S pt only, cons V–XI	OTAR
A324		[183?]	–	'No 20'; names, notes 1843	OTAR(P)
	CAMBRIDGE				
A325	22.2.1791	[1791]	James Rankin copy Lt Augustine Prevost	'B14' '453'; Petite Nation R with notes on navigability, marshes; FN 235	OTNR (SR 8918)
A326		–.–.1791	James Rankin copy D.W. Smith	'11' 'office copy'; names, South Nation R with falls; 80 ch	OTNR (SR 97872)
A327		–.–.1791	James Rankin copy W.C.	'C9'; includes Petite Nation R to Ottawa R and notes; 80 ch	OTAR
A328		18.8.1792 –.4/8.1794	Exam W. Chewett	'1391' 'C8'; marshes	OTAR
A329		[182?]	Copy J.G. Chewett	Marshes, c & c reserves	OTAR
A330	27.4.1832	[1834]	Duncan McDonell	'B19'; c & c reserves, falls; FN 94	OTNR (SR 701)
	CAMDEN (KENT)				
A331	–	1794	Pat McNiff A. Iredell	'A3' '258'; 2 cons, names; scale n.g.	OTNR (SR 705)
A332		[180?]	[W. Chewett?]	'A2' '34'; rough plan showing purchase lines by Hambly and Iredell, c & c reserves, a few pencilled names, later notes	OTAR(P)

A333		[182?]	Copy J.G.C.	'No 2'; c & c reserves, marshes, names	OTAR(P)
A334	13.7.1832	2.2.1833	Benjamin Springer	'B19' '400'; pt; marshes, c & c blocks; FN 96	OTNR (SR 704)
A335		–.7.1843	Thomas Parke	Survey grid, reserves; scale n.g.	OTAR
	CAMDEN (Lennox and Addington)				
A336	–	–.–.1789 [1790?]	Lewis Kotte [sgd] Samuel Holland SG	'A6'; names, c & c reserves, notes 1794 and 1802	OTAR
A337		[1792?]	–	'33'; glebe, names with some dated 1794–7; scale n.g.	OTAR(P)
A338	15.8.1807	26.12.1807	Sam'l S. Wilmot	'No 4'; names, c & c reserves	OTAR(P)
A339	22.8.1808	27.12.1808	Sam'l S. Wilmot	'B6'; reserves, marshes, town reserve; FN 95	OTNR (SR 702)
A340		[1808?]	[S. Wilmot?]	'1399' 'C3'; cons 1–6; survey grid, Napanee R	OTAR
A341		–.8.1843	Thomas Parke SG	Survey grid, reserves; scale n.g.	OTAR
A342		2.7.1856	E.P. Taché	'Office copy'; outlines of lots	OTNR (SR 703)
	CANONTO, N and S				
A343	5.6.1857	4.9.1857	Francis Jones	'No 2'; S pt; rating of land, relief; FN 1016	OTNR (SR 712)
A344		–.8.1859	Andrew Russell AC	S pt; comments on land, names, later changes	OTAR(P)
A345	26.10.1858	6.7.1859	J.L.P. O'Hanly	'No 6'; N and S pt; rating of land, clearings with names, marshes, rapids, dam; FN 1015	OTNR (SR 711)
A346		–.8.1859	Andrew Russell AC	N pt; comments on land, clearings with names, many later changes	OTAR(P)
	CARADOC				
A347	19.1.1820	16.7.1821	M. Burwell	'No 9'; names, town plot Colborne, c & c reserves, roads; FN 98	OTNR (SR 725)
A348		18.7.1821	M. Burwell	Marshes, c & c reserves, some names	OTAR (Talbot BkE/2)
A349		[1821?]	–	'1392' 'C7'; reserves, marshes, Long Woods Rd; watermark: 'WHATMAN 1820'	OTAR
A350		10.5.1830	M. Burwell	'Q10' '1118' 'Upper and Lower Munsee Villages'; no of wigwams, cornfields, c & c reserves, roads, trails	OTNR (SR 727)
A351		25.11.1830	M. Burwell	'Q34' '1117'; note: 'erroneous see plan Q35' (**A353**); village of Colborne, c & c reserves, marshes	OTAR (SR 726)

	Date of Instructions	Date of Map	Surveyor and Signature	Endorsements and Notes	Location
A352		8.12.1830	Copy J.G.C. W. Chewett ASG	Some names of owners and date of grant, c & c reserves, lots to be allotted by T. Talbot, state of performance of settlement duty, notes	OTAR
A353	29.7.1833	30.7.1834	Henry James Castle	'Q35' '1119'; pt; rd connecting Long Woods Rd with village of Colborne, Indian reserve; scale n.g.; FN 99	OTNR (SR 729)
A354		9.6.1835	Copy Henry Lizars	'C37'; c & c reserves with notes on variations, village of Colborne, mills, Indian lands for sale	OTAR (SR 728)
A355		–.7.1843	Thomas Parke SG	Survey grid, reserves; scale n.g.	OTAR
	CARDEN				
A356	16.2.1858	27.12.1858	John K. Roche	'No 7'; Portage Rd lots (Eldon Twp), marshes; FN 1023	OTNR (SR 714)
A357		7.9.1860	Andrew Russell AC	'Office copy'; names, marshes	OTAR(P)
	CARDIFF				
A358	4.9.1861	31.10.1862	James W. Fitzgerald	'No 22'; pt; free grant lots on Burleigh Rd, marshes, comments on trees and land, relief; FN 1022	OTNR (SR 716)
A359		[1862]	[J. Fitzgerald]	'C15'; pt: lots 1–15; free grant lots on Burleigh Rd, comments on land, contents	OTAR
A360	4.11.1862	10.9.1863	James W. Fitzgerald	'No 27'; residue of twp; marshes, relief, contents; FN 1021	OTNR (SR 715)
A361		16.12.1863	James W. Fitzgerald	'16792/63'; pt: cons XXI–XXIII; marshes, relief	OTNR (SR 10209)
A362		[1863]	[J. Fitzgerald]	'C15'; pt: lots 16–32; marshes, contents	OTAR
A363		16.3.1864	J. Fitzgerald Andrew Russell AC/CL	Names, many later changes, copy	OTAR(P)
	CARDWELL				
A364	9.1.1866	19.11.1866	F.A. Baldwin	Marshes, relief, Parry Sound Rd; FN 1031	OTNR (SR 718)
A365		29.4.1867	A. Russell AC	Names, Parry Sound Rd	OTAR(P)
	CARLOW				
A366	8.4.1865	[7.9.1866]	Charles Fraser Aylsworth	'C29'; clearings with names, marshes, relief; FN 1019	OTNR (SR 720)

	CARRICK				
A367		16.4.1852	John Rolph C/CL	'Projected plan to accomp Instructions'; bearings, dimensions, rd surveys; scale n.g.	OTAR
A368	16.4.1852	26.12.1852	John D. Daniell	'B57'; marsh, rd survey; FN 1020	OTNR (SR 730)
A369		17.5.1854	A.N. Morin C/CL	'No 58'; names	OTAR(P)
	CARTWRIGHT				
A370	24.2.1816	29.2.1816	Sam'l S. Wilmot	'B4' '365'; pt: cons 1–4; relief, marsh, reserves	OTAR (SR 734)
A371		26.8.1816	Sam'l S. Wilmot	'B5' '366'; relief, marshes	OTAR (SR 732)
A372		[1817]	Sam'l S. Wilmot	'B6' '367'; lake, marshes, relief, rice beds, Indian trading point, reserves; FN 102	OTNR (SR 733)
A373		10.3.1820	Thos Ridout	Projected plan for survey, c & c reserves, bearings, instructions	OTAR
A374		–.8.1843	Thomas Parke SG	Includes pt Scugog and Mariposa twps; survey grid, reserves; scale n.g.	OTAR
A375		–.–.1843	–	'No 7'; includes pt Mariposa and Scugog; names, marshes, relief; scale n.g.	OTAR(P)
	CASHEL				
A376	16.5.1860	17.5.1861	Henry A. MacLeod	'C18'; clearings with names, relief, marshes, mill sites, roads; FN 1035	OTNR (SR 739)
A377		–.10.1861	Andrew Russell AC	'Office plan'; names in SW portion	OTAR(P)
	CAVAN				
A378	10.2.1817	19.3.1817	Sam'l S. Wilmot	'B3' '368'; pt: 4 cons; c & c reserves; FN 104	OTNR (SR 744)
A379	2.5.1817	[1817]	Sam'l S. Wilmot	'A3' 'Completion'; names, c & c reserves; FN 104	OTNR (SR 743)
A380		[182?]	Copy J.G. Chewett W.C. SS&D	'C2' '1408'; relief, marshes, c & c reserves	OTAR (SR 742)
A381		[182?]	–	'No 8'; relief, marshes, c & c reserves, names, notes 1829 and 1844	OTAR(P)
A382		–.8.1843	Thomas Parke SG	Survey grid, reserves; scale n.g.	OTAR
	CAVENDISH				
A383	4.4.1861	5.6.1862	M. Lough	'No 19'; marshes; FN 1038	OTNR (SR 746)

	Date of Instructions	Date of Map	Surveyor and Signature	Endorsements and Notes	Location
A384		[1862?]	–	Areas of hardwood, hemlock, and pine, burnt land; scale n.g.	OTAR (SR 4607)
	CAYUGA				
A385	15.11.1830	6.1.1831	Lewis Burwell	'Q51' '1112'; pt; Indian surrender, marshes, mill seat, Delaware Council House and mission school lot, a few names; FN 106	OTNR (SR 748)
A386		6.1.1831 13.9.1833	Lewis Burwell copy J.G.C.	'A5' '34'; pt: 2 cons and village of Cayuga; Delaware Council House and school lot, names	OTNR (SR 747)
A387	23.4.1833 18.4.1833	4.3.1834	Lewis Burwell	'B3'; notes on survey, trails, boundaries of tracts, Indian reserves, village of Cayuga, marshes; 20 ch; FN 107	OTNR (SR 749)
A388		14.5.[1834?]	Lewis Burwell copy J.G.C.	'No 2' 'office plan'; names, village of Cayuga, marshes	OTAR(P)
A389		[1834?]	–	'1396' 'C27' 'C1'; village of Cayuga, Indian reserves, land owned by Augustus Jones, John Huff, and John Dochstader, roads; scale n.g.	OTAR
	CHANDOS				
A390	16.11.1859	7.12.1860	James Fitzgerald	'E6' '3336/61'; boundary line btwn Chandos and Cardiff; comments on the land, exploring lines; FN 892	OTAR (SR 5865)
A391	12.6.1861	31.10.1862	J.W. Fitzgerald	'No 21'; free grant lots on Burleigh Rd, comments on trees and land, marshes, lumber shanty; FN 1041	OTNR (SR 752)
A392		–.–.1862 –.4.1863	James W. Fitzgerald copy Andrew Russell AC	Marshes, roads, names, later changes	OTAR(P)
	CHAPMAN				
A393	24.8.1866	18.6.1867	A.B. Perry	'R41'; outlines of Chapman and Ryerson; relief, marshes, Nipissing Rd line; FN 2467	OTNR (SR 5927)
	CHARLOTTENBURGH				
A394	18.6.1785	1786	P. McNiff	'19'; names, glebe, marshes; scale n.g.	OTAR (SR 86722)

A395		15.12.1789	Lewis Kotte, P. McNiff, W. Chewett copy W. Chewett	'N28' '1022'; includes Kenyon; names, notes on land grants	OTNR (SR 5495)
A396		[179?]	P. McNiff	'19'; 'rec'd from McNiff in 1796'; names; scale n.g.	OTNR (SR 756)
A397	2.4.1791	2.2.1792	W. Chewett	'22'; also includes Kenyon; names, glebes; scale n.g.	OTAR(P)
A398		12.10.1792	W. Chewett	'21'; names	OTAR(P)
A399		29.10.1794	W. Chewett	'No 21'; pt; marshes; scale n.g.	OTNR (SR 761)
A400		25.11.1794	William Chewett	'No 17'; notes on earlier surveys by Kotte, McNiff, Chewett, McDonell, and Rankin, a few names, marshes, road, relief	OTNR (SR 759)
A401	–	8.2.1820	R. Sherwood	'No 7B' '356'; pt: also Lancaster; lots at mouth R aux Raisins; 20 ch	OTNR (SR 760)
A402	17.4.1830	[1830]	Duncan McDonell	'PF41' '769'; pt: cons 7–8; scale n.g.; FN 117	OTNR (SR 757)
A403	1.5.1832	[1833?]	Jn. McGillis	'PF37' '706'; pt: 4 cons incl gore; marsh; scale n.g.; FN 116	OTNR (SR 758)
	CHARLOTTEVILLE				
A404	3.12.1795 28.10.1796	[179?]	[T. Welch?] copy W.C.	'C6'; survey grid, rivers; scale n.g.; FN 119	OTAR
A405		23.1.1814	M. Burwell	Pt; lots along Talbot Rd, other roads, names located by T. Talbot to 1836	OTAR (Talbot BkC/1)
A406	26.5.1837 8.9.1837	–.4.1838	Peter Carroll	'35[?]'; pt; marsh and Turkey Point clearings, Fort Norfolk, road; scale n.g.; FN 120	OTNR (SR 762)
A407		23.5.1838	Peter Carroll copy J.G. Chewett	'No 20'; pt; marsh and Turkey Point, town plot, names	OTAR(P)
A408		–.4.1839 23.11.1843	Peter Carroll copy G.S. Thomas Parke	Pt: front con A, B, and 1; marsh, cleared land, roads, town plot reserve, Fort Norfolk	OTAR
A409		[1843?]	–	'No 11'; c & c reserves, roads, names, notes 1843 and 1848; scale n.g.	OTAR(P)
A410		–.7.1843	Thomas Parke SG	Survey grid, reserves; scale n.g.	OTAR
A411		–.10.1846	CLD	'1387'; survey grid	OTAR
	CHATHAM				
A412	7.5.1798	8.7.1799	[A. Iredell]	'38'; names, adds to 1833; scale n.g.; FN 108	OTAR (SR 772)

	Date of Instructions	Date of Map	Surveyor and Signature	Endorsements and Notes	Location
A413		24.8.1800	Chewett & Ridout ASG	'1384' 'C1'; plan for survey, lines already run and notes, c & c reserves	OTAR
A414	23.8.1809	[1811]	T. Smith	'No 5'; includes 'Baldoon Bay,' names, marshes, town lots, c & c reserve block; FN 333, 334	OTNR (SR 771)
A415		[181?]	Copy W.C.	'No 6' 'Office Plan'; c & c reserves, names, town plot	OTAR(P)
A416		-.7.1843	Thomas Parke SG	Survey grid, reserves; scale n.g.	OTAR
	CHINGUACOUSY				
A417	8.2.1819	25.8.1819	R. Bristol	'A8' '42'; S pt; c & c reserves, names; FN 126	OTNR (SR 768)
A418		27.8.1819	Thos Ridout SG	Projected plan: rear or N half to be surveyed, c & c reserves	OTAR
A419		23.10.1819	Richard Bristol	'B7' '358'; N pt; c & c reserves, marsh; FN 125	OTNR (SR 770)
A420		-.10.1819	Richard Bristol	'B6' '359'; N pt; c & c reserves, marshes, beaver meadow	OTAR (SR 769)
A421		-.10.1819	Richard Bristol	'B8' '357'; N pt; c & c reserves, marsh, beaver meadow, a few names	OTAR (SR 767)
A422		[1819?]	[Richard Bristol?]	'A5' '41'; names, c & c reserves, later adds; scale n.g.	OTAR (SR 2051-A)
A423		-.-.1819	R. Bristol	Diagram: pt: N or rear half; c & c reserves, marshes; scale n.g.	OTAR
A424		[182?]	R. Bristol copy W.C. SS&D	'C5'; c & c reserves, bearings, 'Brampton' added later, pinholes for tracing	OTAR
A425		[182?]	R. Sherwood	Gore; lots 1–17; names, marshes; scale n.g.; FN 675 (OTAR)	OTAR
A426		-.-.1822	T. Ridout SG	'No 51' 'office plan' '1st location made 11 Sept 1819'; names	OTAR(P)
A427		-.7.1843	Thomas [Parke] SG	Survey grid, reserves, pt missing; scale n.g.	OTAR
	CLARENCE				
A428	4.6.1789?	[1791?]	[James Rankin?]	'A15' '44' 'Twp no 5' 'Old Survey'; pt: front cons; names; scale n.g.; FN 21–135	OTAR(P)
A429		14.8.1792 29.4.1795	W. Chewett	'A11' 'Twp no 5'; names on Grand [Ottawa] R; scale n.g.	OTAR (SR 779)

A430	14.3.1820	[1821]	William McDonald	'A20' '353'; c & c reserves, relief, marshes, a few names, tree types; scale n.g.; FN 335	OTNR (SR 777)
A431		[1821?]	Copy J.G. Chewett	Marshes, c & c reserves	OTAR
A432		[1821?]	–	'12'; c & c reserves, names, marsh, some changes; scale n.g.	OTAR(P)
A433		13.1.1857	Joseph Cauchon C/CL	Survey grid, later copy of Wm McDonald's plan	OTAR
	CLARENDON				
A434	12.6.1861	11.8.1862	John Snow	Clearings with names, marshes, roads, mill sites; FN 1051	OTNR (SR 781)
A435		21.3.1864	Andrew Russell AC	Roads, marshes	OTAR (SR 780)
A436		9.5.1865	Andrew Russell AC/CL	Frontenac Rd, names, later changes	OTAR(P)
	CLARKE				
A437	22.2.1791	[179?]	D.W. Smith ASG	'1388' 'C5'; survey grid, reserves, projected plan; 80 ch	OTAR
A438		[179?]	–	'B7' '352'; pt; con lines marked only, outline; scale n.g.	OTAR (SR 782)
A439		6.9.1811	Copy W.C. exam Tho Ridout	'No 9C' 'office plan'; names; 80 ch	OTNR (SR 6307)
A440		12.12.1826	W.C.	'1407' 'C4'; c & c reserves, road, notes on previous surveys	OTAR
A441		–.8.1843	Thomas Parke SG	'C4'; survey grid, reserves; scale n.g.	OTAR
	CLINTON				
A442	–	[1787?]	D.W. Smith ASG	'A6' '46' 'Rec'd from Land Board of Lincoln' 'twp no 5'; names; scale n.g.	OTAR (SR 789)
A443		25.10.1791	Augustus Jones copy Charles Chambers [sgd] Samuel Holland	'No 5'; gore; names	OTNR (SR 787A)
A444	1.7.1794	[1795?]	–	'1386' 'C44' 'C3'; survey grid, pinholes for tracing; scale n.g.	OTAR
A445		[1795?]	D.W. Smith ASG	'A7' '1393'; pt: cons 9–10; names; scale n.g.	OTAR (SR 785)
A446		11.12.1811	Thos Ridout	'A8' '48'; names, notes on survey problems	OTAR (SR 786)
A447		2.2.1832	George Rykert	'707' 'PF11'; gore; names; 20 ch	OTNR (SR 787)
A448		–.8.1846	A.R.	Relief, copy	OTAR (SR 788)

	Date of Instructions	Date of Map	Surveyor and Signature	Endorsements and Notes	Location
	CLYDE				
A449	12.12.1862	17.7.1863	Charles Sproatt	Relief, marshes; FN 1057	OTNR (SR 791)
	COLBORNE				
A450	–	4.9.1835	John McDonald copy D. McDonald	'No 4'; for Canada Co., Falls Reserve; FN 127, 128, 129	OTNR (SR 795)
A451		[1835?]	John McDonald copy D. McDonald	Lot sizes, contents, names on lots for 1st and 2nd surveys E and W division	OTAR (Canada Co. Atlas 4)
	COLCHESTER, N and S				
A452	1790	14.7.1794	Patrick McNiff	'49'; front, lots 33–97; notes by McNiff re original width of lots 1786 and 1790, names; scale n.g.	OTNR (SR 300)
A453		–.–.1797	A. Iredell	'A6'; N pt; names, 2 maps pasted together; scale n.g.; FN 130	OTAR (SR 797)
A454	28.2.1805	[11.5.1805]	Thomas Smith	'No 4'; c & c blocks in N pt, names in S pt, marshes; scale n.g.; FN 134	OTNR (SR 798)
A455		[1805]	Thos. Smith	'No 2' 'X9' '957'; S pt and Gosfield; village reserve, names in front con only, comments on land; scale n.g.	OTAR (SR 796)
A456	17.4.1821	10.2.1832	M. Burwell	'No 3'; names in N pt, marshes, Malden Rd; FN 132	OTNR (SR 799)
A457		10.2.1832	Copy from Mr Burwell's plan	'No 36'; N and S pts; S pt surv by Thos Smith 1805, c & c reserves, marshes, names, village plot, later changes	OTAR(P)
A458		–.7.1843	Thomas Parke SG	'C48'; survey grid, Malden Rd, reserves; scale n.g.	OTAR
	COLLINGWOOD				
A459	–	[1833]	C. Rankin	'B40' '350'; town of Thornbury, c & c reserves, falls, relief; FN 135	OTNR (SR 805)
A460		[1834?]	C. Rankin	'B39'; c & c reserves, names in cons I–IV, marshes, copy	OTAR(P)
A461		[1834?]	C. Rankin copy J.G.C.	'No 5'; names, c & c reserves, notes 1836 and 1837, town plot	OTAR(P)
A462		–.7.1843	Thomas Parke SG	Survey grid, reserves, town of Thornbury; scale n.g.	OTAR

	CORNWALL				
A463	–	1784–1787 15.12.1789	Louis Kotte Patk. McNiff Wm. Chewett	Includes pt Roxborough; names, rapids, marshes, glebe	OTNR (SR 6784)
A464		1784–7	P. McNiff L. Kotte W. Chewett	'3'; cons 1–9; names, town plot, some later changes	OTAR(P)
A465		[1786?]	P. McNiff	'No 1A' '52' 'Rec'd from P. McNiff in 1786'; names, marshes, mills, comments on land; scale n.g.	OTAR (SR 813)
A466		2.2.1791	W. Chewett	Town plot, names, marshes, rapids	OTAR(P)
A467	22.2.1791	[1791] 18.8.1792	[James Rankin] exam W. Chewett	'No 8B' '357'; pt: lots N of R aux Raisin and pt Roxborough; FN 235	OTNR (SR 816)
A468		[1791]	[J. Rankin]	'998'; pt: cons 7–9 Cornwall and cons 10–11 Roxborough; houses, trails, note 'see field notes C52' (i.e., FN 235); scale n.g.	OTAR (SR 815)
A469		2.12.1794	W. Chewett	'No 15C'; relief, marshes, roads, town of Cornwall	OTNR (SR 814)
	CRAMAHE				
A470	25.8.1795	[1796]	A. Greely	'No 11'; c & c reserves, names, later notes 1817, 1829, and 1844, copy; scale n.g.; FN 346	OTAR(P)
A471		[6?].9.1811	Exam Thos Ridout	'A2'; names	OTNR (SR 5024)
A472	29.2.1824	25.11.1824	Richard Birdsall	'B32'; resurvey and correction of E side line, mills; FN 141	OTNR (SR 824)
A473		25.11.1824	Richard Birdsall	'B8'; same as above (**A472**)	OTNR (SR 823)
A474		–.8.1843	Thomas Parke	Survey grid, reserves, shows creation of Brighton [1851]; scale n.g.	OTAR
	CROSBY, N and S				
A475	–	16.6.1795	Lewis Grant	'A2'; S pt: cons 1–3; c & c reserves; FN 1–65	OTNR (SR 837)
A476		20.6.1805	Reuben Sherwood	'B3'; S pt; c & c reserves, a few names, note 1826; 60 ch	OTAR (SR 836)
A477	28.3.1806	[11.12.1806]	[R. Sherwood]	'No 6'; S pt; names, c & c reserves; scale n.g.; FN 143, 144	OTNR (SR 835)
A478		[11.12.1806]	[R. Sherwood]	'No 7'; N pt; c & c reserves, names, scale n.g.; FN 145	OTNR (SR 86725)
A479	10.5.1842	–.7.1842	P.V. Elmore	'709'; N pt: con 10; FN 146	OTNR (SR 834)

	Date of Instructions	Date of Map	Surveyor and Signature	Endorsements and Notes	Location
A480		4.3.1844	R. Sherwood copy SGO	'1589' 'C55'; N pt; survey grid; scale n.g.	OTAR
A481		4.3.1844	R. Sherwood copy Thomas Parke SG	'C56'; S pt; survey grid; scale n.g.	OTAR
	CROWLAND				
A482	20.12.1793	16.5.1795	[Daniel Hazen?] D.W. Smith ASG	'A27' '341'; sent from Exec Comm to SGO, includes Willoughby, some names; scale n.g.	OTNR (SR 2349)
A483		[1795?]	[Sgd] Samuel Holland	'No 4'; glebe, names, Merrittsville, later changes, copy; scale n.g.	OTAR(P)
A484		20.9.1811	Exam Thos Ridout	'A9' '178'; names, Merrittsville	OTNR (SR 841)
A485	–	–.2.1832	John A. Tidey	'PF12' '708'; pt: gore btwn Crowland and Humberstone; 50 ch	OTNR (SR 840)
A486		–.6.1832	John A. Tidey	'B2' '459' 'private survey'; pt: gore btwn Crowland and Humberstone; amendment of PF12 (**A485**); marsh	OTNR (SR 839)
A487	15.9.1832	17.10.1832	C. Rankin	'B1' '345'; gore, ungranted lands, notes on surveys; 20 ch; FN (OTAR)	OTNR (SR 5315)
	CULROSS				
A488	23.6.1848	–.–.1849	Allan Park Brough	'B37'; pt along Durham Rd; marshes, relief, town reserve	OTNR (SR 843)
A489	30.4.1852	–.–.1852	George McPhillips	'B66'; marshes, relief, limestone; FN 1085	OTNR (SR 842)
A490		15.5.1854	A.N. Morin C/CL	'No 57'; names	OTAR(P)
	CUMBERLAND				
A491	4.6.1789?	[179?]	Copy Lt Augustine Prevost [sgd] Samuel Holland	'A12' '56'; pt: front con with names; c & c reserves; scale n.g.	OTAR (SR 846)
A492		14.8.1792 29.8.1795	Exam W. Chewett	'A13' '57' 'Twp no 6'; outline, a few names; scale n.g.	OTAR (SR 845)
A493	24.3.1820	[1820]	Duncan McDonell	'A14' '347'; c & c reserves, marshes, mill, a few names, road; FN 147	OTNR (SR 848)
A494		–.5.1820	Thos. Ridout	A few names, c & c reserves	OTNR (SR 844)

A495		5.5.1821	Duncan McDonell copy J.G.C. Thos Ridout	'18'; c & c reserves, marshes, names, mill	OTAR(P)
A496		[1821?]	Duncan McDonell copy J.G.C.	'10' 'office plan'; c & c reserves, names, marshes, notes 1843, later changes	OTAR(P)
A497		[1821?]	Copy J.G. Chewett	'C58'; marshes, a few names	OTAR
A498		4.2.1829	Copy W.C.	'C5' '1391'; marshes	OTAR (SR 847)
	DALHOUSIE				
A499	23.6.1819	[2.9.1820]	R. Sherwood	'B15' '373'; c & c reserves, marshes; FN 1099	OTNR (SR 854)
A500		[182?]	–	'No 4'; c & c reserves, names, notes 1838 and 1843; scale n.g.	OTAR(P)
A501		–.8.1843	Thomas Parke SG	'D2'; survey grid, reserves; scale n.g.	OTAR
A502		–.11.1848	Copy T. Bouthillier CLD	Pt: lots 1–16 only; survey grid	OTAR
	DALTON				
A503	22.10.1860	20.9.1861	M. Deane	'No 15'; marshes, clearings with names, falls, rapids; FN 1098	OTNR (SR 855)
	DARLING				
A504	6.6.1822	–.–.1822	R. Sherwood	'B3'; c & c reserves, marshes, a few names; FN 148	OTNR (SR 860)
A505		2.5.1823	R. Sherwood copy J.G.C.	'No 28' '67' 'For Land Board Dist Bathurst'; c & c reserves, marshes, names	OTAR (SR 861)
A506		[1823?]	R. Sherwood copy J.G.C.	'No 3'; c & c reserves, names, notes 1843, later changes	OTAR(P)
A507		–.8.1843	Thomas Parke SG	Survey grid, reserves; scale n.g.	OTAR
	DARLINGTON				
A508	1.7.1793	[1793]	Wm Hambly	'A4' 'Protraction' [projection for survey]; names, c & c reserves; scale n.g.; FN 237	OTNR (SR 866)
A509		[1793?]	D.W. Smith	'C3' '1373' 'office copy'; c & c reserves; 80 ch	OTNR (SR 867)
A510		6.9.1811	Exam Thos Ridout	'A16' '68'; c & c reserves, names; scale n.g.	OTAR (SR 865)
A511		1817	[S. Wilmot?] exam Thos Ridout	'No 12' 'office plan'; c & c reserves, names; [FN 101?]	OTAR(P)
A512		–.8.1843	Thomas Parke SG	Survey grid, reserves; scale n.g.	OTAR

	Date of Instructions	Date of Map	Surveyor and Signature	Endorsements and Notes	Location
	DAWN				
A513	22.12.1820	20.7.1821	[Shubal Park]	'No 7'; names; FN 8–387	OTNR (SR 864)
A514		[1821?]	S. Park copy J.G.C.	'No 40' 'office copy'; includes Camden gore, c & c reserves, marshes, names	OTAR(P)
A515		–.7.1843	Thomas Parke SG	'D6'; survey grid, reserves, later add: 'Gore of Camden'; scale n.g.	OTAR
	DELAWARE				
A516	31.1.1798	3.9.1799	Copy W.C.	'1379' 'C12' 'Addition of pt of the 2nd, the 3rd, 4th and 5th surveyed Cons etc'; Delaware village; FN 153	OTAR
A517		[180?]	–	'No 20'; c & c reserves, names, Delaware village, notes 1835, 1842–3, relief; scale n.g.	OTAR(P)
A518		[182?]	Copy J.G.C.	'1378'; c & c reserves, marshes	OTNR (SR 873)
A519		–.7.1843	Thomas Parke SG	Survey grid, reserves; scale n.g.	OTAR
A520	7.3.1867	13.4.1867	Wm McMillan	'D40'; town line btwn Southwold and Indian lands in Delaware; 20 ch; FN 1755	OTNR (SR 872)
	DENBIGH				
A521	27.10.1856	[1857]	Thomas T. Bower	'B58'; pt; bearings; FN 1108	OTNR (SR 875)
A522		5.11.1860	Andrew Russell AC/CL	Addington Rd, names, later changes	OTAR(P)
A523		10.12.1863	J.L.P. O'Hanly	Tree types, trail, pine and hardwood areas	OTAR (SR 7166)
	DENNIS				
A524	25.7.1859	[3.11.1860]	Joseph Wm. Burke	'D13'; boundary, Indian reserve, wooded areas, burnt land; FN 1113	OTNR (SR 877)
A525		4.4.1861	Andrew Russell AC/CL	Indian boundary	OTAR(P)
	DERBY				
A526	8.7.1840	3.12.1840	C. Rankin	'B41'; Derby and Sydenham twps; Sydenham town plot, mill sites, roads, Indian settlement, relief, soundings, marshes; FN 154	OTNR (SR 878)
A527		10.1.1843	Thomas Parke SG	Pt: cons I–III; mill sites, Sydenham town plot, roads, trails	OTAR

A528		13.11.1848	Copy CLD	Survey grid, Sydenham town plot, no of acres	OTAR
	DEREHAM				
A529	29.4.1799	[3.12.1799]	Wm. Hambly	'No 19'; names, reserves; scale n.g.; FN 155	OTNR (SR 881)
A530	14.4.1810	[4.9.1810]	Sam'l S. Wilmot	'A3'; SE quadrant surveyed only, c & c reserves, names; FN 157	OTNR (SR 880)
A531		[182?]	J.G. Chewett	'No 20' 'office copy'; c & c reserves, names, marsh	OTAR (SR 883)
A532	10.1.1832	[1832]	R. Mount	'B4' '370'; c & c reserves, marshes, roads, foundry; FN 156	OTNR (SR 882)
A533		–.7.1843	Thomas Parke SG	'11'; survey grid, reserves; scale n.g.	OTAR
	DIGBY				
A534	31.10.1859	30.7.1860	Michael Deane	'No 8'; beaver meadows, relief, clearings with names; FN 1123	OTNR (SR 894)
A535		16.10.1860	Andrew Russell AC/CL	Names in SW pt	OTAR(P)
	DORCHESTER, N and S				
A536	13.7.1799	[1800]	Wm. Hambly copy W.C.	'C9' '1382'; N pt; c & c reserves; FN 161	OTNR (SR 902)
A537		[180?]	–	'1383' 'C8'; pt: S of Thames R; rivers and lakes, survey grid	OTAR
A538	14.4.1810	17.6.1810	Sam'l S. Wilmot	'No 18'; names, marshes, c & c reserves, survey markers; FN 159	OTNR (SR 901)
A539		[181?]	–	'57'; N pt: cons 1–5 N of Thames R; c & c reserves, names, notes 1816 and 1843; scale n.g.	OTAR(P)
A540		[181?]	Copy J.G. Chewett	'1376' pt: N of Thames R; c & c reserves	OTAR
A541		[181?]	–	'No 17'; S pt: BF and cons 1–4 S of Thames R; c & c reserves, names	OTAR(P)
A542		–.7.1843	Thomas Parke	N pt; survey grid, reserves N of Thames R; scale n.g.	OTAR
A543		–.7.1843	Thomas Parke	N and S pt; cons A, B, I–XIII S of Thames; survey grid, reserves; scale n.g.	OTAR
A544		–.1.1848	Wm Smiley A.R. CLD	'No 52' '129'; pt: con A and B S of Thames R; clergy reserves, mills, roads; scale n.g.; FN 160	OTAR(P)

	Date of Instructions	Date of Map	Surveyor and Signature	Endorsements and Notes	Location
	DOURO				
A545	1.1.1822	16.4.1823	Richard Birdsall	'B9' '404'; c & c reserves, contents, marshes, a few names; FN 162	OTNR (SR 903)
A546		8.8.1825	R. Birdsall copy J.G.C. Thos Ridout	Names, c & c reserves	OTAR
A547		[1825?]	R. Birdsall copy J.G.C.	'No 13' 'office plan'; c & c reserves, names, many changes, notes 1825–45	OTAR(P)
A548		–.7.1843	Thomas Parke	Survey grid, reserves; scale n.g.	OTAR
	DOVER				
A549	2.8.1795	14.11.1795	A. Iredell	'A12' '635'; includes pts of Raleigh, Chatham, and Harwich; 40 lots, formerly the reserve on Thames R (now allotted to existing twps); town of Chatham, names; 20 ch; FN 110	OTNR (SR 905)
A550	14.11.1795	[1797]	A. Iredell	'B2' '3551'; pt of W and E divisions; scale n.g.	OTNR (SR 6700)
A551		[1797?]	A. Iredell	'B3' '402'; pt; lines run; scale n.g.	OTNR (SR 909)
A552	27.4.1804	3.11.1804	[W. Hambly]	'71'; pt; names, c & c reserves, note: 'the unlocated part of this twp reserved for the Earl of Selkirk'; scale n.g.; FN 164	OTNR (SR 907)
A553		[1804?]	William Hambly	'A9'; pt: cons 3–18; marshes, meadows, Lord Selkirk's lands and bldgs; possibly unfinished	OTNR (SR 908)
A554		6.3.1805	A. Iredell	'896'; includes Chatham and Camden twps; outlines; 80 ch	OTNR (SR 904)
A555		[1805?]	Copy W.C.	'71' 'No 8'; names, notes 1829 and others that are faded, many later changes	OTAR(P)
A556		[1805?]	–	'A10' '74'; pt on Thames R; names	OTAR (SR 912)
A557	23.8.1809	[1810]	Thos S[mith]	'A8'; Baldoon settlement, marsh, meadow, earlier survey lines, a few names; scale n.g.; FN 338, 339	OTNR (SR 906)
A558		26.4.1830	C. Rankin	'No 20' 'Pain Cour Block'; lots 1–15, con 2; names; 20 ch; FN 165	OTNR (SR 911)
A559		–.7.1843	Thomas Parke	'D17'; survey grid, reserves; scale n.g.	OTAR

	DOWNIE				
A560	–	4.9.1835 21.1.1839	John McDonald dr H. Lizars	'No 5'; for Canada Co.; contents, road, marshes; FN 166, 167	OTNR (SR 914)
A561		4.9.1838 21.1.1839	John McDonald	I, III survey in 1838, IV survey 1839; contents, names, road	OTAR (Canada Co. Atlas 5)
	DRAPER				
A562	29.4.1857	16.2.1858	John K. Roche	'D No 1'; S pt; roads, portage; scale n.g.; FN 1130	OTNR (SR 916)
A563		24.4.1858	J.K. Roche Andrew Russell AC/CL	'No 2' 'Office Plan'; names, Muskokaville town plot added (1862)	OTAR(P)
A564	16.7.1861	22.8.1862	W.H. Deane	'No 22'; town plot, post office, clearings with names, roads, marsh, relief; FN 1129	OTNR (SR 915)
	DRUMMOND				
A565	24.2.1816	[1816?]	[R. Sherwood?]	'A3' 'Blotter Plan'; Perth settlement, c & c reserves, notes and names 1816 and 1817, patentees with names of regiments or 'Emigrant'; FN 171	OTAR(P)
A566		–.1.1817	R. Sherwood	'B4' '371'; c & c reserves, marshes	OTNR (SR 917)
A567		–.–.1817	R. Sherwood	'1377' 'C2'; c & c reserves, marshes, copy	OTAR
A568		[1817?]	[R. Sherwood?]	'No 5'; town of Perth, c & c reserves, names, notes 1822 and 1833; scale n.g.	OTAR(P)
A569		[1817?]	James H. Powell Secretary & Superintendent	'No 27'; names, c & c reserves, Perth patentees with names of regiments; scale n.g.	OTAR(P)
A570		–.8.1843	Thomas Parke SG	Survey grid, reserves; scale n.g.	OTAR
	DUDLEY				
A571	9.12.1861	15.8.1862	B.W. Gossage	Marshes, relief, Peterson Rd, Burleigh Rd line; FN 1134	OTNR (SR 920)
	DUMFRIES				
A572	–	[1857?]	Thomas Devine Surv in Chief U.C.	'D24'; S pt: con I–VI N of Paris; railways, Glen Morris, relief	OTAR
	DUMMER				
A573	1.1.1822	16.4.1823	Richard Birdsall	'B10'; c & c reserves, marshes, contents; FN 172	OTNR (SR 922)

	Date of Instructions	Date of Map	Surveyor and Signature	Endorsements and Notes	Location
A574		[1823?]	R. Birdsall copy J.G.C.	'78' 'No 14'; c & c reserves, marshes, names, notes 1829 and 1838, later changes	OTAR(P)
A575		–.7.1843	Thomas Parke SG	Survey grid, reserves; scale n.g.	OTAR
	DUNGANNON				
A576	9.12.1856	[1857]	Quintin Johnstone	'No 5'; pt: outlines and subdivision of outer lots; marshes, comments on soil and tree types, Hastings Rd; FN 1139	OTNR (SR 926)
A577		–.–.1861	Andrew Russell AC/CL	Pt: lots laid out along Hastings Rd only; names	OTAR(P)
A578	28.12.1863	25.8.1864	J.L.P. O'Hanly	'D35'; marshes, clearings, roads, Harris Bronson timber location; FN 1140	OTNR (SR 925)
	DUNN				
A579	18.4.1833 23.4.1833	[1834]	[Lewis Burwell]	'D27' 'C6'; includes Sherbrooke Twp; marshes, relief, town of Dunnville, naval depot, Indian lands, drowned land along Grand R, feeder to Welland Canal; scale n.g.; FN 175	OTAR
A580		[1834?]	Lewis Burwell copy J.G.C.	'C22' '1375'; marsh, names of large lot holders, naval depot, Welland Canal feeder	OTAR (SR 929)
A581		[1834?]	Lewis Burwell reduced J.G.C.	'No 6' 'Office Plan'; roads, town of Dunnville, names	OTAR(P)
	DUNWICH				
A582	18.8.1797	[1797–8?]	[W. Parren Lawe]	'No 13' '77'; N pt; c & c reserves, names; scale n.g.; FN 178, 179	OTNR (SR 935)
A583	4.5.1803	[1803]	William Hambly	'No 12'; names, c & c reserves; FN 177	OTNR (SR 931)
A584	8.6.1811	24.10.1811	Mahlon Burwell	Pt: Talbot Rd W with distances; lots; FN 757	OTNR (SR 6676)
A585		[182?]	[M. Burwell?]	'A2'; c & c reserves, names, cert by Thos Talbot 16.3.1821	OTAR (SR 933)
A586		[182?]	–	'1380' 'D28' 'C11'; pt: cons A–D and 1–3 only; survey grid; scale n.g.	OTAR
A587		[182?]	J.G. Chewett	'No 48' 'office copy'; marsh, rivers	OTAR (SR 934)

A588		[182?]	–	'1381' 'C10'; unfinished outline of survey grid; scale n.g.	OTAR
A589	13.7.1832	24.1.1833	Benjamin Springer	'No 14'; c & c reserves, names, former surveys and resurvey; FN 176, 180	OTNR (SR 932)
A590		–.7.1843	Thomas Parke SG	Survey grid, reserves; scale n.g.	OTAR
	DYSART				
A591	19.10.1861	1.8.1862	John James Francis	Marshes, relief, portages, rapids; FN 1142	OTNR (SR 938)
	EASTHOPE, N and S				
A592	–	4.9.1835	John McDonald copy H. Lizars	'No 7'; for Canada Co., Stratford on Avon, contents; FN 182	OTNR (SR 939)
A593		4.9.1835	John McDonald copy H. Lizars	Lot sizes, contents of I–III surveys, names, Stratford	OTAR (Canada Co. Atlas 6)
	EASTNOR				
A594	–	1.1.1857	J. Stoughton Dennis	'E58'; shows Eastnor and pt of Albemarle; town plots of Hardwicke and Adair, relief, marshes; scale n.g.; FN 1146	OTNR (SR 5498)
A595		9.12.1865	Andrew Russell AC/CL	'78'; town plots of Adair and Hardwicke, no of acres but no names; scale n.g.	OTAR(P)
	EDWARDSBURGH				
A596	–	1785–7 15.11.1789	Jeremiah McCarthy, Wm Chewett and Capt Sherwood copy W. Chewett	'1202'; names, Johnstown town plot, sizes; FN 261	OTNR (SR 951)
A597	21.3.1791	–.8.1791	J. Pennoyer	'No 38' '1019' 'Quebec Plan'; resurvey of outline of twp; FN 501, FN 336 (OTAR)	OTNR (SR 948)
A598		29.8.1795	W. Chewett	'80' 'A3'; names, Johnstown, further reserve for town, reserve for seminary; scale n.g.	OTAR(P)
A599		[1795?]	W. Chewett	'80' 'No 9' 'Quebec Plan'; names, conflicting lines for town of Johnstown, reserve for town parks, later changes on shore	OTAR(P)
A600	22.3.1816	24.8.1816	William Fraser	'No 8'; pt: con 9; names; 20 ch; FN (OTAR)	OTNR (SR 946)
A601	6.10.1836	16.7.1838	James West	'B17' '403'; pt: cons 8–9; marshes; FN 187	OTNR (SR 949)

	Date of Instructions	Date of Map	Surveyor and Signature	Endorsements and Notes	Location
A602	9.1.1847	[1848]	[James West]	Plan of subdivision of lots 24–8, con 2 and pt lots 24–30, con 1; cleared land, bldgs, names of owners; 4 ch; FN 186	OTAR
A603		–.7.1848	CLD	Same information and area as map above (**A602**); town plot and park lots to S; 10 ch	OTAR
A604		[1848?]	[James West]	'No 10'; Johnston and reserve for town parks to N, names; scale n.g.	OTAR (SR 947)
A605	25.11.1847	28.2.1849	John Booth copy Wm Campbell	'B18'; lines in cons 5–8 as surv by earlier surveyors with notes, roads, improved lands, bldgs; FN 184, 189	OTAR (SR 950)
A606		28.2.1849	John Booth Wm Campbell	'B18'; resurvey, includes all earlier survey lines in cons 5–8, roads, clearings, houses, mills, village	OTNR (SR 945)
	EGREMONT				
A607	28.8.1845	–.–.1846	Robert W. Kerr	'B25' '641'; pt: cons 2 and 3 and Normanby; Owen Sound Rd, marshes; FN 1152	OTNR (SR 955)
A608		–.9.1846	A.R. CLD	Pt and Normanby; lots along Owen Sound Rd, free grant lots, reserves	OTAR
A609	18.7.1851	[1852]	John D. Daniels	'B59'; clearings, marshes, rd survey; FN 1153	OTNR (SR 954)
A610		6.3.1852	Copy Thomas Devine John Rolph C/CL	'C3' 'No 36'; reserves, roads	OTAR(P)
	EKFRID				
A611	19.1.1820	20.12.1820	M. Burwell	'B5' '376'; c & c reserves, relief, marshes, mill seats, Long Woods Rd; FN 191, 192, 193	OTNR (SR 957)
A612		20.12.1820	M. Burwell	Road, c & c reserves, names of those located by T. Talbot to 1846	OTAR (Talbot BkD/3)
A613		[182?]	[M. Burwell]	'C8' 'No 21' 'Office Plan'; names	OTAR(P)
A614		[182?]	J.G. Chewett	'C13'; marshes, c & c reserves	OTAR
A615		8.12.1830	Copy J.G.C. W. Chewett ASG	Some names with date of location, lots under T. Talbot, c & c reserves, marshes	OTAR
A616		–.7.1843	Thomas Parke SG	Survey grid, reserves; scale n.g.	OTAR

	ELDERSLIE				
A617	8.4.1851	–.–.1851	George McPhillips	'B54'; marshes, road, Paisley town plot; FN 1156	OTNR (SR 958)
A618		7.5.1852	Copy T. Devine John Rolph C/CL	'77' 'No 65'; names, Paisley town plot	OTAR(P)
	ELDON				
A619	1.6.1822	–.–.1825	Henry Ewing	'B13'; c & c reserves, meadows, marshes, mill seat, a few names; FN 194	OTNR (SR 959)
A620		[1825?]	H. Ewing	'No 15' 'office copy'; some names, c & c reserves, marshes	OTAR (SR 961)
A621		20.9.1836	Henry Ewing	'No 18'; pt; Portage Rd lots, names across lots 24–32; scale n.g.; FN 195	OTNR (SR 960)
A622		[1836?]	H. Ewing copy J.G.C.	'78' 'No 16'; c & c reserves, names, notes 1834, 1835, and 1836, Portage Rd, 'vacant lands reserved'	OTAR(P)
A623		[1836?]	[H. Ewing?]	'78' 'No 17'; c & c reserves, names, marshes, Portage Rd, names and notes 1834, 1840s, 1850s	OTAR(P)
A624		12.1.1843	Thomas Parke	'Office copy'; Portage Rd, c & c reserves, vegetation, names	OTNR (SR 6530)
A625		–.7.1843	Thomas Parke	Survey grid, reserves; scale n.g.	OTAR
	ELIZABETHTOWN				
A626	–	9.4.1791	W. Chewett	'No 5'; names, glebe, marshes; scale n.g.	OTAR (SR 963)
A627		29.4.1795 29.8.1795	W. Chewett	'80' 'A4'; names, glebe	OTAR(P)
A628		–.–.1795	Copy Wm Chewett	'80' 'No 21'; c & c reserves, marshes, names, mills	OTAR(P)
A629		[1795?]	–	'No 11' 'District Plan'; marshes, glebe, names; scale n.g.	OTAR (SR 966)
A630	22.11.1797?	22.10.1797	Lewis Grant	'B4' '405'; pt; conflicting survey lines cons 3–9, marshes; 60 ch	OTNR (SR 965)
A631	15.5.1809?	15.6.1810	Reuben Sherwood	'B12'; mills, mill pond; FN 198	OTNR (SR 964)
A632	15.6.1818	6.11.1818	John Booth	'B5' '378'; resurvey, roads, marshes, various types of mills, some other bldgs identified; FN 199	OTNR (SR 967)
A633		–.8.[1843]	Thomas Parke SG	Survey grid, reserves; scale n.g.	OTAR

	Date of Instructions	Date of Map	Surveyor and Signature	Endorsements and Notes	Location
	ELLICE				
A634	–	[–.1.1835] 27.1.1839	John McDonald dr H. Lizars	'No 6'; for Canada Co., contents, marshes, relief; FN 196, 197	OTNR (SR 962)
A635		21.1.1839	John McDonald	Contents of survey cons 6–16, names in S pt, marshes	OTAR (Canada Co. Atlas 7)
A636		30.4.1852	J. McDonald John Rolph C/CL	Shows Ellice and Logan twps; survey lines already run	OTAR
	ELMA				
A637	30.4.1852	19.10.1853	John Grant	'B67'; marshes, relief, clearings, town plot, conflicting survey lines; FN 1157	OTNR (SR 968)
A638		29.5.1854	A.N. Morin C/CL	'79' 'No 35' 'Office Plan'; survey from school lands in N pt, town of 'Towbridge,' names	OTAR(P)
A639		–.6.1854	A.N. Morin C/CL	'E11'; town plot	OTAR
	ELMSLEY				
A640	26.11.1803	[1804]	John Stegmann	'No 13'; names, conflicting survey lines, marshes; FN 341	OTNR (SR 969)
A641		[183?]	Copy J.G.C.	'1367' '12B'; cons I–X; c & c reserves, marshes	OTAR
A642		–.8.1843	Thomas Parke	N pt; cons 4–10, survey grid, reserves; scale n.g.	OTAR
	ELZEVIR				
A643	29.7.1820	24.5.1821	W. Conger	'B7' '377'; c & c reserves, a few names, marshes; FN 246	OTNR (SR 972)
A644		3.9.1821	W. Conger copy Thos Ridout	'N48'; c & c reserves, marshes, lots patented to John Smith	OTAR(P)
A645		[1821?]	W. Conger copy J.G.C.	'79' 'No 7' 'Office Plan'; c & c reserves, names, many later changes	OTAR(P)
A646		–.7.1843	Thomas Parke	Survey grid, reserves; scale n.g.	OTAR
	EMILY				
A647	12.5.1818	31.12.1818	Sam'l S. Wilmot	'B4' '407'; relief, marshes, unfinished; FN 200, 201	OTNR (SR 970)
A648		31.3.1819	Sam'l S. Wilmot	'B12' '408'; relief, marshes, c & c reserves	OTNR (SR 971)

A649		15.4.1819	Copy J.G. Chewett W.C. SS&D Thos Ridout SG	'80' 'No 40' 'Received from the Land Board ... 6 March 1827'; names in S half only, marshes	OTAR(P)
A650		[1819?]	[S. Wilmot?]	'80' 'N19'; c & c reserves, marshes, names, notes 1838, 1844 etc, later changes	OTAR(P)
A651		6.7.1826	Mr Wilmot copy J.G.C. Thos. Ridout	Lots deeded, c & c reserves, later adds in 1820s and 1850s	OTAR (SR 6547)
A652		–.7.1843	Thomas Parke	Survey grid, reserves; scale n.g.	OTAR
	ENNISKILLEN				
A653	13.7.1832	8.1.1833	Eliakim Malcolm [sgd] Lewis Burwell	'B4' '409'; surveyed by Malcolm under Burwell's direction, c & c reserves, marshes; FN 202	OTNR (SR 973)
A654		17.2.1834	Copy J.G.C.	'78' 'No 9'; c & c reserves, marshes, names	OTAR(P)
A655		–.7.1843	Thomas Parke	'E17'; survey grid, reserves; scale n.g.	OTAR
	ENNISMORE				
A656	–	–.–.1822	Andrew Miller	'No 20'; c & c reserves, names; FN 249	OTNR (SR 977)
A657		[1822?]	A. Miller copy W.C.	'80' 'C6'; c & c reserves, marshes, names, formerly Emily gore	OTAR(P)
A658		–.7.1843	Thomas Parke	Survey grid, reserves; scale n.g.	OTAR
	ERAMOSA				
A659	18.6.1819	9.12.1819	Samuel Ryckman	'B2' '410'; c & c reserves, a few names, cliffs along river, marshes; FN 203	OTNR (SR 974)
A660		[1819]	[S. Ryckman?]	'79' 'A13' '94'; location tickets dated 24.12.1819, c & c reserves, names; scale n.g.	OTAR(P)
A661		[1819?]	S. Ryckman copy W.C.	'79' 'No 8' 'Office Plan'; c & c reserves, marshes, names	OTAR(P)
A662		–.7.1843	Thomas Parke SG	Survey grid; scale n.g.	OTAR
	ERIN				
A663	8.2.1819	10.11.1819	Charles Kennedy	'A10'; pt: lots 1–12; c & c reserves, some names, marshes; FN 204	OTNR (SR 975)
A664		[1819?]	[C. Kennedy?]	'81' 'A12' '85'; S pt, lots 1–17; names, c & c reserves, notes 1828 and 1832; scale n.g.	OTAR(P)

	Date of Instructions	Date of Map	Surveyor and Signature	Endorsements and Notes	Location
A665	–.8.1820	5.4.1821	Samuel Ryckman	'B9'; c & c reserves, a few names, beaver meadows and dams, marshes; FN 242	OTNR (SR 976)
A666		[1821?]	[S. Ryckman?]	'81' 'No 7'; c & c reserves, names, notes 1819, 1824, 1830s, 1840s	OTAR(P)
A667		–.11.1842	Robert W. Kerr	Pt; improvements in rd btwn cons 7–8 at lots 10 & 11 and 20 & 21, new line of rd; 12 perches	OTAR
A668		–.7.1843	Thomas Parke SG	Survey grid, reserves; scale n.g.	OTAR
A669		–.11.1846	CLD	Pt: lots 18–32; survey grid	OTAR
A670		8.4.1846	CLD copy A.R. T. Bouthillier	Survey grid	OTAR
	ERNESTOWN				
A671	–	–.–.1783	John Collins copy Wm. Chewett and Chas. Chambers [sgd] Samuel Holland	'No 6'; names, glebe	OTNR (SR 97935)
A672		1784 17.8.1829	[Sgd] W. Chewett ASG	'A No 10' '87'; note indicating plan used in surveying and settling loyalist troops; scale n.g.	OTNR (SR 979)
A673		[179?]	W. Chewett	'AN11' 'Quebec Plan'; names, marshes, reserves, glebe	OTAR(P)
A674		[179?]	–	'81' 'A8' '86'; names, reserves; scale n.g.	OTAR(P)
A675		[179?] 15.3.1811	Alex Aitken exam T. Ridout	'81' 'No 5'; names, reserves, glebe	OTAR(P)
A676		–.8.1843	Thomas Parke SG	'–A'; survey grid, reserves; scale n.g.	OTAR
A677		–.10.1846	D.B. Papineau	'B13'; survey grid, reserves	OTAR (SR 86728)
A678		26.6.1856	E.P. Taché per C/CL	Survey grid	OTAR
	ESCOTT				
A679	30.6.1788	23.12.1794	W. Chewett	'C6' '1st and 2nd Con laid out by Messrs James and Hugh McDonell'; shoreline relief	OTNR (SR 984)
A680		[1796]	[L. Grant]	'A6' '179'; 'True course' of con lines, names; scale n.g.; FN 500	OTAR (SR 982)
A681		[1796]	[L. Grant]	'A7' '89'; glebe, names; scale n.g.	OTAR (SR 983)

A682		9.9.1856	Joseph Cauchon C/CL	'92' 'No 34'; Grenadier Is, lot nos only, later changes; scale n.g.	OTAR(P)
	ESQUESING				
A683	8.2.1819	[–.8.1819] 9.9.1819	Richard Bristol Charles Kennedy	1 map in 2 sections: 'A9' '90'; front pt; c & c reserves; FN 208; 'A11' '91'; rear pt; names; FN 207	OTNR (SR 985)
A684		–.–.1822	Chas Kennedy and Richard Bristol copy W.C. SS&D	'84' 'No 9'; names, some later changes, N half surveyed by Kennedy and S half by Bristol	OTAR(P)
A685		–.7.1843	Thomas Parke SG	Survey grid, reserves; scale n.g.	OTAR
	ESSA				
A686	4.2.1820	19.6.1820	Sam'l Benson	'No 7'; names, c & c reserves; scale n.g.; FN 206	OTNR (SR 980)
A687		19.6.1820	Sam'l M. Benson	'B10'; c & c reserves, marshes; scale n.g.	OTAR (SR 981)
A688		19.6.1820	Samuel Benson	Marshes, c & c reserves, a few names; scale n.g.	OTAR
A689		19.6.1820	Sam'l M. Benson copy J.G. Chewett	'83' 'No 13'; c & c reserves, marshes, names; scale n.g.	OTAR(P)
A690		–.7.1843	Thomas Parke SG	Survey grid, reserves; scale n.g.	OTAR
	ETOBICOKE				
A691	21.3.1795	–.4.1795	Abraham Iredell	'A11' '95'; pt; some names, notes; 20 ch; FN 209	OTNR (SR 995)
A692		20.4.1795	Abraham Iredell	'B11'; S pt; only E half laid out, rest is sketched, notes on survey and type of land; 20 ch	OTAR (SR 993)
A693		[1795?]	Copy W.C.	'A37' '93'; military tract, a few names; 20 ch	OTAR (SR 996)
A694	27.6.1798	[1798]	[Wm Hambly]	'A10'; instructions from D.W. Smith ASG, clergy reserve, names; 20 ch; FN 216	OTNR (SR 989)
A695	25.1.1811	25.2.1811	Sam'l S. Wilmot	'B12'; S pt; Colonel Smith's land, roads, clearings; 20 ch; FN 211	OTNR (SR 992)
A696		[1811?]	W.C.	'A9'; c & c reserves, names, relief, marshes, later notes 1816–17 and 1819; 20 ch	OTAR(P)
A697		[1811?]	–	'No 8'; c & c reserves, names, later changes	OTAR(P)
A698	2.1.1838	19.1.1838	H.J. Castle	Reserve at mouth of Humber, bridge, roads, relief; 1" = 2.6 ch; FN 210	OTNR (SR 997)
A699		–.7.1843	Thomas Parke SG	Survey grid, reserves; scale n.g.	OTAR
A700		2.3.1844	Thomas Parke SG	'1368' 'C32'; survey grid, Dundas St	OTAR

	Date of Instructions	Date of Map	Surveyor and Signature	Endorsements and Notes	Location
A701		20.3.1852	T. Devine John Rolph C/CL	'C72' 'No 20'; 'Humber Park lots' E of Humber R, names, roads; scale n.g.	OTAR(P)
A702		18.4.1857	William Hawkins	Pt; for Mr James Stuck, notes on earlier surveys, 2 copies; 10 ch	OTAR
A703		[1857?]	–	Resurvey of rd allowances; scale n.g.	OTAR
	EUPHRASIA				
A704	–	20.4.1836	J.G. Chewett	'Diagram for the survey ... Euphrasy'; survey grid, reserves; 80 ch	OTAR
A705		–.9.1836	C. Rankin	'No 56'; c & c reserves, names; FN 217	OTNR (SR 1000)
A706		–.9.1836	C. Rankin DS	'B15' 'Plan No 2'; c & c reserve blocks proposed, marshes	OTNR (SR 999)
A707		20.9.[1836?]	C. Rankin	Pt: cons 9–12, lots 1–8 and lots 73–103 on the rd, and cons 1–3 E and W; 80 ch	OTAR
A708		[1836?]	Copy J.G.C.	'1369'; c & c reserves	OTAR
A709		–.7.1843	Thomas Parke SG	Survey grid, reserves; scale n.g.	OTAR
	EYRE				
A710	12.12.1862	28.5.1863	John James Francis	Marshes, relief; FN 1166	OTNR (SR 1003)
	FARADAY				
A711	9.12.1856	[–.12.1857]	Quintin Johnstone	'No 9'; outlines and surveyed outer area subdivided, comments on land and trees, marshes, relief, mill sites, town plot sites; FN 1174, 1906	OTNR (SR 1009)
A712		–.1.1861	Andrew Russell AC/CL	'288'; pt: lots along Hastings Rd only; some names	OTAR(P)
	FENELON				
A713	2.9.1824	23.12.1824	James Kirkpatrick	'No 21' 'Office Plan'; names, c & c reserves, contents; FN 253	OTNR (SR 1016)
A714		[1824?]	[J. Kirkpatrick?]	Names, adds to 1850s, pts missing; scale n.g.	OTAR (SR 1017)
A715		[1824?]	Copy J.G.C.	'290' 'No 22'; c & c reserves, names, marshes, notes 1826–33	OTAR(P)

A716		18.5.1831	Copy J.G.C.	'C7' '3' '175'; c & c reserves, marshes	OTAR (SR 1018)
A717		–.7.1843	Thomas Parke SG	Survey grid, reserves; scale n.g.	OTAR
	FENWICK				
A718	7.11.1859	[1.12.1860]	Joseph Wm Burke	'F14'; Aupaquosh town plot, marshes, burnt land and relief, Indian houses; FN 1177	OTNR (SR 1020)
A719		11.4.1861	Andrew Russell AC/CL	Goulais R town plot, marsh, burnt land	OTAR (SR 1021)
A720		7.2.1862	Andrew Russell AC/CL	'92'; Indian lands, town plot, treed and marshy areas, relief, a few names	OTAR(P)
	FERRIE				
A721	24.8.1866	18.6.1867	A.B. Perry	'F23'; outlines of Ferrie and Croft twps, relief, marshes, comments on land; FN 2467	OTNR (SR 6612)
	FINCH				
A722	1.9.1793	2.6.1794	Wm Chewett	'No 12C' '1364'; glebes, crown reserves, marshes, tree types indicated along outside survey lines, survey conflicts; FN 535	OTNR (SR 1029)
A723	4.5.1803	[1803]	John Stegmann	'16'; names, survey conflicts; FN 399	OTNR (SR 1028)
	FISHER				
A724	28.10.1864	2.11.1865	George B. Kirkpatrick	Mining reserve, Indian reserve boundary, marshes, relief, village of 'Batchewaung'; FN 1182	OTNR (SR 1032)
A725		15.3.1867	A. Russell AC	'86'; Indian lands, marshes, mining lots	OTAR(P)
	FITZROY				
A726	6.6.1822	–.–.1822	R. Sherwood	'B16' '413'; c & c reserves, some names, falls, rapids, marshes; scale n.g.; FN 400	OTNR (SR 1034)
A727		22.5.1823	R. Sherwood copy J.G.C. Thos Ridout SG	'No 29'; c & c reserves, marshes, a few names, area reserved from settlement on L Chaudière	OTAR (SR 1035)
A728		[1823?]	R. Sherwood copy J.G.C.	'C63' 'No 6' '2nd copy'; c & c reserves, names, notes 1843, later changes	OTAR(P)
A729		18.3.1830	R. Sherwood copy W. Chewett ASG	'C63' 'A4'; Fitzroy and Torbolton twps, c & c reserves, names, marshes	OTAR(P)

	Date of Instructions	Date of Map	Surveyor and Signature	Endorsements and Notes	Location
	FLAMBOROUGH, E and W				
A730	–	20.10.1791	Augustus Jones copy J.F. Holland [sgd] Samuel Holland	'B1' 'Twp no 8'; E pt; 5 cons, a few names, Long Beach; scale n.g.	OTAR (SR 1040)
A731	23.5.1793?	[1793?]	[A. Iredell?]	'A5' '102'; E pt; rear lots 1–13 cons 5–10, names; scale n.g.; FN 403	OTAR(P) (SR 1036)
A732		[1793?]	D.W. Smith ASG	'A8'; rec'd from Land Board of Lincoln; shows lots 1–35 in 9 cons Barton and lots 1–14 con 1–3 Flamborough, E and W, names; scale n.g.	OTAR(P)
A733		[1793?]	D.W. Smith ASG	'A4'; Cootes Paradise, some names	OTNR (SR 1041)
A734	16.8.1797	[1797]	[J. Stegmann]	'A3'; c & c reserves, names; scale n.g.; FN 56	OTAR (SR 1037)
A735		[1799]	John Stegmann A. Jones	'Q1' '1051' 'Received by D.W.S. 11.7.1799'; E pt and pt of Nelson; Capt Brant's land, 2 plans; 20 ch; FN 366	OTNR (SR 1039, 1039A)
A736		[180?]	Copy W.C.	'No 10' 'Fair Office Plan'; names, 'Coots Paradise town plot' [Dundas], c & c reserves; scale n.g.	OTAR(P)
A737		19.6.1822 10.3.1847	Copy A. Jones A.R. CLD T. Bouthillier	W pt; lots 16–20 on Dundas St and pt Ancaster Twp, survey posts; 10 ch	OTAR
A738		–.7.1843	Thomas Parke SG	Survey grid, reserves; scale n.g.	OTAR
A739	6.10.1846	[1847?]	Peter Carroll	'B36' '1195'; W pt; lot 19 con 1, Coots Paradise, a few names, Desjardins Canal; 4 ch	OTNR (SR 1038)
	FLOS				
A740	18.8.1821	14.1.1822	John Goessman	'No 10'; names, c & c reserves; FN 405, 418	OTNR (SR 38265)
A741		[182?]	J.G. Chewett	'No 53' 'Office copy'; c & c reserves, some names, marshes, Penetang Rd lots; scale n.g.	OTAR (SR 1045)
A742		–.7.1843	Thomas Parke SG	Survey grid, reserves; scale n.g.	OTAR
	FOLEY				
A743	30.1.1866	6.10.1866	Geo. Stewart	'F22'; marshes, relief, Parry Sound Rd, clearings with names; FN 1191	OTNR (SR 1046)

	FRANKLIN				
A744	24.9.1864	20.7.1865	Henry Lawe	'F21'; marshes, relief, portages; FN 1201	OTNR (SR 1056)
	FRASER				
A745	17.5.1854	[11.4.1855]	J. Robertson	'B48'; shows outlines and pt subdivided, marshes, relief, road, printed title; FN 1200	OTNR (SR 1059)
A746		23.1.1856	Joseph Cauchon CLD	Twp only partially laid out, Petawawa R, winter roads, copy for agent	OTAR (SR 1058)
	FREDERICKSBURGH, N and S				
A747	–	–.–.1784	James Peachey, Lewis Kotte, Henry Holland, Sam'l Tuffe	'No 48' '1009' 'No 9' 'office copy'; names	OTNR (SR 5265)
A748		–.–.1784	James Peachey, L. Kotte, H. Holland, S. Tuffe copy [sgd] S. Holland	'C84' 'No 9'; names, some later changes	OTAR(P)
A749		[1784?]	Copy W. Chewitt	'105' 'A No 13'; 'Twp no 3'and half of 'twp no 4'; names, town plot; scale n.g.	OTAR
A750		[179?]	–	'1366' 'C5'; survey grid, marsh; scale n.g.	OTAR
A751		[179?]	–	'No 8'; names, village, glebe	OTAR(P)
A752	–	–.–.1835	P.V. Elmore	'B53' '713'; pt: cons 2–3; resurvey, notes, orig posts; 20 ch	OTNR (SR 1063)
A753		–.–.1856	CLD J.W.B. E.P. Taché per C/CL	Survey grid	OTAR
	FULLARTON				
A754	–	4.9.1835 –.–.1839	John McDonald dr H. Lizars	'No 8'; shows Fullerton and Hibbert twps, marshes, roads; FN 166, 167	OTNR (SR 1070)
A755		21.1.1839	John McDonald	Contents of survey cons 6–14, roads, some names; FN 166	OTAR (Canada Co. Atlas 8)

	Date of Instructions	Date of Map	Surveyor and Signature	Endorsements and Notes	Location
A756		21.1.1839	John McDonald	'No 8A'; some names	OTAR (SR 1069)
	GAINSBOROUGH				
A757	15.11.1792 14.8.1795	[180?]	–	'No 7'; c & c reserves, names; scale n.g.	OTAR(P)
	GALWAY				
A758	20.4.1857	31.12.1857	M. Deane	'G No 1'; NW pt; beaver meadow; FN 1216	OTNR (SR 1074)
A759		2.5.1858	Andrew Russell AC/CL	'N25–9'; N pt and lots on Bobcaygeon Rd; names	OTAR (SR 5563)
A760	22.6.1859	24.4.1860	William Drennan	'G No 9'; SE pt; marsh, relief, types of trees; FN 1215	OTNR (SR 1075)
A761		10.9.1860	W. Drennan Andrew Russell AC/CL	'1'; names, marshes, Bobcaygeon Rd, a few notes, copy	OTAR (SR 5562)
	GARAFRAXA, E and W				
A762	–.8.1820	8.11.1821	Samuel Ryckman	'B3' '452' 'S26-18'; c & c reserves, some names; FN 815	OTNR (SR 8905)
A763		[1821?]	Samuel Ryckman copy J.G.C.	'94' 'No 13' 'Office Plan'; c & c reserves, names, notes 1844, 1845, 1851	OTAR(P)
A764		–.7.1843	Thomas Parke SG	Survey grid, reserves; scale n.g.	OTAR
A765	8.1.1861	–.5.1867	C.J. Wheelock	'1174/68'; pt: lot 1 con 19; notes on survey lines; scale n.g.	OTNR (SR 5293)
	GEORGINA				
A766	4.11.1817	[6.1.1818]	Duncan McDonell	'No 14'; names; scale n.g.; FN 411, 413	OTNR (SR 1081)
A767		[1818?]	Duncan McDonell	'A12' '106'; c & c reserves, pencilled names; scale n.g.	OTAR (SR 1082)
A768		[1818?]	Copy W.C.	'C8' '1356'; note: 'O.C. 4th March 1819 rescinded by O.C. 15 May 1822,' c & c reserves, town plot site	OTAR (SR 1080)
A769		–.7.1843	Thomas Parke SG	'G5'; survey grid, reserves; scale n.g.	OTAR
	GLAMORGAN				
A770	10.6.1861	18.3.1862	E.R. Ussher	'No 13'; marshes, rapids, falls, relief; FN 1233	OTNR (SR 1102)

	GLANFORD				
A771	6.12.1793	–.1.1794	Augustus Jones	Glanford and pt of Binbrook 'No 11'; c & c reserves, names; FN 366	OTNR (SR 1093)
A772	20.1.1798	[1799] 20.9.1811	John Stegmann exam Thos Ridout	'A25' '107'; includes pt of Binbrook; c & c reserves, names, Grand River Rd; FN 3-289	OTNR (SR 1092)
A773		14.12.1811	[J. Stegmann?] Thos Ridout SG	'98' 'No 12'; names, road	OTAR(P)
A774		–.7.1843	Thomas Parke SG	Survey grid, reserves; scale n.g.	OTAR
	GLENELG				
A775	–	6.3.1846	[A. Vidal?] Andrew Russell S&D CLD	'290' 'No 47'; pt: lots in 3 cons E of Owen Sound Rd only; school lands, names	OTAR(P)
A776		–.6.1850	CLD	Cons I–III, smaller lots either side of Durham Rd, con IV–XV larger lots; projected plan; scale n.g.	OTAR
A777	25.6.1850	30.4.1851	J. Stoughton Dennis	'B53'; marshes, residue, previous surveys, relief; FN 944	OTNR (SR 1103)
A778		9.7.1851	J.S. Dennis copy Thos Devine Andrew Russell C/CL	'290' 'No 33'; Durham Rd, Garafraxa Rd, names	OTAR(P)
	GLOUCESTER				
A779	4.6.1789	[1789?]	–	'A6' '111' 'Township no 7'; front con, names; scale n.g.	OTAR (SR 1109)
A780		14.8.1792 25.8.1795	W. Chewett SS&D exam W. Chewett	'A8' '113' a few names; scale n.g.	OTAR (SR 1107)
A781		[1794?]	J. Stegmann	Survey of twp boundary and front con lines; c & c reserves, names; scale n.g.; FN 854, 14–4	OTNR (SR 1106)
A782	24.3.1820	[1820]	Duncan McDonell	'A5'; marshes, names; FN 414	OTNR (SR 1110)
A783		5.5.1821	D. McDonell copy J.G.C. Thos Ridout	'20' 'For the Land Board'; names, c & c reserves, Rideau Falls; scale n.g.	OTAR (SR 1108)
A784		[1821?]	Duncan McDonell copy J.G.C.	'95' '6'; c & c reserves, names, later changes, marshes, notes 1839, 1843	OTAR(P)
A785		10.5.1857	Copy T.D. CLD T. Bouthillier	'C15'; pt and Osgoode Twp; Long Island, lots, boat channel; 10 ch	OTAR (SR 86738)

	Date of Instructions	Date of Map	Surveyor and Signature	Endorsements and Notes	Location
A786	–	–.10.1857	Wm. McConnell	'13904/58' '108763/62' pt: lots XXI and XXII junction gore; improvements with names, clearings; 8 ch; FN 2202	OTNR (SR 5559)
A787		–.10.1857 6.8.1862	Wm McConnell CLD	Pt: lots 21 and 22 junction gore, plan of subdivision, various claims and names, cleared lands, bldgs; 8 ch	OTNR (SR 1105)
	GODERICH				
A788	26.8.1828	1828–9	David Gibson	'No 9' '1145'; diagram, town of Goderich, roads; FN 416, 417	OTNR (SR 1111)
A789		1828–9	David Gibson	Goderich and Bayfield town plots and Falls Reserve, roads, names, data on relief, etc, for Goderich harbour	OTAR (Canada Co. Atlas 9)
A790		12.8.1861	A.C. Robertson	'No 11'; pt; 'Cut line'	OTNR (SR 1112)
A791		12.8.1861	A.C. Robertson	Altered survey of 'Cut line'; lots 24–7 cons 2–11, lot 83–4 Maitland Con	OTAR (Canada Co. Atlas)
	GOSFIELD, N and S				
A792	–	[1790]	P. McNiff	'A12' '114'; front con, redoubts on lot 8 on E side, names; scale n.g.	OTNR (SR 1120)
A793		[179?]	Copy W.C.	'A14' '116'; lots 1–32	OTAR (SR 1119)
A794		9.7.1800	A. Iredell	'A13'; pt: front con only; a few names; FN 110?	OTNR (SR 1121)
A795	28.2.1805	[1806]	[Thos Smith]	'A15' '117'; pt; c & c blocks, names in front cons; FN 133, 134	OTNR (SR 1124)
A796	17.4.1821	26.3.1823	M. Burwell	'B5'; Talbot Rd, c & c reserves, marshes, trail; FN 420	OTNR (SR 1123)
A797		[1823?]	[M. Burwell]	Talbot Rd, survey grid, marshes	OTAR
A798		[1823?]	Copy J.G. Chewett	'C71' 'No 10' 'Office Plan'; names, marshes, many later changes	OTAR(P)
A799		18.1.1832	Copy J.G.C. W. Chewett ASG	Marshes, c & c reserves, lots granted with names, lots open for location by T. Talbot, trails	OTAR (Talbot BkC/13)
A800		–.7.1843	Thomas Parke SG	Survey grid, reserves; scale n.g.	OTAR
A801		–.2.1848	CLD	'C71' 'No 41' 'Office copy'	OTAR(P)

	GOULBURN				
A802	24.2.1816	–.1.1817	R. Sherwood	'B14' '415'; c & c reserves, marshes; FN 8–74	OTNR (SR 1126)
A803	16.1.1818	2.4.1818	Wilson Conger	'B5'; c & c reserves; FN 419	OTNR (SR 1128)
A804		[182?]	–	'No 30' '118'; names; scale n.g.	OTAR (SR 1127)
A805		[182?]	–	'93' 'No 7' 'Office Plan'; c & c reserves, names, town of Richmond, notes 1843, copy	OTAR(P)
A806		–.9.1846	Copy A.R. CLD	'1363' 'G14'; town of Richmond, survey grid	OTAR
	GOWER, N and S				
A807	25.6.1799	29.11.1799	Lewis Grant	'No 15'; S pt; names, c & c reserves; FN 240, 2–273	OTNR (SR 1134)
A808		[1799?]	[Lewis Grant?]	'No 14'; N pt; reserves, names, pt lost; scale n.g.	OTNR (SR 1133)
A809		1799 21.8.1844	Lewis Grant SGO	'1362'; survey grid	OTAR
A810	18.11.1824	–.–.1824	Reuben Sherwood, Wm. Campbell, Asa Landon	'B14'; N pt; c & c reserves; FN 423, 547	OTNR (SR 1132)
A811	4.5.1830	–.9.1830	James West	'No 16'; S pt; cons 6–9, marshes; FN 421	OTNR (SR 1131)
A812		–.9.1830 21.8.1844	James West	'1361'; S pt; cons 6–9, copy	OTAR (SR 1135)
A813		–.8.1843	Thomas Parke SG	S pt; survey grid, reserves; scale n.g.	OTAR
	GRANTHAM				
A814	–	25.10.1791	Augustus Jones copy [sgd] Sam'l Holland	'No 9'; names; FN 255	OTAR(P)
A815		25.10.1791 30.1.1794	Aug. Jones copy Lewis Grant D.W. Smith	'A14'; names	OTNR (SR 1139)
A816	6.1.1795?	16.7.1795	D.W. Smith M. Dixon	'A13' '120'; names; scale n.g.	OTAR (SR 1138)
A817		24.12.1811	Exam Thos Ridout	'A12' '119'; names	OTAR (SR 1140)
	GRATTAN				
A818	12.4.1851	–.–.1851	John Booth	'B33'; pt: S half 8 cons; beaver ponds, marshes, claims of squatters, Opeongo Rd, relief; scale n.g.; FN 343, 344	OTNR (SR 1144)

	Date of Instructions	Date of Map	Surveyor and Signature	Endorsements and Notes	Location
A819	1.10.1852	20.5.1853	Robert Hamilton	'B42'; clearings with names, roads, timber slides, marshes; FN 1244	OTNR (SR 1142)
A820		20.5.1853	Robert Hamilton	'B41'; pt; town plot, cleared areas, roads, timber slides; scale n.g.	OTAR (SR 1143)
A821		-.10.1853	CLD A.N. Morin C/CL	'97' 'No 45'; names, town plot, later changes, notes 1863	OTAR(P)
A822		12.10.1863	William Bell	'R30'; pt: lots on Ottawa and Opeongo Rd, cleared lands, marshes, roads; 20 ch	OTNR (SR 6504)
	GREENOCK				
A823	23.6.1848	[1850?]	[A. Brough?]	Pt and Kinloss Twp: cons 1–3 N and S of Durham Rd, scale n.g.; FN 746?	OTAR
A824	30.4.1851	[28.8.1852]	R. Walsh	'B55'; earlier survey lines, resurveys, beaver meadows, marshes, 'windfall'; FN 1245	OTNR (SR 1148)
A825		26.5.1854	A.N. Morin C/CL	'No 55'; names, Paisley town plot	OTAR(P)
	GREY				
A826	30.4.1852	-.-.1852	P. Donnelly	'B65'; marshes, town plot, reserves, lots; FN 1246	OTNR (SR 1147)
A827		12.12.1854	P.S. Donnelly A.N. Morin C/CL	'No 68'; names, town of Cranbrooke	OTAR(P)
	GRIFFITH				
A828	1.9.1857	[1859]	Josias Richey	'No 12'; pt: cons I–VII; squatters, improvements, road, 'shutes'; 16 ch; FN 1247	OTNR (SR 1146)
A829		[1859]	Josias Richey	'No 8'; pt; clearings with names, bldgs, roads	OTNR (SR 1145)
A830		-.12.1860	Andrew Russell AC/CL	'94'; names in S and E, many later changes	OTAR(P)
	GRIMSBY				
A831	–	25.10.1791	Augustus Jones	'No 8'; glebe, names, some later changes, copy	OTAR(P)
A832		23.9.1811	Exam Thos Ridout copy W.C.	'1358' 'C9'; gore survey, names; 20 ch	OTAR
A833	28.12.1831	-.11.1832	George Rykert	'B5'; names in con 7; 20 ch; FN 428	OTNR (SR 1154)
A834		28.12.1832	SGO	'1359'; notes on earlier surveys, road; scale n.g.	OTAR

A835		29.5.1841	James Kirkpatrick	'B8' '124'; earlier surveys, 'square' twp and orig cons 9–10	OTNR (SR 1150)
	GUELPH				
A836	[1827]	[1830?]	[John McDonald]	'No 14' '1146'; town plot, types of trees, marshes, roads; FN 429, 430	OTNR (SR 1157)
	GUILFORD				
A837	17.2.1862	6.4.1863	F.A. Baldwin dr A.C. Thomson	'No G13a'; relief, marshes, Peterson Rd; FN 1253	OTNR (SR 1160)
	GWILLIMBURY, E, N, and W				
A838	11.4.1800	[1803?]	John Stegmann	'A14'; N and E pt; names, tamarack and cedar swamp; scale n.g.; FN 4–49	OTNR (SR 1169)
A839		[1803?]	[J. Stegmann]	'A15' '456'; E pt; swamps with tree types, names, relief, c & c and special reserves	OTNR (SR 1164)
A840	26.11.1803	[1804]	William Hambly	'A16'; N pt; remaining pt of twp, names, marshes; FN 432, 435	OTNR (SR 1168)
A841	8.11.1806	10.1.1807	Sam'l S. Wilmot	'B13' '451'; N and E pt; marshes, relief, description; FN 434	OTNR (SR 5804)
A842		[1807?]	–	'No 13'; N pt; c & c reserves, names, later changes	OTAR (P)
A843		[1807?]	Copy W.C.	'C6' '1357'; N pt; marshes, c & c reserves, Yonge St	OTAR (SR 1170)
A844		[181?]	W.C. SS&D	'C7' '1360'; E pt; town of Gwillimbury reserve, c & c reserves, marshes, Yonge St	OTAR (SR 1171)
A845		26.2.[1817?]	Thos Ridout	'No 11'; E pt; marshes, names	OTAR(P)
A846	15.9.1819	12.11.1819	Gabriel Lount	'B14' '417; W pt; c & c reserves, marsh, special reserve, a few names; scale n.g.; FN 345	OTNR (SR 1167)
A847		[1819?]	–	'A13' '126'; W pt; names; scale n.g.	OTAR (SR 1165)
A848		16.6.[1823]	J. Stegmann and G. Lount copy W.C.	W pt; marshes, c & c reserves, names, town plots	OTAR
A849		[1823?]	J. Stegmann and G. Lount copy W.C. SS&D	'No 12'; W pt; names, Amsterdam town plot	OTAR(P)
A850		–.7.1843	Thomas Parke SG	E pt; survey grid, reserves; scale n.g.	OTAR
A851		–.7.1843	Thomas Parke SG	N pt; survey grid, reserves; scale n.g.	OTAR

	Date of Instructions	Date of Map	Surveyor and Signature	Endorsements and Notes	Location
A852		–.7.1843	Thomas Parke SG	W pt; town plot; scale n.g.	OTAR
A853	15.6.1852	–.11.1852	John Ryan	'B55'; W pt; Holland Marsh resurvey, names, roads; FN 1312	OTNR (SR 1166)
A854		–.11.1852 5.12.1854	John Ryan A.N. Morin C/CL	'No 58'; W pt and pt of King Twp; 'Holland Marsh,' timbered and non-timbered marsh, encroachments on patented land, names; scale n.g.	OTAR(P)
	HAGARTY				
A855	30.4.1860	–.8.1862	Robert Hamilton	'No 14'; types of trees, marshes, clearings with names, lumbering; FN 1262, 1263	OTNR (SR 1233)
A856		–.–.1862 9.5.1863	Robert Hamilton Andrew Russell AC	Names, clearings, later changes	OTAR(P)
	HALDIMAND				
A857	25.8.1795	[1796]	[A. Greeley]	'No 20'; names, c & c reserves; 45 ch; FN 346	OTNR (SR 1235)
A858		[1796?]	D.W. Smith ASG	'C8' '1350'; reserves; 80 ch	OTAR (SR 1235(2))
A859		6.9.1811	W.C. exam Thos Ridout SG	'108' 'A8'; names, c & c reserves	OTAR(P)
A860		–.8.1843	Thomas Parke SG	Survey grid, reserves; scale n.g.	OTAR
	HALLOWELL				
A861	–	[179?]	[Alex Aitken?]	'No 15'; names, note by W.C. 22.1.1823 re surveys; scale n.g.	OTNR (SR 1244)
A862		[179?]	Copy W.C.	'133' 'A No 18' 'Quebec Plan'; names; scale n.g.	OTAR
A863		[179?]	Copy [W.C.]	'132' 'A16'; names, note dated 1795; scale n.g.	OTAR
A864	11.11.1809	[10.5.1810]	[John Ryder]	'B8' '447' 'Ryder's plan'; c & c reserves, some names; FN 455	OTNR (SR 6703)
A865		13.7.1812	W. Conger	'Roads and highways now in use'	OTNR (SR 1240)
A866	12.11.1818	17.7.1818	Wilson Conger	'A No 17' '259'; conflicting survey lines at junction of Hallowell and Sophiasburgh twps, names; FN 438, 439	OTNR (SR 1241)
A867		22.1.1823	W.C.	'A No 15' '131'; names, previous surveys by Conger and Elmore; scale n.g.; FN (OTAR)	OTNR (SR 1243)

A868		[1823?]	–	'C11'; c & c reserves; scale n.g.	OTNR (SR 1242)
A869		[1831?]	–	'No 11'; names, notes on survey and later conflicting survey lines 29.6.1831 by J.G.C.	OTAR
A870	19.8.1831	–.–.1833	P.V. Elmore	'B40' '444'; resurvey, marshes, rd allowances; also a transcript OTNR (SR 1239); FN 276	OTNR (SR 6409)
A871		[1833?]	Copy J.G. Chewett	'No 11'; names, later changes	OTAR(P)
A872		–.8.1843	Thomas Parke SG	Survey grid, reserves; scale n.g.	OTAR
	HAMILTON				
A873	23.6.1795	8.12.1797	[A. Root]	'No 25'; c & c reserves, names; 45 ch; FN 819	OTNR (SR 1246)
A874		[1797?]	D.W. Smith ASG	'C9' '1349'; survey grid; 80 ch	OTAR (SR 1250)
A875		[1797?]	Copy W.C.	'134' 'C11'; survey grid	OTAR
A876		14.9.1811	W.C. exam Thos Ridout SG	'106' 'A5'; names, c & c reserves	OTAR(P)
A877		22.8.1821	Richard Birdsall	'B14' '420'; pt: cons 7–9 and shore of Rice Lake	OTNR (SR 1251)
A878		5.11.1834	Copy Henry Lizars	'1346' 'C10'; survey grid, pin holes for tracing	OTAR
A879		3.11.1837	J.G. Chewett dr Henry Lizars J.W. Macaulay [SG]	Marsh; scale n.g.	OTAR (SR 1248)
A880		–.8.1843	Thomas Parke	Survey grid, reserves; scale n.g.	OTAR
A881	18.2.1846 13.5.1846	–.–.1847	J.K. Roche	'B30'; relief, roads, mills, towns of Cobourg and Bewdley; FN 821	OTNR (SR 1245)
A882		[14.1.1867]	E.C. Caddy	'No 31'; Cobourg, Baltimore mills, survey monuments; FN 866	OTNR (SR 5269)
	HARBURN				
A883	15.3.1862	11.12.1862	John James Francis	Peterson Rd, marshes, relief; FN 1271	OTNR (SR 1258)
	HARCOURT				
A884	9.12.1861	1.7.1862	William Drennan	Marshes with types of trees, relief, Peterson Rd; FN 1274	OTNR (SR 1262)
	HARVEY				
A885	14.2.1822	–.–.1822	Andrew Miller	'No 23' '96279'; names, c & c reserves, marshes; FN 1282	OTNR (SR 1276)

	Date of Instructions	Date of Map	Surveyor and Signature	Endorsements and Notes	Location
A886		–.9.1832	J. Huston	'B15' '460'; pt; FN 442	OTNR (SR 1277)
A887		–.7.1843	Thomas Parke SG	Survey grid, reserves; scale n.g.	OTAR
A888	9.1.1864	15.3.1865	Theodore Clementi	'No 28'; cleared land with names, marshes; FN 1281	OTNR (SR 86732)
A889		15.3.1865	Theodore Clementi	'9A'; types of trees, marshes	OTAR (SR 1275)
	HARWICH				
A890	4.2.1796	[31.12.1797]	[A. Iredell]	'138'; pt; pts of map missing; scale n.g.; FN 443	OTNR (SR 1283)
A891		9.7.1800	A. Iredell SGO	'A19' '139'; a few names, reserves, Chatham; scale n.g.; FN 444, 447	OTAR (SR 1279)
A892		[1800?]	[A. Iredell]	'A16' '140'; names, Chatham, indicated as Iredell's plan by A. Russell 1.1.1843, pts of map missing; scale n.g.	OTAR (SR 1280)
A893		[180?]	[W. Chewett?]	'C5' '1348'; Chatham town reserve with glebe and blockhouse; shows a different angle of concessions from Iredell's plan; 80 ch	OTAR (SR 1281)
A894		[180?]	–	'1351' 'C6'; survey grid, c & c reserves, roads, town labelled 'erroneous'	OTAR
A895		[180?]	Copy W.C.	'A18'; Chatham, names, notes 1807, Pointe aux Pins reserve O.C. 28.1.1848, later additions; scale n.g.	OTAR (SR 1284)
A896	18.6.1811 6.10.1815	[1816?]	M. Burwell copy J.G.C.	'A17'; reduced and corrected from Burwell's plan, c & c reserves, Talbot Rd, other roads, names on S pt, marshes, revised cons; 80 ch; FN 445	OTNR (SR 1278)
A897		5.5.1818	Thos Ridout	Pts along Talbot Rd and Raleigh Twp, names, notes about errors in surveys; scale n.g.	OTAR
A898	17.4.1821	31.3.1831	M. Burwell	'No 12'; marshes, roads, names, c & c reserves; FN 448	OTNR (SR 1282)
A899		–.–.1831	M. Burwell copy J.G.C.	'105' 'C4'; marshes, names, some later changes	OTAR(P)
A900		–.7.1843	Thomas Parke SG	Roads, town of Shrewsbury, reserves	OTAR
A901		19.3.1844	Thomas Parke SG copy T.C.J.	'1353' 'C No 30'; roads, marshes; 80 ch	OTAR

A902		–.12.1849	Copy Thos Devine A.R.	'A164'; park lots adjacent to Chatham; 4 ch	OTNR (SR 1286)
A903	2.1.1852	8.3.1852	Albert P. Salter	'B26'; pt: cons 1–5; marshes, Shrewsbury, patented and unpatented lands, clearings, roads; FN 1283, 1284	OTNR (SR 1285)
A904		17.1.1854	T. Devine CLD A.N. Morin C/CL	'105' 'No 42' 'Office copy'; pt: lots 14–24 cons 1–5; names, Talbot Rd, town plot Shrewsbury	OTAR(P)
A905	27.6.1864	8.9.1864	Henry Lawe	'No 15'; Pointe aux Pins at the Rondeau, marshes	OTNR (SR 1983)
	HAVELOCK				
A906	14.5.1862	14.2.1863	William Drennan	Relief, marshes; FN 1286	OTNR (SR 1288)
	HAWKESBURY, E and W				
A907	–	[178?]	[P. McNiff]	'No 3' 'twp No 1 & No 2'; pt: front cons; names	OTAR (SR 1290)
A908		[178?] [ca 1790]	T. Papineau and Pat. McNiff copy Lt Aug Prevost [sgd] Samuel Holland	'141' 'No 9' 'twp no 1 & no 2'; pt: front cons	OTAR
A909		[178?]	–	'No 2' '419' 'B16'; 'Supposed relative situation of the Sigy of Point a l'Original'; also includes Lancaster Twp; 80 ch	OTAR (SR 1293)
A910		11.8.1792 29.8.1795	Exam W. Chewett W. Chewett SS East District	'A10'; pt: front cons; names; scale n.g.	OTAR (SR 1294)
A911		14.8.1792 28.4.1795	Exam W. Chewett W. Chewett SS East District	'A9' '143' 'Township no. 2'; cons 1–4; a few names; scale n.g.	OTAR (SR 1295)
A912	11.10.1796	–.–.1797	Wm. Fortune	'B9' '449'; pt: front; marshes, boundary conflicts with seigneury of Longueuil; FN 348	OTNR (SR 1291)
A913		–.–.1797	W. Fortune	'B10' '442'; 2 cons and BF from Ottawa R, marshes; 20 ch	OTNR (SR 5538)
A914	15.2.1798	[1798]	Wm. Fortune	'No 8'; names	OTNR (SR 1292)
A915		[182?]	Copy J.G. Chewett	A few names	OTAR (SR 1289)
A916		2.12.1826	Thos Ridout SG	'105' '7' 'Office Plan'; names, c & c reserves, many later changes	OTAR(P)

	Date of Instructions	Date of Map	Surveyor and Signature	Endorsements and Notes	Location
	HAY				
A917	–	4.9.1835	John McDonald dr D. McDonald	'No 11'; for Canada Co., lots along boundaries only, contents; FN 452	OTNR (SR 1299)
A918		23.9.1837	John McDonald dr W. Lawson	'No 23' '1147'; marshes, meadow springs, contents; FN 451	OTNR (SR 1300)
A919		23.9.1837	John McDonald dr W. Lawson	Shows present survey of interior block and earlier survey, contents, marshes, a few names	OTAR (Canada Co. Atlas 11)
	HEAD				
A920	24.8.1858 7.12.1858	24.8.1858 11.4.1859	Duncan Sinclair	'No 7' 'No 9'; pt: cons XII–XVII Maria and cons X–XVIII Head; shows Pembroke and Mattawan Rd lots, cleared land, types of trees, some bldgs; FN 1294	OTAR (SR 6568)
	HERRICK				
A921	17.7.1866	[1867]	Quintin Johnstone	'H32'; wooded land, town plot; FN 3797	OTNR (SR 1311)
	HERSCHEL				
A922	11.12.1856	–.10.1858	J.S. Peterson	'B3'; pt; outer lots outline, relief, comments on land, marshes; FN 1291	OTNR (SR 1312)
A923		13.7.1859	CLD Andrew Russell AC	'H20'; pt; subdivision along N and S boundaries and on E along Hastings Rd line, a few names	OTAR
A924	6.8.1864	10.8.1865	A.B. Perry	'No 29'; marsh, relief, clearings; FN 1292	OTNR (SR 1313)
A925		29.4.1867	CLD Andrew Russell AC	'112'; names on S and E pts, many later changes	OTAR(P)
	HIBBERT				
A926	–	21.1.1839	John McDonald	Contents of latest survey cons 6–14, some names, marshes; FN 166	OTAR (Canada Co. Atlas 12)
	HILLIER				
A927	–	[179?]	–	'A1' '11'; pt; names in cons I–III N from L Ontario; scale n.g.	OTAR(P)

A928		[1823?]	Copy W.C.	'No 12'; c & c reserves, names, marshes, notes on the rd allowances, later changes, bearing per Act 1823 (separating Hillier from Ameliasburgh)	OTAR(P)
	HINCHINBROOKE				
A929	18.6.1821	10.6.1824	Sam'l M. Benson	'B10' '421'; marshes, c & c reserves, notes on terrain; FN 454	OTAR (SR 1319)
A930		[1824]	Copy W.C.	'1354' 'C6'; c & c reserves, marshes, note re broken lots 13.10.1824	OTAR
A931		20.9.1826	Sam'l M. Benson	'No 10'; 'Corrected' plan, names, c & c reserves, marshes, mill sites; scale n.g.; FN 453	OTAR (SR 1320)
A932		–.8.1843	Thomas Parke	Survey grid, reserves; scale n.g.	OTAR
A933	14.11.1854	31.5.1856	Thomas Fraser Gibbs	'B55'; cleared land with names, roads, mills, relief, marshes, tree types, contents; FN 1304	OTNR (SR 1321)
A934		16.8.1856	T.F. Gibbs copy J.W.B. CLO Joseph Cauchon C/CL	'111' 'No 51'; names, later changes	OTAR(P)
	HINDON				
A935	19.10.1860	[24.9.1861]	Crosby Brady	'H13'; pt on rivers only; relief, marshes, Bobcaygeon Rd; FN 1303	OTNR (SR 1322)
A936		–.10.1861	CLD Andrew Russell AC	'111'; marshes, roads, a few names, relief, later changes	OTAR(P)
	HOLLAND				
A937	19.9.1845	[31.1.1846]	[C. Rankin]	'B27' '700'; includes Sullivan Twp; Garafraxa Rd and other rd lots; FN 457	OTNR (SR 1325)
A938		–.8.1846	CLD Andrew Russell SS&D	'108' 'No 55' 'Office copy'; Garafraxa Rd lots, outline only	OTAR(P)
A939		–.7.1848	CLD	'108' 'No 20'; pt; Garafraxa Rd lots, names	OTAR(P)
A940		18.11.1848	[C. Rankin] copy A.R. CLD	Pt; lots along Garafraxa Rd; FN 749	OTAR
A941		29.12.1851	Copy T. Devine CLD John Rolph C/CL	'108' 'No 46'; school lands, names, Sydenham Rd lots, Garafraxa Rd survey	OTAR(P)

	Date of Instructions	Date of Map	Surveyor and Signature	Endorsements and Notes	Location
	HOPE				
A942	28.5.1793	[1793?]	[A. Iredell] D.W. Smith	'A7' 'Office copy'; c & c reserves, names, carrying place, house; 80 ch; FN 258	OTNR (SR 1327)
A943		19.9.1811	Copy W.C. exam T. Ridout	'A16'; names	OTAR(P)
A944		–.8.1843	Thomas Parke SG	'H30'; survey grid, reserves; scale n.g.	OTAR
A945	20.5.1845	14.7.1845	John K. Roche	'B28'; pt: cons 6–10; mills, resurvey, improved land; FN 1310	OTNR (SR 1330)
A946		19.7.1845	John K. Roche	'B27' '424' 'No 1'; pt: cons 6–10; relief, marshes, improved land, roads, a few names; scale n.g.	OTNR (SR 1329)
A947		18.8.1845	A.R. T. Bouthillier CLD	'423'; pt showing eight previous surveys and lines cons 6–10	OTNR (SR 1331)
	HORTON				
A948	20.4.1825	–.–.1825	Owen Quinn	'No 8'; falls, rapids, names, cleared land; FN 259	OTNR (SR 1343)
A949		[1825?]	Copy J.G. Chewett	'C3'; names, c & c reserves	OTNR (SR 1344)
A950		22.10.1834	Owen Quinn copy Henry Lizars SGO	'113' 'A6'; names, c & c reserves, clearings	OTAR(P)
A951		–.8.1843	Thomas Parke SG	Survey grid, c & c reserves; scale n.g.	OTAR
	HOUGHTON				
A952	24.3.1809	[1809?]	[M. Burwell?]	'New Tract of Land'; includes Bayham and Malahide twps; lots with names along Talbot Rd as located by T. Talbot, with dates to ca 1816; scale n.g.; FN 513	OTAR (Talbot BkE/8)
A953		6.1.1814	Mahlon Burwell	Pt; lots at N end with names as located by T. Talbot to 1818	OTAR (Talbot BkE/4)
A954		28.6.1819	M. Burwell	Front, lots along Lake Rd	OTAR (Talbot BkD/12)
A955	20.2.1819 15.3.1819	20.11.1819	M. Burwell	'No 24'; c & c reserves, roads, marsh, earlier survey lines and bearing notes, a few names; FN 461	OTNR (SR 1336)
A956		[182?]	M. Burwell copy J.G.C.	'124' 'No 23'; school lands, c & c reserves, marshes, names	OTAR(P)

A957		[182?]	[M. Burwell?]	'B26' '425'; c & c reserves, names	OTAR (SR 1335)
A958		11.9.1823	Thos Ridout SG	Marshes, c & c reserves, most school land reserves, names of people located along front by T. Talbot	OTAR (Talbot BkD/4)
A959		–.7.1843	Thomas Parke SG	Survey grid, reserves; scale n.g.	OTAR
	HOWARD				
A960		28.7.1799	[A. Iredell?]	'A28' '149'; pt (fragment only); some names; scale n.g.; FN 444	OTNR (SR 1339)
A961	8.6.1811	23.9.1811	M. Burwell	Pt: front 2 cons and Orford Twp; names of those located by T. Talbot to 1819	OTAR (Talbot BkD/8)
A962	8.6.1811 6.10.1815	30.11.1816	M. Burwell	Names as located by T. Talbot, c & c reserves; FN 463	OTAR (Talbot BkE/6)
A963		20.12.[1816]	M. Burwell	'A20' '148'; Talbot Rd lots, lots along Thames R, trail, marshes, later note 1817	OTNR (SR 1337)
A964		5.5.1818	T. Ridout	Pt; Talbot Rd, rd to Thames, names	OTAR
A965		[1816?]	–	Pt and Harwich Twp; lots 97–102 and 116–128; names located along Talbot Rd by T. Talbot to 1817; scale n.g.	OTAR (Talbot BkD/11)
A966		[1816?] [17.4.1821?]	M. Burwell copy J.G. Chewett W.C. Thos Ridout	'No 14'; pt; Talbot Rd through twp, names, marshes, c & c reserves, relief	OTAR (SR 1338)
A967	17.4.1821	13.3.1823	M. Burwell	'A21'; trail, marshes, c & c blocks, a few names, Talbot Rd; FN 463	OTNR (SR 1340)
A968		13.3.1823	M. Burwell copy J.G.C.	'113' 'No 13'; c & c reserves, marshes, names, notes 1837 and 1838	OTAR(P)
A969		23.1.1824	M. Burwell Thos Ridout SG	Marshes, c & c reserves, names in middle and E and W pts as located by T. Talbot to 1837, copy	OTAR Talbot BkE/11
A970		–.7.1843	Thomas Parke SG	Survey grid, reserves; scale n.g.	OTAR
	HOWE ISLAND				
A971	7.2.1833	18.3.1833	Frederick Preston Rubidge	'B30'; contents, notes, marsh, clergy reserves, 'Hon. C.W. Grant' and other names; 20 ch; FN 807	OTNR (SR 1345)
A972		5.9.1837	Copy J.G. Chewett SGO	'113' 'No 20'; c & c reserves, names; 20 ch	OTAR(P)
A973		–.8.1843	Thomas Parke SG	Survey grid, reserves; scale n.g.	OTAR

	Date of Instructions	Date of Map	Surveyor and Signature	Endorsements and Notes	Location
A974		29.5.1856	J.W.B. CLD E.P. Taché	Survey grid; 20 ch	OTAR
	HOWICK				
A975		26.4.1852	Copy T.D. CLD John Rolph C/CL	Notes on lines to be surveyed and bearings, projected plan	OTAR
A976	20.8.1852	–.–.1853	H.P. Savigny	'B70'; Fordwich town plot, common school lands, marshes; FN 1264	OTNR (SR 1341)
A977		7.9.1854	CLD A.N. Morin C/CL	'115' 'No 64' 'Office copy'; names, Fordwich town plot	OTAR(P)
	HOWLAND				
A978	16.5.1863	1.8.1864	A. Niven	'No 26'; marshes, clearings; FN 1315	OTNR (SR 1342)
A979		22.10.1867	CLD A. Russell AC	'113'; town plot, lot sizes	OTAR(P)
	HULLETT				
A980	–	4.9.1835 –.10.1837	John McDonald	'No 10' '1149'; contents, mill sites for Canada Co., results of five surveys; FN 59, 196, 465	OTNR (SR 1349)
A981		[1835–7?]	[J. McDonald]	Contents of surveys I–III	OTAR (Canada Co. Atlas 10)
	HUMBERSTONE				
A982	4.3.1794	[1794?]	[T. Welch]	'114' 'No 13'; cons 1–5, glebe, names, notes 1801, 1817, 1818; scale n.g.; FN 466	OTAR(P)
A983		21.10.1811	Thos. Ridout	'No 12', mills, beaver dams, names	OTNR (SR 95570)
	HUMPHREY				
A984	18.1.1866	[1866]	T.F. Gibbs	'H33'; Parry Sound Rd, town plot, relief, marshes; FN 1321	OTNR (SR 1351)
	HUNGERFORD				
A985	3.9.1797	–.–.1797	A. Aitken	'B11' '426'; cons 1–5, marshes	OTAR (SR 1355)

A986		–.–.1797	Alex'r Aitken	'A No 19' '151'; relief, marshes, names	OTNR (SR 1357)
A987		[181?]	Copy W.C.	'C8' '1362'; marshes, relief	OTAR (SR 1354)
A988		25.8.1819	Copy W.C. Thos Ridout	'C7' '1355' 'for the Land Board'; cons 1–5, c & c reserves, relief	OTAR (SR 1353)
A989	18.6.1821	16.2.1822	Sam'l M. Benson	'B13'; pt: cons 5–14; contents, mill sites, beaver meadows, c & c reserves, marshes, windfall; scale n.g.; FN 468	OTNR (SR 1356)
A990		16.3.1822	Sam'l M. Benson	Some names, c & c reserves; scale n.g.	OTAR
A991		15.3.1822	S. Benson Thos Ridout SG	'115' 'No 46'; pt: cons 5–14; c & c reserves, marshes, names, copy	OTAR(P)
A992		[183?]	S. Benson	'115' 'No 13' 'Office Plan'; c & c reserves, names, later changes, notes 1843 and 1852, copy from Aitken and Benson's surveys	OTAR(P)
A993	7.4.1837	31.10.1837	Sam'l M. Benson	'714'; cons 1–4, roads, notes on land; FN 467	OTNR (SR 1352)
A994		–.7.1843	Thomas Parke SG	'H41'; survey grid, reserves; scale n.g.	OTAR
	HUNTINGDON				
A995	18.12.1796	22.8.1797	A. Aitken	'B12' '429'; c & c reserves, marshes, tree types, pt 'not surveyed'	OTNR (SR 1362)
A996		13.12.1797	Alex'r Aitken	'No 14'; names	OTAR (SR 1361)
A997		[180?]	–	'1347' 'C10'; survey grid, outline only; scale n.g.	OTAR
A998	5.3.1831	19.4.1832	Sam'l M. Benson	'B9' '428'; road, relief, marshes; FN 471	OTNR (SR 1363)
A999		–.7.1843	Thomas Parke SG	Survey grid, reserves; scale n.g.	OTAR
	HUNTLEY				
A1000	23.6.1819	[1820]	R. Sherwood	'B6' '427'; c & c reserves, marshy areas; FN 472	OTNR (SR 1364)
A1001		[1820]	R. Sherwood	'No 32' '154'; names, c & c reserves; scale n.g.	OTAR (SR 1365)
A1002		[1820?]	R. Sherwood copy J.G.C.	'No 9'; c & c reserves, names, later adds; scale n.g.	OTAR(P)
A1003		18.3.1830	W. Chewett J.G.C.	'A5'; includes March Twp; marshes, c & c reserves, names; scale n.g.	OTAR(P)
	HURON				
A1004	11.4.185	–.–.1851	E.R. Jones	'B51'; townplot, black ash marshes, beaver meadows; FN 1324	OTNR (SR 1366)

	Date of Instructions	Date of Map	Surveyor and Signature	Endorsements and Notes	Location
A1005		3.2.1852	Copy T.D. CLD Andrew Russell S&D	'117' 'No 63' 'Copied from B51' (**A1004**) 'Common School Lands'; names	OTAR(P)
	INNISFIL				
A1006	–	24.3.1820	Rich'd Birdsall	'No 15'; c & c reserves, names; scale n.g.; FN 474, 475	OTNR (SR 1373)
A1007		24.3.1820	Rich'd Birdsall	'B17' '430'; c & c reserves, marsh, notes on survey; scale n.g.	OTAR (SR 1372)
A1008		[1820?]	Copy J.G.C.	'A17' 'No 54'; names, many later changes, c & c reserves, later notes 1842 and 1844	OTAR(P)
A1009		–.7.1843	Thomas Parke SG	Survey grid, reserves; scale n.g.	OTAR
	JONES				
A1010	29.9.1862	26.7.1864	A.G. Forrest	'No 82'; marshes, improved land with names, roads; FN 1351	OTNR (SR 1386)
A1011		22.10.1867	CLD A. Russell AC	'120'; marshes, names, Ottawa and Opeongo Rd lots	OTAR(P)
	KALADAR				
A1012	29.7.1820	1822 10.6.1824	Henry Ewing	'B14' '435'; c & c reserves, marshes; FN 1355	OTNR (SR 1388)
A1013		[1822?]	Copy J.G. Chewett	'1331'; c & c reserves, marshes, pinholes for tracing	OTAR
A1014		[1822?]	Copy J.G.C.	'No 20'; c & c reserves, note on price of land, a few names	OTAR(P)
A1015		–.8.1843	Thomas Parke SG	Survey grid, reserves; scale n.g.	OTAR
A1016		9.7.1856	J.W.B. CLO E.P. Taché per C/CL	Survey grid	OTAR
A1017	27.6.1857	31.8.1857	A.B. Perry	'B46'; Addington Rd free grant lots, clergy reserves; FN 2228	OTNR (SR 1391)
A1018		31.8.1857 –.10.1857	A.B. Perry Andrew Russell AC/CL	Cons 6–8; free grant lots on Addington Rd, rd line	OTAR (SR 1389)

A1019	20.6.1860	12.4.1861	A.B. Perry	'K No 4'; resurvey, improved land with names, index to field notes, relief, marshes, roads, mill sites; FN 1356	OTNR (SR 1390)
A1020		–.11.1861	Andrew Russell	Names, later changes, roads, cleared land and bldgs	OTAR(P)
	KARS				
A1021	7.11.1859	[1860] 1.12.1861	Joseph Wm Burke	'K3'; Indian lands and village, trails, burnt land; FN 1358	OTNR (SR 1394)
A1022		10.2.1862	Andrew Russell AC	Relief, trails, marshes	OTAR (SR 1393)
	KENNEBEC				
A1023	29.7.1820	1824 20.1.1827	Publius V. Elmore	'B16' Twp no 3'; c & c reserves, marsh, relief, mill site, a few names, notes; FN 260	OTAR (SR 1405)
A1024		11.4.1825	Publius V. Elmore	'B15' '434'; marshes, c & c reserves, relief, note: 'copied 17th Jany 1827 W.C.'	OTAR (SR 1403)
A1025		10.3.1827	P.V. Elmore copy W.C.	'C12'; c & c reserves, relief, marshes, clearings, mill sites	OTAR
A1026		14.10.1834	P.V. Elmore copy Henry Lizars	'No 19' 'Office copy'; tree types, marshes, c & c reserves, names, later changes	OTAR(P)
A1027		–.8.1843	Thomas Parke SG	Survey grid, reserves; scale n.g.	OTAR
	KENYON				
A1028	2.4.1791	9.5.1792	William Chewett Samuel Holland	'23'; names, copy; scale n.g.	OTAR(P)
A1029		27.11.1794	W. Chewett and J. Rankin [copy] W. Chewett	'K3' 'No 20C' '1336'	OTAR
A1030		27.4.–29.8 [ca 1795]	W. Chewett	'20'; 9 cons, also includes Charlottenburgh Twp; names, marshes; scale n.g.	OTNR (SR 1407)
A1031		[ca 1795]	W.C.	'No A5' '156'; names, marshes; scale n.g.	OTAR (SR 1408)
A1032		28.2.1849	Copy T. Devine exam A.R. CLD	'No 26'; includes Roxborough Twp; former St Regis Indian reserve, names; 20 ch	OTAR(P)
	KEPPEL				
A1033	–	[1856]	[C. Rankin]	'B81'; Indian reserves, Sydenham town plot, roads, relief, marshes	OTNR (SR 1409)

	Date of Instructions	Date of Map	Surveyor and Signature	Endorsements and Notes	Location
A1034		[1856?]	C. Rankin	'PH148' 'Caughnawaga Block'; clearings, names of owners; 10 ch	OTNR (SR 4581)
A1035		9.3.1857	J.W.B. Joseph Cauchon C/CL	'No 72'; some lots with names, Indian lands, pt town plot	OTAR(P)
	KINCARDINE				
A1036	28.6.1850	31.1.1851	James W. Bridgland	'B41'; Penetangore town plot, improved land, bldgs, mill, marshes, wooded areas; FN 1370	OTNR (SR 1415)
A1037		30.10.1851	T.D. Andrew Russell	'No 62' 'Office copy'; names, Penetangore town plot, some later changes; scale n.g.	OTAR(P)
	KING				
A1038	20.11.1799	[1800]	John Stegmann	'No 16'; c & c reserves, marsh, names; scale n.g.; FN 3–407	OTNR (SR 1416)
A1039		[180?]	Copy W.C.	'1334' 'C9'; c & c reserves, marshes, relief	OTAR
A1040		[180?]	Copy W.C.	'1333' 'C10'; pt: cons 1–5, 'twp B' and line btwn Markham and Whitchurch for 9 cons; scale n.g.	OTAR
A1041		1.2.1817	Thos Ridout	'No 17'; c & c reserves, names	OTAR(P)
A1042		–.7.1843	Thomas Parke SG	Survey grid, conflicting survey lines, reserves; scale n.g.	OTAR
A1043	–	23.8.1865	Henry MacLeod PLS	'No 7'; resurvey, towns, railways, roads	OTNR (SR 5556)
	KINGSTON				
A1044	11.9.1783	–.–.1783	John Collins	'B43'; names for 7 cons, shows pt of Pittsburgh Twp with names along Cataraqui R, glebe; scale n.g.	OTAR (SR 1419)
A1045		[1783?]	[John Collins]	'A No 20' '159' 'Quebec Plan'; names for 7 cons and in Pittsburgh Twp	OTAR (SR 1420)
A1046		[1783?]	–	'A21'; names, glebe; scale n.g.	OTAR (SR 1423)
A1047		–.–.1783	John Collins copy Francis Morin [sgd] Samuel Holland	'No 18' 'Quebec Plan'; names	OTAR(P)
A1048		[1783?]	–	'B48' '984' 'Twps 1 and 2'; includes Ernestown Twp; glebe, fort, list of names	OTNR (SR 5976)

A1049		[27.10.1783] 9.9.1842	Thomas Parke SG	'1332'; copy with slight variations and different notes of John Collins's plan of 27.10.1783 (**412**); scale n.g.	OTAR
A1050	8.6.1794	25.3.1797	Alex Aitken	'No 17'; town, marshes, a few names	OTNR (SR 1424)
A1051		[1797?]	–	'No 16' 'Office Plan'; names, some later changes including pt Pittsburgh and Storrington twps; scale n.g.	OTAR(P)
A1052		13.3.1827	William Kilborn	Pt: rear half lot no 15, con 2; roads, names of owners; 4 ch	OTAR
A1053	24.8.1831	–.–.1831	Publius V. Elmore	'B17' '432'; E and S boundary lines resurveyed, roads; FN 483	OTNR (SR 1421)
A1054		–.8.[1843]	Thomas Parke SG	Survey grid, reserves; scale n.g.	OTAR
A1055	15.7.1845	23.3.1846	A. Wells	'B42'; pt: W boundary and 'western addition'; FN 836	OTNR (SR 166)
A1056		6.8.1846 31.8.1846	William McMillan R.H. Bonnycastle	Front lots 22–25 con 1, water lots; 2 ch	OTNR (SR 1425)
A1057		20.3.1850	Thomas Fraser and Thomas Burrows	Copy of Aitken's plan of 25.3.1797 (**A1050**), but also shows school sections proposed, some names, town of Kingston	OTAR
	KINLOSS				
A1058	23.6.1848	–.–.1849	Allen Park Brough	'B38'; includes Kincardine Twp; Durham Rd survey, town, marshes, relief; FN 746	OTNR (SR 1414)
A1059		30.4.1852	Copy T.D. John Rolph C/CL	'Projected Plan'; notes on lines to be surveyed, town plot reserve	OTAR
A1060	30.4.1852	–.–.1852	E.R. Jones	'B62'; common school lands, relief, town plot, marshes; FN 1368	OTNR (SR 1426)
A1061		–.–.1852	E.R. Jones	'B63' '993/53'; pt; lakes in cons 1–3, relief; 10 ch	OTNR (SR 1427)
A1062		31.5.1854	A.N. Morin C/CL	'No 61'; names, some later adds	OTAR(P)
	KITLEY				
A1063	11.10.1796	30.10.1797	Lewis Grant	'No 17'; c & c reserves, names; FN 284	OTNR (SR 1430)
A1064		[1797?]	[L. Grant]	'C2' 'C7' '13'; names	OTAR(P)
A1065		[1816]	R. Sherwood	'B15' '436'; c & c reserves, portage; FN 485	OTNR (SR 1431)
A1066		–.8.1843	Thomas Parke SG	Survey grid, reserves; scale n.g.	OTAR

	Date of Instructions	Date of Map	Surveyor and Signature	Endorsements and Notes	Location
	KORAH				
A1067	12.5.1858	24.1.1859	James Johnston	'No 7'; Awenge and Korah twps; village of Ste Marie, Hudson Bay Co. land, burnt land, relief; FN 1379	OTNR (SR 1434)
A1068		2.4.1859	CLD	'129'; Awenge and Korah twps; names, later changes	OTAR(P)
	LAKE				
A1069	15.11.1821	-.-.1822	Henry Ewing	'B20' '438'; c & c reserves, marshes, contents; FN 487	OTNR (SR 1439)
A1070		[1822?]	–	'16'; c & c reserves, marshes	OTAR (SR 1438)
A1071		[1822?]	Henry Ewing copy W.C.	'No 21'; c & c reserves, names, lots returned to CLD for sale 5.8.1842	OTAR(P)
A1072		-.7.1843	Thomas Parke SG	'L2'; survey grid, reserves; scale n.g.	OTAR
	LANARK				
A1073	23.6.1819	[1821]	R. Sherwood	'B8' '461'; c & c reserves, reserves for Lanark village and park lots, marshes; FN 1099	OTNR (SR 1443)
A1074		[1821?]	[R. Sherwood?]	'No 11'; town site, c & c reserves, names and later additions	OTAR(P)
A1075		-.8.1843	Thomas Parke SG	Survey grid, reserves; scale n.g.	OTAR
	LANCASTER				
A1076		1784–5 [179?]	P. McNiff and James McDonell W. Chewitt	'15'; includes Lochiel Twp; notes on province boundary 1806 and 1809, names, later additions	OTAR(P)
A1077	18.6.1785 26.6.1787	-.-.1787	Lt. Jas McDonell	'17'; 12 cons and pt of Charlottenburg; marshes, wooded areas, lots E and W of boundary line; scale n.g.; FN 496	OTNR (SR 1444)
A1078		2.2.1791	W. Chewett	'No 9A'; names, notes on correcting of errors in 1789 and 1790; scale n.g.	OTAR (SR 1445)
A1079		-.-.1792 27.4.1795 29.8.1795	Exam W. Chewett	'No 20' '162'; names, conflicting boundary lines; scale n.g.; FN 492, 493	OTAR (SR 1446)
A1080		-.5.1796	Patrick McNiff	'No 8A' '157'; pt: first 5 cons; names, rec'd by Wm Chewett from McNiff 5.1796; scale n.g.	OTNR (SR 1448)

A1081	–	6.4.1817	Duncan McDonnell	'No 6B' '462'; pt: cons 14–18; notes on survey problems; scale n.g.; FN 494	OTNR (SR 1447)
A1082		27.12.1826	W.C.	'1324' 'Projection'; notes on surveys and conflicting boundary lines, lots according to Quebec Plan	OTNR (SR 1449)
	LANSDOWNE				
A1083		[1788?]	[H. McDonnell?]	'A24'; Lansdowne cons 1–5; names	OTAR(P)
A1084		[1788?]	[H. McDonnell?]	'C7' 'A23'; Lansdowne 13 cons; names, glebe; scale n.g.	OTAR(P)
A1085		26.12.1794	W. Chewett	'C8' '1322'; Lansdowne cons 1–9; cons 1–3 laid out by James and Hugh McDonell, outline	OTAR (SR 1458)
A1086		28.4.1795 29.8.1795	W. Chewett	'A25' '165'; cons 1–9 Lansdowne; names, glebe; scale n.g.	OTAR (SR 1457)
A1087		[179?]	Copy W. Chewett	'C16'; Lansdowne and Escott 'Fair Plan,' outline with lakes, rivers, marshes	OTAR (SR 1455)
A1088		[179?]	W. Chewett?	'1313' 'C9'; Lansdowne front and rear; notes re line run by Mr Grant and on 'Quebec plan'	OTAR
A1089	25.7.1795	9.4.1796	Lewis Grant	'437' 'B7'; pt: Leeds, Lansdowne, and Escott; shows pts surv by L. Grant and Messrs J. and H. McDonell; 80 ch; FN 500, 837	OTAR
A1090		–.–.1811	Reuben Sherwood	'No 18'; front and rear Lansdowne; names, railways, later surveys of islands; FN 731	OTNR (SR 1454)
A1091		[1811?]	[R. Sherwood?]	'A12'; cons 3–11 Lansdowne and pt Escott; names, c & c reserves; scale n.g.	OTAR (SR 1456)
A1092		8.3.1820	T. Ridout SG	'No 31' '166' 'For the Land Board'; pt: cons 6–11 Lansdowne; vacant lots marked	OTAR (SR 1459)
A1093	–.8.1843	Thomas Parke SG	Lansdowne; survey grid, reserves; scale n.g.	OTAR	
	LAVANT				
A1094	6.6.1822	30.12.1823	Wm Graves Reuben Sherwood	'B7' '439'; c & c reserves, marshes, a few names; FN 497	OTNR (SR 1466)
A1095		[1823?]	R. Sherwood copy J.G.C.	'No 10'; c & c reserves, names	OTAR(P)

	Date of Instructions	Date of Map	Surveyor and Signature	Endorsements and Notes	Location
A1096		2.5.1823	R. Sherwood copy J.G.C. Thos Ridout	'No 26' 'For the Land Board'; c & c reserves, very few names; scale n.g.	OTAR(P)
A1097	–.8.1843	Thomas Parke SG	Survey grid, reserves; scale n.g.	OTAR	
	LAXTON				
A1098	24.8.1858	27.12.1858	John K. Roche	'No 2'; relief, marshes; FN 1391	OTNR (SR 1468)
A1099		–.4.1859	Andrew Russell AC/CL	'Office copy'; names, marshes; scale n.g.	OTAR(P)
	LEEDS				
A1100		[1788]	Hugh McDonnell	'A9'; Leeds cons 1–5; originally part of plan from Pittsburgh and Elizabethtown to Lansdowne and the twps 9 and 10; names; scale n.g.	OTAR(P)
A1101	30.6.1788	28.12.1794	W. Chewett	'C11' '1329'; Leeds cons 1–9; relief, only pts of rivers shown, cons 1–3 surv by James and Hugh McDonell [1788]	OTAR (SR 1473)
A1102		[1794?]	Copy W.C.	'C13'; Leeds front and rear; survey grid	OTAR
A1103		[1794?]	[W. Chewett?]	'A10'; District plan, Leeds Twp cons 1–5; names, lots of J. Stone and Sir J. Johnson run at angle to twp layout; scale n.g.	OTAR(P)
A1104		[1794?]	–	'A11' '172'; 5 cons, Leeds; names; scale n.g.	OTAR(P)
A1105		–.4.1795 –.8.1795	[Illegible]	'No 19'; Leeds front and rear; names, many later additions, c & c reserves; scale n.g.	OTAR(P)
A1106	25.7.1795	9.4.1796	Lewis Grant	'437' 'B7'; pt: Leeds, Lansdowne, and Escott; shows pts surv by L. Grant and Messrs J. and H. McDonell; 80 ch; FN 500, 837	OTAR
A1107		29.7.1796	Lewis Grant	'B6'; Leeds; marsh, c & c reserves; FN 500	OTNR (SR 1471)
A1108		[1796?]	Lewis Grant	'A8' '169'; Leeds pt: cons 1–3; names, c & c reserves, 'Thames' R; scale n.g.	OTNR (SR 1474)

A1109		[1796?]	[Chewett copy?]	'C12'; Leeds front and rear; lines as surveyed by Mr Grant, survey grid	OTAR
A1110	15.5.1809?	15.6.181[0]	Reuben Sherwood	'B15' '464'; Leeds; c & c reserves, a few names, marshes; FN 498, 499	OTNR (SR 1470)
A1111		8.3.1820	T. Ridout	'No 30' '173'; Leeds; 'For the Land Board'; N pt cons 4–10; vacant lots marked	OTAR (SR 1472)
A1112		[after 1825]	R. Sherwood copy J.G.C.	'C10'; Leeds front and rear; St Lawrence corrected from Quebec plan; watermark dated '1825'	OTAR
A1113		–.8.1843	Thomas Parke SG	Leeds; survey grid, reserves; scale n.g.	OTAR
	LEFROY				
A1114	9.5.1860	12.7.1861	C.G. Hanning	'L5'; relief, rapids, falls, burnt land, portages; FN 1695	OTNR (SR 1475)
A1115		–.8.1861	CLD Andrew Russell AC	'138'; names, Indian lands, later changes	OTAR(P)
	LIMERICK				
A1116	9.12.1856	[–.12.1857]	Quintin Johnstone	'No 1'; pt; scale n.g.; FN 1399, 1906	OTNR (SR 1483)
A1117		–.–.1860	CLD Andrew Russell AC	'138'; pt; lots along Hastings Rd, a few names	OTAR(P)
A1118	12.5.1862	28.4.1863	Henry MacLeod	'No 7'; residue of twp; improved land, marsh, beaver meadow, Hastings Rd; FN 1400	OTNR (SR 1482)
A1119		–.–.1863 8.7.1863	H. MacLeod CLD	'138' 'No 87' 'Office copy'; names, later changes	OTAR(P)
	LINDSAY				
A1120	–	1.1.1856	J. Stoughton Dennis	'L No 14'; marshes, wooded areas, copy made in 1879; FN 3259	OTNR (SR 86737)
	LOBO				
A1121	19.1.1820	8.8.1820	M. Burwell	'No 26'; c & c reserves, names; FN 502, 503	OTNR (SR 1495)
A1122		8.12.1830	Copy J.G.C. W. Chewett ASG	'L18'; c & c reserves, names, lots under direction of T. Talbot, marshes	OTAR
A1123		–.7.1843	Thomas Parke SG	Survey grid, reserves; scale n.g.	OTAR
A1124		4.9.1844	M. Burwell copy SGO	'1327'; survey grid; copy of Burwell's map of 1820; scale n.g.	OTAR

	Date of Instructions	Date of Map	Surveyor and Signature	Endorsements and Notes	Location
	LOCHIEL				
A1125	–	10.5.1795	W. Chewett	'C21'; notes on previous surveys, boundary line btwn U.C. and L.C.	OTNR (SR 1489)
A1126		[29.8.1795]	[W. Chewett]	'18' 'office copy'; formerly N pt Lancaster, names, reserves; scale n.g.	OTNR (SR 1490)
A1127		[182?]	Copy J.G. Chewett	'No 1'; outlines	OTAR (SR 1491)
A1128	20.9.1822	[1823] 31.8.1827	Angus Cattanach copy W.C.	'No 24'; gore, names, note on provincial boundary, pt not determined 25.9.1827; 20 ch; FN 282	OTAR(P)
A1129		27.12.1826	W.C.	'No 1C' 'Projection'; conflicting survey lines and notes, mills, marshes, similar to **A1130**	OTNR (SR 1487)
A1130		27.12.1826	W.C.	'No 1C' 'Office plan'; conflicting survey lines from Cattanach and McNaughton surveys, notes	OTAR (SR 1488)
	LOGAN				
A1131	–	4.9.1835 21.1.1839	John McDonald dr H. Lizars	'No 12'; cons I–V and XI–XVI; for Canada Co., marshes; FN 196, 197	OTNR (SR 1494)
A1132		21.1.1839	John McDonald	Contents of present survey cons 6–16, marshes, town of Mitchell	OTAR (Canada Co. Atlas 13)
	LONDON				
A1133	–	14.12.1796	A. Iredell	'PF2' '758'; c & c reserves, marshes, notes on trees and water, survey marker; 80 ch	OTAR (SR 1497)
A1134	11.3.1810	21.6.1810	Mahlon Burwell	'A7'; c & c reserves, a few names; FN 15–281, 5–475	OTNR (SR 1496)
A1135		12.9.1818	Thos Ridout SG	Names as located and inscribed by T. Talbot with dates to 1837, c & c reserves, town plot	OTAR (Talbot BkD no 1)
A1136	17.9.1818	31.5.1819	M. Burwell	'B6'; notes on 'New survey method', c & c reserves, marshes, town plot; FN 15–301, 7–241, 506	OTNR (SR 1498)
A1137		31.5.1819 [1819?]	M. Burwell copy	'C41' 'No 25'; copy; c & c reserves, names, town of London E and W of Thames R	OTAR(P)
A1138		–.7.1843	Thomas Parke SG	'L21'; survey grid, reserves; scale n.g.	OTAR
	LONGFORD				
A1139	7.10.1861	18.8.1862	H.J. Cambie	Marshes; FN 1406	OTNR (SR 1500)

	LONGUEUIL				
A1140	–	8.3.1784 4.5.1784	Jos Papineau [sgd] Samuel Holland copy W.C.	'B17' 'E2'; pt: front; notes; 12 1/2 arpents	OTAR (SR 10597)
A1141		18.12.1810	–	'Seigneury of Point à L'Orignal'; certified by Nath H. Tredwell and Wm. Lowe, village of L'Orignal, names; copies of original in Registry office	OTNR (SR 86760, 86761) (photo-reproductions)
A1142		[182?]	Anthony Swalwell	Rough sketch, mills, roads, court-house; scale n.g.	OTAR
A1143		15.10.1831	W. Chewett	'B15' '577' 'Seigneury of Point à l'Orignal'; pt; boundary resurvey, notes on boundary dispute re adjoining twps	OTNR (SR 2065)
A1144		22.7.1833	Jos Fortune Duncan McDonell	'B18'; orig boundary survey and resurvey; 50 ch; FN 14	OTNR (SR 5968)
	LOUGHBOROUGH				
A1145	16.10.1792 23.11.1792	[1796]	Alex'r Aitkin	'B19' '440'; c & c reserves, marshes	OTNR (SR 1507)
A1146		[1796?]	[A. Aitken?]	'C15' '1319'; outlines, water bodies, marshes	OTAR (SR 1506)
A1147		[1796?]	[A. Aitken?]	'No 22'; c & c reserves, names with dates 1794–1846; scale n.g.	OTAR (SR 1508)
A1148	16.1.1832	1.8.1832	C. Rankin	'B18' '441'; c & c reserves, mill sites; FN 508	OTNR (SR 1505)
A1149		1.8.1832	C. Rankin	'No 27' '715'; conflicting survey lines cons 2–7, names of owners	OTNR (SR 1504)
A1150		[1832?]	Copy J.G. Chewett	'C14'; also includes pt of Storrington; names, later changes	OTAR(P)
A1151		–.8.1843	Thomas Parke SG	'L24'; survey grid, reserves; scale n.g.	OTAR
A1152		27.9.1856	J.W.B. CLO. Joseph Cauchon C/CL	Survey grid	OTAR (SR 5488)
	LOUTH				
A1153	–	25.10.1791	Augustus Jones [sgd] Samuel Holland	'No 14'; names, glebe, later changes, copy	OTAR(P)
A1154		[1795?]	[A. Iredell?] D.W. Smith ASG	'A15' 'Received from Land Board'; names; scale n.g.; FN 209	OTAR (SR 1513)
A1155		25.1.1812	Exam Thos Ridout SG	'A16' '176'; names, glebe lots with names of lessees	OTAR (SR 1512)

	Date of Instructions	Date of Map	Surveyor and Signature	Endorsements and Notes	Location
	LUTHER, E and W				
A1156	10.6.1831	1.10.1831	Lewis Burwell	'No 18'; names, c & c reserves, trail, pt noted later as 'erroneous see McPhillips Plan B70' (**A1159**); FN 509	OTNR (SR 1518)
A1157		[1831?]	Copy J.G.C.	Marshes, c & c reserves	OTAR
A1158		–.7.1843	Thomas Parke SG	Survey grid, reserves; scale n.g.	OTAR
A1159	28.9.1854	.–.1855	Geo. McPhillips	'B70'; surveyed in 1854–5; relief, marshes; FN 368	OTNR (SR 1519)
A1160		5.12.1860	Andrew Russell AC/CL	Names, clearings, relief	OTAR(P)
	LUTTERWORTH				
A1161	27.10.1858	–.7.1859	Chas. Unwin	'No 3'; marshes, roads; FN 1416	OTNR (SR 1520)
A1162		13.1.1860	CLD	'141'; names, later changes	OTAR(P)
	LYNDOCH				
A1163		15.4.1857	H.O. Wood	'B57'; lots on boundary with Sebastopol and Brudenell	OTAR (SR 1525)
A1164	12.6.1861	14.8.1862	H.O. Wood	'No 6'; marshes, relief, roads, trail; FN 1420	OTNR (SR 1526)
A1165		–.–.1862 3.6.1863	H.O. Wood copy CLD Andrew Russell AC	'142'; marshes, names, Addington Rd lots, later changes	OTAR(P)
A1166	23.4.1862	–.6.1862	A.B. Perry	'R23' '9760/62'; also includes Brudenell Twp; Addington Rd survey, trees, terrain, clearings with names	OTNR (SR 4593)
	MACAULAY				
A1167	29.4.1857	–.3.1858	John Ryan	'B75'; pt; marshes; FN 1433	OTNR (SR 1531)
A1168		–.3.1858 24.4.1858	John Ryan CLO Andrew Russell AC	'180' 'No 1'; names in S and W pts, road, later changes	OTAR(P)
A1169	7.6.1861	1.8.1862	W.H. Deane	'No 16'; pt; marshes, relief, beaver meadow; FN 1432	OTNR (SR 1532)
A1170		–.–.1862 28.7.1863	W.H. Deane copy T.D. CLD Andrew Russell AC	'180' 'No 20'; pt: lots 6–32 cons 4–13; names, beaver meadows, marsh, later changes	OTAR(P)

	MACDONALD				
A1171	5.5.1860	18.10.1860	Edward Miles	'M No 10'; marshes, cleared land, mining locations; FN 1431	OTNR (SR 1534)
A1172		–.6.1861	CLD Andrew Russell AC	'180'; marshes, relief, Great Northern Rd line, mining location	OTAR(P)
	MADOC				
A1173	14.1.1820	2.6.1820	John Ryder	'A No 28'; names, c & c reserves; FN 510	OTNR (SR 1545)
A1174		[182?]	–	'No 23' 'Office Plan'; c & c reserves, names, later changes, notes 1843	OTAR(P)
A1175		–.7.1843	Thomas Parke SG	Survey grid, reserves; scale n.g.	OTAR
A1176	25.2.1867	16.8.1867	Henry MacLeod	Pt: lots 30–32; conflicting survey lines, clearings, marshes, roads; FN 1443	OTNR (SR 1544)
	MAIDSTONE				
A1177	6.5.1796	[1796?]	A. Iredell	'A24'; c & c reserves, names; FN 110	OTNR (SR 1547)
A1178	17.4.1821	31.12.1824	M. Burwell	'476' 'No 17'; also includes Rochester Twp, c & c reserves, names, later notes Feb 1826; FN 512	OTAR
A1179		[1824?]	M. Burwell copy W.C.	'C16' 'No 34'; also includes Rochester Twp; names, later changes	OTAR(P)
A1180		15.2.1826	Copy J.G.C. Thos Ridout SG	Includes Rochester Twp; marshes, names as located by T. Talbot to 1849	OTAR (Talbot BkC/16)
A1181		–.7.1843	Thomas Parke SG	'M17'; survey grid, reserves, Talbot Rd W and Middle Rd; scale n.g.	OTAR
	MALAHIDE				
A1182	14.4.1810	[1810?]	[M. Burwell?]	'C16' '1796'; c & c reserves, N boundary to be surveyed by Mr Wilmot; FN 514	OTAR (SR 1553)
A1183		[1810?]	[M. Burwell?]	Names located by T. Talbot to 1837, c & c reserves	OTAR (Talbot BkC/14)
A1184		[1810?] 4.4.1820	[M. Burwell] copy Chewett	'No 27'; c & c reserves, names, scale n.g.	OTNR (SR 1552)
A1185		5.5.1818	Thos Ridout SGO	'M18' 'No 4'; c & c reserves, names	OTAR
A1186		8.10.1825	W.C. Thos Ridout	'No 15'; pt, includes Dorchester and Yarmouth twps; c & c reserves, conflicting survey lines	OTNR (SR 1551)
A1187		–.7.1843	Thomas Parke SG	Survey grid, reserves; scale n.g.	OTAR

	Date of Instructions	Date of Map	Surveyor and Signature	Endorsements and Notes	Location
	MALDEN				
A1188	1.9.1793	13.7.1794	Patrick McNiff	'A25' '182'; names, marsh, town plot	OTNR (SR 1554)
A1189	16.12.1795	19.4.1796	A. Iredell	'No 15'; names; FN 110	OTNR (SR 1555)
A1190		[1800?]	Copy W.C.	'Q13' '1054'; proposed fort and town, cessions by Indians including one of 11.9.1800	OTNR (SR 2496)
A1191		[180?]	Copy W.C.	'39'; Amherstburg town boundary added as of 1851, names, later changes	OTAR(P)
A1192	23.12.1831 10.1.1832	8.4.1832	Peter Carroll	'No 16' '475'; pt; crown and clergy blocks, marsh, names, Amherstburg, and military reserve; FN 519	OTNR (SR 1556)
A1193		[1832?]	Copy J.G.C.	'467' 'C8'; also includes 'Huron Reserve'; c & c reserves, marsh, Amherstburg; scale n.g.	OTAR
A1194		-.7.1843	Thomas Parke SG	Survey grid, reserves; scale n.g.	OTAR
A1195		-.10.1846	Copy CLD	Marsh, reserves	OTAR (SR 1557)
	MANVERS				
A1196	24.2.1816	12.11.1816	Sam'l S. Wilmot	'B19' '469'; relief, marshes	OTNR (SR 1561)
A1197		31.12.1816	Sam'l S. Wilmot	'B16'; c & c reserves, relief, a few names; FN 515	OTNR (SR 1560)
A1198		[182?]	-	'No 28'; names, relief, c & c reserves, notes 28 June 1829 and 1844	OTAR(P)
A1199		15.11.1831	Copy J.G.C.	'C12'; c & c reserves, marshes	OTAR
A1200		-.8.1843	Thomas Parke SG	Survey grid, reserves; scale n.g.	OTAR
	MARA				
A1201	14.10.1820	2.1.1821	J.G. Chewett	'No 19'; c & c reserves, names; FN 281	OTNR (SR 1563)
A1202		16.6.1831	Copy J.G.C.	'A19'; c & c reserves, some names	OTAR (SR 1564)
A1203	25.4.1836	16.8.1836	Robert Ross	'B21' '472'; pt; marshes; FN 516	OTNR (SR 1562)
A1204		-.7.1843	Thomas Parke SG	Survey grid, reserves; scale n.g.	OTAR
	MARCH				
A1205	23.6.1819	-.8.1820	R. Sherwood	'B10' '470' 'Twp no 5 Rideau military settlement'; FN 280	OTNR (SR 1566)

A1206		[1820?]	R. Sherwood copy J.G.C.	'C8' 'No 13' 'Office Plan'; c & c reserves, names	OTAR(P)
	MARIPOSA				
A1207	10.3.1820	-.-.1820	Thos. Galbraith	'B17' '465'; c & c reserves, marshes, treed areas; FN 521	OTNR (SR 1568)
A1208		-.-.1820	T. Galbraith	'B18' '466'; c & c reserves, marshes	OTAR (SR 1569)
A1209		4.1.1823	T. Galbraith Thos Ridout	'No 41' 'For the Land Board'; c & c reserves, names, marshes, copy	OTAR(P)
A1210		[1823?]	W.C.	'No 27'; names, c & c reserves	OTAR(P)
A1211		[183?]	Copy [name illegible]	Reserves, marshes, lots deeded, a few names with dates 1855–6	OTAR
A1212		-.7.1843	Thomas Parke SG	Survey grid, reserves; scale n.g.	OTAR
	MARKHAM				
A1213	5.9.1794	[1794?]	Abraham Iredell	'A18' '185'; S pt; c & c reserves, names; FN 257, 734	OTNR (SR 1570)
A1214	19.7.1801	[1801?]	John Stegmann	'B24' '473'; N pt; crown reserves, rivers; scale n.g.; FN 517, 3–310	OTNR (SR 1571)
A1215		[1801?]	Copy W.C.	'1304' 'C12'; c & c reserves, pinholes for tracing; scale n.g.	OTAR
A1216		-.3.1817	Thos Ridout SG	'No 21'; c & c reserves, names	OTAR(P)
A1217		-.7.1843	Thomas Parke SG	Survey grid, reserves; scale n.g.	OTAR
	MARLBOROUGH				
A1218	22.2.1791	-.-.1791	Theodore de Pencier	'A14'; pt; notes on survey, names, glebe, reserve for schoolmaster; FN 14–434	OTNR (SR 1573)
A1219		[1791?]	W. Chewett	'No 20' 'Office Plan'; names, later changes	OTAR(P)
A1220		15.1.1821	R. Sherwood	'A13' '181'; c & c reserves, marshes, a few names; FN 477	OTNR (SR 1578)
A1221		[1821?]	[R. Sherwood?]	'No 32' 'Office plan'; cons 5–10; names, c & c reserves; scale n.g.	OTAR(P)
A1222		-.9.1846	Copy T.D. A.R.	'1308'; Rideau R, marshes	OTAR (SR 1579)

	Date of Instructions	Date of Map	Surveyor and Signature	Endorsements and Notes	Location
	MARMORA				
A1223	[9.6.1819]	[1819]	John Ryder [sgd] Reuben Sherwood	'B22' '471'; c & c reserves, mill seats, a few names; FN 520	OTNR (SR 1575)
A1224		[1819?]	R. Sherwood copy J.G.C.	'162' 'No 24'; c & c reserves, names, later notes and changes 1839 and 1843, marshes	OTAR(P)
A1225		30.1.182[2?]	SGO Thos Ridout	'162' 'No 47'; names, c & c reserves	OTAR(P)
A1226		–.7.1843	Thomas Parke SG	Survey grid, reserves; scale n.g.	OTAR
	MARYBOROUGH				
A1227	31.5.1848	18.1.184[9]	Patrick Callaghan	'B38'; marshes, town reserve; FN 1455	OTNR (SR 1588)
A1228		[1849]	Patrick Callaghan	'B49'; marshes, town reserve	OTNR (SR 1589)
A1229		25.4.1849	T.D. CLD J.H. Price C/CL	'No 45'; names	OTAR(P)
	MARYSBURGH, N and S				
A1230	–	[1784]	John Collins and W. Chewett	'1024' 'N228'; pt: NW Marysburgh and E Sophiasburgh; names	OTNR (SR 5486)
A1231		[179?]	–	'B47'; fragment by East Lake; names; scale n.g.	OTAR
A1232		[179?]	–	'A24'; east pt to Point Pleasant; names along shore; scale n.g.	OTAR
A1233	12.11.1792 11.1.1793	24.12.1796	Alex Aitken	'B23' '455'; nature of shoreline; FN 2–118	OTNR (SR 7027)
A1234		[1796]	[A. Aitken]	'A23'; names; scale n.g.	OTNR (SR 1582)
A1235		[1796]	Alex Aitken	'No 25'; town plot, names, reserves, pts missing	OTNR (SR 1583)
A1236		[1796?]	[A. Aitken?]	'A27'; names	OTAR (SR 1584)
A1237		[1796?]	[A. Aitken?]	'A22' '191'; pt and Sophiasburgh Twp; names; scale n.g.	OTAR (SR 1585)
A1238		[1796?]	Copy W.C.	'No 26'; notes on rd allowances from A. Aitken's plan, names	OTAR(P)
A1239		[1796?]	–	'189' 'A25'; pt and Sophiasburgh Twp; names; scale n.g.	OTAR

A1240		[1796?]	Copy W.C.	'C25'; includes pt Hallowell; survey grid, marshes, relief	OTAR
A1241	–	10.12.1821	W. Conger	Pt: cons 1–2; improvements; scale n.g.; FN 294	OTAR
A1242		–.8.1843	Thomas Parke SG	Survey grid, reserves; scale n.g.	OTAR
A1243		1.9.1856	Sam'l M. Benson	Waupoos Is, names, marshes; 10 ch	OTAR
A1244		–.10.1857	CLD A. Russell AC	'230' 'No 64'; Waupoos Is, names, copy of 'Q89'; 10 ch	OTAR(P)
	MATAWATCHAN				
A1245	15.3.1862	21.8.1862	Edwin H. Kertland	'No 14'; relief, marsh, improvements with names; FN 1465	OTNR (SR 1596)
A1246		[1862?]	–	'Office copy'; some names, later changes	OTAR(P)
A1247		27.11.1864	CLD Andrew Russell	'M32'; pt: cons I–IV; free grant lots on Frontenac Rd	OTAR
	MATCHEDASH				
A1248		[2.6.1836]	J.G. Chewett J. Radenhurst	'Diagram for survey'; c & c reserves, bearings, note dated 2.6.1836; 80 ch	OTAR
A1249	2.6.1836	–.10.1836	James Hamilton	'B18' '47'; c & c reserves, marshes, meadows, a few names; FN 523	OTNR (SR 1592)
A1250		–.10.1836	J. Hamilton copy J.G.C.	'153' 'No 20'; names, marshes, later changes, pt missing	OTAR(P)
A1251		–.7.1843	Thomas Parke SG	Survey grid, reserves; scale n.g.	OTAR
	MATILDA				
A1252	18.6.1785	[1786]	P. McNiff W. Chewett	'A13'; names, glebe and other reserves, mills, rec'd from P. McNiff in 1786; scale n.g.	OTAR (SR 1602)
A1253		[1788?]	Lewis Kotte, Pat McNiff and W. Chewett copy W. Chewett	'1007'; from surveys in 1784–7; names; FN 261?	OTNR (SR 1600)
A1254		15.10.1792	P. McNiff, L. Kotte, and W. Chewett [sgd] Samuel Holland	'1'; from surveys in 1784–7; names, later changes	OTAR(P)
A1255		8.12.1794	Messrs L. Kotte, P. McNiff, and W. Chewett	'9C'; marshes, relief	OTAR (SR 1601)

	Date of Instructions	Date of Map	Surveyor and Signature	Endorsements and Notes	Location
A1256		27.4.1795 29.8.1795	Exam W. Chewett	'196' 'No 2A' 'Land Board'; names, glebe, marshes	OTAR
A1257		[182?]	Copy J.G. Chewett	Survey grid, watermark: 'WHATMAN 18[2?]6'	OTAR
A1258		26.11.1852 24.1.1853	Jas West	'B14' 'Office Copy'; pt: cons 1–3; 20 ch	OTNR (SR 1603)
A1259		31.1.1854	James West A.N. Morin C/CL	'No 25'; pt: cons 1–3; roads, resurvey; 20 ch	OTAR(P)
	MATTAWAN				
A1260	12.8.1861	20.2.1864	L.A. Russell	'No 22'; marshes, relief, trails, improvements; FN 1464	OTNR (SR 1594)
	MCCLURE				
A1261	11.12.1856	–.10.1858	J.S. Peterson	'No 4'; pt; notes on soil and timber, Peterson Rd; FN 1552	OTNR (SR 1615)
A1262		24.1.1861	CLD Andrew Russell AC	'145'; pt; Hastings Rd survey, names	OTAR(P)
	MCDOUGALL				
A1263	3.5.1865 7.9.1865	–.8.1866	J.L.P. O'Hanly	'M27'; Parry Sound village, rivers, lakes, marshes; FN 1557, 2226	OTNR (SR 1625)
A1264		–.8.1866	J.L.P. O'Hanly	'93'; comments on land, Parry Sound village; scale n.g.	OTNR (SR 7152)
A1265		27.3.1867	CLD	'146'; Parry Sound village, roads, marshes, names	OTAR(P)
	MCGILLIVRAY				
A1266	–	4.9.1835 [16.3.1836?]	John McDonald dr D. McDonald	'No 14'; pt; for Canada Co., contents; FN 59	OTNR (SR 1624)
A1267		23.9.1837	John McDonald dr W. Lawson	'No 21'; present and former surveys and unsurveyed areas, for Canada Co.; FN 451	OTNR (SR 1623)
A1268		28.9.1837	John McDonald dr W. Lawson	Cons 6–27; contents of present survey, former surveys and unsurveyed area, some names	OTAR (Canada Co. Atlas)
	MCKAY				
A1269	19.10.1854	9.6.1855	John Robertson	'B51'; twp only partially subdivided, rivers, roads and trails, printed title; FN 1555	OTNR (SR 1629)

A1270		–.8.1855	CLD Joseph Cauchon C/CL	'C13'; rd allowances along Petawawa R	OTAR
A1271		10.4.1856	J.W.B. CLO Joseph Cauchon C/CL	'144' 'No 49'; exploration lines, winter rd, marshes, contents, later changes	OTAR(P)
	MCKENZIE				
A1272	24.8.1866	18.6.1867	A.B. Perry	'M29'; pt; outlines, trees, relief, marshes; FN 2467	OTNR (SR 6548)
	MCKILLOP				
A1273	–	4.2.1833 21.1.1839	John McDonald dr H. Lizars	'No 13' '1154'; for Canada Co., contents; FN 197	OTNR (SR 1633)
A1274		21.1.1839	John McDonald	Cons 6–14; contents of present survey, marshes, some names in cons I–V	OTAR (Canada Co. Atlas 15)
	MCLEAN				
A1275	28.2.1862	27.10.1862	Robert Burns	'No 15'; relief, marshes, falls, rapids; FN 1534	OTNR (SR 1638)
A1276		–.6.1864	CLD Andrew Russell C/CL	'121'; marshes, names, later changes	OTAR(P)
	MCNAB				
A1277		[1824?]	–	Diagram for survey of 'Wilmot' [McNab], c & c reserves, watermark: 'WHATMAN 1818'; 80 ch	OTAR
A1278		–.–.1824	J. McNaughton	'B9' '477'; relief, marshes, c & c reserves, a few names; scale n.g.; FN 541	OTNR (SR 1644)
A1279		[1824?]	J. McNaughton copy W.C.	'No 12' 'Office copy'; c & c reserves, names, later changes	OTAR(P)
A1280		–.8.1843	Thomas Parke SG	Survey grid, reserves; scale n.g.	OTAR
	MEDONTE				
A1281		–.1.1820	W.C.	Diagram for survey	OTAR
A1282	5.2.1820	[1820]	[J.G. Chewett]	'No 22'; names; FN 526	OTNR (SR 1653)
A1283		[182?]	Copy J.G.C.	'1301'; c & c reserves, marshes	OTAR (SR 1652)
A1284		–.7.1843	Thomas Parke SG	Survey grid, reserves; scale n.g.	OTAR
	MELANCTHON				
A1285	4.2.1820	24.8.1825	Hugh Black	'No 23'; E pt; names; FN 315	OTNR (SR 1657)

	Date of Instructions	Date of Map	Surveyor and Signature	Endorsements and Notes	Location
A1286		–.7.1843	Thomas Parke SG	E pt: cons 1–4; reserves; scale n.g.	OTAR
A1287		3.9.1852	T.D. CLD Andrew Russell SS&D	'No 44'; some names on rd lots only	OTAR(P)
A1288	17.3.1853	–.–.1853	David Gibson	'B61'; survey of residue of twp except Sydenham Rd; marshes, relief; FN 1469	OTNR (SR 1656)
A1289		20.7.1854	A.N. Morin C/CL	'No 31'; names mainly in W pt	OTAR(P)
A1290	–	27.4.1858	F.F. Passmore	'35'; cons 1–4; resurvey, notes on survey; 30 ch; FN 525	OTNR (SR 5500)
	MERSEA				
A1291	–	22.6.1799	A. Iredell	'A27'; front; reserve for Point Pelee, trail, Indian cabins, names	OTNR (SR 1660)
A1292	16.3.1806	[1806]	T. Smith DS	'A26' '197'; W pt; names, clergy reserve, improved areas; FN 134	OTNR (SR 1661)
A1293		30.11.1816	M. Burwell	Names as located along Talbot Rd by T. Talbot	OTAR (Talbot BkE/7)
A1294	6.10.1815	20.12.1816	M. Burwell	'No 19'; Talbot Rd, names, marshes, Point Pelee reserve; FN 527	OTNR (SR 1659)
A1295	17.4.1821	27.6.1827 30.6.1827	M. Burwell copy J.G.C. Thos Ridout SG	Marshes, c & c reserves, names located at N end by T. Talbot to 1843; FN 611	OTAR (Talbot BkE/5)
A1296		[1827?]	M. Burwell copy J.G. Chewett W.C.	'C77' 'No 18'; includes Talbot Rd survey, c & c reserves, names, marsh, notes 1827 and 1850s, many later changes	OTAR(P)
A1297		14.3.1836	M. Burwell	'478' 'B9'; marshes, c & c reserves, Talbot Rd survey, copy; FN 527	OTAR
A1298		–.7.1843	Thomas Parke SG	Reserves; scale n.g.	OTAR
	METHUEN				
A1299	–	[–.5.1823]	John Huston	'B20' '479'; c & c reserves, marshes; FN 310	OTNR (SR 1666)
A1300		[1823?]	Copy J.G.C.	'155' 'No 41'; some names, later changes, note re return of vacant lands to C/CL 5.7.1839	OTAR(P)
A1301		–.7.1843	Thomas Parke SG	Reserves, survey grid; scale n.g.	OTAR

	MIDDLETON				
A1302	24.3.1809	6.12.1809	Mahlon Burwell	'B39' '853'; pt; boundary line with Walsingham, Talbot Rd; scale n.g.; FN 528	OTAR (SR 1670)
A1303		[1810]	Mahlon Burwell	'No 28'; Talbot Rd, names; FN 528	OTNR (SR 1668)
A1304		[181?]	–	Talbot Rd with names located by T. Talbot to 1817; scale n.g.	OTAR (Talbot BkC/8)
A1305	26.1.1824	7.2.1825	John McDonald	'B7' '483' c & c reserves, notes on soil and timber, hay marsh, tamarack swamp; FN 529	OTNR (SR 1669)
A1306		[1825?]	[J. Mcdonald?]	Relief, marshes, tree types, trails, names almost illegible; scale n.g.	OTAR (Talbot BkC/10)
A1307		[1825?]	[J. Mcdonald?]	'1297'; Talbot Rd, c & c reserves, pinholes for tracing	OTAR
A1308		[1825?]	John McDonald copy W.C.	'1298' 'C14'; notes on types of timber and soil, marshes, c & c reserves; scale n.g.	OTAR
A1309		–.7.1843	Thomas Parke SG	Survey grid, reserves; scale n.g.	OTAR
A1310		–.11.1846	Copy CLD	'C44'; survey grid, Talbot Rd; scale n.g.	OTAR
	MILLER				
A1311	5.6.1857	–.10.1860	J.S. Harper	'M12'; Frontenac Rd lots, mill sites; FN 1483	OTNR (SR 1671)
A1312		–.10.1861	CLD Andrew Russell AC	'168'; Frontenac Rd lots, some names, later changes	OTAR(P)
	MINDEN				
A1313	23.8.1858	1.7.1859	J.W. Fitzgerald	'No 6'; Minden town plot (shown in 2 proposed locations), relief, marshes, portages; FN 1481	OTNR (SR 1674)
A1314		1.7.1859	Jas. W. Fitzgerald	'No 5'; marshes, relief, Minden town plot, portages, Bobcaygeon Rd	OTAR (SR 1675)
A1315		[186?]	Andrew Russell CLD	'250'; names, Bobcaygeon Rd, town plot, mill sites, portages	OTAR(P)
	MINTO				
A1316		26.4.1852	CLD John Rolph C/CL	Projected plan, lines already surveyed and those to be surveyed	OTAR
A1317	26.4.1852	6.8.1852	C. Rankin	Pt; proposed con A on E boundary for squatters; scale n.g.	OTAR
A1318		17.3.1853	C. Rankin	'B57'; improvements, marshes, treed areas; FN 1484	OTNR (SR 1677)

	Date of Instructions	Date of Map	Surveyor and Signature	Endorsements and Notes	Location
A1319		17.3.1853 2.12.1853	A.N. Morin C/CL C. Rankin	'No 43'; names	OTAR(P)
	MONAGHAN, N and S				
A1320	2.5.1817	3.9.1817	Sam'l S. Wilmot	'A10' '199'; S pt; relief, names; FN 530	OTNR (SR 1679)
A1321	5.1.1818	24.3.1818	Sam'l S. Wilmot	'No 29'; names; FN 373	OTNR (SR 97949)
A1322		[1818?]	–	'A9' '200'; names, marshes, relief; scale n.g.	OTAR (SR 1680)
A1323		–.7.1843	Thomas Parke SG	N pt; town of Peterborough, park lots; scale n.g.	OTAR
A1324		–.8.1843	Thomas Parke SG	Survey grid, reserves; scale n.g.	OTAR
	MONCK				
A1325	7.3.1863	2.5.1864	W.H. Deane PLS	'No 23'; names, relief indicated along survey line, beaver meadows; FN 1489	OTNR (SR 1681)
A1326		31.10.1864	CLD Andrew Russell AC	'294' 'No 25'; names, later changes	OTAR(P)
	MONMOUTH				
A1327	4.9.1861	31.10.1862	James W. Fitzgerald	'No 17'; E pt; free grant lots on Burleigh Rd, comments on soil and timber; FN 1486	OTNR (SR 1685)
A1328	4.11.1862	10.9.1863	James W. Fitzgerald	'No 21'; W pt; relief, swamp; FN 1487	OTNR (SR 1684)
	MONO				
A1329	4.2.1820	19.6.1820	Sam'l M. Benson	'B19' '484'; E pt; c & c reserves, trails, relief, marshes; FN 532	OTNR (SR 1686)
A1330		19.6.1820	Sam'l M. Benson	'A20' 'office plan'; E pt; c & c reserves, some names; scale n.g.	OTAR (SR 1687)
A1331		19.6.[1820]	S.M. B[enson]	Some names, c & c reserves, rock outcrop; scale n.g.	OTAR
A1332		–.–.1821	Hugh Black	'B20' '486; W pt; c & c reserves, names; FN 533	OTNR (SR 1689)
A1333		–.–.1821	Hugh Black	'B22' '485'; W pt; relief, marshes	OTNR (SR 1688)
A1334		[1821?]	–	'No 24'; names, c & c reserves, reference to Hugh Black's survey of 1821	OTAR(P)
A1335		–.7.1843	Thomas Parke SG	Survey grid, reserves; scale n.g.	OTAR

	MONTAGUE				
A1336	11.10.1796	[1794–5] [1797?]	[W. Fortune?] [J. Stegmann?]	'No 21'; c & c reserves, names; FN 3–319, FN 311, 602	OTNR (SR 1690)
A1337		4.11.1819	Copy W.C.	'No 28'; marshes, vacant lots	OTAR (SR 1691)
A1338		18.11.1837	J. Stegmann copy J.G. Chewett	'1' 'No 33' 'Office copy'; marshes, c & c reserves, names	OTAR(P)
A1339		–.8.1843	Thomas Parke SG	Survey grid, reserves; scale n.g.	OTAR
	MONTEAGLE				
A1340	11.12.1856	–.10.1858	J.S. Peterson	'No 13'; W pt and outline; comments on land and timber; FN 1491	OTNR (SR 1693)
A1341		–.1.1861	CLD Andrew Russell AC	'167'; pt; Hastings Rd lots, comments on land and timber	OTAR(P)
A1342	13.6.1861	12.4.1862	J.J. Haslett	'No 13a'; E pt; relief, marshes, mill sites; FN 1492	OTNR (SR 1692)
A1343		30.7.1862	CLD Andrew Russell AC	'294'; Hastings Rd, names, marshes	OTAR(P)
A1344		–.12.1862	J.J. Haslett	'No 18'; pt of 6 cons; beaver ponds, marshes; FN 1493	OTNR (SR 1694)
	MOORE				
A1345	8.4.1829	–.1.1830	R. Mount	'B8' '487'; c & c reserves, list of squatters and improved lands, Indian reserve; FN 537	OTNR (SR 1698)
A1346		[1830?]	Copy J.G.C.	'No 20' 'Office Plan'; marshes, c & c reserves, names, some later changes, town of Corunna	OTAR(P)
A1347		–.7.1843	Thomas Parke SG	Survey grid, reserves; scale n.g.	OTAR
	MORNINGTON				
A1348	30.5.1848	19.12.1848	James W. Bridgland	'B37'; town plot, cedar, tamarack, and black ash swamps, marsh, beaver meadow, clearings; FN 1507	OTNR (SR 1704)
A1349		–.12.1849	T.D. CLD J.H. Price C/CL	'M56'; survey grid, town plot, mill, some small lots shown; scale n.g.	OTAR
A1350		–.1.1850	T.D. J.H. Price C/CL	'No 29'; names, Poole town plot	OTAR(P)
	MORRIS				
A1351	26.10.1847	11.8.1848	A. Wilkinson	'B31'; marshes, relief, rivers; FN 1503, 1504, 1505, 1506	OTNR (SR 1705)

	Date of Instructions	Date of Map	Surveyor and Signature	Endorsements and Notes	Location
A1352		–.2.1849	T.D. CLD J.H. Price C/CL	'No 53'; names	OTAR(P)
	MORRISON				
A1353	25.6.1859	12.8.1860	J.O. Browne	'M No 8'; traverse tables on lakes, free-grant lots along rd, a few names; FN 1499	OTNR (SR 1706)
	MOSA				
A1354	19.1.1820	26.12.1820	M. Burwell	'B8' '488'; c & c reserves, Long Woods Rd, battle site, trails; FN 538	OTNR (SR 1709)
A1355		20.12.1820	M. Burwell	Names located by T. Talbot to 1843, c & c reserves	OTAR (Talbot BkD/14)
A1356		[1820?]	J.G. Chewett	'1300'; c & c reserves, marshes; scale n.g.	OTAR
A1357		8.12.1830	Copy J.G.C. W. Chewett ASG	Marshes, c & c reserves, lots located with names and dates, lots under direction of T. Talbot	OTAR
A1358		[1830?]	M. Burwell copy J.G.C.	'No 29'; names; site of Battle of Longwoods, later endorsements 1843, 1851, and 1853	OTAR(P)
A1359		–.7.1843	Thomas Parke SG	Survey grid, reserves; scale n.g.	OTAR
	MOULTON				
A1360	18.4.1833/ 23.4.1833 16.5.1833	1.1834	Lewis Burwell	'B4'; includes Canborough and Dunn twps; lots, Indian lands, contents of good and saleable lands, marshes, feeder to Welland Canal; 20 ch; FN 175	OTNR (SR 6942)
	MOUNTAIN				
A1361	–	15.4.1791	W. Chewett	'6'; c & c reserves, names	OTAR(P)
A1362	1.9.1793	10.4.1794	W. Chewett	'No 11C'; reserves, types of trees indicated on boundaries; FN 535	OTAR
A1363		[1794?]	Copy W.C.	Marsh, c & c reserves	OTAR
A1364	[25.3.1796]	[12.1796]	John Stegmann	'No 2B' '481'; reserves, marshes; FN 3–340	OTNR (SR 1713)
A1365	22.8.1797	19.6.1798	Lewis Grant	'11B' '482'; reserves, marshes; FN 314	OTNR (SR 1711)
A1366		4.1.1799	Lewis Grant	'No 6A' '203'; reserves, names	OTAR (SR 1714)
A1367	23.1.1834	–.–.1836	James West	'3B' '480'; pt: front cons 10–12; treed areas; FN 534	OTNR (SR 1712)

	MULMUR				
A1368	4.2.1820	–.–.1822	Hugh Black	'A21' c & c reserves, relief, rivers, mill sites, a few names, note: site of 'volcano'; FN 287	OTAR (SR 1720)
A1369		–.–.1822	Hugh Black	'No 25'; names, c & c reserves, later notes	OTNR (SR 1719)
A1370		–.7.1843	Thomas Parke SG	Survey grid, reserves; scale n.g.	OTAR
	MURRAY				
A1371		[179?]	A. Jones DPS	'No 13'; pt; scale n.g.	OTAR (SR 1728)
A1372		[1794]	[L. Grant]	'A7'; outline only; Salmon Creek, Trent R; scale n.g.; FN 539	OTNR (SR 1729)
A1373	3.11.1795	28.2.1800	Copy W.C. Chewett Thos Ridout	'No 31'; alterations to survey, c & c reserves, reserve for canal, names	OTNR (SR 86749)
A1374		24.2.1800 20.9.1811	Copy W.C. Thos Ridout exam	'A11'; names, c & c reserves, reserve for canal, notes re alterations	OTNR (SR 1726)
A1375	[8.11.1815]	[1816]	J. Ryder	'A12' '206'; pt: BF and cons A, B, and C; canal, roads, a few names; scale n.g.; FN 372	OTNR (SR 1727)
A1376		[1816?]	J. Ryder	Pt BF and con I; scale n.g.	OTAR (SR 1730)
A1377		[183?]	–	'No 30'; names, marshes, Trenton town plot, canal reserve	OTAR(P)
A1378		21.12.1839	Copy J.G. Chewett	Pt; shows canal reserve and lots requested for the canal, also pt Cramahe and town of Newcastle; scale n.g.	OTAR
A1379		–.8.1843	Thomas Parke SG	Survey grid, reserves; scale n.g.	OTAR
A1380		[185?]	E.C. Caddy	'K3'; pt; areas of dry and drained land; 5 ch	OTNR (SR 92379)
	MUSKOKA				
A1381	29.4.1857	11.11.185[7]	C. Rankin	'B74'; E pt; undivided block, rd lines; FN 1517	OTNR (SR 1734)
A1382		24.12.1857	Andrew Russell CLD	'161' 'No 46'; names, later changes	OTAR(P)
	NASSAGAWEYA				
A1383	18.6.1819	12.11.1819	Sam'l Ryckman	'B6' '493'; marshes, relief, point of local magnetic attraction, c & c reserves; FN 542	OTNR (SR 1742)
A1384		[1819?]	[S. Ryckman]	'A17' '209'; rear pt; names; scale n.g.	OTAR (SR 1743)
A1385	[8.2.1819?]	20.5.1819	R. Sherwood	'B5' '491'; also includes Nelson Twp; c & c reserves, a few names, relief, 'Gold Mountain'; FN 543	OTNR (SR 1750)

	Date of Instructions	Date of Map	Surveyor and Signature	Endorsements and Notes	Location
A1386		[182?]	Copy J.G. Chewett	'A18'; pt: lots 1–17, also shows lots 1–15 rear pt of Nelson; c & c reserves, names	OTAR(P)
A1387		[182?]	R. Sherwood and S. Ryckman copy W.C. SS&D	'No 15' 'Office Plan'; lots 1–32; names, later changes	OTAR(P)
A1388		–.7.1843	Thomas Parke SG	Survey grid, reserves; scale n.g.	OTAR
	NEEBING				
A1389	10.6.1859	10.7.1860	Thomas W. Herrick	'N No 8'; town plot, park lots, Fort William, trails, Indian reserve, relief, comments on land; FN 1572	OTNR (SR 1744)
A1390		[10.7.1860?]	[T. Herrick?]	'295'; town plot, park lots, pt of Indian reserve surrendered 1859, names, later changes	OTAR(P)
	NELSON				
A1391	31.1.1805	18.6.1806	Sam'l S. Wilmot	'A15' '211' 'Rough Plan'; names, reserves, trails, relief; FN 544	OTAR (SR 1749)
A1392		28.6.1806	Sam'l S. Wilmot	'A16' '212'; Joseph Brant's land, c & c reserves, names, relief	OTNR (SR 1748)
A1393		[182?]	W.C. SS&D	'No 16' 'Office Plan'; names, many later changes, references to Bristol's, Sherwood's, and Wilmot's surveys, town of Wellington Square marked with date 10.5.1831	OTAR(P)
A1394		–.7.1843	Thomas Parke SG	Survey grid, reserves; scale n.g.	OTAR
	NEPEAN				
A1395	1.9.1793	[1794]	[J. Stegmann]	'No 14'; names, c & c reserves, photoreproduction only; scale n.g.; FN 854	OTAR (SR 1753) (photoreproduction)
A1396		[1794?]	[J. Stegmann?]	'No 35' 'Land Board Plan'; names	OTAR (SR 1755)
A1397	–	1823 1824	John McNaughton and Asa La[ndon] under Reuben Sherwood	'B18' '498'; c & c reserves; FN 545, 546, 547	OTNR (SR 1754)
A1398		[1824?]	J. McNaughton and A. Landon copy W.C.	'No 15' '492'; c & c reserves	OTAR (SR 1751)

A1399		18.3.1830	J.G.C. W. Chewett ASG	'C4' 'No 35'; pt in Bytown; c & c reserves, names, later changes	OTAR(P)
A1400	3.6.1853	22.6.1853	Duncan Sinclair Robert Bell	'B43'; pt: lot 39 con A, and BF; reserve; 2 ch; FN 1570	OTNR (SR 1752)
	NIAGARA				
A1401	–	–.–.1787	P.R.F[rey] D.W. Smith	'A18' 'rec'd from Land Board'; names, crown reserve, 'Navy Hall'; 38 ch	OTNR (SR 1761)
A1402		1787 [1794?]	Philip Frey copy Augustus Jones	'A19' '215'; surveyed by Frey in 1787, names; 38 ch; FN 366	OTNR (SR 1759)
A1403		[180?]	–	'898' 'No 2'; pt and Stamford Twp; Niagara town plot, military reserves at Niagara and Queenston, some owners	OTAR (SR 213)
A1404		20.9.1811	Copy W.C. exam Thos Ridout	'C22' '1295'; pt; town of Niagara, names, military reserve	OTNR (SR 1762)
A1405		12.4.1830	W. Chewett ASG	'C20' '1294'; military reserve as surveyed in 1787 with notes on parts surrendered earlier; scale n.g.	OTNR (SR 1760)
A1406		19.12.1855	Edmund DeCew	'B20'; roads, Queenston military reserve; FN 551	OTNR (SR 1758)
	NICHOL				
A1407	–	[1845?]	–	'B8' '1190'; a few names, also includes names in Eramosa, NW pt of twp unsurveyed, watermark: 'J WHATMAN 1841'	OTAR(P)
A1408		–.2.1845	Copy Thos A. Blyth	Names in W half, Elora, Fergus; scale n.g.	OTAR
	NISSOURI, E and W				
A1409	10.9.1819	20.11.1819	Shubal Park	'B20' '599'; c & c reserves, a few names; FN 552	OTNR (SR 1771)
A1410		[1819?]	–	'A5'; c & c reserves, some names; scale n.g.	OTAR(P)
A1411		[182?]	S. Park copy W.C.	'No 30'; names, c & c reserves	OTAR(P)
A1412		–.7.1843	Thomas Parke SG	Survey grid, reserves; scale n.g.	OTAR
A1413		16.3.1844	Copy J.G. Chewett Thomas Parke SG	Marshes, c & c reserves	OTAR (SR 1772)
	NORMANBY				
A1414	–	–.6.1847	CLD Andrew Russell AC	'No 28' 'Office copy'; Owen Sound Rd survey, names	OTAR(P)

	Date of Instructions	Date of Map	Surveyor and Signature	Endorsements and Notes	Location
A1415		17.2.1852	CLD John Rolph C/CL	Projected plan, extensive notes on lines to be surveyed, lines and areas already surveyed	OTAR
A1416	17.2.1852	–.–.1852	D. Gibson	'B58'; marshes, town plot reserve; FN 1585	OTNR (SR 1776)
A1417		–.12.1853	CLD A.N. Morin C/CL	'No 51'; town reserve, mill sites, names	OTAR(P)
	NORWICH, N and S				
A1418	29.4.1799	[3.12.1799]	William Hambly	'No 31'; names; scale n.g.; FN 556	OTNR (SR 1777)
A1419		[1799]	Wm Hambly	'C34'; outline, later note: N pt of gore surveyed by Peter Carroll 1834	OTNR (SR 1779)
A1420	21.4.1834	8.4.1835	Peter Carroll	'PF5' '702'; pt; gore B; FN 555	OTNR (SR 1778)
A1421		[1835?]	Copy J.G. Chewett	C & c reserves	OTAR
A1422		–.7.1843	Thomas Parke SG	Survey grid, reserves; scale n.g.	OTAR
	NOTTAWASAGA				
A1423	9.8.1832	27.2.1833	Thos Kelly	'B24' '489'; pt; mill sites, c & c reserves, area surveyed previous year; FN 553	OTNR (SR 1782)
A1424		[1833?]	T. Kelly	'C14' 'Office copy'; lots improved by settlers under Messrs Bauerman and Tupper (1837), and those improved by Scotch settlers, c & c reserves, names, marshes, town plot Sudbury	OTAR(P)
A1425	23.3.1833	18.8.1833	C. Rankin	'No 26'; formerly Merlin twp, c & c reserves, names, town plot; FN 553, 554	OTNR (SR 1781)
A1426		–.7.1843	Thomas Parke SG	Survey grid, reserves; scale n.g.	OTAR
A1427	–	26.5.1860	Wm Gibbard	Five acre lots on lot 25, cons 8–9; bldgs, names; 4 ch	OTNR (SR 1780)
A1428		23.6.1860	Thos Devine, Head of Surveys Andrew Russell AC	'PH156'; five-acre lots on lot 25, cons 8–9; location map showing irregular lengths of bordering cons, bldgs, some names; 4 ch	OTNR (SR 5528)
A1429		11.3.1864	Wm Gibbard Andrew Russell	Pt: five-acre lots on lot 25, cons 8–9; bldgs, names, copy; scale n.g.	OTAR(P)
	OAKLAND				
A1430	1.9.1796	[30.12.1796]	[Thomas Welch]	'No 32'; names, c & c reserves; scale n.g.; FN 376	OTNR (SR 1791)

A1431		[180?]	Copy W.C.	'1288' 'C20'; marshes, Six Nations Indians' land; scale n.g.	OTAR
A1432		–.7.1843	Thomas Parke SG	Survey grid, reserves; scale n.g.	OTAR
	OAKLEY				
A1433	20.11.1860	15.10.1861	William Murdoch	Mills, falls, marshes, town plot; FN 1595	OTNR (SR 1784)
A1434		–.2.1862	CLD Andrew Russell AC	'173'; town plot, mill sites, names, later changes	OTAR(P)
	OLDEN				
A1435	–	–.–.1826	Publius V. Elmore	'B25' '500' 'Twp no 4'; c & c reserves, mill, marshes, mill seats; FN 845	OTNR (SR 1788)
A1436		Surv 1826	P.V. Elmore copy J.G.C.	'No 28'; c & c reserves, some names, marshes	OTAR(P)
A1437		4.8.18[26?]	Copy J.G. Chewett	'1290'; c & c reserves, marshes, mill sites	OTAR
A1438		–.8.1843	Thomas Parke SG	Survey grid, reserves; scale n.g.	OTAR
A1439		–.8.1843	SGO	Survey grid; scale n.g.	OTAR
A1440		3.7.1856	J.W.B. CLO E.P. Taché per C/CL	Survey grid	OTAR
A1441	4.2.1860	[30.1.1861]	T.F. Gibbs	'O91'; resurvey, improvements, roads; FN 1599	OTNR (SR 1789)
A1442		3.5.1861	CLD Andrew Russell AC	Copy for agent, lakes named, lot lines offset around lakes and rivers	OTAR (SR 1790)
A1443		29.3.1862	CLD	Copy of resurvey, names, roads, clearings	OTAR(P)
	ONEIDA				
A1444	13.8.1841	24.6.1842	William Walker	'Q64'; settled areas, names, bldgs, roads, mills, marshes; FN 567	OTNR (SR 1794)
A1445		24.6.1842 25.7.1842	William Walker copy A. Larue	'No 50'; names, large irregular lots and reserves with descriptions, marshes	OTAR(P)
A1446		24.3.1843	William Walker	'Q67' '1085'; pt; alterations of survey around Plank Rd and other roads, marshes, reserves; 20 ch; FN 568	OTAR(P)
	ONONDAGA				
A1447	14.7.1842	8.10.1842	James Kirkpatrick	'Q62'; contents, a few names, Indian church reserves and villages, improvements, roads; FN 1602	OTNR (SR 1795)

	Date of Instructions	Date of Map	Surveyor and Signature	Endorsements and Notes	Location
A1448		-.-.1842 -.11.1843	James Kirkpatrick copy Thomas Parke SG	'No 42' 'Office copy'; names, roads, town plot, mills, cleared lands	OTAR(P)
A1449		31.1.1853	Lewis Burwell	'Q90'; pt; boundary dispute in Martin Bend opposite Newport; contents; 10 ch	OTNR (SR 1796)
A1450		17.7.1857	Lewis Burwell copy CLD	'No 73' 'Martin Bend'; names and table of no of acres, notes on rd allowance; 10 ch	OTAR(P)
	OPS				
A1451	14.2.1824	-.-.1825	Duncan McDonell	'No 32'; names; FN 570–1	OTNR (SR 1797)
A1452		[1825?]	[D. McDonell?]	Names, c & c reserves, pts missing	OTAR (SR 1799)
A1453		[1825?]	Duncan McDonell copy J.G.C.	'C14'; c & c reserves, marshes, some names	OTAR (SR 1798)
A1454		-.7.1843	Thomas Parke SG	Survey grid, reserves, notes; scale n.g.	OTAR
A1455		-.12.1846	J.P. CLD A.R.	'1291'; survey grid	OTAR
	ORFORD				
A1456	1.9.1793	-.1.1794	P. McNiff	'B22'; pt: lots 1–17 N and S of Thames R, as granted to Moravian Indians, cornfields	OTAR (SR 1802)
A1457		[1794?]	D.W. Smith	'Q6' '1063' 'K18'; pt; boundary of purchase from Indians in 1790, Moravian villages; 2 miles	OTNR (SR 2431)
A1458	8.6.1811	24.10.1811	Mahlon Burwell	'A23'; pt and Howard Twp; Talbot Rd W and Petite Pointe aux Pins in Harwich; some names; FN 757	OTAR (SR 1350)
A1459	13.8.1824	23.9.1825	M. Burwell	'No 21'; pt; Middle Rd, names, Canada Co. land, locations on Thames; FN 559	OTNR (SR 1801)
A1460		23.9.1825	M. Burwell	Reserves, marshes, Talbot Rd, a few names along Middle Rd; scale n.g.	OTAR (Talbot BkD/13)
A1461		[1825?]	Copy J.G. Chewett	'1289' 'C29'; N pt Indian reserve; rd survey, reserves, Talbot Rd	OTAR
A1462		[1825?]	M. Burwell copy J.G. Chewett W.C.	'C12'; pt and Howard Twp; Talbot Rd section, relief, marshes	OTAR

A1463		–.7.1843	Thomas Parke SG	S pt surveyed, Canada Co. lands, other reserves; scale n.g.	OTAR
A1464	–	23.9.1857	Francis H. Lynch	'No 30'; pt and Zone Twp; lands surrendered by Delaware Indians, marshes, Indian reserve; 30 ch	OTNR (SR 1800)
A1465		–.3.1862	CLD Andrew Russell AC	Pt and Zone Twp; Indian reserve, some names, marshes; 30 ch	OTAR(P)
	ORILLIA				
A1466	23.6.1820	[1820]	J.G. Chewett	'No 27'; names, surveyed for Borland and Roe; FN 573	OTNR (SR 1803)
A1467		[1820?]	Copy J.G.C.	'1293'; N pt; c & c reserves, marshes	OTAR (SR 1804)
A1468		[1820?]	Copy J.G.C.	'1292'; S pt; marshes, c & c reserves	OTAR (SR 1805)
A1469		–.7.1843	Thomas Parke SG	Survey grid, reserves; scale n.g.	OTAR
	ORO				
A1470	(5.2.1820)	[1.6.1820?]	J.G. Chewett	'57'; names, c & c reserves; FN 560	OTNR (SR 97937)
A1471		10.6.1831	Copy J.G.C.	'C16'; town plot, c & c reserves, marshes, a few names	OTAR (SR 1807)
A1472		–.7.1843	Thomas Parke SG	Survey grid, reserves; scale n.g.	OTAR
	OSGOODE				
A1473	8.9.1820	27.6.1821	T. Ridout SG	Diagram for survey, c & c reserves, lines to be surveyed	OTAR
A1474		[1822?]	Wm. Macdonald	'3'; includes watercolour view, names, comments on land and trees, marshes; scale n.g.; FN 378	OTNR (SR 1810)
A1475		29.11.1822	Wm. Macdonald Thos Ridout SG	'No 4'; c & c reserves, names, copy	OTAR(P)
A1476		[1822?]	–	'A19' '262'; c & c reserves; scale n.g.	OTAR (SR 1811)
	OSNABRUCK				
A1477	18.6.1785	2.12.1789	W. Chewett	'No 27' '1004' 'office copy'; from surveys 1784–7 by Lewis Kotte, P. McNiff, and Wm Chewett; names; FN 261	OTNR (SR 1818)
A1478		2.2.1791 29.8.1795	W. Chewett	'11'; glebe, marshes, names	OTAR(P)

	Date of Instructions	Date of Map	Surveyor and Signature	Endorsements and Notes	Location
A1479		15.10.179[2?]	W. Chewett copy James Toosey [sgd] Sam Holland	'12'; names, later changes	OTAR(P)
A1480		5.12.1794	W. Chewett	'1283' 'No 16C'; survey grid, marshes, relief, notes on earlier surveys	OTAR
A1481		23.2.1816	Thos Ridout	'No 1'; pt of 3rd con line from Lewis Grant's survey 22.9.1796; scale n.g.	OTAR
A1482	2.2.1826	[1828]	William Browne	'501'; pt: rear cons VI–IX; scale n.g.; FN 297	OTNR (SR 1814)
	OSO				
A1483	29.7.1820	23.1.1827	Publius V. Elmore	'B24' '494'; c & c reserves, marshes, a few names, falls, navigable river; FN 846	OTNR (SR 1818)
A1484		18.10.1834	P.V. Elmore copy Henry Lizars	'No 27' 'Office copy'; c & c reserves, cedar, tamarack, and black alder swamps, mill site, some names	OTAR (SR 1817)
A1485		[1834?]	–	'C16'; c & c reserves, marshes	OTAR (SR 1816)
A1486		–.8.1843	Thomas Parke SG	'O14'; survey grid, reserves; scale n.g.	OTAR
A1487	10.6.1861	19.4.1862	Thomas Gibbs	'No 94'; resurvey, contents, improvements, roads, dams; FN 1605, 1606	OTNR (SR 1819)
A1488		21.11.1862	Andrew Russell AC	Resurvey, names, many later changes	OTAR(P)
A1489		–.3.1864	CLD Andrew Russell AC	Copy of resurvey	OTAR (SR 1815)
	OSPREY				
A1490	11.5.1850	28.1.1851	C. Rankin	'B49'; marshes, a few names, Durham Rd; scale n.g.; FN 379	OTNR (SR 1820)
A1491		–.8.1851	Copy T. Devine S and D	'No 41'; names	OTAR(P)
	OTONABEE				
A1492		29.7.1819	SGO	Projected plan, lines and shore to be surveyed, c & c reserves, town plot reserve; scale n.g.	OTAR
A1493	29.7.1819	8.[12.1819]	R. Birdsall	'No 33'; names; FN 381	OTNR (SR 95571)

A1494		8.12.1819 8.1.1820 6.3.1827	Richard Birdsall Thos Ridout SG	'No 42'; c & c reserves, names, town plot, mill seat, road; scale n.g.	OTAR (SR 1822)
A1495		–.–.1820	[R. Birdsall?]	'2007'; names, c & c reserves, town plot; 7/8 mile	OTAR
A1496		23.10.1829	Jas G. Chewett	C & c reserves, names on lots indicating if deeded, located by Peter Robinson, and if settlement duty performed, marshes	OTAR
A1497		4.11.1834	R. Birdsall copy Henry Lizars	'No 33' 'Office copy'; c & c reserves, names, later changes	OTAR(P)
A1498		–.7.1843	Thomas Parke SG	Survey grid, reserves; scale n.g.	OTAR
	OXFORD (Grenville Co)				
A1499	22.2.1791 21.3.1791	28.3.1791	Lt Aug Prevost [sgd] Samuel Holland copy W. Chewett	'A22' '188'; survey grid, town projected with reserves at falls of Rideau on E side of Oxford and Marlborough twps, glebes; scale n.g.	OTAR (SR 1836)
A1500		–.4–6.1791	Jesse Pennoyer	'A15' '266'; glebes, names, marshes; 1" = 1/2 mile; FN 273	OTNR (SR 1834)
A1501		–.–.1791	J. Pennoyer	'No 33'; includes pt Edwardsburgh; survey grid, marshes, glebe, falls, Rideau R, notes on land, reserves	OTAR (SR 1832)
A1502		–.–.1792	W. Chewett	'No 22'; c & c reserves, names, later changes	OTAR(P)
A1503		28.4.1795	W. Chewett	'No 23'; glebes, names	OTAR(P)
A1504	–	29.8.1795 –.–.1815	Duncan McDonell	'B8' '587'; includes Wolford; survey grid; 80 ch; FN 495	OTAR (SR 1835)
A1505		2.1816	William Graves	'B9' '496'; pt: cons 2–7; roads, reserves, resurvey; FN 563	OTNR (SR 1840)
A1506	6.2.1834	–.–.1836	James West	'B16'; Kemptville, roads, marshes, mills; FN 565	OTNR (SR 1833)
A1507		–.8.1843	Thomas Parke SG	Survey grid, reserves; scale n.g.	OTAR
	OXFORD, E, N, and W (Oxford Co)				
A1508	5.6.1794	[1795?]	Copy W.C.	'C18'; marshes, 'landing' at Upper Forks Thames R, rd to Burlington Bay	OTAR (SR 1841)
A1509	13.12.1797	[1797?]	D.W. Smith	'No 33'; names, c & c reserves, projection for surveyor	OTNR (SR 97934)
A1510	13.7.1799	[1800]	William Hambly	'No 34'; names; FN 161	OTNR (SR 1838)
A1511		[1800?]	Copy W.C.	'1287' 'O20' 'C19'; Ingersoll (added later), marshes; scale n.g.	OTAR

	Date of Instructions	Date of Map	Surveyor and Signature	Endorsements and Notes	Location
A1512		[1800?]	–	'C17'; Ingersoll (added later), reserve for town in E pt [Oxford town plot/Woodstock]	OTAR (SR 1839)
A1513	21.7.1832 3.10.1832	16.1.1833	Lewis Burwell	'B79'; includes Blandford Twp; govt reserves in twp at forks of Thames, improvements of squatters, town plot; 20 ch; FN 63, 770	OTNR (SR 1837)
A1514		[183?]	Copy J.G. Chewett	'O19'; c & c reserves	OTAR
A1515		–.7.1843	Thomas Parke SG	Includes N Dorchester Twp; survey grid, reserves; scale n.g.	OTAR
	PAIPOONGE				
A1516	10.6.1859	10.7.1860	Thomas W. Herrick	'P No 6'; relief, notes on minerals; FN 1572	OTNR (SR 1843)
A1517		4.2.1861	CLD Andrew Russell AC	'305'; names, later changes	OTAR(P)
	PAKENHAM				
A1518	6.6.1822	–.–.1822	John Booth Reuben Sherwood	'B17' '505'; c & c reserves, a few names, marshes; FN 575	OTNR (SR 1844)
A1519		[1822?]	R. Sherwood copy J.G.C.	'No 16'; names, c & c reserves	OTAR(P)
A1520		[1822?]	R. Sherwood copy J.G.C.	'No 31'; c & c reserves, some names	OTAR(P)
A1521		–.8.1843	Thomas Parke SG	Survey grid, reserves; scale n.g.	OTAR
	PALMER				
A1522		5.12.1864	George B. Kirkpatrick	Relief, marshes, mill sites	OTAR (SR 86752)
A1523	5.12.1864	2.11.1865	George B. Kirkpatrick	'P17'; relief, mining location, marshes, mill sites; FN 1618	OTNR (SR 1845)
A1524		30.4.1866	CLD Andrew Russell AC	'182'; relief, marshes, a few names, 'forfeited' most later annulled; scale n.g.	OTAR(P)
	PALMERSTON				
A1525	26.2.1822	[1822?]	Neil Macdonald	'B21' '506'; c & c reserves, rapids, marshes; FN 576	OTNR (SR 1848)
A1526		[1822?]	Neil McDonald	'C17' '1282'; c & c reserves, marshes, mill site, copy	OTAR (SR 1846)

A1527		[1822?]	Copy J.G. Chewett	'1273'; survey grid	OTAR
A1528		–.8.1843	Thomas Parke SG	'P3'; survey grid, reserves; scale n.g.	OTAR
A1529	2.2.1860	27.3.1861	John A. Snow	'B5'; improved land with names, marshes, roads, lumber depots and slides; FN 1617	OTNR (SR 1847)
A1530		–.10.1861	Andrew Russell AC	'C39'; names, later changes	OTAR(P)
	PEEL				
A1531	9.5.1843	–.11.1843	Robert W. Kerr	'B18' '678'; marshes, roads; FN 1632	OTNR (SR 1866)
A1532		–.–.1843 13.1.1844	R.W. Kerr Thomas Parke SG	'No 49' 'Office copy'; names	OTAR(P)
A1533		1843 17.1.1844	R.P. Walker Thomas Parke SG	Rd lots Arthur to Fergus, survey grid	OTAR
A1534		–.12.1846	Copy CLD	'C18' '1274'; rd route	OTAR (SR 1867)
	PELHAM				
A1535	4.6.1794	[1794–5?]	[T. Welch?]	'No 16'; names, later addition shows pt purchased for military purposes in 1838; scale n.g.; FN 847	OTAR(P)
A1536		1811 22.4.1841	Exam Thos Ridout copy J.G.C. K. Cameron ASG	'C13' '1276'; notes on survey lines	OTAR (SR 1869)
	PEMBROKE				
A1537	25.9.1834	4.1.1836	J. McNaughton	'B11' '509'; trails, relief, c & c reserves, contents; FN 577	OTNR (SR 1871)
A1538		4.1.1835[*sic*] 29.1.1836	J. McNaughton copy J.G.C.	'No 17' 'Office copy'; c & c reserves, names	OTAR(P)
A1539		[1836?]	Copy J.G. Chewett	C & c reserves	OTAR
A1540		–.8.1843	Thomas Parke SG	Survey grid, reserves; scale n.g.	OTAR
	PENNEFATHER				
A1541	25.7.1859	[3.11.1860]	Jos Wm Burke	'P7' 'No 2 N Rge XXVI W'; trees, relief; FN 1633	OTNR (SR 1872)
A1542		5.4.1861	CLD Andrew Russell AC	'187'; Indian lands as of 11.10.1866, later changes	OTAR(P)
	PENRYTH				
A1543	9.10.1848	26.9.1849	Albert P. Salter	'LH No 14'; front, traverse lines on St Marie R	OTNR (SR 5499)

	Date of Instructions	Date of Map	Surveyor and Signature	Endorsements and Notes	Location
	PERCY				
A1544	23.6.1795	[1796?]	William Hambly [A. Greely?]	'No 34'; c & c reserves, names, note that con lines run by Greely in 1796; FN 286 (A. Greely), 2–42 (Hambly)	OTNR (SR 1876)
A1545		30.11.1820	W.C.	'C16'; c & c reserves, names, notes on earlier surveys by Hambly and Aaron Greely	OTAR
A1546		[1820?]	W.C.	'A14'; notes on errors by Hambly signed W. Chewett 30.11.1826, names	OTNR (SR 1875)
A1547		–.8.1843	Thomas Parke SG	Survey grid, reserves; scale n.g.	OTAR
	PETAWAWA				
A1548	12.4.1854	13.9.1854	Robert Hamilton	'B47'; pt; lots along river, mill sites, town plot, roads, improvements; FN 1642, 1643	OTNR (SR 1878)
A1549		30.11.1857	Robert Hamilton	'B57'; roads, mill sites, improvements	OTNR (SR 1879)
A1550		17.4.1858	CLD	Names, roads	OTAR(P)
	PICKERING				
A1551	22.2.1791	[1791]	[A. Jones] D.W. Smith ASG	'A22' '245'; names, c & c reserves, formerly 'Edinburgh'; 80 ch; FN 835	OTAR (SR 1885)
A1552	5.8.1797	[1797?]	[A. Jones?]	'C17' '511'; c & c reserves, road	OTAR (SR 1883)
A1553		[180?]	W.C	'C18' 'office copy'; c & c reserves, marshes	OTNR (SR 1884)
A1554		[180?]	W.C.	'No 28'; names, c & c reserves, later changes	OTAR(P)
A1555		2.5.1823	Thos. Ridout	'A23'; c & c reserves, names; scale n.g.	OTAR(P)
A1556		–.7.1843	Thomas Parke SG	Survey grid, reserves; scale n.g.	OTAR
	PITTSBURGH				
A1557	4.6.1787	1787	Alex Aitken	'B50' 'No 56'; 6 cons; names, mill, marsh, Kingston and Pt Henry	OTNR (SR 1892)
A1558		–.–.1787	Alex Aitken [sgd] Samuel Holland	'A30'; names, marshes, copy; scale n.g.	OTAR(P)
A1559		[179?]	[S. Holland?]	'A31' '270'; pt: cons 1–4; names; scale n.g.	OTAR (SR 1890)
A1560		[179?]	–	'A32'; names with dates from 1795; scale n.g.	OTAR(P)

A1561	17.2.1807	12.6.1807	Reuben Sherwood	'B26' '510'; resurvey, conflicting survey lines; scale n.g.; FN 584, 585	OTNR (SR 1889)
A1562		[1807]	Reuben Sherwood	'No 30' 'B26'; names	OTNR (SR 1888)
A1563		–.8.1843	Thomas Parke SG	'P15'; includes Storrington Twp; survey grid, reserves; scale n.g.	OTAR
A1564		28.5.1856	JWB[?] CLD E.P. Taché	Survey grid, reserves	OTAR (SR 1891)
	PLANTAGENET, N and S				
A1565	4.6.1789	[1791]	James Rankin	'A2' '279' 'Quebec Plan'; front con; names, notes on reserved school lands; scale n.g.; FN 235	OTAR (SR 1896)
A1566		29.8.1795	Exam W. Chewett	'A1'; some names; scale n.g.	OTAR (SR 1897)
A1567	11.10.1796	–.–.1797	W. Fortune	'B13' '548'; pt on Grand R; marshes, old survey lines; 20 ch; FN 348?	OTNR (SR 3996)
A1568		[1797?]	W. Fortune	'B12' '508'; pt on Grand R; names, for Edwd Jessup	OTNR (SR 1902)
A1569		[181?]	Copy W.C.	'C3' '1281'; pt: 4 cons; marshes, relief	OTAR (SR 1900)
A1570	8.2.1819	–.–.1820	Wm. Browne	'A3' '277'; middle pt; roads, mill, a few names; scale n.g.; FN 1646	OTNR (SR 1895)
A1571		27.12.1820	Thos Ridout	'19' 'For the Land Board'; c & c reserves, names, marshes, mills, relief	OTAR (SR 1899)
A1572		–.–.1821	Wm. Browne	'B11' '507'; pt to be added, comments on land and trees, a few names; scale n.g.; FN 272	OTNR (SR 1901)
A1573		[182?]	–	'No 27' 'Office Plan'; c & c reserves, names, later changes, bearings according to Fortune and Browne; scale n.g.	OTAR(P)
A1574		[1821?]	Copy J.G. Chewett	Survey grid, a few names, mills, falls	OTAR
A1575		27.1.1829	Copy W.C.	'C4'; mills, relief, marsh, 'Upper Falls'	OTAR (SR 1898)
	PLYMPTON				
A1576	5.6.1829	19.12.1829	C. Rankin	'B11' '515'; cons V–XIII; c & c reserves, notes; FN 301, 1649	OTNR (SR 1910)
A1577		19.12.1829	C. Rankin copy J.G. Chewett	'C14' 'For settlers under Henry Jones'; S pt with notes on N boundary; c & c reserves	OTAR (SR 1904)
A1578		19.12.1829 5.1.1830	C. Rankin copy W. Chewett	Laid out for settlers under Henry Jones, c & c reserves, marshes, notes on survey	OTAR

	Date of Instructions	Date of Map	Surveyor and Signature	Endorsements and Notes	Location
A1579		[1829?]	–	'B12' '513'; marshes, relief, unfinished, watermark: '1826'; scale n.g.	OTAR (SR 1909)
A1580	3.5.1831	–.9.1831	Peter Carroll	'B10' '512'; pt; rd from Caradoc to L Huron (Egremont Rd); FN 190	OTNR (SR 1908)
A1581	21.6.1832	29.12.1832	Peter Carroll	'B13' '514'; c & c reserves, marshes, Erroll, road; FN 586	OTNR (SR 1905)
A1582		[1832?]	[P. Carroll?]	'No 22'; c & c reserves, names	OTAR(P)
A1583		[1832?]	P. Carroll copy J.G.C.	'C13' '1272'; c & c reserves, roads, marshes	OTAR (SR 1906)
A1584		[1832?]	–	'1280'; outline; 100 ch	OTAR (SR 1907)
A1585		–.7.1843	Thomas Parke SG	Survey grid, reserves; scale n.g.	OTAR
	PORTLAND				
A1586	20.5.1790	[179?]	[A. Aitken?]	'A No 29' '281'; names with dates 1794–1818, c & c reserves; scale n.g.	OTAR (SR 1915)
A1587		[1808?]	Chewett and Ridout ASG	Rough plan for survey, reserves; scale n.g.	OTAR
A1588	22.8.1808	[1809]	Sam'l S. Wilmot	'Surveyed by order of F. Gore' 'No 31'; names; FN 587	OTNR (SR 1914)
A1589		–.8.1843	Thomas Parke SG	Survey grid, reserves; scale n.g.	OTAR
A1590	21.1.1862	–.9.1863	A.B. Perry	Con lines XI–XIV; resurvey, survey monuments, marshes, mills	OTAR
	PRINCE				
A1591	2.5.1860	–.–.1860	S.R. Prince	'No 8' 'No 1 N and S, Rge 27 W'; includes Parke Twp; relief; FN 1657	OTNR (SR 1920)
A1592		–.10.1861	CLD	'192'; includes Parke Twp; twps No 1 N and S; names, later changes	OTAR(P)
	PROTON				
A1593	17.3.1853	9.7.1855	David Gibson	'B67'; pt; marsh, trees; FN 1664	OTNR (SR 1923)
A1594		–.2.1856	J.W.B. CLO Joseph Cauchon C/CL	'P22'; includes pt of road survey on NE; survey grid	OTAR

A1595		–.2.1856	C.L.O. Joseph Cauchon C/CL	'P22'; marshes, lacks road survey on NE	OTAR
A1596		–.1.1862	Andrew Russell C/CL	'Office Plan'; names	OTAR(P)
	PUSLINCH				
A1597	28.3.1828 9.5.1828	[1828]	[D. Gibson]	'No 17'; names, per SI of 1828; FN 594	OTNR (SR 1927)
A1598		[1828]	David Gibson	'Y32'; pt; includes pt clergy reserve for Lincoln, Aboukir Rd, marshes; 20 ch	OTNR (SR 86754
A1599		–.–.1828	D. Gibson copy J.G. Chewett	'Y27' '761'; pt; rd line through S block of clergy reserve; scale n.g.	OTAR (SR 1929)
A1600		–.–.1828	David Gibson copy J.G. Chewett	Pt; rd survey, 2 cons E and W of Aboukir Rd, marshes, names, relief; 20 ch	OTAR
A1601		[1828]	–	Title missing, similar to 1828 plan (OTAR) (**A1600**) but names vary; scale n.g.	OTAR
A1602	14.6.1831	–.12.1831	David Gibson	'No 19'; lots 1–13 cons VIII–XI E of Aboukir Rd; town lots in 'Farnham,' names; 20 ch; FN 595	OTNR (SR 86755
A1603		[1831?]	Copy J.G.C.	'No 20' '457'; names, c & c reserves, 'common' lot 6 Con VIII	OTAR (SR 1928)
A1604	21.11.1831	–.1.1832	David Gibson	'No 18'; gore, tract of land btwn Beverly and Puslinch, c & c reserves, names; scale n.g.; FN 593	OTNR (SR 1930)
A1605		27.2.1832	D. Gibson copy J.G.C. W. Chewett ASG	'10064'; marshes, roads, some names	OTAR
A1606		[184?]	–	Aboukir Rd, other roads, settlements, marshes, linen tracing	OTAR
A1607		–.7.1843	Thomas Parke SG	Survey grid, all noted as clergy reserve except for gore; scale n.g.	OTAR
A1608		25.11.1843	Robert W. Kerr	Lots 21 and 22 cons VII and VIII; streams, mill pond, 8 ch	OTAR
	RADCLIFFE				
A1609	26.10.1858	–.–.1858–9	Edwin H. Kertland	'No 53'; Hastings and Opeongo rds, marshes; FN 1672, 1879	OTNR (SR 1932)
A1610		–.7.1860	CLD Andrew Russell AC	Pt: cons I–VII, free-grant lots along Hastings and Opeongo Junction Rd	OTAR

	Date of Instructions	Date of Map	Surveyor and Signature	Endorsements and Notes	Location
A1611	19.10.1860	17.8.1861	Edwin H. Kertland	'R64'; colonization roads, relief, a few names; FN 1671	OTNR (SR 1933)
A1612		-.11.1864	CLD	'193' 'Office copy'; Hastings and Opeongo Junction Rd, free-grant lots, names, later changes	OTAR(P)
	RAGLAN				
A1613	17.5.1865	18.4.1867	Joseph Doupe	'R40'; roads, marshes, relief; FN 1675	OTNR (SR 1934)
A1614		22.10.1867	CLD A. Russell AC	'194'; names, later changes	OTAR(P)
	RAINHAM				
A1615		[1795–7?]	copy W.C.	'1268' 'C15'; road, conflicting survey lines; scale n.g.; FN 223, 386?	OTAR
A1616	–	27.3.1829	W. Chewett ASG J.G.C.	'C14' '1263'; notes on earlier surveys by Hambly and Walsh with conflicting lines	OTNR (SR 1936)
A1617	18.4.1829	[1829]	Samuel Smith	'B6' '522'; mills, marshes, trees, rocky shoreline; FN 596	OTNR (SR 1935)
A1618		[1829?]	[S. Smith?]	'No 17'; c & c reserves, names; scale n.g.	OTAR(P)
A1619		18.4.1829	Samuel Smith Thomas Parke SG	'No 20' 'Office copy'; a few names, nature of shoreline; scale n.g.	OTAR(P)
A1620		-.7.1843	Thomas Parke SG	Survey grid, reserves, notes; scale n.g.	OTAR
A1621		1.8.1859	Sam'l Smith Andrew Russell AC	Survey grid, land granted to Jos Bouchette 1813, copy	OTAR
	RALEIGH				
A1622	4.2.1796?	27.5.1798	A. Iredell	'B15' '520'; S pt; 20 ch; FN 444	OTNR (SR 1940)
A1623		[20.7.1799]	[A. Iredell]	'A29' '284'; pt; names, note: pt of Iredell's map of 20.7.1799 of Raleigh and Tilbury; scale n.g.; FN 13–340, 343	OTNR (SR 1937)
A1624	8.6.1811	8.6.1811	Thos Ridout SG	Area under location and grant, c & c reserves, names of those located by T. Talbot on N side Talbot Rd with dates to 1819	OTAR (Talbot BkD/2)
A1625		20.12.[1816]	M. Burwell	'A30'; pt; Talbot Rd, 2 large c & c reserves in 1 block; FN 597	OTNR (SR 1941)

A1626		[20.12.1816?]	[M. Burwell?]	Pt; Talbot Rd lots, names located by T. Talbot to 1817	OTAR (Talbot BkC/12)
A1627		[1820?]	Copy J.G. Chewett W.C. SS & D	'C16' '1264'; pt; Talbot Rd with mileages, marshes, c & c reserves	OTAR (SR 1938)
A1628	17.4.1821	17.4.1821	Thos Ridout SG copy J.G.C.	Indian land, c & c reserves, marshy areas; scale n.g.	OTAR
A1629		22.2.1823	M. Burwell	'B14'; c & c reserves in a block, a few names, marshes, roads; FN 598	OTNR (SR 1939)
A1630		[1823?]	[M. Burwell?]	'No 23'; names, many later changes; scale n.g.	OTAR(P)
A1631		15.2.1826	Copy J.G.C. Thos Ridout	Marshes, names in middle sections as located by T. Talbot to 1843	OTAR (Talbot BkE/13)
A1632		-.7.1843	Thomas Parke SG	Survey grid, reserves, marsh; scale n.g.	OTAR
	RAMA				
A1633	1.10.1834	3.3.1835	J.W. Keating	'A24'; pt; a few names; FN 312	OTNR (SR 1944)
A1634		3.3.1835 8.4.1835	J.W. Keating copy SGO	'No 30'; cons I–VII, c & c reserves, names, marshes	OTAR(P)
A1635	14.9.1835	-.9/10.1835	C.R[ankin]	'B37' '523'; pt: front con; notes on survey, names; 20 ch	OTNR (SR 1943)
A1636		-.7.1843	Thomas Parke SG	Survey grid; reserves; scale n.g.	OTAR
A1637	22.5.1855	-.-.1855	Chas. Unwin	'B68'; pt; rapids, marshes; FN 1674	OTNR (SR 1945)
A1638		28.4.1856	Joseph Cauchon C/CL	'No 60'; pt; names in cons A–Q, con 1–7 mainly blank	OTAR(P)
A1639	29.9.1860	7.11.1860	James W. Bridgland	'R21'; Rama Is, mining locations, mill; 10 ch; FN 313	OTNR (SR 1942)
A1640		-.12.1860	Andrew Russell AC/CL	Rama Is, village of Washago, names and later changes; 10 ch	OTAR
A1641	27.12.1860	25.7.1861	J. Stoughton Dennis	'R62'; pt; survey of part left unsurveyed by Unwin; rapids; scale n.g.; FN 1673	OTNR (SR 1946)
A1642		[1861?]	–	Pt cons F–G	OTAR (SR 1947)
A1643		-.11.1861	Andrew Russell AC/CLD	Cons G–N, marshes, beaver dam, names, later changes	OTAR(P)
	RAMSAY				
A1644	23.6.1819	25.1.1821	R. Sherwood	'B12' '524'; c & c reserves, rapids and falls, a few names; FN 599	OTNR (SR 1948)
A1645		25?.1.1821	R. Sherwood	Marshes, c & c reserves, names	OTAR

	Date of Instructions	Date of Map	Surveyor and Signature	Endorsements and Notes	Location
A1646		[1821?]	R. Sherwood copy J.G.C.	'No 18'; c & c reserves, names, later changes	OTAR(P)
	RAWDON				
A1647	18.12.1796	21.8.1797	Alex'r Aitken	'B27' '518'; marshes, meadows, tree types, relief indicated for cons 4–13, pts surveyed by others	OTNR (SR 1953)
A1648		Summer 1797	Alex Aitken	'No 32'; c & c reserves, names	OTNR (SR 1955)
A1649		[1797?]	[A. Aitken?]	'A33'; names with dates from 1799; scale n.g.	OTAR(P)
A1650	11.5.1836	8.5.1837	Sam'l M. Benson	'B37' '519'; pt: cons 5–14; comments on land, roads, spring; FN 600	OTNR (SR 1954)
A1651		–.7.1843	Thomas Parke SG	Survey grid, reserves; scale n.g.	OTAR
	REACH				
A1652	18.11.1809	–.–.1810	Sam'l S. Wilmot	'No 31'; names, c & c reserves; FN 601	OTNR (SR 1958)
A1653		[1810?]	[S. Wilmot?]	'C20' '1267'; relief, marshes, Indian footpath, height of land	OTAR (SR 1957)
A1654		[1810?]	W.C.	'C19' '1266'; c & c reserves, marshes, relief	OTAR (SR 1959)
A1655		–.7.1843	Thomas Parke SG	Survey grid, reserves; scale n.g.	OTAR
	RICHARDS				
A1656	30.4.1860	–.8.1862	Robert Hamilton	'R27'; comments on land and timber, relief, marshes; FN 1685	OTNR (SR 1991)
A1657		–.–.1862 18.5.1863	Robert Hamilton CLD Andrew Russell AC	'197'; names in S pt; later changes	OTAR(P)
A1658		16.6.1864	Andrew Russell AC	Shows lakes and rivers actually surveyed, others sketched	OTAR (SR 1951)
	RICHMOND				
A1659	–	–.–.1787	John Collins	'No 25' '999'; names	OTNR (SR 1972)

A1660		[1787]	John Collins copy James Toosey Samuel Holland	'A36' '286'; names	OTAR (SR 1969)
A1661		[1793?]	–	'A34' '288'; con survey lines, some names, prior to **A1662**; scale n.g.	OTAR (SR 1966)
A1662		[1796?]	–	'A35'; '287'; names, some dated 1794–6, con lines differ from **A1661** and **A1660**; scale n.g.	OTAR (SR 1967)
A1663	30.5.1795	10.4.179[7]	Alex Aitken	'B28' '525'; 8 cons	OTNR (SR 1968)
A1664		11.6.1799 31.7.1799	Alex Aitken copy W.C.	'No 33'; c & c reserves, names, later changes	OTAR(P)
A1665	15.4.1831	13.6.1831 22.2.1836	Publius V. Elmore	'No 34'; 2 maps: (1) cons 10–11, c & c reserves, names (2) outline only and roads; FN 276	OTNR (SR 1965)
A1666		–.8.1843	Thomas Parke SG	Survey grid, reserves; scale n.g.	OTAR
A1667		28.6.1856	J.W.B. E.P. Taché for C/CL	Outline, Napanee	OTAR (SR 1971)
A1668		–.10.1857	CLD Andrew Russell AC	'For agent'; pt: cons IX to XI; survey grid	OTAR
A1669		29.9.1862	CLD Andrew Russell AC	Cons IX–XI; copy of pt of office plan, 2 sheets	OTAR
A1670	–.10.1862	5.12.1862	Sam'l M. Benson	'R26'; pt; con 11, names; 20 ch; FN 1684	OTNR (SR 1970)
A1671		27.7.1866	S. Benson A. Russell AC	Con XI; 'erroneous boundary of Tyendinaga,' copy; 20 ch	OTAR
	RIDOUT				
A1672	15.8.1861	28.7.1862	G.Z. Rykert	'R28'; relief, marshes, colonization rd; FN 1688	OTNR (SR 1974)
A1673		–.–.1862 6.5.1863	G.Z. Rykert copy CLD Wm McDougall C/CL	'195'; Bobcaygeon Rd, names	OTAR(P)
A1674		13.1.1863	exam T.D. CLD Andrew Russell AC	'X3–10'; survey grid, lakes, rivers	OTAR
A1675		23.1.1864	Andrew Russell AC	Outline, rivers, lakes	OTAR (SR 1975)
A1676		20.7.1865	Henry Lawe	'R36' '10492/65'; NE pt	OTNR (SR 86757)

	Date of Instructions	Date of Map	Surveyor and Signature	Endorsements and Notes	Location
	ROCHESTER				
A1677	6.5.1796	[1799?]	[A. Iredell]	'A31' '291'; c & c reserves, names; scale n.g.; FN 110, 609	OTNR (SR 1989)
A1678		-.7.1843	Thomas Parke SG	Survey grid, reserves; scale n.g.	OTAR
	ROLPH				
A1679	26.9.1854	11.2.1856	Robert Hamilton	'B50'; roads, names, settlement, town plot; FN 1690	OTNR (SR 1979)
A1680		1.4.1856	CLO Joseph Cauchon C/CL	'195' 'No 48'; town plot reserve, names, later changes	OTAR(P)
	ROMNEY				
A1681	–	27.6.1799	Abraham Iredell	'A33'; front of twp, names, reserves	OTAR (SR 1982)
A1682		8.6.1811	Thos Ridout SG	Lots with names on Talbot Rd as located by T. Talbot to 1829	OTAR (Talbot BkE/9)
A1683	8.6.1811 17.4.1821	1811 24.3.1831	M. Burwell	'B20'; c & c reserves, marshes, Talbot Rd; FN 605, 757	OTNR (SR 1981)
A1684		[182?]	Copy J.G.C.	'No 25'; c & c reserves, notes referring to Burwell's field notes and O.C. 5.10.1818 re reserve of 1 chain along shore, Talbot Rd, some names	OTNR (SR 1980)
A1685		[182?]	M. Burwell copy J.G. Chewett W.C.	'C28' 'No 24'; Talbot Rd, notes on survey and War of 1812, marshes	OTAR(P)
A1686		18.1.1832	M. Burwell Copy J.G.C. W. Chewett	Reserves, marshes, names of those located by T. Talbot to 1836	OTAR (Talbot BkD/7)
A1687		-.7.1843	Thomas Parke SG	Survey grid, reserves; scale n.g.	OTAR
A1688		-.11.1846	Copy CLD	'C40'; Talbot Rd W	OTAR
	ROSE				
A1689	9.5.1860	12.7.1861	C.G. Hanning	'R63' '4483/61'; relief; FN 1695	OTNR (SR 1993)
A1690		-.8.1861	CLD Andrew Russell AC	'196'; names, Salter's Rd line, later note: 'withdrawn from settlement 1943'	OTAR(P)

	ROSS				
A1691	25.9.1834	4.1.1836	J. McNaughton	'B13'; trails, relief, marshes, park lots; FN 606	OTNR (SR 1992)
A1692		4.1.1836 28.1.1836	J.W. McNaughton copy J.G.C.	'No 19'; names, later changes, c & c reserves	OTAR(P)
A1693		[1836?]	Copy J.G. Chewett	'1765' 'C11'; survey grid, roads, trails	OTAR
A1694		–.8.1843	Thomas Parke SG	Survey grid, reserves; scale n.g.	OTAR
	ROXBOROUGH				
A1695	14.2.1791	[1791?]	[J. Rankin]	'A7'; names in first 5 cons only, glebe; scale n.g.; FN 235	OTAR(P)
A1696		[179?]	–	'No 7A' '292' 'Land Board Plan'; pt: cons 10–15; names, clergy reserve block; scale n.g.	OTAR (SR 1998)
A1697		[1791?]	W. Chewett	Names, later changes, some notes dated 1789; scale n.g.	OTAR(P)
A1698	19.3.1827	17.8.1827	Angus Cattanach	'No 1B' '5217'; marshes, notes, contents; FN 608	OTNR (SR 1999)
A1699		27.8.1827 27.9.1827	Angus Cattanach copy W.C.	'1269' 'R19' 'No 19C'; marshes, notes on earlier surveys and conflicting lines	OTAR
	RUSSELL				
A1700	8.9.1820	[1822]	[Wm McDonald]	'B1' '829'; tree types, marsh, c & c reserves; scale n.g.; FN 389	OTNR (SR 2004)
A1701		30.3.1825	Copy J.G.C. Thos Ridout SG	'22' '294' 'For the Land Board'; c & c reserves, marshes, names; scale n.g.	OTAR (SR 2001)
A1702		18.4.1829	Copy T. Ridout SG	'5' 'Office Plan'; c & c reserves, names, some changes, notes re adjacent twp boundaries; scale n.g.	OTAR(P)
A1703	26.3.1859	6.5.1859	H.O. Wood	'No 52'; pt: lots A–C cons VII–X; FN 390	OTNR (SR 2002)
A1704		–.7.1859	Andrew Russell AC CLD	Pt; boundaries with Cambridge, Finch, and Winchester	OTAR (SR 2003)
	RYAN				
A1705	4.7.1866	–.12.1866	Wilson and McGee	'R39'; relief, marshes, mining locations; FN 1700	OTNR (SR 2007)
	RYDE				
A1706	28.12.1860	9.10.1861	R.T. Burns	'R66'; relief, marshes; FN 1701	OTNR (SR 2008)

	Date of Instructions	Date of Map	Surveyor and Signature	Endorsements and Notes	Location
	ST JOSEPH				
A1707	–	21.7.1837	Copy J.G. Chewett SGO	'212' 'No 38' 'Office copy'; pt: lots 1–11 cons 1–12, naval reserves	OTAR(P)
A1708		22.7.1837 1.6.1843	Copy J.G. Chewett Thomas Parke SG	'939'; pt; ' From Treet's Survey'	OTNR (SR 2013)
A1709	20.7.1852	–.2.1856	T.N. Molesworth	'No 20' 'Office copy'; names, town plot, military reserve and Campement d'Ours Is; FN 1793	OTNR (SR 2036)
	ST VINCENT				
A1710	31.12.1834	5.6.1835	C. Rankin	'B27'; c & c reserves, mill site; FN 640	OTNR (SR 2015)
A1711		[1835?]	C. Rankin	'B26' '539'; c & c and other reserves	OTNR (SR 2014)
A1712		[1835?]	–	'No 34' 'Office Plan'; names, later notes 1833–7, c & c reserves; scale n.g.	OTAR(P)
A1713		[1835?]	Copy J.G.C.	'A27' '318'; c & c reserves, names in SE pt only	OTAR(P)
A1714		–.7.1843	Thomas Parke SG	Survey grid, reserves; scale n.g.	OTAR
	SALTER				
A1715	15.5.1860	10.9.1861	Chas Unwin	'S20'; wooded areas, marsh, portages, Hudson's Bay Co. post, northern road line; FN 1706	OTNR (SR 2016)
A1716		29.11.1861	CLD Andrew Russell AC	'199'; 'Office'; twp no 4 S, Hudson's Bay Co. post at La Cloche, roads, portages, names	OTAR(P)
	SALTFLEET				
A1717	–	25.10.1791	Augustus Jones	'34' '1025'; names, twps no 7 and 8 [Saltfleet and Barton]; FN 848	OTNR (SR 2021)
A1718		25.10.1791	Augustus Jones [sgd] Samuel Holland	'No 20'; names, some later changes, copy	OTAR(P)
A1719		25.10.1791 29.3.1795	A. Jones copy J.F. Holland [sgd] Sam'l Holland exam and corrected D.W.S.	'A21' '303'; names	OTNR (SR 2019)

A1720		[1791?]	D.W. Smith	'A20' '3115'; rec'd from Land Board names on N and S pts, relief; scale n.g.	OTAR(P)
A1721	29.4.1799	11.7.179[9]	John Stegmann D.W.S.	'Y25' '809'; pt: Long Beach, lots 26 and 27 belonging to Govt House; road, cornfield, later notes; 20 ch	OTAR (SR 2020)
A1722		25.9.1811	Copy W.C. exam Thos Ridout	'A19' '304'; names	OTAR(P)
	SANDWICH, E, W, and S				
A1723	–	[179?]	P. McNiff	'A42' '297'; W pt; Petite Côte, names, roads, mills; scale n.g.; FN 612	OTAR (SR 2024)
A1724		[1793]	Patrick McNiff	'A37' '245'; E pt: lots 63–154, con 1 and pt of back cons; names; scale n.g.	OTNR (SR 2035)
A1725	–	30.1.1797	A. Iredell	'A36' '295'; W pt; names; FN 130, 610	OTNR (SR 2032)
A1726		18.7.1797	Abraham Iredell copy J.G.C.	'No 27'; W pt; names, town	OTNR (SR 2027)
A1727		[1797?] 9.7.1800	A. Iredell W.C. exam	'A34'; W pt; names; 20 ch	OTNR (SR 2029)
A1728		18.7.1797 9.7.1808	Ab Iredell exam W.C.	'B16' '551'; W pt: lots 1–59; Petite Côte, list of lots with sizes	OTAR (SR 2023)
A1729	5.5.1798?	[1798?]	[A. Iredell?]	'A41' '300'; W pt; Petite Côte, names, adds to 1820; FN 609, 773	OTAR (SR 2031)
A1730		25.5.1798	T. Smith copy W.C.	'C24'; W pt: lots 36–51 on river and property of I.B. Féré in rear; names, a few bldgs; 15 ch	OTAR
A1731		30.12.1800	T. Smith	W pt; lands of Wm Park and Meldrum and Park, names, town plot Sandwich, notes	OTAR(P)
A1732		[1800?]	P. McNiff W. Chewett and Thos Ridout ASG	'A38' '299' 'sketch from the plans of McNiff'; W pt; Petite Côte, names, extensive notes on earlier surveys by McNiff, T. Smith, and claims for land 179?–1801; scale n.g.	OTNR (SR 2030)
A1733		3.7.1803	Abraham Iredell	'A35' '298'; W pt; L'Assomption, names, survey for Hon. James Baby; scale n.g.	OTNR (SR 2033)
A1734		[1803?]	Copy W.C.	'1258' 'C18'; W pt; Petite R to Petite Côte, lines surv by Iredell and McNiff, some rear lots laid out, mills	OTAR
A1735		[1803?]	Copy W.C.	'1257'; W pt; Petite R to Grosse Isle, similar to **A1734** but unfinished	OTAR

	Date of Instructions	Date of Map	Surveyor and Signature	Endorsements and Notes	Location
A1736		23.1.1807	Thos. Smith	'A39' '301'; E pt: lots 63–78, con 1 and corresponding lots back to con 6; names, notes on survey	OTNR (SR 2034)
A1737		17.4.1821	Copy J.G.C. Thos Ridout SG	'1253' 'C17'; survey grid, town of Sandwich, rd line, c & c reserves	OTAR
A1738	17.4.1821	[1823]	[M. Burwell]	'No 28'; S pt; names, town, Talbot Rd; FN 611, 667	OTNR (SR 2028)
A1739		29.11.1824	M. Burwell	Includes Maidstone and Rochester; lots with names as located by T. Talbot along the Talbot Rd and Middle Rd to 1840; FN 11–261	OTAR (Talbot BkE/10)
A1740		[1824?]	M. Burwell	'C20' '1255'; town of Sandwich, roads, notes on earlier surveys, Talbot Rd survey and new survey, pt with indication of terrain, names, copy	OTAR (SR 2026)
A1741		-.-.1824 -.-.1825	M. Burwell copy J.G.C.	'No 26'; names, many later changes, reserved blocks for town of Sandwich; 26 ch	OTAR(P)
A1742		15.2.1826	Copy J.G.C. Thos Ridout SG	Marshes, c & c reserves, names as located by T. Talbot in rear lots to 1836	OTAR (Talbot BkE/3)
A1743		-.7.1843	Thomas Parke SG	Survey grid, reserves; scale n.g.	OTAR
	SARAWAK				
A1744	–	12.6.1857	Edwin H. Kertland	Town plot of Brooke; FN 293, 985	OTNR (SR 2040)
A1745		30.10.1857	CLD Andrew Russell AC	'200' 'No 63' 'Office copy'; town plot of Brooke, Oliphant Rd, bearings, contents	OTAR(P)
A1746		-.9.1861	CLD Andrew Russell AC	'S10'; marshes, relief, town plot of Brooke	OTAR
	SARNIA				
A1747	8.4.1829	30.1.1830	Roswell Mount	'No 29'; c & c reserves, names, Indian reserves, later adds, railways; FN 614	OTNR (SR 2044)
A1748		[1830?]	Copy W.C.	'1248'; c & c reserves, marshes, Indian reserve	OTAR
A1749		10.7.1835	Peter Carroll	'B23' '530'; pt; military reserve, types of trees, marsh	OTNR (SR 5831)
A1750		13.7.1837	Copy J.G. Chewett J.W. Macaulay SG	Indian reserve, marsh, some names	OTAR

A1751	–	10.6.1842 17.8.1842	John O'Mara copy A. Larue Thomas Parke	'1105' 'office copy'; pt; Indian reserve, office copy, town plot; scale n.g.; FN 613	OTNR (SR 2043)
A1752		10.6.1842	John O'Mara	'717'; pt; shows purchase of 2560 acres in the Indian reserve by Malcolm Cameron; scale n.g.	OTAR
A1753		–.7.1843	Thomas Parke SG	Survey grid, reserves, Indian reserve; scale n.g.	OTAR
	SAUGEEN				
A1754		23.12.1850	A. Wilkinson copy A.R.	Diagram for the survey of lots 51–60 cons 1–2, reserve for a town plot; scale n.g.	OTAR
A1755	4.1.1851	–.2.1851	Arch. McNab Exam A.R.	'B42' '515/51'; pt: lots 51–60 btwn Saugeen R and L Huron S of town reserve; 10 ch; FN 615	OTNR (SR 2046)
A1756		23.6.1851	Robert F. Lynn	'S179½'; pt; boundary btwn Arran and Saugeen, Southampton town plot; scale n.g.	OTNR (SR 6742)
A1757	13.1.1851	8.9.1851	Alexander Vidal	'B48'; town plot Southampton, reserve along river; FN 1711	OTNR (SR 2047)
A1758		[1851?]	A. Vidal	'Reduced from Vidal's plan'; Southampton shown laid out, survey grid; scale n.g.	OTAR
	SCARBOROUGH				
A1759	22.2.1791	[179?]	[W.C.?]	'C23' '308'; c & c reserves, road; FN 298 or 835	OTAR (SR 2053)
A1760		25.9.1811	Exam Thos Ridout	'A25'; references to field notes for 1791–3 for survey markers in cons A–D, names; scale n.g.	OTAR(P)
A1761		–.1.1817	Exam Thos Ridout	'No 32' 'Office plan'; c & c reserves, names	OTNR (SR 97957)
A1762	1.3.1833	18.3.1833	John Galbraith	'B25' '532'; 5th con line; FN 268	OTNR (SR 2052)
A1763		–.7.1843	Thomas Parke SG	Survey grid, reserves; scale n.g.	OTAR
A1764	8.8.1862	6.6.1864	F.F. Passmore	'S29'; roads, resurvey; FN 618	OTNR (SR 5561)
	SCOTT				
A1765	10.4.1807	30.6.1807	Sam'l S. Wilmot	'No 33'; c & c reserves, names, comments on land; FN 625	OTNR (SR 2061)
A1766		[182?]	Copy J.G.C.	'1249'; c & c reserves, marshes	OTAR (SR 2060)
A1767		–.7.1843	Thomas Parke SG	Survey grid, reserves; scale n.g.	OTAR

	Date of Instructions	Date of Map	Surveyor and Signature	Endorsements and Notes	Location
	SEBASTOPOL				
A1768	27.5.1856	24.3.1857	John A. Snow	'B54'; Ottawa and Opeongo Rd, improved land, houses indicating settlement, relief, marshes; FN 1718	OTNR (SR 2062)
A1769		–.–.1857 27.5.1857	J. Snow T. Devine CLD E.P. Taché Acting C/CL	'201' 'No 50'; Ottawa and Opeongo Rd lots, names, later changes	OTAR(P)
A1770	4.8.1862	12.11.1863	William Bell	'R31' '15248/63'; pt; lots on Ottawa and Opeongo Rd, cleared land, relief, meadows; 20 ch; FN 2207	OTNR (SR 6581)
	SENECA				
A1771	–	3.10.1842	James Kirkpatrick	'S61'; '1106'; names, tract names, contents, Grand R Navigation Co., towns, Onondaga mission school lot, roads; FN 1720	OTNR (SR 2068)
A1772		–.–.1842	James Kirkpatrick copy Thomas Parke SG	'No 48'; town plot, Onondaga mission school lot, Grand R Navigation Co., roads, irregular lots, names, marshes	OTAR(P)
A1773		24.3.1848	Edmund DeCew	Pt and Canborough and Cayuga twps; lots flooded by Wm Fitches's mill pond, Canboro village; 20 ch	OTAR
A1774	–	24.5.1854	Edm'd DeCew	'Q87' '6042/54'; Fishcarrier Tract, names, village of York; 20 ch	OTNR (SR 2069)
A1775	–	–.3.1859	T.C. Brownjohn	Pt; position of John A. Nelles's land and neighbours E side Grand R, canal; 10 ch	OTAR
	SEYMOUR				
A1776	8.2.1819	–.–.1819	William Browne	'B21' '333'; relief, c & c reserves, marshes, a few names	OTAR (SR 2072)
A1777		[182?]	W. Browne copy W.C. S & D	'No 35'; names, school lands, many later changes; scale n.g.	OTAR(P)
A1778	21.6.1832	1832	Alex Campbell	'B23' '551'; resurvey; FN 621	OTAR (SR 2073)
A1779	8.10.1832	17.8.1833	A. Campbell	'B22'; c & c reserves, a few names, mill sites, trails; FN 622	OTNR (SR 2078)
A1780		[1833?]	A. Campbell copy J.G.C.	'S19'; c & c reserves, names, notes on earlier survey by Wm Browne	OTAR

A1781		-.8.1843	Thomas Parke SG	Survey grid, reserves, varying positions shown for some lines; scale n.g.	OTAR
A1782	25.6.1845	[1846]	[P.V. Elmore]	'No 47' '544'; shows astronomical survey in 1846 and earlier surveys by Campbell and Browne, cleared land, some names; FN 853	OTNR (SR 2076)
A1783		[1846]	P.V. Elmore exam A.R.	'B29' '534'; astronomical resurvey of cons VIII–XII, earlier surveys, improved lots	OTNR (SR 2075)
A1784	30.7.1860	-.-.1860	John J. Haslett	'No 12'; pt: lots XIV–XV, con I; cleared and fenced areas; 4 ch; FN 391	OTNR (SR 2074)
	SHEFFIELD				
A1785	18.6.1821	23.7.1822	Sam'l M. Benson	'B29' '655'; c & c reserves, a few names, marshes; FN 626	OTNR (SR 2094)
A1786		[1822?]	S. Benson copy J.G.C.	'1259' 'S20' 'C22'; c & c reserves, marshes	OTAR
A1787		[1822?]	–	'Office Copy'; survey grid, reserves	OTAR (SR 2093)
A1788		30.3.1825	Thos Ridout SG	'No 35'; c & c reserves, names, many changes	OTAR(P)
A1789		-.8.1843	Thomas Parke SG	Survey grid, reserves; scale n.g.	OTAR
A1790		13.12.1855	F. Lemieux Acting for C/CL	Survey grid	OTAR (SR 2092)
	SHEGUIANDAH				
A1791	14.11.1862	14.9.1864	George McPhillips	'S No 32'; town plot; FN 1735	OTNR (SR 2905)
A1792	20.2.1866	-.9.1866	David O'Keeffe	'S35' '13379/66'; 'windfall,' burnt land, reserve; FN 1734	OTNR (SR 2906)
	SHERBORNE				
A1793	1.10.1861	7.1862	C. Brady	'No 25'; colonization rd, marshes, portages, relief; FN 1737	OTNR (SR 2100)
A1794		18.9.1862	CLD	'205'; names, many later changes, roads showing varying routes	OTAR(P)
	SHERBROOKE (Haldimand Co)				
A1795	–	-.-.1821	J. Burch copy J.G.C.	'1067'; naval reserve, road; 20 ch	OTNR (SR 2103)

	Date of Instructions	Date of Map	Surveyor and Signature	Endorsements and Notes	Location
	SHERBROOKE, N and S (Lanark Co)				
A1796	9.10.1816	–.–.1817	W. Fraser	'B20' '554'; S pt; c & c reserves; scale n.g.; FN 627	OTNR (SR 2104)
A1797	24.2.1816	28.2.1821	R. Sherwood	'B19' '536'; N pt; c & c reserves, marshes; FN 628	OTNR (SR 2101)
A1798		[182?]	[R. Sherwood?]	'No 33' '553'; S pt; c & c reserves, some names; scale n.g.	OTNR (SR 2102)
A1799		–.8.1843	Thomas Parke SG	N pt; survey grid, reserves; scale n.g.	OTAR
A1800		–.8.1843	Thomas Parke SG	S pt; survey grid, reserves; scale n.g.	OTAR
A1801	1.12.1864	14.2.1865	Walter Beatty	'S31'; pt: gore btwn N Crosby and S Sherbrooke, attached to latter, contents; 20 ch; FN 1736	OTNR (SR 5558)
	SHERWOOD				
A1802	30.4.1860	–.8.1862	Robert Hamilton	'No 73' '15658/62'; pt and Burns Twp; outlines, relief, marshes, types of trees; FN 1263	OTNR (SR 6724)
A1803	10.6.1861	25.6.1862	A.G. Forrest	Opeongo Rd, rivers, lakes; FN 1740	OTNR (SR 2106)
A1804		24.11.1865	CLD Andrew Russell AC	'204'; Opeongo Rd lots, roads, names, later changes	OTAR(P)
	SIDNEY				
A1805	–	–.–.1787	Lewis Kotte	'No 38'; names	OTNR (SR 86762)
A1806	–	Summer 1790	A. Aitken	'B33' '560'; pt: cons 4–6; comments on trees and land; 1" = 1/2 mile	OTNR (SR 2206)
A1807		[1790?]	A. Aitken	'A39'; names, a few later adds; scale n.g.	OTAR(P)
A1808	12.12.1831	[1832]	C. Rankin	'P.F.25' '718'; pt: cons 7–9; roads; FN 630	OTNR (SR 2113)
A1809		–.7.1843	Thomas Parke SG	Survey grid, reserves; scale n.g.	OTAR
A1810		–.10.1846	A.R.	'C39' '1260'; copy, outline of lots	OTAR (SR 2114)
A1811		–.10.1846	CLD	'C38' '1256'; same as **A1811**	OTAR (SR 2115)
	SMITH				
A1812	12.5.1818	30.6.1818	Sam'l S. Wilmot	'A15'; marshes, relief, c & c reserves, names; FN 392	OTAR (SR 2122)
A1813		24.9.1818	Sam'l Wilmot	'No 36'; names, c & c reserves	OTNR (SR 2121)

A1814		22.10.1818	Sam'l S. Wilmot	'B24' '541'; pt; 'Street of Communication' in twp, rd survey from R Otonabee to con 7	OTNR (SR 2125)
A1815		15.4.1819	Copy W.C. Thos Ridout SG	'No 43'; names, some later changes, marshes, town plot reserve, c & c reserves, later notes	OTAR(P)
A1816		[1819?]	Copy J.G. Chewett	'C17' 'waters sketched'; c & c reserves, marshes, relief, lakes and rivers named, trails; scale n.g.	OTAR (SR 2126)
A1817	15.1.1830	[23.2.1830]	R. Birdsall	'No 37' '540'; pt resurvey cons 12–16; c & c reserves, relief, settlement; FN 632	OTNR (SR 2124)
A1818		–.7.1843	Thomas Parke SG	Survey grid, reserves, notes; scale n.g.	OTAR
	SNOWDON				
A1819	23.8.1858	5.3.1859	M. Deane	'3523/59'; sketch showing progress of survey, survey grid, rd lots; scale n.g.	OTAR
A1820		6.8.1859	M. Deane	'No 3'; mill reserve; FN 1752	OTNR (SR 2129)
A1821		–.11.1860	CLD Andrew Russell AC	'207'; names, Bobcaygeon Rd lots	OTAR(P)
	SOMBRA				
A1822	–	–.7.1800	A. Iredell exam SGO	Formerly 'Shawanese' Twp, notes on survey, land and trees, Indian villages, some lines not run, village of Baldoon; 80 ch	OTAR (SR 2130)
A1823	6.12.1819	–.3.1820	Thos Smith	'B17'; c & c reserves, names, marsh, village of Baldoon, rivers, other settlement; FN 633	OTNR (SR 5530)
A1824		[1820?]	–	'No 30'; includes Chatham Twp; c & c reserves, names, many later changes, village of Baldoon	OTAR(P)
A1825		–.7.1843	Thomas Parke SG	Survey grid, reserves; scale n.g.	OTAR
	SOMERVILLE				
A1826	26.4.1834	24.10.1835	J. Smith Jr	'B25' '537'; c & c reserves; scale n.g.; FN 634	OTNR (SR 2132)
A1827		[1835?]	Copy J.G.C.	'No 38'; c & c reserves, names; scale n.g.	OTAR(P)
A1828		–.7.1843	Thomas Parke SG	Survey grid, reserves; scale n.g.	OTAR
A1829	23.10.1854	11.7.1855	John Reid	'B41'; pt; FN 1757	OTNR (SR 2134)
A1830	15.11.1854	24.7.1855	M. Deane	'B42'; comments on land; FN 1756	OTNR (SR 2131)
A1831		3.2.1856	Joseph Cauchon C/CL	'No 49'; pt: lots 13–27, cons I–X and con A; no names	OTAR(P)

	Date of Instructions	Date of Map	Surveyor and Signature	Endorsements and Notes	Location
A1832		31.7.1856	J.W.B. Joseph Cauchon C/CL	'No 48' 'Office copy'; names	OTAR(P)
A1833	26.7.1860 13.10.1860	17.11.1860	Geo. A. Stewart	'S18'; pt; insets of 2 mill sites at 2 ch; 40 ch; FN 1758	OTNR (SR 2133)
	SOPHIASBURGH				
A1834	10.–.1785	[178?]	–	'313' 'A38'; N pt and Hallowell Twp; names, town glebe and fortification reserve on Green Pt; scale n.g.	OTAR
A1835		[178?]	Copy Lt Augustine Prevost [sgd] Samuel Holland SG	'321' 'A39'; pt laid out with names, note on accuracy of source maps, portage	OTAR
A1836	22.2.1791	15.4.1797	Alexr Aitkin	'A37'; names, later changes, marshes, note on surveys 22.10.1825 W.C.	OTAR(P)
A1837		[1797?]	W.C.	'1261' 'C23'; includes Hallowell Twp; survey grid, marshes, pinholes for tracing	OTAR
A1838		[1797?]	[Alex Aitken]	'No 37'; names; scale n.g.	OTNR (SR 2135)
A1839		[180?]	–	'No 36'; names, marshes; scale n.g.	OTAR(P)
A1840	20.5.1812	4.7.1812	Willson Conger	'24' '877'; 'Roads and Highways now in use'	OTNR (SR 4746)
A1841	29.8.1833 7.5.1834	29.7.1834	Wm Hawkins	'No 49'; Big Is; names, reserves for schools, wooded areas; 20 ch; FN 60, 234	OTNR (SR 615)
A1842		[1834]	[W. Hawkins]	'1503'; Big Is, forested land, survey grid, bridge; scale n.g.	OTAR
A1843	20.2.1839	–.–.1839	Publius V. Elmore	'B39'; resurvey, location of monuments	OTNR (SR 2136)
A1844		–.8.1843	Thomas Parke SG	Includes Hallowell Twp; survey grid, reserves, notes; scale n.g.	OTAR
A1845	5.4.1864	–.6.1864	A.C. Webb	'S30'; pt; gore D, names; FN 1765	OTNR (SR 2137)
	SOUTHWOLD				
A1846	25.3.1799	[1799?]	[W. Hambly?]	'A11'; names, note re survey of lands from end of con 4 to L Erie for schools, c & c reserves; scale n.g.; FN 638	OTAR(P)

A1847	24.3.1809	–.12.1810	M. Burwell	Reserves, marshes, lots with names on Talbot Rd as located by T. Talbot; FN 513	OTAR (Talbot BkE/1)
A1848		[1810?]	[M. Burwell]	'A10'; c & c reserves, names, note re lot nos on Talbot Rd [sgd] T. Ridout 8.8.1816; scale n.g.	OTNR (SR 2140)
A1849		[1810?]	[M. Burwell]	Names along Talbot Rd, same note as in **A1848**	OTAR (SR 2139)
A1850	15.3.1819	28.6.1819	M. Burwell	'B9' '552'; c & c reserves, names; FN 636	OTNR (SR 2138)
A1851		28.6.1819	[M. Burwell]	Pt; Talbot Rd to L Erie, reserves, names of those located by T. Talbot	OTAR (Talbot BkD/6)
A1852		[1819?]	M. Burwell copy J.G.C.	'No 35' 'Office Plan'; copy of Burwell's plans of 1811 and 1819; names, c & c reserves	OTAR(P)
A1853		23.3.1831	M. Burwell	'No 36'; c & c reserves, names, roads	OTNR (SR 2142)
A1854		–.–.1831	M. Burwell copy J.G.C.	'No 46' 'Office copy'; c & c reserves, a few names, roads, marshes; scale n.g.	OTAR(P)
A1855		–.7.1843	Thomas Parke SG	Survey grid, reserves; scale n.g.	OTAR
	SPRAGGE				
A1856	15.5.1860	10.9.1861	Chas Unwin	'E No 7'; twps 3 and 4 S Range XII W Algona (Spragge and Esten), Esten annulled 1953; marsh; FN 1766	OTNR (SR 2146)
	STAFFORD				
A1857	24.12.1838	[27.1.1841]	[J. Richey]	'B25' '545'; c & c reserves, note on clergy reserve 13.5.1842; scale n.g.; FN 265	OTNR (SR 2149)
A1858		–.–.1841	[J. Richey]	'214' 'No 37' 'No 5'; c & c reserves, names	OTAR(P)
	STAMFORD				
A1859	–	–.10.1791	–	'No 18'; glebe, names, many later changes	OTAR(P)
A1860	–	22.12.1813	Thos Ridout SG	'A21'; names, mills	OTNR (SR 2150)
A1861		[184?]	–	Pt; shows new rd (Clarke St) through lots 190, 191, 193, 223, and across Welland R, names, military reserves; scale n.g.	OTAR
A1862		[184?]	–	Pt: lots 175 and 190; Mr Clark's house and land; scale n.g.	OTAR

	Date of Instructions	Date of Map	Surveyor and Signature	Endorsements and Notes	Location
	STANHOPE				
A1863	22.9.1859	[1860]	G.A. Stewart	'S No 5'; town reserve, lakes, names; FN 1771	OTNR (SR 2151)
	STANLEY				
A1864	–	4.9.1835	John McDonald dr D. McDonald	'No 15' '1157'; for Canada Co.; town plot at Bayfield R, contents; FN 452	OTNR (SR 2152)
A1865		[1835?]	[J. Mcdonald]	Names, Bayfield town plot; scale n.g.	OTAR (Canada Co. Atlas 16)
	STEPHEN				
A1866	–	4.9.1835	John McDonald dr D. McDonald	'No 16' '1155'; pt; only 3 cons and Lake Rd lots laid out, for Canada Co.; FN 59, 451, 452	OTNR (SR 2156)
A1867		23.9.1837	John McDonald dr W. Lawson	'No 22' '1156'; present and former surveys, contents, unsurveyed areas	OTNR (SR 2155)
A1868		23.9.1837	John McDonald dr W. Lawson	Contents of present survey of interior, former survey and an unsurveyed area on Aux Sables R	OTAR (Canada Co. Atlas 17)
	STEPHENSON				
A1869	10.6.1861	21.6.1862	Robert Gilmour	'No 23'; Muskoka Rd, marshes; FN 1776	OTNR (SR 2158)
A1870		–.–.1862 17.7.1863	Robert Gilmour CLD	'214'; names, Muskoka Rd	OTAR(P)
	STORRINGTON				
A1871	–	–.10.1846	CLD	'1247'; shows pts Loughborough, Kingston, and Pittsburgh twps from which Storrington created	OTAR
A1872		19.1.1856	CLD Joseph Cauchon C/CL	Pt; 'formerly part of Pittsburgh', cons 5–15; scale n.g.	OTAR (SR 2165)
A1873		19.1.1856	CLD Joseph Cauchon C/CL	Pt; formerly Kingston Twp	OTAR
A1874		–.1.1856	CLD Joseph Cauchon C/CL	Pt and Loughborough Twp; survey grid	OTAR

	SULLIVAN				
A1875	19.5.1843	20.10.1843	J.S. Dennis	'B16'; high bank, crown reserve, meadow, black ash and cedar swamp; FN 267	OTNR (SR 2175)
A1876		–.1.1844	SGO Thomas Parke SG	Survey grid, Saugeen Rd lots, reserves	OTAR
A1877		–.8.1847	Andrew Russell SS and D CLD	'No 20'; school lands, names	OTAR(P)
A1878		14.11.1848	Copy A.R. CLD	Survey grid, Owen Sound Rd lots; scale n.g.	OTAR
	SUNNIDALE				
A1879	15.8.1831	31.12.1831	Thos Kelly	'B29' '566'; route to twp of 'Merlin,' relief, notes on trees; FN 642, 646	OTNR (SR 2181)
A1880	9.8.1832	27.2.1833	Thos Kelly	'B28'; c & c reserves, portage; FN 644	OTNR (SR 2183)
A1881		[1833?]	Copy J.G.C.	'C56' 'A34' '39?'; c & c reserves, marsh, names, Indian paths	OTAR(P)
A1882	3.6.1834	25.7.1834	Robert Ross	'A62'; 5-acre lots in cons 1–3 W of rd to L Huron; 8 ch; FN 645	OTNR (SR 2185)
A1883		25.7.1834	Robert Ross	'C56' 'No 44'; pt; 5-acre lots on Sunnidale Rd W side cons 1–3; 10 ch	OTAR(P)
A1884		[1834?]	Copy J.G.C.	'1254'; rd lots including five-acre rd lots, town plots of Rippon and Hythe, marsh, c & c reserves	OTAR
A1885		12.6.1837 13.6.1837	Copy J.G. Chewett SGO J.W. Macauley	Five-acre park lots on cons 2–3 W side Sunnidale Rd; 8 ch	OTAR
A1886		–.7.1843	Thomas Parke SG	Survey grid, rd lots, town of Hythe, reserves; scale n.g.	OTAR
	SYDENHAM				
A1887	4.7.1842 25.7.1842	17.12.1842	C.R.	'No 1'; village of Sydenham, relief; FN 650	OTNR (SR 2179)
A1888		17.12.1842	C. Rankin	'No 2' 'No 2 showing suggested alterations'; village of Sydenham, school lands, names, reserves	OTAR(P)
A1889		[1842?]	[C. Rankin?]	Rd survey, military reserves, rd from Oakville, town plot, relief; scale n.g.	OTAR (SR 2180)
A1890		30.6.1843	Thomas Parke SG	Reserves, town of Sydenham, marshes, relief, contents of some lots; scale n.g.	OTAR

	Date of Instructions	Date of Map	Surveyor and Signature	Endorsements and Notes	Location
	TARENTORUS				
A1891	12.5.1858	21.1.1859	Albert Pellew Salter	'No 5'; wooded land, village of 'Ste Marie,' park lots; FN 1810	OTNR (SR 2216)
A1892		28.3.1859	CLD	'216'; twps no 1 N and S Range 25 W, town plot of Sault Ste Marie, names, later changes; scale n.g.	OTAR(P)
	TAY				
A1893	23.6.1820	[1820]	J.G. Chewett	'No 35'; Penetanguishene Rd and military reserve, c & c reserves; FN 652	OTNR (SR 2217)
A1894		[1820?]	J.G. Chewett	'No 35' 'Surveyed for Borland & Roe' 'office copy'; military reserve, names, c & c reserves, later changes	OTAR(P)
A1895		–.7.1843	Thomas Parke SG	Survey grid, reserves, military reserves and naval depot; scale n.g.	OTAR
	TECUMSETH				
A1896	15.6.1819	[1819]	[G. Lount]	'B30' '557'; c & c reserves, marsh; scale n.g.; FN 654	OTNR (SR 2219)
A1897		[182?]	G. Lount copy W.C. SS & D	'A28' '387'; marsh in N pt, names in S pt	OTAR(P)
A1898		–.–.1822	G. Lount copy W.C. Thos Ridout SG	'No 36' 'Office Plan'; names, many later changes	OTAR(P)
A1899	6.9.1832	[1832]	George Lount	'B31' '558'; surv in 1819 and 1832, c & c reserves; FN 653	OTNR (SR 2220)
A1900		–.7.1843	Thomas Parke SG	Survey grid, reserves; scale n.g.	OTAR
	TEHKUMMAH				
A1901	16.5.1863 30.3.1865	30.3.1866	G. Brockitt Abrey	'No 9'; roads, town plot, only partly subdivided; FN 1814	OTNR (SR 2186)
	THOMPSON				
A1902	7.5.1860	–.–.1861	Robert Gilmour	'B6' 'twps 3 and 4 S Range XVI W' (Thompson and Patton); marsh, relief; FN 1818	OTNR (SR 2199)
	THORAH				
A1903	24.1.1820	–.–.1820	J.E. White	'No 37'; names; scale n.g.; FN 657	OTNR (SR 2196)

A1904		8.12.1826	J.E. White Thos Ridout	'No 38'; later notes 1830, 1844, and 1859, names, c & c reserves, some later changes	OTAR(P)
A1905	28.12.1826	–.5.1827	David Gibson	'B32'; c & c reserves, a few names; FN 658	OTNR (SR 2195)
A1906		–.7.1843	Thomas Parke SG	Survey grid, reserves; scale n.g.	OTAR
A1907	19.9.1863	24.11.1863	Geo Gibson	'No 7'; Thorah Is; 10 ch; FN 2141	OTAR(P) (SR 2194)
	THOROLD				
A1908	–	28.1.1794	Augustus Jones copy Lewis Grant D.W. Smith ASG	'A22'; names	OTAR(P)
A1909		[1794?]	D.W. Smith ASG	'A23' '323' 'rec'd from Land Board of Lincoln'; names; scale n.g.	OTAR (SR 2203)
A1910		[1794?]	–	'No 19'; pt; names, glebe, Merrittsville added later; scale n.g.	OTAR (SR 2201)
A1911		24.1.1812	Exam Thos Ridout	'A24' '322'; names	OTNR (SR 2200)
A1912		[182?]	–	'C16' '1246'; outline and lot nos, shows town of Thorold with 1856 boundary, roads	OTAR (SR 2202)
	THURLOW				
A1913	–	–.–.1787	Lewis Kotte	'B45' '997'; 6 cons, names	OTNR (SR 2207)
A1914		–.–.1787 –.5.1792	Lewis Kotte W. Chewett	'No 40'; names, shoreline, later notes by W. Chewett 1831	OTAR(P)
A1915		1787 20.9.1848	Copy TD CLD T. Bouthillier	Copy from Lewis Kotte plan 1787 'Quebec Plan No 40' for court case; scale n.g.	OTAR
A1916		[179?]	–	'A41'; names, some later changes from 1795 on; scale n.g.	OTAR(P)
A1917	8.8.1817	31.12.1817	Sam'l S. Wilmot	'No 49'; lot 4, con 2 in 5-acre park lots; names; 4 ch; FN 395	OTNR (SR 2205)
A1918		23.1.1832	W. Chewett ASG	Diagram for the survey of cons VI–IX, notes on lines to be run and earlier surveys; scale n.g.	OTAR
A1919	1.7.1834	–.–.1835	F.P. Rubidge	Pt; Point Ann, vegetation, clearings, houses, roads; FN 396	OTNR (SR 5487)
A1920		–.7.1843	Thomas Parke SG	Survey grid, reserves; scale n.g.	OTAR

	Date of Instructions	Date of Map	Surveyor and Signature	Endorsements and Notes	Location
A1921		–.10.1846	Copy T.D. CLD	'1245'; outline	OTAR (SR 2204)
	TILBURY, E				
A1922	4.2.1796	28.7.1799 9.6.1800	A. Iredell	'A28'; pt; names, c & c reserves	OTNR (SR 2209)
A1923	17.4.1821	17.4.1821	Copy J.G.C. Thos Ridout SG	C & c reserves, Talbot Rd; scale n.g.	OTAR
A1924		[1824]	[M. Burwell]	'No 32'; lots given to Col Talbot in 1826, c & c reserves, names, roads; FN 664	OTNR (SR 2208)
A1925		[1824?]	M. Burwell	'No 38'; names, some later changes, Middle Rd survey, copy	OTAR(P)
A1926		[1826?]	Copy J.G.C. Thos Ridout	Names located by T. Talbot to 1830s	OTAR (Talbot BkC/15)
A1927		–.7.1843	Thomas Parke SG	Survey grid, reserves, Middle Rd; scale n.g.	OTAR
	TILBURY, W				
A1928	17.4.1821	31.12.1824	M. Burwell	'No 31' '1171'; lots given to Col Talbot in 1826, names; FN 667	OTNR (SR 2210)
A1929		15.2.1826	Copy J.G.C. Thos Ridout SG	Names located by T. Talbot to 1836	OTAR (Talbot BkC/3)
A1930		–.7.1843	Thomas Parke SG	Survey grid, reserves; scale n.g.	OTAR
	TILLEY				
A1931	5.12.1864	6.9.1866	[H. Wilson] CLD A. Russell AC	'217'; Indian land, 'Begleys Copper location'; FN 1821	OTAR(P)
	TINY				
A1932	18.8.1821	[10.1.1823]	[J. Goessman]	'A29'; c & c reserves, new town site, old town site, military and naval reserve, names; FN 418, 665	OTNR (SR 2212)
A1933		[1823?]	Copy J. Goessman	'No 39'; names, military reserves, roads, Penetanguishene, c & c reserves, relief, many later changes, later notes 1842 and 1844	OTAR(P)

A1934		16.6.1829	Copy J.G.C. W. Chewett ASG	C & c reserves, marshes, some names, military reserves and town plot at Penetanguishene; scale n.g.	OTAR
A1935		–.7.1843	Thomas Parke SG	Survey grid, reserves; scale n.g.	OTAR
	TORBOLTON				
A1936	6.6.1822	30.1.1823	R. Sherwood	'B21'; c & c reserves, a few names; FN 668	OTNR (SR 2230)
A1937		[1823?]	R. Sherwood copy J.G.C.	'No 21'; c & c reserves, names, notes 1829 and 1843	OTAR(P)
A1938		2.5.1823	R. Sherwood copy J.G.C. Thos Ridout SG	'No 34'; c & c reserves, names, marshes	OTAR(P)
	TORONTO				
A1939	2.1.1806	1.6.1806	Sam'l S. Wilmot	'A36'; S pt; Mississauga Indian reserve, names; FN 676	OTAR (SR 2225)
A1940		28.6.1806	Sam'l S. Wilmot	'A35'; 5 cons and pt Etobicoke; Indian reserve, names, 'windfall'; FN 569, 677	OTNR (SR 2226)
A1941	8.2.1819	–.4.1819	Richard Bristol	'A30'; N pt; names; scale n.g.; FN 671	OTNR (SR 2227)
A1942		[1819?]	Copy J.G.C.	'C25' '1241'; N pt from Bristol's survey, S pt from Wilmot's survey; Credit reserve, c & c reserves, road	OTAR (SR 2223)
A1943		[1821?]	S. Wilmot J.G. Chewett	'B35' '562'; 'Racey Tract,' pt from Wilmot's traverse of the river in 1806, lots 1–8 in 2 cons N and S of Dundas St; town plot; scale n.g.; FN 672	OTNR (SR 2222)
A1944		20.2.[1821?]	SGO	'No 40' 'Office copy'; Indian reserve survey, Racey Tract, names, many later changes	OTAR(P)
A1945	24.1.1828	[1.3.1828]	John Goessman	'B33'; mill sites in cons 1–2; 20 ch; FN 673	OTNR (SR 2224)
A1946		[1828?]	John Goessman copy J.G.C.	'No 43'; pt of Indian reserve N of Dundas St; c & c reserves, names, mill sites, note dated 1828; 20 ch	OTAR(P)
A1947		19.4.1843	SGO	Pt showing Mississauga Indian reserve, orig reserve and pt surveyed, Port Credit to con II Dundas St	OTAR
A1948		–.7.1843	Thomas Parke SG	Survey grid, reserves; scale n.g.	OTAR
A1949	2.9.1845	14.4.1846	J.S. Dennis	'Q78'; town plot, bldgs, improvements, old survey, Indian village; 20 ch	OTNR (SR 2335)
A1950		14.4.1846 6.12.1854	John Dennis A.N. Morin C/CL	'No 59' 'Indian Reserve River Credit'; names, town plot, 'Old Survey' boundary, copy; 20 ch	OTAR(P)

	Date of Instructions	Date of Map	Surveyor and Signature	Endorsements and Notes	Location
	TORONTO GORE				
A1951	8.2.1819	14.6.1819	R. Sherwood	'B34'; c & c reserves, names; FN 675	OTNR (SR 2228)
A1952		[1819?]	[R. Sherwood?]	'No 41'; names, adds to 1860s; scale n.g.	OTAR (SR 2229)
A1953		28.4.1828	Copy J.G.C. Thos Ridout SG	c & c reserves, lots deeded and those sold with price, names	OTAR
A1954		–.–.1828	Copy J.G. Chewett	'No 42' 'Office copy'; c & c reserves, names	OTAR(P)
A1955		–.7.1843	Thomas Parke SG	Survey grid, reserves; scale n.g.	OTAR
	TOSORONTIO				
A1956	4.2.1820?	–.–.1821	Hugh Black	'No 44'; lots 1–33, cons 1–7; FN 683	OTNR (SR 2231)
A1957		[1821]	Hugh Black	'B36' '567'; c & c reserves, relief, marshes, tree types	OTAR (SR 2233)
A1958		[1821?]	[H. Black]	'1240'; marshes, survey grid	OTAR
A1959		–.7.1843	Thomas Parke SG	Survey grid, reserves; scale n.g.	OTAR
A1960	22.6.1852	–.7.1852	Hugh P. Savigny	'B53'; gore btwn Tosorontio and Sunnidale; FN 682	OTNR (SR 2232)
	TOWNSEND				
A1961	–	[1793]	William Hambly D.W. Smith ASG	'1239' 'Protraction of the twp'; reserves, twp granted to Andrew Pierce et al 22.3.1793; 20 ch; FN 264	OTAR (SR 2240)
A1962		[1802?]	William Hambly	'A12'; names, c & c reserves; 80 ch	OTNR (SR 2237)
A1963		[1802?] [182?]	William Hambly copy J.G.C.	'No 37'; names, c & c reserves; scale n.g.	OTAR(P)
A1964	12.1.1816	15.1.1824	M. Burwell	'B18' '561'; examination 13th con line; 80 ch; FN 686 (pt 1)	OTNR (SR 2238)
A1965		15.1.1824 9.2.1825	M. Burwell copy J.G.C. Thos Ridout SG	'C22'; resurvey of 13th con line, survey grid; 80 ch	OTAR
A1966	13.10.1826	5.7.1830	M. Burwell	'B10' '564'; resurvey 13th con; FN 686 (pt 2)	OTNR (SR 2239)
A1967		–.7.1843	Thomas Parke SG	Survey grid, reserves; scale n.g.	OTAR
	TRAFALGAR				
A1968	14.2.1806	18.6.1806	Sam'l S. Wilmot	'A24' 'Rough plan'; cons parallel to Dundas St, names, c & c reserves, old Dundas St; FN 689	OTAR(P)

A1969		28.6.1806	Sam'l S. Wilmot	'A22' '330'; pt: five cons; names, roads, relief, c & c reserves, Indian camp; FN 676, 687	OTNR (SR 2242)
A1970	8.2.1819	12.6.1819	Richard Bristol	'B4' '571'; N pt; c & c reserves; FN 688	OTNR (SR 2241)
A1971		[1819?]	[Richard Bristol?]	N pt cons 1–11; c & c reserves, windfall; scale n.g.	OTAR
A1972		[1819?]	Copy W.C. SS & D	'No 21'; names, town of Bronte, c & c reserves, some later changes	OTAR(P)
A1973		[1819?]	Copy J.G. Chewett W. Chewett SS & D	'A23' '329'; cons 1–11 N of Dundas St; c & c reserves, names, Esquesing outlined to N, note 1821	OTAR(P)
A1974		–.7.1843	Thomas Parke SG	Survey grid, reserves; scale n.g.	OTAR
	TUCKERSMITH				
A1975	–	4.9.1835	John McDonald dr H. Lizars	'No 17' '1128'; contents, for Canada Co.; FN 167	OTNR (SR 2245)
A1976		[1835?]	[J. Mcdonald]	Contents of I–III surveys, marshes, names	OTAR (Canada Co. Atlas 18)
	TUDOR				
A1977	–	–.–.1851	P.V. Elmore	'B38'; lots in cons A and B; scale n.g.	OTNR (SR 2247)
A1978	5.12.1856 22.6.1857	[1857]	W.H. Deane	'No 51'; roads, settlement; FN 1828	OTNR (SR 2248)
A1979		3.10.1857	W.H. Deane	'No 52'; pt: lot 67 on Hastings Rd, mill site on Crow R, longitudinal section; 4 ch	OTNR (SR 2249)
A1980	22.9.1862	9.6.1863	Henry A. MacLeod	'No 5'; cons XV–XIX; settlement; FN 1827	OTNR (SR 2250)
	TURNBERRY				
A1981	30.4.1852	30.4.1852	Copy T.D. CLD John Rolph C/CL	Projected plan, notes on lines to be surveyed and surveyors; scale n.g.	OTAR
A1982		–.9.1853 5.1.1854	Wm McClary Charles Fraser exam A.R.	'B68'; beaver meadow, cedar swamp, high bank, proposed town (Wingham); FN 1833, 1834	OTNR (SR 2255)
A1983		–.6.1854	T.D. A.N. Morin C/CL	'No 66'; names, Wingham	OTAR(P)
	TUSCARORA				
A1984	13.8.1841	24.6.1842	William Walker	'Q63' '1101'; names, bldgs, roads; FN 691, 692	OTNR (SR 2256)

	Date of Instructions	Date of Map	Surveyor and Signature	Endorsements and Notes	Location
A1985		24.6.1842 25.7.1842	William Walker copy A. LaRue	'No 20' 'Office copy'; names in W pt and along river, paths, roads, mills, some houses	OTAR(P)
	TYENDINAGA				
A1986	15.2.1820	–.6.1820	R. Sherwood	'No 41'; Mohawk lands, names, later adds	OTNR (SR 2260)
A1987		[1820?]	R. Sherwood	'1242' 'C24'; pt: cons 1–4; c & c reserves, pinholes for tracing, copy	OTAR
A1988		17.7.1835	A. Campbell	'Q35' '569'; Mohawk reserve; FN 693	OTNR (SR 2259)
A1989	21.7.1835	3.6.1835	Sam'l M. Benson	'B34' '570'; S pt; road; FN 2816, 2817	OTNR (SR 2258)
A1990		27.5.1836	Sam'l M. Benson	'B36' '568'; rear pt; c & c reserves, comments on land; FN 694	OTNR (SR 2261)
A1991		[184?]	–	'No 42' 'compiled from four partial plans'; con II S and pt BF; c & c reserve, 'Indian reserve,' marshes, some trees, names in N pt; scale n.g.	OTAR(P)
A1992		–.7.1843	Thomas Parke SG	N pt; survey grid, reserves; scale n.g.	OTAR
A1993		–.7.1843	Thomas Parke SG	S pt; survey grid, reserves; scale n.g.	OTAR
A1994		–.10.1846	copy A.R. CLD	'1243' 'C36' 'office copy'; survey grid	OTAR
A1995		14.8.1862	E.T. CLD Andrew Russell AC	Pt; boundary btwn Tyendinaga and Richmond twps from cons V–X Tyendinaga; 2 sheets	OTAR
	USBORNE				
A1996	–	21.1.1839	John McDonald	'CC' '1159'; roads; FN 66	OTNR (SR 2264)
A1997		21.1.1839	John McDonald	Contents of cons 4–15; some names, roads	OTAR (Canada Co. Atlas 19)
	UXBRIDGE				
A1998	14.11.1804	8.4.1805	Sam'l S. Wilmot	'No 45'; names, c & c reserves; FN 695, 696	OTNR (SR 2266)
A1999		[182?]	Copy J.G.C.	'1238'; c & c reserves, marshes	OTAR (SR 2265)
A2000		–.7.1843	Thomas Parke SG	Survey grid, reserves; scale n.g.	OTAR

	VANKOUGHNET				
A2001	26.4.1866	[1866]	–	Projected plan, notes on lines to be run, section nos; scale n.g.	OTAR
A2002		3.5.1867	George F. Austin	'No 3'; marshes, copper veins, water power; FN 1841	OTNR (SR 2269)
A2003		–.11.1867	CLD A. Russell AC	'226'; names, Indian lands, later changes	OTAR(P)
	VAUGHAN				
A2004	21.8.1798	[1798]	John Stegmann	'No 46'; names, c & c reserves; scale n.g.; FN 3–430	OTNR (SR 2271)
A2005		[181?]	–	'No 55' 'Office copy'; names; scale n.g.	OTAR (SR 2272)
A2006		–.7.1843	Thomas Parke SG	Survey grid, reserves; scale n.g.	OTAR
A2007	–	10.12.1860	J. Stoughton Dennis	'No 2'; shows eight side roads, resurvey; FN 857	OTNR (SR 2270)
	VERULAM				
A2008	1.7.1822?	[1823]	John Huston	'B26'; c & c reserves; scale n.g.; FN 697	OTNR (SR 2274)
A2009		[1823?]	Copy John Huston W.C.	'No 39' 'Office Plan'; names, some changes, notes 1838 and 1851, marshes	OTAR(P)
A2010		[183?]	[J. Reid?]	Names with dates 1840s and 1850s; scale n.g.	OTAR (SR 2275)
A2011		19.7.1836	Copy J.G. Chewett SGO	'1237' 'C18'; marshes, survey grid; scale n.g.	OTAR
A2012		–.7.1843	Thomas Parke SG	Survey grid, reserves; scale n.g.	OTAR
	VESPRA				
A2013	5.2.1820	[1820]	J.G. Chewett	'No 48'; c & c reserves, names, town plot of Kempenfeldt, later adds 1834; FN 703	OTNR (SR 2276)
A2014		16.6.1831	Copy J.G.C.	'No 48'; Kempenfeldt town plot and Barrie town plot, c & c reserves, marshes, names, road	OTAR (SR 2277)
A2015	18.5.1835	–.–.1835	J. Goessmann	'No 47' '573'; c & c reserves, Barrie and another town plot to E, roads, mills, portage routes Nottawasaga R, land classification; FN 700, 701	OTNR (SR 2278)
A2016		–.7.1843	Thomas Parke SG	Survey grid, reserves; scale n.g.	OTAR
	WAINFLEET				
A2017	8.12.1809	[1811?]	[M. Burwell?]	'A25' '227'; names, glebe in centre, notes 1809; scale n.g.	OTAR(P)

	Date of Instructions	Date of Map	Surveyor and Signature	Endorsements and Notes	Location
A2018		[1811]	M. Burwell T.D.	'No 21'; names, mill pond, Welland Canal Co. land, later adds; FN 711	OTNR (SR 2283)
A2019		12.12.1811	Copy W.C. exam Thos Ridout	'A26'; 'Great Cranberry Marsh' (Welland Canal Company), names in other lots	OTAR(P)
	WALLACE				
A2020		30.4.1852	Copy T.D. John Rolph C/CL	Projected plan to accompany SI, notes on lines to be surveyed and surveyors; scale n.g.	OTAR
A2021	30.4.1852	10.4.1855	Eliakim Malcolm	'B75'; lot sizes, marsh, clearings, some bldgs; FN 1851	OTNR (SR 2286)
A2022		23.1.1856	Eliakim Malcolm Joseph Cauchon C/CL	'No 54'; names	OTAR(P)
	WALLBRIDGE				
A2023	24.8.1866	15.5.1867	M. Deane	'No 43'; outlines, marsh, relief, comments on trees and land; FN 2334	OTNR (SR 6585)
	WALPOLE				
A2024	30.11.1795 3.12.1795	[1796?]	[W. Hambly]	'No 20–1'; pt; names, c & c reserves, later adds to 1843; scale n.g.; FN 223	OTNR (SR 97959)
A2025		[1796?]	[W. Hambly]	'No 20–2'; pt; gore, names; scale n.g.	OTNR (SR 97958)
A2026		–.7.1843	Thomas Parke SG	Survey grid, reserves; scale n.g.	OTAR
A2027		–.10.1847	CLD	Outline; later note indicates plan is 'imperfect'	OTAR (SR 2289)
A2028		–.10.1847	CLD	'1222'; survey grid	OTAR
A2029	–	5.4.1851	C. Rankin, Zenas Fell Commissioners	Boundary resurvey of Walpole and Woodhouse twps; scale n.g.	OTAR
	WALSINGHAM				
A2030	1.11.1809	1.8.1815	T. Ridout SG	'1228' 'C25'; relief, survey grid	OTAR
A2031		28.3.1816	Mahlon Burwell	'B19' '574'; resurvey (exam of cons 2–5), notes; FN 707	OTNR (SR 2292)
A2032		[1816?]	–	C & c reserves, names, many later changes; scale n.g.	OTAR(P)
A2033		–.7.1843	Thomas Parke SG	Survey grid, reserves; scale n.g.	OTAR

A2034		25.8.1847	T.W. Walsh	Pt including pt of Houghton Twp; 10 ch	OTAR (SR 2293)
A2035	11.10.1849	19.2.1850	Thos W. Walsh	'B34'; pt; marsh, Long Point; 10 ch; FN 704, 706	OTNR (SR 2294)
A2036		19.2.1850	Thos W. Walsh	'B35'; pt; Long Point with open channel, lots 1–24, con 1, A and B; 40 ch	OTNR (SR 2295)
A2037		[1850?]	CLD	'No 70'; includes Charlotteville Twp; 'Long Point,' names, many later changes; scale n.g.	OTAR(P)
	WARWICK				
A2038	30.5.1831	–.9.1831	Peter Carroll	'B21'; pt; rd survey, c & c reserves; FN 190	OTNR (SR 2302)
A2039	29.5.1832	29.12.1832	Peter Carroll	'B18' '576'; c & c reserves, marshes, main rd; FN 709	OTNR (SR 2301)
A2040		[1832?]	[P. Carroll?]	'1227'; c & c reserves, marshes; scale n.g.	OTAR (SR 2300)
A2041		6.2.1833	Peter Carroll copy J.G. Chewett	'No 34'; names, c & c reserves	OTAR (SR 2303)
A2042		[1833?]	–	'No 33'; c & c reserves, names; scale n.g.	OTAR(P)
A2043		–.7.1843	Thomas Parke SG	Survey grid, reserves; scale n.g.	OTAR
	WATERLOO				
A2044	–	[182?]	–	'B9' '575'; pt; broken lots, in N part and Gore; scale n.g.	OTNR (SR 2306)
	WATT				
A2045	9.8.1864	–.11.1865	T.W. Nash	Names, roads; FN 1860	OTNR (SR 2305)
A2046		11.1865	T.W. Nash	Survey grid	OTAR (SR 2304)
A2047		28.5.1867	CLD A. Russell AC	'230'; names, Parry Sound Rd, later changes	OTAR(P)
	WAWANOSH, E and W				
A2048	1836 and 26.1.1838	–.6.1838	William Hawkins	'B21'; c & c reserves, marshes; FN 710	OTNR (SR 2309)
A2049		3.8.1838	Wm. Hawkins copy J.G. Chewett	'No 50' 'Office copy'; surveyed 1836–8; school lands, c & c reserves, names	OTAR(P)
A2050		[1840?]	copy J.G. Chewett K. Cameron ASG	C & c reserves, marshes	OTAR
A2051		–.7.1843	Thomas Parke SG	Survey grid, reserves; scale n.g.	OTAR

	Date of Instructions	Date of Map	Surveyor and Signature	Endorsements and Notes	Location
A2052		–.12.1847	Copy A.R. CLD T. Bouthillier	Survey grid	OTAR
	WELLESLEY				
A2053	31.3.1843	5.9.1843	William Walker	'B17' '579'; names of owners and settlement prior to survey with lots conflicting; FN 1862, 1863	OTNR (SR 2311)
A2054		–.–.1843 5.1.1844	W. Walker Thomas Parke SG	'No 20'; c & c reserves, names	OTAR(P)
A2055		–.1.1844	Thomas Parke SG	Survey grid	OTAR
A2056	–	19.12.1848	James W. Bridgland	'B50'; pt; gore lots	OTNR (SR 2312)
A2057		22.1.1849	Copy T. Devine CLD	'No 20' '1204'; gore lots, a few names	OTAR(P)
A2058		–.2.1849	Copy T.D. CLD	Gore lots cons I–XV	OTAR
A2059		12.7.1861	Joseph Hobson	'16183/61'; lots 4, 5 in con 10; 6 ch	OTNR (SR 5526)
	WESTMEATH				
A2060	25.9.1834	7.1.1836 8.5.1836	J. McNaughton exam J.G. Chewett	'B22'; roads, portages, adds 1874; FN 712	OTNR (SR 2316)
A2061		[1836?]	Copy J.G. Chewett	Marshes, c & c reserves, trails	OTAR
A2062		[1836?]	J.G. Chewett	'No 22' '233' 'Office Copy'; c & c reserves, names, notes 1837	OTAR(P)
A2063		–.8.1843	Thomas Parke SG	Survey grid, reserves; scale n.g.	OTAR
	WESTMINSTER				
A2064	9.5.1810	–.5/6.1810 24.5.1811	Simon Z. Watson Thos Ridout	'No 41' '335'; pt: front; names, c & c reserves, roads, later adds; FN 303	OTNR (SR 2318)
A2065		24.5.1811	Thos Ridout	Pt: BF and cons 1–2, notes re realigning survey lines, Commissioners Rd; scale n.g.	OTAR (Talbot BkD/9)
A2066		[1811?]	–	Pt; survey along rd leading E–W to mouth of river and rd going S, varying line for E–W rd proposed by Mr Watson	OTAR (Talbot BkD/16)
A2067	13.8.1816	21.12.1820	M. Burwell	'B11' '581'; pt; roads; FN 713	OTNR (SR 2317)
A2068	21.5.1819	5.10.1821	John Bostwick	'B12' '580'; c & c reserves; FN 715	OTNR (SR 2319)

A2069		[1821?]	–	'No 38' 'Office Plan'; notes 1821 and 1843, c & c reserves, names	OTAR(P)
A2070		11.9.1823	Thos Ridout	School lands in S, c & c reserves, names located by T. Talbot	OTAR (Talbot BkC/2)
A2071		–.7.1843	Thomas Parke SG	Survey grid, reserves, roads; scale n.g.	OTAR
	WHITBY				
A2072	14.2.1791 24.4.1795	14.7.1795	A. Jones DPS	'No 52'; names, c & c reserves, later adds; FN 835	OTNR (SR 2321)
A2073		[1795?]	D.W. Smith ASG	'1223' 'C29'; reserves, notes on survey, pinholes for tracing; scale n.g.	OTAR
A2074		[1795?]	W.C. SS and D	'C31'; c & c reserves, roads, pinholes for tracing	OTAR
A2075		[180?]	–	'C30' '1235'; marshes, relief, names in 1st con adjacent to shoreline, adds, harbour of Windsor and town	OTAR (SR 2322)
A2076		–.7.1843	Thomas Parke SG	Survey grid, reserves; scale n.g.	OTAR
	WHITCHURCH				
A2077	22.4.1800 12.7.1802	[–.10.1802]	John Stegmann	'No 49'; names, c & c reserves; scale n.g.; FN 718	OTNR (SR 2324)
A2078		[1802?]	John Stegmann	'B38' '582'; crown reserve, relief, marshes	OTAR (SR 2325)
A2079		[1802?]	Copy W.C.	'A38' '336'; names	OTAR (SR 2326)
A2080		[1802?]	[J. Stegmann?]	'A31'; names with dates 1799–1801; scale n.g.	OTAR (SR 2323)
A2081		[1802?]	Copy W.C.	'1233' 'W18' 'C28'; c & c reserves, marshes, pinholes for tracing	OTAR
A2082		–.7.1843	Thomas Parke SG	Survey grid, reserves; scale n.g.	OTAR
	WICKLOW				
A2083	11.12.1856	–.10.1858	J.S. Peterson	'No 1'; pt; comments on timber and soil, marshes, mill sites; FN 1877	OTNR (SR 2331)
A2084	26.10.1858	–.4.1859	Edwin H. Kertland	'No 11a'; pt; road, mill sites; FN 1878	OTNR (SR 2332)
A2085		–.7.1860	CLD Andrew Russell AC	Pt: cons I–V free-grant lots along Hastings and Opeongo Junction Rd	OTAR
A2086	19.10.1860	27.9.1861	Edwin Henry Kertland	'W20'; roads; 20 ch; FN 1876	OTNR (SR 2330)
A2087		2.1.1862	CLD A. Russell AC	'234'; names, later changes	OTAR(P)

	Date of Instructions	Date of Map	Surveyor and Signature	Endorsements and Notes	Location
	WILBERFORCE				
A2088	11.4.1851	18.8.1851	A. Russell CLD	Pt: cons XII–XVIII; diagram for survey, roads, mills, notes on lines to be run; scale n.g.	OTAR
A2089		1851	J. Robertson PLS	Survey grid, marshes	OTAR (SR 2338)
A2090		–.–.1851 19.8.1852	[J.] Robertson Andrew Russell CLD	'235' 'No 46'; names	OTAR(P)
A2091		1852	John Robertson	'B34' 'In 1296/52' 'office copy'; marshes, later adds; FN 1880	OTNR (SR 2337)
	WILLIAMS, E and W				
A2092	–	24.5.1832 1835	John McDonald exam J.G. Chewett	'No 19' '1160'; pt W of Centre Rd; for Canada Co., contents; FN 720	OTNR (SR 2341)
A2093		24.5.1832 1838	John McDonald exam J.G. Chewett	'No 18' '1161'; pt E of Centre Rd; for Canada Co., contents; 40 ch; FN 719	OTNR (SR 2342)
A2094		[1832?]	[J. Mcdonald?]	Canada Co. stamp: ' 19.2.1947'; pt E of Centre Rd; contents, names; scale n.g.	OTAR (Canada Co. Atlas 20)
A2095		[1832?]	[J. Mcdonald?]	Canada Co. stamp: '19.2.1947; pt W of Centre Rd, contents, some names; scale n.g.	OTAR (Canada Co. Atlas 20)
	WILLIAMSBURGH				
A2096	–	1784–7	Lewis Kotte P. McNiff Wm. Chewett	'No 29' '996'; pt: cons 1–7; names, 'incomplete'	OTNR (SR 2343)
A2097		1784–7	Lewis Kotte P. McNiff Wm. Chewett	'No 26'; alterations to 23.11.1789, names, reserve for glebe and schoolmaster	OTAR (SR 2344)
A2098		2.2.1791	W. Chewett	'No 3A'; notes 1795 and 1836, names, later changes along river; scale n.g.	OTAR(P)
A2099		15.10.1792	Copy W. Chewett [sgd] S. Holland	'4' 'Quebec Plan'; names, notes 1793 and 1843, note: 'no 9th Con'	OTAR(P)
A2100		15.1.1795	W. Chewett	'No 18C' '1232'; notes on survey, marshes	OTNR (SR 2345)
A2101		1796	P. McNiff [sgd] W.C. Chewett	'5' '336' 'Rec'd from McNiff in 1796'; names added at various dates, other adds to 1836; scale n.g.	OTNR (SR 2346)

	WILLOUGHBY				
A2102	20.12.1793 27.5.1795	6.5.1795	D.W. Smith J. Small Thos Ridout	'A27' '341'; includes W Crowland; names; scale n.g.	OTNR (SR 2349)
A2103		[1795?]	–	'60' 'No 22'; names, later changes, note: 'East shore River Niagara sketched'; scale n.g.	OTAR(P)
A2104		24.9.1811	Copy W.C. exam Thos Ridout	'A28' '390'; names	OTNR (SR 2350)
A2105		[182?]	–	'1236'; survey grid outline	OTAR
A2106	13.1.1864	10.3.1864	J. Stoughton Dennis	'No 14' '4002/64'; pt; Navy Is, cleared areas, some bldgs, public right of way along shore; 5 ch	OTNR (SR 7141)
A2107		10.3.1864	J.S. Dennis	'4002/64'; Navy Is; survey grid, treed areas, public right of way, relief; 5 ch	OTAR
	WILMOT				
A2108	6.2.1824	-.-.1824	John Goessman	'B7' '586'; marshes, roads, survey in crown reserve portion, Wilmot; FN 721	OTNR (SR 2351)
A2109		1824 1828	John Goessman copy W.C.	'No 22' 'Crown and Clergy Reserves for the Co of Lincoln'; notes on estimate of acres for Canada Co., names along roads, marshes	OTAR(P)
A2110		[1824?]	J. Goessman	'1225' 'C8'; town plot, copy	OTAR
A2111		[1828]		'Copy of the Diagram for laying out the Crown reservations in ... Wilmot' for John Goessman; scale n.g.	OTAR
A2112	31.5.1828	6.10.1828	John Goessman	'No 23'; for Canada Co., crown reserve blocks not surveyed, names; scale n.g.; FN 722	OTNR (SR 2352)
A2113		[1828?]	Copy J.G. Chewett	'No 24' 'Office copy'; roads, majority of lots (and Kings College patented to Canada Co.), marshes, names	OTAR(P)
A2114		[1828?]	W.C. [copy?]	Unfinished	OTNR (SR 86767)
A2115		29.8.1845	A.R. CLD T. Bouthillier	Survey grid, roads, marshes, pinholes for tracing	OTAR
	WINCHESTER				
A2116	1.9.1793	10.4.1794	W. Chewett SS	'1234' 'W28' 'No 7C'; reserves, marshes, tree types	OTAR
A2117		18.4.1794	W. Chewett	'9'; c & c reserves, names, marshes, later notes 1843	OTAR(P)

	Date of Instructions	Date of Map	Surveyor and Signature	Endorsements and Notes	Location
A2118		[1796?]	John Stegmann	'No 10B' '583'; reserves; FN 3–343	OTNR (SR 2355)
A2119	22.8.1797	10.12.1798	Lewis Grant	'No 4B' '584'; pt; reserves, marshes; FN 291	OTNR (SR 2356)
A2120		4.1.1799	Lewis Grant	'No 4A' '338'; names, reserves	OTNR (SR 2354)
	WINDHAM				
A2121	18.8.1797	18.8.1797	Wm Hambly	'B13' '585'; reserves, marshes, meadows; FN 727	OTNR (SR 2357)
A2122		[180?]	Copy W.C.	'1226' 'C24'; marshes, trails	OTAR
A2123		[180?]	W.C.	'C23'; Indian trails, c & c reserves, names, later changes	OTAR(P)
A2124		[182?]	–	'No 40'; c & c reserves, trails, later changes 1820s, notes 1843; scale n.g.	OTAR(P)
A2125		–.7.1843	Thomas Parke SG	Survey grid, reserves; scale n.g.	OTAR
	WOLFE ISLAND				
A2126	–	[181?]	–	'1219'; outline only, Kingston	OTAR
A2127	10.5.1822	6.10.1822	J.G. Chewett	'No 43'; c & c reserves, names, patents data, later adds; scale n.g.; FN 425, 426	OTNR (SR 86768)
A2128		[1822?]	Copy J.G.C.	'C26' '1218'; outline, c & c reserves, later notes on survey	OTAR (SR 2359)
A2129		–.8.1843	Thomas Parke SG	Survey grid; reserves; scale n.g.	OTAR
	WOLFORD				
A2130	24.9.1795	[1795?]	John Stegmann	'No 24'; names, c & c reserves, many adds to 1845; scale n.g.; FN 2–145, 4–18, 4–23, 4–59	OTNR (SR 2361)
A2131		[182?]	Copy J.G.C.	'1224'; c & c reserves, marshes	OTAR (SR 2360)
A2132		–.8.1843	Thomas Parke SG	Survey grid, reserves; scale n.g.	OTAR
	WOLLASTON				
A2133	9.12.1856	[1857]	Quintin Johnstone	'No 3'; timber, type of land, mill sites; scale n.g.; FN 1882, 1906	OTNR (SR 2363)
A2134		15.7.1859	Andrew Russell AC CLD	'W32'; pt; subdivision along Hastings Rd lots and lots 1–5 cons I–XVI	OTAR

A2135		–.–.1860	Andrew Russell AC	Pt; Hastings Rd survey only, names	OTAR(P)
A2136	16.11.1863	30.7.1864	John A. Snow	'No 39'; mill sites, timber, terrain, photoreproduction; scale n.g.; FN 1883	OTNR (SR 2362)
A2137		29.4.1867	Henry Lawe A. Russell AC	Names, roads, some later changes	OTAR(P)
	WOODHOUSE				
A2138	15.7.1795 28.10.1796	[1796?]	–	'No 42'; c & c reserves, names, many adds, notes 1816, 1822, and 1836; scale n.g.; photoreproduction in OTNR (SR 2365)	OTAR(P)
A2139		[180?]	Copy W.C.	'1220' 'C26'; survey grid, notes on survey	OTAR
A2140		–.7.1843	Thomas Parke SG	Survey grid, reserves; scale n.g.	OTAR
A2141	7.9.1845	7.3.1846	Verified Thos W. Walsh exam A.R.	'1193'; boundary btwn Woodhouse and Walpole; 20 ch; FN 229	OTNR (SR 2366)
A2142		5.4.1851	C. Rankin, Zenas Fell Commissioners	'B43'; boundary btwn Woodhouse and Walpole	OTNR (SR 2367)
	WOOLWICH				
A2143	–	29.1.1808	A. Jones	'B10'; names	OTNR (SR 2368)
	WYLIE				
A2144	29.8.1863 17.10.1863	12.10.1863 10.11.1863 22.12.1863	W.J. MacDonald	Endorsed dates: '4.1.1864' '5.2.1864'; 6 progress diagrams for the survey of the twp; scale n.g.	OTAR
A2145		14.4.1864	W.J. Macdonald	'No 35'; relief, marshes, mill sites, settlers and clearings; FN 1887	OTNR (SR 2370)
	YARMOUTH				
A2146	11.7.1799	–.1.1800	A. Jones	'B15' '588'; marshes, timber, school reserves; FN 305	OTNR (SR 2373)
A2147		13.8.1802	[A. Jones?]	A few names along the front, later names located by T. Talbot to 1836	OTAR (Talbot BkC/5)
A2148	24.3.1809	[1809?]	[M. Burwell?]	Pt; Talbot Rd, names to 1816; FN 513	OTAR (Talbot BkC/6)
A2149		7.1.1814	Mahlon Burwell	Relief, marshes, names on the front and along Talbot Rd located by T. Talbot	OTAR (Talbot BkC/4)

	Date of Instructions	Date of Map	Surveyor and Signature	Endorsements and Notes	Location
A2150		[1814?]	–	'A13' '389'; cons 1–6; names, a few later changes; scale n.g.	OTAR(P)
A2151		[1814?]	–	'No 43'; names, c & c reserves	OTNR (SR 2374)
A2152		[1814?]	[M. Burwell?]	Includes Southwold Twp; N branch Talbot Rd, trails, names located by T. Talbot to 1818; scale n.g.	OTAR (Talbot BkC/7)
A2153	15.3.1819	10.12.1819	M. Burwell	'B14' '389' 'School twp'; pt N of Talbot Rd; town of St Thomas, c & c reserves; FN 728	OTNR (SR 2372)
A2154		10.12.1819	M. Burwell	School twp, c & c reserves, town of St Thomas	OTAR (Talbot BkC/11)
A2155		[1819?]	[M. Burwell?]	'No 44'; c & c reserves, school lands in N pt, names, notes 1819	OTAR(P)
A2156		11.9.1823	Thos Ridout SG	Pt from Edgware Rd N; c & c reserves, rest reserved for school lands, names of those located by T. Talbot	OTAR (Talbot BkD/5)
A2157		–.7.1843	Thomas Parke SG	Survey grid, reserves, Edgware Rd, Talbot Rd; scale n.g.	OTAR
	YONGE				
A2158	–	1787 [179?]	[Sgd] Samuel Holland copy W. Chewett	'A17'; includes Escott; names; scale n.g.	OTAR(P)
A2159		[179?]	–	'A16'; pt Yonge front and rear; names, note re direction con lines should run; scale n.g.	OTAR (SR 2384)
A2160		[179?]	–	'A21' '392' 'District Plan'; pt Yonge front and rear; District Plan, names, reserves; scale n.g.	OTAR (SR 2383)
A2161	25.7.1794	–.9.1794	Lewis Grant	'B11' '590'; pt: lots 7–8 con 1 and BF Yonge; marshes, mill sites; 10 ch	OTNR (SR 2378)
A2162		Autumn 1794	Lewis Grant	'A20'; pt Yonge front and rear; names, mill, road, burying ground, improvements	OTAR (SR 2379)
A2163		14.12.1794	Lewis Grant	'B10'; Yonge front and rear; a few names, mills, marshes, rivers, lakes, later adds; FN 302	OTNR (SR 2382)
A2164		14.12.1794 31.10.1795	Lewis Grant	'A18'; pt Yonge front and rear; names, roads, Jessup's mill, burying ground, copy; FN 729, 732	OTAR (SR 2381)
A2165		[1795?]	Copy W.C.	'C15' '1216'; pt Yonge front and rear; Jessup's mill, Toniata R, outline, burying ground	OTAR (SR 2377)

A2166		28.3.1795	W. Chewett	'A19'; c & c reserves, names; scale n.g.	OTAR(P)
A2167		[1795?]	–	'C17' '1217'; Yonge and Escott; conflicting survey lines, outline, discrepancy btwn 'Quebec Plan' and Grant's plan; scale n.g.	OTAR (SR 2376)
A2168	–	8.3.1820	T. Ridout	'No 27' '342' 'For the Land Board'; pt rear of Yonge and Escott; cons 8–10, town of Johnstown	OTAR (SR 2380)
A2169		8.3.1820	Thos. Ridout	'No 26' 'For the Land Board'; pt Escott and rear of Yonge and Escott; some names, vacant land	OTAR (SR 2375)
A2170		–.8.[1843]	Thomas Parke SG	Includes Escott; survey grid, reserves; scale n.g.	OTAR
	YORK				
A2171	22.2.1791	[1791]	[A. Jones]	'Y30' '847' 'Township of Dublin'; front line only, shoreline, marsh; scale n.g.; FN 835	OTNR (SR 2391)
A2172		[1791]	A. Jones copy W.C.	'No 14' '848' 'Plan of the front line of Dublin (now York)'; lots 1–35, soundings in harbour; scale n.g.	OTAR (SR 2389)
A2173		[1791]	A. Jones	'Y30'; front line only 'Township of Dublin,' 'Toronto Fort'; copy; scale n.g.	OTAR
A2174	26.6.1793	[1793?]	[A. Aitken] W.C.	'A34' 'Copied from Aitken plan'; names, town plot, Castle Frank 'old fort'; 20 ch; FN 298, 366	OTNR (SR 2388)
A2175	29.10.1796	[1797?]	–	'A33' 'office plan'; names, later changes, c & c reserves; scale n.g.	OTNR (SR 10903)
A2176		[1797?]	[W.C.?]	'A3?' '32?'; names, notes 1798, 1799, 1800, 1812, and 1815	OTAR(P)
A2177		[180?]	John Stegmann copy W.C.	'A86'; lots 15–16 BF; transcript copy made in 1935; scale n.g.	OTAR (SR 2386)
A2178		–.7.1843	Thomas Parke SG	Survey grid, reserves; scale n.g.	OTAR
A2179	–	11.10.1867	F.F. Passmore	Peninsula in front of lots 5–7, first con from Bay for Mr Samuel Hill; 4 ch	OTNR (SR 2390)
	ZONE				
A2180		17.2.1821	T. Ridout SG	Diagram for survey, c & c reserves, notes on lines already surveyed; scale n.g.	OTAR
A2181	27.2.1821	4.2.1823	M. Burwell	'No 35'; includes W Euphemia; names, notes to 1851, notes on patents; scale n.g.; FN 741	OTNR (SR 2398)
A2182		4.2.1823	M. Burwell	'1215' 'C23'; c & c reserves, marshes, Indian village, Moravian village, copy; scale n.g.	OTAR

	Date of Instructions	Date of Map	Surveyor and Signature	Endorsements and Notes	Location
A2183		[1823?]	M. Burwell	Note 27.12.1820 to reserve all lots under 100 acres, c & c reserves and lots located by T. Talbot in N pt, names to 1840, copy	OTAR (Talbot BkE/12)
A2184		18.6.1830	M. Burwell	'Q20' '1098'; W Orford; old Indian village, site of battle (War of 1812), c & c reserves, boundary of reserve for Moravian Indian village	OTNR (SR 2395)
A2185	2.11.1837	22.10.1838	M. Burwell A. McIntosh copy J.G. Chewitt	Lots 1–14, cons I–XI; Moravian Tract, 26,005 acre Indian reserve, villages, notes; scale n.g.; FN 10–655	OTAR
A2186		23.7.1843	M. Burwell Thomas Parke SG	'No 35' '1214' 'Office copy'; plank rd as boundary, salt spring, oil spring	OTAR (SR 2397)
A2187		–.7.1843	Thomas Parke SG	Survey grid, reserves; scale n.g.	OTAR
A2188	23.7.1845	17.9.1845	B. Springer	'B24' '591'; Indian reserve and crown land, also plan of gore; 20 ch; FN 737, 738, 740	OTNR (SR 2396)
	ZORRA				
A2189	29.9.1819	11.5.1820	Shubel Park	'1516'; c & c reserves, marshes; FN 296	OTNR (SR 2399)
A2190		11.5.1820	–	'A14'; c & c reserves, marshes, names	OTAR(P)
A2191		[1820?]	S. Park copy J.G.C. T. Ridout SG	'No 45' 'Office plan'; names, later changes, notes 1843	OTAR(P)
A2192		[1820?]	–	C & c reserves, marshes; scale n.g.	OTNR (SR 5995)
A2193		–.7.1843	Thomas Parke SG	Survey grid, reserves; scale n.g.	OTAR

Appendix B

Registered Subdivision Plans

	Date of Survey	Date of Regist.	Surveyor	Owner	Description and Notes	Location
	ABERFOYLE					
B1	22.1.58	18.7.60	Francis Kerr	Estate of G. Schatz	Pt NE1/2 lot 22, 7th con, twp Puslinch; lots on both sides Dundas St, bldgs identified; transcript; 2 ch	Wellington 61 R.P.119
	(ABOYNE)					
B2	17.8.55	29.12.56	E.H. Kertland	Messrs Allan & Geddes	For description see **1101**	Wellington 21 R.P.88
	ACTON					
B3	15.8.56	–	Winter & Howitt	Wilbur F. Adams	Queen St to Bower St, rail station to Main St; 2 ch	Halton 20 no R.P.#
B4	4.5.57	26.5.57	Winter & Livingston	James Dickson	'James Dickson's Survey,' G.T.R. west to Scene St, north of Main St; 3/4 ch	Halton 20 R.P.25
B5	3.10.57	17.10.57	Henry Winter	Jas Young	Queen St to Mill St, G.T.R. to Wellington St and beyond; 1 ch	Halton 20 R.P.28
B6	8.4.58	27.1.59	Winter & Abrey	Adams Family	Lots east to Guelph St and Queen St north to East Bower St, owners, mill ponds; 2 ch	Halton 20 R.P.31
B7	25.2.61	29.12.65	Henry Winter	Municipal Council Esquesing Twp	Compiled plan; G.T.R. and station, lots on both sides Main St to Havelock St and btwn Queen and East Bower sts; 3 ch	Halton 20 R.P.31 Acton
	ADELAIDE TWP					
B8	–.5.55	13.9.55	Beattie & Bay	John McRoberts & James Cousins	Lots 9 and 10, 1st con N.E.R., twp Adelaide; Egremont Rd north to Victoria St, Mount Cashell St to Adelaide St; 3 ch	Middlesex 33 R.P.86
B9	29.9.65	30.9.65	Wm McMillan	David Glass	North pts lots 9 and 10, 1st con N.E.R., twp Adelaide; 3 ch	Middlesex 33 R.P.205
	AILSA CRAIG					
B10	30.8.60	25.4.61	H. Carew Boulton	David Craig	SW pt lot 25, 5th con, twp McGillivray; east of Centre Rd, G.T.R. and Craigs Station to rd allowance btwn McGillivray and Williams; 100 ft	Middlesex 33 R.P.183
B11	–	27.12.61	Henry C. Boulton	William G. Shipley	Lots along town line McGillivray and Williams; 100 ft	Middlesex 33 R.P.170

B12	30.6.62	8.7.62	H. Carew Boulton	William G. Shipley	Lots along town line McGillivray/ Williams, east of side-rd btwn lots 25 and 26; 100 ft	Middlesex 33 R.P.174
B13	–	30.5.65	B. Springer	William G. Shipley	Lots along town line and George St, west of side-rd btwn lots 25 and 26; 100 ft	Middlesex 33 R.P.204 Co
	ALEXANDRIA					
B14	30.[12?].52	17.8.57	Duncan McDonnell, John McNaughton	Donald Alexander MacDonald	Areas south of Garry R and Military Rd N, Kenyon St, Ottawa St and Mile Plot, surveyed by J. McNaughton 1829; bldgs, bridge; 2 ch	Glengarry 14 R.P.1
B15	13.9.58	4.5.59	John McNaughton	Episcopal Corp. Diocese Kingston & Separate School Board no 10	'Johnstown,' north pt lot 37, 1st con, twp Lochiel east of Military Rd; public hwy north to Victoria St, 'St James Square'; 1.75 ch	Glengarry 14 R.P.2
	(ALGIERS town plot)					
B16	–.5.56	4.2.57	John Denison	John N. Ancil, John Rose, Christopher Blattner	S1/2 lot 22, west Con Lake Rd, S1/2 lot 22, east Con and north pt lot 23, east Con Lake Rd, twp Stanley; 2 ch	Huron 22 R.P.142
	ALLENFORD					
B17	22.10.67	24.6.68	C. Rankin, A. Sproat	Messrs Jas Allen & Cooper	Lots 10 and 11, con A, twp Amabel; Sauble R to Alice St, Albert St to Elizabeth St; 132 ft	Bruce 3 R.P.53
	ALLISTON					
B18	–	19.8.58	Henry Creswicke	George Fletcher	Victoria St to Albert St, west of Alma St; 3 ch	Simcoe 51 R.P.65
B19	13.6.67	5.7.67	Edmund Seager	Charles Cowen	Lot 1, XV con, twp Tecumseth; King St to Paris St, Wellington St to Victoria St, owners; 1.75 ch	Simcoe 51 R.P.122
	(ALMA) (Huron Co)					
B20	6.5.56	24.1.57	Kertland & Gilkison	E. Dinsley	Pt lot 6, Huron Rd, con I, twp Hullett; Clinton St to Byers St, Edward St to Morris St; 2 ch	Huron 22 R.P.140

	Date of Survey	Date of Regist.	Surveyor	Owner	Description and Notes	Location
	ALMA (Wellington Co)					
B21	23.1.61	16.3.61	Joseph Wm Burke	Alexander McCrea, Thomas Graham & James Graham	Pt lot I, con I, twp Pilkington and lot 22, con 14, twp Peel; Hannah St to Simpson St, Raglan St, Church and Pelliser sts, bldgs, drawings of 3 churches; 2 ch	Wellington 61 R.P.134
	ALMONTE					
B22	31.7.49	[26.1.50?]	James Richey	Edward Mitcheson	'Victoria,' NE1/2 lot 15, 9th con, twp Ramsay; Queen St to Proving Line and Mill St, Mississippi R; 1.5 ch	Lanark 26 R.P.Almonte 1
B23	–.5.50	[4.6.50?]	Joseph M.O. Cromwell	Daniel Shipman	'Ramsayville,' pt NE1/2 lot 15, 9th con, twp Ramsay; Bridge and Mill sts, bldgs, owners; 2 ch	Lanark 26 R.P.Almonte 'Ramsayville'
B24	–.6.54	3.8.54	Joseph M.O. Cromwell	Edward Mitcheson	'Waterford,' pt NE1/2s lots 15 and 16, 9th con, twp Ramsay; Main, Prince's, and Union sts, bldgs identified, mills and bridges; 1 ch	Lanark 26 R.P.162
B25	–.9.59	5.12.59	Joseph M.O. Cromwell	Estate of Matthew Anderson	Pt NE1/2s lots 14 and 15, 9th con, twp Ramsay; James St to Bridge St, B & O Ry to County St, owners; 2 ch	Lanark 26 R.P.Almonte 182
B26	14.5.60	12.9.60	Joseph M.O. Cromwell	Estate of Matthew Anderson	Lots on Brougham, Clyde, and Martin sts by river, bridge; 2 ch	Lanark 26 R.P.Almonte 109
B27	–.10.60	11.2.61	Joseph M.O. Cromwell	William Riddell	Bridge St to Albert St and along Water St, owners, station-house; 1 ch	Lanark 26 R.P.Almonte 140
B28	–	5.4.61	Josias Richey	Estate of R.S. Henderson	Lots Ottawa St to Adelaide St, Martin St to Florence St, some lots on Bridge St btwn Maitland St, station ground and Clyde St; bldgs; 2.5 ch	Lanark 26 R.P.Almonte 167
B29	–	14.5.61	Josias Richey	Smith Coleman	Mill St and all streets on island, bldgs identified, detailed plan; 1 ch	Lanark 26 R.P.Almonte 189
B30	–.7.61	16.8.61	Josias Richey	John Baird	Bridge St to Charles St, Colbourne St to Mill St; 1 ch	Lanark 26 R.P.Almonte 216

B31	10.4.63	29.4.63	George F. Austin	J. James & Jane McLean	Park lots 1–6, Block A and lot 3 Block C, pt of SW1/2 lot 16, 10th con, twp Ramsay; Albert St to Ottawa St, Florence St to rd allowance beyond James St, some owners; 1 ch	Lanark 26 R.P.Almonte 251
B32	–	23.6.65	W.J. Macdonald	Thomas Tennant	Pt lot 15, 9th con, twp Ramsay; Wesley and Water sts and along B & O Ry Co. property, North Lanark Agricultural Society showgrounds; 66 ft	Lanark 26 R.P.Almonte 30
B33	–	22.8.65	W.J. Macdonald	George Patterson	Pt lot 15, 10th con, twp Ramsay; Paterson and George sts, south of Ottawa St; 66 ft	Lanark 26 R.P. Almonte 41
B34	16.1.67	18.4.67	Andrew Bell	B. & W. Rosamond & Co.	'Coleman's Island,' pt E1/2 lot 16, 9th con, twp Ramsay; streets, bldgs, owners; 80 ft	Lanark 26 R.P.208
B35	–.7.67	16.9.67	Joseph M.O. Cromwell	James H. Wylie	Pts NE 1/2s lots 15 and 16 on Main St north of Mississippi R, 9th con, twp Ramsay; ry bridge, grist mill; 1 ch	Lanark 26 R.P. Almonte 294
	ALTON					
B36	–.11.57	30.1.58	Charles J. Wheelock	John Morris et al.	For description see **1109**	Peel 43 R.P.Cal-5
	ALTONA					
B37	–.11.55	10.10.57	George McPhillips	David Reesor	Lot 1, 2nd con, twp Uxbridge; Main St, 2nd con, Line and Front sts, inn and school; 2 ch	Durham 40 R.P.H-50062
	AMELIASBURG					
B38	24.4.51	–	John O. Conger	Owen Roblin	'Roblin's Mills,' lot 81, 3rd con, twp Ameliasburgh; streets unnamed; 1 ch	Prince Edward 47 R.P.Amelias-burgh 1
B39	–.10.66	22.8.69	D. Williams	Municipal Council of Ameliasburgh	'Roblin's Mills,' lots 81 and 82, 3rd con, twp Ameliasburgh; Roblins Lake to pond, Main and Coleman sts, Hector to Tailor St, Valley St, mills; 2 ch	Prince Edward 47 R.P. 'Roblins Mills' 1
	AMHERSTBURG					
B40	–	10.2.51	A.P. Salter	Thomas Park	Lots east of Dalhousie to King St on both sides Park St; transcript; 60 ft	Essex 12 R.P.3

	Date of Survey	Date of Regist.	Surveyor	Owner	Description and Notes	Location
B41	27.8.53	26.11.59	John A. Wilkinson	John Bell	Pt lot 2, 1st con, twp Malden; Perry, Brock and Simcoe sts; transcript; 0.5 ch	Essex 12 R.P.157
B42	6.11.66	21.12.66	Samuel Brodie	Arthur Rankin	Dalhousie St, Sandwich Rd, North St to Richmond St, asylum reserve; transcript; 1 ch	Essex 12 R.P.2
	AMHERST ISLAND					
B43	27.3.67	13.8.67	William Perceval	Robert Perceval Maxwell	Shows streets and lots; 20 ch	Lennox 29 R.P.62
	(AMSTERDAM)					
B44	–	[55?]	George Lount	Thompson Smith	Amsterdam and annexed village of Manheim; certified by Crown Lands Dept Nov 1846 with addition of ry; 2 ch	York 65 R.P.'Manheim'
	ANCASTER					
B45	–.6.67	[19.6.67?]	David Chas O'Keeffe	Eyre Thuresson	Pt lot 46, 2nd con, twp Ancaster; Ontario St to Picton St; 66 ft	Wentworth 62 R.P.326 (old 53)
	ANCASTER TWP					
B46	29.6.42	–	Thos Allen Blyth	William Allan	Lots 7th con bounded by Glanford and Indian lands; 20 ch	Wentworth 62 R.P.351 (old 20)
	ANDREWSVILLE					
B47	–.9.60	23.1.62	John Burchill	Messrs R. & S. Andrews	Lot 2, con A, twp Montague; Water St on Rideau R to William St, Main St to Harriet St; 80 ft	Lanark 27 R.P.380
	ANGUS					
B48	–	24.4.57	Henry Creswicke	J.B. Curtis	Lot 30, 3rd con, and lot 29, 2nd con, twp Essa; from O S & H Railroad south along Curtis St to Mill St; 3 ch	Simcoe 51 R.P.57
	(ANNAN)					
B49	18.10.56	18.10.56	Molesworth & Weatherald	Herbert Dixon	For description see **1139**	Huron 22 R.P.143

	APPIN					
B50	22.1.56	3.3.56	John O'Mara	Hugh Rankin	'Ekfrid-Centre,' pt N1/2 lot 13, 1st con, twp Ekfrid; lots on Queen, Stewart, Broad, Thames and Elgin sts; photoreproduction; 200 ft	Middlesex 34 R.P.103
B51	-.-.56	10.1.57	B. Springer	Lachlin McTaggart	'Ekfrid-Centre,' west angle lot 12 S1/2, 1st con, twp Ekfrid; Ekfrid St to South St, Thames St to Argyle St; photoreproduction; 1 ch	Middlesex 34 R.P.130
B52	8.4.57	30.10.58	B. Springer	Duncan Dewar	'Argyle,' NW pt lot 12, 1st con, twp Ekfrid; Waterloo St to G.W.R., Wellington St to Thames St, bldgs identified; plan later cancelled; photoreproduction; 80 ft	Middlesex 34 R.P.154
B53	-.5.61	23.7.61	B. Springer	Dugald S. Mackellar	N1/2 lot 12, 1st con, twp Ekfrid; Dugald St to Thames St, Waterloo St to Front Ave; photoreproduction; 2 ch	Middlesex 34 R.P.168
	APPLETON					
B54	-.10.67	26.3.68	Joseph M.O. Cromwell	William Wilson	SW1/2 lot 3, south side Mississippi R, 10th con, twp Ramsay; Wilson St fronting SW branch of river btwn Princess and William sts; 1 ch	Lanark 26 R.P.Appleton 288
	ARDEN					
B55	10.11.64	14.8.68	M.B. Rombough	M.B. Rombough	'Clarendon,' lot 14, 9th con, twp Kennebec; Ann to John St, con rd to King St, bldgs; 2 ch	Frontenac 13 R.P.45
B56	5.4.65	14.8.68	M.B. Rombough	–	Lot 14, 8th con, twp Kenebec; streets named; 2 ch	Frontenac 13 R.P.46(2)
	ARKONA					
B57	7.10.54	[7.10.54?]	B. Springer	John Smith	'Bosanquet,' south angle lot 6 in South Boundary con, twp Bosanquet; King St to Wellington St, Waterloo St to North St; transcript; 2 ch	Lambton 25 R.P.1 Arkona
B58	25.8.55	[25.8.55?]	B. Springer	Neal Eastman & Jonathan Smith	'Bosanquet,' south end lot 5, South Boundary con, twp Bosanquet; Union St to King St, Smith St to Ann St; 1 ch	Lambton 25 R.P.2 Arkona

	Date of Survey	Date of Regist.	Surveyor	Owner	Description and Notes	Location
B59	29.4.56	1.7.56	B. Springer	C. Crawford	'Bosanquet,' SW pt lot 5, South Boundary con, twp Bosanquet; King St to Union St, North St to Centre St; 1 ch	Lambton 25 R.P.3 Arkona
B60	–	3.4.58	P.V. Elmore	Utter, Eastman, et al.	Lots 4–7 including South Boundary Bosanquet; plan missing	Lambton 25 R.P.4 Arkona
B61	–.–.63	15.8.65	Alexander Davidson	Neal Eastman	Lot 5, South Boundary Bosanquet; King St to Water St, Smith St to Ann St; 1.5 ch	Lambton 25 R.P.5 Arkona
	ARNPRIOR					
B62	17.6.54	14.12.54	John A. Snow	Daniel McLachlin	Elgin to Ottawa St, Harrington to Albert St; mill, timber slides, etc; 264 ft	Renfrew 49 R.P.7
B63	26.4.58	3.5.58	W.J. Mcdonald	Estate Hugh McGonigal	Lot 4, 13th con, twp McNab; 13/14 con line to Mahan St; Petre to Patrick St; B & O Ry; 2 ch	Renfrew 49 R.P.12
B64	–	14.11.65	W.J. Mcdonald	McGonigal Estate	E1/2 lot 4, con 3, twp McNab; McGonigal St to beyond B & O Ry, Patrick St to Flat Rapid Rd; 2 ch	Renfrew 49 R.P.19
	ARTHUR					
B65	4.7.57	7.7.57	W. & A. Boultbee	Timothy Carroll	1 ch	Wellington 60 R.P.83
B66	17.12.57	17.12.57	William Boultbee	Andrew Mitchell	South of Frances St around Conestoga R, mill pond, mill, reserve; see also **1144**; transcript; 2 ch	Wellington 60 no R.P.#
	ARVA					
B67	[6.1.50?]	4.7.55	Wm McMillan	Edward & Catherine Mathews	'Village of St John's,' S1/2 pt lot 16, 7th con, twp London; north of Church St, Main St to Elgin St; 1 ch	Middlesex 33 R.P.85 Co
	ASHGROVE					
B68	1.10.64	–	G. Brockitt Abrey	Prepared for Township of Esquesing	At corner lots 10 and 11, con VIII, twp Esquesing; 2 ch	Halton 20 no R.P.#

	ATHENS					
B69	–.8.53	[14.9.53?]	Henry Lillie	–	West pt and 'Farmersville' (Athens), lots 13 and 14, 7th and 8th cons, twp Yonge; travelled roads, bldgs; 24 ch	Leeds 28 R.P.106
B70	8.12.60?	20.12.60	Walter Beatty	Prepared for Council Rear of Yonge & Escott	Village of 'Farmersville,' lots 13 and 14, VIII and IX cons, twp Yonge; Church St to Prince St, George St to Henry St; 2 ch	Leeds 28 R.P.115
	AURORA					
B71	9.3.43	9.5.67	Robert Ford Lynn	W.B. Jarvis Estate	Front pt lot 80, 1st con, twp King; west of Yonge St, mill pond and race; 4 ch	York 65 R.P.9
B72	28.5.53	20.1.55	Robert F. Lynn	Richard Matchell	'Village of Match-ville,' pt lot 81 1st con, Whitchurch; east side Yonge St to Toronto & Huron Railroad, lots on both sides Centre St; 200 links	York 65 R.P.107
B73	–.6.53	11.8.53	George McPhillips	John Mosley	Formerly 'Machell's Corners,' lot 80, 1st con Whitchurch; east of Yonge St, to Ross St, Metcalf St to Wellington St, bldgs identified; 2 ch	York 65 R.P.68
B74	–.9.53	11.8.53	George McPhillips	Walter McKenzie	Formerly Machell's Corners, lot 80, 1st con Whitchurch; east of Ross St, resubdivision of pt of **B73**; 2 ch	York 65 R.P.80
B75	–.4.54	21.10.54	George McPhillips	J.S. Shortt & Eliza McNally	Lot 80, 1st con King; major roads, type of trees, relief, mills and mill sites; 2 ch	York 65 R.P.102
B76	–.11.56	12.8.57	George McPhillips	John Mosley	Lot 80, 1st con Whitchurch; Wellington St to Thomas St, Ross St to Seat St; 2 ch	York 65 R.P.212
B77	–	29.1.58	Dennis & Gossage	James & Lackie	Pt lot 81, 1st con east of Yonge St, twp Whitchurch; both sides Centre St; 2 ch	York 65 R.P.231
B78	12.2.63	14.2.63	Hallen & Wilson	J.T. Gurnett	Pt lot 79, 1st con, twp Whitchurch; east of Yonge St to Gurnett and Victoria sts; stream, relief, tannery, residence, stables; 60 links	York 65 Plan 1B
B79	19.5.63	4.7.63	Hallen & Wilson	Wm Mosley	Pt lot 80, 1st con, twp King; west of Yonge St to Mill St, Wellington St to Tyler St, several bldgs identified; 1 ch	York 65 R.P.2
B80	1.8.65	1.8.65	Hallen & Wilson	Chas Doan	Pt lot 81, east of Yonge St, 1st con, twp Whitchurch; Wellington St to Maple St, Yonge St to Spruce St; 1 ch	York 65 R.P.5

	Date of Survey	Date of Regist.	Surveyor	Owner	Description and Notes	Location
B81	–.5.67	3.11.69	George McPhillips	John Mosley	Lot 80, 1st con, twp Whitchurch; Wellington to Thomas St east of Ross St; 4 ch	York 65 R.P.17
	AYLMER					
B82	24.11.54	27.3.55	Jesse P. Ball	[Mr Van Patten?]	North pts lots 83, 84, and 85 south of Talbot Rd E and south pts lots 83, 84, and 85 north of Talbot Rd E, twp Malahide; Wellington St to Victoria St, South St to North St and Cat Fish Creek; 2 ch	Elgin 11 no R.P.#
	AYR					
B83	[1852?]	–	James Black	James Black	McDonald Block, twp N Dumfries; Gibson St to Hall St, east of Northumberland St, Wm McDonald's original boundary; 1 ch	Waterloo 67 R.P.553
B84	23.4.52	24.11.53	James Black	John Hall	'Village of Jedburgh,' twp N Dumfries; Smiths Creek, Ayr mill pond, and Stanley St in Ayr to Main and Hall sts in Jedburgh, several bldgs identified; 2 ch	Waterloo 67 R.P.555
B85	–.5.53	4.9.55	James Black	William Bruce	Bruce lots S1/2 lot 36, 8th con, twp N Dumfries; lots btwn branches of Smiths Creek, lots along road to Blenheim; 2 ch	Waterloo 67 R.P.554
	BADEN					
B86	–.–.55	[5.56?]	M.C. Schofield	Jacob Beck	G.T.R. line and station, mill pond, streets, bldgs; 2 ch	Waterloo 58 R.P.627
	(BALAKLAVA)					
B87	8.3.60	14.5.60	E.H. Kertland	John Shennan	For description see **1149**	Bruce 3 R.P.29
	BALDERSON					
B88	–.11.64	30.12.65	John Morris	Clark & Bothwell	'Village of Clarkville,' W1/2 lot 1, 7th con, twp Drummond; boundary btwn Drummond and Bathurst twps to Bothwell St, 8th con line to Clark St; 1 ch	Lanark 27 R.P.125

	(BALENTRA)					
B89	26.7.51	12.2.52	Wm R. Rombough	John & Robert Grange	East front lot 4, 6th con, twp Sheffield; Salmon R to William St, John St to Mill St close to Tamworth; 2 ch	Lennox 29 R.P.32
B90	–	6.4.61	Wm R. Rombough	James C. Bell	Pt west front lot 4, 7th con, twp Sheffield; east to Ottawa Rd, John St to Mill St; 1 ch	Lennox 29 R.P.31
	BALLINAFAD					
B91	21.7.60	26.9.60	Winter & Abrey	John Appelbe	$SW_{1/2}$ lot 1, 8th con, twp Erin; transcript; 1 ch	Wellington 61 R.P.129
B92	25.2.61	29.12.65	Henry Winter, Winter & Abrey	Prepared for Twp of Esquesing	Compiled plan; 1 ch	Halton 20 no R.P.#
	(BANNOCKBURN)					
B93	25.3.56	3.4.56	Charles L. Davies	John Wanless	Lot 24 north of Bayfield Rd on south branch Bayfield R, twp Stanley; bldgs identified; 3 ch	Huron 22 R.P.Stanley 3
	BARRIE					
B94	9.4.51	3.1.53	Hugh P. Savigny	John Bingham	Pt lot 22, 4th con, twp Vespra; lots east of mill pond on both sides John St; 2 ch	Simcoe 51 R.P.13
B95	–.–.52	7.7.53	Wm Gibbard	W.C. Ross	Lot 23, 5th con, twp Vespra; btwn Anne and Bayfield sts from Donald St to Ridout and Strathy [sts?]; 3 ch	Simcoe 51 R.P.17
B96	23.2.53	8.7.53	Wm Gibbard	Charles [B?]	Louisa St to Ann Eliza St, Berczy St to Harriet and Melanie sts; 2 ch	Simcoe 51 R.P.18
B97	22.4.53	3.9.53	Robert Ross	Charles Thompson	Broken lot 26, 5th con, and broken lot 26, 6th con, twp Vespra; gore from Tiffin St bounded on east by Bradford St; 4 ch	Simcoe 51 R.P.15
B98	25.7.53	25.7.53	Hugh P. Savigny	James Patton	$W_{1/2}$ lot 21, 4th con, twp Vespra; area east of mill pond; 2 ch	Simcoe 51 R.P.19
B99	–.–.53	29.3.54	Hugh P. Savigny	John Ross	Pt lot 25, 5th con, twp Vespra; bay to Sanford St, river to Rose (later Brock) St; 2 ch	Simcoe 51 R.P.22
B100	–.–.53	19.2.55	Hugh P. Savigny	Wm Baldwin	'Baldwin's Allendale,' $N_{1/2}$ lot 8, 14th con, twp Innisfil; both sides of ry line, bounded by Baldwin and Tiffin sts, freight station, Cumberland St and Essa Rd; 4 ch	Simcoe 51 R.P.29

	Date of Survey	Date of Regist.	Surveyor	Owner	Description and Notes	Location
B101	–.–.53	27.6.56	Hugh P. Savigny	Thos Milburn	'Allendale,' N1/2 lot 9, 14th con, twp Innisfil; ry station and reserve, east of Reed St, Fleming St to bay; 2 ch	Simcoe 51 R.P.40
B102	23.1.54	20.2.55	Robert Ross	Jacob Jacobs	N1/2 lot 7, 14th con, twp Innisfil; 'Jacob's Allendale' west of Baldwin St to Centre and Main sts, north to Tiffin St; 4 ch	Simcoe 51 R.P.30
B103	1.8.54	4.8.54	Robert Ross	S.M. Sanford	North pt lot 26, 5th con, twp Vespra; SE of Ross (later Brock) St; 4 ch	Simcoe 51 R.P.25
B104	23.11.54	–	Wm Gibbard	Jas Patton & Henry Hatton Gowan	W1/2 lots 23 and 24, 4th con, twp Vespra; east of Bayfield St, north of Worsley and James sts; photoreproduction; 2.5 ch	Simcoe 51 R.P.31
B105	–.–.54	[54?]	–	Perry Estate	Donald St to beyond Perry St, Anne St to Cole St; 2 ch	Simcoe 51 R.P.27
B106	–	4.11.56	Henry Creswicke	James Patton	West pt lot 22, 3rd con, twp Vespra; area beyond Duckworth St, Hayter's House; 3 ch	Simcoe 51 R.P.50
B107	1.8.57	–	W. Sanders	T. Demmery	At Barrie Station, twp Innisfil; area from ry to Essa Rd on Kempenfelt Bay; 80 ft	Simcoe 51 R.P.5a
B108	19.11.58	–.1.60	Henry Creswicke	Hon James Patton	Area at Market Sq, Penetang, Berczy, Mulcaster and Peel sts; 1 ch	Simcoe 51 R.P.78
B109	3.1.62	4.1.62	Henry Creswicke	Hon James Patton	Resubdivision of lot 9 north of Dunlop St; 66 ft	Simcoe 51 R.P.85
B110	5.9.63	7.9.63	Henry Creswicke	Henry Bammel, Alvis Boys	NE pt W1/2 lot 23, 4th con, Vespra; Wellington St at Owen St, Farm Block A; 2 ch	Simcoe 51 R.P.94
B111	–.–.66	28.7.66	W. Sanders	William Roe	'Roe's Block,' SE1/4 lot 23, 4th con, twp Vespra; lots on Penetanguishene Rd, Anne Eliza (later James) St, Melinda St, landowners; 3 ch	Simcoe 51 R.P.108
B112	–.6.66	30.10.66	W. Sanders	Prepared for Town of Barrie	Pt 'Betridge Estate'; Water St to Dunlop St, Duckworth St to Sampson St, relief, bldgs identified; 1 ch	Simcoe 51 R.P.113

B113	–.6.66	30.10.66	W. Sanders	Prepared for Town of Barrie	'Bingham Block,' W1/2 lot 22, 4th con, twp Vespra; 4th and 5th con line to beyond Berczy St, Collier St to Rose St; 3 ch	Simcoe 51 R.P.114
B114	–.6.66	–	W. Sanders	Prepared for Town of Barrie	'Edgar Block,' east pt lot 24, 5th con, twp Vespra; btwn Ross St and Bay and from Owen St to Bradford St, bldgs identified; 2 ch	Simcoe 51 R.P.115
B115	17.5.67	27.6.67	Henry Creswicke	Dalton McCarthy the Younger & Archibald C. Thomson	E1/2 lot 23, 5th con, twp Vespra, alteration of **B95** (1852); Bayfield St to Ecole's St at Rose St; 4 ch	Simcoe 51 R.P.121
B116	–.–.67	12.12.67	Henry Creswicke	Sarah Trooman	Area around James, Mulcaster, Peel, and Penetanguishene sts; 1 ch	Simcoe 51 R.P.124
	BARTON TWP					
B117	–.–.55	25.3.59	Thomas A. Blyth	David Hess	Pt lot 14, 6th con, twp Barton; east of Hamilton and Port Dover Rd, south of Hess St to 7th Con Rd; 3 ch	Wentworth 62 R.P.292 (old 25)
B118	10.10.67	5.2.68	Thomas A. Blyth	William Cook Estate	Pt lots 1 and 2, 7th and 8th cons, twp Barton; irregular lots; 4 ch	Wentworth 62 R.P.294 (old 58)
	BATTERSEA					
B119	19.11.52	26.8.59	A.B. Perry	Henry Van Luven	'Rockville,' lots 10 and 11, 9th con, twp Storrington; Main and Wellington sts at Cross and Factory sts; 4 mills; bridge; 2 ch	Frontenac 13 R.P.27
B120	20.8.62	13.9.62	S.O. McGuin	Henry Van Luven	Lots 10 and 11, 9th con, twp Storrington (formerly Pittsburg?/Loughborough); bldgs identified; scale n.g.	Frontenac 13 R.P.34
	BAYFIELD					
B121	4.9.35	–	J. McDonald	Baron de Tuyll	Town and estate of Bayfield, twps Goderich and Stanley; transcript copied 2.12.41; 5 ch	Huron 22 R.P.144
B122	10.4.56	18.4.56	John Denison	Neel MacTavish	'St Andrews Bayfield'; River St to Argyle St, Bayfield Rd to rd allowance btwn ranges C and D; 3 ch	Huron 22 R.P.299

	Date of Survey	Date of Regist.	Surveyor	Owner	Description and Notes	Location
B123	22.9.56	23.9.56	Molesworth & Weatherald	John Hamilton J.P.	For description see **1162**	Huron 22 R.P.145
B124	–	17.12.56	Molesworth & Weatherald	Messrs Stark & Hamilton	For description see **1164**	Huron 22 R.P.146
B125	–	13.5.57	Molesworth & Weatherald	Joshua Calloway	West pt lot 4, Bayfield con, twp Goderich; note on auction sale, mills, streets in north end, see also **1161**; 4 ch	Huron 22 R.P.541
B126	–	14.3.60	Molesworth & Weatherald	Prepared for Town of Bayfield	Cameron St to Bayfield R, L Huron to Sarnia St, Clangregor Sq; 4 ch	Huron 22 R.P.147
B127	20.12.61	21.12.61	John Denison	Charlotte Henrietta de Tuyll	New roads, ranges A, B, D, and E, twp Stanley; south of river, Bayfield R to Bayfield Rd, Main St to East; 6 ch	Huron 22 R.P.148
B128	12.4.64	13.4.64	John Denison	Dr Woods	Cameron St to Euphemia and Main sts; 2 ch	Huron 22 R.P.149
	BAYHAM					
B129	11.10.59	14.10.59	Jesse P. Ball	Nicholas Spore, Caleb Cook, Harlinde Orton	'Richmond,' north pts lots 110 and 111 south of Talbot Rd E, and south pts lots 111 and 112 north of Talbot Rd E, twp Bayham; bldgs, reserves, owners; 2 ch	Elgin 11 R.P.22
	BEACHBURG					
B130	–	21.9.54	J.S. Brown	Abel & David Beach	Pt lot 9, 5th con, twp Westmeath; bldgs by Bytown and Pembroke Rd are identified; 2 ch	Renfrew 49 R.P.6
	BEACHVILLE					
B131	19.12.53	–	Wm Smiley	H.F. Martin	Pt BF lots 21 and 22, 2nd con, twp N Oxford; Thames R to G.W.R. line, lots on river and Oxford St, mill; 2 ch	Oxford 41 R.P.37
B132	25.8.54	–	Wm Smiley	Thomas Youngs	North pt $W_{1/2}$ lot 8, BF con, twp W Oxford at south side Woodstock and London Stone Rd; 1 ch	Oxford 41 R.P.51

B133	29.5.55	–	Wm Smiley	H.F. Martin & W. Henry	NW pt lot 8, BF con, twp W Oxford; Zorra St to Water St, Woodstock and Ingersoll Stone Rd to Thames R; 2 ch	Oxford 41 R.P.115A
B134	22.8.55	–	Wm Smiley	Wright Farnsworth	'Wrightville,' SW and NW pt of N and S1/2s lot 21, 1st con, twp N Oxford; lots north of gravel rd from Beachville to Embro; 2 ch	Oxford 41 R.P.96
B135	11.6.56	–	J. Stoughton Dennis	J.E. Thompson	Pt lots 20 and 21, 1st and 2nd cons, twp N Oxford; Embro St to Beachville Ave, William St to Brook St and Thames R; 132 ft	Oxford 41 R.P.75
B136	–.–.56	[30.1.60?]	Wm Smiley	M.L. Green	NE pt lot 8, BF con, twp W Oxford; Zorra St at Main St; 1 ch	Oxford 41 R.P.121
B137	6.4.57	–	Wm Smiley, Cyrus Carroll asst	H.F. Martin	NW pt lot 8, BF con, twp W Oxford; from Thames R to Hook and Zorra sts; 1-ch bar	Oxford 41 R.P. 115
B138	21.5.57	[1.11.60?]	Wm Smiley	Stewart Canfield	North pt lot 9, BF con, W Oxford twp; lots front on Main St; 1 ch	Oxford 41 R.P.127
B139	25.5.60	–	Cyrus Carroll	Prepared for Municipal Council	Lots 20 and 21, 1st and 2nd cons, twp N Oxford; William St to Thames R, Martin St to Beachville Ave, G.W.R.; 3 ch	Oxford 41 R.P.141
B140	–.–.63	–	Wm Smiley	Prepared for Municipal Council	Compiled plan; lots btwn Thames R and Main St, some south; cultural detail; transcript; 4 ch	Oxford 41 R.P.154
	BEARBROOK					
B141	7.7.66	5.11.66	R. Sparks	Thomas Wilson	'Wilsonville,' pt lot 20, 4th con, twp Cumberland; lots on con rd allowance and rd from Foubertville to Duncanville, sketches of bldgs; 2 ch	Russell 50 R.P.Wilsonville
	BEAVERTON					
B142	20.7.59	30.7.59	James McCallum, Jr	Neil Gordon	Lot 14, 6th con, twp Thorah; along Mara Rd; 1 ch	Durham 40 R.P.(Beaverton)

	Date of Survey	Date of Regist.	Surveyor	Owner	Description and Notes	Location
	BELFAST					
B143	-.-.57	30.3.58	Molesworth & Weatherald	Joseph Alton	'Altonville,' lot 12, 10th and 11th cons, lot 13, 10th con, twps Wawanosh and Ashfield; Rachel St to Henry St, Market St to John St; 2 ch	Huron 22 R.P.141
	BELFOUNTAIN					
B144	-.-.46	8.7.53	Hugh Black	J. McCurdy	Credit R west branch to Main St; grist mill; 16 perches	Peel 43 R.P.Cal-2
	BELLE RIVER					
B145	12.10.58	22.10.58	O. Bartley	Charles Baby	'Rochester,' lot A east of Belle R, twp Rochester; Tecumseh St to South St at G.W.R., depot, Maple St to Hickory St; transcript; 50 ft	Essex 12 R.P.39
B146	[-.2.67?]	12.2.67	O. Bartley	C.S. Chisholm	'Chisholme,' west pt lot A, 1st con, twp Rochester; Lake St to Broadway, Belle R to Eleventh St, G.W.R. station; transcript; 100 ft	Essex 12 R.P.158
B147	28.6.67	28.6.67	O. Bartley	Captain M. Robarsh	Pt lot A, 1st con, twp Maidstone; Maidstone St to G.W.R., Ontario St to Belle R, mill; transcript; 30 ft	Essex 12 R.P.27
	BELLEVILLE					
B148	-.10.19	14.5.50	Henry Smith	William Bell	Lot 7, 2nd con, twp Thurlow; owners; 10 ch	Hastings 21 R.P.3B
B149	5.12.32	25.8.51	Samuel M. Benson	'Town of Moira Plan'	Pt lot 3, 1st con, twp Thurlow; Moira R to Ann and Bridge sts, owners; 2 ch	Hastings 21 R.P.14
B150	20.5.40	25.6.40	Samuel M. Benson	G. Taylor & W. Taylor	S1/2 lot 5, 1st con, twp Thurlow; Dundas St to Hotel St, John St to Ann St, survey description; 2 ch	Hastings 21 R.P.1
B151	–	31.8.44	John Emerson	'Jones Plan'	Pt lot 5, 1st con, twp Thurlow; Moira R to Front, Francis to Johnson St; 2 ch	Hastings 21 R.P.2
B152	-.-.44	25.11.49	J.J. Haslett	Commercial Bank	Pt lot 2, 1st con, twp Thurlow; Dundas and Ann sts; 3 ch	Hastings 21 R.P.9

B153	–.8.44	22.11.49	John J. Haslett	Edmund Murney	Pt lot 2, 1st con, twp Thurlow; lots on Catharine, Henry, Ontario, and Murney sts, some bldgs and owners; 3 ch	Hastings 21 R.P.20
B154	–.–.45	23.3.47	Samuel M. Benson	Asa Yeomans	Pt N1/2 lot 1 1st con, twp Thurlow; William and Lewis sts; (plan missing, see Plan R-594, photoreproduction)	Hastings 21 R.P.75
B155	–.–.45	22.11.49	John J. Haslett	Edmund Murney	Pt lot 6, 1st con, twp Thurlow; lots on Emily, Albion, Elizabeth, Victoria sts, 'Canniffs Estate'; 2 ch	Hastings 21 R.P.15
B156	–.–.46	30.10.46	John J. Haslett	G.B. Spencer	Pt lots 33 and 34, town of Belleville; btwn Front and Pinnacle sts, bldgs, some owners; 20 ft	Hastings 21 R.P.99
B157	–.10.46	19.11.53	John J. Has[lett?]	James Spence	Pt lots 36 and 37, 1st con, twp Sidney; lots on 2nd con Sidney; 2 ch	Hastings 21 R.P.67
B158	20.5.47	–	Samuel M. Benson	Alexander O. Petrie	Pt lot 12, east side Front St, west side Pinnacle St; 40 ft	Hastings 21 R.P.68
B159	–.5.47	–.10.49	John J. Haslett	Wellington Murney	Pt lot 1, 1st con, twp Thurlow; Bridge St W to the north, lots on both sides Yeomans St; 2 ch	Hastings 21 R.P.4 [1847]
B160	7.6.47	7.6.47	Samuel M. Benson	John Way Maybee	Pt BF lot 5, 1st con, twp Thurlow; both sides John St, a few owners; 1 ch	Hastings 21 R.P.17
B161	–.3.48	3.4.48	John J. Haslett	Joseph Shuter & Robert Charles Wilkins	'Wilkin's Block,' lots 22 and 23, west side Pinnacle St at Bridge St; 24 ft	Hastings 21 R.P.35
B162	–.3.48	3.4.48	John J. Haslett	Joseph Shuter & Robert Charles Wilkins	'Shuter's Block,' lot 16, west side Pinnacle St; 30 links	Hastings 21 R.P.16B
B163	–.–.48	24.4.49	John J. Haslett	G.W. Myers	Pt lots 9 and 10, 2nd con, twp Thurlow; several owners; 4 ch	Hastings 21 R.P.4 [1848]
B164	–.–.[5?]	–	John Emerson	St Thomas Church	Lots granted to rector; drawn from original crown grant, Rear to Church St; 1 ch	Hastings 21 R.P.69
B165	–.3.50	24.9.50	John J. Haslett	Robert Wilkins	'Wilkins Block,' lots 22 and 23, west side Pinnacle St; market-place to Bridge St, Pinnacle St W, several owners, bldgs; 20 ft	Hastings 21 R.P.10

	Date of Survey	Date of Regist.	Surveyor	Owner	Description and Notes	Location
B166	6.5.50	–	John J. Haslett	'Bell's Block'	Lot 5, east side Pinnacle St; 20 ch	Hastings 21 R.P.13B
B167	–.7.50	10.9.51	P.V. Elmore	B. & J. Row & B. Hunt	'Meyres Common,' north pt lots 1–5, 1st con, twp Thurlow; resurvey of Philip Short's' 1848 plan; Moira R to Colborne St, Park St to con line; 2 ch	Hastings 21 R.P.12A
B168	–.9.50	22.10.50	John J. Haslett	John Ross	'Ham's Block,' lot 26, east side Front St; bldgs; 10 ft	Hasting 21 R.P.22 (3rd)
B169	1.10.50	1.10.50	John J. Haslett	For County of Hastings	'Ham's Block,' south side Dundas St; John St at Dundas St, owners, burying ground; 50 links	Hastings 21 R.P.22
B170	19.12.50	19.12.50	Samuel M. Benson	Jabez Kellogg	'MacNab Block,' pt lot 33, east side Front St and pt lot 33, west side Pinnacle St; 2 ch	Hastings 21 R.P.21
B171	–.12.50	9.8.51	John J. Haslett	Thomas Coleman	'Coleman's Block,' north of Moira St; Moira R to Queen St, Victoria St to Front St, mill dam; 3 ch	Hastings 21 R.P.25
B172	–.–.50	26.3.51	John J. Haslett	Samuel Stevens	'Steven's Block,' west pt lot 4, 3rd con, twp Thurlow; 2/3 Con Rd to road from 3rd con, twp Sidney, Victoria to Park St, bldgs; 2 ch	Hastings 21 R.P.3A
B173	–.5.51	5.5.51	John Emerson	Edmund Murney	'Murney's Plot,' pt lot 5, 1st con, twp Thurlow; Bay of Quinte to Edmund St, John St to Main St; 2 ch	Hastings 21 R.P.24
B174	12.7.51	5.6.52	Samuel M. Benson	Joseph Shuter	Lot 15, west side Pinnacle St and lot 15, east side Front St; Front St to Pinnacle St south of Dundas St; 32 ft	Hastings 21 R.P.18
B175	31.7.51	24.10.51	Samuel M. Benson	Phillip F. Canniff	'Wellington Plot,' pt lot 6, 2nd con, twp Thurlow; east side Moira R, Byron St, road from Belleville to Canniffs Mills; 1 ch	Hastings 21 R.P.45
B176	–.7.51	6.7.52	John Emerson	Estate of James Canniff	'Victoria,' pt lot 6, 2nd con, twp Thurlow; road from Belleville to Canniffs Mills; 1 ch	Hastings 21 R.P.47

B177	–.–.51	14.6.51	John J. Haslett	John Grier	'The Globe Property,' north of Bleakers Grove; Strachan St to Second Con St, Front St to Colbourne St; 2 ch	Hastings 21 R.P.11B
B178	–.–.51	6.8.51	John J. Haslett	Edmund Murney	'Murney's Block,' north side Bridge St; Bridge St to Catharine St, Octavia St to Isabel St; 1 ch	Hastings 21 R.P.8 (2nd)
B179	–.–.51	25.9.51	John J. Haslett	William Fitzgibbon	'Fitzgibbon's Block,' north side Bridge St, west side Yeomans St; 30 ft	Hastings 21 R.P.60
B180	24.1.52	31.1.53	Samuel M. Benson	Charles S. Ross	Pt lot 23, east side Front St, south side Bridge St; several owners; 20 ft	Hastings 21 R.P.31
B181	–.5.52	19.5.52	John J. Haslett	John Reid	'Reid's Block,' lots 55 and 56, north side George St according to 1845 plan of lot 1, 1st con, twp Thurlow; George St; 40 links	Hastings 21 R.P.7
B182	–.–.52	2.6.52	John J. Haslett	'Hutton's Block'	Lots 37 and 38, 1st con, twp Sidney; Charlotte St to Joseph St, both sides William St, Town Line St; 3 ch	Hastings 21 R.P.6
B183	13.9.52	28.10.52	Samuel M. Benson	James Canniff	Pt lot 6, 2nd con, twp Thurlow; Moira R to plank rd to Canniffs Mills; 1 ch	Hastings 21 R.P.50
B184	–.–.52	28.10.52	John J. Haslett	Henry Easton & Jane A. Easton	'Easton Block,' btwn Harriet and Earl sts; Victoria St to Coleman St; 40 ft	Hastings 21 R.P.23
B185	–.–.52	14.11.52	John J. Haslett	William Davenport	Lot 24, west side Pinnacle St; 10 ft	Hastings 21 R.P.8
B186	–.4.53	9.3.54	John Emerson	James Canniff	'Moira,' lot 6, 2nd con, twp Thurlow; Moorman St to George St, both sides McDonald St, some sales and prices on one copy; 2 original plans; 1 ch	Hastings 21 R.P.10
B187	15.5.53	18.7.53	John J. Haslett	'Phippen's Block'	Lot 7, 2nd con, twp Thurlow; James and John sts; 1 ch	Hastings 21 R.P.19A
B188	–.7.53	29.9.53	H.H. Horsey	C.L. Herchmer	'Herchmer Plot,' E1/2 lot 9 and W1/2 lot 10, 1st con, twp Thurlow; Kingston Rd to 1/2 Con Rd, both sides Albert Rd; 4 ch	Hastings 21 R.P.65
B189	4.8.53	27.8.53	Samuel M. Benson	William Tossell	'Tossell's Block,' lots 10–13, south side Bridge St W on pt S1/2 lot 1, 1st con, twp Thurlow; Bridge St to William St; 60 ft	Hastings 21 R.P.29
B190	–.–.53	6.8.53	John J. Haslett	'Greenshields Block'	Lot 69, north side Dundas St; both sides John and Dundas sts; 30 ft	Hastings 21 R.P.32

	Date of Survey	Date of Regist.	Surveyor	Owner	Description and Notes	Location
B191	-.-.53	29.8.53	John J. Haslett	Wm Ponton	'Ponton's Block,' lots 21 and 22, south side Bridge St; William St to Bridge St W; 30 ft	Hastings 21 R.P.27
B192	-.-.53	12.9.53	John J. Haslett	John Booth	'Booth's Block,' lots 7–9, 14, south side Bridge St, east side Wellington St; 30 ft	Hastings 21 R.P.28
B193	-.-.53	13.9.53	John J. Haslett	G.E. Henderson	'Henderson's Block,' lots 59, 60, 67, 70, east side Wellington St; Wellington, Henry, Dundas, and George sts; 40 ft	Hastings 21 R.P.30
B194	-.-.53	2.11.53	John J. Haslett	E.P. Russell	'Russell's Block,' pt Globe Property north of 'Bleackers Grove'; Front St at Strachan St, bldgs, some owners; 20 ft	Hastings 21 R.P.33
B195	-	-.-.53	John Emerson	Roach Bullen	'Zoar,' pt W1/2 lot 7, 1st con, twp Thurlow; both sides William St; 5 ch	Hastings 21 R.P.51
B196	-.-.54	11.3.54	John J. Haslett	C.G. Lewis & R.C. Wilkins	Lots 21 and 22, east side Pinnacle St; both sides Benjamin St; 10 ft	Hastings 21 R.P.34
B197	-.5.54	-	Publius V. Elmore	William H. Ponton & William Breakenridge	Lot 38, 1st con, twp Sidney; Joseph St btwn William and Townline St; 1 ch	Hastings 21 R.P.63
B198	-.-.54	8.7.54	John J. Haslett	E.H. Coleman	Pt 'Coleman's Estate'; btwn Mill St and Moira R, numerous bldgs identified; 20 ft	Hastings 21 R.P.26
B199	-.-.54	4.8.54	John J. Haslett	Peter Robertson	'Robertson's Block,' lots 71 and 71a, north side Dundas St; btwn Townline and Wellington sts, later cancelled; 52 ft	Hastings 21 R.P.62
B200	-.-.54	[7.8.54?]	John J. Haslett	Salyer Reeds Estate	Pt lots 7–9, 4th con, twp Thurlow; lots along plank rd, bldgs; 3 ch	Hastings 21 R.P.61
B201	-.-.54	7.11.54	John J. Haslett	Breakenridge, Walton, LeVesconte & Henderson	'Reynold's Block,' lots 38 and 39, west side Pinnacle St, and lot 38, east side Front St; Mill St at Pinnacle and Front sts; 20 ft	Hastings 21 R.P.71
B202	-.-.54	16.1.55	William Wallbridge	E.H. Coleman	Lot 10, 'Coleman Block,' pt lot 3, 1st con, twp Thurlow; Moira St to Harriett St, Albert to Coleman St; 1 ch	Hastings 21 R.P.72
B203	-.-.55	16.4.64	John J. Haslett	James Spence	Pt E1/2 lot 36, 1st con, twp Sidney; James St, Peter St to 2nd Con St, G.T.R.; 1 ch	Hastings 21 R.P.101

B204	–.1.56	30.1.56	Publius V. Elmore	R.J. Everitt	Lot 2, west side Park St, 2nd con, twp Thurlow; plank rd to Park St, both sides College (Donald) St; 1 ch	Hastings 21 R.P.80
B205	–.7.56	12.9.56	John Emerson	A.L. Smith & C.G. LeVesconte	Pt lot 6, 1st con, twp Thurlow; Bridge St to Pine St, Charles St to Reed St; 1.5 ch	Hastings 21 R.P.87
B206	–.8.56	9.9.56	John Emerson	M. Foster	'Foster's Town Plot,' pt lot 6, 1st con, twp Thurlow; Bay of Quinte to Bridge St, Henry St to Foster and Matilda sts, a few owners; photoreproduction; 150 links	Hastings 21 R.P.85
B207	–.12.56	18.5.57	John Emerson	A.L. Smith	NE corner lot 6, 1st con, twp Thurlow; gravel rd from Belleville to G.T.R. depot and Northcott St, Hambly St and 2nd Con Rd; 1 ch	Hastings 21 R.P.19
B208	–.5.57	1.7.57	Horsey & Nash	Messrs Jackson, Peto, Brassey & Betts	'Terrace Block,' pt E1/2 lot 7, 1st con, twp Thurlow; Brassey St to Con Rd, Betts St to Peto St, G.T.R. ground; 1 ch	Hastings 21 R.P.91
B209	–.10.57	2.1.58	John Emerson	Asa Yeomans	'Yeoman's Plan B,' pt lot 1, 1st con, twp Thurlow; Union and Railroad sts btwn Hutton and Frank sts; 2 ch	Hastings 21 R.P.92B
B210	–.10.59	–	John Emerson	Horace Yeomans	'Yeoman's Plan B,' Block C and pt Block B; both sides Elmer St; resubdivision of plan above; 2 ch	Hastings 21 R.P.92
B211	26.4.61	9.5.61	Samuel M. Benson	William Dafoe	Coulter St to Mill St west of Dafoe St; 20 ft	Hastings 21 R.P.98
B212	24.5.61	–.–.64	Innes & Macleod	J.W.D. Moodie	Catherine St btwn and on Sinclair and Dunbar sts; 2 ch	Hastings 21 R.P.102
B213	9.2.63	27.2.63	Publius V. Elmore (dr by Philip Short)	Tobias Blecker	Pt W1/2 lot 7, 1st con, twp Thurlow; inset showing original subdivision of lot; Bridge St to G.T.R., both sides Blecker St; 3.5 ch	Hastings 21 R.P.100
B214	25.10.63	26.10.63	Henry A. MacLeod	Jno. Ross	'Lemoine Lands,' lots 1 and 2, 2nd con, twp Thurlow; Sidney to Lemoine St, College to beyond Mary St; 6 ch	Hastings 21 R.P.22 (2nd)
B215	26.5.64	–.–.65	[Henry Horsey?]	Dunbar Moodie	Bridge St to Catherine St along Sinclair St; photoreproduction; 2 ch	Hastings 21 R.P.109
B216	1.6.64	20.10.64	Samuel M. Benson	James Canniff	Pt lots 5 and 6, 2nd con, twp Thurlow; Moira R to James St, a few bldgs and owners identified; 3 ch	Hastings 21 R.P.103

	Date of Survey	Date of Regist.	Surveyor	Owner	Description and Notes	Location
B217	–.6.64	29.9.65	Samuel M. Benson	Revd Thomas Campbell	Pt lot 27, pt N1/2 lot 28, pt S1/2 lot 29, east side Front St, lot 26 and pt lot 27, west side Pinnacle St; Front St to Pinnacle St at Campbell St, surrounding owners identified; 40 ft	Hastings 21 R.P.108
B218	19.1.65	19.1.65	Innes & MacLeod	Robert Read	Lots 1 and 1 east side Ann St north of Dundas St, and pt lot 6, 1st con, twp Thurlow; 50 links	Hastings 21 R.P.106
B219	2.6.66	2.6.66	Innes & MacLeod	Agnes Fitzgibbon	Pt lot 2, 1st con, twp Thurlow; both sides Dunbar St; 2 ch	Hastings 21 R.P.113
B220	–	9.4.67	William Wallbridge, Innes & Simpson	Robert Gordon	'Coleman Block,' lot 7; Harriett St to Earl St, Coleman St to Front St; 1 ch	Hastings 21 R.P.117
	BELL EWART					
B221	29.2.64	29.3.64	John Stoughton Dennis	James McIntyre, Adam Crooks	'Bell Ewart Lake,' pt lots 23–25, 4th con, twp Innisfil; Cumberland St to Maple St, Cameron St to Cooks Bay; Northern Ry land and station; 4 ch	Simcoe 51 R.P.96
	BELLROCK					
B222	9.6.53	13.7.53	William R. Rombough	William Pomero	Pt lots 19 and 20, 11th con, and lot 19, 10th con, twp Portland; some bldgs and owners identified; 2 ch	Frontenac 13 R.P.31 (4)
	BELMONT					
B223	9.6.53	13.7.53	William Robinson	William Barker	'McLaren's Farm,' lot 1, 7th con, twp Westminster; west of Port Stanley Rd, north of baseline Westminster; 3 ch	Middlesex 33 R.P.29
B224	29.11.55	4.1.56	Jesse P. Ball	Thomas Nugent	'Late Plymouth,' south and west pts lot 24, 6th con, twp Dorchester; NE corner Main and Union sts; 2 ch	Middlesex 33 R.P.97
B225	6.10.64	8.11.64	Jesse P. Ball	Thomas Nugent	South pt lot 24, 6th con, twp North Dorchester, and NE pt lot 1, 7th con, twp Westminster, NW pt lot 24, 7th con, twp S Dorchester; Washburn St to Cherry St, West St, Victoria St, graveyard; 2 ch	Middlesex 33 R.P.198

	BELMORE					
B226	–.–.67	19.3.67	Cyrus Carroll	Elizabeth Irwin	Lot 1, con C, twp Turnberry; Culross to Gowan St, west of Howick St to Irwin St; 2 ch	Huron 22 R.P.164
	BELWOOD					
B227	1.9.60	10.9.60	William Grain	George Douglas Ferguson & John Watt	'Village of Douglas,' lots 62–5 on Dobbin and North sts; lot 11, 7th con, twp W Garafraxa; 100 ft	Wellington 61 R.P.125
	(BENDERVILLE town plot)					
B228	15.8.56	16.8.56	W. Boultbee	G.H. Bender	For description see **1177**	Wellington 60 no R.P.#
	BENMILLER					
B229	–.–.54	20.4.54	T.N. Molesworth	B. Miller	'Village of Colborne,' pt lot 1, 1st con, eastern division, twp Colborne; Miller, Main, and Maitland sts, bldgs identified; 2 ch	Huron 22 R.P.205
B230	1.9.63	23.10.63	Thomas Weatherald	Daniel S. Miller	'Village of Colborne,' Blocks A and B; Maitland St to Maitland R, road deviation, bldgs identified; 2 ch	Huron 22 R.P.206
	BERVIE					
B231	1.12.58	28.2.60	Latham B. Hamlin	Nicoll McIntyre	Pt lot 50, range 15, S Durham Rd, twp Kincardine; Edwin St to Durham St, Lawson Lane to Nicol St, bldgs identified; 2 ch	Bruce 3 R.P.26
	BERWICK					
B232	8.4.58	27.1.60	George Bruce	Riverside Cooperative Cheese Manufacturing Assoc.	Beaver St to mill pond, Union St to creek, bldgs identified; 1 ch	Stormont 52 R.P.2
	BETHANY					
B233	–.–.58	30.9.60	William Wallbridge	M. McAllister, J. Byers, J. Wilson, W. Gibson	Pts lots 24, 7th and 8th cons, twp Manvers; James, Young, John, Wilson, and Queen sts to Gore St, Port Hope, Lindsay & Beaverton R.R., a few bldgs; 2 ch	Port Hope 9 R.P.Manvers 5

	Date of Survey	Date of Regist.	Surveyor	Owner	Description and Notes	Location
B234	11.12.67	13.12.67	M. Deane	Christopher Fell	Pt lot 23, 7th and 8th cons, twp Manvers; 2 ch	Port Hope 9 R.P.Manvers 6
B235	25.12.67	–	M. Lough	Josias Wilson	Pt W1/2 of NW1/4 lot 24, 7th con, twp Manvers; King and Queen sts; a few owners; 2 ch	Port Hope 9 R.P.Manvers 3
	BIDDULPH TWP					
B236	–.7.61	16.7.61	Samuel Peters	Dennis Sutton	Pt lot 23, 1st con, twp Biddulph; east of town line Biddulph/McGillivray; 4 ch	Middlesex 33 R.P.184
	(BINGHAMSVILLE town plot)					
B237	28.10.56	9.1.57	Kertland & Gilkison	T. Bingham	Pt lot 26, 10th con, twp Hullett; Maitland R to King St, Main St to Robert St, bldgs identified; 2 ch	Huron 22 R.P.Hullett 3
	BIRR					
B238	–.11.56	16.1.57	Leather & Robinson	James MacDonald	'Town of Silverwood,' lot 16, 12th con, twp London; 4 unnamed streets (later cancelled) running north and south, east of Proof Line Rd; 2 ch	Middlesex 33 R.P.132
	BISHOPGATE					
B239	26.6.46	–	Lewis Burwell	George Washington Whitehead & Russel Smith	SE corner lot 1, 6th con, twp Burford; Smith, Whitehead, and Brock sts, Burford plank rd; 1 ch	Brant 2 R.P.51
B240	5.8.57	26.3.58	Lewis Burwell	Charles S. Perley	NE corner lot 1, 7th con, twp Burford; Elizabeth, Charles, and Perley sts, rd allowance btwn cons 6 and 7; 1 ch	Brant 2 R.P.51A
	BLAIR					
B241	30.9.57	–	James Pollock	Charles Allan & James Geddes to Messrs Caldwell	Pts lots 4 and 5 Richard Beasley's Lower Block, west side Grand R, twp Waterloo; streets north and south of Main St to Preston St btwn Centre St and road to Preston, bldgs identified, pt of village as laid out by E.H. Kertland; 2 ch	Waterloo 67 R.P.580

	BLANSHARD TWP					
B242	9.3.55	11.12.60	J.K. Clendinen	John Cook & George Thom	Division of lot 29, E and W1/2s South Boundary con, twp Blanshard; owners; 3.6 ch	Perth 44 R.P.297
B243	–	8.10.56	J.K. Clendinen	Archd McCallum	Lot 37, Thames Con, twp Blanshard; 4 ch	Perth 44 R.P.295
B244	28.12.58	6.1.59	W. Graeme Tomkins	James Remato	Pt lot 16 east of Mitchell Rd, twp Blanshard	Perth 44 R.P.296
	BLENHEIM					
B245	11.5.52	1.6.67	Richard Parr	M. Little	Pt lot 10, 1st con west of Communication Rd, twp Harwich; Regent St to Ellen St, Little St to Chatham St, note: north pt staked out in 1844 by Parr; 2 ch	Kent 24 R.P.91
B246	12.11.66	12.1.67	Thomas Malcolm	For Municipality	Compiled plan of town; Regent St to MacGregor St, Little St to Lumley St, bldgs identified; 2 ch	Kent 24 R.P.88
B247	–	1.3.67	James Johnston	E. Larwell & G. Thomas	Ellen to Regent St, Little to street west of it, streets west of Chatham St, bldgs; 2 ch	Kent 24 R.P.89
B248	–	1.6.67	A.P. Salter	John Jackson	Pt lot 10 east of Communication Rd, twp Harwich; John St to Talbot St, Chatham St to Hall St; 2 ch	Kent 24 R.P.90
	BLOOMINGTON					
B249	–.11.67	24.11.69	G. & W. McPhillips	James M. Patterson	8th con, twp Whitchurch; 2 ch	York 65 R.P.18
	BLOOMSBURG					
B250	185?6?	–	–	–	Pt lot 4, 11th con, twp Townsend; Main St to mill pond, unfinished, unregistered; scale n.g.	Norfolk 37 R.P.40A
	BLUEVALE					
B251	–	6.8.57	William Rath	Jacob Cantelon	Pt lot 31, 1st con, twp Turnberry; Elizabeth St to Orange St, side rd to Victoria St; 2 ch	Huron 22 R.P.165

	Date of Survey	Date of Regist.	Surveyor	Owner	Description and Notes	Location
B252	–	18.3.57	Andrew Bay	Alexander Duncan	Lots 29 and 30, 1st con, twp Turnberry; Clyde St to Georges St, Maitland St to Green St; 1.5 ch	Huron 22 R.P.166
	BLYTH					
B253	7.12.55	29.12.55	William Perceval	David McDonald	Lot 42, 1st con, twp Wawanosh, and S1/2 lot 1, 9th con, twp Morris; Wilson St to Mill St, Wellington to 1/2 con line, twp Wawanosh; 4 ch	Huron 22 R.P.168
B254	–.6.60	28.9.60	William Ralph	Lucius McConnell	Pt lots 1 and 2, 10th con, twp Morris; Wilson St to Morris St, McConnell St to Westmoreland St, bldgs and owners identified; 3 ch	Huron 22 R.P.169
	BOBCAYGEON					
B255	–.2.62	26.2.62	Michael Deane	Thomas Need & Jabez Thurston Reeve	Formerly 'Rokeby,' lot 15, 10th con, twp Verulam; John St south of river and btwn East and Portland sts, bldgs identified; 4 ch	Victoria 57 R.P.11
B256	2.12.67	6.2.68	John D. Evans	Johanna Brown, Samuel McClelland, Thos Taylor, et al.	Subdivision of lot 4, west side Bolton St, owners; 20 ft	Victoria 57 R.P.20
	(BODMIN)					
B257	7.1.59	22.1.59	Andrew Bay	John Mitchell	Lot 9, 5th con, twp Morris; Maitland R to Charlotte St, bldgs; 2 ch	Huron 22 R.P. Morris 2
	BOLSOVER					
B258	–.12.64	15.2.65	George Gibson	Duncan E. McRa[e]?	On Talbot R; along King St btwn Ontario St and Talbot St, bldgs identified; 2 ch	Victoria 57 R.P.15
	BOLTON					
B259	10.3.52	10.4.52	Thomas Chevalier Prosser	Henry Nunn	E1/2 lot 7, 7th con, twp Albion; Humber R, Nunn St and King Rd, bldgs identified, cleared land; 2 ch	Peel 43 R.P.ALB-2

B260	–	22.8.56	Thomas Chevalier Prosser	James Johnson, John Tindale, M. & Saml Bolton, et al.	For description see **1184**	Peel 43 R.P.ALB-4
B261	21.2.60	28.2.60	Thomas Chevalier Prosser	Charles Bolton	Lot 8, 7th con, twp Albion; Humber R to Hemlock St, Union St to beyond James St, bldgs, owners; 2 ch	Peel 43 R.P.BOL-1
B262	10.4.60	25.7.61	Thomas Chevalier Prosser	Walford Estate	Lot 8, 7th con, twp Albion; Queen St to Brick Lane, King St to beyond Willow St, owners; 1 ch	Peel 43 R.P.BOL-2
B263	–	29.2.64	Robert Walsh	Alexander Buist	E1/2 lot 10, 6th con, twp Albion; 7th con line and side-road btwn lots 10 and 11, new road over Humber R, bldgs identified; 2 ch	Peel 43 R.P.BOL-3
	BORNISH					
B264	9.7.56	29.9.56	Samuel Peters	J.G. Harper	'Dalgetty,' lot 11 west of Centre Rd, twp Williams; Main St to William St, King St west to Nelson St; cancelled by **B2810**; 198 ft	Middlesex 33 R.P.119
	BOSANQUET TWP					
B265	27.3.62	1.7.65	William Rath	For Canada Co.	Pt of twps Bosanquet, Stephen, and McGillivray; copy, surveyed under instructions from Canada Co.; topography, vegetation, L Burwell, L Smith, R aux Sables (Ausable); 40 ch	Middlesex 33 R.P.240
B266	27.3.62	7.7.65	William Rath	For Canada Co.	Pt cons 1 and 2, twp Bosanquet; plan missing	Lambton 25 R.P.Bosanquet 5
	BOTHWELL					
B267	10.9.55	1.6.67	John Stoughton Dennis	George Brown	Lots 11 and 12 and pt lot 13, 9th con, twp Zone; G.W.R. to Cherry St, Marianne St to Jane St; photoreproduction; 3 ch	Kent 24 R.P.141
B268	–	22.2.66	Unwin & Dyas	Bothwell Land & Petroleum Co. Ltd	Pt lots 4–10 north of Longwoods Rd and pt lots 11 and 12, 9th con, twp Zone; lots on Peter St and btwn Hope St, Con Rd, and G.W.R. on NW side; 4 ch	Kent 24 R.P.142

	Date of Survey	Date of Regist.	Surveyor	Owner	Description and Notes	Location
B269	13.3.66	14.3.66	Unwin & Dyas	E.B. Adams	'Adam's Addition,' W Bothwell, pt lot 10, 8th con, twp Zone; Oil Ave to Franklin St, both sides G.W.R., bldgs; 1 ch	Kent 24 R.P.163
B270	12.4.66	19.4.66	Unwin & Dyas	E.B. Adams	'Adams Addition,' W Bothwell, altered version of plan above, Eva St added west of Franklin St at G.W.R.; 1 ch	Kent 24 R.P.164
B271	1.9.66	20.10.66	Sherman Malcolm	Adin McIntyre	SE1/4 lot 11, 8th con, twp Zone; Main St to McIntyre St, Marseilla St to Oil Ave; 1 ch	Kent 24 R.P.160
	BOWMANVILLE					
B272	21.8.51	20.4.52	John Grant	'Grant's Plan'	Pt lots 11–13, 1st con, twp Darlington; Pine St to Wellington St, Chapel St to Liberty St; 2.5 ch	Newcastle 10 R.P.'Grant's Plan'
B273	19.2.56	6.3.56	George Stewart	Lockhart & Simpson	Odell St to Fourth St, Lamb St to High St; 2 ch	Newcastle 10 R.P.Bowmanville 'Lockhart & Simpson'
B274	1.8.56	3.10.56	Thomas Wallis Herrick	John Hutcheson	N1/2 lot 9, 1st con, twp Darlington; streets not identified, south of rd allowance cons 1 and 2; 66 ft	Newcastle 10 R.P.Bowmanville
B275	3.10.56	10.10.56	Thomas Wallis Herrick	J. Porter, S.B. Bradshaw, M. Porter	South pt lot 9, 2nd con, twp Darlington; Mann St to beyond Porter St, Winstanley St, Bradshaw St, and con line; 2 ch	Newcastle 10 R.P.'Porter & Bradshaw'
B276	15.11.56	28.5.57	Thomas Wallis Herrick	A. Wilson, R. Armour & George Mearns	Pt lot 11, BF con, twp Darlington; river to Liberty St, G.T.R. to baseline, bldgs; 100 ft	Newcastle 10 R.P.Bowmanville 'Wilson Armour & Mearns'
B277	16.2.57	3.3.57	L.H. Shortt	William Hambly	Pt lot 12, 2nd con, twp Darlington; Elgin St, Hambly St, con rd and side-rd lots 12 and 13; 3 ch	Newcastle 10 R.P.Bowmanville 'Hambly'
B278	14.4.58	4.5.58	L.H. Shortt	John Smart	'Smart Estate,' pt lot 9, 1st con, and lots 9 and pt 10, BF con, twp Darlington; L Ontario to Eighth St, river and swamp to Mearns Ave, bldgs, owners, G.T.R., Harbour Co. property; 3 ch	Newcastle 10 R.P.Bowmanville 'Smart'

	BOXGROVE					
B279	–.6.50	19.8.50	George McPhillips	Joseph Tomlinson, Wm E. Beebe	'Village of Sparta,' 8th and 9th cons, twp Markham; bldgs and owners identified; 4 ch	Toronto 64 R.P.19
	BRADFORD					
B280	22.11.49	26.11.49	John Ryan	James Drury	West of Simcoe St, south of Holland St; 1.25 ch	Simcoe 51 R.P.11
B281	4.6.52	3.11.56	John Ryan	William Soles	South pt lot 15, 7th con, twp W Gwillimbury; Holland St to John St, bldgs identified; 2 ch	Simcoe 51 R.P.49
B282	10.11.52	4.1.53	Hugh P. Savigny	Wilson Stoddart	Pt lot 16, 7th con, twp W Gwillimbury; NE of Barrie and Holland sts; 2 ch	Simcoe 51 R.P.14
B283	14.10.56	7.4.57	William Hawkins	William Hawkins	Pt lot 15, 8th con, twp W Gwillimbury; North and South John sts north of Bradford, owners, includes note of 21.11.58 altering plan; 132 ft	Simcoe 51 R.P.56
B284	–.1.57	11.11.67	John Ryan	For 'Town of Bradford'	Compiled plan, all surveys and names, certified by all surveyors and some owners, O S & H Ry, Amsterdam in SE, owners and bldgs identified; 3 ch	Simcoe 51 R.P.122A
B285	11.10.59	8.11.59	William Hawkins	William Hawkins	Pt lot 15, 7th con, W Gwillimbury; btwn Barry and Church sts and above Queen St, grammar school lot; 2 ch	Simcoe 51 R.P.77
B286	–.10.65	1.3.66	S.W. Hallen	Estate of John Ryan; James Stoddart & James W. Barry	'Block B,' Barrie St west to Church St, Queen St to beyond David St; 1.5 ch	Simcoe 51 R.P.105
B287	–.–.65	–	Henry Creswicke	Wilson Stoddart	Pt lot 16; NE from Holland and Barrie sts, various surveys shown; 2 ch	Simcoe 51 R.P.106
B288	25.4.66	16.11.66	William Hawkins	William Hawkins	North of Queen St and from Toronto St to Church St; 2 ch	Simcoe 51 R.P.117
	BRAMPTON					
B289	1.4.48	27.2.49	Jno. Stoughton Dennis	George Wright	Etobicoke R and Centre Rd to Elizabeth St, north to Nelson St, owners; 1.5 ch	Peel 43 R.P.BR1 (12)

	Date of Survey	Date of Regist.	Surveyor	Owner	Description and Notes	Location
B290	22.7.50	–	J.S. Dennis	Geo. Wright et al.	Compiled plan; east and west of Hurontario St, John St to Ellen St, owners; transcript; 3 ch	Peel 43 R.P.BR2
B291	–	10.4.52	Chisholm Miller	William Gardner	'Block 41'; Nelson St west to beyond California St, Ann St to Union St, distillery; 1/2 ch	Peel 43 R.P.BR3 (10)
B292	–.6.53	4.1.54	Chisholm Miller	George Wright	Lot 6, west twp Chinguacousy; West St to Hurontario St, Market St to Nelson St, G.T.R. and station; transcript; 2 ch	Peel 34 R.P. BR4
B293	1.3.54	9.5.54	T.C. Prosser	John Lynch et al.	'Railway Block & Wellington Block'; Toronto, Guelph & Sarnia Railroad to Church and King sts; 2 ch	Peel 43 R.P.BR5
B294	20.5.54	26.6.54	T.C. Prosser	John Elliott	East of side-rd btwn lots 5 and 6; 2 ch	Peel 43 R.P.BR6
B295	2.3.54	1.9.55	Chisholm Miller	–	'Washington Block,' pt lot 7, 1st con west, twp Chinguacousy; west of Hurontario St, south to David St; 1 ch	Peel 43 R.P.BR8
B296	20.8.55	25.8.55	Chisholm Miller	John Elliott	'Elliott Block,' pt E1/2 lot 5, 1st con, west pt lot 5, 1st con east of Hurontario St, twp Chinguacousy; Victoria [Queen] St to South Wellington St, Elliott St to Mary St; 2 ch	Peel 43 R.P.BR7
B297	–.11.55	7.2.56	Charles Unwin	Samuel Patterson	For description see **1189**	Peel 43 R.P.BR9
B298	4.4.56	18.4.56	F.F. Passmore	John Vodden	'Vodden Block,' Hurontario St east to beyond Hannah St; 28 ft	Peel 43 R.P.BR10
B299	9.6.56	26.12.56	Bristow, Fitzgerald & Spencer	John Guest	Lot 4, 1st con east of Hurontario St; east of Hurontario St, south of Guest St; 40 ft	Peel 43 R.P.BR11
B300	1.4.59	8.7.59	A. Scott	Vodden Estate	'Vodden Estate,' pt lot 7, 1st con, east of Centre Rd, twp Chinguacousy; north of Vodden St, east of Hurontario St, Etobicoke R, topography, burying ground; 2 ch	Peel 43 R.P.BR12

B301	–.2.61	8.1.62	A. Scott	Geo. Wright Estate	Pt lot 1 on 'J.S. Dennis Plan,' pt lot 6, 1st con E.H.S., twp Chinguacousy; north of Queen St, east of Hurontario St; 20 ft	Peel 43 R.P.BR14
B302	–.–.62	6.6.62	A. Scott	A.F. Scott	Resubdivision of Block G on plan above; Nelson St to Church St, Centre St to Hemlock St; 1.5 ch	Peel 43 R.P.BR15
B303	10.10.66	31.10.66	A. Scott	For the Bank of Montreal	Pts lot 5, 1st con W.H.S., twp Chinguacousy, pt village lot 13; resubdivision of pt of **B296**; Hurontario St to Elizabeth St, one side Queen St; 132 ft	Peel 43 R.P.BR16
B304	14.6.67	27.11.67	A. Scott	John Elliott	Pt E1/2 lot 5, 1st con W.H.S., twp Chinguacousy; south of Queen St, south Wellington St west of Hurontario St; 2 ch	Peel 43 R.P.BR17
	BRANCHTON					
B305	10.9.55	[13.10.55?]	James Pollock	William Rosebrugh	Galt branch G.W.R., south to Albert St, west to Jane St; 2 ch	Waterloo 67 R.P.608
B306	2.8.56	–	James Pollock	William Rosebrugh	Pt lot 4, 7th con, twp N Dumfries; Galt Branch G.W.R. south to Mary St, west to Jane St, bldgs identified; 132 ft	Waterloo 67 R.P.608 (2nd)
	BRANTFORD					
B307	pre-1849	[11.4.51?]	Lewis Burwell	Sarah Lefferty	Terrace St to Colbourne St, Alfred St to Rawdon St, several owners, brewery; photoreproduction; 2 ch	Brant 2 R.P.2.5
B308	18.3.57	9.19.62	Lewis Burwell	James Weymes	Lots 1 and 2, south side Grey St, Market St; photoreproduction; 20 ft	Brant 2 R.P.20
B309	21.11.51	30.3.53	Lewis Burwell	Sarah J. Lefferty	North of Colbourne St, Rawdon to canal basin; Grand R Navigation Co. land, relief; photoreproduction; 2 ch	Brant 2 R.P.2
B310	7.9.53	10.11.53	Lewis Burwell	James Cockshutt	'Eagle's Nest Tract,' lot 22; Newport to Market St and Greenwich St; photoreproduction; 2 ch	Brant 2 R.P.16 2
B311	15.11.53	5.5.54	Lewis Burwell	Edward Chant & Henry Chant	Block D; west side Sydenham St to St John St, Usher St to Buffalo, Brantford & Goderich R.R.; photoreproduction; 1 ch	Brant 2 R.P.3

	Date of Survey	Date of Regist.	Surveyor	Owner	Description and Notes	Location
B312	12.4.54	4.10.55	O. Robinson	Henry Hyde	'Hyde Place'; pt of proposed continuation of Terrace-hill St, several owners; photoreproduction; .5 ch	Brant 2 R.P.5
B313	1.5.54	14.4.57	Lewis Burwell	Emily A. Milliken	Both sides Buffalo, Brantford & Goderich R.R., Duke to Wadsworth St, West St to Waterloo St, Wilkins St to Buffalo St, Main St to West St; photoreproduction; 66 ft	Brant 2 R.P.17
B314	3.5.54	2.10.55	O. Robinson	Mary Gillin	'Block 11d G east of Wilkes Tract'; Chatham St to Sheridan St, Murray St to Peel St; photoreproduction; 1 ch	Brant 2 R.P.14
B315	16.5.54	19.7.54	Orpheus Robinson	John A. Wilkes	'Wilkes Tract'; Darling St to Buffalo Brantford & Goderich R.R., Charlotte St to Canning St; photoreproduction; 2 ch	Brant 2 R.P.21
B316	16.8.54	23.8.54	Orpheus Robinson	Frederick T. Wilkes	'Eagle Place,' west pt lot 2 in 'Eagle's Nest Tract'; Dover, Erie, Mohawk, and 3rd–5th sts, notes on roads to connect new survey areas for public thoroughfare, Grand R Navigation Co.; 4 ch	Brant 2 R.P.36
B317	23.9.54	10.10.54	Lewis Burwell	Joseph Lister, William L. Billing & George Sterling	'Echo Place,' south pt lot 38, 4th con and lot 24 south of Hamilton Rd, twp Brantford; both sides Hamilton Rd around James and William sts, bldgs, owners; 2 ch	Brant 2 R.P.39
B318	29.6.55	5.4.56	Lewis Burwell	George S. Wilkes	'Holmedale'; west limit to Crescent St, Seneca St to Buffalo, Brantford & Goderich R.R.; 4 ch	Brant 2 R.P.46
B319	1.12.55	1.12.55	S. Peters	J. Puleston	Pt lot D, 4th con, twp Brantford; Hamilton Rd to Grey St and Buffalo, Brantford R.R., Puleston St to Schram St and beyond, bldgs; 1.5 ch	Brant 2 R.P.28
B320	–	[13.3.56]	[O. Robinson]	[Geo. S. Wilkes]	'Bushhill & Oakley Park'; lots 26–30, 3rd con, twp Brantford; Grand R to road from St George to Brantford, Oakley park and Elm St to Toll Gate Rd; plan missing (see **1197**)	Brant 2 R.P.31

B321	–.9.56	7.11.56	O. Robinson	G. Gilbert & W.J. Fenton	Pt 'Smith and Kerby Tract'; Belmont St to north limit of town, Sydenham St to Stanley St, inset location map shows rest of town, Buffalo & L Huron Ry; photoreproduction; 40 ft	Brant 2 R.P.7
B322	14.4.57	2.6.74	Lewis Burwell	Stephen J. Jones	Wilkins St to Buffalo St, Main St to Washington St; 40 ft	Brant 2 R.P.44A
B323	9.6.57	2.9.57	Lewis Burwell	Robert Danson & James State	Sydenham St to High St both sides Princess St; photoreproduction; 40 ft	Brant 2 R.P.15
B324	–.–.57	19.6.57	T. Cheesman	Frederick T. Wilkes	For description see **1198**	Brant 2 R.P.35 (2nd)
B325	–.–.57	21.3.66	Thomas Cheesman, D. Johnson	A.K. Smith	North Ward; Dumfries to Smith St, Napolean, Kerby, and Egerton sts, 18 lots mill to Spring St surveyed by D. Johnson PLS 29.4.62; photoreproduction; 2 ch	Brant 2 R.P.9A
B326	13.2.58	31.8.58	Lewis Burwell	James Cockshutt	'Brantford Water-Side'; Grand R and canal basin, Greenwich St to Newport St to Market St, lands of Grand R Navigation Co., some owners; photoreproduction; 60 ft	Brant 2 R.P.16 1
B327	–	30.6.58	O. Robinson	George S. Wilkes	Lots east and west of St George Rd; Chestnut St to Buffalo & L Huron R.R., Florence St to James St; photoreproduction; 150 ft	Brant 2 R.P.13
B328	–	31.7.58	O. Robinson	J.D. Clement	Lot 'G' west of 'Wilkes Tract'; Charlotte St to Clarence St, Grey St to Buffalo & L Huron R.R.; 40 ft	Brant 2 R.P.23
B329	14.5.61	29.5.61	O. Robinson	John Robinson	Lots 1 and 2, north side Marlborough St, pt lot 1 south of Grey St, Block M, east side West St; photoreproduction; 13.2 ft	Brant 2 R.P.19
B330	17.5.61	28.5.61	Lewis Burwell	Estate of Daniel M. Gilkison	South pt of 'Brant Farm' on west side Grant R; Brunswick St to Oxford St, Gilkison St near Grand R to York St, Spencer's Brewery; photoreproduction; 2 ch	Brant 2 R.P.11
B331	12.2.62	4.3.62	O. Robinson	Hugh & Thomas Spencer	Southwest pts of tract formerly known as SE pt 'Brant Farm,' west side Grand R; 5 ch	Brant 2 R.P.22

	Date of Survey	Date of Regist.	Surveyor	Owner	Description and Notes	Location
B332	26.11.63	8.12.63	Lewis Burwell	John Brunskill	Front of N1/2 of 'Brant Farm'; Oxford St to Brant St, Grand R to Burford St, owners; photoreproduction; 4 ch	Brant 2 R.P.8
	BRANTFORD TWP					
B333	23.1.56	24.1.56	Lewis Burwell	Phillip C. Van Brocklin	South pt of grant to 'Hiram Phelps' on south side Grand R, twp Brantford; owners; 4 ch	Brant 2 R.P.28
B334	18.6.58	[23.5?.61]	Lewis Burwell	John Campbell Shipman, Messrs Batty	'Batty Farm,' lots 30–2, con I, twp Brantford; owners; 10 ch	Brant 2 R.P.158
B335	1.7.61	22.1.62	Lewis Burwell	Thomas Grimshaw	'Kerr Tract,' Block 5, twp Brantford; owners, swamps, main rds; 10 ch	Brant 2 R.P.41
B336	16.4.63	2.5.63	Lewis Burwell	Thomas Racey	Front pt lot 3, 1st con west side Mount Pleasant Rd, twp Brantford; 2 ch	Brant 2 R.P.24
	BRESLAU					
B337	15.1.58	–	James Pollock	Joseph Erb	Lot 114 of Upper Block, twp Waterloo; Berlin St to Ford St, Erb St to Preston St, G.T.R. line and station, mill pond, Grand R; 2 ch	Waterloo 58 R.P.588
	BREWERS MILLS					
B338	1.8.65	5.6.72	T.W. Nash	'Ordnance Lands'	S pt lot 25, 8th con, twp of Pittsburg; lots along Kingston and Phillipsville Macadamized Rd; 3 ch	Frontenac 13 R.P.53
	(BRIDGEND PLACE)					
B339	10.3.63	2.5.63	William J. Macdonald	William J. Macdonald	West pt Block C, West Division, twp Colborne; east of Maitland R, north of gravel rd, relief, cemetery; 4 ch	Huron 22 R.P.180
	BRIDGENORTH					
B340	13.12.54	24.1.55	George A. Stewart	Thomas Ward	Prince's St to Chemong or Mud Lake, Communication Rd on east; 3 ch	Peterborough 45 R.P.4 Smith

	BRIGHT					
B341	27.10.62	–	William Smith	G. Baird	Formerly 'Plattsville Station,' twp Blenheim; Buffalo & L Huron R.R. to Archibald St east of Main St, bldgs identified; 1 ch	Oxford 41 R.P.152
	BRIGHTON					
B342	14.10.48	7.6.64	Michael Deane	Estate of Thomas D. Sandford	Pt lot 1, 2nd con, twp Cramahe; Dundas, Sandford, and Chapel sts; 4 ch	Northumberland 38 R.P.20 (Brighton)
B343	–.6.53	7.6.56	J.S. Peterson	Ira R. Proctor	Lot 2, 2nd con, twp Brighton; Dundas St to beyond Proctor St, Factory St to beyond Victoria St, owners; 1 ch	Northumberland 38 R.P.8 (Brighton)
B344	[1.7.53?]	–	John J. Haslett	A.C. Singleton	'Singleton's Block,' pt lot 35, con A, twp Brighton; Dundas St to George St, Chapel St to both sides Ontario St; 2 ch	Northumberland 38 R.P.'Singleton Block'
B345	–.10.53	12.4.55	J.S. Peterson	William Butler	Lot 1, 1st con, twp Brighton; William St to Dundas St, Prince Edward St to Division St; 2 ch	Northumberland 38 R.P.10 (Brighton)
B346	–.10.53	15.12.64	J.S. Peterson	William Butler	Lots 34 and 35, 1st con, twp Brighton; Lampton St to rd allowance Cramahe/Murray, Harbour, Baldwin, and Prince Edward sts; 1 ch	Northumberland 38 R.P.23 (Brighton)
B347	–.11.54	7.6.56	J.S. Peterson	–	Ontario St to Railroad St, Dundas St to G.T.R. depot ground; 5/6 ch	Northumberland 38 R.P.7 (Brighton)
B348	20.4.61	7.12.61	J.S. Peterson	A.C. Singleton	W1/2 lot 35, con A, twp Brighton; Danford Rd, gravel rd, Block 1 conveyed prior to 3.1852; 5 ch	Northumberland 38 R.P.15 (Brighton)
B349	–.12.63	24.12.63	A.C. Webb	J. Ham Perry	Pt lot 35, con B, twp Brighton; G.T.R. to new gravel rd to Trenton, Oliphant St to both sides Percy Ave; 2 ch	Northumberland 38 R.P.18 (Brighton)

	Date of Survey	Date of Regist.	Surveyor	Owner	Description and Notes	Location
B350	25.4.64	25.7.64	George A. Stewart	Commercial Bank of Canada	Lots 3 and 4, 1st con, twp Brighton; both sides G.T.R., bldgs, owners; 4 ch	Northumberland 38 R.P.21 (Brighton)
B351	27.6.65	3.1.66	Michael Deane	Estate Thomas D. Sandford	Lot 1, 2nd con, twp Cramahe; Dundas St north along Kingsley Ave and Chapel St; 4 ch	Northumberland 38 R.P.26 (Brighton)
B352	-.10.66	27.4.67	A.C. Webb	Town of Brighton	Compilation map; inset map of east side Prince Edward St btwn Elizabeth and Dundas sts, detailed lots, streets, some owners; transcript; 4 ch	Northumberland 38 R.P.28 (Brighton)
	BRISBANE					
B353	-.-.54	10.7.54	John Moore	Thomas J. Bush	'Bristol,' pt E1/2 lot 13, 7th con, W1/2 lot 13, 8th con, twp Erin; St Paul St to James St on both sides Guelph Rd; 1 ch	Wellington 61 R.P.63
	BROCKVILLE					
B354	[ca 1824]	-	John Booth, Henry Lillie	Dr E. Hubbell, David & Daniel Jones, Mrs Charland, et al.	Pt lots 12 and 13, 1st con, 'Elizabethtown'; mill pond to Dunhams Rd btwn lots 13 and 14 and present travelled road, some owners, copy made by Henry Lillie 185?; transcript; 2 ch	Leeds 28 R.P.124
B355	1.1.45	13.7.67	Charles Booth	Estate of Hon. Charles Jones	Pt lot 10 and E1/2 lot 11, 1st con, twp Elizabethtown on north side of Pearl St; James St to rd allowance btwn cons 1 and 2, Ormond St to Bethune St, copy made in 1867; transcript; 4 ch	Leeds 28 R.P.9
B356	-.1.48	-	-	Samuel Reynolds	King St to James St west of Bartholomew St, owners; transcript; 80 ft	Leeds 28 R.P.104
B357	-.5.53	19.6.72	Chas Booth?, Samuel Hazelwood	Estate of Ormond Jones	Pearl St and btwn George and Park sts; copy of original; transcript; 50 ft	Leeds 28 R.P.20
B358	28.11.53	-	Francis Jones	-	Pt W1/2 lot 9, 1st con west of Bartholomew, south of Charles St; plan missing	Leeds 28 R.P.107

B359	1.12.53	9.8.62	Francis Jones	Estate of Ormond Jones	Main St to Pine St, Market St to Garden St, owners; 20 ft	Leeds 28 R.P.2
B360	[185?]	–	John Booth, Henry Lillie	Robinson, Easton & estate of William Matthie	Pt front 1/2s lots 14 and 15, 1st con, 'Elizabethtown'; Queens Hwy to G.T.R., Oak St to Maple St, Sheppard's Mill pond, relief, owners; 100 ft	Leeds 28 R.P.108
B361	5.5.54	24.10.71	Henry Lillie	Ormond Jones	E1/2 lot 17, 1st con, twp Elizabethtown; Kingston Rd to 2nd con rd, lots off Centre St, bldgs; 200 ft	Leeds 28 R.P.17
B362	10.12.57	–	Henry Lillie	Estate of Dr Hubbell	Pts lots 12 and 13, 1st con, twp Elizabethtown; G.T.R. and Delhi St to Havelock St west of Perth St, mill pond, grist mill; 80 ft	Leeds 28 R.P.109
B363	–.5.59	19.8.72	Francis Jones	Anson Jones	Park lots XII-XV in lot 10, 1st con, twp Elizabethtown; G.T.R. to Maple Ave, Park Ave to Elm Ave; 100 ft	Leeds 28 R.P.24
B364	–.10.59	18.8.64	–	Andrew Norton Buell	William St to Brockville & Ottawa Ry, Pearl St to G.T.R. grounds and station; transcript; 100 ft	Leeds 28 R.P.7
B365	21.10.61	12.11.62	Henry Lillie	Estate of Billa Flint	Pt lots 12, 13, and 14, 1st con, twp Elizabethtown; Lincoln St to rd allowance btwn cons 1 and 2, Russell St to Victoria macadamized rd; transcript; 2 ch	Leeds 28 R.P.4
B366	–.–.63	–	Jno. Killalley, Samuel Hazelwood	Estate of James Crawford	First Ave to North Augusta Rd, King St north to 2nd con rd, G.T.R. cuts through area, owners, Crawford house and park; transcript; 4 ch	Leeds 28 R.P.136
B367	6.5.67	13.7.67	–	Mrs Florella Jones	Pt park lot 5; east of Park St, lots on both sides Charles St, south of G.T.R.; 48 ft	Leeds 28 R.P.8
	BROOKLIN					
B368	2.11.4[4?]	29.1.52	John Shier	John Magee	'Winchester,' SW pt lot 22, 6th con, twp Whitby; 6th Con Rd north to George St, Duke St west to Queen St; 2 ch	Durham 40 R.P.H-50054
B369	30.7.51	4.11.51	John Shier	Campbell & Way Plan	Pt lots 23 and E1/2 24, 6th con, twp Whitby; Queen St west to Baldwin and Price sts, 6th con rd to Way St, mill; 2 ch	Durham 40 R.P.H-50052

	Date of Survey	Date of Regist.	Surveyor	Owner	Description and Notes	Location
B370	3.12.56	10.12.56	John Shier	'B.F. Perry's Plan'	Pt lot 23, 6th con, twp Whitby; George St to North St, Queen St west to Colston Ave; 2 ch	Durham 40 R.P.H-50053
	BROUGHAM					
B371	–.5.57	31.8.57	George McPhillips	Gould, Woodruff, et al.	Lots 18 and 19, 5th and 6th cons, twp Pickering; John St north to Martin St, Spring St west to North St, bldgs identified, owners; 2 ch	Durham 40 R.P.Pickering
	BROWNSVILLE					
B372	22.2.56	[25.2.56?]	Jesse P. Ball	Brown & P. Brinton, et al.	South pts lot 21 and 22, 10th con, north pts lots 21 and 22, 11th con, twp Dereham; Hincks St east to Rolph St, Ann St to Sophia St; 2 ch	Oxford 41 R.P.66
	BRUCEFIELD					
B373	29.6.57	25.7.57	A. Bay	Hugh Mustard & John Armstrong	Lot 30, 1st con, twp Tuckersmith, lot 16, 1st con, twp Stanley; both sides London Rd and Bayfield Mill Rd; 2 ch	Huron 22 R.P.182
B374	–.3.60	14.3.60	John Denison	Village of Brucefield	Lots XV and XVI, 1st con, twp Stanley; lots on London Rd and rd allowance btwn lots XV and XVI; 2 ch	Huron 22 R.P. 185
B375	7.1.67	5.2.67	A. Bay	J. Macdonald	Lot XXXI, 1st con, London Rd, twp Tuckersmith; 2 ch	Huron 22 R.P.181
	BRUSSELS					
B376	–	1.2.56	A. Bay	William Ainlay	'Ainlaysville,' lot 1, 10th con, twp Grey; Turnberry St to Victoria St, Thomas St to Queen St, mill reserve; 4 ch	Huron 22 R.P.187
B377	–	30.3.59	A. Bay	Thomas Halliday	'Ainlaysville,' lot XXX, 6th con, twp Morris; Turnberry St to Halliday St, Hawkes St to rd allowance btwn cons V and VI, Maitland R; 2 ch	Huron 22 R.P.188

B378	15.9.65	9.11.65	Cyrus Carroll	John L. Knechtel	'Ainlaysville,' lot 1, 10th con, twp Grey, lots south side William St, north of Mill St, east of Turnberry St; 3 ch	Huron 22 R.P.189
	BURFORD TWP					
B379	26.1.51	28.10.52	William Smiley	Jacob Smith	Pt southwest pt lot 1, 6th con, twp Burford; 1 ch	Brant 2 R.P.50
	BURLINGTON					
B380	17.6.54	21.7.54	Henry Winter	D. Torrance	'Wellington Square'; L Ontario north to Caroline St, Brant St to Martha St, schedule of owners; part of plan missing; 2 ch	Halton 20 R.P.12
B381	20.6.64	17.6.67	G. Brockitt Abrey	Corporation of Nelson	For description see **1214**	Halton 20 R.P.39
	BURRITTS RAPIDS					
B382	–.11.49	28.12.50	William Campbell	Stephen Burritt	E1/2 lot 26, 1st con, twp Marlborough; bounded by Centre, Broadway, Water, Rideau sts, dam; 1 ch	Ottawa-Carleton 5 R.P.2
B383	19.10.50	22.10.50	William Campbell	Henry Burritt	Pt lot 5, 1st con, twp Oxford; Queen's Hwy and Rideau Canal to Rideau R btwn Oxford and Henry sts, mill; 80 links	Grenville 15 R.P.Oxford 3
B384	–.5.53	10.2.54	William Campbell	Daniel Burritt	W1/2 lot 25, 1st con, twp Marlborough; lots on Broadway, Centre, Bridge sts; burial ground, park lot; 1 ch	Ottawa-Carleton 5 R.P.4
	BUXTON					
B385	1.12.59	1.6.67	A.P. Salter & Co.	G.W. Brodie	Pt lot 8, 12th con south of Middle Rd, twp Raleigh; Victoria to King St, Charlotte St to George St; 1 ch	Kent 24 R.P.176
	BYNG					
B386	7.9.65	5.1.66	Henry Lawe	Estate of Samuel Street & Estate of William Hamilton Merritt	'Haldimand,' lot 16 and pt lots 15 and 17, 1st con north and south of Dunnville and Dover Rd, along Sulphur Creek and Grand R, Welland Canal lands; 4 ch	Haldimand 18 R.P.14473 Card 9

	Date of Survey	Date of Regist.	Surveyor	Owner	Description and Notes	Location
	CAINSVILLE					
B387	31.10.64	15.3.67	Lewis Burwell, Quintin Johnstone	Town of Brantford	Lots 1–36 at junction of canal and Grand R, owners, Oneida Mission School; 4 ch	Brant 2 R.P.29
	CAISTORVILLE					
B388	21.9.54	10.10.54	Edmund DeCew	–	Lot 20, 1st and 2nd con, twp Caistor; Binbrook St to David St east of Seneca St, Wesleyan church, later corrections on Binbrook St (25.9.55); 2 ch	Niagara 30 R.P.26 Co
B389	28.4.56	29.1.57	Edmund DeCew	W.J. Stevenson	E1/2 lot XX, 1st con, twp Caistor; Binbrook, York, and John sts; 1 ch	Niagara 30 R.P.25 Co
	CALEDON					
B390	–.9.51	–.4.54	Chisholm Miller	James Neelands	'Charles Town' from west of Hurontario St to east, John St south to beyond Brock St; 2 ch	Peel 43 R.P.Cal-3
B391	30.5.65	5.8.65	A.B. Scott	Thomas Bell	'Charleston,' east pt S1/2 lot 16, 1st con, twp Caledon; west of Hurontario St, McFaul, George, and John sts; 1.5 ch	Peel 43 R.P.Cal-7
	CALEDON EAST					
B392	–.6.55	14.6.55	T.C. Prosser	James Munsie	'Paisley,' SE1/4 lot 4, con VI, twp Caledon; 1 ch	Peel 43 R.P.CAL-4
B393	14.10.63	4.12.63	R.W. Hermon	Rebecca Greer & Sons	'Paisley,' west pt lot 21, 1st con, twp Albion; lots on town line (6th) and side-rd btwn lots 20 and 21; 1 ch	Peel 43 R.P.ALB-5
	CALEDON TWP					
B394	–.2.61	8.3.61	A.B. Scott	Isaac Hunter	Pt lot 3, 1st con, twp Caledon; east of Hurontario St at Credit R; 2.5 ch	Peel 43 R.P.Cal-6
	CALEDONIA SPRINGS					
B395	–	13.3.39	Andrew Russell	–	Pt lot 20, con I, twp Caledonia; site of springs; plan for Richmond Sq and various bldgs, i.e., assembly rooms; bridges, inset map: route from Montreal to Caledonia; 100 ft	Prescott 46 R.P.2

	CAMBRAY					
B396	7.5.61	10.6.61	W.H. Deane	Joseph Wilkinson	E1/2 lot 5, 1st con, twp Fenelon; Lindsay St west to beyond Pine St, Mill St to beyond Oak St; 2 ch	Victoria 57 R.P.9
B397	–	1.6.61	Robert T. Burns	James Roy	Hill St to con rd, Campbell St south to side line; 50 ft	Victoria 57 R.P.8
	CAMDEN EAST					
B398	–.9.44	27.4.55	G. Clapp	James Williams	Pt lot 25, 1st con, twp Camden; several streets unnamed; 4 ch	Lennox 29 R.P.21
	CAMDEN TWP (L and A)					
B399	20.12.60	–.2.61	S.O. McGuin	William Thomas Madden	Lot 17, 1st con, twp Camden; lots south of Newburgh on Newburgh Rd, Township Line, and Centre St; 4 ch	Lennox 29 R.P.23
	CAMPBELLFORD					
B400	–.–.55	11.2.57	J.J. Haslett	Robert C. Wilkins	Pt lots 8 and 9 in 5th and 6th cons; twp Seymour; plan missing	Northumberland 38 R.P.22 (Campbellford)
B401	[1.10.56?]	[–.10.57?]	P.V. Elmore	Kirchhoffer & Cockburn	Lots X and XI, VI con, twp Seymour; lots on George St to Elmore St, Second St to beyond Market St, route of planned Grand Junction R.R. and station; 2 ch	Northumberland 38 R.P.'Campbell-ford'
B402	6.5.65	8.5.65	C.F. Caddy	Kirchhoffer et al.	Water lots on George and Front sts on both sides Trent R, bldgs, grist mill; 2 ch	Northumberland 38 R.P.24 (Campbellford)
B403	–.–.67	25.1.67	C.F. Caddy	H. Rowed	Lot 10, 7th con, twp Seymour; Queen St to Kent St and Trent R, Nelson to Wellington St; 2 ch	Northumberland 38 R.P.27 (Campbellford)
	CAMPBELLVILLE					
B404	28.3.54	10.7.54	Henry Winter	Colin Campbell	On both sides Nelson St, Mary St to Queen St; 1 ch	Halton 20 R.P.11

	Date of Survey	Date of Regist.	Surveyor	Owner	Description and Notes	Location
	CANBORO					
B405	24.7.60	30.8.60	Edmund & John DeCew	Thomas Birdsall, John Folmsbee	Lots XIV and XV, 1st and 2nd cons, twp Canborough; east to Indiana/Canborough St, west to beyond Oswego and Birdsall sts, sawmill; 2 ch	Haldimand 18 R.P.8851 Card 7
	CANBOROUGH TWP					
B406	15.5.58	20.6.59	Andrew Hood	'Ebenezer Society'	Pts lots 6 and 7, 2nd con, twp Canborough; west of Robinson Rd, bldgs, list of purchasers; 10 ch	Haldimand 18 R.P.7573 Card 8
	CANNIFTON					
B407	[–.1.48?]	–.–.48	John Emerson	Joseph Canniff	Pt lots 5 and 6, 3rd con, twp Thurlow; road to Canniff Mills to Gunton St, owners; 2 ch	Hastings 21 R.P.36
B408	–.11.49	4.12.49	John Emerson	Joseph Canniff	'Canniff-ville,' pt lots 5 and 6, 2nd con, twp Thurlow; streets unnamed; 2 ch	Hastings 21 R.P.46
B409	–.3.56	13.1.57	John Emerson	Jonas Canniff	'Canniffville,' pt lots 5 and 6, 2nd con, twp Thurlow; along Moira R below 3rd con rd, streets unnamed; 2 ch	Hastings 21 R.P.90
B410	–.–.56	10.6.68	P.V. Elmore, John J. Haslett	Jonas Canniff	Lots 5–7, 3rd con, twp Thurlow; Letty St to Thomas St, Philean St to Division St, owners names; 3 ch	Hastings 21 R.P.124
	CANNING					
B411	22.7.56	31.8.56	Thomas Allchin	Barbara & William Young	NW1/4 lot 4, 1st con, twp Blenheim; G.W.R. lands to Young St, west of Canning Rd; 1 ch	Oxford 41 R.P.112
B412	19.9.60	13.12.60	Cyrus Carroll	Township of Blenheim	Lot 4, 1st and 2nd cons, twp Blenheim; compiled plan from R.P.112 and R.P. 165; west of Nith R btwn Main, James, John, and Mill sts and btwn Elizabeth, Young, Jane, and Marcy sts; 3 ch	Oxford 41 R.P.122
B413	–.–.[66]	7.7.66?	John Maxwell	R.C. Mudge	Both sides Concession St to Elizabeth St, river, John St, etc, Main St to James St, bldgs, mill dams and proposed race; 3 ch	Oxford 41 R.P.165

	CANNINGTON					
B414	11.6.[50?]	5.11.50	John Grant	Alexander Munro	Lot 20, 11th con, twp Brock; road btwn cons 11 and 12 to Park St, Albert St west to mill pond; 2 ch	Durham 40 R.P.H-50055
	CARADOC TWP					
B415	1.10.55	7.12.55	Leather & Robinson	Captain Agassiz	Lot 21, 1st range south of Longwoods Rd; photoreproduction; 3 ch	Middlesex 34 R.P.90
B416	–	20.10.56	B. Springer	L.J. Agassiz	S1/2 lot 20 south of Longwoods Rd; photoreproduction; 4 ch	Middlesex 34 R.P.121
	CARDINAL					
B417	[18.10.48?]	18.10.48	James West	James Jessup	'Elgin'; canal and lock on St Lawrence, north to Dundas St, Lewis St to Jessup St, descriptive promotion of town; 81 ft	Grenville 15 R.P.(Elgin) Cardinal Edwards 7
B418	–	2.4.50	William Tracy	–	'Lewisville'; Queens Hwy to canal, William St to beyond Henry St, owners; 1.5 ch	Grenville 15 R.P.Edwards 11 (Cardinal)
B419	31.1.60	6.3.60	James West	James Jessup	'Elgin'; amended version of **B417** showing new street from James St to George St and alteration of lots 176–9; 80 ft	Grenville 15 R.P.Edwards-burgh 14
B420	22.3.60	4.6.60	James West	William T. Benson	'Elgin'; a revised verison of plan above, New St to Victoria St; 80 ft	Prescott 46 R.P.Edwards-burgh 16
	CARLETON PLACE					
B421	25.6.59	7.7.59	Joseph M.O. Cromwell	William Murphy	Rear of NE1/2 lot 14, 12th con, twp Beckwith; rd allowance Beckwith/Ramsay to William St, Baines St to Bridge St, owners; 24 ft	Lanark 26 R.P.Carleton Place 194
B422	–.10.60	14.11.60	John Morris	William Murphy	Front 1/2 of E1/2 lot 14, con XII, twp Beckwith; Bridge St to Brockville & Ottawa R.R., Mill St to XII St, owners, market reserve; 1 ch	Lanark 26 R.P.Carleton Place 272

	Date of Survey	Date of Regist.	Surveyor	Owner	Description and Notes	Location
	CARLISLE (Middlesex Co)					
B423	16.1.50	29.1.51	B. Springer	George Shipley	NW end lot 29, 1st con, twp Williams; mill race, mill yard, Shipley's Grist Mill, owners; 2 ch	Middlesex 33 R.P.8
B424	–.7.55	14.6.62	S. Peters	Duncan Stewart	South pt lot 29 and southeast pt lot 28, 2nd con, twp E Williams; Neil St to Bruce St, Church St to West St; 3 ch	Middlesex 33 R.P.172
	CARLISLE (Wentworth Co)					
B425	–.6.52	17.7.52	Robert W. Kerr	George Abrey	William St to Main St west of 8/9 con rd; similar to **B427**; 2 ch	Wentworth 62 R.P.341 (old 24)
B426	23.10.58	26.10.58	J. Mackintosh	Andrew Patten	North end lot 7, 8th con, twp E Flamborough; on same sheet as survey of pt of Hamilton (**B988**); 2 ch	Wentworth 62 R.P.295 (17 and 17a)
B427	1.3.61	–	G. Brockitt Abrey	George Abrey	William St to Main St west of 8/9 con rd; 2 ch	Wentworth 62 R.P.340 (old 24)
	CARLSBAD SPRINGS					
B428	25.10.64	5.2.66	H.O. Wood	Stephen Minions	'Cathartick,' N1/2 lot 3, con VII, twp Gloucester; Way and Russell sts, Minion N and Spring St, bldgs; 1 ch	Ottawa-Carleton 5 R.P.19
	CASTLETON					
B429	14.1.54	–	J. Keeler	J.A. Keeler	Lots 33 and 34, 7th con, twp Cramahe; con 6/7 rd allowance to Haldimand Rd and Pine St, Old Percy Rd to Pine St, pond, saw and grist mill; 3 ch	Northumberland 38 R.P.3 (Castleton)
	CATHCART					
B430	30.1.50	29.7.57	William Smiley	Stephen Bunker	'Sidenham,' pt SE1/4 lot 17, 5th con, twp Burford; lots on King, Mill, Mary, Margaret, and David sts; 1 ch	Brant 2 R.P.53 (Cathcart)
B431	17.9.66	21.11.66	William Smiley	A. McDonald	North pt lot 15 and northwest pt lot 14, 6th con, twp Burford; 4 ch	Brant 2 R.P.53 (2nd Cathcart)

	CAYUGA					
B432	22.12.53	18.9.54	Edmund DeCew	James Cockshutt	'Victoria Place,' lot 28, 1st con, north side Talbot Rd, twp N Cayuga; east of town of Cayuga; 4 ch	Haldimand 18 R.P.2915 Card 46
B433	29.3.64	31.10.64	Edmund DeCew	'Corporation of Village of Cayuga'	'Market Block'; King and Ottawa sts, Talbot Rd and Cayuga St, market sq, town hall; 1 ch	Haldimand 18 R.P.13255 Card 4
B434	25.3.67	[20.4.71?]	Edmund DeCew	'Indian Department'	West of Grand R, Philip St to Dixon St, some owners; 4 ch	Haldimand 18 no R.P.#
	(CAYUGA HEIGHTS town plot)					
B435	8.12.52	[26.12.52?]	Lewis Burwell	Joseph Thomas	East pt lot E, con IV, twp Brantford; owners; 1 ch	Brant 2 R.P.33
	CENTREVILLE (Lennox Co)					
B436	26.8.50	21.10.50	Wm R. Rombough	James F. Hawley	Front of lot 25, 6th con, twp Camden E; con rd allowance to Mudlake Rd, macadamized rd to Brock St; 1 ch	Lennox 29 R.P.18
	CENTREVILLE (Oxford Co)					
B437	–.5.47	–	Wm McClary	David Doty	Pts lots 15 and 16, BF con, twp Oxford W; Factory St to Picton St, King St to Brock St, mill race and pond; 1 ch	Oxford 41 R.P.12
B438	–.–.48	–	Wm McClary	David Doty	Pts lots 15 and 16, BF con, twp Oxford W; sawmill pond, lathe pond, grist mill pond to East St, lots along North Mill St and Mill St btwn Queen and Brock sts; 1 ch	Oxford 41 R.P.28
B439	10.5.54	–	Wm Smiley	Thomas Elliott	North pt of E1/2 lot 15, BF con, twp W Oxford; Stone Rd (King St) and Victoria St; 1 ch	Oxford 41 R.P.42
B440	–.–.63	–	Wm Smiley	'Township of West Oxford'	Lots 15 and 16, BF con, twp W Oxford; Mill St to Victoria St, North Mill St to Thames St, Main St to Brock St, Ingersoll to Woodstock Stone Rd, grist mill, school house; 2 ch	Oxford 41 R.P.155
	(CENTREVILLE town plot) (Middlesex Co)					
B441	7.7.59	7.3.65	R. Gilmour	Frederick Parr	Pt N1/2 lot 17, 2nd range, twp Mosa; Parr St to Haggarty St; photoreproduction; 1 ch	Middlesex 34 R.P.203

	Date of Survey	Date of Regist.	Surveyor	Owner	Description and Notes	Location
	CHARLESTON					
B442	–.7.35	–	John Booth	–	Lots 21 and 22, 9th con, twp Yonge; Wiltsie to St Andrews St, Fly St to Rock St, lots laid out in previous survey by J.R. White; 100 ft	Leeds 28 R.P.103
	CHATHAM					
B443	9.7.37	–	John A. Wilkinson	Robert S. Woods	Pt lot 1, 1st con, twp Chatham; Thames R to Head St, Baldoon St to Chatham St, owners; 2 ch	Kent 24 R.P.1
B444	–.–.45	10.5.52	Richard Parr	M. Stuart Woods	'Chatham North,' front of lot 1, 1st con, twp Chatham; Thames R to Head St, Baldoon St to Chatham St, bldgs, 'resurveyed in 1845'; 2 ch	Kent 24 R.P.2
B445	28.3.49	–	Richard Parr	–	Lots on William, Park, and Wellington sts; 2 ch	Kent 24 R.P.105 1/2
B446	–.12.49	–	Richard Parr	Church of England	'Clergy Reserve'; Murray St to Gaol St, Adelaide St to Princess St, registry office, gaol and court-house; 2 ch	Kent 24 R.P.5
B447	24.5.52	26.7.52	Richard Parr	–	Compilation map from survey notes of 1845–7 and 1849; Third St to Fourth St, King St to unnamed street, bldgs, owners; 2 ch	Kent 24 R.P.4A
B448	–.5.52	1.6.68	Richard Parr	M. Stuart Woods	'Chatham North,' pt lot 1, 1st con, twp Chatham; Head St to Forest St, St Clair St to Elizabeth St; 2 ch	Kent 24 R.P.3
B449	10.5.53	1.6.67	A.P. Salter	'Presbyterian Church'	Lots bounded by Adelaide, Park, William, and Wellington sts, subdivision of Presbyterian church reserve; 1/2 ch	Kent 24 R.P.7
B450	–.7.53	1.6.67	Richard Parr	William Price, Daniel S. Dobson & George Kirk	Wesleyan Methodist church land; at corner Gaol and Prince sts bounded by grammar school land and Agricultural Society ground; 1 ch	Kent 24 R.P.6

B451	25.3.54	18.4.54	Salter & Jones	Louise Read et al.	Pt lot 24, 1st con, twp Dover E; Cross St to Head St, Louise St to Robert St, owners; 1 ch	Kent 24 R.P.8
B452	19.5.54	1.6.67	A.P. Salter	George Thomas & James Beatty	SE1/2 park lots 1 and 2; St George St to William St, Wade St to 2nd con rd; 40 ft	Kent 24 R.P.9
B453	4.11.54	7.11.54	A.P. Salter	Thomas McCrae	Park lot 10 and pt park lot 9; Park St to Gray St, Rond Eau gravel rd to Robertson St; 1 ch	Kent 24 R.P.10
B454	-.-.[54]	-	Richard Parr, Salter and Jones	George Thomas & Robert Stuart Woods	For description see **1248**	Kent 24 R.P.4
B455	23.2.5[5?]	27.3.55	A.P. Salter	Ingram Taylor	Pt lot 2, 1st con, twp Chatham; Catherine St to Park St, Thames R to Head St; 2 ch	Kent 24 R.P.11
B456	10.12.55	11.3.56	A.P. Salter	J.B. Williams	Lot 40; Colbourne, Seaton, and Princess sts; 26 ft	Kent 24 R.P.13
B457	[12.11.56?]	1.6.67	A.P. Salter & Co.	Rev Archibald Campbell	Pt lot 2, 2nd con, twp Harwich; Park Ave to Arnold St, Sinclair St to Wilkinson St; 1 ch	Kent 24 R.P.12
B458	25.11.56	1.6.67	A.P. Salter & Co.	Town of Chatham	Wellington St to town line Harwich/Raleigh and Raleigh and Park sts; common school and playground, church lands; 1 ch	Kent 24 R.P.14
B459	5.9.59	[5.9.59?]	T. Chisholm Livingston	George Jameson	Subdivision of lot 33, corner Prince and Colborne sts; 1/2 ch	Kent 24 R.P.15
B460	23.6.65	1.9.70	Arthur Jones	R.K. Payne et al.	Lots 130 and 131, Block C, corner Wellington and Raleigh sts; transcript; 40 links	Kent 24 R.P.21
B461	15.7.65	7.11.65	A.P. Salter	Capt W.H. Smith	Lots 82 and 83, market block and Wellington St, owners; 40 ft	Kent 24 R.P.16
	CHATHAM TWP					
B462	15.9.57	1.6.67	A.P. Salter	J.B. Williams	NW1/2 lot 1, 5th con, twp Chatham; Kentucky St bisects area; 2.56 ch	Kent 24 R.P.229

	Date of Survey	Date of Regist.	Surveyor	Owner	Description and Notes	Location
	CHELTENHAM					
B463	–.6.59	8.7.59	W. Sanders	E. Haines	Pt lot 29, IV con W.H.S., twp Chinguacousy; owners, bldgs on Main St, dam, grist mill, bridge, sawmill, reserve for foundry; 66 ft	Peel 43 R.P.CH6
	CHERRY VALLEY					
B464	–	5.12.67	Geo. A. Simpson	For Municipal Council	Pt lots 1 and 2, 1st con, south side East Lake, twp Athol; Main St; 2 ch	Prince Edward 47 R.P.Cherry Valley I
	CHESTERVILLE					
B465	15.10.52	7.3.66	William Tracy	John P. Crysler	Lot 18, 4th con, twp Winchester; Queen St to King St, Emma St to Water St, list of contents of blocks; 2 ch	Dundas 8 R.P.11
	CHINGUACOUSY TWP					
B466	17.5.39	17.6.40	C. Rankin	James Alderson & William Wilkinson	Dispute over property line; shows incorrect line by McCartney and correct line by Callaghan on lot 8 affecting lots 7 and 9; 10 ch	Peel 43 R.P.CH2
	CHIPPAWA					
B467	7.7.53	8.7.53	James W. Fell	James Cummings	Chippawa Creek and Welland R east to Welland St, Francis St to Niagara St, owners, bldgs, church lots, bridges, steam grist mill; transcript; 2 ch	Niagara 59 R.P.1
	CHURCHVILLE					
B468	1.6.55	14.8.56	James W. Bridgland	E. Wiman	W1/2 lot 14, 3rd con E.H.S., twp Toronto; at Credit R on both sides Church St; 1 ch	Peel 43 R.P.TOR6

	CLANDEBOYE					
B469	12.6.52	12.6.52	Wm McMillan, A.N. Holmes	James Charles Maiklin	'Ireland,' both sides Hodgin St, Logan to Harbourn, Flanagan to St Patrick St; 10 rods	Middlesex 33 R.P.178
B470	13.1.55	2.3.55	Leather & Robinson	J. Shanly	'Ireland'; James to Hodgins St, St Patrick St and further east; 1 ch	Middlesex 33 R.P.179
B471	27.7.55	30.7.55	Samuel Peters	D. Bell & M. Seger	'Ireland,' lot 24, twp Biddulph; Flanagan St to St Patrick St, both sides Cathcart St; 3 ch	Middlesex 33 R.P.180
B472	-.-.55	17.1.57	S. Peters	R. Hodgson	'Ireland,' front pt lot 20, 1st con, twp McGillivray; Hodgin St to James St, Flanagan St to Hodgson St, market grounds; 1.5 ch	Middlesex 33 R.P.181
B473	-.4.57	13.5.57	Davies & MacLeod	James Barber	'Ireland'; Cathcart St to Water St, Stanley St to Flanagan St, bldgs, steam grist mill; amended by **B236**; 2 ch	Middlesex 33 R.P.182
	CLAREMONT					
B474	17.1.56	18.1.56	W.E. Yarnold	Mrs William Dow	SE corner lot 19, 9th con, twp Pickering; rd allowance btwn cons 8 and 9 north to David St, rd allowance btwn lots 18 and 19 west to William St; 1 ch	Durham 40 R.P.Pickering
	CLAYTON					
B475	-.6.55	21.11.55	Joseph M.O. Cromwell	'Estate of Hon. James Wylie & Sen. William G. Wylie'	'Clifton,' SW1/2 lot 23, 2nd con, twp Ramsay; Indian R to Raglan St, rd allowance btwn cons 1 and 2 to Louis St, owners, school reserves; 1 ch	Lanark 26 R.P. Clayton 248
	CLEARVILLE					
B476	-.5.58	1.6.67	John O'Mara	Samuel Burns	Talbot St to Burns St, St Andrews St to Wellington St; 4 ch	Kent 24 R.P.167
	CLIFFORD					
B477	-	26.1.57	E.H. Kertland	Charles Allen & Jas Geddes	For description see **1257**	Wellington 60 R.P.78

	Date of Survey	Date of Regist.	Surveyor	Owner	Description and Notes	Location
	CLINTON					
B478	–.5.50	27.9.60	Joseph Kirk	J. Rattenbury	Joseph St to Cayley St, North St to East St, alteration by Thom. Weatherald 31.3.64; 5 ch	Huron 22 R.P.327
B479	–.1.53	10.8.53	Joseph Kirk	William Shipley	Huron Rd to Shipley St to Albert St; 2 ch	Huron 22 R.P.328
B480	18.4.54	22.4.54	T.N. Molesworth	Joseph Whitehead	Pt lot 24, con 1, twp Hullet; along Railway Terrace north of Prince's St, plan of town to south; 4 ch	Huron 22 R.P.329
B481	25.9.55	25.9.55	William Perceval	Thomas F. Rance & Samuel H. Rance	Pt lot XXIV, 1st con, twp Hullet; Mill St to Charles St, Railway Terrace to Elm St; 2 ch	Huron 22 R.P.330
B482	25.9.55	7.11.57	William Perceval	Gilbert Griffin	'Inkerman Terrace,' pt lot XXIII, 1st con, twp Hullett; Ontario St to Range St; 4 ch	Huron 22 R.P.334
B483	29.10.55	3.11.55	William Perceval	W. & E. Smart & A. & K. Bache	Lots 22 and 23, Huron Rd Con, twp Goderich; Buffalo, Brantford & Goderich Ry to Newton St, Maitland St to North St, Church Sq, College Sq; 4 ch	Huron 22 R.P.331
B484	26.6.56	31.10.56	Kertland & Gilkison	William Rattenbury	Subdivision of town lot 177; Huron Rd and Baseline, inset location map; 30 ft	Huron 22 R.P.332
B485	4.9.56	27.10.57	A. Bay	'Estate of James Gordon'	Victoria St to King St, Bayfield R to Cutter St; 2 ch	Huron 22 R.P.333
B486	17.1.60	18.2.60	A. Bay	Issac Rattenbury	Town lots 15, 16, 45, and 46; north of Isaac St, btwn Mary St and Huron Rd; 20 ft	Huron 22 R.P.335
B487	30.9.61	9.3.63	A. Bay	James Crombie	Lots 252-4, 274–6; below Princess St; 1 ch	Huron 22 R.P.338
B488	24.12.61	4.2.62	A. Bay	William Shipley	Pt lot XXIV, Huron Rd Con, twp Goderich; John St to Huron St, John St to Charles St, North St to Shipley St, Queen St to Albert St; 2 ch	Huron 22 R.P.336
B489	–.10.62	29.1.63	A. Bay	Isaac Rattenbury	Lot 1, Huron Rd Con, twp Goderich; Buffalo & L Huron Ry to St Joseph St, North St to King St; 2 ch	Huron 22 R.P. 337

B490	19.1.63	10.7.63	A. Bay	'Estate of William Rattenbury'	Victoria St to Prince's St, Ontario St and East St; 3 ch	Huron 22 R.P.339
B491	17.11.63	11.3.64	A. Bay	'Estate of James Gordon'	Lots 292–4, 'Gordon Estate' on London Rd; .5 ch	Huron 22 R.P.340
B492	28.11.65	26.12.65	A. Bay	James Crombie	Lots 252–4, 273–6, and pt lots 280–90; Princess St; 1 ch	Huron 22 R.P.341
	CLINTON TWP					
B493	20.9.56	5.1.57	Andrew Hood	Various owners	Lots 1–4, cons II and III, twp Clinton; shows boundaries and ownership of various lots; 5 ft	Niagara 30 R.P.21 Co
	COBOURG					
B494	–	1.10.24	–	F.A. LaRocque	[Hibernia-Division St] south of King St; L Ontario to East Spring St and South King St; photoreproduction; 4 ch	Northumberland 39 R.P.Instrument 1163
B495	–	13.11.32	F.P. Rubidge	–	Pt lot 18, con A, and lot 18, BF con B; L Ontario to King St, Ontario St to Hibernia St, owners; 4 ch	Northumberland 39 R.P.Instrument 2788
B496	3.8.37	2.7.39	George Sanders	T.D. Campbell et al.	Pt lot 17, broken con A, twp Hamilton; Blocks A–G south of Seminary St, owners; 160 ft	Northumberland 39 R.P.Instrument 5571
B497	12.6.39	14.6.39	Alfred Rubidge	'Abraham Crouter's Plan'	Lot 18, broken con A, twp Hamilton; Furnace St to beyond Academy St, owners	Northumberland 39 R.P.Instrument 5548
B498	–.–.41	29.9.41	F.P. Rubidge	–	Lot 16, BF con A, twp Hamilton; King St to Spencer St, Division St to line btwn lots 15 and 16, owners, Victoria College and land; 4 ch	Northumberland 39 R.P.Instrument 6480
B499	–.–.41	11.11.41	F.P. Rubidge	–	Lot 16, BF con B, twp Hamilton; L Ontario to King St, Division St to Church St, owners, bldgs; 2 ch	Northumberland 39 R.P.Instrument 6480

	Date of Survey	Date of Regist.	Surveyor	Owner	Description and Notes	Location
B500	–	23.1.44	George Sanders	'Burnet Property'	Tay to King St, lines btwn lots XIX and XX to Ontario St; 2 ch	Northumberland 39 R.P.Instrument 7133
B501	–	–.–.44	John K. Roche	–	Lot 20, BF con, and south pt lot 20, con A, twp Hamilton; L Ontario to Kingston Rd, line btwn lots 20 and 21 to line btwn lots 19 and 20, mill, mill pond, and race; 3 ch	Northumberland 39 R.P.Instrument 7457
B502	–	–.–.44	John K. Roche	–	North pt lot 20, con A, twp Hamilton; St Andrews St to Port Hope Rd and junction with line btwn lots 20 and 21; 3 ch	Northumberland 39 R.P.Instrument 7461
B503	2.7.45	2.7.45	J.K. Roche	–	Pt lot 20, con A, twp Hamilton; Kingston Rd to St Andrews St, line btwn lots 20 and 21 to Sinclair St; scale n.g.	Northumberland 39 R.P.Instrument 7684
B504	17.11.5?	–	George Sanders	'Estate of J. Connell'	Seminary St to Furnace St, Victoria St to Ball St; 200 links	Northumberland 39 R.P.Cobourg O
B505	–.6.56	25.9.81	E.C. Caddy	George M. Clark	Lots on Cottesmore Ave btwn King St and past G.T.R.; 2 ch	Northumberland 39 R.P.Cobourg 11
B506	–.–.56	22.7.56	E.C. Caddy	Mr Hayles	Lot 17, 1st con, twp Hamilton; White and Division sts, owners; 1 ch	Northumberland 39 R.P.Cobourg 3
B507	26.11.56	[26.11.56?]	Dennis & Boulton	Thomas Galt	Pt lots 17 and 18, con A, twp Hamilton; station to Campbell St, Division St to side-road btwn lots 18 and 19, bldgs; 132 ft	Northumberland 39 R.P.Cobourg 9
B508	10.6.57	[10.6.57?]	John K. Roche	Buck, Gravely & McKay	For description see **1263**	Northumberland 39 R.P.Cobourg 10
B509	28.10.57	[28.10.57?]	E.C. Caddy	Hon G.S. Boulton	Division St to Cobourg & Peterborough R.R., Seminary St to G.T.R. depot, foundry; 2 ch	Northumberland 39 R.P.Cobourg 13

B510	–	25.10.58	E.C. Caddy	Major D. Campbell	Pt lot 14, con A, twp Hamilton; btwn Fraser St, G.T.R., Darcy, and Major sts; 132 ft	Northumberland 39 R.P.Cobourg 6
B511	–.3.59	16.4.59	R.C.P. Brown	W. & D. Burnet	Pt lot XIX, BF con A, twp Hamilton; Block N, L Ontario to G.T.R., other streets, mill pond, bridges; 5 ch	Northumberland 39 R.P.Instrument 829
B512	–	13.12.61	–	Hon. G.S. Boulton	King St to G.T.R., rd allowance 14/15 to division line btwn lots 15 and 16, glebe, owners; 2 ch	Northumberland 39 R.P.Cobourg 18
B513	–	9.6.66	John K. Roche	Sidney Smith	King, Burnham, West, Chapel, John, and College sts, G.T.R. and station, Cobourg & Peterborough R.R. and station, relief, mill ponds, court-house; 5 ch	Northumberland 39 R.P.Cobourg 12
	COLBORNE					
B514	14.1.54	[14.1.54?]	J. Keeler	J.A. Keeler	Lot 31, 1st con, and 31–3, 2nd con, twp Cramahe; south of King St to Park St, Ontario St to rd allowance 30/31, 2nd con, bldgs, owners, churches; 3 ch	Northumberland 38 R.P.4 (Colborne)
B515	10.6.54	31.8.54	J. Keeler	J.M. Merriman	Lot 28, 2nd con, twp Cramahe; Kingston Rd and Furnace St, owners; 3 ch	Northumberland 38 R.P.5 (Colborne)
B516	–.8.56	27.9.56	P.V. Elmore	William Coulson	Lot 32, 1st con, twp Cramahe; G.T.R. to Coulson St, Ontario St to Division St; 2 ch	Northumberland 38 R.P.9 (Colborne)
B517	–.8.56	2.6.57	P.V. Elmore	Norman Bennett	Lot 32, 1st con, twp Cramahe; G.T.R. and station ground to Bennett St, Ontario St to Division St; 2 ch	Northumberland 38 R.P.11 (Colborne)
B518	–.–.57	–	–	'Merriman Property'	Merriman, Spring, and Grover sts, attached auction notice for 7.7.57; 2 ch	Northumberland 38 R.P. 'Merriman Prop' (Colborne)
B519	–.8.61	26.8.61	R.C.P. Brown	George Goslee	Pt lot XXX, con II, twp Cramahe; Old Post Rd to Kingston, owners; 2 ch	Northumberland 38 R.P.14 (Cramahe)

	Date of Survey	Date of Regist.	Surveyor	Owner	Description and Notes	Location
B520	–.9.62	15.12.63	J.H. Reid	Town of Colborne	Compiled plan; William St to Park St, Ontario St to Colton St, mill pond, mills, owners; transcript; 4 ch	Northumberland 38 R.P.'Reid Plan' 17
B521	–.4.64	28.5.64	A.C. Webb	J.M. Grover	North pt lot XXX, con 1, twp Cramahe; King St south to Napier St, Elgin St to beyond Kensington Ave, bldgs, G.T.R.; 4 ch	Northumberland 38 R.P.19 'Grover Plan' (Colborne)
	COLCHESTER S TWP					
B522	–.–.24	28.11.78	C. Rankin	James Wood	Lots 7–10, 2nd and 3rd cons, twp Colchester; prairie, wooded area; transcript of original; 10 ch	Essex 12 R.P.202
	COLDWATER					
B523	14.3.56	9.7.56	W.E. Yarnold	William Proudfoot & J.T. Bush	'Drumlanrig,' pt lot 24, 12th con, twp Medonte, and pt W1/2 lot 1, 12th con, twp Tay; north of Coldwater village, owners, shipyard reserve twp Tay; 3 ch	Simcoe 51 R.P.41
B524	16.7.57	12.10.57	Hugh Savigny	George Copeland	Pt lot 22, 12th con, twp Medonte; area south of Sturgeon Bay Rd along Orillia and Coldwater Rd, mill pond, mill bridges; 2 ch	Simcoe 51 R.P.16
	COLLINGWOOD					
B525	3.6.53	30.6.53	John Tully	John S. Wallace	Terminus of Northern R.R. area from road to harbour to Toronto St and from Wellington St east to Victoria St; plan damaged; 4 ch	Simcoe 51 R.P.39
B526	–.6–7.55	7.5.56	William Gibbard	George Jackson	Hume St north beyond Francis St, Albert St to Hurontario St, market block; 3 ch	Simcoe 51 R.P.39
B527	–.10.55	28.4.59	William Gibbard	B.W. Smith	Lots 43 and 44, 9th con, twp Nottawasaga; area from harbour to 5th St, Hurontario St to beyond Elm St, high water mark; area surveyed for Joel Underwood; 3 ch	Simcoe 51 R.P.73

B528	–.3.56	26.3.56	William Gibbard	Joel Underwood	Pt BF lot 44, IX con, twp Nottawasaga; north of Second St to water, Birch St to Spruce St; 2 ch	Simcoe 51 R.P.38
B529	6.4.56	21.10.56	William Gibbard	Messrs McMaster, Paterson, Hamilton & Robinson	N1/2 lot 42, 8th con, twp Nottawasaga; east of railroad to Hurontario St, south of Hume St to beyond Hamilton St, reserve for ry, owners; 3 ch	Simcoe 51 R.P.48
B530	6.5.56	23.1.57	William Gibbard	Messrs Blackburn & Faulkner	Lots 9–12, 19, and 10 in S1/2 lot 40, 10th con, twp Nottawasaga; Tecumseth St to Douglas St, Ann St to Nile St; 50 ft	Simcoe 51 R.P.51
B531	14.6.56	1.9.56	William Gibbard	David Reesor	Lot 42, 9th con, twp Nottawasaga; Hurontario St west to High St, 5th St to 10th St, owners, park reserve; 3 ch	Simcoe 51 R.P.45
B532	21.7.56	16.8.56	John Tully	Francis Lewis	Terminus of Ont Simcoe & Huron R.R., SE corner lot 40, 11th con, twp Nottawasaga; Tecumseth St to George St west of Princess St, inset location map; 1.5 ch	Simcoe 51 R.P.44
B533	15.9.56	24.3.57	William Gibbard	Messrs McMaster, Patterson, Hamilton & Robinson	St Clair St to bay, Hurontario St and ry boundary on west, market block, high water line, mill reserve; pt missing; 100 ft	Simcoe 51 R.P.55
B534	10.10.56	13.10.56	Arthur Bristow	J.P. Cummins	S1/2 lot 44, twp Nottawasaga, Alma St; 3 ch	Simcoe 51 R.P.47
B535	3.3.57	10.3.57	John Tully	[John S. Wallace?]	Pt lot 46, 11th con, twp Nottawasaga; south of St Thomas St, west of Elgin St; 31.5 ft	Simcoe 51 R.P.53
B536	29.9.63	29.12.64	John Fleming	Joseph Robinson	N1/2 lot 43, 8th con, twp Nottawasaga; alteration to **B533**, Victoria and Albert sts, Napolean and Turkish crescents, Alma Circus, and Huron, Nelson, Wellington, and Simcoe crescents and circuses altered into rectangular survey grid; 200 ft	Simcoe 51 R.P.95
B537	6.6.67	20.6.67	John Fleming	Mrs Gibbard	S1/2 lot 41, 9th con, twp Nottawasaga; west of Hurontario St; 4 ch	Simcoe 51 R.P.120
	COLUMBUS					
B538	–.3.62	19.12.62	William E. Yarnold	For Municipal Council	'Municipal Plan,' 6th and 7th cons, twp Whitby; along Church and Simcoe sts; 3 ch	Durham 40 R.P.H-50017

	Date of Survey	Date of Regist.	Surveyor	Owner	Description and Notes	Location
	CONESTOGO					
B539	–.1.57	[–.2.57?]	Schofield & Hobson	Charles Hendry, Geo. D. Wilson, David Musselman, et al.	Elgin St to Grand R, King St to Glasgow St, mill pond; 2 ch	Waterloo 58 R.P.601
B540	22.6.57	[22.6.57?]	Schofield & Hobson	Soloman Kaufman	King St to Feodore St, Kaufman St to William St; 1 ch	Waterloo 58 R.P.600
	CONSECON					
B541	–.–.53	1.12.67	C.E. Rankin, J.J. Haslett	S. Greenshields, Son & Co.	'A true copy from Congers Plan'; lots for sale on Store St, Clark's reserve, Bay, Main, Victoria, and other streets; scale n.g.	Prince Edward 47 R.P.Consecon 1
	COOKSTOWN					
B542	–.–.47	7.10.59	Archibald McNab	'Perry Estate'	S1/2 lot 1, 1st con, twp Innisfil; NE of King and Queen sts; printed title; 3 ch	Simcoe 51 R.P.76
B543	1.8.54	11.4.55	Robert Ross	William Evans	East BF lot 1, 11th con, twp Essa; NW of King and Queen sts; 2 ch	Simcoe 51 R.P.32
B544	10.8.58	10.8.58	Henry Creswicke	John Armstrong	Park lot 7, pt lot 1, 1st con, twp Innisfil; further subdivision of **B542** east of King St; 1.57 ch	Simcoe 51 R.P.64
B545	–.–.63	14.2.63	William Sanders	James Summers	Pt lot 1, 1st con, twp Innisfil; English church, bldgs; 1 ch	Simcoe 51 R.P.90
B546	–.10.64	19.10.64	William Sanders	John Hamilton	Lot 1, 15th con, twp W Gwillimbury; bldgs, owners; 1.5 ch	Simcoe 51 R.P.99
	COOKSVILLE					
B547	–.–.58	1.3.61	William Sanders	S.G. Ogden	Lot 16, 1st con north of Dundas St, twp Toronto; Dundas St north to Milton [Melissa St] west of Centre Rd, bldgs, owners, school, hall; 2 ch	Peel 43 R.P.TOR8
	COPETOWN					
B548	–	[4.10.56?]	T.A. Blyth	Samuel C. Ridley	For description see **1283**	Wentworth 62 R.P. 342 (old 33)

	CORBYVILLE					
B549	–.4.53	2.6.53	John Emerson	Ann Tapson	'Tapson,' pt lot 8, 3rd con, twp Thurlow; mill reserve by Moira R, 'Episcopal Methodist Parsonage lot'; 1 ch	Hastings 21 R.P.44
	CORNWALL					
B550	2.4.58	24.10.67	Thomas S. Rubidge, John S. Bruce	–	'Cornwall Glebe lot,' G.T.R. north of Cornwall with station yard, owners; transcript; 200 ft	Stormont 52 R.P.6A
B551	19.10.63	19.10.63	John S. Bruce	Loyal Orange Primary Lodge 880	'Cornwall Glebe lot,' same as **B550**; 200 ft	Stormont 52 R.P.6
	CORNWALL TWP					
B552	25.2.41	14.2.42	James West	–	Lot ?, pt 3rd con, twp Cornwall; plan missing	Stormont 52 R.P.1
	COURTLAND					
B553	–	–	Walsh & Mercer	–	Lots on Talbot, Main, Steam, Jane, and Union sts; 1.5 ch	Norfolk 37 R.P.14A
	CRAIGHURST					
B554	–.–.59	14.2.63	Henry Creswicke	James Patton	Lot 41, 1st con, twp Medonte; 3 ch	Simcoe 51 R.P.91
	CRANBROOK					
B555	11.5.57	19.2.62	A. Bay	William Tanner	'Tannersville,' lot XV, XIIth con, twp Grey; South St to Parliament St, Albert St to Presbytery St; 2 ch	Huron 22 R.P.305
	(CRANSFORD)					
B556	8.12.56	3.8.57	T.N. Molesworth	William Harris	Pt lot 7, IV con, east division twp Ashfield, and deviation of rd allowance btwn lots 6 and 7, IV con; Nine Mile R, mills, races, dams, bldgs; 4 ch	Huron 22 R.P.209
	CREDITON					
B557	17.2.64	4.7.64	P.K. Hyndman	'Estate of Jacob Rath'	Lot 11, con VI, twp Stephen; owners; 3 ch	Huron 22 R.P.210

	Date of Survey	Date of Regist.	Surveyor	Owner	Description and Notes	Location
B558	3.6.67	4.12.67	A. Bay	John Parsons, William Sweet, et al.	Lots X and XI, VI and VII cons, twp Stephen; 2 ch	Huron 22 R.P.211
	CREEMORE					
B559	-.-.61	9.7.62	William Sanders	Edward Webster	Pt lots 9 and 8, 4th and 5th cons, twp Nottawasaga; detailed map, bridges, mills, mill race, dams, bldgs, English church, owners, relief; 4 ch	Simcoe 55 R.P.88
	CREWSONS CORNERS					
B560	10.11.53	–	Charles Kennedy	George Ryckman	'Ryckmantown,' pt NE1/2 lot 1, 7th con, twp Eramosa; G.T.R.; transcript; 2 ch	Wellington 61 R.P.71
	CROSSHILL					
B561	1.9.62	[1.9.62?]	Moses McFadden	'Estate of Hugh Hutchison'	King to Queen St west of Hutchison St; another survey shown south of King St to Gunn St; printed title; 2 ch	Waterloo 58 R.P.616
	(CROTON)					
B562	-.-.56	–	Walsh & Mercer	H.E. Fisher	Lot 41, II con south of Talbot St, twp Middleton; con rd, Mill, Main, Hill, and Prospect sts, inset: 'Croton West'; 1.5 ch	Norfolk 37 R.P.18A
	CROWLAND TWP					
B563	16.4.60	23.2.61	Jacob Misener	'Estate of Eli Doan'	Pt lots 11 and 12 and gore, 7th con, twp Crowland; owners, farm lots; 2 ch	Niagara 59 R.P.926 (Old Crowland 1)
	CROYDON					
B564	23.6.53	25.2.60	William R. Rombough	John M. Williams	Front of lot 14, 8th con, twp Camden; Victoria and Ascension sts, river, Union and Front sts along Salmon R; 2 ch	Lennox 29 R.P.14
	CRUMLIN					
B565	–	19.8.52	Samuel Peters	Charles Priddle	Nissouri Hotel; part of plan missing; 5 ch	Middlesex 33 R.P.17

	CULLODEN					
B566	5.11.55	[5.11.55]	Jesse P. Ball	Brown, Smith & Regan	Pts of north pts lots 21 and 22, 9th con, and south pts lots 21 and 22, 8th con, twp Dereham; Chapel St to North St, East St to West St; 2 ch	Oxford 41 R.P.120
	CUMBERLAND					
B567	11.5.57	–	William McConnell	Amable Faubert	'Faubertville,' pt lot 14, con I, twp Cumberland; market to Queen St, Commercial St to St Peter St, bldgs; photoreproduction; 1 ch	Russell 50 R.P.Faubertville
B568	–.–.62	26.3.79	R. Sparks	Amable Faubert	'Faubertville,' pt lot 14, 1st con O.S., twp Cumberland; Sparks to Queen St, East to West St; 66 ft	Russell 50 R.P.Faubertville
	(CUMMINSVILLE)					
B569	2.7.57	8.7.57	Winter & Livingston	Titus G. Cummins	Pt lot 8, con II, twp Nelson; on Limestone Creek west of grist mill, woollen factory, tannery, Rachel St to Ann St, river to George St, some lots projected only; printed title; 1 ch	Halton 20 R.P.26
	CYRVILLE					
B570	12.12.66	25.12.66	R. Sparks	M. & J. Cyr	Pt lot 27, 2nd con, Ottawa Front, twp Gloucester; rd allowance to George St, St Laurent Blvd, Michael St; 2 ch	Carleton 5 R.P.23
	DALHOUSIE MILLS					
B571	14.7.60	14.7.60	A. Cattanach	James Thayer	Pt lots 8 and 9, 8th con, twp Lancaster; notes on original survey 1830, owners, mill pond and dam, Delisle R; 66 ft	Glengarry 14 R.P.13
	DARBYVILLE					
B572	19.11.56	17.3.57	Winter & Howitt	Easterbrook & Darby	Both sides Nelson and Nassagaweya Rd at rd allowance btwn lots 20 and 21, cons 3 and 4, twp Nassagaweya; 1 ch	Halton 20 R.P.24

	Date of Survey	Date of Regist.	Surveyor	Owner	Description and Notes	Location
	DARLINGTON TWP					
B573	2.11.56	4.12.56	–	George Haines	South pt lot 7, 1st con, twp Darlington; lots btwn Baseline and Kingston Rd, btwn Side Rd, lots VI and VII, and road in lot 7; 4 ch	Newcastle 10 R.P.'Haines' Darlington
B574	7.11.56	8.11.56	T.W. Herrick	F. Cubitt	Lot 7, BF, twp Darlington; Baseline to G.T.R., sideline btwn lots 6 and 7 and street west of line; 5 ch	Newcastle 10 R.P.'Cubitt' Darlington
B575	23.3.57	[23.3.57?]	Lawrence H. Shortt	Wm Pinch	Pt lot 14, 3rd con, twp Darlington; side-rd allowance and 1st to 4th sts; 2 ch	Newcastle 10 R.P.'Pinch' Darlington
	DAWN TWP					
B576	–.4.61	[16.4.61?]	E.R. Jones	William Kelly	East pt lot 34, 7th con, and lots 33 and 34, 8th con, and lot 34, 9th con, and west pt lot 34, 10th con, twp Dawn; 8 ch	Lambton 25 R.P.Dawn 2
B577	–.4.61	26.7.61	G.P. Liddy	Messrs Winslow & Patchin	West pt lot 34, 7th con, twp Dawn; later cancelled; 2 ch	Lambton 25 R.P.Dawn 3
B578	5.4.66	10.4.66	Henry Smith	A. Farewell	E1/2 lot 32, con 8, twp Dawn; 3 ch	Lambton 25 R.P.Dawn 5
B579	18.6.66	19.6.66	Henry Smith	R.A. Alger	Lot 31, con 9, twp Dawn; inset map shows location of wells and well bldg; 4 ch	Lambton 5 R.P.Dawn 6
	(DEAL town plot)					
B580	14.8.65	12.5.66	Alexander McIntosh, A.P. Salter	C. Smith	Lot 145, twp Raleigh; L Erie to Victoria St, Albert St by 'Ditch' to Raleigh, Centre St; 1.25 ch	Kent 24 R.P.181
	(DEELMAGE CITY town plot)					
B581	15.12.65	31.1.66	A.C. Webb	Owen Deelmage	Pt lot 22, 11th con, twp Percy; plan missing	Northumberland 38 R.P.25

	DELAWARE					
B582	–	3.5.54	Benjamin Springer	George Tiffany	BF lots 4 and 5, 1st con, twp Delaware; Commissioners Rd to Pleasant St, river to York and Wellington sts; photoreproduction; 4 ch	Middlesex 34 R.P.47
B583	–	17.2.55	B. Springer	Dr A. Francis	Pt park lots II and V; King St E to Wellington St E, Prince Albert St to Victoria St; photoreproduction; 1 ch	Middlesex 34 R.P.83
	DELAWARE WEST					
B584	14.9.54	14.4.60	Benjamin Springer	Joseph Dain	East pt lot 23 and lot 24 north of Longwoods Rd, twp Caradoc; King St west to Thames, Adelaide St to Thames; photoreproduction; 2 ch	Middlesex 34 R.P.160 1/2
	DELHI					
B585	29.7.51	–	Thomas Walsh	–	'Fredericksburg,' pt lot 188, north of Talbot Rd E; laid out btwn Talbot Rd and 12th con, Windham Twp; 4 ch	Norfolk 37 R.P.16A
	DELTA					
B586	30.6.65	–	W. Beatty	For Municipal Council of Bastard & Burgess	Compiled plan; lots on streets off Main and King sts, owners; 2 ch	Leeds 28 R.P.116
	DEMORESTVILLE					
B587	6.10.66	5.6.76	Charles E. Rankin	For Municipal Council	River to James St, Thomas St to South St, bldgs, mills, 2 graveyards; 3 ch	Prince Edward 47 R.P. Demorestville 1
	DESERONTO					
B588	26.8.37	4.9.51	G.S. Clapp	John Culbertson	'Diseronca,' Bay of Quinte to Belleville-Kingston Rd, 1st St to 7th St, wharf; 4 ch	Hastings 21 R.P.43
B589	9.12.56	7.5.57	G.S. Clapp	Archibald Culbertson	E1/2 lot 38, BF 1st con, twp Tyendinaga; Main St to road to Napanee, steam mill to St George St; 2 ch	Hastings 21 R.P.84

	Date of Survey	Date of Regist.	Surveyor	Owner	Description and Notes	Location
	DINSLEY TERRACE					
B590	–.11.54	16.3.55	William Perceval	Edward Dinsley	Pt lot 36, 1st con, twp Stanley; 2 ch	Huron 22 R.P.225
	DOON					
B591	–.–.57	[29.12.57?]	Schofield & Hobson	Hon. Adam Ferrie	Streets named, mill pond, various mills, vegetation, businesses identified; 2 ch	Waterloo 58 R.P.578
	DORADO					
B592	–.–.56	9.3.58	William Smith	C. Cosens	Lots along Elma St btwn Grey and Perth sts, Moss Inn, Maitland R; 2 ch	Perth 44 R.P.281
	DORCHESTER					
B593	–.–.53–4	10.6.54	Samuel Peters	P. Hunter	'Frampton,' pt lot 9, 4th con, twp N Dorchester; north of Thames R, south of G.W.R.; 2 ch	Middlesex 33 R.P.52
	DORCHESTER N TWP					
B594	–.–.55	5.3.60	William Ralph	Messrs William & Peter McClary	Lot XI and W1/2 lot XII, 1st con south of Thames R, twp N Dorchester; Elgin Rd and area to east; 1 ch	Middlesex 33 R.P.158 Co
B595	30.12.56	23.1.57	Samuel Peters	Charles G. Moore	N1/2 lot 13, 2nd con, twp N Dorchester; north of Thames R; 3 ch	Middlesex 33 R.P.133 Co
B596	–.–.60	9.3.63	William Ralph	William McClary	E1/2 lot XV and SW1/4 lot XIV, 1st con, twp N Dorchester south of Thames R; park lots; 4 ch	Middlesex 33 R.P.185 Co
	DOUGLAS					
B597	4.3.53	30.9.53	J.S. Harper	J.G. Malloch	Lots 3–5, 8th con, twp Bromley; Robertson St to High St, Queen St to Edward St, mills, slides, squares; 4 ch	Renfrew 49 R.P.1
B598	–.4.60	1.8.60	William J. McDonald	Robert R. Smith	Pt lot 5, 9th con, twp Bromley; Smith to Cameron St, Elizabeth St to Queen St, burying ground; 2 ch	Renfrew 49 R.P.15

	DOVER TWP					
B599	–.5.66	23.9.68	Charles Fraser	M. McLear	'Baldoon Farm'; west of Sydenham R, east of Chenail Ecarté, old house sites, windmills, burying grounds, etc; 4 ch	Kent 24 R.P.208
	DOWNIE TWP					
B600	27.8.57	10.9.58	Alfred Howitt	–	Road btwn con lines VI and VII and VII and IX, twp Downie; lots, houses, bearings, distances, certified by adjacent owners; 5 ch	Perth 44 R.P.301
B601	1.4.59	–	Joseph G. Kirk	–	Alteration of road in cons IX and X, Gore of Downie; bearings, position, original rd allowance; 5 ch	Perth 44 R.P.302
B602	4.9.63	18.3.64	Joseph G. Kirk	Thomas White & Thomas G. Thomson	Mill ground and road alterations, lot 18, con VII, twp Downie; description, bearings, distances; 3 ch	Perth 44 R.P.303
	DRAYTON					
B603	10.4.60	6.6.60	Edwin H. Kertland	Messrs Hambly & Wales	Main St south to Queen St, Union St to beyond King St, bridges, mill property; 2 ch	Wellington 60 R.P.4
B604	18.6.61	16.7.61	Joseph W. Burke	John Dales	Lot I, con X, twp Peel; south side Main St east of Union and John sts; 2 ch	Wellington 60 R.P.3 (142)
B605	13.6.62	13.6.62	W.H.L. Lapenotiere	J. Ferrie	Main St to Canistoga R, Wellington St east to beyond Elm St; 2 ch	Wellington 60 R.P.1 (149)
B606	20.9.64	9.1.65	Lapenotiere & Bolger	For Municipal Council	Queen St to Canistoga R, Wellington St to Union St and beyond; 3 ch	Wellington 60 R.P.9 (162?)
	DRESDEN					
B607	5.11.45	1.6.67	Richard Parr	D.R. Van Allen	Pt lot 4, 5th con, twp Dawn; Main St to St John St, George St to Metcalfe St and Sydenham R; 2 ch	Kent 24 R.P.127
B608	–.–.52	1.6.67	Richard Parr	D.R. Van Allen	Pt lot 4, 4th con, Gore Camden; Queen St to Metcalfe St to St George St; 2 ch	Kent 24 R.P.128
B609	8.5.55	1.6.67	Samuel Smith	William Wright	'Fairport,' pt lot 3, Vth con, twp Dawn; copy by A.P. Salter, Sydenham St to Main St, North St to Sydenham R; 2 ch	Kent 24 R.P.131

	Date of Survey	Date of Regist.	Surveyor	Owner	Description and Notes	Location
B610	26.10.64	21.7.65	William R. Rombough	Carscallen & Thorey	'North Dresden,' pt lot 4, 4th con, Gore Camden; Camden St to Richmond St btwn James and St George sts; 2 ch	Kent 24 R.P.130
B611	–.–.64 and 66	5.3.67	William R. Rombough	Carscallen & Thorey	'North Dresden,' pt lot 4, 4th con, Camden W Gore; Sydenham R to Richmond St, Rufus St to St George St; 2 ch	Kent 24 R.P.130
B612	–	1.6.67	Salter & Jones	Corporation of Dresden	'Fairport,' pts lots 4, 4th con, and lots 3 and 4, 5th con, Camden Gore; compiled plan, Sydenham St to Metcalfe Ave, West St to Victoria St, 'strangers burying ground'; 2 ch	Kent 24 R.P.126
	DRUMBO					
B613	11.10.51	–	James Black	Henry Munro	Oxford St north to Hope St, Wilmot St east to Jackson St, bldgs; 2 ch	Oxford 41 R.P.22
B614	17.8.57	[15.9.57?]	Thomas Allchin	Maitland Fisher	For description see **1295**	Oxford 41 R.P.104
B615	5.5.59	–	Thomas Allchin	Henry Muma	Oxford St to Buffalo & L Huron R.R. grounds and Jarvis St, lots on both sides Wilmot St btwn Mill and Mechanic sts; 2 ch	Oxford 41 R.P.117
B616	1.9.60	–	Cyrus Carroll	Corporation of Blenheim Township	Lot 13, 16th con, and lots 12 and 13, 7th con, twp Blenheim; South St to Buffalo & L Huron R.R. and Jarvis St, Henry St to Wilmot St; 3 ch	Oxford 41 R.P.123
B617	29.8.61	[30.8.61?]	Cyrus Carroll	Henry Muma	Pt lots 12 and 13, 7th con, twp Blenheim; South St to Railway and Jarvis sts, Henry St to Wilmot St; 2 ch	Oxford 41 R.P.135
B618	7.7.62	[7.7.62?]	W.G. Wonham	Henry Muma	Oxford St to Buffalo & L Huron R.R. and Jarvis St, Mill St to Mechanic St; 2 ch	Oxford 41 R.P.138
	DRYSDALE					
B619	–.–.56	22.10.56	John Denison	Messrs Robert Drysdale & James McDonald	'Drysdaleville,' S1/2 lot 25, W Lake Rd Con, and pt lot 30, and SE corner lot 25, W Lake Rd Con, twp Stanley; 2 ch	Huron 22 R.P.226

	DUART					
B620	5.6.57	1.6.67	John O'Mara	Thomas Carswell	'Dun-Eden,' pt lot 5, north side Ridge Rd, twp Orford; bounded by Ridge Rd, St Andrews Rd, Dundas St, Inverara Rd, and Wallace St; 3 ch	Kent 24 R.P.170
	DUBLIN					
B621	11.11.61	12.11.61	A. Bay	J. Whitehead	'Carronbrook,' lots XV and XVI, 1st con, twp Hibbert; Buffalo & L Huron R.R. bisects lots; 2 ch	Perth 44 R.P.314
	DUMFRIES N TWP					
B622	19.12.54	9.4.61	James Pollock	Adam Ainslie	S1/2 lot 6, 12th con, twp N Dumfries; owners; 2 ch	Waterloo 67 R.P.609 (2nd)
	DUNDAS					
B623	–.–.37	–	Robert W. Kerr	Estate of Richard Hatt	Copy 11.4.51, Head St to York St, Mill St to Mountain St, specific mills, proposed mill sites; transcript; scale n.g.	Wentworth 62 R.P.1443 2 pts
B624	–.3.52	–	H. McMahon	St James Church	'Coot's Paradise,' Main St to canal basin, Morden's Creek to North St, church survey; 100 ft	Wentworth 62 R.P.1464 (formerly Dun 22)
B625	7.9.55	9.1.56	J. MacIntosh	Messrs Allan & Mathieson	Freestone Quarry to Park St, Sydenham St to Princess St; 2 ch	Wentworth 62 R.P.1446 (formerly Dun 4)
B626	28.5.56	31.5.56	Bristow, Fitzgerald & Spencer	J. Leslie	Pt lots 13 and 14, 1st con, twp Flamborough W; along Mountain St btwn Market and Brock sts; 132 ft	Wentworth 62 R.P.1446 (formerly Dun 24)
B627	30.6.57	9.11.57	Thomas A. Blyth	Hon. Sir A.N. MacNab, Hon. W. Cayley	Station to Park St, York Rd to Sydenham Rd, owners, cemetery; 120 ft	Wentworth 62 R.P.1447 (formerly Dun 5)
B628	13.8.62	[13.8.62?]	Walter G. Bellair	Rev William McMurray	Hatt St to King St, Foundry St to McMurray St; 30 ft	Wentworth 62 R.P.1453 (formerly Dun 11)

	Date of Survey	Date of Regist.	Surveyor	Owner	Description and Notes	Location
	DUNGANNON					
B629	17.1.56	17.1.56	William Perceval	William Mallough	Pt lot 12, 4th con, twp Ashfield; James St to Albert St off Southampton St; 2 ch	Huron 22 R.P.227
B630	19.3.57	19.3.57	Molesworth & Weatherald	William McMath	Albert St to James St, Southampton St to William St; 1 ch	Huron 22 R.P.228
	DUNN TWP					
B631	10.5.49	22.1.50	Andrew Hood	Hugh Earl	'Earl Tract,' 1st, 2nd, and 3rd cons south of Dunnville and Dover Rd, twp Dunn; near Haldimand Village and north of Grand R, lot descriptions, relief; 10 ch	Haldimand 18 R.P.518A Card 10
B632	7.9.65	5.1.66	Henry Lawe	Estate of William H. Merritt et al.	'Haldimand Tract,' lots 13–16 and west pt of lot 17, 2nd con, and pt of lots 13–17, 1st con south of Dunnville and Dover Rd, and pts of lots 13–16, 1st con north of Dunnville and Dover Rd, twp Dunn; south of Haldimand Village on Grand R; 10 ch	Haldimand 18 R.P.14472 Card 10
	DUNNVILLE					
B633	2.4.53	6.3.54	Andrew Hood	Hezekiah Davis	Lot 4, north side Canal St E, and lots 1 and 2, north side Lock St and along Chestnut St; 30 ft	Haldimand 18 R.P.2539 Card 21
B634	20.2.56	16.2.59	Andrew Hood	William H. Merritt et al.	Lots I-V on Canal St W; brick store; 20 ft	Haldimand 18 R.P.7135 Card 22
	DUNTROON					
B635	24.1.58	6.4.58	William Gibbard	Rev John Campbell	NW1/4 lot 24, 8th con, twp Nottawasaga; east of Hurontario St, reserves, streets named; 2 ch	Simcoe 51 R.P.62
B636	26.7.61	10.1.62	T.C. Prosser	Angus & Archibald Bell	'South Bowmore,' pt lot XXV, VIII con, twp Nottawasaga; east of Hurontario St, north of Simcoe St; 1 ch	Simcoe 51 R.P.86

	DURHAM					
B637	[19.7.53?]	[19.7.53?]	John D. Daniell	A. & W. Hunter	Pt lot 24, 1st con, twp Bentinck and Glenelg; William St to Owen Sound Rd, Durham Rd to Jackson St; 102 ft	Grey 17 R.P.501
B638	–.7.54	24.8.55	David Gibson	John Edge	Pt lot 25, 1st con, twp Glenelg; Lambton St to Durham Rd, Garafraxa Rd to Rock St, several mills; 4 ch	Grey 17 R.P.502
B639	2.7.55	8.8.55	Edwin H. Kertland	John Moodie	Lots on 3rd division lot XXVII, 1st con, twp Glenelg (Old Survey); 2 ch	Grey 17 R.P.504
B640	2.7.55	8.8.55	Edwin H. Kertland	George Jackson	Lots on 2nd division lot XXVII, 1st con, twp Bentinck; Garafraxa Rd to Countess St, east and west of South St; 4 ch	Grey 17 R.P.505
B641	2.7.55	8.8.55	Edwin H. Kertland	Charles Vollett	Lots on 2nd division lot XXVII, 1st con, twp Glenelg; Garafraxa Rd, owners; 4 ch	Grey 17 R.P.507
B642	9.7.55	8.8.55	Edwin H. Kertland	Thomas Brown	Lots on 1st division lot XXVII, 1st con, twp Bentinck (Old Survey); Garafraxa Rd to Saugeen west of South St; 2 ch	Grey 17 R.P.506
B643	22.1.56	25.2.56	Edwin H. Kertland	William Hunter	Lots on 2nd and 3rd divisions of lot 24, 1st con, twp Bentinck; Owen Sound Rd to Park St, Durham Rd to John St, owners; 165 ft	Grey 17 R.P.508
B644	26.2.56	1.3.56	Edwin H. Kertland	William Hunter	Lots on 3rd division lot 23 and 1st division lot 24, 1st con, twp Bentinck; Owen Sound Rd to Park St, Markham St to Wyndham St; approx 165 ft	Grey 17 R.P.509
B645	4.10.56	23.11.57	William R. Rombough	John G. Davidson	Lots on 1st division lot XXVII, 1st con, twp Glenelg; Garafraxa Rd to Brock St, Elizabeth St to South St E; 1 ch	Grey 17 R.P.510
	EASTHOPE N TWP					
B646	1.7.55	31.7.55	John Tully	Ned Carruthers	For description see **1079**	Perth 44 R.P.279
B647	–.–.56	30.6.58	William Smith	James Dougherty	Lot 22, 13th con, twp N Easthope; 2 ch	Perth 44 R.P.289
B648	–.4.57	–	Joseph G. Kirk	–	Lot 45, 3rd con, twp N Easthope; 4 ch	Perth 44 R.P.288

	Date of Survey	Date of Regist.	Surveyor	Owner	Description and Notes	Location
	EASTHOPE S TWP					
B649	[11.2.59?]	14.2.59	Joseph G. Kirk	Thomas Towers	Pt lot 41 and 42, con VI, twp S Easthope; 100 acres, mill pond; 4 ch	Perth 44 R.P.320
B650	6.5.61?	30.5.61	Joseph G. Kirk	John Wilson	Lot 40, 1st con, twp S Easthope; G.T.R., travelled road; 4 ch	Perth 44 R.P.321
B651	1.10.61?	18.3.62	Joseph Kirk	David Tracksell	Pt lot 20, 1st con, twp S Easthope; south of G.T.R. grounds; 2 ch	Perth 44 R.P.323
	EASTONS CORNERS					
B652	-.4.50	24.3.52	William Campbell	Samuel S. Easton	W1/2 lot 24, 2nd con, twp Wolford; along Elgin, Beaver, and Ann sts, Main and Henry sts; 50 ft	Grenville 15 R.P.Wolford 2
B653	-.7.54	2.8.55	John Burchill	George Henry & J. Easton, Julie Denaent	Rear pt lot 25, 2nd con, twp Wolford; along Queen's Hwy btwn Beaver and Henry sts; 50 ft	Grenville 15 R.P.Wolford 3
B654	–	3.7.58	John Burchill	George Easton	Pt lot 25, 2nd con, twp Wolford; along Queens Hwy, Baldwin, and Henry sts; 160 ft	Grenville 15 R.P.Wolford 4
	EASTWOOD					
B655	27.10.56	[27.10.56?]	W.G. Wonham	Messrs Vansittart & Cottle	Pt lot 8, 1st con, twp E Oxford; Dundas St to G.W.R. and Brantford and Ingersoll Rd, both sides East St; 2 ch	Oxford 41 R.P.90
B656	28.11.56	[28.11.56?]	W.G. Wonham	Thomas Phelan	E1/2 lot 9, 1st con, twp E Oxford; Dundas St to G.W.R., Broadway St to Phelan St; 2 ch	Oxford 41 R.P.91
	EDEN MILLS					
B657	[30.10.52?]	30.10.52	–	Adam Lind Argo	'Eden,' pt lot 1, 2nd con, twp Eramosa; Main St to Speed R; 2 ch	Wellington 61 R.P.67
B658	-.8.54	26.10.54	Francis Kerr	H. Hartop	'Eden,' south side of river on Mill, York, and Cedar sts, grist and sawmill; 4 ch	Wellington 61 R.P.68

B659	14.12.55	14.12.55	William Haskins	Henry Hartop & John A. Davidson	'Eden,' pt lot 1, 2nd con, twp Eramosa; road btwn Eramosa and Nassagaweya twps to Eramosa branch of Speed R, SE of Elm St, mills and ponds; 1 ch	Wellington 61 R.P.69
	EGANVILLE					
B660	19.2.[59?]	23.3.63	Forrest & Thistle	Estate of John Egan	Pt lots 18 and 19, con VIII, twp Wilberforce, lots 20 and 21, con XXI, twp Grattan; copied by William Bell PLS, Alice St to Campbell St, Raglan and Paul sts to Maple and Church sts, church reserves, mills, slide, sawlog pond; 2 ch	Renfrew 49 R.P.16
	EGMONDVILLE					
B661	–	8.9.57	Molesworth & Weatherald	C.L. Van Egmond	Lots 10 and 11, II and III con, twp Tuckersmith; Raglan St to Victoria St, William and Dunlop sts to mill pond, bldgs; 3.2 ch	Huron 22 R.P.232
	ELDORADO					
B662	2.1.67	2.3.67	C.F. Aylsworth	John Moore	NE1/4 lot 17, 5th con, twp Madoc; lots on Centre, John, and Charles sts; 2 ch	Hastings 21 R.P.114
B663	–.3.67	–.3.67	C.F. Aylsworth	John Moore	NE1/4 lot 17, 5th con, twp Madoc; a correction to **B662**, John and Charles sts extended further away from Hastings St; 2 ch	Hastings 21 R.P.115
B664	[–.11.67?]	4.12.67	Murdoch, Reid & Unwin	Hugh R. Fletcher & T.D. Ledyard	For description see **1303**	Hastings 21 R.P.121
	ELIZABETHTOWN TWP					
B665	7.11.59	–	Francis Jones	A.P. Colton	Pt of rear 1/2 lot VI, 1st con, twp Elizabethtown; lots on G.T.R.; transcript; 1 ch	Leeds 28 R.P.112
	ELIZABETHVILLE					
B666	–.–.[5?]	–	–	John McMurtry	Mill pond to Church St, King St to William St, bldgs identified, Episcopal church; 1 ch	Port Hope 9 R.P.Hope 6

	Date of Survey	Date of Regist.	Surveyor	Owner	Description and Notes	Location
	ELMIRA					
B667	–.–.61	–.–.[62?]	M.C. Schofield	Joel Good	Lots on both sides King and Mill sts btwn Arthur and Park sts; 2 ch	Waterloo 58 R.P.559
B668	7.7.62	[7.7.62?]	James Pollock	'Jonas Wenger'	Lot 88, German Company Tract, twp Woolwich; south of Church St SE and on both sides Arthur St, owners; 2 ch	Waterloo 58 R.P.560
B669	19.5.66	[19.5.66?]	James Pollock	Robert Kenning	Lot 89, German Company Tract, twp Woolwich; lots on both sides Factory St, north of Church St, east of Arthur St; 2 ch	Waterloo 58 R.P. 558
	ELORA					
B670	12.7.51	12.7.51	Edwin H. Kertland	–	For description see **1305**	Wellington 61 R.P.56
B671	–.6.54	26.3.57	J. Mackintosh	James Mathieson	Lot 18, 11th con, twp Nichol; btwn Sophia and Mathieson sts; 4 ch	Wellington 61 R.P.76
B672	–.–.56	20.5.59	Edwin H. Kertland	–	For description see **1309**	Wellington 61 R.P.111
B673	14.6.58	–	J.W. Burke	W.P. Newman	Lot 21, west side of Geddes St; 1 ch	Wellington 61 R.P.101
B674	20.6.59	2.7.59	J.W. Burke	Messrs Mathieson & Allan	Pt lot 18, con XI, twp Nichol; Colbourne St to Mathieson St, Elora and Saugeen Rd to Irvine St; 4 ch	Wellington 61 R.P.112
	EMBRO					
B675	16.12.33	[10.2.54?]	Peter Carroll, W.G. Wonham	Isaac Buchanan	Copied in 1854; Commissioner St to St Andrews St, Huron Rd to north branch of Thames, mill and mill pond; 2 ch	Oxford 41 R.P.39
B676	7.9.53	–	William Smiley	James & George Adams	Pt SE1/4 lot 12, 4th con, twp West Zorra; Huron St to Elgin St, James St to Union St; 1 ch	Oxford 41 R.P.134
B677	17.9.53	30.1.54	William Smiley	John D. Dent	Pt NW pt of NW1/4 lot 11, 5th con, twp Zorra; rd allowance btwn cons 4 and 5 to Sutherland St, along John St; 1 ch	Oxford 41 R.P.38

B678	7.2.54	–	J.K. Clendinen	John D. Dent	Thames R to con line south of Commissioners St; 2 ch	Oxford 41 R.P.145
B679	12.11.55	–	William Smiley	George Duncan	NE pt lot 11, 4th con, twp Zorra; John, Elgin, and Huron sts, owners; 1 ch	Oxford 41 R.P.133
B680	14.12.55	–	William Smiley	Jacob Hodginson	NE pt lot 12, 4th con, twp West Zorra; Maria St to Huron St, North St to Elizabeth St; 1 ch	Oxford 41 R.P.69
B681	–.–.[5?]	–	William McMillan	Messrs Colin Munroe, Levi Fowler & James Ferguson	For description see **1310**	Oxford 41 R.P.131
B682	20.11.56	[20.11.56?]	Leather & Robinson	Messrs J. Ferguson, C. Munroe & L. Fowler	For description see **1311**	Oxford 41 R.P.81
B683	27.3.66	19.4.66	William Smiley	Donald Matheson	NW pt lot 12, 5th con, twp West Zorra; Thames and mill pond to St Andrews and Huron sts; 4 ch	Oxford 41 R.P.164
	EMBRUN					
B684	1.12.63	10.4.66	H.O. Wood	D.J. Bonchere?	Lot 8, 8th con, twp Russell; Roy St and Castor R btwn 7 and 8 con rd and centre of 8th con, bldgs identified; 100 ft	Russell 50 R.P.Embrun
	ENNISKILLEN TWP					
B685	–.9.60	–	P.S. Donnelly	C.G. Bruce	Pt lot 17, 1st con, twp Enniskillen; 4 ch	Lambton 25 R.P.Enniskillen 2
B686	5.7.61	7.7.63	James Pollock	J.H.E. Akins & G.E. Fuller	S1/2 of E1/4 lot 15, 4th con, twp Enniskillen; later cancelled; 2 ch	Lambton 25 R.P.Enniskillen 5
B687	13.7.61	[13.7.61?]	James Pollock	Julia A. Macklem	Lot XIX, 1st con, twp Enniskillen; streets laid out but unnamed; 3 ch	Lambton 25 R.P.Enniskillen 3
B688	–.10.65	13.2.66	E.R. Jones	Mr Fox et al.	Pt SE1/4 lot 14, 3rd con, twp Enniskillen; Black Creek, plank rd; 2 ch	Lambton 25 R.P.Enniskillen 6
B689	–.12.65	23.5.66	J.J. Francis	William Bauborn	E1/2 of W1/2 lot 14, 3rd con, twp Enniskillen; relief, creek, etc; 2 ch	Lambton 25 R.P.Enniskillen 11 1/2
B690	–.1.66	19.2.66	E.R. Jones	Messrs Shannon, Kelly & Bruce	W1/2 lot 20, 1st con, twp Enniskillen; Cross and Centre sts; 2 ch	Lambton 25 R.P.Enniskillen 7

	Date of Survey	Date of Regist.	Surveyor	Owner	Description and Notes	Location
B691	–.1.66	5.3.66	J.J. Francis	Messrs Bruce, Ives & Dunham	Lot 15, 1st con, twp Enniskillen, and lots 32 and 33, 7th con, twp Dawn; A St to 9th St, County Rd to rd btwn cons 6 and 7; 4 ch	Lambton 25 R.P.Enniskillen 71/2 (Dawn 4)
B692	21.4.66	23.3.66	Henry Smith	Henry Howland	NW1/4 lot 14, IX con, twp Enniskillen; relief, treed areas, inset map shows region with oil wells, company names and/or landowners, 2 ch	Lambton 25 R.P.Enniskillen 8
B693	–.4.66	26.4.66	E.R. Jones	Messrs Thurber & Fox	N1/2 lot 14, 1st con, twp Enniskillen; 4 ch	Lambton 25 R.P.Enniskillen 10
B694	–	18.5.66	George Gibson	Alexander H. Morrison & Mr Griffin	Lot 16, 12th con, twp Enniskillen; Bear Creek, oil wells; 4 ch	Lambton 25 R.P.Enniskillen 11
B695	28.5.66	26.5.66	Henry Smith	Messrs Ellis & Howland	Lot 15, con 8, twp Enniskillen; bldgs; 4 ch	Lambton 25 R.P.Enniskillen 12
B696	–.5.66	28.6.66	George Gibson	William Richardson	N1/2 lot 13, 9th con, twp Enniskillen; Durham Creek, oil wells, owners; 4 ch	Lambton 25 R.P.Enniskillen 13
B697	11.8.66	19.4.67	William McMillan	Henry Swift & David Garth	Lot 22, 3rd con, twp Enniskillen; 200 ft	Lambton 25 R.P.Enniskillen 17
B698	9.11.66	30.11.66	Henry Smith	Todd & Elmons	E1/2 lot 22, 2nd con, twp Enniskillen; Black Creek, owners; 4 ch	Lambton 25 R.P.Enniskillen 14
B699	4.3.67	14.3.67	George Gibson	A.R. Ball	SE1/4 lot 11, 12th con, twp Enniskillen; oil wells; 4 ch	Lambton 25 R.P.Enniskillen 16
	ENNOTVILLE					
B700	28.3.55	21.1.59	Edwin H. Kertland	John McLaren	Lot 10, 6th con, twp Nichol; McLaren, Henry, Main, and Margarette sts, bldgs; 2 ch	Wellington 61 R.P.109

	ENTERPRISE					
B701	9.12.54	4.3.65	William R. Aylsworth	Jackson, Jackson & Dopking	Pts lots XXXVII and XXXVIII, con VII, and pt lot 37, con VIII, twp Camden; South St to Concession Rd, West St to Ann St; 132 ft	Lennox 29 R.P.2
	EPSOM					
B702	–.9.60	14.2.61	W.E. Yarnold	For Municipal Council	Lots 6 and 7, 7th con, twp Reach; King St north to beyond Byron St, Brock St to Palace St, owners; 2 ch	Durham 40 R.P.H-50027
	ERBSVILLE					
B703	–.–.61	[12.9.61?]	Joseph Hobson	Samuel Erb	Lot 45, Upper Block, twp Waterloo; mill pond, water lots, King and Waterloo sts; resurvey; 2 ch	Waterloo 58 R.P.575
	ERIN					
B704	15.11.52	–	Charles Kennedy	–	For description see **1312**	Wellington 61 R.P.61
B705	–.4.58	28.6.58	Charles J. Wheelock	'Estate of Daniel McMillan'	Pt lot 15, 10th con, twp Erin; Main St to Wheelock St, rd allowance btwn lots 14 and 15 and 15 and 16; 2 ch	Wellington 61 R.P.102
B706	–.4.5[8?]	24.12.58	Charles J. Wheelock	John S. Shingler	Pt lot 13, 10th con, twp Erin; 1 ch	Wellington 61 R.P.107
B707	–.–.61	28.10.63	C.J. Wheelock	Thomas Brown	Pt E1/2 lot 15, 9th con, twp Erin; Antrim St to rd allowance btwn cons 9 and 10; 2 ch	Wellington 61 R.P.157
B708	–.6.65	2.12.65	C.J. Wheelock	Charles McMillan	E1/2 lot 15, 9th con, twp Erin, north of mill privilege, pond, and Church St W; transcript; 2 ch	Wellington 61 R.P.167
	ERIN TWP					
B709	–.10.62	18.1.65	C.J. Wheelock	William Clark	Pt lot 12, 9th and 10th cons, twp Erin; 2 ch	Wellington 61 R.P.165
	ERINDALE					
B710	10.7.50	9.4.57	W.F. Brown	–	'Springfield,' lots 4–6, 1st range SE of Dundas St, Credit Reserve; Thompson St to river, [Nanticoke] St to Proudfoot St,	Peel 42 R.P.TOR7

	Date of Survey	Date of Regist.	Surveyor	Owner	Description and Notes	Location
					owners, Credit R west, grist mill, mill race; 2 ch	
B711	8.5.62	29.12.62	F.F. Passmore	'Magrath Family'	Pt lot 6, 1st and 2nd range, 'Racey Tract,' north of Dundas St; road, cleared areas; 2 ch	Peel 43 R.P.TOR9
	ERINSVILLE					
B712	31.9.54	7.1.55	William R. Rombough	John Murphy	West front lot 9, 4th con, twp Sheffield; Ottawa Rd, Tullow and Thomas sts; 1 ch	Lennox 29 R.P.16
	ERNESTOWN					
B713	4.7.56	15.7.56	A.B. Perry	John Link	'Linkville,' lot 19, 2nd con, twp Ernestown; 2nd con rd to Victoria St, John St to King St, station grounds G.T.R.; 2 ch	Lennox 29 R.P.13A
	ERNESTOWN TWP					
B714	3.5.54	24.6.54	A.B. Perry	'Episcopal Methodist Church'	Pt lot 5, 4th con, twp Ernestown; lots on both sides Centre Ave btwn church, parsonage, and public cemetery; 2 rods	Lennox 29 R.P.13
	ETOBICOKE TWP					
B715	11.6.47	15.10.47	John Stoughton Dennis	John Gurbb	'St Andrews,' (later Thistletown); lots mainly along Albion Plank Rd; 2 ch	Toronto 64 R.P.6
B716	16.10.47	25.11.47	John Stoughton Dennis	John Chew	Subdivision of lot V, Vth con, twp York; lots along Weston Plank Rd, Centre, and Elgin sts, Humber R; 3 ch	Toronto 64 R.P.7
B717	12.10.49	9.6.51	James McCallum, Jr	John P. Delahaye	'Claireville,' pt lot 40, 4th con, twp Etobicoke; 2 ch	Toronto 64 R.P.28
B718	–.7.50	5.1.54	John Stoughton Dennis	James Henderson	'Etobicoke,' lots D, E, and F and pts lots C and G on L Ontario and lots 1 and 2, 2nd range from Humber R, south of Mill Reserve; Mimicoke Creek; 4 ch	Toronto 64 R.P.83
B719	10.5.51	27.4.53	John Tully	Watkins Gamble	'Milton on the Humber,' 10th con, BF (Lambton), twp Etobicoke; south of Dundas St btwn plank rd to Milton Mills and con B, owners; 2 ch	Toronto 64 R.P.26

B720	17.8.54	23.4.55	Robert F. Lynn	Estate of Duncan Murchinson	'Lambton West'; lots 10 and 11, con C, south division BF Etobicoke; along Dundas St, owners, mills, bridge, post office; 2 ch	Toronto 64 R.P.116
B721	14.1.56	29.7.56	J.O. Browne	J. Lukin Robinson	'Etobicoke,' subdivision of lots C–F and lot 1, 2nd range from Humber R, south of Mill Reserve; north and south from Lakeshore Rd, estate in detail; further subdivision of **B718**; 4 ch	Toronto 64 R.P.164
B722	1.10.56	13.10.56	J. Stoughton Dennis	John & W. Arnold	Subdivision of lots 20 and 21, con C fronting on Humber R, twp Etobicoke; area west of Humber R and G.T.R. station btwn River St and rd allowance btwn lots 21 and 22; 3 ch	Toronto 64 R.P.174
B723	6.11.56	12.12.56	J. Stoughton Dennis	John Arnold	Subdivision of park lots 131–3 of lot 20, con B, on Humber R; Arnold St to Bridge St, Elora to River St; 100 ft	Toronto 64 R.P.186
B724	1.1.57	19.3.58	J. Stoughton Dennis	John A. Donaldson	'Lambton,' lot 11, con C, and pts lots 10, cons B and C, twp Etobicoke; Humber R west and north from Dundas Rd, ravine land, relief; 400 ft	Toronto 64 R.P.234
B725	3.5.62	9.5.62	F.F. Passmore	J. Lukin Robinson	Alteration of plan R.P.164 (14.1.56) to close Windsor St; area south of Hamilton & Toronto Ry along Manchester, Southampton, Hanover, and Coventry sts	Toronto 64 R.P.63
	EVERTON					
B726	17.8.57	19.8.57	William Haskins	Messrs Everts & Stewart	Pts lots 11 and 12, 7th con, twp Eramosa; Wellington St to north of Albert St, Stewart St to Evert St, bldgs, mills, etc; 2 ch	Wellington 61 R.P.70
	EXETER					
B727	–.5.55	3.8.55	William Robinson	Carling & Co.	Waterloo St to Huron and North sts, various subdivision surveys named; 3 ch	Huron 22 R.P.357
B728	20.9.55	24.9.55	William Robinson	T. Gidley	Pt lot XXII, 1st con, twp Stephen; Sanders St to Victoria St, Marlborough to Main St; 132 ft	Huron 22 R.P.358
B729	–.5.56	3.7.56	Leather & Robinson	George McConnell	Lots btwn Andrew, Main, Hill, and North sts, bldgs; 3 ch	Huron 22 R.P.359

	Date of Survey	Date of Regist.	Surveyor	Owner	Description and Notes	Location
B730	9.9.56	17.9.57	William Robinson	Richard Taylor	Pt W1/2 lot XVI, 1st con, twp Usborne; John St to North St, Bodmin St to Andrew St; 3 ch	Huron 22 R.P.Exeter 360
B731	20.1.63	20.2.63	John Macdonald	Donald McDonald & Estate of Alexander Macdonald	'Francestown,' lot 1, 1st con, twp Hay, and lots XXVII and XXV, 1st con, twp Stephen; bldgs, mill pond, mill race; 4 ch	Huron 22 R.P.120
B732	29.2.64	3.3.64	P.K. Hyndman	Andrew McConnell	Pt lot 20, con 1, twp Usborne; 2 ch	Huron 22 R.P.Exeter 361
	FAIRPORT					
B733	17.8.48	6.10.48	John Shier	Richard Gardner	Lot 23, BF, twp Pickering; Commerce St to Bay St, Queen St to L Ontario; 2 ch	Durham 40 R.P.(Pickering)
	FANSHAWE					
B734	3.1.55	7.12.55	Samuel Peters	W.W. Street	Lot 8, 4th con, twp London; park lots, relief, house, barn; 4 ch	Middlesex 33 R.P.91
	FENELON FALLS					
B735	-.-.54	7.3.55	Edward C. Caddy	James Wallis	For description see **1324**	Victoria 57 R.P.19P
B736	26.9.64 6.1.65	5.7.66	E.C. Caddy, M. Deane	T.S. Stayner	North of river, east to Maryboro Lodge, south of Francis St, west of Block E	Victoria 57 R.P.17
	FERGUS					
B737	9.6.50	23.6.60	W. Grain	John Perry	'Woodside Survey,' pt lot 21, con 15, twp Nichol; from Garafraxa St along Perry and Woodside sts; 2 ch	Wellington 61 R.P.117
B738	11.5.54	25.5.54	Milton Schofield	James Webster	Eramosa Rd to Forfar St, Nichol/Garafraxa rd allowance to Tower St, churches, squares; transcript; 200 ft	Wellington 61 R.P.55
B739	1.11.55	1.11.55	William Haskins	John Platt	Park lot 12, NW side Grand R, town of Fergus; Owen Sound Rd to St John St, north of Forfar St; 50 ft	Wellington 61 R.P.60

B740	–.–.56	22.9.57	Henry Strange	Hon. Adam Ferguson, G.D. Ferguson & John Watt	Fergus and 'South Kinnettles'; Garafraxa Rd to beyond Elora St, Tower St to con rds 14 and 15; transcript; 4 ch	Wellington 61 R.P.77
B741	10.8.57	8.11.58	Edwin H. Kertland	James Perry	Pt lot 21, con 15, twp Nichol on north side Grand R; lots on Owen Sound Rd; 2 ch	Wellington 61 R.P.104
B742	17.12.58	23.12.58	Edwin H. Kertland	James Mathieson & Charles Allen	Union St to other side of Grand R and Hill St, Lamond St to St Patrick St, bldgs, proposed bridges; 4 ch	Wellington 61 R.P.106
B743	8.2.63	4.3.63	W. Grain	A.D. Ferrier	'Belsyde Survey'; Scotland St to beyond Thistle St, Belsyde Ave to Union St; 3 ch	Wellington 61 R.P.154
	FERMOY					
B744	–.8.67	30.11.67	John Bignell	Henrietta Hunt	Streets named; 1 ch	Frontenac 13 R.P.43 (7)
	FEVERSHAM					
B745	29.10.61	2.11.[61?]	T.C. Prosser	Edward Horton	Lots 16 and 17, 9th con, twp Osprey; Beaver R, Victoria and Wellington sts, mill pond; 4 ch	Grey 17 R.P.231
	FINGAL					
B746	–.10.56	21.1.57	A. Driscoll	R. Blackwood	Pt lot 19, north side Talbot Rd E, twp Southwold; east of Union Rd to Argyle St; 2 ch	Elgin 11 R.P.14
B747	–.10.56	25.2.67	Alfred Driscoll	L. Fowler	Pt lot 19, north side Talbot Rd E, twp Southwold; lots on both sides Mill St, west of Union Rd; 5 ch	Elgin 11 R.P.31
B748	–.10.56	10.6.67	A. Driscoll	A. Wood	Pt lot 19, south side Talbot Rd E, twp Southwold; lots along Centre St from Queen St to Cawnpore St; 4 ch	Elgin 11 R.P.33
	FITZROY HARBOUR					
B749	22.6.58	21.3.59	John Robertson	Alexander Shirreff	Lots 23 and 24, 10th con, twp Fitzroy; Carp R to Ottawa R, Wilson St to Park St, church reserves, mill ponds, dams; 4 ch	Ottawa-Carleton 5 R.P.9

	Date of Survey	Date of Regist.	Surveyor	Owner	Description and Notes	Location
	FLAMBOROUGH W TWP					
B750	–.5.67	14.11.67	James Mackintosh	Estate of Harker Lyons	Park lots, pt of lots 18, 19, and 20, 1st con, twp W Flamborough; G.T.W. to York Rd, graveyard; 4 ch	Wentworth 62 R.P.196 (old 54)
	FLEETWOOD					
B751	3.5.58	[3.5.58?]	Thomas J. Dennehy	Thomas Russell et al.	Lots on Queens, Mill, and McFalls sts; 1 ch	Port Hope 9 R.P.Manvers 10
	FLESHERTON					
B752	26.11.60	[26.11.60]	–	William K. Flesher	Pts lots 150 and 151, 1st range west of Toronto and Sydenham Rd, twp Artemisia; Toronto, Durham, Collingwood, Hill, and Springs sts; 2 ch	Grey 17 R.P.32
B753	14.7.65	[8.5.67?]	William Spry	Mary & [?] Munshaw or William Wright	Pt lot 151, 1st range, NE of Toronto and Sydenham Rd, twp Artemesia; Sydenham and Toronto St; 2 ch	Grey 17 R.P.30
	FLINTON					
B754	–.9.59	18.5.74	John Emerson	Hon. B. Flint	Pt lots 21 and 22, 4th con, twp Kaladar; Edward St to Holden St, John St to Holton St; 2 ch	Lennox 29 R.P.32A
	FLORENCE					
B755	–	–.–.60	Robert Johnson	–	Pt lots 16 and 17, cons 1 and 14, twp Euphemia; Victoria St to Fansher St, Sydenham R to Alfred and Charles sts, owners; transcript; 2 ch	Lambton 25 R.P.Euphemia 1
B756	1.9.66	11.4.67	William McClary	Adam Hope & Co.	Pt lot 16, 14th con, twp Dawn; Sydenham R to Union St and river to Main St; 88 ft	Lambton 25 R.P.Euphemia 2
	FONTHILL					
B757	11.3.52	13.3.52	C.K. Fell	Thomas Canby	'Temperanceville'; Church St to West Canborough St and Pelham St; trancript; 2 ch	Niagara 59 R.P.715 (old Pelham 1)

	FOREST					
B758	–.6.58	[1.6.58?]	B. Springer	Timothy Ressiguie	East pt lot 30, 14th con, twp Plympton; Watt St to Wellington St, Washington St to Main St; 1 ch	Lambton 25 R.P.Forest 1
B759	–.4.59	–	Alex Davidson	Timothy Ressiguie	E1/2 lot 30, 14th con, twp Plympton; George St to Wellington St, Union St to Main St, G.T.R.; 1 ch	Lambton 25 R.P.Forest 2
B760	–.–.63	–	Alexander Davidson	T Ressiguie	3rd plan, E1/2 lot 30, 14th con, twp Plympton; George St, G.T.R. to Queen St, Union St to Main St; 1.5 ch	Lambton 25 R.P.Forest 3
B761	–.–.64	27.3.65	Alexander Davidson	B. Holdsworth	West pt lot 3, 8th con, twp Warwick; lots btwn G.T.R. and King St and on Main St; 1 ch	Lambton 25 R.P.Forest 4
B762	–.11.67	3.12.67	A. Davidson	Benjamin Holdsworth	NW pt lot 3, VIII con, twp Warwick; G.T.R. to John St, Main St to Albert St; 2 ch	Lambton 25 R.P.Forest 18
	FOREST MILLS					
B763	26.8.[53?]	13.10.53	G.S. Clapp	–	'McKitrick Town,' W1/2 lot 14, 7th con, twp Richmond; Napanee-Sheffield Rd to West St, James St to Salmon R; 4 ch	Lennox 29 R.P.15
	FORT ERIE					
B764	29.1.54	13.8.57	Andrew Hood	N. Forsyth	Front pt lot 2, 1st con, twp Bertie; terminus Buffalo, Brantford & Goderich Ry west to Goderich St, John St to Forsyth, bldgs, owners; 1 ch	Niagara 59 R.P.503 (old Ft Erie 2)
B765	1.7.54	1.7.54	Andrew Hood	W.A. Thomson & John W. Denis	Front pt lot 3 and south pt lot 4, 1st con, twp Bertie; Niagara R to Aberdeen St and beyond Catherine St west to Murray St, owners, depot, ferry house, custom-house; 3 ch	Niagara 59 R.P.502 (old Ft ERie 1)
B766	5.10.55	19.2.59	Andrew Hood	A. Douglas & William Wallace	Front pt lot 2 and north pt lot 1, 1st con, twp Bertie; Niagara R to bluff, Ordnance Reserve to rd allowance btwn lots 2 and 3, B.B. & G. R.R. Co. lands with engine house; see also **1345**; 2 ch	Niagara 59 R.P.504 (old Ft Erie 3)

	Date of Survey	Date of Regist.	Surveyor	Owner	Description and Notes	Location
B767	–.–.57	–	–	Hon. H.A. Murray, J. Wadsworth & Cap. C.A. Murray	Lots along Garrison Rd and Bertie St, Murray Battery and Waterloo sts, terminus B.B. & G. Ry with passenger depot and engine house, mill; plan attached to deed no 5184, 1857; 3 ch	Niagara 59 no R.P.#
B768	1.6.58	14.3.61	Andrew Hood	'Town of Fort Erie'	Gilmore St to Fort, Niagara R to Erie St, relief, B.B. & G. Ry bldgs, estates and landscaping; 200 ft	Niagara 59 R.P.505 (Ft Erie old 4)
B769	–.10.61	23.2.63	George Z. Rykert	Hamilton V. Thornhill	South pts lot 5, 1st and 2nd cons, twp Bertie; bldgs, relief, vegetation; transcript; 4 ch	Niagara 59 R.P.347 (orig Bertie 1)
	FRANKFORD					
B770	19.9.37	29.4.51	Gilbert S. Clapp	–	Trent R to King St, Ann St to Adelaide St, mill pond, bridge; 4 ch	Hastings 21 R.P.48
B771	23.12.52	10.3.55	J.S. Peterson	John Lee	Lot 6, 5th con, twp Sidney; park lots either side of Belleville and Division sts, reserve for Church of England parsonage; 2 ch	Hastings 21 R.P.73
B772	–.4.53	20.10.55	J.S. Peterson	Mr Roblin	Sidney St to Adelaide St, Park St to King St, mill pond; 4 ch	Hastings 21 R.P.78
B773	–.5.55	29.12.56	J.S. Peterson	Patrick Turley	Trent R to Main St, John St to Bridge St, Roman Catholic church; 2 ch	Hastings 21 R.P.88
B774	–.5.55	11.4.57	J.S. Peterson	Jacob Finkle	Lot 7, 5th con, twp Sidney; Fountain St to Inkerman St, Raglan St to Cottage St, Junction R.R.; 2.5 ch	Hastings 21 R.P.89
	FRANKVILLE					
B775	7.6.34	–	John Booth	Benjamin F. Wilson	Rear 1/2 lot 21, 8th con, and front 1/2 lot 21, 9th con, twp Kitley; Perth St, Church St at James, King and Union sts; 200 ft	Leeds 28 R.P.Frankville 102
	FREELTON					
B776	–.2.56	19.6.56	J. Mackintosh	–	Lot 7, 9th con, twp West Flamborough; West St to Mill St south to Queen St; 2 ch	Wentworth 62 R.P.330 (old 42)

	FROOMFIELD					
B777	27.3.54	–	P.D. Salter	Froome Talfourd	St Clair R to Cross St, boundary btwn lots 70 and 71 on south; transcript; 2 ch	Lambton 25 R.P.Moore 4
B778	–.–.56	–	P.V. Elmore	J.F. Davis	Lot 72, front con, twp Moore; Front, Frederick, Charlotte, and Davis sts; mill creek, dock, bridge; 2 ch	Lambton 25 R.P.Moore 6
B779	16.7.59	[16.7.59?]	P.S. Donnelly	Richard Bertrand	Front St to Creek, lots on both sides Richard St; transcript; 51 ft	Lambton 25 R.P.Moore 8
	FULLARTON					
B780	27.1.64	26.2.64	William Rath	John & James Woodley	'Summervale,' pt lots 11 and 12, West Mitchell Rd con, twp Fullarton; at intersection of Thames and Mitchell Rds; 2 ch	Perth 44 R.P.306
	GALETTA					
B781	21.9.50	–	James Richey	James Hubbell	'Hubbells Falls,' E1/2 lot 21, 5th con, twp Fitzroy; on Mississippi R; scale n.g.	Ottawa-Carleton 5 R.P.1
	GALT					
B782	3.9.49	[8.10.51?]	James Pollock	William Dickson	Compilation map; Grand R to Sprague's Rd and St Andrew St, Forbes St to Waterloo St, owners, bldgs identified, English church, St Andrews church and burial ground; 1 ch	Waterloo 67 R.P.456
B783	7.5.50	–	James Pollock	'Estate of Hon Robert Dickson'	Grand R to Wellington St, Colborne St to Simcoe St, lots south of river on Main St btwn Bridge and Waterloo sts, owners, relief, Galt mills, canal; 2 ch	Waterloo 67 R.P.444
B784	8.9.51	[30.11.58?]	James Pollock	Adam Ainslie	Samuelston St to Hunter, Dundas, and Waterloo sts; 2 ch	Waterloo 67 R.P.440
B785	21.5.52	–	James Black	Robert Forbes	Block B, west side of West Main St, rd allowance btwn cons 11 and 10 to Forbes St; 1 ch	Waterloo 67 R.P.481
B786	–.–.52	–	James Black	J. Mackenzie	'Mackenzie Block,' Union St to John St, Elgin St to Chalmers St; 2 ch	Waterloo 67 R.P.443

	Date of Survey	Date of Regist.	Surveyor	Owner	Description and Notes	Location
B787	2.11.53	15.11.53	James Black	J. Mackenzie	Bruce St to road btwn cons 10 and 11, Chestnut St to Cameron St; 1 ch	Waterloo 67 R.P.441
B788	–	8.11.54	Alexander W. Simpson	James Webster	Pt lot 2, 11th con, twp North Dumfries, east side Grand R; Dundas and Waterloo macadamized rd to Simcoe St, Arthur and Kerr sts, Queen St to Samuelston St; transcript; 100 ft	Waterloo 67 R.P.447
B789	–.–.54	11.8.71	James Pollock	William Osborne	N pt lot 3, 10th con, twp North Dumfries, west side Grand R; Osborne St to Grand R, Cedar St to Victoria Ave; 2 ch	Waterloo 67 R.P.451
B790	7.6.55	7.6.55	James Pollock	–	Plan of Mill and Hawthorn sts; bldgs, owners, resurvey; 1 ch	Waterloo 67 R.P.483
B791	–.–.55	13.10.58	James Black	Andrew Elliott	'Elliot Block'; Grand R to East St, rd allowance btwn cons 10 and 11 to South St, ry and station; 3 ch	Waterloo 67 R.P.445
B792	27.5.56	[27.5.56?]	James Pollock	J. Mackenzie	Pine and McNaughton sts to Pollock Ave, Spruce and Oak sts, Presbyterian burying ground; 1 ch	Waterloo 67 R.P.442
B793	12.8.56	19.3.57	James Pollock, J. Cradock Simpson del	Walter Scott	'Sandy knowl,' pt lot 10, 12th con, twp North Dumfries; Waverly and Scott sts, road from Galt to Guelph, cleared areas, bldgs; 2 ch	Waterloo 67 R.P.610
B794	1.7.67	10.8.67	James Pollock	John Davidson	'Pollock Place,' pt lot 11, con 12, twp North Dumfries; btwn Pond lots and Hunter, Dundas, and Waterloo sts, macadamized rd, grammar school lot; 2 ch	Waterloo 67 R.P.448
	GANANOQUE					
B795	6.6.53	–	W. Deane	W.S. & J.L. Macdonald	Pts lots XI-XV and BFs, 1st con, twp Leeds; west side of river to Maple St; transcript; 11/2 ch	Leeds 28 R.P.105
B796	1.4.58	[1.4.58?]	W.H. Deane	Hon. John Macdonald	Pts lots 13, 14, and 15, 1st con, twp Leeds; Gananoque R to Herbert St, Emma St to St Lawrence R, bridge, based upon earlier surveys 2.5.42; 3 ch	Leeds 28 R.P.110

B797	15.11.58	–	W.H. Deane	W.S. Macdonald	Both sides Gananoque R, Stone and Mill sts to Brock St, inset map, bldgs identified, shows subdivision on **B795** with changes; transcript; 11/2 ch	Leeds 28 R.P.111
B798	21.2.60	[21.2.60?]	William Perceval	Trust & Loan Co. Upper Canada	Lots 8–13, BF and 1st con, twp Leeds; rural lots; transcript?; 4 ch	Leeds 28 R.P.113
B799	25.5.63	1.4.71	Walter Beatty	William Brough	Pt 'Block B' both sides Hickory St btwn King and First sts; 1 ch	Leeds 28 R.P.16
B800	12.10.64	10.9.67	Walter Beatty	For Municipal Corporation	'Block O,' village lots 630–6 and 1037–9; Stone and Pine sts to Gananoque R, Market Square, mill reserve; 1 ch	Leeds 28 R.P.11 Block O
B801	–	25.4.67	Walter Beatty	–	Plan of boundaries of town; 4 ch	Leeds 28 R.P.Gananoque
B802	19.7.67	15.8.67	Walter Beatty	–	Subdivision of 'Water lot E' west of Market St; Cryslers wharf, warehouses; 1 ch	Leeds 28 R.P.10
	GEORGETOWN					
B803	–.1.54	–	Chisholm Miller	–	For description see **1364**	Halton 20 no R.P.#
B804	–.5.54	–	George McPhillips	David Reesor	Area north of original survey of Georgetown, sawmills, north Glenwilliams on Credit R, bldgs identified; 4 ch	Halton 20 R.P.10
B805	31.5.55	–	Chisholm Miller	Robert Cavanagh	Pt lot 20, 9th con, twp Esquesing; Ann St, proposed road to G.T.R. station, mill pond and sawmill on branch Credit R; 2 ch	Halton 20 R.P.9-2
B806	1.10.57	[17.10.]57	Henry Winter	Messrs Young & Barber	Charles St to Main St, Joseph St to Wesleyan St; 2 ch	Halton 20 R.P.27
B807	22.10.57	26.10.57	Henry Winter	Philo W. Dayfoot	From Georgetown station of G.T.R. to John St; 2 ch	Halton 20 R.P.29
B808	7.6.59	16.6.59	Winter & Abrey	Morris Kennedy	Btwn G.T.R., John, Water, and Mill sts and rd allowance btwn cons 8 and 9; 2 ch	Halton 20 R.P.32
B809	9.7.59	12.7.59	T.C. Livingston	John Kennedy	Photoreproduction; 1 ch	Halton 20 R.P.33
B810	4.8.59	11.6.65	T.C. Livingston	George Kennedy	Pt lot 18, 9th con, twp Esquesing; G.T.R. station to Livingston St, over to Main St; 4 ch	Halton 20 R.P.37

	Date of Survey	Date of Regist.	Surveyor	Owner	Description and Notes	Location
	GILFORD					
B811	–.–.67	16.?.67	Henry Creswicke	Charles Wilson	N1/2 lot 21, 14th con, twp W Gwillimbury; Main St to Thomas St, Northern R.R. to sideline; 3 ch	Simcoe 51 R.P.123
	GLEN ALLAN					
B812	19.11.55	–	Edwin H. Kertland	David Ghent	For description see **1366**	Wellington 60 R.P.62
B813	22.1.57	6.2.57	Edwin H. Kertland	Archibald MacDonald	For description see **1367**	Wellington 60 R.P.60
B814	1.4.62	3.4.62	Moses McFadden	'John Vernon'	N pt of W1/2 lot 6, 2nd con, twp Peel; rd allowance btwn cons 2 and 3 to George St and along Vernon St; 3 ch	Wellington 60 R.P.61 (146)
B815	4.7.64	9.1.65	W.H.L. LaPenotiere, Francis Bolger	Municipal Council of Peel	Compiled plan, Wellesley St to rd allowance btwn lots VI and VII, north of Main St W to line btwn cons III and IV, south of Main St E to Wellesley St, relief, some bldgs identified; 3 ch	Wellington 60 R.P.63
	GLENCOE					
B816	–.6.57	29.3.60	B. Springer	A.P. McDonald & Randolph Ross	N1/2 lot XXIV, 1st con, twp Ekfrid, and S1/2 lot 1, 2nd con, twp Mosa, north of Longwoods Rd; South St to North St, Walker St to Victoria St, bldgs, Glencoe Station; photoreproduction; 2 ch	Middlesex 34 R.P.159
	GLEN MAJOR					
B817	–	8.11.60	John Shier	Aaron Sharrard	'Glen Sharrard,' lot 2, 7th con, twp Uxbridge; lots along Queen St; 2 ch	Durham 40 R.P.15369 (Uxbridge Twp)
	GLEN MILLER					
B818	–.9.54	–	J.S. Peterson	D.M. Gilkison	For description see **1368**	Hastings 21 R.P.111

B819	–.7.65	6.5.66	William Hawkins	Alexander Jacke	'St Albans,' pt lot A, 2nd con, twp Sidney; shows same area as R.P.111 but a different lot layout; 1 1/2 ch	Hastings 21 R.P.111A
	GLEN ROSS					
B820	–.7.59	5.8.59	–	J. Stevenson & Joseph Way	Front lots 8–10, 9th con, twp Sidney; Bay St to John St, Green St to Way St on Trent R, public park; 2 ch	Hastings 21 R.P.94
	GLEN TAY					
B821	–.10.67	29.7.68	John Morris	John Hargreaves	Pt lot 20, 2nd con, twp Bathurst; South, Perth, Mill, and North sts on both sides Tay R, owners, some bldgs identified; 1 ch	Lanark 27 R.P.97
	GLEN WILLIAMS					
B822	1.10.64	–	Winter & Abrey	Township of Esquesing	Compiled plan, earlier surveys located, streets named; 3 ch	Halton 20 no R.P.#
	GODERICH					
B823	–.9.44	–	J.G. Kirk	Canada Co.	Britannia Rd to river and harbour, a few bldgs identified; 4 ch	Huron 22 R.P.Goderich 1
B824	–	16.10.51	T.N. Molesworth	William Reed	'Reedsville'; Elizabeth St to Eldon St, York St to Blake St; 2 ch	Huron 22 R.P.453
B825	–	16.7.52	T.N. Molesworth	Robert Parke	Pt lot 1, Maitland con, twp Goderich; area NE of Britannia Rd at Maitland Rd, Walnut St to Maple St; 4 ch	Huron 22 R.P.454
B826	–.6.53	26.6.57	William Perceval	Charles Hutchinson, Isaac Salkeld	Park lots 2 and 3 south of Britannia Rd; north of Thomas St, Wright St to Elizabeth St, inset shows Goderich and harbour; 2 ch	Huron 22 R.P.459
B827	13.12.54	3.1.55	William Perceval	Maurice B. Seymour	Lot 10, con A, town of Goderich; Huron St to Jones St on both sides Elizabeth St; 2 ch	Huron 22 R.P.455
B828	20.6.55	20.6.55	William Perceval	John Gordon	Town lots 330, 377, and 378; along Toronto and Elgin sts and btwn there and Picton St; 30 ft	Huron 22 R.P.456
B829	–.1.56	16.5.56	T.N. Molesworth	Ira Lewis	For description see **1384**	Huron 22 R.P.Goderich 6

	Date of Survey	Date of Regist.	Surveyor	Owner	Description and Notes	Location
B830	10.9.56	12.9.56	J. Macdonald	Canada Co.	Surveys for Canada Co.; Britannia Rd to Maitland R, L Huron to river; transcript; 4 ch	Huron 22 R.P.457
B831	1.5.57	8.6.57	Molesworth & Weatherald	Messrs R. & T. Macindoe Robertson	For description see **1385**	Huron 22 R.P.458
B832	–	25.8.57	Molesworth & Weatherald	Cameron & Keays	Park lots VI, VII, and IX, con A, town of Goderich; Britannia Rd to Blake and Baldwin sts, McDonald St to Gibbons St, Bayfield Rd to Hincks St; 2 ch	Huron 22 R.P.460
B833	–.–.59	10.3.59	Molesworth & Weatherald	William Bennett Rich	Park lots XVII and XVIII, con C, town of Goderich; Bennett St to Rich St west of Eldon St; 2 ch	Huron 22 R.P.461
B834	–	6.6.59	T.N. Molesworth, copied W. Armstrong	Canada Company	'Goderich Harbour'; shows property sold by Canada Co. to Buffalo and Lake Huron Ry Co., relief, island; 4 ch	Huron 22 R.P.462
B835	–	27.2.65	Thomas Weatherald	George Wilson	Pt park lot 108, Maitland con, town of Goderich; Huron Rd to Mary St, Walnut St to Maple St; 2 ch	Huron 22 R.P.463
	GODERICH TWP					
B836	–.6.54	23.8.54	William Perceval	J. Hillyard Cameron	Subdivision of pt lot 4, Lake Shore con, twp Goderich; Buffalo, Brantford & Goderich R.R. line; 4 ch	Huron 22 R.P.538
B837	–.6.55	13.11.55	William Perceval	Smith Whittier	Subdivision of lots 6 and 7, con B, and lot 8, con 5, twp Goderich; 4 ch	Huron 22 R.P.540
B838	–.7.55	[12.7.55?]	William Perceval	Lewis & Galt	Subdivision of lot 10, 1st con, twp Goderich; 4 ch	Huron 22 R.P.539
B839	30.7.58	5.8.58	Molesworth & Weatherald	John Longworth	Subdivision of lot V, Maitland con, twp Goderich; Buffalo & Lake Huron Ry depot, bldgs; 4 ch	Huron 22 R.P.542
B840	12.8.61	23.10.61	A.C. Robertson	Authorized by Canada Co.	Resurvey of 'Cut line,' lots 24–7, 2nd–9th cons; lots 26 and 27, 10th con; lot 27, 11th con; lots 83 and 84, Maitland con, twp Goderich; 40 ch	Huron 22 R.P.544

B841	10.5.65	31.5.65	Libert Chandler	Trust & Loan Co. of Upper Canada	Lot 10, 1st con, twp Goderich; resurvey, Bayfield Rd to L Huron; 4 ch	Huron 22 R.P.545
	GORMLEY					
B842	–.11.56	5.11.59	George McPhillips	James? Gormley	'Gormley Corners,' lot 35, 3rd con, twp Markham; bldgs; 2 ch	Toronto 64 R.P.254
	GORRIE					
B843	15.5.56	15.11.56	William Rath	Edward Leech & Brothers and George & Robert Greer	For description see **1390**	Huron 22 R.P.276
	(GOUROCK)					
B844	–.2.56	30.6.56	Henry Strange	Edward Lowry	'Sweaborg,' pt lot IV, Division B, SE of Waterloo Rd; Waterloo Rd to Graham St, Lowry St to McConnell St, cancelled in 1883; 1 ch	Wellington 61 R.P.46
	GRAFTON					
B845	–.–.55	24.2.56	Edward C. Caddy	Campbell & Pym	Pt lot 21, 1st con, twp Haldimand; lots along road to Kingston and road btwn lots 22 and 21, Frank and Charles sts, owners; 2 ch	Northumberland 39 R.P.Haldimand 4
B846	–	7.1.59	W. Boulton	–	Lot 23, 1st con, twp Haldimand; Air and Charlotte sts, road from Cobourg to Kingston, bldgs, owners; 4 ch	Northumberland 39 R.P.Haldimand 7
	GRANTHAM TWP					
B847	–.2.59	11.2.59	George Z. Rykert	'Estate of David Emmett'	Pt lot 10, 5th con, twp Grantham; Queenston and Grimsby macadamized rd and rd allowance to 10 Mile Creek, subdivided into 9 parcels, owners; 4 ch	Niagara 30 R.P.38 Co
B848	–.2.59	11.2.59	George Z. Rykert	Estate of David Emmett	Same areas as plan above but shows different lot layout; 4 ch	Niagara 30 R.P.39 Co

	Date of Survey	Date of Regist.	Surveyor	Owner	Description and Notes	Location
	(GRANTON) (Huron Co)					
B849	–.–.60	14.3.60	John Denison	'Township of Stanley'	Lots XXX and XXXI, 1st con, twp Stanley; 'Mr Thomas Grant's Survey,' lots along London Rd, owners; 2 ch	Huron 22 R.P.248
	GRANTON (Middlesex Co)					
B850	30.1.67	10.6.67	A. Niven	Alexander & James Grant	Pts lots 24, cons 12 and 13, twp Biddulph; Head St to G.T.R., King St to Queen St, bldgs identified, owners; 3 ch	Middlesex 33 R.P.221 Co
	GREENBANK					
B851	–.9.60	14.2.61	W.E. Yarnold	Township of Reach	'Municipal Plan,' lots 12 and 13, 10th and 11th cons, twp Reach; along King and Centre sts, owners; 2 ch	Durham 40 R.P.16115 (Reach)
	GRIMSBY					
B852	20.12.33	–	George A. Ball	–	Lots on 'the Stony flat 40 mile creek'; along Main, Depot, and Adelaide sts, owners; transcript; 2 ch	Niagara 30 R.P.36 Co
B853	16.9.54	–.1.55	–	Robert F. Nelles	NE corner lot 4, 1st con and BF, twp Grimsby; esplanade at lake to G.W.R., along Fanning Ave; 132 ft	Niagara 30 R.P.33 Co
B854	–	18.5.58	George Rykert	Messrs Nelles	Adelaide St to Victoria Ave by Depot St; 1/2 ch	Niagara 30 R.P.20 Co
	GUELPH					
B855	–.–.47	–	Francis Kerr	G.S. Tiffany	Woolwich St to Strange St, Clarence St to Kerr St, house of John Wilson, Esq.; 2 ch	Wellington 61 R.P.17
B856	–.–.[5?]	–	Henry Strange	–	'Priory Block'; Woolwich St to Speed R, Market St W, bldgs; transcript; 1 ch	Wellington 61 R.P.16
B857	16.12.54	19.12.54	Francis Kerr	G.S. Tiffany	For description see **1402**	Wellington 61 R.P.18
B858	30.4.55	5.2.56	Francis Kerr	John Thorp	Lots 59 and 60; on both sides Thorp St btwn Woolwich St and Speed R, court-house, G.T.R. station; 11/2 ch	Wellington 61 R.P.26

B859	26.5.55	31.5.55	Francis Kerr	John Pipe	'Pipe Lot,' pt lot B, Division A; Woolwich St to Speed R, Clarence St to London Rd, some bldgs identified; transcript; 2 ch	Wellington 61 R.P.31
B860	–.–.55	20.6.56	Henry Strange	Mr Buckland	Lots 1–6 and 1/2 lot 7, Range Division A; London Rd to Elliott St, road extension to Paisley Block, north to beyond Sussex St, Buckland residence, plan later amended; 11/2 ch	Wellington 61 R.P.30
B861	–.6.55	15.6.59	Francis Kerr	W.M. Nicholson	Lots 27, 28, 33, and 34; btwn Surrey and Waterloo sts and Grant and Huskisson sts, some bldgs identified; transcript; 2 ch	Wellington 61 R.P.41
B862	1.7.55	19.7.55	Milton C. Schofield, J. Hobson	George Harvey	Pt lot 4, Division F; York Rd to Eramosa branch of Speed R; 4 ch	Wellington 61 R.P.19
B863	–.7.55	22.8.55	Milton C. Schofield, J. Hobson	James McCartney	Woolwich Rd to Cardigan St, London Rd NW; 1 ch	Wellington 61 R.P.21
B864	–.8.55	16.11.55	Milton C. Schofield, Frederick J. Chadwick	John Thorp	Park lots 7–10 and pt lot 4, Division F of George Harvey's survey; York Rd to Eramosa branch of Speed R, Hooper to Hood St; 2 ch	Wellington 61 R.P.25
B865	5.9.55	12.9.55	Frederick J. Chadwick, Milton C. Schofield	A.R. McDonald	G.T.R. to Paisley Rd, Glengarry St to west limit of town; 1 ch	Wellington 61 R.P.20
B866	–.9.55	24.9.55	Milton C. Schofield, J. Hobson	Francis Shanly	Park lot 50; Cambridge St to Cork St, Yorkshire to Glasgow St; 50 ft	Wellington 61 R.P.22
B867	–.9.55	3.10.55	Milton C. Schofield, Fred J. Chadwick	J.J. Kingsmill	Paisley St to Mount St, Alma St to Edinburgh St; 2 ch	Wellington 61 R.P.23
B868	11.10.55	7.1.56	John McDonald	Canada Co.	Compiled plan, streets named, market-place, burying ground, churches; transcript; 4 ch	Wellington 61 R.P.8
B869	16.10.55	22.10.55	William Haskins	Reverend Arthur Palmer	Pt of 'Tyrcathlen'; Queen and Palmer sts to Speed R, 'proposed bridge' at Grange St; 66 ft	Wellington 61 R.P.32
B870	25.10.55	25.10.55	Milton C. Schofield, dr by J. Hobson	Adam J. Fergusson	Market St to Paisley St, Fleet St and Yorkshire St to Edinburgh St; 132 ft	Wellington 61 R.P.27
B871	25.10.55	9.11.55	Milton C. Schofield	John Thorp	For description see **1404**	Wellington 61 R.P.24

	Date of Survey	Date of Regist.	Surveyor	Owner	Description and Notes	Location
B872	–.10.55	1.3.56	Milton C. Schofield	John Neeve	Waterloo St to Surrey St, Grant to Neeve St; 1 ch	Wellington 61 R.P.33
B873	–.11.55	10.11.56	Milton C. Schofield, A.W. Simpson	George J. Grange	Paisley Rd to Inkerman St, Alma St to Edinburgh St, G.T.R. and station, Galt & Guelph Ry and station; 200 ft	Wellington 61 R.P.28
B874	11.12.55	11.12.55	Francis Kerr	Edwin Hubbard	Lots btwn Dublin, Norfolk, London, and Norwich sts and on both sides Woolwich Rd; transcript; 2 ch	Wellington 61 R.P.35
B875	11.12.55	15.12.55	Francis Kerr, dr by Fred J. Chadwick	John Arnold	Park lots 4–6, 11–13, 26–9, 36 and 37, 48 and 49; Gladwin St to Suffolk St, Glasgow St to Edinburgh St; see also **1401**; 2 ch	Wellington 61 R.P.29
B876	–.–.55	[3.7.56?]	Milton C. Schofield	Hon. J.A. Macdonald	York Rd to Speed R, 'Present Travelled Rd' on east to Crawford St and river, on back: altered plan on both sides Cross St east of Neeve St; 2 ch	Wellington 61 R.P.113
B877	–.–.55	27.1.57	Francis Kerr	John Galt	Both sides G.T.R. btwn York Rd and Paisley Block Rd, owners; 3 ch	Wellington 61 R.P.53
B878	31.7.56	31.7.56	William Haskins	Estate of Robert Thompson	Pt E1/2s lots 1 and 2, 2nd con, Division G; Speed R to Charles St, west of Dundas Rd to Mary St, Victoria Place, bridge, tannery, mill race; 1 ch	Wellington 61 R.P.37
B879	–	8.9.56	William Haskins	William D.P. Jarvis & Robert Scott	Lots in IIIrd range, Division A; on both sides Augusta and Amelia sts btwn rd allowance ranges III/IV and road ranges II/III; 1 ch	Wellington 61 R.P.36
B880	–.8.56	9.5.57	Henry Strange	Estate of Charles McTague	Park lots I–IV, 1st range, SW of Woolwich Rd, Division A; London Rd to beyond McTague St, Globe St to Woolwich Rd; 1 ch	Wellington 61 R.P.105
B881	25.9.56	31.12.58	Henry Strange	Messrs John Emslie & Company	Park lots LXVI–LXX; Market St to Bristol St, Fleet St to Edinburgh Rd; transcript; 2 ch	Wellington 61 R.P.42
B882	7.10.56	28.10.56	Schofield & Hobson	William Alexander	Paisley Block Rd to other side of Alexander St on both sides G.T.R.; 2 ch	Wellington 61 R.P.54

B883	18.10.56	20.10.56	Henry Strange	Estate of James Oliver	Lot D, Division A; Waterloo Rd to Speed R, Edinburgh Rd to Roland St; 2 ch	Wellington 61 R.P.34
B884	-.-.56	9.5.57	William Haskins	Estate Charles McTague	Pt SW1/2S lots 1–3, 3rd con, Division G; subdivision of lot 3, 3rd con, is R.P.50; 2 ch	Wellington 61 R.P.39 and 50
B885	-.12.56	15.7.56	Francis Kerr	John Mitchell	King St to Perth St, west of Eramosa Rd to Spring St, foundry, George's Mill; transcript; 2 ch	Wellington 61 R.P.40
B886	-.12.56	21.10.57	Francis Kerr	George Sylvester Tiffany	Pt 'Priory Grounds'; Woolwich Rd to Duke St, Grange St to bridge; 2 ch	Wellington 61 R.P.94
B887	-.12.57	12.11.58	Francis Kerr	Estate of Peter McTague	Lots 5–8 on both sides Mont St btwn Glebe and Woolwich sts; transcript; 132 ft	Wellington 61 R.P.38
B888	23.1.58	30.1.58	Francis Kerr	St Andrews Chur ch	Pt of 'Scotch Glebe; Edinburgh Rd to Woolwich Rd; 3 ch	Wellington 61 R.P.98
B889	11.3.58	18.3.58	Francis Kerr	A.J. Fergusson	Lots on east side Speed R btwn Bridge St and Eramosa Rd, bldgs; 2 ch	Wellington 61 R.P.99
B890	1.10.58	27.8.60	Schofield & Hobson	James Webster	Lots 9–15, 1st range, and pt lot 2, BF Division F; Metcalfe St to Speed R, Eramosa Rd to north limit of town; 3 ch	Wellington 61 R.P.121
B891	2.10.59	25.11.59	Francis Kerr, W.R. Turner	George S. Grange	Alteration to Blocks A, B, C around ry station btwn Alma and Edinburgh sts, Inkerman and Paisley sts; 200 ft	Wellington 61 R.P.115
B892	9.7.60	-.7.60	William Haskins	John Thorp	BF lot 1 and SE pt BF lot 2, 1st range, Division F; west of Metcalfe St, Wellington Place, names of large lot owners, bldgs; 1 ch	Wellington 61 R.P.120
B893	14.9.60	17.9.60	Frederick J. Chadwick, A.W. Simpson	John Macdonald	'Albert Place,' lots 7 and 8, 1st range, and west pt lot 6, BF of Division F; Speed R to Metcalfe St, Palmer St to Eramosa Rd; 3 ch	Wellington 61 R.P.127
B894	15.9.60	17.9.60	Frederick J. Chadwick	J. Macdonald	Lots 1–3, east side of Eramosa Rd, and lots 6–8, 2nd range, Division F; park lots, Metcalfe St to rd allowance btwn 2nd and 3rd ranges, Grange St to Eramosa Rd; transcript; 4 ch	Wellington 61 R.P.128
B895	5.11.60	5.11.60	Frederick J. Chadwick	George McK. Stewart	Eramosa Rd to Delhi St; 2 ch	Wellington 61 R.P.133

	Date of Survey	Date of Regist.	Surveyor	Owner	Description and Notes	Location
B896	23.1.61	23.2.61	Thomas W. Cooper	William & Joseph Dyson	Park lot B; Wellington St to Speed R to Dundas Rd, bldgs; 1 ch	Wellington 61 R.P.136
B897	–.3.61	20.4.61	Francis Kerr	Edwin Hubbard	Pt lot 34; Woolwich Rd to Speed R, west of side-rd, Goldies grist mill; 1 ch	Wellington 61 R.P.139
B898	–.–.61	9.9.61	Francis Kerr	G. Palmer	Park lots 87, 91, 93, and 94; Norfolk St to Speed R, Norwich St to London Rd; 2 ch	Wellington 61 R.P.144
B899	–	19.9.61	Thomas W. Cooper	G. Palmer	Park lots 23 and 24; at Suffolk St and along Glasgow and Chambers sts; 1 ch	Wellington 61 R.P.145
B900	–	15.1.62	Frederick J. Chadwick	George M. Stewart	King St to Delhi St, Spring St to Derry St; 1 ch	Wellington 61 R.P.146
B901	12.4.62	12.4.62	Francis Kerr	St Andrews Church	Glebe lot; Woolwich Rd to Edinburgh Rd; 3 ch	Wellington 61 R.P.148
B902	–.7.62	6.9.62	Thomas W. Cooper	Henry A. Kirkland	Part lots 14–16; south of London Rd btwn Yorkshire and Glasgow sts, bldgs; 1 ch	Wellington 61 R.P.152
B903	2.10.62	22.12.62	Frederick J. Chadwick	Henry Hatch	Park lot 25; Dublin and Suffolk sts; 1 ch	Wellington 61 R.P.153
B904	30.5.63	3.8.62	Frederick J. Chadwick	Henry Hatch	Amended map of park lot 25 and plan above; Dublin St at Suffolk St; 1 ch	Wellington 61 R.P.156
B905	29.11.64	10.12.64	Frederick J. Chadwick	John MacDonald	On both sides G.T.R. east of Queen St and along Duke, Elizabeth, and Grange sts, canal; 3 ch	Wellington 61 R.P.161
B906	–.10.65	25.7.68	Thomas W. Cooper	St Andrews Church	Pt of Glebe, lots 23, 24, 25, range I; 2 ch	Wellington 61 R.P.172
	GUELPH TWP					
B907	–.–.54	6.7.60	Henry Strange	Thomas Keating	Pt lots I and II, 1st con, Division E; Waterloo Rd to Napoleon St west of Con Rd; 1 ch	Wellington 61 R.P.52
B908	[11.10.55?]	–	[Canada Co.]	–	Pt of Division A; Speed R to Edinburgh Rd, possibly copied from Canada Co. plan (see **B868**); 6 ch	Wellington 61 R.P.43
B909	11.10.56	23.3.57	Henry Strange	John C. Chadwick	Park lots in 'Ballinard,' lot B, Division E, twp Guelph; Galt & Guelph Ry; 2 ch	Wellington 61 R.P.47

B910	–	3.4.57	William Haskins	William Griffiths	Park lots in lot 11, 3rd con, Division D, twp Guelph; owners; 4 ch	Wellington 61 R.P.45
B911	–.1.57	17.4.57	Francis Kerr	J.T. Leslie	Park lots on lot 5, 7th con, Division C, twp Guelph; 2 ch	Wellington 61 R.P.48
B912	–.3.61	12.12.65	Milton C. Schofield, dr by Fred Chadwick	James Webster & David Allan	'The Rocks,' alteration in survey of lots 3–5, 1st con, and lot 3, 2nd con, Division C, twp Guelph; on York Rd by Speed R, relief; 4 ch	Wellington 61 R.P.61 and 168
B913	21.12.65	22.12.65	Frederick J. Chadwick	County of Wellington	'Chipchase Farm,' lots 1 and 2, 3rd con, Division D, twp Guelph; west of Woolwich Rd; 6 ch	Wellington 61 R.P.169
	GWILLIMBURY N TWP					
B914	–.–.65	31.8.65	Dennis & Gossage	T. Sibbald	Broken lot 15, 2nd con, N Gwillimbury; earlier surveys; 3 ch	York 65 R.P.6
	HALIBURTON					
B915	12.9.67	15.10.67	C. Hanning, E.R. Ussher	Canadian Land & Emigration Co.	Streets, relief, mill reserve, swamp; 4 ch	Haliburton 19 no R.P.#
	HALLOWELL TWP					
B916	5.11.52	–	John O. Conger	Estate of Joseph Terwilleyar	Pt lots 7–9, 3rd con, Military Tract, twp Hallowell; owners; 10 ch	Prince Edward 47 R.P.Hallowell 8
B917	7.8.52	18.12.77	John K. Roche, H.J. & W.H. Browne	University of Toronto	Gore K; owners, treed and cleared areas, bldgs; certified copy of original at OTU; 10 ch	Prince Edward 47 R.P.Hallowell 2
B918	7.8.52	18.12.77	John K. Roche, H.J. & W.H. Browne	University of Toronto	Block B; owners, cleared and wooded lands; certified copy of original at OTU; 10 ch	Prince Edward 47 R.P.Hallowell 3
B919	30.12.52	18.12.77	John K. Roche, H.J. & W.H. Browne	University of Toronto	Gore G; owners; certified copy of original at OTU; 10 ch	Prince Edward 47 R.P.Hallowell 1
B920	30.12.52	20.12.81	John K. Roche, H.J. & W.H. Browne	University of Toronto	Gore H; cleared, wooded, and marsh land, owners; certified copy of original at OTU; 6 ch	Prince Edward 47 R.P.Hallowell 4

	Date of Survey	Date of Regist.	Surveyor	Owner	Description and Notes	Location
	HAMILTON					
B921	13.8.34	–	H.J. Castle	James Hughson	Lots on Burlington Bay; bay to Brock St, James St to beyond John St, bldgs, wharfs, owners, water lots; 2 ch	Wentworth 62 R.P.misc 7 drawer 1 (old plan 19)
B922	16.12.34	–	Lewis Burwell	Allan N. MacNab & John Strachan	Lot 15, 1st con with BF on Burlington Bay, and pt lot 15, 2nd con, twp Barton; bay to Sheaffe St btwn James St and bay, marshy area; transcript; 2 ch	Wentworth 62 R.P.127
B923	13.7.38	–	Lewis Burwell	Hamilton, Ferguson, Kirkendall, et al.	Lots 12–16, 2nd and 3rd cons, twp Barton; Court House Sq at John St, Methodist chapel and school, owners; 2 ch	Wentworth 62 R.P.misc 9 drawer 3
B924	24.8.38	–	Thomas A. Blyth	Sir Allan MacNab	William St to beyond Mills St, Cherry St to Division St; owners, same as **R.P.1436**, which is a copy of this plan; scale n.g.	Wentworth 62 R.P.misc 16 drawer 4
B925	3.10.38	–	Thomas A. Blyth	James Mills	Queen St to Lock St, Main St to York St; 2 ch	Wentworth 62 R.P.1435
B926	–.9.45	27.5.57	Thomas A. Blyth	John Stinson	James St to Hughson St, Stuart St to Union St; 60 ft	Wentworth 62 R.P.24 (old 20)
B927	3.4.46	–	Thomas A. Blyth	Thomas Stinson	Lots on both sides East Market St at Mary St; 66 ft	Wentworth 62 R.P.7 (old 39)
B928	–.–.46?	–	Thomas A. Blyth	Daniel Kelly	Similar to **B934** but reserve not shown, 'E and J Moore' is written across in pencil; 132 ft	Wentworth 62 R.P.38 (old 54)
B929	24.8.47	27.2.52	Thomas A. Blyth	Richard Beasley	Main St south to William St, Lock St to Dundurn St, owners, reserves; 100 ft	Wentworth 62 R.P.244 (old 29?)
B930	–.8.47	–	Thomas A. Blyth	Estate of Thomas Taylor	James St to McNab St, Colborne St S; 132 ft	Wentworth 62 R.P.8 (old 40)
B931	27.10.47	–	Thomas A. Blyth	H.B. Wilson	Wellington St to east limit of city and beyond, King St to Peel St, Peel St in wrong position; 100 ft	Wentworth 62 R.P.223 (1st version)
B932	26.11.47	–	Thomas A. Blyth	Thomas Stinson	Lots along Margaret St btwn Main and King sts; 50 ft	Wentworth 62 R.P.227 (old 37)

B933	28.12.47	–	Thomas A. Blyth	Thomas Stinson	King St to Main St east of Wellington St and chapel ground; 50 ft	Wentworth 62 R.P.6 (old 38)
B934	–.–.47	–	Thomas A. Blyth	E. & J.F. Moore	King St to Rebecca St and reserve, Mary St to Wellington St, owners; 132 ft	Wentworth 62 R.P.36 (old 59)
B935	–.7.49	–	Thomas A. Blyth	Andrew Miller	York St, James St to MacNab St; 40 ft	Wentworth 62 R.P.misc 12 drawer 4
B936	–.–.[49?]	–	–	Andrew Miller	Lots btwn King, York, James, and MacNab sts; similar to **B935**; scale n.g.	Wentworth 62 R.P.50 (old 22)
B937	–.–.5?	–	T.A. Blyth	Allan Napier McNab	Lot 19, 3rd con, twp Barton; rivers, ravines, owners; 4 ch	Wentworth 62 R.P.1434
B938	–.–.5?	–	Thomas A. Blyth	James Cahill	West of Wentworth St, lots along Shaw St; 50 ft	Wentworth 62 R.P.1429
B939	[pre 50]	–	–	Robert Walker, Samuel Nash, W.T. Sunley, et al.	'Kirkendall Survey,' pt of block btwn King, Market, MacNab, and Park sts, owners; 20 ft	Wentworth 62 R.P.53 (old 55)
B940	–.9.50	–	Robert Kerr	Thomas Stinson	Lots 1 and 2, corner of King and Princess sts, St Mary's Ward and lots at corner King and Margaret sts, St Georges Ward; 72 ft	Wentworth 62 R.P.46 (old 19 and 19A)
B941	1.12.50	8.4.52	Thomas A. Blyth	Michael Aikman	Lot 10, 2nd con, and lot 10, 3rd con, twp Barton; Wentworth St to Burlington St and beyond, Barton St to summit of mountain, relief; 3 ch	Wentworth 62 R.P.26 (old 22)
B942	25.10.51	–	Thomas A. Blyth	Sir Allan Napier McNab	Burlington Bay to Sheaffe St, Bay St to James St, marshy area; similar to **B922**; 132 ft	Wentworth 62 R.P.misc 13? drawer 2
B943	–	–.–.51	Thomas A. Blyth	David Kirkendall	Pt of 'David Kirkendall Survey'; Bay St to James St, King St to Mulberry St; scale n.g.	Wentworth 62 R.P.39
B944	–.3.52	–	R.W. Kerr, copy Charles J. Fraser	P. Hess	Main St to Miles St, Caroline St to Queen St, property coloured red owned by Hess at death; 6 ch	Wentworth 62 R.P.121 (old 49)
B945	–.3.53	5.11.53	Thomas A. Blyth	J.H. Cameron	Bay south to Barton St, Wellington St to Victoria St, G.W.R., bldgs, shoreline; 100 ft	Wentworth 62 R.P.254 (old 36)
B946	10.6.53	–.1.54	Thomas A. Blyth	R.J. Hamilton	N pt lot 13, 4th con, twp Barton; summit of mountain to Barton St, west of Wellington St, owners; 2 ch	Wentworth 62 R.P.212 (old 48)

	Date of Survey	Date of Regist.	Surveyor	Owner	Description and Notes	Location
B947	13.6.53	–	Robert W. Kerr	Robert Chisholm(?)	Pt lot 11, 3rd con, twp Barton; Main St to mountain; owners; 2 ch	Wentworth 62 R.P.misc 18 drawer 2 (old 25)
B948	16.12.[5]3	–	Thomas A. Blyth	Robert Land	Lots 32–9, 56–63; Cannon St to Barton St, Wellington St to Emerald St; 104 ft	Wentworth 62 R.P.1433
B949	[19.12.53]	19.12.53	–	Messrs Kerr, McLaren & Streets	Markland St to Bold St, Bowery St to Queen St; later deleted and replaced by **B958**; 100 ft	Wentworth 62 R.P.256
B950	28.12.53	–	Thomas A. Blyth	Richard Bull	Pt 'Robert Land's Survey,' block btwn Robert St, Cannon St, Victoria Ave, and East Ave; Robert St to Cannon St, Wellington St to Emerald St; 104 ft	Wentworth 62 R.P.4 (old 30)
B951	–	10.1.54	–	J. Ruthven	Lots on (1) Park St to James St, Sheaffe to Mulberry St, (2) Catherine St to Mary St at Henry St, (3) Queen St to Hess St, Hunter St to Bold St, and (4) Mills St at Auror[*sic*] (now Ford) St, bldgs, estates, landscaping, St Mary's Church; 60 ft	Wentworth 62 R.P.230 (old 34)
B952	12.1.54	[12.1.54?]	Thomas A. Blyth	R.P. Street	Park lots in lots 6 and 7, 4th con, and pt lot 7, 3rd con, twp Barton; mountain to Fennel Ave, lots along Upper Gage; 3 ch	Wentworth 62 R.P.296 (old 28)
B953	28.1.54	–	Thomas A. Blyth	Peter Ferguson	Cannon St to Rebecca St, Wellington St to Mary St; 100 ft	Wentworth 62 R.P.255
B954	15.2.54	28.4.54	Edmund DeCew	'W.A. Park'	'Park's Survey,' lot IX, 1st con, twp Barton; Wentworth St to Sherman Ave, Barton St to Ontario St, G.W.R., Sherman's Inlet east of city; 2 ch	Wentworth 62 R.P.126 (old 61)
B955	–.4.54	24.1.59	Thomas A. Blyth	Walter H. Dickson	King St to Dundurn Castle and Burlington Bay btwn Dundurn and Railway (now Locke) sts, Dundurn Castle and grounds, G.W.R. property; photoreproduction of transcript; scale n.g.	Wentworth 62 R.P.41

B956	–.9.54	2.6.55	Thomas A. Blyth	Messrs W.L. Billings & F.W. Fearman	Lots on Maple Ave south of Duke St; 50 ft	Wentworth 62 R.P.2 (old 31)
B957	–.11.54	28.7.56	Thomas A. Blyth	Willoughby A. Nicolls	North end lot 19, 4th con, twp Barton; south limit of Hamilton to 2 streets beyond Dundurn St to Halloran St; 2 ch	Wentworth 62 R.P.35 (old 60)
B958	13.11.54	18.11.54	Thomas A. Blyth	Archibald Kerr & John Brown	Pt lot 16, 3rd con, twp Barton; bounded by Queen, Hess, Bold, and Markland sts; amendment of **B949** (1853); 100 ft	Wentworth 62 R.P.152 (old 52)
B959	–.–.54	5.3.58	Thomas A. Blyth	V.H. Tisdale	King St to Wilson St, Steven St to Emerald St; 50 ft	Wentworth 62 R.P.125 (old 7)
B960	19.1.55	19.1.55	–	William Leggo & Alfred Patrick	Lots on Amelia and Tirzah sts bounded by Queen St Rd, 'Proposed Road to Ancaster,' owners; 132 ft	Wentworth 62 R.P.29 (old 26)
B961	–.1.55	12.3.55	Thomas A. Blyth	Michael Aikman	Wentworth St to Burlington St, Main St to King St; 100 ft	Wentworth 62 R.P.27 (old 23)
B962	–.1.55	18.10.55	Thomas A. Blyth	A. Logie, W. Griffin & J.D. Pringle	Lots 216, 217, 220, 221, and pts 212 and 213 and lots 77–88; Herkimer St to Concession Rd, MacNab St to Bowery St, owners; 50 ft	Wentworth 62 R.P.40 (old 56)
B963	18.6.55	–	Thomas A. Blyth	Dr Billings & Joseph Lister	Wentworth St to Williams St btwn G.W.R. and Barton St; 100 ft	Wentworth 62 R.P.3 (old 32)
B964	1.9.55	–	Thomas A. Blyth	Michael Aikman	Main St to King St, Burlington St and east, owners; 100 ft	Wentworth 62 R.P.97 (old 72)
B965	13.9.55	14.11.55	Thomas A. Blyth	G.W. Burton and R. & J.R. Martin	Park lots in pt lot 10, 5th con, twp Barton; Fennel Ave to Mohawk Rd, east of Upper Wentworth St; 4 ch	Wentworth 62 R.P.290 (old 33)
B966	15.11.55	17.1.56	William Boultbee	John Applegarth et al.	Lots 71 and 72, corner of John and Peel sts in 'George Hamilton's Survey'; 30 ft	Wentworth 62 R.P.28 (old 25)
B967	28.11.55	5.12.55	Thomas A. Blyth	George Duggan	Mills St to Peel St, Aurora St to Cherry St; 50 ft	Wentworth 62 R.P.31 (old 41)
B968	[–.–.55?]	–	T.A. Blyth	Wm Leggo	For description see **1438**	Wentworth 62 R.P.124
B969	1.7.56	4.7.56	Thomas A. Blyth	Samuel Zimmerman	Estate of 'Judge Taylor' MacNab St to James St, Colborne St; 40 ft	Wentworth 62 R.P.37 (old 44)

	Date of Survey	Date of Regist.	Surveyor	Owner	Description and Notes	Location
B970	1.7.56	16.7.56	Thomas A. Blyth	J.T. Gilkison	Sherman's Inlet and Burlington Bay west to Wentworth St and south to Munro St; 2 ch	Wentworth 62 R.P.32 (old 45)
B971	1.7.56	16.7.56	Thomas A. Blyth	J.T. Gilkison	'Hon. John H. Cameron Survey,' park lots 13–22; Victoria Ave to Emerald St, Barton St to South St and G.W.R.; 100 ft	Wentworth 62 R.P.33 (old 46)
B972	12.7.56	12.7.56	Bristow, Fitzgerald & Spencer	Messrs Spohn & Start	'Hess Place'; Market St to King St, Hess St to Caroline St; 100 ft	Wentworth 62 R.P.5 (old 35)
B973	[30.7.56?]	30.7.56	William Boultbee	M. Rossin & Bros	Lots at John and Peel sts and on Hughson St at back of Christ's Church, bldgs; 16 ft	Wentworth 62 R.P.25 (old 27)
B974	–.8.56	2.1.57	Thomas A. Blyth	Robert Kneeshaw	'Brick Yard Track in Springers Survey,' lots 3 and 4 on Hannah and Cherry sts; 20 ft	Wentworth 62 R.P.30 (old 12)
B975	–.8.56	11.6.57	Thomas A. Blyth	Sir A.N. MacNab	Park lot 3, York St; lots on both sides Locomotive St; 40 ft	Wentworth 62 R.P.23 (old 19)
B976	–.9.56	26.1.57	Thomas A. Blyth	Charles Allan	Pt N1/2 lots 11 and 12, 5th con, twp Barton; Upper Wentworth St to Upper Wellington St, lots along Mountain Dr and South St; 2 ch	Wentworth 62 R.P.231 (old 17)
B977	–	1.10.56	Thomas A. Blyth	Hon. M. Cameron	Pt of 'Beasley Farm'; area east of Paradise Rd, King St to 5th St, trees, relief; 100 ft	Wentworth 62 R.P.34 (old 13)
B978	30.10.56	3.5.58	Thomas A. Blyth	John Hill	Front of lot 11, 4th con, twp Barton; 4 ch	Wentworth 62 R.P.291 (old 21)
B979	–.11.56	12.7.57	Thomas A. Blyth, copy by J.H. Caddy	Sir A.N. MacNab	Btwn Railway St and Inchbury St, St Mary's Lane to York St, also a similar copy in OOAMA; 1 ch	Wentworth 62 R.P.228 (old 11)
B980	30.4.57	–	William Boultbee	Messrs Holden & Papps	Lots on both sides Grove St east of Liberty St, and along Aurora St south of Mills St to Jane St; location map; 20 ft	Wentworth 62 R.P.120 (old 61)
B981	18.6.57	12.6.57	Thomas A. Blyth	Estate of William Blaikie	Park lots in pt of lots 29–32, 1st con, twp Saltfleet; G.W.R. to Brampton St, Parkdale Ave to Woodward Ave and beyond, owners; 4 ch	Wentworth 62 R.P.308 (14) and OHMA (Map 7610)

B982	10.11.57	11.11.57	Thomas A. Blyth	Allan N. MacNab	Pt lot 19, 2nd con, twp Barton; Jones St south to King St, Dundurn St to west of Breadalbane; 2 ch	Wentworth 62 R.P.42 (old 4)
B983	5.2.58	10.3.58	Thomas A. Blyth	Thomas Stinson	Ida St to Main St, Burris St to Burlington Ave; 70 ft	Wentworth 62 R.P.225 (old 18 and 18a)
B984	15.2.58	10.3.58	Thomas A. Blyth	Thomas Stinson	King St north to Wilson St, east of Steven St, market house site; 66 ft	Wentworth 62 R.P.43 (old 8)
B985	15.2.58	10.3.58	Thomas A. Blyth	Thomas Stinson?	Park lot 2 in 'Michael Aikman's Survey' of lot 10, 2nd con, twp Barton; Wellington St to King St, on one side of Burlington St; 50 ft	Wentworth 62 R.P.46 (old 19 and 19a)
B986	18.5.58	28.6.[7?]	Thomas A. Blyth	Estate of James Mills	North pt lot 17, 4th con, twp Barton; south of Hamilton, west of Queen St; 2 ch	Wentworth 62 R.P.60 (old 21)
B987	6.8.58	–	Thomas A. Blyth, Samuel Ryckman	Estate of George & Robert J. Hamilton	King St to Mountain Rd, James St to Ferguson St; transcript; 2 ch	Wentworth 62 R.P.1431
B988	23.10.58	26.10.58	Thomas A. Blyth	Walter Muirhead	Pt of lot 16, V con, twp Barton; on same sheet as survey of Carlisle (**B426**); 3 ch	Wentworth 62 R.P.295 (old 17 and 17a)
B989	26.11.58	27.11.58	Thomas A. Blyth	Estate of James Mills	Lots 4, 6, 10, corner of Main and Railway sts; Market St to Main St, Railway St to Peter St; 50 ft	Wentworth 62 R.P.225 (old 18 and 18a)
B990	19.7.59	13.1.60	Thomas A. Blyth	E.M. Harris & W.A. Park	Park lots on Mountain Cres, supersedes **B976**; Wellington St to Upper Wentworth St, Fennel St to Mountain Dr, estate of late Joseph Kirkendall; 3 ch	Wentworth 62 R.P.123 (old 27)
B991	26.9.59	–	–	Mary E. Crooks et al.	Lots on corner of George and Aurora sts; 20 ft	Wentworth 62 R.P.45
B992	12.4.60	–	William Boultbee	O. Springer	Compiled plan, lot 13, 3rd con, twp Barton; Division St to Walnut St, Main St to rd allowance btwn 3rd and 4th cons; 2 ch	Wentworth 62 R.P.48 (old 28)
B993	11.12.60	12.12.60	Thomas A. Blyth	Hiram Clarke	Block lying btwn Victoria Ave, Wellington, Clarke, and Duke sts, owners; 66 ft	Wentworth 62 R.P.44 (old 32)
B994	1.2.61	[1.2.61?]	Thomas A. Blyth	Estate of James Mills	2nd block and 3rd range in 'James Mills Survey'; Lock St to Pearl St, Broadway St to Little James St; 50 ft	Wentworth 62 R.P.47 (old 25)

	Date of Survey	Date of Regist.	Surveyor	Owner	Description and Notes	Location
B995	15.4.64	18.4.64	Thomas A. Blyth	James D. Mackay	Lots 46 and 10 on corner of Main and Railway sts in 'Late James Mills Survey'; 50 ft	Wentworth 62 R.P.150 (old 35 1/2)
B996	11.6.64	14.6.64	William Haskins	William Davey	Pt of block bounded by Lock, Pearl, Little, Main, and Broadway sts; 20 ft	Wentworth 62 R.P.57 (old 36)
B997	5.6.65	8.12.66	Thomas A. Blyth	David Murray	Pt lot 8 in 'Sir A.N. MacNab Survey' of lot 17, 1st (2nd) con, twp Barton; along Railway St; 26 1/4 ft	Wentworth 62 R.P.229 (old 21)
B998	14.9.65	5.12.65	Thomas A. Blyth	John Ferguson	Pt of 'Ferguson Property'; Elgin St to Mary St, Barton St to Cannon St; 100 ft	Wentworth 62 R.P.55 (old 46)
B999	–	20.12.64	Thomas A. Blyth	J.D. Pringle	Pt 'Beasley Property'; King St north to Market St, lots on both sides Walnut St; 40 ch	Wentworth 62 R.P.52 (old 47)
B1000	23.5.66	21.5.66	William Haskins	Commercial Bank of Canada	Pt lot 13, 2nd con, twp Barton; NW corner Wellington and King sts; 20 ft	Wentworth 62 R.P.214 (old 50)
B1001	18.6.67	[11.10.67?]	Thomas A. Blyth	Estate of P.H. Hamilton	Duke St to Bold St, Bond St to MacNab St; 50 ft	Wentworth 62 R.P.1432 (old 57) and OHMA (Map 7459, 7545)
B1002	13.7.67	–	Thomas A. Blyth	Estate of Andrew Stevens	King St to mountain, east of Emerald St, owners; 3 ch	Wentworth 62 R.P.misc 17 dr 2 (old 21)
B1003	–.9.67	[3.9.67?]	Thomas A. Blyth	Estate of George Sylvester Tiffany	Block btwn Queen, Hess, Napier, and Market sts in 'the late Peter Hesse's Survey'; 100 ft	Wentworth 62 R.P.54 (old 52)
	HAMILTON TWP					
B1004	–	5.3.67	E.C. Caddy	–	A resurvey of twp, town limits of Cobourg, bearings, monuments located; 10 ch	Northumberland 39 R.P. Hamilton 14

	HAMPTON					
B1005	24.12.56	5.1.57	L.H. Shortt	B.F. Perry	Lot 18, 5th con, twp Darlington; Simpson Ave to Waldron Estate, Scugog Rd to Waldron St; 2 ch	Newcastle 10 R.P.Perry (Darlington)
B1006	31.1.57	14.4.57	L.H. Shortt	L. Ormiston	Lot 1, 5th con, twp Darlington; on both sides Scugog Rd, Division, Liberty, Temperance, Washington, Alma, and Ormistown sts, bldgs; 3 ch	Newcastle 10 R.P.Ormiston (Darlington)
	HANOVER					
B1007	–	9.2.58	William R. Rombough	A.Z. Gottwals	Pt lots 3–5, 1st con south of Durham Rd, twp Bentinck; Durham Rd to David and Sophia sts, Mary St to Mattin St; 1 ch	Grey 17 R.P.700
B1008	–.–.60	31.1.61	Schofield & Hobson	H.P. Adams & A.Z. Gottwals	Durham Rd to Saugeen R, rd allowance btwn Grey and Bruce cos to Victoria St, owners; 3 ch	Grey 17 R.P.701
B1009	–.–.60	1.5.61	Schofield & Hobson	H.P. Adams	Durham Rd to Saugeen R, California St east to rd allowance btwn Grey and Bruce cos, mills; 3 ch	Grey 17 R.P.700
B1010	16.12.61	11.4.62	William Hawkins	H. Buttenhorn	Pt lot 2 south of Durham Rd, twp Bentinck; David St to Durham Rd on both sides Victoria St	Grey 17 R.P.762
B1011	20.2.62	23.3.66	William R. Rombough	John Hahn et al.	Pt lots 73 and 74, 1st con south of Durham Rd and lot 73 north of Durham Rd, twp Brant; Saugeen R to co line, Ann St to above Durham Rd, relief; 2 ch	Grey 17 R.P.772
	HARLEY					
B1012	15.4.57	13.5.57	John A. Tidey	Stephen Coon	'Derby,' lot 13, 9th con, twp Burford; lots btwn Middle and Victoria sts, Main St beyond George and Elgin sts; 99 ft	Brant 2 R.P.54 (bottom)
B1013	16.4.57	15.6.57	John A. Tidey	Sarah Higson	'Derby,' lot 12, 9th con, twp Burford; lots on Middle St above Main St, owners; 99 ft	Brant 2 R.P.54 (top)
	HARPURHEY					
B1014	30.4.47	7.9.50	David Smith, J.W. McDonald	William Chalk	Huron Rd and North St, bldgs, owners; 4 ch	Huron 22 R.P.251

	Date of Survey	Date of Regist.	Surveyor	Owner	Description and Notes	Location
B1015	26.8.50	–	Joseph G. Kirk	Copps & Gouinlock	Pt lot 15, 1st con, twp Tuckersmith; lots along Huron Rd, Presbyterian church; 2 ch	Huron 22 R.P.250
B1016	11.9.54	11.9.54	William Rath	I. Lewis, I. Galt, C. Widder, R.H. Lowe	Pt lot 14, 1st con, 'Huron Rd Survey; twp Tuckersmith; B.B. & G Ry depot; 2 ch	Huron 22 R.P.252
B1017	–	28.12.55	Joseph G. Kirk	George Worsley	Pt lot 16, 1st con, twp Tuckersmith; on both sides B.B. & G. Ry, partial resurvey by A. Bay (28.4.56) on back; 1 ch	Huron 22 R.P.253
B1018	–	14.7.56	A. Bay	Edward Cash	'Cash's Survey,' lot 15, 1st con, twp Tuckersmith; William St to Ann St, Grace St to Old Huron Rd; 1 1/2 ch	Huron 22 R.P.254
B1019	–	30.7.56	A. Bay	William Fowler	Lot XIII, 1st con, twp Tuckersmith; 1 ch	Huron 22 R.P.255
B1020	–	4.3.57	A. Bay	Robert Hays	Lot XXX, 1st con, twp Tuckersmith; 3 ch	Huron 22 R.P.249
B1021	–	8.12.60	William Rath	William Chalk	Pt north pt lot 16, 1st con, twp Tuckersmith; Old Huron Rd and Huron Rd, ry depot; 2 ch	Huron 22 R.P.256
B1022	27.4.61	27.4.61	A.C. Robertson	Miss Mackenzie	Btwn B. & L.H.R. station grounds and Huron Rd; 2 ch	Huron 22 R.P.257
	HARRINGTON WEST					
B1023	7.8.56	–	William Smiley	David L. Demorest, J. Fraser	'Harrington,' pt lots 30 and 31, 2nd con, twp W Zorra; David St to Thames R and Charlotte St, West St to East St, bldgs, owners, mill pond; 2 ch	Oxford 41 R.P.87
	HARRISBURG					
B1024	–.–.55	9.10.55	Quintin Johnstone	A.M. Vrooman	'Vroomenia,' pt N1/2 lot 1, 1st con, twp S Dumfries; Brant St to James St, King, Main, and Queen sts, G.W. & Galt R.R., owners; 2 ch	Brant 2 R.P.73
B1025	12.10.55	12.10.55	Quintin Johnstone	Francis A. Marshall	'Vroomenia,' amends plan above (**B1024**) for lots on King, Main, Queen, Ryall, and James sts; 2 ch	Brant 2 R.P.74

B1026	24.11.55	17.1.56	James Pollock	Messrs J. & D.M. Osborne	'Dumfries' (Fairchild's Creek); Wellington Ave to Gore of Beverly Twp, Elgin St to Brant St, Galt Preston & Guelph Ry and G.W.R. and stations; 132 ft	Brant 2 R.P.63
B1027	11.1.56	15.1.56	W.G. Wonham	James Ryall	'Dumfries' (late Fairchild's Creek), lot 1, 1st con, twp S Dumfries; Burlington, Main, King, and Ontario sts; 30 ft	Brant 2 R.P.64
B1028	2.6.56	12.8.56	James Pollock	Messrs J. & D.M. Osborne	For description see **1452**; amended plan that relates to **B1026**, **B1029**	Brant 2 R.P.65 (2nd)
B1029	21.10.63	22.10.63 16.8.64	Thomas A. Blyth	A. Vrooman, Laurason & Laurason	Two plans amending **B1026**; Gore of Beverly to Victoria Ave, G.W.R. to Brant St, bldgs of Galt Preston & Guelph Ry; plans similar except for registration dates; 2 ch	Brant 2 R.P.65 and 71
	HARRISTON					
B1030	[-.-.59?]	3.1.67	E.H. Kertland	Thomas Hartley, John Webb & Arch Harrison	For description see **1453**	Wellington 60 R.P.26
	HARROWSMITH					
B1031	11.9.54	18.3.[5?]	William R. Rombough	Moses Spike	'Spikes Corners,' fronts of lots 7 and 6, 5th con, twp Portland; 2 ch	Frontenac 13 R.P.20
	(HARTFIELD)					
B1032	15.9.56	31.10.56	Henry Strange	Thomas Card	Pts lots XIX-XXII, 2nd con, Division D, twp Guelph; later cancelled; 2 ch	Wellington 61 R.P.49
	HARWICH					
B1033	–	1.6.67	A.P. Salter	Alexander McKay	Pt lots XIX on both sides of town line; Prince St to James St, King St to George St, bldgs; 88 ft	Kent 24 R.P.198
	HARWOOD					
B1034	–	12.4.55	Edward C. Caddy	Trustee R. Sinclair	Town plot of Harwood, Rice Lake, twp Hamilton; lots Front St to Park St, ry ground to rd allowance IX con, ry bridge; 3 ch	Northumberland 39 R.P.Hamilton 2

	Date of Survey	Date of Regist.	Surveyor	Owner	Description and Notes	Location
	HASTINGS (Northumberland Co)					
B1035	2.7.51	15.12.63	John Reid	James Crooks	Lot 4, 8th con, twp Asphodel; Front St to Queen St, 7/8 Con Rd to Nelson St, mills, locks, slide; possibly similar to R.P.1 (missing); 2 ch	Northumberland 38 R.P.17 (Hastings)
B1036	[24.3.60?]	30.3.61	J.S. Peterson	Timothy Coughlin & Henry Foulds	E1/2 lot 4, 7th con, twp Asphodel, and W1/2 lot 5, 8th con, twp Asphodel; Albert to Front St, William St to Hope St, Division St to John St, bldgs identified; 3 ch	Northumberland 38 R.P.13 (Hastings)
B1037	–.11.61	9.10.68	Thomas J. Dennehy	Henry Foulds & Timothy Coughland	For description see **1456**	Northumberland 38 R.P.33 (Hastings)
B1038	–.8.62	15.6.63	J. Russ	Henry Foulds	Pt lots 12, 13, 14 in 12th con and lot 14 in 11th con, twp Percy; Water St to King St, streets off gravel rd, Clyde St to Elgin St, bldgs; 3 ch	Northumberland 38 R.P.16 (Hastings)
	(HASTINGS town plot) (Wellington Co)					
B1039	[ca 1858]	–	William Boultbee	G.H. Bender	For description see **1457**	Wellington 60 no R.P.#
	HAWKESBURY					
B1040	–.8.25	–	Anthony Swalwell	Thomas Mears	BF, 1st con, West Division of Hawkesbury; roads, relief, vegetation, bldgs	Prescott 75 no R.P.#
B1041	13.10.38	–	Duncan McDonell	–	Pts BF, lots 11–12, and E1/2 lot 13, con 1, twp W Hawkesbury; plan missing	Prescott 46 R.P.1
B1042	–	13.6.54	Robert Hamilton	–	Pts BF, lots 9–11, con 1, twp W Hawkesbury; plan missing	Prescott 46 R.P.4
	HAWKESVILLE					
B1043	–.7.56	–	John Grant	Gabriel Hawke	For description see **1461**	Waterloo 58 R.P.626A

B1044	–.–.62	3.2.66	Moses McFadden	John Hawke	Pt lot 2, con 12, E.S. Wellesley; streets, mill and mill pond, mill race; 4 ch	Waterloo 58 R.P.626
	HAYDON					
B1045	30.1.55	3.7.55	John Smart	James Shepherd, Charles Bates, et al.	'Charlesville,' lot 14, 8th con, twp Darlington; King, Moon, Nelson, and Church sts and rd allowance 8th con, mill pond and race, bldgs; 2 ch	Newcastle 10 R.P.'Charlesville' (Darlington)
	HEIDELBERG					
B1046	19.10.58	–	Schofield & Hobson	John Meyer	John St to King St east of Queen St; 1 ch	Waterloo 58 R.P.603
	HESPELER					
B1047	16.6.46	15.12.48	James Black	Robert Forbes	'New-Hope'; lots along Queen St, owners, mill pond, bldgs; transcript; 1 ch	Waterloo 67 no R.P.#
B1048	–.–.57	–.10.58	Schofield & Hobson	David Rife	'New-Hope'; lots mainly along Queen, Cooper, and Galt sts; 3 ch	Waterloo 67 R.P.541
B1049	27.12.58 –.6.62	–	M.C. Schofield & J. Hobson	M. Bergey, Henry Wanner & Robt Forbes	Speed R to Galt and Cooper sts, owners, notes re alterations to plan in 1859; 2 ch	Waterloo 67 R.P.540
	HILLSBOROUGH BEACH					
B1050	–.6.66	21.6.66	A. Davidson	John Jones	'Hillsboro,' lots L and L1, front con, twp Plympton; Main St; 1 ch	Lambton 25 R.P.Plympton 7
	HILLSBURGH					
B1051	–.–.[5?]	–	Henry Strange	Nazareth Hill	Pt lots XXV and XXVI, 8th con, and pt lot XXV, 7th con, twp Erin; east of Orangeville St, north of town line btwn cons VII and VIII; transcript; 3 ch	Wellington 61 R.P.62
B1052	–.10.57	28.10.57	Francis Kerr	George Henshaw	Pt W1/2 lot 23, 8th con, twp Erin; bldgs; 2 ch	Wellington 61 R.P.95
B1053	–.11.62	3.7.63	C.J. Wheelock	William How	Pt lot 23, 7th con, twp Erin; Main St to William St; 1.75 ch	Wellington 61 R.P.155

	Date of Survey	Date of Regist.	Surveyor	Owner	Description and Notes	Location
	HOLLAND LANDING					
B1054	17.8.53	4.10.53	Henry White	T.H. Lloyd	'St Albans,' Yonge St to river, Queen St to Bradford, relief, owners; 1 ch	York 65 R.P.76
B1055	16.10.54	16.10.54	J.O. Browne	J. Lukin Robinson	'St Albans,' subdivision of lots CVI and CVII, E Gwillimbury; area east of Yonge St at Beverly Mills, mill pond to Newmarket St, North St to mill pond, lots extend east to 2nd con line, note re part on **B1057**; approx 3 ch	York 65 R.P.98
B1056	7.7.55	25.1.56	William Hawkins	Messrs T.J. O'Neill & T.N. Gibbs	Lot 110, 1st con west of Yonge St, twp E Gwillimbury; north of Holland Landing, Yonge St to Northern R.R. and beyond to 2nd Con Rd, north and south of Centre St, inset location map, auction notice, owners, relief, clearings, toll-house; 4 ch	York 65 R.P.143
B1057	11.7.55	6.3.56	J.O. Browne	J. Lukin Robinson	Subdivision of lot 107, twp E Gwillimbury; Yonge St at Sharon St north to con line, Ont Simcoe Huron R.R. to North St, bldgs along Yonge St; 4 ch	York 65 R.P.149
B1058	18.4.60	25.9.60	Henry White	For Municipal Council	Compiled plan; sources listed, very detailed, bldgs, owners, reserves, vegetation, streets; 4 ch	York 65 R.P.258
	HOLLEN					
B1059	3.6.53	2.8.62	Edwin H. Kertland	William Mendell	Lots 18 and 16, 5th con, twp Maryborough; Canistoga R and mill property, High St to Jane St, Church St to Elgin St; 2 ch	Wellington 60 R.P.71
B1060	29.9.64	8.10.64	LaPenotiere & Bolger	William F. Mendell	Elgin St west to Wellington St, Raglan St north to King St, further streets laid out, mills, churches, school property, burial ground; 3 ch	Wellington 60 R.P.69

	HOLMESVILLE					
B1061	–	11.1.61	T.N. Molesworth	Jonas Copp	Pt lot XII, Huron Rd con, twp Goderich; Huron Rd to Buffalo, Brantford & Goderich R.R.; 2 ch	Huron 22 R.P.543
	HOPE TWP					
B1062	–	13.7.52	–	–	S1/4 lot 11, 2nd con, twp Hope; 2 ch	Port Hope 9 R.P.Hope 5
B1063	–	15.1.61	–	–	For description see **401**; based on plan above	Port Hope 9 R.P.Hope 9
B1064	9.8.54	11.11.54	E.C. Caddy	William Butterfield	Pt lot IX, 2nd con, twp Hope; lots along rd allowance btwn cons 8 and 9; 3 ch	Port Hope 9 R.P.Hope 11
B1065	9.6.55	–.6.55	George A. Stewart	Peter Robertson	'Clifton Grove,' pt lot 10, 1st con, twp Hope; west of Toronto Rd, bldgs; 50 ft	Port Hope 9 R.P.Hope 14
B1066	–.10.57	–	–	W.E. Butterfield	S1/2 lot 8, 4th con, twp Hope; adjacent owners indicated; 12 rods	Port Hope 9 R.P.7 Hope Twp
B1067	12.2.61	14.2.61	George A. Stewart	J. Boyce	Lot 4, 2nd con, twp Hope; shows positions of new and old channels of Smiths Creek; 1 ch	Port Hope 9 R.P.Hope 12
B1068	18.8.65	18.8.65	M. Lough	Estate of John T. Williams	Subdivision of pt lot 10, 2nd con, twp Hope; along rd allowance btwn lots 10 and 11, bldgs; 2 ch	Port Hope 9 R.P.Hope 13
	(HOPKINSBURG town plot)					
B1069	10.4.58	10.4.58	Andrew Miller	Estate of Ephraim Hopkins	Main St to Stoney Creek, L Ontario to Catherine St, owners; 1 ch	Wentworth 62 R.P.1430 (old 9)
	HORNBY					
B1070	1.10.61	29.12.65	G. Brockitt Abrey	For Municipal Council	Baseline of Esquesing Twp and rd allowance of lot 1, con VIII; 2 ch	Halton 20 no R.P.#
	(HUSTON)					
B1071	21.5.60	12.3.61	J.W. Burke	Walter P. & Edward H. Newman	'Hustonville,' pt lots E1/2 11 and W1/2 12, con 8, twp Marysborough; Bridge St to Market St, beyond Tromanhiser St to Wallace St, mill property, church; 2 ch	Wellington 60 R.P.68
B1072	8.6.61	1.7.61	J.W. Burke	John Huston	'Hustonville,' W1/2 lot 12, con VIII, twp Marysborough; 2 ch	Wellington 60 R.P.73(141)

	Date of Survey	Date of Regist.	Surveyor	Owner	Description and Notes	Location
	INGERSOLL					
B1073	–.1.48	28.11.48	William McClary W.G. Wonham	Daniel Carroll	Pt lot 19, BF con, twp W Oxford; Thames R south to Commissioners Rd, Carroll St to side-rd 18/19, lots A and B btwn John and McCarthy sts laid out in 1856; 2 ch	Oxford 41 R.P.13
B1074	10.3.51	–	O. Bartley	John Carnegie	'Carnegietown,' lot XI, con IV, twp N Oxford; Thames St to John St, Thames R to beyond Bell St, G.W.R. depot, Roman Catholic church; 2 ch	Oxford 41 R.P.18
B1075	31.9.51	–	W.G. Wonham	Estate of Edward Mathews	NE1/2 lot XX, con 1, twp W Oxford; along Canterbury and Wellington sts, north and east of mill pond and mill dam; 1 ch	Oxford 41 R.P.23
B1076	–.–.51	31.10.51	W.G. Wonham	Estate of Edward Mathews	Lots 1 and 2, north side of King St and west of Thames St; 30 ft	Oxford 41 R.P.24
B1077	1.1.52	–	W.G. Wonham	McKeand Bros & Company	Park lots on pt lots IX and X, IV con, twp N Oxford; Thames north to Haines St, lots along McKeand and Victoria sts, G.W.R.; 3 ch	Oxford 41 R.P.27
B1078	18.5.52	[18.5.52?]	W.G. Wonham	R.H. Carroll	Lot XIX, BF con, twp W Oxford; south of Commissioners Rd, east of Port Burwell Rd; 66 ft	Oxford 41 R.P.40
B1079	25.6.53	–	W.G. Wonham	–	Pt lot 21, BF con, twp W Oxford; Queen St to Wonham St, Thames R to Anne St, mill pond; 1.5 ch	Oxford 41 R.P.31
B1080	17.9.53	–	W.G. Wonham	Estate of Charles Ingersoll	Catherine St to Thames R, Whiting St to Wellington St; 2 ch	Oxford 41 R.P.150
B1081	28.11.53	[28.11.53?]	W.G. Wonham	Daniel Carroll	Lot XII, 4th con, twp N Oxford; Thames R to King Solomon St, Mutual St to rd allowance btwn lots XII and XIII, G.W.R.; 2 ch	Oxford 41 R.P.41
B1082	–.–.53	–	W.G. Wonham	J.C. Macklin & W.W. Street	Pt lots XXIII and XXIV, 1st con, and lot XXIII, BF con, twp W Oxford; Thames R to South St, Ingersoll St to West St, bldgs, relief; 3 ch	Oxford 41 R.P.44

B1083	2.1.54	–	W.G. Wonham	Elisha Hall	Pt lot 19, 1st con, twp W Oxford; Harris St to Hall and Frank sts, Canterbury St to Tunis St; 2 ch	Oxford 41 R.P.84
B1084	13.7.54	–	W.G. Wonham	John Elliott	Lots 7–17, east side of John St on lot 11, con 4, twp N Oxford; Thames St to John St north of Bell St; 33 ft	Oxford 41 R.P.46
B1085	11.11.54	–	W.G. Wonham	David Canfield	N pt lot XVIII, BF con, twp W Oxford; macadamized rd and east of rd allowance btwn lots 18 and 19; 2 ch	Oxford 41 R.P.54
B1086	5.3.55	–	W.G. Wonham	John Carnegie	Lot 11, 4th con, twp N Oxford; Thames R to Raglan St, Union St to Mutual St, Roman Catholic church, G.W.R.; 2 ch	Oxford 41 R.P.95
B1087	21.6.55	–	W.G. Wonham	Henry Crotty	Pt lot X, 4th con, twp N Oxford; Thames R and G.W.R. depot to Innis St, Union St to Cashel St; 2 ch	Oxford 41 R.P.79
B1088	24.8.55	–	W.G. Wonham	–	Pt lot 11, 3rd con, twp N Oxford; Hale St to Howard Ave, gravel rd to Davy St; 2 ch	Oxford 41 R.P.64
B1089	13.12.55	–	William Smiley	David Taylor	Park lot 1 in D. Canfield survey (**B1085**); lots SE of Stone Rd and rd allowance btwn lots 18 and 19; 1 ch	Oxford 41 R.P.67
B1090	28.12.55	–	William Smiley	Herkamer Daggart & Nicholas Taylor	Subdivision of park lots 2 and 3, in D. Canfield survey (**B1085**); Cherry St to Queen St and along Taylor St; 1 ch	Oxford 41 R.P.68
B1091	14.4.56	–	W.G. Wonham	Charles P. Hall	Park lot 4, east and west side of Oxford St, at Catherine St and near Thames St; 1 ch	Oxford 41 R.P.72
B1092	22.4.56	–	W.G. Wonham	James Smart	Park lot 6, D. Canfield's survey (**B1085**); .75 ch	Oxford 41 R.P.169
B1093	1.10.56	–	W.G. Wonham	J. Barnett	King St to Charles St, Wonham St to Barnett St; 40 ft	Oxford 41 R.P.78
B1094	9.10.56	–	W.G. Wonham	Neil McKay	Lot 23, BF con, twp W Oxford; James St to macadamized rd west of Ingersoll St; 1 ch	Oxford 41 R.P.83
B1095	29.10.56	–	W.G. Wonham	Thomas Brown	Park lot 5, south side Catherine St; lots along Catherine, Oxford, and Thames sts; 1 ch	Oxford 41 R.P.88

	Date of Survey	Date of Regist.	Surveyor	Owner	Description and Notes	Location
B1096	18.11.56	–	W.G. Wonham	John Brown & John J. Mackenzie	Ingersoll and Thamesford Gravel Rd to Haines St and Jura Lane, Crusoe Ave to Castel St; 150 ft	Oxford 41 R.P.82
B1097	20.11.56	–	W.G. Wonham	John Fish	Lots along Victoria St btwn Thames and John sts, north of G.W.R. station ground; 1 ch	Oxford 41 R.P.85
B1098	19.1.57	–	W.G. Wonham	W.G. Wonham, John Height (Trustees)	Lot 17, BF con, twp W Oxford; on either side of Thames R and Brantford and Ingersoll Gravel Rd, Alfred St to Adolphus St; 2 ch	Oxford 41 R.P.92
B1099	11.5.57	[5.8.69?]	W.G. Wonham	Willard Eastwood	Lots in park lot 12 south of Haines St; 1 ch	Oxford 41 R.P.?
B1100	–.–.57	[25.6.57?]	W.G. Wonham	G.T. Jarvis	Lot 13 and pt lot 14, con 4, twp N Oxford; Thames R to rd allowance btwn cons 3 and 4, Pemberton St to Murray St; 2 ch	Oxford 41 R.P.102
B1101	–.–.57	[16.7.57?]	W.G. Wonham	James Harris	Pt lots XX and XXI, 1st con, twp W Oxford; Cross St to rd allowance btwn cons 1 and 2 east of Union St; 3 ch	Oxford 41 R.P.107
B1102	11.8.57	–	W.G. Wonham	Messrs Benson & Merritt	King St to Charles St, Thames St to Mill St, grist mill, distillery plot; 60 links	Oxford 41 R.P.109
B1103	5.9.57	–	W.G. Wonham	C.P. Hall	No 2 plan of park lot 4 and pt lot 3 on west side Oxford St at Catherine St; 1 ch	Oxford 41 R.P.103
B1104	14.1.58	–	W.G. Wonham	E. Doty	Park lot 1 south of Ann St btwn Thames St and Oxford St; 66 ft	Oxford 41 R.P.106
B1105	–.–.58	[15.10.58?]	W.G. Wonham	H. Taylor	Park lot 1, 'Ingersoll Survey'; Anne St to Cottage St btwn Thames St and Oxford St; 66 ft	Oxford 41 R.P.113
B1106	–	29.5.60	Cyrus Carroll	'The Kneeshaw Estate'	Lot 11, 3rd con, twp N Oxford; Hale St to Howard St, Ingersoll Gravel Rd to Davy St; 4 ch	Oxford 41 R.P.142
B1107	22.4.65	–	W.G. Wonham	James R. Benson	Charles St to King St, Oxford St to Church St; 2 ch	Oxford 41 R.P.156

B1108	–.–.65	[2.9.65?]	W.G. Wonham	Robert Kneeshaw	Pt lot 11, 3rd con, twp N Oxford; Hale St to Milton St, Davy St to Ingersoll Gravel Rd; 132 ft	Oxford 41 R.P.161
	INGLESIDE					
B1109	29.12.55	4.4.65	George Bruce	George Crawford	'Wales,' pt lot 7, 1st con, twp Osnabruck; Railroad and Broadway sts to boundary btwn Crawford and Stuart sts, Main St to Crawford St, owners; 50 ft	Stormont 52 R.P.5
	INKERMAN					
B1110	30.10.60	20.2.67?	James West	Robert Lowery	Pt lot 18, 3rd con, twp Mountain; lots on Mountain, Sullivan, Sarah, Queen, and Margaret sts, bldgs, mill pond, grist mill; 45 ft	Dundas 8 R.P.14
	INNERKIP					
B1111	28.9.51	–	William Smiley	George Lee	Lots 9 and 10, 17th con, twp Zorra, and lot 8, 6th con, twp Blandford; 4 ch	Oxford 41 R.P.21
B1112	8.11.53 12.7.56	[8.11.53?] [12.7.56?]	William Smiley	Charles Vincent	East pt of W1/2 lot 10, 17th con, twp E Zorra; Coleman St to Blandford St, Burton St to side-rd btwn lots 10 and 11; 1856 certification is for lots btwn Balsam St, side-rd, Blandford and Coleman sts; photo-reproduction; 2 ch	Oxford 41 R.P.35
B1113	10.2.55	12.11.56	William Smiley	A. Thompson	Town lots north pt lot 9 and south pt lot 10, 17th con, twp E Zorra; on both sides Thames R and on Blandford St and road btwn cons 16 and 17; 4 ch	Oxford 41 R.P.80
B1114	31.5.55	8.6.55	W.G. Wonham	S.G. Swan & John Lee	Side-rd btwn lots 10 and 11 to Alma St, Blandford St to Inkerman St; 2 ch	Oxford 41 R.P.59
B1115	–.10.57	[–.–.58?]	William Smiley	Estate of George Lee	Lots 9 and 10, 17th con, twp E Zorra, and lot 8, 6th con, twp Blandford; Blandford St to Thames R, George St to Harwood St, mills, trees, relief; 4 ch	Oxford 41 R.P.111
	INNISFIL TWP					
B1116	23.4.53	3.9.53	Robert Ross	Charles Thompson	Park lots on east pt of N1/2 lot 7, 13th con, twp Innisfil; 4 ch	Simcoe 51 R.P.21

	Date of Survey	Date of Regist.	Surveyor	Owner	Description and Notes	Location
B1117	23.4.53	5.9.53	Robert Ross	Charles Thompson	Park lots on W1/2 lot 6, 14th con, twp Innisfil; 4 ch	Simcoe 51 R.P.20
B1118	2.3.57	13.3.57	Henry Creswicke	John Arnold	Park lots on lot 23, 3rd con, twp Innisfil; Front and Centre sts; 4 ch	Simcoe 51 R.P.54
B1119	–.5.57	20.11.58	William Sanders	Hon. James Patton	Park lots on lot 6, 12th and 13th cons, twp Innisfil; Essa Rd, owners, houses; 6 ch	Simcoe 51 R.P.67
B1120	20.8.64	27.8.64	William Sanders	Estate of John Pratt	N1/2 lot 16, 11th con, twp Innisfil; 7 lots, houses, English church; 6 ch	Simcoe 51 R.P.98
	INNISVILLE					
B1121	–.6.51	26.7.51	Joseph M.O. Cromwell	James Ennis, Sr & James Ennis, Jr	'Ennisville,' lot 20, 11th con, twp Drummond; Main St on both sides Mississippi R, mills, bldgs, dam, bridge, owners; 2 ch	Lanark 27 R.P.124
	INVERARY					
B1122	[16.9.55?]	16.9.55	Thomas Fraser	Jas Campbell	'Inverary'; Earl St to Victoria St, Wellington St to Division St; scale n.g.	Frontenac 13 R.P.24
	INVERMAY					
B1123	–.1.56	4.3.58	Archibald McNab	William A. Corbett & Hiram Kilbourne	For description see **1480**	Bruce 3 R.P.15
	IONA					
B1124	–.12.49	21.3.50	Charles Fraser	Duncan McCormick et al.	Iona and Elliottville, pt lot 1 south of Back St, twp Southwold, and pt lot C, VII and VIII cons, twp Dunwich; 2 ch	Elgin 11 R.P.3A
	IROQUOIS					
B1125	1.3.56	20.3.56	Thomas S. Rubidge	James Hodges	'Matilda,' centre pt lot 21, 1st con, twp Matilda; St Lawrence to Third St, East St to West St, G.T.R., owners; 200 ft	Dundas 8 R.P.4
B1126	27.3.57	–	D.R. Brown	Messrs Brouse, Coons & Carman	Front pt W1/4 lots 21–3, 1st con, twp Matilda; St Lawrence to ry, Albert St to Mary St, bldgs; 2 ch	Dundas 8 no R.P.#

B1127	–.4.58	29.11.72	James West	Messrs Peter & Mathew Carman	Front lot 24, 1st con, twp Matilda; canal to G.T.R., Brock St to John St; 100 ft	Dundas 8 R.P.21
	(IRVINEDALE town plot)					
B1128	12.3.61	9.8.61	Henry Strange	Thomas M. Valentine	Lot 9, 15th con, twp Nichol on Owen Sound Rd and Logan St; 2 ch	Wellington 61 R.P.143
	JANETVILLE					
B1129	12.5.65	31.5.65	M. Deane	John McDermid	Pt of lot V, XIII con, twp Manvers; 2 ch	Port Hope 9 R.P.Manvers 7
	JASPER					
B1130	–.5.62	27.8.88	John Burchill	Ambrose Olmstead	'Albune,' lot 4, 4th con, twp Kitley; Queens Hwy to Maple St, John St to William St; 60 ft	Leeds 28 R.P.95
	JERSEY					
B1131	8.10.58	8.11.58	B.W. Gossage	Hiram Moore	Pts lots 8 and 9, BF of 3rd con, twp N Gwillimbury; Elizabeth and Matilda sts, Emily and Olivia sts, bldgs, steam and sawmill; 100 ft	York 65 R.P.245
	JORDAN					
B1132	–	–	George Rykert	–	Lots along Main St and twp rd allowance; 2 ch	Niagara 30 R.P.3 Co
	JORDAN STATION					
B1133	–	29.4.56	Hiram Johnson	Solomon Secord	'Bridgeport,' pt lots 17 and 18, 2nd range, twp Louth; 20 Mile Creek to Ontario St, Chestnut St to beyond William St; 80 ft	Niagara 30 R.P.41 Co
	KARS					
B1134	6.6.57	11.6.57	H.O. Wood	Adam J. Eastman	'Wellington'; east end lot 23, 1st con, twp N Gower; Wellington St to Ann St, Rideau St to Waterloo and Nelson sts; 100 ft	Ottawa-Carleton 5 R.P.7
	(KATESVILLE)					
B1135	22.8.56	25.8.56	Walsh & Mercer	Alexander Campbell	For description see **1487**	Middlesex 34 R.P.116

	Date of Survey	Date of Regist.	Surveyor	Owner	Description and Notes	Location
	KEENANSVILLE					
B1136	18.9.56	30.7.60	Robert Walsh	Robert Keenan et al.	Lots 13 and 14, 7th con, twp Adjala; various estates, streets named, mill pond, grist mill and tail race; 2 ch	Simcoe 51 R.P.80
	KEENE					
B1137	–	6.3.47	James Bird	Thomas Carr	Pt lot 12, 7th con, twp Otonabee; High St at Main St; 1 ch	Peterborough 45 R.P.R-7 Otonabee
B1138	–.6.49	23.6.49	John Reid	T. Short	SE1/4 lot 13, 7th con, twp Otonabee; Main and High sts; 2 ch	Peterborough 45 R.P.R-7 Otonabee
B1139	21.3.53	21.3.53	–	'Burnham's Plan'	High St to Mill St, river with sawmill and grist mill, Bridge St to north of 3rd St; 4 ch	Peterborough 45 R.P.R-9 Otonabee
B1140	2.9.54	3.2.55	John Reid	T. Short	Lots on both sides Main St west of High St; 2 ch	Peterborough 45 R.P.R-10 Otonabee
	KELVIN					
B1141	13.10.56	28.12.56	Eliakim Malcolm	Cornelius H. Forman	Pt lot 12, 14th con, twp Burford; on Forman, King, and Pearl sts; 1/2 ch	Brant 2 R.P.52
B1142	24.6.59	13.11.59	Sherman Malcolm	George Forman	Pt lot 12, 14th con, twp Burford; lots on Cedar, King, and Forman sts; 1 ch	Brant 2 R.P.52 Kelvin
B1143	15.4.61	13.6.61	Eliakim Malcolm	Adeline Forman	Pt lot 13, 14th con, twp Burford; lots on middle of town line, Forman St and on unnamed street; 2 ch	Brant 2 R.P.53 Kelvin
	KEMPTVILLE					
B1144	–.6.36	–	Copied by Francis Jones	–	South Kemptville, pt lot 25, 3rd con, twp Oxford; lots east of Hurd St along Oxford St, river; 2 ch	Grenville 15 R.P.Oxford 2
B1145	–.6.44	–	Francis Jones	–	Pt South Kemptville; lots north of south branch Rideau R; 2 ch	Grenville 15 R.P.Oxford 6

B1146	–.–.5?	–	–	–	River to North St, West St to James St, streets east of this to river, wooded and swampy areas; 5 ch	Grenville 15 R.P.Kemptville 1
B1147	25.4.50	–	Francis Jones	Revd Henry Patton	North Kemptville, North St to con rd, Rideau St to James St; 2 ch	Grenville 15 R.P.Kemptville 2
B1148	29.4.50	16.6.50	Francis Jones	Revd Henry Patton	'Kemptville Centre,' south branch Rideau R to Main St, Alfred St to Harriet St, owners; 55 links	Grenville 15 R.P.Kemptville 3
B1149	18.5.55	–	John Burchill	Revd Henry Patton	Pt 'Kemptville Centre,' pt lot 26, 3rd con, twp Oxford; Main St to Alma St, Alfred St to Rideau St, cottage plot, burial ground and church; 80 ft	Grenville 15 R.P.Kemptville 4
B1150	22.9.55	11.3.56	Francis Jones	Francis Jones	For description see **1488**	Grenville 15 R.P.Kemptville 5 and 6
B1151	2.12.56	27.12.56	John Burchill	Revd Henry Sheiler	'Elliottville,' lot 28, 3rd con, twp Oxford; lots along James, Main, and Centre sts and along river, mill pond; 100 ft	Grenville 15 R.P.Kemptville 7
B1152	10.7.57	13.7.57	Sandford Fleming	James R. Bradbury	Pt lots 28 and 29, 3rd con, twp Oxford; Ottawa & Prescott Ry to Gower St across south branch Rideau R, James St east to Court St, proposed market square and fairground; 200 ft	Grenville 15 R.P.Kemptville 8
B1153	28.10.59	9.1.60	John Burchill	Edwin Hurd	'West Kemptville,' lot 25, 3rd con, twp Oxford; Main St to Queens Hwy, Hurd St to Church St, 2 reserves; 100 ft	Grenville 15 R.P.Oxford 5
B1154	–	1.3.59	William Wagner	H.O. Burritt	Pt lot 27, IIIrd con, twp Oxford; Prescott St to Park St, Ottawa St to Victoria St; 100 ft	Grenville 15 R.P.Kemptville 9
B1155	20.11.60	5.2.61	John Burchill	Alfred Holmes	SE pt lot 27, 3rd con, twp Oxford; Queens Hwy to Van Buren St, County Rd east to Joseph St and Ottawa Prescott Ry; 60 ft	Grenville 15 R.P.Kemptville 10
	KERWOOD					
B1156	19.12.59	23.4.61	Samuel Peters	J.I. McKenzie	E1/2 lot 6 and W1/2 lot 7, 5th con, south of Egremont Rd, twp Adelaide; Grace to Mackenzie St, Clyde to Havelock St, north of London and Port Sarnia Ry; 198 ft	Middlesex 30 R.P.165 Co

	Date of Survey	Date of Regist.	Surveyor	Owner	Description and Notes	Location
	KILBRIDE					
B1157	17.9.53	10.8.54	Samuel Peters	Messrs Panton & Baker	Pt lot 9 in con II, twp Nelson; new survey, East St to Blessington St, Jane St to rd allowance btwn cons 2 and 3, owners, 2 ponds, 2 sawmills; 3 ch	Halton 20 R.P.13
	KILWORTH					
B1158	14.3.49	27.12.49	B. Springer	John Woodhall	Thames R to Elgin St and road btwn lots B and C, owners; photoreproduction; 2 ch	Middlesex 34 R.P.2
	KINBURN					
B1159	13.2.57	21.4.57	A. Bay	Michael C. Patterson & Francis H. Scholes	Lots V and VI, VIth con, twp Hullett; Union St to Cedar St, Jane St to Hamilton St; 1 ch	Huron 22 R.P.279 and 279A
	KINCARDINE					
B1160	–.6.56	29.8.56	John Denison	William Sutton [et al.]	'Williamsburgh,' lots 12 and 13, con A, twp Kincardine; L Huron to Goderich and Saugeen Rd, King St to Broadway St; 4 ch	Bruce 3 R.P.4
B1161	1.9.57	18.9.57	L.B. Hamlin	Messrs Culbey & Montgomery	'Penetangore,' park lots on pt lots 16 and 17, con A, twp Kincardine, inset location map (40 ch); 2 ch	Bruce 3 R.P.10
	KING CITY					
B1162	30.1.55	7.2.55	J. Stoughton Dennis	George Beatty	Lots 3, 4, and 5, 4th con, twp King; on both sides Ont, Simcoe & Huron Ry line and station, diagram of park lots; 71 ft	York 65 R.P.109
	KING TWP					
B1163	21.8.39	17.6.40	Charles Rankin	–	Shows difference btwn old line btwn 8th and 9th cons, twp King, and that run by Mr Callaghan; 30 ch	York 65 R.P.4
B1164	22.9.39	17.6.40	Charles Rankin	Jacob Snyder & Seneca Weller	Pt of 8th con, lots 5 and 6; re a disputed boundary; 10 ch	York 65 R.P.1A

KINGSTON

B1165	–.3.20	7.11.59	John Ryder	Smith Bartlett	N pt W1/2 lot 22, 1st con, twp Kingston; copy of original	Frontenac 13 R.P.D4
B1166	18.4.22	26.3.63	W.H. Kilborn	Rectory of Kingston	Church lot G; King St to Clarence St, school lot, copy of original; 28 ft	Frontenac 13 R.P.D3
B1167	–.7.37	21.1.56	Thos Burrowes	James B. Clark	Pt N1/2 lot 4, twp Kingston; Montreal Rd along Parke St; copy of earlier, lost plan; 2 ch	Frontenac 13 R.P.B26
B1168	–.–.4?	–	W.H. Kilborn	Town of Kingston	Water to North St, west to West St; original lot nos to 439, some names of owners, military reserve, fort, bldgs; 3 ch	Frontenac 13 R.P.A5
B1169	–.–.4?	–	James W. Benn	Town of Kingston	Compiled plan; water to Avenue St and govt ground, north to 3 streets above North St, college, artillery ground; scale n.g.	Frontenac 13 R.P.A1
B1170	17.6.41	22.3.47	William H. Kilborn	John McLean	Park lots on front of farm lot 5, west side Cataraqui R, twp Kingston; 3 ch	Frontenac 13 R.P.15
B1171	7.8.41	30.4.51	W.H. Kilborn	Queens College	Queens College ground, SW1/4 lot 21, 1st con; King, Union, Johnson, and College sts, lots on both sides College St; 4 ch	Frontenac 13 R.P.B11
B1172	14.9.41	14.8.55	W.H. Kilborn	Estate of John S. Cartwright	Rear lot 24, 1st con, twp Kingston; Old Rd to Loughborough Rd to Albert St; 1 ch	Frontenac 13 R.P.A13
B1173	–.10.41	1.5.50	George Bruce	Hon. John Macaulay	'Arthur-Place'; Stuart St to Union St, Barrie St to Arch St, owners; 1 ch	Frontenac 13 R.P.A4
B1174	2.4.42	–	James W. Benn	Estate of Richard Ellerbeck	E1/2 lot 21, 1st con, twp Kingston; Union St to Cross St, lots on both sides Elizabeth St, owners; 1 ch	Frontenac 13 R.P.B20
B1175	18.6.42	–	P.V. Elmore	W.H. Boulton, Esq.	W1/2 of E1/2 lot 22, 1st con, twp Kingston; Union St to Front St, lots along Beverly St; 2 ch	Frontenac 13 R.P.B15
B1176	14.10.42	3.3.43	James W. Benn	John Counter, Thos Kirkpatrick	Pt lot 22, 1st con, twp Kingston; lots along Victoria St btwn Johnson and Store sts; 2.5 ch	Frontenac 13 R.P.A8
B1177	29.11.42	26.2.86	W.H. Kilborn	Thomas Rogers	Front lot 24, 1st con, twp Kingston; north side extension of Church St at Grass St; 1.5 ch	Frontenac 13 R.P.A19

	Date of Survey	Date of Regist.	Surveyor	Owner	Description and Notes	Location
B1178	–.9.44	–	James W. Benn	Kingston Twp	Road built by petition of S.B. Harrison and others; area of Union, Centre, Store, and Johnson sts, Queens College, Provincial Penitentiary lands; 5 ch	Frontenac 13 R.P.A10
B1179	–.10.46	–	A.W. Wells, D.B. Papineau & A. [Russell]	–	Pt of west addition to Kingston; roads, lots; 40 ch	Frontenac 13 R.P.9
B1180	–	22.3.47	George Bruce	John McLean	West side Cataraqui R; 3 ch	Frontenac 13 R.P.14
B1181	30.10.47	11.9.54	Wm H. Kilborn	Estate of Chas Stuart	Subdivision of pt farm lot A; Montreal St to Division St north of Picard St, owners, table of lots sold; 200 ft	Frontenac 13 R.P.B30
B1182	15.1.50	30.8.50	Thomas Fraser Gibbs	John Counter	Park lot II and pt lot 25; Bagot St to Clergy St, Johnson St W, bldgs, addition of lots 17–20, A and B 20.8.50; 2 ch	Frontenac 13 R.P.B27
B1183	16.9.50	4.6.51	Thomas Fraser Gibbs	John McLean	SE pt lot 1, Cataraqui con; Grove Orchard, Cataraqui, and River sts; 2 ch	Frontenac 13 R.P.B3
B1184	13.7.52	17.12.52	Thomas Fraser Gibbs	John Alex Macdonald	'Minnes Tract'; Princess to Jenkins Lane, Colborne and Third sts; 2 ch	Frontenac 13 R.P.C18
B1185	17.11.52	–	Thomas F. Gibbs	Francis Manning Hill	For description see **1541**	Frontenac 13 no R.P.#
B1186	29.12.52	8.1.53	A.B. Perry	Smith Bartlett	'Williamsville,' 'Bartlett's Farm'; pt W1/2 lot 22, 1st con; Princess St and Concession Rd, similar to **B1166**; 2 ch	Frontenac 13 R.P.C17
B1187	–	9.1.53	–	Smith Bartlett	W1/2 lot 22, 1st con, twp Kingston; lots on Centre St and Parke St to Store St; similar to plan below but less detailed; 2 ch	Frontenac 13 R.P.A7
B1188	–	9.1.53	–	Smith Bartlett	W1/2 lot 22, 1st con, twp Kingston, 'Bartlett Farm'; on both sides of Centre St btwn Front and Store sts, owners, drawings of bldgs; 2 ch	Frontenac 13 R.P.A3
B1189	9.3.54	6.4.54	Thomas Fraser Gibbs	Archibald John Macdonell	SE pt lot 22, 1st con, twp Kingston; Union St to King St, Collingwood and Beverley sts, bldgs, owners, brewery, wharfs; 4 ch	Frontenac 13 R.P.B4

B1190	15.5.54	7.6.54	Thomas Fraser Gibbs	Arch. John Macdonell	Lots on Collingwood, Nelson, Princess, Johnson, and Union sts, bldgs; 4 ch	Frontenac 13 R.P.A2
B1191	5.6.54	13.6.54	Thomas Fraser Gibbs	A.J. Macdonell	West pt lot 22; Union St to Princess St, Collingwood and Nelson sts west to Centre and Regent sts, bldgs, some owners; 4 ch	Frontenac 13 R.P.B23
B1192	7.7.54	18.10.58	Wm H. Kilborn	Hon. Geo. H. Markland	East side of Patrick St btwn George and John sts; 2 copies (one unregistered); 33 ft	Frontenac 13 R.P.C30
B1193	4.8.54	5.8.54	Thomas Fraser Gibbs	–	'Ellerbeck Farm,' E1/2 lot 21; King St to Park St; printed; 6 ch	Frontenac 13 R.P.B31
B1194	14.11.54	16.11.54	Thomas F. Gibbs	John Flanigan	Pt lot XVIII, 1st con, twp Kingston; south of Bath Rd, west of Main and King sts, owners, bldgs; 4 ch	Frontenac 13 R.P.20
B1195	–.5.55	27.6.55	Thomas Fraser Gibbs	Samuel Taylor	SE pt lot 20, 1st con, 'Portsmouth'; King St to Union St along Alvington Ave, owners, estate houses; 2 ch	Frontenac 13 R.P.22
B1196	–.9.55	6.9.55	Thomas Fraser Gibbs	Maxwell Strange	SE pt lot 19 and SW pt lot 20, 2nd con, twp Kingston; Bath Rd, Princess St, Waterloo to Inkerman St; 2 ch	Frontenac 13 R.P.23
B1197	1.–.56?	[–.–.67?]	Thomas F. Gibbs	James Hopkirk	For description see **1546**	Frontenac 13 R.P.47
B1198	23.6.56	1.8.56	Thomas Fraser Gibbs	John Creighton	Pt lot 24 bounded by Barrie, Stuart, George, and O'Kill sts; 1 ch	Frontenac 13 R.P.A20
B1199	19.9.56	19.1.57	–	P.C. Murdock	W1/2 lot 1 west of Great Cataraqui R; Division, Thomas, Russell, Joseph sts; 2 ch	Frontenac 13 R.P.B7
B1200	22.11.58	8.10.59	Wm Perceval	Sir Chas J. Stuart	Pt lot A on M. Ferguson Tract; Plum St to Princess St, Division St to Barrie St, description of property by W.H. Kilborn 30.12.54; 1 ch	Frontenac 13 R.P.A9
B1201	22.11.58	9.6.62	Wm Perceval	Sir Chas J. Stuart	Same as plan above but less complete; 1 ch	Frontenac 13 R.P.A11
B1202	–	1.7.62	E.H. Kertland	Estate of John McLean	Lots 103–14 and 15 of town survey; Barrack and Wellington sts, govt yard, A.C. Chewett & Co., owners and leasees; 25 ft	Frontenac 13 R.P.A6
B1203	16.7.62	4.8.62	T.W. Nash	John D. Macdonald	Lot D of town survey; Wellington St to Rideau St, bldgs; 33 ft	Frontenac 13 R.P.D30

	Date of Survey	Date of Regist.	Surveyor	Owner	Description and Notes	Location
B1204	23.2.63	3.3.64	T.W. Nash	Patrick Donnelly	Pt lot 24, at Barrie and Earl sts; 33 ft	Frontenac 13 R.P.B2
B1205	4.12.63	–	Geo. B. Kirkpatrick	Jane McLeod, John Torrance, P. McGrogan	Street allowance from Centre St to Beverly St btwn Union and King sts, owners, wharf; 4 ch	Frontenac 13 R.P.D14
B1206	1.1.64	–	Geo. B. Kirkpatrick	John Stuart Smyth	Pt lot A, twp Kingston; btwn Patrick, James, and Carlisle sts; 1 ch	Frontenac 13 R.P.A16
B1207	8.2.64	11.2.65	T.W. Nash	R.J. Cartwright	Rear of BF of lot 17, 1st con, twp Kingston; Front St to Hall St; 1 ch	Frontenac 13 R.P.6
B1208	4.4.67	5.11.69	T.W. Nash	Thos Paton et al.	Water lot 22 btwn G.T.R. and Ontario St; 20 ft	Frontenac 13 R.P.C1
B1209	8.6.67	8.6.67	T.W. Nash	James Alexander McDowall	'Stuartsville'; N pt lot 24, 1st con, twp Kingston; lots btwn 6th St and York Rd west of Division St; 1 ch	Frontenac 13 R.P.C11
	KINGSVILLE					
B1210	29.1.50	19.4.50	John A. Wilkinson	Andrew Stewart, James King, Richard Herington	Mill Creek to Mill St, Prince Albert St to Spruce St, English church, Methodist church, boundaries of surveys for different owners; transcript; 2 ch	Essex 12 R.P.184 and 185
	(KINNETTLES)					
B1211	–.9.55	7.1.56	Milton C. Schofield	Alexander Harvey	S pt BF lot 8, 14th con north of Grand R; relief, market sq; 3 ch	Wellington 61 R.P.57
	KITCHENER					
B1212	7.10.1851	–	Moses Springer	Benjamin Eby, Joseph Schneider, David Weber, et al.	'Berlin'; Church St to Pine St, Lancaster St to Young St; later part of R.P.365; 4 ch	Waterloo 58 no R.P.#
B1213	10.10.54	–	Joseph Hobson	George John Grange	'Berlin,' streets and lots on both sides G.T.R., Strange St to Lancaster St, Queen St to Shanly St, owners; 264 ft	Waterloo 58 R.P.374, 375, 376, 377
B1214	20.4.55	[–.7.55?]	Milton C. Schofield	John Hoffman	Pts of lots 1, 18, and 49, Upper Block, twp Waterloo, along South and Mill sts; 4 ch	Waterloo 58 R.P.384

B1215	14.5.55	–	Milton C. Schofield	Estate of Henry Eby	Village lots 4 and pt lot 12, south of King St, and pt twp lot 17, Upper Block, twp of Waterloo; 1 ch	Waterloo 58 R.P.367
B1216	12.6.55	–	Milton C. Schofield	Estate of Henry Eby	Pt lot 17, Upper Block; lots along Albert (now Madison St) and Moyer St; 1 ch	Waterloo 58 R.P.368
B1217	–.10.55	–	Milton C. Schofield	Estate of Frederick Gaukel	Pt twp lot 3 and village lot 16, pts twp lots 16 and 17 and pts lot 17, Upper Block of G.C.T.; streets; 2 ch	Waterloo 58 R.P.379–82
B1218	4.12.55	3.3.56	Milton C. Schofield	Gabriel Bowman	Lots on Young and King sts; 16 ft	Waterloo 58 R.P.362
B1219	–.2.56	[–.2.56?]	Milton C. Schofield	Frank Evans Marcon	Lots on Weber, Water, and Victoria sts; 25 ft	Waterloo 58 R.P.389
B1220	–.12.56	[16.12.56?]	Schofield & Hobson	P.N. Tagge et al.	'Bridgeport,' compiled plan, twp Waterloo; streets named, relief, vegetation, creeks, mills and mill ponds; 2 ch	Waterloo 58 R.P.577
B1221	–.8.57	–	Schofield & Hobson	C.G. Tisdale, John Atkinson	'Edenburgh,' '(German Mills),' pt of original Bechtel Tract; streets named; 2 ch	Waterloo 58 R.P.586
B1222	21.11.57	–	Schofield & Hobson	Andreas Schmidt	Frederick and Lancaster sts; 1 ch	Waterloo 58 R.P.392
B1223	–.–.57	[–.2.58?]	Schofield & Hobson	Estate of Charles H. Ahrens	Lots on Queen and Weber sts; 80 links	Waterloo 58 R.P.360
B1224	–.–.57	[–.2.58?]	Schofield & Hobson	Estate of Charles H. Ahrens	Lots 1, 2, and 3 of twp lot 3, Upper Block, German Co. Tract; Queen St, Weber, and David Ahren sts, possibly extension or revision of plan above; 80 links	Waterloo 58 R.P.360–1
B1225	–.–.57	[–.2.59?]	Schofield & Hobson	Estate of Christian Enslin	Pt lot 2, Upper Block, G.C.T., lot 33 of Eby Estate on both sides Weber St; 80 links	Waterloo 58 R.P.372
B1226	–.–.58	[–.9.58?]	Schofield & Hobson	C.K. Nahrgang	Foundry to Queen St, owners; 1 ch	Waterloo 58 R.P.391
B1227	–.10.58	–	Schofield & Hobson	Estates of Joseph E. Schneider & Benjamin Eby	Resurvey of pt of twp lots 2 and 17, Upper Block, G.C.T.; David St to Cedar St, Church St to junction of Frederick and Lancaster sts, owners; 2 ch	Waterloo 58 R.P.364, 393, 394

	Date of Survey	Date of Regist.	Surveyor	Owner	Description and Notes	Location
B1228	–.5.59	–	Schofield & Hobson	David Weber, Abraham C. Weber & Christian Eby	Pts twp lots 3, 4, 16, Upper Block, G.C.T.; 3 areas, Frederick St to Water St, King St to Pine St, Cameron to Cedar St west of Weber St; on both sides of Ahrens and Wilhelm sts; 3 ch	Waterloo 58 R.P.365–99, 400–1
B1229	–.–.59	[24.12.59?]	Milton C. Schofield	Geo. J. Grange	Amended survey of **B1213** (1854); 264 ft	Waterloo 58 R.P.378
B1230	–.–.59	–	–	Geo. & Levy Gaukel et al.	Pt of Frederick Gaukel's survey (**B1217**) (1855), lots on King btwn Queen and Foundry sts; 100 links	Waterloo 58 R.P.383
B1231	–.–.60	[1.10.60?]	Joseph Hobson	Estate of Moritz Hund	Pt of Bechtel Tract; 3 ch	Waterloo 58 R.P.576
B1232	–.–.61	[8.6.61?]	Joseph Hobson	Estate of Christian Eby	Pt lot 18 G.C.T.	Waterloo 58 R.P.371
B1233	–.–.61	[28.6.61?]	Joseph Hobson	Estate of Christian Eby; Wm Moyer; Jacob Shantz	Pt lots 17 and 18, G.C.T.; Preston & Berlin Ry, Albert, Moyer, Hawkins, and Church sts, owners; 2 ch	Waterloo 58 R.P.366, 390, 395
B1234	–.–.62	[16.1.62?]	Joseph Hobson	John Brubacher & Elias Eby & Estate of Christian Eby	King St to Weber St, Cedar St to Cameron St, and lots off Lancaster and south side Frederick St; 2 ch	Waterloo 58 R.P.363, 369, 370
B1235	–.–.62	[7.3.63?]	Joseph Hobson	Estate of Benjamin Weber	Pt lots 16 and 21, G.C.T.; on both sides G.T.R., owners; 3 ch	Waterloo 58 R.P.402
B1236	2.4.63	–	Joseph Hobson	D. Shoemaker	Lots at Duke and Queen sts; 1 ch	Waterloo 58 R.P.396
B1237	13.9.64	27.1.65	Joseph Hobson	Estate of Balthazar Krug	Lots 6–10 and pt lot 5 'David Weber's Survey'; Weber and Frederic sts; 80 links	Waterloo 58 R.P.388
	KLEINBURG					
B1238	25.2.48	15.3.48	John Stoughton Dennis	Andrew Mitchell	Lot 24, 8th con, twp Vaughan; lots along King Rd and road to 10th con by Kline's Mill, road to Stegmann's Mill, sawmills, owners, school lots; 2 ch	Toronto 64 R.P.9
B1239	25.6.48	27.2.49	John Stoughton Dennis	Andrew Mitchell	'Mount Vernon,' lots as indicated on plan above; school lot on King Rd; 2 ch	Toronto 64 R.P.11

B1240	1.4.55	7.6.65	J. Stoughton Dennis	John Gartshore	'Mount Vernon,' pt lot 24, 8th con, twp Vaughan; King Rd to Napier St and beyond to Humber R, north and south of John St, relief; 1 ch	Toronto 64 R.P.275
B1241	3.1.56	5.8.57	J. Stoughton Dennis	J. Mahaffy	East of Kleinburg and Kleine's Rd north of Vaughan Plank Rd; 2 ch	Toronto 64 R.P.210
B1242	22.6.57	8.10.62	Robert Walsh	Robert Samuel Cheffy, M.D.	Pt lot 24, 8th con, twp Vaughan; west of Vaughan Plank Rd, north of Kleine's Rd, owners; 2 ch	Toronto 64 R.P.268
	KOMOKA					
B1243	21.5.54	11.7.54	Benjamin Springer	Patrick Hamilton Geddes	'Wellington,' E pt N1/2 lot 4, 2nd con, twp Lobo; north of G.W.R., west of Main St; 2 ch	Middlesex 33 R.P.55
B1244	–.5.55	11.5.55	James Pollock	Ira Spaulding	Lot 5, 2nd con, twp Lobo, east of Main St, south of G.W.R./Port Sarnia Branch and north of Superior Ave; 200 ft	Middlesex 33 R.P.76
B1245	27.2.56	9.4.56	James Pollock	Ira Spaulding	Main St north to G.W.R. grounds, Concession Ave to Superior Ave; 200 ft	Middlesex 33 R.P.109
B1246	15.4.56	16.4.58	B. Springer	Benjamin Smith	'Wellington,' N angle lot 4, 1st con, twp Lobo; King St to George St, Main St to Washington St; 2 ch	Middlesex 33 R.P.152 Co
B1247	–.–.56	9.8.56	Samuel Peters	Samuel Drake	S1/2 lot 5, 3rd con, twp Lobo; Concession Ave NW to John St, Clarendon St to Main St; 200 ft	Middlesex 33 R.P.113
	LAKEFIELD					
B1248	29.5.49	9.7.50	John Reid	Mr Burnham	Broken lot 17, 8th con, twp Douro; Otonabee R to Regent St, Bridge St to Reid St; 2 ch	Peterborough 45 R.P.N-1 Lakefield
B1249	25.3.59	28.3.59	V.M. Clementi	Mr Burnham	Lot 17, 8th con, twp Douro, and lot 27, 8th con, twp Smith; both sides Otonabee R, 8th Concession St north to park lots 1–3 on west side and to King St on east side, owners, mills, dam; 2 ch	Peterborough 45 R.P.2 Lakefield
B1250	15.10.60	7.11.60	Theodore & V.M. Clementi	W.C. Nicholls	Lot XVI, con VIII, twp Douro; Otonabee R to line btwn cons 7 and 8 and sideline btwn cons 16 and 17; 2 ch	Peterborough 45 R.P.N-3 Lakefield

	Date of Survey	Date of Regist.	Surveyor	Owner	Description and Notes	Location
B1251	27.2.61	27.2.61	V.M. Clementi	T.J. Nelson	Pt lot XXVII, con VII, twp Smith; 8th Concession St to Nelson St; 2 ch	Peterborough R.P.N-4 Lakefield
B1252	–.–.63	26.9.67	John Reid	George Preston	Front of SW1/4 lot 26, 8th con, twp Smith; east of River Rd and along Concession Rd; 1 ch	Peterborough 45 R.P.11–0 Smith
B1253	–	11.2.63	Theodore Clementi	Sam & Robert A. Strickland	Resurvey Block C; Smith St to George St, Clementi St to Otonabee R; 1 ch	Peterborough 45 R.P.N-5 Lakefield
B1254	–	13.9.65	Theodore Clementi	Mr Ermatinger	Pt lot XVII, con VII, twp Douro; on both sides Ermatinger St; 3 ch	Peterborough 45 R.P.6 Lakefield
	LAKEPORT					
B1255	14.1.54	14.3.55	Joseph Keeler	J.A. Keeler	'Colborne Harbour,' lot 35, 1st con, twp Cramahe, and lots 1 and 2, cons B and C, twp Haldimand; btwn Lake Shore Rd and L Ontario, Ontario St to Pine St, mill pond and various mills, limestone quarry; 3 ch	Northumberland 39 R.P.Haldimand 1
	LAKESIDE					
B1256	14.6.55	–	W.G. Wonham	David Doty	Brock St east to Queen St, King St south to Doty St; 2 ch	Oxford 41 R.P.61
	LAMBETH					
B1257	29.4.53	18.6.53	Samuel Peters	G. Jackson	'St Andrews,' lot 70, east side of north branch of Talbot Rd, twp Westminster; 1 ch	Middlesex E 33 R.P.27
	LANCASTER					
B1258	–.–.54	3.9.57	John S. Bruce	John McLennan & Duncan McDougal, trustees	Compiled plan, lot 38, 1st con, twp Lancaster; Duncan St north to Thomas St, military rd east to Wood and Head sts; 2 ch	Glengarry 14 R.P.37

B1259	1.12.56	10?.1.57	Tom S. Rubidge	James Hodges	'New Lancaster'; Beech St to Cedar St, boundary btwn Lancaster and Charlottenburg twps to Elm St, G.T.R. and bldgs; 100 ft	Glengarry 14 R.P.31
B1260	4.8.57	-.-.57	Tom S. Rubidge	James Hodges	'New Lancaster,' east pt lots K and L, 1st con, twp Charlottenburg; Cedar St to Beech St btwn twp boundary and west to beyond Elm St, G.T.R. and bldgs; 100 ft	Glengarry 14 R.P.15
B1261	29.8.57	4.9.57	John S. Bruce	John McLennan & Duncan McDougal, trustees	'Kirk Town,' pt lot 38, 1st con, twp Lancaster; St Lawrence R to Church St, along King and Calvin sts, church; 2 ch	Glengarry 14 R.P.36
B1262	4.9.65	28.9.65	John S. Bruce	D.A. Macdonald	'New Lancaster,' east pt lots K and L, 1st con, twp Charlottenburg; railroad north to Birch St btwn Military Rd and street beyond Albert St; 60 ft	Glengarry 14 R.P.16
	LANG					
B1263	12.9.50	27.12.50	John Reid	'Short's First Plan'	'Allandale,' W1/2s lots 18 and 19, 6th con, twp Otonabee; South St to North St, mill pond with flour mill, sawmill, dam, tail race; 2 ch	Peterborough 45 R.P.R-11
B1264	1.8.53	1.10.53	John Reid	J.C. Humphries	'East Allandale,' E1/2 lot 18, 6th con, twp Otonabee; Indian R with mill dam and mills to North St and Otonabee St; 1 ch	Peterborough 45 R.P.R-12 Otonabee
B1265	13.6.62	13.6.62	A.H. Macdougall	John Byram	Pt lot 19, 6th con, twp Otonabee; along Athol St; 1 ch	Peterborough 45 R.P.R-13 Otonabee
	LASKAY					
B1266	–	30.8.56	George McPhillips	David Reesor	Town and park lots, 6th con, twp King; from line btwn lots 3 and 4 to pt lot 5, area west of 6th con line or Main St, bldgs, mills; 2 ch	York 65 R.P.167
	LEAMINGTON					
B1267	17.5.59	28.4.60	A. Wilkinson	John A. Wilkinson	Lot 6, 2nd con, twp Mersea; John St to Talbot Rd W, Glebe to Erie St, owners; transcript; 100 ft	Essex 12 R.P.174

	Date of Survey	Date of Regist.	Surveyor	Owner	Description and Notes	Location
B1268	19.9.65	10.10.67	A. Wilkinson	John McGaw	Lot 244, south on Talbot Rd W, twp Mersea; Erie St to McGaw St, Talbot Rd W to Mill St; transcript; 1 ch	Essex 12 R.P.170
B1269	22.9.65	10.11.67	A. Wilkinson	John A. Wilkinson	Lot 244, north on Talbot Rd W, twp Mersea; Erie St to lot 243, Clark St to Talbot Rd W; transcript; 1 ch	Essex 12 R.P.175
	LEFROY					
B1270	1.12.53	6.9.54	George W. Phillips	John Goodfellow	Town lots, N1/2 lot 21, 3rd con, twp Innisfil; at O.S. & Huron R.R. station; sale notice; 2 ch	Simcoe 51 R.P.24
B1271	3.12.64	3.12.64	William Sanders	John Goodfellow	Alteration of plan above; Northern Ry and station ground, bldgs on lots at corner Essa St and Front St; 1 ch	Simcoe 51 R.P.100
B1272	8.12.66	13.12.66	Henry Creswicke	Henry Grose	Lots around Concession St to Northern Rd; 2 ch	Simcoe 51 R.P.118
	LEITH					
B1273	–.–.54	[1.7.54?]	William Smith	John Telfer	John St to Owen Sound and Huron St, Leith Walk to Brant St, mills, owners; photoreproduction; 2 ch	Grey 16 R.P.Leith
	(LIGHTBURNE)					
B1274	13.8.66	13.2.67	F.F. Passmore	Seely, Knock & Lightburne	Pt lot I, con 8, twp Enniskillen; Sarnia Plank Rd, Elmhurst and Cardwell sts; later cancelled; 66 ft	Lambton 25 R.P.Enniskillen 15
	LIMEHOUSE					
B1275	1.10.64	[29.12.65?]	G. Brockitt Abrey	Twp of Esquesing	Compilation plan; Bescoby's survey, W. Shank's survey, J. Meredith's survey, etc; 3 ch	Halton 20 no R.P.#
	LINDSAY					
B1276	28.7.52	29.9.52	D. Macdonnell	A.J. Macdonell	Park lots on lot XIX, Vth con, and lot XIX, VIth con, twp Ops; Adelaide St to Brock	Victoria 57 R.P.8P

					St across Scugog R, George St to Mary St; 4 ch	
B1277	2.11.52	19.1.53	F.F. Passmore	F.F. Carruthers	South of Durham St btwn Adelaide and Brock sts; 4 ch	Victoria 57 R.P.9P
B1278	6.3.54	9.5.54	John K. Roche	William F. Harper et al.	Lots 20 and 21, 6th con, twp Ops; Lindsay St to Verulam St, below Melbourne St to above Queen St, ry depot and route; 4 ch	Victoria 57 R.P.15P
B1279	30.5.54	16.6.54	William Proudfoot	Bank of Upper Canada Lindsay Land Co.	Lots 20 and 21, 6th con, twp Ops; Queen St to Durham St, Lindsay St to Verulam St; scale n.g.	Victoria 57 R.P.10P
B1280	1.8.54	29.8.54	M. Deane	G.M. Roche & Robert Lang	Park lots I, XIV, XX, XXVII, and XXVIII on lots XX and XXI, VIth con, twp Ops; King St N to (3rd) St, Lindsay St to St Paul St; 4 ch	Victoria 57 R.P.11P
B1281	27.12.55	1.7.56	M. Deane	Revd J.J. Chisholm	Park lots X and H; George St to Mary St, Lindsay St to Wolfe St; 2 ch	Victoria 57 R.P.2P
B1282	24.6.56	28.6.56	–	John Knowlson et al.	Park lots 1, 2, 14, 15, 27, 28 on NW pt lot XXI, VIth con, twp Ops; Kent St north across Scugog R and mills to Queen St, Lindsay St to St Patrick St; 2 ch	Victoria 57 R.P.12P
B1283	22.1.57	–	William Proudfoot	–	Lots 20 and 21, 6th con, twp Ops; Durham St to Colbourne St, Verulam St to 5th St beyond Lindsay St, mills, dams, races, market square, ry and depot; scale n.g.	Victoria 57 no R.P.#
B1284	15.1.57	17.1.57	Edward Haycock	R.N. Waddell	Lot XXII and E1/2 lot XXIII, 5th con, and lots XXII and XXIII, 6th con, twp Ops; Colborne St to Eglinton and Dermot sts, Angeline St to Verulam St, Ph. L and B Railway (lumber) station; 4 ch	Victoria 57 R.P.1
B1285	21.5.57	–	W.H. Deane	Reverend J.J. Chisholm	Park lots Y and I.I on lot 19, 6th con, twp Ops; Scugog R to Wolfe and George sts; 2 ch	Victoria 57 R.P.2
B1286	19.10.59	15.11.59	M. Deane	Henry Baldwin	Park lots 8 and 9 west of Adelaide St; Kent St to Henry St, Adelaide St west for two streets; 1 ch	Victoria 57 R.P.4

	Date of Survey	Date of Regist.	Surveyor	Owner	Description and Notes	Location
B1287	–.–.60	[17.10.61?]	M. Deane	For Municipal Corporation	For description see **1564**Victoria 57 R.P.10	
B1288	–	1.4.61	Robert T. Burns	G.M. Roche	Lot 5 south of Kent St at William St; 20 ft	Victoria 57 R.P.6
B1289	1.4.64	1.4.64	W.H. Deane	T. Kennan	Park lots 13 and 14 west of Albert St; Waverly Ave btwn Adelaide and Albert sts; 1 ch	Victoria 57 R.P.13
B1290	6.9.64	19.11.64	W.H. Deane	William McDonnell & Thomas Kennan	Boundary btwn lots on lot 2, south of Peel St; 10 ft	Victoria 57 R.P.14
	LINWOOD					
B1291	–.–.61	[9.5.61?]	Moses McFadden	James & Francis Wright, David Walker, James Scott, John Brown	West pt twp Wellesley; Adelaide to Alfred St, Sarah St to Jane St, mill ponds, steam sawmill, inset location map; 2 ch	Waterloo N 58 R.P.614
	LISTOWEL					
B1292	14.5.57	14.5.57	John Grant	James Barber, Samuel Davidson, Wm Dodd, John A. Tremain	1st con, twps Wallace and Elma; Alma St to Inkerman St, Barber St to William St, mill properties; 2 ch	Perth 44 R.P.148
B1293	15.6.63	20.7.66	R.W. Herman	John Banning	Lot 26, 1st con, twp Wallace; on both sides Inkerman and Victoria sts; 1 ch	Perth 44 R.P.152
B1294	6.7.63	23.2.64	R.W. Herman	Samuel Davidson	Lot 24, 1st con, twp Wallace; Main St to Maitland R, Wallace St; 2 ch	Perth 44 R.P.149
B1295	27.5.64	17.1.65	R.W. Herman	–	Park lots on N1/2 lot 38, 1st con, twp Elma; 2 ch	Perth 44 R.P.150
B1296	31.7.64	15.4.65	R.W. Herman	D.D. Campbell	Pt lot 25, 1st con, twp Wallace; Wallace St to Division St, north of Main St to Penelope St; 2 ch	Perth 44 R.P.151
	LIVERPOOL					
B1297	6.6.53	6.5.54	F.F. Passmore	Edward Shortiss	For description see **1566**	Durham 40 R.P.H-50057

B1298	20.2.63	28.12.65	F.F. Passmore	G. & A. Bostwick	Pt lot 24, con 1, twp Pickering; 4 ch	Durham 40 R.P.H-50058
	LLOYDTOWN					
B1299	27.7.66	25.2.67	Robert Walsh	W.B. Jarvis	Lots 30, 31, and 32, 9th con, twp King; Front St to Queen and Victoria sts, 10th con line east to Church and Main sts, mills, waste races; 1.5 ch	York 65 R.P.8
	LOBO					
B1300	–.8.55	28.9.55	William McMillan	Henry F. Edwards	Area north of Sarnia Rd, houses, toll-house, blacksmith's shop, etc; 2 ch	Middlesex 33 R.P.89
	LOBO TWP					
B1301	11.11.63	13.1.65	B. Springer	John Grey	Park lots on SE1/2 lot 2, 3rd con, twp Lobo; 2 ch	Middlesex 33 R.P.201
	LONDESBOROUGH					
B1302	–	2.9.57	Kertland & Gilkison	T. Hagyard	Lots 25 and 26, 11th con, twp Hullett; King St to Trueman St, Main St to Victoria St; 1 ch	Huron 22 R.P.285
B1303	6.5.60	1.9.60	A. Bay	Thomas Hagyard	Lot XXVI, XI con, twp Hullett; King St at Main St; 1 ch	Huron 22 R.P.286
	LONDON					
B1304	6.5.30	25.9.54	Roswell Mount	George J. Goodhue	South addition; Bathurst St north to Hitchcock St and river to beyond Richmond St, relief; 3 ch	Middlesex 33 R.P.61W
B1305	18.5.32	2.11.76	Peter Carroll	George J. Goodhue & John Kent	Additions; area east of north and east branches of Thames R to Mark Lane btwn Lichfield and King sts, relief; 3 ch	Middlesex 33 R.P.199 1/2W
B1306	–.–.44	8.1.58	William McClary	County Council of Middlesex	'Jail Block,' lots 1–5, north side North St and lots 1–5, south side Duke St, Duke St to North St, Wellington St to Waterloo St; 1 ch	Middlesex 33 R.P.151

	Date of Survey	Date of Regist.	Surveyor	Owner	Description and Notes	Location
B1307	-.12.45	30.3.69	William McClary	Alexander Griffith & Bros	SE1/4 lot 12, 2nd con, twp London; 3 ch	Middlesex 33 R.P.251
B1308	-.5.47	5.12.74	William McClary	George J. Goodhue	Park lot btwn Regent and Huron sts; 2 ch	Middlesex 33 R.P.197W
B1309	-.4.48	9.12.63	William McClary	John Kent	Lots 1 and 2 and pt lot 3, east side Wharncliffe Rd; btwn Wharncliffe and north branch of Thames and along Centre St; 3 ch	Middlesex 33 R.P.191LW
B1310	-.5.49	5.6.58	William McClary	G.J. Goodhue	Park lot btwn Regent and Victoria sts, east of Wharncliffe Rd; 2 ch	Middlesex 33 R.P.148
B1311	-.4.50	18.5.50	William McClary	Jeremiah Hill	Broken park lots 4 and 5, east side Wharncliffe Hwy and west of north branch of Thames R, 2nd con, twp London; Oxford, Centre, and Mill sts; 2 ch	Middlesex 33 R.P.5W
B1312	–	24.1.51	William McMillan	Rev B. Cronyn	Area from Oxford St to north of Grosvenor St, east of Adelaide St; 2 ch	Middlesex 33 R.P.7
B1313	-.6.51	14.11.53	William McClary	D.J. Hughs	Pt lots 6 and 7, Fullerton St, and lots 6 and 7, Hiscock St, east of Talbot St; 40 ft	Middlesex 33 R.P.39W
B1314	16.5.51	25.5.51	William McClary	Charles Henry	N1/2 lot 12, 1st con, twp London; Oxford St to Rattle St, Hill St to Adelaide St; 2 ch	Middlesex 33 R.P.166
B1315	16.9.51	13.11.51	Samuel Peters	Messrs Mellish & Russell	Pt lot 25, BF con, twp Westminster; east branch of Thames R to Bridge and Clarke sts, Wellington Bridge; 1.25 ch	Middlesex 33 R.P.11 (4th)
B1316	20.9.51	6.10.51	Samuel Peters	Mrs J.L. Monsarrat	'Belfield Farm,' s1/2 lot 12, 3rd con, twp London; on both sides Belfield St; 3 ch	Middlesex 33 R.P.9
B1317	17.11.51	10.5.52	Samuel Peters	William Barker	S1/2 lot 11, 2nd con, twp London; around Sydenham and Barker sts; 3 ch	Middlesex 33 R.P.14
B1318	8.12.51	18.2.56	William McClary	Estate of Edward Matthews	Pt lot 10, north side Dundas St; lots east of Richmond St, north of Dundas St; 10 ft	Middlesex 33 R.P.102W
B1319	1.12.51	1.12.51	Samuel Peters	J.H. Cameron	Alteration of original survey by Wm McClary; Great Market to Duke St, Colborne St to William St, bldgs; 100 ft	Middlesex 33 R.P.12E
B1320	-.-.51	2.5.71	Samuel Peters, William McClary	John Wilson	Thames to Sarnia St, 'new water course,' Ann to John St, relief; 1.5 ch	Middlesex 33 R.P.183

B1321	14.5.52	1.8.53	Samuel Peters	J. Franklin	'Caddy Property,' lots 49–51; north of Duke St btwn Cartwright and Maitland sts; 40 ft	Middlesex 33 R.P.31E
B1322	22.5.52	6.4.53	Samuel Peters	Messrs Renwick & Thomson	Lots along Mount Pleasant and Oxford sts; 2 ch	Middlesex 33 R.P.22W
B1323	28.5.52	6.5.54	Samuel Peters	Charles Henry	Pt lot 12, 2nd con, twp London; 1.5 ch	Middlesex 33 R.P.49
B1324	–.5.52	23.10.78	William McClary	Estate of John Wilson	Park lot 1 south of Victoria St; east of Wharncliffe Hwy to Gt Talbot St; 2 ch	Middlesex 33 R.P.202
B1325	–.6.52	20.3.53	Samuel Peters	Estate of F. Magill	Lots on York, Gray, and Horton sts; 30 ft	Middlesex 33 R.P.21E
B1326	–.–.52	28.8.52	Samuel Peters	Messrs Macklin & Moore	Lots 6 and 7, 1st con, twp London, 1st–3rd sts; 3 ch	Middlesex 33 R.P.19
B1327	–.10.52	[20.7.63?]	Samuel Peters, W.B. Leather	W. Barker	Burlington St to George St, Oxford St to James St, bldgs, alteration to plan by W.B. Leather increasing lot sizes on Burlington; 40 ft	Middlesex 33 R.P.162
B1328	9.11.52	16.5.55	Samuel Peters	Rev C. Brough	S1/2 lot 9, 3rd con, twp London; east and west of Hale St; 3 ch	Middlesex 33 R.P.77
B1329	–.–.52	1.3.70	Samuel Peters	S. Morrill	SE pt lot 5, con A, twp London; along Thames and gravel rd to Hamilton; 4 ch	Middlesex 33 R.P.267
B1330	19.1.53	23.4.53	Samuel Peters	Messrs W. & D. Glass	Pt lot 25, BF con, twp Westminster, along Bridge St west of Thames, owners; 1.25 ch	Middlesex 33 R.P.23 (4th)
B1331	31.5.53	31.5.53	Samuel Peters	Messrs H.C.R. Becker, G. Macbeth, L. Ridout & J.G. Horne	Pt lot 6 east of Wharncliffe Hwy, twp Westminster; north branch of Thames R to Stanley St, east branch of Thames R to Wharncliffe Hwy, relief, G.W.R.; 1.5 ch	Middlesex 33 R.P.26 (4th)
B1332	16.6.53	20.6.53	Samuel Peters	Messrs T. Scatcherd & J. Daniell	James St to Grosvenor St, George St to Burlington St; 80 ft	Middlesex 33 R.P.28W
B1333	24.6.53	18.7.53	William Robinson	Messrs Smith & Glen	Pt N1/2 lot 12, 1st con, twp London; on both sides of Pall Mall, east of Adelaide St; 1 ch	Middlesex 33 R.P.30E
B1334	2.7.53	21.6.54	Samuel Peters	Rev B. Cronyn	Bond St to Dundas St E, William St to Adelaide St, bldgs; 90 ft	Middlesex 33 R.P.41E
B1335	7.7.53	18.8.54	Samuel Peters	Samuel Peters	Duke St to E North St, west of William St to Peters Ave; 60 ft	Middlesex 33 R.P.59E

	Date of Survey	Date of Regist.	Surveyor	Owner	Description and Notes	Location
B1336	8.8.53	[12.9.53?]	Samuel Peters	George B. Scott	E Dundas St to E North St, west of William St; 40 ft	Middlesex 33 R.P.36E
B1337	12.8.53	16.8.53	Samuel Peters	S.S. Pomroy	N1/2 lot 11, 2nd con, twp London; cleared land north and south of Park St; 3 ch	Middlesex 33 R.P.32
B1338	21.8.53	18.8.53	William Robinson	Joseph F. Rolfe	Pt lot 25, BF con, twp Westminster, btwn Stanley Rd and Hamilton St, owners; 66 ft	Middlesex 33 R.P.33 (4th)
B1339	31.8.53	12.5.54	Leather & Robinson	William Hale	Park lots on lot VIII, con C, twp London; south of Governors Rd to G.W.R., east and west of Hale St, sold at auction; 4 ch	Middlesex 33 R.P.50
B1340	-.8.53	6.11.54	Leather & Robinson	Col Askin	Lots on north side Oxford St; Port Sarnia Rd to Thames R, St James St to Oxford St, relief; 2 ch	Middlesex 33 R.P.65W
B1341	-.-.53	8.9.68	Samuel Peters	Messrs E. Adams & W. Elliot	S1/2 lot 21, 2nd con, twp London; G.W.R., cleared and wooded areas; 3 ch	Middlesex 33 R.P.243
B1342	9.9.53	22.10.53	Samuel Peters	David Main	Pt lot 27, 1st con, twp Westminster; south of Commissioner's Rd on both sides main St; 1.5 ch	Middlesex 33 R.P.37
B1343	28.10.53	28.10.53	William McMillan	John Scanlon	Lot 3, con A, twp London; north of William St, east of Phillip St, owners, travelled road, relief of Thames shoreline; 4 ch	Middlesex 33 R.P.38
B1344	10.2.54	13.2.54	William Robinson	Peter McCann	Park lots 4 and 5 east of Wharncliffe Hwy; along Centre St, owners; 1 ch	Middlesex 33 R.P.43LW
B1345	10.2.54	13.3.55	Samuel Peters	Rev B. Cronyn	Duke St to E Dundas St, William St to Adelaide St, bldgs; 60 ft	Middlesex 33 R.P.73E
B1346	13.3.54	13.3.54	Samuel Peters	Sam A. Peters	Leasehold property on E Dundas St to E King St, Adelaide St to Lyle St; 80 ft	Middlesex 33 R.P.44 (3rd)
B1347	30.3.54	30.3.54	William Robinson	John Scanlon	Nelson St to Trafalgar St, Maitland St to William St; 1 ch	Middlesex 33 R.P.45E
B1348	27.4.54	10.6.54	Samuel Peters	Rev B. Cronyn	Leasehold property, E Dundas St to E King St, Adelaide St to Lyle St, addition to **B1346**; 80 ft	Middlesex 33 R.P.51 (3rd)
B1349	27.4.54	15.8.54	Samuel Peters	J.B. Strathy	Cheapside to Grosvenor St, George St to Burlington St, owners; 80 ft	Middlesex 33 R.P.57W

B1350	–.4.54	[28.7.54?]	Samuel Peters	Samuel Peters	'Bridgetown,' Thames R to Wharncliffe Rd, Blackfriars St to Oxford St, distillery, mill, cattle shed; 2 ch	Middlesex 33 R.P.58LW
B1351	–.5.54	15.6.54	Leather & Robinson	Messrs Scanlon & Palmer	Pt lot XXVII, 1st con, twp Westminster; Commissioner's Rd east and west of Upper Queen St, inset location map; 3 ch	Middlesex 33 R.P.53
B1352	22.5.54	12.8.54	Samuel Peters	David C. Farrar	Lots on Paul St west of Wharncliffe Hwy, owners; 120 ft	Middlesex 33 R.P.56W
B1353	1.6.54	24.6.57	William Robinson	B. Calvin	Plan of Bathurst St, Horton St, Simcoe St, Grey St, and Clifford St as laid out on east side Adelaide St and btwn G.W.R. and Hamilton Rd in pt lot 12, con C, twp London; 132 ft	Middlesex 33 R.P.143
B1354	5.7.54	6.7.54	Samuel Peters	T. Wilcock	Pall Mall and Adelaide St; 50 ft	Middlesex 33 R.P.54E
B1355	1.8.54	4.10.54	Leather & Robinson	Capt Pattinson	Pt lot XVI, IIIrd con, twp London; btwn Huron St and Thames R; 2 ch	Middlesex 33 R.P.62
B1356	6.9.54	7.9.54	Samuel Peters	Messrs Nash & Ashton	Regent St to Victoria St, William St to Adelaide St; 80 ft	Middlesex 33 R.P.60E
B1357	4.10.54	9.11.54	William Robinson	L. Lawrason	Lots on both sides Maitland St btwn Duke and Dundas sts; 66 ft	Middlesex 33 R.P.66E
B1358	10.10.54	19.10.55	Samuel Peters	Messrs Raynard & Shaw	Wellington and Clarke sts, SE section to Thames R, relief; 80 ft	Middlesex 33 R.P.95 (4th)
B1359	11.10.54	26.9.70	Samuel Peters	Col Renwick & J.E. & J.S. Thomson	Oxford St to Piccadilly St, Sarnia St to Wellington St; 50 ft	Middlesex 33 R.P.180
B1360	20.10.54	30.10.54	William McMillan	Denis O'Brien	Pt lots 5 and 6 west of Wharncliff Hwy, twp Westminster; Thames R to ry, Centre and Kent sts, bldgs, trees; 2 ch	Middlesex 33 R.P.63W
B1361	31.10.54	1.11.54	Leather & Robinson	George McGumm	Lots IV and V east of Wharncliff Hwy, twp London; along Gunn St west of river and north of line btwn cons 1 and 2; 30 ft	Middlesex 33 R.P.64LW
B1362	10.11.54	21.11.54	William Robinson	James Glen	Pt lot XXVII, 1st con, twp Westminster; south of Commissioner's Rd E, west of Upper Queen St; 2 ch	Middlesex 33 R.P.68

	Date of Survey	Date of Regist.	Surveyor	Owner	Description and Notes	Location
B1363	22.11.54	29.11.54	Samuel Peters	Robert A. Hill	N1/2 lot 7, con C, twp London; south of Dundas St on both sides Hill and Buck sts; 3 ch	Middlesex 33 R.P.69
B1364	–.–.54	15.4.61	Samuel Peters	Charles Henry	Pt lot 12, 1st con, twp London; on both sides Charles St, north of Pall Mall; 1.75 ch	Middlesex 33 R.P.164 (3rd)
B1365	29.1.55	30.6.55	Leather & Robinson	Robert Webster	Lot 8, 3rd con, twp London; east and west of Webster St and north and south of William St; 3 ch	Middlesex 33 R.P.82
B1366	8.3.55	12.12.55	Samuel Peters	George Nickels	Lots on NE corner Waterloo and E Hill sts; 15 ft	Middlesex 33 R.P.107E
B1367	2.5.55	28.9.69	Samuel Peters	W. Rowland	Lot 10 north of E Simcoe St, west of Colborne St; 30 ft	Middlesex 33 R.P.176(E)
B1368	8.5.55	9.5.55	Leather & Robinson	John Scanlon	N pt lot IX, con C, twp London; north of G.W.R., south of Governors Rd, cleared areas; 4 ch	Middlesex 33 R.P.74
B1369	–.5.55	21.6.55	Leather & Robinson	Isaac Webster	N1/2 lot VII, IIIrd con, twp London; north and south of Ann St; 2 ch	Middlesex 33 R.P.79
B1370	11.6.55	14.10.65	Samuel Peters	Mr Gumb	Pt lot 24, BF con, twp Westminster; Thames on north, rd allowance btwn lots 24 and 25 on west; 1.5 ch	Middlesex 33 R.P.206
B1371	24.6.55	9.2.61	William Robinson	Messrs James Oliver-Noble, R. Oliver & William Pollard	Pt lot XI, cons B and C, twp London; Hamilton Rd, road from Westminster to Smith St; 1 ch	Middlesex 33 R.P.163
B1372	29.6.55	3.7.55	Leather & Robinson	Robert Webster	Pt lot VI south side of King St; SW corner King and Clarence sts; 20 ft	Middlesex 33 R.P.84W
B1373	26.7.55	17.9.55	Leather & Robinson	Mr Tigert	Lots on Grosvenor and Matilda sts west of William St; 37 ft	Middlesex 33 R.P.87E
B1374	26.7.55	8.10.56	Leather & Robinson	C. Hennessy	Lots 8–11 on south side of Mill St; Mill St to John St west of George St; 30 ft	Middlesex 33 R.P.123
B1375	11.8.55	16.10.55	Leather & Robinson	James Moir	'Kent Property,' pt lot III; Wharncliff Hwy to street on east; 66 ft	Middlesex 33 R.P.94LW

B1376	–.9.55	21.9.55	Samuel Peters	A. Proudfoot	SE corner Maitland and Piccadilly sts; 40 ft	Middlesex 33 R.P.88E
B1377	–.10.55	5.6.58	William McClary	George Jervis Goodhue	Pt lot 12, 2nd con, twp London; Centre and Adelaide sts; 3 ch	Middlesex 33 R.P.149
B1378	7.11.55	13.12.56	Leather & Robinson	Erwin Simpson	Resurvey of pt lot 1, BF con, twp Westminster; Port Stanley Rd west and north of Centre St; 2 ch	Middlesex 33 R.P.108
B1379	6.12.55	–.12.55	Samuel Peters	W. Winslow	Pt lot 7 east of Wortley Rd, twp Westminster; 30 ft	Middlesex 33 R.P.92
B1380	22.12.55	10.1.56	William Robinson	Thomas Cronyn	Lots 3 and 4, north side of Dundas St at Wellington St; 20 ft	Middlesex 33 R.P.98W
B1381	–.–.55	24.9.56	Samuel Peters	D.B. Strathy	On both sides Raglan St btwn Lichfield and John sts, owners; 50 ft	Middlesex 33 R.P.118
B1382	–.–.55	–.–.56	Leather & Robinson	Mr Rich	Pt lot B west of Wharncliffe Hwy; con line to Caroline St west of Proof Line Rd, Perkins Tavern and Brewery; 80 ft	Middlesex 33 R.P.126
B1383	–.–.55	6.6.57	Samuel Peters	W. & J. Carling	Colborne St to Maitland St, Piccadilly St to Pall Mall, owners; 99 ft	Middlesex 33 R.P.141
B1384	–.–.55	3.5.61	Samuel Peters	E.W. Hyman	James St to Oxford St, Burlington St to Wellington St; 80 ft	Middlesex 33 R.P.159
B1385	–.–.55	11.4.64	Leather & Robinson	Samuel Stanfield, John & Wm Carling, Wm Hale, et al.	Lots 23–7; west side Wellington St and east side Burlington St; Grosvenor St to St James St, Burlington St to Wellington St; 60 ft	Middlesex 33 R.P.163
B1386	–.–.55	15.12.68	Samuel Peters	J.L. Williams	East Grey St to East South St, lots along Colborne St; 80 ft	Middlesex 33 R.P.172
B1387	–.–.55	2.9.69	Samuel Peters	J. Salter	Bond St to Duke St, William St to Maitland St; 80 ft	Middlesex 33 R.P.177(E)
B1388	–.1.56	12.2.56	Samuel Peters	London Co. Grammar School	Duke St to E North St, Wellington St to Church St, school reserve on Church St; 40 ft	Middlesex 33 R.P.101W
B1389	8.4.56	7.6.56	William Robinson	Messrs Evans & Thompson	Cheapside to Grosvenor St, Wellington St to Waterloo St, gravel pit; 1 ch	Middlesex 33 R.P.106E
B1390	–.4.56	31.5.56	Charles L. Davies	Charles Hutchison	South pt lot 12, con C; Nightingale Ave to road to Hamilton east of Adelaide St; 150 ft	Middlesex 33 R.P.110 (3rd)

	Date of Survey	Date of Regist.	Surveyor	Owner	Description and Notes	Location
B1391	3.5.56	31.12.56	–	P.G. Norris & J. Wells	Oxford St to Piccadilly St west of Waterloo St; 40 ft	Middlesex 33 R.P.129
B1392	–.5.56	28.6.56	Leather & Robinson	Rev C. Brough	Maitland St to William St, Great Market St to Bond St; 60 ft	Middlesex 33 R.P.114
B1393	–.5.56	[8.7.56?]	Leather & Robinson	Duncan Campbell	Lot 1, east side of Wharncliffe Rd, and lot 1, west of Center St, twp London; Center St to Wharncliffe from Blackfriars Bridge Rd; 40 ft	Middlesex 33 R.P.111
B1394	–.6.56	2.4.57	William McClary	William Irwin	Lot 1, broken park lots 4 and 5, east side Wharncliffe Hwy, 2nd con, twp London; Centre and Irwin sts; 30 ft	Middlesex 33 R.P.139
B1395	–.6.56	20.8.56	William Robinson	J.G. Mountford	Pt S1/2 lot X, 1st con, twp London; north of Governors Rd to Burderop St east and west of Nightingale St; 2 ch	Middlesex 33 R.P.115
B1396	–	13.2.57	A. Bay	John Battie	Lots G and H and lots 9 and 10, con B, twp London; Elgin St to East St south of Hamilton Rd; 2 ch	Middlesex 33 R.P.137
B1397	–	13.2.57	A. Bay	United Presbyterian Church	Lots 1 and 2 and pt 3, west side Colborne St; Bond to Hope St west of Colborne St; 1 ch	Middlesex 33 R.P.136
B1398	20.8.58	18.11.58	Samuel Peters	Rev J. Bailey	'William Street,' Fullarton St to North St, Richmond St to Talbot St; 2 ch	Middlesex 33 R.P.156
B1399	–.–.58	17.6.69	Samuel Peters	London & Port Sarnia Ry Co.	Lots 6–11 south of East Bathurst St and lots 6–10 and pt 11 north of East Horton St; East Bathurst St to East Horton St, Waterloo St to Colborne St; 60 ft	Middlesex 33 R.P.175(E)
B1400	10.4.60	9.2.66	Samuel Peters	Thomas Kent	John St to Litchfield St west of Sarnia St; 99 ft	Middlesex 33 R.P.167
B1401	19.9.60	24.9.60	Samuel Peters	Isaac Webster	Pt lots 16 and 17 south of East Dundas St; Maitland St to west of East Dundas St, bldgs; 10 ft	Middlesex 33 R.P.157
B1402	22.7.61	23.7.61	William Robinson	John Crombie, Adam Murray, Alex Smith, et al.	Lots on Colborne, Bond, and Hope sts; owners; 40 ft	Middlesex 33 R.P.158

B1403	18.2.62	20.6.62	William McClary	Estate of Elizabeth Coombs	Lot XXI, north side King St; 12 ft	Middlesex 33 R.P.160
B1404	15.10.62	[21.10.62?]	Samuel Peters	M. Meston et al.	Pt of 'Kent Property'; Thames to Talbot St, John St to Lichfield St, relief; 80 ft	Middlesex 33 R.P.161
B1405	14.2.63	12.9.64	A. Bay	James Heavey	Lots; Regent St to Victoria St, Waterloo St to Grafton St; 1 ch	Middlesex 33 R.P.165
B1406	15.10.63	17.10.63	William Robinson	Duncan Campbell	Lot 2, east side Wharncliffe Rd, and lot 2, west side of Centre St (formerly known as pt of 'Kent Property'); 40 ft	Middlesex 33 R.P.186 1/2
B1407	17.5.64	26.5.64	William McClary	Thomas Kent	Park lot 1, bounded on north by Blackfriars Rd and on west by Centre St; Thames and mill dam to Blackfriars Rd and Centre St; 1 ch	Middlesex 33 R.P.197 1/2(W)
B1408	14.6.64	7.11.64	Samuel Peters	J. Kent	Thames at Blackfriars Bridge, Lichfield St, Ridout to Talbot St, owners; 60 ft	Middlesex 33 R.P.164(W)
B1409	29.11.64	10.5.66	Samuel Peters	Thomas Kent	Thames north branch to Talbot St, Barton to Lichfield, relief along shores; 60 ft	Middlesex 33 R.P.166(W)
B1410	-.-.66	11.5.67	Samuel Peters	Grammar & Common School	'College Block to be leased'; Duke to North St, Church St to Wellington St, school reserve, owners, 'U.P. Church'; 50 ft	Middlesex 33 R.P.169(W)
B1411	-.12.66	15.1.67	William Robinson	Corporation of the City of London	Lots 4 and 5 and N1/2 lot 3 on east side Waterloo St north of Bond; Market St to Bond St, Waterloo St to Colborne St; 1 ch	Middlesex 33 R.P.168(E)
B1412	21.9.67	25.2.69	B. Springer	Diocese of Huron	S pt lot 15, 3rd con, twp London; Thames mill race and reserve, residence of Archdeacon Brough; 2 ch	Middlesex 33 R.P.250 Co
	LONDON TWP					
B1413	5.8.52	19.8.52	Samuel Peters	Angus McDougall	S pt lot 3, 1st con, twp London; north of Governors Rd, Lorne and Argyle sts, later notes added; 2 ch	Middlesex 33 R.P.18 Co
B1414	26.8.52	13.9.53	Samuel Peters	Messrs Macklin & Street	North pt lot 5, con C, twp London; Governors Rd S; 2.5 ch	Middlesex 33 R.P.35 Co
B1415	-.-.52	19.6.71	Samuel Peters	Thomas Whitchurch	Lot 7 and pt lot 6, con A, twp London; east branch of Thames R to rd allowance btwn cons A and B, plank rd to Hamilton; 3 ch	Middlesex 33 R.P.286 Co

	Date of Survey	Date of Regist.	Surveyor	Owner	Description and Notes	Location
B1416	13.6.53	13.6.53	William Robinson	Mr Bogue	SW pt lot 18, 3rd con, twp London; auction notice; 2 ch	Middlesex 33 R.P.25 Co
B1417	24.5.53	5.5.54	William McMillan	William Rowland	S1/2 lot 23, 3rd con, twp London; cleared and treed areas, bldgs; 3 ch	Middlesex 33 R.P.48 Co
B1418	-.-.53	31.12.53	Samuel Peters	Colonel Ball	Pt lot 16, 3rd con, twp London; south of Goderich to London Rd and west branch of Thames R, mill and mill property; 2 ch	Middlesex 33 R.P.40 Co
B1419	-.-.53	10.6.69	Samuel Peters	John McDougall	North pt lot 4, 1st con, twp London; 3 ch	Middlesex 33 R.P.260 Co
B1420	-.8.54	5.7.62	Leather & Robinson	Mr Dalton	S1/2 of S1/2 lot XVII, 4th con, twp London; river with bridge; 2 ch	Middlesex 33 R.P.173 Co
B1421	-.-.54	15.9.66	Samuel Peters	Mrs Proudfoot	S1/2 lot 20, 2nd con, twp London; park lots; 3 ch	Middlesex 33 R.P.216 Co
B1422	17.1.55	9.2.55	Leather & Robinson	John Gamble Horne	W1/2 lot XV, 5th con, twp London; 2 ch	Middlesex 33 R.P.72 Co
B1423	5.5.55	15.6.55	Samuel Peters	W.C. Freeman	SE1/4 lot 23, 1st con, twp London; 2 ch	Middlesex 33 R.P.78 Co
B1424	-.-.56	29.9.56	Charles L. Davies	Messrs W.W. Street & A. Lefroy	N1/2 lot 7, con IV, twp London; 3 ch	Middlesex 33 R.P.120 Co
B1425	30.10.58	30.10.58	W.A. Pigott	W. Blake	Resurvey of S1/2 of N1/2 lot 4, con A, twp London; 3 ch	Middlesex 33 R.P.155 Co
B1426	29.10.59	30.4.60	Samuel Peters	Samuel Thornton	Pt lot 25, BF con, twp London; Thames R, barn, dwelling; 3 ch	Middlesex 33 R.P.161 Co
B1427	-.11.60	11.12.60	Samuel Peters	Bank of British North America	Lot 10, 3rd con, twp London; old channel of river; 3 ch	Middlesex 33 R.P.162 Co
	(LONG ISLAND LOCKS)					
B1428	-.9.60	18.1.61	John Burchill	Edmund Burritt	'Long Island Locks' lot 25, BF on Rideau con, twp Gloucester; Chestnut St at river to Cedar St, Olive St to Queen's Hwy, owners; 80 ft	Ottawa-Carleton 5 R.P.13
	LONGWOOD					
B1429	10.1.55	10.1.55	B. Springer	William Middlemiss	'Middleton,' lot 2, 2nd con, twp Caradoc; East St to South St below G.W.R., lots on	Middlesex 34 R.P.71

					Victoria St and on Front St north of ry btwn William and Waterloo sts; photoreproduction; 2 ch	
B1430	6.7.57	3.12.57	B. Springer	Dennis Corchran	'Middleton,' west side of N1/2 lot 3, IInd con, twp Caradoc; both sides Huron St btwn Front St and line btwn cons 2 and 3; photoreproduction; 100 ft	Middlesex 34 R.P.146
B1431	15.4.58	28.6.58	B. Springer	Wm Middlemiss	'Middleton,' N1/2 lot 2, 2nd con, twp Caradoc; lots on Chatham St, bldgs on G.W.R. station ground; photoreproduction; 2 ch	Middlesex 34 R.P.150
	LONSDALE					
B1432	-.-.54	7.2.54	William Wallbridge	John Lazire	Pt lot 32, 3rd con, twp Tyendinaga; mill pond, bldgs, streets named; 4 ch	Hastings 21 R.P.41
B1433	-.4.55	16.6.55	P.V. Elmore	James Lazier	S pt lot XXXII, 3rd con, twp Tyendinaga; Salmon R to Main St, West St to Centre St, mills identified; 2 ch	Hastings 21 R.P.74
	LORETTO					
B1434	28.7.66	20.3.68	Robert Walsh	Patrick Derham	Lot 15, 5th/6th con, twp Adjala; streets laid out west of Main St and south of Queen St, survey notes; 2 ch	Simcoe 51 R.P.125
	L'ORIGNAL					
B1435	30.5.50	16.9.50	Robert Hamilton	–	Compiled plan; streets named, bldgs, owners, grist and sawmills; 2 ch	Prescott 46 R.P.3
	LOUGHBOROUGH TWP					
B1436	10.3.42	[26.8.42?]	A.B. Perry	District of Midland	Boundary survey of 1st and 2nd cons, twp Loughborough; inset map (western boundary), detailed legend on survey posts, bearings, owners; 12 ch	Frontenac 13 R.P.1
	LOUISVILLE					
B1437	17.7.35	23.6.38	Lewis Burwell	John Sharp	Kent St to Bridge St, river to Spring St, owners, mill reserves, shipyards; 2 ch	Kent 24 R.P.142B

	Date of Survey	Date of Regist.	Surveyor	Owner	Description and Notes	Location
	LOUTH TWP					
B1438	30.9.63	5.10.63	Edgar Berryman	Estate of Jacob Gould	Owners; 5 ch	Niagara 30 R.P.59 Co
B1439	–	1.4.64	–	H. Mittelberger	Lots 1 and 2, 3rd con, twp Louth; owners with list of sales; 264 ft	Niagara 30 R.P.34 Co
	LOWVILLE					
B1440	10.1.57	13.1.57	James Cleaver	James Cleaver	Pt lot 7, 3rd con, twp Nelson, new survey; Nelson Rd, part of planned Nassagaweya Rd, owners; 2 ch	Halton 20 R.P.22
	LUCAN					
B1441	21.9.63	22.10.63	A. Bay	Donald McDonald	'Marystown,' pts lots 6 north and south of road to London Proof Line, twp Biddulph; Market St to G.T.R., Main St to rd allowance btwn cons 4 and 5, market sq; 3 ch	Middlesex 33 R.P.188 Co
B1442	4.8.63	22.10.63	A. Bay	Peter Butler, Sr	Pt lot 5 south of Biddulph Gravel Rd; G.T.R. to Main St west to Water St; 1.5 ch	Middlesex 33 R.P.187 Co
B1443	11.8.65	12.2.66	A. Bay	J. MacDonald	Park lots on lot VI south of gravel rd, twp Biddulph; G.T.R. south and east to con rd btwn lots VI and VII; 3 ch	Middlesex 33 R.P.210 Co
B1444	11.8.65	12.2.66	A. Bay	Peter Butler	Pt lots V and VI north of Biddulph Gravel Rd east to Beach St, lots along Market St; 2 ch	Middlesex 33 R.P.211 Co
B1445	7.6.66	21.6.66	J.O. Browne	Donald [Mc?]Donald	Lot 6 north of road to London Proof Line, twp Biddulph; Market St to G.T.R., Main St to rd allowance btwn cons 4 and 5; 3 ch	Middlesex 33 R.P.213 Co
B1446	4.6.67	7.6.67	J.O. Browne	Donald McDonald	Lot 6 north of road to London Proof Line; lots north of Duchess St; 3 ch	Middlesex 33 R.P.220 Co
	LUCKNOW					
B1447	–.–.58	21.9.58	Molesworth & Weatherald	James Somerville	Campbell St to Gouch St, Stauffer St to Walter St, mills; 2 ch	Bruce 3 R.P.20

B1448	16.1.61	20.4.61	Libert Chandler	James Somerville	Pt N1/2 lot 13, XIV con, twp Wawanosh; Campbell St to Willoughby St, Ross St to Havelock St; 1.5 ch	Bruce 3 R.P.31
B1449	1.7.63	4.3.68	L.B. Hamlin	James Somerville	Canning St to Campbell St, Ross St to Havelock St; large mill site; 2 ch	Bruce 3 R.P.49
B1450	1.7.63	2.10.63	L.B. Hamlin	Messrs Rookledge & Somerville	Pts lots 61 and 62, 1st con, twp Kinloss; Campbell St to Rose St, Albert St to river, bldgs; 2 ch	Bruce 3 R.P.36
B1451	26.7.65	15.2.66	James Warren	James Somerville	Gough St to Ludgard St, mill pond to Nine Mile R west branch; 2 ch	Bruce 3 R.P.43
B1452	22.8.66	11.9.66	James Warren	Messrs Rookledge & Somerville	Alteration of **B1450** in Albert St and park lots 37, 49, and 50; Albert, Rose, and Hamilton sts; 2 ch	Bruce 3 R.P.46
	LYN					
B1453	–.–.54–9	[31.3.60?]	John Booth	Messrs Richard Coleman, James Coleman & Richard Coleman, Jr	Lots 28, 29, and 30, 3rd con, twp Elizabethtown; plan spans years from 1854–9; rd allowance btwn cons 2 and 3 to Fly St, Church St to James St, Lyn branch G.T.R., owners, mills; 150 ft	Leeds 28 R.P.114
	LYNDEN					
B1454	15.11.55	27.10.56	W. Robinson	Estate of Barnabas Howard	S1/2 lot 13, 1st con, twp Beverly; Dundas St to G.W.R., along Howard St; 3 ch	Wentworth 62 R.P.197 (old 16)
	LYNDHURST					
B1455	26.8.65	29.5.76	W. Beatty	Estate of Hons Charles & Jonas Jones	Lots 2 and 3, 10th con, twp Lansdowne; east of mill ponds btwn Edward and Charles sts, bldgs, reserve lots with privilege for canal; 3 ch	Leeds 28 R.P.38
	LYNEDOCH					
B1456	–	–	Thomas Walsh	–	Brock St to Simcoe St and bridge, XIII con Rd to Union St, North St to Bostwick St	Norfolk 37 R.P.5A
	MADOC					
B1457	–.5.50	30.7.50	P.V. Elmore	Uriah Seymour	'Hastings,' W1/2 lot 1, VI con, twp Madoc; Cooper and Division sts to road to Marmora, park lots to McNab St, bldgs, mill pond; 2 ch	Hastings 21 R.P.13A

	Date of Survey	Date of Regist.	Surveyor	Owner	Description and Notes	Location
B1458	10.8.64	30.12.64	C.F. Aylsworth	Horace Seymour	'Hastings,' E1/2 lot 1, VII con, twp Madoc; Division St to Elgin St, Park St to Victoria St; 2 ch	Hastings 21 R.P.104
B1459	24.9.64	–	Innes & MacLeod	Mr Russell	'Hastings,' north pt; Division St to Park St, Deer Creek to beyond Nelson St; 2 ch	Hastings 21 R.P.105
B1460	27.3.67	16.4.67	C.F. Aylsworth	Charles Kirk	'Hastings' (south pt), lot 12, 14th con, twp Huntingdon; Seymour St to Sarah St, Durham St to Charles St; 1.5 ch	Hastings 21 R.P.118
B1461	4.4.67	4.4.67	C.F. Aylsworth	R.M. Norman	'Norman Hill' subdivision of park lots 1 and 2, Russell Estate, W1/2 lot 2, 6th con, twp Madoc; Donald, Campbell, Frances, and Charles sts; 1.5 ch	Hastings 21 R.P.119
	MAITLAND					
B1462	24.3.65	13.5.65	Henry Lillie	George C. Longley	Lot 30, 1st con, twp Augusta; Main or King St to Sarah St, George St to Church St; 1 ch	Grenville 15 R.P.Augusta 3
B1463	30.6.65	3.7.65	Henry Lillie	George C. Longley	Park lots, west side of side-rd on lot 30, 1st con, twp Augusta; Church St north from King St beyond G.T.R. to rd allowance btwn cons 1 and 2; 4 ch	Grenville 15 R.P.Augusta 6
	MALDEN TWP					
B1464	20.8.63	24.8.63	O. Bartley	Susan A. Duff	SW pt lot 21, con 11, twp Malden; Duff St to River St, Amherstburg St near Detroit R; transcript; 1 ch	Essex 12 R.P.155
	(MALTA)					
B1465	1.1.56	12.1.56	J.S. Dennis	Mr MacGregor	Town plot on lots 34–9, Lake Range or con A, twp Bruce; Cayley St to MacGregor St, Front St to lakeshore; 3 ch	Bruce 3 R.P.1
	MALTON					
B1466	5.10.55	24.10.55	J.S. Dennis	J.S. Dennis et al.	NE1/2 lot XI, VI con east of Hurontario St, twp Toronto; Beverly St to Holderness St, Cattrick St to plank rd, G.T.R. station and grounds, bldgs; 100 ft	Peel 43 R.P.TOR4

MANCHESTER (Huron Co)

B1467	–.11.54	30.12.54 24.4.55	William Perceval, T. Weatherald	Eneas Elkin	Pt lot 45, 14 con, twp Hullett; Maitland Terrace to Egmont St, Elgin St to George St; addition in Apr 1855; 2 ch	Huron 22 R.P.289
B1468	19.7.58	14.10.58	William Rath	George Fulton	Pt lots 27 and 28, 1st con, twp Wawanosh; Goderich St to Sebastopol St, Elizabeth St to Loftus St, Maitland R, bldgs; 2 ch	Huron 22 R.P.291
B1469	1.1.67	5.2.67	A. Bay	J. Macdonald	Park lots on lot XXVII, 1st con, twp Wawanosh; 1 ch	Huron 22 R.P.292

MANCHESTER (Ontario Co)

B1470	20.11.58	26.1.60	W.E. Yarnold	Messrs Ewers, Pewson & Fitchett	Lots XIII, IVth and Vth cons, twp Reach; Brock St east to May St on both sides King St, owners; 2 ch	Durham 40 R.P.H-50023

MANDAUMIN

B1471	–.9.56	10.2.57	P.S. Donnelly	Scott Hyde & Hill	Town plot on NW pt lot 1, 2nd con, twp Plympton; G.W.R. Sarnia branch, Julia St to Oak St and on both sides Victoria St; 100 ft	Lambton 25 R.P.Plympton 4

MANILLA

B1472	15.6.57	27.7.57	F.C. McCallum	W. & T. Coulthard	Subdivision of pt lot 24, 8th con, twp Brock; Simcoe St to Ontario St, Brock St to Mill St; 2 ch	Durham 40 R.P.H-50051

MANOTICK

B1473	30.9.62	2.5.65	George F. Austin	Arthur McEwen	Pt lot 8, twp Long Island; Island St to Rideau R, Bridge St and Arthur St; 1 ch	Ottawa-Carleton 5 R.P.17MAN
B1474	–.9.62	26.11.62	George F. Austin	M.K. Dickinson & Co.	Pt lots 1 and 2, con A, twp North Gower, and lots 8 and 9, twp Long Island; Tighe St to west branch Rideau R, Highway to Island St, bldgs, key plan added later; 1 ch	Ottawa-Carleton 5 R.P.15MAN
B1475	–.1.63	9.11.65	Joseph M.O. Cromwell	Richard Tighe the Elder & John & Richard Tighe the Younger	Lot 2, BF or con A, twp North Gower; Rideau R to Anne St, Catherine St to Tighe St, bldgs; 66 ft	Ottawa-Carleton 5 R.P.18NG

	Date of Survey	Date of Regist.	Surveyor	Owner	Description and Notes	Location
	MAPLE					
B1476	18.8.53	17.9.53	J.O. Browne	Robert G. Dalton	For description see **1613**	Toronto 64 R.P.72
B1477	–	17.9.53	–	Thomas Holmes	For description see **1614**	Toronto 64 R.P.73
B1478	2.10.53	3.11.53	J.S. Dennis	Thomas Holmes	Lot 21, 3rd con, twp Vaughan; shows same information as plan above with slightly different dimensions, reserve of bldgs on lot 1; 2 ch	Toronto 42 R.P.79
	(MARBLE VILLAGE town plot)					
B1479	–	17.1.56	–	Rowland Wingfield	Rear of lot 10 and S1/2 lot 11, 1st con, twp Anderdon; some park lots, stone quarry; transcript; 150 ft	Essex 12 R.P.12
	MARCHMONT					
B1480	–	20.5.59	William Sanders	S.P. Powley	W1/2 lot 2, 1st con, twp Orillia; bldgs, Accommodation Rd or Mill St to Powley St, Indian reserve; 2 ch	Simcoe 51 R.P.74
	MARIATOWN					
B1481	3.2.45	–	–	Multiple owners	Pt lot 36, 1st con, twp Williamsburg; Kings Hwy to St Lawrence R, Mill St to beyond Cherry St; scale n.g.	Dundas 8 R.P.1
	MARKDALE					
B1482	14.6.66	14.6.66	Wm Spry	Mark Armstrong	On lot 101, ranges I SW and NE Toronto and Sydenham Rd; lots on Mill, Brown, Mark, and Sydenham sts, bldgs with names of businesses and owners; 2 ch	Grey 17 R.P.552
	MARKHAM					
B1483	–.5.50	5.8.50	George McPhillips	Municipal Corporation	Compilation map, VII and VIII cons, twp Markham; mill ponds, bldgs, distilleries, mills, factories, owners, etc; 4 ch	Toronto 64 R.P.18

B1484	–.4.56	6.6.56	George McPhillips	Joseph Reesor	Lots along Albert St; 4 ch	Toronto 64 R.P.157
B1485	–.9.56	9.10.56	George McPhillips	A. Barker	Town lots in pt lot 9, 8th con, twp Markham; Rouge R and mill pond east of Mill St btwn Nelson and Rouge sts; 2 ch	Toronto 64 R.P.173
B1486	4.11.56	4.11.56	H. Northcote	Estate of Chester F. Hall	151 lots and 22 park lots in village; Markham to Joseph St and Maple St to Park St and 9th Con Rd; 125 ft	Toronto 64 R.P.180
B1487	14.1.59	22.1.59	George McPhillips	David Reesor	Subdivision of lots 5 and 14–17; Main St, Foundry Lane, Peer, and Wilson sts; 2 ch	Toronto 64 R.P.247
	MARMORA					
B1488	–.9.49	29.12.[49?]	J.J. Haslett	Marmora Foundry Co.	Pt lots 7–9, 4th con, twp Marmora; Crow R to Hays St, Madoc St to Nathan St, mills, forge, store, bldgs; see also plan below; 2 ch	Hastings 21 R.P.5
B1489	18.9.49	18.9.54	J.J. Haslett	Marmora Foundry Co.	Pt lots 7–9, 4th con, twp Marmora; Madoc St to Nathan St, John's St to Harp St, bldgs; see also plan above; 2 ch	Hastings 21 R.P.70
B1490	–.6.55	27.8.56	P.V. Elmore	Marmora Foundry Co.	Lots VI and VII, IV con, twp Marmora; Burstall St to Forsyth St, Madoc St to Evans St, bldgs; 2 ch	Hastings 21 R.P.83
	MARSDEN					
B1491	–.3.52	11.3.52	Francis Kerr	E. Murton	Pt lot 14, 2nd con, Division D, twp Guelph; Mr Blythe's Tavern; 1 ch	Wellington 61 R.P.44
	MARSVILLE					
B1492	–.10.58	2.11.58	Charles J. Wheelock	Estate of Gerrard Dunbar	Pt W1/2 lot 5, 14th con, twp Garafraxa; north of road from Fergus to Orangeville and along Gerrard St; 1.5 ch	Dufferin 7 R.P.103
	MARTINTOWN					
B1493	–.9.60	12.7.65	Duncan McDonnell, John S. Bruce	Estate of Duncan McMartin	North pt E1/2 lot 26, 1st con, twp Charlottenburg, south side R aux Raisins; Mary St, Dundas St to river; 1 ch	Glengarry 14 R.P.2 (Martintown)

	Date of Survey	Date of Regist.	Surveyor	Owner	Description and Notes	Location
	MARYSBURGH N TWP					
B1494	16.8.42	18.10.79	P.V. Elmore, H.J. & O. Browne	University of Toronto	Gore A; owners; copy of original; 20 ch	Prince Edward 47 R.P.N Marysburgh 3
	MAXWELL					
B1495	20.7.66	14.9.66	Peter S. Gibson	Charles D. Maginn	'Charlestown,' pt lot XI, VII con, twp Osprey; lots on gravel rd and Charles St; 2 ch	Grey 17 R.P.262
	MCDONALDS CORNERS					
B1496	10.8.59	8.2.60	John Morris	Messrs McLean, Anderson, Struthers & Scott	E1/2s lots 7 and 8, IX con, twp Dalhousie, N Sherbrooke St, Mississippi St; 2 ch	Lanark 26 McDonalds Corners
	MEADOWVALE					
B1497	1.7.56	1.7.56	Arthur Bristow	F. Silverthorne	Pts E1/2s lots 11 and 12, 3rd con west of Hurontario St, N division, twp Toronto; btwn Credit R and mill pond, bldgs, swamp; 1.60 links	Peel 43 R.P.TOR-5
	MEAFORD					
B1498	25.1.53	–	Hugh Savigny	Jesse Purdy	South pt of village on lot 15, 5th con, twp St Vincent; Boucher St to Mill Rd, Seymour St to William St; 2 ch	Grey 16 R.P.71
B1499	–.–.56	9.7.59	Thomas Donovan	William Stephenson	Subdivision of pt lot XVII, con V, twp St Vincent; Bayfield St to Cook St, Parker St to William St, owners; transcript; 4 ch	Grey 16 R.P.74
B1500	7.8.59	13.3.62	Thomas Donovan	C.R. Sing	Pt lot XV, 4th con, twp St Vincent; St Vincent St near Boucher St, later amendment included; transcript; 1 ch	Grey 16 R.P.77
B1501	9.2.63	12.2.63	Thomas Donovan	Cyrus R. Sing	Subdivision of lot XV, W1/2 VI con, twp St Vincent; btwn Miller St and Big Head R; 3 ch	Grey 16 R.P.139

B1502	3.3.64	30.6.64	Thomas Donovan	J. Stewart	Subdivision of lot XIX; Sykes and Nelson sts, owners; transcript; 30 ft	Grey 16 R.P.84
B1503	12.3.64	16.3.64	Thomas Donovan	Wesleyan Church	Subdivision of lot XIX; Nelson St to Trowbridge St at Sykes St, owners; 30 ft	Grey 16 R.P.83
B1504	19.10.67	29.5.68	Robert F. Lynn	Cyrus R. Sing	Park lots, subdivision of NE pt lot XVI, VI con, twp St Vincent; transcript; 4 ch	Grey 16 R.P.79
	(MEHRING town plot)					
B1505	17.2.63	[17.2.63?]	Joseph Hobson	Daniel Mehring	Pt lot 3, 5th con, E Section, twp Wellesley; 4 ch	Waterloo 58 R.P.617
	MELBOURNE					
B1506	8.5.58	13.7.58	B. Springer	Messrs Miller, Clarke, McNutty, Robinson	Lot 1, north and south of Longwoods Rd, twp Caradoc, and lot 1, north and south of Longwoods Rd, twp Ekfrid; Peter St to Victoria St, Clark St to East St, owners, tavern; photoreproduction; 2 ch	Middlesex 34 R.P.151
	MELROSE					
B1507	7.11.55	23.11.55	Leather & Robinson	Rev W. Wilkinson	N1/2 lot XXII, Vth con, twp London; east from town line btwn London and Lobo; 3 ch	Middlesex 33 R.P.96 Co
	MERRICKVILLE					
B1508	16.3.46	22.8.50	William Campbell	Messrs Mirrick, Aaron, et al.	Pt lots 8 and 9, con A, twp Wolford; Main St to Wallace St, Elgin St to Patrick St; 100 ft	Grenville 15 R.P.Merrickville 1
B1509	–.4.49	[16.3.50?]	John Booth	William Mirrick	'North Mirickville,' lots 8 and 9, con B, twp Montague; on both sides Mill and Montague sts btwn Orchard and Brook sts; 60 ft	Grenville 15 R.P.Merrickville 2
B1510	11.2.59	14.3.59	William Wagner	Dr P.H. Church	Pt lot 8, BF A, twp Wolford; Ruggles St east to Julia St, Main St to Drummond St; 100 ft	Grenville 15 R.P.Merrickville 3
B1511	22.10.63	18.12.63	John Burchill	Municipal Corporation	Compilation plan, lots 8 and 9, cons A and B, twp Montague, and park lots on lots 8–10, con A, twp Wolford; James St to North and Maria sts, Frederick St to Erskine and Marion sts, Rideau R and Canal, mill, dam, pond; 100 ft	Grenville 16 R.P.Merrickville 4

	Date of Survey	Date of Regist.	Surveyor	Owner	Description and Notes	Location
	METCALFE (Carleton Co)					
B1512	9.2.55	14.5.55	John A. Snow	Adam Baker & Joseph Allan	Lots 21, 7th and 8th cons, twp Osgoode; Victoria St to Russell St, Hume St to York St; 2 ch	Ottawa-Carleton 5 R.P.5
	(METCALFE town plot) (Middlesex Co)					
B1513	4.7.51	13.8.52	B. Springer	Robert L. Johnston	NE1/4 lot 3, 11th con, twp Metcalfe; Richmond St to East St, South Wellington St to Sydenham R, grist mill and dam, sawmill, reserve; photoreproduction; 2 ch	Middlesex 34 R.P.16
	MIDDLEPORT					
B1514	2.11.52	2.11.52	William Smith	John L. Hager	Grand R to Hager St, Yowell St to David St, bldgs, owners; 1 ch	Brant 2 R.P.99
	MILFORD					
B1515	-.-.67	10.5.67	George A. Simpson	Municipal Council	Pt lot 245, 1st con south of Black R, and pt lots 25 and 26, 1st con north of Black R, twp Marysburgh, Old Rd, Main, Philip, Spring, and King sts; 2 ch	Prince Edward 47 R.P.Milford 1
	MILLBANK					
B1516	-.-.57	-	-	Messrs Rutherford & Smith	For description see **1622**	Perth 44 R.P.260
B1517	-.12.57	2.7.58	Schofield & Hobson	John Smith	Wellington St to mill pond, Stratford St to Mornington St, mills; 2 ch	Perth 44 R.P.261
	MILLBRIDGE					
B1518	28.3.67	4.4.67	C.F. Aylsworth	R.M. Norman	Grant lot 21 E and 21 W Hastings Rd, twp Tudor; Mill St to Anne St, Hastings St to Norman St; 1.25 ch	Hastings 21 R.P.116
B1519	21.4.67	24.4.67	C.F. Aylsworth	I.P. Potter	Grant lots XIX and XX, west side Hastings Rd, twp Tudor; Jordan R to Mill St, Parker St to Hastings Rd; 2 ch	Hastings 21 R.P.120

MILLBROOK

B1520	18.6.52	24.7.52	John Reid	–	Lot 20, 6th con, twp Cavan; mill pond and mills, lots; 3 ch	Port Hope 9 R.P.Cavan 14
B1521	5.5.54	22.9.54	John Reid	William Wallace	Pt lot 12, 5th con, twp Cavan; Centre and Union sts, rd btwn cons 4 and 5; 1 ch	Port Hope 9 R.P.Cavan 9
B1522	12.5.54	12.3.57	John Reid	James Douglas	Front W1/2 lot 11, 5th con, twp Cavan; Con Rd on both sides Port Hope & Lindsay R.R. line; 1 ch	Port Hope 9 R.P.Cavan 11
B1523	5.5.55	19.5.55	John K. Roche	Joseph A. Graham & T.M. Sowden	Lot 13, 5th con, twp Cavan; Main St on east side; owners; 2 ch	Port Hope 9 R.P.Cavan 4
B1524	30.12.56	5.10.76	John K. Roche	Mr Hunter	Pt lot 10, 5th con, twp Cavan; lots on Queen, Hunter, and Cavan sts; 1 ch	Port Hope 9 R.P.Cavan 18
B1525	19.9.56	23.9.56	John Reid	R. Hughes	SW pt lot 10, 4th con, twp Cavan; both sides Port Hope & Lindsay R.R. above mill pond; 2 ch	Port Hope 9 R.P.Cavan 12
B1526	4.5.56	21.5.60	John Reid	James Deyell	Lot 12, IV con, twp Cavan; lots on Anne and Deyell sts and Mall St, Factory Pond, mill pond and flour mill; 2 ch	Port Hope 9 R.P.Cavan 2
B1527	28.6.56	21.1.71	John Reid	William Sowden	Pt W1/2 lot 12, con V, twp Cavan; 1 ch	Port Hope 9 R.P.Cavan 6
B1528	–.6.56	–	John Reid	William Sowden	NE pt lot 10 and NW pt lot 11, 4th con, twp Cavan; on both sides George St backing on Port Hope & Lindsay R.R. line, owners; 1 ch	Port Hope 9 R.P.Cavan 5
B1529	2.8.61	[2.8.61?]	–	Robert Armstrong	Pt lot 13, Vth con, twp Cavan; lots on Kells, Bank, and King sts and Middle Rd; creek, mill race, carding mill, owners; 2 ch	Port Hope 9 R.P.Cavan 10
B1530	14.10.63	4.12.63	M. Lough	–	Pt W1/2 lot 12, Vth con, twp Cavan; Millbrook & Peterborough R.R., owners, English church; 2 ch	Port Hope 9 R.P.Cavan 13
B1531	6.2.64	20.2.64	George A. Stewart	Estate of James Deyell	Pts lot 11 and 12, IVth con, twp Cavan; lots along Ann and Frederick sts, owners, all bldgs in centre pt of village shown; 2 ch	Port Hope 9 R.P.Cavan 3
B1532	13.7.64	28.10.65	William Murdoch	Thomas Hutchinson	Pt E1/2 lot 12, 5th con, twp Cavan; on Ann St, Centre Union, middle rd line, and con line; 2 ch	Port Hope 9 R.P.Cavan 8

	Date of Survey	Date of Regist.	Surveyor	Owner	Description and Notes	Location
	MILL GROVE					
B1533	22.11.58	[22.11.58?]	Thomas A. Blyth	Edward Lafferty et al.	Pt lot 19, IV con, twp Flamborough W; 1 ch	Wentworth 62 R.P.332 (old 26)
	MILLTOWN					
B1534	–	19.10.52	John J. Haslett	David Smith	Pt N1/2 lot 11, 1st con, twp Tyendinaga; Catherine St, Main St, and Church St to Salmon R, mill dam, mills, furnace, tannery; 1 ch	Hastings 21 R.P.40
B1535	–.–.60	25.3.61	J.J. Haslett	N.W. Lazier	Pt lot 10, 1st con, twp Tyendinaga; Main St to G.T.R., Anna St to Leonard St and Bridge St, bldgs; 2 ch	Hastings 21 R.P.97
	MILTON					
B1536	9.5.51	18.9.51	Hugh Black	Mathias Teetzel	Lot 13, 2nd con, twp Trafalgar; Oak St to Pearl St, Fulton St to Ontario St; 2 ch	Halton 20 R.P.3
B1537	31.5.53	6.6.53	Charles Unwin	Dr Charles Gardner	Pt lot 13, 2nd con, twp Trafalgar; Main St east to beyond Mary St, Charles St south, owners; 1 ch	Halton 20 R.P.5
B1538	27.6.53	5.7.53	Charles Unwin & Hugh Black	John Mar[tin]	Lots on Main and Mill sts btwn James and Elizabeth sts; 2 ch	Halton 20 R.P.6
B1539	31.3.54	5.6.54	Henry Winter	M. Teetzel	Main St to Oak St beyond Prince St, proposed alteration in course of Sixteen Mile Creek and pt of former course, post office, Milton Iron Works, Steam Flouring Mills; 2 ch	Halton 20 R.P.9
B1540	4.5.54	23.5.54	Henry Winter	H. Foster	Robert St to Main St, Foster St to Bronte St, court-house and gaol; 2 ch	Halton 20 R.P.7
B1541	7.5.55	7.5.55	Henry Winter	John Martin	Park lots; Bronte St to Garden Lane and mill pond, Mill St to mill pond, cemetery; 2 ch	Halton 20 R.P.17
B1542	29.5.55	21.10.56	Henry Winter	'M. Teetzel Survey'	Subdivision of Block I in Teetzel's survey; Pearl St to Main St, Charles St, Commercial St; 28-ft bar	Halton 20 R.P.20

B1543	27.5.56	29.5.56	Henry Winter	John Martin	Subdivision of park lots 1–3 in John Martin's survey; Mill St to Grove St, Bronte St to Elizabeth St; 1 ch	Halton 20 R.P.18
B1544	9.12.56	13.12.56	Winter & Howitt	Charles Gardner	Subdivision of lots II–IV and XX in Dr Gardiner's survey; Main St to Mary St, west of Charles St, bldgs, owners; 25 ft	Halton 20 R.P.21
B1545	26.6.60	8.7.61	Henry Winter	Richard Montgomery	Subdivision of lots 23 and 24, Block V, John Martin's survey; north of Main St at Martin St, owners; 50 ft	Halton 20 R.P.36
B1546	24.12.67	15.1.68	G. Brockitt Abrey	Municipality of Milton	Compilation plan; Ontario St to Bronte St, Robert St to Woodward Ave, mill pond, market sq, etc, all previous surveys shown; 3 ch	Halton 20 R.P.41
	MINDEN					
B1547	24.9.66	–	A. Russell, Asst Commr Crown Lands Dept	–	Streets named; copy of survey by R.T. Burns 1860; 2 ch	Haliburton 19 R.P.Minden
	MITCHELL					
B1548	–.–.55	18.5.55	Joseph Kirk	J.W. & C. James	Park lot 27; Alma to Adelaide St, St David's St; 1 ch	Perth 44 R.P.336
B1549	10.6.56	13.6.56	William Rath	J. Peterson, G. & W. Hennick	Park lots 20 and 21; Waterloo and St George St by mill pond; 1 ch	Perth 44 R.P.337
B1550	20.6.57	14.12.63	William Rath	Charles Thom	Park lot 26; Huron Rd to B. & L.H. Ry; 2 ch	Perth 44 R.P.342
B1551	–.–.58	13.3.58	William Rath	George Ullyot	Park lot 39; 1 ch	Perth 44 R.P.338
B1552	–.–.59	–.2.59	Joseph Kirk	Canada Co. plan	Town of Mitchell; 4 ch	Perth 44 R.P.339
B1553	29.11.61	16.1.62	Joseph Kirk	Elizabeth Jackson	Lot 26, 2nd con, twp Fullarton; 4 ch	Perth 44 R.P.307
B1554	11.6.62	1.11.62	William Rath	Canada Co.	Lots 23, 28, and 29, 1st con, twp Fullerton; bisected by B. & L.H. Ry; 4 ch	Perth 44 R.P.341
B1555	7.11.65	5.12.65	William Rath	Joseph Whitehead	Park lot XXVIII; 2 ch	Perth 44 R.P.343

	Date of Survey	Date of Regist.	Surveyor	Owner	Description and Notes	Location
	MONAGHAN TWP					
B1556	5.12.66	6.12.66	T.B. Clementi	'Bradburn's Plan'	Pt lot VI, con XII, N Monaghan; owners; 4 ch	Peterborough 45 Plan 15Q Monaghan
	MONO CENTRE					
B1557	27.10.60	9.8.66	R.W. Herman	Alexander Laidlaw	Lots east of 2/3 Con Rd; bldgs, owners; 12 ch	Dufferin 7 R.P.109 (Mono)
	MONO MILLS					
B1558	2.9.55	6.5.56	P. Callaghan	Richard Holmes	'Market Hill Village' east of 6th line; lots along Simcoe, Richmond, and Church sts; 2 ch	Peel 43 R.P.ALB-3
	MOORETOWN					
B1559	–.–.53	–	P.S. Donnelly	I.F. Baby & Co.	'Moore'; west pt lot 36, Front Con, twp Moore; St Clair R to Sophia St, William St to St James St; transcript; 1 ch	Lambton 25 R.P.Moore 3
B1560	–.1.56	[–.1.56?]	P.S. Donnelly	William Vidal	Vidal St to St Clair R, William St to St James St; transcript; 80 ft	Lambton 25 R.P.Moore 7
B1561	–.8.59	[31.8.59?]	P.S. Donnelly	William R. Wright	St Clair R to Emily St on both sides Napoleon St; transcript; 66 ft	Lambton 25 R.P.Moore 9
B1562	28.6.60	9.1.56?	P.S. Donnelly	John Stewart	St Clair R to Emily St, Victoria St to William St; 1 ch	Lambton 25 R.P.Moore 10
	MORPETH					
B1563	22.4.56	23.4.56	A.P. Salter	William Sheldon	Main St to Park St, Talbot St to Erie St; 2 ch	Kent 24 R.P.85
B1564	6.6.56	1.6.67	William McMillan	Levi Fowler	Lot 92, north Talbot Rd W, twp Howard; Talbot St to Kent St, Main St to Mill St; 4 ch	Kent 24 R.P.86
B1565	–	1.6.67	Messrs Salter & Johnston	Multiple owners	Pts lots 91 and 92, north and south of Talbot Rd, twp Howard; Bagot St to Mill St, Erie St to Kent St, lots on Main St; 5 ch	Kent 24 R.P.87

B1566	–.–.67	1.6.67	–	L. Cushing & J. Arnold	Front of lot 92, south on Talbot Rd W, twp Howard; owners; 42 ft	Kent 24 R.P.227
B1567	–.–.67	1.6.67	A.P. Salter	Wm Sheldon	Pt lot 91, south on Talbot Rd W, twp Howard; Bagot St to Main St, Talbot St north to Erie St, owners; 2 ch	Kent 24 R.P.84B
	MORRISBURG					
B1568	9.5.55	12.7.55	Francis Jones	T.W.H. Bedstead	E1/2 lot 30, 1st con, twp Williamsburgh; Queens Hwy to Ellen St, Church St to Maple St; 1 ch	Dundas 8 R.P.2
B1569	–.9.55	1.10.55	James West	Jesse W. Ross	W1/2 lot 30, 1st con, twp Williamsburgh; Queens St to G.T.R. and Railway Ave, gravel rd to Victoria St; 80 ft	Dundas 8 R.P.3
B1570	1.3.56	20.3.56	T.S. Rubidge	James Hodges	W1/2 lot 31, 1st con, twp Williamsburgh; canal to G.T.R., High St and St Lawrence St, owners; 200 ft	Dundas 8 R.P.5
B1571	3.6.56	3.6.56	William Tracy	W. Casselman	E1/2 lot 32, 1st con, twp Williamsburgh; highway to ry, lots on 5th St; 8 perches	Dundas 8 R.P.7
B1572	31.8.57	8.9.57	William Tracy	Samuel Rossiter	E1/2 lot 30, 1st con, twp Williamsburgh; Water St at canal and mill race to Rossiter St, Rose St to Lock St; 4 ch	Dundas 8 R.P.6
B1573	18.10.58	15.2.59	William Tracy	Chaffey's Block	W1/2 lot 30, 1st con, twp Williamsburgh; Canal St to Main St, Union St to Division St; 50 ft	Dundas 8 R.P.8
B1574	10.11.58	10.8.59	William Tracy	Isaac Eacutt	E1/2 lot 32, 1st con, twp Williamsburgh; Canal St to Main St, lots on both sides William St; 50 ft	Dundas 8 R.P.9
B1575	3.6.64	7.5.66	George Bruce	T.W.H. Bedstead	E1/2 lot 30, 1st con, twp Williamsburgh; lots on Church, Elizabeth, Bedstead, and Maud sts; 160 ft	Dundas 8 R.P.12
B1576	28.4.65	28.4.65	Tom S. Rubidge	Thomas S. Rubidge	'Hodges Block'; Queens St to G.T.R., High St to St Lawrence St, reserve areas, partial alteration and cancellation of **B1570**; 200 ft	Dundas 8 R.P.10
B1577	1.9.66	7.9.66	T.S. Rubidge	Janet McKenzie	'Rossiter Block'; canal to G.T.R., St Lawrence St to Nine Mile Rd, owners, fairgrounds; 200 ft	Dundas 8 R.P.13
B1578	6.8.67	[6.8.67?]	George Bruce	Timothy W.H. Bedstead	E1/2 lot 30, 1st con, twp Williamsburgh; lots on Church St at G.T.R.; 160 ft	Dundas 8 R.P.15

	Date of Survey	Date of Regist.	Surveyor	Owner	Description and Notes	Location
	MORRISTON					
B1579	24.9.53	24.9.53	Hugh Black	Donald W. Edwards	'Elgin,' SE pt of SW pt lot 31, 8th con, twp Puslinch; 2 ch	Wellington 61 R.P.72
B1580	–.12.53	11.2.54	Francis Kerr	Alvis Ops	Lot 31, 8th con, twp Puslinch; on Brock Rd, store, warehouse; 2 ch	Wellington 61 R.P.73
B1581	–.–.59	6.10.59	Francis Kerr, Wilson R. Turner del	Alex Och	Subdivision of part lots 1–6 and pt alterations in town lots; lots south of Badenoch St and east of Queen St; 2 ch	Wellington 61 R.P.114
B1582	28.11.60	19.12.60	J. Mackintosh	Municipal Council of Morriston	Compilation plan; Fisher St to James and Queen sts on both sides Badenoch St; 1948 transcript; 2 ch	Wellington 61 R.P.135
	MORTON					
B1583	10.8.57	18.8.57	Henry Lillie	George Morton	Lot 1, 5th con, twp S Crosby; Queens Hwy to Water St and White Fish R, all bldgs, description advertising village; transcript; 2 ch	Leeds 28 R.P.1
	MOSA TWP					
B1584	2.10.65	23.10.65	Thomas W. Dyas	Richard Brierly et al.	Lot 24, 1st range north of Longwoods Rd, twp Mosa; photoreproduction; 3 ch	Middlesex 34 R.P.207
B1585	1.12.65	8.1.66	Unwin & Dyas	E.B. Adams	N1/2 lot 28 and pt lot 29, 1st range north of Longwoods Rd, twp Mosa; inset map shows owners, location, relief, location of oil wells; photoreproduction; 4 ch	Middlesex 34 R.P.208
B1586	7.2.66	8.2.66	Unwin & Dyas	Charles L. Amos	S1/2 lot 26, 2nd range north of Longwoods Rd, twp Mosa; 2 ch	Middlesex 34 R.P.209
B1587	–.3.66	31.8.66	Unwin, Dyas & Forneri	Messrs Thayer & Hall	'Allen Farm,' lot 30, range I south of Longwoods Rd, twp Mosa; bldgs, oil wells; photoreproduction; 1.5 ch	Middlesex 34 R.P.214
B1588	28.8.66	31.8.66	Unwin, Dyas & Forneri	Messrs Thayer & Hall	Pt lot 29, 1st range north of Longwoods Rd, twp Mosa; lands of International Petroleum Co. of Detroit; photoreproduction; 3 ch	Middlesex 34 R.P.215

B1589	3.9.66	10.4.67	C.C. Forneri	Messrs Tisdale, Freeman & Pierce	Pt lot 27, 1st range south of Longwoods Rd, twp Mosa; photoreproduction; 2 ch	Middlesex 34 R.P.219
	MOSSLEY					
B1590	20.9.56	7.2.57	William McClary	James Spring	Pt lot 12, 3rd con, twp Dorchester south of Thames R; east of North Elgin Rd; 2 ch	Middlesex 33 R.P.134 Co
	MOUNT ALBERT					
B1591	1.3.67	14.5.67	James McCallum, Jr	Thomas Rear	Pt lot XII, VIII con, twp East Gwillimbury; Centre Rd to Gould Lane, mill pond; 1 ch	York 65 R.P.10
	MOUNT BRYDGES					
B1592	25.1.55	24.1.55	Samuel Peters	J. London	N1/2 lot 18, 2nd con, twp Caradoc; Church St to 3rd Con Rd, Queen St to London St, G.W.R.; photoreproduction; 2 ch	Middlesex 34 R.P.70
B1593	9.5.55	9.5.55	Samuel Peters	J.W. Emerson	Rd allowance cons 2 and 3 to Victoria St, Prince St to Provincial St, Market Sq; 3 ch	Middlesex 34 R.P.75
B1594	22.11.55	8.3.56	Samuel Peters	H.C.R. Becher & John Wilson	Lot 19, 2nd con, twp Caradoc; Dickson St to rd btwn cons 2 & 3, Harris St to McKinstry St, G.W.R. reserved areas; photoreproduction; 4 ch	Middlesex 34 R.P.112
B1595	-.-.56	1.4.57	Samuel Peters	J.W. Emerson	S1/2 lot 18, 2nd con, twp Caradoc; William St to Thomas St, Church St to Caradoc St; 2 ch	Middlesex 34 R.P.138
B1596	11.3.62	4.4.62	Wm Robinson	Jeremiah London	Lots on both sides Adelaide St above and below G.W.R., bldgs; 2 ch	Middlesex 34 R.P.171
B1597	6.5.64	25.5.64	Samuel Peters	Jeremiah London	Pt N1/2 lot 18, 2nd con, twp Caradoc; on both sides Adelaide St and on Bowan, Railroad, King, Hartman, and Queen sts, on both sides G.W.R. line; photoreproduction; 2 ch	Middlesex 34 R.P.196
B1598	30.8.64	11.11.64	Samuel Peters	H.C.R. Becher & Hon. J. Wilson	Pt lot 19, 2nd con, twp Caradoc; road btwn cons 2 and 3 to Tom St, lots on Harris, Beattie, Radcliff, Buchanan, and Gourlay sts on both sides G.W.R., amended plan; 4 ch	Middlesex 34 R.P.199

	Date of Survey	Date of Regist.	Surveyor	Owner	Description and Notes	Location
	MOUNT ELGIN					
B1599	5.5.51	–	W.G. Wonham	Adam Tripp	N1/2 lot 10, 5th con, twp Dereham; lots along front 5th con and Tillsonburg Rd; 1 ch	Oxford 41 R.P.25
	MOUNT FOREST					
B1600	1.12.55	26.1.57	E.H. Kertland	Allan McAllan	For description see **1636**	Wellington 60 R.P.16 (1)
B1601	–.–.64	29.6.64	Hugh Wilson	John Foster	Pt lot 33, 1st con, twp Normanby; Sligo St to Duke St north of town plot, Perth St to Main St, bldgs; 2 ch	Wellington 60 R.P.17 (8)
	MOUNT PLEASANT (Brant Co)					
B1602	27.10.55	17.11.56	O. Robinson	Thomas Eadie	Front lot 4, 1st range east of Mt Pleasant Rd, twp Brantford; North St, 1st St E, Mt Pleasant Rd; 2 ch	Brant 2 R.P.47
B1603	25.11.55	15.3.58	Sherman Malcolm	Russel Hardy	Pt lot 4, west side Mt Pleasant Rd; lots on Russel St; 1.33 ch	Brant 2 R.P.48
	MOUNT PLEASANT (Durham Co)					
B1604	–.5.54	23.2.55	Thos Dennehy, George A. Stewart	Messrs G. Workman, G. Jamison, A. Webster, T. Best	Boucher St to mill pond, High St to Workman St, tannery and factory lots; copy of plan by Dennehy; 2 ch	Port Hope 9 R.P.Cavan 17
	NAPANEE					
B1605	–.–.50	6.5.50	John Ryder	John C. Clark	'Clarkville,' W1/2 lot 20, 7th con, twp Fredericksburgh; macadamized rd to Napanee R, streets not named; 2 ch	Lennox 29 R.P.12
B1606	30.8.59	–	A.B. Perry	R.L. Cartwright	Compilation plan; Napanee R to Graham St and G.T.R. line and station, Hessford St to ry; also shows Cartwrightville to east of ry: First St to Church St, road to Camden and Newburgh St to Centre St and beyond, bldgs, notes on earlier surveys and verifications; 3 ch	Lennox 29 R.P.82

B1607	1.5.61	–	Samuel Benson	–	Bridge St to Dundas St; Robinson St to West St; 66 ft	Lennox 29 R.P.28
B1608	–.12.61	–	Samuel Benson	A. Campbell	Park lots on pt lot 20, 7th con, twp Fredericksburgh; Chamberlain Rd btwn rd to Kingston and rd btwn cons 6 and 7, owners; 3 ch	Lennox 29 R.P.19
B1609	–.10-63	–	A.B. Perry	–	Lots on Centre St north of Graham St; Thomas St to G.T.R depot, Robert St to John St, bldgs at depot; 2 ch	Lennox 29 R.P.27
B1610	–.2.67	–	A.B. Perry	–	Lots btwn Donald and Union and Dundas and Thomas sts; contents; 2 ch	Lennox 29 R.P.30
B1611	8.7.67	20.6.67	R.O. Walsh	Trust & Loan Co. of Upper Canada	W1/2 lot 20 south of madadamized rd, 7th con, twp Fredericksburgh; lots on Chamberlain Rd; 4 ch	Lennox 29 R.P.26
	NAPIER					
B1612	29.9.57	29.9.58	Charles L. Davies	John Arthurs	Pt lot 3, 6th con, twp Metcalf; lots on Sydenham R to Clover St, High Market St to Curry St, bldgs, owners, market and court-house reserves; photoreproduction; 2 ch	Middlesex 34 R.P.145
B1613	29.1.59	17.5.59	B. Springer	Robert L. Johnston	NE1/4 lot 3, 7th con, and SE pt lot 3, 6th con, twp Metcalf; Victoria St to Robert St, Ridout St to Duke St, grist and sawmill; photoreproduction; 2 ch	Middlesex 34 R.P.156
	NELSON					
B1614	26.2.55	17.9.70	Thomas A. Blyth	J.D. Pringle	For description see **1645**	Halton 20 R.P.48
	NEUSTADT					
B1615	1.11.59	14.3.60	Hugh Wilson	David Winkler	Pt lots 1–3, 13th con, twp Normandy; Jacob and William sts to Queen St, Forler St to mill pond, bldgs, owners; 2 ch	Grey 17 R.P.161
	(NEW ABERDEEN)					
B1616	–.6.56	–	Schofield & Hobson	George Davidson	For description see **1646**	Waterloo 58 R.P.640

	Date of Survey	Date of Regist.	Surveyor	Owner	Description and Notes	Location
	NEWBORO					
B1617	20.10.63	1.4.64	Henry Lillie	John Kilborn & Benjamin Tett	Pt of 'Newboro'; plan missing	Leeds 28 R.P.6
	NEWBRIDGE					
B1618	24.10.64	5.9.67	C. Carroll	William Spence	'Spencetown,' lot 31, 4th con, twp Howick; Mill St; 3 ch	Huron 22 R.P.297
	NEWBURGH					
B1619	4.12.47	–.12.48	A.B. Perry	–	Lot 17, 2nd con, twp Camden; Baldwin St to 2nd con rd, Brock, Durham, and East sts, Main St to East St; 2 ch	Lennox 29 R.P.7
B1620	–.–.48	–.12.48	–	–	Lots on Mill, Centre, Water, and Store sts; scale n.g.	Lennox 29 R.P.8
B1621	2.11.50	20.7.55	A.B. Perry	Isaac B. Aylsworth	Lot 17, 2nd con, twp Camden E; North St to 2nd Con Rd, Main St to East St, owners; 2 ch	Lennox 29 R.P.9
B1622	8.11.50	24.7.52	A.B. Perry	Homer Spencer	SW pt lot 17, 2nd con, twp Camden; Durham St to 2nd Con Rd, Main St to Brock St; 1 ch	Lennox 29 R.P.5
B1623	23.11.50	6.3.51	A.B. Perry	Cephas H. Miller	SE pt lot 16, 2nd con, twp Camden; 2nd Con Rd to Baldwin St, Church St, Main St, Wesleyan Methodist church; 1 ch	Lennox 19 R.P.6
B1624	11.9.54	12.1.58	William R. Rombough	Cephas H. Miller	Front lot 16, 2nd con, twp Camden; 2nd Con Rd to Baldwin St, Academy St to Church St, drawing of Academy; 1 ch	Lennox 29 R.P.3
B1625	23.9.54	12.1.55	William R. Rombough	–	Rear lot 17, 1st con, twp Camden; Napanee R with 2 mill dams and pond, bridges, mills, con rd to Grove St, Main St to Madden St, owners; 1 ch	Lennox 29 R.P.56
B1626	–.6.60	27.2.61	A.B. Perry	Thomas Midden	Lots 17 and 18, 1st con, twp Camden south of river; Napanee R to road to Clarks Mills, Main St to Earl St; 2 ch	Lennox 29 R.P.4
B1627	–.12.61	21.6.62	W.R. Aylsworth	Richard Williams	N1/2 of S1/2 lot 16, 1st con, twp Camden; Centre Rd and travelled rd, owners; 3 ch	Lennox 29 R.P.11

	NEWBURY					
B1628	27.3.54	5.4.54	John O'Mara	John Tucker	'New Town,' pt N1/2 lot 17, 2nd con, twp Mosa; Tucker, Broadway, Hagerty, Dundas, and York sts, 2 mill plots, inset map (village limits); photoreproduction; 20 ch	Middlesex 34 R.P.46
B1629	31.7.54	17.11.54	John O'Mara	Robert Thompson	Queen St to beyond Elgin St, James St to Durham St; photoreproduction; 2 ch	Middlesex 34 R.P.67
B1630	4.9.56	25.9.58	John O'Mara	John Tucker	Dundas St to Henry St, Broadway St to Market St, market ground, 2 mill plots; photoreproduction; 2 ch	Middlesex 34 R.P.153
B1631	-.-.57	10.1.57	William McMillan	Thomas Webster	Lot 18, 2nd con, twp Mosa; Brock St to G.W.R., Jane St to Hagarty St, reserve for court-house and foundry; 100 ft	Middlesex 34 R.P.131
	NEWCASTLE					
B1632	-.-.64	-	C.G. Hanning	Hon. George Boulton	Arthur St to North St, L Ontario to Monro St, mill pond, bridge, mill, etc; 4 ch	Newcastle 10 'Newcastle'
	NEW DUNDEE					
B1633	-.-.63	-.-.63	James Black	F.G.Millar	Lot 6, 3rd con, Block A, twp Wilmot; Bridge St to mill pond, Queen St to mill property, grist and sawmill; 1.5 ch	Waterloo 58 R.P.628
	NEW GLASGOW					
B1634	19.7.55	9.5.67	Samuel Peters	Sir Richard Airey	'Airey,' Balaklava St to Talbot St, Furnival Rd to Alma St; 1.5 ch	Elgin 11 R.P.32
	NEW HAMBURG					
B1635	-.-.4?	-	Brown?	-	'New Hamburgh'; Bleams Rd to Huron St, Water, Peel, and Jacob sts; some names	Waterloo 58 no R.P.#
B1636	-.-.45	-	Robert W. Kerr	Absalom Shade	'Hamburgh,' twp Wilmot; Smith's Creek, bounded by Peel St, Bleams Rd, Huron St, and Streets B and C, mills, names of owners; 2 ch	Waterloo 58 no R.P.#
B1637	30.12.53	[30.12.53?]	William Rath	Messrs William Scott & William Henry Allen	Pt lot 23 north of Bleam's Rd, twp Wilmot; Victoria St to Shade St, Elizabeth St to Derby St; 2 ch	Waterloo 58 R.P.533

	Date of Survey	Date of Regist.	Surveyor	Owner	Description and Notes	Location
B1638	1.12.54	[1.12.54?]	Milton C. Schofield	George Davidson	Catherine St to Victoria St and on both sides G.T.R., James St to Bleam's Rd; 3 ch	Waterloo 58 R.P.532A
B1639	15.9.56	–	Bristow & Fitzgerald	D.G. Macdonald	For description see **1652**	Waterloo 58 R.P.532B
B1640	20.9.60	[20.9.60?]	Joseph Hobson	William Moyer	Pt lot 24 north of Bleam's Rd, twp Wilmot; Moyer St and G.T.R. west of river; 3 ch	Waterloo 58 R.P.532
	NEWINGTON					
B1641	22.11.66	16.4.68	John S. Bruce	J.N. Dixon	Pt lot 7, 8th con, twp Osnabruck; bldgs, sawmill, proposed headrace; 2 ch	Stormont 52 R.P.7
	NEW LOWELL					
B1642	–.–.66	15.11.66	W. Sanders	Messrs Jacques, Hay & Co.	Lot 10, 4th con, twp Sunnidale; Clarendon St east to Northern R.R., from river to Windham St, factory and other bldgs, ry grounds; 2 ch	Simcoe 51 R.P.116
	NEWMARKET					
B1643	5.4.33	8.5.50	George Lount	Eli Gorham	SW pt lot 33, 2nd con, twp Whitchurch; lots on both sides King St, owners; 1 ch	York 65 R.P.15
B1644	–.7.53	[–.7.53?]	William Gibbard	George Lount	Town lots; Erie St to Niagara St, Ontario St to Huron St, Ontario Simcoe & Huron R.R. line; 2 ch	York 65 R.P.78
B1645	–.12.53	[–.12.53?]	William Gibbard	W.A. Clarke	Lots on both sides mill pond and Ontario Simcoe & Huron R.R., bldgs, reserves; 2 ch	York 65 R.P.85
B1646	8.5.54	30.10.54	F.F. Passmore	W.A. Clarke	Area west of Queen St, villa lots at west end along Timothy, Cedar, and Lydia sts; 2 ch	York 65 R.P.103
B1647	27.10.54	19.3.55	William Henry	Messrs Srigley	Lot 34, 2nd con, twp Whitchurch; along Srigley St btwn Prospect and Queen sts; 4 ch	York 65 R.P.113
B1648	7.5.55	14.6.55	J.S. Dennis	[Messrs Srigley?]	West pt lot 35, 2nd con, twp Whitchurch; O.S. & H. R.R. station, line, Holland R, old mill to Robinson St, Victoria St to	York 65 R.P.125

					town line E Gwillimbury and Whitchurch; 66 ft	
B1649	–.10.55	24.9.57	John Ryan	Mordecai Millard	Pt lots 94 and 95, con 1, twp Whitchurch; Ontario St to Tecumseth St, Niagara St to Northern R.R. and Holland R, bldgs; 12 ch	York 65 R.P.222
B1650	17.2.62	25.2.62	S.W. Hallen	George Lount	Northern R.R. and Holland R to Niagara St, Ontario St to Huron St, bldgs; 2 ch	York 65 R.P.262
B1651	23.7.63	24.11.63	S.W. Hallen	William Roe	Main St to Second St, Water St to Timothy St, Northern Ry; 60 ft	York 65 R.P.4A
B1652	21.5.67	23.5.67	S.W. Hallen	Mrs L.M. Gamble	Lot 96, con I, twp E Gwillimbury; Huron St north to Charles St, Northern Ry west to Main St and old road; 2 ch	York 65 R.P.11
B1653	30.11.67	26.12.68	S.W. Hallen	'Botsford Estate'	Pt lot 94, con I, twp Whitchurch; Botsford St to Timothy St, Main St to Church St; 65 ft	York 65 R.P.13
B1654	30.11.67	26.12.68	S.W. Hallen	'Botsford Estate'	Pt lot 94, con I, twp Whitchurch; on both sides Botsford St; 50 ft	York 65 R.P.14
B1655	30.11.67	26.12.68	S.W. Hallen	'Botsford Estate'	Pt lot 94, con I, twp Whitchurch; Northern Ry to Main St on both sides Dominion St, 'Christian Church'; 66 ft	York 65 R.P.15
	NEWPORT					
B1656	31.1.56	2.2.56	O. Robinson	Thaddeus & George J. Smith	West side Grand R; streets; 2 ch	Brant 2 R.P.37
	NEWTON ROBINSON					
B1657	[1.4.47?]	1.4.47	Robert Walsh	Thomas Cooke	'Newton Robinson,' east pt broken lot 24, 15th con, twp Tecumseth; a few lots; 1 ch	Simcoe 51 R.P.10
	NIAGARA FALLS					
B1658	11.4.51	3.12.53	J.W. Fell	Falls Company	Dunn St to Lundy's Lane and west to road btwn lots 142 and 143 and 160 and 161, twp Stamford; owners, ry, relief; transcript; 3 ch	Niagara 59 R.P.1 (old Stamford 1)
B1659	15.6.54	1.7.54	James Pollock	Samuel Zimmerman & James Oswald	Pt town plot 'Elgin,' lots 92 and 93, twp Stamford; Morrison St to Bridge St and Niagara R to St Lawrence Ave, N.F. Suspension Bridge, market block; transcript; 100 ft	Niagara 59 R.P.999 (old N.F. Town 2)

	Date of Survey	Date of Regist.	Surveyor	Owner	Description and Notes	Location
B1660	[16.7.55]	8.8.55	James W. Fell	Buchanan, Bender	Pt lots 111 and 128, twp Stamford; lots btwn river and Erie & Ont Ry; 1.25 ch	Niagara 59 R.P.274 (old N.F. Town 3)
B1661	-.9.55	9.10.55	J.W. Fell	Estate of Major Leonard	'Drummond Hill,' pt lots 125 and 131, twp Stamford; Lundy's Lane to rd allowance btwn lots 125 and 131, England St to Leonard St, owners; transcript; 2 ch	Niagara 59 R.P.2 (old Stamford 2)
B1662	20.11.55	25.3.56	James Pollock	Messrs McMicken & Dickson	'Drummondville'; Portage Rd to Stanley St, Lundy's Lane to Summer St, owners; 2 ch	Niagara 59 R.P.3 (old Stamford 3)
B1663	15.2.56	15.9.5[6?]	J.W. Fell	P. Bender	'Elgin,' pt lot 92, twp Stamford; along plank rd and Bridge St; 100 ft	Niagara 59 R.P.275 (old N.F. Town 4)
B1664	19.8.56	2.12.56	J.S. Dennis	J. Adam & Francis H. [?]	'Victoria Terrace,' pt lots 127 and 128, twp Stamford; layout for terrace with park reserve in middle of Carriage Dr, lots on both sides later deleted; 40 ft	Niagara 59 R.P.277 (old N.F. 8)
B1665	29.10.56	31.10.56	James Pollock	A.C. Crysler & J.H. Fairbank	Pt 'Clifton'; Simcoe St on both sides, Niagara R to 1st Con St, south of Erie & Ontario R.R.; 100 ft	Niagara 59 R.P.276 (old Town 5)
B1666	-.-.56	22.11.56	James Pollock	R.G. Benedict & Co.	Pt 'Clifton'; transcript; 100 ft	Niagara 59 R.P.1000 (old N.F. Town 6)
B1667	2.7.57	22.7.57	James Pollock	R.G. Benedict & Co.	Pt 'Clifton,' town plot, blocks 45 and 46; Raglan St and Nelson St east of 1st Con St; later deleted; 100 ft	Niagara 59 R.P.278 (old N.F. Town 278)
B1668	16.11.64	13.5.65	Dennis & Gossage	F.H. Heward	'Victoria Terrace,' pts lots 128 and 129, twp Stamford; Carriage Dr around park reserve with lots on both sides; 50 ft	Niagara 59 R.P.279 (old Town 9)
	NIAGARA-ON-THE-LAKE					
B1669	9.5.23	-.5.23	Claudius Shaw	–	Original town plot; lots 1–412, churchyard, Mississauga Reserve, relief, some streets, military reserve, Crook's Wharf, King's Wharf; 6 ch	Niagara 30 R.P.10 Co

	NIAGARA TWP					
B1670	4.9.55	–.2.56	Edmund De Cew	Municipal Council	Pt of Niagara Twp including Queenston, roads, some boundaries verified; 40 ch	Niagara 30 R.P.28 Co
	NICHOL TWP					
B1671	–.10.55	[–.10.55?]	Milton C. Schofield, J. Hobson del	Robert Garven	Lot 18, 15th con, twp Nichol; 3 ch	Wellington 61 R.P.87
B1672	–.–.55?	–	W.H. Barker	William Moorehead	Lot 19, 15th con, twp Nichol; owners, swampy area btwn cons XIV and XV and Owen Sound Rd; 3 ch	Wellington 61 R.P.71
	NILE					
B1673	–.–.63	12.5.63	Thomas Weatherald	James Stewart	Lot 1, con XI, Western Division, twp Colborne; sawmill property; 2 ch	Huron 22 R.P.295
	NILESTOWN					
B1674	–.–.56	10.2.57	William McMillan	Messrs Putnam & Lane	Lots along Hamilton and Elgin Rd and Dorchester and Westminster town line; 2 ch	Middlesex 33 R.P.135 Co
	NITHBURG					
B1675	2.6.53	16.12.53	Moses Springer	James Brown	Lot 17, 12th con, twp NE Hope; mill pond to Queen St, Wellesley boundary to Main St, mill yard, tannery, market sq; 2 ch	Perth 44 R.P.276
B1676	–.–.56	4.3.58	William Smith	James Brown	Western pt Huron St to mill pond, lots on Erie, Ontario, and Simcoe sts; 2 ch	Perth 44 R.P.277
	NORHAM					
B1677	–.–.55	12.8.55	J. Russ	John Sparrow & N. Hercheimer	'North & South Centreville,' lot 17, 2nd con, twp Percy; lots on Harvey, Raglan, road to Colborne, road to Seymour, and Puffer St; 2 ch	Northumberland 38 R.P.6 (Percy)
B1678	–.6.67	18.4.68	David Williams	Municipal Council of Norham	Lot 17, 2nd con, twp Percy; gravel rd to Puffer St to Sparrow St, new con line to John St, bldgs; 2 ch	Northumberland 38 R.P.30 (Percy)

	Date of Survey	Date of Regist.	Surveyor	Owner	Description and Notes	Location
	NORMANDALE					
B1679	10.7.52	–	Thomas W. Walsh	–	Plank rd and Harbour Co. plot and wharf, lots on Main, Caroline, Hill, and Vittoria sts; 2 ch	Norfolk 37 R.P.4A
	NORTH AUGUSTA					
B1680	17.11.55	11.9.57	John Burchill	Hiram H. Bellamy	Lot 33, 8th con, twp Augusta; Brockville and N Augusta Co Rd to intersection of Mill St and Mirickville and Maitland Co Rd, mill pond and plot; 60 ft	Grenville 15 R.P.Augusta 3
B1681	–.9.63	13.10.63	John Burchill	L.H. Bellamy	Lots 32–4, 8th con, twp Augusta; alteration of plan above; south branch Rideau R to Marion St and Queens Hwy, lots along Merrickville and Maitland Rd, mill plot; 100 ft	Grenville 15 R.P.Augusta 4
	NORTH GOWER					
B1682	4.9.51	3.5.52	Francis Jones	Wm Craig	Lots on Main, Craig, Andrews, and Green sts; 60 ft	Ottawa-Carleton 5 R.P.3
	NORVAL					
B1683	26.12.56	19.1.57	Bristow & Fitzgerald	Thomas Foster	Pt W1/2 lot 10, 11th con, twp Esquesing; John to Queen St, Toronto and Guelph Plank Rd west to James St; 80 links	Halton 20 R.P.23
B1684	–.11.60	–	A.B. Scott	'Saint Dennys Survey'	Pt NE1/4 lot 10, 11th con, twp Esquesing; below Toronto and Guelph Plank Rd; 1 ch	Halton 20 R.P.38
B1685	1.10.64	[1.10.64?]	Winter & Abrey	For Township of Esquesing	Compilation plan; earlier surveys shown, streets named; 4 ch	Halton 20 no R.P.#
B1686	12.4.67	21.4.87	C. Miller, A. McNab	William Clay	'Upper Norval,' pt lot 15, 11th con, twp Esquesing; G.T.R. to Queen St, area west of Broadway; 150 links	Halton 20 R.P.77
	NORWICH					
B1687	25.6.49	–	J.A. Tidey	Village of Norwich	'Norwichville'; Otter Creek north to North St and east to Victoria St, owners, bldgs; 3 ch	Oxford 41 R.P.15

B1688	24.11.58	–	J.A. Tidey	Rev Thomas Webster	SW pt lot 9, 4th con, twp N Norwich; Main St to Otter Creek, Woodstock & Pt Dover Rail Co. to Centre St, owners; 99 ft	Oxford 41 R.P.114
B1689	26.11.64	–	William Smiley	Estate of John Steele	'Norwichville,' lot 8, 4th and 5th cons, twp N Norwich; Main St to Otter Creek, Averys Lane to Stover St, bldgs, owners, Methodist Meeting House lot; 99 ft	Oxford 41 R.P.158
	NORWICH TWP					
B1690	12.6.39	–	P. Carroll	–	Boundary line survey btwn lots 4 and 5, 3rd con, twp Norwich; owners, cleared land; 20 ch	Oxford 41 no R.P.#
	NORWOOD					
B1691	15.2.53	23.2.53	Joseph Keeler	J.A. Keeler	Queen St to Wellington St, Oak St to Belmont St, sawmill and grist mill; 4 ch	Peterborough 45 R.P.P-1 Norwood
	NOTTAWA					
B1692	22.3.54	24.2.57	W. Gibbard	Rev Adam Townley & Elizabeth Townley	Lot 36, 8th con, twp Nottawasaga; east of Hurontario St, Queen St to street above Mill St; 1 ch	Simcoe 51 R.P.52
	NOTTAWASAGA TWP					
B1693	31.1.56	12.8.56	W. Gibbard	Douglas G. MacDonald	S1/2 lot 40, 10th con, twp Nottawasaga; Tecumseth St north to George St, High St west to Princess St, owners, cleared land, bldgs, swampy areas; 3 ch	Simcoe 51 R.P.43
B1694	9.4.56	7.8.56	W. Gibbard	J.M. Heath	S1/2 lot 47, 11th con, twp Nottawasaga; lots west of Cranberry L, streets laid out; 3 ch	Simcoe 51 R.P.42
B1695	–.4.57	3.6.57	W. Gibbard	J.H. Richardson & H. Wittrock	Subdivision of lots 63, 64, 67, and 68, S1/2 lot 40, 10th con, twp Nottawasaga; Alexander St to Durham St; 40 ft	Simcoe 51 R.P.59
	OAKVILLE					
B1696	[2.6.37?]	12.1.50	Robert W. Kerr	Estate of Wm Chisholm	Bond St to Shedden St, owners, relief, mill dam, shipyard, reserves for Scotch church, George's Sq, public cemetery; 4 ch	Halton 20 R.P.1

	Date of Survey	Date of Regist.	Surveyor	Owner	Description and Notes	Location
B1697	2.6.56	12.8.56	Henry Winter	Messrs Smith & Romain	From the water to Colborne St, Allen St to Second St; 70 ft	Halton 20 R.P.19
B1698	11.2.61	11.6.61	Henry Winter	George K. Chisholm	Three sections: Reynolds St to Allen St, south of Division St, Palmer to Randal St, refers to earlier survey of lots 91 and 92 by Robert W. Kerr 1.8.36; 100 ft	Halton 20 R.P.34
B1699	11.2.61	11.6.61	Henry Winter	John A. Chisholm	Subdivision of pt lots XII and XIII, con III, S.D. St, twp Trafalgar; Division St to Spruce St, plank rd to Allen St; 100 ft	Halton 20 R.P.35
	OAKWOOD					
B1700	22.1.53	28.9.53	William Galbraith	Thomas Mark	Lots along King and Eldon sts; 1 ch	Victoria 57 R.P.13P
B1701	–.8.56 15.5.57	[–.8.56?] [15.5.57?]	Thomas J. Dennehy	[W?] A. McLaughlin	Plan 1, lot 17, 8th con, twp Mariposa; Taylor St W and King St south to Alma St; plan 2, lot 16, 8th con, town hall and hotel on Elm St at King St and lots on north; 1 ch	Victoria 57 no R.P.#
B1702	–.–.61	11.5.61	Robert T. Burns	A.A. McLaughlin	King St to Alma St, King St south to Flora St and north to Albert St, on both sides Eldon St; 3 ch	Victoria 57 R.P.7
B1703	22.2.66	2.5.66	M. Deane	N.W. Pearson	Subdivision of SW3/4 lot 16, 9th con, twp Mariposa; east of Eldon St and north of King St; 3 ch	Victoria 57 R.P.16
	ODESSA					
B1704	5.7.50	14.9.50	A.B. Perry	–	'Mill Creek,' E1/2 lot 31, 4th con, twp Ernestown; South St to North St, Bridge St at river to Durham St, contents; 2 ch	Lennox 29 R.P.25
B1705	–.11.50	13.3.51	A.B. Perry	P.D. & J.K. Booth	'Millcreek,' pt lot 32, 4th con, twp Ernestown; Mud Lake Rd, Factory St, Gore St and Mill St, bldgs, mill creek, mill ponds, dams, bridges, mills; 2 ch	Lennox 29 R.P.79

OIL SPRINGS

B1706	–.4.61	31.5.61	E.R. Jones	W.E. Sanborn	Subdivision of lot 18, 2nd con, twp Enniskillen; bldgs; photoreproduction; 2 ch	Lambton 25 R.P.Oil Springs 4
B1707	29.6.61	[29.6.61?]	James Pollock	Presquisle and Canada Oil Company	Subdivision of N1/2 of E1/4 lot 18, II con, twp Enniskillen; relief; 2 ch	Lambton 25 R.P.Oil Springs 1
B1708	11.9.61	26.9.61	S. Peters	'William's Oil Lands'	Subdivision of lots 16 and 18, 1st and 2nd cons, twp Enniskillen; 250 ft	Lambton 25 R.P.Oil Springs 2 (Enniskillen 4)
B1709	3.10.61	[3.10.61?]	J.O. Browne	Mr Matthews	Subdivision of E1/2 lot 19, con II, twp Enniskillen; oil wells; 3 ch	Lambton 25 R.P.Oil Springs 3
B1710	29.6.63	4.7.63	E.R. Jones	W. Shiriff	Front pt lot 18, 3rd con, twp Enniskillen; Main St, lots btwn Shiriff and Johnson sts, bldgs, a few oil wells; 100 ft	Lambton 25 R.P.Oil Springs 5
B1711	9.7.64	17.9.64	E.R. Jones	Ivin Dunham Bruce et al.	Subdivision of W1/2 lot 16, 3rd con, twp Enniskillen; relief; 3 ch	Lambton 25 R.P.Oil Springs 6
B1712	–.12.65	14.2.66	E.R. Jones	Enniskillen Petroleum & Refining Co.	Subdivision of pt W1/2 lot 18, 2nd con, twp Enniskillen; lots on Young, Duryee, James sts and rd allowance btwn cons 2 and 3; 100 ft	Lambton 25 R.P.Oil Springs 7
B1713	28.3.66	7.4.66	Henry Carre	Messrs James Grey & Standish O'Grady	'O'Keef's Subdivision,' NW pt lot 16, 2nd con, twp Enniskillen; Lawrence St to Main St, Elliott St to Elizabeth St; 100 ft	Lambton 25 R.P.Oil Springs 8
B1714	–.–.66	23.4.66	Henry Smith	Enniskillen Petroleum & Refinery	Subdivision 3, range B, and subdivisions 4 and 5, ranges C, D, E, lot 18, con 2, twp Enniskillen; Young St to Sanborn St, lots south of Wolseley St, relief; 66 ft	Lambton 25 R.P.Oil Springs 9
B1715	12.5.66	14.5.66	Henry Smith	Albert Clark	Main St to Isabell St, Merchant St to Irene St; 33 ft	Lambton 25 R.P.Oil Springs 10
B1716	26.5.66	31.5.66	Henry Smith	Owen & James Kelly	Subdivision of pt lot 1, range A in subdivision of pt lot 18, con 2, twp Enniskillen; south side Main St east of Sanborn St; 20 ft	Lambton 25 R.P.Oil Springs 11

	Date of Survey	Date of Regist.	Surveyor	Owner	Description and Notes	Location
B1717	30.5.66	9.10.66	F.F. Passmore	Messrs Ives, Dunham & Bruce et al.	Subdivision W1/2 lot XVI, con III, twp Enniskillen; lots near bldgs of Wyoming Rock Oil Co. office, refinery; 1 ch	Lambton 25 R.P.Oil Springs 12
B1718	23.10.66	27.10.66	Henry Smith	Wyoming Petroleum Co.	Subdivision of E1/2 lot 16, con 3, twp Enniskillen; Main St to Tenth St, Bruce St to Prospect Ave, refineries located and named, relief; 3 ch	Lambton 25 R.P.Oil Springs 13
	OMEMEE					
B1719	1.7.57	2.7.67	George Stewart	N. Kirchoffer, T.C. Clarke, T.R. & M. Merritt, T.M. & Jas R. Benson, et al.	Port Hope, Lindsay & Beaverton R.R.; 4th Con St north to 5th Con St, King St east to Park St, ry grounds and station, Greenwood Park, owners; 200 ft	Victoria 57 R.P.19
B1720	1.10.62	13.10.62	M. Lough	–	Port Hope, Lindsay & Beaverton R.R. east to Dixon St north and south of King St to mill pond and Distillery St and Elm St; 4 ch	Victoria 57 R.P.12
B1721	18.4.67	29.4.67	Crosbie Brady	A. McQuade	Subdivision of SW1/4 lot 6, 4th con, twp Emily; area north of King St on both sides Orange St; 2 ch	Victoria 57 R.P.18
	ONEIDA TWP					
B1722	26.3.44	[26.3.44?]	Edmund De Cew	'Tiffany Block'	Caledonia Rd and bridge near York to farther up Grand R, Townsend Rd; transcript; 10 ch	Haldimand 18 R.P.49
B1723	20.1.55	13.6.60	Edmund De Cew	Robert Anderson & Martindale & Pearts	Lot 1; along and back from Grand R; 16 ch	Haldimand 18 R.P.8716 Oneida
	ONONDAGA					
B1724	1.5.50	15.3.53	John Jackson	Grand R Navigation Co.	Grand R north side Front St; towing path; 2 ch	Brant 2 R.P.101
B1725	4.5.54	–	O. Robinson	John Merrill	Pt broken lot 41, 3rd con, twp Onondaga east of Fairchilds Creek; Brantford St to John St, Main St to beyond Centre St; photoreproduction; 2 ch	Brant 2 R.P.100

B1726	28.9.55	1.10.55	O. Robinson	George C. Thomas & Alexander Hawley	SE pt broken lot 23, range east of Fairchilds Creek and pt river lot 41, 3rd con east of Fairchilds Creek; owners, Brantford St to Carrier St, Grant R to Main St; 2 ch	Brant 2 R.P.98
B1727	30.11.55	[15.6.57?]	O. Robinson	Messrs J.B. Racey & George H.M. Johnson	Pt of south pt river lot 42, con III east of Fairchilds Creek, twp Onondaga; lots along Johnston and Brantford sts, Centre Lane and rd allowance btwn lots 42 and 43, B. & L.H. Ry Co.; 2 ch	Brant 2 R.P.102
B1728	5.6.57	12.6.57	O. Robinson	John Merrill	Pts river lot 41, con III east of Fairchild's Creek, twp Onondaga; Brantford St to Buffalo & L.H. Ry, lots east and west of Centre St; 2 ch	Brant 2 R.P.103
	ORANGEVILLE					
B1729	15.10.51	[15.10.51?]	Chisholm Miller	Orange Lawrence	Main St south to beyond Church St, Wellington St and about 2 streets on either side, owners, bldgs, mill and mill reserve; 2 ch	Dufferin 7 R.P.58
B1730	21.7.56	17.7.57	J. Stoughton Dennis	Jesse Ketchum, Jr	Lot 1, 1st con west of Hurontario St, twp Mono; Broadway Ave to 3rd Ave, 4th St E to 1st St; 3 ch	Dufferin 7 R.P.159
B1731	–.2.57	2.6.57	Charles J. Wheelock	James B. House	Pt lot 1, con E, twp Garafraxa; Wellington St to Sarah St and James St, Mary St; 50 ft	Dufferin 7 R.P.59
B1732	22.12.57	9.6.58	Charles J. Wheelock	Messrs John M. & Jabez Smith	Pt lot 2, con E, twp Garafraxa; 15 ft	Dufferin 7 R.P.100
B1733	–.–.60	22.8.78	Charles J. Wheelock	A. Wilcox	Subdivision of pt E1/2 lot 2, 2nd con, west of Hurontario St, twp Mono; 2 ch	Dufferin 7 R.P.275
B1734	–.12.60	24.1.61	Charles Wheelock	Twp of Garafraxa	Pt lots 1 and 2, con E, and pt lot 1, con F, twp Garafraxa; rd allowance btwn cons D and E, btwn Main St and rd allowance Wellington/Peel cos, Credit R, Presbyterian church; 3 ch	Dufferin 7 R.P.138
B1735	–.10.61	2.9.68	Charles J. Wheelock	William McMaster	Subdivision of lot 10, block 5, twp Garafraxa; Water St to Main St, brick store; 50 links	Dufferin 7 R.P.173

	Date of Survey	Date of Regist.	Surveyor	Owner	Description and Notes	Location
	ORCHARD					
B1736	1.1.59	6.5.62	William R. Rombough	John Orchard	'Orchardville,' subdivision of pt of 2nd and 3rd division of lot 13, 1st con, twp Egremont; lots on Garafraxa Rd, John and Thomas sts, fairground; 1 ch	Grey 17 R.P.120
	ORFORD TWP					
B1737	8.1.66	22.2.66	Unwin & Dyas	Charles Bennett	For description see **1015**	Kent 24 R.P.169
B1738	30.1.66	–.6.66	Unwin & Dyas	Messrs Fletcher & Black	Pt 'Grant Farm,' lot 25, con XIV, twp Orford; relief; 4 ch	Kent 24 R.P.168
B1739	24.3.66	5.7.66	Samuel Brodie	Messrs Behn & Prince	Lot 22, con XV, twp Orford; relief, inset location map, owners; 3 ch	Kent 24 R.P.166
B1740	4.4.66	31.1.67	Thomas W. Dyas	Messrs Lester et al.	'McQueen Farm' and pt 'Bennett Farm,' lot 25 and pt lot 24, 15th con, twp Orford; 4 ch	Kent 24 R.P.174
B1741	23.6.66	10.11.66	Unwin, Dyas & Forneri	William McMillan	Subdivision of lot 21, con XV, twp Orford; 4 ch	Kent 24 R.P.172
B1742	5.11.66	14.11.66	C.C. Forneri	Leonard B. Vough	'Johnstone Farm,' lot 26, con XV, twp Orford; 4 ch	Kent 24 R.P.173
	ORILLIA					
B1743	29.12.55	5.11.55	Dennis & Boulton	Messrs Skelton & Patton	Area west of St Andrews St and south of Mill Rd; 2 ch	Simcoe 51 R.P.35
B1744	1.10.56	2.10.56	Henry Creswicke	James Dalls	Park lots pt W1/2 lot 9, 4th con, twp S Orillia; 3 ch	Simcoe 51 R.P.46
B1745	–.–.57	24.4.57	Henry Creswicke	Allan Gardener	Lot 9, 5th con, twp S Orillia; King St to Mississaga St, West St to lake, some lots; originally surveyed by Messrs Scott & McLean, resurveyed by Creswicke; 3 ch	Simcoe 51 R.P.58
B1746	–.3.58	–	W. Sanders	Gerald Alley	E1/2 lot 9, 4th con, twp Orillia; area SW of Chemong St and north of Barrie and Oro sts, owners, burying ground reserve; 2 ch	Simcoe 51 R.P.63

	ORLEANS					
B1747	–.–.58	9.9.58	W. McConnell	College of Bytown	'St. Joseph,' lots 1 and 2, con 1, twp Gloucester; lots on St Joseph and Ottawa sts, Cumberland St to St Anne St, bldgs; 2 ch	Ottawa-Carleton 5 R.P.8GL
B1748	9.6.59	14.5.59	H.O. Wood	François Dupuis	'St. Joseph,' lot 3, con 1, twp Gloucester; Scott St to Ottawa St, Dupuis St to St John St, bldgs; 2 ch	Ottawa-Carleton 5 R.P.10GL
	ORONO					
B1749	21.2.65	–	C.G. Hanning	Denison Douglas, Eldad Johns, Joseph Tucker, et al.	Two plans; lots and streets from con line to gravel rd, lots on Main, Church, Mill sts, mill pond, river, bldgs; 3 ch	Newcastle 10 R.P.Orono Plan (Clarke Twp)
	ORWELL					
B1750	26.7.52	13.8.52	Jesse P. Ball	Edward C. Beckett & Daniel Graves	'Temperanceville,' lot 74 south of Talbot Rd E, twp Malahide; Talbot Rd south to Main St, Mill, Church, and Cross sts; 2 ch	Elgin 11 R.P.15A (Middlesex)
B1751	17.11.54	7.8.55	Jesse P. Ball	John Tuttle	'Temperanceville,' south pt lot 73 north of Talbot Rd E, twp Yarmouth; South St to west limit of lot 73, Talbot Rd past John St; 2 ch	Elgin 11 R.P.2431
	OSCEOLA					
B1752	–.5.57	25.7.59	James Lyons	A. McLaren	Fitzpatrick St to Division St, Pembroke Ave to beyond Mill St, mills, mill ponds, church reserve; 3 ch	Renfrew 49 R.P.14
	OSHAWA					
B1753	31.12.53	2.4.55	John Shier	Charles Arkland	King St to Maple St, Simcoe St to Celina St; 2 ch	Durham 40 R.P.H-50005 (Oshawa)
B1754	10.10.54	2.4.55	John Shier	J.B. Warren	Front lots 11 and 12, 2nd con, twp Whitby; Mechanics St to Simcoe St, King St to Brock St, mill race, Methodist burying ground; 2 ch	Durham 40 R.P.H-50002 (Oshawa)
B1755	5.3.55	2.4.55	John Shier	Mr McGrigor	Lot 11, 1st con, twp Whitby; McGrigor St to King St, Simcoe St to Centre St; 2 ch	Durham 40 R.P.H-50004 (Oshawa)

	Date of Survey	Date of Regist.	Surveyor	Owner	Description and Notes	Location
B1756	–.–.55	2.4.55	John Shier	William Kerr	SW pt lot 10, 2nd con, twp Whitby; King and Simcoe sts; 2 ch	Durham 40 R.P.H-50003 (Oshawa)
B1757	30.4.55	4.5.55	John Shier	Edward Arkland	SW pt lot 10, 1st con, twp Whitby; Base Line Rd north to Jackson Ave, Simcoe St to Peto St; 1 ch	Durham 40 R.P.H-50006 (Oshawa)
B1758	–.–.61	4.3.61	John Shier	J.B. Warren	Amended plan lots 11 and 12, 2nd con, twp Whitby; lots coloured are amended from **B1754**; 2 ch	Durham 40 R.P.H-50007 (Oshawa)
B1759	–.6.62	19.12.62	W.E. Yarnold	Municipality of East Whitby	'Harmony,' 1st and 2nd cons, twp E Whitby; intersection of King and Queen sts; 4 ch	Durham 40 R.P.H-50000 (Oshawa)
B1760	1.8.64	6.9.65	John Shier	John B. Warren	Lot 11, 2nd con, twp Whitby; Brock St to Louisa St west of Simcoe St; 2 ch	Durham 40 R.P.H-50010 (Oshawa)
B1761	22.8.64	9.11.64	John Shier	Samuel Hall	Lot 10, 2nd con, twp Whitby; btwn Bond and Colborne sts at rd allowance btwn lots 10 and 11; 3 ch	Durham 40 R.P.H-50008 (Oshawa)
B1762	6.6.65	14.6.65	John Shier	Thomas Conant	West side lot 10, BF con, twp E Whitby; Cedardale Pond to Norquon Rd; 2 ch	Durham 40 R.P.H-50009 (Oshawa)
B1763	–	7.4.66	Unwin & Jack	J.W. Gamble	For description see **1719**	Durham 40 R.P.H-50001 (Oshawa)
B1764	13.4.66	14.5.66	John Shier	Samuel Hall	Pt lot 10, 2nd con, twp Whitby; Colborne St to Elgin St, Simcoe St E; 2 ch	Durham 40 R.P.H-50011 (Oshawa)
B1765	29.6.67	13.7.67	John Shier	Thomas Conant	Lot 10, BF con, twp E Whitby; road to Oshawa harbour to Station St; 2 ch	Durham 40 R.P.H-50012 (Oshawa)
B1766	13.7.67	27.7.67	John Shier	William Kerr	Lot 10, 2nd con, twp Whitby; Bond St to Colborne St, Simcoe St to Ontario St and beyond; 2 ch	Durham 40 R.P.H-50013 (Oshawa)

B1767	5.10.67	9.10.67	John Shier	James Gibbons	Subdivision of park lots 9, 10, 11, and lots 11 and 12, fronting west side Church St on 'Warren's Plan'; Brock St at Church St; 2 ch	Durham 40 R.P.H-50014 (Oshawa)
B1768	14.10.67	13.12.67	John Shier	John McGrigor	Town and park lots on pt lot 11, 1st con, and lots 1–3 and Block P on 'McGrigor's Plan'; Monck St to Simcoe St, Lloyd St to Elm St, creek and mill race; 2 ch	Durham 40 R.P.H-50015
B1769	30.10.67	19.2.68	John Shier	R.G. McGrigor	Pt lot 11, 1st con, twp Whitby; mill pond to Simcoe St, Royal St to Hall St; 2 ch	Durham 40 R.P.H-50016
	OTONABEE TWP					
B1770	2.12.52	8.1.55	John Reid	Mr Orde	Park lots west pt lot 26, 11th con, twp Otonabee; Rice Lake Rd; 3 ch	Peterborough 45 R.P.Otonabee 2
B1771	18.7.60	5.11.60	John Reid	Estate of Charles Anderson	Bldgs shown, Otonabee R at Rice Lake; 4 ch	Peterborough 45 R.P.Otonabee 3
B1772	–.–.63	1.12.63	Theodore Clementi	W.C. Downer	Pt lot 26, con 13, twp Otonabee; 2 ch	Peterborough 45 R.P.Otonabee 4
	OTTAWA					
B1773	23.8.45	–	Donald Kennedy	John LeBreton	Lot 40, con A, twp Nepean; 1st con Ottawa; Front to Montreal and Amelia sts, Broad St to Rideau Front, owners, relief; transcript; 125 links	Ottawa-Carleton 5 R.P.2
B1774	29.3.55	27.6.61	Donald Kennedy, William Wagner	Estate of Hon. Thomas Mackay	'New Edinburgh,' pt lot 3, Gore of Gloucester; Perth St to Ottawa St, Rideau R to McKay St; 2 ch	Ottawa-Carleton 5 R.P.15NE
B1775	–.4.56	11.12.65	James Slater	R.C. Diocese of Ottawa	Subdivision of villa lot A on Water St and on south side Cathcart St and on east side King St and subdivision of villa lots 1–3 on north side Park St; lots on King, Water, and Park sts by Rideau R; 1 ch	Ottawa-Carleton 4 R.P.1223
B1776	28.4.57	4.5.57	John Booth, Robert Bell	Louis J. Besserer	Resurvey of pt 1st con, twp Nepean, fronting on Ottawa R, resurveyed lines and posts; scale n.g.	Ottawa-Carleton 5 R.P.6
B1777	17.6.57	4.2.58	John A. Snow	James Rochester	Lot 39, 1st con, Ottawa Front, twp Nepean; Napier St to Cedar St btwn Division and Preston sts; 2.5 ch	Ottawa-Carleton 5 R.P.13

	Date of Survey	Date of Regist.	Surveyor	Owner	Description and Notes	Location
B1778	1.10.[57]	4.3.58	John Snow	George Lang	'Lang Block' subdivision of lot 7 north side Rideau St, lot 6 north side Rideau St, and lot 1 north side of King St; 40 ft	Ottawa-Carleton 5 R.P.5
B1779	–	[17.6.58?]	James D. Slater	Mr Besserer	Lot C, con D; Theodore St to Rideau St, Ottawa St to Rideau R, bldgs; transcript; 2 ch	Ottawa-Carleton 4 R.P.6
B1780	13.6.59	2.7.59	Geo. F. Austin	Hugh Torney	Continuation of 'Victoria Village'; S1/2 front lot 20 Junction Gore, twp Gloucester; Rideau St to Front St, hwy to Rideau St; 2 ch	Ottawa-Carleton 5 R.P.11GL
B1781	5.8.59	1.12.59	Robert Sparks	G.H. Preston	Subdivision of Blocks 119, 125, and 120, in lot 59, 1st con, Ottawa Front; Poplar St to Pine St, Division St to Rochester St; 66 ft	Ottawa-Carleton 5 R.P.14A
B1782	18.8.59	14.10.59	George F. Austin	Charles O'Connor	Pt lot letter B, con C, Rideau Front; Rideau Canal to Concession Rd, owners; 1 ch	Ottawa-Carleton 5 R.P.12A
B1783	–.6.60	22.1.67	George F. Austin, W.C. Thistle	Joseph Aumond	Subdivision of water lot 1, letter O; lots on Cathcart, Sussex, and Bolton sts on Ottawa R, relief, Phoenix Wharf; 30 ft	Ottawa-Carleton 5 R.P.2015
B1784	12.7.60	6.8.60	George F. Austin	Lyman Perkins	Pt lot 40, 1st con, twp Nepean; Nelson St to Division St; 30 links	Ottawa-Carleton 5 R.P.7LEB
B1785	29.8.60	2.10.60	George F. Austin	A. Main	Theodore St to Wilbrod St, King St to Chapel St, bldgs; 32 ft	Ottawa-Carleton 5 R.P.8BESS
B1786	17.9.60	23.3.61	Robert Sparks	G.F. Preston	Subdivision of Block 126 as shown in subdivision of lot 39, 1st con, Ottawa Front, twp Nepean; Division St to Rochester St, Balsam St to Pine St; 1 ch	Ottawa-Carleton 5 R.P.16ROCH
B1787	29.11.60	11.12.65	J.L. O'Hanly	Roman Catholic Corp.	'Cathedral Block,' park lots 6–8 north side Ottawa St, 6–8 south side Park St; Park St to Ottawa St, St Joseph St to Notre Dame St; 30 ft	Ottawa-Carleton 5 R.P.1222

B1788	26.9.61	28.8.62	Robert Sparks	Janet Anderson	Subdivision of N1/2 lot 36, 1st con, twp Nepean; lots on both sides Richmond Rd, owners; 2 ch	Ottawa-Carleton 5 R.P.14HT
B1789	21.11.61	17.12.61	W.R. Thistle	French Canadian Institute	Subdivision of park lot 1 and W1/2 lot 2, south side Park St, Lower Ottawa; on Park and Napoleon sts at King St; 20 ft	Ottawa-Carleton 5 R.P.9
B1790	–.12.62	21.1.63	Austin & Thistle	R.W. Scott & J. McEllhinny	Subdivision of villa lot 9 north Ottawa St and 9 and F south Park St; Rideau R to Ottawa St and Parliament St; lots on Park and Robson sts; 20 ft	Ottawa-Carleton 5 R.P.11
B1791	–.1.63	11.6.[63]	George F. Austin	Charles Chapman	Subdivision of pt park lot 52 (Col By Estate); Henry St to Frank St east of Esther St; 66 ft	Ottawa-Carleton 5 R.P.12BY
B1792	20.3.63	24.3.69	James D. Slater	Estate of N. Sparks	Lot C, con C; Nicholas St and beyond by canal basin to Con Rd B and C, Wellington St to Maria St; 2 ch	Ottawa-Carleton 5 R.P.3922
B1793	25.8.63	2.12.70	W.R. Thistle	Mrs Mary Fraser	'Fraserfield,' subdivision of east pt lot 1, con B, R Front, twp Nepean; Con B/C Rd to Dows Lake; 1st con, lot 40 to lot K, lots on Bronson, Wallace, Duncan, inset location map; 66 ft	Ottawa-Carleton 5 R.P.28SHER
B1794	–.–.64	2.5.64	Thomas C. Keefer	Thomas McKay	'New Edinburgh,' pt lots 3 and 4, Gore of Gloucester; Rideau R to Mackay St, Ottawa St to Victoria St; 2 ch	Ottawa-Carleton 5 R.P.17NE
B1795	18.5.64	27.5.69	Robert Sparks	Ralph W. Mutchmor	Subdivision of east pt lot I, con C, twp Nepean; off Rideau Canal; 2 ch	Ottawa-Carleton 5 R.P.24OE
B1796	28.5.64	4.1.65	John McLatchie	J. Salmon	Pt Block 3 on subdivision of Front 1/2 lot 36, 1st con O.F., twp Nepean; 30 ft	Ottawa-Carleton 5 R.P.16HT
B1797	18.7.64	2.10.67	George F. Austin	Hon. Judge Small	Subdivision of pt lot 40, 1st con, twp Nepean; lots on Lebreton and Sophia sts; 70 ft	Ottawa-Carleton 5 R.P.2545
B1798	16.9.64	19.3.66	Robert Sparks	Estate of John Mutchmer	Subdivision of west pt lot 1, con C, twp Nepean; Rideau Canal to Craig St, rd allowance to Centre St; 2 ch	Ottawa-Carleton 5 R.P.26085

	Date of Survey	Date of Regist.	Surveyor	Owner	Description and Notes	Location
B1799	7.12.64	19.3.66	George Austin	Thomas Fuller & John Honey	North side Richmond Rd, twp Nepean; owners, large lots; 3 ch	Ottawa-Carleton 5 R.P.20
B1800	-.-.64	22.6.66	Robert Sparks	T.G. Anderson	Subdivision of Block 1, lot 36, 1st con, twp Nepean; lots on present-day Parkdale and Anderson sts; 1 ch	Ottawa-Carleton 5 R.P.21HT
B1801	20.6.65	5.7.65	Forrest & Thistle	Messrs Featherston & Ryan	Subdivision of villa lot 5, North Ottawa St, and lot 5, South Park St; lots on continuation of Gloucester St, Ottawa to Park St; 30 ft	Ottawa-Carleton 5 R.P.887
B1802	28.7.66	29.5.67	Duncan Sinclair	Estate of Proud & Wood	Pt lot D, con D, twp Nepean, Rideau Front; Ottawa, Wilbrod, and Theodore sts; 20 ft	Ottawa-Carleton 5 R.P.2275
B1803	8.10.66	-.11.67	John A. Snow	Samuel Booth	'Rockville,' pt lot 23, 1st con, 1st range, twp Gloucester, Ottawa Front; Montreal Rd to river, George St to Carson's Rd, cultural detail, relief, trees; 1 ch	Ottawa-Carleton 5 R.P.22
B1804	8.8.67	8.8.68	Thistle & Baldwin	William Kehoe	Subdivision of pts lot D, cons C and D, twp Nepean, pt of canal reservation; canal reserve to Nicholas Rd, Theodore St to rd allowance btwn cons C and D; 50 links	Ottawa-Carleton 5 R.P.3350
B1805	14.8.67	3.4.68	Thistle & Baldwin	'By' Estate	Subdivision of pt lot D, con C, twp Nepean; Elgin St to Percy St, Biddy St to Maria St; 2 ch	Ottawa-Carleton 5 R.P.2996
B1806	2.9.67	20.5.70	George F. Austin	Mrs Jane Eccles	Pt W1/2 lot 40, 1st con, twp Nepean; lots on Bell, Lebreton, and Eccles sts; 2 ch	Ottawa-Carleton 5 R.P.4908
B1807	24.9.67	11.7.70	George F. Austin	Miss Louise Lelievre	Pt W1/2 lot 40, 1st con, twp Nepean; lots on both sides of Lebreton and Louisa sts; 132 ft	Ottawa-Carleton 5 R.P.25LEB
B1808	21.11.67	18.9.68	Duncan Sinclair	Campbell & Ross	Lot 10 'Snow's Survey,' pt subdivision of lot 39, 1st con, Ottawa Front, twp Nepean; lots on Maple St, Division St, and Concession Rd; 66 ft	Ottawa-Carleton 5 R.P.20

B1809	6.12.67	18.2.68	Duncan Sinclair	George Stirling	Subdivision of villa lot 3, south side Park St, and N1/2 of villa lot 3, north side Ottawa St; lots on Rose, Napoleon, and Park sts; 16.5 ft	Ottawa-Carleton 5 R.P.2879
	OTTERVILLE					
B1810	27.4.54	–	John A. Tidey	Bullock & Cromwell	North St to Norfolk St, Elgin St to York St; bldgs, owners, cultural detail; 3 ch	Oxford 41 R.P.43
B1811	1.8.56	[12.4.61?]	John A. Tidey	Mr Levi Walker	Park lots, lot 13, 9th con, twp Norwich; lots along James, Cherry, Mill, and Main sts, cleared land, burying ground, Friends Meeting House; 3 ch	Oxford 41 R.P.129
B1812	7.3.57	–	Walsh & Mercer	J.G. Williams	Lots on Norfolk, Brockville, Alma, Dover, and Pine sts, bldgs; 150 ft	Oxford 41 R.P.97
B1813	–.–.[57?]	–	Charles L. Beard	Gilbert Moore	For description see **1775**	Oxford 41 no R.P.#
	OWEN SOUND					
B1814	–.–.54	7.7.55	F.F. Passmore	John McNab	For description see **1783**	Grey 16 R.P.2
B1815	–.–.54	13.–.60	Archibald McNab	John Mills	Park lot 8 btwn Terrace and Charlotte sts south of Patterson St; transcript; 1 ch	Grey 16 R.P.21
B1816	25.1.55	16.2.55	Chisholm Miller	A.M. Stephens	Sydenham R to Dease and Newbury sts, bridge on Poulett St; 2 ch	Grey 16 R.P.1
B1817	15.9.55	21.9.55	C. Rankin	Charles Paynter	Park lot IX, east side West St; lots on Paynter St btwn West St and Sydenham R; transcript; 2 ch	Grey 16 R.P.4
B1818	–.–.55	[23.10.55?]	–	William Hodgson	Subdivision of lot 13, west side Murdoch St; lots on Union and Murdoch sts; transcript; 30 ft	Grey 16 R.P.7
B1819	15.12.55	11.2.56	John O. Conger	Thomas Scott	Lots 1 and 2, south side Division St and west side Scrope St; lots on Division and Scrope sts; 24 ft	Grey 16 R.P.5
B1820	–.–.56	[27.2.56?]	Archibald McNab	James R. Bradbury	Subdivision of park lot 2, 4th con, range east of Garafraxa Rd; lots on Toronto, Maitland, and Division sts; transcript; 1 ch	Grey 16 R.P.8

	Date of Survey	Date of Regist.	Surveyor	Owner	Description and Notes	Location
B1821	–.3.56	16.7.56	Archibald McNab	W.C. Boyd	Subdivision of park lots 1–3 north and 2 and 3 south of Baring St; lots on Campbell St to Eliza St, Boyd St to Gravel St; transcript; 1 ch	Grey 16 R.P.9
B1822	–.3.56	7.12.70	Archibald McNab	William A. Stephens	Subdivision of lot 12 east of Marsh St and lot 12 west of Water St; transcript; 50 links	Grey 16 R.P.26
B1823	–.6.56	24.9.56	Archibald McNab	William Beattie	Subdivision of part lot 3, 1st range west of river; lots on Beattie Ave and Poulett St; transcript; 2 ch	Grey 16 R.P.11
B1824	–.6.56	27.10.58	Archibald McNab	James Hamilton	Subdivision of pt lot 4 north of Baring St and east of Church St; lots on Elizabeth St to Baring St; 1 ch	Grey 16 R.P.19
B1825	–.7.56	5.8.56	C. Rankin	William Bradbury	Subdivision of park lot 2, 1st range west of river; lots on Regent St btwn river and Government Rd, inset location map; transcript; 100 ft	Grey 16 R.P.10
B1826	1.8.56	14.9.66	Thomas Donovan	T. Gladwin Hurd	Subdivision of park lot 10, 10th range, twp Sydenham; James to John St, William to George St; transcript; 3 ch	Grey 16 R.P.22
B1827	–.–.56	14.11.56	Archibald McNab	A.M. Stephens	Subdivision of lots 13 and 14 east of Marsh St, twp Sydenham; lots on Marsh, Russell sts; transcript; 33 ft	Grey 16 R.P.12
B1828	31.1.57	16.2.57	C. Rankin	Ezra Brown	Park lot 11, 2nd range west of river; bearings, pt sold to grammar school; 1 ch	Grey 16 R.P.13
B1829	–.–.57	14.2.57	Archibald McNab	William Miller	Subdivision of park lot 9, 2nd range west of river; lots from Front to Scott St, Union to Jackson St; transcript; 1 ch	Grey 16 R.P.17
B1830	14.5.57	14.5.57	–	John Frost	Subdivision of pt mill reserve; lots on Poulett, Albert, and Victoria sts; 1 ch	Grey 16 R.P.15
B1831	–.5.57	[4.8.57?]	Henry Strange	G.D. Fergusson & John Watt	Subdivision of lots 13–16 south of Union St; lots on Union and Brown sts; transcript; 25 ft	Grey 16 R.P.14
B1832	4.8.57	15.9.57	Henry Strange	Ferguson & Watt & Co.	Subdivision of park lots 5–7, 1st range east of Garafraxa Rd; lots on Huron, Ontario, Erie sts; 100 ft	Grey 16 R.P.16

B1833	–.–.58	6.1.80	Archibald McNab	Estate of Alexander McNab	Subdivision of park lot 11; lots on Mary Jane St; 1.5 ch	Grey 16 R.P.34
B1834	28.2.59	8.7.59	Rankin & Spry	R. Jonas Williams	Subdivision of park lot 10, 2nd range west of river; Terrace St to Scott St, Baker St to Frost St, owners; transcript; 100 ft	Grey 16 R.P.18
B1835	3.9.61	2.11.61	C. Rankin	A.R.R. Mulholland	Subdivision of lots 4–6, east side Hill St, pt of endowment of St George's Church; lots btwn Hill, Pell, and Division sts; transcript; 20 ft	Grey 16 R.P.31
B1836	20.8.62	25.8.62	Archibald McNab	John Lee	Amended plan of subdivision of pt lot 8, east side Stephens St; transcript; 26 ft	Grey 16 R.P.20
B1837	14.10.67	20.4.78	William Spry	Estate of Ezra Brown	Lots 1 and 2 east side Poulett St; transcript; 20 ft	Grey 16 R.P.30
	OXFORD MILLS					
B1838	–.11.43	6.7.54	John Burchill	Messrs Aaron Merrick & Richey Waugh	W1/2 lot 17, 5th con, twp Oxford; Quarry St south of Rideau R to Prince St, con rd to Bridge St, sawmill, grist mill, mill pond; 100 ft	Grenville 15 R.P.Oxford 4
	OXFORD N TWP					
B1839	12.2.56	[12.2.56?]	W.G. Wonham	John McNab	Lot 8, 4th con, twp N Oxford; Thames R and G.W.R. and Victoria St to rd allowance btwn cons 3 and 4, lots on both sides McNab St; 3 ch	Oxford 41 R.P.89
B1840	3.6.57	[3.6.57?]	W.G. Wonham	John McNab	Lot 8, 4th con, twp N Oxford; Thames R to Ingersoll and Thamesford Gravel Rd, O'Connell St to McNab St, streets laid out later west of James St; 3 ch	Oxford 41 R.P.94
B1841	5.6.60	[5.6.60?]	C. Carroll	Municipal Council	'McNab Estate,' lot 8, 4th con, twp N Oxford; Thames R and G.W.R. to Ingersoll and Thamesford Gravel Rd, O'Connell St to McNab St; 3 ch	Oxford 41 R.P.143
	OXLEY					
B1842	–.–.53	24.10.55	Richard Parr	Messrs Thomas Salmoni & John Ridsdale	'Oxford,' pt lot 54, twp Colchester; L Erie to Bond St, Derby St to York St, several bldgs, mill; transcript; 2 ch	Essex 12 R.P.188

	Date of Survey	Date of Regist.	Surveyor	Owner	Description and Notes	Location
	PAISLEY					
B1843	–.–.57	2.11.57	Robert Johnson	Samuel T. Rowe	Alma St to Teeswater and Saugeen R, James St to Regent St S, relief, mills; 2 ch	Bruce 3 R.P.12
B1844	–.–.57	23.12.57	Robert Gilmour	Simon Orchard	Subdivision of pt lot 6, con A, twp Elderslie, and pt park lots 1–4 on Queen St N and pt park lot 5, Queen St N, George St N, and Nelson St N; Queen St N to Saugeen R, Cambridge St to North St, mills; 2 ch	Bruce 3 R.P.13
B1845	31.5.60	5.6.60	Robert Gilmour	E.C. Dowling	Subdivision of lot 35, west side Queen St N, and pt park lots 15, Cambridge and North sts; 1 ch	Bruce 3 R.P.28
B1846	–.–.65	13.12.65	Robert Gilmour	Samuel Rowe	Subdivision of lot 25, west side Queen St S; lots on Rowe St; 30 ft	Bruce 3 R.P.39
B1847	–.–.65	27.12.65	Robert Gilmour	Samuel T. Rowe	Subdivision of lots XXXI and XXXII, west side Queen St N, being 3rd subdivision of pt of village; Teeswater to Church St, lots on Victoria St N; 1 ch	Bruce 3 R.P.40
B1848	–.–.65	30.12.65	Arthur Bristow	S. Orchard	Subdivision of pt lot XVI, con A, east side Elora and Saugeen Rd; Saugeen R to North St, Elora and Saugeen Rd to George St, owners, tannery, marshes; 1.5 ch	Bruce 3 R.P.41
B1849	–.–.65	30.12.65	Robert Gilmour	Simon Orchard	'Orchard's 2nd Subdivision'; George St N to Queen St N, Saugeen R to Orchard St; 2 ch	Bruce 3 R.P.42
	PAKENHAM					
B1850	–.8.55	22.3.56	John Robertson	Andrew Dickson	Lots on Graham and Victoria sts, Mississippi R to Dalkeith St, bldgs, cultural detail; 2 ch	Lanark 26 R.P.Pakenham 167
B1851	–.8.58	4.10.58	J.M.O. Cromwell	Andrew Dickson	Lots on Isabella St, Renfrew St, pt Jessie St, and Railway Tract; Dalkeith St to Victoria St, Brockville & Ottawa Ry to Renfrew St, bridge, dam, bldgs; 2 ch	Lanark 26 R.P.Pakenham 314

	(PALMERSTON town plot)					
B1852	14.7.56	29.7.56	Bristow, Fitzgerald & Spencer	Lennox B. Boyle	Twp of Luther; Pendarvis St to Empire St, Edinburgh St to Portland St; 2 ch	Wellington 60 no R.P.#
	PARIS					
B1853	30.9.58	23.3.59	Jesse P. Ball	Robert Rosebrugh	North pt lots 12 and 13, 1st con, twp Brantford; Dundas St to Catherine St, Grand R to Chapel St, owners; 2 ch	Brant 2 R.P.109
B1854	-.-.60	23.1.60	P. Gardner	Archibald Kerr & Charles Whittlaw	Subdivision of E1/2 lot 32, 2nd con, twp S Dumfries; lots on both sides Oak Ave, owners; 3 ch	Brant 2 R.P.67
	PARKHILL					
B1855	-.8.61	9.10.61	Alexander Davidson	William Kelly	'West-Wood,' north pt lot 6, XIX con, twp W Williams; lots along King St at Main St; 1 ch	Middlesex 33 R.P.169 Co
B1856	28.10.61	16.10.62	William McMillan	Thomas Elliot	'Westwood,' pt lot 7, 19th and 20th cons, twp Williams; lots along Peter, Front, King sts, and Prince St S and Westwood St; 2 ch	Middlesex 33 R.P.176 Co
B1857	-.4.64	13.5.64	David C. O'Keefe	Charles McKinnon	Pt north pt lot 16, con 19, twp W Williams; Queen St to Main St, south of Broadway St; 1 ch	Middlesex 33 R.P.194 Co
B1858	-.9.64	20.12.64	George McPhillips	David Reesor	Mill St to Broad St west of McGillivray St; 1 ch	Middlesex 33 R.P.200 Co
B1859	-.11.64	24.1.64	Alexander Davidson	William Hastings	Lot 5, XX con, twp W Williams; G.T.R. north to William St, east of Main St; 1.5 ch	Middlesex 33 R.P.202 Co
B1860	1.6.67	7.5.68	Alexander Davidson	Charles McKinnon	Park lots, pt lot 6, XVIII con, twp W Williams; Columbia St to Argyle St east of Queen St; 2 ch	Middlesex 33 R.P.236 Co
B1861	-.-.67	22.6.67	Alexander Davidson	William Hastings	Lot 5, XX con, twp W Williams; G.T.R. to William St, lots east of Main St to Pearl St; 1.5 ch	Middlesex 33 R.P.222 Co
B1862	-.6.67	24.9.69	S. James	Hon. David Reesor	Lots on William, Emily, and Station sts; 2 ch	Middlesex 33 R.P.261 Co
B1863	-.12.67	15.2.68	Alexander Davidson	Charles McKinnon	Pt N1/2 lot 6, XIX con, twp W Williams; Queen St to Main St, lots along John St; 1 ch	Middlesex 33 R.P.231 Co

	Date of Survey	Date of Regist.	Surveyor	Owner	Description and Notes	Location
	PEFFERLAW					
B1864	12.9.57	31.3.58	James McCallum, Jr	George Johnson	Lot 23, twp Georgina; Simcoe St to mill pond on Black R, grist and sawmill, bldgs, dam; 3 ch	York 65 R.P.237
	PELEE ISLAND					
B1865	1.11.66	9.8.69	A. Wilkinson	McCormicks et al.	Lots, marshes, owners; 20 ch	Essex 12 R.P.35
B1866	–	21.8.67	A. Wilkinson	Wm McCormick et al.	Similar to plan above (R.P.35) but different notes on lots; transcript; 20 ch	Essex 12 R.P.38
	PEMBROKE					
B1867	–.–.53	23.2.54	P.J. Robertson	Alex Moffat	Pt lot 35, Front or 2nd con; Allumette L to Renfrew St, Muskrat R to Elgin St, bldgs; 2 ch	Renfrew 49 R.P.2
B1868	–.4.55	21.12.55	J. McNaughton	John Supple	Pt lots 32–4, 2nd con, twp Pembroke; Pembroke St to Allumette L, Muskrat R to William St, grist and sawmill, timber slide; 1 ch	Renfrew 49 R.P.10
B1869	–.5.55	21.12.55	J. McNaughton	James Miller, Sr	Pt lot 16, 1st con, twp Pembroke; Berlin St to Water St on Allumette L, James St to School St, relief; 2 ch	Renfrew 49 R.P.9
B1870	–.5.55	8.–.58	J.W. McNaughton	Peter White	Pt lot 31, 2nd con, twp Pembroke; Pembroke St to Allumette L btwn Peter and Cecilia sts; 2 ch	Renfrew 49 R.P.13
B1871	–.4.56	29.3.70	James Lyons	William McAdam	'Campbelltown'; Pembroke Terrace, Mary St to Rankin St, owners, bldgs, relief; 100 ft	Renfrew 49 R.P.26
B1872	–.–.65	20.6.65	William Bell	Alexander Moffat	Lot 35, Front con, twp Pembroke; Mary St to Allumette L, Henry St to Muskrat R, grist, sawmill, and slide; 2 ch	Renfrew 49 R.P.17
B1873	–.6.65	19.9.65	William Bell	Peter White	Pt lots 30 and 31, 2nd con, twp Pembroke; Pembroke St to Allumette L, Peter St to Elizabeth St, churches, dwelling; 1.3 ch	Renfrew 49 R.P.18

B1874	18.5.67	10.6.67	William Bell	Rev John Gillie	Pt lot 29, Front con, twp Pembroke; btwn Pembroke and Ottawa Rd and Ottawa R; 1 ch	Renfrew 49 R.P.20
	PENETANGUISHENE					
B1875	–.–.65	25.9.65	J.O. Browne	Messrs N.H. Beatty & John Leys	Subdivision of E1/2 lot 115, con I, twp Tay; Dunlop St to Beatty St, Edward St to rd allowance btwn lots 115 and 116; 1.2 ft	Simcoe 51 R.P.101
	PERTH					
B1876	–.12.51	5.2.52	J.M.O. Cromwell	John G. Malloch	Pt park lots 2 and 4, NE1/2 and SE1/2 park lot 3, in SW1/2 lot 2, 2nd con, twp Drummond; lots on Mary, Isabella, Boulton, Queen, D'Arcy, Drummond, Victoria, and King sts, owners; 100 ft	Lanark 27 R.P.161
B1877	–.–.56	20.5.56	John Morris	Hon. William Morris	Lots 1 and 2, north side Craig St, and lots 1 and 2, south side Hervy St; Wilson, Craig, Gore, and Hervey sts; 40 ft	Lanark 27 R.P.141
B1878	–.10.58	1.11.58	Joseph M.O. Cromwell	Estate of Rev John H. McDonagh	Park lot 2, NE1/2 lot 1, 2nd con, twp Drummond; Leslie St to St Mary St, Wilson St to Tay R; 1 ch	Lanark 27 R.P.155
	(PERU)					
B1879	1.10.64	–	G. Brockitt Abrey	Twp of Esquesing	Pt lot 2, cons I and II; river, mill pond; 2 ch	Halton 20 no R.P.#
	PETERBOROUGH					
B1880	–.–.43	9.7.50	Richard Birdsall	Zachary Burnham	Pt lots 29 and 30, 13th con, twp Otonabee; Little L to Elizabeth St, Otonabee R to line btwn cons 12 and 13, bldgs; 2 ch	Peterborough 45 R.P.Ashb 2
B1881	25.11.52	26.11.52	John Reid	Mr Rubidge	'Rubidge's Plan,' park lot 1, 13th con, twp Monaghan; lots on Sherbrook St west of Park St; 2 ch	Peterborough 45 R.P.22
B1882	2.12.53	6.5.56	John Reid	Mr Cluxton	Park lot XII, lot 13, 13th con, twp Monaghan; along Hopkins Ave west of Park St; 2 ch	Peterborough 45 R.P.25
B1883	6.12.53	17.12.56	John Reid	P. Dennistowns	SE pt lot 16, 1st con, twp Smith; Smith St to River Rd, Otonabee R; never laid out; 1 ch	Peterborough 45 R.P.16

	Date of Survey	Date of Regist.	Surveyor	Owner	Description and Notes	Location
B1884	28.3.54	15.6.54	John Reid	Mr Perry	Park lot 20, lot 15, con 12, twp Monaghan; 2 ch	Peterborough 45 R.P.Monaghan 4Q
B1885	–.3.54	21.6.55	Edward C. Caddy	G. Boulton	Pts lots 30 and 31, con 13, twp Otonabee; Otonabee R to Armour Rd south to Warsaw St; 2 ch	Peterborough 45 R.P.S-3A Ashburnham
B1886	17.5.54	11.3.55	John Reid	Mr Dunsford	Lots 5–7 btwn Dublin and Edinburgh sts and west of George St, Dublin St to Edinburgh St, Aylmer St to George St; 1 ch	Peterborough 45 R.P.2 (30)
B1887	17.5.55	31.5.55	M. Deane	Mr Roache	Subdivision of park lot VIII, lot XIV, XIIth con, twp Monaghan; at Park St to Little L along rd allowance; 2 ch	Peterborough 45 R.P.24
B1888	–.5.55	9.6.55	Thomas Dennehy	'Woodland St Plan'	Pt N1/2 lot 12, 13th con, twp Monaghan; along Woodlands St; 1.5 ch	Peterborough 45 R.P.Monaghan 7
B1889	–.–.55	21.9.55	–	[Anglican] 'Church Warden's Plan'	Clergy lot 7 north of Murray and east of Aylmer St; Aylmer St to old burial ground, Murray St to McDonnell St; 40 ft	Peterborough 45 R.P.3 (34)
B1890	–.–.55	2.12.55	E.C. Caddy	John Langton	'Blythe Mills,' Otonabee R and mill pond at River Rd and Water St; 2 ch	Peterborough 45 R.P.14
B1891	20.2.56	20.2.56	John Reid	Henry Benson	Lots 15 and 16, 1st con, twp Smith; Water St and River Rd to George St, schedule of lots; 2 ch	Peterborough 45 R.P.15
B1892	–.3.57	10.11.57	John Reid	Stafford F. Kirkpatrick	For description see **1826**	Peterborough 45 R.P.9Q Monaghan
B1893	–.–.57	2.6.57	A. Driscoll	Rev Mark Burnham	Pt lots 29 and 30, con XIII, twp Otonabee; river to Stewart St, Douro St to Maria St, Peterboro & Cobourg Ry; 2 ch	Peterborough 45 R.P.S-4A Ashburnham
B1894	–.–.57	24.1.60	Alfred Driscoll	Rev M. Burnham	Pt lots 29 and 30, 13th con, twp Otonabee; Cobourg & Peterboro Ry and station to Concession St, Elizabeth St to Maria St; 2 ch	Peterborough 45 R.P.S-6A Ashburnham
B1895	14.12.57	3.12.60	John Reid	Mr Otty	Subdivision of lot 12, 12th con, twp Monaghan; 4 ch	Peterborough 45 R.P.11Q

B1896	–.–.59	18.8.59	George A. Stewart	Auburn Estate	Otonabee R to Douro Rd to boundary line, 'contemplated canal for mill purposes as located in 1849'; 4 ch	Peterborough 45 R.P.19 City and Ashb 5
B1897	11.10.59	12.11.59	John Reid	W. Clurton	Park lot 8, pt lot 14, 12th con, twp Monaghan; Lake St, Park St to Little L, Port Hope & Peterboro Ry; 2 ch	Peterborough 45 R.P.26
B1898	6.8.62	6.8.62	A.H. McDougall	Mr Jeffrey	Subdivision of lots 22 and 23 south of London St, lots 22 and 23 north of McDonnell St and west of George St; Park St to Gilchrist St, London St to McDonnell St; 2 ch	Peterborough 45 R.P.4
B1899	–.–.62	8.9.62	Theodore Clementi	J.J. Henthorn	Lot 1 east of George and north of Hunter St; corner George and Hunter sts; 1/5 ch	Peterborough 45 R.P.5
B1900	18.12.62	20.12.62	–	W.S. Conger, C.A. Weller	Park lot 2, lot 14, XII con, twp Monaghan; lots along Princess St btwn George and Park sts; 68 ft	Peterborough 45 R.P.27
B1901	31.3.63	31.3.63	John Reid	Mr McDonnell	Park lot 13 in lot 13, 13th con, twp Monaghan; Park St and west of town plot; 3 ch	Peterborough 45 R.P.28
B1902	–.9.63	16.2.64	Theodore Clementi	Peterborough Town Trust	Subdivision of corporation reserve; Park St to Little L, Lake St to Townsend St; 2 ch	Peterborough 45 R.P.6
B1903	1.9.64	1.9.64	Theodore Clementi	Peterborough Town Trust	Correction of R.P.6 above; marshy land at NE end George St, Townsend St; 2 ch	Peterborough 45 R.P.7 (50)
B1904	–.–.64	25.11.64	A.H. Macdougall	A. Smith	Pt lot 1, 12th con, twp Douro; River Rd east to con line; 3 ch	Peterborough 45 R.P.6 Douro
B1905	–.–.65	25.4.65	John Reid, A.H. Macdougall	Mrs J.K. Roche	Park lot 7, pt lot 14, 12th con, twp Monaghan; Park St to Little L, centre line of ry; 1.25 ch	Peterborough 45 R.P.29
B1906	–.–.66	18.6.67	Theodore Clementi	Estate of Judge Hall, Hon. John A. MacDonald	'Beavermead Property'; pt lots 26–8, cons 12 and 13, twp Otonabee; Little L and Otonabee R to E Cobourg & Peterboro Ry, bldgs; 4 ch	Peterborough 45 R.P.S-7A Ashb (Otonabee 5)
B1907	28.5.67	20.6.67	George A. Stewart	Mr Brown	Subdivision of pt lots 1, 12th and 13th cons, twp Douro; Peterboro & Chemong Ry to Douro Rd; 2 ch	Peterborough 45 R.P.30 (Ashb 8)
B1908	6.12.67	31.12.67	George A. Stewart	Samuel Dickson	'Mill Property'; along Otonabee R at Dickson's Dam btwn London and Hunter sts, Junction Ry, sawmills, cultural detail; 100 ft	Peterborough 45 R.P.8

	Date of Survey	Date of Regist.	Surveyor	Owner	Description and Notes	Location
	PETROLIA					
B1909	7.12.65	28.12.66	A. McDonell	Alfred B. Wood	Petrolia St to Mumford St, Holland St to County Rd; 66 ft	Lambton 25 R.P.Petrolia 16
B1910	9.2.66	10.2.66	A. McDonell	Messrs Chamberlain & Smiley	NW pt lot 15, 10th con, twp Enniskillen; on both sides Kintail St btwn Petrolia and Third sts; 1 ch	Lambton 25 R.P.Petrolia 2
B1911	19.2.66	24.2.66	Henry Smith	Messrs Smiley & Parson	Subdivision of pt S1/2 lot 14, con 12, twp Enniskillen; Toronto Rock Oil Co. and Maple Leaf Oil Co. lands, relief; photoreproduction; 1.5 ch	Lambton 25 R.P.Petrolia 3
B1912	24.2.66	16.6.66	A. McDonell	Warren Toley	Lot 15, 10th con, twp Enniskillen; Petrolia to 3rd St and Derby St on both sides Mutual Ave; 1 ch	Lambton 25 R.P.Petrolia 10
B1913	–.3.66	7.3.66	A. McDonell	Messrs Chamberlain & Smiley	NE1/2 lot 14, con 12, N1/2 range A and B; plan missing	Lambton 25 R.P.Petrolia 4
B1914	7.3.66	16.3.66	A. McDonell	E.H. Thompson	Subdivision of NE pt lot 15, 12th con, twp Enniskillen; photoreproduction; scale n.g.	Lambton 25 R.P.Petrolia 5 (Enniskillen 52)
B1915	9.3.66	14.3.66	A.B. Scott	Alfred Fletcher	Subdivision of E1/2 lot 13, 12th con, twp Enniskillen; 4 ch	Lambton 25 R.P.Petrolia 7 (Enniskillen 9)
B1916	10.3.66	23.3.66	A. McDonell	Hon. Donald MacDonald	N1/2 lot 14, con X, twp Enniskillen; Petrolia St to Sixth St, Bear Creek to Fourth St, relief; 2 ch	Lambton 25 R.P.Petrolia 6
B1917	–.3.66	30.4.66	A. McDonell	Crescent Petroleum Assn of New York & Canada	Oil and village lots, subdivision of lot 13, 10th con, twp Enniskillen; Bear Creek, relief, oil wells and refineries; 5 ch	Lambton 25 R.P.Petrolia 9
B1918	–.3.66	25.5.66	E.R. Jones	Messrs G.W. Woods & J.H. Eakins	Subdivision of pt lot 15, 11th con, twp Enniskillen; rd allowance btwn cons X and XI to North St; 100 ft	Lambton 25 R.P.Petrolia 8
B1919	–.3.66	13.9.66	Walter G. Bellair	Messrs Joseph Price & George Lowe Reid	S1/2 lot 14, 9th con, twp Enniskillen; 2 ch	Lambton 25 R.P.Petrolia 13

B1920	1.6.66	16.6.66	George Gibson	George Moore	E1/2 of W1/2 lot 15, 10th con, twp Enniskillen; lots on Mutual Ave, Third St, Petrolia St; 4 ch	Lambton 25 R.P.Petrolia 11
B1921	12.7.66	14.2.67	A. McDonell	William Noyes	Subdivision of pt lots 14 and 15, con XII, twp Enniskillen; 2 ch	Lambton 25 R.P.Petrolia 18
B1922	23.7.66	6.8.66	A. McDonell	George England	'McDonald's Reserve,' Petrolia St to Pearl and Third sts, England Ave to First Ave, bldgs; 1 ch	Lambton 25 R.P.Petrolia 12
B1923	6.10.66	5.11.66	A. McDonell	Michael Jeffers	W1/2 lot XII, XIth con, twp Enniskillen; lots on Petrolia St; 3 ch	Lambton 25 R.P.Petrolia 14
B1924	14.11.66	3.12.66	George Gibson	C. Brown	Subdivision of N1/2 lot 11, con 11, twp Enniskillen; drawings of oil wells and refineries; 3 ch	Lambton 25 R.P.Petrolia 15
B1925	22.1.67	14.2.67	Smith & Nicholl	Messrs Case, Fairbanks & Reid	Pt lot XIII, con XI, twp Enniskillen; G.W.R., lots on Station, Railroad, and Petrolia sts, bldgs; 40 ft	Lambton 25 R.P.Petrolia 17
B1926	23.1.67	15.6.67	Smith & Nicholl	Messrs Luce & Thomas	Pt lot XII, con X, twp Enniskillen; lots on Wingfield St south of Petrolia St and G.W.R. station; 1 ch	Lambton 25 R.P.Petrolia 23
B1927	29.1.67	15.2.67	George Gibson	Mr Winsor	SE1/4 lot 11, 11th con, twp Enniskillen; 2 ch	Lambton 25 R.P.Petrolia 19
B1928	11.4.67	16.4.67	Walter G. Bellair	George L. Reid	Subdivision of S1/2 lot 14, 10th con, twp Enniskillen; 1st Ave, north branch Durham Creek; 3 ch	Lambton 25 R.P.Petrolia 20
B1929	-.-.67	11.5.67	E.R. Jones	Hartford Oil Co.	Subdivision of pt E1/2 lot 14, 11th con, twp Enniskillen; lots on rd allowance btwn cons X and XI and btwn 2 streets, refinery grounds; 100 ft	Lambton 25 R.P.Petrolia 21
B1930	29.5.67	30.5.67	George Gibson	Andrew Elliott	Subdivision of E1/2 lot XII, XIth con, twp Enniskillen; Petrolia St to Andrew St, park lots to north, ry station to Centre St and beyond; 2 ch	Lambton 25 R.P.Petrolia 22
B1931	2.11.67	26.12.67	Passmore & Nicholl	Mr Woods	Subdivision of pt lot XIII, Xth con, twp Enniskillen; lots on Walnut St and side-road btwn lots 12 and 13, relief; 1 ch	Lambton 25 R.P.Petrolia 24

	Date of Survey	Date of Regist.	Surveyor	Owner	Description and Notes	Location
	PETWORTH					
B1932	–.6.64	5.10.64	S.O. McGuin	John Stevenson	Lot 19, 6th con, twp Portland; streets named, bldgs, owners; 2 ch	Frontenac 13 R.P.16
	PICTON					
B1933	–.–.[33?]	–	William McDonald	Rev William Macaulay	For description see **1830**	Prince Edward 47 R.P.Picton 1
B1934	–.4.42	[18.4.42?]	W. Conger	Estate of Matthew Patterson	Pt lot 2; lots on Main St, subdivided among heirs; 1 ch	Prince Edward 47 R.P.Picton 4
B1935	15.11.48	–	J.O. Conger	Messrs Davis & Yarwood	Pt lot A; Ferguson St to river; 1 ch	Prince Edward 47 R.P.Picton 5
B1936	27.12.49	14.2.50	J.O. Conger	Hon. Robert Wilkins	Pt lot A, twp Hallowell; lots on road to Wellington, Agnes, and Armden sts, owners; 1 ch	Prince Edward 47 R.P.Picton 6
B1937	–.8.50	–	J.O. Conger	Hon. John McDonald	Main St to Hill St, Water St to Division St, brewery, storehouse, wharf; 1 ch	Prince Edward 47 R.P.Picton 3
B1938	24.10.57	–.8.57	–	Mary Coleman, Catherine Ferguson	Lot A, 1st con north of Carrying Place, and pt lots 23 and 24, 3rd con, Military Tract; lots on Main and Washburn sts, East Lake Rd, Ferguson St, owners, mill pond, sawmill, bldgs; 120 ft	Prince Edward 47 R.P.Picton 2
B1939	10.11.57	10.11.57	J.O. Conger	Alexander Patterson	Pt lot 2, 1st con, twp Hallowell; King, Centre, and Paul sts, owners; 1 ch	Prince Edward 47 R.P.Picton 13
B1940	–.–.59	1.11.59	–	Phillip Low	N1/2 lot 20, 1st con, twp Hallowell, E.C.P.; lots off Main St on Phillip, Low, John, Robinson, and Maitland sts; scale n.g.	Prince Edward 47 R.P.Picton 19
B1941	–.–.5?	–	–	Miss Rebecca Washburn	Pt N1/2 lot A, twp Hallowell; lots on Washburn, Simeon, and Rebecca sts, owners; 1.25 ch	Prince Edward 47 R.P.Picton 7

B1942	10.6.61	10.6.61	J.O. Conger	J.R. Austin	Pt lot 22, 3rd con, Military Tract, twp Hallowell; Main St to Henry, Rogers, and Talbot sts; 1 ch	Prince Edward 47 R.P.Picton 8
B1943	20.6.61	–	J.O. Conger	W.T. Yarwood	Pt lot 22, 3rd con, Military Tract, twp Hallowell; lots on East Lake Rd south of Main St, owners; 4 ch	Prince Edward 47 R.P.Picton 6
B1944	17.7.61	–	J.O. Conger	John P. Roblin	Pt lot 22, 3rd con, Military Tract, twp Hallowell; lots on road north and west of East Lake Rd, owners; 4 ch	Prince Edward 47 R.P.Picton 7
B1945	9.10.61	–	J.O. Conger	Mary Ferguson, estate of Catherine Ferguson	Lots on Mary and Ferguson sts, owners as divided by will; 2 ch	Prince Edward 47 R.P.Picton 12
B1946	–.–.[61?]	9.4.72	J.O. Conger	Frederick Hare & Barbary Toby	Lots on Mary St, Ontario St, and Grove St, owners; see also plan above; 1 ch	Prince Edward 47 R.P.Picton 10
B1947	10.4.63	–	J.O. Conger	Multiple owners	Lots on East Lake Rd and Spring St, owners	Prince Edward 47 R.P.Picton 9
B1948	11.10.64	26.10.64	M. Lough	–	Subdivision W1/2 lot 2, 1st con, N.C.P., twp Hallowell; King St to con line, village lots along Paul, Centre, Elm, Princess, and Queen sts, larger lots NW, bldgs, owners, Agricultural Society; 5 ch	Prince Edward 47 R.P.Picton 14
	PILKINGTON TWP					
B1949	25.8.57	11.5.61	E.H. Kertland	Rev Arthur Palmer	For description see **1087**	Wellington 61 R.P.140
	(PIUSVILLE town plot)					
B1950	–.–.48	12.12.49	P.D. Salter	James & Elizabeth Kevill	Lot 25 north of Malden Rd; King St to Victoria St, Malden Rd to Kevill St; transcript; 4 ch	Essex 12 R.P.31
	PLANTAGENET					
B1951	9.2.58	4.2.62	W. McConnell	Peter McMartin	'Hattville,' pt lot 11, Old Survey, twp N Plantagenet; on Nation R, West St to Water St, Nation St to river, bldgs, owners, mills, Roman Catholic church, town hall; transcript; 2 ch	Prescott 46 R.P.6

	Date of Survey	Date of Regist.	Surveyor	Owner	Description and Notes	Location
	PLATTSVILLE					
B1952	10.9.51	–	James Black	Samuel Platt	Albert St to Odd St and Smiths Creek, Victoria St to Wilmot St; 2 ch	Oxford 41 R.P.57
B1953	12.10.53	–	Thomas Allchin	Thomas Shortis	Sarah St to Albert and Odd sts, Tecumseth St to Wilmot St, mills, cultural detail; 2 ch	Oxford 41 R.P.33
B1954	–.–.57	[–.–.64]	Schofield & Hobson, T. Weatherald	Samuel Platt	Albert St to Young and Odd sts, Platt St to mill pond and Smith's Creek or Nith R, cultural detail; 2 ch	Oxford 41 R.P.162
B1955	29.6.59	–	James Black	Thomas Workman	North pt lot 18, 12th con, twp Blenheim, 'Workman Block'; Workman St to Albert St, Douro St crossing Smith's Creek to Louisa St; 2 ch	Oxford 41 R.P.116
B1956	29.10.60	–	Cyrus Carroll	Blenheim Twp Corporation	Compilation plan, lots 18 and 19, 12th and 13th cons, twp Blenheim; Elizabeth St to Young St, Tecumseth St to Louisa and Platt sts; 3 ch	Oxford 41 R.P.124
	POINT EDWARD					
B1957	[29.10.64?]	5.1.65	Henry A.F. Macleod	Charles J. Brydges	'Huron'; Alexandra Ave to G.T.R. and new ordnance reserve, Sarnia station ground to Albert St, proposed Sarnia branch of G.T.R.; 2 ch	Lambton 25 R.P.Point Edward 1
	PORT ALBERT					
B1958	[29.2.56?]	12.9.56	William Perceval	William Barrett	Subdivision of park lots 5 and 6, range G east of London Rd; lots on William and Anne sts at London Rd, inset location map; 2 ch	Huron 22 R.P.137
B1959	[21.2.57?]	6.2.60	William Perceval	John Hawkins, Jr	Subdivision of park lots 6 and 7 north of Melbourne St; Melbourne St to North St, Harrison St to Drury Lane, owners; 2 ch	Huron 22 R.P.138
	PORT BOLSTER					
B1960	5.5.55	1.8.55	James McCallum, Jr	John G. Bolster	Pt lot XXX, con VIII, twp Georgina; Gardiner and King sts to L Simcoe; 1 ch	York 65 R.P.129

B1961	18.1.58	2.4.59	F.C. McCallum	George G. Green & Denis Nolan	Pt lot XXV, VIIth and VIIIth cons, twp Georgina; King St to Frederick St, Alice St to lake, owners; 3 ch	York 65 R.P.251
	(PORT BRUCE) (Bruce Co)					
B1962	8.1.56	9.[1].56	O. Bartley	George Butchart	Lots 29–33, lots A and B, con VI; streets named; 4 ch	Bruce 3 R.P.3
	PORT BRUCE (Elgin Co)					
B1963	30.10.54?	1.3.55	Jesse P. Ball	Lindley Moore et al.	Lots 4–6, 1st con, twp Malahide; L Erie to Bruce St, Victoria St to East St, lighthouse, market sq; 3 ch	Elgin 11 R.P.5
	PORT BURWELL					
B1964	–.–.[34?]	15.6.69	Mahlon Burwell	Mahlon Burwell	Waterloo St to L Erie, Strachan St to Chatham St, canal, dam, owners; notes on dates of subdivisions by L. Burwell; 186 ft	Elgin 11 no R.P.#
B1965	24.6.56	27.6.56	Jesse P. Ball	Lewis Burwell	L Erie to Bridge St to Ericus St, Chatham St to Victoria St, Otter Creek, market sq; 3 ch	Elgin 11 R.P.12
B1966	30.4.66	17.5.66	Jesse P. Ball	George Backhouse	Pt SW pt lot 13, 1st con, twp Bayham; L Erie to William St, Victoria St to Elizabeth St; 3 ch	Elgin 11 R.P.30
	PORT COLBORNE					
B1967	8.12.47	25.2.58	Andrew Hood	W.H. Merritt, Jr	Extension of west pt Port Colborne, 1st con, twp Humberstone; Welland Canal to Catherine St, north from Buffalo & L Huron Ry and Princess St; 2 ch	Niagara 59 R.P.989
B1968	–.–.53	27.1.53	Andrew Hood	William Hamilton Merritt et al.	Pt lots 27 and 28, 1st con, twp Humberstone; on both sides Welland Canal at L Erie, east to Catherine St, bldgs, proposed basin; 2 ch	Niagara 59 R.P.987
B1969	–.–.53	25.6.53	George Z.	William Hamilton Merritt	Amends R.P.987 above, pt lot 28, 1st con, twp Humberstone; King St to Catherine St, Adelaide St to Elgin St; transcript; 2 ch	Niagara 59 R.P.988
B1970	6.7.53	8.7.53	James W. Fell	Abraham Neff et al.	'Petersburg'; lots along Main St W and E and Thompson St, owners, canal; transcript; 1.35 ch	Niagara 59 R.P.762

	Date of Survey	Date of Regist.	Surveyor	Owner	Description and Notes	Location
B1971	11.12.54	16.12.54	Andrew Hood	County of Welland	Lot 27, 1st con, twp Humberstone; Fares St west to Welland Canal, L Erie to Killaly St, relief; 2 ch	Niagara 59 R.P.843
B1972	22.3.56	12.5.57	James W. Fell	John Thompson	'Petersburg,' pt lot 28, 2nd con; Thompson St to George St, Canal St to rd allowance btwn lots 28 and 29, owners; 1.35 ch	Niagara 59 R.P.763
B1973	18.5.60	27.9.60	E. & J. De Cew	Lewis G. Carter	Lot 29, 1st con, twp Humberstone; west of Elm St, lots along Ash St, owners; 2 ch	Niagara 59 R.P.844
B1974	22.12.60	15.1.61	Henry Ross, Jacob Misener	John McGillivray	'Petersburg'; lots along Welland Canal and rd allowance north of rd allowance btwn cons 1 and 2, Welland R.R. to Port Colborne; 2 ch	Niagara 59 R.P.764
B1975	–.5.63	30.12.65	John De Cew	C.H. Carter	South pt lot XXIX, 1st con, twp Humberstone; Sugarloaf St near L Erie to municipal bldg west of Elm St; 2 ch	Niagara 59 R.P.845
	PORT CREDIT					
B1976	15.5.57	15.8.57	Bristow & Fitzgerald	W.N. Rutledge	Area south of Toronto & Hamilton Ry, south of Credit R and gravel rd from Port Credit to Indian Village, church property; 75 links	Peel 43 R.P.PC3
	PORT DALHOUSIE					
B1977	–.–.51	–	–	–	L Ontario to canal and pond, harbour west to Church St; 4 ch	Niagara 30 R.P.13 Co
B1978	–.5.64	1.8.64	George Z. Rykert	Multiple owners Compiled plan?	L Ontario to canal and ry depot, harbour and canal entrance west to Church (now Johnston) St, canal bldgs; 2 ch	Niagara 30 R.P.7 Co
	PORT DOVER					
B1979	11.9.35	–	Lewis Burwell	–	L Erie to Union St, Clark St to Colin St, Lynn R; 4 ch	Norfolk 37 R.P.21A
B1980	–.–.46	–	Thomas Allchin	[Israel W. Powell?]	Streets; plan damaged and illegible	Norfolk 37 R.P.22A

B1981	–.–.56	–	Walsh & Mercer	–	L Erie to Pattersons Creek, Alma St to Inkerman St, swampy grounds; 2.5 ch	Norfolk 37 R.P.23A
	PORT ELGIN					
B1982	2.3.57	22.8.57	Kertland & Sproat	Messrs Stafford, Shantz, Hilker, Bricker & Seffert	Catherine St to Elizabeth St, L Huron to Lehnen St, public reserves; 3 ch	Bruce 3 R.P.11
B1983	4.2.67	14.3.67	A. Sproat	Benjamin Shantz	Subdivision of farm lot 11, con IX, and lots 11–13, con VIII, twp Saugeen; mill creek; 4 ch	Bruce 3 R.P.47
	PORT ELMSLEY					
B1984	–.4.54	10.7.62	Joseph M.O. Cromwell	H.N. Sherwood	Front pts lots 12 and 13, 7th con, twp N Elmsley; lots on Sherwood, Perth, Sykes, Shaw, and Mill sts on an island, mills, dams, rapids, bldgs; 2 ch	Lanark 27 R.P.289
	(PORT HEAD town plot)					
B1985	–.–.56	20.9.56	John Denison	Capt D. Rowan	Lots XXXI–XXXV, con A on L Huron; south Harbour St to Rowan St, Queen St to King St; 3 ch	Bruce 3 R.P.5
	PORT HOPE					
B1986	–.–.37	–	J. Huston	'Shaw & Armour Old Plan'	Walton St to Kings St and Shaw Lane, bldgs, owners; replaced by **B1986**; 40 ft	Port Hope 9 R.P.PH13
B1987	22.11.44	13.12.44	John K. Roche	Messrs Waddell & Gilmour	Btwn Walton and Peter sts and Queen and Mill sts, mills, bridge; 65 ft	Port Hope 9 R.P.PH14
B1988	–.–.47	1.9.47	–	Messrs Shaw & Armour	Subdivision of lot 18; Mill St to King St, Shaw St to Ward St, owners, drawings of 6 houses on lots; replaces **B1988**; 30 ft	Port Hope 9 R.P.PH8
B1989	20.12.47	–	John K. Roche	Mr Fraser	Pt lots 56, 70, and 71; Walton St to Cavan St, bldgs; 16 ft	Port Hope 9 R.P.PH12
B1990	1.11.48	6.11.48	David Drope	Dennis Riorden	Margaret, Ellen, Riordan, and Caroline sts, owners; 93 ft	Port Hope 9 R.P.PH3
B1991	–.–.49	2.11.50	John K. Roche	Estate of John D. Smith	North to con line at Walker and Ashford sts, rd allowance btwn lots 4 and 5 to Choate St, streets named; transcript; 3 ch	Port Hope 9 R.P.Smith Plan

	Date of Survey	Date of Regist.	Surveyor	Owner	Description and Notes	Location
B1992	3.8.50	–	John K. Roche	–	Subdivision of town lot 55; lots on John St, bldgs; 50 links	Port Hope 9 R.P.PH19
B1993	20.3.52	27.3.52	John K. Roche	University of Toronto	Lot 4, 1st and BF cons, twp Hope; Peter St to Molson St, Hope St to Nelson St; transcript; 2 ch	Port Hope 9 R.P.PH11
B1994	–.–.52	2.11.52	J.K. Roche	Hon. G. Moffatt	Pt lot 17; lots on Ward St through to Harcourt St, bldgs; 50 ch	Port Hope 9 R.P.PH22
B1995	15.9.54	20.9.54	John K. Roche	John McDermott & James Walsh	Subdivision of pt park lots 74 and 75; Cavan Rd to rd allowance btwn lots VI and VII, lots on both sides Bedford St; 2 ch	Port Hope 9 R.P.PH18
B1996	8.11.54	8.11.65	John K. Roche	McDermott & Walsh	Pt lot 4, 1st con, twp Hope; Ward St to College St, Hope St to Nelson St; 2 ch	Port Hope 9 R.P.PH16
B1997	24.4.55	25.4.55	George A. Stewart	Dennis Riordan	Subdivision of pt park lot 36; Ellen to Margaret St, Martha to Hope St, owners; 80 ft	Port Hope 9 R.P.PH4
B1998	28.11.55	–.11.55	George A. Stewart	Messrs H. Meredith, J. Hagerman, R. Wallace, F. Beamish	Park lot 38; Cavan St to Sydenham St, lots on both sides Howard St, Smith's Creek; 1 ch	Port Hope 9 R.P.PH23
B1999	–	[28.11.56?]	George A. Stewart	Thomas Merritt, John Smart, Thomas Benson	Subdivision of pt park lot 66; Walton to Sherborne and Augusta sts, on both sides Thomas St; 60 ft	Port Hope 9 R.P.PH9
B2000	11.7.57	7.11.57	John K. Roche	Thomas Ridout	Subdivision of lot 8, BF and 1st con, twp Hope; lots on Bramley St to Park St btwn lot lines; photoreproduction; 2 ch	Port Hope 9 R.P.Ridout Plan
B2001	–.–.5?	–	John K. Roche	–	Subdivision of pt lot 33; lots on Ward and Harcourt sts and Port Hope and Rice Lake Rd; 1 ch	Port Hope 9 R.P.PH20
B2002	–.–.5?	–	–	Mr Moffat	'Protestant Hill,' pt town lot 34, 'Moffat Plan'; lots along Parcours, Lees St, and High Rd, owners, bldgs, distillery, piggery; 40 ft	Port Hope 9 R.P.PH17
B2003	6.11.58	[6.11.58?]	George A. Stewart	Estate of John Halton	Lots on Hope and Princess sts, owners; 20 ft	Port Hope 9 R.P.PH15

B2004	21.11.66	4.4.77	George A. Stewart	Estate of John Williams	Subdivision of park lot 60; Hayward St to Base Line, Smith St to Pine St, owners; 50 ft	Port Hope 9 R.P.PH10
B2005	21.11.66	4.4.77	George A. Stewart	Estate of John Williams	Subdivision of pt lot 9, 1st con; Ridout St to Jocelyn St, Victoria St to Toronto St, bldgs; photoreproduction; 150 ft	Port Hope 9 R.P.Hope 'Stewart Plan'
	PORT LAMBTON					
B2006	5.3.50	[5.3.50?]	Phillip S. Donnelly	Phillys S. Down	North pt lot F, 6th con, and south pt lot G, 7th con, twp Sombra; Front St to Hill St, John St to Moore St, owners; photoreproduction; 1 ch	Lambton 25 R.P.Sombra 2
	PORTLAND					
B2007	–.8.43	12.4.73	George Bruce	Prepared for Inspector, Registry Offices	Eastwater St to 3rd con, Campbell St to Queen St, 'lands permanently drowned by Rideau Canal Co', owners, steamboat landing; 120 ft	Leeds 28 R.P.27
	PORT NELSON					
B2008	–	–	–	–	Ontario St west about 4 streets, L Ontario to Fourth St; 2 ch	Halton 20 no R.P.#
	PORT PERRY					
B2009	–.10.45	2.1.55	John Shier	Peter Perry	'Scugog,' lot 19, 6th con, twp Reach; Water St along L Scugog west to rd allowance btwn lots 18 and 19, south of L Scugog to Cinderella St; 2 ch	Durham 40 R.P.Port Perry
B2010	24.8.49	23.2.52	John Shier	Reuben Crandell	'Borelia,' lots 17–18, 6th con, twp Reach; lots along Simcoe and Queen sts; 2 ch	Durham 40 R.P.H-50019
B2011	1.7.54	5.12.54	J.S. Dennis	John Cameron	Lot 18 and pt lot 19, 6th con, twp Reach; L Scugog to Simcoe St, Casimir St to Cotton St; 3 ch	Durham 40 R.P.H-50020
	(PORT POWELL town plot)					
B2012	10.12.53?	16.8.55	William Gibbard	[Illegible]	'Port Powell'; pier and Murray St on shore, 2 more streets, Ridout St to Bleeker St; 4 ch	Simcoe 51 R.P.33

	Date of Survey	Date of Regist.	Surveyor	Owner	Description and Notes	Location
	PORT ROBINSON					
B2013	3.9.52	11.10.52	L.J. Leslie	Board of Works	Lot 203, BF 203 and 202, twp Thorold; Chippawa R to lot 6 along Welland Canal, canal to Chippawa Creek, towing paths, old and new canals and locks; 2 ch	Niagara 59 R.P.(Thorold Twp 1)
B2014	–.–.53	10.4.61	J. Misener	Samuel Hill	Pt lot 213, twp Thorold; old canal to Main St, Hill St to Carl St; 2 ch	Niagara 59 R.P.Pt Rob 4
B2015	6.2.54	3.3.54	James W. Fell	Duncan McFarland	Pt lot 202 and BF, twp Thorold; Chippawa Creek to canal and to Margaret St, canal cut to Chippawa Creek, sawmill, owners, old and new canals, church lot; transcript; 3 ch	Niagara 59 R.P.(Thorold Twp 2)
B2016	–.11.65	30.12.65	–	Welland Canal	Canal property, lots A–G; Chippawa Creek, lots along Front St, unnamed street and old canal; 1 ch	Niagara 59 R.P.Pt Rob (Thorold Twp old 5)
	PORT RYERSE					
B2017	–.–.5?	–	–	E.P. Ryerse	Pts lots 2 and 3, BF twp Woodhouse; mill pond to Wellington and Brock sts, ravine to Cove St, mill bridge; wharves	Norfolk 37 R.P.58A
B2018	–.–.5?	–	Thomas W. Walsh	–	Ryerse land to wharves, Yonge's Creek to Wellington St; 2 ch	Norfolk 37 R.P.59A
	PORTSMOUTH					
B2019	–.6.60	10.6.62	T.W. Nash	'Richardson Block'	Pt western division of SE1/4 lot 19, 1st con, twp Kingston; north of Union St, east of Main St, bldgs, owners, limestone quarry, springs; 1 ch	Frontenac 13 R.P.17
	PORT STANLEY					
B2020	17.11.42	–	Daniel Hanvey	Divisees of Joseph Smith	Lot 16, south of Lake Rd, twp Southwold; L Erie to Lake Rd, lot 15 to Yarmouth twp, relief by shading; 2 ch	Elgin 11 no R.P.#

B2021	–	24.12.52	D. Hanvey	Estate of Joseph Smith	Lots 14–16, 2nd con north of Lake Rd, twp Southwold; Elgin St to Fingal St, Main and Talbot sts to Mill St, Kettle Creek, owners, relief; 2 ch	Elgin 11 R.P.20A
B2022	7.10.56	22.3.61	Charles L. Davies	Messrs Bostwick & Warren	Pt lot 1, 1st con, twp Yarmouth; Matilda St to Hill St west of East St; 2 ch	Elgin 11 R.P.24
	PORT UNION					
B2023	–.10.55	29.2.56	F.F. Passmore	John Pearce	Lot 35, con B, BF, twp Pickering; bounded by Scarborough Twp, G.T.R. on lakeshore, and road from Highland Creek, bldgs; 2 ch	Durham 40 R.P.(Pickering Twp)
	PRESCOTT					
B2024	17.5.49	15.6.60	James West	Estate of Hamilton Walker	North of Wood St and along Walker St, owners; 2 ch	Grenville 15 R.P.Prescott 5
B2025	–.11.54	5.12.70	James West	Ormond Jones	Wood St to Eliza St, Susan St to Ward St, owners; 50 ft	Grenville 15 R.P.Prescott 10
B2026	–.2.57	3.3.57	James West	James & H.D. Jessup	Pt of lots 2–5, 1st con, twp Augusta; St Lawrence R to Wood St, Sophia St to East St; 2 ch	Grenville 15 R.P.Prescott 2
B2027	–.6.57	23.9.57	James West	James & N.O. Jessup	St Lawrence St, lots on Laire, Josephine, Jessup, Hyde, and Clarendon sts, and on Railway Ave in area north of King St btwn St Lawrence and West sts; 2 ch	Grenville 15 R.P.Prescott 3
B2028	14.9.59	15.9.59	James West	John Reid	Lot 18, north side King St; King St at George St; 30 ft	Grenville 15 R.P.Prescott 4
B2029	15.6.60	25.10.61	James West	Estate of Hamilton Walker	Subdivision; Park St to Scott St above G.T.R., lots along Walker St; 80 ft	Grenville 15 R.P.Prescott 6
B2030	–.10.60	1.12.62	James West	H.D. Jessup	Pt lot 4, 1st con, twp Augusta; James St to Railway Ave, St Lawrence to West St; 2 ch	Grenville 15 R.P.Prescott 7
B2031	19.10.64	20.10.64	James West	H.D. Jessup	Pt W1/2 lot 4 and pt E1/2 lot 5, 1st con, twp Augusta; James St to G.T.R., St Lawrence St to Sophia St; 2 ch	Grenville 15 R.P.Prescott 8

	Date of Survey	Date of Regist.	Surveyor	Owner	Description and Notes	Location
	PRESTON					
B2032	1.8.50	[2.4.51?]	James Pollock	John Erb and later owners	Compilation; pt lots 1–3, BF 'Beasley Block,' east side Grand R, twp Waterloo; Grand R north to William St, Laurel St and mill pond SW to Hamilton St, Dover St to Bishop St, bldgs, owners, mill, mill race; 4 ch	Waterloo 67 R.P.521
B2033	1.8.50	29.4.51	James Pollock	Jacob Rose, Jr (originally John Erb)	Hamilton St to King St, John St west to mill race, old course of creek shown, owners, township hall; 1 ch	Waterloo 67 R.P.523
B2034	14.12.55	[14.5.56?]	James Pollock	George Lowe Reid	Lots near ry station; sections along Victoria Ave, Hespler St, and back to connect to Victoria Ave; also printed version without additions (see **1890**); 50 ft	Waterloo 67 R.P.526 and 526(2)
B2035	11.7.57	[11.7.57?]	James Pollock	Otto Klotz	'Klotz's Block'; ms version of R.P.528 below (printed); 2 ch	Waterloo 67 R.P.528(2)
B2036	[–.–.57?]	–	–	–	For description see **1893**	Waterloo 67 R.P.524
B2037	12.7.58	[12.7.58?]	James Pollock	John Brown	Queen St to Concession Rd, Brown St to Chestnut and Cedar sts, relief; 132 ft	Waterloo 67 R.P.531
B2038	7.8.58	[5.10.58?]	James Pollock	Joseph Erb	Preston & Berlin Ry to Speed R and Cyrus St, bldgs along Main St, owners, mill pond and mill races; 2 ch	Waterloo 67 R.P.522
B2039	–.–.59	[9.3.59?]	N. Booth, James Pollock	–	For description see **1891(2)**	Waterloo 67 R.P.520
B2040	–.4.59	11.4.59	James Pollock	George L. Reid	Queen St to con rd beyond Galt & Guelph Ry, Brown St to Union St, owners; 132 ft	Waterloo 67 R.P.527
B2041	–.–.62	2.11.63	James Pollock	Otto Klotz	Amendments to some lots and North St; from plan **B2035**; 2 ch	Waterloo 67 R.P.528(2)
B2042	28.12.66	25.1.67	James Pollock	Municipality of Preston	Grand R to Speed R and north, Cyrus St NW of Speed R to Galt & Guelph Ry and NE and beyond, list of owners (past and present); 4 ch	Waterloo 67 no R.P.#

	PRICEVILLE					
B2043	22.2.64	24.7.66	William Rombough	Mr McDonald	Lots on Artemesia St, Durham Rd, Kincardine St, and Collingwood Rd, mills, mill pond; 1.5 ch	Grey 17 R.P.11
	PRINCE ALBERT					
B2044	–.4.55	2.7.55	John Shier	A. Farewell	East pt lot 16 and north pt lot 17, 5th con, twp Reach; south of Scugog St to beyond Victoria St, Pine St to Queen St; 3 ch	Durham 40 R.P.(Port Perry) (H-50022?)
B2045	14.9.59	26.10.59	W.E. Yarnold	Estate of Andrew Laing	Lot 16, 5th con, twp Reach; west of Simcoe St, north of King St; 25 ft	Durham 40 R.P.H-50024
B2046	–.9.60	14.2.61	W.E. Yarnold	A. Farewell	Lots 16 and 17, 4th and 5th cons, twp Reach; lots along Simcoe and King sts, owners; transcript; 3 ch	Durham 40 R.P.H-50025
B2047	–.–.67	11.3.68	John Shier	A. Farewell	Amends R.P.(Port Perry); town and park lots; Scugog St south to Victoria St and beyond, Pine St to Queen St; 3 ch	Durham 40 R.P.31013 (Port Perry)
	PRINCETON					
B2048	20.7.36	–	J.P. Ball	–	Pt lot 13, 1st con, twp Blenheim; Dundas St to King St, Pine St to line btwn lots 12 and 13; 2 ch	Oxford 41 no R.P.#
B2049	27.8.51	–	William Smiley	Thomas Grinton	NE pt lot 13, 1st con, twp Blenheim; on Middle Town Line and rd allowance btwn cons 1 and 2; 1 ch	Oxford 41 R.P.20
B2050	29.9.55	–	William Smiley	C.O. Closter	NE pt lot 13, 1st con, twp Blenheim; Roper St to Palmer St, Main St to Murray St; 1.5 ch	Oxford 41 R.P.146
B2051	–.–.55	15.8.55 4.10.61	W.G. Wonham	W.A. & Mary Gissing	Elgin St to Cowan St, Middle Town Line to McQueen St, G.W.R. and depot, a few lots added as per later certification; 2 ch	Oxford 41 R.P.65
B2052	–.–.56	[–.9.56?]	W.G. Wonham	Manuel Freeman	Dundas St to G.W.R. depot, Wonham St to Middle Town Line and McQueen St, bldgs; 2 ch	Oxford 41 R.P.99
B2053	22.11.60	–	Cyrus Carroll	Township of Blenheim	Lots 12 and 13, 1st con, twp Blenheim; Dundas St to Roper St, Wonham St to McQueen and Murray sts; 3 ch	Oxford 41 R.P.151

	Date of Survey	Date of Regist.	Surveyor	Owner	Description and Notes	Location
B2054	10.10.61?	–	W.G. Wonham	Manuel Freeman	Dundas St to Victoria St, Middle Town Line east to Wonham St; cancels pt of **B2052**; 2 ch	Oxford 41 R.P.136
	PUSLINCH TWP					
B2055	24.11.56	24.3.57	Francis Kerr	Thomas C. Kerr	Subdivision of lot 8, 7th con, twp Puslinch; transcript; 4 ch	Wellington 61 R.P.74
	PUTNAM					
B2056	–.11.63	10.12.63	William McClary	Thomas Putman	'Putmanville,' pt lot IV, con B, twp N Dorchester; lots along Main, Marshall, Thames, and Malahide sts, mill pond; 2 ch	Middlesex 33 R.P.192
	QUEENSTON					
B2057	–.–.[3?]	10.5.93	–	–	King St to Front St, York St to river; 100 ft	Niagara 30 R.P.37
B2058	–.12.57	27.1.64	George Rykert	Estate of Robert Hamilton	Lots 5, 6, 41, and 52, twp Niagara; Erie & Ontario Ry, Accommodation Rd, owners, pt cleared, notes on division of land by court order 10.10.58; 4 ch	Niagara 30 R.P.16 Co
	(RACEY VALE town plot)					
B2059	10.3.66	18.4.66	A.P. Salter	James B. Racey	For description see **1911**	Kent 24 R.P.171
	RAGLAN					
B2060	–.6.62	19.12.62	W.E. Yarnold	Municipality of Raglan	Village in 8th and 9th cons, twp E Whitby; lots along Simcoe and Alma sts; 3 ch	Durham 40 R.P.H-50018
	RATHO					
B2061	–.1.66	–	William Smith	J. Williams	Villa lots on lot 6, 12th con, twp Blandford; Bank St to Buffalo & L Huron R.R. depot, Hughes St to King St; 1 ch	Oxford 41 R.P.163

	RAVENNA					
B2062	–.–.65	24.11.71	Robert F. Lynn	George Walter, Sr	NE pt lot 15, 9th con, twp Collingwood; Walter and Benton sts and rd allowances; transcript; 2 ch	Grey 61 R.P.114
	REDNERSVILLE					
B2063	4.6.36	[3.5.51?]	Willson Conger, John O. Conger	John & Owen Roblin	'Melbourne,' pt lots 75 and 76; Ameliasburgh con I; Bay St to South St, West St to East St; 1 ch	Prince Edward 47 R.P.Rednersville 'Melbourne'
B2064	–.[10.56]	22.8.67	David Williams	Municipality of Rednersville	Lots 75 and 76, 1st con, twp Ameliasburgh; Bay of Quinte to South St, East St to Redner St, Roblin's and Radner's bldgs; 2 ch	Prince Edward 47 R.P.Rednersville 1
	RENFREW					
B2065	–.6.49	29.8.54	J.S. Harper	Jonah Sadler	SE1/2 lot 11, 1st con, twp Horton; Albert St to Sadler St, Elizabeth St to creek, mill creek and 2 bridges; 2 ch	Renfrew 49 R.P.4
B2066	20.2.51?	6.3.54	J.S. Harper	Mr Plante	W1/2 lot 11, 2nd con, twp Horton; Horton St to Plante St, Renfrew Ave east to Hall Ave; 2 ch	Renfrew 49 R.P.3
B2067	16.3.54	28.7.55	J.S. Harper	Frances Hincks	Lots 13, 1st and 2nd cons, twp Horton; Bonnechere R to Bruce St, east to Bourette St, relief, mills, etc; 2 ch	Renfrew 49 R.P.8
B2068	–.2.57?	24.2.57	Duncan Sinclair	J.L. McDougall	Anne St to Lochiel St, Patrick St to Bonnechere Rd; 2 ch	Renfrew 49 R.P.11
	RENTON					
B2069	4.7.59	–	Thomas W. Walsh	–	Simcoe St to Havelock St, Queen St to Boston St; 1 ch	Norfolk 37 R.P.39A
	RICHMOND HILL					
B2070	–.9.56	–	George McPhillips	James Langstaff	Lot 48, 1st con, twp Vaughan; north of Mill St and lots on both sides Lucas St, owners; 1 ch	Toronto 64 R.P.269

	Date of Survey	Date of Regist.	Surveyor	Owner	Description and Notes	Location
B2071	–.9.57	31.3.68	George McPhillips	John Arnold	Lot 46, 1st con, twp Vaughan; west of Yonge St around Arnold St and further south; 4 ch	Toronto 64 R.P.286
	RICHWOOD					
B2072	–.–.57	[22.4.58?]	James Black	Robert Kennedy	Buffalo & L Huron R.R. to Head St and King St; 1 ch	Oxford 41 R.P.110
	RIDGETOWN					
B2073	29.4.52	1.6.67	Samuel Smith	Richard Marsh	North pt lot 9, front of 10th cons, twp Howard; Marsh St and Middle or Ridge Rd; 1 ch	Kent 24 R.P.65
B2074	[28.7.56?]	1.6.67	A.P.Salter	Henry Marsh	Lot 9, 10th con, twp Howard; Main St to David St, Marsh St to Maple (formerly Thomas) St, market-place; 1 ch	Kent 24 R.P.63
B2075	[30.12.56?]	1.6.67	A.P. Salter	J. Watson	Pt lot 9, 9th con, twp Howard; Main St to Queen St, Walnut St to Water St; 1 ch	Kent 24 R.P.64
B2076	–.–.67	1.6.67	Messrs Salter & Johnston	Ebenezer Colby et al.	Pts lots 9 and 10, 9th and 10th cons, twp Howard; Thomas St to Nelson St, Queen St to David St; 2 ch	Kent 24 R.P.62
B2077	–.–.56	30.8.67	Thomas Scane	Municipal Corporation of Ridgetown	Pt lot 9, 10th con, twp Howard; lots on William St at Erie St and btwn William and Main sts; 2 ch	Kent 24 R.P.66
	RIDGEVILLE					
B2078	31.7.53	14.3.54	Charles K. Fell	Isaac P. Willson	Lots along Con Rd, First and South sts; 1 ch	Niagara 59 R.P.693
	RIVERSDALE					
B2079	20.1.56	[–.1.57?]	E.H. Kertland	G. Cromar	Pt lots 29 and 30, 1st con, twp Greenock; Teesdale St to Christopher St, James St to Sylvan St, inset location map; 2 ch	Bruce 3 R.P.6

	ROCKFORD					
B2080	–.–.[5?]	–	–	–	Lot 21, 10th con, twp Townsend; 32 lots laid out on Durham, Main, Dundas, and Oxford sts	Norfolk 38 R.P.38A
	ROCKWOOD					
B2081	–.–.53	21.3.55	T.C. Prosser	John Harris	Pt W1/2 lot 4, 5th con, twp Eramosa; on both sides of Main St; transcript; 2 ch	Wellington 61 R.P.65
B2082	–.10.56	25.7.62	H. Strange	H. Strange	For description see **1919**	Wellington 61 R.P.150 and 64
B2083	–.–.57	14.5.57	Francis Kerr	William Horne	New Rd and Mill St; 1 ch	Wellington 61 R.P.66
	ROMNEY					
B2084	[19.10.61?]	26.10.61	Salter & Jones	Mr Williams	Lot 6, 2nd con, twp Romney; Middleton St to Talbot St, Harbour St to Lake St, Two Creeks east branch; 2 ch	Kent 24 R.P.187
	ROSEDALE					
B2085	24.11.59	6.1.59	John Burchill	Alvin Rose	'Roseville,' lot 21, 2nd con, twp Montague; Rose's Creek to Farmer St, Prince St to Rideau St, bldgs; 60 ft	Lanark 27 R.P.246
	ROSEMOUNT					
B2086	–.4.61	10.6.61	William Sanders	Hugh Morrison	SE pt lot 1, 8th con, twp Mulmur; lots along Commercial St near Victoria and Albert sts, bldgs, store, tavern; 1 ch	Dufferin 7 R.P.84
B2087	–.–.62	20.8.62	Edmund Seager	Joshua Tate	Lots south of Mulmur/Mono twp line and west of Mono/Adjala twp line; 2 ch	Dufferin 7 R.P.68
	ROSSMORE					
B2088	–.10.50	5.6.73	J.J. Haslett	–	'Wilkinsville,' pt lots 60 and 61, 1st con, twp Ameliasburgh; Ridley St to Robert St, Bay of Quinte to Charles St, bldgs, wharves; 2 ch	Prince Edward 47 R.P.Rossmore 4

	Date of Survey	Date of Regist.	Surveyor	Owner	Description and Notes	Location
	ROTHSAY					
B2089	27.11.55	26.1.57	E.H. Kertland	Messrs Allan & Geddes	For description see **1921**	Wellington 60 R.P.70
	(ROXBURGH town plot)					
B2090	5.8.56?	17.11.57	A. Bay	Robert Dickson	Lot XXX, con III, twp McKillop; lots along William, Scott, and James sts, mill pond; 45 ft	Huron 22 R.P.296
	RUSSELL					
B2091	-.-.53	[19.3.53?]	D.R. Brown	James Turnbull & wife	'Duncansville'; Castor St to Castor R, Con Rd to Duncan St, owners, bldgs, mill; 1 ch	Russell 50 R.P.Duncansville
B2092	25.10.64?	15.8.65	H.O. Wood	W.Z. Helmer	'Duncansville,' east end lot 11, con 2, twp Russell; II/III con rd to Parallel St, Castor R to Main St, bldgs, owners; 1 ch	Russell 50 R.P.Duncansville
	RUTHVEN					
B2093	29.10.60	7.4.66	A. Wilkinson	Michael Wigle	Lot 9, 2nd con, twp Gosfield; lots on Main St, Queen St, Prince, and Wigle sts; transcript; 2 ch	Essex 12 R.P.183
B2094	25.9.67	27.9.69	A. Wilkinson	Henry M. Wigle	Lot 10, 2nd con, twp Gosfield; Elgin St to Albert St, Main St to Lark St; 1 ch	Essex 12 R.P.182
	ST CATHARINES					
B2095	-.-.36	-	Robert A. Maingy	-	For description see **1922**	Niagara 30 R.P.77 City
B2096	-.-.40	-	Francis Hall	Henry Mittleberger	'Plot Grove Estate'; Lake St to James and Academy sts; 1 ch	Niagara 30 R.P.11 City
B2097	-.4.43	-	-	John Young	Academy St to Court St, St Paul St to King St; 66 ft	Niagara 30 R.P.76 City
B2098	-.4.44	10.5.71	George Rykert	Estate of Dr F.L. Converse	East side St Paul St to Welland Canal across mill race, owners; 40 ft	Niagara 30 R.P.41 City
B2099	29.6.47	29.6.49	-	Messrs William Woodruff, Daniel	'Shipman Tract'; Academy St to St Paul St, Ontario St to beyond William St;	Niagara 30 R.P.23 City

				Haynes, William Hamilton Merritt	transcript; 120 ft	
B2100	–	[14.6.52?]	–	Messrs William Woodruff, Daniel Haynes, William Hamilton Merritt	Alteration of R.P.23; pt of tract south of St Paul's St; transcript; 10 ft	Niagara 30 R.P.18 City
B2101	25.10.55	16.1.56	George Rykert	A.K. Boomer	James St to Mary St, St Paul St to Academy St, owners; 50 ft	Niagara 30 R.P.7 City
B2102	–.–.55	–	George Rykert	H. Mittleberger	Welland Ave east to Maple St, Chestnut St to Lake St, owners; 2 ch	Niagara 30 R.P.12 City
B2103	–.–.55?	–	–	A.E. Rykert	For description see **1924**	Niagara 30 no R.P.#
B2104	–	28.5.56	George Rykert	Benjamin Shenston	S1/2 lot 16, 4th con, twp Grantham; Carlton and Wood sts; 2 ch	Niagara 30 R.P.23 Co
B2105	–	[–.10.57?]	–	J.C. Rykert	For description see **1924(2)**	Niagara 30 R.P.74A City (2 sheets)
B2106	–.–.[5?]	–	–	Messrs Phelps & Merritt	Clark and James sts to intersection of Academy and Queenston sts, King's St to beyond North St; 2 ch	Niagara 30 R.P.24 City
B2107	–.3.60?	12.5.60	George Rykert	–	Pt lot 15, 4th con, twp Grantham; 2 ch	Niagara 30 R.P.22 Co
B2108	–.9.60	4.10.60	George Rykert	Mr Laurie	Pt lot 15, 3rd con, twp Grantham; Vine St to Scott St, Laurie Block; 100 ft	Niagara 30 R.P.29 Co
B2109	25.3.62	24.4.67	Edgar Berryman	James Dougan	'Dougan-Turner Plan'; Queenston St to Niagara and Church sts; 30 ft	Niagara 30 R.P.13 City
B2110	26.5.62	6.12.71	Edgar Berryman	–	Subdivision of lot 12, 5th con, twp Grantham; east of Grantham Ave; 3.75 ch	Niagara 30 R.P.32
B2111	22.9.62	19.8.65	Edgar Berryman	Messrs W.L. Copeland & Calvin Brown	'St Catharines House Property'; at Ontario St and St Paul's St; diagram altering boundary attached to plan; 30 ft	Niagara 30 R.P.33 City
B2112	30.12.63	20.12.63	Edgar Berryman & George Rykert	James Dougan	Welland Ave to Welland Ry and Wall St, Elm Ave, station; 66 ft	Niagara 30 R.P.8 City
B2113	–.–.66	26.11.66	George Rykert	J.G. Currie	'Nugent Property'; Pelham Rd, G.W.R., and St Paul St, bldgs; 50 ft	Niagara 30 R.P.34 City

	Date of Survey	Date of Regist.	Surveyor	Owner	Description and Notes	Location
B2114	–.–.66	28.11.66	George Rykert	Estate of Susan Adams	Subdivision; Welland Canal to Ontario St, lots along Yates St, owners; 1 ch	Niagara 30 R.P.3 City
B2115	–.–.[66?]	–	George Rykert	Jacob Hainer	West end of town; Parmelia St to St Paul St, G.W.R. to Macdonald St, owners; 1 ch	Niagara 30 R.P.35 City
B2116	–.–.67	2.2.67	George Rykert	Eli Gregory	Lots on Welland Ave, York St to Welland Ave and Lake St, owners; 66 ft	Niagara 30 R.P.20 City
B2117	–	1.6.67	Edward Gardiner	Calvin Brown	Pt lots XIX and XX, con VIII, twp Grantham; Lincoln Ave to Pelham turnpike rd; 2 ch	Niagara 30 R.P.24 City
B2118	–	10.7.67	George Rykert	James Taylor	Subdivision; Yates to St John St and west of Ann St; 33 ft	Niagara 30 R.P.40 City
B2119	–	12.7.67	Edward Gardiner	William Wiley	S1/2 lot XVI, Vth con, twp Grantham; Welland Ave to Russell Ave, Geneva St to Niagara St, Welland Ry, county gaol; 2 ch	Niagara 30 R.P.19 City
B2120	17.10.67?	25.11.67	George Rykert	William McGivern	East limit of town to Ida St, north of road to Niagara and Queenston; 1 ch	Niagara 30 R.P.42 City
B2121	–	23.11.67	–	John Page	W1/2 lot 15, 6th con, twp Grantham; John St west to beyond Page St, Welland Ave south to Queenston St, owners; 200 ch	Niagara 30 R.P.38 City
	ST CLEMENTS					
B2122	–.–.57	[6.2.57?]	[Schofield & Hobson]	Maslin Ruff	SW corner of line btwn lots 2 and 3 and cons 7 and 8; lots on both sides Ruff St; 2 ch	Waterloo 58 R.P.620
B2123	–	[11.8.60?]	James Pollock	John Funk	Lot 2, con VIII, twp Wellesley; St Clement St to beyond Funk St, Main St to beyond Lidy St; 3 ch	Waterloo 58 R.P.619
B2124	–.–.61	[9.10.61?]	Joseph Hobson	Joseph Freyburger, Martin Snyder	'St Clemens'; lots along Joseph and Church sts, Roman Catholic church lot; 2.5 ch	Waterloo 58 R.P.618
	ST HELENS					
B2125	21.1.57?	22.1.57	Molesworth & Weatherald	Henry Mathers	Maitland to Mary-Anne St, William to Henry St, owners, bldgs; 2 ch	Huron 22 R.P.301

B2126	–	2.5.60	Molesworth & Weatherald	William Gordon	Pt lot 18, con XI and X, and pt lot 19, con XI and X, twp Wawanosh; William to Henry St, Maitland to Mary-Anne St; 2 ch	Huron 22 R.P.300
	ST JACOBS					
B2127	19.12.54?	15.1.55	Moses Springer	Messrs John B. Bowman, Jacob C. Snyder, et al.	Princess St to Main St on both sides King St to Young St and Queen St, cultural detail; 2 ch	Waterloo 58 R.P.604
	ST JOSEPH					
B2128	–.10.56	17.3.57	John Denison	William Coe	'Lakeview,' N1/2 lot 11, W con, twp Hay, and S1/2 lot 11, E con, Lake Rd; streets, Johnston's Mill; 2.5 ch	Huron 22 R.P.283
	ST MARYS					
B2129	–	24.9.53	J.K. Clendenin	George Tracy	Lot 20, 17th con, twp Blanshard; Thames R to Wellington St at Washington and Berlin sts; 2 ch	Perth 44 R.P.204
B2130	13.2.55?	20.2.55	J.K. Clendenin	W.P. Smith	Subdivision of park lot 5 north of Queen St; Queen St to Trout Creek at Charles St; 40 ft	Perth 44 R.P.205
B2131	30.3.55?	18.4.55	J.K. Clendenin	Charles Ingersoll	Queen St to Elgin St, Salina St to Thomas St; 200 ft	Perth 44 R.P.207
B2132	[6.6.55?]	12.9.56	Messrs Beattie & Bay	Rev J.J.A. Proudfoot	S1/2 lot 15, Thames Con, twp Blanshard; Thames R to Frances St, John St to James St; 2 ch	Perth 44 R.P.212
B2133	24.8.55?	12.9.55	J.K. Clendenin	J.O. Hutton	Pt lot 23, Thames Con, twp Blanshard; Thames R to Salina St, both sides Westover St; 1 ch	Perth 44 R.P.206
B2134	3.10.55	21.7.56	J.K. Clendenin	Rev Mr Warner	Pt lot 24, Thames Con, twp Blanshard; Warner St btwn Elgin and Queen sts; 1 ch	Perth 44 R.P.211
B2135	13.2.56?	1.4.56	J.K. Clendenin	Thomas Christie	Queen St to beyond Christie St, Elizabeth St to Ingersoll St; 90 ft	Perth 44 R.P.210
B2136	16.2.56?	15.2.56	J.K. Clendenin	William Moscrip	Subdivision of park lot 1, south side Queen St, pt lot 18, 18th con, twp Blanshard; Queen St to Jones St at Brock St; 40 ft	Perth 44 R.P.209

	Date of Survey	Date of Regist.	Surveyor	Owner	Description and Notes	Location
B2137	9.9.56?	7.10.56	J.K. Clendenin	James Dunn	Lot south of Queen St on lot 24, Thames Con, twp Blanshard; Queen St to Elgin St, lots along Carroll St; 44 ft	Perth 44 R.P.213
B2138	23.10.56	8.11.58	J.K. Clendenin, Alfred Howitt	Thomas Birtch	Lot 15, Thames Con, twp Blanshard; Thames R to Queen St, lots on Birtch and Elgin sts to Queen, Raglan, and Pelissier sts; 4 ch	Perth 44 R.P.217
B2139	26.12.56?	26.1.57	J.K. Clendenin	Edward Long	'Tycharnia Block,' pt lot XIX, con XVIII, twp Blanshard; Victoria to Park St, lots btwn Thames Ave and Thames R; 40 ft	Perth 44 R.P.214
B2140	31.8.57?	3.9.57	William Drennan	William Veal Hutton	Pt lots 17 and 18, con 17, twp Blanshard; Water St to Thames St, lots on Thames and Marden sts, Victoria Bridge from end of Queen St, mill race and mills; 100 ft	Perth 44 R.P.229
B2141	20.4.58?	20.4.58	Alfred Howitt	James Ingersoll	Subdivision of lot 21, Thames Con, twp Blanshard; Queen St to Inglis St, west of Thames R to Ingersoll St; 3 ch	Perth 44 R.P.216
B2142	20.9.58?	14.10.58	Fitzgerald & Drennan	David Glass	Lot 15 and pt lots 14 and 16, con XVIII, and pt lot 16, con XVII, twp Blanshard; Alice St to G.T.R., James St to Head St, London branch of G.T.R.; 2 ch	Perth 44 R.P.215
B2143	–.1.59	–	William G. Tomkins	Andrew Forresters	Lot 16, con XVII, twp Blanshard; lots on Water St and btwn there and Thames R; 100 ft	Perth 44 R.P.220
B2144	1.2.59?	–	W.G. Tomkins	George Tracey	Pt lots 19 and 20, con XVII, twp Blanshard; lots along G.T.R. St Mary's and London branch; 2 ch	Perth 44 R.P.218
B2145	–.4.59?	3.5.59	W.G. Tomkins	George Tracey	Pt lots 19 and 20, con XVII, twp Blanshard; St Maria St to Elizabeth St, Church St to James St, bldgs, owners, G.T.R. London and St Mary's branch; 2 ch	Perth 44 R.P.219
B2146	13.12.59?	26.10.60	W.G. Tomkins	John Smith	Subdivision of park lots 2 and 3, north side Queen St, on lot 17, 18th con, and lot 2, south side Queen St, and lot 2, south side Jones St on lot 18, 18th con, twp	Perth 44 R.P.221

					Blanshard; Queen St to Elgin St, mainly west of Waterloo St; 1 ch	
B2147	–.–.[5?]	3.4.55	William Carroll	–	Lot 24, Thames Con, twp Blanshard; Queen St to Thomas St, Carroll St; 4 ch	Perth 44 R.P.208
B2148	–.–.[5?]	–	J.K. Clendenin	Lauriston Crittenden, George Tracey & James Ingersoll	Lots 19 and 20, 17th con; Front St to St Paul St, Thomas St to Charles St, mill pond and dam; 4 ch	Perth 44 R.P.203
B2149	–	27.11.60	John M. McGrigor	William Hunter	Mill race and Thames R to Water St bounded by W. Hutton's property and G.T.R.; 40 ft	Perth 44 R.P.222
B2150	22.1.61?	23.1.61	Alexander Niven	George Tracy	Lot 12 west side of Church; park at Church St, Free church; 60 ft	Perth 44 R.P.223
B2151	12.2.61?	12.3.61	W. Robinson	David Glass	Lot XV and pt lot XIV and XVI, con XVIII, and pt lot XVI, con XVII, twp Blanshard; lots along G.T.R. at Carling St, ry bldgs; 2 ch	Perth 44 R.P.224
B2152	9.8.61	12.10.61	John M. McGrigor	Thomas Birtch	Plan of Thomas St; transcript; 132 ft	Perth 44 R.P.226
B2153	–	30.8.62	J.K. Clendenin	James Ingersoll	Elgin to Widder St, Thames St to Charles St, cemetery; 3 ch	Perth 44 R.P.225
B2154	–.–.62	19.6.67	John M. McGrigor	Robert Birtch	Lot 18, 19th con, twp Blanshard; Queen St to Elgin St, lots along Cain, Jones, and Jinklin sts; 2 ch	Perth 44 R.P.228
B2155	–.–.63	26.5.65	A. Niven	John J.A. Proudfoot	S1/2 lot 15, Thames Con, twp Blanshard; lots along Emily St; 3 ch	Perth 44 R.P.227
	ST THOMAS					
B2156	–.–.2?	–	–	Messrs Rapelje & Goodhue & Lee	Area around Talbot St btwn Pleasant and Church sts according to Rapelje's and Goodhue and Lee's surveys; 2 ch	Elgin 11 no R.P.#
B2157	–.–.[5?]	–	Daniel Hanvey	–	Talbot St north to block beyond Spring St, St George St east to lot 3, IX con, cemetery, possibly the plan amended by **B2170**; 2 ch	Elgin 11 no R.P.#
B2158	14.12.53	28.12.53	Daniel Hanvey	Municipality of St Thomas	Kettle Creek to Lawrence St, gravel rd on south, relief; 2 ch	Elgin 11 R.P.1

	Date of Survey	Date of Regist.	Surveyor	Owner	Description and Notes	Location
B2159	–	[1.7.54?]	Daniel Hanvey	Messrs White, Mitchell & Southwick	For description see **1934**	Elgin 11 R.P.3
B2160	–.1.54	4.11.59	Daniel Hanvey	Benjamin Drake	Amended plan of pt lot 47, south on Talbot Rd E, known as pt lot 2, 8th con, twp Yarmouth; Prince Albert St to Talbot St, Port Stanley St to Elgin St, relief; 132 ft	Elgin 11 R.P.23
B2161	–.–.54	26.12.55	Samuel Peters	James Blackwood	Mill pond to Kettle Creek, grist mill, woollen factory, old mill, relief; 1 ch	Elgin 11 R.P.10
B2162	–.–.54	30.1.56	Samuel Peters	James Blackwood	NE corner London and Talbot rds; 50 ft	Elgin 11 R.P.11
B2163	17.8.55	29.8.65	Daniel Hanvey	William Lipsey	Pt lot 47, north on Talbot Rd E, known as lot 2, 9th con, twp Yarmouth; lots along North, St George, Davis, and First sts, Kettle Creek and ravine with marshes, owners, cemetery; 66 ft	Elgin 11 R.P.28
B2164	–.–.55	26.12.55	Samuel Peters	James Blackwood	Lots south of Talbot St, house; 1 ch	Elgin 11 R.P.9
B2165	–.9.56	23.6.57	Alfred Driscoll	E. Horton	Pt lot 4, 7th con, twp Yarmouth; lots east of London & Pt Stanley Ry along Sinclair and St Frances sts, south of con rd to Ermatinger St; 100 ft	Elgin 11 R.P.16
B2166	–.9.56	–	Daniel Hanvey	R. Luke & J. Stanton	Beech St to river, Maple St west to gravel rd; proposed line of Gt Southern Ry, relief, 2 copies; 100 ft	Elgin 11 no R.P.#
B2167	–.–.57	15.12.58	L. Burwell, D. Hanvey & S. Peters	Messrs Doyle & Wilcox	Lots 13 and 15 known as the Doyle and Wilcox lots; lots on Talbot Rd E west of Stanley St and north of Centre St; 2 ch	Elgin 11 R.P.21
B2168	–.9.56	23.12.56	T.W. Dobbie	E.W. Harris	Talbot St to Curtis St west of Pearl St; 40 ft	Elgin 11 R.P.13
B2169	–.–.56	26.2.58	S. Peters	Messrs Ross, Moore & McIntyre	West pt lot 4, 8th con, twp Yarmouth; Ross St to Port Stanley Ry, Talbot St to McIntyre St, relief; 132 ft	Elgin 11 R.P.19

B2170	–.–.57	12.6.57	Daniel Hanvey	James Thomas Curtis	Amended plan, south end lot 2, 9th con, twp Yarmouth; Talbot St to Kettle Creek east to East St, cemetery; 2 ch	Elgin 11 R.P.15
B2171	2.5.63?	2.5.63	Daniel Hanvey	E. Horton et al	Amends **B2165**, pt lot 4, 7th con, twp Yarmouth; lots along Frances St, Ermatinger St, and Sinclair St east of London & Pt Stanley Ry; 100 ft	Elgin 11 R.P.27
B2172	–.–.[60?]	–	A.G. Saunders	Multiple owners	Barwick St to road to Pt Stanley, Ross St to town line and beyond on west, relief, Kettle Creek, court-house, school, church; 400 ft	Elgin 11 no R.P.#
	ST WILLIAMS					
B2173	13.7.52	–	Thomas W. Walsh	J.B. Hutchinson	Lots mainly along Concession St or Queen St and Town Line St; 3 ch	Norfolk 37 R.P.1A
	SALEM (Hastings Co)					
B2174	–.–.54	1.2.55	William Wallbridge	James Jamieson	Lot 12, 8th con, twp Thurlow; Mill to Jamieson St, mill pond to old road and St Andrews St, mill, bldgs; 2 ch	Hastings 21 R.P.17 (2nd)
	SALEM (Wellington Co)					
B2175	18.4.56	20.2.57	E.H. Kertland	Messrs Wissler, Erb & Keith	Town line Pilkington/Nichol to above Robert St, Wissler St to Mathieson St; transcript of printed map; 2 ch	Wellington 61 R.P.75
B2176	–.3.64	11.1.65	R.M. Newman	Sem Wissler	Subdivision of pt lot 17, 11th con, twp Nichol; Elora Cemetery, Cemetery Ave; 2 ch	Wellington 61 R.P.164
	SALFORD					
B2177	–.–.52	[18d.8.52?]	W.G. Wonham	–	'Manchester,' lot XIV, 1st and 2nd cons, twp Dereham; lots along Ingersoll and Port Burwell Rd and rd allowance btwn cons 1 and 2; 1 ch	Oxford 41 R.P.30
	SANDWICH E TWP					
B2178	3.4.52	14.9.53	P.D. Salter	Trustees of African M.E. Church	Lots 142 and 143, 3rd con, twp Sandwich; size and position of original lots corrected; transcript; 10 ch	Essex 12 R.P.65

	Date of Survey	Date of Regist.	Surveyor	Owner	Description and Notes	Location
B2179	25.–.59	15.1.62	O. Bartley	Municipality of Sandwich East	Road line btwn Pellette and Lauzon lines; lots, owners, near Detroit R; transcript; 8 ch	Essex 12 R.P.59
	SARNIA					
B2180	5.10.36	–	Alexander McIntosh & John A. Wilkinson	–	River to Christina St, George St to Harris St, owners; transcript; 1 ch	Lambton 25 R.P.Sarnia 1
B2181	–.5.44	–.7.47	Alex Vidal	Messrs Laforge, Caughette, Brandymore, et al.	Subdivision of lot 16, Front Con, twp Sarnia; boundaries of various owners' lots; 2 ch	Lambton 25 R.P.Sarnia Twp (mem 8498)
B2182	–.3.47	9.7.47	A. Vidal & John O'Mara	Durand property	Three plans: (1) pts lots 22 and 23, VIIth con, and lots 65–9, Front Con; (2) pts lots 72 and 73, Front Con; (3) pt lot 74, Front Con, twp Sarnia; Durand property, 5 ch; 3.5 ch; 1 ch	Lambton 25 R.P.2A Sarnia
B2183	8.11.54?	11.11.54	P.D. Salter	Estate of Henry Jones	For description see **1946**	Lambton 25 R.P.Sarniatown 3
B2184	15.5.55	[3.6.56?]	P.D. Salter	William Taylor	'Taylor's Block'; Victoria and Taylor sts; transcript; 18.5 ft	Lambton 25 R.P.4 Sarnia
B2185	–.–.53–6	14.12.64	A. Vidal & E.R. Jones	Messrs Vidal, Salter & Farrell	St Clair R to East St, London Rd to Cromwell and Wellington sts, bldgs; transcript; 3 ch	Lambton 25 R.P.14 Sarnia
B2186	–.–.56	13.8.56	E.R. Jones	John Cameron	'Robertsville,' pt lot 21, 7th con, twp Sarnia; Lake Rd to Cameron's Plot, con rd to John St, owners; 4 ch	Lambton 25 R.P.Sarnia 114
B2187	–	31.10.56	J. Stoughton Dennis	Stewart & Schwieger	Pt lots 72 and 73, Front Con, and lot 21, 6th con, twp Sarnia; London Rd to Nelson St, Clark St to Heath St; 3 ch	Lambton 25 R.P.Sarnia 115
B2188	28.4.57	–	E.R. Jones	Messrs Drake & Scott	Subdivision of lot C, north side London Rd; London Rd to Durand St, lots on both sides Derby St; transcripts; 1 ch	Lambton 25 R.P.Sarnia 7
B2189	–.5.57	15.7.59	B. Springer	Adolphus Mahon	Park lot B (pt of Durand property) north of London Rd; Durand St to London Rd,	Lambton 25 R.P.Sarnia 8

					lots on both sides James St, inset location map; transcript; 60 ft	
B2190	–.–.57	22.12.59	P.V. Elmore	F. Davis	Pt farm lot 76, Front Con, twp Sarnia; Victoria to East St on both sides Davis St; transcript; 2 ch	Lambton 25 R.P.Sarnia 9
B2191	–.–.57	27.8.67	P.V. Elmore	Hon. M. Cameron	'Laforge Orchard'; Francis and Christina sts and Federal Lane, church, post office; 1/2 ch	Lambton 25 R.P.16
B2192	–.12.58	25.10.61	E.R. Jones	Peter Porter	Subdivision of park lots 23 and 24 north of London Rd, London Rd to Durand St, lots off Milton St; 1 ch	Lambton 25 R.P.Sarnia 11
B2193	–.1.61	30.7.61	E.R. Jones	Messrs Cameron, Copeland, Mackenzie, Leys & Belchamber	Resurvey; Lochiel to Cromwell St, Front St to Christina St; transcript; 50 ft	Lambton 25 R.P.Sarnia 10
B2194	–	22.10.62	E.R. Jones	Messrs McCord & Taylor	Maxwell St to Durand St, Christina St to Charlotte St, burial ground; transcript; 2 ch	Lambton 25 R.P.Sarnia 12
B2195	–	[5.3.63?]	E.R. Jones	Messrs Stewart, Vidal & Schwieger	Pt lots 72 and 73, Front Con, and lot 21, 6th con, twp Sarnia; 3 ch	Lambton 25 R.P.Sarnia 116
	SARNIA TWP					
B2196	–.–.62	28.5.62	Alex Davidson	Municipality of Sarnia	Bed of L Wawanosh, subdivided, rd allowances, drain; photoreproduction; 4 ch	Lambton 25 R.P.Sarnia Twp 7
	SCARBOROUGH TWP					
B2197	–.–.53	2.4.55	J.O. Browne	–	'Highland Creek,' subdivision of pt lot VII, con I, twp Scarborough; at corner of Kingston and Danforth rds, bldgs; 1 ch	Toronto 64 R.P.114
B2198	–	3.1.56	F.F. Passmore	Isaac Stoner	For description see **1956**	Toronto 64 R.P.142
B2199	–.1.57	28.8.57	George McPhillips	David Reesor	'Malvern,' lot 18, 3rd con, twp Scarborough; Scarborough St north to Adelaide St, Markham St east to Malvern St, park reserve and fairground, 'Speed the Plough Inn'; 2 ch	Toronto 64 R.P.217

	Date of Survey	Date of Regist.	Surveyor	Owner	Description and Notes	Location
B2200	25.5.66	29.5.66	Gossage & Wadsworth	A.C. Knowles & Richard Knowles	Subdivision S1/2 and NE1/4 lot 7, 2nd con, twp Scarborough; owners; 5 ch	Toronto 64 R.P.279
	SCHOMBERG					
B2201	15.1.58	20.8.60	Robert Walsh	Thomas Brown	'Brownsville,' E1/2 lots 33 and 34, 9th con, twp King; resurvey of village, lots along Main and King sts, mill pond, index of owners; 2 ch	York 65 R.P.267
	SCOTLAND					
B2202	24.2.54	21.2.56	E. Malcolm	Eliakim Malcolm	Pt west pt lot 1, 2nd con, twp Oakland; Simcoe, Church, Queen, Malcolm, and Louisa sts, reserves for schools and churches, names; also 2nd plan for lots on Brant and Whitney sts (printed); 1 ch; 4 ch	Brant 2 R.P.86 pts 1 and 2
	SEAFORTH					
B2203	26.4.56?	30.10.56	A. Bay	George Sparling	Lot XXV, 1st con, twp McKillop; Huron Rd to George St, lots on both sides William St; 6.5 ch	Huron 22 R.P.385
B2204	1.11.59?	9.7.60	William Rath	George Sparling	Lot 25, 1st con, twp McKillop; north of Huron Rd; 1 ch	Huron 22 R.P.386
B2205	6.4.63?	7.4.63	A. Bay	Edgar James	Lot XI, 1st con, twp Tuckersmith; Main St to beyond Jarvis St on both sides Buffalo & L Huron Ry; 2 ch	Huron 22 R.P.387
B2206	–.12.66	18.12.66	G. & W. McPhillips	James Beattie & Samuel Stark	Lot XXVI, 1st con, twp McKillop; Goderich St to North St, West St to Main St, school site; 2 ch	Huron 22 R.P.388
B2207	–.6.67	11.6.67	G. & W. McPhillips	E.J. Jarvis	Subdivision of Blocks C, D, and N on lot XI, 1st con, twp Tuckersmith; lots on Huron, High, and Ord sts north of ry ground; 2 ch	Huron 22 R.P.389
	SEELYS BAY					
B2208	2.9.61?	19.5.63	W. Beatty	T.H. Russell	Pt lot 4, con VII, twp Leeds; Bay St to Adelaide St, Park St to Kingston and Phillipsville macadamized rd; 2 ch	Leeds 28 R.P.5

	SELBY					
B2209	15.10.56	26.5.60	G.S. Clapp	John McKim	Lots 21 and 22, 4th con, and lot 21, 5th con, twp Richmond; lots laid out at crossroads of con rd and Napanee and Sheffield Rd; 2 ch	Lennox 29 R.P.24
B2210	11.11.57	2.1.[?]	W.R. Rombough	Joseph Thompson	Subdivision W1/2 lot 22, 5th con, twp Richmond; lots on Sheffield Rd, Church St, and con rd allowance, village and park lots; 2 ch	Lennox 29 R.P.78
	SHAKESPEARE					
B2211	5.11.53?	10.11.53	William Rath	Alexander Mitchell	Lot 20, 1st con, twp S Easthope; Huron Rd to South St, Side Rd to Tannahill St; 2.5 ch	Perth 44 R.P.331
B2212	8.11.53?	28.12.53	William Rath	Catherine Thompson	'Bellview,' pt lot 21, 1st con, twp S Easthope; Huron Rd to Catherine St, West St to Sideroad; 2.5 ch	Perth 44 R.P.332
B2213	4.2.54?	10.2.54	William Rath	Estate of Hugh Thompson	'Bellview,' pt lot 21, 1st con, twp S Easthope; Side Rd to West St, Huron St to Catherine St; 2.5 ch	Perth 44 R.P.333
B2214	–.6.55	17.7.55	Charles Davies	John Galt	SW corner of village near station; 3 ch	Perth 44 R.P.334
B2215	–.–.56	[27.4.57?]	Schofield & Hobson	John Galt	Pt lots 22 and 23, SW Shakespeare on both sides of station; 4 ch	Perth 44 no R.P.#
B2216	17.8.63	30.4.64	F.J. Chadwick	Thomas Galt	North of G.T.R. to Huron Rd, William St to West St; 3 ch	Perth 44 R.P.335
	SHANNONVILLE					
B2217	–.9.55	13.11.55	P.V. Elmore	Robert Clarke	'North Shannonville,' south pt of North Range lot 6, 1st con south of Slash Rd, twp Tyendinaga; Front St to Rear St, King St to Queen St, G.T.R.; 2 ch	Hastings 21 R.P.79
B2218	–.1.56	3.3.56	P.V. Elmore	L.A. Appleby	'Quinte,' lot 5, 1st con, twp Tyendinaga; Omar St to St Arnaud St, Station St to King St, G.T.R. station ground; 2 ch	Hastings 21 R.P.81
	SHANTY BAY					
B2219	–.–.64	20.12.65	Henry Creswicke	Edward G. O'Brien	Streets named, alterations; 2 ch	Simcoe 51 R.P.104

	Date of Survey	Date of Regist.	Surveyor	Owner	Description and Notes	Location
	(SHANTZ)					
B2220	13.6.55	–.7.55	Milton C. Schofield, Joseph Hobson	John Galt	Queen St to Reist St, Bowman St to Miller St, G.T.R. running east to west; 3 ch	Waterloo 58 R.P.572
B2221	–.–.61	24.4.61	M.C. Schofield	John Galt	Amends plan above (R.P.572); 3 ch	Waterloo 58 R.P.573
B2222	11.9.63?	15.3.64	Fred J. Chadwick	Thomas Galt	Amended plan of village; 3 ch	Waterloo 58 R.P.574
	SHERBROOKE TWP					
B2223	2.11.54?	27.6.55	Andrew Hood	Silas Hardison	'Montresser lot,' at Broad Creek; at Welland Canal, Lake Shore Rd, sawmill, bridge, lumber yard; 1 ch	Haldimand 18 R.P.3516
	(SIDDALSVILLE)					
B2224	24.12.49	25.4.50	B. Springer	John Siddall	Lots 24 and 25, 3rd con, twp Lobo; cancelled 7.4.1965, streets named, mill creek and pond, carding mill; 2 ch	Middlesex 33 R.P.4
	SIDNEY TWP					
B2225	–.1.53	15.1.53	P.V. Elmore	Elijah Ketchison	W1/2 lot 31, 2nd con, twp Sidney; Ketcheson Block; 4 ch	Hastings 21 R.P.49
B2226	–.9.56	26.11.56	P.V. Elmore	R.J. Everett	Park lots, south pt lot 38, Vth con, twp Sidney; con rd to Public Rd, lots on line btwn Sidney and Thurlow twps; 3 ch	Hastings 21 R.P.86
	SIMCOE					
B2227	–.–.56	–	–	Municipal Corporation of Simcoe	Metcalfe and Dean sts to mill pond, John St to Norfolk St, court-house sq, market sq, boundary of town amended; subdivided by T. Walsh 29.11.72; scale n.g.	Norfolk 37 R.P.27A
B2228	[–.–.5?6?]	–	T. Walsh	Messrs Wilson & Walsh	John St to Mill St; lands purchased by Woodstock & L Erie Ry Co. for depot and station; 2.5 ch	Norfolk 37 no R.P.#

	SINCLAIRVILLE					
B2229	–.11.49	6.8.68	Edmund De Cew	–	East pt lot 30 and pt lot 31, west side Welland R, 10th con, twp Binbrook; Indian line rd allowance to road X/IX con, Welland R to mill pond in lot 29, old bed of Buckhorn Creek; 2 ch	Wentworth 62 R.P.312
	SINGHAMPTON					
B2230	–.–.56	7.11.56	William Gibbard	Andrew Yuill	'Kelvin,' east pt lot 9, con A, twp Osprey; lots on Clyde, Union, Bell, Yuill, and Queen sts; 2 ch	Grey 17 R.P.261
B2231	31.12.56	26.2.63	Thomas Donovan	Cyrus R. & Josiah R. Sing	Lot 18, 12th con, twp Nottawasaga; Collingwood St to Mad R, Melancthon St to Mill St; related to **B2232**; 2 ch	Simcoe 51 R.P.92
B2232	–.–.56	4.3.63	Thomas Donovan	Cyrus R. & Josiah R. Sing	For description see **1972**	Grey 17 R.P.251
	SMITHS FALLS					
B2233	–.7.58	22.2.76	Joseph M.O. Cromwell	Estate of John Crawford	Pt lot 19, 4th con, twp Montague; Chambers St, Rideau Ave, owners; 4 ch	Lanark 27 R.P.1184
	SOMBRA					
B2234	3.4.54	–	P.D. Salter	Thomas Forsyth	Formerly 'St Louis'; St Clair R to East St, North St to King St, areas south of rd allowance btwn cons 11 and 12; transcript; 2 ch	Lambton 25 R.P.Sombra 3
	SONYA					
B2235	15.4.61	3.11.63	W.E. Yarnold	A. Farewell	Lots XXIII and XXIV, XIIIth con, twp Reach; Nonquon R to Isabella St, Coryell St to Henrietta St; 3 ch	Durham 40 R.P.H-50028
	SOPHIASBURGH TWP					
B2236	–.7.40	–	P.V. Elmore	Multiple owners	'Gore B' subdivided, owners; 10 ch	Prince Edward 47 R.P.Sophias-burgh 1

	Date of Survey	Date of Regist.	Surveyor	Owner	Description and Notes	Location
	SOUTHAMPTON					
B2237	–	7.3.57	Francis H. Lynch	J. McNab	Subdivision of park lot 8, north and south of High St; 20 ft	Bruce 3 no R.P.#
B2238	1.12.58	9.12.58	Francis H. Lynch	T. Huss	Subdivision of park lot 17, east side Anglesea St; lots on Wellington, Elm, and Beech sts; 1 ch	Bruce 3 R.P.22
B2239	29.17.58	6.2.61	Francis H. Lynch	T. Leys	Subdivision of park lot 15, Grenville St, and lots 15 and 16, west side Anglesea St; Marpeth St to Wellington St, Grenville St to Anglesea St; 1 ch	Bruce 3 R.P.30
B2240	10.6.58	[16.7.58?]	Alexander Sproat	Thomas Godfrey	Subdivision of farm lot 10, con XIV, twp Saugeen; Cayley St; 4 ch	Bruce 3 R.P.19
B2241	3.9.59	[5.9.59?]	Sproat & Hawkins	John Eastwood	Subdivision of lot 8, North High St; lots on Albert and High sts; 33 ft	Bruce 3 R.P.24
B2242	–	29.11.59	F.H. Lynch-Staunton	O. Martyn	Subdivision of park lot 18, east side Norfolk St; Norfolk to Martyn and Galway sts and off Peel St; 1 ch	Bruce 3 R.P.25
B2243	23.4.61?	6.7.61	Alexander Sproat	Messrs Godfrey, Sproat & McNabb	Subdivision of lots 9–12, North High St; lots on High, Union, Victoria, and Albert sts; 30 ft	Bruce 3 R.P.33
B2244	5.1.63?	12.1.63	A. Sproat	Patrick Hamilton	Subdivision of lots A and B, North Clarendon St; 30 ft	Bruce 3 R.P.34
B2245	14.1.63?	27.6.63	A. Sproat	Alexander Angus	Subdivision of lot 8, South High St; lots on Albert and High sts; 33 ft	Bruce 3 R.P.35
B2246	19.10.63?	7.11.63	A. Sproat	Hamilton Tennent	Subdivision of lot VI, south side High St; 2 ch	Bruce 3 R.P.37
B2247	24.8.66?	10.9.66	A. Sproat	Mr Torrance	Subdivision of lot VI, North High St; 40 ft	Bruce 3 R.P.45
	SOUTHWOLD TWP					
B2248	14.8.61	3.12.67	T.W. Dobbie	C.C. Abbott	Pt lot 45 north of Talbot Rd E, twp Southwold; Kettle Creek, lots off Port Stanley to London gravel rd, relief; 4 ch	Elgin 11 R.P.34

	SPARTA					
B2249	27.2.54?	9.10.55	Jesse P. Ball	Hiram Kepp et al.	North pt lot 21 and NW pt lot 22, 3rd con, and south pt lot 21, 4th con, twp Yarmouth; on both sides King St btwn South and North sts, owners; 2 ch	Elgin 11 R.P.7
	SPENCERVILLE					
B2250	1.3.50	21.3.50	Francis Jones	David Spencer	Lot 26, 6th con, twp Edwardsburgh; Petit Nation R to Centre St, North St to South St; 1 ch	Grenville 15 R.P.Edwardsburgh 10
B2251	–.11.54	16.4.55	William Campbell	David Spencer	Pt E1/2 lot 27, 6th con, twp Edwardsburgh; Water St to macadamized rd, Cedar St to Cherry St; 1 ch	Grenville 15 R.P.Edwardsburgh 12
	SPEYSIDE					
B2252	6.1.58	22.1.58	Henry Winter	Peter Cruikshank	Pt lots 15 and 16, 2nd con, twp Esquesing, on north and south sides Cruikshank St west of Ontario St; 2 ch	Halton 20 R.P.30
	SPRINGFIELD					
B2253	16.7.57?	11.2.58	Jesse P. Ball	Mark Hornby et al.	NE pt lot 20, 9th con, and west pt lot 21, 10th con, twp Malahide, and south pt lot 6, 12th con, twp S Dorchester; Main St, East St to Mill St, mill block; 2 ch	Elgin 11 R.P.18
	SPRINGFORD					
B2254	2.2.53	–	John A. Tidey	Dyer Willcox	Main St to Temperance St, West St to Prospect St; 2 ch	Oxford 41 R.P.32
	STAFFA					
B2255	–	27.5.56	William Rath	Isaac B. Aylsworth & Charles Tiffin	'Hibbert,' pt lots 15 and 16, 9th con, twp Hibbert; two parts of survey, streets, reserve, burial ground; 2 ch	Perth 44 R.P.312
	STANLEYVILLE					
B2256	9.7.65	11.12.65	John Morris	Michael Stanley	E1/2 lot 15, 8th con, twp N Burgess; lots on IX con line to Church and Stanley sts, Roman Catholic church, owners, town hall; 1 ch	Lanark 27 R.P.250

	Date of Survey	Date of Regist.	Surveyor	Owner	Description and Notes	Location
	STAYNER					
B2257	–	18.12.58	Henry Creswicke	John Ewart	'Nottawasaga,' lot 24, 2nd con, twp Nottawasaga; south of Sunnidale Rd and Main St, west of Phillips Rd, O.S.H.R. station ground, bldgs, mill reserve, market sq; extension of survey made by Charles Lount; 3 ch	Simcoe 51 R.P.68
B2258	–	30.3.59	Henry Creswicke	Gideon Phillips	Lot 24, 1st con, twp Nottawasaga; east of Phillips St on both sides Sunnidale St; 3 ch	Simcoe 51 R.P.71
B2259	–.–.63	14.11.65	H. Creswicke	T.A. Stayner	Resurvey of pt 'Garibaldi Town plot,' lots 24 and 25, 3rd con, twp Nottawasaga; area west of line btwn Quebec and Montreal sts, pond, bldgs; 3 ch	Simcoe 51 R.P.103
B2260	–.–.63	14.11.65	Henry Creswicke, Jr	T.A. Stayner	SE1/4 lot 25, 2nd con, twp Nottawasaga; north of Main St to creek, east of Scott St, relief; 2 ch	Simcoe 51 R.P.102
B2261	9.6.66?	12.6.66	Charles Unwin	Donald McEachern	Subdivision of lot 26 south of Main St, twp Nottawasaga; Main St to corner Oak and William sts; 60 ft	Simcoe 51 R.P.107
	STEPHEN TWP					
B2262	31.12.57	31.12.57	A. Bay	–	Deviation road through lots XX and XXI, Vth con, twp Stephen; 2 ch	Huron 22 R.P.119
	STEWARTTOWN					
B2263	–.–.46	–	Charles Kennedy	William Appelbe	[Partially obliterated], 9 lots, pt W1/2 lot ?, 8th con, twp Esquesing; 2 ch	Halton 20 R.P.52
B2264	–	[25.2.61?]	Henry Winter	Twp of Esquesing	Compilation plan of D. Stewart's and W. Appelbe's surveys; Main St south to John St and Young St, mill pond; 3 ch	Halton 20 no R.P.#
	STIRLING					
B2265	–.5.49	7.11.49	John J. Haslett	Edward Fidler	'Rawdon,' pt E1/2 lot 11, 1st con, twp Rawdon; Front St to beyond Victoria St, North St to burying ground, owners, mill dam, saw and grist mills; 1 ch	Hastings 21 R.P.59

B2266	–.12.49	8.5.50	John J. Haslett	Ebenezer Allan	Pt lot 12, 1st con, twp Rawdon; Front St to Church St, lots on both sides Allan St; 1 ch	Hastings 21 R.P.56
B2267	–.12.49	6.12.51	John J. Haslett	Joseph Green	Pt lot 12, 1st con, twp Rawdon; Front St to Church St, Marmora Rd to Annis St; 1 ch	Hastings 21 R.P.52
B2268	–.–.49	10.6.50	John J. Haslett	Henry Hawkins	'Rawdon,' north end lot 23, 9th con, twp Sidney; Front St to Rawdon Creek, Emma St to John St, bldgs; 1 ch	Hastings 21 R.P.54
B2269	–.5.50	4.6.50	P.V. Elmore	Nicholas Lake	'Rawdon,' W1/2 lot XI, con I, twp Rawdon; Front St to Rear St east and west of Emily St, bldgs; 1 ch	Hastings 21 R.P.15
B2270	–.10.52	17.2.53	John Emerson	Edward Fidler	John St to Wellington St; lots on John, Gore, Victoria, Albert, North, and Wellington sts; 1 ch	Hastings 21 R.P.37
B2271	–.–.52	28.10.52	John J. Haslett	James Ross	Lot 23, 9th con, twp Sidney; Emma St to John St, Front St to beyond Elizabeth St, park lots on both sides Henry St, inset map; 2 ch	Hastings 21 R.P.16A
B2272	–.–.53	25.7.53	John J. Haslett	T.J. Higgins	Pt lot 13, 1st con, twp Rawdon; lots on Marmora St above Front and Church sts; 1 ch	Hastings 21 R.P.42
B2273	–.9.53	22.9.53	John Emerson	Edward Fidler	North pt lot 10 and E1/2 lot 11, 1st con, twp Rawdon; park lots; 4 ch	Hastings 21 R.P.38
B2274	2.11.53?	20.11.53	John Emerson	John Canniff, Jr	Rear lot 4, 3rd con, twp Thurlow; plank rd to John St; 3 ch	Hastings 21 R.P.58
B2275	–.–.53	7.1.54	John J. Haslett	Zach Wheeler & P.R. Weaver	Pt lots 19 and 20, 9th con, twp Sidney; Weaver to Front St, Peter and James sts; 80 ft	Hastings 21 R.P.39
B2276	–.–.53	9.1.54	John J. Haslett	E. Allan	Pt lot 12, 1st con, twp Rawdon; similar to **B2266** but more lots on west side Allan St north of Church St; 1 ch	Hastings 21 R.P.57
B2277	–.–.55	21.9.55	J. Emerson	H. Greenshields	Subdivision of park lots I, XII, XIII, XIV, and XXVII; lots mainly on Wellington, Raglan, Edward to Henry sts; scale n.g.	Hastings 21 R.P.77
B2278	–.–.59	7.1.60	J.J. Haslett	James Ross	Lot 23, 9th con, twp Sidney; James St to Front St, Emma St to John St, Rawdon Creek, inset map (park lots); 2 ch	Hastings 21 R.P.95

	Date of Survey	Date of Regist.	Surveyor	Owner	Description and Notes	Location
B2279	–.1.60	24.1.60	John Emerson	Edward Fidler	North pt lot 10 and E1/2 lot 11, 1st con, twp Rawdon; Front St to beyond Matilda St, North St to beyond William St; scale n.g.	Hastings 21 R.P.96
	STOCO					
B2280	4.1.51	25.9.51	William R. Rombough	Phillip Huffman	Lot 14, 8th con, twp Hungerford by Maria R; 2 ch	Hastings 21 R.P.55
	STONEY CREEK					
B2281	15.1.35	–	William Holley	Stephen Jones	Jones St, road to Hamilton; 50 ft	Wentworth 62 R.P.192
B2282	7.5.56	[8.8.65?]	T.A. Blyth	Henry Sanders	For description see **1985**	Wentworth 62 R.P.309
	STONEY POINT					
B2283	20.11.61?	20.11.61	O. Bartley	P. Desjardins	Pt lots 8 and 9, BF con, twp Tilbury W; lots on Tecumseh St, St Joseph St to Tecumseh St, on both sides G.W.R. depot grounds, transcript; 40 ft	Essex 12 R.P.152
	STOUFFVILLE					
B2284	–.12.52	2.4.53	George McPhillips	Municipal Corporation	Compiled plan; lot 35, 9th con, twp Markham, and lot 1, 9th con, twp Whitchurch; owners, cultural detail; 4 ch	Toronto 64 R.P.51
B2285	–.10.57	25.1.58	George McPhillips	William Pringle & S.R. Wright	Lot 1, 9th con, twp Whitchurch; Main St to North St, 10th con line to West St; 4 ch	York 65 R.P.230
B2286	6.7.63	5.8.63	J.J. McKenna	S.R. Wright	Resurvey pt lot 1, 9th con, twp Whitchurch; Main St to North St, 10th con line to Stouffer St; 2 ch	York 65 R.P.3
	STRATFORD					
B2287	–	3.11.51	Joseph Kirk	W.F. McCulloch	Park lots 430–5 and pt 429; Mornington Rd to mill pond, St George St to James St; 4 ch	Perth 44 R.P.68

B2288	31.7.52?	15.9.52	Joseph G. Kirk	W.F. McCulloch	Lots btwn York and Ontario sts; Ontario St to Avon R, mills and bridge, Erie Rd to Church St; 1 ch	Perth 44 R.P.66
B2289	–	26.3.53	F.F. Passmore	William Mackenzie	St Patrick St south to unnamed street beyond Guelph St, Nelson St to beyond Niles St; 4 ch	Perth 44 R.P.53
B2290	–	26.3.53	F.F. Passmore	William Mackenzie	St Patrick St to Cambria and Guelph sts, Nelson St to beyond Niles St; 4 ch	Perth 44 R.P.55
B2291	8.4.53	15.4.53	J.O. Browne	William Mackenzie	Subdivision of park lots; Thomas St to St George St, Caledonia Rd to Britannia Rd; 80 ft	Perth 44 R.P.52
B2292	2.9.53	–	J.O. Browne	–	For description see **1991**	Perth 44 no R.P.#
B2293	19.9.54?	12.10.54	Joseph G. Kirk	Canada Company	Compilation plan; Gore St to Princess St, Front St to John St; transcript; 4 ch	Perth 44 R.P.20
B2294	–.12.54	28.2.55	Joseph G. Kirk	J.C.W. Daly	Subdivision of park lot 426; Princess St, Wellesley St west to Daly St; 1 ch	Perth 44 R.P.73
B2295	1.5.55?	2.5.55	Joseph G. Kirk	John A. McCarthy	Park lot 436; Brittania St to Princess St, Mornington Rd to Earl St; 1 ch	Perth 44 R.P.70
B2296	3.7.55?	13.7.55	John Tully	John Arnold & James Lukin Robinson	For description see **1996**	Perth 44 R.P.47
B2297	–.–.55	27.8.55	Joseph G. Kirk	Joseph G. Kirk	Lots along Waterloo St and from Brunswick to Rebecca St and creek; 1.5 ch	Perth 44 R.P.27
B2298	–.8.55	20.12.55	C.L. Davies	Mr Linton	Pt park lot 452; Gore St north to St David St, Dounie Rd to Victoria St, G.T.R.; see also plan below; 1 ch	Perth 44 R.P.25
B2299	–.8.55	–	John O'Grady	–	For description see **1995**	Perth 44 no R.P.#
B2300	–	26.10.55	Joeph G. Kirk	Messrs Kermott & Strong	'Mill Block'; Huron St along Avon R to mill pond at Court St, St Michaels St to York St; 60 ft	Perth 44 R.P.65
B2301	–.–.55	28.12.55	Joseph Kirk	Jarvis	Pt lot 45, twp N Easthope; shows extension of road, owners; 2 ch	Perth 44 R.P.78
B2302	–.–.56	16.4.56	Joseph Kirk	Jarvis	Pt lot 45, 1st con, twp N Easthope; lots north of Ontario St and side-road btwn lots 45 and 46; 2 ch	Perth 44 R.P.79

	Date of Survey	Date of Regist.	Surveyor	Owner	Description and Notes	Location
B2303	–.–.56	24.4.57	Schofield & Hobson	John Galt	Niles to Front St, Shakespeare St to Guelph St, G.T.R. and Buffalo & L Huron Ry; 1 ch	Perth 44 R.P.53
B2304	26.10.56	30.10.56	Kertland & Gilkison	G. Funck	Subdivision of park lot 450; Cambria, Nelson, Gore, and G.T.R.; 1 ch	Perth 44 R.P.83
B2305	–.–.57	24.3.57	Schofield & Hobson	George F. Granger	Subdivision of pt park lot 457 and park lot 460; Guelph St to Grange St, Niles St to Dounie Rd; 2 ch	Perth 44 R.P.75
B2306	–.5.57?	13.5.57	Joseph G. Kirk	Samuel Monteith	Erie Rd to Church St, Galt St south to G.T.R.; 1 ch	Perth 44 R.P.40
B2307	26.5.57?	1.7.57	W.G. Wonham	George Alexander	Park lot 448; Cambria St south 2 streets, Vincent St to Birmingham St; 1 ch	Perth 44 R.P.38
B2308	–.–.57	4.6.57	Joseph G. Kirk	John P. Vivian	Pt park lot 458; Brunswick St to Rebecca St, Niles St to Front St; 1 ch	Perth 44 R.P.21
B2309	–.9.57?	9.6.58	Joseph Kirk	Thomas Cawston	Subdivision of pt lot 3, 1st con, twp Downie; Huron St to Avon St, John St west 2 streets; 2 ch	Perth 44 R.P.42
B2310	–	3.10.57	–	Robinson	Subdivision of park lots 438 and 439; James St to John St, Britannia St to Princess St; later cancelled; 1 ch	Perth 44 R.P.81
B2311	9.4.59?	18.4.59	Joseph G. Kirk	Sharman	Front lot 3, 1st con, twp Ellice; Huron St to Hibernia St, John St to Huntingdon St; 2 ch	Perth 44 R.P.63
B2312	19.4.59?	23.8.59	Joseph G. Kirk	Mr McLagan	Subdivision of pt lot 47, 2nd con, twp S Easthope; south of South St, east of Dounie St, and north of road btwn cons II and III; 4 ch	Perth 44 R.P.14
B2313	–	2.5.60	Sandford Fleming	T. Lukin Robinson	Resubdivision of pt R.P.47; Front St to beyond Main St, Ontario St to G.T.R. and Buffalo, Brantford & Goderich Ry; 4 ch	Perth 44 R.P.48
B2314	25.3.61?	25.3.61	Joseph G. Kirk	Mr McLagan	Lot 47, 2nd con, twp S Easthope; south of south boundary of town and B. & L.H. Ry; 4 ch	Perth 44 R.P.15

B2315	12.4.61	20.4.61	Joseph G. Kirk	John Sharman	Subdivision of lot 3, 1st con, twp Ellice; Huron St to Hibernia St; 2 ch	Perth 44 R.P.60
B2316	9.10.61	18.10.61	Joseph Kirk	Edgar John Jarvis	Subdivision of park lot 1; north of Huron Rd and east of side-rd lots 45 and 46; 1 ch	Perth 44 R.P.80
B2317	–.2.62	[–.4.62?]	F. Kerr & M.C. Schofield	G.J. Grange, G.M. Stewart & F. Shanly	Park lots 457 and 460; Guelph St to Grange St, Dounie Rd to Niles St; 2 ch	Perth 44 R.P.76
B2318	–.7.62	12.8.63	Joseph G. Kirk	Mr Sharpe	Pt lot 3, 1st con, twp Dounie; Avon R to Avon St, west of John St, bldgs, B. & L.H. Ry; 3 ch	Perth 44 R.P.43
B2319	22.6.64	24.6.64	Joseph G. Kirk	John Holmes	Subdivision of park lot 447; St Davids St to Cambria St, St Vincent St to Birmingham St; 1 ch	Perth 44 R.P.84
B2320	30.6.65?	1.7.65	Joseph Kirk	Maurice Kylie	Pt lot 47, 1st con, twp S Easthope; B. & L.H. Ry to Street 1, Front St east to Street 2; 2 ch	Perth 44 R.P.49
B2321	8.3.66?	25.9.68	Joseph Kirk	Maurice Kylie	Subdivision of pt lot 47, 1st con, twp S Easthope; Street 1 to Street 2, Front St to Street 3, B. & L.H. Ry; 2 ch	Perth 44 R.P.50
	STRATHALLAN					
B2322	3.6.56	–	W.G.Wonham	Charles Allan	'Alma'; lots along Oxford St and Woodstock and Huron gravel rd crossed by Queen St; 1 ch	Oxford 41 R.P.74
	(STRATHALLAN town plot)					
B2323	24.12.58?	11.10.60	Edwin H. Kertland	Charles Allan	Lots 19 and 20, 16th con, twp Nichol, bldgs; 3 ch	Wellington 61 R.P.132
	STRATHROY					
B2324	–.12.53	3.10.55	P.S. Donnelly	Messrs Keefer & Frank	Newmarket to Sydenham R, Arthur St, Carradoc and Adelaide Rd, market sq, G.W.R., mill property, relief; 2 ch	Middlesex 34 R.P.93
B2325	–.12.53	9.4.63	P.S. Donnelly	John Frank	North St to Front St below Sydenham R; photoreproduction; 2 ch	Middlesex 34 R.P.186
B2326	–.2.56?	3.4.56	Charles L. Davies	James Keefer	Addition to G.W.R. depot; lots on Beech St and on both sides Adelaide St btwn Maitland Terrace and High St, lots on Argyle and Buchannan sts; 4 ch	Middlesex 34 R.P.104

	Date of Survey	Date of Regist.	Surveyor	Owner	Description and Notes	Location
B2327	22.4.56?	26.4.56	Charles L. Davies	Messrs Reid & Gregory	Subdivision of streets, town line to High St, Lothian Ave to Fullarton Ave; photoreproduction; 1.5 ch	Middlesex 34 R.P.105
B2328	–.–.56	24.7.62	S. Peters	A.H. Kittredge	NW pt lot 12, 10th con, twp Caradoc; depot on Sarnia Branch G.W.R. with lots to north; photoreproduction; 2 ch	Middlesex 34 R.P.175
B2329	–.–.56	5.12.67	Charles L. Davies	Messrs Blackburn	Pt lot 12, 10th con, twp Caradoc; Sarnia branch of G.W.R. to town line, on both sides Head St; photoreproduction; 2 ch	Middlesex 34 R.P.226
B2330	28.3.57?	6.4.57	Charles L. Davies	Thomas C. Gregory	NE pt lot 13, con X, twp Caradoc; G.W.R. to High St, Lothian Ave to beyond Centre Ave, Church Cres; photoreproduction; 264 ft	Middlesex 34 R.P.140
B2331	–.6.57	26.1.58	H. Low	William B. Munn	Pt N1/2 lot 14, 10th con, twp Caradoc; town line btwn Caradoc and Adelaide to beyond High St, Egerton Ave to York St; photoreproduction; 2 ch	Middlesex 34 R.P.147
B2332	–.–.57	24.6.57	Hamilton Low	B.F. Perry	Pt NW1/4 lot 13, 10th con, twp Caradoc; G.W.R. to town line Caradoc and Adelaide, side-rd btwn lots 12 and 13 to Zimmerman Ave; photoreproduction; 2 ch	Middlesex 34 R.P.142
B2333	–.6.61	–	William McMillan	Trust & Loan Company of Upper Canada	Pt lot 10, 10th con, twp Caradoc; streets unnamed; photoreproduction; 4 ch	Middlesex 34 R.P.167
B2334	5.8.62	21.11.62	Samuel Peters	G. Lowe Reid	Pt NW1/4 lot 12, 10th con, twp Caradoc; Princess St to County Rd; south of G.W.R. depot; bldgs; photoreproduction; 2 ch	Middlesex 34 R.P.177
B2335	6.8.62	[3.9.62?]	Samuel Peters	George Lowe Reid	Resurvey of lots on North, Maria, Emily, and Front sts; photoreproduction; 1 ch	Middlesex 34 R.P.175 1/2
B2336	22.10.63?	22.10.63	Nathaniel Low	Messrs Johnston, Winslow & Zimmerman	Lot 22, 5th con, twp Adelaide; Metcalfe St to side-rd btwn lots 21 and 22 and rd allowance btwn cons 4 and 5, G.W.R.; photoreproduction; 2 ch	Middlesex 34 R.P.189
B2337	21.8.66?	22.9.66	William McMillan	Messrs Kettridge & Althouse	South pt lots 23 and 24, 4th con, twp Adelaide south of Egremont Rd; Front St	Middlesex 34 R.P.217

					to town line btwn Caradoc and Adelaide, Arthur St to beyond E Front St; photoreproduction; 2 ch	
B2338	10.10.67	3.12.67	George P. Liddy	James English	Pt lot 12, 10th con, twp Caradoc; lots on both sides Henry St at Caradoc St; 2 ch	Middlesex 34 R.P.225
B2339	30.10.67?	5.11.67	Charles L. Davies, B. Springer	James Keefer	High St to Keefer St, Princess St to Adelaide St; photoreproduction; 2 ch	Middlesex 34 R.P.224
	STREETSVILLE					
B2340	–	21.4.53	Hugh Black	John Barnhart	Pt E1/2 lot 4, 5th con west of Hurontario St; lots along Broadway, Pearl, Tannery, and Crumbie sts to Mullet Creek; 2 ch	Peel 43 R.P.Str 1
B2341	23.2.56	8.5.56	Bristow, Fitzgerald & Spencer	Messrs Hyde & Rutledge	Subdivision of pts lot 5, 4th and 5th cons west of Hurontario St; Ontario St north to rd allowance btwn lots V and VI, Credit R to John St, cultural detail along river, bldgs, owners; 2 ch	Peel 43 R.P.Str 2
B2342	26.4.56	14.7.56	Bristow, Fitzgerald & Spencer	T. Street	Queen St to Church St, bldgs, cultural detail; 2 ch	Peel 43 R.P.Str 3
B2343	6.5.56?	9.6.57	Bristow, Fitzgerald & Spencer	G. Doherty	Pt lot 3, 4th con west of Hurontario St; lots along George St, cultural detail; 1.5 ch	Peel 43 R.P.Str 5
B2344	16.7.56?	18.8.56	Bristow, Fitzgerald & Spencer	Multiple owners	Compilation plan, pts lots 1–7, 4th con, and pts lots 1–7, 5th con west of Hurontario St; owners, mills; 4 ch	Peel 43 R.P.Str 4
	SUMMERHILL					
B2345	–.2.56	22.5.57	William Perceval	Joseph Armstrong	Lot 33, 7th con, twp Hullett; Ontario to Maitland St, Cayley to Erie St; 2 ch	Huron 22 R.P.304
	SUNNYSIDE					
B2346	14.7.53	26.3.62	J. Stoughton Dennis	John Tully	Villa lots on lot III, 1st con, twp Tay; east of Penetanguishene Rd, relief, owners; 4 ch	Simcoe 51 R.P.87
	SUTTON					
B2347	–.8.48	21.12.50	Henry White	J.O. Bourchier	Black R to North St and NE to West St, market-place; 1 ch	York 65 R.P.25
B2348	1.7.57?	13.8.57	Charles Unwin	J.O. Bourchier	Lots 1 and 2, 7th con, twp Georgina; Simcoe St west to town line btwn	York 65 R.P.213

	Date of Survey	Date of Regist.	Surveyor	Owner	Description and Notes	Location
					Georgina and N Gwillimbury, 7th con line to 8th con line, streets named, cultural detail, owners; 3 ch	
	SWEABURG					
B2349	28.12.55	[14.11.56?]	William Smiley	Calvin Martin	SE pt lot 5, 3rd con, twp W Oxford; Arnold St to William St, Norwich St to Church St; 2 ch	Oxford 41 R.P.93
B2350	–.–.63	–	William Smiley	For Municipal Council	SE pt lot 5, 3rd con, twp W Oxford; Arnold St to William St, Norwich St to Solon St; 2 ch	Oxford 41 R.P.153
	SYDENHAM					
B2351	–	22.12.46	James William Benn	Messrs George M. Yarker & William Holditch	Streets named, owners, bldgs; scale n.g.	Frontenac 13 R.P.19
	SYDENHAM TWP					
B2352	28.2.56?	28.2.56	–	Hiram Kilbourn	Subdivision of N1/2 lot 8, 12th con, twp Sydenham; lots btwn Garafraxa Rd and 11th con line; transcript; scale n.g.	Grey 16 R.P.147
	SYLVAN					
B2353	–.5.58	6.12.68	B. Springer	William Channer	East pt lots 16 and 17, XXI con W.C.R., twp W Williams; King St to Nelson St, west of Main St; 1 ch	Middlesex 33 R.P.248 Co
	TAMWORTH					
B2354	–	4.3.50	William R. Rombough	C. Wheeler	West front, lots 5 and 6, 7th con, twp Sheffield; on both sides Salmon R, lots on Ottawa, Bridge St, and macadamized rd; 2 ch	Lennox 29 R.P.35
B2355	13.8.52	–	William R. Rombough	C. Wheeler?	Amends earlier plan, east front lot 5, 6th con, and west front lots 5 and 6, 7th con, twp Sheffield; Neely St to macadamized rd, Peel St to Bagot St, Water St; 2 ch	Lennox 29 R.P.35B

B2356	–.5.62	–.3.63	William R. Aylsworth	Reuben N. Neely	Lot 5, 6th con, twp Sheffield; Front St to Addington Rd, West Rd to Concession Rd and Salmon R, owners; 2 ch	Lennox 29 R.P.34
B2357	11.5.64	6.7.64	William R. Rombough	C. Wheeler	Lots 5 and 6, 7th con, twp Sheffield; Salmon R, lots on Addington Rd, Water and John sts, Adelaide to Ottawa St, con rd to Rear St; 2 ch	Lennox 29 R.P.33
	TARA					
B2358	17.5.58?	28.5.58	Thomas H. Lynch	Mr Berford	Subdivision of lots 31 and 32, 8th con, twp Arran; Sable R, Park Rd to Post Rd, rd allowance con 8/9 to Alexander St; 4 ch	Bruce 3 R.P.18
B2359	10.11.58?	26.11.58	Alexander Sproat	S. Berford	Subdivision of lots 31 and 32, con 9, twp Arran; Brook St to North St, Post Rd to Park Rd; 4 ch	Bruce 3 R.P.21
B2360	–	[24.3.59?]	C. Rankin	John Hamilton	Lot 30, 8th con, twp Arran; lots on Hamilton St to Saugeen Rd, Mary Ann St to Matilda St; 4 ch	Bruce 3 R.P.23
B2361	22.11.60?	18.1.61	Alexander Sproat	John M. Lumsden	Pt farm lots 29 and 30, con VIII, twp Arran; 2 ch	Bruce 3 R.P.29
	TEESWATER					
B2362	–.–.56	13.4.58	George McPhillips	Messrs Brown, Gibson, Hadwin, Fulford	Lots 15 and 16, 6th and 7th cons, twp Culross; Marcy St to Mitchell St, Marion St to Richmond St; 2 ch	Bruce 3 R.P.16
	TEETERVILLE					
B2363	[–.–.5?]	–	T.W. Walsh	–	Pt lots 13 and 14, Vth con, twp Windham; 1 ch	Norfolk 37 R.P.57A
	TERRA COTTA					
B2364	12.8.57	3.[9.57?]	Fitzgerald & Drennan	Henry Tucker	West pt of E1/2 lot 27, 6th con, twp Chinguacousy W.H.S., area west of Credit R, lots along Mill and High sts, mills, race, bldgs; 60 ft	Peel 43 R.P.CH5
	THAMESFORD					
B2365	–.–.54	31.3.55	Samuel Peters	J.G. Horne	Formerly 'St Andrews,' addition to W1/2 lot 1, 11th con, twp Nissouri; Dundas St to	Oxford 41 R.P.56

	Date of Survey	Date of Regist.	Surveyor	Owner	Description and Notes	Location
					St Andrews St, con rd to St Patrick St; 3 ch	
B2366	–	[–.5.54?]	A.H. Connor	Mrs Margaret Brock	Pt lot 22, 1st con, twp N Oxford; lots on Middleton St south of Dundas St; 2 ch	Oxford 41 R.P.45
B2367	5.1.58?	6.1.58	W.G. Wonham	Joel & Eleazer MacCarty	Dundas St to Washington St, Wallace St to George St, mill pond, Anglican church; transcript; 3 ch	Oxford 41 R.P.105
B2368	18.5.60	–	Cyrus Carroll	For Municipal Council	Lots 22 and 23, 1st con, twp N Oxford; Dundas St to rd allowance btwn cons 1 and 2, Middleton St to gravel rd to Ingersoll; transcript (scale enlarged to 3 ch); 4 ch	Oxford 41 R.P.140
	THAMESVILLE					
B2369	–.4.52	1.6.67	Richard Parr	Mary E. Wallace	Pt lot 12, front con, twp Howard; G.W.R. to above Orchard St, William St to Thames R; 2 ch	Kent 24 R.P.147
B2370	4.6.55?	1.6.67	John O'Mara	David Sherman	'Tecumseh'; pt E1/2 lot 15, con B, twp Camden; ry depot and track to Sherman St, Victoria St to Lomila St N; 2 ch	Kent 24 R.P.143
B2371	4.5.56?	1.6.67	John O'Mara	David Sherman	For description see **2003**	Kent 24 R.P.144
	THEDFORD					
B2372	–.9.58	27.8.59	B. Springer	Nelson E. Southworth & William Layman	Pt W1/2 lot 20 and pt W1/2 lot 21, 3rd con, twp Bosanquet; King St to Louisa and Elizabeth sts, Anne St to Nelson St, G.T.R. station; 3 ch	Lambton 25 R.P.Thedford 1
	THORNBURY					
B2373	–.12.55	25.11.65	William Gibbard	Messrs Olmstead & Shortis	'Mill Reserve'; lots along Mill St to Beaver R and Bridge and Louisa sts, other streets, bldgs, owners; transcript; 100 ft	Grey 16 R.P.101

B2374	–.–.62	17.12.62	John A. Fleming	Samson Webb	Subdivision of lot 5, corner of Bruce and Alfred sts; lots on Alfred and Bruce sts; transcript; 1 ch	Grey 16 R.P.100
B2375	1.7.63	19.2.66	Robert F. Lynn	William Jubez Marsh	Park lot 5, town Thornbury; 18 lots on Alice and Bruce sts; transcript; 50 ft	Grey 16 R.P.99
	THORNHILL					
B2376	12.11.47	12.12.48	John Tully	Mr Griffiths	Pt lot 29, 1st con east of Yonge St, twp Markham; lots south of plank rd and north and south of Elgin St, owners, sales information; 200 ft	Toronto 64 R.P.8
B2377	13.9.53	16.9.53	David Gibson	Wellington Frizzell	Subdivision of pt lot XXX east of Yonge St; along John and Colborne sts, owners; 2 ch	Toronto 64 R.P.71
	THORNTON					
B2378	–.–.57	1.11.58	William Sanders	William Stoddart	East pt lot 16, 11th con, twp Essa; area west of Barrie St and north of Robert St; 2 ch	Simcoe 51 R.P.66
B2379	–.–.59	6.8.59	Henry Creswicke	Aaron Walker	Lot 1, 7th con, twp Innisfil; lots east of town line, owners; 132 ft	Simcoe 51 R.P.75
B2380	2.11.66?	8.2.67	Henry Creswicke	William Stoddart	Lot 16, 11th con, twp Essa; area NW of Robert St and Barrie St (later name); 3 ch	Simcoe 51 R.P.119
	THOROLD					
B2381	–.–.52	1.6.52	George Z. Rykert	George Keefer	Front St to West St, South St and south town boundary to St David's St, owners, bldgs, mills, cotton factory; transcript; 100 ft	Niagara 59 R.P.889
B2382	1.11.52	24.6.53	George Z. Rykert	Dr Rolls	Front St east to Chapel St, Water St to Bridge Ave; transcript; 2 ch	Niagara 59 R.P.890
B2383	10.12.55?	12.12.55	George Z. Rykert	H. Mittelburger	For description see **2007**	Niagara 59 R.P.892
B2384	–.–.60	–	Thomas C. Keefer	Multiple owners	Detailed plan; Beaver Dam Rd to G.W.R. lines and old Welland Ry, Chapel St north to Russell St, all bldgs, owners, relief, locks; 200 ft	Niagara 59 no R.P.#

	Date of Survey	Date of Regist.	Surveyor	Owner	Description and Notes	Location
B2385	22.5.62	3.11.62	Zenas Fell	D. Hoover	Pt lot XV; Chapel St east to Wellington St, Peter St north to Regent St, Welland Ry; 1.3 ch	Niagara 59 R.P.893
B2386	–.–.67	18.9.67	George Z. Rykert	John Keefer	St David St to line btwn Grantham and Thorold twps, Queen St to Welland St, owners, details along Welland Canal, cultural detail; 2 ch	Niagara 59 R.P.894
	(THORPVILLE town plot)					
B2387	–.–.56	21.10.57	Schofield & Hobson	John Thorp	For description see **2009**	Wellington 61 R.P.93
	THURLOW TWP					
B2388	–.4.53	19.7.53	P.V. Elmore	Robert Findlay	Park lots, south pt lot 10, 3rd con, twp Thurlow; 4 ch	Hastings 21 R.P.53
B2389	–.8.53	28.9.53	H.H. Horsey	Messrs Walton & LeVesconte	'Bininger Plot,' lot 9, 3rd con, and pt lots 9 and 10, 2nd con, twp Thurlow; Park Rd to rd 3/4 con, sideline road to Belleville Rd; 4 ch	Hastings 21 R.P.66
B2390	8.1.66?	3.2.66	Henry Carre	Ann S. Ridley	$W_{1/2}$ lot 4, con II, twp Thurlow; pt park lots 6 and 5; 50 ft	Hastings 21 R.P.110
	TILLSONBURG					
B2391	–.–.54	[1.9.54?]	Jesse P. Ball	Tillson & Bloomfield	Pts lots III, IV, V, XII con, twp Dereham; John Pound St to Wolf St, Harvey St to London Rd and Brock St, mills, tannery, post office; 3 ch	Oxford 41 R.P.60
B2392	–.11.57	[20.10.58?]	T.W. Dobbie	Rev R. Rogers & A. McLean	Ann St and Gourie St; 1 ch	Oxford 41 R.P.118
B2393	–.–.59	[1.9.59?]	J.P. Vansittart	Thomas Hardy	Pt lot 5, 11th con, twp Dereham; lots on Niagara, John, and Railway sts on both sides Oxford St; 3 ch	Oxford 41 R.P.119
B2394	23.5.65	–	T.W. Dobbie	E.D. Tillson	Resurvey, pts lots 4 and 5, 12th con, twp Dereham; rd allowance btwn cons 1 and 2 to London Rd/Bunker Hill St, Cranberry	Oxford 41 R.P.160A

					St to Washington Grand Ave, owners, relief, mill ponds; transcripts; 200 ft	

TORONTO

B2395	–.–.[2?]	–	–	Thomas Stoyell	Lot St to King St, Ontario St to Parliament St, subdivision of land purchased from D.W. Smith, 2 maps on 1 sheet; 2 ch	Toronto 63 R.P.7A
B2396	–.–.[2?]	–	–	Hospital Trustees	Subdivision of hospital block C; Richmond St to Adelaide St, Victoria St to Church St; transcript; 1 ch	Toronto 63 R.P.8A
B2397	–.–.29	[7.6.31?]	J.G. Chewett	Hon. George Crookshank	Pt lot H, twp York; south of Lot St, west of Peter St; 80 ft	Toronto 63 R.P.1B
B2398	26.1.31	–	J.G. Chewett	Hon. William Dummer Powell	Subdivision of lot 12, twp York; area from Lot St to college grounds and from College Ave and Hon. J.B. Robinson property west to D. Boulton property, owners; 120 ft	Toronto 63 R.P.1
B2399	[–.–.34]	–	–	–	'Terauley,' 12-acre block in front of park lots 9 and 10, twp York; Lot St to Macauley Lane, Yonge St to Elizabeth St, later called Macaulaytown, owners; transcript; 1.25 ch	Toronto 63 R.P.6A
B2400	–.–.[34]	16.5.57	Copy? by J.O. Browne	John Strachan	Lots along McGill, Anne, and Carleton sts btwn Yonge and Church sts; 37 ft	Toronto 63 R.P.203
B2401	19.5.36	[19.5.36?]	J.G. Chewett	–	Area from Yonge St to beyond Church St and from Lot St to Richmond St, date on transcript; 55 ft	Toronto 63 R.P.3A
B2402	–.9.36	[23.10.50?]	Robert Lynn	Hon. Peter McGill	425 building lots, block marked 1–4, lying btwn Church, Gould, Victoria, and Gerrard sts; estate on Lot St through to Shuter; transcript; 132 ft	Toronto 63 R.P.22A
B2403	–.–.37	23.11.70	Thomas Young	Home District	Reserve for gaol and court-house; Toronto St to Church St, King St to Newgate St, St Andrews Church, Wesleyan Methodist Chapel, Home District gaol and court-house, ground plan of all 4 bldgs; transcript; 27 ft	Toronto 63 R.P.D87

	Date of Survey	Date of Regist.	Surveyor	Owner	Description and Notes	Location
B2404	–.–.39	8.11.39	Thomas Young	John Strachan	Park lots 9 and 10, 1st con from bay, twp York; Yonge St to Sayre St, lots on Pine and St Agnes sts, bldgs, owners; 50 ft	Toronto 63 R.P.2A
B2405	–.–.3?	–	J.G. Chewett	D'Arcy Boulton	Subdivision of park lots 13 and 14 fronting on Lot St; lots on Beverly, John, William, Henry, and Lot sts; transcript; 60 ft	Toronto 63 R.P.C2
B2406	[7.11.40]	–	–	–	Lots btwn Richmond, Newgate (Adelaide), Church, and New sts, 2 schoolhouses; transcript; 66 ft	Toronto 63 R.P.9A
B2407	–.[ca 40]	–	–	Hon. C.A. Hagerman	Subdivision of pt park lot 10, twp York; btwn Sayre and Elizabeth sts and btwn Agnes and Albert sts, Osgoode and Louisa sts named; 1 ch	Toronto 63 R.P.13A
B2408	–.–.[40?]	6.3.56	J.O. Browne	J. Lukin Robinson	Subdivision of park lot XI; Park Lane to Sayre St, Elm St to Osgoode St; 40 ft	Toronto 63 R.P.147
B2409	–.1.41	–	Thomas Young	City of Toronto	Water lots; Berkeley St to York St, present shoreline, description of lots; transcript; 160 ft	Toronto 63 R.P.5A
B2410	25.5.43	17.5.52	Robert Lynn	Samuel Ridout	Pt park lot 4, 42 lots; Lot St to Carlton St and lots laid out along Seaton St, park lots in area east and west of Yonge and Parliament sts; 2.5 ch	Toronto 63 R.P.41
B2411	–.5.43	14.2.54	John Howard	John Strachan	Pt of block bounded by Front, Simcoe, Wellington, and York sts; 40 ft	Toronto 63 R.P.86
B2412	–.–.44	17.4.51	John G. Howard	John Y. Bown	Amelia St south to Elm St, Sumach St to Parliament St; original and 2 transcripts; 66 ft	Toronto 63 R.P.26
B2413	–.–.45	22.2.45	J.G. Howard	Thomas G. Ridout	W1/3 lot 4, 1st con from bay, twp York; Sherbourne to Parliament St, East St to Carlton St; 250 ft	Toronto 63 R.P.4A
B2414	–.4.45	6.5.53	Robert F. Lynn	George Bilton	Lots; College Ave to Yonge St, Edward St to College St, owners, Fleming's Garden, Logan's Garden; 103 ft	Toronto 63 R.P.60

B2415	–.8.45	25.4.63	Robert Lynn	Jesse Ketchum	13 lots, pt lot 25, con 2 from bay in Yorkville; Humber Rd, McMurrich and Yonge sts; 40 ft	Toronto 63 R.P.27OY
B2416	–.9.45	26.6.50	John G. Howard	Anne Macdonell	Lots btwn Richmond, Adelaide, Duncan, and Simcoe sts; 40 ft	Toronto 63 R.P.17
B2417	–.3.46	26.2.53 26.4.53	John G. Howard	Estate of Chief Justice Powell	Park lot 12; College Ave to William, Dummer, and Murray sts, lots and bldgs on estate, shows creek, racket court, bowling green, walks, cemetery, etc; the two plans are identical; 66 ft	Toronto 63 R.P.49 and 55
B2418	16.7.46	17.9.50	Robert Lynn	Charles Wallis Heath	'Deer Park,' front of lot 21, 3rd con from bay, twp York; lots on Heath St, area west of Yonge St, north of St Clair Ave, price of lots, road to pottery; 100 ft	Toronto 63 R.P.20
B2419	12.10.46	8.3.69	Robert Lynn	Estate of John Bishop	Lots on town lot 11, north side Adelaide St, Bishop's bldgs and stables; 20 ft	Toronto 63 R.P.D57
B2420	–.–.46	27.9.53	John Stoughton Dennis	J.M. Strachan	'Crookshank Block,' park lot XXI, 1st con from bay; Queen St to north city limit, lots on both sides Clinton, Strachan, and Bishop sts, owners; 132 ft	Toronto 63 R.P.75
B2421	–.–.47	–	John S. Dennis	James M. Strachan	'Strachan Plan,' pt lot 11, 1st con, twp York; Kingston Rd north to beyond Methuen St, lots on both sides Clifford St; transcript; 198 ft	Toronto 63 R.P.'Strachan Plan'
B2422	–.–.[47?]	–.–.[47?]	John G. Howard	S.P. Jarvis	Lots btwn Gerrard, Queen, Mutual, and George sts, owners, prices of lots; 2.4-ch bar	Toronto 63 R.P.10A
B2423	18.8.49	31.7.51	J.O. Browne	Hon. William Allan	Duchess St north to Queen St, lots on both sides Caroline St; 5 ch	Toronto 63 R.P.29
B2424	[–.11.49]	–	J. Stoughton Dennis	Hon. John Elmsley	'Clover Hill Estate,' lots btwn Yonge, St Cuthbert's, St Mary's, and St Alban's sts; Barnstable Villa, church reserve, St Joseph's Place; 62 ft	Toronto 63 R.P.13
B2425	–.–.49	12.11.55	F.F. Passmore	George H. White	Area west of Yonge St and south of Concession Rd, lots on both sides North St, owners; 1 ch	Toronto 63 R.P.139

	Date of Survey	Date of Regist.	Surveyor	Owner	Description and Notes	Location
B2426	[12.1.50]	22.11.52	J.O. Browne	John A. MacAulay	Pt park lots IX and X, Queen St to Agnes St, Yonge St to the Hagerman Estate beyond Terauley St, plan of Church of Holy Trinity; 43 ft	Toronto 63 R.P.45
B2427	27.2.50	–	J.O. Browne	William Allan	Lots on Queen and Caroline sts, St David's Ward, area south and west of Queen and Caroline sts to George St, water course, relief; 25 ft	Toronto 63 R.P.14
B2428	9.4.50	1.6.50	J.O. Browne	J. Lukin Robinson	Pt park lot XI; Christopher St to Elm St, Park Lane by College Ave to Sayre St, see also **B2431**; 40 ft	Toronto 63 R.P.16
B2429	14.5.50	17.5.70	John Tully	Mrs Lucy Brock	Park lot 30, 1st con from bay, twp York; smaller lots along Dundas St and Lakeshore Rd; transcript; 4 ch	Toronto 63 R.P.300
B2430	[22.5.50]	2.10.50	John Tully	Trustees of the Hospital Endowment	Lots; Queen St south to Adelaide, Brock St to St Andrews market, bldgs; 50 ft	Toronto 63 R.P.21
B2431	[1.6.50]	22.4.61	J.O. Browne	J. Lukin Robinson	Pt park lot XI; College Ave to Sayre St, Christopher St to Elm St, see also **B2428**; 40 ft	Toronto 63 R.P.D14
B2432	30.7.50	19.11.51	John G. Howard	Sara Ann Fitzgerald	Lots north side Wellington St east of York St, owners; 12.5 ft	Toronto 63 R.P.33
B2433	–.–.50	14.12.50	–	–	Subdivision of park lot XI; Avenue St to Christopher St, Park Lane to Sayre St; 40 ft	Toronto 63 R.P.24
B2434	6.5.51	21.5.51	William Robinson	John Harper	Spadina Ave to George Denison's Land, Augusta St to beyond Victoria St W and property belonging to John Ritchey; approx 30 ft	Toronto 63 R.P.27
B2435	–.5.51	11.9.51	John G. Howard	Rev E. Baldwin	Pt park lot 3, 1st con from bay, twp York; Carlton St to Winchester St, Parliament St to McMahon St, owners; 75 ch	Toronto 63 R.P.31
B2436	2.12.51	[2.12.51?]	J. Stoughton Dennis	Estate of Alexander Wood	Subdivision of park lots 7 and 8, 1st con from bay, twp York; Maitland to Wood St, Yonge St to Church St; 50 ft	Toronto 63 R.P.34

B2437	24.1.52	24.1.52	John G. Howard	Hon. H.J. Boulton	Adelaide to King St, York St to Simcoe St; 24 ft	Toronto 63 R.P.35
B2438	20.4.52	–.4.53	F.F. Passmore	Powell Estate	Pt of estate; north and east of Front and York sts, owners; 100 ch	Toronto 63 R.P.52
B2439	25.5.52	11.8.52	G.P. Liddy	Estate of John Hugill	'Yorkville'; lots on Severn St at Yonge St; 33 ft	Toronto 63 R.P.42
B2440	28.5.52	26.10.52	J.G. Howard	William Wakefield	Garden and villa lots; Bellevue Place btwn Strachan and Bishop sts north to lots on both sides Clinton St; 6.6 ft	Toronto 63 R.P.43
B2441	3.8.52	6.10.60	John G. Howard	T.G. Hurd, E.E.W. Hurd & J. Esten	'Garrison Reserve'; Hospital St to Queen St, Tecumseth St on west; 13 ft	Toronto 63 R.P.D8
B2442	22.8.52	26.1.53	F.F. Passmore	Estate of James Browne	Lot 4, 1st con from bay, twp York; area from Don and Danforth plank rd south to Lake, Kingston Rd, owners; 256 ft	Toronto 63 R.P.47
B2443	1.10.52	15.12.52	G.P. Liddy	R.A. Parker	'Yorkville,' pt lot 21, 2nd con from bay, twp York; area west of Yonge St and south of William (Yorkville) St, owners; 40 ft	Toronto 63 R.P.46
B2444	30.10.52	30.10.52	John G. Howard	John G. Howard	NW pt park lot 4, 1st con from bay, twp York; west of Sherbourne St, north of East St, owners; 26 ft	Toronto 63 R.P.44
B2445	12.2.53	29.4.53	John G. Howard	Samuel Rossin et al.	For description see **2097**	Toronto 63 R.P.57
B2446	25.2.53	25.2.53	J.S. Dennis	Estate of William Dummer Powell	Subdivision of lot 25, 3rd con from bay, twp of York; relief; 5 ch	Toronto 64 R.P.53
B2447	1.4.53	14.5.53	J.O. Browne	Sam B. Harman	Subdivision of lot XXI, 2nd con from bay, twp York; 4 ch	Toronto 63 R.P.61
B2448	20.4.53	2.5.53	F.F. Passmore	Estate of James Browne	Wharf and water lots; wharf at Esplanade btwn Church and Scott sts, owners, fences, Bank of Montreal, Wellington Hotel, stage office; 1 ch	Toronto 63 R.P.58
B2449	–	17.5.53	J.H. Livingston	Estate of M.R. Leonard	'St Davids Ward'; George St to Jarvis St north of Shuter St, owners; 10 ft	Toronto 63 R.P.62
B2450	20.5.53	20.5.53	Robert F. Lynn	James Charles	Pt of rear pt park lots 7 and 8, 1st con, twp York; lots along Gloucester St, owners; 1/3 ch	Toronto 63 R.P.63

	Date of Survey	Date of Regist.	Surveyor	Owner	Description and Notes	Location
B2451	27.5.53	19.9.53	J. Stoughton Dennis	James M. Strachan & W.J. Fitzgerald	'Crookshank Estate,' pts park lots 18–20, 1st con from bay, twp York; Hope St to Bathurst St, College St to Queen St, owners; 99 ft	Toronto 63 R.P.74
B2452	6.6.53	21.11.53	Robert F. Lynn	Rev James Harris	North pt park lots 7 and 8, 1st con from bay, twp York; lots north of Gloucester St btwn Yonge and Church sts; 70 ft	Toronto 63 R.P.81
B2453	24.6.53	15.8.53	William Robinson	C. Thompson	Pt lot 20, 3rd con from bay, twp York; area east of Yonge St around Centre St, Don R with mills and pond, bldgs; 2 ch	Toronto 63 R.P.67
B2454	1.7.53	4.7.53	J. Stoughton Dennis	G.T. Denison	'Bellevue Estate,' subdivision of front pt, being park lot 17 and E1/2 lot 18, 1st con from bay, twp York; Queen St to St Patrick St, Spadina Ave west to Maria Ave, owners; 99 ft	Toronto 63 R.P.65
B2455	–.8.53	23.8.53	D. Gibson	John Sleigh	'Yorkville,' pt lot 21, II con from bay, twp York; area west of Yonge St, north and south of Sydenham St, area to south marked 'Potter's Field' and to north marked 'Fairbanks'; 60 ft	Toronto 63 R.P.69
B2456	17.8.53	31.8.53	Robert F. Lynn	Walter McKenzie	'Yorkville,' pt lot 21, 2nd con from bay, twp York; on both sides of Bellair's St btwn Sydenham and William sts; 40 ft	Toronto 63 R.P.70Y
B2457	–.8.53	5.10.54	David Gibson	James Cockshutt	Section C of military reserve; west side Tecumseth St btwn Queen and Richmond sts, bldgs; 20 ft	Toronto 63 R.P.91
B2458	–.9.53	27.9.54	William Hawkins	M.P. Hayes	Villa lots; Don and Danforth Rd to L Ontario, subdivision of lot 4 on both sides of a road, Kingston Rd, owners, revision of **B2442**; 3 ch	Toronto 63 R.P.90
B2459	13.9.53	21.1.54	William Thomas, John G. Howard	Hospital Trust	Lots fronting on King, Peter, Adelaide, John, and Widmer sts, King St to Adelaide St, John St to Peter St; 30 ft	Toronto 63 R.P.84
B2460	25.9.53	24.11.54	William Thomas, John G. Howard	Edward D. McMahon	Lots on Beech St btwn McMahon and Seaton sts; 60-ft bar	Toronto 63 R.P.82

B2461	4.10.53	5.10.53	John Tully	Rev E. Baldwin	Winchester St to Nassau St, Parliament St to McMahon St; 48 ft	Toronto 63 R.P.77
B2462	–.–.[ca 53]	–	F.F. Passmore	William Lilley, Alex Leith, Charles Romain & Thomas Hayes	Subdivision of lots 1–8, Section II of military reserve; Richmond St to Adelaide St, Portland St to market sq; 20 ft	Toronto 63 R.P.64
B2463	–.–.53	4.9.63	J.O. Browne	James Lukin Robinson	Subdivision pt lot V, 2nd con from bay, twp York; Don and Danforth Rd and area north of it, lots along unnamed rd; 250 ch	Toronto 63 R.P.271
B2464	–.[3.54]	1.3.55	J. Stoughton Dennis	Estate of G.T. Denison	Subdivision of pt park lots 17 and 18, 1st con from bay; College St to north city limit, Lippincott to Borden St; 2 ch	Toronto 63 R.P.112
B2465	18.5.54	9.10.54	J. Stoughton Dennis	James M. Strachan, W.J. Fitzgerald	'Crookshank Estate,' pt park lots 18–20 north of College St, College St to north city limit, Hope St to Lippincott St; transcript; 120 ft	Toronto 63 R.P.93
B2466	8.6.54	9.6.54	[J. Stoughton Dennis]	F.W. Jarvis et al.	'Denison Estate,' subdivision of pt park lot 17 north of College St, College St to north city limit, Borden to Major St; 100 ft	Toronto 63 R.P.87
B2467	22.6.54	17.1.55	J. Stoughton Dennis	W.S. Durie	Pt park lot 16; College St at Spadina Ave, lots along Robert St, Crescent Gardens; 66 ft	Toronto 63 R.P.106
B2468	6.7.54	23.2.57	J. Stoughton Dennis	Estate of Col Givens	Pt park lot 24; south of Cecil St, Cedar St east of Dundas St; 50 ft	Toronto 63 R.P.194
B2469	15.7.54	28.7.54	J. Stoughton Dennis	M.R. Vankoughnet	Pt of park lot 16 on Queen St; Queen St and lots on both sides Van Auley St north from Queen; 40 ft	Toronto 63 R.P.88
B2470	17.7.54	–	J.O. Browne	John Beverly Robinson, Jr	Subdivision of pt park lot 20; south of Dundas St btwn Ontario and Lumley sts; transcript; 49 ft	Toronto 63 R.P.89
B2471	19.7.54	21.7.73	J.O. Browne	C. Robinson, Stephen Howard, W.G. Schreiber	Subdivision of lots 4, 5, 6, 119, 120–2, 137–9, 140, 157, 160, 177, 180, pt of **B2451**; Hope to Lumley St, Dundas to College St; transcript; scale n.g.	Toronto 63 R.P.D152
B2472	9.8.54	26.12.54	J. Stoughton Dennis	Messrs Boulton & Salter	BF lots 14 and pt lot 15; Queen St to Front St E, east of Don R to D'Arcy St, G.T.R., proposed canal, plan oriented to the south, sale notice by auction; transcript; 132 ft	Toronto 63 R.P.105

	Date of Survey	Date of Regist.	Surveyor	Owner	Description and Notes	Location
B2473	23.8.54	27.3.57	J.O. Browne	Estate of George Shaw	Subdivision of W1/2 lot 28, 2nd con from bay, twp York; area around Davenport Rd, owners; 4 ch	Toronto 63 R.P.197
B2474	16.10.54	16.10.54	J.O. Browne	J. Lukin Robinson	Subdivision of lot XII, 1st con from bay, twp York; from bay to con rd above lots F and G, Kingston Turnpike Rd, swampy land; 4 ch	Toronto 63 R.P.96
B2475	16.10.54	16.10.54	J.O. Browne	J. Lukin Robinson	Subdivision of pt park lot X; Czar and Sullivan sts at University St; 80 ft	Toronto 63 R.P.97
B2476	16.10.54	16.10.54	J.O. Browne	J. Lukin Robinson	Subdivision of park lot XVI; lots btwn Victoria and Augustus sts west of Spadina Ave; 80 ft	Toronto 63 R.P.99
B2477	16.10.54	16.10.54	J.O. Browne	J. Lukin Robinson	South of Queen St E, east of George St, creek and ravine; 25 ft	Toronto 63 R.P.100
B2478	16.10.54	16.10.54	J.O. Browne	J. Lukin Robinson	Subdivision of lot III, 2nd con from bay, twp York; from east branch of Don R to 2nd con line, Dawes Tavern; 4 ch	Toronto 63 R.P.101
B2479	–.10.54	29.10.55	J.O. Browne	William Rees	Brock St to Portland St, Queen St W south to King St W, St Andrews or Western Market Sq, King St Arcade; 52 ft	Toronto 63 R.P.135
B2480	28.12.54	28.12.54	J. Stoughton Dennis	G. Duggan, Jr	For description see **2107**	Toronto 63 R.P.104 (now in OTAR)
B2481	15.1.55	7.2.55	J. Stoughton Dennis	Hon. J.H. Cameron	Subdivision of north pt lots 14 and 15, 1st con from bay; Don and Danforth Plank Rd, bldgs, owners, tavern, slaughter-house; 2 ch	Toronto 63 R.P.110
B2482	–.–.55	25.1.55	Donald McDonald, Charles Unwin	Trustees of the Toronto Hospital	South pts lot 16 and BF park lots 1 and 2, 1st con from bay, twp York; Don R to Parliament, Elm St to harbour, market-place, Trinity Church land; transcript drawn from earlier plans; 2 ch	Toronto 63 R.P.108
B2483	10.2.55	9.3.55	J. Stoughton Dennis	Samuel Thompson	'Carlton,' subdivision of pt lot 34, 2nd con from bay, twp York; area east of Weston plank rd and north of Davenport Rd; bldgs; 2 ch	Toronto 63 R.P.111

B2484	2.4.55	15.8.55	Sandford Fleming	Thomas G. Ridout	Pt W1/3 park lot 4; Carlton St south to Wilton Cres, lots on east side Sherbourne; 100 ft	Toronto 63 R.P.132
B2485	10.4.55	7.8.55	Charles Unwin	Mr Coates	Pt park lot 17; St Patrick St and Denison Ave to Augusta Ave; 30 ft	Toronto 63 R.P.131
B2486	10.4.55	18.8.56	F.F. Passmore	W. Wilson	North of Richmond, west of Bathurst, ordnance ground; 33 ch	Toronto 63 R.P.165
B2487	14.4.55	7.4.68	Sandford Fleming	J.G. Brown, Sandford Fleming, S.M. Jarvis	For description see **2112**	Toronto 63 R.P.D41
B2488	23.4.55	26.4.55	Charles Unwin	James Francis	Pt park lot 2; King and Pine sts, bldgs; 20 ft	Toronto 63 R.P.117
B2489	3.5.55	22.5.55	J.O. Browne	Estate of William Allen	Subdivision of town lot 2 and pt lot 3, south side Queen St and north side Duchess St; Queen, Ontario, Duchess, and Caroline sts; 49 ft	Toronto 63 R.P.124
B2490	–	8.5.55	F.F. Passmore	A.H. St Germain	Park lot 2; revision of **B2488**, bldgs; 20 ft	Toronto 63 R.P.118
B2491	9.5.55	10.4.56	J.O. Browne	Charles Robinson	Subdivision of park lot XVIII, being subdivision of lots 129 and 130 of 'Crookshank Estate' or **B2451**; Bathurst to Lippincott St, lots btwn and along unnamed st; 50 ft	Toronto 63 R.P.121
B2492	–	9.5.55	F.F. Passmore	Robert I. Turner	'Bracondale Hill Estate,' pt lot XXVII, 2nd con from bay, twp York; area from Charles St north to con rd, Mutual St west to Christie St, bldgs, owners; 3 ch	Toronto 63 R.P.119
B2493	9.5.55	18.5.55	J.O. Browne	Charles Robinson	'Crookshank Estate,' subdivision of lots 3 and 4 of **B2451**; Markham St to Ontario St, lots laid out along Robinson St; 50 ft	Toronto 63 R.P.123
B2494	18.5.55	10.5.55	J.O. Browne	Charles Robinson	'Crookshank Estate,' subdivision of lots 24–35, 48, and 52 of pt of **B2465**; north city limits to Herrick St, Bathurst St to Lippincott St; 50 ft	Toronto 63 R.P.120
B2495	11.5.55	16.5.55	Charles Unwin	Dr Small	Pt BF park lot 2; King, Parliament, Palace, and Trinity sts, Trinity Church, parsonage, schoolhouse, bldgs, Trinity Church land; 30 ft	Toronto 63 R.P.122

	Date of Survey	Date of Regist.	Surveyor	Owner	Description and Notes	Location
B2496	6.6.55	24.12.70	F.F. Passmore	Mr Sproule	Pt Block I adjoining military reserve; lots on north side Richmond St and south side Queen St; 29 ft	Toronto 63 R.P.D89
B2497	8.6.55	17.9.55	J.O. Browne	G.W. Allan	Subdivision of park lot 5; Bloor St to Isabella St, Huntley St to Sherbourne St, estate of S.P. Jarvis with bldgs, owners, blockhouse; 100 ft	Toronto 63 R.P.132A
B2498	19.6.55	25.6.55	Charles Unwin	Messrs E.E.W. Hurd, J.J. Hayes, Charles Robertson, William Hind, D. MacDonald	Pt Section K, military reserve; lots on King, Adelaide, Tecumseth, and West sts; 20 ft	Toronto 63 R.P.126
B2499	–.–.55	29.8.67	F.F. Passmore	W.H. Draper	For description see **2114**	Toronto 63 R.P.D37
B2500	1.7.55	1.3.58	J. Stoughton Dennis	Messrs Bolton & Salter	Subdivision of lot 14, 1st con from bay, twp York; north of Kingston Rd btwn Boulton and DeGrassi sts, G.T.R. Co. lands; 40 ch	Toronto 63 R.P.233
B2501	2.7.55	20.7.55	Robert F. Lynn	James Wheeler	9 lots btwn Elizabeth, Sayer, and Albert sts; 10 ft	Toronto 63 R.P.128
B2502	10.7.55	11.7.55	Charles Unwin	F.W. Jarvis	Pt park lot 4; north of Queen St, east of Sherbourne St to McMahon St, estates, owners; 40 ft	Toronto 63 R.P.127
B2503	–	2.8.55	Charles Unwin	Robert Alway	'Yorkville,' subdivision of pt lot 21, 2nd con from bay, twp York; lots at SE corner of Davenport Place and plank rd, bldgs; 20 ft	Toronto 63 R.P.130
B2504	13.8.55	24.6.56	Dennis & Boulton	Charles C. Small	Subdivision of pt park lot 3; Beech St btwn McMahon and Parliament sts; 40 ft	Toronto 63 R.P.160
B2505	1.9.55	1.9.55	J.O. Browne	A.M. Clark	Subdivision of park lots 9 and 10; College Ave and Clarendon Place north to Breadalbane St and btwn Yonge St, Survey Place, Elmsley Villa, Stanley Cres; 60 ft	Toronto 63 R.P.132C
B2506	1.9.55	20.10.55	J.O. Browne	John E. & R.E. Playter	Subdivision of lot XI, 2nd con, twp York; lots on both sides John St above 2nd con	Toronto 63 R.P.134

					line btwn Ellerbeck and Sarah sts, bldgs, mill road; 150 ft	
B2507	4.9.55	8.10.55	J.G. Howard	Consumers Gas Co.	Lots on King St E; 13-ft bar	Toronto 63 R.P.133
B2508	18.10.55	25.4.56	John Tully	Robert O'Hara & Walter O'Hara	'Brockton' at junction G.T.R. and Ontario Simcoe & Huron Union Ry; to Clarendon Rd; printed by J. Ellis; 4 ch	Toronto 63 R.P.152
B2509	19.10.55	19.12.55	J.O. Browne	George H. White	Subdivision of park lot 7; along Church St btwn Charles and Isabella sts, later annotations; 42 ft	Toronto 63 R.P.140
B2510	3.11.55	9.11.55	Robert F. Lynn	Messrs Gibson & Bugg	Central pt park lots 9 and 10, 1st con from bay, twp York; Sayer St to Yonge St, mainly on north side Gerrard St, Sullivan's house, related to **B2513**; 40 ft	Toronto 63 R.P.136
B2511	12.12.55	3.1.56	J. Stoughton Dennis	S. Thompson	Pt 'Carlton,' lot 34, 2nd con, twp York; Weston plank rd to Laughton Ave, Davenport Rd north to rd allowance btwn cons 2 and 3, lots also on Carlton, Queen, and King sts; 3 ch	Toronto 63 R.P.141
B2512	13.12.55	6.3.56	J.O. Browne	G.W. Allan	Subdivision of park lots 5 and 6; Wilton Cres north to Gerrard St, George St to Sherbourne St; 60 ft	Toronto 63 R.P.150
B2513	1.1.56	21.2.56	Robert F. Lynn	Messrs Gibson & Bugg	Central pt park lots 9 and 10, 1st con from bay; bounded by Yonge St, Hon. J.B. McAulay, Waltons Estate, and Fleming Garden; lots along Gerrard St and from Yonge St west to Sayer St, owners, related to **B2510**; 40 ft	Toronto 63 R.P.145
B2514	10.1.56	21.3.56	Charles Unwin	Mr McMahon	'McMahon property,' pt park lot 4; Carleton St to Queen St, George St to Parliament St, owners; 2 ch	Toronto 63 R.P.D2
B2515	18.2.56	6.3.56	J.O. Browne	J. Lukin Robinson	Subdivision of lot XI, Wellington and Front sts; Front St to Wellington St along Windsor St; 29 ft	Toronto 63 R.P.146
B2516	18.2.56	7.3.56	J.O. Browne	J. Lukin Robinson	Subdivision of lots 1–16, Block K, military reserve; Niagara St to Tecumseth St, Adelaide St to Richmond St; 5 ft	Toronto 63 R.P.148

	Date of Survey	Date of Regist.	Surveyor	Owner	Description and Notes	Location
B2517	20.2.56	20.2.56	J.O. Browne	Hospital Endowment	'Hospital Estate,' subdivision of lots 27–31; area bounded by Elm, Sumach, and Spruce sts; 30-ft bar	Toronto 63 R.P.144
B2518	17.3.56	22.3.56	J.G. Howard	George Ridout	Wellington St to King St, John St to Dorset St and government grounds, bldgs on John and Dorset sts; 25 ft	Toronto 63 R.P.151
B2519	28.3.56	25.6.68	John Tully	Hospital Endowment	Lots on Queen, Brock, and Adelaide sts; St Andrews market, owners; 50 ft	Toronto 63 R.P.D46
B2520	9.4.56	21.7.56	F.F. Passmore	Charles Romain	Adelaide St to King St, lots along Brant St; 30 ft	Toronto 63 R.P.161
B2521	11.4.56	1.5.56	Sandford Fleming	James Henderson	Pt park lot 14, 1st con from bay, twp York; area north of Kingston Rd and along Boulton and DeGrassi sts, G.T.R. route and property, bldgs; 50 ft	Toronto 63 R.P.153
B2522	29.4.56	7.5.56	J.O. Browne	J. Lukin Robinson	Subdivision of lots 12–14, north side Richmond St; Richmond St to Queen St, John St to Simcoe St, lots btwn Duncan and Simcoe sts; 40 ft	Toronto 63 R.P.155
B2523	6.5.56	7.5.56	J.O. Browne	J. Lukin Robinson	Subdivision of park lot 10; area btwn Sayre and Terauley sts and College Ave and Hayter St, trees; 40 ft	Toronto 63 R.P.154
B2524	14.5.56	14.5.56	F.F. Passmore	Martin Scanlan	Subdivision of east pt lot 8, hospital reserve at Pine and Park sts; bldgs, estate; 20 ft	Toronto 63 R.P.156
B2525	–	1.6.56	J.O. Browne	A.M. Clark	'Elmsley Villa Estate,' subdivision of park lots 9 and 10; College Ave to Breadalbane St, Yonge St to Surrey St; 60 ft	Toronto 63 R.P.159
B2526	5.6.56	3.12.56	Sandford Fleming	Hon. Christopher Widmer	For description see **2117**	Toronto 63 R.P.185
B2527	18.6.[56?]	16.7.58	Charles Unwin	J.D. Ridout	Pt park lot XVIII; Queen St to Elizabeth St, Denison Ave to Bathurst St, 2 bldgs; 60 ft	Toronto 63 R.P.232
B2528	21.6.56	28.4.57	J.O. Browne	J. Lukin Robinson	Subdivision of park lot XXI; Strachan St to Bishop St and along Wilton and Herbert sts; 100 ft	Toronto 63 R.P.199

B2529	25.6.56	21.11.56	F.F. Passmore	Roman Catholic Diocese of Toronto	King St to Queen St, Pine St to Park St; 66 ft	Toronto 63 R.P.183
B2530	–.6.56	13.10.56	Sandford Fleming	George H. Cheney	For description see **2120**	Toronto 63 R.P.175
B2531	15.7.56	9.9.56	J. Stoughton Dennis	William George Draper and Charles Jones	Subdivision of lots 14 and 15, Wellington Place, and lot 5, Ontario Terrace, Section A of garrison reserve; Front St to Wellington St, Portland St to Draper St; 50 ft	Toronto 63 R.P.171
B2532	22.7.56	23.7.56	H. Northcote	William Hayden	Park lots 7 and 8, 1st con from bay, twp York; Yonge St to Church St, Charles St to Hayden St, lots on both sides Hayden; 50 ft	Toronto 63 R.P.163
B2533	1.8.56	25.8.56	J. Stoughton Dennis	John Mayor	'Runnymeade Estate,' pts lots 39 and 40, IInd con from bay, twp York; Davenport and Dundas sts btwn Jane and Victoria [Clendennan] sts; 4 ch	Toronto 63 R.P.166
B2534	11.8.56	25.8.57	H. Northcote	George S. Ross	At corner of Duchess and Parliament sts; transcript; 20 ft	Toronto 63 R.P.215
B2535	22.8.56	6.9.56	Robert F. Lynn	John Gibson	Pt park lot 10, 1st con from bay, twp York; Terauley St to Elizabeth St along Hagerman St; 20 ft	Toronto 63 R.P.169
B2536	–	2.9.56	J. Stoughton Dennis	John Boyd	Subdivision of pt park lot 2; Parliament and Oak sts; 50 ft	Toronto 63 R.P.168
B2537	8.9.56	8.9.56	John Tully	Robert O'Hara	'Brockton,' villa lots 1–13 on 'O'Hara estate'; Lakeshore Rd at Sorauren St crossed by Toronto and Hamilton Ry; 4 ch	Toronto 63 R.P.170
B2538	16.9.56	6.11.56	Sandford Fleming	John G. Brown	For description see **2124**	Toronto 63 R.P.181
B2539	–.10.56	1.10.56	J. Stoughton Dennis	Sophia Dalton	Pt park lot 15; east of Spadina Ave to Huron St, College St to Division St; 50 ft	Toronto 63 R.P.176
B2540	1.10.56	6.11.58	J.O. Browne	J.O. Browne	'Crookshank Estate,' subdivision of lots 201 and 202; College St btwn Lumley and Ontario sts, further subdivision of **B2465**; 20 ft	Toronto 63 R.P.244
B2541	1.10.56	5.1.57	J. Stoughton Dennis	Charles Romain & William P. Howland	Subdivision of SW pt lot XXV, con 2 from bay, twp York; north city limits to Wells St, Brunswick west to Bathurst St; 100 ft	Toronto 63 R.P.191

	Date of Survey	Date of Regist.	Surveyor	Owner	Description and Notes	Location
B2542	–	30.10.56	Charles Unwin	Mary H. Ridout	South pt park lot 4; north of Queen St btwn Sherbourne and McMahon sts, Humphreys and Unwin estates; 40 ft	Toronto 63 R.P.177
B2543	31.10.56	4.11.56	John Tully	F. Collins	'Yorkville'; Yonge St at Davenport Rd, lots along Scollard St, bldgs; 50 ft	Toronto 63 R.P.179
B2544	–.–.56	12.12.56	John Tully	W. O'Hara	'Brockton'; Lakeshore Rd btwn Roncesvalles and Sorauren sts, a corrected version of **B2537**; 4 ch	Toronto 63 R.P.187
B2545	28.11.56	13.12.56	J.O. Browne	Joshua Crawford	Subdivision of pt lot 15, 1st con from bay, twp York; area east of Don R btwn Monro St and Mill Rd and along Crawford St, bldgs; 40 ft	Toronto 63 R.P.188
B2546	5.12.56	11.4.59	J. Stoughton Dennis	W.B. Phillips	'Clover Hill Estate,' pt lots 9 and 10, 1st con from bay, twp York; area from Yonge St west to St Cuthberts St and from St Marys St to St Albans St, a corrected version of **B2424**; 4 ch	Toronto 63 R.P.D3
B2547	3.1.57	7.1.57	Thomas Wallis Herrick	Fred W. Jarvis	Subdivision of lots 36–8 and pt lot 39, being pt park lot 8; lots at corner of Gould and Victoria sts; 20 ft	Toronto 63 R.P.192
B2548	3.1.57	16.2.57	Sandford Fleming	Thomas G. Ridout	Subdivision of W1/3 park lot 4; Carlton to Beech St and east of Sherbourne St, owners, amends **B2424**; 100 ft	Toronto 63 R.P.193
B2549	18.1.57	3.3.57	Charles Unwin	R. Wright	'Gore Vale Estate'; old and new north city limits south to Durham St, lots along Lambton and Surrey sts south of Bloor, west of Clinton; 50 ft	Toronto 63 R.P.196
B2550	–	27.2.57	F.F. Passmore	J. Wickson	'Yorkville'; lots along New Kent Rd (Alcorn Ave) west of Yonge St; 68 ft	Toronto 63 R.P.195
B2551	19.3.57	14.7.58	Bristow & Fitzgerald	F.F. Carruthers	'Yorkville'; east of Yonge St, SW pt lot 19, 2nd con from bay, twp York; owners, roads, ravine, houses, 'Rosedale Villa'; 40 ft	Toronto 63 R.P.241
B2552	14.4.57	18.4.57	Sandford Fleming	Thomas Brunskill	North pt park lot 3; McMahon St to Parliament St, East St to Nassau St; 100 ft	Toronto 63 R.P.198

B2553	16.4.57	3.7.57	John Tully	J. Bugg & R. Robinson	For description see **2130**	Toronto 63 R.P.208
B2554	–	29.4.57	F.F. Passmore	Mrs Bright	Pt lots 12 and 13, 1st con from bay, twp York; area south of Danforth Rd; 1.25 ch	Toronto 63 R.P.200
B2555	5.5.57	8.5.57	J.O. Browne	John Strachan	Subdivision of block lying btwn Wellington and Front sts; Simcoe St to York St; 46 ft	Toronto 63 R.P.201
B2556	7.5.57	13.5.57	J.O. Browne	William Rees	'Crookshank Estate,' lot I and pt lot II; along Robinson St btwn Bathurst and Markham sts, subdivision of pt of **B2451**; 20 ft	Toronto 63 R.P.202
B2557	13.5.57	12.8.57	John Ross Jack	J. Thomas Dick	Pt lot 8, Section C, military reserve; west side of Bathurst St btwn Queen and Richmond sts; 60 ft	Toronto 63 R.P.211
B2558	–.–.57	13.5.65	Charles Unwin	John Leys	Pt park lot 24; Harrison St to Dundas St, Denison St to Shaw St; 100 ft	Toronto 63 R.P.D29
B2559	1.6.57	11.6.57	Charles J. Wheelock	Jesse Ketchum, Jr	'Eglinton,' park and villa lots; area east of Yonge St at [Blythwood Rd] Victoria Ave; 'longitudinal section showing the available fall for proposed mill,' later annotations; 200 ft	Toronto 63 R.P.205
B2560	–.6.57	8.3.70	H. Northcote	William Sharpe	Pt park lots 7 and 8; btwn Yonge and Church sts and north side Maitland St; 60 ft	Toronto 63 R.P.D67
B2561	16.6.57	17.6.57	J. Ross Jack	Matthew Walton et al.	Subdivision of pt park lots IX and X, 1st con from bay, twp York; Yonge St to Sayer St, Gerrard St to Elm St; 60 ft	Toronto 63 R.P.206
B2562	17.6.57	21.7.57	Sandford Fleming	A. Brunel	'Military Reserve,' lots 1 and 3, Section I; Wellington Place to Front St, Brock St W, lanes; 16 ft	Toronto 63 R.P.209
B2563	30.7.57	12.9.57	J. Stoughton Dennis	James McMacklin et al.	Subdivision of pt lot 26, 2nd con from bay; Bathurst St to Hope St, London St to Hammond St, Seaton Sq; 100 ft	Toronto 63 R.P.219
B2564	–	15.8.57	John Ross Jack	Estate of John & George Ernest	Subdivision of lot 10, BF 1st con from bay, twp York; Ashbridges Bay to con rd, Leslie St to Lake St; 4 ch	Toronto 63 R.P.214

	Date of Survey	Date of Regist.	Surveyor	Owner	Description and Notes	Location
B2565	24.8.57	25.8.57	Charles Unwin	Samuel G. Ridout	Pt park lot 4; Sherbourne to Seaton St, Carlton to Gerrard, residences of S.G. Ridout and Sullivan, further subdivision of **B2410**; 40 ft	Toronto 63 R.P.216
B2566	29.8.57	17.6.59	Unwin & Jack	Matthew Walton et al.	Subdivision of pt park lots IX and X, 1st con from bay, twp York; Gerrard St to Elm St and Yonge St west to Sayer St, some areas subdivided earlier on **B2561**; 60 ft	Toronto 63 R.P.D4
B2567	3.9.57	26.8.69	John Tully	John O'Donaghue	For description see **2129**	Toronto 63 R.P.D62
B2568	3.9.57	23.9.57	John Tully	W. Hannah	Frank St to Amelia St near Sumach St, 2 houses shown; 40 ft	Toronto 63 R.P.221
B2569	5.9.57	19.9.57	John Tully	J. Bugg	Lots on Albert, Louisa, and Terauley sts; 20 ft	Toronto 63 R.P.220
B2570	8.9.57	12.9.57	John Tully	W. Murphy	Lots on South Park and Palace sts; Palace St to South Park St, east of East St to Elizabeth St; 33 ft	Toronto 63 R.P.218
B2571	–	9.10.57	J.O. Browne, F.F. Passmore	J. Lukin Robinson	Subdivision of park lot X, new survey of lot 15 on **B2510**; North St btwn Charles St and con line; 25 ft	Toronto 63 R.P.224
B2572	10.10.57	10.10.57	Sandford Fleming	Thomas Ridout & Collingwood Schreiber	Subdivision of hospital lots 14–26 and pt 27, south side of Palace St, and lots 17–25 and pts 26 and 27, north side of Front St in east end of city; Palace St to Front St, Don R to Cherry St, G.T.R.; 80 ft	Toronto 63 R.P.225
B2573	–.–.57	14.10.57	John K. Roche	Estate of Thomas Bright	Lots 19 and 20, north side King St E, south side Queen St, and west side Sumach St, and lots 13 and 14 (old survey), north side King St; bldgs, Roman Catholic church property; 65 ft	Toronto 63 R.P.226
B2574	–.–.57	5.11.57	John K. Roche	Estate of Thomas Bright	Lots 22, 23, and 24, including marsh to Don R, being pt of hospital reserve; area btwn River St and Don R north of Queen St; 26 ft	Toronto 63 R.P.227

B2575	5.11.57	5.11.57	Charles Unwin	John Ridout	Subdivision of pt park lot 4; Seaton St to George St, Carlton St to Wilton Cres around Moss Park, botanical gardens, bldgs; 200 ft	Toronto 63 R.P.229
B2576	21.4.58	26.8.58	Unwin & Jack	J.W. Gamble	Lots on Edward St btwn Yonge and Sayer sts; 50 ft	Toronto 63 R.P.243
B2577	22.6.58	6.9.65	J.O. Browne	William Rees	'Cambria Dock Estate'; Esplanade and Railway Ave west of Simcoe St, survey remarks by D.P.S. Browne on broken area left btwn north boundary of lots and high watermark, 15.7.65; 10 ft	Toronto 63 R.P.D31
B2578	7.7.58	9.7.58	Unwin & Jack	J.D. Humphreys	Lots on Seaton and Beech sts; Sherbourne St to Seaton St, Moss Pk and Wilton Cres on west side, house, trees; 32 ft	Toronto 63 R.P.239
B2579	7.7.58	9.7.58	Unwin & Jack	J.D. Humphreys	Lots on Queen and Sumach sts; area NW of Queen and Sumach sts; 30 ft	Toronto 63 R.P.240
B2580	7.7.58	9.8.58	Northcote & Cooper	Thomas Elliot	'Yorkville,' 'McIntosh Property'; pt park lot 21, 2nd con from bay, twp York; west of Yonge St to boundary of glebe, owners; 25 ft	Toronto 63 R.P.242
B2581	14.2.59	1.4.59	John Tully	Walter O'Hara	Pt lot 34, 1st con from bay, twp York; Dundas St and G.T.R.; 4 ch	Toronto 63 R.P.250
B2582	-.-.59	4.3.59	Charles J. Wheelock	James Dobson	'Yorkville'; lots along William St west of Yonge St, market sq, owners; 50 ft	Toronto 63 R.P.248Y
B2583	8.3.59	16.3.59	Sandford Fleming	Hon. George W. Allan	Subdivision of pt park lots VIII and VII, 1st con from bay, twp York; Charles St to Isabella St and Yonge St east to Church St; 50 ft	Toronto 63 R.P.D1
B2584	-.-.59	19.3.59	F.F. Passmore	J.P. Cummings	Pt lot 21, con 2 from bay, twp York; Yonge St to Davenport Rd with lots along Beverly St; 132 ft	Toronto 63 R.P.249Y
B2585	12.5.59	1.7.59	F.F Passmore, Charles Unwin, Robert Dalton	MacDonell Estate	'MacDonell Estate'; Richmond St to Adelaide St, John St to Simcoe St, partition of lands among members of MacDonell family and tenants; transcript; 66 ft	Toronto 63 R.P.D5
B2586	12.5.59	12.7.59	Charles Unwin, F.F. Passmore, Robert G. Dalton	MacDonell Estate	'MacDonell Estate,' pt park lot 28, 1st con from bay, twp York; lots on Gladstone Ave north and south of Dundas St, owners; 2 ch	Toronto 63 R.P.D6

	Date of Survey	Date of Regist.	Surveyor	Owner	Description and Notes	Location
B2587	–.–.59	16.9.59	F.F. Passmore	Brent Neville	Pt NW pt lot 9, 1st con from bay, twp York; lots btwn Don and Danforth Rd and G.T.R.; 4 ch	Toronto 63 R.P.253
B2588	21.11.59	1.8.60	John Tully	Samuel G. Wood	'Brockton,' park lot 30, 1st con from bay, twp York; Lakeshore Rd to con rd, G.T.R. and Ont., Simcoe Huron Union Ry; 4 ch	Toronto 63 R.P.256
B2589	28.11.59	16.12.59	Unwin & Miles	Mrs Radenhurst	Lots on Queen, Parliament, and Sydenham sts; transcript; 20 ft	Toronto 63 R.P.D7
B2590	30.11.59	14.9.60	John Tully	John McMurrich	'Playter Farm,' building and park lots for sale; plank rd from Sarah St to 4th Ave north of Don and Danforth Rd; 288 ft	Toronto 63 R.P.257
B2591	1.5.60	28.11.60	F.F. Passmore	Baldwin & Ross Families	'Baldwin Estate,' pt park lots 15 and 16, 1st con from bay; Robert St to Beverly St and con rd [Bloor] to Queen St; 3 ch	Toronto 63 R.P.D10
B2592	–.–.60	22.5.60	J.O. Browne	Messrs O'Neill & Carroll	Subdivision of pt lot 15, 1st con from bay, twp York; Mill St to Monro St, Kingston Rd north and east of Don R, owners; 40 ft	Toronto 63 R.P.255
B2593	3.10.60	9.10.60	F.F. Passmore	Mr West	'Yorkville,' lots on Davenport Rd; west of Davenport Rd and on both sides New St, owners; 24 ft	Toronto 63 R.P.259
B2594	25.10.60	31.10.60	John Tully	Estate of John Romney	SW corner of Winchester and Sumach sts; owners, cottage, see also **B2412**; 20-ft bar	Toronto 63 R.P.D9
B2595	19.11.60	5.12.60	Unwin & Miles	Samuel G. Ridout	Park lot 4, [NW] corner of Seaton and Gerrard sts; house; 30 ft	Toronto 63 R.P.D11
B2596	25.2.61	4.3.61	W.H. Ellis	Trinity Church	'Trinity Church Property'; Palace, Parliament, King, and Trinity sts, owners, Trinity Church and schoolhouse; 30 ft	Toronto 63 R.P.D12
B2597	2.4.61	2.4.61	Unwin & Miles	R.B. Denison	'Belle Vue Estate'; Lippincott St to Grosvenor St, College St to Denison Ave, reservation fortress on Bellevue Ave; 75 ft	Toronto 63 R.P.D13
B2598	12.6.61	9.11.61	John Tully	Estate of W.B. Crew	Subdivision on Duchess St at Berkeley St; ground-plan of house, garden, yard, pond, fowl house, aviary, kitchen garden; 10 ft	Toronto 63 R.P.D19

B2599	27.7.61	–.9.61	John Tully	Estate of W.B. Crew	SW angle of Pine and Oak sts; 2 bldgs with ground-plans; 20 ft	Toronto 63 R.P.D16
B2600	2.9.61	–.9.61	–	John Ritchey	Pt park lot 16, 1st con from bay, twp York; Spadina Ave west to Vanauley St, Agnes St to Saint Andrews St, creek; 40 ft	Toronto 63 R.P.D15
B2601	14.10.61	30.4.62	Unwin & Miles	J. Elmsley	'Clover Hill Estate'; alteration of St Joseph's St; Yonge St to Cuthbert St on north side St Joseph's St; 80 ft	Toronto 63 R.P.D22
B2602	1.11.61	13.11.61	Sandford Fleming	University of Toronto	Lots on College St north to university grounds, east of Queens Park, relief, trees, asylum, medical school, observatory, etc, area proposed for botanic gardens, Queens Park leased to City for public park 1.1.59; 2 ch	Toronto 63 R.P.D18
B2603	23.12.61	21.7.62	Dennis & Gossage	M.C. Cameron et al.	Lot 24, 3rd con from bay, twp York; bldgs, owners; 4 ch	Toronto 63 R.P.266
B2604	8.1.62	13.1.62	H. Northcote	G.S. Ross	Corner of Sydenham and McMahon sts; 10 ft	Toronto 63 R.P.D20
B2605	–	9.4.62	Charles Unwin	Mrs S. Ridout	New subdivision of lots 2–7; north and west of Queen and Seaton sts, alteration of R.P.177 (30.10.56); 10 ft	Toronto 63 R.P.D21
B2606	27.6.62	28.6.62	B.W. Gossage	D.L. McPherson	'Yorkville,' 'McIntosh Property,' pt park lot 21, 2nd con from bay, twp York; cancellation of **B2580**; 4 links	Toronto 63 R.P.265
B2607	–	21.8.62	William H. Ellis	Mary E. Jones	Subdivision of pt of Front park lot 23, 1st con from bay, twp York; Queen St to Maitland St, Bond St to [Shaw] St; 50 ft	Toronto 63 R.P.D23
B2608	–.–.62	28.11.62	B.W. Gossage	Hon. H.J. Boulton	Pt lot 5 west side Bay St south of Wellington St; 40 ft	Toronto 63 R.P.D24
B2609	–	28.4.63	Charles Unwin	Estate of George Taylor Denison	Pt S1/2 park lots 25, 26, and 27; Bloor St to Queen St btwn Dundas St and west city limit; 4 ch	Toronto 63 R.P.D25
B2610	11.5.63	18.5.63	John Tully	John Mulholland	Lots on Mutual and Dalhousie sts north of Queen St E; warehouses, Presbyterian church; 20 ft	Toronto 63 R.P.D26
B2611	1.8.63	26.11.69	J.O. Browne	–	Appendix to **B2512** showing extension of lane btwn Sherbourne and Pembroke sts north of Wilton Cres; 60 ft	Toronto 63 R.P.D64

	Date of Survey	Date of Regist.	Surveyor	Owner	Description and Notes	Location
B2612	2.11.63	27.1.69	John Tully	Arthur Whitesides	Pt park lot 1, 1st con from bay, twp York; SW corner of North Park and Sumach sts, cottages, stable; 13 ft	Toronto 63 R.P.D56
B2613	16.3.64	8.4.64	J.O. Browne	M.H. Dixon, Jr	Subdivision of pt park lot 9; College Ave to Hayter St, Yonge St to Terauley St, Wykeham Lodge, Parkes Factory; 50 ft	Toronto 63 R.P.D27
B2614	–	15.7.64	Henry McLeod	G.W.R. Co.	'Pound House Block' btwn Peter and Brock sts south of Front St; 50 ft	Toronto 63 R.P.D28
B2615	11.8.64	15.7.65	J.O. Browne	G. Allan	Subdivision of pt park lot 5; Gloucester St to Carleton St, Sherbourne to Wellesley Place, Homewood House and grounds and horticultural grounds; 60 ft	Toronto 63 R.P.D30
B2616	18.10.64	6.2.65	Dennis & Gossage	Joseph C. Morrison	Subdivision of 'Rose Estate,' lot 16, 2nd con from Bay, twp York; east of Yonge St along Inglewood Dr, vegetation, relief; 4 ch	Toronto 63 R.P.274
B2617	31.12.64	20.1.66	Dennis & Gossage	John C. Griffith Executor	Subdivision of lot 17, 2nd con, and lot 20, 3rd con from bay, twp York; lots along Clarence St east of Yonge St, Thompson Ave and Charles St east of Yonge and north of Bloor, relief, ravine; 4 ch	Toronto 63 R.P.277
B2618	23.8.65	28.8.65	John Tully	Walter O'Hara	Villa lots at 'Brockton,' NW corner lot 34, 1st con from bay, twp York; lots along Dundas St backing on Alhambra on one side north to rd allowance btwn 1st and 2nd cons from bay; transcript; 4 ch	Toronto 63 R.P.276
B2619	22.3.66	24.3.66	Henry Northcote	W.J. Harper	'Yorkville,' pt lot 21, 2nd con from bay, twp York; west of Yonge St, south of Baldwin St; 15.6 ft	Toronto 63 R.P.278
B2620	11.6.66	[11.8.66?]	Dennis & Gossage	–	Subdivision of 'Robinson Heward Farm,' lot 12, BF, 1st con from bay, twp York; south of Kingston Rd, owners, swampy lands; 1 ch	Toronto 63 R.P.D81
B2621	–	18.10.66	F.F. Passmore	Estate of Miss Baldwin	Subdivision of lot 8, north side King St, and lot 8, south side Adelaide St east of York St; 40 ft	Toronto 63 R.P.D32

B2622	16.10.66	18.10.66	F.F. Passmore	–	'Baldwin Estate,' pt park lots 14–16, 1st con from bay, twp York; Queen St to con rd [Bloor St], Beverly St and university grounds west to Robert St and Denison Estate; 3 ch	Toronto 63 R.P.D33
B2623	22.10.66	–	Henry Northcote	John Harper	Subdivision of lots 11 and 12, north side Charles (formerly Frank) St, being pt park lot 1, 1st con from bay, twp York; 15 ft	Toronto 63 R.P.D34
B2624	9.5.67	3.7.67	Robert F. Lynn	James Fleming	45 building lots on Elm St, pt park lot 9; Elm St to Edward St, Yonge St to Terauley St; 40 ft	Toronto 63 R.P.D36
B2625	21.5.67	1.6.67	B.W. Gossage	Stephen Heward et al.	Subdivision of pt lot XXVI, 2nd con from bay, twp York; Hope St to Bathurst St, Seaton St to Hammond St; 2 ch	Toronto 63 R.P.281
B2626	24.6.67	24.9.67	Gossage & Wadsworth	Estate of William Small	'Berkeley Estate,' subdivision of pts lots 6, 7, and 8, 1st con from bay, twp York; Kingston Rd to G.T.R., mill pond, 'Serpentine,' Berkeley Church property; 3 ch	Toronto 63 R.P.282
B2627	27.6.67	2.7.67	Gossage & Wadsworth	–	'Townsley Estate,' subdivision of pt of south side Isabella St; cites earlier unregistered plan by Arthur Wells; 50 ft	Toronto 63 R.P.D35
B2628	4.7.67	7.8.69	Gossage & Wadsworth	Estate of George Taylor Denison	Subdivision of pt park lot XXIX, 1st con from bay, twp York; Lakeshore Rd to Dundas St btwn 2 rd allowances, Northern Ry, G.T.R.; transcript; 3 ch	Toronto 63 R.P.294
B2629	16.9.67	25.1.68	J.O. Browne	–	Appendix to **B2613**; revised subdivision of pts park lots 9 and 10; College Ave to Hayter St, Terauley St to Yonge St, bldgs, Parkes Factory, Wykeham Lodge and estate; 50 ft	Toronto 63 R.P.D42
B2630	4.10.67	–	C. Rankin	James E. Small	Subdivision of south pt park lot III; Queen St to Sydenham St, Parliament St to McMahon, possibly laid out before 1850, original plan lost; 100 ft	Toronto 63 R.P.D38
B2631	–.10.67	17.2.68	Wadsworth & Unwin	Estate of Robert Riddell	Subdivision of N1/2 lot 18, IIIrd con from bay, twp York; lots east of Yonge St along William St, inset map; 3 ch	Toronto 63 R.P.284

	Date of Survey	Date of Regist.	Surveyor	Owner	Description and Notes	Location
B2632	20.11.67	26.11.67	Wadsworth & Unwin	Thomas Gelly & William Caxley	Subdivision of lots 1 and 2, north side Duke St and south side Duchess St; burial ground on Duchess St; 30 ft	Toronto 63 R.P.D39
B2633	–	3.12.67	H.C. Boulton	–	Subdivision of lots 7–12, pt **B2412**; Amelia to Winchester St west of Sumach St; 25 ft	Toronto 63 R.P.D40
	(TRAFALGAR town plot)					
B2634	–.9.56	–	Henry Strange	Robert Porter	Pt lot VII, 1st con, Division E, twp Guelph; listed as 'incomplete' in registry office; 2 ch	Wellington 61 R.P.51
	TRENTON					
B2635	–.–.34	26.7.55	F.P. Rubidge (J.J. Haslett)	Robert C. Wilkins	At mouth of Trent R; Cummins St to Robertson St, Ragg St to Pinnacle St, bldgs; 2 ch	Hastings 21 R.P.76
B2636	–.8.53	27.9.53	J.S. Peterson	Estate of Adam Henry Meyers	Town plot, pt lot 2, 1st con, twp Murray; originally called Hanover, Trent R to Metcalfe St and rd allowance btwn lots 2 and 3; 2 ch	Hastings 21 R.P.6 (2)
B2637	21.9.53	4.10.53	John Stoughton Dennis	John Strachan	'Trenton East,' lot P, Gore of Sidney; Trent St to Hemans and Chestnut sts, Bay to con rd allowance, Gilmour & Co. land, additions by surveyor; 3 ch	Hastings 21 R.P.64
B2638	–.8.55	25.6.56	J.S. Peterson	J.F. Flindall	Lot 1, BF, twp Sidney; Bay of Quinte to King St on both sides Distillery St, distillery, malt-house, bldgs; 2 ch	Hastings 21 R.P.82
B2639	10.2.65	9.8.65	James Macleod	'Hawley Estate'	'Hawley Estate,' pt of Water St to King St, Bridge St to Concession Rd, bldgs; 1 ch	Hastings 21 R.P.107
B2640	–.7.65	15.3.66	William Hawkins	John Howcutt	Pt lot A, 1st con, gore of Sidney, Queen St to Birch St, Trent St to beyond Trenton St; 2 ch	Hastings 21 R.P.112
B2641	–	10.12.67	D. Williams	G. Francis	Pt lot 1, 1st con, twp Murray; Spring St to Dominion St, Marmora St to line btwn Sidney and Murray twps; 2 ch	Hastings 21 R.P.122

	TUCKERSMITH TWP					
B2642	22.11.54	6.2.55	William Perceval	Wm Moore	Subdivision of N1/2 lot 49, 1st con, twp Tuckersmith; 2 ch	Huron 22 R.P.132
	TULLAMORE					
B2643	24.11.56	4.5.57	Bristow & Fitzgerald	I.M. Chafee	Pt lot 17, con VIII, gore of Toronto, and pt lot 17, con VI east of Hurontario St, twp Chinguacousy; King St and King William St, bldgs, owners, cultural detail; 66 ft	Peel 43 R.P.CH4
B2644	20.11.56	4.5.57	Messrs Bristow & Fitzgerald	I.M. Chafee	For description see **2149** (the printed version of **B2643**)	Peel 43 TORG2
	TWEED					
B2645	–	21.11.49	John Emerson	Felix Gabourie	'Georgetown,' pt lot 11, 9th con, twp Hungerford; 2 streets on edge of L Sloco; 2 ch	Hastings 21 R.P.11A
B2646	–.9.50	–.9.50	John Emerson	James Jamison	Pt lot 11, 10th con, twp Hungerford; Jamison St to Bridge St, Metcalfe St to Moira R, mill, dam, bridge; 2 ch	Hastings 21 R.P.12B
B2647	18.5.59	17.8.59	John Emerson	Felix Gabourie	'Georgetown,' lot 11, 9th con, twp Hungerford; lots on Hungerford Rd; scale n.g.	Hastings 21 R.P.93
	TYRCONNELL					
B2648	–.4.48	31.3.55	B. Springer	George MacBeth	Lots 8 and 9, 10th cons, twp Dunwich; L Erie to High St, Queen St to Talbot St, relief, bridges, dam; 4 ch	Elgin 11 R.P.6
B2649	–.–.55	26.12.55	Samuel Peters	James Blackwood	Lots 8 and 9, 9th and 10th cons, twp Dunwich; L Erie north to Derby and Deveron sts, line btwn lots 7 and 8 to Queen and Clyde sts, relief, owner's residence; 264 ft	Elgin 11 R.P.8
	UDORA					
B2650	24.10.56	31.10.56	F.C. McCallum	Thomas Bolster	Lots XXI and XXII, 1st con, twp Georgina; Black R to Mill St, lots on Victoria and York sts and town line btwn Scott and Georgina sts; 2 ch	York 65 R.P.178

	Date of Survey	Date of Regist.	Surveyor	Owner	Description and Notes	Location
	UNION (Elgin Co)					
B2651	–.11.51	23.2.52	Charles Fraser	Charles Fraser	Pt village, twp Yarmouth; Colborne St and gravel rd to limit btwn lots 4 and 5, road to Sparta on line btwn cons III and IV to Washington St; 2 ch	Elgin 11 R.P.13A
	UNION (Essex Co)					
B2652	31.7.51	30.8.51	P.D. Salter	Margaret & Winelle Wigle	Pt lot 9, front, twp Gosfield; company store on L Erie, lots from Main St to Duke St on both sides Wellington St; transcript; 2 ch	Essex 12 R.P.30
B2653	12.12.54	3.5.55	Philip S. Donnelly	Winellee M. Wigle	Pt lot 9, twp Gosfield; Main St to Duke St, Raglan St to Wellington St; transcript; 2 ch	Essex 12 R.P.30(2)
B2654	26.5.62	13.12.62	A. Wilkinson	James Dougall	Lot 9, 1st con, twp Gosfield; resurvey and altered, L Erie and Main St to Duke St, Wellington St to Raglan St; transcript; 100 ft	Essex 12 R.P.28
	(UNION town plot) (Wellington Co)					
B2655	18.11.57	28.1.58	Francis Kerr	Silas Edwards	Pt lots 9 and 10, 10th con, Division C, twp Guelph; grist mill on Speed R; 2 ch	Wellington 61 R.P.97
	UNIONVILLE					
B2656	–.8.56	24.12.56	George McPhillips	–	E1/2 lot 11, 5th con, twp Markham; Auburn St to Union St, Pavillion and Euclid sts, bldgs; 2 ch	Toronto 64 R.P.190
	UTICA					
B2657	–.9.60	14.2.61	W.E. Yarnold	Municipal Corp. Twp Reach	Lots 6 and 7, 5th con, and lot 6, 4th con, twp Reach; lots along King and Brock sts, owners; 2 ch	Durham 40 R.P.H-50026
	UTOPIA					
B2658	–.–.56	–	H.P. Savigny	James Magee	'Essa Station,' east pt lot 30, 5th con, twp Essa; Magee's sawmill and bldgs on river, R.R. depot, not certified; 2 ch	Simcoe 51 R.P.68A Essa

	UXBRIDGE					
B2659	10.5.48	12.8.51	John Shier	Joseph Gould	'Gouldville,' NE pt lot 29, 6th con, twp Uxbridge; lots along Mill St and along road from Toronto to Pickering; 2 ch	Durham 40 R.P.(Uxbridge town)
B2660	1.6.52	15.9.55	James McCallum, Jr	William Hamilton	Pt lots 30 and 31, 6th con, twp Uxbridge; lots along Stouffville Rd and Mill St, Black R, mill pond, bounded by Victoria St, cultural detail; 2 ch	Durham 40 R.P.(Uxbridge Twp)
B2661	1.3.56	25.5.61	James McCallum, Jr	John P. Plank	Pt lots XXX and XXXI, 7th con, twp Uxbridge; Main St, Black R, lots along Brock St, bldgs; 3 ch	Durham 40 R.P.H-50061 (16851 Uxbridge)
B2662	9.3.56	25.11.59	James McCallum, Jr	Joseph Bascom	Pt lot XXX, 6th con, twp Uxbridge; lots along King and Bascom sts to mill pond; 2 ch	Durham 40 R.P.13303 (Uxbridge Twp)
B2663	10.4.56	3.7.56	John Shier	Joseph Gould	E1/2 lots 29–31, 6th con, twp Uxbridge; lots as laid out by J. Gould (1848) and W. Hamilton (1852), mills, relief, streets named; 3 ch	Durham 40 R.P.(Uxbridge Twp)
B2664	–.6.62	4.3.63	John J. McKenna	Richard Bell	Lot 29, 7th con, twp Uxbridge; east of Main St, lots along Reach and Bell sts; 2 ch	Durham 40 R.P.H-50060
B2665	7.5.64	12.7.64	James McCallum, Jr	J.C. Widdifield	Lots on SW1/4 lot 34, 7th con, twp Uxbridge; 2.8 ch	Durham 40 R.P.H-50063
	VANDECAR					
B2666	5.2.57	25.1.64	W.G. Wonham	Seymour Sage	'Sageville,' Matilda to Edwin St south of Concession St; 2 ch	Oxford 41 R.P.126
	VANKLEEK HILL					
B2667	–.12.59	16.2.60	Peter W. McLaren	Mun Corp. of W Oxbury on behalf of original owners	Pt lots 8–10, con 5, and pts lots 9 and 10, con 6, twp Hawkesbury; Wall St to Higginson St, High St to Head St; 1 ch	Prescott 46 R.P.5
	VARNA					
B2668	–.4.56	3.6.56	John Denison	Donald Gordon, John Crawford & James Wanless	Pt lot 18 and 19 north and south Bayfield Rd Con, twp Stanley; notes on location of plot; 3 ch	Huron 22 R.P.307

	Date of Survey	Date of Regist.	Surveyor	Owner	Description and Notes	Location
B2669	–.3.60	14.3.60	John Denison	Township of Stanley	Pt lot 18 north and south and pt lot 19 south of Bayfield Rd Con, twp Stanley; owners; 2.5 ch	Huron 22 R.P.308
	VARNEY					
B2670	14.6.56	19.6.56	Edwin Henry Kertland	Thomas Sirr	Lot 3, 1st con, twp Normanby; Garafraxa Rd to Field St, mill pond with bldgs to Thomas St; 2 ch	Grey 17 R.P.155
	VAUGHAN TWP					
B2671	–.–.[53]	20.8.53	J.S. Dennis	Rowland Burr	'Burrlington & Ellis Burgh,' subdivision of pt lot 31, con IX, twp Vaughan; Humber R, sawmill; 4 ch	Toronto 64 R.P.132B
B2672	–.9.55	13.11.55	George McPhillips	David Chapman	Lot 28, 1st con, twp Vaughan; owners, orchard, barn, house; 4 ch	Toronto 64 R.P.137
	VENTNOR					
B2673	–.5.59	13.5.61	William Campbell	Josiah Levi & Edward Adams	'Adams,' lot 15, 7th con, and lots 15 and 16, 8th con, twp Edwardsburgh; Edward St below Petite Nation R to Harold St on north side, lots along Mill St, 2 sawmills, mill race, grist mill, flume; 1 ch	Grenville 15 R.P.Edwards-burgh 15
	VERNONVILLE					
B2674	–	11.12.60	E.C. Caddy	C.H. Vernon	Albert St to Victoria St, St George St to beyond North St; 2 ch	Northumberland 39 R.P.Haldimand 8
	VERONA					
B2675	8.5.58	31.1.63	A.B. Perry	S. Shibley	Lots IX and X, 10th con, twp Portland; streets named, Napanee R, marsh and drowned land; 2 ch	Frontenac 13 R.P.22 (35)

	VICTORIA					
B2676	10.10.56	20.11.56	Bristow & Fitzgerald	Andrew Crawford	Lot 27 east and west of Centre Rd; Queen St on north, lots on both sides Main St and along Adelaide and Elizabeth sts; 1 ch	Peel 43 R.P.CH3
	VICTORIA SQUARE					
B2677	–.11.56	27.11.56	George McPhillips	William G. Kingston	Union St to Victoria St btwn Elgin and Albert sts, bldgs; 1 ch	Toronto 64 R.P.184
	VIENNA					
B2678	31.3.51	–	Jesse P. Ball	Samuel Garnsey	Pt central pt lot XV, 3rd con, twp Bayham; Big Otter Creek to plank rd, lots along North, North Centre, and East sts, plank rd, reserves, owners; 2 ch	Elgin 11 no R.P.#
B2679	–.–.53	11.2.54	Jesse P. Ball	Thomas & S. Edison	Pt central pt lot 15 and south and west pt lot 14, 3rd con, twp Bayham; Big Otter Creek to road btwn lots 13 and 14; 2 ch	Elgin 11 R.P.2
B2680	16.3.54	15.6.54	Jesse P. Ball	Alum Marr	South pt lot 13, 3rd con, twp Bayham; King St north to Big Otter Creek, west limit to Union St; 2 ch	Elgin 11 no R.P.#
B2681	28.11.54	2.12.54	Jesse P. Ball	Municipality of Vienna	North pt lots 12–16, 2nd con, and south pts lots 12–16, 3rd con, twp Bayham; Vienna St on south, Centre St to Main St, bridges, reserved lots; 4 ch	Elgin 11 R.P.4
B2682	26.3.56	7.10.67	Jesse P. Ball	David Stillwell	NE pt lot 15, 3rd con, twp Bayham; Mill Rd to rd allowance btwn cons 3 and 4, west of plank rd, owners; 2 ch	Elgin 11 R.P.17
	VILLA NOVA					
B2683	15.7.55	–	Thomas W. Walsh	Estate of W. Walker	Pt lot 18, cons 8 and 9, twp Townsend; river with mill and tannery, bldgs, graveyard; 2 ch	Norfolk 37 R.P.41A
	VROOMANTON					
B2684	12.6.55	13.8.56	James McCallum, Jr	James Vrooman & Nathaniel Bolster	Lots along King and Brock sts and by mill pond, sawmill; 2 ch	Durham 40 R.P.H-50050
B2685	31.8.59	1.2.60	J.C. McCallum	Thomas Bolster	Subdivision of pt lots 6 and 7, 7th con, twp Brock; 2 ch	Durham 40 R.P.13718 (Brock Twp)

	Date of Survey	Date of Regist.	Surveyor	Owner	Description and Notes	Location
B2686	4.7.62	5.3.63	J.C. McCallum, Jr	Thomas Bolster	Lots 6 and 7, 7th con, twp Brock; 8th con line south to King St, Simcoe St west to Nelson St, alteration of earlier plan 11.8.56; 2 ch	Durham 40 R.P.H-50049
	WAINFLEET					
B2687	15.10.56	5.6.58	Andrew Hood	Mr Graybill	'Marsville,' NE pt lot 19, 3rd con, twp Wainfleet; lots north of Welland Canal feeder to Hartwell St, bldgs around mill reserve; 2 ch	Niagara 59 R.P.985 (old Wainfleet 1)
B2688	–.–.[6?]	–	–	Edward Lee	'Marshville,' lots adjoining village in 3rd con, twp Wainfleet; lots south of Welland Canal feeder along Brown St and another street, owners, bldgs, old grist mill, land owned by Welland Co.; 2 ch	Niagara 59 R.P.986 (old plan 0)
	WALKERTON					
B2689	4.12.55	29.2.56	Edwin H. Kertland	Thomas Bilkie	Lot 23, 1st con south of Durham Rd, twp Brant; 2 ch	Bruce 3 R.P.2
B2690	4.2.57	26.2.57	Edwin H. Kertland	Joseph Walker & William Walker	Saugeen R south to South St, west to Elizabeth St, east to George St; 4 ch	Bruce 3 R.P.7
B2691	29.7.57	19.8.57	William R. Rombough	William Hall	Subdivision of lots 24 and 25, 1st con south of Durham Rd, twp Brant; Durham Rd to Princess St, Elizabeth St to Mary St; 2 ch	Bruce 3 R.P.9
B2692	26.12.57	[1.1.58?]	Francis Kerr	James Boulton	Lots on Mary and Queen to Duke St, Boulton and Church and Bay sts, several other streets and bldgs shown; 2 ch	Bruce 3 R.P.14
B2693	11.2.58	11.5.58	Sproat & Hawkins	Joseph Walker	Lots on Durham and Victoria sts to Saugeen R; 2 ch	Bruce 3 R.P.17
B2694	–.11.63	7.12.63	M.C. Schofield	James Hodgert	Subdivision of pt lot 29, 1st con, twp Brant north of Durham Rd; north of Queen and Boulton sts, owners; 3 ch	Bruce 3 R.P.38

	WALLACEBURG					
B2695	–.3.48	1.6.68	Richard Parr	J.H. Bates	'Batehampton,' pt lots 11 and 12, 1st con, twp Sombra; Marion St to Sydenham R, Amelia St to Jane St, owners; 2 ch	Kent 24 R.P.110
B2696	–.6.50	1.6.67	Richard Parr	W. & W. Eberts	Pt lot 13, 2nd con, twp Sombra; King St to Sydenham R, Murray St to Princess St; approx 22 ft	Kent 24 R.P.112
B2697	22.5.51	23.6.51	P.S. Donnelly	James Baby	'Babyville,' Baldwin St to Camp St, Elgin St to James St; 100 ft	Kent 24 R.P.111
B2698	–.3.53	1.6.67	P.S. Donnelly	James Baby	'Babyville,' James St at Sydenham R to Elgin St, Lisgar St to Camp St; 100 ft	Kent 24 R.P.114A
B2699	18.11.54	–	A.P. Salter	W. & W. Eberts	'Wallaceburgh North,' pt lot 13, con 2, twp Sombra; Margaret Ave to Ellen St, Collins St to Dundas St; 1.5 ch	Kent 24 R.P.117
B2700	17.11.56	1.6.67	A.P. Salter & Co.	Hy Myers Marsh	Subdivision, King St to George St, Murray St to Victoria St; 2 ch	Kent 24 R.P.115
B2701	–.4.57	[25.4.57?]	P.S. Donnelly	Alexander McKay	Continuation of town; Sydenham R to James St btwn Oak and west limit of town; 80 ft	Kent 13 R.P.113
B2702	8.12.56	21.1.67	Charles Fraser	Municipal Council	Compilation plan; includes surveys of McKay, Johnson, Baby, Langstaff, Eberts, and Marsh; 200 ft	Kent 24 R.P.118
B2703	–.5.66	[16.7.66?]	Charles Fraser	Alexander Vical	'Babyville,' compilation plan of whole town; corrections made in a few lots, James St to above Wall St, Lisgar St to north branch Sydenham R and Emily St; 100 ft	Kent 24 R.P.116
	WALLACETOWN					
B2704	–.–.56	10.9.58	William McMillan	Alexander Rose	Pt lot XII, cons VII and VIII, twp Dunwich; Queen St to Wallace St, Currie St to Gordon St; 2 ch	Kent 11 R.P.20
	WALSINGHAM					
B2705	1.8.64	–	T.W. Walsh	Stephen D. Brown	'Brownstown,' N1/2 lot 13, con V, and S1/2 lot 13, con VI, twp Walsingham; lots from Main St to South St, Morgan St to Brown St, showground and town hall site; 2.5 ch	Norfolk 37 R.P.48A

	Date of Survey	Date of Regist.	Surveyor	Owner	Description and Notes	Location
	WALTERS FALLS					
B2706	–	14.5.63	Archibald McNab	John Matheson	Lots on Alma, Front, and Victoria sts and river; photoreproduction; 3 ch	Grey 16 R.P.123
	WALTON					
B2707	20.2.66	7.3.67	A. Bay	John Hewitt	Lot 1, 13th con, twp Grey; lots on High, King, Patrick, and Queen sts, mill block; 1 ch	Huron 22 R.P.310
B2708	–.9.67	21.12.67	George McPhillips	Thomas Lurax	Lot XXX, 10th con, twp Morris; lots along rd allowance btwn Morris and Grey twps, Walton Hotel; 2 ch	Huron 22 R.P.312
	WANSTEAD					
B2709	–.–.57	1.2.60	E.R. Jones	Alexander Scott	'Lambton,' lot 26, 2nd con, twp Plympton; 1st–4th sts, Scott St to Henderson St; 3 ch	Lambton 25 R.P.Plympton 6
B2710	–.9.58	8.2.59	E.R. Jones	Henry C.R. Beecher	Lot 25, 2nd con, twp Plympton; 1st–5th sts; Woodford St, G.W.R. station grounds; 3 ch	Lambton 25 R.P.Plympton 5
	WARDSVILLE					
B2711	15.3.50	31.1.54	John O'Mara	Talbot S. & John Ward	'Ward Plot,' George St to Main St, Hagerty St to King St; photoreproduction; 2 ch	Middlesex 34 R.P.42
B2712	4.7.51	7.12.67	William Smiley	Kennedy Parker & Co, J.W.A. Skinner	Adjoining SE pt BF lot 16, 1st range south of Long Woods Rd, twp Mosa; 1st tier of lots south of Main St and graveyard from old survey, Main St to McNab St, Creek St to Mill St, mill race; transcript; 1.5 ch	Middlesex 34 R.P.227
B2713	16.8.52	9.12.57	John O'Mara	Mr Davis	'Davis Plot,' Thames R to Main St, Davis St to O'Mara St, church, school plot; transcript; 2 ch	Middlesex 34 R.P.127
B2714	29.5.55	23.1.67	B. Springer	Henry R. Archer	SE pt lot 17, 1st range north of Long Woods Rd, twp Mosa; lots on Main and William sts and on Hagerty Rd btwn William and Mill sts, town hall; photoreproduction; 2 ch	Middlesex 34 R.P.218

B2715	29.7.57	31.7.57	John O'Mara	James Ward	Pt S1/2 lot 16, 1st range north of Longwoods Rd, twp Mosa, and west pt of S1/2 lot 16 showing schoolhouse site; bounded by Victoria, Wellington, and Queen sts; photoreproduction; 2 ch	Middlesex 34 R.P.144
B2716	30.5.67	24.9.67	John O'Mara	Talbot S. & J. Ward	Pt lot 16, 1st range north of Longwoods Rd, twp Mosa; George St to Victoria St, Hagerty Rd to Queen St, grammar school land; photoreproduction; 2 ch	Middlesex 34 R.P.223
	WARKWORTH					
B2717	21.5.51	3.1.52	J.S. Peterson	Jonathan Reeso	'Percy,' lots on Church, Main, Deuter, and East sts, owners; 1 ch	Northumberland 38 R.P.2 (Percy)
B2718	5.5.57	12.6.57	E.C. Caddy	Messrs Fleury Le Mesurier, Tilstons et al.	'Percy,' pt lot 16, 3rd con, twp Percy; Mill St south 4 blocks, lots on Walter and George sts, bldgs; 2 ch	Northumberland 38 R.P.12 (Percy)
B2719	–.7.67	–.4.68	David Williams	Municipal Council	Lots 16 and 17, 3rd con, twp Percy; Mill and Church sts to rd allowance btwn cons 2 and 3, West St to East St, relief, bldgs, churches, school, town hall; 2 ch	Northumberland 38 R.P.29 (Percy)
	(WARRINGTON)					
B2720	–.–.58–9	27.4.59	William Gibbard	John McWatt, John Dewe & Margaret Sutherland	Pt lots 22 and 23, 1st con, twp Nottawasaga; William St to James St, Huron St to beyond Erie St, mills and bldgs; 3 ch	Simcoe 51 R.P.72
	WARSAW					
B2721	9.2.53	2.6.53	John Reid	–	From boundary btwn Douro and Dummer to road to Norwood by Indian R and mill pond, flour mill, carding mill, sawmill, dam; 3 ch	Peterborough 45 R.P.H2 Dummer
	WARWICK					
B2722	–.1.55	29.11.55	P.D. Salter	David Rogers	Front pt lot 10, 1st con north of Egremont Rd, twp Warwick; Burwell St to Egremont Rd; 3 ch	Lambton 25 R.P.Warwick 4

	Date of Survey	Date of Regist.	Surveyor	Owner	Description and Notes	Location
B2723	13.9.55	28.9.55	A. Bay	Thomas Rothwell	Lot XXVIII, 1st con south of Egremont Rd, twp Warwick; Egremont Rd to Dame St, side-rd btwn lots 27 and 28 to Meath St; 2 ch	Lambton 25 R.P.Warwick 3
	WASHINGTON					
B2724	-.11.51	–	James Black	Arthur John Robertson	Pt lots 12 and 13, 12th con, twp Blenheim; lots along Washington and Wilmot sts, owners; 2 ch	Oxford 41 R.P.100
B2725	12.9.60	–	Cyrus Carroll	Twp Corp. of Blenheim	Compiled plan; lots 12 and 13, 12th and 13th cons, twp Blenheim; lots along Washington and Wilmot sts; 3 ch	Oxford 41 R.P.125
	WATERDOWN					
B2726	26.8.54	–	Henry Winter	–	Ransom St to James St, John St to beyond Union St, very detailed, owners, dams, bridges, mill races; 2 ch	Wentworth 62 R.P.Waterdown (old 47)
B2727	1.6.55	28.6.56	Henry Winter	Messrs McMonnies & Stocks	Dundas St to rd allowance btwn cons 3 and 4, east of Mill St; 2 ch	Wentworth 62 R.P.Waterdown (old 58)
B2728	30.8.56	–	Winter & Howitt	Messrs McMonnies & Stocks	Church St to Wellington St, Mill St to side-rd line 5/6; 2 ch	Wentworth 62 R.P.Waterdown (old 18)
	WATERLOO					
B2729	-.-.55	[-.7.55?]	Milton C. Schofield	John Hoffman	Pts lots 14 and 15, twp Waterloo; btwn Park and Mary sts, mill pond to Green St, owners, Mount Hope Cemetery, Mill Sq; 4 ch	Waterloo 58 R.P.385
B2730	-.-.56	[-.1.57?]	Schofield & Hobson	Messrs Jacob C. & Elias Snider	Pt lot 14, Upper Block, German Co. Tract; Albert St to Erb St, Erb St to Church and Elgin sts; 2 ch	Waterloo 58 R.P.491
B2731	-.-.57	[-.9.57?]	Schofield & Hobson	Menno Snyder	Menno St to Foundry St, Erb St to Weaver St; 80 ft	Waterloo 58 R.P.495

B2732	–.–.58	[–.4.58?]	Schofield & Hobson	Estate of Frederick Mussleman	Frederick St to Schneider St east of King St, owners; 2 ch	Waterloo 59 R.P.494
B2733	–.–.59	[9.11.59?]	M.C. Schofield	Estate of John Diller	Pt lot 6, Upper Block, G.C.T.; 3 ch	Waterloo 58 R.P.493
B2734	–.–.61	[26.8.61?]	Joseph Hobson	David D. Bowman	Subdivision of pt lot 15, Upper Block, G.C.T., lots along Union, Bowman, and David sts; 2 ch	Waterloo 58 R.P.403
B2735	–.–.64	19.10.64	Joseph Hobson	Jacob C. Snider & Elias Snider	Lots west of King St; 80 links	Waterloo 58 R.P.492
B2736	–.–.66	5.6.67	Joseph Hobson	Estate of Jacob C. Snider	Pt lot 23, north of Erb St; 4 ch	Waterloo 58 R.P.496
B2737	–.–.67	14.3.68	James Pollock	Thomas C. Kerr	Subdivision of park lots 204 and 407 of John Hoffman's survey (**B2729**); William St west of Caroline St; 2 ch	Waterloo 58 R.P.497
	WATERLOO TWP					
B2738	21.6.54	[19.11.78?]	Noah Bowman	Michael Bergey	Pts lot 6, cons 3 and 4, twp Waterloo; owners, copy of instrument 14834; transcript; 200 ft	Waterloo 58 R.P.600
B2739	–.9.57	–	Francis Kerr	Mr Bergey	Subdivision of pt lot 12, 3rd con, Lower Block, twp Waterloo; 2 ch	Waterloo 58 R.P.590
B2740	16.11.58	–	James Pollock	Joseph Erb	Pt lot 54, Upper Block, twp Waterloo; 4 ch	Waterloo 58 R.P.589
B2741	–.–.61	[8.5.61?]	M.C. Schofield	Martin Schiedel	Pt lot 56 and twp lot 72, Upper Block, G.C.T., twp Waterloo; 3 ch	Waterloo 58 R.P.584
B2742	–.–.62	[5.11.62?]	Joseph Hobson	William Mayer	Subdivision of pt lots 84 and 106, Upper Block, twp Waterloo; on both sides Berlin and Guelph Rd and Preston and Freiburg Rd, owners; 4 ch	Waterloo 58 R.P.582
B2743	–.–.63	[18.8.63?]	Joseph Hobson	William Mayer	Subdivision of pt lot 110, G.C.T., twp Waterloo; 4 ch	Waterloo 58 R.P.583
B2744	–.–.63	13.1.64	Joseph Hobson	John Brubacher	Subdivision of lot 148, G.C.T., twp Waterloo; on both sides Huron Rd east of Wilmot Twp boundary; 4 ch	Waterloo 58 R.P.585

	Date of Survey	Date of Regist.	Surveyor	Owner	Description and Notes	Location
	WATFORD					
B2745	–.–.59?	5.3.59	Charles L. Davies	George L. Reid	Pt lots 18 and 19, 5th con south of Egremont Rd, twp Warwick; G.W.R. to Huron St, Warwick St to Main St, station bldgs; 2 ch	Lambton 25 R.P.Watford 1
B2746	16.10.65	21.10.65	T.C. Brownjohn	George L. Reid	Addition to pt lots 18 and 19, 5th con, twp Warwick; area below and above Sarnia branch G.W.R. north to Simcoe St, Warwick St to beyond Main St, owners; 2 ch	Lambton 25 R.P.Watford 2
B2747	25.10.65	8.11.65	Thomas Charles Brownjohn	Charles Wilson	Pt E1/2 lot 18, 5th con, twp Warwick; Mill St to Rachel St, West St to Main St; 100 ft	Lambton 25 R.P.Watford 3
B2748	–.11.67	23.10.68	Alexander Davidson	John & David Ross	NE pt lot 18, Vth con south of Egremont Rd, twp Warwick; Simcoe St to rd allowance btwn cons 4 and 5 west of Main St; 1.5 ch	Waterloo 25 R.P.Watford 4
	(WAUBUNO)					
B2749	–.–.55	11.12.56	William McClary	T.G. Ridout	For description see **2160**	Middlesex 33 R.P.128
	WELLAND					
B2750	–.9.45	22.6.53	J.W. Fell	Duncan McFarland & John Donaldson	'Merrittsville Aqueduct,' old canal to road to Port Robinson New Stone Aqueduct, Welland R to Division St, owners; transcript; 1.25 ch	Niagara 59 R.P.551 (old Welland 2)
B2751	30.2.53	30.4.53	Edmund De Cew	James Shotwell	'Merrittville,' lot 248, twp Thorold; Welland R to Elgin St, Shotwell to Aqueduct St, mills, factory, warehouse; transcript; 2 ch	Niagara 59 R.P.549 (old Welland 1)
B2752	11.9.54	22.9.54	Zenas Fell	W.A. Bald	Pt lot 26, con V, twp Crowland; Jane St to Main St, Welland Canal to Denistown St; transcript; 1 ch	Niagara 59 R.P.552 (old Welland 3)
B2753	29.9.55	30.10.55	Zenas Fell	T. Burgar	'Merritville,' pt lot XXIV, con IV, and lot XXIV, con V, twp Crowland; aqueduct and	Niagara 59 R.P.553 (old

					canal to Division and Burgar sts, county bldgs, proposed market sq, see also **B2761**; transcript; 2 ch	Welland 4)
B2754	28.12.55	29.12.55	Jacob Misener	John Dunigan	'Diagram No. 2'; river and old channel of canal to unnamed con rd beyond Elizabeth St, Aqueduct St to Shotwell St; transcript; 2 ch	Niagara 59 R.P.550 (old Welland 5)
B2755	16.9.56	28.10.56	Jacob Misener	N.T. Fitch & J. Lamount	Map 3, subdivision of lots 84 and 87 on **B2754**; along Elm, Locust, and Pine sts and Main St to Aqueduct St; 2 ch	Niagara 59 R.P.554 (old Welland 6)
B2756	31.12.56	4.3.57	Henry T. Ross, Jacob Misener	N.T. Fitch & Jacob Griffith	Map 4; Park St to Young St, east of Canal St; transcript; 2 ch	Niagara 59 R.P.555 (old Welland 7)
B2757	3.4.57	8.2.58	Henry Ross, Jacob Misener	Thomas Burgar	'Merrittville,' lot 24, 5th con, twp Crowland; Cross St to Burgar St, Main St to Randolph St, market sq; 2 ch	Niagara 59 R.P.558 (old Welland 10)
B2758	–.5.57	20.9.61	Henry T. Ross, Jacob Misener	Moses Bett	Jane St to Merritt St, Denistown St to Welland Canal, owners; transcript; 2 ch	Niagara 59 R.P.560 (old Welland 12)
B2759	–.8.57	26.11.57	Henry T. Ross, Jacob Misener	Jesse Stoner	'Merrittville,' Jane St to Welland R, William St to Denistown St and beyond; transcript; 2 ch	Niagara 59 R.P.556 (old Welland 8)
B2760	16.1.58	8.2.58	Henry T. Ross, Jacob Misener	Thomas Burgar	'Merrittville,' lot 24, con V, twp Crowland; Welland R to Welland St, Burgar St to rd allowance, lots along Welland and Randolph sts; 2 ch	Niagara 59 R.P.557 (old Welland 9)
B2761	16.1.58	4.3.58	Henry T. Ross, Jacob Misener	N.T. Fitch	Con rd to Main St, east of canal to Canal St; continuation of **B2753**; 2 ch	Niagara 59 R.P.559 (old Welland 11)
B2762	–.4.59	25.8.64	Henry T. Ross, Jacob Misener	T. Burgar	Main St to Dorothy St btwn road to Port Robinson and ry, owners; 2 ch	Niagara 59 R.P.561 (old Welland 13)
B2763	–.–.59	20.5.59	Henry T. Ross, Jacob Misener	Archibald L. Cumming	Lot 28, twp Thorold; Dorcas St to Schofield St, plank rd to Chippawa Rd; transcript; 1 ch	Niagara 59 R.P.644 (old Thorold Twp 3)

	Date of Survey	Date of Regist.	Surveyor	Owner	Description and Notes	Location
	WELLANDPORT					
B2764	-.10.57	15.10.59	J.W. Fell	William Hitch	Pt lots 15 and 16, 1st con, twp Gainsborough; Quadrant St and Welland R to Victoria St and beyond Welland R to Beaver Creek, owners, schoolhouse lot, steam sawmill, store, bridge; 100 ft	Niagara 30 R.P.4 Co
	WEST FRANKLIN					
B2765	12.5.63	10.2.68	S.W. Hallen	Messrs Isaac & Aaron P. Tod	Lot 6, con 7, twp E Gwillimbury; 2 ch	York 65 R.P.12
	WESTMINSTER TWP					
B2766	15.8.53	19.8.53	Samuel Peters	C. Hutchinson	Pt lots 17 and 18, BF con, twp Westminster; Centre St, Hill St; later cancelled; 3 ch	Middlesex 33 R.P.34
B2767	17.5.55	25.6.55	Messrs Beattie & Bay	Thomas Fleming	Lots 17 and 18, 1st con, twp Westminster; street with lots fronting on pond; 2 ch	Middlesex 33 R.P.80 Co
B2768	-.6.55	24.10.59	Samuel Peters	Rev H. Massingberd	Pt lot 29, 1st con, twp Westminster; swampy areas, Commissioner's Rd S; 2 ch	Middlesex 33 R.P.157 Co
B2769	14.6.55	29.3.64	S. Peters	John Hutton	Pt lot 32, 1st con, twp Westminster; 1st con/BF to Commissioner's Rd, West St to John St; 3 ch	Middlesex 33 R.P.193 Co
B2770	26.6.55	26.6.55	Charles L. Davies	E.T. Ledyard	Pt lot 37, con B, twp Westminster; detailed drawing of cottage; 3 ch	Middlesex 33 R.P.81 Co
B2771	28.1.56	30.1.56	Leather & Robinson	Francis M. Palmer	Lot IX, con VIII, twp Westminster; park lots; 3 ch	Middlesex 33 R.P.100 Co
B2772	-.9.56	5.12.56	William McClary	Estate of A.S. Odell	Pt lot 24 south of Commissioners Rd, 1st con, twp Westminster; south of Commissioners Rd east of gravel rd; 1 ch	Middlesex 33 R.P.125 Co
B2773	5.11.56	8.11.56	Leather & Robinson	Capt Hennessy	Pt S1/2 lot XXX, 1st con, twp Westminster; east of London and Port Stanley Rd, south of Commissioner's Rd; 2 ch	Middlesex 33 R.P.124 Co
	WEST MONKTON					
B2774	3.3.57	21.3.57	Kertland & Gilkison	E. Winstanley	For description see **2161**	Perth 44 R.P.272

B2775	13.4.57	8.6.57	Kertland & Gilkison	E. Winstanley	Lots 16 and 17, 18th con, and lot 16, 17th con, twp Elma; Maddison St to Queen St, Winstanley St to Toronto St, mill property, market sq; 3 ch	Perth 44 R.P.273
	WESTPORT					
B2776	–.–.5?	–	T.T. Bower	George Crawford	Pt lot 11, 6th con, twp N Crosby; Rideau L to Church St, Rideau St to Bedford St; transcript; 1 ch	Leeds 28 R.P.135
	WESTWOOD					
B2777	5.8.56	7.5.57	John Reid	Mr Westwood	Lot 11, 2nd con, twp Asphodel; lots along rd allowance btwn lots 10 and 11, Ouse R, saw and flour mills, church; 3 ch	Peterborough 45 R.P.C-7 Asphodel
	WEXFORD					
B2778	30.4.60	21.12.60	Francis Jones	Mr Gainfort	'New Wexford,' front pt lots 36 and 37, 1st con, twp Edwardsburgh; Water St to Scott St, Railway St to Shanley St; 65 ft	Grenville 15 R.P.Edwardsburgh 13
	WHITBY					
B2779	–.–.4?	–.–.77	John Shier	'John Scadding'	'John Scadding Plan,' lots 26 and 27, BF con; plan missing but shown on Municipal Plan 75 (2.7.78)	Durham 40 R.P.H-50035
B2780	–.11.46	9.5.54	John Shier	Peter Perry	Lots 25–7, 2nd con, twp Whitby; Dundas St to Chestnut St, Kent St to Pine St; 2 ch	Durham 40 R.P.(Whitby Town)
B2781	–.5.54	1.9.54	John Shier	Asa Werden	N1/2 lots 26 and 27, 1st con, twp Whitby; Dundas St to Burns St, Henry St to Peel St; 3 ch	Durham 40 R.P.(Whitby Town)
B2782	–.9.54	7.7.55	John Shier	Francis Keller	Pt S1/2 lot 26, 1st con, twp Whitby; east of Brock St, lots along St Peter and St Lawrence sts; 2 ch	Durham 40 R.P.H-50034
B2783	–.10.54	6.8.55	John Shier	Messrs Farewell, Wallace & Keller	For description see **2168**	Durham 40 R.P.H-50045
B2784	30.12.54	27.3.55	William E. Yarnold	Mary Ann Tincombe	Pt lot 21, 1st con, twp Whitby; G.T.R. line north to Miller St btwn Henry and Centre sts; 2 ch	Durham 40 R.P.H-50039

	Date of Survey	Date of Regist.	Surveyor	Owner	Description and Notes	Location
B2785	26.5.55	26.5.55	John Shier	John Radenhurst	SE1/4 lot 27, 1st con, twp Whitby; King St to Third St, Brock St, plank rd to Centre St; 3 ch	Durham 40 R.P.H-50047
B2786	26.5.55	–	John Shier	John Radenhurst	For description see **2169**	Durham 40 no R.P.#
B2787	–	16.10.55	John Shier	William Thorndike	N1/2 lot 23, 1st con, twp Whitby; Dundas St to Pitt St, west of Hopkins St; 3 ch	Durham 40 R.P.(Whitby Town)
B2788	12.11.55	15.11.55	John Shier	J. Ham. Perry	S1/2 lots 25 and 26, 2nd con, twp Whitby; Dundas St to Beech St, Brock St to York St; 3 ch	Durham 40 R.P.(Whitby Town)
B2789	8.12.55	9.7.57	John Shier	Asa Werden	Subdivision of S1/2 town lots 31 and 32 west of Brock St, 6th double range, lots 17 and 18 east of Brock St, 7th double range, lots 13–16, 31, and 32 west of Brock St and lots 1, 2, 17, and 18 east of Brock St, 8th double range, laid out on N1/2 lots 26 and 27, 1st con, twp Whitby; Burns to St John St, Green to Byron St; 2 ch	Durham 40 R.P.H-50033 and H-50038
B2790	15.3.56	16.5.56	John Shier	Robert E. Perry	E1/2 lot 27, 2nd con, twp Whitby; Chestnut St to Poplar St, Brock St to Centre St; 3 ch	Durham 40 R.P.(Whitby Town)
B2791	6.5.56	16.5.56	John Shier	J.H. Perry	Pt lots 27 and 28, 2nd con, twp Whitby; Dundas St to Beech St, High St to Kent St; 3 ch	Durham 40 R.P.(Whitby Town)
B2792	24.9.56	24.9.56	John Shier	Mr Gerries	Subdivision of park lots 36 and 37 on lot 29, 2nd con, twp Whitby; Nelson St to Cochrane St, lots along Bonaccord St; 1.5 ch	Durham 40 R.P.H-50045
B2793	24.9.56	24.9.56	John Shier	James H. Gerries	Subdivision of lots 37 and 38 north of Dundas St, west of Byron St; 30 ft	Durham 40 R.P.H-50030
B2794	24.9.56	24.9.56	John Shier	James H. Gerries	Subdivision of lots 17 and 18, 2nd tier, 5th double range east of Brock St; at corner of Brock and St John sts; 33 ft	Durham 40 R.P.H-50031

B2795	10.11.56	4.6.57	J. Stoughton Dennis	Thomas Galt	North pt lots 25 and 26, BF con, twp Whitby; King St to Watson St, John St to Whitby St, bldgs, G.T.R. and station; 100 ft	Durham 40 R.P.H-50036
B2796	26.3.61	28.3.61	John Shier	Messrs Annes & Lowe	NE pt lot 28, 1st con, twp Whitby; Maria St to Dundas St, Frances St to Henry St; 2 ch	Durham 40 R.P.H-50046 (16432 Whitby)
B2797	–	24.8.64	Edward Webb	John Kerr, Jr	North of Dundas St btwn Palace and Euclid sts, bldgs; 1 ch	Durham 40 R.P.H-50040
B2798	11.7.65	25.7.65	John Shier	Wm Laing, Robert & James Campbell	Subdivision of lots 10–13, Perry's Block, North Ward, being pt S1/2 lot 26, 2nd con, twp Whitby; at Brock and Dundas sts; 30 ft	Durham 40 R.P.H-50041
B2799	21.12.65	22.2.66	John Shier	Estate of Ezra Annes	North pt lot 28, 1st con, twp Whitby; Dundas St S to Harriet St, Annes St to Henry St; 3 ch	Durham 40 R.P.26917 (Whitby)
B2800	18.1.66	22.1.66	John Shier	William Laing et al.	Subdivision of town lots 1 and 2, 1st double range east of Brock St; 20 ft	Durham 40 R.P.H-50041
	WHITE LAKE					
B2801	–.–.52	25.10.52	James Richey	Allan McNab	Pt lot 6, 3rd and 4th cons, twp [McNab]; Main and Allan sts at Waba L and Creek, owners; scale n.g.	Renfrew 49 R.P.5
	WHITEVALE					
B2802	–.–.57	22.1.57	John Shier	Truman P. White	'Major,' pt of lots 31 and 32, 4th and 5th cons, twp Pickering; lots along Main St, later amended, see also **B2803**; 2 ch	Durham 40 R.P.H-50056
B2803	–.6.60	30.6.60	John Shier	T.P. White	Amends plan above by cancelling some lots; 2 ch	Durham 40 R.P.H-50056(2)
	WIDDER					
B2804	–.–.55	[10.1.56?]	Samuel Peters	Donald McDonald	Lots 17 and 18, 1st con, and lots 18 and 19, 2nd con, twp Bosanquet; Blyth St to Henry St, Whitby St to Bosanquet St, relief; 2 ch	Lambton 25 R.P.Bosanquet 2
B2805	12.2.57	2.4.57	B. Springer	Isaac Decker	Pt lots 18 and 19, 2nd con, twp Bosanquet; Temperance St to Burwell St, Frank St to Church St; 1 ch	Lambton 25 R.P.Bosanquet 4

	Date of Survey	Date of Regist.	Surveyor	Owner	Description and Notes	Location
	(WILBEY town plot)					
B2806	–.–.61	[8.6.61?]	Joseph Hobson	Estate of Christian Shantz	Pt lot 16 north of Erbs Rd, Main St to Nith St; 1.5 ch	Waterloo 58 R.P.630
	WILKESPORT					
B2807	–.5.54	9.11.55	P.S. Donnelly	H.A. Wilkes	NW pt lot 16, 12th con, twp Sombra; north branch Sydenham R to Queen St; 1 ch	Lambton 25 R.P.Sombra 4
B2808	28.8.65	3.4.68	Henry Winter	William Kimball	'Kimball,' pt S1/2 lot 14, 13th con, twp Sombra; Wellington to Main St, William St to George St; 2 ch	Lambton 25 R.P.Sombra 5
	(WILLBROOK)					
B2809	10.4.54	9.10.54	T.C. Prosser	Wesley C. Wise	W1/2 lot 7, 2nd con, twp Nelson; Twelve Mile Creek with sawmill, Hill St to River St, Main St, bldgs; 2 ch	Halton 20 R.P.14
	WILLIAMS TWP					
B2810	17.4.60	19.4.60	Samuel Peters	J.G. Harper	Lot 11, west side Centre Rd, twp Williams; plan cancels R.P.119 (**B264**) for Dalgetty; 3 ch	Middlesex 33 R.P.160 Co
	WILLIAMSTOWN					
B2811	–.7.63	15.10.63	John S. Bruce	–	Pt lots 49 and 50 north of R aux Raisins and pt lot 4 south of R aux Raisins, twp Charlottenburgh; flour mill, sawmill, church, fairgrounds; 4 ch	Glengarry 14 R.P.18
	WILMOT TWP					
B2812	27.8.60	–	James Black	Messrs Jacob S. Gingerich, Daniel Cressman & Ulrich Steiner	N1/2s lots 10, 11, 12 and S1/2 lot 12, 1st con, Block A, twp Wilmot; 4 ch	Waterloo 58 R.P.631
B2813	–.–.60	[9.1.61?]	Joseph Hobson	Estate of Henry King	Subdivision of S1/2 lot 8, 1st con, Block A south of G.C.T., twp Wilmot; owners; 3 ch	Waterloo 59 R.P.632

WINDSOR

B2814	30.6.35	26.11.67	John A. Wilkinson	Charles Baby	Park lot C; Peter St to Baby St, north and south of Mill St; transcript; 66 ft	Essex 12 R.P.48
B2815	23.9.35	30.6.51	John A. Wilkinson	Augustus Tregent by his attn Patrick Tregent	South Detroit; Main St and Detroit R to park lots back of St George St, lots on both sides McDougall St; 66 ft	Essex 12 R.P.106
B2816	7.7.52	8.7.56	Albert P. Salter	Arthur Rankin	Pt lot 86, front con, twp Sandwich; on both sides Mercer St btwn Sandwich and L'Assumption sts; 50 ft	Essex 12 R.P.123
B2817	16.11.52	31.12.52	John A. Wilkinson	Messrs Langlois, Laserliss, Trudell	Park lot H; Detroit R to Cross St, Huron Church Line to South St, some bldgs sketched; transcript; 4 ch	Essex 12 R.P.54
B2818	-.-.53	-.-.53	P.S. Donnelly	Estate of F. Baby	Detroit R to London St, River St to Ferry St; transcript; 1 ch	Essex 12 R.P.120
B2819	4.8.53	5.1.54	–	Estate of Alex Langlois	E1/2 lot 91; twp Sandwich; partly illegible; transcript; 11/2 arpents	Essex 12 R.P.147
B2820	3.9.53	[11.7.67?]	John A. Wilkinson	John Prince	Pt Indian reserve; Main St to Detroit R, Chewett St to Detroit St, owners; transcript; 1 ch	Essex 12 R.P.41
B2821	-.11.53	10.1.54	P.S. Donnelly	Vilae Ouellette	Pt lot 81 or 82, 1st con, twp Sandwich; Detroit R and Sandwich St to Chatham St, lots on both sides Ouellette St; transcript; 1 ch	Essex 12 R.P.84
B2822	-.11.53	27.12.53	P.S. Donnelly	S.S. McDonell	Pt lot 82 or 83, 1st con, twp Sandwich; lots along Goyeau St; transcript; approx 117 ft	Essex 12 R.P.93
B2823	20.12.53	–	P.S. Donnelly	S.S. McDonell	Lot 82 or 83, 1st con, twp Sandwich; from river to Park St, on both sides Goyeau, sale notice, descriptions; transcript of printed map based on **B2822**; 75 ft	Essex 12 R.P.92
B2824	20.12.53	27.12.53	P.S. Donnelly	S.S. McDonell	Pt lot 82 or 83, 1st con, twp Sandwich; on both sides Goyeau St btwn Sandwich and Park sts, profile, see also **B2822–3**; transcript; 66 ft	Essex 12 R.P.91
B2825	-.6.54	1.9.54	P.S. Donnelly	William Kissock	Subdivision of lots A and D, NE side McDougall St, lots along McDougall St from St George St; transcript; 40 ft	Essex 12 R.P.108

	Date of Survey	Date of Regist.	Surveyor	Owner	Description and Notes	Location
B2826	–.7.54	6.1.55	P.S. Donnelly	W.G. Hall	Front pt lot 84, 1st con, twp Sandwich; lots on both sides Windsor Ave btwn Sandwich St and Barrack Sq; transcript; 50 ft	Essex 12 R.P.94
B2827	–.7.54	6.1.55	P.S. Donnelly	W.G. Hall	Rear pt lot 84, 1st con, twp Sandwich; lots along Windsor Ave; transcript; 124 ft	Essex 12 R.P.96
B2828	16.10.54	9.1.69	A.P. Salter	S.S. MacDonell	Pt lot LXXXVII, con I, twp Sandwich; Grand Coulee to Tuscarora St with lots on both sides Howard Ave; transcript; 2 ch	Essex 12 R.P.127
B2829	7.9.55	3.11.55	Leather & Robinson	Alfred Baby	Pt lot LXXIX, 1st con, twp Sandwich; west of Windsor St btwn London and Park sts; transcript perhaps of printed plan; 48 ft	Essex 12 R.P.78
B2830	13.9.55	17.9.55	J.A. Wilkinson	Wm A. Ritchie	Pt lot 87; lots along Howard Ave south of Grand Coulee; transcipt; 2 ch	Essex 12 R.P.128
B2831	–.–.56	14.5.56	Bartley & Pinney	J. Dougall & C. Hunt	Extension, pt lot 78, 1st con, twp Sandwich; Detroit R to park lot 3, lots on both sides Bruce Ave; transcript; 100 ft	Essex 12 R.P.77
B2832	24.5.56	8.7.56	O. Bartley	A. Rankin	Subdivision of pt lot 86, twp Sandwich; Sandwich St to Erie St, lots on both sides Mercer and Victoria sts, Alma Cres, and St Clair Circus; transcript; 3 ch	Essex 12 R.P.122
B2833	20.6.[56?]	12.5.73	Bartley & Pinney	Louis Horace Davenport	'Davenport Estate,' Detroit R to Sandwich St west of Ferry St; transcript; 20 ch	Essex 12 R.P.90
B2834	24.3.58	27.3.58	O. Bartley	W.P. Campbell	Lots A and D, east side McDougall St; lots along McDougall St at St George St; transcript; 34 ft	Essex 12 R.P.107
B2835	24.12.59	16.2.60	Alexander Wilkinson	E. Carson & E. Salter	'Narcisse A. Jennette Estate,' lots 76–8, 1st con, twp Sandwich; Detroit R and Sandwich St to Peltier's Coulee, owners; transcript; 2 ch	Essex 12 R.P.75
B2836	24.8.60	14.5.61	O. Bartley	Josiah Strong	Lot G, west side MacDougall St, pt lot 85, con I, twp Sandwich; transcript; 20 ft	Essex 12 R.P.109
B2837	6.8.61	6.8.61	William Scott	Municipal Council	Plan of roads around public park; Windsor Ave at Park St; transcript; 300 ft	Essex 12 R.P.95

B2838	10.12.62	16.12.62	O. Bartley	James Dougall	Pt lot 80; 'Dougall's Nursery,' Chatham to Elliott St, Pelissier St to Windsor St, inset shows Chatham St to river, Ferry St to Bruce Ave; transcript; 60 ft	Essex 12 R.P.81
B2839	28.6.64	18.5.67	O. Bartley	John O'Connor, Sr	Lots XLIV, XLIII, LIV, LIII, and lot C according to survey of lot LXXXV, con 1, twp Sandwich; Detroit R to St George St, lots on both sides McDougall St; transcript; 100 ft	Essex 12 R.P.111
B2840	–.6.64	22.8.64	A. Wilkinson	Benjamin Marantette	Subdivision of pt lots 89, 1st and 2nd cons, twp Sandwich; south of Sandwich St, owners; transcript; 4 ch	Essex 12 R.P.140
B2841	24.7.64	6.12.64	O. Bartley	Alexander Crawford	Pt lot LXXV, con 1, twp Sandwich; Sandwich St on Detroit R south, lots along Crawford Ave; transcript; 60 ft	Essex 12 R.P.70
B2842	4.7.67	5.7.67	O. Bartley	P. Conway	Subdivision of park lot III, twp Sandwich; transcript; 40 ft	Essex 12 R.P.112
B2843	28.8.67	28.11.67	O. Bartley	Mark Richards	Subdivision of park lot E, twp Sandwich; transcript; 30 ft	Essex 12 R.P.113
	WINGHAM					
B2844	19.11.66	7.12.66	A. Bay	E. Foley	Park lots VI, VII, VIII; lots on Josephine St; 1 ch	Huron 22 R.P.411
B2845	17.6.67	24.6.67	A. Bay	Mary Cornyn	Park lots III, IV, and V; lots on Josephine St; 1 ch	Huron 22 R.P.412
B2846	23.5.67	17.10.67	A. Bay	Charles & Mary Ann Scott	Subdivision of pt Block B and lots 344 and 345; lots on Scott and Josephine sts; 2 ch	Huron 22 R.P.413
	WINONA					
B2847	–.–.55?	–	–	Hon. J. Willson	'Ontario Village' esplanade, lake to G.W.R., West St to East St, pier, hotel; 4 ch	Wentworth 62 R.P.310
	WINTERBOURNE					
B2848	–.–.54	–	M. Schofield	W.H. Lanphier	For description see **2196**	Waterloo 58 R.P.A-12
B2849	–.–.55	–	M.C. Schofield	Sheriff Davidson	For description see **2197**	Waterloo 58 R.P.598 (copy in A-20)

	Date of Survey	Date of Regist.	Surveyor	Owner	Description and Notes	Location
B2850	28.4.55	–	J. Mackintosh	Messrs Allan & Mathieson	For description see **2198**	Waterloo 59 R.P.598
	WOLFE ISLAND TWP					
B2851	18.6.43	15.6.73	Thos F. Gibbs	–	Lots 10 and 11, con 4, and Bear Point	Frontenac 13 R.P.58
B2852	28.5.58	7.12.58	William Perceval	John Hitchcock	'Marysville,' streets named; 1-ch bar	Frontenac 15 R.P.26(13)
B2853	1.8.65	3.6.66	T.W. Nash	Lucinda C. Burrows & George T. Barrett	North pt lot A; streets named; 1 ch	Frontenac 15 R.P.40(5)
	WOLVERTON					
B2854	–	[9.8.52?]	James Black	Enos Wolverton	Smith's Creek to Washington St, River St to James St, mill race, bridge, market sq; 3 ch	Oxford 41 R.P.29
	WOODSTOCK					
B2855	–.–.42	10.10.56	O. Bartley	Rev Bettridge	George St to Dundas St, Riddell St to York St, Bettridge Sq; 100 ft	Oxford 41 R.P.76
B2856	–.12.48	–	William Smiley	Henry Finkle	North pt lot 21, 1st con, twp E Oxford; Finkles Mill pond to Dundas St, Finkle St to beyond Metcalfe St; 1 ch	Oxford 41 R.P.14
B2857	29.6.50	–	O. Bartley	Elizabeth Dawson & Richard Morris	Lot XVIII, con 1, twp E Oxford; lots fronting on Dundas St; 20 ft	Oxford 41 R.P.16
B2858	31.3.51	–	William Smiley	Messrs Archibald & Hamilton Burtch	NW pt lot 19, 1st con, twp E Oxford; G.W.R. depot to Dundas St, Chapel St to Young St; 1 ch	Oxford 41 R.P.19
B2859	–	[24.7.51?]	W.G. Wonham	Levi H. Perry	N1/2 lot XXI, 1st con, twp E Oxford; Dundas St to G.W.R., Adelaide to Perry St; 2 ch	Oxford 41 R.P.26
B2860	16.11.52	[9.5.66?]	W.G. Wonham, William Smiley	John Hatch	Lot XX, 1st con, twp E Oxford; G.W.R. depot north to Dundas St, Wellington St to Bay St, several additions made 14.4.54, 18.8.64, 1.11.64; 90 ft	Oxford 41 R.P.34

B2861	17.11.53	–	William Smiley	Pelham Teeple	'East Woodstock,' north pt W1/2 lot 18, 1st con, twp E Oxford; G.W.R. to Dundas St, Oxford St to Teeple St; 66 ft	Oxford 41 R.P.36
B2862	27.6.54	–	William Smiley	John Finkle	NW pt lot 20, 1st con, twp E Oxford; Finkles Mill pond and G.W.R. to Dundas St, lots along Finkle and Metcalfe sts; 1 ch	Oxford 41 R.P.47
B2863	6.9.54	[14.9.54?]	William Smiley	John Lindsay	Park lots on NE pt lot 19, 2nd con, twp E Oxford; Concession St to West St, Oxford St to Woodstock and Pt Dover Ry; 2 ch	Oxford 41 R.P.48
B2864	12.9.54	[16.10.55?]	W.G. Wonham	Col A.W. Light	Macadamized rd, Cedar Creek and Dundas St to Phelan St west of Mill St, G.W.R.; 2 ch	Oxford 41 R.P.55
B2865	20.9.54	–	W.G. Wonham	Thomas J. Cottle	Dundas St to Vincent St, Riddell St to Huron St; 3 ch	Oxford 41 R.P.49
B2866	–.–.54	–	W.G. Wonham	W.S. & R.N. Lights	Pt lot XXI, 1st con, twp E Oxford; mill pond and G.W.R. to Simcoe St, Mill St to Finkle St; 2 ch	Oxford 41 R.P.52
B2867	–.–.54	–	W.G. Wonham	Deedes & De Blaquiere [Survey?]	Pt lot 20, twp Blandford; Dundas St to Canterbury St, Riddell St to York St, sq btwn Princes and Adelaide sts; 100 ft	Oxford 41 R.P.50
B2868	–.–.54	–	W.G. Wonham	Joseph Hatch	Dundas St to Simcoe St, lots along Reeve and Metcalfe sts; later certification re adjustments to lots on Reeve St for the market; 45 ft	Oxford 41 R.P.53
B2869	–.4.55	–	W.G. Wonham	James Hatch	Pt lot 18, 1st con, twp E Oxford; Maud St to Woodstock and Norwich gravel rd, G.W.R. to con line; 3 ch	Oxford 41 R.P.73
B2870	–.6.55 2.11.66	–	William Smiley & Schofield	Henry J. Burtch	Lot 19, 1st con, twp E Oxford; Erie and Woodstock R.R. to Cedar St, east of G.W.R. to Walter and Railway sts, additions to plans; 2 ch	Oxford 41 R.P.63
B2871	–.9.55 7.5.57	–	W.G. Wonham	Nelson Bendyshe	Dundas St, Grace St and con line to Vincent St, Huron St to High St and Marlboro St; 3 ch	Oxford 41 R.P.62
B2872	15.9.56 29.10.57	–	W.G. Wonham	William Spencer	Park lots; rear of 1st con to Joint St and river, Mill St to Finkle St, streets and lots north of Spencer St added in later certification; 2 ch	Oxford 41 R.P.77

	Date of Survey	Date of Regist.	Surveyor	Owner	Description and Notes	Location
B2873	-.-.56	27.1.59	W.G. Wonham & William Smiley	Messrs Lights	Dundas St to Bowers St, Mill St W, G.W.R., cabinet factory; transcript; 4 ch	Oxford 41 R.P.86
B2874	9.3.57	–	W.G. Wonham	Henry de Blaquiere	Park lot 1, 3rd range; Vincent St to Henry St, Riddle St to Graham St; 1 ch	Oxford 41 R.P.98
B2875	-.-.57	11.8.57	William Smith	Messrs Wilson, Douglas & Kintrea	'Douglasville,' G.W.R. to north of Dundas St, lots along Lamport St, similar to **B2877**; 3 ch	Oxford 41 R.P.101
B2876	-.-.57	[25.5.57?]	W.G. Wonham	Wm Brearley, Sr & Jr	Pt lot 18, 1st con, twp E Oxford; Dundas St to G.W.R., lots along Stafford St; 2 ch	Oxford 41 R.P.108
B2877	-.-.57	–	Samuel Peters, William Smith	Estate of Joseph Clarke	Along Clarke St north of Dundas St, owners; 150 ft	Oxford 41 R.P.174
B2878	-.-.5?	26.2.63	T? Shenston	Thomas Appelton	'Shenston's Survey,' NW pt lot 18, 1st con, twp E Oxford; bounded by Dundas, Hincks, and Commercial sts; 33 ch	Oxford 41 R.P.144
B2879	-.-.5?	21.10.54	O. Bartley	Rev W. Bettridge	S1/4 lot 20, con I, twp Blandford; Dundas St to Prince's St, Riddel St to York St, Bettridge Sq; 100 ft	Oxford 41 R.P.11
B2880	25.3.61	–	W.G. Wonham	Church Wardens	Lots on Dundas, Graham, and Light sts; 40 ft	Oxford 41 R.P.130
B2881	13.5.63	–	William Smiley	Messrs Barwick & Beard	North pt Gore, twp W Oxford; Dundas St to Park Row, G.W.R., lots along Main St; 2 ch	Oxford 41 R.P.157
B2882	1.4.64	1.7.65?	W.G. Wonham	Daniel Penman	Pt lot 26, 1st con, twp E Oxford; Victoria St to Dover St, Dover Lane to G.W.R.; 100 ft	Oxford 41 R.P.160
	WOODVILLE					
B2883	14.11.59	–	William Galbraith	Alex. Stewart	W1/2 of W1/2 lot 1, 3rd con, twp Eldon; lots along Argyle and Queen sts at Nappadale St, description of lots; 1 ch	Victoria 57 R.P.3
B2884	9.3.61	9.3.61	George Gibson	E.R. Irish, A. Stewart, J. Ferguson, J. Morison	Argyle St south to John St, Nappadale St east past Union St, bldgs; 2 ch	Victoria 57 R.P.5

	(WORSOW town plot)					
B2885	26.12.53	30.1.54	Edmund De Cew	James Cockshutt	Lot 49, 1st con, south side Talbot Rd, twp N Cayuga; lots along Talbot Rd and rd allowance to east; 2 ch	Haldimand 18 R.P.2426
	WROXETER					
B2886	6.8.60	17.8.60	A. Bay	James Patton	Lots XXVI–XXVIII, con A, twp Howick; Maitland R, mill pond; 3 ch	Huron 22 R.P.315
	WYEBRIDGE					
B2887	–.–.59	19.1.60	Henry Creswicke	Angus Grant	'Macville on-the-Wye,' lot 94, 1st con, twp Tiny; mill site; 3 ch	Simcoe 51 R.P.79
B2888	–.–.64	27.7.64	Alex W. Simpson	Angus Grant	'Macville on-the-Wye,' E1/2 lots 93 and 94, 1st con, W.P.R., twp Tiny; mills, English church, river lots, relief; 3 ch	Simcoe 51 R.P.97
	WYOMING					
B2889	–	–.8.56 13.12.56	–	C.W. Robertson & Marshall Mackay	E1/2 lot 15 and W1/2 lot 16, con 2; plan missing	Lambton 25 R.P.Wyoming 1
B2890	12.5.62	12.1.63	W.G. Wonham	William Spencer	Lots 15 and 16, 2nd con, twp Plympton; Zone to Superior St, London to Toronto St, G.W.R. station; transcript; 132 ft	Lambton 25 R.P.Wyoming 2
	WYTON STATION					
B2891	28.4.53	5.5.53	William McMillan	John Scatcherd	Pt NW corner lot 10, 2nd con, twp Nissouri W; 1 ch	Middlesex 33 R.P.24 Co
B2892	14.1.56	17.1.56	William McMillan	John Scatcherd	Pt of lot X, 2nd con, twp Nissouri W; west of Talbot St, north of High St; 5 ch	Middlesex 33 R.P.99 Co
	YARKER					
B2893	24.12.49	9.6.51	A.B. Perry	Samuel Scott	'Simcoe,' lot 41, 1st con, twp Camden E; lots on Water, Bridge, Branch, and School sts, description of lots, bldgs, foundry, sawmill, machine shop; 2 ch	Lennox 29 R.P.22
B2894	8.8.63	12.2.63	William R. Rombough	–	'Simcoe,' E1/2 lots 41 and 42, 1st con, twp Camden; lots on Colebrook, Bridge, Mill, Centre, and Ridge sts, owners; 1 ch	Lennox 29 R.P.27A

	Date of Survey	Date of Regist.	Surveyor	Owner	Description and Notes	Location
	YORK TWP					
B2895	18.7.46	28.10.46	J.S. Dennis	Woodberry Card	'Weston,' subdivision of west pt lot VII, con V, twp York; lots along Albion or Weston Plank Rd and Church St, owners, Humber R; 2 ch	Toronto 64 R.P.5
B2896	17.10.48	20.3.52	John Stoughton Dennis	J.A. Donaldson	'Plan A ... Weston,' lot 6, con V, twp York; north side Weston Plank Rd, owners; 2 ch	Toronto 64 R.P.38
B2897	20.11.52	6.5.63	F.F. Passmore	Estate of James Browne	Subdivision of south pt lot 27, 3rd con, twp York; area south of Yorkville and Vaughan Plank Rd, bldgs, orchard land parcels; 4 ch	Toronto 64 R.P.59
B2898	9.2.53	19.2.53	J. Stoughton Dennis	John Lawrence	'Weston,' pt lot VII, con V, twp York; lots north of Weston Plank Rd and east of Church St, owners; 200 ft	Toronto 64 R.P.48
B2899	3.3.53	5.3.53	John Stoughton Dennis	John A. Donaldson	'Weston,' east pt lot 6, Vth con from Yonge St, twp York; Toronto & Guelph Ry line, area north of side-rd btwn lots 5 and 6, owners; 300 ft	Toronto 64 R.P.50
B2900	–.8.53	5.10.54	David Gibson	James Cockshutt	'Sabden & Wibsey,' front and rear of N1/2 lot V, con II W, twp York; lots near plank rd, con III, called 'Sabden' and con II rd called 'Wibsey'; 2 ch	Toronto 64 R.P.92
B2901	16.10.54	16.10.54	J.O. Browne	J. Lukin Robinson	Subdivision of lot II, 2nd con from bay, twp York; north of Don and Danforth Plank Rd, Dawes Tavern, relief, owners, bldgs, creeks; 2 ch	Toronto 64 R.P.94
B2902	16.10.54	16.10.54	J.O. Browne	J. Lukin Robinson	Subdivision of N1/2 lot VIII, 2nd con from bay, twp York; 4 ch	Toronto 64 R.P.95
B2903	1.1.55	9.10.57	J. Stoughton Dennis	J. Stoughton Dennis & Thomas Shortis	'Weston,' pt lot 6, Vth con west of Yonge St, twp York; area northeast of John St and Weston plank rd, G.T.R. station; 1 ch	Toronto 64 R.P.223
B2904	9.3.55	2.4.55	J. Stoughton Dennis	J.H. Cameron & H.W. Boulton	'Sandhurst,' subdivision of pt lot 28, 3rd con from bay, twp York; south of	Toronto 64 R.P.115

					Yorkville and Vaughan Plank Rd, lots along Hilton and Kennedy sts; 4 ch	
B2905	14.8.55	22.11.55	Dennis & Boulton	Thomas Clarkson & James G. Worts	'Helliwell Mill Property'; south of Don Mills Rd, mill bldgs, dam, head-race, paper mill, grist mill, houses, mill property boundary; 3 ch	Toronto 64 R.P.138
B2906	13.6.56	22.7.56	J. Stoughton Dennis	E.C. Fisher	'Balmoral,' W1/2 lot 5, 3rd con west of Yonge St, twp York; Main St to Fisher St, Balmoral St to Gray St btwn Weston and Toronto Ry station ground; 2 ch	Toronto 64 R.P.162
B2907	22.8.56	24.9.56	Sandford Fleming	Sandford Fleming	Lot 6, 4th con west of Yonge St, twp York; east of village of Weston, relief, bldgs, trees; 3 ch	Toronto 64 R.P.172
B2908	–.10.56	22.12.56	George McPhillips	William Nichols	'Newton Brook,' SW1/4, lot 24, 1st con east of Yonge St, twp York; 2 ch	Toronto 64 R.P.189
B2909	–	7.11.56	J. Stoughton Dennis	William Tyrrell	'Weston,' subdivision of pt lot 7, the 'Porter Farm,' and lot 6, lots 70–80, the 'Donaldson Farm,' 5th con, twp York; King St, Beech St NE of Weston plank rd; 3 ch	Toronto 64 R.P.182
B2910	26.11.56	22.6.57	Bristow & Fitzgerald	Angus Blue	Pt S1/2 lot 16, 1st con east of Yonge St, twp York; houses, mills, and businesses; 3 ch	Toronto 64 R.P.207
B2911	20.5.57	29.5.57	J. Stoughton Dennis	John & W. Hogg	Pt lot 11, I con east, and lot 11, 1st con west of Yonge St, twp York; bldgs, flour mills; 100 ft	Toronto 64 R.P.204
B2912	26.5.57	19.3.58	J. Stoughton Dennis	John A. Donaldson	'Weston,' pt lot 16, 5th con west of Yonge St, twp York; south and east of Humber R, relief by hachures; 2 ch	Toronto 64 R.P.236
B2913	1.8.57	20.6.62	B.W. Gossage	J.S. Dennis	'Weston,' villa lots 67 and 68 fronting on street north of station ground on **B2899**; North Station St to Elai St, Maria St to east; 60 links	Toronto 64 R.P.264
B2914	1.10.57	19.3.58	J. Stoughton Dennis	John A. Donaldson	'Weston,' at intersection north limit John St and west limit of North Station St on lot VI, Vth con west of Yonge St, twp York; 30 ft	Toronto 64 R.P.235

	Date of Survey	Date of Regist.	Surveyor	Owner	Description and Notes	Location
B2915	7.10.57	16.10.57	Charles Unwin	Anne Jane Seymour & Jane Seymour	Subdivision of SW pt lot 25, 3rd con from bay, twp York; Seymour St btwn Stewart and Powell sts; 3 ch	Toronto 64 R.P.228
B2916	7.10.57	14.4.58	Dennis & Gossage	Misses Thompson	Subdivision of pt lot 35, 3rd con from bay, twp York; Weston Plank Rd to Union St, Albert St to rd allowance, hotel, toll-house, barn and shed; 40 ft	Toronto 63 R.P.238
B2917	14.4.58	3.4.61	Lindsay & Miles	Joseph Holly	'Weston,' lot 8, 5th con, BF twp York; area btwn Weston Plank Rd and G.T.R., see also **B2919**; 60 links	Toronto 64 R.P.261
B2918	6.11.58	11.11.58	B.W. Gossage	Messrs J. & W. Hogg	Pt lot 10, 1st con east of Yonge St, twp York; lots along Yonge and Old Yonge sts, Mill St and side-rd btwn lots 10 and 11, dam, mill pond, school lot, owners; 100 ft	Toronto 64 R.P.246
B2919	21.6.59	25.6.59	Edward Miles	Rev W.A. Johnson	'Weston,' pt lot 8, 5th con, twp York; parsonage lot on Rectory Rd btwn Weston plank rd and G.T.R., school lot; 1 ch	Toronto 64 R.P.252
B2920	7.11.62	7.5.64	John James Francis	W.R. Wadsworth	Pt lot VI, Vth con west of Yonge St, lying west of North Station St and south of John St; G.T.R. station, owners; 100 ft	Toronto 64 R.P.272
B2921	1.8.[64?]	6.9.64	J. Stoughton Dennis	William Tyrrell	'Weston,' pt lot VII, Vth con west of Yonge St, twp York; east of G.T.R., north of King St to Church St, bounded on east by Elm St and Porter farm, owners, bldgs, landscaping; 2 ch	Toronto 64 R.P.273
B2922	4.12.67	20.2.68	Wadsworth & Unwin	Estate of Joseph Dennis	Subdivision of lot 1, 4th con west of Yonge St, twp York; along Weston gravel rd and G.T.R., Black Creek ravine, relief; 4 ch	Toronto 64 R.P.285
	(ZETLAND)					
B2923	24.4.62	17.3.66	A.C. Robertson	William Beckett	Lots 17 and 18, con B, twp Turnberry; Beckett to Wellington St, John to William, west of Maitland R, relief, bridges; 2 ch	Huron 22 R.P.319

	ZONE TWP					
B2924	15.7.65	–	Thomas W. Dyas	Howard Smith	'Pepper Farm,' lot XIX, River Range; Thames R to Longwoods Rd, Pepper well sketched; 5 ch	Kent 24 R.P.151
B2925	–.9.65	10.10.65	Thomas W. Dyas	Messrs Charles A. Eldridge, Cheyes A. Darling, Francis C. McCarty & Frederick O. Thorpe	'Whitehead Farm,' lot 2, north side Longwoods Rd; 4 ch	Kent 24 R.P.152
B2926	–.2.66	5.5.66	William G. McGeorge	Neil Johnson & James Duff	Oil lots, E1/2 lot 6, VIth con, G.W.R.; 2 ch	Kent 24 R.P.154
B2927	23.2.66	8.3.66	Unwin & Dyas	McCarty et al.	'Colville Farm,' lot 21, River Range; owners, leasee, relief; 3 ch	Kent 24 R.P.153
B2928	10.5.66	16.5.66	Unwin & Dyas	William G.E. Pope	'Swalwell Farm,' lot 17, River Range; relief; see also **B2933**; 2 ch	Kent 24 R.P.155
B2929	18.5.66	26.5.66	A.P. Salter	W.G.E. Pope	'McRitchie Farm,' W1/2 lot 20 south of Longwoods Rd; inset location map, relief, drawings of oil wells; 3 ch	Kent 24 R.P.157
B2930	15.6.66	27.6.66	Unwin, Dyas & Forneri	Bothwell C.W. Land & Petroleum Co. Ltd	Subdivision of pt lots 13 and 14, River Range; 4 ch	Kent 24 R.P.158
B2931	28.6.66	9.11.66	Sherman Malcolm	Joseph C. Nile	'Niles Petroleum Farm,' lots 16 and 17, north of Longwoods Rd; area west of Bothwell, owners, relief, G.W.R., sketches of oil wells; 4 ch	Kent 24 R.P.162
B2932	17.7.66	22.9.66	Unwin, Dyas & Forneri	W.G.E. Pope	'Atwill Farm,' pt E1/2 lot 20, River Range; under lease, Pope's Well and others, relief; 1.6 ch	Kent 24 R.P.159
B2933	20.11.66	24.11.66	Unwin & Dyas	Messrs Williams, Wells, Conro, C.L. Forneri	For description see **1016**	Kent 24 R.P.161
	ZURICH					
B2934	–.–.58	1.12.58	Molesworth & Weatherald	Frederick Knell	Pt lots XX and XXI, XIth con, twp Hay; Edward St to Mary St, John St to rd allowance btwn cons X and XI, mills; 2 ch	Huron 22 R.P.320
B2935	30.5.67	14.6.67	A. Bay	Lewis Vauthier	Lot XXI, 10th con, twp Hay; east side of 'Cranberry Marsh'; 1.5 ch	Huron 22 R.P.321

Appendix C

Nautical Charts

1815–16 Reconnaissance Survey of the Lakes

The first comprehensive reconnaissance surveys of the Great Lakes and St Lawrence R were made in 1815 and accompanied a report by Sir Edward Owen on the naval establishment in Canada, recommendations on improvement of transport from Montreal to Kingston, and defence of the line of navigation through the lakes. The main report is no 82 from Sir Edward Owen to John Wilson Croker of 25 Nov 1815 (GBLpro CO 42/171 87ff and 172). Other reports, such as Lt Vidal's 'Journal from Long Point to Point Pelee' of July 1815 and Reuben Sherwood's report on the communication from the Bay of Quinte to L Simcoe via Rice L and his investigation of the Rideau R of 22 June 1815, are enclosed in other dispatches by Sir Edward Owen in the volume cited. Additional information for some sheets came from Capt W.F.W. Owen's 1817 report, 'Proceedings and Report on the Surveys and Plans of the Lakes of Canada' (GBTAUh Owen 1817); the maps accompanying the various reports are listed below by the numbers endorsed on the sheets: C1 to C4 of the St Lawrence R accompanied Sir E. Owen's reports 36, 37, and 48 of 30 June 1815 (GBLpro CO 42/171). C5–C50 originally accompanied report 82 in vol 172 cited above; copies of most maps with the same titles and all by E.E. Vidal are found in a folder entitled 'Plans etc of Lakes in Canada Communicated by Commodore Owen' (GBTAUh (P23 Aa1)) (photoreproductions in OOAMA).

C1

'No 2' [Sketch of part of the St Lawrence River from above Long Sault Island to Point à Bodet]
Ms 38 x 56 cm Scale not given Endorsements: 'In Sir E. Owen's No 37, In 15604 of 1816 S.P. Col. Canada vol 141/2' 'Appl ... to ... Nos 36 and 37'
A rough sketch with proposed locations of locks; a close copy is found in GBTAUh (P27); (*PRO Cat* 1572).
GBLpro (MR 643/3) GBTAUh (P27)

C2

[No 2a?] Sketch of the St Lawrence between Cornwall and St Regis June 1815 by Captain W.F.W. Owen R.N.
Ms 35 x 91 cm 1" to 600 yds Endorsements: [as in C1 with] 'vol 141/4'
Shows points where readings of latitude were taken between Massena Pt and Little Regis Is; also a copy in GBTAUh (P27); (*PRO Cat* 1572).
GBLpro (MR 643/2) GBTAUh (P27)

C3

'No 3' [Sketch of the St Lawrence River from Brockville to Point Barbu]
32 x 65 cm 1" to 2 miles Endorsements: 'Applicable to Nos 36 and 37' [see no '36 37'] 'enclosure to Sir E. Owen's no 36 of 30 June 1815.'
'Rapids and valley which appears favourable for a canal to pass Pt Barbu' shown east of Johnston; notes about points for locks, batteries; Ft Wellington shown east of 'better situation for a work'; a similar map with a few more place names is in GBTAUh (P27); (*PRO Cat* 1571).
GBLpro (MPG 480 (2)) GBTAUh (P27)

C4

[No 4] [Sketch of the St Lawrence River from Kingston to Brockville]
Ms 38 x 94 cm 1" to 1 mile Endorsements: 'In 15604 of 1816; In No 48 from Sir E.'
Notes on location of the channel and adds of islands and parts of shoreline to finish plan; names of twps, rivers, and islands; also a copy in GBTAUh (P27); (*PRO Cat* 1574).
GBLpro (MPG 481) GBTAUh (P27)

C5

'No 1' [Chart of area from Kingston to Grand Isle [Wolfe Is] and Sacketts Harbour]
Ms 78 x 53 cm Scale not given Endorsements: 'Report no 1 – 82'
A rough sketch with soundings in Kingston harbour and to Grand Island; 'Simcoe' Is [Forrest Is] (*PRO Cat* 1525).
GBLpro (MPG 48)

C6

'No 2' Chart of Kingston Harbour and Entrances thereto from Lake Ontario drawn by J. Harris Master H.M.S. Pc Regent
Ms 58 x 87 cm 1" to 1/3 mile
A rough sketch from Amherst Is to Point Frederick; soundings; Cataraqui Bridge and military post; points marked are not keyed on map; (*PRO Cat* 1481).
GBLpro (MPG 49)

C7

'No 3' [Chart of area from Little Sandy Bay to Carlton Island]
Ms 49 x 108 cm Scale not given
A rough sketch; soundings; points marked along shore of Bay of Quinte not keyed; 'Mohawk Settlement'; (*PRO Cat* 1526).
GBLpro (MPG 50)

C8

'No 4' Survey of the North Shore of Lake Ontario taken in the Years 1783 and 1789 by Messrs Kotte and La Force
Ms 73 x 235 cm Approx 1" to 1 2/3 miles
A rough copy of the north half of **9** (1789) showing the same districts, cos, and general information, but with a few names of creeks added; sand-bars across harbours shown; (*PRO Cat* 1515).
GBLpro (MPG 51)

C9
'No 5' The Upper Gap between Amherst Island and Prince Edward County and the Netley's Gap Between the False Ducks on Lake Ontario 20th June 1815 By Captain W.F.W. Owen R.N.
Ms 94 x 74 cm 1" to 1/2 geog mile
Soundings from Amherst Is to Bay of Quinte; a small part added to the map showing Little Duck Is; (*PRO Cat* 1517).
GBLpro (MPG 52)

C10
'No 6' Plan of Nicholas and Egg Islands and the adjacent Coast on Lake Ontario with Soundings Shoals, etc. by T. Chillingworth Master of H.M. Ship St Lawrence 1815 Copy E.E. Vidal
Ms 74 x 161 cm 1" to 440 yds
Includes 'West Lake by Sandbanks'; soundings; point 'U' not keyed; (*PRO Cat* 1520).
GBLpro (MPG 53)

C11
'No 7' Plan of Presqu'Isle on Lake Ontario with Soundings in feet, shoals etc. by T. Chillingworth. Augt 1815. Copy [Sgd] E.E. Vidal
Ms 60 x 116 cm 1" to 500 yds
Shows 'Carrying Place to the Bay of Quinte' with blockhouse and bldgs along the trail; (*PRO Cat* 1518).
GBLpro (MPG 54)

C12
'No 8' Sketch of the River Nen (or Rush) on Lake Ontario
Ms 60 x 45 cm Scale not given
Shows soundings, channel and cliffs, and nature of shoreline; (*PRO Cat* 1524).
GBLpro (MPG 55)

C13
'No 9' Sketch of Duffin's Creek on Lake Ontario by T. Chillingworth – 1815
Ms 58 x 43 cm Scale not given
Soundings, nature of bottom and banks; (*PRO Cat* 1451).
GBLpro (MPG 56)

C14
'No 10' [Chart of the Harbour of York] Copy [Sgd] E.E. Vidal.
Ms 37 x 118 cm 1" to 20 chains
Shows the area from the Humber R to east of the Don R; soundings for the shore and around island; shows Garrison reserve, fort, and old French fort; Dundas St [Queen St] as the north boundary of the town; Castle Frank, House of Assembly, and blockhouse at the east end; mainly a copy of Bouchette's plans (**2013**) with the addition of soundings; (*PRO Cat* 1603).
GBLpro (MPG 57)

C15
[No 11] Plan of Burlington Bay on Lake Ontario with Soundings &c By T. Chillingworth, Master of H.M. Ship St Lawrence. 1815.
Ms 62 x 105 cm 11/4" to 1/2 nautical mile
Inset: 'Sketch of the Outlet of Burlington Lake'; from Sixteen Mile Creek on the north to Forty Mile Creek on the south shore; nature of bottom and shoreline; settlements along shore; fortification on Burlington Height; 'Brandt's Indian Chief' noted in Nelson Twp; also an undated copy with same title in GBTAUh (E432 Aa2); (*PRO Cat* 1441).
GBLpro (MPG 58) GBTAUh (E432 Aa2)

C16
'No 12' Plan of the River Niagara from Queenston June 1815. T. Chillingworth.
Ms 131 x 62 cm 1" to 400 yds
Inset: 'Fort Niagara'; shows Fort George, Mississauga, Niagara, and Niagara town plot; soundings; nature of shoreline; inset of American fort shows nature of defences and use of bldgs; (*PRO Cat* 1508).
GBLpro (MPG 59)

C17
'No 13' Plan of the Coast from Mississaga to Four Mile Creek by T. Chillingworth: Master R.N. 1815 (Copy) (E.E. Vidal) No 13
Ms 36 x 70 cm 1" to 250 yds
Shows the area from Fort Mississauga to Four Mile Creek on L Ontario; triangulation lines; soundings; note on point 'Q' at Niagara with a view to landing stores; (*PRO Cat* 1519).
GBLpro (MPG 60)

C18
[No] '14' Sketch of the 18 and 20 Mile Creeks on Lake Ontario by T. Chillingworth
Ms 68 x 74 cm 1" to 200 yds
Soundings, nature of shoreline, sandbanks, marshy areas; (*PRO Cat* 1523).
GBLpro (MPG 61)

C19
[No 15] Map of the Niagara District in Upper Canada, by Lieutenant W.A. Nesfield, drawn partly from Survey & from documents obtained from the Qr Mr Genls Department
Ms 56 x 82 cm Approx 1" to 3 miles
Shows roads, villages, forts, mills, houses and names of some settlers, battle sites of the War of 1812; an important general map also listed under Niagara region (see no **713**); (*PRO Cat* 1390).
GBLpro (MPG 62)

C20
'No 16' Sketch of the Position on the Chippewa and of the Roads and Principal Settlements on the Chippewa and Lyon's Creek

Ms 36 x 39 cm 1" to 1 mile Watermark: 'J WHATMAN 1809'
From the Chippewa R to the Short Hills area; shows roads, mills, names of settlers; (*PRO Cat* 1445).
GBLpro (MPG 63)

C21
'No 17' Sketch of Grand River Lake Erie by Captn W.F.W. Owen and of Mohawk Bay by Commodore Sir E. Owen 1815. Copy E.E. Vidal
Ms 144 x 38 cm Scale not given
Soundings, names of settlers, various points located; 'C' near Mohawk Bay proposed for building, etc; (*PRO Cat* 1463).
GBLpro (MPG 64)

C22
'No 18' Running Sketch of Grand River with Mohawk Bay Lake Erie – Copy. E.E. Vidal
Ms 45 x 152 cm Scale not given
Soundings marked up river; marsh; farms and names of settlers; 'Lord Selkirks land said to be still mortgaged to the Indians'; note that Mohawk Bay not properly surveyed and mention of preserving lines of Mr Harris; three points marked including 'C' proposed for building; (*PRO Cat* 1464).
GBLpro (MR 22)

C23
[No 18b] A Plan of Long Point Bay and Turkey-Point Harbour, Lake Erie Surveyed by J. Harris R.N. July 1815 Lieut A.T.E. Vidal, fecit (Signed) W.F.W. Owen. Copy E.E. Vidal
Ms 82 x 126 cm 1" to 1000 yds
A rough sketch showing soundings, marshes, treed areas, sand, roads, settlements; (*PRO Cat* 1496).
GBLpro (MR 22(2)) GBTAUh

C24
'No 19' [Map of the area from Grand River to Detroit River and Lake St Clair]
Ms 47 x 125 cm Scale not given
Shows roads, twps, settlements, windmills on the Detroit R; between Charlotteville and Woodhouse twps stars marked along road but not keyed; road shown along shore between Point Pelee and Port Talbot; (*PRO Cat* 1387).
GBLpro (MPG 65)

C25
'No 20' Plan of the Islands at the West End of Lake Erie from their Latitudes and Bearings August 1815. Signed W.F.W. Owen
Ms 22 x 31 cm 1" to 4 miles
Shows Point Pelee, Point Pelee Is, Cunningham Is, and Sandusky Is; (*PRO Cat* 1453).
GBLpro (MPG 66)

C26
'No 22' A Sketch of the Communication between Erie and Huron by T.S. of Sandwich U.C.
Ms 44 x 59 cm 1" to 2 miles
The word Sandwich has been crossed out and Huron inserted; from Point Pelee to Turkey Is; soundings; points marked but not keyed; (*PRO Cat* 2537).
GBLpro (MPG 68)

C27
'No 23' [Chart of Lake and River St Clair] Copy [Sgd] E.E. Vidal
Ms 48 x 61 cm Scale not given
Shows ship channels at the entry of the St Clair R; soundings; names of rivers; settlements; points T, U, V, X, Y, Z are marked but not keyed; (*PRO Cat* 1565).
GBLpro (MPG 69)

C28
'No 24' River Detroit The Outline copied from a Plan in the Engineer's Drawing Room at Quebec to which the Soundings are filled in from the Observations of Captn W.F.W. Owen and his Assistants Sandwich, 20th Augt 1815. (Signed) W.F.W. Owen. (Copy) E.E. Vidal
Col ms 166 x 37 cm Scale not given
'The Soundings being taken in different boats are laid down in the same number of colours to prevent Confusion'; (*PRO Cat* 2536); two copies in GBTAUh both lack signature of Vidal and 'River Detroit' in title, and 'La Grande Isle aux Dindes' is not named.
GBLpro (MPG 70) GBTAUh (194 Aa1)

C29
'No 25' A Plan of part of the District of Hesse ... Delineated from Actual Surveys made in the years 1788 & 1790 by Patrick McNiff Depy Surveyr.
Ms 52 x 264 cm 1" to 40 chains
Based on no **908**; (*PRO Cat* 1456).
GBLpro (MPG 71)

C30
'No 26' Eye Sketch River Ruscum ... (Signed) J. Harris
Ms 36 x 21 cm 1 1/2" to 1/4 mile
Note: 'A small River ... affords shelter for Batteaux if the Bridge were removed from its mouth – it was only navigable about 2 miles when I was up it in August 1815'; area is east of the Detroit R and emptying into L St Clair; soundings; house and fields; (*PRO Cat* 1563).
GBLpro (MPG 72)

C31
'No 27' Eye Sketch of Big Bear River by J. Harris Master R.N. 1815
Ms 26 x 24 cm Approx 1 2/3" to 1 mile
Soundings; point 'X' not keyed; (*PRO Cat* 1595).
GBLpro (MPG 73(1))

C32
'No 27[b]' Eye Sketch of the Coast from the Detroit River to the River Thames and Chenail Écarté to the River St Clair – also up Big Bear River. 1815 (Signed) J. Harris. (Copy) E.E. Vidal
Ms 28 x 50 cm Scale not given
Soundings along coast; marshy areas; 'Baldoon' and 'Lord Selkirks land' marked; Sydenham R and Bear Creek; (*PRO Cat* 1564).
GBLpro (MPG 73(2))

C33
'No 28' River St Clair from the old Ship Channel to the Rapids. Surveyed Captn W.F.W. Owen 1815
Ms 38 x 592 cm 1" to 100 fathoms Watermark: 'J WHATMAN 1809'
Soundings, swamps; a large detailed survey; (*PRO Cat* 1567).
GBLpro (MPG 74)

C34
[No 29a] A Chart of the Eastern Coasts of Lake Huron and its relative connexion with some of the principal places on the other Lakes. Nov. 1815 (Signed) W.F.W. Owen Copy. E.E. Vidal
Ms 52 x 65 cm 61/2" to 1° latitude
Shows the area from Fort Erie to the St Clair R and north to the Bruce Peninsula and Matchedash and the east shore of Georgian Bay; relief, nature of shoreline; a rough sketch; described as 12 in W.F.W. Owen's 'Proceedings ...' (1817) with note: 'this chart will require some corrections from later observation'; (*PRO Cat* 1470).
GBLpro (MPG 75(4))

C35
'No 29B' A Plan of the Straits from Lake Huron into the Manitoolin Lake from the Open Gat to Cabots Head from a Survey made 26th 27th and 28th Septr 1815 (Signed) W.F.W. Owen Copy E.E. Vidal
Ms 46 x 66 cm 1" to 1 mile [geog?]
Shoreline and relief shown from below Cabots Head to islands and Cape Hurd; soundings; notes on navigation; described in W.F.W. Owen's 'Proceedings ...' (1817) as 13 and 'determined only by astronomical observations'; (*PRO Cat* 1589).
GBLpro (MPG 75(3))

C36
'No 29C' A Draft of the Coast of Little Cabotia from Cape Liverpool to Point Rich 4 Novr 1815 (Signed) W.F.W. Owen Copy E.E. Vidal
Ms 52 x 59 cm 1" to 21/3 sea miles
Various bays, sounds, relief along shoreline; soundings; (*PRO Cat* 1588).
GBLpro (MPG 75(1))

C37
'No 29D' Chart of Nottawasaga Bay and Penetanguishene Harbour
Ms 65 x 93 cm Scale not given
Soundings; place names; winter road from Kempenfelt Bay to Penetanguishene; military establishment at the latter; a survey line from L Simcoe 'traced in from Mr Wilmot's survey of 1812'; also an untitled plan 'by Lt Poyntz' of approx 1" to 2 miles Watermark: '1812' (GBTAUh (191 Aa2)); probably 15 in Owen's 'Proceedings ...' (1817) with note: 'entirely founded on astronomical observations and a transit survey'; (*PRO Cat* 1592).
GBLpro (MPG 75(5)) GBTAUh (191 Aa2)

C38
'No 29E' A Plan of the Harbour of Pennetengushene taken October 1815: by Captn Wm Owen R.N.
Ms 64 x 47 cm 1" to 300 yds
Soundings; on the southeast shore 'Remains of the Log Huts for the proposed Establishment'; (PRO Cat 1535); 16 in Owen's 'Proceedings ...' (1817) with note: 'intended to be surveyed again the winter of 1817 and 18'; also a copy with same title and date but without Owen's name in GBTAUh.
GBLpro (MPG 75(2)) GBTAUh (B784 Aa1)

C39
'No 30' Plan of the Scite [*sic*] proposed as a new Post to which the Garrison of Michilimakinac may be removed 1815. Copy E.E. Vidal
Ms 99 x 116 cm 1" to 100 fathoms
Shows a harbour on the southwest side of Manitoulin Is; soundings; also a copy without date and names in GBTAUh (*PRO Cat* 2540).
GBLpro (MPG76) GBTAUH (B781 Aa1)

C40
'No 33' [Sketch of the Communication between York and Penetanguishene Harbour via Lake Simcoe]
Ms 126 x 47 cm Scale not given
A copy of the maps from Simcoe's journey of 1793 (**317**) with additional notes; notes on portages, Indian purchases, 'Mr Cowan's house,' 'Gwyllims-bury' and twps south of it located; (*PRO Cat* 1591).
GBLpro (MPG 79)

C41
[No] '34' Plan by actual survey of the street of Communication between Kempenfeldt Bay on Lake Simcoe and Pennetengushene Harbour on Lake Huron; and one Concession on each side thereof; made out at the particular request of Angus Shaw Esq. Agent to the North West Company. Yonge Street 15th Augt 1812 (Signed) Saml S. Wilmot Surveyor
Ms 97 x 68 cm 1" to 80 chains
A copy of no **334(3)**; (*PRO Cat* 1590).
GBLpro (MPG 80)

C42
[No 35] Front Part of the Town of Gwyllimsbury
Ms 37 x 88 cm 1" to 4 chains
Shows the east branch of the Holland R, marshy land; lots laid out along old Yonge St with jog to

new Yonge St; probably copied from part of Wilmot's 1811 plan (see no **1416**); (*PRO Cat* 1466).
GBLpro (MPG 81)

C43
'No 36' [Water communications between the Bay of Quinte and the Talbot River]
Ms 117 x 50 cm Scale not given
Shows rivers, lakes, rapids, falls, many place-names; accompanied by Capt Reuben Sherwood's 'Report of navigation ...' 22 June 1815 to Col Myers which keys the points shown on the map; (GBLpro CO42/171) (PRO Cat 1389); also a copy with the same title in GBTAUh (P 27).
GBLpro (MPG 82(4)) GBTAUh (P27)

C44
'No 37' [Map of the Rideau River]
Ms 49 x 69 cm 1" to 4 miles
Accompanied by Capt Reuben Sherwood's reports of 15 Feb 1815 to Col Myers Dy QM Gen with fuller explanation of obstacles to navigation in the river (GBLpro CO 42/171) falls, rapids, mills, twps, etc; (*PRO Cat* 1388).
GBLpro (MPG 82(3))

C45
[No] '36 37' [i.e. 37b?] [The St Lawrence River from Howe Island to Brockville] Memorandum. This Sketch is laid down from Actual Survey; (the South Shore the whole of the Islands and Ship Channel excepted) by Captain Sherwood D.A.Q.M.G. Qr Mr Genls Office Montreal April 11th 1815. Copy
Ms 28 x 98 cm 1" to 1 mile
Islands named; track of ships investigating the area; soundings; names of places and of settlers along the shore; (*PRO Cat* 1573).
GBLpro (MPG 82(2))

C46
'No 40'[a] Kettle Creek, an eye sketch Signed. Alexr T.E. Vidal 1815 Copy E.E. Vidal
Ms 30 x 20 cm 5" to 1 mile
Accompanied by 'Abstract of Lieutenant Vidal's Journal from Long Point to Point Pelee from the 23d to 30th July 1815,' 4pp; notes and description of the creek, shoreline, trees, channel, etc; also a copy with same title sgd 'A.T.E. Vidal 1815 W.F.W. Owen' in GBTAUh; (*PRO Cat* 1475).
GBLpro (MPG 83(2)) GBTAUh (E428 Aa2)

C47
'No 40'[b] Otter River an Eye Sketch whilst rowing up it. [Sgd] A.T.E. Vidal (Signed) W.F.W. Owen Copy E.E.Vidal
Ms 36 x 29 cm 4" to 1 mile
Notes on river and navigation; soundings; notes on settlement and names of settlers; also accompanied by abstract of Vidal's journal as noted in 40a above; (PRO Cat 1440); a copy with the same title sgd 'A.T.E. Vidal 1815 W.F.W. Owen' in GBTAUh; (*PRO Cat* 1440).
GBLpro (MPG 83(3)) GBTAUh (E429 Aa2)

C48
'No 41' Sketch of Fort Erie Roadstead the commencement of Lake Erie with the Soundings Shoals &c. Copy E.E. Vidal
Ms 35 x 40 cm 1" to 1/2 mile
Soundings; fort; storehouses; Buffalo Creek; oriented to the south; (*PRO Cat* 1458).
GBLpro (MPG 84)

C49
'No 42' Sketch of the Straits of St Mary between Lake Huron and Lake Superior by A. Brice Lieut. Rol Engr
Ms 60 x 74 cm 1" to 2 1/4 miles
The plan appears to have been copied from Bryce's sketch of 1798 (see no **847**) and includes his note on the survey; a later note has been added locating a boundary between Manitoulin and St Joseph Is: 'it is said the Americans intend to claim a line in this direction as their boundary'; (*PRO Cat* 1585).
GBLpro (MPG 85)

C50
'No 45' A Chart of the Straits of St Mary's and Michilimackinac containing the Water Communication between the three Great Lakes. viz. Superior Huron & Michigan. Copy [Sgd] E.E. Vidal
Ms 43 x 36 cm 1" to 2 1/3 marine leagues
A rough sketch; a few rapids and falls shown; islands; (*PRO Cat* 1586).
GBLpro (MPG 87)

Miscellaneous Early Manuscript Charts

C51 *[179?]*
Survey of Part of the River Thames Copied from a Plan in the Royl Engineers Drawing Room
Ms 51 x 80 cm Scale not given
Copied from surveys made in the 1790s.
GBTAUh (E431 Aa2)

C52 *1811*
[Georgian Bay] [Sgd] N[?]te Poyntz fecit 1811 Abt
Ms 52 x 75 cm Approx 1" to 10 miles
Inset: 'Penetanguishene Harbour' 2 1/2" to 5 miles'; a crude chart showing eastern coastline of Georgian Bay south to Penetanguishene.
GBTAUh (190 Aa2)

C53 *1814*
A Chart of the Channels leading into Kingston Harbour 1814
Ms 46 x 66 cm Approx 1" to 1/2 mile
A detailed survey with soundings; also another copy in same location with watermark '1809.'
GBTAUh (192 Aa2)

C54 *[ca 1814]*
[Lake Ontario by Capt Connor etc]
Ms 51 x 143 cm Approx 1" to 4 miles Watermark: '1814'
Soundings; place-names; also another copy in the same location.
GBTAUh (189 Aa2)

C55 *1815*
A Plan of Kingston Harbour Navy Bay and Hamilton Cove Lake Ontario ... By T. Chillingworth Master HMS St Lawrence 1815
Ms 57 x 121 cm 1" to 100 yards
A comprehensive and important survey showing the Naval Yard in great detail; soundings; topographic information along shore; also a second copy in same location with a little less detail for dockyard.
GBTAUh (182 Aa2)

C56 *1815*
A Plan of His Majesty's Naval Yard Kingston Point Frederick Upper Canada America in the Year 1815
Col ms 57 x 47 cm 1" to 160 feet
A detailed plan of the dockyard with bldgs; shows the following ships: *Star, Prince Regent, Saint Lawrence, Princess Charlotte, Charwell, Psyche, Montreal; Duke Kent Hull* not in same position as on C55.
GBTAUh (193 Aa1)

C57 *1815*
Plan of the River Ouse or Grande River with part of Mohawk Bay Surveyed by John Harris Master R.N. May 1815
Ms 66 x 77 cm 1" to 400 yds
A few soundings; houses with names of inhabitants; note indicates mouth of river was 130 yds wide in May and in Nov only 53 yds wide; probably 2nd item listed in W.F.W. Owen's 'Proceedings ...' (1817) 81.
GBTAUh (E427 Aa2)

1816–25 The Survey of the Lakes

The Survey of the Great Lakes was commenced in 1816 under the direction of Capt W.F.W. Owen and completed in 1825 by Lt Henry Bayfield; the first instruction to begin the survey was issued on 5 Nov 1815 by Sir E. Owen to Capt W.F.W. Owen: 'It is desirable that a complete Survey shall be made ... of every part of the river and Lake of the Thousand Islands as low as the Galop Rapids, as well as of the three lakes, Ontario, Erie and Huron' (OOA RG 8 I vol 370); on 14 June 1817 Owen was ordered to return to England and Lt Bayfield assumed command; Bayfield's 'Notes re Survey of the Great Lakes 1816–1825' include instructions on procedures for the survey and are found in the Bayfield Papers (OOA MG 24 F28 vol 2). The ms charts resulting from the surveys are listed below grouped by the progress of the survey from the St Lawrence R to L Superior; (Harris; Wolter (ongoing research); McKenzie, xiii–xxvii).

ST LAWRENCE RIVER 1816

C58
Index to the Survey of the Head of the River Saint Lawrence, made by order of The Right Honorable The Lords Commissioners of the Admiralty, in the Year 1816. under the Direction of Captain Wm Fitz Wm Owen R.N. [Sgd] W.F.W. Owen, Geo. D. Cranfield Lieut 90th Lt Infy Pxt and Scripst
Col ms Approx 117 x 260 cm 11/2" to 1000 fathoms
Shows the area from Edwardsburg Twp to beyond Kingston and south to Sacketts Harbour; shows towns, roads, and houses along shore; swampy areas; shoals, soundings; no sheet lines for larger scale maps shown; 'a complete plan of the head of the River St Lawrence in 19 sheets Scale 1/12000' was noted in W.F.W. Owen's 'Proceedings ...' (1817), 85, as finished 'and lodged in the office here,' and the index described here is noted as a reduction from it; however these plans have not been found; photoreproduction in OOAMA (V11/418).
GBTAUh (B788Aa 3h)

Related maps

(2)
Index to the Survey ... Owen R.N. Copied from a Map borrowed from the Admiralty. [Sgd] S.B. Howlett Inspector General's Office February 6th 1828.
Col ms 53 x 247 cm 1" to approx 666.6 fathoms
Endorsements: stamps 'B O' 'IGF'
A copy, without soundings, of (1) above; (Holmden 1232).
OOAMA

LAKE ONTARIO 1816–18

C59
Chart of Lake Ontario Surveyed by Order of the Right Honorable Lords Commissioners of the Admiralty In 1816 By Captn W.F.W. Owen, R.N. and His Assistants Messrs A.T.E. Vidal, and H.W. Bayfield, Lieuts R.N. and Mr Harris, Master.
Col ms 93 x 175 cm 1" to 1 mile of longitude or 1:216,000
Remarks: 'The Roads and Rivers on the American side and the interior have been added from De Witt, Bouchette and Chewit for the purpose of General information and are by no means to be considered as forming a part of the Survey'; a sheet showing the survey of the back communica-

tion between Lakes Ontario and Huron has been pasted over part of the north shore – a reduced version of the plans listed below; soundings are shown in Burlington Bay, the Bay of Quinte, and the St Lawrence R; Yonge St, Dundas St, Kingston Rd, and roads to the Rideau shown; relief, nature of shoreline; similar to D8029/1 see below; photoreproduction in OOAMA (V11/414).
GBTAUh (B674)

Related maps

(2) [Chart of Lake Ontario] Reduced from a Survey by the Admiralty in 1816. Reduced by S.B. Howlett Inspector General's Office 30th April 1828.
Col ms 47 x 76 cm Scale not given Endorsements: stamp 'B O'
A reduction of (1) with the same information and the same note about sources; (Holmden 1909).
OOAMA

C60
Chart of Lake Ontario on a 1/4 of an Inch to a mile of Longitude from the Surveys made by Order of the Lords Commissioners of the Admiralty
Col ms in 14 sheets 73 x 180 cm or smaller 1" to 1 mile of longitude Watermark: 'J WHATMAN 1816'
Shows index lines for the 14 detailed sheets, which are filed together as a set; attribution in the GBTAUh catalogue: 'Roughs Capt. Owen'; sheets I–VII No cover the north shore of L Ontario and sheets I–VII So cover the south shore; the scale is not given but was probably .833 inches to 1 mile or 1:65,432 as described in W.F.W. Owen's 'Proceedings ...' (1817, 85); sheets II and III No and sheet VI So, which cover the northeast shore of the lake and part of the north shore of the Niagara Peninsula, were missing in 1879; shoreline, soundings, places, a few roads, etc.
GBTAUh (D8029/1, 4–9, 11–15)

C61
Survey of Part of the North Coast of Lake Ontario Including the Bay of Quinté and Newcastle Harbour by Captain W.F.W. Owen R.N. In the Years 1816 & 1817. Sheet 1 ... 2 ... 3 ... 4
4 mss Sizes vary 1" to .66 nautical miles
The four sheets fit together to cover coast from Amherst Is to Newcastle Harbour; there is also another chart in same location 'Survey of part of Lake Ontario from Grenadier Id to Henderson including Sacketts harbour ... 1816.'
GBTAUh (L3210 Aa2)

C62
Chart of the Prince Edward's or South Bay. Lake Ontario Surveyed by Lieut H.W. Bayfield and Mr J. Harris Master R.N. Under the direction of Capt W.F.W. Owen R.N. A.D. 1816. G.D. Cranfield Lieut 90th L.I. fecit
Col ms 62 x 97 cm 1" to 2000 ft Watermark: 'JAMES WHATMAN TURKEY MILL KENT 1814'
Shows [Prince Edward Bay], Waupoos Is, The Drakes [False Ducks Is]; soundings; shoreline shown by shading.
GBTAUh (C124 Aa1)

C63
Plan of Newcastle Harbour Lake Ontario Copied from a Plan in the Rl Engineers Office Quebec 29th August 1815 [Sgd] G. Nicolls Lt Col. Comg RE
Col ms 42 x 81 cm 2" to 1 mile
This plan was probably used in the making of the survey and had some information added to it; 'Directions for Sailing into the Harbour of Newcastle by Lieut Paxton of the Provincial Navy'; shows the coast of Presqu'isle and east to Prince Edward Co; soundings at harbour mouth; planned location of town shown.
GBTAUh (B780 Aa1)

C64
Plan of Newcastle Harbour Lake Ontario Surveyed by Mr J. Harris Master R.N. under the Direction of Captain W.F.W. Owen R.N. [Sgd] W.F.W. Owen. Kingston U.C. 2nd January 1817. Geo Darley Cranfield Lieut 90th Light Infy Pinxt and [illegible]
Col ms 59 x 65 cm 1" to 1000 ft
A more detailed plan of the harbour alone with relief shown by colour wash; soundings; treed areas, clearings; sandy, marshy, and rocky shores.
GBTAUh (B779 Aa1)

C65
Plan of Gananoqui Surveyed in April 1817 by Lieut E.A. Smith 70th Regt
Col ms 38 x 57 cm 1" to 500 ft
An attractive plan with relief, treed areas, mills, barracks, blockhouse, and other bldgs shown; road; possibly drafted later as it is not listed in W.F.W. Owen's 'Proceedings ...' (1817).
GBTAUh (C123 Aa1)

C66
Plan of Kingston and its vicinity. The Shores and Measures by Lieutenant A.T.E. Vidal Royal N. under the Direction of Captain Wm Fitz Wm Owen R.N. The Town and Works from a Survey by Lieut H.L. Renny Rl Engineers and the Soundings by Actg Lieut Wm [*sic*] Bayfield Royal Navy [Sgd] W.F.W. Owen Captn Geo. Cranfield fecit
Col ms 114 x 70 cm 1" to 500 ft
Inset: 'Plan of Point Frederick with the proposed Alterations for the Dock-Yard Establishment' 1" to 250 ft; also 'Continuation of the Cataraqui to the Mills same scale'; completed by 1817 as it is listed in W.F.W. Owen's 'Proceedings ...' (1817), 85); an attractive plan with relief by colour wash, wooded areas, fort and all in town shown; the inset shows fortifications, and stone and wooden bldgs, all named; bldgs to be torn down; nine ships shown in dockyard.
GBTAUh (B718 50c)

C67
Plan of York. Lake Ontario. Surveyed under the Direction of Captain W.F.W. Owen R.N. By Lieutenant H.W. Bayfield R. Navy Geo. D. Cranfield Lieut 90th Lt Infy fecit
Col ms 45 x 52 cm 1" to 1000 ft Watermark: 'J WHATMAN 1813'
Probably completed later in 1817 as listed as 'finished but not arrived' in W.F.W. Owen's 'Proceedings ...' (1817, 86); an attractive plan showing relief by hachures, treed areas, marsh, sand and shingle beaches; remarks: 'The Town is copied from a Plan in the Surveyor General's Office' (and similar to **2040–1**, shows streets and major bldgs including 'Civil Government Houses,' 'Government House,' and 'House of Assembly'; gaol, church, and public school; bridges shown over creeks and road connections.
GBTAUh (B778 Aa1)

C68
Plane Projection of the North Channel and Bay of Quinté Lake Ontario Surveyed from Measures on the Ice in the Winters of 1816 & 17 By Lieuts Vidal and Bayfield, Mr J. Harris Master, and Mr A.B. Becher Midn R.N. Under the direction of Captain W.F.W. Owen R.N. [Sgd] W.F.W. Owen. A.B. Becher Pinxit et Scripst
Col ms in 4 sheets Approx 117 x 386 cm 1" to 666.6 yds or approx 1:24,000
Shows the area from Kingston and the Cataraqui R to the mouth of the Trent R; shows north channel only; relief by colour wash; swamps; soundings; possibly part missing at the west end beyond Carrying Place as a plan of the Bay of Quinte at 1:24,000 in 6 sheets is listed in W.F.W. Owen's 'Proceedings ...' (1817); the sheet from Kingston to Ernestown is in a different hand; photoreproduction in OOAMA.
GBTAUh (B774)

C69
Sketch of the Water Communication between Kingston and the Ottawa. By Captain Otty of the Royal Navy and Lieutenant Jebb Rl Engineers Kingston 1st August 1816 Geo. Cranfield H.O. Kingston U.C. 4 August 1816 [Sgd] W.F.W. Owen Captain
Col ms 81 x 221 cm 1" to 1 geog mile
Endorsements: 'Sept 30 '16 to Hydrographer'
Listed in W.F.W. Owen's 'Proceedings ...' (1817) as 'Sketch of the Rideau communication' with note that no astronomical observations or accurate surveys were made; similar to no **465**.
GBTAUh (B782)

C70
Measured Sketch of the back Communication between Lakes Ontario and Huron by Captain W.F.W. Owen R.N. Geo. Darley Cranfield Lieutt 90th Light Infantry Pinxt et Script Kingston 12th August 1817
Ms in 10 sheets Ea 80 x 60 cm or smaller 1" to 500 fathoms
Shows relief, soundings in navigable areas of rivers, lakes; main roads; houses shown along the river system; trails including Indian trail from Rice L; listed in W.F.W. Owen's 'Proceedings ...' (1817), 86; photoreproduction in OOAMA.
GBTAUh (B787/1–10)

C71
Measured Sketch of the Water Communication between The Bay of Quinté and Lake Huron, by the Rice Lake &c&c From the Lower Falls of the River Trent, to its mouth by Lt Cranfield D.A.Q.M.G. the Remainder by Captn W.F.W. Owen R.N. and Lieutt Smith 70th Regiment in the Years 1816 and 1817. Copied from the Original Surveys by Lieutt G.D. Cranfield 90th Light Infy Quebec 6th May 1818.
Col ms in 5 sections Ea 75 x 155 cm or smaller 1" to 1000 yds Watermark: 'JAMES WHATMAN TURKEY MILLS KENT 1814'
Each sheet has a running title 'Water Communication between the Bay of Quinte and Lake Huron' and sheets are numbered 'No 1' to 'No 5'; 'No 2' includes 'Remarks on the Percy Portage surveyed by Lieutt Smith 70th Regt'; some different trails and notes than **C70**, but also generally more notes and more survey points marked; there is also a tracing of 'No 1' in OOAMA; (Holmden 1510).
OOAMA (NMC 17006)

Related maps

(2)
Measured Sketch ... Copied from the Original Surveys by Lieut G.D. Cranfield 90th Regt Infy Quebec 6th May 1816 [i.e. 1818]
Col ms in 8 sheets Ea 66 x 87 cm or smaller 1" to 1000 yds Endorsements (on each sheet): 'Capt Owens R.N. Communication leading from the mouth of the River Trent, towards Penetanguishene'
Similar to plan above but laid out on more sheets and the title is given on the first sheet only; also in OTAR are copies on tracing paper of 'No 2 Water Communication between the Bay of Quinte and Lake Huron' and 'No 3' [without title] from the set in OOAMA (see above).
OTAR (SR 7067; 7111; 7134; 7763–9)

NIAGARA RIVER, LAKE ERIE, AND LAKE ST CLAIR 1817–18

C72
Index to the Survey of the River Niagara Made by Order of the Right Honorable The Lords Commissioners of the Admiralty In the Year 1817. Under the direction of Captain Wm Fitz Wm Owen. R.N.
Col ms 61 x 94 cm 1" to 4000 ft
Shows relief by colour wash, soundings, details of shoreline, and rocky areas; Queenston, 'Newark' [Niagara] are shown and main roads; no sheet lines are shown for the larger survey; the larger

scale sheets are described in Owen's 'Proceedings ...' (1817), 87, as 11 sheets at 1:12,000, from Fort Mississauga to Snake Hill above Fort Erie 'the whole distance carefully levelled and triangled from Bases measured on the Road including Sketches of Chippewa and Tonawenda on 1:24,000 Altho' a complete drawing has not been made of this yet the plan is as complete as it can be made' photoreproduction in OOAMA; the large scale plans have not been found.
GBTAUh (B785)

C73
A Survey of the River Niagara ... Captain William Fitz William Owen R.N. Copy [sgd] J Nightingale 23d Feby 1836
Col ms 57 x 99 cm 1" to 4000 ft Endorsements: stamp 'B↑O'
Shows the same information as **C72** but the relief is more sketchily depicted; (Holmden 2083).
OOAMA (NMC 21729)

C74
Lake Erie on Mercator's projection surveyed by order of the Lord's Commissioners of the Admiralty by Lieut Henry Wy. Bayfield Royal Navy in the summers of 1817 and 1818. [Sgd] Henry Wy Bayfield
Ms 94 x 200cm Approx 20" to 1° latitude
'N.B. In the Survey of the South Coast I was assisted by Lieut Henry Renny Royal Engineers the coast of the head of the Lake from Amherstburgh round to Sandusky was surveyed by him alone. Mr P.E. Collins Mids accompanied me during the whole of the Survey. The shoals etc. in the entrance of the River Niagara are taken from Captain W.F.W. Owens Survey of that River. The soundings are in feet. The Coast everywhere wooded except where the clearances are shown by a single line. To finish the Survey of the Lake it requires to be sounded generally. Several shoals in the head of the Lake mentionned to exist by report have been searched for but not found'; an outline plan with indication of the nature of the shore and rivers and some place-names; photoreproduction in OTUM.
GBTAUh (B223a)

C75
Lake Erie on Mercator Projection 12 Sheets Surveyed by Order of the Lords Commissioners of the Admiralty by Lieut Henry Wy Bayfield Royal Navy
Ms in 12 sheets Ea approx 65 x 98 cm or 98 x 65 cm 1" to 1° latitude Watermark: 'J WHATMAN 1816' on several sheets Endorsements: 'Received from Commodore Barrie 26th July 1820' stamp 'HO'
'The Soundings are in feet as also the estimated height of the cliffs'; other notes are the same as those on **C74** except the note 'Mr P.E. Collins Midn attached to the Surveying Department also accompanied me both in 1817 and 1818 [Sgd] Henry Wy Bayfield'; the rough sheets are numbered: north coast nos 2–6, south coast nos 2–6, a sheet 3d, and no 1 showing both north and south coast; note on north no 3: 'Long Point said to belong to the Crown H.W.B. Should be reserved Signed R. Barrie'; the soundings have now been completed since **C74** was made and added to the detailed sheets.
GBTAUh (B716 Aa1/1–11; B716/121d)

C76
Survey of Lake Erie in the Years 1817 and 1818 By Lieut Henry W. Bayfield R.N. Drawn by Mr George Alexr Frazer Mate and Draughtsman
Col ms 69 x 126 cm 10" to 1° latitude
Endorsements: stamp 'HO'
A more finished plan of the survey of L Erie and includes 11 insets; insets on the Canadian side: 'Survey of the Inner and Outer Bays of Long Point' 1" to 7.8 nautical miles; 'Survey of the entrance of the River Niagara' 1 1/2" to 4000 ft, 'Survey of the mouth of the River Detroit which connects Lakes Erie and St Clair' 1" to 4000 ft, 'Survey of Mohawk Bay' 3" to 2000 yds; relief, vegetation along shore, clearings, soundings, forts, towns; comments on bottom and shoreline; the printed chart (**C114**) was prepared from this plan; (*OHIM* 6.14).
GBTAUh (B223 15i)

Related maps

(**2**) (Copy) Survey of Lake Erie in the Years 1817 and 1818 by Lieut Henry W. Bayfield R.N., ... Copied by J. Nightingale 9th Jany 1828.
Col ms 52 x 121 cm 10" to 1° latitude Watermark: 'J GREEN & SONS 1826' Endorsements: stamp 'B↑O
Includes the inset for Niagara R and Detroit R copied from plan above.
OOAMA (NMC 16713)

C77
Running Track Survey of the River St Clair August 1817 by Lieut H.W. Bayfield R.N. Assisted by Lieut H. Renny R.E. [Sgd] H.W. Bayfield Lieut and Surveyor
Ms 59 x 27 cm 1" to 1 nautical mile Endorsements: stamp 'HO'
Shows the area from Chenail Ecarté to L Huron; soundings; nature of shoreline.
GBTAUh (E 487 Aa2)

C78
Track Survey of the Lake St Clair by Lieut H.W. Bayfield R.N. Assisted by Lieut H. Renny R.E. Augt 1817 [Sgd] H.W. Bayfield Lieut and Surveyor
Col ms 34 x 38 cm 1" to 2 nautical miles
Endorsements: stamp 'HO'
Shows the nature of the shoreline and ship channels.
GBTAUh (E486 Aa2)

LAKE HURON 1817–22

C79

Part of Lake Huron on Mercator's Projection Surveyed by Order of the Lords Commissioners of the Admiralty by Lieut Henry Wy Bayfield Royal Navy assisted by Lieut Henry Renny Royal Engineers in Sept 1817. [Sgd] Henry W. Bayfield Lieut R.N.
Ms Size unknown Scale not given
Shows the west part of L Huron with the entrance to L Michigan; probably joins with a sheet to the east, possibly sheet below or similar plan; outlines of shore; soundings, relief.
GBTAUh (B715 Aa1 M)

C80

[North part of Lake Huron including North Channel]
Ms 63 x 99 cm Scale not given
Shows area from Cape Hurd to Falls of St Mary; soundings; entered in GBTAUh catalogue May 1834 as 'Survey Copy from Cp Byfld.'
GBTAUh (H953 Aa2)

C81

[Detailed manuscript roughs (plans) of Lake Huron]
34 mss (some col) Size varies [approx 1" to 1 mile]
GBTAUh E347/1–10 15f are as follows: [east coast]: 'East Coast Lake Huron No 5 Surveyed July 1820 by Lieut H.W. Bayfield R.N. and Mr P.E. Collins Midsn & Assistant Surveyor' and 'East Coast of Lake Huron No 6 Surveyed in June 1819 by ...' and [the south part of the Grand Manitoulin]; these three sheets cover the Bruce Peninsula from the Fishing Islands past Cape Hurd to the north shore; [north coast]: 'North Coast of Lake Huron No 5 Surveyed in 1819 and 1821 by Lieut H.W. Bayfield R.N. Surveyor and Mr P.E. Collins Midsn & Assistant Surveyor' and 'North Coast Lake Huron No 6 Surveyed in 1819 and 1822 by ...' and 'North Coast ...No 7 ... No 8 ... No 9 ... [same date as No 6]' and 'North Coast Lake Huron No 10 Surveyed in 1817 and 1822 by ...'; these six sheets show the north shore of L Huron and the relevant parts of Manitoulin Is; sheet 9 includes Drummond Is and Portlock Harbour; sheet 10 shows the area from the Falls of St Mary to the north part of St Joseph Is; sheet 5 joins east coast no 6 and sheet 10 joins west coast no 8 [U.S.].

GBTAUh E346/1-24 8d: (1) R St Mary from the falls to L George 'No 21'; (2) Neebish Is 'No 20'; (3) St Joseph Is and C. 'No 24'; (4) St Joseph Is 'No 21'; (5) Triton Shoal to Drummond Island 'No 5'; (6) 1st Manitoulin and 2nd Manitoulin Is and Grand Manitoulin 'No 17' with note about triangulation of 1819 and 1822 sgd 'HWB'; (7) Port Collier, Drummond Is 'No 19'; (8) Mississauga R ... to the east 'No 6'; (9) Grand Manitoulin Is 'No 15'; (10) N Coast of Lake Huron centred on the Is of La Cloche 'No 14'; (11–12) Grand Manitou Is 'No 23' ... 'No 7'; (13) Grand Manitoulin including Manitoulin Gulf; (14) 4th Manitoulin to Cabots Head 'No 4'; (15) east coast of L Huron 'No 22'; (16) Rapids of St Clair to Cape Ipperwash ... 'No 11'; (17) vicinity of Squaw Is 'No 81'; (18) 'Lake Huron NE Coast Original Projection Surveyed in 1820.1 by [Sgd] Lieut Henry Wy Bayfield R.N. and his Assistant Mr Philip Collins Mate' shows the mouths of the French River and the Bustard Islands (OHIM 6.15); (19) northeast coast of L Huron 'No 1'; (20) northeast coast of L Huron north of Watches Islet 'No 3'; (21) southern part of Georgian Bay from Christian Is to Prince William Henry Is including Penetanguishene Harbour 'No 12'; (23) Gloucester Bay 'No 13'; (24) Cape Chin to Owen Sound 'No 9'; (22) appears to be missing; some sheets show triangulation lines.
GBTAUh (E347/1–10 15f; E346/1–24 8d)

C82

Survey of Lake Huron By Lieut Henry Wy Bayfield. R.N. assisted by Mr Philip. Ed Collins. Mid. in the Years 1819, 20, 21 and 22. Drawn By Mr George Alexr Frazer Mate and Draughtsman.
Ms 144 x 145cm Approx 14" to 1° latitude
Endorsements: stamps 'HO' '348 MNo.2' GBL accession stamp '6 Nov 1874'
A more finished plan of the hydrographic survey and probably the plan from which the printed charts were prepared; soundings, nature of shoreline, relief; rivers, place-names; spot heights; soundings with red are noted as from the 'Remark Books of His Majesty's Schooners Surprize and Huron' 'The Black Meridians are of relative Longitude from Point Edward.'
GBL (Add Mss 31358.A)

C83

Survey of Penetanguishene Harbour Lake Huron by Lieut H.W. Bayfield, R.N.
Ms 44 x 27 cm 1" to 1200 ft
Soundings; nature of shoreline; there is also a plan 'Penetanguishene Harbour Lake Huron [Sgd] Henry Wy Bayfield' GBTAUh (E352 Aa2)).
GBTAUh (L3210 Aa2 E352 Aa2)

C84

Survey of St Joseph's North Channel Lake Huron made in August 1822 by Lieut Henry W. Bayfield R.N. Surveyor and his assistant Mr P.E. Collins Midn
Col ms 54 x 92 cm 1" to 500 fathoms
Endorsements: stamp 'H O'
Shows the north side of St Joseph Is with details on the shoreline; soundings.
GBTAUh (E349 Aa2)

C85

Rattle Snake Harbour Lake Huron [Sgd] H.W. Bayfield Lt & Surveyor
Col ms 31 x 27 cm 2" to 500 fathoms
Endorsements: stamp 'H O'
Shows the 'Fourth Manitoulin or Fitzwilliam

Island' [southeast end of Manitoulin Is] with Rattlesnake Harbour, Wall Is and Owen Channel; relief; soundings.
GBTAUh (E350 Aa2)

C86
Port Collier Drummond Island Surveyed in October 1817 by Lieut Henry Wy Bayfield R.N.
Ms 61 x 44 cm 1" to 1000 ft
Soundings; relief by shading.
GBTAUh (E354 Aa2)

C87
The Narrows of the Manitoulin Straits the only channel for Vessels to the Northward of the Manitoulin Islds [and] Entrance of the Manitoulin Gulf [Both sgd] H.W. Bayfield
2 mss on 1 sheet 9 x 13 cm 1" to 350 or 250 fathoms
GBTAUh (E351 Aa2)

LAKE SUPERIOR 1816, 1823–5

C88
North Coast of Lake Superior No 2 Surveyed in 1823 by Lieut Henry Wy Bayfield, Royal Navy and his assistant Mr Philip E. Collins Midsh [Sgd] H.W. Bayfield Lieut & Surveyor 'E 478' [and] North Coast of Lake Superior No 3 Surveyed in 1823 and 1825 by ... Surveyor
2 mss 72 x 56 cm and 62 x 62 cm 5 3/4" to 10' latitude Endorsements (both ms): stamp 'HO'; GBTAUh endorsement 'E478 Aa2' almost obliterated
Provenance: transferred to OOAMA by Canadian Hydrographic Service in 1964; sheets 2 and 3 show the area from Nipigon Bay and Ile St Ignace west to Thunder Bay and the Grand Portage and Pigeon R; soundings; relief by hachures and wash; types of rock; grid for copying; rivers, place-names, etc; fairly finished maps; nos 1, 2, and 3 are noted in GBTAUh catalogues as being sent to the Canadian Hydrographer 15 Feb 1912, but sheet 1 has not been found.
OOAMA (NMC 21807–8)

C89
Survey of Lake Superior by Lieut Henry Wy Bayfield, R.N. assisted by Mr Philip. Ed Collins, Mid. Between the Years 1823 and 25. Drawn by Mr George Alexr Frazer, Mate. H.W.B.
Ms 93 x 186 cm Approx 2" to 10' latitude
Endorsements: stamp 'E477' 'H O'
Provenance: transferred to OOAMA by Canadian Hydrographic Service in 1964; a more finished plan with grid over part for tracing; probably the plan from which the printed charts were prepared; relief and details of nature of shoreline; soundings; rivers, places named; a few comments on minerals.
OOAMA (NMC 17418)

C90
Survey of the Coast of Lake Superior between Thunder Point and the old Grand Portage in the Winter of 1816 & 17 by A.B. Becher R.N.
Ms 90 x 163 cm 1" to 1 nautical mile
Inset: 'A Survey of Pigeon River on the Ice in March 1817 by A.B. Becher R.N.' 3" to 1/2 nautical mile; three views from various baselines; list of English place-names and French equivalents; described in W.F.W. Owen's 'Proceedings ...' (1817) as '36.'
GBTAUh (B775 1d)

C91
Survey of the River Kaminitiquoia in Decr 1816 by A.B. Becher R.N.
Col ms 57 x 130 cm 1 1/2" to 1/4 mile Endorsements: 'No 37' '1/12000'
'View of Fort William from the River'; these and plans below are from Becher's reconnaissance surveys with Lord Selkirk in 1816 when the survey was under the direction of Capt W.F.W. Owen; this plan is listed as no 37 and described in Owen's 'Proceedings ...' (1817), 87; the scale appears to be slightly different from that recorded in Owen's report; relief by grey wash; triangulation up the river; Fort William and bldgs; the attractive view of Fort William shows the Hudson's Bay Co. post, canoes, and river.
GBTAUh (B800 49b)

C92
Part of the River St Mary from the Falls to Lake George Surveyed in 1825 by Lieut Henry Wy Bayfield and his assistant Mr. P.E. Collins Midn.
Ms 35 x 59 cm 1" to 500 fathoms
The first part of the river with soundings and topographical details; (OHIM 6.19).
GBTAUh (E353 Aa2)

C93
River St Marys From the Rapids to the entrance of Lake Superior surveyed in July 1825 by ... [Sgd] Henry W Bayfield
Ms 41 x 64 cm 1" to 500 fathoms
Notes on the falls; soundings, topography.
GBTAUh (E480 Aa2)

Miscellaneous Later Surveys

C94 *1839*
A Resurvey of the Inner and Outer Bays of Long Point shewing the New Channel by John Harris R.N. late Assistant Surveyor to Capt W.F.W. Owen in 1815.16 & 17 Long Point 24th May 1839
Ms 59 x 71 cm Approx 1" to 1 nautical mile
Endorsements: stamp 'HO, 27 Ju 39'
A detailed survey with soundings and topograhical detail along shore; 'Site of the old Lighthouse undermined by the water' and a note about a proper position for light to southwest; probably a

final draft for the published chart issued in 1839 (see **C129**).
GBTAUh (L1703 Aa2)

C95 *[186?]*
Sheet III – North America – River St Lawrence above Montreal – Montreal to Farrens Pt. Reduced from a plan of the River St Lawrence in the Office of Public Works Toronto 1856
Ms 62 x 95 cm Approx 1.75" to 1 mile
Shows lights with a note indicating some in different positions from Admiralty list, sgd 'William Chimmo 10 July 66'; shows stations for gunboats of the 1st and 2nd Divisions with a note: 'On the recent occasion only four out of the seven were employed' [sgd] 'J. Hope [?] Vice Admiral'; a note indicates these were final drawings for the production of printed charts, 'stations not for insertion when engraved' (see **C124**).
GBTAUh (D9323/1 Tf)

Related maps

(2) *[186?]*
Sheet IV – North America – River St Lawrence above Farrens Pt Canal – Farrens Pt to Prescott. Reduced From a plan of the River St Lawrence in the Office of Public Works Toronto 1856
Ms 74 x 95 cm Approx 1.75" to 1 mile
Stations 4–7 as described on sheet above are on this sheet; charts are based on (**550**).
GTBAUh (D9323/2 Tf)

1828–67 Printed Charts

The printed charts from the survey of the Great Lakes were published from 1828 on and most went through several major and minor revisions before 1867. All charts show soundings, usually in feet, relief by hachures along shores, notes on the nature of the shoreline, mouths of rivers, falls, etc, notes on types of rock and tree, place-names. Small-scale charts also generally include the longitude and latitude markings in the margin, a north arrow and compass, and a note on the variation of the compass.

The main group of charts is arranged by chart numbers, first assigned in the 1839 Admiralty Chart Catalogue; although many of the charts were first published in 1828, the chart numbers appear to have been added only after 1839; the numbers were assigned to the charts already in existence, but in the order listed in the catalogue (roughly from L Superior east to the St Lawrence R); later charts were given the next higher number or given numbers of withdrawn charts in random order and these are listed at the end. In addition, many charts were reissued between editions, a fact that can be determined from watermarks, agency statements, and printed chart numbers and prices; for further information users should consult David and Campbell (1984).

No 320 (Sheet 1)

C96 *1828*
Survey / of / LAKE SUPERIOR. / BY / LIEUT. HENRY WY. BAYFIELD, R.N. / Assisted by Mr. Philip Ed. Collins, Mid. / between the Years 1823 & 1825. / Sheet 1 // London Published according to Act of Parliament at the Hydrographical Office of the Admiralty 18th June 1828. // J. & C. Walker Sculpt.
Print (engrav) 88 x 60 cm 13" to 1° latitude
Inset: 'Track Survey / of the / RIVER ST LOUIS. / BY Mr Philip Ed Collins, Mid. / under the direction of Lieut H.W. Bayfield, R.N.' approx 1" to 1 nautical mile; Hydrographical Office stamp 'Price 5s.'; relief along shoreline by hachures; notes on rock types and terrain; harbours and landing places; north arrow and variation of compass marked; shows area from head of the lake to Pigeon R.
GBTAUh OOAMA OTMCL USDLC

Later editions and states

(2) *[ca 1846]*
Additions as follows: sheet no '320'; 'Soundings are in feet'; 'Price Three s.'
GBTAUh OOAMA

(3) *1863*
[Imprint changed]: London Published ... 18th June 1828. Corrections to 1861. Novr 1863. Sold by J.D. Potter Agent for the Admiralty Charts 31 Poultry and 11 King St. Tower Hill / 320A
'Price Two Shillings'; variation of the compass in 1860; land stipple added.
OOAMA OTAR

No 320 (Sheet 2)

C97 *1828*
LAKE SUPERIOR. / SHEET 2. // London Published according to Act of Parliament at the Hydrographical Office of the Admiralty 1st September 1828. // J. & C. Walker Sculpt.
Print (engrav) 88 x 61 cm Approx 12.5" to 1° latitude
Hydrographical Office stamp '5s.'; shows area from Pigeon R to about the Slate Islands.
GBTAUh OOAMA OTMCL

Later editions and states

(2) *[ca 1846]*
Additions as follows: chart no '320'; 'Price Three s.'
GBTAUh

(3) *[1860?]*
[Added to imprint] ... / Sold by J.D. Potter Agent for the Admiralty Charts 31 Poultry and 11 King Street Tower Hill. ... / 320B

'Price Two Shillings'; insets added: 'ONTONAGON HARBOUR / From the United States Survey – 1859' 1" to 2.1 cables; 'AGATE HARBOUR / From the United States Survey / 1858' 1" to 3 cables; 'MARQUETTE HARBOUR / From the United States Survey. 1859' approx 1" to 2 cables; land stipple added.
GBTAUh

(4) *1863*
[Added to imprint]: ... 1st September 1828. Corrections to 1861. Novr 63 ...
OOAMA OTAR

No 320 (Sheet 3)

C98 *1828*
LAKE SUPERIOR. / SHEET III. // London Published according to Act of Parliament at the Hydrographical Office of the Admiralty 15th September 1828. // J. & C. Walker Sculpt.
Print (engrav) 87 x 60 cm Approx 12.5" to 1° latitude
Inset: 'Track Survey / of the / PIC RIVER, / by / Mr Philip E. Collins Midsn. / & Assistant Surveyor under the direction of / Lieut H.W. Bayfield' 1" to 500 fathoms; shows the northeastern side of the lake; Hydrographical Office stamp: 'Price 5s.'
GBTAUh OOAMA OTMCL

Later editions and states

(2) *[1846]*
Additions as follows: chart no '320'; 'Price Three s.'
GBTAUh

(3) *1863*
[Additions to imprint]: London ... 15th September 1828. Corrections Novr 1863. Sold by J.D. Potter Agent for the Admiralty Charts 31 Poultry and 11 King Street Tower Hill. ... 320C
'Price Two shillings'; land stipple added; variation of the compass as of 1860.
OOAMA OTAR

No 321

C99 *1828*
Chart / of part of the / NORTH COAST OF LAKE SUPERIOR, / FROM / Grand Portage Bay to Hawk Islet, / INCLUDING / ISLE ROYALE, / Surveyed by / Lieut Henry Wy Bayfield R.N. / and his Assistant MR PHILIP E. COLLINS, Midn R.N. // London Published according to Act of Parliament at the Hydrographical Office of the Admiralty 5th May 1828. // J. & C. Walker Sculpt.
Print (engrav) 63 x 94 cm 5" to 10' latitude [5" to 1 nautical mile?]
Inset: 'Track Survey / of the / RIVER KAMINISTIQUI-A, / IN / Thunder Bay.' 1" to 500 fathoms; printed stamp of Hydrographical Office and 'Price 5 S.'; shows the area from 88° to 90° W from about Nipigon Bay to Grand Portage; soundings; nature of shoreline; relief; types of rock.
GBTAUh

Later editions and states

(2) [184?]
Chart no '321' added at bottom below imprint.
GBTAUh

(3) *[ca 1846]*
Additions as follows: 'Price Three S.'; hand stamped statement added after the imprint: 'Sold by R.B. Bate, 21, Poultry, for the Lords Commissrs of the Admiralty, by their Appointment.'
OOAMA

(4) *1863*
[Imprint changed]: London ... 5th May 1828. Corrections 1861. 1863 / Sold by J.D. Potter Agent for the Admiralty Charts 31 Poultry & 11 King Street Tower Hill.
Stipple added; international boundary partly shown.
OOAMA

No 322

C100 *1828*
Chart / of that Part of the / NORTH COAST OF LAKE SUPERIOR / that includes / NEEPIGON & BLACK BAYS. / Surveyed by / Lieut Henry Wy Bayfield, R.N. / and his assistant / Mr Philip E. Collins, Mid. R.N. / 1823 // London Published according to Act of Parliament at the Hydrographical Office of the Admiralty 5th July 1828. // J. & C. Walker. Sculpt
Print (engrav) 63 x 79 cm 5" to 10' latitude
Printed stamp of Hydrographical Office and 'Price 4s.'; shows the area from 87° 30' to 89° W; soundings, etc; north arrow; variation of compass.
GBTAUh

Later editions and states

(2) *[ca 1846]*
Additions as follows: chart no '322' at bottom below imprint; watermark (USDLC and OOAMA copies): 'RUSE & TURNER 1844'; 'Price Two s. Sixp.'; GBTAUh has an earlier or later state with 'Price Two shillings.'
USDLC GBTAUh OOAMA

(3) *1861*
[Imprint changed]: London ... 5th July 1828. Corrections 1861. / Sold by J.D. Potter Agent for the Admiralty Charts 31 Poultry & 11 King Street Tower Hill
Note added on chart: 'Magnetic variation 1861 decreasing about 4' annually.
OOAMA

(4) *1863*
[Imprint changed]: ... Corrections 1861. Novr 1863.
GBTAUh OOAMA

No 323

C101 *1828*
Chart / of Part of the / NORTH COAST OF LAKE SUPERIOR, / FROM / Small Lake Harbour to Peninsula Harbour. / Surveyed by / LIEUT HENRY WY BAYFIELD, R.N. / assisted by / Mr Philip E. Collins, Midn / 1823 // London Published according to Act of Parliament at the Hydrographical Office of the Admiralty 22d July 1828. // J. & C. Walker Sculpt.
Print (engrav) 47 x 62 cm 5" to 10' latitude
Printed stamp of Hydrographical Office and 'Price 3s.'; soundings, nature of shoreline; shows area from 86° 30' to 87° 40' W.
GBTAUh

Later editions and states

(2) *[ca 1846]*
Additions as follows: chart no '323' at bottom right below imprint; watermark: 'RUSE & TURNER 1846'; 'Price Two s.'
USDLC OOAMA GBTAUh

(3) *1861*
[Imprint changed]: London ... 22d July 1828. Corrections to 1861. / Sold by J.D. Potter, Agent for the Admiralty Charts, 31 Poultry, & 11 King Street Tower Hill.
Magnetic variation given as of 1861
OOAMA

No 324

C102 *1828*
A Survey of / ST MARY'S RIVER / From the Rapids to the entrance of Lake Superior. / by / LIEUT HENRY WY BAYFIELD R.N. / and / Mr Philip E. Collins Midn Assistant. / 1825. // London Published according to Act of Parliament at the Hydrographical Office of the Admiralty 13th Feby 1828. // J. & C. Walker Sculpt.
Print (engrav) 28 x 46 cm 1 1/2" to 1000 fathoms [1.5" to 1 nautical mile?]
No graticule is shown on the chart; GBTAUh has state with 'Price 1s.'
OOAMA GBTAUh

Later editions and states

(2) *[ca 1846]*
Additions as follows: chart no '324' at bottom right below imprint; printed stamp of Hydrographical Office and 'Price 1s.'; 'Lake Superior' added to water area.
USDLC

(3) *(1864)*
NORTH AMERICA / RIVER ST MARY / BETWEEN LAKES HURON & SUPERIOR / From / EAST NEEBISH TO POINT IROQUOIS / FROM THE UNITED STATES COAST SURVEY / 1853–57 // Published at the Admiralty 16th Novr 1864, under the Superintendence of Captn G.H. Richards, R.N. – Hydrographer. / Sold by J.D. Potter, Agent for the Admiralty Charts, 31 Poultry, & 11 King St Tower Hill. // Engraved by J. & C. Walker // 324
Print (engrav) 62 x 80 cm 2" to 1 1/4 miles
Inset: 'HEAD OF ST MARY RIVER / CONTINUATION / from / ROUND ID POINT TO POINT IROQUOIS'; a new chart in the same no but based on the U.S. survey; shows more detail than the earlier charts particularly by indicating wooded areas; more soundings; navigation routes and lights fixed and flashing are also shown; gives sailing directions for the area; derived from U.S. charts nos 13 and 14 of 1857.
OOAMA

No 325

C103 *1828*
A Survey of / ST MARY'S RIVER / FROM THE FALLS TO LAKE GEORGE, / by / LIEUT HENRY WY BAYFIELD R.N. / and / Mr Philip E. Collins Midn and Assistant. / 1825. // London Published according to Act of Parliament at the Hydrographical Office of the Admiralty 18th Augt 1828. // J. & C. Walker Sculpt.
Print (engrav) 30 x 59 cm 1" to 500 fathoms [2" to 1 nautical mile?]
No graticule is given; printed stamp of Hydrographical Office and 'Price 2s.'
GBTAUh

Later editions and states

(2) *[184?]*
Additions as follows: chart no '325' at bottom below imprint.
OTAR USDLC OOAMA GBTAUh

(3) *1863*
[Imprint changed]: Corrections to 1861. 1863. / Sold by J.D. Potter, Agent for the Admiralty Charts 31 Poultry & 11 King Street Tower Hill.
Land stipple added; 'Price One Shilling.'
GBTAUh

(4) *(1864)*
NORTH AMERICA / RIVER ST MARY / BETWEEN LAKES HURON & SUPERIOR / from / THE ENTRANCE OF MUD LAKE TO THE EAST NEEBISH / FROM THE UNITED STATES COAST SURVEY / 1853–58 // London, Published at the Admiralty 16th Novr 1864 under the Superintendence of Captn. G.H. Richards, R.N. Hydrographer. / Sold by J.D. Potter, Agent for the Admiralty Charts, 31 Poultry & 11 King St Tower Hill. // Engraved by J. & C. Walker. // 325
Print (engrav) 62 x 61 cm 3" to approx 2 miles
A new chart based on the U.S. survey; shows more detailed information about wooded areas along shore and more soundings; navigation routes and lights shown; derived from U.S. chart no 14 of 1858 (**C134**).
OOAMA

No 326

C104 *1828*
A Survey / OF / ST JOSEPH'S NORTH CHANNEL / LAKE HURON, / BY / Lieut Henry W. Bayfield R.N. / Assisted by MR P.E. COLLINS Midn / 1822. // London Published according to Act of Parliament at the Hydrographical Office of the Admiralty 10th March 1828. // J. & C. Walker Sculpt.
Print (engrav) 46 x 61 cm 1.5" to 1 nautical mile
Inset: 'The / SHIP / NEEBISH RAPID' 1" to 200 fathoms; shows the area from L George and Sugar Is south to Neebish Is and Mud L and east to St Joseph Is; printed stamp of Hydrographical Office and 'Price 3s.'
OOAMA GBTAUh

Later editions and states

(2) *[ca 1846]*
Additions as follows: chart no '326' at bottom right below imprint; watermark on LC copy '...WHATMAN 184[3?]'; 'Price 2s.'; 'Lake Huron' added to water area.
OTAR GBTAUh USDLC

(3) *1865*
A Survey / OF / ST JOSEPH'S NORTH CHANNEL / FROM / LAKE GEORGE TO LAKE HURON / BY / Lieut Henry W. Bayfield R.N. / Assisted by MR P.E. COLLINS Midn / 1822. / The Channel from Mud L to L George is reduced from the United States Survey 1853–57 // London Published according to Act of Parliament at the Hydrographical Office of the Admiralty 10th March 1828. – Corrections to 1861. July 63. Jan 65. / Sold by J.D. Potter, Agent for the Admiralty Charts, 31 Poultry, & 11 King Street, Tower Hill // J. & C. Walker Sculpt. // 326
From the same plate as (2) above; extensive revisions to the Mud L/L George area.
OOAMA

No 327 (Sheet I)

C105 *1828*
LAKE HURON / SHEET I. / SURVEYED BY CAPTN H.W. BAYFIELD R.N. / 1822
Print (engrav) 63 x 48 cm 14 1/4" to 1° latitude [.2" to 1 nautical mile?]
Shows St Mary's R to western Manitoulin and south to Thunder Bay, Michigan; no copy of an 1828 state has been found but since the chart was listed in the Admiralty Chart Catalogue of 1839, a state earlier than 1848 must exist; title and imprint not verified.
Original not located

Later editions and states

(2) *1848*
[Imprint changed]: London Published according to Act of Parliament at the Hydrographic Office of the Admiralty, June 13th 1848./ Sold by R.B. Bate Agent for the Admiralty Charts 21 Poultry // J. & C. Walker, Sculpt // 327
Printed stamp of Hydrographic Office with 'F B' and 'Price 2s.'; OTAR copy has watermark: '...WHATMAN 184[?]'; USDLC copy has watermark 'WHATMAN 1856' and the additions of lighthouses on the U.S. side; one OOAMA copy has ms revisions and date '1856'; GBTAUh has state with 'Price Eighteen pence.'
OTAR USDLC OOAMA GBTAUh

No 327 (Sheet II)

C106 *1828 [184?]*
LAKE HURON / SHEET II. / SURVEYED BY H.W. BAYFIELD R.N. / 1822. // London Published according to Act of Parliament at the Hydrographic Office of the Admiralty 1828 / Sold by R.B. Bate Agent for the Admiralty Charts 21 Poultry // J. & C. Walker Sculpt // 327
Print (engrav) 63 x 48 cm 14.5" to 1° latitude
Printed stamp of Hydrographic Office with 'F.B.' and 'Price 2 shillings'; shows the area from the north shore of L Huron to part of the Bruce Peninsula; one NMC copy has ms revisions and date '1856'; an earlier state has not been found.
OTAR USDLC OOAMA

No 327 (Sheet III)

C107 *1828*
LAKE HURON. / SHEET III. // London Published according to Act of Parliament at the Hydrographical Office of the Admiralty 29th Sept 1828. // J. & C. Walker Sculpt
Print (engrav) 63 x 47 cm 14.5" to 1° latitude
Shows the Georgian Bay area; printed stamp of Hydrographical Office and 'Price 3s.'
GBTAUh

Later editions and states

(2) *[ca 1846]*
SHEET III. / SURVEYED BY CAPTN. H.W. BAYFIELD, R.N. 1822. // London ...
Additions as follows: chart no '327' and 'Price 2s.'; (*OHIM* 6.16?).
OOAMA GBTAUh

(3) *[1848?]*
[Added below imprint in larger type]: Sold by R.B. BATE, 21 Poultry, For the Lords Commissrs of the Admiralty, by their Appointment.
The price has been changed by hand to '2/6' (USDLC); there is a copy of (2) in OOAMA with ms revisions and date changed to '1848' and below it 1856 which suggests the LC copy was published in either of these two years.
USDLC

(4) *1863*
CANADA WEST / LAKE HURON. / GEORGIAN BAY / SURVEYED BY CAPTN H.W. BAYFIELD, R.N. 1822 // London Published according to Act of

Parliament at the Hydrographical Office of the Admiralty 29th Sept 1828. Corrections to 1861. June 63. /Sold by J.D. Potter Agent for the Admiralty Charts, 31 Poultry & 11 King St Tower Hill // J. & C. Walker Sculpt. 327
The title has been changed but the map is from the same plate.
GBTAUh

(5) *1864–5*
[Revised dates added to imprint]: ... Corrections to 1861. June – 63. Decr 64.
OOAMA copy has 'March 65' added in ms and the compass variation statement is dated '1865.'
OOAMA

No 327 (Sheet IV)

C108 *1828*
LAKE HURON. / SHEET IV. // London Published according to Act of Parliament at the Hydrographical Office of the Admiralty 25th July 1828. // J. & C. Walker Sculpt.
Print (engrav) 63 x 47 cm 14.5" to 1° latitude
Shows Sagana Bay and the U.S. coast of L Huron; printed stamp of Hydrographical Office; 'Price 2s.'
GBTAUh

Later editions and states

(2) *[ca 1839]*
[Added to title]: 'SURVEYED BY CAPTN. H.W. BAYFIELD R.N. / 1822'...
Chart no '327' added below the imprint; one OOAMA copy has ms adds of lights.
OTAR OOAMA GBTAUh

(3) *[184?]*
[Added below imprint]: Sold by R.B. BATE, 21 Poultry for the Lords Commssrs of the Admiralty, by their Appointment.
Price changed in ms by the stamp to '2/6d.'
USDLC

(4) *1863*
[Added to imprint]: Corrections to 1861. June 63 / Sold by J.D. Potter Agent for the Admiralty Charts 31 Poultry & 11 King St Tower Hill ... Price Eighteen pence
Land stipple added.
GBTAUh

No 327 (Sheet V)

C109 *1828*
LAKE HURON. / SHEET V. // London Published according to Act of Parliament at the Hydrographical Office of the Admiralty 8th Sept. 1828. // J. & C. Walker Sculpt.
Print (engrav) 63 x 47 cm 13.75" to 1° latitude
Shows the south part of L Huron north to the Sauble R; printed stamp of Hydrographical Office and 'Price 2s.'
GBTAUh OOAMA (NMC 119995)

Later editions and states

(2) *[184?]*
[Added to title]: SURVEYED BY CAPTN. H.W. BAYFIELD, R.N. 1822.
Chart no '327' added below the imprint; 'Price 2s.'
USDLC OOAMA GBTAUh

(3) *[184?]*
[Added below imprint]: Sold by R. B. Bate, 21 Poultry, for the Lords Commissrs of the Admiralty, by their Appointment.
Price below stamp changed in ms to '2/6.'
USDLC

(4) *1863*
[Added to imprint]: Corrns June 1863. / Sold by J.D. Potter, Agent for the Admiralty Charts, 31 Poultry & 11 King St Tower Hill
Land stipple added; 'Price Eighteen pence.'
GBTAUh

No 328

C110 *1828*
LAKE HURON / PORT COLLIER, / BY / Lieut. H.W. Bayfield R.N. / 1817 // London Published according to Act of Parliament at the Hydrographical Office of the Admiralty 31st May 1828. // J. & C. Walker Sculpt.
Print (engrav) 30 x 21 cm 1" to 2000 ft
Shows the port on Drummond Is with soundings; shoals, etc; 'Price 6d.'
GBTAUh

Later editions and states

(2) *[184?]*
Chart no '328' added.
GBTAUh OOAMA

(3) *1861*
[Added to imprint]: ... 31st May 1828. Corrections to 1861. / Sold by J.D. Potter Agent for the Admiralty Charts, 31 Poultry & 11 King Street. Tower Hill
The magnetic variation statement is dated 1861 and stippling has been added to the land areas; some soundings from U.S. 'Survey of 1854.'
GBTAUh

(4) *1863*
[Added after 1861 in imprint]: 63
OOAMA

No 329

C111 *1828*
LAKE HURON / RATTLE SNAKE HARBOUR, / BY / Lieut. H.W. Bayfield R.N. // London Published according to Act of Parliament at the Hydrographical Office of the Admiralty 3d June 1828. // J. & C. Walker Sculpt.
Print (engrav) 29 x 22 cm 2" to 500 fathoms
'Price 6d.'
GBTAUh

Later editions and states

(2) *[184?]*
Chart no '329 added below imprint.
OOAMA GBTAUh

(3) *1863*
[Added to imprint]: Corrtns 1861. June 63
Compass variation statement is dated '1861'; land stipple added.
OOAMA GBTAUh

No 330

C112 *1828*
Track Survey / of the / LAKE & RIVER ST CLAIR. / By / Lieut. H.W. Bayfield R.N. Assisted by Lieut H. Renny R.E. in August 1818. // London Published according to Act of Parliament at the Hydrographical Office of the Admiralty 23d April 1828. // J. & C. Walker Sculpt.
Print (engrav) 53 x 29 cm 1" to 2.25 nautical miles
Longitude/latitude readings at various points along river and lake; printed stamp of the Hydrographical Office; 'Price 1s. 6d.'
GBTAUh

Later editions and states

(2) *[184?]*
Chart no '330' added at the bottom.
OTAR USDLC GBTAUh

(3) *1861*
[Added below imprint]: Sold by J.D. Potter Agent for the Admiralty Charts 31 Poultry & 11 King St Tower Hill
Compass variation statement is dated '1861'; 'Price sixpence.'
OOAMA GBTAUh

No 331

C113 *1828*
A Survey / of the / RIVER DETROIT. / FROM LAKE ST CLAIR to A & B. / BY / Capt. W.F.W. Owen & Assistants. / in 1815. / Continued from A.B. to Lake Erie, By Lieut. H.W. Bayfield in 1817 // London Published according to Act of Parliament at the Hydrographical Office of the Admiralty 12th April 1828. // J. & C. Walker Sculpt.
Print (engrav) 59 x 28 cm 1" to 1 nautical mile
Also shows settlements, bldgs, line of treed areas; 'Price 2s.'
GBTAUh

Later editions and states

(2) *[184?]*
A Survey / of the / RIVER DETROIT. / FROM LAKE ERIE TO LAKE ST CLAIR / BY ... in 1815 ... // ...
Chart no '331' added below imprint; 'Continued ... Bayfield in 1817' deleted from title and 'A' and 'B' deleted from chart; also a copy at GBTAUh (L5725 Aa3) with ms adds dated 20 April 1846 showing an American naval depot.
GBTAUh (L5725 Aa3) OOAMA

(3) *1863*
[Added to imprint]: 61. Corrections June 1863. / Sold by J.D. Potter, Agent for the Admiralty Charts 31 Poultry & 11 King Street Tower Hill
Land stipple added; some soundings added from 'U.S. chart 1853.'
GBTAUh

No 332

C114 *1828*
A Survey of / LAKE ERIE; / in the Years 1817 & 1818, / By / LIEUT HENRY W. BAYFIELD, R.N. // London Published according to Act of Parliament at the Hydrographical Office of the Admiralty 19th May 1828. // J. & C. Walker Sculpt.
Print (engrav) 60 x 91 cm 10" to 1° latitude
Includes insets on the American side: 'Put IN BAY,' 'MIAMIS BAY,' 'CAYANOGA RIVER Mouth,' 'Mouth of River Segnan,' 'Presqu'Isle Harbour' and 'Grand River'; printed stamp of Hydrographical Office and 'Price 5s.'
GBTAUh

Later editions and states

(2) *[ca 1846]*
[Added after imprint]: Sold by R.B. Bate Agent for the Admiralty Charts 21 Poultry.
Chart no '332' added below imprint; LC copy has a watermark: '... WHATMAN ... 1851,' which suggests a later printing without further changes; GBTAUh has a state without Bate imprint but with 'Price 3s.' and also a copy with ms corrections by Lt Tyssen dated 15 May 1846 (GBTAUh (L5126 Aa3)).
USDLC GBTAUh (L5126 Aa3) OOAMA

(3) *1861*
[Bate statement removed from imprint and the following added]: ... 19th May 1828. Corrections 1861. / Sold by J.D. Potter Agent for the Admiralty Charts 31 Poultry & 11 King St Tower Hill
'Price 3 shillings'; land stipple added.
OOAMA GBTAUh

(4) *1863*
[Date added to imprint]: ... 1861. 63
GBTAUh

(5) *(1864)*
NORTH AMERICA / LAKE ERIE / COMPILED FROM THE SURVEYS OF LIEUT. HENRY W. BAYFIELD R.N. 1817, 1818 AND FROM THE UNITED STATES SURVEYS – 1849. // London Published at the Admiralty 8th July 1864 by Capt. G.H. Richards Hydrographer, / Sold by J.D. Potter Agent for the Admiralty Charts 31 Poultry and 11 King Street Tower Hill // Engraved [by J. & C. Walker] // 332
Print (engrav) 65 x 97 cm 10.75" to 1° latitude
Inset: 'ENTRANCE TO RONDEAU HARBOUR / By Mr A. Wise 1861' 1" to 400 ft; the sheet has been redrawn to incorporate the results of the U.S. survey and to remove the insets of U.S. bays and

add some for Canada; railways are shown and a stipple is used for the land; lower right corner missing in OOAMA copy; partly derived from **C131**; (Holmden 1886; Karpinski 871).
OOAMA

No 333

C115 *1828*
Survey of MOHAWK BAY / Lake Erie / BY LIEUT H.W. BAYFIELD R.N. // London, Published according to Act of Parliament at the Hydrographical Office of the Admiralty 29th March 1828. // J. & C. Walker Sculpt.
Print (engrav) 23 x 26 cm 1" to approx 670 yds or 7" to 1 nautical mile
From Pt Selkirk to Barbed Pt; printed stamp of Hydrographical Office; 'Price 6d.'
GBTAUh

Later editions and states

(2) *[184?]*
Chart no '333' added in the bottom margin.
OTAR OOAMA GBTAUh

(3) *1863*
[Added to imprint]: ... 29th March 1828. Corrections 1861. 63 / Sold by J.D. Potter Agent for the Admiralty Charts 31 Poultry & 11 King St Tower Hill
The compass diagram has been redrawn, more detail is given for lighthouse on island, and the magnetic variation statement is dated '1861'; 'Price Sixpence.'
OOAMA GBTAUh

No 334

C116 *1828*
LAKE ERIE / INNER AND OUTER BAYS / of LONG POINT. / BY / Lieut Henry W. Bayfield, R.N. / in 1818. // London Published according to Act of Parliament at the Hydrographical Office of the Admiralty 8th March 1828. // J. & C. Walker Sculpt.
Print (engrav) 90 x 43 cm 7" to 1 nautical mile
Printed Hydrographical Office stamp and 'Price 1s.'
USDLC GBTAUh

No 336

C117 *1828*
Survey / of the RIVER NIAGARA. / Made under the direction of / CAPTN WM FITZ WM OWEN, in the Year 1817. // London Published according to Act of Parliament at the Hydrographical Office of the Admiralty 7th May 1828. // J. & C. Walker Sculpt.
Print (engrav) 62 x 42 cm 1" to 1.1 nautical miles
Inset: 'Survey / of the Entrance of the / RIVER NIAGARA / from / Lake Erie. / by Lieut H.W. Bayfield R.N.' approx 1" to 950 yds; printed stamp of Hydrographical Office; 'Price 3s'; also shows roads with some names of settlers at various points; town of 'Newark.'
GBTAUh

Later editions and states

(2) *[184?]*
Chart no '336' added; one state in OOAMA has the watermark 'J WHATMAN 1828' and statement of variation of the compass at Ft Niagara; the other state lacks this information but has a more detailed engraving for the compass rose.
GBTAUh OOAMA

(3) *1863*
[Revisions to imprint statement]: ... 7th May 1828. 61. Corrections 1863 / Sold by J.D. Potter Agent for the Admiralty Charts 31 Poultry & 11 King St Tower Hill.
Inset added: 'BUFFALO HARBOUR / ENLARGED' 1" to 40 cables; a note indicates that inset and some soundings 'from the United States Survey corrected to 1856'; railways have been added; the compass rose has been moved; more places and rivers shown; Niagara enlarged.
OOAMA

No 337

C118 *1828*
Plan / OF / YORK HARBOUR / Lake Ontario. / Surveyed under the Direction of / CAPTN. W.F.W. OWEN, R.N. / BY Lieut, (now Commander) H.W. Bayfield, R.N. / Drawn by Geo. D. Cranfield. Lieut. 90th. Lt. Infy. // London Published according to Act of Parliament at the Hydrographical Office of the Admiralty 28th April 1828. J. & C. Walker Sculpt.
Print (engrav) 25 x 28 cm 1" to 1800 ft Watermark: 'J WHATMAN TURKEY MILL 1827'
Printed stamp of the Hydrographical Office and 'Price 6d'; note indicates 'the Town is copied from a Plan in the Surveyor Generals Office'; the plan is based on the ms plan of 1817 (**C67**) but has been oriented to the north and the town is shown in more finished form; 'Town of York' named on map.
GBTAUh

Later editions and states

(2) *[184?]*
Plan / of / TORONTO HARBOUR, / Lake Ontario. / Surveyed under the Direction of / CAPTN W.F.W. OWEN, R.N. / By Lieutt now Commander H.W. Bayfield R.N. / Drawn by Geo. D. Cranfield, Lieut 90th Lt Infy. // London, Published according to Act of Parliament at the Hydrographical Office of the Admiralty 28th April 1828. // J. & C. Walker, Sculpt // 337
Print (engrav) 25 x 28 cm 1" to 1800 ft

Printed stamp of the Hydrographical Office and 'Price 6d.'; town is named 'Town of Toronto'; revision to title and addition of printed chart no '337.'
OOAMA GBTAUh

Related maps

(3) *1848*
[Additions to imprint]: ... 28th April 1828. Additions to 1848. / Sold by R.B. Bate Agent for the Admiralty Charts 21 Poultry.
Shows area reclaimed for wharves, depths; 'Queens Wharf light H.'
OOAMA

(4) *1861*
[Changes to imprint]: ... 1848. Corrections to 1861. / Sold by J.D. Potter Agent for the Admiralty Charts 31 Poultry & 11 King Street Tower Hill
Ms notes indicate corrected to 1861 by Capt J. Blythsea; shows the breakthrough of the eastern channel with soundings; the longitude/latitude of Queens Wharf is given by 'Lieut Ashe's Electric connection with Quebec 1859.'
GBTAUh (D6178 f 21)

(5) *1863*
[Revisions to imprint]: ... Additions to 1848. Corrections to 1861. Decr 1863.
Compass rose redrawn with circle and 'City of Toronto'; railways, wharves added; more bldgs shown; the magnetic variation is noted in 1861; new soundings shown around Gibraltar Point.
OOAMA

No 338

C119 *1828*
A Survey / of the / RIVER ST. LAWRENCE, / FROM / Lake Ontario to the Galop Rapids, / BY / CAPN W.F.W. OWEN, R.N. / 1826 / SHEET 1. // London Published according to Act of Parliament at the Hydrographical Office of the Admiralty 16th July 1828. // J. & C. Walker Sculpt.
Print (engrav) 63 x 46 cm 11/2" to 1 nautical mile
Printed stamp of the Hydrographical Office and 'Price 3s.'
GBTAUh

Later editions and states

(2) *[184?]*
A Survey / of the / RIVER ST LAWRENCE, / FROM / Lake Ontario to the Galop Rapids, / IN FIVE SHEETS / BY / CAPTN W.F.W. OWEN, R.N. / 1818 / SHEET I. // London Published ... 16th July 1828. // J. & C. Walker Sculpt. // 338
The title has been changed and chart no has been added; 'Price 3s.'; shows the Kingston area to part of Wolfe Is and Grenadier Is.
GBTAUh

(3) *[ca 1846]*
Additions as follows: Price changed to 2s.
OOAMA USDLC

(4) *1863*
[Revisions to imprint]: ... 16th July 1828. Corrections 1861. May 63. / Sold by J.D. Potter, Agent for the Admiralty Charts, 31 Poultry & 11 King Street Tower Hill ...
Price 'Eighteenpence'; land stipple added; magnetic variation statement dated '1861.'
GBTAUh

(5) *1863*
[Revisions to imprint]: ... 16th July 1828. Corrections 1861. Dec 63. / Sold by J.D. Potter, ... 338a
The latitude/longitude for Kingston is given 'by Electric Telegraph from Cambridge Obsy. U.S.'; compass rose moved and redrawn; railways added; lighthouse on Snake Is added.
OOAMA

Sheet II

C120 *1828*
RIVER ST LAWRENCE. / SHEET II. // London Published according to Act of Parliament at the Hydrographical Office of the Admiralty 12th Augt 1828. // J. & C. Walker Sculpt //
Print (engrav) 61 x 46 cm 11/2" to 1 nautical mile
Watermark: '... WHATMAN 1828'
Printed stamp of the Hydrographical Office and 'Price 3s.'; Oak Pt, Wolfe Is, to Grindstone Is.
GBTAUh

Later editions and states

(2) *[ca 1846]*
Watermark: '... 1845'
Chart no '338' added; 'Price 2s.'
GBTAUh USDLC OOAMA

(3) *1863*
[Revisions to imprint]: ... 12th Aug 1828. -61. Corrections Dec. 63. / Sold by J.D. Potter, Agent for the Admiralty Charts 31 Poultry & 11 King Street Tower Hill. // J. & C. Walker Sculpt // 338b
Railways, Rock Is light, and land stipple added; price 'Eighteenpence.'
OOAMA GBTAUh

Sheet III

C121 *1828*
RIVER ST LAWRENCE. / SHEET III. // London Published according to Act of Parliament at the Hydrographical Office of the Admiralty 22d Augt 1828. // J. & C. Walker Sculpt
Print (engrav) 61 x 46 cm 11/2" to 1 nautical mile
Watermark: '...WHATMAN ... 1828'
Printed stamp Hydrographical Office and 'Price 3s.'; from Navy Is to Broughton Is near Mallorytown.
GBTAUh

Later editions and states

(2) *[ca 1846]*
Chart no '338' added; 'Price 2s.'
GBTAUh OOAMA USDLC

(3) *1863*
[Revisions to imprint]: ... 22d Augt 1818. Corrections to 1861. Decr 63. / Sold by J.D. Potter, Agent for the Admiralty Charts, 31 Poultry, & 11 King Street Tower Hill. ... // 338c
Railways added; compass rose moved and re-drawn; Sunken Rock light and land stipple added; price 'Eighteenpence.'
OOAMA GBTAUh

Sheet IV

C122 *1828*
RIVER ST LAWRENCE. / SHEET IV. // London Published according to Act of Parliament at the Hydrographical Office of the Admiralty 9th Augt 1828. // J. & C. Walker Sculpt
Print (engrav) 62 x 44 cm 1 1/2" to 1 nautical mile
Watermark: '... WHATMAN ... 1828'
Printed stamp of the Hydrographical Office and 'Price 3s.'; 'Tonnewanta' or Jones Creek to Maitland.
GBTAUh

Later editions and states

(2) *[ca 1846]*
Chart no '338' added; watermark: 'RUSE & TURNERS 1845'
GBTAUh OOAMA USDLC

(3) *1863*
[Revisions to imprint]: ... 9th Augt 1818. Corrections to 1861. Decr 63. / Sold by J.D. Potter Agent for the Admiralty Charts 31 Poultry & 11 King Street Tower Hill. // J. & C. Walker Sculpt. // 338d
Railways and land stipple added; a light added on one of the islands; Price 'Eighteenpence.'
GBTAUh OOAMA

Sheet V

C123 *1828*
RIVER ST LAWRENCE. / SHEET V. // London Published according to Act of Parliament at the Hydrographical Office of the Admiralty 5th Augt 1828. // J. & C. Walker Sculpt
Print (engrav) 43 x 39 cm 1 1/2" to 1 nautical mile
Watermark: '... WHATMAN 1828'
Printed stamp of the Hydrographical Office and 'Price 3s.'; Maitland to Galop Rapids.
GBTAUh

Later editions and states

(2) *[ca 1846]*
Chart no '338' added; 'Price 2s.'
GBTAUh OOAMA USDLC

(3) *1863*
[Revisions to imprint]: ... 5th Augt 1828. 61. Dec 63. / Sold by J.D. Potter Agent for the Admiralty Charts 31 Poultry and 11 King Street Tower Hill // J. & C. Walker Sculpt // 338e
Railways and land stipple added; light added at Ogdensburg; price 'Eighteenpence.'
GBTAUh OOAMA

No 259a

C124 *1866*
NORTH AMERICA / RIVER ST LAWRENCE / MONTREAL TO FARRENS PT / From a Plan in the Office of Public Works / TORONTO / 1856 / Montreal to Lachine Rapids From the Survey of Captn H.W. Bayfield 1858. // London, Published at the Admiralty Sept 29th 1866 under the superintendance of Captain G.H. Richards, R.N.: F.R.S. Hydrographer. / Sold by J.D. Potter, Agent for the Admiralty Charts, 31 Poultry & 11 King Street, Tower Hill. // Engraved by Davies & Bryer // 259a
Print (engrav) 65 x 98 cm Approx 1" to 1 nautical mile
Printed stamp: 'Hydrographic Office G.H.R.'; 'Price Two Shillings'; based on **547** and **550**.
GBTAUh OOAMA

Related maps

(2) No 259b
NORTH AMERICA / RIVER ST LAWRENCE / FARRENS PT TO KINGSTON / From a Plan in the Office of Public Works / TORONTO / 1856 / Gallops Rapid to Kingston from the Survey of Captain Owen, R.N. 1818. // London – Published at the Admiralty, Sep 28th 1866; under the Superintendance of Captain G.H. Richards; R.N.: F.R.S. Hydrographer. / Sold by J.D. Potter, Agent for the Admiralty Charts, 31 Poultry & 11 King Street Tower Hill. // Engraved by Davies & Bryer // 259b
Print (engrav) 74 x 97 cm Approx 1/2" to 1 nautical mile
Printed stamp 'Hydrographic Office G.H.R.'; price 'Two Shillings'; based on **547** and **550**.
GBTAUh OOAMA

No 407

C125 *1863*
UPPER CANADA – PLAN OF PORTS IN LAKE HURON // London – Published at the Admiralty 7th Octr 1863 / Sold by J.D. Potter, Agent for the Admiralty Charts 31 Poultry & 11 King Street Tower Hill // Engraved under the direction of Capt. G.A. Bedford R.N. // Engraved by J. & C. Walker // 407
Print (engrav) 3 maps on 1 sheet 65 x 48 cm
The plans are as follows: 'GEORGIAN BAY / PENETANGUISHENE / HARBOUR / SURVEYED BY LIEUTT HENRY W. BAYFIELD, R.N. / 1822.' 3" to 1/2 sea mile; 'GEORGIAN BAY / COLLINGWOOD HARBOUR / SURVEYED BY MR Wm GIBBARD, C.E. / April 1858' 4.5" to 5 cables; 'GODERICH HARBOUR / SURVEYED BY MR F.A. WISE / July 1861' 1.5" to 1 cable.
OOAMA

Later editions and states

(2) *1865*
[Revisions to imprint]: ... 7th Octr 1863. Corrections Feb 1865. / Sold by J.D. Potter ...
OOAMA

No 490

C126 *1864*
NORTH AMERICA / LAKE ERIE / WEST END / FROM THE UNITED STATES COAST SURVEY / 1849 // London Published at the Admiralty 15th Sept 1864, under the Superintendence of Captn G.H. Richards R.N., Hydrographer. / Sold by J.D. Potter, Agent for the Admiralty Charts 31 Poultry, & 11 King Street Tower Hill. / Engraved by J. & C. Walker
Print (engrav) 68 x 83 cm .6" to 1 nautical mile
Inset: 'Continuation of Detroit River upon the same scale'; printed stamp: 'Hydrographic Office G.H.R.'; from the Detroit R to Point Pelee on the north shore, and south shore to Sandusky; lights and buoys are shown; chart no possibly trimmed off; derived from **C130**.
OOAMA

No 519

C127 *1865*
NORTH AMERICA / LAKE HURON / FROM THE UNITED STATES COAST SURVEY, 1856–60 / The Canadian Coast From Captn H.W. Bayfields Survey, 1822. // London [Published] at the Admiralty 14th Feby 1865, under the Superintendence of Captn [G.H.] Richards, R.N. Hydrographer. / Sold by J.D. Potter, Agent for the Admiralty Charts, 31 Poultry & 11 King St [Tower Hill] // Engraved by J. & C. Walker
Print (engrav) 99 x 67 cm 10.75" to 1° latitude
OOAMA copy has small parts missing; cross sections; similar to other U.S. charts and partly derived from **C135–6**; (Karpinski 877).
OOAMA

No 1152

C128 *1838*
LAKE ONTARIO / AND THE / BACK COMMUNICATION WITH LAKE HURON / Surveyed by / CAPTN W.F.W. OWEN R.N. 1817. // 1152 // Published according to Act of Parliament at the Hydrographic Office of the Admiralty April 12th 1838: / Sold by R.B. Bate Agent for the Admiralty Charts 21 Poultry // J. & C. Walker Sculpt
Print (engrav) hand col 63 x 92 cm Scale not given [.2" to 1 nautical mile]
Printed stamp 'Hydrographic Office F.B.' and in ms: 'Price 5s'; based on **C71**; shows Toronto incorrectly oriented, Belleville and Windsor [Whitby]; major roads and places; Niagara R extends beyond outer border.
GBTAUh

Later editions and states

(2) *[1846?]*
Change: 'Price Three Shils'; also a copy with ms corrections by Cdr Powell 20 Apr 1845 (GBTAUh (L5128 Aa3)).
GBTAUh GBTAUh (L5128 Aa3)

(3) *1851*
[Revisions to imprint]: ... April 12th 1838: / Sold by J.D. Potter Agent for the Admiralty Charts 31 Poultry. / Corrected to 1851. ... 1152
Rochester R drawn beyond inner margin; chart no '1152' added.
OOAMA OTAR USDLC

(4) *1861*
[Revisions to imprint]: '1861' replaces '1851'
The title has been moved to the upper centre of sheet; compass roses redrawn; 'By Lieut. Ashe's Telegraphic Communication with Cambridge Observatory U.S. in 1859, the Longitude of this Chart is about 5' too westerly.'
OOAMA

No 1235

C129 *1839*
NORTH AMERICA / LAKE ERIE / LONG POINT BAY / Shewing the New Channel recently broken through the Isthmus / BY MR JOHN HARRIS R.N. / 1839. // 1235 // Published according to Act of Parliament at the Hydrographic Office of the Admiralty August 17th 1839 / Sold by R.B. Bate Agent for the Admiralty Charts 21 Poultry. // J. & C. Walker Sculpt.
Print (engrav) 29 x 35 cm Approx 1" to 2 sea miles
Watermark: '1837'
Printed stamp: 'Hydrographic Office F.B. Price 9d.'; a copy of the plan was also enclosed in a letter from Capt Wm Sanderson R.N. to A.M. O'Ferrall Admiralty of 7 Nov 1839 complaining of a hazard in the area (GBLpro CO 42/465 p 59).
GBTAUh GBLpro (CO 42/465 p 59)

Later editions and states

(2) *[ca 1841]*
'Price 1s'; also a copy with ms adds about new channel dated 20 Apr 1846 (GBTAUh (L5124 Aa3)).
GBTAUh GBTAUh (L5124 Aa3) OOAMA USDLC

(3) *1863*
[Revisions to imprint]: ... August 17th 1839. Corrections to 1861. June 63 / Sold by J.D. Potter Agent for the Admiralty Charts 31 Poultry 11 King St Tower Hill.
The Dover lighthouse and a light at North Foreland have been added; magnetic variation statement dated '1861'; land stipple added; 'Price Sixpence.'
GBTAUh OOAMA

1852–67 U.S. Survey of the Northern and Northwestern Lakes

Printed charts from the U.S. survey of the northern and northwestern lakes were published from surveys of American waters made by the U.S. Corps of Topographical Engineers. Surveys of U.S. harbours were made from the 1820s to 1840s; however, the surveys of the northern and northwestern lakes did not begin until 1841 and the first published chart was in 1852; only charts that show substantial parts of Canada West are included here; the charts are arranged by date of publication since chart numbers are not printed on the charts and do not seem to have been assigned until later (the chart numbers were assigned in date order and charts 1–30 were first published before 1867) (Wolter, ongoing research). In addition, some maps related to the U.S. survey of the lakes and covering Canadian waters were produced to accompany U.S. Congress Senate documents from 1842–3 to 1867 (see Karpinski 727–9, 731, 799, 832, 834–8, 852–4, 862, 886–7).

C130 *1852*
WEST END OF LAKE ERIE / AND DETROIT RIVER / From Surveys under the direction of the / TOPOGRAPHICAL BUREAU OF THE WAR DEPARTMENT / in obedience to Acts of Congress requiring the / SURVEY OF THE NORTHERN AND NORTH WESTERN LAKES / Triangulation by Lieut. J.N. MACOMB, L.C. WOODRUFF, J.W. GUNNISON & E.P. SCAMMON Corps Topl Engrs / and Messrs R.W. BURGESS, J.F. PETERS & J.H. FORSTER Assistants / under the orders of / LIEUT. COL. JAMES KEARNEY / Corps Topl Engrs 1849 // Reduction for Engraving by John Lambert Draughtsman and Engraved by W. Smith / under the direction of Capt T.J. Lee Corps Topl Engrs Washington May 1852.
Print (engrav) 92 x 72 cm 1:120,000
Printed stamp: 'Survey of the Lakes 1852'; includes Point Pelee to Detroit R and to L St Clair; 'Detroit River from Surveys by Lieuts J.N. Macomb & W.H. Warner Corps Topl Engrs in 1840' '41 & 42'; soundings; table of water levels; sailing directions and sailing lines; notes on shoreline; [chart no 2]; (Karpinski 790).
OTAR USDLC

C131 *1853*
LAKE ERIE / Compiled from Surveys made under the direction of the / BUREAU OF TOPOGRAPHICAL ENGINEERS, WAR DEPARTMENT. / in obedience to Acts of Congress requiring the / SURVEY OF THE NORTHERN AND NORTH WESTERN LAKES, / and from reliable information. / 1849. / Reduction for Engraving by John Lambert Draughtsman / under the Direction of Capt. T.J. Lee, Corps Topl. Engrs. / Washington 1853.
Print (engrav) 60 x 98 cm 1:400,000
Printed stamp: 'Survey of the Lakes T.E. 1852'; soundings; nature of shoreline; sailing directions; OTAR copy (SR 7170) has ms notes on longitude/latitude; [chart no 1 dated 1852 in Cat]; (Karpinski 792).
OTAR (SR 7170) USDLC OSINH

C132 *1854*
SKETCH / of the Navigation through / EAST NEEBISH RAPIDS / RIVER ST MARY / From Surveys by Capt E.P. Scammon Corps Topl Engrs / W.H. HEARDING and C.S. COLE Assistants / under the direction of Capt J.N. MACOMB Corps Topl Engrs / 1853. Reduced for engraving by F. Herbst Draughtsman / Engraved by W.H. Dougal / under the direction Capt T.J. Lee Corps Topl Engrs / Washington February / 1854
Print (engrav) 48 x 36 cm 1:15,000
Soundings; nature of shoreline; sailing directions; [chart no 5]; (Karpinski 796).
OTAR OTUTF USDLC

C133 *1857*
CHART No 1 OF / RIVER Ste MARIE / From / POINT IROQUOIS TO EAST NEEBISH / Surveyed under the direction of / Captain J.N. MACOMB Topl Engrs / in 1853, 1854, 1855. / with additions to date under the orders of / Captain G.G. MEADE Topl Engrs / 1857 // SURVEY OF THE NORTHERN AND NORTH WESTERN LAKES / made in obedience to Acts of Congress and under the direction of / THE BUREAU OF TOPOGRAPHICAL ENGINEERS OF THE WAR DEPARTMENT // Reduced for Engraving by J.U. Mueller Assistant Engraved by W.H. Dougal
Print (engrav) 62 x 89 cm 1:40,000
Printed stamp: 'Survey of the Lakes T E 1853'; soundings; sailing directions and sailing lines; lighthouses; nature of the shoreline; magnetic declination; [chart no 13 dated as 1858 in Cat]; (Karpinski 821).
OTAR USDLC

C134 *1858*
CHART No 2 OF / RIVER STE MARIE / including the part / FROM THE ENTRANCE OF MUD LAKE TO THE EAST NEEBISH / Surveyed under the direction of / Captain J.N. MACOMB Topl Engrs / in 1853 and 1854. / Reduction for engraving under the direction of / Captain G.G. MEADE Topl Engrs / in 1858 // SURVEY OF THE NORTHERN AND NORTH WESTERN LAKES / made in obedience to Acts of Congress and under the direction of / THE BUREAU OF TOPOGRAPHICAL ENGINEERS OF THE WAR DEPARTMENT ... Reduced drawing by J.U. Müller U.S.L.S. Engraved by W.H. Dougal
Print (engrav) 62 x 62 cm 1:40,000
Printed stamp: 'Survey of the Lakes T.E. 1858'; soundings; sailing lines; sailing directions; shoreline detail; table of magnetic declinations; notes; [chart no 14]; (Karpinski 827).
OTAR USDLC

C135 *1860*
GENERAL CHART OF / LAKE HURON / Projected from trigonometrical Surveys under the orders of / Captain G.G. MEADE Topl Engrs / and from other reliable information / 1860 // SURVEY OF THE NORTHERN AND NORTH WESTERN LAKES / made in obedience to Acts of Congress and under the direction of / THE BUREAU OF TOPOGRAPHICAL ENGINEERS OF THE WAR DEPARTMENT // Reduction for Engraving by J.U. Mueller Assistant U.S.L.S. Electrotype No 1 Engraved by W.H. Dougal
Print (electrotype) 89 x 66 cm 1:400,000
Note about authorities; harbours of refuge; dangers; water table; list of lighthouses; profiles of coastlines; extensive notes; [chart no 22].
OTAR USDLC

C136 *1861*
SOUTHEND OF LAKE HURON / AND / HEAD OF THE ST. CLAIR RIVER / Projected from a trigonometrical Survey executed under the orders of / CAPT. GEO. G. MEADE TOP. ENGRS. / in 1859. // SURVEY OF THE NORTHERN AND NORTH WESTERN LAKES / Made in obedience to acts of Congress and under the direction of / THE BUREAU OF TOPOGRAPHICAL ENGINEERS OF THE WAR DEPARTMENT // Reduction for engraving by Asst. Joshua Barney, Engraved by William H. Dougal.
Print (engrav) 70 x 66 cm 1:120,000
Printed stamp: 'SURVEY OF THE LAKES T.E. 1861'; inset: 'HEAD OF ST. CLAIR RIVER / SHOWING THE ANCHORAGE GROUND' 1:16,000; notes on sources; water table; harbours; anchorages; dangers; [chart no 23]; (Karpinski 855).
OTUTF USDLC

Appendix D

International Boundary Surveys

Preliminary Boundary Surveys – South

D1 *[1817–18]*
[Chart of the River Cataraqui from St Regis to Pointe au Pins] Map 1
Col ms in 6 sheets Ea 58 x 72 cm or smaller 1" to 400 yds
One of four map sets made from surveys by David Adams and David Thompson, American and British astronomical surveyors, under the Treaty of Ghent, Articles 6 and 7, originally enclosed in Commissioner Ogilvy's report to Castlereagh 15 Jan 1819 (GBLpro CO 6/5); the accompanying letter indicates that map 1 is from 1817 and maps 2–4 below are from 1818; the maps are attractive surveys of the St Lawrence with towns, villages, and twps shown on both sides of the river; a legend keys the routes used by British and American craft; some survey baselines are marked and some triangulation lines with points numbered; map 1 shows different lines for 45° N latitude by Ellicot and Thompson and shows 'Chryslers Farm and Mill'; many place-names are in French; the shapes of many islands are poor and clearly predate the full survey; maps 2 and 3 are in the same hand; a complete set of transcripts of maps in GBLpro CO 6/5 is found in OOAMA (MG11 CO 6/5); (*PRO Cat* 1570).
GBLpro (CO 700 Canada 77A/1)

The other maps are as follows

(2) *[1818]*
Chart of the River Cataraqui From Point-au-Pin to the Lower End of Wells's Island Map 2
Col ms in 10 sheets Ea 72 x 66 cm or smaller 1" to 400 yds
Shows area from Matilda Twp to Grenadier Is and Brockville; Fort Wellington and Johnstown are shown with bldgs; photoreproduction in OOAMA (NMC 4811); (*OHIM* 6.21).
GBLpro (CO 700 Canada 77A/2)

(3) *[1818]*
Chart of the River Cataraque from the Lower end of Wells's Island to the Lower ends of Grand Isle and Howe Island Map 3
Col ms 108 x 182 cm 1" to 400 yds
Shows the area from Yonge to Leeds twps and includes Grindstone Is.
GBLpro (CO 700 Canada A/3)

(4) *[1818]*
Chart of the River Cataraqui from the Lower End of Grand Isle and Howe Island to the Head of Grand Isle and Lower End of Isle Tonty Map 4
Col ms in 6 sheets Ea approx 163 x 54 cm or smaller 1" to 400 yds
Shows the area from Pittsburg to Kingston twps and the islands at the entrance to L Ontario; shows Kingston in detail with bldgs and fortifications at Point Frederick and Point Henry; photoreproduction in OOAMA (NMC 51862).
GBLpro (CO 700 Canada 77A/4)

D2 *[1819]*
[The northeast end of Lake Ontario] Map 5
Col ms in 3 sheets 292 x 257 cm 1" to 400 yds
One of the four maps from surveys by David Thompson and William Bird; originally enclosed in Acting Commissioner Hale's report to Joseph Planta of 20 Jan 1820 in which he was transmitting surveys made during the previous summer under the Treaty of Ghent, Article 6 (GBLpro CO 6/5 maps 5–8); the maps show triangulation lines and numbered points; relief along shorelines; (*PRO Cat* 1527).
GBLpro (MR 851)

The other maps are as follows

(2) *[1819]*
[From the Mouth of the Niagara River to the Grand Island and from Strawberry Island to Lake Erie]
Map 6 ... 7 ... 8
3 col mss Sizes vary 1" to 400 yds
(*PRO Cat* 1510, 1511).
GBLpro (MPG 126; 127)

D3 *[1820]*
[The Detroit River Map no 9]
Col ms 68 x 158 cm Scale not given
This and the maps in (2) below were originally enclosed in Anthony Barclay's report to Lord Londonderry of 27 June 1821 transmitting maps of the previous season's work under Article 6 (GBLpro CO 6/5 maps 9–12); shows triangulation lines and numbered points; relief along shore; Sandwich, Detroit, and Amherstburg shown in detail; (*PRO Cat* 2539).
GBLpro (MPG 128)

Related maps

(2) *[1820]*
[Map of the north channel L Huron from Cockburn Island to St Joseph and Drummond islands]
Col ms in 3 sheets Size varies Scale not given
Inset (on east sheet): 'A sketch of the channel between Manitoulin & Cockburn Island'; Barclay describes the three sketches as 'Incoherent sections of Lake Huron not capable of affording much information'; (*PRO Cat* 1471, 1472).
GBLpro (MR 864–5)

D4 *[1821]*
No I [Map of the St Lawrence River from Upper Long Sault to Barnhart's Island] [Sgd] David Thompson Astr Surveyor to the Board under the 6th and 7th Articles of the Treaty of Ghent
Col ms Size not known 1" to 400 yds
Originally enclosed in Barclay to Londonderry 18 Jan 1822 to illustrate the principle used in locating the boundary around islands in the St Lawrence (GBLpro FO 5/170 f 177); shows the boundary decided under Article 6 which ceded Barnhart's Is to the U.S.

Other maps from the same source show contentious parts of other sections of the boundary.
GBLpro (FO 5/170 f 177)

Related maps

(2) *[1821]*
No II [Map of the Detroit River] [Sgd] David Thompson ...
Col ms Size not known 1" to 400 yds
The map shows the disagreement over the possession of three islands in Detroit R.
GBLpro (FO 5/170 f 175)

(3) *[1821]*
No III [Map of the islands in the entrance to the St Clair River] [Sgd] David Thompson ...
Col ms Size not known 1" to 400 yds
The map was used to illustrate the principle used to decide the main channel in the St Clair R and the relationship to the Detroit R dispute.
GBLpro (FO 5/170 f 179)

(4) *[1822]*
[Plan of the Detroit River]
Col ms Size not known 1" to 400 yds
Enclosed in Barclay's letter to Londonderry 9 Feb 1822 to show areas where the commissioners could not agree on the boundary around various islands as keyed in ff 184–6 of Barclay's letter (GBLpro FO 5/170 f 227); the letter also included a copy of the map of L Huron showing the boundary, which is similar to the official maps (see **D5(15)**).
GBLpro (FO 5/170 f 225)

Official Boundary Maps – South

D5 *[1817–22, 1822]* British
[Surveys made under Article 6 of the Treaty of Ghent showing the boundary between Upper Canada and the United States from Cornwall to St Mary's River]
50 col mss bound in atlas Sizes vary Most at 1" to 400 yds unless otherwise noted
The atlas was probably the one used for the zincographed ed of 1871 because of note: 'Returned by Ordnance Survey Office Southampton February 18 1871'; originally accompanied (GBLpro FO 925/1916); all sheets are sgd as on the first sheet unless otherwise indicated; a note by John Bigsby indicates that A, 5.2, and 7.3 were added later; each sheet shows the boundary, triangulation lines, and sometimes relief; (*PRO Cat* 167).

The sheets are as follows

(1)
[Printed title]: Declaration and Decision of the Commissioners of Great Britain and the United States under the VIth Article of the Treaty of Ghent of 1814, respecting Boundaries. Signed at Utica, 18th June 1822. with note from 'State Papers vol IX p 791'

(2)
Contents of the Portfolio

(3)
[Index to sheets added later on the following map]: 'A Map of the Located Districts in the Province of Upper Canada ... London ... James Wyld ... 1838' [see **43(6)**]

1.1 The First Section No I Iroquois or St Lawrence 1817 [Sgd] Anthony Barclay, Peter B. Porter Commissioners; David Thompson, William A. Bird, Surveyors under the 6 & 7 Articles of the Treaty of Ghent. Drawn from the composed models of D.P. Adams Esqr Surveyor by C. Schwarz. [Endorsed on back]: 'Filed 4th of June 1819 by order of the Board ... under the 6th & 7th Articles Treaty of Ghent ...' [Bug Is to Sheek Is]

1.2 ... No II Iroquois or St Lawrence ... [Long Sault to Chrysler Is]

1.3 ... No III Iroquois or St Lawrence ... [Goose-Neck Is to 'Pointe aux Pins']

2.1 The Second Section No I Iroquois or St Lawrence 1818 ... ['Point au Iroquois' to Chimney Point]

3.1 The Third Section No I Iroquois or St Lawrence 1818 ... [Johnstown to Point au Tremble]

3.2 ... No II Iroquois or St Lawrence ... [Boundary between Elizabethtown/Augusta twps to Hammond/Hague twps]

4.1 The Fourth Section No I Iroquois or St Lawrence ... [Gull Is to Grenadier Is]

5.1 The Fifth Section No I Iroquois or St Lawrence ... [Rowe's Is to Kingston]

5.2 ... No II Iroquois or St Lawrence ... [Grindstone Is to pt Howe Is] [Sketch]: 'Les 1000 Iles' C.A. LeSueur delineavit

6.1 The Sixth Section No I Iroquois or St Lawrence Grande Isle 1818 ... [Howe Is to Grand Is]

6.2 ... No II ...

7.1 The Seventh Section No I Northeast end of Lake Ontario 1819

7.2 The Fifth [*sic*] Section No II Northeast end of Lake Ontario 1819 ...

7.3 ... No III ...
A Ontario 1819 ... [Northeast corner of L Ontario]
B Copy of a Chart of Lake Ontario the Head of the River St Lawrence etc Surveyed by the Hydrographic Department under the direction of Capt W.F.W. Owen R.N. in the Years 1815, 1816 & 1817. Copied D.Q.M. Generals Office Quebec 9th May 1822 (Sign'd) Wm R Dickson D A Q M G (Sign'd) R C M Cockburn Lieut. Col & D.Q.M.G. [Sgd] E.W. Bridges. Scale not given

8.1 The Eighth Section No I Niagara 1819. ... [L Ontario to Queenston]

8.2 ... No II Niagara ... [To Chippewa and Fort Schlosser]

9.1 The Ninth Section No I Niagara 1819. ... [Grand Is]

9.2 ... No II Niagara ... [Grand Is to L Erie]

10.1 The Tenth Section No I South West End of Lake Erie 1821 ...
1" to 1.12 miles

10.2 Part of the Third or Lake Erie Section of the Survey of 1819

11.1 The Eleventh Section No I Detroit 1820 ... [L Erie to Fighting Is]

11.2 ... No II Detroit ... [Fighting Is to R Rouge]

11.3 ... No III Detroit ... [Sandwich to L St Clair]

12.1 The Twelfth Section No I Lake St Clair 1821 ...
A Lake St Clair
B Channels of Lake St Clair ...
C North Shore of St Clair from Point Huron in the Lake to the Head of Chenaille Ecarte in the River
D Channels of Lake St Clair ...

13.1 The Thirteenth Section No I River St Clair 1821 ...

14.1 [Northwest part of Lake Huron] ...

15.1 The Fifteenth Section No 1 Lake Huron 1820 & 21 ...
Notes indicate that part is from actual survey, part of the Bruce Peninsula from surveys of Capt Owen, and part from the map of 'Mr William Smyth and are not to be depended upon.'
A [Eastern and western straits of Manitou Island] ...
B [Drummond Island] ...
[C?] ['Isles à la Crosse'] ...
D.1 St Josephs ...
D.2 [Part of St Joseph] ...
[D.3?] [Lake Huron] I – XII
Twelve sheets untitled and unsigned.
GBLpro (FO 925/1916)

D6 *[1817–1821, 1822]* American
[Surveys made under Article 6 of the Treaty of Ghent ... Cornwall to St Mary's River]
50 col mss Sizes vary Ea 1" to 400 yds
Sheets I, VI, VIII, and IX endorsed 4 July 1818 or 4 June 1819 and sgd by Order of the Board of Commissioners; the sheets are similar to the British set but in a different hand and sgd differently; all sheets are as sgd on the first sheet unless otherwise noted; each sheet in two parts.

The sheets are as follows:

No I Iroquois or St Lawrence 1817. We certify this to be a true map of part of the Boundary designated by the sixth article of the Treaty of Ghent from actual Survey by order of the Board [Sgd] Peter B. Porter Anthony Barclay Commissioners, William A. Bird, David Thompson, Surveyors ...

No II Iroquois or St Lawrence 1817 ...

No III Iroquois or St Lawrence 1817 ...

No IV Iroquois or St Lawrence 1818 ...

No V Iroquois or St Lawrence 1818 ... C.A.L.S Del.

No VI Iroquois or St Lawrence 1818 ... C.A. Le Sueur Del.

No VII Iroquois or St Lawrence 1818 ...

No VIII Iroquois or St Lawrence 1818 ...

No IX Iroquois or St Lawrence 1818 ...

No X Iroquois or St Lawrence 1818 ...

[11] Lake Ontario copied from the Survey made in the years 1815–16 & 17 by Capt W.F.W. Owen of H.B. Majesty's Royal Navy

[12] Ontario 1819 ...
1" to 1 nautical mile

[13] No I Niagara 1819 ...

[14] No II Niagara 1819 ...

[15] The Second Section of the Survey of 1819 ...

[16] No IV Niagara 1819 ...

[17] Lake Erie That part west of Point Pele and Sandusky including all the islands is reduced from the actual surveys made by Order of the Commissioners

[18] [Southwest end of Lake Erie] ...

[19] No I Detroit 1820 ...

[20] No II Detroit 1820 ...

[21] No III Detroit 1820 ...

[22] Lake St Clair ...
1" to 1 nautical mile

[23] [River St Clair] ...

[24] The Fifteenth Section No I Lake Huron 1820 & 21, We certify this to be a true Map (the black lines only included) of part of the Boundary ... with the same note as that on the British map

[25] [Drummond Island to St Joseph Island] ... J. Ferguson del.
1" to 1 nautical mile
USDNA (RG 76 series 31)

Preliminary Boundary Surveys – North

D7 *[182?]*
[Map showing the various boundary positions for the area between Lake Superior and the Lake of the Woods]
Ms 206 x 302 cm Scale not given Endorsements: stamp 'BW'
Shows the 'Boundary offered by the British Commission through this broken communication' [Pigeon R route] and the U.S. position via the Kaministiquia R; shows the Mississippi R and boundary line per the 1783 treaty through Fond Du Lac at the end of L Superior and the St Louis R system; conflicting lines also shown for the northwest angle of the Lake of the Woods; notes on routes and connections.
OOAMA

D8 *[182?, 1842?]*
[Map of Lake Superior] [Sgd] David Thompson Astronomer and Surveyor 6th & 7th Articles of the Treaty of Ghent
Col ms Size not known 1" to 7.5 geog miles
Shows a careful delineation of the coastline and relief from the boundary surveys conducted by Thompson; shows the mouth of the R St Louis and the boundary line demanded by the British commissioner [1825]; the final boundary 'by Lord Ashburton' [1842] has been added later; notes on the nature of the shoreline and navigation are also given and sgd by Thompson; photoreproduction in OOAMA (NMC 16808).
GBL (Add Mss 27363e)

D9 *[1824]*
Sketch Map of Lake of the Woods
Col ms Size not known 1" to 4 miles
Enclosed in Barclay to Canning 10 March 1824 describing two possible northwest points for the Lake of the Woods boundary (GBLpro FO 5/187 f 235); the map shows earlier boundary lines and the 49th parallel N latitude; there is also an untitled map showing the same information, endorsed '5029 Canada Encl. 3 Received December 16 1824 in Mr Plantas's' (letter of 14 Dec 1824) (GBLpro CO 42/201); (*PRO Cat* 1621).
GBLpro (FO 5/187 f235; MPG 486)

D10 *[1824–6]*
[Map of three water routes connecting Lake Superior and Lake of the Woods] Sketched from my survey in 1798. [Sgd] David Thompson
Ms 85 x 106 cm Scale not given
This and the two maps below are from the Dr Johann Tiarks Papers (OOAMA MG24M); shows water routes via the Kaministiquia R, Pigeon R, and the St Louis R to the Lake of the Woods; (Tiarks Collection map 15).
OOAMA (NMC 11695)

Related maps

(2) *[1824?]*
[Maps of the water route from Lake Superior to Lake of the Woods via the Pigeon River] [Sgd] Samuel Thompson Assistant Surveyor
5 mss Ea 81 x 154 cm or smaller [Approx 1" to 1 mile] Watermark: '...1820'
Most of the sheets of a major survey of this water route; the western sheets are numbered 1–4 and the eastern sheet is numbered 'No 7'; (Tiarks Collection maps 1–5).
OOAMA (NMC 51718; 51713)

(3) *[1825?]*
[Map of the mouth of the River St Louis and the west end of Lake Superior]
Ms 41 x 52 cm [Approx 1" to 1 mile] Watermark: '...1817'
Probably prepared in 1825 when Barclay prepared a case for the British for this most southerly boundary position (Classen 104–9); (Tiarks Collection map 12).
OOAMA (NMC 51710)

D11 *[1826?]*
A General Map of the Country North West of Lake Superior ... [Sgd] Saml Thompson Draftsman & Asst Surveyor
Ms 100 x 119 cm Scale not given
Originally from commission reports (GBLpro FO 303/29); note on front describes surveys: 'The route from the Kaministiquia River to Lac a la Croix is laid down upon this map from Surveys made by Mr Ferguson and myself in the summer of 1824 and the route by the Pigeon River to Lake Namekan is reduced from our surveys of 1823–24 signed George W. Whistler Draftsman & Ass. Surveyor.' [and] 'The southern route from Lake Saisaginega to the East end of Lac a la Croix and from the west end of Lac a la Croix thro' Loon Lake to Lac Namekan is laid down upon this Map from Surveys made by Mr D. Thompson and myself in the Summers of 1823 & 24 and the routes by the Riviere St Louis to Sand Point Lake is reduced from my Survey of 1825. [Sgd] Saml Thompson ...'; rapids and portages shown; (*PRO Cat* 1402).
GBLpro (MPK 57)

D12 *[1826?]*
[Map of the Neebish channels, George Island, and the St Mary's River]
Ms in 4 sheets 136 x 327 cm [Approx 1" to 400 yds] Watermarks: '...1817...1821'
Shows the islands in the river but no boundary is shown; (Tiarks Collection maps 6–9); there is also an untitled map in OOAMA (NMC 24756) sgd

'David Thompson Astronomer and Surveyor under the 6th and 7th Articles of the Treaty of Ghent' showing the British and American claims in the area and endorsed with a 'BW' stamp.
OOAMA (NMC 51717; 24756)

D13 *[1826]*
[Untitled maps relating to disputed areas of the northern boundary between Lake Huron and Lake Superior]
5 col mss Sizes vary Scales vary
The first map of the area from Drummond's Is to St Mary's R was enclosed in Barclay's no 5 to Canning 27 Feb 1826 discussing three points of difference between the Commissioners for the Neebish channels (GBLpro FO 5/215; MR 427(1)); the second map '[Sgd] Samuel Thompson Draftsman...' is of the same area but is noted as replacing the earlier incorrect plan and was enclosed in Barclay's no 21 to Joseph Planta of 28 Oct 1826 (GBLpro FO 5/215; MR 427(3)); this plan names St Tammany's and 'St George's or Sugar Islands' and shows the boundary around St Joseph Is; the other three maps enclosed in the 2nd report show the water connection from L Superior to Lake of the Woods with the boundary in the latter (MR 427(2, 4, 5)); (*PRO Cat* 1579, 1580, 1396, 1622); there is also a plan of the St Mary's R from Drummond Is showing the 'termination of Boundary line under the 6th Article of the Treaty of Ghent' and islands in dispute in Canning's no 19, 1826 (GBLpro FO 115/46) (*PRO Cat* 1578); and also 'Map of the Neebish Channels and Islands exhibiting the Water Communications in dispute between the British and American Commissioners under the 6th & 7th Articles of the Treaty of Ghent. Reduced from a Copy of the Survey made by Order of the Commissioners' in report filed in (GBLpro FO 925/1422) (*PRO Cat* 1581).
GBLpro (MR 427(1–5); MPK 117; FO 925/1422)

Official Boundary Maps: North

D14 *[1818–26, 1826]* British
[Surveys made under Article 7 of the Treaty of Ghent showing the boundary between Canada and the United States from St Mary's River to Lake of the Woods]
34 col mss bound in atlas Sizes vary 1" to 400 yds unless otherwise noted; Endorsements: 'America ms. vol 240' 'General Sir Henry Lefroy 14/Nov/82'
The boundary is not shown on the first four maps as the line was not settled until 1842 (Classen, 110) and the boundary is only shown on some of the other maps; all the maps are sgd as in No 1 unless indicated otherwise; David Thompson's field notes for the 1817–25 survey under Articles 6 and 7 are in OTAR (MU2968–82); (*PRO Cat* 1393)

The contents are as follows

[On sheet at front of volume] 'A Descriptive List of Maps prepared under the 7th article ... the following are signed by Mr Thompson Principal Surveyor to the Board ... [nos 1–26] ...' 'the following maps are signed by Mr James Ferguson as principal Surveyor to the Board ... [nos 27–34]' Extract from Journal sent home by A.W. Barclay 22 July 1828. Such maps as were not completed at the last meeting ... are hereby filed as of October 23 1826 ... two complete sets of the above maps were delivered to each of the Commissioners'

No 1 [St Tammany Island] a true Map of part of the Survey under the 7 Article of the Treaty of Ghent, made by order of the Commissioners [Sgd] Anthony Barclay, Peter B. Porter, Commissioners, David Thompson, Surveyor, under the 6 & 7 Articles of the Treaty of Ghent Filed as of the 23d October 1826 By order of the Board October 22d 1827 ... [Sgd] S. Thompson Draftsman & Asst. Surveyor.

No 2 [Tammany Island to 'South George or Sugar Island'] ...

No 3 [Middle George or Sugar Island] ...

No 4 [north part of George or Sugar Island] ...

No 5 [Sault Ste Marie, boundary shown] ...

No 6 [West part of St Mary's R, boundary shown]

No 7 [Entrance into Lake Superior, boundary shown]

No VIII [Lake Superior] ...
scale not given; the boundary is shown to the east end of Isle Royale only.

No 9 [Mouth of St Louis River] ...

No 10 [River St Louis] ...

No 11 [River St Louis and Rivière aux Embaras] ...

No 12 [Lesser Vermilion River, Vermilion Lake, and Greater Vermilion River] ...

No 13 [Pigeon River to Mountain Lake] ...

No 14 [Arrow Lake to Gun Flint Lake and Knife Lake] ...

[No 14a Lake Kasieganagan] 'A true Copy of the Map made ... by James Ferguson American Principal Surveyor ... being intended to exhibit the Course for a proposed boundary ... in the Journal of the Board ... 23d day of October 1826 [Sgd] David Thompson ... Commissioners'
No boundary is shown.

No 15 [Passoomenan ... to Lac LaCroix] ...

[No 15a Lac Lacroix] ... [as in 14a] ... James Ferguson ... to exhibit the Course of a proposed boundary

No 16 [Greater Vermilion River to Sand Point Lake] ...

No 17 [Nameukan River] ...

No 18 [Rainy Lake, boundary shown in west part]

No 19 [Rainy River, boundary shown]

No 20 [Rainy River, boundary shown]

No 21 [North Rainy Lake to Spawning River] ...

No 22 [Sakahagan Lake] ...

No 23 [East part of Lake of the Woods] ...

No 24 [Lake of the Woods, boundary shown]

No 25 [Lake of the Woods with the northwestern point marked, boundary shown]

No 26 [North part of Lake of the Woods] ...

[No 27 Isle St Tammany and Isle St George] A true map of part of the survey under the Seventh Article ... J. Ferguson Surveyor to the Commissioners George W. Whistler Draftsman & Assistant Surveyor
1" to 1/2 geog mile

[No 28 'Saut de Sainte Marie' to 'Point Iroquois'] ...
1" to 1/2 geog mile
Boundary shown

[No 29 Lake Superior from Isle Royale to the entrance of the Pigeon River] ...
1" to 1 geog mile

[No 30 Arrow River and Pigeon River] ...

[No 31 Moose Lake to Flint Lake] ...

[No 32 Lake Saisaginegan] ...

[No 33 Sturgeon Lake] ...

[No 34 Rivière Maligne, Lac LaCroix, Lake Namekan] ...
GBLpro (FO 925/1920)

D15 *[1818–26, 1842]* British
[Surveys made under Article 7 of the Treaty of Ghent and under the Webster-Ashburton Treaty of 9 Aug 1842 from St Mary's River to the Lake of the Woods]
36 col mss Sizes vary Scales vary, 1" to 400 yds or as noted

Maps are similar to preceding set but the final boundary established by the 1842 treaty has been added; the Treaty of Ghent boundary is shown in blue and red and that determined under the Webster-Ashburton Treaty is in brown; triangulation lines; no boundary is shown on sheets IX–XII or on some of the western sheets not sgd by Ashburton and Webster; sheets 27–34, which cover the first part and are similar to those in preceding set (D14), are by the American surveyors; the boundary as of the 1842 treaty is shown on the St Mary's R area (in which George Is went to the U.S.) and along the Pigeon R system (Classen, 110).
(*PRO Cat* 1397)

The sheets are as follows

No I [St Tammanay Island] A true Map of Part of the Survey under the 7th Article of the Treaty of Ghent made by order of the Commissioners [Sgd] Anthony Barclay, Peter B. Porter Commissioners; David Thompson Surveyor, under the 6th & 7th Articles of the Treaty of Ghent. Filed by order of the Board October 23d 1826 [Sgd] ... S. Thompson Draftsman & Asst Surveyor

No II [St Tammanay Island and 'North George or Sugar Island'] map of Boundary agreed to by Treaty August 9 1842 [Sgd] Ashburton, Daniel Webster ... A true Map ...

No III [Middle George or Sugar Island] Map of Boundary ... 1842 ...

No IV [North part of George or Sugar Island] Map of Boundary ... 1842 ...

No V [St Mary's River] A true map ...

No VI [West part of St Mary's River] A true map ...

No VII [Entrance to Lake Superior] A true map ...

No VIII [Lake Superior] Map of Boundary ... 1842 ... A true map ...

No IX [Mouth of River St Louis] ... A true map ...

No X [River St Louis] ... a true map ...

No XI [River St Louis and Rivière aux Embaras] ... a true map ...

No XII [Upper Vermilion River and Lake Vermilion] ... a true map

No XIII [Lake Superior, Pigeon River to Mountain Lake] Map of the Boundary ... 1842 ...

[No 14A Lake Kaseiganagah] a true Copy of the Map made ... by James Ferguson ... to exhibit the course of a certain line ... described by the British Commissioner for a Proposed Boundary ... Map of Boundary agreed to by Treaty August 9 1842 [Sgd] Ashburton, Daniel Webster

No XIV [Arrow Lake to Knife Lake] ... Map of Boundary ... 1842

[No 15A Lac La Croix] A true Copy ... [as in 14A] ...

No XV [Sakahagan Lake to Lac La Croix] ... Map of Boundary ... 1842 ...

No XVI [Lac La Croix to Sand Point Lake] ... Map of Boundary ... 1842

No XVII [Nameukan River] ... a true map ...

No XVIII [Rainy Lake] ... Map of boundary ... 1842 ...

No XIX [Rainy Lake, Rainy River] ... a true map ...

No XX [Rainy River] ... a true map ...

No XXI [Rainy Lake to Spawning River] ... a true map ...

No XXII [North part of Rainy Lake to southeast part Lake of the Woods] ... a true map ...

No XXIII [part of Lake of the Woods] ... a true map ...

No XXIV [Lake of the Woods] ... a true map ...

No XXV [Lake of the Woods and southwestern point] ... a true map ...

No XXVI [North part of Lake of the Woods] ... a true map ...

[No 27 Isle St Tammany and Isle Sainte George] We certify this to be a true map ... J. Ferguson Surveyor to the Commissioners ... October 23d 1826 ... George W. Whistler ... Map of the Boundary ... 1842

[No 28 Saut de Saint Marie to Point Iroquois] A true map ... George M. Whistler ...

[No 29 Lake Superior from Isle Royale to Pigeon River] ... J. Ferguson Surveyor ... George W. Whistler U.S. Artillery Draftsman & Assist Surveyor.
Shows 1842 boundary.

[No 30 Pigeon River to Sagagan] ... J. Ferguson ... George W. Whistler. Shows 1842 boundary

[No 31 Moose Lake to Flint Lake] ... J. Ferguson ... George W. Whistler.
Shows 1842 boundary.

[No 32 Lake Saisaginegan] ... J. Ferguson ... George W. Whistler.
Shows 1842 boundary.

[No 33 Sturgeon Lake] ... J. Ferguson ... George W. Whistler

[No 34 Lac à la Croix] ... J. Ferguson ... George W. Whistler. Shows 1842 boundary.
GBLpro (FO 925/1919)

D16 *[1818–26, 1842]* American
[Surveys made under Article 7 of the Treaty of Ghent and under the Webster-Ashburton Treaty of 9 Aug 1842 from St Mary's River to Lake of the Woods]
24 col mss Sizes vary Mainly 1" to 400 yds or as noted; scale not given for some sheets
Most sheets show the boundary by the Treaty of Ghent; the western sheets and those at the eastern end show the boundary as determined in 1842; the set is similar to the British set preceding (**D15**), including a supplementary set of eight maps showing the parts of the boundary settled in 1842.

The sheets are as follows

No I [St Tammany Island and St Joseph Island] [Sgd] S. Thompson Draftsman & Asst Surveyor ... I hereby certify this map is a True Copy of the original filed by order of the Board of Commissioners under the 6th & 7th Articles of the Treaty of Ghent [Sgd] S. Thompson Draftsman & Surveyor. A true Map of part of the Survey, under the 7th Article of the Treaty of Ghent made by Order of the Commissioners [Sgd] Peter B. Porter, Anthony Barclay Commissioners, David Thompson Surveyor under the 6th & 7th Articles of the Treaty of Ghent Filed as of the 23rd October 1826 By Order of the Board October 22nd 1827

No II [St Joseph's to George or Sugar Island] ... Map of the boundary agreed upon by Treaty August 9th 1842 [Sgd] Daniel Webster, Ashburton

No III [Lake George] Boundary under the Treaty of Washington ... [signatures, etc, as in No II]

No IV [Lake George to Sugar Rapids] Boundary under the Treaty of Washington ... [as in No II]

No V ['Sault Ste Marie' to Pointe aux Pins] ... [as in No I]

No VI [River Ste Marie] ... [as in No I]

No VII [River Ste Marie to Lake Superior] ... [as in No I]

No VIII [Lake Superior] ... [as in No II]

No IX [River St Louis to Lake Superior] ... [as in No I]

No X [River St Louis continuedd] ... [as in No I]

No XI [River St Louis continuedd] ... [as in No I]

No XII [Vermilion Rriver and Lake] ... [as in No I]

No XIII [Lake Superior, Pigeon River to Mountain Lake] ... [as in No II]

No XIV [Arrow Lake to Knife Lake] ... [as in No II] A true copy of the map ... by James Ferguson American Principal Surveyor ... intended to exhibit the course of a certain line described by the British Commissioner for a Proposed Boundary ... 23rd October 1826 [Sgd] David Thompson ... Peter Porter, Anthony Barclay ... Map of boundary agreed to ... August 9th 1842 ...
[Inset: Kaseiganagah Lake enlarged]

No XV [Knife Lake to Lac La Croix] ... [as in No II]
[Inset: Lac LaCroix enlarged]

No XVI [Sheet missing]

No XVII [River Nameukan] ... [as in No I]

No XVIII [Sheet missing]

No XIX [Rainy Lake to Rainy River] ... [as in No I]

No XX [Rainy River] ... [as in No I]

No XXI [Part of Rainy Lake] ... [as in No I]

No XXII [Part of Rainy Lake] ... [as in No I]

No XXIII [Part of Lake of the Woods] ... [as in No I]

No XXIV [South part of Lake of the Woods] ... [as in No I]

No XXV [Lake of the Woods with the northwestern point] ... [as in No I]
Shows boundary.

No XXVI [north part of Lake of the Woods] ... [as in No I]
Shows boundary.
USDNA (RG 76 series 33)

Related maps

(**2**) *[1826, 1842]*
No 1 Map of the River Sainte Marie Surveyed by order of The Honorable The Commissioners under the 6th and 7th articles of the Treaty of Ghent [Sgd] George W. Whistler U.S. Artillery Draftsman and Assist Surveyor. A true map of part of the Survey under the Seventh Article of the Treaty of Ghent made by order of the Commissioners [Sgd] Peter B. Porter Anthony Barclay Commissioners under the 6th & 7th articles of the Treaty of Ghent [Sgd] J Ferguson Surveyor to the Commissioners Filed by Order of the Board October 23rd 1826 ... Map of the Boundary agreed upon by Treaty August 9th 1842 [Sgd] Daniel Webster, Ashburton

8 mss Sizes vary 2" to 1 geog mile
The first sheet of an additional set of eight maps showing the parts of the boundary finally settled in 1842; relief shown by formlines, hachures, and some shading; the other sheets are as follows

No 2 Continuation of the Map of the River Sainte Marie

No 3 Map of Isle Royale in Lake Superior with the adjacent shores and Islands

No 4 [to No 8] Map of a part of Certain Surveys along the Water Communications Northward of Lake Superior Commencing at the mouth of the Pigeon R and extending westward to Lake Namekan ...
USDNA (RG 76 series 33, supplementary maps 1–8)

Copies of Boundary Surveys and Later Maps

D17 *[1817–26]*
[Copies of surveys made under Articles 6 and 7 of the Treaty of Ghent from Cornwall to Lake of the Woods]
90 col mss in 3 vols Sizes vary Ea at 1" to 400 yds or smaller
Endorsements: stamp 'Department of Lands & Forests, Surveys'
Probably the official set owned by David Thompson since his is the only signature on the maps and many of his maps and papers were acquired by the Crown Lands Dept in the mid-nineteenth century (see note to **D24**); covers the north and south sections; sheets are very similar to the official surveys except for sheet numbering; sheet XXV is missing.

The sheets are as follows
No I Iroquois or St Lawrence A true map of part of the Survey of the 6th Article of the Treaty of Ghent by order of the Commissioners [Sgd] David Thompson Astronomer & Surveyor Henry G. Thompson, Drftsman

No II–XXI [St Lawrence River to the entrance to Lake Ontario sgd as in No I]

No XXII A true Copy of the Map of the naval Survey of Lake Ontario by Capt Owen ...

No XXIII–L [Niagara River, Lake Erie, to St Clair River] ...

Sheets from here on lack the signature of Henry Thompson.
No LI–LXX [St Clair River to Lake George] ... including No LII [Lake Huron] ... a true map (of the black lines included) of part of the Boundary designated by the Sixth Article of the Treaty of Ghent from actual Survey by order of the Board [Sgd] David Thompson Astronomer and Surveyor under the 6th and 7th Articles of the Treaty of Ghent.

No LXXI–LXXV [St Mary's River to Lake Superior] ...

No LXXVI–LXXXVII [River St Louis, Vermilion River and Lake, Pigeon River to Gunflint Lake]

No LXXXVIII–XC [Lake of the Woods] ...

[Arrow Lake to Crooked Lake] Sheets 2 ... 3 ... 4 ... [on each sheet]:

A true map of part of the Survey under the 7th Article of the Treaty of Ghent ... (Signed Anthony Barclay, Peter B. Porter, David Thompson ... October 23rd 1826 ... a true copy of the original maps [Sgd] David Thompson.
A note on map 4 by a line along the Vermilion R indicates the line is 'the Boundary demanded by the British Commissioner.'
OTAR

Related maps

(2) There is also a copy of the map for L Superior by Barclay, Porter, and David Thompson 'Filed by order of the Board October 23d 1826 ...,' which includes pencil grid lines for copying (OTAR (SR 6457)). In addition, there is a set of 59 sheets (two sheets missing) covering the whole boundary, signed by Peter B. Porter and Anthony Barclay, commissioners, and William A. Bird and David Thompson, surveyors, in the Buffalo and Erie County Historical Society (Peter B. Porter Papers); a set of tracings was made in 1824 by J.J. Bigsby, the British secretary to the board, consisting of 33 sheets of the southern part of the survey under Article 6, all certified by Bigsby and later given to the Royal Geographical Society (N. America S/14); a copy of the map of 'Lake Ontario' and one of the 'Lake Erie' sheet, both showing boundaries, are in GBLpro FO 925/1918(1–2); (*PRO Cat* 1454, 1522).
OTAR GBLpro (FO 925/1918(1–2)) GBLrg (N.A.S/14) USNBuHi

D18 *1823*
[Map of part of the St Lawrence River showing the boundary between Sheek's Island and Barnhart's Island] Copy by James G. Chewett A.D.
Col ms 50 x 90 cm 1" to 10 chains
Originally enclosed in Capt Barrie to Maitland of 25 Oct 1823 and further enclosed in Maitland to Bathurst no 118 of 9 Feb 1824 (OOA RG 7 G12 V13 no 118); shows soundings, rocks; a few bldgs and points marked but not keyed; concern about giving Barnhart's Is to the Americans and preserving a British-controlled passage for navigation was demonstrated in this map and those below (Classen, 102).
OOAMA (NMC 24755)

Related maps

(2) *1823*
A Sketch of that Part of the St. Lawrence forming Barnhart's Island, in the Township of Cornwall and Province of Upper Canada: shewing that if that Island is ceded to the United States the Navigation of the River may be controlled by the State of New York by Wm. Browne, D.S. 1823.
Col ms 46 x 64 cm 1" to 40 perches
Shows a rough survey of the two islands with the boundary; 'Village of Milleroches'; roads; notes on navigation; point marked where boats must ascend on the U.S. side; (Holmden 3897).
OOAMA (NMC 14115)

(3) *[1823?]*
[Map of Sheeks and Barnhart's islands] ... The Boundary is laid down according to the Survey of the Commissioners under the Treaty of Ghent. No 1 (Signed) Wm Macdonald D.S. Copied by J.G. Chewett
Col ms 54 x 94 cm 4" to 1 mile
Insets: 'Moulinette Rapids' and 'Milleroche Rapids' both at 1" to 5 chains; 'View taken from the North Shore'; also shows bldgs in Cornwall, Moulinette, and Milleroches.
OTAR (SR 8873)

D19 *1824, 1828*
[Copies of boundary surveys for Article 6 of the Treaty of Ghent from Cornwall to Lake George made by Lt Piers and R.S.M. Bouchette]
22 col mss Sizes vary Ea 1" to 400 yds or smaller
All sheets show relief along shorelines, the boundaries, and towns with a rough street layout and bldgs.

The sheets are as follows

(1) Plan of the River Cataraqui from the Island of St Regis to Isle au Rapid Plat drawn by Lieut Piers, Royl Staff Corps, 1824. (Signed) Anthy Barclay Peter B. Porter, Commissioners David Thompson, Wm A. Bird, Surveyors under the 6th & 7th Articles of the Treaty of Ghent
Watermark: 'JAMES WHATMAN ... 1819'
Endorsements: '415/1' stamp 'CREOC'
Also another plan OOAMA (NMC 24757) with the same title, marked '(Copy)' and further sgd 'Commanding Royal Engineer's Office, Quebec, May 23rd, 1828' and endorsed: 'Sheet No 8 East' 'AA54' and stamps 'IGF' 'B↑O' (Holmden 3901).
OOAMA (NMC 24754; 24757)

(2) Plan of the River Iroquois or St Lawrence from Johnstown to Sucker Creek. Drawn by R.S.M. Bouchette 1824 (Signed) ... [as in 1]
Watermark: 'JAMES WHATMAN ... 1817'
Endorsements: '415/2'; stamp 'CREOC'
Also another plan in OOAMA (NMC 16858) with the same title, marked '(Copy)' and further sgd ... [as in 1] '22nd May 1828'; watermark: 'JAMES WHATMAN ... 1823'; endorsements: 'Sheet No 7 East' 'AA53' and stamps 'IGF' 'BO' (Holmden 3907).
OOAMA (NMC 16869; 16858)

(3) Plan of the St Lawrence from Johnstown to Tp of Hague drawn by Lieut Piers, Royal Staff Corp's. (Signed) ... [as in 1] (Copy) [Sgd] Commanding Royal Engineer's Office Quebec May 24th 1828
Watermark: 'JAMES WHATMAN ... 1823'
Endorsements: 'Sheet No 6 East' 'AA 52'; stamps 'IGF' 'B↑O'
The original sheet by Piers has not been found; (Holmden 3906).
OOAMA (NMC 16859)

(4) Plan of the River Iroquois or St Lawrence from Hammond to Augusta 1818. Drawn by R.S.M. Bouchette 1824 (Signed) ... [as in 1] [Sgd] (Copy) Commanding Royal Engineers Office, Quebec, 24th May 1828.
Watermark: 'WHATMAN ... 1820' Endorsements: 'Sheet No 5 East' 'AA51'; stamps 'IGF' 'B↑O'
The original sheet by Bouchette has not been found; (Holmden 3905).
OOAMA (NMC 16855)

(5) Plan of the St Lawrence from Tar Island to Budlings Mills 1818. Drawn by Lieut Piers, Royl Staff Corps (Signed) ... [as in 1]
Watermark: 'JAMES WHATMAN ... [18]19'
Endorsements: '415/5'; stamp 'CREOC'
Also another plan in OOAMA (NMC 24751) with the same title marked '(Copy)' and further signed '... [as in 1] May 20th, 1828'; watermark: ' ... WHATMAN ... 1820'; endorsements: 'Sheet No 4 East' and stamps 'IGF' 'B↑O' (Holmden 1230).
OOAMA (NMC 24750–1)

(6) Plan of part of the Iroquois or St Lawrence 1818. Drawn by R.S.M. Bouchette, 1824. (Signed) ... [as in 1] (Copy) [Sgd] ... [as in 1] 24th May 1828. Commanding Royal Engineer Canada
Watermark: 'JAMES WHATMAN ... 1823'
Endorsements: 'Sheet No 3 East' 'AA 49'; stamps 'IGF' 'B↑O'
The original plan by Bouchette has not been found; (Holmden 3904).
OOAMA (NMC 16856)

(7) Plan of part of the Iroquois or St Lawrence. [Grindstone Is to Howe Is] 1818. Drawn by R.S.M. Bouchette (Signed) ... [as in 1]
Watermark: 'JAMES WHATMAN ... 1819'
Endorsements: '415/7' stamp 'CREOC'
Also another plan in OOAMA (NMC 14291) of the same title, marked '(Copy)' and further signed '... [as in 1] 21st May, 1828.'; watermark: '... WHATMAN ... 1823'; endorsements: 'Sheet No 2 East' 'AA48' and stamps 'IGF' 'B↑O' (Holmden 3895).
OOAMA (NMC 16862; 14291)

(8) Plan of the River St Lawrence from Howe Island to Lake Ontario. Drawn by Lieut Piers Royl Staff Corps (Signed) ... [as in 1]
Watermark: 'JAMES WHATMAN ... 1819'
Endorsements: '415/8'; stamp 'CREOC'; the untitled north sheet of this map with the same watermark and endorsed: 'CREOC' 'No 415/81' '277–7' is in OTAR.

Also another plan in OOAMA (NMC 43339) with the same title marked '(Copy)' and further signed '... [as in 1] ... 19th May 1828'; two sheets, watermark (on both sheets): ' ... WHATMAN ... 1820'; endorsements: 'Sheet No 1 North' 'No 1' 'Sheet No 1 South' 'No 2' 'AA47' and stamps 'IGF' 'B↑O' (Holmden 2563, 1231); despite title the north sheet covers the same area as (9) below; the north sheets show Kingston with streets and bldgs.
OOAMA (NMC 27192; 43339) OTAR

(9) Plan of Part of Lake Ontario, Bay of Quente etc. Drawn by R.S.M. Bouchette (Signed) ... [as in 1]
1" to 800 yds col ms in 3 sheets
Watermark: 'JAMES WHATMAN ... 1819'
Endorsements: '415/9' stamp 'CREOC'
OOAMA (NMC 16857)

(10) Plan of the Niagara from Beaver Island to Navy Island, survey of 1819. Drawn by R.S.M. Bouchette (Signed) ... [as in 1]
Watermark: '... WHATMAN ... 1819' Endorsements: '415/ '; stamp: 'CREOC'
OOAMA (NMC 17926)

(11) Plan of the River Niagara from Lake Erie to Grand Island, Survey of 1819. Drawn by R.S.M. Bouchette. (Signed) ... [as in 1]
Watermark: 'JAMES WHATMAN ... 1819'
Endorsements: '415/ ' stamp 'CREOC'
OOAMA (NMC 16860)

(12) Plan of the south West End of Lake Erie 1821. Drawn by R.S.M. Bouchette 1824. (Signed) ... [as in 1]
Watermark: '... WHATMAN ... 1819' Endorsements: '415/ '; stamp 'CREOC'
OOAMA (NMC 16732)

(13) Plan of the Detroit from Lake Erie to River Rouge Drawn by Lieut. Piers Royal Staff Corps. 1820. (Signed) ... [as in 1]
Watermark: '... WHATMAN ... 1819' Endorsements: '415/ ' stamp 'CREOC'
OOAMA (NMC 14289)

(14) Plan of the Detroit River from Sandwich to Lake St Clair, 1820. Drawn by R.S.M. Bouchette 1824. (Signed) ... [as in 1]
Watermark: '... WHATMAN ... 1819' Endorsements: '415/ '; stamp 'CREOC'
OOAMA (NMC 16861)

(15) Plan of Lake St Clair. Drawn by R.S.M. Bouchette, 1824. (Signed) ... [as in 1]
1" to 1 geog mile Watermark: '... WHATMAN ... 1819' Endorsements: '415/ '; stamp 'CREOC'
OOAMA (NMC 16870)

(16) Plan of Lake Huron, 1820–21. Drawn by R.S.M. Bouchette. (Signed) ... [as in 1]
1" to 7.1 miles Watermark: 'WHATMAN ... 1819' Endorsements: '415/ '; stamp 'CREOC'
Notes indicate that some lines are from actual survey by Thompson and Bird, others from Capt Owen (see App C), and most from earlier map **(30(3))**; plan is similar to 15.1 and [24] in official boundary surveys (**D5, D6**).
OOAMA (NMC 24753)

(17) Plan of the St Lawrence [*sic*] from the Manitoulin Islands to Lake George. Drawn by R.S.M. Bouchette, 1824. (Signed) ... [as in 1]
1" to 1 geog mile Watermark: 'WHATMAN ... 1819'
Endorsements: '415/ '; stamp 'CREOC'
Shows north shore of Lake Huron.
OOAMA (NMC 16871)

D20 *[1827?]*
A Map exhibiting the Water Communications from Isle Royale to Lac La Pluie in Controversy between the British & American Commissioners under the 6th & 7th Article of the Treaty of Ghent: Reduced from a Copy of the survey made by Order of the Commissioners
Ms 57 x 76 cm 1" to 7 geog miles
Enclosed in commission reports GBLpro (FO 925/1423); shows the Pigeon R and Kaministiquia R systems; (*PRO Cat* 1403).
GBLpro (FO 925/1423)

D21 *1828*
LETTER / FROM / THE SECRETARY OF STATE, / Transmitting, pursuant to a resolution of the House of Representatives, of the nineteenth ultimo, / A COPY OF THE MAPS AND REPORT / OF THE / COMMISSIONERS UNDER THE TREATY OF GHENT, / FOR ASCERTAINING THE / NORTHERN AND NORTHWESTERN BOUNDARY / BETWEEN / THE UNITED STATES AND GREAT BRITAIN. / March 18, 1828. / Read, and laid upon the table. / WASHINGTON: PRINTED BY GALES & SEATON / 1828
[4] p 8 maps on [4] pp, prints (liths) Sizes vary Scales vary
Includes selected maps of the L Erie, Detroit R, and Drummond Is section of the boundary under Article 6 showing problems in determining boundary position; (*Bib Can* 7191; Goggin 31; Karpinski 664–8).

The sheets are as follows

P[3] [Introduction and description of the boundary]

[1] South West End of Lake Erie We certify this to be a true map of part of the Boundary designated by the Sixth Article of the Treaty of Ghent from actual survey by Order of the Board. Peter B. Porter Anth. Barclay Commissioners William A. Bird David Thompson Surveyors Under the 6th & 7th Articles of the Treaty of Ghent. // On Stone by James Eddy / Pendleton's Lithography, Boston.

[2] No. 1 Detroit 1820 ... [as in 1] [L Erie to Fighting Is]

[3] No. 2 / DETROIT. / 1820 ... [as in 1] [Fighting Is to R Rouge]
[4] No. 3 / DETROIT / 1820 ... [as in 1 except lacks engraving statement] [Sandwich to L St Clair]

[5] Lake St Clair .... [as in 1]

[6] [River St Clair] ...... [as in 1]

[7] [Drummond Island to St Joseph Island] ... [as in 1]

[8] THE / FIFTEENTH SECTION / No 1 / LAKE HURON / 1820 & 1821 ... [as in 1]
OOAMA OTMCL USDNA (RG 76 series 32 no 138)

D22 *[183?]*
[Map of the St Lawrence River from St Regis to Prescott; certified as a true copy of this part of the boundary survey] David Thompson Ast and Surveyor for the 6th & 7th Articles of the Treaty of Ghent
5 col mss Sizes vary Ea 1" to 400 yds Watermark: 'JAMES WHATMAN ... 1832' Endorsements: stamp 'BW'
Triangulation lines shown across the river; distances between points.
OOAMA (NMC 16863)

D23 *1835*
OHIO / BOUNDARY / No. III / South bend of Lake Erie: / Map exhibiting the position occupied / in the determination of the most Southwardly / point of the Boundary line between / THE / United States & Canada. / Surveyed under the direction of Capt A. Talcot, / U.S. Engineers; / by / Lieuts Wash. Hood. Robt E. Lee / DRAWN BY / Lieut W. Hood / 1835 [Sgd in facsimile] A. Talcott Capt Engs
Print (lith) 48 x 114 cm 1" to 1000 ft
Inset: 'POINT PELE, / UPPER CANADA. / Map exhibiting the second position occupied / in the determination of the most southwardly / point of the Boundary line between the / UNITED STATES & CANADA / Surveyed under the direction of / Capt Andrew Talcott, U.S. Engineers, by Lieuts W. Hood & R.E. Lee, U.S.A. / 1835.' 1" to 1000 ft; in U.S. Congress, House of Representatives, 24th Congress 1st session (1835–6), Executive Documents, House Document no 59 (cited in Karpinski 686); triangulation points; relief of shoreline, sandbanks, wooded areas; (*PRO Cat* 2774).
GBLpro (FO 925/1443)

D24 *[ca 1837–40]*
Map of the Niagara River, shewing the boundary-line between Canada and the United States As Surveyed in pursuance of the Sixth Article of the Treaty of Ghent: – Compiled by J.G. Chewett principally from a Set of the Plans of Survey lodged in this Office by David Thompson Esquire Astronomer and Surveyor for the Commissioners on the part of Great Britain
Col ms 60 x 98 cm Scale not given
Shows the boundary line in detail; twps with survey grid; canals including Welland Canal; military reserves; railway between Buffalo and Niagara Falls; also a copy with the same title '[Sgd] Copy J.G. Chewett Surveyor Genls Office Toronto 10th July 1840' in OOAMA (NMC 24758) (Holmden 3914); these and plans below are copies made by J.G. Chewett.
OTAR (SR 5931) OOAMA (NMC 24758)

Related maps

(2) *1838*
Copy from Mr Thompsons Plans of the Boundary line between Upper Canada & the United States [Sgd] J.G. Chewett S.G. Office 4th Jany 1838
Ms 49 x 69 cm 1" to 400 yds
Shows the boundary in the Niagara R between Grand Is and Niagara Falls.
OTAR (SR 81005)

(3) *1837*
Sketch shewing the Boundary line designated by Order of the Board under the 6th Article of the Treaty of Ghent laid down from Plans by David Thompson Esquire Astronomer and Surveyor under the 6th and 7th Articles [Sgd] J G Chewitt Surveyor Genls Office Toronto 18th July 1837. Surveyor Generals Office Toronto 18th July 1837 [Sgd] J.W. Macaulay Surv Genl
Col ms on tracing paper 130 x 57 cm scale not given
Shows the boundary through the islands at the southwest end of L Erie.
OTMCL

(4) *[1838?]*
Map of the Waters between Lakes Erie & Huron shewing the boundary line between Canada and the United States As Surveyed in pursuance of the Sixth Article of the Treaty of Ghent: – Compiled by J.G. Chewett, principally from a Set of Plans of Survey lodged in this Office by David Thompson Esquire Astronomer and Surveyor for the Commissioners on the part of Great Britain
Col ms 193 x 64 cm Scale not given Endorsements: '1037'
Shows the boundary in detail, twps and survey grid, rivers and settlements marked; shows Sarnia, Enniskillen, Moore, Dawn, and Sombra twps all surveyed in the 1830s and Corunna (laid out in 1836).
OTAR (SR 6635)

D25 *1840*
[Map of Lake Superior and the water communications to Lake of the Woods and Red River] [To] His excellency the Right Honorable Charles Poulett Thomson Governor General Montreal 11th May 1840 [Sgd] David Thompson late Astronomer and Surveyor under the 6th and 7th Articles of the Treaty of Ghent. Henry G. Thompson Sculpts
Col ms in 4 sheets 90 x 244 cm Scale not given Endorsements: stamp 'BW'
Shows relief, rivers, lakes etc; shows boundary as of 1783, the U.S. claims for the northern Kaministiquia route, the British claim for the Pigeon R route; shows height of land, notes on portages and lengths, boundary shown in Lake of the Woods.
OOAMA (NMC 24773)

D26 [*ca 1845*]
A True Map of Part of the Survey under the 7th Article of the Treaty of / Ghent: by order of the Commissioners. / Anthony Barclay, Peter B. Porter, Commissioners / David Thompson Surveyor, October 23rd. 1826. / ... / A true Copy of the original Map / David Thompson / MATTHEW'S LITH.
4 prints (liths) Sizes vary Ea 11/4" to 1 mile
Shows the boundary in the St Mary's R around George Is, and from L Superior along the Pigeon R, to Arrow L, Crooked L to Rainy L, indicating the final decisions established by the Webster-Ashburton Treaty of 1842; sheet 1 not held by OOAMA.
OOAMA (NMC 24761–3) OTAR

D27 *1850*
[Lake Superior to Lake of the Woods] Copy of an approximate Map of Mr Thompson's (Ast. under 6.7. A.T. Ghent) from his survey of 1822.
7 col mss Size varies Scale not given
Endorsements: 'Given to me by Mr Astronomer Thompson & by me presented to the Royl Geogr Socy of London [Sgd] J.I. Bigsby ... Feb: 1850'
Title varies on other sheets but all presented by Bigsby, a secretary to the commission, to GBLrg in Feb 1850; various copies of sheets showing river and lake connections by the Pigeon R to Lake of the Woods; boundary sometimes shown; notes on geology and rock types, portages and navigability of rivers.
GBLrg (Can S/S19; S21–4)

Appendix E

Towns of Upper Canada Arranged by County

ALGOMA

Garden River
Goulais Bay
Hilton Beach
(St Joseph town plot)
Sault Ste Marie

BRANT

Bishopgate
Brantford
Cainsville
Cathcart
(Cayuga Heights town plot)
Harley
Harrisburg
Kelvin
Middleport
Mount Pleasant
Newport
Onondaga
Paris
St George
Scotland
(Tuscarora town plot)

BRUCE

Allenford
(Balaklava)
Bervie
(Cheviot)
(Hardwicke town plot)
Inverhuron
Invermay
Kincardine
Lockerby
Lucknow
Lurgan
(Lurgan town plot)
(Malta)
Oliphant
Paisley
(Port Bruce)
Port Elgin
(Port Head town plot)
Riversdale
Southampton
Tara
Teeswater
Walkerton
Wiarton

CARLETON

Burritts Rapids
Carlsbad Springs
Cyrville
Fitzroy Harbour
Galetta
Kars
(Long Island Locks)
Manotick
Metcalfe
North Gower
Orleans
Ottawa
Richmond

DUFFERIN

Marsville
Mono Centre
Orangeville
Rosemount

DUNDAS

Chesterville
Inkerman
Iroquois
Mariatown
Morrisburg

DURHAM

Bethany
Bowmanville
Elizabethville
Fleetwood
Hampton
Haydon
Janetville
Millbrook
Mount Pleasant
Newcastle
Orono
Port Britain
Port Hope

ELGIN

Aylmer
Bayham
Fingal
Iona
New Glasgow
Orwell
Port Bruce
Port Burwell
Port Stanley
Port Talbot
St Thomas
Sparta
Springfield
Tyrconnell
Union
Vienna

ESSEX

Amherstburg
Belle River
Colchester
Kingsville
Leamington
(Marble Village town plot)
Oxley
(Piusville town plot)
Ruthven
Stoney Point
Union
Windsor

FRONTENAC

Arden
Battersea
Bellrock
Brewers Mills
Cataraqui
Fermoy
Harrowsmith
Inverary
Kingston
Petworth
Portsmouth
Sydenham
Verona

GLENGARRY

Alexandria
Dalhousie Mills
Lancaster
Martintown
Williamstown

GRENVILLE

Burritts Rapids
Cardinal
Eastons Corners
Johnstown
Kemptville
Maitland
Merrickville
(New Oswegatchie)
North Augusta
Oxford Mills
(Plumbport townplot)
Prescott
Spencerville
Ventnor
Wexford

GREY

Ayton
(Cape Rich)
Durham
Eugenia
Feversham
Flesherton
Hanover

Leith
Markdale
Maxwell
Meaford
Neustadt
Orchard
Owen Sound
Priceville
Ravenna
Thornbury
Traverston
(Vail Point town plot)
Varney
Walters Falls
Williamsford

HALDIMAND

Byng
Caledonia
Canboro
Canfield
Cayuga
Dunnville
(Indiana)
Port Maitland
(Worsow town plot)

HALIBURTON

Haliburton
Minden

HALTON

Acton
Ashgrove
Bronte
Burlington
Campbellville
(Cumminsville)
Darbyville
Georgetown
Glen Williams
Hornby
Kilbride
Limehouse
Lowville
Milton
Nelson
Norval
Oakville
(Peru)
Port Nelson
Speyside
Stewarttown
(Willbrook)

HASTINGS

Belleville
Cannifton
Corbyville
Deseronto
Eldorado
Frankford
Glen Miller
Glen Ross
Lonsdale
Madoc
Marmora
Millbridge
Milltown
Salem
Shannonville
Stirling
Stoco
Trenton
Tweed

HURON

(Algiers town plot)
(Alma)
(Annan)
(Bannockburn)
Bayfield
Belfast
Belmore
Benmiller
(Binghamsville town plot)
Bluevale
Blyth
(Bodmin)
(Bridgend Place)
Brucefield
Brussels
Clinton
Cranbrook
(Cransford)
Crediton
Dinsley Terrace
Drysdale
Dungannon
Egmondville
Exeter
Fordwich
Goderich
Gorrie
(Granton)
Harpurhey
Holmesville
Kinburn
Londesborough
Manchester
Newbridge
Nile
Port Albert
(Roxburgh town plot)
St Helens
St Joseph
Saltford
Seaforth
Summerhill
Varna
Walton
Wingham
Wroxeter
(Zetland)
Zurich

KENT

(Antrim)
Blenheim
Bothwell
Buxton
Chatham
Clearville
(Deal town plot)
Dresden
Duart
Harwich
Louisville
Moraviantown
Morpeth
(Racey Vale town plot)
Ridgetown
Romney
Shrewsbury
Thamesville
Wallaceburg
Wallacetown

LAMBTON

Alvinston
Arkona
Corunna
Errol
Florence
Forest
Froomfield
Hillsborough Beach
(Lightburne)
Mandaumin
Mooretown
Oil Springs
Petrolia
Point Edward
Port Franks
Port Lambton
Sarnia
Sombra
Thedford
Wanstead
Warwick
Watford
Widder
Wilkesport
Wyoming

LANARK

Almonte
Andrewsville

Appleton
Balderson
Carleton Place
Clayton
Franktown
Glen Tay
Innisville
Lanark
McDonalds Corners
Pakenham
Perth
Port Elmsley
Rosedale
Smiths Falls
Stanleyville

LEEDS

Athens
Brockville
Charleston
Delta
Frankville
Gananoque
Jasper
Lyn
Lyndhurst
Morton
Newboro
Portland
Seelys Bay
Westport

LENNOX AND ADDINGTON

Adolphustown
Amherst Island
(Balentra)
Camden East
Centreville
Croydon
Enterprise
Erinsville
Ernestown
Flinton
Forest Mills
Napanee
Newburgh
Odessa
Sandhurst
Selby
Tamworth
Yarker

LINCOLN

Caistorville
Grimsby
Jordan
Jordan Station
Niagara-on-the-Lake
Port Dalhousie
Queenston
St Catharines
Wellandport

MANITOULIN

Little Current
Sheguiandah

MIDDLESEX

Adelaide
Ailsa Craig
Appin
Arva
Belmont
Birr
Bornish
Carlisle
(Centreville town plot)
Clandeboye
(Colborne)
Crumlin
Delaware
Delaware West
Dorchester
Fanshawe
(Forestville town plot)
Glencoe
Granton
(Katesville)
Kerwood
Kilworth
Komoka
Lambeth
Lobo
London
Longwood
Lucan
Melbourne
Melrose
(Metcalfe town plot)
Mossley
Mount Brydges
Napier
Newbury
Nilestown
Parkhill
Putnam
(Siddalsville)
Strathroy
Sylvan
Wardsville
(Waubuno)
Wyton Station

MUSKOKA

Muskoka Falls

NORFOLK

Bloomsburg
(Charlotteville)
Courtland
(Croton)
Delhi
Lynedoch
Normandale
Port Dover
Port Ryerse
Renton
Rockford
St Williams
Simcoe
Teeterville
Villa Nova
Walsingham

NORTHUMBERLAND

Brighton
Campbellford
Castleton
Cobourg
Colborne
(Deelmage City town plot)
Grafton
Harwood
Lakeport
(Newcastle town plot)
Norham
(Seymour town plot)
Vernonville
Warkworth

ONTARIO

Altona
Atherley
Beaverton
Brooklin
Brougham
Cannington
Claremont
Columbus
Epsom
Fairport
Glen Major
Greenbank
Liverpool
Manchester
Manilla
Oshawa
Port Perry
Port Union
Prince Albert
Raglan
Sonya
Utica
Uxbridge

Vroomanton
Whitby
Whitevale

OXFORD

Beachville
Bright
Brownsville
Canning
Centreville
Culloden
Drumbo
Eastwood
Embro
Harrington West
Ingersoll
Innerkip
Lakeside
Mount Elgin
Norwich
Otterville
Plattsville
Princeton
Ratho
Richwood
Salford
Springford
Strathallan
Sweaburg
Thamesford
Tillsonburg
Vandecar
Washington
Wolverton
Woodstock

PARRY SOUND

Rosseau

PEEL

Alton
Belfountain
Bolton
Brampton
Caledon
Caledon East
Cheltenham
Churchville
Cooksville
Erindale
(Indian Village, Credit River)
Malton
Meadowvale
Mono Mills
Port Credit
Streetsville
Terra Cotta
Tullamore
Victoria

PERTH

Dorado
Dublin
Fullarton
Gowanstown
Listowel
Millbank
Mitchell
Nithburg
Poole
St Marys
Shakespeare
Staffa
Stratford
Trowbridge
West Monkton

PETERBOROUGH

Bridgenorth
Hastings
(Hiawatha town plot)
Keene
Lakefield
Lang
Norwood
Peterborough
Warsaw
Westwood

PRESCOTT

Caledonia Springs
Hawkesbury
L'Orignal
Plantagenet
Vankleek Hill

PRINCE EDWARD

Ameliasburg
Cherry Valley
Consecon
Demorestville
Milford
Picton
Rednersville
Rossmore

RENFREW

Arnprior
Beachburg
Douglas
Eganville
Osceola
Pembroke
Petawawa
Renfrew
White Lake

RUSSELL

Bearbrook
Cumberland
Embrun
Russell

SIMCOE

Alliston
Angus
Avening
Barrie
Bell Ewart
Bradford
(Bristol)
Coldwater
Collingwood
Cookstown
Craighurst
Creemore
Duntroon
Gilford
Hawkestone
(Hythe town plot)
Keenansville
Lefroy
Loretto
Marchmont
New Lowell
Newton Robinson
Nottawa
Orillia
Penetanguishene
(Port Powell)
(Rippon town plot)
Shanty Bay
Singhampton
Stayner
(Sudbury town plot)
Sunnyside
Thornton
Utopia
(Warrington)
Wyebridge

STORMONT

Berwick
Cornwall
Ingleside
(Milleroches)
Newington

THUNDER BAY

Fort William

VICTORIA

Bobcaygeon
Bolsover

Cambray
Fenelon Falls
Kirkfield
Lindsay
Oakwood
Omemee
Woodville

WATERLOO

Ayr
Baden
Blair
Branchton
Breslau
Conestogo
Crosshill
Doon
Elmira
Erbsville
Galt
Hawkesville
Heidelberg
Hespeler
Kitchener
Linwood
(Mehring town plot)
(New Aberdeen)
New Dundee
New Hamburg
Preston
St Clements
St Jacobs
(Shantz)
Waterloo
(Wilbey town plot)
Winterbourne

WELLAND

Chippawa
Cooks Mills
Fonthill
Fort Erie
Merritton
Niagara Falls
Port Colborne
Port Robinson
Ridgeville
Thorold
Wainfleet
Welland

WELLINGTON

Aberfoyle
(Aboyne)
Alma
Arthur
Ballinafad
(Ballinard town plot)
Belwood
(Benderville town plot)
Brisbane
Clifford
Crewsons Corners
Drayton
Eden Mills
Elora
Ennotville
Erin
Everton
Fergus
Glen Allan
(Gourock)
Guelph
Harriston
(Hartfield)
(Hastings town plot)
Hillsburgh
Hollen
(Huston)
(Irvinedale town plot)
(Kinnettles)
Marsden
Minto
Morriston
Mount Forest
(Palmerston town plot)
Rockwood
Rothsay
Salem
(Strathallan town plot)
(Thorpville town plot)
(Trafalgar town plot)
(Union town plot)

WENTWORTH

(Abbotsford town plot)
Ancaster
Carlisle
Copetown
Dundas
Freelton
Hamilton
(Hopkinsburg town plot)
(Inverness town plot)
Lynden
Mill Grove
Sinclairville
Stoney Creek
Waterdown
Winona

YORK

(Amsterdam)
Aurora
Bloomington
Boxgrove
Etobicoke Twp
Gormley
(Gwillimbury town plot)
Holland Landing
Jersey
Keswick
King City
Kleinburg
Laskay
Lloydtown
Maple
Markham
Mount Albert
Newmarket
Pefferlaw
Pine Grove
Port Bolster
Richmond Hill
Scarborough Twp
Schomberg
Stouffville
Sutton
Thornhill
Toronto
Udora
Unionville
Victoria Square
West Franklin
(Windham town plot)
York Twp

Name Index

Subject Index

Title Index